# TIME
# ALMANAC
# 2013

## POWERED BY

### ENCYCLOPÆDIA
# Britannica®

www.britannica.com

Jacob E. Safra, *Chairman of the Board*
Jorge Aguilar-Cauz, *President*

Chicago · London · New Delhi · Paris · Seoul · Sydney · Taipei · Tokyo

© 2012 BY ENCYCLOPÆDIA BRITANNICA, INC. All rights reserved.

All TIME material copyright © 2012 Time Inc. All rights reserved.

Front cover photo credits. Earth: Henrik Jonsson/iStockphoto. Insets, left to right: Streeter Lecka—Getty Images; NASA—JPL; Brendan Smialowski—AFP—Getty Images; Chip Somodevilla—Getty Images; AFP—Getty Images; Andreas Solaro—AFP—Getty Images. Back cover photo credits. Left to right: Alex Wong—Getty Images; Clive Brunskill—Getty Images; Kevork Djansezian—Getty Images; Scott Olson—Getty Images; 20th Century Fox—Moviepix—Getty Images

ISBN-10: 1-61893-019-2; ISBN-13: 978-1-61893-019-4  Hardcover
ISBN-10: 1-60320-940-9; ISBN-13: 978-1-60320-940-3  Paperback
International Standard Serial Number: 0073-7860

No part of this work may be reproduced or utilized in any form or by any means, electronic or mechanical, including photocopying, recording, or by any information storage and retrieval system, without permission in writing from the publisher.

ENCYCLOPÆDIA BRITANNICA ALMANAC 2013

Britannica.com may be accessed on the Internet at http://www.britannica.com. For information on group and bulk sales, please send an e-mail to books@eb.com.

*(Trademark Reg. U.S. Pat. Off.) Printed in U.S.A.*

If you would like to order any of our hardcover Collector's Edition books, please call us at 1-800-327-6388 (Monday through Friday, 7:00 A.M.–8:00 P.M. or Saturday, 7:00 A.M.–6:00 P.M. Central Time).

## Learning That Works

*by Joe Klein, TIME*

Clyde McBride is one of those everyday saints who, without much fanfare, go about the work of changing, and sometimes saving, the lives of children. He teaches agricultural science on the Navajo reservation in Kayenta AZ. He's a memorable-looking fellow, with his cowboy hat, horsehide tie, and a body like a giant sack of flour perched on tiny toothpick legs. His most notable characteristic, though, is his persistence. When a new school superintendent arrived in town a few years ago, McBride parked himself on the guy's doorstep. "He came in and gave me the 'I have a dream' speech," says superintendent Harry Martin. "I told him I'd think about it, but he wouldn't let me think about it. He was bugging me three, four times a week about it."

McBride's dream was a state-of-the-art agricultural-sciences building with two veterinary operating theaters—one for small animals and one for large ones—to train Navajo kids to be veterinary aides and technicians and perhaps even to start a few of them down the road to becoming veterinarians. "I thought it was a waste of money and time," Martin told me. "I'm an old English teacher. I was very skeptical about vocational education. We needed to be drilling them on basic skills. But McBride said he'd make a believer out of me. And he did."

Two years later, with the US$2.4 million agricultural-and-technical-sciences building up and running, Martin says, "It's without doubt the best program we have. It's an alternative way to teach them math, science and reading. They love it. They're attentive, working hard, hands on."

McBride imports veterinarians from around the country to visit the reservation and work with the 226 students, who assist in both operating theaters, prepping animals for surgery and learning how to suture, draw blood, and give injections. The veterinary clinic has become a valued resource on the reservation, but more than that, the academic results have been spectacular. "Nearly every one of these kids passed the state comprehensive test we give to 17-year-olds in Arizona," Martin told me. "Less than about 40% of my non-vocational-education students passed."

### The Bad Old Days

Vocational education used to be where you sent the dumb kids or the supposed misfits who weren't suited for classroom learning. It began to fall out of fashion about 40 years ago, in part because it became a civil rights issue: voc-ed was seen as a form of segregation, a convenient dumping ground for minority kids in Northern cities. "That was a real problem," former New York City schools chancellor Joel Klein told me. "And the voc-ed programs were pretty awful. They weren't training the kids for specific jobs or for certified skills. It really was a waste of time and money."

Unfortunately, the education establishment's response to the voc-ed problem only made things worse. Over time, it morphed into the theology that every child should go to college (a four-year liberal-arts college at that) and therefore every child should be required to pursue a college-prep course in high school. The results have been awful. High school dropout rates continue to be a national embarrassment. And most high school graduates are not prepared for the world of work. The unemployment rate for recent high school graduates who are not in school is a stratospheric 33%. The results for even those who go on to higher education are brutal: four-year colleges graduate only about 40% of the students who start them, and two-year community colleges graduate less than that, about 23%.

"College for everyone has become a matter of political correctness," says Diane Ravitch, a professor of education at New York University. "But according to the Bureau of Labor Statistics, less than a quarter of new job openings will require a bachelor of arts degree. We're not training our students for the jobs that actually exist." Meanwhile, the US has begun to run out of welders, glaziers, and auto mechanics—the people who actually keep the place running.

In Arizona and more than a few other states, that is beginning to change. Indeed, the old notion of vocational education has been stood on its head. It's now called career and technical education (CTE), and it has become a pathway that even some college-bound advanced-placement students are pursuing. About 27% of the students in Arizona opt for the tech-ed path, and they are more likely to score higher on the state's aptitude tests, graduate from high school, and go on to higher education than those who don't. "It's not rocket science," says Sally Downey, superintendent of the spectacular East Valley Institute of Technology in Mesa AZ, 98.5% of whose students graduate from high school. "It's just finding something they like and teaching it to them with rigor."

Actually, it's a bit more than that: it's developing training programs that lead to jobs or recognized certification, often in partnership with local businesses. The vehicles in the auto shop at East Valley, for example, look a lot different from the old jalopies that kids in my high school used to work on. There are 40 late-model cars and the latest in diagnostic equipment, donated by Phoenix auto dealers, who are desperate for trained technicians. "If you can master the computer-science and electronic components," Downey says, "you can make over US$100,000 a year as an auto mechanic."

Arizona has another, rather unusual advantage. Its state education superintendent, John Huppenthal, went to high school in Tucson on the voc-ed track. "It was considered the path for losers, but I didn't know any better," says Huppenthal, a Republican who was elected to the statewide post. "I came from a family of machinists. I didn't know anybody who'd gone to college, and I was happy in wood shop. I remember making a chess set, a very complicated project that really made mathematics come alive for me." He also happened to be a state-champion wrestler with pretty good test scores, and his coach encouraged him to study engineering at Northern Arizona University. "I really believe that some form of CTE is essential for a world-class education," he says. "Most students respond better to a three-dimensional learning process. It's easier to learn engineering by actually building a house—which my family did when I was a kid, by the way—than sitting in a classroom figuring out the process in the abstract. Some students can respond to two-dimensional learning, but most respond better when it's hands on. Every surgeon needs to know how to sew, saw and drill."

Precise statistics are sparse; it's difficult to keep track of students after they leave high school. But Carolyn Warner, a former Arizona schools chancellor, says tech-track students "are more focused, so they're more likely to graduate from two- and four-year colleges. Those who graduate from high school with a certificate technical expertise in a field like auto repair or welding are certainly more likely to find jobs."

Still, Huppenthal finds vocational school is a tough sell to the state's education establishment. "It doesn't have the prestige of a college-prep course," he says, "and it costs a lot more than two-dimensional education to do it right." Traditionally, Democrats have tended to be opposed on ideological grounds. They're the strongest believers in college for everyone. Republicans are reluctant to spend the money on state-of-the-art equipment like the veterinary center on the Navajo reservation, although some concede that CTE programs that prepare students for actual jobs are a good idea. "It's like walking in a hurricane," says Huppenthal. "You know where you want to be going, but the winds keep pushing you off course."

## Battling False Conceptions

Yet if the winds of change are blowing, CTE is beginning to produce its own weather systems—human tornadoes like McBride and Downey, the superintendent at East Valley, who is smart and extremely pushy, constantly working the business community in Phoenix for help in starting training programs. There are 28 programs on her campus, with more coming. There are firefighter, police, and EMT programs; a state-of-the-art kitchen for culinary-services training; and welding (which can pay US$48 per hour), aeronautics, radio-station, marketing, and massage-therapy instruction. "We have a lot of resorts around here," Downey explains, "and our students often work part-time as masseurs to earn money for college."

Almost all of these courses lead to professional certificates in addition to high school diplomas, and many of the students are trained by employers for needed technical specialties. None of her 3,200 students are full-time. They spend half a day, usually afternoons, at East Valley and receive academic training at 35 different home high schools in the mornings.

"Look at this," Downey says as she shows me a fully stocked medical laboratory. "We got US$1.5 million from Veterans Affairs to run a program for surgical assistants, and they gave us a teacher to teach it." The premedical and nursing students here are dressed in scrubs. Downey barges into a classroom and begins polling the students. "How many of you are going on to some form of higher education?" Almost everyone's hand goes up. "How many of you are taking advanced-placement programs in your home high schools?" A scattering of hands. "How many of you have had to make sacrifices to come here?" Again, a forest of hands. Most of the sacrifices involve hours of travel and having to give up ex-

tracurricular activities. "And how many of you were discouraged from doing this by your local high schools?" About half. The home high schools tend to have the standard biases against vocational education—that it's a waste of time, that it takes away from the academic experience.

"The public school system also has a civic purpose," says Jonathan Zimmerman, an education historian at New York University, citing a common academic argument against vocational education. "You're not just preparing people to work. You're preparing people to be citizens. In a democracy, you need citizens who can think critically." But people with jobs, especially skilled jobs, tend to be better citizens than those without them. And the teamwork involved in the training programs at East Valley and on the Navajo reservation tends to help create a sense of community.

"In my home high school, you're sitting in a room with 30 other students who don't care, trying to pay attention to a teacher who doesn't care," says Aaron Pietryga, who is training to become a firefighter. "But [East Valley] is like my family. Most of the kids at my home school don't have any idea what I'm doing in the afternoon, and when I explain it to them, they say, 'Wow, you're doing all that cool stuff, and you're going to college. Why didn't I know about that?'"

## "Let Them Drink"

On a recent chilly morning at the Navajo reservation, McBride was giving Huppenthal and me a hands-on tour of his veterinary facility. Husband-and-wife veterinarians from Pittsburgh had volunteered their services for a few days and were spaying a dog in the small-animal operating theater, with the help of students in blue surgical scrubs. "They're very good," says Sharon Wirtz, one of the vets. "They have an exceptional feel for this, especially with the larger animals," like sheep and horses. Students were suturing bananas and injecting oranges with red dye for practice. Recently a pack of wild dogs attacked some sheep on the reservation, and McBride took some students to care for them. "Some of these kids suture better than I do," he says. "It brings tears to my eyes."

But his real triumph wasn't in teaching the Navajo the technical skills. These students also knew how to make an impression; they had learned the soft skills necessary to be good employees. They looked you in the eye, introduced themselves, and shook your hand (which was universally true at East Valley as well). This was striking, given the history of depression and despair on the reservation. "These kids are thirsty. All you've got to do," McBride says, eyes brimming, "is let them drink.

Fast-growing fields that do not require a bachelor's degree: likely growth in demand, 2012 to 2020.

| | |
|---|---|
| Masonry helpers | 60% |
| Veterinary technicians | 52% |
| Iron/rebar workers | 49% |
| Physical-therapy assistants | 46% |
| Medical sonographers | 44% |
| Dental hygienists | 38% |
| Radiology technicians | 28% |
| Registered nurses | 26% |

Source: Bureau of Labor Statistics

# E-Readers and Tablets: The New Frontier in Technology

*by Michael Ray*

Two high-tech items once regarded as the playthings of early gadget adopters and the technorati had clearly broken into the mainstream in 2011. Electronic reading devices, or e-readers, and tablet computers were ubiquitous throughout the year, with the market's two leading products—the Amazon Kindle and the Apple iPad—posting especially impressive numbers. In March, Apple Inc. CEO Steve Jobs returned from a medical leave of absence to unveil the iPad 2, a slimmer, faster model of the popular tablet. Debuting less than a year after its predecessor had essentially created the tablet computer market, the iPad 2 incorporated front and rear cameras for the capturing of video and still images, an enhancement that allowed it to perform as an all-in-one video-conferencing device. Both the iPad and the iPad 2 sold well in spite of a soft global economy—consumers purchased more than 25 million of the devices within the first nine months of the year, and they were available in more than 90 countries.

Tablets on the whole were estimated to represent about 15% of the personal computing market in 2011, an increase of more than 300% over the previous year and a bright spot in an otherwise sluggish sales period for computer hardware. This was outstanding news for Apple, and the company posted a string of record-setting quarterly earning statements that put it on track to easily surpass US$100 billion in revenue for the year. Such attractive numbers drew a host of imitators to the burgeoning tablet market, but they did little more than compete for second place behind the iPad juggernaut. Hewlett-Packard debuted its Touchpad tablet with much fanfare in July only to discontinue it a month later. BlackBerry manufacturer Research in Motion and mobile phone giant Motorola fared little better with their tablet offerings, which approached the iPad in price but not in popularity. In terms of quality, only Sony Corp.'s Tablet S and Samsung's Galaxy Tab series could credibly compete with the iPad, but their sales remained a dim shadow of Apple's throughout the year.

Compared with the iPad, the Kindle, which debuted in 2007, was an established presence in the consumer electronics market. Improvements to Amazon's e-reader had made it progressively lighter and sturdier, and later models possessed a longer battery life and antiglare screens that made reading easier in less-than-ideal lighting conditions. Seeking to capture market share at the expense of per-unit sales returns, Amazon slashed prices on its entry-level Kindles, with the cheapest models dipping below the psychologically significant US$100-price point. Amazon sought to make up for the low (or even negative) profit margins on these units through the sale of content at Amazon.com's online store. This tactic appeared to bear fruit; Amazon in May announced that it currently sold more Kindle titles than traditional hardcover and softcover books combined. Analysts estimated that more than 300 million Kindle e-books were sold in 2011 alone, and that figure was projected to more than double in 2012. The Amazon Web site offered nearly one million titles in the proprietary Kindle format, and American Kindle owners could borrow virtual books from more than 10,000 public libraries through the OverDrive distribution service.

Amazon-created applications had previously allowed iPhone and iPad owners to read Kindle titles on their Apple devices, but Amazon staked its own claim on the Apple-dominated tablet market in November with the debut of the Kindle Fire. Bowing with a price point below US$200, the Fire featured a roughly 18-cm (7-in) color LCD touchscreen and an extensive library of Amazon-supplied media content. Interest in the device was so intense that Amazon registered more than 2,000 presales per hour in the weeks prior to its release. Although it was dubbed an "iPad killer" by some in the media, it lacked many of the features that defined a true tablet computer,

> *Amazon in May announced that it currently sold more Kindle titles than traditional hardcover and softcover books combined.*

leading critics to dub it a "tablet lite." Brick-and-mortar bookseller Barnes & Noble challenged Amazon in the color e-reader market with its Nook Tablet. Although more expensive than the Fire, it featured more storage and a crisper display than Amazon's offering. Released within days of each other, both devices operated on Google's Android operating system platform, and each made use of Wi-Fi technology to allow Web surfing and the streaming of audio and video content (indeed, the Fire's limited storage space was mitigated by its extensive reliance on Internet-based "cloud" technology to provide users with virtual storage). As the Fire and the Nook were a fraction of the cost of even a first-generation iPad, the two devices came to define the entry-level tablet market. They also fueled a marketing war between Amazon and Barnes & Noble as the two retailers attempted to secure exclusive licensing agreements with publishers and application developers. One notable deal, which granted Amazon the exclusive right to distribute the digital versions of 100 of DC Comics' most popular graphic novels, led Barnes & Noble to pull the physical copies of the books from its shelves. Weeks later Barnes & Noble announced a partnership with DC rival Marvel Comics. The tug-of-war demonstrated not only the commitment of Amazon and Barnes & Noble to their respective devices but also the desire of traditional publishers to see their products prominently displayed in the emerging e-book and tablet paradigm.

*Michael Ray is an Assistant Editor for Encyclopædia Britannica.*

# The Culmination of the US Space Shuttle Program

*by John M. Logsdon*

On 21 Jul 2011, the 30-year-old US space shuttle program reached its end when the final shuttle, *Atlantis*, landed at NASA's Kennedy Space Center after having concluded a 12-day mission. It was the 135th launch in a flight program that began with the launch of the first space shuttle on 12 Apr 1981 and comprised four test flights, 129 operational missions, and two flights that were cut short by catastrophic accidents, each resulting in the death of the seven-person crew. Though the space shuttle program achieved significant accomplishments, a number of promises remained unfulfilled.

Each space shuttle consisted of three elements: the shuttle orbiter, the winged vehicle that accelerated into orbit, carried out its mission, and then glided to a runway landing; the external tank, the large cigar-shaped body that carried the system's extremely cold liquid hydrogen and liquid oxygen fuel and burned up as it reentered the atmosphere after it was jettisoned a few minutes after liftoff; and two solid rocket boosters that attached to the sides of the external tank and provided most of the lifting power during the first two minutes after launch, after which they separated and fell into the ocean, from which they were recovered to be refurbished and reused. After the solid rockets were jettisoned, three main engines on the rear of the orbiter accelerated the orbiter to its orbital speed of 28,000 km/hr (17,500 mph).

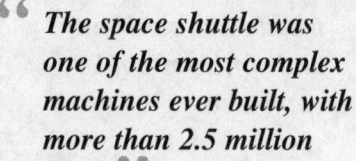

> **The space shuttle was one of the most complex machines ever built, with more than 2.5 million parts.**

Six shuttle orbiters were built. The first, *Enterprise,* was a test vehicle not intended for space travel. On the basis of a letter-writing campaign, it was named after the spacecraft in the television series *Star Trek.* The other orbiters were named after research ships. The first to fly, *Columbia,* engaged in 27 successful missions before breaking up on reentry on 1 Feb 2003. A piece of the external tank's insulation foam had punched a hole in the orbiter's wing two minutes after launch; this allowed the heat of reentry 16 days later to melt the wing's internal structure. The next, *Challenger,* flew nine missions before it broke up 73 seconds after launch on 28 Jan 1986, after its fuel ignited as a solid rocket booster failed because of a faulty rubber O-ring. *Discovery* flew the most, completing 39 missions between 1984 and 2011; *Atlantis* performed 33 missions, beginning in 1985, including the final shuttle mission in July 2011. *Endeavour* replaced *Challenger* and had 25 flights between 1992 and 2011. The five orbiters carried 355 different people (306 men and 49 women) from the US and 15 other countries into orbit; many of those people made multiple trips to space.

The space shuttle was one of the most complex machines ever built, with more than 2.5 million parts. The shuttle orbiter was 37 m (122 ft) long and had a wingspan of 24 m (78 ft); its payload bay measured 5 × 18 m (15 × 60 ft). Its heaviest payload, the Chandra X-ray Observatory and its upper stage and support equipment (launched in 1999), weighed

some 25 tons at launch. When attached to its external tank, the shuttle stood 56 m (184 ft) high; it weighed up to 2 million kg (4.5 million lb) on liftoff. The shuttle could fly only to low Earth orbit, ranging from 185 to 640 km (115 to 400 mi) above the planet. On most missions it carried a crew of seven. Prior to the *Challenger* accident, the shuttle was thought safe enough to carry passengers such as politicians and a teacher.

The space shuttle, with its large payload bay, orbital maneuvering capability, and robotic arm, was capable of many different operations in space. It carried various spacecraft, including communications satellites and probes to Jupiter and Venus, to Earth orbit for launch to their final orbits. The shuttle served as an orbiting laboratory, carrying out many onboard experiments. It retrieved satellites that were launched into incorrect orbits and returned them to Earth for relaunch. It also carried out classified missions for the national security community.

Among the space shuttle's most notable achievements were:

- Five missions to the Hubble Space Telescope—the first one to install the corrective optics that allowed Hubble to operate at full capability despite a misshapen primary mirror and the others to give it additional capabilities and to extend its life
- Nine dockings (1995–98) with the Russian space station Mir as a first step in US-Russian cooperation in human spaceflight
- Thirty-seven flights between 1998 and 2011 to assemble and provision the International Space Station

The space shuttle set a precedent for international cooperation in human spaceflight. Canada contributed the robotic arm, and Europe provided a small laboratory—Spacelab—that could be carried in the shuttle's payload bay.

Despite these significant accomplishments, the space shuttle program did not fulfill many of the promises made by its proponents to gain program approval. When Pres. Richard Nixon announced in 1972 that the US would develop the shuttle, he envisioned that the reusable vehicle would "revolutionize transportation into near space, by routinizing it." The shuttle was very difficult to operate safely, however. It remained experimental, and its complexity carried inherent safety risks. In 1972 NASA estimated that a shuttle mission would cost US$10.5 million (US$54.7 million in 2010 dollars); the average cost was US$775 million in 2010 dollars. The total shuttle program cost through development and 135 flights was US$113.7 billion (US$209.1 billion in 2010 dollars, or US$1.55 billion per flight). The shuttle was projected to fly as many as 55 missions annually, but the most shuttle launches in one year (1985) turned out to be nine. When the space shuttle was retired, there was not an immediate replacement for its crew-carrying capability.

# The Arab Spring: The End of the Beginning

*by Mark Almond*

No one could say for certain what Tunisian street vendor Mohamed Bouazizi was thinking when he set fire to himself on 17 Dec 2010, but he probably could not have imagined that his action would spark in his own country a Jasmine Revolution, which in 2011 evolved into a wider revolt that became known throughout the world as the Arab Spring. His self-immolation galvanized citizens in North Africa and the Middle East to protest against government repression and corruption and in the process bring about the downfall of three heads of state (Tunisia, Egypt, and Libya). As reports of his desperate act soon spread far beyond Tunisia, various media—satellite television news, mobile phones, and social networking Web sites—turned a local suicide viral. What made Bouazizi's self-destructive response to an alleged shakedown by a local policewoman so electrifying was the sense among residents across the Arab world that it could have happened to them.

**The Unrest.** Even prior to Bouazizi's death, public protests had erupted in Tunisia. Local corruption as well as rumors of corruption at the top echelons of the government combined to destabilize the 23-year-old regime of Pres. Zine al-Abidine Ben Ali. Like other de facto presidents for life, Ben Ali favored family members' involvement in government affairs. The Trabelsi extended family of his wife, Leila, reportedly had fingers in every pie, and this association had corroded the authority of the regime. Within a month of Bouazizi's lighting himself on fire, Ben Ali and his family had fled into exile. This development broke the decadeslong logjam in the Arab world, as some of the world's longest-serving rulers suddenly faced real challenges to their leadership. Only a few months earlier in Surt, Libya, Muammar al-Qaddafi, in power there since 1969, had hosted Ben Ali, along with Egyptian Pres. Hosni Mubarak (head of state since 1981) and Yemeni Pres. ʻAli ʻAbd Allah Salih (in power since 1978).

The contrast between the aging rulers and their very young populace was striking. Listening to the dreary litany of praise and the rambling speeches of a "leader for life" was becoming intolerable for teenagers and twentysomethings whose parents had heard the same voice addressing them at that age. Demographic pressure was a constant from Morocco to Yemen, but inside the regimes discontent with family rule was growing. The very longevity of Arab leaders made the succession issue increasingly urgent. Older loyalists were irritated by the emergence of presidential sons, who not only were much younger than they were but also seemed to want to combine the pleasures of a playboy lifestyle with an accelerated promotion to the top.

What proved disastrous for the rulers was the unwillingness of previously loyal generals to deploy tanks against protesters in a crisis. Mubarak had faced serious protests prior to late January 2011, but he had never lacked tools of repression. That month, however, his longtime defense minister, Mohamed Hussein Tantawi, turned against Mubarak and sent tanks to Cairo's Tahrir Square to protect demonstrators from Mubarak's police. The military's refusal to back Mubarak was rooted in tensions over Mubarak's grooming of his son Gamal as his successor as well as a push by Gamal's friends to advance their business interests at the expense of the Egyptian army's vast economic empire.

Both Ben Ali and Mubarak had alienated the generals by fostering their own clans, especially by promoting the prospect of turning the authoritarian republic into a dynastic regime by passing the presidency to a son. Qaddafi's fostering of his son Sayf al-Islam as heir apparent turned his old comrades in arms, notably Minister of the Interior Abdel Fattah Younis, into enemies when the crisis broke out in Libya only a week after the fall of Mubarak on 11 February.

The prolonged violence in Libya, Syria, and Yemen reflected the role of clan loyalties and religious affiliation in helping to entrench regimes that faced considerable opposition. Though Qaddafi's was the weakest—owing to his eccentric rule that had left him without an effective military—defectors from his ramshackle forces had little to rely on to organize resistance to him.

> **His self-immolation galvanized citizens in North Africa and the Middle East to protest against government repression and corruption....**

Without NATO intervention, Qaddafi would probably have retained control over Libya, but his flamboyant televised threats to pursue the rebels in Benghazi "*zanga zanga*" ("from alley to alley") backfired because they raised the spectre in the Western media of a massacre. Already unpopular with the other members of the Arab League—and also with Iran for sectarian reasons—Qaddafi had no friends in the international community. When Libyan diplomats at the UN peeled away and called on the international community to step in, France and Britain in particular were ready to heed calls for "humanitarian intervention."

NATO, aware of the primitive level of Qaddafi's armaments and seeing evidence of desertion by senior figures such as Younis, used air power to protect Libyan civilians from Qaddafi's loyalists. Though NATO had confidence that Qaddafi's regime was already imploding, its combined forces, local rebels, and special forces from Arab states took from mid-March until late August to capture the capital, Tripoli. It was another two months before NATO airstrikes drove Qaddafi out of his final stronghold—his birthplace, Surt—and to a grisly fate at the hands of rebel forces. The prolonged nature of the struggle for power in Libya indicated that Qaddafi had a significant minority of support and that many Libyans stood aside unsure of whom to support. Infighting among Qaddafi's enemies raised the specter of civil war between them once the "Brother Leader" was gone. Libya lacked the religious mosaic of a country such as Syria. Libya's regional and tribal divisions meant that rivalries among

Qaddafi's opponents were pronounced even as they struggled against his regime.

Protests in Syria began soon after the Libyan crisis turned into an armed conflict. Although Syrian Pres. Bashar al-Assad's uncle Rif'at played the role of regime insider-turned-dissident from his exile in London, few Syrians respected the man whom many held responsible for having directed the brutal suppression of the uprising in Hamah some 30 years earlier. The absence of senior regime defectors meant that the Syrian regime maintained effective coordination over the state machine, whereas Qaddafi had relied on ad-hoc leadership by his sons, clan members, and a few mercenaries.

Although the West had deep security and economic ties in the Gulf states, it chose not to exert hard pressure on monarchies there to move toward democracy. When Bahrain's Sunni monarchy came under pressure from largely Shi'ite pro-democracy activists imitating the tactics employed by Egyptian demonstrators in Tahrir Square, it received active military support from Saudi forces. Saudi Arabia, which had a restive Shi'ite population in its eastern province, saw a risk of spillover from Bahrain's Shi'ite majority if protests there succeeded. The fact that Bahrain hosted the US 5th Fleet and was an ally against Iran led US politicians to downplay the repression there and to emphasize King Hamad ibn 'Isa al-Khalifah's public declarations in favor of reform rather than the heavy hand of his security forces.

The Gulf states supported opposition to the would-be republican dynasts but carefully protected their own monarchies. Oil and gas revenues gave them the resources to buy social peace—at least in the short term. Although Qatar's emir, Sheikh Hamad ibn Khalifah Al Thani, both funded the al-Jazeera satellite TV network (its reports stimulated more protests) and sent troops to support the rebellion against Qaddafi, at home he offered only to "consult" his own subjects on government policy. The fall of the secular dictators Ben Ali and Mubarak left the Sunni Gulf monarchs in a much stronger position in the Arab League, which they used to legitimize calls for intervention against Libya and sanctions on Syria.

**Religious Overtones.** The motive for the oil-rich monarchs to promote political change seemed to have been less political than religious. Saudi and Qatari financial backing and satellite media openly promoted political parties associated with the Muslim Brotherhood in North Africa and Syria. Their hope, presumably, that the triumph of such parties in any new democracy would cement a Saudi-style Islamic social order was one of the reasons secular people, non-Muslim religious minorities, and Shi'ites reluctantly backed regimes that were similar to that of Assad's.

The reluctance of the Shi'ite-led Iraqi government to follow its US ally in denouncing the Assad regime baffled Washington. It was not just that prominent Iraqis from the prime minister down were given asylum in Syria prior to 2003 as refugees escaping Iraqi leader Saddam Hussein. The main enemies of the post-Saddam democracy in Iraq were precisely the armed Sunni Muslim radicals whom Baghdad saw as the vanguard of the anti-Assad movement. Given that Syria's Alawites were seen in the same negative light by Sunnis as other Shi'ites—and were also allies of Iran—the regional struggle for power between the Wahhabi Sunni regime in Saudi Arabia and the Shi'ite

Islamic Republic of Iran was threatening to erupt into a regional religious civil war.

The proponents of a secular democracy in Syria as the alternative to the secular Ba'thist dictatorship led by the Alawite Assad clan appeared to be hopelessly squeezed between the extremes. Other religious minorities, such as Christians and Druze, seemed to fear a Muslim Brotherhood regime and remained loyal to Assad. Over the border in Lebanon, an alliance made up of Shi'ite Hezbollah, Christians, and Druze had a parliamentary majority and rejected Arab League sanctions on Syria.

The other major regional player was Turkey. After initially denouncing foreign intervention, Turkish Prime Minister Recep Tayyip Erdogan became a vocal critic of Qaddafi's regime and a proponent of NATO intervention. Erdogan also became fiercely critical of Assad's regime. Erdogan's Justice and Development Party (AKP) was widely seen as the model for an Islamic democratic movement in the Arab world. The AKP's electoral successes since 2002 were based on its successful handling of the economy (even during a worldwide crisis), and its characterization as an Islamic party gave it particular appeal to the religious-based opposition to secular dictatorships in the Arab world. The AKP model seemed to offer a reassuring mix of constitutional government, economic competence, and respect for the religious sentiments of the majority.

Tensions between Christian Copts and Muslims became acute in 2011 after Mubarak's fall. Although the crowds in Tahrir Square and Alexandria included prominent Coptic supporters of democratization, so-called Salafists—or Wahhabi extremist groups—denounced them as an alien and un-Islamic element. Disputes over new church-building projects spiraled out of control into street clashes, with more than 30 people killed in October.

**Outlook.** Although it was probably too early to give a final verdict on the meaning of the Arab Spring, it was clear that it reenergized political engagement in the region, both by many of the people who actually lived there and by powerful actors such as the US and its NATO allies. Given the region's oil reserves and the tensions surrounding Arab-Israeli and Arab-Iranian relations, the importance of the permutations of the eventual outcome could not be exaggerated.

In 2011, decades of authoritarian stability in the Arab world came to an end. Three alternatives beckoned: the advance of democracy, a return to another kind of authoritarian regime, or chaos. The teeming population of frustrated young people had had their ambitions and hopes raised, but the economic sources of their frustration had worsened in the previous 12 months. Clan and religious structures might prove stronger than the appeal of new nationwide democratic arrangements. The very drama of political revolution has worsened the economies, especially in Egypt and Tunisia, which are highly dependent on tourism and foreign investment. Past new democratic dawns had floundered when economic downturns destroyed the consensus for change. Successful Muslim democracies, such as Turkey and Malaysia, had enjoyed decades of peace to build up their economic foundations. Impatience for rapid change on all fronts after decades of authoritarian immobility could undermine the hopes of the Arab Spring, ironically, because it expressed the popular mood for complete change—now.

*Mark Almond is a Visiting Professor in International Relations at Bilkent University, Ankara, Turkey, and a member of the University of Oxford's History Faculty.*

# Chronology, July 2011–June 2012

*A day-by-day listing of important and interesting events, adapted from Britannica Book of the Year. See also Disasters.*

## July 2011

**1 Jul** An Exxon Mobil oil pipeline near Billings MT ruptures, spilling as much as 1,000 bbl of oil into the flooding Yellowstone River.

▸ The Las Conchas wildfire in New Mexico, the largest in the state's history, is reported to have consumed more than 41,700 ha (103,000 ac) and to be only 3% contained.

▸ Proposed constitutional changes that slightly liberalize the government in Morocco are overwhelmingly approved in a popular referendum.

**2 Jul** Finance ministers of the euro-zone countries announce that the next installment of aid for Greece, €12 billion (US$17.4 billion), will be released.

▸ In an upset, Petra Kvitova of the Czech Republic defeats Russian Mariya Sharapova to take her first All-England (Wimbledon) women's tennis championship; the following day Novak Djokovic of Serbia wins the men's title for the first time when he defeats Rafael Nadal of Spain.

**3 Jul** In legislative elections in Thailand, the For Thais party, headed by Yingluck Shinawatra, sister of deposed prime minister Thaksin Shinawatra, wins in a landslide.

**4 Jul** In response to the growing threat of famine in North Korea, the European Union announces the release of US$14.5 million in emergency food aid.

▸ Thailand's victorious For Thais party announces that it has formed a coalition with four other parties, and the country's military declares that it will not intervene in the election results.

**5 Jul** In a Florida case that has riveted the public, Casey Anthony is found not guilty of the murder of her daughter, Caylee, who disappeared in 2008 at the age of two and whose decomposed body was found in December of that year; the public is outraged.

▸ Officials in China acknowledge that an oil spill from an offshore drilling rig in the Bohai Sea that occurred in early June and was first officially revealed on 1 July has spread over 830 sq km (320 sq mi).

**6 Jul** Rebels in Libya take control of the town of Qawalish from government forces, while the battle for Misurata continues.

▸ The International Olympic Committee president, Jacques Rogge, announces the selection of P'yongch'ang (Pyeongchang), South Korea, as the location of the Winter Games of 2018.

**7 Jul** News Corp. announces that it is shutting down the popular British tabloid *The News of the World,* which is at the center of a burgeoning phone-hacking scandal.

▸ The US Environmental Protection Agency issues new rules to go into effect in 2012 to reduce particulate emissions from power plants in 28 states that cause smog and acid rain.

**8 Jul** The US Department of Labor reports that the unemployment rate in June rose to 9.2% and that the economy's growth was anemic, with only 18,000 nonfarm jobs added.

▸ The space shuttle *Atlantis,* carrying astronauts Chris Ferguson, Doug Hurley, Doug Magnus, and Rex Walheim, takes off on the final space shuttle mission.

**9 Jul** In a ceremony in the capital city of Juba, the new country of South Sudan formally becomes independent, and Salva Kiir Mayardit is sworn in as president; the first country to recognize it is Sudan.

**10 Jul** Russia wins the Fédération Internationale de Volleyball World League championship in men's volleyball in Gdansk, Poland, defeating Brazil to take its second World League title.

**11 Jul** Organized groups of supporters of Syria's government attack the American and French embassies in Damascus; the US and France have both expressed support for antigovernment protesters.

▸ Ryu So-Yeon of South Korea scores a three-stroke victory over her countrywoman Seo Hee-Kyung in a three-hole playoff to win the US Women's Open golf tournament in Colorado Springs CO.

**12 Jul** US Pres. Barack Obama presents the Medal of Honor to Sgt. First Class Leroy Arthur Petry, who has served two combat tours in Iraq and six in Afghanistan, for his bravery in a battle in Afghanistan in 2008.

**13 Jul** The embattled News Corp. announces the withdrawal of its vaunted bid to buy full control of the satellite television company British Sky Broadcasting, known as BSkyB.

**14 Jul** A plan to ask the United Nations to admit Palestine as a full member is approved by the Arab League.

▸ South Sudan becomes the 193rd member of the United Nations.

**15 Jul** The United States recognizes the rebel Transitional National Council as the legitimate government of Libya.

**16 Jul** US Pres. Barack Obama meets privately in the White House with the Dalai Lama, the spiritual leader of Tibet, despite objections from China.

**17 Jul** It is reported that the movie *Harry Potter and the Deathly Hallows: Part 2* took in US$168.6 million in its opening weekend, surpassing *The Dark Knight*'s ticket sales in 2008 to set a new US record.

▸ Japan beats the US 3–1 on penalty kicks to win the FIFA Women's World Cup in association football (soccer).

▸ Darren Clarke of Northern Ireland defeats American golfers Phil Mickelson and Dustin Johnson by three strokes to win the British Open golf tournament at Royal St. George's in Sandwich, England.

**18 Jul** US Pres. Barack Obama nominates Richard Cordray, formerly attorney general of Ohio, to head the new Consumer Financial Protection Bureau, which begins operations three days later.

**19 Jul** In Homs, Syria, government forces open fire on funeral processions for the 10 protesters who were killed the previous day; at least 15 people are killed.

**20 Jul** Egypt's interim government sets out a complex plan for legislative elections to take place in the fall; the vote will occur in several stages, and half the members will be elected in a winner-take-all system and half in a proportional-representation system.

**21 Jul** The leaders of the member countries of the euro zone agree on an extensive plan to rescue the economy of Greece; the plan will also offer debt relief to both Ireland and Portugal.

▸ The space shuttle program comes to an end with the landing at Kennedy Space Center in Florida of *Atlantis* after the completion of its final mission.

**22 Jul** In Norway a powerful car bomb damages buildings in Oslo and kills 7 people, and hours later at a Labour Party youth summer camp on the island of Utoya, a man guns down at least 68 people.

▸ Mission scientists for NASA announce that the Mars Science Laboratory, a rover known as Curiosity, will have as its destination the Gale Crater, near the planet's equator; the rover is scheduled to launch later in 2011 and to reach Mars in August 2012.

**23 Jul** Anders Behring Breivik, described as a right-wing fundamentalist Christian who abhors multiculturalism, is charged in Norway with both the massacre on Utoya Island and the bombing in Oslo.

---

QUOTE OF THE MONTH

❝ *[He] turned a youth paradise into hell.* ❞

—Norwegian Prime Minister Jens Stoltenberg, describing the previous day's massacre at a youth camp on Utoya Island, 23 July

---

**24 Jul** In Argentina, Uruguay defeats Paraguay 3–0 to win its record 15th Copa América, the South American championship in association football (soccer).

▸ Australian cyclist Cadel Evans wins the Tour de France.

**25 Jul** The Vatican recalls its ambassador to Ireland in response to an Irish government report that said, among other things, that the Vatican had encouraged Roman Catholic clergy to ignore guidelines adopted in 1996 that included mandatory reporting of sexual abuse of children by clergy members to civil authorities.

**26 Jul** The Millennium Challenge Corporation, a US government agency, freezes a planned US$350 million grant to Malawi because of that government's reaction to recent protests.

**27 Jul** The British government recognizes the rebel National Transitional Council as the legitimate government of Libya and expels Libyan diplomats in London representing the current government.

**28 Jul** At the FINA swimming world championships in Shanghai, American Ryan Lochte sets a new world record in the men's 200-m individual medley of 1 min 54 sec; it is the first world record achieved since the banning of high-tech swimming suits in January 2010.

**29 Jul** The US Department of Commerce issues revised figures showing that GDP grew at a rate of 0.4% in the first fiscal quarter of 2011 and 1.3% in the second quarter and that the 2008–09 recession had been deeper than earlier figures indicated.

▸ With the chief executives of the major automobile manufacturers by his side, US Pres. Barack Obama announces new rules for gas mileage that will require mileage in new cars to improve incrementally to reach an average fuel efficiency of 54.5 mi per gal by 2025.

**30 Jul** In Roses, Spain, elBulli, regarded as one of the top restaurants in the world and a lodestar in contemporary cuisine, serves its final meal; it is expected to open as a foundation for experimental cooking in 2014.

**31 Jul** After weeks of brinksmanship, US congressional leaders and Pres. Barack Obama reach an accord on a framework for a budget deal that Republican leaders require before agreeing to increase the government's borrowing limit.

▸ Taiwanese golfer Yani Tseng captures the Women's British Open golf tournament for the second consecutive year with a four-stroke win over American Brittany Lang.

# August 2011

**1 Aug** A report is published online by a team of astronomers who, with the use of the Herschel space telescope, became the first to see an oxygen molecule (consisting of two oxygen atoms joined by a double bond) in space; the molecule was found in a star-forming region in the constellation Orion.

**2 Aug** A bill to reduce government spending and raise the debt ceiling is signed into law in Washington DC.

**3 Aug** In Cairo former Egyptian president Hosni Mubarak goes on trial on charges of corruption and of complicity in the killing of antigovernment protesters; the trial is televised.

▸ Syrian armed forces move into Hamah, the center of some of the biggest antigovernment demonstrations, killing many as the government moves to crush the opposition.

**4 Aug** Stock markets in the US experience their biggest drop in two years as the Dow Jones Industrial Average loses 4.31% of its value and the Standard & Poor's 500-stock index falls by 4.78%.

▸ The US government gives conditional approval to a plan of the Shell Oil Co. to drill for oil in the Beaufort Sea, north of Alaska.

**5 Aug** The rating agency Standard & Poor's for the first time ever downgrades the risk rating of US debt from AAA to AA+ in a controversial move; the agency cites political unpredictability in a statement.

▸ The US Department of Labor reports that the unemployment rate in July dropped to 9.1% and that the number of nonfarm jobs added to the economy was 117,000.

**6 Aug** A small protest march against the killing of a local man by police in the Tottenham section of London explodes into a large riot with looting and fighting against riot police.

▸ The militant organization al-Shabaab withdraws from Mogadishu, ceding control of the Somalian capital to the transitional government.

**7 Aug** Pender Harbour, under jockey Luis Contreras, wins the Breeders' Stakes race at Woodbine in Toronto, the final leg of the Canadian Triple Crown in Thoroughbred horse racing; Contreras also rode the winners in the first two legs of the Triple Crown.

**8 Aug** Rioters in London set fire to a Sony Corp. warehouse that is a distribution hub for independent record labels in Britain and Ireland, destroying untold numbers of CDs and other record stock.

▸ The Standard & Poor's 500-stock index loses 6.7% of its value, and the Dow Jones Industrial Average falls 634 points (5.6%), closing below 11,000 points for the first time in 2011.

**9 Aug** Some 10,000 police officers patrol the streets of London in an effort to end the riots, looting, and arson of the past three nights, but elsewhere in England, including Birmingham, Manchester, and Liverpool, such mayhem escalates.

**10 Aug** North Korean and South Korean military forces exchange artillery fire near Yeonpyeong Island.

▸ James H. Billington, the US librarian of Congress, names Philip Levine the country's 18th poet laureate; Levine succeeds W.S. Merwin.

**11 Aug** The Standard & Poor's 500-stock index rises 4.6% after having fallen 4.4% the previous day in a display of unprecedented volatility that is also affecting markets in Europe.

▸ Yingluck Shinawatra takes office as Thailand's first female prime minister.

**12 Aug** Italian Prime Minister Silvio Berlusconi, after an emergency cabinet meeting, announces a new austerity package that includes tax increases and cuts in local government.

**13 Aug** Rebel forces in Libya seize control of much of the city of Al-Zawiyah; the road through Al-Zawiyah is an important supply route for Tripoli.

**14 Aug** At the Atlanta Athletic Club golf course in Johns Creek GA, Keegan Bradley of the US defeats his countryman Jason Dufner in a three-hole playoff to win the PGA championship tournament.

▸ The 52nd Edward MacDowell Medal for outstanding contributions to the arts is awarded to American playwright Edward Albee at the MacDowell Colony in Peterborough NH.

**15 Aug** The energy company Royal Dutch Shell reveals that a leak from an oil rig off the eastern coast of Scotland has spilled some 206,700 liters (54,600 gal) of oil into the North Sea.

▸ The Internet company Google announces its planned acquisition of Motorola Mobility Holdings, which will allow Google to add smartphones and tablet computers to its portfolio.

**16 Aug** Voters in Seattle approve a large highway tunnel project to run under downtown; the tunnel is expected to be completed in late 2015.

**17 Aug** The Special Tribunal for Lebanon, an international court created by the UN and the government of Lebanon, issues indictments of four members of the militant organization Hezbollah for the 2005 assassination of Lebanese Prime Minister Rafiq al-Hariri.

**18 Aug** The US for the first time calls for Syrian Pres. Bashar al-Assad to step down and announces robust sanctions; Canada, France, Germany, the UK, and the EU also call for Assad's resignation.

**19 Aug** Belarus suspends its agreement, made in December 2010, to give up its store of highly enriched uranium in return for financial aid from the US.

▸ In Myanmar (Burma), opposition leader Aung San Suu Kyi meets for the first time with Pres. Thein Sein.

**20 Aug** It is reported that Shane Bauer and Joshua Fattal, American hikers who were arrested in July 2009 after having apparently strayed across the Iraqi border into Iran, have been sentenced to eight years in prison for spying.

**21 Aug** Afghanistan's Independent Election Commission announces that nine candidates in the 2010 legislative election who had been disqualified after winning will have their seats restored; they will be seated in place of the candidates who were elevated earlier.

**22 Aug** Rebel forces in Libya march into Tripoli and declare victory over Muammar al-Qaddafi, to general jubilation, though Qaddafi's whereabouts are unknown, and he has not surrendered.

---

QUOTE OF THE MONTH

❝ *We congratulate the Libyan people for the fall of Muammar al-Qaddafi and call on the Libyan people to go into the street to protect the public property. Long live free Libya.* ❞

—mass text message from Libya's National Transitional Council on the fall of Tripoli, 22 August

---

▸ The UN reports that a cattle raid by ethnic Murle against Nuer villages in eastern South Sudan on 18 August resulted in the theft of some 30,000 cattle and the deaths of more than 600 people, a far greater death toll than initially believed.

**23 Aug** Rebels in Libya seize Bab al-ʿAziziyyah, the Tripoli compound of deposed ruler Muammar al-Qaddafi, though in a radio address Qaddafi insists that he will continue to fight for control of the country.

▸ A shallow 5.8-magnitude earthquake with its epicenter in Mineral VA rattles much of eastern North America; the National Cathedral and the Washington Monument in Washington DC are among the damaged structures.

**24 Aug** An unmanned Russian Progress cargo spaceship carrying food and fuel for the International Space Station crashes shortly after takeoff from the Baikonur space center in Kazakhstan.

**25 Aug** Members of a drug cartel set fire to a casino in Monterrey, Mexico; at least 52 people die in the blaze.

**26 Aug** A suicide car bomber destroys much of the UN headquarters building in Abuja, Nigeria, in a massive blast that kills at least 21 people; the Islamic militant organization Boko Haram claims responsibility.

▸ In Monaco the Spanish club Barcelona defeats F.C. Porto of Portugal 2–0 to win the European Super Cup in association football (soccer).

**27 Aug** The Transitional National Council, the internationally recognized governing body of Libya, for the first time releases the names of all of its members; the council has grown from 31 to 40 members, and its chairman, Mustafa Abdel-Jalil, says that it plans to expand to 80.

**28 Aug** In Erin WI, Kelly Kraft is the winner of the US men's amateur golf championship.

▸ With a bases-loaded single hit by Nick Pratto, the Ocean View team from Huntington Beach CA defeats the team from Hamamatsu City, Japan, 2–1 to win baseball's 65th Little League World Series in Williamsport PA.

**29 Aug** Japanese Minister of Finance Yoshihiko Noda is chosen by the ruling Democratic Party to succeed Naoto Kan as prime minister; the legislature elects him prime minister the following day.

**30 Aug** The American oil company Exxon Mobil signs an agreement with Russian state-owned oil company Rosneft that will allow Exxon to explore for oil in the Russian Arctic; in exchange, Rosneft will be permitted to participate in Exxon projects in the US.

**31 Aug** The High Court in Australia rules that a government agreement signed in July to send mi-

grants who arrived by boat to Malaysia violates Australian law.

▶ US military forces in Iraq mark the first month in which no American soldier was killed; 4,465 US troops have died in the Iraq War since it began in March 2003, and roughly 48,000 troops are serving in Iraq.

# September 2011

**1 Sep** Libya's rebel-led government extends by one week the deadline for loyalists of deposed ruler Muammar al-Qaddafi to surrender, and Qaddafi releases an audio recording declaring that Surt is now the capital of Libya.

**2 Sep** The US Department of Labor reports that the unemployment rate in August remained at 9.1%; the economy did not see any net increase in jobs.

▶ It is reported that violence between Christians and Muslims over the past week in Jos, Nigeria, has left at least 21 people dead.

**3 Sep** The government of South Sudan announces that the capital of the country will be moved from Juba to Ramciel.

▶ George Lee Andrews makes his 9,382nd and final performance in the Broadway musical *The Phantom of the Opera*, a record run; for most of the 23 years, he played the part of Monsieur André.

**4 Sep** At the world track and field championships in Taegu, South Korea, the Jamaican team anchored by Usain Bolt breaks the world record in the 4 × 100 relay with a time of 37.04 sec.

**5 Sep** The UN declares that the famine in Somalia has spread to the Bay region and that hundreds of people a day are dying of starvation.

**6 Sep** A wildfire in Bastrop county, Texas, has destroyed some 550 homes, making it the most destructive fire in Texas history; it is one of dozens of wildfires that have burned more than 47,900 ha (118,400 ac) in the state.

▶ English recording artist P.J. Harvey, who in 2001 became the first female winner of the Mercury Prize for best album by a British or an Irish artist, wins the 2011 Mercury Prize for her album *Let England Shake*; she is the first person to win a second Mercury Prize.

**7 Sep** Germany's Constitutional Court rules that Germany has the legal right to participate in financial rescue packages for weaker members of the euro zone; it also requires that future bailouts be approved by a legislative committee.

**8 Sep** Mahmoud Jibril, the head of Libya's Transitional National Council's Executive Board and the country's de facto prime minister, makes his first public appearance in Tripoli to speak at a news conference.

▶ The US National Park Service signs an agreement to expand the 44,100-ha (109,000-ac) Petrified Forest National Park in Arizona by 10,700 ha (26,500 ac) with the long-sought purchase of private ranchland adjoining the park.

**9 Sep** *Science* magazine publishes a report by Lee Berger of the University of Witwatersrand in South Africa in which he posits the revolutionary claim that recently discovered fossils of *Australopithecus sediba* show that the species was likely a direct ancestor of *Homo* species.

▶ China's state news agency reports that more than 14 million people, most of them in southwestern China, lack adequate drinking water as a result of a long-lasting drought.

**10 Sep** Masked Marvel, ridden by William Buick, wins the St. Leger Thoroughbred horse race at Doncaster, England.

**11 Sep** Samantha Stosur of Australia defeats American Serena Williams in an upset to win the women's US Open tennis championship; the following day Novak Djokovic of Serbia defeats Rafael Nadal of Spain to take the men's title.

▶ In golf's biennial Walker Cup competition in Aberdeen, Scotland, Great Britain and Ireland defeat the US for the first time since 2003 with a 14–12 victory.

**12 Sep** The UN Human Rights Council announces the appointment of a three-person panel to investigate human rights abuses in Syria and estimates the number of protesters killed in Syria to date to be 2,600.

**13 Sep** The US Census Bureau releases figures showing that in 2010 some 46.2 million Americans lived below the poverty level, 2.6 million more than the previous year, and that the poverty rate was 15.1%; also, the median household income declined 2.3% from the previous year.

**14 Sep** The Hague Civil Court orders the Dutch government to compensate the widows of seven men who were executed in Rawagedeh in western Java in 1947 during Indonesia's fight for independence from the Netherlands.

**15 Sep** Turkey agrees to host a US-made radar system as part of the NATO missile defense shield program.

▶ Astronomers working with the Kepler planet-hunting spacecraft launched by NASA in 2009 announce the discovery of a planet circling a double-star system in the constellation Cygnus; the planet, named Kepler 16b, is informally called Tattooine for the planet with two suns in the 1977 movie *Star Wars*.

**16 Sep** A South Korean government official declares that envoys from North and South Korea have scheduled a meeting to discuss restarting six-country talks on dealing with North Korea's nuclear-weapons program.

**17 Sep** Fighting erupts between Yemeni security forces and militias aligned with the antigovernment movement in Sanaa.

**18 Sep** The major Swiss bank UBS releases a statement explaining how it had failed to notice rogue trading that resulted in a loss of US$2.3 billion; former trader Kweku M. Adoboli has been charged in the incident.

▶ The Emmy Awards are presented in Los Angeles: winners include the television shows *Modern Family* and *Mad Men* and the actors Jim Parsons, Kyle Chandler, Melissa McCarthy, Julianna Margulies, Ty Burrell, Peter Dinklage, Julie Bowen, and Margo Martindale.

**19 Sep** Hundreds of civilians flee Surt, Libya; battles between rebel forces and those loyal to deposed leader Muammar al-Qaddafi have raged for five days.

▸ New York Yankees pitcher Mariano Rivera notches his 602nd career save in a win over the Minnesota Twins, setting a Major League Baseball record.

**20 Sep** The end of "Don't Ask, Don't Tell" in the US military goes into effect; henceforward openly gay and lesbian people are permitted to serve.

▸ Burhanuddin Rabbani, the head of Afghanistan's High Peace Council and a former president of the country, is assassinated by a suicide bomber who pretended to be a peace negotiator for the Taliban.

**21 Sep** Greece's government announces further and deeper austerity measures in an effort to qualify for international aid.

▸ Shane Bauer and Joshua Fattal, American hikers who unintentionally crossed the border from Iraq into Iran in July 2009 and had been jailed in Iran ever since, are released from prison and leave Iran.

**22 Sep** The US ceremonially reopens its embassy in Tripoli, Libya; the embassy had been abandoned in February.

▸ Pope Benedict XVI makes his first state visit to Germany; he addresses the country's legislature and later celebrates mass for some 60,000 people in Berlin's Olympic Stadium.

---

**QUOTE OF THE MONTH**

*❝ If it is true, then we truly haven't understood anything about anything. ❞*

—CERN theorist Alvaro De Rújula, commenting on the anticipated announcement regarding neutrinos' exceeding the speed of light, 22 September

---

**23 Sep** CERN particle physics researchers in Geneva report that they have measured neutrinos traveling faster than the speed of light; if the result is borne out by further investigation, it would violate the special theory of relativity.

▸ Palestinian leader Mahmoud Abbas formally requests that Palestine be admitted to the United Nations in a speech before the General Assembly.

**24 Sep** Police appear to use pepper spray without provocation at a demonstration by a group of activists who have occupied Zuccotti Park in New York City since 17 September in the genesis of a growing protest movement called Occupy Wall Street, which is against the influence of financial interests on government at the expense of ordinary people.

**25 Sep** King ʿAbd Allah of Saudi Arabia for the first time grants women the right to vote and to hold office beginning with the next elections, scheduled for 2015; he also says that women may be appointed to the Consultative Council.

▸ Patrick Makau of Kenya wins the Berlin Marathon with a time of 2 hr 3 min 38 sec, a new record time for completing a marathon; Florence Kiplagat of Kenya is the fastest woman, with a time of 2 hr 19 min 44 sec.

**26 Sep** For the first time in the battle for Surt, Libya, forces of the new government succeed in taking control of part of the city.

**27 Sep** Greece's legislature passes a law to establish the first property tax in the country; the tax will affect about 80% of Greek households and will be a large burden to many of them.

▸ Australia lifts its ban on service in combat roles by women in the armed services.

**28 Sep** Jeff Bezos, head of the online retailer Amazon.com, introduces the Kindle Fire, a tablet computer intended to compete with Barnes & Noble's Nook Color and Apple's iPad.

**29 Sep** Germany's legislature approves the expansion of the fund available to bail out euro-zone countries with high debt levels; all 17 euro-zone countries must approve the measure, but Germany's is among the most crucial votes.

**30 Sep** A US CIA drone strike in Yemen kills the American-born cleric Anwar al-Awlaki, who is believed to be a top leader of al-Qaeda in the Arabian Peninsula and to be behind several anti-American plots.

▸ Japan cancels evacuation advisories for an area encompassing five towns outside the 19-km (12-mi) exclusion zone around the stricken Fukushima Daiichi nuclear power plant, which suffered meltdowns after the 11 March earthquake and tsunami.

# October 2011

**1 Oct** The Geelong Cats defeat the Collingwood Magpies 18.11 (119)–12.9 (81) in the Australian Football League Grand Final and thus win the AFL title.

**2 Oct** The Marshall Islands passes a law creating the largest shark sanctuary in the world; it encompasses 1,900,500 sq km (750,000 sq mi) in the Pacific Ocean.

▸ The German filly Danedream, ridden by Andrasch Starke, wins the Prix de l'Arc de Triomphe Thoroughbred horse race by five lengths in spite of long odds against her.

**3 Oct** A court in Perugia, Italy, overturns the 2009 convictions of American student Amanda Knox and her former boyfriend, Raffaele Sollecito of Italy, for the 2007 murder of Knox's British roommate, Meredith Kercher; the case has aroused high emotions in all the countries concerned.

▸ The Nobel Prize for Physiology or Medicine is awarded to Canadian immunologist Ralph Stein-

man, who died three days earlier, and to American immunologist Bruce Beutler and French immunologist Jules Hoffmann for their discoveries concerning the response of the immune system to infection.

**4 Oct** The American rare-earth-producing company Molycorp announces that it has found a significant deposit of heavy rare-earth minerals in southern California; 99% of the world's heavy rare earths are produced in China.

▸ In Stockholm the Nobel Prize for Physics is awarded to American astrophysicist Saul Perlmutter and to American-born Australian astronomer Brian Schmidt and American astronomer Adam Riess for their unexpected discovery that the universe is expanding at an accelerating rate, an indication of the existence of dark energy.

**5 Oct** The Nobel Prize for Chemistry is awarded to Dan Shechtman of Israel for his discovery of quasicrystals, in which the arrangement of atoms exhibits regular but nonrepeating patterns.

**6 Oct** Both the European Central Bank and the Bank of England leave their benchmark interest rates unchanged, but the Bank of England expands its program of quantitative easing in an effort to shore up the British economy.

▶ The Nobel Prize for Literature is awarded to Swedish poet Tomas Tranströmer.

**7 Oct** The Nobel Peace Prize is awarded to Liberian Pres. Ellen Johnson Sirleaf, Liberian peace activist Leymah Gbowee, and Yemeni liberal Islamist antigovernment activist Tawakkul Karman.

▶ The US Department of Labor reports that the unemployment rate in September remained at 9.1% and that the economy as a whole added 103,000 nonfarm jobs.

▶ The Minnesota Lynx defeat the Atlanta Dream 73–67 in game three to sweep the best-of-five final series and win the Women's National Basketball Association championship.

**8 Oct** Leeds gains a 32–16 victory over St. Helens to win the British rugby league Super League Grand Final.

**9 Oct** With his third-place finish in the Japanese Grand Prix (won by Jenson Button of Britain), German driver Sebastian Vettel secures his second successive Formula One automobile racing drivers' championship.

▶ The Chicago Marathon is won by Moses Mosop of Kenya, with a time of 2 hr 5 min 37 sec; the women's victor for the third year in a row is Liliya Shobukhova of Russia, with a time of 2 hr 18 min 20 sec.

**10 Oct** An American research company releases a study showing that median income fell 6.7% in the period after the official end of the recession (June 2009 to June 2011) in the US; during the recession (December 2007 to June 2009), it fell only 3.2%.

▶ The Nobel Memorial Prize in Economic Sciences goes to American economists Thomas Sargent and Christopher Sims for their independent work on methodology for discovering how government policies affect and are affected by the broad economy.

**11 Oct** Israel and the Palestinian organization Hamas announce that they have agreed to an exchange of more than 1,000 Palestinian prisoners for Gilad Shalit, an Israeli soldier who was captured by Hamas in June 2006.

**12 Oct** The US Congress ratifies free-trade agreements with South Korea, Colombia, and Panama that were signed in 2006; they are the first such accords approved since 2007.

**13 Oct** Slovakia's legislature approves the expansion of the euro rescue fund; it is the last of the 17 member countries whose agreement was required.

**14 Oct** Indian Prime Minister Manmohan Singh signs an agreement with Pres. Thein Sein of Myanmar (Burma) expanding cooperation in trade and oil and gas exploration; India also extends credits for infrastructure projects in Myanmar.

**15 Oct** In a planned day of protest against the financial system and economic inequality, demonstrations take place in cities throughout the world, including New York City, Berlin, London, Tokyo, Sydney, and Rome, where rioting breaks out.

**16 Oct** Hundreds of troops of Kenya's armed forces enter Somalia to fight against the al-Shabaab militants.

**17 Oct** A US official says that US military advisers are to be stationed in Uganda to help hunt down the guerrilla group the Lord's Resistance Army.

**18 Oct** The Man Booker Prize goes to British writer Julian Barnes for his novel *The Sense of an Ending*.

▶ The owner of a wild-animal menagerie in Zanesville OH releases the animals and then commits suicide; by the following day local authorities have had to kill nearly all the animals—including 17 lions, 18 Bengal tigers, wolves, bears, and monkeys.

**19 Oct** In Tokyo the Japan Art Association awards the Praemium Imperiale to Japanese conductor Seiji Ozawa, British sculptor Anish Kapoor, American painter Bill Viola, British actress Dame Judi Dench, and Mexican architect Ricardo Legorreta.

**20 Oct** After a convoy attempting to flee Surt, Libya, is stopped by NATO air strikes, former Libyan leader Muammar al-Qaddafi is found hiding in a drainage ditch and is killed.

---

**QUOTE OF THE MONTH**

❝ *It is the end of tyranny and dictatorship. Qaddafi has met his fate.* ❞

—Abdel Hafez Ghoga, spokesman for Libya's Transitional National Council, on the death of former Libyan leader Muammar al-Qaddafi, 20 October

---

▶ The Basque separatist organization ETA formally renounces armed struggle and appeals for dialogue with the governments of Spain and France.

**21 Oct** US Pres. Barack Obama announces that the US military will leave Iraq by the end of 2011; the date was specified in the 2008 status of forces agreement, and negotiations to extend the deadline were unsuccessful.

▶ A Mexican commercial truck enters the US for the first time since the 1994 passage of the North American Free Trade Agreement following the resolution of safety concerns to the satisfaction of US Department of Transportation.

**22 Oct** In Melbourne long-shot filly Pinker Pinker wins the W.S. Cox Plate under jockey Craig Williams.

**23 Oct** New Zealand defeats France 8–7 to win the Rugby Union World Cup final in Auckland, New Zealand.

▶ The 14th annual Mark Twain Prize for American Humor is awarded to Will Ferrell in a ceremony at the John F. Kennedy Center for the Performing Arts in Washington DC.

**24 Oct** Syria withdraws its ambassador to the US in response to the departure two days earlier of Robert Ford, the US ambassador to Syria; Ford, who spoke out against the Syrian government crackdown on antigovernment protests, was said to fear for his safety.

**25 Oct** The US Congressional Budget Office releases a report saying that income inequality in the US has grown significantly in the past 30 years, with government policies doing less to prevent the phenomenon; the after-tax income of the wealthiest fifth of the population in 2007 was higher than that of the remaining four-fifths together.

▶ The last B53 nuclear bomb in the US arsenal is dismantled in Texas; the nine-megaton bomb was put into service in 1962 and was far and away the largest remaining bomb in the US nuclear arsenal.

**26 Oct** Mustafa Abdel-Jalil, chairman of Libya's Transitional National Council, says in an interview that he has asked NATO to keep air patrols and military advisers in the country through the end of the year.

**27 Oct** European Union leaders meeting in Brussels reach an agreement that requires banks to accept a 50% loss on their loans to Greece; they also consent to the outline of a comprehensive plan to shore up the euro.

▸ The US Department of Commerce estimates that the country's economy grew at an annual rate of 2.5% in the third quarter, a distinct improvement over the previous quarter.

**28 Oct** British Prime Minister David Cameron announces that the Commonwealth has approved changes that will allow the oldest child, rather than only the oldest son, of the British monarch to inherit the throne and that will, for the first time since 1701, permit the monarch to be married to a member of the Roman Catholic Church.

▸ In the World Series, the St. Louis Cardinals defeat the Texas Rangers 6–2 in game seven to win the Major League Baseball championship for the 11th time; St. Louis slugger David Freese is named the Series MVP.

**29 Oct** Australia's national carrier, Qantas Airways, grounds its entire fleet in an employee lockout; the airline and its employees have been engaged in a prolonged labor dispute.

**30 Oct** Tens of thousands of people attend an antigovernment rally in Lahore, Pakistan, led by former cricket star Imran Khan.

**31 Oct** UNESCO approves full membership for Palestine, which becomes the 195th member of the organization.

▸ The UN estimates that the world population has reached seven billion, though it does not identify a specific infant as the seven-billionth person born; the world population reached six billion in 1999.

# November 2011

**1 Nov** Dunaden wins Australia's Melbourne Cup Thoroughbred horse race by a nose over Red Cadeaux.

**2 Nov** Pakistan's government chooses to normalize trade relations with India to increase trade between the countries.

▸ A spokesman for the African Union reveals that Djibouti will contribute some 850 troops to AU peacekeeping forces in Somalia; the organization hopes to increase the number of peacekeepers, who currently are all from Uganda and Burundi, to as many as 20,000.

▸ The Dorothy and Lillian Gish Prize is awarded to American modern dance choreographer Trisha Brown.

**3 Nov** A new law is announced in Cuba that will for the first time permit citizens and permanent residents to buy and sell real estate without first seeking government approval.

▸ Shenzhou 8, an unmanned space capsule, successfully docks with the module Tiangong I some 320 km (200 mi) above Earth in a new milestone for China's space program.

**4 Nov** The US Department of Labor reports that the unemployment rate in October fell to 9%, though the economy as a whole added only 80,000 nonfarm jobs.

▸ The General Assembly of the International Union of Pure and Applied Physics announces names for the three most recently discovered elements: darmstadtium (Ds), roentgenium (Rg), and copernicium (Cn).

**5 Nov** Jerry Sandusky, a former defensive coordinator for the respected football team of Pennsylvania State University and the head of a foundation for at-risk children, is arraigned on charges of having sexually abused eight boys.

▸ The Breeders' Cup Classic Thoroughbred horse race is won by Drosselmeyer, under jockey Mike Smith; the four-year-old colt charged from 10th place for the victory at Churchill Downs in Louisville KY.

**6 Nov** Geoffrey Mutai of Kenya wins the New York City Marathon with a time of 2 hr 5 min 6 sec, and Ethiopia's Firehiwot Dado is the fastest woman, with a time of 2 hr 23 min 15 sec.

▸ Nicol David of Malaysia wins a record sixth squash World Open championship with her defeat of Jenny

Duncalf of Britain, while Nick Matthew of the UK wins a second consecutive men's title when he defeats Gregory Gaultier of France.

**7 Nov** The US and Bolivia agree to restore diplomatic relations; ties were broken in 2008 when Bolivian Pres. Evo Morales expelled the US ambassador and drug-enforcement agents.

**8 Nov** The International Atomic Energy Agency releases a report laying out evidence that led it to conclude that Iran has engaged in activity related to the development of nuclear weaponry.

▸ The video game *Call of Duty: Modern Warfare 3* goes on sale and in the next 24 hours sets a new record for sales in the US and the UK of US$400 million.

**9 Nov** The Atlantic States Marine Fisheries Commission votes to reduce by as much as 37% the allowable catch of menhaden, a vital forage fish that is harvested for use in fertilizer, bait, and animal and fish feed; the population of the fish is at 10% of historic levels.

▸ Legendary head football coach Joe Paterno of Pennsylvania State University is fired and Graham Spanier resigns as university president in the fallout from the pedophile scandal surrounding former assistant coach Jerry Sandusky; Paterno is faulted for having failed to act adequately when accusations against Sandusky came to his attention.

**10 Nov** Jefferson county in Alabama files for bankruptcy protection; it is the largest US municipality ever to have taken this step.

**11 Nov** A helicopter ferrying officials from Mexico City to Cuernavaca, Mexico, crashes, killing all eight aboard, including Interior Secretary Francisco Blake Mora, who is a leading figure in the government's fight against drug traffickers, four other ministry employees, and three members of the country's air force.

**12 Nov** The Arab League agrees to suspend Syria's membership effective in four days if Syria has not by then adhered to the requirements of a peace agreement.

▸ According to Iranian officials, as members of the Revolutionary Guard transport munitions at a military base outside Bidganeh, Iran, an accidental explosion occurs that kills at least 17 members of the guard; one of those killed, however, is Brig. Gen.

Hassan Moghaddam, a commander in the country's missile-development program.

**13 Nov** Finnish driver Jari-Matt Latvala wins the Wales Rally GB; nonetheless, French driver Sébastien Loeb, who left the race at stage 18 after a collision, secures the drivers' championship in World Rally Championship racing for a record eighth time.

**14 Nov** The US Supreme Court agrees to rule on the constitutionality of the health care reform act that was signed into law in 2010; oral arguments are to be heard by March 2012.

▸ Emirates Airlines, based in Dubayy, agrees to purchase fifty 777-300ER airplanes from the American manufacturer Boeing, with options for the purchase of an additional 20 aircraft; it is the biggest deal in Boeing's history.

**15 Nov** Police in New York City forcibly clear the two-month-old encampment of Occupy Wall Street protesters from Zuccotti Park, though the protests continue; authorities in cities throughout the US are grappling with how to handle similar encampments.

**16 Nov** US Pres. Barack Obama and Australian Prime Minister Julia Gillard announce an agreement to station 2,500 US Marines in Australia.

▸ In Washington DC the Congressional Gold Medal is awarded to pioneering astronauts John Glenn, Neil Armstrong, Buzz Aldrin, and Michael Collins.

**17 Nov** The UN-backed tribunal charged with trying architects of the murderous Khmer Rouge regime in Cambodia for crimes against humanity recommends that the defendant Ieng Thirith, the highest-ranked woman in the Khmer Rouge government, be released because she suffers from dementia.

**18 Nov** Tahrir Square in Cairo fills with tens of thousands of protesters who demand the end of military rule; they are enraged over the military's insistence that it retain primacy in the new constitution.

---

---

▸ Aung San Suu Kyi agrees to reregister her political party, the National League for Democracy, in Myanmar (Burma).

**19 Nov** A Loya Jirga (grand council) called by Afghan Pres. Hamid Karzai endorses his call for American troops to remain in the country on a long-term basis, subject to restrictions as to their activities.

**20 Nov** It is reported that hundreds of Ethiopian troops, supported by personnel carriers and tanks, have entered Somalia to fight the militant al-Shabaab insurgents.

▸ The Fukuoka SoftBank Hawks defeat the Chunichi Dragons 3–0 in game seven to win baseball's Japan Series.

▸ After a win in the final auto race of the season, the Ford 400 in Homestead FL, Tony Stewart is crowned winner of the NASCAR drivers' championship; he also won the title in 2002.

▸ The Los Angeles Galaxy wins the Major League Soccer title with a 1–0 victory over the Houston Dynamo in the MLS Cup.

**21 Nov** In the US a bipartisan congressional "super committee" that was charged with finding US$1.2 trillion in deficit reductions on pain of triggering unpopular automatic budget cuts declares that it has failed to agree on a plan.

**22 Nov** Prime Minister Yousaf Raza Gilani of Pakistan accepts the resignation of Husain Haqqani as ambassador to the US; Haqqani has been accused of having sought American help to prevent a possible military coup in Pakistan, and he is replaced the following day by Sherry Rehman.

▸ American Samoa, which began playing association football (soccer) in international matches in 1994, defeats Tonga 2–1 in a prequalifying match for the 2014 World Cup; it is the team's first-ever victory after a series of 30 frustrating losses.

**23 Nov** In Riyadh, Saudi Arabia, Pres. ʿAli ʿAbd Allah Salih of Yemen signs an agreement transferring power to his vice president; the agreement nonetheless allows Salih to retain the title of president until the next election.

**24 Nov** The Arab League tells Syria that it must agree within 24 hours to allow international monitors to enter the country or face sanctions, and the European Union issues a statement saying that there is urgent need for civilians in Syria to be protected.

**25 Nov** Australia's minister of immigration, Chris Bowen, announces that henceforth asylum seekers who arrive by sea in Australia may receive bridge visas that would allow them to live and work in the country while they await judgment on their applications.

**26 Nov** Officials in Pakistan say that NATO air strikes the previous night struck two military posts near the country's northwestern boundary with Afghanistan, killing at least 25 Pakistani soldiers, and Pakistan shuts down NATO supply routes into Afghanistan as an expression of its outrage.

▸ NBA owners and players reach a tentative agreement in their long-running labor dispute that will allow them to begin a shortened basketball season on 25 December.

**27 Nov** The Arab League imposes economic sanctions against Syria because of the country's failure to comply with the terms of a peace treaty that it agreed to on 2 November and its refusal to accept international observers to monitor its compliance.

▸ The British Columbia Lions capture the 99th Canadian Football League Grey Cup, defeating the Winnipeg Blue Bombers 34–23.

▸ The Japan Cup Thoroughbred horse race is won by the filly Buena Vista, ridden by Yasunari Iwata.

**28 Nov** The first phase of legislative elections in Egypt gets under way with a large turnout; the final phase is scheduled for January 2012.

**29 Nov** Hundreds of Iranian students attack and ransack the British embassy in Tehran.

**30 Nov** US Secretary of State Hillary Rodham Clinton arrives in Myanmar (Burma) for the first visit to that country by a US secretary of state since 1955.

▸ A massive one-day strike in Britain encompasses tens of thousands of public employees protesting against austerity measures.

# December 2011

**1 Dec** Yemen's political opposition declares that it has reached an agreement with the country's ruling party on the makeup of an interim government to rule until elections, which are scheduled for February 2012.

**2 Dec** The Community of Latin American and Caribbean States (CELAC), a new regional grouping with 33 member countries, holds its first summit meeting in Caracas.

▸ The US Department of Labor reports that the unemployment rate in November fell to 8.6%, its lowest level since March 2009, and that 120,000 nonfarm jobs were created; the rate of participation in the workforce, however, fell by 0.2%.

**3 Dec** A battle takes place in Syria's Idlib province between security forces and defectors from the armed services; at least 15 individuals are killed, including people from both sides of the fighting and civilians.

**4 Dec** Iranian officials say that the country's military has shot down an American stealth drone that was spying in eastern Iran.

▸ Spain defeats Argentina 3–1 to win its fifth Davis Cup in men's international team tennis.

▸ The annual Kennedy Center Honors are presented in Washington DC to film actress Meryl Streep, musical theater performer Barbara Cook, pop singer and songwriter Neil Diamond, cellist Yo-Yo Ma, and saxophonist Sonny Rollins.

**5 Dec** The advocacy group Global Witness withdraws from the Kimberley Process program, saying that the decision by the Kimberley Process to certify diamonds from Zimbabwe's Marange fields undercuts its mission of preventing the sale of diamonds that generate profits for groups that engage in violence.

▸ Britain's Turner Prize is presented in Gateshead, England, to Scottish sculptor Martin Boyce; his winning entry is a piece in which gallery pillars and a library table are reimagined as a fanciful forest.

**6 Dec** Elio Di Rupo of the Francophone Socialist Party is sworn in as prime minister of Belgium 18 months after elections; he is the country's first French-speaking leader in some 30 years.

**7 Dec** A member of Egypt's ruling council tells a group of American and British journalists that the military will control the writing of the constitution to protect the country from the Islamist majority that the legislature appears likely to have.

**8 Dec** The European Central Bank for the second time in recent weeks lowers its key interest rate by a quarter point, to 1%.

**9 Dec** In a summit meeting in Brussels, the member countries of the European Union agree to a new pact to bind the union closer and allow greater EU oversight of the budgets of member countries; only the UK declines to sign on.

**10 Dec** *The New England Journal of Medicine* reports online that a team of medical researchers testing gene therapy for the form of hemophilia called hemophilia B have treated six people, all of whom saw notable improvement in a successful trial.

▸ Steer roper Trevor Brazile is crowned winner of the all-around cowboy world championship for a record ninth time at the Wrangler National Finals Rodeo in Las Vegas.

**11 Dec** The first legislative elections to be held in more than 10 years in Côte d'Ivoire take place peacefully.

**12 Dec** Canada announces its intention to withdraw from the Kyoto Protocol agreement to reduce emissions of greenhouse gases.

▸ Fatou Bensouda of The Gambia is chosen to succeed Luis Moreno-Ocampo of Argentina as chief prosecutor of the International Criminal Court in June 2012; she has been the court's deputy prosecutor since 2004 and previously served as attorney general and as minister of justice in The Gambia.

**13 Dec** Violence between security forces and antigovernment demonstrators leaves at least 32 people dead in Syria, 19 of them civilians in Idlib province trying to block a military convoy.

**14 Dec** The day after Israeli settlers in the West Bank attacked an Israeli army base, Israeli Prime Minister Benjamin Netanyahu declares that Israeli right-wing militants will henceforth be subject to the same lengthy administrative detentions that Palestinian militants endure.

▸ For the first time in three years, OPEC, at a meeting in Vienna, agrees to raise its production target; the new target is 30 million bbl per day.

**15 Dec** In a small ceremony at the airport in Baghdad, US Secretary of Defense Leon Panetta declares an official end to the war that the US began in Iraq in 2003.

▸ After hearing reports that Qatar is discussing hosting peace talks for Afghanistan that include Taliban militants, Afghanistan withdraws its ambassador to Qatar.

**16 Dec** The World Trade Organization accepts Russia's application to become a member; the following day Samoa and Montenegro are also approved.

▸ The online gaming company Zynga, maker of popular games played on the social network Facebook, begins trading on the NASDAQ stock exchange.

**17 Dec** The Iraqi National Accord (al-Iraqiyyah) political bloc announces that it is boycotting Iraq's legislature.

**18 Dec** The final convoy of US soldiers, with 110 vehicles and about 500 troops, crosses out of Iraq into Kuwait.

▸ In Yokohama, FC Barcelona of Spain, led by Argentine international Lionel Messi, defeats Santos FC of Brazil 4–0 to take the FIFA Club World Cup championship.

**19 Dec** North Korea's official news media announce that the country's leader, Kim Jong Il, died on 17 December while on a train.

▸ Syria signs an agreement with the Arab League to allow outside observers into the country to monitor its compliance with a peace agreement; the observer mission is to last for one month.

**20 Dec** Thousands of women march in Tahrir Square in Cairo to express outrage over the brutal treatment of women demonstrators by armed forces in recent days; videos have emerged showing military officers beating, stripping, and kicking women.

**21 Dec** Activists in Syria report that the government has intensified its campaign against protesters in northwestern Syria and has over the past three days killed at least 160 people.

▸ The European Central Bank makes three-year, 1%-interest loans of €489 billion (US$640 billion) to 523 European banks in hopes of easing the financial crisis in Europe.

**22 Dec** Legislation to set up an independent anticorruption agency is introduced in India's legislature.

**23 Dec** Opposition leader Aung San Suu Kyi formally registers the National League for Democracy political party for participation in future elections in Myanmar (Burma).

**24 Dec** Nigerian officials say that two days of fighting between government forces and those of the Islamic militant group Boko Haram in Damaturu, in northeastern Nigeria, have left at least 50 people dead and that 11 more people died in a shoot-out in Maiduguri.

**25 Dec** In Madala, Nigeria, a bomb attack by the Boko Haram Islamic militant group on St. Theresa Catholic Church kills at least 38 worshippers; two other churches also suffer attacks.

**26 Dec** At least 30 people are killed in the Syrian government siege of Homs, and 50 members of the Arab League observer mission arrive in Damascus.

**27 Dec** Afghan Pres. Hamid Karzai withdraws his objections to the opening of a Taliban office in Qatar; the purpose of the office is to make it possible to safely engage in peace talks with representatives of the Taliban.

**28 Dec** A wave of strikes at state agencies spreads through Yemen; workers demand the removal of bosses who have ties to the country's government and are accused of corruption.

**29 Dec** Kim Jong-Eun is publicly declared the supreme leader in North Korea during a memorial ceremony for Kim Jong Il.

> ### QUOTE OF THE MONTH
>
> *❝ Respected Comrade Kim Jong-Eun is now supreme leader of our party, military, and people.* ❞
>
> —Kim Yong-Nam, president of North Korea's legislature, announcing Kim Jong-Eun's ascension to power, 29 December

▶ The Turkish military says that a strike that was intended to be against Kurdish militants in northern Iraq instead killed 35 Turkish cigarette smugglers; pro-Kurdish rioting takes place in Istanbul and elsewhere in response.

▶ Samoa spends its final day in the same time zone as American Samoa, where it has been since 1892; it moves one time zone to the west, across the International Date Line, making the following day 31 December.

**30 Dec** At the last bell of the year at the New York Stock Exchange, the Dow Jones Industrial Average shows a rise of 5.5% since the beginning of the year, whereas the Standard & Poor's 500-stock index posts a decrease of 0.003% for the year.

**31 Dec** The final vessels cross the finish line in the 2011 Sydney Hobart Yacht Race in Australia; two days earlier the first-to-finish line honors were awarded to *Investec Loyal,* and the overall winner was declared to be *Loki.*

# January 2012

**1 Jan** The 88-member Arab Parliament recommends that the Arab League end its observer mission to Syria, saying that the mission has failed to prevent the killing of citizens by the Syrian government.

▶ Iran's nuclear agency announces that its scientists have for the first time produced a nuclear fuel rod, which it says has been inserted into the core of the country's research nuclear reactor.

**2 Jan** Thousands of people rally outside the National Opera in Budapest to protest Hungary's new constitution, which went into effect the previous day, as undermining democracy in the country.

**3 Jan** A spokesman for the Taliban in Afghanistan announces that the militant extremist organization has reached a preliminary agreement to set up a political office in Qatar; it is hoped that such an office will make peace negotiations possible.

**4 Jan** US Pres. Barack Obama appoints Richard Cordray director of the new Consumer Financial Protection Bureau.

**5 Jan** Local officials in South Sudan say that ethnic violence between the Lou Nuer and the Murle peoples in the past two weeks has left at least 3,000 people dead; the figure has not been confirmed.

**6 Jan** The US Department of Labor reports that the unemployment rate for December 2011 fell from 8.7% to 8.5% and that the economy added 200,000 nonfarm jobs.

**7 Jan** Nigerian authorities say that the previous day the Islamic militant group Boko Haram killed at least 33 people in assorted attacks in Nigeria, including attacks on a meeting hall, a beauty parlor, and a church.

▶ Martial law that has been in place since 2009 is lifted in Fiji, but new restrictions are also announced.

**8 Jan** Iranian newspapers publish a report stating that the head of the country's nuclear agency said in an interview that a new underground nuclear-enrichment facility near Qom will shortly become operational.

**9 Jan** Tens of thousands of protesters march in several cities in Nigeria while a general strike shuts down business in much of the country, all in response to the sudden ending of government fuel subsidies, which has caused the price of fuel to double in the past week.

▶ The University of Alabama defeats Louisiana State University 21–0 in college football's Bowl Championship Series title game in New Orleans to win the NCAA Football Bowl Subdivision championship.

**10 Jan** The Naandi Foundation, an independent charity in India, releases a report based on a survey of 73,000 households that found that though the levels of malnutrition in the country have fallen by 20% in the past seven years, some 42% of children in India under the age of five nonetheless suffer from malnutrition.

**11 Jan** The government of Mexico reports that 47,515 people died in drug-related violence between December 2006 and September 2011 and that though the figure for the first nine months of 2011 is 11% higher than that for the first nine months of 2010, the rate of annual increase is the lowest yet.

**12 Jan** The government of Myanmar (Burma) signs a cease-fire agreement with the Karen National Union, the group of ethnic Karen rebels who have been fighting for autonomy for decades.

▶ Officials in Iran express anger and outrage over the killing the previous day of Mostafa Ahmadi Roshan, deputy director of a uranium-enrichment plant at Natanz.

**13 Jan** Myanmar (Burma) releases 651 political prisoners, including leaders of student protests in 1988 and of antigovernment protests in 2007 as well as a former prime minister; hours later the US announces that it will restore diplomatic relations with the country.

▶ A Mediterranean cruise ship, the *Costa Concordia,* carrying some 4,200 passengers and crew members runs aground and capsizes off Italy's Giglio Island; at least 25 people are killed and 7 are missing.

**14 Jan** Ma Ying-jeou is elected to a second term of office as president of Taiwan.

**15 Jan** At the Golden Globe Awards in Beverly Hills CA, best picture honors go to *The Descendants* and *The Artist;* best director goes to Martin Scorsese for *Hugo.*

▶ The Dakar Rally concludes in Lima; the winners are French driver Stéphane Peterhansel in a Mini Countryman automobile, Frenchman Cyril Despres on a KTM motorcycle, Dutch driver Gérard de Rooy in an Iveco truck, and Argentina's Alejandro Patronelli in a Yamaha ATV.

▶ Osku Palermaa of Finland defeats American Ryan Shafer to become the first international bowler and the first two-hander to win the Professional Bowlers Association World Championship, the first major championship of the season.

**16 Jan** At Thoroughbred horse racing's 2011 Eclipse Awards, Havre de Grace is named Horse of the Year; it is the third consecutive year that the honor has been awarded to a female.

**17 Jan** US Secretary of the Interior Ken Salazar announces a ban on the import of Burmese pythons, two species of African pythons, and yellow anacondas; the Florida Everglades have been overrun by enormous pythons that are thought to have been released by pet owners.

▶ The centenary of the arrival at the South Pole of the British expedition led by Robert F. Scott is celebrated with a cricket game at the South Pole played by a team of British scientists against an international team of scientists; the British team wins.

**18 Jan** A protest takes place on the Internet to oppose legislation before the US Congress that is intended to curtail online piracy—that is, illegal dissemination of copyrighted material; Web-based companies say that the language of the two bills is too broad, and the bills are later withdrawn.

**19 Jan** The photographic supply and imaging company Eastman Kodak Co. files for bankruptcy protection.

▶ The International Maritime Bureau reports that the number of Somali pirate attacks in 2011 rose to 237 from the previous year's 219 but that only 28 of those attacks were successful, as against 49 in 2010.

**20 Jan** In response to objections from the EU and the IMF, from which Hungary seeks financial aid, Prime Minister Viktor Orban announces his abandonment of a plan to merge the country's central bank with its regulator of financial markets.

**21 Jan** It is reported that two teams of scientists whose research into how avian influenza viruses mutate to move from animal hosts to human ones and how they become transmissible has led them to produce a more-contagious virus have chosen to

suspend their research in order that fears that such an enhanced virus could escape the laboratory may be addressed.

**22 Jan** Pres. 'Ali 'Abd Allah Salih of Yemen leaves the country for medical treatment in the US, leaving power in the hands of his vice president, 'Abd Rabbuh Mansur Hadi; it is unclear whether he intends to return.

---

**QUOTE OF THE MONTH**

❝ *I feel sorry for you and invite you to return to your house and start with a new page with the new leadership.* ❞

—Pres. 'Ali 'Abd Allah Salih of Yemen addressing protesters before departing for the US, 22 January

---

▶ Croatia holds a referendum on joining the European Union; the result is resoundingly positive.

▶ The first-ever Winter Youth Olympic Games conclude in Innsbruck, Austria; 70 national delegations participated in the 10-day sporting event, in which 372 medals were awarded, with Germany the top winner.

**23 Jan** The upper house of France's legislature approves a bill that makes it a crime to deny officially recognized genocides, including—to the great ire of Turkey—the 1915 Armenian genocide.

▶ In the field of children's literature, the Newbery Medal is awarded to Jack Gantos for his novel *Dead End in Norvelt,* and Chris Raschka wins the Caldecott Medal for his picture book *A Ball for Daisy.*

**24 Jan** In his state of the union address, US Pres. Barack Obama outlines proposals intended to create greater equality of opportunity for workers and to improve the long-term economy.

**25 Jan** Alex Salmond, first minister of Scotland, lays out his schedule for a referendum on independence to be held in late 2014; British Prime Minister David Cameron holds that the Scottish Parliament is not empowered to approve a referendum.

▶ The Japanese government releases figures showing that the country in 2011 experienced an overall trade deficit for the first time since 1980.

▶ US Navy Seals raid a pirate encampment in Hiimo Gaabo, Somalia, killing nine gunmen and rescuing American aid worker Jessica Buchanan and Danish aid worker Poul Hagen Thisted; both were working for the Danish Refugee Council when they were kidnapped in October 2011.

**26 Jan** The city of Jalalabad and four districts in eastern Afghanistan are ceremonially turned over from NATO to the control of the Afghan army; it is about the 20th such turnover so far.

**27 Jan** After meeting with Afghan Pres. Hamid Karzai, French Pres. Nicolas Sarkozy announces that French troops will be withdrawn from Afghanistan by the end of 2013, a year earlier than the rest of NATO troops are to leave; the scheduled drawdown for 2012 is also increased.

**28 Jan** The Arab League suspends its observer mission in Syria, saying that the intensification of Syria's campaign against the antigovernment protesters has made it too dangerous for the monitors to remain in the country.

▶ Belarusian Victoria Azarenka defeats Mariya Sharapova of Russia to win the Australian Open women's tennis championship; the following night at 1:37 AM, Novak Djokovic of Serbia overcomes Spaniard Rafael Nadal to take the men's title in a record-breaking 5-hour 53-minute final match.

▶ Top awards at the Sundance Film Festival in Park City UT go to *Beasts of the Southern Wild, The House I Live In, Valley of Saints,* and *Searching for Sugar Man.*

**29 Jan** The Iraqi National Accord (al-Iraqiyyah) political bloc announces that it will end its boycott, begun in mid-December 2011, of the country's legislature.

▶ Officials in Sudan and China report that Sudanese rebels allied with South Sudan have kidnapped some 29 Chinese road workers in the border state of South Kordofan.

**30 Jan** An EU summit meeting in Brussels produces an agreement on fiscal discipline within the euro zone that is signed by all the member states except the UK and the Czech Republic.

▶ The World Trade Organization rules that China's system of quotas and export taxes on nine industrial minerals is illegal and must be dismantled.

**31 Jan** In testimony before the Senate Intelligence Committee on threats to the US, Director of National Intelligence James R. Clapper, Jr., points to Iran, cyberattacks, and violence in Mexico as among the biggest concerns.

▶ The US Food and Drug Administration approves a drug that targets a genetic mutation that causes one form of cystic fibrosis; it is the first drug to target the cause of the disease.

# February 2012

**1 Feb** In Port Said, Egypt, after the home association football (soccer) team defeats the country's top team in an upset, fans of the Port Said team rush the field, attacking fans and members of the losing team and setting off a stampede; at least 73 people die in the melee.

▶ The social network Facebook files for what is expected to be the biggest-ever initial public offering (IPO) of technology stock.

**2 Feb** For the first time in more than 20 years, the UK names its ambassador to Somalia; Matt Baugh will be based in Kenya because of security concerns in Somalia.

▶ The US Centers for Disease Control and Prevention recommends that boys aged 11–21 be vaccinated against human papillomavirus (HPV); previously the recommendation for vaccination was for girls only.

**3 Feb** Inspectors from the International Atomic Energy Agency depart Iran after a three-day visit during which they were denied access to people and places that had raised concern in the West that Iran might be planning to build nuclear weapons.

▶ The US Department of Labor reports that the unemployment rate in January fell to 8.3% and that a fairly robust 243,000 new jobs were added to the economy.

**4 Feb** The Syrian government intensifies its attack against the inhabitants of Homs, while in the UN Security Council, China and Russia veto a resolution supporting a peace plan for Syria that was put forward by the Arab League.

▶ The United Nations reports that 3,021 Afghan civilians died in war-related violence in 2011, an 8% increase over the previous year and the highest annual figure so far in the 10-year-old war.

**5 Feb** Political leaders in Greece agree to new spending cuts in response to pressure from the European Commission, the European Central Bank, and the International Monetary Fund.

▶ In Indianapolis the New York Giants defeat the New England Patriots 21–17 to win the National Football League's Super Bowl XLVI.

**6 Feb** In spite of a 7–0 loss to the Aragua Tigres (Tigers) of Venezuela in the final game of the round-robin tournament, the Escogido Leones (Lions) of the Dominican Republic win baseball's Caribbean Series.

▶ The Court of Arbitration for Sport strips Spanish cyclist Alberto Contador of his 2010 victory in the Tour de France and retroactively bans him from cycling for two years beginning in January 2011.

**7 Feb** Hours after a police mutiny began, Mohamed Nasheed resigns as president of Maldives in an apparent coup; he is succeeded by Vice Pres. Mohammed Waheed Hassan.

▶ Thousands of workers in Greece engage in a general strike in protest against a proposed austerity package that focuses on cutting wages.

**8 Feb** The five biggest American banks agree to a US$25 billion settlement; the bulk of the funds are intended to help homeowners struggling to stay in homes with mortgages that cost more than the current values of the properties.

▶ The head of the Russian Antarctic Expedition reports that after 10 years of drilling through ice, scientists at the Vostok Research Station have reached the large body of fresh water known as Lake Vostok 3,769 m (12,366 ft) below the surface of the ice; it is the first contact with a freshwater lake on the frozen continent.

**9 Feb** Political leaders in Greece agree to an austerity plan that will, among other things, cut the minimum wage by 22% and freeze private-sector wages.

▶ The US Nuclear Regulatory Commission approves the building of two new nuclear reactors at the Vogtle nuclear plant in Georgia; they are the first nuclear reactors to be authorized since 1978.

**10 Feb** Afghan investigators say that they have found that a NATO air strike two days earlier that killed eight young people who were herding sheep was directed at the boys because of misinformation given to French troops in the area.

**11 Feb** British authorities arrest a police officer, an armed services member, an official of the Ministry of Defense, and five prominent staff members of the News Corp. flagship paper *The Sun* in a widening bribery investigation.

**12 Feb** At the Grammy Awards in Los Angeles, the top winner is British soul singer Adele, who wins six awards, including both song of the year and record of the year for "Rolling in the Deep" and album of the year for *21;* best new artist is alternative band Bon Iver.

▶ Zambia wins the Africa Cup of Nations in association football (soccer) for the first time when it defeats Côte d'Ivoire 8–7 in a penalty shoot-out in the final match in Libreville, Gabon.

**13 Feb** Pakistan's Supreme Court indicts Prime Minister Yousaf Raza Gilani on charges of contempt of court for his failure to obey court orders to pursue corruption charges against Pres. Asif Ali Zardari.

▶ The technology company Apple Inc. announces that the independent outside auditor Fair Labor Association has at Apple's request begun to review working conditions at plants where Apple products and parts are manufactured.

**14 Feb** The Bank of Japan announces a plan to inject money into the economy in hopes of reaching 1% inflation after the economy shrank at a rate of 2.3% in the final quarter of 2011.

▶ Palacegarden Malachy, a Pekingese, wins Best in Show at the Westminster Kennel Club's 136th dog show.

**15 Feb** The Islamic extremist organization Boko Haram attacks a federal prison in Koton Karifi, Nigeria, and frees 119 inmates.

**16 Feb** The UN General Assembly approves a nonbinding resolution condemning the Syrian government's crackdown on the protest movement and calling on Syrian Pres. Bashar al-Assad to relinquish power.

**17 Feb** French citizens line up at banks to convert French francs to euros on the final day that such an exchange can be made; francs become worthless the following day.

**18 Feb** Foxconn Technologies, a major electronics manufacturer that is based in Taiwan and has several factories in China, announces that it will significantly raise wages at its Chinese factories and reduce overtime hours.

▶ A referendum is held in Latvia on a constitutional amendment to add Russian to Latvian as an official state language; the proposed amendment is defeated.

**19 Feb** The journal *Nature Nanotechnology* reports that scientists at Indiana's Purdue University and at Australia's University of New South Wales have created a working transistor from one phosphorous atom in a silicon crystal substrate; this is seen as a major advance and a step toward quantum computing.

▶ The Italian film *Cesare deve morire* (*Caesar Must Die*), directed by Paolo and Vittorio Taviani, wins the Golden Bear at the Berlin International Film Festival.

**20 Feb** The US and Mexico sign the Transboundary Agreement on oil drilling in the Gulf of Mexico; the accord allows for joint inspection of oil rigs belonging to either country and may open up a large area for deep-sea drilling.

**21 Feb** Rioting takes place outside Bagram Air Base in Afghanistan after American NATO workers were found the previous night disposing of copies of the Qur'an by incineration, which is regarded by Muslims as an act of desecration.

▶ Saudi Arabia names an ambassador to Iraq, restoring the diplomatic relations that were severed in 1990 after Iraq invaded Kuwait.

▶ The *Proceedings of the National Academy of Sciences of the United States of America* publishes a report by a team of Russian scientists who say that they have successfully grown live campion plants from fruits of a 32,000-year-old plant that was found buried in permafrost in northeastern Siberia.

**22 Feb** During the Syrian government bombardment of Homs, a building serving as a media center for the opposition is targeted, and 22 people there, including American journalist Marie Colvin and French photographer Rémi Ochlik, are killed in the violence.

▶ Prime Minister François Fillon of France orders that the term *mademoiselle,* indicating an unmarried woman, cease to be used on government forms.

**23 Feb** A series of coordinated bomb and gun attacks throughout Iraq result in the deaths of at least 40 people, some 25 of them in Baghdad.

**24 Feb** Violent protests in Afghanistan over the burning of copies of the Qur'an by American military personnel continue; at least 24 people have died in the protests so far.

**25 Feb** A two-day meeting of the finance ministers of the Group of 20 countries with developed and emerging economies begins in Mexico City; a major focus of the meeting is the size of the European Union's emergency stabilization fund.

**26 Feb** A referendum on a new constitution is staged in Syria; the following day the government announces that the new document, which ends one-party rule and sets a limit of two seven-year terms of office for the president, received a 90% approval.

▶ At the 84th Academy Awards presentation, Oscars are won by, among others, *The Artist* (best picture) and its director, Michel Hazanavicius, and the actors Jean Dujardin, Meryl Streep, Christopher Plummer, and Octavia Spencer.

**27 Feb** Chinese architect Wang Shu is named winner of the 2012 Pritzker Architecture Prize; among his works, which use old and traditional materials in forms that honor but do not copy the past, is the history museum in Ningbo, China.

▶ In Daytona Beach FL, the 54th running of the Daytona 500 NASCAR race, already delayed by a full day because of rain, is won by Matt Kenseth after a further lengthy delay that occurred when in the 160th lap a car hit a jet-dryer truck that then exploded in flames.

**28 Feb** The international police organization Interpol announces the arrest of 25 people from four countries who are thought to be members of the Internet hacking collective Anonymous and are suspected of planning cyberattacks against government and business targets.

▶ The Dow Jones Industrial Average closes above 13,000 points, a level it had not reached since 19 May 2008.

**29 Feb** North Korea unexpectedly announces that in return for food aid from the US, it will suspend its uranium-enrichment program and nuclear testing and will allow nuclear inspectors to monitor its activity.

▶ The stock market valuation of the technology company Apple Inc. passes US$500 billion; it is only the sixth American company ever to have achieved that distinction.

▶ James Murdoch resigns as chairman of News International, the British newspaper arm of the media conglomerate News Corp., which is at the center of a phone-hacking and bribery scandal.

# March 2012

**1 Mar** Syrian government forces rout the rebel Revolutionary Brigades of Baba Amr in Homs.

▸ Serbia officially becomes a candidate country for membership in the European Union.

**2 Mar** Legislative elections take place in Iran; the government reports a 64% turnout, and allies of supreme leader Ayatollah Sayyed Ali Khamenei win a large majority of seats.

**3 Mar** Syrian antigovernment activists report that the government's military offensive against the city of Hamah has intensified; also, the government is preventing workers from the International Committee of the Red Cross from entering Homs.

**4 Mar** After four years as Russia's prime minister, former president Vladimir Putin is elected to a six-year term as president of Russia, as was expected.

**5 Mar** An activist group, Invisible Children, posts online an informative video, *KONY 2012,* about the brutal Ugandan militia group the Lord's Resistance Army, and the video goes hugely viral in the US within days, prompting donations to the group and calls for action.

**6 Mar** The maiden flight of a new twice-weekly Turkish Airlines service to Mogadishu, Somalia, lands safely at the war-torn city's airport; Turkish Airlines is the first major commercial carrier to serve the country in more than 20 years.

▸ The American energy company Chevron declares that a fire that followed an explosion caused by a buildup of gas pressure on the *KS Endeavor* gas-exploration drilling rig off the southeastern coast of Nigeria has burned itself out after 46 days; the rig was destroyed, and two workers on it were killed.

**7 Mar** A report is presented to a physics conference stating that researchers at the Fermi National Accelerator Laboratory in Batavia IL have found a bump in their data that might be evidence of the long-sought Higgs boson; the finding coincides with a similar discovery, announced in December 2011, by researchers at the Large Hadron Collider near Geneva.

**8 Mar** British Queen Elizabeth II begins her Diamond Jubilee tour of the UK with a visit to Leicester, England, where she takes in a cultural dance performance and a fashion parade.

▸ In New York City the winners of the National Book Critics Circle Awards are announced as Edith Pearlman for *Binocular Vision: New and Selected Stories* (fiction), Maya Jasanoff for *Liberty's Exiles: American Loyalists in the Revolutionary World* (nonfiction), John Lewis Gaddis for *George F. Kennan: An American Life* (biography), Mira Bartók for *The Memory Palace: A Memoir* (autobiography), Laura Kasischke for *Space, in Chains* (poetry), and Geoff Dyer for *Otherwise Known as the Human Condition: Selected Essays and Reviews* (criticism).

**9 Mar** Greece enters debt restructuring, in effect defaulting on its debt; under the deal the bulk of its remaining debt will be held by the European Central Bank, the IMF, and individual European countries.

▸ The US Department of Labor reports that the unemployment rate in February remained at 8.3% and that 227,000 new jobs were added to the economy.

**10 Mar** A 340-ton granite boulder arrives in Los Angeles to become part of the planned art installation *Levitated Mass* by Michael Heizer at the Los Angeles County Museum of Art; the boulder's journey began in Riverside CA, where it was quarried, in February.

**11 Mar** In a horrific case of mass murder, an apparently deranged US Army sergeant leaves his base in Afghanistan's Kandahar province and goes door-to-door in nearby villages, shooting and killing 17 residents.

▸ The All-England Open men's badminton championship is won by Lin Dan of China after Lee Chong Wei of Malaysia retires with an injury; Li Xuerui of China defeats her countrywoman Wang Yihan to win the women's title.

**12 Mar** Both antigovernment activists and the Syrian government report that dozens of people in Homs were massacred overnight; the activists say that government forces were responsible, and the government blames "terrorist armed groups."

▸ The civil rights division of the US Department of Justice tells Texas that it may not enforce its new law requiring voters to present state-issued photo identification, saying that the law would have an adverse effect on Hispanic voters.

**13 Mar** Encyclopædia Britannica announces that the 2010 printing of its 32-volume printed set will, after 244 years, be the final one and that henceforth the reference publisher will focus on online and mobile publishing and on creating educational materials for schools.

▸ The Nasdaq composite stock index closes at 3039.88, its first close above 3000 since 2000.

**14 Mar** The member countries of the euro zone formally approve a plan for a second financial bailout of Greece and authorize the release of the first installment of the funds.

▸ The International Criminal Court issues its first verdict; it finds Thomas Lubanga, leader of a rebel militia in the Democratic Republic of the Congo, guilty of having recruited children under the age of 15 and of having used them in war.

▸ Dallas Seavey wins the Iditarod Trail Sled Dog Race, crossing under the Burled Arch in Nome AK after a 1,570-km (975-mi) journey that took him 9 days 4 hours 29 minutes 26 seconds; Seavey, at age 25, is the youngest person to have won the annual race.

**15 Mar** Bo Xilai is removed as Communist Party chief of Chongqing, China; it is later reported that Bo was making plans to obstruct a corruption investigation that involved members of his family.

▸ US government officials say that the country intends to resume sending military aid to Egypt; the US has supplied such assistance for some 30 years but suspended it in 2011 over human rights concerns during the revolution.

▸ The US$250,000 A.M. Turing Award for excellence in computer science is granted to Judea Pearl for his contributions to artificial intelligence, including work on processing information under uncertainty and on machine learning about causality.

**16 Mar** Rowan Williams announces that he will resign as archbishop of Canterbury and senior bishop of the Anglican Communion at the end of the year; he intends to be a theologian at the University of Cambridge.

**17 Mar** With its 16–9 defeat of France on the final day of competition, Wales wins the Six Nations Rugby Union championship with a 5–0 record.

▶ At the World Cup skiing finals in Schladming, Austria, American Lindsey Vonn sets a record for most World Cup points won by a female competitor in a season (1,980); the previous record (1,970), set in 2006, was held by Janica Kostelic of Croatia.

**18 Mar** For the first time in more than two decades, the Somali National Theatre in Mogadishu opens; some 1,000 people attend a program consisting of a play, music, and comedy performances.

**19 Mar** Australia's Senate passes a 30% tax on windfall profits in iron and coal mining; the money will go to pensions and public works, among other priorities.

▶ Laurent Kasper-Ansermet resigns from the joint UN-Cambodian Khmer Rouge war-crimes tribunal, saying that his investigations were being impeded by the Cambodian government; Kasper-Ansermet replaced another judge on the tribunal who had resigned in October 2011 for similar reasons.

**20 Mar** The Association of Southeast Asian Nations reveals that Myanmar (Burma) has invited representatives from all the other member countries to monitor legislative elections in the country that are scheduled for 1 April.

▶ The state attorney in Florida's Seminole county announces that he will open an investigation, to run parallel with one opened the previous day by the US Department of Justice, into the February shooting death in Sanford of Trayvon Martin, an unarmed teenager, by George Zimmerman, a neighborhood watch volunteer; Zimmerman, who claimed self-defense under Florida law, was not arrested at the time of the shooting, and outrage has spread throughout the country.

**21 Mar** The UN Security Council endorses a peace plan for Syria presented by UN and Arab League envoy Kofi Annan.

▶ The National Football League suspends New Orleans Saints coach Sean Payton for a full year as punishment for a program in which players were offered rewards for injuring opponents; other penalties assessed include the indefinite suspension of former Saints defensive coordinator Gregg Williams, who designed the bounty program.

**22 Mar** Pres. Amadou Toumani Touré of Mali is overthrown by disaffected soldiers apparently led by Capt. Amadou Haya Sanogo; it is announced that the constitution has been suspended and that the reason for the coup is the government's failure to deal adequately with a Tuareg insurgency in the north.

---

**QUOTE OF THE MONTH**

❝ *The situation is very serious, and absolutely chaotic. It's a very, very big step back for democracy.* ❞

—Soumaïla Cissé, a candidate in Mali's presidential election that was scheduled for April, commenting on the coup that had just taken place in Mali, 22 March

---

▶ In Ireland the Mahon Tribunal issues a report after 15 years of hearings into possible government corruption involving bribery and land developers in the 1980s and '90s; the tribunal found rampant and widespread corruption and raises suspicion about former prime minister Bertie Ahern.

**23 Mar** A new concentrated operation to eliminate the Ugandan rebel group the Lord's Resistance Army is announced by the African Union; the operational headquarters are to be located in South Sudan, and the troops are to be drawn from the four countries in which the LRA has been active.

▶ *The Hunger Games,* a movie version of the best-selling novel by Suzanne Collins, opens at midnight in theaters throughout the US; it goes on to earn US$155 million in its opening weekend in North America, setting a new record for a spring release.

**24 Mar** Syrian antigovernment activists report that shelling by government forces in Homs continues and that the town of Saraqeb, in Idlib province, has come under attack.

**25 Mar** Golfer Tiger Woods wins the Arnold Palmer Invitational golf tournament, his 72nd PGA tour title and his first since 13 Sep 2009.

▶ *Yokozuna* Hakuho defeats *sekiwake* Kakuryu in a play-off to win the Emperor's Cup at the Haru Basho (spring grand sumo tournament) in Osaka.

▶ American film director James Cameron travels in a minisubmarine to the lowest point in the Mariana Trench, in the western Pacific Ocean, at 10.9 km (6.8 mi) below the ocean surface, the lowest point on Earth; the feat has been achieved only one other time, in 1960.

**26 Mar** After a three-day visit to Mexico, Pope Benedict XVI makes the second-ever papal visit to Cuba, where he is greeted by Cuban Pres. Raúl Castro and celebrates mass before some 200,000 people in Santiago de Cuba.

▶ The winner of the PEN/Faulkner Award for Fiction is announced as Julie Otsuka for her novel *The Buddha in the Attic.*

**27 Mar** The Economic Community of West African States (ECOWAS), in an emergency meeting, suspends Mali's membership and arranges a standby peacekeeping force.

**28 Mar** The Dalai Lama is named the winner of the annual Templeton Prize, which honors a living person who has contributed to affirming life's spiritual dimension, for his work promoting cross-cultural understanding and nonviolence.

**29 Mar** A three-day summit of the Arab League gets under way in Baghdad; the last summit of the organization was in March 2010 in Libya.

▶ In a budget speech, Canadian Minister of Finance Jim Flaherty announces that the Royal Canadian Mint will cease making and distributing pennies later in the year.

**30 Mar** Finance ministers of the member countries of the euro zone, known as the Eurogroup, agree to maintain a fund of about €800 billion (about US$1 trillion), to be available to bail out members if necessary.

▶ Officials in Wisconsin announce that a recall election against Gov. Scott Walker will take place in June; in early 2011 Walker ignited the ire of some voters by supporting and signing legislation to weaken public unions.

**31 Mar** The Freedom and Justice Party, the political arm of the Muslim Brotherhood, nominates Khairat al-Shater as its candidate for the presidency of Egypt; it previously vowed not to contest the election.

▶ Monterosso, from the stables of the ruler of Dubayy, wins the Dubai World Cup, the world's richest horse race.

# April 2012

**1 Apr** Elections are held in Myanmar (Burma) for about 10% of the seats in the lower house of the legislature; the vast majority of those seats are won by the opposition National League for Democracy, with one seat going to iconic democracy advocate Aung San Suu Kyi.

▸ Amadou Haya Sanogo, leader of the recent coup in Mali, declares that he will reinstate the constitution and hold a convention to appoint an interim government to organize elections; also, Tuareg rebels seize control of the ancient city of Timbuktu.

**2 Apr** The US Supreme Court rules that the constitutional ban on unreasonable search does not preclude the strip search of anyone who has been arrested and is to enter a jail's general population, even if the arrest is for a minor offense and even if there is no reasonable cause for the search.

▸ The NCAA championship in men's basketball is won by the University of Kentucky, which defeats the University of Kansas 67–59; the following day Baylor University, with a record of 40–0, defeats the University of Notre Dame 80–61 to win the women's title.

**3 Apr** The British satellite broadcasting company BSkyB announces the resignation of James Murdoch as its chairman; this amounts to a withdrawal from British media for Murdoch.

**4 Apr** At a ceremony at Somalia's newly reopened National Theater in Mogadishu, a bomb explodes during a speech by Prime Minister Abdiweli Mohamed Ali; four people, including two sports officials, are killed.

**5 Apr** A derelict Japanese squid trawler that was set adrift by the tsunami triggered by the Japanese earthquake of 11 Mar 2011 and drifted to the waters off Alaska is scuttled by the US Coast Guard, which determined that the boat posed a hazard to ships in the area.

**6 Apr** The US Department of Labor reports that the unemployment rate in March decreased to 8.2% but that the economy added only a disappointing 120,000 nonfarm jobs.

▸ The last play written by Tennessee Williams, *In Masks Outrageous and Austere*, which has never been performed before, opens in previews Off-Broadway at the Culture Project.

**7 Apr** The contestants in the 158th University Boat Race are in a tight race when a protester swims into the path of the boats, and the race is halted; when it resumes 31 minutes later, Cambridge is the victor; Cambridge now leads the series 81–76.

**8 Apr** Pakistani Pres. Asif Ali Zardari meets in New Delhi with Indian Prime Minister Manmohan Singh; it is the first state visit to India by a Pakistani head of state since 2005.

▸ Bubba Watson of the US wins the Masters golf tournament in Augusta GA after defeating South African Louis Oosthuizen on the second hole in a sudden-death play-off.

**9 Apr** The online social network Facebook announces its purchase for about US$1 billion in cash and stock of Instagram, a popular network that makes it easy to add special effects to photographs taken with mobile phones and to share the photos.

**10 Apr** An administrative court in Egypt issues a preliminary injunction that suspends the committee chosen to write a new constitution, because the members appointed by the legislature are not political outsiders, as they are required to be.

▸ Pres. Evo Morales of Bolivia rescinds a contract previously granted to a Brazilian construction company to build a controversial road through the Amazon.

**11 Apr** The US Food and Drug Administration announces new rules that will require farmers to get a prescription from a veterinarian in order to feed antibiotics to livestock; antibiotics have been routinely fed to farm animals, a practice that has contributed to an increase in antibiotic-resistant bacteria.

**12 Apr** A military coup takes place in Guinea-Bissau shortly before a planned presidential runoff election; the front-runner, Prime Minister Carlos Gomes Júnior, who is a champion of military reform, is taken prisoner.

▸ A project to use all of the world's supplies of a new and relatively low-cost vaccine against cholera gets under way in Haiti, where an outbreak has killed more than 7,000 people since it began about 18 months earlier.

**13 Apr** In honor of the centenary of the birth of Kim Il-Sung, North Korea's first leader, the country launches a rocket carrying a satellite in spite of opposition from the West, which regards the launching as a test of a long-range missile; the rocket disintegrates shortly after liftoff.

**14 Apr** The UN Security Council votes unanimously in favor of sending as many as 30 military observers to Syria to monitor the carrying-out of the terms of a cease-fire agreement there.

▸ In a ceremony in Cleveland OH, the Rock and Roll Hall of Fame inducts musicians Donovan, Laura Nyro, and Freddie King, the bands Guns N' Roses, Red Hot Chili Peppers, and the Beastie Boys, and the backing bands the Small Faces/Faces, the Crickets, the Famous Flames, the Midnighters, the Comets, the Blue Caps, and the Miracles; producers Don Kirshner, Cosimo Matassa, Tom Dowd, and Glyn Johns are also honored.

▸ Neptune Collonges, ridden by Daryl Jacob, comes from behind to win by a nose over Sunnyhillboy in the Grand National steeplechase horse race at the Aintree course in Liverpool, England.

**15 Apr** In London *Matilda the Musical* wins a record seven Laurence Olivier Awards: best new musical, best director, best actress in a musical, best actor in a musical, best set design, best sound design, and best theater choreographer.

**16 Apr** Jim Yong Kim, president of Dartmouth College, is named the next president of the World Bank.

▸ In New York City the winners of the 2012 Pulitzer Prizes are announced: two awards go to the *New York Times*, which wins for explanatory reporting and for international reporting; winners in arts and letters include Tracy K. Smith in poetry and Kevin Puts in music, but no award is given in fiction.

▸ The 116th Boston Marathon is won by Wesley Korir of Kenya with a time of 2 hr 12 min 40 sec; the fastest woman is Sharon Cherop of Kenya, who posts a time of 2 hr 31 min 50 sec.

**17 Apr** The African Union responds to the military coup in Guinea-Bissau by suspending the country's membership.

▸ Shareholders of the banking company Citigroup vote against a proposed pay package totaling US$15 million for Vikram S. Pandit, the bank's CEO, as being higher than is warranted.

▸ W.S. Di Piero is named the winner of the 2012 Ruth Lilly Poetry Prize.

**18 Apr** Officials of the US and NATO finalize agreements to gradually have Afghan forces take over the task of fighting insurgents in Afghanistan, to keep some international military presence there after US troops depart in 2014, and to assist with the financial support of Afghan forces; other details of the transition remain to be worked out.

▸ Pat Summitt, who has early-onset Alzheimer disease, retires as head coach of the women's basketball team at the University of Tennessee after a 38-year career in which her team won eight national championships; Summitt holds the NCAA record for most basketball victories.

**19 Apr** In Paris an international meeting on Syria is convened at which French Pres. Nicolas Sarkozy contends that Syrian Pres. Bashar al-Assad is lying to the international community; the peace agreement that held briefly is collapsing under increasing violence.

**20 Apr** At a meeting in Washington DC, Christine Lagarde, managing director of the International Monetary Fund, reveals that the fund has increased its lending capacity by more than US$430 billion, to be used if necessary for the euro-zone debt crisis.

**21 Apr** The UN Security Council increases the number of cease-fire monitors to be sent to Syria to 300.

**22 Apr** In France's presidential election, Socialist candidate François Hollande wins 28.5% of the vote to incumbent Nicolas Sarkozy's 27.1%; a runoff election will take place on 6 May.

▸ Wilson Kipsang of Kenya wins the London Marathon with a time of 2 hr 4 min 44 sec, and Mary Keitany of Kenya is the fastest woman in the race, with a time of 2 hr 18 min 37 sec.

**23 Apr** Iran disconnects several major Persian Gulf oil terminals from the Internet in an attempt to counter a cyberattack on the Ministry of Petroleum and on oil-related companies.

▸ The Swiss-based foods giant Nestlé announces its purchase of Pfizer Nutrition, the infant-nutrition branch of the pharmaceutical company Pfizer, for the staggering sum of US$11.85 billion; global sales of baby food have been increasing at an annual rate of 10%.

**24 Apr** The Supreme Court of the Philippines rules that about half of Hacienda Luisita, the 4,000-ha (10,000-ac) estate belonging to the family of Pres. Benigno S. Aquino III, must be redistributed among some 6,000 farming families; large family estates have long been identified as a cause of entrenched inequality in the country.

**25 Apr** The British government releases figures showing that the economy shrank by 0.2% in the first quarter of 2012, which means that the UK is now, for the second time in three years, in recession.

**26 Apr** Former Liberian president and strongman Charles G. Taylor is convicted by an international tribunal of crimes against humanity and war crimes for his support of a militia that committed atrocities in Sierra Leone in 1996–2002.

▸ The upper house of Argentina's legislature overwhelmingly approves an initiative by Pres. Cristina Fernández de Kirchner to expropriate control of the oil and gas company YPF SA, which is owned by the Spanish energy company Repsol.

**27 Apr** The military rulers of Guinea-Bissau release presidential candidate Carlos Gomes Júnior and interim president Raimundo Pereira, and they are flown to Côte d'Ivoire; the junta also agrees to a plan by the Economic Community of West African States to deploy some 600 soldiers to Guinea-Bissau to ensure a return to democracy.

▸ The US Department of Commerce releases a preliminary report stating that the country's economy grew by 2.2% in the first quarter of 2012, a lower rate than had been hoped for and less than the figure for the final quarter of 2011.

**28 Apr** The first private operator of high-speed domestic trains in Europe, Nuovo Trasporto Viaggiatori, begins operations with a luxury train, the Italo, that travels from Naples to Milan and back at up to 300 km/hr (186 mph).

**29 Apr** American boxer Paul Malignaggi wins the World Boxing Association welterweight title by technical knockout over the previously undefeated Vyacheslav Senchenko of Ukraine.

**30 Apr** UN Secretary-General Ban Ki-Moon addresses the national legislature of Myanmar (Burma), encouraging the lawmakers to continue on their road to democracy.

# May 2012

**1 May** In Kabul, US Pres. Barack Obama and Afghan Pres. Hamid Karzai sign an agreement on relations between the countries after US troops leave Afghanistan in 2014.

▸ The military junta ruling Mali regains control after an attempted countercoup that began the previous day.

**2 May** In a historic moment for Myanmar (Burma), iconic pro-democracy leader Aung San Suu Kyi is sworn in as a member of the country's legislature, as are other members of her National League for Democracy party.

▸ Eurostat reports that overall unemployment in the 17 member countries of the euro zone rose to 10.9% in March; it was 9.9% a year earlier.

▸ The only version of the Edvard Munch work *The Scream* that is in private hands, an 1895 pastel, is sold at auction by Sotheby's for US$119.9 million, by far the highest amount ever paid for a work of art at auction.

**3 May** Haiti's Chamber of Deputies approves the appointment of Laurent Lamothe as prime minister.

▸ At the National Magazine Awards presentation in New York City, *Time* is named Magazine of the Year; general-excellence award winners are *Inc.*, *Bloomberg Businessweek*, *House Beautiful*, *IEEE Spectrum*, and *O, the Oprah Magazine*.

**4 May** Tens of thousands of people rally in Aleppo, Syria, to protest the sudden forcible closing of Aleppo University the previous day; government forces fire on the demonstrators, reportedly killing at least four of them.

▶ The US Department of Labor reports that in April the economy added only 115,000 nonfarm jobs and that some 342,000 jobless Americans stopped looking for work, resulting in the decline of the official unemployment rate to 8.1%.

**5 May** I'll Have Another, a 15–1 long shot ridden by Mario Gutiérrez, comes from the number 19 post position to win the Kentucky Derby by 1½ lengths over favorite Bodemeister.

**6 May** François Hollande of the Socialist Party narrowly defeats incumbent Nicolas Sarkozy to win election as president of France.

---

QUOTE OF THE MONTH

**"** *Austerity need not be Europe's fate.* **"**

—Socialist Party candidate François Hollande on his election as president of France, 6 May

---

**7 May** Widely boycotted legislative elections are held in Syria, though violence continues; the government bills the elections as a step toward reform.

**8 May** Dmitry Medvedev is confirmed as prime minister of Russia the day after Vladimir Putin's inauguration as the country's president.

▶ Sweden's Polar Music Prize Foundation announces that the winners of the Polar Music Prize are American singer-songwriter Paul Simon and American cellist Yo-Yo Ma.

**9 May** US Pres. Barack Obama, in a televised interview with ABC reporter Robin Roberts, declares himself to be in favor of the right of same-sex couples to marry.

▶ In a battle between two Spanish association football (soccer) teams, Madrid's Club Atlético defeats Athletic Club Bilbao 3–0 to win the UEFA Europa League title in Bucharest, Romania.

**10 May** JPMorgan Chase, the biggest American bank, discloses that it has lost more than US$2 billion in a derivatives trade that was part of a failed hedging strategy.

▶ The journal *Science* publishes online a report on the remains of a Mayan village in the Petén region of Guatemala where a house was found that appears to have been the studio of a scribe and that contains a rich archive of calendrical and astronomical calculations that were previously seen only in the Dresden Codex.

**11 May** The discoveries of scientists studying the observations made by NASA's Dawn spacecraft, which has been orbiting the asteroid Vesta since July 2011, are published in the journal *Science;* the protoplanet has some 2,000 craters and an iron core and is expected to yield a good deal of new information about the solar system.

**12 May** Manchester City defeats the Queens Park Rangers 3–2 to win the English Premier League title in association football (soccer); it was Manchester City's first title since 1968.

**13 May** Scott Thompson steps down after four months as CEO of the Internet services company Yahoo! Inc. in a scandal relating to his inflated academic credentials.

**14 May** Battle for control of the rebel-held Syrian city of Rastan, near Homs, leaves some 23 Syrian sol-

diers dead; also, for the third successive day, fighting related to the Syrian conflict takes place in Tripoli, Lebanon.

▶ The US National Oceanic and Atmospheric Administration reports that six populations of fishes, including haddock in the Gulf of Maine and Chinook salmon off the coast of northern California, have returned to healthy population levels as a result of catch limits.

**15 May** A team of UN cease-fire monitors in Khan Sheikhoun, Syria, is caught in the cross fire when Syrian government forces open fire on demonstrators; some 20 people are reportedly killed, but no monitors are injured.

**16 May** The UN releases a report stating that annual worldwide deaths from pregnancy and childbirth dropped from more than 543,000 in 1990 to about 287,000 in 2010; the greatest improvement was in East Asia.

**17 May** The US-Korea Institute at Johns Hopkins University, Baltimore MD, reports that satellite imagery indicates that North Korea has resumed work on a new experimental light-water reactor in Yongbyon, which is believed to be part of the country's nuclear-weapons program.

▶ The US Census Bureau releases information stating that in the 12 months ended in July 2011, 49.6% of US births were non-Hispanic whites, the first time the figure for that demographic has dropped below half; minorities, including African Americans, Hispanics, and Asians, accounted for 50.4% of American births.

**18 May** At the beginning of a summit of the Group of Eight industrialized countries at Camp David, Maryland, the New Alliance for Food Security and Nutrition is introduced; it is a consortium of more than 45 companies, ranging from large multinational food producers to small local exporters, that will invest in projects to help poor farmers increase production.

▶ The online social network Facebook's public trading debut on Nasdaq, the biggest listing on the exchange, results in no significant change in the company's valuation, contrary to high expectations; mistakes by Nasdaq are thought to have been partially responsible.

**19 May** In association football (soccer), Chelsea FC of Britain defeats Bayern Munich of Germany 4–3 in a penalty shoot-out to win the UEFA Champions League title in Munich.

▶ Kentucky Derby winner I'll Have Another edges out Bodemeister to win the Preakness Stakes, the second event in US Thoroughbred horse racing's Triple Crown.

**20 May** Russia defeats Slovakia 6–2 to win the men's International Ice Hockey Federation world championship in Helsinki, Finland.

**21 May** In Mali protesters—angered by an agreement reached the previous day in which junta leader Capt. Amadou Haya Sanogo will step down and be treated as a former head of state and Dioncounda Traoré will remain interim president for a year—invade the presidential palace and beat Traoré.

**22 May** The SpaceX rocket Falcon 9 lifts off from the Kennedy Space Center at Cape Canaveral, Florida, and places the capsule Dragon into orbit; Dragon is to dock with the International Space Station, taking it cargo, in a demonstration that SpaceX, a private company, is able to fulfill a contract to fly cargo missions to and from the space station.

**23 May** Millions of Egyptians line up for their first chance to choose a new president as the election gets under way.

▶ Hundreds of people are arrested in Canada's Quebec province after a violent protest in Montreal and Quebec city against large increases in university tuition; the protests began in February and have grown in response to government attempts to end them.

**24 May** A post from Xinhua, the Chinese news agency, on the country's official Web site, quotes an economist as saying that the sudden and widespread slowdown in the country's economy has been noted by policy makers.

▶ As part of her Diamond Jubilee, Britain's Queen Elizabeth II launches a Web site on which the complete personal journals of Queen Victoria are available; the project is a collaboration between the Bodleian Libraries at the University of Oxford, the Royal Archives, and the online research platform ProQuest.

**25 May** Activists in Syria report that government forces have attacked Houla, an area in Homs province, and massacred at least 100 civilians—men, women, and children.

▶ Brazilian Pres. Dilma Rousseff vetoes 12 parts of a bill to open significant portions of protected forest areas to major agricultural concerns, including the most controversial provision, which would have granted amnesty to landowners who engaged in illegal deforestation.

**26 May** Paolo Gabriele, the butler of Pope Benedict XVI, is formally charged with having illegally possessed and disseminated private documents in a scandal stemming from the publication in January and February of documents that indicated corruption in the awarding of Vatican work contracts and revealed disagreements on the management of the Vatican bank.

▶ In Baku, Azerbaijan, Swedish singer Loreen wins the Eurovision Song Contest with her song "Euphoria"; the runner-up is Buranovskiye Babushki of Russia, who offer the number "Party for Everybody."

**27 May** The UN Security Council issues a unanimous statement condemning Syria's government for its role in the 25 May massacre of at least 100 civil-

ians, including nearly 50 children, in the Houla area of Homs province.

▶ The 96th Indianapolis 500 automobile race is won by Dario Franchitti of Scotland; it is his third victory in the event.

▶ Ryder Hesjedal of Canada wins the Giro d'Italia (Tour of Italy) bicycle race by 16 seconds over Joaquim Rodríguez of Spain.

▶ The French-German-Austrian film *Amour* wins the Palme d'Or at the Cannes Festival in France.

**28 May** The Kolkata Knight Riders defeat defending champions Chennai Super Kings to win their first Indian Premier League title in Twenty20 cricket.

**29 May** The US and nine other countries, including Australia, the UK, France, and Germany, expel Syrian diplomats from their countries to express their displeasure over the 25 May massacre in Houla.

▶ US Pres. Barack Obama awards the Presidential Medal of Freedom to, among others, former Supreme Court justice John Paul Stevens, former secretary of state Madeleine Albright, Mercury astronaut and former senator John Glenn, novelist Toni Morrison, and musician Bob Dylan.

**30 May** The Special Court for Sierra Leone, an international tribunal, sentences former Liberian president Charles G. Taylor to 50 years in prison for the war crimes in Sierra Leone of which he was convicted in April.

▶ Fire officials in New Mexico say that the Whitewater-Baldy Complex wildfire in the Gila National Forest, which was started by a lightning strike on 9 May, has grown to become the biggest wildfire in New Mexico's history, having burned 68,907 ha (170,272 ac), and is still uncontained.

▶ Madeline Miller wins the Orange Prize, an award for fiction written by women and published in the UK, for her first novel, *The Song of Achilles*.

**31 May** India's government releases estimates that the country's economy grew 6.5% during the fiscal year that ended in March, down from 8.4% the previous year and its slowest rate of growth in almost 10 years.

▶ The Dragon cargo capsule built by SpaceX splashes down in the Pacific Ocean after a successful mission to take supplies to and retrieve experiment samples and remove garbage from the International Space Station.

# June 2012

**1 Jun** The US Department of Labor reports that the unemployment rate in May rose to 8.2%; the economy added only 69,000 nonfarm jobs.

▶ A referendum held in Ireland on the European Union fiscal-stability agreement that was signed in January results in approval; at least 12 of the 17 euro-zone countries must ratify the pact for it to go into effect.

**2 Jun** A judge in Egypt finds former president Hosni Mubarak guilty of having been an accessory to the killing of unarmed protesters during the 2011 uprising that led to the end of his rule, saying that Mubarak failed to prevent the killing; Mubarak is sentenced to life in prison.

▶ The Derby at Epsom Downs in Surrey, England, is won by five lengths by Camelot, ridden by Joseph O'Brien and trained by Aidan O'Brien; Camelot earlier won the Two Thousand Guineas and thus has victories in the first two legs of the British Thoroughbred horse racing Triple Crown.

**3 Jun** The celebration of the Diamond Jubilee of British Queen Elizabeth II culminates with a pageant consisting of a flotilla of some 1,000 boats, including a barge bearing the royal family, which makes its way down the River Thames through London.

**4 Jun** A suicide car bomber attacks the Baghdad office of the Shi'ite organization that administers Shi'ite mosques and other religious sites; at least 18 people are killed.

**5 Jun** Wisconsin Gov. Scott Walker, a Republican, is returned to office in a recall election, defeating Democratic challenger Tom Barrett, mayor of Milwaukee.

▶ It is reported that a team from Museum of London Archaeology has found a portion of the Curtain Theatre in the Shoreditch area of London; the theater was built in 1577 and was used by William Shakespeare to stage his plays in 1597–99, before the opening of the Globe Theatre.

**6 Jun** Opposition activists in Syria report that a pro-government militia has massacred some 78 people in the village of Qubeir in Hamah province.

**7 Jun** Syrian government forces block UN monitors who are attempting to investigate allegations that a massacre took place in the village of Qubeir, northwest of Hamah city; the unarmed observers come under fire.

▸ James H. Billington, the US librarian of Congress, names Natasha Trethewey the country's 19th poet laureate; Tretheway succeeds Philip Levine.

**8 Jun** The US Pentagon reports that the rate of suicide among active-duty military members has increased in 2012 to approximately one a day, which surpasses the rate of battle deaths.

**9 Jun** Mariya Sharapova of Russia defeats Italian Sara Errani to win the women's French Open tennis title and complete a career Grand Slam; two days later Rafael Nadal of Spain defeats Novak Djokovic of Serbia to capture the men's championship for a record seventh time.

▸ American Timothy Bradley wins a World Boxing Organization welterweight title fight against Manny Pacquiao of the Philippines in a controversial split decision; most ringside observers believe that Pacquiao won the match.

▸ Union Rags, with jockey John Velazquez aboard, wins the Belmont Stakes, the last event in American Thoroughbred horse racing's Triple Crown; Kentucky Derby and Preakness winner I'll Have Another was retired the previous day after having suffered an injured tendon.

**10 Jun** The 66th Tony Awards ceremony takes place in New York City; winners include *Clybourne Park*, *Once* (which takes eight awards), Arthur Miller's *Death of a Salesman*, and *The Gershwins' Porgy and Bess* and actors James Corden, Nina Arianda, Steve Kazee, and Audra McDonald.

▸ Feng Shanshan of China captures the LPGA championship golf tournament in Pittsford NY by two strokes; she is the first Chinese golfer to win on the LPGA Tour.

▸ In Nairn, Scotland, Britain and Ireland defeats the US 10½–9½ to win the Curtis Cup in women's team golf for the first time since 1996.

**11 Jun** The Nobel Foundation announces that because of investment losses that have shrunk the foundation's endowment, the amount of money to be given to future Nobel laureates will be decreased by about 20%.

▸ A coroner in Australia issues a final ruling that the infant Azaria Chamberlain was killed by a dingo when she was on a camping trip with her parents in 1980; previous inquests had resulted in open verdicts in spite of evidence (found after the baby's mother was convicted of her murder) showing that a dingo was the culprit.

▸ The Los Angeles Kings defeat the New Jersey Devils 6–1 in game six to win the Stanley Cup, the National Hockey League championship trophy, for the first time ever; goalie Jonathan Quick wins the Conn Smythe Trophy, awarded to the most valuable player during the play-offs.

**12 Jun** The government of Yemen declares that its forces have regained control of the cities of Zinjibar and Jaar from militants affiliated with al-Qaeda.

**13 Jun** Shinya Yamanaka of Japan, who found a way to reprogram ordinary human cells to turn them into pluripotent stem cells, which can become any type of cell in the body, and Linus Torvalds of Finland, who created the open-source computer operating system Linux, are awarded the Millennium Technology Prize in Finland.

▸ Matt Cain of the San Francisco Giants pitches the 22nd perfect game in Major League Baseball history when he strikes out 14 batters in his team's 10–0 victory over the Houston Astros; the 21st perfect game was pitched on 21 April by Philip Humber of the Chicago White Sox.

**14 Jun** Egypt's Supreme Constitutional Court, whose composition remains the same as it was before the revolution, rules that the election of the legislature in March was invalid because some candidates who ran as individuals had in fact affiliated with a party and that former prime minister Ahmad Shafiq must remain on the ballot for the runoff presidential election.

▸ The journal *Science* publishes online a report by archaeologists who used a uranium-thorium dating technique to find that some of the cave art at El Castillo and Altamira, in northern Spain, dates to at least 40,800 years ago, quite a bit earlier than was previously thought and close to the time that modern humans first lived in Europe.

**15 Jun** Egypt's military government shuts down the newly elected legislature and declares its intention to issue its own interim constitution in what many describe as a military coup.

---

---

▸ The International IMPAC Dublin Literary Award is granted to British author Jon McGregor for his 2010 novel *Even the Dogs*.

▸ A 1597 Wyfliet atlas is returned to the Royal Library of Sweden; it was found in New York City, where a man had purchased it at a Sotheby's auction in 2003, and is the first to be recovered of at least 56 rare books that librarian Anders Burius stole before his thievery was detected in 2004.

**16 Jun** The UN suspends its observer mission in Syria, saying that the escalating violence has made it too dangerous for the unarmed monitors to patrol.

▸ In Oslo, Aung San Suu Kyi of Myanmar (Burma) accepts the Nobel Peace Prize that she was awarded in 1991 and gives her Nobel address, in which she speaks to the need to reduce suffering in the world.

**17 Jun** The military government of Egypt issues an interim constitution that dramatically decreases the power of the president and gives the authority to pass laws and create a budget to the ruling council.

▸ Webb Simpson secures a one-stroke victory over fellow American Michael Thompson and Graeme McDowell of Northern Ireland to win the US Open golf tournament in San Francisco.

▸ In the 80th running of the 24 Hours of Le Mans endurance automobile race, the Audi team—consisting of André Lotterer of Germany, Marcel Fässler of Switzerland, and Benoît Tréluyer of France—takes the victory, completing 378 laps; it is the first time a hybrid-powered vehicle has won the race.

**18 Jun** China's Shenzhou 9 space capsule, carrying astronauts Jing Haipeng, Liu Wang, and Liu Yang, the country's first female astronaut, successfully docks with the Tiangong 1 space lab in a milestone for China's space program.

**19 Jun** In a televised speech to the country, Pres. Thein Sein of Myanmar (Burma) announces a series of reforms to open the economy, including decreasing government involvement in most economic sectors.

▸ The Maryland Racing Commission declares that Secretariat ran the 1973 Preakness Stakes in a record 1 min 53 sec, after a panel reviewed footage of the race and determined the new time; Secretariat already held the record for the Kentucky Derby and Belmont Stakes Thoroughbred horse races.

**20 Jun** The election commission in Egypt announces that it will postpone naming the winner of the runoff presidential election; observers expected that the results would be released on 21 June.

**21 Jun** The Miami Heat defeats the Oklahoma City Thunder 121–106 in game five of the best-of-seven Finals tournament to secure the team's second National Basketball Association championship; LeBron James of the Heat is named Finals MVP.

▸ In a review of the 9 June welterweight fight between Manny Pacquiao and Timothy Bradley, a panel of World Boxing Organization judges unanimously scores the fight for Pacquiao; the official result, a split decision for Bradley, is not affected.

**22 Jun** Former Pennsylvania State University assistant football coach Jerry Sandusky is found guilty of having sexually abused 10 young boys.

▸ The 2012 winners of the Kyoto Prize are announced: computer scientist Ivan E. Sutherland (advanced technology), molecular cell biologist Yoshinori Ohsumi (basic sciences), and literary critic Gayatri Chakravorty Spivak (arts and philosophy).

**23 Jun** In Troon, Scotland, Alan Dunbar becomes the third golfer from Northern Ireland to have won the British Amateur Championship.

▸ The Australian mare Black Caviar comes in a short head in front of Moonlight Cloud in the Diamond Jubilee Stakes at Royal Ascot in Berkshire, England, in her 22nd consecutive victory.

**24 Jun** Artist Michael Heizer's installation *Levitated Mass*, featuring a 340-ton boulder atop a channel in a field of decomposed granite, opens to the public at the Los Angeles County Museum of Art.

**25 Jun** Spain formally requests financial assistance for its banking sector from the European Union, and Cyprus indicates that it plans to request aid as well.

▸ The Folger Shakespeare Library editions of the works of William Shakespeare for the first time become available as e-books.

**26 Jun** The British House of Commons agrees to the renaming of the clock tower of London's Houses of Parliament in honor of the Diamond Jubilee of Queen Elizabeth II; the tower, which is commonly called Big Ben, is to be officially known as Elizabeth Tower.

**27 Jun** The British bank Barclays agrees to pay some US$450 million to settle accusations that it manipulated interest rates, including the London Interbank Offered Rate (LIBOR), in order to increase its own profits.

▸ In Belfast, Northern Ireland, Queen Elizabeth II of Britain publicly shakes hands with Martin McGuinness, the deputy first minister of Northern Ireland's power-sharing government and a former commander in the Irish Republican Army.

▸ Scientists studying the recently discovered hominin species *Australopithecus sediba* report their findings that the diet of that species, unlike that of contemporaneous hominin species, probably consisted mostly of leaves, fruit, and tree bark.

**28 Jun** The US Supreme Court rules constitutional the provision of the Affordable Care Act that penalizes individuals who fail to acquire health insurance, but it strikes down provisions intended to push states into expanding Medicaid programs to cover more of the poor.

**29 Jun** Syrian opposition groups report that well over 100 civilians were killed the previous day, most of them as a result of a government assault on Douma, a suburb of Damascus.

▸ At a summit of the member countries of the euro zone, agreements are made to consider establishing a single banking supervisory agency for the euro zone and to allow bailout funds to be lent directly to undercapitalized banks rather than being added to the national debt of countries receiving assistance.

**30 Jun** Witnesses in Timbuktu, Mali, say that Islamic militants who took control of the area have begun destroying mausoleums of Sufi saints—sites that are considered an important part of the city's cultural heritage.

# Disasters

*Listed here are major disasters between July 2011 and June 2012. The list includes natural and nonmilitary mechanical disasters that claimed 15 or more lives and/or resulted in significant damage to property.*

## July 2011

**5 Jul** Off Tunisia. A boat carrying mostly Somali migrants to Saudi Arabia catches fire about four hours after its departure from Sudan and sinks in the Red Sea; some 200 passengers drown.

**8 Jul** Democratic Republic of the Congo. A Hewa Bora Airways passenger plane crashes as it attempts to land in bad weather at Kisangani; at least 70 of those aboard are killed.

**10 Jul** Russia. A riverboat dating from 1955 that is carrying families on a Volga River cruise sinks in the Kuybyshev Reservoir; 122 of the passengers, including 28 children, lose their lives.

**10 Jul** Uttar Pradesh, India. A passenger train bound for New Delhi derails about 120 km (75 mi) from Lucknow; at least 69 passengers perish.

**11 Jul** Bangladesh. An open truck carrying dozens of boys returning to their school from an association football (soccer) match goes off the road and flips into a roadside canal; at least 44 of the schoolboys drown in the canal.

**17 Jul** Ecuador. The government bans the sale of alcohol for three days in response to a spate of methyl alcohol poisoning from the consumption of bootleg liquor that left at least 21 people dead.

23 Jul Near Wenzhou, China. A high-speed train plows into another train that has stalled on the tracks in a horrific accident in which at least six cars derail and 40 people are killed.

26 Jul Morocco. A C-130 troop transport aircraft of the Royal Moroccan Air Force crashes into a mountain near the city of Guelmim; 80 of those aboard perish in the country's worst air disaster since 1973.

27 Jul South Korea. Mud slides caused by heavy rainfall crush parts of a resort village in Chuncheon and homes on a hillside in southern Seoul, killing at least 29 people; at least 59 people die as a result of the rains throughout the country.

# August 2011

9 Aug Comoros. A passenger ferry traveling from Moroni on Grande Comore to Anjouan hits rocks and capsizes; more than 50 people are drowned.

22 Aug Uttar Pradesh, India. A truck carrying devotees to a temple in Ballia district overturns into a water-filled ditch; at least 41 passengers perish.

28 Aug US. Hurricane Irene churns up the eastern seaboard for a second day, leaving flooding, destroyed homes and damaged property, and about 40 people dead in its wake.

29 Aug Uganda. Landslides following heavy rain cause the deaths of at least 40 people in the eastern Bulambuli district.

31 Aug New York City. The city medical examiner reports that 19 people died as a result of excessive heat in the city in late July and August.

# September 2011

4 Sep Western and central Japan. Massive flooding results when Typhoon Talas makes landfall; at least 40 people are killed, and dozens more are said to be missing.

7 Sep Yaroslavl, Russia. A chartered passenger plane carrying most of the Yaroslavl Lokomotiv professional ice hockey team crashes during take-off; 44 of the 45 people aboard, including all of the team members—many of whom are former National Hockey League players—die in the disaster.

10 Sep Off Zanzibar, Tanzania. Authorities say that an overloaded ferry traveling from Zanzibar to Pemba Island overturned and capsized and that more than 200 of the passengers died.

12 Sep Nairobi, Kenya. As people rush to collect gasoline spilling from a burst pipeline, sparks blow onto the gasoline, which explodes, incinerating more than 100 people and destroying many homes.

18 Sep Himalayas. A 6.9-magnitude earthquake centered in the Indian state of Sikkim causes damage in northeastern India, Nepal, and the Chinese region of Tibet; more than 100 people are reported to have died.

19 Sep Pakistan. UN and Pakistani sources say that monsoon rains have brought catastrophic flooding to Sindh province, where more than 220 people have died and 665,000 homes have been damaged or destroyed.

26 Sep Northeastern India. At least 80 people are said to have lost their lives in flooding resulting from monsoon rains, many of them killed by the collapse of building walls.

27 Sep Philippines. Typhoon Nesat pummels the country, resulting in the deaths of at least 52 people, many of them in Manila.

27 Sep Northern and eastern Thailand. A Thai newspaper reports that flooding from strong monsoon rains has caused at least 158 deaths in the area.

30 Sep South Asia. It is reported that weeks of flooding along the Mekong River caused by unusually heavy rains has left at least 150 people in Cambodia and southern Vietnam dead, the vast majority of them in Cambodia.

# October 2011

13 Oct Cambodia. It is reported that the death toll from flooding resulting from monsoon rains has reached at least 247.

13 Oct Nepal. A crowded bus goes off a mountain highway and falls into the Sun Kosi River below; at least 42 of those aboard die.

16 Oct Central America. Officials say that a week of heavy rains has led to flooding and landslides in which at least 81 people perished, at least 28 of them in Guatemala, 32 in El Salvador (which experiences record amounts of rain), 13 in Honduras, and 8 in Nicaragua.

20 Oct Myanmar (Burma). Flash flooding carries away some 300 homes and leaves at least 147 people dead in Pakokku. The flooding occurs when a river overflows as a result of torrential rain, part of the unusually intense monsoon season in Southeast Asia.

23 Oct Eastern Turkey. A 7.1-magnitude earthquake brings destruction to the area, causing devastation in the cities of Van and Ercis; at least 534 people perish, and hundreds of buildings are reduced to rubble.

25 Oct Thailand. The death toll from catastrophic flooding in Thailand rises to 366, and floodwaters begin to encroach on Bangkok, breaching barriers that were constructed to protect the city's domestic airport.

# November 2011

5 Nov Manizales, Colombia. Heavy rains cause a landslide that sweeps away homes and kills at least 48 residents.

8 Nov Thailand. The death toll from more than three months of flooding reaches 527; floodwaters continue to inundate much of Bangkok.

**8 Nov** Haridwar, India. At a religious festival, as thousands of Hindu pilgrims surge forward to make offerings, a stampede occurs when some people fall while those behind continue to push forward; some 20 people succumb.

**9 Nov** Southeastern Turkey. At least 40 people perish and numerous buildings (including two hotels) are destroyed in Van province in a 5.7-magnitude earthquake; it is the second temblor in two weeks in the area.

**15 Nov** Gansu province, China. A nine-seat van carrying 62 preschoolers has a head-on collision with a coal truck in Qingyang; the bus driver, a teacher, and at least 21 children are killed.

# December 2011

**9 Dec** Kolkata (Calcutta). A fire breaks out in the basement of an upscale private hospital, and at least 94 patients expire.

**15 Dec** West Bengal, India. An investigation is ordered after mass deaths result from the drinking of bootleg intoxicants that contain methyl alcohol; at least 170 people are fatally poisoned.

**17 Dec** Indonesia. A wooden Indonesian boat full of would-be migrants to Australia sinks in stormy weather off the coast of Java and breaks up; hundreds are missing and feared dead.

**17 Dec** Southern Philippines. Tropical storm Washi hits farther south than most storms, causing flash flooding and devastation on the island of Mindanao; more than 1,000 people die, and hundreds remain unaccounted for at the end of the year.

**18 Dec** Off Sakhalin Island, Russia. As two ships tow a Russian drilling platform toward a new assignment in the middle of a winter storm, the platform sinks; four bodies are found, and 49 of those on the platform are missing and assumed to have drowned.

# January 2012

**1 Jan** Kenya. A ferry traveling from Lamu to the Kenyan mainland sinks in the Indian Ocean after colliding with a cargo boat; more than 20 passengers are feared lost.

**5 Jan** Mindanao island, Philippines. After several days of rain, a landslide in Compostela Valley province buries a village and crushes at least 36 people; the area has been undermined by unregulated gold mining.

**13 Jan** Off Giglio Island, Italy. The *Costa Concordia*, a cruise ship with some 4,200 people aboard, runs aground and capsizes; 32 passengers are killed. The ship's captain, who escaped early in the ordeal, becomes a pariah and faces criminal charges.

**24 Jan** Papua New Guinea. At least 25 people are buried alive in Southern Highlands province by a huge landslide; it is thought that excavations for a natural gas project may have set off the disaster.

**25 Jan** Rio de Janeiro. Three office buildings collapse, leaving at least 17 people dead, with the remaining 7 missing presumed dead; work being done without permits is considered a possible culprit in the disaster.

**28 Jan** Lima, Peru. A fire races through an unlicensed alcohol- and drug-rehabilitation center that is said to be overcrowded and to treat its clients in a punitive manner; at least 27 people die in the conflagration.

**29 Jan** Florida, US. Extremely low visibility caused by fog and smoke from a brush fire on Interstate Highway 75 south of Gainesville results in a multicar pileup involving at least five cars and six tractor-trailers; 11 people are killed.

# February 2012

**2 Feb** Off the northern coast of Papua New Guinea. The MV *Rabaul Queen*, a ferry carrying more than 300 passengers, sinks; more than 200 are rescued, leaving some 100 people missing.

**5 Feb** Europe. It is reported that extreme cold over the past several days, with temperatures as low as −22 °C (−8 °F), has left at least 131 people dead in Ukraine, 53 dead in Poland, 11 in Italy, 5 in France, and 3 in Hungary; many of those who succumbed were homeless.

**5 Feb** Dominican Republic. A boat carrying would-be migrants from the Dominican Republic sinks, and 17 bodies are found in the sea.

**6 Feb** Philippines. A 6.9-magnitude earthquake buries the village of Planas on Negros Island; at least 15 people are killed, with some 70 believed to be missing.

**6 Feb** Lahore, Pakistan. An illegal pharmaceutical manufacturing facility in a residential area collapses after an explosion in the basement; at least 23 people in the building are killed.

**8 Feb** Afghanistan. A three-month-old baby becomes the 24th child in the past month to have frozen to death in camps outside Kabul housing refugees from the war.

**14 Feb** Comayagua, Honduras. A fire of unknown cause breaks out at an overcrowded prison; by the time it is extinguished several hours later, at least 360 of the prison's 852 inmates have succumbed.

**19 Feb** Ecuador. In the northern part of the country, a passenger bus goes off the road and over a cliff; at least 29 people perish.

**22 Feb** Buenos Aires. A commuter train traveling at 26 km/hr (16 mph) hits the barrier of the platform as it enters Once station, crumpling the first two cars and killing at least 51 passengers.

# March 2012

**2 Mar** US. Tornadoes spin out of a large storm system and cut a swath of destruction through the American Midwest and South, leaving at least 39 people dead in Indiana, Kentucky, Ohio, Alabama, and Georgia; the Indiana towns of Marysville and Henryville are particularly hard-hit.

**3 Mar** Poland. Two passenger trains collide head-on outside Szczekociny, killing at least 16 passengers and injuring a further 58; it is unclear why the trains were on the same track.

**3 Mar** Guinea. A truck carrying people from Moribadou to a weekly market in Beyla goes into a ravine when its brakes fail; as many as 50 people die.

**4 Mar** Brazzaville, Republic of the Congo. A series of powerful explosions, touched off by a barracks fire in a weapons depot, collapses several nearby buildings and leaves more than 246 people dead.

**5 Mar** Afghanistan. An avalanche buries the village of Sherin Nazim in Badakhshan province, killing at least 50 of its 200 residents.

**6 Mar** Madagascar. Officials say that Cyclone Irina, which struck the country's southeastern coast nine days earlier, left at least 65 people dead and some 70,000 homeless; two weeks before that, 35 people were killed and 240,000 displaced by Cyclone Giovanna.

**12 Mar** Afghanistan. An avalanche engulfs a village in Nuristan province; at least 45 people perish; it is the second fatal avalanche in the country in the past several days.

**13 Mar** Valais, Switzerland. A bus carrying children from a Belgian school home after a ski excursion crashes into the wall of a tunnel, destroying the front third of the bus and killing at least 28 people.

**13 Mar** Bangladesh. A ferry collides with a cargo boat in the Meghna River and sinks; at least 139 people perish.

**16 Mar** Kabul, Afghanistan. A Turkish military helicopter goes down onto a three-story house; at least 12 of the service members on the helicopter and 2 civilians inside the house perish.

**20 Mar** Uttar Pradesh, India. A van attempts to cross railroad tracks at an unguarded crossing and is struck by a train; at least 15 of the van passengers are crushed to death.

## April 2012

**2 Apr** Siberia. A UTair turboprop plane carrying 43 people crashes shortly after takeoff from Tyumen, Russia, and breaks apart; 31 of those aboard are killed.

**7 Apr** Kashmir. On the Siachen Glacier, at the disputed border between India and Pakistan, an avalanche traps and buries at least 124 Pakistani soldiers and 14 civilians stationed at a battalion headquarters that is crushed by the snow.

**15 Apr** Punjab state, India. A four-story blanket factory in the city of Jalandhar suddenly collapses, burying dozens of workers; 23 of them are crushed to death.

**20 Apr** Pakistan. A Bhoja Air Boeing 737-200 flying from Karachi to Islamabad during a thunderstorm crashes into a wheat field outside Islamabad; all 127 people aboard perish.

**20 Apr** Veracruz state, Mexico. On a winding highway near Alamo, the trailer of a tractor-trailer truck comes loose and strikes a passenger bus carrying farm workers; the bus overturns, and at least 43 passengers are killed.

**30 Apr** Eastern India. Dozens of people perish when a ferry capsizes on the rain-swollen Brahmaputra River during a storm; authorities say that at least 100 are dead and many more are missing.

## May 2012

**7 May** Northern Afghanistan. Flash flooding resulting from spring melting of an unusually heavy snowpack drowns 23 people who are celebrating a wedding.

**9 May** Afghanistan. A French aid group reveals that a survey conducted in March found that at least 100 children in refugee camps in Afghanistan died of exposure during the harsh winter, far more than had previously been reported.

**21 May** Albania. One of two buses carrying university students on a trip to Saranda goes off a mountain cliff near Himarë and falls some 80 m (260 ft); 13 passengers, 11 of them students, lose their lives.

**22 May** Andhra Pradesh state, India. The Hampi Express passenger train plows into a freight train that was stationary on the tracks in Penukonda, causing the deaths of at least 25 passengers in three cars of the Bangalore-bound train.

**28 May** Qatar. At least 19 people die in a fire in the opulent Villaggio Mall in Doha; the conflagration appears to have started in a children's play area and to have spread.

**Late May** Emilia-Romagna region, Italy. Two earthquakes—a 6.0-magnitude one on 20 May and a 5.8-magnitude one on 29 May—leave at least 24 people dead and crumble scores of buildings, doing incalculable damage to many historically important structures dating to the Renaissance and earlier.

## June 2012

**3 Jun** Nigeria. A Dana Air MD-83 passenger jet crashes in a residential neighborhood of Lagos, tearing through several buildings on its way down; all 153 people on board and an unknown number of city residents are killed.

**11 Jun** Northern Afghanistan. Two earthquakes in the Hindu Kush mountains, measured at magnitudes 5.4 and 5.7, cause a landslide that buries some two dozen houses in a village; some 100 people are feared to have lost their lives.

**21 Jun** Off the coast of Christmas Island. A fishing boat carrying would-be migrants to Australia sinks south of the Indonesian island of Java. A massive rescue effort is mounted, and, though 109 passengers are rescued, some 90 people are feared lost.

**24 Jun** Guerrero state, Mexico. A passenger bus carrying people to a political rally in Buenavista de Cuellar goes off a road in wet conditions and overturns in a ravine; at least 32 passengers perish.

**29 Jun** Northeastern India. It is reported that more than 2,000 villages have been flooded as a result of ongoing heavy monsoon rains and that at least 80 people have died so far; hundreds of thousands are trapped.

# People

## The TIME 100, 2012: The World's Most Influential People

*by the staff of TIME*

Each year the editors of TIME designate 100 individuals as the most influential persons of the year. The magazine's designation is not a commendation; it is a recognition of a person's influence, whether for good or for ill.

### BREAKOUTS

**Jessica Chastain** The actress turned heads in the films *The Help*, *The Debt*, and *The Tree of Life*.

**Viola Davis** The veteran actress won new fame at 46 for her powerful role in *The Help*.

**Novak Djokovic** The witty Serb won three major tourneys in 2011 to become No. 1 on the court.

**Ali Ferzat** Embracing the Syrian people's struggles, the political cartoonist speaks truth to power.

**E.L. James** The mother of two made kinky erotica mainstream with her *Fifty Shades of Grey* trilogy.

**Anthony Kennedy** The associate justice wields the swing vote on the Supreme Court. That's influence.

**Salman Khan** The computer whiz's online classroom, khanacademy.org, offers a top-shelf education—for free.

**Jeremy Lin** The New York Knicks' overnight sensation proved a smart Asian-American could star in the NBA.

**Louis CK** The popular comedian helms the FX hit *Louie*—and blazed the trail for online comedy.

**Christian Marclay** His acclaimed art film *The Clock* stitches together 24 hours of movie time-checks.

**Ben Rattray** His Web site, Change.org, helps people tell their stories and focus attention on issues.

**René Redzepi** The foraging chef's restaurant, Noma, put Norway on the map of global cuisine.

**Rihanna** The hot young singer from Barbados shines with her hard-working take on modern pop.

**Marco Rubio** The US senator from Florida, a second-generation Cuban immigrant, hopes to be the new face of the GOP.

**Raphael Saadiq** The former Tony! Toni! Toné! singer is reinventing the classic sound of soul music.

**Tim Tebow** The fiercely competitive quarterback freely expresses his strong Christian convictions.

**Yani Tseng** The young Taiwanese golfer is the world's No. 1 ranked female player and the future of a growing LPGA.

**Kristen Wiig** The SNL comic wrote and starred in the hit *Bridesmaids*, opening new doors for women in film.

### PIONEERS

**Cami Anderson** The education reformer took her radical vision for improving schools from New York City to Newark.

**Marc Andreessen** The creator of the first popular Web browser is one of Silicon Valley's venture-capital seers.

**José Andrés** Spain's great tapas chef is a celebrated food advocate, promoter, philanthropist, and artist.

**Anonymous** This leaderless Internet hive brain hacks into the digital domains of authority, encouraging public scrutiny.

**Ali Babacan and Ahmet Davutoglu** Turkey's deputy prime minister for economy and foreign minister campaign for progress in the Arab world.

**Preet Bharara** New York City's gutsy prosecutor takes on Wall Street firms, drug runners, and hackers, ensuring justice for all.

**Sarah Burton** The British designer took up the mantle of the late Alexander McQueen—and soared.

**Pete Cashmore** The man behind the visionary site Mashable uses digital platforms to make lives better.

**Maryam Durani** The owner-operator of a Kandahar radio station offers a forum for Afghan women.

**Asghar Farhadi** The Iranian filmmaker's Oscar-winning movie *A Separation* put a human face on his complex nation.

**Ron Fouchier** The gutsy virologist introduced the bird-flu virus into labs to help scientists fight future deadly outbreaks.

**Rached Ghannouchi** The scholar-politician returned from exile to steer Tunisia on a moderate path.

**Anjali Gopalan** The Indian-born US activist works to advance gay rights in her native land.

**Robert Grant** The professor of medicine helped discover new drugs that lower the risk of contracting and spreading HIV.

**Freeman Hrabowski** As president, he turned the humble University of Maryland, Baltimore County, into a scientific powerhouse.

**Samira Ibrahim** The Egyptian executive, 25, sued the military for subjecting female protesters to a "virginity test."

**Andrew Lo** The management professor's novel way to analyze financial markets: as messy biological systems.

**Dulce Matuz** At 27, the longtime US resident helped promote a path to citizenship for her fellow undocumented immigrants.

**Alexey Navalny** The Russian activist's network documents corruption in Vladimir Putin's regime.

**Sharmeen Obaid-Chinoy** The Pakistani director's documentary film *Saving Face* exposed acid-related violence against women.

**Elinor Ostrom** The Nobel Prize-winning economist is pioneering new ways to avoid misuse of shared resources.

**Ann Patchett** The brilliant author of *State of Wonder* opened a bookstore in Nashville to promote reading.

**Ai-jen Poo** The labor activist of Taiwanese descent has led the campaign to improve the lives of US domestic workers.

**Hans Rosling** The visionary health statistician turns simple numbers into an eye-opening profile of the future of the human race.

**Donald Sadoway** The MIT engineering professor's work with batteries is creating a new vision of the future of energy.

**Henrik Schärfe** The Danish professor challenged the status quo with his doppelganger robot, Geminoid-DK.

**Manal al-Sharif** The divorced mother of two led protests to allow Saudi women to drive cars—then was jailed and shamed.

**Barbara Van Dahlen** Her organization Give an Hour mobilizes volunteers to ensure the mental health of US military families.

## MOGULS

**Eike Batista** Brazil's richest man is helping reinvent Rio de Janeiro for the Olympics.

**Sara Blakely** Her innovative, slimming underwear line, Spanx, has flourished. Next up: girdles for men.

**Warren Buffett** The wealthy, humble investor is a globally admired philanthropist.

**Chen Lihua** An entrepreneur, a diplomat, and a patron of the arts champions Chinese culture.

**Tim Cook** Soft-spoken, humble, and intense, Apple's new maestro is filling Steve Jobs's big shoes.

**Ray Dalio** The Bridgewater hedge fund manager exhibits prescience and sound judgment.

**Daniel Ek** His creation, Spotify, is revolutionizing the music business for artists and audiences.

**Harold Hamm** He built a small oil company into a powerhouse of new technology, spinning off jobs and becoming a philanthropist.

**Chelsea Handler** TV's risk-taking female comic is creating a media empire of her own.

**Virginia Rometty** IBM's first woman boss is a market visionary and an advocate for corporate responsibility.

**Sheryl Sandberg** Facebook's thoughtful, energetic COO is creating positive change on a global scale.

**Hamad bin Jassim bin Jaber al-Thani** Qatar's prime minister and foreign minister has elevated his nation's influence in the Arab world.

**Alice Walton** The Wal-Mart heir opened a magnificent museum of American art in Arkansas.

**Harvey Weinstein** The producer won an Oscar for *The Artist* and champions independent film.

## LEADERS

**Bashar Assad** Syria's president cracked down on reform, exposing himself as a ruthless enemy of his people.

**Mamata Banerjee** The Indian political reformer led a movement that finally removed sclerotic communist rule in West Bengal.

**Fatou Bensouda** The Gambian jurist became the first African woman to assume the top job at an international judicial tribunal.

**Iftikhar Chaudhry** The head of Pakistan's Supreme Court has squared off against his nation's prime minister, president, and intelligence agencies.

**Andrew Cuomo** New York State's gutsy governor fought teachers' unions, lowered business taxes, and stood up for gay rights.

**Cardinal Timothy Dolan** The Roman Catholic archbishop of New York bodily led his church into the US political arena.

**Mario Draghi** The president of the European Central Bank, an Italian pragmatist and skillful negotiator, faces a host of crises.

**Maria das Graças Silva Foster** The new boss of Brazil's Petrobras is the first woman to run a major global oil-and-gas company.

**Walter Isaacson** The journalist has enlightened readers with powerful biographies on Franklin, Einstein, and Jobs.

**Goodluck Jonathan** Nigeria's new leader has fought corruption, while promoting good governance and peace in West Africa.

**Ayatollah Ali Khamenei** Iran's aging cleric is the Middle East's longest-serving dictator.

**Kim Jong Un** Will North Korea's new leader continue the regime's autarky and saber rattling at the expense of prosperity?

**Christine Lagarde** France's former finance minister will lead the International Monetary Fund during the euro zone crisis.

**Erik Martin** He is the force behind Reddit, a hive-mind Web site that covers the news in new ways.

**Mario Monti** The fate of Europe rests on the shoulders of Italy's gutsy prime minister, who takes on vested interests.

**Benjamin Netanyahu** Israel's prime minister is a strong, determined leader whose concerns over Iran's intentions may well prove prescient.

**Barack Obama** The president appeared smart, steady, and trustworthy: his GOP foes did not. And he took out Osama bin Laden.

**Mullah Mohammad Omar** The fugitive leader of the Taliban is reemerging as a leader, even as NATO troops leave Afghanistan.

**Ron Paul** The Texas congressman, a libertarian, is a rarity: a straight-talking politician who hews to his beliefs.

**Cecile Richards** Planned Parenthood's chief stands for women's right to health care and reproductive freedom.

**Mitt Romney** He has excelled in business, as Olympics boss, and as governor of Massachusetts. Can he win the White House?

**Dilma Rousseff** The onetime activist, now the president of Brazil, is tackling social inequality and reaching out to Brazil's neighbors.

**Juan Manuel Santos** Colombia's president leads his nation's battle against poverty and inequality.

**Portia Simpson Miller** Jamaica's first female prime minister is an advocate for gay civil rights who hopes to break her nation's ties to Britain.

**U Thein Sein** The new president of Myanmar (Burma) has presided over his nation's unexpected transition to democracy.

**Wang Yang** The Communist Party boss of Guangdong province is a reformer who fights corruption and promotes democracy.

**Xi Jinping** China's presumptive next president will tackle a stumbling economy, party corruption, and eroding political stability.

**Sheik Moktar Ali Zubeyr** is the purported leader of al-Shabaab, an Islamic militia that continues to destabilize ailing Somalia.

## ICONS

**Adele** Britain's soulful, candid singer conquered the world with her old-school album *21*.

**Catherine, duchess of Cambridge, and Pippa Middleton** Commoners moving effortlessly up Britain's snobby social ladder, they are avatars of inspiration.

**Hillary Clinton** The secretary of state has strengthened US relationships with allies, rallied other nations to deal with Libya and other rogue states, and inspired women around the globe.

**Stephen Colbert** The character he plays on TV's *The Colbert Report* devastates political foes in hilarious, unanswerable fashion.

**Claire Danes** Playing a CIA analyst on TV's *Homeland*, she offered a surprising, nuanced, finely calibrated class in acting.

**Matt Lauer** NBC's master of the morning *Today* broadcast is cool, relaxed, capable, and informed.

**Angela Merkel** Germany's chancellor holds sway over much of Europe, fighting against economic collapse.

**Lionel Messi** Argentina's soccer star dazzled again, scoring a record five Champions League goals in one game.

**Oscar Pistorius** The indomitable double-amputee sprinter from South Africa won the right to compete in the London Olympics.

**Tilda Swinton** The brilliant, daring Anglo-Scots actress is a powerful advocate for international cinema.

# Celebrities and Newsmakers

*These mini-biographies are intended to provide background information about people in the news. See also the Obituaries (below) for recently deceased persons.*

**50 Cent** (Curtis Jackson; 6 Jul 1976, Jamaica, Queens NY), American hard-core rapper and actor.

**Shawn A-in-chut Atleo** (16 Jan 1967?), Canadian First Nations activist; national chief of the Assembly of First Nations from 2009.

**Eva Aariak** (Arctic Bay, NT [now in NU], Canada), Canadian politician; premier of Nunavut from 2008.

**Mahmoud (Ridha) Abbas** (nom de guerre Abu Mazen; 26 Mar 1935, Zefat, British Palestine), Palestinian politician; chairman of the Palestine Liberation Organization executive committee from 2004 and cofounder (with Yasir Arafat) of the Fatah movement; he served as the first prime minister of the Palestinian Authority and was its president from 2005.

**Mohamed Ould Abdel Aziz** (1956, Akjoujt, Mauritania), Mauritanian military leader; chairman of the high council of state, 2008–09, and president from 2009.

**Paula (Julie) Abdul** (19 Jun 1962, San Fernando CA), American pop singer, choreographer, and TV personality.

**Abdullah** ('Abdullah ibn 'Abd al-'Aziz al-Sa'ud; 1923, Riyadh, Saudi Arabia), Saudi royal; king of Saudi Arabia from 2005.

**Abdullah II** ('Abd Allah ibn al-Husayn; 30 Jan 1962, Amman, Jordan), Jordanian royal; king of Jordan from 1999.

**George Abela** (22 Apr 1948, Qormi, Malta), Maltese politician; president of Malta from 2009.

**Neil Abercrombie** (26 Jun 1938, Buffalo NY), American politician (Democrat); governor of Hawaii from 2010.

**Tuanku Mizan Zainal Abidin ibni al-Marhum Sultan Mahmud** (22 Jan 1962, Kuala Terengganu, Malaysia), Malaysian politician; *yang di-pertuan agong* (head of state) of Malaysia, 2001 and 2006–11.

**J(effrey) J(acob) Abrams** (27 Jun 1966, New York NY), American producer and director.

**Jill (Ellen) Abramson** (19 Mar 1954, New York City NY), American journalist; executive editor of the *New York Times* from 2011.

**Chinua Achebe** (Albert Chinualumogu Achebe; 16 Nov 1930, Ogidi, Nigeria), Nigerian novelist and poet.

**Amy (Lou) Adams** (20 Aug 1974, Aviano, Italy), American stage and film actress.

**Gerry Adams** (Gerard Adams; Irish: Gearóid Mac Ádhaimh; 6 Oct 1948, West Belfast, Northern Ireland), Irish resistance leader; president of Sinn Féin, the political wing of the Irish Republican Army, from 1983.

**Adele** (Adele Laurie Blue Adkins; 5 May 1988, West Norwood, England), English soul and jazz singer.

**János Áder** (9 May 1959, Csorna, Hungary), Hungarian politician; president of Hungary from 2012.

**Aravind Adiga** (1974, India), Indian writer.

**Ben(jamin Geza) Affleck** (15 Aug 1972, Berkeley CA), American actor, writer, and director.

**Isaias Afwerki** (2 Feb 1946, Asmara, Ethiopia [now in Eritrea]), Eritrean independence leader, secretary-general of the Provisional Government, and first president of Eritrea, from 1993.

**Christina (Maria) Aguilera** (18 Dec 1980, Staten Island NY), American pop singer and TV personality.

**Mahmoud Ahmadinejad** (28 Oct 1956, Garmsar, Iran), Iranian politician; president of Iran from 2005.

**Sheikh Sharif Sheikh Ahmed** (25 Jul 1964, Somalia), Somali politician; nominally president of Somalia from 2009.

**Jeannot Ahoussou-Kouadio** (6 Mar 1951, Raviart, Côte d'Ivoire), Ivorian politician; prime minister of Côte d'Ivoire from 2012.

**Martti Ahtisaari** (23 Jun 1937, Viipuri, Finland [now Vyborg, Russia]), Finnish politician; president of Finland, 1994–2000, and winner of the 2008 Nobel Peace Prize.

**Ai Weiwei** (18 May 1957, Beijing, China), Chinese artist and activist.

**Daniel Francis Akerson** (21 Oct 1948, California), American corporate executive; CEO (from 2010) and chairman (from 2011) of General Motors Corp.

**Akihito** (original name Tsugu Akihito; era name Heisei; 23 Dec 1933, Tokyo, Japan), Japanese royal; emperor of Japan from 1989.

**Akil Akilov** (1944, Tajikistan?), Tajik politician; prime minister of Tajikistan from 1999.

**Jessica (Marie) Alba** (28 Apr 1981, Pomona CA), American TV and film actress.

**Albert II** (Albert Félix Humbert Théodore Christian Eugène Marie of Saxe-Coburg-Gotha; 6 Jun 1934, Brussels, Belgium), Belgian royal; king of Belgium from 1993.

**Albert II** (Albert Alexandre Louis Pierre; 14 Mar 1958, Monaco), Monegasque prince and ruler of Monaco from 2005.

**Sherman J. Alexie, Jr.** (7 Oct 1966, Wellpinit, Spokane Indian Reservation, Washington), American poet and novelist who writes of his Native American upbringing; recipient of the Pen/Faulkner Award for Fiction in 2010.

**Monica Ali** (20 Oct 1967, Dacca, Pakistan [now Dhaka, Bangladesh]), Bangladeshi-born British writer.

**Muhammad Ali** (Cassius Marcellus Clay, Jr.; 17 Jan 1942, Louisville KY), American boxer, the first to win the heavyweight championship three times.

**Samuel A. Alito, Jr.** (1 Apr 1950, Trenton NJ), American jurist; associate justice of the US Supreme Court from 2006.

**Ilham Aliyev** (Ilham Geidar ogly Aliev; 24 Dec 1961, Baku, USSR [now in Azerbaijan]), Azerbaijani politician; prime minister of Azerbaijan briefly in 2003 and president from October 2003.

**Paul G. Allen** (21 Jan 1953, Mercer Island WA), American corporate executive; cofounder (1975) of Microsoft Corp. and owner of several professional sports teams.

**Thad Allen** (16 Jan 1949, Tucson AZ), American military leader; commandant of the US Coast Guard (2006–10); he coordinated the federal response to Hurricane Katrina (2005) and the Deepwater Horizon oil spill (2010).

**Woody Allen** (Allen Stewart Konigsberg; 1 Dec 1935, Brooklyn NY), American filmmaker and actor.

**Isabel Allende** (2 Aug 1942, Lima, Peru), Chilean writer in the magic realist tradition.

**Pedro Almodóvar (Caballero)** (24 Sep 1949, Calzada de Calatrava, Spain), Spanish film director specializing in melodrama.

**Alois** (Alois Philipp Maria Prince von und zu Liechtenstein; 11 Jun 1968, Zürich, Switzerland), Liechtenstein crown prince.

**Marin Alsop** (16 Oct 1956, New York NY), American conductor and jazz violinist; music director of the Baltimore Symphony Orchestra from 2007; she was the first woman to head a major American orchestra.

**Norov Altankhuyag** (?, Mongolia?), Mongolian politician; prime minister of Mongolia from 2012.

**David Alward** (2 Dec 1959, Beverly MA), American-born Canadian politician (Progressive Conservative); premier of New Brunswick from 2010.

**Yukiya Amano** (9 May 1947, Japan), Japanese international official; director general of the International Atomic Energy Agency from 2009.

**James F. Amos** (12 Nov 1946), American military officer; commandant of the US Marine Corps from 2010.

**Paul Thomas Anderson** (26 Jun 1970, Studio City CA), American film director.

**Wes Anderson** (1 May 1969, Houston TX), American film director.

**Tadao Ando** (13 Sep 1941, Osaka, Japan), Japanese architect; recipient of the 1995 Pritzker Prize.

**Marc Andreessen** (9 Jul 1971, Cedar Falls IA), American computer innovator; developer of Netscape.

**Andrew** (Andrew Albert Christian Edward Mountbatten-Windsor; 19 Feb 1960, Buckingham Palace, London, England), British prince; second son of Queen Elizabeth II and Prince Philip, duke of Edinburgh; and duke of York.

**Criss Angel** (Christopher Nicholas Sarantakos; 19 Dec 1967, Long Island NY), American magician and illusionist.

**Maya Angelou** (Marguerite Annie Johnson; 4 Apr 1928, St. Louis MO), American poet.

**Jennifer Aniston** (Jennifer Linn Anistassakis; 11 Feb 1969, Sherman Oaks CA), American TV and film actress.

**Kofi (Atta) Annan** (18 Apr 1938, Kumasi, Gold Coast [now Ghana]), Ghanaian diplomat; UN secretary-general, 1997–2006; corecipient, with the UN, of the 2001 Nobel Peace Prize.

**Anne** (Anne Elizabeth Alice Louise Mountbatten-Windsor; 15 Aug 1950, Clarence House, London, England), British princess; daughter of Queen Elizabeth II and Prince Philip, duke of Edinburgh.

**Andrus Ansip** (1 Oct 1956, Tartu, USSR [now in Estonia]), Estonian politician; prime minister of Estonia from 2005.

**Carmelo Anthony** (29 May 1984, New York NY), American pro basketball forward.

**Kenny Anthony** (8 Jan 1951, Saint Lucia), Saint Lucia politician; prime minister of Saint Lucia, 1997–2006 and from 2011.

**Marc Anthony** (Marco Antonio Muñiz; 16 Sep 1968, Spanish Harlem, New York NY), American singer.

**Judd Apatow** (6 Dec 1967, Syosset NY), American filmmaker.

**Benigno Aquino III** (8 Feb 1960, Manila, Philippines), Filipino politician; president of the Philippines from 2010.

**Nabil al-Araby** (15 Mar 1935, Egypt), Egyptian secretary-general of the League of Arab States from 2011.

**Giorgio Armani** (11 Jul 1934, Piacenza, Italy), Italian fashion designer.

**Billie Joe Armstrong** (17 Feb 1972, Rodeo CA), American punk-rock vocalist and guitarist (for Green Day).

**Lance Armstrong** (18 Sep 1971, Plano TX), American cyclist.

**Raja Pervez Ashraf** (26 Dec 1950, Sanghar, Pakistan), Pakistani politician; prime minister of Pakistan from 2012.

**Bashar al-Assad** (11 Sep 1965, Damascus, Syria), Syrian politician; president of Syria from 2000.

**Julian Assange** (3 Jul 1971, Townsville, QLD, Australia), Australian computer programmer; founder of WikiLeaks, the media organization and Web site that releases classified or otherwise privileged information.

**Almazbek Atambayev** (17 Sep 1956, Arashan, Kyrgyzstan), Kyrgyz politician; president of Kyrgyzstan from 2011.

**Kate Atkinson** (1951, York, England), British author.

**Abdul Rahman ibn Hamad al-Attiyah** (1950, Qatar), Qatari international official; secretary-general of the Gulf Cooperation Council, 2002–11.

**Margaret (Eleanor) Atwood** (18 Nov 1939, Ottawa, ON, Canada), Canadian poet, novelist, and critic.

**Aung San Suu Kyi** (19 Jun 1945, Rangoon, Burma [now Yangon, Myanmar]), Burmese human rights activist and politician; recipient in 1991 of the Nobel Peace Prize.

**David Axelrod** (22 Feb 1953, New York NY), American political consultant (Democrat).

**Jean-Marc Ayrault** (25 Jan 1950, Maulévrier, France), French politician; prime minister of France from 2012.

**Mykola Azarov** (17 Dec 1947, Kaluga, Russia), Russian-born Ukrainian politician; prime minister of Ukraine from 2010.

**(Verónica) Michelle Bachelet (Jeria)** (29 Sep 1951, Santiago, Chile), Chilean politician (Socialist); president of Chile, 2006–10; head of UN Women from 2010.

**Michele Bachmann** (6 Apr 1956, Waterloo IA), American politician (Republican); member of the US House of Representatives from 2007.

**Bob Baffert** (13 Jan 1953, Nogales AZ), American trainer of Thoroughbred racehorses.

**(Josiah) Voreque ("Frank") Bainimarama** (27 Apr 1954, Kiuva, Fiji), Fijian military leader; self-appointed acting prime minister of Fiji from 2007.

**Sheila (Colleen) Bair** (3 Apr 1954, Wichita KS), American businesswoman; chair of the Federal Deposit Insurance Corporation (FDIC), 2006–11.

**Kurmanbek Bakiyev** (1 Aug 1949, Masadan, Kirghiz SSR, USSR [now Teyyit, Kyrgyzstan]), Kyrgyz politician; president of Kyrgyzstan, 2005–10.

**John E(lias) Baldacci** (30 Jan 1955, Bangor ME), American politician (Democrat); governor of Maine, 2003–11.

**Alec Baldwin** (Alexander Rae Baldwin III; 3 Apr 1958, Massapequa NY), American film and TV actor.

**Christian (Charles Philip) Bale** (30 Jan 1974, Haverfordwest, Pembrokeshire, Wales), British film actor.

**Robert Ballard** (30 Jun 1942, Wichita KS), American oceanographer and marine geologist; he discovered the wreck of the *Titanic* in 1985.

**Steven A. Ballmer** (24 Mar 1956, Detroit? MI), American corporate executive; CEO of Microsoft Corp. from 2000.

**Ban Ki-moon** (13 Jun 1944, Umsong, Japanese-occupied Korea [now in South Korea]), Korean government and international official; secretary-general of the United Nations from 2007.

**Eric Bana** (Eric Banadinovich; 9 Aug 1968, Melbourne, VIC, Australia), Australian actor.

**Joyce Banda** (12 Apr 1950, Malemia, Malawi), Malawian politician; vice president of Malawi, 2009–12, and president from 2012.

**Rupiah Banda** (13 Feb 1937, Gwanda, Zimbabwe), Zambian politician; president of Zambia from 2008.

**Russell Banks** (28 Mar 1940, Newton MA), American novelist.

**Tyra Banks** (4 Dec 1973, Los Angeles CA), American model, actress, and TV show host.

Banksy (1974?, Bristol?, England), British graffiti artist.

Haley (Reeves) Barbour (22 Oct 1947, Yazoo City MS), American politician (Republican); governor of Mississippi, 2004–12.

Javier (Ángel Encinas) Bardem (1 Mar 1969, Las Palmas, Canary Islands, Spain), Spanish film actor.

Daniel Barenboim (15 Nov 1942, Buenos Aires, Argentina), Israeli pianist and conductor; recipient of a Praemium Imperiale in 2007.

Sacha (Noam) Baron Cohen (13 Oct 1971, Hammersmith, London, England), British comedian and actor.

José Manuel Durão Barroso (23 Mar 1956, Lisbon, Portugal), Portuguese politician; prime minister of Portugal, 2002–04, and president of the European Commission from 2004.

Dean (Oliver) Barrow (2 Mar 1951, Belize City, British Honduras [now Belize]), Belizean politician (United Democratic Party); prime minister of Belize from 2008.

Dave Barry (3 Jul 1947, Armonk NY), American humorist, newspaper columnist, and author.

Drew Barrymore (Andrew Blythe Barrymore; 22 Feb 1975, Culver City CA), American film actress and producer.

Bartholomew I (Dimitrios Archontonis; 29 Feb 1940, Imbros [now Gokceada], Turkey), Eastern Orthodox archbishop of Constantinople and ecumenical patriarch from 1991.

Richard Barton (2 Jun 1967, New Canaan CT), American Internet entrepreneur (Expedia.com, Zillow.com).

Jaume Bartumeu Cassany (10 Nov 1954, Andorra), Andorran chief executive, 2009–11.

Carol (Ann) Bartz (29 Aug 1948, Winona MN), American corporate executive; CEO and president of Yahoo! Inc., 2009–11.

Traian Basescu (4 Nov 1951, Basarabi, Romania), Romanian politician; president of Romania from 2004.

Omar Hassan Ahmad al-Bashir (1944, Hosh Bannaga, Anglo-Egyptian Sudan), Sudanese military leader; president of Sudan from 1989.

Muhammad Salim Basindwah (January 1935, Aden, Yemen), Yemeni politician; prime minister of Yemen from 2011.

Sükhbaataryn Batbold (1963), Mongolian businessman and politician; prime minister of Mongolia, 2009–12.

Robert Battle (1973, Florida), American dancer and choreographer; artistic director of the Alvin Ailey American Dance Theater from 2011.

Michael (Benjamin) Bay (17 Feb 1965, Los Angeles CA), American director and producer of action films.

Beatrix (31 Jan 1938, Soestdijk, Netherlands), Dutch royal; queen of the Netherlands from 1980.

Glenn Beck (10 Feb 1964, Mount Vernon WA), American conservative TV and radio commentator and author.

David (Robert) Beckham (2 May 1975, Leytonstone, East London, England), British association football (soccer) player.

Victoria Beckham (Victoria Caroline Adams; 7 Apr 1975, Goff's Oak, Hertfordshire, England), British pop singer ("Posh Spice" of the Spice Girls) and designer.

Kate Beckinsale (26 Jul 1973, London, England), British actress.

Mike Beebe (Michael Dale Beebe; 28 Dec 1946, Amagon AR), American politician (Democrat); governor of Arkansas from 2007.

Bill Belichick (William Stephen Belichick; 16 Apr 1952, Nashville TN), American football coach.

Zine al-Abidine Ben Ali (3 Sep 1936, Hammam-Sousse, French Tunisia), Tunisian politician; president of Tunisia, 1987–2011.

Benedict XVI (Joseph Alois Ratzinger; 16 Apr 1927, Marktl am Inn, Bavaria, Germany), German Roman Catholic churchman; pope from 2005.

Raymond Benjamin (24 Nov 1945, Alexandria, Egypt), French international official; secretary-general of the International Civil Aviation Organization from 2009.

Regina (Marcia) Benjamin (26 Oct 1956, Mobile AL), American physician; US surgeon general from 2009.

Alan Bennett (9 May 1934, Leeds, England), British dramatist and writer.

Robert (Julian) Bentley (3 Feb 1943, Columbiana AL), American doctor and politician (Republican); governor of Alabama from 2011.

Gurbanguly Berdymukhammedov (29 Jun 1957, Bararab, USSR [now in Turkmenistan]), Turkmen politician; president of Turkmenistan from 2006.

Sali (Ram) Berisha (15 Oct 1944, Tropojë, Albania), Albanian cardiologist and politician (Democratic Party); president of Albania, 1992–97, and prime minister from 2005.

Silvio Berlusconi (29 Sep 1936, Milan, Italy), Italian businessman and politician; prime minister of Italy, 1994–95, 2001–06, and 2008–11.

Ben(jamin Shalom) Bernanke (13 Dec 1953, Augusta GA), American economist; chairman of the Board of Governors of the Federal Reserve System from 2006.

Tim(othy J.) Berners-Lee (8 Jun 1955, London, England), British inventor of the World Wide Web and director of the World Wide Web Consortium from 1994.

Halle (Maria) Berry (14 Aug 1968, Cleveland OH), American film actress and model.

Tarcisio Cardinal Bertone (2 Dec 1934, Romano Canavese, Italy), Italian Roman Catholic churchman; secretary of state of the Vatican from 2006.

Andris Berzins (10 Dec 1944, Latvia), Latvian politician; president of Latvia from 2011.

Steve(n Lynn) Beshear (21 Sep 1944, Dawson Springs KY), American politician (Democrat); governor of Kentucky from 2007.

Bruce A(lan) Beutler (29 Dec 1957, Chicago IL), American immunologist; winner of the 2011 Nobel Prize for Physiology or Medicine.

Vjekoslav Bevanda (1956, Mostar, Yugoslavia [now Bosnia and Herzegovina]), Bosnia and Herzegovinian politician; prime minister of Bosnia and Herzegovina from 2012.

Beyoncé (Knowles) (4 Sep 1981, Houston TX), American R&B singer and actress.

Jeffrey P. Bezos (12 Jan 1964, Albuquerque NM), American corporate executive; founder and CEO of Amazon.com from 1995.

Baburam Bhattarai (1954, Nepal?), Nepalese politician; prime minister of Nepal from 2011.

Bhumibol Adulyadej (Rama IX; 5 Dec 1927, Cambridge MA), Thai royal; king of Thailand from 1946.

Joe Biden (Joseph Robinette Biden, Jr.; 20 Nov 1942, Scranton PA), American politician (Democrat); senator from Delaware, 1973–2009, and vice president of the US from 2009.

Justin (Drew) Bieber (1 Mar 1994, Stratford, ON, Canada), Canadian pop singer.

Jessica (Claire) Biel (3 Mar 1982, Ely MN), American TV and film actress.

Kathryn Bigelow (27 Nov 1951, San Carlos CA), American film director; she was the first woman to win an Academy Award for best director.

**Paul Biya** (13 Feb 1933, Mvomeka'a, Cameroon), Cameroonian politician; president of Cameroon from 1982.

**Jack Black** (28 Aug 1969, Hermosa Beach CA), American film actor and comic rock musician.

**Rod Blagojevich** (Milorad R. Blagojevich; 10 Dec 1956, Chicago IL), American politician (Democrat); governor of Illinois, 2003–09; he was impeached on corruption allegations that included the attempted sale of US Pres. Barack Obama's vacated Senate seat, and in 2012 he began serving a 14-year prison sentence.

**Tony Blair** (Anthony Charles Lynton Blair; 6 May 1953, Edinburgh, Scotland), British politician (Labour); prime minister of the UK, 1997–2007, and special envoy to the Middle East thereafter.

**Cate Blanchett** (Catherine Elise Blanchett; 14 May 1969, Melbourne, VIC, Australia), Australian film actress.

**Rebecca M. Blank** (19 Sep 1955, Columbia MO), American economist; acting US secretary of commerce in 2011 and in 2012.

**Mary J. Blige** (11 Jan 1971, New York NY), American hip-hop soul singer.

**Amy Bloom** (1953, New York NY), American writer.

**Harold (Irving) Bloom** (11 Jul 1930, New York NY), American literary critic.

**Orlando Bloom** (13 Jan 1977, Canterbury, Kent, England), British film actor.

**Michael R. Bloomberg** (14 Feb 1942, Medford MA), American businessman and politician (independent); mayor of New York City from 2002.

**Emil Boc** (6 Sep 1966, Rachitele, Romania), Romanian politician; prime minister of Romania, 2008–12.

**Andrea Bocelli** (22 Sep 1958, Lajatico, Italy), Italian operatic tenor.

**John A(ndrew) Boehner** (17 Nov 1949, Cincinnati OH), American politician (Republican); representative from Ohio from 1991, House majority leader (2006) and speaker of the House from 2011.

**Irina Bokova** (12 Jul 1952, Bulgaria), Bulgarian diplomat and politician; director general of UNESCO from 2009.

**Charles F(rank) Bolden, Jr.** (19 Aug 1946, Columbia SC), American astronaut; administrator of NASA from 2009.

**Haji Hassanal Bolkiah Mu'izzadin Waddaulah** (15 Jul 1946, Brunei Town [now Bandar Seri Begawan], Brunei), Bruneian royal; sultan of Brunei from 1967.

**Usain Bolt** (21 Aug 1986, Montego Bay, Jamaica), Jamaican sprinter.

**Barry (Lamar) Bonds** (24 Jul 1964, Riverside CA), American baseball player who broke the all-time home run record in 2007; in 2011 he was found guilty of obstruction of justice for his grand jury testimony concerning steroid use, and he served 30 days of house arrest.

**(Thomas) Yayi Boni** (1952, Tchaourou, French Dahomey [now Benin]), Beninese politician (independent); president of Benin from 2006.

**Jon Bon Jovi** (John Francis Bongiovi, Jr.; 2 Mar 1962, Perth Amboy NJ), American rock singer, musician, and songwriter.

**Bono** (Paul David Hewson; also known as Bono Vox; 10 May 1960, Dublin, Ireland), Irish rock vocalist (for U2) as well as a human rights activist and mediator.

**Boiko Borisov** (13 Jun 1959), Bulgarian politician; prime minister of Bulgaria from 2009.

**Umberto Bossi** (19 Sep 1941, Cassano Magnano, Italy), Italian politician and leader of the separatist Northern League, 1991–2012.

**Kate Bosworth** (Catherine Anne Bosworth; 2 Jan 1983, Los Angeles CA), American film and TV actress.

**Anthony (Michael) Bourdain** (25 Jun 1956, New York NY), American chef, author, and TV personality.

**Jean Bourgain** (28 Feb 1954, Ostend, Belgium), Belgian mathematician; winner of the 1994 Fields Medal and the 2012 Crafoord Prize in Mathematics.

**Abdelaziz Bouteflika** (2 Mar 1937, Tlemcen, Algeria), Algerian politician, diplomat, and president of Algeria from 1999.

**Dési(ré Delano) Bouterse** (13 Oct 1945, Domburg, Dutch Guiana [now Suriname]), Surinamese politician; president of Suriname from 2010.

**Martin Boyce** (1967, Hamilton, Scotland), Scottish sculptor; winner of the 2011 Turner Prize.

**Danny Boyle** (20 Oct 1956, Manchester, England), British film director.

**François Bozizé** (14 Oct 1946, Mouila, French Equatorial Africa [now in Gabon]), Central African Republic politician; president of the Central African Republic from 2003.

**Tom Brady** (Thomas Brady; 3 Aug 1977, San Mateo CA), American professional football quarterback.

**Zach(ary Israel) Braff** (6 Apr 1975, South Orange NJ), American TV and film actor.

**Lakhdar Brahimi** (1 Jan 1934, Algeria), Algerian statesman, diplomat, and international official.

**Serge Brammertz** (17 Feb 1962, Eupen, Belgium), Belgian jurist; prosecutor for the International Tribunal for the Former Yugoslavia from 2008.

**Russell Brand** (4 Jun 1975, Grays, Essex, England), British comedian and actor.

**Richard (Charles Nicholas) Branson** (18 Jul 1950, Shamley Green, Surrey, England), British entrepreneur who founded the Virgin empire in 1973.

**Terry E. Branstad** (17 Nov 1946, Leland IA), American politician (Republican); governor of Iowa from 2011.

**Ryan (Joseph) Braun** (17 Nov 1983, Mission Hills CA), American professional baseball player; winner of the National League MVP Award in 2011.

**Anthony Braxton** (4 Jun 1945, Chicago IL), American avant-garde reed player and composer.

**Phil(ip Norman) Bredesen** (21 Nov 1943, Oceanport NJ), American politician (Democrat); governor of Tennessee, 2003–11.

**Abigail (Kathleen) Breslin** (14 Apr 1996, New York NY), American actress.

**Jan(ice K.) Brewer** (26 Sep 1944, Hollywood CA), American politician (Republican), governor of Arizona from 2009.

**Stephen (Gerald) Breyer** (15 Aug 1938, San Francisco CA), American jurist; associate justice of the US Supreme Court from 1994.

**Sergey (Mikhaylovich) Brin** (21 Aug 1973, Moscow, USSR [now in Russia]), Russian-born computer scientist and Internet entrepreneur who cofounded (1998) the Google Internet search engine.

**Matthew Broderick** (21 Mar 1962, New York NY), American actor.

**Martin Brodeur** (6 May 1972, Montreal, QC, Canada), French Canadian ice-hockey player; in 2009 he became the all-time winningest goalie in the National Hockey League.

**Wallace S. Broecker** (29 Nov 1931, Chicago IL), American geochemist, a specialist in climate change; recipient of a National Medal of Science in 1996 and a Crafoord Prize in 2006.

**Josh (J.) Brolin** (12 Feb 1968, Los Angeles CA), American film and TV actor.

**Kix Brooks** (Leon Eric Brooks; 12 May 1955, Shreveport LA), American country-and-western singer.

(Troyal) Garth Brooks (7 Feb 1962, Tulsa OK), American country-and-western singer.

Pierce (Brendan) Brosnan (16 May 1953, Navan, County Meath, Ireland), Irish actor.

Dan Brown (22 Jun 1964, Exeter NH), American novelist.

Jerry Brown (7 Apr 1938, San Francisco CA), American politician (Democrat); governor of California, 1975–83, and from 2011.

Tina Brown (Christina Hambley Brown; 21 Nov 1953, Maidenhead, England), English American magazine editor and writer.

Sam Brownback (12 Sep 1956, Garnett KS), American politician (Republican); member of the US House of Representatives (1995–96) and US Senate (1996–2011); governor of Kansas from 2011.

Jerry Bruckheimer (21 Sep 1945, Detroit MI), American film and TV producer.

Kobe Bryant (23 Aug 1978, Philadelphia PA), American basketball player.

Phil Bryant (8 Dec 1954, Moorhead MS), American politician (Republican); governor of Mississippi from 2012.

Quentin Bryce (1942, Brisbane, QLD, Australia), Australian politician; governor-general of Australia from 2008.

Bill Bryson (1951, Des Moines IA), American-born journalist and travel writer.

John Bryson (24 Jul 1943, New York NY), American businessman; US secretary of commerce, 2011–12.

Patrick J(oseph) Buchanan (2 Nov 1938, Washington DC), American conservative journalist.

Christopher (Taylor) Buckley (1952, New York NY), American satiric novelist and magazine editor.

Warren (Edward) Buffett (30 Aug 1930, Omaha NE), American investor; CEO of Berkshire Hathaway Inc. from 1965; one of the world's richest people.

James J(oseph) Bulger ("Whitey"; 3 Sep 1929, Boston MA), American mob boss and fugitive; captured in 2011.

Sandra (Annette) Bullock (26 Jul 1964, Arlington VA), American film actress.

Gisele (Caroline Nonnenmacher) Bündchen (20 Jul 1980, Horizontina, Brazil), Brazilian fashion model.

Mark Burnett (17 Jul 1960, Myland, East London, England), English-born American reality-TV-show producer.

Ken(neth Lauren) Burns (29 Jul 1953, Brooklyn NY), American documentary filmmaker.

Sarah Burton (1975?, England), British fashion designer; creative director of Alexander McQueen from 2010.

Tim(othy William) Burton (25 Aug 1958, Burbank CA), American film director and writer.

Steve Buscemi (13 Dec 1957, Brooklyn NY), American film actor.

Barbara Bush (Barbara Pierce; 8 Jun 1925, Rye NY), American first lady; wife of US Pres. George W. Bush (married 6 Jan 1945).

George H(erbert) W(alker) Bush (12 Jun 1924, Milton MA), American statesman; vice president of the US, 1981–89, and 41st president, 1989–93; father of US Pres. George W. Bush.

George W(alker) Bush (6 Jul 1946, New Haven CT), American politician (Republican); 43rd president of the US, 2001–09; son of US Pres. George H.W. Bush.

Laura Bush (Laura Lane Welch; 4 Nov 1946, Midland TX), American first lady; wife of US Pres. George W. Bush (married 5 Nov 1977).

Mangosuthu Gatsha Buthelezi (27 Aug 1928, Mahlabatini, Natal, Union of South Africa [now KwaZulu Natal province, South Africa), South African Zulu chief, the founder (1975) and leader of the Inkatha Freedom Party.

Gerard (James) Butler (13 Nov 1969, Glasgow, Scotland), British actor.

A.S. Byatt (Antonia Susan Drabble; 24 Aug 1936, Sheffield, England), English literary critic and novelist.

(Mary) Rose Byrne (24 Jul 1979, Balmain, Sydney, NSW, Australia), Australian actress.

Nicolas Cage (Nicholas Kim Coppola; 7 Jan 1964, Long Beach CA), American film actor.

Cai Guo Qiang (8 Dec 1957, Quanzhou, Fujian province, China), Chinese installation artist.

Herman Cain (13 Dec 1945, Memphis TN), American businessman and politician (Republican).

Matt Cain (1 Oct 1984, Dothan AL), American professional baseball starting pitcher; he pitched a perfect game for the San Francisco Giants in June 2012, only the 22nd player in MLB history to do so.

Santiago Calatrava (28 Jul 1951, Valencia, Spain), Spanish architect.

Felipe (de Jesús) Calderón (Hinojosa) (18 Aug 1962, Morelia, Mexico), Mexican politician (National Action Party); president of Mexico from 2006.

Micheline Calmy-Rey (7 Aug 1945, Sion, Switzerland), Swiss politician; president of Switzerland in 2007 and 2011.

Eddie Baza Calvo (29 Aug 1961, Tamuning, Guam), Guamanian politician (Republican); governor of Guam from 2011.

Felix Perez Camacho (30 Oct 1957, Camp Zama, Japan), Guamanian politician (Republican); governor of Guam, 2003–11.

David (William Donald) Cameron (9 Oct 1966, London, England), British politician (Conservative); prime minister of the United Kingdom from 2010.

James Cameron (16 Aug 1954, Kapuskasing, ON, Canada), Canadian film director whose credits include Titanic (1997) and Avatar (2009); he was also involved in underwater exploration.

Camilla (Camilla Parker Bowles; Camilla Shand; 17 Jul 1947, London, England), British duchess of Cornwall and celebrity; wife of Charles, prince of Wales (married 9 Apr 2005).

Louis C. Camilleri (1955, Alexandria, Egypt), American corporate executive; chairman and CEO of Philip Morris International from 2008.

Gordon Campbell (12 Jan 1948, Vancouver, BC, Canada), Canadian politician (Liberal); premier of British Columbia, 2001–11, and High Commissioner to the United Kingdom of Great Britain and Northern Ireland from 2011.

Naomi Campbell (22 May 1970, London, England), British runway and photographic model.

Eric Cantor (6 Jun 1963, Richmond VA), American politician (Republican); member of the US House of Representatives from 2001 and majority leader from 2011.

Don(ald L.) Carcieri (16 Dec 1942, East Greenwich RI), American banker and politician (Republican); governor of Rhode Island, 2003–11.

Steve(n John) Carell (16 Aug 1962, Concord MA), American comic actor.

Drew (Allison) Carey (23 May 1958, Cleveland OH), American comic TV actor and game-show host.

Mariah Carey (27 Mar 1970, Huntington, Long Island, NY), American pop singer.

Peter (Philip) Carey (7 May 1943, Bacchus Marsh, VIC, Australia), Australian author.

**Carl XVI Gustaf** (Carl Gustaf Folke Hubertus; 30 Apr 1946, Stockholm, Sweden), Swedish royal; king from 1973.

**Jay Carney** (22 May 1965?, Washington DC), American journalist and media official; White House press secretary from 2011.

**Robert A. Caro** (30 Oct 1935, New York NY), American biographer.

**Caroline** (Caroline Louise Margaret Grimaldi; 23 Jan 1957, Monte Carlo, Monaco), Monegasque princess, the elder daughter of Prince Rainier III and Princess Grace.

**Jim Carrey** (James Eugene Carrey; 17 Jan 1962, Newmarket, ON, Canada), Canadian-born American comic actor.

**Helena Bonham Carter** (26 May 1966, London, England), British film and TV actress.

**Jimmy Carter** (James Earl Carter, Jr.; 1 Oct 1924, Plains GA), American statesman; 39th president of the US, 1977–81, and recipient of the 2002 Nobel Peace Prize.

**Marsh(all N.) Carter** (1940, Washington DC?), American corporate executive; chairman of the New York Stock Exchange from 2005.

**Rosalynn Carter** (18 Aug 1927, Plains GA), American first lady; wife of US Pres. Jimmy Carter (married 7 Jul 1946).

**David Caruso** (7 Jan 1956, Forest Hills NY), American actor.

**James Carville, Jr.** (25 Oct 1944, Carville LA), American political strategist and commentator.

**George W. Casey, Jr.** (22 Jul 1948, Sendai, Japan), American military officer; chief of staff of the US Army, 2007–11.

**Pete Cashmore** (18 Sep 1985, Scotland), Scottish blogger; founder of the blog Mashable.

**Fidel (Alejandro) Castro (Ruz)** (13 Aug 1926, near Birán, Cuba), Cuban revolutionary; leader of Cuba, 1959–2008; he became a defiant symbol of communist revolution in Latin America.

**Raúl (Modesto) Castro (Ruz)** (3 Jun 1931, near Birán, Cuba), Cuban revolutionary leader and politician; acting president of Cuba from 2006, following the illness of his brother Fidel, and president from 2008.

**Helio Castroneves** (10 May 1975, São Paulo, Brazil), Brazilian race-car driver.

**Catherine, duchess of Cambridge** (Catherine Elizabeth Middleton; 9 Jan 1982, Reading, Berkshire, England), British consort of Prince William (married 29 April 2011), duke of Cambridge and second in line to the British throne.

**Aníbal (António) Cavaco Silva** (15 Jul 1939, Boliqueime, Algarve, Portugal), Portuguese politician; prime minister of Portugal, 1985–95, and president from 2006.

**Roberto Cavalli** (15 Nov 1940, Florence, Italy), Italian fashion designer.

**Michael Cera** (7 Jun 1988, Brampton, ON, Canada), Canadian actor.

**Vinton G(ray) Cerf** (23 Jun 1943, New Haven CT), American computer scientist known as the "father of the Internet."

**Michael Chabon** (24 May 1963, Washington DC), American novelist and short-story writer.

**Lincoln D. Chafee** (26 Mar 1953, Warwick RI), American politician (Independent); governor of Rhode Island from 2011.

**Riccardo Chailly** (20 Feb 1953, Milan, Italy), Italian orchestra conductor; music director of the Leipzig Opera, 2005–08, and Leipzig's Gewandhaus Orchestra from 2005.

**John T. Chambers** (23 Aug 1949, Cleveland OH), American corporate executive; CEO (from 1995) and chairman (from 2006) of Cisco Systems, Inc.

**Jackie Chan** (Chan Kwong-Sang; 7 Apr 1954, Hong Kong), Chinese actor and director of martial arts films.

**Margaret Chan** (1947, Hong Kong), Hong Kong–born public health officer; director general of the World Health Organization from 2007.

**Dave Chappelle** (David Chappelle; 24 Aug 1973, Washington DC), American comedian and actor.

**Jean Charest** (John James Charest; 24 Jun 1958, Sherbrooke, QC, Canada), French Canadian politician; leader of the Quebec Liberal Party from 1998 and premier of Quebec from 2003.

**Charlene, princess of Monaco** (Charlene Lynette Wittstock; 25 Jan 1978, Bulawayo, Zimbabwe), South African consort of Prince Albert II of Monaco (married 1 Jul 2011).

**Charles** (Charles Philip Arthur George Mountbatten-Windsor; 14 Nov 1948, Buckingham Palace, London, England), British prince of Wales; the eldest son of Queen Elizabeth II and Prince Philip, duke of Edinburgh; and heir apparent to the throne.

**Jessica Chastain** (24 Mar 1977, Sacramento CA), American actress.

**Hugo Chávez (Frías)** (28 Jul 1954, Sabaneta, Venezuela), Venezuelan military leader and politician; president of Venezuela from 1999.

**Don Cheadle** (29 Nov 1964, Kansas City MO), American film and TV actor.

**Chen Chun** (Sean Chen; 13 Oct 1949, Taiwan?), Taiwanese politician; president of the Executive Yuan (premier) from 2012.

**Dick Cheney** (Richard Bruce Cheney; 30 Jan 1941, Lincoln NE), American politician (Republican); US secretary of defense, 1989–93, and vice president of the US, 2001–09.

**Ron Chernow** (?, ?), American historian and author; his *Washington: A Life* won the 2011 Pulitzer Prize for biography.

**Kenny Chesney** (26 Mar 1968, Luttrell TN), American country-and-western singer.

**Dale Chihuly** (20 Sep 1941, Tacoma WA), American glass artist.

**Lee Child** (Jim Grant; 1954, Coventry, West Midlands, England), English author of thrillers.

**Laura Chinchilla** (28 Mar 1959, San José, Costa Rica), Costa Rican politician; first female president of Costa Rica from 2010.

**Fujio Cho** (1937, Tokyo, Japan), Japanese corporate executive; chairman of Toyota Motor Corp. from 2005.

**Deepak Chopra** (22 Oct 1946, New Delhi, British India), Indian-born American endocrinologist, alternative-medicine advocate, and best-selling author.

**Choummaly Sayasone** (6 Mar 1936, Attapu province, French Indochina [now in Laos]), Laotian political official; general secretary of the Lao People's Revolutionary Party from 2006, and president of Laos from 2006.

**Chris Christie** (6 Sep 1962, Newark NJ), American lawyer and politician (Republican); governor of New Jersey from 2010.

**Perry (Gladstone) Christie** (21 Aug 1943, Nassau, Bahamas, British West Indies), Bahamian politician; prime minister of the Bahamas, 2002–07, and again from 2012.

**Dimitris Christofias** (29 Aug 1946, Kato Dhikomo, British Cyprus), Cypriot politician; president of Cyprus from 2008.

**Steven Chu** (28 Feb 1948, St. Louis MO), American physicist; corecipient of the 1997 Nobel Prize for Physics; US secretary of energy from 2009.

**Ralph J(ohn) Cicerone** (2 May 1943, New Castle PA), American electrical engineer and atmospheric scientist; president of the National Academy of Sciences from 2005.

**Tom Clancy** (Thomas L. Clancy, Jr.; 12 Apr 1947, Baltimore MD), American best-selling novelist.

**James R. Clapper, Jr.** (c. 1941), American military leader; US director of national intelligence from 2010.

**Eric Clapton** (Eric Patrick Clapp; 30 Mar 1945, Ripley, Surrey, England), British guitarist, singer, and songwriter.

**Christy Clark** (20 Oct 1965, Burnaby, BC, Canada), Canadian politician (Liberal); premier of British Columbia from 2011.

**Helen Clark** (26 Feb 1950, Hamilton, New Zealand), New Zealand politician (Labour); prime minister of New Zealand, 1999–2008, and first female administrator of the United Nations Development Programme from 2009.

**Kelly Clarkson** (24 Apr 1982, Burleson TX), American pop singer and TV personality.

**Patricia (Davies) Clarkson** (29 Dec 1959, New Orleans LA), American stage, film, and TV actress.

**John (Marwood) Cleese** (27 Oct 1939, Weston-super-Mare, England), British comic actor.

**Nick Clegg** (Nicholas William Peter Clegg; 7 Jan 1967, Chalfont St. Giles, Buckinghamshire, England), British politician (Liberal Democrats); deputy prime minister of the United Kingdom from 2010.

**Van Cliburn** (Harvey Lavan Cliburn, Jr.; 12 Jul 1934, Shreveport LA), American pianist.

**Bill Clinton** (William Jefferson Blythe III; 19 Aug 1946, Hope AR), American statesman; 42nd president of the US, 1993–2001.

**Hillary Rodham Clinton** (Hillary Diane Rodham; 26 Oct 1947, Chicago IL), American politician (Democrat); senator from New York, 2001–09, unsuccessful candidate for president of the US in 2008, and US secretary of state from 2009; wife of US Pres. Bill Clinton.

**George Clooney** (6 May 1961, Lexington KY), American film and TV actor.

**Glenn Close** (19 Mar 1947, Greenwich CT), American film and stage actress.

**G(erald) Wayne Clough** (24 Sep 1941, Douglas GA), American educator and executive; secretary of the Smithsonian Institution from 2008.

**Diablo Cody** (Brooke Busey; 14 Jun 1978, Chicago IL), American stripper-turned-writer; author of scripts for TV and film.

**Paulo Coelho** (24 Aug 1947, Rio de Janeiro, Brazil), Brazilian novelist.

**Ethan Coen** (21 Sep 1958, St. Louis Park MN), American filmmaker.

**Joel Coen** (29 Nov 1955, St. Louis Park MN), American filmmaker.

**J(ohn) M(axwell) Coetzee** (9 Feb 1940, Cape Town, Union of South Africa), South African novelist and critic; recipient of the 2003 Nobel Prize for Literature.

**Leonard Cohen** (21 Sep 1934, Montreal, QC, Canada), Canadian singer and songwriter.

**Stephen Colbert** (13 May 1964, Charleston SC), American TV commentator and satirist; host of *The Colbert Report* from 2005.

**Ornette Coleman** (9 Mar 1930, Fort Worth TX), American jazz saxophonist, composer, and bandleader.

**Toni Collette** (Antonia Collette; 1 Nov 1972, Sydney, NSW, Australia), Australian film and TV actress.

**Billy Collins** (1941, New York NY), American poet; poet laureate of the US, 2001–03.

**Francis S. Collins** (14 Apr 1950, Staunton VA), American physician, geneticist, and medical administrator; director of the National Institutes of Health from 2009.

**Suzanne Collins** (1963?), American author of the young adult trilogy *Hunger Games*.

**Álvaro Colom (Caballeros)** (15 Jun 1951, Guatemala City, Guatemala), Guatemalan politician (National Union for Hope); president of Guatemala, 2008–12.

**Sean Combs** ("Puffy"; Puff Daddy; P. Diddy; Diddy; 4 Nov 1970, Harlem, New York NY), American rap artist, impresario, fashion mogul, and actor.

**Common** (Lonnie Rashid Lynn, Jr.; Common Sense; 13 Mar 1972, Chicago IL), American hip-hop artist and actor.

**Blaise Compaoré** (1951, Ziniane, Upper Volta [now Burkina Faso]), Burkinabe politician; president of Burkina Faso from 1987.

**Alpha Condé** (4 Mar 1938, Boke, Guinea), Guinean politician; president of Guinea from 2011.

**Jennifer Connelly** (12 Dec 1970, Round Top NY), American fashion model and film actress.

**(Thomas) Sean Connery** (25 Aug 1930, Edinburgh, Scotland), Scottish film actor.

**Alberto Contador** (6 Dec 1982, Pinto, Spain), Spanish cyclist; winner of the 2007 and 2009 Tours de France; his 2010 Tour victory was voided after he was found guilty of doping.

**Dane (Jeffrey) Cook** (18 Mar 1972, Boston MA), American comedian and actor.

**Timothy D. Cook** (1 Nov 1960, Robertsdale AL), American corporate executive; CEO of Apple Computer from 2011.

**Anderson (Hays) Cooper** (3 Jun 1967, New York NY), American TV journalist.

**Bradley Cooper** (5 Jan 1975, Philadelphia PA), American TV and film actor.

**Chris(topher W.) Cooper** (9 Jul 1951, Kansas City MO), American film and TV actor.

**Francis Ford Coppola** (7 Apr 1939, Detroit MI), American film director, writer, and producer.

**Sofia Coppola** (14 May 1971, New York NY), American film director, writer, actress, and designer; daughter of director Francis Ford Coppola.

**Tom Corbett** (Thomas; 17 Jun 1949, Philadelphia PA), American attorney and politician (Republican); governor of Pennsylvania from 2011.

**Rich(ard) Cordray** (3 May 1959, Columbus OH), American politician (Democrat) and lawyer; director of the US Consumer Financial Protection Bureau from 2012.

**Chick Corea** (Armando Anthony Corea; 12 Jun 1941, Chelsea MA), American jazz pianist, composer, and bandleader.

**Patricia Cornwell** (Patricia Daniels; 9 Jun 1956, Miami FL), American author of mystery novels.

**Rafael (Vicente) Correa (Delgado)** (6 Apr 1963, Guayaquil, Ecuador), Ecuadorian politician; president of Ecuador from 2007.

**Uwe Corsepius** (9 Aug 1960, Berlin, Germany), German economist and public official; secretary-general of the Council of the European Union from 2011.

**Jon (Stevens) Corzine** (1 Jan 1947, Willey's Station IL), American politician (Democrat); senator from New Jersey, 2001–06, and governor, 2006–10; CEO of the brokerage firm MF Global Holdings, 2010–11.

**Bill Cosby** (William Henry Cosby, Jr.; 12 Jul 1937, Philadelphia PA), American comedian, actor, and author.

**Bob Costas** (Robert Quinlan Costas; 22 Mar 1952, New York NY), American TV sportscaster and host.

**Kevin (Michael) Costner** (18 Jan 1955, Lynwood CA), American film actor and director.

**Marion Cotillard** (30 Sep 1975, Paris, France), French actress.

**Tom Coughlin** (Thomas Richard Coughlin; 31 Aug 1946, Waterloo NY), American football coach.

**Katie Couric** (7 Jan 1957, Arlington VA), American TV journalist.

**Simon (Phillip) Cowell** (7 Oct 1959, Brighton, East Sussex, England), British record producer and TV personality.

**Brian Cowen** (Irish: Brian Ó Comhain; 10 Jan 1960, Tullamore, County Offaly, Ireland), Irish politician (Fianna Fáil); prime minister of Ireland, 2008–11.

**Courteney (Bass) Cox** (15 Jun 1964, Birmingham AL), American TV and film actress.

**Paula Cox** (?, Bermuda?), Bermudan politician; prime minister of Bermuda from 2010.

**Tony Cragg** (1949, Liverpool, England), British sculptor and installation artist; recipient of a Praemium Imperiale in 2007.

**Daniel (Wroughton) Craig** (2 Mar 1968, Chester, Cheshire, England), British stage and movie actor who played James Bond in films from 2006.

**Bryan Cranston** (7 Mar 1956, San Fernando Valley, California), American actor.

**Charlie Crist** (Charles Joseph Crist, Jr.; 24 Jul 1956, Altoona PA), American politician (Independent); governor of Florida, 2007–11.

**Russell (Ira) Crowe** (7 Apr 1964, Wellington, New Zealand), New Zealand–born Australian film actor.

**Tom Cruise** (Thomas Cruise Mapother IV; 3 Jul 1962, Syracuse NY), American actor.

**Nilo Cruz** (1962?, Matanzas, Cuba), Cuban-born American playwright.

**Penélope Cruz (Sánchez)** (28 Apr 1974, Madrid, Spain), Spanish film actress.

**Chet Culver** (Chester John Culver; 25 Jan 1966, Washington DC), American politician (Democrat); governor of Iowa, 2007–11.

**Andrew Cuomo** (6 Dec 1957, New York NY), American politician (Democrat); governor of New York since 2011.

**Ann Curry** (19 Nov 1956?, Guam), American TV journalist.

**John (Paul) Cusack** (28 Jun 1966, Evanston IL), American film actor.

**Mirko Cvetkovic** (16 Aug 1950, Zajecar, Yugoslavia [now in Serbia]), Serbian politician; prime minister of Serbia, 2008–12.

**Miley (Ray) Cyrus** (Destiny Hope Cyrus; 23 Nov 1992, Franklin TN), American TV and film actress and singer.

**Sprent Dabwido** (1972, Nauru), Nauruan politician; president of Nauru from 2011.

**Ivica Dacic** (1 Jan 1966, Prizren, Yugoslavia [now in Kosovo]), Serbian politician; prime minister of Serbia from 2012.

**Dalai Lama** (the 14th Dalai Lama, Tenzin Gyatso; original name Lhamo Dhondrub; 6 Jul 1935, Takster, Amdo province, Tibet [now Tsinghai province, China]), Tibetan spiritual leader and ruler-in-exile (1959–2011); head of the Tibetan Buddhists; recipient of the 1989 Nobel Peace Prize; winner of the 2012 Templeton Prize.

**Richard M(ichael) Daley** (24 Apr 1942, Chicago IL), American politician (Democrat); mayor of Chicago, 1989–2011.

**William M(ichael) Daley** (9 Aug 1948, Chicago IL), American businessman and government official; US secretary of commerce, 1997–2000, and White House chief of staff, 2011–12.

**Jack Dalrymple** (16 Oct 1948, Minneapolis MN), American businessman and politician (Republican); governor of North Dakota from 2010.

**Matt(hew Page) Damon** (8 Oct 1970, Cambridge MA), American film actor.

**Claire (Catherine) Danes** (12 Apr 1979, New York NY), American actress.

**Michael Daniel** (?, ?), American public official; cybersecurity coordinator for the US government from 2012.

**Lee Daniels** (24 Dec 1959, Philadelphia PA), American film director and producer.

**Mitch(ell Elais) Daniels, Jr.** (7 Apr 1949, Monongahela PA), American businessman and politician (Republican); director of the US Office of Management and Budget, 2001–03, and governor of Indiana from 2005.

**Edwidge Danticat** (19 Jan 1969, Port-au-Prince, Haiti), Haitian-born American author.

**Dennis Daugaard** (11 Jun 1953, Sioux Falls SD), American politician (Republican); governor of South Dakota from 2011.

**Larry David** (2 Jul 1947, Brooklyn NY), American actor and writer.

**Shani Davis** (13 Aug 1982, Chicago IL), American speed skater; first black athlete to win an individual Winter Olympics gold medal.

**Viola Davis** (11 Aug 1965, Saint Matthews SC), American actress.

**Daniel (Michael Blake) Day-Lewis** (29 Apr 1957, London, England), British film actor.

**Pierre de Boissieu** (1945), French statesman; secretary-general of the Council of the European Union, 2009–11.

**Robert De Niro** (17 Aug 1943, New York NY), American film actor.

**(John) Nathan Deal** (25 Aug 1942, Millen GA), American politician (Republican); governor of Georgia from 2011.

**Howard (Brush) Dean III** (17 Nov 1948, New York NY), American physician and politician (Democrat); governor of Vermont, 1991–2003, and chairman of the Democratic National Committee, 2005–09.

**Idriss Déby Itno** (1952, Fada, Chad, French Equatorial Africa [now in Chad]), Chadian politician; president of Chad from 1990.

**Paula Deen** (Paula Ann Hiers; 19 Jan 1947, Albany GA), American TV cook and cookbook author.

**Ellen DeGeneres** (26 Jan 1958, Metairie LA), American comedian and TV personality.

**John P. deJongh, Jr.** (13 Nov 1957, St. Thomas, US Virgin Islands), Virgin Islander politician (Democrat); governor of the US Virgin Islands from 2007.

**Benicio Del Toro** (19 Feb 1967, San Turce, Puerto Rico), American film actor.

**Bertrand Delanoë** (30 May 1950, Tunis, French Tunisia), French politician (Socialist); mayor of Paris from 2001.

**Don DeLillo** (20 Nov 1936, New York NY), American postmodernist novelist.

**Michael S. Dell** (23 Feb 1965, Houston TX), American businessman; founder of Dell Computer Corp. and its CEO, 1984–2004 and again from 2007.

**Martin E. Dempsey** (1952, Bayonne NJ), American military leader; chairman of the Joint Chiefs of Staff from 2011.

**Patrick Dempsey** (13 Jan 1966, Lewiston ME), American film and TV actor.

**Judi Dench** (Judith Olivia Dench; 9 Dec 1934, York, England), British stage, TV, and film actress; recipient of a 2011 Praemium Imperiale.

**Nick Denton** (24 Aug 1966, Hampstead, London, England), British founder of Gawker Media.

**Johnny Depp** (John Christopher Depp II; 9 Jun 1963, Owensboro KY), American film actor.

**Kiran Desai** (3 Sep 1971, New Delhi, India), Indian-born American novelist; her *The Inheritance of Loss* won the 2006 Booker Prize.

**Hailemariam Desalegn** (1965, Ethiopia?), Ethiopian politician; prime minister of Ethiopia from 2012.

**Zooey (Claire) Deschanel** (17 Jan 1980, Los Angeles CA), American actress.

**Frankie Dettori** (Lanfranco Dettori; 15 Dec 1970, Milan, Italy), Italian-born English jockey.

**Darrell Dexter** (10 Sep 1957, Halifax, NS, Canada), Canadian politician (Nova Scotia New Democratic Party); premier of Nova Scotia from 2009.

**Ikililou Dhoinine** (1962), Comoran politician; president of Comoros from 2011.

**Cameron (Michelle) Diaz** (30 Aug 1972, San Diego CA), American model and actress.

**Junot Díaz** (31 Dec 1968, Santo Domingo, Dominican Republic), Dominican Republic–born American writer.

**Kate DiCamillo** (25 Mar 1965, Philadelphia PA), American author of children's books.

**Leonardo (Wilhelm) DiCaprio** (11 Nov 1974, Los Angeles CA), American film actor.

**Joan Didion** (5 Dec 1934, Sacramento CA), American author and journalist.

**Vin Diesel** (Mark Vincent; 18 Jul 1967, New York NY), American film actor.

**Matt Dillon** (18 Feb 1964, New Rochelle NY), American film actor.

**Jamie Dimon** (James Dimon; 13 Mar 1956, New York NY), American executive; president and CEO of JP-Morgan Chase & Co. from 2005.

**Peter Dinklage** (11 Jun 1969, Morristown NJ), American actor.

**Céline Dion** (30 Mar 1968, Charlemagne, QC, Canada), French Canadian pop singer.

**El Hadji Diouf** (15 Jan 1981, Dakar, Senegal), Senegalese association football (soccer) star for French and English clubs and for the Senegalese national team.

**Jacques Diouf** (1 Aug 1938, Saint-Louis, French West Africa [now in Senegal]), Senegalese international official; director general of the Food and Agriculture Organization of the UN, 1994–2011.

**Novak Djokovic** (22 May 1987, Belgrade, Serbia), Serbian tennis player.

**E(dgar) L(aurence) Doctorow** (6 Jan 1931, New York NY), American novelist.

**Mick Dodson** (Michael James Dodson; 10 Apr 1950, Katherine, NT, Australia), Australian Aboriginal leader and activist; he was named Australian of the Year for 2009.

**Gary Doer** (31 Mar 1948, Winnipeg, MB, Canada), Canadian politician (New Democratic Party of Manitoba); premier of Manitoba, 1999–2009, and Canadian ambassador to the US from 2009.

**Timothy M(ichael) Dolan** (6 Feb 1950, St. Louis MO), American Roman Catholic church leader; archbishop of New York from 2009.

**Domenico Dolce** (13 Aug 1958, Polizzi Generosa, near Palermo, Italy), Italian fashion designer and partner of Stefano Gabbana.

**Valdis Dombrovskis** (5 Aug 1971, Riga, Latvia), Latvian politician; prime minister of Latvia from 2009.

**Plácido Domingo** (21 Jan 1941, Madrid, Spain), Spanish-born Mexican operatic tenor.

**John (Joseph) Donahoe II** (1960, US?), American executive; president and CEO of eBay from 2008.

**Patrick R. Donahoe** (?, Pennsylvania?), American postal executive; CEO and postmaster general of the US Postal Service from 2010.

**Tom Donilon** (Thomas E. Donilon), American political consultant and public official; US national security advisor from 2010.

**Vincent (Phillip) D'Onofrio** (30 Jul 1959, Brooklyn NY), American TV and film actor.

**Landon Donovan** (4 Mar 1982, Ontario CA), American association football (soccer) player.

**Shaun Donovan** (24 Jan 1966, New York NY), American architect and government official; US secretary of housing and urban development from 2009.

**Jack Dorsey** (4 Apr 1977, St. Louis MO), American entrepreneur; cofounder of Twitter.

**José Eduardo dos Santos** (28 Aug 1942, Luanda, Portuguese Angola), Angolan statesman and president of Angola from 1979.

**Denzil L. Douglas** (14 Jan 1953, St. Paul's, Saint Kitts, British West Indies [now in Saint Kitts and Nevis]), West Indian politician; prime minister of Saint Kitts and Nevis from 1995.

**Gabby Douglas** (Gabrielle Douglas; 31 Dec 1995, Virginia Beach VA), American gymnast; gold-medal winner at the 2012 London Olympics.

**James H. Douglas** (21 Jun 1951, Springfield MA), American politician (Republican); governor of Vermont, 2003–11.

**Michael Douglas** (25 Sep 1944, New Brunswick NJ), American film actor and producer.

**Rita (Frances) Dove** (28 Aug 1952, Akron OH), American writer and teacher; poet laureate of the US, 1993–95.

**Maureen Dowd** (14 Jan 1952, Washington DC), American journalist and op-ed columnist for the *New York Times*.

**Robert Downey, Jr.** (4 Apr 1965, New York NY), American actor.

**Jim Doyle** (James Edward Doyle; 23 Nov 1945, Washington DC), American politician (Democrat); governor of Wisconsin, 2003–11.

**Mario Draghi** (3 Sep 1947, Rome, Italy), Italian economist; president of the European Central Bank from 2011.

**Dr. Dre** (Andre Young; 18 Feb 1965, Los Angeles CA), American rap musician and impresario, considered a pioneer of gangsta rap.

**Deborah Drattell** (1956, Brooklyn NY), American composer of operas.

**Matt Drudge** (27 Oct 1967), American Internet journalist; editor of the Drudge Report.

**David (William) Duchovny** (7 Aug 1960, New York NY), American TV and film actor.

**Gustavo (Adolfo) Dudamel (Ramírez)** (26 Jan 1981, Barquisimeto, Venezuela), Venezuelan conductor; music director of the Los Angeles Philharmonic from 2009.

**Robert W. Dudley** (1955, Queens NY), American corporate executive; group chief executive of BP PLC from 2010.

**Hilary (Ann Lisa) Duff** (28 Sep 1987, Houston TX), American TV and film actress and pop singer.

**Carol Ann Duffy** (23 Dec 1955, Glasgow, Scotland), British poet; first woman to serve as poet laureate of Britain, from 2009.

**Jean (Edmond) Dujardin** (19 Jun 1972, Rueil-Malmaison, France), French actor.

**Mike Duke** (Michael T. Duke; ?, ?), American corporate executive; president and CEO of Wal-Mart from 2009.

**Arne Duncan** (6 Nov 1964, Chicago IL), American education administrator; US secretary of education from 2009.

**Tim(othy Theodore) Duncan** (25 Apr 1976, St. Croix, US Virgin Islands), American professional basketball player.

**Kathy Dunderdale** (Kathleen Mary Margaret Warren Dunderdale; February 1952, Burin, Newfoundland and Labrador, Canada), Canadian politician (Progressive Conservative); premier of Newfoundland and Labrador from 2010.

**Lena Dunham** (13 May 1986, New York City NY), American actress, director, and writer.

**Ronnie (Gene) Dunn** (1 Jun 1953, Coleman TX), American country-and-western singer.

**Kirsten (Caroline) Dunst** (30 Apr 1982, Point Pleasant NJ), American film actress.

**Ann E. Dunwoody** (January 1953, Fort Belvoir VA), US general; first woman to reach (2008) four-star status in the US military.

**Kevin Durant** (29 Sep 1988, Washington DC), American basketball player.

**Robert Duvall** (5 Jan 1931, San Diego CA), American actor, producer, and screenwriter.

**Bob Dylan** (Robert Allen Zimmerman; 24 May 1941, Duluth MN), American singer and songwriter; he received a special citation from the Pulitzer Prize committee in 2008.

**Freeman (John) Dyson** (15 Dec 1923, Crowthorne, Berkshire, England), British-born American physicist and educator.

**James Dyson** (2 May 1947, Cromer, Norfolk, England), British inventor.

**Steve Earle** (Stephen Fain Earle; 17 Jan 1955, Fort Monroe VA), American country singer, guitarist, songwriter, and novelist.

**(Ralph) Dale Earnhardt, Jr.** (10 Oct 1974, Concord NC), American NASCAR race-car driver.

**Clint(on) Eastwood, Jr.** (31 May 1930, San Francisco CA), American film actor and moviemaker.

**Roger Ebert** (18 Jun 1942, Urbana IL), American film critic.

**Marcelo (Luis) Ebrard (Casaubon)** (10 Oct 1959, Mexico City, Mexico), Mexican politician (Party of the Democratic Revolution); head of government of the Federal District (mayor of Mexico City) from 2006.

**Umberto Eco** (5 Jan 1932, Alessandria, Italy), Italian literary critic, novelist, and semiotician.

**Marian Wright Edelman** (6 Jun 1939, Bennettsville SC), American attorney and civil rights advocate who founded the Children's Defense Fund.

**Edward** (Edward Anthony Richard Louis Mountbatten-Windsor; 10 Mar 1964, Buckingham Palace, London, England), British prince; third son of Queen Elizabeth II and Prince Philip, duke of Edinburgh; and earl of Wessex.

**Tuiatua Tupua Tamasese Efi** (1 Mar 1938, Samoa?), Samoan royal; O le Ao o le Malo (elective monarch) of Samoa from 2007.

**Zac Efron** (18 Oct 1987, San Luis Obispo CA), American TV and film actor.

**Jennifer Egan** (1962, Chicago IL), American author; her *A Visit from the Goon Squad* won the 2011 Pulitzer Prize for fiction.

**Dave Eggers** (8 Jan 1970, Chicago IL), American author, screenwriter, and graphic artist; founder of *McSweeney's*, a media company that publishes books, magazines, and Web sites, from 1998.

**Mohamed ElBaradei** (Muhammad al-Baradei; 17 Jun 1942, Cairo, Egypt), Egyptian international official; director general of the International Atomic Energy Agency, 1997–2009.

**Tsakhiagiyn Elbegdorj** (30 Mar 1963, Zereg, Mongolia), Mongolian politician (Democratic Party); prime minister of Mongolia, 1998 and 2004–06, and president from 2009.

**Olafur Eliasson** (1967, Copenhagen, Denmark), Danish installation artist.

**Elizabeth II** (Elizabeth Alexandra Mary Windsor; 21 Apr 1926, London, England), British royal; queen of the United Kingdom of Great Britain and Northern Ireland from 1952.

**Lawrence J(oseph) Ellison** (17 Aug 1944, Chicago IL), American corporate executive; founder and CEO of Oracle Corp. from 1977.

**James Ellroy** (Lee Earle Ellroy; 4 Mar 1948, Los Angeles CA), American mystery writer.

**Ernie Els** (Theodore Ernest Els; 17 Oct 1969, Johannesburg, South Africa), South African golfer.

**Mike Eman** (Michiel; 1 Sep 1961, Oranjestad, Aruba), Aruban politician; prime minister of Aruba from 2009.

**Rahm Emanuel** (29 Nov 1959, Chicago IL), American politician (Democrat); congressman from Illinois, 2003–09, White House chief of staff, 2009–10, mayor of Chicago from 2011.

**Eminem** (Marshall Bruce Mathers III; 17 Oct 1973, St. Joseph MO), American hip-hop artist.

**Emmanuel III Delly** (Emmanuel-Karim Delly; 6 Oct 1927, Telkaif, Iraq), Iraqi churchman; patriarch of Babylonia and the Chaldeans (leader of the Chaldean Catholic Church) from 2003 and Roman Catholic cardinal from 2007.

**Anne Enright** (11 Oct 1962, Dublin, Ireland), Irish writer; her novel *The Gathering* was awarded the 2007 Man Booker Prize.

**Recep Tayyip Erdogan** (26 Feb 1954, Istanbul, Turkey), Turkish politician (Justice and Development Party); prime minister of Turkey from 2003.

**Dervis Eroglu** (1938), Turkish Cypriot politician; president of the Turkish Republic of Northern Cyprus from 2010.

**Béji Caïd Essebsi** (1926, ?), Tunisian politician; interim prime minister of Tunisia in 2011.

**Melissa Etheridge** (29 May 1961, Leavenworth KS), American rock singer and songwriter.

**Samuel Eto'o (Fils)** (10 Mar 1981, Nkon, Cameroon), Cameroonian association football (soccer) player; he was voted African Footballer of the Year in 2003, 2004, 2005, and 2010.

**John Fahey** (New York City NY), American executive; president and CEO of the National Geographic Society, 1998–2010, and chairman of the board and CEO from 2011.

**Richard D. Fairbank** (18 Sep 1950, Menlo Park CA), American corporate executive; founder, chairman, and CEO of Capital One Financial Corp. from 1988.

**Edie Falco** (Edith Falco; 5 Jul 1963, Brooklyn NY), American film and TV actress.

**Mary Fallin** (9 Dec 1954, Warrensburg MO), American politician (Republican); governor of Oklahoma from 2011.

**Jimmy Fallon** (James Thomas Fallon, Jr.; 19 Sep 1974, Brooklyn NY), American comedian and talk-show host.

**(Hannah) Dakota Fanning** (23 Feb 1994, Conyers GA), American film actress.

**Abdirahman Mohamed Farole** (1945, Italian Somaliland [now in Somalia]), Somali politician; president of the secessionist republic of Puntland from 2009.

**Louis (Abdul) Farrakhan** (Louis Eugene Walcott; 11 May 1933, Bronx NY), American leader of the Nation of Islam (Black Muslims) from 1978.

**Colin (James) Farrell** (31 May 1976, Dublin, Ireland), Irish actor.

**Suzanne Farrell** (Roberta Sue Ficker; 16 Aug 1945, Cincinnati OH), American ballet dancer.

**Michael Fassbender** (2 Apr 1977, Heidelberg, Germany), German actor.

**Anthony S(tephen) Fauci** (24 Dec 1940, Brooklyn NY), American public-health physician and AIDS researcher; director of the National Institute of Allergy and Infectious Diseases from 1984; won a Presidential Medal of Freedom in 2008.

**(Catharine) Drew Gilpin Faust** (18 Sep 1947, New York NY), American educator and historian; president of Harvard University from 2007.

**Werner Faymann** (4 May 1960, Vienna, Austria), Austrian politician (Social Democrat); chancellor of Austria from 2008.

**Salam Fayyad** (1952, near Tulkarm, Jordan [West Bank]), Palestinian politician (Third Way); prime minister of the Palestinian Authority from 2007.

**Roger Federer** (8 Aug 1981, Basel, Switzerland), Swiss tennis player who has won the most Grand Slam tournaments in men's professional tennis history.

**Felipe** (Felipe de Borbón y Grecia; 30 Jan 1968, Madrid, Spain), Spanish royal, prince of Asturias, and heir to the Spanish throne.

**Julian (Alexander) Fellowes** (17 Aug 1949, Cairo, Egypt), British actor, writer, and producer.

**Dennis Fentie** (8 Nov 1950, Edmonton, AB, Canada), Canadian politician; premier of Yukon, 2002–11.

**Alex Ferguson** (31 Dec 1941, Glasgow, Scotland), association football (soccer) coach.

**Craig Ferguson** (17 May 1962, Glasgow, Scotland), British film and TV actor; host of TV's *The Late Late Show* from 2005.

**Sarah (Margaret) Ferguson** (15 Oct 1959, London, England), British celebrity; duchess of York after her marriage (23 Jul 1986) to Prince Andrew; they divorced in 1996.

**Cristina (Elisabet) Fernández (Wilhelm) de Kirchner** (19 Feb 1953, La Plata, Argentina), Argentine politician; president of Argentina, following her husband, Néstor Kirchner, from 2007.

**Leonel Fernández (Reyna)** (26 Dec 1953, Santo Domingo, Dominican Republic), Dominican politician; president of the Dominican Republic, 1996–2000 and 2004–12.

**(John) Will(iam) Ferrell** (16 Jul 1967, Irvine CA), American comedian and actor.

**America (Georgine) Ferrera** (18 Apr 1984, Los Angeles CA), American film and TV actress.

**Tina Fey** (Elizabeth Stamatina Fey; 18 May 1970, Upper Darby PA), American comedian, writer, and actress.

**Robert Fico** (15 Sep 1964, Topolcany, Czechoslovakia [now in Slovakia]), Slovak politician (Social Democrat); prime minister of Slovakia, 2006–10 and again from 2012.

**Sally (Margaret) Field** (6 Nov 1946, Pasadena CA), American comic and dramatic actress.

**Ralph (Nathaniel) Fiennes** (22 Dec 1962, Suffolk, England), British dramatic actor.

**Harvey (Forbes) Fierstein** (6 Jun 1954, Brooklyn NY), American playwright and actor.

**Vlad Filat** (6 May 1969, Lapusna, Moldova), Moldovan politician; prime minister of Moldova from 2009.

**François Fillon** (4 Mar 1954, LeMans, France), French politician; prime minister of France, 2007–12.

**David (Leo) Fincher** (28 Aug 1962, Denver CO), American film director.

**Harvey V. Fineberg** (15 Sep 1945, Pittsburgh PA), American public-health physician and medical administrator; president of the Institute of Medicine from 2002.

**Colin Firth** (10 Sep 1960, Grayshott, Hampshire, England), British actor.

**Heinz Fischer** (9 Oct 1938, Graz, Austria), Austrian politician (Social Democrat); president of Austria from 2004.

**Allison Fisher** (24 Feb 1968, Cheshunt, Hertfordshire, England), British pocket-billiards champion.

**Isla (Lang) Fisher** (3 Feb 1976, Muscat, Oman), British film actress.

**Benígno (Repeki) Fitial** (27 Nov 1945, Saipan, Northern Mariana Islands), Northern Marianas politician (Covenant Party); governor of the Northern Mariana Islands from 2006.

**Patrick Fitzgerald** (22 Dec 1960, New York NY), American special prosecutor in a number of high-profile cases; US attorney for the Northern District of Illinois, 2001–12.

**Tim Flannery** (28 Jan 1956, Melbourne, VIC, Australia), Australian zoologist and environmentalist; he was named Australian of the Year for 2007.

**Vince Flynn** (6 Apr 1966, St. Paul MN), American author of thrillers.

**Mohamed Said Fofana** (?, Guinea?), Guinean politician; prime minister of Guinea from 2010.

**Ken Follett** (pseudonyms Zachary Stone and Simon Myles; 5 Jun 1949, Cardiff, Wales), British author of political thrillers and historical novels.

**Eric Foner** (?, ?), American historian, educator, and author; his *The Fiery Trial: Abraham Lincoln and American Slavery* won the 2011 Pulitzer Prize for history.

**Jorge Carlos Fonseca** (20 Oct 1950), Cape Verdean politician; president of Cape Verde from 2011.

**Harrison Ford** (13 Jul 1942, Chicago IL), American film actor.

**Rob(ert) Ford** (28 May 1969?, Etobicoke, ON, Canada?), Canadian politician (Progressive Conservative); mayor of Toronto from 2010.

**Tom Ford** (27 Aug 1961, Austin TX), American fashion designer and film director.

**William Clay Ford, Jr.** (3 May 1957, Detroit MI), American businessman; executive chairman of Ford Motor Co. from 2006.

**Diego Forlán** (19 May 1979, Montevideo, Uruguay), Uruguayan association football (soccer) player; won the Golden Ball award in the 2010 FIFA World Cup.

**William Forsythe** (1949, New York NY), American ballet dancer, choreographer, and director.

**Luis G. Fortuño** (31 Oct 1960, San Juan PR), Puerto Rican politician; governor of Puerto Rico from 2009.

**Jodie Foster** (Alicia Christian Foster; 19 Nov 1962, Los Angeles CA), American film actress and director.

**Norman (Robert) Foster** (1 Jun 1935, near Manchester, England), British architect; recipient of the 1999 Pritzker Prize and a 2002 Praemium Imperiale.

**Megan (Denise) Fox** (16 May 1986, Rockwood TN), American actress.

**Jamie Foxx** (Eric Bishop; 13 Dec 1967, Terrell TX), American actor and comedian.

**Don Francisco** (Mario Kreutzberger; 28 Dec 1940, Talca, Chile), Chilean-born American TV personality; host of the popular show *Sábado Gigante* on the Spanish-language Univision channel.

**(Luis) Federico Franco (Gómez)** (23 Jul 1962, Asunción, Paraguay), Paraguayan politician; president of Paraguay from 2012.

**James (Edward) Franco** (19 Apr 1978, Palo Alto CA), American actor.

**Al Franken** (21 May 1951, New York NY), American comedian, writer, and politician; senator from Minnesota from 2009.

**Missy Franklin** (10 May 1995, Pasadena CA), American swimmer; gold-medal winner at the 2012 London Olympics.

**Jonathan Franzen** (17 Aug 1959, Western Springs IL), American author.

**Frederik** (Frederik André Henrik Christian; 26 May 1968, Copenhagen, Denmark), Danish crown prince.

**Morgan Freeman** (1 Jun 1937, Memphis TN), American theater and film actor.

**Dawn French** (11 Oct 1957, Holyhead, Wales), British actress, comedian, and writer.

**Dave Freudenthal** (David Duane Freudenthal; 12 Oct 1950, Thermopolis WY), American politician (Democrat); governor of Wyoming, 2003–11.

**Thomas L. Friedman** (20 Jul 1953, Minneapolis MN), American journalist and author; foreign-affairs columnist for the *New York Times*.

**Janus Friis** (1976, Denmark), Danish Internet entrepreneur; codeveloper of Joost, a popular program for receiving TV broadcasts on a personal computer, and Skype, which allows users to make phone calls over the Internet.

**(Carlos) Mauricio Funes (Cartagena)** (18 Oct 1959, San Salvador, El Salvador), Salvadoran journalist and politician; president of El Salvador from 2009.

**Stefano Gabbana** (14 Nov 1962, Milan, Italy), Italian fashion designer and partner of Domenico Dolce.

**John Lewis Gaddis** (1941, Cotulla TX), American educator and writer; his *George F. Kennan: An American Life* won the 2012 Pulitzer Prize for biography or autobiography.

**Zach Galifianakis** (1 Oct 1969, Wilkesboro NC), American actor.

**John Galliano** (Juan Carlos Antonio Galliano Guillen; 28 Nov 1960, Gibraltar), British fashion designer and designer in chief at Christian Dior, 1996–2011.

**Sonia Gandhi** (Sonia Maino; 9 Dec 1947, Turin, Italy), Italian-born Indian widow of Rajiv Gandhi and a political force in India.

**James Gandolfini** (18 Sep 1961, Westwood NJ), American actor.

**Gabriel (José) García Márquez** (6 Mar 1928, Aracataca, Colombia), Colombian novelist and short-story writer, a figure in the magic realism movement in Latin American literature; recipient of the 1972 Neustadt Prize and the 1982 Nobel Prize for Literature.

**Alan García (Pérez)** (23 May 1949, Lima, Peru), Peruvian politician; president of Peru, 1985–90 and 2006–11.

**Andrew Garfield** (20 Aug 1983, Los Angeles CA), English actor.

**Jennifer (Anne) Garner** (17 Apr 1972, Houston TX), American TV and film actress.

**Kevin (Maurice) Garnett** (19 May 1976, Mauldin SC), American professional basketball player.

**Eldar Gasimov** (1989, Baku, Azerbaijan), Azerbaijani singer; winner (as part of the duo Ell/Nikki, with Nigar Jamal) of the 2011 Eurovision Song Contest.

**Ivan Gasparovic** (27 Mar 1941, Poltar, Czechoslovakia [now in Slovakia]), Slovak politician; president of Slovakia from 2004.

**Bill Gates** (William Henry Gates III; 28 Oct 1955, Seattle WA), American computer programmer, businessman, philanthropist, and cofounder of Microsoft Corp.; he has been named the world's richest person by *Forbes* numerous times.

**Melinda Gates** (Melinda French; 15 Aug 1964, Dallas TX), American philanthropist; cofounder of the Bill & Melinda Gates Foundation.

**Robert M(ichael) Gates** (25 Sep 1943, Wichita KS), American government official; CIA director, 1991–93, and US secretary of defense, 2006–11.

**Joachim Gauck** (1940, Rostock, Germany), German politician; president of Germany from 2012.

**Jean-Paul Gaultier** (24 Apr 1952, Arcueil, France), French fashion designer.

**Laurent Gbagbo** (31 May 1945, Gagnoa, French West Africa [now in Côte d'Ivoire]), Ivorian politician; president of Côte d'Ivoire, 2000–11; in 2011 he was arrested, charged with crimes against humanity by the International Criminal Court.

**Leymah Gbowee** (1972, Liberia), Liberian peace activist; winner of the 2011 Nobel Peace Prize.

**Haile Gebrselassie** (18 Apr 1973, Assela, Ethiopia), Ethiopian long-distance runner and world record holder in the marathon.

**Frank Gehry** (Frank Owen Goldberg; 28 Feb 1929, Toronto, ON, Canada), Canadian-born American architect and designer; recipient of the 1989 Pritzker Prize.

**Timothy (Franz) Geithner** (18 Aug 1961, New York NY), American public official; US secretary of the treasury from 2009.

**Julius Genachowski** (19 Aug 1962), American businessman and public official; chairman of the Federal Communications Commission (FCC) from 2009.

**Reinhard Genzel** (24 Mar 1952, Bad Homburg vor der Höhe, West Germany [now Germany]), German astrophysicist; winner of the 2012 Crafoord Prize in Astronomy.

**Francis (Eugene) Cardinal George** (16 Jan 1937, Chicago IL), American Roman Catholic churchman; archbishop of Chicago from 1997 and cardinal from 1998.

**Leo W. Gerard** (1947?, Sudbury, ON, Canada), Canadian labor leader; international president of the United Steelworkers International from 2001.

**Richard (Tiffany) Gere** (31 Aug 1949, Philadelphia PA), American film actor.

**Valery (Abisalovich) Gergiev** (2 May 1953, Moscow, USSR [now in Russia]), Russian conductor; artistic and general director of the Mariinsky Theatre from 1996 and principal conductor of the London Symphony Orchestra from 2007.

**Ricky (Dene) Gervais** (25 Jun 1961, Reading, Berkshire, England), British comedian and actor.

**Mohamed Ghannouchi** (18 Aug 1941, Al-Hamma, French Tunisia), Tunisian politician; prime minister of Tunisia, 1999–2011.

**Andrea Ghez** (1965, New York NY), American astrophysicist; winner of the 2012 Crafoord Prize in Astronomy.

**Robert Ghiz** (21 Jan 1974, Charlottetown, PE, Canada), Canadian politician (Liberal); premier of Prince Edward Island from 2007.

**Paul (Edward Valentine) Giamatti** (6 Jun 1967, New Haven CT), American actor.

**Frida Giannini** (1972, Rome, Italy), Italian fashion designer; creative director at Gucci from 2006.

**Jim Gibbons** (James Arthur Gibbons; 16 Dec 1944, Sparks NV), American politician (Republican); governor of Nevada, 2007–11.

**Robert Gibbs** (29 Mar 1971, Auburn AL), American political consultant and media official; White House press secretary, 2009–11.

**Mel (Columcille Gerard) Gibson** (3 Jan 1956, Peekskill NY), Australian American actor, producer, and director.

**Gabrielle Giffords** (8 Jun 1970, Tucson AZ), American politician (Democrat); served in the US House of Representatives (2007–12); survived an assassination attempt in 2011.

**(Makhdoom Syed) Yousaf Raza Gilani** (9 Jun 1952, Karachi, Pakistan), Pakistani politician (PPP); prime minister of Pakistan, 2008–12.

**Alan Gilbert** (23 Feb 1967, New York NY), American violinist and conductor; music director of the New York Philharmonic from 2009.

**João Gilberto (do Prado Pereira de Oliveira)** (10 Jun 1931, Juazeiro, Bahia state, Brazil), Brazilian bossa-nova singer, songwriter, and guitarist.

**Julia Gillard** (29 Sep 1961, Barry, Vale of Galmorgan, Wales), Australian politician (Labor); the first female Australian prime minister from 2010.

**Tony Gilroy** (Anthony Joseph Gilroy; 11 Sep 1956, New York NY), American screenwriter and director.

**Newt(on Leroy) Gingrich** (17 Jun 1943, Harrisburg PA), American politician (Republican), author, and TV commentator; speaker of the US House of Representatives, 1995–98.

**Ruth Bader Ginsburg** (15 Mar 1933, Brooklyn NY), American jurist; associate justice of the US Supreme Court from 1993.

**Nikki Giovanni** (Yolande Cornelia Giovanni, Jr.; 7 Jun 1943, Knoxville TN), American poet.

**Rudy Giuliani** (Rudolph William Giuliani; 28 May 1944, Brooklyn NY), American politician (Republican); mayor of New York City, 1994–2002.

**Ira Glass** (3 Mar 1959, Baltimore MD), American radio broadcaster, creator (1995) and host of *This American Life* on public radio and later also on cable TV.

**Philip Glass** (31 Jan 1937, Baltimore MD), American minimalist composer.

**Savion Glover** (19 Nov 1973, Newark NJ), American dancer and choreographer.

**Louise (Elisabeth) Glück** (22 Apr 1943, New York NY), American poet; US poet laureate, 2003–04.

**Faure (Essozimna) Gnassingbé (Eyadéma)** (6 Jun 1966, Afagnan, Togo), Togolese politician; president of Togo in February 2005 and again from May 2005.

**Jean-Luc Godard** (3 Dec 1930, Paris, France), French film director.

**Whoopi Goldberg** (Caryn Elaine Johnson; 13 Nov 1955, New York NY), American comedian, film actress, and TV talk-show host.

**(Orette) Bruce Golding** (5 Dec 1947, Clarendon, Jamaica, British West Indies), Jamaican politician; prime minister of Jamaica, 2007–11.

**Carlos Gomes, Jr.** (19 Dec 1949, Bolama, Portuguese Guinea [now Guinea-Bissau]), Guinea-Bissauan politician; prime minister of Guinea-Bissau, 2004–05 and 2009–12.

**José Horacio Gomez** (26 Dec 1951, Monterrey, Mexico), American Roman Catholic churchman; archbishop of Los Angeles from 2011.

**Ralph E. Gonsalves** (8 Aug 1946, Colonarie, Saint Vincent, British West Indies [now in Saint Vincent and the Grenadines]), West Indian politician; prime minister of Saint Vincent and the Grenadines from 2001.

**Alejandro González Iñárritu** (15 Aug 1963, Mexico City, Mexico), Mexican film director.

**Lawrence Gonzi** (1 Jul 1953, Valletta, Malta), Maltese politician (Nationalist); prime minister of Malta from 2004.

**Roger Goodell** (19 Feb 1959, Jamestown NY), American sports executive; commissioner of the National Football League from 2006.

**Allegra Goodman** (1967, Brooklyn NY), American writer, notably on Jewish themes.

**Doris Kearns Goodwin** (4 Jan 1943, Brooklyn NY), American historian, biographer, and TV commentator.

**Al(bert Arnold) Gore, Jr.** (31 Mar 1948, Washington DC), American statesman and environmental advocate; vice president of the US, 1993–2001, and corecipient of the 2007 Nobel Peace Prize.

**Ryan (Thomas) Gosling** (12 Nov 1980, London, ON, Canada), Canadian TV and film actor.

**Michael Gove** (26 Aug 1967, Edinburgh, Scotland), British politician (Conservative); secretary of state for education from 2010.

**(Allen) Kelsey Grammer** (21 Feb 1955, St. Thomas, US Virgin Islands), American TV actor, writer, and producer.

**Michael Grandage** (2 May 1962, Yorkshire, England), British theater director; artistic director of London's Donmar Warehouse (2002–12) and of the Michael Grandage Company from 2012.

**Jennifer Granholm** (Jennifer Mulhern; 5 Feb 1959, Vancouver, BC, Canada), Canadian-born American attorney, politician (Democrat), and TV talk-show host; governor of Michigan, 2003–11.

**Hugh Grant** (9 Sep 1960, London, England), British film actor.

**Günter (Wilhelm) Grass** (16 Oct 1927, Danzig, Germany [now Gdansk, Poland]), German poet, novelist, playwright, sculptor, and printmaker; recipient of the 1999 Nobel Prize for Literature.

**Michael Graves** (9 July 1934, Indianapolis IN), American postmodernist architect and housewares designer.

**José Graziano da Silva** (17 Nov 1949, ?), Brazilian teacher and public official; director general of the Food and Agriculture Organization of the UN from 2011.

**Richard Greenberg** (1958, Long Island NY), American playwright.

**Stephen Greenblatt** (7 Nov 1943, Boston MA), American scholar; his *The Swerve: How the World Became Modern* won the 2012 Pulitzer Prize for general nonfiction.

**Brian Greene** (9 Feb 1963, New York NY), American physicist and expert on string theory.

**Paul Greengrass** (13 Aug 1955, Cheam, Surrey, England), British film director.

**Alan Greenspan** (6 Mar 1926, New York NY), American monetary policy maker; chairman of the Board of Governors of the Federal Reserve System, 1987–2006.

**Christine Gregoire** (Christine O'Grady; 24 Mar 1947, Auburn WA), American politician (Democrat); governor of Washington from 2005.

Grégoire III Laham (Lutfi Laham; 15 Dec 1933, Daraya, Syria), Syrian church leader; patriarch of Antioch in the Greek Melkite Catholic Church from 2000.

Philippa Gregory (9 Jan 1954, Nairobi, Kenya), British historical novelist.

Brad Grey (1958?, Bronx NY), American talent agent, producer, and film executive; chairman and CEO of Paramount Motion Picture Group from 2005.

Ólafur Ragnar Grímsson (14 May 1943, Ísafjörður, Iceland), Icelandic politician; president of Iceland from 1996.

John Grisham (8 Feb 1955, Jonesboro AR), American lawyer and best-selling novelist.

Matt(hew Abram) Groening (15 Feb 1954, Portland OR), American cartoonist and creator (1989) of TV's The Simpsons.

Dave Grohl (David Eric Grohl; 14 Jan 1969, Warren OH), American rock drummer, guitarist, and singer (for Nirvana and Foo Fighters).

Jon Gruden (17 Aug 1963, Sandusky OH), American professional football coach and television commentator.

Martin Gruenberg (?, ?), American businessman; acting chair of the Federal Deposit Insurance Corporation (FDIC) from 2011.

Nikola Gruevski (31 Aug 1970, Skopje, Yugoslavia [now in Macedonia]), Macedonian politician; prime minister of Macedonia from 2006.

Dalia Grybauskaite (1 Mar 1956, Vilnius, USSR [now in Lithuania]), Lithuanian politician; president of Lithuania from 2009.

(Edward Michael) Bear Grylls (7 Jun 1974, Isle of Wight), British survival expert and TV star.

Armando (Emílio) Guebuza (20 Jan 1943, Marrupula, Portuguese Mozambique), Mozambican politician; secretary-general of the Frelimo political party from 2002 and president of Mozambique from 2005.

Ismail Omar Guelleh (27 Nov 1947, Diré-Dawa, Ethiopia), Djiboutian politician; president of Djibouti from 1999.

Guillaume (Guillaume Jean Joseph Marie; 11 Nov 1981, Château de Betzdorf, Luxembourg), Luxembourgian grand duke, prince of Nassau and Bourbon-Parma, and heir to the throne.

Ozzie Guillen (Oswaldo José Guillen Barrios; 20 Jan 1964, Ocumare del Tuy, Venezuela), Venezuelan-born professional baseball manager.

Abdullah Gul (29 Oct 1950, Kayseri, Turkey), Turkish economist and politician; prime minister of Turkey, 2002–03, and president from 2007.

Tim(othy) Gunn (29 Jul 1953, Washington DC), fashion consultant and TV personality.

José Ángel Gurría Treviño (8 May 1950, Tampico, Tamaulipas state, Mexico), Mexican economist; secretary-general of the Organisation for Economic Co-operation and Development from 2006.

Xanana Gusmão (José Alexandre Gusmão; 20 Jun 1946, Laleia, Portuguese Timor [now East Timor (Timor-Leste)]), Timorese independence leader; first president of independent East Timor, 2002–07, and prime minister from 2007.

António (Manuel de Oliveira) Guterres (30 Apr 1949, Lisbon, Portugal), Portuguese politician (Socialist); prime minister, 1995–2002, and UN high commissioner for refugees from 2005.

Savannah Guthrie (27 Dec 1971, Tucson AZ), American TV journalist and news anchor.

Buddy Guy (George Guy; 30 Jul 1936, Lettsworth LA), American blues guitarist and singer.

Gyanendra Bir Bikram Shah Dev (7 Jul 1947, Kathmandu, Nepal), Nepalese king, last monarch of Nepal, 2001–08.

Jake Gyllenhaal (Jacob Benjamin Gyllenhaal; 19 Dec 1980, Los Angeles CA), American film actor.

Haakon (Haakon Magnus; 20 Jul 1973, Oslo, Norway), Norwegian crown prince and heir to the throne.

'Abd Rabbuh Mansur Hadi (1945, Thukain, Yemen), Yemeni politician; vice president of Yemen, 1994–2012, and president from 2012.

Zaha Hadid (31 Oct 1950, Baghdad, Iraq), Iraqi-born architect; recipient of the 2004 Pritzker Prize.

William Hague (28 Mar 1961, Rotherham, Yorkshire, England), British politician (Conservative); foreign secretary from 2010.

Hilary Hahn (27 Nov 1979, Lexington VA), American violinist.

Stelios Haji-Ioannou (14 Feb 1967, Athens, Greece), Greek entrepreneur who created the easyGroup holding company, which includes easyJet.

(Nimrata) Nikki R(andhawa) Haley (20 Jan 1972, Bamberg SC), American politician (Republican); governor of South Carolina from 2011.

Donald (Andrew) Hall, Jr. (20 Sep 1928, New Haven CT), American poet, essayist, and critic; US poet laureate, 2006–07.

Michael C. Hall (1 Feb 1971, Raleigh NC), American actor.

Tarja (Kaarina) Halonen (24 Dec 1943, Helsinki, Finland), Finnish politician; president of Finland, 2000–12.

Josh Hamilton (21 May 1981, Raleigh NC), American professional baseball player.

Jon(athan Daniel) Hamm (10 Mar 1971, St. Louis MO), American actor.

Herbie Hancock (Herbert Jeffrey Hancock; 12 Apr 1940, Chicago IL), American Grammy Award-winning jazz keyboardist and composer.

Chelsea Handler (25 Feb 1975, Livingston NJ), American comedian, author, and TV talk-show host.

Daniel Handler (pseudonym Lemony Snicket; 28 Feb 1970, San Francisco CA), American children's book author.

Michael Haneke (23 Mar 1942, Munich, Germany), Austrian film director.

Tom Hanks (Thomas Jeffrey Hanks; 9 Jul 1956, Concord CA), American film actor and director.

Sean (Patrick) Hannity (30 Dec 1961, New York NY), American conservative commentator and talk-show host.

Hans Adam II (14 Feb 1945, Vaduz, Liechtenstein), Liechtenstein royal; prince of Liechtenstein from 1989.

Harald V (21 Feb 1937, Skaugum, Norway), Norwegian royal; king of Norway from 1991.

Marcia Gay Harden (14 Aug 1959, La Jolla CA), American film, stage, and TV actress.

Stephen (Joseph) Harper (30 Apr 1959, Toronto, ON, Canada), Canadian politician (Conservative); prime minister of Canada from 2006.

Padraig Harrington (31 Aug 1971, Dublin, Ireland), Irish golfer.

Ed(ward Allen) Harris (28 Nov 1950, Englewood NJ), American film and stage actor and director.

Neil Patrick Harris (15 Jun 1973, Albuquerque NM), American actor.

Harry (Henry Charles Albert David Mountbatten-Windsor; 15 Sep 1984, London, England), British prince of Wales; son of Charles and Diana, prince and princess of Wales, and third in line to the British throne.

**Mary Hart** (Mary Johanna Harum; 8 Nov 1950, Madison SD), American actress and cohost of *Entertainment Tonight* on TV, 1982–2011.

**Sheikh Hasina Wazed** (28 Sep 1947, Tungipara, India [now in Bangladesh]), Bangladeshi politician; prime minister of Bangladesh, 1996–2001 and again from 2009.

**Bill Haslam** (23 Aug 1958, Knoxville TN), American politician (Republican); governor of Tennessee from 2011.

**Robert Hass** (1 Mar 1941, San Francisco CA), American poet; US poet laureate, 1995–97.

**Anne (Jacqueline) Hathaway** (12 Nov 1982, Brooklyn NY), American film actress.

**Stephen W. Hawking** (8 Jan 1942, Oxford, Oxfordshire, England), British theoretical physicist, a specialist in cosmology and quantum gravity.

**Salma Hayek (Jiménez)** (2 Sep 1966, Coatzacoalcos, Veracruz state, Mexico), Mexican-born actress.

**Todd Haynes** (2 Jan 1961, Los Angeles CA), American film director, producer, and screenwriter.

**Michel Hazanavicius** (29 Mar 1967, Paris, France), French director and screenwriter.

**Seamus (Justin) Heaney** (13 Apr 1939, near Castledawson, Northern Ireland), Irish poet; recipient of the 1995 Nobel Prize for Literature.

**Hugh M. Hefner** (9 Apr 1926, Chicago IL), American magazine publisher (*Playboy*).

**Katherine (Marie) Heigl** (24 Nov 1978, Washington DC), American model and TV and film actress.

**Dave Heineman** (David Eugene Heineman; 12 May 1948, Falls City NE), American politician (Republican); governor of Nebraska from 2005.

**Ed Helms** (24 Jan 1974, Atlanta GA), American actor.

**Chris Hemsworth** (11 Aug 1983, Melbourne, VIC, Australia), Australian actor.

**Liam Hemsworth** (13 Jan 1990, Melbourne, VIC, Australia), Australian actor.

**Henri** (16 Apr 1955, Château de Betzdorf, Luxembourg), grand duke of Luxembourg from 2000.

**(Charles) Brad(ford) Henry** (10 Jun 1963, Shawnee OK), American politician (Democrat); governor of Oklahoma, 2003–11.

**Thierry (Daniel) Henry** (17 Aug 1977, Châtillon, near Paris, France), French association football (soccer) player.

**Gary R(ichard) Herbert** (7 May 1947, American Fork UT), American politician (Republican); governor of Utah from 2009.

**Felix Hernandez** (8 Apr 1986, Valencia, Venezuela), Venezuelan professional baseball starting pitcher; he pitched a perfect game for the Seattle Mariners in August 2012, only the 23rd player in MLB history to do so.

**Seymour M(yron) Hersh** (8 Apr 1937, Chicago IL), American investigative reporter and writer.

**Jacques Herzog** (19 Apr 1950, Basel, Switzerland), Swiss architect; corecipient of the 2001 Pritzker Prize and of a Praemium Imperiale in 2007.

**John Hickenlooper** (6 Feb 1952, Narbeth PA), American politician (Democrat); governor of Colorado from 2011.

**Michael D. Higgins** (18 Apr 1941, Limerick, Ireland), Irish politician and human rights activist; president of Ireland from 2011.

**Tommy Hilfiger** (Thomas Jacob Hilfiger; 24 Mar 1951, Elmira NY), American fashion designer.

**Faith Hill** (Audrey Faith Perry; 21 Sep 1967, Jackson MS), American country singer.

**Paris Hilton** (17 Feb 1981, New York NY), American heiress and socialite.

**Sam(uel Archibald Anthony) Hinds** (27 Dec 1943, Mahaicony, British Guiana [now Guyana]), Guyanese politician; president of Guyana in 1997 and prime minister, 1992–97, 1997–99, and again from 1999.

**Kazuo Hirai** (?, Japan), Japanese business executive; president and CEO of Sony Corp. from 2012.

**Emile (Davenport) Hirsch** (13 Mar 1985, Palms CA), American film actor.

**Damien Hirst** (1965, Bristol, England), British artist.

**Susan Hockfield** (1951, Chicago IL), American neuroscientist; president of the Massachusetts Institute of Technology from 2004.

**David Hockney** (9 Jul 1937, Bradford, Yorkshire, England), British painter, draftsman, printmaker, photographer, and stage designer.

**John (Henry) Hoeven III** (13 Mar 1957, Bismarck ND), American politician (Republican); governor of North Dakota, 2000–10.

**James P(hillip) Hoffa** (19 May 1941, Detroit MI), American labor leader; general president of the International Brotherhood of Teamsters from 1999.

**Dustin Hoffman** (8 Aug 1937, Los Angeles CA), American film and stage actor.

**Jules Hoffmann** (2 Aug 1941, Echternach, Luxembourg), French immunologist; winner of the 2011 Nobel Prize for Physiology or Medicine.

**Philip Seymour Hoffman** (23 Jul 1967, Fairport NY), American stage and film actor and theater director.

**Hulk Hogan** (Terry Gene Bollea; 11 Aug 1953, Augusta GA), American professional wrestler and actor.

**Eric (Himpton) Holder (Jr.)** (21 Jan 1951, New York NY), American lawyer; US attorney general from 2009.

**John (Paul) Holdren** (1 Mar 1944, Sewickley PA), presidential science adviser and director of the Office of Science and Technology Policy from 2009.

**François Hollande** (12 Aug 1954, Rouen, France), French socialist politician; president of France from 2012.

**Katie Holmes** (Kate Noelle Holmes; 18 Dec 1978, Toledo OH), American TV, film, and stage actress.

**Andrew (Michael) Holness** (22 Jul 1972, Spanish Town, Jamaica), Jamaican politician; prime minister of Jamaica, 2011–12.

**Tom Hooper** (Thomas George Hooper; 1972, London, England), British TV and film director.

**(Philip) Anthony Hopkins** (31 Dec 1937, Margam, Wales), British film and stage actor.

**Nick Hornby** (17 Apr 1957, Redhill, Surrey, England), British novelist and journalist.

**Khaled Hosseini** (4 Mar 1965, Kabul, Afghanistan), Afghan-born American novelist.

**Dwight Howard** (8 Dec 1985, Atlanta GA), American basketball player.

**Ken Howard** (28 Mar 1944, El Centro CA), American actor; president of the Screen Actors Guild from 2009.

**Ron Howard** (1 Mar 1954, Duncan OK), American TV and film actor and director.

**Terrence (Dashon) Howard** (11 Mar 1969, Chicago IL), American TV and film actor.

**Hu Jintao** (25 Dec 1942, Jixi, Anhui province, China), Chinese statesman; general secretary of the Communist Party of China from 2002 and president of China from 2003.

**Mike Huckabee** (Michael Dale Huckabee; 24 Aug 1955, Hope AR), American politician (Republican) and political commentator; governor of Arkansas, 1996–2007.

**Quiara Alegría Hudes** (?, ?), American playwright; her *Water by the Spoonful* won the 2012 Pulitzer Prize for drama.

**Jennifer (Kate) Hudson** (12 Sep 1981, Chicago IL), American soul and gospel singer and film actress.

**Arianna Huffington** (Ariana Stassinopoulos; 1950, Athens, Greece), Greek-born American political commentator, syndicated newspaper columnist, and author; cofounder of The Huffington Post.

**Felicity (Kendall) Huffman** (9 Dec 1962, Bedford NY), American TV and film actress.

**Robert (Studley Forrest) Hughes** (28 Jul 1938, Sydney, NSW, Australia), Australian art critic and author.

**Ollanta Humala** (27 Jun 1962, Lima, Peru), Peruvian military official and politician; president of Peru from 2011.

**Philip Humber** (21 Dec 1982, Nacogdoches TX), American professional baseball starting pitcher; he pitched a perfect game for the Chicago White Sox in April 2012, only the 21st player in MLB history to do so.

**Hun Sen** (4 Apr 1951, Kampong Cham province, Cambodia), Cambodian politician; prime minister of Cambodia from 1985.

**Jon M(eade) Huntsman, Jr.** (26 Mar 1960, Palo Alto CA), American businessman (Huntsman Family Holdings), politician (Republican), and philanthropist; governor of Utah, 2005–09, and US ambassador to China, 2009–11.

**Nicholas Hytner** (7 May 1956, Didsbury, near Manchester, England), British theater director; artistic director of the National Theatre from 2003.

**Ice Cube** (O'Shea Jackson; 15 Jun 1969, Los Angeles CA), American rapper, songwriter, and actor.

**Ice-T** (Tracy Morrow; 16 Feb 1958, Newark NJ), American hip-hop artist and actor.

**Ieronymos II** (Ioannis Liapis; 1938, Oinofyta, Greece), Greek Orthodox churchman; archbishop of Athens and all Greece from 2008.

**Ekmeleddin Ihsanoglu** (26 Dec 1943, Cairo, Egypt), Turkish professor of history; secretary-general of the Organisation of the Islamic Conference from 2005.

**Toomas Hendrik Ilves** (26 Dec 1953, Stockholm, Sweden), Estonian diplomat; president of Estonia from 2006.

**Jeffrey R(obert) Immelt** (19 Feb 1956, Cincinnati OH), American corporate executive; CEO of the General Electric Co. from 2001 and chairman of the President's Council on Jobs and Competitiveness from 2011.

**Hubert (Alexander) Ingraham** (4 Aug 1947, Pine Ridge, Bahamas, British West Indies), Bahamian politician; prime minister of the Bahamas, 1992–2002 and 2007–12.

**José Miguel Insulza** (2 Jun 1943, Santiago, Chile), Chilean government official (Socialist); secretary-general of the Organization of American States from 2005.

**Valentin Inzko** (22 May 1949, Klagenfurt, Austria), Austrian diplomat; high representative for Bosnia and Herzegovina from 2009.

**John (Winslow) Irving** (2 Mar 1942, Exeter NH), American novelist and short-story writer.

**Bill Irwin** (11 Apr 1950, Santa Monica CA), American actor and choreographer.

**Walter Isaacson** (20 May 1952, New Orleans LA), American corporate executive and biographer; chairman and CEO of the Cable News Network (CNN), 2001–03, and president and CEO of the Aspen Institute from 2003.

**Kazuo Ishiguro** (8 Nov 1954, Nagasaki, Japan), Japanese-born British novelist.

**Shintaro Ishihara** (30 Sep 1932, Kobe, Japan), Japanese author and nationalist politician; governor of Tokyo from 1999.

**Takanobu Ito** (29 Aug 1953), Japanese businessman; president and CEO of Honda Motor Co. from 2009.

**Toyo Ito** (1941, Seoul, South Korea), South Korean architect; recipient of a Praemium Imperiale in 2010.

**Gjorge Ivanov** (2 May 1960, Valandovo, Yugoslavia [now in Macedonia]), Macedonian politician; president of Macedonia from 2009.

**Jonathan Ive** (1967, London, England), British designer; head of industrial design at Apple Inc.

**Bakir Izetbegovic** (28 Jun 1956, Sarajevo, Yugoslavia [now in Bosnia and Herzegovina]), Bosnia and Herzegovinian politician; chairman of the presidency of the republic from 2012.

**Hugh (Michael) Jackman** (12 Oct 1968, Sydney, NSW, Australia), Australian film and stage actor.

**Alan (Eugene) Jackson** (17 Oct 1958, Newnan GA), American country-and-western singer and guitarist.

**Janet (Damita Jo) Jackson** (16 May 1966, Gary IN), American singer and film and TV actress.

**Jesse (Louis) Jackson** (8 Oct 1941, Greenville SC), American civil rights leader, minister, and politician.

**Lisa P(erez) Jackson** (8 Feb 1962, Philadelphia PA), American public official; administrator of the US Environmental Protection Agency from 2009.

**Peter Jackson** (31 Oct 1961, Pukerua Bay, New Zealand), New Zealand film director and producer.

**Phil(ip Douglas) Jackson** (17 Sep 1945, Deer Lodge MT), American basketball player and coach.

**Samuel L(eroy) Jackson** (21 Dec 1948, Washington DC), American film actor.

**Marc Jacobs** (9 Apr 1963, New York NY), American fashion designer.

**Bharrat Jagdeo** (23 Jan 1964, Unity village, Demarara, Guyana), Guyanese politician; president of Guyana, 1999–2011.

**Mick Jagger** (Michael Philip Jagger; 26 Jul 1943, Dartford, Kent, England), British rock musician and lead singer for the Rolling Stones.

**Thorbjørn Jagland** (5 Nov 1950, Drammen, Norway), Norwegian politician; secretary-general of the Council of Europe from 2009.

**Atifete Jahjaga** (20 Apr 1975, Rashkoc, Kosovo), Kosovar law enforcement official and politician; president of Kosovo from 2011.

**Helmut Jahn** (4 Jan 1940, Nürnberg, Germany), German-born architect.

**Nigar Jamal** (7 Sep 1980, Baku, Azerbaijan), Azerbaijani singer; winner (as part of the duo Ell/Nikki, with Eldar Gasimov) of the 2011 Eurovision Song Contest.

**E(rika) L(eonard) James** (?, ?), British author of erotica (the Fifty Shades trilogy).

**LeBron James** (30 Dec 1984, Akron OH), American professional basketball player.

**Judith (Ann) Jamison** (10 May 1944, Philadelphia PA), American dancer and choreographer; artistic director of the Alvin Ailey American Dance Theater (1989–2011).

**Yahya Jammeh** (Alphonse Jamus Jebulai Jammeh; 25 May 1965, Kanilai village, Gambia), Gambian politician; president of Gambia from 1994.

**Janez Jansa** (17 Sep 1958, Ljubljana, Yugoslavia [now in Slovenia]), Slovenian politician; prime minister of Slovenia from 2012.

**Mariss Jansons** (14 Jan 1943, Riga, Latvia), Latvian-born American director; conductor of the Royal Concertgebouw Orchestra of Amsterdam from 2004.

**Jim Jarmusch** (22 Jan 1953, Akron OH), American avant-garde filmmaker.

**Neeme Järvi** (7 Jun 1937, Tallinn, Estonia), Estonian conductor; chief conductor of the Hague Philharmonic from 2005.

**D(isanayaka) M(udiyanselage) Jayaratne** (4 Jun 1931), Sri Lankan politician; prime minister of Sri Lanka from 2010.

**Jay-Z** (Shawn Corey Carter; 4 Dec 1970, Brooklyn NY), American rapper.

**Hamadi Jebali** (1949, Sousse, Tunisia), Tunisian engineer and politician; interim prime minister of Tunisia from 2011.

**Katharine Jefferts Schori** (26 Mar 1954, Pensacola FL), American church leader; presiding bishop of the US Episcopal Church from 2006.

**Derek (Sanderson) Jeter** (26 Jun 1974, Pequannock NJ), American baseball player.

**Bobby Jindal** (Piyush Jindal; 10 Jun 1971, Baton Rouge LA), American politician (Republican); governor of Louisiana from 2008.

**Scarlett Johansson** (22 Nov 1984, New York NY), American film and stage actress.

**Elton John** (Reginald Kenneth Dwight; 25 Mar 1947, Pinner, Middlesex, England), British singer, composer, and pianist.

**Jasper Johns** (15 May 1930, Augusta GA), American painter and graphic artist, a pioneer of Pop art.

**(Alexander) Boris (de Pfeffel) Johnson** (19 Jun 1964, New York NY), American-born British journalist, editor (*Spectator*), and MP (Conservative); mayor of London from 2008.

**Chad (Javon) Johnson** (Chad Ochocinco; 9 Jan 1978, Miami FL), American professional football player.

**Denis Johnson** (1949, Munich, West Germany), American novelist, short-story writer, and poet.

**Dwayne (Douglas) Johnson** ("The Rock"; 2 May 1972, Hayward CA), American professional wrestler-turned-actor.

**Robert L. Johnson** (8 Apr 1946, Hickory MS), American entrepreneur; founder (1980) of BET (Black Entertainment Television).

**Ellen Johnson Sirleaf** (29 Oct 1938, Monrovia, Liberia), Liberian government and international official; winner of the 2011 Nobel Peace Prize and president of Liberia from 2006.

**David Johnston** (28 Jun 1941, Sudbury, ON, Canada), Canadian educator and legal scholar; governor-general of Canada from 2010.

**Angelina Jolie (Voight)** (4 Jun 1975, Los Angeles CA), American film actress and philanthropist.

**Goodluck Jonathan** (20 Nov 1957, Otuoke, Nigeria), Nigerian politician; vice president of Nigeria, 2007–10, and president from 2010.

**Bill T. Jones** (William Tass Jones; 15 Feb 1952, Steuben county NY), American dancer, choreographer, and director.

**Carwyn Jones** (1967, Swansea, Wales), Welsh politician; first minister of Wales from 2009.

**Edward P(aul) Jones** (5 Oct 1950, Washington DC), American short-story writer and novelist.

**James Earl Jones** (Todd Jones; 17 Jan 1931, Arkabutla MS), American actor.

**January Jones** (5 Jan 1978, Sioux Falls SD), American actress.

**Norah Jones** (30 Mar 1979, New York NY), American jazz-pop vocalist and pianist.

**Quincy (Delight) Jones, Jr.** (14 Mar 1933, Chicago IL), American jazz and pop arranger, composer, and producer.

**Tommy Lee Jones** (15 Sep 1946, San Saba TX), American actor.

**Michael (Jeffrey) Jordan** (17 Feb 1963, Brooklyn NY), American basketball player; he was voted ESPN's Athlete of the Century and is believed by many to be the best basketball player in history; he became majority owner of the NBA Charlotte Bobcats in 2010.

**Ivo Josipovic** (28 Aug 1957, Zagreb, Yugoslavia [now in Croatia]), Croatian politician; president of Croatia from 2010.

**Juan Carlos I** (Juan Carlos Alfonso Victor María de Borbón y Borbón; 5 Jan 1938, Rome, Italy), Spanish royal; king from 1975.

**Juanes** (Juan Esteban Aristizábal Vásquez; 9 Aug 1972, Medellín, Colombia), Colombian singer, songwriter, and guitarist.

**Anerood Jugnauth** (29 Mar 1930, Mauritius), Mauritian politician; prime minister of Mauritius, 1982–95 and 2000–03, and president, 2003–12.

**Jean-Claude Juncker** (9 Dec 1954, Rédange-sur-Attert, Luxembourg), Luxembourgian politician; prime minister of Luxembourg from 1995.

**Alain Juppé** (15 Aug 1945, Mont-de-Marsan, France), French politician; prime minister of France, 1995–97, and foreign minister, 1993–95, and from 2011.

**Joseph Kabila** (4 Jun 1971, Sud-Kivu province, Democratic Republic of the Congo), Congolese politician; president of the Democratic Republic of the Congo from 2001.

**Ismail Kadare** (28 Jan 1938, Gjirokastër, Albania), Albanian novelist and poet; recipient of the first Man Booker International Prize, in 2005.

**Paul Kagame** (23 Oct 1957, Gitarama, Ruanda-Urundi [now Rwanda]), Rwandan politician; president of Rwanda from 2000.

**Elena Kagan** (28 Apr 1960, New York NY), American lawyer and educator; dean of Harvard Law School (2003–09); solicitor general of the United States (2009–10); associate justice of the US Supreme Court from 2010.

**Robert E(lliot) Kahn** (23 Dec 1938, Brooklyn NY), American computer scientist, a key developer of the network that became the Internet; recipient of a Japan Prize in 2008.

**Tim(othy Michael) Kaine** (26 Feb 1958, St. Paul MN), American politician (Democrat); governor of Virginia, 2006–10, and chairman of the Democratic National Committee, 2009–11.

**Kaká** (Ricardo Izecson dos Santos Leite; 22 Apr 1982, Brasília, Brazil), Brazilian association football (soccer) player; he was voted World Player of the Year by FIFA in 2007.

**Ingvar Kamprad** (1926, Småland province, Sweden), Swedish businessman; founder of the home-furnishing company IKEA.

**Naoto Kan** (10 Oct 1946, Ube, Yamaguchi prefecture, Japan), Japanese politician (Democratic Party of Japan); prime minister of Japan, 2010–11.

**Anish Kapoor** (1954, Bombay [now Mumbai], India), Indian-born British sculptor; recipient of a Praemium Imperiale in 2011.

**Radovan Karadzic** (19 Jun 1945, Petnjica, Yugoslavia [now in Montenegro]), Bosnian Serb politician and president of Republika Srpska (Bosnia and Herzegovina), 1992–96; he was wanted as a war criminal and was arrested in 2008.

**Donna Karan** (Donna Faske; 2 Oct 1948, Forest Hills NY), American fashion designer.

**Kim(berly Noel) Kardashian** (21 Oct 1980, Los Angeles CA), American socialite and reality TV star.

**Islam Karimov** (30 Jan 1938, Samarkand, USSR [now in Uzbekistan]), Uzbek politician; president of Uzbekistan from 1990.

**Tawakkul Karman** (7 Feb 1979, Ta'izz, Yemen), Yemini women's rights activist; winner of the 2011 Nobel Peace Prize.

**Mel(vin Alan) Karmazin** (24 Aug 1943, New York NY), American media executive; CEO of Sirius XM Radio (formerly Sirius Satellite Radio) from 2004.

**Hamid Karzai** (24 Dec 1957, Karz, Afghanistan), Afghan statesman; president of Afghanistan from 2001.

**John Kasich** (13 May 1952, McKees Rocks PA), American politician (Republican); governor of Ohio from 2011.

**Garry Kasparov** (Garri Kimovich Kasparov; original name Garri or Harry Weinstein; 13 Apr 1963, Baku, USSR [now in Azerbaijan]), Azerbaijani-born Russian chess champion of the world, 1985–2000, and political activist.

**Jyrki Katainen** (14 Oct 1971, Siilinjärvi, Finland), Finnish politician; prime minister of Finland from 2011.

**Jeffrey Katzenberg** (21 Dec 1950, New York NY), American film producer; CEO of DreamWorks Animation SKG from 2004.

**Diane Keaton** (Diane Hall; 5 Jan 1946, Los Angeles CA), American actress and director.

**Keb' Mo'** (Kevin Moore; 3 Oct 1951, Los Angeles CA), American blues musician.

**Garrison Keillor** (Gary Edward Keillor; 7 Aug 1942, Anoka MN), American humorist and writer best known for his long-running radio variety show, *A Prairie Home Companion*.

**Toby Keith (Covel)** (8 Jul 1961, Clinton OK), American country-and-western singer.

**Bill Keller** (18 Jan 1949), American journalist; managing editor of the *New York Times*, 1997–2001, and executive editor, 2003–11.

**Tim(othy J.) Keller** (1950, Pennsylvania), American churchman and author; founding pastor (1989) of Redeemer Presbyterian Church, New York City.

**William M. Kelso** (30 Mar 1941, Chicago IL), American archaeologist; director of archaeology for the Jamestown Rediscovery Project.

**Thomas (Michael) Keneally** (pseudonym William Coyle; 7 Oct 1935, Sydney, NSW, Australia), Australian novelist.

**Anthony (McCleod) Kennedy** (23 Jul 1936, Sacramento CA), American jurist; associate justice of the US Supreme Court from 1988.

**Enda Kenny** (24 Apr 1951, Castlebar, Ireland), Irish politician (Fine Gael); prime minister of Ireland from 2011.

**R(ichard) Gil Kerlikowske** (1949, Fort Myers FL), American law enforcement official; director of national drug control policy ("drug czar") from 2009.

**Lee Kernaghan** (15 Apr 1964, Corryong, VIC, Australia), Australian country singer; he was named Australian of the Year for 2008.

**John F(orbes) Kerry** (11 Dec 1943, Fitzsimmons Army Hospital [now in Aurora CO]), American politician (Democrat) and senator from Massachusetts from 1985.

**John (Phillip) Key** (9 Aug 1961, Auckland, New Zealand), New Zealand politician (National Party); prime minister of New Zealand from 2008.

**Alicia Keys** (Alicia Augello Cook; 25 Jan 1981, New York NY), American R&B singer and pianist.

**Hamad ibn Isa al-Khalifah** (28 Jan 1950, Bahrain), Bahraini sheikh; emir and chief of state from 1999; he proclaimed himself king in 2002.

**(Seretse Khama) Ian Khama** (27 Feb 1953, Bechuanaland [now Botswana]), Botswanan military officer; president of Botswana from 2008.

**Hojatolislam Sayyed Ali Khamenei** (15 Jul 1939, Meshed, Iran), Iranian Shi'ite clergyman and politician who served as president, 1981–89, and as that country's *rahbar*, or leader, from 1989.

**Jhalanath Khanal** (20 May 1950, Sakhejung, Nepal), Nepalese politician; prime minister of Nepal, 2011.

**Mwai Kibaki** (15 Nov 1931, Gatuyaini village, Central province, Kenya), Kenyan politician; president of Kenya from 2002.

**Angelique Kidjo** (14 Jul 1960, Ouidah, Dahomey [now Benin]), Beninese pop singer.

**Nicole (Mary) Kidman** (20 Jun 1967, Honolulu HI), American-born Australian actress.

**Anselm Kiefer** (8 Mar 1945, Donaueschingen, Germany), German Neo-Expressionist painter.

**Salva Kiir Mayardit** (1952?, Sudan?), South Sudanese politician; president of South Sudan from 2011.

**Jakaya (Mrisho) Kikwete** (7 Oct 1950, Msoga, British Tanganyika [now in Tanzania]), Tanzanian military officer and government official; president of Tanzania from 2005.

**Val (Edward) Kilmer** (31 Dec 1959, Los Angeles CA), American film actor.

**Jeong H. Kim** (1961, Seoul, South Korea), Korean-born American electronics industry executive who was founder (1992) of Yurie Systems, Inc., and president of Alcatel-Lucent's Bell Labs from 2005.

**Jim Yong Kim** (1959, Seoul, Korea), Korean physician and health expert; president of Dartmouth, 2009–12; director of the World Bank from 2012.

**Kim Jong-Eun** (1983?, North Korea), North Korean political official; successor to his father, Kim Jong Il, as leader of North Korea from 2011.

**Jimmy Kimmel** (13 Nov 1967, Brooklyn NY), American comedian and TV talk-show host.

**B.B. King** (Riley B. King; 16 Sep 1925, Itta Bena, near Indianola MS), American blues guitarist and singer.

**Bob King** (18 Aug 1946, Michigan), American labor leader; president of the United Automobile Workers from 2010.

**Larry King** (Lawrence Harvey Zeiger; 19 Nov 1933, Brooklyn NY), American TV journalist.

**Stephen (Edward) King** (pseudonym Richard Bachman; 21 Sep 1947, Portland ME), American writer of novels combining horror, fantasy, and science fiction.

**Stephenson King** (13 Nov 1958, Saint Lucia, British West Indies?), West Indian politician (United Workers Party); prime minister of Saint Lucia, 2007–11.

**Barbara Kingsolver** (8 Apr 1955, Annapolis MD), American author and political activist; winner of the 2010 Orange Prize for Fiction for *The Lacuna*.

**Galway Kinnell** (1 Feb 1927, Providence RI), American poet.

**Michael Kinsley** (9 Mar 1951, Detroit MI), American political commentator and editor.

**Kirill I** (20 Nov 1946, Leningrad, USSR [now St. Petersburg, Russia]), Russian Orthodox patriarch of Moscow and All Russia from 2009.

**Ron Kirk** (1954, Austin TX), American politician (Democrat); mayor of Dallas, 1995–2001, and US trade representative from 2009.

**John A. Kitzhaber** (5 Mar 1947, Colfax WA), American politician (Democrat); governor of Oregon from 2011.

**Mari Kiviniemi** (27 Sep 1968, Seinäjoki, Finland), Finnish politician; prime minister of Finland, 2010–11.

**Vaclav Klaus** (19 Jun 1941, Prague, Czechoslovakia [now in the Czech Republic]), Czech politician who served as prime minister of the Czech Republic, 1992–97, and president of the Czech Republic for one month in 1993 and again from 2003.

**Calvin (Richard) Klein** (19 Nov 1942, Bronx NY), American fashion designer.

**Miroslav Klose** (9 Jun 1978, Opole, Poland), German association football (soccer) player.

**Heidi Klum** (1 Jun 1973, Bergisch Gladbach, West Germany), German American supermodel and TV-show host.

**Bobby Knight** (Robert Montgomery Knight; 25 Oct 1940, Massillon OH), American basketball coach and TV commentator; one of the winningest coaches in men's collegiate basketball.

**Keira Knightley** (26 Mar 1985, Teddington, London, England), British film actress.

**Ken Kobayashi** (14 Feb 1949, Japan), Japanese businessman; president and CEO of Mitsubishi Corp. from 2010.

**Samuel Kobia** (20 Mar 1947, Miathene, British Kenya), Kenyan Methodist church leader; general secretary of the World Council of Churches, 2004–09.

**Charles (de Ganahl) Koch** (1 Nov 1935, Wichita KS), American business executive, co-owner of Koch Industries and financial supporter of libertarian and conservative causes.

**David (Hamilton) Koch** (3 May 1940, Wichita KS), American business executive, co-owner of Koch Industries and financial supporter of libertarian and conservative causes.

**Bronisław Komorowski** (4 Jun 1952, Oborniki Slaskie, Poland), Polish politician; president of Poland from 2010.

**Zeljko Komsic** (20 Jan 1964, Sarajevo, Yugoslavia [now in Bosnia and Herzegovina]), Bosnia and Herzegovinian politician; chairman of the presidency of the republic, 2007–08, 2009–10, and 2011–12.

**Yusef Komunyakaa** (29 Apr 1947, Bogalusa LA), American poet.

**Konoé Tadateru** (8 May 1939, Japan), Japanese international official; president of the International Federation of Red Cross and Red Crescent Societies from 2009.

**Maxim Kontsevich** (25 Aug 1964, Khimki, USSR [now in Russia]), Russian mathematician; recipient of the Fields Medal in 1998 and a Crafoord Prize in 2008.

**Joseph Kony** (1961?, Odek, Uganda), Ugandan rebel commander; leader of the Lord's Resistance Army.

**Rem Koolhaas** (17 Nov 1944, Rotterdam, Netherlands), Dutch architect; recipient of the 2000 Pritzker Prize.

**Jeff Koons** (21 Jan 1955, York PA), American Pop-art painter and sculptor.

**Dean (Ray) Koontz** (9 Jul 1945, Everett PA), American novelist.

**Ted Kooser** (Theodore Kooser; 25 Apr 1939, Ames IA), American poet; US poet laureate, 2004–06.

**Ernest Bai Koroma** (2 Oct 1953, Makeni, British Sierra Leone), Sierra Leonean politician; president of Sierra Leone from 2007.

**Michael (David) Kors** (Karl Anderson, Jr.; 1959, Merrick, Long Island NY), American fashion designer.

**Jadranka Kosor** (1 Jul 1953, Pakrac, Yugoslavia [now in Croatia]), Croatian politician; prime minister of Croatia, 2009–11.

**Jon Krakauer** (12 Apr 1954, Brookline MA), American author of nonfiction.

**Alison Krauss** (23 Jul 1971, Decatur IL), American bluegrass fiddle player and singer.

**Lenny Kravitz** (26 May 1964, Brooklyn NY), American rock musician and actor.

**Gidon Kremer** (27 Feb 1947, Riga, USSR [now in Latvia]), Latvian-born violinist and conductor.

**William Kristol** (23 Dec 1952, New York NY), American editor and columnist.

**Alan B. Krueger** (17 Sep 1960, New Jersey?), American economist; chairman of the Council of Economic Advisers from 2011.

**Paul Krugman** (28 Feb 1953, New York NY), American economist and journalist; winner of the 2008 Nobel Prize for Economics.

**Andrius Kubilius** (8 Dec 1956, Vilnius, USSR [now in Lithuania]), Lithuanian politician; prime minister of Lithuania, 1999–2000 and again from 2008.

**Dennis J. Kucinich** (8 Oct 1946, Cleveland OH), American politician (Democrat); mayor of Cleveland, 1977–79; congressman from Ohio from 1997.

**Ted Kulongoski** (Theodore R. Kulongoski; 5 Nov 1940, Missouri), American politician (Democrat); governor of Oregon, 2003–11.

**Yayoi Kusama** (22 Mar 1929, Matsumoto, Nagano prefecture, Japan), Japanese artist; recipient of a 2006 Praemium Imperiale.

**Tony Kushner** (16 Jul 1956, New York NY), American playwright.

**Shia LaBeouf** (11 Jun 1986, Los Angeles CA), American actor.

**Lady Gaga** (Stefani Joanne Angelina Germanotta; 28 Mar 1986, Yonkers NY), American singer.

**Christine Lagarde** (1 Jan 1956, Paris, France), French lawyer; managing director of the International Monetary Fund from 2011.

**Emeril (John) Lagasse** (15 Oct 1959, Fall River MA), American TV chef, restaurateur, and media personality.

**Karl Lagerfeld** (10 Sep 1938, Hamburg, Germany), German-born French fashion designer.

**Ray LaHood** (6 Dec 1945, Peoria IL), American politician (Republican); congressman from Illinois, 1995–2009, and US secretary of transportation from 2009.

**Anthony Lake** (1939), American diplomat and author; executive director of UNICEF from 2010.

**Guy Laliberté** (1959, Quebec city, QC, Canada), Canadian circus performer and founder of Cirque du Soleil.

**Edward S. Lampert** (19 Jul 1962, Roslyn NY), American business executive; founder (1988) of ESL Investments and chairman of Sears Holdings Corp. from 2005.

**Pascal Lamy** (8 Apr 1947, Levallois-Perret, Paris, France), French financial and government official; EU trade commissioner, 1999–2004, and director general of the World Trade Organization from 2005.

**Rocco Landesman** (20 Jul 1947, St. Louis MO), American theater producer; chairman of the US National Endowment for the Arts from 2009.

**Mitch Landrieu** (16 Aug 1960, New Orleans LA), American politician (Democrat); mayor of New Orleans from 2010.

**Diane Lane** (22 Jan 1965, New York NY), American film actress.

**Nathan Lane** (Joseph Lane; 3 Feb 1956, Jersey City NJ), American stage and film actor.

**Helmut Lang** (10 Mar 1956, Vienna, Austria), Austrian fashion designer.

**Jessica Lange** (20 Apr 1949, Cloquet MN), American film, stage, and TV actress.

**Frank Langella** (1 Jan 1940, Bayonne NJ), American film actor.

**Anthony M. LaPaglia** (31 Jan 1959, Adelaide, SA, Australia), Australian film and TV actor.

**Lewis H. Lapham** (8 Jan 1935, San Francisco CA), American liberal political commentator and editor of *Harper's Magazine,* 1976–81 and 1983–2006.

**Irwin LaRocque** (?, Dominica), Dominican public official; secretary-general of the Caribbean Community (CARICOM) from 2011.

**Lyndon (Hermyle) LaRouche, Jr.** (8 Sep 1922, Rochester NH), American economist, populist politician, and perennial presidential candidate.

**John Lasseter** (12 Jan 1957, Hollywood CA), American animator and director; chief creative officer at Pixar Animation Studios from 2006.

**Matt(hew Todd) Lauer** (30 Dec 1957, New York NY), American TV journalist and news anchor.

**Ralph Lauren** (Ralph Lifshitz; 14 Oct 1939, New York NY), American fashion designer.

**(James) Hugh (Calum) Laurie** (11 Jun 1959, Oxford, England), British TV and film actor.

**Taylor Lautner** (11 Feb 1992, Grand Rapids MI), American actor.

**Sergey (Viktorovich) Lavrov** (21 Mar 1950, Moscow, USSR [now in Russia]), Russian politician; Russian foreign minister from 2004.

**Jude Law** (29 Dec 1972, Blackheath, London, England), British stage and screen actor.

**Jennifer (Shrader) Lawrence** (15 Aug 1990, Louisville KY), American film and TV actress.

**Martin Lawrence** (16 Apr 1965, Frankfurt am Main, West Germany), American TV actor and comedian.

**Nigella (Lucy) Lawson** (6 Jan 1960), British cook and author of food-related books.

**John le Carré** (David John Moore Cornwell; 19 Oct 1931, Poole, Dorset, England), English spy novelist.

**Jean-Marie Gustave Le Clézio** (13 Apr 1940, Nice, France), French author; winner of the 2008 Nobel Prize for Literature.

**Ursula K(roeber) Le Guin** (21 Oct 1929, Berkeley CA), American science-fiction and fantasy writer.

**Meave Leakey** (28 Jul 1942, London, England), British-born Kenyan paleoanthropologist.

**Richard (Erskine Frere) Leakey** (19 Dec 1944, Nairobi, Kenya), Kenyan physical anthropologist, paleontologist, conservationist, and politician.

**Ang Lee** (23 Oct 1954, P'ing-Tung county, Taiwan), Taiwanese-born film director.

**Jason (Michael) Lee** (25 Apr 1970, Orange CA), American skateboarder and film and TV actor.

**Spike Lee** (Shelton Lee; 20 Mar 1957, Atlanta GA), American film director.

**Stan Lee** (Stanley Martin Lieber; 28 Dec 1922, New York NY), American comic-book artist; creator of Spider-Man and other superheroes.

**Lee Hsien Loong** (10 Feb 1952, Singapore), Singaporean politician and economic expert; prime minister of Singapore from 2004.

**Lee Kun Hee** (9 Jan 1942, Uiryung, Japanese-occupied Korea [now in South Korea]), South Korean corporate executive; chairman of the Samsung Group, 1987–2008 and again from 2010.

**Lee Myung Bak** (19 Dec 1941, Osaka, Japan), South Korean politician; mayor of Seoul, 2002–06, and president of South Korea from 2008.

**John Leguizamo** (22 Jul 1964, Bogotá, Colombia), Colombian-born American comedian and actor.

**Dennis Lehane** (4 Aug 1966, Dorchester, Boston MA), American crime novelist.

**Jim Lehrer** (James C. Lehrer; 19 May 1934, Wichita KS), American TV journalist and author.

**Annie Leibovitz** (Anna-Lou Leibovitz; 2 Oct 1949, Westbury CT), American portrait photographer and photojournalist.

**Jay Leno** (James Douglas Muir Leno; 28 Apr 1950, Short Hills NJ), American comedian and TV talk-show host.

**Melissa (Chessington) Leo** (14 Sep 1960, New York NY), American film and TV actress.

**Paul LePage** (9 Oct 1948, Lewiston ME), American politician (Republican); governor of Maine from 2011.

**Robert Lepage** (12 Dec 1957, Quebec, QC, Canada), Canadian actor, director, and playwright.

**Doris Lessing** (Doris May Thaler; 22 Oct 1919, Kermanshah, Persia [now Bakhtaran, Iran]), British novelist and short-story writer; recipient of the 2007 Nobel Prize for Literature.

**Jonathan (Allen) Lethem** (19 Feb 1964, Brooklyn NY), American novelist, short-story writer, and essayist.

**Letsie III** (David Mohato; 17 Jul 1963, Morija, Basutoland [now Lesotho]), Lesotho royal; king of Lesotho, 1990–95 and again from 1996.

**David (Michael) Letterman** (12 Apr 1947, Indianapolis IN), American TV talk-show host.

**Tracy Letts** (4 Jul 1965, Tulsa OK), American playwright and actor whose *August: Osage County* won the 2008 Pulitzer Prize for drama.

**James Levine** (23 Jun 1943, Cincinnati OH), American conductor and pianist; music director of the Metropolitan Opera from 1976 and of the Boston Symphony Orchestra, 2004–11.

**Philip Levine** (10 Jan 1928, Detroit MI), American poet; poet laureate of the US for 2011–12.

**Bernard-Henri Lévy** (5 Nov 1948, Béni-Saf, French Algeria), Algerian-born French media darling and author of best-selling "enhanced nonfiction" books.

**Eugene Levy** (17 Dec 1946, Hamilton, ON, Canada), Canadian comic actor and writer.

**Jacob J. Lew** (29 Aug 1955, New York NY), American economist; director of the US Office of Management and Budget, 1998–2001, and 2010–12; White House chief of staff from 2012.

**(Diane) Monique Lhuillier** (1971, Cebu, Philippines), American couturier.

**Jet Li** (Li Lian Jie; 26 Apr 1963, Beijing, China), Chinese-born *wushu* (acrobatic martial arts) champion and film actor.

**Li Na** (26 Feb 1982, Wuhan, Hubei, China), Chinese tennis player.

**Daniel Libeskind** (12 May 1946, Lodz, Poland), Polish-born Israeli American architect.

**Nicklas (Erik) Lidström** (28 Apr 1970, Västerås, Sweden), Swedish ice-hockey defenseman.

**Joseph I. Lieberman** (24 Feb 1942, Stamford CT), American politician (Independent Democrat); senator from Connecticut from 1989.

**Gordon Darcy Lilo** (28 Aug 1965, Solomon Islands), Solomon Islands politician; prime minister of the Solomon Islands from 2011.

**Rush Limbaugh** (12 Jan 1951, Cape Girardeau MO), American radio talk-show host and conservative commentator.

**Laura Linney** (5 Feb 1964, New York NY), American film and stage actress.

**John Lithgow** (19 Oct 1945, Rochester NY), American film and TV actor.

**Lucy (Alexis) Liu** (2 Dec 1968, Jackson Heights, Queens NY), American TV and film actress.

**Liu Xiaobo** (28 Dec 1955, Changchun, China), Chinese human rights activist; recipient of the 2010 Nobel Peace Prize.

**Nicholas (Joseph Orville) Liverpool** (9 Sep 1934, Dominica, British West Indies), West Indian politician; president of Dominica from 2003.

**Kenneth Livingstone** (17 Jun 1945, Lambeth, London, England), British politician (Labour); mayor of London, 2000–08.

**LL Cool J** (James Todd Smith; 14 Jan 1968, Queens NY), American hip-hop artist and actor.

**Andrew Lloyd Webber** (22 Mar 1948, London, England), British composer of stage musicals; recipient of a Praemium Imperiale in 1995 and a 2006 Kennedy Center Honor.

**Porfirio Lobo (Sosa)** (22 Dec 1947, Trujillo, Honduras), Honduran politician; president of Honduras from 2010.

**Ryan Lochte** (3 Aug 1984, Daytona Beach FL), American swimmer.

**Gary Locke** (21 Jan 1950, Seattle WA), American politician (Democrat); governor of Washington, 1997–2005, US secretary of commerce, 2009–11, and US ambassador to China from 2011.

**Keith Alan Lockhart** (7 Nov 1959, Poughkeepsie NY), American conductor of the Boston Pops from 1993.

**Christopher Loeak** (11 Nov 1952, Ailinglaplap, Marshall Islands), Marshallese politician; president of the Marshall Islands from 2012.

**John Logan** (24 Sep 1961, Chicago IL), American screenwriter and playwright.

**Lindsay (Morgan) Lohan** (2 Jul 1986, New York NY), American actress and film starlet.

**Jonah Tali Lomu** (12 May 1975, Auckland, New Zealand), New Zealand rugby winger.

**Letitia A. Long** (1959?, Annapolis MD), American intelligence official; director of the National Geospatial-Intelligence Agency from 2010, the first female to head one of the major US intelligence agencies.

**Richard Long** (1945, Bristol, England), British sculptor; recipient of a Praemium Imperiale in 2009.

**Eva (Jacqueline) Longoria** (15 Mar 1975, Corpus Christi TX), American TV actress.

**Jennifer Lopez** (24 Jul 1970, Bronx NY), American pop singer, actress, and fashion designer.

**Loreen** (Lorine Zineb Noka Talhaoui; 16 Oct 1983, Stockholm?, Sweden), Swedish singer; winner of the 2012 Eurovision Song Contest.

**Sophia Loren** (Sofia Villani Scicolone; 20 Sep 1934, Rome, Italy), Italian film actress; recipient of a Praemium Imperiale in 2010.

**Peter Löscher** (17 Sep 1957, Villach, Austria), Austrian corporate executive; president and CEO of Siemens AG from 2007.

**Louis C.K.** (Louis Szekely; 12 Sep 1967, Washington DC), American comedian, writer, director, and producer.

**Julia Louis-Dreyfus** (13 Jan 1961, New York NY), American actress.

**Henri Loyrette** (31 May 1952, Neuilly-sur-Seine, France), French museum curator; director of the Louvre from 2001.

**George (Walton) Lucas, Jr.** (14 May 1944, Modesto CA), American film producer.

**Fernando (Armindo) Lugo (Méndez)** (30 May 1951, San Pedro del Paraná, Paraguay), Paraguayan Roman Catholic bishop; president of Paraguay, 2008–12.

**Baz(mark Anthony) Luhrmann** (17 Sep 1962, near Sydney, NSW, Australia), Australian film and stage director and producer.

**Alyaksandr (Hrygorevich) Lukashenka** (30 Aug 1954, Kopys, Vitebsk oblast, Belorussian SSR, USSR [now Belarus]), Belarusian politician; president of Belarus from 1994.

**Igor Luksic** (14 Jun 1976, Bar, Montenegro), Montenegrin politician; prime minister of Montenegro from 2010.

**Luiz Inácio Lula da Silva** (27 Oct 1945, Garanhuns, Pernambuco state, Brazil), Brazilian labor leader and politician (Workers' Party); president of Brazil, 2003–11.

**Marian Lupu** (20 Jun 1966, Balti, USSR [now Moldova]), Moldovan politician; president of Moldova, 2010–12.

**Jane Lynch** (14 Jul 1960, Dolton IL), American film and television actress.

**John (H.) Lynch** (25 Nov 1952, Waltham MA), American businessman and politician (Democrat); governor of New Hampshire from 2005.

**Yo-Yo Ma** (7 Oct 1955, Paris, France), American cellist.

**Ma Ying-jeou** (Ma Yingjiu; 13 Jul 1950, Hong Kong), Taiwanese politician and government official; mayor of Taipei, 1998–2006, and president of Taiwan from 2008.

**Lorin Maazel** (6 Mar 1930, Neuilly, France), French-born American conductor and violinist.

**Gloria (Macaraeg) Macapagal Arroyo** (5 Apr 1947, San Juan, Philippines), Philippine politician; president of the Philippines, 2001–10.

**Seth MacFarlane** (26 Oct 1973, Kent CT), American writer, director, actor, and creator of animated TV shows.

**Rachel Maddow** (1 Apr 1973, Castro Valley CA), American liberal television commentator.

**Madonna** (Madonna Louise Veronica Ciccone; 16 Aug 1958, Bay City MI), American singer, songwriter, actress, and entrepreneur.

**John Dramani Mahama** (29 Nov 1958, Bole-Bamboi district, Ghana), Ghanaian politician; interim president of Ghana from 2012.

**Bill Maher** (20 Jan 1956, New York NY), American TV comedian and personality.

**Roger Michael Cardinal Mahony** (27 Feb 1936, Hollywood CA), American Roman Catholic churchman; archbishop of Los Angeles, 1985–2011, and cardinal from 1991.

**Mohammed ibn Rashid al-Maktum** (1949, Dubai, British Trucial States [now in United Arab Emirates]?), UAE sheikh; crown prince from 1995 and ruler of Dubai from 2006.

**Tuilaepa Sailele Malielegaoi** (14 Apr 1945, Lepa, Samoa), Samoan politician; prime minister of Samoa from 1998.

**Nuri (Kamal) al-Maliki** (Jawad al-Maliki; Abu Isra; 1 Jul 1950, near Karbala, Iraq), Iraqi politician (Shi'ite); prime minister of Iraq from 2006.

**Evgeni Malkin** (31 Jul 1986, Magnitogorsk, Russia), Russian ice-hockey player.

**John (Gavin) Malkovich** (9 Dec 1953, Christopher IL), American film actor and filmmaker.

**Dannell P(atrick) Malloy** (21 Jul 1955, Stamford CT), American lawyer and politician (Democrat); governor of Connecticut from 2011.

**David (George Joseph) Malouf** (20 Mar 1934, Brisbane, QLD, Australia), Australian poet and novelist.

**David (Alan) Mamet** (30 Nov 1947, Chicago IL), American playwright, director, and screenwriter.

**Nelson (Rolihlahla) Mandela** (18 Jul 1918, Umtata, Cape of Good Hope, Union of South Africa [now Mthatha, South Africa]), South African black nationalist leader and statesman; he was a political prisoner, 1962–90, president of South Africa (1994–99), and corecipient of the 1993 Nobel Peace Prize.

**Barry Manilow** (Barry Alan Pincus; 17 Jun 1946, Brooklyn NY), American pop singer and songwriter.

**Michael (Kenneth) Mann** (5 Feb 1943, Chicago IL), American film director.

**Bradley Manning** (17 Dec 1987, Crescent OK), US Army intelligence analyst; accused of providing the Web site WikiLeaks with hundreds of thousands of classified documents.

**Eli(sha Nelson) Manning** (3 Jan 1981, New Orleans LA), American pro football quarterback.

**Peyton (Williams) Manning** (24 Mar 1976, New Orleans LA), American pro football quarterback.

**Hilary Mantel** (6 Jul 1952, Hadfield, Derbyshire, England), English writer; winner of the 2009 Man Booker Prize.

**(Patricia) Rooney Mara** (17 Apr 1985, Bedford NY), American actress.

**Sergio Marchionne** (17 Jun 1952, Chieti, Italy), Italian Canadian businessman; CEO of Fiat SpA and Chrysler Group LLC.

**Margrethe II** (Margrethe Alexandrine Thorhildur Ingrid; 16 Apr 1940, Copenhagen, Denmark), Danish royal; queen of Denmark from 1972.

**Julianna Margulies** (8 Jun 1966, Spring Valley NY), American actress.

**Mariza** (Mariza Nunes; 1974?, Mozambique), Portuguese fado singer.

**Mary Ellen Mark** (20 Mar 1940, Philadelphia PA), American photojournalist.

**Jack Markell** (26 Nov 1940, Newark DE), American politician (Democrat); governor of Delaware from 2009.

**Branford Marsalis** (26 Aug 1960, Breaux Bridge LA), American jazz saxophonist and bandleader.

**Wynton Marsalis** (18 Oct 1961, New Orleans LA), American jazz trumpeter and composer.

**Yann Martel** (25 Jun 1963, Salamanca, Spain), Spanish-born Canadian novelist.

**Michel (Joseph) Martelly** (12 Feb 1961, Port-au-Prince, Haiti), Haitian musician and politician; president of Haiti from 2011.

**Antoni Martí Petit** (1963, Escaldes-Engordany, Andorra), Andorran chief executive from 2011.

**Chris Martin** (2 Mar 1977, Exeter, England), British musician; pianist and vocalist for Coldplay.

**George R.R. Martin** (20 Sep 1948, Bayonne NJ), American author of the fantasy series *A Song of Ice and Fire*.

**Steve Martin** (14 Aug 1945, Waco TX), American comedic actor, screenwriter, playwright, and author.

**Ricardo (Alberto) Martinelli (Berrocal)** (11 Mar 1952, Panama City, Panama), Panamanian politician; president of Panama from 2009.

**Susana Martinez** (14 Jul 1959, El Paso TX), American attorney and politician (Republican); governor of New Mexico from 2011.

**Mary** (Mary Donaldson; 5 Feb 1972, Hobart, TAS, Australia), Australian-born marketing executive and crown princess of Denmark; wife of Crown Prince Frederik (married 14 May 2004).

**Moncef Marzouki** (1945, ?), Tunisian politician; president of Tunisia from 2011.

**Masako** (Masako Owada; 9 Dec 1963, Tokyo, Japan), Japanese royal; princess consort of Crown Prince Naruhito (married 9 Jun 1993).

**Mathilde** (Mathilde d'Udekem d'Acoz; 21 Jan 1973, Uccle, Belgium), Belgian royal; princess consort of Prince Philippe (married 4 Dec 1999), heir to the throne.

**Dave Matthews** (David John Matthews; 9 Jan 1967, Johannesburg, South Africa), American rock musician (of the Dave Matthews Band).

**James Mattis** (1950?, Pullman WA), American military leader; commander of US Central Command from 2010.

**Máxima** (Máxima Zorreguieta Cerruti; 17 May 1971, Buenos Aires, Argentina), Argentine-born Dutch investment banker and princess consort of Crown Prince Willem-Alexander (married 2 Feb 2002).

**Misty (Erie) May-Treanor** (30 Jul 1977, Los Angeles CA), American beach volleyball player; gold-medal winner at the 2012 London Olympics.

**John (Clayton) Mayer** (16 Oct 1977, Bridgeport CT), American singer and songwriter.

**Marissa Mayer** (30 May 1975, Wausau WI), American corporate executive; CEO and president of Yahoo! Inc. from 2012.

**Thom Mayne** (19 Jan 1944, Waterbury CT), American architect; recipient of the 2005 Pritzker Prize.

**Floyd Mayweather, Jr.** ("Pretty Boy"; 24 Feb 1977, Grand Rapids MI), American boxing champion in several weight classes, from lightweight to super welterweight.

**Kiran Mazumdar-Shaw** (1954?, Bangalore [now Bengaluru], India), Indian business executive; founder (1978) of Biocon India, India's first biotechnology company.

**Mary (Patricia) McAleese** (27 Jun 1951, Belfast, Northern Ireland), Irish politician; president of Ireland, 1997–2011.

**James (Andrew) McAvoy** (21 Apr 1979, Glasgow, Scotland), British actor.

**John (Sidney) McCain III** (29 Aug 1936, Panama Canal Zone), American politician (Republican); senator from Arizona from 1987.

**Cormac McCarthy** (Charles McCarthy, Jr.; 20 Jul 1933, Providence RI), American novelist in the Southern gothic tradition.

**Melissa (Ann) McCarthy** (26 Aug 1970, Plainfield IL), American actress.

**(James) Paul McCartney** (18 Jun 1942, Liverpool, England), British singer, songwriter, and former member of the Beatles.

**Stella (Nina) McCartney** (13 Sep 1971, London, England), British fashion designer.

**Matthew McConaughey** (4 Nov 1969, Uvalde TX), American actor.

**(Addison) Mitch(ell) McConnell (Jr.)** (20 Feb 1942, Tuscumbia AL), American politician (Republican); senator from Kentucky from 1985, Senate whip, 2003–07, and Senate minority leader from 2007.

**David McCullough** (7 Jul 1933, Pittsburgh PA), American biographer and historian.

**Audra (Ann) McDonald** (3 Jul 1970, West Berlin, West Germany [now in Berlin, Germany]), American theater actress.

**Robert F(rancis) McDonnell** (15 Jun 1954, Philadelphia PA), American politician (Republican); governor of Virginia from 2010.

**Frances McDormand** (23 Jun 1957, Chicago IL), American film actress.

John (Patrick) McEnroe, Jr. (16 Feb 1959, Wiesbaden, West Germany), American tennis player and TV sportscaster.

Reba McEntire (28 Mar 1954, McAlester OK), American country singer and TV and film actress.

Ian (Russell) McEwan (21 Jun 1948, Aldershot, England), British novelist.

Patrick McGorry (1952?, Dublin, Ireland), Australian psychiatrist and educator; he was named Australian of the Year for 2010.

Phil(lip C.) McGraw (1 Sep 1950, Vinita OK), American talk-show host, author, and psychologist-educator.

(Samuel) Tim(othy) McGraw (1 May 1967, Delhi LA), American country-and-western singer and actor.

Dalton McGuinty (19 Jul 1955, Ottawa, ON, Canada), Canadian lawyer and politician (Liberal); premier of Ontario from 2003.

Rory McIlroy (4 May 1989, Holywood, Northern Ireland), Northern Irish golfer.

Kevin McKenzie (29 Apr 1954, Burlington VT), American ballet dancer, choreographer, and director.

Simon McKeon (1955?, Australia), Australian banker, yachtsman, and philanthropist; he was named Australian of the Year for 2011.

Beverley McLachlin (7 Sep 1943, Pincher Creek, AB, Canada), Canadian Supreme Court justice from 1989 and chief justice from 2000.

Bob McLeod (?, ?), Canadian politician; premier of the Northwest Territories from 2011.

Vince(nt Kennedy) McMahon (Jr.) (24 Aug 1945, Pinehurst NC), American wrestling promoter; owner of World Wrestling Entertainment, Inc., from 1982.

Larry McMurtry (3 Jun 1936, Wichita Falls TX), American novelist.

W. James McNerney, Jr. (22 Aug 1949, Providence RI), American corporate executive; chairman of the board, president, and CEO of the Boeing Co. from 2005.

James M. McPherson (11 Oct 1936, Valley City ND), American historian of slavery and the antislavery movement.

Ian McShane (29 Sep 1942, Blackburn, Lancashire, England), British film and TV actor.

Jon Meacham (1969, Chattanooga TN), American author, political commentator, and editor.

Matt Mead (11 Mar 1962, Jackson WY), American politician (Republican); governor of Wyoming from 2011.

Russell (Charles) Means (10 Nov 1939, Pine Ridge SD), American Sioux activist.

Fouad Mebazaa (15 Jun 1933, Tunis, Tunisia), Tunisian politician; president of Tunisia, 2011.

Danilo Medina (Sánchez) (10 Nov 1951, Arroyo Cano, Dominican Republic), Dominican politician; president of the Dominican Republic from 2012.

Dmitry (Anatolyevich) Medvedev (14 Sep 1965, Leningrad, USSR [now St. Petersburg, Russia]), Russian lawyer and politician; president of Russia, 2008–12, and prime minister from 2012.

Zubin Mehta (29 Apr 1936, Bombay, British India [now Mumbai, India]), Indian orchestral conductor; music director of the Israel Philharmonic from 1977.

John Mellencamp (Johnny Cougar; John Cougar Mellencamp; 7 Oct 1951, Seymour IN), American singer and songwriter.

Eva Mendes (5 Mar 1974, Miami FL), American model and film actress.

Sam(uel Alexander) Mendes (1 Aug 1965, Reading, England), British stage and film director.

Paulo Mendes da Rocha (25 Oct 1928, Vitória, Espírito Santo state, Brazil), Brazilian architect and professor; recipient of the 2006 Pritzker Prize.

Fradique de Menezes (1942), Sao Tome and Principe politician; president of Sao Tome and Principe, 2001–03 and 2003–11.

Angela Merkel (Angela Dorothea Kasner; 17 Jul 1954, Hamburg, West Germany), German politician (Christian Democratic Union); chancellor of Germany from 2005.

W(illiam) S(tanley) Merwin (30 Sep 1927, New York NY), American poet and translator; US poet laureate for 2010–11.

Lionel (Andrés) Messi (24 Jun 1987, Rosario, Argentina), Argentine association football (soccer) player; he was voted World Player of the Year by FIFA in 2009, 2010, and 2011.

Mette-Marit (Mette-Marit Tjessem Høiby; 19 Aug 1973, Kristiansand, Norway), Norwegian royal; princess consort of Crown Prince Haakon (married 25 Aug 2001).

Pierre de Meuron (8 May 1950, Basel, Switzerland), Swiss architect; corecipient of the 2001 Pritzker Prize and of a Praemium Imperiale in 2007.

Stephenie Meyer (24 Dec 1973, Hartford CT), American author of fiction for young adults.

Jonathan Rhys Meyers (Jonathan Michael Francis O'Keefe; 27 Jul 1977, Dublin, Ireland), Irish film actor.

M.I.A. (Maya Arulpragasam; 18 Jul 1975, London, England), British-born Sri Lankan singer and rapper.

Michael (Michael Hohenzollern-Sigmaringen; ruled as Mihai I; 25 Oct 1921, Sinaia, Romania), Romanian king, 1927–30 (under regency) and 1940–47.

Jillian Michaels (18 Feb 1974, Los Angeles CA), American fitness expert and TV personality.

Lorne Michaels (Lorne Michael Lipowitz; 17 Nov 1944, Toronto, ON, Canada), Canadian-born TV and film producer.

James (Alix) Michel (16 Aug 1944, Mahe Island, Seychelles), Seychelles politician; president of Seychelles from 2004.

Lea Michele (29 Aug 1986, Bronx NY), American actress.

Michiko (Michiko Shoda; 20 Oct 1934, Tokyo, Japan), Japanese royal; empress consort of Emperor Akihito (married 10 Apr 1959).

Phil(ip Alfred) Mickelson (16 Jun 1970, San Diego CA), American professional golf player.

Pippa Middleton (Philippa Charlotte; 6 Sep 1983, England), British socialite; sister of Catherine, duchess of Cambridge.

Bette Midler (1 Dec 1945, Honolulu HI), American comedian, singer, and actress.

Zoran Milanovic (30 Oct 1966, Zagreb, Yugoslavia [now in Croatia]), Croatian politician; prime minister of Croatia from 2011.

David (Wright) Miliband (15 Jul 1965, London, England), British politician (Labour); foreign secretary, 2007–10.

Dennis Miller (3 Nov 1953, Pittsburgh PA), American television comedian, radio talk-show host, and writer.

Sienna (Rose) Miller (28 Dec 1981, New York NY), American-born British stage and film actress.

Sue Miller (29 Nov 1943, Chicago IL), American novelist.

Nicki Minaj (Onika Tanya Maraj; 8 Dec 1982?, Saint James, Trinidad and Tobago?), Trinidadian hip-hop artist.

**Kylie (Ann) Minogue** (28 May 1968, Melbourne, VIC, Australia), Australian actress and pop singer.

**Thomas Mirow** (6 Jan 1953, Paris, France), French government official; president of the European Bank for Reconstruction and Development from 2008.

**Helen Mirren** (Ilyena Lydia Mironoff; 26 Jul 1945, Chiswick, London, England), British stage, TV, and film actress.

**Joni Mitchell** (Roberta Joan Anderson; 7 Nov 1943, Fort Macleod, AB, Canada), Canadian singer, songwriter, and painter.

**Efthimios E. Mitropoulos** (30 May 1939, Piraeus, Greece), Greek international official; secretary-general of the International Maritime Organization, 2004–12.

**Lakshmi (Narayan) Mittal** (15 Jun 1950, Sadulpur, Rajasthan state, India), Indian-born British steel magnate.

**Satoshi Miura** (3 Apr 1944, Japan?), Japanese corporate executive; CEO and president of Nippon Telephone & Telegraph from 2007.

**Ratko Mladic** (12 Mar 1943, Kalinovik village, Bosnia, Yugoslavia [now in Bosnia and Herzegovina]), Bosnian Serb military officer sought as a war criminal; he was captured in 2011.

**Mo'Nique** (Mo'Nique Imes-Hicks; 11 Dec 1967, Woodlawn MD), American comedian and actress.

**Thomas S(pencer) Monson** (21 Aug 1927, Salt Lake City UT), American church leader; president of the Church of Jesus Christ of Latter-day Saints from 2008.

**Mario Monti** (19 Mar 1943, Varese, Italy), Italian economist and politician; prime minister from 2011.

**Alan Moore** (18 Nov 1953), British author and creator of graphic novels.

**Demi Moore** (Demetria Gene Guynes; 11 Nov 1962, Roswell NM), American film actress.

**Julianne Moore** (Julie Anne Smith; 3 Dec 1960, Fort Bragg NC), American film actress.

**Lorrie Moore** (Marie Lorena Moore; 13 Jan 1957, Glens Falls NY), American short-story writer and novelist.

**Michael Moore** (23 Apr 1954, Davison MI), American film director, author, and political activist.

**(Juan) Evo Morales (Ayma)** (26 Oct 1959, Orinoca, Bolivia), Bolivian farm-union leader; president of Bolivia from 2006.

**Jason Moran** (21 Jan 1975, Houston TX), American jazz pianist and bandleader.

**Luis Moreno Ocampo** (4 Jun 1952, Buenos Aires, Argentina), Argentine lawyer; the first chief prosecutor of the International Criminal Court, from 2003.

**Piers Morgan** (Piers Stefan Pughe-Morgan; 30 Mar 1965, Guildford, Surrey, England), British journalist and TV talk-show host.

**Manny Mori** (Emanuel Mori; 1948, Chuuk state?, Micronesia), Micronesian politician; president of Micronesia from 2007.

**Mark Morris** (29 Aug 1956, Seattle WA), American dancer and choreographer.

**Matthew Morrison** (30 Oct 1978, Fort Ord CA), American actor.

**Toni Morrison** (Chloe Anthony Wofford; 18 Feb 1931, Lorain OH), American novelist; recipient of the 1993 Nobel Prize for Literature.

**Mohammed (Mohammed) Morsi (ʿIssa al-ʿAyyat)** (20 Aug 1951, Sharqiyyah Governorate, Egypt), Egyptian engineer and politician (Muslim Brotherhood); president of Egypt from 2012.

**Viggo (Peter) Mortensen** (20 Oct 1958, New York NY), American film actor.

**Walter Mosley** (12 Jan 1952, Los Angeles CA), American writer of science fiction and mystery novels.

**Kate Moss** (16 Jan 1974, Addiscombe, Surrey, England), British model.

**Andrew Motion** (26 Oct 1952, London, England), English poet, teacher, editor, and biographer; poet laureate of Britain, 1999–2009.

**Kgalema (Petrus) Motlanthe** (19 Jul 1949, Johannesburg, Union of South Africa), South African politician (African National Congress); president of South Africa, 2008–09, and deputy president from 2009.

**Markos Moulitsas (Zúniga)** ("Kos"; 11 Sep 1971, Chicago IL), American populist journalist and blogger; founder and editor of the Daily Kos blog from 2002.

**Amr Muhammad Moussa** (3 Oct 1936, Cairo, Egypt), Egyptian secretary-general of the League of Arab States, 2001–11.

**Bill Moyers** (Billy Don Moyers; 5 Jun 1934, Hugo OK), American TV journalist, former government official, and author.

**Brian T. Moynihan** (9 Oct 1959, Marietta OH), American businessman; president and CEO of Bank of America from 2010.

**Mswati III** (19 Apr 1968, Swaziland), Swazi royal; king of Swaziland from 1986.

**(Muhammed) Hosni Mubarak** (4 May 1928, Al-Minufiyah governorate, Egypt), Egyptian politician; president of Egypt, 1981–2011.

**Robert S(wan) Mueller III** (7 Aug 1944, New York NY), American government official; FBI director from 2001.

**Robert (Gabriel) Mugabe** (21 Feb 1924, Kutama, Southern Rhodesia [now Zimbabwe]), Zimbabwean politician; the first prime minister (1980–87) of the reconstituted state of Zimbabwe and president from 1987.

**Muhammad VI** (Muhammad ibn al-Hassan; 21 Aug 1963, Rabat, Morocco), Moroccan royal; king from 1999.

**Ali Muhammad Mujawar** (1953, Shabwah, British-protected Aden [now in Yemen]), Yemeni politician; prime minister of Yemen, 2007–11.

**José (Alberto) Mujica (Cordano)** (20 May 1935, Montevideo, Uruguay), Uruguayan politician (Broad Front); president of Uruguay from 2010.

**Pranab Mukherjee** (11 Dec 1935, Mirati village, West Bengal, British India), Indian politician (Indian National Congress); president of India from 2012.

**Siddhartha Mukherjee** (1971?, India), Indian-born cancer physician and researcher; his *The Emperor of All Maladies: A Biography of Cancer* won the 2011 Pulitzer Prize for general nonfiction.

**Alan Mulally** (4 Aug 1945, Oakland CA), American businessman; president and CEO of Ford Motor Co. from 2006.

**Paul Muldoon** (20 Jun 1951, Portadown, Northern Ireland), Irish-born American poet.

**Mike Mullen** (Michael Glenn Mullen; 4 Oct 1946, Los Angeles CA), American military leader; chairman of the Joint Chiefs of Staff, 2007–11.

**Herta Müller** (17 Aug 1953, Nitchidorf, Romania), Romanian-born German writer; winner of the 2009 Nobel Prize for Literature.

**Thomas Müller** (13 Sep 1989, Weilheim, West Germany), German association football (soccer) player; won the Golden Boot award in the 2010 FIFA World Cup.

**Carey Mulligan** (28 May 1985, London, England), British actress.

**Alice Munro** (Alice Anne Laidlaw; 10 Jul 1931, Wingham, ON, Canada), Canadian short-story writer; recipient of the 2009 Man Booker International Prize.

**(Keith) Rupert Murdoch** (11 Mar 1931, Melbourne, VIC, Australia), Australian-born British newspaper publisher and media entrepreneur; founder of the global media holding company News Corporation Ltd.

**Eddie Murphy** (3 Apr 1961, Brooklyn NY), American comedian and film actor.

**Cormac Murphy-O'Connor** (24 Aug 1932, Reading, Berkshire, England), British church leader; archbishop of Westminster (leader of the Roman Catholic Church in the UK), 2000–09, and cardinal, 2001–09.

**Andy Murray** (15 May 1987, Glasgow, Scotland), Scottish tennis player; gold-medal winner at the 2012 London Olympics.

**Narayana Murthy** (20 Aug 1946, Kolar, British India), Indian international business executive and pioneer in India's high-tech industry; cofounder of Infosys Technologies Ltd., a technology and consulting firm.

**Yoweri (Kaguta) Museveni** (15 Aug 1944, Mbarra district, Uganda), Ugandan politician; president of Uganda from 1986.

**Pervez Musharraf (Nish-i-Imtiaz)** (11 Aug 1943, New Delhi, British India), Pakistani military leader and politician; head of Pakistan's government, 1999–2001, and president of Pakistan, 2001–08.

**Riccardo Muti** (28 Jul 1941, Naples, Italy), Italian conductor; music director of La Scala Orchestra in Milan, 1986–2005; music director of the Chicago Symphony Orchestra from 2010.

**Mike Myers** (25 May 1963, Scarborough, ON, Canada), Canadian comedian and actor.

**James Nachtwey** (14 Mar 1948, Syracuse NY), American news photographer.

**Rafael Nadal (Parera)** (3 Jun 1986, Manacor, Mallorca, Spain), Spanish tennis player.

**Khalifah ibn Zayid al-Nahyan** (1948?, Al-ʿAyn, Abu Dhabi, British Trucial States [now United Arab Emirates]), UAE sheikh; ruler of Abu Dhabi and president of the United Arab Emirates from 2004.

**Ratu Epeli Nailatikau** (5 Jul 1941), Fijian politician; president of Fiji from 2009.

**V(idiadhar) S(urajprasad) Naipaul** (17 Aug 1932, Chaguanas, Trinidad, British West Indies [now in Trinidad and Tobago]), Trinidadian-born British writer; recipient of the 2001 Nobel Prize for Literature.

**Datuk Seri Najib Tun Razak** (23 Jul 1953, Kuala Lipis, Malaysia), Malaysian politician; prime minister of Malaysia from 2009.

**Giorgio Napolitano** (29 Jun 1925, Naples, Italy), Italian politician (Communist); president of Italy from 2006.

**Janet Napolitano** (29 Nov 1957, New York NY), American politician (Democrat); governor of Arizona, 2003–09, and US secretary of homeland security from 2009.

**Naruhito** (23 Feb 1960, Tokyo, Japan), Japanese crown prince.

**Nas** (Nasir bin Olu Dara Jones; "Nasty Nas"; "Nas Escobar"; 14 Sep 1973, Queens NY), American hip-hop artist.

**Mohamed Nasheed** (17 May 1967, Male, Maldives), Maldivian politician; president of Maldives, 2008–12.

**Sayyed Hassan Nasrallah** (31 Aug 1960, Borj Hammoud, Beirut, Lebanon), Lebanese Islamic extremist military leader; secretary-general of Hezbollah from 1992.

**Taslima Nasrin** (25 Aug 1962, Mymensingh, Bangladesh), Bangladeshi Islamic feminist writer.

**S(ellapan) R(amanathan) Nathan** (3 Jul 1924, Singapore?), Singaporean politician; president of Singapore, 1999–2011.

**Bruce Nauman** (6 Nov 1941, Fort Wayne IN), American sculptor and installation and performance artist.

**Nursultan Nazarbayev** (6 Jul 1940, Chemolgan, USSR [now in Kazakhstan]), Kazakh politician; president of Kazakhstan from 1990.

**Youssou N'Dour** (1 Oct 1959, Dakar, French West Africa [now in Senegal]), Senegalese singer and songwriter.

**Petr Necas** (19 Nov 1964, Uherské Hradiste, Czechoslovakia [now in Czech Republic]), Czech politician; prime minister of the Czech Republic from 2010.

**Liam Neeson** (William Neeson; 7 Jun 1952, Ballymena, Northern Ireland), British film actor.

**Willie (Hugh) Nelson** (30 Apr 1933, Fort Worth TX), American songwriter and guitarist.

**Madhav Kumar Nepal** (9 Mar 1953, Gaur, Nepal), Nepalese politician; prime minister of Nepal, 2009–11.

**Nerses Bedros XIX** (Boutros Tarmouni; 17 Jan 1940, Cairo, Egypt), Armenian churchman; patriarch of the Catholic Armenians from 1999.

**Benjamin Netanyahu** (21 Oct 1949, Tel Aviv [now Tel Aviv–Yafo], Israel), Israeli politician; prime minister of Israel, 1996–99 and again from 2009.

**Randy Newman** (Randall Stuart Newman; 28 Nov 1943, Los Angeles CA), American songwriter, singer, and pianist.

**Marc Newson** (1963, Sydney, NSW, Australia), Australian industrial designer.

**Thandie Newton** (Thandiwe Newton; 6 Nov 1972, Zambia), Zambian-born British TV and film actress.

**Teodoro Obiang Nguema Mbasogo** (1942, Acoacan, Río Muni [now Equatorial Guinea]), Equatorial Guinean politician; president of Equatorial Guinea from 1979.

**Nguyen Minh Triet** (8 Oct 1942, Ben Cat district, French Indochina [now in Vietnam]), Vietnamese politician; president of Vietnam, 2006–11.

**Nguyen Tan Dung** (17 Nov 1949, Ca Mau, French Indochina [now in Vietnam]), Vietnamese politician; prime minister of Vietnam from 2006.

**Manuel Serifo Nhamadjo** (1958), Guinea-Bissauan politician; acting president of Guinea-Bissau from 2012.

**Vincent Gerard Nichols** (8 Nov 1945, Crosby, Merseyside, England), British church leader; archbishop of Westminster (leader of the Roman Catholic Church in the UK) from 2009.

**Jack Nicholson** (John Joseph Nicholson; 22 Apr 1937, Neptune NJ), American film actor.

**Sauli (Väinämö) Niinistö** (24 Aug 1948, Salo, Finland), Finnish politician; president from 2012.

**Tomislav Nikolic** (15 Feb 1952, Kragujevac, Yugoslavia [now in Serbia]), Serbian politician; president of Serbia from 2012.

**Bujar (Faik) Nishani** (29 Sep 1966, Durrës, Albania), Albanian politician; president of Albania from 2012.

**Ryue Nishizawa** (7 Feb 1966, Kanagawa prefecture, Japan), Japanese architect; corecipient of the 2010 Pritzker Prize.

Jay Nixon (Jeremiah W. Nixon; 13 Feb 1956, De Soto MO), American politician (Democrat); governor of Missouri from 2008.

Pierre Nkurunziza (18 Dec 1963, Ngozi province, Burundi), Burundian Hutu rebel leader; president of Burundi from 2005.

Ronald K(enneth) Noble (1957?, New Jersey), American law professor and government official; secretary-general of Interpol from 2000.

Yoshihiko Noda (1957, Funabashi, Japan), Japanese politician; prime minister of Japan from 2011.

Christopher (Jonathan James) Nolan (30 Jul 1970, London, England), British film director.

Indra Nooyi (28 Oct 1955, Madras [now Chennai], Tamil Nadu state, India), Indian-born American businesswoman; chairman and CEO of PepsiCo from 2007.

Norodom Sihamoni (14 May 1953, Phnom Penh, Cambodia), Cambodian royal; king of Cambodia from 2004.

Norodom Sihanouk (Preah Baht Samdach Preah Norodom Sihanuk Varman; 31 Oct 1922, Phnom Penh, Cambodia), Cambodian king, 1941–55 and 1993–2004; head of state, 1960–70 and 1991–93.

Bruce Norris (16 May 1960, Texas), American playwright; his Clybourne Park won the 2011 Pulitzer Prize for drama.

Chris Noth (13 Nov 1954, Madison WI), American film and TV actor.

Lynn Nottage (1964, Brooklyn NY), American playwright.

Jean Nouvel (12 Aug 1945, Fumel, France), French architect; recipient of a Praemium Imperiale in 2001 and the 2008 Pritzker Prize.

Dirk Nowitzki (19 Jun 1978, Würzburg, West Germany [now Germany]), German basketball player.

Michael A(nthony) Nutter (29 Jun 1957, Philadelphia PA), American politician (Democrat); mayor of Philadelphia from 2008.

Joyce Carol Oates (16 Jun 1938, Lockport NY), American novelist, short-story writer, and essayist.

Barack (Hussein) Obama (II) (4 Aug 1961, Honolulu HI), American politician (Democrat); 44th president of the US, from 2009, and winner of the 2009 Nobel Peace Prize.

Michelle Obama (Michelle LaVaughn Robinson; 17 Jan 1964, Chicago IL), American first lady; wife of Pres. Barack Obama (married 3 Oct 1992).

Téa Obreht (1985, Yugoslavia), Serbian American author; winner of the 2011 Orange Prize for Fiction for The Tiger's Wife.

Conan O'Brien (18 Apr 1963, Brookline MA), American TV talk-show host.

Piermaria J. Oddone (26 Mar 1944, Arequipa, Peru), Peruvian-born American experimental particle physicist and administrator; director of the Fermi National Accelerator Laboratory from 2005.

Raila (Amollo) Odinga (7 Jan 1945, Maseno, Nyanza province, British Kenya), Kenyan politician (Liberal Democratic); prime minister of Kenya from 2008.

Kenzaburo Oe (31 Jan 1935, Ose, Ehime prefecture, Japan), Japanese novelist; recipient of the 1994 Nobel Prize for Literature.

Apollo (Anton) Ohno (22 May 1982, Seattle WA), American short-track speed skater; he was the most decorated American athlete in the history of Winter Olympics.

Monique Ohsan Bellepeau (1942, Mauritius), Mauritian politician; vice president of Mauritius, 2010–12, and acting president in 2012.

Masahiro Okafuji (c. 1950, Japan?), Japanese businessman; president and CEO of ITOCHU Corp. from 2010.

Keith Olbermann (27 Jan 1959, New York NY), American TV sportscaster and commentator.

Claes (Thure) Oldenburg (28 Jan 1929, Stockholm, Sweden), Swedish-born Pop-art sculptor.

Sharon Olds (19 Nov 1942, San Francisco CA), American poet.

Jamie Oliver (27 May 1975, Essex, England), British chef and TV personality.

Ehud Olmert (30 Sep 1945, Binyamina, British Palestine [now in Israel]), Israeli politician (Kadima); prime minister of Israel, 2006–09.

Ashley (Fuller) Olsen (13 Jun 1986, Sherman Oaks CA), American former child star, fashion designer, and a marketing phenomenon in modeling, films, TV, and music videos.

Mary-Kate Olsen (13 Jun 1986, Sherman Oaks CA), American former child star, fashion designer, and a marketing phenomenon in modeling, films, TV, and music videos.

Timothy (David) Olyphant (20 May 1968, Honolulu HI), American actor.

Martin (Joseph) O'Malley (18 Jan 1963, Washington DC), American politician (Democrat); mayor of Baltimore, 1999–2007, and governor of Maryland from 2007.

Sean Patrick Cardinal O'Malley (29 Jun 1944, Lakewood OH), American Roman Catholic churchman; archbishop of Boston from 2003; cardinal from 2006.

(Philip) Michael Ondaatje (12 Sep 1943, Colombo, British Ceylon [now Sri Lanka]), Canadian novelist and poet.

Shaquille (Rashaun) O'Neal (6 Mar 1972, Newark NJ), American basketball center.

Michael E. O'Neill (?, ?), American business executive; chairman of Citigroup from 2012.

Peter (Charles Paire) O'Neill (13 Feb 1965, Pangia District, Australian-mandated Territory of Papua and New Guinea [now Papua New Guinea), Papua New Guinean politician; prime minister of Papua New Guinea from 2011.

Viktor Orbán (31 May 1963, Alcsútdoboz, Hungary), Hungarian politician; prime minister of Hungary, 1998–2002, and from 2010.

Bill O'Reilly (William James O'Reilly, Jr.; 10 Sep 1949, New York NY), American TV journalist and talk-show host.

Suze Orman (5 Jun 1951, Chicago IL), American financial adviser and best-selling author.

(José) Daniel Ortega (Saavedra) (11 Nov 1945, La Libertad, Nicaragua), Nicaraguan guerrilla leader and politician; president of Nicaragua, 1984–90 and again from 2007.

Babatunde Osotimehin (February 1949, Nigeria), Nigerian public health official; executive director of the UN Population Fund from 2011.

Joel Osteen (5 Mar 1963, Houston TX), American evangelist; head of the Lakewood Church in Houston.

Paul S. Otellini (12 Oct 1950, San Francisco CA), American corporate executive; president of Intel Corp. from 2002 and CEO from 2005.

Peter (Seamus) O'Toole (2 Aug 1932, Connemara, County Galway, Irish Free State), British stage and film actor.

Butch Otter (Clement Leroy Otter; 3 May 1942, Caldwell ID), American politician (Republican); governor of Idaho from 2007.

**Roza Otunbayeva** (23 Aug 1950, Osh, Kirghiz SSR, USSR [now in Kyrgyzstan], Kyrgyz politician; head of the interim government of Kyrgyzstan, 2010–11.

**Alassane Ouattara** (1 Jan 1942, Dimbokro, Côte d'Ivoire, French West Africa), Ivorian politician; president of Côte d'Ivoire from 2010.

**Alexander (Mikhailovich) Ovechkin** (17 Sep 1985, Moscow, USSR [now in Russia]), Russian professional hockey player.

**Hisashi Owada** (18 Sep 1932, Niigata, Japan), Japanese jurist; president of the International Court of Justice, 2009–12.

**Clive Owen** (3 Oct 1964, Keresley, Coventry, Warwickshire, England), British actor.

**Amos Oz** (4 May 1939, Jerusalem, British Palestine), Israeli novelist, short-story writer, and essayist.

**Mehmet Oz** (11 Jun 1960, Cleveland OH), American cardiac surgeon, TV medical expert, and author.

**Seiji Ozawa** (1935, Shenyang, Japanese-occupied China), Japanese conductor; recipient of a Praemium Imperiale in 2011.

**Cynthia Ozick** (17 Apr 1928, New York NY), American novelist, short-story writer, and playwright.

**Rajendra K. Pachauri** (20 Aug 1940, Nainital, Uttar Pradesh [now in Uttarakhand state], British India), Indian businessman; head of the Intergovernmental Panel on Climate Change from 2002.

**Al(fredo James) Pacino** (25 Apr 1940, New York NY), American film actor.

**Manny Pacquiao** (17 Dec 1978, Kibawe, Mindanao, Philippines), Filipino politician and boxing champion in numerous weight classes.

**Larry Page** (Lawrence Edward Page; 1972, East Lansing MI), American computer scientist and Internet entrepreneur who cofounded (1998) the Google Internet search engine.

**Borut Pahor** (2 Nov 1963, Postojna, Yugoslavia [now in Slovenia]), Slovenian politician; prime minister of Slovenia, 2008–12.

**Brad Paisley** (28 Oct 1972, Glen Dale WV), American contemporary country-and-western singer.

**Ian (Richard Kyle) Paisley** (6 Apr 1926, Armagh, County Armagh, Northern Ireland), Northern Irish Protestant leader and politician; first minister of Northern Ireland, 2007–08.

**Sarah Palin** (Sarah Heath; 11 Feb 1964, Sandpoint ID), American politician (Republican); governor of Alaska, 2006–09, and the Republican nominee for vice president in 2008.

**Gwyneth Paltrow** (28 Sep 1972, Los Angeles CA), American film and stage actress.

**Orhan Pamuk** (7 Jun 1952, Istanbul, Turkey), Turkish novelist; winner of the 2006 Nobel Prize for Literature.

**Leon Panetta** (28 Jun 1938, Monterey CA), American politician; director of the Office of Management and Budget, 1993–94, White House chief of staff, 1994–97, director of the CIA, 2009–11, and secretary of defense from 2011.

**Paola** (Paola dei Principi Ruffo di Calabria; 11 Sep 1937, Forte dei Marmi, Italy), Italian-born Belgian royal; queen consort of King Albert II (married 2 Jul 1959).

**Lucas Papademos** (11 Oct 1947, Athens, Greece), Greek economist; prime minister of Greece, 2011–12.

**George Papandreou** (16 Jun 1952, St. Paul MN), American-born Greek politician; prime minister of Greece, 2009–11.

**Karolos Papoulias** (4 Jun 1929, Ioannina, Greece), Greek politician; president of Greece from 2005.

**Anna (Helene) Paquin** (24 Jul 1982, Winnipeg, MB, Canada), New Zealand film and TV actress.

**Sara Paretsky** (8 Jun 1947, Ames IA), American mystery writer.

**Nick Park** (Nicholas Wulstan Park; 6 Dec 1958, Preston, Lancashire, England), British film animator.

**Mary-Louise Parker** (2 Aug 1964, Fort Jackson SC), American actress on stage, in film, and on television.

**Sarah Jessica Parker** (25 Mar 1965, Nelsonville OH), American TV and film actress.

**Trey Parker** (Randolph Severn Parker III; 19 Oct 1969, Conifer CO), American writer, actor, and producer; cocreator of the TV comedy series *South Park* and the Broadway musical *The Book of Mormon.*

**Mark Parkinson** (24 Jun 1957, Wichita KS), American politician (Democrat); governor of Kansas, 2009–11.

**Suzan-Lori Parks** (10 May 1963, Fort Knox KY), American playwright.

**Sean R. Parnell** (19 Nov 1962, Hanford CA), American politician (Republican); governor of Alaska from 2009.

**Anja Pärson** (25 Apr 1981, Umeå, Sweden), Swedish downhill skier.

**Jim Parsons** (James Joseph Parsons; 24 Mar 1973, Houston TX), American actor.

**Richard D(ean) Parsons** (4 Apr 1949, Bedford-Stuyvesant, Brooklyn NY), American corporate executive; CEO of Time Warner (formerly AOL Time Warner), 2002–07, and chairman of Citigroup, 2009–12.

**Dolly (Rebecca) Parton** (19 Jan 1946, Locust Ridge TN), American country-and-western singer, songwriter, and actress.

**Amy Pascal** (1959, Los Angeles CA), American film executive; chairman of Sony Pictures Entertainment Motion Picture Group from 2003 and cochairman of Sony Pictures Entertainment from 2006.

**Darrell Pasloski** (1960/61, Canada?), Canadian politician; premier of Yukon from 2011.

**Pedro Passos Coelho** (1964, Coimbra, Portugal), Portuguese politician; prime minister of Portugal from 2011.

**Ann Patchett** (2 Dec 1963, Los Angeles CA), American novelist.

**David A. Paterson** (20 May 1954, Brooklyn NY), American politician (Democrat); governor of New York, 2008–11.

**Pratibha Patil** (19 Dec 1934, Jalgaon, British India), Indian politician; the country's first female president, 2007–12.

**Danica (Sue) Patrick** (25 Mar 1982, Beloit WI), American race-car driver.

**Deval (Laurdine) Patrick** (31 Jul 1956, Chicago IL), American politician (Democrat); governor of Massachusetts from 2007.

**Robert Pattinson** (13 May 1986, London, England), British actor.

**Ron(ald Ernest) Paul** (20 Aug 1935, Pittsburgh PA), American physician and libertarian politician; congressman from Texas from 1997.

**Tim(othy James) Pawlenty** (27 Nov 1960, St. Paul MN), American politician (Republican); governor of Minnesota, 2003–11.

**(Constantine) Alexander Payne** (20 Feb 1961, Omaha NE), American director, screenwriter, and producer.

**Pelé** (Edson Arantes do Nascimento; 23 Oct 1940, Três Corações, Minas Gerais state, Brazil), Brazilian association football (soccer) legend.

Scott Pelley (28 Jul 1957, San Antonio TX), American TV journalist and news anchor.

Cesar Pelli (12 Oct 1926, Tucumán, Argentina), Argentine architect.

Nancy Pelosi (Nancy D'Alesandro; 26 Mar 1940, Baltimore MD), American politician (Democrat); congresswoman from California from 1987, House Democratic leader, 2003–07, speaker of the House, 2007–11, and minority leader from 2011.

Sean (Justin) Penn (17 Aug 1960, Santa Monica CA), American film actor and director.

Murray Perahia (19 Apr 1947, New York NY), American concert pianist.

Bev(erly Eaves) Perdue (14 Jan 1947, Grundy VA), American politician (Democrat); governor of North Carolina from 2009.

Sonny Perdue (George Ervin Perdue III; 20 Dec 1946, Perry GA), American agribusinessman and politician (Republican); governor of Georgia, 2003–11.

Shimon Peres (Shimon Perski; 2 Aug 1923, Wolozyn, Poland [now Valozhyn, Belarus]), Israeli statesman; prime minister of Israel, 1984–86 and 1995–96, and president from 2007; he won the Nobel Peace Prize in 1994 for his efforts to work with the Palestinian Liberation Organization.

Otto (Fernando) Pérez (Molina) (1 Dec 1950, Guatemala City, Guatemala), Guatemalan politician and army official; president of Guatemala from 2012.

Saul Perlmutter (1959, Champaign-Urbana IL), American physicist; winner of the 2011 Nobel Prize for Physics.

Grayson Perry (24 Mar 1960, Chelmsford, Essex, England), British artist; recipient of the 2003 Turner Prize.

Katy Perry (Katheryn Elizabeth Hudson; 25 Oct 1984, Santa Barbara CA), American pop singer.

Rick Perry (James Richard Perry; 4 Mar 1950, West Texas), American politician (Republican); governor of Texas from 2000.

Tyler Perry (Emmitt Perry, Jr.; 13 Sep 1969, New Orleans LA), American playwright, actor, screenwriter, and director.

Kamla Persad-Bissessar (22 Apr 1952, Siparia, Trinidad, British West Indies [now in Trinidad and Tobago]), Trinidadian politician; prime minister of Trinidad and Tobago from 2010.

David (Howell) Petraeus (7 Nov 1952, Cornwall-on-Hudson NY), American military leader; commander of Multinational Force Iraq, 2007–08, US Central Command, 2008–10, and US and NATO forces in Afghanistan, 2010–11; director of the CIA from 2011.

Michael Phelps (30 Jun 1985, Baltimore MD), American swimmer; the most decorated medallist in Olympic history.

Philip (Prince Philip of Greece and Denmark; 10 Jun 1921, Corfu, Greece), British duke of Edinburgh; prince consort of Queen Elizabeth II (married 20 Nov 1947).

Danny Philip (1951, Solomon Islands?), Solomon Islands politician; prime minister of the Solomon Islands, 2010–11.

Philippe (Philippe Leopold Louis Marie; 15 Apr 1960, Brussels, Belgium), Belgian royal; duke of Brabant and crown prince of Belgium.

Susan Philipsz (1965, Glasgow, Scotland), Scottish artist; winner of the 2010 Turner Prize.

(Matthew) Ryan Phillippe (10 Sep 1974, New Castle DE), American TV and film actor.

Ellen (Philpotts-) Page (21 Feb 1987, Halifax, NS, Canada), Canadian TV and film actress.

Renzo Piano (14 Sep 1937, Genoa, Italy), Italian architect; winner of the 1998 Pritzker Prize and the 2002 UIA Gold Medal for Architecture.

T(homas) Boone Pickens (22 May 1928, Holdenville OK), American billionaire oilman; advocate of aggressive investment in alternative energy.

Jodi Picoult (19 May 1966, Nesconset NY), American author.

Navanethem Pillay (23 Sep 1941, Durban, Union of South Africa), South African judge; UN high commissioner for human rights from 2008.

Sebastián Piñera (1 Dec 1949, Santiago, Chile), Chilean politician (National Renewal); president of Chile from 2010.

Jean Ping (24 Nov 1942, Omboué, French Gabon), Gabonese statesman; UN General Assembly president, 2004, and chairman of the Commission of the African Union from 2008.

Pink (Alecia Beth Moore; 8 Sep 1979, Doylestown PA), American pop singer.

Jada Pinkett Smith (Jada Koren Pinkett; 18 Sep 1971, Baltimore MD), American actress and singer.

Robert Pinsky (20 Oct 1940, Long Branch NJ), American poet and critic; poet laureate of the US, 1997–2000.

Manuel Pinto da Costa (1937), Sao Tome and Principe politician; president of Sao Tome and Principe, 1975–91, and from 2011.

Pedro (Verona Rodrigues) Pires (April 1934, Ilha do Fogo, Cape Verde), Cape Verdean politician; president of Cape Verde, 2001–11.

Oscar Pistorius (22 Nov 1986, Johannesburg, South Africa), South African sprinter; first amputee to compete in track and field in the Olympics, and first to reach an Olympic final.

Surin Pitsuwan (28 Oct 1949, Nakhon Si Thammarat, Thailand), Thai intellectual and government official; secretary-general of the Association of Southeast Asian Nations from 2008.

(William) Brad(ley) Pitt (18 Dec 1963, Shawnee OK), American film actor.

Rosen Plevneliev (14 May 1964, Gotse Delchev, Bulgaria), Bulgarian politician; president of Bulgaria from 2012.

(Arthur) Christopher (Orme) Plummer (13 Dec 1929, Toronto, ON, Canada), Canadian actor.

Yevgeny (Viktorovich) Plushchenko (also spelled Evgeni Plushenko; 3 Nov 1982, Solnechny, USSR [now in Russia]), Russian figure skater.

Amy Poehler (16 Sep 1971, Burlington MA), American actress and comedian on TV and in films.

Hifikepunye (Lucas) Pohamba (18 Aug 1935, Okanghudi, South West Africa [now Namibia]), Namibian independence leader and politician; president of Namibia from 2005.

Sidney Poitier (20 Feb 1927?, Miami FL), Bahamian American stage and film actor and director.

Roman Polanski (Raimund Liebling; 18 Aug 1933, Paris, France), Polish film director, scriptwriter, and actor.

Judit Polgár (23 Jul 1976, Budapest, Hungary), Hungarian chess grand master.

Maurizio Pollini (1942, Milan, Italy), Italian pianist; recipient of a Praemium Imperiale in 2010.

Victor Ponta (20 Sep 1972, Bucharest, Romania), Romanian politician; prime minister from 2012.

Gregg Popovich (28 Jan 1949, East Chicago IN), American professional basketball coach.

**Natalie Portman** (Natalie Hershlag; 9 Jun 1981, Jerusalem, Israel), American film actress.

**Zac(hary E.) Posen** (24 Oct 1980, Brooklyn NY), American fashion designer.

**Earl A. ("Rusty") Powell III** (24 Oct 1943, Spartanburg SC), American museum official; director of the National Gallery of Art in Washington DC from 1992.

**Samantha Power** (1970, Ireland), Irish-born American writer and political adviser; foreign-policy adviser to the National Security Council from 2009.

**Miuccia Prada** (1949, Milan, Italy), Italian fashion designer.

**René (García) Préval** (17 Jan 1943, Port-au-Prince, Haiti, Haitian); politician; president of Haiti, 1996–2001, and 2006–11.

**André (George) Previn** (6 Apr 1929, Berlin, Germany), German-born American pianist, composer, and conductor.

**Richard Price** (12 Oct 1949, Bronx NY), American novelist and screenwriter.

**Reince Priebus** (18 Mar 1972, Kenosha WI), American attorney and politician (Republican); chairman of the Republican National Committee from 2011.

**Prince** (Prince Rogers Nelson; 7 Jun 1958, Minneapolis MN), American singer and songwriter.

**E(dna) Annie Proulx** (22 Aug 1935, Norwich CT), American writer.

**(José) Albert(o) Pujols** (16 Jan 1980, Santo Domingo, Dominican Republic), Dominican baseball player.

**Rajkeswur Purryag** (12 Dec 1947, Camp Fouquereaux, Mauritius), Mauritian politician; president of Mauritius from 2012.

**Georgi Purvanov** (28 Jun 1957, Kovachevtsi, Bulgaria), Bulgarian politician; president of Bulgaria, 2002–12.

**Vladimir (Vladimirovich) Putin** (7 Oct 1952, Leningrad, USSR [now St. Petersburg, Russia]), Russian intelligence officer; prime minister of Russia, 1999–2000 and 2008–12, and president, 1999–2008 and from 2012.

**Kevin Puts** (3 Jan 1972, St. Louis MO), American composer; his *Silent Night: Opera in Two Acts* won the 2012 Pulitzer Prize for music.

**(Sayyid) Qabus ibn Sa'id** (18 Nov 1940, Salalah, Oman), Omani head of state; sultan of Oman from 1970 and prime minister from 1972.

**Thomas Quasthoff** (9 Nov 1959, Hildesheim, West Germany), German bass-baritone.

**Queen Latifah** (Dana Elaine Owens; 18 Mar 1970, Newark NJ), American rap musician, film actress, and TV personality.

**Anna (Marie) Quindlen** (8 Jul 1953, Philadelphia PA), American political commentator and author.

**Pat Quinn** (16 Dec 1948, Hinsdale IL), American politician (Democrat); governor of Illinois from 2009.

**Daniel Radcliffe** (23 July 1989, Fulham, London, England), British film and stage actor.

**Paula Radcliffe** (17 Dec 1973, Northwich, Cheshire, England), British marathon runner.

**Iveta Radicová** (7 Dec 1956, Bratislava, Czechoslovakia [now in Slovakia]), Slovak politician; prime minister of Slovakia, 2010–12.

**Nebojsa Radmanovic** (1 Oct 1949, Gracanica, Yugoslavia [now in Bosnia and Herzegovina]), Bosnia and Herzegovinian politician; chairman of the presidency of the republic, 2008–09, and 2010–11.

**Aishwarya Rai** (1 Nov 1973, Mangalore, Karnataka state, India), Indian beauty queen and film actress.

**Béchara Raï** (25 Feb 1940, Lebanon), Lebanese (Maronite Catholic) patriarch of Antioch and all the East from 2011.

**Sam(uel M.) Raimi** (23 Oct 1959, Franklin MI), American cult filmmaker.

**Rain** (Jeong Ji-hoon; 25 Jun 1982, Seoul, South Korea), Korean pop singer and actor.

**Mahinda Rajapakse** (18 Nov 1945, British Ceylon [now Sri Lanka]), Sri Lankan politician; prime minister of Sri Lanka, 2004–05, and president from 2005.

**Raj Rajaratnam** (15 Jun 1957, Colombo, Sri Lanka), Sri Lankan-born businessman and founder of Galleon Group, a hedge-fund firm in New York; convicted of insider trading in 2011.

**Andry Rajoelina** (30 May 1974), Malagasy politician; president of Madagascar from 2009.

**Mariano Rajoy (Brey)** (27 Mar 1955, Santiago de Compostela, Spain), Spanish politician (Popular Party); prime minister of Spain from 2011.

**Imomali Rakhmon** (5 Oct 1952, Dangara, Tadzhik SSR, USSR [now Tajikistan]), Tajik politician; president of Tajikistan from 1992.

**José Ramos-Horta** (26 Dec 1949, Dili, Portuguese Timor [now East Timor (Timor-Leste)]), Timorese nationalist leader; prime minister of East Timor, 2006–07, and president, 2007–12; corecipient of the 1996 Nobel Peace Prize.

**Donald Ramotar** (22 Oct 1950, Caria Caria, Guyana), Guyanese politician; president of Guyana from 2011.

**Gordon (James) Ramsay** (8 Nov 1966, Glasgow, Scotland), British chef and TV personality.

**Rania al-Abdullah** (Rania al-Yaseen; 31 Aug 1970, Kuwait), Kuwaiti-born Jordanian royal; queen consort of King Abdullah II (married 10 Jun 1993).

**Ian Rankin** (28 Apr 1960, Cardenden, Fife, Scotland), British crime novelist.

**Noomi Rapace** (Noomi Norén; 28 Dec 1979, Hudiksvall, Sweden), Swedish actress.

**Phylicia Rashad** (Phylicia Ayers-Allen; 19 Jun 1948, Houston TX), American TV and stage actress and director.

**Anders Fogh Rasmussen** (26 Jan 1953, Ginnerup, Denmark), Danish politician; prime minister of Denmark, 2001–09, and secretary-general of NATO from 2009.

**Lars Løkke Rasmussen** (15 May 1964, Vejle, Denmark) Danish politician; prime minister of Denmark, 2009–11.

**Simon (Denis) Rattle** (19 Jan 1955, Liverpool, England), British orchestra conductor; principal conductor and artistic director of the Berlin Philharmonic from the 2002–03 season.

**Marc Ravalomanana** (1949, near Atananarivo, French Madagascar), Malagasy politician; president of Madagascar, 2002–09

**Rachael (Domenica) Ray** (25 Aug 1968, Cape Cod MA), American TV cook and cookbook author.

**Alison M. Redford** (7 Mar 1965, Kitimat, BC, Canada), Canadian politician (Progressive Conservative); premier of Alberta from 2011.

**(Charles) Robert Redford, Jr.** (18 Aug 1937, Santa Monica CA), American film actor and director.

**Vanessa Redgrave** (30 Jan 1937, London, England), British stage and screen actress and political activist.

**Joshua Redman** (1 Feb 1969, Berkeley CA), American jazz saxophone player.

**Sumner Redstone** (Sumner Murray Rothstein; 27 May 1923, Boston MA), American media executive.

**Martin J(ohn) Rees** (23 Jun 1942, York, England), British astronomer royal; recipient of the Templeton Prize in 2011.

**Keanu (Charles) Reeves** (2 Sep 1964, Beirut, Lebanon), American actor.

**Steve Reich** (3 Oct 1936, New York NY), American composer.

**Harry Reid** (2 Dec 1939, Searchlight NV), American politician (Democrat); senator from Nevada from 1987, Senate leader from 2005.

**John C(hristopher) Reilly** (24 May 1965, Chicago IL), American stage and film actor.

**Rob Reiner** (6 Mar 1947, Bronx NY), American actor, director, writer, and producer.

**(John) Fredrik Reinfeldt** (4 Aug 1965, Österhaninge, Sweden), Swedish politician (Moderate Party); prime minister of Sweden from 2006.

**Manfred Reinke** (?, Germany?), German scientist; executive secretary of the Antarctic Treaty system from 2009.

**Jason Reitman** (19 Oct 1977, Montreal, QC, Canada), Canadian actor, director, and writer.

**M(argaret) Jodi Rell** (Mary Carolyn Reavis; 16 Jun 1946, Norfolk VA), American politician (Republican); governor of Connecticut, 2004–11.

**Edward (Gene) Rendell** (5 Jan 1944, New York NY), American politician (Democrat); mayor of Philadelphia, 1992–2000, and governor of Pennsylvania, 2003–11.

**Ruth Rendell** (Baroness Rendell of Babergh; pseudonym Barbara Vine; 17 Feb 1930, London, England), British mystery novelist.

**Jeremy Renner** (7 Jan 1971, Modesto CA), American actor.

**Ryan Reynolds** (23 Oct 1976, Vancouver, BC, Canada), Canadian film actor.

**Yasmina Reza** (1 May 1959, Paris, France), French playwright.

**Christina Ricci** (12 Feb 1980, Santa Monica CA), American film actress.

**Anne Rice** (Howard Allen O'Brien; pseudonyms A.N. Roquelaure and Anne Rampling; 4 Oct 1941, New Orleans LA), American Gothic novelist.

**(George) Maxwell Richards** (1931, San Fernando, Trinidad, British West Indies [now in Trinidad and Tobago]), Trinidadian chemical engineer and university professor; president of Trinidad and Tobago from 2003.

**Keith Richards** (18 Dec 1943, Dartford, Kent, England), British rock guitarist and singer (for the Rolling Stones).

**Bill Richardson** (William Blaine Richardson; 15 Nov 1947, Pasadena CA), American politician (Democrat); governor of New Mexico, 2003–11.

**Nicole Richie** (15 Sep 1981, Berkeley CA), American celebrity entertainer and fashion designer.

**Gerhard Richter** (9 Feb 1932, Dresden, Germany), German Capitalist Realist artist.

**Adam G(uy) Riess** (16 Dec 1969, Washington DC), American astronomer; winner of the 2011 Nobel Prize for Physics.

**Rihanna** (Robyn Rihanna Fenty; 20 Feb 1988, Saint Michael parish, Barbados), West Indian pop singer and actress.

**Robert R. Riley** (3 Oct 1944, Ashland AL), American politician (Republican); governor of Alabama, 2003–11.

**LeAnn Rimes** (28 Aug 1982, Jackson MS), American country-and-western singer.

**Kelly Ripa** (2 Oct 1970, Stratford NJ), American talk-show host and actress.

**Bill Ritter** (August William Ritter, Jr.; 6 Sep 1956, Denver CO), American politician (Democrat); governor of Colorado, 2007–11.

**Tim Robbins** (16 Oct 1958, West Covina CA), American actor.

**Cecil E(dward) Roberts, Jr.** (31 Oct 1946, Kayford WV), American labor leader; president of the United Mine Workers of America from 1995.

**John G(lover) Roberts** (27 Jan 1955, Buffalo NY), American jurist; chief justice of the US from 2005.

**Julia Roberts** (Julie Fiona Roberts; 28 Oct 1967, Smyrna GA), American film actress.

**Nora Roberts** (Eleanor Marie Robertson; 10 Oct 1950, Silver Spring MD), American novelist.

**Marilynne Robinson** (1947, Sandpoint ID), American author.

**Peter (David) Robinson** (29 Dec 1948, Belfast, Northern Ireland), Northern Irish Protestant loyalist politician; first minister of Northern Ireland from 2008.

**Chris Rock** (7 Feb 1966, Georgetown SC), American stand-up comedian and actor.

**Kid Rock** (Robert James Ritchie; 17 Jan 1971, Romeo MI), American rap-rock artist.

**Andy Roddick** (30 Aug 1982, Omaha NE), American tennis player.

**Aaron Rodgers** (2 Dec 1983, Chico CA), American professional football player.

**Alex Rodriguez** (27 Jul 1975, New York NY), American baseball player.

**Narciso Rodríguez** (January 1961, New Jersey), American fashion designer.

**Robert (Anthony) Rodriguez** (20 Jun 1968, San Antonio TX), Mexican American filmmaker.

**Seth Rogen** (15 Apr 1982, Vancouver, BC, Canada), Canadian film actor.

**James E. Rogers** (20 Sep 1947, Birmingham AL), American corporate executive; president and CEO (from 2006) and chairman of the board (from 2007) of Duke Energy.

**Richard (George) Rogers** (23 Jul 1933, Florence, Italy), British architect; recipient of a Praemium Imperiale in 2000 and the Pritzker Prize in 2007.

**Jacques Rogge** (2 May 1942, Ghent, Belgium), Belgian Olympic yachtsman, surgeon, and sports executive; president of the International Olympic Committee from 2001.

**Floyd Roland** (23 Nov 1961, Inuvik, NT, Canada), Canadian politician; premier of the Northwest Territories, 2007–11.

**Sonny Rollins** (Theodore Walter Rollins; 7 Sep 1930, Harlem, New York NY), American jazz saxophonist.

**Ray Romano** (21 Dec 1957, Queens NY), American comic actor.

**Virginia M. Rometty** ("Ginni"; 1957/1958, ?), American business executive; president and CEO of the International Business Machines (IBM) Corp. from 2012.

**(Willard) Mitt Romney** (12 Mar 1947, Bloomfield MI), American businessman, sports executive, and politician (Republican); governor of Massachusetts, 2003–07.

**Tony Romo** (21 Apr 1980, San Diego CA), American pro football quarterback.

**Cristiano Ronaldo (dos Santos Aveiro)** (5 Feb 1985, Funchal, Madeira, Portugal), Portuguese association football (soccer) player; he was voted World Player of the Year by FIFA in 2008.

**Charlie Rose** (5 Jan 1942, Henderson NC), American TV journalist and interviewer.

**Derrick Rose** (4 Oct 1988, Chicago IL), American basketball player.

**Philip (Milton) Roth** (19 Mar 1933, Newark NJ), American novelist and short-story writer; winner of the 2011 International Man Booker.

**Mike Rounds** (Marion Michael Rounds; 24 Oct 1954, Huron SD), American politician (Republican); governor of South Dakota, 2003–11.

**Mickey Rourke** (16 Sep 1952, Schenectady NY), American actor.

**Dilma (Vana) Rousseff** (14 Dec 1947, Belo Horizonte, Brazil), Brazilian politician (Workers' Party); president of Brazil from 2011.

**Karl Rove** (25 Dec 1950, Denver CO), American right-wing political operative, consultant, and commentator; former chief strategist for Pres. George W. Bush.

**J(oanne) K(athleen) Rowling** (31 Jul 1965, Chipping Sodbury, near Bristol, Gloucestershire, England), British author, creator of the Harry Potter series.

**Taur Matan Ruak** (José Maria de Vasconcelos; 10 Oct 1956, Osso Huna, Portuguese Timor [now East Timor (Timor-Leste)]), Timorese politician; president of East Timor from 2012.

**Rick Rubin** (Frederick Jay Rubin; 10 Mar 1963, Lido Beach NY), American record producer.

**Marco Rubio** (28 May 1971, Miami FL), American politician (Republican); senator from Florida from 2011.

**Kevin (Michael) Rudd** (21 Sep 1957, Nambour, QLD, Australia), Australian politician (Labor); prime minister of Australia, 2007–10.

**Geoffrey Rush** (6 Jul 1951, Toowoomba, QLD, Australia), Australian film actor; he was named Australian of the Year in 2012.

**(Ahmed) Salman Rushdie** (19 Jun 1947, Bombay, British India [now Mumbai, India]), Anglo-Indian novelist.

**Richard Russo** (15 Jul 1949, Johnstown NY), American author; winner of the 2002 Pulitzer Prize for fiction.

**Mark Rutte** (14 Feb 1967, The Hague, Netherlands), Dutch politician (People's Party for Freedom and Democracy); prime minister of the Netherlands from 2010.

**John Rutter** (24 Sep 1945, London, England), British composer and conductor; founder (1981) and leader of the Cambridge Singers.

**Kay Ryan** (11 Sep 1945, San Jose CA), American poet; recipient of the 2004 Ruth Lilly Poetry Prize and US poet laureate (2008–10); her *The Best of It* won the 2011 Pulitzer Prize for poetry.

**Paul Ryan** (29 Jan 1970, Janesville WI), American politician (Republican); member of the US House of Representatives from 1999.

**Winona Ryder** (Winona Laura Horowitz; 29 Oct 1971, Winona MN), American film actress.

**Mikhail Saakashvili** (21 Dec 1967, Tbilisi, USSR [now in Georgia]), Georgian politician; president of Georgia, 2004–07 and from 2008.

**Charles Saatchi** (9 Jun 1943, Baghdad, Iraq), Iraqi-born British advertising executive and art patron.

**Sabah al-Ahmad al-Jabir Al Sabah** (1929?, Kuwait city, Kuwait), Kuwaiti sheikh; emir from 2006.

**Jeffrey D(avid) Sachs** (5 Nov 1954, Detroit MI), American economist; involved in efforts to eradicate poverty on a global scale.

**Muqtada al-Sadr** (1974, Al-Najaf, Iraq), Iraqi Shiʿite Muslim cleric, one of the most powerful political figures in Iraq in the early 21st century.

**Ken Salazar** (2 Mar 1955, Alamosa CO), American lawyer and politician (Democrat); senator from Colorado, 2005–09, and US secretary of the interior from 2009.

**Sebastião (Ribeiro) Salgado** (8 Feb 1944, Aimorés, Minas Gerais state, Brazil), Brazilian photographer.

**ʿAli ʿAbdallah Salih** (21 Mar 1942, Beit al-Ahmar, Yemen), Yemeni politician; president of Yemen (Sanʿa), 1978–90, and of the unified Yemen, 1990–2012.

**Macky Sall** (11 Dec 1961, Fatick, Senegal), Senegalese politician; prime minister of Senegal, 2004–07, and president from 2012.

**Alex(ander Elliot Anderson) Salmond** (31 Dec 1954, Linlithgow, Scotland), Scottish politician (Scottish National Party); first minister of Scotland from 2007.

**Esa-Pekka Salonen** (30 Jun 1958, Helsinki, Finland), Finnish conductor; musical director of the Los Angeles Philharmonic, 1992–2009, and principal conductor and artistic adviser of the Philharmonia Orchestra, London, from 2008.

**Antonis (Konstantinou) Samaras** (23 May 1951, Athens, Greece), Greek politician; prime minister of Greece from 2012.

**Andy Samberg** (David Andrew Samberg; 18 Aug 1978, Berkeley CA), American comedian and actor.

**Ahmed Abdallah Sambi** (5 Jun 1958, Mutsamudu, Anjouan, French Comoro Islands), Comoran Muslim religious leader; president of Comoros, 2006–11.

**Adam Sandler** (9 Sep 1966, Brooklyn NY), American comic actor.

**Brian Sandoval** (5 Aug 1963, Redding CA), American politician (Republican); governor of Nevada from 2011.

**Jerry Sandusky** (Gerald Arthur Sandusky; 26 Jan 1944, Washington PA), American collegiate football coach; convicted in 2012 of sexually abusing young boys.

**Mark Sanford** (Marshall Clement Sanford, Jr.; 15 Jan 1960, Fort Lauderdale FL), American politician (Republican); governor of South Carolina, 2003–11.

**Truong Tan Sang** (21 Jan 1949, My Hanh, Vietnam), Vietnamese politician; president of Vietnam from 2011.

**Lobsang Sangay** (1968, Darjiling, India), Tibetan scholar and political leader; prime minister in the Tibetan Central Administration (the Tibetan government-in-exile) from 2011.

**Malam Bacai Sanhá** (5 May 1947, Darsalame, Portuguese Guinea [now Guinea-Bissau]), Guinea-Bissauan politician; president of Guinea-Bissau, 2009–12.

**Johan (Alexander) Santana (Araque)** (13 Mar 1979, Tovar, Venezuela), Venezuelan pro baseball starting pitcher.

**Rick Santorum** (10 May 1958, Winchester VA), American politician (Republican); member of the US House of Representatives, 1991–95, and Senate, 1995–2007.

**Juan Manuel Santos Calderón** (10 Aug 1951, Bogotá, Colombia), Colombian politician; finance minister (2000–02), defense minister (2006–09), and president of Colombia from 2010.

**Cristina Saralegui** (29 Jan 1948, Havana, Cuba), Cuban-born American Spanish-language TV talk-show host.

**Susan Sarandon** (Susan Abigail Tomalin; 4 Oct 1946, New York NY), American actress.

**Thomas J(ohn) Sargent** (19 Jul 1943, Pasadena CA), American economist; winner of the 2011 Nobel Prize for Economics.

Serzh (Azati) Sarkisyan (30 Jun 1954, Stepanakert, Nagorno-Karabakh autonomous oblast, USSR [now in Azerbaijan]), Armenian politician; prime minister of Armenia, 2007–08, and president from 2008.

Tigran Sarkisyan (29 Jan 1960, Kirovakan, USSR [now Vanadzor, Armenia]), Armenian economist and politician; prime minister of Armenia from 2008.

Nicolas Sarkozy (Nicolas Paul-Stéphane Sarközy de Nagy-Bocsa; 28 Jan 1955, Paris, France), French conservative politician; interior minister, 2005–07, and president of France, 2007–12.

Denis Sassou-Nguesso (1943, Edou, French Equatorial Africa [now in the Republic of the Congo]), Congolese politician; president of the Republic of Congo, 1979–92 and again from 1997.

Michael Sata (Chilufya) (6 Jul 1937, Mwikulu, Northern Rhodesia [now Zambia]), Zambian politician; president from 2011.

al-Walid ibn Talal ibn Abdulaziz al-Saud (1954, Riyadh, Saudi Arabia), Saudi prince and billionaire businessman.

Dan Savage (7 Oct 1964, Chicago IL), American author, columnist, and gay-rights activist.

Diane K. Sawyer (Lila Sawyer; 22 Dec 1945, Glasgow KY), American TV journalist and news anchor.

Antonin Scalia (11 Mar 1936, Trenton NJ), American jurist; associate justice of the US Supreme Court from 1986.

Joe Scarborough (Charles Joseph Scarborough; 9 Apr 1963, Atlanta GA), American conservative TV host and commentator.

Mary L. Schapiro (19 Jun 1955, New York NY), American finance administrator; chairman of the Securities and Exchange Commission from 2009.

Brian P. Schmidt (24 Feb 1967, Missoula MT), American Australian astronomer; winner of the 2011 Nobel Prize for Physics.

Eric E. Schmidt (1955?), American computer scientist and corporate executive; CTO of Sun Microsystems, Inc., 1983–97, chairman and CEO of Novell, Inc., 1997–2001, and chairman of Google, Inc., from 2001.

Pál Schmitt (13 May 1942, Budapest, Hungary), Hungarian politician; president of Hungary, 2010–12.

Julian Schnabel (26 Oct 1951, Brooklyn NY), American Neo-Expressionist artist and film director.

Howard Schultz (19 Jul 1953, Brooklyn NY), American businessman; CEO of Starbucks Corp. from 1987.

Philip Schultz (1945, Rochester NY), American poet.

Michael Schumacher (3 Jan 1969, Hürth-Hermülheim, West Germany), German Formula 1 race-car driver.

Arnold (Alois) Schwarzenegger (30 Jul 1947, Thal bei Graz, Austria), Austrian-born American bodybuilder, film actor, and politician (Republican); governor of California, 2003–11.

Brian (David) Schweitzer (4 Sep 1955, Havre MT), American politician (Democrat); governor of Montana from 2005.

David Schwimmer (2 Nov 1966, Astoria, Queens NY), American TV, film, and stage actor.

Jon Scieszka (8 Sep 1954, Flint MI), American author of books for children.

John Scofield (26 Dec 1951, Dayton OH), American jazz electric guitarist, composer, and bandleader.

Martin Scorsese (17 Nov 1942, Flushing, Long Island NY), American film director, writer, and producer.

Rick Scott (1 Dec 1952, Bloomington IL), American businessman and politician (Republican); governor of Florida from 2011.

Ridley Scott (30 Nov 1937, South Shields, Durham, England), British film director and producer.

Kristin Scott Thomas (24 May 1960, Redruth, Cornwall, England), British actress.

Ryan (John) Seacrest (24 Dec 1974, Atlanta GA), American TV program host (American Idol) and radio personality.

Seal (Sealhenry Olusegun Olumide Samuel; 19 Feb 1963, Kilburn, London, England), British soul singer.

Sean Paul (Ryan Francis Henriques) (8 Jan 1973, St. Andrew, Jamaica), Jamaican reggae and rap musician.

Kathleen Sebelius (Kathleen Gilligan; 15 May 1948, Cincinnati OH), American politician (Democrat); governor of Kansas, 2003–09, and US secretary of health and human services from 2009.

Amy Sedaris (29 Mar 1961, Endicott NY), American comic actress and writer.

David Sedaris (26 Dec 1956, Johnson City NY), American writer and humorist.

Kyra (Minturn) Sedgwick (19 Aug 1965, New York NY), American film and TV actress.

Jason (Jordan) Segel (18 Jan 1980, Los Angeles CA), American actor and writer.

Ivan G. Seidenberg (1947?, Bronx NY), American corporate executive; CEO of Verizon Communications from 2002.

Thein Sein (20 Apr 1945), Burmese military officer; prime minister of Myanmar (Burma), 2007–11, and president from 2011.

Jerry Seinfeld (Jerome Seinfeld; 29 Apr 1954, Brooklyn NY), American comic and TV personality.

Kazuyo Sejima (29 Oct 1956, Mito, Japan), Japanese architect; corecipient of the 2010 Pritzker Prize.

Koji Sekimizu (3 Dec 1952, Yokohama, Japan), Japanese public official; secretary-general of the International Maritime Organization from 2012.

Bud Selig (Allan H. Selig; 30 Jul 1934, Milwaukee WI), American sports executive; Major League Baseball commissioner from 1998.

Greg Selinger (c. 1951), Canadian politician; premier of Manitoba from 2009.

Paul Sereno (11 Oct 1957, Aurora IL), American paleontologist.

Richard Serra (2 Nov 1939, San Francisco CA), American minimalist sculptor of large outdoor works; recipient of a Praemium Imperiale in 1994.

Nasrallah Pierre Cardinal Sfeir (Nasrallah Boutros Pierre Sfeir; 15 May 1920, Reyfoun, Lebanon), Lebanese (Maronite Catholic) patriarch of Antioch and all the East, 1986–2011, and Roman Catholic cardinal from 1994.

Tuanku Abdul Halim Muadzam Shah ibni al-Marhum Sultan Badlishah (28 Nov 1927, Istana Anak Bukit, Malaysia), Malaysian politician; yang di-pertuan agong (head of state), 1970–75, and from 2011.

Shakira (Shakira Isabel Mebarak Ripoll; 2 Feb 1977, Barranquilla, Colombia), Colombian-born pop singer.

Tony Shalhoub (Anthony Marcus Shalhoub; 9 Oct 1953, Green Bay WI), American TV and film actor.

John Patrick Shanley (1950, Bronx NY), American screenwriter and playwright.

Mariya (Yuryevna) Sharapova (19 Apr 1987, Nyagan, USSR [now in Russia]), Russian tennis player.

Kamalesh Sharma (30 Sep 1941), Indian diplomat; secretary-general of the Commonwealth from 2008.

**Al Sharpton** (3 Oct 1954, New York NY), American politician (Democrat), political activist, civil rights leader, and TV host.

**William Shatner** (22 Mar 1931, Montreal, QC, Canada), Canadian TV actor.

**Daniel Shechtman** (24 Jan 1941, Palestine [now Tel Aviv-Yafo, Israel), Israeli chemist; winner of the 2011 Nobel Prize for Chemistry.

**Charlie Sheen** (Carlos Irwin Estevez; 3 Sep 1965, New York NY), American film and TV actor.

**Martin Sheen** (Ramon Estevez; 3 Aug 1940, Dayton OH), American stage, film, and TV actor.

**Judith Sheindlin** (21 Oct 1942, Brooklyn NY), American TV judge (of *Judge Judy*).

**Sam(uel) Shepard (Rogers)** (5 Nov 1943, Fort Sheridan IL), American playwright and actor.

**Cindy Sherman** (Cynthia Morris Sherman; 19 Jan 1954, Glen Ridge NJ), American photographer.

**Sviatoslav Shevchuk** (5 May 1970, Stryy, USSR [now Ukraine]), Ukrainian Greek Catholic Church leader; major archbishop of Kyiv-Halyc from 2011.

**Yingluck Shinawatra** (21 Jun 1967, San Kamphaeng, Thailand), Thai politician; prime minister of Thailand from 2011.

**Eric K. Shinseki** (28 Nov 1942, Lihue HI), American army officer; US secretary of veterans affairs from 2009.

**Masaaki Shirakawa** (27 Sep 1949, Kitakyushu, Japan), Japanese banker; governor of the Bank of Japan from 2008.

**Vandana Shiva** (5 Nov 1952, Dehra Dun, Uttar Pradesh [now in Uttarakhand] state, India), Indian biologist and social activist against the "biological theft" of the resources of poor countries by the richer ones.

**Peter Shumlin** (24 Mar 1956, Brattleboro VT), American politician (Democrat); governor of Vermont from 2011.

**Than Shwe** (2 Feb 1933, Kyaukse, Burma [now Myanmar]), Burmese military officer; head of government in Myanmar, 1992–2003, and chairman of the State Peace and Development Council (head of state), 1992–2011.

**M(anoj) Night Shyamalan** (6 Aug 1970, Pondicherry, India), Indian-born film director, screenwriter, and producer.

**Gabourey Sidibe** (6 May 1983, Brooklyn NY), American actress.

**Jóhanna Sigurðardóttir** (4 Oct 1942, Reykjavik, Iceland), Icelandic politician; prime minister of Iceland from 2009.

**(David) Derek Sikua** (10 Sep 1959, Guadalcanal province, British-protected Solomon Islands), Solomon Islands politician; prime minister of Solomon Islands, 2007–10.

**Haris Silajdzic** (1 Oct 1945, Sarajevo, Yugoslavia [now in Bosnia and Herzegovina]), Bosnia and Herzegovinian politician; chairman of the presidency of the republic in 2008 and 2010.

**Ahmed Mohamed Silanyo** (1936), Somali politician; president of the secessionist Republic of Somaliland from 2010.

**Sarah (Kate) Silverman** (1 Dec 1970, Bedford NH), American comedian, TV actress, and writer.

**Silvia** (Silvia Renate Sommerlath; 23 Dec 1943, Heidelberg, Germany), Swedish royal and social activist; queen consort of King Carl XVI Gustaf (married 19 Jun 1976).

**Charles Simic** (9 May 1938, Belgrade, Yugoslavia [now in Serbia]), Yugoslav-born American poet; US poet laureate, 2007–08.

**Russell Simmons** (4 Oct 1957, Queens NY), American hip-hop impresario and cofounder of Def Jam Records.

**Jessica Simpson** (10 Jul 1980, Dallas TX), American pop singer and actress.

**Lorna Simpson** (13 Aug 1960, Brooklyn NY), American multimedia artist.

**Portia Simpson Miller** (12 Dec 1945, Wood Hall, Jamaica), Jamaican politician; prime minister, 2006–07 and again from 2012.

**Christopher A(lbert) Sims** (21 Oct 1942, Washington DC), American economist; winner of the 2011 Nobel Prize for Economics.

**Hammerskjoeld Simwinga** (17 Nov 1964, Isoka, Zambia), Zambian environmentalist; recipient of the 2007 Goldman Environmental Prize for Africa.

**Manmohan Singh** (26 Sep 1932, Gah, Punjab, British India [now in Pakistan]), Indian economist; prime minister of India from 2004.

**Gary Sinise** (17 Mar 1955, Blue Island IL), American TV and film actor and director.

**(Sayyid) Ali (Hussaini) al-Sistani** (4 Aug 1930?, near Meshed, Iran), Iranian Shiʿite Muslim cleric.

**Alexander (Johan Hjalmar) Skarsgård** (25 Aug 1976, Stockholm, Sweden), Swedish film and TV actor.

**Jeffrey S. Skoll** (16 Jan 1965, Montreal, QC, Canada), Canadian entrepreneur; cofounder of eBay and the founder (1999) and chairman of the philanthropic Skoll Foundation.

**Leonard (Edward) Slatkin** (1 Sep 1944, Los Angeles CA), American conductor; music director of the Detroit Symphony Orchestra from 2008.

**Carlos Slim (Helú)** (28 Jan 1940, Mexico City, Mexico), Mexican investor; head of Grupo Carso, SA de CV, and chairman and CEO of the national telephone monopoly, Teléfonos de México (Telmex); he was named the world's richest person by *Forbes* each year since 2010.

**Tavis Smiley** (13 Sep 1964, Gulfport MS), American advocacy journalist on radio and TV.

**Alexander McCall Smith** (24 Aug 1948, Bulawayo, Southern Rhodesia [now Zimbabwe]), British author of crime novels and works for children.

**Anna Deavere Smith** (18 Sep 1950, Baltimore MD), American playwright, actress, and professor.

**Marc (Kelly) Smith** (195?, Chicago IL), American performance poet; originator of the poetry slam.

**Michael W. Smith** (7 Oct 1957, Kenova WV), American Christian singer.

**Patti (Lee) Smith** (30 Dec 1946, Chicago IL), American musician, poet, and visual artist.

**Stephen Smith** (12 Dec 1955, Narrogin, WA, Australia), Australian politician (Labor); Australian foreign minister, 2007–10, trade minister, 2010, and defense minister from 2010.

**Tracy K. Smith** (16 Apr 1972, ?), American author; her *Life on Mars* won the 2012 Pulitzer Prize for Poetry.

**Will(ard Christopher) Smith, Jr.** (25 Sep 1968, Philadelphia PA), American rapper and actor.

**Zadie Smith** (Sadie Smith; 27 Oct 1975, Willesden Green, London, England), British novelist.

**Snoop Dogg** (Snoop Lion; Calvin Broadus; 20 Oct 1972, Long Beach CA), American gangsta rap musician.

**Gary (Sherman) Snyder** (8 May 1930, San Francisco CA), American poet.

**Rick Snyder** (19 Aug 1958, Battle Creek MI), American businessman and politician (Republican); governor of Michigan from 2011.

**José Sócrates (Carvalho Pinto de Sousa)** (6 Sep 1957, Vilar de Maçada, Portugal), Portuguese civil engineer and politician (Socialist); prime minister of Portugal, 2005–11.

**Steven Soderbergh** (14 Jan 1963, Atlanta GA), American film director.

**Sofia** (Princess Sophie of Greece; Sofia de Grecia y Hannover; 2 Nov 1938, Athens, Greece), Spanish royal; queen consort of King Juan Carlos I (married 12 May 1962).

**Hilda Solis** (20 Oct 1957, Los Angeles CA), American politician (Democrat); congresswoman from California, 2001–09, and US secretary of labor from 2009.

**Hope (Amelia) Solo** (30 Jul 1981, Richland WA), American association football (soccer) player.

**Michael (Thomas) Somare** (9 Apr 1936, Rabaul, Australian-mandated New Guinea [now Papua New Guinea]), Papua New Guinean politician; prime minister of Papua New Guinea, 1975–80, 1982–85, 2002–11, and in opposition from 2011.

**Juan (Octavio) Somavia** (21 Apr 1941, Chile), Chilean international official; director general of the International Labour Organization from 1999.

**Stephen (Joshua) Sondheim** (22 Mar 1930, New York NY), American composer and lyricist for musical theater.

**Sang-Hyun Song** (21 Dec 1941, Japanese-occupied Korea [now in South Korea]), South Korean jurist; president of the International Criminal Court from 2009.

**Sonja** (Sonja Haraldsen; 4 Jul 1937, Oslo, Norway), Norwegian royal; queen consort of King Harald V (married 29 Aug 1968).

**Sophie** (Sophie Helen Rhys-Jones; 20 Jan 1965, Oxford, England), British royal; wife of Prince Edward (married 19 Jun 1999) and countess of Wessex.

**Aaron Sorkin** (9 Jun 1961, Scarsdale NY), American screenwriter, playwright, and TV producer.

**Guillaume Soro** (8 May 1972, Kofiplé, Côte d'Ivoire), Ivorian politician; prime minister of Côte d'Ivoire, 2007–12.

**Sonia (Maria) Sotomayor** (25 Jun 1954, Bronx NY), American jurist; associate justice of the US Supreme Court from 2009.

**David H(ackett) Souter** (17 Sep 1939, Melrose MA), American jurist; associate justice of the US Supreme Court, 1990–2009.

**Eduardo Souto de Moura** (25 Jul 1952, Porto, Portugal), Portuguese architect; winner of the 2011 Pritzker Prize.

**Wole Soyinka** (Akinwande Oluwole Soyinka; 13 Jul 1934, Abeokuta, Nigeria), Nigerian playwright, poet, novelist, and critic; recipient of the 1986 Nobel Prize for Literature.

**Kevin Spacey** (Kevin Matthew Fowler; 26 Jul 1959, South Orange NJ), American stage and film actor; artistic director of the Old Vic theater in London from 2003.

**Nicholas Sparks** (31 Dec 1965, Omaha NE), American novelist.

**Britney (Jean) Spears** (2 Dec 1981, Kentwood LA), American pop singer and celebrity.

**Octavia (Lenora) Spencer** (25 May 1972, Montgomery AL), American actress.

**W(inston) Baldwin Spencer** (8 Oct 1948), West Indian politician; prime minister of Antigua and Barbuda from 2004.

**Steven Spielberg** (18 Dec 1947, Cincinnati OH), American film director and producer.

**Nikola Spiric** (4 Sep 1956, Drvar, Yugoslavia [now in Bosnia and Herzegovina]), Bosnia and Herzegovinian politician; prime minister of Bosnia and Herzegovina, 2007–12.

**Eliot (Laurence) Spitzer** (10 Jun 1959, Riverdale, Bronx NY), American attorney, politician (Democrat), and TV host; governor of New York, 2007–08.

**Marc (J.W.) Sprenger** (30 Jul 1962, Netherlands?), Dutch public health official; director of the European Centre for Disease Prevention and Control (ECDC) from 2010.

**Bruce Springsteen** (23 Sep 1949, Freehold NJ), American rock singer and songwriter.

**(Michael) Sylvester (Enzio) Stallone** ("Sly"; 6 Jul 1946, New York NY), American film actor and director.

**Albert Starr** (1 Jun 1926, New York NY), American cardiovascular surgeon and inventor of an artificial heart valve; recipient of a 2007 Lasker Medical Prize.

**James G. Stavridis** (15 Feb 1955, West Palm Beach FL), American military official; Supreme Allied Commander, Europe (SACEUR) from 2009 and commander of the US European Command from 2009.

**Danielle (Fernande Schuelein-) Steel** (14 Aug 1947, New York NY), American romance novelist.

**Michael Steele** (19 Oct 1958, Andrews AFB, Prince George's county MD), American politician (Republican); first African American chairman of the Republican National Committee, 2009–11.

**Gwen Stefani** (3 Oct 1969, Fullerton CA), American rock and pop vocalist.

**Gregg Steinhafel** (1955), American businessman; president of Target Corp. from 1999 and its CEO from 2008.

**Frank P(hilip) Stella** (12 May 1936, Malden MA), American painter.

**Ed Stelmach** (11 May 1951, Lamont, AB, Canada), Canadian politician (Progressive Conservative); premier of Alberta, 2006–11.

**Stephanie** (Stéphanie Marie Elizabeth Grimaldi; 1 Feb 1965, Monaco), Monegasque princess; the youngest child of Prince Rainier III and Grace Kelly.

**Marcus Stephen** (1 Oct 1969, Nauru?), Nauruan weight lifter and politician; president of Nauru, 2007–11.

**Howard Stern** (12 Jan 1954, Roosevelt NY), American radio and TV personality.

**John Paul Stevens** (20 Apr 1920, Chicago IL), American jurist; associate justice of the US Supreme Court, 1975–2010.

**Jon Stewart** (Jonathan Stewart Leibowitz; 28 Nov 1962, New York NY), American actor, writer, and comedian; anchor of TV's *The Daily Show* from 1999.

**Kristen Stewart** (9 April 1990, Los Angeles CA), American actress.

**Patrick Stewart** (13 Jul 1940, Mirfield, Yorkshire, England), British actor.

**Ben Stiller** (30 Nov 1965, New York NY), American comedian, actor, and film director.

**Sting** (Gordon Matthew Sumner; 2 Oct 1951, Wallsend, Newcastle upon Tyne, England), British singer, songwriter, and actor.

**Jens Stoltenberg** (16 Mar 1959, Oslo, Norway), Norwegian economist and politician (Norwegian Labor Party); prime minister of Norway, 2000–01 and from 2005.

**Biz Stone** (Christopher Isaac Stone; 10 Mar 1974, Massachusetts), American entrepreneur; cofounder of Twitter.

**Emma Stone** (Emily Jean Stone; 6 Nov 1988, Scottsdale AZ), American actress.

**Matt Stone** (Matthew Richard Stone; 26 May 1971, Houston TX), American writer, actor, and producer; cocreator of the TV comedy series *South Park* and the Broadway musical *The Book of Mormon*.

**Oliver (William) Stone** (15 Sep 1946, New York NY), American director, writer, and producer.

**Tom Stoppard** (Tomas Straussler; 3 Jul 1937, Zlin, Moravia, Czechoslovakia [now in the Czech Republic]), Czech-born British playwright and screenwriter.

**Dominique Strauss-Kahn** (25 Apr 1949, Neuilly-sur-Seine, France), French politician (Socialist); managing director of the International Monetary Fund, 2007–11.

**Jack Straw** (John Whitaker Straw; 3 Aug 1946, Brentwood, Essex, England), British politician; home secretary, 1997–2001, foreign secretary, 2001–06, and secretary of state for justice and lord high chancellor, 2007–10.

**Meryl Streep** (Mary Louise Streep; 22 Jun 1949, Summit NJ), American film actress.

**Barbra Streisand** (Barbara Joan Streisand; 24 Apr 1942, Brooklyn NY), American singer, actress, and film director.

**Ted Strickland** (4 Aug 1941, Lucasville OH), American politician (Democrat); governor of Ohio, 2007–11.

**Howard Stringer** (19 Feb 1942, Cardiff, Wales), Welsh-born business executive; chairman and CEO of Sony Corp., 2005–12.

**Susan Stroman** (17 Oct 1954, Wilmington DE), American theater director.

**Elizabeth Strout** (6 Jan 1956, Portland ME), American author.

**Freundel Stuart** (27 Apr 1951, St. Philip, Barbados), Barbadian politician; prime minister of Barbados from 2010.

**Hiroshi Sugimoto** (1948, Tokyo, Japan), Japanese photographer; recipient of a Praemium Imperiale in 2009.

**Arthur Ochs Sulzberger, Jr.** (22 Sep 1951, Mount Kisco NY), American newspaper executive; publisher of the *New York Times* from 1992 and chairman from 1997.

**Pat Summitt** (Patricia Head; 14 Jun 1952, Henrietta TN), American women's basketball coach; the winningest coach in NCAA basketball history.

**Rashid Sunyaev** (Rashid [Aliyevich] Syunyayev; 1 Mar 1943, Tashkent, USSR [now in Uzbekistan]), Russian astrophysicist; director of the Max Planck Institute for Astrophysics from 1995; recipient of the 2000 Bruce Medal and a 2008 Crafoord Prize.

**Subra Suresh** (c. 1957, Mumbai, India), Indian-born engineer and educator; director of the National Science Foundation from 2010.

**Kiefer Sutherland** (William Frederick Dempsey George Sutherland; 21 Dec 1966, London, England), Canadian film and TV actor.

**Ichiro Suzuki** (22 Oct 1973, Kasugai, Aichi prefecture, Japan), Japanese baseball player.

**Hilary Swank** (30 Jul 1974, Lincoln NE), American film actress.

**Taylor Swift** (13 Dec 1989, Reading PA), American country singer.

**Tilda Swinton** (Katherine Matilda Swinton; 5 Nov 1960, London, England), British actress.

**Wanda Sykes** (7 Mar 1964, Portsmouth VA), American comedian and actress.

**Boris Tadic** (15 Jan 1958, Sarajevo, Yugoslavia [now in Bosnia and Herzegovina]), Serbian politician and government official; president of Serbia, 2004–12.

**Jalal Talabani** (1933, Kalkan, Iraq), Iraqi Kurdish politician; president of Iraq from 2005.

**Tony Tan** (7 Feb 1940, British Singapore), Singaporean politician; president of Singapore from 2011.

**Terence Tao** (17 Jul 1975, Adelaide, SA, Australia), Australian American mathematician; winner of the 2012 Crafoord Prize in Mathematics.

**Quentin (Jerome) Tarantino** (27 Mar 1963, Knoxville TN), American film director and screenwriter.

**Marc Tarpenning** (1 Jun 1964, Sacramento CA), American entrepreneur and cofounder of Tesla Motors.

**Ratan (Naval) Tata** (28 Dec 1937, Bombay, British India [now Mumbai, India]), Indian corporate executive; chairman of the Tata Group and its several subsidiary companies.

**Channing (Matthew) Tatum** (26 Apr 1980, Cullman AL), American actor.

**Audrey Tautou** (9 Aug 1978, Beaumont, France), French film actress.

**John Tavener** (28 Jan 1944, London, England), British composer.

**Julie Taymor** (15 Dec 1952, Newton MA), American theater and film director.

**Tim Tebow** (Timothy Richard Tebow; 14 Aug 1987, Makati City, Philippines), American professional football player.

**Willy Telavi** (?, Tuvalu?), Tuvaluan politician; prime minister of Tuvalu from 2010.

**Oscar Temaru** (1 Nov 1944, Faaa, Tahiti, French Polynesia), French Polynesian politician; president of French Polynesia, 2004, 2005–06, 2007–08, 2009, and from 2011.

**Mario Testino** (30 Oct 1954, Lima, Peru), Peruvian fashion photographer.

**Hashim Thaci** (24 Apr 1969, Buroja, Yugoslavia [now in Kosovo]), Kosovar politician; prime minister of Kosovo from 2008.

**John A. Thain** (26 May 1955, Antioch IL), American financial official; CEO of the New York Stock Exchange, 2004–07, and the last CEO of Merrill Lynch, 2007–09.

**Thongsing Thammavong** (12 Apr 1944, Laos), Laotian politician; prime minister of Laos from 2010.

**Hamad ibn Khalifah al-Thani** (1950, Doha, Qatar), Qatari sheikh; emir of Qatar from 1995.

**Twyla Tharp** (1 Jul 1941, Portland IN), American dancer, director, and choreographer.

**Charlize Theron** (7 Aug 1975, Benoni, South Africa), South African actress.

**Thich Nhat Hanh** (11 Oct 1926, central Vietnam), Vietnamese Buddhist monk, pacifist, and teacher.

**Lyonchen Jigme (Yoeser) Thinley** (1952, Bumthang district, Bhutan), Bhutanese prime minister, 1998–99, 2003–04, and again from 2008.

**Clarence Thomas** (23 Jun 1948, Pinpoint community, near Savannah GA), American jurist; associate justice of the US Supreme Court from 1991.

**Michael Tilson Thomas** (21 Dec 1944, Hollywood CA), American conductor and composer; music director of the San Francisco Symphony from 1995.

**Tillman (Joseph) Thomas** (13 Jun 1945, Hermitage, St. Patrick, Grenada, British West Indies), West Indian politician; prime minister of Grenada from 2008.

**Emma Thompson** (15 Apr 1959, London, England), British film actress.

**Robert Thomson** (11 Mar 1961, Echuca, VIC, Australia), Australian journalist; editor of *The Times* of London, 2002–07, and managing editor of *The Wall Street Journal* from 2008.

**Helle Thorning-Schmidt** (14 Dec 1966, Denmark), Danish politician; prime minister of Denmark from 2011.

**Billy Bob Thornton** (4 Aug 1955, Hot Springs AR), American director and actor.

**Uma (Karuna) Thurman** (29 Apr 1970, Boston MA), American film actress.

**Rex W. Tillerson** (23 Mar 1952, Wichita Falls TX), American petroleum company executive; chairman and CEO (from 2006) of Exxon Mobil Corp.

**Timbaland** (Timothy Z. Mosley; 10 Mar 1972, Norfolk VA), American R&B and rap composer, record producer, and performer.

**Justin (Randall) Timberlake** (31 Jan 1981, Memphis TN), American pop singer and actor.

**Nicolae Timofti** (22 Dec 1948, Ciutulesti, Moldova), Moldovan politician; president of Moldova from 2012.

**Sakata Tojuro** (31 Dec 1931, Kyoto, Japan), Japanese Kabuki actor; recipient of a 2008 Praemium Imperiale.

**Earl Ray Tomblin** (15 Mar 1952, Logan county WV), American politician (Democrat); governor of West Virginia from 2010.

**Peter Tomka** (1 Jun 1956, Banska Bystrica, Slovakia), Slovakian jurist; president of the International Court of Justice from 2012.

**Anote Tong** (1952), Kiribati politician; president of Kiribati from 2003.

**Gaston Tong Sang** (7 Aug 1949, Bora-Bora, Tahiti, French Polynesia), French Polynesian politician; president of French Polynesia, 2006–07, 2008–09, and 2009–11.

**Bamir Topi** (24 Apr 1957, Tiranë, Albania), Albanian biologist and politician; president of Albania, 2007–12.

**Johnson Toribiong** (1946, Airai, US-occupied Palau), Palauan politician; president of Palau from 2009.

**Daniel Tosh** (29 May 1975, Germany), American comedian and TV actor.

**Amadou Toumani Touré** (4 Nov 1948, Mpoti, French Sudan [now in Mali]), Malian politician; president of Mali, 1991–92 and 2002–12.

**Hamadoun Touré** (3 Sep 1953, French Sudan [now Mali]), Malian international official; secretary-general of the International Telecommunication Union from 2007.

**Tomas Tranströmer** (15 Apr 1931, Stockholm, Sweden), Swedish poet; winner of the 2011 Nobel Prize for Literature.

**Dioncounda Traoré** (1942, Kati, French Sudan [now Mali]), Malian politician; interim president of Mali from 2012.

**Randy Travis** (Randy Traywick; 4 May 1959, Marshville NC), American country-and-western singer, songwriter, and actor.

**John (Joseph) Travolta** (18 Feb 1955, Englewood NJ), American TV and film actor.

**Natasha Trethewey** (26 Apr 1966, Gulfport MS), American poet; poet laureate of the US for 2012–13.

**Jean-Claude Trichet** (20 Dec 1942, Lyons, France), French banker, governor of the Banque de France, 1993–2003, and president of the European Central Bank, 2003–11.

**Libby Trickett** (Lisbeth Lenton; 28 Jan 1985, Townsville, QLD, Australia), Australian swimmer.

**Lars von Trier** (30 Apr 1956, Copenhagen, Denmark), Danish film director and cinematographer.

**Calvin Trillin** (5 Dec 1935, Kansas City MO), American author, commentator, and occasional poet.

**Travis Tritt** (9 Feb 1963, Marietta GA), American country-and-western singer.

**Robert L. Trivers** (19 Feb 1943, Washington DC), American evolutionary biologist and sociobiologist; recipient of a 2007 Crafoord Prize.

**Garry R. Trudeau** (21 Jul 1948, New York NY), American cartoonist; creator of the durable *Doonesbury* syndicated comic strip.

**Richard L. Trumka** (24 Jul 1949, Nemacolin PA), American labor leader; president of the AFL-CIO from 2009.

**Donald (John) Trump** (14 Jun 1946, New York NY), American real-estate developer and reality-TV personality.

**Morgan Tsvangirai** (10 Mar 1952, Gutu, Southern Rhodesia [now Zimbabwe]), Zimbabwean labor leader and politician; head of the Movement for Democratic Change (from 1999), the main opposition leader to the regime of Pres. Robert Mugabe, and prime minister of Zimbabwe in a historic power-sharing agreement from 2009.

**Togiola T(alalei) A. Tulafono** (28 Feb 1947, Aunu'u Island, American Samoa), American Samoan politician (Democrat); governor of American Samoa from 2003.

**Tommy Tune** (28 Feb 1939, Wichita Falls TX), American musical-comedy dancer and actor.

**Tupou VI** (Tupouto'a Lavaka; 12 Jul 1959, Nuku'alofa, Tonga), Tongan royal; king of Tonga from 2012.

**Danilo Turk** (19 Feb 1952, Maribor, Yugoslavia [now in Slovenia]), Slovenian law professor and diplomat; president of Slovenia from 2007.

**Ted Turner** (Robert Edward Turner III; 19 Nov 1938, Cincinnati OH), American TV executive, yachtsman, and philanthropist; the founder of Turner Broadcasting System (TBS) and Cable News Network (CNN).

**John Turturro** (27 Feb 1957, Brooklyn NY), American stage, film, and TV actor.

**Donald (Franciszek) Tusk** (22 Apr 1957, Gdansk, Poland), Polish politician (Civic Platform); prime minister of Poland from 2007.

**Desmond (Mpilo) Tutu** (7 Oct 1931, Klerksdorp, South Africa), South African Anglican cleric who in 1984 received the Nobel Peace Prize for his role in the opposition to apartheid in South Africa.

**Olav Fykse Tveit** (24 Nov 1960), Norwegian theologian; general secretary of the World Council of Churches from 2010.

**Anne Tyler** (25 Oct 1941, Minneapolis MN), American novelist and short-story writer.

**Steven Tyler** (Steven Tallarico; 26 Mar 1948, New York NY), American singer (Aerosmith) and TV personality.

**Yuliya (Volodymyrivna) Tymoshenko** (27 Nov 1960, Dnipropetrovsk, USSR [now in Ukraine]), Ukrainian businesswoman and politician (Yuliya Tymoshenko Bloc); prime minister of Ukraine, 2005 and 2007–10.

**(Alfred) McCoy Tyner** (Sulaimon Saud; 11 Dec 1938, Philadelphia PA), American jazz pianist and composer.

**Carrie Underwood** (10 Mar 1983, Muskogee OK), American country singer.

**Mihai-Razvan Ungureanu** (22 Sep 1968, Iasi, Romania), Romanian politician; prime minister in 2012.

**Keith (Lionel) Urban** (26 Oct 1967, Whangerei, New Zealand), New Zealand–born Australian country singer.

**Usher** (Usher Raymond IV; 14 Oct 1978, Chattanooga TN), American R&B singer.

**Herman Van Rompuy** (31 Oct 1947, Etterbeek, Belgium), Belgian politicián (Christian Democratic and Flemish); prime minister of Belgium, 2008–09; president of the European Council from 2010.

**Gus van Sant** (24 Jul 1952, Louisville KY), American film director.

**Mario Vargas Llosa** (28 Mar 1936, Arequipa, Peru), Peruvian writer; recipient of the 2010 Nobel Prize for Literature.

**Harold (Eliot) Varmus** (18 Dec 1939, Oceanside NY), American virologist; corecipient of the 1989 Nobel Prize for Physiology or Medicine; director of the National Institutes of Health, 1993–99, and director of the National Cancer Institute from 2010.

**Vince(nt Anthony) Vaughn** (28 Mar 1970, Minneapolis MN), American actor.

**Eddie Vedder** (Edward Louis Severson III; 23 Dec 1964, Evanston IL), American rock vocalist and songwriter (for Pearl Jam).

**Abhisit Vejjajiva** (3 Aug 1964, Newcastle upon Tyne, England), Thai politician; prime minister of Thailand, 2008–11.

**Maxim Vengerov** (Maksim Aleksandrovich Vengerov; 20 Aug 1974, Novosibirsk, USSR [now in Russia]), Russian-born concert violinist.

**J. Craig Venter** (14 Oct 1946, Salt Lake City UT), American geneticist and researcher into the human genome; he was the founder of Celera Genomics and the J. Craig Venter Institute.

**Justin (Brooks) Verlander** (20 Feb 1983, Manakin Sabot VA), American professional baseball player; winner of both the Cy Young and American League MVP awards in 2011.

**Donatella Versace** (2 May 1955, Reggio di Calabria, Italy), Italian fashion designer; creative director at the Versace design house from 1997.

**Ben Verwaayen** (11 Feb 1952, Driebergen, Netherlands), Dutch corporate executive; CEO of Alcatel-Lucent from 2008.

**Charles M. Vest** (9 Sep 1941, Morgantown WV), American scientist and educator; president of the Massachusetts Institute of Technology, 1990–2004, and president of the National Academy of Engineering from 2007.

**Jack Vettriano** (Jack Hoggan; 17 Nov 1951, St. Andrews, Fife, Scotland), British painter.

**Victoria** (Victoria Ingrid Alice Desirée; 14 Jul 1977, Stockholm, Sweden), Swedish crown princess and duchess of Västergötland.

**David Villa** (3 Dec 1981, Tuilla, Spain), Spanish association football (soccer) player.

**Antonio Villaraigosa** (Antonio Ramón Villar, Jr.; 23 Jan 1953, East Los Angeles CA), American politician (Democrat); mayor of Los Angeles from 2005.

**Tom Vilsack** (13 Dec 1950, Pittsburgh PA), American politician (Democrat); governor of Iowa, 1999–2007, and US secretary of agriculture from 2009.

**Bill Viola** (William Viola; 25 Jan 1951, New York City NY), American video artist; recipient of a Praemium Imperiale in 2011.

**Diana Vishneva** (Diana Viktorovna Vishnyova; 13 Jun 1976, Leningrad, USSR [now St. Petersburg, Russia]), Russian ballerina with the Mariinsky Ballet and, from 2003, the American Ballet Theatre.

**Lindsey Vonn** (Lindsey Kildow; 18 Oct 1984, St. Paul MN), American Alpine skier.

**Peter Voser** (29 Aug 1958, Switzerland), Swiss businessman; CEO of Royal Dutch Shell from 2009.

**Filip Vujanovic** (1 Sep 1954, Belgrade, Yugoslavia [now in Serbia]), Montenegrin politician; president of the Republic of Montenegro, before and after its independence, 2002–03 (acting) and again from 2003.

**Abdoulaye Wade** (29 May 1926, Kébémer, French West Africa [now in Senegal]), Senegalese politician; president of Senegal, 2000–12.

**Dwyane Wade** (17 Jan 1982, Chicago IL), American professional basketball player.

**Mohamed Waheed Hassan** (3 Jan 1953, Maldives), Maldivian politician; president of Maldives from 2012.

**Mark (Robert Michael) Wahlberg** (5 Jun 1971, Dorchester, Boston MA), American actor.

**Rufus Wainwright** (22 Jul 1973, Rhinebeck NY), Canadian singer and songwriter.

**Ted Waitt** (18 Jan 1963, Sioux City IA), American computer executive and philanthropist; cofounder of Gateway Inc. in 1985 and chairman and president of the charitable Waitt Family Foundation from 1993.

**Derek (Alton) Walcott** (23 Jan 1930, Castries, Saint Lucia, British West Indies), West Indian poet and playwright; recipient of the 1992 Nobel Prize for Literature.

**Jimmy (Donal) Wales** (7 Aug 1966, Huntsville AL), American entrepreneur and Internet publisher; founder of *Wikipedia*.

**Alice (Malsenior) Walker** (9 Feb 1944, Eatonton GA), American novelist, poet, and short-story writer.

**Scott Walker** (2 Nov 1967, Colorado Springs CO), American politician (Republican); governor of Wisconsin from 2011.

**Brad Wall** (24 Nov 1965, Swift Current, SK, Canada), Canadian businessman and politician (Progressive Conservative); premier of Saskatchewan from 2007.

**Mark Walport** (1953, England), British immunologist; director of the Wellcome Trust from 2003.

**Kerri (Lee) Walsh** (15 Aug 1978, Santa Clara CA), American beach volleyball player; gold-medal winner at the 2012 London Olympics.

**Barbara (Ann) Walters** (25 Sep 1931, Boston MA), American television personality, broadcast journalist, and interviewer.

**Alice L. Walton** (c. 1949), American heiress of part of the Wal-Mart fortune.

**Jim C. Walton** (c. 1948), American business executive; chairman and CEO of the Arvest Bank Group.

**Christoph Waltz** (4 Oct 1956, Vienna, Austria), Austrian actor.

**Vera Wang** (27 Jun 1949, New York NY), American fashion designer.

**Jigme Khesar Namgyal Wangchuk** (21 Feb 1980, Thimphu, Bhutan), Bhutanese royal; king from 2006.

**Shane Keith Warne** (13 Sep 1969, Ferntree Gully, VIC, Australia), Australian cricketer, a spin bowler named one of *Wisden*'s Five Cricketers of the Century.

**Rick Warren** (1954, San Jose CA), American evangelist minister.

**Denzel Washington, Jr.** (28 Dec 1954, Mount Vernon NY), American film, stage, and TV actor.

**Kerry Washington** (31 Jan 1977, Bronx NY), American actress.

**Debbie Wasserman Schultz** (Deborah Wasserman Schultz; 27 Sep 1966, Long Island NY), American politician (Democrat); representative of Florida from 2005 and chairman of the Democratic National Committee from 2011.

**Alice Waters** (28 Apr 1944, Chatham NJ), American locavore chef and restaurant owner (Chez Panisse, Berkeley CA).

**John Waters** (22 Apr 1946, Baltimore MD), American filmmaker.

**Bubba Watson** (Gerry Lester Watson, Jr.; 5 Nov 1978, Bagdad FL), American professional golfer.

**Emma (Charlotte Duerre) Watson** (15 Apr 1990, Paris, France), British film actress.

**John S. Watson** (c. 1957), American business executive; chairman and CEO of Chevron Corp. from 2010.

**Naomi Watts** (28 Sep 1968, Shoreham, Kent, England), Australian film actress.

**Karrie Webb** (21 Dec 1974, Ayr, QLD, Australia), Australian golfer.

**Andrew (Thomas) Weil** (8 Jun 1942, Philadelphia PA), American physician and champion of alternative medicine.

**Bob Weinstein** (18 Oct 1954, Queens NY), American film executive; cofounder, with his brother Harvey Weinstein, of Miramax Films and the Weinstein Company.

**Harvey Weinstein** (19 Mar 1952, Queens NY), American film executive; cofounder, with his brother Bob Weinstein, of Miramax Films and the Weinstein Company.

**Rachel Weisz** (7 Mar 1971, London, England), British film actress.

**Florence (Mary Leontine) Welch** (28 Aug 1986, London, England), English songwriter and singer (Florence and the Machine).

**Wen Jiabao** (September 1942, Tianjin, China), Chinese geologist and party and state official; premier of China from 2003.

**Jann S. Wenner** (7 Jan 1946, New York NY), American journalist; originator (1967) and publisher of *Rolling Stone* magazine.

**Kanye West** (8 Jun 1977, Atlanta GA), American rapper and music producer.

**Guido Westerwelle** (27 Dec 1961, Bad Honnef, Germany), German politician (Free Democrat); vice-chancellor of Germany, 2009–11, and foreign minister from 2009.

**Randy Weston** (Randolph Edward Weston; 6 Apr 1926, Brooklyn NY), American jazz pianist and composer.

**Vivienne Westwood** (Vivienne Swire; 8 Apr 1941, Tintwistle, Derbyshire, England), British fashion designer.

**Forest (Steven) Whitaker** (15 Jul 1961, Longview TX), American film actor and director.

**Betty (Marion) White** (17 Jan 1922, Oak Park IL), American actress.

**Jack White** (John Anthony Gillis; 9 Jul 1975, Detroit MI), American alternative-rock guitarist, drummer, vocalist (for the White Stripes, the Raconteurs, and the Dead Weather), songwriter, and record producer.

**Shaun White** (3 Sep 1986, San Diego CA), American snowboarder.

**John Edgar Wideman** (14 Jun 1941, Washington DC), American novelist.

**Eveline Widmer-Schlumpf** (16 Mar 1956, Switzerland), Swiss lawyer and politician; president of Switzerland from 2012.

**Kristen (Carroll) Wiig** (22 Aug 1973, Canandaigua NY), American comedian, actress, and screenwriter.

**Richard (Purdy) Wilbur** (1 Mar 1921, New York NY), American poet associated with the New Formalist movement; poet laureate of the US, 1987–88.

**Tom Wilkinson** (Thomas Jeffery Wilkinson, Jr.; 12 Dec 1948, Leeds, West Yorkshire, England), British character actor.

**George F(rederick) Will** (4 May 1941, Champaign IL), American conservative political commentator and columnist.

**Willem-Alexander** (27 Apr 1967, Utrecht, Netherlands), Dutch crown prince.

**William** (William Arthur Philip Louis Mountbatten-Windsor, duke of Cambridge; 21 Jun 1982, London, England), British prince of Wales; son of Charles and Diana, prince and princess of Wales, and second in line to the British throne.

**Aaron S. Williams** (Illinois), American public official; director of the Peace Corps from 2009.

**Brian (Douglas) Williams** (5 May 1959, Elmira NY), American TV journalist and news anchor.

**C(harles) K(enneth) Williams** (4 Nov 1936, Newark NJ), American poet.

**Evan Williams** (31 Mar 1972, Nebraska), American entrepreneur; cofounder of Twitter.

**John Williams** (24 Apr 1941, Melbourne, VIC, Australia), Australian-born classical guitarist.

**John (Towner) Williams** (8 Feb 1932, Queens NY), American conductor and composer of movie sound tracks.

**Lucinda Williams** (26 Jan 1953, Lake Charles LA), American contemporary folk and country singer and songwriter.

**Michelle (Ingrid) Williams** (9 Sep 1980, Kalispell MT), American actress.

**Pharrell Williams** ("Skateboard P"; 5 Apr 1973, Virginia Beach VA), American hip-hop artist, songwriter, and producer.

**Robbie Williams** (Robert Peter Maximillian Williams; 13 Feb 1974, Tunstall, Stoke-on-Trent, Staffordshire, England), British singer.

**Robin Williams** (21 Jul 1952, Chicago IL), American comedian and actor.

**Rowan (Douglas) Williams** (14 Jun 1950, Swansea, Wales), Welsh-born Anglican clergyman; archbishop of Canterbury—considered the senior bishop in the Anglican Communion—from 2003.

**Serena Williams** (26 Sep 1981, Saginaw MI), American tennis player and clothing designer.

**Vanessa (Lynn) Williams** (18 Mar 1963, Tarrytown NY), American singer and actress.

**Venus Williams** (17 Jun 1980, Lynwood CA), American tennis player and businesswoman.

**Bruce Willis** (Walter Bruce Willison; 19 Mar 1955, Idar-Oberstein, West Germany), American actor.

**Brian Wilson** (20 Jun 1942, Inglewood CA), American pop music songwriter and producer (for the Beach Boys); recipient of a 2007 Kennedy Center Honor.

**Luke (Cunningham) Wilson** (21 Sep 1971, Dallas TX), American actor.

**Owen (Cunningham) Wilson** (18 Nov 1968, Dallas TX), American actor.

**Robert Wilson** (4 Oct 1941, Waco TX), American avant-garde theater director.

**Oprah Winfrey** (29 Jan 1954, Kosciusko MS), American TV personality; host and producer of *The Oprah Winfrey Show*, 1985–2011.

**Kate Winslet** (5 Oct 1975, Reading, England), British film actress.

**Anna Wintour** (3 Nov 1949, London, England), British-born fashion magazine editor, editor in chief of American *Vogue* from 1988.

**(Laura Jean) Reese Witherspoon** (22 Mar 1976, Baton Rouge LA), American film actress.

**Edward Witten** (26 Aug 1951, Baltimore MD), American mathematician and specialist in superstring theory; recipient of the 1990 Fields Medal and a 2008 Crafoord Prize.

**Patricia A(nn) Woertz** (17 Mar 1953, Pittsburgh PA), American corporate executive; CEO of Archer Daniels Midland from 2006.

**Girma Wolde-Giorgis** (December 1924, Addis Ababa, Ethiopia), Ethiopian military officer; president of Ethiopia from 2001.

**Nathan Wolfe** (24 Aug 1970, Detroit MI), American virologist and professor, a specialist in the transfer of viruses from animals to humans.

**Tom Wolfe** (Thomas Kennerly Wolfe, Jr.; 2 Mar 1930, Richmond VA), American novelist, journalist, and social commentator.

**Tobias (Jonathan Ansell) Wolff** (19 Jun 1945, Birmingham AL), American writer.

**Stevie Wonder** (Steveland Judkins; Steveland Morris; 13 May 1950, Saginaw MI), American pop songwriter and singer.

**Elijah (Jordan) Wood** (28 Jan 1981, Cedar Rapids IA), American film actor.

**Tiger Woods** (Eldrick Woods; 30 Dec 1975, Cypress CA), American golfer.

**Klaus Wowereit** (1 Oct 1953, West Berlin, West Germany [now in Berlin, Germany]), German politician (Social Democratic Party); mayor of Berlin from 2001.

**Stephen Wozniak** (11 Aug 1950, San Jose CA), American electrical engineer; cofounder of Apple Computer Corp. (now Apple Inc.).

**Wu Den-yih** (30 Jan 1948, Caotun, Taiwan), Taiwanese politician; president of the Executive Yuan (premier), 2009–12.

**Jason Wu** (27 Sep 1982, Taipei, Taiwan), Taiwan-born fashion designer.

**Christian Wulff** (19 Jun 1959, Osnabrück, West Germany), German politician; president of Germany, 2010–12.

**Ken Wyatt** (1953?, Australia), Australian physician and politician; the first Aboriginal man elected to the Australian House of Representatives (in 2010).

**Xavi** (Xavier Hernández Creus; 25 Jan 1980, Terrassa, Spain), Spanish association football (soccer) player.

**Ram Baran Yadav** (4 Feb 1948, Sapahi, Dhanukha, Nepal), Nepalese politician; the first president of Nepal, from 2008.

**Shinya Yamanaka** (4 Sep 1962, Osaka, Japan), Japanese physician and stem-cell researcher; recipient of a 2009 Lasker Medical Prize.

**Yang Jiechi** (May 1950, Shanghai, China), Chinese foreign minister from 2007.

**Viktor Yanukovych** (9 Jul 1950, Yenakiyeve, Ukraine), Ukrainian politician; president of Ukraine from 2010.

**Susilo Bambang Yudhoyono** (9 Sep 1949, Pacitan, East Java, Indonesia), Indonesian military officer; president of Indonesia from 2004.

**Muhammad Yunus** (28 Jun 1940, Chittagong, East Bengal, British India [now in Bangladesh]), Bangladeshi economist specializing in microcredit and founder of the Grameen Bank; corecipient of the 2006 Nobel Peace Prize.

**Sadi Yusuf** (1934, near Basra, Iraq), Iraqi-born poet.

**Adam Zagajewski** (21 Jun 1945, Lwow, Poland [now Lviv, Ukraine]), Polish poet, novelist, and essayist.

**José Luis Rodríguez Zapatero** (4 Aug 1960, Valladolid, Spain), Spanish politician (Socialist Workers Party); prime minister of Spain, 2004–11.

**Asif Ali Zardari** (21 Jul 1956, Nawabshah, Pakistan), Pakistani politician and widower of Benazir Bhutto; cochairman of the Pakistan People's Party from 2007 and president of Pakistan from 2008.

**Valdis Zatlers** (22 Mar 1955), Latvian politician; president of Latvia, 2007–11.

**Ayman al-Zawahiri** (19 Jun 1951, Maadi, Egypt), Egyptian-born physician and militant Islamic extremist; leader of the al-Qaeda organization from 2011.

**Abdul Latif bin Rashid al-Zayani** (Al-Muharraq, Bahrain), Bahraini government official; secretary-general of the Gulf Cooperation Council from 2011.

**Jurelang Zedkaia** (13 Jul 1950, Majuro Atoll, Marshall Islands), Marshallese politician; president of the Marshall Islands, 2009–12.

**(José) Manuel Zelaya (Rosales)** (20 Sep 1952, Catacamas, Honduras), Honduran politician (Liberal Party); president of Honduras, 2006–09.

**Sam Zell** (Samuel Zielonka; 28 Sep 1941, Chicago IL), American real-estate tycoon.

**Renée (Kathleen) Zellweger** (25 Apr 1969, Katy TX), American actress.

**Robert Zemeckis** (14 May 1952, Chicago IL), American film director.

**Niklas Zennström** (1966, Sweden), Swedish Internet entrepreneur; codeveloper of Joost, a popular program for receiving TV broadcasts on a personal computer, and Skype, software for communication over the Internet.

**Catherine Zeta-Jones** (Catherine Jones; 25 Sep 1969, Swansea, West Glamorgan, Wales), Welsh-born actress.

**Zhang Ziyi** (9 Feb 1979, Beijing, China), Chinese actress.

**Zhou Long** (8 Jul 1953, Beijing, China), Chinese composer; his opera *Madame White Snake* won the 2011 Pulitzer Prize for music.

**Jeffrey Zients** (?, ?), American business executive; acting director of the US Office of Management and Budget from 2012.

**George Zimmerman** (1983, Virginia), American underwriter who in 2012 fatally shot Trayvon Martin, an African American teenager, igniting a nationwide controversy that focused on racism and Stand Your Ground laws.

**Mary (Alice) Zimmerman** (23 Aug 1960, Lincoln NE), American stage director.

**Slavoj Zizek** (21 Mar 1949, Ljubljana, Yugoslavia [now in Slovenia]), Slovenian political philosopher and social critic.

**Robert B. Zoellick** (25 Jul 1953, Evergreen Park IL), American businessman and government official; US trade representative, 2001–05, deputy secretary of state, 2005–06, and president of the World Bank, 2007–12.

**Mark Zuckerberg** (14 May 1984, Dobbs Ferry NY), American Internet entrepreneur; founder and CEO of Facebook, a social networking Web site.

**Mortimer B. Zuckerman** (4 Jun 1937, Montreal, QC, Canada), Canadian-born American publisher, columnist, and editor in chief of *U.S. News & World Report.*

**Jacob (Gedleyihlekisa) Zuma** (12 Apr 1942, Inkandla, Natal, Union of South Africa [now in KwaZulu Natal province, South Africa]), South African politician; deputy president of South Africa, 1999–2005, president of the African National Congress from 2007, and president of South Africa from 2009.

**Peter Zumthor** (26 Apr 1943, Basel, Switzerland), Swiss architect; recipient of the 2009 Pritzker Prize.

# Obituaries

*Death of notable people since 1 Jul 2011*

**Richard Adler** (3 Aug 1921, New York NY—21 Jun 2012, Southampton, Long Island NY), American composer and lyricist who achieved Broadway stardom with his songwriting partner, Jerry Ross, with the Tony Award-winning musicals *The Pajama Game* (1954) and *Damn Yankees* (1955); Adler also wrote classical works, including the Pulitzer Prize-nominated *Yellowstone Overture* (1980), and he produced Pres. John F. Kennedy's 1962 birthday tribute, at which Marilyn Monroe crooned "Happy Birthday, Mr. President."

**Ramiz Alia** (18 Oct 1925, Shkoder, Albania—7 Oct 2011, Tirana, Albania), Albanian politician who, as president of Albania (1982–92) and head of the country's communist party (1985–91), instituted mild reforms in that previously isolated country by expanding ties with its European neighbors, initiating limited economic reforms, and relaxing the communists' tight grip on Albanian society.

**Svetlana Alliluyeva** (Svetlana Iosifovna Stalina; Lana Peters; 28 Feb 1926, Moscow, Russia, USSR—22 Nov 2011, Richland county, Wisconsin), Russian-born daughter of Soviet ruler Joseph Stalin who caused an international sensation when she defected to the US in 1967 and subsequently published two volumes of memoirs describing her life as Joseph Stalin's youngest child and the events surrounding her defection.

**Francisco Xavier do Amaral** (1937, Turiscai, Portuguese Timor—6 Mar 2012, Dili, East Timor [Timor-Leste]), East Timorese independence leader and politician who was the first president of East Timor (1975–78) during its fight for independence from colonial Portugal and then from invading Indonesia.

**Amarillo Slim** (Thomas Austin Preston, Jr.; 31 Dec 1928, Johnson AR—29 Apr 2012, Amarillo TX), American gambler who became a colorful and astute poker player who became an international celebrity with the advent in 1970 of the World Series of Poker (WSOP), which featured his favorite game, Texas Hold'em; he captured titles in five WSOP events, and in 1992 he was inducted into the Poker Hall of Fame.

**John Arden** (26 Oct 1930, Barnsley, Yorkshire, England—28 Mar 2012, Galway, Ireland), British playwright who was one of the most important playwrights to emerge in mid-20th-century Britain; his plays mix poetry and songs with colloquial speech in a boldly theatrical manner and involve strong conflicts purposely left unresolved.

**Neil (Alden) Armstrong** (5 Aug 1930, Wapakoneta OH—25 Aug 2012, Cincinnati OH), American astronaut who blasted off in the Apollo 11 vehicle toward the Moon on 16 Jul 1969 (with fellow astronauts Edwin ["Buzz"] Aldrin, Jr., and Michael Collins), and on 20 July Armstrong (the commander of the mission) exited the *Eagle* landing module and became the first person to step onto the Moon—his famous words, "That's one small step for [a] man, one giant leap for mankind," adroitly encapsulated the incredible feat, but in the excitement of the moment, Armstrong skipped the "a" in the statement that he had prepared; Armstrong was awarded the Presidential Medal of Freedom in 1969.

**Eve Arnold** (Eve Cohen; 21 Apr 1912, Philadelphia PA—4 Jan 2012, London, England), American-born photojournalist who was best known for her candid images that provided glimpses of the intimate moments of celebrities on movie sets, including those of Paul Newman, Joan Crawford, and Elizabeth Taylor but particularly ones featuring Marilyn Monroe; she received a National Book Award for *In China* (1980), and she was the recipient in 1980 of the lifetime achievement award of the American Society of Magazine Photographers; she was made honorary OBE in 2003.

**Nick(olas) Ashford** (4 May 1941, Fairfield SC—22 Aug 2011, New York NY), American lyricist and singer who created an amazing songbook together with composer Valerie Simpson (his wife from 1974) that spanned such genres as soul, rhythm and blues, and funk; some of the duo's most memorable tunes include "Cry like a Baby" (1964, Aretha Franklin), "Ain't No Mountain High Enough" (1967, Marvin Gaye and Tammi Terrell; 1970, Diana Ross), "Didn't You Know (You'd Have to Cry Sometime)" (1969, Gladys Knight and the Pips), "I'm Every Woman" (1978, Chaka Khan), and their own single "Solid (as a Rock)," which became a number one international sensation in 1984.

**Stan(ley) Barstow** (28 Jun 1928, Horbury, West Yorkshire, England—1 Aug 2011, Port Talbot, Wales), British novelist who achieved enormous success with his first book, *A Kind of Loving* (1960; filmed 1962; stage play 1970); Barstow was one of several young British writers (including Alan Sillitoe, John Braine, and others collectively known as the Angry Young Men) who achieved immediate success in the 1950s and '60s with their unsentimental depiction of working-class life.

**Ahmed Ben Bella** (25 Dec 1916?, Marnia, French Algeria [now Maghnia, Algeria]—11 Apr 2012, Algiers, Algeria), Algerian nationalist politician who steered his country toward a socialist economy as a leader of the Algerian War of Independence against France and as the first prime minister (1962–63) and first elected president (1963–65) of the Algerian republic.

**Jan Berenstain** (Janice Marian Grant; 26 Jul 1923, Philadelphia PA—24 Feb 2012, Solebury PA), American writer of children's stories who was the coauthor with her husband, Stan (and, after his death in 2005, with their son Michael), of some 300 books that feature the everyday lives of the Berenstain Bears, a close-knit ursine family of four, whose illustrated adventures mirror real experiences of the real-life Berenstains and deal humorously but honestly with such concerns as safety, money management, emotional troubles, and peer pressure.

**Maeve Binchy** (28 May 1940, Dalkey, County Dublin, Ireland—30 Jul 2012, Dublin, Ireland), Irish journalist and author who penned compelling and often witty best-selling novels and short stories, many of which explore small-town Irish life, though one of her best known, *Circle of Friends* (1990; film 1995), is set at a university in Dublin; she also wrote several plays for the stage and television.

**Pedro (Rodriguez) Borbón** (2 Dec 1946, Mao, Valverde, Dominican Republic—4 Jun 2012, Pharr TX), American baseball player who used his dependable arm to make a club record 531 appearances with the Cincinnati Reds (1970–78) and lead the team to back-to-back World Series victories (1975, 1976); he finished his 12-year career with an earned run average of 3.52. In 2010 Borbón was elected into the Reds Hall of Fame.

**Juan María Bordaberry Arocena** (17 Jun 1928, Montevideo, Uruguay—17 Jul 2011, Montevideo, Uruguay), Uruguayan politician who was president of Uruguay (1972–76), but his administration quickly devolved into a military dictatorship that lasted more than a decade; in 2006 he was arrested and charged with having had involvement in human rights violations; convicted in 2010, Bordaberry was serving a 30-year sentence under house arrest at the time of his death.

**Tomás Borge Martínez** (13 Aug 1930, Matagalpa, Nicaragua—30 Apr 2012, Managua, Nicaragua), Nicaraguan revolutionary and politician who was a founder (1961) and leader of the Sandinista National Liberation Front, the rebel group that overthrew (1979) Pres. Anastasio Somoza Debayle and thereby ended the 43-year dictatorship of the Somoza family.

**Ernest Borgnine** (Ermes Effron Borgnino; 24 Jan 1917, Hamden CT—8 Jul 2012, Los Angeles CA), American actor who portrayed characters ranging from brutish thugs to hapless everymen and was especially remembered for his Academy Award-winning best-actor performance as the sensitive butcher looking for love in *Marty* (1955), the commander of a Navy PT boat in the television sitcom *McHale's Navy* (1962–66; film 1964), and the brutal Sgt. Fatso Judson in the military drama *From Here to Eternity* (1953); in 2011, Borgnine was honored with a lifetime achievement award from the Screen Actors Guild.

**F(rederick) Herbert Bormann** (24 Mar 1922, New York NY—7 Jun 2012, North Branford CT), American ecologist who led a research team that in the early 1970s discovered the presence and harmful effects of acid rain in North America; he was elected to the National Academy of Sciences in 1973.

**Butch Bouchard** (Émile Bouchard; 4 Sep 1919, Montreal, QC, Canada—14 Apr 2012, Brossard, QC, Canada), Canadian hockey player who was an imposing defenseman (1941–56) for the Montreal Canadiens and helped the team capture four Stanley Cups (1944, 1946, 1953, and 1956), the last two while he served (1948–56) as the much-beloved team captain; he was inducted into the Hockey Hall of Fame in 1966.

**Ray Douglas Bradbury** (22 Aug 1920, Waukegan IL—5 Jun 2012, Los Angeles CA), American author who crafted highly imaginative science-fiction and fantasy short stories and novels that often blend social criticism or nostalgia for the past with an awareness of the hazards of runaway technology; he was perhaps best known for *The Martian Chronicles* (1950; filmed for television in 1980), an episodic "novel" of interconnected stories, which was generally considered a science-fiction classic in its depiction of materialistic Earth Men's exploitation and corruption of an idyllic Martian civilization, and *Fahrenheit 451* (1951; film, 1966), a dystopian novel about a near-future world in which it is illegal to own or read a book. In 2007 the Pulitzer Prize Board awarded Bradbury a Special Citation for his distinguished career.

**Andrew (James) Breitbart** (1 Feb 1969, Los Angeles CA—1 Mar 2012, Los Angeles CA), American political Internet publisher who skewered liberal targets, frequently with the use of undercover videos; his vigorous online campaigns made him a hero to many on the political right, though in some cases he was shown to have used deceptive or inaccurate sources.

**Helen Gurley Brown** (18 Feb 1922, Green Forest AR—13 Aug 2012, New York NY), American author and editor who expounded on the merits of unmarried life in her first book, the best-selling *Sex and the Single Girl* (1962), which shocked American readers with the notion that unmarried women not only engaged in sexual relations but also enjoyed them; she also raised eyebrows as the editor in chief (1965–97) of the glossy women's magazine *Cosmopolitan.*

**Lesley Brown** (1946?, England?—6 Jun 2012, Bristol, England), British personality who attracted international attention after giving birth on 25 Jul 1978 to her daughter Louise Joy Brown, the world's first "test-tube baby."

**Frank (Randolph) Cady** (8 Sep 1915, Susanville CA—8 Jun 2012, Wilsonville OR), American actor who portrayed Sam Drucker, the genial shopkeeper from the television sitcoms *Petticoat Junction* (1964–70) and *Green Acres* (1965–71); his character also made brief appearances in *The Beverly Hillbillies* (1962–71).

**Adolfo Calero** (Adolfo Calero Portocarrero; 22 Dec 1931, Managua, Nicaragua—2 Jun 2012, Managua, Nicaragua), Nicaraguan lawyer and militant group leader who was the public face of, and influential lobbyist for, the Contras, the US-backed rebels fighting to overthrow the Marxist-oriented Sandinista government in Nicaragua; during the Iran-Contra Affair in the mid-1980s, he cooperated with Lieut. Col. Oliver North to raise clandestine funds for the Contras' activities and to buy weapons, despite passage in 1984 of a US law that banned direct or indirect US military aid to the Contras.

**Alfonso Cano** (Guillermo León Sáenz Vargas; 22 Jul 1948, Bogotá, Colombia—4 Nov 2011, mountains of Cauca state, Colombia), Colombian Marxist guerrilla leader who led (2008–11) the Revolutionary Armed Forces of Colombia (FARC), the country's largest rebel group.

**Don Carter** (Donald James Carter; "Mr. Bowling"; 29 Jul 1926, St. Louis MO—5 Jan 2012, Miami FL), American bowler who was a powerhouse competitive tenpin bowler who perfected an inimitable, unorthodox right-handed backswing (he bent his elbow) that catapulted him to stardom on the Professional Bowlers Association (PBA) tour; he was a founding member (1958) and the first president of the PBA, and he held six Bowler of the Year titles (1953–54, 1957–58, 1960, and 1962); in 1970 bowling writers crowned him the best bowler of all time.

**Gary (Edmund) Carter** ("The Kid"; 8 Apr 1954, Culver City CA—16 Feb 2012, Palm Beach Gardens FL), American baseball player who represented a dual threat at home plate while playing (1974–92) major league baseball (MLB), notably for the Montreal Expos (1974–84, 1992) and the New York Mets (1985–89); he was a powerhouse clutch hitter (he won five Silver Slugger Awards) and a rifle-armed catcher (he captured three Gold Gloves). He was an 11-time All Star and 2-time (1981 and 1984) All Star MVP, and he was inducted in 2003 into the National Baseball Hall of Fame in Cooperstown NY as an Expo.

**Robert Lee Carter** (11 Mar 1917, Caryville FL—3 Jan 2012, New York NY), American civil rights lawyer and judge who worked as a member of the NAACP, fighting racial discrimination in education and housing—in particular, doing work to develop the legal theory that was used to support the 1954 Brown v. Board of Education of Topeka case, in which the US Supreme Court ultimately outlawed separate public schools for black and white students.

**Jimmy Castor** (James Walter Castor; 23 Jan 1940, New York NY—16 Jan 2012, Henderson NV), American musician and songwriter who crooned hits that spanned genres ranging from doo-wop to soul; his works were sampled in nearly 3,000 songs by artists such as Kanye West and the Spice Girls.

**John (Angus) Chamberlain** (16 Apr 1927, Rochester IN—21 Dec 2011, New York NY), American sculptor, painter, printmaker, and filmmaker who was an Abstract Expressionist who created works that were typified by Mr. Press (1961), a construction of fragments from automobiles, crumpled and jammed together to create an effect of isolated, frozen movement.

**Giorgio Chinaglia** (24 Jan 1947, Carrara, Italy—1 Apr 2012, Naples FL), Italian footballer who thrilled association football (soccer) fans as one of the sport's greatest goal scorers and a leading star in the 1970s of the North American Soccer League (NASL); he retired in 1983, having scored more NASL goals than any other player in the league's history, and he was inducted into the National Soccer Hall of Fame in 2000.

**John Christopher** (Christopher Samuel Youd; 16 Apr 1922, Knowsley, Lancashire, England—3 Feb 2012, Bath, England), British writer who crafted dystopian science-fiction novels for a young-adult audience, most notably the Tripods trilogy—The White Mountains (1967), The City of Gold and Lead (1967), and The Pool of Fire (1968)—and a prequel, When the Tripods Came (1988).

**Dick Clark** (Richard Wagstaff Clark; 30 Nov 1929, Bronxville NY—18 Apr 2012, Santa Monica CA), American television personality and businessman who was best remembered as the youthful-looking host of American Bandstand (1957–87), the television dance show that captivated teenagers with its mix of lip-synched performances, interviews, and a "Rate-a-Record" segment; he also became a TV fixture as the host of The (New) $25,000 Pyramid, TV's Bloopers & Practical Jokes, and ABC's New Year's Rockin' Eve; he became one of pop music's most important tastemakers as exposure on American Bandstand or his prime-time program, The Dick Clark Show, generated countless hits; among the many awards programs that Dick Clark Productions produced was the American Music Awards, which he created.

**Charles (Wendell) Colson** ("Chuck"; 16 Oct 1931, Boston MA—21 Apr 2012, Falls Church VA), American political and religious figure who was a close political aide (1969–73) to US Pres. Richard Nixon and was the reputed mastermind behind the campaign of "dirty tricks" advanced to discredit the president's opponents that culminated in the Watergate scandal; Colson was tried and convicted (1974) for having obstructed justice in an elaborate cover-up staged to hide the activities that took place to destroy the credibility of Pentagon analyst Daniel Ellsberg (who in 1971 had leaked the Pentagon Papers to the New York Times); Colson was the recipient in 1993 of the US$1 million Templeton Prize for Progress in Religion.

**Marie (Catherine) Colvin** (12 Jan 1956, Oyster Bay, Long Island NY—22 Feb 2012, Homs, Syria), American journalist who reported on the effects of war on civilian populations, repeatedly placing herself in harm's way with the beleaguered populations to bring their stories and the horror of war to light in a clear-eyed but often heartrending manner; she was known especially for her reporting in 1999 from conflicts in East Timor (Timor-Leste) and the Russian republic of Chechnya and from the war in Kosovo in the late 1990s.

**Don Cornelius** (27 Sep 1936, Chicago IL—1 Feb 2012, Los Angeles CA), American television host and producer who created, produced, and hosted the groundbreaking and iconic music and dance television show Soul Train (1970–2006), which introduced to audiences throughout the country not only up-and-coming black musicians, many of whom gained their first national exposure on the show, but also youthful African American fashions, hairstyles, and dance moves.

**Norman (Lewis) Corwin** (3 May 1910, Boston MA—18 Oct 2011, Los Angeles CA), American radio writer, producer, and director who captivated a generation of American listeners in the 1930s and '40s with moving and eloquent radio plays that earned him the nickname "the poet laureate of radio"; he was best known for the broadcasts We Hold These Truths (1941) and On a Note of Triumph (1945), and he received a Peabody Award (1941); he was inducted into the Radio Hall of Fame in 1993.

**John Cowles, Jr.** (27 May 1929, Des Moines IA—17 Mar 2012, Minneapolis MN), American newspaper executive and philanthropist who was a significant supporter of the arts and cultural life in the Minneapolis area; he was instrumental in the establishment in Minneapolis of the Guthrie Theater (1963), the Hubert H. Humphrey Metrodome sports stadium (1982), and the Cowles Center for Dance and the Performing Arts (2011).

**Harry (Eugene) Crews** (7 Jun 1935, Alma GA—28 Mar 2012, Gainesville FL), American novelist who won a cult following for his offbeat and bleakly comic tales rooted in the Southern Gothic tradition.

**Ann Elizabeth Curtis** (Ann Elizabeth Curtis Cuneo; 6 Mar 1926, San Francisco CA—26 Jun 2012, San Rafael CA), American swimmer who dominated her sport during the 1940s, with three Olympic medals and five world records, as well as 34 national titles and 56 American records; her achievements earned her the 1944 Sullivan Award, making her the first woman and the first swimmer to win that prestigious amateur athletics honor; she was inducted into the International Swimming Hall of Fame in 1966 and elected to the International Women's Sports Hall of Fame in 1985.

**John Howard Davies** (9 Mar 1939, London, England—22 Aug 2011, Blewbury, Oxfordshire, England), British actor, producer, and director who was a child star in post-World War II Britain, playing the title roles in director David Lean's Oliver Twist (1948), The Rocking Horse Winner (1949), and Tom Brown's Schooldays (1951); he later became a director and producer and went on to become the head (1977–82) of BBC Comedy, responsible—at least in part—for such hit comedy TV shows as Monty Python's Flying Circus, Fawlty Towers, and No Job for a Lady.

**Al Davis** (Allen Davis; 4 Jul 1929, Brockton MA—8 Oct 2011, Oakland CA), American football coach and sports executive who was indelibly identified with the Oakland Raiders football franchise for more than four decades (1966–2011), first as its maverick coach and general manager and then as part owner and from 1976 full owner; the Raiders won three Super Bowls (1977, 1981, and 1984) of the five it played and from 1963 to 1985 accrued an unmatched overall record of 229–91–11; Davis was inducted into the Pro Football Hall of Fame in 1992.

**Richard Dawson** (Colin Lionel Emm; 20 Nov 1932, Gosport, Hampshire, England—2 Jun 2012, Los Angeles CA), British actor and television game-show host who costarred as RAF Corp. Peter Newkirk in the American TV sitcom *Hogan's Heroes* (1965–71), set in a World War II prisoner-of-war (POW) camp, but he achieved far greater renown as the host (1976–85; 1994–95) of the long-running game show *Family Feud*, a show based on contestants' ability to guess the answers that studio audience members had given to a series of questions. Dawson's personal charm and witty banter (along with his penchant for kissing all of the women contestants) made *Family Feud* one of TV's hottest syndicated game shows, broadcast as many as 11 times a week, and reportedly made Dawson one of TV's highest-paid celebrities.

**Miguel de la Madrid Hurtado** (12 Dec 1934, Colima, Mexico—1 Apr 2012, Mexico City, Mexico), Mexican politician who served (1982–88) as president of Mexico during an economic crisis (with inflation topping 100% and unemployment reaching 25%); he was reviled for imposing strict austerity measures to counter the crisis and for his ineffectual response to the devastating 1985 earthquake in Mexico City that claimed some 10,000 lives; he was nonetheless credited with moving the country toward a free-market economy.

**Shelagh Delaney** (25 Nov 1939, Salford, Lancashire, England—20 Nov 2011, Suffolk, England), British playwright who won critical acclaim and popular success at age 19 with the London production of her first play, *A Taste of Honey* (1958).

**John Demjanjuk** (Ivan Demjanjuk; 3 Apr 1920, Makharintsy, Ukraine, USSR—17 Mar 2012, Bad Feilnbach, Germany), Ukrainian-born accused war criminal who became an international cause célèbre as he spent more than 30 years fighting allegations that he was "Ivan the Terrible," a Nazi guard who operated the gas chambers at the Treblinka extermination camp in Poland during World War II; he was convicted in Germany in May 2011 on more than 28,000 counts of being an accessory to murder at the Sobibor extermination camp and sentenced to a five-year prison term.

**Rauf Denktash** (27 Jan 1924, Paphos, British Cyprus—13 Jan 2012, Nicosia [Lefkosa], Turkish Republic of Northern Cyprus), Turkish Cypriot politician who battled throughout his career for a two-state solution to the sectarian division on the island of Cyprus and thus for international recognition of the self-proclaimed (1983) Turkish Republic of Northern Cyprus (TRNC), of which he served as the de facto head of state (under various titles) from February 1973 until he retired in April 2005.

**Angelo Dundee** (Angelo Mirena, Jr.; 30 Aug 1921, Philadelphia PA—1 Feb 2012, Clearwater FL), American boxing trainer and manager who trained such illustrious world champion boxers as Muhammad Ali (formerly Cassius Clay), Carmen Basilio, George Foreman, Sugar Ray Leonard, Jimmy Ellis, Luis Rodríguez, José Nápoles, Sugar Ramos, Ralph Dupas, and Willie Pastrano.

**Duck Dunn** (Donald Dunn; 24 Nov 1941, Memphis TN—13 May 2012, Tokyo, Japan), American musician who played bass (mid-1960s–1971 and periodically thereafter) with Booker T. and the MG's; the racially integrated group was inducted into the Rock and Roll Hall of Fame in 1992.

**Honeyboy Edwards** (David Edwards; 28 Jun 1915, near Shaw MS—29 Aug 2011, Chicago IL), American blues singer who was the last of the Mississippi Delta bluesmen to have come of age in the 1930s; the recording of a 2004 concert with Pinetop Perkins, Henry Townsend, and Robert Lockwood, Jr.—*Last of the Great Mississippi Bluesmen: Live in Dallas*—won a Grammy Award in 2008 for best traditional blues album, and Edwards also received a Grammy in 2010 for lifetime achievement.

**Nora (Louise) Ephron** (19 May 1941, New York NY—26 Jun 2012, New York NY), American author, screenwriter, and film director who captured the essence of romantic comedy in film classics that featured biting wit and strong female characters, most notably *When Harry Met Sally...* (1989) and *Sleepless in Seattle* (1993), which earned Ephron, respectively, her second and third Academy Award nominations for best original screenplay (*Silkwood* [1983] won Ephron her first Oscar nomination).

**Chris Ethridge** (John Christopher Ethridge II; 10 Feb 1947, Meridian MS—23 Apr 2012, Meridian MS), American musician and songwriter who played bass for the Flying Burrito Brothers, a band that launched the development of country rock; he coauthored several songs with bandmate Gram Parsons, including "Hot Burrito #1," "Hot Burrito #2," and "She."

**Horst Faas** (28 Apr 1933, Berlin, Germany—10 May 2012, Munich, Germany), German photojournalist who captured the fear, suffering, and exhaustion of war in images taken for the Associated Press (AP) during the Vietnam War and other international conflicts; in the process, he won two Pulitzer Prizes—in 1965 for combat pictures taken in Vietnam and in 1972 for photos shot in rebellious East Pakistan (now Bangladesh); as the AP's chief of photography in Asia (1962–74), he was responsible for the distribution and publication of such iconic images as Eddie Adams's photograph of a South Vietnamese officer shooting a Viet Cong prisoner in the head and Hyung Cong ("Nick") Ut's of a naked little girl running toward the camera, screaming as she tries to escape from a napalm attack.

**James Farentino** (James Ferrantino; 24 Feb 1938, Brooklyn NY—24 Jan 2012, Los Angeles CA), American actor who was a handsome and suave leading man who was best remembered for his TV series roles as an attorney (*The Bold Ones: The Lawyers;* 1969–72), a doctor (*Dynasty;* 1981–82), and a father (*ER;* 1996) and for his performance in the film *The Pad and How to Use It* (1966); Farentino earned a Golden Globe award in 1967.

**Betty Ford** (Elizabeth Anne Bloomer; 8 Apr 1918, Chicago IL—8 Jul 2011, Rancho Mirage CA), American first lady who was the outspoken wife of US Pres. Gerald R. Ford and the cofounder (1982) and chair (1982–2005) of the Betty Ford Center, a facility dedicated to helping people recover from drug and alcohol dependence; Ford compiled a remarkably independent record as first lady, voicing public support for such issues as *Roe* v. *Wade*—the US Supreme Court decision that legalized abortion—and the Equal Rights Amendment (ERA), then up for ratification in several state legislatures; *Newsweek* magazine later named her Woman of the Year, and she was the recipient of a Presidential Medal of

Freedom (1991) and corecipient (1999) with her husband of a Congressional Gold Medal.

**Frank Benjamin Foster, III** (23 Sep 1928, Cincinnati OH—26 Jul 2011, Chesapeake VA), American jazz artist who played robust bop tenor saxophone solos in the Count Basie Orchestra and also composed arrangements that were essential in creating the modern Basie style in the 1950s; two years after Basie's death, Foster led the Basie Orchestra (1986–95), which won Grammy Awards in 1987 and 1990, and in 2002 Foster was named a National Endowment for the Arts Jazz Master.

**Itamar Augusto Cautiero Franco** (28 Jun 1930, at sea off the coast of Brazil—2 Jul 2011, São Paulo, Brazil), Brazilian politician who served as vice president (1990–92) and president (1992–95) of Brazil, but he was a quiet, intensely private man who shunned most public meetings and avoided difficult decisions, and he proved to be unable to cope with government corruption scandals and inflation of up to 6,000%.

**Joe Frazier** (Smokin' Joe; 12 Jan 1944, Beaufort SC—7 Nov 2011, Philadelphia PA), American boxer who reigned (16 Feb 1970-22 Jan 1973) as world heavyweight boxing champion until he was beaten by George Foreman at Kingston, Jamaica, but was probably best remembered for the bruising bouts he fought against Muhammad Ali, including "The Fight of the Century," held in New York City's Madison Square Garden on 8 Mar 1971 and the "Thrilla in Manila" on 1 Oct 1975; Frazier was inducted into the International Boxing Hall of Fame in 1990.

**Lucian (Michael) Freud** (8 Dec 1922, Berlin, Germany—20 Jul 2011, London, England), British artist who brought a sometimes shocking realism to his figurative paintings, notably his work in portraiture and the nude; Freud—a grandson of Sigmund Freud—often highlighted and undercut the erotics of the female nude, opting out of the idealizing tendencies of much of the history of Western art, and beginning in the 1980s, he was increasingly drawn toward what could be called extreme body types; he was a Companion of Honour (1983) and a member of the Order of Merit (1993).

**Jonathan Frid** (John Herbert Frid; 2 Dec 1924, Hamilton, ON, Canada—14 Apr 2012, Hamilton, ON, Canada), Canadian actor who gained fame playing the vampire Barnabas Collins in the American gothic daytime serial *Dark Shadows* (1966–71); the character was introduced in 1967 as the series added a supernatural element to its plotline.

**Carlos Fuentes** (11 Nov 1928, Panama City, Panama—15 May 2012, Mexico City, Mexico), Mexican novelist, short-story writer, playwright, critic, and diplomat who was one of the foremost Mexican writers of the 20th century and the winner of the 1987 Cervantes Prize, the most prestigious Spanish-language literary award; of his more than 30 books, his best known include *La muerte de Artemio Cruz* (1962; *The Death of Artemio Cruz*) and *Gringo viejo* (1985; *The Old Gringo*; film 1989).

**Paul Fussell, Jr.** (22 Mar 1924, Pasadena CA—23 May 2012, Medford OR), American literary scholar and social historian who delved into the horrors of war and the cultural impact of conflict, most notably in *The Great War and Modern Memory* (1975), which critically examined art and literature prior to and after World War I; in 1976 that volume won the National Book Award.

**Ben Gazzara** (Biagio Anthony Gazzara; 28 Aug 1930, New York NY—3 Feb 2012, New York NY), American actor who enjoyed a career of more than 60 years in show business; on Broadway he originated the role of Brick in the 1955 production of Tennessee Williams's *Cat on a Hot Tin Roof,* and he appeared in films such as *The Strange One* (1957), *Anatomy of a Murder* (1959), and *Saint Jack* (1979); he also won an Emmy Award for the movie *Hysterical Blindness* (2002).

**Robin (Hugh) Gibb** (22 Dec 1949, Douglas, Isle of Man—20 May 2012, London, England), British-born singer-songwriter who joined with his fraternal twin, Maurice, and their older brother, Barry, to form the Bee Gees, one of the most successful pop groups ever; the music of the Bee Gees (shortened from Brothers Gibb) featured close high-pitched three-part harmonies, a strong bass line, and detailed orchestrations, and the trio secured a string of hit records, an estimated 200 million albums sold, and seven Grammys, including a Lifetime Achievement Award (2000) and a Legend Award (2003); they were the first band to receive the latter honor. The brothers were inducted into the Rock and Roll Hall of Fame in 1997 and were made CBE in 2002.

**Jean Giraud** (Jean Henri Gaston Giraud; Gir; Moebius; 8 May 1938, Nogent-sur-Marne, France—10 Mar 2012, Paris, France), French graphic artist who gained near-legendary status among aficionados for his densely drawn, detailed graphic evocations of the American West (which he drew over the signature "Gir") and especially for his breathtaking science-fiction explorations (signed "Moebius").

**Kiro (Blagoje) Gligorov** (3 May 1917, Stip, Kingdom of Serbia [now in Macedonia]—1 Jan 2012, Skopje, Macedonia), Macedonian politician who, as president (1991–99), steered his country through the difficult transition from a constituent republic within Yugoslavia to an independent state officially known as the Former Yugoslav Republic of Macedonia, the only Yugoslav republic to accomplish secession without civil war; he handled often bitter negotiations with Greece, which opposed the new republic's use of the name Macedonia.

**Florence Green** (Florence Beatrice Patterson; 19 Feb 1901, London, England—4 Feb 2012, King's Lynn, Norfolk, England), British servicewoman who was the last known veteran of World War I.

**Andy Griffith** (Andrew Samuel Griffith; 1 Jun 1926, Mount Airy NC—3 Jul 2012, Manteo NC), American actor who specialized in portraying homespun characters, notably the kindly sheriff of the idyllic fictional town of Mayberry in the television sitcom *The Andy Griffith Show* (1960-68) and a genial yet wily defense attorney in the dramatic series *Matlock* (1986–95); he won a Grammy Award in 1997 for best Southern gospel, country gospel, or bluegrass gospel album for *I Love to Tell the Story—25 Timeless Hymns,* and in 2005 he was awarded the Presidential Medal of Freedom.

**Greg (Norman) Ham** (27 Sep 1953, Melbourne, VIC, Australia—found dead 19 Apr 2012, Carlton North, VIC, Australia), Australian musician who played keyboards and woodwinds in the pop band Men at Work; he was best known for his saxophone riffs on "Who Can It Be Now?" and his flute part on "Down Under," both of which were singles from the band's phenomenally successful debut album, *Business as Usual* (1982).

**Marvin (Frederick) Hamlisch** (2 Jun 1944, New York City NY—6 Aug 2012, Los Angeles CA), American composer and conductor who displayed remarkable versatility in a stylistically diverse corpus; he was best known, however, for his many film scores and for his Pulitzer Prize-winning play *A Chorus Line* (1975; film 1985), which won nine Tony Awards, including best musical production and best score, and ultimately became one of the longest-running Broadway musicals of all time; his most successful works were his original music for *The Way We Were* (1973), which won Oscars for best original song and best dramatic score, and his arrangement of Scott Joplin ragtime music for *The Sting* (1973), which won an Oscar for best musical adaptation (his music for those films also won several Grammy Awards). Hamlisch also won several Emmy Awards and composed theme music for a number of TV programs, such as *Good Morning America*.

**Oscar Handlin** (29 Sep 1915, Brooklyn NY—20 Sep 2011, Cambridge MA), American historian and educator who examined immigration and other social topics in American history in such notable works as the Pulitzer Prize-winning *The Uprooted* (1951).

**Vaclav Havel** (5 Oct 1936, Prague, Czechoslovkia [now in Czech Republic]—18 Dec 2011, Hradcek, Czech Republic), Czech playwright, political dissident, and politician who was president of Czechoslovakia (1989–92) and of the Czech Republic (1993–2003) after having been a prominent participant in the liberal reforms of 1968 (the Prague Spring) and a leader in the human rights movement after the Soviet clampdown on Czechoslovakia that year.

**Heavy D** (Dwight Errington Myers; 24 May 1967, Mandeville, Jamaica—7 Nov 2011, Los Angeles CA), American rapper and actor who drew fans with energetic lyrics embedded with jokes about his hefty frame and inspiring optimism; his many hits, such as "Gyrlz, They Love Me" (1989) and "Now That We Found Love" (1991), incorporated the soulful smoothness of rhythm and blues into hip-hop.

**Robert Hegyes** (7 May 1951, Perth Amboy NJ—26 Jan 2012, Edison NJ), American actor who was best known for playing Juan Epstein, a member of a group of high school misfits dubbed the Sweathogs in the television sitcom *Welcome Back, Kotter* (1975–79).

**Levon Helm** (Mark Lavon Helm; 26 May 1940, Elaine AR—19 Apr 2012, New York NY), American musician who provided a bottom-heavy, versatile beat as drummer and contributed clear evocative tones as a vocalist for the seminal roots-rock group the Band; he later enjoyed an encore career that netted him three Grammy Awards in the early 21st century. Helm was recruited by rockabilly singer Ronnie Hawkins to tour with him in Canada in his backup band, the Hawks, who struck out on their own in 1963 and two years later were hired by Bob Dylan to back him up on a tour showcasing his new, more rock-oriented direction; by 1968, with the release of *Music from Big Pink*, the Hawks had become the Band; in 1994 Helm was inducted into the Rock and Roll Hall of Fame as a member of the Band.

**Sherman (Alexander) Hemsley** (1 Feb 1938, Philadelphia PA—24 Jul 2012, El Paso TX), American actor who charmed television audiences in the 1970s and '80s as the irascible George Jefferson on the sitcom *All in the Family* and the hit spin-off *The Jeffersons*.

**Reginald (Charles) Hill** (3 Apr 1936, West Hartlepool, Durham, England—12 Jan 2012, near Ravenglass, Cumbria, England), British novelist who created the Yorkshire crime-fighting police team of Superintendent Andrew Dalziel and Sergeant (later Detective Inspector) Peter Pascoe in two dozen detective novels over a 40-year span—from their introduction in *A Clubbable Woman* (1970) through *Midnight Fugue* (2009); Hill received the Crime Writers Association's Golden Dagger for *Bones and Silence* (1990) and the Diamond Dagger for lifetime achievement in 1995.

**Christopher (Eric) Hitchens** (13 Apr 1949, Portsmouth, England—15 Dec 2011, Houston TX), British American author, critic, and bon vivant who proffered trenchant polemics on politics, religion, and other topics that positioned him at the forefront of public intellectual life in the late 20th and early 21st centuries; with the publication of *God Is Not Great: How Religion Poisons Everything* (2007), he moved to the forefront of the modern atheist movement.

**Harri Hermanni Holkeri** (6 Jan 1937, Oripää, Finland—7 Aug 2011, Helsinki, Finland), Finnish politician who devoted his life to a political career that culminated in his service as prime minister of Finland (1987–91) and his role in brokering (alongside Canadian Gen. John de Chastelain and American diplomat George J. Mitchell) the 1998 Good Friday Agreement that achieved peace in Northern Ireland; Holkeri also was elected president of the UN General Assembly for 2000 and in 2003–04 was a UN special representative in Kosovo.

**Celeste Holm** (29 Apr 1917, Brooklyn NY—15 Jul 2012, New York NY), American actress who originated the role of flirtatious Ado Annie Carnes in the Broadway musical *Oklahoma!* (1943) and was forever remembered for her rendition of the play's showstopping song "I Cain't Say No."

**Whitney Houston** (9 Aug 1963, Newark NJ—11 Feb 2012, Beverly Hills CA), American singer and actress who reigned as a pop diva during the mid-1980s and early 1990s and amassed global sales in excess of 86 million copies with the release of her first four albums; her debut album, *Whitney Houston* (1985), yielded three number one songs; Houston was the daughter of Emily ("Cissy") Houston—whose vocal group, the Sweet Inspirations, sang backup for Aretha Franklin—and the cousin of singer Dionne Warwick. In 1992 Houston married singer Bobby Brown and made her motion-picture debut in *The Bodyguard;* the film featured her powerful rendition of Dolly Parton's "I Will Always Love You," which stayed at number one for 14 weeks, and the film soundtrack dominated the Grammys the following year, with Houston winning the awards for album of the year, record of the year, and best female pop vocal performance. In 1998 Houston released *My Love Is Your Love,* which earned her another Grammy Award.

**Andrew Fielding Huxley** (22 Nov 1917, London, England—30 May 2012, Cambridge, England), British physiologist who was the corecipient (with Alan Lloyd Hodgkin and John Carew Eccles) of the 1963 Nobel Prize for Physiology or Medicine; Huxley's work centered on nerve and muscle fibers and dealt particularly with the chemical phenomena involved in the transmission of nerve impulses; he was admitted to the Royal Society in 1955 and later served (1980–85) as its president, and he was knighted in 1974 and appointed to the Order of Merit in 1983.

**Eiko Ishioka** (12 Jul 1938, Tokyo, Japan—21 Jan 2012, Tokyo, Japan), Japanese designer who won accolades in the worlds of theater, film, and advertising for her sensual and compelling designs; her many honors included an Academy Award, a

Grammy Award, and two Tony Award nominations; in addition, she was director of costume design of the opening ceremonies of the 2008 Olympic Games in Beijing.

**Etta James** (Jamesetta Hawkins; 25 Jan 1938, Los Angeles CA—20 Jan 2012, Riverside CA), American singer who, as a multifaceted singer, could harness the powerful vocals she used for soul, blues, and rhythm and blues numbers to caress such 1960s ballads as "All I Could Do Was Cry," "I'd Rather Go Blind," and the sensuous "At Last," which became her signature song; after signing (1960) with Chess Records, James became its first major female star, and her artistry was recognized with four Grammy Awards, including one in 2003 for lifetime achievement, as well as induction into the Rock and Roll Hall of Fame (1993), the Blues Hall of Fame (2001), and the Grammy Hall of Fame (1999 and 2008).

**Bill Jenkins** (William Tyler Jenkins; "Grumpy"; 22 Dec 1930, Philadelphia PA—29 Mar 2012, Paoli PA), American drag racer who captured 13 National Hot Rod Association (NHRA) titles and earned induction in 2008 into the International Motorsports Hall of Fame not only because of his driving skills but also because of his many mechanical innovations, including improved engines, front-end suspension systems, and a slick-shift manual transmission.

**Steve Jobs** (Steven Paul Jobs; 24 Feb 1955, San Francisco CA—5 Oct 2011, Palo Alto CA), American entrepreneur who, as the audacious cofounder of Apple Computer, Inc. (from 2007 Apple Inc.), was a charismatic pioneer of the personal computer (PC) and the visionary behind the creation and innovative marketing of the Macintosh PC (1984), which inaugurated the practical application of the user-friendly graphical interface that Jobs first saw demonstrated (1979) at Xerox Corp.'s Palo Alto Research Center; other breakthrough consumer products developed by Apple under Jobs's leadership include the colorful egg-shaped iMac PC (1998), the stylish laptop iBook (1999), the iPod compact MP3 music player and iTunes digital jukebox software (both 2001), the iTunes Music Store (2003), the iPhone smartphone (2007), and the iPad tablet computer (2011); he bought (1986) the computer-graphics firm Pixar Animation Studios, which he built into a major animation studio (Pixar's IPO in 1995 made Jobs a billionaire).

**Davy Jones** (David Thomas Jones; 30 Dec 1945, Manchester, England—29 Feb 2012, Stuart FL), British actor and singer who became an international sensation in the late 1960s as the front man and lone Englishman in the American pop group the Monkees; though the foursome—Jones, former child actor Micky Dolenz, and musicians Mike Nesmith and Peter Tork—began as a fictional band created specifically for the American sitcom *The Monkees* (1966–68), the quartet turned into a genuine pop music phenomenon. The show's zany comedy, innovative music videos, and catchy pop tunes earned it an Emmy Award as best comedy in 1967 while Jones's baby face, English accent, and smooth vocals on such hits as "Daydream Believer," "A Little Bit Me, a Little Bit You," and "Valleri" brought him heartthrob status among teenage girls.

**Kathryn Joosten** (Kathryn Joostyn; Kathryn Rausch; 20 Dec 1939, Chicago IL—2 Jun 2012, Los Angeles CA), American actress who held feature roles in television as the gossipy neighbor Karen McCluskey in *Desperate Housewives* (2005–12), which earned her two Emmy awards (2005, 2008) and a

third nomination in 2010, and the sharp-tongued secretary to the President, Dolores Landingham, in *The West Wing* (1999–2002).

**Ahmed Wali Karzai** (1961, Karz, Kandahar province, Afghanistan—12 Jul 2011, Kandahar, Afghanistan), Afghani government official who was perceived by many as a symbol of corruption in Afghanistan as the controversial younger half brother of Afghan Pres. Hamid Karzai and a predominant power broker in Afghanistan who wielded almost complete control over the country's southern provinces.

**Nicholas (deBelleville) Katzenbach** (17 Jan 1922, Philadelphia PA—8 May 2012, Skillman NJ), American lawyer and government official who served as deputy attorney general (1962–64) under Pres. John F. Kennedy and attorney general (1965–66) and undersecretary of state (1966–69) under Pres. Lyndon B. Johnson; Katzenbach was involved in the vanguard of the civil rights movement and in the escalation of the Vietnam War; he gained bipartisan support for passage of the landmark Civil Rights Act of 1964 and the Voting Rights Act of 1965, both of which he helped draft.

**Bil Keane** (William Keane; 5 Oct 1922, Philadelphia PA—8 Nov 2011, Paradise Valley AZ), American cartoonist who celebrated the humorous side of family life in the lighthearted one-panel comic *The Family Circus*, which debuted in 1960 and eventually appeared in nearly 1,500 newspapers.

**David Kelly** (11 Jul 1929, Dublin, Ireland—12 Feb 2012, Dublin, Ireland), Irish actor who was a reliable character actor for more than 50 years on the Dublin stage, in movies, and on television programs, but to international audiences he was best known for portraying broadly comic Irishmen, notably the amiably feckless contractor O'Reilly on the classic BBC TV sitcom *Fawlty Towers* (1975) and on the big screen as Grandpa Joe in *Charlie and the Chocolate Factory* (2005); his most acclaimed stage role was in the Irish premiere (1959) of Samuel Beckett's *Krapp's Last Tape* and in the 1991 revival of that play, in which the tapes used onstage were actually recorded during his 1959 performances.

**Mary Richardson Kennedy** (Mary Kathleen Richardson; 4 Oct 1959, NJ—found dead 16 May 2012, Bedford NY), American personality who provoked close media speculation with her turbulent marriage to Robert F. Kennedy, Jr.

**Kim Jong Il** ("Dear Leader"; 16 Feb 1941, Siberia, Russia, USSR—17 Dec 2011, North Korea?), North Korean supreme leader who was the son of North Korean Premier and Korean Workers' (communist) Party (KWP) Chairman Kim Il-Sung and successor to his father as the authoritarian ruler (1994–2011) of North Korea; Kim Jong Il's leadership of the country was marked by severe famine (1990s) and the acquisition of nuclear weapons technology.

**Rodney (Glen) King** (2 Apr 1965, Sacramento CA—17 Jun 2012, Rialto CA), American personality who was an African American construction worker whose videotaped beating by white Los Angeles Police Department (LAPD) officers in March 1991 (and the officers' subsequent treatment by the courts) sparked violent race riots and fueled a charged debate about civil rights and the US justice system; his car was pulled over for speeding by four LAPD officers, and he attempted to escape on foot, but after being chased down, he was repeatedly kicked, struck with batons, and stunned with Tasers, and he sustained serious injuries, including skull fractures and facial paralysis. Under public pressure the officers were brought to trial in 1992, but the jury acquitted three, and a mistrial was declared for the fourth, spurring some of the worst riots in US history, resulting in more than 50 dead and an estimated US$1 billion in damages in the area of South Los Angeles.

**Thomas Kinkade** (19 Jan 1958, Sacramento CA—6 Apr 2012, Monte Sereno CA), American artist who built a successful commercial industry with his light-infused paintings that featured cottages, bridges, gardens, and Americana scenes infused with the warm glow of sunlight, and he accordingly trademarked the moniker "Painter of Light"; the nostalgic quality of Kinkade's paintings, which were reproduced in the thousands, made him wildly popular with the general public, and he became one of the most highly collected living artists, though he was often derided by critics who considered his work to be kitschy.

**Jerry Leiber** (Jerome Leiber; 25 Apr 1933, Baltimore MD—22 Aug 2011, Los Angeles CA), American songwriter and record producer who wrote the lyrics for many enduring songs of the 1950s and '60s; he and partner Mike Stoller (who created the tunes) were perhaps the most successful writers and producers of the 1950s, with hits such as "Hound Dog," recorded by Willie Mae ("Big Mama") Thornton, "Yakety Yak" by the Coasters, and songs for Elvis Presley movies, including *Love Me Tender* (1956) and *Jailhouse Rock* (1957); in 1987 the pair were inducted into the Rock and Roll Hall of Fame.

**Mark (Edward) Lenzi** (4 Jul 1968, Huntsville AL—9 Apr 2012, Greenville NC), American diver who won the Olympic gold medal in the 1992 Games and the bronze in the 1996 Games for the 3-meter springboard; he was the first to score over 100 points in a single dive (1991) and the first American to complete the difficult forward 4½ somersault in a national competition (1989).

**George (Smith) Lindsey** (17 Dec 1928, Fairfield AL—6 May 2012, Nashville TN), American actor who portrayed the grinning Goober, the affable but dimwitted gas-station attendant and mechanic who appeared on three television series, *The Andy Griffith Show* (1964–68), *Mayberry R.F.D.* (1968–71), and *Hee-Haw* (1971–93).

**Andrew (Maurice) Love** (21 Nov 1941, Memphis TN—12 Apr 2012, Memphis TN), American saxophonist who lent his riffs to more than 80 gold and platinum records with his musical partner, white trumpeter Wayne Jackson; the two played backup during the 1960s for such Stax Records artists as Wilson Pickett, Aretha Franklin, and Otis Redding, and later the duo, performing (1969–2004) as the Memphis Horns, became a stalwart backup for such superstars as Neil Diamond, Elvis Presley, James Taylor, Willie Nelson, Billy Joel, Buddy Guy, and Al Green. In 2012 the Memphis Horns were the recipients of a Grammy Award for lifetime achievement.

**John Mackey** (24 Sep 1941, New York NY—6 Jul 2011, Baltimore MD), American football player who starred in the NFL in the 1960s and early '70s and was the prototype of the modern tight end—a receiver who possessed the speed to run deep patterns as well as the power to run over tacklers; he served (1970–73) as president of the NFL Players Association, and he was elected to the Pro Football Hall of Fame in 1992.

**Edoardo Mangiarotti** (7 Apr 1919, Renate, Italy—25 May 2012, Milan, Italy), Italian fencer who was one of the most successful performers in the history of fencing, in both foil and épée—over a 40-year career, he secured 13 Olympic medals (6 gold) in five Summer Games between 1936 and 1960; in 2003 the International Olympic Committee awarded him a Platinum Wreath, calling him "the most decorated athlete in *all* Olympic sports in the history of the Olympics."

**Ante Markovic** (25 Nov 1924, Konjic, Kingdom of Serbs, Croats, and Slovenes [now in Bosnia and Herzegovina]—28 Nov 2011, Zagreb, Croatia), Yugoslav businessman and politician who, as the last premier (1989–91) of the Socialist Federal Republic of Yugoslavia, failed to prevent the outbreak of violence between the constituent republics and the breakup of the country into independent states.

**Jim Marshall** (James Charles Marshall; 29 Jul 1923, London, England—5 Apr 2012, Milton Keynes, Buckinghamshire, England), British inventor who developed, with musician Ken Bran and engineer Dudley Craven, a powerful amplifier that delivered the raw, throaty sound that rock guitarists, among them Pete Townshend of the Who and Jimi Hendrix, sought; in 2003 Marshall was appointed OBE.

**Tony Martin** (Alvin Morris; Anthony Martin; 25 Dec 1913, San Francisco CA—27 Jul 2012, Los Angeles CA), American pop singer and movie actor who was one of the most celebrated all-around entertainers of his era, noted for his handsome visage and smooth baritone voice; he made guest appearances on radio and television and hosted the TV variety program *The Tony Martin Show* (1954–56).

**John McCarthy** (4 Sep 1927, Boston MA—24 Oct 2011, Stanford CA), American mathematician and computer and cognitive scientist who coined the term *artificial intelligence* (AI) in 1955 and was a pioneer in that field; his main research in AI involved the formalization of commonsense knowledge; his major honors were the A.M. Turing Award (1971), the Kyoto Prize (1988), and the National Medal of Science (1990).

**Barney McKenna** (Bernard Noel McKenna; "Banjo Barney from Donnycarney"; 16 Dec 1939, Dublin, Ireland—5 Apr 2012, Howth, Ireland), Irish musician who contributed his raspy voice and dazzling tenor banjo playing to the folk band the Dubliners, a pivotal group credited with influencing younger Irish performers such as U2, the Pogues, and Sinead O'Connor.

**Ralph (Angus) McQuarrie** (13 Jun 1929, Gary IN—3 Mar 2012, Berkeley CA), American conceptual artist who created production paintings from a script by film director George Lucas that resulted in the look of *Star Wars* (1977) and its first two sequels, *The Empire Strikes Back* (1980) and *Return of the Jedi* (1983); his work informed the appearance of the villainous Darth Vader and of the robots C-3PO and R2-D2 as well as many locations in the movies; McQuarrie shared an Academy Award for best visual effects for his work on *Cocoon* (1985).

**Abdelbaset Ali Mohmed al-Megrahi** (1 Apr 1952, Tripoli, Libya—20 May 2012, Tripoli, Libya), Libyan national who was the only person to be convicted in the 1988 Pan Am flight 103 bombing (also known as the Lockerbie bombing), in which 270 people died; he was sentenced to a minimum jail term of 27 years, but in 2008, while serving his term in a Scottish prison, he was diagnosed with terminal prostate cancer, and Scottish authorities, presented with doctors' opinions that he had only three months to live, opted in August 2009 to release Megrahi—a decision that rankled US authorities, particularly after he was received in Libya with a hero's welcome and then survived for almost three more years.

**John (Evans) Atta Mills** (21 Jul 1944, Tarkwa, Ghana—24 Jul 2012, Accra, Ghana), Ghanaian politician and scholar who, as president of Ghana from January 2009, set about to improve the socioeconomic situation of ordinary Ghanaians, introduced an austerity program in which he promised steep cuts in government spending, and instituted policies to eliminate four cabinet ministries and reduce the size of the presidential convoy; he also presided over the commencement in late 2010 of the country's first commercial oil production.

**Harry Morgan** (Harry Bratsburg; 10 Apr 1915, Detroit MI—7 Dec 2011, Los Angeles CA), American actor who was best known for his television work, particularly as the gruff but kindhearted Col. Sherman T. Potter (1975–83) on *M\*A\*S\*H*, for which he won an Emmy Award for best supporting actor in 1980; he also costarred as Officer Bill Gannon (1967–70) on *Dragnet 1967*.

**Bingu wa Mutharika** (Brighton Webster Ryson Thom; 24 Feb 1934, Thyolo, Nyasaland [now Malawi]—5 Apr 2012, Lilongwe, Malawi), Malawian economist and politician who was elected president of Malawi in 2004; he set out to eliminate corruption, streamline spending, and reform Malawi's moribund agricultural sector, ending the country's dependence on food aid.

**LeRoy Neiman** (LeRoy Joseph Runquist; 8 Jun 1921, St. Paul MN—20 Jun 2012, New York NY), American artist who achieved tremendous popularity and commercial success through his vividly colored impressionistic paintings that documented public life; best known as a sports artist, he covered the Olympics five times, and he was named an official artist for the Winter Games in Lake Placid NY (1980) and in Sarajevo, Yugoslavia (now in Bosnia and Herzegovina; 1984), and for the 1984 Summer Games in Los Angeles.

**John (Reginald) Neville** (2 May 1925, London, England—19 Nov 2011, Toronto, ON, Canada), British-born Canadian actor and director who achieved stardom with his natural and wide-ranging performances in Shakespearean plays and, as artistic director, revivified several Canadian theaters; in 1972 he moved to Canada, taking the helm at the Stratford Shakespeare Festival (1986–89); he was made OBE (1965) and an Officer of the Order of Canada (2006).

**Patricia (Mary) Neway** (30 Sep 1919, Brooklyn NY—24 Jan 2012, East Corinth VT), American opera singer who lent her wide-ranging intense soprano vocals and dramatic stage presence to scores of operas during her 15 years (1951–66) at the New York City Opera; she was indelibly remembered, however, for creating the Broadway roles of Magda Sorel in Gian Carlo Menotti's *The Consul* (1950) and of the Mother Abbess in Rodgers and Hammerstein's *The Sound of Music* (1960); for the latter performance, which included her soaring rendition of "Climb Ev'ry Mountain," she won a Tony Award as best featured actress in a musical.

**Nguyen Cao Ky** (8 Sep 1930, Son Tay, Vietnam—23 Jul 2011, Kuala Lumpur, Malaysia), South Vietnamese military and political leader who was the flamboyant and vehemently anticommunist commander of South Vietnam's air force (1963–65) and the country's premier (1965–67) following the June 1965 military coup in which he unseated the government of Premier Phan Huy Quat.

**Johnny Otis** (John Alexander Veliotes; 28 Dec 1921, Vallejo CA—17 Jan 2012, Altadena CA), American bandleader, drummer, singer, and promoter who was instrumental in furthering the careers of such important rhythm-and-blues performers as Big Mama Thornton, Little Willie John, Little Esther Phillips, and Etta James, with whom he wrote the smash hit "Roll with Me Henry" (retitled "The Wallflower"); in 1994 Otis was inducted into the Rock and Roll Hall of Fame.

**Cotton Owens** (Everett Owens; 21 May 1924, Union SC—7 Jun 2012, Spartanburg SC), American auto-racing pioneer who gained renown for having won 47 NASCAR premier-series races as a driver and then as a car owner; he earned the nickname "King of the Modifieds" for his success in the Modified Division championships in the early 1950s and then went on to win nine times in the NASCAR top circuit as a driver. In 1998 Owens was named one of NASCAR's 50 Greatest Drivers, and he was one of five individuals chosen to be inducted into the 2013 NASCAR Hall of Fame.

**Joe Paterno** (Joseph Vincent Paterno; "JoePa"; 21 Dec 1926, Brooklyn NY—22 Jan 2012, State College PA), American football coach who was the iconic and beloved longtime (1966–2011) head coach at Pennsylvania State University (Penn State) and held the record for career victories (409) in Division I college football and the record for career coaching victories in bowl games (24), but his final season was marred by a scandal involving former assistant coach Jerry Sandusky, who in 2011 was arrested and charged with 40 counts of sexual abuse of boys between 1994 and 2009; Paterno led Penn State to consecutive undefeated seasons in 1968 and 1969 and another in 1973, and Penn State won its first national championship of the Paterno era in 1982 and added another—as well as a fourth undefeated season—in 1986. In January 2002, Paterno became the first active coach in 20 years to receive the Amos Alonzo Stagg Award, the highest honor given by the American Football Coaches Association, and in 2007 he was inducted into the College Football Hall of Fame.

**John (Adolphus) Payton** (27 Dec 1946, Los Angeles CA—22 Mar 2012, Baltimore MD), American civil rights lawyer who was a tireless advocate for equality as president and director-counsel (from 2008) of the NAACP Legal Defense and Educational Fund; in the late 1990s he defended the University of Michigan's decision to consider race as a factor for admission, and he later argued before the US Supreme Court in support of the practice.

**Eddie Perkins** (3 Mar 1937, Clarksdale MS—10 May 2012, Chicago IL), American boxer who was a crafty pugilist who recorded 74 wins (21 by knockout), 20 losses, and 2 draws during his 19-year professional career and reigned as WBA (14 Sep–15 Dec 1962) and WBA and WBC (15 Jun 1963–18 Jan 1965) light welterweight champion; he was inducted into the World Boxing Hall of Fame in 2006 and into the International Boxing Hall of Fame in 2008.

**Matthew (James) Perry, Jr.** (3 Aug 1921, Columbia SC—29 Jul 2011, Columbia SC), American lawyer and judge who worked tirelessly to advance the legal status of African Americans during the civil rights movement, arguing several cases before the US Supreme Court; his most significant case was *Edwards* v. *South Carolina* (1963), which upheld

African Americans' right to engage in protest marches and which was cited in at least 70 other US Supreme Court cases.

**Pete Pihos** (Peter Louis Pihos; "The Golden Greek"; 22 Oct 1923, Orlando FL—16 Aug 2011, Winston-Salem NC), American football player who was a mainstay of the NFL's Philadelphia Eagles for nine years (1947–55) and helped the team achieve unprecedented back-to-back NFL championship titles; he led the NFL in receptions for three seasons (1953–55) and in touchdown catches once (1953), and he was inducted into both the College (1966) and the Pro (1970) Football Hall of Fame.

**Ferdinand Alexander Porsche** ("Butzi"; 11 Dec 1935, Stuttgart, Germany—5 Apr 2012, Salzburg, Austria), German automobile designer who was the grandson of automobile pioneer Ferdinand Porsche and the creator of the original model and design drawings for the Porsche 911—that iconic sports car, offered for sale in 1964, became one of the auto manufacturer's most successful and enduring models; it was still in production, in its seventh incarnation, in 2012.

**Muammar al-Qaddafi** (1942, near Surt, Libya—20 Oct 2011, Surt, Libya), Libyan de facto head of state who ruled Libya for more than four decades, from 1 Sep 1969, when he seized control of the government in a military coup that deposed King Idris, until he was ousted in August 2011; a devout Muslim and ardent Arab nationalist, he rose steadily through the military ranks, all the while plotting with fellow officers to overthrow the Libyan monarchy. After the 1969 coup Qaddafi was named commander in chief of the armed forces and chairman of Libya's new governing body; his government became known for financing a broad spectrum of revolutionary or terrorist groups, including its purported involvement in the destruction of a civilian airliner in 1988 over Lockerbie, Scotland, which triggered UN and US sanctions that were not fully lifted until 2003 following Qaddafi's announcement that Libya would cease its unconventional-weapons program. In early 2011, anti-Qaddafi protests broke out in Libya—the regime attempted to violently suppress the insurgency, but opposition forces gradually took control of the country; Qaddafi was killed by rebel forces in his hometown, one of the last remaining loyalist strongholds.

**Burhanuddin Rabbani** (1940, Faizabad, Badakhshan, Afghanistan—20 Sep 2011, Kabul, Afghanistan), Afghan Islamic scholar and political leader who instituted strict Islamic laws as the president (1992–96) of Afghanistan but was driven into exile after the rise of the even more fundamentalist Taliban.

**Jerry Ragovoy** (Jordan Ragovoy, Norman Margulies, Norman Meade; 4 Sep 1930, Philadelphia PA—13 Jul 2011, New York NY), American songwriter and record producer who wrote some of the best-known rock-and-roll songs of the 1960s, including "Time Is on My Side," recorded by the Rolling Stones (1964), and several of Janis Joplin's hits, notably "Piece of My Heart" and "Try (Just a Little Bit Harder)."

**Jim Rathmann** (Royal Richard Rathmann; 16 Jul 1928, Alhambra CA—23 Nov 2011, Palm Bay FL), American race-car driver who set a record in 1959 for the fastest-ever Indy car race (clocking an average speed of 170 mph) at the first and only such race at Daytona (FL) Speedway; months later he won the grueling 1960 Indianapolis 500; Rathmann was inducted into the Auto Racing Hall of Fame in 1993 and the Motorsports Hall of Fame in 2007.

**Herb(ert) Reed** (7 Aug 1928, Kansas City MO—4 Jun 2012, Danvers MA), American singer who was the last surviving member of the Platters, a vocal ensemble that he cofounded in the early 1950s and that went on to become one of the foremost close-harmony doo-wop singing groups of the early days of rock and roll as well as one of the first African American groups to achieve crossover popularity on the mainstream music charts; the group was inducted into the Rock and Roll Hall of Fame in 1990.

**Adrienne (Cecile) Rich** (16 May 1929, Baltimore MD—27 Mar 2012, Santa Cruz CA), American poet, scholar, and critic who demonstrated a stylistic transformation from formal, well-crafted but imitative poetry to a more personal and powerful style; throughout the 1960s and '70s, her increasing commitment to the women's movement and to a feminist cause, and after openly acknowledging her homosexuality, lesbian aesthetic politicized much of her later poetry; she turned down the National Medal of Arts in 1997, and she was awarded the Bollingen Prize in 2003.

**Sally Kristen Ride** (26 May 1951, Encino CA—23 Jul 2012, La Jolla CA), American astronaut who became the first American woman in space when she rocketed into orbit (18 Jun 1983) aboard the shuttle orbiter *Challenger;* she served on a second space mission aboard *Challenger* in October 1984.

**Cliff Robertson** (Clifford Parker Robertson III; 9 Sep 1923, La Jolla CA—10 Sep 2011, Stony Brook NY), American actor who enjoyed a creditable career onstage and on television but was best remembered by moviegoers for his portrayal of Lieut. John F. Kennedy in *PT 109* (1963) and for his Academy Award-winning title role in *Charly* (1968).

**Jerry Robinson** (Sherrill David Robinson; 1 Jan 1922, Trenton NJ—7 Dec 2011, New York NY), American comic book artist who was credited with the creation (together with writer Bill Finger, 1940) of the ghoulish Joker, the ultimate comic book villain and nemesis of Batman, and Batman's ward and sidekick, Robin, the Boy Wonder, as well as such characters in the Caped Crusader franchise as Alfred (Bruce Wayne's butler) and the evildoer Two-Face.

**Andy Rooney** (Andrew Aitken Rooney; 14 Jan 1919, Albany NY—4 Nov 2011, New York NY), American journalist and essayist who was best known for his curmudgeonly commentaries (1978–2011) that aired at the end of the television news program *60 Minutes;* his segment, which usually featured his splenetic—and drily humorous—complaints about the vagaries of modern life, earned him three Emmy Awards (1979, 1981, and 1982) as well as a lifetime achievement Emmy in 2003.

**Barney Rosset** (Barnet Lee Rosset, Jr.; 28 May 1922, Chicago IL—21 Feb 2012, New York NY), American publisher who, as the head of Grove Press (1951–85), repeatedly and successfully challenged obscenity laws, championed avant-garde authors, and was regarded as one of the most important and groundbreaking American publishers of the 20th century; under his direction Grove in 1959 published an unexpurgated edition of D.H. Lawrence's novel *Lady Chatterley's Lover* (1928), and the 1961 publication of Henry Miller's *Tropic of Cancer* (1934) led to a 1964 US Supreme Court ruling permitting the book to be published and sold.

**F(rank) Sherwood Rowland** ("Sherry"; 28 Jun 1927, Delaware OH—10 Mar 2012, Corona del Mar CA),

American chemist who shared the 1995 Nobel Prize for Chemistry with chemists Mario Molina and Paul Crutzen for research on the depletion of Earth's ozone layer; working with Molina, Rowland discovered that man-made chlorofluorocarbon (CFC) propellants accelerate the decomposition of the ozonosphere, which protects Earth from ultraviolet radiation, and their findings eventually brought about international changes in the chemical industry.

**Ken Russell** (Henry Kenneth Alfred Russell; 3 Jul 1927, Southampton, Hampshire, England—27 Nov 2011, Lymington, Hampshire, England), British filmmaker who gained international acclaim for *Women in Love* (1969); the visual beauty of the film and its tasteful handling of erotic scenes won the approval of public and critics alike and earned Russell best director nominations from the Academy Awards and the Golden Globes.

**Ann Rutherford** (Therese Ann Rutherford; 2 Nov 1917, Vancouver, BC, Canada—11 Jun 2012, Beverly Hills CA), Canadian-born American actress who appeared in sisterly roles in the film classic *Gone with the Wind* (1939) and in *Pride and Prejudice* (1940); Rutherford's defining role, however, was that of Polly Benedict, the love interest of Andy Hardy, in the series of movies (in the late 1930s and early '40s) in which she costarred with Mickey Rooney.

**Malam Bacai Sanhá** (5 May 1947, Darsalame, Portuguese Guinea [now in Guinea-Bissau]—9 Jan 2012, Paris, France), Guinea-Bissauan politician who brought a certain level of stability to his country when he was elected president in the aftermath of the March 2009 assassination of Pres. João Bernardo Vieira; Sanhá was ultimately unable to control drug trafficking, official corruption, and violent crime, however.

**Vidal Sassoon** (17 Jan 1928, London, England—9 May 2012, Los Angeles CA), British hairstylist and entrepreneur who revolutionized women's hairstyling in the 1950s and '60s when he introduced short "wash-and-wear" hair that did not demand the weekly trips to the salon and hours of care at home commonly required by the then-prevalent heavily teased and sprayed bouffant styles; his emphasis on precise scissor cuts and stark geometric angles was influenced by his lifelong interest in architecture as well as by his desire to create simple styles that complemented each woman's individual bone structure and natural hair texture. In the 1970s Sassoon established salons, as well as hairdressing schools, in Europe and North America, and he personally marketed his eponymous hair- and skin-care products in television commercials enhanced by the catchy slogan "If you don't look good, we don't look good"; he was made CBE in 2009.

**Oscar Luigi Scalfaro** (9 Sep 1918, Novara, Italy—29 Jan 2012, Rome, Italy), Italian politician who brought a reputation for honesty and traditional moral leadership to his position as the president of Italy (1992–99) during a period of political instability in the country; at the end of his term, he was appointed senator for life.

**Earl (Eugene) Scruggs** (6 Jan 1924, Flint Hill NC—28 Mar 2012, Nashville TN), American bluegrass banjoist who perfected a banjo-picking technique (the "Scruggs style") that helped to popularize the five-string banjo; he and his longtime (1948–69) partner, guitarist Lester Flatt, became one of the great bluegrass bands, and Flatt & Scruggs were inducted into the Country Music Hall of Fame in 1985; in 1991 they were—with Bill Monroe—the first inductees into the International Bluegrass Hall of Fame. In 2008 Scruggs received a Grammy Lifetime Achievement Award.

**Junior Seau** (Tiaina Baul Seau, Jr.; 19 Jan 1969, San Diego CA—2 May 2012, Oceanside CA), American football player who was a formidable and intense linebacker who played for 20 seasons with such NFL teams as the New England Patriots (2006–09), the Miami Dolphins (2003–05), and the San Diego Chargers (1990–2002), which he helped to the Super Bowl in 1994, the team's only appearance in that championship game; Seau, who was named to the Pro Bowl 12 times, had a career total of 545 tackles and 56.5 sacks, and he was also named NFL Man of the Year in 1994.

**Lee Roy Selmon** (20 Oct 1954, Eufaula OK—4 Sep 2011, Tampa FL), American football player who was a hard-hitting, imposing defensive end who was credited with 23 sacks during his professional NFL career (1976–84) with the Tampa Bay Buccaneers; he played college football at the University of Oklahoma, and he helped the team capture national championships in 1974 and 1975—in 1976 he received the Lombardi trophy as the top college lineman. He was inducted into the College Football Hall of Fame in 1988 and the Pro Football Hall of Fame in 1995.

**Maurice (Bernard) Sendak** (10 Jun 1928, Brooklyn NY—8 May 2012, Danbury CT), American artist and writer who illustrated more than 80 children's books, notably the trilogy made up of *Where the Wild Things Are* (1963; winner of the 1964 Caldecott Medal), *In the Night Kitchen* (1970), and *Outside over There* (1981), all featuring a menagerie of sometimes frightening monsters and goblins that magically invade the dream lives and imaginations of children; he was awarded the National Medal of Arts in 1996.

**Anthony Shadid** (26 Sep 1968, Oklahoma City OK—16 Feb 2012, eastern Syria), American journalist who spent his career as a foreign correspondent covering developments in the Middle East for the *Boston Globe* (2001–03), the *Washington Post* (2003–09), and the *New York Times* (2009–12) newspapers, often at considerable personal peril; for his incisive reporting in Iraq, he won Pulitzer Prizes in 2004 and 2010.

**John (Malchase David) Shalikashvili** (27 Jun 1936, Warsaw, Poland—23 Jul 2011, Tacoma WA), Polish-born American army officer who served as supreme allied commander of NATO forces in Europe (1992–93) and as chairman of the US Joint Chiefs of Staff (1993–97); he was the first immigrant—as well as the first soldier to rise from the enlisted ranks—to hold the top command in the US military; he was a vocal critic of the military's "Don't Ask, Don't Tell" policy regarding gay and lesbian members of the military.

**Yitzhak Shamir** (Yitzhak Jazernicki, Yezernitzky, Yizernitsky, or Ysernitzky; 15 Oct 1915, Ruzinoy, Poland, Russian Empire [now Ruzhany, Belarus]—30 Jun 2012, Tel Aviv–Yafo, Israel), Polish-born Zionist leader and Israeli politician who was the hard-line prime minister of Israel three times: 1983–84, 1986–90, and 1990–92.

**Carroll (Hall) Shelby** (11 Jan 1923, Leesburg TX—10 May 2012, Dallas TX), American race-car driver and builder who was the visionary designer of innovative high-performance racing cars, notably the Shelby Cobra and the Ford GT40, and he was responsible in the commercial sector for the reintroduction of several Mustang-based Shelby cars; he had a successful racing career of his own—he earned accolades as Sports Ilustrated's Sports Car Driver of the Year in 1956 and Driver of the Year in 1957, and he was the winning codriver for Aston Martin in the 1959 Le Mans race.

**Robert Bernard Sherman** (19 Dec 1925, Brooklyn NY—5 Mar 2012, London, England), American songwriter who delighted moviegoers with dozens of catchy songs and film scores, all created with his younger brother, Richard Sherman; their quintessential work was for Walt Disney Productions—notably in the film Mary Poppins (1964), for which they won an Academy Award (and a Grammy Award) for best score as well as an Oscar for the song "Chim Chim Cher-ee," and the ubiquitous theme-park song "It's a Small World (After All)." The Shermans were inducted into the Songwriters Hall of Fame in 2005 and were awarded the National Medal of Arts in 2008.

**Fred Shuttlesworth** (Freddie Lee Robinson; 18 Mar 1922, Mount Meigs AL—5 Oct 2011, Birmingham AL), American civil rights leader who established (1957), with Martin Luther King, Jr., and others, the Southern Christian Leadership Council (SCLC) and worked to end segregation in the South; for his efforts—which included challenging segregated schools and buses and participating in sit-ins and in the Freedom Rides of the early 1960s—Shuttlesworth received the Presidential Citizens Medal in 2001.

**Joe Simon** (Hymie Simon; Joseph Henry Simon; 11 Oct 1913, Rochester NY—14 Dec 2011, New York NY), American cartoonist who created (together with Jack Kirby) a cast of superheroes that included Captain America, Manhunter, and Boy Commandos; a longtime copyright battle with Marvel Comics over Captain America was settled out of court in 2003, and Simon finally saw the superhero featured on the big screen in Captain America: The First Avenger (2011).

**Willie Smith** ("Big Eyes"; 19 Jan 1936, Helena AR—16 Sep 2011, Chicago IL), American blues musician who was the drummer in the Muddy Waters band primarily in the early 1960s and the '70s; Smith was the drummer on four Grammy Award-winning albums during that period, and his final album, Joined at the Hip (2010), recorded with pianist Pinetop Perkins, won the 2010 Grammy Award for best traditional blues album.

**Margie Stewart** (Margery Stewart; Margie Stewart Johnson; 14 Dec 1919, Wabash IN—26 Apr 2012, Burbank CA), American actress and pinup girl who was selected by the US Army as its official and only World War II poster girl—her wholesome image was emblazoned on 12 posters (94 million copies were made), and the first set bore the caption "Please...get there and BACK!" and a cautionary tagline, "Be careful what you say or write."

**Bert Sugar** (Herbert Randolph Sugar; 7 Jun 1936, Washington DC—25 Mar 2012, Mount Kisco NY), American sportswriter who delighted boxing fans for more than three decades as a flamboyant repository of boxing knowledge and legend; a popular raconteur as well as a vivid and passionate writer and television and radio commentator, he was easily recognized around boxing venues with his ever-present fedora and cigar, and he was inducted into the International Boxing Hall of Fame in 2005.

**Hubert Sumlin** (November 1931, near Greenwood MS—4 Dec 2011, Wayne NJ), American blues musician who was the principal guitar player for bluesman Howlin' Wolf for more than 20 years; Sumlin's complex, inventive leads served as a counterpoint to Wolf's raw vocals in some of Wolf's biggest hits, including "Smokestack Lightnin'" (1956), "Wang Dang Doodle" (1960), and "Killing Floor" (1964), and he appeared on most of the recordings that Wolf made for Chess Records. Sumlin later joined Muddy Waters's band in 1956, but the strain of touring with Waters drove Sumlin to return to Wolf, where he stayed until Wolf's death in 1976. A Rolling Stone magazine poll of the 100 greatest guitarists of all time ranked Sumlin number 43.

**Donna Summer** (LaDonna Adrian Gaines; 31 Dec 1948, Boston MA—17 May 2012, Naples FL), American singer-songwriter who reigned as the "Queen of Disco" during the 1970s with her steamy vocals on such chart-topping classics as "Love to Love You Baby" and "I Feel Love" but transcended that genre and won five Grammy Awards for vocal performances that covered rock ("Hot Stuff"), inspirational ("He's a Rebel" and "Forgive Me"), dance music ("Carry On"), and rhythm and blues ("Last Dance," her signature song, from the film Thank God It's Friday [1978]); she also scored big hits with "MacArthur Park" and "No More Tears (Enough Is Enough)," a duet with Barbra Streisand.

**Censu Tabone** (Vincent Tabone; 30 Mar 1913, Victoria, Gozo, British Malta—14 Mar 2012, San Giljan, Malta), Maltese ophthalmologist and politician who was the reform-minded fourth president of Malta (1989–94) and a respected physician who worked both at home and across Asia on behalf of WHO in an attempt to control and eradicate the destructive eye disease trachoma.

**Dorothea (Margaret) Tanning** (25 Aug 1910, Galesburg IL—31 Jan 2012, New York NY), American painter and writer who was a prominent Surrealist, but her artistic career was overshadowed by that of her famous husband, German painter and sculptor Max Ernst; her own dreamlike imagery, however, was considered more Gothic in nature than surreal; after Tanning and Ernst married in 1946, the couple moved to Sedona AZ, where they hosted a bohemian crowd of visitors, including writers Truman Capote and Dylan Thomas.

**Tupou V** (King Siaosi [George] Tupou V; Siaosi Taufa'ahau Manumataongo Tuku'aho Tupou; 4 May 1948, Nuku'alofa, Tongatapu island, British-protected Tonga—18 Mar 2012, Hong Kong), Tongan monarch who relinquished the absolute power that he initially held and oversaw Tonga's transformation into a constitutional monarchy as well as its first democratic parliamentary elections in 2010.

**Cy Twombly** (Edwin Parker Twombly, Jr.; 25 Apr 1928, Lexington VA—5 Jul 2011, Rome, Italy), American painter, draftsman, and sculptor who pursued some early experiments in an Abstract Expressionist vein before developing the calligraphic and sometimes graffiti-like repetitive and scumbled marks and gestures on canvas and paper for which he was best known.

**Jack Twyman** (John Kennedy Twyman; 21 May 1934, Pittsburgh PA—30 May 2012, Cincinnati OH), American basketball player who was one of the best pure-shooting forwards in the NBA while playing (1955–66) for the Rochester (from 1957 Cincinnati) Royals; in 823 games played he scored 15,840 points (an average of 19.2 points per game) and snapped up 5,424 rebounds, making him one of the all-time leaders in offense;

Twyman was inducted into the Basketball Hall of Fame in 1983.

**Barry (Forster) Unsworth** (10 Aug 1930, Wingate, Durham, England—5 Jun 2012, Perugia, Italy), British novelist who explored morality and greed in his historical fiction and re-created past worlds through vivid prose and meticulous research; he was the corecipient (with Michael Ondaatje) of the Booker Prize in 1992 for his novel *Sacred Hunger; Pascali's Island* (1980; film 1988) and *Morality Play* (1995; filmed as *The Reckoning*, 2003) were also short-listed for the Booker Prize.

**Gore Vidal** (Eugene Luther Gore Vidal, Jr.; 3 Oct 1925, West Point NY—31 Jul 2012, Los Angeles CA), American novelist, playwright, and essayist who was noted for his irreverent and intellectually adroit novels, his outspoken political opinions, and the witty and satiric observations that made him a popular guest on television talk shows; in *United States: Essays, 1952–1992* (1993; National Book Award) he incisively analyzed contemporary American politics and government.

**Janice (Elaine) Voss** (8 Oct 1956, South Bend IN—6 Feb 2012, Scottsdale AZ), American astronaut who was one out of six women to have travelled into space five times, spending 49 days in orbit from 1993 to 2000.

**Mike Wallace** (Myron Leon Wallace; 9 May 1918, Brookline MA—7 Apr 2012, New Canaan CT), American television journalist who was noted for his aggressive, bruising style during his interrogational interviews on the long-running television program *60 Minutes*, for which he served as coeditor (1968–2006); he helped develop the format for *60 Minutes*, pioneering the "ambush interview," in which he appeared on the scene with cameras in tow, and he grilled a slew of subjects, including Watergate coconspirator John Ehrlichman, Iranian leaders Ayatollah Ruhollah Khomeni and Mahmoud Ahmadinejad, Palestinian leader Yasir Arafat, African American Muslim leader Malcolm X, and euthanasia advocate Jack Kevorkian. Wallace earned 21 Emmy Awards, 5 DuPont-Columbia journalism awards, and 5 Peabody Awards.

**Doc Watson** (Arthel Lane Watson; 3 Mar 1923, Stony Fork, near Deep Gap NC—29 May 2012, Winston-Salem NC), American musician and singer who introduced a flat-picking style that elevated the acoustic guitar from a rhythmically strummed background instrument to a leading role in bluegrass, country, folk, and rock music, notably during the folk-music revival of the 1960s. Between 1973 and 2006 Watson won eight Grammys, including a lifetime achievement award (2004), and he received the National Medal of Arts from US Pres. Bill Clinton in 1997.

**Kitty Wells** (Muriel Ellen Deason; 30 Aug 1919, Nashville TN—16 Jul 2012, Madison TN), American singer and songwriter who was the first female star of country music and scored hits with "It Wasn't God Who Made Honky Tonk Angels" (1952), "Release Me" (1954), and "I Can't Stop Loving You" (1958). She was inducted into the Country Music Hall of Fame in 1976, and she was presented with a Lifetime Achievement Award at the Grammys in 1991.

**Dan Wheldon** (Daniel Clive Wheldon; 22 Jun 1978, Emberton, Buckinghamshire, England—16 Oct 2011, Las Vegas NV), British race-car driver who won the 2011 Indianapolis 500 after having captured both that race and the overall Indy Racing League (IRL) drivers' championship in 2005.

**Reed Whittemore** (Edward Reed Whittemore II; 11 Sep 1919, New Haven CT—6 Apr 2012, Kensington MD), American educator and poet who penned free-flowing ironic verse and twice served (1964–65 and 1984–85) as consultant in poetry to the Library of Congress (now poet laureate consultant in poetry).

**Nicol Williamson** (14 Sep 1936, Hamilton, Scotland—16 Dec 2011, Amsterdam, Netherlands), British actor who earned the approbation "the greatest English actor of his generation."

**Tom Wilson** (Thomas Albert Wilson; 1 Aug 1931, Grant Town WV—16 Sep 2011, Cincinnati OH), American cartoonist who was the creator of the hapless rotund cartoon character Ziggy, a short, bald everyman whose wry and self-deprecating comments framed life's tribulations; Wilson spent more than 35 years as an artist at American Greetings Corp., where he helped to develop such characters as Strawberry Shortcake and the Care Bears, and he shared an Emmy Award in 1983 for the Christmas special *Ziggy's Gift*.

**Amy (Jade) Winehouse** (14 Sep 1983, London, England—found dead 23 Jul 2011, London, England), British singer-songwriter who skyrocketed to fame with her critically acclaimed multiple Grammy Award-winning album *Back to Black* (2006), but her tempestuous love life and substance-abuse problems stalled her recording career even as they made her a favorite subject of tabloid journalism.

**John Wood** (5 Jul 1930, Derbyshire, England—6 Aug 2011, Chipping Campden, Gloucestershire, England), British actor who played an enormous variety of roles to great effect but was best known for his work in plays by Shakespeare and by British playwright Tom Stoppard; Wood won a Tony for his portrayal of Henry Carr in Stoppard's *Travesties* (1976), a part that was written for him; he was made CBE in 2007.

**Orlando (Vernada) Woolridge** (16 Dec 1959, Bernice LA—31 May 2012, Mansfield LA), American basketball player who scored thousands of baskets with acrobatic alley-oop passes and soaring slam dunks during his 13 seasons (1981–94) in the National Basketball Association; the powerful offensive player played for eight teams, most notably the Chicago Bulls (1981–86), New Jersey Nets (1986–88), and Los Angeles Lakers (1988–90).

**Adam (Nathaniel) Yauch** (MCA; 5 Aug 1964, Brooklyn NY—4 May 2012, New York NY), American rapper and musician who was a cofounder and member, with Michael ("Mike D") Diamond and Adam ("Adrock") Horovitz, of the groundbreaking and widely admired hip-hop band Beastie Boys, whose punk-rap fusion evolved from clownishness to experimentation to rap with a social message; in addition, Yauch started (1994) the Milarepa Fund, which produced the Tibetan Freedom Concert series; two of the band's albums won Grammy Awards (*Hello Nasty* in 1998 for best alternative music performance and *The Mix-up* in 2007 for best pop instrumental album), and Beastie Boys were inducted into the Rock and Roll Hall of Fame in 2012.

**Abdullahi Yusuf Ahmed** (15 Dec 1934, Barta, Puntland region, Somalia—23 Mar 2012, Abu Dhabi, UAE), Somali warlord and political leader who was the autocratic president of Somalia's semiautonomous region of Puntland (1998–2001; 2002–04) until Somalia's parliament in exile elected him president of the Transitional Federal Government (then based in Nairobi).

# Awards

## TIME's Top 100 Films

There's nothing like a list to stimulate a strong discussion, so in the hopes of striking a few sparks among movie lovers, TIME asked its long-time film critics Richard Corliss and Richard Schickel to compile a list of the 100 greatest films ever made. Of course, the discussions that followed between the two critics were entirely civil at all times. Below, the films and the year they were released.

### A–C
Aguirre: The Wrath of God (1972)
The Apu Trilogy (1955, 1956, 1959)
The Awful Truth (1937)
Baby Face (1933)
Bande à part (1964)
Barry Lyndon (1975)
Berlin Alexanderplatz (1980)
Blade Runner (1982)
Bonnie and Clyde (1967)
Brazil (1985)
Bride of Frankenstein (1935)
Camille (1936)
Casablanca (1942)
Charade (1963)
Children of Paradise (1945)
Chinatown (1974)
Chungking Express (1994)
Citizen Kane (1941)
City Lights (1931)
City of God (2002)
Closely Watched Trains (1966)
The Crime of Monsieur Lange (1936)
The Crowd (1928)

### D–F
Day for Night (1973)
The Decalogue (1989)
Detour (1945)
The Discreet Charm of the Bourgeoisie (1972)
Dodsworth (1936)
Double Indemnity (1944)
Dr. Strangelove or: How I Learned To Stop Worrying and Love the Bomb (1964)
Drunken Master II (1994)
E.T.: The Extra-Terrestrial (1982)
8 1/2 (1963)
The 400 Blows (1959)
Farewell My Concubine (1993)
Finding Nemo (2003)
The Fly (1986)

### G–J
The Godfather, Parts I and II (1972, 1974)
The Good, the Bad, and the Ugly (1966)
Goodfellas (1990)
A Hard Day's Night (1964)
His Girl Friday (1940)
Ikiru (1952)
In a Lonely Place (1950)
Invasion of the Body Snatchers (1956)
It's a Gift (1934)
It's a Wonderful Life (1946)

### K–M
Kandahar (2001)
Kind Hearts and Coronets (1949)
King Kong (1933)
The Lady Eve (1941)
The Last Command (1928)
Lawrence of Arabia (1962)
Léolo (1992)
The Lord of the Rings (2001, 2002, 2003)
The Man with a Camera (1929)
The Manchurian Candidate (1962)
Meet Me in St. Louis (1944)
Metropolis (1927)
Miller's Crossing (1990)
Mon oncle d'Amérique (1980)
Mouchette (1967)

### N–P
Nayakan (1987)
Ninotchka (1939)
Notorious (1946)
Olympia, Parts 1 and 2 (1938)
On the Waterfront (1954)
Once upon a Time in the West (1968)
Out of the Past (1947)
Persona (1966)
Pinocchio (1940)
Psycho (1960)
Pulp Fiction (1994)
The Purple Rose of Cairo (1985)
Pyaasa (1957)

### Q–S
Raging Bull (1980)
Schindler's List (1993)
The Searchers (1956)
Sherlock, Jr. (1924)
The Shop Around the Corner (1940)
Singin' in the Rain (1952)
The Singing Detective (1986)
Smiles of a Summer Night (1955)
Some Like It Hot (1959)
Star Wars (1977)
A Streetcar Named Desire (1951)
Sunrise (1927)
Sweet Smell of Success (1957)
Swing Time (1936)

### T–Z
Talk to Her (2002)
Taxi Driver (1976)
Tokyo Story (1953)
A Touch of Zen (1971)
Ugetsu (1953)
Ulysses' Gaze (1995)
Umberto D (1952)
Unforgiven (1992)
White Heat (1949)
Wings of Desire (1987)
Yojimbo (1961)

# TIME's Person of the Year, 1927–2011

Every year since 1927, TIME has named a Person of the Year, identifying the individual who has done the most to affect the news in the past twelve months. The designation is often mistaken for an honor, but the magazine has always pointed out that inclusion on the list is not a recognition of good works (like the Nobel Peace prize, for example), but rather a reflection of the sheer power of one's actions, whether for good or for ill. Hence, both Adolf Hitler and Ayatollah Ruhollah Khomeini were chosen Person of the Year at the time when their actions commanded the attention of the world. Below, the complete list of Persons of the Year.

| | |
|---|---|
| 1927 | Charles Lindbergh |
| 1928 | Walter Chrysler |
| 1929 | Owen Young |
| 1930 | Mahatma Gandhi |
| 1931 | Pierre Laval |
| 1932 | Franklin Delano Roosevelt |
| 1933 | Hugh Johnson |
| 1934 | Franklin Delano Roosevelt |
| 1935 | Haile Selassie |
| 1936 | Wallis Simpson |
| 1937 | Chiang Kai-Shek and Soong Mei-ling |
| 1938 | Adolf Hitler |
| 1939 | Joseph Stalin |
| 1940 | Winston Churchill |
| 1941 | Franklin Delano Roosevelt |
| 1942 | Joseph Stalin |
| 1943 | George Marshall |
| 1944 | Dwight Eisenhower |
| 1945 | Harry Truman |
| 1946 | James F. Byrnes |
| 1947 | George Marshall |
| 1948 | Harry Truman |
| 1949 | Winston Churchill ("Man of the Half-Century") |
| 1950 | The American Fighting-Man (representing US troops fighting in the Korean War; first abstract chosen) |
| 1951 | Mohammed Mossadegh |
| 1952 | Queen Elizabeth II |
| 1953 | Konrad Adenauer |
| 1954 | John Foster Dulles |
| 1955 | Harlow Curtice |
| 1956 | Hungarian Freedom Fighter (representing the citizens' uprising against Soviet domination) |
| 1957 | Nikita Khrushchev |
| 1958 | Charles De Gaulle |
| 1959 | Dwight Eisenhower |
| 1960 | US Scientists (represented by Linus Pauling, Isidor Rabi, Edward Teller, Joshua Lederberg, Donald A. Glaser, Willard Libby, Robert Woodward, Charles Draper, William Shockley, Emilio Segrè, John Enders, Charles Townes, George Beadle, James Van Allen, and Edward Purcell) |
| 1961 | John F. Kennedy |
| 1962 | Pope John XXIII |
| 1963 | Martin Luther King, Jr. |
| 1964 | Lyndon Johnson |
| 1965 | William Westmoreland |
| 1966 | The Generation Twenty-Five and Under (representing American youth) |
| 1967 | Lyndon Johnson |
| 1968 | Apollo 8 Astronauts Frank Borman, Jim Lovell, and William Anders |
| 1969 | The Middle Americans (representing the American electorate's turn to the right) |
| 1970 | Willy Brandt |
| 1971 | Richard Nixon |
| 1972 | Richard Nixon and Henry Kissinger |
| 1973 | John Sirica |
| 1974 | King Faisal |
| 1975 | American Women (represented by Betty Ford, Carla Hills, Ella Grasso, Barbara Jordan, Susie Sharp, Jill Conway, Billie Jean King, Susan Brownmiller, Addie Wyatt, Kathleen Byerly, Carol Sutton, and Alison Cheek) |
| 1976 | Jimmy Carter |
| 1977 | Anwar el-Sadat |
| 1978 | Deng Xiaoping |
| 1979 | Ayatollah Ruhollah Khomeini |
| 1980 | Ronald Reagan |
| 1981 | Lech Walensa |
| 1982 | The Computer (first non-human abstract chosen; termed "Machine of the Year") |
| 1983 | Ronald Reagan and Yuri Andropov |
| 1984 | Peter Ueberroth |
| 1985 | Deng Xiaoping |
| 1986 | Corazon Aquino |
| 1987 | Mikhail Gorbachev |
| 1988 | Endangered Earth ("Planet of the Year") |
| 1989 | Mikhail Gorbachev ("Man of the Decade") |
| 1990 | George H.W. Bush |
| 1991 | Ted Turner |
| 1992 | Bill Clinton |
| 1993 | The Peacemakers (represented by Nelson Mandela and F.W. de Klerk [South Africa] and Yasir Arafat and Yitzhak Rabin [Middle East]) |
| 1994 | Pope John Paul II |
| 1995 | Newt Gingrich |
| 1996 | David Ho |
| 1997 | Andy Grove |
| 1998 | Bill Clinton and Kenneth Starr |
| 1999 | Jeffrey P. Bezos |
| 2000 | George W. Bush |
| 2001 | Rudolph Giuliani |
| 2002 | The Whistleblowers (represented by Cynthia Cooper of Worldcom, Sherron Watkins of Enron, and Coleen Rowley of the FBI) |
| 2003 | The American Soldier (representing US troops fighting in Iraq and Afghanistan) |
| 2004 | George W. Bush |
| 2005 | The Good Samaritans (represented by Bono [Paul Hewson], Bill Gates, and Melinda Gates) |
| 2006 | You (representing the new age of user-generated Internet content) |
| 2007 | Vladimir Putin |
| 2008 | Barack Obama |
| 2009 | Ben Bernanke |
| 2010 | Mark Zuckerberg |
| 2011 | The Protester |

# Nobel Prizes

The Alfred B. Nobel Prizes are regarded as the world's most prestigious awards given for intellectual achievement. They are awarded annually from a fund bequeathed for that purpose by the Swedish inventor and industrialist Alfred Nobel and administered by the Nobel Foundation. Nobel's will established five of the six prizes: those for physics, chemistry, literature, physiology or medicine, and peace. The prize for economic sciences was added in 1969. Each year thousands of invitations are sent out to members of scholarly institutions, scientists, Nobel laureates, members of national legislatures, and others, requesting nominations. The country given is the citizenship of the recipient at the time that the award was made. Prizes may be withheld in years when no worthy recipient can be found or when the world situation (e.g., World War II) prevents the gathering of information needed to reach a decision. A cash award of SEK 10 million (about US$1,440,000) and a commemorative medal are given.

**Nobel Foundation Web site:** <http://nobelprize.org>.

## Physics

| YEAR | WINNER(S) | COUNTRY | ACHIEVEMENT |
|------|-----------|---------|-------------|
| 1901 | Wilhelm Conrad Röntgen | Germany | discovery of X-rays |
| 1902 | Hendrik Antoon Lorentz | Neth. | investigation of the influence |
|      | Pieter Zeeman | Neth. | of magnetism on radiation |
| 1903 | Henri Becquerel | France | discovery of spontaneous radioactivity |
|      | Marie Curie | France | investigations of radiation phenomena |
|      | Pierre Curie | France | discovered by Becquerel |
| 1904 | John William Strutt (Lord Rayleigh) | UK | discovery of argon |
| 1905 | Philipp Lenard | Germany | research on cathode rays |
| 1906 | J.J. Thomson | UK | research into the electrical conductivity of gases |
| 1907 | A.A. Michelson | US | spectroscopic and metrological investigations |
| 1908 | Gabriel Lippmann | France | photographic reproduction of colors |
| 1909 | Ferdinand Braun | Germany | development of |
|      | Guglielmo Marconi | Italy | wireless telegraphy |
| 1910 | Johannes Diederik van der Waals | Neth. | research concerning the equation of state of gases and liquids |
| 1911 | Wilhelm Wien | Germany | discoveries regarding laws governing heat radiation |
| 1912 | Nils Dalén | Sweden | invention of automatic regulators for lighting coastal beacons and light buoys |
| 1913 | Heike Kamerlingh Onnes | Neth. | investigation into the properties of matter at low temperatures; production of liquid helium |
| 1914 | Max von Laue | Germany | discovery of diffraction of X-rays by crystals |
| 1915 | Lawrence Bragg | UK | analysis of crystal structure |
|      | William Bragg | UK | by means of X-rays |
| 1917 | Charles Glover Barkla | UK | discovery of the characteristic X-radiation of elements |
| 1918 | Max Planck | Germany | discovery of the elemental quanta |
| 1919 | Johannes Stark | Germany | discovery of the Doppler effect in positive ion rays and the division of spectral lines in the electric field |
| 1920 | Charles Édouard Guillaume | Switz. | discovery of anomalies in alloys |
| 1921 | Albert Einstein | Switz. | work in theoretical physics |
| 1922 | Niels Bohr | Denmark | investigation of atomic structure and radiation |
| 1923 | Robert Andrews Millikan | US | work on the elementary charge of electricity and on the photoelectric effect |
| 1924 | Karl Manne Georg Siegbahn | Sweden | work in X-ray spectroscopy |
| 1925 | James Franck | Germany | discovery of the laws governing the |
|      | Gustav Hertz | Germany | impact of an electron upon an atom |
| 1926 | Jean Perrin | France | work on the discontinuous structure of matter |
| 1927 | Arthur Holly Compton | US | discovery of the wavelength change in diffused X-rays |
|      | C.T.R. Wilson | UK | method of making visible the paths of electrically charged particles |
| 1928 | Owen Willans Richardson | UK | work on electron emission by hot metals |
| 1929 | Louis-Victor de Broglie | France | discovery of the wave nature of electrons |
| 1930 | Chandrasekhara Venkata Raman | India | discovery of Raman effect, light wavelength variation that occurs when a light beam is deflected by molecules |
| 1932 | Werner Heisenberg | Germany | creation of quantum mechanics |
| 1933 | P.A.M. Dirac | UK | introduction of wave equations |
|      | Erwin Schrödinger | Austria | in quantum mechanics |
| 1935 | James Chadwick | UK | discovery of the neutron |
| 1936 | Carl David Anderson | US | discovery of the positron |
|      | Victor Francis Hess | Austria | discovery of cosmic radiation |
| 1937 | Clinton Joseph Davisson | US | experimental demonstration of the interference |
|      | George Paget Thomson | UK | phenomenon in crystals irradiated by electrons |

## Physics (continued)

| YEAR | WINNER(S) | COUNTRY | ACHIEVEMENT |
|---|---|---|---|
| 1938 | Enrico Fermi | Italy | disclosure of artificial radioactive elements produced by neutron irradiation |
| 1939 | Ernest Orlando Lawrence | US | invention of the cyclotron |
| 1943 | Otto Stern | US | discovery of the magnetic moment of the proton |
| 1944 | Isidor Isaac Rabi | US | resonance method for the registration of various properties of atomic nuclei |
| 1945 | Wolfgang Pauli | Austria | discovery of the exclusion principle of electrons |
| 1946 | Percy Williams Bridgman | US | discoveries in the domain of high-pressure physics |
| 1947 | Edward V. Appleton | UK | discovery of the Appleton layer in the upper atmosphere |
| 1948 | Patrick M.S. Blackett | UK | discoveries in the domain of nuclear physics and cosmic radiation |
| 1949 | Hideki Yukawa | Japan | prediction of the existence of mesons |
| 1950 | Cecil Frank Powell | UK | photographic method of studying nuclear processes; discoveries concerning mesons |
| 1951 | John D. Cockcroft | UK | work on the transmutation of atomic nuclei by accelerated particles |
| | Ernest T.S. Walton | Ireland | |
| 1952 | Felix Bloch | US | discovery of nuclear magnetic resonance in solids |
| | E.M. Purcell | US | |
| 1953 | Frits Zernike | Neth. | method of phase-contrast microscopy |
| 1954 | Max Born | UK | statistical studies of atomic wave functions |
| | Walther Bothe | W.Ger. | invention of the coincidence method |
| 1955 | Polykarp Kusch | US | measurement of the magnetic moment of the electron |
| | Willis Eugene Lamb, Jr. | US | discoveries in the hydrogen spectrum |
| 1956 | John Bardeen | US | investigations on semiconductors and the invention of the transistor |
| | Walter H. Brattain | US | |
| | William B. Shockley | US | |
| 1957 | Tsung-Dao Lee | China | discovery of violations of the principle of parity, the symmetry between phenomena in coordinate systems |
| | Chen Ning Yang | China | |
| 1958 | Pavel Alexeyevich Cherenkov | USSR | discovery and interpretation of the Cherenkov effect, which indicates that electrons emit light as they pass through a transparent medium at a speed higher than the speed of light in that medium |
| | Ilya Mikhaylovich Frank | USSR | |
| | Igor Yevgenyevich Tamm | USSR | |
| 1959 | Owen Chamberlain | US | confirmation of the existence of the antiproton |
| | Emilio Segrè | US | |
| 1960 | Donald A. Glaser | US | development of the bubble chamber |
| 1961 | Robert Hofstadter | US | determination of the shape and size of atomic nucleons |
| | Rudolf Ludwig Mössbauer | W.Ger. | discovery of the Mössbauer effect, a nuclear process permitting the resonance absorption of gamma rays |
| 1962 | Lev Davidovich Landau | USSR | contributions to the understanding of condensed states of matter |
| 1963 | J. Hans D. Jensen | W.Ger. | development of the shell model theory of the structure of the atomic nuclei |
| | Maria Goeppert Mayer | US | |
| | Eugene Paul Wigner | US | principles governing the interaction of protons and neutrons in the nucleus |
| 1964 | Nikolay G. Basov | USSR | work in quantum electronics leading to the construction of instruments based on maser-laser principles |
| | Aleksandr M. Prokhorov | USSR | |
| | Charles Hard Townes | US | |
| 1965 | Richard P. Feynman | US | work in quantum electrodynamics, which describes mathematically all interactions of light with matter and of charged particles with one another |
| | Julian Seymour Schwinger | US | |
| | Shin'ichiro Tomonaga | Japan | |
| 1966 | Alfred Kastler | France | discovery of optical methods for studying Hertzian resonances in atoms |
| 1967 | Hans Albrecht Bethe | US | discoveries concerning the energy production of stars |
| 1968 | Luis W. Alvarez | US | work with elementary particles, in particular the discovery of resonance states |
| 1969 | Murray Gell-Mann | US | classification of elementary particles and their interactions |
| 1970 | Hannes Alfvén | Sweden | work in magnetohydrodynamics and in antiferromagnetism and ferrimagnetism |
| | Louis-Eugène-Félix Néel | France | |
| 1971 | Dennis Gabor | UK | invention of holography |
| 1972 | John Bardeen | US | development of the theory of superconductivity, the disappearance of electrical resistance in various solids when they are cooled below certain temperatures |
| | Leon N. Cooper | US | |
| | John Robert Schrieffer | US | |
| 1973 | Leo Esaki | Japan | experimental discoveries in tunneling in semiconductors and superconductors |
| | Ivar Giaever | US | |
| | Brian D. Josephson | UK | predictions of supercurrent properties |
| 1974 | Antony Hewish | UK | work in radio astronomy |
| | Martin Ryle | UK | |

## Physics (continued)

| YEAR | WINNER(S) | COUNTRY | ACHIEVEMENT |
|---|---|---|---|
| 1975 | Aage N. Bohr | Denmark | work on the atomic nucleus |
| | Ben R. Mottelson | Denmark | that paved the way for nuclear |
| | James Rainwater | US | fusion |
| 1976 | Burton Richter | US | discovery of new class of |
| | Samuel C.C. Ting | US | elementary particles (psi, or J) |
| 1977 | Philip W. Anderson | US | contributions to understanding the |
| | Nevill F. Mott | UK | behavior of electrons in |
| | John H. Van Vleck | US | magnetic, noncrystalline solids |
| 1978 | Pyotr L. Kapitsa | USSR | research in magnetism and low-temperature physics |
| | Arno Penzias | US | discovery of cosmic microwave background |
| | Robert Woodrow Wilson | US | radiation, providing support for the big-bang theory |
| 1979 | Sheldon Lee Glashow | US | contributions to the theory of the |
| | Abdus Salam | Pakistan | unified weak and electromagnetic |
| | Steven Weinberg | US | interactions of subatomic particles |
| 1980 | James Watson Cronin | US | demonstration of the simultaneous violation of both |
| | Val Logsdon Fitch | US | charge-conjugation and parity-inversion symmetries |
| 1981 | Nicolaas Bloembergen | US | applications of lasers |
| | Arthur L. Schawlow | US | in spectroscopy |
| | Kai M.B. Siegbahn | Sweden | development of electron spectroscopy |
| 1982 | Kenneth G. Wilson | US | analysis of continuous phase transitions |
| 1983 | Subrahmanyan Chandrasekhar | US | contributions to understanding the evolution and devolution of stars |
| | William A. Fowler | US | studies of nuclear reactions key to the formation of chemical elements |
| 1984 | Simon van der Meer | Neth. | discovery of subatomic particles W and Z, |
| | Carlo Rubbia | Italy | which supports the electroweak theory |
| 1985 | Klaus von Klitzing | W.Ger. | discovery of the quantized Hall effect, permitting exact measurements of electrical resistance |
| 1986 | Gerd Binnig | W.Ger. | development of the scanning tunneling |
| | Heinrich Rohrer | Switz. | electron microscope |
| | Ernst Ruska | W.Ger. | development of the electron microscope |
| 1987 | J. Georg Bednorz | W.Ger. | discoveries of superconductivity in |
| | Karl Alex Müller | Switz. | ceramic materials |
| 1988 | Leon Max Lederman | US | research in |
| | Melvin Schwartz | US | subatomic |
| | Jack Steinberger | US | particles |
| 1989 | Hans Georg Dehmelt | US | development of methods to isolate atoms |
| | Wolfgang Paul | W.Ger. | and subatomic particles for study |
| | Norman Foster Ramsey | US | development of the atomic clock |
| 1990 | Jerome Isaac Friedman | US | discovery of |
| | Henry Way Kendall | US | atomic |
| | Richard E. Taylor | Canada | quarks |
| 1991 | Pierre-Gilles de Gennes | France | discovery of general rules for behavior of molecules |
| 1992 | Georges Charpak | France | invention of a detector that traces subatomic particles |
| 1993 | Russell Alan Hulse | US | identification of |
| | Joseph H. Taylor, Jr. | US | binary pulsars |
| 1994 | Bertram N. Brockhouse | Canada | development of |
| | Clifford G. Shull | US | neutron-scattering techniques |
| 1995 | Martin Lewis Perl | US | discovery of the tau subatomic particle |
| | Frederick Reines | US | discovery of the neutrino subatomic particle |
| 1996 | David M. Lee | US | discovery of |
| | Douglas D. Osheroff | US | superfluidity in |
| | Robert C. Richardson | US | isotope helium-3 |
| 1997 | Steven Chu | US | process of |
| | Claude Cohen-Tannoudji | France | cooling and trapping atoms with |
| | William D. Phillips | US | laser light |
| 1998 | Robert B. Laughlin | US | discovery of fractional quantum Hall effect, showing |
| | Horst L. Störmer | US | that electrons in a low-temperature magnetic field can |
| | Daniel C. Tsui | US | form a quantum fluid with fractional electric charges |
| 1999 | Gerardus 't Hooft | Neth. | study of the quantum structure |
| | Martinus J.G. Veltman | Neth. | of electroweak interactions |
| 2000 | Zhores I. Alferov | Russia | development of fast semiconductors |
| | Herbert Kroemer | Germany | for use in microelectronics |
| | Jack S. Kilby | US | development of the integrated circuit (microchip) |
| 2001 | Eric A. Cornell | US | achievement of Bose-Einstein condensation in dilute |
| | Wolfgang Ketterle | Germany | gases of alkali atoms; early fundamental studies of |
| | Carl E. Wieman | US | the properties of the condensates |

## Physics (continued)

| YEAR | WINNER(S) | COUNTRY | ACHIEVEMENT |
|------|-----------|---------|-------------|
| 2002 | Raymond Davis, Jr. | US | pioneering contributions to astrophysics, in particular the detection of cosmic neutrinos |
| | Masatoshi Koshiba | Japan | |
| | Riccardo Giacconi | US | pioneering contributions to astrophysics, which have led to the discovery of cosmic X-ray sources |
| 2003 | Alexei A. Abrikosov | US/Russia | pioneering contributions to the theory of superconductors and superfluids |
| | Vitaly L. Ginzburg | Russia | |
| | Anthony J. Leggett | UK/US | |
| 2004 | David J. Gross | US | discovery of asymptotic freedom in the theory of the strong interaction |
| | H. David Politzer | US | |
| | Frank Wilczek | US | |
| 2005 | Roy J. Glauber | US | contributions to quantum theory of optical coherence |
| | John L. Hall | US | contributions to the development of laser-based precision spectroscopy, including the optical frequency comb technique |
| | Theodor W. Hänsch | Germany | |
| 2006 | John C. Mather | US | discovery of the blackbody form and variability of cosmic microwave background radiation |
| | George F. Smoot | US | |
| 2007 | Albert Fert | France | discovery of Giant Magnetoresistance (large resistance changes in materials composed of alternating layers of various metallic elements), a nanotechnology application |
| | Peter Grünberg | Germany | |
| 2008 | Makoto Kobayashi | Japan | research on the origin of the broken symmetry in subatomic physics that predicts three families of quarks |
| | Toshihide Maskawa | Japan | |
| | Yoichiro Nambu | US | discovery of spontaneous broken symmetry in subatomic physics |
| 2009 | Charles K. Kao | UK/US | contributions in the transmission of light in fiber optics |
| | Willard S. Boyle | Canada/US | invention of the CCD sensor |
| | George E. Smith | US | |
| 2010 | Andre Geim | Neth. | experiments with the two-dimensional material graphene |
| | Konstantin Novoselov | UK/Russia | |
| 2011 | Saul Perlmutter | US | discovery of the accelerating expansion of the universe through observations of distant supernovae |
| | Adam G. Riess | US | |
| | Brian P. Schmidt | US/Australia | |

## Chemistry

| YEAR | WINNER(S) | COUNTRY | ACHIEVEMENT |
|------|-----------|---------|-------------|
| 1901 | Jacobus H. van 't Hoff | Neth. | discovery of the laws of chemical dynamics and osmotic pressure |
| 1902 | Emil Fischer | Germany | work on sugar and purine syntheses |
| 1903 | Svante Arrhenius | Sweden | theory of electrolytic dissociation |
| 1904 | William Ramsay | UK | discovery of inert gas elements |
| 1905 | Adolf von Baeyer | Germany | work on organic dyes and hydroaromatic compounds |
| 1906 | Henri Moissan | France | isolation of fluorine; introduction of the Moissan furnace |
| 1907 | Eduard Buchner | Germany | discovery of noncellular fermentation |
| 1908 | Ernest Rutherford | UK | investigations into the disintegration of elements and the chemistry of radioactive substances |
| 1909 | Wilhelm Ostwald | Germany | pioneer work on catalysis, chemical equilibrium, and reaction velocities |
| 1910 | Otto Wallach | Germany | pioneer work in alicyclic combinations |
| 1911 | Marie Curie | France | discovery of radium and polonium; isolation of radium |
| 1912 | Victor Grignard | France | discovery of the Grignard reagents |
| | Paul Sabatier | France | method of hydrogenating organic compounds |
| 1913 | Alfred Werner | Switz. | work on the linkage of atoms in molecules |
| 1914 | Theodore W. Richards | US | accurate determination of various atomic weights |
| 1915 | Richard Willstätter | Germany | research in plant pigments, especially chlorophyll |
| 1918 | Fritz Haber | Germany | synthesis of ammonia |
| 1920 | Walther Hermann Nernst | Germany | work in thermochemistry |
| 1921 | Frederick Soddy | UK | investigation into the chemistry of radioactive substances and the occurrence and nature of isotopes |
| 1922 | Francis William Aston | UK | work with mass spectrographs; formulation of the whole-number rule |
| 1923 | Fritz Pregl | Austria | method of microanalysis of organic substances |
| 1925 | Richard Zsigmondy | Austria | elucidation of the heterogeneous nature of colloidal solutions |
| 1926 | Theodor H.E. Svedberg | Sweden | work on disperse systems |
| 1927 | Heinrich Otto Wieland | Germany | research into the constitution of bile acids |
| 1928 | Adolf Windaus | Germany | research into the constitution of sterols |
| 1929 | Hans von Euler-Chelpin | Sweden | investigations into the fermentation of sugars and the enzyme action involved |
| | Arthur Harden | UK | |

# Chemistry (continued)

| YEAR | WINNER(S) | COUNTRY | ACHIEVEMENT |
|------|-----------|---------|-------------|
| 1930 | Hans Fischer | Germany | hemin, chlorophyll research; synthesis of hemin |
| 1931 | Friedrich Bergius | Germany | } invention and development of |
| | Carl Bosch | Germany | } chemical high-pressure methods |
| 1932 | Irving Langmuir | US | discoveries and investigations in surface chemistry |
| 1934 | Harold C. Urey | US | discovery of heavy hydrogen |
| 1935 | Frédéric and Irène Joliot-Curie | France | synthesis of new radioactive elements |
| 1936 | Peter Debye | Neth. | work on dipole moments and diffraction of X-rays and electrons in gases |
| 1937 | Norman Haworth | UK | research on carbohydrates and vitamin C |
| | Paul Karrer | Switz. | research on carotenoids, flavins, and vitamins |
| 1938 | Richard Kuhn (declined) | Germany | carotenoid and vitamin research |
| 1939 | Adolf Butenandt (declined) | Germany | work on sexual hormones |
| | Leopold Ruzicka | Switz. | work on polymethylenes and higher terpenes |
| 1943 | Georg Charles von Hevesy | Hungary | use of isotopes as tracers in chemical research |
| 1944 | Otto Hahn | Germany | discovery of the fission of heavy nuclei |
| 1945 | Artturi Ilmari Virtanen | Finland | invention of the fodder preservation method |
| 1946 | John Howard Northrop | US | } preparation of enzymes and |
| | Wendell M. Stanley | US | } virus proteins in pure form |
| | James B. Sumner | US | discovery of enzyme crystallization |
| 1947 | Robert Robinson | UK | investigation of alkaloids and other plant products |
| 1948 | Arne Tiselius | Sweden | research on electrophoresis and adsorption analysis; discoveries concerning serum proteins |
| 1949 | William Francis Giauque | US | behavior of substances at extremely low temperatures |
| 1950 | Kurt Alder | W.Ger. | } discovery and development of |
| | Otto Paul Hermann Diels | W.Ger. | } diene synthesis |
| 1951 | Edwin M. McMillan | US | } discovery of and research on |
| | Glenn T. Seaborg | US | } transuranium elements |
| 1952 | A.J.P. Martin | UK | } development of partition |
| | R.L.M. Synge | UK | } chromatography |
| 1953 | Hermann Staudinger | W.Ger. | work on macromolecules |
| 1954 | Linus Pauling | US | study of the nature of the chemical bond |
| 1955 | Vincent du Vigneaud | US | first synthesis of a polypeptide hormone |
| 1956 | Cyril N. Hinshelwood | UK | } work on the kinetics of |
| | Nikolay N. Semyonov | USSR | } chemical reactions |
| 1957 | Alexander Robertus Todd | UK | work on nucleotides and nucleotide coenzymes |
| 1958 | Frederick Sanger | UK | determination of the structure of the insulin molecule |
| 1959 | Jaroslav Heyrovsky | Czech. | discovery and development of polarography |
| 1960 | Willard Frank Libby | US | development of radiocarbon dating |
| 1961 | Melvin Calvin | US | study of chemical steps that take place during photosynthesis |
| 1962 | John C. Kendrew | UK | } determination of the structure of |
| | Max Ferdinand Perutz | UK | } hemoproteins |
| 1963 | Giulio Natta | Italy | } research into the structure and synthesis of polymers |
| | Karl Ziegler | W.Ger. | } in the field of plastics |
| 1964 | Dorothy M.C. Hodgkin | UK | determination of the structure of biochemical compounds essential in combating pernicious anemia |
| 1965 | R.B. Woodward | US | synthesis of sterols, chlorophyll, and other substances |
| 1966 | Robert S. Mulliken | US | work concerning chemical bonds and the electronic structure of molecules |
| 1967 | Manfred Eigen | W.Ger. | } studies of |
| | Ronald G.W. Norrish | UK | } extremely fast |
| | George Porter | UK | } chemical reactions |
| 1968 | Lars Onsager | US | work on the theory of thermodynamics of irreversible processes |
| 1969 | Derek H.R. Barton | UK | } work in determining the actual three-dimensional |
| | Odd Hassel | Norway | } shape of molecules |
| 1970 | Luis Federico Leloir | Argentina | discovery of sugar nucleotides and their role in the biosynthesis of carbohydrates |
| 1971 | Gerhard Herzberg | Canada | research in the structure of molecules |
| 1972 | Christian B. Anfinsen | US | fundamental contributions to the study of ribonuclease |
| | Stanford Moore | US | } fundamental contributions |
| | William H. Stein | US | } to enzyme chemistry |
| 1973 | Ernst Otto Fischer | W.Ger. | } studies in the field of |
| | Geoffrey Wilkinson | UK | } organometallic chemistry |
| 1974 | Paul J. Flory | US | studies of long-chain molecules |
| 1975 | John W. Cornforth | UK | } work in |
| | Vladimir Prelog | Switz. | } stereochemistry |

## Chemistry (continued)

| YEAR | WINNER(S) | COUNTRY | ACHIEVEMENT |
|---|---|---|---|
| 1976 | William N. Lipscomb, Jr. | US | studies on the structure of boranes |
| 1977 | Ilya Prigogine | Belgium | widening the scope of thermodynamics |
| 1978 | Peter Dennis Mitchell | UK | formulation of a theory of energy transfer processes in biological systems |
| 1979 | Herbert Charles Brown | US | } introduction of compounds of boron and |
| | Georg Wittig | W.Ger. |   phosphorus in the synthesis of organic substances |
| 1980 | Paul Berg | US | first preparation of a hybrid DNA |
| | Walter Gilbert | US | } development of chemical and |
| | Frederick Sanger | UK |   biological analyses of DNA structure |
| 1981 | Kenichi Fukui | Japan | } orbital symmetry interpretation |
| | Roald Hoffmann | US |   of chemical reactions |
| 1982 | Aaron Klug | UK | determination of the structure of biological substances |
| 1983 | Henry Taube | US | study of electron transfer reactions |
| 1984 | Bruce Merrifield | US | development of a method of polypeptide synthesis |
| 1985 | Herbert A. Hauptman | US | } development of a way to map the |
| | Jerome Karle | US |   chemical structure of small molecules |
| 1986 | Dudley R. Herschbach | US | } development of methods |
| | Yuan T. Lee | US |   for analyzing basic |
| | John C. Polanyi | Canada |   chemical reactions |
| 1987 | Donald J. Cram | US | } development of molecules |
| | Jean-Marie Lehn | France |   that can link with |
| | Charles J. Pedersen | US |   other molecules |
| 1988 | Johann Deisenhofer | W.Ger. | } discovery of structure |
| | Robert Huber | W.Ger. |   proteins needed |
| | Hartmut Michel | W.Ger. |   in photosynthesis |
| 1989 | Sidney Altman | US | } discovery of certain |
| | Thomas Robert Cech | US |   basic properties of RNA |
| 1990 | Elias James Corey | US | development of retrosynthetic analysis for synthesis of complex molecules |
| 1991 | Richard R. Ernst | Switz. | improvements in nuclear magnetic resonance spectroscopy |
| 1992 | Rudolph A. Marcus | US | explanation of how electrons transfer between molecules |
| 1993 | Kary B. Mullis | US | } invention of techniques for |
| | Michael Smith | Canada |   gene study and manipulation |
| 1994 | George A. Olah | US | development of techniques to study hydrocarbon molecules |
| 1995 | Paul Crutzen | Neth. | } explanation of processes |
| | Mario Molina | US |   that deplete Earth's |
| | F. Sherwood Rowland | US |   ozone layer |
| 1996 | Robert F. Curl, Jr. | US | } discovery of new |
| | Harold W. Kroto | UK |   carbon compounds |
| | Richard E. Smalley | US |   called fullerenes |
| 1997 | Paul D. Boyer | US | } explanation of the enzymatic |
| | John E. Walker | UK |   conversion of adenosine triphosphate |
| | Jens C. Skou | Denmark | discovery of sodium-potassium-activated adenosine triphosphatase |
| 1998 | Walter Kohn | US | development of the density-functional theory |
| | John A. Pople | UK | development of computational methods in quantum chemistry |
| 1999 | Ahmed H. Zewail | Egypt/US | study of the transition states of chemical reactions using femtosecond spectroscopy |
| 2000 | Alan J. Heeger | US | } discovery of plastics |
| | Alan G. MacDiarmid | US |   that conduct |
| | Hideki Shirakawa | Japan |   electricity |
| 2001 | William S. Knowles | US | } work on chirally catalyzed |
| | Ryoji Noyori | Japan |   hydrogenation reactions |
| | K. Barry Sharpless | US | work on chirally catalyzed oxidation reactions |
| 2002 | John B. Fenn | US | } development of soft desorption ionization methods |
| | Koichi Tanaka | Japan |   for mass spectrometric analyses of biological macromolecules |
| | Kurt Wüthrich | Switz. | development of nuclear magnetic resonance spectroscopy for determining the three-dimensional structure of biological macromolecules in solution |
| 2003 | Peter Agre | US | } cell membrane channel |
| | Roderick MacKinnon | US |   discoveries |
| 2004 | Aaron Ciechanover | Israel | } discovery of |
| | Avram Hershko | Israel |   ubiquitin-mediated |
| | Irwin Rose | US |   protein degradation |

## Chemistry (continued)

| YEAR | WINNER(S) | COUNTRY | ACHIEVEMENT |
|---|---|---|---|
| 2005 | Yves Chauvin | France | development of the |
| | Robert H. Grubbs | US | metathesis method in |
| | Richard R. Schrock | US | organic synthesis |
| 2006 | Roger D. Kornberg | US | studies of the molecular basis of eukaryotic transcription |
| 2007 | Gerhard Ertl | Germany | studies of chemical processes on solid surfaces |
| 2008 | Martin Chalfie | US | discovery and development |
| | Osamu Shimomura | US | of GFP, the green |
| | Roger Y. Tsien | US | fluorescent protein |
| 2009 | Venkatraman Ramakrishnan | US | studies of the structure |
| | Thomas A. Steitz | US | and function |
| | Ada E. Yonath | Israel | of the ribosome |
| 2010 | Richard F. Heck | US | development of palladium-catalyzed |
| | Ei-ichi Negishi | Japan | cross couplings for |
| | Akira Suzuki | Japan | organic synthesis |
| 2011 | Dan Shechtman | Israel | discovery of quasicrystals |

## Physiology or Medicine

| YEAR | WINNER(S) | COUNTRY | ACHIEVEMENT |
|---|---|---|---|
| 1901 | Emil von Behring | Germany | work on serum therapy |
| 1902 | Ronald Ross | UK | discovery of how malaria enters an organism |
| 1903 | Niels Ryberg Finsen | Denmark | treatment of skin diseases with light |
| 1904 | Ivan Petrovich Pavlov | Russia | work on the physiology of digestion |
| 1905 | Robert Koch | Germany | tuberculosis research |
| 1906 | Camillo Golgi | Italy | work on the structure |
| | Santiago Ramón y Cajal | Spain | of the nervous system |
| 1907 | Alphonse Laveran | France | discovery of the role of protozoa in diseases |
| 1908 | Paul Ehrlich | Germany | work on |
| | Élie Metchnikoff | Russia | immunity |
| 1909 | Emil Theodor Kocher | Switz. | work on aspects of the thyroid gland |
| 1910 | Albrecht Kossel | Germany | researches in cellular chemistry |
| 1911 | Allvar Gullstrand | Sweden | work on dioptrics of the eye |
| 1912 | Alexis Carrel | France | work on the vascular suture; the transplantation of organs |
| 1913 | Charles Richet | France | work on anaphylaxis |
| 1914 | Robert Bárány | Austria-Hungary | work on vestibular apparatus |
| 1919 | Jules Bordet | Belgium | work on immunity factors in blood serum |
| 1920 | August Krogh | Denmark | discovery of the capillary motor-regulating mechanism |
| 1922 | A.V. Hill | UK | discoveries concerning heat production in muscles |
| | Otto Meyerhof | Germany | work on metabolism of lactic acid in muscles |
| 1923 | Frederick G. Banting | Canada | discovery of |
| | J.J.R. Macleod | UK | insulin |
| 1924 | Willem Einthoven | Neth. | discovery of the electrocardiogram mechanism |
| 1926 | Johannes Fibiger | Denmark | contributions to cancer research |
| 1927 | Julius Wagner-Jauregg | Austria | work on malaria inoculation in dementia paralytica |
| 1928 | Charles-Jules-Henri Nicolle | France | work on typhus |
| 1929 | Christiaan Eijkman | Neth. | discovery of the antineuritic vitamin |
| | Frederick Gowland Hopkins | UK | discovery of growth-stimulating vitamins |
| 1930 | Karl Landsteiner | US | discovery of human blood groups |
| 1931 | Otto Warburg | Germany | discovery of the nature of the respiratory enzyme |
| 1932 | Edgar Douglas Adrian | UK | discoveries regarding |
| | Charles Scott Sherrington | UK | the functions of neurons |
| 1933 | Thomas Hunt Morgan | US | discoveries concerning chromosomal heredity functions |
| 1934 | George Richards Minot | US | discoveries concerning |
| | William P. Murphy | US | liver treatment |
| | George H. Whipple | US | for anemia |
| 1935 | Hans Spemann | Germany | discovery of the organizer effect in embryos |
| 1936 | Henry Dale | UK | work on the chemical |
| | Otto Loewi | Germany | transmission of nerve impulses |
| 1937 | Albert Szent-Gyorgyi | Hungary | work on biological combustion |
| 1938 | Corneille Heymans | Belgium | discovery of the role of sinus and aortic mechanisms in respiration regulation |
| 1939 | Gerhard Domagk (declined) | Germany | discovery of the antibacterial effect of Prontosil |
| 1943 | Henrik Dam | Denmark | discovery of vitamin K |
| | Edward Adelbert Doisy | US | discovery of the chemical nature of vitamin K |
| 1944 | Joseph Erlanger | US | research on differentiated |
| | Herbert S. Gasser | US | functions of nerve fibers |

## Physiology or Medicine (continued)

| YEAR | WINNER(S) | COUNTRY | ACHIEVEMENT |
|---|---|---|---|
| 1945 | Ernst Boris Chain | UK | discovery of |
| | Alexander Fleming | UK | penicillin and its |
| | Howard Walter Florey | Australia | curative value |
| 1946 | Hermann J. Muller | US | production of mutations by X-ray irradiation |
| 1947 | Carl and Gerty Cori | US | discovery of how glycogen is catalytically converted |
| | Bernardo A. Houssay | Argentina | discovery of the pituitary hormone function in sugar metabolism |
| 1948 | Paul Hermann Müller | Switz. | discovery of properties of DDT |
| 1949 | António Egas Moniz | Portugal | discovery of therapeutic value in leucotomy for psychoses |
| | Walter Rudolf Hess | Switz. | discovery of the function of the interbrain |
| 1950 | Philip Showalter Hench | US | research on adrenal cortex |
| | Edward Calvin Kendall | US | hormones, their structure, and |
| | Tadeus Reichstein | Switz. | their biological effects |
| 1951 | Max Theiler | South Africa | yellow fever discoveries |
| 1952 | Selman A. Waksman | US | discovery of streptomycin |
| 1953 | Hans Adolf Krebs | UK | discovery of the citric-acid cycle |
| | Fritz Albert Lipmann | US | discovery of coenzyme A metabolism |
| 1954 | John Franklin Enders | US | cultivation of the |
| | Frederick C. Robbins | US | poliomyelitis virus in |
| | Thomas H. Weller | US | tissue cultures |
| 1955 | Axel H.T. Theorell | Sweden | discoveries concerning oxidation enzymes |
| 1956 | André F. Cournand | US | discoveries concerning |
| | Werner Forssmann | W.Ger. | heart catheterization and |
| | Dickinson W. Richards | US | circulatory changes |
| 1957 | Daniel Bovet | Italy | production of synthetic curare |
| 1958 | George Wells Beadle | US | discovery of the genetic regulation |
| | Edward L. Tatum | US | of chemical processes |
| | Joshua Lederberg | US | discoveries concerning genetic recombination |
| 1959 | Arthur Kornberg | US | work on producing nucleic |
| | Severo Ochoa | US | acids artificially |
| 1960 | Macfarlane Burnet | Australia | discovery of acquired immunity to |
| | Peter B. Medawar | UK | tissue transplants |
| 1961 | Georg von Békésy | US | discovery of functions of the inner ear |
| 1962 | Francis H.C. Crick | UK | discoveries concerning |
| | James Dewey Watson | US | the molecular structure |
| | Maurice Wilkins | UK | of DNA |
| 1963 | John Carew Eccles | Australia | study of the transmission |
| | Alan Hodgkin | UK | of impulses along |
| | Andrew F. Huxley | UK | a nerve fiber |
| 1964 | Konrad Bloch | US | discoveries concerning |
| | Feodor Lynen | W.Ger. | cholesterol and fatty-acid metabolism |
| 1965 | François Jacob | France | discoveries concerning |
| | André Lwoff | France | regulatory activities |
| | Jacques Monod | France | of the body cells |
| 1966 | Charles B. Huggins | US | research on causes and |
| | Peyton Rous | US | treatment of cancer |
| 1967 | Ragnar Arthur Granit | Sweden | discoveries about chemical |
| | Haldan Keffer Hartline | US | and physiological visual |
| | George Wald | US | processes in the eye |
| 1968 | Robert William Holley | US | deciphering |
| | Har Gobind Khorana | US | of the |
| | Marshall W. Nirenberg | US | genetic code |
| 1969 | Max Delbrück | US | research and discoveries |
| | A.D. Hershey | US | concerning viruses and |
| | Salvador Luria | US | viral diseases |
| 1970 | Julius Axelrod | US | discoveries concerning |
| | Ulf von Euler | Sweden | the chemistry of |
| | Bernard Katz | UK | nerve transmission |
| 1971 | Earl W. Sutherland, Jr. | US | discoveries concerning the action of hormones |
| 1972 | Gerald M. Edelman | US | research on the chemical |
| | Rodney Robert Porter | UK | structure of antibodies |
| 1973 | Karl von Frisch | Austria | discoveries in |
| | Konrad Lorenz | Austria | animal behavior |
| | Nikolaas Tinbergen | UK | patterns |
| 1974 | Albert Claude | US | research on the structural |
| | Christian René de Duve | Belgium | and functional organization |
| | George E. Palade | US | of cells |

## Physiology or Medicine (continued)

| YEAR | WINNER(S) | COUNTRY | ACHIEVEMENT |
|---|---|---|---|
| 1975 | David Baltimore | US | discoveries concerning the interaction between |
| | Renato Dulbecco | US | tumor viruses and the genetic |
| | Howard Martin Temin | US | material of the cell |
| 1976 | Baruch S. Blumberg | US | studies of the origin and |
| | D. Carleton Gajdusek | US | spread of infectious diseases |
| 1977 | Roger C.L. Guillemin | US | research on pituitary |
| | Andrew Victor Schally | US | hormones |
| | Rosalyn S. Yalow | US | development of radioimmunoassay |
| 1978 | Werner Arber | Switz. | discovery and application |
| | Daniel Nathans | US | of enzymes that |
| | Hamilton O. Smith | US | fragment DNA |
| 1979 | Allan M. Cormack | US | development of |
| | Godfrey N. Hounsfield | UK | the CAT scan |
| 1980 | Baruj Benacerraf | US | investigations of genetic |
| | Jean Dausset | France | control of the response of the |
| | George Davis Snell | US | immune system to foreign substances |
| 1981 | David Hunter Hubel | US | discoveries concerning the processing of visual |
| | Torsten Nils Wiesel | Sweden | information by the brain |
| | Roger Wolcott Sperry | US | discoveries concerning cerebral hemisphere functions |
| 1982 | Sune K. Bergström | Sweden | discoveries concerning the biochemistry |
| | Bengt I. Samuelsson | Sweden | and physiology of |
| | John Robert Vane | UK | of prostaglandins |
| 1983 | Barbara McClintock | US | discovery of mobile plant genes that affect heredity |
| 1984 | Niels K. Jerne | Denmark | theory and development |
| | Georges J.F. Köhler | W.Ger. | of a technique |
| | César Milstein | UK/ | for producing |
| | | Argentina | monoclonal antibodies |
| 1985 | Michael S. Brown | US | discovery of cell receptors relating to |
| | Joseph L. Goldstein | US | cholesterol metabolism |
| 1986 | Stanley Cohen | US | discovery of chemical agents |
| | Rita Levi-Montalcini | Italy | that help regulate the growth of cells |
| 1987 | Susumu Tonegawa | Japan | study of genetic aspects of antibodies |
| 1988 | James Black | UK | development of new |
| | Gertrude Belle Elion | US | classes of drugs for |
| | George H. Hitchings | US | combating disease |
| 1989 | J. Michael Bishop | US | study of cancer-causing |
| | Harold Varmus | US | genes called oncogenes |
| 1990 | Joseph E. Murray | US | development of kidney and |
| | E. Donnall Thomas | US | bone-marrow transplants |
| 1991 | Erwin Neher | Germany | discovery of how cells |
| | Bert Sakmann | Germany | communicate, as related to diseases |
| 1992 | Edmond H. Fischer | US | discovery of a class of enzymes |
| | Edwin Gerhard Krebs | US | called protein kinases |
| 1993 | Richard J. Roberts | UK | discovery of "split," or |
| | Phillip A. Sharp | US | interrupted, genetic structure |
| 1994 | Alfred G. Gilman | US | discovery of cell signalers |
| | Martin Rodbell | US | called G-proteins |
| 1995 | Edward B. Lewis | US | identification of genes |
| | Christiane Nüsslein-Volhard | Germany | that control the body's |
| | Eric F. Wieschaus | US | early structural development |
| 1996 | Peter C. Doherty | Australia | discovery of how the immune |
| | Rolf M. Zinkernagel | Switz. | system recognizes virus-infected cells |
| 1997 | Stanley B. Prusiner | US | discovery of the prion, a type of disease-causing protein |
| 1998 | Robert F. Furchgott | US | discovery that nitric oxide |
| | Louis J. Ignarro | US | acts as a signaling molecule in |
| | Ferid Murad | US | the cardiovascular system |
| 1999 | Günter Blobel | US | discovery that proteins help govern cellular organization |
| 2000 | Arvid Carlsson | Sweden | discovery of how signals |
| | Paul Greengard | US | are transmitted between nerve |
| | Eric Kandel | US | cells in the brain |
| 2001 | Leland H. Hartwell | US | discovery of key |
| | R. Timothy Hunt | UK | regulators of |
| | Paul M. Nurse | UK | the cell cycle |
| 2002 | Sydney Brenner | UK | discoveries concerning how genes |
| | H. Robert Horvitz | US | regulate and program organ |
| | John E. Sulston | UK | development and cell death |
| 2003 | Paul C. Lauterbur | US | discoveries concerning magnetic |
| | Peter Mansfield | UK | resonance imaging |

## Physiology or Medicine (continued)

| YEAR | WINNER(S) | COUNTRY | ACHIEVEMENT |
|---|---|---|---|
| 2004 | Richard Axel | US | discoveries of odorant receptors and the |
| | Linda B. Buck | US | organization of the olfactory system |
| 2005 | Barry J. Marshall | Australia | discovery of the bacterium Helicobacter pylori and its |
| | J. Robin Warren | Australia | role in peptic ulcer disease and gastritis |
| 2006 | Andrew Z. Fire | US | discovery of RNA interference: gene silencing |
| | Craig C. Mello | US | by double-stranded RNA |
| 2007 | Mario R. Capecchi | US | discoveries of principles for introducing |
| | Martin J. Evans | UK | specific gene modifications |
| | Oliver Smithies | US | using embryonic stem cells |
| 2008 | Françoise Barré-Sinoussi | France | discovery of the human |
| | Luc Montagnier | France | immunodeficiency virus (HIV) |
| | Harald zur Hausen | Germany | research supporting the theory that human papillomaviruses cause cervical cancer |
| 2009 | Elizabeth H. Blackburn | US/Australia | discovery of the protection |
| | Carol W. Greider | US | of chromosomes by telomeres |
| | Jack W. Szostak | US | and the enzyme telomerase |
| 2010 | Robert G. Edwards | UK | development of the technique of in vitro fertilization |
| 2011 | Bruce A. Beutler | US | discoveries concerning the activation of innate |
| | Jules A. Hoffmann | Luxembourg | immunity |
| | Ralph M. Steinman (posthumously) | Canada | discovery of the dendritic cell and its role in adaptive immunity |

## Literature

| YEAR | WINNER(S) | COUNTRY | FIELD |
|---|---|---|---|
| 1901 | Sully Prudhomme | France | poetry |
| 1902 | Theodor Mommsen | Germany | history |
| 1903 | Bjørnstjerne Martinus Bjørnson | Norway | prose fiction, poetry, drama |
| 1904 | José Echegaray y Eizaguirre | Spain | drama |
| | Frédéric Mistral | France | poetry |
| 1905 | Henryk Sienkiewicz | Poland | prose fiction |
| 1906 | Giosuè Carducci | Italy | poetry |
| 1907 | Rudyard Kipling | UK | poetry, prose fiction |
| 1908 | Rudolf Christoph Eucken | Germany | philosophy |
| 1909 | Selma Lagerlöf | Sweden | prose fiction |
| 1910 | Paul Johann Ludwig von Heyse | Germany | poetry, prose fiction, drama |
| 1911 | Maurice Maeterlinck | Belgium | drama |
| 1912 | Gerhart Hauptmann | Germany | drama |
| 1913 | Rabindranath Tagore | India | poetry |
| 1915 | Romain Rolland | France | prose fiction |
| 1916 | Verner von Heidenstam | Sweden | poetry |
| 1917 | Karl Gjellerup | Denmark | prose fiction |
| | Henrik Pontoppidan | Denmark | prose fiction |
| 1918 | Erik Axel Karlfeldt (declined) | Sweden | poetry |
| 1919 | Carl Spitteler | Switzerland | poetry, prose fiction |
| 1920 | Knut Hamsun | Norway | prose fiction |
| 1921 | Anatole France | France | prose fiction |
| 1922 | Jacinto Benavente y Martínez | Spain | drama |
| 1923 | William Butler Yeats | Ireland | poetry |
| 1924 | Wladyslaw Stanislaw Reymont | Poland | prose fiction |
| 1925 | George Bernard Shaw | Ireland | drama |
| 1926 | Grazia Deledda | Italy | prose fiction |
| 1927 | Henri Bergson | France | philosophy |
| 1928 | Sigrid Undset | Norway | prose fiction |
| 1929 | Thomas Mann | Germany | prose fiction |
| 1930 | Sinclair Lewis | US | prose fiction |
| 1931 | Erik Axel Karlfeldt (posthumously) | Sweden | poetry |
| 1932 | John Galsworthy | UK | prose fiction |
| 1933 | Ivan Alekseyevich Bunin | USSR | poetry, prose fiction |
| 1934 | Luigi Pirandello | Italy | drama |
| 1936 | Eugene O'Neill | US | drama |
| 1937 | Roger Martin du Gard | France | prose fiction |
| 1938 | Pearl Buck | US | prose fiction |
| 1939 | Frans Eemil Sillanpää | Finland | prose fiction |
| 1944 | Johannes V. Jensen | Denmark | prose fiction |
| 1945 | Gabriela Mistral | Chile | poetry |
| 1946 | Hermann Hesse | Switzerland | prose fiction |
| 1947 | André Gide | France | prose |

## Literature (continued)

| YEAR | WINNER(S) | COUNTRY | FIELD |
|---|---|---|---|
| 1948 | T.S. Eliot | UK | poetry, criticism |
| 1949 | William Faulkner | US | prose fiction |
| 1950 | Bertrand Russell | UK | philosophy |
| 1951 | Pär Lagerkvist | Sweden | prose fiction |
| 1952 | François Mauriac | France | poetry, prose fiction, drama |
| 1953 | Winston Churchill | UK | history, oration |
| 1954 | Ernest Hemingway | US | prose fiction |
| 1955 | Halldór Laxness | Iceland | prose fiction |
| 1956 | Juan Ramón Jiménez | Spain | poetry |
| 1957 | Albert Camus | France | prose fiction, drama |
| 1958 | Boris L. Pasternak (declined) | USSR | prose fiction, poetry |
| 1959 | Salvatore Quasimodo | Italy | poetry |
| 1960 | Saint-John Perse | France | poetry |
| 1961 | Ivo Andric | Yugoslavia | prose fiction |
| 1962 | John Steinbeck | US | prose fiction |
| 1963 | George Seferis | Greece | poetry |
| 1964 | Jean-Paul Sartre (declined) | France | philosophy, drama |
| 1965 | Mikhail A. Sholokhov | USSR | prose fiction |
| 1966 | S.Y. Agnon | Israel | prose fiction |
|  | Nelly Sachs | Sweden | poetry |
| 1967 | Miguel Ángel Asturias | Guatemala | prose fiction |
| 1968 | Yasunari Kawabata | Japan | prose fiction |
| 1969 | Samuel Beckett | Ireland | prose fiction, drama |
| 1970 | Aleksandr I. Solzhenitsyn | USSR | prose fiction |
| 1971 | Pablo Neruda | Chile | poetry |
| 1972 | Heinrich Böll | West Germany | prose fiction |
| 1973 | Patrick White | Australia | prose fiction |
| 1974 | Eyvind Johnson | Sweden | prose fiction |
|  | Harry Martinson | Sweden | prose fiction, poetry |
| 1975 | Eugenio Montale | Italy | poetry |
| 1976 | Saul Bellow | US | prose fiction |
| 1977 | Vicente Aleixandre | Spain | poetry |
| 1978 | Isaac Bashevis Singer | US | prose fiction |
| 1979 | Odysseus Elytis | Greece | poetry |
| 1980 | Czeslaw Milosz | US | poetry |
| 1981 | Elias Canetti | Bulgaria | prose |
| 1982 | Gabriel García Márquez | Colombia | prose fiction, journalism, social criticism |
| 1983 | William Golding | UK | prose fiction |
| 1984 | Jaroslav Seifert | Czechoslovakia | poetry |
| 1985 | Claude Simon | France | prose fiction |
| 1986 | Wole Soyinka | Nigeria | drama, poetry |
| 1987 | Joseph Brodsky | US | poetry, prose |
| 1988 | Naguib Mahfouz | Egypt | prose fiction |
| 1989 | Camilo José Cela | Spain | prose fiction |
| 1990 | Octavio Paz | Mexico | poetry, prose |
| 1991 | Nadine Gordimer | South Africa | prose fiction |
| 1992 | Derek Walcott | Saint Lucia | poetry |
| 1993 | Toni Morrison | US | prose fiction |
| 1994 | Kenzaburo Oe | Japan | prose fiction |
| 1995 | Seamus Heaney | Ireland | poetry |
| 1996 | Wislawa Szymborska | Poland | poetry |
| 1997 | Dario Fo | Italy | drama |
| 1998 | José Saramago | Portugal | prose fiction |
| 1999 | Günter Grass | Germany | prose fiction |
| 2000 | Gao Xingjian | France | prose fiction, drama |
| 2001 | V.S. Naipaul | UK | prose fiction |
| 2002 | Imre Kertész | Hungary | prose fiction |
| 2003 | J.M. Coetzee | South Africa | prose fiction |
| 2004 | Elfriede Jelinek | Austria | prose fiction, drama |
| 2005 | Harold Pinter | UK | drama |
| 2006 | Orhan Pamuk | Turkey | prose fiction |
| 2007 | Doris Lessing | UK | prose fiction, social criticism |
| 2008 | Jean-Marie Gustave Le Clézio | France/Mauritius | prose fiction, essays |
| 2009 | Herta Müller | Germany | poetry, prose |
| 2010 | Mario Vargas Llosa | Peru | poetry, prose |
| 2011 | Tomas Tranströmer | Sweden | poetry |

## Peace

| YEAR | WINNER(S) | COUNTRY |
|---|---|---|
| 1901 | Henri Dunant | Switzerland |
| | Frédéric Passy | France |
| 1902 | Élie Ducommun | Switzerland |
| | Charles-Albert Gobat | Switzerland |
| 1903 | Randal Cremer | UK |
| 1904 | Institute of International Law | (founded 1873) |
| 1905 | Bertha, Freifrau von Suttner | Austria-Hungary |
| 1906 | Theodore Roosevelt | US |
| 1907 | Ernesto Teodoro Moneta | Italy |
| | Louis Renault | France |
| 1908 | Klas Pontus Arnoldson | Sweden |
| | Fredrik Bajer | Denmark |
| 1909 | Auguste-Marie-François Beernaert | Belgium |
| | Paul-H.-B. d'Estournelles de Constant | France |
| 1910 | International Peace Bureau | (founded 1891) |
| 1911 | Tobias Michael Carel Asser | The Netherlands |
| | Alfred Hermann Fried | Austria-Hungary |
| 1912 | Elihu Root | US |
| 1913 | Henri-Marie Lafontaine | Belgium |
| 1917 | International Committee of the Red Cross | (founded 1863) |
| 1919 | Woodrow Wilson | US |
| 1920 | Léon Bourgeois | France |
| 1921 | Karl Hjalmar Branting | Sweden |
| | Christian Lous Lange | Norway |
| 1922 | Fridtjof Nansen | Norway |
| 1925 | Austen Chamberlain | UK |
| | Charles G. Dawes | US |
| 1926 | Aristide Briand | France |
| | Gustav Stresemann | Germany |
| 1927 | Ferdinand-Édouard Buisson | France |
| | Ludwig Quidde | Germany |
| 1929 | Frank B. Kellogg | US |
| 1930 | Nathan Söderblom | Sweden |
| 1931 | Jane Addams | US |
| | Nicholas Murray Butler | US |
| 1933 | Norman Angell | UK |
| 1934 | Arthur Henderson | UK |
| 1935 | Carl von Ossietzky | Germany |
| 1936 | Carlos Saavedra Lamas | Argentina |
| 1937 | Robert Gascoyne-Cecil | UK |
| 1938 | Nansen International Office for Refugees | (founded 1931) |
| 1944 | International Committee of the Red Cross | (founded 1863) |
| 1945 | Cordell Hull | US |
| 1946 | Emily Greene Balch | US |
| | John R. Mott | US |
| 1947 | American Friends Service Committee | US |
| | Friends Service Council | UK |
| 1949 | John Boyd Orr | UK |
| 1950 | Ralph Bunche | US |
| 1951 | Léon Jouhaux | France |
| 1952 | Albert Schweitzer | France |
| 1953 | George C. Marshall | US |
| 1954 | Office of the United Nations High Commissioner for Refugees | (founded 1951) |
| 1957 | Lester B. Pearson | Canada |
| 1958 | Dominique Pire | Belgium |
| 1959 | Philip John Noel-Baker | UK |
| 1960 | Albert John Luthuli | South Africa |
| 1961 | Dag Hammarskjöld (posthumously) | Sweden |
| 1962 | Linus Pauling | US |

| YEAR | WINNER(S) | COUNTRY |
|---|---|---|
| 1963 | International Committee of the Red Cross | (founded 1863) |
| | League of Red Cross Societies | (founded 1919) |
| 1964 | Martin Luther King, Jr. | US |
| 1965 | United Nations Children's Fund | (founded 1946) |
| 1968 | René Cassin | France |
| 1969 | International Labour Organisation | (founded 1919) |
| 1970 | Norman Ernest Borlaug | US |
| 1971 | Willy Brandt | West Germany |
| 1973 | Henry Kissinger | US |
| | Le Duc Tho (declined) | North Vietnam |
| 1974 | Seán MacBride | Ireland |
| | Eisaku Sato | Japan |
| 1975 | Andrey Dmitriyevich Sakharov | USSR |
| 1976 | Mairéad Corrigan | Northern Ireland |
| | Betty Williams | Northern Ireland |
| 1977 | Amnesty International | (founded 1961) |
| 1978 | Menachem Begin | Israel |
| | Anwar el-Sadat | Egypt |
| 1979 | Mother Teresa | India |
| 1980 | Adolfo Pérez Esquivel | Argentina |
| 1981 | Office of the United Nations High Commissioner for Refugees | (founded 1951) |
| 1982 | Alfonso García Robles | Mexico |
| | Alva Myrdal | Sweden |
| 1983 | Lech Walesa | Poland |
| 1984 | Desmond Tutu | South Africa |
| 1985 | International Physicians for the Prevention of Nuclear War | (founded 1980) |
| 1986 | Elie Wiesel | US |
| 1987 | Oscar Arias Sánchez | Costa Rica |
| 1988 | United Nations Peace-keeping Forces | |
| 1989 | Dalai Lama | Tibet |
| 1990 | Mikhail Gorbachev | USSR |
| 1991 | Aung San Suu Kyi | Myanmar (Burma) |
| 1992 | Rigoberta Menchú | Guatemala |
| 1993 | F.W. de Klerk | South Africa |
| | Nelson Mandela | South Africa |
| 1994 | Yasir Arafat | Palestinian territories |
| | Shimon Peres | Israel |
| | Yitzhak Rabin | Israel |
| 1995 | Pugwash Conferences | (founded 1957) |
| | Joseph Rotblat | UK |
| 1996 | Carlos Filipe Ximenes Belo | East Timor |
| | José Ramos-Horta | East Timor |
| 1997 | International Campaign to Ban Landmines | (founded 1992) |
| | Jody Williams | US |
| 1998 | John Hume | Northern Ireland |
| | David Trimble | Northern Ireland |
| 1999 | Doctors Without Borders | (founded 1971) |
| 2000 | Kim Dae Jung | Republic of Korea |
| 2001 | Kofi Annan | Ghana |
| | United Nations | (founded 1945) |
| 2002 | Jimmy Carter | US |

## Peace (continued)

| YEAR | WINNER(S) | COUNTRY | YEAR | WINNER(S) | COUNTRY |
|------|-----------|---------|------|-----------|---------|
| 2003 | Shirin Ebadi | Iran | 2007 | Albert Arnold (Al) Gore, Jr. | US |
| 2004 | Wangari Maathai | Kenya | (cont.) | | |
| 2005 | Mohamed ElBaradei | Egypt | 2008 | Martti Ahtisaari | Finland |
| | International Atomic | (founded 1957) | 2009 | Barack H. Obama | US |
| | Energy Agency | | 2010 | Liu Xiaobo | China |
| 2006 | Muhammad Yunus | Bangladesh | 2011 | Leymah Gbowee | Liberia |
| | Grameen Bank | (founded 1976) | | Tawakkul Karman | Yemen |
| 2007 | Intergovernmental Panel | (founded 1988) | | Ellen Johnson Sirleaf | Liberia |
| | on Climate Change | | | | |

## Economics

| YEAR | WINNER(S) | COUNTRY | ACHIEVEMENT |
|------|-----------|---------|-------------|
| 1969 | Ragnar Frisch | Norway | work in |
| | Jan Tinbergen | Neth. | econometrics |
| 1970 | Paul Samuelson | US | work in scientific analysis of economic theory |
| 1971 | Simon Kuznets | US | extensive research on the economic growth of nations |
| 1972 | Kenneth J. Arrow | US | contributions to general economic |
| | John R. Hicks | UK | equilibrium theory and welfare theory |
| 1973 | Wassily Leontief | US | development of input-output analysis |
| 1974 | Friedrich von Hayek | UK | pioneering analysis of the interdependence of |
| | Gunnar Myrdal | Sweden | economic, social, and institutional phenomena |
| 1975 | Leonid V. Kantorovich | USSR | contributions to the theory of |
| | Tjalling C. Koopmans | US | optimum allocation of resources |
| 1976 | Milton Friedman | US | work in consumption analysis and economic stabilization |
| 1977 | James Edward Meade | UK | contributions to the theory |
| | Bertil Ohlin | Sweden | of international trade |
| 1978 | Herbert A. Simon | US | study of decision-making in economic organizations |
| 1979 | Arthur Lewis | UK | research into analyses of economic processes |
| | Theodore W. Schultz | US | in developing nations |
| 1980 | Lawrence Robert Klein | US | creation of empirical models of business fluctuations |
| 1981 | James Tobin | US | portfolio-selection theory of investment |
| 1982 | George J. Stigler | US | studies of economic effects of governmental regulation |
| 1983 | Gerard Debreu | US | mathematical proof of the supply-and-demand theory |
| 1984 | Richard Stone | UK | development of national income accounting systems |
| 1985 | Franco Modigliani | US | analyses of household savings and financial markets |
| 1986 | James M. Buchanan, Jr. | US | development of the public-choice theory bridging economics and political science |
| 1987 | Robert Merton Solow | US | contributions to the theory of economic growth |
| 1988 | Maurice Allais | France | study of the theory of markets and efficient resource use |
| 1989 | Trygve Haavelmo | Norway | development of statistical techniques for economic forecasting |
| 1990 | Harry M. Markowitz | US | study of financial |
| | Merton H. Miller | US | markets and investment |
| | William F. Sharpe | US | decision making |
| 1991 | Ronald Coase | US | application of economic principles to the study of law |
| 1992 | Gary S. Becker | US | application of economic theory to social sciences |
| 1993 | Robert William Fogel | US | contributions to |
| | Douglass C. North | US | economic history |
| 1994 | John C. Harsanyi | US | development |
| | John F. Nash | US | of game |
| | Reinhard Selten | Germany | theory |
| 1995 | Robert E. Lucas, Jr. | US | incorporation of rational expectations in macroeconomic theory |
| 1996 | James A. Mirrlees | UK | contributions to the theory of incentives under |
| | William Vickrey (posthumously) | US | conditions of asymmetric information |
| 1997 | Robert C. Merton | US | method for determining the value of |
| | Myron S. Scholes | US | stock options and other derivatives |
| 1998 | Amartya Sen | India | contribution to welfare economics |
| 1999 | Robert A. Mundell | Canada | analysis of optimum currency areas and of policy under different exchange-rate regimes |
| 2000 | James J. Heckman | US | development of methods of statistical |
| | Daniel L. McFadden | US | analysis of individual and household behavior |
| 2001 | George A. Akerlof | US | analyses of |
| | A. Michael Spence | US | markets with asymmetric |
| | Joseph E. Stiglitz | US | information |

## Economics (continued)

| YEAR | WINNER(S) | COUNTRY | ACHIEVEMENT |
|------|-----------|---------|-------------|
| 2002 | Daniel Kahneman | US/Israel | psychological study of economic decision making |
|      | Vernon L. Smith | US | establishment of laboratory experiments for empirical economic analysis of alternative market mechanisms |
| 2003 | Robert F. Engle | US | methods of analysis of economic time series with time-varying volatility |
|      | Clive W.J. Granger | UK | methods of analysis of economic time series with common trends |
| 2004 | Finn E. Kydland | Norway | macroeconomic analysis of the time consistency of economic policy and the driving forces behind business cycles |
|      | Edward C. Prescott | US | |
| 2005 | Robert J. Aumann | Israel/US | enhancement of the understanding of conflict and cooperation through game-theory analysis |
|      | Thomas C. Schelling | US | |
| 2006 | Edmund S. Phelps | US | analysis of intertemporal tradeoffs in macroeconomics |
| 2007 | Leonid Hurwicz | US | research that |
|      | Eric S. Maskin | US | laid the foundations |
|      | Roger B. Myerson | US | of mechanism design theory |
| 2008 | Paul Krugman | US | research into trade patterns and location of economic activity |
| 2009 | Elinor Ostrom | US | research in economic governance, especially the commons |
|      | Oliver E. Williamson | US | analysis of economic governance, especially the boundaries of the firm |
| 2010 | Peter A. Diamond | US | analysis of financial markets containing search frictions |
|      | Dale T. Mortensen | US | |
|      | Christopher A. Pissarides | UK/Cyprus | |
| 2011 | Thomas J. Sargent | US | empirical research on cause and effect in the macroeconomy |
|      | Christopher A. Sims | US | |

# Special Achievement Awards

## Kennedy Center Honors

The Kennedy Center Honors are bestowed annually by the John F. Kennedy Center for the Performing Arts in Washington DC. They salute several artists each year for lifetime achievement in the performing arts.
**Web site:** <www.kennedy-center.org/programs/specialevents/honors/>.

| YEAR | NAME | FIELD | YEAR | NAME | FIELD |
|------|------|-------|------|------|-------|
| 1978 | Marian Anderson | opera singer | 1983 | Katherine Dunham | dancer, choreographer |
|      | Fred Astaire | dancer, actor | | Elia Kazan | theater and film director |
|      | George Balanchine | choreographer | | Frank Sinatra | singer, actor |
|      | Richard Rodgers | composer | | James Stewart | actor |
|      | Arthur Rubinstein | pianist | | Virgil Thomson | composer, music critic |
| 1979 | Aaron Copland | composer | 1984 | Lena Horne | singer, actress |
|      | Ella Fitzgerald | jazz singer | | Danny Kaye | actor, comedian |
|      | Henry Fonda | actor | | Gian Carlo Menotti | composer |
|      | Martha Graham | dancer, choreographer | | Arthur Miller | playwright |
|      | Tennessee Williams | playwright | | Isaac Stern | violinist |
| 1980 | Leonard Bernstein | conductor | 1985 | Merce Cunningham | dancer, choreographer |
|      | James Cagney | actor | | Irene Dunne | actress |
|      | Agnes de Mille | dancer, choreographer | | Bob Hope | entertainer, actor |
|      | Lynn Fontanne | actress | | Alan Jay Lerner | playwright, lyricist |
|      | Leontyne Price | opera singer | | Frederick Loewe | composer |
| 1981 | Count Basie | jazz pianist | | Beverly Sills | opera singer |
|      | Cary Grant | actor | 1986 | Lucille Ball | actress |
|      | Helen Hayes | actress | | Ray Charles | soul musician |
|      | Jerome Robbins | dancer, choreographer | | Hume Cronyn | actor |
|      | Rudolf Serkin | pianist | | Jessica Tandy | actress |
| 1982 | George Abbott | theater producer, director, writer | | Yehudi Menuhin | violinist |
|      | | | | Antony Tudor | choreographer |
|      | Lillian Gish | actress | 1987 | Perry Como | singer |
|      | Benny Goodman | swing musician | | Bette Davis | actress |
|      | Gene Kelly | dancer, actor | | Sammy Davis, Jr. | singer, dancer, entertainer |
|      | Eugene Ormandy | conductor | | | |

## Kennedy Center Honors (continued)

| YEAR | NAME | FIELD |
|------|------|-------|
| 1987 (cont.) | Nathan Milstein | violinist |
| | Alwin Nikolais | choreographer |
| 1988 | Alvin Ailey | dancer, choreographer |
| | George Burns | actor, comedian |
| | Myrna Loy | actress |
| | Alexander Schneider | violinist, conductor |
| | Roger L. Stevens | arts administrator |
| 1989 | Harry Belafonte | folk singer, actor |
| | Claudette Colbert | actress |
| | Alexandra Danilova | ballet dancer |
| | Mary Martin | actress, singer |
| | William Schuman | composer |
| 1990 | Dizzy Gillespie | jazz musician |
| | Katharine Hepburn | actress |
| | Risë Stevens | opera singer |
| | Jule Styne | composer |
| | Billy Wilder | film director |
| 1991 | Roy Acuff | country musician |
| | Betty Comden | theater and film writer |
| | Adolph Green | theater and film writer |
| | Fayard Nicholas | dancer |
| | Harold Nicholas | dancer |
| | Gregory Peck | actor |
| | Robert Shaw | conductor |
| 1992 | Lionel Hampton | swing musician |
| | Paul Newman | actor |
| | Joanne Woodward | actress |
| | Ginger Rogers | dancer, actress |
| | Mstislav Rostropovich | musician, conductor |
| | Paul Taylor | dancer, choreographer |
| 1993 | Johnny Carson | television entertainer |
| | Arthur Mitchell | dancer, choreographer |
| | Georg Solti | conductor |
| | Stephen Sondheim | composer, lyricist |
| | Marion Williams | gospel singer |
| 1994 | Kirk Douglas | actor |
| | Aretha Franklin | soul singer |
| | Morton Gould | composer |
| | Harold Prince | theater director, producer |
| | Pete Seeger | folk musician |
| 1995 | Jacques d'Amboise | dancer, choreographer |
| | Marilyn Horne | opera singer |
| | B.B. King | blues musician |
| | Sidney Poitier | actor |
| | Neil Simon | playwright |
| 1996 | Edward Albee | playwright |
| | Benny Carter | jazz musician |
| | Johnny Cash | country musician |
| | Jack Lemmon | actor |
| | Maria Tallchief | ballet dancer |
| 1997 | Lauren Bacall | actress |
| | Bob Dylan | singer, songwriter |
| | Charlton Heston | actor |
| | Jessye Norman | opera singer |
| | Edward Villella | dancer, choreographer |
| 1998 | Bill Cosby | actor, comedian |
| | Fred Ebb | lyricist |
| | John Kander | composer |
| | Willie Nelson | country musician |
| | André Previn | pianist, composer, conductor |
| | Shirley Temple Black | actress, diplomat |
| 1999 | Victor Borge | pianist, comedian |
| | Sean Connery | actor |
| | Judith Jamison | dancer, choreographer |
| | Jason Robards | actor |
| | Stevie Wonder | singer, songwriter |

| YEAR | NAME | FIELD |
|------|------|-------|
| 2000 | Mikhail Baryshnikov | dancer |
| | Chuck Berry | musician |
| | Plácido Domingo | opera singer |
| | Clint Eastwood | actor, director |
| | Angela Lansbury | actress |
| 2001 | Julie Andrews | actress |
| | Van Cliburn | pianist |
| | Quincy Jones | music producer, composer |
| | Jack Nicholson | actor |
| | Luciano Pavarotti | opera singer |
| 2002 | James Earl Jones | actor |
| | James Levine | conductor |
| | Chita Rivera | musical theater performer |
| | Paul Simon | singer |
| | Elizabeth Taylor | actress |
| 2003 | James Brown | musician |
| | Carol Burnett | actress |
| | Loretta Lynn | musician |
| | Mike Nichols | director |
| | Itzhak Perlman | musician |
| 2004 | Warren Beatty | film actor, director |
| | Ossie Davis | actor, writer, producer, director |
| | Ruby Dee | actress, writer |
| | Elton John | musician |
| | Joan Sutherland | opera singer |
| | John Williams | composer |
| 2005 | Tony Bennett | singer |
| | Suzanne Farrell | dancer, teacher |
| | Julie Harris | actress |
| | Robert Redford | film actor, director, producer |
| | Tina Turner | singer, actress |
| 2006 | Zubin Mehta | conductor |
| | Dolly Parton | singer, actress |
| | William "Smokey" Robinson | singer |
| | Steven Spielberg | film director, producer |
| | Andrew Lloyd Webber | composer |
| 2007 | Leon Fleisher | pianist, conductor |
| | Steve Martin | actor, writer |
| | Diana Ross | singer, actress |
| | Martin Scorsese | film director |
| | Brian Wilson | composer, singer |
| 2008 | Roger Daltrey | singer, composer, actor |
| | Morgan Freeman | actor |
| | George Jones | country musician |
| | Barbra Streisand | singer, actress, director, producer, writer |
| | Twyla Tharp | dancer, choreographer |
| | Pete Townshend | musician, composer |
| 2009 | Mel Brooks | writer, actor, director, producer, composer |
| | Dave Brubeck | pianist, composer |
| | Grace Bumbry | opera singer |
| | Robert De Niro | actor, director, producer |
| | Bruce Springsteen | singer, songwriter |
| 2010 | Merle Haggard | singer, songwriter |
| | Jerry Herman | composer, lyricist |
| | Bill T. Jones | dancer, choreographer, theater director |
| | Paul McCartney | singer, songwriter, musician |
| | Oprah Winfrey | television host, producer, actress |

## Kennedy Center Honors (continued)

| YEAR | NAME | FIELD |
|------|------|-------|
| 2011 | Barbara Cook | singer |
| | Neil Diamond | singer, songwriter |
| | Sonny Rollins | saxophonist, composer |

| YEAR | NAME | FIELD |
|------|------|-------|
| 2011 (cont.) | Meryl Streep | actress |
| | Yo-Yo Ma | cellist |

## National Medal of Arts

The National Medal of Arts, awarded annually since 1985 by the National Endowment for the Arts and the president of the United States, honors artists and art patrons for remarkable contributions to American arts. Nominations are garnered from the public and various arts fields and reviewed by the National Council on the Arts. The winners are selected by the president.

Web site: <www.nea.gov/honors/medals/medalists_year.html>.

| YEAR | NAME | FIELD |
|------|------|-------|
| 1985 | Elliott Carter, Jr. | composer |
| | Dorothy Buffum Chandler | patron |
| | Ralph Ellison | writer |
| | José Ferrer | actor |
| | Martha Graham | dancer, choreographer |
| | Hallmark Cards, Inc. | patron |
| | Lincoln Kirstein | patron |
| | Paul Mellon | patron |
| | Louise Nevelson | sculptor |
| | Georgia O'Keeffe | painter |
| | Leontyne Price | opera singer |
| | Alice Tully | patron |
| 1986 | Marian Anderson | opera singer |
| | Frank Capra | film director |
| | Aaron Copland | composer |
| | Willem de Kooning | painter |
| | Dominique de Menil | patron |
| | Agnes de Mille | dancer, choreographer |
| | Exxon Corp. | patron |
| | Seymour H. Knox | patron |
| | Eva Le Gallienne | actress, producer |
| | Alan Lomax | ethnomusicologist |
| | Lewis Mumford | architectural critic |
| | Eudora Welty | writer |
| 1987 | Romare Bearden | painter |
| | J.W. Fisher | patron |
| | Ella Fitzgerald | singer |
| | Armand Hammer | patron |
| | Sydney and Frances Lewis | patrons |
| | Howard Nemerov | writer, scholar |
| | Alwin Nikolais | choreographer |
| | Isamu Noguchi | sculptor |
| | William Schuman | composer |
| | Robert Penn Warren | writer |
| 1988 | Brooke Astor | patron |
| | Saul Bellow | writer |
| | Sydney J. Freedberg | art historian, curator |
| | Francis Goelet | patron |
| | Helen Hayes | actress |
| | Gordon Parks | filmmaker, photographer, writer |
| | I.M. Pei | architect |
| | Jerome Robbins | dancer, choreographer |
| | Rudolf Serkin | pianist |
| | Roger L. Stevens | arts administrator |
| | Obert C. Tanner | patron |
| | Virgil Thomson | composer, music critic |
| 1989 | Leopold Adler | historic preservationist, civic leader |
| | Dayton Hudson Corp. | patron |
| | Katherine Dunham | dancer, choreographer |
| | Alfred Eisenstaedt | photojournalist |

| YEAR | NAME | FIELD |
|------|------|-------|
| 1989 (cont.) | Martin Friedman | museum director |
| | Leigh Gerdine | civic leader, patron |
| | Dizzy Gillespie | jazz musician |
| | Walker K. Hancock | sculptor |
| | Vladimir Horowitz[1] | pianist |
| | Czeslaw Milosz | writer |
| | Robert Motherwell | painter |
| | John Updike | writer |
| 1990 | George Abbott | theater producer, director, writer |
| | Hume Cronyn | actor, director |
| | Merce Cunningham | dancer, choreographer |
| | Jasper Johns | painter, sculptor |
| | B.B. King | blues musician |
| | David Lloyd Kreeger | patron |
| | Jacob Lawrence | painter |
| | Harris and Carroll Sterling Masterson | patrons |
| | Ian McHarg | landscape architect |
| | Beverly Sills | opera singer |
| | Southeastern Bell Corp. | patron |
| | Jessica Tandy | actress |
| 1991 | Maurice Abravanel | conductor, music director |
| | Roy Acuff | country musician |
| | Pietro Belluschi | architect |
| | J. Carter Brown | museum director |
| | Charles "Honi" Coles | tap dancer |
| | John O. Crosby | opera director, conductor |
| | Richard Diebenkorn | painter |
| | R. Philip Hanes, Jr. | patron |
| | Kitty Carlisle Hart | actress, singer |
| | Pearl Primus | choreographer, anthropologist |
| | Isaac Stern | violinist |
| | Texaco Inc. | patron |
| 1992 | AT&T | patron |
| | Marilyn Horne | opera singer |
| | Allan Houser | sculptor |
| | James Earl Jones | actor |
| | Minnie Pearl | Grand Ole Opry performer |
| | Robert Saudek | television producer, museum director |
| | Earl Scruggs | banjo player |
| | Robert Shaw | conductor |
| | Billy Taylor | jazz pianist |
| | Robert Venturi and Denise Scott Brown | architects |
| | Lila Wallace– Reader's Digest Fund | patron |
| | Robert Wise | film director |

## National Medal of Arts (continued)

| YEAR | NAME | FIELD |
|------|------|-------|
| 1993 | Walter and Leonore Annenberg | patrons |
| | Cabell "Cab" Calloway | jazz musician |
| | Ray Charles | soul musician |
| | Bess Lomax Hawes | folklorist, musician |
| | Stanley Kunitz | poet |
| | Robert Merrill | opera singer |
| | Arthur Miller | playwright |
| | Robert Rauschenberg | painter |
| | Lloyd Richards | theater director |
| | William Styron | writer |
| | Paul Taylor | dancer, choreographer |
| | Billy Wilder | film director, writer |
| 1994 | Harry Belafonte | folksinger, actor |
| | Dave Brubeck | jazz musician |
| | Celia Cruz | salsa singer |
| | Dorothy DeLay | violin instructor |
| | Julie Harris | actress |
| | Erick Hawkins | dancer, choreographer |
| | Gene Kelly | dancer, actor |
| | Pete Seeger | folk musician |
| | Catherine Filene Shouse | patron |
| | Wayne Thiebaud | painter |
| | Richard Wilbur | poet |
| | Young Audiences | arts organization |
| 1995 | Licia Albanese | opera singer |
| | Gwendolyn Brooks | poet |
| | B. Gerald and Iris Cantor | patrons |
| | Ossie Davis and Ruby Dee | actors |
| | David Diamond | composer |
| | James Ingo Freed | architect |
| | Bob Hope | entertainer |
| | Roy Lichtenstein | painter |
| | Arthur Mitchell | dancer, choreographer |
| | William S. Monroe | bluegrass musician |
| | Urban Gateways | arts education organization |
| 1996 | Edward Albee | playwright |
| | Boys Choir of Harlem | choir |
| | Sarah Caldwell | opera conductor |
| | Harry Callahan | photographer |
| | Zelda Fichandler | theater founder, director |
| | Eduardo "Lalo" Guerrero | Chicano musician |
| | Lionel Hampton | swing musician |
| | Bella Lewitzky | dancer, choreographer |
| | Vera List | patron |
| | Robert Redford | actor, film director |
| | Maurice Sendak | illustrator, writer |
| | Stephen Sondheim | composer, lyricist |
| 1997 | Louise Bourgeois | sculptor |
| | Betty Carter | jazz singer |
| | Agnes Gund | patron |
| | Daniel Urban Kiley | landscape architect |
| | Angela Lansbury | actress |
| | James Levine | opera conductor, pianist |
| | MacDowell Colony | artists' colony |
| | Tito Puente | jazz and mambo musician |
| | Jason Robards | actor |
| | Edward Villella | dancer, choreographer |
| | Doc Watson | folk and country musician |

| YEAR | NAME | FIELD |
|------|------|-------|
| 1998 | Jacques d'Amboise | dancer, choreographer |
| | Antoine "Fats" Domino | rock-and-roll musician |
| | Ramblin' Jack Elliott | folk musician |
| | Frank O. Gehry | architect |
| | Barbara Handman | patron |
| | Agnes Martin | painter |
| | Gregory Peck | actor |
| | Roberta Peters | opera singer |
| | Philip Roth | writer |
| | Sara Lee Corp. | patron |
| | Steppenwolf Theatre Company | arts organization |
| | Gwen Verdon | actress, dancer |
| 1999 | Irene Diamond | patron |
| | Aretha Franklin | soul singer |
| | Michael Graves | architect, designer |
| | The Juilliard School | performing arts school |
| | Norman Lear | television producer, writer |
| | Rosetta LeNoire | actress, theater founder |
| | Harvey Lichtenstein | arts administrator |
| | Lydia Mendoza | Tejano musician |
| | Odetta | folksinger |
| | George Segal | sculptor |
| | Maria Tallchief | ballet dancer |
| 2000 | Maya Angelou | poet, writer |
| | Eddy Arnold | country musician |
| | Mikhail Baryshnikov | dancer, dance company director |
| | Benny Carter | jazz musician |
| | Chuck Close | painter |
| | Horton Foote | dramatist |
| | Lewis Manilow | patron |
| | National Public Radio cultural programming division | broadcaster |
| | Claes Oldenburg | sculptor |
| | Itzhak Perlman | violinist |
| | Harold Prince | theater director |
| | Barbra Streisand | singer, actress |
| 2001 | Alvin Ailey Dance Foundation | modern dance company and school |
| | Rudolfo Anaya | writer |
| | Johnny Cash | country musician |
| | Kirk Douglas | actor |
| | Helen Frankenthaler | painter |
| | Judith Jamison | dancer, choreographer |
| | Yo-Yo Ma | cellist |
| | Mike Nichols | theater and film director |
| 2002 | Florence Knoll Bassett | designer, architect |
| | Trisha Brown | dancer, choreographer |
| | Philippe de Montebello | museum director |
| | Uta Hagen | actress, educator |
| | Lawrence Halprin | landscape architect |
| | Al Hirschfeld[1] | artist, caricaturist |
| | George Jones | singer, songwriter |
| | Ming Cho Lee | painter, stage designer |
| | William "Smokey" Robinson, Jr. | singer, songwriter |
| 2003 | Austin City Limits | television show |
| | Beverly Cleary | children's book author |
| | Rafe Esquith | arts educator |

## National Medal of Arts (continued)

| YEAR | NAME | FIELD |
|---|---|---|
| 2003 (cont.) | Suzanne Farrell | dancer, artistic director, arts educator |
| | Buddy Guy | blues musician |
| | Ron Howard | actor, director, writer |
| | Mormon Tabernacle Choir | choir |
| | Leonard Slatkin | conductor |
| | George Strait | singer, songwriter |
| | Tommy Tune | director, actor |
| 2004 | Andrew W. Mellon Foundation | patron |
| | Ray Bradbury | writer |
| | Carlisle Floyd | opera composer |
| | Frederick "Rick" Hart[1] | sculptor |
| | Anthony Hecht[1] | poet |
| | John Ruthven | painter |
| | Vincent Scully | architectural historian |
| | Twyla Tharp | dancer, choreographer |
| 2005 | Louis Auchincloss | writer |
| | James DePreist | conductor |
| | Paquito D'Rivera | musician |
| | Robert Duvall | actor |
| | Leonard Garment | arts advocate |
| | Ollie Johnston | animator, artist |
| | Wynton Marsalis | musician, educator |
| | Dolly Parton | singer, songwriter |
| | Pennsylvania Academy of the Fine Arts | arts academy |
| | Tina Ramirez | dancer, choreographer |
| 2006 | William Bolcom | composer |
| | Cyd Charisse | dancer |
| | Roy R. DeCarava | photographer |
| | Wilhelmina C. Holladay | patron |
| | Interlochen Center for the Arts | music school |
| | Erich Kunzel | conductor |
| | Preservation Hall Jazz Band | jazz ensemble |
| | Gregory Rabassa | translator |
| | Viktor Schreckengost | industrial designer |
| | Dr. Ralph Stanley | bluegrass musician |
| 2007 | Morten Lauridsen | composer |
| | Lionel Hampton International Jazz Festival | music competition, festival |
| | N. Scott Momaday | author, poet |
| | Roy R. Neuberger | patron |
| | R. Craig Noel | theater director |
| | Les Paul | guitarist, inventor |
| | Henry Steinway | patron |

| YEAR | NAME | FIELD |
|---|---|---|
| 2007 (cont.) | George Tooker | painter |
| | Andrew Wyeth | painter |
| 2008 | Olivia de Havilland | actress |
| | Fisk Jubilee Singers | choral ensemble |
| | Ford's Theatre Society | theater, museum |
| | Hank Jones | jazz musician |
| | José Limón Dance Foundation | dance company |
| | Stan Lee | comic book writer |
| | Jesús Moroles | sculptor |
| | Presser Foundation | patron |
| | Sherman Brothers | songwriters |
| 2009 | Bob Dylan | singer, songwriter |
| | Clint Eastwood | director, actor |
| | Milton Glaser | graphic designer |
| | Maya Lin | artist, designer |
| | Rita Moreno | singer, dancer, actress |
| | Jessye Norman | soprano |
| | Oberlin Conservatory of Music | conservatory |
| | Joseph P. Riley, Jr. | patron |
| | School of American Ballet | ballet school |
| | Frank Stella | painter, sculptor |
| | Michael T. Thomas | conductor |
| | John Williams | composer, conductor |
| 2010 | Robert Brustein | theater critic, producer, playwright, educator |
| | Van Cliburn | pianist, music educator |
| | Mark di Suvero | sculptor |
| | Donald Hall | poet |
| | Jacob's Pillow Dance Festival | dance festival |
| | Quincy Jones | musician, music producer |
| | Harper Lee | writer |
| | Sonny Rollins | jazz musician |
| | Meryl Streep | actress |
| | James Taylor | singer, songwriter |
| 2011 | Will Barnet | painter, printmaker |
| | Rita Dove | poet, author |
| | Al Pacino | actor, director, producer |
| | Emily Rauh Pulitzer | patron, philanthropist |
| | Martin Puryear | sculptor |
| | Mel Tillis | singer, songwriter |
| | André Watts | pianist |
| | United Service Organizations | human service organization for US military |

[1]*Awarded posthumously.*

## Spingarn Medal

*The National Association for the Advancement of Colored People (NAACP) presents the medal for distinguished achievement among African Americans. The medal is named for early NAACP activist Joel E. Spingarn.*

| YEAR | NAME | FIELD |
|---|---|---|
| 1915 | Ernest Everett Just | marine biologist |
| 1916 | Charles Young | army officer |
| 1917 | Harry Thacker Burleigh | singer, composer |
| 1918 | William Stanley Braithwaite | poet, literary critic |

| YEAR | NAME | FIELD |
|---|---|---|
| 1919 | Archibald Henry Grimké | lawyer, diplomat, social activist |
| 1920 | W.E.B. Du Bois | sociologist, social activist |
| 1921 | Charles S. Gilpin | actor |

# Spingarn Medal (continued)

| YEAR | NAME | FIELD |
|---|---|---|
| 1922 | Mary Burnett Talbert | civil rights activist |
| 1923 | George Washington Carver | agricultural chemist |
| 1924 | Roland Hayes | singer, composer |
| 1925 | James Weldon Johnson | diplomat, anthologist |
| 1926 | Carter G. Woodson | historian |
| 1927 | Anthony Overton | businessman |
| 1928 | Charles W. Chesnutt | writer |
| 1929 | Mordecai W. Johnson | minister, university president |
| 1930 | Henry Alexander Hunt | educator, government official |
| 1931 | Richard B. Harrison | actor |
| 1932 | Robert Russa Moton | educator, civil rights leader |
| 1933 | Max Yergan | civil rights leader |
| 1934 | William T.B. Williams | educator |
| 1935 | Mary McLeod Bethune | educator, social activist |
| 1936 | John Hope (posthumously) | educator |
| 1937 | Walter White | civil rights leader |
| 1938 | no medal awarded | |
| 1939 | Marian Anderson | opera singer |
| 1940 | Louis T. Wright | surgeon, civil rights leader |
| 1941 | Richard Wright | writer |
| 1942 | A. Philip Randolph | labor and civil rights leader |
| 1943 | William H. Hastie | lawyer, judge |
| 1944 | Charles Richard Drew | surgeon, research scientist |
| 1945 | Paul Robeson | actor, singer, social activist |
| 1946 | Thurgood Marshall | lawyer, US Supreme Court justice |
| 1947 | Percy L. Julian | chemist |
| 1948 | Channing H. Tobias | civil rights leader |
| 1949 | Ralph Bunche | diplomat, scholar |
| 1950 | Charles Hamilton Houston (posthumously) | lawyer |
| 1951 | Mabel Keaton Staupers | nurse, social activist |
| 1952 | Harry T. Moore (posthumously) | civil rights activist, educator |
| 1953 | Paul R. Williams | architect |
| 1954 | Theodore K. Lawless | dermatologist, philanthropist |
| 1955 | Carl Murphy | journalist, civil rights activist |
| 1956 | Jackie Robinson | baseball player |
| 1957 | Martin Luther King, Jr. | civil rights leader |
| 1958 | Daisy Bates and the Little Rock Nine | school integration activists |
| 1959 | Duke Ellington | jazz musician |
| 1960 | Langston Hughes | writer |
| 1961 | Kenneth Bancroft Clark | educator |
| 1962 | Robert C. Weaver | economist, government official |
| 1963 | Medgar Evers (posthumously) | civil rights activist |
| 1964 | Roy Wilkins | civil rights leader |
| 1965 | Leontyne Price | opera singer |
| 1966 | John H. Johnson | publisher |

| YEAR | NAME | FIELD |
|---|---|---|
| 1967 | Edward W. Brooke III | lawyer, US senator |
| 1968 | Sammy Davis, Jr. | singer, dancer, entertainer |
| 1969 | Clarence M. Mitchell, Jr. | civil rights lobbyist |
| 1970 | Jacob Lawrence | painter |
| 1971 | Leon H. Sullivan | minister, civil rights activist |
| 1972 | Gordon Parks | filmmaker, photographer, writer |
| 1973 | Wilson C. Riles | educator |
| 1974 | Damon Keith | lawyer, judge |
| 1975 | Hank Aaron | baseball player |
| 1976 | Alvin Ailey | dancer, choreographer |
| 1977 | Alex Haley | writer |
| 1978 | Andrew Young | civil rights leader |
| 1979 | Rosa Parks | civil rights activist |
| 1980 | Rayford W. Logan | educator, writer |
| 1981 | Coleman A. Young | labor activist, politician |
| 1982 | Benjamin E. Mays | educator, minister |
| 1983 | Lena Horne | singer, actress |
| 1984 | Thomas Bradley | politician |
| 1985 | Bill Cosby | actor, comedian |
| 1986 | Benjamin L. Hooks | civil rights leader, government official |
| 1987 | Percy Ellis Sutton | civil rights activist, politician |
| 1988 | Frederick Douglass Patterson (posthumously) | educator |
| 1989 | Jesse Jackson | minister, politician, civil rights leader |
| 1990 | L. Douglas Wilder | politician |
| 1991 | Colin Powell | army general, government official |
| 1992 | Barbara Jordan | lawyer, politician |
| 1993 | Dorothy I. Height | social activist |
| 1994 | Maya Angelou | poet |
| 1995 | John Hope Franklin | historian, educator |
| 1996 | A. Leon Higginbotham | lawyer, judge, historian, scholar |
| 1997 | Carl T. Rowan | journalist, commentator |
| 1998 | Myrlie Evers-Williams | civil rights activist |
| 1999 | Earl G. Graves | publisher |
| 2000 | Oprah Winfrey | television host, media personality |
| 2001 | Vernon E. Jordan, Jr. | lawyer, civil rights activist |
| 2002 | John Lewis | politician, civil rights activist |
| 2003 | Constance Baker Motley | judge, lawyer, civil rights activist |
| 2004 | Robert L. Carter | judge, lawyer, civil rights activist |
| 2005 | Oliver W. Hill | lawyer, civil rights activist |
| 2006 | Benjamin S. Carson | physician |
| 2007 | John Conyers, Jr. | politician |
| 2008 | Ruby Dee | actress, writer |
| 2009 | Julian Bond | statesman, civil rights activist |
| 2010 | Cicely Tyson | actress |
| 2011 | Frankie Muse Freeman | lawyer, civil rights activist |

# Science Honors

## Fields Medal

The Fields Medal, officially known as the International Medal for Outstanding Discoveries in Mathematics, is granted every four years to between two and four mathematicians for outstanding or groundbreaking research. It is traditionally given to mathematicians under the age of 40. Prize: Can$15,000 (about US$15,300).

| YEAR | NAME | PRIMARY RESEARCH |
|---|---|---|
| 1936 | Lars Ahlfors | Riemann surfaces |
| | Jesse Douglas | Plateau problem |
| 1950 | Laurent Schwartz | functional analysis |
| | Atle Selberg | number theory |
| 1954 | Kunihiko Kodaira | algebraic geometry |
| | Jean-Pierre Serre | algebraic topology |
| 1958 | Klaus Roth | number theory |
| | René Thom | topology |
| 1962 | Lars Hörmander | partial differential equations |
| | John Milnor | differential topology |
| 1966 | Michael Atiyah | topology |
| | Paul Cohen | set theory |
| | Alexandre Grothendieck | algebraic geometry |
| | Stephen Smale | topology |
| 1970 | Alan Baker | number theory |
| | Heisuke Hironaka | algebraic geometry |
| | Sergey Novikov | topology |
| | John Thompson | group theory |
| 1974 | Enrico Bombieri | number theory |
| | David Mumford | algebraic geometry |
| 1978 | Pierre Deligne | algebraic geometry |
| | Charles Fefferman | classical analysis |
| | Gregory Margulis | Lie groups |
| | Daniel Quillen | algebraic K-theory |
| 1983 | Alain Connes | operator theory |
| | William Thurston | topology |
| | Shing-Tung Yau | differential geometry |
| 1986 | Simon Donaldson | topology |
| | Gerd Faltings | Mordell conjecture |
| | Michael Freedman | Poincaré conjecture |

| YEAR | NAME | PRIMARY RESEARCH |
|---|---|---|
| 1990 | Vladimir Drinfeld | algebraic geometry |
| | Vaughan Jones | knot theory |
| | Shigefumi Mori | algebraic geometry |
| | Edward Witten | superstring theory |
| 1994 | Jean Bourgain | analysis |
| | Pierre-Louis Lions | partial differential equations |
| | Jean-Christophe Yoccoz | dynamical systems |
| | Yefim Zelmanov | group theory |
| 1998 | Richard Borcherds | mathematical physics |
| | William Gowers | functional analysis |
| | Maksim Kontsevich | mathematical physics |
| | Curt McMullen | chaos theory |
| 2002 | Laurent Lafforgue | number theory and analysis |
| | Vladimir Voevodsky | algebraic geometry |
| 2006 | Andrei Okounkov | algebraic geometry |
| | Grigory Perelman (declined) | Ricci flow |
| | Terence Tao | prime numbers, nonlinear equations |
| | Wendelin Werner | mathematics of critical phenomena |
| 2010 | Elon Lindenstrauss | measure rigidity in ergodic theory |
| | Ngo Bao Chau | proof of the Fundamental Lemma |
| | Stanislav Smirnov | statistical physics |
| | Cédric Villani | Boltzmann equation |

## National Medal of Science

The National Medal of Science was established by Congress in 1959. Awarded annually since 1962 by the National Science Foundation, it recognizes notable achievements in mathematics, engineering, and the physical, natural, social, and behavioral sciences.
**National Science Foundation Web site:** <www.nsf.gov/od/nms/medal.jsp>.

| YEAR | NAME | FIELD |
|---|---|---|
| 1962 | Theodore von Karman | aerospace engineering |
| 1963 | Luis W. Alvarez | physics |
| | Vannevar Bush | electrical engineering |
| | John Robinson Pierce | communications engineering |
| | Cornelius Barnardus van Niel | biology |
| | Norbert Wiener | mathematics |
| 1964 | Roger Adams | chemistry |
| | Othmar Herman Ammann | civil engineering |
| | Theodosius Dobzhansky | genetics |
| | Charles Stark Draper | aerospace engineering |
| | Solomon Lefschetz | mathematics |
| | Neal Elgar Miller | psychology |
| | H. Marston Morse | mathematics |
| | Marshall Warren Nirenberg | biochemistry |

| YEAR | NAME | FIELD |
|---|---|---|
| 1964 (cont.) | Julian Seymour Schwinger | physics |
| | Harold C. Urey | chemistry |
| | Robert Burns Woodward | chemistry |
| 1965 | John Bardeen | physics |
| | Peter J.W. Debye | physical chemistry |
| | Hugh L. Dryden | physics |
| | Clarence L. Johnson | aerospace engineering |
| | Leon M. Lederman | physics |
| | Warren K. Lewis | chemical engineering |
| | Francis Peyton Rous | pathology |
| | William W. Rubey | geology |
| | George Gaylord Simpson | paleontology |
| | Donald D. Van Slyke | chemistry |
| | Oscar Zariski | mathematics |
| 1966 | Jacob A.B. Bjerknes | meteorology |
| | Subrahmanyan Chandrasekhar | astrophysics |

## National Medal of Science (continued)

| YEAR | NAME | FIELD |
|------|------|-------|
| 1966 (cont.) | Henry Eyring | chemistry |
| | Edward F. Knipling | entomology |
| | Fritz Albert Lipmann | biochemistry |
| | John Willard Milnor | mathematics |
| | William C. Rose | biochemistry |
| | Claude E. Shannon | mathematics, electrical engineering |
| | John H. Van Vleck | physics |
| | Sewall Wright | genetics |
| | Vladimir Kosma Zworykin | electrical engineering |
| 1967 | Jesse W. Beams | physics |
| | Francis Birch | geophysics |
| | Gregory Breit | physics |
| | Paul Joseph Cohen | mathematics |
| | Kenneth S. Cole | biophysics |
| | Louis P. Hammett | chemistry |
| | Harry F. Harlow | psychology |
| | Michael Heidelberger | immunology |
| | George B. Kistiakowsky | chemistry |
| | Edwin Herbert Land | physics |
| | Igor I. Sikorsky | aircraft design |
| | Alfred H. Sturtevant | genetics |
| 1968 | Horace A. Barker | biochemistry |
| | Paul D. Bartlett | chemistry |
| | Bernard B. Brodie | pharmacology |
| | Detlev W. Bronk | biophysics |
| | J. Presper Eckert, Jr. | engineering, computer science |
| | Herbert Friedman | astrophysics |
| | Jay L. Lush | livestock genetics |
| | Nathan M. Newmark | civil engineering |
| | Jerzy Neyman | statistics |
| | Lars Onsager | chemistry |
| | B.F. Skinner | psychology |
| | Eugene Paul Wigner | mathematical physics |
| 1969 | Herbert C. Brown | chemistry |
| | William Feller | mathematics |
| | Robert J. Huebner | virology |
| | Jack Kilby | electrical engineering |
| | Ernst Mayr | biology |
| | Wolfgang K.H. Panofsky | physics |
| 1970 | Richard Dagobert Brauer | mathematics |
| | Robert H. Dicke | physics |
| | Barbara McClintock | genetics |
| | George E. Mueller | physics |
| | Albert Bruce Sabin | medicine, vaccine development |
| | Allan R. Sandage | astronomy |
| | John C. Slater | physics |
| | John Archibald Wheeler | physics |
| | Saul Winstein | chemistry |
| 1971 | no recipients named | |
| 1972 | no recipients named | |
| 1973 | Daniel I. Arnon | biochemistry |
| | Carl Djerassi | chemistry |
| | Harold E. Edgerton | electrical engineering, photography |
| | Maurice Ewing | geophysics |
| | Arie Jan Haagen-Smit | biochemistry |
| | Vladimir Haensel | chemical engineering |
| | Frederick Seitz | physics |
| | Earl W. Sutherland, Jr. | biochemistry |
| | John Wilder Tukey | statistics |

| YEAR | NAME | FIELD |
|------|------|-------|
| 1973 (cont.) | Richard T. Whitcomb | aerospace engineering |
| | Robert Rathbun Wilson | particle physics |
| 1974 | Nicolaas Bloembergen | physics |
| | Britton Chance | biophysics |
| | Erwin Chargaff | biochemistry |
| | Paul J. Flory | physical chemistry |
| | William A. Fowler | nuclear astrophysics |
| | Kurt Gödel | mathematics |
| | Rudolf Kompfner | physics |
| | James Van Gundia Neel | genetics |
| | Linus Pauling | chemistry |
| | Ralph Brazelton Peck | geotechnical engineering |
| | Kenneth Sanborn Pitzer | physical chemistry |
| | James Augustine Shannon | physiology |
| | Abel Wolman | sanitary engineering |
| 1975 | John W. Backus | computer science |
| | Manson Benedict | nuclear engineering |
| | Hans Albrecht Bethe | theoretical physics |
| | Shiing-shen Chern | mathematics |
| | George B. Dantzig | mathematics |
| | Hallowell Davis | physiology |
| | Paul Gyorgy | medicine, vitamin research |
| | Sterling Brown Hendricks | chemistry |
| | Joseph O. Hirschfelder | chemistry |
| | William Hayward Pickering | physics |
| | Lewis H. Sarett | chemistry |
| | Frederick Emmons Terman | electrical engineering |
| | Orville Alvin Vogel | research agronomy |
| | Wernher von Braun | aerospace engineering |
| | E. Bright Wilson, Jr. | chemistry |
| | Chien-Shiung Wu | physics |
| 1976 | Morris Cohen | materials science |
| | Kurt Otto Friedrichs | mathematics |
| | Peter C. Goldmark | communications engineering |
| | Samuel Abraham Goudsmit | physics |
| | Roger Charles Louis Guillemin | physiology |
| | Herbert S. Gutowsky | chemistry |
| | Erwin W. Mueller | physics |
| | Keith Roberts Porter | cell biology |
| | Efraim Racker | biochemistry |
| | Frederick D. Rossini | chemistry |
| | Verner E. Suomi | meteorology |
| | Henry Taube | chemistry |
| | George Eugene Uhlenbeck | physics |
| | Hassler Whitney | mathematics |
| | Edward O. Wilson | biology |
| 1977 | no recipients named | |
| 1978 | no recipients named | |
| 1979 | Robert H. Burris | biochemistry |
| | Elizabeth C. Crosby | neuroanatomy |
| | Joseph L. Doob | mathematics |
| | Richard P. Feynman | theoretical physics |

## National Medal of Science (continued)

| YEAR | NAME | FIELD |
|---|---|---|
| 1979 (cont.) | Donald E. Knuth | computer science |
| | Arthur Kornberg | biochemistry |
| | Emmett N. Leith | electrical engineering |
| | Herman F. Mark | chemistry |
| | Raymond D. Mindlin | mechanical engineering |
| | Robert N. Noyce | computer science |
| | Severo Ochoa | biochemistry |
| | Earl R. Parker | materials science |
| | Edward M. Purcell | physics |
| | Simon Ramo | electrical engineering |
| | John H. Sinfelt | chemical engineering |
| | Lyman Spitzer, Jr. | astrophysics |
| | Earl Reece Stadtman | biochemistry |
| | George Ledyard Stebbins | botany, genetics |
| | Victor F. Weisskopf | physics |
| | Paul Alfred Weiss | biology |
| 1980 | no recipients named | |
| 1981 | Philip Handler | biochemistry |
| 1982 | Philip W. Anderson | physics |
| | Seymour Benzer | molecular biology |
| | Glenn W. Burton | genetics |
| | Mildred Cohn | biochemistry |
| | F. Albert Cotton | chemistry |
| | Edward H. Heinemann | aerospace engineering |
| | Donald L. Katz | chemical engineering |
| | Yoichiro Nambu | theoretical physics |
| | Marshall H. Stone | mathematics |
| | Gilbert Stork | organic chemistry |
| | Edward Teller | nuclear physics |
| | Charles Hard Townes | physics |
| 1983 | Howard L. Bachrach | biochemistry |
| | Paul Berg | biochemistry |
| | E. Margaret Burbidge | astronomy |
| | Maurice Goldhaber | physics |
| | Herman H. Goldstine | computer science |
| | William R. Hewlett | electrical engineering |
| | Roald Hoffmann | chemistry |
| | Helmut E. Landsberg | climatology |
| | George M. Low | aerospace engineering |
| | Walter H. Munk | oceanography |
| | George C. Pimentel | chemistry |
| | Frederick Reines | physics |
| | Wendell L. Roelofs | chemistry, entomology |
| | Bruno B. Rossi | astrophysics |
| | Berta V. Scharrer | neuroscience |
| | John Robert Schrieffer | physics |
| | Isadore M. Singer | mathematics |
| | John G. Trump | electrical engineering |
| | Richard N. Zare | chemistry |
| 1984 | no recipients named | |
| 1985 | no recipients named | |
| 1986 | Solomon J. Buchsbaum | physics |
| | Stanley Cohen | biochemistry |
| | Horace R. Crane | physics |
| | Herman Feshbach | physics |
| | Harry Gray | chemistry |
| | Donald A. Henderson | medicine, public health |
| | Robert Hofstadter | physics |
| | Peter D. Lax | mathematics |
| | Yuan Tseh Lee | chemistry |
| | Hans Wolfgang Liepmann | aerospace engineering |

| YEAR | NAME | FIELD |
|---|---|---|
| 1986 (cont.) | T.Y. Lin | civil engineering |
| | Carl S. Marvel | chemistry |
| | Vernon B. Mountcastle | neurophysiology |
| | Bernard M. Oliver | electrical engineering |
| | George Emil Palade | cell biology |
| | Herbert A. Simon | social science |
| | Joan A. Steitz | molecular biology |
| | Frank H. Westheimer | chemistry |
| | Chen Ning Yang | theoretical physics |
| | Antoni Zygmund | mathematics |
| 1987 | Philip Hauge Abelson | physical chemistry |
| | Anne Anastasi | psychology |
| | Robert Byron Bird | chemical engineering |
| | Raoul Bott | mathematics |
| | Michael E. DeBakey | heart surgery |
| | Theodor O. Diener | plant pathology |
| | Harry Eagle | cell biology |
| | Walter M. Elsasser | physics |
| | Michael H. Freedman | mathematics |
| | William S. Johnson | chemistry |
| | Har Gobind Khorana | biochemistry |
| | Paul C. Lauterbur | chemistry |
| | Rita Levi-Montalcini | neurology |
| | George E. Pake | research, physics |
| | H. Bolton Seed | civil engineering |
| | George J. Stigler | economics |
| | Walter H. Stockmayer | chemistry |
| | Max Tishler | chemistry |
| | James Alfred Van Allen | physics |
| | Ernst Weber | electrical engineering |
| 1988 | William O. Baker | chemistry |
| | Konrad E. Bloch | biochemistry |
| | David Allan Bromley | physics |
| | Michael S. Brown | molecular genetics |
| | Paul C.W. Chu | physics |
| | Stanley N. Cohen | genetics |
| | Elias James Corey | chemistry |
| | Daniel C. Drucker | engineering education |
| | Milton Friedman | economics |
| | Joseph L. Goldstein | molecular genetics |
| | Ralph E. Gomory | mathematics, research |
| | Willis M. Hawkins | aerospace engineering |
| | Maurice R. Hilleman | vaccine research |
| | George W. Housner | earthquake engineering |
| | Eric Kandel | neurobiology |
| | Joseph B. Keller | mathematics |
| | Walter Kohn | physics |
| | Norman Foster Ramsey | physics |
| | Jack Steinberger | physics |
| | Rosalyn S. Yalow | medical physics |
| 1989 | Arnold O. Beckman | chemistry |
| | Richard B. Bernstein | chemistry |
| | Melvin Calvin | biochemistry |
| | Harry G. Drickamer | chemistry, physics |
| | Katherine Esau | botany |
| | Herbert E. Grier | aerospace engineering |
| | Viktor Hamburger | biology |
| | Samuel Karlin | mathematics |
| | Philip Leder | genetics |
| | Joshua Lederberg | genetics |

## National Medal of Science (continued)

| YEAR | NAME | FIELD |
|---|---|---|
| 1989 (cont.) | Saunders Mac Lane | mathematics |
| | Rudolph A. Marcus | chemistry |
| | Harden M. McConnell | chemistry |
| | Eugene N. Parker | theoretical astrophysics |
| | Robert P. Sharp | geology |
| | Donald C. Spencer | mathematics |
| | Roger Wolcott Sperry | neurobiology |
| | Henry M. Stommel | oceanography |
| | Harland G. Wood | biochemistry |
| 1990 | Baruj Benacerraf | pathology, immunology |
| | Elkan R. Blout | chemistry |
| | Herbert W. Boyer | biochemistry, genetics |
| | George F. Carrier | mathematics |
| | Allan MacLeod Cormack | physics |
| | Mildred S. Dresselhaus | physics |
| | Karl August Folkers | chemistry |
| | Nick Holonyak, Jr. | electrical engineering |
| | Leonid Hurwicz | economics |
| | Stephen Cole Kleene | mathematics |
| | Daniel E. Koshland, Jr. | biochemistry |
| | Edward B. Lewis | genetics |
| | John McCarthy | computer science |
| | Edwin Mattison McMillan | nuclear physics |
| | David G. Nathan | pediatrics |
| | Robert V. Pound | physics |
| | Roger R.D. Revelle | oceanography |
| | John D. Roberts | chemistry |
| | Patrick Suppes | philosophy, statistics education |
| | E. Donnall Thomas | medicine |
| 1991 | Mary Ellen Avery | pediatrics |
| | Ronald Breslow | chemistry |
| | Alberto P. Calderon | mathematics |
| | Gertrude B. Elion | pharmacology |
| | George H. Heilmeier | electrical engineering |
| | Dudley R. Herschbach | chemistry |
| | G. Evelyn Hutchinson | zoology |
| | Elvin A. Kabat | immunology |
| | Robert W. Kates | geography |
| | Luna B. Leopold | hydrology, geology |
| | Salvador Luria | biology |
| | Paul A. Marks | hematology, cancer research |
| | George A. Miller | psychology |
| | Arthur L. Schawlow | physics |
| | Glenn T. Seaborg | nuclear chemistry |
| | Folke K. Skoog | botany |
| | H. Guyford Stever | aerospace engineering |
| | Edward C. Stone | physics |
| | Steven Weinberg | nuclear physics |
| | Paul C. Zamecnik | molecular biology |
| 1992 | Eleanor J. Gibson | psychology |
| | Allen Newell | computer science |
| | Calvin F. Quate | electrical engineering |
| | Eugene M. Shoemaker | planetary geology |
| | Howard E. Simmons, Jr. | chemistry |
| | Maxine F. Singer | biochemistry, administration |
| | Howard Martin Temin | virology |
| | John Roy Whinnery | electrical engineering |

| YEAR | NAME | FIELD |
|---|---|---|
| 1993 | Alfred Y. Cho | electrical engineering |
| | Donald J. Cram | chemistry |
| | Val Logsdon Fitch | particle physics |
| | Norman Hackerman | chemistry |
| | Martin D. Kruskal | mathematics |
| | Daniel Nathans | microbiology |
| | Vera C. Rubin | astronomy |
| | Salome G. Waelsch | molecular genetics |
| 1994 | Ray W. Clough | civil engineering |
| | John Cocke | computer science |
| | Thomas Eisner | chemical ecology |
| | George S. Hammond | chemistry |
| | Robert K. Merton | sociology |
| | Elizabeth F. Neufeld | biochemistry |
| | Albert W. Overhauser | physics |
| | Frank Press | geophysics, administration |
| 1995 | Thomas Robert Cech | biochemistry |
| | Hans Georg Dehmelt | physics |
| | Peter M. Goldreich | astrophysics |
| | Hermann A. Haus | electrical engineering |
| | Isabella L. Karle | chemistry |
| | Louis Nirenberg | mathematics |
| | Alexander Rich | molecular biology |
| | Roger N. Shepard | psychology |
| 1996 | Wallace S. Broecker | geochemistry |
| | Norman Davidson | chemistry, molecular biology |
| | James L. Flanagan | electrical engineering |
| | Richard M. Karp | computer science |
| | C. Kumar N. Patel | electrical engineering |
| | Ruth Patrick | limnology |
| | Paul Samuelson | economics |
| | Stephen Smale | mathematics |
| 1997 | William K. Estes | psychology |
| | Darleane C. Hoffman | chemistry |
| | Harold S. Johnston | chemistry |
| | Marshall N. Rosenbluth | theoretical plasma physics |
| | Martin Schwarzschild | astrophysics |
| | James Dewey Watson | genetics, biophysics |
| | Robert A. Weinberg | cancer research |
| | George W. Wetherill | planetary science |
| | Shing-Tung Yau | mathematics |
| 1998 | Bruce N. Ames | biochemistry, cancer research |
| | Don L. Anderson | geophysics |
| | John N. Bahcall | astrophysics |
| | John W. Cahn | materials science |
| | Cathleen Synge Morawetz | mathematics |
| | Janet D. Rowley | medicine, cancer research |
| | Eli Ruckenstein | chemical engineering |
| | George M. Whitesides | chemistry |
| | William Julius Wilson | sociology |
| 1999 | David Baltimore | virology, administration |
| | Felix E. Browder | mathematics |
| | Ronald R. Coifman | mathematics |
| | James Watson Cronin | particle physics |
| | Jared Diamond | physiology |
| | Leo P. Kadanoff | theoretical physics |
| | Lynn Margulis | microbiology |
| | Stuart A. Rice | chemistry |
| | John Ross | chemistry |

## National Medal of Science (continued)

| YEAR | NAME | FIELD |
|---|---|---|
| 1999 (cont.) | Susan Solomon | atmospheric science |
| | Robert M. Solow | economics |
| | Kenneth N. Stevens | electrical engineering, speech |
| 2000 | Nancy C. Andreasen | psychiatry |
| | John D. Baldeschwieler | chemistry |
| | Gary S. Becker | economics |
| | Yuan-Cheng B. Fung | bioengineering |
| | Ralph F. Hirschmann | chemistry |
| | Willis Eugene Lamb, Jr. | physics |
| | Jeremiah P. Ostriker | astrophysics |
| | Peter H. Raven | botany |
| | John Griggs Thompson | mathematics |
| | Karen K. Uhlenbeck | mathematics |
| | Gilbert F. White | geography |
| | Carl R. Woese | microbiology |
| 2001 | Andreas Acrivos | chemical engineering |
| | Francisco J. Ayala | molecular biology |
| | George F. Bass | nautical archaeology |
| | Mario R. Capecchi | genetics |
| | Marvin L. Cohen | materials science |
| | Ernest R. Davidson | chemistry |
| | Raymond Davis, Jr. | chemistry, astrophysics |
| | Ann M. Graybiel | neuroscience |
| | Charles D. Keeling | oceanography |
| | Gene E. Likens | ecology |
| | Victor A. McKusick | medical genetics |
| | Calyampudi R. Rao | mathematics, statistics |
| | Gabor A. Somorjai | chemistry |
| | Elias M. Stein | mathematics |
| | Harold Varmus | virology, administration |
| 2002 | Leo L. Beranek | engineering |
| | John I. Brauman | chemistry |
| | James E. Darnell | cell biology |
| | Richard L. Garwin | physics |
| | James G. Glimm | mathematics, statistics |
| | W. Jason Morgan | geophysics |
| | Evelyn M. Witkin | genetics |
| | Edward Witten | mathematical physics |
| 2003 | J. Michael Bishop | microbiology |
| | G. Brent Dalrymple | geology |
| | Carl R. de Boor | mathematics |
| | Riccardo Giacconi | astrophysics |
| | R. Duncan Luce | cognitive science |
| | John M. Prausnitz | chemical engineering |
| | Solomon H. Snyder | neuroscience |
| | Charles Yanofsky | molecular biology |
| 2004 | Kenneth J. Arrow | economics |
| | Norman E. Borlaug | agriculture |
| | Robert N. Clayton | geochemistry |
| | Edwin N. Lightfoot | engineering |
| | Stephen J. Lippard | chemistry |
| | Phillip A. Sharp | molecular biology, biochemistry |

| YEAR | NAME | FIELD |
|---|---|---|
| 2004 (cont.) | Thomas E. Starzl | medicine |
| | Dennis P. Sullivan | mathematics |
| 2005 | Jan D. Achenbach | mechanical engineering |
| | Ralph A. Alpher | astronomy |
| | Gordon H. Bower | psychology |
| | Bradley Efron | statistics |
| | Anthony S. Fauci | immunology |
| | Tobin J. Marks | chemistry |
| | Lonnie G. Thompson | glaciology |
| | Torsten N. Wiesel | neurobiology |
| 2006 | Hyman Bass | mathematics |
| | Marvin H. Caruthers | genetic engineering |
| | Rita R. Colwell | marine microbiology |
| | Peter B. Dervan | organic chemistry |
| | Nina V. Fedoroff | molecular biology |
| | Daniel Kleppner | atomic physics |
| | Robert S. Langer | medical research |
| | Lubert Stryer | biochemistry |
| 2007 | Fay Ajzenberg-Selove | nuclear physics |
| | Mostafa A. El-Sayed | laser dynamics |
| | Leonard Kleinrock | Internet technology |
| | Robert J. Lefkowitz | receptor biology |
| | Bert W. O'Malley | molecular biology |
| | Charles P. Slichter | condensed-matter physics |
| | Andrew J. Viterbi | wireless communications |
| | David J. Wineland | ionic physics |
| 2008 | Berni Alder | physical sciences |
| | Francis S. Collins | biology |
| | Joanna S. Fowler | chemistry |
| | Elaine Fuchs | biology |
| | James E. Gunn | physical sciences |
| | Rudolf E. Kálmán | engineering |
| | Michael I. Posner | behavioral and social sciences |
| | JoAnne Stubbe | chemistry |
| | J. Craig Venter | biology |
| 2009 | Yakir Aharonov | physical sciences |
| | Stephen J. Benkovic | chemistry |
| | Esther M. Conwell | physical sciences |
| | Anne Marye Fox | chemistry |
| | Susan Lee Lindquist | biology |
| | Mortimer Mishkin | behavioral and social sciences |
| | David Mumford | mathematics, computer science |
| | Stanley Prusiner | biology |
| | Warren Washington | physical sciences |
| | Amnon Yariv | engineering |
| 2010 | Jacqueline K. Barton | molecular biology |
| | Ralph L. Brinster | genetics |
| | Shu Chien | bioengineering |
| | Rudolf Jaenisch | molecular biology |
| | Peter J. Stang | molecular chemistry |
| | Richard A. Tapia | mathematics |
| | Srinivasa S.R. Varadhan | mathematics |

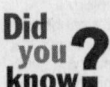

**Did you know?** The Council of the European Union has named one or more European Capitals of Culture yearly since 1985. With this designation comes qualification for the EU's Melina Mercouri International Prize, which is given to reward actions to safeguard the world's major cultural landscapes. It comes with a €1.5 million (US$1.9 million) award. The European Capitals of Culture for 2012 are Guimarães, Portugal, and Maribor, Slovenia; Marseille-Provence, France, and Košice, Slovakia, have been named for 2013.

# Nature, Science, Medicine, & Technology

## The Golden Age of Gas

### by Bryan Walsh, TIME

The global energy picture used to be simple. There were producers (oil giants like Saudi Arabia and natural gas titans like Russia), and they sold to consumers (industrial nations like the US, China, and Germany). It was a precarious situation, one that left consumers vulnerable to high prices and producers at risk of low prices, yet no one expected it to change anytime soon.

But it has, thanks largely to an advanced drilling process that sounds like a network-TV curse word: fracking. The technique, which involves the use of explosives, chemicals, and millions of gallons of water to create tiny fractures in shale thousands of feet underground, has unlocked new supplies of natural gas long considered too difficult and expensive to tap. In the US, where fracking (short for hydraulic fracturing) originated as the product of wildcat drillers and government researchers, it has transformed the industry, revitalizing domestic drilling and producing so much natural gas that US prices for the fuel fell to a 10-year low early in 2012.

Now Europe and China—which together have more than twice the US's estimated shale-gas reserves—are following suit, investing billions of dollars in shale-gas drilling. China announced in March 2012 it's aiming to produce 6.5 billion cubic meters of shale gas by 2015, and the same month the state-owned China National Petroleum Corp. signed a production-sharing agreement with Shell on shale gas. Europe is moving more slowly, though countries like gas-rich Poland are already drilling. The investments could change the global energy landscape by reducing the world's dependence on Middle Eastern and African resources.

"The US has given a major present to international energy with shale gas," Fatih Birol, chief economist of the International Energy Agency (IEA), told TIME in a 2012 interview. The question now is whether China and Europe can overcome the complex network of environmental, technical, and political hurdles now holding back their efforts.

### To Frack or Not to Frack

A little more than a decade after energy experts predicted the US would need to import liquefied natural gas (LNG) to offset declining domestic production, American companies are swimming in so much shale gas, they're lobbying Washington to allow LNG exports. But the US isn't the only place with fracking potential; shale gas is proving so abundant, the IEA has predicted that the world could be entering a golden age of gas, in which inexpensive natural gas replaces coal as the electricity source of choice. Energy-hungry Europe and China have two of the richest shale-gas reserves; China's is potentially the largest in the world.

But just because the gas is there doesn't mean it will be tapped. The shale-gas push in the US has been slowed by environmental concerns over fracking—chiefly the possibility of groundwater pollution—which will only intensify in politically greener and more crowded Europe. France and Bulgaria have already banned fracking for environmental reasons.

In China there are other obstacles. Its shale gas is buried more deeply, making development more expensive. State-owned Chinese companies lack fracking expertise. And while the richest reserves are found in relatively unpopulated areas—a plus—those lands tend to lack the water and pipelines needed to frack. China's geology could prove more challenging as well if, as in Britain, concerns arise about earthquakes and other problems attributable to drilling. The independent British company Cuadrilla Resources began drilling wells in northwestern England but suspended operations in 2011 after two small earthquakes were detected near the sites. Cuadrilla later released a report that said fracking likely caused the quakes. British environmentalists are warning about the groundwater contamination allegedly caused by fracking in the US. And although the estimates of British shale-gas reserves are impressive, they are preliminary. No one will know how much gas is economically recoverable until companies start drilling.

### Frack On

There are reasons for Europe and China to persist. Shale gas could allow former Soviet-bloc states like Poland, Romania, and Ukraine, which are highly dependent on Russian natural gas, to break free of Moscow, which has used energy as a political weapon. Russia is clearly worried—so worried that its president, Vladimir Putin, has been singing environmentalists' tune about the dangers of fracking. In Poland, which has the largest reserves in Europe, the government has offered more than 100 shale-gas concessions to mostly foreign energy companies. "Poland wants to get rid of Russian gas," says Anne-Sophie Corbeau, the IEA's senior gas expert. "They're getting a lot more support from the population than you're seeing in other countries."

Authoritarian China doesn't need that popular support; the government is encouraging state-owned oil companies to partner with experienced international players like Shell. "We completed 11 wells last year [2011]. We hope to effectively double that this year," Shell chief financial officer Simon Henry told reporters in April 2012.

Fracking a well, as any roughneck will tell you, is as much art as science. It was always going to take time to adapt the US experience abroad—and it may not take in every country. But fracking is here to stay, scrambling a global energy picture that had long seemed settled. There's no guarantee it will be golden, but we're definitely entering the age of gas.

# Time

## Time Zone Map

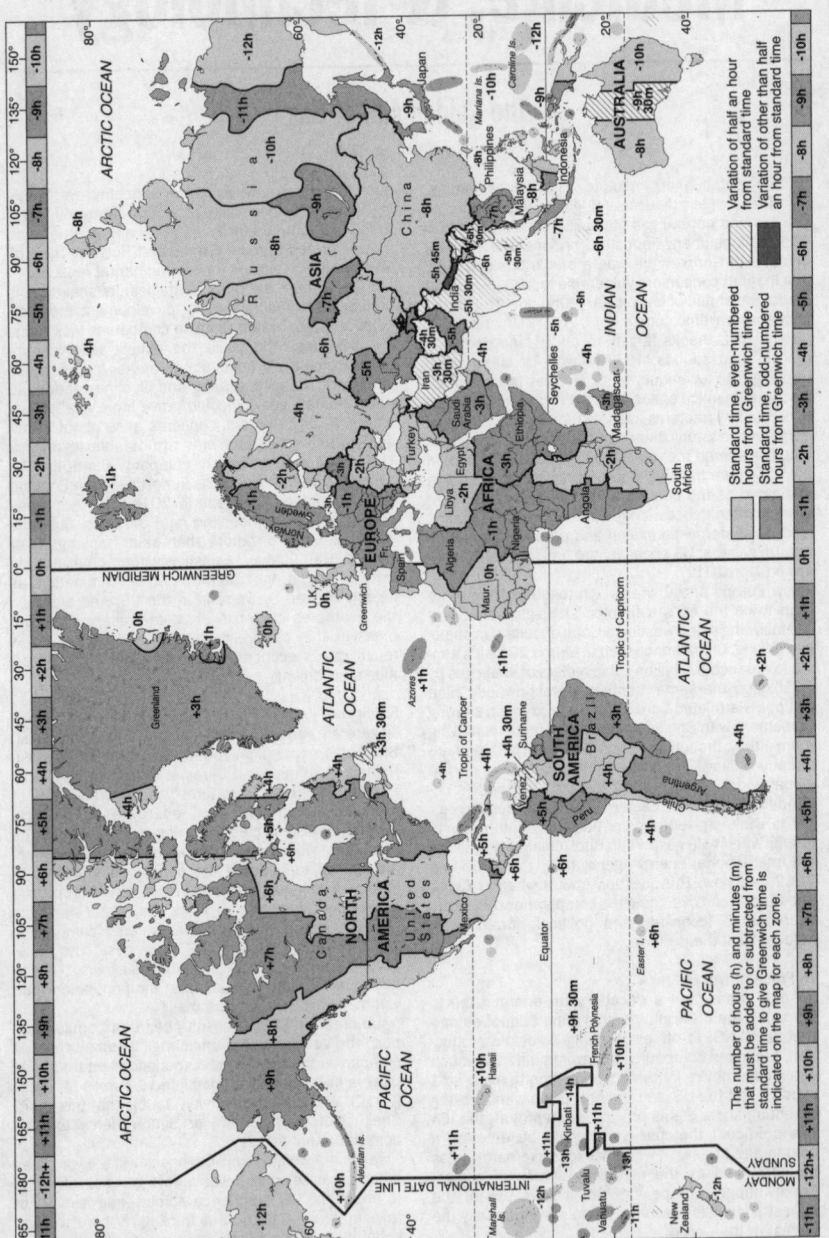

Based on data from HM Nautical Almanac Office

## Daylight Saving Time

Also called **summer time**, **daylight saving time** is a system for uniformly advancing clocks to extend daylight hours during conventional waking time in the summer. In the Northern Hemisphere, clocks are usually set ahead one hour in late March or in April and are set back one hour in late September or in October; most Southern Hemisphere countries that observe daylight saving time set clocks ahead in October or November and reset them in March or April. Whereas equatorial and tropical countries do not observe daylight saving time because daylight hours stay about the same from season to season, Kyrgyzstan and Iceland observe it year-round.

The practice was first suggested in a whimsical essay by **Benjamin Franklin** in 1784. In 1907 an Englishman, William Willett, campaigned for setting the clock ahead by 80 minutes in four moves of 20 minutes each on the first four Sundays in April and reversing this on the first four Sundays in September. In 1909 the British House of Commons rejected a bill to advance the clock by one hour in the spring and return to Greenwich Mean (standard) Time in the autumn.

Several countries, including Australia, Great Britain, Germany, and the United States, adopted **daylight saving time** during World War I to conserve fuel by reducing the need for artificial light. During World War II, clocks were kept continuously advanced by an hour in some nations—for instance, in the US from 9 Feb 1942 to 30 Sep 1945—and England used "double summer time" during part of the year, advancing clocks two hours from the standard time during the summer and one hour during the winter months.

In 2005 the US Congress changed the law governing daylight saving time, moving the start of it from the first Sunday in April to the second Sunday in March, while moving the end date from the last Sunday in October to the first Sunday in November starting in 2007. However, it is not observed in Hawaii, American Samoa, Guam, Puerto Rico, the Virgin Islands, the Northern Mariana Islands, or the state of Arizona (except Navajo reservations).

## Julian and Gregorian Calendars

The **Julian calendar**, also called the Old Style calendar, is a dating system established by Julius Caesar as a reform of the Roman republican calendar. Caesar, advised by the Alexandrian astronomer Sosigenes, made the new calendar solar, not lunar, and he took the length of the solar year as 365¼ days. The year was divided into 12 months, all of which had either 30 or 31 days except February, which contained 28 days in common (365-day) years and 29 in every fourth year (a leap year, of 366 days). Because of misunderstandings, the calendar was not established in smooth operation until AD 8. Further, Sosigenes had overestimated the length of the year by 11 minutes 14 seconds, and by the mid-1500s, the cumulative effect of this error had shifted the dates of the seasons by about 10 days from Caesar's time. This inaccuracy led **Pope Gregory XIII** to reform the Julian calendar. His **Gregorian calendar**, also called the New Style calendar, is still in general use. Gregory's proclamation in 1582 restored the calendar to the seasonal dates of AD 325, an adjustment of 10 days. Although the amount of regression was some 14 days by Pope Gregory's time, Gregory based his reform on restoration of the vernal equinox, then falling on 11 March, to the date (21 March) it had in AD 325, the time of the Council of Nicaea. Advancing the calendar 10 days after 4 Oct 1582, the day following being reckoned as 15 October, effected the change.

The Gregorian calendar differs from the Julian only in that no century year is a leap year unless it is exactly divisible by 400 (e.g., 1600, 2000). A further refinement, the designation of years evenly divisible by 4,000 as common (not leap) years, will keep the Gregorian calendar accurate to within one day in 20,000 years.

## Jewish Calendar

The **Jewish calendar** is lunisolar—i.e., regulated by the positions of both the Moon and the Sun. It consists usually of 12 alternating lunar months of 29 and 30 days each (except for Heshvan and Kislev, which sometimes have either 29 or 30 days), and totals 353, 354, or 355 days per year. The average lunar year (354 days) is adjusted to the solar year (365¼ days) by the periodic introduction of leap years in order to assure that the major festivals fall in their proper season. The leap year consists of an additional 30-day month called **First Adar**, which always precedes the month of (Second) Adar. (During leap year, the Adar holidays are postponed to Second Adar.) A leap year consists of either 383, 384, or 385 days and occurs seven times during every 19-year period (the so-called Metonic cycle). Among the consequences of the lunisolar structure are these: (1) The number of days in a year may vary considerably, from 353 to 385 days. (2) The first day of a month can fall on any day of the week, that day varying from year to year. Consequently, the days of the week upon which an annual Jewish festival falls vary from year to year despite the festival's fixed position in the Jewish month. The months of the Jewish calendar and their Gregorian equivalents are as follows:

| JEWISH MONTH | GREGORIAN MONTH(S) | JEWISH MONTH | GREGORIAN MONTH(S) |
|---|---|---|---|
| Tishri | September–October | Nisan | March–April |
| Heshvan, or Marheshvan | October–November | Iyyar | April–May |
| Kislev | November–December | Sivan | May–June |
| Tevet | December–January | Tammuz | June–July |
| Shevat | January–February | Av | July–August |
| Adar | February–March | Elul | August–September |

# Muslim Calendar

The **Muslim calendar** (also called the **Islamic calendar**, or **Hijrah**) is a dating system used in the Muslim world that is based on a year of 12 months. Each month begins with the sighting of the crescent of the new moon as it emerges from eclipse. The **months** of the Muslim calendar are Muharram, Safar, Rabi I, Rabi II, Jumada I, Jumada II, Rajab, Sha'ban, Ramadan, Shawwal, Dhu al-Qa'dah, and Dhu al-Hijjah.

In the standard Muslim calendar the months are alternately 30 and 29 days long except for the 12th month, Dhu al-Hijjah, the length of which is varied in a 30-year cycle intended to keep the calendar in step with the true phases of the Moon. In 11 years of this cycle, Dhu al-Hijjah has 30 days, and in the other 19 years it has 29. Thus the year has either 354 or 355 days. No months are intercalated, so that the named months do not remain in the same seasons but retrogress through the entire solar, or seasonal, year (of about 365.25 days) every 32.5 solar years.

There are some exceptions to this calendar in the Muslim world. Turkey uses the Gregorian calendar, while Iran has a Muslim calendar that is based on a solar year. The Iranian calendar still begins from the same dating point as other Muslim calendars—that is, some 10 years prior to the death of Muhammad in AD 632. Thus, the Gregorian year AD 2013 corresponds to the Hijrah years of AH 1434–35.

# Chinese Calendar

The **Chinese calendar** is a dating system used concurrently with the Gregorian (Western) calendar in China and Taiwan and in neighboring countries (e.g., Japan). The calendar consists of 12 months of alternately 29 and 30 days, equal to 354 or 355 days, or approximately 12 full lunar cycles. Intercalary months have been inserted to keep the calendar year in step with the solar year of about 365 days. **Months** have no names but are instead referred to by numbers within a year and sometimes also by a series of 12 animal names that from ancient times have been attached to years and to hours of the day.

The calendar also incorporates a **meteorologic cycle** that contains 24 points, each beginning one of the periods named. The establishment of this cycle required a fair amount of astronomical understanding of Earth as a celestial body. Modern scholars acknowledge the superiority of pre-Sung **Chinese astronomy** (at least until about the 13th century AD) over that of other, contemporary nations.

The **24 points** within the meteorologic cycle coincide with points 15° apart on the ecliptic (the plane of Earth's yearly journey around the Sun or, if it is thought that the Sun turns around Earth, the apparent journey of the Sun against the stars). It takes about 15.2 days for the Sun to travel from one of these points to another (because the ecliptic is a complete circle of 360°), and the Sun needs 365¼ days to finish its journey in this cycle. Supposedly, each of the 12 months of the year contains two points, but, because a lunar month has only 29½ days and the two points share about 30.4 days, there is always the chance that a lunar month will fail to contain both points, though the distance between any two given points is only 15°. If such an occasion occurs, the intercalation of an extra month takes place. For instance, one may find a year with two "Julys" or with two "Augusts" in the Chinese calendar. In fact, as mentioned above, the exact length of the month in the Chinese calendar is either 30 days or 29 days—a phenomenon that reflects its lunar origin.

| SOLAR TERMS—CHINESE (ENGLISH EQUIVALENTS) | GREGORIAN DATE (APPROXIMATE) | LUNAR MONTH (CORRESPONDENCE OF LUNAR AND SOLAR MONTHS APPROXIMATE) |
|---|---|---|
| Lichun (spring begins) | 5 February | 1—tiger |
| Yushui (rain water) | 19 February | |
| Jingzhe (excited insects) | 5 March | 2—rabbit/hare |
| Chunfen (vernal equinox) | 20 March | |
| Qingming (clear and bright) | 5 April | 3—dragon |
| Guyu (grain rains) | 20 April | |
| Lixia (summer begins) | 5 May | 4—snake |
| Xiaoman (grain fills) | 21 May | |
| Mangzhong (grain in ear) | 6 June | 5—horse |
| Xiazhi (summer solstice) | 21 June | |
| Xiaoshu (slight heat) | 7 July | 6—sheep/ram |
| Dashu (great heat) | 23 July | |
| Liqiu (autumn begins) | 7 August | 7—monkey |
| Chushu (limit of heat) | 23 August | |
| Bailu (white dew) | 8 September | 8—chicken/rooster |
| Qiufen (autumn equinox) | 23 September | |
| Hanlu (cold dew) | 8 October | 9—dog |
| Shuangjiang (hoar frost descends) | 24 October | |
| Lidong (winter begins) | 8 November | 10—pig/boar |
| Xiaoxue (little snow) | 22 November | |
| Daxue (heavy snow) | 7 December | 11—rat |
| Dongzhi (winter solstice) | 22 December | |
| Xiaohan (little cold) | 6 January | 12—cow/ox |
| Dahan (severe cold) | 20 January | |

## Chinese Calendar (continued)

| CHINESE NEW YEAR | GREGORIAN DATE | ANIMAL | CHINESE NEW YEAR | GREGORIAN DATE | ANIMAL |
|---|---|---|---|---|---|
| 4705 | 18 Feb 2007 | pig/boar | 4712 | 31 Jan 2014 | horse |
| 4706 | 7 Feb 2008 | rat | 4713 | 19 Feb 2015 | sheep/ram |
| 4707 | 26 Jan 2009 | cow/ox | 4714 | 9 Feb 2016 | monkey |
| 4708 | 14 Feb 2010 | tiger | 4715 | 28 Jan 2017 | rooster |
| 4709 | 3 Feb 2011 | rabbit/hare | 4716 | 16 Feb 2018 | dog |
| 4710 | 23 Jan 2012 | dragon | 4717 | 5 Feb 2019 | boar |
| 4711 | 10 Feb 2013 | snake | 4718 | 25 Jan 2020 | rat |

## Religious and Traditional Holidays

The word holiday comes from "holy day," and it was originally a day of dedication to religious observance; in modern times a holiday may be of either religious or secular commemoration. All dates in this article are Gregorian.

**Jewish holidays**—The major holidays are the Pilgrim Festivals: **Pesah** (Passover), **Shavuot** (Feast of Weeks, or Pentecost), and **Sukkoth** (Tabernacles); and the High Holidays: **Rosh Hashana** (New Year) and **Yom Kippur** (Day of Atonement).

Pesah commemorates the Exodus from Egypt and the servitude that preceded it. As such, it is the most significant of the commemorative holidays, for it celebrates the very inception of the Jewish people—i.e., the event that provided the basis for the covenant between God and Israel. The term Pesah refers to the paschal (Passover) lamb sacrificed on the eve of the Exodus, the blood of which marked the Jewish homes to be spared from God's plague. Leaven (se'or) and foods containing leaven (hametz) are neither to be owned nor consumed during Pesah. Aside from meats, fresh fruits, and vegetables, it is customary to consume only those foods prepared under rabbinic supervision and labeled "kosher for Passover." The unleavened bread (matzo) consists entirely of flour and water. On the eve of Pesah families partake of the seder, an elaborate festival meal. The table is bedecked with an assortment of foods symbolizing the passage from slavery (e.g., bitter herbs) into freedom (e.g., wine). Pesah will begin at sundown on 25 March and end on 2 April in 2013. (All Jewish holidays begin at sundown.)

A distinctive **Rosh Hashana** observance is the sounding of the ram's horn (shofar) at the synagogue service. Symbolic ceremonies, such as eating bread and apples dipped in honey, accompanied by prayers for a "sweet" and propitious year, are performed at the festive meals. In 2013 Rosh Hashana will begin at sundown on 4 September and will end on 6 September. **Yom Kippur** is a day when sins are confessed and expiated and man and God are reconciled. It is the holiest and most solemn day of the Jewish year. It is marked by fasting, penitence, and prayer. Working, eating, drinking, washing, anointing one's body, engaging in sexual intercourse, and donning leather shoes are all forbidden. Yom Kippur begins at sundown on 13 September in 2013.

Though not as important theologically, the feast of **Hanukkah** has become socially significant, especially in Western cultures. Hanukkah commemorates the rededication (164 BCE) of the Second Temple of Jerusalem after its desecration three years earlier. Though modern Israel tends to emphasize the military victory of the general Judas Maccabeus, the distinctive rite of lighting the menorah also recalls the Talmud story of how the small supply of nondesecrated oil—enough for one day—miraculously burned in the Temple for eight full days until new oil could be obtained. During Hanukkah, in addition to the lighting of the ceremonial candles, gifts are exchanged and children play holiday games. The festival occurs 8 through 16 Dec 2012, subsequently spanning 27 November through 5 Dec 2013.

**Christian holidays**—The major holidays celebrated by nearly all Christians are **Easter** and **Christmas**.

**Easter** celebrates the Resurrection of Jesus on the third day after his Crucifixion. In the Christian liturgical year, Easter is preceded by the period of **Lent**, the 40 days (not counting Sundays) before Easter, which traditionally were observed as a period of penance and fasting. Lent begins on **Ash Wednesday**, a day devoted to penitence. Holy Week precedes **Easter Sunday** and includes **Maundy Thursday**, the commemoration of Jesus' last supper with his disciples; **Good Friday**, the day of his Crucifixion; and **Holy Saturday**, the transition between Crucifixion and Resurrection. Easter shares with Christmas the presence of numerous customs, some of which have little to do with the Christian celebration of the resurrection but clearly derive from folk customs. In 2013 the Western churches (nearly all Christian denominations) will observe Ash Wednesday on 13 February and Easter on 31 March. For Eastern Orthodox Christians, Lent begins on 18 March in 2013.

**Christmas** commemorates the birth of Jesus Christ. Since the early part of the 20th century, Christmas has also become a secular family holiday, observed by non-Christians, devoid of Christian elements, and marked by an increasingly elaborate exchange of gifts. In this secular Christmas celebration, a mythical figure named Santa Claus plays the pivotal role. Christmas is held on 25 December in most Christian cultures but occurs on the following 7 January in some Eastern Orthodox churches.

**Islamic holidays**—**Ramadan** is the holy month of fasting for Muslims. The Islamic ordinance prescribes abstention from evil thoughts and deeds as well as from food, drink, and sexual intercourse from dawn until dusk throughout the month. The beginning and end of Ramadan are announced when one trustworthy witness testifies before the authorities that the new moon has been sighted; a cloudy sky may therefore delay or prolong the fast. The end of the fast is celebrated as the feast of 'Id al-Fitr. Ramadan is scheduled to begin on 8 July in 2013 and 'Id al-Fitr on 7 August of that year (all Islamic holidays begin at sundown). The Muslim New Year, **Hijrah**, is on 14 November in 2012 and 3 November in 2013.

## Religious and Traditional Holidays (continued)

After 'Id al-Fitr, the second major Islamic festival is 'Id al-Adha, observed on 14 through 18 October in 2013. Throughout the Muslim world, all who are able to sacrifice sheep, goats, camels, or cattle and then divide the flesh equally among themselves, the poor, and friends and neighbors to commemorate the ransom of Ishmael with a ram. This festival falls at the end of the hajj, the pilgrimage to the holy city of Mecca in Saudi Arabia, which every adult Muslim of either sex must make at least once in his or her lifetime.

'Ashura was originally designated in AD 622 by Muhammad as a day of fasting from sunset to sunset, probably patterned on the Jewish Day of Atonement, Yom Kippur. Among the Shi'ites, 'Ashura is a major festival that commemorates the death of Husayn (Hussein), son of 'Ali and grandson of Muhammad. It is a period of expressions of grief and of pilgrimage to Karbala (the site of Husayn's death, in present-day Iraq). 'Ashura is on 23 November in 2012 and 12 November in 2013.

**Buddhist holidays**—Holidays practiced by a large number of Buddhists are *uposatha* days and days that commemorate events in the life of the Buddha.

The four monthly holy days of ancient Buddhism continue to be observed in the Theravada countries of Southeast Asia. These *uposatha* days—the new moon and full moon days of each lunar month and the eighth day following the new and full moons—have their origin, according to some scholars, in the fast days that preceded the Vedic soma sacrifices.

The three major events of the Buddha's life—his birth, Enlightenment, and entrance into final nirvana—are commemorated in all Buddhist countries but not everywhere on the same day. In the Theravada countries the three events are all observed together on **Vesak**, the full moon day of the sixth lunar month, which usually occurs in May. In Japan and other Mahayana countries, the three anniversaries of the Buddha are observed on separate days (in some countries the birth date is 8 April, the Enlightenment date is 8 December, and the death date is 15 February).

**Chinese holidays**—The **Chinese New Year** is celebrated with a big family meal, and presents of cash are given to children in red envelopes. In 2013 the Chinese New Year will be on 10 February.

During the **Chinese Moon Festival**, on the 15th day of the 8th month of the lunar calendar, people return to their homes to visit with their family. The traditional food is moon cakes, round pastries stuffed with food such as red bean paste. The Moon Festival will occur on 19 September in 2013.

**Japanese holidays**—The Japanese celebrate **7-5-3 day** (Shichi-go-san no hi), in which parents bring children of those ages to the Shinto shrine to pray for their continued health. This day is held on 15 November.

In mid-July (or mid-August, in some areas) the Japanese celebrate **Bon** (also known as Bon Matsuri, or Urabon). The festival honors the spirits of deceased householders and of the dead generally. Memorial stones are cleaned, community dances are performed, and paper lanterns and fires are lit to welcome the dead and to bid them farewell at the end of their visit. The Shinto New Year, **Gantan-sai**, is celebrated on 1–3 January.

**Hindu holidays**—**Dussehra** celebrates the victory of Rama over Ravana, the symbol of evil on earth. In 2013 Dussehra falls on 14 October. **Diwali** is a festival of lights devoted to Laksmi, the goddess of wealth. During the festival, small earthenware lamps filled with oil are lit and placed in rows along the parapets of temples and houses and set adrift on rivers and streams. Diwali is on 3 November in 2013. **Maha-sivaratri**, the most important sectarian festival of the year for devotees of the Hindu god Shiva, occurs on 10 March in 2013. **Holi** is a spring festival, probably of ancient origin. Participants throw colored waters and powders on one another, and, on this day, the usual restrictions of caste, sex, status, and age are disregarded. It will be on 27 March in 2013.

**Sikh holidays**—Sikhs observe all festivals celebrated by the Hindus of northern India. In addition, they celebrate the birthdays of the first and the last Gurus and the martyrdom of the fifth (Arjun) and the ninth (Tegh Bahadur). In 2013 **Guru Nanak Dev Sahib's birthday** is celebrated on 17 November, and that of **Guru Gobind Singh Sahib** is celebrated on 5 January in 2014. On 16 June in 2014 **Arjun's martyrdom** is observed. *Kachi lassi* (sweetened milk) is offered to passersby to commemorate his death. On 24 November in 2014 the **martyrdom of Guru Tegh Bahadur** is observed.

**Baha'i holidays**—The Baha'i New Year (**Naw Ruz**) in 2013 will fall on 20 March (all Baha'i holidays begin at sundown). Other important observances include the **declaration of the Bab** (22 May), the **Baha Ullah's birth** (11 November), and **Ascension** (28 May).

**Zoroastrian holidays**—**Noruz** (New Year) is on 21 March for 2013, and the 28th of that month is **Khordad Sal**, the birth of the prophet Zarathustra.

**African American holiday**—**Kwanzaa** (Swahili for "First Fruits") is celebrated each year from 26 December to 1 January and is patterned after various African harvest festivals. Maulana Karenga, a black-studies professor, created Kwanzaa in 1966 as a nonreligious celebration of family and social values. Each day of Kwanzaa is dedicated to one of seven principles: unity (*umoja*), self-determination (*kujichagulia*), collective responsibility (*ujima*), cooperative economics (*ujamaa*), purpose (*nia*), creativity (*kuumba*), and faith (*imani*).

 **Did you know?**

Rinderpest, or cattle plague, officially became only the second disease in history to be eradicated. The disease, described as the equivalent of measles in cattle, was responsible for deaths in herds catastrophic enough to cause famines in previous centuries. On 28 Jun 2011, the United Nations Food and Agriculture Organization declared the disease eradicated. Only smallpox previously had been so designated.

## Perpetual Calendar

The perpetual calendar is a type of dating system that makes it possible to find the correct day of the week for any date over a wide range of years. Aspects of the perpetual calendar can be found in the Jewish religious and the Julian calendars, and some form of it has appeared in many proposed calendar reforms.

To find the day of the week for any Gregorian or Julian date in the perpetual calendar provided in this table, first find the proper dominical letter (one of the letters A through G) for the year in the upper table. Leap years have two dominical letters, the first applicable to dates in January and February, the second to dates in the remaining months. Then find the same dominical letter in the lower table, in whichever column it appears opposite the month in question. The days then fall as given in the lowest section of the column.

| YEAR | CENTURY | | | | | | | | | | | |
|---|---|---|---|---|---|---|---|---|---|---|---|---|
| | JULIAN CALENDAR | | | | | | | GREGORIAN CALENDAR | | | | |
| | 0 / 700 / 1400 | 100 / 800 / 1500* | 200 / 900 | 300 / 1000 | 400 / 1100 | 500 / 1200 | 600 / 1300 | 1500** | 1600 / 2000 | 1700 / 2100 | 1800 / 2200 | 1900 / 2300 |
| 0 | DC | ED | FE | GF | AG | BA | CB | ... | BA | C | E | G |
| 1 29 57 85 | B | C | D | E | F | G | A | F | G | B | D | F |
| 2 30 58 86 | A | B | C | D | E | F | G | E | F | A | C | E |
| 3 31 59 87 | G | A | B | C | D | E | F | D | E | G | B | D |
| 4 32 60 88 | FE | GF | AG | BA | CB | DC | ED | CB | DC | FE | AG | CB |
| 5 33 61 89 | D | E | F | G | A | B | C | A | B | D | F | A |
| 6 34 62 90 | C | D | E | F | G | A | B | G | A | C | E | G |
| 7 35 63 91 | B | C | D | E | F | G | A | F | G | B | D | F |
| 8 36 64 92 | AG | BA | CB | DC | ED | FE | GF | ED | FE | AG | CB | ED |
| 9 37 65 93 | F | G | A | B | C | D | E | C | D | F | A | C |
| 10 38 66 94 | E | F | G | A | B | C | D | B | C | E | G | B |
| 11 39 67 95 | D | E | F | G | A | B | C | A | B | D | F | A |
| 12 40 68 96 | CB | DC | ED | FE | GF | AG | BA | GF | AG | CB | ED | GF |
| 13 41 69 97 | A | B | C | D | E | F | G | E | F | A | C | E |
| 14 42 70 98 | G | A | B | C | D | E | F | D | E | G | B | D |
| 15 43 71 99 | F | G | A | B | C | D | E | C | D | F | A | C |
| 16 44 72 | ED | FE | GF | AG | BA | CB | DC | ... | CB | ED | GF | BA |
| 17 45 73 | C | D | E | F | G | A | B | ... | A | C | E | G |
| 18 46 74 | B | C | D | E | F | G | A | ... | G | B | D | F |
| 19 47 75 | A | B | C | D | E | F | G | ... | F | A | C | E |
| 20 48 76 | GF | AG | BA | CB | DC | ED | FE | ... | ED | GF | BA | DC |
| 21 49 77 | E | F | G | A | B | C | D | ... | C | E | G | B |
| 22 50 78 | D | E | F | G | A | B | C | ... | B | D | F | A |
| 23 51 79 | C | D | E | F | G | A | B | ... | A | C | E | G |
| 24 52 80 | BA | CB | DC | ED | FE | GF | AG | ... | GF | BA | DC | FE |
| 25 53 81 | G | A | B | C | D | E | F | ... | E | G | B | D |
| 26 54 82 | F | G | A | B | C | D | E | C | D | F | A | C |
| 27 55 83 | E | F | G | A | B | C | D | B | C | E | G | B |
| 28 56 84 | DC | ED | FE | GF | AG | BA | CB | AG | BA | DC | FE | AG |

| MONTH | DOMINICAL LETTER | | | | | | |
|---|---|---|---|---|---|---|---|
| January, October | A | B | C | D | E | F | G |
| February, March, November | D | E | F | G | A | B | C |
| April, July | G | A | B | C | D | E | F |
| May | B | C | D | E | F | G | A |
| June | E | F | G | A | B | C | D |
| August | C | D | E | F | G | A | B |
| September, December | F | G | A | B | C | D | E |
| 1 8 15 22 29 | Sunday | Saturday | Friday | Thursday | Wednesday | Tuesday | Monday |
| 2 9 16 23 30 | Monday | Sunday | Saturday | Friday | Thursday | Wednesday | Tuesday |
| 3 10 17 24 31 | Tuesday | Monday | Sunday | Saturday | Friday | Thursday | Wednesday |
| 4 11 18 25 | Wednesday | Tuesday | Monday | Sunday | Saturday | Friday | Thursday |
| 5 12 19 26 | Thursday | Wednesday | Tuesday | Monday | Sunday | Saturday | Friday |
| 6 13 20 27 | Friday | Thursday | Wednesday | Tuesday | Monday | Sunday | Saturday |
| 7 14 21 28 | Saturday | Friday | Thursday | Wednesday | Tuesday | Monday | Sunday |

*On and before 1582, 4 October only.    **On and after 1582, 15 October only.

Source: Smithsonian Physical Tables, 9th edition, rev. 2003.

## Civil Holidays

| DAY | EVENT |
| --- | --- |
| 1 January | New Year's Day, the first day of the modern calendar (various countries) |
| 20 January | Inauguration Day, for quadrennial inauguration of US president |
| 26 January | Australia Day, commemorates the establishment of the first British settlement in Australia |
| 3rd Monday in January | Martin Luther King Day, for birth of US civil rights leader |
| 2nd new moon after winter solstice (at the earliest 21 January and at the latest 19 February) | New Year, for Chinese lunar year, inaugurating a 15-day celebration |
| 6 February | Waitangi Day, for Treaty of Waitangi, granting British sovereignty (New Zealand) |
| 11 February | National Foundation Day, for founding by first emperor (Japan) |
| 14 February | St. Valentine's Day, celebrating the exchange of love messages and named for either of two 3rd-century Christian martyrs (various) |
| 3rd Monday in February | Presidents' Day, Washington-Lincoln Day, or Washington's Birthday, for birthdays of US Presidents George Washington and Abraham Lincoln |
| 8 March | International Women's Day, celebration of the women's liberation movement |
| 17 March | St. Patrick's Day, for patron saint of Ireland (Ireland and various) |
| 21 or 22 March | Vernal Equinox Day, for beginning of spring (Japan) |
| 25 March | Independence Day, for proclamation of independence from the Ottoman Empire (Greece) |
| 4th Sunday in Lent | Mothering Day (UK) |
| 1 April | April Fools' Day, or All Fools' Day, day for playing jokes, falling one week after the old New Year's Day of 25 March (various) |
| 5 April | Qingming, for sweeping tombs and honoring the dead (China) |
| 7 April | World Health Day, for founding of World Health Organization |
| 22 April | Earth Day, for conservation and reclaiming of the natural environment (various) |
| 25 April | ANZAC Day, for landing at Gallipoli (Australia/New Zealand/Samoa/Tonga) |
| 29 April | Green Day, national holiday for environment and nature (Japan) |
| 30 April | Queen's Birthday, for Queen Beatrix's investiture and former queen Juliana's birthday (The Netherlands) |
| 1 May | May Day, celebrated as labor day or as festival of flowers (various) |
| 3 May | Constitution Memorial Day, for establishment of democratic government (Japan) |
| 5 May | Children's Day, honoring children (Japan/Republic of Korea) |
| 5 May | Cinco de Mayo, anniversary of Mexico's victory over France in the Battle of Puebla (Mexico) |
| 8/9 May | V-E Day, or Liberation Day, for end of World War II in Europe (various) |
| 2nd Sunday in May | Mother's Day, honoring mothers (US) |
| Monday on or preceding 25 May | Victoria Day, for Queen Victoria's birthday (Canada) |
| 30 or last Monday in May | Memorial Day, or Decoration Day, in honor of the deceased, especially the war dead (US) |
| 2 June | Anniversary of the Republic, for referendum establishing republic (Italy) |
| 5 June | Constitution Day (Denmark) |
| 6 June | National Day, for Gustav I Vasa's ascension to the throne and adoption of Constitution (Sweden) |
| 10 June | Portugal's Day, or Camões Memorial Day, anniversary of Luis de Camões's death |
| 14 June | Flag Day, honoring flag (US) |
| 3rd Saturday in June | Queen's Official Birthday, for Queen Elizabeth II (UK/New Zealand) |
| 3rd Sunday in June | Father's Day, honoring fathers (US) |
| 23 June | National Day, for Grand Duke Jean's official birthday (Luxembourg) |
| 23–24 June | Midsummer Eve and Midsummer Day, celebrating the return of summer (various European) |
| last Sunday in June | Gay and Lesbian Pride Day, final day of weeklong advocacy of rights of gay men and lesbians (international) |
| 1 July | Canada Day (formerly Dominion Day), for establishment of dominion |
| 4 July | Independence Day, for Declaration of Independence from Britain (US) |
| 12 July | Orangemen's Day, or Orange Day, anniversary of the Battle of the Boyne (Northern Ireland) |
| 14 July | Bastille Day, for fall of the Bastille and onset of French Revolution (France) |
| 21 July | National Day, for separation from The Netherlands (Belgium) |
| 1 August | National Day, anniversary of the founding of the Swiss Confederation (Switzerland) |
| 6 August | Hiroshima Day, for dropping of atomic bomb (Japan) |
| full-moon day of 8th lunar month | Chusok, harvest festival (Republic of Korea) |
| 1st Monday in September | Labor Day, tribute to workers (US/Canada) |
| 15 September | Respect-for-the-Aged Day, for the elderly (Japan) |
| 16 September | Independence Day, for independence from Spain (Mexico) |
| 23 or 24 September | Autumnal Equinox Day, for beginning of autumn; in honor of ancestors (Japan) |

## Civil Holidays (continued)

| DAY | EVENT |
|---|---|
| two weeks ending on 1st Sunday in October | Oktoberfest, festival of food and drink, formerly commemorating marriage of King Louis (Ludwig) I (Germany) |
| 3 October | Day of German Unity, for reunification of Germany |
| 5 October | Republic Day, for founding of the republic (Portugal) |
| 12 or 2nd Monday in October | Hispanic Day, Columbus Day, Discovery Day, or Day of the Race, for Christopher Columbus's discovery of the New World on behalf of Spain (Spain and various) |
| 2nd Monday in October | Thanksgiving Day, harvest festival (Canada) |
| 24 October | United Nations Day, for effective date of UN Charter (international) |
| 26 October | National Day, for end of postwar occupation and return of sovereignty (Austria) |
| 31 October | Halloween, or All Hallows' Eve, festive celebration of ghosts and spirits, on eve of All Saints' Day (various) |
| 5 November | Guy Fawkes Day, anniversary of the Gunpowder Plot to blow up the king and Parliament (UK) |
| 11 November | Armistice Day, Remembrance Day, or Veterans Day, honoring participants in past wars and recalling the Armistice of World War I (various) |
| 23 November | Labor Thanksgiving Day, honoring workers (Japan) |
| 4th Thursday in November | Thanksgiving Day, harvest festival (US) |
| 16 December | Day of Reconciliation, for promoting national unity (South Africa) |
| 23 December | Emperor's Birthday, for birthday of Emperor Akihito (Japan) |
| 26 December | Boxing Day, second day of Christmas, for giving presents to service people (various) |
| 31 December | New Year's Eve, celebration ushering out the old year and in the new year (various) |

# The Universe

## Astronomical Constants

| QUANTITY | SYMBOL | VALUE |
|---|---|---|
| astronomical unit | AU | length of the semimajor axis of the Earth's orbit around the Sun—149,597,870 km (92,955,808 mi) |

measures large distances in space; equals the average distance from the Earth to the Sun

| | | |
|---|---|---|
| parsec | pc | one parsec equals 3.26 light-years |

measures the distance at which the radius of the Earth's orbit subtends an angle of one second of arc

| | | |
|---|---|---|
| light-year | ly | $9.46089 \times 10^{12}$ km ($5.8787 \times 10^{12}$ mi) |

measures the distance traveled by light moving in a vacuum in the course of one year

| | | |
|---|---|---|
| speed of light (in a vacuum) | c | $2.99792458 \times 10^{10}$ cm per sec (186,282 mi per sec) |

| | | |
|---|---|---|
| mass of the Sun | Sun $M$. | $1.989 \times 10^{30}$ kg (330,000 times the mass of the Earth) |

| | | |
|---|---|---|
| radius of the Sun | Sun $R$. | $6.96 \times 10^{8}$ m (109 times the radius of Earth) |

| | | |
|---|---|---|
| Earth's mean radius | | 6,378 km (3,963 mi) |

| | | |
|---|---|---|
| mean solar day (on Earth) | | 24 h 3 min 56.55 sec of mean sideral time |

the interval between two successive passages of the Sun across the same meridian is a solar day; in practice, since the rate of the Sun's motion varies with the seasons, use is made of a fictitious Sun that always moves across the sky at an even rate

| | | |
|---|---|---|
| tropical (or solar) year (on Earth) | | 365.256 days |

the time required for the Earth's orbital motion to return the Sun's position to the spring equinoctial point

| | | |
|---|---|---|
| synodic month (on Earth) | | 29.53 days |

the time required for the Moon to pass through one complete cycle of phases

## Definitions of Astronomical Positions

A conjunction is an apparent meeting or passing of two or more celestial bodies. For example, the Moon is in conjunction with the Sun at the phase of new Moon, when it moves between the Earth and Sun and the side turned toward the Earth is dark. Inferior planets—those with orbits smaller than the Earth's (namely, Venus and Mercury)—have two kinds of conjunctions with the Sun. An **inferior conjunction** occurs when the planet passes approximately between Earth and Sun; if it passes exactly between them, moving across the Sun's face as seen from Earth, it is said to be in transit (see below). A **superior conjunction** occurs when Earth and the other planet are on opposite sides of the Sun, but all three bodies are again nearly in a straight line. Superior planets, those having orbits larger than the Earth's, can have only superior conjunctions with the Sun.

When celestial bodies appear in opposite directions in the sky they are said to be in **opposition**. The Moon, when full, is said to be in opposition to the Sun (the Earth is then approximately between them). A superior planet (one with an orbit farther from the Sun than Earth's) is in opposition when Earth passes between it and the Sun. The opposition of a planet is a good time to observe it, because the planet is then at its nearest point to the Earth and in its full phase. The inferior planets, Venus and Mercury, can never be in opposition to the Sun.

When a celestial body as seen from the Earth makes a right angle with the direction of the Sun it is said to be in **quadrature**. The Moon at first or last quarter is said to be at east or west quadrature, respectively. A superior planet is at west quadrature when its position is 90° west of the Sun.

The east–west coordinate by which the position of a celestial body is ordinarily measured is known as the **right ascension**. Right ascension in combination with **declination** defines the position of a celestial object. Declination is the angular distance of a body north or south of the celestial equator. North declination is considered positive and south, negative. Thus, +90° declination marks the north celestial pole, 0° the celestial equator, and −90° the south celestial pole. The symbol for right ascension is the Greek letter α (alpha) and for declination the lowercase Greek letter Δ (delta).

The angular distance in celestial longitude separating the Moon or a planet from the Sun is known as **elongation**. The greatest elongation possible for the two inferior planets is about 48° in the case of Venus and about 28° in that of Mercury. Elongation may also refer to the angular distance of any celestial body from another around which it revolves or from a particular point in the sky; e.g., the extreme east or west position of a star with reference to the north celestial pole.

The point at which a planet is closest to the Sun is called the **perihelion**, and the most distant point in that planet's orbit is the **aphelion**. The term helion refers specifically to the Sun as the primary body about which the planet is orbiting.

**Occultation** refers to the obscuring of the light of an astronomical body, most commonly a star, by another astronomical body, such as a planet or a satellite. Hence, a solar eclipse is the occultation of the Sun by the Moon. From occultations of stars by planets, asteroids, and satellites, astronomers are able to determine the precise sizes and shapes of the latter bodies in addition to the temperatures of planetary atmospheres. For example, astronomers unexpectedly discovered the rings of Uranus during a stellar occultation on 10 Mar 1977.

A complete or partial obscuring of a celestial body by another is an **eclipse**; these occur when three celestial objects become aligned. The Sun is eclipsed when the Moon comes between it and the Earth; the Moon is eclipsed when it moves into the shadow of the Earth cast by the Sun. Eclipses of natural or artificial satellites of a planet occur as the satellites move into the planet's shadow. When the apparent size of the eclipsed body is much smaller than that of the eclipsing body, the phenomenon is known as an **occultation** (see above). Examples are the disappearance of a star, nebula, or planet behind the Moon, or the vanishing of a natural satellite or space probe behind some body of the solar system. A **transit** (see above) occurs when, as viewed from the Earth, a relatively small body passes across the disk of a larger body, usually the Sun or a planet, eclipsing only a very small area: Mercury and Venus periodically transit the Sun, and a satellite may transit its planet.

When an object orbiting the Earth is at the point in its orbit that is the greatest distance from the center of the Earth, this point is known as **apogee**; the term is also used to describe the point farthest from a planet or a satellite (as the Moon) reached by an object orbiting it. **Perigee** is the opposite of apogee.

The difference in direction of a celestial object as seen by an observer from two widely separated points is termed **parallax**. The measurement of parallax is used directly to find the distance of the body from the Earth (geocentric parallax) and from the Sun (heliocentric parallax). The two positions of the observer and the position of the object form a triangle; if the base line between the two observing points is known and the direction of the object as seen from each has been measured, the apex angle (the parallax) and the distance of the object from the observer can be determined.

An **hour angle** is the angle between an observer's meridian (a great circle passing over his head and through the celestial poles) and the hour circle (any other great circle passing through the poles) on which some celestial body lies. This angle, when expressed in hours and minutes, is the time elapsed since the celestial body's last transit of the observer's meridian. The hour angle can also be expressed in degrees, 15° of arc being equal to one hour.

## Constellations

From the earliest times the star groups known as **constellations**, the smaller groups (parts of constellations) known as **asterisms**, and, also, **individual stars** have received names connoting some meteorological phenomena or symbolizing religious or mythological beliefs. At one time it was held that the constellation names and myths were of Greek origin, but it is now thought that they are primarily of Semitic or even pre-Semitic origin and that they came to the Greeks through the Phoenicians.

## Constellations (continued)

The Alexandrian astronomer **Ptolemy** lists the names and orientation of 48 constellations in his *Almagest*, and, with but few exceptions, they are identical with those used at the present time. The majority of the remaining 40 constellations that are now accepted were added by European astronomers in the 17th and 18th centuries. In the 20th century the delineation of precise boundaries for all 88 constellations was undertaken by a committee of the International Astronomical Union.

| NAME | GENITIVE | MEANING | NOTES |
|---|---|---|---|
| **Constellations described by Ptolemy: the zodiac** | | | (First-magnitude stars are given in italics in this column) |
| Aries | Arietis | Ram | |
| Taurus | Tauri | Bull | *Aldebaran* is the constellation's brightest star. Taurus also contains the Pleiades star cluster and the Crab Nebula. |
| Gemini | Geminorum | Twins | The brightest stars in Gemini are Castor and *Pollux*. |
| Cancer | Cancri | Crab | Cancer contains the well-known star cluster Praesepe. |
| Leo | Leonis | Lion | *Regulus* is the brightest star in Leo. |
| Virgo | Virginis | Virgin | *Spica* is the brightest star in Virgo. |
| Libra | Librae | Balance | |
| Scorpius | Scorpii | Scorpion | *Antares* is the brightest star of Scorpius. |
| Sagittarius | Sagittarii | Archer | The center of the Milky Way Galaxy lies in Sagittarius, with the densest star clouds of the galaxy. |
| Capricornus | Capricorni | Sea-goat | |
| Aquarius | Aquarii | Water-bearer | |
| Pisces | Piscium | Fishes | |
| **Other Ptolemaic constellations** | | | |
| Andromeda | Andromedae | Andromeda (an Ethiopian princess of Greek legend) | The constellation's most notable feature is the great spiral galaxy Andromeda (also called M31). |
| Aquila | Aquilae | Eagle | The brightest star in Aquila is *Altair*. |
| Ara | Arae | Altar | |
| Argo Navis | Argus Navis | the ship *Argo* | Argo Navis is now divided into smaller constellations that include Carina, Puppis, Pyxis, and Vela. |
| Auriga | Aurigae | Charioteer | The brightest star in Auriga is *Capella*. The constellation also contains open star clusters M36, M37, and M38. |
| Boötes | Boötis | Herdsman | *Arcturus* is the brightest star in Boötes. |
| Canis Major | Canis Majoris | Greater Dog | *Sirius* is the brightest star in Canis Major. |
| Canis Minor | Canis Minoris | Smaller Dog | *Procyon* is the brightest star in Canis Minor. |
| Cassiopeia | Cassiopeiae | Cassiopeia was a legendary queen of Ethiopia | Tycho's nova, one of the few recorded supernovae in the Galaxy, appeared in Cassiopeia in 1572. |
| Centaurus | Centauri | Centaur (possibly represents Chiron) | *Alpha Centauri* in Centaurus contains Proxima, the nearest star to the Sun. |
| Cepheus | Cephei | Cepheus (legendary king of Ethiopia) | Delta Cephei was the prototype for cepheid variables (a class of variable stars). |
| Cetus | Ceti | Whale | Mira Ceti was the first recognized variable star. |
| Corona Austrina | Coronae Austrinae | Southern Crown | |
| Corona Borealis | Coronae Borealis | Northern Crown | |
| Corvus | Corvi | Raven | |
| Crater | Crateris | Cup | |
| Cygnus | Cygni | Swan | Cygnus contains the asterism known as the Northern Cross; the constellation's brightest star is *Deneb*. |
| Delphinus | Delphini | Dolphin | Delphinus contains the asterism known as Job's Coffin. |
| Draco | Draconis | Dragon | Draco contains the star Thuban, which was the polestar in 3000 BC. |
| Equuleus | Equulei | Little Horse | |
| Eridanus | Eridani | River Eridanus or river god | *Achernar* is the brightest star in Eridanus. |
| Hercules | Herculis | Hercules (Greek hero) | Hercules contains the great globular star cluster M13. |
| Hydra | Hydrae | Water Snake | |
| Lepus | Leporis | Hare | |
| Lupus | Lupi | Wolf | |

## Constellations (continued)

| NAME | GENITIVE | MEANING | NOTES |
|---|---|---|---|
| **Other Ptolemaic constellations (continued)** | | | |
| Lyra | Lyrae | Lyre | The brightest star in Lyra is *Vega*. In some 10,000 years, *Vega* will become the polestar. Lyra also contains the Ring Nebula (M57). |
| Ophiuchus | Ophiuchi | Serpent-bearer | |
| Orion | Orionis | Hunter | *Rigel* is the brightest star in Orion; M42 (the Great Nebula) resides in Orion. |
| Pegasus | Pegasi | Pegasus (winged horse) | The constellation contains stars of the Great Square of Pegasus. |
| Perseus | Persei | Perseus (legendary Greek hero) | |
| Piscis Austrinus | Piscis Austrini | Southern Fish | The brightest star in Piscis Austrinus is *Fomalhaut*. |
| Sagitta | Sagittae | Arrow | |
| Serpens | Serpentis | Serpent | |
| Triangulum | Trianguli | Triangle | The constellation contains M33, a nearby spiral galaxy. |
| Ursa Major | Ursae Majoris | Great Bear | The seven brightest stars of this constellation are the Big Dipper (also called the Plough). |
| Ursa Minor | Ursae Minoris | Lesser Bear | Ursa Minor contains Polaris (the north polestar). |
| **Southern constellations, added c. 1600** | | | |
| Apus | Apodis | Bird of Paradise | |
| Chamaeleon | Chamaeleontis | Chameleon | |
| Dorado | Doradus | Swordfish | The most notable object in Dorado is the Large Magellanic Cloud. |
| Grus | Gruis | Crane | |
| Hydrus | Hydri | Water Snake | |
| Indus | Indi | Indian | |
| Musca | Muscae | Fly | |
| Pavo | Pavonis | Peacock | |
| Phoenix | Phoenicis | Phoenix (mythical bird) | |
| Triangulum Australe | Trianguli Australis | Southern Triangle | |
| Tucana | Tucanae | Toucan | The most notable object in Tucana is the Small Magellanic Cloud. |
| Volans | Volantis | Flying Fish | |
| **Constellations of Bartsch, 1624** | | | |
| Camelopardalis | Camelopardalis | Giraffe | |
| Columba | Columbae | Dove | |
| Monoceros | Monocerotis | Unicorn | |
| **Constellations of Hevelius, 1687** | | | |
| Canes Venatici | Canum Venaticorum | Hunting Dogs | The constellation contains M51 (the Whirlpool Galaxy). |
| Lacerta | Lacertae | Lizard | |
| Leo Minor | Leonis Minoris | Lesser Lion | |
| Lynx | Lyncis | Lynx | |
| Scutum | Scuti | Shield | Scutum contains the Scutim star cloud in the Milky Way. |
| Sextans | Sextantis | Sextant | |
| Vulpecula | Vulpeculae | Fox | Vulpecula contains M27 (the Dumbbell Nebula). |
| **Ancient asterisms that are now separate constellations** | | | |
| Carina | Carinae | Keel [of the *Argo*, a legendary ship] | The brightest star in Carina is *Canopus*. |
| Coma Berenices | Comae Berenices | Berenice's Hair | The constellation contains both a coma (star cluster) and the north galactic pole (a point that lies perpendicular to the Milky Way). |
| Crux | Crucis | [Southern] Cross | |
| Puppis | Puppis | Stern [of the *Argo*] | |
| Pyxis | Pyxidis | Compass [of the *Argo*] | |
| Vela | Velorum | Sails [of the *Argo*] | |

## Constellations (continued)

| NAME | GENITIVE | MEANING | NOTES |
|---|---|---|---|
| Southern constellations of Lacaille, c. 1750 | | | |
| Antlia | Antliae | Pump | |
| Caelum | Caeli | [Sculptor's] Chisel | |
| Circinus | Circini | Drawing Compasses | |
| Fornax | Fornacis | [Chemical] Furnace | |
| Horologium | Horologii | Clock | |
| Mensa | Mensae | Table [Mountain] | |
| Microscopium | Microscopii | Microscope | |
| Norma | Normae | Square | |
| Octans | Octantis | Octant | Octans contains the south celestial pole. |
| Pictor | Pictoris | Painter's [Easel] | |
| Reticulum | Reticuli | Reticle | |
| Sculptor | Sculptoris | Sculptor's [Work-shop] | Sculptor contains the south galactic pole. |
| Telescopium | Telescopii | Telescope | |

## Astrology: The Zodiac

*Signs of the zodiac are popularly used for divination as well as for designation of constellations.*

| NAME | SYMBOL | DATES | SEX/NATURE | TRIPLICITY | HOUSE | EXALTATION |
|---|---|---|---|---|---|---|
| Aries the Ram | ♈ | 21 Mar–19 Apr | masculine/moving | fire | Mars | Sun (19°) |
| Taurus the Bull | ♉ | 20 Apr–20 May | feminine/fixed | earth | Venus | Moon (3°) |
| Gemini the Twins | ♊ | 21 May–21 Jun | masculine/common | air | Mercury | |
| Cancer the Crab | ♋ | 22 Jun–22 Jul | feminine/moving | water | Moon | Jupiter (15°) |
| Leo the Lion | ♌ | 23 Jul–22 Aug | masculine/fixed | fire | Sun | |
| Virgo the Virgin | ♍ | 23 Aug–22 Sep | feminine/common | earth | Mercury | Mercury (15°) |
| Libra the Balance | ♎ | 23 Sep–23 Oct | masculine/moving | air | Venus | Saturn (21°) |
| Scorpius the Scorpion | ♏ | 24 Oct–21 Nov | feminine/fixed | water | Mars | |
| Sagittarius the Archer | ♐ | 22 Nov–21 Dec | masculine/common | fire | Jupiter | |
| Capricorn the Goat | ♑ | 22 Dec–19 Jan | feminine/moving | earth | Saturn | Mars (28°) |
| Aquarius the Water Bearer | ♒ | 20 Jan–18 Feb | masculine/fixed | air | Saturn | |
| Pisces the Fish | ♓ | 19 Feb–20 Mar | feminine/common | water | Jupiter | Venus (27°) |

## Classification of Stars

The spectral sequence O–M represents stars of essentially the same chemical composition but of different temperatures and atmospheric pressures. Stars belonging to other, more rare types of spectral classifications differ in chemical composition from those stars classified under the O–M scheme.

Each spectral class is additionally subdivided into 10 spectral types. For example, spectral class A is subdivided into spectral types A0–A9 with 0 being the hottest and 9 the coolest. (Spectral class O is unusual in that it is subdivided into O4–O9.) Between two stars of the same spectral type, the more luminous star will also be larger in diameter. Thus the Yerkes system of luminosity also tells something of a star's radius, with Ia being the largest and V the smallest. Approximately 90% of all stars are main-sequence, or type V, stars.

Based upon these systems, the Sun would be a G2 V star (a yellow, relatively hot dwarf star).

| SPECTRAL CLASS | COLOR | APPROXIMATE SURFACE TEMP (°C) | EXAMPLES |
|---|---|---|---|
| O | blue | 30,000 or greater | these stars are relatively rare |
| B | blue-white | 20,000 to 30,000 | Rigel, Alpha Crucis, Beta Crucis |
| A | white | 10,000 to 20,000 | Sirius, Vega, Fomalhaut |
| F | yellow-white | 7,000 to 10,000 | Canopus, Procyon |
| G | yellow | 6,000 to 7,000 | Sun |
| K | orange | 4,500 to 6,000 | Arcturus, Aldebaran |
| M | red | 3,000 to 4,500 | Betelgeuse, Antares |

**LUMINOSITY CLASSES (BASED UPON THE YERKES SYSTEM)**

| | |
|---|---|
| Ia | most luminous supergiants |
| Ib | luminous supergiants |
| II | bright giants |
| III | normal giants |
| IV | subgiants |
| V | main-sequence stars (dwarfs) |

# Astronomical Phenomena for 2013

*Source:* The Astronomical Almanac for the Year 2013.

| MONTH | DAY | HOUR (GMT) | EVENT | MONTH | DAY | HOUR (GMT) | EVENT |
|---|---|---|---|---|---|---|---|
| January | 2 | 05 | Earth at perihelion | April | 3 | 05 | last quarter |
| | 5 | 04 | last quarter | | 7 | 01 | Neptune 6° S of Moon |
| | 5 | 20 | Spica 0°6 N of Moon[1] | | 8 | 10 | Mercury 7° S of Moon |
| | 7 | 01 | Saturn 4° N of Moon | | 10 | 10 | new moon |
| | 10 | 10 | Moon at perigee | | 12 | 19 | Pluto stationary |
| | 10 | 12 | Venus 3° S of Moon | | 14 | 18 | Jupiter 2° N of Moon |
| | 11 | 20 | new moon | | 15 | 22 | Moon at apogee |
| | 13 | 12 | Mars 6° S of Moon | | 18 | 00 | Mars in conjunction with Sun |
| | 14 | 17 | Neptune 6° S of Moon | | 18 | 13 | first quarter |
| | 17 | 05 | Uranus 5° S of Moon | | 19 | 21 | Mercury 2° S of Uranus |
| | 18 | 09 | Mercury in superior conjunction | | 25 | 00 | Spica 0°004 S of Moon[1] |
| | 19 | 00 | first quarter | | 25 | 20 | full moon[2] |
| | 22 | 03 | Jupiter 0°5 N of Moon[1] | | 26 | 02 | Saturn 4° N of Moon |
| | 22 | 11 | Moon at apogee | | 27 | 20 | Moon at perigee |
| | 27 | 05 | full moon | | 28 | 08 | Saturn at opposition |
| | 27 | 18 | Vesta stationary | May | 2 | 11 | last quarter |
| | 30 | 16 | Jupiter stationary | | 4 | 07 | Neptune 6° S of Moon |
| February | 2 | 02 | Spica 0°3 N of Moon[1] | | 7 | 00 | Uranus 4° S of Moon |
| | 3 | 10 | Saturn 3° N of Moon | | 10 | 00 | new moon[2] |
| | 3 | 14 | last quarter | | 10 | 21 | Pallas in conjunction with Sun |
| | 4 | 17 | Ceres stationary | | 11 | 21 | Mercury in superior conjunction |
| | 7 | 12 | Moon at perigee | | 12 | 13 | Jupiter 3° N of Moon |
| | 8 | 21 | Mercury 0°3 N of Mars | | 13 | 14 | Moon at apogee |
| | 10 | 07 | new moon | | 18 | 05 | first quarter |
| | 11 | 18 | Mercury 5° S of Moon | | 18 | 10 | Venus 6° N of Aldebaran |
| | 13 | 16 | Uranus 4° S of Moon | | 21 | 01 | Mercury 7° N of Aldebaran |
| | 16 | 21 | Mercury greatest elongation E (18°) | | 22 | 11 | Spica 0°005 S of Moon[1] |
| | 17 | 21 | first quarter | | 23 | 10 | Saturn 4° N of Moon |
| | 18 | 12 | Jupiter 0°9 N of Moon[1] | | 25 | 04 | full moon[2] |
| | 18 | 22 | Vesta 0°3 N of Moon[1] | | 25 | 04 | Mercury 1°4 N of Venus |
| | 19 | 06 | Moon at apogee | | 26 | 02 | Moon at perigee |
| | 19 | 11 | Saturn stationary | | 27 | 10 | Mercury 2° N of Jupiter |
| | 21 | 07 | Neptune in conjunction with Sun | | 28 | 21 | Venus 1°0 N of Jupiter |
| | 22 | 19 | Mercury stationary | | 31 | 14 | Neptune 6° S of Moon |
| | 25 | 20 | full moon | | 31 | 19 | last quarter |
| March | 1 | 07 | Spica 0°1 N of Moon[1] | June | 3 | 08 | Uranus 4° S of Moon |
| | 2 | 15 | Saturn 3° N of Moon | | 7 | 18 | Neptune stationary |
| | 4 | 13 | Mercury in inferior conjunction | | 8 | 16 | new moon |
| | 4 | 22 | last quarter | | 9 | 22 | Moon at apogee |
| | 5 | 23 | Moon at perigee | | 10 | 11 | Venus 5° N of Moon |
| | 10 | 16 | Neptune 6° S of Moon | | 10 | 23 | Mercury 6° N of Moon |
| | 11 | 20 | new moon | | 12 | 17 | Mercury greatest elongation E (24°) |
| | 16 | 21 | Mercury stationary | | 13 | 13 | Juno stationary |
| | 18 | 01 | Jupiter 1°5 N of Moon | | 16 | 17 | first quarter |
| | 19 | 03 | Moon at apogee | | 18 | 20 | Spica 0°1 S of Moon[1] |
| | 19 | 17 | first quarter | | 19 | 16 | Jupiter in conjunction with Sun |
| | 20 | 11 | equinox | | 19 | 17 | Saturn 4° N of Moon |
| | 24 | 18 | Jupiter 5° N of Aldebaran | | 20 | 18 | Mercury 1°9 S of Venus |
| | 27 | 09 | full moon | | 21 | 05 | solstice |
| | 28 | 15 | Spica 0°005 S of Moon[1] | | 23 | 01 | Venus 5° S of Pollux |
| | 28 | 17 | Venus in superior conjunction | | 23 | 11 | Moon at perigee |
| | 29 | 01 | Uranus in conjunction with Sun | | 23 | 12 | full moon |
| | 29 | 20 | Saturn 3° N of Moon | | 25 | 23 | Mercury stationary |
| | 31 | 04 | Moon at perigee | | 27 | 21 | Neptune 6° S of Moon |
| | 31 | 22 | Mercury greatest elongation W (28°) | | | | |

## Astronomical Phenomena for 2013 (continued)

| MONTH | DAY | HOUR (GMT) | EVENT |
|---|---|---|---|
| June (continued) | 30 | 05 | last quarter |
| | 30 | 15 | Uranus 4° S of Moon |
| July | 2 | 00 | Pluto at opposition |
| | 5 | 15 | Earth at aphelion |
| | 6 | 12 | Mars 4° N of Moon |
| | 7 | 01 | Moon at apogee |
| | 8 | 07 | new moon |
| | 9 | 04 | Saturn stationary |
| | 9 | 19 | Mercury in inferior conjunction |
| | 10 | 23 | Venus 7° N of Moon |
| | 16 | 03 | first quarter |
| | 16 | 04 | Spica 0°3 S of Moon[1] |
| | 17 | 01 | Saturn 3° N of Moon |
| | 18 | 00 | Uranus stationary |
| | 20 | 14 | Mercury stationary |
| | 21 | 20 | Moon at perigee |
| | 22 | 05 | Venus 1°2 N of Regulus |
| | 22 | 06 | Mars 0°8 N of Jupiter |
| | 22 | 18 | full moon |
| | 25 | 06 | Neptune 6° S of Moon |
| | 27 | 22 | Uranus 3° S of Moon |
| | 29 | 18 | last quarter |
| | 30 | 09 | Mercury greatest elongation W (20°) |
| August | 3 | 09 | Moon at apogee |
| | 3 | 22 | Jupiter 4° N of Moon |
| | 4 | 01 | Juno at opposition |
| | 4 | 11 | Mars 5° N of Moon |
| | 5 | 03 | Mercury 7° S of Pollux |
| | 5 | 09 | Mercury 4° N of Moon |
| | 6 | 04 | Vesta in conjunction with Sun |
| | 6 | 22 | new moon |
| | 10 | 02 | Venus 5° N of Moon |
| | 12 | 09 | Spica 0°6 S of Moon[1] |
| | 13 | 08 | Saturn 3° N of Moon |
| | 14 | 11 | first quarter |
| | 18 | 01 | Ceres in conjunction with Sun |
| | 19 | 01 | Moon at perigee |
| | 19 | 12 | Mars 6° S of Pollux |
| | 21 | 02 | full moon |
| | 21 | 15 | Neptune 6° S of Moon |
| | 24 | 07 | Uranus 3° S of Moon |
| | 24 | 21 | Mercury in superior conjunction |
| | 27 | 02 | Neptune at opposition |
| | 28 | 10 | last quarter |
| | 31 | 00 | Moon at apogee |
| | 31 | 17 | Jupiter 4° N of Moon |
| September | 2 | 10 | Mars 6° N of Moon |
| | 5 | 12 | new moon |
| | 5 | 13 | Venus 1°8 N of Spica |
| | 8 | 15 | Spica 0°8 S of Moon[1] |
| | 8 | 21 | Venus 0°4 N of Moon[1] |
| | 9 | 17 | Saturn 2° N of Moon |
| | 12 | 17 | first quarter |
| | 15 | 17 | Moon at apogee |
| | 17 | 23 | Neptune 6° S of Moon |
| | 19 | 11 | full moon |
| | 20 | 00 | Venus 4° S of Saturn |
| September (continued) | 20 | 05 | Pluto stationary |
| | 20 | 15 | Uranus 3° S of Moon |
| | 20 | 16 | Juno stationary |
| | 22 | 21 | equinox |
| | 24 | 19 | Mercury 0°8 N of Spica |
| | 27 | 04 | last quarter |
| | 27 | 18 | Moon at apogee |
| | 28 | 09 | Jupiter 5° N of Moon |
| October | 1 | 06 | Mars 7° N of Moon |
| | 3 | 14 | Uranus at opposition |
| | 5 | 01 | new moon |
| | 6 | 22 | Mercury 3° S of Moon |
| | 7 | 04 | Saturn 1°9 N of Moon |
| | 8 | 12 | Venus 5° S of Moon |
| | 9 | 10 | Mercury greatest elongation E (25°) |
| | 10 | 19 | Mercury 5° S of Saturn |
| | 10 | 23 | Moon at perigee |
| | 11 | 23 | first quarter |
| | 13 | 02 | Juno 0°9 N of Moon[1] |
| | 14 | 22 | Mars 1°0 N of Regulus |
| | 15 | 06 | Neptune 6° S of Moon |
| | 16 | 16 | Venus 1°6 N of Antares |
| | 17 | 21 | Uranus 3° S of Moon |
| | 19 | 00 | full moon[2] |
| | 21 | 15 | Mercury stationary |
| | 25 | 14 | Moon at apogee |
| | 25 | 22 | Jupiter 5° N of Moon |
| | 27 | 00 | last quarter |
| | 30 | 01 | Mars 6° N of Moon |
| November | 1 | 08 | Venus greatest elongation E (47°) |
| | 1 | 20 | Mercury in inferior conjunction |
| | 2 | 07 | Spica 0°8 S of Moon[1] |
| | 3 | 13 | new moon[2] |
| | 6 | 09 | Moon at perigee |
| | 6 | 12 | Saturn in conjunction with Sun |
| | 7 | 01 | Venus 8° S of Moon |
| | 7 | 07 | Jupiter stationary |
| | 10 | 06 | first quarter |
| | 10 | 14 | Mercury stationary |
| | 11 | 11 | Neptune 6° S of Moon |
| | 13 | 22 | Neptune stationary |
| | 14 | 03 | Uranus 3° S of Moon |
| | 17 | 15 | full moon |
| | 18 | 03 | Mercury greatest elongation W (19°) |
| | 22 | 05 | Jupiter 5° N of Moon |
| | 22 | 10 | Moon at apogee |
| | 25 | 19 | last quarter |
| | 26 | 04 | Mercury 0°3 S of Saturn |
| | 27 | 16 | Mars 6° N of Moon |
| | 29 | 17 | Spica 0°9 S of Moon[1] |
| December | 1 | 10 | Saturn 1°3 N of Moon[1] |
| | 3 | 00 | new moon |
| | 4 | 10 | Moon at perigee |
| | 6 | 00 | Venus 8° S of Moon |
| | 6 | 19 | Venus greatest illuminated extent |
| | 8 | 17 | Neptune 6° S of Moon |

## Astronomical Phenomena for 2013 (continued)

| MONTH | DAY | HOUR (GMT) | EVENT | MONTH | DAY | HOUR (GMT) | EVENT |
|---|---|---|---|---|---|---|---|
| December | 9 | 15 | first quarter | December | 21 | 17 | solstice |
| (continued) | 11 | 07 | Uranus 3° S of Moon | (continued) | 25 | 14 | last quarter |
| | 17 | 09 | full moon | | 26 | 03 | Mars 5° N of Moon |
| | 18 | 02 | Uranus stationary | | 27 | 03 | Spica 1°1 S of Moon[1] |
| | 19 | 07 | Jupiter 5° N of Moon | | 29 | 01 | Saturn 0°9 N of Moon[1] |
| | 20 | 00 | Moon at apogee | | 29 | 06 | Mercury in superior conjunction |
| | 20 | 20 | Venus stationary | | | | |

[1]Occultation.    [2]Eclipse.

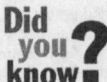

**Did you know?** A project featuring collaboration between scientists from the National Herbarium in the Iraqi Ministry of Agriculture and botanists at the Kew Gardens was restarted in late 2011 after more than 25 years. *The Flora of Iraq,* a planned nine-volume work, was begun in 1960, and the last publication occurred in 1985. Political considerations forced the cessation of the project, which has three planned volumes remaining. Between 3,300 and 3,500 species of Iraqi flora will have been catalogued and described upon completion of the work.

## Morning and Evening Stars

*This table gives the morning and evening stars for autumn 2012 through 2013. The morning and evening stars are actually planets visible to the naked eye during the early morning and at evening twilight.*

| PLANET | MORNING STAR | EVENING STAR |
|---|---|---|
| Mercury | 24 Nov 2012–2 Jan 2013; 11 Mar–4 May, 19 Jul–16 Aug, 8 Nov–12 Dec 2013 | 22 Sep–12 Nov 2012; 31 Jan–26 Feb, 19 May–1 Jul, 4 Sep–27 Oct 2013 |
| Venus | 22 Sep 2012–16 Feb 2013 | 7 May–31 Dec 2013 |
| Mars | 20 Jun–31 Dec 2013 | 1 Jan–9 Feb 2013 |
| Jupiter | 22 Sep–3 Dec 2012; 4 Jul–31 Dec 2013 | 3 Dec 2012–5 Jun 2013 |
| Saturn | 12 Nov 2012–28 Apr 2013; 24 Nov–31 Dec 2013 | 22 Sep–8 Oct 2012; 28 Apr–20 Oct 2013 |
| Uranus | 22 Sep–late December 2012; mid-April–late September 2013 | late December 2012–early March 2013; early October–late December 2013 |
| Neptune | mid-March–late August 2013 | late November 2012–early February 2013; late August–late November 2013 |

## Characteristics of Celestial Bodies

*Mean orbital velocity indicates the average speed at which a planet orbits the Sun unless otherwise specified. Inclination of orbit to ecliptic indicates the angle of tilt between a planet's orbit and the plane of Earth's orbit (essentially the plane of the solar system). Orbital period indicates the planet's sidereal year (in Earth days except where noted). Rotation period indicates the planet's sidereal day (in Earth days except where noted). Inclination of equator to orbit indicates the angle of tilt between a planet's orbit and its equator. Gravitational acceleration is a measure of the body's gravitational pull on other objects. Escape velocity is the speed needed at the surface to escape the planet's gravitational pull. Eccentricity of orbit is a measure of the circularity or elongation of an orbit; 0 indicates circular orbits, and closer to 1 more elliptical ones.*

**Sun**
diameter (at equator): 1.39 million km (863,705 mi)
mass (in $10^{20}$ kg): 19.8 billion
density (mass/volume, in kg/m³): 1,408
mean orbital velocity: the Sun orbits the Milky Way's center at around 220 km/sec (136.7 mi/sec)
orbital period: the Sun takes approximately 250 million Earth years to complete its orbit around the Milky Way's center
rotation period: 25–36 Earth days

gravitational acceleration: 275 m/sec² (902.2 ft/sec²)
escape velocity: 618.02 km/sec (384.01 mi/sec)
mean temperature at visible surface: 5,527 °C (9,980 °F)
probes and space missions: US—Pioneer 5–9, launched 1960–68; Skylab, 1973; Genesis, 2001; Solar Dynamics Observatory, 2010; Japan—Yohkoh, 1991; US/European Space Agency (ESA)—Ulysses, 1990–2009; SOHO, 1995.

## Characteristics of Celestial Bodies (continued)

**Mercury**
average distance from the Sun: 58 million km (36 million mi)
diameter (at equator): 4,879 km (3,032 mi)
mass (in $10^{20}$ kg): 3,300
density (mass/volume, in kg/m³): 5,427
eccentricity of orbit: 0.206
mean orbital velocity: 47.9 km/sec (29.7 mi/sec)
inclination of orbit to ecliptic: 7.0°
orbital period: 88 Earth days
rotation period: 58.6 Earth days
inclination of equator to orbit: probably 0°
gravitational acceleration: 3.7 m/sec² (12.1 ft/sec²)
escape velocity: 4.3 km/sec (2.7 mi/sec)
mean temperature at surface†: 167 °C (333 °F)
satellites: none known
probes and space missions: US—Mariner 10, 1973; Messenger, 2004.

**Venus**
average distance from the Sun: 108.2 million km (67.2 million mi)
diameter (at equator): 12,104 km (7,521 mi)
mass (in $10^{20}$ kg): 48,700
density (mass/volume, in kg/m³): 5,243
eccentricity of orbit: 0.007
mean orbital velocity: 35.0 km/sec (21.8 mi/sec)
inclination of orbit to ecliptic: 3.4°
orbital period: 224.7 Earth days
rotation period: 243.0 Earth days (retrograde)
inclination of equator to orbit: 177.4°
gravitational acceleration: 8.9 m/sec² (29.1 ft/sec²)
escape velocity: 10.4 km/sec (6.4 mi/sec)
mean temperature at surface†: 464 °C (867 °F)
satellites: none known
probes and space missions: USSR—Venera 1–16, 1961–83; Vega 1 and 2, 1984; US—Mariner 2, 5, and 10, 1962, 1967, and 1973; Pioneer Venus Orbiter and Pioneer Venus Multiprobe, 1978; Galileo, 1989; Magellan, 1989; US/ESA—Cassini-Huygens, 1997; ESA—Venus Express, 2005.

**Earth**
average distance from the Sun: 149.6 million km (93 million mi)
diameter (at equator): 12,756 km (7,926 mi)
mass (in $10^{20}$ kg): 59,800
density (mass/volume, in kg/m³): 5,515
eccentricity of orbit: 0.017
mean orbital velocity: 29.8 km/sec (18.5 mi/sec)
inclination of orbit to ecliptic: 0.00°
orbital period: 365.26 days
rotation period: 23 hours, 56 minutes, and 4 seconds of mean solar time
inclination of equator to orbit: 23.4°
gravitational acceleration: 9.8 m/sec² (32.1 ft/sec²)
escape velocity: 11.2 km/sec (7.0 mi/sec)
mean temperature at surface†: 15 °C (59 °F)
satellites: 1 known—the Moon.

**Moon (of Earth)**
average distance from Earth: 384,401 km (238,855.7 mi)
diameter (at equator): 3,475 km (2,159 mi)
mass (in $10^{20}$ kg): 730
density (mass/volume, in kg/m³): 3,340
eccentricity of orbit: orbital eccentricity of Moon around Earth is 0.055

mean orbital velocity: the Moon orbits Earth at 1.0 km/sec (0.64 mi/sec)
inclination of orbit to ecliptic: 5.1°
orbital period: the Moon revolves around Earth in 27.32 Earth days
rotation period: the Moon rotates on its axis every 27.32 Earth days (synchronous with orbital period)
inclination of equator to orbit: 6.7°
gravitational acceleration: 1.6 m/sec² (5.3 ft/sec²)
escape velocity: 2.4 km/sec (1.5 mi/sec)
mean temperature at surface†: daytime: 107 °C (224.6 °F); nighttime: −153 °C (−243.4 °F)
probes and space missions: USSR, US, ESA, Japan, China—collectively about 70 missions since 1959, including 9 manned missions by the US. On 20 Jul 1969 humans first set foot on the Moon, from NASA's Apollo 11.

**Mars**
average distance from the Sun: 227.9 million km (141.6 million mi)
diameter (at equator): 6,794 km (4,222 mi)
mass (in $10^{20}$ kg): 6,420
density (mass/volume, in kg/m³): 3,933
eccentricity of orbit: 0.094
mean orbital velocity: 24.1 km/sec (15 mi/sec)
inclination of orbit to ecliptic: 1.9°
orbital period: 687 Earth days (1.88 Earth years)
rotation period: 24.6 Earth hours
inclination of equator to orbit: 24.9°
gravitational acceleration: 3.7 m/sec² (12.1 ft/sec²)
escape velocity: 5.0 km/sec (3.1 mi/sec)
mean temperature at surface†: −65 °C (−85 °F)
satellites: 2 known—Phobos and Deimos
probes and space missions: US—Mariner 4, 6, 7, and 9, 1964–71; Viking 1 and 2, 1975; Mars Global Surveyor, 1996; Mars Pathfinder, 1996; 2001 Mars Odyssey, 2001; Mars Exploration Rovers, 2003; Mars Reconnaissance Orbiter, 2005; USSR—Mars 2–7, 1971–73; Phobos 1 and 2, 1988; ESA—Mars Express, 2003; Phoenix, 2007.

**Jupiter**
average distance from the Sun: 778.6 million km (483.8 million mi)
diameter (at equator): 142,984 km (88,846 mi)
mass (in $10^{20}$ kg): 18.99 million
density (mass/volume, in kg/m³): 1,326
eccentricity of orbit: 0.049
mean orbital velocity: 13.1 km/sec (8.1 mi/sec)
inclination of orbit to ecliptic: 1.3°
orbital period: 11.86 Earth years
rotation period: 9.9 Earth hours
inclination of equator to orbit: 3.1°
gravitational acceleration: 23.1 m/sec² (75.9 ft/sec²)
escape velocity: 59.5 km/sec (37.0 mi/sec)
mean temperature at surface†: −110 °C (−166 °F)
satellites: at least 62 moons—including Callisto, Ganymede, Europa, and Io—plus rings
probes and space missions: US—Pioneer 10 and 11, 1972–73; Voyager 1 and 2, 1977; Galileo, 1989; Ulysses, 1990; Juno, 2011; US/ESA—Cassini-Huygens, 1997.

**Saturn**
average distance from the Sun: 1.433 billion km (890.8 million mi)
diameter (at equator): 120,536 km (74,897 mi)
mass (in $10^{20}$ kg): 5.68 million

## Characteristics of Celestial Bodies (continued)

density (mass/volume, in kg/m³): 687
eccentricity of orbit: 0.057
mean orbital velocity: 9.7 km/sec (6 mi/sec)
inclination of orbit to ecliptic: 2.5°
orbital period: 29.43 Earth years
rotation period: 10.66 Earth hours
inclination of equator to orbit: 26.7°
gravitational acceleration: 9.0 m/sec² (29.4 ft/sec²)
escape velocity: 35.5 km/sec (22.1 mi/sec)
mean temperature at surface†: −140 °C (−220 °F)
satellites: at least 62 moons—including Titan—plus rings
probes and space missions: US—Pioneer 11, 1973; Voyager 1 and 2, 1977; US/ESA—Cassini-Huygens, 1997.

### Uranus
average distance from the Sun: 2.872 billion km (1.784 billion mi)
diameter (at equator): 51,118 km (31,763 mi)
mass (in 10²⁰ kg): 868,000
density (mass/volume, in kg/m³): 1,270
eccentricity of orbit: 0.046
mean orbital velocity: 6.8 km/sec (4.2 mi/sec)
inclination of orbit to ecliptic: 0.8°
orbital period: 84.01 Earth years
rotation period: 17.2 Earth hours (retrograde)
inclination of equator to orbit: 97.8°
gravitational acceleration: 8.7 m/sec² (28.5 ft/sec²)
escape velocity: 21.3 km/sec ( 13.2 mi/sec)
mean temperature at surface†: −195 °C (−320 °F)
satellites: at least 27 moons, plus rings
probes and space missions: US—Voyager 2, 1977.

### Neptune
average distance from the Sun: 4.495 billion km (2.793 billion mi)
diameter (at equator): 49,528 km (30,775 mi)
mass (in 10²⁰ kg): 1.02 million
density (mass/volume, in kg/m³): 1,638
eccentricity of orbit: 0.009
mean orbital velocity: 5.48 km/sec (3.40 mi/sec)
inclination of orbit to ecliptic: 1.8°
orbital period: 164.79 Earth years
rotation period: 16.1 Earth hours
inclination of equator to orbit: 28.3°
gravitational acceleration: 11.0 m/sec² (36.0 ft/sec²)
escape velocity: 23.5 km/sec (14.6 mi/sec)
mean temperature at surface†: −200 °C (−330 °F)
satellites: at least 13 moons, plus rings
probes and space missions: US—Voyager 2, 1977.

### Pluto
average distance from the Sun: 5.910 billion km (3.67 billion mi); Pluto lies within the Kuiper belt and can be considered its largest known member
diameter (at equator): 2,344 km (1,485 mi)
mass (in 10²⁰ kg): 125
density (mass/volume, in kg/m³): about 2,000
eccentricity of orbit: 0.249
mean orbital velocity: 4.72 km/sec (2.93 mi/sec)
inclination of orbit to ecliptic: 17.2°
orbital period: 248 Earth years
rotation period: 6.4 Earth days (retrograde)
inclination of equator to orbit: 122.5°
gravitational acceleration: 0.6 m/sec² (1.9 ft/sec²)

escape velocity: 1.1 km/sec (0.7 mi/sec)
mean temperature at surface†: −225 °C (−375 °F)
satellites: 5 known—including Charon
probes and space missions: US—New Horizons, 2006.

### asteroids
(several hundred thousand small rocky bodies, about 1,000 km [610 mi] or less in diameter, that orbit the Sun primarily between the orbits of Mars and Jupiter)
distance from the Sun: between approximately 300 million km (190 million mi) and 600 million km (380 million mi), with notable outliers
estimated mass (in 10²¹ kg): 2.3
probes and space missions: US—Galileo, 1989; Ulysses, 1990; NEAR Shoemaker, 1996; Deep Space 1, 1998; Stardust, 1999; Dawn, 2007; US/ESA—Cassini-Huygens, 1997; Japan—Hayabusa, 2003–2010; ESA—Rosetta, 2004.

### Comet 1P/Halley
distance from the Sun at closest point of orbit: 87.8 million km (54 million mi); farthest distance from the Sun: 5.2 billion km (3.2 billion mi).
diameter (at equator): 16 x 8 x 8 km (9.9 x 4.9 x 4.9 mi)
density (mass/volume, in kg/m³): possibly as low as 200
eccentricity of orbit: 0.967
inclination of orbit to ecliptic: 18°
orbital period: 76.1 to 79.3 Earth years; the next appearance will be 2061. The comet's orbit is retrograde.
rotation period: 52 Earth hours
probes and space missions: USSR—Vega 1 and 2, 1984; ESA—Giotto, 1985; Japan—Sakigake and Suisei, 1985.

### Comet Hale-Bopp
distance from the Sun at closest point of orbit: 136 million km (84.5 million mi); farthest distance from the Sun: 74.7 billion km (46.4 billion mi).
eccentricity of orbit: 0.995
orbital period: 4,000 Earth years; last closest pass of Sun was on 31 Mar 1997.

### Kuiper belt
(a huge flat ring located beyond Neptune containing residual icy material from the formation of the outer planets)
average distance from the Sun (main concentration): 4.5–7.5 billion km (2.8–4.7 billion mi)
mass: scientists estimate there may be as many as 100,000 icy, cometlike bodies of a size greater than 100 km in the Kuiper belt; the belt is estimated to have a mass of 6,000 x 10²⁰ kg.
probes and space missions: US—New Horizons, 2006.

### Oort cloud
(an immense, roughly spherical cloud of icy, cometlike bodies inferred to orbit the Sun at distances roughly 1,000 times that of the orbit of Pluto)
average distance from the Sun: 3–7 trillion km (1.9–4.3 trillion mi)
mass: some trillions of the cloud's icy objects have an estimated total mass of at least 600,000 x 10²⁰ kg (10 times the mass of Earth).

†For celestial bodies with no surface, temperature given is at a level in the atmosphere equal to 1 bar of pressure.

## Solar System Superlatives

**Largest planet:** Jupiter (142,984 km [88,846 mi] diameter); all of the other planets in the solar system could fit inside Jupiter.

**Largest moon:** Jupiter's moon Ganymede (5,268 km [3,273 mi] diameter).

**Smallest planet:** Mercury (4,879 km [3,032 mi] diameter).

**Smallest moons:** Jupiter and Saturn both have numerous satellites that are smaller than 10 km (6 mi) in diameter.

**Planet closest to the Sun:** Mercury (average distance from the Sun 58 million km [36 million mi]).

**Planet farthest from the Sun:** Neptune (average distance from the Sun 4.50 billion km [2.79 billion mi]); Pluto, demoted to a dwarf planet in 2006, was the farthest planet from the Sun for all but 20 years of its 248-year orbital period.

**Planet with the most eccentric (least circular) orbit:** Mercury (eccentricity of 0.206).

**Moon with the most eccentric orbit:** Neptune's moon Nereid (eccentricity of 0.75).

**Planet with the least eccentric orbit:** Venus (eccentricity of 0.007).

**Moon with the least eccentric orbit:** Saturn's moon Tethys (eccentricity of 0.0001).

**Planet most tilted on its axis:** Uranus (axial tilt of 98° from its orbital plane).

**Planets with the most moons:** Jupiter and Saturn (at least 62).

**Planets with the fewest moons:** Mercury and Venus (none).

**Planet with the longest day:** Venus (1 day on Venus equals 243 Earth days).

**Planet with the shortest day:** Jupiter (1 day on Jupiter equals 9.9 Earth hours).

**Planet with the longest year:** Neptune (1 year on Neptune equals 165 Earth years).

**Planet with the shortest year:** Mercury (1 year on Mercury equals 88 Earth days).

**Fastest orbiting planet:** Mercury (47.9 km/sec [29.7 mi/sec] mean orbital velocity).

**Slowest orbiting planet:** Neptune (5.48 km/sec [3.40 mi/sec] mean orbital velocity).

**Hottest planet:** Venus (464 °C [867 °F] average temperature); although Mercury is closer to the Sun, Venus is hotter because Mercury has no atmosphere, whereas the atmosphere of Venus traps heat via a strong greenhouse effect.

**Coldest planet:** Neptune (−220 °C [−364 °F] average temperature).

**Brightest visible star in the night sky:** Sirius (apparent visual magnitude −1.46).

**Brightest planet in the night sky:** Venus (apparent visual magnitude −4.5 to −3.77).

**Densest planet:** Earth (density of 5,515 kg/m³).

**Least dense planet:** Saturn (density of 687 kg/m³); Saturn in theory would float in water.

**Planet with strongest gravity:** Jupiter (more than twice the gravitational force of Earth at an altitude at which one bar of atmospheric pressure is exerted).

**Planet with weakest gravity:** Mars (slightly more than one-third the gravitational force of Earth).

**Planet with the largest mountain:** Mars (Olympus Mons, an extinct volcano, stands some 21 km [13 mi] above the planet's mean radius and 540 km [335 mi] across).

**Planet with the deepest valley:** Mars (Valles Marineris, a system of canyons, is some 4,000 km [2,500 mi] long and from about 2 to 9 km [1 to 5.6 mi] deep).

**Largest known impact crater:** Valhalla, a crater on Jupiter's moon Callisto, has a bright central area that is about 600 km (370 mi) across, with concentric ridges extending about 1,500 km (900 mi) from the center. (The largest crater on Earth believed to be of impact origin is the Vredefort ring structure in South Africa, which is about 300 km [190 mi] across.)

## The Sun

The Sun is the star around which Earth and the other components of the solar system revolve. It is the dominant body of the system, constituting more than 99% of the system's entire mass. The Sun, at least 90% hydrogen by number of atoms, is the source of an enormous amount of energy produced during the conversion of hydrogen atoms to helium. This energy provides Earth with the light and heat necessary to support life. STEREO, launched in 2006, gave the first view of the entire Sun in February of 2011. Together with NASA's Solar Dynamics Observatory (launched in 2010), STEREO will reveal the Sun's entire surface and atmosphere over the next seven years. The geologic record of Earth and the Moon reveals that the Sun was formed about 4.5 billion years ago.

The Sun is classified as a G2 V star, where G2 stands for the second hottest stars of the yellow G class—of surface temperature about 5,500 °C (10,000 °F)—and V represents a main sequence, or dwarf, star, the typical star for this temperature class (see also "Classification of Stars"). The Sun exists in the outer part of the Milky Way Galaxy and was formed from material that had been processed inside other stars and supernovas.

The mass of the Sun is 743 times the total mass of all the planets in the solar system and 330,000 times that of Earth. All the planetary and interplanetary gravitational phenomena are negligible effects in comparison to the gravitational force exerted by the Sun. Under the force of gravity, the mass of the Sun presses inward, and to keep the star from collapsing, the central pressure outward must be great enough to support its weight. The Sun's core, which occupies approximately 25% of the star's radius, has a density about 100 times that of water (roughly 6 times that at the center of Earth), but the temperature at the core is at least 15 million °C (27 million °F), so the central pressure is at least 10,000 times greater than that at the center of Earth. In this environment atoms are stripped of their electrons, and at this high temperature the bare nuclei collide to produce the nuclear reactions that are responsible for generating the energy vital to life on Earth.

The temperature of the Sun's surface is so high that no solid or liquid can exist; the constituent materials are predominantly gaseous atoms, with a very small number of molecules. As a result, there is no fixed surface. The surface viewed from Earth, the photosphere, is approximately 400 km (250 mi) thick and

## The Sun (continued)

is the layer from which most of the radiation reaches us; the radiation from below the photosphere is absorbed and reradiated, while the emission from overlying layers drops sharply, by about a factor of six every 200 km (124 mi).

While the temperature of the Sun drops from 15 million °C (27 million °F) at the core to around 5,500 °C (10,000 °F) at the photosphere, it begins to rise in the chromosphere, a layer several thousand kilometers thick. Temperatures there range from 4,200 °C (7,600 °F) to 100,000 °C (180,000 °F). Above the chromosphere is a comparatively dim, extended halo called the corona, which has a temperature of 1 million °C (1.8 million °F) and reaches far past the planets. Beyond a distance of around 3.5 million km (2.2 million mi) from the Sun, the corona flows outward at a speed (near Earth) of 400 km/sec (250 mi/sec); this flow of charged particles is called the solar wind.

Superposed on the Sun's stable energy, however, is an 11-year cycle of magnetic activity manifested by regions of transient strong magnetic fields called sunspots. The largest sunspot can be seen on the solar surface even without a telescope.

## Mercury

Mercury is the planet closest to the Sun, revolving around it at an average distance of 58 million km (36 million mi). In Sumerian times, some 5,000 years ago, it was already known in the night sky. In classical Greece the planet was called Apollo when it appeared as a morning star and Hermes, for the Greek equivalent of the Roman god Mercury, when it appeared as an evening star.

Mercury's orbit lies inside the orbit of the Earth and is more elliptical than those of most of the other planets. At its closest approach (perihelion), Mercury is only 46 million km (28.5 million mi) from the Sun, while its greatest distance (aphelion) approaches 70 million km (43.5 million mi). Mercury orbits the Sun in 88 Earth days at an average speed of 48 km per second (29.8 mi per sec), allowing it to overtake and pass Earth every 116 Earth days (synodic period).

Because of its proximity to the Sun, the surface of Mercury can become extremely hot. High temperatures at "noon" may reach 400 °C (755 °F) while the "predawn" lowest temperature is −173 °C (−280 °F). Mercury's equator is almost exactly in its orbital plane (its spin-axis inclination is nearly zero), and thus Mercury does not have seasons as does the Earth. Because of its elliptical orbit and a peculiarity of its rotational period (see below), however, certain longitudes experience cyclical variations in temperatures on a "yearly" as well as on a "diurnal" basis.

Mercury is about 4,879 km (3,032 mi) in diameter, the smallest of the planets. Mercury is only a bit larger than the Moon. Its mass, as measured by the gravitational perturbation of the path of the Mariner 10 spacecraft during close flybys in 1974–75, is about one-eighteenth of the mass of the Earth. Escape velocity, the speed needed to escape from a planet's gravitational field, is about 4.3 km per second (2.7 mi per second)—compared with 11.2 km per sec (7 mi per sec) for the Earth.

The mean density of Mercury, calculated from its mass and radius, is about 5.43 grams per cubic cm, nearly the same as that of the Earth (5.52 grams per cubic cm).

Photographs relayed by the Mariner 10 spacecraft showed that Mercury spins on its axis (rotates) once every 58.646 Earth days, exactly two-thirds of the orbital period of 87.9694 Earth days. This observation confirmed that Mercury is in a 3:2 spin-orbit tidal resonance—i.e., that tides raised on Mercury by the Sun have forced it into a condition that causes it to rotate three times on its axis in the same time it takes to revolve around the Sun twice. The 3:2 spin-orbit coupling combines with Mercury's eccentric orbit to create very unusual temperature effects.

Although Mercury rotates on its axis once every 58.646 Earth days, one rotation does not bring the Sun back to the same part of the sky, because during that time Mercury has moved partway around the Sun. A solar day on Mercury is 176 Earth days (exactly two Mercurian years).

Whereas Mercury's low escape velocity and high surface temperatures permit only a thin atmosphere, called the exosphere, ion emissions were found to be active there during the MESSENGER spacecraft's 2009 flyby, which also revealed energy buildup in Mercury's magnetic tail and volcanic activity that proved to be younger than previously documented. In March 2011, MESSENGER became the first craft to orbit Mercury.

## Venus

Venus is the second planet from the Sun and the planet whose orbit is closest to that of the Earth. When visible, Venus is the brightest planet in the sky. Viewed through a telescope, it presents a brilliant, yellow-white, essentially featureless face to the observer. The obscured appearance results because the surface of the planet is hidden from sight by a continuous and permanent cover of clouds.

Venus's orbit is the most nearly circular of that of any planet, with a deviation from perfect circularity of only about 1 part in 150. The period of the orbit—that is, the length of the Venusian year—is 224.7 Earth days. The rotation of Venus is unusual in both its direction and speed. Most of the planets in the solar system rotate in a counterclockwise direction when viewed from above their north poles; Venus, however, rotates in the opposite, or retrograde, direction. Were it not for the planet's clouds, an observer on Venus's surface would see the Sun rise in the west and set in the east.

Venus spins on its axis slowly, taking 243 Earth days to complete one rotation. Venus's spin and orbital periods are nearly synchronized with the Earth's orbit such that Venus presents almost the same face toward the Earth when the two planets are at their closest.

Venus is nearly the Earth's twin in terms of size and mass. Venus's equatorial diameter is about 95% of the Earth's diameter, while its mass is 81.5% of that of the Earth. The similarities to the Earth in size and mass also produce a similarity in density; Venus's density is 5.24 grams per cubic cm, as compared with 5.52 for the Earth.

## Venus (continued)

A planet's rotation generally causes a slight flattening at the poles and bulging at the equator, but Venus's very slow rotation rate allows it to maintain its highly spherical shape.

Composed of 96.5% carbon dioxide and 3.5% nitrogen, Venus's atmosphere is the most massive of all the terrestrial planets (Mercury, Venus, Earth, and Mars). The surface's atmospheric pressure varies with the surface elevation but averages about 90 bars, or 90 times the atmospheric pressure at the Earth's surface. This is the same pressure found at a depth of about one kilometer in the Earth's oceans. Temperatures range between −45 °C (−49 °F) and 500 °C (932 °F); the average temperature is 464 °C (867 °F).

Recent photos from the European Space Agency's Venus Express spacecraft revealed lava flows dating from as little as several hundred years ago, causing scientists to deem it "geologically active."

## Earth

Earth is the third planet in distance outward from the Sun. It is the only planetary body in the solar system that has conditions suitable for life, at least as known to modern science.

The average distance of Earth from the Sun—149.6 million km (93 million mi)—is designated as the distance of the unit of measurement known as the AU (astronomical unit). Earth orbits the Sun at a speed of 29.8 km (18.5 mi) per second, making one complete revolution in 365.26 days. As it revolves around the Sun, Earth spins on its axis and rotates completely once every 23 hr 56 min 4 sec. Earth has a single natural satellite, the Moon.

The fifth largest planet of the solar system, Earth has a total surface area of roughly 510.1 million sq km (197 million sq mi), of which about 29%, or 148 million square km (57 million square mi), is land. Oceans and smaller seas cover the balance of the surface. Earth is the only planet known to have liquid water. Together with ice, the liquid water constitutes the hydrosphere. Seawater makes up more than 98% of the total mass of the hydrosphere and covers about 71% of Earth's surface. Significantly, seawater constituted the environment of the earliest terrestrial life forms.

Earth's atmosphere consists of a mixture of gases, chiefly nitrogen (78%) and oxygen (21%). Argon makes up much of the remainder of the gaseous envelope, with trace amounts of water vapor, carbon dioxide, and various other gases also present. Earth's structure consists of an inner core of nearly solid iron, surrounded possibly by a liquid outer layer (proposed by geoscientists in 2010) and successive layers of molten metals and solid rock, and a thin layer at the surface comprising the continental crust.

Earth is surrounded by a magnetosphere, a region dominated by Earth's magnetic field and extending upward from about 140 km (90 mi) in the upper atmosphere. In the magnetosphere, the magnetic field of Earth traps rapidly moving charged particles (mainly electrons and protons), the majority of which flow from the Sun (as solar wind). If it were not for this shielding effect, such particles would bombard the terrestrial surface and destroy life. High concentrations of the trapped particles make up two doughnut-shaped zones called the Van Allen radiation belts. These belts play a key role in certain geophysical phenomena, such as auroras.

## The Moon

The Moon is the sole natural satellite of Earth. It revolves around the planet from west to east at a mean distance of about 384,400 km (238,900 mi). The Moon is less than one-third the size of Earth, having a diameter of only about 3,475 km (2,159 mi) at its equator. The Moon shines by reflecting sunlight, but its albedo—i.e., the fraction of light received that is reflected—is only 0.073.

The Moon rotates about its own axis in about 27.32 days, which is virtually identical to the time it takes to complete its orbit around Earth. As a result, the Moon always presents nearly the same face to Earth. The rate of actual rotation is uniform, but the arc through which the Moon moves from day to day varies somewhat, causing the lunar globe (as seen by a terrestrial observer) to oscillate slightly over a period nearly equal to that of revolution.

The surface of the Moon has been a subject of continuous telescopic study from the time of Galileo's first observation in 1609. The Italian Jesuit astronomer Giovanni B. Riccioli designated the dark areas on the Moon as seas (maria), with such fanciful names as Mare Imbrium ("Sea of Showers") and Mare Nectaris ("Sea of Nectar"). During the centuries that followed the publication of these early studies, more detailed maps and, eventually, photographs were produced. A Soviet space probe photographed the side of the Moon facing away from Earth in 1959. By the late 1960s, the US Lunar Orbiter missions had yielded close-up photographs of the entire lunar surface. On 20 Jul 1969, Apollo 11 astronauts Neil Armstrong and Edwin ("Buzz") Aldrin set foot on the Moon. US explorations continued with GRAIL, the twin solar-powered spacecraft launched in late 2011 to map the Moon's gravitational field. Equipped with student-run instruments, the spacecraft also retrieved images for scientific study by middle schoolers.

Craters, which measure up to about 200 km (320 mi) or more in diameter, are scattered over the surface in great profusion and often overlap one another. Meteorites hitting the lunar surface at high velocity produced most of the large craters. Many of the smaller ones—those measuring less than 1 km (0.6 mi) across—appear to have been formed by explosive volcanic activity, however. The Moon's maria have relatively few craters. These lava outpourings spread over vast areas after most of the craters had already been formed.

Various theories for the Moon's origin have been proposed. At the end of the 19th century, the English astronomer Sir George H. Darwin advanced a hypothesis stating that the Moon had been originally part of Earth but had broken away as a result of tidal gravitational action and receded from the planet. This was proved unlikely in the 1930s. A theory that arose dur-

## The Moon (continued)

ing the 1950s postulated that the Moon had formed elsewhere in the solar system and was then later captured by Earth. This idea was also proved to be physically implausible and was dismissed. Today, most investigators favor an explanation known as the giant-impact hypothesis, which postulates that a Mars-sized body struck proto-Earth early in the history of the solar system. As a result, a cloud of fragments from both bodies was ejected into orbit around Earth, and this later accreted into the Moon.

## Moon Phases, 2012–2013

As the Moon orbits Earth, more or less of the half of the Moon illuminated by the Sun is visible on Earth. During the lunar month the Moon's appearance changes from dark (the new moon) to being illuminated more and more on the right side (waxing crescent, first quarter, and waxing gibbous) to the full disc being illuminated (the full moon). The phases of the Moon are completed by the Moon being illuminated less and less on the left side (waning gibbous, last quarter, and waning crescent) and end with another new moon. This cycle takes place over a period of around 29 days; the time from new moon to new moon is referred to as a lunation.

The phases of the Moon are caused by the positions of the Sun in relationship to the Moon. Thus, when the Sun and the Moon are close in the sky a dark new moon is the result (the Sun is lighting the half of the Moon not visible to Earth). When the Sun and the Moon are at opposition (in opposite parts of the sky) the full moon occurs (the Sun illuminates fully the half of the Moon seen on Earth). When the Sun and the Moon are at about a 90-degree angle, one sees either a first quarter or a last quarter moon.

The dates for the new moon, first quarter, full moon, and last quarter for late June 2012–December 2013 are given in the table below.

| MONTH | NEW MOON | FIRST QUARTER | FULL MOON | LAST QUARTER |
|---|---|---|---|---|
| June 2012 | 19 | 27 | (3 July) | (11 July) |
| July 2012 | 19 | 26 | (2 August) | (9 August) |
| August 2012 | 17 | 24 | 31 | (8 September) |
| September 2012 | 16 | 22 | 30 | (8 October) |
| October 2012 | 15 | 22 | 29 | (7 November) |
| November 2012 | 13 | 20 | 28 | (6 December) |
| December 2012 | 13 | 20 | 28 | (5 January) |
| January 2013 | 11 | 18 | 27 | (3 February) |
| February 2013 | 10 | 17 | 25 | (4 March) |
| March 2013 | 11 | 19 | 27 | (3 April) |
| April 2013 | 10 | 18 | 25 | (2 May) |
| May 2013 | 10 | 18 | 25 | 31 |
| June 2013 | 8 | 16 | 23 | 30 |
| July 2013 | 8 | 16 | 22 | 29 |
| August 2013 | 6 | 14 | 21 | 28 |
| September 2013 | 5 | 12 | 19 | 27 |
| October 2013 | 5 | 11 | 18 | 26 |
| November 2013 | 3 | 10 | 17 | 25 |
| December 2013 | 3 | 9 | 17 | 25 |

## Mars

Mars is the fourth planet in order of average distance from the Sun and the seventh in order of diminishing size and mass. It orbits the Sun once in 687 Earth days and spins on its axis once every 24 Earth hours and 37 minutes.

Because of its blood-red color, Mars has often been associated with warfare and slaughter. It is named for the Roman god of war; as far back as 3,000 years ago, Babylonian astronomer-astrologers called the planet Nergal for their god of death and pestilence. The Greeks called it Ares for their god of battle; the planet's two satellites, Phobos (Fear) and Deimos (Terror), were later named for the two sons of Ares and Aphrodite.

Mars moves around the Sun at a mean distance of approximately 1.52 times that of Earth from the Sun. Because the orbit of Mars is relatively elongated, the distance between Mars and the Sun varies from 206.6 to 249.2 million km (128.4 to 154.8 million mi). Mars completes a single orbit in roughly the time in which Earth completes two. At its closest approach, Mars is less than 56 million km (34.8 million mi) from Earth, but it recedes to almost 400 million km (248.5 million mi). Mars is a small planet. Its equatorial radius is about half that of Earth, and its mass is only one-tenth the terrestrial value.

The axis of rotation is inclined to the orbital plane at an angle of 24.9°, and, as on Earth, the tilt gives rise to seasons. The Martian year consists of 668.6 Martian solar days (called sols). The orientation and eccentricity of the orbit (eccentricity denotes how much the orbit deviates from a perfect circle: the more elongated, the more eccentric) leads to seasons that are quite uneven in length. The Martian atmosphere is mainly composed of carbon dioxide. It is very thin (less than 1% of Earth's atmospheric pressure). Evidence suggests that the atmosphere was much denser in the remote past and that water was once much more abundant at the surface. Only small amounts of water are found in the lower atmosphere today, occasionally forming thin ice clouds at high altitudes and, in several localities, morning ice fogs. Mars's polar caps consist of frozen

## Mars (continued)

carbon dioxide and water ice. Observations confirm that water ice also is present under large areas of the Martian surface and hint that liquid water may have flowed in geologically recent times.

The characteristic temperature in the lower atmosphere is about $-70$ °C ($-100$ °F). Unlike that of Earth, the total mass (and pressure) of the atmosphere experiences large seasonal variations, as carbon dioxide "snows out" at the winter pole.

The surface of Mars shows the massive extinct volcano Olympus Mons, which stands some 21 km (13 mi) above the planet's mean radius and is 540 km (335 mi) across, and Valles Marineris, a system of canyons, is some 4,000 km (2,500 mi) long and from about 2 to 9 km (1 to 5.6 mi) deep.

Discovered in 1877 by Asaph Hall of the United States Naval Observatory, Phobos and Deimos, Mars' two satellites, are small and cannot be seen from all locations on the planet because of their size, proximity to the planet, and near-equatorial orbits. Little was known about these bodies until observations were made by NASA's orbiting Mariner 9 spacecraft nearly a century later. Further observations by the European Space Agency's Mars Express spacecraft uncovered evidence in 2010 that suggests that Phobos was formed when rocks blasted into space from a comet or meteorite collision with Mars and clumped together.

In November 2011, soon after the mission of the Mars Exploration Rover Spirit was declared successfully complete, NASA launched Curiosity to continue seeking clues concerning possible previous life and present microbial life on the Red Planet. During its planned two-year fact-finding mission, Curiosity was set to analyze the environment with greater depth by way of samples drilled from rocks and gathered from the ground.

---

In 2010, the International Year of Biodiversity, the United Kingdom declared a 210,000 sq mi (545,000 sq km) protection zone in the Chagos islands, creating the world's largest marine reserve. Included in the reserve is the Great Chagos Bank, the largest living coral structure. The Indian Ocean archipelago is home to an enormous variety of coral and fish species, and the designation banned industrial commercial fishing and deep-sea mining.

---

## Jupiter

Jupiter is the most massive of the planets and is fifth in average distance from the Sun. When ancient astronomers named the planet Jupiter for the ruler of the gods in the Greco-Roman pantheon, they had no idea of the planet's true dimensions, but the name is appropriate, for Jupiter is larger than all the other planets combined. It has a narrow ring system and at least 64 known satellites, 3 larger than Earth's Moon. Jupiter also has an internal heat source—i.e., it emits more energy than it receives from the Sun. This giant has the strongest magnetic field of any planet, with a magnetosphere so large that, if it could be seen from Earth, its apparent diameter would exceed that of the Moon. Jupiter's system is the source of intense bursts of radio noise, at some frequencies occasionally radiating more energy than the Sun.

Of particular interest concerning Jupiter's physical properties is its low mean density of 1.33 grams per cubic cm—in contrast with Earth's 5.52 grams/cm³—coupled with the large dimensions and mass and the short rotational period. The low density and large mass indicate that Jupiter's composition and structure are quite unlike those of Earth and the other inner planets, a deduction that is supported by detailed investigations of the giant planet's atmosphere and interior.

Jupiter has no solid surface; the transition from the atmosphere to its highly compressed core occurs gradually at great depths. The close-up views of Jupiter from the Voyager spacecraft revealed a variety of cloud forms, with a predominance of elliptical features reminiscent of cyclonic and anticyclonic storm systems on Earth. All these systems are in motion, appearing and disappearing on time scales dependent on their sizes and locations. Also observed to vary are the pastel shades of various colors present in the cloud layers—from the tawny yellow that seems to characterize the main layer, through browns and blue-grays, to the well-known salmon-colored Great Red Spot, Jupiter's largest, most prominent, and longest-lived feature.

Because Jupiter has no solid surface, it has no topographic features, and latitudinal currents dominate the planet's large-scale circulation. The lack of a solid surface with physical boundaries and regions with different heat capacities makes the persistence of these currents and their associated cloud patterns all the more remarkable. The Great Red Spot, for example, moves in longitude with respect to Jupiter's rotation, but it does not move in latitude.

The Voyager 1 spacecraft verified the existence of a ring system surrounding Jupiter when it crossed the planet's equatorial plane. Subsequently, images from the Galileo spacecraft revealed that the ring system consists principally of four concentric components whose boundaries are associated with the orbits of Jupiter's four innermost moons. The ring system is composed of large numbers of micrometer-sized particles that produce strong forward scattering of incident sunlight. The presence of such small particles requires a source, and the association of the ring boundaries with the four moons makes the source clear. The particles are thought to be generated by impacts on these moons (and on still smaller bodies within the main part of the ring) by micrometeoroids, cometary debris, and possibly volcanically produced material from Jupiter's moon Io.

A direct, invisible wave motion was detected in one of Jupiter's jet streams through studies of images taken by the Cassini spacecraft. Meanwhile, in late 2011, NASA's Juno spacecraft was launched on a six-year journey to study Jupiter in detail, in hopes of gaining a greater revelation of the planet's origin and evolution.

# Jovian Moons

The satellites orbiting Jupiter are numerous; there are at least 64 Jovian moons and likely additional ones to be discovered.

The first objects in the solar system discovered by means of a telescope (by Galileo in 1610) were the four brightest moons of Jupiter. Now known as the Galilean satellites, they are (in order of increasing distance from Jupiter) Io, Europa, Ganymede, and Callisto. Each is a unique world in its own right. Callisto and Ganymede, for example, are as large as or larger than the planet Mercury, but, while Callisto's icy surface is ancient and heavily cratered from impacts, Ganymede's appears to have been extensively modified by internal activity. Europa may still be geologically active, and evidence points to an ocean of liquid water, and possibly even life, beneath its frozen surface. Io is the most volcanically active body in the solar system; its surface is a vividly colored landscape of erupting vents, pools and solidified flows of lava, and sulfurous deposits.

Data for the first 16 known Jovian moons (discovered 1610–1979) are summarized below. The orbits of the inner eight satellites have low inclinations (they are not tilted relative to the planet's equator) and low eccentricities (their orbits are relatively circular). The orbits of the outer eight have much higher inclinations and eccentricities, and four of them are retrograde (they are opposite to Jupiter's spin and orbital motion around the Sun). The innermost four satellites are thought to be intimately associated with Jupiter's ring and are the sources of the fine particles within the ring itself.

Beginning in 1999 some 47 tiny moons (including one seen in 1975 and then lost) were discovered photographically in observations from Earth. All have high orbital eccentricities and inclinations and large orbital radii; nearly all of the orbits are retrograde. Rough size estimates based on their brightness place them between 2 and 8 km (1.2 and 5 mi) in diameter. They were assigned provisional numerical designations on discovery; many also have received official names.

In the table, "sync" denotes that the orbital period and rotational period are the same, or synchronous. Hence, the moon always keeps the same face toward Jupiter. "R" following the orbital period indicates a retrograde orbit. Unspecified quantities are unknown.

| NAME (DESIGNATION) | MEAN DISTANCE FROM JUPITER | DIAMETER | MASS ($10^{17}$ KG)[1] | DENSITY (GRAMS/CM³) | ORBITAL PERIOD (EARTH DAYS) | ROTATIONAL PERIOD (EARTH DAYS) |
|---|---|---|---|---|---|---|
| Metis (JXVI) | 128,000 km (80,000 mi) | 43 km (27 mi) | [1] | | 0.295 | sync |
| Adrastea (JXV) | 129,000 km (80,000 mi) | 16 km (10 mi) | [0.07] | | 0.298 | sync |
| Amalthea (JV) | 181,400 km (113,000 mi) | 167 km (104 mi) | 20.8 | 0.86 | 0.498 | sync |
| Thebe (JXIV) | 221,900 km (138,000 mi) | 99 km (62 mi) | [15] | | 0.675 | sync |
| Io (JI) | 421,800 km (262,000 mi) | 3,643 km (2,264 mi) | 893,200 | 3.53 | 1.769 | sync |
| Europa (JII) | 671,100 km (417,000 mi) | 3,122 km (1,940 mi) | 480,000 | 3.01 | 3.551 | sync |
| Ganymede (JIII) | 1,070,400 km (665,000 mi) | 5,262 km (3,270 mi) | 1,482,000 | 1.94 | 7.155 | sync |
| Callisto (JIV) | 1,882,700 km (1,170,000 mi) | 4,821 km (2,996 mi) | 1,076,000 | 1.83 | 16.69 | sync |
| Leda (JXIII) | 11,165,000 km (6,938,000 mi) | 20 km (12 mi) | [0.11] | | 240.92 | |
| Himalia (JVI) | 11,461,000 km (7,122,000 mi) | 170 km (106 mi) | 42 | 1.3–2.4 | 250.56 | 0.4 |
| Lysithea (JX) | 11,717,000 km (7,281,000 mi) | 36 km (22 mi) | [0.63] | | 259.2 | |
| Elara (JVII) | 11,741,000 km (7,296,000 mi) | 86 km (53 mi) | [8.7] | | 259.64 | 0.5 |
| Ananke (JXII) | 21,276,000 km (13,220,000 mi) | 28 km (17 mi) | [0.3] | | 629.77 R | |
| Carme (JXI) | 23,404,000 km (14,543,000 mi) | 46 km (29 mi) | [1.3] | | 734.17 R | |
| Pasiphae (JVIII) | 23,624,000 km (14,679,000 mi) | 60 km (37 mi) | [3] | | 743.63 R | |
| Sinope (JIX) | 23,939,000 km (14,875,000 mi) | 38 km (24 mi) | [0.7] | | 758.9 R | |

[1]Quantities given in brackets are poorly known.

## Jovian Ring

Jupiter's complex ring was discovered and first studied by the twin Voyager spacecraft during flybys of the planet in 1979 and further elucidated by images from the Galileo spacecraft in 1996–97. The ring consists of four main components: an outer gossamer ring, whose outer radius coincides with the orbital radius of the Jovian moon Thebe (222,000 km; 137,900 mi); an inner gossamer ring bounded on its outer edge by the orbit of Amalthea (181,000 km; 112,500 mi); the main ring, extending inward some 6,000 km (3,730 mi) from the orbits of Adrastea (129,000 km; 80,160 mi) and Metis (128,000 km; 79,540 mi); and a halo of particles with a thickness of 20,000 km (12,430 mi) that extends from the main ring inward to a radius of about 92,000 km (57,170 mi). For comparison, Jupiter's visible surface lies at a radius of about 71,500 km (44,430 mi) from its center. The moons involved with the ring are believed to supply the fine particles that compose it.

## Saturn

Saturn is the sixth planet in order of average distance from the Sun and the second largest of the planets in mass and size. Its dimensions are almost equal to those of Jupiter, while its mass is about a third as large; it has the lowest mean density of any object in the solar system.

Both Saturn and Jupiter resemble stellar bodies in that the light gas hydrogen dominates their bulk **chemical composition**. Saturn's atmosphere is 91% hydrogen by mass and is thus the most hydrogen-rich atmosphere in the solar system. Saturn's structure and **evolutionary history**, however, differ significantly from those of its larger counterpart. Like the other giant planets—Jupiter, Uranus, and Neptune—Saturn has extensive satellite and ring systems, which may provide clues to its origin and evolution. The planet has at least 62 moons, including the second largest in the solar system. Saturn's dense and extended rings, which lie in its equatorial plane, are the most impressive in the solar system.

Saturn has a variety of **rotation periods**, with periods from 10 hours 10 minutes near the equator to about 30 minutes longer at latitudes higher than 40°. The rotation period of Saturn's deep interior can be determined from the rotation period of the magnetic field, which is presumed to be rooted in an outer core of hydrogen compressed to a metallic state. The "surface" of Saturn that is seen through telescopes and in spacecraft images is actually a complex layer of clouds.

The **atmosphere** of Saturn shows many smaller-scale time-variable features similar to those found in that of Jupiter, such as red, brown, and white spots; bands; eddies; and vortices. The atmosphere generally is less active than Jupiter's on a small scale. In October 2010, dark clouds in the atmosphere, produced by soot and other carbon products created by lightning strikes on methane, were evidenced by Cassini, a NASA probe launched in 1997. In December 2010, Cassini began documenting a giant storm that continued to rage for nearly a year. At its peak the storm encircled the entire planet, covering some 4 billion square km (1.5 billion square mi), and produced more than 10 lightning flashes per second.

## Saturnian Moons

At least 62 natural satellites are known to circle Saturn. Data for the first 18 Saturnian moons (discovered 1655–1990) are summarized below. The satellites closest to Saturn are regular, meaning that their orbits are fairly circular and not greatly inclined (tilted) with respect to the planet's equator. All of the satellites in the table except **Phoebe** are regular.

**Titan** is Saturn's largest moon and the only satellite in the solar system known to have clouds (some of which were reported in early 2011 to consist of ice particles) and a dense atmosphere (composed mostly of nitrogen and methane). Enveloped in a reddish haze, it is thought to be composed of complex organic compounds produced by the action of sunlight on its clouds and atmosphere. That organic molecules may have been settling out of the haze onto Titan's surface for much of its history has caused scientists to speculate that life may have evolved there. Observations by the Cassini-Huygens spacecraft showed Titan to have a varied surface sculpted by rains of hydrocarbon compounds, flowing liquids, wind, impacts, and possibly volcanic and tectonic activity. In 2012, Cassini photographed large methane "lakes" near Titan's equator.

The European Space Agency's Herschel space observatory captured evidence that the planet's chemical makeup is directly influenced by an all-encompassing vapor circle formed by water ejected from **Enceladus**.

Because of **Hyperion's** highly irregular shape and eccentric orbit, it does not rotate stably about a fixed axis but rotates chaotically, alternating between periods of tumbling and seemingly regular rotation.

Images and data from Cassini have led astronomers to conclude that **Iapetus's** two-tone surface comes from falling dust from another Saturnian satellite, forming a dark side, versus the lighter side, caused by ice.

Between 2000 and 2005, about 30 tiny moons occupying various (mostly distant) orbits were discovered. Like the numerous outer moons of Jupiter, nearly all of the recent finds around Saturn belong to the irregular class. More than half of them are in retrograde orbits (they move opposite to Saturn's spin and orbital motion around the Sun).

In the table, "sync" denotes that the orbital period and rotational period are the same, or synchronous. Hence, the moon always keeps the same face toward Saturn. Unspecified quantities are unknown.

| NAME (DESIGNATION) | MEAN DISTANCE FROM SATURN | DIAMETER | MASS ($10^{17}$ KG) | DENSITY (GRAMS/CM³) | ORBITAL PERIOD (EARTH DAYS) | ROTATIONAL PERIOD (EARTH DAYS) |
|---|---|---|---|---|---|---|
| Pan (SXVIII) | 133,580 km (83,000 mi) | 20 km (12 mi) | 0.049 | 0.36 | 0.575 | |
| Atlas (SXV) | 137,670 km (85,540 mi) | 33 km (21 mi) | 0.066 | 0.44 | 0.602 | |

## Saturnian Moons (continued)

| NAME (DESIGNATION) | MEAN DISTANCE FROM SATURN | DIAMETER | MASS ($10^{17}$ KG) | DENSITY (GRAMS/CM³) | ORBITAL PERIOD (EARTH DAYS) | ROTATIONAL PERIOD (EARTH DAYS) |
|---|---|---|---|---|---|---|
| Prometheus (SXVI) | 139,380 km (86,610 mi) | 98 km (61 mi) | 1.59 | 0.48 | 0.603 | |
| Pandora (SXVII) | 141,720 km (88,060 mi) | 84 km (52 mi) | 1.37 | 0.5 | 0.629 | |
| Epimetheus (SXI) | 151,410 km (94,080 mi) | 119 km (74 mi) | 5.3 | 0.69 | 0.694 | sync |
| Janus (SX) | 151,460 km (94,110 mi) | 179 km (112 mi) | 19 | 0.63 | 0.695 | sync |
| Mimas (SI) | 185,540 km (115,290 mi) | 396 km (246 mi) | 373 | 1.15 | 0.942 | sync |
| Enceladus (SII) | 238,040 km (147,910 mi) | 504 km (313 mi) | 1,076 | 1.61 | 1.37 | sync |
| Tethys (SIII) | 294,670 km (183,100 mi) | 1,066 km (662 mi) | 6,130 | 0.97 | 1.888 | sync |
| Telesto (SXIII)* | 294,710 km (183,120 mi) | 23 km (14 mi) | 0.07 | | 1.888 | |
| Calypso (SXIV)* | 294,710 km (183,120 mi) | 20 km (12 mi) | 0.04 | | 1.888 | |
| Dione (SIV) | 377,420 km (234,520 mi) | 1,124 km (698 mi) | 10,970 | 1.48 | 2.737 | sync |
| Helene (SXII)† | 377,420 km (234,520 mi) | 32 km (20 mi) | 0.25 | | 2.737 | |
| Rhea (SV) | 527,070 km (327,510 mi) | 1,528 km (949 mi) | 22,900 | 1.23 | 4.518 | sync |
| Titan (SVI) | 1,221,870 km (759,230 mi) | 5,152 km (3,201 mi) | 1,342,000 | 1.88 | 15.95 | sync |
| Hyperion (SVII) | 1,500,880 km (932,600 mi) | 286 km (178 mi) | 55 | 0.54 | 21.28 | chaotic |
| Iapetus (SVIII) | 3,560,840 km (2,212,600 mi) | 1,470 km (913 mi) | 17,900 | 1.08 | 79.33 | sync |
| Phoebe (SIX) | 12,947,780 km (8,045,380 mi) | 214 km (133 mi) | 83 | 1.63 | 550.31 (retrograde) | 0.4 |

*Telesto and Calypso occupy the same orbit as Tethys but about 60° ahead and behind, respectively.
†Helene occupies the same orbit as Dione but about 60° behind.

## Saturnian Rings

Saturn's rings have intrigued astronomers ever since they were discovered telescopically by Galileo in 1610, and their mysteries have only deepened since they were photographed and studied by Voyager 1 and 2 in the early 1980s. In October 2009, researchers announced the discovery of a giant Saturnian ring that lies far beyond the planet's other rings. Sighted through NASA's Spitzer Space Telescope, it is the largest known planetary ring in the solar system, beginning about 6 million km (about 3.7 million mi) from Saturn and stretching outward another 12 million km (7.5 million mi). In April 2011, researchers posited that ripples in Saturn's inner rings were caused by debris from a comet collision some 30 years ago. The **particles** that make up the rings are composed primarily of water ice and range from dust specks to house-sized chunks. The rings exhibit a great amount of structure on many scales, from the broad **A, B, and C rings** visible from Earth down to myriad narrow component ringlets. Odd structures resembling spokes, braids, and spiral waves are also present. Some of this detail is explained by gravitational interaction with a number of Saturn's 62 moons, but much of it remains unaccounted for.

Numerous **divisions** or gaps are seen in the major ring regions. A few of the more prominent ones are named for famous astronomers who were associated with studies of Saturn.

The major rings and divisions, listed outward from Saturn, are given below. For comparison, Saturn's visible surface lies at a radius of about 60,300 km (37,500 mi).

| RING (OR DIVISION) | RADIUS OF RING'S INNER EDGE | WIDTH | COMMENTS |
|---|---|---|---|
| D ring (Guerin division) | 67,000 km (41,630 mi) | 7,500 km (4,700 mi) | visible only in reflected light |
| C ring (Maxwell division) | 74,490 km (46,290 mi) | 17,500 km (10,900 mi) | also called Crepe ring |
| B ring (Cassini division, Huygens gap) | 91,980 km (57,150 mi) | 25,500 km (15,800 mi) | brightest ring; Cassini division is the largest ring gap |
| A ring | 122,050 km (75,840 mi) | 14,600 km (9,100 mi) | the outermost ring visible from Earth |

## Saturnian Rings (continued)

| RING (OR DIVISION)<br>(Encke division) | RADIUS OF RING'S INNER EDGE | WIDTH | COMMENTS<br>located within the A ring,<br>near its outer edge |
|---|---|---|---|
| F ring | 140,220 km (87,130 mi) | 30–500 km (20–300 mi) | faint, narrowest major ring |
| G ring | 166,000 km (103,150 mi) | 8,000 km (5,000 mi) | faint |
| E ring | 180,000 km (111,850 mi) | 300,000 km (186,400 mi) | faint |

## Uranus

Uranus is the seventh planet in order of distance from the Sun and the first found with the aid of a telescope. Its low density and large size place it among the four giant planets, all of which are composed primarily of hydrogen, helium, water, and other volatile compounds and which thus are without solid surfaces. Absorption of red light by methane gas gives the planet a blue-green color. The planet has at least 27 satellites, ranging up to 789 km (490 mi) in radius, and 13 narrow rings.

Uranus spins on its side; its rotation axis is tipped at an angle of 98° relative to its orbit axis. The 98° tilt is thought to have arisen during the final stages of planetary accretion when bodies comparable in size to the present planets collided in a series of violent events that knocked Uranus onto its side.

Although Uranus is nearly featureless, extreme contrast enhancement of images taken by the Voyager spacecraft reveals faint bands oriented parallel to circles of constant latitude. Apparently the rotation of the planet and not the distribution of absorbed sunlight controls the cloud patterns.

Wind is the motion of the atmosphere relative to the rotating planet. At high latitudes on Uranus, as on the Earth, this relative motion is in the direction of the planet's rotation. At low (that is, equatorial) latitudes, the relative motion is in the opposite direction. On the Earth these directions are called east and west, respectively, but the more general terms are prograde and retrograde. The winds that exist on Uranus are several times stronger than are those of the Earth. The wind is 200 m (656 ft) per second (prograde) at a latitude of 55° S and 110 m (360.8 ft) per second (retrograde) at the equator. Neptune's equatorial winds are also retrograde, although those of Jupiter and Saturn are prograde. No satisfactory theory exists to explain these differences.

Uranus has no large **spots** like the Great Red Spot of Jupiter or the Great Dark Spot of Neptune. Since the giant planets have no solid surfaces, the spots represent atmospheric storms. For reasons that are not clear, Uranus seems to have the smallest number of storms of any of the giant planets. Most of the mass of Uranus (roughly 80%) is in the form of a liquid core made primarily of icy materials (water, methane, and ammonia).

Uranus was discovered in 1781 by the English astronomer **William Herschel**, who had undertaken a survey of all stars down to eighth magnitude—i.e., those about five times fainter than stars visible to the naked eye. Herschel suggested naming the new planet the Georgian Planet after his patron, King George III of England, but the planet was eventually named according to the tradition of naming planets for the gods of Greek and Roman mythology; Uranus is the father of Saturn, who is in turn the father of Jupiter.

After the discovery, Herschel continued to observe the planet with larger and better telescopes and eventually discovered its two largest satellites, Titania and Oberon, in 1787. Two more satellites, Ariel and Umbriel, were discovered by the British astronomer William Lassell in 1851. The names of the four satellites come from English literature—they are characters in works by Shakespeare and Pope—and were proposed by Herschel's son, John Herschel. A fifth satellite, Miranda, was discovered by Gerard P. Kuiper in 1948. The tradition of naming the satellites after characters in Shakespeare's and Pope's works continues to the present.

## Uranian Moons and Rings

Uranus has 27 known **satellites** forming three distinct groups: 13 small moons orbiting quite close to the planet, 5 large moons located somewhat farther out, and finally, another 9 small and much more distant moons. The members of the first two groups are in nearly circular orbits with low inclinations with respect to the planet.

The densities of the four largest satellites, **Ariel, Umbriel, Titania,** and **Oberon,** suggest that they are about half (or more) water ice and the rest rock. Oberon and Umbriel are heavily scarred with large impact craters dating back to the very early history of the solar system, evidence that their surfaces probably have been stable since their formation. In contrast, Titania and Ariel have far fewer large craters, indicating relatively young surfaces shaped over time by internal geological activity. **Miranda,** though small compared with the other major moons, has a unique jumbled patchwork of varied surface terrain revealing surprisingly extensive past activity.

The 5 major moons were **discovered** telescopically from Earth between 1787 and 1948. Ten of the 13 innermost moons, with radii of about 10–80 km (6–50 mi), were found in Voyager 2 images. The rest of the moons, with radii of 5–81 km (3–50 mi), were detected in Earth-based observations between 1997 and 2003; the orbital motion of nearly all of the outermost moons is retrograde (opposite to the direction of Uranus's spin and revolution around the Sun).

Thirteen narrow rings are known to encircle Uranus, with radii from 41,837 to 51,149 km (25,996 to 31,783 mi), for the most part within the orbits of the innermost moons. For comparison, Uranus's visible surface lies at a radius of about 25,600 km (15,900 mi). The ring system was first detected in 1977 during Earth-based observations of Uranus. Subsequent observations from Earth and images from Voyager 2 and the Hubble Space Telescope clarified the number and other features of the rings.

In the table, "sync" denotes that the orbital period and rotational period are the same, or synchronous. Hence, the moon always keeps the same face toward Uranus.

## Uranian Moons and Rings (continued)

| NAME (DESIGNATION) | MEAN DISTANCE FROM URANUS | DIAMETER | MASS ($10^{20}$ KG) | DENSITY (GRAMS/CM$^3$) | ORBITAL PERIOD (EARTH DAYS) | ROTATIONAL PERIOD (EARTH DAYS) |
|---|---|---|---|---|---|---|
| Miranda (V) | 129,900 km (80,720 mi) | 471 km (293 mi) | 0.66 | 1.2 | 1.413 | sync |
| Ariel (I) | 190,900 km (118,620 mi) | 1,158 km (719 mi) | 13.5 | 1.67 | 2.52 | sync |
| Umbriel (II) | 266,000 km (165,280 mi) | 1,169 km (727 mi) | 11.7 | 1.4 | 4.144 | sync |
| Titania (III) | 436,300 km (271,100 mi) | 1,578 km (980 mi) | 35.2 | 1.71 | 8.706 | sync |
| Oberon (IV) | 583,500 km (362,570 mi) | 1,523 km (946 mi) | 30.1 | 1.63 | 13.46 | sync |

## Neptune

Neptune is the eighth planet in average distance from the Sun. It has 13 known satellites. It was named for the Roman god of the sea, whose trident serves as the planet's astronomical symbol.

Neptune's **distance** from the Sun varies between 29.8 and 30.4 astronomical units (AUs). Its **diameter** is about four times that of Earth, but because of its great distance Neptune cannot be seen from Earth without the aid of a telescope. Neptune's deep blue **color** is due to the absorption of red light by methane gas in its atmosphere. It receives less than half as much sunlight as Uranus, but heat escaping from its interior makes Neptune slightly warmer than the latter. The heat released may also be responsible for Neptune's stormier **atmosphere**, which exhibits the fastest winds seen on any planet in the solar system.

Neptune's **orbital period** is 164.8 Earth years. It has not completely circled the Sun since its discovery in 1846, so some refinements in calculations of its orbital size and shape are still expected. The planet's orbital eccentricity of 0.009 means that its orbit is very nearly circular; among the planets in the solar system, only Venus has a smaller eccentricity. Neptune's seasons (and the seasons of its moons) are therefore of nearly equal length, each about 41 Earth years in duration. The length of Neptune's day, as determined by Voyager 2, is 16.11 Earth hours.

As with the other giant planets of the outer solar system, Neptune's atmosphere is composed predominantly of hydrogen and helium. The **temperature** of Neptune's atmosphere varies with altitude. A minimum temperature of about −223 °C (−369 °F) occurs at pressure near 0.1 bar. The temperature increases with altitude to about 477 °C (891 °F) at 2,000 km (1,240 mi, which corresponds to a pressure of $10^{-11}$ bar) as measured from the one-bar level and remains uniform above that altitude. It also increases with depth to about 6,730 °C (12,140 °F) near the center of the planet.

As is the case with several of the other large planets, the **winds** on Neptune are constrained to blow generally along lines of constant latitude and are relatively invariable with time. Winds on Neptune vary from about 100 m/sec (328 ft/sec) in an easterly (prograde) direction near latitude 70° S to as high as 700 m/sec (2,300 ft/sec) in a westerly (retrograde) direction near latitude 20° S.

The high winds and relatively large contribution of escaping internal heat may be responsible for the observed turbulence in Neptune's visible atmosphere. Two large dark ovals are clearly visible in images of Neptune's southern hemisphere taken by Voyager 2 in 1989, although they are not present in Hubble Space Telescope images made two years later. The largest, called the **Great Dark Spot** because of its similarity in latitude and shape to Jupiter's Great Red Spot, is comparable to the entire Earth in size. It was near this feature that the highest wind speeds were measured. Atmospheric storms such as the Great Dark Spot may be centers where strong upwelling of gases from the interior takes place.

Neptune's mean **density** is about 30% of Earth's; nevertheless, it is the densest of the giant planets. Neptune's greater density implies that a larger percentage of its interior is composed of melted ices and molten rocky materials than is the case for the other gas giants.

## Neptunian Moons and Rings

Neptune has at least 13 natural satellites, but Earth-based observations had found only 2 of them, Triton in 1846 and Nereid in 1949, before Voyager 2 flew by the planet in 1989. The spacecraft observed 5 small moons orbiting close to Neptune and verified the existence of a 6th that had been detected from Earth in 1981. Data for these 8 moons are summarized in the table below. In 2002–03, 5 additional small moons (diameters roughly 30–60 km [20–40 mi]) were discovered telescopically from Earth; they all occupy highly inclined and elliptical orbits that are comparatively far from Neptune.

**Triton** is Neptune's only large moon and the only large satellite in the solar system to orbit its planet in the retrograde direction (opposite the planet's rotation and orbital motion around the Sun). Thus, as is also suspected of the solar system's other retrograde moons, Triton likely was captured by its planet rather than formed in orbit with its planet from the solar nebula. Its density (2 grams/cm$^3$) suggests that it is about 25% water ice and the rest rock. Triton has a tenuous atmosphere, mostly of nitrogen. Its varied icy surface, imaged by Voyager 2, contains giant faults and dark markings that have been interpreted as the product of geyserlike "ice volcanoes" in which the eruptive material may be gaseous nitrogen and methane. Nereid has the most elliptical orbit of any planet or moon in the solar system; it also is probably a captured object.

## Neptunian Moons and Rings (continued)

Neptune's system of six faint rings, with radii from about 42,000 to 63,000 km (26,000–39,000 mi), straddles the orbits of its 4 innermost moons. (Neptune's visible surface lies at a radius of 24,800 km, or 15,400 mi.) The outermost ring, named Adams, is unusual in that it contains several clumps, or concentrations of material, that before Voyager 2's visit had been interpreted incorrectly as independent ring arcs. What created and has maintained this structure has not yet been fully explained; it has been suggested that the clumps resulted from the relatively recent breakup of a small moon and are being temporarily held together by the gravitational effects of the nearby moon Galatea.

In the table, "sync" denotes that the orbital period and rotational period are the same, or synchronous. Hence, the moon always keeps the same face toward Neptune.

| NAME (DESIGNATION) | MEAN DISTANCE FROM NEPTUNE | DIAMETER | MASS ($10^{20}$ KG) | DENSITY (GRAMS/CM³) | ORBITAL PERIOD (EARTH DAYS) | ROTATIONAL PERIOD (EARTH DAYS) |
|---|---|---|---|---|---|---|
| Naiad (III) | 48,227 km (29,967 mi) | 67 km (42 mi) | 0.002 | | 0.294 | |
| Thalassa (IV) | 50,075 km (31,115 mi) | 83 km (52 mi) | 0.004 | | 0.312 | |
| Despina (V) | 52,526 km (32,638 mi) | 151 km (94 mi) | 0.02 | | 0.335 | |
| Galatea (VI) | 61,953 km (38,496 mi) | 175 km (109 mi) | 0.04 | | 0.429 | |
| Larissa (VII) | 73,548 km (45,701 mi) | 195 km (121 mi) | 0.05 | | 0.555 | |
| Proteus (VIII) | 117,647 km (73,102 mi) | 420 km (261 mi) | 0.5 | | 1.122 | |
| Triton (I) | 354,800 km (220,462 mi) | 2,707 km (1,682 mi) | 214 | 2.061 | 5.877 (retrograde) | sync |
| Nereid (II) | 5,513,400 km (3,425,868 mi) | 340 km (211 mi) | 0.3 | | 360.147 | |

## Pluto

Pluto is named for the god of the underworld in Roman mythology. It was long considered the planet normally farthest from the Sun, but on 24 Aug 2006, the International Astronomical Union announced that it was downgrading the status of Pluto to a dwarf planet. The key criterion in this classification was that Pluto, which orbits in the cluttered, icy Kuiper belt, had not cleared the neighborhood around its orbit. This was a controversial decision sure to be revisited.

Pluto has five natural satellites, Charon, Hydra, Nix, and unnamed moons discovered in mid-2011 and in mid-2012. Because Charon's diameter is more than half the size of Pluto's and they orbit around a common center of gravity, it was common to speak of the Pluto-Charon system as a double planet. Charon, named for the boatman in Greek mythology who carried the souls of the dead across the river Styx, was discovered in 1978, while Hydra and Nix were both first seen in 2005. The New Horizons spacecraft, launched in January 2006 and scheduled to arrive at Pluto in 2015, will search for yet more new satellites.

Pluto is so distant (its average distance from the Sun is 39.6 astronomical units, or AU) that sunlight traveling at 299,792 km/sec (186,282.1 mi/sec) takes more than five hours to reach it. An observer standing on the dwarf planet's surface would see the Sun as an extremely bright star in the dark sky, providing Pluto with only 1/1600 the amount of sunlight reaching the Earth.

Pluto has a diameter less than half that of Mercury; it is about two-thirds the size of the Moon. Pluto's physical characteristics are unlike those of any of the planets. Pluto resembles most closely Neptune's icy satellite Triton, which implies a similar origin for these two bodies. Most scientists now believe that Pluto and Charon are large icy planetesimals left over from the formation of the giant outer planets of the solar system. Accordingly, Pluto can be interpreted to be the largest known member of the Kuiper belt (which, as discussed, includes the outer part of Pluto's orbit). Observations of Pluto show that it appears slightly red, though not as red as Mars or Io. Thus, the surface of Pluto cannot be composed simply of pure ices. Its overall reflectivity, or albedo, ranges from 0.3 to 0.5, as compared with 0.1 for the Moon and 0.8 for Triton.

The surface temperature of Pluto has proved very difficult to measure. Observations made from the Infrared Astronomical Satellite suggest values in the range of −228 to −215 °C (−379 to −355 °F), whereas measurements at radio wavelengths imply a range of −238 to −223 °C (−397 to −370 °F). The temperature certainly must vary over the surface, depending on the local reflectivity and solar zenith angle. There is also expected to be a seasonal decrease in incident solar energy by a factor of roughly three as Pluto moves from perihelion to aphelion.

The detection of methane ice on Pluto's surface made scientists confident that it had an atmosphere before one was actually discovered. The atmosphere was finally detected in 1988 when Pluto passed in front of a star as observed from the Earth. The light of the star was dimmed before disappearing entirely behind Pluto during the occultation. This proved that a thin, greatly distended atmosphere was present. Because that atmosphere must consist of vapors in equilibrium with their ices, small changes in temperature will have a large effect on the amount of gas in the atmosphere.

# Measurements and Numbers

## International System of Units (SI)

Rapid advances in science and technology in the 19th and 20th centuries fostered the development of several overlapping systems of units of measurements as scientists improvised to meet the practical needs of their disciplines. The **General Conference on Weights and Measures** was chartered by international convention in 1875 to produce standards of physical measurement based upon an earlier international standard, the meter-kilogram-second (MKS) system. The convention calls for regular General Conference meetings to consider improvements or modifications in standards, an International Committee of Weights and Measures elected by the Conference (meets annually), and several consultative committees. **The International Bureau of Weights and Measures** (Bureau International des Poids et Mesures) at Sèvres, France, serves as a depository for the primary international standards and as a laboratory for certification and intercomparison of national standard copies.

The 1960 **International System** (universally abbreviated as **SI**, from *système international*) builds upon the MKS system. Its **seven basic units**, from which other units are derived, are currently defined as follows: the **meter**, defined as the distance traveled by light in a vacuum in 1/299,792,458 second; the **kilogram** (about 2.2 pounds avoirdupois), which equals 1,000 grams as defined by the international prototype kilogram of platinum-iridium in the keeping of the International Bureau of Weights and Measures; the **second**, the duration of 9,192,631,770 periods of radiation associated with a specified transition of the cesium-133 atom; the **ampere**, which is the current that, if maintained in two wires placed one meter apart in a vacuum, would produce a force of $2 \times 10^{-7}$ newton per meter of length; the **candela**, defined as the intensity in a given direction of a source emitting radiation of frequency $540 \times 10^{12}$ hertz and that has a radiant intensity in that direction of 1/683 watt per steradian; the **mole**, defined as containing as many elementary entities of a substance as there are atoms in 0.012 kilogram of carbon-12; and the **kelvin**, which is 1/273.16 of the thermodynamic temperature of the triple point (equilibrium among the solid, liquid, and gaseous phases) of pure water.

**International Bureau of Weights and Measures** Web site: <www.bipm.org/en/home>.

## Elemental and Derived SI Units and Symbols

| Quantity | SI Units | | |
|---|---|---|---|
| | UNIT | FORMULA/EXPRESSION IN BASE UNITS | SYMBOL |
| **elemental units** | | | |
| length | meter | — | m |
| mass | kilogram | — | kg |
| time | second | — | s |
| electric current | ampere | — | A |
| luminous intensity | candela | — | cd |
| amount of substance | mole | — | mol |
| thermodynamic temperature | kelvin | — | K |
| | | | |
| **derived units** | | | |
| acceleration | meter/second squared | $m/s^2$ | |
| area | square meter | $m^2$ | |
| charge | coulomb | $A \times s$ | C |
| Celsius temperature | degree Celsius | K | °C |
| density | kilogram/cubic meter | $kg/m^3$ | |
| electric field strength | volt/meter | $V/m$ | |
| electrical potential | volt | $W/A$ | V |
| energy | joule | $N \times m$ | J |
| force | newton | $kg \times m/s^2$ | N |
| frequency | hertz | $s^{-1}$ | Hz |
| illumination | lux | $lm/m^2$ | lx |
| inductance | henry | $V \times s/A$ | H |
| kinematic viscosity | square meter/second | $m^2/s$ | |
| luminance | candela/square meter | $cd/m^2$ | |
| luminous flux | lumen | $cd \times sr$ | lm |
| magnetic field strength | ampere/meter | $A/m$ | |
| magnetic flux | weber | $V \times s$ | Wb |
| magnetic flux density | tesla | $Wb/m^2$ | T |
| plane angle | radian | $m \times m^{-1}=1$ | rad |
| power | watt | $J/s$ | W |
| pressure | pascal (newton/square meter) | $N/m^2$ | Pa |
| resistance | ohm | $V/A$ | Ω |
| stress | pascal (newton/square meter) | $N/m^2$ | Pa |
| velocity | meter/second | $m/s$ | |
| viscosity | newton-second/square meter | $N \times s/m^2$ | |
| volume | cubic meter | $m^3$ | |

## Conversion of Metric Weights and Measures

conversions accurate within 10 parts per million

inches × 25.4[1] = millimeters; millimeters × 0.0393701 = inches
feet × 0.3048[1] = meters; meters × 3.28084 = feet
yards × 0.9144[1] = meters; meters × 1.09361 = yards
miles (statute) × 1.60934 = kilometers; kilometers × 0.621371 = miles (statute)
square inches × 6.4516[1] = square centimeters; square centimeters × 0.155000 = square inches
square feet × 0.0929030 = square meters; square meters × 10.7639 = square feet
square yards × 0.836127 = square meters; square meters × 1.19599 = square yards
acres × 0.404686 = hectares[2]; hectares[2] × 2.47105 = acres
cubic inches × 16.3871 = cubic centimeters; cubic centimeters × 0.0610237 = cubic inches
cubic feet × 0.0283168 = cubic meters; cubic meters × 35.3147 = cubic feet
cubic yards × 0.764555 = cubic meters; cubic meters × 1.30795 = cubic yards
quarts (liquid) × 0.946353 = liters[2]; liters[2] × 1.05669 = quarts (liq)
gallons × 0.00378541 = cubic meters; cubic meters × 264.172 = gallons
ounces (avdp)[3] × 28.3495 = grams; grams × 0.0352740 = ounces (avdp)[3]
pounds (avdp)[3] × 0.453592 = kilograms; kilograms × 2.20462 = pounds (avdp)[3]
horsepower × 0.745700 = kilowatts; kilowatts × 1.34102 = horsepower

[1]Exact.    [2]Common term not used in SI.    [3]avdp = avoirdupois.
Source: National Institute of Standards and Technology.

## Tables of Equivalents: Metric System Prefixes

prefixes designating multiples and submultiples

| PREFIX | SYMBOL | FACTOR BY WHICH UNIT IS MULTIPLIED | | EXAMPLES |
|---|---|---|---|---|
| exa- | E | $10^{18}$ | = 1,000,000,000,000,000,000 | |
| peta- | P | $10^{15}$ | = 1,000,000,000,000,000 | |
| tera- | T | $10^{12}$ | = 1,000,000,000,000 | |
| giga- | G | $10^{9}$ | = 1,000,000,000 | gigabyte (GB) |
| mega- | M | $10^{6}$ | = 1,000,000 | megaton (Mt) |
| kilo- | k | $10^{3}$ | = 1,000 | kilometer (km) |
| hecto-, hect- | h | $10^{2}$ | = 100 | hectare (ha) |
| deca-, dec- | da | 10 | = 10 | decastere (das) |
| | | | 1 | |
| deci- | d | $10^{-1}$ | = 0.1 | decigram (dg) |
| centi-, cent- | c | $10^{-2}$ | = 0.01 | centimeter (cm) |
| milli- | m | $10^{-3}$ | = 0.001 | milliliter (ml) |
| micro-, micr- | μ | $10^{-6}$ | = 0.000001 | microgram (μg) |
| nano- | n | $10^{-9}$ | = 0.000000001 | nanosecond (ns) |
| pico- | p | $10^{-12}$ | = 0.000000000001 | |
| femto- | f | $10^{-15}$ | = 0.000000000000001 | |
| atto- | a | $10^{-18}$ | = 0.000000000000000001 | |

## Cooking Measurements

| MEASURE | CONVENTIONAL EQUIVALENTS[1] | METRIC EQUIVALENT |
|---|---|---|
| drop | 1/60 teaspoon | 0.08 ml |
| dash | 1/8 teaspoon | 0.62 ml |
| teaspoon | 8 dashes; 1/3 tablespoon; 1/6 fluid ounce | 4.93 ml |
| tablespoon | 3 teaspoons; 1/2 fluid ounce | 14.79 ml |
| ounce (weight) | 1/16 pound | 28.35 g |
| fluid ounce (volume) | 2 tablespoons | 29.57 ml |
| dram | 1/8 fluid ounce | 3.70 ml |
| cup | 8 fluid ounces; 16 tablespoons; 1/2 pint | 236.59 ml |
| pound | 16 ounces | 453.6 g |
| pint | 16 fluid ounces; 2 cups; 1/2 quart | 473.18 ml |
| quart | 32 fluid ounces; 4 cups; 2 pints; 1/4 gallon | 946.36 ml |
| gallon | 128 fluid ounces; 16 cups; 8 pints; 4 quarts | 3.785 l |
| peck | 2 gallons | 7.57 l |
| bushel | 8 gallons; 4 pecks | 30.28 l |

[1]All ounce measurements are in US ounces or fluid ounces.

## Spirits Measures

*Many specific volumes have varied over time and from place to place, but the proportional relationships within families of measures have generally remained the same. All ounce measures are in US fluid ounces.*

| MEASURE | CONVENTIONAL EQUIVALENTS | METRIC EQUIVALENT |
|---|---|---|
| pony | 0.75 oz = ¾ shot= ½ jigger | 22.17 ml |
| shot/ounce/finger | 1 oz = 1⅓ ponies = ⅔ jigger | 29.57 ml |
| jigger | 1.5 oz = 2 ponies = 1½ shots | 44.36 ml |
| double | 2 oz = 2 shots | 59.15 ml |
| triple | 3 oz = 3 shots | 88.72 ml |
| pint | 16 oz = ⅝ fifth = ½ quart | 473.2 ml |
| bottle (champagne or other wine) | about 25.5 oz or ⅙ imperial gallon | 750 ml (industry standard) |
| fifth | 25.6 oz = ⅘ quart = ⅕ gallon | 757.1 ml |
| quart | 32 oz = ½ magnum = ¼ gallon | 946.3 ml |
| magnum | 2 bottles (champagne or other wine) | 1.5 l |
| magnum | 64 oz = 2 quarts = ½ gallon | 1.893 l |
| yard | 80 oz = 5 pints | 2.365 l |
| gallon/double magnum | 128 oz = 4 quarts = 5 fifths = 2 magnums | 3.785 l |
| imperial gallon | 1.20 gallons = ⅖ barn gallon | 4.546 l |
| ale/beer gallon | 1.22 gallons | 4.620 l |
| barn gallon | 2½ imperial gallons | 11.37 l |
| half keg | 5 gallons (type varies) | varies |
| keg | 10 gallons (type varies) | varies |
| British bottle | 126 bottles = 21 imperial gallons | 95.47 l |
| barrel (wine) | 126 quarts = 31½ gallons | 119.2 l |
| barrel (ale/beer) | 144 quarts = 36 gallons | 136.3 l |
| British hogshead (ale/beer) | 54 imperial gallons = ½ butt (ale/beer) = ¼ tun (ale/beer) | 245.5 l |
| British hogshead (wine) | 63 imperial gallons = ½ butt (wine) = ¼ tun (wine) | 286.4 l |
| butt/pipe (ale/beer) | 108 imperial gallons = ½ tun (ale/beer) | 491.0 l |
| butt/pipe (wine) | 126 imperial gallons = ½ tun (wine) | 572.8 l |
| tun (ale/beer) | 216 imperial gallons = 4 British hogsheads (ale/beer) = 2 butts (ale/beer) | 982.0 l |
| tun (wine) | 252 imperial gallons = 12 British bottles = 2 butts (wine) | 1,146 l |

## Playing Cards Chances

### Blackjack

Number of two-card combinations in a 52-card deck (where aces equal 1 or 11 and face cards equal 10) for each number between 13 and 21

Approximate chances of various hands reaching or exceeding 21

| TOTAL WITH TWO CARDS | POSSIBLE COMBINATIONS FROM 52 CARDS |
|---|---|
| 21 | 64 |
| 20 | 136 |
| 19 | 80 |
| 18 | 86 |
| 17 | 96 |
| 16 | 86 |
| 15 | 96 |
| 14 | 102 |
| 13 | 118 |

| TOTAL IN HAND BEFORE DEAL (TWO OR MORE CARDS) | CHANCE OF REACHING A COUNT OF 17 TO 21 (%) | CHANCE OF EXCEEDING 21 | |
|---|---|---|---|
| | | ONE CARD (%) | ANY NUMBER OF CARDS (%) |
| 16 | 38 | 62 | 62 |
| 15 | 42 | 54 | 58 |
| 14 | 44 | 46 | 56 |
| 13 | 48 | 38 | 52 |

### Poker

Number of ways to reach and odds of reaching various five-card combinations on a single deal (52-card deck, no wild cards)

| HAND | NUMBER OF COMBINATIONS | ODDS OF RECEIVING ON A SINGLE DEAL |
|---|---|---|
| royal flush | 4 | 1 in 649,740 |
| straight flush | 36 | 1 in 72,193 |
| four of a kind | 624 | 1 in 4,165 |
| full house | 3,744 | 1 in 694 |
| flush | 5,108 | 1 in 509 |
| straight | 10,200 | 1 in 255 |
| three of a kind | 54,912 | 1 in 47 |
| two pairs | 123,552 | 1 in 21 |
| one pair | 1,098,240 | 1 in 2 |

## Roman Numerals

Seven numeral-characters compose the Roman numeral system. When a numeral appears with a line above it, it represents the base value multiplied by 1,000. However, because Roman numerals are now seldom utilized for values beyond 4,999, this convention is no longer in use.

| ARABIC | ROMAN | ARABIC | ROMAN | ARABIC | ROMAN | ARABIC | ROMAN |
|---|---|---|---|---|---|---|---|
| 1 | I | 15 | XV | 60 | LX | 800 | DCCC |
| 2 | II | 16 | XVI | 70 | LXX | 900 | CM |
| 3 | III | 17 | XVII | 80 | LXXX | 1,000 | M |
| 4 | IV | 18 | XVIII | 90 | XC | 1,001 | MI |
| 5 | V | 19 | XIX | 100 | C | 1,002 | MII |
| 6 | VI | 20 | XX | 101 | CI | 1,003 | MIII |
| 7 | VII | 21 | XXI | 102 | CII | 1,900 | MCM |
| 8 | VIII | 22 | XXII | 103 | CIII | 2,000 | MM |
| 9 | IX | 23 | XXIII | 200 | CC | 2,001 | MMI |
| 10 | X | 24 | XXIV | 300 | CCC | 2,002 | MMII |
| 11 | XI | 25 | XXV | 400 | CD | 2,100 | MMC |
| 12 | XII | 30 | XXX | 500 | D | 3,000 | MMM |
| 13 | XIII | 40 | XL | 600 | DC | 4,000 | MMMM or M$\overline{\text{V}}$ |
| 14 | XIV | 50 | L | 700 | DCC | 5,000 | $\overline{\text{V}}$ |

## Mathematical Formulas

*The ratio of the circumference of a circle to its diameter is $\pi$ (3.141592653589793238462643383279..., generally rounded to 22/7 or 3.1416). It occurs in various mathematical problems involving the lengths of arcs or other curves, the areas of surfaces, and the volumes of many solids.*

| | SHAPE | ACTION | FORMULA |
|---|---|---|---|
| circumference | circle | multiply diameter by $\pi$ | $\pi d$ |
| area | circle | multiply radius squared by $\pi$ | $\pi r^2$ |
| | rectangle | multiply height by length | $hl$ |
| | sphere surface | multiply radius squared by $\pi$ by 4 | $4\pi r^2$ |
| | square | length of one side squared | $s^2$ |
| | trapezoid | parallel side length A + parallel side length B multiplied by height and divided by 2 | $(A+B)h/2$ |
| | triangle | multiply base by height and divide by 2 | $hb/2$ |
| volume | cone | multiply base radius squared by $\pi$ by height and divide by 3 | $br^2\pi h/3$ |
| | cube | length of one edge cubed | $a^3$ |
| | cylinder | multiply base radius squared by $\pi$ by height | $br^2\pi h$ |
| | pyramid | multiply base area by height and divide by 3 | $hb/3$ |
| | sphere | multiply radius cubed by $\pi$ by 4 and divide by 3 | $4\pi r^3/3$ |

## Large Numbers

The American system of numeration for denominations above one million was modeled on a French system, but subsequently the French system changed to correspond to the German and British systems. In the American system each of the denominations above 1,000 millions (the American *billion*) is 1,000 times the preceding one (one trillion = 1,000 billions; one quadrillion = 1,000 trillions). In the British system the first denomination above 1,000 millions (the British *milliard*) is 1,000 times the preceding one, but each of the denominations above 1,000 milliards (the British *billion*) is 1,000,000 times the preceding one (one trillion = 1,000,000 billions; one quadrillion = 1,000,000 trillions). In recent years, however, British usage has reflected widespread and increasing use of the values of the American system.

Source: Merriam-Webster, Inc., *Merriam-Webster's Collegiate Dictionary*, 11th ed., 2003.

| AMERICAN NAME | VALUE IN POWERS OF TEN | NUMBER OF ZEROS | BRITISH NAME | VALUE IN POWERS OF TEN | NUMBER OF ZEROS |
|---|---|---|---|---|---|
| billion | $10^9$ | 9 | billion | $10^{12}$ | 12 |
| trillion | $10^{12}$ | 12 | trillion | $10^{18}$ | 18 |
| quintillion | $10^{18}$ | 18 | quintillion | $10^{30}$ | 30 |
| septillion | $10^{24}$ | 24 | septillion | $10^{42}$ | 42 |
| quattuordecillion | $10^{45}$ | 45 | quattuordecillion | $10^{84}$ | 84 |
| googol | $10^{100}$ | 100 | googol | $10^{100}$ | 100 |
| centillion | $10^{303}$ | 303 | centillion | $10^{600}$ | 600 |
| googolplex | $10^{googol}$ | googol | googolplex | $10^{googol}$ | googol |

## Periodic Table of the Elements

The periodic table arranges the elements into groups (vertically) of elements sharing common physical and chemical characteristics and into periods (horizontally) of sequentially increasing atomic number and electron-shell configuration. Elements 113, 115, 117, and 118 have been created experimentally and have temporary names. Atomic weights in parentheses indicate the number of the most stable isotope of a radioactive element.

| 1 | 2 | 3 | 4 | 5 | 6 | 7 | 8 | 9 | 10 | 11 | 12 | 13 | 14 | 15 | 16 | 17 | 18 |
|---|---|---|---|---|---|---|---|---|---|---|---|---|---|---|---|---|---|
| 1 H | | | | | | | | | | | | | | | | | 2 He |
| 3 Li | 4 Be | | | | | | | | | | | 5 B | 6 C | 7 N | 8 O | 9 F | 10 Ne |
| 11 Na | 12 Mg | | | | | | | | | | | 13 Al | 14 Si | 15 P | 16 S | 17 Cl | 18 Ar |
| 19 K | 20 Ca | 21 Sc | 22 Ti | 23 V | 24 Cr | 25 Mn | 26 Fe | 27 Co | 28 Ni | 29 Cu | 30 Zn | 31 Ga | 32 Ge | 33 As | 34 Se | 35 Br | 36 Kr |
| 37 Rb | 38 Sr | 39 Y | 40 Zr | 41 Nb | 42 Mo | 43 Tc | 44 Ru | 45 Rh | 46 Pd | 47 Ag | 48 Cd | 49 In | 50 Sn | 51 Sb | 52 Te | 53 I | 54 Xe |
| 55 Cs | 56 Ba | 57 La | 72 Hf | 73 Ta | 74 W | 75 Re | 76 Os | 77 Ir | 78 Pt | 79 Au | 80 Hg | 81 Tl | 82 Pb | 83 Bi | 84 Po | 85 At | 86 Rn |
| 87 Fr | 88 Ra | 89 Ac | 104 Rf | 105 Db | 106 Sg | 107 Bh | 108 Hs | 109 Mt | 110 Ds | 111 Rg | 112 Cn | 113 Uut | 114 Fl | 115 Uup | 116 Lv | 117 Uus | 118 Uuo |

**Lanthanide Series**

| 58 Ce | 59 Pr | 60 Nd | 61 Pm | 62 Sm | 63 Eu | 64 Gd | 65 Tb | 66 Dy | 67 Ho | 68 Er | 69 Tm | 70 Yb | 71 Lu |
|---|---|---|---|---|---|---|---|---|---|---|---|---|---|

**Actinide Series**

| 90 Th | 91 Pa | 92 U | 93 Np | 94 Pu | 95 Am | 96 Cm | 97 Bk | 98 Cf | 99 Es | 100 Fm | 101 Md | 102 No | 103 Lr |
|---|---|---|---|---|---|---|---|---|---|---|---|---|---|

| Element | Symbol | Atomic no. | Atomic weight |
|---|---|---|---|
| Actinium | Ac | 89 | (227) |
| Aluminum | Al | 13 | 26.98154 |
| Americium | Am | 95 | (243) |
| Antimony | Sb | 51 | 121.760 |
| Argon | Ar | 18 | 39.948 |
| Arsenic | As | 33 | 74.92160 |
| Astatine | At | 85 | (210) |
| Barium | Ba | 56 | 137.327 |
| Berkelium | Bk | 97 | (247) |
| Beryllium | Be | 4 | 9.01218 |
| Bismuth | Bi | 83 | 208.98040 |
| Bohrium | Bh | 107 | (272) |
| Boron | B | 5 | 10.811 |
| Bromine | Br | 35 | 79.904 |
| Cadmium | Cd | 48 | 112.411 |
| Calcium | Ca | 20 | 40.078 |
| Californium | Cf | 98 | (251) |
| Carbon | C | 6 | 12.0107 |
| Cerium | Ce | 58 | 140.116 |
| Cesium | Cs | 55 | 132.90545 |
| Chlorine | Cl | 17 | 35.453 |
| Chromium | Cr | 24 | 51.9961 |
| Cobalt | Co | 27 | 58.93320 |
| Copernicium | Cn | 112 | (285) |
| Copper | Cu | 29 | 63.546 |
| Curium | Cm | 96 | (247) |
| Darmstadtium | Ds | 110 | (281) |
| Dubnium | Db | 105 | (268) |
| Dysprosium | Dy | 66 | 162.500 |
| Einsteinium | Es | 99 | (252) |
| Erbium | Er | 68 | 167.259 |
| Europium | Eu | 63 | 151.964 |
| Fermium | Fm | 100 | (257) |
| Flerovium | Fl | 114 | (289) |
| Fluorine | F | 9 | 18.99840 |
| Francium | Fr | 87 | (223) |
| Gadolinium | Gd | 64 | 157.25 |
| Gallium | Ga | 31 | 69.723 |
| Germanium | Ge | 32 | 72.64 |
| Gold | Au | 79 | 196.96657 |
| Hafnium | Hf | 72 | 178.49 |
| Hassium | Hs | 108 | (270) |
| Helium | He | 2 | 4.00260 |
| Holmium | Ho | 67 | 164.93032 |
| Hydrogen | H | 1 | 1.00794 |
| Indium | In | 49 | 114.818 |
| Iodine | I | 53 | 126.90447 |
| Iridium | Ir | 77 | 192.217 |
| Iron | Fe | 26 | 55.845 |
| Krypton | Kr | 36 | 83.798 |
| Lanthanum | La | 57 | 138.90547 |
| Lawrencium | Lr | 103 | (262) |
| Lead | Pb | 82 | 207.2 |
| Lithium | Li | 3 | 6.941 |
| Livermorium | Lv | 116 | (293) |
| Lutetium | Lu | 71 | 174.967 |
| Magnesium | Mg | 12 | 24.3050 |
| Manganese | Mn | 25 | 54.93805 |
| Meitnerium | Mt | 109 | (276) |
| Mendelevium | Md | 101 | (258) |
| Mercury | Hg | 80 | 200.59 |
| Molybdenum | Mo | 42 | 95.94 |
| Neodymium | Nd | 60 | 144.242 |
| Neon | Ne | 10 | 20.1797 |
| Neptunium | Np | 93 | (237) |
| Nickel | Ni | 28 | 58.6934 |
| Niobium | Nb | 41 | 92.90638 |
| Nitrogen | N | 7 | 14.0067 |
| Nobelium | No | 102 | (259) |
| Osmium | Os | 76 | 190.23 |
| Oxygen | O | 8 | 15.9994 |
| Palladium | Pd | 46 | 106.42 |
| Phosphorus | P | 15 | 30.97376 |
| Platinum | Pt | 78 | 195.084 |
| Plutonium | Pu | 94 | (244) |
| Polonium | Po | 84 | (209) |
| Potassium | K | 19 | 39.0983 |
| Praseodymium | Pr | 59 | 140.90765 |
| Promethium | Pm | 61 | (145) |
| Protactinium | Pa | 91 | 231.03588 |
| Radium | Ra | 88 | (226) |
| Radon | Rn | 86 | (222) |
| Rhenium | Re | 75 | 186.207 |
| Rhodium | Rh | 45 | 102.90550 |
| Roentgenium | Rg | 111 | (280) |
| Rubidium | Rb | 37 | 85.4678 |
| Ruthenium | Ru | 44 | 101.07 |
| Rutherfordium | Rf | 104 | (267) |
| Samarium | Sm | 62 | 150.36 |
| Scandium | Sc | 21 | 44.9559 |
| Seaborgium | Sg | 106 | (271) |
| Selenium | Se | 34 | 78.96 |
| Silicon | Si | 14 | 28.0855 |
| Silver | Ag | 47 | 107.8682 |
| Sodium | Na | 11 | 22.98977 |
| Strontium | Sr | 38 | 87.62 |
| Sulfur | S | 16 | 32.065 |
| Tantalum | Ta | 73 | 180.94788 |
| Technetium | Tc | 43 | (98) |
| Tellurium | Te | 52 | 127.60 |
| Terbium | Tb | 65 | 158.92535 |
| Thallium | Tl | 81 | 204.3833 |
| Thorium | Th | 90 | 232.03806 |
| Thulium | Tm | 69 | 168.93421 |
| Tin | Sn | 50 | 118.710 |
| Titanium | Ti | 22 | 47.867 |
| Tungsten (wolfram) | W | 74 | 183.85 |
| Ununoctium | Uuo | 118 | (294) |
| Ununpentium | Uup | 115 | (288) |
| Ununseptium | Uus | 117 | (292) |
| Ununtrium | Uut | 113 | (284) |
| Uranium | U | 92 | 238.02891 |
| Vanadium | V | 23 | 50.9415 |
| Xenon | Xe | 54 | 131.293 |
| Ytterbium | Yb | 70 | 173.04 |
| Yttrium | Y | 39 | 88.90585 |
| Zinc | Zn | 30 | 65.409 |
| Zirconium | Zr | 40 | 91.224 |

# Applied Science

## Chemistry

Chemistry is the science that deals with the properties, composition, and structure of substances (defined as elements and compounds), the transformations that they undergo, and the energy that is released or absorbed during these processes. Every substance, whether naturally occurring or artificially produced, consists of one or more of the hundred-odd species of atoms that have been identified as elements. Although these atoms, in turn, are composed of more elementary particles, they are the basic building blocks of chemical substances; there is no quantity of oxygen, mercury, or gold, for example, smaller than an atom of that substance. Chemistry, therefore, is concerned not with the subatomic domain but with the properties of atoms and the laws governing their combinations and with how the knowledge of these properties can be used to achieve specific purposes.

## Physics

Physics is the science that deals with the structure of matter and the interactions between the fundamental constituents of the observable universe. The basic physical science, its aim is the discovery and formulation of the fundamental laws of nature. In the broadest sense, physics (from the Greek *physikos*) is concerned with all aspects of nature on both the macroscopic and submicroscopic levels. Its scope of study encompasses not only the behavior of objects under the action of given forces but also the nature and origin of gravitational, electromagnetic, and nuclear force fields. Its ultimate objective is the formulation of a few comprehensive principles that bring together and explain all such disparate phenomena. Physics can, at base, be defined as the science of matter, motion, and energy. Its laws are typically expressed with economy and precision in the language of mathematics.

## Weight, Mass, and Density

Mass, strictly defined, is the quantitative measure of inertia, the resistance a body offers to a change in its speed or position when force is applied to it. The greater the mass of a body, the smaller the change produced by an applied force. In more practical terms, it is the measure of the amount of material in an object, and in common usage is often expressed as weight. However, the mass of an object is constant regardless of its position, while weight varies according to gravitational pull.

In the International System of Units (SI; the metric system), the kilogram is the standard unit of mass, defined as equaling the mass of the international prototype of the kilogram, currently a platinum-iridium cylinder kept at Sèvres, near Paris, France; it is roughly equal to the mass of 1,000 cubic centimeters of pure water at the temperature of its maximum density. In the US customary system, the unit is the slug, defined as the mass which a one pound force can accelerate at a rate of one foot per second per second, which is the same as the mass of an object weighing 32.17 pounds on the earth's surface.

Weight is the gravitational force of attraction on an object, caused by the presence of a massive second object, such as the Earth or Moon. Weight is the product of an object's mass and the acceleration of gravity at the point where the object is located. A given object will have the same mass on the Earth's surface, on the Moon, or in the absence of gravity, while its weight on the Moon would be about one sixth of its weight on the Earth's surface, because of the Moon's smaller gravitational pull (due in turn to the Moon's smaller mass and radius), and in the absence of gravity the object would have no weight at all.

Weight is measured in units of force, not mass, though in practice units of mass (such as the kilogram) are often substituted because of mass's relatively constant relation to weight on the Earth's surface. The weight of a body can be obtained by multiplying the mass by the acceleration of gravity. In SI, weight is expressed in newtons, or the force required to impart an acceleration of one meter per second per second to a mass of one kilogram. In the US customary system, it is expressed in pounds.

Density is the mass per unit volume of a material substance. It offers a convenient means of obtaining the mass of a body from its volume, or vice versa; the mass is equal to the volume multiplied by the density, while the volume is equal to the mass divided by the density. In SI, density is expressed in kilograms per cubic meter.

# Communications

## Introduction to the Internet

The Internet is a dynamic collection of computer networks that has revolutionized communications and methods of commerce by enabling those networks around the world to interact with each other. Sometimes referred to as a "network of networks," the Internet was developed in the United States in the 1970s but was not widely used by the general public until the early 1990s. By the end of 2011 some 2.27 billion people, or roughly 33% of the world's population, were estimated to be regular users of the Internet. It is estimated that at least half of the world's population had some form of Internet access

## Introduction to the Internet (continued)

in 2011, and it is assumed that wireless access will continue to play a growing role.

The Internet supports human communication via electronic mail (**e-mail**), social networks, real-time "chat rooms," instant messaging (IM), newsgroups, and audio and video transmission and allows people to work collaboratively at many different locations. It supports access to information by many applications, including the **World Wide Web**, which uses text and graphical presentations. Publishing has been revolutionized, as whole novels and reference works are available on the Web, and online periodicals are also common. The Internet has attracted a large and growing number of "e-businesses" (including subsidiaries of traditional "brick-and-mortar" companies) that carry out most of their sales and services over the Internet.

While the precise structure of the future Internet is not yet clear, many directions of growth seem apparent. One is the increased availability of wireless access, enabling better real-time use of Web-managed information. Another future development is toward higher backbone and network access speeds. Backbone data rates of 10 billion bits (10 gigabits) per second are readily available today, but data rates of 1 trillion bits (1 terabit) per second or higher will eventually become commercially feasible. At very high data rates, high-resolution video, for example, would occupy only a small fraction of available bandwidth, and remaining bandwidth could be used to transmit auxiliary information about the data being sent, which in turn would enable rapid customization of displays and prompt resolution of certain local queries.

Communications connectivity will be a key function of a future Internet as more machines and devices are interconnected. In June 2011 the Internet Corporation for Assigned Names and Numbers approved the expansion of domains, allowing for Internet addresses to be tailored to a company or organization's brand, such as .pepsi, but at a hefty application fee of $185,000 and an annual fee of $25,000. The approval of a top-level domain for pornographic sites (.xxx) earlier in 2011 ended a 10-year battle with conservative and religious groups. IPv6, the Internet Engineering Task Force's 128-bit IP address standard protocol that was introduced in 1998, was scheduled to launch 6 Jun 2012, with several major companies, including AT&T and Comcast, welcoming the transition from the 32-bit IPv4. Testing of the HTML5 standard continued through 2012 with the World Wide Web Consortium aiming for a 2014 launch date.

## Growth of Internet Use

*Source: International Telecommunication Union, ICT Indicators Database.*

| YEAR | US USERS | WORLD USERS | YEAR | US USERS | WORLD USERS |
|------|----------|-------------|------|----------|-------------|
| 2002 | 167,197,000 | 679,819,000 | 2007 | 212,080,000 | 1,364,000,000 |
| 2003 | 172,250,000 | 790,121,000 | 2008 | 220,142,000 | 1,560,000,000 |
| 2004 | 201,661,000 | 934,953,000 | 2009 | 227,719,000 | 1,746,000,000 |
| 2005 | 203,824,000 | 1,022,000,000 | 2010 | 239,894,000 | 2,013,000,000 |
| 2006 | 206,098,000 | 1,150,000,000 | 2011 | 245,203,000 | 2,265,000,000 |

## Cell Phone Subscribers Worldwide, 2011

*Source: International Telecommunication Union, ICT Indicators Database.*

| COUNTRY | SUBSCRIBERS | SUBSCRIBERS PER 1,000 RESIDENTS | COUNTRY | SUBSCRIBERS | SUBSCRIBERS PER 1,000 RESIDENTS |
|---------|-------------|--------------------------------|---------|-------------|--------------------------------|
| China | 986,253,000 | 732 | Philippines | 87,256,000 | 920 |
| India | 893,863,000 | 720 | Bangladesh | 85,000,000 | 565 |
| United States | 331,600,000 | 1,059 | Egypt | 83,425,000 | 1,011 |
| Russia | 256,117,000 | 1,793 | United Kingdom | 81,612,000 | 1,308 |
| Brazil | 242,232,000 | 1,232 | Thailand | 78,668,000 | 1,132 |
| Indonesia | 236,800,000 | 977 | France | 66,300,000 | 1,050 |
| Japan | 129,868,000 | 1,027 | Turkey | 65,322,000 | 887 |
| Vietnam | 127,318,000 | 1,434 | South Africa | 64,000,000 | 1,268 |
| Pakistan | 108,895,000 | 616 | Iran | 56,043,000 | 749 |
| Germany | 108,700,000 | 1,323 | Ukraine | 55,567,000 | 1,230 |
| Nigeria | 95,167,000 | 586 | Argentina | 55,000,000 | 1,349 |
| Mexico | 94,565,000 | 824 | Saudi Arabia | 53,706,000 | 1,912 |
| Italy | 92,300,000 | 1,518 | **world** | **5,972,000,000** | **857** |

## Growth of Cell Phone Use in the US

*Number of cellular mobile telephone subscribers in the US, 2000–2011. Source: CTIA-The Wireless Association Annualized Wireless Industry Survey Results, December 1985–December 2011.*

| YEAR | SUBSCRIBERS | YEAR | SUBSCRIBERS | YEAR | SUBSCRIBERS | YEAR | SUBSCRIBERS |
|------|-------------|------|-------------|------|-------------|------|-------------|
| 2000 | 109,478,031 | 2003 | 158,721,981 | 2006 | 233,040,781 | 2009 | 290,941,191 |
| 2001 | 128,374,512 | 2004 | 182,140,362 | 2007 | 255,395,599 | 2010 | 310,996,629 |
| 2002 | 140,766,842 | 2005 | 207,896,198 | 2008 | 270,333,881 | 2011 | 331,594,848 |

# Aerospace Technology
## Space Exploration

Three men were the first scientists to conceive pragmatically of spaceflight: the Russian **Konstantin Tsiolkovsky**, the American **Robert Goddard**, and the German **Hermann Oberth**. By the end of World War II, the German development of rocket propulsion for aircraft and guided missiles (notably the V-2) had reached a high level. After the war the US and its allies fell heir to the technical knowledge of rocket power developed by the Germans. The technical director of the German missile effort, **Wernher von Braun**, and some 150 of his top aides surrendered to US troops. Most immigrated to the US, where they assembled and launched V-2 missiles that had been captured and shipped there. The USSR carried out an unpublicized but extensive and likely similar program; Britain and France conducted smaller programs.

In both the US and the USSR the development of **military missile technology** was essential to the achievement of satellite flight. Preparations for the International Geophysical Year (IGY, 1957–58) stimulated discussion of the possibility of launching **artificial Earth satellites** for scientific investigations. Both the US and the USSR became determined to prepare scientific satellites for launching during the IGY. While the US was still developing a space launch vehicle, the USSR startled the world by placing **Sputnik 1** in orbit on 4 Oct 1957. This was followed a month later by **Sputnik 2**, which carried a live dog. The failure by the US to launch its small payload on 6 Dec 1957 heightened that country's political discomfiture in view of its supposed advanced status in science. Following debates on the necessity of achieving parity, the US government established the **National Aeronautics and Space Administration (NASA)** in 1958. Since that time, NASA has conducted virtually all major aspects of the US space program.

The first successful US satellite, **Explorer 1**, was launched about four months after Sputnik 1. During the next decades the two countries participated in a space race, conducting thousands of successful launches of spacecraft of all varieties including scientific-research, communications, meteorological, remote-sensing, military-reconnaissance, early-warning, and navigation satellites, lunar and planetary probes, and manned craft. The USSR launched the first human, **Yury Gagarin**, into orbit around Earth on 12 Apr 1961. On 20 July 1969, the US landed two men, **Neil Armstrong** and **Edwin ("Buzz") Aldrin**, on the surface of the Moon as part of the **Apollo 11** mission. On 12 Apr 1981, the 20th anniversary of manned space flight, the US launched the first reusable manned space transportation system, the **space shuttle**. Since the 1960s various European countries, Japan, India, China, and other countries have formed their own agencies for space exploration and development. The **European Space Agency (ESA)** consists of 18 member states. Private corporations, too, offer space launches for communications and remote-sensing satellites.

In the post-Apollo decades, while the US focused much of its manned space program on the shuttle, the USSR concentrated on launching a series of increasingly sophisticated Earth-orbiting **space stations**, beginning with the world's first in 1971. Station crews, who were carried up in two- and three-person spacecraft, carried out mostly scientific missions while gaining experience in living and working for long periods in the space environment. After the USSR was dissolved in 1991, its space program was continued by Russia on a much smaller scale owing to economic constraints. The US launched a space station in 1973 using surplus Apollo hardware and conducted shuttle missions to a Russian station, Mir, in the 1990s. In 1998, at the head of a 16-country consortium and with Russia as a major partner, the US began in-orbit assembly of the **International Space Station (ISS)**, using the shuttle and Russian expendable launch vehicles to ferry the facility's modular components and crews into space. In addition to manned and unmanned lunar exploration, space exploration programs have included deep-space robotic missions to the planets, their moons, and smaller bodies such as comets and asteroids. Also important has been the development of unmanned space-based astronomical observatories, which allow observation of near and distant cosmic objects above the filtering and distorting effects of Earth's atmosphere.

**Significant space programs and missions:**

**Sputnik** (Russian for "fellow traveler")
**Years launched:** 1957–58. **Country or space agency:** USSR. **Designation:** 1 through 3 (first series). **Not manned. Events of note:** Sputnik 1 was the first satellite to be successfully launched into space, and Sputnik 2 carried a small dog named Laika ("Barker").

**Vanguard**
**Years launched:** 1958–59. **Country or space agency:** US. **Designation:** 1 through 3. **Not manned. Events of note:** The first attempted Vanguard launch, hastily mounted in December 1957 after the USSR's Sputnik successes, failed with the launch vehicle's explosion.

**Explorer**
**Years launched:** 1958–75. **Country or space agency:** US. **Designation:** 1 through 55. **Not manned. Events of note:** Explorer 1, the first successful US satellite, discovered Earth's inner radiation belt.

**Pioneer**
**Years launched:** 1958–78. **Country or space agency:** US. **Designation:** 1 through 13. **Not manned. Events of note:** Pioneer 10 was the first spacecraft to travel through the asteroid belt, to fly by Jupiter, and to escape the solar system; Pioneer 11 was the first to visit Saturn.

**Luna** (Russian for "Moon")
**Years launched:** 1959–76. **Country or space agency:** USSR. **Designation:** 1 through 24. **Not manned. Events of note:** Luna 2 was the first spacecaft to crash-land on the lunar surface; Luna 3 took the first photographs of the Moon's far side; three Lunas (16, 20, and 24) returned with samples of lunar soil.

**Vostok** (Russian for "east")
**Years launched:** 1961–63. **Country or space agency:** USSR. **Designation:** 1 through 6. **Manned. Events of note:** The first man in space and to orbit Earth was Soviet cosmonaut Yury Gagarin in Vostok 1, launched

on 12 April 1961. Vostok 6 was launched with Valentina Tereshkova, the first woman in space, in 1963.

## Mercury
**Years launched:** 1961–63 (manned missions). **Country or space agency:** US. **Designation:** Mercury spacecraft had program designations, but they were better known by the individual names bestowed on them, such as *Freedom 7*, to honor the seven NASA astronauts chosen for the program. **Events of note:** Some 20 preliminary unmanned Mercury missions took place between 1959 and 1961. Of the six manned missions, *Freedom 7* was launched in 1961 with Alan Shepard (the first American in space) aboard, and *Friendship 7* in 1962 with John Glenn (the first American to orbit Earth).

## Ranger
**Years launched:** 1961–65. **Country or space agency:** US. **Designation:** 1 through 9. **Not manned. Events of note:** Ranger 4 was the first US spacecraft to crash-land on the Moon; the last three Rangers returned thousands of images of the lunar surface before crashing on the lunar surface as planned.

## Mariner
**Years launched:** 1962–73. **Country or space agency:** US. **Designation:** 1 through 10. **Not manned. Events of note:** Various Mariners in the program flew by Venus, Mercury, and Mars. Mariner 9 mapped Mars in detail from orbit, becoming the first spacecraft to orbit another planet. Mariner 10 was the first spacecraft to have visited the vicinity of Mercury.

## Voskhod (Russian for "sunrise" or "ascent")
**Years launched:** 1964–65. **Country or space agency:** USSR. **Designation:** 1 and 2. **Manned. Events of note:** Voskhod 1 was the first spacecraft to carry more than one person; Aleksey Leonov performed the first space walk, from the Voskhod 2 spacecraft, on 18 Mar 1965.

## Gemini
**Years launched:** 1965–66. **Country or space agency:** US. **Designation:** 1 through 12. **Manned. Events of note:** Ten two-person manned missions followed two unmanned test flights. Gemini 8 was the first spacecraft to rendezvous and dock with another craft. The Gemini program showed that astronauts could live and work in space for the time needed for a round-trip to the Moon.

## Lunar Orbiter
**Years launched:** 1966–67. **Country or space agency:** US. **Designation:** 1 through 5. **Not manned. Events of note:** Five consecutive spacecraft made detailed photographic surveys of most of the Moon's surface, providing the mapping essential for choosing landing sites for the manned Apollo missions.

## Soyuz (Russian for "union")
**Years launched:** 1967–present. **Country or space agency:** USSR. **Designation:** 1 through 40 (first series). Three subsequent series of upgraded spacecraft received the additional suffix letters T, TM, or TMA and were renumbered from 1. **Manned. Events of note:** On 24 Apr 1967 cosmonaut Vladimir Komarov conducted the inaugural test flight (Soyuz 1) of this multiperson transport craft but died returning to Earth after the parachute system failed, becoming the first fatality during a spaceflight. Soyuz 11 ferried the crew of the first space station, Salyut 1. Soyuz TM-2 made the inaugural manned flight of this TM upgrade while transporting the second crew of the Mir

space station. Soyuz TM-31 carried up the International Space Station's first three-man crew.

## Apollo
**Years launched:** 1968–72 (manned missions). **Country or space agency:** US. **Designation:** 7 through 17. **Events of note:** Several unmanned test flights preceded 11 manned Apollo missions, including two in Earth orbit (7 and 9), two in lunar orbit (8 and 10), one lunar flyby (13), and six lunar landings (11, 12, and 14–17) in which a total of 12 astronauts walked on the Moon. Apollo 11, crewed by Neil Armstrong, Michael Collins, and Buzz Aldrin, was the first mission to land humans on the Moon, on 20 Jul 1969. Apollo 13, planned as a lunar landing mission, experienced an onboard explosion en route to the Moon; after a swing around the Moon, the crippled spacecraft made a harrowing but safe return to Earth with its crew, James Lovell, John Swigert, and Fred Haise. The landing missions collectively returned almost 382 kg (842 lb) of lunar rocks and soil for study.

## Salyut (Russian for "salute")
**Years launched:** 1971–82. **Country or space agency:** USSR. **Designation:** 1 through 7 (two designs). **Manned. Events of note:** Salyut 1, launched 19 Apr 1971, was the world's first space station; its crew, cosmonauts Georgy Dobrovolsky, Vladislav Volkov, and Viktor Patsayev, died returning to Earth when their Soyuz spacecraft depressurized. Salyut 6 operated as a highly successful scientific space platform, supporting a series of crews over a four-year period.

## Skylab
**Year launched:** 1973. **Country or space agency:** US. **Manned. Events of note:** Skylab, based on the outfitted and pressurized upper stage of a Saturn V Moon rocket, was the first US space station. Three successive astronaut crews carried out solar astronomy studies, materials-sciences research, and biomedical experiments on the effects of weightlessness.

## Apollo-Soyuz
**Year launched:** 1975. **Countries or space agencies:** US and USSR. **Manned. Events of note:** As a sign of improved US-Soviet relations, an Apollo spacecraft carrying three astronauts docked in Earth orbit with a Soyuz vehicle carrying two cosmonauts. It was the first cooperative multinational space mission.

## Viking
**Year launched:** 1975. **Country or space agency:** US. **Designation:** 1 and 2. **Not manned. Events of note:** Both probes traveled to Mars, released landers, and took photographs of large expanses of Mars from orbit. The Viking 1 lander transmitted the first pictures from the Martian surface; both landers carried experiments designed to detect living organisms or life processes but found no convincing signs of life.

## Voyager
**Year launched:** 1977. **Country or space agency:** US. **Designation:** 1 and 2. **Not manned. Events of note:** Both Voyager spacecraft flew past Jupiter and Saturn, transmitting measurements and photographs; Voyager 2 went on to Uranus in 1986 and then to Neptune. Both craft continued out of the solar system, with Voyager 1 overtaking Pioneer 10 in 1998 to become the most distant human-made object in space.

## space shuttle (Space Transportation System, or STS)
**Years launched:** 1981–2011. **Country or space**

agency: US. **Designation:** Individual missions were designated STS with a number (and sometimes letter) suffix, though the orbiter spacecraft themselves were reused. **Manned. Events of note:** The first flight of a manned space shuttle, STS-1, was on 12 Apr 1981 with the orbiter *Columbia*. The other original operational orbiters were *Challenger, Discovery,* and *Atlantis*. During shuttle mission STS-51-L, *Challenger* exploded after liftoff on 28 Jan 1986, killing all seven astronauts aboard, including a private citizen, Christa McAuliffe; the orbiter *Endeavour* was built as a replacement vehicle. Space shuttle missions were used to deploy satellites, space observatories, and planetary probes; to carry out in-space repairs of orbiting spacecraft; and to take US astronauts to the Russian space station Mir. Beginning in 1998 a series of shuttle missions ferried components, supplies, and crews to the International Space Station during its assembly and operation. In 2003 the orbiter *Columbia* disintegrated while returning from a space mission, claiming the lives of its seven-person crew, including Ilan Ramon, the first Israeli astronaut to go into space.

### Giotto
**Year launched:** 1985. **Country or space agency:** ESA. **Not manned. Events of note:** This first deep-space probe launched by ESA made a close flyby of Halley's Comet, collecting data and transmitting images of the icy nucleus. It was then redirected to a second comet, using a gravity-assist flyby of Earth, the first time that a spacecraft coming back from deep space had made such a maneuver.

### Mir (Russian for "peace" and "world")
**Years launched:** 1986–96. **Country or space agency:** USSR/Russia. **Manned. Events of note:** The core of this modular space station was launched on 20 Feb 1986; five additional modules were added over the next decade to create a large, versatile space laboratory. Although intended for a five-year life, it supported human habitation between 1986 and 2000, including an uninterrupted stretch of occupancy of almost 10 years, and it hosted a series of US astronauts as part of a Mir–space shuttle cooperative endeavor. In 1995 Mir cosmonaut Valery Polyakov set a space endurance record of nearly 438 days.

### Magellan
**Year launched:** 1989. **Country or space agency:** US. **Not manned. Events of note:** Magellan was the first deep-space probe deployed by the space shuttle. During four years in orbit above Venus, it mapped some 98% of the surface of the planet with radar at high resolution. At the end of its mission, it was sent on a gradual dive into the Venusian atmosphere, where it measured various properties before burning up.

### Galileo
**Year launched:** 1989. **Country or space agency:** US. **Not manned. Events of note:** Galileo released an atmospheric probe into the Jovian system and then went into orbit around Jupiter for an extended study of the giant planet and its Galilean moons. Among many discoveries, Galileo found evidence of a liquid-water ocean below the moon Europa's icy surface.

### NEAR Shoemaker (Near Earth Asteroid Rendezvous)
**Year launched:** 1996. **Country or space agency:** US. **Not manned. Events of note:** This spacecraft was the first to orbit a small body (the Earth-approaching asteroid Eros) and then to touch down on its surface. It studied Eros for a year with cameras and instruments and then made a soft landing and transmitted gamma-ray data from the surface for more than two weeks.

### Mars Pathfinder
**Year launched:** 1996. **Country or space agency:** US. **Not manned. Events of note:** This was the first spacecraft to land on Mars since the 1976 Viking missions; the lander and its robotic surface rover, Sojourner, together successfully collected 17,000 images and other data.

### Cassini-Huygens
**Year launched:** 1997. **Countries or space agencies:** US and ESA. **Not manned. Events of note:** Consisting of an orbiter (Cassini) and a descent probe (Huygens), the spacecraft traveled to the Saturnian system. En route it flew by Jupiter and returned detailed images. Cassini then established an orbit around Saturn for several years of studies, while the Huygens probe parachuted through the atmosphere of the moon Titan, transmitting data during its descent and from the moon's surface.

### International Space Station (ISS)
**Years launched:** 1998–present. **Countries or space agencies:** US, Russia, ESA, Canada, Japan, and Brazil. **Manned. Events of note:** A large complex of habitat modules and laboratories, the ISS was assembled in Earth orbit by means of space-shuttle and Proton and Soyuz rocket flights that brought components, crews, and supplies. The first component, called Zarya, was launched on 20 Nov 1998. The ISS received its first resident crew on 2 Nov 2000.

### Chandra X-Ray Observatory
**Year launched:** 1999. **Country or space agency:** US. **Not manned. Events of note:** The world's most powerful X-ray telescope, it revolves in an elliptical orbit around Earth, delivering roughly 1,000 observations of the universe annually.

### 2001 Mars Odyssey
**Year launched:** 2001. **Country or space agency:** US. **Not manned. Events of note:** This spacecraft was launched to study Mars from orbit and serve as a communications relay for future landers. Some of its data suggested the presence of huge subsurface reservoirs of frozen water in both polar regions.

### Mars Express
**Year launched:** 2003. **Country or space agency:** ESA. **Not manned. Events of note:** The spacecraft's lander, Beagle 2, which was designed to examine the rocks and soil for signs of past or present life, failed to establish radio contact after presumably reaching the Martian surface.

### Mars Exploration Rovers
**Year launched:** 2003. **Country or space agency:** US. **Designation:** Spirit and Opportunity. **Not manned. Events of note:** Twin six-wheeled robotic rovers, each equipped with cameras, a microscopic imager, a rock-grinding tool, and other instruments, landed on opposite sides of Mars. Both rovers found evidence of past water; particularly dramatic was the discovery by Opportunity of rocks that appeared to have been laid down at the shoreline of an ancient body of salty water.

### Deep Impact
**Year launched:** 2005. **Country or space agency:** US. **Not manned. Events of note:** Deep Impact was the first

spacecraft designed to study the interior composition of a comet. It released an instrumented impactor into the path of Comet Tempel 1's icy nucleus. A high-resolution camera and other apparatuses on the flyby portion of the probe studied the impact and the resulting crater.

## Mars Reconnaissance Orbiter
**Year launched: 2005. Country or space agency: US. Not manned. Events of note:** It carries the most powerful camera ever flown on a space mission. The Orbiter is an important communications link between other spacecraft, Mars, and Earth.

## Phoenix
**Year launched: 2007. Country or space agency: US. Not manned. Events of note:** Phoenix was the first spacecraft designed to measure water (ice) on a planet other than Earth. It was equipped with robotic arms and sophisticated sensors to dig under the surface of Mars, collect soil samples, and analyze them. It landed on the surface of Mars on 25 May 2008 and quickly established communications with Earth. Before the end of its planned three-month experiment, Phoenix verified the presence of water (ice) in the Martian subsurface.

## Lunar Crater Observation and Sensing Satellite
**Year launched: 2009. Country or space agency: US. Not manned. Events of note:** The objective of the Lunar Crater Observation and Sensing Satellite (LCROSS) was to confirm the presence of water (ice) in a crater in the permanent shadow on the Moon's south pole. On 9 Oct 2009, LCROSS conducted experiments that successfully uncovered water on the Moon.

## Kepler
**Year launched: 2009. Country or space agency: US. Not manned. Events of note:** Kepler's mission is to locate and identify terrestrial planets (those one-half to twice the size of Earth) in the habitable zone of their stars. As of mid-2012, Kepler had positively identified 61 planets. In April 2012, the mission was extended into 2016.

## CryoSat-2
**Year launched: 2010. Country or space agency: ESA. Not manned. Events of note:** CryoSat-2 is charged with measuring precisely the thickness of the marine ice in the polar oceans and the ice sheets covering Greenland and Antarctica.

# Space Exploration Firsts

| EVENT | DETAILS | COUNTRY OR AGENCY | DATE ACCOMPLISHED |
|---|---|---|---|
| first person to study in detail the use of rockets for spaceflight | Konstantin Tsiolkovsky | Russia | late 19th–early 20th centuries |
| first launch of a liquid-fueled rocket | Robert Goddard | US | 16 Mar 1926 |
| first launch of the V-2 ballistic missile, the forerunner of modern space rockets | Wernher von Braun | Germany | 3 Oct 1942 |
| first artificial Earth satellite | Sputnik 1 | USSR | 4 Oct 1957 |
| first animal launched into space | dog Laika aboard Sputnik 2 | USSR | 3 Nov 1957 |
| first spacecraft to hard-land on another celestial object (the Moon) | Luna 2 | USSR | 14 Sep 1959 |
| first applications satellite launched | TIROS 1 (weather observation) | US | 1 Apr 1960 |
| first recovery of a payload from Earth orbit | Discoverer 13 | US | 11 Aug 1960 |
| first piloted spacecraft to orbit Earth | Vostok 1 (piloted by Yury Gagarin) | USSR | 12 Apr 1961 |
| first US citizen in space | Alan Shepard on Freedom 7 | US | 5 May 1961 |
| first piloted US spacecraft to orbit Earth | Friendship 7 (piloted by John Glenn) | US | 20 Feb 1962 |
| first active communications satellite | Telstar 1 | US | 10 July 1962 |
| first data transmitted to Earth from vicinity of another planet (Venus) | Mariner 2 | US | 14 Dec 1962 |
| first woman in space | Valentina Tereshkova on Vostok 6 | USSR | 16 Jun 1963 |
| first satellite to operate in geostationary orbit | Syncom 2 (telecommunications satellite) | US | 26 Jul 1963 |
| first space walk | Aleksey Leonov on Voskhod 2 | USSR | 18 Mar 1965 |
| first spacecraft pictures of Mars | Mariner 4 | US | 14 Jul 1965 |
| first spacecraft to soft-land on the Moon | Luna 9 | USSR | 3 Feb 1966 |
| first death during a space mission | Vladimir Komarov on Soyuz 1 | USSR | 24 Apr 1967 |
| first humans to orbit the Moon | Frank Borman, James Lovell, and William Anders on Apollo 8 | US | 24 Dec 1968 |
| first human to walk on the Moon | Neil Armstrong on Apollo 11 | US | 20 Jul 1969 |
| first unmanned spacecraft to carry lunar samples back to Earth | Luna 16 | USSR | 24 Sep 1970 |
| first soft landing on another planet (Venus) | Venera 7 | USSR | 15 Dec 1970 |
| first space station launched | Salyut 1 | USSR | 19 Apr 1971 |
| first spacecraft to orbit another planet (Mars) | Mariner 9 | US | 13 Nov 1971 |
| first spacecraft to soft-land on Mars | Mars 3 | USSR | 2 Dec 1971 |
| first spacecraft to fly by Jupiter | Pioneer 10 | US | 3 Dec 1973 |
| first international docking in space | Apollo and Soyuz spacecraft | US/USSR | 17 Jul 1975 |
| first pictures transmitted from the surface of Mars | Viking 1 | US | 20 Jul 1976 |
| first spacecraft to fly by Saturn | Pioneer 11 | US | 1 Sep 1979 |
| first reusable spacecraft launched and returned from space | space shuttle Columbia | US | 12–14 Apr 1981 |

## Space Exploration Firsts (continued)

| EVENT | DETAILS | COUNTRY OR AGENCY | DATE ACCOMPLISHED |
|---|---|---|---|
| first spacecraft to fly by Uranus | Voyager 2 | US | 24 Jan 1986 |
| first spacecraft to make a close flyby of a comet's nucleus | Giotto at Halley's Comet | European Space Agency (ESA) | 13 Mar 1986 |
| first spacecraft to fly by Neptune | Voyager 2 | US | 24 Aug 1989 |
| first large optical space telescope launched | Hubble Space Telescope | US/ESA | 25 Apr 1990 |
| first spacecraft to orbit Jupiter | Galileo | US | 7 Dec 1995 |
| first spacecraft to orbit and land on an asteroid | NEAR Shoemaker at the asteroid Eros | US | 14 Feb 2000– 12 Feb 2001 |
| first piloted Chinese spacecraft to orbit Earth | Shenzhou 5, piloted by Yang Liwei | China | 15 Oct 2003 |
| first privately funded human spaceflight (to 100 km [62 mi] height) | SpaceShipOne, piloted by Michael W. Melvill | US (private venture) | 21 Jun 2004 |
| first spacecraft to strike a comet's nucleus and study its interior composition | Deep Impact at Comet Tempel 1 | US | 4 Jul 2005 |
| first spacecraft designed to measure water (ice) on a planet other than Earth | Phoenix | US | 5 Jun 2008 |
| first private spacecraft launched and returned from space orbit | Dragon | SpaceX | 8 Dec 2010 |

# Air Travel

## Flight History

Humanity has been fascinated with the possibility of flight for millennia—there are historical references to a Chinese kite that used a rotary wing as a source of lift from as early as about AD 400. Toys using the principle of the helicopter were known during the Middle Ages. Near the end of the 15th century, Leonardo da Vinci made drawings pertaining to flight. In the 1700s experiments were made with the ornithopter, a machine with flapping wings.

The history of successful flight begins with the hot-air balloon. Two French brothers, Joseph and Étienne Montgolfier, experimented with a large cell contrived of paper in which they could collect heated air. On 19 Sep 1783 the Montgolfiers sent aloft a balloon with a rooster, a duck, and a sheep, and on 21 November the first manned flight was made. Balloons gained importance as their flights ranged for hundreds of miles, but they were essentially unsteerable.

Count Ferdinand von Zeppelin spent much of his retired life working with balloons, particularly on the steering problem. Hydrogen and illuminating gas eventually replaced hot air, and a motor was mounted on a bag filled with gas that had been fitted with propellers and rudders. It was Zeppelin who first saw clearly that maintaining a steerable shape was essential. On 2 Jul 1900 Zeppelin undertook the first experimental flight of what he called an airship. The development of the dirigible went well until the docking procedure at Lakehurst NJ on 6 May 1937, when the Hindenburg burst into flames and exploded, with a loss of 36 lives. Public reaction made further development futile.

It should be noted that neither balloons nor dirigibles had produced true flight: what they had done was harness the dynamics of the atmosphere to lift a craft off the ground, using what power (if any) they supplied primarily to steer. The first scientific exposition of the principles that ultimately led to the successful flight with a heavier-than-air device came in 1843 from Sir George Cayley, who is regarded by many as the father of fixed-wing flight. He built a successful man-carrying glider that came close to permitting real flight. His work was built upon in the experiments on gliders from the late 1800s by Otto Lilienthal of Germany and Octave Chanute of the US.

The American brothers Wilbur and Orville Wright by 1902 had developed a fully practical biplane glider that could be controlled in every direction. Fitting a small engine and two propellers to another biplane, the Wrights on 17 Dec 1903 made the world's first successful flight of a man-carrying, engine-powered, heavier-than-air craft at a site near Kitty Hawk NC.

World War I (1914–18) further accelerated the expansion of aviation. Initially used for aerial reconnaissance, aircraft were soon fitted with machine guns and bombs; military aircraft with these types of armaments became known, respectively, as fighters and bombers.

By the 1920s the first small commercial airlines had begun to carry mail, and the increased speed and range of aircraft made nonstop flights over the world's oceans, poles, and continents possible. In the 1930s more efficient monoplane aircraft with all-metal fuselages and retractable undercarriages became standard. Aircraft played a key role in World War II (1939–45), developing in size, weight, speed, power, range, and armament. The war marked the high point of piston-engined propeller craft while also introducing the first aircraft with jet engines, which could fly at higher speeds. Jet-engined craft became the norm for fighters in the late 1940s and proved their superiority as commercial transports beginning in the '50s. The high speeds and low operating costs of jet airliners led to a massive expansion of commercial air travel in the second half of the 20th century.

The next great aviation innovation was the ability to fly at supersonic speeds. The first supersonic aircraft—a Bell XS-1 rocket-powered plane piloted by Maj. Charles E. Yeager of the US Air Force—broke the sound barrier on 14 Oct 1947 at 1,066 km/hr (662 mph) and attained a top speed of 1,126 km/hr (700 mph).

## Flight History (continued)

The first supersonic passenger-carrying commercial airplane, the Concorde, was built jointly in Great Britain and France and was in regular commercial service between 1976 and 2003. In the 21st century aircraft manufacturers strove to produce larger planes. A huge new passenger airliner, the double-decker Airbus A380, with a passenger capacity of 555 (40% greater than the next largest airplane), began commercial flights in late October 2007. The Boeing 787 Dreamliner has a capacity of 330 but a range of 3,050 nautical miles, making it more fuel-efficient than the A380. The first Dreamliner was delivered to All Nippon Airways in September 2011, and the plane's first commercial flight took place the following month.

## Airlines in the US: Best On-Time Arrival Performance

Data for 2011.
Source: US Department of Transportation, February 2012.

| RANK | AIRLINE | % OF ALL FLIGHTS | RANK | AIRLINE | % OF ALL FLIGHTS | RANK | AIRLINE | % OF ALL FLIGHTS |
|---|---|---|---|---|---|---|---|---|
| 1 | Hawaiian Airlines | 92.8 | 7 | United Airlines | 80.2 | 13 | American Eagle Airlines | 76.3 |
| 2 | Alaska Airlines | 88.2 | 8 | US Airways | 79.8 | | | |
| 3 | Airtran Airways | 84.4 | 9 | SkyWest Airlines | 79.3 | 14 | Atlantic Southeast Airlines | 75.2 |
| 4 | Mesa Airlines | 83.7 | 10 | Frontier Airlines | 79.2 | | | |
| 5 | Delta Airlines | 82.3 | 11 | American Airlines | 77.8 | 15 | ExpressJet Airlines | 74.7 |
| 6 | Southwest Airlines | 81.3 | 12 | Continental Airlines | 77.1 | | | |

## World's Busiest Airports

Ranked by total aircraft movement (takeoffs and landings), 2011.
Source: Airports Council International, <www.airports.org>.

| RANK | AIRPORT | SERVES | AIRPORT CODE | TOTAL MOVEMENTS |
|---|---|---|---|---|
| 1 | Hartsfield-Jackson Atlanta International Airport | Atlanta GA | ATL | 923,991 |
| 2 | O'Hare International Airport | Chicago IL | ORD | 875,798 |
| 3 | Dallas/Fort Worth International Airport | Dallas/Fort Worth TX | DFW | 646,803 |
| 4 | Denver International Airport | Denver CO | DEN | 628,784 |
| 5 | Los Angeles International Airport | Los Angeles CA | LAX | 603,912 |
| 6 | Charlotte Douglas International Airport | Charlotte NC | CLT | 539,842 |
| 7 | Beijing Capital International Airport | Beijing, China | PEK | 533,253 |
| 8 | McCarran International Airport | Las Vegas NV | LAS | 531,538 |
| 9 | George Bush Intercontinental Airport | Houston TX | IAH | 528,725 |
| 10 | Paris Charles de Gaulle International Airport | Paris, France | CDG | 514,059 |
| 11 | Frankfurt Airport | Frankfurt, Germany | FRA | 487,162 |
| 12 | Heathrow Airport | London, UK | LHR | 480,931 |
| 13 | Phoenix Sky Harbor International Airport | Phoenix AZ | PHX | 461,989 |
| 14 | Philadelphia International Airport | Philadelphia PA | PHL | 448,129 |
| 15 | Detroit Metropolitan Wayne County Airport | Detroit MI | DTW | 443,028 |
| 16 | Amsterdam Airport Schiphol | Amsterdam, Netherlands | AMS | 437,074 |
| 17 | Minneapolis–St. Paul International Airport | Minneapolis/St. Paul MN | MSP | 434,401 |
| 18 | Madrid Barajas International Airport | Madrid, Spain | MAD | 429,381 |
| 19 | Toronto Pearson International Airport | Toronto, ON, Canada | YYZ | 428,312 |
| 20 | Munich International Airport | Munich, Germany | MUC | 409,956 |
| 21 | John F. Kennedy International Airport | New York NY | JFK | 407,783 |
| 22 | Newark Liberty International Airport | Newark NJ | EWR | 405,763 |
| 23 | San Francisco International Airport | San Francisco CA | SFO | 403,564 |
| 24 | Miami International Airport | Miami FL | MIA | 394,572 |
| 25 | Tokyo International Airport | Tokyo, Japan | HND | 378,914 |

# Meteorology

## World Temperature Extremes

| REGION | highest recorded air temperature | | | lowest recorded air temperature | | |
|---|---|---|---|---|---|---|
| | PLACE (ELEVATION) | °F | °C | PLACE (ELEVATION) | °F | °C |
| Africa | Al-'Aziziyah, Libya (112 m [367 ft]; 13 Sep 1922) | 136.0 | 57.8 | Ifrane, Morocco (1,635 m [5,364 ft]; 11 Feb 1935) | −11.0 | −23.9 |

## World Temperature Extremes (continued)

| REGION | highest recorded air temperature | | | lowest recorded air temperature | | |
|---|---|---|---|---|---|---|
| | PLACE (ELEVATION) | °F | °C | PLACE (ELEVATION) | °F | °C |
| Antarctica | Lake Vanda, 77° 32″ S 161° 40″ E (99 m [325 ft]; 5 Jan 1974) | 59.0 | 15.0 | Vostok, 78° 27″ S, 106° 52″ E (3,420 m [11,220 ft]; 21 Jul 1983) | −128.6 | −89.2 |
| Asia | Tirat Zevi, Israel (−300 m [−984 ft]; 22 Jun 1942) | 129.0 | 53.9 | Oymyakon, Russia (806 m [2,644 ft]; 6 Feb 1933) | −89.9 | −67.7 |
| Australia | Cloncurry, QLD (193 m [633 ft]; 16 Jan 1889) | 127.5 | 53.1 | Charlotte Pass, NSW (1,780 m [5,840 ft]; 29 Jun 1994) | −8.0 | −22.2 |
| Europe | Sevilla, Spain (39 m [128 ft]; 4 Aug 1881) | 122.0 | 50.0 | Ust-Shchuger, Russia (85 m [279 ft]; date unknown) | −67.0 | −55.0 |
| North America | Greenland Ranch, Death Valley, California (−54 m [−177 ft]; 10 Jul 1913) | 134.5 | 56.9 | Snag, YT, Canada (646 m [2,119 ft]; 3 Feb 1947) | −81.0 | −62.8 |
| South America | Rivadavia, Argentina (205 m [672 ft]; 11 Dec 1905) | 120.0 | 48.9 | Colonia, Sarmiento, Argentina (268 m [879 ft]; 1 Jun 1907) | −27.0 | −32.8 |
| Tropical Pacific | Echague, Luzon, Philippines (78 m [256 ft]; date unknown) | 105.0 | 40.6 | Haleakala, Hawaii (2,972 m [9,751 ft]; date unknown) | 18.0 | −7.8 |

# Indexes

## Wind Chill Index

*The wind chill index is based upon a formula that determines how cold the atmosphere feels by combining the temperature and wind speed and applying other factors. For more information, see <www.nws.noaa.gov/om/windchill/index.shtml>.*

| | CALM | TEMPERATURE (°F) | | | | | | | | | | | | | |
|---|---|---|---|---|---|---|---|---|---|---|---|---|---|---|---|
| | | 40 | 35 | 30 | 25 | 20 | 15 | 10 | 5 | 0 | −5 | −10 | −15 | −20 | −25 | −30 |
| | 5 | 36 | 31 | 25 | 19 | 13 | 7 | 1 | −5 | −11 | −16 | −22 | −28 | −34 | −40 | −46 |
| | 10 | 34 | 27 | 21 | 15 | 9 | 3 | −4 | −10 | −16 | −22 | −28 | −35 | −41 | −47 | −53 |
| | 15 | 32 | 25 | 19 | 13 | 6 | 0 | −7 | −13 | −19 | −26 | −32 | −39 | −45 | −51 | −58 |
| | 20 | 30 | 24 | 17 | 11 | 4 | −2 | −9 | −15 | −22 | −29 | −35 | −42 | −48 | −55 | −61 |
| WIND | 25 | 29 | 23 | 16 | 9 | 3 | −4 | −11 | −17 | −24 | −31 | −37 | −44 | −51 | −58 | −64 |
| SPEED | 30 | 28 | 22 | 15 | 8 | 1 | −5 | −12 | −19 | −26 | −33 | −39 | −46 | −53 | −60 | −67 |
| (MPH) | 35 | 28 | 21 | 14 | 7 | 0 | −7 | −14 | −21 | −27 | −34 | −41 | −48 | −55 | −62 | −69 |
| | 40 | 27 | 20 | 13 | 6 | −1 | −8 | −15 | −22 | −29 | −36 | −43 | −50 | −57 | −64 | −71 |
| | 45 | 26 | 19 | 12 | 5 | −2 | −9 | −16 | −23 | −30 | −37 | −44 | −51 | −58 | −65 | −72 |
| | 50 | 26 | 19 | 12 | 4 | −3 | −10 | −17 | −24 | −31 | −38 | −45 | −52 | −60 | −67 | −74 |
| | 55 | 25 | 18 | 11 | 4 | −3 | −11 | −18 | −25 | −32 | −39 | −46 | −54 | −61 | −69 | −75 |
| | 60 | 25 | 17 | 10 | 3 | −4 | −11 | −19 | −26 | −33 | −40 | −48 | −55 | −62 | −69 | −76 |

## Heat Index

*The Heat Index shows the effects of the combination of heat and humidity. Apparent temperature is the temperature as it feels to your body. For more information see <www.jeonet.com/heat.htm>.*

| relative humidity | AIR TEMPERATURE (°F) | | | | | | | | | | |
|---|---|---|---|---|---|---|---|---|---|---|---|
| | 70 | 75 | 80 | 85 | 90 | 95 | 100 | 105 | 110 | 115 | 120 |
| | | | | | apparent temperature | | | | | | |
| 0% | 64 | 69 | 73 | 78 | 83 | 87 | 91 | 95 | 99 | 103 | 107 |
| 10% | 65 | 70 | 75 | 80 | 85 | 90 | 95 | 100 | 105 | 111 | 116 |
| 20% | 66 | 72 | 77 | 82 | 87 | 93 | 99 | 105 | 112 | 120 | 130 |
| 30% | 67 | 73 | 78 | 84 | 90 | 96 | 104 | 113 | 123 | 135 | 148 |
| 40% | 68 | 74 | 79 | 86 | 93 | 101 | 110 | 123 | 137 | 151 | |
| 50% | 69 | 75 | 81 | 88 | 96 | 107 | 120 | 135 | 150 | | |
| 60% | 70 | 76 | 82 | 90 | 100 | 114 | 132 | 149 | | | |
| 70% | 70 | 77 | 85 | 93 | 106 | 124 | 144 | | | | |
| 80% | 71 | 78 | 86 | 97 | 113 | 136 | 157 | | | | |
| 90% | 71 | 79 | 88 | 102 | 122 | 150 | 170 | | | | |
| 100% | 72 | 80 | 91 | 108 | 133 | 166 | | | | | |

## Ultraviolet (UV) Index

The Ultraviolet (UV) Index predicts the intensity of the sun's ultraviolet rays. It was developed by the National Weather Service and the US Environmental Protection Agency to provide a daily forecast of the expected risk of overexposure to the sun. The Index is calculated on a next-day basis for dozens of cities across the US. Other local conditions, such as cloud cover, are taken into account in determining the UV Index number. UV Index numbers are: 0–2 (minimal exposure); 3–4 (low exposure); 5–6 (moderate exposure); 7–9 (high exposure); and 10 and over (very high exposure).

Some simple precautions can be taken to reduce the risk of sun-related illness: limit time in the sun between 10 AM and 4 PM, when rays are generally the strongest; seek shade whenever possible; use a broad spectrum sunscreen with an SPF of at least 15; wear a wide-brimmed hat and, if possible, tightly woven, full-length clothing; wear UV-protective sunglasses; avoid sunlamps and tanning salons; and watch for the UV Index daily. The UV Index should not be used by seriously sun-sensitive individuals, who should consult their doctors and take additional precautions regardless of the exposure level.

# Hurricanes

## Hurricane and Tornado Classifications

The **Saffir/Simpson Hurricane Wind Scale**[1] is used to rank tropical cyclones.

**Category 1.** *Barometric pressure:* 28.91 in or more; *wind speed:* 74–95 mph; *damage:* minimal.

**Category 2.** *Barometric pressure:* 28.50–28.91 in; *wind speed:* 96–110 mph; *damage:* extensive.

**Category 3.** *Barometric pressure:* 27.91–28.47 in; *wind speed:* 111–130 mph; *damage:* devastating.

**Category 4.** *Barometric pressure:* 27.17–27.88 in; *wind speed:* 131–155 mph; *damage:* catastrophic.

**Category 5.** *Barometric pressure:* less than 27.17 in; *wind speed:* 155 mph or more; *damage:* catastrophic.

**Tornado classifications.**
Tornadoes are assigned specific values on the Fujita Scale,or F-Scale, of tornado intensity established by meteorologist T. Theodore Fujita.
Categories:

**F0.** *Wind speed:* 40–72 mph; *damage:* light.

**F1.** *Wind speed:* 73–112 mph; *damage:* moderate.

**F2.** *Wind speed:* 113–157 mph; *damage:* considerable.

**F3.** *Wind speed:* 158–206 mph; *damage:* severe.

**F4.** *Wind speed:* 207–260 mph; *damage:* devastating.

**F5.** *Wind speed:* 261–318 mph; *damage:* incredible.

[1]*Published by permission of Herbert Saffir, consulting engineer, and Robert Simpson, meteorologist. The scale was revised in early 2010 to remove hurricane-related data, such as storm surge and flooding. Damage estimates are in part affected by building codes and duration and direction of high winds.*

## Hurricane Names

*Source: National Hurricane Center.*

In 1953, the National Hurricane Center developed a list of given names for Atlantic tropical storms. This list is now maintained by the World Meteorological Organization (WMO). Until 1979 only women's names were used, but since then men's and women's names have alternated. There are six lists currently in rotation, so names can be reused every six years. Any country affected by a hurricane, however, can request that its name be retired for ten years. Also, if a storm has been particularly destructive, the WMO can remove it from the list and replace it with a different name.

## Deadliest Hurricanes in the US

Listed below, in order of number of deaths, are the 25 deadliest hurricanes to hit the US or its territories in 1851–2012. Hurricane names are given in parentheses after the location, when applicable.

Note: ranking numbers 10 and 20 on the list are repeated due to the equal number of fatalities in separate hurricanes. Source: National Hurricane Center. <www.nhc.noaa.gov/pdf/nws-nhc-6.pdf>.

| | HURRICANE LOCATION | YEAR | CATEGORY | DEATHS |
|---|---|---|---|---|
| 1 | Galveston TX | 1900 | 4 | 8,000[1] |
| 2 | NC; SC; Puerto Rico | 1899 | 3 | 3,419 |
| 3 | Lake Okeechobee, Florida | 1928 | 4 | 2,500[2] |
| 4 | Cheniere Caminada LA | 1893 | 4 | 2,000[3] |
| 5 | southeastern LA; MS (Katrina) | 2005 | 3 | 1,200 |
| 6 | Sea Islands, South Carolina and Georgia | 1893 | 3 | 1,000[4] |
| 7 | Puerto Rico; US Virgin Islands | 1867 | 3 | 811 |
| 8 | Puerto Rico | 1852 | 1 | 800 |
| 9 | GA; SC | 1881 | 2 | 700 |
| 10 | Last Island, Louisiana | 1856 | 4 | 600[3] |

## Deadliest Hurricanes in the US (continued)

| HURRICANE LOCATION | YEAR | CATEGORY | DEATHS | HURRICANE LOCATION | YEAR | CATEGORY | DEATHS |
|---|---|---|---|---|---|---|---|
| 10 New Orleans LA | 1915 | 3 | 600[3] | 19 Galveston TX | 1915 | 4 | 275 |
| 12 southwestern LA; northern TX (Audrey) | 1957 | 4 | 416 | 20 MS; southeastern LA; VA (Camille) | 1969 | 5 | 256 |
| 13 Florida Keys | 1935 | 5 | 408 | 20 New England | 1938 | 3 | 256 |
| 14 northeastern US | 1944 | 3 | 390[3] | 22 US Virgin Islands; Puerto Rico | 1932 | 2 | 225 |
| 15 FL; MS; AL | 1926 | 4 | 372 | | | | |
| 16 Grand Isle LA | 1909 | 3 | 350 | 23 northeastern US (Diane) | 1955 | 1 | 184 |
| 17 Puerto Rico (San Felipe) | 1928 | 5 | 312 | 24 GA; SC; NC | 1898 | 4 | 179 |
| 18 Florida Keys; southern TX | 1919 | 4 | 287 | 25 TX | 1875 | 3 | 176 |

[1]Death toll may have been as high as 12,000.   [2]Death toll may have been as high as 3,000.   [3]Including those lost at sea.   [4]Death toll may have been as high as 2,000.

## Costliest Hurricanes in the US

Listed below, in order of the highest monetary damage figures in constant 2012 US dollars, are the 25 costliest hurricanes to hit the US or its territories in 1900–2012. Locations of the damaged areas are given in parentheses after the hurricane name. Note that figures for Hurricanes Hugo and Georges reflect the damage done by those storms both on the US mainland and on its Caribbean territories. Source: National Hurricane Center.

<www.nhc.noaa.gov/pdf/nws-nhc-6.pdf>.

| RANK | HURRICANE (LOCATION) | YEAR | CATEGORY | ESTIMATED DAMAGE (US$), NOT ADJUSTED | DAMAGE IN CONSTANT 2012 US DOLLARS |
|---|---|---|---|---|---|
| 1 | Katrina (southeastern FL; southeastern LA; MS) | 2005 | 3 | 108,000,000,000 | 126,900,300,000 |
| 2 | Andrew (southeastern FL; southeastern LA) | 1992 | 5 | 26,500,000,000 | 43,344,000,000 |
| 3 | Ike (TX; LA) | 2008 | 2 | 29,520,000,000 | 31,463,500,000 |
| 4 | Wilma (southern FL) | 2005 | 3 | 21,007,000,000 | 24,683,300,000 |
| 5 | Ivan (AL; northwestern FL) | 2004 | 3 | 18,820,000,000 | 22,862,800,000 |
| 6 | Charley (southwestern FL) | 2004 | 4 | 15,113,000,000 | 18,359,500,000 |
| 7 | Irene (NC) | 2011 | 3 | 15,800,000,000 | 16,118,800,000 |
| 8 | Hugo (SC; USVI; PR) | 1989 | 4 | 8,000,000,000 | 14,805,000,000 |
| 9 | Rita (southwestern LA; northern TX) | 2005 | 3 | 12,037,000,000 | 14,143,500,000 |
| 10 | Allison (northern TX) | 2001 | TS[1] | 9,000,000,000 | 11,661,800,000 |
| 11 | Frances (FL) | 2004 | 2 | 9,507,000,000 | 11,549,200,000 |
| 12 | Agnes (FL; northeastern US) | 1972 | 1 | 2,100,000,000 | 11,528,800,000 |
| 13 | Betsy (southeastern FL; southeastern LA) | 1965 | 3 | 1,420,500,000 | 10,348,400,000 |
| 14 | Floyd (mid-Atlantic US; northeastern US) | 1999 | 2 | 6,900,000,000 | 9,504,200,000 |
| 15 | Jeanne (FL) | 2004 | 3 | 7,660,000,000 | 9,305,500,000 |
| 16 | Georges (USVI; PR; FL; MS; AL) | 1998 | 3 | 6,365,000,000 | 8,960,900,000 |
| 17 | Camille (MS; southeastern LA; VA) | 1969 | 5 | 1,420,700,000 | 8,883,400,000 |
| 18 | Opal (northwestern FL; AL) | 1995 | 3 | 5,142,000,000 | 7,742,600,000 |
| 19 | Frederic (AL; MS) | 1979 | 3 | 2,300,000,000 | 7,270,000,000 |
| 20 | Diane (northeastern US) | 1955 | 1 | 831,700,000 | 7,121,500,000 |
| 21 | Isabel (mid-Atlantic US) | 2003 | 2 | 5,370,000,000 | 6,697,300,000 |
| 22 | Fran (NC) | 1996 | 3 | 4,160,000,000 | 6,084,300,000 |
| 23 | Celia (southern TX) | 1970 | 3 | 930,000,000 | 5,500,400,000 |
| 24 | (New England) | 1938 | 3 | 308,000,000 | 5,012,700,000 |
| 25 | Gustav (LA) | 2008 | 2 | 4,618,000,000 | 4,922,000,000 |

[1]Of tropical storm intensity but included because of high damage.

**Did you know?** A bottle of champagne recovered from a shipwreck sold for a record amount in June 2011. The Veuve Clicquot champagne, which was cargo on a ship that sank off of Finland's Åland islands in the 19th century, was one of 160 bottles recovered from the wreck. It was sold for some US$42,000. Also found were bottles of beer thought to be the oldest still-drinkable beer in existence.

# Geologic Disasters

## Measuring Earthquakes

The seismologists Beno Gutenberg and Charles Francis Richter introduced measurement of the seismic energy released by earthquakes on a magnitude scale in 1935. Each increase of one unit on the scale represents a 10-fold increase in the magnitude of an earthquake. Seismographs are designed to measure the different components of seismic waves, such as wave type, intensity, and duration. This table shows the typical effects of earthquakes in various magnitude ranges. For further information, see <crack.seismo.unr.edu/ftp/pub/louie/class/100/magnitude.html>.

| MAGNITUDE | EARTHQUAKE EFFECTS |
|---|---|
| Less than 3.5 | Generally not felt, but recorded. |
| 3.5–5.4 | Often felt, but rarely causes damage. |
| Less than 6.0 | At most, slight damage to well-designed buildings. Can cause major damage to poorly constructed buildings over small regions. |
| 6.1–6.9 | Can be destructive in areas up to about 100 km (62 mi) across where people live. |
| 7.0–7.9 | Major earthquake. Can cause serious damage over larger areas. |
| 8 or greater | Great earthquake. Can cause serious damage in areas several hundred km across. |

## Major Historical Earthquakes

*Magnitudes given for pre-20th-century events are generally estimations from intensity data. In cases where no magnitude is available, the earthquake's maximum intensity, written as a Roman numeral from I to XII, is given. Most fatality data are estimates.*

| YEAR (AD) | AFFECTED AREA | MAGNITUDE OR INTENSITY | DEATHS | YEAR (AD) | AFFECTED AREA | MAGNITUDE OR INTENSITY | DEATHS |
|---|---|---|---|---|---|---|---|
| 365 | Knossos, Crete, Greece | XI | 50,000 | 1906 | off the coast of Ecuador | 8.8 | 1,000 |
| 526 | Antioch, Syria | unknown | 250,000 | 1906 | Valparaíso, Chile | 8.2 | 20,000 |
| 844 | Damascus, Syria | VIII | 50,000 | 1906 | San Francisco CA | 7.9 | 700 |
| 847 | Damascus, Syria | X | 70,000 | 1907 | southwestern Tajikistan | 8.0 | 12,000 |
| 847 | Mosul, Iraq | unknown | 50,000 | 1908 | Messina, Italy | 7.5 | 110,000 |
| 856 | Damghan, Iran | unknown | 200,000 | 1912 | Sea of Marmara, Turkey | 7.8 | 2,800 |
| 893 | Daipur, India | unknown | 180,000 | 1915 | Avezzano, Italy | 7.0 | 32,610 |
| 893 | Ardabil, Iran | unknown | 150,000 | 1920 | Gansu province, China | 8.5 | 200,000 |
| 893 | Caucasus | unknown | 82,000 | 1923 | Tokyo; Yokohama, Japan | 7.9 | 142,800 |
| 1042 | Palmyra, Syria | X | 50,000 | 1927 | Qinghai province, China | 7.6 | 40,900 |
| 1138 | Aleppo, Syria | unknown | 230,000 | 1933 | Sanriku, Japan | 8.4 | 2,990 |
| 1201 | Upper Egypt or Syria | IX | 1,100,000 | 1935 | Quetta, Pakistan | 7.5 | 20,000 |
| 1268 | Cilicia, Turkey | unknown | 60,000 | 1939 | Erzincan, Turkey | 7.8 | 32,700 |
| 1290 | Chihli, China | unknown | 100,000 | 1939 | Chillán, Chile | 7.8 | 28,000 |
| 1556 | Shaanxi province, China | 8.0 | 830,000 | 1944 | Tonankai, Japan | 8.1 | 998 |
| | | | | 1944 | San Juan, Argentina | 7.4 | 8,000 |
| 1667 | Shemakha, Azerbaijan | unknown | 80,000 | 1945 | off the coast of Pakistan | 8.0 | 4,000 |
| | | | | 1946 | Nankaido, Japan | 8.1 | 1,362 |
| 1668 | Shandong province, China | XII | 50,000 | 1948 | Ashgabat, Turkmenistan | 7.3 | 176,000 |
| 1693 | Sicily, Italy | 7.5 | 93,000 | 1950 | China-India border, near Myanmar (Burma) | 8.7 | 574 |
| 1703 | Jeddo, Japan | unknown | 200,000 | 1960 | Puerto Montt, Chile | 9.5 | 5,700 |
| 1727 | Tabriz, Iran | unknown | 77,000 | 1960 | Agadir, Morocco | 5.7 | 10,000–15,000 |
| 1730 | Hokkaido, Japan | unknown | 137,000 | | | | |
| 1731 | Beijing, China | unknown | 100,000 | 1964 | Prince William Sound, Alaska | 9.2 | 131 |
| 1739 | China | X | 50,000 | 1968 | Khorasan, Iran | 7.3 | 12,000 |
| 1755 | Lisbon, Portugal; Spain; Morocco | 8.7 | 62,000 | 1970 | northern Peru | 7.9 | 70,000 |
| | | | | 1970 | Yunnan province, China | 7.5 | 10,000 |
| 1755 | Kashan, Iran | unknown | 40,000 | 1972 | Fars, Iran | 7.1 | 5,054 |
| 1780 | Tabriz, Iran | 7.7 | 200,000 | 1972 | Managua, Nicaragua | 6.2 | 10,000 |
| 1783 | Calabria, Italy | unknown | 50,000 | 1974 | Yunnan province, China | 6.8 | 20,000 |
| 1811 | New Madrid MO | 8.6 | unknown | 1974 | North-West Frontier Province, Pakistan | 6.2 | 5,300 |
| 1812 | Caracas, Venezuela | 9.6 | 26,000 | | | | |
| 1835 | northern Japan | 7.6 | 28,300 | 1975 | Liaoning province, China | 7.0 | 2,000 |
| 1868 | Arica, Chile | 9.0 | 25,000 | 1976 | Mindanao, Philippines | 7.9 | 8,000 |
| 1868 | Ecuador; Colombia | 7.7 | 70,000 | 1976 | Tangshan, China | 7.5 | 242,000 |
| 1883 | Java, Indonesia | unknown | 100,000 | 1976 | Guatemala City, Guatemala | 7.5 | 23,000 |
| 1896 | Sanriku, Japan | 8.5 | 27,000 | 1976 | Turkey-Iran border | 7.3 | 5,000 |
| 1905 | Kangra, India | 7.5 | 19,000 | 1977 | Bucharest, Romania | 7.2 | 1,500 |

## Major Historical Earthquakes (continued)

| YEAR (AD) | AFFECTED AREA | MAGNITUDE OR INTENSITY | DEATHS |
|---|---|---|---|
| 1978 | Khorasan, Iran | 7.8 | 15,000 |
| 1980 | Ech-Cheliff (El-Asnam), Algeria | 7.7 | 5,000 |
| 1980 | southern Italy | 6.5 | 3,114 |
| 1985 | Michoacán state, Mexico | 8.1 | 9,500 |
| 1988 | Gyumri (Leninakan), Armenia | 6.8 | 25,000 |
| 1990 | Luzon, Philippines | 7.7 | 1,621 |
| 1990 | Rasht, Iran | 7.4 | 50,000 |
| 1991 | northern India | 6.8 | 2,000 |
| 1992 | Flores, Indonesia | 7.5 | 2,500 |
| 1993 | Latur, India | 6.2 | 9,748 |
| 1995 | Sakhalin Island, Russia | 7.1 | 1,989 |
| 1995 | Kobe, Japan | 6.9 | 5,502 |
| 1997 | eastern Iran | 7.3 | 1,567 |
| 1998 | Feyzabad, Afghanistan | 6.6 | 4,000 |
| 1999 | Taiwan | 7.7 | 2,400 |
| 1999 | Izmit, Turkey | 7.4 | 17,118 |
| 2001 | Gujarat state, India | 8.0 | 20,023 |
| 2002 | Hindu Kush mountains, Afghanistan | 6.1 | 1,000 |
| 2003 | northern Algeria | 6.8 | 2,266 |
| 2003 | Bam, Iran | 6.6 | 26,000 |

| YEAR (AD) | AFFECTED AREA | MAGNITUDE OR INTENSITY | DEATHS |
|---|---|---|---|
| 2004 | off the western coast of Sumatra, Indonesia | 9.0 | 227,898 |
| 2005 | northern Sumatra, Indonesia | 8.6 | 1,313 |
| 2005 | Kashmir, Pakistan | 7.6 | 80,000 |
| 2006 | Bantul, Indonesia | 6.3 | 5,749 |
| 2007 | off the coast of central Peru | 8.0 | 514 |
| 2008 | eastern Sichuan province, China | 7.9 | 87,587 |
| 2009 | southern Sumatra, Indonesia | 7.5 | 1,117 |
| 2009 | central Italy | 6.3 | 295 |
| 2010 | off the western coast of Chile, near Maule | 8.8 | 521 |
| 2010 | southern Haiti, near Port-au-Prince | 7.0 | 85,000–316,000 |
| 2010 | southern Qinghai province, China | 6.9 | 2,968 |
| 2011 | off the northeastern coast of Honshu, Japan | 9.0 | 19,300 |
| 2011 | Ercis-Van, Turkey | 7.2 | 570 |
| 2011 | Christchurch, New Zealand | 6.3 | 180 |
| 2012 | off the northwestern coast of Sumatra, Indonesia | 8.6 | 5 |

## Tsunami

A tsunami is a catastrophic ocean wave, usually caused by a submarine earthquake occurring less than 30 mi (50 km) beneath the seafloor, with a magnitude greater than 6.5. Underwater or coastal landslides or volcanic eruptions also may cause a tsunami. The often-used term tidal wave is a misnomer: the wave has no connection with the tides. After the earthquake or other generating impulse, a train of simple, progressive oscillatory waves is propagated great distances at the ocean surface in ever-widening circles, much like the waves produced by a pebble falling into a shallow pool. In deep water, the wavelengths are enormous, about 60 to 125 mi (100 to 200 km), and the wave heights are very small, only 1 to 2 ft (0.3 to 0.6 m). The resulting wave steepness is extremely low; coupled with the waves' long periods that vary from five minutes to an hour, this enables normal wind waves and swell to completely obscure the waves in deep water. Thus, a ship in the open ocean experiences the passage of a tsunami as an insignificant rise and fall. As the waves approach the continental coasts, friction with the increasingly shallow bottom reduces the velocity of the waves. The period must remain constant; consequently, as the velocity lessens, the wavelengths become shortened and the wave amplitudes increase, coastal waters rising as high as 100 feet (30 m) in 10 to 15 minutes. By a poorly understood process, the continental shelf waters begin to oscillate after the rise in sea level. Between three and five major oscillations generate most of the damage; the oscillations cease, however, only several days after they begin. Occasionally, the first arrival of a tsunami at a coast may be a trough, the water receding and exposing the shallow seafloor.

## Deadly Volcano Eruptions

*Casualty figures are approximate.*

| VOLCANO (LOCATION) | YEAR | CASUALTIES |
|---|---|---|
| Tambora (Indonesia) | 1815 | 92,000[1] |
| Krakatoa (Indonesia) | 1883 | 36,000[1] |
| Pelée (Martinique) | 1902 | 30,000 |
| Ruiz (Colombia) | 1985 | 25,000[2] |
| Etna (Italy) | 1669 | 20,000 |
| Unzen (Japan) | 1792 | 15,000 |
| Kelud (Indonesia) | 1586 | 10,000 |
| Laki (Iceland) | 1783 | 9,000 |
| Kelud (Indonesia) | 1919 | 5,000 |
| Vesuvius (Italy) | 79 | 3,360 |
| Awu (Indonesia) | 1711 | 3,200 |
| Raung (Indonesia) | 1638 | 3,000 |

| VOLCANO (LOCATION) | YEAR | CASUALTIES |
|---|---|---|
| Raung (Indonesia) | 1730 | 3,000 |
| Lamington (Papua New Guinea) | 1951 | 3,000 |
| Awu (Indonesia) | 1856 | 2,800 |
| Taal (Philippines) | 1906 | 1,500 |
| Taal (Philippines) | 1911 | 1,300 |
| Etna (Italy) | 1536 | 1,000 |
| Paricutín (Mexico) | 1949 | 1,000 |
| Purace (Colombia) | 1949 | 1,000 |
| Pinatubo (Philippines) | 1991 | 350 |
| Merapi (Indonesia) | 2010 | 153 |
| El Chichón (Mexico) | 1982 | 100 |
| St. Helens (Washington) | 1980 | 57 |

[1]Includes tsunami triggered by eruption.  [2]Includes mudflow triggered by eruption.

# Civil Engineering

## The Seven Wonders of the Ancient World

The seven wonders of the ancient world were considered to be the preeminent architectural and sculptural achievements of the Mediterranean and Middle East. Although different lists exist, the classic list contains the following:

**Pyramids of Giza.** The oldest of the wonders and the only one substantially in existence today, the pyramids of Giza were erected c. 2575–c. 2465 BC on the west bank of the Nile River in northern Egypt. The designations of the pyramids—Khufu, Khafre, and Menkaure—correspond to the kings for whom they were built. Khufu (also called the Great Pyramid) is the largest of the three, the length of each side at the base averaging 230 m (755 ft). According to Herodotus, the Great Pyramid took 20 years to construct and demanded the labor of 100,000 men.

**Hanging Gardens of Babylon.** A series of landscaped terraces ascribed to either Queen Sammu-ramat (810–783 BC) or King Nebuchadrezzar II (c. 605–c. 562 BC), the gardens were built within the walls of the royal palace at Babylon (in present-day southern Iraq). They did not actually "hang" but were instead roof gardens laid out on a series of ziggurat terraces that were irrigated by pumps from the Euphrates River.

**Statue of Zeus.** An ornate figure of Zeus on his throne, this wonder was completed about 430 BC by Phidias of Athens after eight years of work. It was placed in the huge Temple of Zeus at Olympia in western Greece. The statue, almost 12 m (40 ft) high and plated with gold and ivory, represented the god sitting on an elaborate throne ornamented with ebony, ivory, gold, and precious stones. On his outstretched right hand was a statue of Nike (Victory), and in the god's left hand was a scepter on which an eagle was perched.

**Temple of Artemis.** The great temple was built by Croesus, king of Lydia, in about 550 BC and was rebuilt after being burned by a madman named Herostratus in 356 BC. The artemesium was famous not only for its great size (over 110 by 55 m [350 by 80 ft]) but also for the magnificent works of art that adorned it. It was destroyed by invading Goths in AD 262, and though it was never rebuilt, copies survive of the famous statue of Artemis in it. This early representation stands stiffly straight, with her hands extended outward. The original was made of gold, ebony, silver, and black stone.

**Mausoleum of Halicarnassus.** This monumental tomb of Mausolus, the tyrant of Caria in southwestern Asia Minor, was built between about 353 and 351 BC by Mausolus' sister and widow, Artemisia. According to the description of Pliny the Elder, the monument, designed by the architect Pythius (Pytheos), was almost square, with a total periphery of 125 m (411 ft). It was bounded by 36 columns, and the top formed a pyramid surmounted by a marble chariot. Fragments of the mausoleum's sculpture are preserved in the British Museum. The mausoleum was probably destroyed by an earthquake, and the stones were reused in local buildings.

**Colossus of Rhodes.** This huge bronze statue was built at the harbor of Rhodes in ancient Greece in commemoration of the raising of the siege of Rhodes (305–304 BC). The sculptor was Chares of Lyndus. The Colossus was said to be 32 m (105 ft) high, making it technically impossible that it could have straddled the harbor entrance, as was popularly believed. The Colossus took 12 years to build (c. 294–282 BC) and was toppled by an earthquake about 225 BC.

**Pharos of Alexandria.** This lighthouse, the most famous of the ancient world, was built by Sostratus of Cnidus about 280 BC on the island of Pharos off Alexandria, and it is said to have been more than 100 m (350 ft) high. It is the archetype of all lighthouses since. The lighthouse was destroyed by an earthquake in the 1300s. In 1994 a large amount of masonry blocks and statuary, thought to be wreckage from the lighthouse, was found in the waters off Pharos.

## Tallest Buildings in the World

*Building height equals the distance from the level of the lowest significant, open-air, pedestrian entrance to the architectural top of the building, including spires but not including antennas, signage, or flag poles. Only buildings that have been completed or are scheduled to be completed in 2012 are included in this table.*
*Source: Council on Tall Buildings and Urban Habitat.*

| RANK | BUILDING | CITY | YEAR COMPLETED | HEIGHT IN FT/M | STORIES |
|------|----------|------|----------------|----------------|---------|
| 1 | Burj Khalifa | Dubai, UAE | 2010 | 2,717/828 | 163 |
| 2 | Makkah Royal Clock Tower Hotel | Mecca, Saudi Arabia | 2012 | 1,972/601 | 120 |
| 3 | Taipei 101 | Taipei, Taiwan | 2004 | 1,667/508 | 101 |
| 4 | Shanghai World Financial Center | Shanghai, China | 2008 | 1,614/492 | 101 |
| 5 | International Commerce Centre | Hong Kong, China | 2010 | 1,588/484 | 108 |
| 6 | Petronas Tower 1 | Kuala Lumpur, Malaysia | 1998 | 1,483/452 | 88 |
| 6 | Petronas Tower 2 | Kuala Lumpur, Malaysia | 1998 | 1,483/452 | 88 |
| 8 | Zifeng Tower | Nanjing, China | 2010 | 1,476/450 | 66 |
| 9 | Willis Tower (Sears Tower) | Chicago IL | 1974 | 1,450/442 | 108 |
| 9 | Kingkey 100 | Shenzhen, China | 2011 | 1,450/442 | 100 |
| 11 | Guangzhou International Finance Center | Guangzhou, China | 2010 | 1,440/439 | 103 |
| 12 | Trump International Hotel & Tower | Chicago IL | 2009 | 1,388/423 | 98 |
| 13 | Jin Mao Building | Shanghai, China | 1999 | 1,381/421 | 88 |
| 14 | Princess Tower | Dubai, UAE | 2012 | 1,355/413 | 101 |
| 14 | Al Hamra Firdous Tower | Kuwait City, Kuwait | 2011 | 1,355/413 | 77 |

## Tallest Buildings in the World (continued)

| RANK | BUILDING | CITY | YEAR COMPLETED | HEIGHT IN FT/M | STORIES |
|---|---|---|---|---|---|
| 16 | Two International Finance Centre | Hong Kong, China | 2003 | 1,352/412 | 88 |
| 17 | 23 Marina | Dubai, UAE | 2012 | 1,289/393 | 90 |
| 18 | CITIC Plaza | Guangzhou, China | 1996 | 1,280/390 | 80 |
| 19 | Shun Hing Square | Shenzhen, China | 1996 | 1,260/384 | 69 |
| 20 | Empire State Building | New York NY | 1931 | 1,250/381 | 102 |
| 21 | Elite Residence | Dubai, UAE | 2012 | 1,247/380 | 87 |
| 22 | Central Plaza | Hong Kong, China | 1992 | 1,227/374 | 78 |
| 23 | Bank of China Tower | Hong Kong, China | 1989 | 1,204/367 | 70 |
| 24 | Bank of America Tower | New York NY | 2009 | 1,201/366 | 55 |
| 25 | Almas Tower | Dubai, UAE | 2008 | 1,181/360 | 68 |

## Longest Span Structures in the World by Type

### Bridges

| SUSPENSION | LOCATION | YEAR OF COMPLETION | MAIN SPAN (M) |
|---|---|---|---|
| Akashi Kaikyo | Kobe–Awaji Island, Japan | 1998 | 1,991 |
| part of eastern link between islands of Honshu and Shikoku | | | |
| Xihoumen | Zhoushan archipelago, China | 2009 | 1,650 |
| links Jintang and Cezi islands | | | |
| Store Baelt (Great Belt) | Zealand–Funen, Denmark | 1998 | 1,624 |
| part of link between Copenhagen and mainland Europe | | | |
| Yi Sun-sin | Gwangyang–Yeosu, South Korea | 2012 | 1,545 |
| world's fourth longest suspension bridge | | | |
| Runyang South | Zhenjian–Jiangsu, China | 2005 | 1,490 |

| CABLE-STAYED (STEEL) | | | |
|---|---|---|---|
| Russky | Vladivostok–Russky Island, Russia | 2012 | 1,104 |
| Sutong | Nantong, China | 2008 | 1,088 |
| longest main span, highest main-bridge tower, and deepest foundation piers for a cable-stayed bridge | | | |
| Stonecutters (Angchuanzhou) | Tsing Yi–Sha Tin, Hong Kong | 2009 | 1,018 |
| links growing areas of Northeast New Territories and Kowloon, Hong Kong | | | |
| Edong | Huangshi–Huanggang, China | 2009 | 926 |
| alleviates congestion on Huangshi Yangtze Bridge | | | |
| Tatara | Onomichi–Imabari, Japan | 1999 | 890 |
| part of western link between islands of Honshu and Shikoku | | | |

| ARCH | | | |
|---|---|---|---|
| **steel** | | | |
| Chaotianmen | Chongqing, China (across the Yangtze) | 2009 | 552 |
| world's longest steel-arch bridge | | | |
| Lupu | Shanghai, China | 2003 | 550 |
| crosses Huangpujiang (Huangpu River) between central Shanghai and Pudong New District | | | |
| New River Gorge | Fayetteville WV | 1977 | 518 |
| provides road link through scenic New River Gorge National River area | | | |
| **concrete** | | | |
| Wanxian | Sichuan province, China | 1997 | 425 |
| crosses Chang Jiang (Yangtze River) in Three Gorges area | | | |
| Krk-1 | Krk island, Croatia | 1980 | 390 |
| links scenic Krk island with mainland Croatia | | | |
| Jialing | Sichuan province, China | 2012 | 364 |
| crosses the Jialing River | | | |

| CANTILEVER | | | |
|---|---|---|---|
| **steel truss** | | | |
| Québec | Quebec City, QC, Canada | 1917 | 549 |
| provides rail crossing over St. Lawrence River | | | |
| Forth | Edinburgh–North Queensferry, Scotland | 1890 | 2 spans, each 521 |
| provides rail crossing over Firth of Forth | | | |
| Minato | Osaka–Amagasaki, Japan | 1974 | 510 |
| carries road traffic across Osaka's harbor | | | |

## Longest Span Structures in the World by Type (continued)

| | LOCATION | YEAR OF COMPLETION | MAIN SPAN (M) |
|---|---|---|---|
| **CANTILEVER (CONTINUED)** | | | |
| **prestressed concrete** | | | |
| Shibanpo-2 | Chongqing, China | 2006 | 330 |
| world's longest prestressed-concrete box girder bridge | | | |
| Stolmasundet | Austevoll, Norway | 1998 | 301 |
| links islands of Stolmen and Sjelbörn south of Bergen | | | |
| Raftsundet | Lofoten, Norway | 1998 | 298 |
| crosses Raft Sound in arctic Lofoten islands | | | |
| | | | |
| **BEAM** | | | |
| **steel truss** | | | |
| Ikitsuki Ohashi | Nagasaki prefecture, Japan | 1991 | 400 |
| connects islands of Iki and Hirado off northwest Kyushu | | | |
| Astoria | Astoria OR | 1966 | 376 |
| carries Pacific Coast Highway across Columbia River between Oregon and Washington | | | |
| Francis Scott Key | Baltimore MD | 1977 | 366 |
| spans Patapsco River at Baltimore harbor | | | |
| **steel plate and box girder** | | | |
| Presidente Costa e Silva | Rio de Janeiro state, Brazil | 1974 | 300 |
| crosses Guanabara Bay between Rio de Janeiro and suburb of Niterói | | | |
| Neckartalbrücke-1 | Weitingen, Germany | 1978 | 263 |
| carries highway across Neckar River valley | | | |
| Brankova (Sava-1) | Belgrade, Serbia | 1956 | 261 |
| provides road crossing of Sava River between Old and New Belgrade | | | |
| | | | |
| **MOVABLE** | | | |
| **vertical lift** | | | |
| Arthur Kill | Elizabeth NJ–New York NY | 1959 | 170 |
| provides rail link between port of Elizabeth and Staten Island | | | |
| Cape Cod Canal | Cape Cod MA | 1935 | 166 |
| provides rail crossing over waterway near Buzzard's Bay | | | |
| Delair | Delair NJ–Philadelphia PA | 1960 | 165 |
| provides rail link across Delaware River between Philadelphia and southern Jersey Shore | | | |
| **swing span** | | | |
| Al-Firdan (El-Ferdan) | Suez Canal, Egypt | 2001 | 340 |
| provides road and rail link between Sinai Peninsula and eastern Nile delta region | | | |
| Santa Fe | Fort Madison IA–Niota IL | 1927 | 160 |
| provides road and rail crossing of Mississippi River | | | |
| Kaiser-Wilhelm-Brücke | Wilhelmshaven, Germany | 1907 | 159 |
| crosses the Wupper River | | | |
| | | | |
| **BASCULE** | | | |
| South Capitol Street/Frederick Douglass Memorial | Washington DC | 1949 | 118 |
| carries road traffic over Anacostia River | | | |
| Sault Sainte Marie | Sault Sainte Marie MI–Ontario, Canada | 1941 | 102 |
| connects rail systems of United States and Canada | | | |
| Charles Berry | Lorain OH | 1940 | 101 |
| carries road traffic over Black River | | | |
| Market Street/Chief John Ross | Chattanooga TN | 1917 | 94 |
| carries road traffic over Tennessee River | | | |
| | | | |
| **Causeways** (fixed link over water only) | | | |
| Qingdao Jiaozhou Bay | Jiaozhou Bay, Shandong province, China | 2011 | 42,500 |
| world's longest transoceanic bridge or causeway | | | |
| Lake Pontchartrain-2 | Metairie–Mandeville LA | 1969 | 38,422 |
| carries northbound road traffic from suburbs of New Orleans to north lakeshore | | | |
| Lake Pontchartrain-1 | Mandeville–Metairie LA | 1956 | 38,352 |
| carries southbound road traffic from north lakeshore to suburbs of New Orleans | | | |
| Hangzhou Bay Transoceanic | near Jiaxing–near Cixi, China | 2008 | 36,000 |
| important component of China's East Coast Superhighway | | | |
| King Fahd | Bahrain–Saudi Arabia | 1986 | 24,950 |
| carries road traffic across Gulf of Bahrain in Persian Gulf | | | |

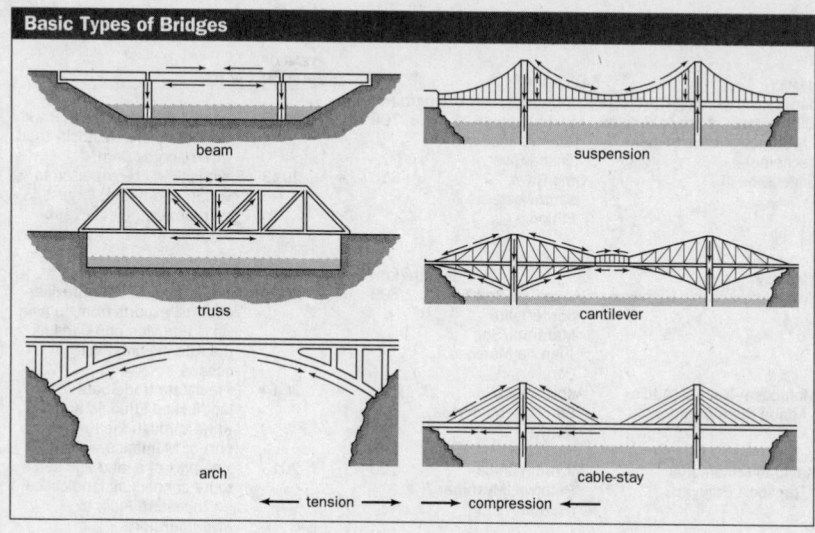

**Basic Types of Bridges**

beam

suspension

truss

cantilever

arch

cable-stay

← tension →     → compression ←

## Notable Civil Engineering Projects (in progress or completed as of July 2012)

| NAME | LOCATION | | YEAR OF COMPLETION | NOTES |
|---|---|---|---|---|
| **airports** | | **terminal area (sq m)** | | |
| New Doha International (phases 1 and 2) | near Doha, Qatar | 465,000 | 2013 | Being built on 22 sq km of Persian Gulf landfill; new departures terminal opened in June 2011 |
| Muscat International | west of Muscat, Oman, near Al-Sib | 332,000 | 2014 | Terminal expanded |
| Frankfurt Airport (new Terminal 3) | Frankfurt am Main, Germany | 106,700 | 2015 | To increase passenger capacity at Europe's 2nd busiest airport by half |
| **bridges** | | **length (main span; m)** | | |
| Hong Kong–Zhuhai Crossing | Hong Kong to China link (via Macau) (in Pearl River estuary) | c. 50 km | 2016 | To include world's largest sea bridge (c. 30 km) and world's longest immersed tube tunnel (5.6 km) |
| Hangzhou Bay #2 (Jia-Shao) | between Jiaxing and Shaoxing, China | 2,680 | 2012 | Will be world's longest all-span cable-stayed bridge |
| San Francisco–Oakland Bay (East Span) | Yerba Buena Island–Oakland CA | 611 | 2013 | To be world's longest self-anchored suspension span |
| **buildings** | | **height (m)** | | |
| Ping An Finance Centre | Shenzhen, China | 660 | 2015 | To be among the world's 10 tallest buildings |
| Shanghai Tower | Shanghai | 632 | 2014 | To be the tallest building in China |
| 1 World Trade Center (Freedom Tower) | New York City | "1,776 ft" (541.3 m) | 2013 | Complex to include 6 new buildings, a memorial, and a museum |
| **dams and hydrologic projects** | | **crest length (m)** | | |
| Diamer-Bhasha | on Indus River near Diamer, Pakistan | 1,169 | 2019 | To be world's highest concrete dam; would satisfy all of Pakistan's current electricity needs and regulate water level of the flood-prone Indus River |

## Notable Civil Engineering Projects (in progress or completed as of July 2012) (continued)

| NAME | LOCATION | | YEAR OF COMPLETION | NOTES |
|------|----------|--|------------|-------|
| **dams and hydrologic projects (continued)** | | **crest length (m)** | | |
| Xiluodu (part of upper Yangtze hydropower development scheme) | 184 km upriver of Yibin, China, on Jinsha River | 700 | 2015 | First of 4-dam scheme that will generate more electricity than Three Gorges Dam |
| Gilgel Gibe III | Omo River, southwestern Ethiopia | 610 | 2013 | Electricity will be exported to Sudan and Kenya; largest hydropower project in sub-Saharan Africa |
| **highways** | | **length (km)** | | |
| South Interoceanic Highway | Iñapari (at Brazilian border)–Ilo/Matarani/San Juan de Marcona, Peru | 2,603 | 2012 | To be paved road for Brazilian imports/exports from/to Asia via 3 Peruvian ports; to link the Atlantic and Pacific oceans |
| Mombasa–Nairobi–Addis Ababa Road Corridor | Addis Ababa, Ethiopia–Mombasa, Kenya | 1,284 | 2014 | To facilitate trade between landlocked Ethiopia and the world through the Kenyan port of Mombasa |
| Kaladan Multimodal Transport Project | Mizoram, India–Patetwa, Myanmar (Burma) | 129 | 2013 | To be part of a land and sea route connecting landlocked northeastern India to Myanmar ports |
| **canals and floodgates** | | **length (m)** | | |
| Southern Delivery System (phase I) | Pueblo Reservoir to Colorado Springs and Denver suburbs | 100,000 | 2016 | To provide needed water from the Arkansas River to Colorado Springs and Denver |
| Panama Canal Expansion | between Panama City and Colón, Panama | — | 2014 | Will include new wider and longer 3-chamber locks, doubling the canal's capacity and allowing the passage of world's biggest container ships |
| South-to-North Water Transfer Project (Middle Route) | Danjiangkou Reservoir (on Haijiang River) to Beijing | — | 2014 | Water will be canalized north to drought-prone Beijing area; total length of canal-pipeline system will be more than 1,273 km |
| **railways (heavy)** | | **length (km)** | | |
| Xinqiu–Bayan Ul Railway | Xinqiu, Liaoning–Bayan Ul, Inner Mongolia, China | 487 | 2012? | To be used for coal transport; future 230-km link to Mongolian border expected |
| Lhasa–Xigaze railway | Lhasa–Xigaze, Tibet, China | 253 | 2015 | Extension of the world's highest railroad will include 29 tunnels |
| North Luzon Railway System project (phase 1) | Caloocan (north Metro Manila)–Clark international airport, Philippines | 82 | 2013? | To accelerate development of central Luzon |
| **railways (high speed)** | | **length (km)** | | |
| Turkish High-Speed | Ankara–Istanbul | 533 | 2013 | To connect capital with largest city; 212-km Ankara–Konya section inaugurated 23 Aug. 2011 |
| Illinois High-Speed | Chicago–St. Louis | 460 | 2015? | To cut travel time between Chicago and St. Louis by one-third |
| Haramain High Speed Rail Project (phase II) | Mecca–Medina, Saudi Arabia | 444 | 2013? | To connect the holy cities of Mecca and Medina with Jeddah and King Abdullah Economic City in Rabigh |

## Notable Civil Engineering Projects (in progress or completed as of July 2012) (continued)

| NAME | LOCATION | YEAR OF COMPLETION | NOTES |
|---|---|---|---|
| **subways/metros/light rails** | **length (km)** | | |
| Namma Metro (Phase I) | Bangalore (Bengaluru), India | 42.3 | 2013 | 2 lines to be built |
| Circle MRT | Singapore | 35.7 | 2012 | To be longest fully automated metro in the world |
| Tel Aviv Mass Transit (Red Line) | Petah Tikva–Bat Yam (suburban Tel Aviv) | 22.5 | 2017 | To be Tel Aviv's first subway system; will link north and south suburbs through downtown |
| **tunnels** | **length (m)** | | |
| Brenner Base Tunnel | Innsbruck, Austria–Fortezza, Italy | 55,392 | 2015 | To be the longest underground railway tunnel in the world; more than 19 km of tunnel had been completed by year-end 2011 |
| Alimineti Madhava Reddy Project | Krishna River to Nalgonda district, Andhra Pradesh state, India | 43,500 | 2012 | To provide irrigation and drinking water to drought-prone Nalgonda; will be the world's longest tunnel without intermediate access |
| Bay Tunnel Project | Menlo Park–Newark CA | 8,047 | 2015 | To replace San Francisco-area water system and make it quake resistant |

*1 m=3.28 ft; 1 km=0.62 mi*

---

**Did you know?**

Several famous people have had newly discovered plants or animals named after them in recent years. Beyoncé Knowles inspired the name of a new Australian horsefly, *Scaptia (Plinthina) beyonceae* in 2012. The previous year the children's cartoon character SpongeBob SquarePants lent his name to *Spongiforma squarepantsii*, a Bornean mushroom species. Reggae pioneer Bob Marley received a posthumous honor in July 2012 with the naming of a new crustacean, *Gnathia marleyi*, weeks after Britain's Prince Charles was honored for his environmental work with the naming of an Ecuadoran frog, *Hyloscirtus princecharlesi*.

---

# Life on Earth
## Taxonomy

**T**axonomy is the classification of living and extinct organisms. The term is derived from the Greek *taxis* ("arrangement") and *nomos* ("law") and refers to the methodology and principles of systematic botany and zoology by which the various kinds of plants and animals are arranged in hierarchies of superior and subordinate groups.

Popularly, classifications of living organisms arise according to need and are often superficial; for example, although the term fish is common to the names shellfish, crayfish, and starfish, there are more anatomical differences between a shellfish and a starfish than there are between a bony fish and a human. Also, vernacular names vary widely. Biologists have attempted to view all living organisms with equal thoroughness and thus have devised a formal classification. A formal classification supports a relatively uniform and internationally understood nomenclature, thereby simplifying cross-referencing and retrieval of information.

Carolus Linnaeus, who is usually regarded as the founder of modern taxonomy and whose books are considered the beginning of modern botanical and zoological nomenclature, drew up rules for assigning names to plants and animals and was the first to use binomial nomenclature consistently, beginning in 1758. Classification since Linnaeus has incorporated newly discovered information and more closely approaches a natural system, and the process of clarifying relationships continues to this day. The table below shows the seven ranks that are accepted as obligatory by zoologists and botanists and sample listings for animals and plants.

| | ANIMALS | PLANTS |
|---|---|---|
| Kingdom | Animalia | Plantae |
| Phylum/Division | Chordata | Tracheophyta |
| Class | Mammalia | Pteropsida |
| Order | Primates | Coniferales |

## Taxonomy (continued)

| | ANIMALS | PLANTS |
|---|---|---|
| Family | Hominidae | Pinaceae |
| Genus | Homo | Pinus |
| Species | Homo sapiens (human) | Pinus strobus (white pine) |

## Names of the Male, Female, Young, and Group of Selected Animals

| ANIMAL | MALE | FEMALE | YOUNG | GROUP |
|---|---|---|---|---|
| ape | male | female | baby | shrewdness |
| bear | boar | sow | cub | sleuth, sloth |
| deer | buck, stag | doe | fawn | herd |
| donkey | jack, jackass | jennet, jenny | colt, foal | drove, herd |
| ferret | hob | jill | kit | business, fesynes |
| fox | reynard | vixen | kit, cub, pup | skulk, leash |
| giraffe | bull | doe | calf | herd, corps, tower |
| hamster | buck | doe | pup | horde |
| hippopotamus | bull | cow | calf | herd, bloat |
| horse | stallion, stud | mare, dam | foal, colt (male), filly (female) | stable, harras, herd, team (working) string or field (racing) |
| human | man | woman | baby, infant, toddler | clan (related), crowd, family (closely related), community, tribe |
| lion | lion | lioness | cub | pride |
| mouse | buck | doe | pup, pinkie, kitten | horde, mischief |
| pig | boar | sow | piglet, shoat, farrow | drove, herd, litter (of pups), sounder |
| quail | cock | hen | chick | bevy, covey, drift |
| rhinoceros | bull | cow | calf | crash |
| seal | bull | cow | pup | herd, pod, rookery, harem |
| sheep | buck, ram | ewe, dam | lamb, lambkin, cosset | drift, drove, flock, herd, mob, trip |
| turkey | tom | hen | poult | rafter |
| whale | bull | cow | calf | gam, grind, herd, pod, school |

## Forests of the World

*This table shows the 20 countries or dependencies that lost the most forest area between 1995 and 2010 and those that gained the most, as well as forest losses or gains by continent. 1 hectare (ha) = .01 sq km, .004 sq mi.*  Source: State of the World's Forests 2011. **Web site:** <www.fao.org/forestry>.

| COUNTRY/AREA | LAND AREA ('000 HA) | TOTAL FOREST IN 1995 ('000 HA) | TOTAL FOREST IN 2010 ('000 HA) | PERCENTAGE OF LAND AREA IN 2010 (%) | % CHANGE 1995–2010 |
|---|---|---|---|---|---|
| Togo | 5,439 | 1,245 | 287 | 5.3 | −76.95 |
| Djibouti | 2,318 | 22 | 6 | 0.3 | −72.73 |
| Kazakhstan[1] | 269,970 | 10,504 | 3,309 | 1.2 | −68.50 |
| Comoros | 186 | 9 | 3 | 1.6 | −66.67 |
| Uzbekistan[1] | 42,540 | 9,119 | 3,276 | 7.7 | −64.08 |
| Mauritania | 103,070 | 556 | 242 | 0.2 | −56.47 |
| Niger | 126,670 | 2,562 | 1,204 | 1.0 | −53.01 |
| Sao Tome and Principe | 96 | 56 | 27 | 28.1 | −51.79 |
| Vanuatu | 1,219 | 900 | 440 | 36.1 | −51.11 |
| Uganda | 19,710 | 6,104 | 2,988 | 15.2 | −51.05 |
| Singapore | 70 | 4 | 2 | 2.9 | −50.00 |
| Libya | 175,954 | 400 | 217 | 0.1 | −45.75 |
| Burundi | 2,568 | 317 | 172 | 6.7 | −45.74 |
| Ghana | 22,754 | 9,022 | 4,940 | 21.7 | −45.24 |
| Nicaragua | 12,034 | 5,560 | 3,114 | 25.9 | −44.00 |
| Namibia | 82,329 | 12,374 | 7,290 | 8.9 | −41.09 |
| Greece | 12,890 | 6,513 | 3,903 | 30.3 | −40.07 |
| Nigeria | 91,077 | 13,780 | 9,041 | 9.9 | −34.39 |
| Belize | 2,281 | 1,962 | 1,393 | 61.1 | −29.00 |
| Albania | 2,740 | 1,046 | 776 | 28.3 | −25.81 |
| Yemen | 52,797 | 9 | 549 | 1.0 | +6,000.00 |
| Seychelles | 46 | 4 | 41 | 89.1 | +925.00 |
| Iraq | 43,737 | 83 | 825 | 1.9 | +893.98 |
| St. Lucia | 61 | 5 | 47 | 77.0 | +840.00 |
| Somalia | 62,734 | 754 | 6,747 | 10.8 | +794.83 |

## Forests of the World (continued)

| COUNTRY/AREA | LAND AREA ('000 HA) | TOTAL FOREST IN 1995 ('000 HA) | TOTAL FOREST IN 2010 ('000 HA) | PERCENTAGE OF LAND AREA IN 2010 (%) | % CHANGE 1995–2010 |
|---|---|---|---|---|---|
| Lesotho | 3,036 | 6 | 44 | 1.4 | +633.33 |
| Iran | 162,855 | 1,544 | 11,075 | 6.8 | +617.29 |
| Eritrea | 10,100 | 282 | 1,532 | 15.2 | +443.26 |
| United Arab Emirates | 8,360 | 60 | 317 | 3.8 | +428.33 |
| Gambia | 1,000 | 91 | 480 | 48.0 | +427.47 |
| Haiti | 2,756 | 21 | 101 | 3.7 | +380.95 |
| Saudi Arabia | 214,969 | 222 | 977 | 0.5 | +340.09 |
| Grenada | 34 | 4 | 17 | 50.0 | +325.00 |
| Swaziland | 1,720 | 146 | 563 | 32.7 | +285.62 |
| Australia | 768,230 | 40,908 | 149,300 | 19.4 | +264.97 |
| Bahamas | 1,001 | 158 | 515 | 51.4 | +225.95 |
| Niue | 26 | 6 | 19 | 73.1 | +216.67 |
| Mauritius | 203 | 12 | 35 | 17.2 | +191.67 |
| El Salvador | 2,072 | 105 | 287 | 13.9 | +173.33 |
| Iceland | 10,025 | 11 | 30 | 0.3 | +172.73 |
| South America | 1,756,239 | 870,594 | 864,351 | 49.2 | −0.72 |
| Europe | 2,213,507 | 145,988 | 1,005,001 | 45.4 | +588.41 |
| Oceania | 848,655 | 90,695 | 191,384 | 22.6 | +110.02 |
| North and Central America | 2,132,999 | 536,529 | 705,393 | 33.1 | +31.47 |
| Africa | 2,964,388 | 520,237 | 674,419 | 22.8 | +29.64 |
| Asia | 3,093,763 | 474,172 | 592,512 | 19.2 | +24.96 |
| World | 13,009,550 | 3,454,382 | 4,033,060 | 31.0 | +16.75 |

[1]Was a part of the USSR in 1995 but is now an independent country.

# Geology

## The Continents

*Figures given are approximate. Area and population as of 2011. Highest and lowest points listed are all given in relation to sea level.*

| CONTINENT | POPULATION | AREA | % OF TOTAL LAND AREA[1] | HIGHEST/LOWEST POINT |
|---|---|---|---|---|
| Africa | 1,050,581,000 | 30,171,372 sq km 11,649,228 sq mi | 20.1 | Mt. Kilimanjaro (Tanzania): 5,895 m (19,340 ft) Lake Assal (Djibouti): −157 m (−515 ft) |
| Antarctica | N/A | 14,200,000 sq km 5,500,000 sq mi | 9.5 | Vinson Massif: 4,892 m (16,050 ft) Bentley Subglacial Trench: −2,500 m (−8,200 ft) |
| Asia | 4,174,999,000 | 31,846,885 sq km 12,296,185 sq mi | 21.2 | Mt. Everest (China/Nepal): 8,850 m (29,035 ft) Dead Sea (Israel/Jordan): −400 m (−1,312 ft) |
| Europe | 740,914,300 | 23,064,078 sq km 8,905,139 sq mi | 15.4 | Mont Blanc (France/Italy/Switzerland); 4,807 m (15,771 ft) Caspian Sea (Russia): −27 m (−90 ft) |
| North America | 546,209,900 | 24,396,779 sq km 9,419,650 sq mi | 16.2 | Mt. McKinley (Alaska): 6,194 m (20,320 ft) Death Valley (California): −86 m (−282 ft) |
| Australia (and Oceania) | 36,314,100 | 8,525,389 sq km 3,291,672 sq mi | 5.7 | Jaya Peak (Indonesia): 5,030 m (16,500 ft) Lake Eyre (Australia): −15 m (−50 ft) |
| South America | 389,967,500 | 17,808,893 sq km 6,876,050 sq mi | 11.9 | Mt. Aconcagua (Argentina/Chile): 6,959 m (22,834 ft) Valdés Peninsula (Argentina): −40 m (−131 ft) |

[1]Together, the continents make up about 29.2% of the Earth's surface.

# Geologic Time Scale

| Eon | Era | Period | Epoch | Age | mya[1] |
|---|---|---|---|---|---|
| Phanerozoic | Cenozoic | Quaternary | Holocene | Tarantian | 0.0117 |
| | | | Pleistocene | "Ionian" | 0.126 |
| | | | | Calabrian | 0.781 |
| | | | | Gelasian | 1.806 |
| | | Neogene | Pliocene | Piacenzian | 2.588 |
| | | | | Zanclean | 3.600 |
| | | | Miocene | Messinian | 5.332 |
| | | | | Tortonian | 7.246 |
| | | | | Serravallian | 11.608 |
| | | | | Langhian | 13.82 |
| | | | | Burdigalian | 15.97 |
| | | | | Aquitanian | 20.43 |
| | | Paleogene | Oligocene | Chattian | 23.03 |
| | | | | Rupelian | 28.4 ± 0.1 |
| | | | Eocene | Priabonian | 33.9 ± 0.1 |
| | | | | Bartonian | 37.2 ± 0.1 |
| | | | | Lutetian | 40.4 ± 0.2 |
| | | | | Ypresian | 48.6 ± 0.2 |
| | | | Paleocene | Thanetian | 55.8 ± 0.2 |
| | | | | Selandian | 58.7 ± 0.2 |
| | | | | Danian | ~61.1 |
| | Mesozoic | Cretaceous | Upper | Maastrichtian | 65.5 ± 0.3 |
| | | | | Campanian | 70.6 ± 0.6 |
| | | | | Santonian | 83.5 ± 0.7 |
| | | | | Coniacian | 85.8 ± 0.7 |
| | | | | Turonian | ~88.6 |
| | | | | Cenomanian | 93.6 ± 0.8 |
| | | | Lower | Albian | 99.6 ± 0.9 |
| | | | | Aptian | 112.0 ± 1.0 |
| | | | | Barremian | 125.0 ± 1.0 |
| | | | | Hauterivian | 130.0 ± 1.5 |
| | | | | Valanginian | ~133.9 |
| | | | | Berriasian | 140.2 ± 3.0 |

| Eon | Era | Period | Epoch | Age | mya[1] |
|---|---|---|---|---|---|
| Phanerozoic | Mesozoic | Jurassic | Upper | Tithonian | 145.5 ± 4.0 |
| | | | | Kimmeridgian | 150.8 ± 4.0 |
| | | | | Oxfordian | ~155.6 |
| | | | Middle | Callovian | 161.2 ± 4.0 |
| | | | | Bathonian | 164.7 ± 4.0 |
| | | | | Bajocian | 167.7 ± 3.5 |
| | | | | Aalenian | 171.6 ± 3.0 |
| | | | Lower | Toarcian | 175.6 ± 2.0 |
| | | | | Pliensbachian | 183.0 ± 1.5 |
| | | | | Sinemurian | 189.6 ± 1.5 |
| | | | | Hettangian | 196.5 ± 1.0 |
| | | Triassic | Upper | Rhaetian | 199.6 ± 0.6 |
| | | | | Norian | 203.6 ± 1.5 |
| | | | | Carnian | 216.5 ± 2.0 |
| | | | Middle | Ladinian | ~228.7 |
| | | | | Anisian | 237.0 ± 2.0 |
| | | | Lower | Olenekian | ~245.9 |
| | | | | Induan | ~249.5 |
| | Paleozoic | Permian | Lopingian | Changhsingian | 251.0 ± 0.4 |
| | | | | Wuchiapingian | 253.8 ± 0.7 |
| | | | Guadalupian | Capitanian | 260.4 ± 0.7 |
| | | | | Wordian | 265.8 ± 0.7 |
| | | | | Roadian | 268.0 ± 0.7 |
| | | | Cisuralian | Kungurian | 270.6 ± 0.7 |
| | | | | Artinskian | 275.6 ± 0.7 |
| | | | | Sakmarian | 284.4 ± 0.7 |
| | | | | Asselian | 294.6 ± 0.8 |
| | | Carboniferous | Pennsylvanian[2] Upper | Gzhelian | 299.0 ± 0.8 |
| | | | | Kasimovian | 303.4 ± 0.9 |
| | | | Pennsylvanian[2] Middle | Moscovian | 307.2 ± 1.0 |
| | | | Pennsylvanian[2] Lower | Bashkirian | 311.7 ± 1.1 |
| | | | Mississippian[2] Upper | Serpukhovian | 318.1 ± 1.3 |
| | | | Mississippian[2] Middle | Visean | 328.3 ± 1.6 |
| | | | Mississippian[2] Lower | Tournaisian | 345.3 ± 2.1 |

| Eon | Era | Period | Epoch | Age | mya[1] |
|---|---|---|---|---|---|
| Phanerozoic | Paleozoic | Devonian | Upper | Famennian | 359.2 ± 2.5 |
| | | | | Frasnian | 374.5 ± 2.6 |
| | | | Middle | Givetian | 385.3 ± 2.6 |
| | | | | Eifelian | 391.8 ± 2.7 |
| | | | Lower | Emsian | 397.5 ± 2.7 |
| | | | | Pragian | 407.0 ± 2.8 |
| | | | | Lochkovian | 411.2 ± 2.8 |
| | | Silurian | Pridoli | | 416.0 ± 2.8 |
| | | | Ludlow | Ludfordian | 418.7 ± 2.7 |
| | | | | Gorstian | 421.3 ± 2.6 |
| | | | Wenlock | Homerian | 422.9 ± 2.5 |
| | | | | Sheinwoodian | 426.2 ± 2.4 |
| | | | Llandovery | Telychian | 428.2 ± 2.3 |
| | | | | Aeronian | 436.0 ± 1.9 |
| | | | | Rhuddanian | 439.0 ± 1.8 |
| | | Ordovician | Upper | Hirnantian | 443.7 ± 1.5 |
| | | | | Katian | 445.6 ± 1.5 |
| | | | | Sandbian | 455.8 ± 1.6 |
| | | | Middle | Darriwilian | 460.9 ± 1.6 |
| | | | | Dapingian | 468.1 ± 1.6 |
| | | | Lower | Floian | 471.8 ± 1.6 |
| | | | | Tremadocian | 478.6 ± 1.7 |
| | | Cambrian[3] | Furongian | Stage 10 | 488.3 ± 1.7 |
| | | | | Stage 9 | ~492.0 |
| | | | | Paibian | ~496.0 |
| | | | Series 3 | Guzhangian | ~499.0 |
| | | | | Drumian | ~503.0 |
| | | | | Stage 5 | ~506.5 |
| | | | Series 2 | Stage 4 | ~510.0 |
| | | | | Stage 3 | ~515.0 |
| | | | Terreneuwian | Stage 2 | ~521.0 |
| | | | | Fortunian | ~528.0 |

| Eon | Era | Period | mya[1] |
|---|---|---|---|
| Proterozoic | Neoproterozoic | Ediacaran | 542.0 |
| | | Cryogenian | ~635.0 |
| | | Tonian | 850.0 |
| | Mesoproterozoic | Stenian | 1,000.0 |
| | | Ectasian | 1,200.0 |
| | | Calymmian | 1,400.0 |
| | Paleoproterozoic | Statherian | 1,600.0 |
| | | Orosirian | 1,800.0 |
| | | Rhyacian | 2,050.0 |
| | | Siderian | 2,300.0 |
| Archean | Neoarchean | | 2,500.0 |
| | Mesoarchean | | 2,800.0 |
| | Paleoarchean | | 3,200.0 |
| | Eoarchean | | 3,600.0 |
| | Hadean (informal) | | 4,000.0 |
| | | | 4,600.0 |

(Precambrian spans the Proterozoic, Archean, and Hadean (informal).)

[1] Millions of years ago.
[2] Both the Mississippian and Pennsylvanian time units are formally designated as subperiods within the Carboniferous Period.
[3] Several Cambrian unit age boundaries are informal and are awaiting ratified definitions.

Published with permission from the International Commission on Stratigraphy (ICS). International chronostratigraphic units, ranks, names, and formal status are approved by the ICS and ratified by the International Union of Geological Sciences (IUGS).
Source: 2009 International Stratigraphic Chart produced by the ICS.

# Geography

## Largest Islands of the World

| NAME AND LOCATION | REGION | AREA[1] | |
| | | SQ MI | SQ KM |
| --- | --- | --- | --- |
| Greenland | North America | 836,330 | 2,166,086 |
| New Guinea, Papua New Guinea/Indonesia | Oceania | 309,000 | 800,000 |
| Borneo, Indonesia/Malaysia/Brunei | Asia | 292,000 | 755,000 |
| Madagascar | Africa | 226,662 | 587,051 |
| Baffin, Nunavut, Canada | North America | 195,928 | 507,451 |
| Sumatra, Indonesia | Asia | 170,233 | 446,687 |
| Great Britain, UK | Europe | 88,394 | 228,938 |
| Honshu, Japan | Asia | 87,992 | 227,898 |
| Victoria, Northwest Territories/Nunavut, Canada | North America | 83,896 | 217,291 |
| Ellesmere, Nunavut, Canada | North America | 75,767 | 196,236 |
| Celebes, Indonesia | Asia | 74,845 | 193,847 |
| South Island, New Zealand | Oceania | 58,776 | 152,229 |
| Java, Indonesia | Asia | 49,926 | 129,307 |
| North Island, New Zealand | Oceania | 44,872 | 116,219 |
| Cuba | North America | 42,427 | 109,886 |
| Newfoundland, Canada | North America | 42,031 | 108,860 |
| Luzon, Philippines | Asia | 40,420 | 104,688 |
| Iceland | Europe | 39,769 | 103,000 |
| Mindanao, Philippines | Asia | 36,537 | 94,630 |
| Ireland, Ireland/UK | Europe | 32,590 | 84,408 |

[1]Area given may include small adjoining islands. Conversions for rounded figures may be rounded to the nearest hundred.

## Highest Mountains of the World by Region

*"I" in the name of a peak refers to the highest in a group of numbered peaks of the same name.*

| NAME AND LOCATION | HEIGHT IN M | HEIGHT IN FT | YEAR FIRST CLIMBED |
| --- | --- | --- | --- |
| **Africa** | | | |
| Kilimanjaro (Kibo peak), Tanzania | 5,895 | 19,340 | 1889 |
| Kenya (Batian peak), Kenya | 5,199 | 17,058 | 1899 |
| Margherita, Ruwenzori Range, Dem. Rep. of the Congo/Uganda | 5,119 | 16,795 | 1906 |
| Ras Dejen, Simen Mtns., Ethiopia | 4,533 | 14,872 | 1841 |
| **Antarctica** | | | |
| Vinson Massif, Sentinel Range, Ellsworth Mtns. | 4,897 | 16,066 | 1966 |
| Tyree, Sentinel Range, Ellsworth Mtns. | 4,852 | 15,919 | 1967 |
| Shinn, Sentinel Range, Ellsworth Mtns. | 4,801 | 15,751 | 1966 |
| Gardner, Sentinel Range, Ellsworth Mtns. | 4,573 | 15,003 | 1966 |
| **Asia** | | | |
| Everest (Chomolungma), Himalayas, China/Nepal | 8,848 | 29,028 | 1953 |
| K2 (Godwin Austen) (Chogori), Karakoram Range, Pakistan/China | 8,611 | 28,251 | 1954 |
| Kanchenjunga I, Himalayas, Nepal/India | 8,586 | 28,169 | 1955 |
| Lhotse I, Himalayas, Nepal/China | 8,516 | 27,940 | 1956 |
| **Caucasus** | | | |
| Elbrus, Russia | 5,642 | 18,510 | 1874 |
| Dykhtau, Russia | 5,204 | 17,073 | 1888 |
| Koshtantau, Russia | 5,151 | 16,900 | 1889 |
| Shkhara, Russia/Georgia | 5,068 | 16,627 | 1888 |
| **Europe** | | | |
| Mont Blanc, Alps, France/Italy/Switzerland | 4,807 | 15,771 | 1786 |
| Dufourspitze, Monte Rosa Massif, Alps, Switzerland/Italy | 4,634 | 15,203 | 1855 |
| Dom (Mischabel), Alps, Switzerland | 4,545 | 14,911 | 1858 |
| Weisshorn, Alps, Switzerland | 4,505 | 14,780 | 1861 |

## Highest Mountains of the World by Region (continued)

| NAME AND LOCATION | HEIGHT IN M | HEIGHT IN FT | YEAR FIRST CLIMBED |
|---|---|---|---|
| **North America** | | | |
| McKinley, Alaska Range, Alaska | 6,194 | 20,320 | 1913 |
| Logan, St. Elias Mtns., Yukon, Canada | 5,951 | 19,524 | 1925 |
| Citlaltépetl (Orizaba), Cordillera Neo-Volcánica, Mexico | 5,610 | 18,406 | 1848 |
| St. Elias, St. Elias Mtns., Alaska/Canada | 5,489 | 18,008 | 1897 |
| | | | |
| **Oceania** | | | |
| Jaya (Sukarno) (Carstensz), Sudirman Range, Indonesia | 5,030 | 16,500[1] | 1962 |
| Pilimsit (Idenburg), Sudirman Range, Indonesia | 4,800 | 15,750[1] | 1962 |
| Trikora (Wilhelmina), Jayawijaya Mtns., Indonesia | 4,750 | 15,580[1] | 1912 |
| Mandala (Juliana), Jayawijaya Mtns., Indonesia | 4,700 | 15,420[1] | 1959 |
| | | | |
| **South America** | | | |
| Aconcagua, Andes, Argentina/Chile | 6,959 | 22,831 | 1897 |
| Ojos del Salado, Andes, Argentina/Chile | 6,893 | 22,615 | 1937 |
| Bonete, Andes, Argentina | 6,872 | 22,546 | 1913 |
| Mercedario, Andes, Argentina/Chile | 6,770 | 22,211 | 1934 |

[1]Conversions rounded to the nearest 10 ft.

## Major Caves and Cave Systems of the World by Continent

*Source: Bob Gulden, National Speleological Society.*

| NAME AND LOCATION | DEPTH[1] | | LENGTH[2] | |
|---|---|---|---|---|
| | FT | M | MI | KM |
| **Africa** | | | | |
| Ifflis, Algeria | 3,839 | 1,170 | 1.2 | 2.0 |
| Boussouil, Algeria | 2,641 | 805 | 2.0 | 3.2 |
| Tafna (Bou Ma'za), Algeria | N/A | N/A | 11.4 | 18.4 |
| Tamdoun, Morocco | N/A | N/A | 11.4 | 18.4 |
| | | | | |
| **Asia** | | | | |
| Krubera, Georgia | 7,188 | 2,191 | 8.2 | 13.2 |
| Sarma, Georgia | 5,774 | 1,760 | 4.0 | 6.4 |
| Air Jernih, Malaysia | 1,165 | 355 | 117.5 | 189.1 |
| Shuanghe Dongqun, China | 1,946 | 593 | 79.5 | 128.0 |
| | | | | |
| **Australia (and Oceania)** | | | | |
| Neide-Muruk, Papua New Guinea | 4,127 | 1,258 | 10.6 | 17.0 |
| Ellis, New Zealand | 3,366 | 1,026 | 20.8 | 33.4 |
| Bullita, Northern Territory, Australia | 75 | 23 | 74.8 | 120.4 |
| Bulmer, New Zealand | 2,477 | 755 | 41.0 | 66.0 |
| | | | | |
| **Europe** | | | | |
| Lamprechtsofen Vogelschacht, Austria | 5,354 | 1,632 | 23.6 | 38.0 |
| Gouffre Mirolda–Lucien Bouclier, France | 5,335 | 1,626 | 8.1 | 13.0 |
| Optimisticheskaya, Ukraine | 49 | 15 | 144.2 | 232.0 |
| Hölloch, Switzerland | 3,079 | 939 | 123.2 | 198.2 |
| | | | | |
| **North America** | | | | |
| Cuicateco, Mexico | 4,869 | 1,484 | 16.3 | 26.2 |
| Huautla, Mexico | 4,839 | 1,475 | 38.6 | 62.1 |
| Mammoth–Flint Ridge, Kentucky | 379 | 116 | 390.0 | 627.6 |
| Jewel, South Dakota | 632 | 193 | 157.4 | 253.2 |
| | | | | |
| **South America** | | | | |
| Collet, Brazil | 2,201 | 671 | N/A | N/A |
| Pumacocha, Peru | 2,093 | 638 | N/A | N/A |
| Boa Vista, Brazil | 164 | 50 | 63.7 | 102.5 |
| Barriguda, Brazil | 200 | 61 | 18.6 | 30.0 |

[1]Below highest entrance.     [2]Explored portion of cave.

## Major Deserts of the World by Continent

| NAME AND LOCATION | AREA | | NAME AND LOCATION | AREA | |
|---|---|---|---|---|---|
| | SQ KM | SQ MI | | SQ KM | SQ MI |
| **Africa** | | | **Australia (continued)** | | |
| Sahara, northern Africa | 8,600,000 | 3,320,000 | Great Sandy, northern Western Australia | 400,000 | 150,000 |
| Kalahari, southwestern Africa | 930,000 | 360,000 | Gibson, Western Australia | 156,000 | 60,000 |
| Namib, southwestern Africa | 135,000 | 52,000 | Simpson, Northern Territory | 143,000 | 55,000 |
| Libyan, Libya, Egypt, and Sudan | N/A | N/A | **North America** | | |
| | | | Great Basin, southwestern US | 492,000 | 190,000 |
| **Asia** | | | Chihuahuan, northern Mexico | 450,000 | 175,000 |
| Arabian, southwestern Asia | 2,330,000 | 900,000 | Sonoran, southwestern US and Baja California | 310,800 | 120,000 |
| Gobi, Mongolia and northeastern China | 1,300,000 | 500,000 | Mojave, southwestern US | 65,000 | 25,000 |
| Rubʻ al-Khali, southern Arabian Peninsula | 650,000 | 250,000 | **South America** | | |
| Karakum, Turkmenistan | 350,000 | 135,000 | Patagonian, southern Argentina | 673,000 | 260,000 |
| **Australia** | | | Atacama, northern Chile | 140,000 | 54,000 |
| Great Victoria, Western and South Australia | 647,000 | 250,000 | | | |

## Major Volcanoes of the World by Continent

| NAME AND LOCATION | ELEVATION | | FIRST RECORDED ERUPTION | MOST RECENT ERUPTION |
|---|---|---|---|---|
| | M | FT | | |
| **Africa** | | | | |
| Kilimanjaro, Tanzania[1] | 5,895 | 19,340 | N/A | N/A |
| Teide (Tenerife), Canary Islands | 3,715 | 12,188 | N/A | 1909 |
| Nyiragongo, Democratic Republic of the Congo | 3,470 | 11,384 | 1884 | 2011 |
| Nyamulagira, Democratic Republic of the Congo | 3,058 | 10,033 | 1865 | 2012 |
| **Antarctica** | | | | |
| Erebus, Ross Island | 3,794 | 12,447 | 1841 | 2011 |
| Melbourne, Victoria Land | 2,732 | 8,963 | N/A | c. 1750 |
| Belinda, Montagu Island | 1,370 | 4,495 | N/A | 2007 |
| Darnley, Sandwich Islands | 1,100 | 3,609 | 1823 | 1956 |
| **Asia and Australia (and Oceania)** | | | | |
| Klyuchevskaya, Kamchatka, Russia | 4,835 | 15,863 | 1697 | 2011 |
| Mauna Kea, Hawaii | 4,205 | 13,796 | N/A | c. 2460 BC |
| Mauna Loa, Hawaii | 4,170 | 13,681 | N/A | 1984 |
| Kerinci, Sumatra, Indonesia | 3,800 | 12,467 | 1838 | 2009 |
| **Europe** | | | | |
| Etna, Italy | 3,350 | 10,991 | N/A | 2012 |
| Eyjafjallajökull, Iceland | 1,666 | 5,466 | 920 | 2010 |
| Hekla, Iceland | 1,491 | 4,892 | 1104 | 2000 |
| Vesuvius, Italy | 1,281 | 4,203 | 79 | 1944 |
| **North America** | | | | |
| Pico de Orizaba (Citlaltépetl), Mexico | 5,675 | 18,619 | N/A | 1846 |
| Popocatépetl, Mexico | 5,426 | 17,802 | 1345 | 2012 |
| Rainier, Washington | 4,392 | 14,409 | N/A | 1894 |
| Shasta, California | 4,317 | 14,162 | 1786 | 1786 |
| **South America** | | | | |
| Guallatiri, Chile | 6,071 | 19,918 | 1825 | 1960 |
| Tupungatito, Chile | 6,000 | 19,685 | 1829 | 1987 |
| Cotopaxi, Ecuador | 5,911 | 19,393 | 1532 | 1940 |
| Láscar, Chile | 5,592 | 18,346 | 1848 | 2007 |

[1]Includes three dormant volcanoes (Kibo, Mawensi, and Shira) that have not erupted in historic times.

## Oceans and Seas

Earth is generally recognized to contain five major oceans: the Pacific, Atlantic, Indian, Arctic, and Southern oceans. The boundaries of each ocean are largely defined by the continents that frame them. The southern portions of the Pacific, Atlantic, and Indian oceans and their tributary seas that surround Antarctica are often referred to as the Southern Ocean. However, water properties, ocean currents, and biological populations are not constrained by these boundaries. Indeed, many researchers do not recognize them either.

The surface areas and volumes of water contained in the oceans and major marginal seas are shown in the table. Figures for the Southern Ocean are not included, however, because no official boundaries exist at present.

| | AREA | | VOLUME | |
|---|---|---|---|---|
| | SQ KM | SQ MI | CU KM | CU MI |
| **Pacific Ocean** | | | | |
| without marginal seas | 165,250,000 | 63,800,000 | 707,600,000 | 169,900,000 |
| with marginal seas | 179,680,000 | 69,370,000 | 723,700,000 | 173,700,000 |
| **Atlantic Ocean** | | | | |
| without marginal seas | 82,440,000 | 31,830,000 | 324,600,000 | 77,900,000 |
| with marginal seas | 106,460,000 | 41,100,000 | 354,700,000 | 85,200,000 |
| **Indian Ocean** | | | | |
| without marginal seas | 73,440,000 | 28,360,000 | 291,000,000 | 69,900,000 |
| with marginal seas | 74,920,000 | 28,930,000 | 291,900,000 | 70,100,000 |
| **Arctic Ocean** | 14,090,000 | 5,440,000 | 17,000,000 | 4,100,000 |
| Gulf of Mexico and Caribbean Sea | 4,320,000 | 1,670,000 | 9,600,000 | 2,300,000 |
| Mediterranean and Black Seas | 2,970,000 | 1,150,000 | 4,200,000 | 1,000,000 |
| Bering Sea | 2,304,000 | 890,000 | 3,330,000 | 800,000 |
| Hudson Bay | 1,230,000 | 470,000 | 160,000 | 40,000 |
| North Sea | 570,000 | 220,000 | 50,000 | 10,000 |
| Baltic Sea | 420,000 | 160,000 | 20,000 | 5,000 |
| Irish Sea | 100,000 | 40,000 | 6,000 | 1,000 |
| English Channel | 75,000 | 29,000 | 4,000 | 1,000 |

| | AVERAGE DEPTH | | |
|---|---|---|---|
| | M | FT | DEEPEST POINT |
| **Pacific Ocean** | | | |
| without marginal seas | 4,280 | 14,040 | Mariana Trench |
| with marginal seas | 4,030 | 13,220 | (11,034 m; 36,201 ft) |
| **Atlantic Ocean** | | | |
| without marginal seas | 3,930 | 12,890 | Puerto Rico Trench |
| with marginal seas | 3,330 | 10,920 | (8,380 m; 27,493 ft) |
| **Indian Ocean** | | | |
| without marginal seas | 3,960 | 12,990 | Sunda Deep of the Java |
| with marginal seas | 3,900 | 12,790 | Trench (7,450 m; 24,442 ft) |
| **Arctic Ocean** | 1,205 | 3,950 | (5,502 m; 18,050 ft) |
| Gulf of Mexico and Caribbean Sea | 2,220 | 7,280 | Cayman Trench (7,686 m; 25,216 ft) |
| Mediterranean and Black Seas | 1,430 | 4,690 | Ionian Basin (4,900 m; 16,000 ft) |
| Bering Sea | 1,440 | 4,720 | Bowers Basin (4,097 m; 13,442 ft) |
| Hudson Bay | 128 | 420 | (867 m; 2,846 ft) |
| North Sea | 94 | 310 | Skagerrak (700 m; 2,300 ft) |
| Baltic Sea | 55 | 180 | Landsort Deep (459 m; 1,506 ft) |
| Irish Sea | 60 | 200 | Mull of Galloway (175 m; 576 ft) |
| English Channel | 54 | 180 | Hurd Deep (172 m; 565 ft) |

## Major Natural Lakes of the World

*Conversions for figures may have been rounded, thousands to the nearest hundred and hundreds to the nearest ten.*

| NAME | LOCATION | AREA SQ MI | AREA SQ KM | NAME | LOCATION | AREA SQ MI | AREA SQ KM |
|---|---|---|---|---|---|---|---|
| Caspian Sea | Central Asia | 149,200 | 386,400 | Tanganyika | eastern Africa | 12,700 | 32,900 |
| Superior | Canada/US | 31,700 | 82,100 | Great Bear | Canada | 12,096 | 31,328 |
| Victoria | eastern Africa | 26,828 | 69,484 | Nyasa (Malawi) | eastern Africa | 11,430 | 29,604 |
| Huron | Canada/US | 23,000 | 59,600 | Great Slave | Canada | 11,030 | 28,568 |
| Michigan | US | 22,300 | 57,800 | Erie | Canada/US | 9,910 | 25,667 |

## Longest Rivers of the World by Continent

*This list includes both rivers and river systems. Conversions of rounded figures may be rounded to the nearest 10 or 100 miles or kilometers.*

| NAME | OUTFLOW | LENGTH | |
| | | MI | KM |
| --- | --- | --- | --- |
| **Africa** | | | |
| Nile | Mediterranean Sea | 4,132 | 6,650 |
| Congo | South Atlantic Ocean | 2,900 | 4,700 |
| Niger | Gulf of Guinea | 2,600 | 4,200 |
| Zambezi | Mozambique Channel | 2,200 | 3,540 |
| **Asia** | | | |
| Yangtze | East China Sea | 3,915 | 6,300 |
| Yenisey-Baikal-Selenga | Kara Sea | 3,442 | 5,539 |
| Huang He (Yellow) | Gulf of Chihli | 3,395 | 5,464 |
| Ob-Irtysh | Gulf of Ob | 3,362 | 5,410 |
| **Europe** | | | |
| Volga | Caspian Sea | 2,193 | 3,530 |
| Danube | Black Sea | 1,770 | 2,850 |
| Ural | Caspian Sea | 1,509 | 2,428 |
| Dnieper | Black Sea | 1,367 | 2,200 |
| **North America** | | | |
| Mississippi-Missouri-Jefferson | Gulf of Mexico | 3,710 | 5,971 |
| Mackenzie-Slave-Peace | Beaufort Sea | 2,635 | 4,241 |
| Missouri-Jefferson | Mississippi River | 2,540 | 4,088 |
| St. Lawrence–Great Lakes | Gulf of St. Lawrence | 2,500 | 4,000 |
| **Australia** | | | |
| Darling | Murray River | 1,702 | 2,739 |
| Murray | Great Australian Bight | 1,572 | 2,530 |
| Murrumbidgee | Murray River | 1,050 | 1,690 |
| Lachlan | Murrumbidgee River | 930 | 1,500 |
| **South America** | | | |
| Amazon-Ucayali-Apurímac | South Atlantic Ocean | 4,000 | 6,400 |
| Paraná | Río de la Plata | 3,032 | 4,880 |
| Madeira-Mamoré-Guaporé | Amazon River | 2,082 | 3,352 |
| Juruá | Amazon River | 2,040 | 3,283 |

# Preserving Nature

## US National Parks

*Dates in parentheses indicate when the area was first designated a national park, in most cases under a different name. Web site: <www.nps.gov/parks.html>.*

| PARK | LOCATION | DESIGNATION DATE | SQ MI | SQ KM |
| --- | --- | --- | --- | --- |
| Acadia | Bar Harbor ME | 1929 (1919) | 74 | 192 |
| American Samoa | American Samoa | 1993 | 14 | 36 |
| Arches | Moab UT | 1971 | 120 | 311 |
| Badlands | southwestern South Dakota | 1978 | 379 | 982 |
| Big Bend | curve of the Rio Grande river, Texas | 1944 | 1,252 | 3,243 |
| Biscayne | near Miami FL | 1980 | 270 | 699 |
| Black Canyon of the Gunnison | near Montrose CO | 1999 | 43 | 112 |
| Bryce Canyon | Bryce Canyon, Utah | 1928 (1924) | 56 | 145 |
| Canyonlands | near Moab UT | 1964 | 527 | 1,366 |
| Capitol Reef | near Torrey UT | 1971 | 379 | 982 |
| Carlsbad Caverns | near Carlsbad NM | 1930 | 73 | 189 |
| Channel Islands | Ventura CA | 1980 | 75 | 194 |
| Congaree | Hopkins SC | 2003 | 34 | 88 |
| Crater Lake | Crater Lake OR | 1902 | 286 | 741 |
| Cuyahoga Valley | near Cleveland and Akron OH | 2000 | 51 | 133 |
| Death Valley | Death Valley, California and Nevada | 1994 | 5,219 | 13,518 |
| Denali | central Alaska | 1980 (1917) | 9,492 | 24,584 |
| Dry Tortugas | Key West FL | 1992 | 101 | 262 |
| Everglades | southern Florida | 1947 | 2,358 | 6,107 |

## US National Parks (continued)

| PARK | LOCATION | DESIGNATION DATE | SQ MI | SQ KM |
|------|----------|------------------|-------|-------|
| Gates of the Arctic | Bettles AK | 1980 | 13,238 | 34,287 |
| Glacier | northwest Montana | 1910 | 1,584 | 4,102 |
| Glacier Bay | Gustavus AK | 1980 | 5,130 | 13,287 |
| Grand Canyon | Grand Canyon, Arizona | 1919 | 1,902 | 4,927 |
| Grand Teton | Moose WY | 1950 (1929) | 484 | 1,255 |
| Great Basin | near Baker NV | 1986 | 121 | 313 |
| Great Sand Dunes | Mosca CO | 2004 | 132 | 343 |
| Great Smoky Mountains | Tennessee and North Carolina | 1934 | 815 | 2,110 |
| Guadalupe Mountains | Salt Flat TX | 1972 | 135 | 350 |
| Haleakala | Kula, Maui HI | 1960 (1916) | 47 | 121 |
| Hawaii Volcanoes | near Hilo HI | 1961 (1916) | 328 | 849 |
| Hot Springs | Hot Springs AR | 1921 | 9 | 22 |
| Isle Royale | Houghton MI | 1940 | 893 | 2,314 |
| Joshua Tree | near Palm Springs CA | 1994 | 1,591 | 4,120 |
| Katmai | near King Salmon AK | 1980 | 7,385 | 19,128 |
| Kenai Fjords | Seward AK | 1980 | 1,047 | 2,711 |
| Kings Canyon | near Three Rivers CA | 1940 (1890) | 722 | 1,869 |
| Kobuk Valley | Kotzebue AK | 1980 | 2,672 | 6,920 |
| Lake Clark | Port Alsworth AK | 1980 | 6,297 | 16,309 |
| Lassen Volcanic | Mineral CA | 1916 | 166 | 430 |
| Mammoth Cave | Mammoth Cave, Kentucky | 1941 | 83 | 214 |
| Mesa Verde | near Cortez and Mancos CO | 1906 | 81 | 211 |
| Mount Rainier | near Ashford WA | 1899 | 368 | 954 |
| North Cascades | near Marblemount WA | 1968 | 1,069 | 2,769 |
| Olympic | near Port Angeles WA | 1938 | 1,442 | 3,734 |
| Petrified Forest | Arizona | 1962 | 146 | 379 |
| Redwood | Crescent City CA | 1968 | 172 | 445 |
| Rocky Mountain | near Estes Park and Grand Lake CO | 1915 | 415 | 1,076 |
| Saguaro | Tucson AZ | 1994 | 143 | 370 |
| Sequoia | near Three Rivers CA | 1890 | 631 | 1,635 |
| Shenandoah | near Luray VA | 1935 | 311 | 805 |
| Theodore Roosevelt | Medora ND (south unit); near Watford City ND (north unit) | 1978 (1947) | 110 | 285 |
| Virgin Islands | St. John, US Virgin Islands | 1956 | 23 | 59 |
| Voyageurs | International Falls MN | 1975 | 341 | 883 |
| Wind Cave | near Hot Springs SD | 1903 | 44 | 115 |
| Wolf Trap | Vienna VA | 2002 | 130 acres | |
| Wrangell–St. Elias | near Copper Center AK | 1980 | 20,587 | 53,320 |
| Yellowstone | Idaho, Montana, and Wyoming | 1872 | 3,468 | 8,983 |
| Yosemite | in the Sierra Nevada, California | 1890 | 1,189 | 3,081 |
| Zion | Springdale UT | 1919 | 229 | 593 |

# Health

## Worldwide Health Indicators

*Column data as follows: **Life expectancy** in 2005; **Doctors** = persons per doctor[1]; **Infant mortality** per 1,000 births in 2005; **Water** = percentage (%) of population with access to safe drinking water in 2004; **Food** = percentage (%) of the FAO recommended minimum in 2004[2].*

| REGION/BLOC | LIFE EXPECTANCY | | DOCTORS | INFANT MORTALITY | WATER | FOOD |
|-------------|------|--------|---------|-----------|-------|------|
| | MALE | FEMALE | | | | |
| **World** | **66.0** | **70.0** | **730** | **38.3** | **83** | **118** |
| | | | | | | |
| **Africa** | **51.8** | **53.8** | **2,560** | **78.4** | **64[3]** | **103** |
| Central Africa | 49.8 | 50.2 | 12,890 | 96.1 | 46[3] | 80 |
| East Africa | 46.9 | 48.2 | 13,620 | 86.7 | 50[3] | 86 |
| North Africa | 67.2 | 71.0 | 890 | 39.2 | 91 | 125 |
| Southern Africa | 47.8 | 51.2 | 1,610 | 55.1 | 85[3] | 119 |
| West Africa | 47.7 | 49.7 | 6,260 | 94.3 | 65[3] | 109 |
| | | | | | | |
| **Americas** | **71.5** | **77.6** | **520** | **17.1** | **91[3]** | **129** |
| Anglo-America[4] | 75.0 | 80.4 | 370 | 6.2 | 100[3] | 140 |
| Canada | 76.7 | 83.6 | 540 | 4.8 | 100 | 136 |
| United States | 74.8 | 80.1 | 360 | 6.4 | 100 | 141 |

## Worldwide Health Indicators (continued)

| REGION/BLOC | LIFE EXPECTANCY MALE | LIFE EXPECTANCY FEMALE | DOCTORS | INFANT MORTALITY | WATER | FOOD |
|---|---|---|---|---|---|---|
| **Americas (continued)** | | | | | | |
| Latin America | 69.4 | 76.0 | 690 | 23.6 | 91 | 123 |
| Caribbean | 67.5 | 71.6 | 380 | 29.4 | 79[3] | 118 |
| Central America | 67.9 | 73.7 | 950 | 21.4 | 88[3] | 106 |
| Mexico | 72.7 | 77.6 | 810 | 12.6 | 97 | 134 |
| South America | 68.9 | 76.2 | 710 | 26.3 | 86[3] | 122 |
| Andean Group | 69.4 | 75.6 | 830 | 23.5 | 86[3] | 108 |
| Brazil | 67.7 | 75.9 | 770 | 30.7 | 90 | 132 |
| Other South America | 72.1 | 79.4 | 410 | 17.5 | 82[3] | 120 |
| **Asia** | **67.2** | **70.3** | **970** | **39.6** | **81[3]** | **116** |
| Eastern Asia | 71.2 | 75.0 | 610 | 22.3 | 78[5] | 121 |
| China | 70.4 | 73.7 | 620 | 25.2 | 77 | 123 |
| Japan | 78.6 | 85.6 | 530 | 2.7 | 100 | 110 |
| Republic of Korea | 71.7 | 79.3 | 740 | 6.4 | 92 | 123 |
| Other Eastern Asia | 71.7 | 77.3 | 500 | 13.8 | 94[3] | 93 |
| South Asia | 63.3 | 64.6 | 2,100 | 60.5 | 85[6] | 108 |
| India | 63.6 | 65.2 | 1,920 | 56.3 | 86 | 112 |
| Pakistan | 64.7 | 65.5 | 1,840 | 76.2 | 91 | 100 |
| Other South Asia | 60.4 | 60.5 | 5,080 | 71.0 | 85[3] | 97 |
| Southeast Asia | 66.8 | 71.9 | 3,120 | 33.9 | 82 | 123 |
| Southwest Asia | 67.3 | 71.9 | 610 | 35.5 | 85[3] | 118 |
| Central Asia | 61.0 | 68.9 | 330 | 54.0 | 82[3] | 99 |
| Gulf Cooperation Council | 73.4 | 77.5 | 620 | 12.7 | 95[3] | 117 |
| Iran | 68.6 | 71.4 | 1,200 | 41.6 | 94 | 131 |
| Other Southwest Asia | 67.6 | 71.9 | 690 | 31.6 | 82[3] | 119 |
| **Europe** | **71.0** | **79.1** | **300** | **7.2** | **98[3]** | **130** |
| European Union (EU) | 75.5 | 81.8 | 290 | 4.8 | 100[3] | 137 |
| France | 76.7 | 83.8 | 330 | 3.6 | 100 | 142 |
| Germany | 75.8 | 82.0 | 290 | 4.1 | 100 | 131 |
| Italy | 77.6 | 83.2 | 180 | 5.9 | 100[3] | 151 |
| Spain | 76.7 | 83.2 | 240 | 4.4 | 100 | 138 |
| United Kingdom | 75.9 | 81.0 | 720 | 5.1 | 100 | 137 |
| Other EU | 73.6 | 80.3 | 320 | 5.2 | 100[3] | 133 |
| Non-EU[7] | 78.5 | 83.5 | 480 | 3.8 | 100[3] | 131 |
| Eastern Europe | 62.3 | 73.8 | 290 | 11.7 | 95[3] | 119 |
| Russia | 59.9 | 73.3 | 240 | 11.5 | 97 | 117 |
| Ukraine | 62.2 | 74.0 | 330 | 10.0 | 96 | 120 |
| Other Eastern Europe | 67.3 | 74.7 | 370 | 13.4 | 84[3] | 121 |
| **Australia** | **78.5** | **83.3** | **400** | **4.7** | **100** | **116** |
| **Oceania** | **74.5** | **79.4** | **480** | **14.7** | **50[8]** | **117** |
| Pacific Ocean Islands | 68.3 | 73.3 | 770 | 30.1 | 67[3] | 118 |

[1]Latest data available for individual countries.    [2]The Food and Agriculture Organization of the United Nations (FAO) calculates this percentage by dividing the caloric equivalent to the known average daily supply of foodstuffs for human consumption in a given country by its population, thus arriving at a minimum daily per capita caloric intake. The higher the percentage, the more calories consumed.    [3]Data for 2000.    [4]Includes Canada, the US, Greenland, Bermuda, and St. Pierre and Miquelon.    [5]Does not include Japan.    [6]Includes Iran.    [7]Western Europe only; includes Andorra, Faroe Islands, Gibraltar, Guernsey, Iceland, Isle of Man, Jersey, Liechtenstein, Monaco, Norway, San Marino, and Switzerland.    [8]Does not include New Zealand.

## Causes of Death, Worldwide, by Region

Global estimates for 2002 as published in the World Health Organization (WHO) World Health Report 2004. Regions are as defined by the WHO. Numbers are in thousands ('000).

| LEADING CAUSES OF DEATH | ALL CATE-GORIES (%) | ALL CATE-GORIES | REGION AFRI-CA | REGION AMER-ICAS | REGION EASTERN MEDITER-RANEAN | REGION EUROPE | REGION SOUTHEAST ASIA | REGION WESTERN PACIFIC |
|---|---|---|---|---|---|---|---|---|
| 1 Ischemic heart disease | 12.6 | 7,208 | 332 | 921 | 538 | 2,373 | 2,039 | 993 |
| 2 Cerebrovascular disease | 9.7 | 5,509 | 359 | 452 | 227 | 1,447 | 1,059 | 1,957 |
| 3 Lower respiratory infections | 6.8 | 3,884 | 1,104 | 223 | 348 | 280 | 1,453 | 471 |

## Causes of Death, Worldwide, by Region (continued)

| LEADING CAUSES OF DEATH | ALL CATE-GORIES (%) | ALL CATE-GORIES | AFRICA | AMER-ICAS | EASTERN MEDITER-RANEAN | EUROPE | SOUTHEAST ASIA | WESTERN PACIFIC |
|---|---|---|---|---|---|---|---|---|
| 4 HIV disease | 4.9 | 2,777 | 2,095 | 103 | 44 | 36 | 436 | 61 |
| 5 Chronic obstructive pulmonary disease | 4.8 | 2,748 | 117 | 241 | 95 | 261 | 656 | 1,375 |
| 6 Perinatal conditions | 4.3 | 2,462 | 554 | 175 | 303 | 65 | 1,012 | 349 |
| 7 Diarrheal diseases | 3.2 | 1,798 | 707 | 57 | 259 | 16 | 604 | 154 |
| 8 Tuberculosis | 2.7 | 1,566 | 348 | 46 | 138 | 69 | 599 | 366 |
| 9 Malaria | 2.2 | 1,272 | 1,136 | 1 | 59 | 0 | 65 | 11 |
| 10 Trachea, bronchus, and lung cancers | 2.2 | 1,243 | 17 | 231 | 27 | 366 | 174 | 427 |
| 11 Road traffic accidents | 2.1 | 1,192 | 195 | 135 | 133 | 127 | 296 | 304 |
| 12 Diabetes mellitus | 1.7 | 988 | 80 | 253 | 55 | 142 | 263 | 192 |
| 13 Hypertensive heart disease | 1.6 | 911 | 60 | 135 | 97 | 179 | 152 | 284 |
| 14 Self-inflicted injuries | 1.5 | 873 | 34 | 63 | 34 | 163 | 246 | 331 |
| 15 Stomach cancer | 1.5 | 850 | 34 | 74 | 21 | 157 | 63 | 500 |
| 16 Cirrhosis of the liver | 1.4 | 786 | 54 | 105 | 67 | 171 | 204 | 185 |
| 17 Nephritis and nephrosis | 1.2 | 677 | 99 | 102 | 65 | 76 | 169 | 165 |
| 18 Colon and rectum cancers | 1.1 | 622 | 20 | 109 | 15 | 228 | 63 | 186 |
| 19 Liver cancer | 1.1 | 618 | 45 | 37 | 15 | 66 | 61 | 394 |
| 20 Measles | 1.1 | 611 | 311 | 0 | 70 | 6 | 196 | 28 |
| 21 Violence | 1.0 | 559 | 134 | 146 | 26 | 73 | 113 | 66 |
| 22 Congenital anomalies | 0.9 | 493 | 56 | 58 | 83 | 38 | 149 | 108 |
| 23 Breast cancer | 0.8 | 477 | 35 | 89 | 27 | 150 | 93 | 82 |
| 24 Esophagus cancer | 0.8 | 446 | 22 | 32 | 16 | 48 | 82 | 245 |
| 25 Inflammatory heart disease | 0.7 | 404 | 42 | 67 | 37 | 101 | 76 | 81 |

## Ten Leading Causes of Death in the US, by Age

*Preliminary data for 2010. Numbers in thousands. Rates per 100,000 population. Numbers are based on weighted data rounded to the nearest individual, so category percentages and rates may not add to totals given.* Source: National Vital Statistics Report, <www.cdc.gov/nchs>.

| CAUSE | NUMBER | RATE | % |
|---|---|---|---|
| **ALL AGES** | | | |
| 1 Diseases of heart | 595,444 | 192.9 | 24.1 |
| *Ischemic heart disease* | 378,270 | 122.5 | 15.3 |
| *Heart failure* | 57,696 | 18.7 | 2.3 |
| 2 Malignant neoplasms | 573,855 | 185.9 | 23.3 |
| *Neoplasms of the trachea, bronchus, and lung* | 158,135 | 51.2 | 6.4 |
| *Neoplasms of the colon, rectum, and anus* | 52,540 | 17.0 | 2.1 |
| *Neoplasms of the breast* | 41,360 | 13.4 | 1.7 |
| 3 Chronic lower respiratory diseases | 137,789 | 44.6 | 5.6 |
| 4 Cerebrovascular diseases | 129,180 | 41.8 | 5.2 |
| 5 Accidents | 118,043 | 38.2 | 4.8 |
| *Motor-vehicle accidents* | 35,080 | 11.4 | 1.4 |
| 6 Alzheimer disease | 83,308 | 27.0 | 3.4 |
| 7 Diabetes mellitus | 68,905 | 22.3 | 2.8 |
| 8 Nephritis, nephrotic syndrome, and nephrosis | 50,472 | 16.3 | 2.0 |
| 9 Influenza and pneumonia | 50,003 | 16.2 | 2.0 |
| 10 Intentional self-harm (suicide) | 37,793 | 12.2 | 1.5 |
| All other causes | 621,140 | 201.2 | 25.2 |
| **All causes, all ages** | **2,465,932** | **798.7** | **100** |

| CAUSE | NUMBER | RATE | % |
|---|---|---|---|
| **1–4 YEARS** | | | |
| 1 Accidents | 1,367 | 8.4 | 31.7 |
| *Motor-vehicle accidents* | 444 | 2.7 | 10.3 |
| *All other accidents* | 923 | 5.7 | 21.4 |
| 2 Congenital malformations, deformations, and chromosomal abnormalities | 495 | 3.0 | 11.5 |

| CAUSE | NUMBER | RATE | % |
|---|---|---|---|
| **1–4 YEARS (CONTINUED)** | | | |
| 3 Assault (homicide) | 367 | 2.3 | 8.5 |
| 4 Malignant neoplasms | 343 | 2.1 | 8.0 |
| 5 Diseases of heart | 156 | 1.0 | 3.6 |
| 6 Influenza and pneumonia | 83 | 0.5 | 1.9 |
| 7 Septicemia | 60 | 0.4 | 1.4 |
| 8 Nonmalignant/unknown neoplasms | 58 | 0.4 | 1.3 |
| 9 Cerebrovascular diseases | 52 | 0.3 | 1.2 |
| 9 Conditions of perinatal origin | 52 | 0.3 | 1.2 |
| All other causes | 1,275 | 7.8 | 29.6 |
| **All causes, 1–4 years** | **4,308** | **26.5** | **100** |

| CAUSE | NUMBER | RATE | % |
|---|---|---|---|
| **5–14 YEARS** | | | |
| 1 Accidents | 1,626 | 4.0 | 30.8 |
| *Motor-vehicle accidents* | 895 | 2.2 | 17.0 |
| *All other accidents* | 731 | 1.8 | 13.9 |
| 2 Malignant neoplasms | 913 | 2.2 | 17.3 |
| 3 Congenital malformations, deformations, and chromosomal abnormalities | 292 | 0.7 | 5.5 |
| 4 Intentional self-harm (suicide) | 273 | 0.7 | 5.2 |
| 5 Assault (homicide) | 254 | 0.6 | 4.8 |
| 6 Diseases of heart | 180 | 0.4 | 3.4 |
| 7 Chronic lower respiratory diseases | 128 | 0.3 | 2.4 |
| 8 Cerebrovascular diseases | 85 | 0.2 | 1.6 |
| 9 Nonmalignant/unknown neoplasms | 83 | 0.2 | 1.6 |
| 10 Influenza and pneumonia | 69 | 0.2 | 1.3 |
| All other causes | 1,371 | 3.3 | 26.0 |
| **All causes, 5–14 years** | **5,274** | **12.9** | **100** |

## Ten Leading Causes of Death in the US, by Age (continued)

| CAUSE | NUMBER | RATE | % |
|---|---|---|---|
| **15–24 YEARS** | | | |
| 1 Accidents | 12,015 | 27.5 | 40.7 |
| *Motor-vehicle accidents* | 7,209 | 16.5 | 24.4 |
| *All other accidents* | 4,806 | 11.0 | 16.3 |
| 2 Assault (homicide) | 4,651 | 10.7 | 15.8 |
| 3 Intentional self-harm (suicide) | 4,559 | 10.5 | 15.5 |
| 4 Malignant neoplasms | 1,594 | 3.7 | 5.4 |
| 5 Diseases of heart | 984 | 2.3 | 3.3 |
| 6 Congenital malformations, deformations, and chromosomal abnormalities | 401 | 0.9 | 1.4 |
| 7 Cerebrovascular diseases | 187 | 0.4 | 0.6 |
| 8 Influenza and pneumonia | 179 | 0.4 | 0.6 |
| 9 Pregnancy, childbirth, and the puerperium | 162 | 0.4 | 0.5 |
| 10 Diabetes mellitus | 161 | 0.4 | 0.5 |
| All other causes | 4,611 | 10.6 | 15.6 |
| **All causes, 15–24 years** | **29,504** | **67.6** | **100** |
| **25–44 YEARS** | | | |
| 1 Accidents | 28,149 | 34.3 | 25.1 |
| *Motor-vehicle accidents* | 10,420 | 12.7 | 9.3 |
| *All other accidents* | 17,729 | 21.6 | 15.8 |
| 2 Malignant neoplasms | 15,389 | 18.7 | 13.7 |
| 3 Diseases of heart | 13,447 | 16.4 | 12.0 |
| 4 Intentional self-harm (suicide) | 12,119 | 14.8 | 10.8 |
| 5 Assault (homicide) | 6,674 | 8.1 | 5.9 |
| 6 Chronic liver disease and cirrhosis | 2,900 | 3.5 | 2.6 |
| 7 HIV disease | 2,638 | 3.2 | 2.4 |
| 8 Cerebrovascular diseases | 2,396 | 2.9 | 2.1 |
| 9 Diabetes mellitus | 2,365 | 2.9 | 2.1 |
| 10 Influenza and pneumonia | 1,146 | 1.4 | 1.0 |
| All other causes | 24,954 | 30.4 | 22.2 |
| **All causes, 25–44 years** | **112,177** | **136.6** | **100** |
| **45–64 YEARS** | | | |
| 1 Malignant neoplasms | 159,379 | 195.6 | 32.3 |
| 2 Diseases of heart | 103,812 | 127.4 | 21.0 |

| CAUSE | NUMBER | RATE | % |
|---|---|---|---|
| **45–64 YEARS (CONTINUED)** | | | |
| 3 Accidents | 32,667 | 40.1 | 6.6 |
| *Motor-vehicle accidents* | 9,655 | 11.8 | 2.0 |
| *All other accidents* | 23,011 | 28.2 | 4.7 |
| 4 Chronic lower respiratory diseases | 18,616 | 22.8 | 3.8 |
| 5 Chronic liver disease and cirrhosis | 18,348 | 22.5 | 3.7 |
| 6 Diabetes mellitus | 17,224 | 21.1 | 3.5 |
| 7 Cerebrovascular diseases | 16,565 | 20.3 | 3.4 |
| 8 Intentional self-harm (suicide) | 14,912 | 18.3 | 3.0 |
| 9 Nephritis, nephrotic syndrome, and nephrosis | 7,306 | 9.0 | 1.5 |
| 10 Septicemia | 6,957 | 8.5 | 1.4 |
| All other causes | 97,590 | 119.8 | 19.8 |
| **All causes, 45–64 years** | **493,376** | **605.4** | **100** |
| **65 YEARS AND OVER** | | | |
| 1 Diseases of heart | 476,519 | 1,183.4 | 26.5 |
| 2 Malignant neoplasms | 396,173 | 983.8 | 22.1 |
| 3 Chronic lower respiratory diseases | 117,856 | 292.7 | 6.6 |
| 4 Cerebrovascular diseases | 109,764 | 272.6 | 6.1 |
| 5 Alzheimer disease | 82,438 | 204.7 | 4.6 |
| 6 Diabetes mellitus | 49,123 | 122.0 | 2.7 |
| 7 Influenza and pneumonia | 42,824 | 106.3 | 2.4 |
| 8 Nephritis, nephrotic syndrome, and nephrosis | 41,995 | 104.3 | 2.3 |
| 9 Accidents | 41,160 | 102.2 | 2.3 |
| *Motor-vehicle accidents* | 6,376 | 15.8 | 0.4 |
| *All other accidents* | 34,784 | 86.4 | 1.9 |
| 10 Septicemia | 26,322 | 65.4 | 1.5 |
| All other causes | 412,446 | 1,024.3 | 23.0 |
| **All causes, 65 years and over** | **1,796,620** | **4,461.7** | **100** |

# HIV/AIDS

Acquired immunodeficiency syndrome, or AIDS, is a fatal transmissable disorder of the **immune system** that is caused by the human immuno-deficiency virus (HIV). HIV was first isolated in 1983. In most cases, HIV slowly attacks and destroys the immune system, leaving the infected individual vulnerable to malignancies and infections that eventually cause death. AIDS is the last stage of HIV infection, during which time these diseases arise. An average interval of 10 years exists between infection with HIV and development of the conditions typical of AIDS. **Pneumonia** and **Kaposi sarcoma** are two of the most common diseases seen in AIDS patients.

HIV is contracted through semen, vaginal fluid, breast milk, blood, or other body fluids containing blood. Health care workers may come into contact with other body fluids that may transmit the HIV virus, including amniotic and synovial fluids. Although it is a transmissable virus, it is not contagious and cannot be spread through coughing, sneezing, or casual physical contact. Other **sexually transmitted diseases**, such as genital herpes, may increase the risk of contracting HIV through sexual contact.

The main **cellular target** of HIV is a special class of white blood cells critical to the immune system known as T4 helper cells. Once HIV has entered, it can cause these cells to function poorly or to die. A hallmark of the onset of AIDS is a drastic reduction in the number of helper T cells in the body. Two predominant strains of the virus, designated HIV-1 and HIV-2, are known. Worldwide the most common strain is HIV-1, with HIV-2 more common primarily in western Africa; the two strains act in a similar manner, but the latter causes a form of AIDS that progresses much more slowly.

**Diagnosis** is made on the basis of blood tests approved by the Centers for Disease Control and Pre-

## HIV/AIDS (continued)

vention that may be administered by a health professional. Alternately, a home collection kit may be purchased. Although no vaccine has yet been approved and no cure has been found that can prevent HIV infection, a new germ-destroying gel has shown promise in women aged 18–40 years old, and several **drugs**, including azidothymidine (AZT), are now used to slow the development of AIDS. **Protease inhibitors**, such as ritonavir and indinavir, have been shown to block the development of AIDS, at least temporarily. Protease inhibitors are most effective when used in conjunction with two different reverse transcriptase inhibitors—the so-called triple-drug therapy.

HIV/AIDS is a major problem in developing countries, particularly sub-Saharan Africa. The most recent UN report states that at the end of 2009, as many as 33.3 million people were estimated to be living with HIV. In 2009 alone, as many as 2.6 million contracted the disease and some 1.8 million died of it.

For confidential information on HIV/AIDS, call 1-800-CDC-INFO.
**Internet resources:** <www.unaids.org/en/default-.asp>; <www.cdc.gov/hiv>.

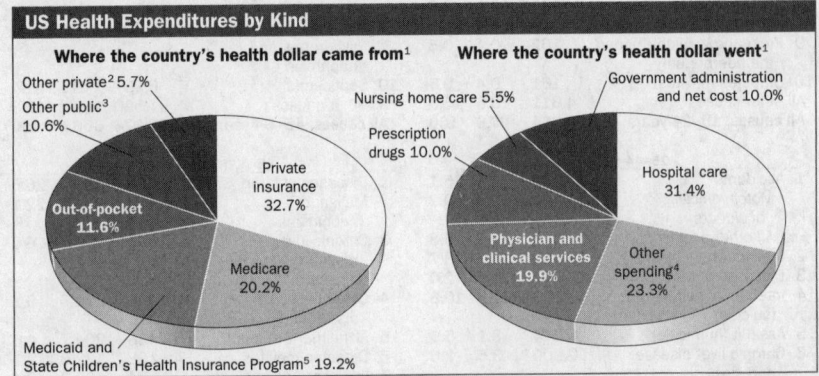

### US Health Expenditures by Kind

**Where the country's health dollar came from**[1]

- Other private[2] 5.7%
- Other public[3] 10.6%
- Out-of-pocket 11.6%
- Private insurance 32.7%
- Medicare 20.2%
- Medicaid and State Children's Health Insurance Program[5] 19.2%

**Where the country's health dollar went**[1]

- Nursing home care 5.5%
- Prescription drugs 10.0%
- Government administration and net cost 10.0%
- Hospital care 31.4%
- Physician and clinical services 19.9%
- Other spending[4] 23.3%

[1] Calendar year 2010. Detail may not add to 100% because of rounding.
[2] Other private includes industrial in-plant, privately funded construction, and non-patient revenues, including philanthropy.
[3] Other public includes programs such as workers' compensation, public health activity, Substance Abuse and Mental Health Services Administration, Indian Health Service, state and local hospital subsidies, and school health.
[4] Other spending includes dentist and other professional services, home health care, durable medical equipment, over-the-counter medicines and sundries, other nondurable medical products, ambulance providers, and research and construction.
[5] Medicaid and State Children's Health Insurance Program includes US Department of Defense and US Department of Veterans Affairs.
Source: Centers for Medicare and Medicaid Services, Office of the Actuary, National Health Statistics Group.

## Sexually Transmitted Diseases (STDs)

Sexually transmitted diseases (STDs) are usually passed from person to person by direct sexual contact. They may also be transmitted from a mother to her child before or at birth or, less frequently, may be passed from person to person in nonsexual contact. STDs usually initially affect the genitals, the reproductive tract, the urinary tract, the oral cavity, the anus, or the rectum, but they may mature in the body to attack various organs and systems. Following are some of the major STDs:

**Syphilis** was first widely reported by European writers in the 16th century, and a virtual epidemic swept Europe around the year 1500. Syphilis is spread through direct contact with a syphilis sore (chancre); development of this sore is the first stage of the disease. The second stage manifests itself as a rash on the palms and the bottoms of the feet. In the last stage, symptoms disappear, but the disease remains in the body and may damage internal organs and lead to paralysis, blindness, dementia, and even death. For individuals infected less than a year, a single dose of penicillin will cure the disease. Larger doses are needed for those who have had it for a longer period of time.

**Gonorrhea**, a form of urethritis (an infection and inflammation of the urethra), is one of the most common STDs. Although spread through sexual contact, the gonorrhea infection can also be spread to other parts of the body after touching the infected area. Men manifest symptoms, which include discharge and a burning sensation when urinating, more often than women. If gonorrhea is left untreated, women may develop pelvic inflammatory disease (PID) and men may become infertile. The disease can also spread to the blood or joints and is potentially life threatening.

**Chlamydia**, another form of urethritis, can be transmitted during vaginal, anal, or oral sex. Since there are frequently no symptoms, most infected individuals do not know they have the disease until complications develop. Untreated chlamydia can cause pain during urination or sex in men and PID in women. Antibiotics can successfully treat the disease.

**Genital herpes**, a disease that became especially widespread in the 1960s and 1970s, often presents minimal symptoms upon infection. The most common sign, however, is blistering in the genital area; outbreaks can occur over many years but generally decrease in severity and number. Genital herpes is

## Sexually Transmitted Diseases (STDs) (continued)

caused by the herpes simplex viruses type 1 (HSV-1) and type 2 (HSV-2). The former causes infections on and around the mouth but may be spread through the saliva to the genitals; the latter is transmitted during sexual contact with someone who has a genital infection. The HSV-2 infection can cause problems for people with suppressed immune systems and for infants who contract the disease upon delivery. Herpes can also leave individuals more susceptible to HIV infection and make those carrying the disease more infectious. A variety of treatments, including antiviral medications, have been used to help manage genital herpes, but currently there is no cure for the disease.

**Internet resource:** <www.cdc.gov/nchhstp>.

# Diet and Exercise

## US Food and Drug Administration (FDA)

*The FDA is a division of the US Department of Health and Human Services.* **FDA Web site:** <www.fda.gov>.

**Mission:** To promote and protect the public health by helping safe and effective products reach the market in a timely way and monitoring products for continued safety after they are in use. **History:** The FDA celebrated its 100th anniversary in 2006, having been created by the passing of the Food and Drugs Act, or Wiley Act, in 1906. The Food, Drug, and Cosmetic Act of 1938 then brought cosmetics and medical devices under the authority of the FDA. The Food and Drug Administration Act of 1988 officially established the body as an agency of the Department of Health and Human Services, with a commissioner of food and drugs appointed by the president with the consent of the Senate. **Locations:** Rockville, College Park, and Silver Spring MD, the last of which is to be the eventual headquarters for all departments. **Commis-** **sioner of Food and Drugs:** Margaret Hamburg. **Budget:** FY 2013 (requested) US$4.5 billion. **Functions:** The FDA is the agency of the US federal government authorized by Congress to inspect, test, approve, and set safety standards for foods and food additives, drugs, chemicals, cosmetics, and household and medical devices. Generally, the FDA is empowered to prevent untested products from being sold and to take legal action to halt the sale of undoubtedly harmful products or of products that involve a health or safety risk. Through court procedure, the FDA can seize products and prosecute the persons or firms responsible for legal violation. FDA authority is limited to interstate commerce. The agency cannot control prices nor directly regulate advertising except of prescription drugs and medical devices.

## Body Mass Index (BMI)

The BMI is a measure expressing the relationship of weight to height determined by dividing body weight in kilograms by the square of height in meters (for convenience, the information has been converted to standard US measurements in the table below). It is more highly correlated with body fat than any other indicator of height and weight. The National Institutes of Health recommend using the BMI scale to help assess the risk of diseases and disabilities associated with an unhealthy weight. Due to the increasing incidence of obesity in the US, the table has been expanded to include a range of BMI numbers above 39, which indicate that a person is "extremely obese." **Source:** <www.nhlbi.nih.gov>.

| HEIGHT (INCHES) | BODY WEIGHT (POUNDS) | | | | | | | | | | | | | | | | | | | | | |
|---|---|---|---|---|---|---|---|---|---|---|---|---|---|---|---|---|---|---|---|---|---|---|
| 58 | 91 | 96 | 100 | 105 | 110 | 115 | 119 | 124 | 129 | 134 | 138 | 143 | 148 | 153 | 158 | 162 | 167 | 172 | 177 | 181 | 186 |
| 59 | 94 | 99 | 104 | 109 | 114 | 119 | 124 | 128 | 133 | 138 | 143 | 148 | 153 | 158 | 163 | 168 | 173 | 178 | 183 | 188 | 193 |
| 60 | 97 | 102 | 107 | 112 | 118 | 123 | 128 | 133 | 138 | 143 | 148 | 153 | 158 | 163 | 168 | 174 | 179 | 184 | 189 | 194 | 199 |
| 61 | 100 | 106 | 111 | 116 | 122 | 127 | 132 | 137 | 143 | 148 | 153 | 158 | 164 | 169 | 174 | 180 | 185 | 190 | 195 | 201 | 206 |
| 62 | 104 | 109 | 115 | 120 | 126 | 131 | 136 | 142 | 147 | 153 | 158 | 164 | 169 | 175 | 180 | 186 | 191 | 196 | 202 | 207 | 213 |
| 63 | 107 | 113 | 118 | 124 | 130 | 135 | 141 | 146 | 152 | 158 | 163 | 169 | 175 | 180 | 186 | 191 | 197 | 203 | 208 | 214 | 220 |
| 64 | 110 | 116 | 122 | 128 | 134 | 140 | 145 | 151 | 157 | 163 | 169 | 174 | 180 | 186 | 192 | 197 | 204 | 209 | 215 | 221 | 227 |
| 65 | 114 | 120 | 126 | 132 | 138 | 144 | 150 | 156 | 162 | 168 | 174 | 180 | 186 | 192 | 198 | 204 | 210 | 216 | 222 | 228 | 234 |
| 66 | 118 | 124 | 130 | 136 | 142 | 148 | 155 | 161 | 167 | 173 | 179 | 186 | 192 | 198 | 204 | 210 | 216 | 223 | 229 | 235 | 241 |
| 67 | 121 | 127 | 134 | 140 | 146 | 153 | 159 | 166 | 172 | 178 | 185 | 191 | 198 | 204 | 211 | 217 | 223 | 230 | 236 | 242 | 249 |
| 68 | 125 | 131 | 138 | 144 | 151 | 158 | 164 | 171 | 177 | 184 | 190 | 197 | 203 | 210 | 216 | 223 | 230 | 236 | 243 | 249 | 256 |
| 69 | 128 | 135 | 142 | 149 | 155 | 162 | 169 | 176 | 182 | 189 | 196 | 203 | 209 | 216 | 223 | 230 | 236 | 243 | 250 | 257 | 263 |
| 70 | 132 | 139 | 146 | 153 | 160 | 167 | 174 | 181 | 188 | 195 | 202 | 209 | 216 | 222 | 229 | 236 | 243 | 250 | 257 | 264 | 271 |
| 71 | 136 | 143 | 150 | 157 | 165 | 172 | 179 | 186 | 193 | 200 | 208 | 215 | 222 | 229 | 236 | 243 | 250 | 257 | 265 | 272 | 279 |
| 72 | 140 | 147 | 154 | 162 | 169 | 177 | 184 | 191 | 199 | 206 | 213 | 221 | 228 | 235 | 242 | 250 | 258 | 265 | 272 | 279 | 287 |
| 73 | 144 | 151 | 159 | 166 | 174 | 182 | 189 | 197 | 204 | 212 | 219 | 227 | 235 | 242 | 250 | 257 | 265 | 272 | 280 | 288 | 295 |
| 74 | 148 | 155 | 163 | 171 | 179 | 186 | 194 | 202 | 210 | 218 | 225 | 233 | 241 | 249 | 256 | 264 | 272 | 280 | 287 | 295 | 303 |
| 75 | 152 | 160 | 168 | 176 | 184 | 192 | 200 | 208 | 216 | 224 | 232 | 240 | 248 | 256 | 264 | 272 | 279 | 287 | 295 | 303 | 311 |
| BMI | 19 | 20 | 21 | 22 | 23 | 24 | 25 | 26 | 27 | 28 | 29 | 30 | 31 | 32 | 33 | 34 | 35 | 36 | 37 | 38 | 39 |
| | | | NORMAL | | | | | | OVERWEIGHT | | | | | | OBESE | | | | | | |

## My Plate Food Guide

In 2011 the USDA released an update of its food-pyramid guide to a healthy diet, changing the pyramid graphic to a dinner plate. It is designed to help individuals get proper nutrients while at the same time consuming the appropriate amount of calories necessary to maintain healthy weight. The 2011 revision also provides information about exercise and weight loss. Diets should be low in added sugars, salt, saturated fat, and cholesterol and moderate in overall fat.

**Find your balance between food and physical activity:**

- Be sure to stay within your daily calorie needs.
- Be physically active for at least 30 minutes most days of the week.
- About 60 minutes a day of physical activity may be needed to prevent weight gain.
- For sustaining weight loss, at least 60 to 90 minutes a day of physical activity may be required.
- Children and teenagers should be physically active for 60 minutes every day or most days.

**Recommended daily intake**
These amounts are appropriate for individuals who get less than 30 minutes per day of moderate physical activity, beyond normal daily activities. Those who are more physically active may be able to consume more because they may have greater calorie needs.

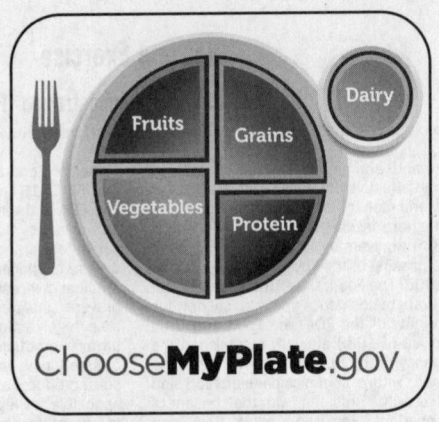

ChooseMyPlate.gov

| | Grains | Vegetables | Fruits | Fats and Oils—limit your intake | Dairy | Protein Foods |
|---|---|---|---|---|---|---|
| **Children** 2–3 years old | 3 ounce equivalents[1] | 1 cup[2] | 1 cup[3] | | 2 cups[4] | 2 ounce equivalents[5] |
| **Children** 4–8 years old | 5 ounce equivalents[1] | 1.5 cups[2] | 1–1.5 cups[3] | | 2.5 cups[4] | 4 ounce equivalents[5] |
| **Girls** 9–13 years old | 5 ounce equivalents[1] | 2 cups[2] | 1.5 cups[3] | | 3 cups[4] | 5 ounce equivalents[5] |
| **Boys** 9–13 years old | 6 ounce equivalents[1] | 2.5 cups[2] | 1.5 cups[3] | | 3 cups[4] | 5 ounce equivalents[5] |
| **Girls** 14–18 years old | 6 ounce equivalents[1] | 2.5 cups[2] | 1.5 cups[3] | | 3 cups[4] | 5 ounce equivalents[5] |
| **Boys** 14–18 years old | 8 ounce equivalents[1] | 3 cups[2] | 2 cups[3] | | 3 cups[4] | 6.5 ounce equivalents[5] |
| **Women** 19–30 years old | 6 ounce equivalents[1] | 2.5 cups[2] | 2 cups[3] | | 3 cups[4] | 5.5 ounce equivalents[5] |
| **Men** 19–30 years old | 8 ounce equivalents[1] | 3 cups[2] | 2 cups[3] | | 3 cups[4] | 6.5 ounce equivalents[5] |
| **Women** 31–50 years old | 6 ounce equivalents[1] | 2.5 cups[2] | 1.5 cups[3] | | 3 cups[4] | 5 ounce equivalents[5] |
| **Men** 31–50 years old | 7 ounce equivalents[1] | 3 cups[2] | 2 cups[3] | | 3 cups[4] | 6 ounce equivalents[5] |
| **Women** 51+ years old | 5 ounce equivalents[1] | 2 cups[2] | 1.5 cups[3] | | 3 cups[4] | 5 ounce equivalents[5] |
| **Men** 51+ years old | 6 ounce equivalents[1] | 2.5 cups[2] | 2 cups[3] | | 3 cups[4] | 5.5 ounce equivalents[5] |

[1] 1 slice of bread, 1 cup of ready-to-eat cereal, or ½ cup of cooked rice, cooked pasta, or cooked cereal can be considered as 1 ounce equivalent from the grains group.

[2] 1 cup of raw or cooked vegetables or vegetable juice or 2 cups of raw leafy greens can be considered as 1 cup from the vegetables group.

[3] 1 cup of fruit or 100% fruit juice or ½ cup of dried fruit can be considered as 1 cup from the fruits group.

[4] 1 cup of milk, yogurt, or soy milk, 1½ ounces of natural cheese, or 2 ounces of processed cheese can be considered as 1 cup from the dairy group.

[5] 1 ounce of meat, poultry, or fish, ¼ cup cooked beans, 1 egg, 1 tablespoon of peanut butter, or ½ ounce of nuts or seeds can be considered as 1 ounce equivalent from the protein foods group.

Source: USDA.

## Nutrient Composition of Selected Fruits and Vegetables

Values shown are approximations for 100 grams (3.57 oz.). Foods are raw unless otherwise noted. **Source:** USDA Nutrient Data Laboratory. kcal: kilocalorie; g: gram; mg: milligram; IU: international unit.

| | ENERGY (KCAL) | WATER (G) | CARBO-HYDRATE (G) | PROTEIN (G) | FAT (G) | VITAMIN A (IU) | VITAMIN C (MG) | THIAMINE (MG) | RIBO-FLAVIN (MG) | NIACIN (MG) |
|---|---|---|---|---|---|---|---|---|---|---|
| **Fruits** | | | | | | | | | | |
| Apple | 59 | 83.93 | 15.25 | 0.19 | 0.36 | 53 | 5.7 | 0.017 | 0.014 | 0.077 |
| Avocado | 161 | 74.27 | 7.39 | 1.98 | 15.32 | 61 | 7.9 | 0.108 | 0.122 | 1.921 |
| Banana | 92 | 74.26 | 23.43 | 1.03 | 0.48 | 81 | 9.1 | 0.045 | 0.100 | 0.540 |
| Blueberries | 56 | 84.61 | 14.13 | 0.67 | 0.38 | 100 | 13.0 | 0.048 | 0.050 | 0.359 |
| Cherries (sweet) | 72 | 80.76 | 16.55 | 1.20 | 0.96 | 214 | 7.0 | 0.050 | 0.060 | 0.400 |
| Grapes | 67 | 81.30 | 17.15 | 0.63 | 0.35 | 100 | 4.0 | 0.092 | 0.057 | 0.300 |
| Grapefruit | 32 | 90.89 | 8.08 | 0.63 | 0.10 | 124 | 34.4 | 0.036 | 0.020 | 0.250 |
| Lemon | 29 | 88.98 | 9.32 | 1.10 | 0.30 | 29 | 53.0 | 0.040 | 0.020 | 0.100 |
| Orange | 47 | 86.75 | 11.75 | 0.94 | 0.12 | 205 | 53.2 | 0.087 | 0.040 | 0.282 |
| Peach | 43 | 87.66 | 11.10 | 0.70 | 0.09 | 535 | 6.6 | 0.017 | 0.041 | 0.990 |
| Pear | 59 | 83.81 | 15.11 | 0.39 | 0.40 | 20 | 4.0 | 0.020 | 0.040 | 0.100 |
| Pineapple | 49 | 86.50 | 12.39 | 0.39 | 0.43 | 23 | 15.4 | 0.092 | 0.036 | 0.420 |
| Plum | 55 | 85.20 | 13.01 | 0.79 | 0.62 | 323 | 9.5 | 0.043 | 0.096 | 0.500 |
| Raspberries | 49 | 86.57 | 11.57 | 0.91 | 0.55 | 130 | 25.0 | 0.030 | 0.090 | 0.900 |
| Strawberries | 30 | 91.57 | 7.02 | 0.61 | 0.37 | 27 | 56.7 | 0.020 | 0.066 | 0.230 |
| **Vegetables** | | | | | | | | | | |
| Asparagus[1] | 24 | 92.20 | 4.23 | 2.59 | 0.31 | 539 | 10.8 | 0.123 | 0.126 | 1.082 |
| Beans (snap, green) | 31 | 90.27 | 7.14 | 1.82 | 0.12 | 668 | 16.3 | 0.084 | 0.105 | 0.752 |
| Broccoli | 28 | 90.69 | 5.24 | 2.98 | 0.35 | 1,542 | 93.2 | 0.065 | 0.119 | 0.638 |
| Cabbage | 25 | 92.15 | 5.43 | 1.44 | 0.27 | 133 | 32.2 | 0.050 | 0.040 | 0.300 |
| Carrot | 43 | 87.79 | 10.14 | 1.03 | 0.19 | 28,129 | 9.3 | 0.097 | 0.059 | 0.928 |
| Cauliflower | 25 | 91.91 | 5.20 | 1.98 | 0.21 | 19 | 46.4 | 0.057 | 0.063 | 0.526 |
| Collards[1] | 26 | 91.86 | 4.90 | 2.11 | 0.36 | 3,129 | 18.2 | 0.040 | 0.106 | 0.575 |
| Corn (sweet, yellow)[1] | 108 | 69.57 | 25.11 | 3.32 | 1.28 | 217 | 6.2 | 0.215 | 0.072 | 1.614 |
| Mushroom[1] | 27 | 91.08 | 5.14 | 2.17 | 0.47 | 0 | 4.0 | 0.073 | 0.300 | 4.460 |
| Onion[1] | 44 | 87.86 | 10.15 | 1.36 | 0.19 | 0 | 5.2 | 0.042 | 0.023 | 0.165 |
| Pepper (sweet, red) | 27 | 92.19 | 6.43 | 0.89 | 0.19 | 5,700 | 190.0 | 0.066 | 0.030 | 0.509 |
| Potato[2] | 93 | 75.42 | 21.56 | 1.96 | 0.10 | 0 | 12.8 | 0.105 | 0.021 | 1.395 |
| Spinach | 22 | 91.58 | 3.50 | 2.86 | 0.35 | 6,715 | 28.1 | 0.078 | 0.189 | 0.724 |
| Sweet potato[2] | 103 | 72.85 | 24.27 | 1.72 | 0.11 | 21,822 | 24.6 | 0.073 | 0.127 | 0.604 |
| Tomato (red) | 21 | 93.76 | 4.64 | 0.85 | 0.33 | 623 | 19.1 | 0.059 | 0.048 | 0.628 |

[1]Boiled. [2]Baked.

## Nutritional Value of Selected Foods

Values shown are approximations. Source: Home and Garden Bulletin No. 72, USDA. kcal: kilocalorie; g: gram; mg: milligram; oz: ounce; fl oz: fluid ounce.

| FOOD | AMOUNT | GRAMS | ENERGY (KCAL) | CARBO-HYDRATE (G) | PROTEIN (G) | TOTAL FAT (G) | SATU-RATED FAT (G) | CALCIUM (MG) | IRON (MG) | SODIUM (MG) |
|---|---|---|---|---|---|---|---|---|---|---|
| **Beverages** | | | | | | | | | | |
| Beer | 12 fl oz | 360 | 150 | 13 | 1 | 0 | 0 | 14 | 0.1 | 18 |
| Cola, regular | 12 fl oz | 369 | 160 | 41 | 0 | 0 | 0 | 11 | 0.2 | 18 |
| Cola, diet (w/aspartame and saccharine) | 12 fl oz | 355 | 0 | 0 | 0 | 0 | 0 | 14 | 0.2 | 32 |
| Coffee, brewed | 6 fl oz | 180 | 0 | 0 | 0 | 0 | 0 | 4 | 0 | 2 |
| Wine, table, red | 3.5 fl oz | 102 | 75 | 3 | 0 | 0 | 0 | 8 | 0.4 | 5 |
| **Dairy** | | | | | | | | | | |
| Butter, salted | 4 oz | 113 | 810 | 0 | 1 | 92 | 57.1 | 27 | 0.2 | 933 |
| Cheese, American (pasteurized, processed) | 1 oz | 28.35 | 105 | 0 | 6 | 9 | 5.6 | 174 | 0.1 | 406 |
| Cottage cheese, small curd | 8 oz | 210 | 215 | 6 | 26 | 9 | 6 | 126 | 0.3 | 850 |
| Cream cheese | 1 oz | 28.35 | 100 | 1 | 2 | 10 | 6.2 | 23 | 0.3 | 84 |
| Cream, sour | 8 oz | 230 | 495 | 10 | 7 | 48 | 30 | 268 | 0.1 | 123 |
| Eggs, cooked, fried | 1 egg | 46 | 90 | 1 | 6 | 7 | 1.9 | 25 | 0.7 | 162 |
| Ice cream, vanilla, 11% fat | 8 oz | 133 | 270 | 32 | 5 | 14 | 8.9 | 176 | 0.1 | 116 |
| Milk, whole, 3.3% fat | 8 oz | 244 | 150 | 11 | 8 | 8 | 5.1 | 291 | 0.1 | 120 |

## Nutritional Value of Selected Foods (continued)

| FOOD | AMOUNT | GRAMS | ENERGY (KCAL) | CARBO-HYDRATE (G) | PROTEIN (G) | TOTAL FAT (G) | SATU-RATED FAT (G) | CALCIUM (MG) | IRON (MG) | SODIUM (MG) |
|---|---|---|---|---|---|---|---|---|---|---|
| **Dairy (continued)** | | | | | | | | | | |
| Milk, low fat, 2% fat | 8 oz | 244 | 120 | 12 | 8 | 5 | 2.9 | 297 | 0.1 | 122 |
| Milk, skim | 8 oz | 245 | 85 | 12 | 8 | 0 | 0.3 | 302 | 0.1 | 126 |
| Yogurt, plain, low fat | 8 oz | 227 | 145 | 16 | 12 | 4 | 2.3 | 415 | 0.2 | 159 |
| **Fats, oils** | | | | | | | | | | |
| Margarine, hard, 80% fat | 0.5 oz | 14 | 100 | 0 | 0 | 11 | 2.2 | 4 | 0 | 132 |
| Olive oil | 0.5 oz | 14 | 125 | 0 | 0 | 14 | 1.9 | 0 | 0 | 0 |
| Vegetable shortening | 0.5 oz | 13 | 115 | 0 | 0 | 13 | 3.3 | 0 | 0 | 0 |
| **Fish** | | | | | | | | | | |
| Fish sticks, frozen | 1 piece | 28 | 70 | 4 | 6 | 3 | 0.8 | 11 | 0.3 | 53 |
| Ocean perch, breaded, fried | 1 piece | 85 | 185 | 7 | 16 | 11 | 2.6 | 31 | 1.2 | 138 |
| Oysters, raw | 8 oz | 240 | 160 | 8 | 20 | 4 | 1.4 | 226 | 15.6 | 175 |
| Salmon, baked, red | 3 oz | 85 | 140 | 0 | 21 | 5 | 1.2 | 26 | 0.5 | 55 |
| Shrimp, fried | 3 oz | 85 | 200 | 11 | 16 | 10 | 2.5 | 61 | 2 | 384 |
| Tuna, canned, white, in water | 3 oz | 85 | 135 | 0 | 30 | 1 | 0.3 | 17 | 0.6 | 468 |
| **Fruits, fruit products** | | | | | | | | | | |
| Applesauce, canned, sweetened | 8 oz | 255 | 195 | 51 | 0 | 0 | 0.1 | 10 | 0.9 | 8 |
| Pineapple, canned, heavy syrup | 8 oz | 255 | 200 | 52 | 1 | 0 | 0 | 36 | 1 | 3 |
| Raisins | 8 oz | 145 | 435 | 115 | 5 | 1 | 0.2 | 71 | 3 | 17 |
| Watermelon | 1 piece | 482 | 155 | 35 | 3 | 2 | 0.3 | 39 | 0.8 | 10 |
| **Grains** | | | | | | | | | | |
| Bagels, plain | 1 bagel | 68 | 200 | 38 | 7 | 2 | 0.3 | 29 | 1.8 | 245 |
| Bread, rye, light | 1 slice | 25 | 65 | 12 | 2 | 1 | 0.2 | 20 | 0.7 | 175 |
| Bread, white | 1 slice | 25 | 65 | 12 | 2 | 1 | 0.3 | 32 | 0.7 | 129 |
| Bread, whole wheat | 1 slice | 28 | 70 | 13 | 3 | 1 | 0.4 | 20 | 1 | 180 |
| Cereal, Cheerios | 1 oz | 28.35 | 110 | 20 | 4 | 2 | 0.3 | 48 | 4.5 | 307 |
| Cereal, Kellogg's Corn Flakes | 1 oz | 28.35 | 110 | 24 | 2 | 0 | 0 | 1 | 1.8 | 351 |
| Cereal, Lucky Charms | 1 oz | 28.35 | 110 | 23 | 3 | 1 | 0.2 | 32 | 4.5 | 201 |
| Cereal, Post Raisin Bran | 1 oz | 28.35 | 85 | 21 | 3 | 1 | 0.1 | 13 | 4.5 | 185 |
| Cake, white, w/white frosting, commercial | 1 piece | 71 | 260 | 42 | 3 | 9 | 2.1 | 33 | 1 | 176 |
| Cheesecake | 1 piece | 92 | 280 | 26 | 5 | 18 | 9.9 | 52 | 0.4 | 204 |
| Chocolate chip cookies, commercial | 4 cookies | 42 | 180 | 28 | 2 | 9 | 2.9 | 13 | 0.8 | 140 |
| Doughnuts, cake, plain | 1 doughnut | 50 | 210 | 24 | 3 | 12 | 2.8 | 22 | 1 | 192 |
| English muffins, plain | 1 muffin | 57 | 140 | 27 | 5 | 1 | 0.3 | 96 | 1.7 | 378 |
| Oatmeal, instant, cooked, w/salt | 8 oz | 234 | 145 | 25 | 6 | 2 | 0.4 | 19 | 1.6 | 374 |
| Popcorn, air-popped, unsalted | 8 oz | 8 | 30 | 6 | 1 | 0 | 0 | 1 | 0.2 | 0 |
| Rice, brown, cooked | 8 oz | 195 | 230 | 50 | 5 | 1 | 0.3 | 23 | 1 | 0 |
| Rice, white, instant, cooked | 8 oz | 165 | 180 | 40 | 4 | 0 | 0.1 | 5 | 1.3 | 0 |
| **Meat, poultry** | | | | | | | | | | |
| Bacon, regular, cooked | 3 slices | 19 | 110 | 0 | 6 | 9 | 3.3 | 2 | 0.3 | 303 |
| Chicken, breast, roasted | 3 oz | 86 | 140 | 0 | 27 | 3 | 0.9 | 13 | 0.9 | 64 |
| Chicken, drumstick, floured, fried | 1.7 oz | 49 | 120 | 1 | 13 | 7 | 1.8 | 6 | 0.7 | 44 |
| Ham, roasted, lean and fat | 3 oz | 85 | 205 | 0 | 18 | 14 | 5.1 | 6 | 0.7 | 1009 |
| Hamburger | 4-oz patty | 174 | 445 | 38 | 25 | 21 | 7.1 | 75 | 4.8 | 763 |
| Lamb chops, braised, lean | 1.7 oz | 48 | 135 | 0 | 17 | 7 | 2.9 | 12 | 1.3 | 36 |
| Turkey, roasted | 8 oz | 140 | 240 | 0 | 41 | 7 | 2.3 | 35 | 2.5 | 98 |
| **Nuts, legumes, seeds** | | | | | | | | | | |
| Peanuts, oil-roasted, unsalted | 8 oz | 145 | 840 | 27 | 39 | 71 | 9.9 | 125 | 2.8 | 22 |
| Peanut butter | 0.5 oz | 16 | 95 | 3 | 5 | 8 | 1.4 | 5 | 0.3 | 75 |
| Tofu | 1 piece | 120 | 85 | 3 | 9 | 5 | 0.7 | 108 | 2.3 | 8 |

## Nutritional Value of Selected Foods (continued)

| FOOD | AMOUNT | GRAMS | ENERGY (KCAL) | CARBO-HYDRATE (G) | PROTEIN (G) | TOTAL FAT (G) | SATU-RATED FAT (G) | CALCIUM (MG) | IRON (MG) | SODIUM (MG) |
|---|---|---|---|---|---|---|---|---|---|---|
| **Sauces, dressings, condiments** | | | | | | | | | | |
| Catsup | 0.5 oz | 15 | 15 | 4 | 0 | 0 | 0 | 3 | 0.1 | 156 |
| Cheese sauce w/milk, from mix | 8 fl oz | 279 | 305 | 23 | 16 | 17 | 9.3 | 569 | 0.3 | 1565 |
| Mayonnaise | 0.5 oz | 14 | 100 | 0 | 0 | 11 | 1.7 | 3 | 0.1 | 80 |
| Mustard, yellow | 0.17 oz | 5 | 5 | 0 | 0 | 0 | 0 | 4 | 0.1 | 63 |
| Salad dressing, French | 0.5 oz | 16 | 85 | 1 | 0 | 9 | 1.4 | 2 | 0 | 188 |
| Salad dressing, Italian, low calorie | 0.5 oz | 15 | 5 | 2 | 0 | 0 | 0 | 1 | 0 | 136 |
| | | | | | | | | | | |
| **Sugars, sweets, miscellaneous snacks** | | | | | | | | | | |
| Chocolate, dark, sweet | 1 oz | 28.35 | 150 | 16 | 1 | 10 | 5.9 | 7 | 0.6 | 5 |
| Potato chips | 10 chips | 20 | 105 | 10 | 1 | 7 | 1.8 | 5 | 0.2 | 94 |
| Pudding, chocolate, instant | 4 oz | 130 | 155 | 27 | 4 | 4 | 2.3 | 130 | 0.3 | 440 |
| Sugar, brown | 8 oz | 220 | 820 | 212 | 0 | 0 | 0 | 187 | 4.8 | 97 |
| Sugar, white, granulated | 8 oz | 200 | 770 | 199 | 0 | 0 | 0 | 3 | 0.1 | 5 |

## Reading Food Labels

The FDA requires most food manufacturers to provide standardized information about certain nutrients. Within strict guidelines the nutritional labels are designed to **aid the consumer in making informed dietary decisions** as well as to **regulate claims made by manufacturers** about their products.

The percent daily value is based on a 2,000-calorie-per-day diet. Some larger packages will have listings for both 2,000-calorie and 2,500-calorie diets. For products that require additional preparation before eating, such as dry cake mixes, manufacturers often provide two columns of nutritional information, one with the values of the food as purchased, the other with the values of the food as prepared.

The FDA selects mandatory label components (see sample label at right) based on current understanding of nutrition concerns, and **component order on the label is consistent with the priority of dietary recommendations.** Components that may appear in addition to the mandatory components are limited to the following: calories from saturated fat, polyunsaturated fat, monounsaturated fat, potassium, soluble fiber, insoluble fiber, sugar alcohol (for example, the sugar substitutes xylitol, mannitol, and sorbitol), other carbohydrate (the difference between total carbohydrate and the sum of dietary fiber, sugars, and sugar alcohol if declared), percent of vitamin A present as beta-carotene, and other essential vitamins and minerals. Any of these optional components that form the basis of product claims, fortification, or enrichment must appear in the nutrition facts. In 2006 labels were required to specify amounts of trans fatty acids.

Certain key descriptions are also regulated by the FDA. They include the following, in amounts per serving:

Low fat: 3 g or less
Low saturated fat: 1 g or less
Low sodium: 140 mg or less
Low cholesterol: 20 mg or less and 2 g or less of saturated fat
Low calorie: 40 calories or less

*Dietary Guidelines for Americans, 2010*
**Web site:** <www.health.gov/dietaryguidelines>.

# Nutrition Facts

Serving Size 1 Bar (40g)

**Amount Per Serving**

**Calories** 170          Calories from Fat 60

**% Daily Value***

| | |
|---|---|
| **Total Fat** 7g | **11%** |
| Saturated Fat 3g | **15%** |
| Trans Fat 0g | |
| **Cholesterol** 0mg | **0%** |
| **Sodium** 160mg | **7%** |
| **Total Carbohydrate** 24g | **8%** |
| Dietary Fiber 3g | **12%** |
| Sugars 10g | |
| **Protein** 5g | |

Vitamin A **2%**  •  Vitamin C **2%**
Calcium **20%**  •  Iron **8%**

*Percent Daily Values are based on a 2,000 calorie diet. Your daily values may be higher or lower depending on your calorie needs:

| | | Calories: | 2,000 | 2,500 |
|---|---|---|---|---|
| Total Fat | Less than | | 65g | 80g |
| Sat Fat | Less than | | 20g | 25g |
| Cholesterol | Less than | | 300mg | 300mg |
| Sodium | Less than | | 2,400mg | 2,400mg |
| Total Carbohydrate | | | 300g | 375g |
| Dietary Fiber | | | 25g | 30g |

Calories per gram:
Fat 9  •  Carbohydrate 4  •  Protein 4

# Ways To Burn 150 Calories

Values shown are approximations. Activities are listed from more to less vigorous—the more vigorous an activity, the less time it takes to burn a calorie. When specific distances are given, the activity must be performed in the time shown (for example, one must run 1.5 miles in 15 minutes to burn 150 calories).

| ACTIVITY | DURATION (MINUTES) |
| --- | --- |
| Climbing stairs | 15 |
| Shoveling snow | 15 |
| Running 1.5 miles (10 minutes/mile) | 15 |
| Jumping rope | 15 |
| Bicycling 4 miles | 15 |
| Playing basketball | 15–20 |
| Playing wheelchair basketball | 20 |
| Swimming laps | 20 |
| Performing water aerobics | 30 |
| Walking 2 miles (15 minutes/mile) | 30 |

| ACTIVITY | DURATION (MINUTES) |
| --- | --- |
| Raking leaves | 30 |
| Pushing a stroller 1.5 miles | 30 |
| Dancing fast | 30 |
| Shooting baskets | 30 |
| Walking 1.75 miles (20 minutes/mile) | 35 |
| Gardening (standing) | 30–45 |
| Playing touch football | 30–45 |
| Playing volleyball | 45 |
| Washing windows or floors | 45–60 |
| Washing and waxing a car or boat | 45–60 |

**Did you know?**

The United Nations International Strategy for Disaster Reduction and the Centre for Research on the Epidemiology of Disasters issued a joint release revealing that earthquakes were the deadliest disasters in the first decade of the 21st century. According to the study cited, of the more than 780,000 people killed in disasters between 2000 and 2009, almost 60 percent perished in earthquakes. The most severe earthquake during this period was the 2008 temblor in Sichuan, China, which killed as many as 87,000 people.

## Target Heart Rate Training Zones

Measuring **target heart rate** involves monitoring your pulse periodically as you exercise. To use the Target Heart Rate chart:

1. Calculate your maximum heart rate by subtracting your age from 220.
2. Determine your target heart rate zone (50–70% of your maximum heart rate).
3. While exercising, monitor your pulse regularly. Count the number of beats for 10 seconds, then multiply by 6 to determine in what zone you are working.

The American Heart Association recommends using the target heart rate scale when participating in more vigorous athletic activity, such as jogging or aerobics. If your activity is moderate or taking your pulse is too bothersome, a "talk test" can be used as a substitute. If you can converse with someone with minimal effort, you are not working too hard. Alternately, if you can sing without difficulty, you are not working hard enough.

Note: For optimal cardiovascular fitness, you should work toward the middle of your 50 and 70% zones. Always check with your physician before starting any fitness routine, especially if you have heart or respiratory concerns.

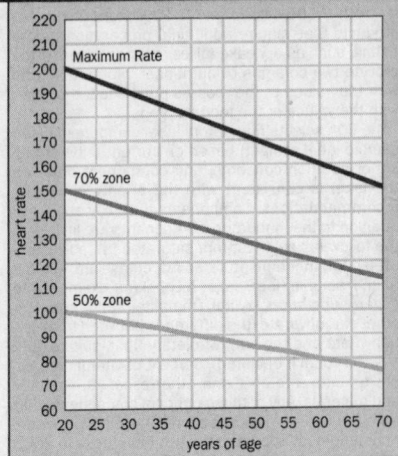

## Meet Kim Jong Un

*by Bill Powell, TIME*

North Korea is a cocktail of poisonous elements: autocratic, repressive, isolated, and poor. Its regime is dangerous not only to its people but also to the rest of the world. North Korea, notes South Korean scholar Cheong Seong-chang, is "a Stalinist monarchy" where bloodlines, and only bloodlines, determine who the next dictator will be—no matter how young or inexperienced that person may be.

Nearly 30,000 US troops help defend the North's prosperous, democratic brethren in the South against a 1.2 million-member army, most of it arrayed within 30 miles (50 km) of the demilitarized zone. Over the past decade, despite crippling economic sanctions imposed by most of the outside world, North Korea has defiantly developed and tested nuclear weapons and the long-range missiles needed to deliver them. Western intelligence agencies estimate that Pyongyang possesses eight to 12 nuclear weapons. The hard truth is that North Korea is Asia's last remaining Cold War trip wire.

This is the country now ostensibly helmed by young Kim Jong Un, nearing 30 by most accounts, the grandson of Kim Il Sung, the founder of the Democratic People's Republic of Korea (DPRK). In Korean, Kim Il Sung was called Suryong (Great Leader), a virtually godlike figure. When he died in 1994, his eldest son, Kim Jong Il, then 52, continued the dynasty. With Kim Jong Il's death in December 2011 at age 69, it is Kim Jong Un's turn.

Whether and to what extent North Korea will change under Kim Jong Un is a matter of greatest consequence to the global balance of power. It's not even clear if he is calling the shots in Pyongyang. The only sure thing for now is that Kim Jong Un is the least-known and understood leader ever of a nuclear-armed nation.

Kim Jong Un was Kim Jong Il's third son, the second with a woman described as his consort. Ko Young Hui was an ethnic Korean born in Osaka, Japan, who died in 2004 of breast cancer. She and her family had returned to North Korea in the early '60s. Back then, Japanese-born Koreans were the lowest of the low in North Korea's quasi-caste system. But Ko, who became a dancer after attending a prestigious art school in Pyongyang, caught the eye of the Dear Leader. In 1981 she gave birth to a boy, Kim Jong Chul; Kim Jong Un was born two years later. In North Korea, Ko's birthplace is a closely guarded secret, as is the fact that some of her kin still live in Japan.

In the mid-1990s, like his older male siblings, Kim Jong Un moved to Switzerland. He stayed with a family assigned to the North Korean embassy in Bern and for the first two years of his life there studied German and English. In 1998, under the pseudonym Pak Un and the pretext of being the son of a diplomat, he enrolled in seventh grade at Schule Liebefeld-Steinhölzli, a public school in the suburb of Liebefeld.

Despite the deception surrounding his true identity, the boy lived what his fellow students say was a normal life. He stayed in a nondescript apartment block about a 10-minute walk from school, and his love affair with basketball intensified. At a time when Michael Jordan was dominating the NBA, Kim became a big fan of the Chicago Bulls, says onetime classmate Joao Micaelo, now a chef in Vienna.

In 2000, just after he had started ninth grade, Kim left school abruptly and headed back home. For much of the next decade, Kim Jong Un's life is even more of a blank, other than the fact that he attended the Kim Il Sung Military Academy in Pyongyang (senior-thesis topic: guidance systems for artillery).

When Kim Jong Il suffered a stroke in 2008, Kim Jong Un's older brother Kim Jong Chul was most often cited as the likely heir, given that Kim Jong Nam, the eldest, had embarrassed himself in Tokyo seven years earlier: he and his family were detained for trying to get into Japan on fake passports, supposedly to visit Tokyo Disneyland. The stroke concentrated the Dear Leader's mind. A successor had to be named. But his father viewed Kim Jong Chul as too reticent. In one account, the Dear Leader once declared that Kim Jong Chul "resembles a girl"—hardly an asset in male-dominated North Korea.

That left only one choice. As it happened, as he moved into his late 20s, Kim Jong Un developed a striking resemblance to his grandfather Kim Il Sung. In a society mesmerized by personality cults, "that meant a lot," says North Korean defector Lee Sung Bak, who was a government bureaucrat. On 27 Sep 2010, Kim Jong Un at 27 was named a four-star general in the Korean People's Army and appointed vice chairman of the Central Military Commission, making him second in command of the country's most powerful institution. With his father's wishes made plain, there was never any doubt that Kim Jong Un's ascension would be smooth.

Today everyone in a position of power in North Korea is at least twice Kim Jong Un's age and vastly more experienced. But they will nonetheless snap off salutes to him. Any deviation has meant at minimum a sentence in North Korea's notorious gulag and at worst death. Two issues are critical for North Korea. Will it liberalize its economy, as its chief patron China did more than 30 years ago, and finally allow its citizens to get at least a whiff of the prosperity that surrounds them in East Asia? And will it give up its pariah status as a rogue nuclear state in return for economic and diplomatic blandishments to help reinvent the country?

A man who knew his father and who has dealt with the leadership in Pyongyang waves the question away. To ask it, he suggests, is to misunderstand the regime. The system needs the dynasty to persist because without it, the entire edifice of power in North Korea could collapse. In that sense, Kim Jong Un is a necessary front man. But the notion that he will pull all the policy strings, stay abreast of palace intrigues, and tell senior cadres and military officers what to do is "a fantasy," says the insider. "He's just a boy. He is soft." Indeed, Kim is already showing the influence of his stay in the West. Unlike his father, he has acknowledged that he is married, and he has shown off his stylish wife, Ri Sol-ju, to the public.

Will Kim Jong Un prove to be too soft? As an NBA fan, he probably knows that in pro basketball, soft is the one thing you do not want to be. And his life now is no game.

# Countries of the World

The information about the countries of the world that follows has been assembled and analyzed by *Encyclopædia Britannica* editors from hundreds of private, national, and international sources. Included are all the sovereign states of the world. The historical background sketches have been adapted, augmented, and updated from *Britannica Concise Encyclopedia* and the statistical sections from *Britannica World Data*, which is published annually in conjunction with the *Britannica Book of the Year*. The section called Recent Developments also has been adapted from material appearing in recent issues of the yearbook, as well as from other sources inside and outside Britannica. The locator maps have been prepared by Britannica's cartography department. Several countries, including those with the largest economies, are given expanded coverage in this section.

All information is the latest available to Britannica. It must be understood that in many cases it takes several years for the various countries or agencies to gather and process statistics—the most current data available will normally be dated several years earlier.

A few definitions of terms used in the articles may be useful. **GDP** (gross domestic product) is the total value of goods and services produced in a country during a given accounting period, usually a year. Typically the value is given in current prices of the year indicated. **GNI** (gross national income) is essentially GDP plus income from foreign transactions minus payments made outside the country. **Imports** are material goods legally entering a country (or customs area) and subject to customs regulations. The value of goods imported is given free on board (**f.o.b.**) unless otherwise specified; the value of goods exported and imported f.o.b. is calculated from the cost of production and excludes the cost of transport. The principal alternate basis for valuation of goods in international trade is that of cost, insurance, and freight (**c.i.f.**); its use is restricted to imports, as it comprises the principal charges needed to bring the goods to the customs house in the country of destination. **Exports** are material goods legally leaving a country and subject to customs regulations. Valuation of goods exported is virtually always f.o.b.

## Afghanistan

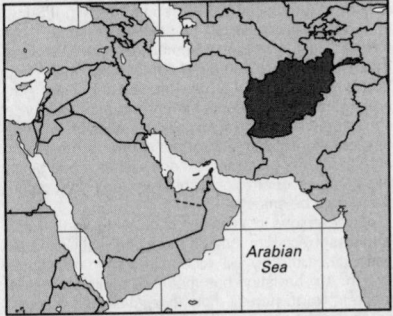

*Arabian Sea*

**Official name:** Islamic Republic of Afghanistan (Jomhuri-ye Eslami-ye Afghanestan [Dari (Persian)]; Da Afghanestan Eslami Jamhuriyat [Pashto]). **Form of government:** Islamic republic with two legislative houses (House of Elders [102]; House of the People [249]). **Head of state and government:** President Hamid Karzai (from 2002). **Capital:** Kabul. **Official languages:** Dari (Persian); Pashto; six additional languages have local official status per the 2004 constitution. **Official religion:** Islam. **Monetary unit:** 1 (new) afghani (Af) = 100 puls; valuation (2 Jul 2012) US$1 = Af 48.24.

### Demography

**Area:** 252,072 sq mi, 652,864 sq km. **Population** (2011): 26,442,000. **Density** (2011): persons per sq mi 104.9, persons per sq km 40.5. **Urban** (2006): 21.5%. **Sex distribution** (2006): male 51.14%; female 48.86%. **Age breakdown** (2006): under 15, 44.6%;

15–29, 26.7%; 30–44, 16.0%; 45–59, 8.6%; 60–74, 3.5%; 75 and over 0.6%. **Ethnolinguistic composition** (2004): Pashtun 42%; Tajik 27%; Hazara 9%; Uzbek 9%; Chahar Aimak 4%; Turkmen 3%; other 6%. **Religious affiliation** (2004): Sunni Muslim 82%; Shi'i Muslim 17%. **Major cities** (2006): Kabul 2,536,300; Herat 349,000; Kandahar (Qandahar) 324,800; Mazar-e Sharif 300,600; Jalalabad 168,600. **Location:** southern Asia, bordering Uzbekistan, Tajikistan, China, Pakistan, Iran, and Turkmenistan.

### Vital statistics

**Birth rate** per 1,000 population (2006): 46.6 (world avg. 20.3). **Death rate** per 1,000 population (2006): 20.3 (world avg. 8.5). **Total fertility rate** (avg. births per childbearing woman; 2006): 6.69. **Life expectancy** at birth (2006): male 43.2 years; female 43.5 years.

### National economy

**Budget** (2006–07). *Revenue:* Af 155,394,000,000 (grants 78.1%; taxes on international trade 8.5%; nontax revenue 5.1%). *Expenditures:* Af 163,884,-000,000 (economic affairs 47.3%; general administration 10.9%; public order 9.1%; defense 7.8%). **Gross national income** (2007): US$10,137,000,000 (US$373 per capita). **Public debt** (external, outstanding; 2007): US$1,961,000,000. **Production** (metric tons except as noted). *Agriculture and fishing* (2006–07): wheat 3,363,000, barley 364,000, rice 361,000, opium poppy (2007) 8,200 (93% of world production); livestock (number of live animals) 9,259,000 sheep, 6,746,000 goats, 174,000 camels; fisheries production (2005) 1,000 (from aquaculture, none). *Mining and quarrying:* salt (2007) 123,000; chromite 6,800; gemstones, n.a.; marble, n.a. *Manufacturing* (value added in Af

---

*1 metric ton = about 1.1 short tons;    1 kilometer = 0.6 mi (statute);    1 metric ton-km cargo = about 0.68 short ton-mi cargo;    c.i.f.: cost, insurance, and freight;    f.o.b.: free on board*

'000,000; 2005–06): food products 48,575; chemical products 1,206; cement, bricks, and ceramics 809. *Energy production (consumption):* electricity (kW-hr; 2006–07) 916,900,000 (483,600,000); coal (metric tons; 2006) 33,000 (33,000); crude petroleum, n.a. (none); petroleum products (metric tons; 2006) none (186,000); natural gas (cu m; 2006) 20,000,000 (20,000,000). **Population economically active** (2006): total 8,207,000; activity rate of total population 31.5% (participation rates: ages 15–64, 60.3; female 23.1; unemployed [January 2009] 33%). **Selected balance of payments data.** Receipts from (US$'000,000): tourism (1998) 1.0; foreign direct investment (2005–07 avg.) 268; official development assistance (2007) 3,951.

## Foreign trade

**Imports** (2006–07; c.i.f.): US$2,744,000,000 (machinery and apparatus 19.4%; household items and medicine 12.0%; food products 12.0%; base and fabricated metals 10.0%; mineral fuels 9.3%). *Major import sources* (2005–06): Japan 16.8%; Pakistan 15.9%; China 12.8%; Russia 9.2%; Uzbekistan 8.3%. **Exports** (2006–07; f.o.b.): US$416,000,000 (carpets and handicrafts 45.0%; dried fruits 30.3%; fresh fruits 9.4%; skins 5.5% [exports of illegal opiates equalled US$4,000,000,000 in 2007]). *Major export destinations* (2005–06): Pakistan 77.6%; India 6.0%; Russia 3.4%; UAE 2.9%.

## Transport and communications

**Transport.** *Railroads* (2006): route length 10 km. *Roads* (2006): total length 42,150 km (paved 29%). *Vehicles* (2005): passenger cars 41,000; trucks and buses 100,000. *Air transport* (2004–05): passenger-km 681,000,000; metric ton-km cargo 20,624,000. **Communications,** in total units (units per 1,000 persons). Telephone landlines (2008): 101,000 (3.7); cellular telephone subscribers (2008): 7,899,000 (290); personal computers (2006): 1,400 (4); total Internet users (2007): 580,000 (21); broadband Internet subscribers (2007): 500 (0.02).

## Education and health

**Literacy** (2006): total population ages 15 and over literate 28.1%; males 43.1%; females 12.6%. **Health** (2007): physicians 4,900 (1 per 5,000 persons); hospital beds 10,290 (1 per 2,381 persons); infant mortality rate per 1,000 live births (2006) 160.2.

## Military

**Total active duty personnel** (April 2009): 82,780 (army 100%); foreign troops (April 2009): 42-country NATO-sponsored security and development force 58,400, of which US 26,200, UK 8,300, Germany 3,500, Canada 2,800, France 2,800, Italy 2,400. **Military expenditure as percentage of GDP** (2007): 1.6%; per capita expenditure US$6.

## Background

The area was part of the Persian empire in the 6th century BC and was conquered by Alexander the Great in the 4th century BC. Hindu influence entered with the Hephthalites and Sasanians; Islam became entrenched about AD 870, during the rule of the Saffarids. Afghanistan was divided between the Mughal empire of India and the Safavid empire of Persia until the 18th century, when other Persians under Nadir Shah took control. Great Britain and Russia fought several wars in the area in the 19th century. From the 1930s Afghanistan had a stable monarchy; it was overthrown in the 1970s. The rebels' intention was to institute Marxist reforms, but the reforms sparked rebellion, and troops from the USSR invaded to establish order. Afghan guerrillas prevailed, and the Soviet Union withdrew in 1988–89. In 1992 an Islamic republic was established, and in 1996 the Taliban militia took power and enforced a harsher Islamic order. The militia's unwillingness to extradite Osama bin Laden and members of his al-Qaeda militant organization following the September 11 attacks in 2001 led to military conflict with the US and allied nations and the overthrow of the Taliban, and a multinational force to occupy the country in the early 21st century.

## Recent Developments

Despite the presence of 130,000 NATO and US troops in Afghanistan in 2011, the level of violence throughout the country did not decline. August was, in fact, the deadliest month for US forces since the invasion in 2003. As the 2014 deadline for the departure of international forces neared, NATO focused on training Afghan army and police forces and gradually transferring security responsibilities to them. Insurgent activity became more frequent in the north and in Kabul, and the Haqqani network, an arm of the Taliban with bases in Pakistan and links to al-Qaeda, was particularly adept at carefully planned and executed assaults. Encouraged by his Western allies, Pres. Hamid Karzai pressed ahead with a reconciliation program. The High Peace Council, founded in 2010 to engage the Taliban, attempted to draw opposition figures into dialogue. Throughout the year talks continued between the Afghan and US governments over a formal agreement regulating the status of US forces in the country following Afghanistan's assumption of responsibility for its own security. A Loya Jirga, or assembly of national leaders, agreed in November that permanent US military bases ought to be allowed for up to 10 years.

**Internet resource:** <www.cso.gov.af>.

# Albania

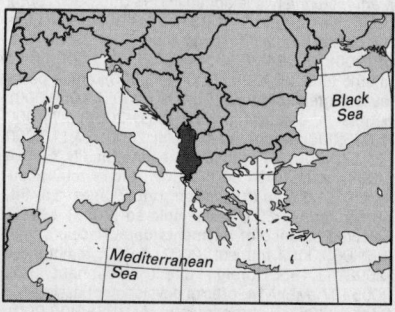

**Official name:** Republika e Shqipërisë (Republic of Albania). **Form of government:** unitary multiparty republic with one legislative house (Assembly [140]).

**Head of state:** President Bamir Topi (from 2007). **Head of government:** Prime Minister Sali Berisha (from 2005). **Capital:** Tirana (Tiranë). **Official language:** Albanian. **Official religion:** none. **Monetary unit:** 1 lek = 100 qindarka; valuation (2 Jul 2012) US$1 = 109.73 leks.

## Demography

**Area:** 11,082 sq mi, 28,703 sq km. **Population** (2011): 3,196,000. **Density** (2011): persons per sq mi 288.4, persons per sq km 111.3. **Urban** (2004) 44.5%. **Sex distribution** (2007): male 49.78%; female 50.22%. **Age breakdown** (2005): under 15, 25.3%; 15–29, 26.4%; 30–44, 19.9%; 45–59, 16.2%; 60–74, 9.2%; 75–84, 2.5%; 85 and over, 0.5%. **Ethnic composition** (2000): Albanian 91.7%; Greek 2.3%; Aromanian 1.8%; Rom 1.8%; other 2.4%. **Traditional religious groups** (2005): Muslim 68%, of which Sunni 51%, Bektashi 17%; Orthodox 22%; Roman Catholic 10%. **Major cities** (2001): Tirana (Tiranë) 343,078; Durrës 99,546; Elbasan 87,797; Shkodër 82,455; Vlorë 77,691. **Location:** southeastern Europe, bordering Montenegro, Kosovo, Macedonia, Greece, and the Mediterranean Sea.

## Vital statistics

**Birth rate** per 1,000 population (2008): 11.4 (world avg. 20.3). **Death rate** per 1,000 population (2008): 5.1 (world avg. 8.5). **Total fertility rate** (avg. births per childbearing woman; 2008): 1.40. **Life expectancy** at birth (2008): male 72.9 years; female 77.8 years.

## National economy

**Budget** (2006). *Revenue:* 229,444,000,000 leks (tax revenue 89.6%; nontax revenue 6.9%; grants 3.5%). *Expenditures:* 258,816,000,000 leks (social security and welfare 25.7%; transport and communications 11.8%; education 10.7%; general administration 10.3%; health 9.2). **Gross national income** (2008): US$12,057,000,000 (US$3,840 per capita). **Public debt** (external, outstanding; end of 2007): US$2,150,000,000. **Production** (metric tons except as noted). *Agriculture and fishing* (2006): alfalfa for forage and silage 2,962,000, corn (maize) 245,400, wheat 230,900; livestock (number of live animals) 1,830,000 sheep, 940,000 goats, 634,000 cattle; fisheries production 7,699 (from aquaculture 26%). *Mining and quarrying* (2006): chromium ore 50,000. *Manufacturing* (value added in US$'000,000; 2005): basic chemical products 33; textiles 33; base metals 32. *Energy production (consumption):* electricity (kWhr; 2006) 5,094,000,000 (5,705,000,000); lignite (metric tons; 2006) 92,000 (105,000); crude petroleum (barrels; 2008) 2,190,000 ([2005] 2,950,000); petroleum products (metric tons; 2006) 271,000 (1,033,000); natural gas (cu m; 2006) 17,170,000 (17,170,000). **Population economically active** (2006): total 1,084,000; activity rate of total population 34.6% (participation rates: ages 15–64, 53.7%; female 39.6%; unemployed [2008] 13.0%). **Selected balance of payments data.** Receipts from (US$'000,000): tourism (2007) 1,002; remittances (2008) 1,495; foreign direct investment (FDI; 2005–07 avg.) 414; official development assistance (2007) 305. Disbursements for (US$'000,000):

tourism (2007) 923; remittances (2008) 10; FDI (2005–07 avg.) 10.

## Foreign trade

**Imports** (2007; c.i.f.): 379,887,000,000 leks (machinery and apparatus 14.2%; food products 12.4%; chemical products 8.8%; refined petroleum products 7.1%; motor vehicles 6.4%; electricity 5.9%; clothing and wearing apparel 5.5%; iron and steel 5.3%). *Major import sources:* Italy 27.1%; Greece 14.6%; Turkey 7.3%; China 6.6%; Germany 5.5%. **Exports** (2007; f.o.b.): 97,456,000,000 leks (clothing and wearing apparel 26.9%; footwear 21.0%; metal ore and scrap 11.6%; mineral fuels 7.5%; locks and safes 4.4%). *Major export destinations:* Italy 68.1%; Greece 8.3%; Serbia (including Kosovo) 6.7%; China 2.6%; Germany 2.4%.

## Transport and communications

**Transport.** *Railroads* (2007): operational route length 399 km; passenger-km 51,000,000; metric ton-km cargo 53,000,000. *Roads* (2002): total length 18,000 km (paved 39%). *Vehicles* (2007): passenger cars 237,932; trucks and buses 89,151. *Air transport* (2005; Albanian Air only): passenger-km 152,000,000. **Communications,** in total units (units per 1,000 persons). Telephone landlines (2008): 316,000 (100); cellular telephone subscribers (2008): 3,141,000 (989); personal computers (2007): 120,000 (38); total Internet users (2006): 471,000 (150); broadband Internet subscribers (2008): 36,000 (11).

## Education and health

**Educational attainment** (2001). Population ages 20 and over having: no formal schooling/incomplete primary education 7.8%; primary 55.6%; lower secondary 2.7%; upper secondary 17.9%; vocational 8.8%; university 7.2%. **Literacy** (2006): total population ages 15 and over literate 98.7%. **Health:** physicians (2004) 3,699 (1 per 845 persons); hospital beds (2007) 9,191 (1 per 346 persons); infant mortality rate per 1,000 live births (2008) 6.0; undernourished population (2002–04) 200,000 (6% of total population based on the consumption of a minimum daily requirement of 1,980 calories).

## Military

**Total active duty personnel** (November 2008): 14,295. **Military expenditure as percentage of GDP** (2008): 1.1%; per capita expenditure US$73.

## Background

The Albanians are descended from the Illyrians, an ancient Indo-European people who lived in central Europe and migrated south by the beginning of the Iron Age. Of the two major Illyrian migrating groups, the Gegs (Ghegs) settled in the north and the Tosks in the south, along with Greek colonizers. The area was under Roman rule by the 1st century BC; after 395 AD it was connected administratively to Constantinople. Turkish invasion began in the 14th century and continued into the 15th century; though the national

---

*1 metric ton = about 1.1 short tons; 1 kilometer = 0.6 mi (statute); 1 metric ton-km cargo = about 0.68 short ton-mi cargo; c.i.f.: cost, insurance, and freight; f.o.b.: free on board*

hero, Skanderbeg, was able to resist them for a time, after his death (1468) the Turks consolidated their rule. The country achieved independence in 1912 and was admitted into the League of Nations in 1920. It was briefly a republic in 1925–28 and then became a monarchy under Zog I, whose initial alliance with Benito Mussolini led to Italy's invasion of Albania in 1939. After the war a socialist government under Enver Hoxha was installed. Gradually Albania cut itself off from the nonsocialist international community and eventually from all nations, including China, its last political ally. By 1990 economic hardship had produced antigovernment demonstrations, and in 1992 a noncommunist government was elected and Albania's international isolation ended. In the late 20th and early 21st centuries, Albania continued to experience economic uncertainty and ethnic turmoil, the latter involving Albanian minorities in Serbia and Macedonia.

### Recent Developments

Albania's economy stabilized somewhat in 2011, as GDP growth in the third quarter was 2.6% greater than in the same period in 2010. Unemployment dropped slightly but held at 13.3% in the third quarter. The annual inflation rate was 3.5%, while the value of the country's exports rose by 22.7%. Despite the progress, the European Union made clear that Albania was not yet ready to attain candidate status.

Internet resource: <www.instat.gov.al>.

# Algeria

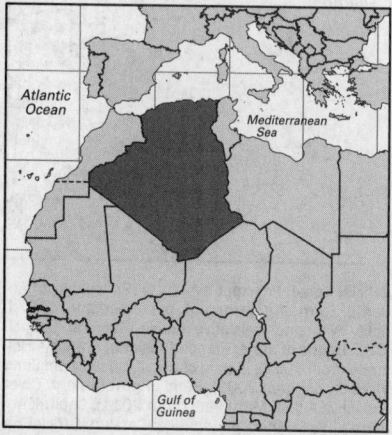

**Official name:** Al-Jumhuriyah al-Jazairiyah al-Dimuqratiyah al-Sha'biyah (Arabic) (People's Democratic Republic of Algeria). **Form of government:** multiparty republic with two legislative houses (Council of the Nation [144; includes 48 nonelected seats appointed by the president]; National People's Assembly [462]). **Head of state:** President Abdelaziz Bouteflika (from 1999). **Head of government:** Prime Minister Ahmed Ouyahia (from 2008). **Capital:** Algiers. **Official languages:** Arabic; Tamazight is designated as a national language. **Official religion:** Islam.

**Monetary unit:** 1 Algerian dinar (DA) = 100 centimes; valuation (2 Jul 2012) US$1 = DA 79.04.

## Demography

**Area:** 919,595 sq mi, 2,381,741 sq km. **Population** (2011): 36,649,000. **Density** (2011): persons per sq mi 39.9, persons per sq km 15.4. **Urban** (2010): 66.5%. **Sex distribution** (2008): male 50.52%; female 49.48%. **Age breakdown** (2007): under 15, 27.2%; 15–29, 32.1%; 30–44, 21.8%; 45–59, 11.9%; 60–74, 5.2%; 75–84, 1.5%; 85 and over, 0.3%. **Ethnic composition** (2000): Algerian Arab 59.1%; Berber 26.2%, of which Arabized Berber 3.0%; Bedouin Arab 14.5%; other 0.2%. **Religious affiliation** (2000): Muslim 99.7%, of which Sunni 99.1%, Ibadiyah 0.6%; Christian 0.3%. **Major cities** (2005): Algiers 1,532,000 (urban agglomeration [2007] 3,354,000); Oran 724,000; Constantine 475,000; Annaba (2004) 410,700; Batna (2004) 285,800. **Location:** northern Africa, bordering the Mediterranean Sea, Tunisia, Libya, Niger, Mali, Mauritania, Western Sahara, and Morocco.

## Vital statistics

**Birth rate** per 1,000 population (2007): 17.1 (world avg. 20.3). **Death rate** per 1,000 population (2007): 4.6 (world avg. 8.5). **Total fertility rate** (avg. births per childbearing woman; 2007): 1.86. **Life expectancy** at birth (2007): male 71.9 years; female 75.2 years.

## National economy

**Budget** (2007). *Revenue:* DA 3,688,500,000,000 (hydrocarbon revenue 75.8%; nonhydrocarbon revenue 24.2%). *Expenditures:* DA 3,092,700,-000,000 (current expenditures 54.1%; capital expenditures 45.9%). **Public debt** (external, outstanding; 2007): US$3,756,000,000. **Production** (metric tons except as noted). *Agriculture and fishing* (2006): wheat 2,687,930, potatoes 2,180,961, barley 1,235,880, dates 491,188, olives 364,733; livestock (number of live animals) 19,615,730 sheep, 3,754,590 goats; fisheries production 146,050 (from aquaculture, negligible). *Mining and quarrying* (2006): iron ore 1,996,000; phosphate rock 1,510,000; zinc (metal content) 572; liquid helium 15,000,000 cum. *Manufacturing* (value added in US$'000,000; 2005): food products and beverages 1,230; fabricated metal products 880; refined petroleum products and manufactured gas 720. *Energy production (consumption):* electricity (kW-hr; 2006) 35,226,-000,000 (35,308,000,000); coal (metric tons; 2006) none (948,000); crude petroleum (barrels; 2008) 485,000,000 ([2006] 148,550,000); petroleum products (metric tons; 2006) 38,294,000 (10,364,000); natural gas (cu m; 2006) 84,900,-000,000 (28,153,000,000). **Gross national income** (2008): US$146,365,000,000 (US$4,260 per capita). **Population economically active** (2006): total 10,109,600; activity rate of population 30% (participation rates: ages 15–64 [2004] 74%; female 16.9%; unemployed [June 2008] 12.3%. **Selected balance of payments data.** Receipts from (US$'000,000): tourism (2007) 219; remittances (2008) 2,202; foreign direct investment (FDI; 2005–07 avg.) 1,514; official development assistance (2007) 390. Disbursements for (US$'000,000): tourism (2007) 377; FDI (2005–07 avg.) 116.

## Foreign trade

**Imports** (2006; c.i.f.): US$21,456,000,000 (food products and live animals 16.9%; nonelectrical machinery 16.0%; iron and steel 12.9%; motor vehicles 11.1%). *Major import sources:* France 20.4%; Italy 8.8%; China 8.0%; Germany 6.9%; US 6.6%. **Exports** (2006; f.o.b.): US$54,613,000,000 (crude petroleum 55.6%; natural gas 27.7%; manufactured gas 7.4%; refined petroleum products 7.2%). *Major export destinations:* US 27.2%; Italy 17.1%; Spain 11.0%; France 8.4%; Canada 6.6%.

## Transport and communications

**Transport.** *Railroads* (2004): route length 3,973 km; (2003) passenger-km 946,000,000; metric ton-km cargo 2,041,000,000. *Roads* (2004): total length 108,302 km (paved 70%). *Vehicles* (2005): passenger cars 1,905,892; trucks and buses 1,068,520. *Air transport* (2007; Air Algérie only): passenger-km 3,162,000,000; metric ton-km cargo 2,420,000. **Communications,** in total units (units per 1,000 persons). Telephone landlines (2008): 3,068,000 (88); cellular telephone subscribers (2007): 27,562,000 (814); personal computers (2007): 377,000 (11); total Internet users (2007): 3,500,000 (103); broadband Internet subscribers (2007): 287,000 (8.4).

## Education and health

**Educational attainment** (1998). Percentage of economically active population ages 6 and over having: no formal schooling 30.1%; primary education 29.9%; lower secondary 20.7%; upper secondary 13.4%; higher 4.3%; other 1.6%. **Literacy** (2005): total population ages 15 and over literate 76.3%; males literate 84.5%; females literate 68.0%. *Health:* physicians (2003) 36,347 (1 per 877 persons); hospital beds (2004) 55,089 (1 per 588 persons); infant mortality rate per 1,000 live births (2007) 29.8; undernourished population (2002–04) 1,400,000 (4% of total population based on the consumption of a minimum daily requirement of 1,870 calories).

## Military

**Total active duty personnel** (November 2008): 147,000 (army 86.4%, navy 4.1%, air force 9.5%). **Military expenditure as percentage of GDP** (2007): 3.3%; per capita expenditure US$126.

## Background

Phoenician traders settled the area early in the 1st millennium BC; several centuries later the Romans invaded, and by AD 40 they had control of the Mediterranean coast. The fall of Rome in the 5th century led to invasion by the Vandals and later by Byzantium. The Islamic invasion began in the 7th century; by 711 all of northern Africa was under the control of the Umayyad caliphate. Several Islamic Berber empires followed, most prominently the Almoravid (c. 1054–1130), which extended its domain to Spain,

and the Almohad (c. 1130–1269). The Barbary Coast pirates, operating in the area, had menaced Mediterranean trade for centuries, and France seized this pretext to enter Algeria in 1830. By 1847 France had established control in the region, and by the late 19th century it had instituted civil rule. Popular movements resulted in the bloody Algerian War (1954–62); independence was achieved following a referendum in 1962. Beginning in the 1990s, Islamic fundamentalist opposition to secular rule led to an outbreak in civil violence between the army and various Islamic extremist groups.

## Recent Developments

Sporadic local rioting betrayed Algerians' frustration with endless examples of maladministration and official incompetence in 2011. In mid-April Pres. Abdelaziz Bouteflika pledged to amend the constitution, inviting political parties to submit their proposals for amendments to a parliamentary committee. The proposed reforms were greeted with general disappointment and rejected even by parties within the president's coalition. Terrorist violence continued throughout northern rural Algeria in 2011, culminating in an attack on the military academy at Cherchell in August in which 18 persons died.

**Internet resource:** <www.algeria.com>.

# Andorra

**Official name:** Principat d'Andorra (Principality of Andorra). **Form of government:** parliamentary coprincipality with one legislative house (General Council [28]). **Heads of state:** French President François Hollande (from 2012); Bishop of Urgell, Spain, Joan Enric Vives Sicília (from 2003). **Head of government:** Chief Executive Antoni Martí Petit (from 2011). **Capital:** Andorra la Vella. **Official language:** Catalan. **Official religion:** none. **Monetary unit:** 1 euro (€) = 100 cents; valuation (2 Jul 2012) US$1 = €0.79 (Andorra uses the euro as its official currency, even though it is not a member of the EU).

## Demography

**Area:** 179 sq mi, 464 sq km. **Population** (2011): 85,600. **Density** (2011): persons per sq mi 478.2, persons per sq km 184.5. **Urban** (2003): 93%. **Sex distribution** (2005): male 52.16%; female 47.84%. **Age breakdown** (2007): under 15, 14.6%; 15–29, 19.0%; 30–44, 29.1%; 45–59, 20.8%; 60–74, 10.3%; 75–84, 4.2%; 85 and over, 2.0%. **Ethnic composition** (by nationality; 2007): Andorran 36.7%; Spanish 33.0%; Portuguese 16.3%; French 6.3%; British 1.3%; Argentinian 0.8%; Moroccan 0.6%; other 5.0%. **Religious affiliation** (2000): Roman Catholic 89.1%; other Christian 4.3%; Muslim 0.6%; Hindu 0.5%; nonreligious 5.0%; other 0.5%. **Major towns** (2007): Andorra la Vella 21,556; Escaldes-Engordany 16,475; Encamp 8,704. **Location:** southwestern Europe, between France and Spain.

## Vital statistics

**Birth rate** per 1,000 population (2007): 10.0 (world avg. 20.3). **Death rate** per 1,000 population (2007): 2.8 (world avg. 8.5). **Total fertility rate** (avg. births per childbearing woman; 2007): 1.17. **Marriage rate** per 1,000 population (2007): 3.1. **Life expectancy** at birth (2007): male 80.4 years; female 85.4 years.

## National economy

**Budget** (2006). *Revenue:* €340,500,000 (indirect taxes 75.7%; property income 4.3%; other taxes and income 20.0%). *Expenditures:* €340,500,000 (current expenditures 53.5%; development expenditures 46.5%). **Production.** *Agriculture and fishing* (2006): tobacco 315 metric tons; other traditional crops include hay, potatoes, and grapes; livestock (number of live animals; 2007) 2,058 sheep, 1,478 cattle, 847 horses. *Quarrying:* small amounts of marble are quarried. *Manufacturing* (2006): manufactured goods include cigarettes, furniture, food products and beverages, newspapers and magazines, and worked metals. *Energy production (consumption):* electricity (kW-hr; 2006) 73,900,000 ([2007] 577,000,000). **Population economically active** (2007): total 43,234; activity rate of total population 55% (participation rates: ages 15–64 [2003] 75.1%; female 46.6%; unemployed, n.a.). **Selected balance of payments data.** Disbursements for (US$'000,-000): remittances (2001–02) 12. **Gross national income** (2007): US$3,250,000,000 (US$43,504 per capita). **Public debt** (2007): US$573,000,000.

## Foreign trade

**Imports** (2007): €1,396,000,000 (machinery and apparatus 26.4%; food products and beverages 16.2%; motor vehicles 9.2%; wearing apparel and knitwear 9.1%; perfumes, cosmetics, and soaps 7.7%; mineral fuels 6.7%). *Major import sources:* Spain 58.7%; France 18.8%; Germany 5.1%; Italy 3.3%; Japan 2.7%. **Exports** (2007): €93,000,000 (electrical machinery and apparatus 25.0%; motor vehicles 18.5%; optical equipment, photographic equipment, and other precision instruments 10.9%; iron and steel products 6.8%; perfumes, cosmetics, and soaps 3.7%). *Major export destinations:* Spain 61.6%; France 16.2%; Germany 15.7%; Italy 2.2%.

## Transport and communications

**Transport.** *Railroads:* none. *Roads* (1999): total length 269 km (paved 74%). *Vehicles* (2007): passenger cars 51,889; trucks and buses 5,395. **Communications,** in total units (units per 1,000 persons).

Telephone landlines (2008): 37,000 (444); cellular telephone subscribers (2008): 64,000 (766); total Internet users (2008): 59,000 (705); broadband Internet subscribers (2008): 21,000 (247).

## Education and health

**Literacy:** resident population is virtually 100% literate. **Health** (2006): physicians 244 (1 per 327 persons); hospital beds 208 (1 per 385 persons); infant mortality rate per 1,000 live births (2006–07) 2.4; undernourished population, n.a.

## Military

**Total active duty personnel:** none. France and Spain are responsible for Andorra's external security; the police force is assisted in alternate years by either French gendarmerie or Barcelona police. Andorra has no defense budget.

## Background

Andorra's independence is traditionally ascribed to Charlemagne, who recovered the region from the Muslims in 803. It was placed under the joint suzerainty of the French counts of Foix and the Spanish bishops of the See of Urgell in 1278, and it was subsequently governed jointly by the Spanish bishop of Urgell and the French head of state. This feudal system of government, the last in Europe, lasted until 1993, when a constitution was adopted that transferred most of the coprinces' powers to the Andorran General Council, a body elected by universal suffrage. Andorra has long had a strong affinity with Catalonia; its institutions are based in Catalonian law, and it is part of the diocese of the See of Urgell (Spain). The traditional economy was based on sheep raising, but tourism has been very important since the 1950s. Andorra joined the United Nations (1993) and the Council of Europe (1994).

## Recent Developments

In 2011 the economic downturn led to changes in Andorra's tax structure, including the proposed introduction of a business tax in 2012 and a sales tax in 2013. Even a theretofore widely resisted income tax appeared to be in the offing.

**Internet resource:** <www.estadistica.ad>.

# Angola

**Official name:** República de Angola (Republic of Angola). **Form of government:** unitary multiparty republic with one legislative house (National Assembly [220, excluding 3 unfilled seats reserved for Angolans living abroad]). **Head of state and government:** President José Eduardo dos Santos (from 1979). **Capital:** Luanda. **Official language:** Portuguese. **Official religion:** none. **Monetary unit:** 1 kwanza (AOA) = 100 cêntimos; valuation (2 Jul 2012) US$1 = kwanza 95.36.

## Demography

**Area:** 481,354 sq mi, 1,246,700 sq km. **Population** (2011): 19,618,000. **Density** (2011): persons per sq mi 40.8, persons per sq km 15.7. **Urban** (2011):

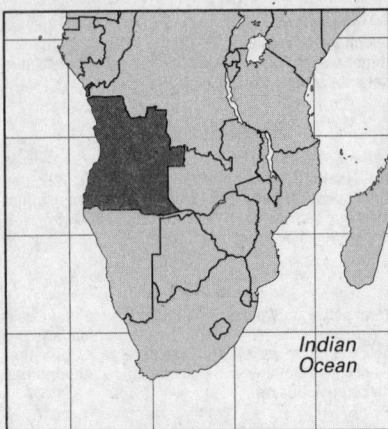

*Indian
Ocean*

59.2%. **Sex distribution** (2007): male 50.51%; female 49.49%. **Age breakdown** (2007): under 15, 43.7%; 15–29, 27.1%; 30–44, 16.2%; 45–59, 8.5%; 60–74, 3.9%; 75–84, 0.6%; 85 and over, negligible. **Ethnic composition** (2000): Ovimbundu 25.2%; Kimbundu 23.1%; Kongo 12.6%; Lwena (Luvale) 8.2%; Chokwe 5.0%; Kwanyama 4.1%; Nyaneka 3.9%; Luchazi 2.3%; Ambo (Ovambo) 2.0%; Mbwela 1.7%; Nyemba 1.7%; mixed race (Eurafrican) 1.0%; white 0.9%; other 8.3%. **Religious affiliation** (2006): Roman Catholic 55%; independent Christian 30%, of which African indigenous 25%, Brazilian evangelical 5%; Protestant 10%; Muslim 0.7%; traditional beliefs/other 4.3%. **Major cities** (2004): Luanda (urban agglomeration; 2005) 2,766,000; Huambo 173,600; Lobito 137,400; Benguela 134,500; Namibe 132,900. **Location**: southern Africa, bordering the Democratic Republic of the Congo (DRC), Zambia, Namibia, and the Atlantic Ocean; the exclave of Cabinda on the Atlantic Ocean borders the Republic of the Congo and the DRC.

## Vital statistics

**Birth rate** per 1,000 population (2007): 44.5 (world avg. 20.3). **Death rate** per 1,000 population (2007): 24.8 (world avg. 8.5). **Total fertility rate** (avg. births per childbearing woman; 2007): 6.27. **Life expectancy** at birth (2007): male 36.7 years; female 38.6 years.

## National economy

**Budget** (2006). *Revenue:* US$20,966,000,000 (petroleum revenue 80.1%; nonpetroleum revenue 19.9%). *Expenditures:* US$14,269,000,000 (current expenditures 71.8%; development expenditures 28.2%). **Production** (metric tons except as noted). *Agriculture and fishing* (2006): cassava 8,810,000, sweet potatoes 685,000, potatoes 593,000, oil palm fruit 291,233; livestock (number of live animals) 4,150,000 cattle, 2,050,000 goats, 780,000 pigs; fisheries production 213,948 (from aquaculture, none). *Mining and quarrying* (2007): diamonds 9,702,000 carats; granite 46,000 cu m. *Manufacturing* (2005): fuel oil 609,000;

diesel fuel 461,000; jet fuel 290,000. *Energy production (consumption):* electricity (kW-hr; 2006) 2,959,000,000 (2,959,000,000); crude petroleum (barrels; 2008) 694,980,000 ([2006] 15,883,000); petroleum products (metric tons; 2006) 1,821,000 (2,075,000); natural gas (cu m; 2006) 793,000,000 (793,000,000). **Selected balance of payments data.** Receipts from (US$'000,000): tourism (2006) 75; foreign direct disinvestment (2005–07 avg.) –947; official development assistance (2007) 241. Disbursements for (US$'000,000): tourism (2006) 148; remittances (2008) 603; foreign direct investment (2005–07 avg.) 247. **Gross national income** (2008): US$62,113,000,000 (US$3,450 per capita). **Public debt** (external, outstanding; 2007): US$10,474,-000,000. **Population economically active** (2006): total 7,246,000; activity rate of total population 43.8% (participation rates: ages 15–64, 82.8%; female 46.7%; unemployed, n.a.).

## Foreign trade

**Imports** (2006): US$10,776,000,000 (consumer goods 60.3%; capital goods 28.8%; intermediate goods 10.9%). *Major import sources* (2005): South Korea 20.5%; Portugal 13.4%; US 12.5%; South Africa 7.4%; Brazil 7.0%. **Exports** (2005): US$31,817,000,000 (crude petroleum 94.2%; diamonds 3.6%; refined petroleum products 0.9%). *Major export destinations* (2005): US 39.8%; China 29.6%; France 7.8%; Chile 5.4%; Taiwan 4.4%.

## Transport and communications

**Transport.** *Railroads* (2008): route length of lines in operation 750 km; (2006; Benguela Railway only) passenger-km 69,900,000; (2006; Benguela Railway only) metric ton-km cargo 510,000. *Roads* (2006): total length 72,000 km (paved 25%). *Vehicles* (2001): passenger cars 117,200; trucks and buses 118,300. *Air transport*: passenger-km (2004) 479,000,000.

## Education and health

**Literacy** (2006): percentage of population ages 15 and over literate 67.4%; males literate 82.9%; females literate 54.2%. **Health:** physicians (2004) 1,165 (1 per 9,890 persons); hospital beds (2005) 1,170 (1 per 10,000 persons); infant mortality rate per 1,000 live births (2007) 184.4; undernourished population (2002–04) 4,800,000 (35% of total population based on the consumption of a minimum daily requirement of 1,800 calories).

## Military

**Total active duty personnel** (November 2008): 107,000 (army 93.5%, navy 0.9%, air force 5.6%). **Military expenditure as percentage of GDP** (2008): 3.9%; per capita expenditure US$194.

## Background

An influx of Bantu-speaking peoples in the 1st millennium AD led to their dominance in the area by c. 1500. The most important Bantu kingdom was the Kongo; south of the Kongo was the Ndongo kingdom

*1 metric ton = about 1.1 short tons;    1 kilometer = 0.6 mi (statute);    1 metric ton-km cargo = about 0.68 short ton-mi cargo;    c.i.f.: cost, insurance, and freight;    f.o.b.: free on board*

of the Mbundu people. Portuguese explorers arrived in 1483 and over time gradually extended their rule. Angola's frontiers were largely determined with other European nations in the 19th century, but not without severe resistance by the indigenous peoples. Its status as a Portuguese colony was changed to that of an overseas province in 1951. Resistance to colonial rule led to the outbreak of fighting in 1961, which led ultimately to independence in 1975. Rival factions continued fighting after independence; although a peace accord was reached in 1994, forces led by Jonas M. Savimbi continued to resist government control. The killing of Savimbi in February 2002 changed the political balance and led to the signing of a cease-fire agreement in Luanda in April that effectively ended the civil war.

### Recent Developments

The rise of oil revenue and foreign investment throughout 2011 ensured Angola's robust economic growth. Real GDP growth was forecast to peak at 8.5% in 2012. Meanwhile, the capital, Luanda, gained the dubious reputation of being the world's most expensive city for political, diplomatic, and commercial elites. In stark contrast, the gap between the wealthy minority and the poor majority grew wider, with few signs of government success in ameliorating socioeconomic problems.

Internet resource: <www.angola.org>.

# Antigua and Barbuda

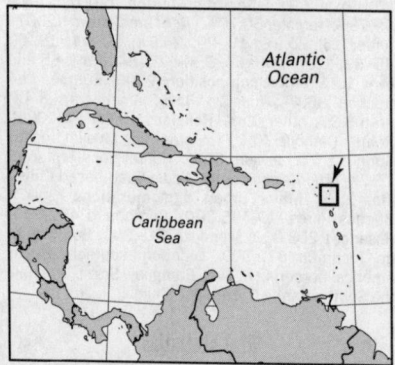

Atlantic
Ocean

Caribbean
Sea

Official name: Antigua and Barbuda. Form of government: constitutional monarchy with two legislative houses (Senate [17]; House of Representatives [19]). Head of state: British Queen Elizabeth II (from 1952), represented by Governor-General Louise Lake-Tack (from 2007). Head of government: Prime Minister Baldwin Spencer (from 2004). Capital: Saint John's. Official language: English. Official religion: none. Monetary unit: 1 Eastern Caribbean dollar (EC$) = 100 cents; valuation (2 Jul 2012) US$1 = EC$2.70.

### Demography

Area: 171 sq mi, 442 sq km. Population (2011): 91,400. Density (2011): persons per sq mi 534.5, persons per sq km 206.8. Urban (2003): 37.7%. Sex distribution (2007): male 47.61%; female 52.39%. Age breakdown (2001): under 15, 27.6%; 15–29, 23.6%; 30–44, 23.3%; 45–59, 16.0%; 60–74, 6.7%; 75–84, 2.1%; 85 and over, 0.7%. Ethnic composition (2000): black 82.4%; US white 12.0%; mulatto 3.5%; British 1.3%; other 0.8%. Religious affiliation (2001): Christian 74%, of which Anglican 23%, independent Christian 23%, other Protestant (including Methodist, Moravian, and Seventh-day Adventist) 28%; Rastafarian 2%; atheist/nonreligious 5%; other/unknown 19%. Major settlements (2006): Saint John's 25,300; All Saints 2,550; Liberta 1,680. Location: islands in the eastern Caribbean Sea.

### Vital statistics

Birth rate per 1,000 population (2007): 17.0 (world avg. 20.3); (2001) within marriage 25.7%. Death rate per 1,000 population (2007): 6.4 (world avg. 8.5). Total fertility rate (avg. births per childbearing woman; 2007): 2.09. Life expectancy at birth (2007): male 71.9 years; female 75.7 years.

### National economy

Budget (2007). *Revenue:* EC$718,300,000 (tax revenue 91.4%, of which taxes on international transactions 38.3%, taxes on income and profits 14.0%; current nontax revenue 5.1%; grants 2.8%; development revenue 0.7%). *Expenditures:* EC$923,800,000 (current expenditures 78.3%, of which transfers and subsidies 21.7%; development expenditures 21.7%). Production (metric tons except as noted). *Agriculture and fishing* (2007): mangoes, mangosteens, and guavas 1,430, melons 840, tomatoes 395, "Antiguan Black" pineapples 210; livestock (number of live animals) 19,000 sheep, 14,500 cattle; fisheries production (2006) 3,092 (from aquaculture, none). *Mining and quarrying:* crushed stone for local use. *Manufacturing:* manufactures include cement, bricks, and tiles, handicrafts, alcoholic and nonalcoholic beverages, and jams and jellies. *Energy production (consumption):* electricity (kW-hr; 2006) 116,000,000 (116,000,000); petroleum products (metric tons; 2006) none (139,000). Population economically active (2001): total 39,564; activity rate of total population 51.5% (participation rates: ages 15–64, 77.0%; female 50%; unemployed [2005] 4%). Gross national income (2008): US$1,165,000,000 (US$13,620 per capita). Public debt (external, outstanding; December 2007): US$615,400,000. Selected balance of payments data. Receipts from (US$'000,000): tourism (2007) 338; remittances (2008) 26; foreign direct investment (2005–07 avg.) 326; official development assistance (2007) 4. Disbursements for (US$'000,000): tourism (2007) 51; remittances (2008) 2.

### Foreign trade

Imports (2007): US$573,000,000 (machinery and apparatus 20.3%; manufactured goods 16.3%; food products and live animals 15.0%; motor vehicles 8.1%; refined petroleum products 6.2%). *Major import sources:* US 58.2%; UK 6.4%; Japan 4.3%; Netherlands Antilles 4.2%; Trinidad and Tobago 3.9%. Exports (2007): US$99,000,000 (refined petroleum products 57.6%; telecommunications equipment 6.6%; generators 3.0%; sails 2.9%). *Major export destinations:* Netherlands Antilles 30.9%; US 23.5%; Barbados 8.2%; Dominica 6.1%; UK 4.2%.

## Transport and communications

**Transport.** *Roads* (2002): total length 1,165 km (paved 33%). *Air transport* (2006): passenger-km 118,200,000; metric ton-km cargo 200,000. **Communications,** in total units (units per 1,000 persons). Telephone landlines (2008): 38,000 (450); cellular telephone subscribers (2008): 137,000 (1,616); total Internet users (2008): 65,000 (769); broadband Internet subscribers (2008): 13,000 (149).

## Education and health

**Educational attainment** (2001). Percentage of population ages 25 and over having: no formal schooling 0.6%; incomplete primary education 2.6%; complete primary 27.9%; secondary 43.6%; higher (not university) 14.4%; university 10.9%. **Literacy** (2003): percentage of total population ages 15 and over literate 85.8%. **Health:** hospital beds (2009) 211 (1 per 420 persons); infant mortality rate per 1,000 live births (2007) 18.8.

## Military

**Total active duty personnel** (November 2008): a 170-member defense force (army 73.5%, navy 26.5%) is part of the Eastern Caribbean regional security system. **Military expenditure as percentage of GDP** (2007): 0.5%; per capita expenditure US$61.

## Background

Christopher Columbus visited Antigua in 1493 and named it after a church in Seville, Spain. It was colonized in 1632 by English settlers, who imported African slaves to grow tobacco and sugarcane. Barbuda was colonized by the English in 1678. In 1834 its slaves were emancipated. Antigua (with Barbuda) was part of the British colony of the Leeward Islands from 1871 until that colony was defederated in 1956. The islands achieved full independence in 1981.

## Recent Developments

In 2011 Antigua and Barbuda began to experience the crime upsurge that had troubled so many Caribbean territories, facilitated by what the national security minister described as "the proliferation of illegal firearms and ammunition." In March the country also found itself on the list of countries in the region criticized by the US State Department in its 2011 International Narcotics Control Strategy Report for not taking sufficient steps to control financial crime.

**Internet resource:** <www.ab.gov.ag>.

# Argentina

**Official name:** República Argentina (Argentine Republic). **Form of government:** federal republic with two legislative houses (Senate [72]; Chamber of Deputies [257]). **Head of state and government:** President Cristina Fernández de Kirchner (from 2007), assisted by Cabinet Chief Juan Manuel Abal Medina (from 2011). **Capital:** Buenos Aires. **Official**

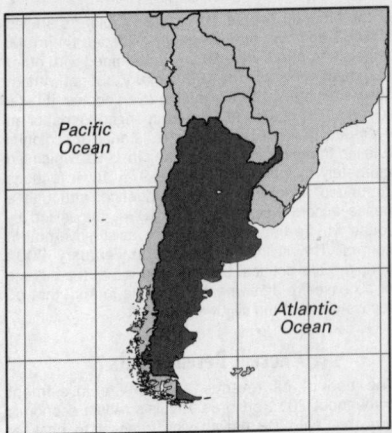

language: Spanish. **Official religion:** none (Roman Catholicism has special status and receives financial support from the state). **Monetary unit:** 1 peso (ARS) = 100 centavos; valuation (2 Jul 2012) US$1 = ARS 4.53.

## Demography

**Area:** 1,073,520 sq mi, 2,780,403 sq km. **Population** (2011): 40,365,000. **Density** (2011): persons per sq mi 37.6, persons per sq km 14.5. **Urban** (2009): 92.2%. **Sex distribution** (2007): male 49.23%; female 50.77%. **Age breakdown** (2007): under 15, 25.9%; 15–29, 24.9%; 30–44, 19.2%; 45–59, 15.4%; 60–74, 9.8%; 75–84, 3.6%; 85 and over, 1.2%. **Ethnic composition** (2000): European extraction 86.4%; mestizo 6.5%; Amerindian 3.4%; Arab 3.3%; other 0.4%. **Religious affiliation** (2005): Roman Catholic 70%; Protestant 9%; Muslim (mostly Sunni) 1.5%; Jewish 0.8%; nonreligious/unknown 16.2%; other (significantly Middle East–based Christian) 2.5%. **Major urban agglomerations** (2007): Buenos Aires 12,795,000; Córdoba 1,452,000; Rosario 1,203,000; Mendoza 918,000; San Miguel de Tucumán 832,000. **Location:** southern South America, bordering Bolivia, Paraguay, Brazil, Uruguay, the South Atlantic Ocean, and Chile.

## Vital statistics

**Birth rate** per 1,000 population (2007): 18.3 (world avg. 20.3). **Death rate** per 1,000 population (2007): 7.5 (world avg. 8.5). **Total fertility rate** (avg. births per childbearing woman; 2007): 2.39. **Life expectancy** at birth (2007): male 72.9 years; female 79.6 years.

## National economy

**Budget** (2008). *Revenue:* ARS 169,463,000,000 (indirect taxes 57.1%; social security contributions 23.7%; direct taxes 12.9%). *Expenditures:* ARS 161,486,000,000 (current expenditures 88.2%, of which social security 41.2%, debt service 11.9%, economic development 9.4%; capital expenditures 11.8%). **Public debt** (external, outstanding; 2007):

---

*1 metric ton = about 1.1 short tons; 1 kilometer = 0.6 mi (statute); 1 metric ton-km cargo = about 0.68 short ton-mi cargo; c.i.f.: cost, insurance, and freight; f.o.b.: free on board*

US$66,110,000,000. **Gross national income** (2008): US$287,160,000,000 (US$7,200 per capita). **Production** (metric tons except as noted). *Agriculture and fishing* (2007): soybeans 45,500,000, alfalfa (2006) 38,783,332, corn (maize) 21,775,364, sunflower seeds 3,500,000, maté 270,000; livestock (number of live animals) 50,750,000 cattle, 12,450,000 sheep, 3,680,000 horses; fisheries production (2006) 1,184,713 (from aquaculture, negligible). *Mining and quarrying* (2006): boron 533,535; copper (metal content) 180,144; silver 248,227 kg; gold 44,131 kg. *Manufacturing* (value added in US$'000,000; 2002): food products 10,152, of which vegetable oils and fats 3,864; base metals 4,031; industrial and agricultural chemical products 2,770; refined petroleum products 2,514. *Energy production (consumption):* electricity (kW-hr; 2007) 104,448,000,000 ([2006] 117,555,000,000); coal (metric tons; 2006) 427,000 (1,254,000); crude petroleum (barrels; 2008) 241,400,000 ([2006] 202,307,000); petroleum products (metric tons; 2006) 26,785,000 (22,541,000); natural gas (cu m; 2007) 59,484,000,000 ([2006] 45,641,000,000). **Selected balance of payments data.** Receipts from (US$'000,000): tourism (2007) 4,314; remittances (2008) 691; foreign direct investment (FDI; 2005–07 avg.) 5,341. Disbursements for (US$'000,000): tourism (2007) 3,921; remittances (2008) 732; FDI (2005–07 avg.) 1,542. **Population economically active** (2006): total 11,089,700; activity rate of total population 46.2% (participation rates: ages 15–64, 68.5%; female 43.4%; unemployed [April 2007–March 2008] 8.1%).

## Foreign trade

**Imports** (2007; c.i.f.): US$44,707,000,000 (machinery and apparatus 30.3%; chemical products 18.5%; motor vehicles 15.0%; mineral fuels 6.0%). *Major import sources:* Brazil 32.8%; US 11.9%; China 11.4%; Germany 4.8%; Mexico 3.0%. **Exports** (2007; f.o.b.): US$55,780,000,000 (soybean animal foodstuffs 10.3%; motor vehicles 9.5%; cereals 9.3%; crude petroleum 8.4%; soybean oil 7.9%; soybeans 6.2%). *Major export destinations:* Brazil 18.8%; China 9.3%; US 7.8%; Chile 7.5%; Spain 3.7%.

## Transport and communications

**Transport.** *Railroads* (2006): route length 30,818 km; (2005) passenger-km 8,327,000,000; (2001) metric ton-km cargo 12,262,000,000. *Roads* (2003): total length 231,374 km (paved 30%). *Vehicles* (2005): passenger cars 5,230,000; trucks and buses 1,775,000. *Air transport* (2007): passenger-km 14,616,000,000; metric ton-km cargo 130,668,000. **Communications,** in total units (units per 1,000 persons). Telephone landlines (2008): 9,631,000 (241); cellular telephone subscribers (2008): 46,509,000 (1,166); personal computers (2006): 3,500,000 (90); total Internet users (2008): 11,212,000 (281); broadband Internet subscribers (2008): 3,185,000 (80).

## Education and health

**Educational attainment** (2001). Percentage of population ages 15 and over having: no formal schooling 3.7%; incomplete primary education 14.2%; complete primary 28.0%; secondary 37.1%; some higher 8.3%; complete higher 8.7%. **Literacy** (2005): percentage of total population ages 15 and over literate

97.5%. **Health:** physicians (2005) 120,978 (1 per 319 persons); hospital beds (2004) 76,446 (1 per 500 persons); infant mortality rate per 1,000 live births (2007) 12.1; undernourished population (2002–04) 1,200,000 (3% of total population based on the consumption of a minimum daily requirement of 1,940 calories).

## Military

**Total active duty personnel** (November 2008): 76,000 (army 54.5%, navy 26.3%, air force 19.2%). **Military expenditure as percentage of GDP** (2008): 0.7%; per capita expenditure US$50.

## Background

Little is known of Argentina's indigenous population before the Europeans' arrival. The area was explored for Spain by Sebastian Cabot in 1526–30; by 1580, Asunción, Santa Fe, and Buenos Aires had been settled. At first attached to the Viceroyalty of Peru (1620), it was later included with regions of modern Uruguay, Paraguay, and Bolivia in the Viceroyalty of the Río de la Plata, or Buenos Aires (1776). With the establishment of the United Provinces of the Río de la Plata in 1816, Argentina achieved its independence from Spain, but its boundaries were not set until the early 20th century. In 1943 the government was overthrown by the military; Col. Juan Perón took control in 1946. He in turn was overthrown in 1955. He returned to power in 1973 after two decades of turmoil. His second wife, Isabel, became president on his death in 1974 but lost power after a military coup in 1976. The military government tried to take the Falkland Islands (Islas Malvinas) in 1982 but was defeated by the British, with the result that the government returned to civilian rule in 1983. The government of Raúl Alfonsín worked to end the human rights abuses that characterized the former regimes. Hyperinflation led to public riots and Alfonsín's electoral defeat in 1989; his Peronist successor, Carlos Menem, instituted laissez-faire economic policies. Under a succession of interim presidents, Argentina experienced one of its worst economic collapses at the beginning of the 21st century. Néstor Kirchner won the 2003 presidential elections and helped to stabilize the economy. Four years later his wife became the country's first elected female president.

## Recent Developments

Despite Argentina's booming economy, concerns grew in 2011 over inflation. The official inflation rate was 9.5% in December, but some international financial organizations believed the figure to be more than twice that. In November the Spanish energy firm Repsol announced that its Argentinian subsidiary YPF had found almost 1 billion bbl of shale oil in the Neuquén province. In February 2012, however, YPF reported results of further testing that pointed to a reserves figure of closer to 23 billion bbl. If the estimates proved accurate, Argentina, already possessing the third most known shale reserves in the world, was poised to double its oil and gas production in the next 10 years. In May the Argentine government controversially nationalized YPF.

**Internet resource:** <www.indec.mecon.ar>.

# Armenia

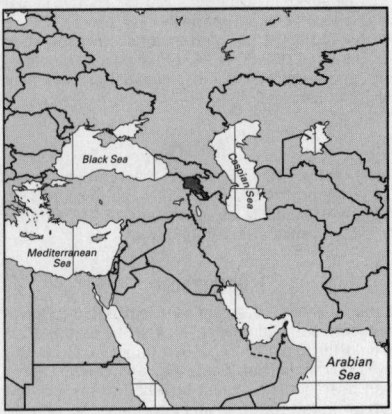

**Official name:** Hayastani Hanrape-tut'yun (Republic of Armenia). **Form of government:** unitary multiparty republic with a single legislative house (National Assembly [131]). **Head of state:** President Serzh Sarkisyan (from 2008). **Head of government:** Prime Minister Tigran Sarkisyan (from 2008). **Capital:** Yerevan. **Official language:** Armenian. **Official religion:** none (the Armenian Apostolic Church [Armenian Orthodox Church] has special status per 1991 religious law). **Monetary unit:** 1 dram (AMD) = 100 luma; valuation (2 Jul 2012) US$1 = 418.00 drams.

## Demography

**Area:** 11,484 sq mi, 29,743 sq km; in addition, about 13% of neighboring Azerbaijan (including the 1,700-sq-mi [4,400-sq-km] geographic region of Nagorno-Karabakh [Armenian: Artsakh]) has been occupied by Armenian forces since 1993. **Population** (2011): 3,100,000. **Density** (2011): persons per sq mi 269.9, persons per sq km 104.2. **Urban** (2009): 64.0%. **Sex distribution** (2007): male 48.38%; female 51.62%. **Age breakdown** (2005): under 15, 20.9%; 15–29, 27.2%; 30–44, 19.5%; 45–59, 17.9%; 60–74, 10.2%; 75–84, 3.8%; 85 and over, 0.5%. **Ethnic composition** (2001): Armenian 97.9%; Kurdish 1.3%; Russian 0.5%; other 0.3%. **Religious affiliation** (2005): Armenian Apostolic (Orthodox) 72.9%; Roman Catholic 4.0%; Sunni Muslim 2.4%; other Christian 1.3%; Yazidi 1.3%; other/nonreligious 18.1%. **Major cities** (2007): Yerevan 1,107,800; Gyumri 147,000; Vanadzor 105,000; Vagharshapat 57,300; Hrazdan 52,900. **Location:** western Transcaucasia, bordering Georgia, Azerbaijan, Iran, and Turkey.

## Vital statistics

**Birth rate** per 1,000 population (2007): 12.4 (world avg. 20.3). **within marriage** 64.5%. **Death rate** per 1,000 population (2007): 8.3 (world avg. 8.5). **Total fertility rate** (avg. births per childbearing woman; 2006): 1.30. **Life expectancy** at birth (2006): male 70.0 years; female 76.4 years.

## National economy

**Budget** (2007). *Revenue:* AMD 588,080,000,000 (tax revenue 82.3%, of which VAT 42.2%, tax on profits 12.8%, income tax 8.0%, excise tax 7.1%; nontax revenue 17.7%). *Expenditures:* AMD 634,-735,000,000 (defense 15.1%; education and science 15.0%; social security 9.9%; public administration 9.8%; police 8.2%; health 7.4%). **Public debt** (external, outstanding; 2007): US$1,272,000,000. **Gross national income** (2008): US$10,320,-000,000 (US$3,350 per capita). **Production** (metric tons except as noted). *Agriculture and fishing* (2007): potatoes 540,000, tomatoes 250,000, grapes 200,000; livestock (number of live animals) 620,200 cattle, 587,200 sheep; fisheries production (2006) 1,406 (from aquaculture 75%). *Mining and quarrying* (2005): copper concentrate (metal content) 16,256; molybdenum (metal content) 3,030; gold (metal content) 1,400 kg. *Manufacturing* (value of production in AMD '000,000; 2007): food products and beverages 208,733; base metals 122,269; construction materials 40,207; 320,000 carats of cut diamonds were processed in 2004. *Energy production (consumption):* electricity (kW-hr; 2008) 6,114,000,000 ([2006] 5,145,000,000); coal (metric tons; 2005), none (negligible); petroleum products (metric tons; 2005) none (320,000); natural gas (cu m; 2005) none (1,596,000,000). **Population economically active:** total (2006) 1,181,300; activity rate of total population (2001) 49.5% (participation rates: ages 15–64 [2001] 72.1%; female 45.7%; unemployed [2008] 6.3%). **Selected balance of payments data.** Receipts from (US$'000,000): tourism (2007) 305; remittances (2008) 1,062; foreign direct investment (FDI; 2005–07 avg.) 451; official development assistance (2007) 352. Disbursements for (US$'000,000): tourism (2007) 294; remittances (2008) 185.

## Foreign trade

**Imports** (2007; c.i.f.): US$3,053,000,000 (machinery and apparatus 14.0%; food products 12.4%; refined petroleum products 7.4%; natural gas 7.4%; iron and steel 6.7%; motor vehicles 5.7%; diamonds 5.4%; gold 4.3%). *Major import sources:* Russia 15.8%; Ukraine 8.2%; Kazakhstan 7.9%; China 6.3%; France 4.9%. **Exports** (2007; f.o.b.): US$1,121,000,000 (ferroalloys 21.0%; cut diamonds 14.0%; nonferrous metals 11.6%, of which unrefined copper 5.9%, aluminum foil 3.3%; wine and brandy 10.3%; copper ore and concentrates 7.9%). *Major export destinations:* Russia 17.7%; Germany 15.0%; Netherlands 13.9%; Belgium 8.9%; Georgia 6.2%.

## Transport and communications

**Transport** (2007). *Railroads:* length 732 km; passenger-km 23,900,000; metric ton-km cargo 770,500,000. *Roads:* length 7,515 km (paved 68%). *Air transport* (Armavia airlines only): passenger-km 993,600,000; metric ton-km cargo 6,100,000. **Communications,** in total units (units per 1,000 persons). Telephone landlines (2005): 537,000 (180); cellular telephone subscribers (2007): 1,876,000 (611); personal computers (2007): 980,000 (319); total Internet users (2006): 173,000 (57); broadband Internet subscribers (2006): 2,000 (0.3).

## Education and health

**Educational attainment** (2001). Percentage of population ages 25 and over having: no formal schooling 0.7%; primary education 13.0%; completed secondary and some postsecondary 66.0%; higher 20.3%. **Literacy** (2006): total population ages 15 and over literate 99.4%; male 99.7%; female 99.2%. **Health** (2007): physicians 12,251 (1 per 264 persons); hospital beds 13,126 (1 per 246 persons); infant mortality rate per 1,000 live births 10.8; undernourished population (2002–04) 700,000 (24% of total population based on the consumption of a minimum daily requirement of 1,980 calories).

## Military

**Total active duty personnel** (November 2008): 42,080 (army 94.7%; air force 5.3%); Russian troops (November 2008) 3,210. **Military expenditure as percentage of GDP** (2008): 3.2%; per capita expenditure US$132.

## Background

Armenia is a successor state to a historical region in southwestern Asia. Historical Armenia's boundaries have varied considerably, but the region extended over what is now northeastern Turkey and the Republic of Armenia. The area was later conquered by the Medes and the Macedonians and still later allied with the Roman Empire. Armenia adopted Christianity as its national religion in AD 303. It came under the rule of the Ottoman Turks in 1514. Over the next centuries, as parts were ceded to other rulers, nationalism arose among the scattered Armenians; by the late 19th century it was causing widespread disruption. Fighting between Turks and Russians escalated when part of Armenia was ceded to Russia in 1878, and it continued through World War I, leading to Armenian deaths on a genocidal scale. With the Turkish defeat, the Russian-controlled part of Armenia was set up as a Soviet republic in 1921. Armenia became a constituent republic of the USSR in 1936. With the latter's dissolution in the late 1980s, Armenia declared its independence in 1991. It fought Azerbaijan for control over Nagorno-Karabakh until a cease-fire in 1994. About one-fifth of the population left the country beginning in 1993 because of an energy crisis. Political tension escalated, and in 1999 the prime minister and some legislators were killed in a terrorist attack on the legislature.

## Recent Developments

Armenian-Turkish relations remained strained in 2011. Pres. Serzh Sarkisyan threatened twice to annul the protocols signed in October 2009 on the normalization of bilateral relations if Ankara continued to tie the ratification of the protocols to progress toward resolving the Nagorno-Karabakh conflict. In July, Turkish Prime Minister Recep Tayyip Erdogan demanded an apology from President Sarkisyan for remarks that Erdogan asserted were an Armenian claim on Turkish territory.

**Internet resource:** <www.armstat.am/en>.

# Australia

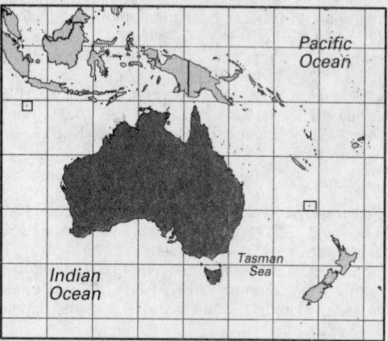

**Official name:** Commonwealth of Australia. **Form of government:** federal parliamentary state (formally a constitutional monarchy) with two legislative houses (Senate [76]; House of Representatives [150]). **Head of state:** British Queen Elizabeth II (from 1952), represented by Governor-General Quentin Bryce (from 2008). **Head of government:** Prime Minister Julia Gillard (from 2010). **Capital:** Canberra. **Official language:** English. **Official religion:** none. **Monetary unit:** 1 Australian dollar ($A) = 100 cents; valuation (2 Jul 2012) US$1 = $A 0.98.

## Demography

**Area:** 2,973,952 sq mi, 7,702,501 sq km. **Population** (2011): 22,651,000. **Density** (2011): persons per sq mi 7.6, persons per sq km 2.9. **Urban** (2005): 88.2%. **Sex distribution** (2008): male 50.09%; female 49.91%. **Age breakdown** (2008): under 15, 18.7%; 15–29, 20.8%; 30–44, 22.0%; 45–59, 20.0%; 60–74, 12.2%; 75–84, 4.5%; 85 and over, 1.8%. **Ethnic composition** (2007): white and others not elsewhere classified 90.2%; Asian (excluding Middle Eastern) 7.3%; aboriginal 2.5%. **Religious affiliation** (2006): Christian 63.9%, of which Roman Catholic 25.6%, Anglican Church of Australia 18.7%, Uniting Church 5.7%, Presbyterian 2.9%, Orthodox 2.6%, Baptist 1.6%, Lutheran 1.3%; other Christian 5.5%; Buddhist 2.1%; Muslim 1.7%; Hindu 0.7%; Jewish 0.4%; no religion 18.7%; other 12.5%. **Major urban centers (metropolitan areas)** (2006): Sydney 3,641,422 (4,119,191); Melbourne 3,371,888 (3,592,590); Brisbane 1,676,389 (1,763,132); Perth 1,256,035 (1,445,077); Adelaide 1,040,719 (1,105,840); Gold Coast 454,436 (541,675); Newcastle 288,732 (493,467); Canberra 356,120 (368,128); Gosford 282,726 (n.a.); Wollongong 234,482 (263,535); Sunshine Coast 184,662 (209,578); Hobart 128,577 (200,524); Geelong 137,220 (160,992); Townsville 128,808 (143,330); Cairns 98,349 (122,731); Toowoomba 95,265 (114,480); Darwin 66,291 (105,990). **Place of birth** (2006): 70.9% native-born; 29.1% foreign-born, of which Europe 10.5% (UK 5.2%, Italy 1.0%, Greece 0.6%, Germany 0.5%, Netherlands 0.4%, Poland 0.3%), Asia and Middle East 7.3% (China [including Hong Kong] 1.4%, Vietnam 0.8%, India 0.7%), New Zealand 2.0%, Africa, the Americas, and other 9.3%. **Location:** Oceania, continent between the Indian Ocean and the South Pacific Ocean. **Mobility** (1999). Population ages 15 and over living in the same residence as in 1998: 84.4%; different residence between states, regions, and neighborhoods 15.6%. **Immigration** (2006–07): permanent immigrants admitted 140,148, from New Zealand 17.1%, UK 16.6%, India 9.6%, China 8.6%, Philippines 4.0%, South Africa 2.9%, Vietnam 2.2%, Malaysia 2.1%, Sri Lanka 1.9%, Sudan 1.8%. **Emigration** (2006–07): 72,100, to New Zealand 19.3%, UK 18.2%, US 10.0%, Hong Kong 7.5%. **Refugee arrivals** (2006–07) 13,017.

## Vital statistics

**Birth rate** per 1,000 population (2007–08): 13.6 (world avg. 20.3); (2006) within marriage 67.3%. **Death rate** per 1,000 population (2007–08): 6.7 (world avg. 8.5). **Total fertility rate** (avg. births per childbearing woman; 2007–08): 1.93. **Life expectancy** at birth (2008): male 79.2 years; female 84.0 years.

## Social indicators

**Quality of working life.** Average workweek (2007): 34.6 hours. Working 50 hours a week or more (2006) 22.5%. Annual rate per 100,000 workers for: accidental injury and industrial disease (2006) 1,070; death (2006) 2.0. Proportion of employed persons insured for damages or income loss resulting from: injury 100%; permanent disability 100%; death 100%. Working days lost to industrial disputes per 1,000 employees (2006): 22. Means of transportation to work (2003): private automobile 74.5%; public transportation 12.0%; motorcycle, bicycle, and foot 5.7%. Discouraged job seekers (2006): 52,900 (0.5% of labor force). **Educational attainment** (2005). Percentage of population ages 15–64 having: no formal schooling and incomplete secondary education 48.5%; completed secondary and postsecondary, technical, or other certificate/diploma 28.9%; bachelor's degree 14.2%; incomplete graduate and graduate degree or diploma 5.4%; unknown 3.0%. **Social participation.** Eligible voters participating in last national election (2007): 94.8%; voting is compulsory. Trade union membership in total workforce (2006): 20.3%. Volunteerism rate of population ages 18 and over (2006) 34.1%. **Social deviance** (2007). Offense rate per 100,000 population for: murder 1.2; sexual assault 94.1; assault 839; auto theft 364; burglary and housebreaking 1,182; robbery 85.6, of which armed robbery 36.5. Incidence per 100,000 in general population of: prisoners 129; suicide (2006) 8.7. **Material well-being** (2005). Households possessing: refrigerator 99.9%; washing machine 96.4%; dishwasher 41.5%; automobiles per 1,000 population (2006) 544.

## National economy

**Gross national income** (2008): US$862,461,000,000 (US$40,350 per capita). **Budget** (2007–08). *Revenue:* $A 303,713,000,000 (tax revenue 94.2%, of which income tax 41.5%, indirect tax 25.6%, corporate taxes 21.3%; nontax revenue 5.8%). *Expenditures:* $A 280,108,000,000 (social security and welfare 34.9%; health 15.8%; economic services 7.4%; general administration 7.2%; education 6.6%; defense 6.3%; interest on public debt 1.3%). **Public debt** (December 2008):

US$106,300,000,000. **Production** (metric tons except as noted). *Agriculture and fishing* (2006–07): sugarcane 36,000,000, wheat 10,822,000, barley 4,257,000, grapes 1,530,000, sorghum 1,283,000, potatoes 1,212,000, oats 748,000, rapeseed 573,000, oranges 461,000, tomatoes 296,000, cotton lint 282,000, carrots 271,000, lettuce 271,000, apples 270,000, bananas 213,000; livestock (number of live animals) 85,711,000 sheep, 28,037,000 cattle, 2,605,000 pigs; fisheries production (2006) 241,456 (from aquaculture 20%); aquatic plants production 15,504 (from aquaculture, none). *Mining and quarrying* (metric tons except as noted; 2006): iron ore (metal content) 170,933,000 (world rank: 2), bauxite 62,307,000 (world rank: 1), ilmenite 2,377,000 (world rank: 1), zinc (metal content) 1,362,000 (world rank: 2), copper (metal content) 879,000 (world rank: 5), lead (metal content) 686,000 (world rank: 2), rutile 232,000 (world rank: 1), nickel (metal content) 185,000 (world rank: 3), cobalt (metal content) 7,400 (world rank: 3), opal (value of production) $A 50,000,000 (world rank: 1), diamonds 21,915,000 carats (world rank: 2), gold 247,000 kilograms (world rank: 4). *Manufacturing* (value added in $A '000,000; 2006–07): base metals 15,158; food products 14,455; machinery and apparatus 10,538; fabricated metal products 9,076; transportation equipment 9,003; chemical products 6,831; beverages and tobacco products 5,787; bricks, cement, and ceramics 5,019. **Population economically active** (July 2007): total 10,952,000; activity rate of total population 52.5% (participation rates: ages 15 and over, 65.0%; female [2006] 45.0%; unemployed [June 2008] 4.2%). *Energy production (consumption):* electricity (kW-hr; 2007) 227,496,000,000 ([2005] 251,120,000,000); coal (metric tons; 2006) 267,490,000 (36,371,000); lignite (metric tons; 2006) 102,825,000 (105,548,000); crude petroleum (barrels; 2006–07) 171,900,000 ([2006] 206,566,000); petroleum products (metric tons; 2006) 29,979,000 (36,211,000); natural gas (cu m; 2007) 37,211,000,000 ([2006] 29,256,000,000). **Selected balance of payments data.** Receipts from (US$'000,000): tourism (2007) 22,405; remittances (2008) 4,638; foreign direct investment (FDI; 2005–07 avg.) 4,236. Disbursements for (US$'000,000): tourism (2007) 14,244; remittances (2008) 2,997; FDI (2005–07 avg.) 4,441.

## Foreign trade

**Imports** (2005–06): $A 167,603,000,000 (machinery and apparatus 29.3%, of which telecommunications equipment 5.8%, office machinery and data-processing equipment 5.3%, electrical machinery 4.8%; transportation equipment 15.8%, of which motor vehicles 12.2%; crude and refined petroleum 12.7%; chemical products 6.1%, of which medicines and pharmaceuticals 4.3%; textiles and wearing apparel 3.9%). *Major import sources* (2006–07): China 15.0%; US 13.8%; Japan 9.6%; Singapore 5.6%; Germany 5.1%; UK 4.1%; Thailand 4.0%; Malaysia 3.7%; South Korea 3.3%; New Zealand 3.1%. **Exports** (2005–06): $A 151,792,000,000 (mineral fuels 24.9%, of which coal [all forms] 16.0%, petroleum products and natural gas 8.9%; food products and

---

*1 metric ton = about 1.1 short tons;  1 kilometer = 0.6 mi (statute);  1 metric ton-km cargo = about 0.68 short ton-mi cargo;  c.i.f.: cost, insurance, and freight;  f.o.b.: free on board*

beverages 12.0%, of which meat 4.4%, cereals 3.2%; iron ore 8.2%; aluminum and aluminum ore 6.9%; gold 4.8%; machinery and apparatus 4.1%; transportation equipment 3.5%). *Major export destinations* (2006–07): Japan 19.4%; China 13.6%; South Korea 7.8%; US 5.8%; New Zealand 5.6%; UK 3.7%; Taiwan 3.7%; Singapore 2.7%; Indonesia 2.5%; Thailand 2.5%.

## Transport and communications

**Transport.** *Railroads* (2006): route length 38,550 km; passengers carried (2004–05) 616,270,000; passenger-km (2004–05) 11,200,000,000; metric ton-km cargo (2004–05) 182,990,000,000. *Roads* (2004): total length 810,641 km (paved 42%). *Vehicles* (2008): passenger cars 11,848,326; trucks and buses 2,880,647. *Air transport* (2006): passenger-km 82,128,000,000; metric ton-km cargo 2,347,000,000. **Communications,** in total units (units per 1,000 persons). Telephone landlines (2008): 9,370,000 (437); cellular telephone subscribers (2008): 22,120,000 (1,032); personal computers (2006): 15,671,000 (757); total Internet users (2008): 11,900,000 (555); broadband Internet subscribers (2008): 5,140,000 (240).

## Education and health

**Literacy** (2006): total population literate, virtually 100%. **Health:** physicians (2006) 55,063 (1 per 375 persons); hospital beds (2005–06) 80,828 (1 per 254 persons); infant mortality rate per 1,000 live births (2007–08): 4.1; undernourished population (2002–04) less than 2.5% of total population.

## Military

**Total active duty personnel** (November 2008): 54,747 (army 50.2%, navy 24.1%, air force 25.7%); troops deployed abroad (November 2008): 2,858, of which to Afghanistan 1,080, to East Timor 750. **Military expenditure as percentage of GDP** (2007): 2.2%; per capita expenditure $961.

## Background

Australia has long been inhabited by Aborigines, who arrived on the continent 40,000–60,000 years ago. Estimates of the population at the time of European settlement in 1788 range from 300,000 to more than 1,000,000. Widespread European knowledge of Australia began with 17th-century explorations. The Dutch landed in 1616 and the British in 1688, but the first large-scale expedition was that of James Cook in 1770, which established Britain's claim to Australia. The first English settlement, at Port Jackson (1788), consisted mainly of convicts and seamen; convicts were to make up a large proportion of the incoming settlers. By 1859 the colonial nuclei of all Australia's states had been formed, but with devastating effects on the Aborigines, whose population declined sharply with the introduction of European diseases and weaponry. Britain granted its colonies limited self-government in the mid-19th century, and Australia achieved federation in 1901. Australia fought alongside the British in World War I, notably at Gallipoli, and again in World War II, defending against the occupation of Australia by the Japanese. It joined the US in the Korean and Vietnam wars. Since the 1960s the government has sought to deal more fairly with the Aborigines, and a loosening of immigration restrictions has led to a more heterogeneous population. Constitutional links allowing British interference in government were formally abolished in 1968, and Australia has assumed a leading role in Asian and Pacific affairs. During the 1990s it experienced several debates about giving up its British ties and becoming a republic.

## Recent Developments

In 2011, Australian Prime Minister Julia Gillard's political authority was undermined by her government's response to the number of unauthorized asylum seekers arriving by boat from Southeast and Central Asia. Gillard attempted to create an offshore processing system, in which the claims of refugees seeking asylum would be assessed in a third country. After the High Court ruled in August that Gillard's plan to exchange refugees with Malaysia was invalid, the government announced that refugees arriving by sea would be processed onshore and could live in the country while their claims were considered. The government's popularity was also harmed by its pursuit of a carbon emissions tax for reducing greenhouse gas emissions, a measure that was largely unpopular with voters. Nevertheless, the bill eventually passed in November. Later that month the lower house of parliament passed a second major reform, the Minerals Resource Rent Tax, which was to be levied on 30% of the so-called superprofits made by large iron-ore and coal-mining companies. The proposal for the tax sparked a fierce debate between mining companies—which argued that it would damage the country's most profitable economic sector—and those who believed that the massive profits of the largest miners should be used to help the country's overall fiscal position. The proposal was passed by the upper house in March 2012. US Pres. Barack Obama visited in November, and he pledged an enhanced US presence in the Asia-Pacific region and a permanent presence of up to 2,500 US Marines in northern Australia. China reacted angrily to what it identified as an expansion of US military alliances in the region, reinforcing the diplomatic challenge facing Gillard's government as it attempted to balance its priorities between its closest military ally, the US, and its largest trading partner, China.

**Internet resource:** <www.abs.gov.au>.

# Austria

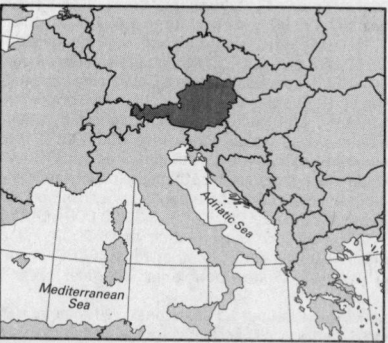

**Official name:** Republik Österreich (Republic of Austria). **Form of government:** federal state with two legislative houses (Federal Council [62]; National Council [183]). **Head of state:** President Heinz Fischer (from 2004). **Head of government:** Chancellor Werner Faymann (from 2008). **Capital:** Vienna. **Official language:** German. **Official religion:** none. **Monetary unit:** 1 euro (€) = 100 cents; valuation (2 Jul 2012) US$1 = €0.79.

## Demography

**Area:** 32,386 sq mi, 83,879 sq km. **Population** (2011): 8,419,000. **Density** (2011): persons per sq mi 260.0, persons per sq km 100.4. **Urban** (2005): 66.5%. **Sex distribution** (2007): male 48.66%; female 51.34%. **Age breakdown** (2007): under 15, 15.5%; 15–29, 18.7%; 30–44, 23.3%; 45–59, 20.3%; 60–74, 14.3%; 75–84, 6.0%; 85 and over, 1.9%. **Population composition by country of birth** (2007): 84.8%; former Serbia and Montenegro 2.3%; Germany 2.2%; Turkey 1.9%; Bosnia and Herzegovina 1.6%; Poland 0.7%; Romania 0.7%; other 5.8%. **Religious affiliation** (2001): Christian 81.5%, of which Roman Catholic 73.7%, Protestant (mostly Lutheran) 4.7%, Orthodox 2.2%; Muslim 4.2%; nonreligious 12.0%; other 0.3%; unknown 2.0%. **Major cities** (2007): Vienna 1,677,867; Graz 250,653; Linz 189,069; Salzburg 149,201; Innsbruck 118,362. **Location:** central Europe, bordering the Czech Republic, Slovakia, Hungary, Slovenia, Italy, Switzerland, Liechtenstein, and Germany.

## Vital statistics

**Birth rate** per 1,000 population (2008): 9.3 (world avg. 20.3); within marriage 61.2%. **Death rate** per 1,000 population (2008): 9.0 (world avg. 8.5). **Total fertility rate** (avg. births per childbearing woman; 2008): 1.41. **Life expectancy** at birth (2008): male 77.6 years; female 83.0 years.

## National economy

**Budget** (2007). *Revenue:* €113,942,000,000 (tax revenue 66.4%, of which income taxes 30.5%, taxes on products 27.1%; social security contributions 33.6%). *Expenditures:* €131,126,000,000 (social protection 41.6%; health 15.5%; general administration 14.2%; education 10.7%; economic affairs 9.6%). **Public debt** (December 2007): US$220,517,000,000. **Production** (metric tons except as noted). *Agriculture and fishing* (2006): sugar beets 2,493,097, corn (maize) 1,471,668, wheat 1,396,300; livestock (number of live animals) 3,160,382 pigs, 2,002,143 cattle; fisheries production 2,863 (from aquaculture 87%). *Mining and quarrying* (2006): iron ore (metal content) 650,000; manganese (metal content) 16,000; tungsten 1,300. *Manufacturing* (value added in €'000,000; 2006): nonelectrical machinery and apparatus 6,250; fabricated metal products 5,550; food products and beverages 3,900. *Energy production (consumption):* electricity (kW-hr; 2008) 66,792,000,000 ([2006] 70,295,000,000); coal (metric tons; 2007) none (4,161,000); lignite (metric tons; 2006) none (753,000); crude petroleum (barrels; 2008)

5,660,000 ([2006] 59,642,000); petroleum products (metric tons; 2006) 7,259,000 (12,106,000); natural gas (cu m; 2008) 1,686,000,000 ([2006] 9,584,000,000). **Population economically active** (2007): total 4,213,500; activity rate of total population 51.4% (participation rates: ages 15–64 [2006] 73.7%; female 45.5%; unemployed [March 2008–February 2009] 6.0%). **Gross national income** (2008): US$386,044,000,000 (US$46,260 per capita). **Selected balance of payments data.** Receipts from (US$'000,000): tourism (2007) 18,754; remittances (2008) 3,237; foreign direct investment (FDI; 2005–07 avg.) 15,882. Disbursements for (US$'000,000): tourism (2007) 10,566; remittances (2008) 3,356; FDI (2005–07 avg.) 17,414.

## Foreign trade

**Imports** (2007; c.i.f.): €114,010,000,000 (machinery and apparatus 23.6%; chemical products 10.9%; motor vehicles and parts 10.6%; crude petroleum 6.3%; food products 5.3%). *Major import sources:* Germany 41.5%; Italy 6.9%; Switzerland 4.2%; China 4.0%; US 3.3%. **Exports** (2007; f.o.b.): €114,400,-000,000 (machinery and apparatus 28.6%, of which electrical machinery 6.9%, general industrial machinery 6.5%; motor vehicles and parts 10.9%; chemical products 9.5%; iron and steel 6.1%; fabricated metal products 4.9%). *Major export destinations:* Germany 30.1%; Italy 8.9%; US 5.1%; Switzerland 4.4%; France 3.6%.

## Transport and communications

**Transport.** *Railroads* (2006; federal railways only): route length (2007) 5,656 km; passenger-km 8,646,000,000; metric ton-km cargo 17,871,-000,000. *Roads* (2003): total length 133,718 km (paved 100%). *Vehicles* (2007): passenger cars 4,245,583; trucks and buses 363,043. *Air transport* (2007): passenger-km 17,412,000,000; metric ton-km cargo 453,756,000. **Communications,** in total units (units per 1,000 persons). Telephone landlines (2008): 3,342,000 (400); cellular telephone subscribers (2008): 10,816,000 (1,296); personal computers (2006): 5,027,000 (607); total Internet users (2008): 4,950,000 (593); broadband Internet subscribers (2008): 1,792,000 (215).

## Education and health

**Educational attainment** (2007). Percentage of population ages 15 and over having: compulsory education through age 14, 28.3%; apprentice training/intermediate technical 48.2%; academic secondary/higher technical 13.9%; university 9.6%. **Literacy:** virtually 100%. **Health** (2007): physicians 20,318 (1 per 410 persons); hospital beds 57,646 (1 per 144 persons); infant mortality rate per 1,000 live births (2008) 3.7; undernourished population (2002–04) less than 2.5% of total population.

## Military

**Total active duty personnel** (November 2008): 34,900 (army 80.8%, air force 19.2%). **Military expenditure as percentage of GDP** (2008): 0.7%; per capita expenditure US$330.

---

*1 metric ton = about 1.1 short tons;    1 kilometer = 0.6 mi (statute);    1 metric ton-km cargo = about 0.68 short ton-mi cargo;    c.i.f.: cost, insurance, and freight;    f.o.b.: free on board*

## Background

Settlement in Austria goes back some 3,000 years, when Illyrians were probably the main inhabitants. The Celts invaded c. 400 BC and established Noricum. The Romans arrived after 200 BC and established the provinces of Raetia, Noricum, and Pannonia; prosperity followed and the population became Romanized. With the fall of Rome in the 5th century AD, many tribes invaded, including the Slavs; they were eventually subdued by Charlemagne, and the area became ethnically Germanic. The distinct political entity that would become Austria emerged in 976 with Leopold I of Babenberg as margrave. In 1278 Rudolf I of the Holy Roman Empire (formerly Rudolf IV of Habsburg) conquered the area; Habsburg rule lasted until 1918. While in power the Habsburgs created a kingdom centered on Austria, Bohemia, and Hungary. The Napoleonic Wars brought about the creation of the Austrian Empire (1804) and the end of the Holy Roman Empire (1806). Count von Metternich tried to assure Austrian supremacy among Germanic states, but war with Prussia led Austria to divide the empire into the Dual Monarchy of Austria-Hungary. Nationalist sentiment plagued the kingdom, and the assassination of Francis Ferdinand by a Serbian nationalist in 1914 triggered World War I, which destroyed the Austro-Hungarian Empire. In the postwar carving up of Austria-Hungary, Austria became an independent republic. It was annexed by Nazi Germany in 1938 and joined the Axis powers in World War II. The republic was restored in 1955 after 10 years of Allied occupation. Austria became a member of the European Union in 1995. After a half-century of military neutrality, Austria was one of the few members of the EU that was not a member of NATO at the outset of the 21st century.

## Recent Developments

In May 2011 Austria opened its labor market to citizens of the eight central and eastern European states that had joined the EU in 2004. Workers from those countries helped to fill a void in skilled labor in certain sectors. The economy grew, and by year's end Austria boasted the lowest unemployment rate in the EU. Exports recovered strongly in early 2011 as the country's largest export market—Germany—staged a strong economic revival. Export growth slowed in the second half of the year, however, as Germany's economy stalled and fiscal tightening hampered growth throughout the euro zone.

Internet resource: <www.statistik.at/web_en>.

# Azerbaijan

**Official name:** Azerbaycan Respublikasi (Republic of Azerbaijan). **Form of government:** unitary multiparty republic with a single legislative house (National Assembly [125]). **Head of state and government:** President Ilham Aliyev (from 2003), assisted by Prime Minister Artur Rasizade (from 2003). **Capital:** Baku (Baki). **Official language:** Azerbaijanian. **Official religion:** none. **Monetary unit:** 1 (new) manat (AZN) = 100 gopik; valuation (2 Jul 2012) free rate, US$1 = AZN 0.78.

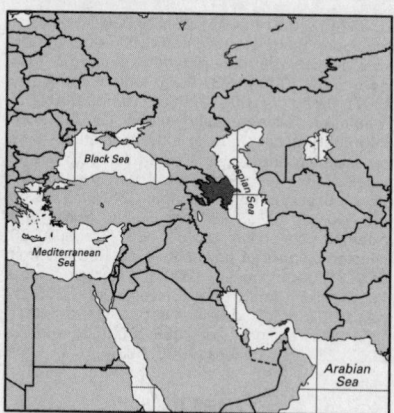

## Demography

**Area:** 33,436 sq mi, 86,600 sq km. **Population** (2011): 9,150,000. **Density** (2011): persons per sq mi 273.7, persons per sq km 105.7. **Urban** (2010): 54.1%. **Sex distribution** (2007): male 49.34%; female 50.66%. **Age breakdown** (2006): under 15, 26.3%; 15–29, 27.9%; 30–44, 22.7%; 45–59, 14.1%; 60–74, 6.7%; 75–84, 1.9%; 85 and over, 0.4%. **Ethnic composition** (1999): Azerbaijani 90.6%; Lezgian (Dagestani) 2.2%; Russian 1.8%; Armenian 1.5%; other 3.9%. **Religious affiliation** (2005): Muslim 87.0%, of which Shiʿi 52.8%, Sunni 34.2%; nonreligious/other 13.0%. **Major cities** (2007): Baku 1,145,000 (urban agglomeration 1,892,000); Ganca 307,500; Sumqayit (Sumgait) 268,800; Mingacevir (Mingechaur) 95,500; Qaracuxur 74,700. **Location:** eastern Transcaucasia, bordering Russia, the Caspian Sea, Iran, Turkey, Armenia, and Georgia.

## Vital statistics

**Birth rate** per 1,000 population (2007): 17.7 (world avg. 20.3); within marriage 88.2%. **Death rate** per 1,000 population (2007): 6.3 (world avg. 8.5). **Total fertility rate** (avg. births per childbearing woman; 2007): 2.30. **Life expectancy** at birth (2007): male 69.7 years; female 75.1 years.

## National economy

**Budget** (2007). *Revenue:* AZN 7,949,000,000 (tax revenue 70.9%, of which corporate taxes 30.9%, VAT 14.8%, income tax 7.4%, social security contributions 6.9%; nontax revenue [all petroleum fund revenues] 29.1%). *Expenditures:* AZN 7,356,000,000 (current expenditures 62.5%; development expenditures 37.5%). **Production** (metric tons except as noted). *Agriculture and fishing* (2006): wheat 1,460,303, potatoes 999,343, barley 399,737, seed cotton 130,123, persimmons 124,485; livestock (number of live animals) 7,304,431 sheep, 2,148,108 cattle; fisheries production 4,093 (from aquaculture 3%). *Mining and quarrying* (2005): limestone 1,256,000. *Manufacturing* (value of production in AZN '000,000; 2007): refined petroleum products 1,634; food, beverages, and tobacco products 1,457; base and fabricated metals 398. *Energy production (consumption):* electricity (kW-hr; 2007)

20,337,000,000 ([2006] 25,429,000,000); crude petroleum (barrels; 2007) 303,000,000 ([2006] 53,972,000); petroleum products (metric tons; 2006) 7,183,000 (3,931,000); natural gas (cu m; 2007) 9,606,000,000 ([2006] 10,662,000,000). **Population economically active** (2005): total 3,906,500; activity rate of total population 46.3% (participation rates: ages 15–61 [male], 15–56 [female] 71.8%; female 47.7%; unemployed [2007] 6.5%). **Gross national income** (2008): US$33,-232,000,000 (US$3,830 per capita). **Public debt** (external, outstanding; 2007): US$1,748,000,000. **Selected balance of payments data.** Receipts from (US$'000,000): tourism (2007) 178; remittances (2008) 1,554; foreign direct investment (2005–07 avg.) 1,537; official development assistance (2007) 225. Disbursements for (US$'000,000): tourism (2007) 264; remittances (2008) 593.

## Foreign trade

**Imports** (2007; c.i.f.): US$5,712,000,000 (machinery and apparatus 30.7%, of which civil engineering equipment and parts 6.2%; food products 11.5%, of which cereals 5.8%; motor vehicles 11.3%; iron and steel products 8.7%; chemical products 7.5%). *Major import sources:* Russia 17.6%; Turkey 10.9%; Germany 8.2%; Ukraine 8.2%; UK 7.2%. **Exports** (2008; f.o.b.): US$47,756,000,000 (crude petroleum 92.5%; refined petroleum products 4.3%; aluminum alloys 0.3%; boats and floating structures 0.3%). *Major export destinations* (2007): Turkey 17.4%; Italy 15.5%; Russia 8.7%; Iran 7.2%; Indonesia 6.4%.

## Transport and communications

**Transport.** *Railroads* (2007): length 2,122 km; passenger-km 1,108,000,000; metric ton-km cargo 10,375,000,000. *Roads* (2004): total length 59,141 km (paved 49%). *Vehicles* (2007): passenger cars 616,853; trucks and buses 138,483. *Air transport* (2007): passenger-km 1,764,000,000; metric ton-km cargo 11,892,000. **Communications**, in total units (units per 1,000 persons). Telephone landlines (2008): 1,318,000 (151); cellular telephone subscribers (2008): 6,548,000 (750); personal computers (2007): 207,000 (24); total Internet users (2007): 1,036,000 (122); broadband Internet subscribers (2008): 60,000 (6.9).

## Education and health

**Educational attainment** (1999). Percentage of population ages 25 and over having: primary education 4.1%; some secondary 9.3%; secondary 50.1%; vocational 4.2%; some higher 0.9%; higher 13.3%. **Literacy** (2007): 99.4%. **Health** (2007): physicians 32,400 (1 per 252 persons); hospital beds 68,100 (1 per 49 persons); infant mortality rate per 1,000 live births 11.6; undernourished population (2003–05) 100,000,000 (12% of total population based on the consumption of a minimum daily requirement of 1,920 calories).

## Military

**Total active duty personnel** (November 2008): 66,940 (army 84.9%, navy 3.3%, air force 11.8%).

**Military expenditure as percentage of GDP** (2008): 2.5%; per capita expenditure US$154.

## Background

Azerbaijan adjoins the Iranian region of the same name, and the origin of their respective inhabitants is the same. By the 9th century AD the area had come under Turkish influence, and in ensuing centuries it was fought over by Arabs, Mongols, Turks, and Iranians. Russia acquired the territory of what is now independent Azerbaijan in the early 19th century. After the Russian Revolution of 1917, Azerbaijan declared its independence; it was subdued by the Red Army in 1920 and became a Soviet Socialist Republic. It declared independence from the collapsing Soviet Union in 1991. Azerbaijan has two geographic peculiarities. The exclave Nakhichevan is separated from the rest of Azerbaijan by Armenian territory. Nagorno-Karabakh, which lies within Azerbaijan and is administered by it, has a Christian Armenian majority. Azerbaijan and Armenia went to war over both territories in the 1990s, causing great economic disruption. Though a cease-fire was declared in 1994, the political situation remained unresolved in the 21st century.

## Recent Developments

Six visits to the region by the Organization for Security and Co-operation in Europe's Minsk Group and two meetings between the Armenian and Azerbaijani presidents mediated by Russian Pres. Dmitry Medvedev yielded little progress toward resolving the Nagorno-Karabakh conflict in 2011. In July talks began on the terms for extending Russia's use of the Gabala radar station in central Azerbaijan beyond 2012. In October Azerbaijan was elected a nonpermanent member of the UN Security Council.

**Internet resource:** <www.azstat.org/indexen.php>.

# Bahamas, The

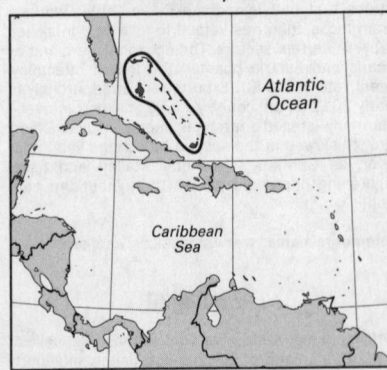

**Official name:** The Commonwealth of The Bahamas. **Form of government:** constitutional monarchy with two legislative houses (Senate [16]; House of Assembly [38]). **Head of state:** British Queen Elizabeth

---

*1 metric ton = about 1.1 short tons;    1 kilometer = 0.6 mi (statute);    1 metric ton-km cargo = about 0.68 short ton-mi cargo;    c.i.f.: cost, insurance, and freight;    f.o.b.: free on board*

II (from 1952), represented by Governor-General Sir Arthur Foulkes (from 2010). **Head of government:** Prime Minister Perry Christie (from 2012). **Capital:** Nassau. **Official language:** English. **Official religion:** none. **Monetary unit:** 1 Bahamian dollar (B$) = 100 cents; valuation (2 Jul 2012) US$1 = B$1.00.

## Demography

**Area:** 5,382 sq mi, 13,939 sq km. **Population** (2011): 360,000. **Density** (2011): persons per sq mi 66.9, persons per sq km 25.8. **Urban** (2009): 83.9%. **Sex distribution** (2008): male 48.71%; female 51.29%. **Age breakdown** (2008): under 15, 26.0%; 15–29, 24.4%; 30–44, 23.9%; 45–59, 16.8%; 60–74, 7.1%; 75–84, 1.5%; 85 and over, 0.3%. **Ethnic composition** (2007): local black/mixed race 74%; Haitian 15%; white/European 11%. **Religious affiliation** (2000): Baptist 35.4%; Anglican 15.1%; Roman Catholic 13.5%; other Protestant/independent Christian 32.3%; other/nonreligious 3.7%. **Major cities and towns** (2006): Nassau 231,500; Freeport 47,100; West End 12,900. **Location:** chain of islands in the Caribbean Sea, southeast of Florida.

## Vital statistics

**Birth rate** per 1,000 population (2006): 13.9 (world avg. 20.3); (2000) within marriage 43.2%. **Death rate** per 1,000 population (2006): 5.3 (world avg. 8.5). **Total fertility rate** (avg. births per childbearing woman; 2006): 2.18. **Life expectancy** at birth (2006): male 62.2 years; female 69.0 years.

## National economy

**Budget** (2008–09). *Revenue:* B$1,569,300,000 (tax revenue 90.3%, of which taxes on international trade and transactions 48.6% [including import duties 32.8%, excise taxes 14.9%], business and professional licenses 7.1%, property taxes 6.2%; nontax revenue 9.7%). *Expenditures:* B$1,672,900,000 (education 19.0%; health 16.6%; general administration 16.6%; public order 11.2%; interest on public debt 9.9%; public works and water supply 7.0%). **Public debt** (external, outstanding; September 2008): US$833,800,000. **Production** (metric tons except as noted). *Agriculture and fishing* (2006): sugarcane 55,500, fruits 33,472; livestock (number of live animals; 2007) 3,000,000 chickens; fisheries production (mainly lobsters, crayfish, and conch) 10,620 (from aquaculture, negligible). *Mining and quarrying* (2006): salt 1,150,000; aragonite 1,100. *Manufacturing* (value of export production in B$'000; 2007): polystyrene 142,200; organic chemical products 84,562; rum 20,282. *Energy production (consumption):* electricity (kW-hr; 2006–07) 2,149,000,000 ([2006] 2,090,000,000); petroleum products (metric tons; 2006) none (693,000). **Gross national income** (2007): US$7,042,000,000 (US$21,021 per capita). **Population economically active** (2007): total 186,105; activity rate of total population 56.2% (participation rates: ages 15–64, 76.2%; female 48.5%; unemployed [February 2009; New Providence only] 12.1%). **Selected balance of payments data.** Receipts from (US$'000,000): tourism (2007) 2,187; remittances, n.a.; foreign direct investment (2005–07 avg.) 1,067. Disbursements for (US$'000,000): tourism (2007) 377; remittances (2008) 143.

## Foreign trade

**Imports** (2007; c.i.f.): B$3,103,000,000 (refined petroleum products 19.2%; machinery and apparatus 14.0%; food products 12.9%; chemical products 9.0%; motor vehicles 6.2%). *Major import sources:* US 88.5%; Netherlands Antilles 2.8%; Venezuela 2.1%; Japan 1.1%. **Exports** (2007; f.o.b.): B$670,000,000 (refined petroleum products 25.0%; polystyrene 21.2%; organic chemical products 12.7%; crayfish 12.1%; aragonite 5.3%; rum 2.9%). *Major export destinations:* US 71.6%; Canada 5.7%; Netherlands 5.6%; France 4.9%; Germany 2.4%.

## Transport and communications

**Transport.** *Railroads:* none. *Roads* (2002): total length 2,717 km (paved 57%). *Vehicles* (2002): passenger cars 112,900; trucks and buses 19,200. *Air transport* (2006): passenger-km 275,700,000; metric ton-km cargo 600,000. **Communications,** in total units (units per 1,000 persons). Telephone landlines (2008): 133,000 (393); cellular telephone subscribers (2008): 358,000 (1,058); total Internet users (2008): 142,000 (420); broadband Internet subscribers (2008): 34,000 (101).

## Education and health

**Educational attainment** (2000). Percentage of population ages 15 and over having: no formal schooling 1.5%; primary education 8.7%; incomplete secondary 19.9%; complete secondary 53.7%; incomplete higher 8.1%; complete higher 7.1%; not stated 1.0%. **Literacy** (2005): total percentage ages 15 and over literate 95.8%; males literate 95.0%; females literate 96.7%. **Health** (2003): physicians 523 (1 per 602 persons); hospital beds 1,068 (1 per 295 persons); infant mortality rate per 1,000 live births (2006) 16.3; undernourished population (2002–04) 25,000 (8% of total population based on the consumption of a minimum daily requirement of 1,940 calories).

## Military

**Total active duty personnel** (November 2008): 860 (paramilitary coast guard 100%). **Military expenditure as percentage of GDP** (2007): 0.8%; per capita expenditure US$175.

## Background

The islands were inhabited by Lucayan Indians when Christopher Columbus sighted them on 12 Oct 1492. He is thought to have landed on San Salvador (Watling) Island. The Spaniards made no attempt to settle but carried out slave raids that depopulated the islands; when English settlers arrived in 1648 from Bermuda, the islands were uninhabited. They became a haunt of pirates, and few of the ensuing settlements prospered. The islands enjoyed some prosperity following the American Revolution, when Loyalists fled the US and established cotton plantations. The islands were a center for blockade runners during the American Civil War. Not until the development of tourism after World War II did permanent economic prosperity arrive. The Bahamas was granted internal self-government in 1964 and became independent from Britain in 1973.

## Recent Developments

In early 2011, US petroleum distributor Buckeye Partners purchased The Bahamas Oil Refining Co. storage terminal in Grand Bahama for US$1.7 billion with plans to increase capacity from 21.6 million bbl to 45.0 million. In May The Bahamas and Cuba agreed on the delimitation of their respective exclusive economic zones to help facilitate offshore oil exploration.

Internet resource: <http://statistics.bahamas.gov.bs>.

# Bahrain

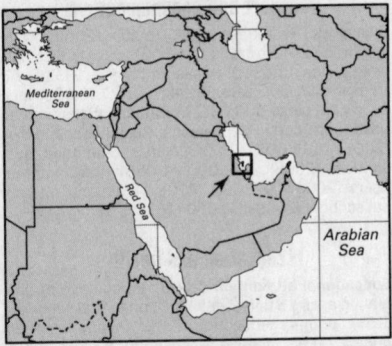

**Official name:** Mamlakat al-Bahrayn (Kingdom of Bahrain). **Form of government:** constitutional monarchy with two legislative houses (Shura Council [40]; Council of Representatives [40]). **Head of state:** King Sheikh Hamad ibn ʿIsa al-Khalifah (from 2002). **Head of government:** Prime Minister Sheikh Khalifah ibn Sulman al-Khalifah (from 1970). **Capital:** Manama. **Official language:** Arabic. **Official religion:** Islam. **Monetary unit:** 1 Bahraini dinar (BD) = 1,000 fils; valuation (2 Jul 2012) US$1 = BD 0.38.

## Demography

**Area:** 292 sq mi, 757 sq km. **Population** (2011): 1,325,000. **Density** (2011): persons per sq mi 4,537.7, persons per sq km 1,750.3. **Urban** (2009): 88.5%. **Sex distribution** (2007): male 60.82%; female 39.18%. **Age breakdown** (2007): under 15, 21.1%; 15–29, 29.1%; 30–44, 31.7%; 45–59, 14.3%; 60–74, 2.8%; 75–84, 0.7%; 85 and over, 0.3%. **Ethnic composition** (2000): Bahraini Arab 63.9%; Indo-Pakistani 14.8%, of which Urdu 4.5%, Malayali 3.5%; Persian 13.0%; Filipino 4.5%; British 2.1%; other 1.7%. **Religious affiliation** (2000): Muslim 82.4%, of which Shiʿi 58%, Sunni 24%; Christian 10.5%; Hindu 6.3%; other 0.8%. **Major urban areas** (2001): Manama (2007) 157,000; Muharraq 91,307; Al-Rifaʿ 79,550; Madinat Hamad 52,718; Al-ʿAli 47,529. **Location:** the Middle East, archipelago in the Persian Gulf, east of Saudi Arabia.

## Vital statistics

**Birth rate** per 1,000 population (2007): 15.4 (world avg. 20.3). **Death rate** per 1,000 population (2007): 2.2 (world avg. 8.5). **Total fertility rate** (avg. births per childbearing woman; 2007): 2.00. **Life expectancy** at birth (2005): male 71.7 years; female 76.8 years.

## National economy

**Budget** (2006). *Revenue:* BD 1,839,600,000 (petroleum and natural gas revenue 77.0%; other 23.0%). *Expenditures:* BD 1,558,500,000 (current expenditures 70.7%; development expenditures 29.3%). **Public debt** (2008): US$6,530,000,000. **Production** (metric tons except as noted). *Agriculture and fishing* (2007): dates 15,500, tomatoes 2,250, onions 1,300; livestock (number of live animals) 41,000 sheep, 26,500 goats, 470,000 chickens; fisheries production (2006) 15,596 (from aquaculture, negligible). *Manufacturing* (value added in BD 000,000; 2007): petroleum products 436.8; aluminum 263.3; other metal industries 115.2. *Energy production (consumption):* electricity (kW-hr; 2008) 11,657,000,000 ([2006] 9,822,000,000); crude petroleum (barrels; 2008) 66,900,000 ([2006] 94,428,000); petroleum products (metric tons; 2006) 11,110,000 (1,447,000); natural gas (cu m; 2008) 15,241,000,000 ([2006] 7,890,000,000). **Gross national income** (2007): US$14,022,000,000 (US$12,935 per capita). **Population economically active** (2005): total 350,000; activity rate of total population 48.3% (participation rates: ages 15 and over 67.0%; female 23.2%; unemployed [Bahrainis only; October 2008] 3.6%). **Selected balance of payments data.** Receipts from (US$'000,000): tourism (2007) 1,105; foreign direct investment (FDI; 2005–07 avg.) 1,907. Disbursements for (US$'000,000): tourism (2007) 479; remittances (2008) 1,483; FDI (2005–07 avg.) 1,261.

## Foreign trade

**Imports** (2007; c.i.f.): US$11,515,000,000 (crude petroleum 50.9%; machinery and apparatus 10.0%; motor vehicles 7.9%; aluminum oxide 5.8%; food products and live animals 4.0%). *Major import sources* (2006; excluding petroleum): Japan 11.9%; Saudi Arabia 11.6%; Australia 8.3%; China 8.2%; US 7.1%. **Exports** (2007; f.o.b.): US$13,665,000,000 (refined petroleum products 79.1%; aluminum [all forms] 9.0%; urea 2.4%; iron ore agglomerates 1.4%; methanol 1.3%). *Major export destinations* (2006; excluding petroleum): Saudi Arabia 20.9%; US 9.3%; India 6.8%; Singapore 6.5%; Qatar 3.9%.

## Transport and communications

**Transport.** *Railroads:* none. *Roads* (2003): total length 3,498 km (paved 79%). *Vehicles* (2007): passenger cars 275,389; trucks and buses 44,075. *Air transport* (2007; Gulf Air only): passenger-km 13,999,000,000; metric ton-km cargo 498,000,000. **Communications,** in total units (units per 1,000 persons). Telephone landlines (2008): 220,000 (196); cellular telephone subscribers (2008): 1,400,000 (1,247); personal computers (2004): 121,000 (147); total Internet users (2007): 250,000 (241); broadband Internet subscribers (2008): 93,000 (83).

---

*1 metric ton = about 1.1 short tons;   1 kilometer = 0.6 mi (statute);   1 metric ton-km cargo = about 0.68 short ton-mi cargo;   c.i.f.: cost, insurance, and freight;   f.o.b.: free on board*

## Education and health

**Educational attainment** (2001). Percentage of population ages 15 and over having: no formal education 24.0%; primary education 37.1%; secondary 26.4%; higher 12.5%. **Literacy** (2005): percentage of population ages 15 and over literate 90.0%; males literate 92.6%; females literate 86.4%. **Health** (2007): physicians 2,225 (1 per 467 persons); hospital beds 2,043 (1 per 509 persons); infant mortality rate per 1,000 live births (2007) 8.3.

## Military

**Total active duty personnel** (November 2008): 8,200 (army 73.2%, navy 8.5%, air force 18.2%); US troops in Bahrain (November 2008): 1,324. **Military expenditure as percentage of GDP** (2008): 2.6%; per capita expenditure US$509.

## Background

The area has long been an important trading center and is mentioned in Persian, Greek, and Roman references. It was ruled by Arabs from the 7th century AD but was then occupied by the Portuguese in 1521–1602. Since 1783 it has been ruled by the Khalifah family, though through a series of treaties its defense remained a British responsibility from 1820 to 1971. After Britain withdrew its forces from the Persian Gulf (1968), Bahrain declared its independence in 1971. It served as a center for the allies in the Persian Gulf War (1990–91). Since 1994 it has experienced bouts of political unrest, mainly among its large Shiʻite population. Constitutional revisions, ratified in 2002, made Bahrain a constitutional monarchy and enfranchised women.

## Recent Developments

The Bahraini Shiʻite opposition rose up against the Sunni-led regime in February 2011. In response the Bahraini government declared martial law and allowed 1,000 soldiers and 500 policemen from Saudi Arabia and the United Arab Emirates to help to keep the peace. The unrest left at least 33 people dead. Confident that it had quelled the rebellion and under pressure from the US, the Bahraini government lifted martial law in June and called for a dialogue with Shiʻite leaders.

**Internet resource:**
<www.cio.gov.bh/cio_eng/default.aspx>.

# Bangladesh

**Official name:** Gana Prajatantri Bangladesh (People's Republic of Bangladesh). **Form of government:** unitary multiparty republic with one legislative house (Parliament [350]). **Head of state:** President Zillur Rahman (from 2009). **Head of government:** Prime Minister Sheikh Hasina Wazed (from 2009). **Capital:** Dhaka. **Official language:** Bengali (Bangla). **Official religion:** Islam. **Monetary unit:** 1 Bangladesh taka (Tk) = 100 paisa; valuation (2 Jul 2012) US$1 = Tk 81.82.

## Demography

**Area:** 56,977 sq mi, 147,570 sq km. **Population** (2011): 142,875,000. **Density** (2011): persons per

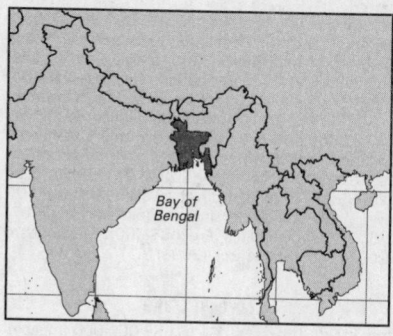

sq mi 2,507.6, persons per sq km 968.2. **Urban** (2009): 27.6%. **Sex distribution** (2006): male 51.21%; female 48.79%. **Age breakdown** (2005): under 15, 33.8%; 15–29, 30.5%; 30–44, 19.5%; 45–59, 10.6%; 60–74, 4.6%; 75–84, 0.9%; 85 and over, 0.1%. **Ethnic composition** (1997): Bengali 97.7%; tribal 1.9%, of which Chakma 0.4%, Saontal 0.2%, Marma 0.1%; other 0.4%. **Religious affiliation** (2005): Muslim (nearly all Sunni) 88.3%; Hindu 10.5%; Buddhist 0.6%; Christian (mostly Roman Catholic) 0.3%; other 0.3%. **Major cities (metropolitan areas)** (2008): Dhaka 7,000,940 (12,797,394); Chittagong 2,579,107 (3,858,093); Khulna 855,650 (1,388,425); Rajshahi 472,775 (775,495); Sylhet 463,198. **Location:** South Asia, bordering India, Myanmar (Burma), and the Bay of Bengal.

## Vital statistics

**Birth rate** per 1,000 population (2006): 20.6 (world avg. 20.3). **Death rate** per 1,000 population (2006): 5.6 (world avg. 8.5). **Total fertility rate** (avg. births per childbearing woman; 2006): 2.41. **Life expectancy** at birth (2006): male 64.4 years; female 66.0 years.

## National economy

**Budget** (2007–08). *Revenue:* Tk 605,400,000,000 (tax revenue 79.3%, of which VAT 28.1%, taxes on income and profits 18.8%, import duties 15.4%; nontax revenue 20.7%). *Expenditures:* Tk 936,100,000,000 (current expenditures 55.8%, of which interest on domestic debt 11.3%, education 9.2%, agriculture 6.5%; development expenditures 24.0%; other 20.2%). **Public debt** (external, outstanding; 2007): US$20,151,000,000. **Production** (metric tons except as noted). *Agriculture and fishing* (2007–08): paddy rice 28,931,000, potatoes 5,762,000, sugarcane 4,983,656, jute 832,000, rapeseed 227,930, allspice (2005) 138,000, ginger 57,000; livestock (number of live animals; 2007) 52,500,000 goats, 25,300,000 cattle; fisheries production (2006) 2,328,545 (from aquaculture 38%). *Mining and quarrying* (2007): granite 1,500,000; marine salt 360,000. *Manufacturing* (value added in Tk '000,000,000; 2004–05): marine products 28.6; medicines and pharmaceuticals 23.0; refined petroleum products 22.9. *Energy production (consumption):* electricity (kW-hr; 2007) 22,572,000,000 ([2006] 23,703,000,000); coal (metric tons; 2007) 1,000,000 (700,000); crude petroleum (barrels; 2007 2,100,000 ([2006] 9,949,000); petroleum products (metric tons; 2006) 884,000 (3,462,000);

natural gas (cu m; 2007) 15,225,000,000 ([2006] 15,488,000,000). **Population economically active** (2004–05): total 49,461,000; activity rate of total population 36.0% (participation rates: ages 15–64, 59.7%; female 24.5%; unemployed or underemployed [2008] 38%). **Gross national income** (2008): US$82,569,000,000 (US$520 per capita). **Selected balance of payments data.** Receipts from (US$'000,000): tourism (2007) 76; remittances (2008) 8,979; foreign direct investment (2005–07 avg.) 768; official development assistance (2007) 1,502. Disbursements for (US$'000,000): tourism (2007) 156; remittances (2008) 3.

## Foreign trade

**Imports** (2006; c.i.f.): US$15,688,000,000 (machinery and apparatus 21.3%; refined petroleum products 10.9%; food products 9.6%; textile yarn and fabrics 9.2%; cotton 5.4%). *Major import sources:* China 16.4%; India 12.0%; Kuwait 9.3%; Japan 5.7%; South Korea 4.2%. **Exports** (2006; f.o.b.): US$11,697,000,000 (knitted or woven clothing and accessories 71.1%; dyed woven fabrics 5.9%; shrimp 4.1%; leather 2.1%; textile yarn 2.0%). *Major export destinations* (2006): US 26.7%; Germany 15.0%; UK 9.0%; China 6.6%; France 6.1%.

## Transport and communications

**Transport.** *Railroads* (2002): route length 2,768 km; passenger-km 3,970,000,000; metric ton-km cargo 908,000,000. *Roads* (2003): total length 239,226 km (paved 10%). *Vehicles* (2005–06): passenger cars 97,450; trucks and buses 113,329. *Air transport* (2007; Biman Bangladesh Airlines only): passenger-km 4,186,000,000; metric ton-km cargo 116,140,000. **Communications**, in total units (units per 1,000 persons). Telephone landlines (2008): 1,345,000 (8.7); cellular telephone subscribers (2008): 44,640,000 (290); personal computers (2006): 3,050,000 (22); total Internet users (2007): 500,000 (3.5); broadband Internet subscribers (2007): 44,000 (0.3).

## Education and health

**Educational attainment** (2004). Percentage of population ages 25 and over having: no formal schooling 48.8%; incomplete primary education 17.9%; complete primary 7.7%; incomplete secondary 15.1%; complete secondary or higher 10.5%. **Literacy** (2006): total population ages 15 and over literate 53.7%; males literate 58.5%; females literate 48.8%. **Health** (2006): physicians 44,632 (1 per 3,110 persons); hospital beds 51,044 (1 per 2,719 persons); infant mortality rate per 1,000 live births 45.0; undernourished population (2002–04) 44,000,000 (30% of total population based on the consumption of a minimum daily requirement of 1,780 calories).

## Military

**Total active duty personnel** (November 2008): 157,053, of which UN peacekeepers 8,028 (army 80.3%, navy 10.8%, air force 8.9%). **Military expenditure as percentage of GDP** (2007): 1.5%; per capita expenditure US$7.

## Background

In its early years Bangladesh was known as Bengal. When the British left the subcontinent in 1947, the area that was East Bengal became the part of Pakistan called East Pakistan. Bengali nationalist sentiment increased after the creation of an independent Pakistan. In 1971 violence erupted; some one million Bengalis were killed, and millions more fled to India, which finally entered the war on the side of the Bengalis, ensuring West Pakistan's defeat. East Pakistan became the independent nation of Bangladesh. Little of the devastation caused by the war has been repaired, and political instability, including the assassinations of two presidents, has continued. In addition, the low-lying country has been repeatedly battered by natural disasters, notably tropical storms and flooding.

## Recent Developments

Bangladesh was affected monetarily in 2011 in the wake of the Arab Spring revolts that swept across the Middle East. Some two-thirds of Bangladesh's recorded remittances were derived from laborers working in that region, especially Saudi Arabia, and they accounted for 12% of Bangladesh's total GDP. Fortunately, the country's textile industry was booming, with an annual increase of 40% recorded in the previous eight months to March, and this US$14 billion rise helped to offset the revenue lost by the decline in remittances.

**Internet resource:** <www.bbs.gov.bd>.

# Barbados

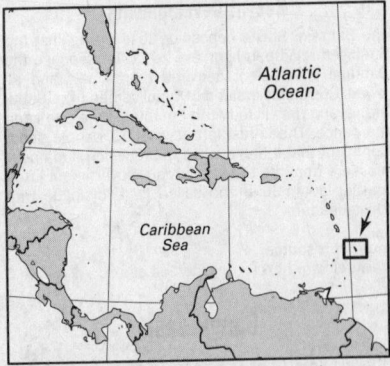

**Official name:** Barbados. **Form of government:** constitutional monarchy with two legislative houses (Senate [21]; House of Assembly [30]). **Head of state:** British Queen Elizabeth II (from 1952), represented by Governor-General Sir Elliot Belgrave (from 2012). **Head of government:** Prime Minister Freundel Stuart (from 2010). **Capital:** Bridgetown. **Official language:** English. **Official religion:** none. **Monetary unit:** 1 Barbados dollar (Bds$) = 100 cents; valuation (2 Jul 2012) US$1 = Bds$2.00.

*1 metric ton = about 1.1 short tons;    1 kilometer = 0.6 mi (statute);    1 metric ton-km cargo = about 0.68 short ton-mi cargo;    c.i.f.: cost, insurance, and freight;    f.o.b.: free on board*

## Demography

**Area:** 166 sq mi, 430 sq km. **Population** (2011): 277,000. **Density** (2011): persons per sq mi 1,668.7, persons per sq km 644.2. **Urban** (2009): 43.7%. **Sex distribution** (2007): male 48.36%; female 51.64%. **Age breakdown** (2007): under 15, 19.8%; 15–29, 22.4%; 30–44, 24.7%; 45–59, 20.2%; 60–74, 8.7%; 75–84, 3.1%; 85 and over, 1.1%. **Ethnic composition** (2000): local black 87.1%; mixed race 6.0%; British expatriates 4.3%; US white 1.2%; Indo-Pakistani 1.1%; other 0.3%. **Religious affiliation** (2000): Christian 72.5%, of which Anglican 28.3%, Pentecostal 18.7%, Adventist 5.5%, Methodist 5.1%; Rastafarian 1.1%; Muslim 0.7%; Hindu 0.3%; nonreligious 17.3%; other/unknown 8.1%. **Major urban areas** (2006): Bridgetown 98,700; Speightstown 3,600; Oistins 2,300. **Location:** island at the eastern edge of the Caribbean Sea where it adjoins the North Atlantic Ocean, northeast of Venezuela.

## Vital statistics

**Birth rate** per 1,000 population (2007): 12.8 (world avg. 20.3). **Death rate** per 1,000 population (2007): 8.5 (world avg. 8.5). **Total fertility rate** (avg. births per childbearing woman; 2007): 1.68. **Life expectancy** at birth (2007): male 71.2 years; female 75.8 years.

## National economy

**Budget** (2006–07). *Revenue* (current revenue only): Bds$2,156,000,000 (tax revenue 95.8%, of which VAT 30.1%, corporate taxes 20.6%, income tax 13.8%, import duties 6.8%; nontax revenue 4.2%). *Expenditures:* Bds$2,351,000,000 (current expenditures 89.1%, of which education 19.0%, general public service 15.7%, debt payments 14.0%, health 12.2%; development expenditures 10.9%). **Production** (metric tons except as noted). *Agriculture and fishing* (2006): sugarcane (2007) 354,000, sweet potatoes 2,000, coconuts 1,950, okra 1,550; livestock (number of live animals) 19,000 pigs, 10,800 sheep, 3,400,000 chickens; fisheries production 1,974 (from aquaculture, none). *Mining and quarrying* (2006): limestone 1,900,000, clay and shale 145,000. *Manufacturing* (2007): cement 294,184, raw sugar 34,700, rum (2005) 132,000 hectolitres; other manufactures include industrial chemical products, electronics, garments, and wooden furniture. *Energy production (consumption):* electricity (kW-hr; 2007) 924,000,000 (924,000,000); crude petroleum (barrels; 2007) 303,000 ([2006] negligible); petroleum products (metric tons; 2006) 1,000 (252,000); natural gas (cu m; 2007) 21,100,000 ([2006] 26,857,000). **Population economically active** (December 2005): total 145,800; activity rate of total population 53.1% (participation rates: ages 15 and over, 69.0%; female 49.5%; unemployed [July–September 2008] 8.4%. **Gross national income** (2007): US$3,580,000,000 (US$12,178 per capita). **Public debt** (external, outstanding; December 2006): US$799,400,000. **Selected balance of payments data.** Receipts from (US$'000,000): tourism (2006) 967; remittances (2008) 168; foreign direct investment (FDI; 2005–07 avg.) 68; official development assistance (2007) 14. Disbursements for (US$'000,000): tourism (2006) 105; remittances (2008) 40; FDI (2005–07 avg.) 11.

## Foreign trade

**Imports** (2007; c.i.f.): US$1,299,000,000 (machinery and apparatus 24.4%; manufactured goods 18.0%; food products 15.6%; chemical products 11.3%; motor vehicles 7.8%). *Major import sources:* US 43.7%; UK 7.8%; Trinidad and Tobago 7.7%; Japan 4.5%; Canada 4.4%. **Exports** (2007; f.o.b.): US$314,000,000 (crude petroleum 21.9%; food products 15.3%, of which raw sugar 6.0%; rum 10.8%; machinery and apparatus 7.8%; medicines 7.7%; fabricated metal products 5.7%). *Major export destinations:* Trinidad and Tobago 27.8%; US 14.2%; UK 9.1%; St. Lucia 6.6%; Jamaica 5.3%.

## Transport and communications

**Transport.** *Railroads:* none. *Roads* (2006): total length 1,650 km (paved virtually 100%). *Vehicles* (2004): passenger cars 92,195; trucks and buses 8,597. *Air transport* (2003): metric ton-km cargo 200,000. **Communications,** in total units (units per 1,000 persons). Telephone landlines (2006): 140,000 (501); cellular telephone subscribers (2006): 237,000 (847); personal computers (2005): 40,000 (148); total Internet users (2007): 280,000 (997); broadband Internet subscribers (2006): 55,000 (202).

## Education and health

**Educational attainment** (2003). Percentage of employed labor force having: no formal schooling 0.5%; primary education 14.9%; secondary 58.7%; technical/vocational 5.4%; university 19.6%; other/unknown 0.9%. **Literacy** (2003): total population ages 15 and over literate 99.7%. **Health** (2007): physicians (2003) 369 (1 per 751 persons); hospital beds 630 (1 per 446 persons); infant mortality rate per 1,000 live births 13.2; undernourished population (2002–04) less than 2.5% of total population.

## Military

**Total active duty personnel** (November 2008): 610 (army 82.0%, navy 18.0%). **Military expenditure as percentage of GDP** (2008): 0.8%; per capita expenditure US$106.

## Background

The island of Barbados was probably inhabited by Arawak Indians who originally came from South America. Spaniards may have landed by 1518, and by 1536 they had apparently wiped out the Indian population. Barbados was settled by the English in the 1620s. Slaves were brought in to work the sugar plantations, which were especially prosperous in the 17th–18th centuries. The British Empire abolished slavery in 1834, and all the slaves in Barbados were freed by 1838. In 1958 Barbados joined the West Indies Federation. When the latter dissolved in 1962, Barbados sought independence from Britain; it achieved it and joined the Commonwealth in 1966.

## Recent Developments

Barbados obtained a US$10 million loan from the Inter-American Development Bank in February 2011 for initiatives in photovoltaics and energy efficiency.

The country was already a leader in renewable energy through its widespread use of solar energy in water heating.

Internet resource: <www.barstats.gov.bb>.

# Belarus

Official name: Respublika Belarus (Republic of Belarus). Form of government: republic with two legislative houses (Council of the Republic [64]; House of Representatives [110]). Head of state and government: President Alyaksandr H. Lukashenka (from 1994), assisted by Prime Minister Mikhail Myasnikovich (from 2010). Capital: Minsk. Official languages: Belarusian; Russian. Official religion: none (a 2003 concordat grants the Belarusian Orthodox Church privileged status). Monetary unit: Belarusian rubel (Br); valuation (2 Jul 2012) US$1 = Br 8,365.00.

## Demography

Area: 80,153 sq mi, 207,595 sq km. Population (2011): 9,472,000. Density (2011): persons per sq mi 118.2, persons per sq km 45.6. Urban (2011): 75.1%. Sex distribution (2007): male 46.67%; female 53.33%. Age breakdown (2005): under 15, 15.7%; 15–29, 23.9%; 30–44, 22.0%; 45–59, 20.3%; 60–74, 12.5%; 75–84, 4.9%; 85 and over, 0.7%. Ethnic composition (1999): Belarusian 81.2%; Russian 11.4%; Polish 3.9%; Ukrainian 2.4%; Jewish 0.3%; other 0.8%. Religious affiliation (2007): nonreligious/atheist 50.0%; Belarusian Orthodox 40.0%; Roman Catholic 7.0%; other Christian 1.0%; Jewish 0.6%; other 1.4%. Major cities (2005): Minsk 1,741,000; Homyel 481,500; Mahilyow 367,700; Vitsyebsk 343,600; Hrodna 318,600. Location: eastern Europe, bordering Latvia, Russia, Ukraine, Poland, and Lithuania.

## Vital statistics

Birth rate per 1,000 population (2008): 11.1 (world avg. 20.3); within marriage 79.9%. Death rate per 1,000 population (2008): 13.8 (world avg. 8.5). Total fertility rate (avg. births per childbearing woman;

2008): 1.42. Life expectancy at birth (2008): male 64.7 years; female 76.5 years.

## National economy

Budget (2007). Revenue: Br 37,167,000,000 (taxes on goods and services 34.2%; social security contributions 30.3%; taxes on trade 16.9%; corporate taxes 6.1%; other taxes 4.8%; nontax revenue 7.7%). Expenditures: Br 36,748,000,000 (social protection 32.9%; economic affairs 25.0%; general administration 23.8%). Public debt (external, outstanding; 2007): US$2,338,000,000. Population economically active (2007): 4,525,200; activity rate of total population 46.6% (participation rate [1999]: ages 15–64, 69.7%; female 52.8%; officially/unofficially unemployed [2008] 1.0%/15–20%). Production (metric tons except as noted). Agriculture and fishing (2007): potatoes 8,744,000, sugar beets 3,626,000, barley 1,911,000, rapeseed 240,000; livestock (number of live animals) 4,007,000 cattle, 3,598,000 pigs; fisheries production (2006) 5,050 (from aquaculture 82%). Mining and quarrying (2005): potash 4,844,000; peat 2,408,000. Manufacturing (2007): fertilizers 5,880,000; cement 3,820,000; crude steel (2005) 2,076,000. Energy production (consumption): electricity (kW-hr; 2007) 31,800,000,000 ([2006] 36,171,000,000); coal (metric tons; 2006) none (132,000); crude petroleum (barrels; 2007) 12,800,000 ([2006] 154,800,000); petroleum products (metric tons; 2006) 17,882,000 (5,622,000); natural gas (cu m; 2006) 219,000,000 (20,779,000,000). Gross national income (2008): US$52,117,000,000 (US$5,380 per capita). Selected balance of payments data. Receipts from (US$'000,000): tourism (2007) 324; remittances (2008) 448; foreign direct investment (2005–07 avg.) 810; official development assistance (2007) 83. Disbursements for (US$'000,000): tourism (2007) 606; remittances (2008) 142.

## Foreign trade

Imports (2007; c.i.f.): US$28,693,000,000 (crude petroleum 25.2%; nonelectrical machinery 11.0%; base and fabricated metals 10.6%; chemical products 9.0%; natural gas 7.3%). Major import sources: Russia 60.0%; Germany 7.6%; Ukraine 5.3%; Poland 2.9%; China 2.8%. Exports (2007; f.o.b.): US$24,275,-000,000 (refined petroleum products 31.4%; machinery and apparatus 12.9%; motor vehicles 8.0%; food products 6.9%, of which dairy products 3.8%; potassium chloride 5.6%; iron and steel 4.9%). Major export destinations: Russia 36.6%; Netherlands 17.6%; UK 6.3%; Ukraine 6.1%; Poland 5.1%.

## Transport and communications

Transport. Railroads (2007): length (2002) 5,533 km; passenger-km 9,366,000,000; metric ton-km cargo 47,933,000,000. Roads (2005): total length 94,797 km (paved 89%). Vehicles (2005): passenger cars 1,771,398. Air transport (2007): passenger-km 975,000,000; metric ton-km cargo 66,000,000. Communications, in total units (units per 1,000 persons). Telephone landlines (2007): 3,672,000 (379); cellular telephone subscribers (2007): 6,960,000 (717); personal computers (2007): 78,000 (80);

---

1 metric ton = about 1.1 short tons;    1 kilometer = 0.6 mi (statute);    1 metric ton-km cargo = about 0.68 short ton-mi cargo;    c.i.f.: cost, insurance, and freight;    f.o.b.: free on board

broadband Internet subscribers (2006): 11,000 (1.2).

## Education and health

**Literacy** (2007): total population ages 15 and over literate 99.7%. **Health** (2007): physicians 46,900 (1 per 207 persons); hospital beds 108,900 (1 per 89 persons); infant mortality rate per 1,000 live births (2008) 4.5; undernourished population (2002–04) 400,000 (4% of total population based on the consumption of a minimum daily requirement of 1,970 calories).

## Military

**Total active duty personnel** (November 2008): 72,940 (army 40.6%, air force and air defense 24.9%, centrally controlled units 34.5%). **Military expenditure as percentage of GDP** (2008): 1.2%; per capita expenditure US$70.

## Background

While Belarusians share a distinct identity and language, they did not enjoy political sovereignty until the late 20th century. The territory that is now Belarus underwent partition and changed hands often; as a result its history is entwined with those of its neighbors. In medieval times the region was ruled by Lithuanians and Poles. Following the Third Partition of Poland, it was ruled by Russia. After World War I, the western part was assigned to Poland, and the eastern part became Soviet Russian territory. After World War II, the Soviets expanded what had been the Belorussian SSR by annexing more of Poland. Much of the area suffered radiation contamination from the Chernobyl accident in 1986, forcing many to evacuate. Belarus declared its independence in 1991 and later joined the Commonwealth of Independent States. Amid increasing political turmoil in the 1990s, it moved toward closer union with Russia but continued to struggle economically and politically at the start of the 21st century.

## Recent Developments

Belarus experienced a difficult year in 2011 as it dealt with spiraling inflation, a currency crisis, shortages of basic products, and heightened international criticism of the country's record on human rights. The Belarusian economy reportedly grew by at least 8.0% from January to September, and industrial production rose by 10.6%. Inflation, however, skyrocketed by more than 74.0% over that same period. The summer was marked by youth protests organized through social media and dubbed a "revolution by social network." The government responded by blocking the organizer's Web sites, and a protest rally on 8 October was undermined by mass arrests of potential participants the day prior to the event.

**Internet resource:**
<www.belstat.gov.by/homep/en/main.html>.

## Belgium

**Official name:** Koninkrijk België (Dutch); Royaume de Belgique (French); Königreich Belgien (German)

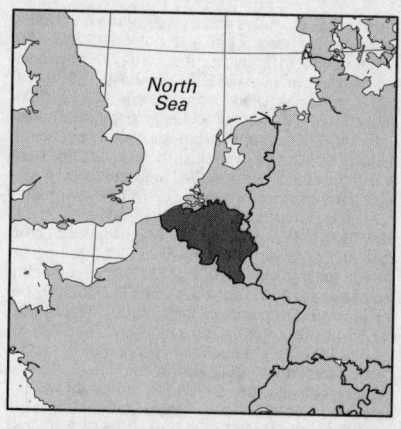

(Kingdom of Belgium). **Form of government:** federal constitutional monarchy with two legislative houses (Senate [71]; House of Representatives [150]). **Head of state:** King Albert II (from 1993). **Head of government:** Prime Minister Elio Di Rupo (from 2011). **Capital:** Brussels. **Official languages:** Dutch; French; German. **Official religion:** none. **Monetary unit:** 1 euro (€) = 100 cents; valuation (2 Jul 2012) US$1 = €0.79.

## Demography

**Area:** 11,787 sq mi, 30,528 sq km. **Population** (2011): 10,971,000. **Density** (2011): persons per sq mi 930.8, persons per sq km 359.4. **Urban** (2009): 97.4%. **Sex distribution** (2007): male 48.98%; female 51.02%. **Age breakdown** (2005): under 15, 17.1%; 15–29, 18.4%; 30–44, 22.0%; 45–59, 20.5%; 60–74, 14.0%; 75–84, 6.4%; 85 and over, 1.6%. **National composition** (2007): Belgian 90.9%, of which Flemish-speaking 53.6%, French-speaking 36.4%, German-speaking 0.9%; Italian 1.6%; French 1.2%; Dutch 1.2%; Moroccan 0.7%; other 4.4%. **Religious affiliation** (2000): Roman Catholic 57%; undefined Christian 15%; Muslim 4%; nonreligious 17%; other 7%. **Major cities/urban agglomerations** (2007): Brussels 148,873/1,831,496; Antwerp 472,071/ 955,338; Liège 190,102/641,591; Gent 237,250/423,320; Charleroi 201,593/405,236. **Location:** western Europe, bordering the Netherlands, Germany, Luxembourg, France, and the North Sea.

## Vital statistics

**Birth rate** per 1,000 population (2008): 11.7 (world avg. 20.3); within marriage 58.0%. **Death rate** per 1,000 population (2007): 9.5 (world avg. 8.5). **Total fertility rate** (avg. births per childbearing woman; 2008): 1.82. **Life expectancy** at birth (2008): male 77.5 years; female 83.5 years.

## National economy

**Budget** (2007). *Revenue:* €160,393,000,000 (social security contributions 28.8%; income tax 23.3%; taxes on goods and services 23.1%). *Expenditures:* €161,154,000,000 (social insurance benefits 46.3%, of which health 12.8%; wages 24.1%; interest on debt 7.8%; capital expenditure 5.9%). **Production**

(metric tons except as noted). *Agriculture and fishing* (2007): sugar beets 5,746,892; potatoes 2,877,685, wheat 1,480,710, chicory roots 361,305; livestock (number of live animals) 6,270,000 pigs, 2,639,700 cattle; fisheries production (2006) 24,219 (from aquaculture 5%). *Mining and quarrying* (2007): marble 340,000. *Manufacturing* (value added in €'000,000; 2007): chemical products 9,228; base and fabricated metals 8,174; food products, beverages, and tobacco products 6,257. *Energy production (consumption)*: electricity (kW-hr; 2007) 88,278,000,000 ([2005] 93,248,000,000); hard coal (metric tons; 2007) none (5,371,000); lignite (metric tons; 2006) 29,000 (313,000); crude petroleum (barrels; 2007) none ([2005] 235,000,000); petroleum products (metric tons; 2006) 28,114,000 (17,514,000); natural gas (cu m; 2007) none ([2006] 21,922,000,000). **Population economically active** (2006): total 4,647,200; activity rate 44.2% (participation rates: ages 15–64, 58.8%; female 44.4%; unemployed [2008] 7.1%). **Gross national income** (2008): US$474,467,000,000 (US$44,330 per capita). **Public debt** (September 2008; federal only): US$398,900,000,000. **Selected balance of payments data.** Receipts from (US$'000,000): tourism (2007) 10,898; remittances (2008) 9,280; foreign direct investment (FDI; 2005–07 avg.) 46,439. Disbursements for (US$'000,000): tourism (2007) 17,268; remittances (2008) 3,689; FDI (2005–07 avg.) 46,284.

## Foreign trade

**Imports** (2007; c.i.f.): US$413,371,000,000 (machinery and apparatus 13.9%; mineral fuels 11.5%; motor vehicles and parts 10.9%; base and fabricated metals 8.5%; medicines 8.0%; organic chemical products 7.3%). *Major import sources:* Germany 17.8%; Netherlands 17.6%; France 11.2%; UK 6.3%; US 5.3%. **Exports** (2007; f.o.b.): US$430,822,000,000 (machinery and apparatus 12.3%; motor vehicles and parts 11.4%; medicines 11.0%; food products 6.9%; mineral fuels 6.6%; organic chemical products 6.5%; iron and steel 6.0%; plastic products 5.1%; diamonds 4.2% [world's leading exporter]). *Major export destinations:* Germany 19.7%; France 16.7%; Netherlands 11.9%; UK 7.6%; US 5.6%.

## Transport and communications

**Transport.** *Railroads* (2006): route length 3,233 km; passenger-km 9,607,000,000; metric ton-km cargo 8,442,000,000. *Roads* (2004): total length 150,567 km (paved 78%). *Vehicles* (2006): passenger cars 4,976,286; trucks and buses 638,579. *Air transport* (2007; Brussels Airlines only): passenger-km 7,542,000,000; metric ton-km cargo 80,668,000. **Communications,** in total units (units per 1,000 persons). Telephone landlines (2008): 4,457,000 (416); cellular telephone subscribers (2008): 11,822,000 (1,104); personal computers (2006): 3,977,000 (377); total Internet users (2007): 7,006,000 (659); broadband Internet subscribers (2008): 2,962,000 (277).

## Education and health

**Educational attainment** (2002). Percentage of population ages 25 and over having: no formal schooling through lower-secondary education 39%; upper secondary/higher vocational 33%; university 28%. **Health:** physicians (2007) 38,402 (1 per 278 persons); hospital beds (2005) 70,795 (1 per 148 persons); infant mortality rate per 1,000 live births (2008) 3.4; undernourished population (2002–04) less than 2.5% of total population.

## Military

**Total active duty personnel** (November 2008): 38,844 (army 36.7%, navy 4.2%, air force 18.9%, medical service 4.9%, joint service 35.3%); foreign forces at NATO headquarters (November 2008): US 1,301; UK 400. **Military expenditure as percentage of GDP** (2007): 1.1%; per capita expenditure US$471.

## Background

Inhabited in ancient times by the Belgae, a Celtic people, the area was conquered by Caesar in 57 BC; under Augustus it became the Roman province of Gallia Belgica. Conquered by the Franks, it later broke up into semi-independent territories, including Brabant and Luxembourg. By the late 15th century AD, the territories of the Netherlands, of which the future Belgium was a part, had gradually united and passed to the Habsburgs. In the 16th century, it was a center for European commerce. The basis of modern Belgium was laid in the southern Catholic provinces that split from the northern provinces after the Union of Utrecht in 1579. Overrun by the French and incorporated into France in 1801, it was reunited to Holland and with it became the independent Kingdom of the Netherlands in 1815. After the revolt of its citizens in 1830, it became the independent Kingdom of Belgium. Under Léopold II it acquired vast lands in Africa. Overrun by the Germans in World Wars I and II, Belgium was the scene of the Battle of the Bulge. Internal discord led to legislation in the 1970s and 1980s that created three nearly autonomous regions in accordance with language distribution: Flemish Flanders, French Wallonia, and bilingual Brussels. In 1993 it became a federation comprising the three regions, which gained greater autonomy at the outset of the 21st century. It is a member of the European Union.

## Recent Developments

Belgium was locked in political stalemate throughout almost the whole of 2011 as efforts to form a coalition government came to naught. The deadlock was finally broken on 6 December, when the Francophone Socialist Party leader, Elio Di Rupo, was sworn in as prime minister. Di Rupo was the first premier from Belgium's French-speaking community since 1979. The breakthrough was only achieved after a succession of senior politicians had failed in numerous attempts since the June 2010 election to forge an agreement between political parties. In all, it took 541 days to form the coalition, which earned Belgium an unwelcome designation in the Guinness World Records as the country without a government for the longest period in peacetime.

**Internet resource:** <http://statbel.fgov.be/en>.

---

*1 metric ton = about 1.1 short tons;    1 kilometer = 0.6 mi (statute);    1 metric ton-km cargo = about 0.68 short ton-mi cargo;    c.i.f.: cost, insurance, and freight;    f.o.b.: free on board*

# Belize

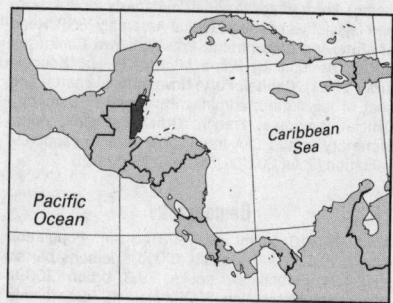

Caribbean Sea

Pacific Ocean

**Official name:** Belize. **Form of government:** constitutional monarchy with two legislative houses (Senate [13]; House of Representatives [32]). **Head of state:** British Queen Elizabeth II (from 1952), represented by Governor-General Colville Young (from 1993). **Head of government:** Prime Minister Dean Barrow (from 2008). **Capital:** Belmopan. **Official language:** English. **Official religion:** none. **Monetary unit:** 1 Belize dollar (BZ$) = 100 cents; valuation (2 Jul 2012) US$1 = BZ$1.90.

## Demography

**Area:** 8,867 sq mi, 22,965 sq km. **Population** (2011): 322,000. **Density** (2011): persons per sq mi 36.3, persons per sq km 14.0. **Urban** (2008): 51.4%. **Sex distribution** (2008): male 49.95%; female 50.05%. **Age breakdown** (2007): under 15, 38.9%; 15–29, 29.4%; 30–44, 17.7%; 45–59, 8.9%; 60–74, 3.8%; 75–84, 1.1%; 85 and over, 0.2%. **Ethnic composition** (2004): mestizo (Spanish-Indian) 48.4%; Creole (predominantly black) 27.0%; Mayan Indian 10.0%; Garifuna (black-Carib Indian) 5.7%; white 3.9%, of which Mennonite 3.2%; East Indian 3.0%; Chinese 0.9%; other 1.1%. **Religious affiliation** (2000): Roman Catholic 49.6%; Protestant 31.8%, of which Pentecostal 7.4%, Anglican 5.3%, Seventh-day Adventist 5.2%, Mennonite 4.1%; other Christian 1.9%; nonreligious 9.4%; other 7.3%. **Major cities** (2008): Belize City 65,200; San Ignacio/Santa Elena 19,100; Belmopan 18,100; Orange Walk 16,300; Dangriga 12,000. **Location:** Central America, bordering Mexico, the Caribbean Sea, and Guatemala.

## Vital statistics

**Birth rate** per 1,000 population (2007): 28.3 (world avg. 20.3); (1997) within marriage 40.3%. **Death rate** per 1,000 population (2007): 5.7 (world avg. 8.5). **Total fertility rate** (avg. births per childbearing woman; 2007): 3.52. **Life expectancy** at birth (2007): male 66.4 years; female 70.1 years.

## National economy

**Budget** (2007). *Revenue:* BZ$765,477,000 (tax revenue 75.2%, of which taxes on goods and services 30.3%, taxes on international trade 22.8%, taxes on income and profits 21.3%; grants 11.4%; nontax revenue 9.7%; other 3.7%). *Expenditures:* BZ$794,-758,000 (current expenditures 80.0%; capital expenditures 20.0%). **Production** (metric tons except as noted). *Agriculture and fishing* (2007): sugarcane

(2008) 1,017,000, oranges 213,100, bananas (2008) 79,200, plantain 41,000, papayas (2008) 28,900; livestock (number of live animals) 58,500 cattle, 1,600,000 chickens; fisheries production (2006) 11,788 (from aquaculture 65%). *Mining and quarrying* (2006): limestone 287,000; sand and gravel 219,000 cu m. *Manufacturing* (value added in US$'000,000; 2007): food products and beverages (significantly citrus concentrate, flour, sugar, and beer) 77.2; textiles, wearing apparel, and footwear 3.6; other (including crude petroleum extraction) 64.3. *Energy production (consumption):* electricity (kW-hr; 2006) 191,000,000 (220,000,000); crude petroleum (barrels; 2007) 1,100,000 (n.a.); petroleum products (metric tons; 2006) none (272,000). **Population economically active** (2005): total 110,786; activity rate of total population 38.2% (participation rates: ages 15–64, 64.2%; female 36.7%; unemployed [2008] 8.1%). **Gross national income** (2008): US$1,186,000,000 (US$3,820 per capita). **Public debt** (external, outstanding; December 2008): US$954,100,000. **Selected balance of payments data.** Receipts from (US$'000,000): tourism (2007) 291; remittances (2008) 78; foreign direct investment (2005–07 avg.) 114; official development assistance (2007) 23. Disbursements for (US$'000,000): tourism (2007) 43; remittances (2008) 29.

## Foreign trade

**Imports** (2007; c.i.f.): US$684,300,000 (refined petroleum products 14.3%; manufactured goods 11.9%; machinery and apparatus 11.7%; food products 9.9%; chemical products 7.5%; motor vehicles 5.8%). *Major import sources:* US 33.9%; Cuba 11.4%; Panama 9.7%; Mexico 9.6%; Guatemala 6.9%). **Exports** (2007; f.o.b.): US$266,600,000 (food products 63.2%, of which orange juice 19.6%, raw cane sugar 16.5%, bananas 7.8%, frozen crustaceans 7.6%, papayas and melons 4.9%; crude petroleum 26.9%). *Major export destinations:* US 26.8%; UK 18.0%; Panama 14.3%; Costa Rica 11.8%; Netherlands 7.8%.

## Transport and communications

**Transport.** *Railroads:* none. *Roads* (2006): total length 3,007 km (paved 19%). *Vehicles* (2003): passenger cars 36,952; trucks and buses 7,380. *Air transport* (2001; Belize international airport only): passenger arrivals 256,564, passenger departures 240,900; cargo loaded 186 metric tons, cargo unloaded 1,272 metric tons. **Communications,** in total units (units per 1,000 persons). Telephone landlines (2008): 31,000 (97); cellular telephone subscribers (2008): 160,000 (497); personal computers (2002): 35,000 (132); total Internet users (2007): 32,000 (111); broadband Internet subscribers (2008): 7,700 (24).

## Education and health

**Educational attainment** (2000). Percentage of population ages 25 and over having: no formal schooling 36.6%; primary education 40.9%; secondary 11.7%; postsecondary/advanced vocational 6.4%; university 3.8%; other/unknown 0.6%. **Literacy** (2003): total population ages 15 and over literate 76.9%; males literate 77.1%; females literate 76.7%. **Health:** physicians (2006) 263 (1 per 1,140 persons); hospital beds (2005) 436 (1 per 665 persons); infant mortality rate per 1,000 live births (2007) 21.2; undernourished population (2002–04) 10,000 (4% of total population based on the consumption of a minimum daily requirement of 1,810 calories).

## Military

**Total active duty personnel** (November 2008): 1,050 (army 100%); foreign forces (2008): British army 30. **Military expenditure as percentage of GDP** (2007): 1.4%; per capita expenditure US$58.

## Background

The area was inhabited by the Maya 300 BC–AD 900; the ruins of their ceremonial centers, including Caracol and Xunantunich, can still be seen. The Spanish claimed sovereignty from the 16th century but never tried to settle Belize, though they regarded as interlopers the British who did. British logwood cutters arrived in the mid-17th century; Spanish opposition was finally overcome in 1798. When settlers began to penetrate the interior they met with Indian resistance. In 1871 British Honduras became a crown colony, but an unfulfilled provision of an 1859 British-Guatemalan treaty led Guatemala to claim the territory. The situation had not been resolved when Belize was granted its independence in 1981. Although Guatemala officially recognized the territory's independence in 1991, a British force, stationed there to ensure the new country's security, was not withdrawn until 1994.

## Recent Developments

Belize's economic growth between January and September 2011 edged up to 2.7%, compared with 1.8% in the same period in 2010. The critical agricultural sector (especially the banana and sugarcane crops) was impacted by extreme weather and fiscal problems. Earnings from exports for the first 10 months of the year totalled more than US$604 million, an increase of 7.8%.

**Internet resource:** <www.statisticsbelize.org.bz>.

# Benin

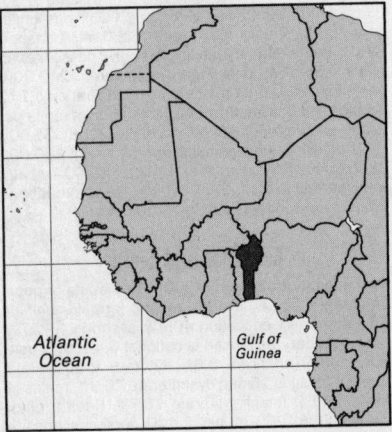

*Atlantic Ocean*     *Gulf of Guinea*

**Official name:** République du Bénin (Republic of Benin). **Form of government:** multiparty republic with one legislative house (National Assembly [83]). **Head of state and government:** President Yayi Boni (from 2006), assisted by Prime Minister Pascal Koupaki (from 2011). **Capital:** Porto-Novo (official capital and seat of legislature; administrative seat in Cotonou). **Official language:** French. **Official religion:** none. **Monetary unit:** 1 CFA franc (CFAF) = 100 centimes; valuation (2 Jul 2012) US$1 = CFAF 521.26.

## Demography

**Area:** 44,310 sq mi, 114,763 sq km. **Population** (2011): 9,100,000. **Density** (2011): persons per sq mi 205.4, persons per sq km 79.3. **Urban** (2009): 41.6%. **Sex distribution** (2008): male 49.99%; female 50.01%. **Age breakdown** (2008): under 15, 45.5%; 15–29, 27.3%; 30–44, 15.7%; 45–59, 7.4%; 60–74, 3.4%; 75–84, 0.6%; 85 and over 0.1%. **Ethnic composition** (2002): Fon 39.2%; Adjara 15.2%; Yoruba (Nago) 12.3%; Bariba 9.2%; Fulani 7.0%; Somba (Otomary) 6.1%; Yoa-Lokpa 4.0%; other 7.0%. **Religious affiliation** (2002): Christian 42.8%, of which Roman Catholic 27.1%, Protestant 5.4%, indigenous Christian 5.3%; Muslim 24.4%; traditional beliefs 23.3%, of which Vodou (voodoo) 17.3%; nonreligious 6.5%; other 9.5%. **Major urban localities** (2006): Cotonou 719,912; Porto-Novo 255,878; Godomey 187,836; Parakou 178,304; Abomey-Calavi 75,226. **Location:** western Africa, bordering Burkina Faso, Niger, Nigeria, the Atlantic Ocean, and Togo.

## Vital statistics

**Birth rate** per 1,000 population (2008): 39.8 (world avg. 20.3). **Death rate** per 1,000 population (2008): 9.7 (world avg. 8.5). **Total fertility rate** (avg. births per childbearing woman; 2008): 5.58.

## National economy

**Budget** (2007). *Revenue:* CFAF 634,000,000,000 (tax revenue 70.3%; nontax revenue 16.0%; grants 13.7%). *Expenditures:* CFAF 585,400,000,000 (current expenditures 65.6%; development expenditures 34.4%, of which externally financed expenditures 19.3%). **Public debt** (external, outstanding; 2007): US$852,000,000. **Gross national income** (2008): US$5,951,000,000 (US$690 per capita). **Production** (metric tons except as noted). *Agriculture and fishing* (2007): cassava 2,525,000, yams 2,240,000, corn (maize) 900,000, seed cotton 313,500, oil palm fruit 275,000, cashews 41,500; livestock (number of live animals) 1,900,000 cattle, 1,439,600 goats; fisheries production (2006) 38,436 (from aquaculture, 1%). *Mining and quarrying* (2006): clay 21,000, gold 20 kg. *Manufacturing* (value added in US$'000,000; 1999): food products 74; textiles 42; beverages 36. *Energy production (consumption):* electricity (kW-hr; 2006) 128,000,000 (718,000,000); crude petroleum (barrels; 2005) 137,000 (negligible); petroleum products (metric tons; 2006) none (972,000). **Population economically active** (2006): total 3,539,000; activity rate of total population 40.4% (participation rates: ages 15–64, 72.9%; female 40.3%; unemployed, n.a.). **Selected balance of payments data.** Receipts from (US$'000,000): tourism (2007) 118; re-

---

*1 metric ton = about 1.1 short tons;*    *1 kilometer = 0.6 mi (statute);*    *1 metric ton-km cargo = about 0.68 short ton-mi cargo;*    *c.i.f.: cost, insurance, and freight;*    *f.o.b.: free on board*

mittances (2008) 271; foreign direct investment (2005–07 avg.) 51; official development assistance (2007) 470. Disbursements for (US$'000,000): tourism (2007) 35; remittances (2008) 67.

## Foreign trade

**Imports** (2005; c.i.f.): US$898,700,000 (food products 26.2%, of which rice 11.2%, poultry cuts 4.7%; refined petroleum products 13.7%; machinery and apparatus 7.4%; electricity 6.3%; motor vehicles 4.7%; cement clinker 4.4%). *Major import sources:* France 18.4%; China 8.8%; Ghana 7.2%; Côte d'Ivoire 6.9%; Thailand 6.7%. **Exports** (2005; f.o.b. [excludes reexports—notably petroleum and food products particularly from Nigeria and Niger—valued at US$253,000,000]): US$288,200,000 (cotton 58.0%; food products 12.0%, of which cashews 6.9%; cigarettes 6.7%). *Major export destinations:* China 36.2%; India 6.9%; Nigeria 5.8%; Niger 5.2%; Indonesia 3.6%.

## Transport and communications

**Transport.** *Railroads* (2006): length 578 km; passenger-km (2005) 17,000,000; metric ton-km cargo 28,900,000. *Roads* (2004): total length 19,000 km (paved 9.5%). *Vehicles* (2003): passenger cars 135,700; trucks and buses 19,200. *Air transport* (2003): metric ton-km cargo 7,000,000. **Communications,** in total units (units per 1,000 persons). Telephone landlines (2007): 110,000 (14); cellular telephone subscribers (2008): 3,435,000 (403); personal computers (2007): 58,000 (7); total Internet users (2008): 550,000 (64); broadband Internet subscribers (2007): 2,000 (0.2).

## Education and health

**Educational attainment** (2002). Percentage of population ages 15 and over having: no formal schooling 63.5%; primary education 18.7%; secondary 15.9%; postsecondary 1.9%. **Literacy** (2005): total percentage of population ages 15 and over literate 43.2%; males literate 58.8%; females literate 28.4%. **Health:** physicians (2003) 1,013 (1 per 7,135 persons); hospital beds (2001) 590 (1 per 11,238 persons); infant mortality rate per 1,000 live births (2008) 66.2; undernourished population (2002–04) 800,000 (12% of total population based on the consumption of a minimum daily requirement of 1,800 calories).

## Military

**Total active duty personnel** (November 2008): 4,750, of which UN peacekeepers 1,178 (army 90.5%, navy 4.2%, air force 5.3%). **Military expenditure as percentage of GDP** (2007): 0.9%; per capita expenditure US$7.

## Background

In southern Benin, the Dahomey, or Fon, established the Abomey kingdom in 1625. In the 18th century, the kingdom became known as Dahomey when it expanded to include Allada and Ouidah, where French forts had been established in the 17th century. In 1857 the French reestablished themselves in the area, and eventually fighting ensued. In 1894 Dahomey became a French protectorate; it was incorporated into the federation of French West Africa in 1904. It achieved independence in 1960. The area called Dahomey was renamed Benin in 1975. Its chronically weak economy produced tension between laborers and the government into the 21st century.

## Recent Developments

There were concerns in 2011 that severe floods, which had devastated Benin's always fragile economy in late 2010, would cause further damage in 2011 as the Ouémé River began rising to record levels again in August. It was reported in early 2012, however, that the erratic rains had not adversely affected the country's major food crops.

**Internet resource:** <www.benintourism.org>.

# Bhutan

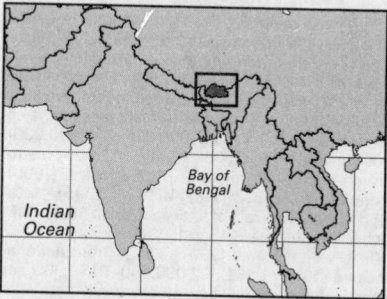

**Official name:** Druk-Yul (Kingdom of Bhutan). **Form of government:** constitutional monarchy with two legislative houses (National Council [25]; National Assembly [47]). **Head of state:** King Jigme Khesar Namgyal Wangchuk (from 2006). **Head of government:** Prime Minister Lyonchen Jigmi Thinley (from 2008). **Capital:** Thimphu. **Official language:** Dzongkha (a Tibetan dialect). **Official religion:** none (Mahayana Buddhism is the spiritual heritage of Bhutan according to the 2008 constitution). **Monetary unit:** 1 ngultrum (Nu) = 100 chetrum; valuation (2 Jul 2012) US$1 = Nu 55.60 (the Indian rupee is also accepted as legal tender).

## Demography

**Area:** 14,824 sq mi, 38,394 sq km. **Population** (2011): 701,000. **Density** (2011): persons per sq mi 47.3, persons per sq km 18.3. **Urban** (2010): 34.7%. **Sex distribution** (2008): male 52.50%; female 47.50%. **Age breakdown** (2008): under 15, 30.9%; 15–29, 31.9%; 30–44, 18.6%; 45–59, 10.6%; 60–74, 6.3%; 75–84, 1.5%; 85 and over, 0.2%. **Ethnic composition** (2005): Bhutia (Ngalops) 50%; Nepalese (Gurung) 35%; Sharchops 15%. **Religious affiliation** (2005): Buddhist 74%; Hindu 25%; Christian 1%. **Major towns** (2005): Thimphu 79,185; Phuntsholing 20,537; Gelaphu 9,199. **Location:** southern Asia, bordering China and India.

## Vital statistics

**Birth rate** per 1,000 population (2008): 20.6 (world avg. 20.3). **Death rate** per 1,000 population (2008):

7.5 (world avg. 8.5). **Total fertility rate** (avg. births per childbearing woman; 2008): 2.48. **Life expectancy** at birth (2008): male 64.8 years; female 66.4 years.

## National economy

**Budget** (2007–08). *Revenue:* Nu 20,481,000,000 (grants 40.7%; nontax revenue 33.0%, of which dividends and transfers 28.4%; tax revenue 23.7%, of which corporate taxes 9.2%; other 2.6%). *Expenditures:* Nu 22,223,000,000 (capital expenditures 52.3%; current expenditures 47.7%). **Public debt** (external, outstanding; July 2008): US$779,900,000. **Production** (metric tons except as noted). *Agriculture and fishing* (2007): corn (maize) 94,500, rice 69,000, potatoes 57,000, ginger 7,350, nutmeg, mace, and cardamom 5,800, mustard seed 4,500; livestock (number of live animals) 385,000 cattle, (2005) 45,538 yaks, 26,000 horses; fisheries production (2006) 300 (from aquaculture, negligible). *Mining and quarrying* (2007): limestone 560,000; dolomite 440,000; gypsum 165,000; ferrosilicon 21,000. *Manufacturing* (value of sales in Nu '000,000; 2007): ferroalloys 1,886; cement 1,664; chemical products 1,406; wood board products (2006) 382. *Energy production (consumption):* electricity (kW-hr; 2006) 3,357,000,000 (739,000,000); coal (metric tons; 2006) 98,000 (52,000); petroleum products (metric tons; 2006) none (51,000). **Population economically active** (2005): total 256,895; activity rate of total population 38.2% (participation rates: ages 15–64, 62.7%; female 36.6%; officially unemployed [2007] 3.7%). **Gross national income** (2008): US$1,302,000,000 (US$1,900 per capita). **Selected balance of payments data.** Receipts from (US$'000,000): tourism (2007) 30; remittances (2007) 1.5; foreign direct investment (2005–07 avg.) 31; official development assistance (2007) 89.

## Foreign trade

**Imports** (2007; c.i.f.): Nu 24,658,000,000 (machinery and apparatus 17.7%; food products and beverages 16.3%; mineral fuels 16.0%; precious stones and precious metals 10.8%; base and fabricated metals 9.2%; palm oil 6.9%). *Major import sources:* India 69.4%; Indonesia 6.0%; Singapore 5.1%; Russia 3.4%; South Korea 3.0%. **Exports** (2007; f.o.b.): Nu 27,859,000,000 (electricity to India 36.0%; unrecorded media [magnetic discs] 16.0%; copper wire 11.8%; ferroalloys 5.3%; information technology software 4.8%; vegetable fats and oils 4.5%). *Major export destinations:* India 81.6%; Hong Kong 9.9%; Thailand 3.9%; Singapore 2.5%; Bangladesh 1.7%.

## Transport and communications

**Transport.** *Railroads:* none. *Roads* (2006): total length 4,545 km (paved 55%). *Vehicles* (2003): passenger cars 10,574; trucks and buses 3,852. *Air transport* (2004): passenger-km 69,000,000; metric ton-km cargo (including the weight of passengers and mail) 6,000,000. **Communications,** in total units (units per 1,000 persons). Telephone landlines (2008): 27,000 (40); cellular telephone subscribers

(2008): 251,000 (368); personal computers (2005): 13,000 (16); total Internet users (2008): 40,000 (59); broadband Internet subscribers (2008): 2,100 (3.1).

## Education and health

**Educational attainment** (2007). Percentage of head of household population having: no formal schooling 73.2%; incomplete/complete primary education 16.5%; incomplete/complete secondary 5.5%; higher 4.8%. **Literacy** (2007): total population ages 6 and over literate 55.5%; males literate 65.7%; females literate 45.9%. **Health** (2006): physicians 150 (1 per 4,428 persons); hospital beds 1,133 (1 per 586 persons); infant mortality rate per 1,000 live births (2008) 51.9.

## Military

**Total active duty personnel** (2006): about 6,000 (army 100%). **Military expenditure as percentage of GDP** (2005): 1.0%; per capita expenditure US$11.

## Background

Bhutan's mountains and forests long made it inaccessible to the outside world, and its feudal rulers banned foreigners until well into the 20th century. In 1865 it came under British influence, and in 1910 it agreed to be guided by Britain in its foreign affairs. India took over Britain's role in 1949, and China's 1950 occupation of neighboring Tibet further strengthened Bhutan's ties with India. The apparent Chinese threat made Bhutan's rulers aware of the need to modernize, and it embarked on a program to build roads and hospitals and to create a system of secular education. The transition from an absolute monarchy to a parliamentary democracy was completed in March 2008, and a new constitution was promulgated in July.

## Recent Developments

In 2011 Bhutan completed the transformation of its political process, continuing with reforms initiated by the abdication of King Jigme Singye Wangchuck in 2006 and the promulgation of a new constitution in 2008. The country's first local government elections were conducted on 27 July. In his annual report to the parliament in July, Prime Minister Lyonchen Jigmi Thinley predicted that Bhutan's economy would continue to grow by 9–10% annually until 2015.

**Internet resource:** <www.nsb.gov.bt>.

# Bolivia

**Official name:** Estado Plurinacional de Bolivia (Plurinational State of Bolivia). **Form of government:** unitary multiparty republic with two legislative houses (Chamber of Departmental Representatives [36]; Chamber of Deputies [130]). **Head of state and government:** President Evo Morales (from 2006). **Capitals:** La Paz (executive and legislative); Sucre (judicial). **Official languages:** Spanish and 36 indigenous

---

*1 metric ton = about 1.1 short tons;    1 kilometer = 0.6 mi (statute);    1 metric ton-km cargo = about 0.68 short ton-mi cargo;    c.i.f.: cost, insurance, and freight;    f.o.b.: free on board*

languages. **Official religion:** none. **Monetary unit:** 1 boliviano (Bs) = 100 centavos; valuation (2 Jul 2012) US$1 = Bs 6.91.

## Demography

**Area:** 424,164 sq mi, 1,098,581 sq km. **Population** (2011): 10.088,000. **Density** (2011): persons per sq mi 23.8, persons per sq km 9.2. **Urban** (2010): 66.4%. **Sex distribution** (2008): male 49.50%; female 50.50%. **Age breakdown** (2008): under 15, 35.9%; 15–29, 29.2%; 30–44, 17.5%; 45–59, 10.8%; 60–74, 4.9%; 75–84, 1.4%; 85 and over, 0.3%. **Ethnic composition** (2006): Amerindian 55%, of which Quechua 29%, Aymara 24%; mestizo 30%; white 15%. **Religious affiliation** (2001): Roman Catholic 78%; Protestant/independent Christian 16%; other Christian 3%, of which Mormon 1.8%; nonreligious 2.5%; other 0.5%. **Major cities** (2001): Santa Cruz 1,116,059 (urban agglomeration [2007] 1,422,000); La Paz 789,585 (urban agglomeration [2007] 1,590,000); El Alto 647,350; Cochabamba 516,683; Oruro 201,230; Sucre 193,873. **Location:** central South America, bordering Brazil, Paraguay, Argentina, Chile, and Peru.

## Vital statistics

**Birth rate** per 1,000 population (2008): 26.5 (world avg. 20.3). **Death rate** per 1,000 population (2008): 7.2 (world avg. 8.5). **Total fertility rate** (avg. births per childbearing woman; 2008): 3.26. **Life expectancy** at birth (2008): male 63.9 years; female 69.4 years.

## National economy

**Budget** (2008). *Revenue:* Bs 58,394,500,000 (sales of hydrocarbons 45.1%; tax income [including royalties on minerals] 36.6%). *Expenditures:* Bs 54,478,200,000 (current expenditures 72.0%; capital expenditures 28.0%). **Production** (metric tons except as noted). *Agriculture and fishing* (2007): sugarcane 6,200,000, soybeans 1,900,000, potatoes 755,000, cassava 373,700, sunflower seeds 170,000, chestnuts (2006) 35,000; additionally, Bolivia was the third largest producer of coca in the world in 2008, producing an estimated 113 metric tons of cocaine; livestock (number of live animals)

8,990,000 sheep, 7,515,000 cattle, 2,490,000 pigs, (2004) 1,900,000 llamas and alpacas; fisheries production (2006) 7,130 (from aquaculture 6%). *Mining and quarrying* (metal content; 2007): zinc 214,050; tin 15,970; tungsten 1,400; silver 530; gold 8,820 kg. *Manufacturing* (value added in Bs '000,000 in constant prices of 1990; 2007): food products 1,792; beverages and tobacco products 766; petroleum products 574. *Energy production (consumption):* electricity (kW-hr; 2007) 5,550,000,000 (4,123,000,000); crude petroleum (barrels; 2007) 15,000,000 ([2006] 20,435,000); petroleum products (metric tons; 2006) 1,847,000 (2,118,000); natural gas (cu m; 2007) 14,301,000,000 ([2006] 1,446,000,000). **Population economically active** (2000): total 3,823,937; activity rate of total population 46.2% (participation rates: ages 15–64, 71.8%; female 44.6%; unemployed [2006] 8% in urban areas). **Gross national income** (2008): US$14,106,000,000 (US$1,460 per capita). **Public debt** (external, outstanding; September 2008): US$2,298,000,000. **Selected balance of payments data.** Receipts from (US$'000,000): tourism (2007) 259; remittances (2008) 927; foreign direct investment (FDI; 2005–07 avg.) 66; official development assistance (2007) 476. Disbursements for (US$'000,000): tourism (2007) 249; remittances (2008) 72.

## Foreign trade

**Imports** (2007; c.i.f.): US$3,522,000,000 (chemical products 17.2%; motor vehicles 13.4%; specialized machinery 8.1%; food products 7.9%; refined petroleum products 7.6%; iron and steel 7.3%). *Major import sources:* Brazil 20.2%; Argentina 16.9%; US 11.7%; Japan 9.4%; China 7.6%. **Exports** (2007; f.o.b.): US$4,812,700,000 (natural gas 41.3%; zinc 14.4%; crude petroleum 5.6%; soybean foodstuffs 4.7%; silver 4.5%; tin 3.7%). *Major export destinations:* Brazil 36.7%; Argentina 8.7%; US 8.6%; Japan 8.5%; Venezuela 5.0%.

## Transport and communications

**Transport.** *Railroads* (2007): route length 3,504 km; (2004) passenger-km 286,000,000; (2004) metric ton-km cargo 1,058,000,000. *Roads* (2004): total length 62,479 km (paved 7%). *Vehicles* (2004): passenger cars 294,000; trucks and buses 173,864. *Air transport* (2006; AeroSur, LAB, and Amaszonas airlines only): passenger-km 1,056,000,000; metric ton-km cargo 7,668,000. **Communications,** in total units (units per 1,000 persons). Telephone landlines (2007): 678,000 (71); cellular telephone subscribers (2008): 4,830,000 (503); personal computers (2006): 224,000 (24); total Internet users (2007): 1,000,000 (106); broadband Internet subscribers (2007): 34,000 (3.6).

## Education and health

**Educational attainment** (2007). Percentage of population ages 19 and over having: no formal schooling 10.7%; some to complete primary education 37.5%; some to complete secondary 27.2%; some to complete higher 24.4%; not specified 0.2%. **Literacy** (2007): total population ages 15 and over literate 90.7%; males literate 96.0%; females literate 86.0%. **Health:** physicians (2004) 3,211 (1 per 2,806 persons); hospital beds (2007) 14,928 (1 per 658 persons); infant mortality rate per 1,000 live births (2008) 45.9; undernourished population (2002–04) 2,000,000 (23% of total population based on the consumption of a minimum daily requirement of 1,780 calories).

## Military

**Total active duty personnel** (November 2008): 46,100 (army 75.5%, navy 10.4%, air force 14.1%). **Military expenditure as percentage of GDP** (2008): 1.4%; per capita expenditure US$27.

## Background

The Bolivian highlands were the location of the advanced Tiwanaku culture in the 7th–11th centuries and, with its passing, became the home of the Aymara, an Indian group conquered by the Incas in the 15th century. The Incas were overrun by the invading Spanish under Francisco Pizarro in the 1530s. By 1600 Spain had established the cities of Charcas (now Sucre), La Paz, Santa Cruz, and what would become Cochabamba and had begun to exploit the silver wealth of Potosí. Bolivia flourished in the 17th century, and for a time Potosí was the largest city in the Americas. By the end of the century, the mineral wealth had dried up. Talk of independence began as early as 1809, but not until 1825 were Spanish forces finally defeated. Bolivia shrank in size when it lost Atacama province to Chile in 1884 at the end of the War of the Pacific and again in 1939 when it lost most of Gran Chaco to Paraguay. One of South America's poorest countries, it was plagued by governmental instability for much of the 20th century. Social and economic tension continued in the early 21st century, fueled by resistance to government efforts to eradicate the growth of coca (from which the narcotic cocaine is derived), by unrest among Bolivia's Indians, and by disagreements over how to exploit the country's vast natural gas reserves.

## Recent Developments

Tension with the US over the illegal cocaine trade coming from Bolivia resurfaced in 2011. René Sanabria Oropeza, the former head of Bolivian antinarcotics efforts, was arrested in Panama in February and sent to Miami, where he pleaded guilty to drug-smuggling charges. In November, however, Bolivia restored diplomatic relations with the US, which had been suspended in 2008 (though the Drug Enforcement Agency [DEA] was not allowed back into the country). Meanwhile, UN drug-control officials maintained that illegal coca growing in Bolivia had increased by 22% since 2008, when Bolivia expelled the DEA.

Internet resource: <www.boliviaweb.com>.

# Bosnia and Herzegovina

**Official name:** Bosna i Hercegovina (Bosnia and Herzegovina). **Form of government:** emerging republic with two legislative houses (House of Peoples [15]; House of Representatives [42]). **Heads of state:** tripartite presidency with 8-month-long rotating chair-

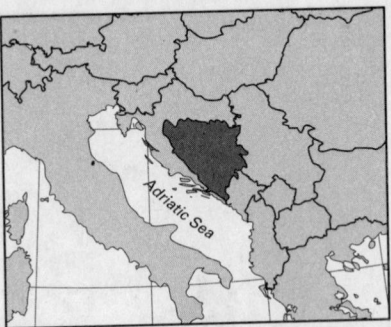

manship (final authority rests with International High Representative Valentin Inzko [from 2009]). **Head of government:** Prime Minister Vjekoslav Bevanda (from 2012). **Capital:** Sarajevo. **Official languages:** Bosnian; Croatian; Serbian. **Official religion:** none. **Monetary unit:** 1 convertible marka (KM; plural maraka) = 100 feninga; valuation (2 Jul 2012) US$1 = KM 1.55 (the euro [€] also circulates as semiofficial legal tender).

## Demography

**Area:** 19,772 sq mi, 51,209 sq km. **Population** (2011): 3,843,000. **Density** (2011): persons per sq mi 194.4, persons per sq km 75.0. **Urban** (2005): 45.7%. **Sex distribution** (2005): male 48.11%; female 51.89%. **Age breakdown** (2005): under 15, 16.6%; 15–29, 22.7%; 30–44, 22.6%; 45–59, 20.4%; 60–74, 13.3%; 75–84, 3.9%; 85 and over, 0.5%. **Ethnic composition** (1999): Bosniak 44.0%; Serb 31.0%; Croat 17.0%; other 8.0%. **Religious affiliation** (2002): Sunni Muslim 40%; Serbian Orthodox 31%; Roman Catholic 15%; Protestant 4%; nonreligious/other 10%. **Major cities** (2005): Sarajevo [2007] 376,000; Banja Luka 165,100; Zenica 84,300; Tuzla 84,100; Mostar 63,500. **Location:** southeastern Europe, bordered by Croatia, Serbia, Montenegro, and the Adriatic Sea.

## Vital statistics

**Birth rate** per 1,000 population (2007): 8.8 (world avg. 20.3); (2006) within marriage 88.4%. **Death rate** per 1,000 population (2007): 9.1 (world avg. 8.5). **Total fertility rate** (avg. births per childbearing woman; 2007): 1.17. **Life expectancy** at birth (2007): male 66.9 years; female 72.5 years.

## National economy

**Budget** (2006). *Revenue:* KM 9,075,000,000 (tax revenue 80.8%, of which VAT/sales tax 29.9%, social security contributions 26.7%, excise tax 11.4%; nontax revenue 13.7%; grants 5.5%). *Expenditures:* KM 8,655,000,000 (current expenditures 86.5%; development expenditures 13.5%). **Gross national income** (2008): US$17,001,000,000 (US$4,510 per capita). **Production** (metric tons except as noted). *Agriculture and fishing* (2007): corn (maize) 635,344, potatoes 387,239, wheat 257,112; livestock (number of live animals) 1,000,000 sheep, 712,000 pigs, 515,000 cattle, in addition, 285,000 beehives; fisheries production 9,625 (from aquaculture 79%). *Mining and quarrying* (2006): iron ore (metal content) 1,700,000; bauxite 816,768; lime 180,000. *Manufacturing* (value of production in KM '000,000; 2006): base and fabricated metals 1,578; food products, beverages, and tobacco products 1,255; wood products 398. *Energy production (consumption):* electricity (kW-hr; 2006) 13,346,000,000 (11,238,000,000); coal (metric tons; 2006) 3,616,000 (4,242,000); lignite (metric tons; 2006) 9,960,000 (9,871,000); petroleum products (metric tons; 2006) none (1,099,000); natural gas (cu m; 2006) none (396,000,000). **Public debt** (external, outstanding; 2007): US$2,981,000,000. **Population economically active** (2007): total 1,196,000; activity rate of total population 36.1% (participation rates: ages 15–64, 52.2%; female 36.5%; unemployed 29.0%). **Selected balance of payments data.** Receipts from (US$'000,000): tourism (2007) 729; remittances (2008) 2,735; foreign direct investment (2005–07 avg.) 1,108; official development assistance (2007) 443. Disbursements for (US$'000,000): tourism (2007) 186; remittances (2008) 70.

## Foreign trade

**Imports** (2007): US$9,720,000,000 (machinery and apparatus 16.8%; food products 11.8%; chemical products 10.5%; refined petroleum products 9.2%; motor vehicles 7.1%; iron and steel 5.2%). *Major import sources:* Croatia 17.6%; Germany 12.5%; Serbia 10.2%; Italy 9.0%; Slovenia 6.4%. **Exports** (2007): US$4,152,000,000 (aluminum 9.7%; fabricated metal products 8.2%; iron and steel 7.1%; metal ore/metal scrap 6.8%; footwear 5.8%; sawn wood 5.7%). *Major export destinations:* Croatia 18.4%; Serbia 13.7%; Italy 13.1%; Germany 12.8%; Slovenia 10.9%.

## Transport and communications

**Transport.** *Railroads* (2005): length 1,028 km; passenger-km 51,396,000; metric ton-km cargo 1,159,000,000. *Roads* (2005): total length 22,419 km (paved [2001] 64%). *Air transport* (2003): passenger-km 47,000,000; metric ton-km 6,000,000. **Communications,** in total units (units per 1,000 persons). Telephone landlines (2008): 1,031,000 (268); cellular telephone subscribers (2008): 3,179,000 (827); personal computers (2007): 246,000 (64); total Internet users (2008): 1,308,000 (340); broadband Internet subscribers (2008): 188,000 (49).

## Education and health

**Educational attainment** (2004). Percentage of population ages 18 and over having: no formal schooling 8.7%; incomplete primary education 11.4%; complete primary 21.4%; incomplete/complete secondary 49.8%; technical/university 8.7%. **Literacy** (2002): total population ages 15 and over literate 94.6%; males literate 98.4%; females literate 91.1%. **Health:** physicians (2005) 5,540 (1 per 694 persons); hospital beds (2004) 11,414 (1 per 337 persons); infant mortality rate per 1,000 live births (2007) 6.8; undernourished population (2002–04) 350,000 (9% of total population based on the consumption of a minimum daily requirement of 2,000 calories).

## Military

**Total active duty personnel** (November 2008): 8,543; EU-sponsored (EUFOR) peacekeeping troops (March 2009): 2,153. **Military expenditure as percentage of GDP** (2008): 1.5%; per capita expenditure US$58.

## Background

Habitation long predates the era of Roman rule, when much of the country was included in the province of Dalmatia. Slav settlement began in the 6th century AD. For the next several centuries, parts of the region fell under the rule of Serbs, Croats, Hungarians, Venetians, and Byzantines. The Ottoman Turks invaded Bosnia in the 14th century, and after many battles it became a Turkish province in 1463. Herzegovina, then known as Hum, was taken in 1482. In the 16th–17th centuries the area was an important Turkish outpost, constantly at war with the Habsburgs and Venice. During this period much of the native population converted to Islam. At the Congress of Berlin after the Russo-Turkish War of 1877–78, Bosnia and Herzegovina was assigned to Austria-Hungary, and it was fully annexed in 1908. Growing Serb nationalism resulted in the 1914 assassination of the Austrian archduke Francis Ferdinand at Sarajevo by a Bosnian Serb, an event that precipitated World War I. After the war the area was annexed to Serbia. Following World War II the twin territory became a republic of communist Yugoslavia. With the collapse of communist regimes in Eastern Europe, Bosnia and Herzegovina declared its independence in 1992; its Serb population objected, and conflict ensued among Serbs, Croats, and Muslims. The 1995 peace accord established a loosely federated government roughly divided between a Muslim-Croat Federation and a Serb Republic (Republika Srpska [RS]). From 1996 to 2002 an EU peacekeeping force was installed there. By the early 21st century, much of the infrastructure damaged during the conflict had been reconstructed, but ethnic tensions remained.

## Recent Developments

In its 2011 progress report on Bosnia and Herzegovina, the European Commission noted "little progress" in reforms necessary for entry to the EU. The acting government in October agreed to implement a list of EU-stipulated steps toward reform of public administration, the judiciary, infrastructure, demining, and assistance to refugees of the 1992–95 war.

**Internet resource:** <www.fzs.ba/Eng/index.htm>.

# Botswana

**Official name:** Republic of Botswana. **Form of government:** multiparty republic with one legislative house (National Assembly [63]). **Head of state and government:** President Ian Khama (from 2008). **Capital:** Gaborone. **Official language:** English (Tswana is the national language). **Official religion:** none. **Monetary unit:** 1 pula (P) = 100 thebe; valuation (2 Jul 2012) US$1 = P 7.65.

## Demography

**Area:** 224,607 sq mi, 581,730 sq km. **Population** (2011): 2,033,000. **Density** (2011): persons per sq

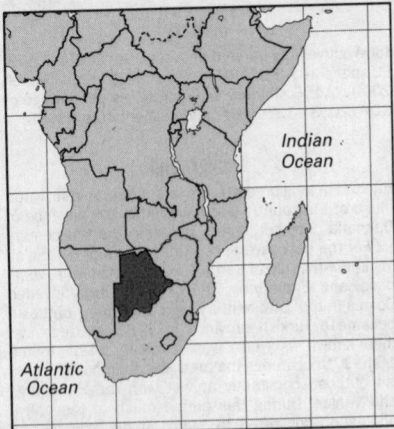

Indian Ocean

Atlantic Ocean

mi 9.1, persons per sq km 3.5. **Urban** (2009): 60.4%. **Sex distribution** (2008): male 49.99%; female 50.01%. **Age breakdown** (2008): under 15, 35.3%; 15–29, 32.9%; 30–44, 17.4%; 45–59, 9.0%; 60–74, 3.9%; 75–84, 1.2%; 85 and over, 0.3%. **Ethnic composition** (2000): Tswana 66.8%; Kalanga 14.8%; Ndebele 1.7%; Herero 1.4%; San (Bushman) 1.3%; Afrikaner 1.3%; other 12.7%. **Religious affiliation** (2005): independent Christian 41.7%; traditional beliefs 35.0%; Protestant 12.8%; Muslim 0.3%; Hindu 0.2%; other 10.0%. **Major cities** (2006): Gaborone 214,400; Francistown 91,800; Molepolole 65,600; Selebi-Pikwe 54,700; Maun 51,600. **Location:** southern Africa, bordered by Namibia, Zimbabwe, and South Africa.

## Vital statistics

**Birth rate** per 1,000 population (2008): 23.2 (world avg. 20.3). **Death rate** per 1,000 population (2008): 8.5 (world avg. 8.5). **Total fertility rate** (avg. births per childbearing woman; 2008): 2.66. **Life expectancy** at birth (2008): male 61.5 years; female 62.1 years.

## National economy

**Budget** (2006–07). *Revenue:* P 27,397,700,000 (tax revenue 92.1%, of which mineral royalties 47.9%, customs duties and excise tax 24.1%, non-mineral income tax 11.2%; nontax revenue 6.3%; grants 1.6%). *Expenditures:* P 19,737,400,000 (general government services including defense 29.2%; education 24.5%; economic services 14.5%; health 11.3%; transfers 10.2%). **Population economically active** (2006): total 651,500; activity rate of total population 35.8% (participation rates: ages 15–59 [2001] 58.1%; female 49.1%; unemployed [2007] 7.5%). **Production** (metric tons except as noted). *Agriculture and fishing* (2007): roots .and tubers 93,000, sorghum 33,000, corn (maize) 12,000, sunflower seeds 7,000; livestock (number of live animals) 3,100,000 cattle, 1,960,000 goats, 300,000 sheep; fisheries production 123 (from aquaculture, none). *Mining and quarrying* (2007): salt 165,710; nickel ore (metal content) 26,532; copper ore (metal con-

tent) 22,589; cobalt (metal content) 356; semi-precious gemstones (mostly agate) 48,000 kg; gold 2,656 kg; diamonds 33,639,000 carats (Botswana is the world's leading producer of diamonds by value). *Manufacturing* (value added in US$'000,-000; 2005): beverages 55; textiles 14; tanned and processed leather 1. *Energy production (consumption):* electricity (kW-hr; 2005) 912,000,000 (2,602,000,000); coal (metric tons; 2007) 828,000 ([2006] 938,000). **Selected balance of payments data.** Receipts from (US$'000,000): tourism (2007) 546; remittances (2008) 148; foreign direct investment (FDI; 2005–07 avg.) 422; official development assistance (2007) 104. Disbursements for (US$'000,000): tourism (2007) 281; remittances (2008) 120; FDI (2005–07 avg.) 53. **Gross national income** (2008): US$12,328,000,000 (US$6,470 per capita). **Public debt** (external, outstanding; 2007): US$380,000,000.

## Foreign trade

**Imports** (2007; c.i.f.): US$3,987,000,000 (machinery and apparatus 18.9%; refined petroleum products 13.7%; motor vehicles 10.6%; food products 10.2%; chemical products 9.2%). *Major import sources:* South Africa 83.5%; China 1.8%; Belgium 1.6%; UK 1.4%; Zimbabwe 1.3%. **Exports** (2007; f.o.b.): US$5,073,000,000 (diamonds 62.5%; nickel matte 15.5%; wearing apparel and accessories 6.7%; copper ore/copper matte 5.8%; textiles 5.0%). *Major export destinations;* UK 65.0%; South Africa 10.2%; Norway 8.1%; Zimbabwe 7.3%; China 1.9%.

## Transport and communications

**Transport.** *Railroads* (2006): route length 888 km; (2003) passenger-km 572,000,000; (2004) metric ton-km cargo 636,700,000. *Roads* (2007; roads maintained by central government only): total length 8,916 km (paved 72%). *Vehicles* (2007): passenger cars 104,926; trucks and buses 105,754. *Air transport* (2007; Air Botswana only): passenger-km 117,700,000. **Communications,** in total units (units per 1,000 persons). Telephone landlines (2008): 142,000 (73); cellular telephone subscribers (2008): 1,486,000 (761); personal computers (2006): 84,000 (45); total Internet users (2008): 80,000 (41); broadband Internet subscribers (2007): 3,500 (1.8).

## Education and health

**Literacy** (2005): total population ages 15 and over literate 81.4%; males literate 78.6%; females literate 84.1%. **Health** (2007): physicians 478 (1 per 3,798 persons); hospital beds 3,704 (1 per 490 persons); infant mortality rate per 1,000 live births (2008) 13.4; undernourished population (2002–04) 600,000 (32% of total population based on the consumption of a minimum daily requirement of 1,860 calories).

## Military

**Total active duty personnel** (November 2008): 9,000 (army 94.4%, air force 5.6%). **Military expenditure as percentage of GDP** (2007): 2.7%; per capita expenditure US$175.

*1 metric ton = about 1.1 short tons;   1 kilometer = 0.6 mi (statute);   1 metric ton-km cargo = about 0.68 short ton-mi cargo;   c.i.f.: cost, insurance, and freight;   f.o.b.: free on board*

## Background

The region's earliest inhabitants were the Khoekhoe and San (Bushmen). Sites were settled as early as AD 190 during the southerly migration of Bantu-speaking farmers. Tswana dynasties, which developed in the western Transvaal in the 13th–14th centuries, moved into Botswana in the 18th century and established several powerful states. European missionaries arrived in the early 19th century, but it was the discovery of gold in 1867 that excited European interest. In 1885 the area became the British Bechuanaland Protectorate. The next year the region south of the Molopo River became a crown colony, and it was annexed by the Cape Colony 10 years later. Bechuanaland itself continued as a British protectorate until the 1960s. In 1966 the Republic of Bechuanaland (later Botswana) was proclaimed an independent member of the British Commonwealth. Independent Botswana tried to maintain a delicate balance between its economic dependence on South Africa and its relations with the surrounding black countries; the independence of Namibia in 1990 and South Africa's rejection of apartheid eased tensions.

## Recent Developments

Botswana's economy was boosted in 2011 by the recovery of the world diamond market in 2010. In September 2011 the government signed a 10-year contract by which De Beers would transfer its worldwide rough diamond collection and sales operations from London to Gaborone by the end of 2013. De Beers also agreed that the government could sell 10% of local diamond production on the world free market.

Internet resource: <www.cso.gov.bw>.

# Brazil

Caribbean Sea

Atlantic Ocean

Pacific Ocean

**Official name:** República Federativa do Brasil (Federative Republic of Brazil). **Form of government:** multiparty federal republic with two legislative houses (Federal Senate [81]; Chamber of Deputies [513]). **Head of state and government:** President Dilma Rousseff (from 2011). **Capital:** Brasília. **Official language:** Portuguese. **Official religion:** none. **Monetary unit:** 1 real (R$; plural reais) = 100 centavos; valuation (2 Jul 2012) US$1 = 1.99 reais.

## Demography

**Area:** 3,287,612 sq mi, 8,514,877 sq km. **Population (2011):** 192,813,000. **Density (2011):** persons per sq mi 58.6, persons per sq km 22.6. **Urban (2010):** 84.3%. **Sex distribution (2005):** male 49.32%; female 50.68%. **Age breakdown (2005):** under 15, 27.6%; 15–29, 27.7%; 30–44, 21.7%; 45–59, 14.1%; 60–74, 6.6%; 75–84, 1.8%; 85 and over, 0.5%. **Racial composition (2000):** white 53.7%; mulatto and mestizo 39.1%; black and black/Amerindian 6.2%; Asian 0.5%; Amerindian 0.4%. **Religious affiliation (2005):** Roman Catholic 65.1%; Protestant 12.7%, of which Assemblies of God 9.2%; independent Christian 10.7%, of which Universal Church of the Kingdom of God 2.2%; Spiritist (Kardecist) 1.3%; Jehovah's Witness 0.7%; African and syncretic religions 0.4%; Muslim 0.4%; nonreligious/other 8.7%. **Major cities (metropolitan areas) (2007):** São Paulo 10,238,500 (19,226,426); Rio de Janeiro 6,093,500 (11,563,302); Belo Horizonte 2,412,900 (5,450,084); Porto Alegre 1,379,100 (3,896,515); Recife 1,533,600 (3,654,534); Salvador 2,891,400 (3,598,454); Brasília 2,348,600 (3,507,662); Fortaleza 2,431,400 (3,436,515); Curitiba 1,797,400 (3,124,596); Campinas 1,022,000 (2,635,261); Belém 1,399,800 (2,043,543); Goiânia 1,236,400 (1,973,892); Manaus 1,602,100 (1,612,475); Vitória 314,000 (1,609,532). **Location:** eastern South America, bordered by Venezuela, Guyana, Suriname, French Guiana, Uruguay, Argentina, Paraguay, Bolivia, Peru, and Colombia. **Families.** Average family size (2005) 3.2; (1996) 1–2 persons 25.2%, 3 persons 20.3%, 4 persons 22.2%, 5–6 persons 23.3%, 7 or more persons 9.0%. **Emigration (2000):** Brazilian emigrants living abroad 1,887,895; in the US 42.3%, in Paraguay 23.4%, in Japan 12.0%. **Immigration (2000):** foreign-born immigrants living in Brazil 683,830; from Europe 56.3%, of which Portugal 31.2%; South/Central America 21.0%; Asia 17.8%, of which Japan 10.4%.

## Vital statistics

**Birth rate** per 1,000 population (2008): 16.4 (world avg. 20.3). **Death rate** per 1,000 population (2008): 6.4 (world avg. 8.5). **Total fertility rate** (avg. births per childbearing woman; 2008): 1.90. **Life expectancy** at birth (2008): male 68.7 years; female 76.0 years.

## Social indicators

**Educational attainment (2005).** Percentage of population ages 25 and over having: no formal schooling or less than one year of primary education 15.0%; 1 to 3 years of primary education 13.7%; complete primary/incomplete secondary 40.2%; complete secondary 18.8%; 1 to 3 years of higher education 3.8%; 4 years or more of higher education 8.0%; unknown 0.5%. **Quality of working life.** Proportion of employed population receiving minimum wage (2002): 53.5%. Number and percentage of children (ages 5–17) working: 5,400,000 (12.6% of age group). **Access to services.** Proportion of urban households having access to (2006): safe public (piped) water supply

93.2%; public (piped) sewage system 66.8%; garbage collection 90.3%. (Rural households have far less access to services.) **Social participation.** Trade union membership in total workforce (2001): 19,500,000. **Social deviance.** *Annual murder rate* per 100,000 population (2005): Brazil 29.6; Rio de Janeiro only (2002) 56; São Paulo only (2002) 54. **Leisure.** Favorite leisure activities include: playing soccer, dancing, practicing *capoeira*, rehearsing all year in neighborhood samba groups for celebrations of Carnival, and competing in water sports, volleyball, and basketball. **Material well-being.** Urban households possessing (2006): electricity 99.7%, color television receiver 94.8%, refrigerator 93.3%, washing machine 42.2%, computer 25.5%, Internet access 19.6%, freezer 16.1%.

## National economy

**Gross national income** (2008): US$1,411,224,000,000 (US$7,350 per capita). **Budget** (2006). *Revenue:* R$543,253,000,000 (tax revenue 72.3%, of which income tax 25.3%, social security contributions 17.0%, VAT on industrial products 5.2%; social welfare contributions 22.7%; other 5.0%). *Expenditures:* R$493,450,000,000 (social security and welfare 30.5%; wages and salaries 19.3%; transfers to state and local governments 17.1%; other 33.1%). **Public debt** (external, outstanding; 2007): US$79,957,000,000. **Production** ('000 metric tons except as noted). *Agriculture and fishing* (2008): sugarcane 648,921, soybeans 59,917, corn (maize) 59,018, cassava 25,878, oranges 18,390, rice 12,100, bananas 7,117, wheat 5,886, seed cotton 3,971, tomatoes 3,934, potatoes 3,676, dry beans 3,461, coffee 2,791, coconuts 2,759, pineapples 2,492, sorghum 1,966, papayas 1,900, cashew apples 1,660, grapes 1,403, dry onions 1,300, mangoes and guavas 1,272, apples 1,121, lemons and limes 1,040, tobacco 850, oil palm fruit 660, maté 436, peanuts (groundnuts) 297, cashews 240, cacao beans 208, sunflower seeds 146, natural rubber 114, garlic 92, pepper 69, Brazil nuts 30; livestock (number of live animals) 175,436,992 cattle, 40,000,000 pigs, 16,500,000 sheep, 5,650,000 horses; fisheries production (2007) 1,072,825 (from aquaculture 27%). *Mining and quarrying* (metric tons; 2007): iron ore (metal content) 235,504,000 (world rank: 1); bauxite 24,800,000 (world rank: 3); kaolin (marketable product) 2,500,000; manganese (metal content) 933,000 (world rank: 5); copper (metal content) 205,728; graphite 76,200 (world rank: 3); nickel (metal content) 58,317; tin (metal content) 10,000 (world rank: 5); tantalum 180 (world rank: 2); gold 49,613 kg; diamonds 182,000 carats. **Population economically active:** September 2006): total 97,528,000; activity rate of total population 52.1% (participation rates: ages 15–64, 73.7%; female 43.7%; unemployed [December 2007–November 2008] 7.9%). **Selected balance of payments data.** Receipts from (US$'000,000): tourism (2007) 4,953; remittances (2008) 5,089; foreign direct investment (FDI; 2005–07 avg.) 22,824; official development assistance (2007) 297. Disbursements for (US$'000,000): tourism (2007) 8,211; remittances (2008) 1,191; FDI (2005–07 avg.) 12,595. *Energy production (consumption):* electricity (kW-hr; 2006) 412,159,000,000 (460,500,000,000); coal (metric tons; 2006) 6,380,000 (21,600,000); crude petroleum (barrels; 2007) 645,800,000 ([2006] 621,888,000); petroleum products (metric tons; 2006) 80,179,000 (74,098,000); natural gas (cu m; 2007) 18,151,000,000 ([2006] 18,609,000,000); ethanol (liters; 2007) 19,000,000,000 (16,700,000,000).

## Foreign trade

**Imports** (2007): US$120,618,000,000 (chemical products 19.0%, of which organic chemicals 5.0%, fertilizers 3.7%, medicines and pharmaceuticals 3.3%; mineral fuels 18.5%, of which crude petroleum 9.9%, refined petroleum products 5.0%; motor vehicles and parts 6.8%; general industrial machinery 5.4%; food products 3.9%; telecommunications equipment 3.7%; power-generating machinery 3.7%). *Major import sources:* US 15.7%; China 10.5%; Argentina 8.6%; Germany 7.2%; Nigeria 4.4%; Japan 3.8%; France 2.9%; Chile 2.9%; South Korea 2.8%; Italy 2.8%. **Exports** (2007): US$160,649,000,000 (food products 19.4%, of which meat 6.9%, coffee 2.1%, animal foodstuffs 2.1%, raw sugar 1.9%; motor vehicles and parts 7.9%; chemical products 6.6%, of which organic chemicals 2.6%; iron ore and concentrates 6.6%; iron and steel 6.3%; crude petroleum 5.5%; soybeans 4.2%; aircraft/spacecraft 3.2%; nonferrous metals 2.9%; power-generating machinery 2.7%; refined petroleum products 2.7%; specialized industrial machinery 2.6%; general industrial machinery 2.4%; wood pulp and waste paper 1.9%). *Major export destinations:* US 15.8%; Argentina 9.0%; China 6.7%; Netherlands 5.5%; Germany 4.5%; Venezuela 2.9%; Italy 2.8%; Chile 2.7%; Mexico 2.7%; Japan 2.7%.

## Transport and communications

**Transport.** *Railroads* (2006): route length 29,605 km; (2005) passenger-km 5,852,000,000; (2005) metric ton-km cargo 154,870,000,000. *Roads* (2004): total length 1,751,868 km (paved [2000] 6%). *Vehicles* (2004): passenger cars 24,936,541; trucks and buses 6,294,502. *Air transport* (2007): passenger-km 52,044,000,000; metric ton-km cargo 1,477,824,000. **Communications,** in total units (units per 1,000 persons). Telephone landlines (2008): 41,141,000 (217); cellular telephone subscribers (2008): 150,641,000 (794); personal computers (2006): 29,340,000 (161); total Internet users (2007): 67,510,000 (360); broadband Internet subscribers (2008): 10,098,000 (53).

## Education and health

**Literacy** (2005): total population ages 15 and over literate 89.0%; males literate 88.7%; females literate 89.2%. **Health** (2005): physicians 505,841 (1 per 356 persons); hospital beds 432,190 (1 per 416 persons); infant mortality rate per 1,000 live births (2008) 23.5; undernourished population (2002–04) 13,100,000 (7% of total population based on the consumption of a minimum daily requirement of 1,900 calories).

---

*1 metric ton = about 1.1 short tons;   1 kilometer = 0.6 mi (statute);   1 metric ton-km cargo = about 0.68 short ton-mi cargo;   c.i.f.: cost, insurance, and freight;   f.o.b.: free on board*

## Military

**Total active duty personnel** (November 2008): 326,435 (army 58.2%, navy 20.5%, air force 21.3%). **Military expenditure as percentage of GDP** (2007): 1.6%; per capita expenditure US$111.

## Background

Little is known about Brazil's early indigenous inhabitants. Though the area was theoretically allotted to Portugal by the 1494 Treaty of Tordesillas, it was not formally claimed by discovery until Pedro Álvares Cabral accidentally touched land in 1500. It was first settled by the Portuguese in the early 1530s on the southeastern coast and at São Vicente (near modern São Paulo); the French and Dutch created small settlements over the next century. A viceroyalty was established in 1640, and Rio de Janeiro became the capital in 1763. In 1808 Brazil became the refuge and the seat of the government of John VI of Portugal when Napoleon invaded Portugal; ultimately the Kingdom of Portugal, Brazil, and the Algarves was proclaimed, and John ruled from Brazil in 1815–21. On John's return to Portugal, his son Pedro I proclaimed Brazilian independence. In 1889 his successor, Pedro II, was deposed, and a constitution mandating a federal republic was adopted. The 20th century saw increased immigration and growth in manufacturing along with frequent military coups and suspensions of civil liberties. Construction of a new capital at Brasília, intended to spur development of the country's interior, worsened the inflation rate. After 1979 the military government began a gradual return to democratic practices, and in 1989 the first popular presidential election in 29 years was held. A severe economic crisis began in the late 1990s, but the country's economy soared in the 21st century, led by the agricultural and energy sectors.

## Recent Developments

On 1 Jan 2011, Dilma Rousseff, a former political prisoner who had been persecuted by the former military regime, was sworn in as the first woman president of Brazil. She outlined a domestic agenda that focused on poverty eradication, political and tax reform, and job creation. The Brazilian economy grew only 2.7% in 2011 after having soared 7.5% in 2010. Measured by the expanded consumer price index, inflation over the year reached 6.56% to exceed the federal government's inflation target of 6.5%. Because the high price of commodities such as sugar and ethanol contributed to inflationary pressures, in April ethanol was subjected to price controls by the National Petroleum Agency. Rousseff subsequently ordered the required levels of ethanol in Brazilian gasoline to be reduced from 25% to 20%. The modest economic growth was still enough to surpass that of the United Kingdom, giving Brazil the world's sixth largest economy.

**Internet resource:** <www.ibge.gov.br/english>.

# Brunei

**Official name:** Negara Brunei Darussalam (State of Brunei Darussalam, Abode of Peace). **Form of government:** monarchy (sultanate) with one advisory house (Legislative Council [29]). **Head of state and**

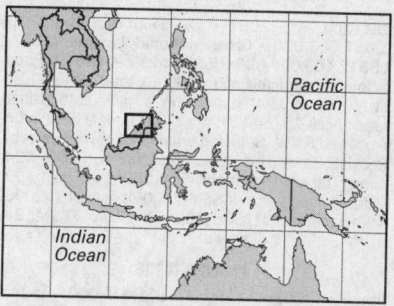

**government:** Sultan and Prime Minister Haji Hassanal Bolkiah Mu'izzadin Waddaulah (from 1967). **Capital:** Bandar Seri Begawan. **Official language:** Malay. **Official religion:** Islam. **Monetary unit:** 1 Brunei dollar (B$) = 100 sen; valuation (2 Jul 2012) US$1 = B$1.27.

## Demography

**Area:** 2,226 sq mi, 5,765 sq km. **Population** (2011): 422,000. **Density** (2011): persons per sq mi 189.6, persons per sq km 73.2. **Urban** (2009): 75.2%. **Sex distribution** (2008): male 53.02%; female 46.98%. **Age breakdown** (2008): under 15, 27.2%; 15–29, 27.7%; 30–44, 25.1%; 45–59, 14.8%; 60–74, 4.1%; 75–84, 0.9%; 85 and over, 0.2%. **Ethnic composition** (2003): Malay 66.6%; Chinese 10.9%; other indigenous 3.6%; other 18.9%. **Religious affiliation** (2006): Muslim 80.4%; Buddhist 7.9%; Christian 3.2%; traditional beliefs/other 8.5%. **Major cities** (2006): Bandar Seri Begawan 67,100; Kuala Belait 32,000; Seria 30,700; Tutong 19,600. **Location:** southeastern Asia, bordering the South China Sea and Malaysia.

## Vital statistics

**Birth rate** per 1,000 population (2007): 16.2 (world avg. 20.3). **Death rate** per 1,000 population (2007): 3.0 (world avg. 8.5). **Total fertility rate** (avg. births per childbearing woman; 2007): 1.70. **Life expectancy** at birth (2007): male 75.2 years; female 77.8 years.

## National economy

**Budget** (2007–08). *Revenue:* B$9,646,000,000 (tax revenue 65.8%, of which taxes on petroleum and natural gas companies 62.5%, import duties 1.6%; nontax revenue 34.2%, of which dividends paid by petroleum companies 18.9%, petroleum and natural gas royalties 10.3%). *Expenditures:* B$5,601,000,000 (current expenditures 80.0%; capital expenditures 20.0%). **Production** (metric tons except as noted). *Agriculture and fishing* (2007): cassava 1,800, rice 1,200, pineapples 990; livestock (number of live animals) 4,580 buffalo, 15,500,000 chickens; fisheries production 2,863 (from aquaculture 22%). *Mining and quarrying:* other than petroleum and natural gas, none except sand and gravel for construction. *Manufacturing* (value added in B$'000,000; 2006–07): liquefied natural gas 1,692; textiles and wearing apparel 122. *Energy production (consumption):* electricity (kW-hr; 2006) 2,948,000,000 (2,656,-000,000); crude petroleum (barrels; 2007) 70,800,000 ([2006] 697,000); petroleum products (metric tons; 2006) 1,207,000 (1,200,000); natural gas (cu m; 2007) 13,219,000,000 ([2006] 1,457,000,000). **Gross national income** (2007): US$12,400,000,000 (US$31,523 per capita). **Population economically active** (2008): total 188,800; activity rate of total population 47.4% (participation rates: ages 15–64 [2001] 65.9%; female 39.4%; unemployed 3.7%). **Selected balance of payments data.** Receipts from (US$'000,000): tourism (2006) 224; foreign direct investment (FDI; 2005–07 avg.) 302. Disbursements for (US$'000,000): tourism (2006) 408; remittances (2008) 405; FDI (2005–07 avg.) 34.

## Foreign trade

**Imports** (2007; c.i.f.): US$2,101,000,000 (machinery, and transportation equipment 41.4%; manufactured goods 21.8%; food products 12.8%). *Major import sources* (2006): Malaysia 21.6%; Singapore 17.4%; Japan 12.8%; US 9.0%; China 7.9%. **Exports** (2007; f.o.b.): US$7,668,000,000 (crude petroleum 66.0%; liquefied natural gas 30.1%; garments 1.5%). *Major export destinations* (2007; for crude petroleum, liquefied natural gas, and garments only): Japan 34.2%; Indonesia 24.7%; Australia 14.0%; South Korea 12.4%; US 5.0%.

## Transport and communications

**Transport.** *Railroads* (2004): length 19 km. *Roads* (2007): total length 3,774 km (paved 76%). *Vehicles* (2003): passenger cars 212,000; trucks and buses (2002) 20,000. *Air transport* (2007): passenger-km 3,720,000,000; metric ton-km cargo 115,536,000. **Communications,** in total units (units per 1,000 persons). Telephone landlines (2006): 80,000 (210); cellular telephone subscribers (2007): 397,000 (997); personal computers (2004): 31,000 (87); total Internet users (2007): 188,000 (488); broadband Internet subscribers (2007): 12,000 (29).

## Education and health

**Educational attainment** (1991). Percentage of population ages 25 and over having: no formal schooling/unknown 17.5%; primary education 43.3%; secondary 26.3%; postsecondary and higher 12.9%. **Literacy** (2004): percentage of total population ages 15 and over literate 92.7%; males literate 95.2%; females literate 90.2%. **Health** (2007): physicians 393 (1 per 1,013 persons); hospital beds 1,068 (1 per 373 persons); infant mortality rate per 1,000 live births 7.6; undernourished population (2002–04) 15,000 (4% of total population based on the consumption of a minimum daily requirement of 1,910 calories).

## Military

**Total active duty personnel** (November 2008): 7,000 (army 70.0%, navy 14.3%, air force 15.7%); British troops 550; Singaporean troops 500. **Military expenditure as percentage of GDP** (2007): 2.8%; per capita expenditure US$880.

## Background

Brunei traded with China in the 6th century AD. Through allegiance to the Javanese Majapahit king-

dom (13th–15th centuries), it came under Hindu influence. In the early 15th century, with the decline of the Majapahit kingdom, many people converted to Islam, and Brunei became an independent sultanate. When Ferdinand Magellan's ships visited in 1521, the sultan of Brunei controlled almost all of Borneo and its neighboring islands. Beginning in the late 16th century, Brunei lost power because of the Portuguese, Dutch, and, later, British activities in the region. By the 19th century, the sultanate of Brunei included Sarawak (present-day Brunei) and part of North Borneo (now part of Sabah). In 1841 a revolt took place against the sultan, and a British soldier, James Brooke, helped put it down; he was later proclaimed governor. In 1847 the sultanate entered into a treaty with Great Britain and by 1906 had yielded all administration to a British resident. Brunei rejected membership in the Federation of Malaysia in 1963, negotiated a new treaty with Britain in 1979, and achieved independence in 1984, with membership in the Commonwealth. Brunei has pursued ways to diversify the economy, notably by encouraging tourism.

## Recent Developments

In 2011, Brunei and Malaysia continued to work on details of a joint resource-exploitation project in the South China Sea. Brunei Shell Petroleum (BSP—50% owned by Royal Dutch Shell PLC) announced a significant new oil discovery in the coastal waters about 100 km (60 mi) offshore. The water depth there was approximately 1,000 m (3,300 ft), which made those hydrocarbon reserves the deepest identified to date by BSP in the Brunei region.

**Internet resource:** <www.depd.gov.bn/home.html>.

# Bulgaria

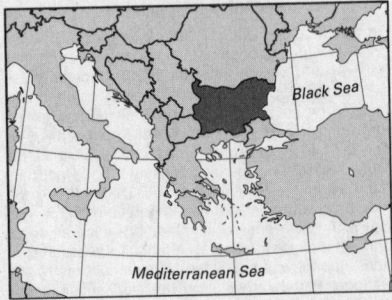

**Official name:** Republika Bulgaria (Republic of Bulgaria). **Form of government:** unitary multiparty republic with one legislative house (National Assembly [240]). **Head of state:** President Rosen Plevneliev (from 2012). **Head of government:** Prime Minister Boiko Borisov (from 2009). **Capital:** Sofia. **Official language:** Bulgarian. **Official religion:** none (the constitution refers to Eastern Orthodoxy as the "traditional" religion). **Monetary unit:** 1 lev (Lv; plural leva) = 100 stotinki; valuation (2 Jul 2012) US$1 = 1.55 leva.

*1 metric ton = about 1.1 short tons;    1 kilometer = 0.6 mi (statute);    1 metric ton-km cargo = about 0.68 short ton-mi cargo;    c.i.f.: cost, insurance, and freight;    f.o.b.: free on board*

## Demography

**Area:** 42,858 sq mi, 111,002 sq km. **Population** (2011): 7,333,000. **Density** (2011): persons per sq mi 171.1, persons per sq km 66.1. **Urban** (2010): 71.4%. **Sex distribution** (2008): male 48.40%; female 51.60%. **Age breakdown** (2007): under 15, 13.4%; 15–29, 20.4%; 30–44, 21.5%; 45–59, 21.2%; 60–74, 16.1%; 75–84, 6.3%; 85 and over, 1.1%. **Ethnic composition** (2001): Bulgarian 83.9%; Turkish 9.4%; Rom (Gypsy) 4.7%; other 2.0%. **Religious affiliation** (2005): Bulgarian Orthodox 81%; Sunni Muslim 12%; Evangelical Protestant 2%; Catholic 1%; other 4%. **Major cities** (2007): Sofia 1,156,796; Plovdiv 345,249; Varna 313,983; Burgas 187,514; Ruse 156,761. **Location:** southeastern Europe, bordering Romania, the Black Sea, Turkey, Greece, Macedonia, and Serbia.

## Vital statistics

**Birth rate** per 1,000 population (2008): 10.2 (world avg. 20.3); (2008) within marriage 48.9%. **Death rate** per 1,000 population (2008): 14.5 (world avg. 8.5). **Total fertility rate** (avg. births per childbearing woman; 2008): 1.48. **Life expectancy** at birth (2008): male 69.5 years; female 76.6 years.

## National economy

**Budget** (2007). *Revenue:* 26,210,000,000 leva (tax revenue 80.6%, of which VAT 30.9%, social insurance 14.6%, excise taxes 14.5%; nontax revenue 12.2%; grants 7.2%). *Expenditures:* 24,389,000,000 leva (current expenditures 81.5%; capital expenditures 17.3%; other 1.2%). **Public debt** (external, outstanding; November 2008): US$5,207,000,000. **Gross national income** (2008): US$41,830,000,000 (US$5,490 per capita). **Production** (metric tons except as noted). *Agriculture and fishing* (2007): wheat 2,390,000, corn (maize) 1,312,900, sunflower seeds 564,447; livestock (number of live animals) 1,635,410 sheep, 1,012,655 pigs, 628,271 cattle; fisheries production 12,929 (from aquaculture 32%). *Mining and quarrying* (2004): copper (metal content) 133,000; zinc (metal content) 17,000; gold 3,818 kg. *Manufacturing* (value added in '000 leva; 2004): refined petroleum products, n.a.; wearing apparel 566; food products 503; nonelectrical machinery and apparatus 485. *Energy production (consumption):* electricity (kW-hr; 2008) 44,423,000,000 (34,684,000,000); coal (metric tons; 2006) 27,000 (4,259,000); lignite (metric tons; 2007) 28,308,000 ([2006] 25,775,000); crude petroleum (barrels; 2006) 205,000 (52,123,000); petroleum products (metric tons; 2006) 6,088,000 (3,944,000); natural gas (cu m; 2008) 213,000,000 (3,806,000,000). **Population economically active** (2008): total 3,504,700; activity rate of total population 46.0% (participation rates: ages 15–64 67%; female 47.0%; unemployed 5.7%). **Selected balance of payments data.** Receipts from (US$'000,000): tourism (2007) 3,131; remittances (2008) 2,634; foreign direct investment (FDI; 2005–07 avg.) 6,620. Disbursements for (US$'000,000): tourism (2007) 1,823; remittances (2008) 74; FDI (2005–07 avg.) 249.

## Foreign trade

**Imports** (2007): US$30,086,000,000 (manufactured goods 20.3%; machinery and apparatus 19.6%; chemical products 8.7%; motor vehicles 8.4%; metal ore and scrap 5.8%). *Major import sources* (2008): Russia 14.5%; Germany 11.8%; Italy 7.9%; Ukraine 7.2%; Romania 5.6%. **Exports** (2007): US$18,576,-000,000 (base and fabricated metals 22.3%, of which copper 9.4%, iron and steel 6.8%; machinery and apparatus 13.0%; refined petroleum products 12.7%; wearing apparel 10.3%; food products 5.5%). *Major export destinations* (2008): Greece 9.9%; Germany 9.2%; Turkey 8.8%; Italy 8.5%; Romania 7.3%.

## Transport and communications

**Transport.** *Railroads* (2004): track length 6,238 km; (2008–09) passenger-km 2,299,000,000; (2008–09) metric ton-km cargo 4,508,000,000. *Roads* (2004): length 44,033 km (paved 99%). *Vehicles* (2005): cars 2,538,000; trucks and buses 371,000. *Air transport* (2007; Hemus Air and Bulgaria Air only): passenger-km 2,001,000,000; metric ton-km cargo 3,400,000. **Communications,** in total units (units per 1,000 persons). Telephone landlines (2008): 2,258,000 (296); cellular telephone subscribers (2008): 10,633,000 (1,395); personal computers (2007): 682,000 (89); total Internet users (2007): 2,368,000 (309); broadband Internet subscribers (2008): 853,000 (112).

## Education and health

**Educational attainment** (2004). Percentage of population ages 25–64 having: no formal schooling to complete primary education 28%; secondary 50%; higher 22%. **Literacy** (2006): total population ages 15 and over literate 98.3%; males 98.7%; females 97.9%. **Health** (2007): physicians 27,756 (1 per 274 persons); hospital beds 48,930 (1 per 155 persons); infant mortality rate per 1,000 live births (2008) 8.6; undernourished population (2002–04) 600,000 (8% of total population based on the consumption of a minimum daily requirement of 1,990 calories).

## Military

**Total active duty personnel** (November 2008): 40,747 (army 46.1%, navy 10.1%, air force 22.9%, central staff 20.9%). **Military expenditure as percentage of GDP** (2007): 2.2%; per capita expenditure US$115.

## Background

Evidence of human habitation in Bulgaria dates from prehistoric times. Thracians were its first recorded inhabitants, dating from c. 3500 BC, and their first state dates from about the 5th century BC; the area was subdued by the Romans, who divided it into the provinces of Moesia and Thrace. In the 7th century AD the Bulgars took the region to the south of the Danube. The Byzantine Empire in 681 formally recognized Bulgar control over the area between the Balkans and the Danube. In the second half of the 14th century, Bulgaria fell to the Turks and ultimately lost its independence. At the end of the Russo-Turkish War (1877–78), Bulgaria rebelled. The ensuing Treaty of San Stefano was unacceptable to the Great Powers, and the Congress of Berlin (1878) resulted. In 1908 the Bulgarian ruler, Ferdinand, declared Bulgaria's independence. After its involvement in the Balkan Wars (1912–13), Bulgaria lost territory. It sided with the Central Powers in World War I and with

Germany in World War II. A communist coalition seized power in 1944, and in 1946 a people's republic was declared. Like other Eastern European countries in the late 1980s, Bulgaria experienced political unrest; its communist leader resigned in 1989. A new constitution proclaiming a republic was implemented in 1991. Bulgaria joined NATO in 2004 and the EU in 2007.

## Recent Developments

Bulgaria and Romania were denied entry into Europe's "borderless" Schengen area in 2011, despite having met the technical requirements for accession. Bulgarian-Russian relations were also strained as the Burgas-Alexandroupolis pipeline project was put on hold after Bulgaria refused to deliver its promised investment in response to the plan's environmental instability. The Bulgarian government also temporarily froze the building of a nuclear plant at Belene because of allegations that the Russian state-owned Rosatom had not provided sufficient documentation on plant equipment environmental-security checks.

Internet resource: <www.nsi.bg/index_en.htm>.

# Burkina Faso

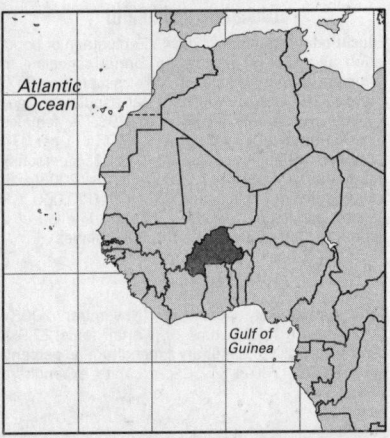

Official name: Burkina Faso. Form of government: multiparty republic with one legislative house (National Assembly [111]). Head of state: President Blaise Compaoré (from 1987). Head of government: Prime Minister Luc Adolphe Tiao (from 2011). Capital: Ouagadougou. Official language: French. Official religion: none. Monetary unit: 1 CFA franc (CFAF) = 100 centimes; valuation (2 Jul 2012) US$1 = CFAF 521.26.

## Demography

Area: 104,543 sq mi, 270,764 sq km. Population (2011): 16,968,000. Density (2011): persons per sq mi 162.3, persons per sq km 62.7. Urban (2009): 24.8%. Sex distribution (2006): male 48.29%; fe-

male 51.71%. Age breakdown (2006): under 15, 46.4%; 15–29, 26.2%; 30–44, 14.3%; 45–59, 7.6%; 60–74, 3.8%; 75–84, 0.9%; 85 and over, 0.3%; unknown 0.5%. Ethnic composition (1995): Mossi 47.9%; Fulani 10.3%; Lobi 6.9%; Bobo 6.9%; Mande 6.7%; Senufo 5.3%; Grosi 5.0%; Gurma 4.8%; Tuareg 3.1%. Religious affiliation (2006): Muslim 60.5%; Roman Catholic 19.0%; traditional beliefs 15.3%; Protestant/independent Christian 4.2%; nonreligious 0.4%; other 0.6%. Major urban localities (2006): Ouagadougou 1,475,223; Bobo-Dioulasso 489,967; Koudougou 88,184; Banfora 75,917; Ouahigouya 73,153. Location: western Africa, bordering Mali, Niger, Benin, Togo, Ghana, and Côte d'Ivoire.

## Vital statistics

Birth rate per 1,000 population (2007): 45.0 (world avg. 20.3). Death rate per 1,000 population (2007): 13.9 (world avg. 8.5). Total fertility rate (avg. births per childbearing woman; 2007): 6.41. Life expectancy at birth (2007): male 50.3 years; female 54.0 years.

## National economy

Budget (2007). *Revenue:* CFAF 618,508,000,000 (tax revenue 65.4%, of which taxes on goods and services 35.2%, taxes on international transactions 12.6%; grants 29.0%; nontax revenue 5.6%). *Expenditures:* CFAF 839,362,000,000 (current expenditures 54.0%; development expenditures 45.8%; other 0.2%). *Production* (metric tons except as noted). *Agriculture and fishing* (2007): sorghum 1,507,000, millet 966,000, seed cotton 690,000, shea nuts (2005) 70,000, bambara beans 40,500, sesame 25,600; livestock (number of live animals) 11,295,000 goats, 7,914,000 cattle, 7,544,000 sheep; fisheries production 10,498 (from aquaculture, 3%). *Mining and quarrying* (2007): gold 2,250 kg; granite 300,000 cu m. *Manufacturing* (value added in CFAF '000,000; 1999): food products, beverages, and tobacco 126,125; textiles 46,217; chemical products 9,335. *Energy production (consumption):* electricity (kW-hr; 2006) 548,000,000 (687,000,000); petroleum products (metric tons; 2006) none (440,000). Population economically active (2006): total 5,412,102; activity rate 38.6% (participation rates: ages 15 and over, 72.7%; female 45.3%; officially unemployed 2.3%). Gross national income (2008): US$7,278,000,000 (US$480 per capita). Public debt (external; 2007): US$1,268,000,000. Selected balance of payments data. Receipts from (US$'000,000): tourism (2006) 53; remittances (2008) 50; foreign direct investment (2005–07 avg.) 223; official development assistance (2007) 930. Disbursements for (US$'000,000): tourism (2006) 55; remittances (2008) 44.

## Foreign trade

Imports (2007; f.o.b. in commodities and c.i.f. in trading partners): CFAF 585,100,000,000 (machinery and apparatus 29.3%; refined petroleum products 24.5%; food products 10.3%). *Major import sources* (2005): France 18.7%; Côte d'Ivoire 18.0%; Togo

---

*1 metric ton = about 1.1 short tons;    1 kilometer = 0.6 mi (statute);    1 metric ton-km cargo = about 0.68 short ton-mi cargo;    c.i.f.: cost, insurance, and freight;    f.o.b.: free on board*

11.4%; Benin 6.8%; Ghana 5.9%. **Exports** (2007): CFAF 296,100,000,000 (raw cotton 55.4%; gold 5.4%; shea nuts 4.6%). *Major export destinations* (2005): Togo 41.1%; Ghana 16.7%; Côte d'Ivoire 10.5%; France 9.8%; Switzerland 9.4%.

## Transport and communications

**Transport.** *Railroads:* route length (2007) 622 km; passenger-km (2003) 9,980,000; metric ton-km cargo (2005) 674,900,000. *Roads* (2006): total length 15,272 km (paved 17%). *Vehicles* (2005): passenger cars 84,161; trucks and buses 38,261. *Air transport* (2005; combined data for Ouagadougou and Bobo-Dioulasso airports): passenger arrivals 134,247, passenger departures 137,373; cargo unloaded 2,837 metric tons, cargo loaded 1,347 metric tons. **Communications,** in total units (units per 1,000 persons). Telephone landlines (2007): 122,000 (8.3); cellular telephone subscribers (2008): 2,553,000 (168); personal computers (2007): 88,000 (6.0); total Internet users (2008): 140,000 (9.2); broadband Internet subscribers (2006): 1,700 (0.1).

## Education and health

**Educational attainment** (2003). Percentage of population ages 25 and over having: no formal schooling or unknown 85.4%; incomplete to complete primary education 7.9%; incomplete to complete secondary 5.5%; higher 1.2%. **Literacy** (2006): percentage of total population ages 15 and over literate 21.1%; males literate 27.9%; females literate 15.4%. **Health** (2007): physicians 441 (1 per 31,634 persons); hospital beds (2006) 12,200 (1 per 1,111 persons); infant mortality rate per 1,000 live births 87.6; undernourished population (2002–04) 2,000,000 (15% of total population based on the consumption of a minimum daily requirement of 1,800 calories).

## Military

**Total active duty personnel** (November 2008): 10,800 (army 59.3%, air force 1.8%, gendarmerie 38.9%). **Military expenditure as percentage of GDP** (2007): 1.3%; per capita expenditure US$7.

## Background

Probably in the 14th century, the Mossi and Gurma peoples established themselves in eastern and central areas of what is now Burkina Faso. The Mossi kingdoms of Yatenga and Ouagadougou existed into the early 20th century. A French protectorate was established over the region (1895–97), and its southern boundary was demarcated through an Anglo-French agreement. It was part of the Upper Senegal–Niger colony and then became a separate colony in 1919. Named Upper Volta, it was constituted an overseas territory within the French Union in 1947, became an autonomous republic within the French Community in 1958, and achieved total independence in 1960. Since then, the country has been ruled primarily by the military and has experienced several coups; following one in 1983, the country received its present name. A new constitution, adopted in 1991, restored multiparty rule; elected government returned in the 1990s. Economic problems plagued the country at the beginning of the 21st century.

## Recent Developments

Although Pres. Blaise Compaoré claimed victory in the Burkina Faso 2010 presidential elections, a tide of demonstrations and strikes swept the country in 2011. Anger over the unexplained death in February of student leader Justin Zongo while under arrest led to violent clashes between security forces and students, resulting in five deaths. Soldiers mutinied in April in Ouagadougou, and there were similar incidents in Pô and Bobo-Dioulasso. That month a new government was formed, headed by Prime Minister Luc Adolphe Tiao.

**Internet resource:** <www.burkina.com>.

# Burundi

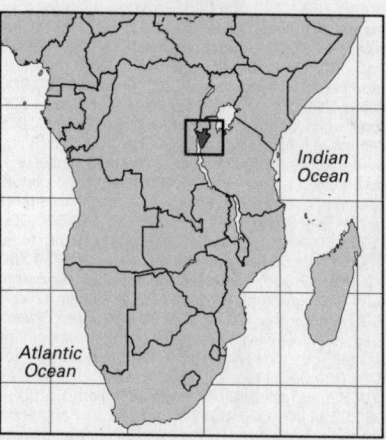

Indian Ocean

Atlantic Ocean

**Official name:** Republika y'u Burundi (Rundi); République du Burundi (French) (Republic of Burundi). **Form of government:** republic with two legislative houses (Senate [41]; National Assembly [106]). **Head of state and government:** President Pierre Nkurunziza (from 2005). **Capital:** Bujumbura. **Official languages:** Rundi; French. **Official religion:** none. **Monetary unit:** 1 Burundi franc (FBu) = 100 centimes; valuation (2 Jul 2012) US$1 = FBu 1,435.55.

## Demography

**Area:** 10,740 sq mi, 27,816 sq km. **Population** (2011): 8,575,000. **Density** (2011): persons per sq mi 798.4, persons per sq km 308.3. **Urban** (2009): 10.7%. **Sex distribution** (2005): male 48.82%; female 51.18%. **Age breakdown** (2005): under 15, 41.4%; 15–29, 30.8%; 30–44, 14.7%; 45–59, 8.7%; 60–74, 3.5%; 75–84, 0.8%; 85 and over, 0.1%. **Ethnic composition** (2000): Hutu 80.9%; Tutsi 15.6%; Lingala 1.6%; Twa Pygmy 1.0%; other 0.9%. **Religious affiliation** (2004): Christian 67%, of which Roman Catholic 62%, Protestant 5%; traditional beliefs 23%; Muslim (mostly Sunni) 10%. **Major city and towns** (2004): Bujumbura 374,152; Gitega 25,500; Ngozi 21,500; Bururi 20,500. **Location:** central Africa, bordering Rwanda, Tanzania, Lake Tanganyika, and the Democratic Republic of the Congo.

## Vital statistics

**Birth rate** per 1,000 population (2005): 35.4 (world avg. 20.3). **Death rate** per 1,000 population (2005): 14.8 (world avg. 8.5). **Total fertility rate** (avg. births per childbearing woman; 2005): 5.04. **Life expectancy** at birth (2005): male 47.8 years; female 50.5 years.

## National economy

**Budget** (2007). *Revenue:* FBu 419,600,000,000 (grants 52.9%; tax revenue 43.5%, of which taxes on goods and services 22.0%, income tax 12.7%, taxes on international trade 8.1%; nontax revenue 3.6%). *Expenditures:* FBu 407,900,000,000 (current expenditures 63.9%; capital expenditures 33.0%; other 3.1%). **Public debt** (external, outstanding; February 2008): US$1,330,000,000. **Production** (metric tons except as noted). *Agriculture and fishing* (2007): bananas 1,600,000, sweet potatoes 835,000, cassava 710,000, taros 62,000, palm oil 12,773; livestock (number of live animals) 750,000 goats, 400,000 cattle, 250,000 sheep; fisheries production 14,200 (from aquaculture 1%). *Mining and quarrying* (2007): columbite-tantalite ore 51,550 kg; gold 2,423 kg. *Manufacturing* (2007): beer 1,289,400 hectoliters; carbonated beverages 294,200 hectoliters; cottonseed oil 51,200 liters. *Energy production (consumption):* electricity (kW-hr; 2007) 117,500,000 (192,600,000); petroleum products (metric tons; 2006) none (58,000); peat (metric tons; 2007) 9,800 ([2000] 12,000). **Selected balance of payments data.** Receipts from (US$'000,000): tourism (2007) 1.3; remittances (2004) 4.1; foreign direct investment (2005–07 avg.) negligible; official development assistance (2007) 466. Disbursements for (US$'000,000): tourism (2007) 104; remittances (2008) negligible. **Gross national income** (2008): US$1,092,000,000 (US$140 per capita). **Population economically active** (2006): total 4,060,000; activity rate of total population 49.7% (participation rates: ages 15–64, 90.5%; female 51.9%; unemployed, n.a.).

## Foreign trade

**Imports** (2007; c.i.f.): US$423,000,000 (refined petroleum products 27.5%; motor vehicles 19.8%; food products 11.0%, of which cereals 7.7%; machinery and apparatus 8.7%; iron and steel 6.4%). *Major import sources:* Saudi Arabia 27.5%; Belgium 11.3%; Uganda 10.7%; Kenya 7.9%; Japan 7.0%. **Exports** (2007; f.o.b.): US$156,200,000 (gold 34.0% [nearly all smuggled from neighboring countries]; coffee 24.6%; motor vehicles 9.2%; black tea 4.2%; raw cane sugar 4.0%; prefabricated buildings 3.0%; hides and skins 2.4%). *Major export destinations:* UAE 34.2%; Switzerland 10.9%; Democratic Republic of the Congo 9.4%; Kenya 7.2%; Rwanda 6.7%.

## Transport and communications

**Transport.** *Railroads:* none. *Roads* (2004): total length 12,322 km (paved 7%). *Vehicles:* passenger cars (2003) 7,000; trucks and buses (2002) 14,400. *Air transport* (2007–08; Bujumbura airport only): passenger arrivals 96,175, passenger departures

62,845; cargo unloaded 2,116 metric tons, cargo loaded 317 metric tons. **Communications,** in total units (units per 1,000 persons). Telephone landlines (2008): 30,000 (3.8); cellular telephone subscribers (2008): 481,000 (60); personal computers (2006): 57,000 (7.0); total Internet users (2008): 65,000 (8.1); broadband Internet subscribers (2008): 200 (0.02).

## Education and health

**Literacy** (2007): percentage of total population ages 15 and over literate 56.1%; males literate 61.4%; females literate 51.1%. **Health:** physicians (2004) 200 (1 per 37,581 persons); hospital beds (2006) 5,663 (1 per 1,429 persons); infant mortality rate per 1,000 live births (2005) 102.0; undernourished population (2002–04) 4,500,000 (66% of total population based on the consumption of a minimum daily requirement of 1,800 calories).

## Military

**Total active duty personnel** (November 2008): 20,000 (army 100%); Burundian troops in Somalia as part of African Union (AU) peacekeeping mission (December 2008): 1,700; South African troops in Burundi representing AU peacekeeping mission (February 2009): 973. **Military expenditure as percentage of GDP** (2007): 7.8%; per capita expenditure US$9.

## Background

Original settlement by the Twa people was followed by Hutu settlement, which occurred gradually and was completed by the 11th century. The Tutsi arrived 300–400 years later; though a minority, they established the kingdom of Burundi in the 16th century. In the 19th century the area came within the German sphere of influence, but the Tutsi remained in power. Following World War I the Belgians took control of the area, which became a UN trusteeship after World War II. Colonial-period conditions had intensified Hutu-Tutsi ethnic animosities, and as independence neared, hostilities flared. Independence was granted in 1962 in the form of a kingdom ruled by the Tutsi. In 1965 the Hutu rebelled but were brutally repressed. The rest of the 20th century saw violent clashes between the two groups. In 2001 a power-sharing transitional government was established, paving the way to the promulgation of a new constitution and the installation of a new government in 2005.

## Recent Developments

After the election boycotts and intermittent violence surrounding the uncontested reelection of Pres. Pierre Nkurunziza in 2010, Burundi struggled to secure its fragile stability and peace during 2011. Concerns over security were heightened amid ongoing grenade attacks as well as threats from the al-Qaeda-linked Somalian militant group al-Shabaab, owing to Burundi's deployment of thousands of troops as part of the African Union's peacekeeping force in Mogadishu, Somalia.

**Internet resource:** <www.burundiembassy-usa.org>.

---

*1 metric ton = about 1.1 short tons;    1 kilometer = 0.6 mi (statute);    1 metric ton-km cargo = about 0.68 short ton-mi cargo;    c.i.f.: cost, insurance, and freight;    f.o.b.: free on board*

# Cambodia

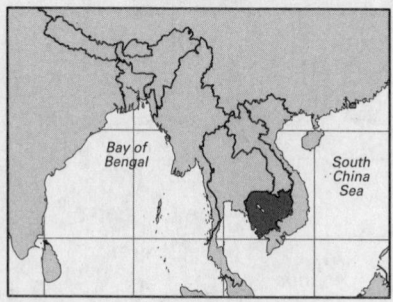

**Official name:** Preahreacheanachakr Kampuchea (Kingdom of Cambodia). **Form of government:** constitutional monarchy with two legislative houses (Senate [61]; National Assembly [123]). **Head of state:** King Norodom Sihamoni (from 2004). **Head of government:** Prime Minister Samdech Hun Sen (from 1998). **Capital:** Phnom Penh. **Official language:** Khmer. **Official religion:** Buddhism. **Monetary unit:** 1 riel (KHR) = 100 sen; valuation (2 Jul 2012) US$1 = 4,098.00 riels.

## Demography

**Area:** 69,898 sq mi, 181,035 sq km. **Population** (2011): 14,702,000. **Density** (2011): persons per sq mi 210.3, persons per sq km 81.2. **Urban** (2008): 19.5%. **Sex distribution** (2008): male 48.51%; female 51.49%. **Age breakdown** (2005): under 15, 36.6%; 15–29, 30.5%; 30–44, 18.4%; 45–59, 9.4%; 60–74, 4.1%; 75–84, 0.9%; 85 and over, 0.1%. **Ethnic composition** (2000): Khmer 85.2%; Chinese 6.4%; Vietnamese 3.0%; Cham 2.5%; Lao 0.6%; other 2.3%. **Religious affiliation** (2000): Buddhist 84.7%; Chinese folk religionist 4.7%; traditional beliefs 4.3%; Muslim 2.3%; Christian 1.1%; other 2.9%. **Major urban areas** (1998): Phnom Penh (2005) 1,364,000; Battambang 124,290; Sisophon 85,382; Siemreap 83,715; Sihanoukville 66,723. **Location:** southeastern Asia, bordering Thailand, Laos, Vietnam, and the Gulf of Thailand.

## Vital statistics

**Birth rate** per 1,000 population (2008): 25.7 (world avg. 20.3). **Death rate** per 1,000 population (2008): 8.2 (world avg. 8.5). **Total fertility rate** (avg. births per childbearing woman; 2008): 3.08. **Life expectancy** at birth (2008): male 59.7 years; female 63.8 years.

## National economy

**Budget** (2007). *Revenue:* KHR 3,280,300,000,000 (tax revenue 58.3%; nontax revenue 17.2%; grants 20.0%; other 4.5%). *Expenditures:* KHR 3,294,700,000,000 (current expenditures 59.7%; development expenditures 40.3%). **Production** (metric tons except as noted). *Agriculture and fishing* (2007): rice 5,995,000, cassava 2,000,000, corn (maize) 380,000, rubber 22,000; livestock (number of live animals) 3,500,000 cattle, 2,790,000 pigs, 775,000 buffalo, (2005) 120,000 crocodiles; fisheries production 514,200 (from aquaculture 7%); aquatic plants production 16,000 (from aquaculture 100%). *Mining and quarrying* (2007): gold, n.a.; gem-

stones, n.a.; salt 76,700. *Manufacturing* (value added in KHR '000,000,000; 2002): wearing apparel 1,808; food products 392; base and fabricated metals 120. *Energy production (consumption):* electricity (kW-hr; 2006) 1,235,000,000 (1,345,000,000); petroleum products (metric tons; 2006) none (1,327,000). **Selected balance of payments data.** Receipts from (US$'000,000): tourism (2007) 1,284; remittances (2008) 325; foreign direct investment (2005–07 avg.) 577; official development assistance (2007) 672. Disbursements for (US$'000,000): tourism (2007) 194; remittances (2008) 164. **Gross national income** (2008): US$8,859,000,000 (US$600 per capita). **Public debt** (external, outstanding; 2007): US$3,537,000,000. **Population economically active** (2004): total 7,557,600; activity rate of total population 55.0% (participation rates: ages 15–64, 82.6%; female 49.4%; registered unemployed 7.1%).

## Foreign trade

**Imports** (2005; c.i.f.): US$4,254,000,000 (retained imports 97.3%; imports for reexport 2.7%). *Major import sources* (2004): Thailand 23.9%; Hong Kong 15.0%; China 13.5%; Singapore 11.5%; Vietnam 7.6%. **Exports** (2005; f.o.b.): US$2,910,000,000 (domestic exports 95.3%, of which garments 77.7%, rice 6.1%, rubber 4.1%, fish 2.6%, sawn timber and logs 0.5%; reexports 4.7%). *Major export destinations* (2004): US 56.2%; Germany 11.5%; UK 7.0%; Canada 4.3%; Vietnam 3.7%.

## Transport and communications

**Transport.** *Railroads* (2004): length 602 km; (2000) passenger-km 45,000,000; (1999) metric ton-km 76,171,000. *Roads* (2004): total length 38,257 km (paved 6%). *Vehicles* (2004): passenger cars 235,298; trucks and buses 35,448. *Air transport* (2005–06): passenger-km 198,000,000; metric ton-km cargo 1,214,000. **Communications,** in total units (units per 1,000 persons). Telephone landlines (2008): 45,000 (3.1); cellular telephone subscribers (2008): 4,237,000 (288); personal computers (2007): 56,000 (4.0); total Internet users (2007): 70,000 (4.8); broadband Internet subscribers (2007): 8,400 (0.6).

## Education and health

**Educational attainment** (2004). Percentage of literate population ages 25 and over having: no formal schooling/unknown 4.6%; incomplete primary education 54.0%; complete primary 23.7%; incomplete secondary 11.3%; secondary/vocational 5.3%; higher 1.1%. **Literacy** (2004): percentage of total population ages 15 and over literate 74.4%; males literate 82.1%; females literate 67.4%. **Health:** physicians (2004) 2,122 (1 per 6,169 persons); hospital beds (2002) 9,800 (1 per 1,405 persons); infant mortality rate per 1,000 live births (2008) 56.6; undernourished population (2002–04) 4,600,000 (33% of total population based on the consumption of a minimum daily requirement of 1,770 calories).

## Military

**Total active duty personnel** (November 2008): 124,300 (army 60.3%, navy 2.3%, air force 1.2%, provincial forces 36.2%). **Military expenditure as percentage of GDP** (2007): 1.6%; per capita expenditure US$10.

## Background

In the early Christian era, what is now Cambodia was under Hindu and, to a lesser extent, Buddhist influence. The Khmer state gradually spread in the early 7th century and reached its height under Jayavarman II and his successors in the 9th–12th centuries, when it ruled the Mekong Valley and the tributary Shan states and built Angkor. Widespread adoption of Buddhism occurred in the 13th century, resulting in a script change from Sanskrit to Pali. From the 13th century Cambodia was attacked by Annam and Siamese city-states and was alternately a province of one or the other. The area became a French protectorate in 1863. It was occupied by the Japanese in World War II and became independent in 1954. Cambodia's borders were the scene of fighting in the Vietnam War from 1961, and in 1970 its northeastern and eastern areas were occupied by the North Vietnamese and penetrated by US and South Vietnamese forces. An indiscriminate US bombing campaign alienated much of the population, enabling the communist Khmer Rouge under Pol Pot to seize power in 1975. Their regime of terror resulted in the deaths of at least one million Cambodians. Vietnam invaded in 1979 and drove the Khmer Rouge into the western hinterlands, but it was unable to effect reconstruction of the country, and Cambodian infighting continued. A peace accord was reached by most Cambodian factions under UN auspices in 1991, and elections were held in 1993. Cambodia joined the Association of Southeast Asian Nations' in 1998.

## Recent Developments

The Khmer Rouge Tribunal (known officially as the Extraordinary Chambers in the Courts of Cambodia) reached another milestone in June 2011 with the start of the joint trial of Khieu Samphan, Nuon Chea, Ieng Sary, and Ieng Thirith, the surviving leaders most identified in the public mind with the brutal 1975–79 regime. Public disagreement between judges and the international prosecutor, leaked documents, and the resignation of UN legal officers complicated the situation. Meanwhile, Kaing Guek Eav (better known as Duch), who in July 2010 had been found guilty against humanity for his actions during the Pol Pot regime and sentenced to 35 years imprisonment, had an appeal rejected. In February 2012, judges increased his sentence to life imprisonment.

**Internet resource:** <www.nis.gov.kh>.

# Cameroon

**Official name:** République du Cameroun (French); Republic of Cameroon (English). **Form of government:** unitary multiparty republic with one legislative house (National Assembly [180]). **Head of state:** President Paul Biya (from 1982). **Head of government:** Prime

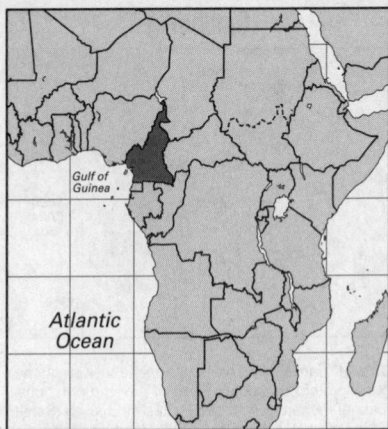

Minister Philemon Yang (from 2009). **Capital:** Yaoundé. **Official languages:** French; English. **Official religion:** none. **Monetary unit:** 1 CFA franc (CFAF) = 100 centimes; valuation (2 Jul 2012) US$1 = CFAF 521.26.

## Demography

**Area:** 183,920 sq mi, 476,350 sq km (includes the 270-sq-mi [700-sq-km] area of Bakassi Peninsula, which was formally ceded by Nigeria to Cameroon in August 2008). **Population** (2011): 20,073,000. **Density** (2011; based on land area): persons per sq mi 111.4, persons per sq km 43.0. **Urban** (2010): 52.0%. **Sex distribution** (2006): male 50.15%; female 49.85%. **Age breakdown** (2006): under 15, 41.5%; 15–29, 29.0%; 30–44, 15.7%; 45–59, 8.8%; 60–74, 4.1%; 75–84, 0.8%; 85 and over, 0.1%. **Ethnic composition** (2006): "western highlanders" 38.0%, including Bamileke 11.5%; "coastal tropical forest peoples" 12.0%, including Bassa 2.5%; "southern tropical forest peoples" 18.0%, including Ewondo (Yaunde) 8.0%; "mostly Islamic central highlanders" 14.0%, including Fulani 8.5%; "mostly traditional believers of central highlands and far north" or "Kirdi" 18.0%, including Mofa 2.5%. **Religious affiliation** (2005): Roman Catholic 27.4%; traditional beliefs 22.2%; Protestant 20.2%; Sunni Muslim 20.0%; nonreligious/other 10.2%. **Major urban areas** (2006): Douala 1,371,400; Yaoundé 1,344,600; Kousséri 476,600; Garoua 461,300; Bamenda 419,400. **Location:** western Africa, bordering Chad, the Central African Republic, the Republic of the Congo, Gabon, Equatorial Guinea, the Bight of Biafra, and Nigeria.

## Vital statistics

**Birth rate** per 1,000 population (2006): 35.6 (world avg. 20.3). **Death rate** per 1,000 population (2006): 13.0 (world avg. 8.6). **Total fertility rate** (avg. births per childbearing woman; 2006): 4.58. **Life expectancy** at birth (2006): male 51.7 years; female 53.0 years.

*1 metric ton = about 1.1 short tons; 1 kilometer = 0.6 mi (statute); 1 metric ton-km cargo = about 0.68 short ton-mi cargo; c.i.f.: cost, insurance, and freight; f.o.b.: free on board*

## National economy

**Budget** (2006). *Revenue:* CFAF 4,472,000,000,000 (grants 59.6%; non-oil revenue 26.0%, of which VAT 10.0%, direct taxes 5.9%, customs duties 4.6%, nontax revenue 2.2%; oil revenue 14.4%). *Expenditures:* CFAF 1,364,000,000,000 (current expenditures 80.4%; capital expenditures 19.6%). **Public debt** (external, outstanding; 2007): US$2,204,000,000. **Gross national income** (2008): US$21,781,000,000 (US$1,150 per capita). **Population economically active** (2006): total 6,857,000; activity rate of total population 37.7% (participation rates: ages 15–64, 64.7%; female 41.2%; unemployed 9.3%, underemployed 68.8%). **Production** (metric tons except as noted). *Agriculture and fishing* (2007): cassava 2,076,000, plantains 1,317,000, oil palm fruit 1,300,000, taro 1,133,000, seed cotton 225,000, cacao 179,239, natural rubber 47,000; livestock (number of live animals) 6,000,000 cattle, 3,800,000 sheep; fisheries production 138,952 (from aquaculture, negligible). *Mining and quarrying* (2007): pozzolana 600,000; limestone 100,000; gold 20,000 kg. *Manufacturing* (value added in US$'000,000; 2002): food products 97; refined petroleum products 88; beverages 78. *Energy production (consumption):* electricity (kW-hr; 2006) 3,900,000,000 (3,320,000,000); crude petroleum (barrels; 2008) 29,700,000 ([2007] 9,500,000); petroleum products (metric tons; 2005) 1,784,000 (932,000); natural gas (cu m; 2006) 20,000,000 (20,000,000). **Selected balance of payments data.** Receipts from (US$'000,000): tourism (2007) 177; remittances (2008) 167; foreign direct investment (2005–07 avg.) 273; official development assistance (2007) 1,933. Disbursements for (US$'000,000): tourism (2007) 318; remittances (2008) 103.

## Foreign trade

**Imports** (2006; c.i.f.): US$3,150,500,000 (crude petroleum 29.4%; chemical products 11.1%; machinery and apparatus 10.9%; cereals 9.0%; motor vehicles 5.8%). *Major import sources:* Nigeria 23.3%; France 17.2%; China 6.3%; Belgium 4.1%; Equatorial Guinea 3.5%. **Exports** (2006; f.o.b.): US$3,576,400,000 (crude petroleum 49.8%; refined petroleum products 11.8%; sawn wood 9.7%; cocoa [all forms] 7.3%; aluminum 4.5%; raw cotton 2.9%; natural rubber 1.8%; coffee 1.8%). *Major export destinations:* Spain 25.9%; Italy 23.1%; France 10.7%; US 6.4%; Netherlands 6.3%.

---

 **Did you know?** Cameroon is home to the goliath frog (*Conraua goliath*), the world's largest frog. Inhabiting the fast-running rivers along the coast, these amphibians can reach longer than one foot in length and weigh more than seven pounds.

---

## Transport and communications

**Transport.** *Railroads* (2005): route length (2006) 987 km; passenger-km 323,000,000; metric ton-km cargo 1,119,000,000. *Roads* (2004): total length 50,000 km (paved 10%). *Vehicles* (2005): passenger cars 175,981; trucks and buses 59,399. *Air transport* (2005): passenger-km 646,000,000; metric ton-km cargo (2001) 23,255,000. **Communications,** in total units (units per 1,000 persons). Telephone landlines (2008): 198,000 (10); cellular telephone subscribers (2008): 6,161,000 (323); personal computers (2006): 194,000 (11); total Internet users (2007): 548,000 (29); broadband Internet subscribers (2007): 400 (0.02).

## Education and health

**Educational attainment** (2004): Percentage of population ages 25 and over having: no formal schooling/unknown 34.3%; primary education 35.3%; secondary 26.2%; higher 4.2%. **Literacy** (2007): percentage of total population ages 15 and over literate 78.8%; males literate 84.6%; females literate 73.2%. **Health** (2004): physicians 2,966 (1 per 5,609 persons); hospital beds 26,487 (1 per 667 persons); infant mortality rate per 1,000 live births (2006) 67.2; undernourished population (2002–04) 4,200,000 (26% of total population based on the consumption of a minimum daily requirement of 1,860 calories).

## Military

**Total active duty personnel** (November 2008): 14,100 (army 88.7%, navy 9.2%, air force 2.1%). **Military expenditure as percentage of GDP** (2007): 1.6%; per capita expenditure US$16.

## Background

The Cameroon area had long been inhabited before European colonization. Bantu speakers from equatorial Africa settled in the south, followed by Muslim Fulani from the Niger River basin, who settled in the north. Portuguese explorers visited in the late 15th century and established a foothold, but they lost control to the Dutch in the 17th century. In 1884 the Germans took control and extended their protectorate over Cameroon. In World War I joint French-British action forced the Germans to retreat, and after the war the region was divided into French and British administrative zones. After World War II the two areas became UN trusteeships. In 1960 the French trust territory became an independent republic. In 1961 the southern part of the British trust territory voted for union with the new republic of Cameroon, and the northern part voted for union with Nigeria. In recent decades economic problems have produced unrest in the country.

## Recent Developments

In apparent response to opposition parties' criticisms of Cameroon's electoral commission, Pres. Paul Biya increased its size by one-half in 2011. The appointments in July followed an earlier reform of the commission that removed its power to determine the final result of any election. Biya easily won reelection in October, garnering more than 77% of the vote. The election, however, was marred by numerous complaints of fraud and irregularities.

**Internet resource:** <www.statistics-cameroon.org>.

# Canada

**Official name:** Canada. **Form of government:** federal multiparty parliamentary state with two legisla-

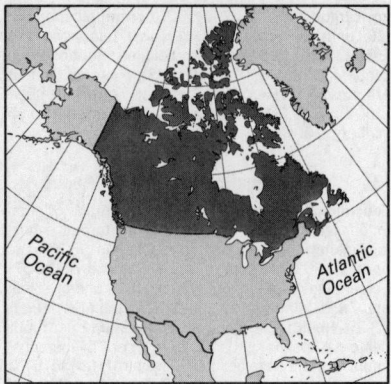

tive houses (Senate [105]; House of Commons [308]). **Head of state:** British Queen Elizabeth II (from 1952), represented by Governor-General David Johnston (from 2010). **Head of government:** Prime Minister Stephen Harper (from 2006). **Capital:** Ottawa. **Official languages:** English; French. **Official religion:** none. **Monetary unit:** 1 Canadian dollar (Can$) = 100 cents; valuation (2 Jul 2012) US$1 = Can$1.02.

## Demography

**Area:** 3,855,103 sq mi, 9,984,670 sq km. **Population** (2011): 34,447,000. **Density** (2011; based on land area): persons per sq mi 9.8, persons per sq km 3.8. **Urban** (2011): 80.7%. **Sex distribution** (2007): male 49.53%; female 50.47%. **Age breakdown** (2007): under 15, 17.0%; 15–29, 20.5%; 30–44, 21.9%; 45–59, 22.0%; 60–74, 12.2%; 75–84, 4.7%; 85 and over, 1.7%. **Population by mother tongue** (2006): English 57.8%; French 22.1%; other 20.1%, of which Chinese languages 3.3%, Italian 1.5%, German 1.5%, Punjabi 1.2%, Spanish 1.2%, Arabic 0.9%, Tagalog 0.9%, Portuguese 0.7%, Polish 0.7%, Urdu 0.5%, Ukrainian 0.5%. **Aboriginal population** (2006): North American Indian 1,172,790 (2.2% of total population); Métis 698,025 (1.3%); Inuit (Eskimo) 50,485 (0.2%); other/multiple 34,500 (0.1%). **Religious affiliation** (2001): Christian 77.1%, of which Roman Catholic 43.2%, Protestant 28.3%, unspecified Christian 2.6%, Orthodox 1.7%, other Christian 1.3%; Muslim 2.0%; Jewish 1.1%; Hindu 1.0%; Buddhist 1.0%; Sikh 0.9%; nonreligious 16.5%; other 0.4%. **Major metropolitan areas** (2006): Toronto 5,113,149; Montreal 3,635,571; Vancouver 2,116,581; Ottawa-Gatineau 1,130,761; Calgary 1,079,310; Edmonton 1,034,945; Quebec 715,515; Winnipeg 694,668; Hamilton 692,911; London 457,720; Kitchener 451,235; St. Catharines–Niagara 390,317. **Location:** northern North America, bordering the Arctic Ocean, the North Atlantic Ocean, the US, and the North Pacific Ocean. **Place of birth** (2006): 80.2% native-born; 19.8% foreign-born, of which Asian 8.1%, European 7.3%, Latin American 1.2%, African 1.2%. **Mobility** (2006). Population living in the same residence as in 2001: 59.1%; different residence, same municipality 22.0%; same province,

different municipality 12.1%; different province 2.9%; different country 3.9%. **Immigration** (2007): permanent immigrants admitted 236,758; from Asia/Pacific 47.6%, of which China 11.4%, India 11.0%, Philippines 8.1%; Africa/Middle East 20.5%; Europe 16.5%; Latin America 10.9%; US 4.4%; refugee population (January 2008) 175,741.

## Vital statistics

**Birth rate** per 1,000 population (2007–08): 11.0 (world avg. 20.3). **Death rate** per 1,000 population (2007–08): 7.2 (world avg. 8.5). **Total fertility rate** (avg. births per childbearing woman; 2006): 1.59. **Life expectancy** at birth (2006): male 76.9 years; female 83.7 years.

## Social indicators

**Educational attainment** (2006). Percentage of population ages 25–64 having: less than complete secondary education 15.5%; complete secondary 23.9%; higher vocational 12.4%; some college/university 25.3%; bachelor's degree 14.6%; beyond bachelor's/master's 7.5%; doctorate 0.8%. **Quality of working life.** Average workweek (2007): 35.6 hours. Annual rate per 100,000 workers for (2006): injury, accident, or industrial illness 1,998; death 5.9. Average days lost to labor stoppages per 1,000 employee-workdays (2001): 0.7. Average round-trip commuting time (2005): 63 minutes; mode of transportation (2006): auto driver 72.3%, auto passenger 7.7%, public transportation 11.0%, walking 6.4%, bicycling 1.3%, other/unknown 1.3%. Labor force covered by a pension plan (2006): 38.1%. **Social participation.** Population over 18 years of age participating in voluntary work (2000): 26.7%. Trade union membership as percentage of civilian labor force (2007) 29.4%. Attendance at religious services on a weekly basis (2006): 17%. **Social deviance** (2007). Offense rate per 100,000 population for: violent crime 929.6, of which battery/aggravated battery/dangerous operation of vehicle 718.5, robbery 89.8, sexual assault 65.0, homicide 1.8; property crime 3,319.7, of which breaking and entering 700.3, auto theft 443.2, fraud 267.7. **Leisure** (1998). Favorite leisure activities (hours weekly): television (2004) 21.4; radio (2005) 19.1; social time 13.3; reading 2.8; sports and entertainment 1.4. **Material well-being** (2006). Households possessing: owned automobile 59.7%; owned truck/van 36.9%; landline telephone only (December 2007) 24.0%; cellular phone (December 2007) 72.4%; air conditioner 48.1%; cable television 65.2%; home computer 75.4%; Internet use from home 68.1%; dishwasher 57.7%.

## National economy

**Gross national income** (2008): US$1,390,040,-000,000 (US$41,730 per capita). **Budget** (2007–08; federal government). *Revenue:* Can$256,575,-000,000 (income tax 46.2%; corporate taxes 16.3%; sales tax 13.8%; contributions to social security 8.5%; other 15.2%). *Expenditures:* Can$242,814,-000,000 (social services 37.0%; defense/police 11.8%; transfers to government subsectors 11.3%; health 10.6%; debt service 8.4%; resource conservation and industrial development 4.5%; foreign af-

*1 metric ton = about 1.1 short tons;    1 kilometer = 0.6 mi (statute);    1 metric ton-km cargo = about 0.68 short ton-mi cargo;    c.i.f.: cost, insurance, and freight;    f.o.b.: free on board*

fairs/international assistance 2.4%; education 2.3%). **Production** (metric tons except as noted). *Agriculture and fishing* (2008): wheat 28,611,100, rapeseed 12,642,900, barley 11,781,400, corn (maize) 10,592,000, potatoes 4,724,460, oats 4,272,600, dry peas 3,571,300, soybeans 3,335,900, linseed 861,100, tomatoes 770,059, apples 393,435, sugar beets 344,700, rye 316,200, dry onions 202,636, canary seed 195,600, mustard seed 161,000, sunflower seeds 112,200, blueberries 94,551, mushrooms and truffles 86,946, grapes 80,959, cranberries 72,642; livestock (number of live animals) 13,895,000 cattle, 13,810,000 pigs, 165,000,000 chickens, 5,880,000 turkeys; fisheries production (2007) 1,174,735 (from aquaculture 14%); aquatic plants production (2006) 11,313 (from aquaculture, none). *Mining and quarrying* (value of production in Can$'000,000; 2007): nickel 9,902 (world rank: 2); copper 4,533; potash 3,142 (world rank: 1); uranium 2,523 (world rank: 1); iron ore 2,512; gold 2,377; zinc 2,087 (world rank: 5); diamonds 1,445; stone 1,333; platinum group 543 (world rank: 3); salt 427 (world rank: 5); cobalt 223 (world rank: 2); gypsum 112 (world rank: 4); ilmenite 816,000 metric tons (world rank: 3); molybdenum (metal content) 6,841 metric tons (world rank: 5). *Manufacturing* (value added in Can$'000,000,000 in constant prices of 2002; 2008): transportation equipment 30.8; food products 19.3; base chemicals, medicines, and soaps 15.6; machinery and apparatus 13.7; fabricated metal products 13.4; base metals 11.8; wood products (excluding furniture) 9.6; paper products 9.5; rubber and plastic products 9.0; information and communication technologies 8.5. **Population economically active** (2006): total 17,825,800; activity rate of total population 55.6% (participation rates: ages 15 and over, 67.5%; female 46.7%; unemployed [January–December 2008] 6.1%). **Public debt** (March 2008): US$477,101,000,000. *Energy production (consumption):* electricity (kW-hr; 2007) 603,180,000,000 ([2005] 604,343,000,000); coal (metric tons; 2007) 32,800,000 ([2005] 15,100,000); lignite (metric tons; 2007) 36,600,000 ([2005] 45,400,000); crude petroleum (barrels; 2008) 946,000,000 (from [in 2007]: the Alberta oil sands 50%, conventional on land sources 38%, offshore Newfoundland in the Atlantic Ocean 12%) ([2006] 641,598,000); petroleum products (metric tons; 2006) 85,832,000 (78,534,000); natural gas (cu m; 2007) 187,000,000,000 (92,900,000,000). **Selected balance of payments data.** Receipts from (US$'000,000): tourism (2007) 15,614; foreign direct investment (FDI; 2005–07 avg.) 66,129. Disbursements for (US$'000,000): tourism (2007) 24,882; FDI (2005–07 avg.) 40,851.

## Foreign trade

**Imports** (2007): Can$408,436,000,000 (machinery and apparatus 25.3%, of which nonelectrical machinery 12.2%; motor vehicles 16.6%, of which cars 6.7%, parts for motor vehicles 5.5%; chemical products 10.3%; crude petroleum 5.9%; food products 4.9%). *Major import sources:* US 54.2%; China 9.4%; Mexico 4.2%; Japan 3.8%; Germany 2.8%; UK 2.8%; South Korea 1.3%; Norway 1.3%. **Exports** (2007): Can$451,043,000,000 (mineral fuels 20.8%, of which crude petroleum 9.3%, natural gas 6.3%; motor vehicles 15.0%, of which cars 8.9%; machinery and apparatus 12.6%; chemical products 8.3%; sawn wood, wood pulp, and paper products 6.4%; food

products 6.2%; base nonferrous metals 5.4%). *Major export destinations:* US 79.0%; UK 2.8%; China 2.1%; Japan 2.0%; Mexico 1.1%; Germany 0.9%; Norway 0.8%; France 0.7%.

## Transport and communications

**Transport.** *Railroads* (2007): length 72,212 km; passenger-km 1,444,656,000; metric ton-km cargo 357,444,000,000. *Roads* (2004): total length 1,408,900 km (paved 35%). *Vehicles* (2005): passenger cars 18,123,885; trucks and buses 785,649. *Air transport* (2007; Air Canada only): passenger-km 74,400,000,000; metric ton-km cargo 1,184,921,000. **Communications**, in total units (units per 1,000 persons). Telephone landlines (2006): 21,000,000 (645); cellular telephone subscribers (2008): 21,455,000 (644); personal computers (2007): 31,051,000 (943); total Internet users (2007): 28,000,000 (852); broadband Internet subscribers (2008): 9,633,000 (289).

## Education and health

**Literacy** (2005): total population ages 15 and over literate virtually 100%. **Health** (2005): physicians (2006) 62,307 (1 per 524 persons); hospital beds 110,113 (1 per 294 persons); infant mortality rate per 1,000 live births 5.4; undernourished population (2002–04) less than 2.5% of total population.

## Military

**Total active duty personnel** (November 2008): 64,371 (army 52.4%, navy 17.0%, air force 30.6%); Canadian troops in Afghanistan as part of the NATO International Security Assistance Force (April 2009): 2,830. **Military expenditure as percentage of GDP** (2007): 1.3%; per capita expenditure US$559.

## Background

Originally inhabited by American Indians and Inuit, Canada was visited about AD 1000 by Scandinavian explorers, whose discovery is confirmed by archaeological evidence from Newfoundland. Fishing expeditions off Newfoundland by the English, French, Spanish, and Portuguese began as early as 1500. The French claim to Canada was made in 1534 when Jacques Cartier entered the Gulf of St. Lawrence. A small settlement was made in Nova Scotia (Acadia) in 1605, and in 1608 Samuel de Champlain founded Quebec. Fur trading was the impetus behind the early colonizing efforts. In response to French activity, the English in 1670 formed the Hudson's Bay Company.

The British-French rivalry for the interior of upper North America lasted almost a century. The first French loss occurred in 1713 at the conclusion of Queen Anne's War (War of the Spanish Succession) when Nova Scotia and Newfoundland were ceded to the British. The Seven Years' War (French and Indian War) resulted in France's expulsion from continental North America in 1763. After the US War of Independence, the population was augmented by Loyalists fleeing the US, and the increasing number arriving in Quebec led the British to divide the colony into Upper and Lower Canada in 1791. The British reunited the two provinces in 1841. Canadian expansionism resulted in the confederation movement of the mid-19th century, and in 1867 the Dominion of Canada, comprising Nova Scotia, New Brunswick, Quebec, and Ontario, came into existence. After confederation, Canada entered a period of westward expansion.

The prosperity that accompanied Canada into the 20th century was marred by continuing conflict between the English and French communities. Through the Statute of Westminster (1931), Canada was recognized as an equal of Great Britain. With the Constitution Act of 1982, the British gave Canada total control over its constitution and severed the remaining legal connections between the two countries. French Canadian unrest continued to be a major concern, with a movement growing for Quebec separatism in the late 20th century. Referendums for more political autonomy for Quebec were rejected in 1992 and 1995, but the issue remained unresolved. In 1999 Canada formed the new territory of Nunavut, and in December 2001, Newfoundland was renamed Newfoundland and Labrador.

## Recent Developments

Canadians went to the polls in 2011 after the parties that collectively held a majority of the seats in the House of Commons—the centrist Liberal Party, the left-wing New Democratic Party (NDP), and the separatist Bloc Québécois—voted in March to find the minority Conservative government in contempt of Parliament for having failed to share information needed to assess proposed legislation. The historic motion marked the first time that the national government of a Commonwealth country had ever been found in contempt of Parliament. The May election resulted in a historic change in the country's political standing, with the Conservatives winning 166 of 308 constituencies and forming a majority government. The Liberals posted the worst result in party history and fell to third place for the first time since Confederation in 1867. The newly emboldened Conservative government reintroduced bills that had been held up by the minority Parliament and tabled new legislation to fulfill long-standing promises. Major initiatives included requiring more fiscal accountability among First Nations (Native American) chiefs and band councillors, abolishing the national long-gun registry, and passing an omnibus crime bill that included among other provisions mandatory minimum sentences for a range of sexual offenses and drug-related crimes. In December Canada announced that it was withdrawing from the Kyoto Protocol, the historic 1997 treaty that attempted to lower greenhouse gas emissions. Canada's accession to the treaty had occurred under a Liberal government, and its exit was expected by many experts under a Conservative one.

Finance Minister Jim Flaherty tabled a new budget in June. Key measures included an austerity plan as well as a pledge to reduce the country's deficit and return to a balanced budget by 2014–15, one fiscal year earlier than originally forecast. In a November budget update, the government once again pushed back the date to the 2015–16 fiscal year in response to a worsening economy. Canada's GDP declined for the first time since 2009 during the second quarter of 2011. Overall, however, it grew 2.6% in 2011. The country's oil sands production continued to be controversial. The industry, centered mainly in the western province of Alberta and thought to be capable of injecting as much as Can$3 trillion (Can$1 = about

US$1) into the economy over the next 25 years, came under attack from environmentalists both in Canada and abroad. In February 2012, the EU voted on a directive that would classify Canada's oil sands crude as more polluting than other oils, a move that Canada vowed to fight. The vote ended in a stalemate, however. In May the government moved to restrict the number of people who could appear before regulatory panels. Thousands had signed up to comment against the proposed Northern Gateway pipeline to ports on the Pacific, intended to facilitate the export of petroleum to the huge markets of Asia. The proposed Keystone pipeline, which would link the oil sands to Texas, was rejected by the US State Department in January over concerns that a portion running through Nebraska could contaminate a major aquifer along its route. In May a new route was submitted for US consideration.

**Internet resource:** <www.statcan.gc.ca>.

# Cape Verde

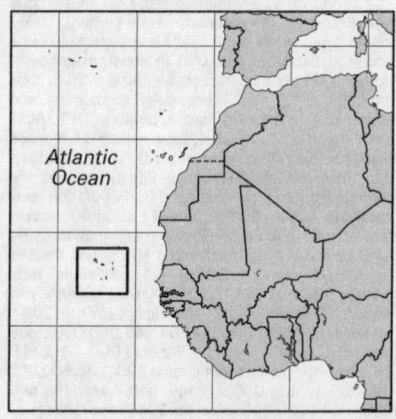

**Official name:** República de Cabo Verde (Republic of Cape Verde). **Form of government:** multiparty republic with one legislative house (National Assembly [72]). **Head of state:** President Jorge Carlos Fonseca (from 2011). **Head of government:** Prime Minister José Maria Neves (from 2001). **Capital:** Praia. **Official language:** Portuguese (Cape Verdean Creole [Crioulo] is the national language). **Official religion:** none. **Monetary unit:** 1 escudo (C.V.Esc.) = 100 centavos; valuation (2 Jul 2012) US$1 = C.V.Esc. 87.66.

## Demography

**Area:** 1,557 sq mi, 4,033 sq km. **Population** (2011): 498,000. **Density** (2011): persons per sq mi 319.8, persons per sq km 123.5. **Urban** (2010): 61.8%. **Sex distribution** (2008): male 47.70%; female 52.30%. **Age breakdown** (2005): under 15, 39.2%; 15–29, 30.2%; 30–44, 16.9%; 45–59, 7.9%; 60–74, 4.4%; 75–84, 1.2%; 85 and over, 0.2%. **Ethnic composition** (2000): Cape Verdean *mestico* (black-white admixture) 69.6%; Fulani 12.2%; Balanta 10.0%; Mandyako

---

*1 metric ton = about 1.1 short tons;    1 kilometer = 0.6 mi (statute);    1 metric ton-km cargo = about 0.68 short ton-mi cargo;    c.i.f.: cost, insurance, and freight;    f.o.b.: free on board*

4.6%; Portuguese white 2.0%; other 1.6%. **Religious affiliation** (2000): Christian 95.1%, of which Roman Catholic 88.1%, Protestant 3.3%, independent Christian 2.7%; Muslim 2.8%; other 2.1%. **Major urban localities** (2009): Praia 125,148; Mindelo 76,650; Santa Maria 18,780; Assomada 13,562; Pedra Badejo 11,348. **Location:** islands in the North Atlantic Ocean, off the coast of western Africa.

## Vital statistics

**Birth rate** per 1,000 population (2007): 25.1 (world avg. 20.3). **Death rate** per 1,000 population (2007): 5.3 (world avg. 8.5). **Total fertility rate** (avg. births per childbearing woman; 2007): 2.89. **Life expectancy** at birth (2007): male 68.3 years; female 73.6 years.

## National economy

**Budget** (2008). *Revenue:* C.V.Esc. 40,129,000,000 (tax revenue 73.7%, of which VAT 29.2%, taxes on income and profits 21.2%, taxes on international transactions 14.7%; grants 16.0%; nontax revenue 6.5%; other 3.8%). *Expenditures:* C.V.Esc. 41,304,000,000 (current expenditures 60.6%; capital expenditures 39.4%). **Public debt** (external, outstanding; December 2006): US$601,000,000. **Gross national income** (2008): US$1,561,000,000 (US$3,130 per capita). **Production** (metric tons except as noted). *Agriculture and fishing* (2007): sugarcane 15,400, corn (maize) 12,000, bananas 6,800; livestock (number of live animals) 217,000 pigs, 115,400 goats, 24,150 cattle; fisheries production 18,328 (from aquaculture, none). *Mining and quarrying* (2007): salt 1,600; pozzolana, n.a. *Manufacturing* (2003): cement 160,000; frozen fish 900; canned fish 200; other manufactured goods include clothing, footwear, and rum. *Energy production (consumption):* electricity (kW-hr; 2006) 252,000,000 (252,000,000); petroleum products (metric tons; 2006) none (100,000). **Population economically active** (2006): total 189,000; activity rate of total population 36.4% (participation rates: ages 15–64, 63%; female 40%; unemployed 18.3%, underemployed 26%). **Selected balance of payments data.** Receipts from (US$'000,000): tourism (2007) 346; remittances (2008) 138; foreign direct investment (2005–07 avg.) 130; official development assistance (2007) 163. Disbursements for (US$'000,000): tourism (2007) 107; remittances (2008) 6.0.

## Foreign trade

**Imports** (2007; c.i.f.): US$737,000,000 (food and agricultural products 20.5%; machinery and apparatus 15.2%; refined petroleum products 9.3%; motor vehicles 8.0%; aircraft and parts 7.2%; chemical products 5.7%). *Major import sources:* Portugal 40.0%; Netherlands 11.5%; France 9.6%; Brazil 6.2%; Spain 4.6%. **Exports** (2007; f.o.b.): US$114,-800,000 (refined petroleum products 49.8%; transport containers 15.8%; fresh fish 8.3%; wearing apparel 5.7%; footwear 4.0%). *Major export destinations:* Côte d'Ivoire 30.7%; Portugal 21.6%; Netherlands 15.2%; Spain 9.1%; France 4.1%.

## Transport and communications

**Transport.** *Railroads:* none. *Roads* (2007): total length 2,250 km (paved [mostly with cobblestones] 78%). *Vehicles* (2003): passenger cars 23,811; trucks and buses 5,032. *Air transport* (2004): passenger-km

725,000,000. **Communications,** in total units (units per 1,000 persons). Telephone landlines (2008): 72,000 (144); cellular telephone subscribers (2008): 278,000 (556); personal computers (2004): 48,000 (102); total Internet users (2008): 103,000 (206); broadband Internet subscribers (2008): 7,400 (15).

## Education and health

**Educational attainment** (1990). Percentage of population ages 25 and over having: no formal schooling/unknown 52.3%; primary 40.9%; incomplete secondary 3.9%; complete secondary 1.4%; higher 1.5%. **Literacy** (2007): total population ages 15 and over literate 79.4%; males literate 87.5%; females literate 72.6%. **Health** (2007): physicians 230 (1 per 2,137 persons); hospital beds 1,016 (1 per 484 persons); infant mortality rate per 1,000 live births 21.7.

## Military

**Total active duty personnel** (November 2008): 1,200 (army 83.3%, air force 8.3%, coast guard 8.4%). **Military expenditure as percentage of GDP** (2007): 0.6%; per capita expenditure US$16.

## Background

When visited by the Portuguese in 1456–60, the islands were uninhabited. In 1460 Diogo Gomes sighted and named Maio and São Tiago, and in 1462 the first settlers landed on São Tiago, founding the city of Ribeira Grande. The city's importance grew with the development of the slave trade, but its wealth attracted pirates so often that it was abandoned after 1712. The prosperity of the Portuguese-controlled islands vanished with the decline of the slave trade in the 19th century but later improved because of their position on the great trade routes between Europe, South America, and southern Africa. In 1951 the colony became an overseas province of Portugal. Many islanders preferred independence, and it was granted in 1975. At one time associated politically with Guinea-Bissau, Cape Verde split from it in the wake of a 1980 coup there.

## Recent Developments

Cape Verde's democratic credentials were enhanced by two elections and a leadership award in 2011. In the February parliamentary election, the African Party for the Independence of Cape Verde gained a majority in the National Assembly. Having reached his term limit, Pedro Pires was not able to stand in the presidential election, which Jorge Carlos Fonseca won in a runoff election. In October Pires was the recipient of the Mo Ibrahim Prize for Achievement in African Leadership, which included a US$5 million award.

**Internet resource:** <www.governo.cv>.

# Central African Republic

**Official name:** République Centrafricaine (Central African Republic). **Form of government:** multiparty republic with one legislative house (National Assembly [105]). **Head of state:** President François Bozizé (from 2003). **Head of government:** Prime Minister Faustin Archange Touadéra (from 2008). **Capital:** Bangui. **Official languages:** French; Sango. **Official**

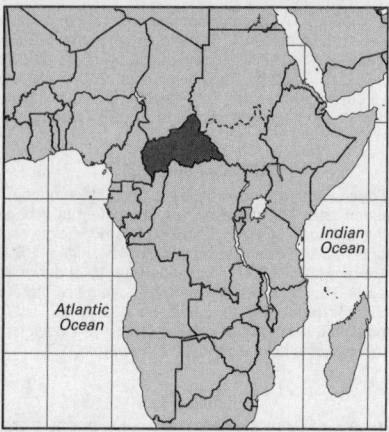

Indian
Ocean

Atlantic
Ocean

**religion:** none. **Monetary unit:** 1 CFA franc (CFAF) = 100 centimes; valuation (2 Jul 2012) US$1 = CFAF 521.26

## Demography

**Area:** 240,324 sq mi, 622,436 sq km. **Population** (2011): 4,950,000. **Density** (2011): persons per sq mi 20.6, persons per sq km 8.0. **Urban** (2009): 38.7%. **Sex distribution** (2007): male 49.44%; female 50.56%. **Age breakdown** (2007): under 15, 41.6%; 15–29, 29.6%; 30–44, 15.1%; 45–59, 7.7%; 60–74, 4.6%; 75–84, 1.2%; 85 and over, 0.2%. **Ethnolinguistic composition** (2004): Gbaya (Baya) 33%; Banda 27%; Mandjia 13%; Sara 10%; Mbum 7%; Ngbaka 4%; other 6%. **Religious affiliation** (2005): Protestant/independent Christian 51%; Roman Catholic 29%; traditional beliefs 10%; Muslim 10%. **Major urban localities** (2003): Bangui 622,771; Bimbo 124,176; Berbérati 76,918; Carnot 45,421; Bambari 41,356. **Location:** central Africa, bordering Chad, Sudan, South Sudan, the Democratic Republic of the Congo, the Republic of the Congo, and Cameroon.

## Vital statistics

**Birth rate** per 1,000 population (2007): 33.5 (world avg. 20.3). **Death rate** per 1,000 population (2007): 18.3 (world avg. 8.5). **Total fertility rate** (avg. births per childbearing woman; 2007): 4.32. **Life expectancy** at birth (2007): male 43.9 years; female 44.1 years.

## National economy

**Budget** (2006). *Revenue:* CFAF 176,300,000,000 (grants 58.4%; tax revenue 34.3%, of which taxes on goods and services 24.3%; nontax revenue 7.3%). *Expenditures:* CFAF 107,200,000,000 (current expenditures 58.3%; development expenditures 41.7%). **Public debt** (external, outstanding; 2007): US$836,-000,000. **Production** (metric tons except as noted). *Agriculture and fishing* (2007): cassava 565,000, yams 346,000, peanuts (groundnuts) 137,000, sesame seeds 40,000, seed cotton (2007–08)

3,355, coffee (2007–08) 1,931; livestock (number of live animals) 3,378,000 cattle, 3,087,000 goats, 805,000 pigs; fisheries production 15,000 (from aquaculture, negligible). *Mining and quarrying* (2007–08): diamonds 326,000 carats (official figure; a roughly equal amount was thought to have been smuggled out of the country). *Manufacturing* (2004): aluminum sheets 184,100; soap 1,800; cigarettes 16,000,000 packets; other manufactures include footwear, textiles, and bicycles. *Energy production (consumption):* electricity (kW-hr; 2007–08) 94,100,000 ([2005] 110,000,000); petroleum products (metric tons; 2006) none (81,000). **Population economically active** (2006): total 1,883,000; activity rate of total population 44.2% (participation rates: ages 15–64, 77.0%; female 45.7%). **Gross national income** (2008): US$1,804,-000,000 (US$410 per capita). **Selected balance of payments data.** Receipts from (US$'000,000): tourism (2005) 4.0; foreign direct investment (2005–07 avg.) 21; official development assistance (2007) 176. Disbursements for (US$'000,000): tourism (2004) 32.

## Foreign trade

**Imports** (2005; c.i.f.): CFAF 98,300,000,000 (refined petroleum products 16.7%; logs and sawn wood 14.8%; food products 13.6%, of which cereals 6.6%; machinery and apparatus 8.6%; motor vehicles 8.3%). *Major import sources* (2007): France 16.6%; Netherlands 13.0%; Cameroon 9.7%; US 6.3%. **Exports** (2007; f.o.b.): CFAF 85,300,000,000 (wood products 49.1%; diamonds 34.9%; coffee 4.9%; cotton 0.5%). *Major export destinations:* Belgium 22.7%; Indonesia 19.3%; Italy 7.7%; France 7.1%; Spain 6.9%.

## Transport and communications

**Transport.** *Railroads:* none. *Roads* (2005): total length (national roads only; much of the 15,600 km local road network is unusable) 10,000 km (paved 7%). *Vehicles* (2006): passenger cars 800; trucks and buses 700. *Air transport* (2003): passenger arrivals (Bangui airport only) 19,250, passenger departures (Bangui airport only) 19,107; metric ton-km cargo 7,000,000. **Communications,** in total units (units per 1,000 persons). Telephone landlines (2006): 12,000 (2.8); cellular telephone subscribers (2008): 154,000 (35); personal computers (2006): 13,000 (3.0); total Internet users (2008): 19,000 (4.3).

## Education and health

**Educational attainment** (1994–95). Percentage of population ages 25 and over having: no formal schooling/unknown 55.1%; at least some primary education 30.5%; at least some secondary education 14.4%. **Literacy** (2007): total population ages 15 and over literate 56.6%; males literate 67.6%; females literate 46.4%. **Health:** physicians (2004) 331 (1 per 11,867 persons); hospital beds (2006) 5,118 (1 per 833 persons); infant mortality rate per 1,000 live births (2007) 83.7; undernourished population (2002–04) 1,700,000 (44% of total population based on the consumption of a minimum daily requirement of 1,800 calories).

---

*1 metric ton = about 1.1 short tons;   1 kilometer = 0.6 mi (statute);   1 metric ton-km cargo = about 0.68 short ton-mi cargo;   c.i.f.: cost, insurance, and freight;   f.o.b.: free on board*

## Military

Total active duty personnel (November 2008): 3,150 (army 63.5%, air force 4.8%, gendarmerie 31.7%). Military expenditure as percentage of GDP (2007): 1.1%; per capita expenditure US$4.

## Background

For several centuries before the arrival of Europeans, the territory was subjected to slave traders. The French explored and claimed central Africa and in 1889 established a post at Bangui. In 1898 they partitioned the colony among commercial concessionaires. United with Chad in 1906 to form the French colony of Ubangi-Shari, it later became part of French Equatorial Africa. It was separated from Chad in 1920 and became an overseas territory in 1946. Named an autonomous republic within the French Community in 1958, the country achieved independence in 1960. In 1966 the military overthrew a civilian government and installed Jean-Bédel Bokassa, who in 1976 declared himself Emperor Bokassa I and renamed the country the Central African Empire. The military again seized power in the 1980s. A new constitution was promulgated in 2004, and a democratically elected government was installed in 2005.

## Recent Developments

The UN continued in 2011 to express its concern at the kidnapping and recruitment of children in the Central African Republic to serve in various rebel armies, including the Lord's Resistance Army (LRA). It was reported that the LRA alone had abducted more than 3,000 people in Central Africa since September 2008. The economy showed some signs of improvement, however, as the agricultural, forestry, and diamond sectors grew. Overall growth was small because of global increases in the price of oil. Health care outside the capital was virtually unobtainable, and the level of poverty remained extremely high.

Internet resource: <www.stat-centrafrique.com>.

## Chad

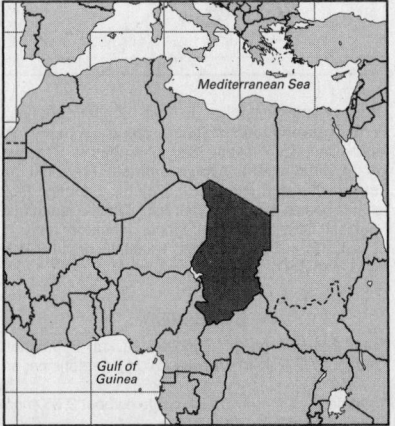

Mediterranean Sea

Gulf of Guinea

## Demography

**Official name:** Jumhuriyah Tshad (Arabic); République du Tchad (French) (Republic of Chad). **Form of government:** unitary republic with one legislative house (National Assembly [188]). **Head of state:** President Idriss Déby (from 1990). **Head of government:** Prime Minister Emmanuel Nadingar (from 2010). **Capital:** N'Djamena. **Official languages:** Arabic; French. **Official religion:** none. **Monetary unit:** 1 CFA franc (CFAF) = 100 centimes; valuation (2 Jul 2012) US$1 = CFAF 521.26.

## Demography

**Area:** 495,755 sq mi, 1,284,000 sq km. **Population** (2011): 12,018,000. **Density** (2011): persons per sq mi 24.2, persons per sq km 9.4. **Urban** (2009): 21.7%. **Sex distribution** (2007): male 47.92%; female 52.08%. **Age breakdown** (2007): under 15, 47.3%; 15–29, 26.4%; 30–44, 13.7%; 45–59, 8.0%; 60–74, 3.8%; 75–84, 0.7%; 85 and over, 0.1%. **Ethnolinguistic composition** (1993): Sara 27.7%; Sudanic Arab 12.3%; Mayo-Kebbi peoples 11.5%; Kanem-Bornu peoples 9.0%; Ouaddaï peoples 8.7%; Hadjeray (Hadjaraï) 6.7%; Tangale (Tandjilé) peoples 6.5%; Gorane peoples 6.3%; Fitri-Batha peoples 4.7%; Fulani (Peul) 2.4%; other 4.2%. **Religious affiliation** (2005): Muslim 57.0%; traditional beliefs 18.8%; Protestant 10.5%; other (significantly Roman Catholic and nonreligious) 13.7%. **Major cities** (2000): N'Djamena (urban agglomeration; 2007) 989,000; Moundou 108,728; Sarh 95,050; Abéché 63,165; Kelo 36,643. **Location:** central Africa, bordered by Libya, Sudan, the Central African Republic, Cameroon, Nigeria, and Niger.

## Vital statistics

**Birth rate** per 1,000 population (2007): 42.4 (world avg. 20.3). **Death rate** per 1,000 population (2007): 16.7 (world avg. 8.6). **Total fertility rate** (avg. births per childbearing woman; 2007): 5.56. **Life expectancy** at birth (2007): male 46.2 years; female 48.3 years.

## National economy

**Budget** (2007). *Revenue:* CFAF 764,900,000,000 (petroleum revenue 73.6%, of which taxes on profits 55.7%, royalties and dividends 17.3%; nonpetroleum tax revenue 24.7%; other 1.7%). *Expenditures:* CFAF 709,300,000,000 (current expenditures 65.4%; development expenditures 34.6%). **Public debt** (external, outstanding; December 2008): US$1,581,000,000. **Production** (metric tons except as noted). *Agriculture and fishing* (2007): rice 1,290,000, sorghum 700,000, millet 550,000, sesame seed 35,300, gum arabic (2006) 25,000; livestock (number of live animals) 6,820,300 cattle, 6,096,390 goats, 2,981,800 sheep, 749,500 camels; fisheries production 70,000 (from aquaculture, none). *Mining and quarrying* (2007): aggregate (gravel) 300,000; natron 12,000; gold 150 kg. *Manufacturing* (2004–05): cotton fiber 88,158; refined sugar 51,823; woven cotton fabrics (2000) 1,000,000 meters. *Energy production (consumption):* electricity (kW-hr; 2006) 95,000,000 (88,300,000); crude petroleum (barrels; 2008) 46,500,000 (n.a.); petroleum products (metric tons; 2006) none (65,000). **Selected balance of payments data.** Receipts from (US$'000,000): tourism (2005) 14; foreign direct investment (2005–07 avg.) 639; official development assistance (2007) 352. Disbursements for (US$'000,000): tourism (2002) 80. **Population economically active** (2006): total 4,179,000; activity rate of total population 39.9% (participation rates: ages 15–64, 74.7%; female 48.8%). **Gross national income** (2008): US$5,916,000,000 (US$530 per capita).

## Foreign trade

**Imports** (2007): CFAF 719,600,000,000 (petroleum sector 39.7%; nonpetroleum private sector 32.9%; public sector 12.0%). *Major import sources:* France 20.4%; Cameroon 16.1%; US 10.9%; China 10.0%; Germany 7.5%. **Exports** (2007): CFAF 1,755,300,-000,000 (crude petroleum 87.0%; live cattle 6.9%; cotton 2.5%; gum arabic 0.9%). *Major export destinations:* US 89.5%; Japan 3.7%; China 3.4%.

## Transport and communications

**Transport.** *Railroads:* none. *Roads* (2006): total length 40,000 km (paved 2%). *Vehicles* (2006): passenger cars 18,867; trucks and buses 28,152. *Air transport* (2001): passenger-km 130,000,000; metric ton-km cargo (2004) 7,000,000. **Communications,** in total units (units per 1,000 persons). Telephone landlines (2006): 13,000 (1.3); cellular telephone subscribers (2008): 1,809,000 (179); personal computers (2006): 19,000 (2.0); total Internet users (2008): 130,000 (13).

## Education and health

**Educational attainment** (2003). Percentage of population ages 25 and over having: no formal schooling 74.5%; primary education 17.4%; secondary education 6.8%; higher education 1.3%. **Literacy** (2007): percentage of total population ages 15 and over literate 53.7%; males literate 61.5%; females literate 46.3%. **Health:** physicians (2004) 345 (1 per 26,370 persons); hospital beds (2005) 3,760 (1 per 2,500 persons); infant mortality rate per 1,000 live births (2007) 102.1; undernourished population (2002–04) 3,000,000 (35% of total population based on the consumption of a minimum daily requirement of 1,810 calories).

## Military

**Total active duty personnel** (November 2008): 25,350 (army 78.9%, air force 1.4%, other 19.7%). **Military expenditure as percentage of GDP** (2007): 1.1%; per capita expenditure US$7.

## Background

About 800 AD the kingdom of Kanem was founded in north-central Africa, and by the early 1200s its borders had expanded to form a new kingdom, Kanem-Bornu, in the northern regions of the area. Its power peaked in the 16th century with its command of the southern terminus of the trans-Sahara trade route to Tripoli. Around this time the rival kingdoms of Baguirmi and Wadai evolved in the south. In the years 1883–93 all three kingdoms fell to the Sudanese adventurer Rabih al-Zubayr, who was in turn pushed out by the French in 1900. Extending their power, the French in 1910 made Chad a part of French Equato-

rial Africa. Chad became a separate colony in 1920 and was made an overseas territory in 1946. The country achieved independence in 1960. This was followed by decades of civil war and frequent intervention by France and Libya, resulting in political instability and a lack of economic development.

## Recent Developments

In February 2011, Chad held parliamentary elections, the first since 2002. Pres. Idriss Déby's Patriotic Salvation Movement won 113 of the 188 seats, but the opposition claimed that there had been widespread fraud. The presidential election was held in April. Déby stood for a fifth term, but the country's main opposition leaders boycotted the election; only two candidates from small parties challenged Déby. After he won nearly 89% of the vote, he was sworn in for another five-year term. Sudanese Pres. Omar al-Bashir attended Déby's inauguration, despite a warrant for his arrest having been issued by the International Criminal Court. Déby continued his rapprochement with Sudan, signing an agreement with that country and the Central African Republic in May.

**Internet resource:** <www.tchad.org/enhome.html>.

# Chile

**Official name:** República de Chile (Republic of Chile). **Form of government:** multiparty republic with two legislative houses (Senate [38]; Chamber of Deputies [120]). **Head of state and government:** President Sebastián Piñera (from 2010). **Capital:** Santiago (legislative bodies meet in Valparaíso). **Official language:** Spanish. **Official religion:** none. **Monetary unit:** 1 peso (Ch$) = 100 centavos; valuation (2 Jul 2012) US$1 = Ch$500.50.

## Demography

**Area:** 291,930 sq mi, 756,096 sq km. **Population** (2011): 17,270,000. **Density** (2011): persons per sq

mi 59.2, persons per sq km 22.8. **Urban** (2009): 86.9%. **Sex distribution** (2008): male 49.46%; female 50.54%. **Age breakdown** (2005): under 15, 24.9%; 15–29, 24.3%; 30–44, 23.0%; 45–59, 16.2%; 60–74, 8.3%; 75–84, 2.5%; 85 and over, 0.8%. **Ethnic composition** (2002): mestizo 72%; white 22%; Amerindian 5%, of which Araucanian (Mapuche) 4%; other 1%. **Religious affiliation** (2002): Roman Catholic 70.0%; Protestant/independent Christian 15.1%; atheist/nonreligious 8.3%; other 6.6%. **Major cities (urban agglomerations)** (2002): Santiago 4,656,690 (5,428,590); Valparaíso 263,499 (803,683); Concepción 212,003 (666,381); La Serena 147,815 (296,253); Antofagasta 285,255. **Location:** southern South America, bordering Peru, Bolivia, Argentina, the South Atlantic Ocean, and the South Pacific Ocean.

## Vital statistics

**Birth rate** per 1,000 population (2006): 14.8 (world avg. 20.3). **Death rate** per 1,000 population (2006): 5.2 (world avg. 8.5). **Total fertility rate** (avg. births per childbearing woman; 2006): 2.00. **Life expectancy** at birth (2006): male 74.8 years; female 80.8 years.

## National economy

**Budget** (2007). *Revenue:* Ch$23,534,000,-000,000 (tax revenue 78.1%; nontax revenue 17.0%; other 4.9%). *Expenditures:* Ch$15,996,-000,000,000 (social protection 28.8%; education 17.2%; health 15.9%; transportation 8.8%; defense 6.5%). **Public debt** (external, outstanding; 2007): US$9,975,000,000. **Population economically active** (2007): total 7,078,000; activity rate of total population 42.5% (participation rates: ages 15–64, 61.7%; female 36.8%; unemployed [November 2007–October 2008] 7.7%). **Production** (metric tons except as noted). *Agriculture and fishing* (2007): grapes 2,350,000, sugar beets 1,806,600, corn (maize) 1,557,100, kiwi fruit 170,000, avocados 167,000; livestock (number of live animals) 4,350,000 cattle, 3,480,000 pigs, 3,420,000 sheep; fisheries production (2006) 4,635,927 (from aquaculture 18%); aquatic plants production 359,770 (from aquaculture 6%). *Mining* (2007): copper (metal content) 5,557,000; iron ore (metal content) 4,195,000; lithium carbonate (2006) 50,035; molybdenum (metal content) 44,900; iodine 15,500; silver 1,936,000 kg; gold 41,500 kg. *Manufacturing* (value added in US$'000,000; 2005): nonferrous base metals 20,677; refined petroleum products 6,245; food products 5,239. *Energy production (consumption):* electricity (kW-hr; 2007) 57,576,000,000 ([2006] 59,840,000,000); coal (metric tons; 2007) 288,000 ([2006] 5,402,000); crude petroleum (barrels; 2008) 963,000 ([2006] 80,800,000); petroleum products (metric tons; 2006) 10,701,000 (9,630,000); natural gas (cu m; 2007) 2,015,000,000 (4,191,000,000). **Gross national income** (2008): US$157,460,000,000 (US$9,400 per capita). **Selected balance of payments data.** Receipts from (US$'000,000): tourism (2007) 1,419; remittances (2008) 3; foreign direct investment (FDI; 2005–07 avg.) 9,600; official development assistance (2007) 120. Disbursements for (US$'000,000): tourism (2007) 1,762; remittances (2008) 6; FDI (2005–07 avg.) 2,963.

## Foreign trade

**Imports** (2007; c.i.f.): US$42,732,000,000 (crude petroleum 22.7%; machinery and apparatus 21.4%; chemical products 11.1%; motor vehicles 9.9%; food products 6.5%). *Major import sources:* US 17.0%; China 11.4%; Brazil 10.5%; Argentina 10.1%; South Korea 7.2%. **Exports** (2007; f.o.b.): US$65,-739,000,000 (refined copper 36.4%; copper ore 20.5%; food products 12.5%, of which fruits 4.0%, fish 3.8%; other base metal ores 5.4%). *Major export destinations:* China 15.2%; US 12.8%; Japan 10.8%; Netherlands 5.9%; South Korea 5.9%.

## Transport and communications

**Transport.** *Railroads* (2006): route length 5,034 km; passenger-km 843,131,000; metric ton-km cargo 3,660,000,000. *Roads* (2003): total length 80,505 km (paved 22%). *Vehicles* (2006): passenger cars 1,514,220; trucks and buses 735,901. *Air transport* (2007): passenger-km 16,056,000,000; metric ton-km cargo 1,294,968,000. **Communications,** in total units (units per 1,000 persons). Telephone landlines (2008): 3,526,000 (214); cellular telephone subscribers (2008): 14,797,000 (899); personal computers (2006): 2,277,000 (141); total Internet users (2008): 5,456,000 (332); broadband Internet subscribers (2008): 1,426,000 (87).

## Education and health

**Educational attainment** (2002). Percentage of population ages 25 and over having: no formal schooling/other 5.4%; incomplete primary education 24.6%; complete primary 8.7%; secondary 43.9%; higher technical 4.9%; university 12.5%. **Literacy** (2006): total population ages 15 and over literate 96.4%. **Health** (2006): physicians 21,100 (1 per 765 persons); hospital beds 37,374 (1 per 432 persons); infant mortality rate per 1,000 live births 7.6; undernourished population (2002–04) 600,000 (4% of total population based on the consumption of a minimum daily requirement of 1,920 calories).

## Military

**Total active duty personnel** (November 2008): 60,560 (army 57.8%, navy 29.4%, air force 12.8%). **Military expenditure as percentage of GDP** (2008): 3.0%; per capita expenditure US$286.

## Background

Originally inhabited by native peoples, including the Mapuche, the Chilean coast was invaded by the Spanish in 1536. A settlement begun at Santiago in 1541 was governed under the Viceroyalty of Peru but became a separate captaincy general in 1778. It revolted against Spanish rule in 1810; its independence was finally assured by the victory of José de San Martín in 1818, and the area was then governed by Bernardo O'Higgins to 1823. In the War of the Pacific against Peru and Bolivia, it won the rich nitrate fields on the coast of Bolivia, effectively forcing that country into a landlocked position. Chile remained neutral in World War I and World War II but severed diplomatic ties with the Axis powers in 1943. In 1970 Salvador Allende was elected president, becoming the first avowed Marxist to be elected chief of state in Latin America. Following economic upheaval, he was ousted in 1973 in a coup led by Gen. Augusto Pinochet, whose military junta for many years harshly suppressed all internal opposition. A national referendum in 1988 rejected Pinochet, and elections held in 1989 returned the country to civilian rule. Chile's economy maintained steady growth through most of the 1990s and in the early 21st century remained one of the strongest in Latin America. In August 2010, 33 miners were trapped 700 m (2,300 ft) below ground in an accident at the San José gold and copper mine in the northern desert. An all-out rescue effort was launched that kept the country and indeed much of the world riveted. On 13 October, to great international jubilation, all 33 miners were safely extracted from the mine.

## Recent Developments

Chile's export-oriented economy maintained a positive balance of trade in 2011 despite the global downturn, facilitated by the government's successful pursuit of free-trade agreements with countries around the globe. Trade continued to increase with China, which remained the largest consumer of Chilean exports; prior to 2007 the US had been the prime destination for Chilean exports. Although Chile had signed free-trade agreements with both countries, China's appetite for Chilean copper was a major factor in that historic shift. Despite Chile's efforts to diversify its exports, however, copper still accounted for about half the country's exports, and its declining price on the international market in 2011 prompted Chile's minister of the economy to predict that the country's economic growth would slow significantly. Although Chile's domestic salmon-farming industry (the second largest in the world) appeared to have recuperated from a 2007 outbreak of infectious salmon anemia, there was a growing consensus that salmon farming might not be sustainable.

Internet resource: <www.ine.cl/?lang=eng>.

# China

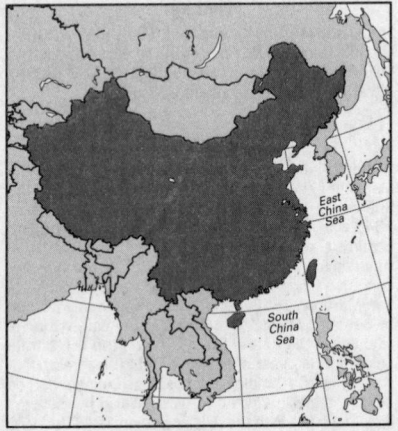

**Official name:** Zhonghua Renmin Gongheguo (People's Republic of China). **Form of government:** single-party people's republic with one legislative house (National People's Congress [3,000]). **Head of state:** President Hu Jintao (from 2003). **Head of government:** Premier Wen Jiabao (from 2003). **Capital:** Beijing (Peking). **Official language:** Mandarin Chinese. **Official religion:** none. **Monetary unit:** 1 renminbi (yuan) (Y) = 10 jiao = 100 fen; valuation (2 Jul 2012) US$1 = Y 6.35.

## Demography

**Area:** 3,696,100 sq mi, 9,572,900 sq km. **Population** (2011): 1,342,274,000. **Density** (2011): persons per sq mi 363.2, persons per sq km 140.2. **Urban** (2010): 46.6%. **Sex distribution** (2008): male 51.47%; female 48.53%. **Age breakdown** (2007): under 15, 17.9%; 15–29, 21.4%; 30–44, 26.8%; 45–59, 20.3%; 60–74, 10.4%; 75–84, 2.7%; 85 and over, 0.5%. **Ethnic composition** (2005): Han (Chinese) 90.95%; Chuang 1.37%; Manchu 0.82%; Yi 0.79%; Hui 0.77%; Miao 0.75%; Uighur 0.74%; Tuchia 0.65%; Tibetan 0.57%; Mongolian 0.49%; Tung 0.28%; Puyi 0.26%; Yao 0.24%; Korean 0.14%; Pai 0.14%; Hani 0.12%; Li 0.11%; Kazakh 0.09%; Tai 0.08%; other 0.64%. **Religious affiliation** (2005): nonreligious 39.2%; Chinese folk-religionist 28.7%; Christian 10.0%, of which unregistered Protestant 7.7%, registered Protestant 1.2%, unregistered Roman Catholic 0.5%, registered Roman Catholic 0.4%; Buddhist 8.4%; atheist 7.8%; traditional beliefs 4.4%; Muslim 1.5%. **Major urban agglomerations** (2007): Shanghai 14,987,000; Beijing 11,106,000; Guangzhou 8,829,000; Shenzhen 7,581,000; Wuhan 7,243,000; Tianjin 7,180,000; Chongqing 6,461,000; Shenyang 4,787,000; Dongguan 4,528,000; Chengdu 4,123,000; Xi'an 4,009,000; Nanjing 3,679,000; Guiyang 3,662,000; Harbin 3,621,000; Changchun 3,183,000; Dalian 3,167,000; Zibo 3,061,000; Hangzhou 3,007,000; Kunming 2,931,000; Taiyuan 2,913,000; Qingdao 2,866,000; Jinan 2,798,000; Zhengzhou 2,636,000; Fuzhou 2,606,000; Changsha 2,604,000; Lanzhou 2,561,000; Xiamen 2,519,000; Jinxi 2,426,000. **Location:** eastern Asia, bordering Mongolia, Russia, North Korea, the Yellow Sea, the East China Sea, the South China Sea, Vietnam, Laos, Myanmar (Burma), India, Bhutan, Nepal, Pakistan, Afghanistan, Tajikistan, Kyrgyzstan, and Kazakhstan. **Mobility** (2007). Population residing in registered enumeration area 90.4%; population not residing in registered enumeration area 9.6%.

## Vital statistics

**Birth rate** per 1,000 population (2008): 12.1 (world avg. 20.3). **Death rate** per 1,000 population (2008): 7.1 (world avg. 8.5). **Total fertility rate** (avg. births per childbearing woman; 2007): 1.77. **Life expectancy** at birth (2007): male 71.3 years; female 74.8 years.

## Social indicators

**Educational attainment** (2007). Percentage of population ages 6 and over having: no formal schooling 8.0%; incomplete/complete primary education 31.8%; some secondary 40.2%; complete secondary 13.4%; some postsecondary through advanced degree 6.6%. **Quality of working life.** Average workweek

---

*1 metric ton = about 1.1 short tons;    1 kilometer = 0.6 mi (statute);    1 metric ton-km cargo = about 0.68 short ton-mi cargo;    c.i.f.: cost, insurance, and freight;    f.o.b.: free on board*

(November 2007): 45.5 hours. Annual rate per 100,000 workers for (2008): death in mining, industrial, or commercial enterprises 2.82. Death toll from work accidents (2008) 91,172. **Access to services.** Percentage of population having access to electricity (2005) 99.4%. Percentage of total (urban, rural) population with safe public water supply (2002) 83.6% (94.0%, 73.0%). Sewage system (1999): total (urban, rural) households with flush apparatus 20.7% (50.0%, 4.3%), with pit latrines 69.3% (33.6%, 86.7%), with no latrine 5.3% (7.8%, 4.1%). **Social participation.** Trade union membership in total labor force (2006): 169,942,200 (22%). Percentage of population who consider themselves religious (2005–06) 31.4%. **Social deviance.** Annual reported arrest rate per 100,000 population (2007) for: thievery 248.0; robbery 22.2; fraud 16.6; injury 12.3; rape 2.4; homicide 1.2. **Material well-being.** Urban households possessing (number per household; 2004): bicycles 1.4; color televisions (2007) 1.4; washing machines 1.0; refrigerators 0.9; air conditioners 0.7; cameras 0.5; computers (2007) 0.5. Rural families possessing (number per household; 2004): bicycles 1.2; color televisions (2007) 0.9; washing machines 0.4; refrigerators 0.2; air conditioners 0.05; cameras 0.04; computers (2007) 0.04.

## National economy

**Gross national income** (2008): US$3,678,488,-000,000 (US$2,770 per capita). **Budget** (2007). *Revenue:* Y 5,132,178,000,000 (tax revenue 88.9%, of which VAT 30.1%, corporate taxes 17.1%, business tax 12.8%, income tax 6.2%; nontax revenue 11.1%). *Expenditures:* Y 4,978,135,000,000 (general administration 17.1%; education 14.3%; social security 10.9%; manufacturing, trade, and finance 8.6%; defense 7.1%; public security/police 7.0%; agriculture and forestry 6.8%; health 4.0%). **Public debt** (external, outstanding; 2007): US$87,653,000,000. **Production** (metric tons except as noted). *Agriculture and fishing* (2007): grains—rice 185,490,000, corn (maize) 151,830,000, wheat 109,860,000; oilseeds—soybeans 15,600,000, peanuts (groundnuts) 13,016,000, rapeseed 10,375,000, sunflower seeds 1,800,000; fruits and nuts—apples 27,500,000, cantaloupes 13,650,000, pears 12,500,000, bananas 7,100,000; other—sugarcane 105,651,000, sweet potatoes 102,000,000, potatoes 72,000,000, cabbage 36,000,000, tomatoes 33,500,000, seed cotton 22,872,000, eggplants 18,000,000, chilies and peppers 14,000,000, garlic 12,000,000, spinach 12,000,000, asparagus 6,250,000, tobacco leaves 2,395,000, tea 1,186,500, silkworm cocoons (2003) 667,000; livestock (number of live animals) 501,475,621 pigs, 197,267,883 goats, 171,961,000 sheep, 116,859,793 cattle, 22,717,000 water buffalo, 4,509,633,000 chickens, 736,912,000 ducks; fisheries production 46,079,311 (from aquaculture 68%); aquatic plants production 10,081,245 (from aquaculture 97%). *Mining and quarrying* (2005; by world rank): metal content of mine output—iron ore 138,000,000 (3), zinc 2,450,000 (1), manganese 1,100,000 (5), lead 1,000,000 (1), copper 740,000 (7), antimony 120,000 (1), tin 110,000 (1), tungsten 61,000 (1), silver 2,500 (3), gold 225 (2); metal ores—bauxite 18,000,000 (3), vanadium 17,000 (1); nonmetals—salt 44,547,000 (2), phosphate rock 9,130,000 (2), magnesite 4,700,000 (1), barite 4,200,000 (1), talc 3,000,000 (1), fluorspar 2,700,000 (1), asbestos 520,000 (2), strontium

140,000 (2). *Energy production (consumption):* electricity (kW-hr; 2008) 3,392,304,000,000 (3,450,200,-000,000); coal (metric tons; 2007) 2,430,000,000 ([2008] 2,740,000,000 [including lignite]); lignite (metric tons; 2007) 120,000 (n.a.); crude petroleum (barrels; 2008) 1,450,000,000 (2,635,000,000); petroleum products (metric tons; 2006) 238,365,000 (256,345,000); natural gas (cu m; 2008) 80,-314,000,000 (80,700,000,000). **Population economically active** (2006): total 792,324,000; activity rate of total population 59.6% (participation rates: ages 15–64, 81.2%; female 45.8%; registered unemployed in urban areas [2008] 4.0%; urban unemployed including migrants [2008] up to 9.0%; rural unemployment is substantial). **Selected balance of payments data.** Receipts from (US$'000,000): tourism (2007) 37,233; remittances (2008) 40,641; foreign direct investment (FDI; 2005–07 avg.) 76,214; official development assistance (2007) 1,439. Disbursements for (US$'000,000): tourism (2007) 29,786; remittances (2008) 5,737; FDI (2005–07 avg.) 18,630.

## Foreign trade

**Imports** (2007; c.i.f.): US$955,956,000,000 (machinery and apparatus 39.4%, of which electronic integrated circuits and micro-assemblies 13.4%, computers and office machines 4.8%, telecommunications equipment and parts 3.7%; chemical products 11.2%, of which organic chemicals 4.0%; mineral fuels 11.0%, of which crude petroleum 8.4%; metal ore and metal scrap 7.3%; optical instruments and apparatus 4.8%). *Major import sources:* Japan 14.0%; South Korea 10.9%; Taiwan 10.6%; China free trade zones 9.0%; US 7.3%; Germany 4.7%; Malaysia 3.0%; Australia 2.7%; Thailand 2.4%; Philippines 2.4%. **Exports** (2007; f.o.b.): US$1,217,776,000,000 (machinery and apparatus 43.0%, of which computers and office machines and parts 13.6%, electrical machinery and electronics 10.6%, telecommunications equipment and parts 8.4%; wearing apparel and accessories 9.5%; chemical products 4.9%; textile yarn, fabrics, and made-up articles 4.6%; iron and steel 4.2%). *Major export destinations:* US 19.1%; Hong Kong 15.1%; Japan 8.4%; South Korea 4.6%; Germany 4.0%; Netherlands 3.4%; UK 2.6%; Singapore 2.4%; Russia 2.3%; India 2.0%.

## Transport and communications

**Transport.** *Railroads* (2008): route length (2007) 78,000 km; passenger-km 777,860,000,000; metric ton-km cargo 2,511,180,000,000. *Roads* (2005): total length 1,930,544 km (paved 82%). *Vehicles* (2007): passenger cars 31,959,900; trucks 10,540,600. *Air transport* (2008): passenger-km 288,280,000,000; metric ton-km cargo 11,960,-000,000. **Communications,** in total units (units per 1,000 persons). Telephone landlines (2008): 340,810,000 (256); cellular telephone subscribers (2008): 641,230,000 (482); personal computers (2007): 75,118,000 (57); total Internet users (2008): 298,000,000 (225); broadband Internet subscribers (2008): 83,366,000 (63).

## Education and health

**Literacy** (2007): total population ages 15 and over literate 91.6%; males literate 95.7%; females literate 87.6%. **Health** (2008): physicians 2,050,000 (1 per 650 persons); hospital beds 3,690,000 (1 per 361 persons); infant mortality rate per 1,000 live births

(2007) 22.9; undernourished population (2002–04) 150,000,000 (12% of total population based on the consumption of a minimum daily requirement of 1,930 calories).

## Military

**Total active duty personnel** (November 2008): 2,185,000 (army 73.2%, navy 11.7%, air force 15.1%). **Military expenditure as percentage of GDP** (2007): 3.0%; per capita expenditure US$97.

## Background

The discovery of Peking man (*Homo erectus*) in 1927 dated the advent of early humans in what is now China to the Middle Pleistocene, about 900,000 to 130,000 years ago. Chinese civilization probably spread from the Huang He (Yellow River) valley, where it existed about 3000 BC. The first dynasty for which there is definite historical material is the Shang (c. 16th century BC), which had a writing system and a calendar. The Zhou overthrew its Shang rulers in the 11th century BC and ruled until the 3rd century BC. Daoism and Confucianism were founded in this era.

A time of conflict, called the Warring States period, lasted from the 5th century BC until 221 BC, when the Qin (Ch'in) dynasty (from whose name China is derived) was established after its rulers had conquered rival states and created a unified empire. The Han dynasty was established in 206 BC and ruled until AD 220. A time of turbulence followed, and Chinese reunification was not achieved until the Sui dynasty was established in 581.

After the founding of the Song dynasty in 960, the capital was moved to the south because of northern invasions. In 1279 this dynasty was overthrown and Mongol (Yuan) domination began. During this time Marco Polo visited Kublai Khan. The Ming dynasty followed the period of Mongol rule and lasted from 1368 to 1644, cultivating antiforeign feelings to the point that China closed itself off from the rest of the world. Peoples from Manchuria overran China in 1644 and established the Qing (Manchu) dynasty. Ever-increasing incursions by Western and Japanese interests led in the 19th century to the Opium Wars, the Taiping Rebellion, and the Sino-Japanese War, all of which weakened the Manchus.

The dynasty fell in 1911, and a republic was proclaimed in 1912 by Sun Yat-sen. The power struggles of warlords weakened the republic. Under Sun's successor, Chiang Kai-shek, some national unification was achieved in the 1920s, but Chiang soon broke with the Communists, who had formed their own armies. Japan invaded northern China in 1937; its occupation lasted until 1945. The Communists gained support after the Long March (1934–35), in which Mao Zedong emerged as their leader.

Upon Japan's surrender at the end of World War II, a fierce civil war began; in 1949 the Nationalists fled to the island of Taiwan and the Communists proclaimed the People's Republic of China. The Communists undertook extensive reforms, but pragmatic policies alternated with periods of revolutionary upheaval, most notably in the Great Leap Forward and the Cultural Revolution. The anarchy, terror, and economic paralysis of the latter led, after Mao's death in 1976, to a turn to moderation under Deng Xiaoping,

who undertook economic reforms and renewed China's ties to the West; the country established diplomatic ties with the US in 1979. The economy has been in transition since the late 1970s, moving from central planning and state-run industries to a mixture of state-owned and private enterprises in manufacturing and services, in the process growing dramatically and transforming Chinese society. Although China was challenged by the Tiananmen Square incident in 1989, its political environment after 1980 was generally stable and included orderly transitions of power to Deng's successors after his death in 1997. Also in 1997, Hong Kong reverted to Chinese rule, and Macau did the same in 1999. A powerful earthquake caused massive destruction and loss of life in Sichuan province in 2008, but later that year Beijing hosted the Summer Olympic Games.

## Recent Developments

In 2011, China consolidated its status as the world's second largest economy, managing significant continued economic growth despite a weak world economy. Its economy grew by 9.2% in 2011, though fourth-quarter growth was the lowest in the last 10 quarters. In November 2011, China set the poverty line for rural residents at nearly US$1 per day (an 80.0% increase), greatly expanding the number of people who qualified for government assistance. In October 2011, 21 provinces and municipalities raised the minimum wage 21.7%, and in January 2012, Sichuan province raised its by 23.4%. As a result, some factories in China continued their exodus to countries with lower manufacturing costs, such as Vietnam. In July 2011, in a case brought by the EU, Mexico, and the United States, the WTO found that the controls China put in 2010 on its export of rare-earth minerals, which are used in developing technologies such as computer and mobile-device components and hybrid and electric cars, violated WTO rules. Nonetheless, in late December China announced that it would again cut its rare-earth export quota, by roughly one quarter. In March 2012, the EU, Japan, and the United States filed another, related complaint with the WTO.

The South China Sea remained a point of contention between China and neighbors such as Vietnam and the Philippines, all of which had territorial claims there. In the summer of 2011, Vietnam complained that Chinese fishing vessels had interfered with oil-exploration activities, while the Philippines asserted that China was building structures on reefs claimed by the Philippines and harassing its oil-exploration activities. China's military demonstrated its ongoing modernization by conducting trial runs of its first aircraft carrier and pointedly testing its new J-20 stealth fighter just before US Secretary of Defense Robert M. Gates visited China in January. Relations with the US were further tested in October when the US Senate passed the Currency Exchange Rate Oversight Reform Act of 2011. Although the US House of Representatives declined to take up the bill because of concerns that it might unleash a trade war, the provisions of the act would allow the US government to impose tariffs on countries such as China that kept their currency value artificially low.

**Internet resource:** <www.stats.gov.cn/english>.

---

*1 metric ton = about 1.1 short tons;    1 kilometer = 0.6 mi (statute);    1 metric ton-km cargo = about 0.68 short ton-mi cargo;    c.i.f.: cost, insurance, and freight;    f.o.b.: free on board*

# Colombia

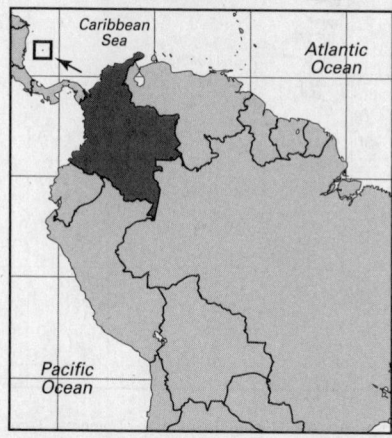

**Official name:** República de Colombia (Republic of Colombia). **Form of government:** unitary multiparty republic with two legislative houses (Senate [102]; House of Representatives [166]). **Head of state and government:** President Juan Manuel Santos Calderón (from 2010). **Capital:** Bogotá. **Official language:** Spanish. **Official religion:** none. **Monetary unit:** 1 peso (Col$) = 100 centavos; valuation (2 Jul 2012) US$1 = Col$1,778.75.

## Demography

**Area:** 440,831 sq mi, 1,141,748 sq km. **Population** (2011): 44,726,000. **Density** (2011): persons per sq mi 101.5, persons per sq km 39.2. **Urban** (2009): 74.8%. **Sex distribution** (2007): male 49.01%; female 50.99%. **Age breakdown** (2007): under 15, 29.8%; 15–29, 25.4%; 30–44, 22.3%; 45–59, 14.4%; 60–74, 6.2%; 75–84, 1.6%; 85 and over, 0.3%. **Ethnic composition** (2006): mestizo 58%; white 20%; mulatto 14%; black 4%; black-Amerindian 3%; Amerindian 1%. **Religious affiliation** (2007): Roman Catholic 80.0%; Protestant/independent Christian 13.5%; Mormon 0.3%; nonreligious 2.0%; other 4.2%. **Major cities** (2007): Bogotá 7,033,914; Medellín 2,248,912; Cali 2,139,535; Barranquilla 1,144,470; Cartagena 871,342. **Location:** northern South America, bordering the Caribbean Sea, Venezuela, Brazil, Peru, Ecuador, the Pacific Ocean, and Panama.

## Vital statistics

**Birth rate** per 1,000 population (2007): 20.2 (world avg. 20.3). **Death rate** per 1,000 population (2007): 5.5 (world avg. 8.5). **Total fertility rate** (avg. births per childbearing woman; 2007): 2.51. **Life expectancy** at birth (2007): male 68.4 years; female 76.2 years.

## National economy

**Budget** (2007). *Revenue:* Col$103,986,000,-000,000 (tax revenue 56.4%, of which taxes on goods and services 26.1%, income tax 16.7%; nontax revenue 39.3%; other 4.3%). *Expenditures:* Col$110,014,000,000,000 (interest on debt 25.1%;

other 74.9%). **Population economically active** (2006): total 20,177,100; activity rate 44.5% (participation rates: ages 12–55, 63.2%; female 43.0%; unemployed [April 2008–March 2009] 11.5%). **Production** (metric tons except as noted). *Agriculture and fishing* (2007): sugarcane 40,000,000, plantains 3,600,000, rice 2,250,000, coffee 710,000; Colombia is a leading producer of coca, with 430 metric tons of illegal cocaine production in 2008; livestock (number of live animals) 26,000,000 cattle, 3,400,000 sheep, 2,500,000 horses; fisheries production 156,100 (from aquaculture 38%). *Mining and quarrying* (2006): nickel (metal content) 94,100; gold 15,700 kg; emeralds 5,734,000 carats. *Manufacturing* (value added in US$'000,000; 2005): processed food products 3,471; refined petroleum products 2,873; medicines, fertilizers, and soaps 1,956. *Energy production (consumption):* electricity (kW-hr; 2006) 51,830,000,000 (52,963,000,000); coal (metric tons; 2007) 71,700,000 (4,480,000); crude petroleum (barrels; 2007) 214,400,000 ([2007] 105,500,000); petroleum products (metric tons; 2006) 13,247,000 (9,442,000); natural gas (cu m; 2006) 6,600,000,000 (9,298,000,000). **Gross national income** (2008): US$207,425,-000,000 (US$4,660 per capita). **Public debt** (external, outstanding; December 2008): US$24,855,-000,000. **Selected balance of payments data.** Receipts from (US$'000,000): tourism (2007) 1,669; remittances (2008) 4,884; foreign direct investment (FDI; 2005–07 avg.) 8,577; official development assistance (2007) 137. Disbursements for (US$'000,000): tourism (2007) 1,537; remittances (2008) 88; FDI (2005–07 avg.) 2,043.

## Foreign trade

**Imports** (2007; c.i.f.): US$32,897,000,000 (machinery and apparatus 26.5%; chemical products 18.5%; motor vehicles 12.0%; base and fabricated metals 9.8%). *Major import sources:* US 26.2%; China 10.1%; Mexico 9.3%; Brazil 7.3%; Venezuela 4.2%. **Exports** (2007; f.o.b.): US$29,991,000,000 (crude petroleum 18.5%; coal 11.1%; refined petroleum products 5.8%; coffee 5.7%; ferronickel 5.6%; wearing apparel and accessories 4.5%; motor vehicles and parts 3.9%; cut flowers 3.7%). *Major export destinations:* US 35.4%; Venezuela 17.4%; Ecuador 4.3%; Switzerland 3.0%; Netherlands 2.8%.

## Transport and communications

**Transport.** *Railroads* (2006): route length 2,030 km; passenger-km (2004) 25,000,000; metric ton-km cargo (2005) 8,236,000,000. *Roads* (2006): total length 164,278 km (paved [2000] 23%). *Vehicles* (2005): cars 1,606,880; trucks and buses 1,079,247. *Air transport* (2007): passenger-km 9,552,000,000; metric ton-km cargo 189,804,000. **Communications,** in total units (units per 1,000 persons). Telephone landlines (2008): 6,820,000 (153); cellular telephone subscribers (2008): 41,365,000 (931); personal computers (2007): 3,513,000 (80); total Internet users (2008): 17,117,000 (385); broadband Internet subscribers (2008): 1,903,000 (43).

## Education and health

**Educational attainment** (2005). Percentage of population ages 25 and over having: no formal schooling/unknown 10.2%; primary education 40.1%; secondary 34.2%; higher 15.5%. **Literacy** (2006): population ages 15 and over literate 92.3%; males literate 92.4%; females literate 92.2%. **Health:** physicians (2006) 51,095 (1 per 849 persons); hospital beds (2004) 50,824 (1 per 833 persons); infant mortality rate per 1,000 live births (2007) 20.1; undernourished population (2002–04) 5,900,000 (13% of total population based on the consumption of a minimum daily requirement of 1,830 calories).

## Military

**Total active duty personnel** (November 2008): 267,231 (army 84.7%, navy 11.5%, air force 3.8%). **Military expenditure as percentage of GDP** (2008): 4.7%; per capita expenditure US$186.

## Background

The Spanish arrived in what is now Colombia c. 1500 and by 1538 had defeated the area's Chibchan-speaking Indians and made the area subject to the Viceroyalty of Peru. After 1740 authority was transferred to the newly created Viceroyalty of New Granada. Parts of Colombia threw off Spanish jurisdiction in 1810, and full independence came after Spain's defeat by Simón Bolívar in 1819. Civil war in 1840 checked development. Conflict between the Liberal and Conservative parties led to the War of a Thousand Days (1899–1903). Years of relative peace followed, but hostility erupted again in 1948; the two parties agreed in 1958 to a scheme for alternating governments. A new constitution was adopted in 1991, but democratic power remained threatened by civil unrest, which continued into the early 21st century and at the violent center of which were powerful drug cartels, leftist guerrillas, and right-wing paramilitary groups.

## Recent Developments

Perhaps the Colombian administration's greatest accomplishment in 2011 was pushing land reform through Congress as a major part of the Victims and Land Restitution Law, a response to the armed conflict between the government, left-wing guerrilla groups, and right-wing paramilitaries that had displaced more than 3 million people. The law, referred to as "historic" by Pres. Juan Manuel Santos, recognized violence in Colombia as the result of an "armed conflict"—a designation that former president Álvaro Uribe had adamantly refused to accept, insisting instead on referring to the ongoing clash as "acts of terrorism." Santos got a major boost when, on 4 November, a military operation killed top Revolutionary Armed Forces of Colombia (FARC) leader Alfonso Cano in the southwestern mountains. In February 2012, FARC announced an end to its practice of kidnappings for ransom and pledged to release all of its captives.

**Internet resource:** <www.dane.gov.co>.

# Comoros

**Official names:** Udzima wa Komori (Comorian); Jumhuriyat al-Qamar al-Muttahidah (Arabic); Union

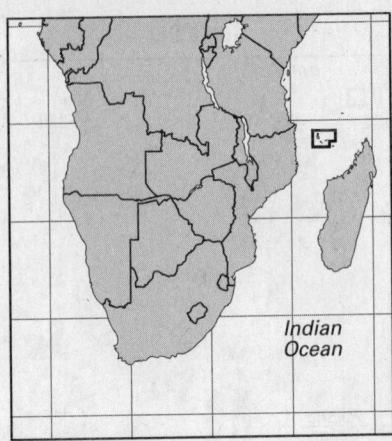

*Indian
Ocean*

des Comores (French) (Union of the Comoros). **Form of government:** republic with one legislative house (Assembly of the Union [33]). **Head of state and government:** President Ikililou Dhoinine (from 2011). **Capital:** Moroni. **Official languages:** Comorian (Shikomor); Arabic; French. **Official religion:** Islam. **Monetary unit:** 1 Comorian franc (CF) = 100 centimes; valuation (2 Jul 2012) US$1 = CF 390.95.

## Demography

**Area:** 719 sq mi, 1,862 sq km. **Population** (2011): 754,000 (excludes Comorians living abroad in France or Mayotte [about 150,000 people]). **Density** (2011): persons per sq mi 1,048.7, persons per sq km 404.9. **Urban** (2008): 28.1%. **Sex distribution** (2006): male 49.61%; female 50.39%. **Age breakdown** (2006): under 15, 42.7%; 15–29, 26.6%; 30–44, 17.8%; 45–59, 8.2%; 60–74, 3.9%; 75 and over, 0.8%. **Ethnic composition** (2000): Comorian (a mixture of Bantu, Arab, Malay, and Malagasy peoples) 97.1%; Makua 1.6%; French 0.4%; other 0.9%. **Religious affiliation** (2005): Muslim (nearly all Sunni) 98.4%; other 1.6%. **Major cities** (2002): Moroni (2007) 46,000; Mutsamudu 21,558; Domoni 13,254; Fomboni 13,053; Tsémbéhou 10,552. **Location:** islands in the western Indian Ocean, between Madagascar and Mozambique.

## Vital statistics

**Birth rate** per 1,000 population (2008): 32.6 (world avg. 20.3). **Death rate** per 1,000 population (2008): 6.3 (world avg. 8.5). **Total fertility rate** (avg. births per childbearing woman; 2006): 5.03. **Life expectancy** at birth (2006): male 60.0 years; female 64.7 years.

## National economy

**Budget** (2007). *Revenue:* CF 33,945,000,000 (tax revenue 49.1%, of which taxes on international trade 17.6%, taxes on goods and services 11.5%; grants 37.7%; nontax revenue 13.2%). *Expenditures:* CF 37,314,000,000 (current expenditures 72.5%, of which interest on debt 2.2%; development

*1 metric ton = about 1.1 short tons;    1 kilometer = 0.6 mi (statute);    1 metric ton-km cargo = about 0.68 short ton-mi cargo;    c.i.f.: cost, insurance, and freight;    f.o.b.: free on board*

expenditures 27.5%). **Public debt** (external, outstanding; 2008): US$277,000,000. **Production** (metric tons except as noted). *Agriculture and fishing* (2007): coconuts 77,000, bananas 65,000, cassava 58,000, cloves 2,500, vanilla 90, ylang-ylang essence 25; livestock (number of live animals) 115,000 goats, 45,000 cattle, 21,000 sheep; fisheries production 16,000 (from aquaculture, none). *Mining and quarrying* (2009): sand, gravel, and crushed stone from coral mining for local construction. *Manufacturing* (2009): products of small-scale industries include processed vanilla and ylang-ylang, cement, handicrafts, soaps, soft drinks, woodwork, and wearing apparel. *Energy production (consumption):* electricity (kW-hr; 2006) 50,600,000 (22,000,000); petroleum products (metric tons; 2006) none (32,000). **Population economically active** (2006): total 348,000; activity rate of total population 42.5% (participation rates: ages 15–64, 73.8%; female 43.1%; unemployed [2005] 13.3%). **Gross national income** (2007): US$425,000,000 (US$680 per capita). **Selected balance of payments data.** Receipts from (US$'000,000): tourism (2006) 27; remittances (2007) 12; foreign direct investment (2005–07 avg.) 1; official development assistance (2007) 44. Disbursements for (US$'000,000): tourism (2006) 11.

### Foreign trade

**Imports** (2007; c.i.f.): CF 49,716,000,000 (refined petroleum products 21.4%; rice 10.4%; meat 6.8%; cement 4.9%; iron and steel 2.3%). *Major import sources* (2005): South Africa 15.4%; France 13.8%; Pakistan 3.1%; Mauritius 3.0%; Belgium-Luxembourg 2.4%. **Exports** (2007; f.o.b.): CF 4,965,000,000 (cloves 57.7%; vanilla 25.7%; ylang-ylang 14.3%). *Major export destinations* (2005): France 73.3%; Germany 10.4%.

### Transport and communications

**Transport.** *Railroads:* none. *Roads* (2004): total length 793 km (paved 70%). *Vehicles* (1996): passenger cars 9,100; trucks and buses 4,950. *Air transport* (2001): passengers arriving or departing Moroni 108,000. **Communications**, in total units (units per 1,000 persons). Telephone landlines (2005): 17,000 (28); cellular telephone subscribers (2007): 40,000 (48); personal computers (2004): 5,000 (6.3); total Internet users (2006): 21,000 (26).

### Education and health

**Educational attainment** (1996). Percentage of population ages 25 and over having: no formal schooling/unknown 73.9%; primary education 11.0%; secondary 15.1%. **Literacy** (2007): total population ages 15 and over literate 57.1%; males literate 64.2%; females literate 50.1%. **Health:** physicians (2004) 48 (1 per 12,417 persons); hospital beds (1995) 1,450 (1 per 342 persons); infant mortality rate per 1,000 live births (2006) 72.9.

### Military

**Total active duty personnel** (2008): the 1,100-member national army is not necessarily accepted by each of the islands; each island also has its own armed security. France provides training for military personnel. **Military expenditure as percentage of GDP** (2005): 3.5%; per capita expenditure US$21.

### Background

The Comoro Islands were known to European navigators from the 16th century. In 1843 France officially took possession of Mayotte and in 1886 placed the other three islands under protection. Subordinated to Madagascar in 1912, Comoros became an overseas territory of France in 1947. In 1961 it was granted autonomy. In 1974 majorities on three of the islands voted for independence, which was granted in 1975. The following decade saw several coup attempts, which culminated in the assassination of the president in 1989. French intervention permitted multiparty elections in 1990, but the country remained in a state of chronic instability. Anjouan and Mohéli seceded from the Comoros federation in 1997. The army took control of the government in 1999. A referendum at the end of 2001 renamed the country the Union of the Comoros and granted the three main islands partially autonomous status.

### Recent Developments

Demobilization efforts in the Comoros stalled in January 2011 when it was revealed that of the roughly 400 weapons used in the 2008 revolt on Anjouan island, only a handful had been turned in. The National Disarmament, Demobilization, and Reintegration Program, organized by the Comorian government with support from the United Nations Development Programme, had begun in June 2010 to disarm former combatants and place them into reskilling and reintegration programs.

Internet resource: <www.comores-online.com/pagegb.htm>.

# Congo, Democratic Republic of the

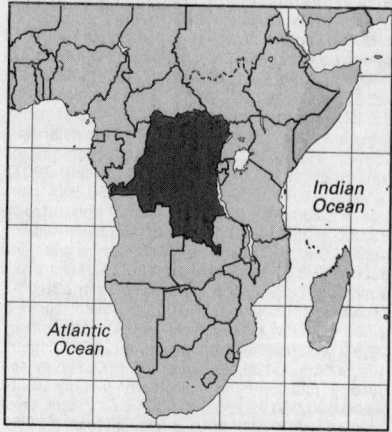

**Official name:** République Democratique du Congo (Democratic Republic of the Congo). **Form of government:** unitary multiparty republic with two legislative houses (Senate [108]; National Assembly [500]). **Head of state:** President Joseph Kabila (from 2001). **Head of government:** Prime Minister Augustin Matata Ponyo Mapon (from 2012). **Capital:** Kinshasa. **Official**

languages: French (Kongo, Lingala, Swahili, and Tshiluba are national languages). Official religion: none. Monetary unit: Congo franc (FC) = 100 centimes; valuation (2 Jul 2012) US$1 = FC 919.32.

## Demography

Area: 905,568 sq mi, 2,345,410 sq km. Population (2011): 67,758,000. Density (2011): persons per sq mi 74.8, persons per sq km 28.9. Urban (2009): 34.6%. Sex distribution (2005): male 49.48%; female 50.52%. Age breakdown (2005): under 15, 47.2%; 15–29, 27.1%; 30–44, 14.2%; 45–59, 7.4%; 60–74, 3.4%; 75–84, 0.6%; 85 and over, 0.1%. Ethnic composition (1983): Luba 18.0%; Kongo 16.1%; Mongo 13.5%; Rwanda 10.3%; Azande 6.1%; Bangi and Ngale 5.8%; Rundi 3.8%; Teke 2.7%; Boa 2.3%; Chokwe 1.8%; Lugbara 1.6%; Banda 1.4%; other 16.6%. Religious affiliation (2004): Roman Catholic 50%; Protestant 20%; Kimbanguist (indigenous Christian) 10%; Muslim 10%; traditional beliefs and syncretic sects 10%. Major urban areas (2004): Kinshasa 7,273,947; Lubumbashi 1,283,380; Mbuji-Mayi 1,213,726; Kananga 720,362; Kisangani 682,599. Location: central Africa, bordering the Central African Republic, South Sudan, Uganda, Rwanda, Burundi, Tanzania, Zambia, Angola, the South Atlantic Ocean, and the Republic of the Congo.

## Vital statistics

Birth rate per 1,000 population (2007): 43.4 (world avg. 20.3). Death rate per 1,000 population (2007): 11.9 (world avg. 8.5). Total fertility rate (avg. births per childbearing woman; 2007): 6.37. Life expectancy at birth (2007): male 51.9 years; female 55.4 years.

## National economy

Budget (2005). Revenue: FC 564,900,000,000 (grants 31.1%; customs and excise taxes 25.7%; direct and indirect taxes 19.7%; petroleum royalties and taxes 17.4%). Expenditures: FC 655,500,-000,000 (current expenditures 65.3%, of which interest on external debt 14.8%; capital expenditures 17.4%; expenditures on demobilization and reintegration 14.8%). Public debt (external, outstanding; 2007): US$10,853,000,000. Production (metric tons except as noted). Agriculture and fishing (2007): cassava 15,000,000, sugarcane 1,550,000, plantains 1,200,000, (2005) pimento and allspice 33,000, coffee 21,300; livestock (number of live animals) 4,000,000 goats, 957,000 pigs; fisheries production 238,970 (from aquaculture 1%). Mining and quarrying (2006): copper (metal content) 130,000; cobalt (metal content) 28,400; tin (metal content) 3,500; silver 67,633 kg; gold 10,000 kg; diamonds 28,540,000 carats. Manufacturing (2004): cement 402,500; flour 199,000; steel 130,000. Energy production (consumption): electricity (kW-hr; 2006) 7,240,000,000 (5,160,000,000); coal (metric tons; 2007) 116,000 (296,000); crude petroleum (barrels; 2008) 7,290,000 (negligible); petroleum products (metric tons; 2006) none (373,000). Gross national income (2008): US$9,843,000,000 (US$150 per capita). Population economically active (2004): total 21,718,000; activity rate 40.0% (participation

rates: ages 15–64, 77.1%; female 41.1%). Selected balance of payments data. Receipts from (US$'000,000): tourism (2005) 1.0; foreign direct investment (2004–06 avg.) 37; official development assistance (2005) 1,828. Disbursements for (US$'000,000): tourism (1997) 7.0.

## Foreign trade

Imports (2005): US$2,465,000,000 (aid-related imports 22.9%; other imports 77.1%). Major import sources (2004): South Africa 18.5%; Belgium 15.6%; France 10.9%; US 6.2%; Germany 5.9%. Exports (2005): US$2,042,000,000 (diamonds 48.4%; crude petroleum 20.0%; cobalt [2004] 15.0%; copper [2004] 3.3%; coffee [2004] 0.9%; gold [2004] 0.7%). Major export destinations: Belgium 42.5%; Finland 17.8%; Zimbabwe 12.2%; US 9.2%; China 6.5%.

## Transport and communications

Transport. Railroads (2003): length (2004) 5,138 km; passenger-km 152,930,000; metric ton-km cargo 506,010,000. Roads (2004): total length 153,497 km (paved 2%). Vehicles (1999): passenger cars 172,600; trucks and buses 34,600. Air transport (1999): passenger-km 263,000,000; metric ton-km cargo 39,000,000. Communications, in total units (units per 1,000 persons). Telephone landlines (2008): 37,000 (0.6); cellular telephone subscribers (2008): 9,263,000 (143); total Internet users (2008): 290,000 (4.5); broadband Internet subscribers (2007): 1,500 (0.02).

## Education and health

Literacy (2003): percentage of total population ages 15 and over literate 65.5%; males literate 76.2%; females literate 55.1%. Health: physicians (2004) 5,827 (1 per 9,585 persons); infant mortality rate per 1,000 live births (2005) 116.5; undernourished population (2002–04) 39,000,000 (74% of total population based on the consumption of a minimum daily requirement of 1,830 calories).

## Military

Total active duty personnel (November 2008): 145,000 (army 79.0%, central staff 9.5%, republican guard 5.0%, air force 2.0%, navy 4.5%); UN peacekeepers (March 2009): 16,600 troops; 1,100 police. Military expenditure as percentage of GDP (2007): 1.7%; per capita expenditure US$3.

## Background

Prior to European colonization, several native kingdoms had emerged in the Congo region, including the 16th-century Luba kingdom and the Kuba federation, which reached its peak in the 18th century. European development began late in the 19th century when King Léopold II of Belgium financed Henry Morton Stanley's exploration of the Congo River. The 1884–85 Berlin West Africa Conference recognized the Congo Free State with Léopold as its sovereign. The growing demand for rubber helped finance the exploitation of the Congo, but abuses against native

1 metric ton = about 1.1 short tons;    1 kilometer = 0.6 mi (statute);    1 metric ton-km cargo = about 0.68 short ton-mi cargo;    c.i.f.: cost, insurance, and freight;    f.o.b.: free on board

peoples outraged Western nations and forced Léopold to grant the Free State a colonial charter as the Belgian Congo in 1908. Independence was granted in 1960, and the country's name was changed to Zaire in 1971. The postindependence period was marked by unrest, culminating in a military coup that brought Gen. Mobutu Sese Seko to power in 1965. Mismanagement, corruption, and increasing violence devastated the infrastructure and economy. Mobutu was deposed in 1997 by Laurent Kabila, who restored the country's name to Democratic Republic of the Congo (DRC). Instability in neighboring countries, an influx of refugees from Rwanda, and a desire for Congo's mineral wealth led to military involvement by various African countries, which fueled existing civil conflict in Congo. Although unrest continued in the beginning of the 21st century, it was somewhat abated by the promulgation in 2003 of a transitional constitution and by the formation of a transitional unity government that included most rebel groups; a new constitution was promulgated and a formal government elected in 2006.

## Recent Developments

Fighting continued in the eastern provinces of the Democratic Republic of the Congo in 2011, stemming from the expansion of the National Congress for the Defense of the People (CNDP), controlled by Tutsi militants. Their quest for more land and greater access to mineral resources was a source of conflict with other ethnic groups and militias in the area. In March 2012, the International Criminal Court issued its first verdict, finding Congolese warlord Thomas Lubanga guilty of war crimes for having forced boys and girls to act as child soldiers during fighting in the country in the early 21st century. In July he was sentenced to 14 years in prison.

Internet resource: <www.bcc.cd>.

# Congo, Republic of the

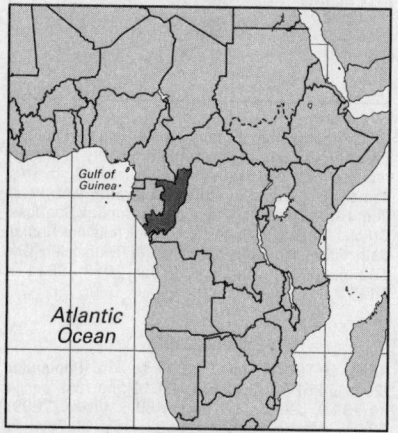

Gulf of Guinea

Atlantic Ocean

**Official name:** République du Congo (Republic of the Congo). **Form of government:** republic with two legislative houses (Senate [72]; National Assembly

[137]). **Head of state and government:** President Denis Sassou-Nguesso (from 1997). **Capital:** Brazzaville. **Official language:** French (Lingala and Monokutuba are national languages). **Official religion:** none. **Monetary unit:** 1 CFA franc (CFAF) = 100 centimes; valuation (2 Jul 2012) US$1 = CFAF 521.26.

## Demography

**Area:** 132,047 sq mi, 342,000 sq km. **Population** (2011): 3,920,000. **Density** (2011): persons per sq mi 29.7, persons per sq km 11.5. **Urban** (2007): 61.0%. **Sex distribution** (2008): male 49.72%; female 50.28%. **Age breakdown** (2008): under 15, 46.1%; 15–29, 27.4%; 30–44, 14.8%; 45–59, 7.4%; 60–74, 3.4%; 75–84, 0.8%; 85 and over, 0.1%. **Ethnic composition** (2000): Kongo 21.2%; Yombe 11.5%; Teke 10.7%; Kougni 8.0%; Mboshi 5.4%; Ngala 4.2%; Sundi 4.0%; other 35.0%. **Religious affiliation** (2005): Roman Catholic 49%; independent Christian 13%; Protestant 11%; Muslim 2%; other (mostly traditional beliefs and nonreligious) 25%. **Major cities** (2007): Brazzaville 1,308,700; Pointe-Noire 647,152; Dolisie 118,562; Nkayi 60,453; Ouesso 26,994. **Location:** west-central Africa, bordering Cameroon, the Central African Republic, the Democratic Republic of the Congo, Angola, the South Atlantic Ocean, and Gabon.

## Vital statistics

**Birth rate** per 1,000 population (2008): 41.8 (world avg. 20.3). **Death rate** per 1,000 population (2008): 12.3 (world avg. 8.5). **Total fertility rate** (avg. births per childbearing woman; 2008): 5.92. **Life expectancy** at birth (2008): male 52.5 years; female 55.0 years.

## National economy

**Budget** (2005). *Revenue:* CFAF 1,300,100,000,000 (petroleum revenue 80.6%; nonpetroleum revenue 16.9%; grants 2.5%). *Expenditures:* CFAF 736,400,000,000 (current expenditures 77.0%, of which interest 20.4%, wages and salaries 17.7%; capital expenditures 23.0%). **Public debt** (external, outstanding; 2006): US$5,328,000,000. **Gross national income** (2008): US$7,134,000,000 (US$1,970 per capita). **Production** (metric tons except as noted). *Agriculture and fishing* (2007): cassava 915,000, sugarcane 550,000, oil palm fruit 90,000; livestock (number of live animals) 290,000 goats, 110,000 cattle, 99,000 sheep; fisheries production 59,966 (from aquaculture, negligible). *Mining and quarrying* (2007): gold 100 kg; diamonds, n.a. *Manufacturing* (2001): residual fuel oil (2000) 206,000; refined sugar 71,814; distillate fuel oils (2000) 62,000. *Energy production (consumption):* electricity (kW-hr; 2006) 453,000,000 (864,000,000); crude petroleum (barrels; 2007) 82,600,000 ([2006] 4,909,000); petroleum products (metric tons; 2006) 625,000 (355,000); natural gas (cu m; 2006) 23,600,000 (23,700,000). **Population economically active** (2006): total 1,482,000; activity rate of total population 40.2% (participation rates: ages 15–64, 69.5%; female 41.3%). **Selected balance of payments data.** Receipts from (US$'000,000): tourism (2007) 54; remittances (2008) 15; foreign direct investment (2005–07 avg.) 473; official development assistance (2007) 127. Disbursements for (US$'000,000): tourism (2007) 168; remittances (2008) 102.

## Foreign trade

**Imports** (2005): CFAF 746,400,000,000 (nonpetroleum sector 85.9%; petroleum sector 14.1%). *Major import sources* (2002): France 26%; US 11%; Italy 8%; Lebanon 6%; Netherlands 5%. **Exports** (2005): CFAF 2,484,300,000,000 (crude petroleum 92.5%; wood products 4.6%; refined petroleum products 1.2%). *Major export destinations* (2002): Taiwan 27%; North Korea 11%; US 10%; South Korea 7%; France 7%.

## Transport and communications

**Transport.** *Railroads* (1998): length 894 km; passenger-km 242,000,000; metric ton-km cargo 135,000,000. *Roads* (2004): total length 17,289 km (paved 5%). *Vehicles:* passenger cars (2002) 30,000; trucks and buses (1997) 15,500. *Air transport* (2002): passenger-km 27,000,000; metric ton-km cargo 3,000,000. **Communications**, in total units (units per 1,000 persons). Telephone landlines (2005): 16,000 (4); cellular telephone subscribers (2008): 1,807,000 (470); personal computers (2006): 17,000 (5); total Internet users (2008): 155,000 (40).

## Education and health

**Educational attainment** (2005). Percentage of population ages 15–49 having: no formal schooling 5.6%; primary education 28.1%; lower secondary 47.2%; upper secondary/higher 19.1%. **Literacy** (2005): total population ages 15 and over literate 87.4%; males literate 92.3%; females literate 82.9%. **Health:** physicians (2000) 540 (1 per 5,745 persons); hospital beds (2001) 5,195 (1 per 623 persons); infant mortality rate per 1,000 live births (2008) 81.7; undernourished population (2003–05) 800,000 (22% of total population based on the consumption of a minimum daily requirement of 1,800 calories).

## Military

**Total active duty personnel** (November 2008): 10,000 (army 80.0%, navy 8.0%, air force 12.0%). **Military expenditure as percentage of GDP** (2007): 1.1%; per capita expenditure US$26.

## Background

In precolonial days the Congo area was home to several thriving kingdoms, including the Kongo, which had its beginnings in the 1st millennium AD. The slave trade began in the 15th century with the arrival of the Portuguese; it supported the local kingdoms and dominated the area until its suppression in the 19th century. The French arrived in the mid-19th century and established treaties with two of the kingdoms, placing them under French protection prior to their becoming part of the colony of French Congo. In 1910 the French possessions were renamed French Equatorial Africa, and Congo became known as Middle (Moyen) Congo. In 1946 Middle Congo became a French overseas territory and in 1958 voted to become an autonomous republic within the French Community. Full independence came two years later. The area has suffered from political instability since independence. Congo's first president was ousted in 1963. A Marxist party, the Congolese Labor Party, gained strength, and in 1968 another coup, led by Maj. Marien Ngouabi, created the People's Republic of the Congo. Ngouabi was assassinated in 1977, and a series of military rulers followed. Fighting between local militias that began in 1997 badly disrupted the economy, and though a 2003 peace agreement largely ended the conflict, sporadic violence continued.

## Recent Developments

In 2011, health issues were a concern in the Republic of the Congo. Congolese citizens welcomed a February announcement that the Global Fund to Fight AIDS, Tuberculosis, and Malaria would provide Congo with US$35 million for the provision of services. However, by June chikungunya, a viral disease related to dengue fever and carried by mosquitoes, had afflicted more than 7,000 people. The country also suffered an outbreak of measles and a cholera epidemic.

**Internet resource:**
<www.embassyofcongo.org/index.html>.

# Costa Rica

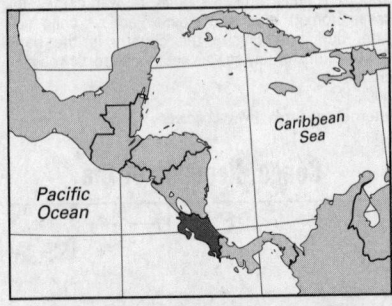

Caribbean Sea

Pacific Ocean

**Official name:** República de Costa Rica (Republic of Costa Rica). **Form of government:** unitary multiparty republic with one legislative house (Legislative Assembly [57]). **Head of state and government:** President Laura Chinchilla (from 2010). **Capital:** San José. **Official language:** Spanish. **Official religion:** Roman Catholicism. **Monetary unit:** 1 Costa Rican colón (₡) = 100 céntimos; valuation (2 Jul 2012) US$1 = ₡498.21.

## Demography

**Area:** 19,730 sq mi, 51,100 sq km. **Population** (2011): 4,577,000. **Density** (2011): persons per sq mi 232.0, persons per sq km 89.6. **Urban** (2009): 63.9%. **Sex distribution** (2006): male 50.76%; female 49.24%. **Age breakdown** (2005): under 15,

---

*1 metric ton = about 1.1 short tons; 1 kilometer = 0.6 mi (statute); 1 metric ton-km cargo = about 0.68 short ton-mi cargo; c.i.f.: cost, insurance, and freight; f.o.b.: free on board*

28.4%; 15–29, 28.1%; 30–44, 21.5%; 45–59, 13.7%; 60–74, 5.9%; 75–84, 1.8%; 85 and over, 0.6%. **Ethnic composition** (2000): white 77.0%; mestizo 17.0%; black/mulatto 3.0%; East Asian (mostly Chinese) 2.0%; Amerindian 1.0%. **Religious affiliation** (2004): Roman Catholic (practicing) 47%; Roman Catholic (nonpracticing) 25%; Evangelical Protestant 13%; nonreligious 10%; other 5%. **Major cities** (2009): San José 356,174; Limón 65,600; Alajuela 50,989; San Francisco 48,036; Cinco Esquinas 43,100. **Location:** Central America, bordering Nicaragua, the Caribbean Sea, Panama, and the North Pacific Ocean.

## Vital statistics

**Birth rate** per 1,000 population (2008): 16.9 (world avg. 20.3); within marriage (2007) 40.1%. **Death rate** per 1,000 population (2008): 4.1 (world avg. 8.5). **Total fertility rate** (avg. births per childbearing woman; 2008): 1.97. **Life expectancy** at birth (2008): male 76.7 years; female 81.7 years.

## National economy

**Budget** (2007). *Revenue:* ₡2,106,400,000,000 (taxes on goods and services 59.1%; income tax 25.2%; taxes on international trade 7.9%). *Expenditures:* ₡2,025,500,000,000 (education 31.8%; interest on debt 20.7%; social protection 16.0%; public order 11.4%; transportation 10.7%). **Public debt** (external, outstanding; 2007): US$3,750,000,000. **Gross national income** (2008): US$27,447,000,000 (US$6,060 per capita). **Production** (metric tons except as noted). *Agriculture and fishing* (2007): sugarcane 4,300,000, bananas 2,240,000, pineapples 1,225,000, green coffee 110,400; livestock (number of live animals) 1,000,000 cattle, 550,000 pigs, 19,500,000 chickens; fisheries production 47,500 (from aquaculture 54%). *Mining and quarrying* (2006): limestone 900,000; gold 1,210 kg. *Manufacturing* (value added in US$'000,000; 2003): food products 734; beverages 188; paints, soaps, and pharmaceuticals 169. *Energy production (consumption):* electricity (kW-hr; 2006) 8,697,000,000 (8,786,000,000); coal (metric tons; 2006) none (60,000); crude petroleum (barrels; 2006) none (4,911,000); petroleum products (metric tons; 2006) 637,000 (2,132,000). **Population economically active** (2008): total 2,059,613; activity rate of total population 45.4% (participation rates: ages 12–59 [2005] 60.8%; female [2005] 36.2%; unemployed 4.9%). **Selected balance of payments data.** Receipts from (US$'000,000): tourism (2007) 2,029; remittances (2008) 635; foreign direct investment (FDI; 2005–07 avg.) 1,409; foreign development assistance (2007) 53. Disbursements for (US$'000,000): tourism (2007) 628; remittances (2008) 271; FDI (2005–07 avg.) 106.

## Foreign trade

**Imports** (2005; c.i.f.): US$9,640,100,000 (machinery and apparatus 34.2%; chemical products 11.0%; mineral fuels 10.5%; plastic products 7.0%; fabricated metal products 6.8%). *Major import sources:* US 40.1%; Japan 5.8%; Mexico 5.0%; Venezuela 4.9%; Ireland 4.5%. **Exports** (2005; f.o.b.): US$7,150,690,000 (machinery and apparatus 29.8%; food products 24.8%, of which bananas 6.8%, pineapples 4.6%, coffee 3.7%; professional and scientific equipment 8.1%; textiles 7.5%; chemical products 6.0%). *Major export destinations:* US 40.2%; Hong Kong 6.8%; Netherlands 6.3%; Guatemala 4.0%; Nicaragua 3.9%.

## Transport and communications

**Transport.** *Railroads* (2004): 278 km. *Roads* (2006): total length 35,983 km (paved 25%). *Vehicles* (2004): passenger cars 620,992; trucks and buses 220,456. *Air transport* (2005; Lacsa [Costa Rican Airlines] only): passenger-km 2,284,000,000; metric ton-km cargo 10,351,000. **Communications**, in total units (units per 1,000 persons). Telephone landlines (2008): 1,438,000 (317); cellular telephone subscribers (2008): 1,887,000 (416); personal computers (2005): 1,000,000 (233); total Internet users (2007): 1,500,000 (336); broadband Internet subscribers (2008): 176,000 (39).

## Education and health

**Educational attainment** (2004). Percentage of population ages 5 and over having: no formal schooling/unknown 12.8%; incomplete primary education 23.3%; complete primary 24.5%; incomplete secondary 18.2%; complete secondary 8.5%; higher 12.7%. **Literacy** (2003): total population ages 15 and over literate 96.0%; males literate 95.9%; females literate 96.1%. **Health:** physicians (2004) 6,600 (1 per 644 persons); hospital beds (2003) 5,908 (1 per 714 persons); infant mortality rate per 1,000 live births (2008) 9.0; undernourished population (2003–05) less than 5% of total population.

## Military

**Paramilitary expenditure as percentage of GDP** (2008): 0.7%; per capita expenditure US$43. The army was officially abolished in 1948. Paramilitary (police) forces (November 2008): 9,800.

## Background

Christopher Columbus landed in Costa Rica in 1502 in an area inhabited by a number of small, independent Indian tribes. These peoples were not easily dominated, and it took almost 60 years for the Spanish to establish a permanent settlement. Ignored by the Spanish crown because of its lack of mineral wealth, the colony grew slowly. Coffee exports and the construction of a rail line improved its economy in the 19th century. It joined the short-lived Mexican Empire in 1821, was a member of the United Provinces of Central America (1823–38), and adopted a constitution in 1871. In 1890 Costa Ricans held what is considered to be the first free and honest election in Central America, beginning a tradition of democracy for which Costa Rica is renowned. In 1987 then president Óscar Arias Sánchez was awarded the Nobel Peace Prize. In the early 21st century, many Costa Ricans looked to increasingly free trade with the US as a solution to the country's economic woes.

## Recent Developments

A long-standing border dispute with Nicaragua was an important issue in 2011 in Costa Rica. The country filed a brief with the International Court of Justice, protesting that Nicaragua's dredging of the San Juan River, which divided the two countries, was a violation of its sovereignty and was causing environmental damage to area wetlands. The court in March handed down a ruling under which Nicaragua was allowed to continue dredging the river, but Costa Rica was permitted to send civilians to monitor potential environmental damage. In December, however, Nicaragua filed a counterclaim, asserting that construction in Costa Rica was resulting in the illegal dumping of sediment into the river.

Internet resource: <www.tourism.co.cr>.

# Côte d'Ivoire

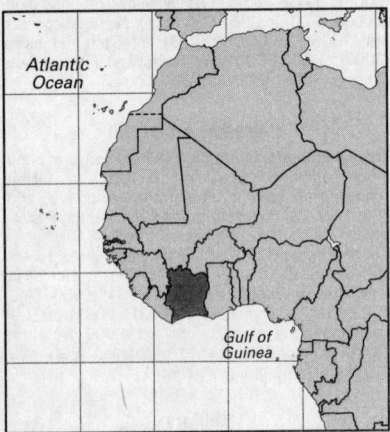

Official name: République de Côte d'Ivoire (Republic of Côte d'Ivoire). Form of government: republic with one legislative house (National Assembly [255]). Head of state and government: President Alassane Ouattara (from 2011), assisted by Prime Minister Jeannot Ahoussou-Kouadio (from 2012). Capital: Yamoussoukro (Abidjan is the de facto capital). Official language: French. Official religion: none. Monetary unit: 1 CFA franc (CFAF) = 100 centimes; valuation (2 Jul 2012) US$1 = CFAF 521.26.

## Demography

Area: 123,863 sq mi, 320,803 sq km. Population (2011): 21,504,000. Density (2011): persons per sq mi 173.6, persons per sq km 67.0. Urban (2008): 49.0%. Sex distribution (2007): male 50.75%; female 49.25%. Age breakdown (2007): under 15, 41.2%; 15–29, 29.2%; 30–44, 16.5%; 45–59, 8.4%; 60–74, 3.9%; 75–84, 0.6%; 85 and over, 0.2%. Ethnolinguistic composition (1998; local population only [in 1998 foreigners constituted 26% of the population]): Akan 42.1%; Mande 26.5%; other 31.4%. Religious affiliation (2005): traditional beliefs 37%; Christian 32%, of which Roman Catholic 17%, Protestant 8%, independent Christian 7%; Muslim 28%; other 3%. Major cities (2005): Abidjan (urban agglomeration) 3,576,000; Bouaké 573,700; Daloa 215,100; Yamoussoukro (2003) 185,600; Korhogo (2003) 115,000. Location: western Africa, bordering Mali, Burkina Faso, Ghana, the Atlantic Ocean, Liberia, and Guinea.

## Vital statistics

Birth rate per 1,000 population (2008): 37.1 (world avg. 20.3). Death rate per 1,000 population (2008): 13.6 (world avg. 8.5). Total fertility rate (avg. births per childbearing woman; 2007): 4.33. Life expectancy at birth (2008): male 50.3 years; female 53.7 years.

## National economy

Budget (2005). Revenue: CFAF 1,566,000,000,000 (tax revenue 79.9%; nontax revenue 14.1%; grants 6.0%). Expenditures: CFAF 1,536,600,000,000 (current expenditures 78.4%; interest on public debt 11.5%; other 10.1%). Public debt (external, outstanding; 2006): US$10,830,000,000. Production (metric tons except as noted). Agriculture and fishing (2007): yams 4,900,000, cassava 2,110,000, plantains 1,590,000, cacao beans 1,300,000, coffee 171,000, cashew nuts 130,000, natural rubber 128,000, fonio 9,700; livestock (number of live animals) 1,523,000 sheep, 1,500,000 cattle; fisheries production 33,416 (from aquaculture 2%). Mining and quarrying (2007): gold 1,243 kg; diamonds 300,000 carats. Manufacturing (value added in CFAF '000,000,000; 1997): food products 156.6, of which cocoa and chocolate 72.4; chemical products 60.2; wood products 55.9; refined petroleum products 46.0. Energy production (consumption): electricity (kW-hr; 2006) 5,510,300 ([2005] 4,181,000,000); crude petroleum (barrels; 2007) 18,800,000 ([2005] 30,000,000); petroleum products (metric tons; 2005) 3,136,000 (974,000); natural gas (cu m; 2005) 1,661,000,000 (1,661,000,000). Population economically active (2006): total 6,937,000; activity rate of total population 36.7% (participation rates: ages 15–64, 66.2%; female 30.5%). Selected balance of payments data. Receipts from (US$'000,000): tourism (2007) 104; remittances (2008) 215; foreign direct investment (2005–07 avg.) 353; official development assistance (2007) 165. Disbursements for (US$'000,000): tourism (2007) 396; remittances (2008) 19. Gross national income (2008): US$20,257,000,000 (US$980 per capita).

## Foreign trade

Imports (2005): CFAF 2,687,000,000,000 (machinery and transportation equipment 40.1%; crude petroleum and refined petroleum products 32.3%; food products 17.0%). Major import sources (2004): France 24.3%; Nigeria 19.2%; UK 4.0%; China 4.0%; Italy 3.8%. Exports (2005): CFAF 3,950,000,000,000 (cacao beans and products 27.5%; crude petroleum and refined petroleum products 26.9%; wood products 3.8%; coffee 2.1%). Major export destinations (2004): US 11.6%; Netherlands 10.3%; France 9.5%; Italy 5.5%; Belgium 4.7%.

## Transport and communications

Transport. Railroads (1999): route length (2004) 660 km; passenger-km 93,100,000; metric ton-km cargo 537,600,000. Roads (2004): total length 80,000 km (paved 8%). Vehicles: passenger cars (2002) 114,000; trucks and buses (2001) 54,900. Air trans-

---

1 metric ton = about 1.1 short tons;    1 kilometer = 0.6 mi (statute);    1 metric ton-km cargo = about 0.68 short ton-mi cargo;    c.i.f.: cost, insurance, and freight;    f.o.b.: free on board

*port* (2002; Abidjan airport only): passenger arrivals and departures 821,400; cargo unloaded and loaded 16,699 metric tons. **Communications**, in total units (units per 1,000 persons). Telephone landlines (2008): 357,000 (18); cellular telephone subscribers (2008): 10,449,000 (533); personal computers (2004): 262,000 (16); total Internet users (2008): 66,000 (34); broadband Internet subscribers (2005): 1,200 (0.07).

## Education and health

**Educational attainment** (1998–99). Percentage of population ages 25 and over having: no formal schooling/unknown 63.0%; primary education 19.4%; secondary 14.3%; higher 3.3%. **Literacy** (2007): percentage of population ages 15 and over literate 55.5%; males literate 65.1%; females literate 45.5%. **Health:** physicians (2004) 2,081 (1 per 8,143 persons); hospital beds (2001) 5,981 (1 per 2,660 persons); infant mortality rate per 1,000 live births (2008) 98.3; undernourished population (2003–05) 2,600,000 (14% of total population based on the consumption of a minimum daily requirement of 1,780 calories).

## Military

**Total active duty personnel** (November 2008): 17,050 (army 38.1%, navy 5.3%, air force 4.1%, presidential guard 7.9%, gendarmerie 44.6%); peacekeeping troops: UN (March 2009) 7,800, French (November 2008): 1,800. **Military expenditure as percentage of GDP** (2007): 1.4%; per capita expenditure US$15.

## Background

Europeans came to the area to trade in ivory and slaves beginning in the 15th century, and local kingdoms gave way to French influence in the 19th century. The French colony of Côte d'Ivoire was founded in 1893, and full occupation took place during 1908–18. In 1946 it became a territory in the French Union; in 1947 the northern part of the country separated and became part of Upper Volta (now Burkina Faso). Côte d'Ivoire peacefully achieved autonomy in 1958 and independence in 1960, when Félix Houphouët-Boigny was elected president. The country's first multiparty presidential elections were held in 1990. Political turmoil has persisted since Houphouët-Boigny died in 1993, and a civil war in 2002 left the country divided into northern and southern sections. Attempts at reconciliation were initiated over the following years, including a 2007 power-sharing agreement signed by both sides.

## Recent Developments

In 2011, Laurent Gbagbo refused to accept defeat in the presidential election held the previous December, despite the fact that Côte d'Ivoire's Independent Electoral Commission had declared that Alassane Ouattara had won. After intense fighting, Gbagbo was captured in April. He was moved to The Hague in November and charged with crimes against humanity by the International Criminal Court. The human and economic cost of the crisis was considerable. Hundreds of thousands of Ivoirians had fled their homes, and it was believed that at least 3,000 had died. Both sides were under investigation for human rights abuses, and the Truth, Reconciliation, and Dialogue Commission was inaugurated in September.

**Internet resource:** <www.ins.ci>.

# Croatia

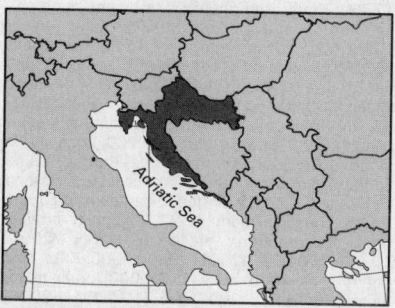

**Official name:** Republika Hrvatska (Republic of Croatia). **Form of government:** multiparty republic with one legislative house (Croatian Parliament [151]). **Head of state:** President Ivo Josipovic (from 2010). **Head of government:** Prime Minister Zoran Milanovic (from 2011). **Capital:** Zagreb. **Official language:** Croatian. **Official religion:** none (Roman Catholicism receives state financial support through concordats with the Vatican). **Monetary unit:** 1 kuna (kn; plural kune) = 100 lipa; valuation (2 Jul 2012) US$1 = kn 5.96.

## Demography

**Area:** 21,851 sq mi, 56,954 sq km. **Population** (2011): 4,287,000. **Density** (2011): persons per sq mi 196.2, persons per sq km 75.3. **Urban** (2008): 57.3%. **Sex distribution** (2006): male 48.17%; female 51.83%. **Age breakdown** (2004): under 15, 16.1%; 15–29, 20.2%; 30–44, 20.9%; 45–59, 20.7%; 60–74, 15.9%; 75–84, 5.3%; 85 and over, 0.9%. **Ethnic composition** (2001): Croat 89.6%; Serb 4.5%; Bosniak 0.5%; Italian 0.4%; Hungarian 0.4%; other 4.6%. **Religious affiliation** (2001): Christian 92.6%, of which Roman Catholic 87.8%, Eastern Orthodox 4.4%; Muslim 1.3%; nonreligious/atheist 5.2%; other 0.9%. **Major cities** (2001): Zagreb 691,724; Split 175,140; Rijeka 143,800; Osijek 90,411; Zadar 69,556. **Location:** southeastern Europe, bordering Slovenia, Hungary, Serbia, Montenegro, Bosnia and Herzegovina, and the Adriatic Sea.

## Vital statistics

**Birth rate** per 1,000 population (2007): 9.4 (world avg. 20.3); within marriage 88.5%. **Death rate** per 1,000 population (2007): 11.8 (world avg. 8.5). **Total fertility rate** (avg. births per childbearing woman; 2007): 1.40. **Life expectancy** at birth (2007): male 72.3 years; female 79.2 years.

## National economy

**Budget** (2007). *Revenue:* kn 108,321,000,000 (tax revenue 59.3%, of which VAT 35.0%, excise taxes 11.2%; social security contributions 34.3%;

nontax revenue 6.0%; grants 0.4%). *Expenditures:* kn 108,008,000,000 (social security and welfare 44.6%; wages and salaries 25.5%; goods and services 4.2%). **Population economically active** (2005): total (1,802,000); activity rate 40.5% (participation rates: ages 15–64, 58.3%; female 45.5%; unemployed [July 2005–June 2006] 12.7%). **Production** (metric tons except as noted). *Agriculture and fishing* (2007): sugar beets 1,582,606, corn (maize) 1,424,599, wheat 950,000, sunflower seeds 54,303; livestock (number of live animals) 1,489,000 pigs, 680,000 sheep, 483,000 cattle; fisheries production (2006) 52,750 (from aquaculture 28%). *Mining and quarrying* (2005): ceramic clay 200,000; ornamental stone 1,000,000 sq m. *Manufacturing* (value added in kn '000,000; 2004): food products and beverages 7,112; refined petroleum products 4,005; chemical products 2,774. *Energy production (consumption):* electricity (kW-hr; 2007) 12,540,000,000 ([2006] 18,052,000,000); coal (metric tons; 2006) none (1,071,000); crude petroleum (barrels; 2007) 6,710,000 ([2006] 34,300,000); petroleum products (metric tons; 2006) 4,537,000 (4,490,000); natural gas (cu m; 2007) 2,713,000,000 ([2006] 2,802,000,000). **Gross national income** (2008): US$60,192,000,000 (US$13,570 per capita). **Public debt** (external, outstanding; 2007): US$14,212,000,000. **Selected balance of payments data.** Receipts from (US$'000,000): tourism (2007) 9,233; remittances (2008) 1,602; foreign direct investment (FDI; 2004–06 avg.) 2,191; official development assistance (2006) 200. Disbursements for (US$'000,000): tourism (2007) 985; remittances (2008) 110; FDI (2004–06 avg.) 267.

## Foreign trade

**Imports** (2007; c.i.f.): US$23,658,000,000 (basic manufactures 20.0%; mineral fuels 15.0%; chemical products 11.0%; motor vehicles and parts 9.3%). *Major import sources:* Italy 16.3%; Germany 14.4%; Russia 9.9%; China 6.2%; Slovenia 6.0%. **Exports** (2007; f.o.b.): US$11,294,000,000 (basic manufactures 15.7%; mineral fuels 12.7%; ships and boats [particularly tankers] 11.5%; chemical products 9.4%; food products 8.0%). *Major export destinations:* Italy 19.2%; Bosnia and Herzegovina 14.4%; Germany 10.1%; Slovenia 8.3%; Austria 6.2%.

## Transport and communications

**Transport.** *Railroads* (2007): length (2004) 2,726 km; passenger-km 1,611,000,000; metric ton-km cargo 3,574,000,000. *Roads* (2005): total length 28,472 km (paved [2003] 85%). *Vehicles* (2008): passenger cars 1,529,271; trucks and buses 175,455. *Air transport* (2007): passenger-km 1,080,000,000; metric ton-km cargo 2,220,000. **Communications,** in total units (units per 1,000 persons). Telephone landlines (2008): 1,851,000 (407); cellular telephone subscribers (2008): 5,924,000 (1,302); personal computers (2004): 842,000 (191); total Internet users (2008): 2,244,000 (493); broadband Internet subscribers (2008): 525,000 (115).

## Education and health

**Educational attainment** (2001). Percentage of population ages 15 and over having: no formal schooling/unknown 3.5%; incomplete primary education 15.8%; primary 21.7%; secondary 47.1%; postsecondary and higher 11.9%. **Literacy** (2003): population ages 15 and over literate 98.5%; males literate 99.4%; females literate 97.8%. **Health** (2005): physicians 8,216 (1 per 541 persons); hospital beds 24,000 (1 per 185 persons); infant mortality rate per 1,000 live births 5.7; undernourished population (2002–04) 300,000 (7% of total population based on the consumption of a minimum daily requirement of 2,010 calories).

## Military

**Total active duty personnel** (November 2008): 18,600 (army 61.2%, navy 10.0%, air force 18.8%, joint staff 10.0%). **Military expenditure as percentage of GDP** (2008): 1.7%; per capita expenditure US$217.

## Background

The Croats, a southern Slavic people, arrived in the area in the 7th century AD and in the 8th century came under Charlemagne's rule. They converted to Christianity soon afterward and formed a kingdom in the 10th century. Most of Croatia was taken by the Turks in 1526; the rest voted to accept Austrian rule. In 1867 it became part of Austria-Hungary, with Dalmatia and Istria ruled by Vienna and Croatia-Slavonia a Hungarian crown land. In 1918, after the defeat of Austria-Hungary in World War I, it joined other southern Slavic territories to form the Kingdom of Serbs, Croats, and Slovenes, renamed Yugoslavia in 1929. During World War II an independent state of Croatia was established by Germany and Italy, embracing Croatia-Slavonia, part of Dalmatia, and Bosnia and Herzegovina; after the war Croatia was rejoined to Yugoslavia as a people's republic. It declared its independence in 1991, sparking insurrections by Croatian Serbs, who carved out autonomous regions with Serbian-led Yugoslav army help; Croatia had taken back most of these regions by 1995 and regained full control of its territory in 2002. With some stability returning, Croatia's economy began to revive in the early 21st century. The country joined NATO in 2009.

## Recent Developments

In June 2011, Croatia provisionally closed negotiations to join the European Union, and on 9 December the country signed the accession treaty that would allow it to become the EU's 28th member in July 2013. This was an achievement that was the culmination of more than a decade's efforts to undertake necessary political and economic reforms, particularly on corruption, which had proved a thorny issue for Bulgaria and Romania. In January 2012 the Croatian public voted to approve joining the EU by a roughly two to one margin.

**Internet resource:** <www.dzs.hr/default_e.htm>.

*1 metric ton = about 1.1 short tons;    1 kilometer = 0.6 mi (statute);    1 metric ton-km cargo = about 0.68 short ton-mi cargo;    c.i.f.: cost, insurance, and freight;    f.o.b.: free on board*

# Cuba

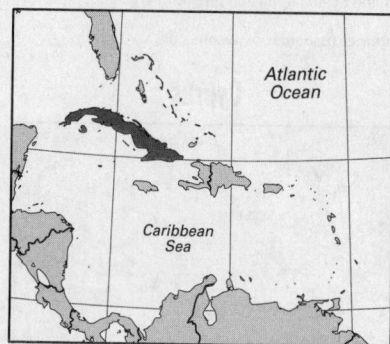

**Official name:** República de Cuba (Republic of Cuba). **Form of government:** unitary socialist republic with one legislative house (National Assembly of the People's Power [614]). **Head of state and government:** President Raúl Castro Ruz (from 2008). **Capital:** Havana. **Official language:** Spanish. **Official religion:** none. **Monetary unit:** 1 Cuban peso (CUP) = 100 centavos; valuation (2 Jul 2012) US$1 = 1.00 CUP.

## Demography

**Area:** 42,426 sq mi, 109,884 sq km. **Population** (2011): 11,240,000. **Density** (2011): persons per sq mi 264.9, persons per sq km 102.3. **Urban** (2009): 75.4%. **Sex distribution** (2008): male 50.09%; female 49.91%. **Age breakdown** (2005): under 15, 19.2%; 15–29, 20.5%; 30–44, 27.6%; 45–59, 17.0%; 60–74, 10.8%; 75–84, 3.6%; 85 and over, 1.3%. **Ethnic composition** (1994): mixed 51.0%; white 37.0%; black 11.0%; other 1.0%. **Religious affiliation** (2005): Roman Catholic 47%; Protestant 5%; nonreligious 22%; other 26% (as much as 70% of the population also practice Santería). **Major cities** (2006): Havana 2,174,790; Santiago de Cuba 425,990; Camagüey 306,702; Holguín 274,805; Santa Clara 208,739. **Location:** island southeast of Florida (US), between the North Atlantic Ocean and the Caribbean Sea.

## Vital statistics

**Birth rate** per 1,000 population (2008): 10.9 (world avg. 20.3). **Death rate** per 1,000 population (2008): 7.6 (world avg. 8.5). **Total fertility rate** (avg. births per childbearing woman; 2008): 1.50. **Life expectancy** at birth (2005–07): male 76.0 years; female 80.0 years.

## National economy

**Budget** (2008). *Revenue:* CUP 42,055,600,000 (tax revenue 61.5%; nontax revenue 38.5%). *Expenditures:* CUP 46,255,600,000 (current revenue 90.3%, of which education 16.2%, health 15.5%, social security contributions 9.5%, public safety and defense 4.4%; capital expenditures 9.7%). **Public debt** (external, outstanding; 2004): US$12,000,000,000. **Production** (metric tons except as noted). *Agriculture and fishing* (2007): sugarcane 11,100,000, tomatoes 640,000, plan-

tains 540,000, tobacco leaves 30,000; livestock (number of live animals) 3,750,000 cattle, 2,765,000 sheep, 1,765,000 pigs; fisheries production 62,144 (from aquaculture 50%). *Mining and quarrying* (2006): nickel (metal content) 75,000; cobalt (metal content) 4,300. *Manufacturing* (2006): cement 1,713,900; steel 257,200; cigarettes (2004) 12,800,000,000 units. *Energy production (consumption):* electricity (kW-hr; 2008) 17,957,100,000 (17,957,100,000); coal (metric tons; 2006) none (11,000); crude petroleum (barrels; 2006) 18,700,000 (39,400,000); petroleum products (metric tons; 2006) 1,861,000 (4,527,000); natural gas (cu m; 2006) 1,085,000,000 (1,085,000,000). **Population economically active** (2008): total 5,027,800; activity rate 44.7% (participation rates: ages 15 and over [2004] 52.3%; female 38.0%; unemployed 1.6%). **Gross national income** (2007): US$51,167,000,000 (US$4,541 per capita). **Selected balance of payments data.** Receipts from (US$'000,000): tourism (2007) 2,141; remittances (2003) 1,200; foreign direct investment (2005–07 avg.) 20; official development assistance (2007) 92.

## Foreign trade

**Imports** (2004; c.i.f.): US$5,610,000,000 (food products 18.4%, of which cereals 8.0%; machinery and apparatus 17.5%; refined petroleum products 12.8%; chemical products 9.6%; crude petroleum 9.4%). *Major import sources* (2006): Venezuela 23.5%; China 16.7%; Spain 9.0%; Germany 6.5%; US 5.1%. **Exports** (2004; f.o.b.): US$2,332,000,000 (nickel oxide 45.5%; food products 19.7%, of which raw cane sugar 11.5%; cigars 8.7%; medicine 6.0%). *Major export destinations* (2006): Netherlands 28.0%; Canada 19.8%; Venezuela 10.7%; China 8.9%; Spain 5.4%.

## Transport and communications

**Transport.** *Railroads* (2003; Cuban Railways only): length 4,226 km; (2001) passenger-km 1,766,600; metric ton-km cargo 806,900,000. *Roads* (2000): total length 60,856 km (paved 49%). *Vehicles* (1998): passenger cars 172,574; trucks and buses 185,495. *Air transport* (2003; Cubana airline only): passenger-km 2,044,000,000; metric ton-km cargo 40,933,000. **Communications**, in total units (units per 1,000 persons). Telephone landlines (2008): 1,104,000 (98); cellular telephone subscribers (2008): 332,000 (29); personal computers (2005): 377,000 (33); total Internet users (2008): 1,450,000 (129); broadband Internet subscribers (2007): 1,900 (0.2).

## Education and health

**Educational attainment** (2002): Percentage of population ages 25 and over having: no formal schooling 14.1%; primary education 17.2%; secondary 26.6%; vocational/teacher training 32.8%; university 9.3%. **Literacy** (2004): total population ages 15 and over literate 96.9%; males literate 97.0%; females literate 96.8%. **Health:** physicians (2006) 70,594 (1 per 160 persons); hospital beds (2004) 70,079 (1 per 160 persons); infant mortality rate per 1,000 live births (2008) 4.7; undernourished population (2003–04) less than 5% of total population.

## Military

**Total active duty personnel** (November 2008): 49,000 (army 77.6%, navy 6.1%, air force 16.3%); US military forces at Naval Base Guantanamo Bay (November 2008): 903. **Military expenditure as percentage of GDP** (2005): 3.8%; per capita expenditure US$151.

## Background

Several Indian groups, including the Ciboney, the Taino, and the Arawak, inhabited Cuba at the time of the first Spanish contact. Christopher Columbus claimed the island for Spain in 1492, and the Spanish conquest began in 1511, when the settlement of Baracoa was founded. The native Indians were eradicated over the succeeding centuries, and African slaves, from the 18th century until slavery was abolished in 1886, were imported to work the sugar plantations. Cuba revolted unsuccessfully against Spain in the Ten Years' War (1868–78); a second war of independence began in 1895. In 1898 the US entered the war; Spain relinquished its claim to Cuba, which was occupied by the US for three years before gaining its independence in 1902. The US invested heavily in the Cuban sugar industry in the first half of the 20th century, and this, combined with tourism and gambling, caused the economy to prosper. In 1958–59 the communist revolutionary Fidel Castro overthrew Cuba's longtime dictator, Fulgencio Batista, and established a socialist state aligned with the Soviet Union, abolishing capitalism and nationalizing foreign-owned enterprises. Relations with the US deteriorated, reaching a low point with the 1961 Bay of Pigs invasion and the 1962 Cuban missile crisis. In 1980 about 125,000 Cubans, including many that their government officially labeled "undesirables," were shipped to the US in what became known as the "Mariel boatlift." When communism collapsed in the USSR, Cuba lost important financial backing and its economy suffered greatly. In the early 21st century, Cuba benefited from a petroleum-trade agreement with Venezuela and eased some of its restrictive economic and social policies. Castro officially stepped down as president in 2008, ending his 49-year rule of Cuba; his younger brother Raúl replaced him as Cuba's leader.

## Recent Developments

Cuba entered the 53rd year of its revolution in 2011 confronted by the urgent necessity for economic reform. Specifically, the government sought to expand nonstate retail and private agricultural sectors, increase the efficiency of state-run enterprises, and lower government expenditures, principally through a reduction of social expenditures and the furlough of some 500,000 state employees. The authorization of licenses in the nonstate retail (*cuenta propia*) sector proceeded steadily. The government authorized local state-run banks to provide start-up loans to small-business entrepreneurs and microcredit grants to farmers. Nearly two million hectares (about five million acres) of vacant state-owned land was leased to about 140,000 small farmers. Moreover, farmers were authorized to bypass inefficient state-controlled distribution systems and sell directly to the public. The government legalized the sale and purchase of

homes and automobiles, as well. Relations with the United States remained largely unchanged, however.

**Internet resource:** <www.one.cu>.

# Cyprus

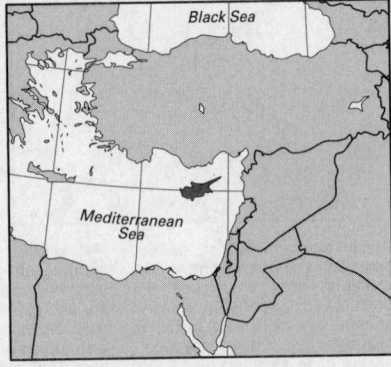

*Two de facto states currently exist on the island of Cyprus: the Republic of Cyprus (ROC), predominantly Greek in character, occupying the southern two-thirds of the island, which is the original and still the internationally recognized de jure government of the whole island; and the Turkish Republic of Northern Cyprus (TRNC), proclaimed unilaterally 15 Nov 1983, on territory originally secured for the Turkish Cypriot population by the 20 Jul 1974 intervention of Turkey. Only Turkey recognizes the TRNC, and the two ethnic communities have failed to reestablish a single state. Provision of separate data below does not imply recognition of either state's claims but is necessitated by the lack of unified data.*

**Area:** 3,572 sq mi, 9,251 sq km. **Population** (2011): 1,118,000 (includes 160,000–170,000 immigrants [mostly from Turkey]; excludes 2,791 British military in the Sovereign Base Areas (SBA) in the ROC and 842 UN peacekeeping troops). **Location:** the Middle East, island in the Mediterranean Sea, south of Turkey.

## Republic of Cyprus

**Official name:** Kipriaki Dhimokratia (Greek); Kibris Cumhuriyeti (Turkish) (Republic of Cyprus). **Form of government:** unitary multiparty republic with one legislative house (House of Representatives [80; 24 seats reserved for Turkish Cypriots are not occupied]). **Head of state and government:** President Dimitris Christofias (from 2008). **Capital:** Lefkosia (Nicosia). **Official languages:** Greek; Turkish. **Monetary unit:** 1 euro (€) = 100 cents; valuation (2 Jul 2012) US$1 = €0.79 (the euro replaced the Cyprus pound [£C] on 1 Jan 2008, at the rate of €1 = £C 0.59).

## Demography

**Area:** 2,276 sq mi, 5,896 sq km (includes 99 sq mi [256 sq km] of British military SBAs and 107 sq mi [278 sq km] of the UN Buffer Zone). **Population**

---

*1 metric ton = about 1.1 short tons;    1 kilometer = 0.6 mi (statute);    1 metric ton-km cargo = about 0.68 short ton-mi cargo;    c.i.f.: cost, insurance, and freight;    f.o.b.: free on board*

(2011): 816,000 (excludes British and UN military forces). **Age breakdown** (2007): under 15, 17.5%; 15–29, 24.0%; 30–44, 21.6%; 45–59, 19.6%; 60–74, 12.2%; 75 and over, 5.1%. **Ethnic composition** (2000): Greek Cypriot 91.8%; Armenian 3.3%; Arab 2.9%, of which Lebanese 2.5%; British 1.4%; other 0.6%. **Religious affiliation** (2001): Greek Orthodox 94.8%; Roman Catholic 2.1%, of which Maronite 0.6%; Anglican 1.0%; Muslim 0.6%; other 1.5%. **Urban areas** (2007): Lefkosia (ROC only) 231,800; Limassol 183,000; Larnaca 81,700.

## Vital statistics

**Birth rate** per 1,000 population (2007): 10.9 (world avg. 20.3). **Death rate** per 1,000 population (2007): 6.8 (world avg. 8.5). **Total fertility rate** (avg. births per childbearing woman; 2007): 1.39. **Life expectancy** at birth (2006–07): male 78.3 years; female 81.9 years.

## National economy

**Budget** (2005). *Revenue:* £C 3,273,700,000 (excises and import duties 41.4%; income tax 22.3%; social security contributions 19.9%). *Expenditures:* £C 3,459,300,000 (current expenditures 91.3%; development expenditures 8.7%). **Gross national income** (2007): US$19,617,000,000 (US$24,940 per capita). **Production** (metric tons except as noted). *Agriculture and fishing* (2008; island of Cyprus): potatoes 131,695, barley 46,806, oranges 43,910, grapes 35,976, grapefruit 26,900, olives 18,025; livestock (number of live animals) 464,900 pigs, 318,400 goats, 267,300 sheep; fisheries production (2007) 4,950 (from aquaculture 51%). *Manufacturing* (value added in US$'000,000; 2005): food products, beverages, and tobacco products 281; cement, bricks, and ceramics 98; base metals and fabricated metal products 67. *Energy production (consumption):* electricity (kW-hr; 2006) 4,652,000,000 (4,652,000,000). **Selected balance of payments data.** Receipts from (US$'000,000): tourism (2007) 2,687; remittances (2008) 279; foreign direct investment (FDI; 2005–07 avg.) 1,590. Disbursements for (US$'000,000): tourism (2007) 1,479; remittances (2008) 577; FDI (2005–07 avg.) 826.

## Foreign trade

**Imports** (2006; c.i.f.): US$7,046,000,000 (refined petroleum products 17.2%; machinery and apparatus 16.4%; motor vehicles 11.0%; food products 9.2%). *Major import sources:* Greece 17.3%; Italy 11.4%; UK 8.9%; Germany 8.9%; Israel 6.2%. **Exports** (2006; f.o.b.): US$1,414,900,000 (refined petroleum products 18.2%; telecommunications equipment 9.9%; motor vehicles 9.8%; vegetables and fruit 8.9%; medicine 8.6%; cigars and cigarettes 4.5%). *Major export destinations:* UK 14.6%; Greece 13.2%; France 7.4%; Germany 4.5%.

## Transport and communications

**Transport.** *Roads* (2004): total length 12,059 km (paved 65%). *Vehicles* (2007): cars 410,936; trucks and buses 120,790. *Air transport* (2008): passenger-km 3,384,000,000; metric ton-km cargo 46,000,000. **Communications,** in total units (island of Cyprus unless otherwise noted; units per 1,000 persons). Telephone landlines (2008): 413,000 (479); cellular telephone subscribers (2008):

1,017,000 (1,177); personal computers (ROC only; 2004): 249,000 (309); total Internet users (2007): 380,000 (445); broadband Internet subscribers (2008): 104,000 (120).

## Education and health

**Educational attainment** (2008). Percentage of population ages 20 and over having: no formal schooling/incomplete primary education 7%; complete primary 18%; secondary 47%; higher education 28%. **Health** (2006): physicians 1,950 (1 per 395 persons); hospital beds 2,864 (1 per 269 persons); infant mortality rate per 1,000 live births (2007) 3.1.

## Military

**Total active duty personnel** (2008): 10,000 (national guard 100%); Greek troops (2008): 950. **Military expenditure as percentage of GDP** (2007): 2.3%; per capita expenditure US$635.

## Turkish Republic of Northern Cyprus

**Official name:** Kuzey Kibris Turk Cumhuriyeti (Turkish) (Turkish Republic of Northern Cyprus). **Capital:** Lefkosa (Nicosia). **Official language:** Turkish. **Monetary unit:** new Turkish lira (YTL); valuation (2 Jul 2012) US$1 = YTL 1.81. **Population** (2011): 302,000 (includes 160,000–170,000 immigrants [mostly from Turkey]; excludes 2,791 British military in the Sovereign Base Areas [SBA] in the ROC and 842 UN peacekeeping troops) (Lefkosa [2006] 49,237; Magusa [Famagusta] [2006] 34,803; Girne [Kyrenia] [2006] 24,122; Güzelyurt [Morphou] [2006] 12,425). **Sex distribution** (2006): male 53.99%; female 46.01%. **Ethnic composition** (2006): Turkish Cypriot/Turkish 96.8%; other 3.2%. **Birth rate** per 1,000 population (2007): 15.0 (world avg. 20.3). **Death rate** per 1,000 population (2007): 6.8 (world avg. 8.5). **Total fertility rate** (avg. births per childbearing woman; 2007) 1.80. **Budget** (2007). *Revenue:* YTL 1,912,021,000 (indirect taxes 29.4%; direct taxes 20.5%; foreign aid 14.8%). *Expenditures:* YTL 2,125,064,000 (social transfers 39.8%; wages and salaries 35.6%; investments 10.7%; defense 5.6%). **Imports** (2004): US$853,100,000 (machinery and transportation equipment 35.7%; food products 9.4%). *Major import sources:* Turkey 60.1%; UK 10.7%. **Exports** (2004): US$62,000,000 (citrus fruits 32.4%; wearing apparel 18.9%). *Major export destinations:* Turkey 46.3%; UK 21.8%. **Health** (2007): physicians 474 (1 per 529 persons); hospital beds 1,380 (1 per 194 persons); infant mortality rate per 1,000 live births 15.0.

## Background

By the late Bronze Age Cyprus had been visited and settled by Mycenaeans and Achaeans, who introduced Greek culture and language, and it became a trading center. By 800 BC Phoenicians had begun to settle there. Ruled over the centuries by the Assyrian, Persian, and Ptolemaic empires, it was annexed by Rome in 58 BC. It was part of the Byzantine Empire in the 4th–12th centuries AD. Cyprus was conquered by the English king Richard I in 1191. A part of the Venetian empire from 1489, it was taken by Ottoman Turks in 1571. In 1878 the British assumed control, and Cyprus became a British crown colony in 1925. It gained independence in 1960. Conflict between Greek and Turkish Cypriots led to the establishment of a UN peacekeeping mission in 1964. In 1974, fearing a movement to unite Cyprus with Greece, Turkish soldiers occupied the northern third of the country, and Turkish Cypriots established a government, which obtained recognition only from Turkey. Conflict has continued to the present, and the UN peacekeeping mission has remained in place. The Republic of Cyprus joined the European Union in 2004 and adopted the euro as its official currency in 2008.

## Recent Developments

Cypriot life was interrupted on 11 Jul 2011 when confiscated contraband ammunition stored at a Greek Cypriot naval base exploded, killing 13 and injuring many. The blast disabled a major power plant, depriving Greek Cyprus of about half of its electricity. In the aftermath the cabinet and military leaders resigned and the ruling coalition collapsed. Emergency measures included rolling blackouts, a strict austerity program to maintain the economy, and, significantly, purchase of power from Turkish Cyprus. The discovery of a large offshore natural gas field was announced in December, however, holding out hope for much-needed revenue in the future.

Internet resource: <www.visitcyprus.com>.

# Czech Republic

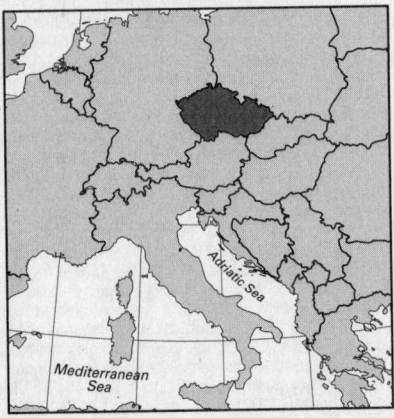

Official name: Ceska republika (Czech Republic). Form of government: unitary multiparty republic with two legislative houses (Senate [81]; Chamber of Deputies [200]). Head of state: President Vaclav Klaus (from 2003). Head of government: Prime Minister Petr Necas (from 2010). Capital: Prague. Official language: Czech. Official religion: none. Monetary unit: 1 koruna (Kc) = 100 haleru; valuation (2 Jul 2012) US$1 = 20.32 Kc.

## Demography

Area: 30,450 sq mi, 78,865 sq km. Population (2011): 10,551,000. Density (2011): persons per sq mi 346.5, persons per sq km 133.8. Urban (2009): 73.5%. Sex distribution (2006): male 48.83%; female 51.17%. Age breakdown (2004): under 15, 14.9%; 15–29, 22.1%; 30–44, 21.3%; 45–59, 22.0%; 60–74, 13.6%; 75–84, 5.2%; 85 and over, 0.9%. Ethnic composition (2001): Czech 90.4%; Moravian 3.7%; Slovak 1.9%; Polish 0.5%; German 0.4%; Silesian 0.1%; Rom (Gypsy) 0.1%; other 2.9%. Religious affiliation (2000): Christian 63.0%, of which Roman Catholic 40.4%, unaffiliated Christian 16.0%, Protestant (mostly Lutheran) 3.1%, independent Christian (mostly independent Catholic [Hussite Church of the Czech Republic]) 2.6%; atheist 5.0%; Jewish 0.1%; nonreligious 31.9%. Major cities (2008): Prague 1,233,211; Brno 370,592; Ostrava 307,767; Plzen 169,273; Liberec 100,914. Location: central Europe, bordering Germany, Poland, Slovakia, and Austria.

## Vital statistics

Birth rate per 1,000 population (2008): 11.5 (world avg. 20.3); within marriage 58.6%. Death rate per 1,000 population (2008): 10.1 (world avg. 8.5). Total fertility rate (avg. births per childbearing woman; 2008): 1.50. Life expectancy at birth (2007): male 73.7 years; female 79.9 years.

## National economy

Budget (2007). Revenue: Kc 1,151,050,000,000 (tax revenue 92.0%, of which social security contributions 45.3%, taxes on goods and services 26.9%, taxes on income and profits 18.8%; grants 4.3%; nontax revenue 3.7%). Expenditures: Kc 1,210,270,000,000 (social security and welfare 33.7%; health 16.1%; education 9.4%; transportation and communications 7.0%; defense 3.8%). Production (metric tons except as noted). Agriculture and fishing (2007): wheat 3,955,437, sugar beets 2,598,676, barley 1,919,712, rapeseed 1,038,400; livestock (number of live animals) 2,741,300 pigs, 1,389,600 cattle; fisheries production 24,723 (from aquaculture 83%). Mining and quarrying (2007): kaolin 3,604,000; feldspar 514,000. Manufacturing (value added in Kc '000,000; 2003): base and fabricated metals 93,380; food products, beverages, and tobacco products 81,440; electrical and optical equipment 70,800. Energy production (consumption): electricity (kW-hr; 2007) 88,187,000,000 ([2006] 71,730,000,000); coal (metric tons; 2007) 12,900,000 ([2005] 9,220,000); lignite (metric tons; 2007) 49,300,000 ([2005] 47,600,000); crude petroleum (barrels; 2006) 2,332,000 (53,800,-000); petroleum products (metric tons; 2006) 5,578,000 (6,761,000); natural gas (cu m; 2007) 223,000,000 ([2006] 10,661,000,000). Population economically active (2007): total 5,198,300; activity rate of total population 50.4% (participation rates: ages 15–64, 69.8%; female 43.6%; unemployed 6.0%). Public debt (external, outstanding; 2004): US$12,020,000,000. Gross national income (2008): US$173,154,000,000 (US$16,600 per capita). Selected balance of payments data. Receipts from (US$'000,000): tourism (2007) 6,637; remittances (2008) 1,415; foreign direct investment (FDI; 2005–07 avg.) 8,931. Disbursements for (US$'000,000): tourism (2007) 3,647; remittances (2008) 3,826; FDI (2005–07 avg.) 927.

---

1 metric ton = about 1.1 short tons;    1 kilometer = 0.6 mi (statute);    1 metric ton-km cargo = about 0.68 short ton-mi cargo;    c.i.f.: cost, insurance, and freight;    f.o.b.: free on board

## Foreign trade

**Imports** (2006; c.i.f.): Kc 2,111,100,000,000 (machinery and apparatus 31.9%; chemical products 10.2%; mineral fuels 9.0%; motor vehicles and parts 8.5%). *Major import sources:* Germany 28.5%; China 6.1%; Russia 6.0%; Poland 5.6%; Slovakia 5.4%. **Exports** (2006; f.o.b.): Kc 2,149,800,000,000 (machinery and apparatus 34.7%, of which computers and office machines and parts 7.8%, general industrial machinery 6.8%; motor vehicles and parts 15.7%; chemical products 5.8%; fabricated metal products 5.5%). *Major export destinations:* Germany 31.9%; Slovakia 8.4%; Poland 5.7%; France 5.5%; Austria 5.1%.

## Transport and communications

**Transport.** *Railroads* (2005): route length (2004) 9,441 km; passenger-km 6,667,000; metric ton-km cargo 14,866,000,000. *Roads* (2006): total length 128,512 km (paved [2004] 100%). *Vehicles* (2005): passenger cars 3,958,708; trucks and buses 435,235. *Air transport* (2008): passenger-km 6,300,000,000; metric ton-km cargo 27,180,000. **Communications,** in total units (units per 1,000 persons). Telephone landlines (2008): 2,278,000 (224); cellular telephone subscribers (2008): 13,780,000 (1,353); personal computers (2004): 5,100,000 (500); total Internet users (2007): 4,400,000 (432); broadband Internet subscribers (2008): 1,760,000 (173).

## Education and health

**Educational attainment** (2001). Percentage of population ages 15 and over having: no formal schooling 0.2%; primary education 21.6%; secondary 68.7%; higher 9.5%. **Literacy** (2001): 99.8%. **Health** (2005): physicians 36,381 (1 per 282 persons); hospital beds 65,022 (1 per 158 persons); infant mortality rate per 1,000 live births (2008) 2.8; undernourished population (2003–05) less than 5% of total population.

## Military

**Total active duty personnel** (November 2008): 24,083 (army 55.5%, air force 20.5%, joint staff 24.0%). **Military expenditure as percentage of GDP** (2008): 1.5%; per capita expenditure US$279.

## Background

Until 1918 the history of what is now the Czech Republic was largely that of Bohemia. In that year the independent republic of Czechoslovakia was born through the union of Bohemia and Moravia with Slovakia. Czechoslovakia came under the domination of the Soviet Union after World War II, and from 1948 to 1989 it was ruled by a communist government. Its growing political liberalization was suppressed by a Soviet invasion in 1968. After communist rule collapsed in 1989–90, separatist sentiments emerged among the Slovaks, and in 1992 the Czechs and the Slovaks agreed to break up their federated state. On 1 Jan 1993 the Czechoslovakian republic was peacefully dissolved and replaced by two new countries, the Czech Republic and Slovakia, with the region of Moravia remaining in the former. In 1999 the Czech Republic entered NATO and in 2004 the EU.

## Recent Developments

The Czech economy grew by a respectable 1% in 2011, boosted by continued strong growth in industrial production (the value of which increased by almost 7%) and exports (the value of which increased by more than 13%). Consumer price inflation—which remained under the Czech National Bank's 2% target band for most of the year—allowed for continued low interest rates, which stood below those of the European Central Bank throughout 2011. Unemployment dropped by February 2012 to just over 9%. In December 2011, however, the world mourned the loss of Czech statesman and intellectual Vaclav Havel, who played a key role in the Velvet Revolution that led to a democratic Czechoslovakia; he served two terms as president of the Czech Republic (1993–2003).

**Internet resource:** <www.czso.cz>.

# Denmark

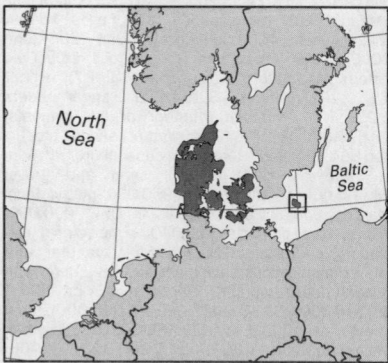

**Official name:** Kongeriget Danmark (Kingdom of Denmark). **Form of government:** constitutional monarchy with one legislative house (Folketing [179]). **Head of state:** Queen Margrethe II (from 1972). **Head of government:** Prime Minister Helle Thorning-Schmidt (from 2011). **Capital:** Copenhagen. **Official language:** Danish. **Official religion:** Evangelical Lutheran. **Monetary unit:** 1 Danish krone (DKK; plural kroner) = 100 øre; valuation (2 Jul 2012) US$1 = DKK 5.91.

## Demography

**Area:** 16,640 sq mi, 43,098 sq km (excludes the Faroe Islands and Greenland). **Population** (2011): 5,574,000. **Density** (2011): persons per sq mi 335.0, persons per sq km 129.3. **Urban** (2008): 86.6%. **Sex distribution** (2008): male 49.57%; female 50.43%. **Age breakdown** (2006): under 15, 18.6%; 15–29, 17.3%; 30–44, 21.9%; 45–59, 20.2%; 60–74, 15.0%; 75–84, 5.1%; 85 and over, 1.9%. **Ethnic composition** (2006): Danish 91.9%; Turkish 0.6%; German 0.5%; Iraqi 0.4%; Swedish 0.4%; Norwegian 0.3%; Bosnian 0.3%; other 5.6%. **Religious affiliation** (2006): Evangelical Lutheran 83.0%; other Christian 1.3%; Muslim 3.7%; nonreligious 5.4%; atheist 1.5%; other 5.1%. **Major urban areas** (2007): Greater Copenhagen 1,153,615; Århus 237,551; Odense 158,163; Ålborg 121,818; Esbjerb 70,880. **Location:** northern Europe, bordering the North Sea, the Baltic Sea, and Germany.

## Vital statistics

**Birth rate** per 1,000 population (2008): 11.8 (world avg. 20.3); within marriage 53.8%. **Death rate** per 1,000 population (2008): 9.9 (world avg. 8.5). **Total fertility rate** (avg. births per childbearing woman; 2008): 1.89. **Life expectancy** at birth (2007–08): male 76.3 years; female 80.7 years.

## National economy

**Budget** (2007). *Revenue:* DKK 694,084,000,000 (taxes on income and profits 44.4%; taxes on goods and services 39.8%). *Expenditures:* DKK 613,412,000,000 (social protection 35.1%; education 11.4%; economic affairs 5.8%; defense 4.3%; health 0.2%). **National debt** (December 2006): US$57,887,000,000. **Population economically active** (2007): total 2,893,200; activity rate of total population 53.0% (participation rates: ages 15–64, 80.2%; female 47.1%; unemployed [July 2005–June 2006] 5.0%). **Production** (metric tons except as noted). *Agriculture and fishing* (2007): wheat 4,519,200, barley 3,104,200, sugar beets 2,255,300; livestock (number of live animals) 13,599,000 pigs, 1,579,000 cattle; fisheries production 684,191 metric tons (from aquaculture 5%). *Mining and quarrying* (2007): sand and gravel 28,600,000 cu m; chalk 1,950,000 metric tons. *Manufacturing* (value of sales in DKK '000,000; 2005): food products 121,040; nonelectrical machinery and apparatus 66,050; computer and telecommunications equipment 49,078. *Energy production (consumption):* electricity (kW-hr; 2007) 37,394,000,000 ([2006] 38,781,000,000); coal (metric tons; 2006) none (9,436,000); crude petroleum (barrels; 2007) 111,300,000 ([2006] 59,111,000); petroleum products (metric tons; 2006) 7,840,000 (6,800,000); natural gas (cu m; 2006) 10,053,000,000 (4,918,000,000). **Gross national income** (2008): US$325,060,000,000 (US$59,130 per capita). **Selected balance of payments data.** Receipts from (US$'000,000): tourism (2007) 6,218; remittances (2008) 1,087; foreign direct investment (FDI; 2005–07 avg.) 9,243. Disbursements for (US$'000,000): tourism (2007) 8,791; remittances (2008) 3,227; FDI (2005–07 avg.) 13,914.

## Foreign trade

**Imports** (2006; c.i.f.): DKK 502,587,000,000 (machinery and apparatus 25.9%; chemical products 10.8%; food products 9.2%; motor vehicles 8.5%). *Major import sources:* Germany 21.5%; Sweden 14.3%; Netherlands 6.2%; UK 5.8%; China 5.3%. **Exports** (2006; f.o.b.): DKK 535,933,000,000 (machinery and apparatus 23.3%, of which general industrial machinery 6.4%, power-generating machinery 4.5%; food products 16.1%, of which meat 5.6%; crude petroleum 9.3%; medicine and pharmaceuticals 7.3%). *Major export destinations:* Germany 15.5%; Sweden 13.8%; UK 8.4%; US 6.0%; Norway 5.7%.

## Transport and communications

**Transport.** *Railroads* (2004): route length 2,644 km; passenger-km 6,132,000,000; metric ton-km cargo 1,976,000,000. *Roads* (2006): total length 72,362 km (paved 100%). *Vehicles* (2006): passenger cars 2,020,013; trucks and buses 508,788. *Air transport* (2008; Danish share of Scandinavian Airlines System): passenger-km 5,316,000,000; metric ton-km cargo (2007) 8,748,000. **Communications,** in total units (units per 1,000 persons). Telephone landlines (2008): 2,487,000 (456); cellular telephone subscribers (2008): 6,551,000 (1,201); personal computers (2004): 3,543,000 (659); total Internet users (2008): 4,630,000 (849); broadband Internet subscribers (2008): 2,006,000 (369).

## Education and health

**Educational attainment** (2004). Percentage of population ages 25–69 having: completed lower secondary or not stated 30.3%; completed upper secondary or vocational 43.9%; undergraduate 19.6%; graduate 6.2%. **Literacy:** 100%. **Health:** physicians (2004) 19,450 (1 per 278 persons); hospital beds (2005) 20,487 (1 per 265 persons); infant mortality rate per 1,000 live births (2008) 4.0; undernourished population (2003–05) less than 5% of total population.

## Military

**Total active duty personnel** (November 2008): 29,550 (army 48.2%, air force 12.1%, navy 11.8%, joint staff 27.9%). **Military expenditure as percentage of GDP** (2008): 1.3%; per capita expenditure US$746.

## Background

The Danes, a Scandinavian branch of the Teutons, settled the area c. the 6th century AD. During the Viking period the Danes expanded their territory, and by the 11th century the united Danish kingdom included parts of what are now Germany, Sweden, England, and Norway. Scandinavia was united under Danish rule from 1397 until 1523, when Sweden became independent; a series of debilitating wars with Sweden in the 17th century resulted in the Treaty of Copenhagen (1660), which established the modern Scandinavian frontiers. Denmark gained and lost various other territories, including Norway, in the 19th and 20th centuries; it went through three constitutions between 1849 and 1915 and was occupied by Nazi Germany in 1940–45. A founding member of NATO (1949), Denmark adopted its current constitution in 1953. It became a member of the European Community in 1973 and of the EU in 1993, but it negotiated exemptions from certain EU provisions in response to some Danes' concerns regarding environmental protection and social welfare. In the early 21st century Denmark's handling of immigrants raised great debate.

## Recent Developments

Ten years of center-right rule in Denmark ended in September 2011, when the center-left opposition "Red Bloc" won a narrow victory in the general elec-

---

*1 metric ton = about 1.1 short tons; 1 kilometer = 0.6 mi (statute); 1 metric ton-km cargo = about 0.68 short ton-mi cargo; c.i.f.: cost, insurance, and freight; f.o.b.: free on board*

tions to the Folketing (parliament), and Helle Thorning-Schmidt became the country's first female prime minister. The new government announced a 10 billion krone (about US$50 billion) growth package to kick-start the economy, including tax and welfare reforms, wage restraint, and improved education and training schemes. The tight immigration policies of the previous government, which had brought Denmark much criticism, were largely set to be relaxed by the new ruling coalition. Asylum seekers, Thorning-Schmidt said, should be treated "with care and respect." On the foreign-policy front, the new government pledged to withdraw Denmark's 750 troops from NATO's International Security Assistance Force in Afghanistan by the end of 2014.

Internet resource: <www.dst.dk/en>.

# Djibouti

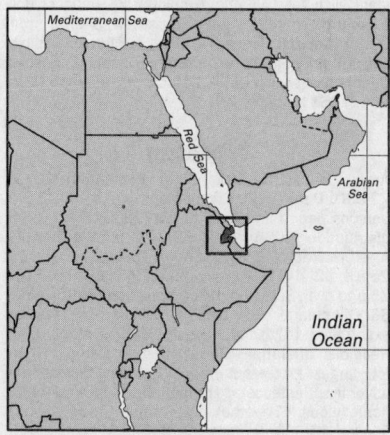

**Official name:** Jumhuriyah Jibuti (Arabic); République de Djibouti (French) (Republic of Djibouti). **Form of government:** multiparty republic with one legislative house (National Assembly [65]). **Head of state and head of government:** President Ismail Omar Guelleh (from 1999). **Capital:** Djibouti. **Official languages:** Arabic; French. **Official religion:** Islam. **Monetary unit:** 1 Djibouti franc (FDJ) = 100 centimes; valuation (2 Jul 2012) US$1 = FDJ 175.95.

## Demography

**Area:** 8,950 sq mi, 23,200 sq km. **Population** (2011): 840,000. **Density** (2011): persons per sq mi 93.9, persons per sq km 36.2. **Urban** (2009): 70.6%. **Sex distribution** (2006): male 51.19%; female 48.81%. **Age breakdown** (2006): under 15, 43.3%; 15–29, 28.0%; 30–44, 13.7%; 45–59, 9.2%; 60–74, 5.1%; 75 and over, 0.7%. **Ethnic composition** (2000): Somali 46.0%; Afar 35.4%; Arab 11.0%; mixed African and European 3.0%; French 1.6%; other/unspecified 3.0%. **Religious affiliation** (2000): Muslim (nearly all Sunni) 94.1%; Christian 4.5%, of which Orthodox 3.0%, Roman Catholic 1.4%; nonreligious 1.3%; other 0.1%. **Major city and towns** (2009): Djibouti (2007) 583,000; Ali Sabieh 23,000; Dikhil 16,700; Arta 11,600. **Location:** the Horn of Africa,

bordering Eritrea, the Red Sea, the Gulf of Aden, Somalia, and Ethiopia.

## Vital statistics

**Birth rate** per 1,000 population (2006): 39.5 (world avg. 20.3). **Death rate** per 1,000 population (2006): 19.3 (world avg. 8.5). **Total fertility rate** (avg. births per childbearing woman; 2006): 5.31. **Life expectancy** at birth (2006): male 41.9 years; female 44.5 years.

## National economy

**Budget** (2005). *Revenue:* FDJ 46,710,000,000 (tax revenue 65.8%, of which indirect taxes 26.3%, direct taxes 24.8%, transit taxes, harbor dues, and other registration fees 14.7%; nontax revenue 17.5%; grants 16.7%). *Expenditures:* FDJ 46,378,000,000 (current expenditures 74.7%; capital expenditures 25.3%). **Public debt** (external, outstanding; February 2006): US$474,000,000. **Production** (metric tons except as noted). *Agriculture and fishing* (2007): lemons and limes 1,800, dry beans 1,500, tomatoes 1,200; livestock (number of live animals) 512,000 goats, 466,000 sheep, 297,000 cattle, 69,000 camels; fisheries production 265 (from aquaculture, none). *Mining and quarrying:* mineral production limited to locally used construction materials such as basalt and evaporated salt (2006) 138,000. *Manufacturing* (2003): products of limited value include furniture, nonalcoholic beverages, meat and hides, light electromechanical goods, and mineral water. *Energy production (consumption):* electricity (kW-hr; 2006) 280,000,000 (280,000,000); petroleum products (metric tons; 2006) none (139,000); natural gas (cu m; 2004) none (4,380,000); geothermal, wind, and solar resources are substantial but largely undeveloped. **Population economically active** (2003): total 299,000; activity rate of total population 39.1% (participation rates: ages 15–64, 69.0%; female 39.5%; unemployed [2006] 60%). **Gross national income** (2008): US$957,000,000 (US$1,030 per capita). **Selected balance of payments data.** Receipts from (US$'000,000): tourism (2006) 9.2; remittances (2008) 29; foreign direct investment (2005–07 avg.) 139; official development assistance (2006) 117. Disbursements for (US$'000,000): tourism (2006) 3.5; remittances (2008) 5.

## Foreign trade

**Imports** (1999; total and commodities data exclude Ethiopian trade via rail): US$152,700,000 (food products and beverages 25.0%; machinery and electric appliances 12.5%; khat 12.2%; refined petroleum products 10.9%; transportation equipment 10.3%). *Major import sources* (2004): Saudi Arabia 21.9%; India 18.7%; China 10.2%; Ethiopia 4.8%; France 4.7%. **Exports** (2001; total and commodities data exclude Ethiopian trade via rail): US$10,200,000 (aircraft parts 24.5%; hides and skins of cattle, sheep, goats, and camels 20.6%; leather products 7.8%; live animals 6.9%). *Major export destinations* (2005): Somalia 66.4%; Ethiopia 21.5%; Yemen 3.4%.

## Transport and communications

**Transport.** *Railroads* (2006): length 100 km; (1999) passenger-km 81,000,000; (2002) metric ton-km cargo 201,000,000. *Roads* (2002): total length

2,890 km (paved 13%). *Vehicles* (2002): passenger cars 15,700; trucks and buses 3,200. *Air transport* (2005): passenger arrivals and departures 219,119; metric tons of freight loaded and unloaded 10,973. **Communications,** in total units (units per 1,000 persons). Telephone landlines (2005): 11,000 (23); cellular telephone subscribers (2007): 45,000 (54); personal computers (2005): 19,000 (41); total Internet users (2006): 11,000 (23); broadband Internet subscribers (2005): 40 (0.09).

## Education and health

**Literacy** (2007): percentage of population ages 15 and over literate 72.2%; males literate 81.2%; females literate 63.8%. **Health:** physicians (2004) 129 (1 per 3,619 persons); hospital beds (2000) 694 (1 per 621 persons); infant mortality rate per 1,000 live births (2006) 102.4; undernourished population (2002–04) 200,000 (24% of total population based on the consumption of a minimum daily requirement of 1,770 calories).

## Military

**Total active duty personnel** (November 2008): 10,450 (army 76.6%, navy 1.9%, air force 2.4%, national security force 19.1%); foreign troops (November 2008): French Foreign Legion 2,850; US 1,900; German 100. **Military expenditure as percentage of GDP** (2007): 1.9%; per capita expenditure US$20.

## Background

Settled around the 3rd century BC by the Arab ancestors of the Afars, Djibouti was later populated by Somali Issas. In AD 825 Islam was brought to the area by missionaries. Arabs controlled the trade in this region until the 16th century; it became the French protectorate of French Somaliland in 1888. In 1946 it became a French overseas territory, and in 1977 it gained its independence. In the late 20th century, the country received refugees from the Ethiopian-Somali war and from civil conflicts in Eritrea. In the 1990s it suffered from political unrest.

## Recent Developments

The tiny yet strategically important Red Sea country of Djibouti faced a severe drought in 2011. The drought, compounded with regional instability, plunged Djibouti—along with its Horn of Africa neighbors Somalia, Kenya, and Ethiopia—into one of the worst famines in decades. More than 13 million people in the region needed urgent humanitarian aid, with close to 120,000 Djiboutians—approximately 15% of the country's population—facing starvation. In February 2012, the IMF announced a US$14 million loan to aid Djibouti's recovery.

**Internet resource:** <www.ministere-finances.dj>.

# Dominica

**Official name:** Commonwealth of Dominica. **Form of government:** multiparty republic with one legislative

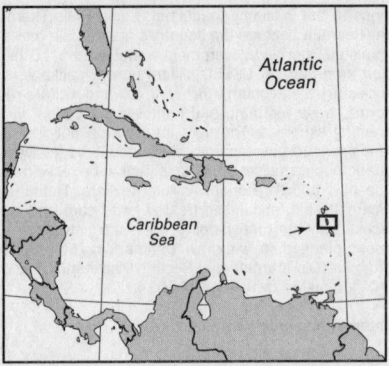

house (House of Assembly [32]). **Head of state:** President Nicholas Liverpool (from 2003). **Head of government:** Prime Minister Roosevelt Skerrit (from 2004). **Capital:** Roseau. **Official language:** English. **Official religion:** none. **Monetary unit:** 1 Eastern Caribbean dollar (EC$) = 100 cents; valuation (2 Jul 2012) US$1 = EC$2.70.

## Demography

**Area:** 290 sq mi, 751 sq km. **Population** (2011): 72,500. **Density** (2011): persons per sq mi 250.0, persons per sq km 96.5. **Urban** (2009): 67.2%. **Sex distribution** (2006): male 50.34%; female 49.66%. **Age breakdown** (2006): under 15, 26.1%; 15–29, 23.8%; 30–44, 27.4%; 45–59, 12.4%; 60–74, 7.0%; 75 and over, 3.3%. **Ethnic composition** (2000): black 88.3%; mulatto 7.3%; black-Amerindian 1.7%; British expatriates 1.0%; Indo-Pakistani 1.0%; other 0.7%. **Religious affiliation** (2001): Roman Catholic 61%; four largest Protestant groups (including Seventh-day Adventist, Pentecostal groups, and Methodist) 28%; nonreligious 6%; other 5%. **Major towns** (2006): Roseau 16,600; Portsmouth 3,600; Marigot 2,900. **Location:** island in the southern Caribbean Sea, south of Guadeloupe and north of Martinique.

## Vital statistics

**Birth rate** per 1,000 population (2006): 15.3 (world avg. 20.3); (1991) within marriage 24.1%. **Death rate** per 1,000 population (2006): 6.7 (world avg. 8.5). **Total fertility rate** (avg. births per childbearing woman; 2006): 1.94. **Life expectancy** at birth (2006): male 72.0 years; female 77.9 years.

## National economy

**Budget** (2008). *Revenue:* EC$467,600,000 (tax revenue 65.7%, of which VAT 24.4%, taxes on international trade and transactions 14.7%, taxes on income and profits 11.1%; grants 27.8%; nontax revenue 6.5%). *Expenditures:* EC$458,300,000 (current expenditures 66.2%, of which wages and salaries 26.2%, transfers 13.9%, debt service 7.2%; development expenditures and net lending 33.8%). **Public debt** (external, outstanding; 2005): US$208,400,000. **Gross national income** (2007): US$310,000,000 (US$4,250 per capita). **Popula-**

---

*1 metric ton = about 1.1 short tons;    1 kilometer = 0.6 mi (statute);    1 metric ton-km cargo = about 0.68 short ton-mi cargo;    c.i.f.: cost, insurance, and freight;    f.o.b.: free on board*

tion economically active (2001): total 27,865; activity rate of total population 40.0% (participation rates: ages 15–64, 64.7%; female 38.9%; unemployed [2002] 25%). **Production** (metric tons except as noted). *Agriculture and fishing* (2007): bananas 30,000, grapefruit and pomelos 17,000, coconuts 12,000; livestock (number of live animals) 13,500 cattle, 9,700 goats, 7,600 sheep; fisheries production 776 (from aquaculture, negligible). *Mining and quarrying:* pumice, limestone, and sand and gravel are quarried primarily for local consumption. *Manufacturing* (value of production in EC$'000; 2004): toilet and laundry soap 24,588; toothpaste 8,774; crude coconut oil (2001) 1,758; other products include fruit juices, beer, garments, bottled spring water, and cardboard boxes. *Energy production (consumption):* electricity (kW-hr; 2006) 85,000,-000 (85,000,000); petroleum products (metric tons; 2006) none (38,000). **Selected balance of payments data.** Receipts from (US$'000,000): tourism (2007) 71; remittances (2008) 30; foreign direct investment (2005–07 avg.) 31; official development assistance (2007) 19. Disbursements for (US$'000,000): tourism (2007) 10; remittances (2008) negligible.

## Foreign trade

**Imports** (2006; c.i.f.): US$166,900,000 (machinery and apparatus 17.1%; food products 15.5%; refined petroleum products 14.2%; chemical products 12.2%; motor vehicles 5.9%). *Major import sources:* US 36.1%; Trinidad and Tobago 22.1%; UK 5.8%; Japan 4.0%; China 3.9%. **Exports** (2006; f.o.b.): US$41,500,000 (food products 32.8%, of which bananas 21.2%; soap 25.3%; dental and oral hygiene preparations 13.5%; stone, sand, and gravel 6.7%). *Major export destinations:* UK 18.6%; Jamaica 15.2%; Antigua and Barbuda 13.0%; France (including overseas departments) 8.2%; Trinidad and Tobago 7.5%.

## Transport and communications

**Transport.** *Railroads:* none. *Roads* (1999): total length 780 km (paved 50%). *Vehicles* (1998): passenger cars 8,700; trucks and buses 3,400. *Air transport* (1997): passenger arrivals and departures 74,100; cargo unloaded 575 metric tons, cargo loaded 363 metric tons. **Communications,** in total units (units per 1,000 persons). Telephone landlines (2004): 21,000 (295); cellular telephone subscribers (2004): 42,000 (589); personal computers (2004): 13,000 (182); total Internet users (2005): 26,000 (372); broadband Internet subscribers (2004): 3,300 (46).

## Education and health

**Educational attainment** (2002). Percentage of population ages 15 and over having: primary education 62%; secondary 31%; vocational/university 7%. **Literacy** (1996): total population ages 15 and over literate, 94.0%. **Health:** physicians (2004) 38 (1 per 1,824 persons); hospital beds (2002) 270 (1 per 257 persons); infant mortality rate per 1,000 live births (2006) 13.7; undernourished population (2003–05) less than 5% of total population.

## Military

**Total active duty personnel** (2006): none (a 300-member police force includes a coast guard unit).

## Background

At the time of the arrival of Christopher Columbus in 1493, Dominica was inhabited by the Caribs. With its steep coastal cliffs and inaccessible mountains, it was one of the last islands to be explored by Europeans, and the Caribs remained in possession until the 18th century; it was then settled by the French and ultimately taken by Britain in 1783. Subsequent hostilities between the settlers and the native inhabitants resulted in the Caribs' near extinction. Incorporated with the Leeward Islands in 1883 and with the Windward Islands in 1940, it became a member of the West Indies Federation in 1958. Dominica became independent in 1978. Offshore banking, a controversial boon to the Dominican economy in the late 20th century, was discontinued early in the 21st century.

## Recent Developments

In April 2011, Dominica signed a US$6.29 million deal with an Icelandic agency to look into developing its geothermal energy resources. Dominica's long-term goal was to build a 120-MW power station that could export power to the neighboring French overseas *départements* of Guadeloupe and Martinique. Exploratory drilling began in December.

**Internet resource:** <www.dominica.gov.dm>.

# Dominican Republic

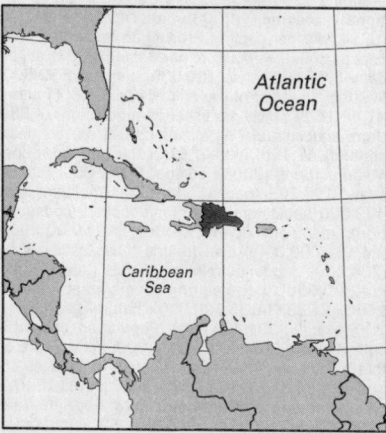

**Official name:** República Dominicana (Dominican Republic). **Form of government:** multiparty republic with two legislative houses (Senate [32]; Chamber of Deputies [183]). **Head of state and government:** President Leonel Fernández Reyna (from 2004). **Capital:** Santo Domingo. **Official language:** Spanish. **Official religion:** none (Roman Catholicism is the state religion per concordat with Vatican City). **Monetary unit:** 1 Dominican peso (RD$) = 100 centavos; valuation (2 Jul 2012) US$1 = RD$39.10.

## Demography

**Area:** 18,792 sq mi, 48,671 sq km. **Population** (2011): 9,440,000. **Density** (2011): persons per sq

mi 502.3, persons per sq km 194.0. **Urban** (2009): 68.5%. **Sex distribution** (2005): male 50.18%; female 49.82%. **Age breakdown** (2002): under 15, 33.5%; 15–29, 26.6%; 30–44, 20.2%; 45–59, 11.7%; 60–74, 5.9%; 75–84, 1.6%; 85 and over, 0.5%. **Ethnic composition** (2003): mulatto 73%; white 16%; black 11%. **Religious affiliation** (2004): Roman Catholic 64.4%; other Christian 11.4%; nonreligious 22.5%; other 1.7%. **Major urban centers** (2002): Santo Domingo 1,887,586; Santiago 507,418; San Pedro de Macorís 193,713; La Romana 191,303; San Cristóbal 137,422. **Location:** eastern two-thirds of the island of Hispaniola, bordered by the North Atlantic Ocean, the Caribbean Sea, and Haiti.

## Vital statistics

**Birth rate** per 1,000 population (2007): 20.4 (world avg. 20.3). **Death rate** per 1,000 population (2007): 3.6 (world avg. 8.5). **Total fertility rate** (avg. births per childbearing woman; 2006): 2.83. **Life expectancy** at birth (2006): male 71.0 years; female 74.5 years.

## National economy

**Budget** (2005). *Revenue:* RD$157,585,000,000 (tax revenue 94.2%, of which taxes on goods and services 49.0%, import duties 24.0%, income taxes 18.8%; nontax revenue 5.8%). *Expenditures:* RD$161,612,000,000 (current expenditures 75.7%; development expenditures 24.3%). **Public debt** (external, outstanding; 2006): US$6,571,000,000. **Gross national income** (2008): US$43,207,000,000 (US$4,390 per capita). **Production** (metric tons except as noted). *Agriculture and fishing* (2007): sugarcane 5,700,000, rice 710,000, bananas 552,500; livestock (number of live animals) 2,210,000 cattle, 47,500,000 chickens; fisheries production 14,689 (from aquaculture 7%). Mining (2007): nickel (metal content) 47,125; marble 6,000 cu m; gold, none. *Manufacturing* (2005): cement 2,779,000; refined sugar 139,203; beer 4,541,000 hectoliters; rum 499,000 hectoliters. *Energy production (consumption):* electricity (kW-hr; 2006) 14,150,000,000 (14,150,000,000); coal (metric tons; 2006) none (704,000); crude petroleum (barrels; 2006) none (14,800,000); petroleum products (metric tons; 2006) 1,936,000 (5,190,000); natural gas (cu m; 2006) none (331,400,000). **Population economically active** (2007): total 4,204,800; activity rate of total population 45.2% (participation rates: ages 15 and over, 64.3%; female 38.7%; unemployed 10.0%). **Selected balance of payments data.** Receipts from (US$'000,000): tourism (2007) 4,082; remittances (2008) 3,487; foreign direct investment (2005–07 avg.) 1,427; official development assistance (2007) 128. Disbursements for (US$'000,000): tourism (2007) 326; remittances (2008) 28.

## Foreign trade

**Imports** (2006): US$8,745,000,000 (consumer goods 50.7%, of which refined petroleum products 21.0%, food products 5.8%; capital goods 15.4%; crude petroleum 10.9%). *Major import sources* (2005): US 50.0%; Colombia 6.2%; Mexico 5.8%. **Exports** (2006): US$6,440,000,000 (reexports of free zones 70.0%, of which wearing apparel 24.8%, electronics 10.3%, jewelry 9.8%; ferronickel 11.0%; mineral fuels 5.6%; raw sugar 1.6%). *Major export destinations* (2005): US 78.9%; Netherlands 2.4%; Mexico 1.9%.

## Transport and communications

**Transport.** *Railroads* (2004): route length 615 km. *Roads* (2002): total length 19,705 km (paved 51%). *Vehicles* (2008): passenger cars 630,815; trucks and buses 383,869. *Air transport:* (1999) passenger-km 4,900,000; (2003) metric ton-km cargo 200,000. **Communications**, in total units (units per 1,000 persons). Telephone landlines (2008): 986,000 (100); cellular telephone subscribers (2008): 7,211,000 (728); personal computers (2007): 331,000 (35); total Internet users (2008): 2,563,000 (259); broadband Internet subscribers (2008): 226,000 (23).

## Education and health

**Educational attainment** (2002). Percentage of population ages 25 and older having: no formal education/unknown 4.1%; incomplete/complete primary education 53.1%; secondary 25.9%; undergraduate 15.9%; graduate 1.0%. **Literacy** (2003): total population ages 15 and over literate 84.7%. **Health** (2005): physicians (public sector only) 12,966 (1 per 730 persons); hospital beds 9,640 (1 per 982 persons); infant mortality rate per 1,000 live births (2006) 29.0; undernourished population (2003–05) 2,000,000 (21% of total population based on the consumption of a minimum daily requirement of 1,840 calories).

## Military

**Total active duty personnel** (November 2008): 49,910 (army 81.0%, navy 8.0%, air force 11.0%). **Military expenditure as percentage of GDP** (2008): 0.6%; per capita expenditure US$30.

## Background

The Dominican Republic was originally part of the Spanish colony of Hispaniola. In 1697 the western third of the island, which later became Haiti, was ceded to France; the remainder of the island passed to France in 1795. The eastern two-thirds of the island was returned to Spain in 1809, and the colony declared its independence in 1821. Within a matter of weeks it was overrun by Haitian troops and occupied until 1844. Since then the country has been under the rule of a succession of dictators, except for short interludes of democratic government, and the US has frequently been involved in its affairs. The termination of the dictatorship of Rafael Trujillo in 1961 led to civil war in 1965 and US military intervention. The country frequently suffered from severe hurricanes, as in 1979 and 1998.

## Recent Developments

Following tradition, the 2012 presidential campaign in the Dominican Republic started early, and the country was awash in propaganda in 2011. Little attention was paid, though, to the Dominican Repub-

*1 metric ton = about 1.1 short tons;   1 kilometer = 0.6 mi (statute);   1 metric ton-km cargo = about 0.68 short ton-mi cargo;   c.i.f.: cost, insurance, and freight;   f.o.b.: free on board*

lic's litany of problems: high unemployment, declining GNP (a reflection of diminished remittances and tourism), 8% inflation, the growth of drug-oriented organized crime, rampant corruption, and chronic and economically debilitating electricity blackouts. Investment in the minerals sector was strong, however, with Canada having overtaken the United States as the principal foreign investor in the Dominican Republic. Moreover, Pres. Leonel Fernández maintained his profile as an activist whose concerns spanned the hemisphere. He engaged constructively with Haiti despite ancient and ongoing grievances concerning illegal Haitian immigration, and he steadily advocated for former Honduran president Manuel Zelaya's return from exile in Santo Domingo.

Internet resource: <http://dominicanrepublic.com>.

# East Timor (Timor-Leste)

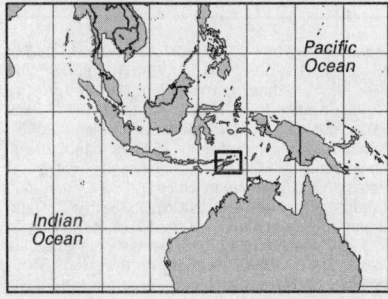

**Official name:** República Democrática de Timor-Leste (Portuguese); Republika Demokratika Timor Lorosa'e (Tetum); (Democratic Republic of Timor-Leste [East Timor]). **Form of government:** republic with one legislative house (National Parliament [65]). **Head of State:** President Taur Matan Ruak (from 2012). **Head of government:** Prime Minister Xanana Gusmão (from 2007). **Capital:** Dili. **Official languages:** Portuguese; Tetum. **Official religion:** none. **Monetary unit:** 1 US dollar (US$) = 100 cents.

## Demography

**Area:** 5,760 sq mi, 14,919 sq km. **Population** (2011): 1,092,000. **Density** (2011): persons per sq mi 189.6, persons per sq km 73.2. **Urban** (2005): 7.8%. **Sex distribution** (2008): male 50.79%; female 49.21%. **Age breakdown** (2008): under 15, 45.0%; 15–29, 25.3%; 30–44, 15.1%; 45–59, 9.6%; 60–74, 4.0%; 75 and over, 1.0%. **Ethnic composition** (1999): East Timorese 80%; other (nearly all Indonesian, and particularly West Timorese) 20%. **Religious affiliation** (2005): Roman Catholic 98%; Protestant 1%; Muslim 1%. **Major urban areas** (2004): Dili 151,026; Los Palos (Lospalos) 12,612; Same 9,966. **Location:** southeast Asia, eastern end of the island of Timor plus an exclave on the western end, bordered by the Timor Sea and Indonesia.

## Vital statistics

**Birth rate** per 1,000 population (2008): 40.9 (world avg. 20.3). **Death rate** per 1,000 population (2008): 10.0 (world avg. 8.5). **Total fertility rate** (avg. births per childbearing woman; 2008): 6.50. **Life expectancy** at birth (2006): male 64.0 years; female 68.7 years.

## National economy

**Budget** (2005–06). *Revenue:* US$485,000,000 (oil and gas revenue 93.1%, of which taxes 74.8%, royalties 15.5%; domestic revenue 6.9%). *Expenditures:* US$93,000,000 (current expenditures 71.3%; capital expenditures 16.9%; previous year spending 11.8%). **Production** (metric tons except as noted). *Agriculture and fishing* (2007): corn (maize) 63,430, cassava 49,720, rice 41,386, coffee 14,000, candlenut (2001) 1,063, cinnamon 75; livestock (number of live animals) 346,000 pigs, 171,000 cattle, 110,000 buffalo; sandalwood exports were formerly more significant; fisheries production 350 (from aquaculture, none). *Mining and quarrying* (2006): commercial quantities of marble are exported. *Manufacturing* (2001): principally the production of textiles, garments, handicrafts, bottled water, and processed coffee. *Energy production (consumption):* electricity (kW-hr; 2006) 320,000,000 (320,000,000); crude petroleum (barrels; 2006) 1,142,000 (negligible); petroleum products (metric tons; 2006) 6,735,000 (97,000). **Population economically active** (2006): total 427,000; activity rate of total population 38% (participation rates: ages 15–64, 71%; female 40%; unemployed [2000] 50%). **Gross national income** (2008): US$2,706,000,000 (US$2,460 per capita). **Selected balance of payments data.** Receipts from (US$'000,000): foreign direct investment (2005–07 avg.) 1; official development assistance (2007) 278.

## Foreign trade

**Imports** (2008): US$268,583,000 (mineral fuels 26.5%; motor vehicles 16.3%; cereals 9.5%; electrical equipment 6.5%; machinery and apparatus 6.5%). *Major import sources:* Indonesia 42.5%; Singapore 17.1%; Australia 13.8%; Vietnam 7.0%; Japan 4.5%. **Exports** (2008): US$49,206,000 (domestic exports 26.2%, of which coffee 25.7%; reexports 73.8%). *Major export destinations* (excluding reexports): Germany 26.9%; US 26.8%; Indonesia 16.6%; Singapore 10.0%; Portugal 6.4%.

## Transport and communications

**Transport.** *Railroads:* none. *Roads* (2005): total length 5,000 km (paved 50%). *Vehicles* (1998): passenger cars 3,156; trucks and buses 7,140. **Communications**, in total units (units per 1,000 persons). Telephone landlines (2003): 2,000 (2.4); cellular telephone subscribers (2007): 69,000 (60); total Internet users (2004): 1,000 (1.1).

## Education and health

**Educational attainment** (2002). Percentage of population ages 15 and over having: no formal education 54.3%, some primary education 14.4%, complete primary 6.2%, lower secondary 10.4%, upper secondary and higher 14.7%. **Literacy** (2005): percentage of population ages 15 and over literate 49%; males literate 54%; females literate 45%. **Health** (2008): physicians 347 (1 per 3,107 persons); hospital beds (1999) 560 (1 per 1,277 persons); infant mortality rate per 1,000 live births 83.5.

## Military

Total active duty personnel (November 2008): 1,286 (army 97%, navy 3%); foreign peacekeeping troops (March 2009): Australian 650; New Zealander 140.

## Background

The Portuguese first settled on the island of Timor in 1520 and were granted rule over Timor's eastern half in 1860. The Timorese political party Fretilin declared East Timor independent in 1975 after Portugal withdrew its troops. It was invaded by Indonesian forces and was incorporated as a province of Indonesia in 1976. The takeover, which resulted in thousands of East Timorese deaths during the next two decades, was disputed by the UN. In 1999 an independence referendum won overwhelmingly; civilian militias, armed by the military and led by local supporters of integration, then rampaged through the province, killing 1,000–2,000 people. The Indonesian parliament rescinded Indonesia's annexation of the territory, and East Timor was returned to its preannexation status as a non-self-governing territory, though this time under UN supervision. Preparation for independence got under way in 2001, with East Timorese voting by universal suffrage in August for a Constituent Assembly of 88 members. Independence was officially declared on 20 May 2002 and was followed by the swearing in of Xanana Gusmão as the first president of the country.

## Recent Developments

East Timor's economy grew rapidly in 2011, with GDP growth forecast at an estimated 8.5%. In the decade following independence, development had slowly led to improved living conditions. The infant mortality rate declined from 79 to 46 per 1,000 live births between 2000 and 2010, and life expectancy rose from 56 to 61. More than 40% of the people remained below the country's poverty line, however, and only half were literate.

Internet resource: <www.dne.mof.gov.tl>.

## Ecuador

Official name: República del Ecuador (Republic of Ecuador). Form of government: unitary multiparty republic with one legislative house (National Assembly [124]). Head of state and government: President Rafael Correa Delgado (from 2007). Capital: Quito. Official language: Spanish (Quechua and Shuar are also official languages for the indigenous peoples). Official religion: none. Monetary unit: 1 US dollar (US$) = 100 cents.

## Demography

Area: 98,985 sq mi, 256,370 sq km. Population (2011): 14,650,000. Density (2011): persons per sq mi 148.0, persons per sq km 57.1. Urban (2009): 66.3%. Sex distribution (2005): male 50.15%; female 49.85%. Age breakdown (2005):

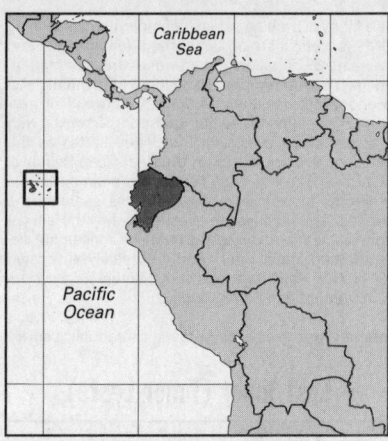

under 15, 32.6%; 15–29, 27.4%; 30–44, 19.5%; 45–59, 12.1%; 60–74, 6.1%; 75–84, 1.8%; 85 and over, 0.5%. Ethnic composition (2000): mestizo 42.0%; Amerindian 40.8%; white 10.6%; black 5.0%; other 1.6%. Religious affiliation (2005): Roman Catholic (practicing) 35%; Roman Catholic (non-practicing) 50%; other (significantly Evangelical Protestant) 15%. Major cities (2003): Guayaquil (urban agglomeration; 2005) 2,387,000; Quito (urban agglomeration; 2005) 1,514,000; Cuenca 303,994; Machala 217,266; Santo Domingo de los Colorados 211,689. Location: northwestern South America, bordering Colombia, Peru, and the Pacific Ocean.

## Vital statistics

Birth rate per 1,000 population (2008): 14.9 (world avg. 20.3). Death rate per 1,000 population (2008): 4.3 (world avg. 8.5). Total fertility rate (avg. births per childbearing woman; 2005): 2.70. Life expectancy at birth (2005): male 71.7 years; female 77.6 years.

## National economy

Budget (2006). Revenue: US$6,895,000,000 (nonpetroleum revenue 75.1%, of which VAT 32.3%, income tax 15.5%, customs duties 9.0%; petroleum export revenue 24.9%). Expenditures: US$7,011,000,000 (current expenditures 76.2%; capital expenditures 23.8%). Production (metric tons except as noted). Agriculture and fishing (2007): sugarcane 7,300,000, bananas 6,130,000, oil palm fruit 2,100,000, plantains 590,000, pyrethrum and dried flowers (2004) 105; livestock (live animals) 5,050,000 cattle, 1,300,000 pigs, 1,050,000 sheep; fisheries production 554,745 (from aquaculture 31%). Mining and quarrying (2007): limestone 5,374,000; gold 3,186 kg. Manufacturing (value added in US$'000,000; 2004): refined petroleum products 1,794; food products 870; beverages 845. Energy production (consumption): electricity (kW-hr; 2006) 14,814,000,000 (16,383,000,000); crude petroleum (barrels; 2007) 187,000,000 ([2006]

---

1 metric ton = about 1.1 short tons;    1 kilometer = 0.6 mi (statute);    1 metric ton-km cargo = about 0.68 short ton-mi cargo;    c.i.f.: cost, insurance, and freight;    f.o.b.: free on board

55,500,000); petroleum products (metric tons; 2006) 7,453,000 (8,218,000); natural gas (cu m; 2006) 687,000,000 (687,000,000). **Population economically active** (2006): total 4,204,800; activity rate of total population 45.2% (participation rates: ages 15–64, 69.6%; female 38.7%; unemployed [March 2006–February 2007] 10.1%). **Public debt** (external, outstanding; December 2006): US$10,108,000,000. **Gross national income** (2008): US$49,105,000,000 (US$3,640 per capita). **Selected balance of payments data.** Receipts from (US$'000,000): tourism (2007) 623; remittances (2008) 3,200; foreign direct investment (2005–07 avg.) 314; official development assistance (2007) 215. Disbursements for (US$'000,000): tourism (2007) 504; remittances (2008) 83.

## Foreign trade

**Imports** (2006; c.i.f.): US$12,114,000,000 (mineral fuels 21.1%; machinery and apparatus 20.0%; chemical products 15.3%; motor vehicles and parts 11.5%; iron and steel 6.0%). *Major import sources* (2008): US 19.0%; Colombia 9.6%; Brazil 4.8%; Japan 3.6%; Mexico 3.5%. **Exports** (2006; f.o.b.): US$12,728,000,000 (crude petroleum 54.5%; bananas and plantains 9.5%; fish 5.4%; shrimp 4.6%; refined petroleum products 3.9%; cut flowers 3.4%). *Major export destinations* (2008): US 45.3%; Peru 9.2%; Chile 8.2%; Colombia 4.2%; Venezuela 3.8%.

## Transport and communications

**Transport.** *Railroads* (2006): route length (2005) 965 km; passenger-km 4,000,000; metric ton-km cargo 2,000. *Roads* (2006): total length 43,670 km (paved 15%). *Vehicles* (2006): passenger cars 519,041; trucks and buses 357,514. *Air transport* (2005): passenger-km 867,100,000; metric ton-km cargo 5,400,000. **Communications,** in total units (units per 1,000 persons). Telephone landlines (2008): 1,910,000 (142); cellular telephone subscribers (2008): 11,595,000 (860); personal computers (2005): 866,000 (65); total Internet users (2008): 1,310,000 (97); broadband Internet subscribers (2008): 35,000 (2.6).

## Education and health

**Educational attainment** (1995). Percentage of population ages 25 and over having: no formal schooling/incomplete primary education 18.8%; complete primary/incomplete secondary 47.2%; complete secondary 16.1%; higher 17.9%. **Literacy** (2003): total population ages 15 and over literate 92.5%; males literate 94.0%; females literate 91.0%. **Health:** physicians (2004) 21,625 (1 per 603 persons); hospital beds (2007) 20,523 (1 per 663 persons); infant mortality rate per 1,000 live births (2008) 16.4; undernourished population (2003–05) 1,900,000 (15% of total population based on the consumption of a minimum daily requirement of 1,770 calories).

## Military

**Total active duty personnel** (November 2008): 57,983 (army 80.2%, navy 12.6%, air force 7.2%). **Military expenditure as percentage of GDP** (2007): 1.8%; per capita expenditure US$57.

## Background

Ecuador was conquered by the Incas in AD 1450 and came under Spanish control in 1534. Under the Spaniards it was a part of the Viceroyalty of Peru until 1740, when it became a part of the Viceroyalty of New Granada. It gained its independence from Spain in 1822 as part of the republic of Gran Colombia, and in 1830 it became a sovereign state. A succession of authoritarian governments ruled into the mid-20th century, and economic hardship and social unrest prompted the military to take a strong role. Border disputes led to war between Peru and Ecuador in 1941; the two fought periodically until agreeing to a final demarcation in 1998. The economy, booming in the 1970s with petroleum profits, was depressed in the 1980s by reduced oil prices and earthquake damage. A new constitution was adopted in 1979. In the 1990s social unrest caused political instability and several changes of heads of state. In a controversial move to help stabilize the economy, the US dollar replaced the sucre as the national currency in 2000. In the early 21st century, Ecuador continued to struggle with political upheaval, social unrest related to indigenous rights and economic policies, and poor economic performance.

## Recent Developments

In February 2011, a judge ordered US-based Chevron Corp. to pay damages of US$8.6 billion and a 10% surcharge to residents of the Ecuadoran Amazon. Plaintiffs in the long-running lawsuit maintained that the region remained heavily polluted after extensive oil production in the 1970s and '80s by Texaco, later taken over by Chevron. Although Chevron was dealt a setback in its appeals in January 2012, the next month a tribunal affiliated with the Permanent Court of Arbitration in The Hague agreed to hear the company's claims.

**Internet resource:** <www.ecuador.com>.

# Egypt

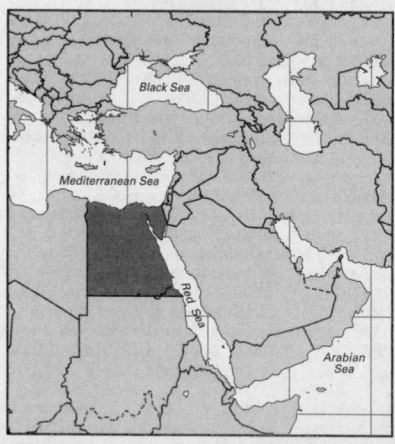

Official name: Jumhuriah Misr al-'Arabiyah (Arab Republic of Egypt). Form of government: interim government. Head of state: President Mohammed Morsi (from 2012). Head of government: Prime Minister Hesham Kandil (from 2012). Capital: Cairo. Official language: Arabic. Official religion: Islam. Monetary unit: 1 Egyptian pound (LE) = 100 piastres; valuation (2 Jul 2012) US$1 = LE 6.06.

## Demography

Area: 386,874 sq mi, 1,002,000 sq km. Population (2011): 82,537,000. Density (2011): persons per sq mi 213.3, persons per sq km 82.4. Urban (2009): 43.0%. Sex distribution (2006): male 51.11%; female 48.89%. Age breakdown (2005): under 15, 33.0%; 15–29, 28.0%; 30–44, 19.8%; 45–59, 12.3%; 60–74, 5.7%; 75 and over, 1.2%. Ethnic composition (2000): Egyptian Arab 84.1%; Sudanese Arab 5.5%; Arabized Berber 2.0%; Bedouin 2.0%; Rom (Gypsy) 1.6%; other 4.8%. Religious affiliation (2000): Muslim 84.4% (nearly all Sunni; Shi'i make up less than 1% of population); Christian 15.1%, of which Orthodox 13.6%, Protestant 0.8%, Roman Catholic 0.3%; nonreligious 0.5%. Major cities (2006): Cairo 6,759,000 ([urban agglomeration; 2007] 11,893,000); Alexandria 4,085,000; Al-Jizah 2,891,000; Shubra al-Khaymah 1,026,000; Port Said 571,000. Location: northern Africa, bordering the Mediterranean Sea, the Gaza Strip, Israel, the Red Sea, Sudan, and Libya.

## Vital statistics

Birth rate per 1,000 population (2008–09): 25.0 (world avg. 20.3). Death rate per 1,000 population (2008–09): 6.3 (world avg. 8.5). Total fertility rate (avg. births per childbearing woman; 2006): 2.83. Life expectancy at birth (2007–08): male 71.0 years; female 74.0 years.

## National economy

Budget (2006–07). Revenue: LE 205,655,000,000 (nontax revenue 42.6%; corporate taxes 23.7%; taxes on goods and services 19.2%). Expenditures: LE 239,602,000,000 (social protection 35.8%; general administration 24.4%; education 11.6%; defense 7.5%. Population economically active (2005): total 22,310,000; activity rate 31.3% (participation rates: ages 15–64 [2001] 46.9%; female 23.3%; unemployed [2008] 8.7%). Production ('000; metric tons except as noted). Agriculture and fishing (2007): sugarcane 16,200, tomatoes 7,550, wheat 7,379, dates 1,130, seed cotton 560, figs 170; livestock ('000; number of live animals) 5,180 sheep, 4,550 cattle, 3,950 buffalo, 120 camels; fisheries production 1,008,007 (from aquaculture 63%). Mining and quarrying (2006): gypsum 3,300; iron ore 2,600; phosphate rock 2,200; salt 1,200; kaolin 416. Manufacturing (value added in US$'000,000; 2002): chemical products 2,823; food products 1,016; textiles and wearing apparel 618. Energy production (consumption): electricity ('000,000 kW-hr; 2008) 128,105 ([2006] 118,058); coal (metric tons; 2006) 25,000

(1,713,000); crude petroleum (barrels; 2008) 241,500,000 ([2006] 205,400,000); petroleum products (metric tons; 2006) 30,700,000 (30,977,000); natural gas (cu m; 2007) 47,488,000,000 (31,800,000,000). Gross national income (2008): US$146,851,000,000 (US$1,800 per capita). Public debt (external, outstanding; 2007): US$26,940,000,000. Selected balance of payments data. Receipts from (US$'000,000): tourism (2007) 9,303; remittances (2008) 9,476; foreign direct investment (FDI; 2005–07 avg.) 8,999; official development assistance (2007) 1,083. Disbursements for (US$'000,000): tourism (2007) 2,446; remittances (2008) 180; FDI (2005–07 avg.) 302.

## Foreign trade

Imports (2007; c.i.f.): US$26,928,000,000 (food products 15.7%, of which wheat 5.8%; machinery and apparatus 14.9%; mineral fuels 14.7%; chemical products 9.8%; iron and steel 4.5%). Major import sources: free zones 15.2%; US 9.5%; Saudi Arabia 8.3%; Germany 6.6%; China 6.0%. Exports (2007; f.o.b.): US$16,101,000,000 (refined petroleum products 25.4%; liquefied natural gas 16.6%; food products 7.7%; crude petroleum 6.5%; iron and steel 4.6%). Major export destinations: free zones 16.3%; India 11.3%; Italy 9.8%; Spain 6.4%; bunkers and ships' stores 6.0%.

## Transport and communications

Transport. Railroads (2005): length 9,525 km; passenger-km 54,853,000,000; metric ton-km cargo 4,234,000,000. Roads (2004): total length 92,370 km (paved 81%). Vehicles: passenger cars (2004) 1,960,000; trucks and buses (2002) 650,000. Inland water (2007): Suez Canal, number of transits 20,384; metric ton cargo 710,098,000. Air transport (2006): passenger-km 10,332,000,000; metric ton-km cargo 323,160,000. Communications, in total units (units per 1,000 persons). Telephone landlines (2008): 12,011,000 (147); cellular telephone subscribers (2008): 41,272,000 (506); personal computers (2007): 3,923,000 (49); total Internet users (2008): 12,569,000 (154); broadband Internet subscribers (2008): 769,000 (9.4).

## Education and health

Educational attainment (2006). Percentage of population ages 10 and over having: no formal schooling 41.6%; incomplete primary education/incomplete secondary 20.7%; complete secondary/some higher 28.1%; university 9.4%; advanced degree 0.2%. Literacy (2001): total population ages 15 and over literate 56.1%; males literate 67.2%; females literate 44.8%. Health: physicians (2006) 161,000 (1 per 451 persons); hospital beds (2007) 185,000 (1 per 393 persons); infant mortality rate per 1,000 live births (2007–08) 16.0; undernourished population (2002–04) 2,600,000 (4% of total population based on the consumption of a minimum daily requirement of 1,900 calories).

1 metric ton = about 1.1 short tons;    1 kilometer = 0.6 mi (statute);    1 metric ton-km cargo = about 0.68 short ton-mi cargo;    c.i.f.: cost, insurance, and freight;    f.o.b.: free on board

## Military

**Total active duty personnel** (November 2008): 468,500 (army 72.6%, navy 3.9%, air force [including air defense] 23.5%). **Military expenditure as percentage of GDP** (2007): 3.5%; per capita expenditure US$58.

## Background

Egypt is home to one of the world's oldest continuous civilizations. Upper and Lower Egypt were united about 3000 BC, beginning a period of cultural achievement and a line of native rulers that lasted nearly 3,000 years. Egypt's ancient history is divided into the Old, Middle, and New Kingdoms, spanning 31 dynasties and lasting to 332 BC. The pyramids date from the Old Kingdom, the cult of Osiris and the refinement of sculpture from the Middle Kingdom, and the era of empire and the Exodus of the Jews from the New Kingdom. An Assyrian invasion occurred in the 7th century BC, and the Persian Achaemenids established a dynasty in 525 BC. The invasion by Alexander the Great in 332 BC inaugurated the Macedonian Ptolemaic period and the ascendancy of Alexandria. The Romans held Egypt from 30 BC to AD 395; later it was placed under the control of Constantinople. Constantine's granting of tolerance in 313 to the Christians began the development of a formal Egyptian (Coptic) church. Egypt came under Arab control in 642 and ultimately was transformed into an Arabic-speaking state, with Islam as the dominant religion. Held by the Umayyad and Abbasid dynasties, in 969 it became the center of the Fatimid dynasty. In 1250 the Mamluks established a dynasty that lasted until 1517, when Egypt fell to the Ottoman Turks. An economic decline ensued, and with it a decline in Egyptian culture. Egypt became a British protectorate in 1914 and received nominal independence in 1922, when a constitutional monarchy was established. A coup overthrew the monarchy in 1952, with Gamal Abdel Nasser taking power. Following three wars with Israel, Egypt, under Nasser's successor, Anwar el-Sadat, ultimately played a leading role in Middle East peace talks. Sadat was succeeded by Hosni Mubarak, who followed Sadat's peace initiatives and in 1982 regained Egyptian sovereignty (lost in 1967) over the Sinai Peninsula. Although Egypt took part in the coalition against Iraq during the Persian Gulf War (1991), it later made peace overtures to Iraq and other countries in the region. Desire for political, economic, and social reform led to a popular uprising of unprecedented proportions in 2011, which forced Mubarak to step down as president and left Egypt's military in control of the country.

## Recent Developments

Several million protesters clashed with security forces in Egypt in 2011, leading to a full-fledged revolution that ousted Pres. Hosni Mubarak and led to his arrest. The Supreme Council of the Armed Forces, a powerful group of military officers, suspended the constitution and dismissed the parliament. Violence left 850 Egyptians dead and 6,000 wounded. A six-decade ban on the Muslim Brotherhood was lifted, and parliamentary elections, held between November 2011 and January 2012, resulted in the Muslim Brotherhood's Freedom and Justice Party winning about 47 percent of the seats.

Egypt held its first free presidential election in May, but the parliament was suspended again in June.

**Internet resource:** <www.capmas.gov.eg/?lang=2>.

# El Salvador

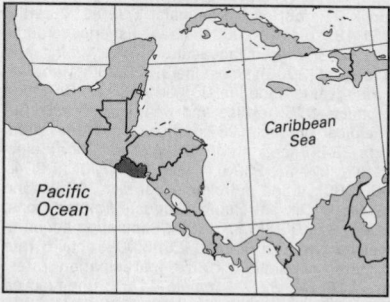

**Official name:** República de El Salvador (Republic of El Salvador). **Form of government:** republic with one legislative house (Legislative Assembly [84]). **Head of state and government:** President Mauricio Funes (from 2009). **Capital:** San Salvador. **Official language:** Spanish. **Official religion:** none (Roman Catholicism, though not official, enjoys special recognition in the constitution). **Monetary unit:** 1 colón (₡) = 100 centavos; valuation (2 Jul 2012) US$1 = ₡8.75 (the US dollar [US$] has also been legal tender since 1 Jan 2001; the colón is rarely in use).

## Demography

**Area:** 8,124 sq mi, 21,040 sq km. **Population** (2011): 6,072,000. **Density** (2011): persons per sq mi 747.4, persons per sq km 288.6. **Urban** (2008): 64.8%. **Sex distribution** (2008): male 47.39%; female 52.61%. **Age breakdown** (2008): under 15, 32.6%; 15–29, 27.2%; 30–44, 18.3%; 45–59, 11.9%; 60–69, 5.0%; 70 and over, 5.0%. **Ethnic composition** (2000): mestizo 88.3%; Amerindian 9.1%, of which Pipil 4.0%; white 1.6%; other/unknown 1.0%. **Religious affiliation** (2005): Roman Catholic 71%; independent Christian 11%; Protestant 10%; Jehovah's Witness 2%; other 6%. **Major cities** (2007): San Salvador 316,090 (urban agglomeration 1,433,000); Santa Ana 245,421; Soyapango 241,403; San Miguel 218,410; Mejicanos 140,751. **Location:** Central America, bordering Guatemala, Honduras, and the North Pacific Ocean.

## Vital statistics

**Birth rate** per 1,000 population (2008): 22.5 (world avg. 20.3); (2003) within marriage 27%. **Death rate** per 1,000 population (2008): 5.9 (world avg. 8.5). **Total fertility rate** (avg. births per childbearing woman; 2006): 3.12. **Life expectancy** at birth (2006): male 67.9 years; female 75.3 years.

## National economy

**Budget** (2007). *Revenue:* US$3,077,600,000 (VAT 53.9%; income tax 31.4%; import duties 6.6%;

grants 1.4%; other 6.7%). *Expenditures:* US$2,-928,900,000 (education 18.4%; defense and public security 18.3%; public health and welfare 9.7%; other 53.6%). **Public debt** (external, outstanding; 2007): US$5,444,000,000. **Production** (metric tons except as noted). *Agriculture and fishing* (2007): sugarcane 5,400,000, corn (maize) 836,695, sorghum 181,694, coffee 94,514; livestock (number of live animals) 1,380,112 cattle, 451,482 pigs, 96,000 horses; fisheries production 52,368 (from aquaculture 7%). *Mining and quarrying* (2006): limestone 1,200,000. *Manufacturing* (value added in US$'000,000; 2004): food products 875; textiles and wearing apparel 262; chemical products 262; refined petroleum products 234. *Energy production (consumption):* electricity (kW-hr; 2006) 5,293,000,000 (5,204,-000,000); crude petroleum (barrels; 2006) none (6,348,000); petroleum products (metric tons; 2006) 811,000 (1,857,000). **Population economically active** (2008): total 2,495,908; activity rate of total population 40.8% (participation rates: ages 16–64, 62.9%; female 41.3%; unemployed 5.9%). **Gross national income** (2008): US$21,-361,000,000 (US$3,480 per capita). **Selected balance of payments data**. Receipts from (US$'000,000): tourism (2007) 847; remittances (2008) 3,804; foreign direct investment (FDI; 2005–07 avg.) 752; official development assistance (2006) 157. Disbursements for (US$'000,-000): tourism (2007) 605; remittances (2008) 29; FDI (2005–07 avg.) 62.

## Foreign trade

**Imports** (2006; c.i.f.): US$7,627,000,000 (food products, beverages, and tobacco 16.2%; imports for re-export 15.8%; machinery and apparatus 14.4%; crude petroleum 13.7%). *Major import sources:* US 40.5%; Guatemala 8.0%; Mexico 7.7%; Brazil 4.0%; Costa Rica 2.9%. **Exports** (2006; f.o.b.): US$3,513,000,000 (reexports [mostly clothing] 45.6%; fabricated metal products 5.9%; coffee 5.4%; distilled spirits 4.5%; paper products 4.2%). *Major export destinations:* US 57.1%; Guatemala 13.0%; Honduras 8.0%; Nicaragua 4.8%; Costa Rica 3.4%.

## Transport and communications

**Transport.** *Railroads* (2007; rail service was suspended in 2005): length 562 km. *Roads* (2002): total length 11,458 km (paved 23%). *Vehicles* (2000): passenger cars 148,000; trucks and buses 250,800. *Air transport* (2005; TACA International Airlines only): passenger-km 8,117,465,000; metric ton-km cargo 37,883,000. **Communications**, in total units (units per 1,000 persons). Telephone landlines (2008): 1,077,000 (155); cellular telephone subscribers (2008): 6,951,000 (1,000); personal computers (2007): 359,000 (52); total Internet users (2007): 763,000 (111); broadband Internet subscribers (2008): 124,000 (18).

## Education and health

**Educational attainment** (2004). Percentage of population over ages 25 having: no formal schooling 22.0%; primary education: grades 1–3 19.1%,

grades 4–6 19.9%; secondary: grades 7–9 13.9%, grades 10–12 14.6%; higher 10.5%. **Literacy** (2008): total population ages 10 and over literate 85.9%; males literate 88.5%; females literate 83.6%. **Health** (2005): physicians 8,670 (1 per 794 persons); hospital beds 4,816 (1 per 1,429 persons); infant mortality rate per 1,000 live births (2004) 10.5; undernourished population (2002–04) 700,000 (11% of total population based on the consumption of a minimum daily requirement of 1,800 calories).

## Military

**Total active duty personnel** (November 2008): 15,500 (army 89.4%, navy 4.5%, air force 6.1%). **Military expenditure as percentage of GDP** (2008): 0.4%; per capita expenditure US$20.

## Background

The Spanish arrived in the area in 1524 and subjugated the Pipil Indian kingdom of Cuzcatlán by 1539. The country was divided into two districts, San Salvador and Sonsonate, both attached to Guatemala. When independence came in 1821, San Salvador was incorporated into the Mexican Empire; upon its collapse in 1823, Sonsonate and San Salvador combined to form the new state of El Salvador within the United Provinces of Central America. From its founding El Salvador experienced political turmoil; powerful economic interests controlled the country through most of the 19th and early 20th centuries but were replaced by a military dictatorship that lasted from 1931 to 1979. Elections held in 1982 set up a new government, but civil war continued throughout the 1980s. Peace accords in 1992 ended the war, but violent crime became a major problem. The country was plagued by inflation and unemployment into the 21st century. In 2006 El Salvador officially entered into the Central America Free Trade Agreement (CAFTA) with the United States.

## Recent Developments

A dispute over environmental damage—specifically water-supply contamination—from gold and silver mining by American and Canadian companies in El Salvador resulted in the government shutdown of some mining operations in 2011. The mining companies claimed that the shutdowns violated the CAFTA-DR agreement. Violence, including a death, ensued, and journalists reporting on the issue received death threats warning them to stop publicizing the dispute.

**Internet resource:** <www.minec.gob.sv>.

# Equatorial Guinea

**Official name:** República de Guinea Ecuatorial (Spanish); République du Guinée Équatoriale (French) (Republic of Equatorial Guinea). **Form of government:** republic with one legislative house (House of People's Representatives [100]). **Head of state and government:** President Teodoro Obiang Nguema Mbasogo (from 1979), assisted by Prime Minister Vicente Ehate Tomi (from 2012). **Capital:** Malabo. **Official lan-

---

*1 metric ton = about 1.1 short tons;　1 kilometer = 0.6 mi (statute);　1 metric ton-km cargo = about 0.68 short ton-mi cargo;　c.i.f.: cost, insurance, and freight;　f.o.b.: free on board*

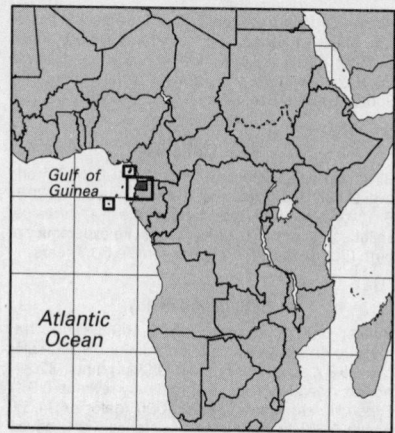

guages: Spanish; French. **Official religion:** none. **Monetary unit:** 1 CFA franc (CFAF) = 100 centimes; valuation (2 Jul 2012) US$1 = CFAF 521.26.

## Demography

**Area:** 10,831 sq mi, 28,051 sq km. **Population** (2011): 720,000. **Density** (2011): persons per sq mi 66.5, persons per sq km 25.7. **Urban** (2011): 39.5%. **Sex distribution** (2008): male 49.57%; female 50.43%. **Age breakdown** (2008): under 15, 42.0%; 15–29, 26.6%; 30–44, 16.6%; 45–59, 8.7%; 60–74, 5.0%; 75–84, 1.0%; 85 and over, 0.1%. **Ethnic composition** (2000): Fang 56.6%; migrant laborers from Nigeria 12.5%, of which Yoruba 8.0%, Igbo 4.0%; Bubi 10.0%; Seke 2.9%; Spaniard 2.8%; other 15.2%. **Religious affiliation** (2000): Roman Catholic 79.9%; Sunni Muslim 4.1%; independent Christian 3.7%; Protestant 3.2%; traditional beliefs 2.1%; nonreligious/atheist 4.9%; other 2.1%. **Major cities** (2003): Malabo 92,900; Bata 66,800; Mbini 11,600. **Location:** western Africa, the mainland portion bordering Cameroon, Gabon, and the Bight of Biafra.

## Vital statistics

**Birth rate** per 1,000 population (2008): 37.1 (world avg. 20.3). **Death rate** per 1,000 population (2008): 9.7 (world avg. 8.5). **Total fertility rate** (avg. births per childbearing woman; 2008): 5.16. **Life expectancy** at birth (2008): male 60.4 years; female 62.1 years.

## National economy

**Budget** (2007). *Revenue:* CFAF 2,308,500,000,000 (oil revenue 90.9%, of which profit sharing 48.9%, royalties 20.3%; non-oil revenue 9.1%, of which tax revenue 3.3%). *Expenditures:* CFAF 1,151,900,-000,000 (infrastructure 43.3%; social services 18.3%; public administration 17.0%). **Public debt** (external, outstanding; 2006): US$156,800,000. **Gross national income** (2008): US$9,875,000,000 (US$14,980 per capita). **Production** (metric tons except as noted). *Agriculture and fishing* (2007): cassava 45,000, sweet potatoes 36,000, oil palm fruit 35,000; livestock (number of live animals) 37,600 sheep, 9,000 goats, 6,100 pigs; fisheries production 3,583 (from aquaculture, none). *Mining and quarry-*

*ing* (2007): gold 200 kg. *Manufacturing* (2004): methanol 1,027,300; processed timber 31,200 cu m. *Energy production (consumption):* electricity (kW-hr; 2006) 29,000,000 (29,000,000); crude petroleum (barrels; 2007) 133,000,000 ([2006] negligible); petroleum products (metric tons; 2006) none (51,000); natural gas (cu m; 2006) 480,000,000 (480,000,000). **Population economically active** (2006): total 193,000; activity rate of total population 38.9% (participation rates: ages 15–64, 69.5%; female 33.7%; unemployed [1998] 30%). **Selected balance of payments data.** Receipts from (US$'000,000): tourism (2005) 5; foreign direct investment (2005–07 avg.) 1,752; official development assistance (2007) 31.

## Foreign trade

**Imports** (2007): CFAF 1,325,000,000,000 (petroleum sector 35.6%; nonpetroleum sector 64.4%). *Major import sources* (2005): US 26.8%; Côte d'Ivoire 21.4%; Spain 13.6%; France 8.8%; UK 7.8%. **Exports** (2007): CFAF 4,893,200,000,000 (crude petroleum 83.1%; methanol 15.9%; timber 0.7%). *Major export destinations* (2005): US 24.6%; China 21.8%; Spain 10.8%; Canada 7.3%; Netherlands 5.2%.

## Transport and communications

**Transport.** *Railroads:* none. *Roads* (2000): total length 2,880 km (paved 13%). *Vehicles* (2002): passenger cars 8,380; trucks and buses 6,618. **Communications,** in total units (units per 1,000 persons). Telephone landlines (2005): 10,000 (20); cellular telephone subscribers (2008): 346,000 (666); personal computers (2004): 7,000 (3.3); total Internet users (2008): 12,000 (23); broadband Internet subscribers (2007): 200 (0.04).

## Education and health

**Literacy** (2006): percentage of total population ages 15 and over literate 87.0%; males literate 93.4%; females literate 80.5%. **Health:** physicians (2004) 101 (1 per 5,020 persons); hospital beds (1998) 907 (1 per 472 persons); infant mortality rate per 1,000 live births (2008) 83.8.

## Military

**Total active duty personnel** (November 2008): 1,320 (army 83.3%, navy 9.1%, air force 7.6%).

## Background

The first inhabitants of the mainland region appear to have been Pygmies. The now-prominent Fang and Bubi reached the mainland region in the 17th-century Bantu migrations. Equatorial Guinea was ceded by the Portuguese to the Spanish in the late 18th century; it was frequented by slave traders, as well as by British, German, Dutch, and French merchants. Independence was declared in 1968, followed by a reign of terror and economic chaos under the dictatorial president Macías Nguema, who was overthrown by a military coup in 1979 and later executed. New constitutions were adopted in 1982 and 1991, but political power remained concentrated in the office of the president. In the early 21st century the standard of living of most people remained low, despite the country's oil wealth.

## Recent Developments

Having been appointed head of the African Union (AU) for 2011, Equatorial Guinea's leader, Teodoro Obiang Nguema Mbasogo, hosted the meeting of AU heads of state in Malabo in June. A state-funded public-relations campaign had tried to challenge the general perception of the country as having one of Africa's most corrupt and repressive regimes, and vast sums were spent on creating a new venue for the meeting so that visitors did not see the squalor in which most of the population continued to live. Obiang's son Teodorin, the favorite to succeed his father, was reported to be building a yacht costing three times what the country spent on health and education annually.

Internet resource:
<www.guineaecuatorialpress.com/?lang=en>.

# Eritrea

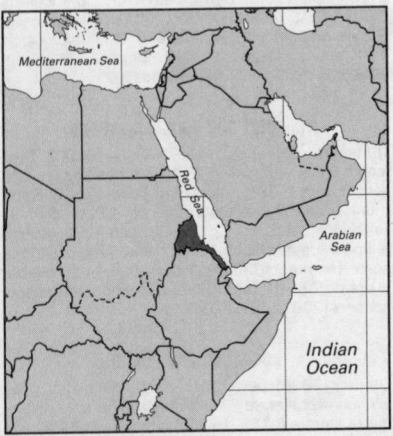

**Official name:** State of Eritrea. **Form of government:** transitional regime with one interim legislative house (transitional National Assembly [150]). **Head of state and government:** President Isaias Afwerki (from 1993). **Capital:** Asmara. **Official language:** none. **Official religion:** none. **Monetary unit:** 1 nakfa (Nfa) = 100 cents; valuation (2 Jul 2012) US$1 = Nfa 15.00.

## Demography

**Area:** 46,774 sq mi, 121,144 sq km. **Population** (2011): 5,415,000. **Density** (2011; based on land area only): persons per sq mi 138.9, persons per sq km 53.6. **Urban** (2009): 21.1%. **Sex distribution** (2006): male 49.84%; female 50.16%. **Age breakdown** (2006): under 15, 44.0%; 15–29, 27.9%; 30–44, 14.3%; 45–59, 8.2%; 60–74, 4.5%; 75 and over, 1.1%. **Ethnolinguistic composition** (2004): Tigrinya (Tigray) 50.0%; Tigré 31.4%; Afar 5.0%; Saho 5.0%; Beja 2.5%; Bilen 2.1%; other 4.0%. **Religious affiliation** (2004): Muslim (virtually all Sunni) 50%; Christian 48%, of which Eritrean Orthodox 40%,

Roman Catholic 5%, Protestant 2%; traditional beliefs 2%. **Major cities** (2003): Asmara 435,000; Keren 57,000; Assab 28,000; Afabet 25,000; Massawa 25,000. **Location:** the Horn of Africa, bordering Sudan, the Red Sea, Djibouti, and Ethiopia.

## Vital statistics

**Birth rate** per 1,000 population (2006): 34.3 (world avg. 20.3). **Death rate** per 1,000 population (2006): 9.6 (world avg. 8.5). **Total fertility rate** (avg. births per childbearing woman; 2006): 5.08. **Life expectancy** at birth (2006): male 57.4 years; female 60.7 years.

## National economy

**Budget** (2002). *Revenue:* Nfa 3,409,800,000 (tax revenue 45.1%, of which import duties 18.1%, sales tax 10.8%, corporate taxes 9.9%; grants 32.8%; nontax revenue 21.2%; extraordinary revenue 0.9%). *Expenditures:* Nfa 6,138,200,000 (defense 34.3%; health 9.6%; humanitarian assistance 7.9%; education 7.6%; debt service 5.7%). **Public debt** (external, outstanding; 2007): US$856,000,000. **Gross national income** (2008): US$1,492,000,000 (US$300 per capita). **Production** (metric tons except as noted). *Agriculture and fishing* (2007): sorghum 130,000, millet 20,000, sesame seeds 19,000; livestock (number of live animals) 2,120,000 sheep, 1,960,000 cattle, 1,720,000 goats, 76,000 camels; fisheries production 1,932 (from aquaculture, none). *Mining and quarrying* (2007): coral 67,332, basalt 45,335, granite 21,394. *Manufacturing* (value added in US$'000,000; 2004): beverages 31; tobacco products 8; furniture 7. *Energy production (consumption):* electricity (kW-hr; 2006) 269,000,000 (269,000,000); petroleum products (metric tons; 2006) none (173,000). **Population economically active** (2006): 1,881,000; activity rate of total population 40.1% (participation rates: ages 15–64, 71.4%; female 41.3%). **Selected balance of payments data.** Receipts from (US$'000,000): tourism (2007) 60; remittances (2003) 150; foreign direct disinvestment (2005–07 avg.) −2; official development assistance (2007) 155.

## Foreign trade

**Imports** (2003; c.i.f.): US$432,800,000 (food products and live animals 40.5%, of which cereals 25.5%; machinery and apparatus 14.8%; motor vehicles 7.3%; chemical products 6.1%). *Major import sources* (2008): Italy 16.9%; UAE 15.7%; China 13.0%; India 9.4%; US 6.7%. **Exports** (2003; f.o.b.): US$6,600,000 (food products and live animals 36.4%, of which fresh fish 22.7%; leather products 10.6%; corals and shells 9.1%). *Major export destinations* (2008): India 31.7%; Italy 18.6%; Kenya 11.9%; China 11.5%; France 5.4%.

## Transport and communications

**Transport.** *Railroads* (2005): route length 306 km. *Roads* (2004): total length 4,000 km (paved 20%). *Vehicles* (1996): automobiles 5,940. *Air transport* (2001; Asmara airport only): passenger arrivals 39,266, passenger departures 46,448; freight loaded 202 metric tons, freight unloaded 1,548 met-

---

*1 metric ton = about 1.1 short tons;    1 kilometer = 0.6 mi (statute);    1 metric ton-km cargo = about 0.68 short ton-mi cargo;    c.i.f.: cost, insurance, and freight;    f.o.b.: free on board*

ric tons. **Communications,** in total units (units per 1,000 persons). Telephone landlines (2008): 40,000 (8.2); cellular telephone subscribers (2008): 109,000 (22); personal computers (2007): 38,000 (8); total Internet users (2008): 150,000 (30).

## Education and health

**Educational attainment** (2002). Percentage of population ages 25 and over having: no formal education/unknown 67.6%, incomplete primary education 16.6%, complete primary 1.3%, incomplete secondary 5.8%, complete secondary 5.7%, higher 3.0%. **Literacy** (2006): total population ages 15 and over literate 61.4%; males literate 72.3%; females literate 50.7%. **Health** (2006): physicians (2004) 215 (1 per 20,791 persons); hospital beds 5,500 (1 per 833 persons); infant mortality rate per 1,000 live births 46.3; undernourished population (2002–04) 3,100,000 (75% of total population based on the consumption of a minimum daily requirement of 1,730 calories).

## Military

**Total active duty personnel** (November 2008): 201,750 (army 99.1%, navy 0.7%, air force 0.2%); mandate for the UN peacekeeping force along the Eritrean-Ethiopian border was terminated in July 2008. **Military expenditure as percentage of GDP** (2003): 24.1%; per capita expenditure US$49.

## Background

As the site of the main ports of the Aksumite empire, Eritrea was linked to the beginnings of the Ethiopian kingdom, but it retained much of its independence until it came under Ottoman rule in the 16th century. From the 17th to the 19th centuries, control of the territory was disputed between Ethiopia, the Ottomans, the kingdom of Tigray, Egypt, and Italy; it became an Italian colony in 1890. Eritrea was used as the base for the Italian invasions of Ethiopia (1896 and 1935–36) and in 1936 became part of Italian East Africa. It was captured by the British in 1941, federated to Ethiopia in 1952, and made a province of Ethiopia in 1962. Thirty years of guerrilla warfare by Eritrean secessionist groups ensued. A provisional Eritrean government was established in 1991, and independence came in 1993. A border war with Ethiopia that began in 1998 ended in an Ethiopian victory in 2000, but boundary disputes with Eritrea's neighbors persisted into the 21st century.

## Recent Developments

Eritrea remained one of the world's poorest countries in 2011, but mining developments brought some hope for progress. Early in the year, Canada-based Nevsun Resources Ltd. announced that it had begun commercial gold production at Bisha mine, which it owned in partnership with the Eritrean government. This coincided with a historic rise in the price of gold, driven by investor concerns about the world's economic health. While Eritrea stood to gain from the newfound mineral wealth, its poor and often tense relations with many other countries became a hindering block.

**Internet resource:** <www.shabait.com>.

# Estonia

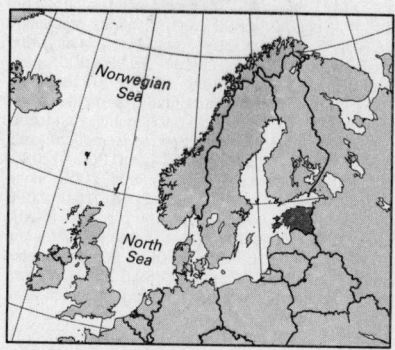

**Official name:** Eesti Vabariik (Republic of Estonia). **Form of government:** unitary multiparty republic with a single legislative house (Riigikogu [101]). **Head of state:** President Toomas Hendrik Ilves (from 2006). **Head of government:** Prime Minister Andrus Ansip (from 2005). **Capital:** Tallinn. **Official language:** Estonian. **Official religion:** none. **Monetary unit:** 1 euro (€) = 100 cents; valuation (2 Jul 2012) US$1 = €0.79.

## Demography

**Area:** 17,462 sq mi, 45,227 sq km. **Population** (2011): 1,340,000. **Density** (2011; based on land area only): persons per sq mi 81.9, persons per sq km 31.6. **Urban** (2009): 68.0%. **Sex distribution** (2008): male 46.05%; female 53.95%. **Age breakdown** (2005): under 15, 15.1%; 15–29, 22.7%; 30–44, 20.5%; 45–59, 20.2%; 60–74, 14.7%; 75–84, 5.7%; 85 and over, 1.1%. **Ethnic composition** (2005): Estonian 68.6%; Russian 25.7%; Ukrainian 2.1%; Belarusian 1.2%; Finnish 0.8%; other 1.6%. **Religious affiliation** (2000): Christian 63.5%, of which unaffiliated Christian 25.6%, Protestant (mostly Lutheran) 17.2%, Orthodox 16.5%, independent Christian 3.3%; nonreligious 25.1%; atheist 10.9%; other 0.5%. **Major cities** (2006): Tallinn 396,852; Tartu 101,965; Narva 66,712; Kohtla-Järve 45,399; Pärnu 44,074. **Location:** eastern Europe, bordering the Gulf of Finland, Russia, Latvia, the Gulf of Riga, and the Baltic Sea.

## Vital statistics

**Birth rate** per 1,000 population (2008): 12.0 (world avg. 20.3); within marriage 40.9%. **Death rate** per 1,000 population (2008): 12.4 (world avg. 8.5). **Total fertility rate** (avg. births per childbearing woman; 2008): 1.66. **Life expectancy** at birth (2008): male 67.6 years; female 79.2 years.

## National economy

**Budget** (2006). *Revenue:* EEK 57,735,000,000 (tax revenue 58.7%, of which taxes on goods and services 46.6%, taxes on income and profits 12.1%; social contributions 20.9%). *Expenditures:* EEK 53,149,000,000 (social protection 30.2%; general administration 17.8%; economic affairs 11.9%; education 8.5%; health 6.6%; defense 5.3%). **Production** (metric tons except as noted). *Agriculture and fishing*

(2007): barley 372,800, wheat 322,000, potatoes 173,700; livestock (number of live animals) 345,800 pigs, 244,800 cattle; fisheries production 98,614 (from aquaculture, negligible). *Mining and quarrying* (2007): oil shale 13,992,000; peat 900,800. *Manufacturing* (value added in US$'000,000; 2006): wood products (excluding furniture) 211; food products 197; printing and publishing 141. *Energy production (consumption):* electricity (kW-hr; 2008) 10,524,000,000 ([2006] 8,758,000,000); coal (metric tons; 2006) none (70,000); lignite (metric tons; 2008) 16,044,000 ([2006] 14,028,000); petroleum products (metric tons; 2006) none (858,000); natural gas (cu m; 2007) none ([2006] 963,000,000). **Population economically active** (2005): total 659,600; activity rate of total population 48.8% (participation rates: ages 15–64, 69.6%; female 50.1%; unemployed [2008] 5.5%). **Gross national income** (2008): US$19,131,000,000 (US$14,270 per capita). **Selected balance of payments data.** Receipts from (US$'000,000): tourism (2007) 1,036; remittances (2008) 422; foreign direct investment (FDI; 2005–07 avg.) 2,345. Disbursements for (US$'000,000): tourism (2007) 670; remittances (2008) 113; FDI (2005–07 avg.) 1,088.

## Foreign trade

**Imports** (2007; c.i.f.): EEK 164,451,000,000 (machinery and apparatus 20.2%; refined petroleum products 11.5%; motor vehicles 11.1%; chemical products 8.6%; food products 5.6%; iron and steel 5.1%). *Major import sources:* Finland 15.9%; Germany 12.8%; Russia 10.2%; Sweden 10.1%; Latvia 7.6%. **Exports** (2006; f.o.b.): EEK 117,121,000,000 (machinery and apparatus 20.1%; refined petroleum products 9.8%; motor vehicles and parts 7.1%; food products 5.6%; sawn wood 5.3%; furniture 4.3%). *Major export destinations:* Finland 18.0%; Sweden 13.3%; Latvia 11.4%; Russia 8.9%; Lithuania 5.8%.

## Transport and communications

**Transport.** *Railroads* (2005): route length (2004) 958 km; passenger-km 246,951,000; metric ton-km cargo 10,629,398,000. *Roads* (2005): total length 57,016 km (paved 23%). *Vehicles* (2005): passenger cars 493,800; trucks and buses 91,400. *Air transport* (2007): passenger-km 756,000,000; metric ton-km cargo 1,044,000. **Communications,** in total units (units per 1,000 persons). Telephone landlines (2008): 498,000 (372); cellular telephone subscribers (2008): 2,524,000 (1,883); personal computers (2007): 700,000 (522); total Internet users (2007): 854,000 (637); broadband Internet subscribers (2008): 318,000 (237).

## Education and health

**Educational attainment** (2000). Percentage of population ages 10 and over having: no formal schooling/incomplete primary education 6.7%; complete primary/lower secondary 31.6%; complete secondary 29.2%; higher vocational 17.5%; undergraduate 12.3%; advanced degree 0.4%; unknown 2.3%. **Health** (2007): physicians 4,504 (1 per 298 persons); hospital beds 7,473 (1 per 179 persons); infant mortality rate per 1,000 live births (2008) 5.0; undernourished population (2002–04) less than 2.5% of total population.

## Military

**Total active duty personnel** (November 2008): 5,300 (army 88.7%, navy 5.7%, air force 5.6%). **Military expenditure as a percentage of GDP** (2008): 1.8%; per capita expenditure US$317.

## Background

The lands on the eastern shores of the Baltic Sea were invaded by Vikings in the 9th century AD, but the Estonians were able to withstand the assaults until the Danes took control in 1219. In 1346 the Danes sold their sovereignty to the Teutonic Order, which was then in possession of Livonia (southern Estonia and Latvia). In the mid-16th century Estonia was once again divided, with northern Estonia capitulating to Sweden and Poland gaining Livonia, which it surrendered to Sweden in 1629. Russia acquired Livonia and Estonia in 1721. Serfdom was abolished, and from 1881 Estonia underwent intensive Russification. In 1918 Estonia obtained independence from Russia, which lasted until the Soviet Union occupied the country in 1940 and forcibly incorporated it into the USSR. Germany held the region (1941–44) during World War II, but the Soviet regime was restored in 1944, after which Estonia's economy was collectivized and integrated into that of the Soviet Union. In 1991, along with other parts of the former USSR, it proclaimed its independence and subsequently held elections. Estonia continued negotiations with Russia to settle their common border, and, along with the other Baltic states, Estonia joined the EU and NATO in 2004.

## Recent Developments

Estonia's economy performed very well in 2011. Not only did Estonia lead all European Union countries in GDP growth rates, but unemployment fell considerably, from 17.3% in 2010 to 12.8% in 2011. Estonia's first year of experience with the euro was positive, despite concerns about participation in the compulsory bailout for Greece and possibly other struggling member states.

**Internet resource:** <www.stat.ee/en>.

# Ethiopia

**Official name:** Federal Democratic Republic of Ethiopia. **Form of government:** federal republic with two legislative houses (House of the Federation [135]; House of Peoples' Representatives [547]). **Head of state:** President Girma Wolde-Giorgis (from 2001). **Head of government:** Prime Minister Hailemariam Desalegn (from 2012). **Capital:** Addis Ababa. **Official language:** none (Amharic is the "working" language). **Official religion:** none. **Monetary unit:** 1 birr (Br) = 100 cents; valuation (2 Jul 2012) US$1 = Br 17.83.

*1 metric ton = about 1.1 short tons;  1 kilometer = 0.6 mi (statute);  1 metric ton-km cargo = about 0.68 short ton-mi cargo;  c.i.f.: cost, insurance, and freight;  f.o.b.: free on board*

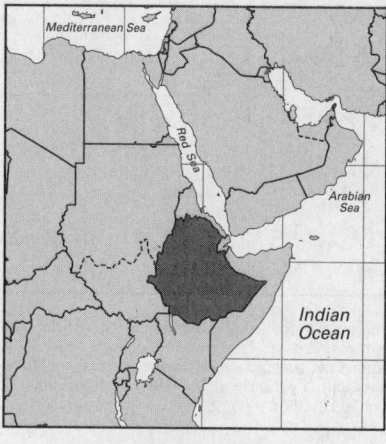

## Demography

**Area:** 410,678 sq mi, 1,063,652 sq km. **Population** (2011): 82,102,000. **Density** (2011): persons per sq mi 199.9, persons per sq km 77.2. **Urban** (2007): 16.2%. **Sex distribution** (2007): male 50.46%; female 49.54%. **Age breakdown** (2007): under 15, 45.0%; 15–29, 28.3%; 30–44, 14.7%; 45–59, 7.2%; 60–74, 3.7%; 75–84, 0.8%; 85 and over, 0.3%. **Ethnic composition** (2007): Oromo 34.5%; Amhara 26.9%; Somali 6.2%; Tigray 6.1%; Sidamo 4.0%; Gurage 2.5%; Welaita 2.3%; other 17.5%. **Religious affiliation** (2007): Orthodox 43.5%; Muslim 33.9%; Protestant 18.6%; traditional beliefs 2.7%; Roman Catholic 0.7%; other 0.6%. **Major cities** (2007): Addis Ababa 2,738,248; Adama (Nazret) 222,035; Dire Dawa 222,000; Mekele 215,546; Gonder 206,987. **Location:** the Horn of Africa, bordering Eritrea, Djibouti, Somalia, Kenya, South Sudan, and Sudan.

## Vital statistics

**Birth rate** per 1,000 population (2008): 44.0 (world avg. 20.3). **Death rate** per 1,000 population (2008): 11.8 (world avg. 8.5). **Total fertility rate** (avg. births per childbearing woman; 2008): 6.17. **Life expectancy** at birth (2008): male 52.5 years; female 57.5 years.

## National economy

**Budget** (2006–07). *Revenue:* Br 30,274,000,000 (tax revenue 57.3%, of which import duties 27.0%, income and profits tax 16.1%, sales tax 9.5%; grants 28.0%; nontax revenue 14.7%). *Expenditures:* Br 35,564,000,000 (capital expenditures 51.7%, of which economic development 32.0%; current expenditures 48.3%, of which education 13.8%, defense 8.4%). **Public debt** (external, outstanding; 2007–08): US$2,753,600,000. **Gross national income** (2008): US$22,742,000,000 (US$280 per capita). **Production** (metric tons except as noted). *Agriculture and fishing* (2007): corn (maize) 4,000,000, wheat 3,000,000, teff (2006–07) 2,437,700, coffee 325,800, maté 260,000, chickpeas 190,000, sesame seeds 164,000; leading producer of beeswax, honey, cut flowers, and khat; livestock (number of live animals) 43,000,000 cattle, 23,700,000 sheep, 18,000,000 goats, 2,300,000 camels, (1998) 3,037 civets; fisheries production 13,253 (from aquaculture, none). *Mining and quarrying* (2007): rock salt 230,000; tantalum 77,000 kg; niobium 12,000 kg; gold 3,400 kg. *Manufacturing* (value added in US$'000,000; 2004): food products 157; beverages 118; bricks, cement, and ceramics 69. *Energy production (consumption):* electricity (kW-hr; 2007–08) 3,530,280,000 ([2005] 2,872,000,000); crude petroleum (barrels; 2005) none (5,640,000); petroleum products (metric tons; 2006) n.a. (1,680,000). **Population economically active** (2005): total 32,158,392; activity rate of total population 50.9% (participation rates: ages 10 and over, 78.4%; female [1999] 45.5%; unemployed 5.0%). **Selected balance of payments data.** Receipts from (US$'000,000): tourism (2007) 177; remittances (2008) 358; foreign direct investment (2005–07 avg.) 355; official development assistance (2007) 2,422. Disbursements for (US$'000,000): tourism (2007) 107; remittances (2008) 15.

## Foreign trade

**Imports** (2006; c.i.f.): US$5,207,000,000 (machinery and apparatus 20.7%; refined petroleum products 19.5%; motor vehicles 14.1%; chemical products 11.0%; food products 6.7%). *Major import sources:* Saudi Arabia 17.9%; China 12.3%; Italy 7.7%; UAE 7.6%; India 5.8%. **Exports** (2006; f.o.b.): US$1,043,000,000 (coffee and khat 40.8%; sesame seeds 15.4%; gum products, cut flowers, and foliage 12.4%; gold 6.2%; leather products 4.2%; chickpeas 3.5%). *Major export destinations:* Germany 12.6%; China 9.7%; Japan 8.4%; Switzerland 6.4%; Saudi Arabia 6.3%.

## Transport and communications

**Transport.** *Railroads* (2003): length 781 km; (2006–07) passenger-km 28,200,000. *Roads* (2007–08): total length 44,359 km (paved [2004] 19%). *Vehicles* (2003): passenger cars 71,311; trucks and buses 65,557. *Air transport* (2008): passenger-km 9,300,000,000; metric ton-km cargo 227,760,000. **Communications,** in total units (units per 1,000 persons). Telephone landlines (2008): 909,000 (11); cellular telephone subscribers (2008): 3,168,000 (37); personal computers (2007): 551,000 (7.0); total Internet users (2008): 360,000 (4.2); broadband Internet subscribers (2007): 300.

## Education and health

**Educational attainment** (2000). Percentage of population ages 15 and over having: no formal schooling 63.8%; incomplete primary education 21.6%; primary 2.6%; incomplete secondary 8.1%; secondary 2.5%; post-secondary 1.4%. **Literacy** (2007): total population ages 15 and over literate 47.5%. **Health:** physicians (2004–05) 1,077 (1 per 66,236 persons); hospital beds (2007–08) 13,145 (1 per 6,062 persons); infant mortality rate per 1,000 live births (2008) 82.6; undernourished population (2003–05) 35,200,000 (46% of total population based on the consumption of a minimum daily requirement of 1,680 calories).

## Military

Total active duty personnel (November 2008): 138,000 (army 97.8%, air force 2.2%); mandate for the UN peacekeeping force along the Eritrean-Ethiopian border was terminated in July 2008. Military expenditure as percentage of GDP (2008): 1.6%; per capita expenditure US$4.

## Background

Ethiopia, the Biblical land of Cush, was inhabited from earliest antiquity and was once under ancient Egyptian rule. Ge'ez-speaking agriculturalists established the kingdom of Da'amat in the 2nd millennium BC. After 300 BC they were superseded by the kingdom of Aksum, whose King Menilek I, according to legend, was the son of King Solomon and the Queen of Sheba. Christianity was introduced in the 4th century AD and became widespread. Ethiopia's prosperous Mediterranean trade was cut off by the Muslim Arabs in the 7th and 8th centuries, and the area's interests were directed eastward. Contact with Europe resumed in the late 15th century with the arrival of the Portuguese. Modern Ethiopia began with the reign of Tewodros II, who began the consolidation of the country. In the wake of European encroachment, the coastal region was made an Italian colony in 1890, but under Emperor Menilek II the Italians were defeated and ousted in 1896. Ethiopia prospered under his rule, and his modernization programs were continued by Emperor Haile Selassie in the 1930s. In 1936 Italy again gained control of the country, and it was held as part of Italian East Africa until 1941, when it was liberated by the British. Ethiopia incorporated Eritrea in 1952. In 1974 Haile Selassie was deposed, and a Marxist government, plagued by civil wars and famine, controlled the country until 1991. In 1993 Eritrea gained its independence, but there were continuing border conflicts with it and neighboring Somalia into the 21st century.

## Recent Developments

Neither Ethiopia nor Eritrea took any steps in 2011 to demarcate their border in line with the 2002 ruling of the Eritrea-Ethiopia Boundary Commission, which Ethiopia had rejected. The Ethiopian military continued to engage in periodic battles with small but persistent domestic armed insurgencies, particularly those in the Somali region of the country. Late in the year, Ethiopia's military also crossed into neighboring Somalia to aid that country in its battle against the Islamic insurgent group al-Shabaab. Although most of the victims were in southern Somalia, Ethiopia experienced drought in some of its arid regions and saw a considerable increase in refugee flows.

Internet resource: <www.csa.gov.et>.

## Fiji

Official name: Republic of the Fiji Islands; Matanitu Tu-Vaka-i-koya ko Viti (Fijian); Fiji Ripablik (Hindustani). Form of government: interim regime. Head of state: President Ratu Epeli Nailatikau (from 2009). Head of government: Prime Minister Voreque Baini-

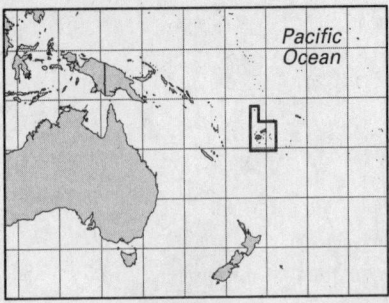

marama (from 2007). Capital: Suva. Official languages: English, Fijian, and Hindustani have equal status per constitution. Official religion: none. Monetary unit: 1 Fiji dollar (F$) = 100 cents; valuation (2 Jul 2012) US$1 = F$1.82.

## Demography

Area: 7,055 sq mi, 18,272 sq km. Population (2011): 852,000. Density (2011): persons per sq mi 120.8, persons per sq km 46.6. Urban (2009): 51.5%. Sex distribution (2007): male 51.02%; female 48.98%. Age breakdown (2007): under 15, 29.0%; 15–29, 27.9%; 30–44, 21.1%; 45–59, 14.5%; 60–74, 6.1%; 75 and over, 1.4%. Ethnic composition (2007): Fijian 56.8%; Indian 37.5%; other Pacific islanders 3.0%, of which Rotuman (Polynesian/other) 1.2%; European/part-European 1.7%; Chinese 0.6%; other 0.4%. Religious affiliation (2007): Christian 64.4%, of which Methodist 34.6%, Roman Catholic 9.1%, Assemblies of God 5.7%; Hindu 27.9%; Muslim 6.3%; other 1.4%. Major urban areas (2007): Nasinu 87,446; Suva 85,691 (urban agglomeration, 241,432); Lautoka 52,220; Nausori 47,604; Nadi 42,284. Location: Oceania, archipelago in the South Pacific Ocean, between Hawaii (US) and New Zealand.

## Vital statistics

Birth rate per 1,000 population (2007): 20.7 (world avg. 20.3). Death rate per 1,000 population (2007): 7.1 (world avg. 8.5). Total fertility rate (avg. births per childbearing woman; 2006): 2.73. Life expectancy at birth (2006): male 67.3 years; female 72.5 years.

## National economy

Budget (2006). Revenue: F$1,373,000,000 (tax revenue 90.7%, of which taxes on goods and services 40.9%, income tax 32.5%; other 9.3%). Expenditures: F$1,530,000,000 (general administration 25.0%; education 22.4%; economic affairs 14.2%; public order 9.4%; health 9.3%; defense 5.4%). Public debt (external, outstanding; June 2009): US$273,000,000. Production (metric tons except as noted). Agriculture and fishing (2007): sugarcane 3,200,000, coconuts 140,000, taro 38,000, cassava 34,500, rice 15,000, ginger 4,300, yaqona (kava) (2006) 2,259; livestock (number of live animals) 315,000 cattle, 4,300,000 chickens; fisheries production (2006) 47,319 (from aquaculture 1%).

1 metric ton = about 1.1 short tons;    1 kilometer = 0.6 mi (statute);    1 metric ton-km cargo = about 0.68 short ton-mi cargo;    c.i.f.: cost, insurance, and freight;    f.o.b.: free on board

*Mining and quarrying* (2005): gold 3,800 kg; silver 1,500 kg. *Manufacturing* (value added in US$'000,000; 2004): food products 63; textiles and wearing apparel 53; beverages 46. *Energy production (consumption):* electricity (kW-hr; 2006) 840,000,000 (841,000,000); coal (metric tons; 2006) none (12,000); petroleum products (metric tons; 2006) none (489,000). **Population economically active** (2007): total 334,787; activity rate of total population 40.0% (participation rates: ages 15–64, 57.0%; female 33.9%; unemployed 8.6%). **Gross national income** (2008): US$3,300,000,000 (US$3,930 per capita). **Selected balance of payments data.** Receipts from (US$'000,000): tourism (2006) 433; remittances (2008) 175; foreign direct investment (2005–07 avg.) 268; official development assistance (2007) 57. Disbursements for (US$'000,000): tourism (2006) 101; remittances (2008) 32.

### Foreign trade

**Imports** (2008; c.i.f.): F$3,601,000,000 (mineral fuels 33.9%; machinery and transportation equipment 20.2%; food products 14.4%). *Major import sources* (2007): Singapore 34.2%; Australia 22.8%; New Zealand 17.7%; China 3.3%; US 3.2%. **Exports** (2008; f.o.b.): F$1,471,000,000 (reexports [mostly refined petroleum products] 33.2%; sugar 16.9%; fish 9.1%; mineral water [2007] 9.1%; wearing apparel 6.9%; lumber 4.0%). *Major export destinations* (2007): Singapore 18.6%; US 14.7%; UK 14.2%; Australia 13.3%; New Zealand 6.9%.

### Transport and communications

**Transport.** *Railroads* (2003; owned by the Fiji Sugar Corporation): length 597 km. *Roads* (1999): total length 3,440 km (paved 49%). *Vehicles* (2005): passenger cars 76,273; trucks and buses 42,311. *Air transport* (2004–05; Air Pacific only): passenger-km 2,360,000,000; metric ton-km cargo 92,108,000. **Communications,** in total units (units per 1,000 persons). Telephone landlines (2007): 108,000 (130); cellular telephone subscribers (2007): 437,000 (524); personal computers (2004): 44,000 (52); total Internet users (2007): 91,000 (110); broadband Internet subscribers (2007): 12,000 (14).

### Education and health

**Educational attainment** (1996). Percentage of population ages 25 and over having: no formal schooling 4.4%; some education 22.3%; incomplete secondary 47.7%; complete secondary 17.0%; some higher 6.7%; university degree 1.9%. **Literacy** (2003): total population ages 15 and over literate 93.7%; males literate 95.5%; females literate 91.9%. **Health** (2007): physicians 318 (1 per 2,622 persons); hospital beds 1,727 (1 per 483 persons); infant mortality rate per 1,000 live births 18.4; undernourished population (2002–04) 40,000 (5% of total population based on the consumption of a minimum daily requirement of 1,920 calories).

### Military

**Total active duty personnel** (November 2008): 3,500 (army 91.4%, navy 8.6%, air force, none); reserve 6,000. **Military expenditure as percentage of GDP** (2007): 1.6%; per capita expenditure US$60.

### Background

Archaeological evidence shows that the islands of Fiji were occupied in the late 2nd millennium BC. The first European sighting was by the Dutch in the 17th century AD; in 1774 the islands were visited by Capt. James Cook, who found a mixed Melanesian-Polynesian population with a complex society. Traders and the first missionaries arrived in 1835. In 1857 a British consul was appointed, and in 1874 Fiji was proclaimed a crown colony. It became independent as a member of the Commonwealth in 1970 and was declared a republic in 1987 following a military coup. Elections in 1992 restored civilian rule. A new constitution was approved in 1997. Coups in 2000 and 2006 created continuing political instability in the early 21st century.

### Recent Developments

Some of the popular support that Fiji's interim administration had earlier enjoyed seemed to erode in 2011. In August the government canceled the Fiji Methodist Church's annual conference after church leaders—active critics of the regime—refused to submit to restrictions on speakers. Organized labor objected to the government's Essential National Industries (Employment) Decree announced in July, which banned strikes and similar actions in key industries. The following month union leaders were detained after a meeting and charged with unlawful assembly.

**Internet resource:** <www.statsfiji.gov.fj>.

# Finland

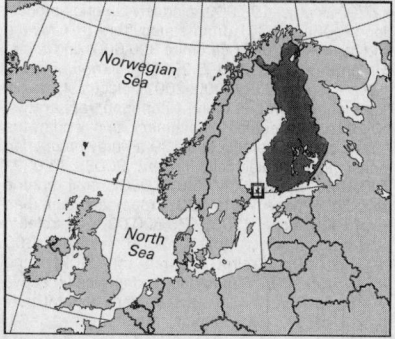

**Official names:** Suomen Tasavalta (Finnish); Republiken Finland (Swedish) (Republic of Finland). **Form of government:** multiparty republic with one legislative house (Parliament [200]). **Head of state:** President Sauli Niinistö (from 2012). **Head of government:** Prime Minister Jyrki Katainen (from 2011). **Capital:** Helsinki. **Official languages:** none (Finnish and Swedish are national [not official] languages). **Official religion:** none. **Monetary unit:** 1 euro (€) = 100 cents; valuation (2 Jul 2012) US$1 = €0.79.

### Demography

**Area:** 130,666 sq mi, 338,424 sq km. **Population** (2011): 5,387,000. **Density** (2011; based on land area only): persons per sq mi 45.9, persons per sq km 17.7. **Urban** (2009): 84.8%. **Sex distribution** (2008): male 49.03%; female 50.97%. **Age breakdown** (2008): under 15, 16.7%; 15–29, 18.8%; 30–44, 19.0%; 45–59, 21.7%; 60–74, 15.9%; 75–84, 5.9%; 85 and over, 2.0%. **Linguistic composition** (2008): Finnish 90.9%; Swedish 5.4%; Russian 0.9%; other 2.8%. **Religious affiliation** (2005): Evangelical Lutheran 83.1%; nonreligious 14.7%; Finnish (Greek) Orthodox 1.1%; Muslim 0.4%; other 0.7%. **Major cities** (2008): Helsinki 576,632 (urban agglomeration [2007] 1,115,000); Espoo 241,565; Tampere 209,552; Vantaa 195,397; Turku 175,582. **Location**: northern Europe, bordering Norway, Russia, the Gulf of Finland, the Baltic Sea, the Gulf of Bothnia, and Sweden.

## Vital statistics

**Birth rate** per 1,000 population (2008): 11.2 (world avg. 20.3); within marriage 59.3%. **Death rate** per 1,000 population (2008): 9.2 (world avg. 8.5). **Total fertility rate** (avg. births per childbearing woman; 2008): 1.85. **Life expectancy** at birth (2008): male 76.3 years; female 83.0 years.

## National economy

**Budget** (2008). *Revenue:* €45,522,000,000 (income and property taxes 34.2%; turnover taxes 33.3%; excise duties 11.0%). *Expenditures:* €45,522,000,000 (social security and health 31.0%; education 15.4%; public debt service 9.3%; agriculture and forestry 6.2%; defense 5.3%). **Public debt** (2008): US$74,700,000,000. **Production** (metric tons except as noted). *Agriculture and fishing* (2007): barley 1,984,000, oats 1,222,000, wheat 797,000; livestock (number of live animals) 1,448,000 pigs, 927,000 cattle, 193,000 reindeer; fisheries production (2006) 162,341 (from aquaculture 8%). *Mining and quarrying* (2006): chromite 320,000; zinc (metal content) 66,109; gold 5,292 kg. *Manufacturing* (value added in €'000,000; 2007): electrical and optical equipment (largely telephone apparatus) 10,291; nonelectrical machinery and apparatus 4,707; chemical products 4,129. *Energy production (consumption):* electricity (kW-hr; 2008) 74,052,-000,000 ([2006] 93,705,000,000); coal (metric tons; 2006) none (7,612,000); crude petroleum (barrels; 2008) none ([2006] 76,800,000); petroleum products (metric tons; 2006) 12,849,000 (10,541,000); natural gas (cu m; 2007) none (4,587,000,000). **Population economically active** (2008): total 2,725,600; activity rate of total population 51.3% (participation rates: ages 15–64, 76.1%; female 47.8%; unemployed [May 2008–April 2009] 8.0%). **Gross national income** (2008): US$255,678,000,000 (US$48,120 per capita). **Selected balance of payments data.** Receipts from (US$'000,000): tourism (2008) 3,127; remittances (2008) 772; foreign direct investment (FDI; 2005–07 avg.) 6,236. Disbursements for (US$'000,000): tourism (2008) 4,350; remittances (2008) 391; FDI (2005–07 avg.) 5,336.

## Foreign trade

**Imports** (2007; c.i.f.): €59,600,000,000 (machinery and apparatus 26.2%; crude petroleum 10.8%;

chemical products 10.1%; motor vehicles and parts 8.5%; metal ore and scrap metal 7.2%). *Major import sources:* Russia 14.1%; Germany 14.0%; Sweden 9.8%; China 7.5%; UK 4.8%. **Exports** (2007; f.o.b.): €65,607,000,000 (telecommunications equipment and parts 13.6%; paper products and cardboard 12.3%; iron and steel 7.8%; specialized machinery 6.7%; refined petroleum products 5.1%; general industrial machinery 5.0%; nonferrous base metals 4.7%). *Major export destinations:* Germany 10.9%; Sweden 10.7%; Russia 10.2%; US 6.4%; UK 5.8%.

## Transport and communications

**Transport.** *Railroads* (2008): route length 5,919 km; passenger-km 4,100,000,000; metric ton-km cargo 10,800,000,000. *Roads* (2008): total length 78,141 km (paved [2005] 65%). *Vehicles* (2005): passenger cars 2,430,345; trucks and buses 363,644. *Air transport* (2007): passenger-km 15,564,000,000; metric ton-km cargo 489,672,000. **Communications,** in total units (units per 1,000 persons). Telephone landlines (2008): 1,650,000 (311); cellular telephone subscribers (2008): 6,830,000 (1,285); personal computers (2007): 2,644,000 (500); total Internet users (2007): 4,169,000 (788); broadband Internet subscribers (2008): 1,617,000 (304).

## Education and health

**Educational attainment** (2003). Percentage of population ages 25 and over having: incomplete upper-secondary education 35.6%; complete upper secondary or vocational 35.8%; higher 28.6%. **Literacy:** virtually 100%. **Health** (2007): physicians 18,843 (1 per 281 persons); hospital beds 36,095 (1 per 147 persons); infant mortality rate per 1,000 live births (2008) 2.6; undernourished population (2002–04) less than 2.5% of total population.

## Military

**Total active duty personnel** (November 2008): 31,900 (army 67.4%, navy 17.9%, air force 14.7%); reserves 237,000. **Military expenditure as percentage of GDP** (2007): 1.3%; per capita expenditure US$596.

## Background

Recent archaeological discoveries have led some to suggest that human habitation in Finland dates back at least 100,000 years. Ancestors of the Sami apparently were present in Finland by about 7000 BC. The ancestors of the present-day Finns came from the southern shore of the Gulf of Finland in the 1st millennium BC. The area was gradually Christianized from the 11th century. From the 12th century Sweden and Russia contested for supremacy in Finland, but by 1323 Sweden ruled most of the country. Russia was ceded part of Finnish territory in 1721; in 1808 Alexander I of Russia invaded Finland, which in 1809 was formally ceded to Russia. The subsequent period saw the growth of Finnish nationalism. Russia's losses in World War I and the Russian Revolution of 1917 set the stage for Finland's independence in 1917. It was defeated by the Soviet Union in the Russo-Finnish War (1939–40) but then sided

---

*1 metric ton = about 1.1 short tons;    1 kilometer = 0.6 mi (statute);    1 metric ton-km cargo = about 0.68 short ton-mi cargo;    c.i.f.: cost, insurance, and freight;    f.o.b.: free on board*

with Nazi Germany against the Soviets during World War II and regained the territory it had lost. Facing defeat again by the advancing Soviets in 1944, it reached a peace agreement with the USSR, ceding territory and paying reparations. Finland's economy recovered after World War II. It joined the EU in 1995.

## Recent Developments

The April 2011 general elections in Finland became a peaceful demonstration of democracy at work. The True Finns, a populist party with an anti-European Union agenda, quadrupled its votes (19.1%) and emerged with 39 seats, up from 5 in 2007. The True Finns' election victory rested mainly on disappointment among voters over the EU, most notably its bailout packages for debt-ridden euro-zone countries such as Greece. Popular opinion saw the share asked of Finland as excessive and regarded the bailouts as a handout to reckless German, British, and French banks, while cautious Finnish banks had refrained from lending to unstable economies.

Internet resource: <www.stat.fi/index_en.html>.

# France

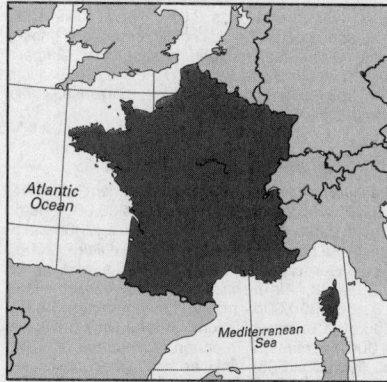

Official name: République Française (French Republic). Form of government: republic with two legislative houses (Senate [348]; National Assembly [577]). Head of state: President François Hollande (from 2012). Head of government: Prime Minister Jean-Marc Ayrault (from 2012). Capital: Paris. Official language: French. Official religion: none. Monetary unit: 1 euro (€) = 100 cents; valuation (2 Jul 2012) US$1 = €0.79.

## Demography

Area: 210,026 sq mi, 543,965 sq km. Population (2011): 63,292,000 (excludes the populations of French Guiana, Guadeloupe, Martinique, and Réunion, totaling 1,903,000 people in mid-2011). Density (2011): persons per sq mi 301.4, persons per sq km 116.4. Urban (2009): 84.6%. Sex distribution (2006): male 48.60%; female 51.40%. Age breakdown (2005): under 15, 18.4%; 15–29, 19.1%; 30–44, 21.1%; 45–59, 20.4%; 60–74, 12.7%; 75–84, 6.3%; 85 and over, 2.0%. Ethnic composition (2000): French 76.9%; Algerian and Moroccan

Berber 2.2%; Italian 1.9%; Portuguese 1.5%; Moroccan Arab 1.5%; Fleming 1.4%; Algerian Arab 1.3%; Basque 1.3%; Jewish 1.2%; German 1.2%; Vietnamese 1.0%; Catalan 0.5%; other 8.1%. Religious affiliation (2004): Roman Catholic 64.3%, of which practicing 8.0%; nonreligious/atheist 27.0%; Muslim 4.3%; Protestant 1.9%; Buddhist 1.0%; Jewish 0.6%; Jehovah's Witness 0.4%; Orthodox 0.2%; other 0.3%. Major cities (urban agglomerations) (2006): Paris 2,181,371 (10,142,977); Marseille 839,043 (1,418,481); Lyon 472,305 (1,417,463); Lille 226,014 (1,016,205); Nice 347,060 (940,017); Toulouse 437,715 (850,873); Bordeaux 232,260 (803,117); Nantes 282,853 (568,743); Toulon 167,816 (543,065); Douai-Lens: Douai (2005) 40,094, Lens (2005) 34,872 (512,462); Strasbourg 272,975 (440,265); Grenoble 156,107 (427,658); Rouen 107,904 (388,798); Valenciennes (2005) 41,506 (355,660); Nancy 105,468 (331,279); Metz 124,435 (322,946); Montpellier 251,634 (318,225); Tours 136,942 (306,974); Saint-Étienne 177,480 (286,400); Rennes 209,613 (282,550). Location: western Europe, bordering the North Atlantic Ocean, Belgium, Luxembourg, Germany, Switzerland, Italy, the Mediterranean Sea, Spain, and Andorra. Immigration: total immigrant population (2004) 4,850,000; immigrants admitted (2002) 205,707, of which North African 30.7%, EU 20.8%, sub-Saharan African 15.2%, Asian 14.1%, other European 11.8%.

## Vital statistics

Birth rate per 1,000 population (2008): 12.9 (world avg. 20.3); (2007) within marriage 48.3%. Death rate per 1,000 population (2008): 8.6 (world avg. 8.5). Total fertility rate (avg. births per childbearing woman; 2008): 2.00. Life expectancy at birth (2008): male 77.6 years; female 84.4 years.

## Social indicators

Educational attainment (2002). Percentage of population ages 25–64 with no formal schooling through lower-secondary education 35%, upper secondary/higher vocational 41%, university 24%. Quality of working life. Legally worked week for full-time employees (2005) 36.0 hours. Rate of fatal injuries per 100,000 insured workers (2004): 3.7. Average days lost to labor stoppages per 1,000 workers (2004): 13. Trade union membership (2003): 1,900,000 (8% of labor force). Access to services (2004). Proportion of principal residences having: electricity 97.4%; indoor toilet 94.6%; indoor kitchen with sink 94.2%; hot water 60.3%; air conditioner 15.4%. Social participation. Population ages 15 and over participating in voluntary associations (1997): 28.0%. Percentage of population who "never" or "almost never" attend church services (2000) 60%; percentage of Roman Catholic population who attend Mass weekly (2003) 12%. Social deviance. Offense rate per 100,000 population (2006) for: murder 1.5, rape 16.0, other assault 269.2; theft (including burglary and housebreaking) 3,403.8. Incidence per 100,000 in general population of: homicide (2001) 0.8; suicide (2001) 16.1. Leisure. Members of sports federations (2007): 16,254,000, of which football (soccer) 2,321,000. Movie tickets sold (2005): 174,200,000. Average daily hours of television viewing for population ages 4 and over (2007): 3.45. Material well-being (2004). Households possessing: automobile (2007) 82%;

color television 95%; personal computer 45%; washing machine 92%; microwave 74%; dishwasher (2001) 39%.

## National economy

**Gross national income** (2008): US$2,702,180,000,000 (US$42,250 per capita). **Budget** (2007). *Revenue:* €369,600,000,000 (tax revenue 80.0%, of which taxes on goods and services 43.6%; social contributions 10.9%; grants 4.5%). *Expenditures:* €411,410,000,000 (social protection 20.0%; education 19.4%; economic affairs 13.8%; debt service 11.1%; defense 8.2%). **Public debt** (2007): US$1,655,000,000,000. **Production** (metric tons except as noted). *Agriculture and fishing* (2008): wheat 39,001,700, sugar beets 30,306,300, corn (maize) 15,818,500, barley 12,171,300, potatoes 6,808,210, grapes 5,664,195, rapeseed 4,719,053, apples 1,940,200, triticale 1,820,950, sunflower seeds 1,607,977, tomatoes 714,635, oats 471,960, dry peas 446,850, lettuce and chicory 420,400, green peas 337,488, string beans 337,488, dry onions 189,992, pears 162,000, mushrooms and truffles 150,450, spinach 143,487, chicory roots 125,475, flax fibre and tow 95,000, kiwi fruit 65,670; livestock (number of live animals) 19,887,458 cattle, 14,805,557 pigs, 8,187,329 sheep, 175,000,000 chickens, 25,253,000 turkeys, 22,848,000 ducks, 420,238 horses; fisheries production (2007) 749,903 (from aquaculture 31%); aquatic plants production (2007) 76,678 (from aquaculture, negligible). *Mining and quarrying* (2006): gypsum 3,500,000; kaolin 300,000; gold 1,500 kg. *Manufacturing* (value added in US$'000,000; 2003): food products 27,023; pharmaceuticals, soaps, and paints 22,675; motor vehicles, trailers, and motor vehicle parts 20,269; fabricated metal products 14,264; general purpose machinery 10,595; plastic products 8,754; medical, measuring, and testing appliances 7,551; aircraft and spacecraft 7,476; publishing 6,911; special purpose machinery 6,605; bricks, cement, and ceramics 5,922; basic chemical products 5,843; base metals 5,547, of which iron and steel 4,117; paper products 5,532; beverages 5,509; furniture 4,218. *Energy production (consumption):* electricity (kW-hr; 2006) 574,473,000,000 (511,138,000,000 [including Monaco]); coal (metric tons; 2007) 168,000 ([2005] 19,069,000); lignite (metric tons; 2006) negligible (36,000 [including Monaco]); crude petroleum (barrels; 2007) 7,430,000 ([2006; including Monaco] 606,000,000); petroleum products (metric tons; 2006 [including Monaco]) 74,659,000 (75,921,000); natural gas (cu m; 2007) 1,079,000,000 ([2006; including Monaco] 49,155,000,000). *Retail trade* (value of sales in €'000,000; 2004): large food stores 162,600; large nonfood stores 136,400; auto repair shops 120,400; pharmacies and stores selling orthopedic equipment 32,600; shops selling bread, pastries, or meat 31,800; small food stores and boutiques 15,300. **Population economically active** (2005): total 27,635,800; activity rate of total population 45.5% (participation rates: ages 15–64, 69.1%; female 46.4%; unemployed [April 2007] 8.2%. **Selected balance of payments data.** Receipts from (US$'000,000): tourism (2007) 54,165; remittances

(2008) 15,133; foreign direct investment (FDI; 2005–07 avg.) 107,025. Disbursements for (US$'000,000): tourism (2007) 36,743; remittances (2008) 4,541; FDI (2005–07 avg.) 153,666.

## Foreign trade

**Imports** (2006; c.i.f. [including Monaco]): US$529,902,000,000 (machinery and apparatus 22.1%, of which electrical machinery and parts 5.4%, general industrial machinery 3.9%, office machines and computers 3.5%; mineral fuels 14.8%, of which crude petroleum 7.5%, refined petroleum products 3.5%; chemical products 12.7%, of which medicines and pharmaceuticals 3.5%; motor vehicles and parts 10.2%; wearing apparel and accessories 3.5%; iron and steel 3.2%). *Major import sources:* Germany 16.3%; Italy 8.5%; Belgium 8.3%; Spain 6.9%; UK 6.1%; China 5.7%; Netherlands 4.1%; Japan 2.4%; Russia 2.4%. **Exports** (2006; f.o.b. [including Monaco]): US$479,013,000,000 (machinery and apparatus 22.1%, of which electrical machinery and parts 6.2%, general industrial machinery 4.8%, power-generating machinery 3.7%, telecommunications equipment 3.1%; chemical products 15.7%, of which medicines and pharmaceuticals 5.1%, perfumery and cosmetics 2.3%; motor vehicles and parts 12.1%; food products 6.1%; aircraft and parts 6.0%; mineral fuels 4.3%; iron and steel 3.7%; alcoholic beverages [mostly wine] 2.4%). *Major export destinations:* Germany 14.5%; Spain 9.9%; Italy 9.1%; UK 8.5%; Belgium 7.4%; US 6.9%; Netherlands 4.1%; Switzerland 2.7%; China 2.1%; Poland 1.8%.

## Transport and communications

**Transport.** *Railroads* (2006): route length (2004) 29,085 km; passenger-km 92,000,000,000; metric ton-km cargo 41,000,000,000. *Roads* (2006): total length 951,500 km (paved 100%). *Vehicles* (2006): passenger cars 30,400,000; trucks and buses 6,262,000. *Air transport* (2008): passenger-km 131,664,000,000; metric ton-km cargo 5,838,300,000. **Communications**, in total units (units per 1,000 persons). Telephone landlines (2008): 35,000,000 (565); cellular telephone subscribers (2008): 57,972,000 (936); personal computers (2007): 40,400,000 (652); total Internet users (2007): 31,571,000 (512); broadband Internet subscribers (2008): 17,691,000 (286).

## Education and health

**Health:** physicians (2007) 212,700 (1 per 291 persons); hospital beds (2004) 457,132 (1 per 132 persons); infant mortality rate per 1,000 live births (2008) 3.6; undernourished population (2002–04) less than 2.5% of total population.

## Military

**Total active duty personnel** (November 2008): 352,771 (army 38.0%, navy 12.5%, air force 16.3%, headquarters staff 1.5%, health services 2.4%, gendarmerie 29.3%). **Military expenditure as percentage of GDP** (2007): 2.4%; per capita expenditure US$980.

*1 metric ton = about 1.1 short tons;   1 kilometer = 0.6 mi (statute);   1 metric ton-km cargo = about 0.68 short ton-mi cargo;   c.i.f.: cost, insurance, and freight;   f.o.b.: free on board*

## Background

Archaeological excavations in France indicate continuous settlement from Paleolithic times. About 1200 BC the Gauls migrated into the area, and in 600 BC Ionian Greeks established several settlements, including one at Marseille. Julius Caesar completed the Roman conquest of Gaul in 50 BC. During the 6th century AD, the Salian Franks ruled; by the 8th century power had passed to the Carolingians, the greatest of whom was Charlemagne. The Hundred Years' War (1337–1453) resulted in the return to France of land that had been held by the British; by the end of the 15th century, France approximated its modern boundaries. The 16th century was marked by the Wars of Religion between Protestants (Huguenots) and Roman Catholics. Henry IV's Edict of Nantes (1598) granted substantial religious toleration, but this was revoked in 1685 by Louis XIV, who helped to raise monarchical absolutism to new heights. In 1789 the French Revolution proclaimed the rights of the individual and destroyed the ancien régime. Napoleon ruled from 1799 to 1814, after which a limited monarchy was restored until 1871, when the Third Republic was created. World War I (1914–18) ravaged the northern part of France. After Nazi Germany's invasion during World War II, the collaborationist Vichy regime governed. Liberated by Allied and Free French forces in 1944, France restored parliamentary democracy under the Fourth Republic. A costly war in Indochina and rising nationalism in French colonies during the 1950s overwhelmed the Fourth Republic. The Fifth Republic was established in 1958 under Charles de Gaulle, who presided over the dissolution of most of France's overseas colonies. In 1981 François Mitterrand became France's first elected Socialist president. At various times from 1986 through the beginning of the 21st century, France balanced a form of divided government known as "cohabitation," with a president and prime minister of different political parties.

## Recent Developments

Although the French economy flatlined in the second quarter of 2011 and saw only tepid growth in the third quarter, it grew by 1.7% for the year, exceeding its 1.4% growth performance of 2010. Both France and Germany began to realize the need for closer integration if the 17 members of the euro zone were to hold together. In a series of Franco-German agreements—often presented as a fait accompli to their euro-zone partners—France accepted Germany's insistence on the euro zone's adoption of pacts on fiscal discipline and competitiveness. In return Germany accepted the French desire for closer budget coordination and tax harmonization among the 17 euro-zone members. France participated in several military interventions. One was in Côte d'Ivoire in support of the UN-backed presidential candidate, Alassane Ouattara, against incumbent Pres. Laurent Gbagbo. Gbagbo claimed that he had won the disputed 2010 election, but the conflict was resolved in April, when pro-Ouattara forces captured and arrested Gbagbo. They were supported by French troops, who acted discreetly in an effort to minimize accusations of neocolonialism in the former French colony. France's bigger commitment was in Afghanistan, but on a visit there in July 2011, French Pres. Nicolas Sarkozy announced that 1,000 French troops would leave by the end of 2012 and the remaining 3,000 by 2014. Despite these commitments, French forces found themselves virtually leading the UN-authorized international intervention in Libya. French planes were among the first to strike military targets associated with Muammar al-Qaddafi's forces in Libya, and France was the first country to recognize the rebel Libyan government.

**Internet resource:** <www.insee.fr/en>.

# Gabon

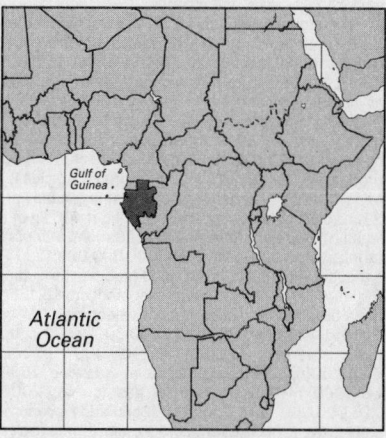

**Official name:** République Gabonaise (Gabonese Republic). **Form of government:** unitary multiparty republic with two legislative houses (Senate [102]; National Assembly [120]). **Head of state:** President Ali Bongo Ondimba (from 2009). **Head of government:** Prime Minister Raymond Ndong Sima (from 2012). **Capital:** Libreville. **Official language:** French. **Official religion:** none. **Monetary unit:** 1 CFA franc (CFAF) = 100 centimes; valuation (2 Jul 2012) US$1 = CFAF 521.26.

## Demography

**Area:** 103,347 sq mi, 267,667 sq km. **Population** (2011): 1,534,000. **Density** (2011): persons per sq mi 14.8, persons per sq km 5.7. **Urban** (2009): 85.6%. **Sex distribution** (2006): male 49.67%; female 50.33%. **Age breakdown** (2005): under 15, 40.0%; 15–29, 28.3%; 30–44, 16.1%; 45–59, 9.3%; 60–74, 4.6%; 75–84, 1.4%; 85 and over, 0.3%. **Ethnic composition** (2000): Fang 28.6%; Punu 10.2%; Nzebi 8.9%; French 6.7%; Mpongwe 4.1%; Teke 4.0%; other 37.5%. **Religious affiliation** (2005): Christian 73%, of which Roman Catholic 45%, Protestant/independent Christian 28%; Muslim 12%; traditional beliefs 10%; nonreligious 5%. **Major urban areas** (2003): Libreville 661,600; Port-Gentil 116,200; Franceville 41,300. **Location:** western Africa, bordering Cameroon, the Republic of the Congo, the South Atlantic Ocean, and Equatorial Guinea.

## Vital statistics

**Birth rate** per 1,000 population (2006): 36.2 (world avg. 20.3). **Death rate** per 1,000 population (2006):

12.3 (world avg. 8.5). **Total fertility rate** (avg. births per childbearing woman; 2006): 4.74. **Life expectancy** at birth (2006): male 53.2 years; female 55.8 years.

## National economy

**Budget** (2006). *Revenue:* CFAF 1,582,600,000,000 (oil revenues 64.0%; taxes on international trade 15.2%; direct taxes 10.0%; indirect taxes 7.2%; other revenues 3.6%). *Expenditures:* CFAF 1,066,300,-000,000 (current expenditures 77.6%, of which transfers 27.3%, wages and salaries 23.7%, debt service 10.9%; capital expenditures 22.4%). **Public debt** (external, outstanding; 2007): US$5,177,000,000. **Gross national income** (2008): US$10,490,000,000 (US$7,240 per capita). **Production** (metric tons except as noted). *Agriculture and fishing* (2007): plantains 275,000, cassava 240,000, sugarcane 220,000, natural rubber 12,000; livestock (number of live animals) 213,000 pigs, 3,100,000 chickens; fisheries production 39,124 (from aquaculture, negligible). *Mining and quarrying* (2005): manganese ore 2,859,000; gold 300 kg (excludes about 400 kg of illegally mined gold smuggled out of Gabon). *Manufacturing* (value added in CFAF '000,000,000; 2004): agricultural products 48.0; wood products (excluding furniture) 31.3; refined petroleum products 18.1. *Energy production (consumption):* electricity (kW-hr; 2006) 1,726,000,000 (1,726,000,000); crude petroleum (barrels; 2007) 83,900,000 ([2006] 5,749,000); petroleum products (metric tons; 2006) 684,000 (497,000); natural gas (cu m; 2006) 126,000,000 (126,000,000). **Population economically active** (2003): total 570,000; activity rate of total population 42.5% (participation rates: ages 15–64, 74.1%; female 43.0%; unemployed 21%). **Selected balance of payments data.** Receipts from (US$'000,000): tourism (2005) 15; remittances (2008) 11; foreign direct investment (FDI; 2005–07 avg.) 199; official development assistance (2006) 31. Disbursements for (US$'000,000): tourism (2004) 214; remittances (2008) 186; FDI (2005–07 avg.) 76.

## Foreign trade

**Imports** (2006; c.i.f.): US$1,725,000,000 (machinery and apparatus 27.6%, of which general industrial machinery 8.8%; food products 13.0%; motor vehicles and parts 9.9%; chemical products 9.2%). *Major import sources:* France 39.9%; Belgium 14.2%; US 7.3%; Cameroon 3.5%; Japan 3.0%. **Exports** (2006; f.o.b.): US$6,015,000,000 (crude petroleum 84.4%; rough wood 5.1%; manganese ore and concentrate 3.1%; veneer and plywood 2.0%; refined petroleum products 1.2%). *Major export destinations:* US 58.4%; China 10.6%; France 7.1%; Singapore 5.3%; Switzerland 2.6%.

## Transport and communications

**Transport.** *Railroads* (2002): route length (2005) 814 km; passenger-km 97,500,000; metric ton-km cargo 1,553,000,000. *Roads* (2004): total length 9,170 km (paved 10%). *Vehicles* (1997): passenger cars 24,750; trucks and buses 16,490. *Air transport* (2002): passenger-km 643,000,000. **Communications,** in total units (units per 1,000 persons). Telephone landlines (2007): 27,000 (18); cellular telephone subscribers (2008): 1,300,000 (963); personal computers (2007): 46,000 (36); total Internet users (2008): 90,000 (68); broadband Internet subscribers (2007): 2,000 (1.3).

## Education and health

**Educational attainment** (2000): no formal schooling 6.2%; incomplete primary and complete primary education 32.7%; lower secondary 41.3%; upper secondary 14.2%; higher 5.6%. **Literacy** (2000): total population ages 15 and over literate 71%; males literate 80%; females literate 62%. **Health** (2003–04): physicians 270 (1 per 5,006 persons); hospital beds 4,460 (1 per 303 persons); infant mortality rate per 1,000 live births (2006) 54.5; undernourished population (2002–04) 60,000 (5% of total population based on the consumption of a minimum daily requirement of 1,850 calories).

## Military

**Total active duty personnel** (November 2008): 4,700 (army 68.1%, navy 10.6%, air force 21.3%); French troops (2008): 800. **Military expenditure as percentage of GDP** (2007): 1.1%; per capita expenditure US$86.

## Background

Artifacts dating from late Paleolithic and early Neolithic times have been found in Gabon, but it is not known when the Bantu speakers who established Gabon's ethnic composition arrived. Pygmies were probably the original inhabitants. The Fang arrived in the late 18th century and were followed by the Portuguese and by French, Dutch, and English traders. The slave trade dominated commerce in the 18th and much of the 19th century. The French then took control, and Gabon was administered (1843–86) with French West Africa. In 1886 the colony of French Congo was established to include both Gabon and the Congo; in 1910 Gabon became a separate colony within French Equatorial Africa. An overseas territory of France from 1946, it became an autonomous republic within the French Community in 1958 and declared its independence in 1960. Rule by a sole political party was established in the 1960s, but discontent with it led to riots in Libreville in 1989. Legalization of opposition parties led to new elections in 1990. The country continued to face economic difficulties despite large revenues from petroleum exports.

## Recent Developments

In February 2011, Gabonese Pres. Ali Ben Bongo Ondimba and Pres. Teodoro Obiang Nguema Mbasogo of Equatorial Guinea met with UN Secretary-General Ban Ki-Moon regarding a border dispute. At stake was the ownership of islands in potentially resource-rich waters in the Gulf of Guinea. They agreed to take their dispute to the International Court of Justice. The two countries cohosted the Africa Cup of Nations association football (soccer) tournament in early 2012.

**Internet resource:** <www.en.legabon.org>.

*1 metric ton = about 1.1 short tons; 1 kilometer = 0.6 mi (statute); 1 metric ton-km cargo = about 0.68 short ton-mi cargo; c.i.f.: cost, insurance, and freight; f.o.b.: free on board*

# Gambia, The

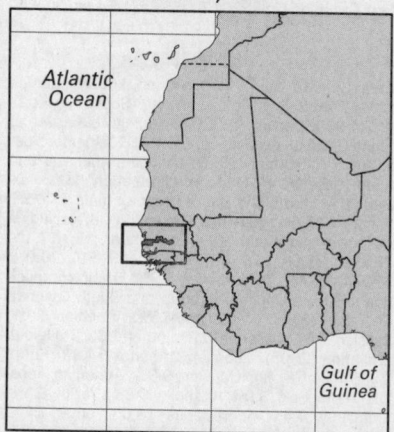

Atlantic Ocean

Gulf of Guinea

**Official name:** Republic of The Gambia. **Form of government:** multiparty republic with one legislative house (National Assembly [53]). **Head of state and government:** President Col. Yahya Jammeh (from 1994). **Capital:** Banjul. **Official language:** English. **Official religion:** none. **Monetary unit:** 1 dalasi (D) = 100 bututs; valuation (2 Jul 2012) US$1 = D 30.99.

## Demography

**Area:** 4,491 sq mi, 11,632 sq km. **Population** (2011): 1,776,000. **Density** (2011): persons per sq mi 395.5, persons per sq km 152.7. **Urban** (2009): 57.4%. **Sex distribution** (2007): male 49.92%; female 50.08%. **Age breakdown** (2007): under 15, 44.1%; 15–29, 26.9%; 30–44, 15.6%; 45–59, 8.8%; 60–74, 3.8%; 75–84, 0.7%; 85 and over, 0.1%. **Ethnic composition** (2003): Malinke 42%; Fulani 18%; Wolof 16%; Diola 10%; Soninke 9%; other 5%. **Religious affiliation** (2005): Muslim 90%; Christian (mostly Roman Catholic) 9%; traditional beliefs/other 1%. **Major cities** (2006): Banjul 33,131 (Greater Banjul [2003] 523,589); Serekunda 335,700; Brikama 80,700; Bakau 45,500; Farafenni 30,400. **Location:** western Africa, bordering Senegal and the North Atlantic Ocean.

## Vital statistics

**Birth rate** per 1,000 population (2007): 39.0 (world avg. 20.3). **Death rate** per 1,000 population (2007): 13.0 (world avg. 8.5). **Total fertility rate** (avg. births per childbearing woman; 2007): 5.2. **Life expectancy** at birth (2006): male 52.3 years; female 56.0 years.

## National economy

**Budget** (2007). *Revenue:* D 3,663,500,000 (tax revenue 82.9%, of which taxes on goods and services 36.7%, taxes on income and profits 24.1%; nontax revenue 11.8%; grants 5.3%). *Expenditures:* D 3,635,000,000 (current expenditures 71.1%, of which interest payments 22.4%; capital expenditures 26.8%; net lending 2.1%). **Production** (metric tons except as noted). *Agriculture and fishing* (2007): millet 160,000, peanuts (groundnuts) 100,000, sorghum 40,000, findo (local cereal; 2005) 600; livestock (number of live animals) 334,000 cattle, 280,000 goats, 150,000 sheep; fisheries production 43,574 (from aquaculture, negligible). *Mining and quarrying* (2007): clay 14,000; sand and gravel are also excavated for local use. *Manufacturing* (value added in US$; 1995): food products and beverages 6,000,000; textiles, wearing apparel, and footwear 750,000; wood products 550,000. *Energy production (consumption):* electricity (kW-hr; 2007) 213,000,000 ([2006] 166,000,000); petroleum products (metric tons; 2006) none (109,000). **Population economically active** (2006): total 754,000; activity rate of total population 45.3% (participation rates: ages 15–64, 77.1%; female 45.6%). **Public debt** (external, outstanding; 2007): US$704,000,000. **Gross national income** (2008): US$653,000,000 (US$390 per capita). **Selected balance of payments data.** Receipts from (US$'000,000): tourism (2007) 75; remittances (2008) 64; foreign direct investment (2005–07 avg.) 60; official development assistance (2007) 72. Disbursements for (US$'000,000): tourism (2007) 7; remittances (2008) 12.

## Foreign trade

**Imports** (2007; c.i.f.): US$262,900,000 (imports for domestic use 70.0%, of which refined petroleum products 10.8%; imports for reexport [principally to Senegal] 30.0%). *Major import sources:* Denmark 14%; US 13%; China 11%; Germany 8%; UK 8%. **Exports** (2007; f.o.b.): US$91,400,000 (reexports 86.3%; peanut [groundnut] oil 3.3%; peanuts [groundnuts] 2.7%; fish 2.0%). *Major export destinations:* reexports (principally to Senegal) 86.3%; domestic exports 13.7%, of which to Senegal 3.5%, to UK 2.7%, to France 1.9%.

## Transport and communications

**Transport.** *Railroads:* none. *Roads* (2004): total length 3,742 km (paved 19%). *Vehicles* (2004): passenger cars 8,109; trucks and buses 2,961. *Air transport* (2001; Yumdum International Airport at Banjul only): passenger arrivals 300,000; passenger departures 300,000; cargo loaded and unloaded 2,700 metric tons. **Communications,** in total units (units per 1,000 persons). Telephone landlines (2008): 49,000 (30); cellular telephone subscribers (2008): 1,166,000 (702); personal computers (2007): 53,000 (33); total Internet users (2008): 114,000 (69); broadband Internet subscribers (2007): 300 (0.2).

## Education and health

**Literacy** (2007): total population ages 15 and over literate 44.9%; males literate 52.3%; females literate 37.8%. **Health:** physicians (2003) 156 (1 per 9,769 persons); hospital beds (2005) 1,221 (1 per 1,250 persons); infant mortality rate per 1,000 live births (2007) 72.0; undernourished population (2002–04) 450,000 (29% of total population based on the consumption of a minimum daily requirement of 1,850 calories).

## Military

**Total active duty personnel** (November 2008): 800 (army 100%). **Military expenditure as percentage of GDP** (2007): 0.6%; per capita expenditure US$2.

## Background

Beginning about the 13th century AD, the Wolof, Malinke, and Fulani peoples settled in different parts of what is now The Gambia and established villages and then kingdoms in the region. European exploration began when the Portuguese sighted the Gambia River in 1455. Britain and France both settled in the area in the 17th century. The British Ft. James, on an island about 20 mi (32 km) from the river's mouth, was an important collection point for the slave trade. In 1783 the Treaty of Versailles reserved the Gambia River for Britain. After the British abolished slavery in 1807, they built a fort at the mouth of the river to block the continuing slave trade. In 1889 The Gambia's boundaries were agreed upon by Britain and France; the British declared a protectorate over the area in 1894. Independence was proclaimed in 1965, and The Gambia became a republic within the Commonwealth in 1970. It formed a limited confederation with Senegal in 1982 that was dissolved in 1989. The country faced severe economic problems that continued into the 21st century.

## Recent Developments

There were widespread reports of human rights abuses against those opposed to The Gambia's Pres. Yahya Jammeh in the November 2011 presidential election. He was reelected with 72% of the vote, though the poll was clouded by accusations of intimidation, fraud, and media bias in favor of Jammeh.

Internet resource: <www.gbos.gm>.

# Georgia

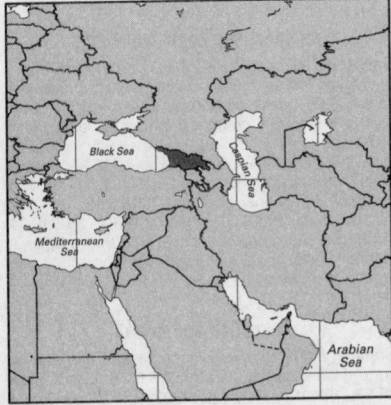

**Official name:** Sakartvelo (Georgia). **Form of government:** unitary multiparty republic with a single legislative house (Parliament [150]). **Head of state and government:** President Mikheil Saakashvili (from 2008), assisted by Prime Minister Vano Merabishvili (from 2012). **Capital:** Tbilisi (T'bilisi). **Official language:** Georgian. **Official religion:** none (special recognition is given to the Georgian Orthodox Church). **Monetary unit:** 1 Georgian lari (GEL) = 100 tetri; valuation (2 Jul 2012) US$1 = 1.64 lari.

## Demography

**Area:** 26,911 sq mi, 69,700 sq km. **Population** (2011; excluding Abkhazia and South Ossetia): 4,474,000. **Density** (2011; excluding Abkhazia and South Ossetia): persons per sq mi 201.1, persons per sq km 77.7. **Urban** (2010; excluding Abkhazia and South Ossetia): 53.0%. **Sex distribution** (2008; excluding Abkhazia and South Ossetia): male 47.45%; female 52.55%. **Age breakdown** (2008; excluding Abkhazia and South Ossetia): under 15, 17.1%; 15–29, 23.9%; 30–44, 20.7%; 45–59, 20.0%; 60–74, 12.4%; 75 and over, 5.9%. **Ethnic composition** (2002; excluding Abkhazia and South Ossetia): Georgian 83.8%; Azerbaijani 6.5%; Armenian 5.7%; Russian 1.5%; Ossetian 0.9%; other 1.6%. **Religious affiliation** (2005): Georgian Orthodox 54.8%; Sunni Muslim 14.5%; Shi'i Muslim 5.0%; Armenian Apostolic (Orthodox) 3.9%; Catholic 0.8%; Yazidi 0.4%; Protestant 0.4%; nonreligious 13.0%; other 7.2%. **Major cities** (2008): Tbilisi (T'bilisi) 1,106,500; Kutaisi 188,600; Batumi 122,200; Rustavi 117,300; Zugdidi 72,100. **Location:** northern Transcaucasia, bordering Russia, Azerbaijan, Armenia, Turkey, and the Black Sea.

## Vital statistics

**Birth rate** per 1,000 population (2008; excluding Abkhazia and South Ossetia): 12.9 (world avg. 20.3); within marriage 65.7%. **Death rate** per 1,000 population (2008; excluding Abkhazia and South Ossetia): 9.8 (world avg. 8.5). **Total fertility rate** (avg. births per childbearing woman; 2007; excluding Abkhazia and South Ossetia): 1.45. **Life expectancy** at birth (2008; excluding Abkhazia and South Ossetia): male 69.3 years; female 79.0 years.

## National economy

**Budget** (2007). *Revenue:* GEL 5,158,600,000 (tax revenue 72.4%, of which VAT 38.3%, social tax 14.0%, corporate taxes 8.4%, excise tax 8.3%; nontax revenue 23.3%; grants 4.3%). *Expenditures:* GEL 5,237,100,000 (defense 28.6%; social security and welfare 14.8%; general public service 14.6%; public order 13.1%; education 7.3%). **Population economically active** (2008): total 1,917,800; activity rate of total population 43.8% (participation rates: ages 15 and over, 62.6%; female 46.4%; unemployed 16.5%). **Production** (metric tons except as noted). *Agriculture and fishing* (2007): potatoes 174,500, grapes 93,000, wheat 92,300, apples 42,500, walnuts 12,400; livestock (number of live animals) 1,318,800 cattle, 509,700 pigs; fisheries production 18,377 (from aquaculture 1%). *Mining and quarrying* (2005): manganese ore 251,800. *Manufacturing* (value of production in US$'000,000; 2006): food products and beverages 95; chemical products 41; cement, bricks, and ceramics 26. *Energy production (consumption):* electricity (kW-hr; 2006) 7,599,000,000 (8,373,000,000); coal (metric tons; 2006) 11,000 (23,000); crude petroleum (barrels; 2007) 357,300 (4,737,700); petroleum products (metric tons; 2006) 4,000 (658,000); natural gas (cu m; 2007) 10,000,000 (1,490,000,000). **Gross national income** (2008): US$10,788,000,000 (US$2,470 per capita). **Public debt** (external, outstanding; March 2009): US$2,170,032,000. **Selected balance of payments data.** Receipts from (US$'000,000): tourism (2007) 385; remittances (2008–09) 907; foreign direct investment (2006–08 avg.) 1,192; official development assistance (2007) 382. Disbursements for (US$'000,000): tourism (2007) 176; remittances (2008–09) 77.

## Foreign trade

**Imports** (2008; c.i.f.): US$6,304,557,300 (mineral fuels 18.5%; motor vehicles 13.9%; food products and beverages 13.7%; nonelectrical machinery 9.1%; electrical machinery 8.2%; chemical products 7.0%). *Major import sources:* Turkey 14.9%; Ukraine 10.4%; Azerbaijan 9.6%; Germany 7.9%; Russia 6.8%. **Exports** (2008; f.o.b.): US$1,496,060,400 (iron and steel 27.4%; food products and beverages [including wine] 16.7%; chemical products 13.6%; mineral fuels 11.3%). *Major export destinations:* Turkey 17.6%; Azerbaijan 13.7%; Ukraine 9.0%; Canada 8.8%; Armenia 8.2%.

## Transport and communications

**Transport.** *Railroads* (2007): 1,559 km; passenger-km 773,900,000; metric ton-km cargo 6,927,500,000. *Roads* (2007): 20,329 km (paved [2006] 39%). *Vehicles* (2008): passenger cars 466,900; trucks and buses 105,100. *Air transport* (2007): passenger-km 474,800,000; metric ton-km cargo 3,600,000. **Communications,** in total units (units per 1,000 persons). Telephone landlines (2008): 556,000 (129); cellular telephone subscribers (2008): 3,283,000 (762); personal computers (2007): 228,000 (52); total Internet users (2008): 388,000 (90); broadband Internet subscribers (2007): 47,000 (11).

## Education and health

**Educational attainment** (2004). Percentage of population ages 15 and over having: no formal education/unknown 1.6%; primary education 4.1%; incomplete secondary 10.5%; secondary 48.2%; incomplete higher 12.3%; higher 23.3%. **Literacy** (2008): virtually 100%. **Health** (2008): physicians 20,253 (1 per 216 persons); hospital beds 14,100 (1 per 310 persons); infant mortality rate per 1,000 live births 17.0; undernourished population (2002–04) 500,000 (9% of total population based on the consumption of a minimum daily requirement of 1,960 calories).

## Military

**Total active duty personnel** (November 2008): 21,150 (army 84.0%, national guard 7.5%, navy 2.3%, air force 6.2%); Russian troops in Abkhazia and South Ossetia (November 2008): 3,800 in each. **Military expenditure as percentage of GDP** (2007): 7.6%; per capita expenditure US$250.

## Background

Ancient Georgia was the site of the kingdoms of Iberia and Colchis, whose wealth was known to the ancient Greeks. The area was part of the Roman Empire by 65 BC and became Christian in AD 337. For the next three centuries it was involved in the conflicts between the Byzantine and Persian empires; after 654 it was controlled by Arab caliphs, who established an emirate in Tbilisi. It was controlled by the Bagratids from the 8th to the 12th century, and the zenith of Georgia's power was reached in the reign of Queen Tamara, whose realm stretched from Azerbaijan to Circassia, forming a pan-Caucasian empire. Invasions by Mongols and Turks in the 13th and 14th centuries disintegrated the kingdom, and the fall of Constantinople (now Istanbul) to the Ottoman Turks in 1453 isolated it from Western Christendom. The next three centuries saw repeated invasions by the Armenians, Turks, and Persians. Georgia sought Russian protection in 1783, and in 1801 it was annexed to Russia. After the Russian Revolution of 1917, the area was briefly independent; in 1921 a Soviet regime was installed, and in 1936 Georgia became the Georgian SSR, a full member of the Soviet Union. In 1990 a noncommunist coalition came to power in the first free elections ever held in Soviet Georgia, and in 1991 Georgia declared independence. In the 1990s, while Pres. Eduard Shevardnadze tried to steer a middle course, internal dissension resulted in conflicts with the northwestern republic of Abkhazia and the northern republic of South Ossetia, and external distrust of Russian motives in the area grew. In 1992 Abkhazia reinstated its 1925 constitution and declared independence, which Georgia refused to recognize. After several weeks of sporadic exchanges of gunfire between Georgian soldiers and rebel forces in South Ossetia, Georgian troops entered the republic on 7 Aug 2008. In response, Russian tanks and troops advanced into South Ossetia on 8 August, bombed the port of Poti and several military bases, and occupied Gori. Several hundred servicemen and civilians died during the fighting, and tens of thousands were forced to flee their homes. Following the deployment of international observers in October, Russian troops withdrew from the conflict zones.

## Recent Developments

Visiting Tbilisi in November 2011, NATO Secretary-General Anders Fogh Rasmussen held out the prospect that Georgia might be offered a Membership Action Plan, a step toward NATO membership, at the alliance's May 2012 summit in Chicago. The European Union formally announced on 5 December that it would begin the talks on a free-trade agreement with Georgia. Under pressure from the US, in November Georgia shelved its longstanding veto of Russia's application for membership in the World Trade Organization in return for the deployment of international inspectors to monitor trade between the Russian Federation and Georgia's breakaway republics of Abkhazia and South Ossetia. GDP grew by 6.5% during the first 10 months of 2011. Annual inflation for January–August was 7.2%. By October Georgia's foreign debt had soared to more than US$4.25 billion.

**Internet resource:** <www.nbg.gov.ge/?lng=eng>.

# Germany

**Official name:** Bundesrepublik Deutschland (Federal Republic of Germany). **Form of government:** federal multiparty republic with two legislative houses (Federal Council [69]; Federal Diet [620; statutory num-

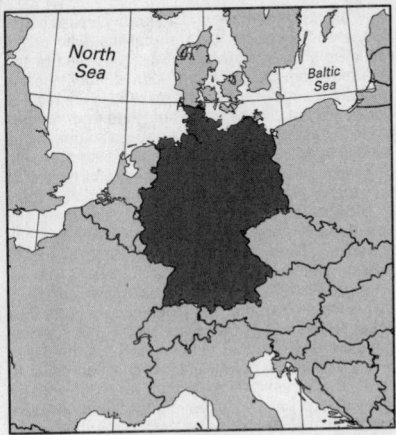

ber is 598]). **Head of state:** President Joachim Gauck (from 2012). **Head of government:** Chancellor Angela Merkel (from 2005). **Capital:** Berlin; some ministries remain in Bonn, the previous capital of West Germany, and the federal supreme court meets in Karlsruhe. **Official language:** German. **Official religion:** none. **Monetary unit:** 1 euro (€) = 100 cents; valuation (2 Jul 2012) US$1 = €0.79.

## Demography

**Area:** 137,879 sq mi, 357,104 sq km. **Population** (2011): 81,604,000. **Density** (2011): persons per sq mi 591.9, persons per sq km 228.5. **Urban** (2008): 84.1%. **Major cities (urban agglomerations)** (2005): Dortmund 588,168 (5,746,018); Essen 585,430 (5,746,018); Duisburg 501,564 (5,746,018); Berlin 3,395,189 (4,200,072); Stuttgart 592,569 (2,625,690); Hamburg 1,743,627 (2,549,339); Munich 1,259,677 (1,940,477); Frankfurt am Main 651,899 (1,915,002); Cologne 983,347 (1,846,241); Mannheim 307,900 (1,579,252); Düsseldorf 574,514 (1,318,512); Nuremberg (Nürnberg) 499,237 (1,030,168); Hannover 515,729 (1,001,580); Saarbrücken 178,914 (942,594); Bonn 312,818 (899,753); Bremen 546,852 (858,488); Wuppertal 359,237 (832,685); Wiesbaden 274,611 (795,725); Dresden 495,181 (695,680); Karlsruhe 285,263 (600,161); Aachen 258,208 (599,676); Bielefeld 326,925 (585,145); Leipzig 502,651 (580,050); Darmstadt 140,562 (531,077). **Location:** central Europe, bordering Denmark, the Baltic Sea, Poland, the Czech Republic, Austria, Switzerland, France, Luxembourg, Belgium, the Netherlands, and the North Sea. **Sex distribution** (2007): male 48.98%; female 51.02%. **Ethnic composition** (by nationality; 2000): German 88.2%; Turkish 3.4% (including Kurdish 0.7%); Italian 1.0%; Greek 0.7%; Serb 0.6%; Russian 0.6%; Polish 0.4%; other 5.1%. **Age breakdown** (2006): under 15, 13.9%; 15–29, 17.6%; 30–44, 22.4%; 45–59, 21.1%; 60–74, 16.7%; 75–84, 6.3%; 85 and over, 2.0%. **Religious affiliation** (2005): Protestant 35.0%, of which Lutheran/Reformed churches 34%; Roman Catholic 32.5%; Sunni Muslim 4.3%; Orthodox 1.7%; New Apostolic 0.5%; Buddhist 0.3%; Jewish 0.2%; nonreligious 18.0%; atheist 2.0%; other 5.5%. **Resident foreign population** (2007): 6,744,900; *region/country of birth:* EU countries 34.7%, of which Italy 7.8%, Poland 5.7%, Greece 4.4%, Austria 2.6%; Turkey 25.4%; Asian countries 12.1%; former Serbia and Montenegro 4.9%; African countries 4.0%; Croatia 3.3%; Russia 2.8%; Bosnia and Herzegovina 2.3%; US 1.5%; other 9.0%. **Population with immigrant background** (2008): 14,800,000 (18% of total population). **Immigration/emigration trends** (2007): foreigners arriving 680,000; Germans departing 165,000.

## Vital statistics

**Birth rate** per 1,000 population (2008): 8.2 (world avg. 20.3); within marriage 68.2%. **Death rate** per 1,000 population (2008): 10.3 (world avg. 8.5). **Total fertility rate** (avg. births per childbearing woman; 2008): 1.37. **Life expectancy** at birth (2008): male 77.2 years; female 82.5 years.

## Social indicators

**Educational attainment** (2006). Percentage of population ages 25–64 having: no formal schooling through primary education 3%; lower secondary 14%; upper secondary 52%; post-secondary non-tertiary 7%; higher vocational 9%; university 14%; advanced degree 1%. **Quality of working life.** Average workweek (2007): 38.4 hours. Annual rate per 100,000 workers (2007) for: injuries or accidents at work 2,803; deaths 2.16. Proportion of labor force insured for damages of income loss resulting from: injury, virtually 100%; permanent disability, virtually 100%; death, virtually 100%. Average days lost to labor stoppages per 1,000 workers (2008): 3.7. **Access to services.** Proportion of dwellings (2002) having: electricity, virtually 100%; piped water supply, virtually 100%; flush sewage disposal (1993) 98.4%; public fire protection, virtually 100%. **Social participation.** Trade union membership in total workforce (2008): 6,441,045 (15.4%). Population "religious"/"deeply religious" (2007): in western Germany 78%/21%; in eastern Germany 36%/8%; 15% of Roman Catholics "regularly" attend religious services. **Social deviance** (2006; excluding eastern Germany except for the former East Berlin). Conviction rate per 100,000 population for: murder, manslaughter, and attempted murder 0.8; sexual abuse of children 3.1; rape 2.7; assault and battery 91.3; theft 195.3; fraud 132.4. **Leisure.** Favorite leisure activities include playing football (soccer; registered participants, 2004) 6,272,804, as well as watching television, using the computer, going to the cinema, attending theatrical and musical performances, visiting museums, and taking part in package tours. **Material well-being** (2008). Households possessing: automobile (2005) 76.8%; refrigerator 98.6%; freezer 52.4%; dishwasher 62.5%; microwave oven 69.6%; washing machine (2004) 95.5%; clothes dryer 38.5%; television (2004) 95.0%; DVD player (2006) 59%; personal computer (2006) 71.6%; Internet access (2006) 57.9%; MP3 player (2006) 23%.

## National economy

**Budget** (2007; general government). *Revenue:* €1,064,730,000,000 (tax revenue 54.5%, of which income tax 21.6%, general taxes on goods and services

---

*1 metric ton = about 1.1 short tons;   1 kilometer = 0.6 mi (statute);   1 metric ton-km cargo = about 0.68 short ton-mi cargo;   c.i.f.: cost, insurance, and freight;   f.o.b.: free on board*

15.6%, excise taxes 6.0%; social security contributions 37.6%; nontax revenue 7.5%; other 0.4%). *Expenditures:* €1,061,590,000,000 (social protection 45.7%; health 14.0%; education 9.1%; economic affairs 7.2%; public debt payments 6.3%; public order 3.5%; defense 2.4%). **Total public debt** (May 2009): US$2,052,-000,000,000. **Production** (metric tons except as noted). *Agriculture and fishing* (2008): wheat 25,988,600, sugar beets 23,002,600, barley 11,967,100, potatoes 11,369,000, rapeseed 5,154,-700, corn (maize) 5,105,900, rye 3,744,200, triticale 2,381,500, grapes 1,428,776, apples 1,046,995, cabbages 806,078, oats 793,200, dry onions 407,602, strawberries 150,854, sunflower seeds 48,900, gooseberries 40,000, hops 39,700, currants 10,587; livestock (number of live animals) 26,686,800 pigs, 12,969,674 cattle, 2,437,000 sheep, 114,625,000 chickens; fisheries production (2007) 293,757 (from aquaculture 15%). *Mining and quarrying* (metric tons; 2006): potash 3,625,000; bentonite 364,000; feldspar 167,332; barite 85,524. *Energy production (consumption):* electricity (kW-hr; 2007) 594,660,000,000 ([2006] 619,784,000,000); coal (metric tons; 2008) 17,200,000 ([2006] 65,500,000); lignite (metric tons; 2008) 175,300,000 ([2006] 176,400,000); crude petroleum (barrels; 2008) 34,100,000 ([2006] 817,800,000); petroleum products (metric tons; 2006) 104,605,000 (100,068,000); natural gas (cu m; 2008) 20,337,000,000 ([2006] 94,772,000,000) (in 2009 Germany was a world leader in the production of wind and solar power). **Gross national income** (2008): US$3,485,674,000,000 (US$42,440 per capita). **Population economically active** (2008): total 41,875,000; activity rate of total population 51.0% (participation rates: ages 15–64, 76.0%; female 45.4%; unemployed [April 2008–March 2009] 8.7%. **Selected balance of payments data.** Receipts from (US$'000,000): tourism (2007) 36,092; remittances (2008) 11,064; foreign direct investment (FDI; 2005–07 avg.) 49,355. Disbursements for (US$'000,000): tourism (2007) 82,966; remittances (2008) 14,976; FDI (2005–07 avg.) 110,338.

## Foreign trade

**Imports** (2007; c.i.f.): US$1,059,308,000,000 (machinery and apparatus 23.0%, of which electrical machinery 6.7%; office machines and computers 4.0%; manufactured goods 14.4%, of which iron and steel 3.6%; mineral fuels 10.5%, of which crude petroleum 5.2%; motor vehicles and parts 8.2%; food products 5.2%; medicines and pharmaceuticals 3.9%). *Major import sources:* France 8.4%; Netherlands 8.3%; China 7.1%; US 5.9%; Italy 5.7%; UK 5.6%; Belgium 5.0%; Austria 4.2%; Switzerland 3.9%; Russia 3.7%. **Exports** (2007; f.o.b.): US$1,328,841,000,000 (machinery and apparatus 28.4%, of which electrical machinery and electronics 7.3%, general industrial machinery 7.0%; transportation equipment 19.0%, of which motor vehicles 16.4%; manufactured goods 14.1%, of which iron and steel, non-ferrous metals, and fabricate metal products 8.6%; chemical products 13.8%, of which medicines and pharmaceuticals 4.2%). *Major export destinations:* France 9.7%; US 7.6%; UK 7.3%; Italy 6.7%; Netherlands 6.4%; Austria 5.4%; Belgium 5.3%; Spain 5.0%; Switzerland 3.8%; Poland 3.7%.

## Transport and communications

**Transport.** *Railroads* (2005): track length 76,473 km (route length 38,206 km); passenger-km 74,946,-000,000; metric ton-km cargo 95,421,000,000. *Roads* (2005): total length 231,480 km (paved [2003] 100%). *Vehicles* (2006): passenger cars 46,090,300; trucks and buses 2,573,100. *Air transport* (2007): passenger-km 206,112,000,000; metric ton-km cargo 8,345,976,000. **Communications,** in total units (units per 1,000 persons). Telephone landlines (2008): 51,500,000 (627); cellular telephone subscribers (2008): 107,245,000 (1,308); personal computers (2007) 53,967,000 (656); total Internet users (2008): 62,500,000 (761); broadband Internet subscribers (2008): 22,600,000 (275).

## Education and health

**Health** (2006): physicians 311,000 (1 per 265 persons); hospital beds 510,767 (1 per 161 persons); infant mortality rate per 1,000 live births (2008) 4.0; undernourished population (2002–04) less than 2.5% of total population.

## Military

**Total active duty personnel** (November 2008): 244,324 (army 65.8%, navy 9.4%, air force 24.8%); German peacekeeping troops abroad (November 2008): 7,300, including 3,300 in Afghanistan; US troops in Germany (November 2008): 40,000; British troops (November 2008): 22,000; French troops (November 2008): 2,800. **Military expenditure as percentage of GDP** (2007): 1.3%; per capita expenditure US$512.

## Background

Germanic tribes entered the region about the 2nd century BC, displacing the Celts. The Romans failed to conquer the region, which became a political entity only with the division of the Carolingian empire in the 9th century AD. The monarchy's control was weak, and power increasingly devolved upon the nobility, organized in feudal states. The monarchy was restored under Saxon rule in the 10th century, and the Holy Roman Empire, centering on Germany and northern Italy, was revived. Continuing conflict between the Holy Roman emperors and the Roman Catholic popes undermined the empire, and its dissolution was accelerated by Martin Luther's revolt in 1517, which divided Germany, and ultimately Europe, into Protestant and Roman Catholic camps, culminating in the Thirty Years' War (1618–48). Germany's population and borders were greatly reduced, and its numerous feudal princes gained virtually full sovereignty. In 1862 Otto von Bismarck came to power in Prussia and over the next decade reunited Germany in the German Empire. It was dissolved in 1918 after the German defeat in World War I. Germany was stripped of much of its territory and all of its colonies. In 1933 Adolf Hitler became chancellor and established a totalitarian state, the Third Reich, dominated by the Nazi Party. Hitler's invasion of Poland in 1939 plunged the world into World War II. Following its defeat in 1945, Germany was divided by the Allied Powers into four zones of occupation. Disagreement with the USSR over the reunification of the zones led to the creation in 1949 of the Federal Republic of Germany (West Germany) and the German Democratic Republic (East Germany). Berlin, the former capital, remained divided. West Germany became a prosperous parliamentary democracy and East Germany a one-party state under Soviet control. The East German Communist government was brought down peacefully in 1989, and Germany was reunited in 1990. After the initial euphoria over unity, the former West Germany sought to incorporate the former East Germany both politically and economically, resulting in heavy financial burdens for the wealthier western Germans. The country continued to move toward deeper political and economic integration with Western Europe through its membership in the European Union.

## Recent Developments

In 2011, Germans saw hopes in the face of signs of economic recovery become obscured by the continuation of the euro-zone crises. The financial emergency in Greece and the ever-increasing need to boost the level of aid to that country caused high levels of strife in the German Bundestag (parliament) and within Chancellor Angela Merkel's governing coalition. Challenges in Germany's Federal Constitutional Court came to a head in September when the court finally rendered the decision that the aid packet to Greece was constitutional. Internally, Germany completed its stringent social security reforms and austerity measures, and the continued economic growth, even with the looming euro crisis, led to some optimism. Economists estimated modest GDP growth of 2.9% in 2011, and unemployment, which had hovered around 9.7% from 1991 to 2010, dropped to 6.8% in December 2011.

Internet resource: <www.destatis.de>.

# Ghana

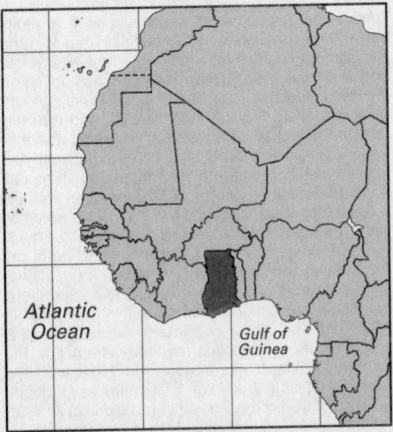

Atlantic Ocean

Gulf of Guinea

**Official name:** Republic of Ghana. **Form of government:** multiparty republic with one legislative house (Parliament [230]). **Head of state and government:** President John Dramani Mahama (from 2012). **Capital:** Accra. **Official language:** English. **Official religion:** none. **Monetary unit:** 1 Ghana cedi (GH¢) = 100 pesewas; valuation (2 Jul 2012) US$1 = GH¢1.94 (the Ghana cedi replaced the cedi [¢] 1 Jul 2007, at the rate of 1 GH¢ = ¢10,000).

## Demography

**Area:** 92,098 sq mi, 238,533 sq km. **Population** (2011): 24,661,000. **Density** (2011): persons per sq mi 267.8, persons per sq km 103.4. **Urban** (2009): 50.7%. **Sex distribution** (2008): male 50.02%; female 49.98%. **Age breakdown** (2008): under 15, 37.7%; 15–29, 29.4%; 30–44, 18.3%; 45–59, 9.5%; 60–74, 4.1%; 75–84, 0.9%; 85 and over, 0.1%. **Ethnic composition** (2000): Akan 41.6%; Mossi 23.0%; Ewe 10.0%; Ga-Adangme 7.2%; Gurma 3.4%; Nzima 1.8%; Yoruba 1.6%; other 11.4%. **Religious affiliation** (2005): Protestant 23.7%; traditional beliefs 21.5%; Sunni Muslim 20.1%; independent Christian 15.9%; Roman Catholic 12.2%; other 6.6%. **Major cities** (2002): Accra (2003) 1,847,432; Kumasi 627,600; Tamale 269,200; Tema 237,700; Obuasi 122,600. **Location:** western Africa, bordering Burkina Faso, Togo, the Atlantic Ocean, and Côte d'Ivoire.

## Vital statistics

**Birth rate** per 1,000 population (2008): 29.4 (world avg. 20.3). **Death rate** per 1,000 population (2008): 9.3 (world avg. 8.5). **Total fertility rate** (avg. births per childbearing woman; 2008): 3.78. **Life expectancy** at birth (2008): male 58.5 years; female 60.8 years.

## National economy

**Budget** (2006). *Revenue:* ¢31,917,680,000,000 (tax revenue 77.2%, of which VAT 18.4%, trade tax 17.0%, petroleum tax 12.8%, income tax 9.7%, corporate tax 9.4%; grants 19.9%; nontax revenue 2.9%). *Expenditures:* ¢38,734,730,000,000 (current expenditures 63.9%, of which transfers 14.7%; debt service 10.2%; capital expenditures 36.1%). **Public debt** (external, outstanding; December 2008): US$3,982,600,000. **Gross national income** (2008): US$15,744,000,000 (US$670 per capita). **Production** (metric tons except as noted). *Agriculture and fishing* (2007): cassava 9,650,000; yams 3,550,000; plantains 2,930,000; cacao beans 690,000; livestock (number of live animals) 3,704,700 goats, 3,420,000 sheep, 1,427,100 cattle; fisheries production 321,875 (from aquaculture, negligible). *Mining and quarrying* (2007): bauxite 748,000; manganese (metal content) 410,000; gold (legal production only) 77,349 kg; gem diamonds 720,000 carats. *Manufacturing* (value added in US$'000,000; 2003): wood products 157; chemical products 115; food products 108; refined petroleum products 55; precious and nonferrous metal products (including gold) 47. *Energy production (consumption):* electricity (kW-hr; 2006) 8,435,000,000 (8,309,000,000); crude petroleum (barrels; 2006) none (12,500,000); petroleum products (metric tons; 2006) 920,000 (1,909,000). **Population economically active** (2006): total 10,218,000; activity rate of total population 44.4% (participation rates: ages 15–64, 73.3%; female 49.4%; unemployed [2001] 20.3%). **Selected balance of payments data.** Receipts from (US$'000,000): tourism (2007) 908; remittances (2008) 128; foreign direct investment (2005–07 avg.) 545; official development assistance (2007) 1,151. Disbursements for (US$'000,000): tourism (2007) 558; remittances (2008) 6.

*1 metric ton = about 1.1 short tons;   1 kilometer = 0.6 mi (statute);   1 metric ton-km cargo = about 0.68 short ton-mi cargo;   c.i.f.: cost, insurance, and freight;   f.o.b.: free on board*

## Foreign trade

**Imports** (2006; c.i.f.): US$5,329,000,000 (machinery and apparatus 19.1%; motor vehicles 14.8%; crude petroleum 12.9%; food products 12.2%; chemical products 10.8%). *Major import sources:* Nigeria 9.6%; China 9.5%; UK 8.9%; US 6.6%; Belgium 5.6%. **Exports** (2006; f.o.b.): US$3,614,000,000 (cocoa 34.3%; gold 31.3%; woven cotton fabrics 6.3%; wood products [excluding furniture] 5.5%). *Major export destinations:* South Africa 25.8%; Burkina Faso 12.6%; Netherlands 11.1%; Switzerland 6.8%; France 4.6%.

## Transport and communications

**Transport.** *Railroads* (2002): route length (2005) 953 km; passenger-km 238,000,000; metric ton-km cargo 168,000,000. *Roads* (2005): total length 57,614 km (paved 15%). *Vehicles* (2006): passenger cars 275,424; trucks and buses 135,819. *Air transport* (2003; Ghana Airways only): passenger-km 906,000,000; metric ton-km cargo 16,630,000. **Communications,** in total units (units per 1,000 persons). Telephone landlines (2008): 144,000 (6); cellular telephone subscribers (2008): 11,570,000 (483); personal computers (2004): 112,000 (5.2); total Internet users (2008): 997,000 (42); broadband Internet subscribers (2008): 17,000 (0.7).

## Education and health

**Educational attainment** (2003). Percentage of population ages 25 and over having: no formal schooling/unknown 41.8%; incomplete primary education 9.6%; primary 3.6%; incomplete secondary 35.0%; secondary 5.4%; higher 4.6%. **Literacy** (2007): total population ages 15 and over literate 65.0%; males literate 71.7%; females literate 58.3%. **Health:** physicians (2004) 3,240 (1 per 6,631 persons); hospital beds (2001) 18,448 (1 per 1,089 persons); infant mortality rate per 1,000 live births (2008) 52.5; undernourished population (2003–05) 1,900,000 (9% of total population based on the consumption of a minimum daily requirement of 1,800 calories).

## Military

**Total active duty personnel** (November 2008): 10,913 (army 74.1%, navy 14.8%, air force 11.1%); UN peacekeepers (November 2008): 2,587. **Military expenditure as percentage of GDP** (2007): 0.7%; per capita expenditure US$5.

## Background

The modern state of Ghana is named after the ancient Ghana empire that flourished until the 13th century AD in the western Sudan, about 800 km (500 mi) northwest of the modern state. The Akan peoples then founded their first states in modern Ghana. Gold-seeking Mande traders arrived by the 14th century, and Hausa merchants arrived by the 16th century. During the 15th century, the Mande founded the states of Dagomba and Mamprussi in the northern half of the region. The Asante, an Akan people, originated in the central forest region and formed a strongly centralized empire that was at its height in the 18th and 19th centuries. European exploration of the region began early in the 15th century, when the Portuguese landed on the Gold Coast; they later established a settlement at Elmina as headquarters for the slave trade. By the mid-18th century the Gold Coast was dominated by numerous forts controlled by Dutch, British, and Danish merchants. Britain made the Gold Coast a crown colony in 1874, and British protectorates over Asante and the northern territories were established in 1901. In 1957 the Gold Coast became the independent state of Ghana. Since independence several political coups have occurred, but the coup of 1981 produced a government that lasted into the 1990s and made a smooth transition into another administration at the beginning of the 21st century.

## Recent Developments

Petroleum production and related activity boosted Ghana's economic growth to 8.9% in 2011. Agriculture also maintained a robust growth rate of more than 5.0%. Cocoa farmers had high yields; despite falling world prices, they benefited from the political turmoil in neighboring Côte d'Ivoire, the world's largest cocoa producer.

**Internet resource:** <www.statsghana.gov.gh>.

# Greece

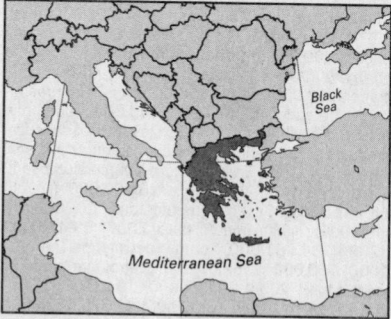

**Official name:** Ellinikí Dhimokratía (Hellenic Republic). **Form of government:** unitary multiparty republic with one legislative house (Hellenic Parliament [300]). **Head of state:** President Karolos Papoulias (from 2005). **Head of government:** Prime Minister Antonis Samaras (from 2012). **Capital:** Athens. **Official language:** Greek. **Official religion:** none (the autocephalous Greek Orthodox Church receives special recognition per the constitution). **Monetary unit:** 1 euro (€) = 100 cents; valuation (2 Jul 2012) US$1 = €0.79.

## Demography

**Area:** 50,949 sq mi, 131,957 sq km. **Population** (2011): 11,372,000. **Density** (2011): persons per sq mi 223.2, persons per sq km 86.2. **Urban** (2005): 60.4%. **Sex distribution** (2006): male 49.51%; female 50.49%. **Age breakdown** (2006): under 15, 14.3%; 15–29, 19.3%; 30–44, 22.9%; 45–59, 19.7%; 60–74, 15.8%; 75–84, 6.6%; 85 and over, 1.4%. **Ethnic composition** (2000; unofficial source; the government states there are no ethnic divisions in Greece): Greek 90.4%; Macedonian 1.8%; Albanian 1.5%; Turkish 1.4%; Pomak 0.9%; Rom (Gypsy) 0.9%; other 3.1%. **Religious affiliation** (2005): Orthodox 90%; Sunni Muslim 5%; Roman Catholic 2%; other 3%. **Major**

cities (2001): Athens 745,514 (urban agglomeration 3,187,734); Thessaloníki 363,987 (urban agglomeration 800,764); Piraeus (Piraiévs) 175,697; Pátrai 161,114; Peristérion 137,918. **Location:** southern Europe, bordering Albania, Macedonia, Bulgaria, Turkey, and the Mediterranean Sea.

## Vital statistics

**Birth rate** per 1,000 population (2008): 10.3 (world avg. 20.3); within marriage 93.5%. **Death rate** per 1,000 population (2008): 9.5 (world avg. 8.5). **Total fertility rate** (avg. births per childbearing woman; 2008): 1.45. **Life expectancy** at birth (2008): male 77.2 years; female 82.2 years.

## National economy

**Budget** (2007). *Revenue:* €89,100,000,000 (tax revenue 51.0%, of which VAT 28.8%, income tax 19.2%; social contributions 35.7%; other revenue 13.3%). *Expenditures:* €95,398,000,000 (social benefits 41.1%; wages and salaries 23.8%; goods and services 10.5%; interest payments 10.4%). **Production** (metric tons except as noted). *Agriculture and fishing* (2007): olives 2,600,000, corn (maize) 1,767,500, tomatoes 1,450,000, oranges 1,000,000, grapes 950,000, peaches and nectarines 700,000; livestock (number of live animals) 8,803,350 sheep, 5,570,885 goats, 1,315,000 beehives; fisheries production 209,356 (from aquaculture 54%). *Mining and quarrying* (2007): bauxite 2,163,000; nickel (metal content) 18,000; marble 150,000 cu m. *Manufacturing* (value added in US$'000,000; 2005): food products and beverages 5,300; textiles 1,950; chemical products 1,750; refined petroleum products and coal derivatives 1,500. *Energy production (consumption):* electricity (kW-hr; 2007) 59,776,000,000 ([2006] 64,991,000,000); coal (metric tons; 2006) none (463,000); lignite (metric tons; 2007) 63,448,000 ([2006] 64,332,000); crude petroleum (barrels; 2006) 760,000 (136,000,000); petroleum products (metric tons; 2006) 20,627,000 (19,158,000); natural gas (cu m; 2006) 16,000,000 (3,275,000,000). **Population economically active** (2007): total 4,917,900; activity rate of total population 44.1% (participation rates: ages 15–64 [2006] 66.9%; female 40.9%; unemployed [April 2007–March 2008] 8.1%). **Gross national income** (2008): US$321,972,-000,000 (US$28,650 per capita). **Public debt** (general government; 2008): US$347,416,000,000. **Selected balance of payments data.** Receipts from (US$'000,000): tourism (2007) 15,550; remittances (2008) 2,687; foreign direct investment (FDI; 2005–07 avg.) 2,629. Disbursements for (US$'000,000): tourism (2007) 3,423; remittances (2008) 1,912; FDI (2005–07 avg.) 3,652.

## Foreign trade

**Imports** (2006; c.i.f.): US$63,739,000,000 (machinery and apparatus 14.4%; crude petroleum 13.1%; food products 8.7%; motor vehicles and parts 8.5%; medicine and pharmaceuticals 5.8%; ships and tankers 5.3%). *Major import sources:* Germany 12.5%; Italy 11.6%; Russia 7.1%; France 5.9%; Netherlands 5.2%. **Exports** (2006; f.o.b.): US$20,943,000,000 (food products 14.0%, of which vegetables and fruit

7.2%; refined petroleum products 12.4%; machinery and apparatus 10.6%; wearing apparel 7.4%; medicine and pharmaceuticals 5.3%; aluminum 4.4%). *Major export destinations:* Germany 11.3%; Italy 11.2%; Bulgaria 6.3%; UK 6.0%; Cyprus 5.3%.

## Transport and communications

**Transport.** *Railroads* (2006): length 2,509 km; passenger-km 1,811,000,000; metric ton-km cargo 662,000,000. *Roads* (2005): total length 34,863 km (paved 93%). *Vehicles* (2007): passenger cars 4,798,530; trucks and buses 1,283,047. *Air transport* (2008): passenger-km 6,612,000,000; metric ton-km cargo 69,660,000. **Communications,** in total units (units per 1,000 persons). Telephone landlines (2008): 5,975,000 (535); cellular telephone subscribers (2008): 13,799,000 (1,235); personal computers (2007): 1,058,000 (94); total Internet users (2008): 3,631,000 (325); broadband Internet subscribers (2008): 1,507,000 (135).

## Education and health

**Educational attainment** (2001). Percentage of population ages 25 and over having: no formal schooling 12.7%; primary education 34.3%; lower secondary 8.5%; upper secondary 25.7%; higher 18.8%. **Literacy** (2007): total population ages 15 and over literate 97.1%; males literate 98.2%; females literate 96.0%. **Health** (2006): physicians (public health institutions only) 21,038 (1 per 436 persons); hospital beds (public health institutions only) 44,307 (1 per 207 persons); infant mortality rate per 1,000 live births (2008) 3.5; undernourished population (2003–05) less than 5% of total population.

## Military

**Total active duty personnel** (November 2008): 156,600 (army 59.7%, navy 12.8%, air force 20.1%, joint staff 7.4%); Greek troops in Cyprus (November 2008): 1,150. **Military expenditure as percentage of GDP** (2007): 2.8%; per capita expenditure US$773.

## Background

The earliest urban society in Greece was the palace-centered Minoan civilization, which reached its height on Crete about 2000 BC. It was succeeded by the mainland Mycenaean civilization, which arose about 1600 BC following a wave of Indo-European invasions. About 1200 BC a second wave of invasions destroyed the Bronze Age cultures, and a dark age followed, known mostly through the epics of Homer. At the end of this time, classical Greece began to emerge (c. 750 BC) as a collection of independent city-states, including Sparta in the Peloponnese and Athens in Attica. The civilization reached its zenith after repelling the Persians at the beginning of the 5th century BC and began to decline after the civil strife of the Peloponnesian War at the century's end. In 338 BC the Greek city-states were taken over by Philip II of Macedon, and Greek culture was spread by Philip's son Alexander the Great throughout his empire. The Romans, themselves heavily influenced by Greek culture, conquered the Greek states in the 2nd century BC. After the fall of Rome, Greece remained part of the Byzan-

*1 metric ton = about 1.1 short tons;    1 kilometer = 0.6 mi (statute);    1 metric ton-km cargo = about 0.68 short ton-mi cargo;    c.i.f.: cost, insurance, and freight;    f.o.b.: free on board*

tine Empire until the mid-15th century AD, when it became part of the expanding Ottoman Empire; it gained its independence in 1832. It was occupied by Nazi Germany during World War II. Civil war followed and lasted until 1949, when communist forces were defeated. In 1952 Greece joined NATO. A military junta ruled the country from 1967 to 1974, when democracy was restored and a referendum declared an end to the Greek monarchy. In 1981 Greece joined the European Community, the first Eastern European country to do so. Upheavals in the Balkans in the 1990s strained Greece's relations with some neighboring states, notably the former Yugoslav entity that took the name Republic of Macedonia.

## Recent Developments

Throughout 2011 Greece struggled to cope with its economic crisis and to implement reforms aimed at averting default. In June Parliament passed a new austerity package that called for €28 billion (about US$41 billion) to be raised over the following five years through tax hikes, public-sector layoffs, and cuts to health care, social benefits, and defense, along with another €50 billion (about US$72 billion) through privatization of public assets. In October eurozone leaders offered a new aid deal of some €130 billion (about US$183 billion). Under this arrangement, private banks agreed to write off 50% of the money Greece owed them. In February 2012, a second €130 billion bailout was offered by the EU and the IMF.

Internet resource:
<www.statistics.gr/portal/page/portal/ESYE>.

# Greenland

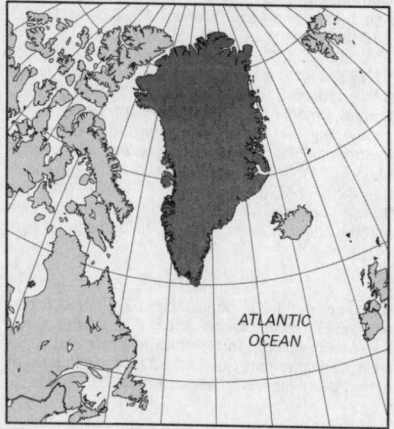

ATLANTIC OCEAN

**Official name:** Kalaallit Nunaat (Greenlandic) (Greenland). **Political status:** self-governing overseas administrative division of Denmark with one legislative house (Parliament [31]). **Head of state:** Danish Queen Margrethe II (from 1972). **Heads of government:** High Commissioner (for Denmark) Mikaela Engell (from 2011); Prime Minister (for Greenland) Kuupik Kleist (from 2009). **Capital:** Nuuk (Godthåb). **Official language:** Greenlandic. **Official religion:** Evangelical Lutheran (Lutheran Church of Greenland). **Monetary**

**unit:** 1 Danish krone (DKK; plural kroner) = 100 øre; valuation (2 Jul 2012) US$1 = DKK 5.91.

## Demography

**Area:** 836,330 sq mi, 2,166,086 sq km. **Population** (2011): 56,700. **Density** (2011; calculated with reference to ice-free area only): persons per sq mi 0.36, persons per sq km 0.14. **Urban** (2010): 84.1%. **Sex distribution** (2008): male 53.05%; female 46.95%. **Age breakdown** (2007): under 15, 23.7%; 15–29, 22.1%; 30–44, 23.3%; 45–59, 20.4%; 60–74, 8.7%; 75 and over, 1.8%. **Ethnic composition** (2008): Inuit (Greenland Eskimo) 89%; Danish and others 11%. **Religious affiliation** (2000): Protestant 69.2%, of which Evangelical Lutheran 64.2%, Pentecostal 2.8%; other Christian 27.4%; other/nonreligious 3.4%. **Major towns** (2008): Nuuk (Godthåb) 15,105; Sisimiut (Holsteinsborg) 5,458; Ilulissat (Jakobshavn) 4,528. **Location:** island in the North Atlantic Ocean, east of northern Canada.

## Vital statistics

**Birth rate** per 1,000 population (2007): 14.9 (world avg. 20.3); (1993) within marriage 29.2%. **Death rate** per 1,000 population (2007): 7.8 (world avg. 8.5). **Total fertility rate** (avg. births per childbearing woman; 2007): 2.28. **Life expectancy** at birth (2006): male 66.4 years; female 73.6 years.

## National economy

**Budget** (general government; 2007). *Revenue:* DKK 8,625,000,000 (block grant from Danish government 44.8%; taxes on income and wealth 33.9%; import duties 6.5%). *Expenditures:* DKK 8,239,000,000 (social welfare 26.0%; education 19.3%; health 12.1%; general administration 11.7%; economic affairs 11.6%). **Production** (metric tons except as noted). *Agriculture, fishing, other marine:* locally grown broccoli, cauliflower, potatoes, and cabbage sold commercially for the first time in 2007; fish catch (2006) 213,600 (of which prawn 132,500, Greenland halibut 44,900, Atlantic cod 10,600, lumpfish 10,000, crab 3,600); number of other marine catch (2006): narwhals 411, minke whales 181, beluga whales 137, porpoises 2,923, seals 187,613, walrus 45; livestock (number of live animals; 2007) 21,704 sheep, 2,441 tame reindeer, 216 horses; number of animals killed (2006) reindeer 15,002, musk ox 2,393, polar bear 118. *Mining* (2007): gold 1,639 kg. *Manufacturing:* principally fish and prawn processing, handicrafts, hides and skins, and ship repair. *Energy production (consumption):* electricity (kW-hr; 2006) 344,000,000 (268,000,-000); petroleum products (metric tons; 2006) none (184,000). **Tourism** (2008): number of overnight stays at hotels 236,913, of which visitors from within Greenland 115,289, from Denmark 79,396, from the US 6,532. **Gross national income** (2007): US$1,834,-000,000 (US$32,429 per capita). **Population economically active** (2003): total 32,119; activity rate of total population 56.5% (participation rates: ages 15–62, 83.5%; female [2006] 48.6%; unemployed [2007; urban only] 6.8%). **Public debt** (2008): none.

## Foreign trade

**Imports** (2007): DKK 3,643,000,000 (mineral fuels [mostly refined petroleum products] 24.2%; machinery and transportation equipment 22.8%; food products 16.4%; manufactured products 13.3%). *Major import sources:* Denmark 70.1%; Sweden 22.6%; Norway 1.7%; Canada 0.9%. **Exports** (2007): DKK 2,322,000,000 (prawn 48.5%; Greenland halibut 19.0%; gold 9.9%; cod 7.7%; crab 1.6%). *Major export destinations:* Denmark 85.1%; Canada 10.0%; Iceland 1.5%; UK 1.2%.

## Transport and communications

**Transport.** *Railroads:* none. *Roads* (1998): total length 150 km (paved 60%). *Vehicles* (2007): passenger cars 4,819; trucks and buses 423. Air transport (2006; Air Greenland A/S only): passenger-km 441,422,000; metric ton-km cargo 49,485,000. **Communications,** in total units (units per 1,000 persons). Telephone landlines (2008): 23,000 (405); cellular telephone subscribers (2008): 56,000 (991); total Internet users (2007): 52,000 (920).

## Education and health

**Educational attainment** (2002). Two-thirds of labor force has no formal education. **Literacy** (2001): total population ages 15 and over literate: virtually 100%. **Health:** physicians (2004) 91 (1 per 626 persons); hospital beds (2005) 411 (1 per 139 persons); infant mortality rate per 1,000 live births (2007) 8.2.

## Military

**Total active duty personnel.** Denmark is responsible for Greenland's defense—Greenlanders are not liable for military service; US Air Force personnel at Thule Air Base (December 2008): 138.

## Background

The Inuit probably crossed to Greenland from North America, along the islands of the Canadian Arctic, from 4000 BC to AD 1000. The Norwegian Erik the Red visited Greenland in 982; his son, Leif Eriksson, introduced Christianity. Greenland came under joint Danish-Norwegian rule in the late 14th century. The original Norse settlements became extinct in the 15th century, but Greenland was recolonized by Denmark. In 1776 Denmark closed the Greenland coast to foreign trade; it was not reopened until 1950. Greenland became part of Denmark in 1953. Home rule was established in 1979. In the early 21st century, the movement for full independence gained support, as did the belief that global warming was responsible for the accelerated melting of the Greenlandic ice.

## Recent Developments

After two years of exploration, Scotland-based Cairn Energy announced in late 2011 that it had failed to discover commercially viable sources of oil or natural gas off Greenland. Just weeks earlier the company had reported that it had spent some £500 million (about US$785 million) on the six completed wells. In early 2012, however, Norway's Statoil purchased a 30.6% stake in one of Cairn's Greenland licenses, reflecting optimism over the future of energy supplies from the island.

**Internet resource:** <www.stat.gl>.

# Grenada

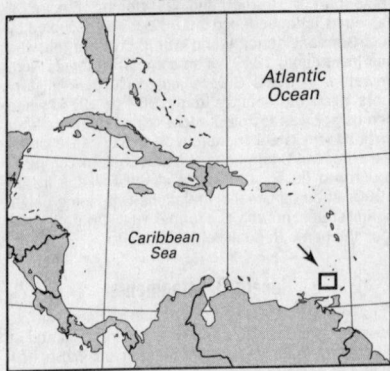

**Official name:** Grenada. **Form of government:** constitutional monarchy with two legislative houses (Senate [13]; House of Representatives [15]). **Head of state:** British Queen Elizabeth II (from 1952), represented by Governor-General Carlyle Glean (from 2008). **Head of government:** Prime Minister Tillman Thomas (from 2008). **Capital:** St. George's. **Official language:** English. **Official religion:** none. **Monetary unit:** 1 Eastern Caribbean dollar (EC$) = 100 cents; valuation (2 Jul 2012) US$1 = EC$2.70.

## Demography

**Area:** 133 sq mi, 344 sq km. **Population** (2011): 108,000. **Density** (2011): persons per sq mi 812.0, persons per sq km 314.0. **Urban** (2009): 30.9%. **Sex distribution** (2008): male 51.96%; female 48.04%. **Age breakdown** (2008): under 15, 32.4%; 15–29, 33.7%; 30–44, 21.6%; 45–59, 8.2%; 60–74, 3.1%; 75 and over, 1.0%. **Ethnic composition** (2000): black 51.7%; mixed 40.0%; Indo-Pakistani 4.0%; white 0.9%; other 3.4%. **Religious affiliation** (2005): Roman Catholic 41%; Protestant (of which significantly Anglican and Seventh-day Adventist) 30%; Rastafarian 5%; nonreligious/other 24%. **Major localities** (2006): St. George's 4,300 (urban agglomeration [2007] 32,000); Gouyave 3,400; Grenville 2,500. **Location:** island between the Caribbean Sea and the Atlantic Ocean, north of Trinidad and Tobago.

## Vital statistics

**Birth rate** per 1,000 population (2008): 18.1 (world avg. 20.3). **Death rate** per 1,000 population (2008): 8.2 (world avg. 8.5). **Total fertility rate** (avg. births per childbearing woman; 2008): 2.30. **Life expectancy** at birth (2008): male 67.1 years; female 70.5 years.

## National economy

**Budget** (2008). *Revenue:* EC$516,100,000 (tax revenue 84.1%, of which tax on international trade 45.5%, corporate taxes 13.8%; grants 10.0%; nontax revenue 5.9%). *Expenditures:* EC$627,500,000 (current expenditures 65.9%, of which wages and salaries 32.0%, transfers 14.9%, debt service 5.6%; capital expenditures 34.1%). **Public debt** (external, outstanding; 2007):

---

*1 metric ton = about 1.1 short tons;    1 kilometer = 0.6 mi (statute);    1 metric ton-km cargo = about 0.68 short ton-mi cargo;    c.i.f.: cost, insurance, and freight;    f.o.b.: free on board*

US$249,740,000. **Gross national income** (2008): US$603,000,000 (US$5,710 per capita). **Production** (metric tons except as noted). *Agriculture and fishing* (2007): sugarcane 7,200, coconuts 7,000, bananas 4,300, nutmeg 2,800, cacao beans 1,000, cinnamon 50, cloves 20; livestock (number of live animals) 13,200 sheep, 7,200 goats, 2,650 pigs; fisheries production 2,407 (from aquaculture, none). *Mining and quarrying:* excavation of limestone, sand, and gravel for local use. *Manufacturing* (value of production in EC$'000; 1997): wheat flour 13,390; soft drinks 9,798; beer 7,072. *Energy production (consumption):* electricity (kW-hr; 2008) 169,568,000 ([2006] 171,000,000); petroleum products (metric tons; 2006) none (78,000). **Population economically active** (2004): total 37,000; activity rate of total population 35% (participation rate: ages 15–64 [1998] 78%; female [1998] 43.5%; unemployed [2005] 18.0%). **Selected balance of payments data.** Receipts from (US$'000,000): tourism (2007) 110; remittances (2008) 64; foreign direct investment (2005–07 avg.) 98; official development assistance (2007) 23. Disbursements for (US$'000,000): tourism (2007) 10; remittances (2008) 4.

## Foreign trade

**Imports** (2006; c.i.f.): US$298,900,000 (machinery and transportation equipment 22.1%; food products and live animals 16.1%; chemical products 9.6%; mineral fuels 5.9%). *Major import sources:* US 39.3%; Trinidad and Tobago 19.2%; UK 5.6%; China 5.3%; Japan 3.9%. **Exports** (2006; f.o.b.): US$25,400,000 (food products and live animals 51.6%, of which fish 14.6%, spices [nearly all nutmeg and mace] 11.0%; machinery and transportation equipment 11.8%; chemical products 4.7%). *Major export destinations:* US 27.6%; Saint Lucia 13.0%; Dominica 9.4%; St. Kitts and Nevis 7.5%; Trinidad and Tobago 7.1%.

## Transport and communications

**Transport.** *Railroads:* none. *Roads* (2000): total length 1,127 km (paved 61%). *Vehicles* (2001): passenger cars 15,800; trucks and buses 4,200. *Air transport* (2001; Point Salines airport only): passengers 331,000; cargo 2,747 metric tons. **Communications,** in total units (units per 1,000 persons). Telephone landlines (2008): 29,000 (276); cellular telephone subscribers (2008): 60,000 (580); personal computers (2004): 16,000 (155); total Internet users (2008): 24,000 (232); broadband Internet subscribers (2008): 10,000 (98).

## Education and health

**Educational attainment** (2001). Percentage of population ages 18 and over having: no formal schooling/unknown 7.6%; primary education 65.1%; secondary 21.7%; higher 5.6%, of which university 1.5%. **Literacy** (2004): total population ages 15 and over literate 98.0%. **Health** (2007): physicians (2006) 96 (1 per 1,111 persons); hospital beds 279 (1 per 385 persons); infant mortality rate per 1,000 live births 11.0; undernourished population (2002–04) 7,000 (7% of total population based on the consumption of a minimum daily requirement of 1,910 calories).

## Military

**Total active duty personnel** (2006): paramilitary and coast guard units only.

## Background

The warlike Carib Indians dominated Grenada when Christopher Columbus sighted the island in 1498 and named it Concepción; they ruled it for the next 150 years. In 1674 it became subject to the French crown and remained so until 1762, when British forces captured it. In 1833 the island's black slaves were freed. Grenada was the headquarters of the government of the British Windward Islands (1885–1958) and a member of the West Indies Federation (1958–62). It became a self-governing state in association with Britain in 1967 and gained its independence in 1974. In 1979 a left-wing government took control in a bloodless coup. Relations with its US-oriented Latin American neighbors became strained as Grenada leaned toward Cuba and the Soviet bloc. In order to counteract this trend, the US invaded the island in 1983; democratic self-government was reestablished in 1984. Grenada's relations with Cuba, once suspended, were restored in 1997.

## Recent Developments

Grenada enhanced its relations with China in 2011. In May a visiting delegation of Chinese business leaders pledged to invest about US$250 million in various areas of the economy, including hotels and cocoa processing.

**Internet resource:** <www.grenadagrenadines.com>.

# Guatemala

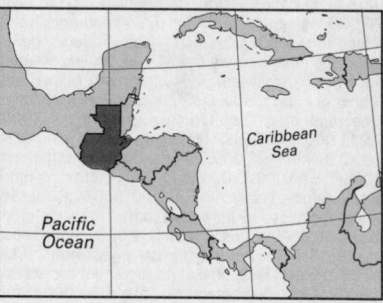

**Official name:** República de Guatemala (Republic of Guatemala). **Form of government:** republic with one legislative house (Congress of the Republic [158]). **Head of state and government:** President Otto Pérez Molina (from 2012). **Capital:** Guatemala City. **Official language:** Spanish. **Official religion:** none. **Monetary unit:** 1 quetzal (Q) = 100 centavos; valuation (2 Jul 2012) US$1 = Q 7.85.

## Demography

**Area:** 42,130 sq mi, 109,117 sq km. **Population** (2011): 14,729,000. **Density** (2011): persons per sq mi 349.6, persons per sq km 135.0. **Urban** (2009): 48.9%. **Sex distribution** (2008): male 48.79%; female 51.21%. **Age breakdown** (2006): under 15, 41.5%; 15–29, 28.6%; 30–44, 14.7%; 45–59, 9.6%; 60–74, 4.4%; 75–84, 1.1%; 85 and over, 0.1%. **Ethnic composition** (2002): mestizo 60.0%; Maya 39.3%, of which Quiché 11.3%, Kekchi 7.6%,

Cakchiquel 7.4%, Mam 5.5%; other 0.7%. **Religious affiliation** (2005): Roman Catholic 57%; Protestant/independent Christian 40%; traditional Mayan religions 1%; other 2%. **Major urban agglomerations** (2002): Guatemala City 942,348; Mixco 277,400; Villa Nueva 187,700; Quetzaltenango 106,700; Escuintla 65,400. **Location:** Central America, bordering Mexico, Belize, the Caribbean Sea, Honduras, El Salvador, and the Pacific Ocean.

## Vital statistics

**Birth rate** per 1,000 population (2007): 29.1 (world avg. 20.3). **Death rate** per 1,000 population (2007): 5.3 (world avg. 8.5). **Total fertility rate** (avg. births per childbearing woman; 2007): 3.70. **Life expectancy** at birth (2007): male 66.7 years; female 73.8 years.

## National economy

**Budget** (2006). *Revenue:* Q 29,102,000,000 (tax revenue 93.6%, of which taxes on goods and services 55.3%; corporate taxes 18.0%; nontax revenue 3.1%). *Expenditures:* Q 33,600,000,000 (general administration 18.8%; education 18.6%; housing 13.8%; transportation 12.8%; public order 9.4%; health 7.7%). **Public debt** (external, outstanding; 2008): US$4,382,400,000. **Production** (metric tons except as noted). *Agriculture and fishing* (2007): sugarcane 18,000,000, corn (maize) 1,100,000, bananas 1,010,000, coffee 216,600, cardamom and nutmeg 19,000; livestock (number of live animals) 2,800,000 cattle, 265,000 sheep, 27,000,000 chickens; fisheries production 33,987 (from aquaculture 48%). *Mining and quarrying* (2007): silver 70,000 kg; gold 7,100 kg. *Manufacturing* (value added in Q '000,000; 2007): food products, beverages, and tobacco products 24,429; textiles, wearing apparel, and footwear 8,340; cement, bricks, and rubber or plastic products 4,284. *Energy production (consumption):* electricity (kW-hr; 2006) 7,911,000,000 (7,832,000,000); coal (metric tons; 2006) none (428,000); crude petroleum (barrels; 2008) 5,670,000 ([2006] 930,000); petroleum products (metric tons; 2006) 23,000 (2,952,000). **Selected balance of payments data.** Receipts from (US$'000,000): tourism (2007) 1,055; remittances (2008) 4,446; foreign direct investment (FDI; 2005–07 avg.) 608; official development assistance (2007) 450. Disbursements for (US$'000,000): tourism (2007) 597; remittances (2008) 18; FDI (2005–07 avg.) 54. **Gross national income** (2008): US$36,634,000,000 (US$2,680 per capita). **Population economically active** (2006): total 5,565,200; activity rate of total population 42.8% (participation rates: ages 15–64, 68.0%; female 38.1%).

## Foreign trade

**Imports** (2007; c.i.f.): US$12,731,000,000 (machinery and apparatus 17.3%; refined petroleum products 15.8%; chemical products 14.8%; food products 9.8%; motor vehicles and parts 7.8%). *Major import sources:* US 34.1%; Mexico 8.8%; China 5.7%; El Salvador 4.8%; South Korea 3.6%. **Exports** (2007; f.o.b.): US$6,900,000,000 (food products 33.0%, of which coffee 8.4%, raw sugar 5.2%, bananas 4.7%; wearing apparel and accessories 20.1%; crude petroleum

3.6%; toiletries and perfumery 3.6%; silver 3.0%). *Major export destinations:* US 42.6%; El Salvador 12.2%; Honduras 8.6%; Mexico 6.7%; Nicaragua 3.9%.

## Transport and communications

**Transport.** *Railroads* (2004): route length 886 km. *Roads* (2002): total length 14,044 km (paved 39%). *Vehicles* (2004): passenger cars 1,328,100; trucks and buses (2000) 53,236. *Air transport* (1999): passenger-km 341,700,000; metric ton-km cargo (2003) 200,000. **Communications,** in total units (units per 1,000 persons). Telephone landlines (2008): 1,449,000 (106); cellular telephone subscribers (2008): 14,949,000 (1,092); personal computers (2005): 262,000 (21); total Internet users (2008): 1,920,000 (143); broadband Internet subscribers (2005): 27,000 (2.1).

## Education and health

**Educational attainment** (2002). Percentage of heads of households having: no formal schooling 33.3%; incomplete/complete primary education 46.1%; incomplete/complete secondary 15.0%; higher 5.6%. **Literacy** (2005): total population ages 15 and over literate 71.8%; males literate 79.1%; females literate 64.6%. **Health** (2005): physicians 12,273 (1 per 1,049 persons); hospital beds 8,894 (1 per 1,429 persons); infant mortality rate per 1,000 live births (2006) 30.8; undernourished population (2002–04) 2,800,000 (22% of total population based on the consumption of a minimum daily requirement of 1,760 calories).

## Military

**Total active duty personnel** (November 2008): 15,500 (army 86.7%, navy 6.4%, air force 6.9%). **Military expenditure as percentage of GDP** (2008): 0.3%; per capita expenditure US$13.

## Background

From simple farming villages dating to 2500 BC, the Maya of Guatemala and the Yucatán developed an impressive civilization. The civilization of the Maya declined after AD 900, and the Spanish began the subjugation of their descendants in 1523. The Central American colonies declared independence from Spain in Guatemala City in 1821, and Guatemala became part of the Mexican Empire until its collapse in 1823. In 1839 Guatemala became an independent republic under the first of a series of dictators who held power almost continuously for the next century. In 1945 a liberal-democratic coalition came to power and instituted sweeping reforms. Attempts to expropriate land belonging to American business interests prompted the US government in 1954 to sponsor an invasion. In the following years Guatemala's social revolution came to an end and most of the reforms were reversed. Chronic political instability and violence thenceforth marked Guatemalan politics; most of the 200,000 deaths that resulted were blamed on government forces. In 1991 the country abandoned its long-standing claims of sovereignty over Belize, and the two established diplomatic relations. It continued to experience violence as guerrillas sought to

*1 metric ton = about 1.1 short tons;   1 kilometer = 0.6 mi (statute);   1 metric ton-km cargo = about 0.68 short ton-mi cargo;   c.i.f.: cost, insurance, and freight;   f.o.b.: free on board*

seize power. A peace treaty was signed in 1996, but labor discontent, widespread crime and poverty, and violations of human rights continued into the 21st century.

### Recent Developments

Guatemala suffered deadly violence by organized-crime gangs during 2011. Crackdowns on gangs in El Salvador, Colombia, and Mexico had pushed criminals from those countries into Guatemala to traffick arms and drugs. In June, US Secretary of State Hillary Clinton visited Guatemala and promised to increase US aid for antidrug efforts in Central America. Cocaine farmers were accused of having destroyed large portions of Guatemala's rainforest to build airstrips, an action that threatened the UNESCO Maya biosphere reserve that included ancient Mayan ruins. In July Pres. Álvaro Colom proposed a "NATO-style" Central American military force to rid the region of gangs.

Internet resource: <www.visitguatemala.com>.

# Guinea

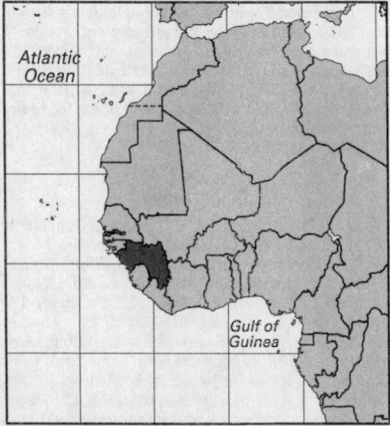

Atlantic Ocean

Gulf of Guinea

**Official name:** République de Guinée (Republic of Guinea). **Form of government:** republic with one advisory body (National Transition Council [155]). **Head of state and government:** President Alpha Condé (from 2010), assisted by Prime Minister Mohamed Saïd Fofana (from 2010). **Capital:** Conakry. **Official language:** French. **Official religion:** none. **Monetary unit:** 1 Guinean franc (FG) = 100 centimes; valuation (2 Jul 2012) US$1 = FG 7,190.01.

### Demography

**Area:** 94,926 sq mi, 245,857 sq km. **Population** (2011): 10,222,000. **Density** (2011): persons per sq mi 107.7, persons per sq km 41.6. **Urban** (2009): 34.9%. **Sex distribution** (2008): male 50.00%; female 50.00%. **Age breakdown** (2008): under 15, 42.9%; 15–29, 26.5%; 30–44, 16.0%; 45–59, 9.2%; 60–74, 4.4%; 75 and over, 1.0%. **Ethnic composition** (2000): Fulani 38.3%; Malinke 25.6%; Susu 12.2%; Kpelle 5.2%; Kisi 4.8%; other 13.9%. **Religious affili-**ation (2005): Muslim (nearly all Sunni) 85%; Christian 8%; traditional beliefs 7%. **Major cities** (2004): Conakry 1,851,800; Kankan 113,900; Labé (2001) 64,500; Kindia (2001) 56,000; Nzérékoré (2001) 55,000. **Location:** western Africa, bordering Guinea-Bissau, Senegal, Mali, Côte d'Ivoire, Liberia, Sierra Leone, and the North Atlantic Ocean.

### Vital statistics

**Birth rate** per 1,000 population (2008): 37.8 (world avg. 20.3). **Death rate** per 1,000 population (2008): 11.3 (world avg. 8.5). **Total fertility rate** (avg. births per childbearing woman; 2008): 5.25. **Life expectancy** at birth (2008): male 55.1 years; female 58.1 years.

### National economy

**Budget** (2008). *Revenue:* FG 3,854,400,000,000 (tax revenue 81.9%, of which taxes on domestic production and trade 29.8%, mining sector revenue taxes 22.0%, taxes on international trade 18.5%; grants 12.7%). *Expenditures:* FG 3,735,600,000,000 (current expenditures 65.2%, of which wages and salaries 23.0%, interest on debt 14.6%; capital expenditures 34.6%; net lending and restructuring 0.2%). **Public debt** (external, outstanding; January 2009): US$3,527,000,000. **Production** (metric tons except as noted). *Agriculture and fishing* (2007): rice 1,401,592, cassava 1,122,171, oil palm fruit 883,000, fonio 243,361, coffee 18,600, cacao beans 15,000; livestock (number of live animals) 4,180,965 cattle, 1,590,400 goats, 1,330,600 sheep; fisheries production 100,000 (from aquaculture, none). *Mining and quarrying* (2008–09): bauxite 16,865,960; gold 508,980 troy oz; diamonds 459,370 carats. *Manufacturing* (2008–09): cement 292,130; flour 21,630; paints 1,340. *Energy production (consumption):* electricity (kW-hr; 2008–09) 683,091,000 ([2006] 836,000,000); petroleum products (metric tons; 2006) none (385,000); natural gas (cu m; 2008–09) 84,460 ([2006] none). **Population economically active** (2007): total 4,500,000; activity rate of total population (2003) 49.0% (participation rates: ages 15 and over, 85.0%; female 47.2%). **Gross national income** (2007): US$3,722,000,000 (US$400 per capita). **Selected balance of payments data.** Receipts from (US$'000,000): tourism (2007) 0.2; remittances (2008) 151; foreign direct investment (2005–07 avg.) 108; official development assistance (2007) 224. Disbursements for (US$'000,000): tourism (2007) 29; remittances (2008) 119.

### Foreign trade

**Imports** (2006): US$942,000,000 (machinery and apparatus 33.7%; refined petroleum products 23.7%; food products 17.5%). *Major import sources:* China 8.6%; France 8.0%; Belgium 4.4%; Côte d'Ivoire 3.5%; India 3.2%. **Exports** (2006): US$1,011,100,000 (bauxite 40.0%; gold 31.6%; alumina 14.0%; diamonds 4.2%; fish 4.2%; coffee 3.1%). *Major export destinations:* Russia 11.6%; Ukraine 9.6%; Spain 9.0%; South Korea 8.8%; US 7.7%.

### Transport and communications

**Transport.** *Railroads* (2008): route length (mostly for bauxite transport) 1,185 km; metric ton-km cargo (1993) 710,000,000. *Roads* (2003): total length

44,348 km (paved 10%). *Vehicles* (2003): passenger cars 47,524; trucks and buses 26,467. *Air transport* (1999): passenger-km 94,000,000; metric ton-km cargo 10,000,000. **Communications,** in total units (units per 1,000 persons). Telephone landlines (2008): 50,000 (5.1); cellular telephone subscribers (2008): 2,600,000 (264); personal computers (2006): 47,000 (5); total Internet users (2008): 90,000 (9.2).

## Education and health

**Educational attainment** of those ages 25 and over having attended school (1999): none/unknown 81.4%; primary education 7.8%; secondary 6.8%; higher 4.0%. **Literacy** (2006): percentage of total population ages 15 and over literate 29.5%; males literate 42.6%; females literate 18.1%. **Health:** physicians (2006) 689 (1 per 13,660 persons); hospital beds (2005) 2,766 (1 per 3,333 persons); infant mortality rate per 1,000 live births (2008) 67.4; undernourished population (2002–04) 2,000,000 (24% of total population based on the consumption of a minimum daily requirement of 1,830 calories).

## Military

**Total active duty personnel** (November 2008): 12,300 (army 69.1%, navy 3.3%, air force 6.5%, gendarmerie 8.1%, republican guard 13.0%). **Military expenditure as percentage of GDP** (2007): 1.1%; per capita expenditure US$5.

## Background

About AD 900 successive migrations of the Susu swept down from the desert and pushed the original inhabitants of Guinea, the Baga, to the Atlantic coast. Small kingdoms of the Susu rose in importance in the 13th century and later extended their rule to the coast. In the mid-15th century, the Portuguese visited the coast and developed a slave trade. In the 16th century, the Fulani established domination over the Fouta Djallon region; they ruled into the 19th century. In the early 19th century, the French arrived and in 1849 proclaimed the coastal region a French protectorate. In 1895 French Guinea became part of the federation of French West Africa. In 1946 it was made an overseas territory of France, and in 1958 it achieved independence. Following a military coup in 1984, Guinea began implementing Westernized government systems. A new constitution was adopted in 1991, and the first multiparty elections were held in 1993. During the 1990s Guinea accommodated several hundred thousand war refugees from neighboring Liberia and Sierra Leone, and conflicts between these countries and Guinea have continued to flare up over the refugee population into the early 21st century.

## Recent Developments

Alpha Condé, Guinea's first democratically elected president since independence, undertook a reform of the security services in 2011. The action won commendation from the United Nations as a model for other West African countries.

**Internet resource:** <www.stat-guinee.org>.

# Guinea-Bissau

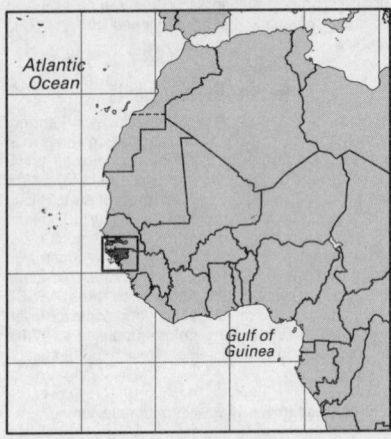

**Official name:** Républica da Guiné-Bissau (Republic of Guinea-Bissau). **Form of government:** transitional with one legislative house (National People's Assembly [102]). **Head of state and government:** President Manuel Serifo Nhamadjo (transitional, from 2012), assisted by Prime Minister Rui Duarte de Barros (transitional, from 2012). **Capital:** Bissau. **Official language:** Portuguese. **Official religion:** none. **Monetary unit:** 1 CFA franc (CFAF) = 100 centimes; valuation (2 Jul 2012) US$1 = CFAF 521.26.

## Demography

**Area:** 13,948 sq mi, 36,125 sq km. **Population** (2011): 1,606,000. **Density** (2011): persons per sq mi 115.1, persons per sq km 44.5. **Urban** (2009): 29.9%. **Sex distribution** (2009): male 48.82%; female 51.18%. **Age breakdown** (2005): under 15, 41.6%; 15–29, 28.1%; 30–44, 16.1%; 45–59, 9.4%; 60–74, 4.1%; 75 and over, 0.7%. **Ethnic composition** (2000): Balante 25.0%; Fulani (locally Fulakunda) 17.1%; Mandyako 12.0%; Malinke 10.0%; Guinean mestiço (Portuguese-black) 9.2%; Pepel 6.3%; nonindigenous Cape Verdean mulatto 1.0%; other 19.4%. **Religious affiliation** (2005): traditional beliefs 49%; Muslim 42%; Christian/other 9%. **Major cities** (2004): Bissau 305,700; Bafatá 15,000; Cacheu 14,000; Gabú 10,000. **Location:** western Africa, bordering Senegal, Guinea, and the North Atlantic Ocean.

## Vital statistics

**Birth rate** per 1,000 population (2005): 37.6 (world avg. 20.3). **Death rate** per 1,000 population (2005): 16.7 (world avg. 8.5). **Total fertility rate** (avg. births per childbearing woman; 2005): 4.93. **Life expectancy** at birth (2005): male 44.8 years; female 48.5 years.

## National economy

**Budget** (2007). *Revenue:* CFAF 53,800,000,000 (grants 50.6%; tax revenue 34.9%; nontax revenue

*1 metric ton = about 1.1 short tons;    1 kilometer = 0.6 mi (statute);    1 metric ton-km cargo = about 0.68 short ton-mi cargo;    c.i.f.: cost, insurance, and freight;    f.o.b.: free on board*

14.5%). *Expenditures:* CFAF 73,700,000,000 (current expenditures 66.9%; capital expenditures 33.1%). **Production** (metric tons except as noted). *Agriculture and fishing* (2008): rice 148,757, cashew nuts 81,000, oil palm fruit 80,000, sugarcane 6,000; livestock (number of live animals) 599,200 cattle, 401,300 pigs; fisheries production (2007) 6,200 (from aquaculture, none). *Mining and quarrying:* small-scale production of clays, limestone, and granite. *Manufacturing* (2003): processed wood 11,000; bakery products 7,900; wood products 4,400. *Energy production (consumption):* electricity (kW-hr; 2006) 66,000,000 (66,000,000); petroleum products (metric tons; 2006) none (91,000). **Selected balance of payments data.** Receipts from (US$'000,000): tourism (2006) 2.8; remittances (2008) 30; foreign direct investment (2005–07 avg.) 11; official development assistance (2007) 123. Disbursements for (US$'000,000): tourism (2006) 16; remittances (2008) 5. **Population economically active** (2006): total 618,000; activity rate of total population 37.5% (participation rates: ages 15–64, 73.0%; female 38.8%). **Public debt** (external, outstanding; 2007): US$730,000,000. **Gross national income** (GNI; 2008): US$386,000,000 (US$250 per capita) (formal economy only; in 2009 most of Guinea-Bissau's income was derived from trafficking South American cocaine into Europe).

## Foreign trade

**Imports** (2007): US$136,000,000 (agricultural products 55.1%, of which refined sugar 12.5%, cereals 11.1%, beverages 7.9%). *Major import sources* (2008): Portugal 25%; Senegal 17%; Pakistan 5%; France 5%; Cuba 4%. **Exports** (2007): US$85,000,000 (cashews 64.3%; refined sugar 11.2%). *Major export destinations* (2008): India 75%; Nigeria 21%.

## Transport and communications

**Transport.** *Railroads:* none. *Roads* (2003): total length 2,755 km (paved 28%). *Vehicles* (2002): passenger cars, trucks, and buses 1,985. *Air transport* (2003): passenger arrivals 17,834, passenger departures 18,528. **Communications,** in total units (units per 1,000 persons). Telephone landlines (2008): 4,600 (3.1); cellular telephone subscribers (2008): 500,000 (333); personal computers (2007): 2,900 (2); total Internet users (2008): 37,000 (25).

## Education and health

**Literacy** (2007): total population ages 15 and over literate 64.6%; males literate 75.1%; females literate 54.4%. **Health** (2005): physicians 188 (1 per 7,522 persons); hospital beds 1,686 (1 per 839 persons); infant mortality rate per 1,000 live births 107.2; undernourished population (2002–04) 600,000 (39% of total population based on the consumption of a minimum daily requirement of 1,800 calories).

## Military

**Total active duty personnel** (November 2008): 6,500 (army 62%, navy 5%, air force 2%, gendarmerie 31%). **Military expenditure as percentage of GDP** (2007): 4.2%; per capita expenditure US$10.

## Background

More than 1,000 years ago the coast of Guinea-Bissau was occupied by iron-using agriculturists. They grew irrigated and dry rice and were also the major suppliers of marine salt to the western Sudan. At about the same time, the region came under the influence of the Mali empire and became a tributary kingdom known as Kaabu. After 1546 Kaabu was virtually autonomous; vestiges of the kingdom lasted until 1867. The earliest overseas contacts came in the 15th century with the Portuguese, who imported slaves from the Guinea area to the offshore Cape Verde Islands. Portuguese control of Guinea-Bissau was marginal despite claims to sovereignty there. The end of the slave trade forced the Portuguese inland in search of new profits. Their subjugation of the interior was slow and sometimes violent; it was not effectively achieved until 1915, though sporadic resistance continued until 1936. Guerrilla warfare in the 1960s led to the country's independence in 1974, but political turmoil continued and the government was overthrown by a military coup in 1980. A new constitution was adopted in 1984, and the first multiparty elections were held in 1994. A destructive civil war in 1998 was followed by military coups in 1999 and 2003, but the coups were followed by elections.

## Recent Developments

In March 2012, Guinea-Bissau held a presidential election, which resulted in a runoff election between Prime Minister Carlos Gomes Júnior and former president Kumba Ialá. Before the runoff election could be held, however, a military coup occurred. The coup was widely condemned—the African Union suspended Guinea-Bissau the next week, and the Economic Community of West African States (ECOWAS) imposed sanctions. In the following weeks, the coup leaders and ECOWAS managed to reach an agreement regarding the restoration of civilian rule, and in May Manuel Serifo Nhamadjo was named president of a transitional government that was intended to restore civilian rule within one year.

**Internet resource:**
<www.republica-da-guine-bissau.org>.

# Guyana

**Official name:** Co-operative Republic of Guyana. **Form of government:** unitary multiparty republic with one legislative house (National Assembly [67]). **Head of state and government:** President Donald Ramotar (from 2011). **Capital:** Georgetown. **Official language:** English. **Official religion:** none. **Monetary unit:** 1 Guyanese dollar (G$) = 100 cents; valuation (2 Jul 2012) US$1 = G$201.21.

## Demography

**Area:** 83,012 sq mi, 214,999 sq km. **Population** (2011): 756,000. **Density** (2011; based on land area only): persons per sq mi 9.9, persons per sq km 3.8. **Urban** (2005): 38.5%. **Sex distribution** (2008): male 50.06%; female 49.94%. **Age breakdown** (2005): under 15, 26.5%; 15–29, 29.7%; 30–44, 23.0%; 45–59, 13.3%; 60–74, 5.6%; 75 and over, 1.9%. **Ethnic composition** (2002): East Indian 43.5%; black 30.2%; mixed race 16.7%; Amerindian 9.2%; other

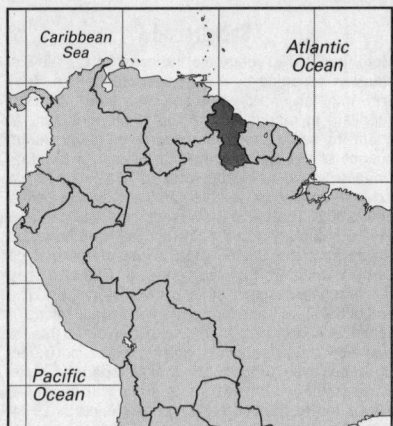

Caribbean Sea
Atlantic Ocean
Pacific Ocean

0.4%. **Religious affiliation** (2002): Christian 57.3%, of which Protestant/independent Christian 48.2% (including Anglican 6.9%), Roman Catholic 8.0%, Jehovah's Witness 1.1%; Hindu 28.4%; Muslim 7.2%; Rastafarian 0.5%; nonreligious 4.3%; other/unknown 2.3%. **Major urban areas** (2006): Georgetown 236,900; Linden 44,900; New Amsterdam 35,700; Corriverton 12,700; Bartica 11,300. **Location:** northern South America, bordering the North Atlantic Ocean, Suriname, Brazil, and Venezuela.

## Vital statistics

**Birth rate** per 1,000 population (2008): 18.5 (world avg. 20.3). **Death rate** per 1,000 population (2008): 7.9 (world avg. 8.5). **Total fertility rate** (avg. births per childbearing woman; 2008): 2.60. **Life expectancy** at birth (2005): male 62.9 years; female 68.3 years.

## National economy

**Budget** (2008): *Revenue:* G$99,513,000,000 (current revenue 82.9%, of which VAT 24.1%, corporate taxes 18.7%, excise tax 13.2%, income tax 12.7%; grants 13.7%). *Expenditures:* G$105,838,000,000 (current expenditures 59.5%; development expenditures 40.5%). **Production** (metric tons except as noted). *Agriculture and fishing* (2007): sugarcane 3,250,000, rice 475,000, coconuts 45,000, cassava (manioc) 29,000, mangoes 12,000; livestock (number of live animals) 130,000 sheep, 110,000 cattle, 21,500,000 chickens; fisheries production 48,100 (from aquaculture 1%), of which shrimp or prawns (2006) 19,860. *Mining and quarrying* (2008): bauxite 1,995,000; gold 8,131 kg; diamonds 169,000 carats. *Manufacturing* (2008): flour 35,700; margarine 1,528; rum 142,000 hectoliters. *Energy production (consumption):* electricity (kW-hr; 2006) 867,000,000 (867,000,000); petroleum products (metric tons; 2006) none (491,000). **Population economically active** (2006): total 279,100; activity rate of total population 37% (participation rates: ages 15–65, 60%; female [2002] 34.1%; unemployed [2002] 11.7%). **Gross national income** (2008): US$1,081,000,000 (US$1,420 per capita). **Public**

debt (external, outstanding; 2008): US$833,000,000. **Selected balance of payments data.** Receipts from (US$'000,000): tourism (2007) 50; remittances (2008) 278; foreign direct investment (2005–07 avg.) 110; official development assistance (2007) 124. Disbursements for (US$'000,000): tourism (2007) 58; remittances (2008) 61.

## Foreign trade

**Imports** (2007; c.i.f.): US$1,028,800,000 (refined petroleum products 22.9%; machinery and apparatus 20.2%; food products 11.3%; chemical products 9.8%). *Major import sources:* Trinidad and Tobago 25.1%; US 25.1%; China 8.5%; UK 6.1%; Netherlands Antilles 3.9%. **Exports** (2007; f.o.b.): US$784,700,000 (gold 20.2%; raw sugar 19.2%; bauxite 12.2%; rice 9.6%; sawn wood 5.0%; shrimp 4.7%; diamonds 4.2%). *Major export destinations:* Canada 21.6%; UK 15.9%; US 14.4%; Barbados 5.9%; Netherlands 5.6%.

## Transport and communications

**Transport.** *Railroads:* none. *Roads* (2000): total length 7,970 km (paved 7%). *Vehicles* (2001): passenger cars 61,300; trucks and buses 15,500. *Air transport* (2001; scheduled traffic only): passenger-km 174,800,000; metric ton-km cargo 1,600,000. **Communications**, in total units (units per 1,000 persons). Telephone landlines (2008): 125,000 (164); cellular telephone subscribers (2005): 281,000 (375); personal computers (2005): 29,000 (39); total Internet users (2008): 205,000 (269); broadband Internet subscribers (2005): 2,000 (2.6).

## Education and health

**Educational attainment** (2002). Percentage of population ages 15 and over having: no formal schooling/unknown 3.4%; primary education 26.0%; secondary 62.1%; post-secondary 3.7%; higher 4.8%. **Literacy** (2005): total population ages 15 and over literate 99.0%; males literate 99.2%; females literate 98.7%. **Health** (2005): physicians 323 (1 per 2,325 persons); hospital beds (2004–05) 1,887 (1 per 401 persons); infant mortality rate per 1,000 live births 33.3; undernourished population (2002–04) 60,000 (8% of total population based on the consumption of a minimum daily requirement of 1,880 calories).

## Military

**Total active duty personnel** (November 2008): 1,100 (army 81.8%, navy 9.1%, air force 9.1%). **Military expenditure as percentage of GDP** (2004): 1.8%; per capita expenditure US$19.

## Background

Guyana was colonized by the Dutch in the 17th century. During the Napoleonic Wars the British occupied the territory and afterward purchased the colonies of Demerara, Berbice, and Essequibo, united in 1831 as British Guiana. The slave trade was abolished in 1807, but emancipation of the 100,000 slaves in the colonies was not completed until 1838. From the 1840s East Indian and Chinese indentured servants

*1 metric ton = about 1.1 short tons; 1 kilometer = 0.6 mi (statute); 1 metric ton-km cargo = about 0.68 short ton-mi cargo; c.i.f.: cost, insurance, and freight; f.o.b.: free on board*

were brought to work the plantations; by 1917 almost 240,000 East Indians had migrated to British Guiana. It was made a crown colony in 1928 and granted home rule in 1953. Political parties began to emerge, developing on racial lines as the People's Progressive Party (largely East Indian) and the People's National Congress (largely black). The PNC formed a coalition government and led the country into independence as Guyana in 1966. In 1970 Guyana became a republic within the Commonwealth; in 1980 it adopted a new constitution. In the last decades of the 20th century, Guyana moved away from the socialist approach first taken following independence. At the beginning of the 21st century, it was still struggling to achieve economic and political stability.

## Recent Developments

Guyana strengthened its sugar industry in recent months. The country obtained a US$16.4 million loan in December 2011 from the EU for developing and increasing sugar production, and an additional US$32.6 million was announced in February 2012.

Internet resource: <www.statisticsguyana.gov.gy>.

# Haiti

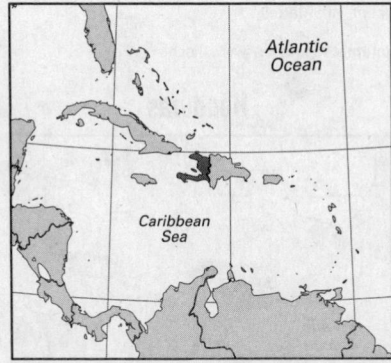

Official name: Repiblik d' Ayiti (Haitian Creole); République d'Haïti (French) (Republic of Haiti). Form of government: republic with two legislative houses (Senate [30]; Chamber of Deputies [99]). Head of state: President Michel Martelly (from 2011). Head of government: Prime Minister Laurent Lamothe (from 2012). Capital: Port-au-Prince. Official languages: Haitian Creole; French. Official religions: Roman Catholicism has special recognition per concordat with the Vatican; Vodou (Voodoo) became officially sanctioned per governmental decree of April 2003. Monetary unit: 1 gourde (G) = 100 centimes; valuation (2 Jul 2012) US$1 = G 42.05.

## Demography

Area: 10,695 sq mi, 27,700 sq km. Population (2011): 9,720,000. Density (2011): persons per sq mi 908.8, persons per sq km 350.9. Urban (2007): 40.1%. Sex distribution (2005): male 49.29%; female 50.71%. Age breakdown (2005): under 15, 42.6%; 15–29, 30.5%; 30–44, 14.2%; 45–59, 7.5%;

60–74, 4.2%; 75 and over, 1.0%. Ethnic composition (2000): black 94.2%; mulatto 5.4%; other 0.4%. Religious affiliation (2003): Roman Catholic 54.7% (about 80% of all Roman Catholics also practice Vodou [Voodoo]); Protestant/independent Christian 28.5%, of which Baptist 15.4%, Pentecostal 7.9%; Vodou (Voodoo) 2.1%; nonreligious 10.2%; other/unknown 4.5%. Major cities (2003): Port-au-Prince 703,023 (urban agglomeration 1,977,036); Carrefour (1999) 336,222; Delmas (1999) 284,079; Cap-Haïtien 111,094; Gonaïves 104,825. Location: western third of the island of Hispaniola, bordered by the North Atlantic Ocean, the Caribbean Sea, and the Dominican Republic.

## Vital statistics

Birth rate per 1,000 population (2007): 27.9 (world avg. 20.3). Death rate per 1,000 population (2007): 9.2 (world avg. 8.5). Total fertility rate (avg. births per childbearing woman; 2007): 3.50. Life expectancy at birth (2007): male 59.1 years; female 62.8 years.

## National economy

Budget (2007). Revenue: G 25,323,750,000 (customs duties 53.1%; sales tax 27.5%; taxes on income and profits 17.8%). Expenditures: G 29,534,070,000 (current expenditures 77.1%, of which wages and salaries 33.9%, transfers 4.2%, interest on public debt 2.3%; capital expenditures 22.9%). Gross national income (2008): US$6,464,000,000 (US$660 per capita). Production (metric tons except as noted). Agriculture and fishing (2007): sugarcane 1,000,000, cassava (manioc) 330,000, bananas 293,000, mangoes 260,000, cacao beans 4,500; livestock (number of live animals) 1,900,000 goats, 1,450,000 cattle, 1,000,000 pigs; fisheries production 10,000 (from aquaculture, none). Mining and quarrying (2007): sand 2,000,000 cu m. Manufacturing (value added in G '000,000 at constant prices of 1986–87; 2002): food products and beverages 484.5; textiles, wearing apparel, and footwear 195.7; chemical and rubber products 63.8. Energy production (consumption): electricity (kW-hr; 2007) 241,990,000 (215,380,000 [excluding December]); petroleum products (metric tons; 2006) none (541,000). Population economically active (2006): total 3,539,000; activity rate of total population 37.5% (participation rates: ages 15–64, 60.4%; female 33.3%; officially unemployed [2003] 32.7%). Public debt (external, outstanding; December 2007): US$1,478,000,000. Selected balance of payments data. Receipts from (US$'000,000): tourism (2007) 140; remittances (2008) 1,300; foreign direct investment (2005–07 avg.) 87; official development assistance (2007) 701. Disbursements for (US$'000,000): tourism (2007) 55; remittances (2008) 96.

## Foreign trade

Imports (2008): US$2,107,750,000 (food products 27.2%; mineral fuels 26.6%; machinery and transportation equipment 8.2%; chemical products 3.5%). Major import sources (2004): US 52.9%; Dominican Republic 6.0%; Japan 2.9%. Exports (2008): US$490,200,000 (reexports to US 86.7%, of which wearing apparel and accessories 85.5%; essential oils 3.7%; mangoes 2.0%; cocoa 1.5%; rock lobster 1.1%). Major export destinations (2004): US 81.8%; Dominican Republic 7.2%; Canada 4.2%.

## Transport and communications

**Transport.** *Railroads:* none. *Roads* (2000): total length 4,160 km (paved 24%). *Vehicles* (1999): passenger cars 93,000; trucks and buses 61,600. **Communications,** in total units (units per 1,000 persons). Telephone landlines (2006): 150,000 (17); cellular telephone subscribers (2008): 3,200,000 (328); personal computers (2007): 499,000 (52); total Internet users (2007): 1,000,000 (104).

## Education and health

**Educational attainment** (2000). Percentage of population ages 25 and over having: no formal education/unknown 46.1%; incomplete primary education 28.9%; primary 5.3%; incomplete secondary 15.6%; secondary 1.8%; higher 2.3%. Literacy (2007): total population ages 15 and over literate 62.1%; males literate 60.1%; females literate 64.0%. **Health:** physicians (1999) 1,910 (1 per 4,000 persons); hospital beds (2000) 6,431 (1 per 1,234 persons); infant mortality rate per 1,000 live births (2007) 71.0; undernourished population (2003–05) 5,300,000 (58% of total population based on the consumption of a minimum daily requirement of 1,860 calories).

## Military

**Total active duty personnel** (2008). The national police force had 2,000 personnel; UN peacekeepers (March 2009): 7,044 troops, 2,011 police.

## Background

Haiti gained its independence when the former slaves of the island rebelled against French rule in 1791–1804. The new republic encompassed the entire island of Hispaniola, but the eastern portion was restored to Spain in 1809. The island was reunited under Haitian Pres. Jean-Pierre Boyer (1818–43); after his overthrow the eastern portion revolted and formed the Dominican Republic. Haiti's government was marked by instability, with frequent coups and assassinations. It was occupied by the US in 1915–34. In 1957 the dictator François ("Papa Doc") Duvalier came to power. Despite an economic decline and civil unrest, Duvalier ruled until his death in 1971. He was succeeded by his son, Jean-Claude ("Baby Doc") Duvalier, who was forced into exile in 1986. Haiti's first free presidential elections, held in 1990, were won by Jean-Bertrand Aristide. He was deposed by a military coup in 1991, after which tens of thousands of Haitians attempted to flee to the US in small boats. The military government stepped down in 1994, and Aristide returned from exile and resumed the presidency. His associate René Préval replaced him in 1995, and in 2000 Aristide reclaimed the presidency, only to be driven from office and out of the country in 2004. An international stabilization mission was established under the leadership of first the US armed forces and then the UN. Economic and political instability continued to plague Haiti in the early 21st century. In January 2010, a powerful earthquake struck the country, causing widespread destruction in Port-au-Prince and the surrounding region. Estimates of the death toll from the quake ranged from 85,000 upward to 316,000—the official Haitian government figure.

## Recent Developments

In 2011 Haiti struggled to recover from the 2010 earthquake. In March Michel Martelly, a singer-turned-politician, won an unprecedented presidential runoff election that attracted fewer than 30% of eligible voters. Martelly's desire to move quickly on campaign promises was delayed by parliamentary rejections of his first two nominations for prime minister. The parliament confirmed his third nominee, Garry Conille, a physician who had also served as chief of staff for UN Special Haiti Envoy Bill Clinton. Conille's government pledged to end the months of political gridlock that had stalled postquake recovery, further disillusioning Haiti's impoverished people—including some 500,000 displaced persons still living in tents in the Port-au-Prince quake zone. Only 43% of a promised US$4.6 billion pledged by international donors for the country's recovery had been disbursed by October. Those funds—applied largely to international contractors and road projects—rendered little tangible change among Haiti's poor, who remained dependent on services of uneven quality provided by nongovernmental organizations and on remittances sent from Haitians living overseas. Conille's administration lasted only until February 2012, however, when he stepped down amid acrimonious disagreement with Martelly.

**Internet resource:** <www.ihsi.ht>.

# Honduras

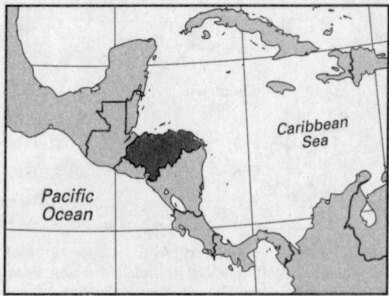

Caribbean Sea

Pacific Ocean

**Official name:** República de Honduras (Republic of Honduras). **Form of government:** multiparty republic with one legislative house (National Congress [128]). **Head of state and government:** President Porfirio Lobo (from 2010). **Capital:** Tegucigalpa. **Official language:** Spanish. **Official religion:** none. **Monetary unit:** 1 lempira (L) = 100 centavos; valuation (2 Jul 2012) US$1 = L 19.06.

## Demography

**Area:** 43,433 sq mi, 112,492 sq km. **Population** (2011): 7,755,000. **Density** (2011): persons per sq mi 178.6, persons per sq km 68.9. **Urban** (2009): 50.8%. **Sex distribution** (2008): male 49.95%; female 50.05%. **Age breakdown** (2005): under 15, 40.5%; 15–29, 29.2%; 30–44, 16.7%; 45–59, 8.6%; 60–74, 3.9%; 75 and over, 1.1%. **Ethnic composition** (2000): mestizo 86.6%; Amerindian 5.5%; black (including Black Carib) 4.3%; white 2.3%; other 1.3%. **Religious affiliation** (2002): Roman Catholic 63%; Evangelical Protestant 23%; other 14%. **Major cities** (2008): Tegucigalpa 967,200; San Pedro Sula 623,100; Choloma 212,400; La Ceiba 167,300; El Progreso 118,200. **Location**: Central America, bordering the Caribbean Sea, Nicaragua, the North Pacific Ocean, El Salvador, and Guatemala.

## Vital statistics

**Birth rate** per 1,000 population (2008): 27.4 (world avg. 20.3). **Death rate** per 1,000 population (2008): 5.6 (world avg. 8.5). **Total fertility rate** (avg. births per childbearing woman; 2008): 3.20. **Life expectancy** at birth (2008): male 67.2 years; female 73.9 years.

## National economy

**Budget** (2008). *Revenue:* L 52,343,000,000 (tax revenue 80.5%; nontax revenue 8.5%; grants 11.0%). *Expenditures:* L 58,650,000,000 (current expenditures 78.7%, of which wages and salaries 41.8%; capital expenditures 21.3%). **Public debt** (external, outstanding; January 2009): US$2,900,000,000. **Production** (metric tons except as noted). *Agriculture and fishing* (2008): sugarcane 5,958,300, oil palm fruit 1,112,118, bananas 910,000, coffee 217,951, tobacco 6,500; livestock (number of live animals) 2,544,888 cattle, 490,000 pigs, 34,000,000 chickens; fisheries production (2007) 67,567 (from aquaculture 81%). *Mining and quarrying* (2007): gypsum (2005) 60,000; zinc (metal content) 38,000; silver 50,000 kg; gold 4,100 kg. *Manufacturing* (value added in L '000,000; 2008): food products, beverages, and tobacco products 21,997; textiles and wearing apparel 15,624; fabricated metal products 4,905. *Energy production (consumption):* electricity (kW-hr; 2008) 6,589,300,000 (6,589,300,000); coal (metric tons; 2006) none (190,000); petroleum products (metric tons; 2006) none (2,256,000). **Selected balance of payments data.** Receipts from (US$'000,000): tourism (2007) 557; remittances (2008) 2,824; foreign direct investment (FDI; 2005–07 avg.) 697; official development assistance (2007) 464. Disbursements for (US$'000,000): tourism (2007) 306; remittances (2008) 2.0; FDI (2005–07 avg.) 1.0. **Population economically active** (2006): total 2,811,800; activity rate of total population 40.0% (participation rates: ages 15 and over, 60.0%; female 34.7%; officially unemployed [2008] 3.5%). **Gross national income** (2008): US$13,026,000,000 (US$1,800 per capita).

## Foreign trade

**Imports** (2008; c.i.f.): US$11,088,100,000 (mineral fuels and lubricants 18.0%; textiles and wearing apparel 17.5%; machinery and electrical equipment 15.4%; food products and live animals 11.9%; chemical products 10.8%; fabricated metal products 7.1%; transportation equipment 5.9%). *Major import sources:* US 40.4%; Guatemala 8.6%; Mexico 5.5%; El Salvador 5.4%; Costa Rica 3.9%. **Exports** (2008; f.o.b.): US$5,984,200,000 (textiles and wearing apparel 49.3%; coffee 10.4%; bananas 6.4%; shrimp 2.4%; tobacco products 2.3%). *Major export destina-*

*tions:* US 40.5%; El Salvador 9.3%; Guatemala 6.9%; Mexico 6.1%; Belgium 5.9%.

## Transport and communications

**Transport.** *Railroads* (2008): serviceable lines 75 km; most tracks are out of use but not dismantled. *Roads* (2008): total length 14,239 km (paved 22%). *Vehicles* (2003): passenger cars 386,468; trucks and buses 113,744. *Air transport* (1995): passenger-km 341,000,000; metric ton-km cargo 33,000,000. **Communications**, in total units (units per 1,000 persons). Telephone landlines (2008): 826,000 (113); cellular telephone subscribers (2008): 6,211,000 (849); personal computers (2007): 143,000 (20); total Internet users (2008): 659,000 (90).

## Education and health

**Educational attainment** (2005–06). Percentage of population ages 25 and over having: no formal schooling/unknown 16.7%; incomplete primary education 37.0%; complete primary 22.7%; secondary 17.6%; higher 6.0%. **Literacy** (2007): total population ages 15 and over literate 83.1%; males literate 82.4%; females literate 83.7%. **Health:** physicians (2006) 5,977 (1 per 1,176 persons); hospital beds (2008) 6,929 (1 per 1,056 persons); infant mortality rate per 1,000 live births (2007) 20.0; undernourished population (2002–04) 1,600,000 (23% of total population based on the consumption of a minimum daily requirement of 1,780 calories).

## Military

**Total active duty personnel** (November 2008): 12,000 (army 69.2%, navy 11.7%, air force 19.1%); US troops (December 2008): 418. **Military expenditure as percentage of GDP** (2008): 0.7%; per capita expenditure US$13.

## Background

Early residents of Honduras were part of the Mayan civilization that flourished in the 1st millennium AD. Christopher Columbus reached Honduras in 1502, and permanent settlement followed. A major war between the Spanish and the Indians broke out in 1537, culminating in the decimation of the Indian population through disease and enslavement. After 1570 Honduras was part of the captaincy general of Guatemala until Central American independence in 1821. Part of the United Provinces of Central America, Honduras withdrew in 1838 and declared its independence. In the 20th century, under military rule, there was constant civil war and some intervention by the US. A civilian government assumed office in 1982. In 2009 Pres. Manuel Zelaya was ousted in a coup—the first military coup in Central America since the end of the Cold War. A military-supported regime held power only until January 2010, when an elected president took office.

## Recent Developments

Former president Manuel Zelaya's return from exile in May 2011 eliminated the final obstacle to Honduras's readmission to the Organization of American States (OAS), from which it had been suspended after Zelaya's removal from power, and in June the OAS voted to readmit Honduras. Despite this, several developments mitigated against foreign investment, not least the spread of violent crime in the country, much of which was related to drug trafficking. Moreover, some 40 people were killed during 2011 in conflicts in the Bajo Aguán region, where farmworkers occupied land that wealthy landowners had purchased in the 1990s under circumstances the farmworkers claimed were illegal.

**Internet resource:** <www.hondurastourism.com>.

# Hong Kong

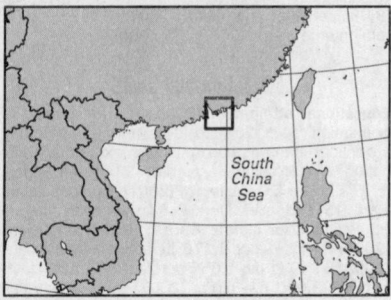

South
China
Sea

**Official name:** Xianggang Tebie Xingzhengqu (Chinese); Hong Kong Special Administrative Region (English). **Political status:** special administrative region of the People's Republic of China with one legislative house (Legislative Council [60]). **Head of state:** Chinese President Hu Jintao (from 2003). **Head of government:** Chief Executive Leung Chun Ying (from 2012). **Government offices:** Central & Western District. **Official languages:** Chinese; English. **Official religion:** none. **Monetary unit:** 1 Hong Kong dollar (HK$) = 100 cents; valuation (2 Jul 2012) US$1 = HK$7.76.

## Demography

**Area:** 426 sq mi, 1,104 sq km. **Population** (2011): 7,125,000. **Density** (2011): persons per sq mi 16,725, persons per sq km 6,454. **Urban** (2009): 100%. **Sex distribution** (2008): male 47.26%; female 52.74%. **Age breakdown** (2008): under 15, 12.8%; 15–29, 20.4%; 30–44, 24.7%; 45–59, 24.9%; 60–74, 11.0%; 75–84, 4.6%; 85 and over, 1.6%. **Ethnic composition** (2006): Chinese 95.0%; Filipino 1.6%; Indonesian 1.3%; assorted Caucasian 0.5%; Indian 0.3%; Nepalese 0.2%; other 1.1%. **Religious affiliation** (2002): nonreligious/non-practitioner of religion 57%; participant of religious practice 43%, of which Protestant 4.5%, Roman Catholic 3.5%, Muslim 1.5%, remainder (mostly Buddhist, Taoist, or Confucianist) 33.5%. **Major built-up areas** (2006): Kowloon 2,019,533; Victoria 981,714; Tuen Mun 488,249; Sha Tin 425,140; Tseung Kwan O 344,872. **Location:** eastern Asia, bordering China and the South China Sea.

## Vital statistics

**Birth rate** per 1,000 population (2008): 11.3 (world avg. 20.3). **Death rate** per 1,000 population (2008):

5.9 (world avg. 8.5). **Total fertility rate** (avg. births per childbearing woman; 2008): 1.06. **Life expectancy** at birth (2008): male 79.4 years; female 85.5 years.

## National economy

**Budget** (2007–08). *Revenue:* HK$358,465,000,000 (earnings and profits taxes 37.3%; indirect taxes 26.9%; capital revenue 22.9%). *Expenditures:* HK$252,400,000,000 (education 21.3%; social welfare 13.8%; health 13.3%; police 11.1%; housing 5.7%; economic services 5.3%). **Public debt** (external, outstanding; January 2007): US$1,673,000,000. **Gross national income** (2008): US$219,255,-000,000 (US$31,420 per capita). **Production** (metric tons except as noted). *Agriculture and fishing* (2007): vegetables 18,900, fruits 1,617; cut flowers are also produced; livestock (number of live animals) 269,100 pigs, 7,273,000 chickens; fisheries production 158,661 (from aquaculture 3%). *Quarrying* (2006): stone and aggregates 6,000,000. *Manufacturing* (value added in HK$'000; 2006): publishing and printed materials 11,954; textiles 5,580; food products 5,548. *Energy production (consumption):* electricity (kW-hr; 2006) 38,613,000,000 (44,982,000,000); coal (metric tons; 2006) none (10,878,000); petroleum products (metric tons; 2006) none (3,432,000); natural gas (cu m; 2006) none (2,322,000,000). **Selected balance of payments data.** Receipts from (US$'000,000): tourism (2007) 13,566; remittances (2008) 355; foreign direct investment (FDI; 2005–07 avg.) 46,190. Disbursements for (US$'000,000): tourism (2007) 15,086; remittances (2008) 394; FDI (2005–07 avg.) 41,789. **Population economically active** (2008): total 3,648,900; activity rate of total population 52.3% (participation rates: ages 15–64, 70.2%; female 46.5%; unemployed [March–May 2009] 5.3%).

## Foreign trade

**Imports** (2008; c.i.f.): HK$3,025,288,000,000 (capital goods 30.2%; consumer goods 26.8%; mineral fuels and lubricants 3.7%; food products 3.2%). *Major import sources:* China 46.6%; Japan 9.8%; Singapore 6.4%; Taiwan 6.3%; US 5.0%. **Exports** (2008; f.o.b.): HK$2,824,151,000,000 (reexports 96.8%, of which capital goods 32.2%, consumer goods 30.6%; domestic exports 3.2%, of which wearing apparel and accessories 0.8%). *Major export destinations:* China 48.5%; US 12.7%; Japan 4.3%; Germany 3.3%.

## Transport and communications

**Transport.** *Railroads* (2003): route length 64 km. *Roads* (2008): total length 2,040 km (paved 100%). *Vehicles* (2008): passenger cars 401,000; trucks and buses 128,000. *Air transport* (2005; Cathay Pacific and Dragonair only): passenger-km 71,595,000,000; metric ton-km cargo 8,026,-729,000. **Communications,** in total units (units per 1,000 persons). Telephone landlines (2008): 4,108,000 (564); cellular telephone subscribers (2008): 11,374,000 (1,563); personal computers (2007): 4,751,000 (686); total Internet users (2008): 4,124,000 (567); broadband Internet subscribers (2008): 1,948,000 (268).

---

*1 metric ton = about 1.1 short tons;    1 kilometer = 0.6 mi (statute);    1 metric ton-km cargo = about 0.68 short ton-mi cargo;    c.i.f.: cost, insurance, and freight;    f.o.b.: free on board*

## Education and health

**Educational attainment** (2008). Percentage of population ages 15 and over having: no formal schooling 5.4%; primary education 18.2%; secondary 46.3%; matriculation 5.4%; nondegree higher 8.2%; higher degree 16.5%. **Literacy** (2000): total population ages 15 and over literate 93.5%; males literate 96.5%; females ·literate 90.2%. **Health** (2005): physicians 11,775 (1 per 588 persons) (additionally, there were 4,848 practitioners of traditional Chinese medicine in Hong Kong at the beginning of 2006); hospital beds 33,939 (1 per 204 persons); infant mortality rate per 1,000 live births (2008) 1.7.

## Military

**Total active duty personnel** (November 2007): 7,000 troops of Chinese military (including elements of army, navy, and air force); Hong Kong residents are exempted from military service.

## Background

The island of Hong Kong and adjacent islets were ceded by China to the British in 1842, and the Kowloon Peninsula and the New Territories were later leased by the British from China for 99 years (1898–1997). A joint Chinese-British declaration, signed on 19 Dec 1984, paved the way for the entire territory to be returned to China, which occurred on 1 Jul 1997. The New Territories constitute more than nine-tenths of the total area. Hong Kong has an excellent natural harbor and is one of the world's major trade and financial centers.

## Recent Developments

Hong Kong remained economically strong in 2011. Its economy grew by an estimated 8.7%, and the unemployment rate dropped to 3.0% by year's end. The value of exports grew by 10.1%. Inflation edged up to 5.3%, however.

**Internet resource:**
<www.censtatd.gov.hk/home/index.jsp>.

# Hungary

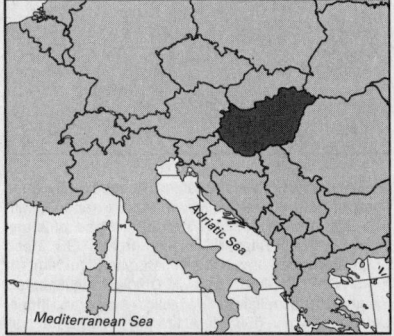

Mediterranean Sea

**Official name:** Magyarország (Hungary). **Form of government:** unitary multiparty republic with one legislative house (National Assembly [386]). Head

of state: President János Áder (from 2012). **Head of government:** Prime Minister Viktor Orbán (from 2010). **Capital:** Budapest. **Official language:** Hungarian. **Official religion:** none. **Monetary unit:** 1 forint (Ft) = 100 filler; valuation (2 Jul 2012) US$1 = Ft 227.00.

## Demography

**Area:** 35,919 sq mi, 93,030 sq km. **Population** (2011): 9,972,000. **Density** (2011): persons per sq mi 277.6, persons per sq km 107.2. **Urban** (2009): 67.7%. **Sex distribution** (2008): male 47.46%; female 52.54%. **Age breakdown** (2008): under 15, 14.9%; 15–29, 19.8%; 30–44, 22.4%; 45–59, 20.8%; 60–74, 14.9%; 75–84, 5.7%; 85 and over, 1.5%. **Ethnic composition** (2000): Hungarian 84.4%; Rom 5.3%; Ruthenian 2.9%; German 2.4%; Romanian 1.0%; Slovak 0.9%; Jewish 0.6%; other 2.5%. **Religious affiliation** (2001): Roman Catholic 51.9%; Reformed 15.9%; Lutheran 3.0%; Greek Catholic 2.6%; Jewish 0.1%; nonreligious 14.5%; other/unknown 12.0%. **Major cities** (2007): Budapest 1,702,297; Debrecen 205,084; Miskolc 171,096; Szeged 167,039; Pécs 156,664. **Location:** central Europe, bordering Slovakia, Ukraine, Romania, Serbia, Croatia, Slovenia, and Austria.

## Vital statistics

**Birth rate** per 1,000 population (2008): 9.9 (world avg. 20.3); within marriage 60.5%. **Death rate** per 1,000 population (2008): 13.0 (world avg. 8.5). **Total fertility rate** (avg. births per childbearing woman; 2008): 1.35. **Life expectancy** at birth (2007): male 69.2 years; female 77.3 years.

## National economy

**Budget** (2006). *Revenue:* Ft 8,653,000,000,000 (social security contributions 34.6%; taxes on goods and services 34.0%; income tax 13.2%). *Expenditures:* Ft 10,710,700,000,000 (social protection 38.0%; economic affairs 12.5%; health 11.6%; public debt 8.6%; education 8.6%; defense 3.1%). **Production** (metric tons except as noted). *Agriculture and fishing* (2007): corn (maize) 8,400,000, wheat 3,988,177, sugar beets 1,676,000, sunflower seeds 1,043,000, Hungarian red paprika (2006) 32,633; livestock (number of live animals) 3,987,000 pigs, 702,000 cattle, 2,708,000 geese; fisheries production 22,888 (from aquaculture 69%). *Mining and quarrying* (2007): bauxite 546,000. *Manufacturing* (value added in US$'000,000; 2005): electrical machinery and apparatus 2,436; food products and beverages 2,363; motor vehicles and parts 2,129; refined petroleum products 1,436. *Energy production (consumption):* electricity ('000,000 kW-hr; 2008) 33,586 ([2006] 43,066); coal ('000 metric tons; 2006) none (1,851); lignite ('000 metric tons; 2008) 9,333 ([2006] 10,184); crude petroleum ('000 barrels; 2008) 5,180 ([2006] 50,700); petroleum products ('000 metric tons; 2006) 6,184 (6,408); natural gas ('000,000 cu m; 2008) 2,691 ([2006] 14,689). **Selected balance of payments data.** Receipts from (US$'000,000): tourism (2007) 4,739; remittances (2008) 2,946; foreign direct investment (FDI; 2005–07 avg.) 6,690. Disbursements for (US$'000,000): tourism (2007) 2,949; remittances (2008) 1,407; FDI (2005–07 avg.) 3,314. **Population economically active** (2008): total 4,208,600; activity rate of total population 41.9% (participation rates: ages 15–64, 61.5%; female 45.7%; unemployed [August 2008–July 2009] 8.7%). **Gross national income** (2008): US$128,581,000,000 (US$12,810 per capita). **Public debt** (2008): US$107,200,000,000.

## Foreign trade

**Imports** (2007; c.i.f.): US$94,660,000,000 (electrical machinery and electronic devices 13.5%; nonelectrical machinery 12.5%; mineral fuels 9.4%; motor vehicles 8.6%). *Major import sources:* Germany 26.8%; Russia 6.9%; Austria 6.1%; China 5.4%; Italy 4.5%. **Exports** (2007; f.o.b.): US$94,591,000,000 (nonelectrical machinery 15.4%, of which engines and parts 8.1%; telecommunications equipment 11.0%; motor vehicles and parts 11.0%; electrical machinery 9.8%). *Major export destinations:* Germany 28.4%; Italy 5.6%; France 4.7%; Austria 4.5%; UK 4.5%.

## Transport and communications

**Transport.** *Railroads* (2008): route length 7,269 km; passenger-km (2007) 8,751,000,000; metric ton-km cargo (2008) 9,817,000,000. *Roads* (2007; national public roads only): total length 31,183 km (paved 99%). *Vehicles* (2008): passenger cars 3,055,000; trucks and buses 442,000. *Air transport* (2007; Malév Hungarian Airlines only): passenger-km (2007) 4,537,000,000; metric ton-km cargo (2008) 17,000,000. **Communications**, in total units (units per 1,000 persons). Telephone landlines (2008): 3,094,000 (308); cellular telephone subscribers (2008): 12,224,000 (1,218); personal computers (2007): 2,574,000 (256); total Internet users (2008): 5,500,000 (548); broadband Internet subscribers (2008): 1,542,000 (154).

## Education and health

**Educational attainment** (2007). Population ages 25–64 having: no formal schooling through lower-secondary education 20%; upper secondary/higher vocational 61%; university 17%; unknown 2%. **Health** (2007): physicians 28,189 (1 per 357 persons); hospital beds 71,902 (1 per 140 persons); infant mortality rate per 1,000 live births (2008) 5.6.

## Military

**Total active duty personnel** (November 2008): 25,207 (army 43.4%, air force 22.5%, joint staff 34.1%). **Military expenditure as percentage of GDP** (2008): 1.2%; per capita expenditure US$161.

## Background

The western part of Hungary was incorporated into the Roman Empire in 14 BC. The Magyars, a nomadic people, occupied the middle basin of the Danube River in the late 9th century AD. Stephen I, crowned in 1000, Christianized the country and organized it into a strong and independent state. Invasions by the Mongols in the 13th century and by the Ottoman Turks in the 14th century devastated the country, and by 1568 the territory of modern Hungary had been divided into three parts: Royal Hungary went to the Habsburgs; Transylvania gained autonomy in 1566 under

the Turks; and the central plain remained under Turkish control until the late 17th century, when the Austrian Habsburgs took over. Hungary declared its independence from Austria in 1849, and in 1867 the dual monarchy of Austria-Hungary was established. Its defeat in World War I resulted in the dismemberment of Hungary, leaving it only those areas in which Magyars predominated. In an attempt to regain some of this lost territory, Hungary cooperated with the Germans against the Soviet Union during World War II. After the war, a pro-Soviet provisional government was established, and in 1949 the Hungarian People's Republic was formed. Opposition to this Stalinist regime broke out in 1956 but was suppressed. Nevertheless, from 1956 to 1988 communist Hungary grew to become the most tolerant of the Soviet-bloc nations of Eastern Europe. It gained its independence in 1989 and soon attracted the largest amount of direct foreign investment in east-central Europe. In 1999 it joined NATO and in 2004 the European Union.

## Recent Developments

In March 2011, the Hungarian government presented plans to reduce public debt from about 80% of GDP to 65–70% by 2015. The government called for cuts in health care, education subsidies, and unemployment benefits to accompany a radical overhaul of the pension system. In September the government adjusted its economic growth forecast from 3.1% of GDP to under 2.0% and announced a new package of austerity measures for 2012. The package included an increase in VAT—with the top bracket rising to 27.0%, the highest rate in the EU—and included a rise in compulsory health insurance contributions and excise taxes, affecting the price of gasoline, alcohol, and tobacco products.

**Internet resource:** <http://portal.ksh.hu>.

# Iceland

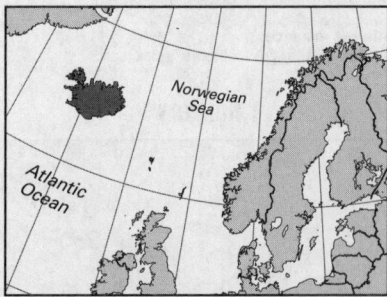

**Official name:** Lýdhveldidh Ísland (Republic of Iceland). **Form of government:** unitary multiparty republic with one legislative house (Althingi [63]). **Head of state:** President Ólafur Ragnar Grímsson (from 1996). **Head of government:** Prime Minister Jóhanna Sigurðardóttir (from 2009). **Capital:** Reykjavík. **Official language:** Icelandic. **Official religion:** Evangelical Lutheran. **Monetary unit:** 1 króna (ISK; plural krónur) = 100 aurar; valuation (2 Jul 2012) US$1 = ISK 125.44.

---

*1 metric ton = about 1.1 short tons;*   *1 kilometer = 0.6 mi (statute);*    *1 metric ton-km cargo = about 0.68 short ton-mi cargo;*    *c.i.f.: cost, insurance, and freight;*    *f.o.b.: free on board*

## Demography

**Area:** 39,769 sq mi, 103,000 sq km. **Population** (2011): 319,000. **Density** (2011): persons per sq mi 8.0, persons per sq km 3.1. **Urban** (2008): 93.1%. **Sex distribution** (2007): male 50.89%; female 49.11%. **Age breakdown** (2007): under 15, 21.0%; 15–29, 22.3%; 30–44, 21.4%; 45–59, 19.2%; 60–74, 10.4%; 75–84, 4.3%; 85 and over, 1.4%. **Ethnic composition** by citizenship (2008): Icelandic 93.2%; European 5.5%, of which Polish 2.7%, Nordic 0.6%; Asian 0.8%; other 0.5%. **Religious affiliation** (2007): Evangelical Lutheran 80.7%; Roman Catholic 2.5%; other Christian 6.8%; other/not specified 10.0%. **Major cities** (2008): Reykjavík 119,547 (urban agglomeration [2007] 195,840); Kópavogur 29,976; Hafnarfjördhur 25,850; Akureyri 17,541; Gardhabær 10,358. **Location:** northern Europe, island between the Greenland Sea, the Norwegian Sea, and the North Atlantic Ocean.

## Vital statistics

**Birth rate** per 1,000 population (2008): 15.2 (world avg. 20.3); within marriage 35.9%. **Death rate** per 1,000 population (2008): 6.3 (world avg. 8.5). **Total fertility rate** (avg. births per childbearing woman; 2008): 2.14. **Life expectancy** at birth (2008): male 79.6 years; female 83.0 years.

## National economy

**Budget** (2007). *Revenue:* ISK 454,588,000,000 (tax revenue 78.4%, of which VAT 42.9%, income tax 31.5%; nontax revenue 21.6%). *Expenditures:* ISK 403,199,000,000 (social security and health 48.8%; education 10.6%; social affairs 9.4%; interest payment 6.9%). **Production** (metric tons except as noted). *Agriculture and fishing* (2007): potatoes 13,000, tomatoes 1,603, hay 1,993,773 cu m; livestock (number of live animals) 454,812 sheep, 70,660 cattle, 41,497 mink; fisheries production (value in ISK '000,000): 80,251, of which cod 29,585, haddock 14,538, redfish 7,646, herring 5,700, saithe 4,263, capelin 4,247, blue whiting 3,022; fisheries production by tonnage 1,404,066 (from aquaculture, negligible). *Mining and quarrying* (2007): pumice 95,000. *Manufacturing* (value of sales in ISK '000,000; 2008): base metals (nearly all aluminum and ferrosilicon) 196,547; preserved and processed fish 162,252; other food products and beverages 72,049. *Energy production (consumption):* electricity (kW-hr; 2007) 11,976,000,000 (11,976,000,000); coal (metric tons; 2006) none (91,000); petroleum products (metric tons; 2006) none (797,000). **Selected balance of payments data.** Receipts from (US$'000,000): tourism (2007) 640; remittances (2008) 46; foreign direct investment (FDI) 2005–07 avg.) 3,385. Disbursements for (US$'000,000): tourism (2007) 1,341; remittances (2008) 100; FDI (2005–07 avg.) 8,180. **Population economically active** (2007): total 181,500; activity rate of total population 58.3% (participation rates: ages 16–64, 87.7%; female 45.5%; unemployed [April–June 2009] 9.1%). **Gross national income** (2008): US$12,702,000,000 (US$40,070 per capita). **Public debt** (December 2008): US$9,906,000,000.

## Foreign trade

**Imports** (2007; c.i.f.): ISK 428,509,000,000 (machinery and apparatus 22.6%; motor vehicles 11.5%; refined petroleum products 8.2%; aircraft and parts 6.6%; food products 6.3%; alumina 4.8%). *Major import sources:* US 13.5%; Germany 12.1%; Sweden 10.0%; Denmark 7.4%; Netherlands 5.6%. **Exports** (2007; f.o.b.): ISK 305,670,000,000 (fresh fish 26.6%; aluminum 26.3%; aircraft 14.6%; dried and salted fish 8.2%; fish foodstuff for animals 3.5%; ferrosilicon 2.6%). *Major export destinations:* Netherlands 21.3%; Germany 13.4%; UK 13.2%; Ireland 7.6%; US 7.5%.

## Transport and communications

**Transport.** *Railroads:* none. *Roads* (2006): total length 13,038 km (paved 33%). *Vehicles* (2007): passenger cars 207,513; trucks and buses 33,038. *Air transport* (2007; Icelandair only): passenger-km 4,252,000; metric ton-km cargo [2005] 121,591,000. **Communications,** in total units (units per 1,000 persons). Telephone landlines (2007): 187,000 (600); cellular telephone subscribers (2007): 348,000 (1,117); personal computers (2005): 142,000 (481); total Internet users (2007): 202,000 (648); broadband Internet subscribers (2008): 100,000 (315).

## Education and health

**Educational attainment** (2007). Percentage of population ages 25–64 having: primary education 3%; lower secondary 33%; upper secondary 23%; postsecondary non-tertiary 11%; higher vocational 4%; university 25%; advanced degree 1%. **Literacy:** virtually 100%. **Health:** physicians (2007) 1,157 (1 per 270 persons); hospital beds (2002) 2,162 (1 per 133 persons); infant mortality rate per 1,000 live births (2008) 2.5; undernourished population (2002–04) less than 2.5% of total population.

## Military

**Total active duty personnel** (November 2008): 130 coast guard (paramilitary) personnel; Iceland has no military. **Coast guard expenditure as percentage of GDP** (2008): 0.3%; per capita expenditure US$109.

## Background

Iceland was settled by Norwegian seafarers in the 9th century and was Christianized by 1000. Its legislature, the Althing, was founded in 930, making it one of the oldest legislative assemblies in the world. Iceland united with Norway in 1262. It became an independent state of Denmark in 1918 but severed those ties to become an independent republic in 1944. Vigdís Finnbogadóttir became the world's first female elected president in 1980.

## Recent Developments

The Icelandic economy began to show signs of an upturn in 2011, on the heels of the sharp contractions it had experienced in recent years. Real GDP increased by an estimated 2.5%, having declined by roughly 4.0% in 2010. Unemployment averaged 7.1% for the year, down slightly from 7.5%. The government continued to be plagued by the losses incurred by foreign depositors when the country's Landsbanki collapsed in 2008. Having compensated their citizens who lost money in the bank's collapse, the British and Dutch governments sought restitution from Iceland.

Internet resource: <www.statice.is>.

# India

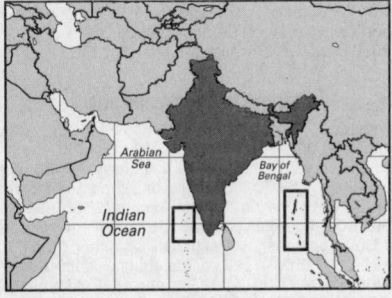

**Official name:** Bharat (Hindi); Republic of India (English). **Form of government:** multiparty federal republic with two legislative houses (Council of States [245], House of the People [545]). **Head of state:** President Pranab Mukherjee (from 2012). **Head of government:** Prime Minister Manmohan Singh (from 2004). **Capital:** New Delhi. **Official languages:** Hindi; English. **Official religion:** none. **Monetary unit:** 1 Indian rupee (₹) = 100 paise; valuation (2 Jul 2012) US$1 = ₹55.60.

## Demography

**Area:** 1,222,559 sq mi, 3,166,414 sq km (excludes 46,660 sq mi [120,849 sq km] of territory claimed by India as part of Jammu and Kashmir but occupied by Pakistan or China). **Population** (2011): 1,216,728,-000. **Density** (2011): persons per sq mi 995.2, persons per sq km 384.3. **Urban** (2011): 31.2%. **Sex distribution** (2008): male 51.87%; female 48.13%. **Age breakdown** (2008): under 15, 30.9%; 15–29, 26.9%; 30–44, 21.2%; 45–59, 13.1%; 60–74, 6.4%; 75–84, 1.3%; 85 and over, 0.2%. **Major cities (urban agglomerations)** (2006 [2007]): Mumbai (Bombay) 12,880,000 (18,978,000); Delhi 11,220,000 (15,926,000); Kolkata (Calcutta) 4,640,000 (14,787,000); Chennai (Madras) 4,350,000 (7,163,000); Bengaluru (Bangalore) 5,100,000 (6,787,000); Hyderabad 3,630,000 (6,376,000); Ahmadabad 3,770,000 (5,375,000); Pune (Poona) 3,040,000 (4,672,000); Surat 3,020,000 (3,842,000); Kanpur 2,900,000 (3,162,000); Jaipur 2,820,000 (2,917,000); Lucknow 2,540,000 (2,695,000); Nagpur 2,270,000 (2,454,000); Patna 1,660,000 (2,158,000); Vadodara (2001) 1,306,227; Bhopal 1,640,000 (1,727,000); Coimbatore (2001) 930,882; Ludhiana 1,580,000 (1,649,000); New Delhi (2001) 302,363. **Location:** southern Asia, bordering Pakistan, China, Nepal, Bhutan, Myanmar (Burma), Bangladesh, and the Indian Ocean. **Linguistic composition** (2001): Hindi

41.03%; Bengali 8.11%; Telugu 7.19%; Marathi 6.99%; Tamil 5.91%; Urdu 5.01%; Gujarati 4.48%; Kannada 3.69%; Malayalam 3.21%; Oriya 3.21%; Punjabi 2.83%; Assamese 1.28%; Maithili 1.18%; Bhili/Bhilodi 0.93%; Santhali 0.63%; Kashmiri 0.54%; Nepali 0.28%; Gondi 0.26%; Sindhi 0.25%; Konkani 0.24%; Dogri 0.22%; Khandeshi 0.20%; Tulu 0.17%; Kurukh/Oraon 0.17%; Manipuri 0.14%; Bodo 0.13%; Khasi 0.11%; Mundari 0.10%; Ho 0.10%; Sanskrit 0.0013%; other 1.41%. Hindi (roughly 66%) and English (roughly 33%) are also spoken as lingua francas. **Castes/tribes** (2001): number of Scheduled Castes (formerly referred to as "Untouchables") 166,635,700; number of Scheduled Tribes (aboriginal peoples) 84,326,240. **Religious affiliation** (2005): Hindu 72.04%; Muslim 12.26%, of which Sunni 8.06%, Shi'i 4.20%; Christian 6.81%, of which independent 3.23%, Protestant 1.74%, Roman Catholic 1.62%, Orthodox 0.22%; traditional beliefs 3.83%; Sikh 1.87%; Buddhist 0.67%; Jain 0.51%; Baha'i 0.17%; Zoroastrian (Parsi) (2000 estimate) 0.02%; nonreligious 1.22%; atheist 0.17%; other 0.43%.

## Vital statistics

**Birth rate** per 1,000 population (2008): 22.8 (world avg. 20.3). **Death rate** per 1,000 population (2008): 8.2 (world avg. 8.5). **Total fertility rate** (avg. births per childbearing woman; 2008): 2.80. **Life expectancy** at birth (2008): male 63.0 years; female 67.0 years.

## Social indicators

**Educational attainment** (2001). Percentage of population ages 25 and over having: no formal schooling 48.1%; incomplete primary education 9.0%; complete primary 22.1%; secondary 13.7%; higher 7.1%. **Quality of working life.** Average workweek (2006): 46.9. Rate of fatal injuries per 100,000 employees (2006) 38. Agricultural workers in servitude to creditors (early 1990s) 10–20%. Children ages 5–14 working as child laborers (2003): 35,000,000 (14% of age group). Percentage of population living below the poverty line (2004–05): 21.7%. **Access to services** (2005–06). Percentage of total (urban, rural) households having access to: electricity for lighting purposes 67.9% (93.1%, 55.7%), kerosene for lighting purposes (2001) 36.9% (8.3%, 46.6%), water closets 24.3% (50.8%, 11.4%), pit latrines 7.9% (7.0%, 8.6%), no latrines 55.3% (16.8%, 74.0%), closed drainage for waste water (2001) 12.5% (34.5%, 3.9%), open drainage for waste water (2001) 33.9% (43.4%, 30.3%), no drainage for waste water (2001) 53.6% (22.1%, 65.8%). Type of fuel used for cooking in households: firewood 54.4% (23.0%, 69.6%), LPG (liquefied petroleum gas) 24.7% (58.7%, 8.2%), dung 10.6% (2.8%, 14.4%), kerosene 3.2% (8.2%, 0.8%), coal 1.9% (4.3%, 0.8%). Source of drinking water: hand pump or tube well 42.8% (21.3%, 53.2%), piped water 24.5% (50.7%, 11.8%), well 9.3% (2.9%, 12.4%), river, canal, spring, public tank, pond, or lake 1.5% (0.8%, 1.8%). **Social participation.** Registered trade unions (2005): 78,465. **Social deviance** (2003). Offense rate per 100,000 population for: murder 3.1; rape 1.5; dacoity (gang robbery) 0.5; theft 23.0; riots 5.4. Rate of suicide per 100,000 population (2007): 10.5. **Material well-being** (2005–06). Total (urban, rural) households possessing: television receivers 44.2% (73.2%, 30.1%), cellular telephones 16.8% (36.3%, 7.4%), scooters, motorcycles, or mopeds 17.2% (30.5%, 10.8%), cars, jeeps, or vans 2.7% (6.1%, 1.0%). Households availing banking services (2001) 35.5% (49.5%, 30.1%).

## National economy

**Gross national income** (2008): US$1,215,485,-000,000 (US$1,070 per capita). **Budget** (2008–09). *Revenue:* ₹9,009,530,000,000 (tax revenue 51.7%, of which corporate taxes 18.3%, income tax 10.0%, excise taxes 9.8%; capital revenue 37.6%; nontax revenue 10.7%). *Expenditures:* ₹9,009,530,000,000 (current expenditures 89.2%, of which public debt payments 21.4%, subsidies 14.3%, defense 8.2%; capital expenditures 10.8%). **Public debt** (external, outstanding; 2007): US$74,419,000,000. **Production** (in '000 metric tons except as noted). *Agriculture and fishing* (2008): sugarcane 348,188, rice 148,260, wheat 78,570, potatoes 34,463, bananas 23,205, corn [maize] 19,290, mangoes 13,649, millet 11,340, seed cotton 11,305, coconuts 10,894, tomatoes 10,261, cassava 9,054, soybeans 9,045, eggplants 8,450, dry onions 8,178, sorghum 7,926, peanuts [groundnuts] 7,338, rapeseed 5,833, chickpeas 5,749, cauliflower 5,015, oranges 4,397, dry beans 3,930, okra 3,497, pigeon peas 3,076, papayas 2,686, lemons and limes 2,429, peas 2,293, apples 2,001, jute 1,846, grapes 1,677, pineapples 1,306, sweet potatoes 1,146, castor beans 1,123, sunflower seeds 1,112, natural rubber 819, tea 805, sesame 666, cashews 665, garlic 645, tobacco 520, ginger 370; livestock (number of live animals) 174,510,000 cattle, 125,732,000 goats, 98,595,000 water buffalo, 64,989,000 sheep, 14,000,000 pigs, 632,000 camels; fisheries production (2007) 7,308 (from aquaculture 46%). *Mining and quarrying* (2007): mica 1.7; iron ore (metal content) 129,000; bauxite 19,221; chromium 3,320; barite 1,000; manganese (metal content) 900; zinc (metal content) 314; lead (metal content) 77.6; copper (metal content) 34.7; silver 79,300 kg; gold 3,000 kg; gem diamonds 15,000 carats. *Manufacturing* (value added in US$'000,000; 2004): chemical products 10,804; base metals 10,109; refined petroleum products 7,214; transportation equipment 6,473; textiles and wearing apparel 5,430; food products 4,300; nonelectrical machinery 3,222; cements, bricks, and ceramics 2,958; other metals 2,120; electrical machinery 1,962. *Energy production (consumption):* electricity (kW-hr; 2008–09) 724,000,000,000 ([2006] 746,829,-000,000); coal (metric tons; 2008–09) 493,220,000 ([2007–08] 502,660,000); lignite (metric tons; 2008–09) 33,364,000 ([2007–08] 34,657,000); crude petroleum (barrels; 2008–09) 254,638,000 ([2007–08] 1,186,382,800); petroleum products (metric tons; 2008–09) 149,519,000 ([2007–08] 140,697,000); natural gas (cu m; 2008–09) 31,804,000,000 ([2007–08] 34,328,000,000). **Population economically active** (2001): total 402,234,724; activity rate of total population 39.1% (participation rates: ages 15–69, 60.2%; female 31.6%; unemployed [2008] 6.8%). **Selected balance of payments data.** Receipts from (US$'000,000): tourism (2007) 10,729; remittances (2008) 51,974; foreign direct investment (FDI; 2006–09 avg.) 30,785; official development assistance (2007) 1,298. Disbursements for (US$'000,000): tourism (2006) 7,352; remittances (2008) 1,580; FDI (2005–07 avg.) 9,823. **Service enterprises** (net value added in ₹'000,000,000; 1998–99): wholesale and retail trade 1,562; finance, real estate, and insurance 1,310; transport and storage 804; community, social, and personal services 763; construction 545.

## Foreign trade

**Imports** (2007–08): US$251,654,000,000 (crude petroleum and refined petroleum products 31.6%; electronics 8.2%; transportation equipment 8.0%; nonelectrical machinery 7.9%; gold 6.6%; chemical products 4.6%; base metals 3.5%; precious stones [significantly diamonds] 3.2%; metal ores [significantly copper ore and concentrates] 3.1%; coal 2.6%). *Major import sources:* China 10.8%; US 8.4%; Saudi Arabia 7.7%; UAE 5.4%; Iran 4.3%; Germany 3.9%; Switzerland 3.9%; Singapore 3.2%; Australia 3.1%; Kuwait 3.1%. **Exports** (2007–08): US$163,132,100,000 (refined petroleum products 17.4%; gems and jewelry [significantly diamonds] 12.1%; textiles and wearing apparel 11.9%; food products, beverages, and tobacco products 11.3%; chemical products 9.1%; machinery and apparatus 5.6%; fabricated metal products 4.3%; transportation equipment 4.3%; iron ore 3.6%). *Major export destinations:* US 12.7%; UAE 9.6%; China 6.6%; Singapore 4.5%; UK 4.1%; Hong Kong 3.9%; Netherlands 3.2%; Germany 3.1%; Belgium 2.6%; Italy 2.4%.

## Transport and communications

**Transport.** *Railroads* (2007–08): route length 63,000 km; passenger-km 735,980,000,000; metric ton-km cargo 511,854,000,000. *Roads* (2002): total length 3,319,644 km (paved 46%). *Vehicles* (2004): passenger cars 9,451,000; trucks and buses 4,516,000. *Air transport* (2008–09): passenger-km 75,932,000,000; metric ton-km cargo 1,071,-000,000. **Communications,** in total units (units per 1,000 persons). Telephone landlines (2008): 37,900,000 (32); cellular telephone subscribers (2008): 346,890,000 (294); personal computers (2007): 38,434,000 (33); total Internet users (2007): 81,000,000 (69); broadband Internet subscribers (2008): 5,280,000 (4.5).

## Education and health

**Literacy** (2007): percentage of total population ages 15 and over literate 66.0%; males literate 76.9%; females literate 54.5%. **Health** (2007): physicians (government hospitals only) 696,700 (1 per 1,696 persons); hospital beds (government hospitals only) 482,500 (1 per 2,449 persons); infant mortality rate per 1,000 live births (2008) 54.0; undernourished population (2002–04) 209,500,000 (20% of total population based on the consumption of a minimum daily requirement of 1,820 calories).

## Military

**Total active duty personnel** (November 2008): 1,281,200 (army 85.8%, navy 4.3%, air force 9.4%, coast guard 0.5%); paramilitary 1,300,586; reserve 1,155,000. **Military expenditure as percentage of GDP** (2008): 2.3%; per capita expenditure US$21.

## Background

Agriculture in India dates back to at least the 7th millennium BC, and an urban civilization, that of the

Indus valley, was established by 2600 BC. Buddhism and Jainism arose in the 6th century BC in reaction to the caste-based society created by the Vedic religion and its successor, Hinduism. Muslim invasions began about AD 1000, establishing the long-lived Delhi sultanate in 1206 and the Mughal dynasty in 1526. Vasco da Gama's voyage to India in 1498 initiated several centuries of commercial rivalry among the Portuguese, Dutch, English, and French. British conquests in the 18th and 19th centuries led to the rule of the British East India Co., and direct administration by the British Empire began in 1858. After Mohandas K. Gandhi helped end British rule in 1947, Jawaharlal Nehru became India's first prime minister, and he, Indira Gandhi (his daughter), and Rajiv Gandhi (his grandson) guided the nation's destiny for all but a few years until 1989. The subcontinent was partitioned into two countries—India, with a Hindu majority, and Pakistan, with a Muslim majority—in 1947. A later clash with Pakistan resulted in the creation of Bangladesh in 1971. In the 1980s and '90s, Sikhs sought to establish an independent state in Punjab, and ethnic and religious conflicts took place in other parts of the country as well. In 2004 Manmohan Singh, a Sikh, became the country's first non-Hindu prime minister. The Kashmir region in the northwest has been a source of constant tension.

## Recent Developments

India entered 2011 on a high note in foreign affairs as a unanimously elected member of the UN Security Council, and in November India captured the Asia-Pacific region's lone seat in the UN Joint Inspection Unit. Prime Minister Manmohan Singh's visit to Dhaka helped strengthen relations with Bangladesh, and a "creeping normalization" of relations with Pakistan enabled Pakistan's beleaguered civilian leadership to approve extending to India the World Trade Organization's most-favored-nation status. Singh participated in the East Asia Summit in Indonesia, and in October he and Myanmar Pres. Thein Sein agreed to bolster ties in several areas, including trade and oil and gas exploration. The possibility of a new strategic partnership between India and Australia was raised in November when the latter signaled its willingness to allow the sale of uranium to New Delhi. In April 2012, India's military tested a nuclear-capable missile with a range large enough to allow India to strike the Chinese cities of Beijing and Shanghai.

Internet resource: <http://mospi.nic.in>.

# Indonesia

Official name: Republik Indonesia (Republic of Indonesia). Form of government: multiparty republic with two legislative houses (Regional Representatives Council [128]; House of Representatives [560]). Head of state and government: President Susilo Bambang Yudhoyono (from 2004). Capital: Jakarta. Official language: Indonesian (Bahasa Indonesia). Official religion: monotheism. Monetary unit: 1 Indonesian rupiah (Rp) = 100 sen; valuation (2 Jul 2012) US$1 = Rp 9,380.00.

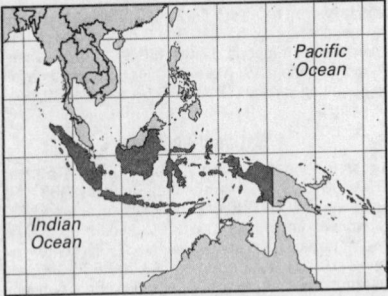

## Demography

Area: 737,815 sq mi, 1,910,931 sq km. Population (2011): 241,343,000. Density (2011): persons per sq mi 327.1, persons per sq km 126.3. Urban (2009): 44.0%. Sex distribution (2006): male 50.01%; female 49.99%. Age breakdown (2006): under 15, 29.1%; 15–29, 27.0%; 30–44, 22.2%; 45–59, 13.5%; 60–74, 6.7%; 75–84, 1.4%; 85 and over, 0.1%. Ethnic composition (2000): Javanese 36.4%; Sundanese 13.7%; Malay 9.4%; Madurese 7.2%; Han Chinese 4.0%; Minangkabau 3.6%; other 25.7%. Religious affiliation (2005): Muslim (excluding syncretists) 55.8%; Neoreligionists (syncretists) 21.2%; Christian 13.2%; Hindu 3.2%; traditional beliefs 2.6%; nonreligious 1.8%; other 2.2%. Major municipalities (2005): Jakarta 8,603,349; Surabaya 2,611,506; Bandung 2,288,570; Medan 2,029,797; Bekasi 1,940,308; Tangerang 1,451,595; Semarang 1,352,869; Depok 1,339,263; Palembang 1,323,169; Makasar 1,168,258. Location: archipelago in southeastern Asia, bordering Malaysia, the Pacific Ocean, Papua New Guinea, the Indian Ocean, and East Timor (Timor-Leste).

## Vital statistics

Birth rate per 1,000 population (2006): 20.1 (world avg. 20.3). Death rate per 1,000 population (2006): 6.3 (world avg. 8.5). Total fertility rate (avg. births per childbearing woman; 2006): 2.41. Life expectancy at birth (2006): male 67.4 years; female 72.4 years.

## National economy

Budget (2005). Revenue: Rp 495,444,000,000,000 (tax revenue 70.0%, of which income tax 35.4%, VAT 20.4%; nontax revenue 30.0%, of which revenue from petroleum 14.7%). Expenditures: Rp 509,419,000,-000,000 (current expenditures 58.5%; regional expenditures 29.5%; developmental expenditures 12.0%). Public debt (external, outstanding; December 2007): US$80,609,000,000. Population economically active (2005): total 106,388,935; activity rate 46.5% (participation rates: ages 16 and over, 66.2%; unemployed 10.3%). Production (metric tons except as noted). Agriculture and fishing (2008): oil palm fruit 85,000,000, rice 60,251,072, sugarcane 26,000,000, cassava 21,593,052, coconuts 19,500,000, corn (maize) 16,323,922, natural rubber 2,921,872, cacao beans 792,761, cloves

1 metric ton = about 1.1 short tons;    1 kilometer = 0.6 mi (statute);    1 metric ton-km cargo = about 0.68 short ton-mi cargo;    c.i.f.: cost, insurance, and freight;    f.o.b.: free on board

80,929, cinnamon 60,000; livestock (number of live animals) 15,805,900 goats, 11,869,200 cattle, 8,355,764 sheep; fisheries production (2007) 6,329,533 (from aquaculture 22%); aquatic plants production (2007) 1,733,705 (from aquaculture 99%). *Mining and quarrying* (2007): bauxite 1,251,000; copper (metal content) 796,000; nickel (metal content) 229,200; silver 268,967 kg; gold 117,851 kg. *Manufacturing* (value added in US$'000,000; 2003): textiles, wearing apparel, and footwear 5,011; tobacco products 4,584; transportation equipment 4,189; food products 3,970; chemical products 3,464; paper products 1,774. *Energy production (consumption):* electricity (kW-hr; 2006) 133,108,000,000 (133,108,000,000); coal (metric tons; 2007) 174,800,000 ([2006] 21,201,000); crude petroleum (barrels; 2007) 357,500,000 ([2006] 329,040,000); petroleum products (metric tons; 2006) 42,347,000 (52,700,000); natural gas (cu m; 2007) 85,200,000,000 (37,700,000,000). **Gross national income** (2008): US$458,159,-000,000 (US$2,010 per capita). **Selected balance of payments data.** Receipts from (US$'000,000): tourism (2007) 5,346; remittances (2008) 6,795; foreign direct investment (FDI; 2005–07 avg.) 6,726; official development assistance (2006) 1,404. Disbursements for (US$'000,000): tourism (2007) 4,446; remittances (2008) 1,766; FDI (2005–07 avg.) 3,519.

## Foreign trade

**Imports** (2005–06; c.i.f.): US$65,712,154,000 (crude petroleum and natural gas 23.7%; machinery and apparatus 16.8%; chemical products 10.4%; base metals 8.8%; transportation equipment 6.5%). *Major import sources* (2006): Singapore 16.4%; China 10.9%; Japan 9.0%; US 6.7%; Saudi Arabia 5.5%. **Exports** (2005–06; f.o.b.): US$78,740,-892,000 (crude petroleum and natural gas 27.4%; rubber products 15.7%; machinery and apparatus 14.5%; textiles 10.8%; base metals 7.0%; paper products 4.2%). *Major export destinations* (2006): Japan 21.6%; US 11.2%; Singapore 8.9%; China 8.3%; South Korea 7.6%.

## Transport and communications

**Transport.** *Railroads* (2007): route length 4,803 km; passenger-km 15,872,000,000; metric ton-km cargo 4,425,000,000. *Roads* (2007): length 396,362 km (paved 56%). *Vehicles* (2007): passenger cars 52,902,100; trucks and buses 4,845,900. *Air transport* (2005): passenger-km 22,986,000,000; metric ton-km cargo (2004) 248,000,000. **Communications,** in total units (units per 1,000 persons). Telephone landlines (2008): 30,378,000 (134); cellular telephone subscribers (2008): 140,578,000 (618); personal computers (2005): 3,285,000 (15); total Internet users (2008): 30,000,000 (132); broadband Internet subscribers (2007): 257,000 (1.1).

## Education and health

**Educational attainment** (2002–03). Percentage of population ages 15–64 having: no schooling or incomplete primary education 19.3%; primary and some secondary 57.2%; complete secondary 19.3%; higher 4.2%. **Literacy** (2007): total population ages 15 and over literate 91.9%; males literate 95.2%; females literate 88.6%. **Health:** physicians (2003) 29,499 (1 per 7,368 persons); hospital beds (2001) 124,834 (1 per 1,697 persons); infant mortality rate per 1,000 live births (2006) 33.3; undernourished population (2003–05) 37,100,000 (17% of total population based on the consumption of a minimum daily requirement of 1,810 calories).

## Military

**Total active duty personnel** (November 2008): 302,000 (army 77.2%, navy 14.9%, air force 7.9%). **Military expenditure as percentage of GDP** (2007): 1.0%; per capita expenditure US$19.

## Background

Proto-Malay peoples migrated to Indonesia from mainland Asia before 1000 BC. Commercial relations were established with China in about the 5th century AD, and Hindu and Buddhist cultural influences from India began to take hold. Arab traders brought Islam to the islands in the 13th century; the religion took hold throughout the islands, except for Bali, which retained its Hindu religion and culture. European influence began in the 16th century, and the Dutch ruled Indonesia from the late 17th century until 1942, when the Japanese invaded. Independence leader Sukarno declared Indonesia's sovereignty in 1945, which the Dutch granted, with nominal union to the Netherlands, in 1949; Indonesia dissolved this union in 1954. The suppression of an alleged coup attempt in 1965 resulted in the deaths of more than 300,000 people the government claimed to be communists, and by 1968 Gen. Suharto had taken power. His government forcibly incorporated East Timor (Timor-Leste) into Indonesia in 1975–76, with much loss of life; East Timor became independent in 2002. In the 1990s the country was beset by political, economic, and environmental problems, and Suharto was deposed in 1998. In 2004 a large tsunami generated by an earthquake off the western coast of Sumatra caused widespread death and destruction.

## Recent Developments

In 2011, Indonesia won plaudits for its impressive economic growth and stable democratic political system. Pres. Susilo Bambang Yudhoyono, in particular, continued to be widely praised by Western leaders for his moderate and statesmanlike leadership. Economically, Indonesia was one of the best-performing countries in Southeast Asia; overall economic growth stood at 6.5%, inflation fell below 5.0%, international investment was strong, and unemployment declined. The size of Indonesia's middle class (estimated by the World Bank to be greater than 80 million) had doubled in seven years, and that group's high-spending behavior fueled robust domestic retail sales and demand. Industries that were previously shrinking, such as footwear and textiles, bounced back strongly. Indonesia's high GDP growth, abundant food and energy, favorable demographic trends, and high consumption patterns led the World Bank to predict that by 2040 the country would rank as one of the fastest-growing economies, along with those of such countries as China, India, and Turkey.

**Internet resource:** <www.bps.go.id/eng>.

# Iran

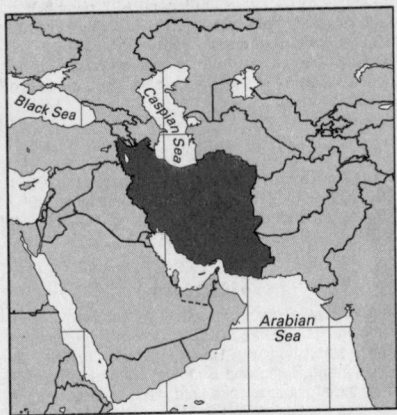

**Official name:** Jomhuri-ye Eslami-ye Iran (Islamic Republic of Iran). **Form of government:** unitary Islamic republic with one legislative house (Islamic Consultative Assembly [290]). **Supreme political/religious authority:** *Rahbar* (Spiritual Leader) Ayatollah Sayyed Ali Khamenei (from 1989). **Head of state and government:** President Mahmoud Ahmadinejad (from 2005). **Capital:** Tehran. **Official language:** Farsi (Persian). **Official religion:** Islam. **Monetary unit:** 1 rial (Rls) = 100 dinars; valuation (2 Jul 2012) US$1 = Rls 12,282.50.

## Demography

**Area** (land area only): 628,874 sq mi, 1,628,777 sq km. **Population** (2011): 75,256,000. **Density** (2011): persons per sq mi 118.3, persons per sq km 45.7. **Urban** (2009–10): 71.8%. **Sex distribution** (2006–07): male 50.88%; female 49.12%. **Age breakdown** (2006–07): under 15, 25.1%; 15–29, 35.4%; 30–44, 20.6%; 45–59, 11.6%; 60–74, 5.4%; 75–84, 1.6%; 85 and over, 0.3%. **Ethnic composition** (2000): Persian 34.9%; Azerbaijani 15.9%; Kurd 13.0%; Luri 7.2%; Gilaki 5.1%; Mazandarani 5.1%; Afghan 2.8%; other 16.0%. **Religious affiliation** (2005): Muslim 98.2% (Shiʿi 86.1%, Sunni 10.1%, other 2.0%); Baha'i 0.5%; Christian 0.4%; Zoroastrian 0.1%; other 0.8%. **Major cities** (2006): Tehran 7,797,520; Mashhad 2,427,316; Esfahan 1,602,110; Tabriz 1,398,060; Karaj 1,386,030. **Location:** the Middle East, bordering the Caspian Sea, Turkmenistan, Afghanistan, Pakistan, the Gulf of Oman, the Persian Gulf, Iraq, Turkey, Azerbaijan, and Armenia.

## Vital statistics

**Birth rate** per 1,000 population (2006–07): 17.8 (world avg. 20.3). **Death rate** per 1,000 population (2006–07): 5.8 (world avg. 8.5). **Total fertility rate** (avg. births per childbearing woman; 2007): 1.83. **Life expectancy** at birth (2007): male 70.0 years; female 72.7 years.

## National economy

**Budget** (2007–08). *Revenue:* Rls 791,199,000,-000,000 (petroleum and natural gas revenue 69.4%; taxes 20.5%, of which taxes on income and profits 12.3%). *Expenditures:* Rls 691,225,000,000,000 (current expenditures 72.8%; development expenditures 21.4%). **Public debt** (external, outstanding; 2007): US$11,146,000,000. **Gross national income** (2007): US$251,486,000,000 (US$3,540 per capita). **Production** (metric tons except as noted). *Agriculture and fishing* (2007): wheat 15,000,000, sugarcane 5,700,000, sugar beets 5,300,000, dates 1,000,000, pistachios 230,000; livestock (number of live animals) 52,220,000 sheep, 25,860,000 goats, 9,776,000 cattle, 146,000 camels; fisheries production 562,424 (from aquaculture 28%). *Mining and quarrying* (2007): iron ore (metal content) 11,000,000; copper ore (metal content) 260,000; chromite 225,000; zinc (metal content) 100,000. *Manufacturing* (value added in US$'000,000; 2005): base metals 3,032; motor vehicles and parts 2,850; refined petroleum products 2,210. *Energy production (consumption):* electricity (kW-hr; 2008) 206,300,000,000 ([2006] 200,794,000,000); coal (metric tons; 2006) 1,520,000 (1,930,000); crude petroleum (barrels; 2008) 1,486,000,000 ([2006] 517,000,000); petroleum products (metric tons; 2006) 75,336,000 (67,265,000); natural gas (cu m; 2007) 111,909,000,000 ([2006] 104,082,000,000). **Population economically active** (2006–07): total 23,469,000; activity rate of total population 33.3% (participation rates: ages 10 and over, 39.4%; female 15.5%; unemployed [October–December 2008] 9.5%). **Selected balance of payments data.** Receipts from (US$'000,000): tourism (2007) 1,486; remittances (2008) 1,115; foreign direct investment (FDI; 2005–07 avg.) 663; official development assistance (2007) 102. Disbursements for (US$'000,000): tourism (2007) 6,002; FDI (2005–07 avg.) 380.

## Foreign trade

**Imports** (2005–06): US$40,969,000,000 (nonelectrical machinery 23.5%; base metals 13.8%; motor vehicles 13.0%; chemical products 10.7%). *Major import sources:* UAE 19.7%; Germany 13.1%; France 6.8%; Italy 6.0%; China 5.5%. **Exports** (2005–06): US$60,013,000,000 (crude petroleum 73.1%; chemical products 5.2%; fruits and nuts 2.2%, of which pistachios 1.4%; wool carpets 0.8%). *Major export destinations:* Japan 16.9%; China 11.9%; Turkey 5.8%; Italy 5.7%; South Korea 5.7%.

## Transport and communications

**Transport.** *Railroads* (2006–07): route length 8,565 km; passenger-km 12,549,000,000; metric ton-km cargo 20,542,000,000. *Roads* (2006–07): length 72,611 km (paved 92%). *Vehicles* (2006–07): passenger cars 920,136; trucks and buses 184,629. *Air transport* (2008; Iran Air, Iran Aseman Airlines, and Mahan Air only): passenger-km 11,760,610,000; metric ton-km cargo 110,843,000. **Communications,** in total units (units per 1,000 persons). Telephone landlines (2008): 24,800,000 (338); cellular telephone subscribers (2008): 43,000,000 (587); personal computers (2007): 7,678,000 (106); total In-

---

*1 metric ton = about 1.1 short tons;   1 kilometer = 0.6 mi (statute);   1 metric ton-km cargo = about 0.68 short ton-mi cargo;   c.i.f.: cost, insurance, and freight;   f.o.b.: free on board*

ternet users (2008): 23,000,000 (314); broadband
Internet subscribers (2008): 300,000 (4.1).

## Education and health

Literacy (2006–07): total population ages 6 and over
literate 84.6%; males literate 88.7%; females literate
80.3%. Health (2006–07): physicians (public sector
only) 29,937 (1 per 2,355 persons); hospital beds
116,474 (1 per 605 persons); infant mortality rate
per 1,000 live births (2007) 29.1; undernourished
population (2002–04) 2,500,000 (4% of total population based on the consumption of a minimum daily
requirement of 1,850 calories).

## Military

Total active duty personnel (November 2008):
523,000 (revolutionary guard corps 23.9%, army
66.9%, navy 3.5%, air force 5.7%). Military expenditure as percentage of GDP (2007): 2.9%; per capita
expenditure US$103.

## Background

Habitation in Iran dates to 100,000 BC, but recorded
history began with the Elamites in 3000 BC. The
Medes flourished from about 728 BC but were overthrown (550 BC) by the Persians, who were in turn
conquered by Alexander the Great in the 4th century
BC. The Parthians created a Greek-speaking empire
that lasted from 247 BC to AD 226, when control
passed to the Sasanians. Arab Muslims conquered
them in 640 and ruled Iran for 850 years. In 1502
the Safavids established a dynasty that lasted until
1736. The Qajars ruled from 1779, but in the 19th
century the country was controlled economically by
the Russian and British empires. Reza Khan seized
power in a coup (1921). His son Mohammad Reza
Shah Pahlavi alienated religious leaders with a program of modernization and Westernization and was
overthrown in 1979; Shi'ite cleric Ruhollah Khomeini
then set up a fundamentalist Islamic republic, and
Western influence was suppressed. The destructive
Iran-Iraq War of the 1980s ended in a stalemate.
Among the most contentious of Iran's foreign policy
issues at the beginning of the 21st century was the
ongoing question of the development of its nuclear
capabilities. Iran insisted that its nuclear pursuits
were intended for peaceful purposes, but the international community, expressing deep suspicion that
Iran's activities included the development of nuclear
weapons, advocated efforts to suspend them.

## Recent Developments

Iran, which rejected any capitulation on its right to produce weapons-grade uranium for peaceful research
purposes, remained embroiled in international disputes in 2011. In November international attention
was focused on Iran's nuclear activities when the International Atomic Energy Agency issued a report pre-
senting evidence that Iran was secretly developing nuclear weapons. Later that month Iranian officials
announced that they were fighting a recently discovered computer worm similar to the Stuxnet worm that
was believed to have been employed in a cyber attack
on Iran's nuclear facilities in 2010. The next day an unexplained explosion at a missile base, which Iran described only as an "accident," killed 17 Revolutionary
Guard members, including the man who was the ar-

chitect of Iran's missile program. As international sanctions continued to affect Iran at year's end, its military
leaders threatened to shut the Strait of Hormuz, the
narrow channel linking the Persian Gulf with the Arabian Sea through which much of the world's petroleum
shipments pass. Although officials later backed away
from the threat, the potential consequences of the
strait's closure—from soaring energy costs to probable
military conflict—were sobering considerations.

Internet resource:
<www.amar.org.ir/Default.aspx?tabid=133>.

# Iraq

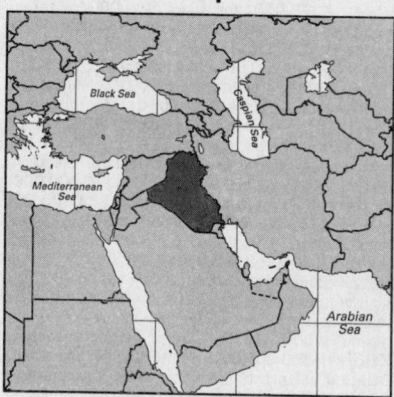

Official name: Al-Jumhuriyah al-ʿIraqiyah (Republic of
Iraq). Form of government: multiparty republic with
one legislative house (Council of Representatives of
Iraq [325]). Head of state: President Jalal Talabani
(from 2005). Head of government: Prime Minister
Nuri al-Maliki (from 2006). Capital: Baghdad. Official
languages: Arabic; Kurdish. Official religion: Islam.
Monetary unit: 1 Iraqi dinar (ID) = 1,000 fils; valuation (2 Jul 2012) US$1 = ID 1,162.00.

## Demography

Area: 167,618 sq mi, 434,128 sq km. Population
(2011): 32,665,000. Density (2011): persons per sq
mi 194.9, persons per sq km 75.2. Urban (2009):
66.3%. Sex distribution (2007): male 50.35%; female 49.65%. Age breakdown (2007): under 15,
43.1%; 15–29, 27.9%; 30–44, 16.4%; 45–59, 8.2%;
60–74, 3.3%; 75 and over, 1.0%. Ethnic composition
(2000): Arab 64.7%; Kurd 23.0%; Turkmen/Azerbai-
jani 6.8%; other 5.5%. Religious affiliation (2000):
Shiʿi Muslim 62.0%; Sunni Muslim 34.0%; Christian
(primarily Chaldean rite and Syrian rite Catholic and
Nestorian) 3.2%; other (primarily Yazidi syncretist)
0.8%. Major urban agglomerations (2007): Baghdad
5,054,000; Mosul 1,316,000; Irbil 926,000; Al-Bas-
rah 870,000; Karkuk (2003) 750,000. Location: the
Middle East, bordering Turkey, Iran, the Persian Gulf,
Kuwait, Saudi Arabia, Jordan, and Syria.

## Vital statistics

Birth rate per 1,000 population (2008): 30.7 (world
avg. 20.3). Death rate per 1,000 population (2008):

5.1 (world avg. 8.5). **Total fertility rate** (avg. births per childbearing woman; 2008): 3.97. **Life expectancy** at birth (2008): male 68.3 years; female 71.0 years.

## National economy

**Budget** (2007). *Revenue:* ID 58,714,000,000,000 (crude oil export revenue 80.3%; oil-related public enterprises 9.8%; grants 4.9%). *Expenditures:* ID 48,153,000,000,000 (current expenditures 79.6%; development expenditures 20.4%). **Public debt** (external, outstanding; September 2009): US$70,000,-000,000–US$120,000,000,000. **Production** (metric tons except as noted). *Agriculture and fishing* (2008): wheat 2,228,000, tomatoes 830,000, potatoes 598,000, dates 440,000; livestock (number of live animals) 6,200,000 sheep, 1,650,000 goats, 1,500,000 cattle, 9,500 camels; fisheries production (2007) 73,589 (from aquaculture 21%). *Mining and quarrying* (2007): salt 25,000. *Manufacturing* (2007): gasoline 19,000,000 barrels; distillate fuels 19,000,000 barrels; residual fuels 58,000,000 barrels. *Energy production (consumption):* electricity (kW-hr; 2006) 31,869,000,000 (33,170,000,000); crude petroleum (barrels; 2008) 884,000,000 ([2006] 178,900,000); petroleum products (metric tons; 2006) 19,703,000 (21,896,000); natural gas (cu m; 2006) 3,408,000,000 (3,408,000,000). **Population economically active** (2006): total 7,002,000; activity rate of total population 24.6% (participation rates: ages 15–64, 43.3%; female 16.8%; unemployed [2009] 18.0%). **Gross national income** (2007): US$69,800,000,000 (US$2,367 per capita). **Selected balance of payments data.** Receipts from (US$'000,000): remittances (2008) 389; foreign direct investment (FDI; 2005–07 avg.) 449; official development assistance (2007) 9,115. Disbursements for (US$'000,000): remittances (2008) 781; FDI (2005–07 avg.) 180.

## Foreign trade

**Imports** (2007): US$18,289,000,000 (private sector imports 55.7%, of which capital goods 41.8%, consumer goods 13.9%; government imports 44.3%, of which refined petroleum products 7.9%). *Major import sources* (2008): Syria 27.6%; Turkey 20.6%; US 11.2%; China 6.2%; Jordan 4.7%. **Exports** (2007): US$39,590,000,000 (crude petroleum 95.4%; refined petroleum products 4.0%; other 0.6%). *Major export destinations* (2008): US 43.5%; Italy 11.0%; South Korea 7.3%; Canada 4.5%; France 4.1%.

## Transport and communications

**Transport.** *Railroads* (2006): route length 580 sq km. *Roads* (2002): total length 45,550 km (paved 84%). *Vehicles* (2001): passenger cars 754,066; trucks and buses 372,241. *Air transport:* n.a. (Iraqi Airways resumed international flights in September 2004 after 14 years of being grounded by war and sanctions). **Communications,** in total units (units per 1,000 persons). Telephone landlines (2008): 1,082,000 (36); cellular telephone subscribers (2009): 17,700,000 (585); total Internet users (2007): 275,000 (9.3).

## Education and health

**Educational attainment** (2004). Percentage of population ages 25 and over having: no formal schooling 28%; incomplete primary education 12%; primary 36%; secondary 9%; higher 15%. **Literacy** (2003): total population ages 15 and over literate 40.4%; males literate 55.9%; females literate 24.4%. **Health** (2008): physicians 16,000 (1 per 1,901 persons); hospital beds (2003) 34,505 (1 per 778 persons); infant mortality rate per 1,000 live births 46.2.

## Military

**Total active duty personnel** (November 2008): 577,056 (army/national guard 32.4%, navy 0.3%, air force 0.3%, ministry of interior/police 67.0%); US forces (August 2009): 130,000.

## Background

Called Mesopotamia in Classical times, the region gave rise to the world's earliest civilizations, including those of Sumer, Akkad, and Babylon. Conquered by Alexander the Great in 330 BC, the area later became a battleground between Romans and Parthians and then between Sasanians and Byzantines. Arab Muslims conquered it in the 7th century AD and ruled until the Mongols took over in 1258. The Ottomans took control in the 16th century and ruled until 1917. The British occupied the country during World War I and created the kingdom of Iraq in 1921. The British occupied Iraq again during World War II. A king was restored following the war, but a revolution ended the monarchy in 1958. Following a series of military coups, the socialist Ba'th Party, led by Saddam Hussein, took control and established totalitarian rule in 1968. The Iran-Iraq War of the 1980s and the Persian Gulf War (precipitated by the Iraqi invasion of Kuwait in 1990) brought heavy casualties and disrupted the economy. The 1990s were dominated by economic and political turmoil. In response to increasingly willful and autocratic behavior by Saddam and the contention that Iraq was in possession of weapons of mass destruction (none were ever found), on 19 Mar 2003 air attacks on Baghdad began, and soon afterward US and British ground forces invaded southern Iraq from Kuwait; within a month most of the country was under the control of coalition forces. Saddam was taken into custody in December. In July 2003 US authorities established an Iraqi Governing Council, and a new interim constitution was agreed upon in late February 2004. Almost immediately after the occupation began, however, various forms of Iraqi opposition arose, and resistance attacks grew in frequency and violence in the years that followed.

## Recent Developments

Security in Iraq in 2011 improved, though some assassinations, political violence, and kidnappings persisted. A notable exception to the improved security situation occurred in September when gunmen, presumably Sunni extremists, stopped a bus carrying Shi'ite pilgrims near the town of Al-Nukhayb and killed 22 men aboard. The incident provoked outrage and calls for revenge among Iraq's Shi'ites. In the summer Usama al-Nujayfi, the Sunni speaker of the Council of

---

*1 metric ton = about 1.1 short tons;    1 kilometer = 0.6 mi (statute);    1 metric ton-km cargo = about 0.68 short ton-mi cargo;    c.i.f.: cost, insurance, and freight;    f.o.b.: free on board*

Representatives, stated that unless conditions for Sunnis improved, they might call for the creation of a Sunni semiautonomous region, similar to that of the Kurds in northern Iraq, which would incorporate at a minimum the three Sunni-dominated governorates of Salah al-Din, Anbar, and Ninawa. Support for a Sunni semiautonomous region gained strength in October when the government arrested hundreds of Sunnis across Iraq after vague accusations of plans for a Ba'thist coup following the withdrawal of US forces. In addition, the government fired 145 faculty and staff members from the University of Tikrit, all of them Sunnis. The government justified the firings by claiming that it was implementing a 2008 de-Ba'thification law that had replaced a decree issued after the US occupation began in 2003.

According to an agreement between Iraq and the United States signed in 2008, all American troops were scheduled to leave the country by the end of 2011. Throughout the year negotiations between the two countries took place over whether to allow some troops to stay in Iraq to train the Iraqi army and security forces. Iraqis firmly rejected the Americans' insistence on legal immunity for any troops left in Iraq. Although some Iraqi factions remained open to the possibility of a continued US military presence, the staunchly anti-American cleric Muqtada al-Sadr, whose political support Prime Minister Nuri al-Maliki required in order to remain in power, used pressure and threats to force a complete US withdrawal from Iraq. After months of internal debate and hesitation, the Iraqi government finally decided to ask the US to withdraw all its troops by the end of the year. The American withdrawal raised questions such as whether Iran would try to fill the vacuum left in Iraq and how Iraqi forces would be trained to use the US equipment purchased by the Iraqi military. In addition, there were fears that sectarian violence might resume. In an effort to address uncertainties related to the American withdrawal, Nuri al-Maliki visited Washington on 12 December for talks with Pres. Barack Obama and his administration. The last remaining US troops left Iraq on 18 December.

Internet resource: <http://cosit.gov.iq/english>.

# Ireland

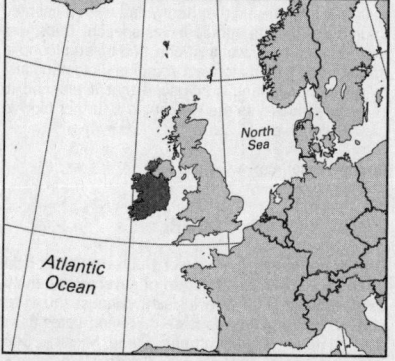

**Official name:** Éire (Irish); Ireland (English). **Form of government:** unitary multiparty republic with two leg-islative houses (Senate [60]; House of Representatives [166]). **Head of state:** President Michael D. Higgins (from 2011). **Head of government:** Prime Minister Enda Kenny (from 2011). **Capital:** Dublin. **Official languages:** Irish; English. **Official religion:** none. **Monetary unit:** 1 euro (€) = 100 cents; valuation (2 Jul 2012) US$1 = €0.79.

## Demography

**Area:** 27,133 sq mi, 70,273 sq km. **Population** (2011): 4,606,000. **Density** (2011): persons per sq mi 169.8, persons per sq km 65.5. **Urban** (2005): 60.5%. **Sex distribution** (2008): male 49.89%; female 50.11%. **Age breakdown** (2008): under 15, 20.6%; 15–29, 23.4%; 30–44, 23.1%; 45–59, 17.5%; 60–74, 10.6%; 75–84, 3.6%; 85 and over, 1.2%. **Ethnic composition** (2000): Irish 95.0%; British 1.7%, of which English 1.4%; Ulster Irish 1.0%; US white 0.8%; other 1.5%. **Religious affiliation** (2006): Roman Catholic 86.8%; Church of Ireland (Anglican) 3.0%; other Christian 2.7%; nonreligious 4.4%; other 3.1%. **Major cities** (2006): Dublin 506,211 (urban agglomeration 1,186,159); Cork 119,418; Galway 72,414; Limerick 52,539; Waterford 45,748. **Location:** western Europe, bordering the UK (Northern Ireland), the Irish Sea, the Celtic Sea, and the North Atlantic Ocean.

## Vital statistics

**Birth rate** per 1,000 population (2008): 16.9 (world avg. 20.3); (2006) within marriage 66.8%. **Death rate** per 1,000 population (2007): 6.4 (world avg. 8.5). **Total fertility rate** (avg. births per childbearing woman; 2007): 2.03. **Life expectancy** at birth (2006): male 76.8 years; female 81.6 years.

## National economy

**Budget** (2005). *Revenue:* €39,849,000,000 (VAT 30.3%; income tax 28.3%; corporate taxes 13.5%). *Expenditures:* €33,496,000,000 (current expenditures 88.4%; capital expenditures 11.6%). *Total public debt* (2008): US$90,000,000,000. **Gross national income** (2008): US$221,158,000,000 (US$49,590 per capita). **Production** (metric tons except as noted). *Agriculture and fishing* (2007): barley 1,125,000, wheat 713,000, potatoes 399,000; livestock (number of live animals) 6,704,000 cattle, 5,522,000 sheep, 1,588,000 pigs; fisheries production 284,246 (from aquaculture 20%). *Mining and quarrying* (2005): zinc ore (metal content) 428,596; lead ore (metal content) 63,810. *Manufacturing* (gross value added in €'000,000; 2005): chemical products 12,000; electrical and optical equipment 7,097; food products, beverages, and tobacco products 6,391. *Energy production (consumption):* electricity (kW-hr; 2007) 27,888,000,000 ([2006] 29,824,000,000); coal (metric tons; 2006) none (2,597,000); crude petroleum (barrels; 2006) none (22,974,000); petroleum products (metric tons; 2006) 3,223,000 (7,384,000); natural gas (cu m; 2007) 498,000,000 ([2006] 4,784,000,000); peat (metric tons; 2006) 4,300,000 (n.a.). **Population economically active** (2005): total 2,014,800; activity rate 48.8% (participation rates: ages 15–64, 70.2%; female 42.3%; unemployed [March 2005–February 2006] 4.4%). **Selected balance of payments data.** Receipts from (US$'000,000): tourism (2007) 6,140; remittances (2008) 643; foreign direct disinvestment (2005–07 avg.) −2,213. Disbursements for

(US$'000,000): tourism (2007) 8,682; remittances (2008) 2,691; foreign direct investment (2005–07 avg.) 16,804.

## Foreign trade

**Imports** (2007; c.i.f.): €62,173,000,000 (machinery and transportation equipment 40.2%, of which office machines and parts 14.8%, motor vehicles 7.0%, electrical machinery 5.2%; chemical products 13.2%; mineral fuels 7.9%; food products 7.2%). *Major import sources* (2006): UK 30.1%; US 11.3%; Germany 8.7%; China 8.3%; Netherlands 4.2%. **Exports** (2007; f.o.b.): €88,581,000,000 (organic chemical products 21.9%; medicinal and pharmaceutical products 16.5%; office machines and parts 14.2%; food products 8.3%). *Major export destinations* (2007): UK 18.7%; US 17.8%; Belgium 14.3%; Germany 7.5%; France 5.8%.

## Transport and communications

**Transport.** *Railroads* (2007): route length (2004) 3,312 km; passenger-km 2,007,065,000; metric ton-km cargo 128,908,000. *Roads* (2003): length 96,602 km (paved 100%). *Vehicles* (2006): passenger cars 1,778,861; trucks 318,604. *Air transport* (2007; Aer Lingus only): passenger-km 14,807,-000,000; metric ton-km cargo 75,400,000. **Communications,** in total units (units per 1,000 persons). Telephone landlines (2008): 2,202,000 (503); cellular telephone subscribers (2008): 5,048,000 (1,503); personal computers (2007): 2,536,000 (582); total Internet users (2008): 2,830,000 (646); broadband Internet subscribers (2008): 891,000 (203).

## Education and health

**Educational attainment** (2006). Percentage of population ages 15–64 having: no formal schooling/primary education 15.1%; some/complete secondary 46.5%; post secondary certificate 9.4%; some higher 9.5%; complete higher 16.8%; unknown 2.7%. **Health:** physicians (2004) 11,141 (1 per 365 persons); hospital beds (2006) 12,051 (publicly funded acute hospitals only) (1 per 352 persons); infant mortality rate per 1,000 live births (2007) 2.9; undernourished population (2002–04) less than 2.5% of total population.

## Military

**Total active duty personnel** (November 2008): 10,460 (army 81.3%, navy 10.5%, air force 8.2%); reserve 14,875. **Military expenditure as percentage of GDP** (2008): 0.5%; per capita expenditure US$303.

## Background

Human settlement in Ireland began about 6000 BC, and Celtic migration dates from c. 300 BC. St. Patrick is credited with Christianizing the country in the 5th century AD. Norse domination began in 795 and ended in 1014, when the Norse were defeated by Brian Boru. Gaelic Ireland's independence ended in 1171, when English King Henry II proclaimed himself overlord of the island. Beginning in the 16th century, Irish Catholic landowners fled religious persecution by the English and were replaced by English and Scottish Protestants. The United Kingdom of Great Britain and Ireland was established in 1801. The Great Famine of the 1840s led over two million people to emigrate and built momentum for Irish Home Rule. The Easter Rising (1916) was followed by the Anglo-Irish War (1919–21), during which the Irish Republican Army used guerrilla tactics to force the British government to negotiate. The signing of the Anglo-Irish Treaty on 6 Dec 1921, when ratified by the Dáil the following month, granted southern Ireland dominion status as the Irish Free State. Internecine struggle between supporters and opponents of the treaty culminated in the Irish Civil War (1922–23). In 1937 the Free State adopted the name Éire (Ireland) and became a sovereign independent country. In 1948 the Dáil passed the Republic of Ireland Act, which took effect in April 1949, declaring Ireland a republic and removing it from the British Commonwealth of Nations. Britain recognized the new status of Ireland but declared that unity with the six counties of Northern Ireland could not occur without consent of the parliament of Northern Ireland. In 1973 Ireland joined the European Economic Community (later the European Community); it is now a member of the EU. The late 20th century was dominated by sectarian hostilities. The Irish government played a pivotal role in winning public support for the Belfast Agreement (1998), which removed Ireland's constitutional claim to the entire island's territory. Ireland continued to play an important consultative role in Northern Ireland, such as helping to negotiate an agreement between the Democratic Union Party and Sinn Féin coalition government in 2010, under which policing and justice powers were to be devolved to Northern Ireland's government.

## Recent Developments

The most unexpected development in 2011 involved a diplomatic row between Ireland and the tiny Vatican City state. In July taoiseach (prime minister) Enda Kenny made a forceful speech criticizing the Vatican for its lack of cooperation with the tribunal set up by the Irish government to investigate child sexual abuse by clergy. He accused the Vatican of having frustrated a lawful inquiry established by a sovereign republic. Kenny, an avowed Catholic, surprised listeners with the vehemence of his arguments. The Vatican's 25-page reply rejected the accusation of hindering the inquiry's work and said that Kenny had misrepresented church documents quoted in his speech. There was no reconciling the two positions, and Ireland found itself at odds with its longest-standing diplomatic ally. In November Ireland announced that it planned to close its embassy to the Vatican, in a further blow to the relationship.

**Internet resource:** <www.cso.ie>.

# Israel

**Official name:** Medinat Yisrael (Hebrew); Dawlat Israil (Arabic) (State of Israel). **Form of government:** multiparty republic with one legislative house (Knesset [120]). **Head of state:** President Shimon Peres (from 2007). **Head of government:** Prime Minister Benjamin Netanyahu (from 2009). **Capital:** Jerusalem is

---

*1 metric ton = about 1.1 short tons; 1 kilometer = 0.6 mi (statute); 1 metric ton-km cargo = about 0.68 short ton-mi cargo; c.i.f.: cost, insurance, and freight; f.o.b.: free on board*

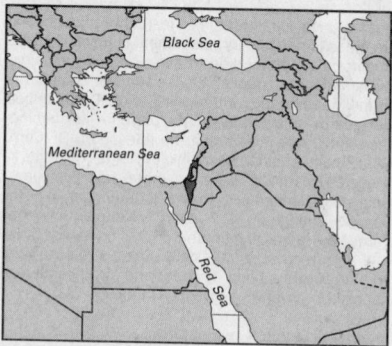

the proclaimed capital of Israel and the actual seat of government, but recognition of its status as capital by the international community has largely been withheld. **Official languages:** Hebrew; Arabic. **Official religion:** none. **Monetary unit:** 1 new (Israeli) sheqel (NIS) = 100 agorot; valuation (2 Jul 2012) US$1 = NIS 3.92.

## Demography

**Area:** 8,357 sq mi, 21,643 sq km (excludes the West Bank and the Gaza Strip). **Population** (2011): 7,450,000. **Density** (2011): persons per sq mi 686.9, persons per sq km 265.2. **Urban** (2011): 91.6%. **Sex distribution** (2008): male 49.44%; female 50.56%. **Age breakdown** (2008): under 15, 28.4%; 15–29, 23.4%; 30–44, 19.4%; 45–59, 15.2%; 60–74, 9.0%; 75–84, 3.5%; 85 and over, 1.1%. **Ethnic composition** (2008): Jewish 75.5%; Arab 20.2%; other 4.3%. **Religious affiliation** (2008): Jewish 75.5%; Muslim 16.8%; Christian 2.1%; Druze 1.7%; other 3.9%. **Major cities** (2008): Jerusalem 763,600; Tel Aviv-Yafo 392,500 (urban agglomeration [2006] 3,040,400); Haifa 264,800 (urban agglomeration [2006] 996,000); Rishon LeZiyyon 226,100. **Location:** Middle East, bordering Lebanon, Syria, Jordan, the West Bank, Egypt, the Gaza Strip, and the Mediterranean Sea.

## Vital statistics

**Birth rate** per 1,000 population (2008): 21.5 (world avg. 20.3). **Death rate** per 1,000 population (2008): 5.4 (world avg. 8.5). **Total fertility rate** (avg. births per childbearing woman; 2008): 2.96. **Life expectancy** at birth (2008): male 79.1 years; female 83.0 years.

## National economy

**Budget** (2007). *Revenue:* NIS 294,399,000,000 (current revenue 67.3%, of which income tax 31.0%, VAT 18.3%; capital revenue 29.2%, of which loans and grants 19.7%). *Expenditures:* NIS 307,-240,000,000 (debt service 32.5%; defense 18.2%; social security and welfare 12.8%; education 11.3%; health 5.5%). **Public debt** (January 2009): US$86,080,000,000. **Gross national income** (2008): US$180,499,000,000 (US$24,700 per capita). **Production** (metric tons except as noted). *Agriculture and fishing* (2008): potatoes 592,001, tomatoes 421,721, oranges 117,804, dates 22,800; livestock (number of live animals) 430,000 sheep, 416,000 cattle; fisheries production (2007)

26,236 (from aquaculture 85%). *Mining and quarrying* (2007): phosphate rock 3,069,000, potash 2,150,000, gypsum 82,974, diamonds 526,000 carats. *Manufacturing* (value added in US$'000,000; 2005): chemical products 3,427; medical, measuring, and testing appliances 2,270; electronics and telecommunications equipment 2,259. *Energy production (consumption):* electricity (kW-hr; 2008) 54,504,000,000 ([2006] 49,967,000,000); coal (metric tons; 2008) none (12,882,000); lignite (metric tons; 2006) 452,000 (452,000); crude petroleum (barrels; 2007) 8,200 ([2006] 73,310,000); petroleum products (metric tons; 2006) 10,687,000 (11,572,000); natural gas (cu m; 2007) 2,758,000,000 ([2008] 1,847,000,000). **Population economically active** (2008): total 2,957,100; activity rate 42.1% (participation rates: ages 15 and over, 56.5%; female 46.6%; unemployed [July 2008–June 2009] 7.0%). **Selected balance of payments data.** Receipts from (US$'000,000): tourism (2007) 3,059; remittances (2008) 1,422; foreign direct investment (FDI; 2005–07 avg.) 9,869. Disbursements for (US$'000,000): tourism (2007) 3,260; remittances (2008) 3,537; FDI (2005–07 avg.) 8,364.

## Foreign trade

**Imports** (2008; c.i.f.) (excluding the import of military goods [equaling US$2,493,000,000 in 2006]): US$65,173,200,000 (machinery and apparatus 19.7%; crude petroleum 16.7%; diamonds 13.6%; chemical products 11.0%; transportation equipment 8.0%). *Major import sources:* US 12.3%; Belgium and Luxembourg 6.8%; China 6.5%; Switzerland 6.1%; Germany 6.0%. **Exports** (2008; f.o.b.): US$61,339,-100,000 (machinery and apparatus 22.4%; chemical products 21.5%; polished diamonds 10.3%; rough diamonds 5.4%; crude petroleum and refined petroleum products 5.0%; professional and scientific equipment 3.6%). *Major export destinations:* US 32.6%; Belgium and Luxembourg 7.6%; Hong Kong 6.8%; India 3.8%; Netherlands 3.3%.

## Transport and communications

**Transport.** *Railroads* (2008): route length 949 km; passenger-km 1,968,000,000, metric ton-km cargo 1,056,000,000. *Roads* (2008): total length 18,096 km (paved 100%). *Vehicles* (2008): passenger cars 1,875,765; trucks and buses 372,268. *Air transport* (2008; El Al only): passenger-km 17,388,000,000; metric ton-km cargo 606,000,000. **Communications,** in total units (units per 1,000 persons). Telephone landlines (2008): 2,900,000 (411); cellular telephone subscribers (2008): 8,982,000 (1,274); personal computers (2004): 5,037,000 (734); total Internet users (2008): 2,106,000 (299); broadband Internet subscribers (2008): 1,600,000 (227).

## Education and health

**Educational attainment** (2007). Percentage of population ages 25–64 having: no formal schooling/unknown 1%; primary 12%; secondary 44%; postsecondary, vocational, and higher 43%. **Literacy** (2004): total population ages 15 and over literate 97.1%; males literate 98.5%; females literate 95.9%. **Health** (2008): physicians (2007) 25,314 (1 per 273 persons); hospital beds 42,178 (1 per 166 persons); infant mortality rate per 1,000 live births 3.8; undernourished population (2002–04) less than 2.5% of total population.

## Military

**Total active duty personnel** (November 2008): 176,500 (army 75.4%, navy 5.4%, air force 19.2%); reserve 565,000. **Military expenditure as percentage of GDP** (2007): 7.2%; per capita expenditure US$1,681.

## Background

The record of human habitation in Israel is at least 100,000 years old. Efforts by Jews to establish a national state there began in the late 19th century. Britain supported Zionism and in 1922 assumed political responsibility for what was Palestine. Migration of Jews there during Nazi persecution led to deteriorating relations with Arabs. In 1947 the UN voted to partition the region into separate Jewish and Arab states, a decision opposed by neighboring Arab countries. The State of Israel was proclaimed in 1948, and Egypt, Transjordan, Syria, Lebanon, and Iraq immediately declared war on it. Israel won this war as well as the 1967 Six-Day War, in which it claimed the West Bank from Jordan and the Gaza Strip from Egypt. Another war with its Arab neighbors followed in 1973, but the Camp David Accords led to the signing of a peace treaty between Israel and Egypt in 1979. Israel invaded Lebanon to quell the Palestine Liberation Organization (PLO) in 1982, and in the late 1980s a Palestinian resistance movement arose in the occupied territories. Peace negotiations between Israel and the Arab states and Palestinians began in 1991. Israel and the PLO agreed in 1993 upon a five-year extension of self-government to the Palestinians of the West Bank and the Gaza Strip. Israel signed a full peace treaty with Jordan in 1994. Israeli soldiers and Lebanon's Hezbollah forces clashed in 1997. Following numerous contentious talks between Israel and Lebanon, Israeli troops abruptly withdrew from Lebanon in 2000, and negotiations between Israel and the Palestinians broke down amid violence that claimed hundreds of lives. In an effort to stem the fighting, Israel in 2005 withdrew its soldiers and settlers from parts of the West Bank and from all of the Gaza Strip, which came under Palestinian control.

## Recent Developments

An unprecedented sequence of popular uprisings, dubbed the "Arab Spring," created regional uncertainty for Israel in 2011. The uprisings, which began in Tunisia in December 2010 and quickly spread across the Arab world, toppled long-standing dictatorships in Tunisia, Egypt, and Libya and precipitated protracted sectarian violence in Syria. Israeli analysts feared that the collapse of the secular dictatorships could bring radical anti-Israeli and anti-Western groups to power. Their biggest fear was that the Islamic extremist Muslim Brotherhood could gain control in Egypt and abrogate the 32-year-old peace treaty with Israel. Relations with Egypt were tense after a cross-border incident in August in which Palestinian militants killed eight Israelis and fled to the Sinai Peninsula. Egyptians were outraged when units of the Israel Defense Forces (IDF) in hot pursuit killed five Egyptian border

guards on Egyptian territory. Ties between Israel and the transitional military government in Egypt were too important for either side to allow an open rift, however. In October, Israel's Defense Minister Ehud Barak formally apologized for the killing of the Egyptian border guards, and the Egyptians played a key behind-the-scenes role in securing the release of IDF Corp. Gilad Shalit, who had been held by Hamas militants in a secret location in Gaza for more than five years. Shalit was handed over to Israeli authorities in October in exchange for 477 jailed Palestinian militants named by Hamas and another 550 to be named by Israel and freed at a later date. Shalit's release was greeted with euphoria in Israel and significantly enhanced Netanyahu's domestic standing.

**Internet resource:** <www.cbs.gov.il>.

# Italy

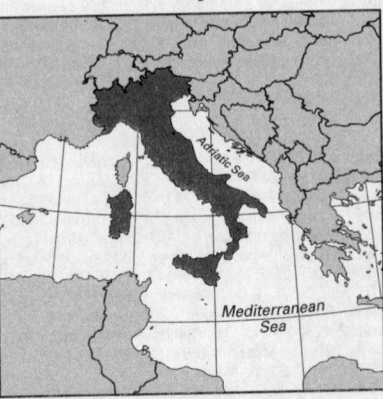

**Official name:** Repubblica Italiana (Italian Republic). **Form of government:** republic with two legislative houses (Senate [321]; Chamber of Deputies [630]). **Head of state:** President Giorgio Napolitano (from 2006). **Head of government:** Prime Minister Mario Monti (from 2011). **Capital:** Rome. **Official language:** Italian (in addition, German is locally official in the region of Trentino–Alto Adige and French is locally official in the region of Valle d'Aosta). **Official religion:** none. **Monetary unit:** 1 euro (€) = 100 cents; valuation (2 Jul 2012) US$1 = €0.79.

## Demography

**Area:** 116,346 sq mi, 301,336 sq km. **Population** (2011): 60,769,000. **Density** (2011): persons per sq mi 522.3, persons per sq km 201.7. **Urban** (2005): 67.6%. **Sex distribution** (2007): male 48.56%; female 51.44%. **Age breakdown** (2007): under 15, 14.1%; 15–29, 16.3%; 30–44, 23.8%; 45–59, 20.1%; 60–74, 16.1%; 75–84, 7.2%; 85 and over, 2.4%. **Ethnolinguistic composition** (2000): Italian 96.0%; North African Arab 0.9%; Italo-Albanian 0.8%; Albanian 0.5%; German 0.4%; Austrian 0.4%; other 1.0%. **Religious affiliation** (2005): Roman Catholic 83%, of which practicing 28%; Muslim 2%; nonreligious/atheist 14%; other 1%. Major cities (urban agglomerations) (2007): Rome 2,718,768 (3,339,000); Milan 1,299,633 (2,945,000); Naples 973,132 (2,250,000); Turin 908,263 (1,652,000); Palermo 663,173 (863,000); Genoa 610,887; Bologna 372,256; Florence 364,710; Bari 322,511; Catania 298,957; Venice 268,993; Verona 264,191; Messina 243,997; Padua 210,173; Trieste 205,356. Location: southern Europe, bordering Switzerland, Austria, Slovenia, the Mediterranean Sea, and France; wholly contained within Italy are the countries of San Marino and Vatican City. Immigration (2007): resident foreigners 3,432,651, of which from EU countries 17.7%, other Europe 23.0%, North African countries 15.2%, other Africa 6.6%, Asian countries 7.7%, other 29.8%.

## Vital statistics

Birth rate per 1,000 population (2008): 9.6 (world avg. 20.3); (2007) within marriage 79.3%. Death rate per 1,000 population (2008): 9.8 (world avg. 8.5). Total fertility rate (avg. births per childbearing woman; 2007): 1.37. Life expectancy at birth (2007): male 78.6 years; female 84.1 years.

## Social indicators

Educational attainment (2007). Percentage of population ages 25 to 64 having: no formal schooling through primary education 15%; lower secondary 33%; upper secondary 37%; university 13%; other 2%. Quality of working life. Average workweek (2008): 34.6 hours. Annual rate per 100,000 workers (2007) for: nonfatal injury 2,647; fatal injury 4. Number of working days lost to labor stoppages per 1,000 workers (2007): 52.6. Material well-being. Rate per 100 households possessing (2008): mobile phone 88.5; personal computer 50.1; Internet access 42.0; satellite dish 30.7. Transport used for work per 100 employees (includes double-counting; 2008): car 75.7%, walking 11.1%, bus 4.9%, motorcycle/motorbike 4.6%, bicycle 3.1%, train 2.9%, underground 2.5%, other 2.9%. Social participation. Trade union membership in total workforce (2004): 30%. Social deviance (2007). Offense rate per 100,000 population for: murder/manslaughter 4.6; rape 8.2; theft 2,756; battery 132.2; robbery 86.2. Access to services (2002). Nearly 100% of dwellings have access to electricity, a safe water supply, and toilet facilities. Leisure (2006). Favorite leisure activities (attendance per 100 people ages 6 and over): cinema 48.9; museum or art exhibition 27.7; sporting events 27.3; discotheque 24.8; archaeological sites or monuments 21.1.

## National economy

Gross national income (2008): US$2,109,075,000,000 (US$35,240 per capita). Budget (2006). Revenue: €672,610,000,000 (taxes on goods and services 27.6%; social security contributions 27.6%; income tax 24.4%; nontax revenue 6.7%; corporate taxes 6.4%). Expenditures: €722,750,000,000 (social protection 37.2%; health 14.4%; economic affairs 12.0%; public debt 9.5%; education 9.2%; defense 2.8%). Public debt (May 2009): US$2,137,581,000,000. Energy production (consumption): electricity (kW-hr; 2008) 316,719,000,000 ([2006] 359,106,000,000); coal (metric tons; 2006) 21,000 (24,806,000); crude petroleum (barrels; 2008) 36,400,000 ([2006] 691,000,000); petroleum products (metric tons; 2006) 89,810,000

(77,681,000); natural gas (cu m; 2008) 9,103,000,000 ([2006] 82,488,000,000). Production (metric tons except as noted). Agriculture and fishing (2008): corn (maize) 9,491,203, wheat 8,855,440, grapes 7,793,301, tomatoes 5,976,912, sugar beets 3,800,000, olives 3,512,660, oranges 2,527,453, apples 2,208,227, potatoes 1,603,828, peaches and nectarines 1,589,118, pears 770,100, artichokes 483,561, kiwi fruit 473,955, sunflower seeds 260,927, hazelnuts 111,841, almonds 118,723; livestock (number of live animals) 9,273,000 pigs, 8,237,000 sheep, 6,283,000 cattle; fisheries production (2007) 465,637 (from aquaculture 38%). Mining and quarrying (2007): limestone 32,953,000; feldspar 4,727,000 [world rank: 1]; marble and travertine 4,643,000; pozzolana 4,000,000 [world rank: 1]. Manufacturing (value added in US$'000,000; 2005): fabricated metal products 34,849; food products 21,119; general purpose machinery 19,782; paints, soaps, pharmaceuticals 14,945; special purpose machinery 13,548; bricks, cement, ceramics 12,684; printing and publishing 10,567; plastic products 9,205; textiles 9,063; motor vehicles and parts 8,533; wearing apparel 8,317; furniture 8,195; iron and steel 7,298; footwear and leather products 6,643. Population economically active (2008): total 25,096,600; activity rate of total population 42.2% (participation rates: ages 15–64, 63.0%; female 40.7%; unemployed [April 2008–March 2009] 7.0%). Selected balance of payments data. Receipts from (US$'000,000): tourism (2007) 42,660; remittances (2008) 3,136; foreign direct investment (FDI; 2005–07 avg.) 33,138. Disbursements for (US$'000,000): tourism (2007) 27,329; remittances (2008) 12,718; FDI (2005–07 avg.) 58,225.

## Foreign trade

Imports (2007; c.i.f.): US$504,582,000,000 (machinery and apparatus 16.4%; chemical products 12.6%; motor vehicles and parts 11.0%; crude petroleum 9.0%; food products 6.4%; iron and steel 5.8%; nonferrous metals 4.0%). Major import sources: Germany 16.7%; France 9.0%; China 5.9%; Netherlands 5.2%; Belgium 4.3%; Spain 4.2%; Libya 3.3%; UK 3.2%; US 3.0%; Switzerland 3.0%. Exports (2007; f.o.b.): US$492,058,000,000 (assorted manufactured goods 20.9%, of which iron and steel 5.2%, fabricated metal products 4.4%; nonelectrical machinery 20.7%, of which general industrial machinery 10.0%, specialized machinery 6.3%; chemical products 10.1%; motor vehicles and parts 8.0%; electrical machinery 5.3%; wearing apparel and accessories 4.6%; food products 4.5%). Major export destinations: Germany 12.8%; France 11.4%; Spain 7.3%; US 6.8%; UK 5.8%; Switzerland 3.7%; Belgium 2.9%; Russia 2.7%; Poland 2.4%; Austria 2.3%.

## Transport and communications

Transport. Railroads: (2007) route length 16,356 km; (2006) passenger-km 46,439,000,000; (2005) metric ton-km cargo 22,760,000,000. Roads (2003): total length 484,688 km (paved 100%). Vehicles (2006): passenger cars 35,297,282; trucks and buses 4,427,846. Air transport (2008; Air One, Alitalia, Livingston S.P.A., and Meridiana airlines only): passenger-km 39,421,000,000; metric ton-km cargo 1,231,000,000. Communications, in total units (units per 1,000 persons). Telephone landlines (2008): 20,031,000 (335); cellular telephone subscribers (2008): 88,580,000 (1,480); personal computers (2007): 21,791,000 (367); total Internet users (2008): 29,118,000 (486); broadband Internet subscribers (2008): 11,283,000 (189).

## Education and health

**Literacy** (2007): total population ages 15 and over literate 98.9%; males literate 99.1%; females literate 98.6%. **Health:** physicians (2006) 215,000 (1 per 274 persons); hospital beds (2005) 234,428 (1 per 250 persons); infant mortality rate per 1,000 live births (2007) 3.8; undernourished population (2002–04) less than 2.5% of total population.

## Military

**Total active duty personnel** (November 2008): 292,983 (army 36.9%, navy 11.6%, air force 14.7%, carabinieri 36.8%); US military forces (December 2008): 9,160. **Military expenditure as percentage of GDP** (2007): 1.8%; per capita expenditure US$635.

## Background

The Etruscan civilization arose in the 9th century BC and was overthrown by the Romans in the 4th–3rd centuries BC. Barbarian invasions of the 4th and 5th centuries AD destroyed the Western Roman Empire. Italy's political fragmentation lasted for centuries but did not diminish its impact on European culture, notably during the Renaissance. From the 15th to the 18th century, Italian lands were ruled by France, the Holy Roman Empire, Spain, and Austria. When Napoleonic rule ended in 1815, Italy was again a grouping of independent states. The Risorgimento successfully united most of Italy, including Sicily and Sardinia, by 1861, and the unification of peninsular Italy was completed by 1870. Italy joined the Allies during World War I, but social unrest in the 1920s brought to power the Fascist movement of Benito Mussolini, and Italy allied itself with Nazi Germany in World War II. Defeated by the Allies in 1943, Italy proclaimed itself a republic in 1946. It was a charter member of NATO (1949) and of the European Community. It completed the process of setting up regional legislatures with limited autonomy in the 1970s. Since World War II it has experienced rapid changes of government but has remained socially stable. It worked with other European countries to establish the European Union.

## Recent Developments

The dramatic downturn in 2011 in the fortunes of Europe's decade-old common currency, the euro, produced a 90-day tidal wave of events in Italy. The country witnessed the collapse of longtime Prime Minister Silvio Berlusconi's government, his replacement by nonpartisan leader Mario Monti, and the introduction of sweeping austerity measures intended to restore debt-ridden Italy's tarnished status within the financially battered European Union. Although Italy represented the euro zone's third largest economy, its debt was estimated at roughly 120% of its GDP. Monti won applause after promising a debt-reduction package intended to balance the Italian budget by 2013. His emergency decrees, dubbed the "Save Italy" package, called for a rise in the retirement age, the introduction of pension reform, the imposition of higher property taxes, and an effort to rein in endemic tax evasion.

Internet resource: <http://en.istat.it>.

# Jamaica

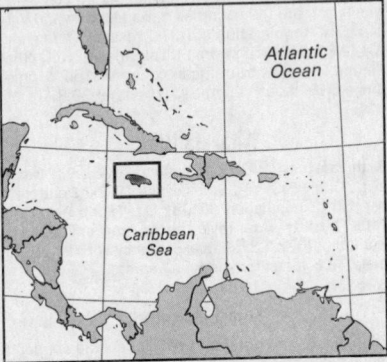

**Official name:** Jamaica. **Form of government:** constitutional monarchy with two legislative houses (Senate [21]; House of Representatives [63]). **Head of state:** British Queen Elizabeth II (from 1952), represented by Governor-General Patrick Allen (from 2009). **Head of government:** Prime Minister Portia Simpson Miller (from 2012). **Capital:** Kingston. **Official language:** English. **Official religion:** none. **Monetary unit:** 1 Jamaican dollar (J$) = 100 cents; valuation (2 Jul 2012) US$1 = J$88.13.

## Demography

**Area:** 4,244 sq mi, 10,991 sq km. **Population** (2011): 2,709,000. **Density** (2011): persons per sq mi 638.3, persons per sq km 246.5. **Urban** (2009): 52.0%. **Sex distribution** (2008): male 49.28%; female 50.72%. **Age breakdown** (2008): under 15, 27.9%; 15–29, 25.0%; 30–44, 23.8%; 45–59, 12.4%; 60–74, 7.1%; 75 and over, 3.8%. **Ethnic composition** (2001): black 91.6%; mixed race 6.2%; East Indian 0.9%; Chinese 0.2%; white 0.2%; other/unknown 0.9%. **Religious affiliation** (2001): Protestant 61.2%, of which Church of God 23.8%, Seventh-day Adventist 10.8%, Pentecostal 9.5%, Roman Catholic 2.6%; other Christian 1.7%; Rastafarian 0.9%; nonreligious 20.9%; other 12.7%. **Major cities** (2006): Kingston 585,300; Spanish Town 148,800; Portmore 103,900; Montego Bay 82,700; Mandeville 47,700. **Location:** island in the Caribbean Sea, south of Cuba.

## Vital statistics

**Birth rate** per 1,000 population (2008): 16.7 (world avg. 20.3). **Death rate** per 1,000 population (2008): 6.3 (world avg. 8.5). **Total fertility rate** (avg. births per childbearing woman; 2008): 2.30. **Life expectancy** at birth (2008): male 71.9 years; female 75.4 years.

*1 metric ton = about 1.1 short tons; 1 kilometer = 0.6 mi (statute); 1 metric ton-km cargo = about 0.68 short ton-mi cargo; c.i.f.: cost, insurance, and freight; f.o.b.: free on board*

## National economy

**Budget** (2008–09). *Revenue:* J$276,199,800,000 (tax revenue 89.1%; nontax revenue 5.8%; grants and other revenue 5.1%). *Expenditures:* J$351,521,-400,000 (public debt service 35.6%; wages and salaries 31.7%; capital expenditures 11.8%). **Production** (metric tons except as noted). *Agriculture and fishing* (2007): sugarcane 2,000,000, coconuts 170,000, oranges 142,000, pimiento and allspice (2005) 10,400, coffee 2,700; livestock (number of live animals) 430,000 cattle, 12,500,000 chickens; fisheries production 22,164 (from aquaculture 25%). *Mining and quarrying* (2008): bauxite 14,697,000; alumina 3,991,000; limestone (2007) 2,950,000; gypsum 238,000. *Manufacturing* (2008): cement 724,600,000; animal feeds (2005) 367,600; sugar 140,000; molasses 62,654; rum [and other distilled spirits] 265,349 hectoliters. *Energy production (consumption):* electricity (kW-hr; 2006) 7,473,000,000 (7,473,000,000); coal (metric tons; 2006) none (32,000); crude petroleum (barrels; 2006) none (7,440,000); petroleum products (metric tons; 2006) 995,000 (3,806,000). **Population economically active** (2008): total 1,302,400; activity rate of total population 48.4% (participation rates: ages 14 and over [2006] 64.6%; female 45.4%; unemployed 10.3%). **Gross national income** (2008): US$13,098,000,000 (US$4,870 per capita). **Public debt** (external, outstanding; May 2009): US$6,297,000,000. **Selected balance of payments data.** Receipts from (US$'000,000): tourism (2008) 1,984; remittances (2008–09) 1,860; foreign direct investment (2006–08 avg.) 1,062; official development assistance (2007) 26. Disbursements for (US$'000,000): tourism (2007) 298; remittances (2008–09) 262; foreign direct disinvestment (2005–07 avg.) –77.

## Foreign trade

**Imports** (2006; c.i.f.): US$5,041,000,000 (crude petroleum 23.6%; machinery and apparatus 15.5%; food products 12.5%; chemical products 11.3%; motor vehicles 6.1%). *Major import sources:* US 36.8%; Trinidad and Tobago 11.5%; Venezuela 10.7%; Japan 4.2%; China 4.1%. **Exports** (2006; f.o.b.): US$1,989,000,000 (alumina 52.3%; refined petroleum products 13.5%; food products 12.0%, of which raw sugar 4.5%, vegetables and fruit 2.9%, coffee 1.5%; alcoholic beverages 4.2%). *Major export destinations:* US 30.4%; Canada 15.6%; China 15.1%; UK 10.3%; Netherlands 7.0%.

## Transport and communications

**Transport.** *Railroads* (2004): route length 201 km. *Roads* (2005): total length 21,532 km (paved 74%). *Vehicles* (2004): passenger cars 357,660; trucks and buses 128,239. *Air transport* (2006; Air Jamaica only): passenger-km 3,907,530,000; metric ton-km cargo 20,192,000. **Communications,** in total units (units per 1,000 persons). Telephone landlines (2008): 317,000 (117); cellular telephone subscribers (2008): 2,723,000 (1,006); personal computers (2005): 179,000 (68); total Internet users (2008): 1,540,000 (569); broadband Internet subscribers (2008): 98,000 (36).

## Education and health

**Educational attainment** (2001). Percentage of population ages 15 and over having: no formal school-ing/unknown 6.7%; primary education 25.5%; secondary 55.5%; higher 12.3%, of which university 4.2%. **Literacy** (2007): population ages 15 and over literate 86.0%; males literate 80.5%; females literate 91.1%. **Health:** physicians (2005) 2,253 (1 per 1,176 persons); hospital beds (2006) 5,326 (1 per 500 persons); infant mortality rate per 1,000 live births (2008) 15.6; undernourished population (2002–04) 250,000 (9% of total population based on the consumption of a minimum daily requirement of 1,930 calories).

## Military

**Total active duty personnel** (November 2008): 2,830 (army 88.3%, coast guard 6.7%, air force 5.0%). **Military expenditure as percentage of GDP** (2007): 1.0%; per capita expenditure US$40.

## Background

The island of Jamaica was settled by Arawak Indians c. AD 600. It was sighted by Christopher Columbus in 1494; Spain colonized it in the early 16th century but neglected it because it lacked gold reserves. Britain gained control in 1655, and by the end of the 18th century Jamaica had become a prized colonial possession due to the volume of sugar produced by slave laborers. Slavery was abolished in the late 1830s, and the plantation system collapsed. Jamaica gained full internal self-government in 1959 and became an independent country within the British Commonwealth in 1962. In the late 20th century, the government nationalized many businesses.

## Recent Developments

The World Bank said in April 2011 that Jamaica could increase its annual GDP by as much as 5.4% if it reduced its crime levels to those of Costa Rica, whose homicide rate was one-fifth that of Jamaica's. The indirect costs of violence, such as victims' stress and lower productivity at work, were cited.

**Internet resource:** <www.statinja.com>.

# Japan

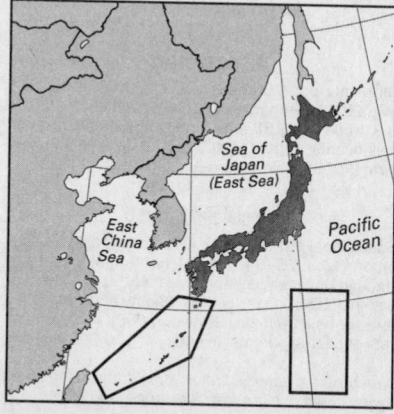

Official name: Nihon, Nippon (Japan). Form of government: constitutional monarchy with a national Diet consisting of two legislative houses (House of Councillors [242]; House of Representatives [480]). Symbol of state: Emperor Akihito (from 1989). Head of government: Prime Minister Yoshihiko Noda (from 2011). Capital: Tokyo. Official language: Japanese. Official religion: none. Monetary unit: 1 yen (¥) = 100 sen; valuation (2 Jul 2012) US$1 = ¥79.34.

## Demography

Area: 145,927 sq mi, 377,950 sq km. Population (2011): 127,937,000. Density (2011): persons per sq mi 876.7, persons per sq km 338.5. Urban (2009): 66.6%. Sex distribution (2009): male 48.72%; female 51.28%. Age breakdown (2009): under 15, 13.4%; 15–29, 16.2%; 30–44, 21.1%; 45–59, 19.4%; 60–74, 19.3%; 75–84, 7.8%; 85 and over, 2.8%. Composition by nationality (2004): Japanese 98.5%; Korean 0.5%; Chinese 0.4%; Brazilian 0.2%; other 0.4%. Immigration/Emigration (2006): permanent immigrants/registered aliens in Japan 2,084,919, from North or South Korea 28.7%, from Taiwan, Hong Kong, Macau, or China 26.9%, from Brazil 15.0%, from the Philippines 9.3%, from Peru 2.8%, from the US 2.5%, from Thailand 1.9%, from Vietnam 1.6%, other 11.3%. Japanese nationals living abroad 1,063,695, in the US 34.8%, in China 11.8%, in Brazil 6.1%, in the UK 5.7%, in Australia 5.6%, in Thailand 3.8%, in Germany 3.2%, other 29.0%. Permanent expatriates (including those with dual nationality) 328,317, of which living in the US 37.6%, in Brazil 19.1%, in Australia 8.5%, in Canada 8.3%. Major cities (2008): Tokyo 8,731,000; Yokohama 3,648,000; Osaka 2,651,000; Nagoya 2,246,000; Sapporo 1,898,000; Kobe 1,533,000; Kyoto 1,467,000; Fukuoka 1,437,000; Kawasaki 1,388,000; Saitama 1,210,000; Hiroshima 1,166,000; Sendai 1,031,000. Major metropolitan areas (2007): Tokyo 35,676,000; Osaka-Kobe 11,294,000; Nagoya 3,230,000; Fukuoka–Kita-Kyushu 2,792,000; Sapporo 2,544,000; Sendai 2,250,000; Hiroshima 2,045,000; Kyoto 1,805,000. Location: eastern Asia, island chain between the North Pacific Ocean and the Sea of Japan. Religious affiliation (2003): Shinto and related beliefs 84.2%; Buddhism and related beliefs 73.6% (many Japanese practice both Shintoism and Buddhism); Christian 1.7%; Muslim 0.1%; other 7.8%. Mobility (2007). Percentage of total population moving: within a prefecture 2.3%; between prefectures 2.0%.

## Vital statistics

Birth rate per 1,000 population (2008): 8.6 (world avg. 20.3). Death rate per 1,000 population (2008): 8.8 (world avg. 8.5). Total fertility rate (avg. births per childbearing woman; 2008): 1.37. Life expectancy at birth (2008): male 79.3 years; female 86.1 years.

## Social indicators

Educational attainment (2007). Percentage of population ages 25–64 having: no formal schooling through upper secondary education 59%; higher vocational 18%; university 23%. Quality of working life. Average hours worked per week (2008): 40.7. Annual rate of deaths/nonfatal injuries per 100,000 workers

(2008): 1.9/177.5. Proportion of labor force insured for damages or income loss resulting from injury, permanent disability, and death (2005): 53.1%. Average man-days lost to labor stoppages per 1,000 workdays (2006): 1.8. Average duration of journey to work (2003): 34.2 minutes. Access to services (2004). Proportion of households having access to: safe public water supply 96.9%; public sewage system 68.0%. Social participation. Adult population working as volunteers at least once in the year (2006) 26.2%. Trade union membership in total workforce (2007): 15.1%. Social deviance (2005). Offense rate per 100,000 population for: homicide 1.0; robbery 3.0; larceny and theft 151.6. Incidence in general population of: drug and substance abuse 0.1. Rate of suicide per 100,000 population (2007): 24.1. Material well-being (2003–04). Households possessing: automobile 81.6%; air conditioner (2002) 87.2%; personal computer 77.5%.

## National economy

Gross national income (2008): US$4,879,171,000,-000 (US$38,210 per capita). Budget (2007–08). Revenue: ¥83,000,000,000,000 (government bonds 30.5%; corporate taxes 20.1%; income tax 19.6%; VAT 12.8%). Expenditures: ¥83,000,000,000,000 (social security 26.2%; debt service 24.3%; public works 8.1%; education and science 6.4%; national defense 5.8%). Public debt (July 2009): US$8,602,560,000,000. Energy production (consumption): electricity (kW-hr; 2008) 990,864,-000,000 ([2007] 959,660,000,000); coal (metric tons; 2007) 1,340,000 ([2006] 179,075,000); crude petroleum (barrels; 2008) 6,180,000 ([2006] 1,461,000,000); petroleum products (metric tons; 2006) 169,502,000 (173,182,000); natural gas (cu m; 2008) 3,864,000,000 ([2006] 92,352,000,000). Composition of energy supply by source (2002): crude oil and petroleum products 49.7%, coal 19.5%, natural gas 13.5%, nuclear power 11.6%, hydroelectric power 3.2%, solar power and other new energy supplies 2.4%, geothermal 0.1%. Population economically active (2008): total 66,620,000; activity rate of total population 52.2% (participation rates: ages 15 and over, 60.3%; female 41.7%; unemployed [September 2008–August 2009] 4.7%). Production (metric tons except as noted). Agriculture and fishing (2007): rice 11,028,750, sugar beets 4,297,000, potatoes 2,800,000, cabbages 2,390,000, sugarcane 1,500,000, green onions 1,265,000, dry onions 1,165,000, tangerines and mandarin oranges 1,066,000, sweet potatoes 968,400, wheat 882,300, apples 840,100, tomatoes 750,300, carrots 750,000, pears 326,400, spinach 302,000, persimmons 244,800, soybeans 226,700, grapes 209,100, taro 195,000, strawberries 193,000, peaches 150,200, chilies 149,600, tea 94,100, mushrooms 67,000, ginger 42,000, kiwi fruit 32,800, chestnuts 22,100, cherries 16,600; livestock (number of live animals) 9,745,000 pigs, 4,423,000 cattle, 284,651,000 chickens; fisheries production (2008) 5,588,000, of which mackerel 514,000, bonito 304,000, squid 291,000, tuna 217,000, pollack 212,000 (from aquaculture [including aquatic plants] 21% [of which laver 338,000, oysters 190,000, yellowtail 158,000, wakame 55,000, pearls 25,000]); whales caught (2005) 815. Mining *and quarrying* (2007): limestone 165,982,000; silica 4,600,000 [world rank: 9]; dolomite 3,655,000; pyrophyllite 345,000; magnesium 12,000; iodine 8,700 [world rank: 2]; silver 11,000 kg; gold 8,869 kg. **Selected balance of payments data.** Receipts from (US$'000,000): tourism (2007) 9,345; remittances (2008) 1,929; foreign direct investment (FDI; 2005–07 avg.) 6,273. Disbursements for (US$'000,000): tourism (2007) 26,511; remittances (2008) 4,743; FDI (2005–07 avg.) 56,532.

## Foreign trade

**Imports** (2006; c.i.f.): ¥67,345,000,000,000 (mineral fuels 27.9%, of which crude petroleum 20.1%, natural gas 5.3%, coal 2.5%; machinery and apparatus 21.1%, of which heavy machinery 4.8%, office machines and computers 4.6%, electronic integrated circuits and micro-assemblies 3.7%; food products 7.4%, of which marine products 2.3%; chemical products 7.1%; metal ores and metal scrap 4.2%; wearing apparel and accessories 4.1%; nonferrous base metals [particularly aluminum and platinum-group] 3.1%; professional and scientific equipment 2.7%; motor vehicles 2.4%). *Major import sources:* China 20.5%; US 12.0%; Saudi Arabia 6.4%; UAE 5.5%; Australia 4.8%; South Korea 4.7%; Indonesia 4.2%; unspecified Asia (probably Taiwan) 3.5%; Germany 3.2%; Thailand 2.9%. **Exports** (2006; f.o.b.): ¥75,214,000,000,000 (machinery and apparatus 39.5%, of which microcircuits and transistors 6.5%, specialized machinery 5.9%, general industrial machinery 5.4%, telecommunications equipment 5.2%, office machines and computers 3.7%, power-generating machinery 3.7%; motor vehicles 21.6%, of which passenger cars 14.6%; chemical products 8.9%; iron and steel 4.6%). *Major export destinations:* US 22.8%; China 14.3%; South Korea 7.8%; unspecified Asia (probably Taiwan) 6.8%; Hong Kong 5.6%; Thailand 3.5%; Germany 3.2%; Singapore 3.0%; UK 2.4%; Netherlands 2.3%.

## Transport and communications

**Transport.** *Railroads* (2007): length (2004) 23,577 km; passenger-km 395,908,000,000; metric ton-km cargo 23,191,000,000. *Roads* (2006): total length 1,197,000 km (paved 79%). *Vehicles* (2008): passenger cars 57,617,000; trucks and buses 16,490,000. *Air transport* (2007): passengers carried 112,543,000; passenger-km 162,954,000,000; metric ton-km cargo 9,449,850,000. **Communications,** in total units (units per 1,000 persons). Telephone landlines (2007): 51,232,000 (401); cellular telephone subscribers (2008): 110,395,000 (864); personal computers (2005): 86,389,000 (675); total Internet users (2007): 88,110,000 (690); broadband Internet subscribers (2008): 30,107,000 (236). *Radio and television broadcasting* (2003): total radio stations 1,612, of which commercial 723; total television stations 15,021, of which commercial 8,276. Commercial broadcasting hours (by percentage of programs): reports—radio 12.3%, television 19.8%; education—radio 2.4%, television 12.3%; culture—radio 13.3%, television 25.1%; entertainment—radio 69.3%, television 37.5%. Advertisements (daily average): radio 149, television 445.

## Education and health

**Literacy:** total population ages 15 and over literate, virtually 100%. **Health** (2006): physicians 275,127 (1 per 464 persons); dentists 95,944 (1 per 1,332 persons); nurses and assistant nurses 1,194,129 (1 per 107 persons); pharmacists 234,429 (1 per 545 persons); midwives (2004) 25,257 (1 per 5,059 persons); hospital beds (2007) 1,620,173 (1 per 79 persons); infant mortality rate per 1,000 live births (2008) 2.6; undernourished population (2002–04) less than 2.5% of total population.

## Military

**Total active duty personnel** (November 2008): 230,300 (army 60.1%, navy 19.1%, air force 19.8%, central staff 1.0%); US troops (December 2008): 34,039 (including 2,850 troops deployed in Afghanistan and Iraq). **Military expenditure as percentage of GDP** (2008): 0.9%; per capita expenditure US$370.

## Background

Japan's history began with the accession of the legendary first emperor, Jimmu, in 660 BC. The Yamato court established the first unified Japanese state in the 4th–5th centuries AD; during this period Buddhism arrived in Japan by way of Korea. For centuries Japan borrowed heavily from Chinese culture, but it began to sever its links with the mainland by the 9th century. In 1192 Minamoto Yoritomo established Japan's first *bakufu,* or shogunate. Unification was achieved in the late 1500s under the leadership of Oda Nobunaga, Toyotomi Hideyoshi, and Tokugawa Ieyasu. During the Tokugawa shogunate, beginning in 1603, the government imposed a policy of isolation. Under the leadership of Emperor Meiji (1868–1912), it adopted a constitution (1889) and began a program of modernization and Westernization. Japanese imperialism led to war with China (1894–95) and Russia (1904–05) as well as to the annexation of Korea (1910) and Manchuria (1931). During World War II, Japan attacked US forces in Hawaii and the Philippines (December 1941) and occupied European colonial possessions in South Asia. In 1945 the US dropped atomic bombs on Hiroshima and Nagasaki, and Japan surrendered to the Allied powers. US postwar occupation of Japan led to a new democratic constitution in 1947. In rebuilding Japan's ruined industrial plant, new technology was used in every major industry. A tremendous economic recovery followed, and Japan became one of the world's wealthiest countries. It was able to maintain a favorable balance of trade despite a long-term economic recession. In March 2011, a severe underwater earthquake off northeastern Japan generated devastating tsunami waves that caused massive destruction and loss of life in coastal areas there.

## Recent Developments

The magnitude-9.0 earthquake and tsunami of 11 March sent shock waves through all aspects of affairs in Japan in 2011. Damage from the temblor was serious, but it paled in comparison with the overwhelming devastation caused by a series of powerful quake-generated tsunami waves, which rushed inland over low-lying areas of the eastern Honshu (Tohoku) coast, sweeping away towns and inundating vast areas of farmland. At the end of the year, some 19,300 people had died or were listed as missing, the bulk of them victims of the tsunami. The most enduring effects of the disaster, however, unfolded at the Fukushima Daiichi nuclear power complex along the coast of Fukushima prefecture, where, following the earthquake and tsunami, the plant's cooling systems failed. That led to partial meltdowns in three reactors and to the release of radioactive materials into the environment. The situation developed into the worst nuclear emergency since the Chernobyl accident in 1986.

The earthquake and tsunami also contributed to dramatic swings in the Japanese economy during 2011. Already operating at close to stall speed at the start of the year, the economy shrank sharply in the first half of the year largely because of the damage to ports, supply networks, and the power grid in northeastern Japan. Also slowing the economy was the loss of electric power produced by nuclear plants as reactors across the country were shut down for inspections and then left off-line. As summer started, with just 17 of Japan's 54 reactors online, the government issued advice to consumers and worked with large employers to reduce electricity consumption in the Tokyo area by 15% during peak daylight hours. With export sectors hit hard by the quake, Japan ran a trade deficit in 2011—its first such deficit in 30 years. By late summer, however, the economy had reversed direction. By the end of the first quarter of 2012, GDP was again growing. Reflecting that recovery, the unemployment rate fell to 4.6% by April 2012. Although the rebound in growth and the decline in unemployment were good news, economic analysts remained worried that the economy faced serious challenges going forward, including slowdowns in Japan's major export markets: Europe, North America, and China.

**Internet resource:**
<www.stat.go.jp/english/index.htm>.

# Jordan

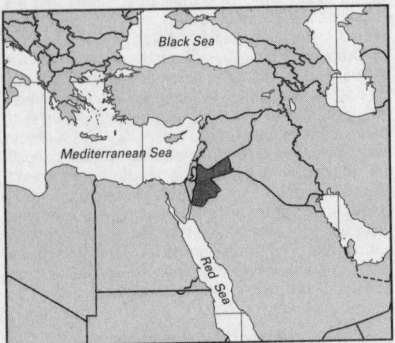

**Official name:** Al-Mamlakah al-Urduniyah al-Hashimiyah (Hashemite Kingdom of Jordan). **Form of government:** constitutional monarchy with two legislative houses (Senate [60]; House of Representatives [120]). **Head of state and government:** King 'Abdullah II (from 1999), assisted by Prime Minister Fayez al-Tarawneh (from 2012). **Capital:** Amman. **Official language:** Arabic. **Official religion:** Islam. **Monetary unit:** 1 Jordanian dinar (JD) = 1,000 fils; valuation (2 Jul 2012) US$1 = JD 0.71.

## Demography

**Area:** 34,277 sq mi, 88,778 sq km. **Population** (2011): 6,180,000. **Density** (2011): persons per sq mi 180.3, persons per sq km 69.6. **Urban** (2009): 78.5%. **Sex distribution** (2008): male 51.05%; female 48.95%. **Age breakdown** (2005): under 15, 37.2%; 15–29, 28.9%; 30–44, 20.7%; 45–59, 8.2%; 60–74, 4.2%; 75–84, 0.7%; 85 and over, 0.1%. **Ethnic composition** (2000): Arab 97.8%, of which Jordanian 32.4%, Palestinian 32.2%, Iraqi 14.0%, Bedouin 12.8%; Circassian 1.2%; other 1.0%. **Religious affiliation** (2005): Sunni Muslim 95%; Christian 3%; other (mostly Shi'i Muslim and Druze) 2%. **Major cities** (2004): Amman 1,036,330; Al-Zarqa 395,227; Irbid 250,645; Al-Rusayfah 227,735; Al-Quwaysimah 135,500. **Location:** the Middle East, bordering Syria, Iraq, Saudi Arabia, the Gulf of Aqaba, Israel, and the West Bank.

## Vital statistics

**Birth rate** per 1,000 population (2007): 28.0 (world avg. 20.3). **Death rate** per 1,000 population (2007): 7.0 (world avg. 8.5). **Total fertility rate** (avg. births per childbearing woman; 2008): 3.50. **Life expectancy** at birth (2008): male 71.6 years; female 74.4 years.

## National economy

**Budget** (2007). *Revenue:* JD 3,971,500,000 (tax revenue 75.4%, of which taxes on goods and services 39.5%, corporate taxes 10.0%, customs duties 9.3%, property taxes 7.7%; nontax revenue 15.5%; grants 8.6%). *Expenditures:* JD 4,540,100,000 (social protection 28.0%; defense 16.7%; education 13.9%; public order 8.8%; economic affairs 7.6%; health 7.1%; public debt 7.1%). **Public debt** (external, outstanding; 2007): US$7,318,000,000. **Production** (metric tons except as noted). *Agriculture and fishing* (2007): tomatoes 550,000, potatoes 170,000, cucumbers 140,000, olives 115,000, eggplants 95,000; livestock (number of live animals) 2,100,000 sheep, 434,000 goats, 25,000,000 chickens; fisheries production 1,015 (from aquaculture 50%). *Mining and quarrying* (2007): phosphate ore 5,552,000; potash 1,796,000; bromine 85,105. *Manufacturing* (value added in US$'000,000; 2006): bricks, cement, and ceramics 423; food products 280; paints, soaps, and pharmaceuticals 260. *Energy production (consumption):* electricity (kW-hr; 2008) 12,682,000,000 ([2006] 11,598,000,000); crude petroleum (barrels; 2007) 9,300 ([2006] 30,900,000); petroleum products (metric tons; 2006) 4,067,000 (4,710,000); natural gas (cu m; 2006) 199,000,000 (2,150,000,000). **Population economically active** (2006): total 1,627,000; activity rate of total population 28.4% (participation rates: ages 15–64, 46.8%; female 17.0%; unemployed [2007] 13.1%). **Gross national income** (2008): US$19,526,000,000 (US$3,310 per capita). **Selected balance of payments data.** Receipts from (US$'000,000): tourism (2007) 2,312; remittances (2007) 3,737; foreign direct investment (FDI; 2005–07 avg.) 2,276; official development assistance (2007) 504. Disbursements for (US$'000,000): tourism (2007) 883; remittances (2007) 479; FDI (2005–07 avg.) 24.

---

*1 metric ton = about 1.1 short tons;    1 kilometer = 0.6 mi (statute);    1 metric ton-km cargo = about 0.68 short ton-mi cargo;    c.i.f.: cost, insurance, and freight;    f.o.b.: free on board*

## Foreign trade

**Imports** (2007; c.i.f.): US$13,531,000,000 (machinery and apparatus 17.4%; crude petroleum 15.3%; food products 13.0%; chemical products 9.3%; motor vehicles and parts 7.2%). *Major import sources:* Saudi Arabia 21.0%; China 9.7%; Germany 7.5%; US 4.7%; Egypt 4.4%. **Exports** (2007; f.o.b.): US$5,700,-000,000 (wearing apparel and accessories 21.3%; fertilizers 14.5%; food products 10.9%, of which tomatoes 3.1%; medicaments 7.5%; telecommunications equipment and parts 5.9%). *Major export destinations:* US 21.8%; Iraq 12.7%; India 8.3%; Saudi Arabia 7.2%; UAE 6.8%.

## Transport and communications

**Transport.** *Railroads* (2004): route length (2006) 506 km; passenger-km 1,000,000; metric ton-km cargo 563,000,000. *Roads* (2005): total length 7,601 km (paved 100%). *Vehicles* (2006): passenger cars 482,042; trucks and buses 216,905. *Air transport* (2006; Royal Jordanian airlines only): passenger-km 5,521,000,000; metric ton-km cargo 210,000,000. **Communications,** in total units (units per 1,000 persons). Telephone landlines (2008): 519,000 (89); cellular telephone subscribers (2008): 5,314,000 (908); personal computers (2007): 383,000 (67); total Internet users (2008): 1,501,000 (257); broadband Internet subscribers (2008): 128,000 (22).

## Education and health

**Educational attainment** (2004). Percentage of population ages 25 and over having: no formal schooling: illiterate 14.0%, literate 4.8%; primary/lower secondary education 36.6%; upper secondary 19.4%; some higher 25.1%, of which advanced degree 2.1%; unknown 0.1%. **Literacy** (2007): percentage of population ages 15 and over literate 92.1%; males literate 95.7%; females literate 88.4%. **Health** (2007): physicians 15,280 (1 per 375 persons); hospital beds 11,029 (1 per 519 persons); infant mortality rate per 1,000 live births (2008) 19.0; undernourished population (2002–04) 300,000 (6% of total population based on the consumption of a minimum daily requirement of 1,810 calories).

## Military

**Total active duty personnel** (November 2008): 100,500 (army 84.6%, navy 0.5%, air force 14.9%). **Military expenditure as percentage of GDP** (2008): 10.6%; per capita expenditure US$332.

## Background

Jordan shares much of its history with Israel, since both occupy the area known historically as Palestine. Much of present-day eastern Jordan was incorporated into Israel under Kings David and Solomon c. 1000 BC. It fell to the Seleucids in 330 BC and to Muslim Arabs in the 7th century AD. The Crusaders extended the kingdom of Jerusalem east of the Jordan River in 1099. Jordan submitted to Ottoman Turkish rule during the 16th century. In 1920 the area comprising Jordan (then known as Transjordan) was established within the British mandate of Palestine. Transjordan became an independent state in 1927, although the British mandate did not end until 1948. After hostilities with the new state of Israel ceased in

1949, Jordan annexed the West Bank of the Jordan River, administering the territory until Israel gained control of it in the Six-Day War of 1967. In 1970–71 Jordan was wracked by fighting between the government and guerrillas of the Palestine Liberation Organization (PLO), a struggle that ended in the expulsion of the PLO from Jordan. In 1988 King Hussein renounced all Jordanian claims to the West Bank in favor of the PLO. In 1994 Jordan and Israel signed a full peace agreement. Upon the death of King Hussein in 1999, his son 'Abdullah took over the throne.

## Recent Developments

The political scene in Jordan in 2011 was dominated by struggles over political reform. In January Jordanian protesters called for reforms to the political system; corruption and unemployment were also key grievances. In August the king announced proposed constitutional reforms, including the establishment of a constitutional court and an independent electoral commission, the prohibition of torture and phone tapping, limitations on the government's ability to dissolve the parliament and pass its own temporary laws, and a reduction in the jurisdiction for the state security court.

**Internet resource:**
<www.dos.gov.jo/dos_home_e/main/index.htm>.

# Kazakhstan

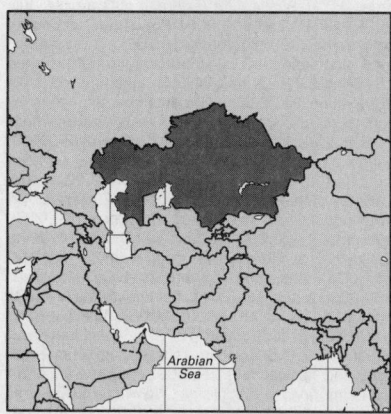

**Official name:** Qazaqstan Respublikasy (Kazakh); Respublika Kazakhstan (Russian) (Republic of Kazakhstan). **Form of government:** unitary republic with two legislative houses (Senate [47]; House of Representatives [107]). **Head of state and government:** President Nursultan Nazarbayev (from 1990), assisted by Prime Minister Karim Masimov (from 2007). **Capital:** Astana. **Official languages:** Kazakh; Russian. **Official religion:** none. **Monetary unit:** 1 tenge (T) = 100 tiyn; valuation (2 Jul 2012) US$1 = T 149.52.

## Demography

**Area:** 1,052,090 sq mi, 2,724,900 sq km. **Population** (2011): 16,560,000. **Density** (2011): persons per sq mi 15.7, persons per sq km 6.1. **Urban** (2009): 54.0%. **Sex distribution** (2008): male 47.59%; female 52.41%. **Age breakdown** (2005): under 15, 23.7%; 15–29, 28.7%; 30–44, 20.7%; 45–59, 16.4%; 60–74, 7.9%; 75–84, 2.3%; 85 and over, 0.3%. **Ethnic composition** (2003): Kazakh 57.2%; Russian 27.2%; Ukrainian 3.1%; Uzbek 2.7%; German 1.6%; Tatar 1.6%; Uighur 1.5%; other 5.1%. **Religious affiliation** (2000): Muslim (mostly Sunni) 42.7%; nonreligious 29.3%; Christian 16.7%, of which Orthodox 8.6%; atheist 10.9%; other 0.4%. **Major cities** (2005): Almaty 1,247,896; Astana 550,-438; Shymkent (Chimkent) 526,140; Qaraghandy (Karaganda) 446,139; Taraz 336,057. **Location:** central Asia, bordering Russia, China, Kyrgyzstan, Uzbekistan, the Aral Sea, Turkmenistan, and the Caspian Sea.

## Vital statistics

**Birth rate** per 1,000 population (2008): 22.6 (world avg. 20.3). **Death rate** per 1,000 population (2008): 9.7 (world avg. 8.5). **Total fertility rate** (avg. births per childbearing woman; 2008): 1.88. **Life expectancy** at birth (2008): male 61.9 years; female 72.6 years.

## National economy

**Budget** (2007). *Revenue:* T 2,895,975,900,000 (tax revenue 81.4%; transfers 8.9%; capital revenue 3.2%). *Expenditures:* T 2,678,280,300,000 (social security 18.8%; education 17.0%; health 11.2%; transportation and communications 10.8%; public order 9.0%). **Public debt** (external, outstanding; July 2009): US$2,254,900,000. **Population economically active** (2008): total 8,415,100; activity rate of total population 53.7% (participation rates: ages 15–64, 78.2%; female 49.6%; unemployed [July 2008–June 2009] 6.7%). **Production** (metric tons except as noted). *Agriculture and fishing* (2008): wheat 12,538,200, potatoes 2,354,400, barley 2,059,000, cotton 317,500; livestock (number of live animals) 16,770,400 sheep and goats, 5,991,600 cattle, 148,300 camels; fisheries production (2007) 41,628 (from aquaculture 1%). *Mining and quarrying* (2006): iron ore 18,600,000; bauxite 4,800,000; chromite 3,600,000 (world rank: 2); copper (metal content) 457,000; zinc (metal content) 400,000; silver 830,000 kg; gold 18,000 kg. *Manufacturing* (value of production in T '000,000; 2008): base metals 1,408,325; food products 757,757; machinery and apparatus 297,501; coke, refined petroleum products, and nuclear fuel 235,309. *Energy production (consumption):* electricity (kW-hr; 2008–09) 77,556,000,000 ([2006] 72,488,000,000); coal (metric tons; 2008–09) 95,011,000 ([2006] 63,765,000); lignite (metric tons; 2008–09) 4,478,000 ([2006] 4,207,000); crude petroleum (barrels; 2008–09) 515,758,000 ([2006] 92,615,000); petroleum products (metric tons; 2006) 11,524,000 (9,048,000); natural gas (cu m; 2008) 33,382,500,000 ([2007] 30,580,000,000). **Gross national income** (2008): US$96,240,000,000 (US$6,140 per capita). **Selected balance of payments data.** Receipts from (US$'000,000): tourism (2007) 1,013; remittances (2008) 192; foreign direct investment (FDI; 2006–08 avg.) 10,337; official development assistance (2007) 202. Disbursements for (US$'000,000): tourism (2007) 1,041; remittances (2008) 3,559; FDI (2005–07 avg.) 876.

## Foreign trade

**Imports** (2008; c.i.f.): US$37,889,000,000 (mineral fuels 15.0%; fabricated metal products 12.4%; transportation equipment 9.3%; machinery and apparatus 7.6%; chemical products 3.6%; iron and steel 3.1%). *Major import sources:* Russia 36.3%; China 12.0%; Germany 6.8%; Ukraine 5.6%; US 5.1%. **Exports** (2008; f.o.b.): US$71,183,500,000 (mineral fuels 72.1%; iron and steel 8.8%; nonferrous metals 6.0%, of which refined copper 4.1%). *Major export destinations:* Italy 16.7%; Switzerland 15.8%; China 10.8%; Russia 8.7%; France 7.6%.

## Transport and communications

**Transport.** *Railroads* (2008): route length 13,700 km; passenger-km 14,130,000,000; metric ton-km cargo 215,110,600,000. *Roads* (2008): total length 93,600 km (paved 90%). *Vehicles* (2007): passenger cars 2,183,100; trucks and buses 442,572. *Air transport:* passenger-km (2008) 5,550,000,000; metric ton-km cargo (2007) 85,700,000. **Communications,** in total units (units per 1,000 persons). Telephone landlines (2008): 3,410,000 (220); cellular telephone subscribers (2008): 14,911,000 (961); total Internet users (2008): 2,300,000 (148); broadband Internet subscribers (2008): 661,000 (43).

## Education and health

**Educational attainment** (1999). Population ages 25 and over having: no formal schooling/some primary education 9.1%; primary education 23.1%; secondary/some postsecondary 57.8%; higher 10.0%. **Literacy** (2007): percentage of total population ages 15 and over literate, virtually 100%. **Health** (2008): physicians 58,945 (1 per 266 persons); hospital beds 120,840 (1 per 130 persons); infant mortality rate per 1,000 live births 20.5; undernourished population (2002–04) 900,000 (6% of total population based on the consumption of a minimum daily requirement of 1,950 calories).

## Military

**Total active duty personnel** (November 2008): 49,000 (army 61.2%, navy 6.1%, air force 24.5%, Ministry of Defense staff 8.2%). **Military expenditure as percentage of GDP** (2007): 1.1%; per capita expenditure US$75.

## Background

Named for its earliest inhabitants, the Kazakhs, the area came under Mongol rule in the 13th century. The Kazakhs consolidated a nomadic empire in the 15th–16th centuries. Under Russian rule by the mid-19th century, it became part of the Kirgiz Autonomous Republic formed by the Soviets in 1920, and in 1925 its name was changed to the Kazakh Autonomous Soviet Socialist Republic. Kazakhstan obtained its independence in 1991. After several years of economic troubles, it began a period of sustained growth, fueled largely by bountiful mineral resources.

*1 metric ton = about 1.1 short tons;   1 kilometer = 0.6 mi (statute);   1 metric ton-km cargo = about 0.68 short ton-mi cargo;   c.i.f.: cost, insurance, and freight;   f.o.b.: free on board*

## Recent Developments

Kazakhstan continued its march toward becoming an industrial power in 2011. In August the minister for industry and new technology announced that in the previous 18 months, 227 industrial projects had been launched in the country, resulting in 29,000 jobs. In July Kazakh officials reported that negotiations over conditions for US and EU firms to enter the Kazakhstan market had been completed, and the country had entered the final stage of preparation for its long-desired goal of accession to the World Trade Organization.

**Internet resource:** <www.eng.stat.kz>.

# Kenya

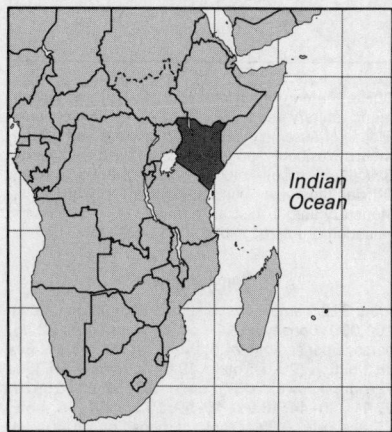

Indian Ocean

**Official name:** Jamhuri ya Kenya (Swahili); Republic of Kenya (English). **Form of government:** unitary multiparty republic with one legislative house (National Assembly [224]). **Head of state and government:** President Mwai Kibaki (from 2002), assisted by Prime Minister Raila Odinga (from 2008). **Capital:** Nairobi. **Official languages:** Swahili; English. **Official religion:** none. **Monetary unit:** 1 Kenya shilling (K Sh) = 100 cents; valuation (2 Jul 2012) US$1 = K Sh 84.05.

## Demography

**Area:** 224,961 sq mi, 582,646 sq km. **Population** (2011): 40,770,000. **Density** (2011): persons per sq mi 181.2, persons per sq km 70.0. **Urban** (2009): 32.3%. **Sex distribution** (2006): male 48.90%; female 51.10%. **Age breakdown** (2006): under 15, 43.1%; 15–29, 30.2%; 30–44, 15.2%; 45–59, 7.0%; 60–74, 3.5%; 75 and over, 1.0%. **Ethnic composition** (2004): Kikuyu 21%; Luhya 14%; Luo 13%; Kalenjin 11%; Kamba 11%; Gusii 6%; Meru 5%; other 19%. **Religious affiliation** (2006): Protestant/independent Christian 66%; Roman Catholic 23%; Muslim 8%; nonreligious 2%; traditional beliefs 1%. **Major cities** (2006): Nairobi 2,864,700; Mombasa 823,500; Nakuru 266,500; Eldoret 227,800; Kisumu 220,000. **Location:** eastern Africa, bordering Ethiopia, Somalia, the Indian Ocean, Tanzania, Uganda, and South Sudan.

## Vital statistics

**Birth rate** per 1,000 population (2006): 39.7 (world avg. 20.3). **Death rate** per 1,000 population (2006): 11.5 (world avg. 8.5). **Total fertility rate** (avg. births per childbearing woman; 2006): 4.91. **Life expectancy** at birth (2006): male 54.3 years; female 54.2 years.

## National economy

**Budget** (2008–09). *Revenue:* K Sh 511,355,-000,000 (tax revenue 85.5%, of which income and profit taxes 39.9%, VAT 24.8%, excise tax 13.7%; nontax revenue 11.0%; grants 3.5%). *Expenditures:* K Sh 621,909,000,000 (current expenditures 74.3%, of which interest payments 8.4%; development expenditures 25.7%). **Production** (metric tons except as noted). *Agriculture and fishing* (2007): sugarcane (2008) 4,991,907, corn (maize) 3,240,000, cassava 850,000, tea (2008) 345,818, pigeon peas 105,000, coffee (2008) 38,705, supplier of cut flowers to EU; livestock (number of live animals) 12,500,000 cattle, 9,300,000 sheep; fisheries production 136,005 (from aquaculture 3%). *Mining and quarrying* (2007): soda ash 386,598; fluorspar 82,000; salt 64,000; tourmaline 8,800 carats; ruby 5,600 carats. *Manufacturing* (value added in US$'000,000; 2006): food products 473; coke oven products (nearly all soda ash) 268; glass and glass products 244. *Energy production (consumption):* electricity (kW-hr; 2008) 5,694,000,000 (5,301,000,000); coal (metric tons; 2006) none (120,000); crude petroleum (barrels; 2006) none (12,800,000); petroleum products (metric tons; 2006) 1,586,000 (3,365,000). **Population economically active** (2006): total 16,944,000; activity rate of total population 46.4% (participation rates: ages 15–64, 82.1%; female 46.5%; unemployed [2008] 40%). **Gross national income** (2008): US$29,541,000,000 (US$770 per capita). **Public debt** (external, outstanding; 2007): US$6,122,-000,000. **Selected balance of payments data.** Receipts from (US$'000,000): tourism (2007) 910; remittances (2008) 1,692; foreign direct investment (FDI; 2005–07 avg.) 267; official development assistance (2007) 1,275. Disbursements for (US$'000,000): tourism (2007) 262; remittances (2008) 16; FDI (2005–07 avg.) 23.

## Foreign trade

**Imports** (2007; c.i.f.): K Sh 605,142,000,000 (crude petroleum 20.9%; machinery and apparatus 16.1%; chemical products 12.8%; motor vehicles 8.5%; food products 6.1%; aircraft 5.6%). *Major import sources:* UAE 14.8%; India 9.4%; China 7.6%; US 7.4%; Japan 6.8%. **Exports** (2007; f.o.b.): K Sh 274,711,000,000 (tea 17.1%; cut flowers 7.7%; wearing apparel and accessories 5.9%; vegetables 5.7%; refined petroleum products 4.0%; coffee 3.8%; soda ash, none). *Major export destinations:* Uganda 12.2%; UK 10.5%; Tanzania 8.1%; Netherlands 8.0%; US 7.0%.

## Transport and communications

**Transport.** *Railroads* (2005): route length 2,778 km; passenger-km 489,000,000; metric ton-km cargo 1,358,000,000. *Roads* (2004): total length 63,265 km (paved 14.8%). *Vehicles* (2004): passenger cars 307,772; trucks and buses 299,317. *Air transport* (2008; Kenya Airways and African Express only): passenger-km 8,829,000,000; metric ton-km cargo 238,451,000. **Communications**, in total units (units per 1,000 persons). Telephone landlines (2008): 252,000 (6.5); cellular telephone subscribers (2008): 16,234,000 (419); personal computers (2007): 529,000 (14); total Internet users (2008): 3,360,000 (87); broadband Internet subscribers (2006): 18,000 (0.5).

## Education and health

**Educational attainment** (1998–99). Percentage of population ages 6 and over having: no formal schooling/unknown 20.2%; primary education 59.0%; secondary 19.7%; university 1.1%. **Literacy** (2000): total population ages 16 and over literate 73.6%; males literate 77.7%; females literate 70.2%. **Health** (2006): physicians (2007) 6,271 (1 per 5,886 persons); hospital beds 51,481 (1 per 714 persons); infant mortality rate per 1,000 live births 59.0; undernourished population (2002–04) 9,900,000 (31% of total population based on the consumption of a minimum daily requirement of 1,840 calories).

## Military

**Total active duty personnel** (November 2008): 24,120 (army 82.9%, navy 6.7%, air force 10.4%). **Military expenditure as percentage of GDP** (2008): 2.1%; per capita expenditure US$17.

## Background

The coastal region of East Africa was dominated by Arabs until it was seized by the Portuguese in the 16th century. The Masai people held sway in the north and moved into central Kenya in the 18th century, while the Kikuyu expanded from their home region in south-central Kenya. The interior was explored by European missionaries in the 19th century. After the British took control, Kenya was established as a British protectorate (1890) and a crown colony (1920). The Mau Mau rebellion of the 1950s was directed against European colonialism. In 1963 the country became fully independent, and a year later a republican government under Jomo Kenyatta was elected. In 1992 Kenyan Pres. Daniel arap Moi allowed the country's first multiparty elections in three decades; however, the government continued to be marked by corruption and mismanagement.

## Recent Developments

One of the provisions of the historic 2010 Kenyan constitution was for the creation of a Supreme Court, which was established in June 2011. Another provision, for the establishment of a new anticorruption agency, was implemented in August. In October Kenya declared war on al-Shabaab (an Islamic militant group) at home and abroad to bring to justice the Somali-based group believed to have orchestrated the kidnappings of tourists in northeastern Kenya. Kenyan troops entered Somalia the next day. It became apparent, however, that the action represented a longer-term strategy, coordinated with Somalia's Transitional Federal Government, to reinforce security in the Somali capital, Mogadishu, and destroy the networks of the rebel militias, pirates, and drugs and

arms traffickers, some with possible links to corrupt officials in Nairobi.

**Internet resource:** <www.knbs.or.ke>.

# Kiribati

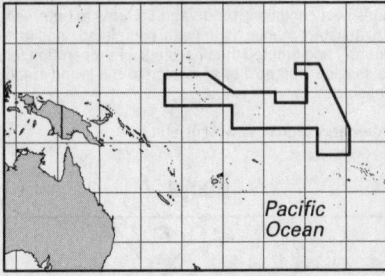

Pacific Ocean

**Official name:** Republic of Kiribati. **Form of government:** unitary republic with one legislative house (House of Assembly [46]). **Head of state and government:** President Anote Tong (from 2003). **Capital:** Bairiki (executive); Ambo (legislative); Betio (judicial). **Official language:** English. **Official religion:** none. **Monetary unit:** 1 Australian dollar ($A) = 100 cents; valuation (2 Jul 2012) US$1 = $A 0.98.

## Demography

**Area:** 312.9 sq mi, 810.5 sq km. **Population** (2011): 101,000. **Density** (2011): persons per sq mi 322.8, persons per sq km 124.6. **Urban** (2009): 43.9%. **Sex distribution** (2007): male 49.64%; female 50.36%. **Age breakdown** (2007): under 15, 38.2%; 15–29, 27.7%; 30–44, 18.0%; 45–59, 10.7%; 60–74, 4.5%; 75 and over, 0.9%. **Ethnic composition** (2000): Micronesian 98.8%; Polynesian 0.7%; European 0.2%; other 0.3%. **Religious affiliation** (2005): Roman Catholic 55.3%; Kiribati Protestant (Congregational) 35.7%; Mormon 3.1%; Baha'i 2.2%; other/nonreligious 3.7%. **Major villages** (2005): Betio 12,509; Bikenibeu 6,170; Teaoraereke 3,939. **Location:** Oceania, islands in the western Pacific Ocean, south of the Hawaiian Islands (US).

## Vital statistics

**Birth rate** per 1,000 population (2007): 30.5 (world avg. 20.3). **Death rate** per 1,000 population (2007): 8.1 (world avg. 8.5). **Total fertility rate** (avg. births per childbearing woman; 2007): 4.12. **Life expectancy** at birth (2007): male 59.4 years; female 65.7 years.

## National economy

**Budget** (2008). *Revenue:* $A 161,700,000 (nontax revenue 24.1%, of which fishing license fees 19.9%; tax revenue 18.4%; grants 57.5%). *Expenditures:* $A 183,000,000 (development expenditures 50.9%; current expenditures 49.1%). **Public debt** (external, outstanding; 2008): US$10,100,000. **Production** (metric tons except as noted). *Agriculture and fishing* (2007): coconuts 110,000, bananas 5,800, taro 2,200; livestock (number of live animals) 12,600 pigs, 480,000 chickens; fisheries production 21,603 (from aquaculture, negligible); aquatic plants (all seaweed) production 1,112 (from aquaculture 100%). *Mining and quarrying:* small amounts of salt. *Manufacturing* (2008): copra 9,135; processed fish, wearing apparel, and handicrafts are also made. *Energy production (consumption):* electricity (kW-hr; 2006) 15,000,000 (15,000,000); petroleum products (metric tons; 2006) none (10,000). **Selected balance of payments data.** Receipts from (US$'000,000): tourism (2001) 3.2; remittances (2008) 9; foreign direct investment (2005–07 avg.) 8; official development assistance (2007) 27. Disbursements for (US$'000,000): tourism (1999) 2.0. **Population economically active** (2005): total 36,969; activity rate of total population 38.8% (participation rates: ages 16 and over, 63.4%; female 45.9%; unemployed 6.1%). **Gross national income** (2008): US$193,000,000 (US$2,000 per capita).

### Foreign trade

**Imports** (2005): $A 96,900,000 (food products 29.6%, of which rice 10.7%, meat 6.4%; refined petroleum products 16.8%; machinery and apparatus 14.6%, of which generators 6.2%; motor vehicles 5.7%). *Major import sources* (2007): Fiji 35.1%; Australia 33.5%; Japan 6.3%; New Zealand 5.9%; China 4.3%. **Exports** (2007): $A 11,655,000 (domestic exports 81.0%, of which crude coconut oil 45.7%, copra and copra cake 14.4%, fish 10.7%, seaweed 1.9%; reexports 19.0%). *Major export destinations* (2005): Australia 22%; Fiji 17%; other Asia (probably Taiwan) 14%; Hong Kong 8%.

### Transport and communications

**Transport.** *Roads* (2000): total length 670 km. *Vehicles* (2004; registered vehicles in South Tarawa only): passenger cars 610; trucks and buses 808. *Air transport:* domestic air service only from 2004. **Communications**, in total units (units per 1,000 persons). Telephone landlines (2008): 4,000 (41); cellular telephone subscribers (2008): 1,000 (10); personal computers (2005): 1,000 (11); total Internet users (2008): 2,000 (21).

### Education and health

**Educational attainment** (2005). Percentage of population ages 5 and over having: no schooling/unknown 9.2%; primary education 40.3%; secondary 47.6%; higher 2.9%. **Literacy** (2001): population ages 15 and over literate 94.0%; males literate 93.0%; females literate 95.0%. **Health:** physicians (2006) 30 (1 per 3,120 persons); hospital beds (2005) 140 (1 per 681 persons); infant mortality rate per 1,000 live births (2007) 45.9; undernourished population (2002–04) 5,000 (7% of total population based on the consumption of a minimum daily requirement of 1,810 calories).

### Military

**Total active duty personnel** (November 2008): none; defense assistance is provided by Australia and New Zealand.

### Background

The islands were settled by Austronesian-speaking peoples before the 1st century AD. In 1765 the British discovered the island of Nikunau; the first permanent European settlers arrived in 1837. In 1916 the Gilbert and Ellice islands and Banaba became a crown colony of Britain; they were later joined by the Phoenix and Line islands. The Ellice Islands declared independence (as Tuvalu) in 1978, and in 1979 the remaining islands became the nation of Kiribati.

### Recent Developments

Kiribati in 2011 remained a strong voice in global forums for small island states facing the catastrophic consequences of climate change. The country scored a coup in September when UN Secretary General Ban Ki-Moon visited and saw firsthand the consequences of climate change and sea-level rise on the low-lying atolls of Kiribati. In February 2012, Pres. Anote Tong entered into negotiations with the government of Fiji to purchase land there in case the islands of Kiribati become uninhabitable.

**Internet resource:** <www.kiribatitourism.gov.ki>.

# Korea, North

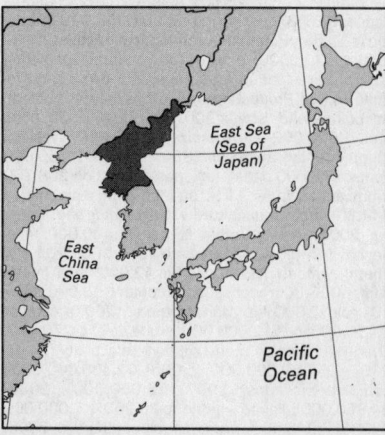

**Official name:** Choson Minjujuui In'min Konghwaguk (Democratic People's Republic of Korea). **Form of government:** unitary single-party republic with one legislative house (Supreme People's Assembly [687]). **Head of state and government:** Supreme Leader Kim Jong-Eun (from 2012). **Capital:** P'yongyang. **Official language:** Korean. **Official religion:** none. **Monetary unit:** 1 (new) North Korean won (W) = 100 chon; valuation (2 Jul 2012) US$1 = 1.30 (new) won (the currency was revalued on 1 Dec 2009; as of this date, 100 (old) North Korean won = 1 (new) North Korean won. The approximate value of the won on the black market in February 2009 was about US$1 = 3,500 [old] won.

### Demography

**Area:** 47,399 sq mi, 122,762 sq km. **Population** (2011): 24,336,000. **Density** (2011): persons per sq mi 513.4, persons per sq km 198.2. **Urban** (2005): 61.6%. **Sex distribution** (2008): male 48.73%; female 51.27%. **Age breakdown** (2007): under 15,

22.1%; 15–29, 23.6%; 30–44, 25.6%; 45–59, 15.5%; 60–74, 11.0%; 75–84, 2.0%; 85 and over, 0.2%. **Ethnic composition** (1999): Korean 99.8%; Chinese 0.2%. **Religious affiliation** (2005): mostly nonreligious/atheist; autonomous religious activities are almost nonexistent. **Major urban agglomerations** (2007): P'yongyang 3,300,000; Namp'o 1,127,000; Hamhung 773,000; Ch'ongjin (1993) 582,480; Kaesong (1993) 334,433. **Location:** eastern Asia, bordering China, Russia, the Sea of Japan (East Sea), the Republic of Korea, and the Yellow Sea.

## Vital statistics

**Birth rate** per 1,000 population (2007): 15.5 (world avg. 20.3). **Death rate** per 1,000 population (2007): 10.4 (world avg. 8.5). **Total fertility rate** (avg. births per childbearing woman; 2007): 1.99. **Life expectancy** at birth (2007): male 60.6 years; female 65.8 years.

## National economy

**Budget** (1999). *Revenue:* 19,801,000,000 [old] won (turnover tax and profits from state enterprises). *Expenditures:* 20,018,200,000 [old] won (1994; national economy 67.8%; social and cultural affairs 19.0%; defense 11.6%). **Population economically active** (2006): total 12,305,000; activity rate of total population 51.9% (participation rates: ages 15–64, 53.7%; female 44.0%). **Production** (metric tons except as noted). *Agriculture and fishing* (2007): rice 2,165,000, potatoes 1,900,000, corn (maize) 1,645,000; livestock (number of live animals) 3,300,000 pigs, 2,760,000 goats, 576,000 cattle; fisheries production 268,700 (from aquaculture 24%); aquatic plants production 444,300 (from aquaculture 100%). *Mining and quarrying* (2007): iron ore (metal content) 1,400,000; magnesite 1,000,000; phosphate rock 300,000; zinc (metal content) 70,000; sulfur 42,000; lead (metal content) 13,000; copper (metal content) 12,000; silver 20; gold 2,000 kg. *Manufacturing* (2007): cement 6,415,000; coke 2,000,000; crude steel 1,279,000. *Energy production (consumption):* electricity (kW-hr; 2007) 25,460,000,000 ([2006] 22,436,000,000); coal (metric tons; 2007) 25,060,000 ([2006] 24,860,000); lignite (metric tons; 2007) 7,000,000 ([2006] 7,946,000); crude petroleum (barrels; 2006) none (2,690,000); petroleum products (metric tons; 2006) 352,000 (701,000). **Public debt** (external, outstanding; 2001): US$12,500,000,000. **Gross national income** (2008): US$24,815,000,000 (US$1,033 per capita). **Selected balance of payments data.** Receipts from (US$'000,000): foreign direct disinvestment (2005–07 avg.) −1; official development assistance (2007) 98.

## Foreign trade

**Imports** (2005): US$2,718,472,000 ([2002; data for commodities exclude trade with South Korea (US$1,525,400,000)] food products, beverages, and other agricultural products 19.3%; mineral fuels and lubricants 15.5%; machinery and apparatus 15.4%; textiles and wearing apparel 10.4%). *Major import sources:* China 39.8%; South Korea 26.3%; Russia 8.2%; Thailand 7.6%; Singapore 2.7%. **Exports** (2005): US$1,338,281,000 ([2002; data for commodities ex-

clude trade with South Korea (US$735,000,000)] live animals and agricultural products 39.3%; textiles and wearing apparel 16.7%; machinery and apparatus 11.6%; mineral fuels and lubricants 9.5%). *Major export destinations:* China 37.3%; South Korea 25.4%; Japan 9.8%; Thailand 9.3%; Russia 0.6%.

## Transport and communications

**Transport.** *Railroads* (2007): length 5,242 km. *Roads* (2007): total length 16,033 mi, 25,802 km (paved [2006] 3%). *Vehicles* (1990): passenger cars 248,000. *Air transport* (2004): passenger-km 39,000,000; metric ton-km cargo (including the weight of mail and passengers) 6,000,000. **Communications,** in total units (units per 1,000 persons). Telephone landlines (2008): 1,180,000 (49).

## Education and health

**Educational attainment** (1987–88). Percentage of population ages 16 and over having attended or graduated from postsecondary-level school: 13.7%. **Literacy** (1997): percentage of total population ages 15 and over literate, 95%. **Health:** physicians (2003) 74,597 (1 per 299 persons); infant mortality rate per 1,000 live births (2007) 53.8; undernourished population (2002–04) 7,600,000 (33% of total population based on the consumption of a minimum daily requirement of 1,900 calories).

## Military

**Total active duty personnel** (November 2008): 1,106,000 (army 85.9%, navy 4.2%, air force 9.9%); reserve 4,700,000. **Military expenditure as percentage of GNI** (2004): 8.1%; per capita expenditure US$80.

## Background

According to tradition, the ancient kingdom of Choson was established in the northern part of the Korean peninsula, probably by peoples from northern China, in the 3rd millennium BC and was conquered by China in 108 BC. The kingdom was ruled by the Yi dynasty from AD 1392 to 1910. That year Korea was formally annexed by Japan. It was freed from Japanese control in 1945, at which time the USSR occupied the area north of latitude 38° N and the US occupied the area south of it. The Democratic People's Republic of Korea was established as a communist state in 1948. North Korea launched an invasion of South Korea in 1950, initiating the Korean War, which ended with an armistice in 1953. Under Kim Il-sung, North Korea became one of the most harshly regimented societies in the world, with a state-owned economy that failed to produce adequate food. In the late 1990s, under Kim Il-sung's successor, Kim Jong Il, the country endured a serious famine; as many as one million Koreans may have died. In October 2006 North Korea conducted an underground nuclear test.

## Recent Developments

The event that overshadowed all others in North Korea in 2011 was the unexpected death of the country's leader, Kim Jong Il, who had been in power officially since 1998. International observers were left waiting to see which of the previously theorized post-Kim scenarios would take shape. Contributing to the uncertainty were instability in the country's economy and in its relationship with South Korea. Further, although Kim's successor, his son Kim Jong-Eun, had been named to a high position on the powerful National Defense Commission in February, he apparently had had little formal experience to prepare him for the country's leadership. Kim Jong-Eun was front and center during the national 10-day mourning period and memorial services. On 29 December Kim Yong-Nam, leader of the Supreme People's Assembly (the national legislature), announced the status of Kim Jong-Eun as "supreme leader," a designation that was believed to indicate his leadership of the military and the Korean Workers' Party. Two days later he was officially named commander of the Korean People's Army.

Internet resource: <www.kcna.co.jp/index-e.htm>.

# Korea, South

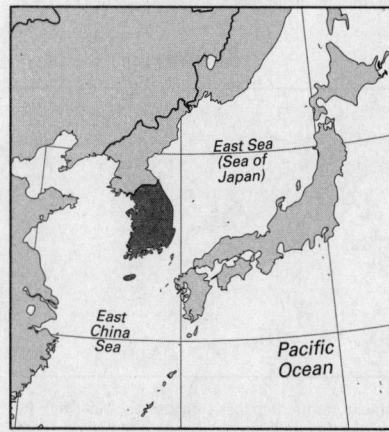

East Sea (Sea of Japan)

East China Sea

Pacific Ocean

**Official name:** Taehan Min'guk (Republic of Korea). **Form of government:** unitary multiparty republic with one legislative house (National Assembly [300]). **Head of state and government:** President Lee Myung Bak (from 2008), assisted by Prime Minister Kim Hwang Sik (from 2010). **Capital:** Seoul. **Official language:** Korean. **Official religion:** none. **Monetary unit:** 1 South Korean won (W) = 100 chon; valuation (2 Jul 2012) US$1 = W 1,146.05.

## Demography

**Area:** 38,486 sq mi, 99,678 sq km. **Population** (2011): 48,755,000. **Density** (2011): persons per sq mi 1,266.8, persons per sq km 489.1. **Urban** (2009): 82.7%. **Sex distribution** (2008): male 50.23%; female 49.77%. **Age breakdown** (2005): under 15, 18.6%; 15–29, 22.5%; 30–44, 26.0%; 45–59, 19.2%; 60–74, 10.7%; 75–84, 2.5%; 85 and over, 0.5%. **Ethnic composition** (2000): Korean 97.7%; Japanese 2.0%; US white 0.1%; Han Chinese 0.1%; other 0.1%. **Religious affiliation** (2005): Christian 43%, of which Protestant 17%, independent Christian 16%, Roman Catholic 9%; traditional beliefs 15%; Buddhist 14%;

New Religionist 14%; Confucianist 10%; other 4%. **Major cities** (2008): Seoul 10,456,034; Pusan 3,596,076; Inch'on 2,741,217; Taegu 2,512,601; Taejon 1,494,951. **Location:** eastern Asia, bordering the Democratic People's Republic of Korea, the Sea of Japan (East Sea), and the Yellow Sea.

## Vital statistics

**Birth rate** per 1,000 population (2008): 9.4 (world avg. 20.3). **Death rate** per 1,000 population (2008): 5.0 (world avg. 8.5). **Total fertility rate** (avg. births per childbearing woman; 2008): 1.19. **Life expectancy** at birth (2007): male 76.1 years; female 82.7 years.

## National economy

**Budget** (2006). *Revenue:* W 209,574,000,000,000 (current revenue 99.3%, of which tax revenue 78.9%, nontax revenue 20.4%; capital revenue 0.7%). *Expenditures:* W 205,928,000,000,000 (current expenditures 84.3%, of which defense 11.4%; capital expenditures 15.7%). **Public debt** (June 2009): US$380,116,000,000. **Production** (metric tons except as noted). *Agriculture and fishing* (2007): rice 5,959,500, cabbages 3,000,000, tangerines, mandarins, satsumas 615,000, persimmons 345,000, garlic 325,000; livestock (number of live animals; 2008) 9,087,000 pigs, 2,876,000 cattle, 119,784,000 chickens; fisheries production 2,464,328 (from aquaculture 25%); aquatic plants production 811,142 (from aquaculture 98%). *Mining and quarrying* (2007): zinc (metal content) 674,400; feldspar 398,513; iron ore (metal content) 163,000; silver (metal content) 1,393,935 kg. *Manufacturing* (value added in US$'000,000; 2006): televisions, radios, telecommunications equipment, and electronic parts 70,085; transportation equipment 52,349, of which automobiles 20,987, automobile parts 16,175, ships and boats 12,771; machinery and apparatus 30,704; chemical products 27,076; iron and steel 20,064; food products 19,928; fabricated metal products 19,172; textiles and wearing apparel 16,913; refined petroleum products 12,161. *Energy production (consumption):* electricity (kW-hr; 2008–09) 425,174,000,000 ([2008] 385,100,000,000); coal (metric tons; 2008–09) 2,604,000 ([2006] 81,003,000); lignite (metric tons; 2006) none (3,706,000); crude petroleum (barrels; 2006) 329,850 (868,150,000); petroleum products (metric tons; 2006) 94,555,000 (55,248,000); natural gas (cu m; 2007) 640,000,000 (37,000,000,000). **Gross national income** (2008): US$1,046,285,000,000 (US$21,530 per capita). **Population economically active** (2009): total 24,525,000; activity rate 50.7% (participation rates: ages 15 and older 61.1%; female 41.3%; unemployed [September 2008–August 2009] 3.3%). **Selected balance of payments data.** Receipts from (US$'000,000): tourism (2007) 5,797; remittances (2008) 3,062; foreign direct investment (FDI; 2005–07 avg.) 3,641. Disbursements for (US$'000,000): tourism (2007) 20,890; remittances (2008) 3,472; FDI (2005–07 avg.) 7,083.

## Foreign trade

**Imports** (2008; c.i.f.): US$435,274,737,000 (mineral fuels 32.7%, of which crude petroleum 24.1%, natural gas 5.7%; machinery and apparatus 23.5%, of which electrical machinery 11.2%; chemical products 8.4%; iron and steel 7.7%). *Major import* *sources:* China 17.7%; Japan 14.0%; US 8.8%; Saudi Arabia 7.8%; UAE 4.4%. **Exports** (2008; f.o.b.): US$422,007,328,000 (machinery and apparatus 34.0%, of which telecommunications equipment 11.7%; electrical equipment 11.7%; transportation equipment 21.4%; chemical products 10.1%; crude petroleum and refined petroleum products 9.1%; professional and scientific equipment 6.0%). *Major export destinations:* China 21.7%; US 11.0%; Japan 6.8%; Hong Kong 4.9%; Singapore 3.9%.

## Transport and communications

**Transport.** *Railroads* (2005): length (2008) 3,381 km; passenger-km 31,004,200,000; metric ton-km cargo 9,336,000,000. *Roads* (2008): total length 103,029 km (paved 78%). *Vehicles* (2006): passenger cars 11,607,000; trucks and buses 4,239,200. *Air transport* (2008): passenger-km 82,236,000,000; metric ton-km cargo 8,786,809,000. **Communications**, in total units (units per 1,000 persons). Telephone landlines (2008): 21,325,000 (443); cellular telephone subscribers (2008): 45,607,000 (947); personal computers (2007): 27,736,000 (578); total Internet users (2008): 34,476,000 (778); broadband Internet subscribers (2008): 15,475,000 (321).

## Education and health

**Educational attainment** (2008). Percentage of population ages 15 and older having: no formal schooling through lower secondary education 31.7%; upper secondary/higher vocational 39.2%; college 9.1%; university 20.0%. **Literacy** (2002): total population ages 15 and over literate 97.9%; males literate 99.2%; females literate 96.6%. **Health** (2008): physicians 95,013 (1 per 507 persons); hospital beds (2006) 417,387 (1 per 114 persons); infant mortality rate per 1,000 live births 3.4; undernourished population (2002–04) less than 2.5% of total population.

## Military

**Total active duty personnel** (November 2008): 692,000 (army 80.9%, navy 9.8%, air force 9.3%); US military forces (January 2009): 24,655. **Military expenditure as percentage of GDP** (2008): 4.0%; per capita expenditure US$594.

## Background

Civilization in the Korean peninsula dates to the 3rd millennium BC. The Republic of Korea was established in AD 1948 in the southern portion of the Korean peninsula. In 1950 North Korean troops invaded South Korea, precipitating the Korean War. UN forces sided with South Korea, while Chinese troops backed North Korea in the war, which ended with an armistice in 1953. The devastated country was rebuilt with US aid, and South Korea prospered in the postwar era, developing a strong export-oriented economy. It experienced an economic downturn in the mid-1990s that affected many Asian economies. Efforts at reconciliation between North and South Korea, including the first-ever summit between their leaders (2000) and reunions of families from both countries, were accompanied by periods of continuing tension.

## Recent Developments

As ever, relations with its northern neighbor made news in South Korea in 2011. In February military representatives from both countries met for talks in the border town of Panmunjom. Little more than a day later, however, the North Korean delegation walked out after the South Koreans pressed for an apology for the sinking of the South Korean ship *Cho-nan* and the shelling of Yonpyong Island, near a disputed maritime border, the previous year. Nevertheless, North Korean leader Kim Jong Il seemed willing to reconvene talks on the North's denuclearization. Nuclear negotiators from both sides met in Bali, Indonesia, in July and in Beijing in September. Tensions continued along the maritime border, however, and in August the two countries briefly exchanged artillery fire near Yonpyong without causing injury. Kim's death on 17 December brought uncertainty as to his country's future direction, but his son and successor, Kim Jong-Eun, indicated some openness to pursuing improvement in inter-Korean relations.

**Internet resource:** <www.kostat.go.kr/eng>.

# Kosovo

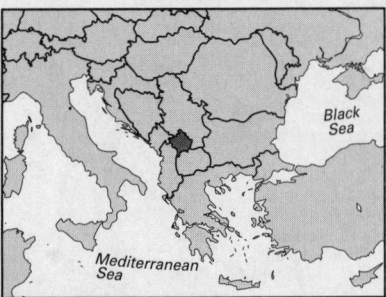

**Official name:** Republika e Kosovës (Albanian); Republika Kosovo (Serbian) (Republic of Kosovo). **Form of government:** multiparty transitional republic with one legislative house (Assembly of Kosovo [120]). **International authority:** UN Interim Administrator Farid Zarif (from 2011), assisted by EU Special Representative Samuel Žbogar (from 2012). **Head of state:** President Atifete Jahjaga (from 2011). **Head of government:** Prime Minister Hashim Thaçi (from 2008). **Capital:** Pristina. **Official languages:** Albanian; Serbian. **Official religion:** none. **Monetary unit:** 1 euro (€) = 100 cents; valuation (2 Jul 2012) US$1 = €0.79 (Kosovo uses the euro as its official currency, even though it is not a member of the EU).

## Demography

**Area:** 4,212 sq mi, 10,908 sq km. **Population** (2011): 1,826,000. **Density** (2011): persons per sq mi 433.5, persons per sq km 167.4. **Urban** (2006): 37%. **Sex distribution** (2007): male 50.52%; female 49.48%. **Age breakdown** (2003): under 15, 32.2%; 15–59, 58.7%; 60 and over, 9.1%. **Ethnic composition** (2008): Albanian 92.0%; Serb 5.3%; other 2.7%.

---

*1 metric ton = about 1.1 short tons;    1 kilometer = 0.6 mi (statute);    1 metric ton-km cargo = about 0.68 short ton-mi cargo;    c.i.f.: cost, insurance, and freight;    f.o.b.: free on board*

Religious affiliation (2006): Muslim (including nominal population) 91.0%; Orthodox 5.5%; Roman Catholic 3.0%; Protestant 0.5%. **Major cities** (2003): Pristina 165,844; Prizren 107,614; Ferizaj 71,758; Mitrovicë (Mitrovica) 68,929; Gjakovë 68,645. **Location:** southeastern Europe, bordering Serbia, Macedonia, Albania, and Montenegro.

## Vital statistics

**Birth rate** per 1,000 population (2008): 16.0 (world avg. 20.3); within marriage 59.8%. **Death rate** per 1,000 population (2008): 3.2 (world avg. 8.5). **Total fertility rate** (avg. births per childbearing woman; 2003): 3.0. **Life expectancy** at birth (2004; Albanian population only): male 69.8 years; female 71.4 years.

## National economy

**Budget** (2007–08). *Revenue:* €2,148,400,000 (tax revenue 79.7%, of which border taxes [including customs duties and VAT] 59.8%, domestic taxes [mostly income and corporate taxes] 19.9%; nontax revenue 20.3%). *Expenditures:* €1,523,000,000 (current expenditures 81.1%; capital expenditures 18.9%). **Production** (metric tons except as noted). *Agriculture and fishing* (2006): wheat 239,464, hay 184,677, corn (maize) 138,248; livestock (number of live animals) 381,995 cattle, 100,814 sheep, 2,337,086 chickens. *Manufacturing* (2006): cement, bricks, and tiles for reconstruction of housing; food products; beverages. *Energy production (consumption):* electricity (kW-hr; 2008) 4,506,000,000 (2,941,000,-000); lignite (metric tons; 2008) 7,842,000 (n.a.). **Gross national income** (2007): US$3,780,000,000 (US$2,117 per capita). **Population economically active** (2007): total 633,000; activity rate of total population 30% (participation rates: ages 15–64, 47%; female 28%; unofficially unemployed [2007] 40%). **Selected balance of payments data.** Receipts from (US$'000,000): tourism (2008) 42; remittances (2008) 785; foreign direct investment (FDI; 2005–07 avg.) 322. Disbursements for (US$'000,000): tourism (2008) 82; remittances (2006) 126; FDI (2006–08 avg.) 15.

## Foreign trade

**Imports** (2008; c.i.f.): €1,927,900,000 (food products and live animals 24.6%; mineral fuels 20.1%; machinery and apparatus 12.2%; base metals 9.3%; chemical products 7.2%; transportation equipment 6.7%). *Major import sources:* Macedonia 18.0%; Serbia 11.1%; Germany 10.2%; Turkey 6.6%; China 6.3%. **Exports** (2008; f.o.b.): €195,900,000 (iron and steel [all forms] 63.3%; food products 11.0%; mineral fuels 9.1%). *Major export destinations:* Belgium 14.3%; Italy 13.0%; India 12.0%; Albania 10.8%; Macedonia 9.9%.

## Transport and communications

**Transport.** *Railroads* (2007): route length 430 km. *Roads* (2008): total length 1,924 km (paved 87%). *Vehicles* (2006): passenger cars 146,744; trucks and buses 20,850. *Air transport* (2007; Pristina airport only): passenger arrivals 483,330; passenger departures 506,962. **Communications**, in total units (units per 1,000 persons). Telephone landlines (2006): 106,000 (60); cellular telephone subscribers (2007): 562,000 (315); total Internet users (2006): 50,000 (28); broadband Internet subscribers (2005): 4,700 (2.3).

## Education and health

**Educational attainment** (2003). Percentage of population ages 25–49 having: no formal schooling 3.5%; incomplete/complete primary 46.0%; incomplete/complete secondary 45.0%; higher 5.5%. **Literacy** (2004): total population ages 15 and over literate 94.1%; males literate 97.3%; females literate 91.3%. **Health:** physicians (2006) 1,534 (1 per 1,368 persons); hospital beds (2005) 5,308 (1 per 387 persons); infant mortality rate per 1,000 live births (2008) 9.7.

## Military

**Total active duty personnel** (February 2010): NATO-led Kosovo Force 10,200.

## Background

The Kingdom of the Serbs, Croats, and Slovenes was created after the collapse of Austria-Hungary at the end of World War I. The country signed treaties with Czechoslovakia and Romania in 1920–21, marking the beginning of the Little Entente. In 1929 an absolute monarchy was established, the country's name was changed to Yugoslavia, and it was divided into regions without regard to ethnic boundaries. Axis powers invaded Yugoslavia in 1941, and German, Italian, Hungarian, and Bulgarian troops occupied it for the rest of World War II. In 1945 the Socialist Federal Republic of Yugoslavia was established; it included the republics of Bosnia and Herzegovina, Croatia, Macedonia, Montenegro, Serbia, and Slovenia. Its independent form of communism under Josip Broz Tito's leadership provoked the USSR. Internal ethnic tensions flared up in the 1980s, causing the country's ultimate collapse. In 1991–92 independence was declared by Croatia, Slovenia, Macedonia, and Bosnia and Herzegovina; the new Federal Republic of Yugoslavia (containing roughly 45% of the population and 40% of the area of its predecessor) was proclaimed by Serbia and Montenegro. Still fueled by long-standing ethnic tensions, hostilities continued into the 1990s. Despite the approval of the Dayton Peace Agreement (1995), sporadic fighting continued and was followed in 1998–99 by Serbian repression and expulsion of ethnic populations in the province of Kosovo. In September–October 2000, the battered nation of Yugoslavia ended the autocratic rule of Pres. Slobodan Milosevic. In April 2001 he was arrested and in June extradited to The Hague to stand trial for war crimes, genocide, and crimes against humanity committed during the fighting in Kosovo. In February 2003 both houses of the Yugoslav federal legislature voted to accept a new state charter and change the name of the country from Yugoslavia to Serbia and Montenegro. Henceforth, defense, international political and economic relations, and human rights matters would be handled centrally, while all other functions would be run from the republican capitals, Belgrade and Podgorica, respectively. The move was seen as an acknowledgment that Serbia and Montenegro had little in common, and a provision was included for both states to vote on independence after three years; Serbia declared its independence in June 2006, shortly after Montenegro severed its federal union with Serbia. From 1999 an autonomous region administered by the UN, Kosovo declared its independence from Serbia on 17 Feb 2008. That December the UN transferred most of its powers of oversight to the EU. In 2010 the International Court of Justice ruled that Kosovo's declaration of independence did not violate international law.

## Recent Developments

Unrest continued in 2011 in northern Kosovo, where ethnic Serbs, backed by the Serbian government, established parallel institutions in defiance of Kosovo's sovereign authority. Negotiations between Serbia and Kosovo continued in an effort to normalize relations between Belgrade and Pristina. At stake was Serbia's candidacy to the EU and Kosovo's place in the international community. Since Kosovo's declaration of independence in 2008, 88 countries had recognized the country.

Internet resource: <http://esk.rks-gov.net/eng>.

# Kuwait

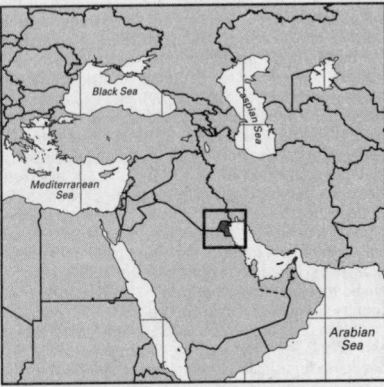

**Official name:** Dawlat al-Kuwayt (State of Kuwait). **Form of government:** constitutional monarchy with one legislative house (National Assembly [65]). **Head of state and government:** Emir Sheikh Sabah al-Ahmad al-Jabir al-Sabah (from 2006), assisted by Prime Minister Sheikh Jabir al-Mubarak al-Hamad al-Sabah (from 2011). **Capital:** Kuwait (city). **Official language:** Arabic. **Official religion:** Islam. **Monetary unit:** 1 Kuwaiti dinar (KD) = 1,000 fils; valuation (2 Jul 2012) US$1 = KD 0.28.

## Demography

**Area:** 6,880 sq mi, 17,818 sq km. **Population** (2011): 3,650,000. **Density** (2011): persons per sq mi 530.5, persons per sq km 204.8. **Urban** (2005): 98.3%. **Sex distribution** (2007): male 59.34%; female 40.66%. **Age breakdown** (2005): under 15, 24.3%; 15–29, 26.8%; 30–44, 34.2%; 45–59, 11.6%; 60–74, 2.7%; 75–84, 0.3%; 85 and over, 0.1%. **Ethnic composition** (2005): Arab 57%, of which Kuwaiti 35%; Bedouin 4%; non-Arab (primarily Asian)

39%. **Religious affiliation** (2005): Muslim 74%, of which Sunni 59%, Shi'i 15%; Christian 13%, of which Roman Catholic 9%; Hindu 10%; Buddhist 3%. **Major cities** (2005): Qalib al-Shuyukh 179,264; Al-Salimiyah 145,328; Hawalli 106,992; Kuwait (city) 32,403 (urban agglomeration [2007] 2,063,000). **Location:** the Middle East, bordering Iraq, the Persian Gulf, and Saudi Arabia.

## Vital statistics

**Birth rate** per 1,000 population (2008): 21.9 (world avg. 20.3). **Death rate** per 1,000 population (2008): 2.3 (world avg. 8.5). **Total fertility rate** (avg. births per childbearing woman; 2008): 2.81. **Life expectancy** at birth (2008): male 76.4 years; female 78.7 years.

## National economy

**Budget** (2006–07). *Revenue:* KD 15,509,300,000 (oil revenue 93.6%; tax revenue 1.9%). *Expenditures:* KD 12,568,700,000 (social security and welfare 29.1%; general public administration 15.8%; oil and electricity 13.4%; defense 10.3%; education 10.1%; health 5.3%). **Public debt** (external, outstanding; 2008): US$7,719,000,000. **Gross national income** (2007): US$125,016,000,000 (US$38,015 per capita). **Production** (metric tons except as noted). *Agriculture and fishing* (2007): tomatoes 55,500, cucumbers and gherkins 35,000, potatoes 23,500, dates 14,500; livestock (number of live animals) 900,000 sheep, 160,000 goats, 28,000 cattle, 5,000 camels; fisheries production 4,721 (from aquaculture 7%). *Mining and quarrying* (2007): sulfur 660,000; lime 50,000. *Manufacturing* (value added in KD '000,000; 2006): refined petroleum products 829; basic chemical products 230; bricks, cement, and tiles 98. *Energy production (consumption):* electricity (kW-hr; 2006) 47,607,000,000 (47,607,-000,000); crude petroleum (barrels; 2008) 979,300,000 ([2006] 331,600,000); petroleum products (metric tons; 2006) 38,505,000 (12,365,000); natural gas (cu m; 2006) 14,064,-000,000 (14,064,000,000). **Population economically active** (2007): total 2,092,509, of which Kuwaiti 15.5%, non-Kuwaiti 84.5%; activity rate of total population 61.6% (participation rates: ages 15–64 [2005] 70.8%; female [2005] 25.2%; unemployed [2006; Kuwaiti nationals only] 4.0%). **Selected balance of payments data.** Receipts from (US$'000,000): tourism (2008) 256; foreign direct investment (FDI; 2005–07 avg.) 160. Disbursements for (US$'000,-000): tourism (2008) 7,571; remittances (2008) 5,558; FDI (2005–07 avg.) 9,184.

## Foreign trade

**Imports** (2007; c.i.f.): KD 5,106,000,000 (industrial requirements 29.1%; machinery and capital equipment 21.4%; durable consumer goods 10.7%; food products and beverages 10.2%). *Major import sources:* Germany 11.5%; US 10.6%; China 10.0%; Japan 8.0%; Italy 6.4%. **Exports** (2007; f.o.b.): KD 18,099,000,000 (crude petroleum 61.5%; refined petroleum products 29.7%; liquefied petroleum gas 3.1%; ethylene products 2.2%). *Major export destinations* (2008): Japan 21%; South Korea 15%; US 10%; Singapore 9%; China 7%.

*1 metric ton = about 1.1 short tons;　1 kilometer = 0.6 mi (statute);　1 metric ton-km cargo = about 0.68 short ton-mi cargo;　c.i.f.: cost, insurance, and freight;　f.o.b.: free on board*

## Transport and communications

**Transport.** *Railroads:* none. *Roads* (2004): total length 5,749 km (paved 85%). *Vehicles* (2004): passenger cars 858,055; trucks and buses 180,940. *Air transport* (2008; Kuwait Airways only): passenger-km 7,447,000,000; metric ton-km cargo 280,346,000. **Communications,** in total units (units per 1,000 persons). Telephone landlines (2008): 541,000 (158); cellular telephone subscribers (2008): 2,907,000 (850); personal computers (2007): 779,000 (237); total Internet users (2008): 1,000,000 (292); broadband Internet subscribers (2005): 25,000 (8.7).

## Education and health

**Educational attainment** (2005). Percentage of population ages 10 and over having: no formal schooling: illiterate 6.2%, literate 37.9%; primary education 12.7%; lower secondary 20.8%; upper secondary 11.7%; some higher 4.1%; completed undergraduate 6.6%. **Literacy** (2005): total population ages 15 and over literate 84.4%; males literate 85.7%; females literate 82.8%. **Health** (2006): physicians 4,775 (1 per 646 persons); hospital beds 5,760 (1 per 535 persons); infant mortality rate per 1,000 live births (2008) 9.2; undernourished population (2002–04) 120,000 (5% of total population based on the consumption of a minimum daily requirement of 1,980 calories).

## Military

**Total active duty personnel** (November 2008): 15,500 (army 71.0%, navy/coast guard 12.9%, air force 16.1%); US troops for Iraqi support (May 2009): 15,000. **Military expenditure as percentage of GDP** (2008): 2.8%; per capita expenditure US$1,441.

## Background

Faylakah Island, in Kuwait Bay, had a civilization dating back to the 3rd millennium BC that flourished until 1200 BC. Greek colonists resettled the island in the 4th century BC. Abd Rahim of the Sabah dynasty became sheikh in AD 1756, the first of a family that continues to rule Kuwait. In 1899, to thwart German and Ottoman influences, Kuwait gave Britain control of its foreign affairs. Following the outbreak of war in 1914, Britain established a protectorate there. In 1961, after Kuwait became independent, Iraq laid claim to it. British troops defended Kuwait, the Arab League recognized its independence, and Iraq dropped its claim. Iraqi forces invaded and occupied Kuwait in 1990, and a US-led military coalition drove them out in 1991. Iraqi forces set fire to most of Kuwait's oil wells, but these were extinguished, and petroleum production soon returned to prewar levels.

## Recent Developments

Although Kuwait avoided the massive popular demonstrations seen in a number of Arab countries in 2011, some youth-led rallies were held to demand political reforms and the eradication of corruption. Early in the year the government tried to mollify the population by distributing 1,000 Kuwaiti dinars (about US$3,650) to each Kuwaiti. Nonetheless, social agitation continued. Relations between Kuwait and Iraq soured in April when Kuwait began to build a megaport on the island of Bubiyan near an inlet that provided Iraq access to the Persian Gulf. In Iraq, which has only a few kilometers of shoreline on the Gulf, public opinion turned against Kuwait over fears that the port would stifle Iraqi trade.

**Internet resource:** <www.cso.gov.kw>.

# Kyrgyzstan

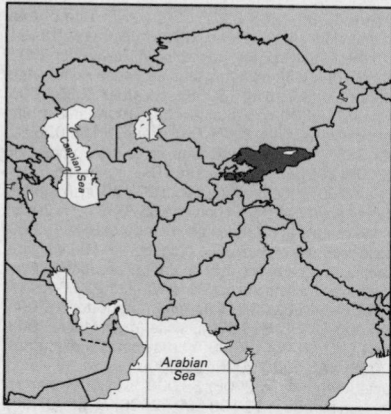

**Official name:** Kyrgyz Respublikasy (Kyrgyz); Respublika Kirgizstan (Russian) (Kyrgyz Republic). **Form of government:** republic with one legislative house (Jogorku Kenesh, or Supreme Council [120]). **Head of state:** President Almazbek Atambayev (from 2011). **Head of government:** Prime Minister Omurbek Babanov (from 2011). **Capital:** Bishkek. **Official languages:** Kyrgyz; Russian. **Official religion:** none. **Monetary unit:** 1 som (KGS) = 100 tyiyn; valuation (2 Jul 2012) US$1 = KGS 47.24.

## Demography

**Area:** 77,199 sq mi, 199,945 sq km. **Population** (2011): 5,168,000. **Density** (2011): persons per sq mi 66.9, persons per sq km 25.8. **Urban** (2009): 35.3%. **Sex distribution** (2008): male 49.34%; female 50.66%. **Age breakdown** (2005): under 15, 31.3%; 15–29, 29.3%; 30–44, 19.9%; 45–59, 12.2%; 60–74, 5.2%; 75–84, 1.9%; 85 and over, 0.2%. **Ethnic composition** (2005): Kyrgyz 67.4%; Uzbek 14.2%; Russian 10.3%; Hui 1.1%; Uighur 1.0%; other 6.0%. **Religious affiliation** (2000): Muslim (mostly Sunni) 60.8%; Christian 10.4%, of which Russian Orthodox 7.7%; nonreligious 21.6%; atheist 6.3%; other 0.9%. **Major cities** (2006): Bishkek 794,300; Osh 224,300; Jalal-Abad 85,100; Karakol 61,900; Tokmok 54,900. **Location:** central Asia, bordering Kazakhstan, China, Tajikistan, and Uzbekistan.

## Vital statistics

**Birth rate** per 1,000 population (2008): 24.1 (world avg. 20.3); (1994) within marriage 83.2%. **Death rate** per 1,000 population (2008): 7.1 (world avg. 8.5). **Total fertility rate** (avg. births per childbearing woman; 2005): 2.69. **Life expectancy** at birth (2007): male 63.6 years; female 72.2 years.

## National economy

**Budget** (2008). *Revenue:* KGS 45,479,000,000 (tax revenue 79.0%, of which VAT 36.4%, customs duties 10.2%, income tax 8.6%; nontax revenue 17.9%; grants 3.1%). *Expenditures:* KGS 36,944,000,000 (education 26.0%; general administration 18.3%; defense and public order 14.8%; social security 12.6%; health 11.8%). **Public debt** (external, outstanding; 2008): US$1,918,000,000. **Population economically active** (2006): total 2,285,000; activity rate of total population 44.1% (participation rates: ages 15–64, 70.4%; female 42.4%; unemployed [November 2007] 8.2%). **Production** (metric tons except as noted). *Agriculture and fishing* (2008): potatoes 1,334,900, wheat 746,200, corn (maize) 462,100; livestock (number of live animals) 3,379,097 sheep, 1,168,026 cattle, 355,533 horses, 338 camels; fisheries production (2007) 141 (from aquaculture 76%). *Mining and quarrying* (2007): mercury 250; gold 10,636 kg. *Manufacturing* (value of production in KGS '000,000; 2008): base metals and fabricated metal products 36,360; food products and tobacco products 11,186; cement, bricks, and ceramics 8,505. *Energy production (consumption):* electricity (kW-hr; 2008) 11,223,000,000 ([2006] 14,561,000,000); coal (metric tons; 2008) 58,000 ([2006] 818,000); lignite (metric tons; 2008) 364,000 ([2006] 436,000); crude petroleum (barrels; 2008) 480,000 ([2006] 516,000); petroleum products (metric tons; 2006) 83,000 (547,000); natural gas (cu m; 2008) 16,000,000 ([2006] 769,000,000). **Gross national income** (2008): US$3,932,000,000 (US$740 per capita). **Selected balance of payments data.** Receipts from (US$'000,000): tourism (2007) 346; remittances (2008) 1,232; foreign direct investment (FDI; 2005–07 avg.) 144; official development assistance (2007) 274. Disbursements for (US$'000,000): tourism (2007) 90; remittances (2008) 196.

## Foreign trade

**Imports** (2007; c.i.f.): US$2,417,000,000 (refined petroleum products 25.2%; machinery and apparatus 14.4%; food products 11.6%; chemical products 10.6%; motor vehicles and parts 4.8%). *Major import sources:* Russia 40.5%; China 14.7%; Kazakhstan 12.9%; Uzbekistan 5.0%; US 4.0%. **Exports** (2007; f.o.b.): US$1,134,200,000 (refined petroleum products 20.8%; gold 19.8%; machinery and apparatus 6.2%; outerwear 5.5%; vegetables 4.2%; glass 3.5%; portland cement 3.5%). *Major export destinations:* Russia 20.7%; Switzerland 19.9%; Kazakhstan 18.0%; Afghanistan 10.4%; Uzbekistan 7.6%.

## Transport and communications

**Transport.** *Railroads* (2007): route length (2008) 470 km; passenger-km 59,900,000; metric ton-km cargo 853,700,000. *Roads* (2000): total length 18,500 km (paved 91%). *Vehicles* (2005): passenger cars 201,430. *Air transport* (2008): passenger-km 585,000,000; metric ton-km cargo 2,314,000. **Communications,** in total units (units per 1,000 persons). Telephone landlines (2008): 494,000 (94); cellular telephone subscribers (2008): 3,394,000 (643); personal computers (2007): 99,000 (19); total Internet users (2008): 850,000 (161); broadband Internet subscribers (2008): 2,900 (0.5).

## Education and health

**Educational attainment** (1999). Percentage of population ages 15 and over having: primary education 6.3%; some secondary 18.3%; completed secondary 50.0%; some postsecondary 14.9%; higher 10.5%. **Literacy** (2006): total population ages 15 and over literate 98.7%. **Health** (2006): physicians 12,710 (1 per 406 persons); hospital beds 26,339 (1 per 196 persons); infant mortality rate per 1,000 live births (2007) 30.6; undernourished population (2002–04) 200,000 (4% of total population based on the consumption of a minimum daily requirement of 1,930 calories).

## Military

**Total active duty personnel** (November 2008): 10,900 (army 78.0%, air force 22.0%); Russian troops (November 2008): 500. **Military expenditure as percentage of GDP** (2007): 1.1%; per capita expenditure US$7.

## Background

The Kyrgyz, a nomadic people of Central Asia, settled in the Tian Shan region in ancient times. They were conquered by Genghis Khan's son Jochi in 1207. The area became part of the Qing empire of China in the mid-18th century. The region came under Russian control in the 19th century, and its rebellion against Russia in 1916 resulted in a long period of brutal repression. Kirgiziya became an autonomous province of the USSR in 1924 and was made the Kirghiz Soviet Socialist Republic in 1936. Kyrgyzstan gained independence in 1991. It subsequently struggled with creating a democratic process and with establishing a stable economy.

## Recent Developments

Unemployment, poverty, and corruption continued to plague Kyrgyzstan in 2011, with little sign of improvement. In September a World Food Programme official reported that the number of families with low levels of food security was increasing and added that the WFP was trying to expand the Food for Work program started in 2010. As part of the effort to improve Kyrgyzstan's poor ratings for corruption, interim president Roza Otunbayeva set up a body to ensure transparency in the use of US rental payments for the facilities at Manas Airport, a major supply base for US forces in Afghanistan. Tensions between ethnic Kyrgyz and ethnic Uzbeks remained strong in the south.

**Internet resource:**
<www.nbkr.kg/index.jsp?lang=ENG>.

# Laos

**Official name:** Sathalanalat Paxathipatai Paxaxon Lao (Lao People's Democratic Republic). **Form of government:** unitary single-party people's republic with one legislative house (National Assembly [132]). **Head of state:** President Choummaly Sayasone (from 2006). **Head of government:** Prime Minister Thongsing Thammavong (from 2010). **Capital:** Vientiane (Viangchan). **Official language:** Lao. **Official religion:**

---

*1 metric ton = about 1.1 short tons; 1 kilometer = 0.6 mi (statute); 1 metric ton-km cargo = about 0.68 short ton-mi cargo; c.i.f.: cost, insurance, and freight; f.o.b.: free on board*

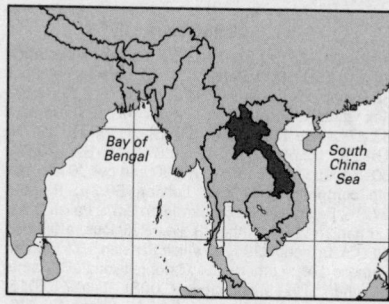

none. **Monetary unit:** 1 kip (KN) = 100 at; valuation (2 Jul 2012) US$1 = KN 7,979.00.

## Demography

**Area:** 91,429 sq mi, 236,800 sq km. **Population** (2011): 6,392,000. **Density** (2011): persons per sq mi 69.9, persons per sq km 27.0. **Urban** (2009): 32.0%. **Sex distribution** (2007): male 49.86%; female 50.14%. **Age breakdown** (2007): under 15, 38.7%; 15–29, 28.9%; 30–44, 17.0%; 45–59, 9.7%; 60–74, 4.3%; 75 and over, 1.4%. **Ethnic composition** (2005): Lao 54.6%; Khmou 10.9%; Hmong 8.0%; Tai 3.8%; Phu Tai (Phouthay) 3.3%; Lue 2.2%; Katang 2.1%; Makong 2.1%; other 13.0%. **Religious affiliation** (2005): traditional beliefs 49%; Buddhist 43%; Christian 2%; nonreligious/other 6%. **Major cities** (2003): Vientiane (Viangchan) 194,200 (urban agglomeration [2007] 745,000); Savannakhet 58,200; Pakxe 50,100; Xam Nua 40,700; Muang Khammouan 27,300. **Location:** southeastern Asia, bordering China, Vietnam, Cambodia, Thailand, and Myanmar (Burma).

## Vital statistics

**Birth rate** per 1,000 population (2008): 34.5 (world avg. 20.3). **Death rate** per 1,000 population (2008): 11.0 (world avg. 8.5). **Total fertility rate** (avg. births per childbearing woman; 2008): 4.50. **Life expectancy** at birth (2008): male 54.1 years; female 58.4 years.

## National economy

**Budget** (2007–08). *Revenue:* KN 7,035,000,000,000 (tax revenue 80.0%, of which turnover tax 17.5%, excise tax 16.9%, tax on mining sector 11.4%, import duties 9.6%; nontax revenue 11.5%; grants 8.5%). *Expenditures:* KN 7,952,000,000,000 (current expenditures 58.1%; capital expenditures 41.9%). **Public debt** (external, outstanding; 2007): US$2,446,000,000. **Population economically active** (2005): total 2,778,000; activity rate of total population 66.6% (participation rates: ages 15–64, 81.3%; female 50.2%; officially unemployed [2005] 2.4%). **Production** (metric tons except as noted). *Agriculture and fishing* (2008): rice 2,710,050, corn (maize) 1,107,780, sugarcane 749,295, natural rubber (hectares; 2006) 11,778; livestock (number of live animals) 2,548,000 pigs, 1,499,000 cattle, 1,155,000 water buffalo, 21,983,000 chickens, 3,200,000 ducks; fisheries production (2007) 104,925 (from aquaculture 74%). *Mining and quarrying* (2007): gypsum 775,000; limestone 750,000; copper (metal

content) 99,040; tin (metal content) 450; gold 4,161 kg. *Manufacturing* (2007): plastic products 7,383; nails 2,168; plywood 952,000,000 sheets. *Energy production (consumption):* electricity (kW-hr; 2008) 3,705,000,000 ([2006] 1,021,000,000); coal (metric tons; 2008) 392,000 ([2006] 305,000); lignite (metric tons; 2006) 319,000 (96,000); petroleum products (metric tons; 2006) none (133,000). **Gross national income** (2008): US$4,674,000,000 (US$750 per capita). **Selected balance of payments data.** Receipts from (US$'000,000): tourism (2008) 275; remittances (2008) 1.0; foreign direct investment (2005–07 avg.) 180; official development assistance (2007) 396. Disbursements for (US$'000,000): remittances (2007) 1.0.

## Foreign trade

**Imports** (2008): US$2,816,100,000 (capital goods 41.6%; crude petroleum 15.0%; materials for garment assembly 5.1%). *Major import sources:* Thailand 68.6%; China 11.3%; Vietnam 4.7%; South Korea 2.5%; Japan 2.5%. **Exports** (2008): US$1,638,600,000 (copper 37.9%; garments 11.6%; timber 8.0%; gold 7.3%; electricity 7.2%). *Major export destinations:* Thailand 34.7%; Vietnam 13.2%; China 8.6%; South Korea 4.5%; UK 3.3%.

## Transport and communications

**Transport.** *Railroads:* none. *Roads* (2007): total length 36,831 km (paved 13%). *Vehicles* (2002): passenger cars, trucks, and buses 315,000. *Air transport* (2007): passenger-km 245,400,000; metric ton-km cargo 200,000. **Communications**, in total units (units per 1,000 persons). Telephone landlines (2008): 98,000 (16); cellular telephone subscribers (2008): 1,822,000 (294); personal computers (2007): 110,000 (18); total Internet users (2008): 130,000 (21); broadband Internet subscribers (2007): 3,600 (0.6).

## Education and health

**Educational attainment** (2005). Percentage of population ages 25 and over having: no formal schooling 32.8%; incomplete primary education 21.6%; complete primary 18.2%; lower secondary 11.4%; upper secondary 6.2%; higher 9.8%. **Literacy** (2005): total population ages 15 and over literate 72.7%; males literate 82.5%; females literate 63.2%. **Health** (2005): physicians 5,000 (1 per 1,129 persons); hospital beds (2007) 6,955 (1 per 838 persons); infant mortality rate per 1,000 live births 79.5; undernourished population (2002–04) 1,100,000 (19% of total population based on the consumption of a minimum daily requirement of 1,730 calories).

## Military

**Total active duty personnel** (November 2008): 29,100 (army 88.0%, air force 12.0%). **Military expenditure as percentage of GDP** (2007): 0.4%; per capita expenditure US$2.

## Background

The Lao people migrated into Laos from southern China after the 8th century AD, displacing indigenous tribes. In the 14th century Fa Ngum founded the first Laotian state, Lan Xang. Except for a period of rule by

Burma (1574–1637), the Lan Xang kingdom ruled Laos until 1713, when it split into three kingdoms. France gained control of the region in 1893. In 1945 Japan seized it and declared Laos independent. The area reverted to French rule after World War II. The Geneva Conference of 1954 unified and granted independence to Laos. Communist forces took control in 1975, establishing the Lao People's Democratic Republic. Laos held its first election in 1989 and promulgated a new constitution in 1991. Although its economy was adversely affected by the mid-1990s Asian monetary crises, it realized a longtime gain in 1997 when it joined the Association of Southeast Asian Nations.

## Recent Developments

A number of high-profile projects encountered serious setbacks in Laos in 2011. In April the start of construction of a much-publicized high-speed rail line, cofinanced by Chinese investors and the Lao government, was postponed to an unspecified date. The project, which was to link Boten (on the border with China) to Vientiane, was delayed allegedly because of concerns over the terms of the contract—one provision of which was for a massive number of Chinese laborers to be hired to work on the line. About a month later, the controversial Xayaboury dam project on the Mekong River in northwestern Laos was also shelved following protests from international nongovernmental organizations and some Southeast Asian governments (including Vietnam) that the dam could have harmful transboundary environmental impacts.

Internet resource: <www.nsc.gov.la>.

# Latvia

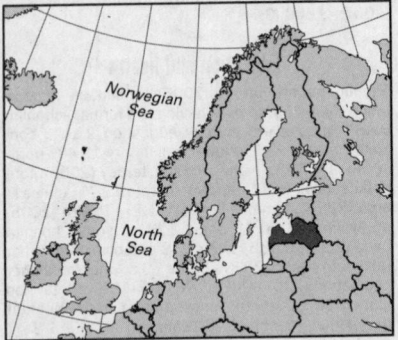

Official name: Latvijas Republika (Republic of Latvia). Form of government: unitary multiparty republic with a single legislative house (Parliament, or Saeima [100]). Head of state: President Andris Berzins (from 2011). Head of government: Prime Minister Valdis Dombrovskis (from 2009). Capital: Riga. Official language: Latvian. Official religion: none. Monetary unit: 1 lats (Ls; plural lati) = 100 santimi; valuation (2 Jul 2012) US$1 = 0.55 Ls.

## Demography

Area: 24,938 sq mi, 64,589 sq km. Population (2011): 2,217,000. Density (2011): persons per sq mi 88.9, persons per sq km 34.3. Urban (2011): 67.5%. Sex distribution (2008): male 46.13%; female 53.87%. Age breakdown (2008): under 15, 13.7%; 15–29, 22.6%; 30–44, 20.8%; 45–59, 20.6%; 60–74, 15.0%; 75–89, 6.9%; 90 and over, 0.4%. Ethnic composition (2008): Latvian 59.3%; Russian 27.8%; Belarusian 3.6%; Ukrainian 2.5%; Polish 2.4%; Lithuanian 1.3%; other 3.1%. Religious affiliation (2005): Orthodox 29%, of which Russian 16%; Roman Catholic 19%; Lutheran 14%; nonreligious 26%; atheist/other 12%. Major cities (2008): Riga 713,016; Daugavpils 104,857; Liepaja 84,747; Jelgava 65,419; Jurmala 55,870. Location: eastern Europe, bordering Estonia, Russia, Belarus, Lithuania, and the Baltic Sea.

## Vital statistics

Birth rate per 1,000 population (2008): 10.6 (world avg. 20.3); within marriage 56.9%. Death rate per 1,000 population (2008): 13.7 (world avg. 8.5). Total fertility rate (avg. births per childbearing woman; 2007): 1.45. Life expectancy at birth (2008): male 67.2 years; female 77.9 years.

## National economy

Budget (2008–09). Revenue: Ls 5,203,700,000 (taxes on products 29.4%; social security contributions 25.3%; income tax 24.7%; VAT 17.4%). Expenditures: Ls 6,602,100,000 (wages and salaries 28.5%; social security and welfare 23.3%; transfers 12.5%). Public debt (external, outstanding; June 2009): US$4,308,600,000. Production (metric tons except as noted). Agriculture and fishing (2008): wheat 989,600, potatoes 673,000, barley 277,000; livestock (number of live animals) 384,000 pigs, 380,000 cattle; fisheries production 158,500 (from aquaculture, negligible). Mining and quarrying (2008): peat 865,500; limestone 515,900; gypsum 349,100. Manufacturing (value added in Ls '000,000; 2008): food products 313.6; wood products (excluding furniture) 270.1; fabricated metal products 131.0. Energy production (consumption): electricity (kW-hr; 2008–09) 4,895,000,000 (7,276,000,000); coal (metric tons; 2008–09) none (137,000); petroleum products (metric tons; 2008–09) none (1,377,000); natural gas (cu m; 2008–09) none (1,573,000,000). Selected balance of payments data. Receipts from (US$'000,000): tourism (2007) 671; remittances (2008) 601; foreign direct investment (FDI; 2005–07 avg.) 1,517. Disbursements for (US$'000,000): tourism (2007) 927; remittances (2008) 58; FDI (2005–07 avg.) 178. Gross national income (2008): US$26,883,000,000 (US$11,860 per capita). Population economically active (2008): total 1,215,800; activity rate of total population 53.7% (participation rates: ages 15–74, 67.7%; female 48.9%; unemployed [July 2008–June 2009] 12.3%).

## Foreign trade

Imports (2008; c.i.f.): Ls 7,527,687,000 (machinery and apparatus 18.3%; mineral fuels 15.6%, of which diesel oil 5.3%; food products and beverages 13.7%;

---

*1 metric ton = about 1.1 short tons;　1 kilometer = 0.6 mi (statute);　1 metric ton-km cargo = about 0.68 short ton-mi cargo;　c.i.f.: cost, insurance, and freight;　f.o.b.: free on board*

transportation equipment 10.7%; base and fabricated metals 10.3%; chemical products 9.7%). *Major import sources:* Lithuania 16.5%; Germany 13.0%; Russia 10.6%; Poland 7.2%; Estonia 7.1%. **Exports** (2008; f.o.b.): Ls 4,428,945,000 (food products and beverages 16.7%; base and fabricated metals 16.7%; wood products 16.6%; machinery and apparatus 12.5%; chemical products 8.4%; textiles and wearing apparel 5.5%). *Major export destinations:* Lithuania 16.7%; Estonia 14.0%; Russia 10.0%; Germany 8.1%; Sweden 6.6%.

## Transport and communications

**Transport.** *Railroads* (2008): length 2,263 km; passenger-km 951,000,000; metric ton-km cargo 19,581,000,000. *Roads* (2008): total length 51,300 km (paved 39%). *Vehicles* (2008): passenger cars 932,800; trucks and buses 140,300. *Air transport* (2008): passenger-km 3,498,000,000; metric ton-km cargo 15,000,000. **Communications,** in total units (units per 1,000 persons). Telephone landlines (2008): 644,000 (285); cellular telephone subscribers (2008): 2,234,000 (989); personal computers (2005): 566,000 (245); total Internet users (2007): 1,252,000 (552); broadband Internet subscribers (2007): 146,000 (64).

## Education and health

**Educational attainment** (2007). Percentage of population ages 15–74 having: none/unknown through complete primary education 26.1%; secondary 25.5%; vocational 30.1%; higher 18.3%. **Literacy** (2007): total population ages 15 and over literate, virtually 100%. **Health** (2008): physicians 8,437 (1 per 268 persons); hospital beds 17,001 (1 per 133 persons); infant mortality rate per 1,000 live births 6.7; undernourished population (2002–04) 70,000 (3% of total population based on the consumption of a minimum daily requirement of 1,960 calories).

## Military

**Total active duty personnel** (November 2008): 5,187 (army 29.4%, navy 13.5%, air force 9.3%, headquarters/administrative/other 47.8%). **Military expenditure as percentage of GDP** (2008): 1.6%; per capita expenditure US$226.

## Background

Latvia was settled by the Balts in ancient times. It was conquered by the Vikings in the 9th century AD and later dominated by its German-speaking neighbors, who Christianized the people in the 12th–13th centuries. By 1230 German rule was established. From the mid-16th to the early 18th century, the region was split between Poland and Sweden, but by the end of the 18th century all of Latvia had been annexed by Russia. Latvia declared its independence after the Russian Revolution of 1917, but in 1940 the Soviet Red Army invaded. Held by Nazi Germany in 1941–44, the country was recaptured by the Soviets and incorporated into the Soviet Union. Latvia gained its independence in 1991 with the breakup of the Soviet Union; subsequently it sought to build ties with Western Europe (becoming a member of both the EU and NATO in 2004), as well as to improve uneasy relations with Russia.

## Recent Developments

Latvia's GDP grew by about 4.5% in 2011. Unemployment rates, though down from their peak of more than 20.0% in 2010, remained stubbornly high throughout the year, averaging roughly 16.0%, and census results suggested that many Latvians were seeking employment abroad. Lawmakers continued to take steps to balance Latvia's budget with the intention of joining the euro zone in 2014. On the international front, Latvian soldiers continued serving in the International Security Assistance Force in Afghanistan, and the parliament extended the force's mandate in December 2011. The people of Latvia, which has a sizable Russian-speaking minority, rejected a bid to make Russian the second official language in a referendum in February 2012.

**Internet resource:** <www.csb.gov.lv/en>.

# Lebanon

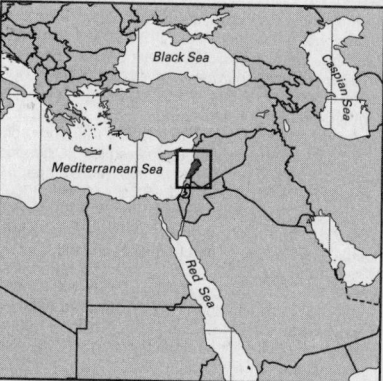

**Official name:** Al-Jumhuriyah al-Lubnaniyah (Lebanese Republic). **Form of government:** unitary multiparty republic with one legislative house (National Assembly [128]). **Head of state:** President Michel Suleiman (from 2008). **Head of government:** Prime Minister Najib Mikati (from 2011). **Capital:** Beirut. **Official language:** Arabic. **Official religion:** none. **Monetary unit:** 1 Lebanese pound (LBP) = 100 piastres; valuation (2 Jul 2012) US$1 = LBP 1,503.50.

## Demography

**Area:** 4,036 sq mi, 10,452 sq km. **Population** (2011): 4,143,000. **Density** (2011): persons per sq mi 1,026.5, persons per sq km 396.4. **Urban** (2005): 86.6%. **Sex distribution** (2008): male 48.97%; female 51.03%. **Age breakdown** (2005): under 15, 27.6%; 15–29, 27.1%; 30–44, 21.7%; 45–59, 13.6%; 60–74, 7.7%; 75–84, 2.0%; 85 and over, 0.3%. **Ethnic composition** (2000): Arab 84.5%, of which Lebanese 71.2%, Palestinian 12.1%; Armenian 6.8%; Kurd 6.1%; other 2.6%. **Religious affiliation** (2005): Muslim 56%, of which Shiʻi 28%, Sunni 28%; Maronite (Eastern-rite Roman Catholic) 22%; Greek Orthodox 8%; Druze 5%; Greek Catholic 4%; other 5%. **Major cities** (2003): Beirut 395,000 (urban agglomeration [2007] 1,846,000)); Tripoli 212,900; Sidon 149,000; Tyre (Sur) 117,100; Al-Nabatiyah

89,400. **Location:** the Middle East, bordering Syria, Israel, and the Mediterranean Sea.

## Vital statistics

**Birth rate** per 1,000 population (2008): 20.2 (world avg. 20.3). **Death rate** per 1,000 population (2008): 5.0 (world avg. 8.5). **Total fertility rate** (avg. births per childbearing woman; 2007): 2.21. **Life expectancy** at birth (2007): male 69.9 years; female 74.2 years.

## National economy

**Budget** (2007). *Revenue:* LBP 8,390,000,000,000 (tax revenue 66.7%, of which taxes on goods and services 34.8%, customs duties 6.7%; nontax revenue 26.5%; grants 5.9%; social contributions 0.9%). *Expenditures:* LBP 12,599,000,000,000 (public debt 37.3%; fuel/electricity 11.2%; defense 9.2%; social protection 7.5%; education 6.9%; health 2.2%). **Public debt** (external, outstanding; July 2009): US$21,294,000,000. **Gross national income** (2008): US$26,297,000,000 (US$6,350 per capita). **Production** (metric tons except as noted). *Agriculture and fishing* (2007): potatoes 490,000, tomatoes 255,000, oranges 195,000, olives 83,000, almonds 27,000; livestock (number of live animals) 495,000 goats, 340,000 sheep, 77,000 cattle; fisheries production 4,614 (from aquaculture 17%). *Manufacturing* (value added in US$'000,000; 1998): food products 345; cement, bricks, and ceramics 212; wood products 188. *Energy production (consumption):* electricity (kW-hr; 2008) 11,188,000,000 ([2007] 10,590,000,000); coal (metric tons; 2006) none (200,000); petroleum products (metric tons; 2006) none (4,009,000). **Population economically active** (2007): total 1,228,800; activity rate of total population 32.7% (participation rates: ages 15–64, 47.6%; female 25.0%; unemployed 9.2%). **Selected balance of payments data.** Receipts from (US$'000,000): tourism (2007) 4,993; remittances (2008) 6,000; foreign direct investment (FDI; 2005–07 avg.) 2,792; official development assistance (2007) 939. Disbursements for (US$'000,000): tourism (2007) 3,114; remittances (2008) 3,022; FDI (2005–07 avg.) 142.

## Foreign trade

**Imports** (2008): US$16,137,000,000 (mineral products [significantly crude petroleum] 26.5%; food products and live animals 13.2%; transportation equipment 10.6%; electrical machinery 10.5%). *Major import sources:* US 11.5%; China 8.6%; France 8.3%; Italy 6.9%; Germany 6.4%. **Exports** (2008): US$3,478,000,000 (precious metal jewelry and stones [significantly gold and diamonds] 16.5%; electrical machinery 15.4%; base and fabricated metals 15.2%; chemical products 12.5%). *Major export destinations:* UAE 10.0%; Switzerland 9.5%; Iraq 7.7%; Syria 6.4%; Saudi Arabia 6.0%.

## Transport and communications

**Transport.** *Railroads:* (2009) 401 km. *Roads* (2005): total length 6,970 km. *Vehicles* (2001): passenger cars 1,370,897; trucks and buses 102,394. *Air transport* (2008; Middle East Airlines only): passenger-km 2,748,000,000; metric ton-km cargo

38,524,000. **Communications,** in total units (units per 1,000 persons). Telephone landlines (2008): 714,000 (170); cellular telephone subscribers (2008): 1,430,000 (341); personal computers (2007): 433,000 (104); total Internet users (2008): 2,190,000 (522); broadband Internet subscribers (2007): 200,000 (48).

## Education and health

**Educational attainment** (2004). Percentage of population ages 4 and over having: no formal education/unknown 13.7%; incomplete primary education 3.2%; primary 54.2%; secondary/vocational 15.5%; upper vocational 1.7%; higher 11.7%. **Literacy** (2005): total population ages 15 and over literate 88.3%; males literate 93.6%; females literate 83.4%. **Health** (2005): physicians 10,538 (1 per 387 persons); hospital beds (2006) 12,037 (1 per 343 persons); infant mortality rate per 1,000 live births 23.6; undernourished population (2002–04) 120,000 (3% of total population based on the consumption of a minimum daily requirement of 1,920 calories).

## Military

**Total active duty personnel** (November 2008): 56,000 (army 96.2%, navy 2.0%, air force 1.8%); estimated strength of Hezbollah (November 2008): 2,000; UN peacekeeping troops (March 2009): 12,261. **Military expenditure as percentage of GDP** (2008): 3.1%; per capita expenditure US$179.

## Background

Much of present-day Lebanon corresponds to ancient Phoenicia, which was settled about 3000 BC. In the 6th century AD, Christians fleeing Syrian persecution settled in what is now northern Lebanon and founded the Maronite Church. Arab tribesmen settled in southern Lebanon and by the 11th century had founded the Druze faith. Lebanon was later ruled by the Mamluks. In 1516 the Ottoman Turks seized control; the Turks ended the local rule of the Druze Shihab princes in 1842. After the massacre of Maronites by Druze in 1860, France forced the Ottomans to form an autonomous province for the Christian area, known as Mount Lebanon. Following World War I, it was administered by the French military, but by 1946 it was fully independent. After the Arab-Israeli War of 1948–49, Palestinian refugees settled in southern Lebanon. In 1970 the Palestine Liberation Organization (PLO) moved its headquarters there and began raids into northern Israel. Political and religious divisions and a growing Palestinian "state within a state" fueled a descent into civil war. In 1976 Syria intervened on behalf of the Christians, and in 1982 Israeli forces attempted to drive Palestinian fighters out of southern Lebanon. Israeli troops had withdrawn from all but a narrow buffer zone in the south by 1985; thereafter, guerrillas from the Lebanese Shi'ite militia Hezbollah clashed with the Israelis regularly. Israeli soldiers completely withdrew from Lebanon in 2000, and Syrian forces disengaged from the country in 2005. In mid-2006 Hezbollah and Israel engaged in a 34-day war, primarily fought in Lebanon, in which more than 1,000 people were killed. Israeli troops subsequently withdrew from most of Lebanon in October 2006.

---

*1 metric ton = about 1.1 short tons;*    *1 kilometer = 0.6 mi (statute);*    *1 metric ton-km cargo = about 0.68 short ton-mi cargo;*    *c.i.f.: cost, insurance, and freight;*    *f.o.b.: free on board*

## Recent Developments

In June 2011, the UN-backed Special Tribunal for Lebanon accused four members of Hezbollah of having assassinated former prime minister Rafiq al-Hariri in Beirut in 2005. Hassan Nasrallah, Hezbollah's leader, refused to cooperate with the tribunal, denouncing it as part of an Israeli and US agenda for Lebanon. In August the government announced that it had been unable to apprehend the suspects, setting the stage for trials in absentia. In February the US Treasury Department accused the Lebanese Canadian Bank of having laundered hundreds of millions of dollars a month for an international drug-trafficking ring associated with Hezbollah. Although the bank denied the allegations, a liquidity problem ensued, forcing the bank to merge with the Lebanese subsidiary of Société Général. Lebanon took over the rotating presidency of the UN Security Council in September, and Pres. Michel Suleiman and Prime Minister Mikati each chaired some of its sessions in New York City.

Internet resource: <www.cas.gov.lb>.

# Lesotho

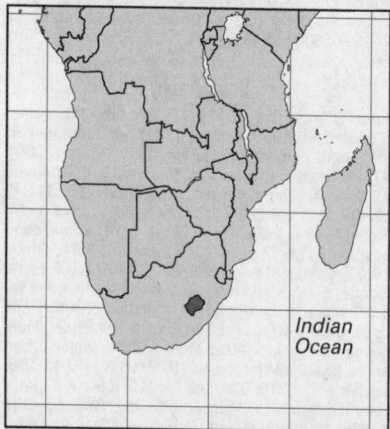

Indian Ocean

**Official name:** Musa oa Lesotho (Sotho); Kingdom of Lesotho (English). **Form of government:** constitutional monarchy with two legislative houses (Senate [33]; National Assembly [120]). **Head of state:** King Letsie III (from 1996). **Head of government:** Prime Minister Motsoahae Thomas Thabane (from 2012). **Capital:** Maseru. **Official languages:** Sotho; English. **Official religion:** Christianity. **Monetary unit:** 1 loti (plural maloti [M]) = 100 licente; valuation (2 Jul 2012) US$1 = M 8.17 (the South African rand is also accepted as legal tender).

## Demography

**Area:** 11,720 sq mi, 30,355 sq km. **Population** (2011): 1,925,000. **Density** (2011): persons per sq mi 164.2, persons per sq km 63.4. **Urban** (2011): 27.6%. **Sex distribution** (2006): male 48.72%; female 51.28%. **Age breakdown** (2006): under 15, 36.2%; 15–29, 31.0%; 30–44, 15.9%; 45–59, 9.9%; 60–74, 5.0%; 75 and over, 2.0%. **Ethnic composition**

(2000): Sotho 80.3%; Zulu 14.4%; other 5.3%. **Religious affiliation** (2000): Christian 91.0%, of which Roman Catholic 37.5%, unaffiliated Christian 23.9%, Protestant (mostly Reformed and Anglican) 17.7%, independent Christian 11.8%; traditional beliefs 7.7%; other 1.3%. **Major urban centers** (2006): Maseru 116,300; Mafeteng 61,600; Hlotse 50,900; Mohale's Hoek 44,500; Maputsoe 32,800. **Location:** southern Africa, surrounded by South Africa.

## Vital statistics

**Birth rate** per 1,000 population (2008): 24.4 (world avg. 20.3). **Death rate** per 1,000 population (2008): 22.3 (world avg. 8.5). **Total fertility rate** (avg. births per childbearing woman; 2008): 3.13. **Life expectancy** at birth (2008): male 41.0 years; female 39.3 years.

## National economy

**Budget** (2007–08). *Revenue:* M 7,169,700,000 (tax revenue 88.3%, of which customs receipts 57.2%, VAT 11.8%, income tax 11.0%; nontax revenue 9.3%; grants 2.4%). *Expenditures:* M 5,334,400,000 (wages and salaries 33.2%; grants 14.5%; transfers 6.2%; debt service 5.5%; social benefits 4.2%). *Production* (metric tons except as noted). *Agriculture and fishing* (2007): potatoes 96,000, corn (maize) 50,800, sorghum 11,200; livestock (number of live animals) 1,025,000 sheep, 715,000 goats, 695,000 cattle; fisheries production 179 (from aquaculture 73%). *Mining and quarrying* (2008): diamonds 216,546 carats. *Manufacturing* (value added in M '000,000; 2007): textiles and wearing apparel 376.8; food products and beverages 59.4; leather products and footwear 30.8. *Energy production (consumption):* electricity (kW-hr; 2006) 200,000,000 (226,000,-000); petroleum products (metric tons; 2003) none (100,000). **Population economically active** (2008): total 788,541; activity rate of total population 38.5% (participation rates: ages 15 and older, 63.5%; female 55.3%; unemployed 22.7%). **Gross national income** (2008): US$2,179,000,000 (US$1,080 per capita). **Public debt** (external, outstanding; January 2009): US$619,000,000. **Selected balance of payments data.** Receipts from (US$'000,000): tourism (2007) 43; remittances (2008) 443; foreign direct investment (2005–07 avg.) 85; official development assistance (2007) 130. Disbursements for (US$'000,000): tourism (2007) 16; remittances (2008) 21.

## Foreign trade

**Imports** (2008; c.i.f.): M 13,237,230,000 ([2006] assorted manufactured goods 40%; food products 24%; chemical products 13%; machinery and transportation equipment 13%). *Major import sources* (2007): other Southern African Customs Union (SACU) countries 76.5%; Asia 21.4%. **Exports** (2008; f.o.b.): M 7,256,070,000 (textiles and wearing apparel 50.4%; diamonds 24.0%; machinery and transportation equipment 14.0%; food products, beverages, and tobacco products 6.6%). *Major export destinations:* other SACU countries 37.7%; North America (mostly US) 35.0%; European Union 24.0%.

## Transport and communications

**Transport.** *Railroads* (2001): length 2.6 km. *Roads* (2006): total length 2,370 km (paved 57%). *Vehicles*

(1996): passenger cars 12,610; trucks and buses 25,000. *Air transport* (1999): passenger-km, negligible (less than 500,000); metric ton-km cargo, negligible. **Communications**, in total units (units per 1,000 persons). Telephone landlines (2008): 65,000 (32); cellular telephone subscribers (2008): 581,000 (284); personal computers (2005): 1,000 (0.5); total Internet users (2008): 73,000 (36); broadband Internet subscribers (2005): 50 (0.02).

## Education and health

**Educational attainment** (2004). Percentage of population ages 25 and over having: no formal education/unknown 18%; incomplete primary education 44%; complete primary 15%; secondary 20%; vocational and higher 3%. **Literacy** (2007): total population ages 15 and over literate 86.5%; males literate 77.1%; females literate 95.6%. **Health:** physicians (2005) 124 (1 per 16,089 persons); hospital beds (2006) 2,618 (1 per 769 persons); infant mortality rate per 1,000 live births (2008) 78.6; undernourished population (2002–04) 250,000 (13% of total population based on the consumption of a minimum daily requirement of 1,850 calories).

## Military

**Total active duty personnel** (November 2008): 2,000 (army 100%). **Military expenditure as percentage of GDP** (2007): 2.3%; per capita expenditure US$20.

## Background

Bantu-speaking farmers created a number of chiefdoms in the area in the 16th century. The most powerful organized the Basotho in 1824 and obtained British protection in 1843 as tension between the Basotho and the South African Boers increased. The area became a British territory in 1868 and was annexed to the Cape Colony in 1871. The colony's effort to disarm the Basotho resulted in revolt in 1880, and four years later it separated from the colony and became a British High Commission Territory. In 1966 it gained independence. A new constitution (1993) ended seven years of military rule. At the beginning of the 21st century, Lesotho suffered from a deteriorating economy and one of the world's highest HIV/AIDS infection rates.

## Recent Developments

In August 2011, government officials from South Africa and Lesotho signed an agreement for the implementation of Phase II of the Lesotho Highlands Water Project. In October a South African company signed a deal with the Lesotho government for a US$15 billion renewable energy venture known as the Lesotho Highlands Power Project, which was expected to generate wind power and hydropower.

**Internet resource:** <www.bos.gov.ls>.

# Liberia

**Official name:** Republic of Liberia. **Form of government:** multiparty republic with two legislative houses

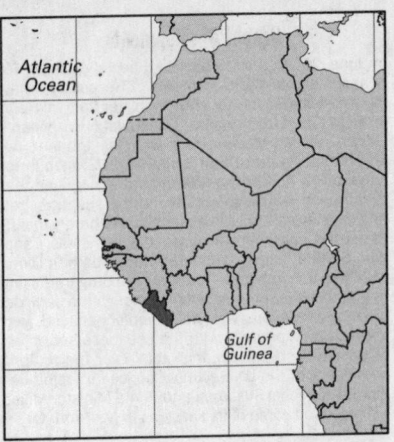

(Senate [30]; House of Representatives [73]). **Head of state and government:** President Ellen Johnson Sirleaf (from 2006). **Capital:** Monrovia. **Official language:** English. **Official religion:** none. **Monetary unit:** 1 Liberian dollar (L$) = 100 cents; valuation (2 Jul 2012) US$1 = L$73.50.

## Demography

**Area:** 37,420 sq mi, 96,917 sq km. **Population** (2011): 3,953,000. **Density** (2011): persons per sq mi 105.6, persons per sq km 40.8. **Urban** (2009): 47.4%. **Sex distribution** (2008): male 50.05%; female 49.95%. **Age breakdown** (2008): under 15, 41.9%; 15–29, 29.1%; 30–44, 16.7%; 45–59, 7.4%; 60–74, 3.4%; 75–84, 1.0%; 85 and over, 0.5%. **Ethnic composition** (2008): Kpelle 20.3%; Bassa 13.4%; Grebo 10.0%; Gio (Dan) 8.0%; Mano 7.9%; Kru 6.0%; Loma (Lorma) 5.1%; Kissi 4.8%; Gola 4.4%; Krahn 4.0%; Vai 4.0%; other 12.1%. **Religious affiliation** (2005): traditional beliefs 40%; Christian (mostly Protestant/independent Christian) 40%; Muslim 20%. **Major urban areas** (2008): Monrovia 1,010,970; Ganta 41,106; Buchanan 34,270; Gbarnga 34,046; Kakata 33,945. **Location:** western Africa, bordering Guinea, Côte d'Ivoire, the North Atlantic Ocean, and Sierra Leone.

## Vital statistics

**Birth rate** per 1,000 population (2007): 43.8 (world avg. 20.3). **Death rate** per 1,000 population (2007): 22.2 (world avg. 8.5). **Total fertility rate** (avg. births per childbearing woman; 2007): 5.94. **Life expectancy** at birth (2007): male 38.9 years; female 41.9 years.

## National economy

**Budget** (2007). *Revenue:* L$10,222,400,000 (customs and excise duties 44.3%; direct taxes 32.1%; indirect taxes 12.6%; maritime revenue 7.6%). *Expenditures:* L$9,498,000,000 (general administration 41.5%; social and community services 19.8%; economic services 6.9%). **Population economically active** (2006): total 1,324,000; activity rate 37.0% (participation rates: ages 15–64, 70.7%; female 39.8%; un-

*1 metric ton = about 1.1 short tons;    1 kilometer = 0.6 mi (statute);    1 metric ton-km cargo = about 0.68 short ton-mi cargo;    c.i.f.: cost, insurance, and freight;    f.o.b.: free on board*

employed [2007] 80%). **Production** (metric tons except as noted). *Agriculture and fishing* (2008): cassava 560,000, sugarcane 265,000, oil palm fruit 183,000, natural rubber 81,000, coffee 3,000, cacao beans 3,000; livestock (number of live animals) 285,000 goats, 241,000 sheep, 199,500 pigs; fisheries production (2007) 16,245 (from aquaculture, none). *Mining and quarrying* (2008): diamonds 60,536 carats; gold 624 kg. *Manufacturing* (value of sales in L$'000; 2007): cement 1,308,767; beer 1,023,734; carbonated beverages 429,776. *International maritime licensing* (registration fees earned; 2007): more than US$12,000,000. *Energy production (consumption):* electricity (kW-hr; 2006) 351,000,000 (351,000,000); petroleum products (metric tons; 2006) none (230,000). **Gross national income** (2008): US$634,000,000 (US$170 per capita). **Public debt** (external, outstanding; 2007): US$910,000,000. **Selected balance of payments data.** Receipts from (US$'000,000): remittances (2007) 303; foreign direct disinvestment (2005–07 avg.) –517; official development assistance (2007) 696. Disbursements for (US$'000,000): remittances (2007) 139; foreign direct investment (2005–07 avg.) 382.

### Foreign trade

**Imports** (2008, excluding December): US$798,000,000 (food products 25.7%, of which rice 15.8%; machinery and transportation equipment 25.6%; refined petroleum products 19.5%). *Major import sources* (2008): South Korea 27%; Singapore 25%; Japan 12%; China 11%. **Exports** (2008, excluding December): US$239,000,000 (rubber products 86.1%; gold 5.1%; diamonds 4.1%; cacao beans and coffee 1.2%). *Major export destinations* (2008): Malaysia 38%; US 16%; Poland 12%; Germany 9%; Belgium 6%.

### Transport and communications

**Transport.** *Railroads* (2009): operational route length, none. *Vehicles* (2002): passenger cars 17,100; trucks and buses 12,800. **Communications,** in total units (units per 1,000 persons). Telephone landlines (2008): 2,000 (0.5); cellular telephone subscribers (2008): 732,000 (193); total Internet users (2008): 20,000 (5.3).

### Education and health

**Educational attainment** (2008). Percentage of population ages 25 and over having: no formal schooling 55.3%; incomplete primary education 7.5%; complete primary 3.3%; incomplete secondary 16.2%; complete secondary 11.3%; vocational 1.2%; higher 5.2%. **Literacy** (2008): total population ages 15 and over literate 54.0%; males literate 65.6%; females literate 42.6%. **Health:** physicians (2009) 122 (1 per 32,418 persons); hospital beds (2001) 2,751 (1 per 1,075 persons); infant mortality rate per 1,000 live births (2007) 149.7; undernourished population (2002–04) 1,700,000 (50% of total population based on the consumption of a minimum daily requirement of 1,820 calories).

### Military

**Total active duty personnel** (November 2008): 2,400; UN peacekeeping troops (August 2009): 10,046. **Military expenditure as percentage of GDP** (2003): 11%; per capita expenditure US$16.

### Background

Africa's oldest republic, Liberia was established as a home for freed American slaves under the American Colonization Society, which founded a colony at Cape Mesurado in 1821. Joseph Jenkins Roberts, Liberia's first nonwhite governor, proclaimed Liberian independence in 1847. In 1980 a coup led by Samuel K. Doe marked the end of the Americo-Liberians' long political dominance over the descendants of indigenous Africans. A destructive civil war consumed the 1990s. A National Transitional Government, supported by UN peacekeeping troops, was established in 2003. Presidential elections were held in 2005, and Ellen Johnson Sirleaf was declared the winner, the first woman to be elected head of state in Africa.

### Recent Developments

The trial of former Liberian president Charles Taylor, charged with crimes against humanity and war crimes, came to a close in March 2011. He was widely considered responsible for Liberia's devastating civil war during the 1990s and for crimes committed during the civil war in neighboring Sierra Leone. The verdict, issued in April 2012, found Taylor guilty on all 11 counts of bearing responsibility for the war crimes and crimes against humanity committed by rebel forces in Sierra Leone, because he had aided and abetted the perpetrators. Taylor's sentence, handed down in May, was for 50 years in prison—effectively a life sentence for the then 64-year-old Taylor, who vowed to appeal.

**Internet resource:**
<www.tlcafrica.com/lisgis/lisgis.htm>.

## Libya

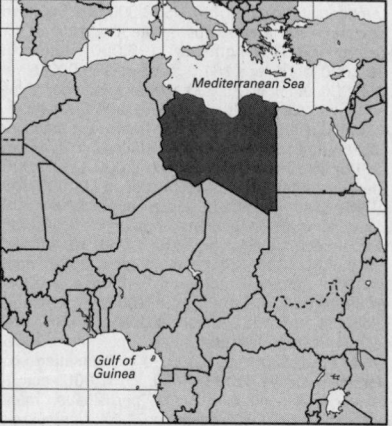

Mediterranean Sea

Gulf of Guinea

**Official name:** Al-Jumhuriyyah al-Libiyyah (Libyan Republic). **Form of government:** interim government with one legislative house (General National Congress [200]). **Head of state:** President of the General National Congress Muhammad al-Megarif (from 2012). **Head of government:** Prime Minister Abdel Rahim al-Keeb (from 2012). **Capital:** Tripoli. **Official language:** Arabic. **Official religion:** Islam.

Monetary unit: 1 Libyan dinar (LD) = 1,000 dirhams; valuation (2 Jul 2012) US$1 = LD 1.25.

## Demography

Area: 647,184 sq mi, 1,676,198 sq km. Population (2011): 6,423,000. Density (2011): persons per sq mi 9.9, persons per sq km 3.8. Urban (2009): 77.7%. Sex distribution (2006): male 51.93%; female 48.07%. Age breakdown (2005): under 15, 30.1%; 15–29, 32.2%; 30–44, 19.8%; 45–59, 11.4%; 60–74, 5.3%; 75–84, 1.0%; 85 and over, 0.2%. Ethnic composition (2000): Arab 87.1%, of which Libyan 57.2%, Bedouin 13.8%, Egyptian 7.7%, Sudanese 3.5%, Tunisian 2.9%; Amazigh (Berber) 6.8%, of which Arabized 4.2%; other 6.1%. Religious affiliation (2000): Muslim (nearly all Sunni) 96.1%; Orthodox 1.9%; Roman Catholic 0.8%; other 1.2%. Major cities (urban agglomerations) (2006 [2007]): Tripoli (Tarabulus) 1,065,405 (2,189,000); Banghazi 670,797 ([2005] 1,113,000); Misratah (2003) 121,669. Location: northern Africa, bordering the Mediterranean Sea, Egypt, Sudan, Chad, Niger, Algeria, and Tunisia.

## Vital statistics

Birth rate per 1,000 population (2005): 26.8 (world avg. 20.3). Death rate per 1,000 population (2005): 3.5 (world avg. 8.5). Total fertility rate (avg. births per childbearing woman; 2005): 3.34. Life expectancy at birth (2005): male 74.3 years; female 78.8 years.

## National economy

Budget (2008). Revenue: LD 72,741,200,000 (oil revenues 88.6%; other 11.4%). Expenditures: LD 44,115,000,000 (development expenditures 65.5%; administrative expenditures 26.9%). Public debt (external outstanding; 2005): US$3,900,000,000. Production (metric tons except as noted). Agriculture and fishing (2007): potatoes 196,000, tomatoes 190,000, dry onions 181,000, dates 175,000, olives 165,000, almonds 25,000; livestock (number of live animals) 4,500,000 sheep, 1,265,000 goats, 130,000 cattle, 47,000 camels; fisheries production 32,161 (from aquaculture 1%). Mining and quarrying (2006): lime 250,000; gypsum 175,000; salt 40,000. Manufacturing (value of production in LD '000,000; 1996): base metals 212; electrical machinery 208; petrochemicals 175. Energy production (consumption): electricity (kW-hr; 2006) 23,992,000,000 (24,025,000,000); coal (metric tons; 2002) none (4,000); crude petroleum (barrels; 2008) 643,800,000 ([2006] 114,800,000); petroleum products (metric tons; 2008) 15,860,000 (10,244,000); natural gas (cu m; 2006) 14,413,000,000 (6,223,000,000). Population economically active (2003): total 2,137,000; activity rate of total population 37.9% (participation rates: ages 15 to 64, 56.7%; female 24.7%; unemployed [2004] 30.0%). Gross national income (2008): US$72,735,000,000 (US$11,590 per capita). Selected balance of payments data. Receipts from (US$'000,000): tourism (2007) 74; remittances (2008) 16; foreign direct investment (2005–07 avg.) 1,864; official development assistance (2007) 19.

Disbursements for (US$'000,000): tourism (2007) 888; remittances (2008) 762.

## Foreign trade

Imports (2004): US$8,768,000,000 (machinery and transportation equipment 48.0%; food products and live animals 14.1%; chemical products 4.0%). Major import sources (2006): Europe 58.7%, of which Italy 9.9%, Germany 8.5%, UK 3.7%; Arab countries 11.3%; Japan 5.7%. Exports (2004): US$20,600,000,000 (hydrocarbons [mostly crude petroleum] 95.7%). Major export destinations (2006): Europe 82.3%, of which Italy 42.5%, Germany 9.8%, Spain 8.5%, France 4.8%; Asian countries 5.4%.

## Transport and communications

Transport. Railroads: none. Roads (2000): total length 83,200 km (paved 57%). Vehicles (2005): passenger cars 1,356,987; trucks and buses 145,935. Air transport (2003): passenger-km 825,000,000; metric ton-km cargo (2001) 259,000. Communications, in total units (units per 1,000 persons). Telephone landlines (2008): 1,033,000 (164); cellular telephone subscribers (2008): 4,828,000 (767); personal computers (2005): 130,000 (21); total Internet users (2008): 323,000 (51); broadband Internet subscribers (2006): 9,600 (1.6).

## Education and health

Literacy (2006): percentage of total population ages 15 and over literate 88.1%; males literate 93.0%; females literate 83.1%. Health: physicians (2004) 7,405 (1 per 775 persons); hospital beds (2002) 21,400 (1 per 256 persons); infant mortality rate per 1,000 live births (2005) 24.6; undernourished population (2002–04) less than 2.5% of total population.

## Military

Total active duty personnel (November 2008): 76,000 (army 65.6%, navy 10.5%, air force 23.7%). Military expenditure as percentage of GDP (2007): 1.1%; per capita expenditure US$113.

## Background

Greeks and Phoenicians settled the area in the 7th century BC. It was conquered by Rome in the 1st century BC and by Arabs in the 7th century AD. In the 16th century, the Ottoman Turks combined Libya's three regions under one regency in Tripoli. In 1911 Italy claimed control of Libya, and by the outbreak of World War II, 150,000 Italians lived there. It became an independent state in 1951. The discovery of oil in 1959 brought wealth to Libya. A decade later a group of army officers led by Muammar al-Qaddafi deposed the king and made the country an Islamic republic. Under Qaddafi's rule it supported the Palestinian Liberation Organization and terrorist groups, bringing protests from many countries, particularly the US. Intermittent warfare with Chad during the 1970s and '80s ended with Chad's defeat of Libya in 1987. International relations in the 1990s were dominated by the consequences of the 1988 bombing of an American airliner over Lockerbie,

1 metric ton = about 1.1 short tons;    1 kilometer = 0.6 mi (statute);    1 metric ton-km cargo = about 0.68 short ton-mi cargo;    c.i.f.: cost, insurance, and freight;    f.o.b.: free on board

Scotland; the US accused Libyan nationalists of the deed and imposed a trade embargo on Libya, endorsed by the UN in 1992. This sanction was lifted in 2003. In 2011 protests against the regime's repressive policies quickly spiraled into civil war. After six months of fighting, Qaddafi was forced from power. He evaded capture for several weeks before being killed by rebel forces in Surt.

## Recent Developments

In 2011, Libya experienced a protracted period of protest and conflict that culminated in a shift to an interim government under the control of the Transitional National Council (TNC) and in the capture and death of the country's longtime ruler Muammar al-Qaddafi. Protests began in late February, after the overthrow of Tunisian leader Zine al-Abidine Ben Ali, but quickly descended into armed conflict. Libya's leader of more than 40 years used the Libyan military as well as mercenaries, mostly from sub-Saharan Africa, in an ultimately unsuccessful attempt to crush the opposition. As civilian casualties mounted, the UN Security Council approved a no-fly zone and other measures to protect civilians from Qaddafi's forces. In addition, the foreign assets of the Libyan government (which totaled more than US$150 billion) were frozen. Despite those efforts, a stalemate persisted for many months, with many thousands of lives lost and extensive internal displacement. In October, after opposition forces had effectively taken over governing Libya, Qaddafi was found and killed by TNC forces. In July 2012, Libyans voted in elections for a new 200-seat assembly that would appoint a new prime minister and draft a constitution.

Internet resource: <www.cbl.gov.ly/eg>.

# Liechtenstein

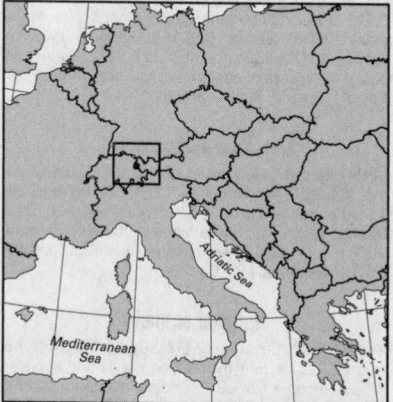

**Official name:** Fürstentum Liechtenstein (Principality of Liechtenstein). **Form of government:** constitutional monarchy with one legislative house (Diet [25]). **Head of state:** Prince Hans Adam II (from 1989). **Head of government:** Prime Minister Klaus Tschütscher (from 2009). **Capital:** Vaduz. **Official language:** German. **Official religion:** none. **Monetary unit:** 1 Swiss franc (CHF) = 100 centimes; valuation (2 Jul 2012) US$1 = CHF 0.95.

## Demography

**Area:** 62.0 sq mi, 160.5 sq km. **Population** (2011): 36,300. **Density** (2011): persons per sq mi 585.5, persons per sq km 226.2. **Urban** (2009): 13.9%. **Sex distribution** (2007): male 49.35%; female 50.65%. **Age breakdown** (2007): under 15, 16.8%; 15–29, 19.9%; 30–44, 22.5%; 45–59, 22.6%; 60–74, 13.1%; 75–84, 3.8%; 85 and over, 1.3%. **Ethnic composition** (2006): Liechtensteiner 66.1%; Swiss 10.3%; Austrian 5.8%; Italian 3.4%; German 3.4%; other 11.0%. **Religious affiliation** (2002): Christian 83.9%, of which Roman Catholic 76.0%, Protestant 7.0%, Orthodox 0.8%; Muslim 4.1%; nonreligious/ other 12.0%. **Major cities** (2007): Schaan 5,690; Vaduz 5,109; Triesen 4,713. **Location:** central Europe, between Austria and Switzerland.

## Vital statistics

**Birth rate** per 1,000 population (2008): 9.9 (world avg. 20.3); within marriage 86.0%. **Death rate** per 1,000 population (2008): 5.8 (world avg. 8.5). **Total fertility rate** (avg. births per childbearing woman; 2008): 1.40. **Life expectancy** at birth (2006): male 78.9 years; female 83.1 years.

## National economy

**Budget** (2007). *Revenue:* CHF 1,010,300,000 (current revenue 98.2%, of which taxes and duties 75.7%, investment income 16.5%; capital revenue and other 1.8%). *Expenditures:* CHF 1,029,200,000 (current expenditures 89.7%, of which wages and salaries 18.2%, financial affairs 17.1%, depreciation on portfolio securities 7.2%; capital expenditures 10.3%). **Public debt:** none. **Tourism** (2007): 59,603 tourist arrivals. **Population economically active** (2007): total 16,193; activity rate of total population 45.3% (participation rates: ages 15 and over [2005] 54.3%; female [2003] 41.4%; unemployed [2007] 2.7%). **Production** (metric tons except as noted). *Agriculture and fishing* (2007): grapes 200; other crops include cereals and apples; livestock (number of live animals) 6,037 cattle, 3,683 sheep, 1,735 pigs; *Manufacturing* (2007): small-scale precision manufacturing includes optical lenses, electron microscopes, electronic equipment, and high-vacuum pumps; metal manufacturing, construction machinery, and ceramics are also important. *Energy production (consumption):* electricity (kW-hr; 2007) 72,273,000 (379,013,000); coal (metric tons; 2004) none ([2003] 13); petroleum products (metric tons; 2004) none (50,000).

## Foreign trade

**Imports** (2007; excludes trade with Switzerland and transshipments through Switzerland): CHF 2,416,000,000 (fabricated metal products and iron and steel 36.8%; machinery and electronic goods 31.9%; mineral fuels and chemical products 15.2%; glass products, ceramics, and textiles 8.5%). *Major import sources:* Germany 40.2%; Austria 36.9%; Italy 5.2%; US 1.8%; France 1.8%. **Exports** (2007; excludes trade with Switzerland and transshipments through Switzerland): CHF 4,182,000,000 (machinery and electronic goods 34.0%; fabricated metal products and precision tools 33.2%; transportation equipment and parts 8.6%; glass products, ceramics, and textiles [including lead crystal and specialized dental products] 7.3%). *Major export destinations:*

Germany 20.0%; US 14.3%; Austria 11.5%; France 9.9%; Italy 6.3%.

## Transport and communications

**Transport.** *Railroads* (2006): length 18.5 km. *Roads* (2007): total length 380 km (paved 100%). *Vehicles* (2007): passenger cars 24,368; trucks and buses 7,532. *Air transport:* the nearest scheduled airport service is through Zürich, Switzerland. **Communications,** in total units (units per 1,000 persons). Telephone landlines (2008): 20,000 (550); cellular telephone subscribers (2008): 34,000 (954); total Internet users (2008): 23,000 (646); broadband Internet subscribers (2007): 14,000 (396).

## Education and health

**Educational attainment** (2000). Percentage of population ages 25 and over having: incomplete compulsory education (schooling to age 16) 3.0%; complete compulsory 22.9%; lower vocational 44.5%; higher vocational, teacher training 13.8%; university 6.6%; unknown 9.2%. **Literacy:** virtually 100%. **Health:** physicians (2005) 79 (1 per 441 persons); hospital beds (1997) 108 (1 per 288 persons); infant mortality rate per 1,000 live births (2006) 5.5.

## Military

**Total active duty personnel:** none; Liechtenstein has had no standing army since 1868; defense is the responsibility of Switzerland. **Military expenditure as percentage of GDP:** none.

## Background

The Rhine plain was occupied for centuries by two independent lordships of the Holy Roman Empire, Vaduz and Schellenberg. The principality of Liechtenstein, consisting of these two lordships, was founded in 1719 and remained part of the Holy Roman Empire. It was included in the German Confederation (1815–66). In 1866 it became independent, recognizing Vaduz and Schellenberg as unique regions forming separate electoral districts. An almost 60-year ruling coalition dissolved in 1997, and the prince won the passage of constitutional reforms in 2003 that greatly strengthened royal power.

## Recent Developments

Liechtenstein was cited in 2011 by the Organisation for Economic Co-operation and Development's Global Forum on Transparency and Information Exchange for Tax Purposes as having made "rapid progress in developing exchange of information mechanisms." The forum noted, however, that Liechtenstein still needed to meet international standards in combating tax evasion and bank secrecy.

**Internet resource:** <www.liechtenstein.li>.

# Lithuania

**Official name:** Lietuvos Respublika (Republic of Lithuania). **Form of government:** unitary multiparty

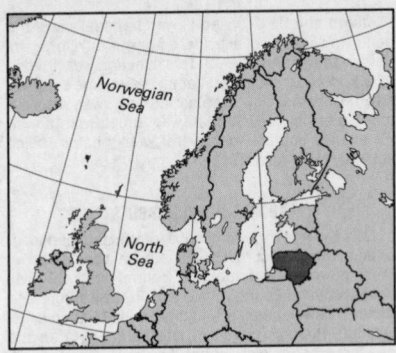

republic with one legislative house (Seimas [141]). **Head of state:** President Dalia Grybauskaite (from 2009). **Head of government:** Prime Minister Andrius Kubilius (from 2008). **Capital:** Vilnius. **Official language:** Lithuanian. **Official religion:** none. **Monetary unit:** 1 litas (LTL; plural litai) = 100 centai; valuation (2 Jul 2012) US$1 = LTL 2.74.

## Demography

**Area:** 25,212 sq mi, 65,300 sq km. **Population** (2011): 3,218,000. **Density** (2011): persons per sq mi 127.6, persons per sq km 49.3. **Urban** (2009): 66.9%. **Sex distribution** (2008): male 46.55%; female 53.45%. **Age breakdown** (2008): under 15, 15.1%; 15–29, 22.7%; 30–44, 21.1%; 45–59, 20.4%; 60–74, 13.8%; 75–84, 5.7%; 85 and over, 1.2%. **Ethnic composition** (2008): Lithuanian 84.1%; Polish 6.1%; Russian 4.9%; Belarusian 1.1%; Ukrainian 0.6%; Jewish 0.1%; other/unknown 3.1%. **Religious affiliation** (2007): Roman Catholic 80.2%; Orthodox 4.9%, of which Old Believers 0.8%; Lutheran/Reformed 0.8%; other Christian 3%; Jewish 0.1%; Muslim 0.1%; nonreligious/other 10.9%. **Major cities** (2008): Vilnius 558,165; Kaunas 352,279; Klaipeda 183,433; Siauliai 126,215; Panevezys 112,619. **Location:** eastern Europe, bordering Latvia, Belarus, Poland, Russia, and the Baltic Sea.

## Vital statistics

**Birth rate** per 1,000 population (2008): 10.4 (world avg. 20.3); within marriage 71.5%. **Death rate** per 1,000 population (2008): 13.1 (world avg. 8.5). **Total fertility rate** (avg. births per childbearing woman; 2008): 1.47. **Life expectancy** at birth (2008): male 66.3 years; female 77.6 years.

## National economy

**Budget** (2007). *Revenue:* LTL 30,067,000,000 (tax revenue 58.4%, of which tax on goods and services 36.8%; income tax 13.0%; social security contributions 30.4%; grants 5.8%; nontax revenue 5.4%). *Expenditures:* LTL 30,933,000,000 (social security and welfare 33.1%; general administration 23.7%; health 11.4%; economic affairs 11.1%; education 6.9%; defense 5.8%). **Gross national income** (2008): US$39,866,000,000 (US$11,870 per capita). **Production** (metric tons except as noted). *Agriculture and*

*1 metric ton = about 1.1 short tons; 1 kilometer = 0.6 mi (statute); 1 metric ton-km cargo = about 0.68 short ton-mi cargo; c.i.f.: cost, insurance, and freight; f.o.b.: free on board*

*fishing* (2007): wheat 1,390,700, barley 1,013,700, sugar beets 799,900; livestock (number of live animals) 1,127,100 pigs, 838,800 cattle; fisheries production 190,890 (from aquaculture 2%). *Mining and quarrying* (2006): limestone 1,776,300; peat 471,400. *Manufacturing* (value added in US$'000,000; 2006): food products and beverages 664, of which dairy products 170; wood products 372; bricks, tiles, and ceramics 192; refined petroleum products 174. *Energy production (consumption):* electricity (kW-hr; 2008) 13,101,000,000 ([2006] 12,054,000,000); coal (metric tons; 2006) none (399,000); crude petroleum (barrels; 2008) 938,000 ([2006] 58,800,000); petroleum products (metric tons; 2006) 7,957,000 (2,486,000); natural gas (cu m; 2006) none (2,926,000,000). **Public debt** (December 2008): US$7,099,000,000. **Population economically active** (2007): total 1,603,100; activity rate of total population 47.6% (participation rates: ages 15–64, 67.9%; female 49.3%; registered unemployed [2008] 5.8%). **Selected balance of payments data.** Receipts from (US$'000,000): tourism (2007) 1,153; remittances (2008) 1,537; foreign direct investment (FDI; 2005–07 avg.) 1,602. Disbursements for (US$'000,000): tourism (2007) 1,143; remittances (2008) 567; FDI (2005–07 avg.) 411.

## Foreign trade

**Imports** (2007; c.i.f.): US$24,445,000,000 (machinery and apparatus 18.1%; mineral fuels 16.2%, of which crude petroleum 9.2%; motor vehicles 14.5%; chemical products 12.6%). *Major import sources:* Russia 18.0%; Germany 15.0%; Poland 10.6%; Latvia 5.5%; Netherlands 4.3%. **Exports** (2007; f.o.b.): US$17,162,000,000 (food products 14.0%; machinery and apparatus 12.8%; refined petroleum products 11.6%; motor vehicles and parts 8.5%; furniture 5.1%; fertilizers 4.9%; wearing apparel and accessories 4.3%). *Major export destinations:* Russia 15.0%; Latvia 12.9%; Germany 10.5%; Poland 6.3%; Estonia 5.8%.

## Transport and communications

**Transport.** *Railroads* (2007): length 2,180 km; passenger-km 408,710,000; metric ton-km cargo 14,372,677,000. *Roads* (2007): total length 80,715 km (paved 88%). *Vehicles* (2007): passenger cars 1,587,903; trucks and buses 140,995. *Air transport* (2007): passenger-km 1,521,700,000; metric ton-km cargo 5,777,000. **Communications**, in total units (units per 1,000 persons). Telephone landlines (2008): 785,000 (234); cellular telephone subscribers (2008): 5,023,000 (1,496); personal computers (2007): 618,000 (183); total Internet users (2008): 1,777,000 (529); broadband Internet subscribers (2008): 590,000 (176).

## Education and health

**Educational attainment** (2005). Percentage of population ages 15 and over having: no schooling through complete primary education 14.7%; lower secondary 18.0%; higher secondary 28.2%; vocational/technical 19.3%; higher 19.8%. **Literacy** (2007): total population ages 15 and over literate 99.7%. **Health** (2008): physicians 13,403 (1 per 250 persons); hospital beds 27,362 (1 per 122 persons); infant mortality rate per 1,000 live births 4.9; undernourished population (2002–04) less than 2.5% of total population.

## Military

**Total active duty personnel** (November 2008): 8,850 (army 83.4%, navy 5.3%, air force 11.3%). **Military expenditure as percentage of GDP** (2008): 1.1%; per capita expenditure US$149.

## Background

Lithuanian tribes united in the mid-13th century to oppose the Teutonic knights. Gediminas, one of the grand dukes, expanded Lithuania into an empire that dominated much of Eastern Europe in the 14th through 16th centuries. In 1386 the Lithuanian grand duke became the king of Poland, and the two countries remained closely associated until Lithuania was acquired by Russia in the Third Partition of Poland in 1795. Occupied by Germany during World War I, it declared its independence in 1918. In 1940 the Soviet Red Army gained control of Lithuania. Germany occupied it again in 1941–44, but the USSR regained control in 1944. With the breakup of the USSR, Lithuania became independent in 1991. It signed a border treaty with Russia in 1997, and it joined the European Union and NATO in 2004.

## Recent Developments

In 2011, Lithuania marked 20 years of independence from the Soviet Union. During the year Lithuania chaired the Organization for Security and Co-operation (OSCE) in Europe, promoting human rights, democracy, and rule of law. Lithuania made a strong economic recovery. Unemployment decreased from 17.8% in 2010 to 15.4%, and real earnings rose by 2.7%, owing to inflation, which increased 3.4%. GDP increased 11.2%, exports rose 28.9%, and industrial production went up by 7.4%.

**Internet resource:** <www.stat.gov.lt/en>.

# Luxembourg

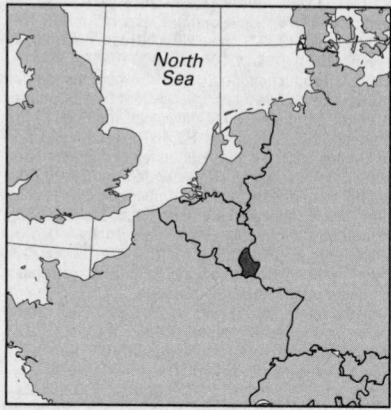

**Official name:** Groussherzogtum Lëtzebuerg (Luxembourgish); Grand-Duché de Luxembourg (French); Grossherzogtum Luxemburg (German) (Grand Duchy of Luxembourg). **Form of government:** constitutional monarchy with one legislative house (Chamber of

Deputies [60]). **Head of state:** Grand Duke Henri (from 2000). **Head of government:** Prime Minister Jean-Claude Juncker (from 1995). **Capital:** Luxembourg. **Official language:** none (Luxembourgish is the national language; French and German are both languages of administration). **Official religion:** none. **Monetary unit:** 1 euro (€) = 100 cents; valuation (2 Jul 2012) US$1 = €0.79.

## Demography

**Area:** 999 sq mi, 2,586 sq km. **Population** (2011): 517,000. **Density** (2011): persons per sq mi 517.5, persons per sq km 199.9. **Urban** (2010): 85.2%. **Sex distribution** (2008): male 49.61%; female 50.39%. **Age breakdown** (2008): under 15, 17.9%; 15–29, 18.7%; 30–44, 24.0%; 45–59, 20.6%; 60–74, 12.2%; 75–84, 5.2%; 85 and over, 1.4%. **Ethnic composition** (nationality; 2008): Luxembourger 56.3%; Portuguese 16.2%; French 5.8%; Italian 3.9%; Belgian 3.4%; German 2.4%; other 12.0%. **Religious affiliation** (2005): Roman Catholic 90%; Protestant 3%; Muslim 2%; Orthodox 1%; other 4%. **Major communes (urban agglomerations)** (2007): Luxembourg 85,467 (125,594); Esch-sur-Alzette 29,515 (72,437); Pétange 15,151 (22,379); Differdange 20,443; Dudelange 18,052. **Location:** western Europe, bordering Belgium, Germany, and France.

## Vital statistics

**Birth rate** per 1,000 population (2008): 11.3 (world avg. 20.3); within marriage 69.8%. **Death rate** per 1,000 population (2008): 7.3 (world avg. 8.5). **Total fertility rate** (avg. births per childbearing woman; 2008): 1.60. **Life expectancy** at birth (2007): male 77.6 years; female 82.7 years.

## National economy

**Budget** (2008; general government [consolidated] budget). *Revenue:* €15,864,000,000 (indirect taxes 33.2%; direct taxes 29.7%; social contributions 27.0%). *Expenditures:* €14,920,300,000 (social benefits 47.7%; development expenditure 9.7%). **Public debt** (2007): negligible. **Gross national income** (2008): US$41,406,000,000 (US$84,890 per capita). **Production** (metric tons except as noted). *Agriculture and fishing* (2008): wheat 97,760, barley 52,816, potatoes 21,756; livestock (number of live animals) 195,855 cattle, 81,407 pigs. *Mining and quarrying* (2007): limited quantities of limestone and slate. *Manufacturing* (value added in €'000,000; 2008): base metals 1,031.9; rubber and plastic products 320.8; fabricated metal products 304.9. *Energy production (consumption):* electricity (kW-hr; 2008–09) 3,508,000,000 ([2006] 7,890,000,000); coal (metric tons; 2006) none (153,000); petroleum products (metric tons; 2006) none (2,498,000); natural gas (cu m; 2007) none (1,403,300,000). **Population economically active** (2008): total 218,100; activity rate of total population 44.6% (participation rates: ages 15–64, 67.0%; female 43.5%; unemployed [September 2008–August 2009] 5.2%). **Selected balance of payments data.** Receipts from (US$'000,000): tourism (2007) 4,009; remittances (2008) 1,737; foreign direct disinvestment (2005–07 avg.) −670. Disbursements from (US$'000,000): tourism (2007) 3,552; remittances (2008) 10,922; foreign direct investment (2005–07 avg.) 21,446.

## Foreign trade

**Imports** (2008; c.i.f.): €17,290,280,000 (transportation equipment 15.5%; mineral fuels 15.2%; machinery and apparatus 14.1%; base and fabricated metals 11.2%; chemical products 9.8%; food products and live animals 7.0%). *Major import sources:* Belgium 34.8%; Germany 29.8%; France 12.7%; Netherlands 6.1%; US 2.4%. **Exports** (2008; f.o.b.): €11,890,410,000 (base and fabricated metals 36.2%; machinery and apparatus 15.9%; chemical products 7.1%; transportation equipment 7.0%; food products and live animals 5.0%). *Major export destinations:* Germany 27.5%; France 17.2%; Belgium 12.8%; Netherlands 6.2%; UK 4.9%.

## Transport and communications

**Transport.** *Railroads* (2008): route length 275 km; passenger-km 316,000,000; metric ton-km cargo 294,000,000. *Roads* (2008): total length 2,894 km (paved 100%). *Vehicles* (2008): passenger cars 329,038; trucks and buses 30,116. *Air transport* (2008; Luxair only): passenger-km 1,368,000,000; metric ton-km cargo, negligible. **Communications,** in total units (units per 1,000 persons). Telephone landlines (2008): 261,000 (542); cellular telephone subscribers (2008): 707,000 (1,471); personal computers (2005): 290,000 (634); total Internet users (2008): 387,000 (805); broadband Internet subscribers (2008): 143,000 (298).

## Education and health

**Educational attainment** (2007). Percentage of population ages 25–64 having: no formal schooling through primary education 18%; lower secondary 9%; upper secondary/higher vocational 47%; higher 26%. **Literacy** (2008): virtually 100% literate. **Health** (2007): physicians 1,672 (1 per 287 persons); hospital beds 2,743 (1 per 175 persons); infant mortality rate per 1,000 live births (2008) 2.0; undernourished population (2002–04) less than 2.5% of total population.

## Military

**Total active duty personnel** (November 2008): 900 (army 100%). **Military expenditure as percentage of GDP** (2007): 0.7%; per capita expenditure US$750.

## Background

At the time of Roman conquest (57–50 BC), Luxembourg was inhabited by a Belgic tribe. After AD 400, Germanic tribes invaded the region. Made a duchy in 1354, it was ceded to the house of Burgundy in 1443 and to the Habsburgs in 1477. In the mid-16th century it became part of the Spanish Netherlands. It was made a grand duchy in 1815. After an uprising in 1830, its western portion became part of Belgium, while the remainder was held by the Netherlands. In 1867 the European powers guaranteed the neutrality and independence of Luxembourg. In the late 19th century it exploited its extensive iron-ore de-

---

*1 metric ton = about 1.1 short tons;   1 kilometer = 0.6 mi (statute);   1 metric ton-km cargo = about 0.68 short ton-mi cargo;   c.i.f.: cost, insurance, and freight;   f.o.b.: free on board*

posits. It was invaded and occupied by Germany in both world wars. It abandoned its neutrality by joining NATO in 1949; it had joined the Benelux Economic Union in 1944. A member of the European Union, its economy has continued to expand. It adopted the euro as its official monetary unit in 1999. On 7 Oct 2000, Grand Duke Jean abdicated power in favor of his son, Crown Prince Henri, after 36 years on the throne.

## Recent Developments

Luxembourg's Prime Minister Jean-Claude Juncker worked tirelessly in 2011 to find some consensus among the euro zone countries to help with the continuing fiscal crisis. As chairman of the Eurogroup, Juncker led finance ministers to approve an additional €12 billion (about US$17.4 billion) installment for the bailout of Greece.

Internet resource: <www.statec.public.lu/en>.

# Macedonia

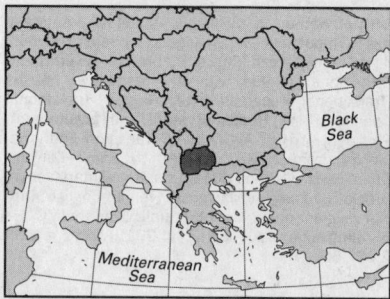

Black Sea

Mediterranean Sea

**Official name:** Republika Makedonija (Macedonian); Republika e Maqedonisë (Albanian) (Republic of Macedonia [member of the UN under the name The Former Yugoslav Republic of Macedonia]). **Form of government:** unitary multiparty republic with one legislative house (Sobranie, or Assembly [123]). **Head of state:** President Gjorge Ivanov (from 2009). **Head of government:** Prime Minister Nikola Gruevski (from 2006). **Capital:** Skopje. **Official languages:** Macedonian; Albanian. **Official religion:** none. **Monetary unit:** 1 denar (MKD) = 100 deni; valuation (2 Jul 2012) US$1 = 48.86 MKD.

## Demography

**Area:** 9,928 sq mi, 25,713 sq km. **Population** (2011): 2,060,000. **Density** (2011): persons per sq mi 207.5, persons per sq km 80.1. **Urban** (2009): 59.2%. **Sex distribution** (2005): male 49.95%; female 50.05%. **Age breakdown** (2005): under 15, 20.5%; 15–29, 23.8%; 30–44, 21.8%; 45–59, 18.8%; 60–74, 11.5%; 75–84, 3.2%; 85 and over, 0.4%. **Ethnic composition** (2002): Macedonian 64.2%; Albanian 25.2%; Turkish 3.9%; Rom (Gypsy) 2.7%; Serbian 1.8%; Bosniak 0.8%; other 1.4%. **Religious affiliation** (2005): Orthodox 65%; Sunni Muslim 32%; Roman Catholic 1%; other (mostly Protestant) 2%. **Major city/municipalities** (2008): Skopje (city) 486,600; Bitola 73,300; Kumanovo 71,700; Prilep 66,000; Tetovo 54,500. **Location:** southeastern Europe, bordering Kosovo, Serbia, Bulgaria, Greece, and Albania.

## Vital statistics

**Birth rate** per 1,000 population (2008): 11.2 (world avg. 20.3); within marriage 87.8%. **Death rate** per 1,000 population (2008): 9.3 (world avg. 8.5). **Total fertility rate** (avg. births per childbearing woman; 2007): 1.46. **Life expectancy** at birth (2007): male 71.1 years; female 75.9 years.

## National economy

**Budget** (2008). *Revenue:* MKD 136,412,000,000 (tax revenue 84.4%, of which social contributions 28.1%, VAT 26.5%, income and profit tax 12.7%, excise taxes 10.5%; nontax revenue 15.6%). *Expenditures:* MKD 140,265,000,000 (current expenditures 85.7%, of which transfers 55.6%, wages and salaries 14.5%, interest 1.9%; capital expenditures 14.3%). **Production** (metric tons except as noted). *Agriculture and fishing* (2007): grapes 225,000, potatoes 192,500, wheat 157,400; livestock (number of live animals) 817,500 sheep, 253,800 cattle; fisheries production 1,218 (from aquaculture 90%). *Mining and quarrying* (metal content; 2007): lead 32,000; zinc 20,000; copper 7,300. *Manufacturing* (value added in US$'000,000; 2006): food products and beverages 297; cement, bricks, and glass products 177; iron and steel (including ferronickel) 103; refined petroleum products 53. *Energy production (consumption):* electricity (kW-hr; 2006) 7,006,-000,000 (8,801,000,000); coal (metric tons; 2006) none (57,000); lignite (metric tons; 2006) 6,639,000 (6,823,000); crude petroleum (barrels; 2006) none (7,821,000); petroleum products (metric tons; 2006) 1,026,000 (893,000); natural gas (cu m; 2006) none (80,000,000). **Population economically active** (2006): total 891,679; activity rate 55.1% (participation rates: ages 15–64, 61.4%; female 39.5%; unemployed 36.0%). **Gross national income** (2008): US$8,432,000,000 (US$4,140 per capita). **Public debt** (external, outstanding; 2007): US$1,520,-000,000. **Selected balance of payments data.** Receipts from (US$'000,000): tourism (2007) 186; remittances (2008) 408; foreign direct investment (2005–07 avg.) 280; official development assistance (2007) 213. Disbursements for (US$'000,000): tourism (2007) 102; remittances (2008) 25.

## Foreign trade

**Imports** (2006; c.i.f.): US$3,763,000,000 (crude petroleum 14.3%; machinery and apparatus 12.2%; iron and steel 9.9%; food products 9.8%; chemical products 9.7%). *Major import sources:* Russia 15.1%; Germany 9.8%; Greece 8.5%; Serbia 7.5%; Bulgaria 6.6%. **Exports** (2006; f.o.b.): US$2,401,000,000 (iron and steel 27.8%, of which flat-rolled products 9.1%, ferronickel 8.4%; wearing apparel and accessories 21.2%; refined petroleum products 8.4%; food products 8.0%; tobacco products 4.7%). *Major export destinations:* Serbia 23.2%; Germany 15.6%; Greece 15.0%; Italy 9.9%; Bulgaria 5.4%.

## Transport and communications

**Transport.** *Railroads* (2007): length (2004) 699 km; passenger-km 109,000,000; metric ton-km cargo 799,000,000. *Roads* (2007): length 13,840 km (paved [2000] 58%). *Vehicles* (2007): passenger cars 248,774; trucks and buses 28,842. *Air transport* (2005; Macedonian Airlines only): passenger-km 266,000,000; metric ton-km cargo 111,000. **Communications,** in total units (units per 1,000 persons). Telephone landlines (2008): 457,000 (224); cellular telephone subscribers (2008): 2,502,000 (123); personal computers (2005): 451,000 (221); total Internet users (2008): 876,000 (429); broadband Internet subscribers (2008): 179,000 (88).

## Education and health

**Educational attainment** (2002). Percentage of population ages 15 and over having: less than full primary education 18.1%; primary 35.0%; secondary 36.9%; postsecondary and higher 10.0%. **Literacy** (2003): total population ages 10 and over literate 96.1%; males literate 98.2%; females literate 94.1%. **Health** (2006): physicians 5,134 (1 per 397 persons); hospital beds 9,343 (1 per 218 persons); infant mortality rate per 1,000 live births (2008) 9.7; undernourished population (2003–05) less than 5% of the total population.

## Military

**Total active duty personnel** (November 2008): 10,890 (army 89.6%, air force 10.4%). **Military expenditure as percentage of GDP** (2008): 2.0%; per capita expenditure US$80.

## Background

Macedonia has been inhabited since before 7000 BC. Part of it was incorporated into a Roman province in AD 29. It was settled by Slavic tribes by the mid-6th century AD. Seized by the Bulgarians in 1185, it was ruled by the Ottoman Empire from 1371 to 1912. The north and center of the region were annexed by Serbia in 1913 and in 1918 became part of what was later known as Yugoslavia. When Yugoslavia was partitioned by the Axis powers in 1941, Yugoslav Macedonia was occupied principally by Bulgaria. Macedonia again became part of Yugoslavia in 1946. After Croatia and Slovenia seceded from Yugoslavia, fear of Serbian dominance drove Macedonia to declare its independence in 1991. Because of Greek objections over using the name of an ancient Greek province, it entered the UN in 1993 as "The Former Yugoslav Republic of Macedonia." It normalized relations with Greece in 1995. Ethnic strife has periodically endangered national stability.

## Recent Developments

Interethnic relations remained largely calm in Macedonia in 2011, despite a violent incident in February in Skopje's Kale fortress, where ethnic Macedonians and Albanians clashed over plans to build a museum in the shape of a church. In mid-October, however, the national census, which was already under way, was canceled after ethnicity-related disagreements over procedures resulted in the resignation of the census commission.

**Internet resource:**
<www.stat.gov.mk/Default_en.aspx>.

# Madagascar

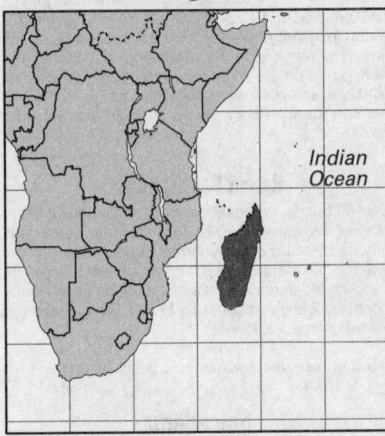

*Indian Ocean*

**Official name:** Repoblikan'i Madagasikara (Malagasy); République de Madagascar (French); Republic of Madagascar (English). **Form of government:** transitional regime with two legislative houses (Transitional Congress [417]; Higher Transitional Council [189]). **Heads of state and government:** President of High Authority of Transition Andry Rajoelina (from 2009), assisted by Prime Minister Omer Beriziky (from 2011). **Capital:** Antananarivo. **Official languages:** Malagasy; French; English. **Official religion:** none. **Monetary unit:** 1 ariary (MGA) = 5 iraimbilanja; valuation (2 Jul 2012) US$1 = MGA 2,207.50.

## Demography

**Area:** 226,658 sq mi, 587,041 sq km. **Population** (2011): 21,307,000. **Density** (2011): persons per sq mi 94.0, persons per sq km 36.3. **Urban** (2009): 29.8%. **Sex distribution** (2005): male 49.72%; female 50.28%. **Age breakdown** (2006): under 15, 44.1%; 15–29, 27.1%; 30–44, 15.7%; 45–59, 8.4%; 60–74, 3.7%; 75–84, 0.9%; 85 and over, 0.1%. **Ethnic composition** (2000): Malagasy 95.9%, of which Merina 24.0%, Betsimisaraka 13.4%, Betsileo 11.3%, Tsimihety 7.0%, Sakalava 5.9%; Makua 1.1%; French 0.6%; Comorian 0.5%; Reunionese 0.4%; other 1.5%. **Religious affiliation** (2005): traditional beliefs 42%; Protestant (significantly Lutheran) 27%; Roman Catholic 20%; Sunni Muslim 2%; other 9%. **Major cities** (2001): Antananarivo 1,403,449; Toamasina 179,045; Antsirabe 160,356; Fianarantsoa 144,225; Mahajanga 135,660. **Location:** island in the Indian Ocean, east of Mozambique.

## Vital statistics

**Birth rate** per 1,000 population (2006): 38.8 (world avg. 20.3). **Death rate** per 1,000 population (2006): 8.7 (world avg. 8.5). **Total fertility rate** (avg. births per childbearing woman; 2006): 5.29. **Life expectancy** at birth (2006): male 59.9 years; female 63.7 years.

---

*1 metric ton = about 1.1 short tons;*    *1 kilometer = 0.6 mi (statute);*    *1 metric ton-km cargo = about 0.68 short ton-mi cargo;*    *c.i.f.: cost, insurance, and freight;*    *f.o.b.: free on board*

## National economy

**Budget** (2007). *Revenue:* MGA 2,251,000,-000,000 (tax revenue 67.76%; grants 31.1%; non-tax revenue 1.3%). *Expenditures:* MGA 2,818,000,-000,000 (current expenditures 50.1%; capital expenditures 49.9%). **Public debt** (external, outstanding; 2007): US$1,425,000,000. **Production** (metric tons except as noted). *Agriculture and fishing* (2007): paddy rice 3,596,000, sugarcane 2,700,000, cassava 2,400,000, cloves (whole and stem) 10,000, vanilla 2,600; livestock (number of live animals) 9,600,000 cattle, 1,610,000 pigs, 3,000,000 geese; fisheries production 159,035 (from aquaculture 7%). *Mining and quarrying* (2007): chromite ore 95,000; graphite 15,000; sapphires 4,700 kg; rubies 920 kg; gold 210 kg (illegally smuggled, 2,000 kg). *Manufacturing* (value in US$'000,000; 2004): beverages 107; wearing apparel 57; fabricated metal products 35. *Energy production (consumption):* electricity (kW-hr; 2006) 1,065,000,000 (1,065,000,000); coal (metric tons; 2006) none (10,000); crude petroleum (barrels; 2006) none (3,518,000); petroleum products (metric tons; 2006) 325,000 (746,000). **Population economically active** (2005): total 9,844,100; activity rate of total population 52.8% (participation rates: ages 15–64, 88.1%; female 49.6%; unemployed 2.8%). **Selected balance of payments data.** Receipts from (US$'000,000): tourism (2007) 262; remittances (2008) 11; foreign direct investment (2005–07 avg.) 459; official development assistance (2007) 892. Disbursements for (US$'000,000): tourism (2007) 94; remittances (2008) 21. **Gross national income** (2008): US$7,766,000,000 (US$410 per capita).

## Foreign trade

**Imports** (2006; c.i.f.): US$1,760,300,000 (refined petroleum products 17.7%; machinery and apparatus 12.8%; food products 11.4%, of which cereals 4.3%; fabrics 9.3%; chemical products 8.6%; motor vehicles 5.0%; wool 4.8%). *Major import sources:* China 17.8%; Bahrain 16.4%; France 13.2%; South Africa 5.7%; US 3.6%. **Exports** (2006; f.o.b.): US$1,008,200,000 (food products and spices 32.4%, of which shrimp 12.0%, vanilla 4.7%, fish 4.4%, cloves 2.7%; wearing apparel and accessories 25.0%; refined petroleum products 7.9%; precious and semi-precious stones 2.6%). *Major export destinations:* France 39.5%; US 15.0%; Germany 6.0%; Italy 4.2%; UK 3.0%.

## Transport and communications

**Transport.** *Railroads* (2000): route length (2003) 901 km; passenger-km 24,471,000; metric ton-km cargo 27,200,000. *Roads* (2000): total length 49,827 km (paved 12%). *Vehicles* (1998): passenger cars 64,000; trucks and buses 9,100. *Air transport* (2007): passenger-km 1,248,000,000; metric ton-km cargo (2006) 18,768,000. **Communications,** in total units (units per 1,000 persons). Telephone landlines (2008): 165,000 (8.6); cellular telephone subscribers (2008): 4,835,000 (253); personal computers (2005): 102,000 (5.5); total Internet users (2008): 316,000 (17); broadband Internet subscribers (2008): 6,200 (0.3).

## Education and health

**Educational attainment** (2003–04). Percentage of population ages 25–59 (male) and 25–49 (female) having: no formal schooling 20.4%; incomplete primary education 33.6%; complete primary 13.2%; incomplete secondary 23.0%; complete secondary 6.4%; higher 3.4%. **Literacy** (2006): percentage of total population ages 15 and over literate 70.7%; males literate 76.5%; females literate 65.3%. **Health** (2004): physicians 1,861 (1 per 9,998 persons); hospital beds 9,303 (1 per 2,000 persons); infant mortality rate per 1,000 live births (2006) 58.5; undernourished population (2002–04) 6,600,000 (38% of total population based on the consumption of a minimum daily requirement of 1,800 calories).

## Military

**Total active duty personnel** (November 2008): 13,500 (army 92.6%, navy 3.7%, air force 3.7%). **Military expenditure as percentage of GDP** (2007): 1.1%; per capita expenditure US$4.

## Background

Indonesians migrated to Madagascar about AD 700. The first European to visit the island was Portuguese navigator Diogo Dias in 1500. Trade in arms and slaves allowed the development of Malagasy kingdoms at the beginning of the 17th century. The Merina kingdom became dominant in the 18th century and in 1868 signed a treaty granting France control over the northwestern coast. In 1895 French troops took the island, and Madagascar became a French overseas territory in 1946. As the Malagasy Republic, it gained independence in 1960. It severed ties with France in the 1970s. A new constitution was adopted in 1992, and the country was named the Republic of Madagascar. The country has since been both politically and economically unstable.

## Recent Developments

While Madagascar remained suspended from the Southern African Development Community (SADC) and the African Union in 2011, the SADC continued to mediate the crisis that had existed since the 2009 de facto coup that brought Andry Rajoelina to power. After a series of SADC talks mediated by former president Joaquim Chissano of Mozambique failed to resolve the dispute, it was announced in September 2011 that the SADC road map to a free and fair election, to be held within a year, had finally been accepted by the main parties in Madagascar. Part of the agreement's terms dictated that former Malagasy president Marc Ravalomanana, who had been living in exile since the coup, would be allowed to return to the Indian Ocean island, despite having been found guilty in absentia of causing civilian deaths and given a life sentence by a Malagasy court during the previous year. In November a unity government was formed by Omer Beriziky, the new prime minister. It was anticipated that the political developments might make possible the return of donor support, which had been cut off after the coup, at a cost to Madagascar of an estimated US$500 million.

**Internet resource:**
<www.madagascar-tourisme.com>.

# Malawi

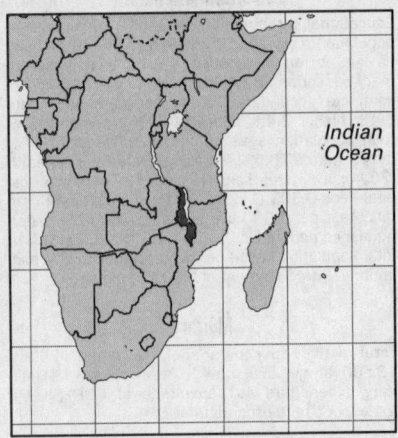

Indian
Ocean

**Official name:** Republic of Malawi. **Form of government:** multiparty republic with one legislative house (National Assembly [193]). **Head of state and government:** President Joyce Banda (from 2012). **Capital:** Lilongwe (the judiciary meets in Blantyre). **Official language:** none. **Official religion:** none. **Monetary unit:** 1 Malawian kwacha (MK) = 100 tambala; valuation (2 Jul 2012) US$1 = MK 270.39.

## Demography

**Area:** 45,747 sq mi, 118,484 sq km. **Population** (2011): 15,381,000. **Density** (2011; based on land area): persons per sq mi 422.6, persons per sq km 163.1. **Urban** (2008): 15.3%. **Sex distribution** (2008): male 48.72%; female 51.28%. **Age breakdown** (2007): under 15, 45.7%; 15–29, 28.4%; 30–44, 14.1%; 45–59, 7.6%; 60–74, 3.5%; 75–84, 0.6%; 85 and over, 0.1%. **Ethnic composition** (2000): Chewa 34.7%; Maravi 12.2%; Ngoni 9.0%; Yao 7.9%; Tumbuka 7.9%; Lomwe 7.7%; Ngonde 3.5%; other 17.1%. **Religious affiliation** (2005): Protestant/independent Christian 55%; Roman Catholic 20%; Muslim 20%; traditional beliefs 3%; other 2%. **Major cities** (2008): Lilongwe 669,021; Blantyre 661,444; Mzuzu 128,432; Zomba 87,366; Kasungu 42,351. **Location:** southeastern Africa, bordering Tanzania, Mozambique, and Zambia.

## Vital statistics

**Birth rate** per 1,000 population (2008): 42.1 (world avg. 20.3). **Death rate** per 1,000 population (2008): 14.9 (world avg. 8.5). **Total fertility rate** (avg. births per childbearing woman; 2008): 5.67. **Life expectancy** at birth (2008): male 48.4 years; female 49.5 years.

## National economy

**Budget** (2008–09). *Revenue:* MK 187,402,000,000 (tax revenue 62.4%, of which VAT 21.0%, excises 9.7%, corporate taxes 8.1%; grants 29.3%; nontax revenue 6.9%; other 1.4%). *Expenditures:* MK 223,502,000,000 (current expenditures 82.0%; capital expenditures 18.0%). **Public debt** (external, outstanding; March 2009): US$664,000,000. **Production** (metric tons except as noted). *Agriculture and fishing* (2007): corn (maize) 3,444,700, sugarcane 2,500,000, cassava 2,150,000, tobacco leaves 118,000, pigeon peas 79,000, tea 39,000, sunflower seeds 5,913; livestock (number of live animals) 1,900,000 goats, 752,000 cattle, 458,000 pigs; fisheries production 68,000 (from aquaculture 2%). *Mining and quarrying* (2007): limestone 31,490; gemstones (significantly rubies and sapphires) 3,710 kg. *Manufacturing* (value added in US$'000,000; 2001): food products 62; beverages 28; chemical products 11. *Energy production (consumption):* electricity (kW-hr; 2006) 1,556,000,000 (1,546,000,000); coal (metric tons; 2007) 58,550 ([2006] 50,000); petroleum products (metric tons; 2006) none (263,000). **Population economically active** (2006): total 5,585,000; activity rate 41.2% (participation rates: ages 15–64, 77.1%; female 50.2%). **Gross national income** (2008): US$4,107,000,000 (US$290 per capita). **Selected balance of payments data.** Receipts from (US$'000,000): tourism (2007) 27; remittances (2008) 1.0; foreign direct investment (2005–07 avg.) 37; official development assistance (2007) 735. Disbursements for (US$'000,000): tourism (2007) 73; remittances (2008) 1.0.

## Foreign trade

**Imports** (2007; c.i.f.): MK 192,833,000,000 (chemical products 27.8%, of which fertilizers 13.7%; refined petroleum products 13.1%; machinery and apparatus 11.8%; motor vehicles 10.4%; food products 5.9%). *Major import sources:* South Africa 29.1%; Mozambique 12.2%; UAE 7.0%; UK 5.0%; India 5.0%. **Exports** (2007; f.o.b.): MK 121,567,000,000 (unmanufactured tobacco 48.7%; corn (maize) 11.5%; raw sugar 7.0%; tea 6.4%; sunflower seeds 3.7%; wearing apparel and accessories 3.7%). *Major export destinations:* Zimbabwe 15.2%; South Africa 14.8%; Belgium 8.0%; UK 6.6%; Germany 5.8%.

## Transport and communications

**Transport.** *Railroads* (2007): route length 797 km; (2004) passenger-km 29,523,000; metric ton-km cargo 18,438,000. *Roads* (2003): total length 15,451 km (paved 45%). *Vehicles* (2001): passenger cars 22,500; trucks and buses 57,600. *Air transport* (2007; Air Malawi only): passenger-km 165,000,000. **Communications,** in total units (units per 1,000 persons). Telephone landlines (2008): 236,000 (16); cellular telephone subscribers (2008): 1,781,000 (122); personal computers (2007): 28,000 (2); total Internet users (2008): 316,000 (22); broadband Internet subscribers (2007): 1,600 (0.1).

## Education and health

**Educational attainment** (2004). Percentage of population ages 25 and over having: no formal education/unknown 33.5%; incomplete primary education 24.2%; complete primary 27.9%; secondary and university 14.4%. **Literacy** (2007): total population ages 15 and over literate 65.9%; males literate 78.1%; females literate 53.9%. **Health** (2008): physicians 260

---

*1 metric ton = about 1.1 short tons;    1 kilometer = 0.6 mi (statute);    1 metric ton-km cargo = about 0.68 short ton-mi cargo;    c.i.f.: cost, insurance, and freight;    f.o.b.: free on board*

(1 per 56,246 persons); hospital beds (2007) 15,658 (1 per 909 persons); infant mortality rate per 1,000 live births 88.1; undernourished population (2002–04) 4,200,000 (35% of total population based on the consumption of a minimum daily requirement of 1,790 calories).

## Military

Total active duty personnel (November 2008): 5,300 (army 100%). Military expenditure as percentage of GDP (2007): 1.7%; per capita expenditure US$3.

## Background

Inhabited since at least 8000 BC, the region was settled by Bantu-speaking peoples between the 1st and the 4th century AD. About 1480 they founded the Maravi Confederacy, which encompassed most of central and southern Malawi. In northern Malawi the Ngonde people established a kingdom about 1600. The slave trade flourished during the 18th–19th centuries. Britain established colonial authority in 1891, and the area became known as Nyasaland in 1907. The colonies of Northern and Southern Rhodesia and Nyasaland formed (1951–53) a federation, which was dissolved in 1963. The next year Malawi achieved independence. In 1966 it became a republic, with Hastings Banda as president. In 1971 Banda was designated president for life, and he ruled until he was defeated in multiparty elections in 1994. A new constitution was adopted in 1995.

## Recent Developments

Malawi's Pres. Bingu wa Mutharika and an ethnic clique consolidated their grip on state institutions in 2011. Meanwhile, the market price of tobacco, the main cash crop, plunged. Civil servants did not receive salaries for months; consumer prices surged; and there were severe shortages of fuel, electricity, and water. Economic troubles were further exacerbated when international donors, concerned with how the government was handling Malawi's economic problems, withheld considerable amounts of aid. In April 2012, however, Mutharika died in office.

Internet resource: <www.nso.malawi.net>.

# Malaysia

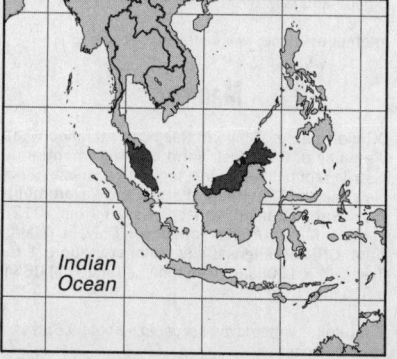

Indian Ocean

Official name: Malaysia. Form of government: federal constitutional monarchy with two legislative houses (Senate [70]; House of Representatives [222]). Head of state: Yang di-Pertuan Agong (Paramount Ruler) Tuanku Abdul Halim Muadzam Shah ibni al-Marhum Sultan Badlishah (from 2011). Head of government: Prime Minister Datuk Seri Najib Tun Razak (from 2009). Capital: Kuala Lumpur (location of the first royal palace and both houses of parliament). Administrative center: Putrajaya (location of the second royal palace, the prime minister's office, and the supreme court). Official language: Malay. Official religion: Islam. Monetary unit: 1 ringgit, or Malaysian dollar (RM) = 100 sen; valuation (2 Jul 2012) US$1 = RM 3.16.

## Demography

Area: 127,724 sq mi, 330,804 sq km. Population (2011): 28,161,000. Density (2011): persons per sq mi 220.5, persons per sq km 85.1. Urban (2009): 71.3%. Sex distribution (2008): male 50.90%; female 49.10%. Age breakdown (2008): under 15, 32.0%; 15–29, 26.6%; 30–44, 20.4%; 45–59, 14.0%; 60–74, 5.6%; 75 and over, 1.4%. Ethnic composition (2008): Malay 50.8%; other indigenous 11.0%; Chinese 22.9%; Indian 6.9%; other citizen 1.2%; noncitizen 7.2%. Religious affiliation (2000): Muslim 60.4%; Buddhist 19.2%; Christian 9.1%; Hindu 6.3%; Chinese folk religionist 2.6%; animist 0.8%; other 1.6%. Major cities (2006): Kuala Lumpur 1,482,400; Subang Jaya 954,300; Klang 936,700; Johor Bahru 838,900; Ipoh 692,200; Putrajaya 55,000. Location: southeastern Asia, on the Malay Peninsula and the northern third of the island of Borneo, bordering Thailand, the South China Sea, Brunei, and Indonesia.

## Vital statistics

Birth rate per 1,000 population (2008): 17.5 (world avg. 20.3). Death rate per 1,000 population (2008): 4.2 (world avg. 8.5). Total fertility rate (avg. births per childbearing woman; 2008): 2.57. Life expectancy at birth (2008): male 72.1 years; female 76.8 years.

## National economy

Budget (2008). Revenue: RM 159,793,000,000 (tax revenue 70.7%, of which corporate taxes 23.6%, taxes on petroleum 15.1%, income tax 9.4%; nontax revenue 29.3%). Expenditures: RM 196,346,-000,000 (current expenditures 78.2%, of which wages and salaries 20.9%; development expenditures 21.8%). Population economically active (2008): total 11,028,100; activity rate 40.8% (participation rates: ages 15–64, 62.6%; female 35.8%; unemployed [April 2008–March 2009] 3.4%). Production (metric tons except as noted). Agriculture and fishing (2008): oil palm fruit 83,000,000, rice 2,384,000, natural rubber 1,072,400, sugarcane 693,850, coconuts 555,120, bananas 530,000, cassava 430,000, cacao beans 30,000; livestock (number of live animals) 790,000 cattle, 131,000 buffalo; fisheries production (2007) 1,783,739 (from aquaculture 19%). Mining and quarrying (2008–09): iron ore 1,023,434; tin (metal content) 2,646; gold 2,427 kg. Manufacturing (value added in RM '000,000; 2006): electrical machinery and electronics 32,017; chemical products 19,035; refined petroleum and coal products 16,577; transportation equipment 6,796. *Energy production (consumption):* electricity (kW-hr; 2008–09) 103,734,200,000 (92,662,100,000); coal (metric tons; 2008–09) 1,433,341 ([2006] 11,143,000); crude petroleum (barrels; 2008–09) 248,239,000 ([2006] 185,607,-500); petroleum products (metric tons; 2008–09) 23,380,000 ([2006] 23,718,000); natural gas (cu m; 2008–09) 56,794,675,000 ([2007] 32,900,-000,000). **Gross national income** (2008): US$188,061,000,000 (US$6,970 per capita). **Public debt** (external, outstanding; 2007): US$18,441,-000,000. **Selected balance of payments data.** Receipts from (US$'000,000): tourism (2007) 12,905; remittances (2008) 1,920; foreign direct investment (FDI; 2006–08 avg.) 7,256; official development assistance (2007) 200. Disbursements for (US$'000,000): tourism (2007) 5,252; remittances (2008) 6,385; FDI (2005–07 avg.) 6,667.

## Foreign trade

**Imports** (2006; c.i.f.): RM 481,000,000,000 (microcircuits and transistors 23.9%; crude petroleum 8.3%; office machines, computers, and parts 7.8%; chemical products 7.8%; base metals 6.8%). *Major import sources:* Japan 13.2%; US 12.5%; China 12.1%; Singapore 11.7%; Thailand 5.5%. **Exports** (2006; f.o.b.): RM 589,367,000,000 (computers, office machines, and parts 17.4%; microcircuits and transistors 15.9%; crude petroleum 8.9%; telecommunications equipment 5.7%; natural gas 4.8%; palm oil 3.2%). *Major export destinations:* US 18.8%; Singapore 15.4%; Japan 8.9%; China 7.2%; Thailand 5.3%.

## Transport and communications

**Transport.** *Railroads* (2008–09): route length (2008) 1,849 km; passenger-km 1,466,892,000; metric ton-km cargo 1,267,935,000. *Roads* (2006): total length 90,127 km (paved 79%). *Vehicles* (2006): passenger cars 7,024,043; trucks and buses 896,570. *Air transport* (2008–09): passenger-km 32,297,000,000; metric ton-km cargo 2,142,-483,000. **Communications,** in total units (units per 1,000 persons). Telephone landlines (2008): 4,292,000 (159); cellular telephone subscribers (2008): 27,743,000 (1,027); personal computers (2006): 6,106,000 (234); total Internet users (2008): 16,903,000 (626); broadband Internet subscribers (2008): 1,302,000 (48).

## Education and health

**Educational attainment** (2002). Percentage of population ages 25–64 having: no formal schooling/unknown 8.4%; primary education 28.7%; lower secondary 20.7%; upper secondary 31.1%; higher 11.1%. **Literacy** (2007): total population ages 15 and over literate 91.9%; males literate 94.2%; females literate 89.6%. **Health** (2008): physicians 25,102 (1 per 1,076 persons); hospital beds (2007) 47,784 (1 per 556 persons); infant mortality rate per 1,000 live births 6.7; undernourished population (2002–04) 600,000 (3% of total population based on the consumption of a minimum daily requirement of 1,850 calories).

## Military

**Total active duty personnel** (November 2008): 109,000 (army 73.4%, navy 12.8%, air force 13.8%). **Military expenditure as percentage of GDP** (2008): 1.9%; per capita expenditure US$146.

## Background

Malaya has been inhabited for 6,000–8,000 years, and small kingdoms existed in the 2nd–3rd centuries AD, when adventurers from India first arrived. Sumatran exiles founded the city-state of Malacca about 1400, and it flourished as a trading and Islamic religious center until its capture by the Portuguese in 1511. Malacca passed to the Dutch in 1641. The British founded a settlement on Singapore Island in 1819, and by 1867 they had established the Straits Settlements, including Malacca, Singapore, and Penang. During the late 19th century the Chinese began to migrate to Malaya. Japan invaded in 1941. Opposition to British rule led to the creation of the United Malays National Organization (UNMO) in 1946, and in 1948 the peninsula was federated with Penang. Malaya gained independence in 1957, and the Federation of Malaysia was established in 1963. Its economy expanded greatly from the late 1970s, and though it experienced the regional economic slump of the mid- to late 1990s, the economy subsequently recovered.

## Recent Developments

Malaysia's GDP grew by an estimated 4.5% in 2011. Almost 35% of Malaysian workers had incomes below the official poverty line, however, and the government announced in April that it was considering instituting a minimum wage. The first meeting of the Global Science and Innovation Advisory Council took place in May. The council advised the government on how best to encourage green development in Malaysia, with a focus on such issues as the handling of industrial waste, water management, and reforestation. A new rare-earth metals refinery being built in Kuantan prompted environmental concerns when engineers associated with the project reported that design and construction flaws could result in radiation leaks. Analysts predicted that the refinery could supply almost one-third of world demand for rare-earth metals (used in many high-technology applications) and could generate more than US$1.7 billion in exports annually.

**Internet resource:** <www.statistics.gov.my>.

# Maldives

**Official name:** Dhivehi Raajjeyge Jumhooriyyaa (Republic of Maldives). **Form of government:** multiparty republic with one legislative house (People's Majlis [77]). **Head of state and government:** President Mohamed Waheed Hassan (from 2012). **Capital:** Male. **Official language:** Dhivehi (Maldivian). **Official religion:** Islam. **Monetary unit:** 1 rufiyaa (Rf) = 100 laari; valuation (2 Jul 2012) US$1 = Rf 15.41.

---

*1 metric ton = about 1.1 short tons;    1 kilometer = 0.6 mi (statute);    1 metric ton-km cargo = about 0.68 short ton-mi cargo;    c.i.f.: cost, insurance, and freight;    f.o.b.: free on board*

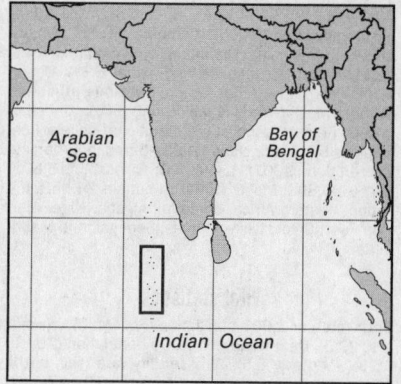

Arabian Sea

Bay of Bengal

Indian Ocean

## Demography

**Area:** 115 sq mi, 298 sq km. **Population** (2011): 325,000. **Density** (2011; based on areas of inhabited islets only): persons per sq mi 6,944, persons per sq km 2,681. **Urban** (2006): 34.7%. **Sex distribution** (2006): male 50.66%; female 49.34%. **Age breakdown** (2006): under 15, 31.1%; 15–29, 33.2%; 30–44, 18.3%; 45–59, 9.2%; 60–74, 5.2%; 75–84, 1.1%; 85 and over, 0.2%; unknown 1.7%. **Ethnic composition** (2000): Maldivian 98.5%; Sinhalese 0.7%; other 0.8%. **Religious affiliation:** virtually 100% Sunni Muslim. **Major islets** (2006): Male 103,693; Hithadhoo 9,465; Fuvammulah 7,636. **Location:** islands in the Indian Ocean, south of India.

## Vital statistics

**Birth rate** per 1,000 population (2008): 22 (world avg. 20.3). **Death rate** per 1,000 population (2008): 3 (world avg. 8.5). **Total fertility rate** (avg. births per childbearing woman; 2006): 2.1. **Life expectancy** at birth (2007): male 72.3 years; female 73.7 years.

## National economy

**Budget** (2008). *Revenue:* Rf 7,757,000,000 (nontax revenue 48.6%, of which resort lease rent 19.5%; tax revenue 43.7%, of which import duties 31.7%; grants 7.2%; other 0.5%). *Expenditures:* Rf 9,789,000,000 (general administration 21.8%; community programs 20.5%; education 15.6%; health 12.8%; police and security 9.1%; defense 5.6%). **Public debt** (external, outstanding; 2008): US$471,700,000. **Production** (metric tons except as noted). *Agriculture and fishing* (2007): vegetables 28,526, bananas 11,000, coconuts 2,625; fisheries production 144,169, of which skipjack tuna 97,342, yellowfin tuna 24,415 (from aquaculture, none). *Mining and quarrying:* coral for construction materials. *Manufacturing:* n.a.; however, major industries include boat building and repairing, coir yarn and mat weaving, coconut and fish processing, lacquerwork, garment manufacturing, and handicrafts. *Energy production (consumption):* electricity (kW-hr; 2008) 301,000,000 ([2006] 212,000,000); petroleum products (metric tons; 2006) none (283,000). **Selected balance of payments data.** Receipts from (US$'000,000): tourism (2007) 586; remittances (2008) 3; foreign direct investment (2005–07 avg.) 13; official development assistance (2007) 37. Disbursements for (US$'000,000): tourism (2007) 92; remittances (2008) 103. **Population economically active** (2006): total 128,836; activity rate of total population 43.1% (participation rates: ages 15–64, 65.8%; female 41.3%; unemployed 14.4%). **Gross national income** (2008): US$1,126,000,000 (US$3,630 per capita).

## Foreign trade

**Imports** (2008; c.i.f.): US$1,388,000,000 (refined petroleum products 22.6%; food products 15.3%; goods for construction 14.1%; transportation equipment and parts 10.4%). *Major import sources:* Singapore 21.3%; UAE 18.0%; India 10.4%; Malaysia 7.7%; Sri Lanka 5.9%. **Exports** (2008; f.o.b.): US$330,500,000 (reexports [mostly jet fuel] 61.6%; fish 37.3%, of which fresh skipjack tuna 16.7%, fresh yellowfin tuna 13.2%, dried fish 3.0%). *Major export destinations* (domestic exports only): Thailand 49.4%; Sri Lanka 9.5%; France 8.8%; Italy 8.3%; UK 7.7%.

## Transport and communications

**Transport.** *Railroads:* none. *Vehicles* (2008): passenger cars 3,917; trucks and buses 2,314. *Air transport* (2008; Male airport only): passenger arrivals 1,275,993, passenger departures 1,264,572; cargo unloaded 20,561 metric tons, cargo loaded 13,029 metric tons. **Communications,** in total units (units per 1,000 persons). Telephone landlines (2008): 47,000 (151); cellular telephone subscribers (2008): 436,000 (1,407); personal computers (2005): 45,000 (152); total Internet users (2008): 72,000 (231); broadband Internet subscribers (2008): 16,000 (51).

## Education and health

**Educational attainment** (2006). Population ages 6 and over 267,283; percentage with bachelor's degree 0.6%, master's degree 0.3%. **Literacy** (2006): total population ages 15 and over literate 93.5%; males literate 92.5%; females literate 94.5%. **Health** (2008): physicians 575 (1 per 539 persons); hospital beds 785 (1 per 395 persons); infant mortality rate per 1,000 live births 11; undernourished population (2002–04) 30,000 (10% of total population based on the consumption of a minimum daily requirement of 1,840 calories).

## Military

**Total active duty personnel** (2006): 2,000-member paramilitary incorporates coast guard duties. **Paramilitary expenditure as percentage of GDP** (2008): 4.9%; per capita expenditure US$139.

## Background

The archipelago was settled in the 5th century BC by Buddhists from Sri Lanka and southern India, and Islam was adopted there in AD 1153. The Portuguese held sway in Male in 1558–73. The islands were a sultanate under the Dutch rulers of Ceylon (now Sri Lanka) during the 17th century. After the British gained control of Ceylon in 1796, the area became a British protectorate, a status formalized in 1887. The islands won full independence from Britain in 1965, and in 1968 a republic was founded. The Maldives joined the Commonwealth in 1982. Its economy has gradually improved, aided by the growth of tourism. A new constitution adopted in 2008 established Islam as the state religion, created greater governmental checks and balances, and allowed women to run for president.

## Recent Developments

Economic issues dominated the political agenda of the Maldives government of Pres. Mohamed Nasheed and the opposition parties in 2011, threatening to cause instability in the country. In May a series of protests erupted in Male against soaring prices after the Maldivian currency, the rufiyaa, was devalued by 20%. The demonstrations allegedly were orchestrated by former president Maumoon Abdul Gayoom's supporters.

Internet resource: <www.planning.gov.mv/en>.

# Mali

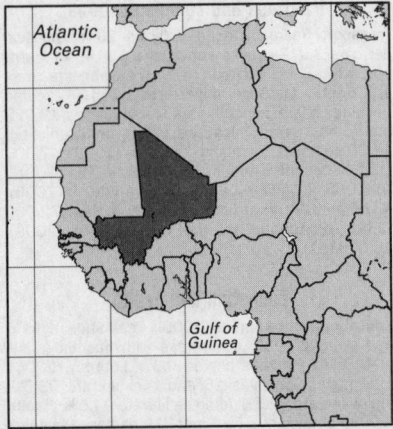

**Official name:** République du Mali (Republic of Mali). **Form of government:** multiparty republic with one legislative house (National Assembly [147]). **Head of state:** President Dioncounda Traoré (interim) (from 2012). **Head of government:** Prime Minister Cheick Modibo Diarra (interim) (from 2012). **Capital:** Bamako. **Official language:** French. **Official religion:** none. **Monetary unit:** 1 CFA franc (CFAF) = 100 centimes; valuation (2 Jul 2012) US$1 = CFAF 521.26.

## Demography

**Area:** 482,077 sq mi, 1,248,574 sq km. **Population** (2011): 15,525,000. **Density** (2011): persons per sq mi 32.2, persons per sq km 12.4. **Urban** (2008): 32.4%. **Sex distribution** (2006): male 49.67%; female 50.33%. **Age breakdown** (2006): under 15, 48.1%; 15–29, 27.7%; 30–44, 12.9%; 45–59, 6.4%;

60–74, 4.1%; 75–84, 0.7%; 85 and over, 0.1%. **Ethnic composition** (2000): Bambara 30.6%; Senufo 10.5%; Fula Macina (Niafunke) 9.6%; Soninke 7.4%; Tuareg 7.0%; Maninka 6.6%; Songhai 6.3%; Dogon 4.3%; Bobo 3.5%; other 14.2%. **Religious affiliation** (2005): Muslim (nearly all Sunni) 90%; Christian (mostly Roman Catholic) 5%; traditional beliefs/nonreligious 5%. **Major cities** (1998): Bamako (urban agglomeration; 2007) 1,494,000; Sikasso 113,803; Ségou 90,898; Mopti 79,840; Koutiala 74,153. **Location:** western Africa, bordering Algeria, Niger, Burkina Faso, Côte d'Ivoire, Guinea, Senegal, and Mauritania.

## Vital statistics

**Birth rate** per 1,000 population (2008): 46.8 (world avg. 20.3). **Death rate** per 1,000 population (2008): 15.3 (world avg. 8.5). **Total fertility rate** (avg. births per childbearing woman; 2008): 6.70. **Life expectancy** at birth (2008): male 49.9 years; female 53.0 years.

## National economy

**Budget** (2008). *Revenue:* CFAF 757,700,000,000 (tax revenue 74.3%; grants 22.4%; nontax revenue 3.3%). *Expenditures:* CFAF 913,500,000,000 (current expenditures 59.8%; capital expenditures 40.2%). **Public debt** (external, outstanding; 2007): US$1,989,000,000. **Selected balance of payments data.** Receipts from (US$'000,000): tourism (2006) 175; remittances (2008) 344; foreign direct investment (2005–07 avg.) 222; official development assistance (2007) 1,017. Disbursements for (US$'000,000): tourism (2006) 120; remittances (2008) 83. **Population economically active** (2004): total 2,598,200; activity rate of total population 23% (participation rates: ages 15–64, 51.1%; female 42.5%; officially unemployed 8.8%). **Production** (metric tons except as noted). *Agriculture and fishing* (2007): millet 1,074,440, rice 955,300, sorghum 907,966, seed cotton 414,965, karite nuts (2005) 85,000, cowpeas 70,000; livestock (number of live animals) 13,010,000 goats, 8,595,000 sheep, 7,917,000 cattle, 476,000 camels; fisheries production 100,640 (from aquaculture 1%). *Mining and quarrying* (2007): salt (2005) 6,000; gold 52,800 kg. *Manufacturing* (2005): beef and veal 98,000; goat meat (2001) 49,000; sheep meat 36,000. *Energy production (consumption):* electricity (kW-hr; 2006) 489,000,000 (489,000,000); petroleum products (metric tons; 2006) none (185,000). **Gross national income** (2008): US$7,360,000,000 (US$580 per capita).

## Foreign trade

**Imports** (2007): CFAF 842,700,000,000 (machinery and apparatus 30.3%; refined petroleum products 28.9%; food products 19.7%). *Major import sources* (2004): France 15.9%; Senegal 12.2%; Côte d'Ivoire 9.4%; Togo 8.5%; Benin 7.4%. **Exports** (2007): CFAF 705,600,000,000 (gold 73.0%; raw cotton and cotton products 15.2%; livestock 4.3%). *Major export destinations* (2004): South Africa 30.9%; Switzerland 20.4%; Senegal 6.3%; China 4.7%; Côte d'Ivoire 4.7%.

---

*1 metric ton = about 1.1 short tons;    1 kilometer = 0.6 mi (statute);    1 metric ton-km cargo = about 0.68 short ton-mi cargo;    c.i.f.: cost, insurance, and freight;    f.o.b.: free on board*

## Transport and communications

**Transport.** *Railroads* (2002): route length (2004) 729 km; passenger-km 196,000,000; metric ton-km cargo 188,000,000. *Roads* (2004): total length 18,709 km (paved 18%). *Vehicles* (2007): passenger cars 86,967; trucks and buses 26,759. **Communications,** in total units (units per 1,000 persons). Telephone landlines (2008): 83,000 (6.5); cellular telephone subscribers (2008): 3,267,000 (257); personal computers (2007): 98,000 (8); total Internet users (2008): 125,000 (9.8); broadband Internet subscribers (2008): 5,300 (0.4).

## Education and health

**Educational attainment** (2001). Population ages 25 and over having: no formal schooling/unknown 82.1%; incomplete primary education 7.7%; complete primary 2.0%; secondary 6.5%; higher 1.7%. **Literacy** (2007): percentage of total population ages 15 and over literate 23.3%; males literate 31.4%; females literate 16.0%. **Health:** physicians (2004) 1,053 (1 per 10,566 persons); hospital beds (2001) 1,664 (1 per 6,203 persons); infant mortality rate per 1,000 live births (2008) 118.1; undernourished population (2003–05) 1,200,000 (11% of total population based on the consumption of a minimum daily requirement of 1,720 calories).

## Military

**Total active duty personnel** (November 2008): 7,350 (army 100%). **Military expenditure as percentage of GDP** (2007): 2.1%; per capita expenditure US$12.

## Background

Inhabited since prehistoric times, the region was situated on a caravan route across the Sahara. In the 12th century, the Malinke empire of Mali was founded on the Upper and Middle Niger. In the 15th century, the Songhai empire in the Timbuktu-Gao region gained control. In 1591 Morocco invaded the area, and Timbuktu remained under the Moors for two centuries. In the mid-19th century, the French conquered the area, which became a part of French West Africa known as the French Sudan. In 1946 it became an overseas territory of the French Union. It was proclaimed the Sudanese Republic in 1958, briefly joined with Senegal (1959–60) to form the Mali Federation, and became the Republic of Mali in 1960. The government was overthrown by military coups in 1968 and 1991. Democratic multiparty elections have been held every five years since 1992.

## Recent Developments

In June 2011 a combined Malian-Mauritanian force attacked an al-Qaeda in the Islamic Maghrib (AQIM) camp in the Wagadou forest. In January 2012, however, an attack by Tuareg rebels in Mali claimed at least 82 lives, and analysts posited that AQIM was involved. After a military coup in March 2012, Mali's constitution was suspended and the government was replaced with the interim National Committee for the Recovery of Democracy and Restoration of the State. In June AQIM-affiliated militants began destroying Sufi shrines in UNESCO-recognized Timbuktu.

**Internet resource:** <www.primature.gov.ml>.

# Malta

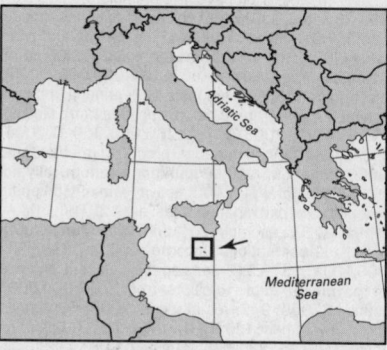

**Official name:** Repubblika ta' Malta (Maltese); Republic of Malta (English). **Form of government:** unitary multiparty republic with one legislative house (Kamra tad-Deputati, or House of Representatives [69; statutory number is 65]). **Head of state:** President George Abela (from 2009). **Head of government:** Prime Minister Lawrence Gonzi (from 2004). **Capital:** Valletta. **Official languages:** Maltese; English. **Official religion:** Roman Catholicism. **Monetary unit:** 1 euro (€) = 100 cents; valuation (2 Jul 2012) US$1 = €0.79 (the euro replaced the Maltese lira [Lm] 1 Jan 2008, at the rate of €1 = Lm 0.43).

## Demography

**Area:** 122 sq mi, 316 sq km. **Population** (2011): 419,000. **Density** (2011): persons per sq mi 3,434.4, persons per sq km 1,325.9. **Urban** (2009): 94.4%. **Sex distribution** (2008): male 49.77%; female 50.23%. **Age breakdown** (2008): under 15, 15.9%; 15–29, 21.6%; 30–44, 19.8%; 45–59, 21.5%; 60–74, 15.1%; 75–84, 4.8%; 85 and over, 1.3%. **Ethnic composition** (2005): Maltese 97.0%; other European 2.3%, of which British 1.2%; other 0.7%. **Religious affiliation** (2004): Roman Catholic 95%, of which practicing 63%; other Christian 0.5%; Muslim 0.7%; nonreligious/atheist 2%; other 1.8%. **Major localities** (2007): Birkirkara 22,241; Mosta 19,018; Qormi 16,625; Zabbar 14,849; Valletta 6,319 (urban agglomeration 81,204). **Location:** islands in the Mediterranean Sea, south of Sicily (Italy).

## Vital statistics

**Birth rate** per 1,000 population (2008): 10.0 (world avg. 20.3); within marriage 74.6%. **Death rate** per 1,000 population (2008): 7.9 (world avg. 8.5). **Total fertility rate** (avg. births per childbearing woman; 2008): 1.43. **Life expectancy** at birth (2008): male 76.7 years; female 82.3 years.

## National economy

**Budget** (2008). *Revenue:* €2,132,200,000 (income tax 34.5%; VAT 21.4%; social security contributions 16.0%; nontax revenue and grants 9.6%). *Expenditures:* €2,365,300,000 (recurrent expenditures 90.1%; capital expenditures 9.9%). **Public debt** (December 2008): US$5,052,000,000. **Production** (metric tons except where noted). *Agriculture and fishing*

(2007): potatoes 25,000, tomatoes 16,600, wheat 9,200; livestock (number of live animals) 73,683 pigs, 19,233 cattle, 1,100,000 chickens; fisheries production 3,783 (from aquaculture 67%). *Mining and quarrying* (2008): salt 6,000, limestone 1,200,000 cu m. *Manufacturing* (value added in US$'000,000; 2005): electronics 153; food products 109; printing and publishing 99. *Energy production (consumption):* electricity (kW-hr; 2006/07) 2,266,000,000 ([2006] 2,296,000,000); petroleum products (metric tons; 2006) none (815,000). **Population economically active** (2006): total 164,400; activity rate of total population 40.5% (participation rates: ages 15–64, 59.1%; female 32.1%; unemployed [April 2008–March 2009] 10.6%). **Gross national income** (2008): US$8,028,-000,000 (US$19,512 per capita). **Selected balance of payments data.** Receipts from (US$'000,000): tourism (2008) 947; remittances (2008) 50; foreign direct investment (2005–07 avg.) 1,170. Disbursements for (US$'000,000): tourism (2008) 435; remittances (2008) 60.

## Foreign trade

**Imports** (2007; c.i.f.): US$4,748,000,000 (machinery and apparatus 33.4%, of which electronic integrated circuits and micro-assemblies 20.0%; refined petroleum products 11.8%; food products 10.9%; chemical products 9.7%). *Major import sources:* Italy 24.9%; UK 14.4%; France 9.1%; Germany 8.4%; US 6.0%. **Exports** (2007; f.o.b.): US$3,067,000,000 (machinery and apparatus 57.4%, of which semiconductor devices 44.6%; medicinal and pharmaceutical products 6.8%; food products 4.8%; printed matter 4.2%; children's toys 3.1%; professional and scientific equipment 3.0%). *Major export destinations:* Germany 13.6%; Singapore 13.6%; France 12.0%; US 11.0%; UK 9.9%.

## Transport and communications

**Transport.** *Railroads:* none. *Roads* (2004): total length 2,254 km (paved 88%). *Vehicles* (2008): passenger cars 222,775; trucks and buses 48,210. *Air transport* (2008; Air Malta only): passenger-km 2,604,000,000; metric ton-km cargo 8,027,000. **Communications,** in total units (units per 1,000 persons). Telephone landlines (2008): 241,000 (586); cellular telephone subscribers (2008): 386,000 (937); personal computers (2005): 67,000 (166); total Internet users (2008): 200,000 (487); broadband Internet subscribers (2008): 99,000 (240).

## Education and health

**Educational attainment** (2005). Percentage of population ages 15 and over having: no formal schooling 2.4%; special education for disabled 0.3%; primary education 25.9%; secondary 45.3%; some postsecondary 16.5%; undergraduate or professional qualification 7.2%; graduate 2.4%. **Literacy** (2005): total population ages 10 and over literate 92.8%; males literate 91.7%; females literate 93.9%. **Health** (2008): physicians 1,374 (1 per 299 persons); hospital beds (2007) 1,967 (1 per 210 persons); infant mortality rate per 1,000 live births 9.9; undernourished population (2002–04) less than 2.5% of total population.

## Military

**Total active duty personnel** (November 2008): 1,954 (armed forces includes air and marine elements); Italian military (November 2008): 49 troops. **Military expenditure as percentage of GDP** (2007): 0.6%; per capita expenditure US$107.

## Background

Inhabited as early as 3800 BC, Malta was ruled by the Carthaginians from the 6th century BC until it came under Roman control in 218 BC. In AD 60 the apostle Paul converted the inhabitants to Christianity. It was under Byzantine rule until the Arabs seized control in 870. In 1091 the Normans defeated the Arabs, and Malta was ruled by feudal lords until it came under the Knights of Malta in 1530. Napoleon seized control in 1798; the British took it in 1800 and returned it to the Knights in 1802. The Maltese protested and acknowledged the British as sovereign, an arrangement ratified in 1814. It became self-governing in 1921 but reverted to a colonial regime in 1936. Malta was severely bombed by Germany and Italy during World War II, and in 1942 it received the George Cross, Britain's highest civilian decoration. In 1964 it gained independence within the Commonwealth and in 1974 became a republic. In 2004 it joined the EU, and it adopted the euro as its official currency in 2008.

## Recent Developments

When the Libyan conflict escalated into full civil war in 2011, Malta became a harbor of refuge and the base for a huge humanitarian mission. In a single week in February, nearly 12,000 people fled from Libya to Malta. Some Libyans wounded in fighting were treated in Malta, and water, food, and medical supplies were sent to Libya from Malta.

**Internet resource:** <www.nso.gov.mt>.

# Marshall Islands

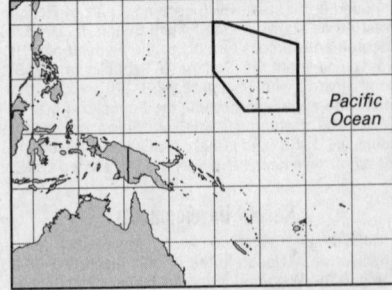

Pacific Ocean

**Official name:** Majol (Marshallese) (Republic of the Marshall Islands). **Form of government:** unitary republic with one legislative house (Nitijela [33]). **Head of state and government:** President Christopher Loeak (from 2012). **Capital:** Majuro. **Official language:** Marshallese (Kajin-Majol). **Official reli-**

---

*1 metric ton = about 1.1 short tons;    1 kilometer = 0.6 mi (statute);    1 metric ton-km cargo = about 0.68 short ton-mi cargo;    c.i.f.: cost, insurance, and freight;    f.o.b.: free on board*

gion: none. **Monetary unit:** 1 US dollar (US$) = 100 cents.

# Demography

**Area:** 70 sq mi, 181 sq km. **Population** (2011): 55,000. **Density** (2011): persons per sq mi 785.7, persons per sq km 303.9. **Urban** (2008): 68.0%. **Sex distribution** (2008): male 50.99%; female 49.01%. **Age breakdown** (2008): under 15, 38.5%; 15–29, 29.6%; 30–44, 16.8%; 45–59, 10.5%; 60–74, 3.6%; 75–84, 0.8%; 85 and over, 0.2%. **Ethnic composition** (2006): Marshallese 92.1%; other Pacific Islanders 1.0%; East Asians 0.5%; US white 0.3%; other 6.1%. **Religious affiliation** (1999): Protestant 85.0%, of which United Church of Christ 54.8%, Assemblies of God 25.8%; Roman Catholic 8.4%; Mormon 2.1%; nonreligious 1.5%; other 3.0%. **Major towns** (1999): Majuro (2004) 20,800; Ebeye 9,345; Laura 2,256. **Location:** Oceania, group of atolls and reefs in the North Pacific Ocean, halfway between Hawaii (US) and Papua New Guinea.

# Vital statistics

**Birth rate** per 1,000 population (2008): 31.5 (world avg. 20.3). **Death rate** per 1,000 population (2008): 4.6 (world avg. 8.5). **Total fertility rate** (avg. births per childbearing woman; 2008): 3.68. **Life expectancy** at birth (2008): male 68.9 years; female 73.0 years.

# National economy

**Budget** (2007). *Revenue:* US$98,900,000 (US government grants 63.6%; tax revenue 25.0%, of which income tax 11.0%, import duties 8.9%; nontax revenue 11.4%). *Expenditures:* US$99,900,000 (current expenditures 79.0%; capital expenditures 21.0%). **Public debt** (external, outstanding; 2008): US$87,000,000. **Production** (metric tons except as noted). *Agriculture and fishing* (2002–03): copra (2007) 5,491, breadfruit 4,536, coconuts 885, pandanus 114; livestock (number of live animals) 12,900 pigs, 86,000 chickens; fisheries production (2006) 42,019, of which skipjack 37,661 (from aquaculture, none). *Mining and quarrying:* for local construction only. *Manufacturing* (2007): copra 5,491; coconut oil and processed (chilled or frozen) fish are important products; the manufacture of handicrafts and personal items (clothing, mats, boats, etc.) by individuals is also significant. *Energy production (consumption):* electricity (kW-hr; 2006) 104,000,000 (104,000,000); petroleum products (metric tons; 2006) none (30,000). **Population economically active** (1999): total 14,677; activity rate of total population 28.9% (participation rates: ages 15–64, 52.1%; female 34.1%; unemployed [2007] 30.9%). **Gross national income** (2008): US$195,000,000 (US$3,270 per capita). **Selected balance of payments data.** Receipts from (US$'000,000): tourism (2007) 4.5; remittances (2005) 0.4; foreign direct investment (FDI; 2005–07 avg.) 272; official development assistance (2007) 52. Disbursements for (US$'000,000): tourism (2006) 0.4; FDI (2005–07 avg.) 24.

# Foreign trade

**Imports** (2006; c.i.f.): US$67,700,000 ([2000] mineral fuels and lubricants 43.6%; machinery and transportation equipment 16.9%; food products, beverages, and tobacco products 10.9%). *Major import sources:* US 45.8%; Australia 8.4%; Japan 8.1%; New Zealand 3.2%; Hong Kong 1.8%. **Exports** (2006–07; f.o.b.): US$20,300,000 ([2005] reexports of diesel fuel 80.9%; crude coconut oil 15.4%). *Major export destinations* (2005): mostly the US.

# Transport and communications

**Transport.** *Roads* (2007): 75 km (only Majuro and Kwajalein have paved roads). *Vehicles* (2004): passenger cars 1,694; trucks and buses 602. *Air transport* (2006; Air Marshall Islands only): passenger-km 31,236,000; metric ton-km cargo 348,000. **Communications,** in total units (units per 1,000 persons). Telephone landlines (2008): 4,400 (73); cellular telephone subscribers (2008): 1,000 (17); personal computers (2005): 4,600 (88); total Internet users (2008): 2,200 (36).

# Education and health

**Educational attainment** (2006). Percentage of population ages 25 and over having: no formal schooling 2.1%; elementary education 28.0%; secondary 55.8%; some higher 7.9%; undergraduate degree 5.1%; advanced degree 1.1%. **Literacy** (2000): total population ages 15 and over literate 92.0%; males literate 92.0%; females literate 92.0%. **Health** (2008): physicians 38 (1 per 1,401 persons); hospital beds (2004) 140 (1 per 411 persons); infant mortality rate per 1,000 live births 26.4.

# Military

The US provides for the defense of the Republic of the Marshall Islands under the 1984 and 2003 compacts of free association; the US Army's premier ballistic missile test site is at Kwajalein.

# Background

The islands were sighted in 1529 by the Spanish navigator Álvaro Saavedra. Germany purchased them from Spain in 1899, and Japan seized them in 1914. During World War II the US took Kwajalein and Enewetak, and the Marshall Islands were made part of a UN trust territory under US jurisdiction in 1947. Bikini and Enewetak atolls served as testing grounds for US nuclear weapons from 1946 to 1958. The country became an internally self-governing republic in 1979. It signed a compact of free association with the US in 1982 and became fully self-governing in 1986. The compact was amended in 2004.

# Recent Developments

The economic woes of the Marshall Islands continued in 2011. For the fourth consecutive year, the Social Security Administration had to sell investments to meet retirees' benefit payments. It was believed that if the trend continued, the fund could be exhausted by 2020.

**Internet resource:** <www.rmiembassyus.org>.

# Mauritania

**Official name:** Al-Jumhuriyah al-Islamiyah al-Muritaniyah (Islamic Republic of Mauritania). **Form of government:** republic with two legislative houses (Senate

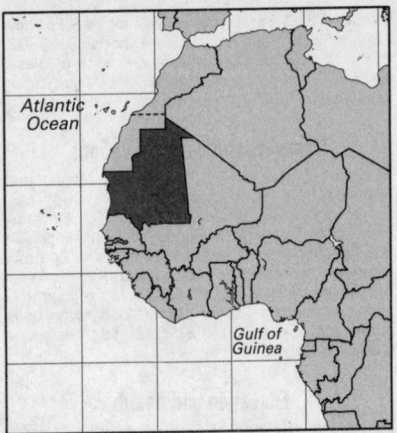

[56]; National Assembly [95]). **Head of state and government:** President Mohamed Ould Abdel Aziz (from 2009), assisted by Prime Minister Moulaye Ould Mohamed Laghdaf (from 2008). **Capital:** Nouakchott. **Official language:** Arabic (Arabic, Fulani, Soninke, and Wolof are national languages). **Official religion:** Islam. **Monetary unit:** 1 ouguiya (UM) = 5 khoums; valuation (2 Jul 2012) US$1 = UM 294.00.

## Demography

**Area:** 398,000 sq mi, 1,030,700 sq km. **Population** (2011): 3,282,000. **Density** (2011): persons per sq mi 8.2, persons per sq km 3.2. **Urban** (2011): 41.5%. **Sex distribution** (2006): male 49.50%; female 50.50%. **Age breakdown** (2006): under 15, 45.6%; 15–29, 27.2%; 30–44, 15.6%; 45–59, 8.0%; 60–74, 3.1%; 75 and over, 0.5%. **Ethnic composition** (2003): black African-Arab-Berber (Black Moor) 40%; Arab-Berber (White Moor) 30%; black African (mostly Wolof, Tukulor, Soninke, and Fulani) 30%. **Religious affiliation** (2000): Sunni Muslim 99.1%; traditional beliefs 0.5%; Christian 0.3%; other 0.1%. **Major cities** (2005): Nouakchott 743,500; Nouadhibou 94,700; Rosso (2000) 48,922; Boghe (2000) 37,531; Adel Bagrou (2000) 36,007. **Location:** northern Africa, bordering Western Sahara, Algeria, Mali, Senegal, and the North Atlantic Ocean.

## Vital statistics

**Birth rate** per 1,000 population (2008): 34.6 (world avg. 20.3). **Death rate** per 1,000 population (2008): 9.3 (world avg. 8.5). **Total fertility rate** (avg. births per childbearing woman; 2008): 4.52. **Life expectancy** at birth (2008): male 57.9 years; female 62.2 years.

## National economy

**Budget** (2005). *Revenue:* UM 131,300,000,000 (tax revenue 57.9%, of which VAT 20.3%, corporate taxes 17.0%; nontax revenue 34.3%, of which fishing royalties 26.9%; grants 7.8%). *Expenditures:* UM 166,100,000,000 (current expenditures 76.2%, of which goods and services 36.5%, wages and salaries 13.5%, defense 10.7%; capital expenditures 23.8%). **Public debt** (external, outstanding; January 2008): US$1,751,000,000. **Production** (metric tons except as noted). *Agriculture and fishing* (2007): rice 77,000, sorghum 58,000, dates 22,000, cowpeas 7,200; livestock (number of live animals) 8,850,000 sheep, 5,600,000 goats, 1,692,000 cattle, 1,600,000 camels; fisheries production 201,588, of which octopuses 11,525 (from aquaculture, none). *Mining and quarrying* (gross weight; 2006–07): iron ore 11,439,000; gypsum (2005) 39,000; copper 5,000. *Manufacturing* (value added in US$'000,000; 1997): food products, beverages, and tobacco products 5.2; machinery, transportation equipment, and fabricated metal products 3.8; bricks, tiles, and cement 1.6. *Energy production (consumption):* electricity (kW-hr; 2006–07) 404,-000,000 (290,000,000); coal (metric tons; 2004) none (7,000); crude petroleum (barrels; 2006–07) 9,600,000 ([2004] 8,830,-000); petroleum products (metric tons; 2006–07) none (431,000). **Selected balance of payments data.** Receipts from (US$'000,000): tourism (2005) 11; remittances (2008) 2; foreign direct investment (2005–07 avg.) 374; official development assistance (2007) 364. Disbursements for (US$'000,000): tourism (1999) 55. **Population economically active** (2006): total 1,238,000; activity rate of total population 39.2% (participation rates: ages 16 and over, 68.8%; female 40.4%; unemployed [2005] 32.5%). **Gross national income** (2007): US$2,636,000,000 (US$840 per capita).

## Foreign trade

**Imports** (2007): US$1,198,800,000 (imports for extractive industries 28.3%; refined petroleum products 23.1%). *Major import sources* (2006): France 11.9%; China 8.2%; US 6.8%; Belgium 6.7%; Italy 5.9%. **Exports** (2007): US$1,342,500,000 (iron ore 39.7%; crude petroleum 23.1%; fish products 15.3%). *Major export destinations* (2006): China 26.3%; Italy 11.8%; France 10.2%; Belgium 6.8%; Spain 6.7%.

## Transport and communications

**Transport.** *Railroads* (2005): route length 697 km; metric ton-km cargo (2000) 7,766,000,000. *Roads* (2006): total length 11,066 km (paved 27%). *Vehicles* (2001): passenger cars 12,200; trucks and buses 18,200. **Communications,** in total units (units per 1,000 persons). Telephone landlines (2008): 76,000 (24); cellular telephone subscribers (2008): 2,092,000 (651); personal computers (2005): 42,000 (14); total Internet users (2006): 100,000 (33); broadband Internet subscribers (2008): 5,900 (1.8).

## Education and health

**Educational attainment** (2000). Percentage of population ages 6 and over having: no formal schooling 43.9%; no formal schooling but literate 2.5%; Islamic schooling 18.4%; primary education 23.2%; lower secondary 5.3%; upper secondary 4.6%; higher technical 0.4%; higher 1.7%. **Literacy** (2007): percentage of total population ages 15 and over literate 43.6%; males literate 53.2%; females

---

*1 metric ton = about 1.1 short tons; 1 kilometer = 0.6 mi (statute); 1 metric ton-km cargo = about 0.68 short ton-mi cargo; c.i.f.: cost, insurance, and freight; f.o.b.: free on board*

literate 34.3%. **Health** (2006): physicians (2005) 477 (1 per 6,212 persons); hospital beds 1,826 (1 per 1,667 persons); infant mortality rate per 1,000 live births (2008) 64.9; undernourished population (2003–05) 200,000 (8% of total population based on the consumption of a minimum daily requirement of 1,790 calories).

## Military

Total active duty personnel (November 2008): 15,870 (army 94.5%, navy 3.9%, air force 1.6%). **Military expenditure as percentage of GDP** (2007): 0.5%; per capita expenditure US$6.

## Background

Inhabited in ancient times by Sanhadja Berbers, in the 11th and 12th centuries Mauritania was the center of the Berber Almoravid movement, which imposed Islam. Arab tribes arrived in the 15th century and formed powerful confederations; the Portuguese also arrived then. France gained control of the coast in 1817 and in 1903 made the territory a protectorate. In 1904 it was added to French West Africa, and later it became a colony. In 1960 Mauritania achieved independence. Its first president was ousted in a 1978 military coup. After a series of military rulers, in 1991 a new constitution was adopted, and multiparty elections were held in 1992. The country faced continued economic hardship and political unrest, including coups, in the late 20th and early 21st centuries.

## Recent Developments

Protests against Mauritania's government, which began in Nouakchott in February 2011, escalated to a "day of rage" held on 25 April. Using tear gas, police prevented demonstrators, who stretched for an estimated half a kilometer through the streets, from entering the main square. Opposition deputies were forcibly kept from joining the march.

**Internet resource:** <http://mauritaniaembassy.us>.

# Mauritius

**Official name:** Republic of Mauritius. **Form of government:** republic with one legislative house (National Assembly [69]). **Head of state:** President Rajkeswur Purryag (from 2012). **Head of government:** Prime Minister Navin Ramgoolam (from 2005). **Capital:** Port Louis. **Official language:** English. **Official religion:** none. **Monetary unit:** 1 Mauritian rupee (Mau Re; plural Mau Rs) = 100 cents; valuation (2 Jul 2012) US$1 = Mau Rs 30.95.

## Demography

**Area:** 788 sq mi, 2,040 sq km. **Population** (2011): 1,288,000. **Density** (2011): persons per sq mi 1,634.5, persons per sq km 631.4. **Urban** (2011): 41.6%. **Sex distribution** (2009): male 49.35%; female 50.65%. **Age breakdown** (2008): under 15, 22.7%; 15–29, 24.6%; 30–44, 23.2%; 45–59, 19.2%; 60–74, 7.7%; 75–84, 2.1%; 85 and over, 0.5%. **Ethnic composition** (2000): Indo-Pakistani 67.0%; Creole (mixed Caucasian, Indo-Pakistani, and African) 27.4%; Chinese 3.0%; other 2.6%. **Religious**

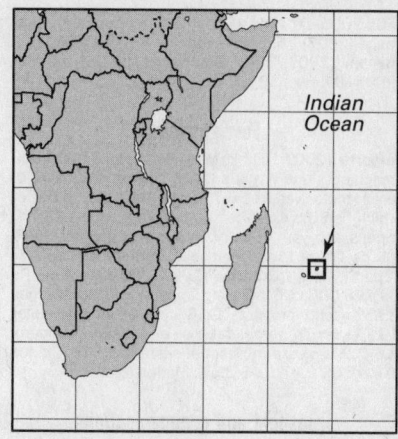

**affiliation** (2000): Hindu 49.6%; Christian 32.2%, of which Roman Catholic 23.6%; Muslim 16.6%; Buddhist 0.4%; other 1.2%. **Major municipalities** (2007): Port Louis 148,939; Beau Bassin–Rose Hill 109,701; Vacoas-Phoenix 106,865; Curepipe 83,754; Quatre Bornes 80,780. **Location:** island in the Indian Ocean, east of Madagascar.

## Vital statistics

**Birth rate** per 1,000 population (2008): 12.9 (world avg. 20.3). **Death rate** per 1,000 population (2008): 7.1 (world avg. 8.5). **Total fertility rate** (avg. births per childbearing woman; 2006): 1.73. **Life expectancy** at birth (2007): male 69.1 years; female 75.8 years.

## National economy

**Budget** (2007–08). *Revenue:* Mau Rs 57,593,500,000 (tax revenue 86.7%, of which taxes on goods and services 46.1%, taxes on trade 11.5%, corporate taxes 10.8%; nontax revenue and grants 13.3%). *Expenditures:* Mau Rs 55,781,200,000 (social security 22.6%; education 14.8%; interest on debt 14.3%; health 8.4%; police and defense 8.1%). **Public debt** (external, outstanding; 2007): US$572,000,000. **Gross national income** (2008): US$8,122,000,000 (US$6,400 per capita). **Production** (metric tons except as noted). *Agriculture and fishing* (2007): sugarcane 4,400,000, tomatoes 13,000, potatoes 13,000; livestock (number of live animals) 28,500 cattle, 10,000,000 chickens; fisheries production 8,476 (from aquaculture 7%). *Mining* (2007): basalt, n.a.; marine salt 6,650. *Manufacturing* (value added in Mau Rs '000,000; 2005): wearing apparel 8,823; food products 6,220; beverages and tobacco products 3,053. *Energy production (consumption):* electricity (kW-hr; 2008) 2,512,000,000 ([2006] 2,350,000,000); coal (metric tons; 2006) none (484,000); petroleum products (metric tons; 2006) none (835,000). **Population economically active** (2004): total 549,600; activity rate of total population 44.5% (participation rates: ages 15 and over, 59.2%; female 35.0%; unemployed [2008] 7.2%). **Selected balance of payments data.** Receipts from (US$'000,000): tourism (2007) 1,304; remittances (2008) 215; foreign direct investment

(FDI; 2005–07 avg.) 162; official development assistance (2007) 75. Disbursements for (US$'000,000): tourism (2007) 361; remittances (2008) 14; FDI (2005–07 avg.) 39.

## Foreign trade

**Imports** (2007; c.i.f.): Mau Rs 121,037,000,000 (machinery and transportation equipment 23.5%, of which motor vehicles 6.7%; food products 16.6%, of which fish 5.8%; refined petroleum products 15.7%; fabrics and yarn 7.4%). *Major import sources:* India 21.2%; China 11.4%; France 10.6; South Africa 7.4%; Japan 3.6%. **Exports** (2007; f.o.b.): Mau Rs 69,708,000,000 (wearing apparel and accessories 35.5%; food products 24.8%, of which raw sugar 13.7%; textile yarns, fabrics, and wearing apparel 2.6%). *Major export destinations:* UK 32.4%; France 10.1%; US 6.4%; UAE 3.5%; Madagascar 2.6%.

## Transport and communications

**Transport.** *Railroads:* none. *Roads* (2005): total length 2,020 km (paved 98%). *Vehicles* (2008): passenger cars 109,500; trucks and buses 61,500. *Air transport* (2005; Air Mauritius only): passenger-km 6,274,000,000; metric ton-km cargo 211,716,000. **Communications,** in total units (units per 1,000 persons). Telephone landlines (2008): 365,000 (285); cellular telephone subscribers (2008): 1,033,000 (807); personal computers (2005): 210,000 (169); total Internet users (2008): 380,000 (297); broadband Internet subscribers (2008): 73,000 (57).

## Education and health

**Educational attainment** (2000). Percentage of population ages 25 and over having: no formal education/unknown 12.8%; primary 44.1%; lower secondary 23.2%; upper secondary/some higher 17.3%; complete higher 2.6%. **Literacy** (2000): percentage of total population ages 12 and over literate 85.1%; males literate 88.7%; females literate 81.6%. **Health** (2008): physicians 1,450 (1 per 875 persons); hospital beds (2007) 3,756 (1 per 336 persons); infant mortality rate per 1,000 live births 14.4; undernourished population (2002–04) 60,000 (5% of total population based on the consumption of a minimum daily requirement of 1,910 calories).

## Military

**Total active duty personnel** (November 2008): none; a 2,000-person paramilitary force includes a 500-person coast guard unit. **Paramilitary expenditure as percentage of GDP** (2008): 0.3%; per capita expenditure US$26.

## Background

The island was visited by the Portuguese in the early 16th century. The Dutch took possession in 1598 and made attempts to settle it (1638–58 and 1664–1710) before abandoning it to pirates. The French East India Company occupied Mauritius in 1721 and administered it until the French government took over in 1767. Sugar production allowed the colony to prosper. The British captured the island

in 1810 and were granted formal control in 1814. In the late 19th century, competition from beet sugar and the opening of the Suez Canal caused an economic decline. After World War II, Mauritius adopted political and economic reforms, and in 1968 it became an independent state within the Commonwealth. In 1992 it became a republic. It has successfully diversified its economy, notably into clothing manufacturing, information technology, and business and financial services.

## Recent Developments

One of Mauritius's core industries, tourism, was tainted after the brutal murder of an Irish tourist in January 2011. Michaela McAreavey was killed by two staff members of the hotel where she was vacationing. Mauritius's US$10 billion economy depended heavily upon tourism. After the implementation of two fiscal-stimulus packages in response to the global economic downturn, however, the Mauritian economy grew almost 4% in 2011.

**Internet resource:** <www.gov.mu/portal/site/cso>.

# Mexico

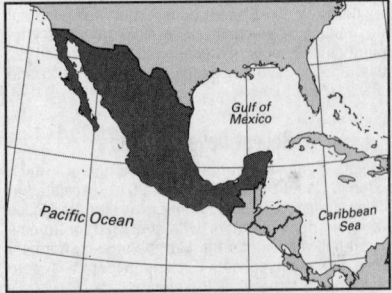

**Official name:** Estados Unidos Mexicanos (United Mexican States). **Form of government:** federal republic with two legislative houses (Senate [128]; Chamber of Deputies [500]). **Head of state and government:** President Felipe Calderón Hinojosa (from 2006). **Capital:** Mexico City. **Official language:** Spanish. **Official religion:** none. **Monetary unit:** 1 Mexican peso (Mex$) = 100 centavos; valuation (2 Jul 2012) US$1 = Mex$13.42.

## Demography

**Area:** 758,450 sq mi, 1,964,375 sq km. **Population** (2011): 114,492,000. **Density** (2011): persons per sq mi 151.0, persons per sq km 58.3. **Urban** (2010): 77.8%. **Sex distribution** (2008): male 49.20%; female 50.80%. **Age breakdown** (2008): under 15, 29.6%; 15–29, 27.0%; 30–44, 21.6%; 45–59, 13.1%; 60–74, 6.4%; 75–89, 2.1%; 90 and over, 0.2%. **Ethnic composition** (2000): mestizo 64.3%; Amerindian 18.0%, of which detribalized 10.5%; Mexican white 15.0%; Arab 1.0%; Mexican black 0.5%; Spaniard 0.3%; US white 0.2%; other 0.7%. **Religious affiliation** (2000): Christian 96.3%, of which Roman

---

*1 metric ton = about 1.1 short tons;  1 kilometer = 0.6 mi (statute);  1 metric ton-km cargo = about 0.68 short ton-mi cargo;  c.i.f.: cost, insurance, and freight;  f.o.b.: free on board*

Catholic 87.0%, Protestant 3.2%, independent Christian 2.7%, unaffiliated Christian 1.4%, other Christian (mostly Mormon and Jehovah's Witness) 2.0%; Muslim 0.3%; nonreligious 3.1%; other 0.3%. **Major cities (urban agglomerations)** (2005 [2007]): Mexico City 8,463,906 (19,028,000); Guadalajara 1,600,894 (4,198,000); Monterrey 1,133,070 (3,712,000); Puebla 1,399,519 (2,195,000); Ecatepec 1,687,549; Toluca 467,712 (1,584,000); Tijuana 1,286,187 (1,553,000); León 1,137,465 (1,488,000); Juárez 1,301,452 (1,343,000); Torreon 548,723 (1,201,000); Ciudad Netzahualcóyotl 1,136,300; San Luis Potosí 685,934 (1,050,000); Querétaro 596,450 (1,032,000); Zapopan 1,026,492; Mérida 734,153 (1,017,000); Mexicali 653,046 (935,000); Aguascalientes 663,671 (927,000); Chihuahua 748,518 (841,000); Culiacán 605,304 (837,000); Saltillo 633,667 (802,000); Naucalpan 792,226; Guadelupe 691,434; Tlalnepantla 674,417; Hermosillo 641,791; Acapulco 616,394. **Location:** southern North America, bordering the US, the Gulf of Mexico, the Caribbean Sea, Belize, Guatemala, and the North Pacific Ocean. **Migration.** Legal Mexican immigrants entering the US in 2004: 173,664; total number of illegal Mexican immigrants in US (2006) 6,600,000.

## Vital statistics

**Birth rate** per 1,000 population (2008): 19.1 (world avg. 20.3); (2003) within marriage 62%. **Death rate** per 1,000 population (2008): 4.8 (world avg. 8.5). **Total fertility rate** (avg. births per childbearing woman; 2008): 2.10. **Life expectancy** at birth (2008): male 74.0 years; female 78.8 years.

## Social indicators

**Educational attainment** (2005). Percentage of population ages 15 and over having: no formal schooling/unknown 10.9%; incomplete primary education 14.3%; complete primary 17.6%; secondary 25.2%; vocational/professional 31.3%; advanced university (master's or doctorate degree) 0.7%. **Access to services** (2005). Proportion of dwellings having: electricity 96.6%; piped water supply 87.8%; piped sewage 84.8%. **Material well-being.** Percentage of households possessing (2005): television 91.0%; refrigerator 79.0%; washing machine 62.7%; computer 19.6%. **Quality of working life** (2008). Average workweek 44.5 hours. Annual rate per 100,000 insured workers for: injury 3,569; death 10. Labor stoppages: 21, involving 13,242 workers. **Social participation.** Trade union membership in total workforce (2000): formal sector only, less than 20%; both formal and informal sectors, 17%. Practicing religious population (1995–97): percentage of adult population attending church services at least once per week 46%. **Social deviance** (2007). Formally registered offense rate per 100,000 population for: murder 6.2; property damage 14.5; rape 4.3; battery 30.2; robbery 69.3; illegal narcotics possession 16.0; fraud 4.4; squatting 3.3; breaking and entering 2.5. Incidence per 100,000 in general population of: alcoholism (2000) 7.6; suicide 4.2.

## National economy

**Gross national income** (2008): US$1,061,444,000,000 (US$9,980 per capita). **Budget** (2008). *Revenue:* Mex$2,857,100,000,000 (nontax revenue 36.9%; tax revenue 34.8%, of which income tax 21.3%; other revenue, from PEMEX state oil company 12.6%, other state-owned organizations or companies 15.7%). *Expenditures:* Mex$2,865,300,000,000 (current expenditures 58.3%; extrabudgetary expenditures 23.2%; capital expenditures 18.5%). **Public debt** (external, outstanding; 2007): US$105,379,000,000. **Production** (metric tons except as noted). *Agriculture and fishing* (2008): sugarcane 51,106,900, corn (maize) 24,320,100, sorghum 6,610,900, oranges 4,306,633, wheat 4,019,400, tomatoes 2,936,773, lemons and limes 2,224,382, bananas 2,159,280, chilies and green peppers 2,054,968, mangoes and guavas 1,855,359, potatoes 1,670,480, dry onions 1,252,441, coconuts 1,246,400, avocados 1,124,565, dry beans 1,122,720, blue agave (2006) 778,000, papayas 638,237, pineapples 685,805, apples 524,755, grapefruit and pomelos 394,865, seed cotton 365,227, grapes 307,478, oil palm fruit 292,499, coffee (green) 265,817; livestock (number of live animals) 32,565,200 cattle, 15,527,600 pigs, 8,831,000 goats, 7,825,000 sheep, 6,350,000 horses, 504,300,000 chickens; fisheries production (2007) 1,496,002 (from aquaculture 10%); aquatic plants production 4,500 (from aquaculture, none). *Mining and quarrying* (2008): fluorspar 980,000 [world rank: 2]; bismuth (metal content) 1,200 [world rank: 2]; silver (metal content) 3,000,000 kg [world rank: 2]; strontium 96,900 [world rank: 3]; lead (metal content) 145,000 [world rank: 5]; zinc (metal content) 460,000 [world rank: 6]; cadmium (metal content) 1,620 [world rank: 6]; gypsum 5,800,000 [world rank: 7]; iron ore (metal content) 12,000,000; sulfur 1,800,000; copper (metal content) 270,000; gold (metal content) 41,000 kg. *Manufacturing* (value added in Mex$'000,000; 2007): food products and beverages 994,797; transportation equipment 146,839, of which motor vehicles 84,137, motor vehicle parts 58,470; mineral fuels 130,233, of which refined petroleum products 121,740; chemical products 125,629, of which pharmaceutical products 58,561; base metals 74,005; bricks, cement, and ceramics 66,932; electrical machinery and equipment 28,962; paper products 28,773; fabricated metal products 26,355; rubber and plastic products 25,690; textiles and wearing apparel 23,195; nonelectrical machinery and apparatus 21,529; electronics 6,442; printing and publishing 6,085; wood products 5,780. *Energy production (consumption):* electricity (kW-hr; 2008) 129,948,000,000 ([2006] 248,872,000,000); coal (metric tons; 2008–09) 10,679,000 ([2006] 1,920,000); lignite (metric tons; 2006) 9,573,000 (14,936,000); crude petroleum (barrels; 2008–09) 913,369,200 ([2006] 495,699,000); petroleum products (metric tons; 2006) 64,836,000 (74,439,000); natural gas (cu m; 2008–09) 74,360,122,000 ([2006] 51,054,509,000). **Population economically active** (2008): total 45,460,000; activity rate of total population 42.6% (participation rates: ages 15–64, 63.6%; female 37.7%; unemployed [April 2008–March 2009] 4.3%). **Selected balance of payments data.** Receipts from (US$'000,000): tourism (2008) 13,289, of which border shoppers only 2,695; remittances (2008) 26,304; foreign direct investment (FDI; 2005–07 avg.) 21,641; official development assistance (2007) 121. Disbursements for (US$'000,000): tourism (2008) 8,526, of which border shoppers only 4,001; FDI (2005–06 avg.) 6,829.

## Foreign trade

**Imports** (2006): US$256,130,000,000 (non-maquiladora sector 65.8%, of which imports for automotive industry 10.9%, special machinery for industries 9.8%, imports for extractive industries 8.2%, electrical and electronic equipment 6.3%, imports for chemical industry 5.6%; maquiladora sector 34.2%, of which electrical and electronic equipment 15.5%). *Major import sources:* US 50.9%; China 9.5%; Japan 6.0%; South Korea 4.2%; Germany 3.7%; Canada 2.9%; Brazil 2.2%; Taiwan 1.9%; Malaysia 1.7%; Italy 1.6%. **Exports** (2006): US$249,997,000,000 (non-maquiladora sector 55.3%, of which motor vehicles and parts 15.1%, crude petroleum 13.9%, special machinery for industries 3.1%, electrical and electronic equipment 2.5%, food products, beverages, and tobacco products 2.4%; maquiladora sector 44.7%, of which electrical and electronic equipment 20.1%, exports of automotive industry 6.1%, professional and scientific equipment 2.6%). *Major export destinations:* US 84.7%; Canada 2.1%; Spain 1.3%; Germany 1.2%; Colombia 0.9%; Venezuela 0.7%; China 0.7%.

## Transport and communications

**Transport.** *Railroads* (2008): route length 26,722 km; passenger-km 147,000,000; metric ton-km cargo 78,872,000,000. *Roads* (2008): total length 360,352 km (paved 35%). *Vehicles* (2007): passenger cars 17,533,245; trucks and buses 8,152,942. *Air transport* (2008): passenger-km 28,514,000,000; metric ton-km cargo 223,958,000. **Communications,** in total units (units per 1,000 persons). Telephone landlines (2008): 20,668,000 (190); cellular telephone subscribers (2008): 75,304,000 (694); personal computers (2006): 14,578,000 (139); total Internet users (2008): 23,260,000 (214); broadband Internet subscribers (2008): 7,597,000 (70).

## Education and health

**Literacy** (2007): total population ages 15 and over literate 92.8%; males literate 94.4%; females literate 91.4%. **Health** (2008): physicians (public health institutions only; 2007) 171,193 (1 per 618 persons); hospital beds (public health institutions only) 84,813 (1 per 1,258 persons); infant mortality rate per 1,000 live births 15.2; undernourished population (2002–04) 5,300,000 (5% of total population based on the consumption of a minimum daily requirement of 1,900 calories).

## Military

**Total active duty personnel** (November 2008): 255,506 (army 73.6%, navy 21.9%, air force 4.5%). **Military expenditure as percentage of GDP** (2007): 0.4%; per capita expenditure US$38.

## Background

Inhabited for more than 20,000 years, Mexico produced great civilizations in AD 100–900, including the Olmec, Toltec, Mayan, and Aztec. The Aztec were conquered in 1521 by Spanish explorer Hernán Cortés, who established Mexico City on the site of the Aztec capital, Tenochtitlán. Francisco de Montejo conquered the remnants of Mayan civilization in the mid-16th century, and Mexico became part of the Viceroyalty of New Spain. In 1821 rebels negotiated a status quo independence from Spain, and in 1823 a new congress declared Mexico a republic. In 1845 the US voted to annex Texas, initiating the Mexican-American War. Under the Treaty of Guadalupe Hidalgo in 1848, Mexico ceded a vast territory in what is now the western and southwestern US. The Mexican government endured several rebellions and civil wars in the late 19th and early 20th centuries. During World War II it declared war on the Axis powers (1942), and in the postwar era it was a founding member of the UN (1945) and the Organization of American States (1948). In 1993 it ratified the North American Free Trade Agreement. The election of Vicente Fox to the presidency in 2000 ended 71 years of rule by the Institutional Revolutionary Party.

## Recent Developments

The extreme violence produced by the country's long-running drug war remained the most prominent issue in Mexico in 2011. The government reported that 47,515 people had died in drug-related violence since the administration of Pres. Felipe Calderón began its assault on drug-trafficking cartels in December 2006. Although the government continued to score notable successes in the capture or killing of cartel leaders, the press reported drug-violence atrocities on a regular basis, and in public-opinion polls, a substantial majority of respondents expressed concerns about worsening public security. In July the Supreme Court ruled that human rights violations committed against civilians by military forces must henceforth come under the jurisdiction of civilian (rather than military) tribunals. The United States continued to provide Mexico with intelligence assistance, equipment, and police training under the terms of the US$1.5 billion multiyear Mérida Initiative. Despite domestic political sensitivities, the Mexican government permitted US Drug Enforcement Agency officers, CIA operatives, and retired US military personnel to operate (albeit without firearms) from a military base in northern Mexico. President Calderón lobbied strenuously for the US government to take tougher measures to block the smuggling of guns into Mexico and reduce US consumption of illegal drugs. After years of political controversy and Mexico's decision in 2009 to impose retaliatory tariffs on imports of US goods and agricultural products valued at up to US$2.5 billion, the US government finally agreed in July to permit Mexican long-distance truckers to operate freely in the United States. The agreement settled the longest-running dispute resulting from the 1994 North American Free Trade Agreement and removed a significant irritant from bilateral relations. In October the first Mexican truck bound for the US interior crossed the border.

**Internet resource:** <www.visitmexico.com>.

---

*1 metric ton = about 1.1 short tons;    1 kilometer = 0.6 mi (statute);    1 metric ton-km cargo = about 0.68 short ton-mi cargo;    c.i.f.: cost, insurance, and freight;    f.o.b.: free on board*

# Micronesia, Federated States of

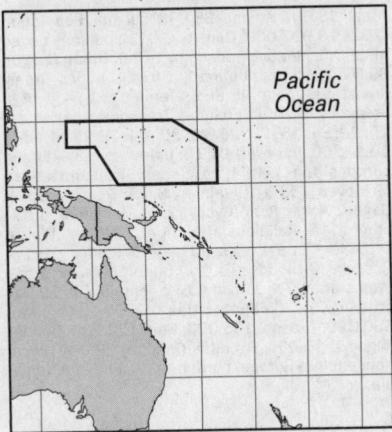

Pacific
Ocean

**Official name:** Federated States of Micronesia. **Form of government:** federal nonparty republic in free association with the US with one legislative house (Congress [14]). **Head of state and government:** President Emanuel Mori (from 2007). **Capital:** Palikir. **Official language:** none (English is the language of the Congress). **Official religion:** none. **Monetary unit:** 1 US dollar (US$) = 100 cents.

## Demography

**Area:** 270.6 sq mi, 700.9 sq km. **Population** (2011): 102,000. **Density** (2011): persons per sq mi 376.9, persons per sq km 145.5. **Urban** (2009): 22.5%. **Sex distribution** (2008): male 50.32%; female 49.68%. **Age breakdown** (2008): under 15, 36.9%; 15–29, 26.9%; 30–44, 17.0%; 45–59, 13.1%; 60–74, 4.7%; 75 and over, 1.4%. **Ethnic composition** (2000): Chuukese/Mortlockese 33.6%; Pohnpeian 24.9%; Yapese 10.6%; Kosraean 5.2%; US white 4.5%; Asian 1.3%; other 19.9%. **Religious affiliation** (2005): Roman Catholic 50%; Protestant 47%; other 3%. **Major towns** (2000): Weno 13,802; Palikir 6,444; Nett 6,158. **Location:** Oceania, island group in the North Pacific Ocean, northeast of New Guinea.

## Vital statistics

**Birth rate** per 1,000 population (2007): 25.5 (world avg. 20.3); (2006) within marriage 83.2%. **Death rate** per 1,000 population (2007): 5.5 (world avg. 8.5). **Total fertility rate** (avg. births per childbearing woman; 2006): 2.68. **Life expectancy** at birth (2007): male 67.4 years; female 68.0 years.

## National economy

**Budget** (2006–07; for consolidated general government). *Revenue:* US$145,200,000 (external grants 63.7%; tax revenue 19.1%; nontax revenue 17.2%, of which fishing access revenue 10.3%). *Expenditures:* US$153,000,000 (current expenditures 91.4%; capital expenditures 8.6%). **Public debt** (external, outstanding; September 2007): US$67,200,000. **Population economically active** (2000): total 37,414;

activity rate of total population 35.0% (participation rates: ages 15–64, 60.7%; female 42.9%; unemployed 22.0%). **Production** (metric tons except as noted). *Agriculture and fishing* (2007): coconuts 41,000, cassava 12,000, sweet potatoes 3,200, betel nuts (2005) 228, kava (*sakau*) n.a.; livestock (number of live animals) 33,000 pigs, 14,000 cattle; fisheries production 16,990, of which significantly skipjack tuna (from aquaculture, negligible); foreign fishing in the Exclusive Economic Zone (200-mile limit; 2007) 111,512 metric tons, of which Taiwanese 53,767 metric tons, Japanese 32,431 metric tons. *Mining and quarrying:* quarrying of sand and aggregate for local construction only. *Manufacturing:* copra and coconut oil are traditionally important products; the manufacture of handicrafts and personal items (garments, mats, boats, etc.) is also important. *Energy production (consumption):* electricity (kW-hr; 2007) 67,300,000 (n.a.). **Gross national income** (2008): US$260,000,000 (US$2,340 per capita). **Selected balance of payments data.** Receipts from (US$'000,000): tourism (2006) 18; remittances (2005) 6.0; foreign direct investment (2005–06 avg.) 0.5; official development assistance (2007) 115. Disbursements for (US$'000,000): tourism (2006) 5.7.

## Foreign trade

**Imports** (2007; c.i.f.): US$142,659,000 (food products and beverages 29.8%; mineral fuels 22.1%; machinery and apparatus 14.4%; transportation equipment 6.0%; chemical products 5.4%). *Major import sources:* US 41.2%; Singapore 8.7%; Japan 8.5%; Hong Kong 6.3%; Australia 4.1%. **Exports** (2007; f.o.b.): US$16,190,000 (tuna 69.9%; betel nuts 13.7%; reef fish 5.2%; cooked food 4.9%; kava 2.6%). *Major export destinations:* Guam 22.5%; US 17.2%; Northern Marianas 4.3%; Japan 4.1%; unspecified 51.2%.

## Transport and communications

**Transport.** *Railroads:* none. *Roads* (2000): total length 240 km (paved 18%). *Vehicles* (2007): passenger cars 3,916; trucks and buses 3,849. *Air transport* (2006; Continental Micronesia only): passenger-km 4,762,000,000; metric ton-km cargo 102,000,000. **Communications,** in total units (units per 1,000 persons). Telephone landlines (2008): 8,700 (79); cellular telephone subscribers (2008): 34,000 (308); personal computers (2005): 6,000 (55); total Internet users (2008): 16,000 (145).

## Education and health

**Educational attainment** (2000). Percentage of population ages 25 and over having: no formal schooling/unknown 13.4%; primary education 37.0%; some secondary 18.3%; secondary 12.9%; some college 18.4%. **Literacy** (2000): total population ages 10 and over literate 72,140 (92.4%); males literate 36,528 (92.9%); females literate 35,612 (91.9%). **Health:** physicians (2005) 62 (1 per 1,774 persons); hospital beds (2006) 365 (1 per 301 persons); infant mortality rate per 1,000 live births (2007) 37.5.

## Military

External security is provided by the US.

## Background

The islands of Micronesia were probably settled by people from eastern Melanesia some 3,500 years ago. Europeans first landed on the islands in the 16th century. Spain took control of the islands in 1886 and then sold them to Germany in 1899. The islands came under Japanese rule after World War I. They were captured by US forces during World War II, and in 1947 they became a UN trust territory administered by the US. The group of islands centered on the Caroline Islands became an internally self-governing federation in 1979. In 1986 the Federated States of Micronesia (FSM) entered into a Compact of Free Association with the US, which was amended in 2003. In the early 21st century, Micronesia found itself threatened by rising water levels.

## Recent Developments

In a move to increase government revenue in 2011, the government of the FSM sold short-term fishing rights in its waters to Papua New Guinea for US$1 million. The agreement was enabled by the FSM's membership in the Parties to the Nauru Agreement (PNA), a consortium of countries whose goals included the extraction of more revenue from member states' tuna fisheries by strictly limiting the access given to deepwater fishing countries.

Internet resource: <www.sboc.fm>.

# Moldova

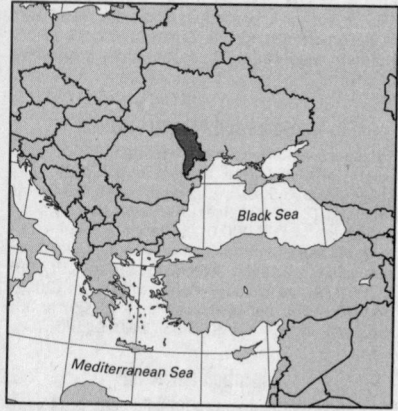

Black Sea

Mediterranean Sea

**Official name:** Republica Moldova (Republic of Moldova). **Form of government:** unitary parliamentary republic with a single legislative house (Parliament [101]). **Head of state:** President Nicolae Timofti (from 2012). **Head of government:** Prime Minister Vlad Filat (from 2009). **Capital:** Chisinau. **Official language:** Moldovan. **Official religion:** none. **Monetary unit:** 1 Moldovan leu (plural lei) = 100 bani; valuation (2 Jul 2012) free rate, US$1 = 12.22 Moldovan lei.

## Demography

**Area:** 13,067 sq mi, 33,843 sq km. **Population** (2011): 3,927,000. **Density** (2011): persons per sq mi 300.5, persons per sq km 116.0. **Urban** (2010): 39.8%. **Sex distribution** (2007; excludes Transdniestria): male 48.06%; female 51.94%. **Age breakdown** (2004; excludes Transdniestria): under 15, 19.1%; 15–29, 26.3%; 30–44, 20.9%; 45–59, 19.1%; 60 and over, 14.3%; unknown 0.3%. **Ethnic composition** (2004; excludes Transdniestria): Moldovan 75.8%; Ukrainian 8.4%; Russian 5.9%; Gagauz 4.4%; Rom (Gypsy) 2.2%; Bulgarian 1.9%; other 1.4%. **Religious affiliation** (2005): Moldovan Orthodox 31.8%; Bessarabian Orthodox 16.1%; Russian Orthodox 15.4%; Sunni Muslim 5.5%; Protestant 1.7%; Jewish 0.6%; nonreligious 19.9%; other 9.0%. **Major cities** (2007): Chisinau 630,300; Tiraspol 155,000; Balti 122,200; Bender (Tighina) 95,000; Rybnitsa (Ribnita) 52,000. **Location:** eastern Europe, bordering Ukraine and Romania.

## Vital statistics

**Birth rate** per 1,000 population (2008): 10.9 (world avg. 20.3); within marriage 77.7%. **Death rate** per 1,000 population (2008): 11.7 (world avg. 8.5). **Total fertility rate** (avg. births per childbearing woman; 2008): 1.28. **Life expectancy** at birth (2008): male 65.6 years; female 73.2 years.

## National economy

**Budget** (2007). *Revenue:* 14,004,000,000 Moldovan lei (tax revenue 75.0%, of which VAT 53.9%; nontax revenue 18.5%; grants 6.5%). *Expenditures:* 14,211,000,000 Moldovan lei (health care 12.9%; education 10.3%; public order 7.5%; social fund transfers 6.2%; transportation and communications 6.0%; interest payments 4.3%; defense 1.9%). **Public debt** (external, outstanding; 2007): US$779,000,000. **Production** (metric tons except as noted). *Agriculture and fishing* (2008): corn (maize) 1,478,560, wheat 1,286,330, sugar beets 960,712, grapes 635,513, sunflower seeds 371,935, walnuts 13,742; livestock (number of live animals) 753,903 sheep, 298,675 pigs, 231,716 cattle; fisheries production (2007) 5,860 (from aquaculture 80%). *Mining and quarrying* (2006): gypsum 725,900. *Manufacturing* (value of production in '000,000 Moldovan lei; 2004; excludes Transdniestria): alcoholic beverages 4,013, of which wine 3,098; food products 3,461; nonmetallic mineral products 1,273. *Energy production (consumption):* electricity (kW-hr; 2006) 3,829,000,000 (7,341,000,000); coal (metric tons; 2006) none (194,000); crude petroleum (barrels; 2006) 29,000 (negligible); petroleum products (metric tons; 2006) none (607,000); natural gas (cu m; 2006) none (2,696,000,000). **Population economically active** (2005; excludes Transdniestria): total 1,422,300; activity rate of total de facto population 39.5% (participation rates: ages 15–64, 53.2%; female 51.5%; unemployed [2008] 4.0%). **Gross national income** (2008; excludes Transdniestria): US$5,338,000,000 (US$1,470 per capita). **Selected balance of payments data.** Receipts from (US$'000,000): tourism

---

*1 metric ton = about 1.1 short tons;    1 kilometer = 0.6 mi (statute);    1 metric ton-km cargo = about 0.68 short ton-mi cargo;    c.i.f.: cost, insurance, and freight;    f.o.b.: free on board*

(2007) 164; remittances (2008) 1,897; foreign direct investment (2005–07 avg.) 299; official development assistance (2007) 269. Disbursements for (US$'000,000): tourism (2007) 213; remittances (2008) 115.

## Foreign trade

**Imports** (2006; c.i.f.): US$2,693,000,000 (machinery and apparatus 13.8%; refined petroleum products 12.6%, chemical products 11.9%, natural gas 8.1%; food products 7.4%). *Major import sources:* Ukraine 19.2%; Russia 15.5%; Romania 12.8%; Germany 7.9%; Italy 7.3%. **Exports** (2006; f.o.b.): US$1,051,000,000 (food products 19.8%, of which cereals 4.3%, walnuts 3.6%; wearing apparel and accessories 19.1%; wine and grape must 15.4%; machinery and apparatus 5.2%). *Major export destinations:* Russia 17.3%; Romania 14.8%; Ukraine 12.2%; Italy 11.1%; Belarus 7.0%.

## Transport and communications

**Transport.** *Railroads* (2007): length 1,154 km; passenger-km 468,000,000; metric ton-km cargo 3,120,000,000. *Roads* (2007): total length 9,337 km (paved 94%). *Vehicles* (2003): passenger cars 252,490; trucks and buses 77,534. *Air transport* (2007): passenger-km 550,000,000; metric ton-km cargo 1,300,000. **Communications,** in total units (units per 1,000 persons). Telephone landlines (2008): 1,115,000 (307); cellular telephone subscribers (2008): 2,420,000 (666); personal computers (2005): 348,000 (83); total Internet users (2008): 800,000 (220); broadband Internet subscribers (2008): 115,000 (32).

## Education and health

**Literacy** (2003): total population ages 15 and over literate 99.1%. **Health** (2008): physicians (excludes Transdniestria) 12,665 (1 per 287 persons); hospital beds (excludes Transdniestria) 21,798 (1 per 167 persons); infant mortality rate per 1,000 live births 12.1; undernourished population (2002–04) 450,000 (11% of total population based on the consumption of a minimum daily requirement of 1,970 calories).

## Military

**Total active duty personnel** (November 2008): 6,000 (army 85.8%, air force 14.2%); opposition forces (excluding Russian troops) in Transdniestria (2008): 7,500; Russian troops in Transdniestria (November 2008): 1,500. **Military expenditure as percentage of GDP** (2008): 0.4%; per capita expenditure US$7.

## Background

Moldova, once part of the principality of Moldavia, was founded by the Vlachs in the 14th century. In the mid-16th century, it was under Ottoman rule. In 1774 it came under Russian control and lost portions of its territory. In 1859 it joined with the principality of Walachia to form the state of Romania, and in 1918 some of the territory it had ceded earlier also joined Romania. Romania was compelled to cede some of the Moldavian area to Russia in 1940, and that area combined with what Russia already controlled to become the Moldavian SSR. In 1991 Moldavia declared independence from the Soviet Union. It adopted the Romanian spelling of Moldova after having legitimized the use of the Roman rather than the Cyrillic alphabet in 1989. It was admitted to the UN in 1992. In 2000 it abandoned its semipresidential form of government to become a parliamentary republic.

## Recent Developments

European Union efforts in 2011 to reinforce Moldova's Western orientation and to limit the gravitational pull of Russia included €78.6 million (about US$104 million) from the EU's bilateral assistance program and a relaxation of visa requirements. There were also a number of visits to Moldova in 2011 by top-level Western diplomats, including US Vice Pres. Joseph Biden and the president of the European Council, Herman Van Rompuy. Meanwhile, relations between the Moldovan Communists and the Russian government remained strained, reducing the likelihood of Moscow's actively contesting EU influence in Moldova.

**Internet resource:**
<www.statistica.md/index.php?l=en>.

# Monaco

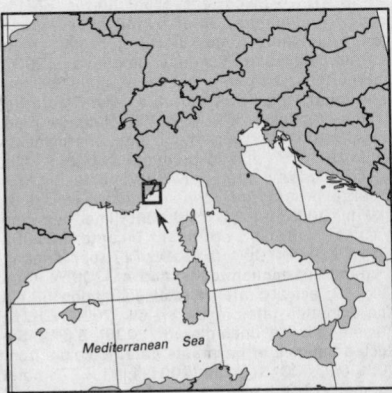

Mediterranean Sea

**Official name:** Principauté de Monaco (Principality of Monaco). **Form of government:** constitutional monarchy with one legislative house (National Council [24]). **Head of state:** Prince Albert II (from 2005). **Head of government:** Minister of State Michel Roger (from 2010), assisted by the Council of Government. **Capital:** no separate area is distinguished as such. **Official language:** French. **Official religion:** Roman Catholicism. **Monetary unit:** 1 euro (€) = 100 centimes; valuation (2 Jul 2012) US$1 = €0.79 (Monaco uses the euro as its official currency, even though it is not a member of the EU).

## Demography

**Area:** 0.78 sq mi, 2.02 sq km. **Population** (2011): 36,000. **Density** (2011): persons per sq mi 46,153.8, persons per sq km 17,821.8. **Urban** (2008): 100%.

**Sex distribution** (2008): male 47.94%; female 52.06%. **Age breakdown** (2008): under 15, 12.8%; 15–29, 12.7%; 30–44, 19.2%; 45–59, 21.8%; 60–74, 19.1%; 75–84, 7.9%; 85 and over, 4.2%; unknown 2.3%. **Ethnic composition** (2008): French 28.4%; Monegasque 21.6%; Italian 18.7%; British 7.5%; Belgian 2.8%; Swiss 2.5%; German 2.5%; US 1.0%; other 15.0% (including Asian countries 2.5%, African countries 2.2%). **Religious affiliation** (2000): Christian 93.2%, of which Roman Catholic 89.3%; Jewish 1.7%; nonreligious and other 5.1%. **Location:** western Europe, bordering the Mediterranean Sea and France.

## Vital statistics

**Birth rate** per 1,000 population (2007): 26.2 (world avg. 20.3); (2005) within marriage 61.4%. **Death rate** per 1,000 population (2007): 14.2 (world avg. 8.5). **Total fertility rate** (avg. births per childbearing woman; 2007): 1.75. **Life expectancy** at birth (2007): male 76.0 years; female 83.9 years.

## National economy

**Budget** (2007). *Revenue:* €845,600,700 (taxes on hotels, banks, and the industrial sector 47.4%; property taxes 12.9%; state-run monopolies 10.0%; customs duties 3.1%). *Expenditures:* €843,119,681 (current expenditures 65.1%; capital expenditures 34.9%). **Production.** *Agriculture and fishing:* limited horticulture and greenhouse cultivation; fisheries production (2007; metric tons) 1 (from aquaculture, none). *Mining and quarrying* (2009): none. *Manufacturing* (value of sales in €'000; 2007): chemical products, cosmetics, perfumery, and pharmaceuticals 364,077; plastic products 266,366; light electronics and precision instruments 86,113. *Energy production (consumption):* electricity (kW-hr; 2001) n.a. (475,000,000 [imported from France]). **Gross national income** (2008): US$6,919,000,000 (US$195,717 per capita). **Population economically active** (2005): total 40,289; activity rate of total population 58.4% (participation rates: ages 17–64 [2000] 61.1%; female 41.4%; unemployed [2000] 3.6%). **Selected balance of payments data.** Receipts from (US$'000,000): tourism (2007) n.a.; 2,773 hotel rooms, 327,985 overnight visitors.

## Foreign trade

**Imports** (2007; excludes trade with France; Monaco has participated in a customs union with France since 1963): €850,202,845 (nonelectrical machinery and apparatus 40.2%; pharmaceuticals, perfumes, wearing apparel, and publishing 19.2%; rubber and plastic products, glass products, construction materials, organic chemical products, and paper products 15.7%; food products 7.4%). *Major import sources:* China 34.9%; Italy 18.6%; Japan 8.5%; UK 7.1%; Belgium 5.3%. **Exports** (2007; excludes trade with France; Monaco has participated in a customs union with France since 1963): €834,108,693 (rubber and plastic products, glass products, construction materials, organic

chemical products, and paper products 39.9%; products of the automobile industry 12.7%; pharmaceuticals, perfumes, wearing apparel, and publishing 12.2%; nonelectrical machinery and apparatus 12.1%). *Major export destinations:* Germany 10.7%; Italy 8.4%; Spain 7.9%; UK 6.6%; Lithuania 5.2%.

## Transport and communications

**Transport.** *Railroads* (2001): length 1.7 km; passengers 2,171,100; cargo 3,357 tons. *Roads* (2007): total length 77 km (paved 100%). *Vehicles* (1997): passenger cars 21,120; trucks and buses 2,770. *Air transport* (2004; charter service of Monacair): passenger-km 414,000. **Communications,** in total units (units per 1,000 persons). Telephone landlines (2008): 35,000 (990); cellular telephone subscribers (2008): 22,000 (622); total Internet users (2008): 22,000 (622); broadband Internet subscribers (2007): 12,000 (348).

## Education and health

**Educational attainment** (2000). Percentage of population ages 17 and over having: primary/lower secondary education 24.7%; upper secondary 27.6%; vocational 12.7%; university 35.0%. **Literacy:** virtually 100%. **Health** (2002): physicians 156 (1 per 207 persons); hospital beds 521 (1 per 62 persons); infant mortality rate per 1,000 live births (2007) 5.2.

## Military

Defense responsibility lies with France according to the terms of the Versailles Treaty of 1919.

## Background

Inhabited since prehistoric times, Monaco was known to the Phoenicians, Greeks, Carthaginians, and Romans. In 1191 the Genoese took possession of it; in 1297 the reign of the Grimaldi family began. The Grimaldis allied themselves with France except for the period 1524–1641, when they were under the protection of Spain. France annexed Monaco in 1793, and it remained under French control until the fall of Napoleon, when the Grimaldis returned. In 1815 it was put under the protection of Sardinia. A treaty in 1861 called for the sale of the towns of Menton and Roquebrune to France and the establishment of Monaco's independence. It joined the UN in 1993. In 1997 the 700-year rule of the Grimaldis, then under Prince Rainier III, was celebrated. Although not a member of the EU, Monaco adopted the euro as its currency in 2002.

## Recent Developments

The Prince Albert of Monaco Foundation continued to work on environmental issues in 2011. A major concern was increasing seawater temperatures, thought to alter the resistance of corals and mollusks to ocean acidification in the Mediterranean Sea.

**Internet resource:** <www.monte-carlo.mc>.

---

*1 metric ton = about 1.1 short tons;    1 kilometer = 0.6 mi (statute);    1 metric ton-km cargo = about 0.68 short ton-mi cargo;    c.i.f.: cost, insurance, and freight;    f.o.b.: free on board*

# Mongolia

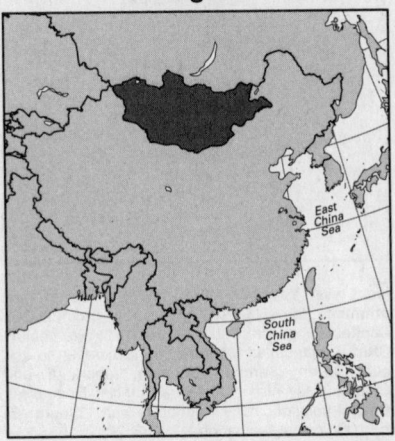

**Official name:** Mongol Uls (Mongolia). **Form of government:** unitary multiparty republic with one legislative house (State Great Hural [76]). **Head of state:** President Tsakhiagiyn Elbegdorj (from 2009). **Head of government:** Prime Minister Sukhbaataryn Batbold (from 2009). **Capital:** Ulaanbaatar (Ulan Bator). **Official language:** Khalkha Mongolian. **Official religion:** none. **Monetary unit:** 1 tugrik (Tug) = 100 mongo; valuation (2 Jul 2012) US$1 = Tug 1,342.00.

## Demography

**Area:** 603,909 sq mi, 1,564,116 sq km. **Population** (2011): 2,765,000. **Density** (2011): persons per sq mi 4.6, persons per sq km 1.8. **Urban** (2010): 63.3%. **Sex distribution** (2004): male 49.60%; female 50.40%. **Age breakdown** (2005): under 15, 28.9%; 15–29, 32.3%; 30–44, 22.6%; 45–59, 10.3%; 60–74, 4.5%; 75–84, 1.1%; 85 and over, 0.3%. **Ethnic composition** (2000): Khalkha Mongol 81.5%; Kazakh 4.3%; Dörbed Mongol 2.8%; Bayad 2.1%; Buryat Mongol 1.7%; Dariganga Mongol 1.3%; Zakhchin 1.3%; Tuvan (Uriankhai) 1.1%; other 3.9%. **Religious affiliation** (2005): traditional beliefs (shamanism) 32%; Buddhist (Lamaism) 23%; Muslim 5%; Christian 1%; nonreligious 30%; atheist/other 9%. **Major cities** (2007): Ulaanbaatar (Ulan Bator) 1,031,200; Erdenet 74,300; Darhan 72,400; Choybalsan (2000) 40,123; Mörön (2000) 28,903. **Location:** north-central Asia, bordering Russia and China.

## Vital statistics

**Birth rate** per 1,000 population (2008): 23.8 (world avg. 20.3); (2001) within marriage 82.2%. **Death rate** per 1,000 population (2008): 5.6 (world avg. 8.5). **Total fertility rate** (avg. births per childbearing woman; 2005): 1.97. **Life expectancy** at birth (2004): male 61.6 years; female 67.8 years.

## National economy

**Budget** (2006). *Revenue:* Tug 1,360,400,000,000 (tax revenue 83.0%, of which income tax 35.0%,

taxes on goods and services 25.9%; nontax revenue 16.6%; other 0.4%). *Expenditures:* Tug 1,237,000,000,000 (economic services 26.1%; social security 20.8%; general administration 19.6%; education 15.6%; health 8.0%; defense and public order 3.7%). **Population economically active** (2004): total 986,100; activity rate of total population 39.3% (participation rates: ages 16–59, 63.7%; female 51.0%; registered unemployed [December 2008] 2.8%). **Production** (metric tons except as noted). *Agriculture and fishing* (2007): hay 930,405, potatoes 114,490, wheat 109,560; livestock (number of live animals) 15,451,700 goats, 14,815,100 sheep, 2,167,900 cattle, 2,114,800 horses, 253,500 camels; fisheries production 185 (from aquaculture, none). *Mining and quarrying* (2007): fluorspar 381,000; copper (metal content) 130,160; molybdenum (metal content) 1,978; gold 17,473 kg. *Manufacturing* (value of production in Tug '000,000; 2006): textiles 93,475; base metals 74,879; food products 71,428. *Energy production (consumption):* electricity (kW-hr; 2006) 3,544,000,000 (3,691,000,000); coal (metric tons; 2006) 1,316,000 (1,316,000); lignite (metric tons; 2006) 6,758,000 (4,301,000); crude petroleum (barrels; 2005) 201,000 (n.a.); petroleum products (metric tons; 2006) none (635,000). **Gross national income** (2008): US$4,411,000,000 (US$1,680 per capita). **Public debt** (external; 2007): US$1,566,000,000. **Selected balance of payments data.** Receipts from (US$'000,000): tourism (2006) 225; remittances (2008) 200; foreign direct investment (2005–07 avg.) 267; official development assistance (2007) 228. Disbursements for (US$'000,000): tourism (2006) 188; remittances (2008) 77.

## Foreign trade

**Imports** (2006; c.i.f.): US$1,489,200,000 (mineral fuels 30.0%; machinery and apparatus 18.2%; food and agricultural products 12.4%; transportation equipment 10.3%). *Major import sources:* Russia 36.6%; China 27.5%; Japan 6.8%; South Korea 5.6%; Kazakhstan 3.5%. **Exports** (2006; f.o.b.): US$1,528,800,000 (copper concentrate 42.7%; gold 18.1%; refined copper 7.2%; combed goat down 5.3%; raw [greasy] cashmere 4.2%; molybdenum 3.2%). *Major export destinations:* China 68.1%; Canada 11.2%; US 7.8%; Russia 2.9%; UK 2.5%.

## Transport and communications

**Transport.** *Railroads* (2006): route length 1,810 km; passenger-km 1,287,000,000; metric ton-km cargo 10,513,000,000. *Roads* (2002): total length 49,250 km (paved 4%). *Vehicles* (2007): passenger cars 110,153; trucks and buses 50,216. *Air transport* (2006): passenger-km 835,800,000; metric ton-km cargo 86,400,000. **Communications,** in total units (units per 1,000 persons). Telephone landlines (2008): 165,000 (63); cellular telephone subscribers (2008): 999,000 (378); personal computers (2005): 340,000 (133); total Internet users (2008): 330,000 (125); broadband Internet subscribers (2007): 7,400 (2.8).

## Education and health

**Educational attainment** (2000). Percentage of population ages 10 and over having: no formal education 11.6%; primary education 23.5%; secondary 46.1%; vocational secondary 11.2%; higher 7.6%. **Literacy** (2004): percentage of total population ages 15 and over literate 97.8%; males 98.0%; females 97.5%. **Health** (2004): physicians 6,590 (1 per 384 persons); hospital beds 18,400 (1 per 138 persons); infant mortality rate per 1,000 live births (2008) 19.6; undernourished population (2003–05) 800,000 (29% of total population based on the consumption of a minimum daily requirement of 1,840 calories).

## Military

**Total active duty personnel** (November 2008): 10,000 (army 89.0%, air force 8.0%, other 3.0%); reserve 137,000. **Military expenditure as percentage of GDP** (2007): 1.1%; per capita expenditure US$16.

## Background

In Neolithic times Mongolia was inhabited by small groups of nomads. During the 3rd century BC it became the center of the Xiongnu empire. Turkic-speaking peoples held sway in the 4th–10th centuries AD. In the early 13th century Genghis Khan united the Mongol tribes and conquered central Asia. His successor, Ogodei, conquered the Chin dynasty of China in 1234. Kublai Khan established the Yuan, or Mongol, dynasty in China in 1279. After the 14th century the Ming dynasty of China confined the Mongols to their homeland in the steppes; later they became part of the Chinese Ch'ing dynasty. Inner Mongolia was incorporated into China in 1644. After the fall of the Ch'ing dynasty in 1911, Mongol princes declared Mongolia's independence from China, and in 1921 Russian forces helped drive off the Chinese. The Mongolian People's Republic was established in 1924 and recognized by China in 1946. The nation adopted a new constitution in 1992 and shortened its name to Mongolia.

## Recent Developments

In 2011, Mongolian Pres. Tsakhiagiin Elbegdorj led visits to Moscow, the United States, and the United Kingdom. Prime Minister Sükhbaataryn Batbold paid official visits to China, including Hong Kong. The mining industry was booming, thanks to high market prices for copper and gold and to China's great demand for coal. Mongolian GDP growth was estimated to reach 9% in 2011. In 2011 Mongolia celebrated the centenary of its declaration of independence and the 2,220th anniversary of the Xiongnu empire, described by President Elbegdorj as the "first state" of the Mongols.

**Internet resource:** <www.nso.mn/v3/index2.php>.

## Montenegro

**Official name:** Crna Gora (Montenegro). **Form of government:** multiparty republic with one legislative house (Parliament [81]). **Head of state:** Pres-

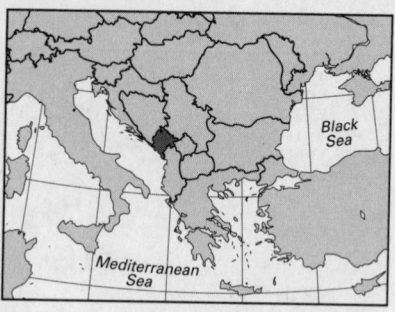

ident Filip Vujanovic (from 2003). **Head of government:** Prime Minister Igor Luksic (from 2010). **Capital:** Podgorica; Cetinje is the old royal capital. **Official language:** Montenegrin (according to the constitution, Serbian, Bosnian, Albanian, and Croatian may also be used as official languages). **Official religion:** none. **Monetary unit:** 1 euro (€) = 100 cents; valuation (2 Jul 2012) US$1 = €0.79 (Montenegro uses the euro as its official currency, even though it is not a member of the EU).

## Demography

**Area:** 5,333 sq mi, 13,812 sq km. **Population** (2011): 620,000. **Density** (2011): persons per sq mi 116.3, persons per sq km 44.9. **Urban** (2011): 63.2%. **Sex distribution** (2006): male 49.28%; female 50.72%. **Age breakdown** (2005): under 15, 19.6%; 15–29, 23.6%; 30–44, 19.8%; 45–59, 19.1%; 60–74, 12.8%; 75–84, 4.3%; 85 and over, 0.8%. **Ethnic composition** (2003): Montenegrin 43.2%; Serb 32.0%; Bosniak/Muslim 11.8%; Albanian 5.0%; undeclared 4.0%; other 4.0%. **Religious affiliation** (2003): Orthodox 70%; Muslim 21%; Roman Catholic 4%; other 5%. **Major settlements** (2003): Podgorica 136,473; Niksic 58,212; Pljevlja 21,377; Bijelo Polje 15,883; Cetinje 15,137. **Location:** southeastern Europe, bordering Bosnia and Herzegovina, Serbia, Kosovo, Albania, the Mediterranean Sea, and Croatia.

## Vital statistics

**Birth rate** per 1,000 population (2008): 13.1 (world avg. 20.3); within marriage 82.6%. **Death rate** per 1,000 population (2008): 9.1 (world avg. 8.5). **Total fertility rate** (avg. births per childbearing woman; 2007): 1.69. **Life expectancy** at birth (2007): male 71.2 years; female 76.1 years.

## National economy

**Budget** (2006). *Revenue:* €582,258,287 (tax revenue 85.8%, of which VAT 44.5%, income tax 12.5%, excise tax 12.4%, taxes on international trade 9.7%; nontax revenue 14.2%). *Expenditures:* €579,780,129 (wages and salaries 27.4%; transfers 20.7%; debt service 20.0%). **Public debt** (external, outstanding; December 2008): US$670,400,000. **Production** (metric tons except as noted). *Agriculture* *and fishing* (2007): potatoes 130,000, grapes 41,000, tomatoes 22,000, tobacco 400; livestock (number of live animals) 249,281 sheep, 114,922 cattle, 13,294 pigs; fisheries production 911 (from aquaculture 1%). *Mining and quarrying* (2007): bauxite 667,053; sea salt 20,000. *Manufacturing* (gross value added in €'000; 2005): base metals and fabricated metal products (mostly of aluminum) 60,766; food products, beverages, and tobacco products 56,607; paper products, publishing, and printing 7,044. *Energy production (consumption):* electricity (kW-hr; 2007) 2,144,000,000 (2,654,000,000 [industrial consumption only]); lignite (metric tons; 2007) 1,195,500 (29,000 [industrial consumption only]). **Population economically active** (2007): total 269,500; activity rate 43.2% (participation rates: ages 16 and over, 52.9%; female 43.0%; unemployed [September 2008–August 2009] 14.1%). **Gross national income** (2008): US$4,008,000,000 (US$6,440 per capita). **Selected balance of payments data.** Receipts from (US$'000,000): tourism (2008) 725; remittances (2006) 100; foreign direct investment (FDI; 2005–07 avg.) 657; official development assistance (2007) 106. Disbursements for (US$'000,000): tourism (2008) 43; FDI (2005–07 avg.) 98.

## Foreign trade

**Imports** (2007; c.i.f.): €2,134,377,900 (mineral fuels 11.6%; motor vehicles 11.4%; nonelectrical machinery and apparatus 9.0%; electrical machinery and apparatus 8.8%; base and fabricated metals 7.1%). *Major import sources:* Serbia 29.9%; Germany 10.0%; Italy 9.8%; Croatia 3.9%; Greece 3.5%. **Exports** (2007; f.o.b.): €599,020,700,000 (aluminum and aluminum products 47.0%; base metals 11.9%; beverages and tobacco products 8.9%; mineral fuels 8.1%). *Major export destinations:* Serbia 28.3%; Italy 27.4%; Greece 12.3%; Hungary 11.1%; Bosnia and Herzegovina 5.1%.

## Transport and communications

**Transport.** *Railroads* (2007): length (2006) 250 km; passenger-km 110,000,000; metric ton-km cargo 184,957,000. *Roads* (2006): total length 7,368 km (paved 64%). *Vehicles* (2007): passenger cars 178,449. *Air transport* (2007): passengers 1,024,491; freight 1,320 metric tons. **Communications,** in total units (units per 1,000 persons). Telephone landlines (2008): 362,000 (577); cellular telephone subscribers (2008): 735,000 (1,171); total Internet users (2008): 294,000 (468); broadband Internet subscribers (2006): 26,000 (42).

## Education and health

**Educational attainment** (2005). Percentage of population ages 15 and over having: no formal education 3.2%; incomplete primary education 6.8%; complete primary 22.5%; secondary 55.0%; higher 12.5%. **Literacy** (2003): total population ages 15 and over literate 97.6%; males literate 99.6%; females literate 95.7%. **Health** (2007): physicians 1,277 (1 per 490 persons); hospital beds 3,948 (1 per 159 persons); infant mortality rate per 1,000 live births (2008) 7.5.

## Military

**Total active duty personnel** (November 2008): 4,500 (army 55.6%, navy 44.4%). **Military expenditure as percentage of GDP** (2007): 2.3%; per capita expenditure US$94.

## Background

The Kingdom of the Serbs, Croats, and Slovenes was created after the collapse of Austria-Hungary at the end of World War I. The country signed treaties with Czechoslovakia and Romania in 1920–21, marking the beginning of the Little Entente. In 1929 an absolute monarchy was established, the country's name was changed to Yugoslavia, and it was divided into regions without regard to ethnic boundaries. Axis powers invaded Yugoslavia in 1941, and German, Italian, Hungarian, and Bulgarian troops occupied it for the rest of World War II. In 1945 the Socialist Federal Republic of Yugoslavia was established; it included the republics of Bosnia and Herzegovina, Croatia, Macedonia, Montenegro, Serbia, and Slovenia. Its independent form of communism under Josip Broz Tito's leadership provoked the USSR. Internal ethnic tensions flared up in the 1980s, causing the country's ultimate collapse. In 1991–92 independence was declared by Croatia, Slovenia, Macedonia, and Bosnia and Herzegovina; the new Federal Republic of Yugoslavia (containing roughly 45% of the population and 40% of the area of its predecessor) was proclaimed by Serbia and Montenegro. Still fueled by long-standing ethnic tensions, hostilities continued into the 1990s. Despite the approval of the Dayton Peace Agreement (1995), sporadic fighting continued and was followed in 1998–99 by Serbian repression and expulsion of ethnic populations in the province of Kosovo. In September–October 2000, the battered nation of Yugoslavia ended the autocratic rule of Pres. Slobodan Milosevic. In April 2001 he was arrested and in June extradited to The Hague to stand trial for war crimes, genocide, and crimes against humanity committed during the fighting in Kosovo. In February 2003 both houses of the Yugoslav federal legislature voted to accept a new state charter and change the name of the country from Yugoslavia to Serbia and Montenegro. Henceforth, defense, international political and economic relations, and human rights matters would be handled centrally, while all other functions would be run from the republican capitals, Belgrade and Podgorica, respectively. A provision was included for both states to vote on independence after three years, and in June 2006 Montenegro's parliament declared the republic's independence, severing some 88 years of union with Serbia.

## Recent Developments

In October 2011 the European Commission recommended that the EU set a date for formal accession talks with Montenegro. The Commission's positive assessment recognized Montenegro for having improved its legislative and institutional framework, its electoral system, and its public administration and judiciary. The country experienced a modest economic recovery and made further progress toward achieving a functioning market economy. Manufacturing output, overall industrial production, and the value of construction projects increased. In November Montenegro signed free-trade agreements with members of the European Free Trade Association (EFTA) and Ukraine that allowed Montenegro to resume its accession negotiations with the World Trade Organization. Montenegrin officials signed separate agreements with Russia and Serbia that called for increased cooperation in tourism, commerce, and energy.

**Internet resource:**
<www.monstat.org/eng/index.php>.

# Morocco

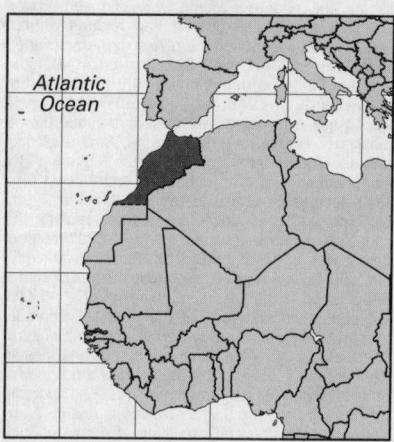

Atlantic Ocean

**Official name:** Al-Mamlakah al-Maghribiyah (Kingdom of Morocco). **Form of government:** constitutional monarchy with two legislative houses (House of Councillors [270]; House of Representatives [395]). **Head of state and government:** King Muhammad VI (from 1999), assisted by Prime Minister Abdelilah Benkirane (from 2011). **Capital:** Rabat. **Official languages:** Arabic; Tamazight. **Official religion:** Islam. **Monetary unit:** 1 Moroccan dirham (DH) = 100 santimat; valuation (2 Jul 2012) US$1 = DH 8.78.

## Demography

**Area:** 268,117 sq mi, 694,420 sq km (includes Western Sahara, annexure of Morocco whose political status has been unresolved since 1991; Western Sahara area: 97,344 sq mi, 252,120 sq km). **Population** (2011; includes Western Sahara, population [2011 est.] 507,000): 32,476,000 (in addition, about 90,000 Western Saharan refugees live in camps near Tindouf). **Density** (2011; includes Western Sahara): persons per sq mi 121.1, persons per sq km 46.8. **Urban** (2009): 57.6%. **Sex distribution** (2008; excludes Western Sahara): male 49.28%; female 50.72%. **Age breakdown** (2008; excludes Western Sahara): under 15, 29.1%; 15–29, 28.6%; 30–44, 21.0%; 45–59, 13.1%; 60–74, 6.0%; 75–84, 1.8%; 85 and over,

0.4%. **Ethnic composition** (2000): Amazigh (Berber) 45%, of which Arabized 24%; Arab 44%; Moors originally from Mauritania 10%; other 1%. **Religious affiliation** (2004): Muslim more than 99% (including Sunni 97%; Shi'i 2%); other less than 1%. **Major urban agglomerations** (2007): Casablanca 3,181,000; Rabat 1,705,000; Fès 1,002,000; Marrakech 872,000; Tangier (2004) 669,685. **Location:** northern Africa, bordering the Mediterranean Sea, the Spanish exclaves of Ceuta and Melilla, Algeria, Mauritania, and the North Atlantic Ocean.

## Vital statistics

**Birth rate** per 1,000 population (2008; excludes Western Sahara): 20.0 (world avg. 20.3). **Death rate** per 1,000 population (2008; excludes Western Sahara): 4.7 (world avg. 8.5). **Total fertility rate** (avg. births per childbearing woman; 2008; excludes Western Sahara): 2.31. **Life expectancy** at birth (2008; excludes Western Sahara): male 72.2 years; female 78.4 years.

## National economy

**Budget.** *Revenue* (2007): DH 167,904,000,000 (VAT 29.6%; corporate taxes 18.1%; income tax 16.5%; nontax revenue 8.8%). *Expenditures* (2007): DH 168,959,000,000 (current expenditures 78.5%; capital expenditures 16.3%). **Public debt** (external, outstanding; 2007): US$15,670,000,000. **Population economically active** (2006): total 10,990,000; activity rate 36.0% (participation rates: ages 15 and over, 51.3%; female [2005] 27.5%; unemployed [April 2008–March 2009] 9.7%). **Production** (metric tons except as noted). *Agriculture and fishing* (2008): wheat 3,769,450, sugar beets 2,925,700, potatoes 1,536,560, olives 765,380, clementines (2006–07) 336,000, grapes 290,794; livestock (number of live animals) 17,077,700 sheep, 2,814,000 cattle, 45,000 camels; fisheries production (2007; roughly 60% of Morocco's fisheries production comes from Atlantic waters off of Western Sahara) 882,079 (from aquaculture, negligible). *Mining and quarrying* (2007): phosphate rock 27,834,000; barite 664,708; fluorite 78,817; zinc (metal content) 68,000; lead (metal content) 44,800; cobalt (metal content) 1,100; silver 246,000 kg. *Manufacturing* (value added in US$'000,000; 2005): food products and beverages 1,467; tobacco products 1,307; wearing apparel 697. *Energy production (consumption):* electricity (kW-hr; 2008) 18,646,000,000 ([2006] 25,190,000,000); coal (metric tons; 2006) none (5,877,000); crude petroleum (barrels; 2007) 81,000 ([2006] 46,000,000); petroleum products (metric tons; 2006) 5,221,000 (7,467,000); natural gas (cu m; 2007) 61,000,000 ([2006] 571,000,000). **Selected balance of payments data.** Receipts from (US$'000,000): tourism (2007) 7,181; remittances (2008) 6,730; foreign direct investment (FDI; 2005–07 avg.) 2,277; official development assistance (2007) 1,090. Disbursements for (US$'000,000): tourism (2007) 880; remittances (2008) 52; FDI (2005–07 avg.) 390. **Gross national income** (2008): US$80,544,000,000 (US$2,580 per capita).

---

1 metric ton = about 1.1 short tons;    1 kilometer = 0.6 mi (statute);    1 metric ton-km cargo = about 0.68 short ton-mi cargo;    c.i.f.: cost, insurance, and freight;    f.o.b.: free on board

## Foreign trade

**Imports** (2008; c.i.f.): DH 321,931,000,000 (mineral fuels 22.2%, of which crude petroleum 9.6%; machinery and apparatus 22.0%; food products and beverages 9.6%). *Major import sources:* France 15.0%; Spain 11.1%; Italy 6.7%; China 5.7%; US 5.0%. **Exports** (2008; f.o.b.): DH 154,493,000,000 (wearing apparel and accessories 16.6%; phosphoric acid 14.6%; phosphate rock 11.2%; fish, shrimp, and octopuses 8.0%; fertilizer 7.1%; electricity distribution equipment 5.8%; vegetables and fruit 5.7%; cannabis is an important illegal export—Morocco was the world's number 2 producer in 2008). *Major export destinations:* France 20.0%; Spain 17.8%; India 6.6%; Brazil 5.1%; Italy 4.7%.

## Transport and communications

**Transport.** *Railroads* (2007): route length (2005) 1,907 km; passenger-km 3,659,000,000; metric ton-km cargo 5,835,000,000. *Roads* (2007): total length 57,799 km (paved 62%). *Vehicles* (2007): passenger cars 1,644,523; trucks and buses 528,175. *Air transport* (2008; Royal Air Maroc only): passenger-km 9,901,000,000; metric ton-km cargo 55,477,000. **Communications,** in total units (units per 1,000 persons). Telephone landlines (2008): 2,991,000 (95); cellular telephone subscribers (2008): 22,816,000 (728); personal computers (2007): 1,115,000 (36); total Internet users (2008): 10,300,000 (329); broadband Internet subscribers (2008): 484,000 (15).

## Education and health

**Educational attainment** (2004). Percentage of population ages 10 and over having: no formal education through incomplete primary education 45.5%; complete primary 40.8%; secondary 8.7%; higher 5.0%. **Literacy** (2007): total population ages 11 and over literate 58.7%; males literate 70.6%; females literate 47.3%. **Health** (2006): physicians 18,248 (1 per 1,678 persons); hospital beds (public hospitals only) 26,649 (1 per 1,149 persons); infant mortality rate per 1,000 live births (2008; excludes Western Sahara) 30.9; undernourished population (2002–04) 1,800,000 (6% of total population based on the consumption of a minimum daily requirement of 1,870 calories).

## Military

**Total active duty personnel** (November 2008): 195,800 (army 89.4%, navy 4.0%, air force 6.6%). **Military expenditure as percentage of GDP** (2008): 3.4%; per capita expenditure US$115.

## Background

The Berbers entered Morocco near the end of the 2nd millennium BC. Phoenicians established trading posts along the Mediterranean during the 12th century BC, and Carthage had settlements along the Atlantic in the 5th century BC. After the fall of Carthage, Morocco became a loyal ally of Rome, and in AD 42 it was annexed by Rome as part of the province of Mauretania. It was invaded by Muslims in the 7th century. Beginning in the mid-11th century, the Almoravids, Almohads, and Marinids ruled successively. After the fall of the Marinids in the mid-15th century, the Sa'dis ruled for a century beginning in 1550. The French fought Morocco over the Algerian boundary in the 1840s, and the Spanish seized part of Moroccan territory in 1859. It was a French protectorate from 1912 until its independence in 1956. In the mid-1970s it reasserted claim to the Western Sahara, and in 1976 Spanish troops withdrew from the region, leaving behind the Algerian-supported Saharan guerrillas of the Polisario movement. Relations with Mauritania and Algeria deteriorated, and fighting over the region continued. Attempts at mediation have repeatedly been made by the international community.

## Recent Developments

In March 2011, Morrocan King Muhammad VI promised comprehensive constitutional reform and appointed a commission, which most opposition leaders boycotted, to draft the legislation. The king nonetheless announced a series of proposals—including an increase in authority for the parliament and the prime minister—in mid-June, to be approved by referendum. The king, however, would remain the highest authority in matters of national security, foreign policy, and religious affairs. Protesters called for a boycott of the referendum, but the reforms were approved by a suspiciously large 98.5% of voters, with a 73.5% turnout.

**Internet resource:** <www.visitmorocco.com>.

# Mozambique

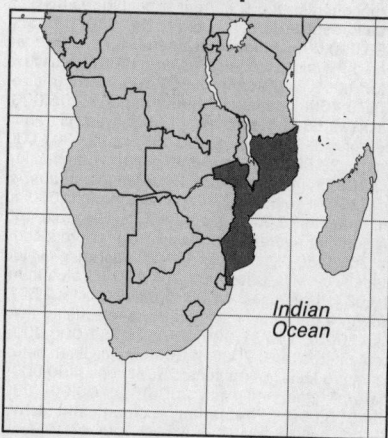

Indian Ocean

**Official name:** República de Moçambique (Republic of Mozambique). **Form of government:** multiparty republic with one legislative house (Assembly of the Republic [250]). **Head of state and government:** President Armando Guebuza (from 2005). **Capital:** Maputo. **Official language:** Portuguese. **Official religion:** none. **Monetary unit:** 1 (new) metical (MTn; plural meticais) = 100 centavos; valuation (2 Jul 2012) US$1 = MTn 27.88 (the [new] metical replaced the [old] metical [MT] on 1 Jul 2006, at the rate of 1 MTn = MT 1,000).

## Demography

**Area:** 308,642 sq mi, 799,380 sq km. **Population** (2011): 22,949,000. **Density** (2011): persons per sq mi 74.4, persons per sq km 28.7. **Urban** (2011): 37.6%. **Sex distribution** (2007): male 47.67%; female 52.33%. **Age breakdown** (2005): under 15, 43.1%; 15–29, 26.8%; 30–44, 16.5%; 45–59, 9.0%; 60–74, 3.9%; 75 and over, 0.7%. **Ethnic composition** (2000): Makuana 15.3%; Makua 14.5%; Tsonga 8.6%; Sena 8.0%; Lomwe 7.1%; Tswa 5.7%; Chwabo 5.5%; other 35.3%. **Religious affiliation** (2005): traditional beliefs 46%; Christian 37%, of which Roman Catholic 19%, Protestant 11%; Muslim 9%; other 8%. **Major cities** (2007): Maputo 1,094,315 (urban agglomeration 1,766,823); Matola 672,508; Nampula 477,900; Beira 431,583; Chimoio 237,278. **Location:** southern Africa, bordering Tanzania, the Indian Ocean, South Africa, Swaziland, Zimbabwe, Zambia, and Malawi.

## Vital statistics

**Birth rate** per 1,000 population (2008): 38.7 (world avg. 20.3). **Death rate** per 1,000 population (2008): 19.5 (world avg. 8.5). **Total fertility rate** (avg. births per childbearing woman; 2006): 5.35. **Life expectancy** at birth (2006): male 41.2 years; female 40.4 years.

## National economy

**Budget** (2008). *Revenue:* MTn 69,107,000,000 (tax revenue 47.3%; grants 45.4%; nontax revenue 7.3%). *Expenditures:* MTn 83,220,000,000 (capital expenditures 48.6%; current expenditures 45.5%). **Public debt** (external, outstanding; 2007): US$2,533,000,000. **Production** (metric tons except as noted). *Agriculture and fishing* (2007): cassava 7,350,000, sugarcane 2,650,000, corn (maize) 1,579,400, peanuts (groundnuts) 105,000, cashews 58,000, tobacco 11,000; livestock (number of live animals) 1,330,000 cattle, 393,000 goats, 28,500,000 chickens; fisheries production 93,108 (from aquaculture 1%). *Mining and quarrying* (2007): bauxite 12,000; limestone 250,000 cu m; tantalite 28,000 kg; garnet 7,200 kg; gold 450 kg (official figures; unofficial artisanal production is 360–480 kg per year). *Manufacturing* (value added in MT '000,000,000; 2003): aluminum 19,067; beverages 4,773; food products 2,577. *Energy production (consumption):* electricity (kW-hr; 2006) 14,737,000,000 (11,751,000,000); coal (metric tons; 2006) 41,000 (negligible); petroleum products (metric tons; 2006) none (490,000); natural gas (cu m; 2006) 2,700,000,000 (84,500,000). **Population economically active** (2003): total 8,981,000; activity rate 47.1% (participation rates: ages 15–64, 84.4%; female 53.8%; unemployed [2004–05] 18.7%). **Gross national income** (2008): US$8,119,000,000 (US$370 per capita). **Selected balance of payments data.** Receipts from (US$'000,000): tourism (2007) 163; remittances (2008) 116; foreign direct investment (2005–07 avg.) 230; official development assistance (2007) 1,777. Disbursements for (US$'000,000): tourism (2007) 180; remittances (2008) 52.

## Foreign trade

**Imports** (2006; c.i.f.): US$2,869,000,000 (machinery and apparatus 14.5%; refined petroleum products 13.1%; food products 11.4%, of which cereals 6.7%; motor vehicles 9.4%). *Major import sources:* South Africa 37.4%; Netherlands 15.8%; India 4.6%; UAE 4.2%; US 3.5%. **Exports** (2006; f.o.b.): US$2,-381,000,000 (aluminum 58.9%; food products 10.2%, of which shrimp 3.6%; electricity 7.5%; natural gas 4.6%; tobacco products 4.6%). *Major export destinations:* Netherlands 59.7%; South Africa 14.1%; Zimbabwe 3.2%; Switzerland 2.2%.

## Transport and communications

**Transport.** *Railroads* (2003): route length (2002) 3,123 km; passenger-km 167,000,000; metric ton-km cargo 1,362,000,000. *Roads* (2000): total length 30,400 km (paved 19%). *Vehicles* (2001): passenger cars 81,600; trucks and buses 76,000. *Air transport* (2007; LAM [Linhas Aéreas de Moçambique] only): passenger-km 440,000,000; metric ton-km cargo 6,000,000. **Communications,** in total units (units per 1,000 persons). Telephone landlines (2008): 78,000 (3.5); cellular telephone subscribers (2008): 4,405,000 (197); personal computers (2005): 283,000 (14); total Internet users (2008): 350,000 (16).

## Education and health

**Educational attainment** (1997). Percentage of population ages 15 and over having: no formal schooling/unknown 79.0%; primary education 18.4%; secondary 2.0%; technical 0.4%; higher 0.2%. **Literacy** (2007): percentage of total population ages 15 and over literate 53.0%; males literate 67.9%; females literate 38.6%. **Health** (2003): physicians 635 (1 per 30,525 persons); hospital beds 16,493 (1 per 1,175 persons); infant mortality rate per 1,000 live births (2006) 112.1; undernourished population (2003–05) 7,500,000 (38% of total population based on the consumption of a minimum daily requirement of 1,800 calories).

## Military

**Total active duty personnel** (November 2008): 11,200 (army 89.3%, navy 1.8%, air force 8.9%). **Military expenditure as percentage of GDP** (2007): 0.7%; per capita expenditure US$3.

## Background

Mozambique was settled by Bantu peoples about the 3rd century AD. Arab traders occupied the coastal region from the 14th century, and the Portuguese controlled the area from the early 16th century. The slave trade later became an important part of the economy. In the late 19th century private trading companies began to administer parts of the inland areas. It became an overseas province of Portugal in 1951. After years of war beginning in the 1960s, the country was granted independence in 1975. It was wracked by civil war in the 1970s and

---

*1 metric ton = about 1.1 short tons;*    *1 kilometer = 0.6 mi (statute);*    *1 metric ton-km cargo = about 0.68 short ton-mi cargo;*    *c.i.f.: cost, insurance, and freight;*    *f.o.b.: free on board*

'80s. In 1990 a new constitution was promulgated, and a peace treaty was signed with the rebels in 1992. The first multiparty elections were held two years later.

## Recent Developments

The government made considerable progress in its economic and social plan in 2011. Real GDP growth stood at 7.4%, backed by increasing foreign investment into minerals and infrastructure megaprojects. In May Brazilian mining conglomerate Vale began coal production in Moatize, which transformed life in a previously neglected area. In October 2011 and again in February 2012, massive gas fields were discovered off the northern coast of Mozambique, leading to increased interest from international mineral companies.

Internet resource: <www.ine.gov.mz>.

# Myanmar (Burma)

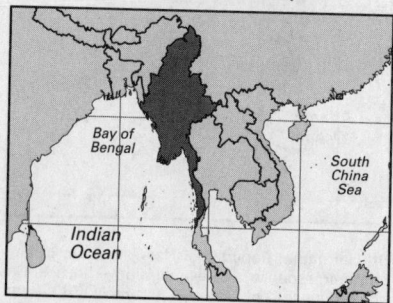

Official name: Pyihtaungsu Thamada Myanmar Naingngandaw (Republic of the Union of Myanmar). Form of government: constitutional republic with two legislative houses (House of Nationalities [224]; House of Representatives [440]). Head of state and government: President Thein Sein (from 2011). Capital: Nay Pyi Taw (Naypyidaw). Official language: Burmese. Official religion: none (the government promotes Theravada Buddhism over other religions). Monetary unit: 1 Myanmar kyat (K) = 100 pyas; valuation (2 Jul 2012) US$1 = K 878.00.

## Demography

Area: 261,228 sq mi, 676,577 sq km. Population (2011): 54,000,000. Density (2011): persons per sq mi 206.7, persons per sq km 79.8. Urban (2008): 32.6%. Sex distribution (2008): male 49.49%; female 50.51%. Age breakdown (2008): under 15, 25.7%; 15–29, 28.6%; 30–44, 23.4%; 45–59, 14.3%; 60–74, 6.2%; 75–89, 1.7%; 90 and over, 0.1%. Ethnic composition (2000): Burman 55.9%; Karen 9.5%; Shan 6.5%; Han Chinese 2.5%; Mon 2.3%; Yangbye 2.2%; Kachin 1.5%; other 19.6%. Religious affiliation (2005): Buddhist 74%; Protestant 6%; Muslim 3%; Hindu 2%; traditional beliefs 11%; other 4%. Major urban agglomerations (2007): Yangon (Rangoon) 4,088,-000; Mandalay 961,000; Nay Pyi Taw 930,000; Mawlamyine (Moulmein) (city population; 2004) 405,800; Pathein (Bassein) (city population;

2004) 215,600. Location: southeastern Asia, bordering China, Laos, Thailand, the Andaman Sea, the Bay of Bengal, Bangladesh, and India.

## Vital statistics

Birth rate per 1,000 population (2008): 17.2 (world avg. 20.3). Death rate per 1,000 population (2008): 9.2 (world avg. 8.5). Total fertility rate (avg. births per childbearing woman; 2008): 1.92. Life expectancy at birth (2008): male 60.7 years; female 65.3 years.

## National economy

Budget (2005–06). Revenue: K 819,534,000,000 (tax revenue 58.2%, of which taxes on goods and services 30.7%, income tax 25.2%; nontax revenue 41.8%). Expenditures: K 1,008,785,000,000 (economic affairs 34.3%; transportation 19.7%; defense 19.6%; education 6.8%; health 2.2%). Public debt (external, outstanding; 2007): US$5,516,000,000. Production (metric tons except as noted). Agriculture and fishing (2007): rice 32,610,000, sugarcane 7,450,000, dry beans 1,765,000, sesame seeds 600,000, pigeon peas 540,000, sunflower seeds 365,000, chickpeas 225,000, garlic 128,000; livestock (number of live animals) 12,500,000 cattle, 6,300,000 pigs, 94,500,000 chickens; fisheries production 2,840,240 (from aquaculture 21%). Mining and quarrying (2008–09): copper (2007; metal content) 14,700; jade 32,311,589 kg; rubies 1,751,355 carats; sapphires 1,313,723 carats; spinel 339,894 carats. Manufacturing (value added in US$'000,000; 2003): nonelectrical machinery and equipment 728; transportation equipment 483; fabricated metal products 254. Energy production (consumption): electricity (kW-hr; 2008–09) 6,654,630,000 ([2006] 6,164,000,000); coal (metric tons; 2006) 1,006,000 (128,000); lignite (metric tons; 2006) 380,000 (111,000); crude petroleum (barrels; 2008–09) 7,058,000 ([2006] 6,035,600); petroleum products (metric tons; 2006) 790,000 (1,633,000); natural gas (cu m; 2008–09) 11,591,300,000 ([2006] 2,119,600,000). Selected balance of payments data. Receipts from (US$'000,000): tourism (2006) 46; remittances (2008) 150; foreign direct investment (2005–07 avg.) 202; official development assistance (2007) 190. Disbursements for (US$'000,000): tourism (2006) 37; remittances (2008) 32. Gross national income (2008): US$28,663,000,000 (US$578 per capita). Population economically active (2008): total 28,361,000; activity rate of total population 57.6% (participation rates: ages 15–64, 79.3%; female 45.5%; officially unemployed 4.9%).

## Foreign trade

Imports (2006–07; c.i.f.): K 16,835,000,000 (mineral fuels 24.8%; nonelectrical machinery and transportation equipment 15.9%; base and fabricated metals 7.0%; synthetic fabrics 6.5%). Major import sources: Singapore 36.5%; China 24.4%; Thailand 10.3%; India 5.3%; Japan 4.9%. Exports (2006–07; f.o.b.): K 30,026,000,000 (natural gas 42.6%; pulses [mostly beans] 11.1%; hardwood 10.0%, of which teak 6.0%; garments 5.3%). Major export destinations: Thailand 48.9%; India 13.7%; Hong Kong 8.2%; China 7.9%; Singapore 3.5%.

## Transport and communications

**Transport.** *Railroads* (2008–09): route length 3,955 km; passenger-km 5,466,155,000; metric ton-km cargo 883,650,000. *Roads* (1999): total length 27,966 km (paved 11%). *Vehicles* (2009): passenger cars 244,609; trucks and buses 79,025. *Air transport* (2007–08): passenger-km 124,885,000; metric ton-km cargo (2006) 245,000,000. **Communications,** in total units (units per 1,000 persons). Telephone landlines (2008): 811,000 (16); cellular telephone subscribers (2008): 367,000 (7.4); personal computers (2005): 400,000 (8.6); total Internet users (2008): 109,000 (2.2); broadband Internet subscribers (2008): 10,000.

## Education and health

**Literacy** (2003): total population ages 15 and over literate 89.7%; males literate 93.7%; females literate 86.2%. **Health** (2004–05): physicians 17,564 (1 per 2,660 persons); hospital beds 34,654 (1 per 1,350 persons); infant mortality rate per 1,000 live births (2008) 49.1; undernourished population (2002–04) 2,400,000 (5% of total population based on the consumption of a minimum daily requirement of 1,820 calories).

## Military

**Total active duty personnel** (November 2008): 406,000 (army 92.4%, navy 3.9%, air force 3.7%).

## Background

Myanmar, until 1989 known as Burma, has long been inhabited, with the Mon and Pyu states dominant between the 1st century BC and the 9th century AD. It was united in the 11th century under a Burmese dynasty that was overthrown by the Mongols in the 13th century. The Portuguese, Dutch, and English traded there in the 16th–17th centuries. The modern Burmese state was founded in the 18th century. It fell to the British in 1885 and became a province of India. It was occupied by Japan in World War II and became independent in 1948. A military coup took power in 1962 and nationalized major economic sectors. In 1990 opposition parties won in national elections, but the army remained in control. Trying to negotiate for a freer government amid the unrest, Aung San Suu Kyi, the National League for Democracy leader, was awarded the Nobel Peace Prize in 1991. She spent extended periods of the 1990s and 2000s under house arrest. The military relinquished authority to a civilian government in 2011.

## Recent Developments

In 2011 Myanmar experienced significant change. Its first civilian president in nearly 50 years, Thein Sein, announced a broad agenda that included social reform, a push against corruption, and promises to respect basic freedoms. Opposition leader Aung San Suu Kyi was permitted to travel around the country. Her party was allowed to open offices, conduct public events without official harassment, and register for the upcoming elections. Suu Kyi ran in the historic legislative election held in April 2012, winning a seat, and her party became the main opposition party in the legislature. The US eased some of its sanctions on Myanmar as a result of this progress, naming an ambassador to the country for the first time since 1988 and allowing some foreign investment.

**Internet resource:** <www.csostat.gov.mm>.

# Namibia

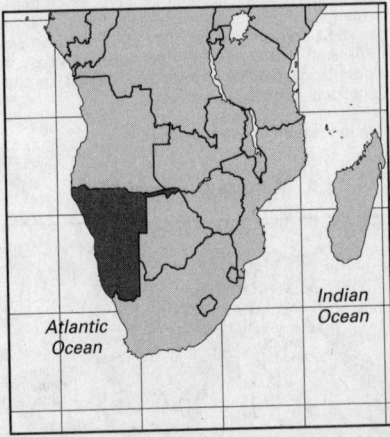

**Official name:** Republic of Namibia. **Form of government:** republic with two legislative houses (National Council [26]; National Assembly [78]). **Head of state and government:** President Hifikepunye Pohamba (from 2005). **Capital:** Windhoek. **Official language:** English. **Official religion:** none. **Monetary unit:** 1 Namibian dollar (N$) = 100 cents; valuation (2 Jul 2012) US$1 = N$8.17.

## Demography

**Area:** 318,193 sq mi, 824,116 sq km. **Population** (2011): 2,324,000. **Density** (2011): persons per sq mi 7.3, persons per sq km 2.8. **Urban** (2009): 37.4%. **Sex distribution** (2006): male 50.13%; female 49.87%. **Age breakdown** (2006): under 15, 38.2%; 15–29, 31.3%; 30–44, 15.6%; 45–59, 9.2%; 60–74, 4.5%; 75 and over 1.2%. **Ethnic composition** (2000): Ovambo 34.4%; mixed race (black/white) 14.5%; Kavango 9.1%; Afrikaner 8.1%; San (Bushmen) and Bergdama 7.0%; Herero 5.5%; Nama 4.4%; Kwambi 3.7%; German 2.8%; other 10.5%. **Religious affiliation** (2000): Protestant (mostly Lutheran) 49.3%; Roman Catholic 17.7%; unaffiliated Christian 14.1%; independent Christian 10.8%; traditional beliefs 6.0%; other 2.1%. **Major urban localities** (2006): Windhoek 277,300; Rundu 62,300; Walvis Bay 54,900; Oshakati 34,900; Swakopmund 26,700. **Location:** southwestern Africa, bordering Angola, Zambia, Botswana, South Africa, and the South Atlantic Ocean.

---

*1 metric ton = about 1.1 short tons;    1 kilometer = 0.6 mi (statute);    1 metric ton-km cargo = about 0.68 short ton-mi cargo;    c.i.f.: cost, insurance, and freight;    f.o.b.: free on board*

## Vital statistics

**Birth rate** per 1,000 population (2008): 25.5 (world avg. 20.3). **Death rate** per 1,000 population (2008): 12.5 (world avg. 8.5). **Total fertility rate** (avg. births per childbearing woman; 2006): 3.06. **Life expectancy** at birth (2006): male 44.5 years; female 42.3 years.

## National economy

**Budget** (2008–09). *Revenue:* N$21,973,000,000 (tax revenue 91.9%, of which customs duties and excises 40.4%, income tax 33.4%, VAT 16.8%; nontax revenue 7.0%; grants 1.1%). *Expenditures:* N$22,469,100,000 (current expenditures 76.9%; capital expenditures 23.1%). **Production** (metric tons except as noted). *Agriculture and fishing* (2007): millet 58,000, corn (maize) 40,000, wheat 10,000, seed cotton 5,200; livestock (number of live animals) 2,700,000 sheep, 2,500,000 cattle, 2,000,000 goats; fisheries production 415,543 (from aquaculture, negligible). *Mining and quarrying* (2007): salt 800,000; fluorite 118,766; zinc (metal content) 52,000; lead (metal content) 11,900; copper (metal content) 8,500; uranium oxide 3,395; amethyst 40,000 kg; silver 30,000 kg; gold 2,600 kg; gem diamonds 2,266,000 carats. *Manufacturing* (value added in N$'000,000; 2006): food products 2,633 (of which fish processing 620, meat processing 101); other manufactures, which include fur products (from Karakul sheep), textiles, carved wood products, and refined metals 2,962. *Energy production (consumption):* electricity (kW-hr; 2006) 1,606,000,000 ([2004] 2,819,000,000). **Selected balance of payments data.** Receipts from (US$'000,000): tourism (2007) 434; remittances (2008) 16; foreign direct investment (2005–06 avg.) 477; official development assistance (2007) 205. Disbursements for (US$'000,000): tourism (2007) 132; remittances (2008) 16; foreign direct disinvestment (2005–07 avg.) −9. **Population economically active** (2006): total 656,000; activity rate of total population 32.0% (participation rates: ages 16 and over, 54.0%; female 43.4%; officially unemployed 5.3%). **Public debt** (external, outstanding; 2006–07): US$2,526,000,000. **Gross national income** (GNI; 2008): US$8,880,000,000 (US$4,200 per capita).

## Foreign trade

**Imports** (2006; c.i.f.): N$21,719,000,000 (refined petroleum products 18.3%; transportation equipment 16.0%; chemical, rubber, and plastic products 12.1%; food products, beverages, and tobacco products 11.5%; machinery and apparatus 9.8%). *Major import sources* (2004): South Africa 85.4%; UK 2.6%; Germany 1.9%; China 1.2%; Zimbabwe 0.8%. **Exports** (2006; f.o.b.): N$20,605,000,000 (diamonds 33.0%; fish 18.2%; other minerals [mainly gold, zinc, copper, lead, and silver] 12.4%; refined zinc 12.2%; meat preparations [mostly beef] 7.8%). *Major export destinations* (2004): South Africa 27.8%; UK 14.9%; Angola 13.8%; US 11.0%; Spain 9.6%.

## Transport and communications

**Transport.** *Railroads:* route length (2006) 2,382 km; (1995–96) passenger-km 48,300,000; (2003–04) metric ton-km 1,247,400. *Roads* (2004): total length 42,237 km (paved 13%). *Vehicles* (2008): passenger cars 107,825; trucks and buses 119,806. *Air transport* (2006; Air Namibia only): passenger-km 1,588,466,000; metric ton-km cargo (2005) 60,429,000. **Communications,** in total units (units per 1,000 persons). Telephone landlines (2008): 140,000 (66); cellular telephone subscribers (2008): 1,052,000 (494); personal computers (2007): 504,000 (240); total Internet users (2008): 114,000 (53); broadband Internet subscribers (2007): 300.

## Education and health

**Educational attainment** (2000). Percentage of population ages 25 and over having: no formal schooling/unknown 26.5%; incomplete primary education 25.5%; complete primary 8.0%; incomplete secondary 24.9%; complete secondary 11.4%; higher 3.7%. **Literacy** (2007): total population ages 15 and over literate 86.6%; males literate 86.5%; females literate 86.7%. **Health:** physicians (2004) 598 (1 per 3,201 persons); hospital beds (2004–05; public sector only) 6,811 (1 per 283 persons); infant mortality rate per 1,000 live births (2006) 48.1; undernourished population (2003–05) 400,000 (19% of total population based on the consumption of a minimum daily requirement of 1,790 calories).

## Military

**Total active duty personnel** (November 2008): 9,200 (army 97.8%, navy 2.2%). **Military expenditure as percentage of GDP** (2008): 4.4%; per capita expenditure US$112.

## Background

Long inhabited by indigenous peoples, Namibia was explored by the Portuguese in the late 15th century. In 1884 it was annexed by Germany as German South West Africa. It was captured in World War I by South Africa, which received it as a mandate from the League of Nations in 1920 and refused to give it up after World War II. A UN resolution in 1966 ending the mandate was challenged by South Africa in the 1970s and '80s. Through long negotiations involving many factions and interests, Namibia achieved independence in 1990. The country has been severely affected by the AIDS epidemic.

## Recent Developments

With the use of nuclear power on the wane worldwide, the price of uranium dropped, but Namibia continued to benefit from the relatively high price of minerals in 2011. The most important news of the year was the announcement in early July that Namibia might have more than 10 billion tons of oil offshore, which would make it one of the largest oil producers on the continent.

**Internet resource:** <www.npc.gov.na/cbs/index.htm>.

# Nauru

**Official name:** Naoero (Republic of Nauru). **Form of government:** republic with one legislative house

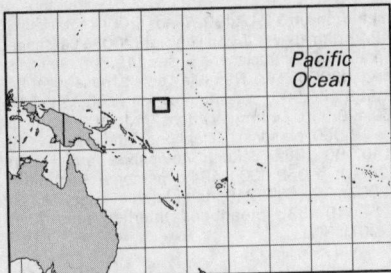

(Parliament [18]). **Head of state and government:** President Sprent Dabwido (from 2011). **Capital:** there is no official capital; government offices are located in Yaren district. **Official language:** none (Nauruan is the national language; English is the language of business and government). **Official religion:** none. **Monetary unit:** 1 Australian dollar ($A) = 100 cents; valuation (2 Jul 2012) US$1 = $A 0.98.

## Demography

**Area:** 8.2 sq mi, 21.2 sq km. **Population** (2011): 9,300. **Density** (2011): persons per sq mi 1,134.1, persons per sq km 438.7. **Urban** (2010): 100%. **Sex distribution** (2006): male 50.78%; female 49.22%. **Age breakdown** (2005): under 15, 37.5%; 15–29, 29.5%; 30–44, 17.8%; 45–59, 11.8%; 60–74, 3.1%; 75 and over, 0.3%. **Ethnic composition** (2006): Nauruan 95.8%; Kiribertese (Gilbertese) 1.5%; Asian 1.4%; other Pacific Islanders 0.3%; other/unknown 1.0%. **Religious affiliation** (2005): Protestant 49%, of which Congregational 29%; Roman Catholic 24%; Chinese folk-religionist 10%; other 17%. **Major cities:** none; population of Yaren urban area (2007) 4,616. **Location:** Oceania, island in the western Pacific Ocean, near the equator east of Papua New Guinea.

## Vital statistics

**Birth rate** per 1,000 population (2009): 29.8 (world avg. 20.3). **Death rate** per 1,000 population (2009): 9.0 (world avg. 8.5). **Total fertility rate** (avg. births per childbearing woman; 2007): 3.4. **Life expectancy** at birth (2008): male 52.5 years; female 58.2 years.

## National economy

**Budget** (2007). *Revenue:* $A 17,751,000 (grants 38.2%; property income 35.3%; sales of goods and services 13.1%; other taxes 13.4%). *Expenditures:* $A 21,769,000. *Total public and private debt* (July 2007): US$854,000,000. **Gross national income** (2008): US$34,933,000 (US$3,650 per capita). **Production** (metric tons except as noted). *Agriculture and fishing* (2007): coconuts 1,800, tropical fruit, coffee, almonds, figs, and pandanus (screw pine) are also cultivated; livestock (number of live animals) 2,900 pigs, 5,000 chickens; fisheries production 39 (from aquaculture, none). *Mining and quarrying* (2007): phosphate rock (gross weight)

45,000 (phosphate extraction, the backbone of the Nauruan economy, halted in 2003 but resumed in 2006; phosphate extraction is expected for the next 5 to 20 years using processing refurbishments). *Manufacturing* (2009): none; virtually all consumer manufactures are imported. *Energy production (consumption):* electricity (kW-hr; 2006) 33,000,000 (33,000,000); petroleum products (metric tons; 2006) none (46,000). **Population economically active** (2002): 3,280; activity rate of total population 32.6% (participation rates: ages 16 and over, 76.7%; female 45.5%; unemployed [2006] 26.7%). **Selected balance of payments data.** Receipts from (US$'000,000): foreign direct investment (2005–07 avg.) 0.67; official development assistance (2007) 26.

## Foreign trade

**Imports** (2005–06): $A 32,300,000 (unspecified [mostly personal material needs] 100%). *Major import sources* (2005): South Korea 48%; US 6%; Germany 5%. **Exports** (2005–06): $A 1,500,000 (phosphate and coral gravel, a by-product of phosphate extraction, virtually 100%). *Major export destinations* (2005): South Korea 30%; Canada 24%.

## Transport and communications

**Transport.** *Railroads* (2001): length 5 km. *Roads* (2004): total length 40 km (paved 73%). *Air transport* (2004): passenger-km 338,000,000; metric ton-km cargo (including weight of passengers and mail) 34,000,000. **Communications,** in total units (units per 1,000 persons). Telephone landlines (2008): 1,800 (188).

## Education and health

**Educational attainment** (2007). Percentage of population ages 15–49 and over having: incomplete/complete primary education 4%; incomplete secondary 71%; complete secondary 17%; more than secondary 8%. **Literacy** (2007): total population ages 15–49 literate 98%; males literate 96.1%; females literate 99.3%. **Health** (2008): physicians 10 (1 per 957 persons); hospital beds 51 (1 per 188 persons); infant mortality rate per 1,000 live births (2003–07) 37.9.

## Military

**Total active duty personnel** (2008): Nauru does not have any military establishment. Its defense is assured by Australia, but no formal agreement exists.

## Background

Nauru was inhabited by Pacific islanders when British explorers arrived in 1798. Annexed by Germany in 1888, in 1919 it was placed under a joint mandate of Britain, Australia, and New Zealand. During World War II it was occupied by the Japanese. Made a UN trust territory under Australian administration in 1947, it gained independence in 1968 and became a member of the Commonwealth and the UN in

---

*1 metric ton = about 1.1 short tons;    1 kilometer = 0.6 mi (statute);    1 metric ton-km cargo = about 0.68 short ton-mi cargo;    c.i.f.: cost, insurance, and freight;    f.o.b.: free on board*

1999. Nauru once had the world's largest concentration of phosphate and became wealthy from mining and processing it. The deposits have been severely depleted, however, and the economy has been converting to fishing activities.

## Recent Developments

By far the most prominent of Nauru's conservation efforts in 2011 was its participation in the expansion of the Nauru Agreement, which sought to protect tuna stocks in the Pacific Ocean. In January the eight partners to the agreement began enforcing quotas on the number of days a particular country's vessels could fish the protected waters and requiring payment for additional days.

**Internet resource:**
<www.naurugov.nr/pages/NBOS.html>.

# Nepal

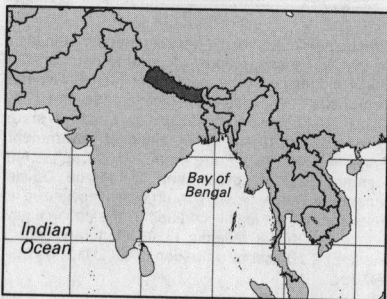

Bay of Bengal

Indian Ocean

**Official name:** Sanghiya Loktantrik Ganatantra Nepal (Federal Democratic Republic of Nepal). **Form of government:** multiparty republic with interim legislature (Constituent Assembly [601]). **Head of state:** President Ram Baran Yadav (from 2008). **Head of government:** Prime Minister Baburam Bhattarai (from 2011). **Capital:** Kathmandu. **Official language:** Nepali. **Official religion:** none. **Monetary unit:** 1 Nepalese rupee (NR; plural NRs) = 100 paisa; valuation (2 Jul 2012) US$1 = NRs 88.95.

## Demography

**Area:** 56,827 sq mi, 147,181 sq km. **Population** (2011): 26,629,000. **Density** (2011): persons per sq mi 468.6, persons per sq km 180.9. **Urban** (2006): 16.7%. **Sex distribution** (2007): male 50.10%; female 49.90%. **Age breakdown** (2005): under 15, 39.0%; 15–29, 27.9%; 30–44, 17.2%; 45–59, 10.2%; 60–74, 4.7%; 75–84, 0.9%; 85 and over, 0.1%. **Ethnic composition** (2000): Nepalese 55.8%; Maithili 10.8%; Bhojpuri 7.9%; Tharu 4.4%; Tamang 3.6%; Newar 3.0%; Awadhi 2.7%; Magar 2.5%; Gurkha 1.7%; other 7.6%. **Religious affiliation** (2001): Hindu 80.6%; Buddhist 10.7%; Muslim 4.2%; Kirat (local traditional belief) 3.6%; Christian 0.5%; other 0.4%. **Major cities** (2001): Kathmandu 671,846; Biratnagar 166,674; Lalitpur 162,991; Pokhara 156,312; Birganj 112,484. **Location:** south-central Asia, bordering China and India.

## Vital statistics

**Birth rate** per 1,000 population (2008): 27.7 (world avg. 20.3). **Death rate** per 1,000 population (2008): 8.3 (world avg. 8.5). **Total fertility rate** (avg. births per childbearing woman; 2007): 3.10. **Life expectancy** at birth (2008): male 63.6 years; female 64.5 years.

## National economy

**Budget** (2007–08). *Revenue:* NRs 104,865,300,000 (tax revenue 81.1%, of which VAT 28.4%, customs duties 20.1%, corporate taxes 12.6%; nontax revenue 18.9%). *Expenditures:* NRs 151,969,500,000 (current expenditures 64.6%, of which education 16.8%, defense 6.7%, health 6.1%; capital expenditures 35.4%). **Production** (metric tons except as noted). *Agriculture and fishing* (2008): rice 4,299,264, sugarcane 2,485,437, potatoes 2,054,817, ginger 176,602, mustard seed 134,286, garlic 32,317, jute 16,988; livestock (number of live animals) 8,135,880 goats, 7,090,714 cattle, 4,496,507 buffalo; fisheries production (2007) 46,779 (from aquaculture 57%). *Mining and quarrying* (2007): limestone 822,042; talc 9,043; marble 22,110 sq m. *Manufacturing* (value added in US$'000,000; 2002): food products 83; textiles and wearing apparel 73; tobacco products 55. *Energy production (consumption):* electricity (kW-hr; 2006) 2,684,000,000 (2,755,000,000); coal (metric tons; 2006) 11,963 (420,000); petroleum products (metric tons; 2006) none (645,000). **Gross national income** (2008): US$11,537,000,000 (US$400 per capita). **Population economically active** (2003): total 9,981,000; activity rate of total population 38.3% (participation rates: ages 15–64, 66.3%; female 41.0%; unofficially unemployed [2004] 42%). **Public debt** (external, outstanding; 2007): US$3,485,000,000. **Selected balance of payments data.** Receipts from (US$'000,000): tourism (2007) 200; remittances (2008) 2,735; foreign direct investment (2005–07 avg.) 0.3; official development assistance (2007) 598. Disbursements for (US$'000,000): tourism (2007) 274; remittances (2008) 4.

## Foreign trade

**Imports** (2006–07; c.i.f.): NRs 191,709,000,000 (basic manufactures [including fabrics, yarns, and wearing apparel] 24.8%; mineral fuels [mostly refined petroleum products] 19.0%; machinery and transportation equipment 18.6%; chemical products 13.5%). *Major import sources* (2006): India 48%; China 13%; UAE 12%; Saudi Arabia 5%; Kuwait 4%. **Exports** (2006–07; f.o.b.): NRs 60,796,000,000 (ready-made garments 9.8%; woolen carpets 9.2%; vegetable ghee 6.8%; thread 6.7%; zinc sheets 5.9%; textiles 5.0%; jute goods 4.5%). *Major export destinations* (2006): India 58%; US 14%; Germany 6%; UK 3%; France 2%.

## Transport and communications

**Transport.** *Railroads* (2006): route length 59 km; passengers carried (2002) 1,600,000; freight handled 22,000 metric tons. *Roads* (2007): total length 17,782 km (paved 30%). *Vehicles* (2007): passenger cars 93,266; trucks and buses 64,959. *Air transport:* passenger-km (2003) 652,000,000; metric ton-km cargo (2005) 7,000,000. **Communications**, in total units (units per 1,000 persons). Telephone landlines (2008): 805,000 (28); cellular telephone subscribers (2008): 4,200,000 (146); personal computers (2005): 132,000 (4.9); total Internet users (2008): 499,000 (17); broadband Internet subscribers (2007): 14,000 (0.5).

## Education and health

**Educational attainment** (2005–06). Percentage of population having: unknown through literate 15.4%; primary education 22.0%; secondary 44.0%; higher 18.6%. **Literacy** (2003–04): total population ages 15 and over literate 48.0%; males literate 64.5%; females literate 33.8%. **Health** (2006): physicians (public health system only) 1,259 (1 per 21,737 persons); hospital beds 9,881 (1 per 2,801 persons); infant mortality rate per 1,000 live births (2007) 48.0; undernourished population (2003–05) 4,000,000 (15% of total population based on the consumption of a minimum daily requirement of 1,760 calories).

## Military

**Total active duty personnel** (November 2008): 69,000 (army 100%). **Military expenditure as percentage of GDP** (2007): 2.1%; per capita expenditure US$6.

## Background

Nepal developed under early Buddhist influence, and dynastic rule dates from about the 4th century AD. It was formed into a single kingdom in 1769 and fought border wars with China, Tibet, and British India in the 18th–19th centuries. Its independence was recognized by Britain in 1923. A new constitution in 1990 restricted royal authority and accepted a democratically elected parliamentary government. The Communist Party of Nepal (Maoist) began an armed insurgency in 1996. Nepal signed trade agreements with India in 1997. On 1 Jun 2001, King Birendra, the queen, and seven other members of the royal family were fatally shot by Crown Prince Dipendra, who then turned the gun on himself. After a historic vote by a constituent assembly in 2008, the monarchy was abolished and Nepal became a multiparty republic.

## Recent Developments

In 2011 the peace process in Nepal came closer to completion following an agreement in November between the four major political parties: the Nepali Congress; Communist Party of Nepal (Unified Marxist-Leninist), or CPN (UML); Unified Communist Party of Nepal (Maoist), or UCPN-M; and Madheshi People's Rights Forum (Democratic). According to the agreement, some 6,500 former rebel combatants were to be integrated into the Nepali military, and other fighters who chose not to remain with the armed forces were to be provided with financial incentives. As well, a truth and reconciliation commission was set up under the agreement.

**Internet resource:** <www.cbs.gov.np>.

# Netherlands

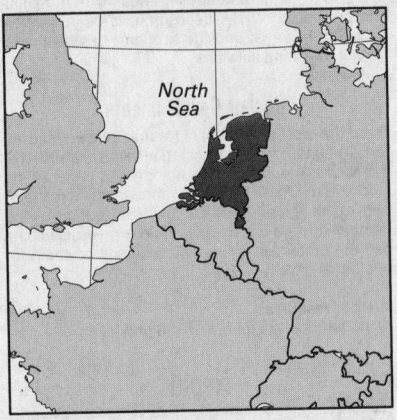

North Sea

**Official name:** Koninkrijk der Nederlanden (Kingdom of the Netherlands). **Form of government:** constitutional monarchy with a parliament (States General) comprising two legislative houses (Senate [75]; House of Representatives [150]). **Head of state:** Queen Beatrix (from 1980). **Head of government:** Prime Minister Mark Rutte (from 2010). **Capital:** Amsterdam. **Seat of government:** The Hague. **Official language:** Dutch (Frisian is officially recognized in Friesland but not legally codified by the national government). **Official religion:** none. **Monetary unit:** 1 euro (€) = 100 cents; valuation (2 Jul 2012) US$1 = €0.79.

## Demography

**Area:** 16,040 sq mi, 41,543 sq km. **Population** (2011): 16,683,000. **Density** (2011; based on land area): persons per sq mi 1,279.0, persons per sq km 493.8. **Urban** (2010): 82.9%. **Sex distribution** (2008): male 49.48%; female 50.52%. **Age breakdown** (2008): under 15, 17.7%; 15–29, 18.2%; 30–44, 21.5%; 45–59, 21.3%; 60–74, 14.5%; 75–84, 5.1%; 85 and over, 1.7%. **Ethnic composition** (by place of origin; 2008): Netherlander 80.0%; from EU countries 5.3%; Indonesian 2.3%; Turkish 2.3%; Surinamese 2.1%; Moroccan 2.1%; Netherlands Antillean/Aruban 0.8%; other 5.1%. **Religious affiliation** (2004): Roman Catholic 30%; Reformed/Lutheran tradition 20%; Muslim 6%; nonreligious/atheist 40%; other 4%. **Major urban agglomerations** (2007): Amsterdam 1,482,287; Rotterdam 1,169,800; The Hague 997,323; Utrecht 592,463; Haarlem 407,521. **Location:** northwestern Europe, bordering the North Sea, Germany, and Belgium.

## Vital statistics

**Birth rate** per 1,000 population (2008): 11.2 (world avg. 20.3); within marriage 58.8%. **Death rate** per 1,000 population (2008): 8.2 (world avg. 8.5). **Total fertility rate** (avg. births per childbearing woman; 2008): 1.77. **Life expectancy** at birth (2008): male 78.4 years; female 82.4 years.

*1 metric ton = about 1.1 short tons;    1 kilometer = 0.6 mi (statute);    1 metric ton-km cargo = about 0.68 short ton-mi cargo;    c.i.f.: cost, insurance, and freight;    f.o.b.: free on board*

## National economy

**Budget** (2007). *Revenue:* €261,628,000,000 (social security contributions 31.3%; indirect taxes 28.3%; direct taxes 26.0%; nontax revenue 7.3%; sales tax 7.1%). *Expenditures:* €259,526,000,000 (current expenditures 92.3%, of which social security and welfare 45.3%; development expenditures 7.7%). **Production** (metric tons except as noted). *Agriculture and fishing* (2007): potatoes 7,200,000, sugar beets 5,400,000, wheat 990,000; flowering bulbs and tubers 80,000 acres (32,400 hectares), of which tulips 27,200 acres (11,000 hectares), cut flowers and plants under glass 10,900 acres (4,400 hectares); livestock (number of live animals) 11,663,000 pigs, 3,763,000 cattle, 1,369,000 sheep; fisheries production 470,363 (from aquaculture 12%). *Mining:* limestone, n.a. *Manufacturing* (value added in €'000,000; 2008): food products, beverages, and tobacco products 16,198; refined petroleum products 8,094; base chemical products and man-made fibers 7,975. *Energy production (consumption):* electricity (kW-hr; 2008) 107,645,000,000 ([2006] 118,192,000,000); coal (metric tons; 2008) none ([2006] 12,683,000); crude petroleum (barrels; 2008) 12,200,000 ([2006] 357,600,000); petroleum products (metric tons; 2006) 61,361,000 (25,334,000); natural gas (cu m; 2008) 79,771,-000,000 ([2006] 50,416,000,000). **Gross national income** (2008): US$824,636,000,000 (US$50,150 per capita). **Public debt** (December 2008): US$392,000,000,000. **Population economically active** (2005): total 8,308,000; activity rate of total population 51% (participation rates: ages 15–64, 75.1%; female 45.1%; unemployed [April 2008–March 2009] 2.8%). **Selected balance of payments data.** Receipts from (US$'000,000): tourism (2007) 13,339; remittances (2008) 3,006; foreign direct investment (FDI; 2005–07 avg.) 51,705. Disbursements for (US$'000,000): tourism (2007) 19,110; remittances (2008) 8,431; FDI (2005–07 avg.) 71,354.

## Foreign trade

**Imports** (2007; c.i.f.): €307,851,000,000 (machinery and apparatus 25.7%, of which office machines, computers, and parts 8.7%; mineral fuels 13.6%, of which crude petroleum 7.0%; chemical products 12.1%; food products 7.0%; motor vehicles 5.4%). *Major import sources:* Germany 20.1%; Belgium 10.8%; China 8.6%; US 7.9%; UK 6.4%. **Exports** (2007; f.o.b.): €348,964,000,000 (machinery and apparatus 26.3%, of which office machines, computers, and parts 8.3%; nonelectrical machinery and equipment 7.3%; chemical products 15.2%; food products 9.8%; refined petroleum products 8.0%). *Major export destinations:* Germany 23.6%; Belgium 11.9%; UK 9.1%; France 8.2%; US 5.0%.

## Transport and communications

**Transport.** *Railroads* (2006): length 2,797 km; passenger-km (2004) 14,097,000,000; metric ton-km cargo (2001) 4,293,000,000. *Roads* (2006): total length 134,981 km (paved 90%). *Vehicles* (2006): passenger cars 7,230,178; trucks and buses 1,064,846. *Air transport* (2007): passenger-km 75,012,000,000; metric ton-km cargo 4,735,-500,000. **Communications**, in total units (units per 1,000 persons). Telephone landlines (2008): 7,324,000 (446); cellular telephone subscribers (2008): 19,927,000 (1,212); personal computers (2007): 14,934,000 (912); total Internet users (2008): 14,273,000 (868); broadband Internet subscribers (2008): 5,756,000 (350).

## Education and health

**Educational attainment** (2007). Percentage of population ages 25–64 having: primary/lower secondary education 27%; upper secondary 39%; higher vocational 2%; university 29%; other 3%. **Health:** physicians (2005) 60,519 (1 per 270 persons); hospital beds (2006) 48,000 (1 per 340 persons); infant mortality rate per 1,000 live births (2008) 3.8.

## Military

**Total active duty personnel** (November 2008): 40,537 (army 53.0%, navy 23.4%, air force 23.6%). **Military expenditure as percentage of GDP** (2007): 1.5%; per capita expenditure US$700.

## Background

Celtic and Germanic tribes inhabited the Netherlands at the time of the Roman conquest. Under the Romans, trade and industry flourished, but by the mid-3rd century AD Roman power had waned, eroded by resurgent German tribes and the encroachment of the sea. A Germanic invasion (406–07) ended Roman control. The Merovingian dynasty followed the Romans but was supplanted in the 7th century by the Carolingian dynasty, which converted the area to Christianity. After Charlemagne's death in 814, the area was increasingly the target of Viking attacks. It became part of the kingdom of Lotharingia, which established an Imperial Church. In the 12th–14th centuries dike building occurred on a large scale. The dukes of Burgundy gained control in the late 14th century. By the early 16th century the Low Countries were ruled by the Spanish Habsburgs. In 1581 the seven northern provinces, led by Calvinists, declared their independence from Spain, and in 1648, following the Thirty Years' War, Spain recognized Dutch independence. The 17th century was the golden age of Dutch civilization. The Dutch East India Company secured Asian colonies, and the country's standard of living soared. In the 18th century the region was conquered by the French and became the Kingdom of Holland under Napoleon (1806). It remained neutral in World War I and declared neutrality in World War II but was occupied by Germany. It joined NATO in 1949, was a founding member of what is now the European Community, and is part of the EU. At the outset of the 21st century the Netherlands benefitted from a strong, highly regulated mixed economy but struggled with the social and economic challenges of immigration.

## Recent Developments

In 2011, the Netherlands avoided massive unemployment and drastic increases in bankruptcies, despite the worldwide economic crisis. The government kept a watchful eye on the European debt crisis and on international developments, recognizing that the Dutch dependence on international trade made the country vulnerable to fluctuations in the world economy. The Netherlands, which ranked 60th in the world by population, had the 16th largest economy and the 8th biggest financial sector and was ranked 5th among investor countries worldwide. Prime Minister Mark Rutte's right-center government announced substantial budget cuts. Before year's end there were plans for additional cuts, including steep progressive cost increases to individuals for health care benefits. The government also announced rollbacks for some government regulations, such as environmental protections, stating that these changes would permit innovation and economic growth. In addition, it acknowledged that the retirement age would need to be raised in the future.

Internet resource: <www.cbs.nl>.

# New Zealand

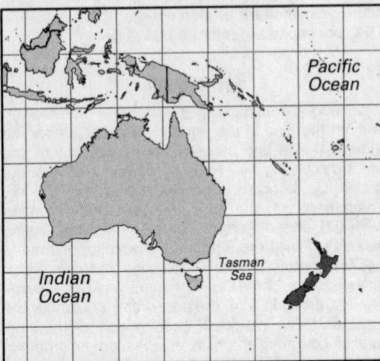

**Official name:** New Zealand (English); Aotearoa (Maori). **Form of government:** constitutional monarchy with one legislative house (House of Representatives [121; statutory number is 120 seats]). **Head of state:** British Queen Elizabeth II (from 1952), represented by Governor-General Sir Jerry Mateparae (from 2011). **Head of government:** Prime Minister John Key (from 2008). **Capital:** Wellington. **Official languages:** English; Maori; New Zealand Sign Language. **Official religion:** none. **Monetary unit:** 1 New Zealand dollar (NZ$) = 100 cents; valuation (2 Jul 2012) US$1 = NZ$1.25.

## Demography

**Area:** 104,515 sq mi, 270,692 sq km. **Population** (2011): 4,407,000. **Density** (2011): persons per sq mi 42.2, persons per sq km 16.3. **Urban** (2010): 86.0%. **Sex distribution** (2006): male 48.96%; female 51.04%. **Age breakdown** (2006): under 15, 21.1%; 15–29, 20.8%; 30–44, 21.8%; 45–59, 19.5%; 60–74, 11.2%; 75 and over, 5.6%. **Ethnic composition** (2006): European 67.6%; Maori (local Polynesian) 14.6%; Asian 9.2%, of which Chinese 3.7%; other Pacific peoples (mostly other Polynesian) 6.9%; other 1.7%. **Religious affiliation** (2006): Chris-

tian 51.1%, of which Anglican 13.3%, Roman Catholic 12.2%, Presbyterian 9.2%, Methodist 2.9%, Maori (indigenous) Christian 1.6%; Hindu 1.6%; Buddhist 1.3%; Muslim 1.0%; nonreligious 31.1%; other 1.0%; unknown 12.9%. **Major urban agglomerations** (2008): Auckland 1,313,200; Christchurch 382,200; Wellington 381,900; Hamilton 197,300; Napier 122,600. **Location:** Oceania, islands between the South Pacific Ocean and the Tasman Sea, southeast of Australia.

## Vital statistics

**Birth rate** per 1,000 population (2008): 15.1 (world avg. 20.3); within marriage 51.9%. **Death rate** per 1,000 population (2008): 6.8 (world avg. 8.5). **Total fertility rate** (avg. births per childbearing woman; 2008): 2.18. **Life expectancy** at birth (2006): male 78.0 years; female 82.2 years.

## National economy

**Budget** (2007). *Revenue:* NZ$65,859,000,000 (tax revenue 85.3%, of which income tax 41.3%; nontax revenue 14.5%; social contributions 0.2%). *Expenditures:* NZ$60,247,000,000 (social protection 33.9%; education 16.7%; health 16.7%; defense 3.2%). **Production** (metric tons except as noted). *Agriculture and fishing* (2007): potatoes 505,000, barley 400,000, apples 380,000, kiwifruit 315,000, grapes 190,000; livestock (number of live animals) 40,000,000 sheep, 9,650,000 cattle; fisheries production 600,868 (from aquaculture 19%); aquatic plants 192 (from aquaculture, none). *Mining and quarrying* (2007): limestone and marl 5,092,000; gold 10,762 kg; silver 10,568 kg. *Manufacturing* (value added in US$'000,000; 2005): food products 4,175; fabricated metal products 1,350; printing and publishing 1,250. *Energy production (consumption):* electricity (kW-hr; 2007–08) 42,728,000,000 ([2006] 37,390,000,000); coal (metric tons; 2007–08) 2,178,000 ([2006] 196,000); lignite (metric tons; 2007–08) 2,855,000 ([2006] 4,783,000); crude petroleum (barrels; 2007–08) 20,607,500 ([2006] 35,016,-000); petroleum products (metric tons; 2007–08) 5,187,000 ([2006] 6,026,000); natural gas (cu m; 2007–08) 4,290,200,000 ([2006] 3,700,-000,000). **Population economically active** (2007): total 2,235,400; activity rate 52.8% (participation rates: ages 15–64, 76.9%; female 46.3%; unemployed [July 2007–June 2008] 3.6%). **Gross national income** (2008): US$119,246,000,000 (US$27,940 per capita). **Selected balance of payments data.** Receipts from (US$'000,000): tourism (2007) 5,406; remittances (2008) 626; foreign direct investment (FDI; 2005–07 avg.) 4,163. Disbursements for (US$'000,000): tourism (2007) 3,066; remittances (2008) 1,202; FDI (2005–07 avg.) 961.

## Foreign trade

**Imports** (2006; c.i.f.): NZ$40,774,000,000 (machinery and apparatus 21.4%; mineral fuels 14.9%; motor vehicles 11.7%; aircraft 4.2%; plastic products 3.8%). *Major import sources:* Australia 20.1%; China 12.2%; US 12.1%; Japan

*1 metric ton = about 1.1 short tons;    1 kilometer = 0.6 mi (statute);    1 metric ton-km cargo = about 0.68 short ton-mi cargo;    c.i.f.: cost, insurance, and freight;    f.o.b.: free on board*

9.1%; Germany 4.4%. **Exports** (2006; f.o.b.): NZ$34,619,000,000 (dairy products 20.6%; beef and sheep meat 12.1%; wood and paper products 9.4%; machinery and apparatus 8.6%; aluminum 4.3%; fish 3.7%; fruit 3.7%). *Major export destinations:* Australia 20.5%; US 13.1%; Japan 10.3%; China 5.4%; UK 4.9%.

## Transport and communications

**Transport.** *Railroads* (2006): route length 4,128 km; metric ton-km cargo (1999–2000) 4,040,000,000. *Roads* (2007): total length 93,748 km (paved 65%). *Vehicles* (2007): passenger cars 2,775,717; trucks and buses 558,412. *Air transport* (2007; Air New Zealand only): passenger-km 28,423,000,000; metric ton-km cargo 906,000,000. **Communications,** in total units (units per 1,000 persons). Telephone landlines (2008): 1,750,000 (414); cellular telephone subscribers (2008): 4,620,000 (1,092); personal computers (2005): 2,077,000 (507); total Internet users (2008): 3,047,000 (720); broadband Internet subscribers (2008): 915,000 (216).

## Education and health

**Educational attainment** (2007). Percentage of population ages 15 and over having: no formal schooling to incomplete primary education 26.8%; primary 9.0%; vocational 29.8%; secondary 15.0%; higher 19.4%. **Literacy:** virtually 100%. **Health:** physicians (2006) 9,547 (1 per 434 persons); hospital beds (2002) 23,825 (1 per 165 persons); infant mortality rate per 1,000 live births (2008) 5.0; undernourished population (2002–04) less than 2.5% of total population.

## Military

**Total active duty personnel** (November 2008): 9,278 (army 51.2%, navy 21.8%, air force 27.0%). **Military expenditure as percentage of GDP** (2008): 1.1%; per capita expenditure US$286.

## Background

Polynesian occupation of New Zealand dates to about AD 1000. First sighted by Dutch explorer Abel Janszoon Tasman in 1642, the main islands were charted by Capt. James Cook in 1769. Named a British crown colony in 1840, the area was the scene of warfare between colonists and native Maori through the 1860s. In 1907 the colony became the Dominion of New Zealand. It administered Western Samoa during 1919–62 and participated in both world wars. New Zealand took a strong stand against nuclear proliferation, since the mid-1980s banning nuclear-powered ships or those carrying nuclear weapons from its waters. There has been a revival of traditional Maori culture and art, and Maori social and economic activism have been central to political developments in the country since the late 20th century.

## Recent Developments

Earthquakes and their aftermaths dominated the events of 'New Zealand in 2011. Following Christchurch's 7.1-magnitude earthquake on 4 Sep 2010, the city sustained months of aftershocks; the strongest of them (magnitude 6.3) struck on 22 Feb 2011, causing more than 180 fatalities, ravaging the central business district, and rendering thousands of residences uninhabitable. Prime Minister John Key declared a state of national emergency in the quake area. Thousands of additional aftershocks, some exceeding magnitude 5.5, were recorded through the end of the year. The Reserve Bank of New Zealand estimated the cost to rebuild the city at NZ$20 billion (US$17 billion), equal to 10% of GDP. In March 2012, it was announced that because of additional damage it had sustained in the aftershocks, the Anglican cathedral was beyond repair and would be demolished.

**Internet resource:** <www.stats.govt.nz>.

# Nicaragua

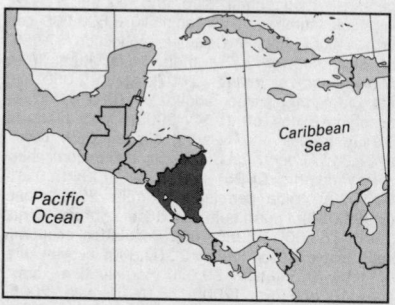

**Official name:** República de Nicaragua (Republic of Nicaragua). **Form of government:** unitary multiparty republic with one legislative house (National Assembly [92]). **Head of state and government:** President Daniel Ortega (from 2007). **Capital:** Managua. **Official language:** Spanish. **Official religion:** none. **Monetary unit:** 1 córdoba (C$) = 100 centavos; valuation (2 Jul 2012) US$1 = C$23.55.

## Demography

**Area:** 50,337 sq mi, 130,373 sq km; land area alone equals 46,464 sq mi, 120,340 sq km. **Population** (2011): 5,870,000. **Density** (2011; based on land area): persons per sq mi 126.3, persons per sq km 48.8. **Urban** (2005): 55.9%. **Sex distribution** (2008): male 50.03%; female 49.97%. **Age breakdown** (2008): under 15, 34.6%; 15–29, 31.3%; 30–44, 19.3%; 45–59, 9.8%; 60–74, 3.1%; 75–84, 0.9%; 85 and over, 1.0%. **Ethnic composition** (2000): mestizo (Spanish/Indian) 63.1%; white 14.0%; black 8.0%; multiple ethnicities 5.0%; other 9.9%. **Religious affiliation** (2005): Roman Catholic 58.5%; Protestant/independent Christian 23.2%, of which Evangelical 21.6%, Moravian 1.6%; nonreligious 15.7%; other 2.6%. **Major cities** (2005): Managua 908,892; León 139,433; Chinandega 95,614; Masaya 92,598; Estelí 90,294. **Location:** Central America, bordering Honduras, the Caribbean Sea, Costa Rica, and the North Pacific Ocean.

## Vital statistics

**Birth rate** per 1,000 population (2008): 23.7 (world avg. 20.3). **Death rate** per 1,000 population (2008):

4.3 (world avg. 8.5). **Total fertility rate** (avg. births per childbearing woman; 2008): 2.63. **Life expectancy** at birth (2008): male 69.1 years; female 73.4 years.

## National economy

**Budget** (2008). *Revenue:* US$1,209,700,000 (tax revenue 92.6%, of which taxes on goods and services 32.7%, taxes on international trade 30.0%, taxes on income and profits 29.8%; nontax revenue 7.4%). *Expenditures:* US$1,641,600,000 (education 20.7%; health 14.4%; economic services 14.4%; defense and public order 11.4%). **Public debt** (external, outstanding; 2007): US$2,144,-000,000. **Production** (metric tons except as noted). *Agriculture and fishing* (2007): sugarcane 4,875,000, corn (maize) 569,948, rice 302,697, peanuts (groundnuts) 116,682, coffee 81,818; livestock (number of live animals) 3,600,000 cattle, 268,000 horses; fisheries production 37,959, of which lobster 3,752 (from aquaculture 30%). *Mining and quarrying* (2007): gold 2,059 kg. *Manufacturing* (value added in C$'000,000 in constant prices of 1994; 2003): food products 1,917; textiles and wearing apparel 969; beverages 713. *Energy production (consumption):* electricity (kW-hr; 2006) 2,958,000,000 (3,011,-000,000); crude petroleum (barrels; 2006) none (5,989,000); petroleum products (metric tons; 2006) 763,000 (1,286,000). **Population economically active** (2006): total 2,204,300; activity rate of total population 39.9% (participation rates: ages 10 and over [2005] 55.0%; female [2005] 35.2%; officially unemployed [2008] 6.1%). **Gross national income** (2008): US$6,126,000,000 (US$1,080 per capita). **Selected balance of payments data.** Receipts from (US$'000,000): tourism (2007) 255; remittances (2008) 818; foreign direct investment (FDI; 2005–07 avg.) 279; official development assistance (2007) 834. Disbursements for (US$'000,000): tourism (2007) 121; FDI (2005–07 avg.) 16.

## Foreign trade

**Imports** (2006; c.i.f.): US$2,741,000,000 (chemical products 16.7%; machinery and apparatus 15.6%; crude petroleum 13.2%; refined petroleum products 10.8%; food products 9.7%). *Major import sources:* US 22.8%; Mexico 14.8%; China 7.6%; Venezuela 6.8%; Costa Rica 5.4%. **Exports** (2006; f.o.b.): US$759,000,000 (coffee 26.4%; cattle meat 10.3%; crustaceans 9.3%; gold 7.7%; raw sugar 6.6%; peanuts [groundnuts] 5.2%). *Major export destinations:* US 46.5%; Mexico 6.2%; Canada 6.0%; Spain 4.5%; Honduras 4.4%.

## Transport and communications

**Transport.** *Railroads* (2004): 6 km. *Roads* (2004): total length 18,669 km (paved [2002] 11%). *Vehicles* (2007): passenger cars 101,899; trucks and buses 187,526. *Air transport* (2000): passenger-km 72,200,000; metric ton-km cargo (2003) 200,000. **Communications,** in total units (units per 1,000 persons). Telephone landlines (2008): 312,000

(55); cellular telephone subscribers (2008): 3,039,000 (536); personal computers (2005): 220,000 (43); total Internet users (2008): 185,000 (33); broadband Internet subscribers (2006): 19,000 (3.6).

## Education and health

**Educational attainment** (2005). Percentage of population ages 10 and over having: no formal schooling/unknown 20.5%; 1–3 years 16.6%; 4–6 years 27.0%; 7–9 years 16.1%; 10–12 years 10.5%; vocational 2.3%; incomplete university 2.6%; complete university 4.4%. **Literacy** (2005): total population ages 15 and over literate 78.0%; males literate 78.1%; females literate 77.9%. **Health** (2003): physicians 2,076 (1 per 2,538 persons); hospital beds 5,030 (1 per 1,047 persons); infant mortality rate per 1,000 live births (2005) 26.4; undernourished population (2003–05) 1,200,000 (22% of total population based on the consumption of a minimum daily requirement of 1,770 calories).

## Military

**Total active duty personnel** (November 2008): 12,000 (army 83.3%, navy 6.7%, air force 10.0%). **Military expenditure as percentage of GDP** (2008): 0.6%; per capita expenditure US$7.

## Background

Nicaragua has been inhabited for thousands of years, most notably by the Maya. Christopher Columbus arrived in 1502, and Spanish explorers discovered Lake Nicaragua soon thereafter. Nicaragua was governed by Spain until 1821, when it declared its independence. It was part of Mexico and then the United Provinces of Central America until 1838, when full independence was achieved. The US intervened in political affairs by maintaining troops there in 1912–33. Ruled by the dictatorial Somoza dynasty from 1936 to 1979, it was taken over by the Sandinistas after a popular revolt. They were opposed by armed insurgents, the US-backed contras, from 1981. The Sandinista government nationalized several sectors of the economy. They lost the national elections in 1990, but Sandinista leader Daniel Ortega returned to power after winning the presidential election of 2006.

## Recent Developments

Despite the ongoing global economic downturn, GDP in Nicaragua was estimated to grow by 4% in 2011. The country experienced strong investment in the energy, manufacturing, mining, and tourism sectors. Moreover, the Inter-American Development Bank authorized approximately US$220 million in loans to Nicaragua for infrastructure development and poverty reduction. Aid of approximately US$500 million from Venezuela, under the auspices of Pres. Hugo Chávez's Bolivarian Alliance for the Peoples of Our America, helped Pres. Daniel Ortega's government make significant investments in food security, housing, education, and health care. High unemploy-

---

*1 metric ton = about 1.1 short tons;*    *1 kilometer = 0.6 mi (statute);*    *1 metric ton-km cargo = about 0.68 short ton-mi cargo;*    *c.i.f.: cost, insurance, and freight;*    *f.o.b.: free on board*

ment (over 7%) and persistent poverty, however, continued to promote emigration and dampen consumer demand.

Internet resource:
<www.visitanicaragua.com/ingles>.

# Niger

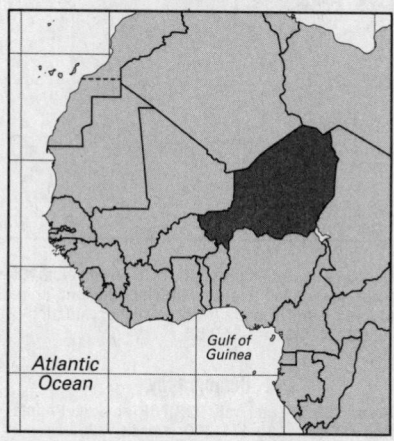

Atlantic Ocean

Gulf of Guinea

**Official name:** République du Niger (Republic of Niger). **Form of government:** republic with one legislative house (National Assembly [113]). **Head of state:** President Mahamadou Issoufou (from 2011). **Head of government:** Prime Minister Brigi Rafini (from 2011). **Capital:** Niamey. **Official language:** French. **Official religion:** none. **Monetary unit:** 1 CFA franc (CFAF) = 100 centimes; valuation (2 Jul 2012) US$1 = CFAF 521.26.

## Demography

**Area:** 489,191 sq mi, 1,267,000 sq km. **Population** (2011): 16,469,000. **Density** (2011): persons per sq mi 33.7, persons per sq km 13.0. **Urban** (2009): 19.8%. **Sex distribution** (2008): male 50.02%; female 49.98%. **Age breakdown** (2008): under 15, 49.6%; 15–29, 25.6%; 30–44, 13.7%; 45–59, 7.2%; 60–74, 3.3%; 75 and over, 0.6%. **Ethnolinguistic composition** (2001): Hausa 55.4%; Zarma-Songhai-Dendi 21.0%; Tuareg 9.3%; Fulani (Peul) 8.5%; Kanuri 4.7%; other 1.1%. **Religious affiliation** (2005): Muslim 90%, of which Sunni 85%, Shiʻi 5%; traditional beliefs 9%; other 1%. **Major cities** (2001): Niamey 707,951 (urban agglomeration [2007] 915,000); Zinder 170,575; Maradi 148,017; Agadez 78,289; Tahoua 73,002. **Location:** western Africa, bordering Algeria, Libya, Chad, Nigeria, Benin, Burkina Faso, and Mali.

## Vital statistics

**Birth rate** per 1,000 population (2008): 52.2 (world avg. 20.3). **Death rate** per 1,000 population (2008): 15.2 (world avg. 8.5). **Total fertility rate** (avg. births per childbearing woman; 2008): 7.83. **Life ex-**

**pectancy** at birth (2008): male 51.0 years; female 53.4 years.

## National economy

**Budget** (2008). *Revenue:* CFAF 584,100,000,000 (tax revenue 48.1%; nontax revenue 27.2%; external aid and grants 24.3%; other 0.4%). *Expenditures:* CFAF 546,000,000,000 (current expenditures 53.1%, of which wages and salaries 15.3%; capital expenditures 46.9%). **Public debt** (external, outstanding; 2008): US$795,000,000. **Selected balance of payments data.** Receipts from (US$'000,000): tourism (2007) 37; remittances (2008) 78; foreign direct investment (2005–07 avg.) 36; official development assistance (2007) 542. Disbursements for (US$'000,000): tourism (2007) 30; remittances (2008) 29; foreign direct disinvestment (2005–07 avg.) −2. **Gross national income** (2008): US$4,823,000,000 (US$330 per capita). **Production** (metric tons except as noted). *Agriculture and fishing* (2008): millet 3,489,400, cowpeas 1,548,000, sorghum 1,311,100, dry onions 373,600, pimento 25,800; livestock (number of live animals) 12,641,500 goats, 10,191,400 sheep, 8,737,400 cattle, 1,630,500 camels; fisheries production (2007) 29,768 (from aquaculture, negligible). *Mining and quarrying* (2008): uranium 2,993; salt (2007) 1,300; gold 2,314 kg. *Manufacturing* (value added in CFAF '000,000; 2008): food products 6,797; paper products, printing, and publishing 2,604; soaps and other chemical products 1,625. *Energy production (consumption):* electricity (kW-hr; 2006) 179,000,000 (535,000,000); coal (metric tons; 2008) 182,912 ([2006] 183,000); petroleum products (metric tons; 2006) none (138,000). **Population economically active** (2006): total 6,139,000; activity rate of total population 42.6% (participation rates: ages 16 and over, 83.5%; female 41.9%).

## Foreign trade

**Imports** (2008): CFAF 501,605,000,000 (food products 25.1%; refined petroleum products 15.5%; machinery and apparatus 15.1%; chemical products 14.9%; transportation equipment 6.8%). *Major import sources:* France 13.7%; China 13.3%; Netherlands 7.6%; US 7.4%; Nigeria 4.9%. **Exports** (2008): CFAF 316,412,000,000 (uranium 62.6%; livestock 23.7%, of which cattle 9.5%; gold 5.6%; onions 4.2%). *Major export destinations:* France 36.8%; Nigeria 25.0%; US 14.2%; Japan 10.4%; Switzerland 5.6%.

## Transport and communications

**Transport.** *Railroads:* none. *Roads* (2008): total length 18,949 km (paved 21%). *Vehicles* (2005): passenger cars 21,360. *Air transport* (2007; Niamey airport only): passenger arrivals 64,904, passenger departures 60,297; cargo unloaded 1,394 metric tons, cargo loaded 149 metric tons. **Communications,** in total units (units per 1,000 persons). Telephone landlines (2008): 65,000 (4.4); cellular telephone subscribers (2008): 1,898,000 (129); personal computers (2005): 10,000 (0.8); total Internet users (2008): 80,000 (5.4); broadband Internet subscribers (2008): 600 (0.04).

## Education and health

**Educational attainment** (2006; Niamey only). Percentage of population ages 25 and over having: no formal schooling/unknown 86.2%; incomplete primary education 6.9%; complete primary 1.0%; incomplete secondary 3.7%; complete secondary 0.4%; higher 0.9%. **Literacy** (2007–08): total population ages 15 and over literate 29.0%; males literate 42.8%; females literate 17.1%. **Health** (2008): physicians (public health institutions only) 427 (1 per 34,548 persons); hospital beds (2007) 2,934 (1 per 4,845 persons); infant mortality rate per 1,000 live births 118.9; undernourished population (2002–04) 3,900,000 (32% of total population based on the consumption of a minimum daily requirement of 1,800 calories).

## Military

**Total active duty personnel** (November 2008): 5,300 (army 98.1%, air force 1.9%). **Military expenditure as percentage of GDP** (2007): 1.0%; per capita expenditure US$3.

## Background

In the territory of Niger, there is evidence of Neolithic culture, and several kingdoms existed there before the colonialists arrived. First explored by Europeans in the late 18th century, it became a French colony in 1922. It became an overseas territory of France in 1946 and gained independence in 1960. The first multiparty elections were held in 1993.

## Recent Developments

In the March 2011 runoff presidential election in Niger, longtime opposition leader Mahamadou Issoufou was victorious. International observers praised the transparency and conduct of the poll. The peaceful transition to democracy was completed in April, when Issoufou took the oath of office. In June most international donors who had frozen development funds announced the resumption of aid programs for Niger. Tens of thousands of Nigeriens who had been working in Libya fled after a revolt against Libyan leader Muammar al-Qaddafi began in February. Nearly 65,000 resided in refugee camps in Niger around the city of Agadez. By August thousands of Qaddafi's African mercenaries were flooding out of Libya into Niger. In November Niger became Africa's newest producer of oil as its first refinery came online, fed by Niger's Agadem oil field. In March 2012, the government signed an agreement to ship petroleum through Chad to a port in Cameroon.

**Internet resource:** <www.stat-niger.org>.

# Nigeria

**Official name:** Federal Republic of Nigeria. **Form of government:** federal republic with two legislative houses (Senate [109]; House of Representatives [360]). **Head of state and government:** President

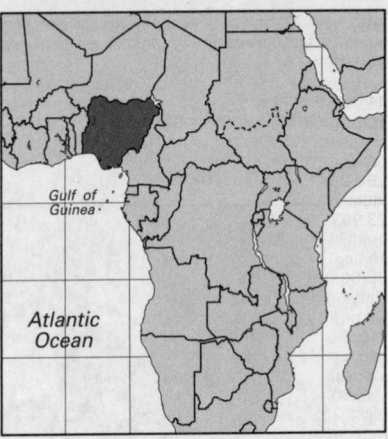

Goodluck Jonathan (from 2010). **Capital:** Abuja. **Official language:** English. **Official religion:** none. **Monetary unit:** 1 naira (N) = 100 kobo; valuation (2 Jul 2012) US$1 = N162.55.

## Demography

**Area:** 356,669 sq mi, 923,768 sq km. **Population** (2011): 162,471,000. **Density** (2011): persons per sq mi 455.5, persons per sq km 175.9. **Urban** (2009): 49.1%. **Sex distribution** (2006): male 50.80%; female 49.20%. **Age breakdown** (2005): under 15, 43.1%; 15–29, 28.2%; 30–44, 15.3%; 45–59, 8.6%; 60–74, 4.0%; 75–84, 0.7%; 85 and over, 0.1%. **Ethnic composition** (2000): Yoruba 17.5%; Hausa 17.2%; Igbo (Ibo) 13.3%; Fulani 10.7%; Ibibio 4.1%; Kanuri 3.6%; Egba 2.9%; Tiv 2.6%; Igbira 1.1%; Nupe 1.0%; Edo 1.0%; Ijo 0.8%; detribalized 0.9%; other 23.3%. **Religious affiliation** (2003): Muslim (predominantly Sunni) 50.5%; Christian 48.2%, of which Protestant 15.0%, Roman Catholic 13.7%, other (mostly independent Christian) 19.5%; other 1.3%. **Major urban agglomerations** (2007): Lagos 9,466,000; Kano 3,140,000; Ibadan 2,628,000; Abuja 1,576,000; Kaduna 1,442,000. **Location:** western Africa, bordering Niger, Chad, Cameroon, the Atlantic Ocean, and Benin.

## Vital statistics

**Birth rate** per 1,000 population (2007): 39.9 (world avg. 20.3). **Death rate** per 1,000 population (2007): 16.8 (world avg. 8.5). **Total fertility rate** (avg. births per childbearing woman; 2007): 5.30. **Life expectancy** at birth (2007): male 46.4 years; female 47.3 years.

## National economy

**Budget** (2008; federal budget). *Revenue:* N2,411,000,000,000 (petroleum revenue 83.3%, of which tax on profits and royalties 39.8%; nonpetroleum revenue 16.7%, of which corporate

---

*1 metric ton = about 1.1 short tons;*    *1 kilometer = 0.6 mi (statute);*    *1 metric ton-km cargo = about 0.68 short ton-mi cargo;*    *c.i.f.: cost, insurance, and freight;*    *f.o.b.: free on board*

taxes 6.3%). *Expenditures:* N2,451,000,000,000 (current expenditures 65.3%; capital expenditures 34.7%). **Production** (metric tons except as noted). *Agriculture and fishing* (2007): cassava 45,750,000, yams 37,150,000, sorghum 10,500,000, peanuts (groundnuts) 3,835,600, cowpeas 3,150,000, cashews 660,000, cacao beans 500,000, melon seeds 488,500, ginger 138,000, sesame seeds 100,000; livestock (number of live animals) 28,583,000 goats, 23,993,500 sheep, 16,258,560 cattle; fisheries production 615,507 (from aquaculture 14%). *Mining and quarrying* (2007): limestone 3,300,000; marble 200,000. *Manufacturing* (value added in N'000,000; 2008): refined petroleum products 44,297; cement 18,036; other unspecified (particularly food products, beverages, and textiles) 543,259. *Energy production (consumption):* electricity (kW-hr; 2006) 23,110,000,000 (23,110,000,000); coal (metric tons; 2007) 530,000 ([2006] 8,000); crude petroleum (barrels; 2008) 767,700,000 ([2006] 43,800,000); petroleum products (metric tons; 2006) 5,319,000 (10,344,000); natural gas (cu m; 2007) 46,046,000,000 ([2006] 10,730,-000,000). **Gross national income** (2008): US$175,622,000,000 (US$1,160 per capita). **Public debt** (external, outstanding; December 2008): US$3,704,000,000. **Population economically active** (2006): total 44,112,000; activity rate 30.5% (participation rates: ages 15–64, 55.5%; female 35.5%; unofficially unemployed [2007] 60%). **Selected balance of payments data.** Receipts from (US$'000,000): tourism (2007) 215; remittances (2008) 9,980; foreign direct investment (FDI; 2005–07 avg.) 10,463; official development assistance (2007) 2,042. Disbursements for (US$'000,000): tourism (2007) 2,444; remittances (2008) 103; FDI (2005–07 avg.) 230.

## Foreign trade

**Imports** (2008): N4,991,000,000,000 (basic manufactures 33.0%; chemical products 25.0%; machinery and transportation equipment 22.0%; food products and live animals 6.0%). *Major import sources* (nonpetroleum imports only [81.6% of all imports]): US 14.4%; China 10.5%; France 9.4%; UK 7.9%; Netherlands 7.4%. **Exports** (2008): N9,495,000,000,000 (crude petroleum 92.2%; other petroleum sector 6.8%; cacao beans 0.3%). *Major export destinations* (crude petroleum exports only): US 23.0%; Spain 9.3%; China 6.0%; Brazil 5.0%; Italy 4.1%.

## Transport and communications

**Transport.** *Railroads* (2005): length (2006) 3,505 km; passenger-km 75,170,000; metric ton-km cargo 18,027,000. *Roads* (2004): total length 193,200 km (paved 15%). *Vehicles* (2007): passenger cars 4,560,000. *Air transport* (2008): passenger-km 2,136,000,000; metric ton-km cargo 7,368,000. **Communications**, in total units (units per 1,000 persons). Telephone landlines (2008): 1,308,000 (8.7); cellular telephone subscribers (2008): 62,989,000 (417); personal computers (2007): 1,182,000 (8); total Internet users (2008): 11,000,000 (73); broadband Internet subscribers (2008): 26,000 (0.2).

## Education and health

**Educational attainment** (2003). Percentage of population ages 25 and over having: no formal schooling/unknown 50.4%; primary education 20.4%; secondary 20.1%; higher 9.1%. **Literacy** (2007): total population ages 15 and over literate 73.1%; males literate 79.4%; females literate 67.0%. **Health** (2005): physicians 42,563 (1 per 3,234 persons); hospital beds 85,523 (1 per 1,609 persons); infant mortality rate per 1,000 live births (2007) 109.0; undernourished population (2002–04) 11,400,000 (9% of total population based on the consumption of a minimum daily requirement of 1,830 calories).

## Military

**Total active duty personnel** (November 2008): 80,000 (army 77.5%, navy 10.0%, air force 12.5%). **Military expenditure as percentage of GDP** (2007): 0.7%; per capita expenditure US$7.

## Background

Inhabited for thousands of years, Nigeria was the center of the Nok culture from 500 BC to AD 200 and of several precolonial empires, including the state of Kanem-Bornu and the Songhai, Hausa, and Fulani kingdoms. Visited in the 15th century by Europeans, it became a center for the slave trade. The area began to come under British control in 1861; by 1903 British rule was total. Nigeria gained independence in 1960 and became a republic in 1963. Ethnic strife soon led to military coups, and military groups ruled the country from 1966 to 1979 and from 1983 to 1999. A civil war between the central government and the former Eastern Region—which seceded and called itself Biafra—began in 1967 and ended in 1970 with Biafra's surrender after widespread starvation and civilian deaths. In 1991 the capital was moved from Lagos to Abuja. The government's execution of environmental activist Ken Saro-Wiwa in 1995 led to international sanctions, and civilian rule was finally reestablished in 1999. Ethnic conflicts continued in the early 21st century, as did violent protests over oil production in the Niger delta. Friction also increased between Muslims and Christians after some of the northern and central states adopted Islamic law.

## Recent Developments

The election campaign that returned Nigerian Pres. Goodluck Jonathan to power in 2011 was generally peaceful, but the rejection of the results by his opponent, former military ruler Muhammad Buhari, sparked violence in which about 800 people were killed, most of whom were Muslim. While religious conflict appeared to be the overt cause of violence, analysts cautioned that the more-important reasons for the violence were stemming from poverty and economic marginalization. Throughout the year many other serious outbreaks of violence occurred in the oil-producing Niger Delta, the Plateau state, where the predominantly Muslim north met the predominantly Christian south, and Borno state. Much of it was caused by the terrorist activities of the fundamentalist Islamic sect Boko Haram. Originally centered in northeastern Borno state, Boko Haram was believed to have links to al-Qaeda in the Islamic Maghrib in Algeria and Niger and al-Shabaab in Somalia. Its militants bombed the UN headquarters in Abuja in August and unleashed coordinated attacks in Borno and Yobe states in November that left an estimated 100 dead. In mid-December the police captured a number of militants and seized a significant amount of arms and bomb-making materials. Militants retaliated with a series of bombings and armed attacks across the northeast and in Abuja on Christmas Day, leaving more than 40 dead and 90,000 displaced. Boko Haram attacks continued in 2012. The organization Human Rights Watch estimated that the group killed 250 in Nigeria in the first month alone, and the estimate had climbed to at least 560 by mid-year.

Internet resource: <http://nigerianstat.gov.ng>.

# Norway

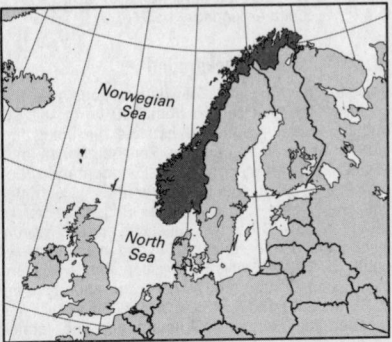

Official name: Kongeriket Norge (Kingdom of Norway). Form of government: constitutional monarchy with one legislative house (Storting, or Parliament [169]). Head of state: King Harald V (from 1991). Head of government: Prime Minister Jens Stoltenberg (from 2005). Capital: Oslo. Official language: Norwegian (Sami is official locally). Official religion: Evangelical Lutheran. Monetary unit: 1 Norwegian krone (NOK; plural kroner) = 100 øre; valuation (2 Jul 2012) US$1 = NOK 5.97.

## Demography

Area: 148,718 sq mi, 385,179 sq km. Population (2011): 4,953,000. Density (2011): persons per sq mi 33.3, persons per sq km 12.9. Urban (2009): 78.8%. Sex distribution (2008): male 49.90%; female 50.10%. Age breakdown (2008): under 15, 19.0%; 15–29, 19.1%; 30–44, 21.7%; 45–59, 19.5%; 60–74, 13.3%; 75–84, 5.1%; 85 and over, 2.3%. Ethnic composition (2008): Norwegian (nonimmigrant) 89.4%; other 10.6%, of which from Europe 4.2%, Asia 3.9%, Africa 1.3%. Religious affiliation (2003): Evangelical Lutheran 85.7%; other Christian 4.5%; Muslim 1.8%; other/nonreligious 8.0%. Major cities (2007): Oslo 560,484 (urban agglomeration 856,915); Bergen 247,746; Trondheim 165,191; Stavanger 119,586; Bærum 108,144. Location: northern Europe, bordering the Barents Sea, Russia, Finland, Sweden, the North Sea, and the Norwegian Sea.

## Vital statistics

Birth rate per 1,000 population (2008): 12.7 (world avg. 20.3); within marriage 45.0%. Death rate per 1,000 population (2008): 8.7 (world avg. 8.5). Total fertility rate (avg. births per childbearing woman; 2008): 1.96. Life expectancy at birth (2008): male 78.3 years; female 83.0 years.

## National economy

Budget (2007). Revenue: NOK 1,146,890,-000,000 (tax revenue 57.5%; nontax revenue 24.5%; social security 18.0%). Expenditures: NOK 736,004,000,000 (social security and welfare 41.5%; general public services 17.5%; health 16.6%; education 5.8%; defense 5.0%; transportation 4.5%). Public debt (June 2009): US$101,447,000,000. Production (metric tons except as noted). Agriculture and fishing (2007): barley 580,000, wheat 380,000, potatoes 380,000; livestock (number of live animals) 2,400,000 sheep, 930,000 cattle; fisheries production 3,209,140 (from aquaculture 26%); aquatic plants production 134,671 (from aquaculture, none). Mining and quarrying (2007): olivine sand 3,000,000, ilmenite concentrate 882,000, iron ore (metal content) 630,000. Manufacturing (value added in NOK '000,000; 2008): machinery and apparatus 55,474; food products, beverages, and tobacco products 34,589; ships and oil platforms 26,139. Energy production (consumption): electricity (kW-hr; 2008) 142,632,000,000 ([2006] 22,518,000,-000); coal (metric tons; 2007) 3,995,000 (1,115,000); crude petroleum (barrels; 2008) 743,700,000 ([2006] 94,800,000); petroleum products (metric tons; 2006) 22,993,000 (11,936,000); natural gas (cu m; 2008) 99,403,-000,000 ([2007] 6,512,000,000). Selected balance of payments data. Receipts from (US$'000,000): tourism (2007) 4,222; remittances (2008) 684; foreign direct investment (FDI; 2005–07 avg.) 4,163. Disbursements for (US$'000,000): tourism (2007) 14,032; remittances (2008) 4,776; FDI (2005–07 avg.) 18,092. Population economically active (2006): total 2,446,000; activity rate of total population 52.5% (participation rates: ages 15–64, 80.8%; female 47.1%; unemployed [July 2008–June 2009] 2.9%). Gross national income (2008): US$415,249,000,000 (US$87,070 per capita).

## Foreign trade

Imports (2007; c.i.f.): NOK 470,681,000,000 (machinery and apparatus 24.8%, of which nonelectrical machinery and equipment 11.6%; base and fabricated metals 10.7%; motor vehicles 10.2%; chemical products 8.6%; metal ore and metal scrap 6.7%). Major import sources: Sweden 14.7%; Germany 13.6%; UK 6.9%; Denmark 6.4%; China 6.0%. Exports (2007; f.o.b.): NOK 799,284,000,000 (crude petroleum 39.9%; natural gas 19.3%; machinery and

---

1 metric ton = about 1.1 short tons;   1 kilometer = 0.6 mi (statute);   1 metric ton-km cargo = about 0.68 short ton-mi cargo;   c.i.f.: cost, insurance, and freight;   f.o.b.: free on board

apparatus 6.8%; refined petroleum products 4.8%; aluminum 4.4%; fish 3.6%; nickel 2.4%). *Major export destinations:* UK 26.2%; Germany 12.3%; Netherlands 10.3%; France 8.0%; Sweden 6.5%.

## Transport and communications

**Transport.** *Railroads* (2007): route length 4,087 km; passenger-km 3,432,000,000; metric ton-km cargo 2,476,000,000. *Roads* (2007): total length 92,920 km (paved 80%). *Vehicles* (2007): passenger cars 2,153,730; trucks and buses 538,225. *Air transport* (2008; SAS [Norwegian part] and Widerøe only): passenger-km 8,194,000,000; metric ton-km cargo 7,646,000. **Communications,** in total units (units per 1,000 persons). Telephone landlines (2008): 1,928,000 (404); cellular telephone subscribers (2008): 5,287,000 (1,109); personal computers (2007): 2,959,000 (629); total Internet users (2008): 4,237,000 (889); broadband Internet subscribers (2008): 1,608,000 (337).

## Education and health

**Educational attainment** (2007). Percentage of population ages 16 and over having: primary and lower secondary education 29.6%; higher secondary 41.3%; higher 24.8%; unknown 4.3%. **Literacy** (2000): virtually 100% literate. **Health:** physicians (2006) 17,523 (1 per 266 persons); hospital beds (2007) 22,882 (1 per 206 persons); infant mortality rate per 1,000 live births (2008) 2.7; undernourished population (2002–04) less than 2.5% of total population.

## Military

**Total active duty personnel** (November 2008): 19,100 (army 34.0%, navy 16.5%, air force 14.2%, central support 31.4%, other 3.9%). **Military expenditure as percentage of GDP** (2008): 1.2%; per capita expenditure US$1,013.

## Background

Several principalities were united into the kingdom of Norway in the 11th century. From 1380 it had the same king as Denmark until it was ceded to Sweden in 1814. The union with Sweden was dissolved in 1905, and Norway's economy grew rapidly. The country remained neutral during World War I, though its shipping industry played a vital role in the conflict. It declared its neutrality in World War II but was invaded and occupied by German troops. Norway is a member of NATO but turned down membership in the EU in 1994. Its economy grew consistently during the 1990s, aided particularly by its North Sea petroleum industry.

## Recent Developments

The Norwegian economy remained strong in 2011. At 3.3% at year's end, unemployment was low, while GDP for mainland Norway grew by 1.6%. Norway's per capita GDP rate was second in Europe only to that of Luxembourg. Two massive oil discoveries, in the Barents and North seas, mitigated Norwegian concerns over the country's declining hydrocarbon reserves. The ecologically vulnerable Lofoten-Vesterålen archipelago was protected from oil and gas exploration for two more years under a compromise reached by the partners in the coalition government. Drilling was, however, allowed in nearby offshore sectors and along the coast of the far northern counties of Troms and Finnmark.

**Internet resource:** <www.ssb.no/english>.

# Oman

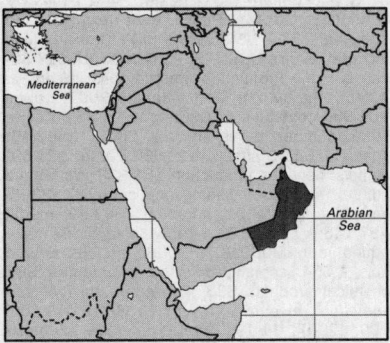

**Official name:** Saltanat 'Uman (Sultanate of Oman). **Form of government:** monarchy with two advisory bodies (State Council [83]; Consultative Council [84]). **Head of state and government:** Sultan (from 1970) and Prime Minister (from 1972) Qabus ibn Sa'id. **Capital:** Muscat (many ministries are located in adjacent Bawshar). **Official language:** Arabic. **Official religion:** Islam. **Monetary unit:** 1 rial Omani (RO) = 1,000 baiza; valuation (2 Jul 2012) US$1 = RO 0.39.

## Demography

**Area:** 119,500 sq mi, 309,500 sq km. **Population** (2011): 2,810,000. **Density** (2011): persons per sq mi 23.5, persons per sq km 9.1. **Urban** (2010): 73.0%. **Sex distribution** (2008): male 50.54%; female 49.46%. **Age breakdown** (2008): under 15, 35.2%; 15–29, 38.5%; 30–44, 16.3%; 45–59, 6%; 60–74, 3.1%; 75 and over, 0.6%. **Ethnic composition** (2000): Omani Arab 48.1%; Indo-Pakistani 31.7%, of which Balochi 15.0%, Bengali 4.4%, Tamil 2.5%; other Arab 7.2%; Persian 2.8%; Zanzibari (blacks originally from Zanzibar) 2.5%; other 7.7%. **Religious affiliation** (2005): Muslim 89%, of which Ibadiyah 75%, Sunni 8%, Shi'i 6%; Hindu 5%; Christian 5%; other 1%. **Major cities** (populations of districts; 2007): Muscat 28,987 (urban agglomeration 620,000); Al-Sib 268,259; Matrah 203,159; Bawshar 193,778; Salalah 185,780. **Location:** the Middle East, bordering the Gulf of Oman, the Arabian Sea, Yemen, Saudi Arabia, and the UAE; the Ru'us al-Jibal exclave occupies the northern tip of the Musandam Peninsula and borders the UAE, the Persian Gulf, and the Strait of Hormuz.

## Vital statistics

**Birth rate** per 1,000 population (2008): 24.2 (world avg. 20.3). **Death rate** per 1,000 population (2008):

2.5 (world avg. 8.5). **Total fertility rate** (avg. births per childbearing woman; 2008): 3.19. **Life expectancy** at birth (2008): male 73.2 years; female 75.4 years.

## National economy

**Budget** (2008). *Revenue:* RO 7,829,400,000 (oil revenue 67.5%; natural gas revenue 11.6%; non-tax revenue 11.0%). *Expenditures:* RO 7,-556,700,000 (current expenditures 58.5%, of which defense 23.5%, education 9.8%, social security and welfare 6.6%, health 3.4%; capital expenditures 30.2%). **Public debt** (external, outstanding; 2006): US$819,000,000. **Gross national income** (2008): US$49,812,200,000 (US$17,884 per capita). **Production** (metric tons except as noted). *Agriculture and fishing* (2007): dates 260,000, tomatoes 41,000, bananas 26,000; livestock (number of live animals; 2008) 1,652,400 goats, 373,500 sheep, 319,900 cattle, 124,500 camels; fisheries production 151,834 (from aquaculture, negligible). *Mining and quarrying* (2008): limestone 3,604,452; chromite 784,082; marble 457,146; gypsum 321,746. *Manufacturing* (value added in US$'000,000; 2006): petroleum products 1,754; cement, bricks, and ceramics 367; chemical products 333. *Energy production (consumption):* electricity (kW-hr; 2008) 16,048,100,-000 ([2007] 11,191,000,000); crude petroleum (barrels; 2008–09) 277,100,000 ([2008] 29,-565,000); petroleum products (metric tons; 2006) 4,172,000 (4,265,000); natural gas (cu m; 2008) 30,288,712,000 (13,460,000,000). **Population economically active** (2007): total 968,782; activity rate of total population 35.5% (participation rates: ages 15–64, 55.2%; female 19.6%; unemployed [2004] 15%). **Selected balance of payments data.** Receipts from (US$'000,000): tourism (2007) 645; remittances (2008) 39; foreign direct investment (FDI; 2005–07 avg.) 1,896. Disbursements for (US$'000,000): tourism (2007) 744; remittances (2008) 5,181; FDI (2005–07 avg.) 377.

## Foreign trade

**Imports** (2008; c.i.f.): RO 8,814,500,000 ([2007] motor vehicles and parts 24.1%; non-electrical machinery and equipment 17.8%; food products and live animals 8.3%; iron and steel 8.2%; chemical products 6.4%). *Major import sources:* UAE 27.2%; Japan 15.6%; US 5.7%; China 4.6%; India 4.5%. **Exports** (2008; f.o.b.): RO 14,503,000,000 (domestic exports 89.5%, of which crude petroleum 58.0%, liquefied natural gas 11.0%, refined petroleum products 6.9%; reexports 10.5%, of which motor vehicles and parts 9.1%). *Major export destinations:* China 28.4%; UAE 10.9%; Japan 8.1%; Thailand 6.7%; South Korea 6.3%.

## Transport and communications

**Transport.** *Railroads:* none. *Roads* (2008): total length 53,556 km (paved 44%). *Vehicles* (2003): passenger cars 308,663; trucks and buses 109,118. *Air transport* (2008; Oman Air only): pas-senger-km 3,551,000,000; metric ton-km cargo 20,000,000. **Communications**, in total units (units per 1,000 persons). Telephone landlines (2008): 274,000 (98); cellular telephone subscribers (2008): 3,219,000 (1,156); personal computers (2006): 180,000 (67); total Internet users (2008): 465,000 (167); broadband Internet subscribers (2008): 32,000 (12).

## Education and health

**Educational attainment** (2003). Percentage of population ages 10 and over having: no formal schooling (illiterate) 15.9%; no formal schooling (literate) 22.3%; primary 35.3%; secondary 17.0%; higher technical 3.3%; higher undergraduate 5.2%; higher graduate 0.7%; other 0.3%. **Literacy** (2007): percentage of total population ages 15 and over literate 84.4%; males literate 89.4%; females literate 77.5%. **Health** (2008): physicians 5,194 (1 per 536 persons); hospital beds 5,473 (1 per 509 persons); infant mortality rate per 1,000 live births 10.3.

## Military

**Total active duty personnel** (November 2008): 42,600 (army 58.7%, navy 9.9%, air force 11.7%, royal household/foreign troops 19.7%). **Military expenditure as percentage of GDP** (2007): 8.1%; per capita expenditure US$1,185.

## Background

Oman has been inhabited for at least 10,000 years. Arabs began migrating there in the 9th century BC. Tribal warfare was endemic until the conversion to Islam in the 7th century AD. It was ruled by Ibadi imams until 1154, when a royal dynasty was established. The Portuguese controlled the coastal areas from about 1507 to 1650, when they were expelled. The Al Bu Sa'id dynasty, founded in the mid-18th century, still rules Oman. Oil was discovered in 1964. In 1970 the sultan was deposed by his son, who began a policy of modernization, and under him the country joined the Arab League and the UN. In the Persian Gulf War, Oman cooperated with the allied forces against Iraq. It subsequently continued to expand its foreign relations.

## Recent Developments

Omani Sultan Qaboos bin Said reacted to what was termed the Arab Spring in 2011 by declaring the complete independence of the state accounting authority, increasing the power of elected officials within the country's national consultative body, and pledging 50,000 new employment opportunities—35,000 in the country's armed forces and the balance in other sectors of the economy. Oman's overall economic situation also benefited from unprecedented pledges of US$10 billion in economic support from Oman's five fellow Gulf Cooperation Council member countries, to be distributed in annual payments spread over the following decade.

**Internet resource:**
<www.omanet.om/english/home.asp>.

---

*1 metric ton = about 1.1 short tons;    1 kilometer = 0.6 mi (statute);    1 metric ton-km cargo = about 0.68 short ton-mi cargo;    c.i.f.: cost, insurance, and freight;    f.o.b.: free on board*

# Pakistan

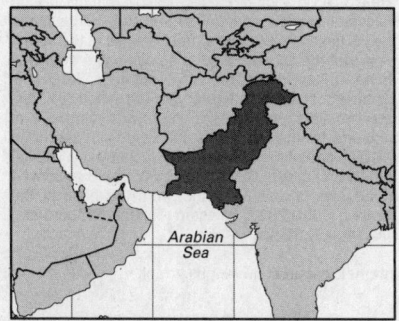

Arabian
Sea

**Official name:** Islamic Republic of Pakistan. **Form of government:** federal republic with two legislative houses (Senate [104]; National Assembly [342]). **Head of state:** President Asif Ali Zardari (from 2008). **Head and government:** Prime Minister Raja Pervez Ashraf (from 2012). **Capital:** Islamabad. **Official language:** none (Urdu is the national language). **Official religion:** Islam. **Monetary unit:** 1 Pakistan rupee (PKR) = 100 paisa; valuation (2 Jul 2012) US$1 = PKR 94.52.

## Demography

*Area data exclude the 33,125-sq-mi (85,793-sq-km) area of Pakistani-administered Jammu and Kashmir (comprising both Azad Kashmir [AK] and Gilgit-Baltistan [GB]); population and density data include Afghan refugees and the 2009 populations of AK (3,890,000) and GB (1,009,000).* **Area:** 307,374 sq mi, 796,096 sq km. **Population** (2011): 187,343,000. **Density** (2011): persons per sq mi 550.2, persons per sq km 212.4. **Urban** (2009): 35.6%. **Sex distribution** (2007): male 51.89%; female 48.11%. **Age breakdown** (2005): under 15, 37.2%; 15–29, 29.9%; 30–44, 16.8%; 45–59, 10.2%; 60–74, 4.7%; 75–84, 1.0%; 85 and over, 0.2%. **Ethnic composition** (2000): Punjabi 52.6%; Pashtun 13.2%; Sindhi 11.7%; Urdu-speaking muhajirs 7.5%; Balochi 4.3%; other 10.7%. **Religious affiliation** (2000): Muslim 96.1%; Christian 2.5%; Hindu 1.2%; others (including Ahmadiyah) 0.2%. **Major urban agglomerations** (2007): Karachi 12,130,000; Lahore 6,577,000; Faisalabad 2,617,000; Rawalpindi 1,858,000; Multan 1,522,000. **Location:** southern Asia, bordering China, India, the Arabian Sea, Iran, and Afghanistan.

## Vital statistics

**Birth rate** per 1,000 population (2008): 25.0 (world avg. 20.3). **Death rate** per 1,000 population (2008): 7.7 (world avg. 8.5). **Total fertility rate** (avg. births per childbearing woman; 2007): 3.13. **Life expectancy** at birth (2007): male 64.3 years; female 64.4 years.

## National economy

**Budget** (2007–08). *Revenue:* PKR 1,368,139,000,000 (tax revenue 75.3%, of which corporate taxes 28.4%, sales taxes 27.4%, customs 11.3%; nontax revenue 24.7%). *Expenditures:* PKR 1,353,660,000,000 (general public service 47.4%; defense 20.3%; economic affairs 5.8%; public order and police 1.8%; education 1.8%). **Public debt** (external, outstanding; June 2008): US$40,243,000,000. **Production** (metric tons except as noted). *Agriculture and fishing* (2007): sugarcane 54,752,000, wheat 23,520,000, rice 8,300,000, seed cotton 6,500,000, mangoes 2,250,000, chickpeas 842,000, sunflower seeds 560,000, dates 510,000; livestock (number of live animals) 53,800,000 goats, 29,600,000 cattle, 27,300,000 buffalo, 900,000 camels; fisheries production (2007–08) 640,000 (from aquaculture 23%). *Mining and quarrying* (2007–08): limestone 30,825,000; rock salt 1,872,000; gypsum 682,000; kaolin (2007) 39,000. *Manufacturing* (value of production in PKR '000,000,000; 2000–01): textiles 321; food products 189; refined petroleum products and coke 94. *Energy production (consumption)* in '000: electricity (kW-hr; 2007–08) 109,021,000 ([2006–07] 72,712,000); coal (metric tons; 2007–08) 3,482 ([2006–07] 7,894); crude petroleum (barrels; 2007–08) 25,610 ([2006] 84,000); petroleum products (metric tons; 2006) 9,793 ([2006–07] 16,847); natural gas (cu m; 2007–08) 40,981,000 ([2006–07] 34,601,000). **Population economically active** (2007): total 50,331,000; activity rate of total population 31.8% (participation rates: ages 15–64, 53.7%; female 20.7%; officially unemployed 5.3%). **Gross national income** (2008): US$162,930,000,000 (US$980 per capita). **Selected balance of payments data.** Receipts from (US$'000,000): tourism (2007) 276; remittances (2008) 7,032; foreign direct investment (FDI; 2005–07 avg.) 3,936; official development assistance (2007) 2,212. Disbursements for (US$'000,000): tourism (2007) 1,593; remittances (2008) 3.0; FDI (2005–07 avg.) 84.

## Foreign trade

**Imports** (2007–08): US$35,417,333,000 (refined petroleum products 17.4%; machinery and apparatus 16.2%; chemical products 14.4%; crude petroleum 12.2%; food products 10.0%). *Major import sources:* UAE 14.5%; Saudi Arabia 10.2%; China 8.6%; Kuwait 6.9%; Singapore 4.8%. **Exports** (2007–08): US$20,122,394,000 (textiles 49.8%, of which woven cotton fabric 11.5%, knitwear 10.5%, bedding 6.9%, ready-made garments 5.5%, cotton yarn 5.3%; rice 5.6%; refined petroleum products 3.7%). *Major export destinations:* US 18.6%; UAE 8.6%; UK 5.3%; Afghanistan 5.1%; Germany 4.1%.

## Transport and communications

**Transport.** *Railroads* (2007): length (2005–06) 11,515 km; passenger-km 25,821,000,000; metric ton-km cargo 5,876,000,000. *Roads* (2007–08): total length 264,853 km (paved 67%). *Vehicles* (2007): passenger cars 1,440,072; trucks and buses 357,455. *Air transport* (2008): passenger-km 13,920,000,000; metric ton-km cargo 319,800,000. **Communications,** in total units (units per 1,000 persons). Telephone landlines (2008): 4,416,000 (25); cellular telephone subscribers (2008): 88,020,000 (497); personal computers (2005): 803,000 (5.2); total Internet users (2008): 18,500,000 (105); broadband Internet subscribers (2008): 168,000 (0.9).

## Education and health

**Literacy** (2006–07): total population ages 15 and over literate 52%; males literate 65%; females literate 38%. **Health** (2007): physicians 127,859 (1 per 1,280 persons); hospital beds (2006) 103,285 (1 per 1,585 persons); infant mortality rate per 1,000 live births 68.0; undernourished population (2003–05) 35,000,000 (23% of total population based on the consumption of a minimum daily requirement of 1,750 calories).

## Military

**Total active duty personnel** (November 2008): 617,000 (army 89.1%, navy 3.6%, air force 7.3%). **Military expenditure as percentage of GDP** (2008): 2.8%; per capita expenditure US$21.

## Background

Pakistan has been inhabited since about 3500 BC. From the 3rd century BC to the 2nd century AD, it was part of the Mauryan and Kushan kingdoms. The first Muslim conquests were in the 8th century AD. The British East India Company subdued the reigning Mughal dynasty in 1757. During the period of British colonial rule, what is now Pakistan was part of India. When the British withdrew in 1947, the new state of Pakistan came into existence by act of the British Parliament. Kashmir remained a disputed territory between Pakistan and India, resulting in full-scale war in 1965 and continued military clashes. Civil war between East Pakistan and West Pakistan resulted in independence for the former, which became Bangladesh, in 1971. Many Afghan refugees migrated to Pakistan during the Soviet-Afghan war in the 1980s. Pakistan elected Benazir Bhutto prime minister in 1988; she was the first woman to head a modern Islamic state. She was ousted in 1990 on charges of corruption and incompetence. During the 1990s border flare-ups with India continued, and Pakistan conducted tests of nuclear weapons. Pakistan's political landscape changed dramatically after the terrorist attacks of September 11. It was quickly determined that they had been staged by the Muslim militant organization al-Qaeda, which was operating out of Afghanistan with the support of the Taliban regime, with which Pakistan had diplomatic relations. As the US prepared to move militarily against both organizations, Pakistan chose to provide support to the US-led coalition. In May 2011, Osama bin Laden—thought to have been the planner of the September 11 attacks— was killed during a raid by US special forces soldiers on a compound in Abbottabad, Pakistan, located less than 100 miles from the capital and in the town that housed the Pakistani military academy.

## Recent Developments

A series of confrontations pushed relations between Pakistan and the United States to new lows in 2011. In April Pakistani officials ordered the departure of 400 US special forces soldiers working in Pakistan as counterterrorism trainers, fearing that the soldiers might also be involved in spying. The administration of Pres. Asif Ali Zardari in May decried the raid in which a US special operations task force killed

Osama bin Laden in a residence in Abbottabad, Pakistan, as a violation of Pakistan's sovereignty. In June Pakistani officials announced that they had ordered the US to vacate Shamsi airfield, a base in the southwest that the US had used in its campaign of armed drone strikes in Pakistan. In November NATO helicopter gunships and fighter aircraft killed 24 Pakistani soldiers posted at the border with Afghanistan, angering Islamabad. Pakistan closed its border to NATO shipments and once again declared the Shamsi airfield off-limits to US drone activity. The US removed all equipment and personnel from the base in December. In July 2012, Pakistan reopened its border to NATO supply trucks.

**Internet resource:** <www.pbs.gov.pk>.

# Palau

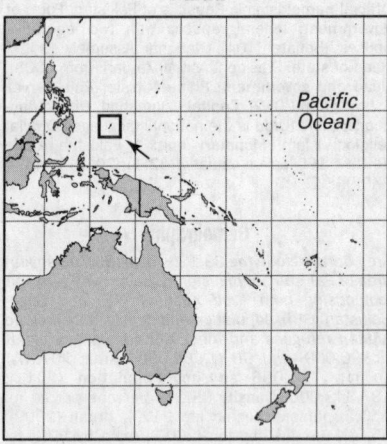

**Official name:** Beluu er a Belau (Palauan); Republic of Palau (English). **Form of government:** republic with two legislative houses (Senate [13]; House of Delegates [16]). **Head of state and government:** President Johnson Toribiong (from 2009). **Capital:** Melekeok. **Official languages:** Palauan; English. **Official religion:** none. **Monetary unit:** 1 US dollar (US$) = 100 cents.

## Demography

**Area:** 188 sq mi, 488 sq km. **Population** (2011): 20,600. **Density** (2011): persons per sq mi 109.6, persons per sq km 42.2. **Urban** (2009): 81.6%. **Sex distribution** (2007): male 53.53%; female 46.47%. **Age breakdown** (2007): under 15, 24.1%; 15–29, 22.8%; 30–44, 28.0%; 45–59, 16.8%; 60–74, 5.3%; 75–84, 2.4%; 85 and over, 0.6%. **Ethnic composition** (2005; population ages 18 and over only): Palauan (Micronesian/Malay/Melanesian admixture) 65.2%; Asian 30.3%, of which Filipino 21.6%, Vietnamese 2.3%; other Micronesian 3.1%; white 1.1%; other 0.3%. **Religious affiliation** (2005; population ages 18 and over only): Roman Catholic 51.0%; Protestant 26.7%; Modekngei (marginal Christian sect) 8.9%;

other Christian 1.8%; other 11.6%. **Major towns** (2005): Koror 10,743; Meyuns 1,153; Kloulklubed 680. **Location:** Oceania, island group in the North Pacific Ocean, east of the Philippines.

## Vital statistics

**Birth rate** per 1,000 population (2007): 12.4 (world avg. 20.3). **Death rate** per 1,000 population (2007): 7.9 (world avg. 8.5). **Total fertility rate** (avg. births per childbearing woman; 2007): 2.00. **Life expectancy** at birth (2008): male 66.3 years; female 72.1 years.

## National economy

**Budget** (2007–08). *Revenue:* US$80,900,000 (grants 48.4%; tax revenue 42.1%; nontax revenue 9.5%). *Expenditures:* US$98,800,000 (current expenditures 77.4%; capital expenditures 22.6%). **Production** (metric tons except as noted). *Agriculture and fishing* (value of sales in US$; 2001): eggs (2003) 638,750, cabbages 116,948, cucumbers 44,009; livestock (number of live animals; 2001) 702 pigs, 21,189 poultry; fisheries production (2007) 1,003 (from aquaculture 2%). *Manufacturing:* includes handicrafts and small items. *Energy production (consumption):* electricity (kW-hr; 2006) 151,000,000 (151,000,000); petroleum products (metric tons; 2006) none (66,000). **Selected balance of payments data.** Receipts from (US$'000,000): tourism (2006) 90; foreign direct investment (FDI; 2005–07 avg.) 1.67; official development assistance (2007) 22. Disbursements for (US$'000,000): tourism (2006) 1.4. **Population economically active** (2005): total 10,203; activity rate of total population 51.3% (participation rates: ages 16 and over, 69.1%; female 39.1%; unemployed 4.2%). **Gross national income** (2008): US$175,000,000 (US$8,650 per capita). **Public debt** (gross external debt; 2006–07): US$22,857,000.

## Foreign trade

**Imports** (2006–07): US$91,287,000 (mineral fuels and lubricants 37.5%; machinery and transportation equipment 17.6%; beverages and tobacco products 14.9%; food products and live animals 9.4%; chemical products 8.7%). *Major import sources:* US 33.2%; Singapore 24.8%; Guam 11.2%; Japan 9.6%; Philippines 7.6%. **Exports** (2006–07): US$10,081,000 (mostly high-grade tuna and garments). *Major export destinations* (2003): Japan 86.7%; Vietnam 5.9%; Zambia 4.6%.

## Transport and communications

**Transport.** *Railroads:* none. *Roads* (2004): total length 61 km (paved 59%). *Vehicles* (2004): passenger cars and trucks 7,247. *Air transport* (2003): passenger arrivals 80,017, passenger departures 78,608. **Communications,** in total units (units per 1,000 persons). Telephone landlines (2008): 7,500 (370); cellular telephone subscribers (2008): 12,000 (592); total Internet users (2007): 5,400 (268); broadband Internet subscribers (2007): 100 (5).

## Education and health

**Educational attainment** (2005). Percentage of population ages 25 and over having: no formal schooling 1.9%; incomplete primary education 9.0%; complete primary 3.9%; incomplete secondary 14.9%; complete secondary 42.2%; some postsecondary 10.0%; vocational 4.1%; higher 14.0%. **Literacy** (2005): total population ages 15 and over literate, virtually 100%. **Health:** physicians (2006) 26 (1 per 771 persons); hospital beds (2004) 135 (1 per 147 persons); infant mortality rate per 1,000 live births (2007) 7.2.

## Military

The US is responsible for the external security of Palau, as specified in the Compact of Free Association of 1 Oct 1994.

## Background

Palau's inhabitants began arriving 3,000 years ago in successive waves from the Indonesian and Philippine archipelagos and from Polynesia. The islands had been under nominal Spanish ownership for more than three centuries when they were sold to Germany in 1899. They were seized by Japan in 1914 and taken by Allied forces in 1944 during World War II. Palau became part of the UN Trust Territory of the Pacific Islands in 1947 and became a sovereign state in 1994; the US provides economic assistance and maintains a military presence in the islands.

## Recent Developments

Palau took steps to protect its wildlife and marine ecosystems in 2011. In January a law passed strictly limiting the hunting of sea turtles. Micronesian leaders also enacted a regional ban in July on the possession or sale of shark fins.

**Internet resource:** <www.palaugov.net/stats>.

# Panama

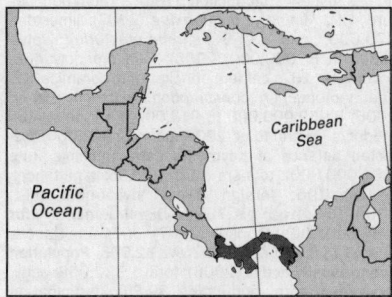

**Official name:** República de Panamá (Republic of Panama). **Form of government:** multiparty republic with one legislative house (National Assembly [71]). **Head of state and government:** President Ricardo Martinelli (from 2009). **Capital:** Panama City. **Official language:** Spanish. **Official religion:** none. **Monetary unit:** 1 balboa (B) = 100 centésimos; valuation (2 Jul 2012) US$1 = B 1.00.

## Demography

**Area:** 28,640 sq mi, 74,177 sq km. **Population** (2011): 3,643,000. **Density** (2011): persons per sq

mi 127.2, persons per sq km 49.1. **Urban** (2010): 74.8%. **Sex distribution** (2007): male 50.43%; female 49.57%. **Age breakdown** (2007): under 15, 29.9%; 15–29, 25.7%; 30–44, 21.9%; 45–59, 13.5%; 60–74, 6.7%; 75 and over, 2.3%. **Ethnic composition** (2000): mestizo 58.1%; black and mulatto 14.0%; white 8.6%; Amerindian 6.7%; Asian 5.5%; other 7.1%. **Religious affiliation** (2008): Roman Catholic 75%; Protestant/independent Christian 20%; Mormon 1%; Jewish 0.3%; Muslim 0.3%; other 3.4%. **Major cities (districts)** (2000): Panama City 415,964 (845,684); San Miguelito 352,936; Colón 52,286 (205,557); Arraiján 63,753 (203,207); La Chorrera 54,823 (153,778). **Location:** Central America, bordering the Caribbean Sea, Colombia, the North Pacific Ocean, and Costa Rica.

## Vital statistics

**Birth rate** per 1,000 population (2007): 20.2 (world avg. 20.3); (2006) within marriage 17.3%. **Death rate** per 1,000 population (2007): 4.4 (world avg. 8.5). **Total fertility rate** (avg. births per childbearing woman; 2007): 2.62. **Life expectancy** at birth (2007): male 73.7 years; female 79.5 years.

## National economy

**Budget** (2007). *Revenue:* B 4,433,000,000 (tax revenue 48.1%, of which indirect taxes 22.5%, income tax 22.2%; nontax revenue 32.9%, of which revenue from Panama Canal 10.5%; capital revenue 16.9%). *Expenditures:* B 4,432,000,000 (current expenditures 78.1%, of which debt servicing 30.7%, education 14.4%, health 13.5%, public order 5.6%; development expenditures 21.9%). **Production** (metric tons except as noted). *Agriculture and fishing* (2007): sugarcane 1,800,000, bananas 440,000, rice 280,000, canteloupes and other melons 130,000, pineapples 71,002; livestock (number of live animals) 1,650,000 cattle, 300,000 pigs, 190,000 horses; fisheries production 215,569 (from aquaculture 4%). *Mining and quarrying* (2007): limestone 270,000; gold 2,059 kg. *Manufacturing* (value added in B '000,000; 2006): food products 468; beverages 167; cement, bricks, and ceramics 82. *Energy production (consumption):* electricity (kW-hr; 2006) 5,962,000,000 (5,913,000,000); petroleum products (metric tons; 2006) none (1,922,000). **Selected balance of payments data.** Receipts from (US$'000,000): tourism (2007) 1,185; remittances (2008) 196; foreign direct investment (FDI; 2005–07 avg.) 1,787. Disbursements for (US$'000,000): tourism (2007) 307; remittances (2008) 198; FDI (2005–07 avg.) 2,095. **Population economically active** (2006): total 1,332,059; activity rate of total population 39.8% (participation rates: ages 15–64, 66.9%; female 37.1%; unemployed [October 2009] 6.6%). **Gross national income** (2008): US$20,973,000,000 (US$6,180 per capita). **Public debt** (external, outstanding; 2007): US$8,267,000,000.

## Foreign trade

**Imports** (2007; c.i.f.) (excludes trade passing through the Colón Free Zone [2007 imports US$7,633,000,000]): US$6,868,000,000 (machinery and apparatus 19.7%; refined petroleum products 17.2%; motor vehicles 11.5%; food products 9.1%; iron and steel 4.2%). *Major import sources:* US 30.8%; free zones 16.0%; Netherlands Antilles 7.1%; China 5.2%; Japan 4.8%. **Exports** (2007; f.o.b.) (excludes trade passing through the Colón Free Zone [2007 reexports US$8,523,000,000, of which textiles and wearing apparel 24.2%; machinery and apparatus 23.9%]): US$1,120,000,000 (fish 24.4%, of which tuna 7.2%; melons and papayas 18.1%; crustaceans and mollusks 10.1%; bananas 10.0%; pineapples 3.8%). *Major export destinations:* US 35.7%; France 10.2%; Sweden 5.6%; China 5.6%; UK 5.5%.

## Transport and communications

**Transport.** *Railroads* (2005; Panama Canal Railway): route length (2007) 77 km; passenger-km 44,734,000,000; metric ton-km cargo 138,104,-000,000. *Roads* (2006): total length 13,365 km (paved 34%). *Vehicles* (2007): passenger cars 436,205; trucks and buses 194,615. Panama Canal traffic (2007–08): oceangoing transits 13,048; cargo 213,081,000 metric tons. *Air transport* (2007; COPA only): passenger-km 7,944,000,000; metric ton-km cargo (2005) 37,226,000. **Communications**, in total units (units per 1,000 persons). Telephone landlines (2008): 496,000 (146); cellular telephone subscribers (2008): 3,805,000 (1,119); personal computers (2007): 154,000 (46); total Internet users (2008): 779,000 (229); broadband Internet subscribers (2008): 158,000 (46).

## Education and health

**Educational attainment** (2000). Percentage of population ages 25 and over having: no formal schooling/unknown 13.8%; primary education 36.4%; secondary 33.9%; undergraduate 14.4%; graduate 1.5%. **Literacy** (2005): total population ages 15 and over literate 93.0%; males literate 93.6%; females literate 92.4%. **Health** (2007): physicians 4,524 (1 per 739 persons); hospital beds 7,689 (1 per 435 persons); infant mortality rate per 1,000 live births 14.7; undernourished population (2002–04) 700,000 (23% of total population based on the consumption of a minimum daily requirement of 1,830 calories).

## Military

**Total active duty personnel** (November 2008): none; a 12,000-member paramilitary includes air and maritime units. **Paramilitary expenditure as percentage of GDP** (2008): 0.9%; per capita expenditure US$66.

## Background

Panama was inhabited by Native Americans when the Spanish arrived in 1501. The first successful Spanish settlement was founded by Vasco Núñez de Balboa in 1510. Panama was part of the Viceroyalty of New Granada until it declared its independence from Spain in 1821 to join the Gran Colombia union. In 1903 it revolted and was recognized by the US, to which it ceded the Canal Zone. The completed

---

*1 metric ton = about 1.1 short tons;    1 kilometer = 0.6 mi (statute);    1 metric ton-km cargo = about 0.68 short ton-mi cargo;    c.i.f.: cost, insurance, and freight;    f.o.b.: free on board*

Panama Canal was opened in 1914; its jurisdiction reverted from the US to Panama in 1999. An invasion by US troops in 1989 overthrew the de facto ruler, Gen. Manuel Noriega. In 2007 a project to expand the canal began.

## Recent Developments

On 21 Oct 2011, US Pres. Barack Obama promulgated a Free Trade Agreement with Panama. This action came days after the deal was ratified by the US Congress but four years after approval by Panama's National Assembly. Panama's economy, the fastest growing in Latin America, expanded by 11.4% (year on year) in the second quarter of 2011. According to one analysis, Panama also had become the region's top recipient of foreign direct investment as a share of GDP.

Internet resource:
<www.visitpanama.com/index.php?lang=en>.

# Papua New Guinea

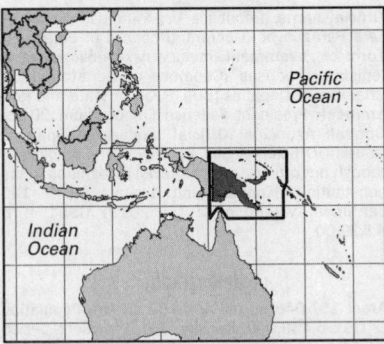

**Official names:** Independent State of Papua New Guinea (English); Gau Hedinarai ai Papua–Matamata Guinea (Hiri Motu); Papua-Niugini (Tok Pisin). **Form of government:** constitutional monarchy with one legislative house (National Parliament [109]). **Head of state:** British Queen Elizabeth II (from 1952), represented by Governor-General Michael Ogio (from 2010). **Head of government:** Prime Minister Peter O'Neill (from 2011). **Capital:** Port Moresby. **Official languages:** English; Hiri Motu; Tok Pisin. **Official religion:** none. **Monetary unit:** 1 kina (K) = 100 toea; valuation (2 Jul 2012) US$1 = K 2.04.

## Demography

**Area:** 178,704 sq mi, 462,840 sq km. **Population** (2011): 6,188,000. **Density** (2011): persons per sq mi 34.6, persons per sq km 13.4. **Urban** (2008): 12.0%. **Sex distribution** (2008): male 51.49%; female 48.51%. **Age breakdown** (2008): under 15, 37.7%; 15–29, 27.2%; 30–44, 19.4%; 45–59, 10.3%; 60–74, 4.5%; 75–84, 0.8%; 85 and over, 0.1%. **Ethnic composition** (1983): New Guinea Papuan 84.0%; New Guinea Melanesian 15.0%; other 1.0%. **Religious affiliation** (2005): Protestant/independent Christian 44%; Roman Catholic 22%; traditional beliefs 34%. **Major cities** (2006): Port Moresby 289,900; Lae 75,600; Arawa

40,300; Mount Hagen 34,900; Popondetta 30,400. **Location:** Oceania, group of islands, including the eastern half of the island of New Guinea, in the South Pacific Ocean near the Equator to the north of Australia, bordering Indonesia.

## Vital statistics

**Birth rate** per 1,000 population (2008): 29.3 (world avg. 20.3). **Death rate** per 1,000 population (2008): 9.6 (world avg. 8.5). **Total fertility rate** (avg. births per childbearing woman; 2008): 3.7. **Life expectancy** at birth (2008): male 55.0 years; female 60.0 years.

## National economy

**Budget** (2008). *Revenue:* K 7,128,000,000 (tax revenue 77.4%, of which corporate taxes 38.0%, income tax 14.8%, excise duties 6.6%; grants 15.8%; nontax revenue 6.8%). *Expenditures:* K 7,003,400,000 (current expenditures 52.0%, of which interest payments 5.3%; capital expenditures 26.9%). **Public debt** (external, outstanding; June 2009): US$1,044,390,000. **Production** (metric tons except as noted). *Agriculture and fishing* (2007): oil palm fruit 1,400,000, bananas 870,000, coconuts 677,000, coffee 75,400, cacao 50,300, natural rubber 4,700; livestock (number of live animals) 1,800,000 pigs; fisheries production 263,960 (from aquaculture, negligible). *Mining and quarrying* (2007): copper (metal content) 169,184; gold 65,000 kg; silver 51,300 kg. *Manufacturing* (value of exports in K '000,000; 2008–09): palm oil 788.8; refined petroleum products 486.5; forest products 367.9. *Energy production (consumption):* electricity (kW-hr; 2007) 2,885,000,000 (2,683,000,000); coal (metric tons; 2004) none (1,000); crude petroleum (barrels; 2008) 13,906,-500 (12,045,000); natural gas (cu m; 2008) 100,000,000 (100,000,000); petroleum products (metric tons; 2006) 842,000 (1,242,000). **Population economically active** (2007): total 3,100,000; activity rate 54.5% (participation rates: ages 15–64 [2000] 73.2%; female 49.2%; officially unemployed [2004] 1.9%). **Gross national income** (2008): US$6,509,000,000 (US$1,010 per capita). **Selected balance of payments data.** Receipts from (US$'000,000): tourism (2005) 3.6; remittances (2008) 13; foreign direct investment (FDI; 2005–07 avg.) 41; official development assistance (2007) 317. Disbursements for (US$'000,000): tourism (2005) 56; remittances (2008) 135; FDI (2005–07 avg.) 5.

## Foreign trade

**Imports** (2008; c.i.f. in commodities and f.o.b. in trading partners): K 8,413,300,000 ([2003] nonelectrical machinery 18.5%; food products 14.8%, of which cereals 7.3%; refined petroleum products 12.9%; transportation equipment 8.8%; chemical products 8.4%; fabricated metal products 6.3%). *Major import sources:* Australia 42.0%; US 22.7%; Singapore 11.3%; Japan 4.7%; China 3.5%. **Exports** (2008): K 15,423,400,000 (gold 30.3%; copper 23.4%; crude petroleum 22.7%; palm oil 6.6%; coffee 3.4%; refined petroleum products 3.3%; logs 3.0%; cocoa 2.2%). *Major export destinations:* Australia 44.3%; Japan 13.3%; Philippines 7.8%; Germany 4.8%; South Korea 4.7%.

## Transport and communications

**Transport.** *Railroads:* none. *Roads* (2000): total length 19,600 km (paved 4%). *Vehicles* (2002): passenger cars 24,900; trucks and buses 87,800. *Air transport:* passenger-km (2006; Air Niugini only) 748,000,000; metric ton-km cargo (2007) 23,000,000. **Communications,** in total units (units per 1,000 persons). Telephone landlines (2008): 60,000 (9.1); cellular telephone subscribers (2008): 600,000 (91); personal computers (2005): 391,000 (64); total Internet users (2008): 120,000 (18).

## Education and health

**Educational attainment** (1990). Percentage of population ages 25 and over having: no formal schooling 82.6%; some primary education 8.2%; completed primary 5.0%; some secondary 4.2%. **Literacy** (2007): total population ages 15 and over literate 57.8%; males literate 62.1%; females literate 53.4%. **Health:** physicians (2005) 750 (1 per 7,849 persons); hospital beds (2000) 14,516 (1 per 371 persons); infant mortality rate per 1,000 live births (2008) 60.0.

## Military

**Total active duty personnel** (November 2008): 3,100 (army 80.6%, maritime element [coastal patrol] 12.9%, air force 6.5%). **Military expenditure as percentage of GDP** (2008): 0.6%; per capita expenditure US$7.

## Background

Papua New Guinea (PNG) has been inhabited since prehistoric times. The Portuguese sighted the coast of New Guinea in 1512. The first colony was founded in 1793 by the British. In 1828 the Dutch claimed the western half as part of the Dutch East Indies. In 1884 Britain annexed the southeastern part and Germany took over the northeastern sector. The British part became the Territory of Papua in 1906 and passed to Australia, which also governed the German sector after World War I. After World War II, Australia governed both sectors as the Territory of Papua and New Guinea. Dutch New Guinea was annexed to Indonesia in 1969. Papua New Guinea achieved independence in 1975 and joined the British Commonwealth. It moved to resolve its war with independence fighters on the island of Bougainville in the 1990s. The decadelong war ended when final terms for peace were negotiated on 1 Jun 2001; Bougainville became an autonomous region in 2005.

## Recent Developments

In September 2011, the media organization WikiLeaks released confidential US diplomatic cables suggesting that Papua New Guinea politicians had enriched themselves with public funds. Although the country received substantial foreign aid—more than US$400 million annually from Australia alone—many hospitals lacked basic medications and equipment.

**Internet resource:** <www.nso.gov.pg>.

# Paraguay

**Official name:** República del Paraguay (Spanish); Tetä Paraguáype (Guaraní) (Republic of Paraguay). **Form of government:** multiparty republic with two legislative houses (Chamber of Senators [45]; Chamber of Deputies [80]). **Head of state and government:** President Federico Franco (from 2012). **Capital:** Asunción. **Official languages:** Spanish; Guaraní. **Official religion:** none (Roman Catholicism, though not official, enjoys special recognition in the constitution). **Monetary unit:** 1 guaraní (₲) = 100 céntimos; valuation (2 Jul 2012) US$1 = ₲ 4,520.00.

## Demography

**Area:** 157,048 sq mi, 406,752 sq km. **Population** (2011): 6,459,000. **Density** (2011): persons per sq mi 41.1, persons per sq km 15.9. **Urban** (2010): 61.4%. **Sex distribution** (2006): male 50.57%; female 49.43%. **Age breakdown** (2006): under 15, 35.4%; 15–29, 28.8%; 30–44, 17.4%; 45–59, 11.4%; 60–74, 5.2%; 75 and over, 1.8%. **Ethnic composition** (2000): mixed (white/Amerindian) 85.6%; white 9.3%, of which German 4.4%, Latin American 3.4%; Amerindian 1.8%; other 3.3%. **Religious affiliation** (2002): Roman Catholic 89.6%; Protestant (including all Evangelicals) 6.2%; other Christian 1.1%; nonreligious/atheist 1.1%; traditional beliefs 0.6%; other/unknown 1.4%. **Major urban areas** (2002): Asunción (2006) 519,361 (urban agglomeration [2007] 1,870,000); Ciudad del Este 222,274; San Lorenzo 204,356; Luque 170,986; Capiatá 154,274. **Location:** central South America, bordering Brazil, Argentina, and Bolivia.

## Vital statistics

**Birth rate** per 1,000 population (2007): 25.0 (world avg. 20.3). **Death rate** per 1,000 population (2007): 5.6 (world avg. 8.5). **Total fertility rate** (avg. births per childbearing woman; 2005): 3.30. **Life expectancy** at birth (2007): male 69.6 years; female 73.8 years.

---

*1 metric ton = about 1.1 short tons;    1 kilometer = 0.6 mi (statute);    1 metric ton-km cargo = about 0.68 short ton-mi cargo;    c.i.f.: cost, insurance, and freight;    f.o.b.: free on board*

## National economy

**Budget** (2006–07): *Revenue:* ₲10,174,723,-000,000 (tax revenue 65.2%, of which VAT 28.5%, income tax 10.9%, taxes on international trade 8.5%; nontax revenue and grants 34.8%). *Expenditures:* ₲9,682,282,000,000 (current expenditures 77.3%, of which wages and salaries 42.9%; capital expenditures 22.7%). **Public debt** (external, outstanding; December 2007): US$2,197,000,000. **Population economically active** (2006): total 2,735,646; activity rate 46.0% (participation rates: ages 15–64 [2002] 61.4%; female 38.5%; unemployed 11.1%). **Production** (metric tons except as noted). *Agriculture and fishing* (2007): cassava 5,100,000, soybeans 3,900,000, sugarcane 3,400,000, maté 87,500, sesame seed 53,000; livestock (number of live animals) 10,000,000 cattle, 1,600,000 pigs, 17,-000,000 chickens; fisheries production 22,100 (from aquaculture 10%). *Mining and quarrying* (2007): dimension stone 70,000; kaolin 66,000. *Manufacturing* (value added in US$'000,000; 2002): food products 253; chemical products 77; beverages 67. *Energy production (consumption):* electricity (kW-hr; 2006) 53,774,000,000 (Paraguay is the world's second largest net exporter of electricity) (8,076,-000,000); petroleum products (metric tons; 2006) negligible (1,201,000). **Gross national income** (2008): US$13,574,000,000 (US$2,180 per capita). **Selected balance of payments data.** Receipts from (US$'000,000): tourism (2007) 102; remittances (2008) 503; foreign direct investment (FDI; 2005–07 avg.) 138; official development assistance (2007) 108. Disbursements for (US$'000,000): tourism (2007) 109; FDI (2005–07 avg.) 6.

## Foreign trade

**Imports** (2006): US$5,254,271,000 (machinery and apparatus 35.9%; mineral fuels 13.2%; transportation equipment 11.5%; chemical products 6.3%; food products, beverages, and tobacco products 6.1%). *Major import sources:* China 27.0%; Brazil 20.0%; Argentina 13.6%; Japan 8.3%; US 6.4%. **Exports** (2006; electricity exports are excluded): US$1,906,367,000 (soybeans 23.0%; meat 22.3%; cereals 11.4%; flour 7.5%; vegetable oils 6.2%; wood products 5.2%). *Major export destinations:* Uruguay 22.0%; Brazil 17.2%; Russia 11.9%; Argentina 8.8%; Chile 6.9%.

## Transport and communications

**Transport.** *Railroads* (2006): operational route length 36 km. *Roads* (2000): total length 29,500 km (paved 51%). *Vehicles* (2007): passenger cars 240,728; trucks 248,086. *Air transport* (2005; Transportes Aéreos del Mercosur only): passenger-km 501,-000,000; metric ton-km cargo, none. **Communications,** in total units (units per 1,000 persons). Telephone landlines (2008): 363,000 (58); cellular telephone subscribers (2008): 5,791,000 (928); personal computers (2005): 460,000 (78); total Internet users (2008): 694,000 (111); broadband Internet subscribers (2008): 94,000 (15).

## Education and health

**Educational attainment** (2003). Percentage of population ages 15 and over having: no formal schooling 4.1%; incomplete primary education 30.2%; complete primary 30.8%; secondary 26.9%; higher 8.0%.

**Literacy** (2005): percentage of total population ages 15 and over literate 94.9%; males literate 95.9%; females literate 93.9%. **Health** (2007): physicians (2005) 5,517 (1 per 873 persons); hospital beds 5,766 (1 per 1,063 persons); infant mortality rate per 1,000 live births 32.4; undernourished population (2003–05) 700,000 (11% of total population based on the consumption of a minimum daily requirement of 1,810 calories).

## Military

**Total active duty personnel** (November 2008): 10,650 (army 71.4%, navy 18.3%, air force 10.3%). **Military expenditure as percentage of GDP** (2008): 0.9%; per capita expenditure US$22.

## Background

Seminomadic tribes speaking Guaraní were in Paraguay long before it was settled by Spain in the 16th and 17th centuries. Paraguay was part of the Viceroyalty of the Río de la Plata until it became independent in 1811. It suffered from dictatorial governments in the 19th century and from the 1865 war with Brazil, Argentina, and Uruguay. The Chaco War with Bolivia over disputed territory was settled primarily in Paraguay's favor by the peace treaty of 1938. Military governments, including that of Alfredo Stroessner, predominated in the mid-20th century until the election of a civilian president, Juan Carlos Wasmosy, in 1993. Paraguay suffered political unrest and a financial crisis beginning in the 1990s and continuing into the 21st century.

## Recent Developments

Even as Paraguay celebrated the bicentennial of its independence from Spain in 2011, the country was faced with economic and social challenges. Large landholders, who produced most of the country's soybeans and beef, blocked government proposals for land redistribution (less than 2% of the population controlled 80% of the country's arable land) and environmental protection. About 19% of Paraguay's population, and 42% of the rural population, lived below the poverty line, but Pres. Fernando Lugo's campaign to improve economic opportunities for the poor largely foundered after soybean producers blocked his efforts to increase taxes. Lugo's administration had limited successes in tackling cocaine trafficking, with a series of large seizures during the year (including one of nearly a ton). Paraguay served as a way station en route from the Andean countries to Africa and Europe.

**Internet resource:** <http://country.paraguay.com>.

# Peru

**Official name:** República del Perú (Spanish) (Republic of Peru). **Form of government:** unitary multiparty republic with one legislative house (Congress [130]). **Head of state and government:** President Ollanta Humala (from 2011), assisted by Prime Minister Juan Jiménez (from 2012). **Capital:** Lima. **Official languages:** Spanish (Quechua and Aymara are official locally). **Official religion:** none (the state recognizes Roman Catholicism as an important element in the historical and cultural development of Peru).

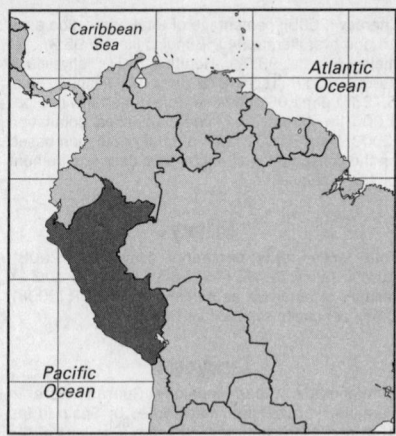

Caribbean Sea

Atlantic Ocean

Pacific Ocean

**Monetary unit:** 1 nuevo sol (S/.) = 100 céntimos; valuation (2 Jul 2012) US$1 = S/. 2.65

## Demography

**Area:** 496,225 sq mi, 1,285,216 sq km. **Population** (2011): 29,249,000. **Density** (2011): persons per sq mi 58.9, persons per sq km 22.8. **Urban** (2007): 75.9%. **Sex distribution** (2007): male 49.68%; female 50.32%. **Age breakdown** (2007): under 15, 30.5%; 15–29, 27.5%; 30–44, 20.4%; 45–59, 12.5%; 60–74, 6.4%; 75–84, 2.0%; 85 and over, 0.7%. **Ethnic composition** (2000): Quechua 47.0%; mestizo 31.9%; white 12.0%; Aymara 5.4%; Japanese 0.5%; other 3.2%. **Religious affiliation** (2005): Roman Catholic 85%, of which practicing weekly 15%; Protestant 7%; independent Christian 4%; other 4%. **Major cities** (2007): Lima (urban agglomeration) 8,472,935; Arequipa 749,291; Trujillo 682,834; Chiclayo 524,442; Piura 377,496. **Location:** western South America, bordering Ecuador, Colombia, Brazil, Bolivia, Chile, and the South Pacific Ocean.

## Vital statistics

**Birth rate** per 1,000 population (2007): 20.2 (world avg. 20.3). **Death rate** per 1,000 population (2007): 6.2 (world avg. 8.5). **Total fertility rate** (avg. births per childbearing woman; 2007): 2.46. **Life expectancy** at birth (2007): male 68.3 years; female 72.0 years.

## National economy

**Budget** (2008). *Revenue:* S/. 68,352,000,000 (tax revenue 85.2%, of which VAT 46.2%, taxes on income and profits 35.3%; nontax revenue 14.8%). *Expenditures:* S/. 60,073,000,000 (current expenditures 76.9%; capital expenditures 14.6%; debt service 8.5%). **Production** (metric tons except as noted). *Agriculture and fishing* (2008): sugarcane 8,228,623, potatoes 3,383,020, rice 2,793,980, quinoa 31,824 (in 2008 Peru ranked second in the world in coca production; an estimated 302 metric tons of cocaine were produced); livestock (number of live animals) 14,580,200 sheep, 5,420,860 cattle, (2007)

4,962,000 llamas and alpacas; fisheries production (2007) 7,250,075 (from aquaculture 1%). *Mining and quarrying* (2008; metal content): iron ore 5,243,000; zinc 1,371,000; copper 1,036,700; lead 317,700; molybdenum 16,100; silver 3,465; gold (all forms) 174,700 kg. *Manufacturing* (value in US$'000,000; 2007): food products 4,066; wearing apparel 1,326; paints, soaps, pharmaceuticals 1,233; refined petroleum products 862. *Energy production (consumption):* electricity (kW-hr; 2006) 27,358,000,000 (27,358,000,000); coal (metric tons; 2007) 127,900 (1,192,000); crude petroleum (barrels; 2008) 28,000,000 ([2006] 56,600,000); petroleum products (metric tons; 2006) 9,193,000 (6,412,000); natural gas (cu m; 2006) 2,249,000,000 (2,249,000,000). **Selected balance of payments data.** Receipts from (US$'000,000): tourism (2007) 1,938; remittances (2008) 2,200; foreign direct investment (FDI; 2005–07 avg.) 3,796; official development assistance (2007) 263. Disbursements for (US$'000,000): tourism (2007) 1,007; remittances (2008) 137; FDI (2005–07 avg.) 470. **Population economically active** (2006): total 13,762,000; activity rate of total population 49.9% (participation rates: ages 15–64, 74.7%; female 44.7%; officially unemployed [metropolitan Lima only; August 2008–July 2009] 8.5%). **Gross national income** (2008): US$114,960,000,000 (US$3,990 per capita). **Public debt** (external, outstanding; 2007): US$19,669,000,000.

## Foreign trade

**Imports** (2007; c.i.f.): US$20,494,000,000 (machinery and apparatus 23.0%; chemical products 14.6%; crude petroleum 13.4%; food products 8.4%; base and fabricated metals 8.3%). *Major import sources:* US 17.7%; China 12.1%; Brazil 9.2%; Ecuador 7.4%; Argentina 5.5%. **Exports** (2007; f.o.b.): US$27,800,000,000 (ores and concentrates 32.3%, of which copper 16.5%, zinc 8.3%, molybdenum 3.5%; gold 15.0%; food products 12.8%, of which fish meal 4.6%; crude petroleum 8.7%; refined copper 8.6%; wearing apparel and accessories 5.1%). *Major export destinations:* US 19.4%; China 10.9%; Switzerland 8.4%; Japan 7.8%; Canada 6.6%.

## Transport and communications

**Transport.** *Railroads* (2006): route length 1,720 km; (2005) passenger-km 125,756,000; metric ton-km cargo 1,164,378,000. *Roads* (2006): total length 78,986 km (paved 14%). *Vehicles* (2007): passenger cars 917,110; trucks and buses 525,277. *Air transport* (2007): passenger-km 6,472,300,000; metric ton-km cargo 148,600,000. **Communications,** in total units (units per 1,000 persons). Telephone landlines (2008): 2,878,000 (101); cellular telephone subscribers (2008): 20,952,000 (734); personal computers (2005): 2,800,000 (103); total Internet users (2008): 7,128,000 (250); broadband Internet subscribers (2008): 726,000 (25).

## Education and health

**Educational attainment** (2005). Percentage of population ages 15 and over having: no formal schooling 11.8%; less than complete primary education

---

*1 metric ton = about 1.1 short tons;    1 kilometer = 0.6 mi (statute);    1 metric ton-km cargo = about 0.68 short ton-mi cargo;    c.i.f.: cost, insurance, and freight;    f.o.b.: free on board*

24.3%; complete primary 11.5%; incomplete secondary 15.3%; complete secondary 19.0%; higher 18.1%. **Literacy** (2005): total population ages 15 and over literate 91.6%; males literate 95.6%; females literate 87.7%. **Health** (2007): physicians 41,788 (1 per 672 persons); hospital beds 44,195 (1 per 635 persons); infant mortality rate per 1,000 live births 30.5; undernourished population (2002–04) 3,300,000 (12% of total population based on the consumption of a minimum daily requirement of 1,820 calories).

## Military

**Total active duty personnel** (November 2008): 114,000 (army 64.9%, navy 20.2%, air force 14.9%). **Military expenditure as percentage of GDP** (2008): 1.1%; per capita expenditure US$47.

## Background

Peru was the center of the Inca empire, which was established about 1230 with its capital at Cuzco. In 1533 it was conquered by Francisco Pizarro, and it was dominated by Spain for almost 300 years as the Viceroyalty of Peru. It declared its independence in 1821, and freedom was achieved in 1824. Peru was defeated in the War of the Pacific with Chile (1879–83). A boundary dispute with Ecuador erupted into war in 1941 and gave Peru control over a larger part of the Amazon basin; further disputes ensued until the border was demarcated again in 1998. The government was overthrown by a military junta in 1968, and civilian rule was restored in 1980. The government of Alberto Fujimori dissolved the legislature in 1992 and promulgated a new constitution the following year. It later successfully combated the Sendero Luminoso (Shining Path) and Tupac Amarú rebel movements. Fujimori won a second term in 1995 and a controversial third term in 2000, but he left office and the country late that year amid allegations of corruption. Fujimori was succeeded by Alejandro Toledo (2001–06), Peru's first democratically elected president of Quechuan ethnicity.

## Recent Developments

Former military officer Ollanta Humala was elected president of Peru in 2011. His basic campaign platform—a commitment to maintaining Peru's rapid economic growth and to sharing that growth with the country's indigenous population—was reflected in his creation of a new Ministry of Development and Inclusion. He also raised mining royalties substantially (with the consent of the international corporation involved) and signed a prior-consultation law that required dialogue with indigenous groups before mining operations could proceed. Peru still faced many difficulties. Its economy depended largely on mineral exports that in turn rested on shifting world prices and the economic well-being of China, the United States, and other more-developed countries. Remnants of the brutal Shining Path insurgency that had paralyzed the country were still active in some remote areas of Peru, and drug production and corruption persisted. In early 2012, however, the government announced that the remaining leaders of the Shining Path, Florindo Flores and Walter Diaz Vega, had been captured by police and military forces.

**Internet resource:** <www.visitperu.com>.

# Philippines

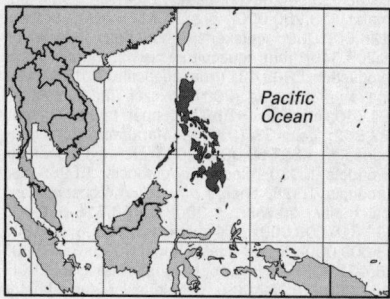

Pacific Ocean

**Official name:** Republika ng Pilipinas (Filipino); Republic of the Philippines (English). **Form of government:** unitary republic with two legislative houses (Senate [24]; House of Representatives [287]). **Head of state and government:** President Benigno Aquino (from 2010). **Capital:** Manila; other government offices and ministries are located in Quezon City and other Manila suburbs. **Official languages:** Filipino; English. **Official religion:** none. **Monetary unit:** 1 Philippine piso (peso; ₱) = 100 sentimos; valuation (2 Jul 2012) US$1 = ₱ 42.04.

## Demography

**Area:** 115,831 sq mi, 300,000 sq km. **Population** (2011): 95,849,000. **Density** (2011): persons per sq mi 827.5, persons per sq km 319.5. **Urban** (2011): 48.8%. **Sex distribution** (2005): male 50.38%; female 49.62%. **Age breakdown** (2005): under 15, 35.6%; 15–29, 28.4%; 30–44, 18.8%; 45–59, 11.2%; 60–74, 4.9%; 75–84, 1.0%; 85 and over, 0.1%. **Ethnic composition** (2000): Tagalog 20.9%; Visayan (Cebu) 19.0%; Ilocano 11.1%; Hiligaynon (Visaya) 9.4%; Waray-Waray (Binisaya) 4.7%; Central Bikol (Naga) 4.6%; Filipino mestizo 3.5%; Pampango 3.1%; other 23.7%. **Religious affiliation** (2005): Roman Catholic 64.9%; independent Christian 17.7%; Muslim 5.1%; Protestant 5.0%; traditional beliefs 2.2%; other 5.1%. **Major cities** (2007): Manila 1,660,714 (National Capital Region 11,553,427); Quezon City 2,679,450; Caloocan 1,378,856; Davao 1,363,337; Cebu City 798,809. **Location:** southeastern Asia, archipelago between the Philippine Sea and the South China Sea, east of Vietnam.

## Vital statistics

**Birth rate** per 1,000 population (2005): 24.1 (world avg. 20.3). **Death rate** per 1,000 population (2005): 5.6 (world avg. 8.5). **Total fertility rate** (avg. births per childbearing woman; 2005): 3.41. **Life expectancy** at birth (2005): male 67.0 years; female 72.9 years.

## National economy

**Budget** (2007). *Revenue:* ₱ 1,047,500,000,000 (tax revenue 89.1%, of which income tax 40.7%, taxes on international trade 20.0%; nontax revenues 10.9%). *Expenditures:* ₱ 1,145,030,000,000 (debt service 24.2%; education 14.3%; transportation and communications 10.0%; public order 5.7%; social protection 4.8%; defense 4.7%; health 1.6%). *Production* (metric tons except as noted). *Agriculture and fishing*

(2007): sugarcane 25,300,000, rice 16,000,000, coconuts 15,580,000; livestock (number of live animals) 13,250,000 pigs, 3,365,000 buffalo, 136,000,000 chickens; fisheries production 3,209,349 (from aquaculture 22%); aquatic plants production 1,505,421 (from aquaculture 100%). *Mining and quarrying* (2007): nickel (metal content) 84,740; chromite 31,592; copper (metal content) 22,862; gold 38,792 kg. *Manufacturing* (value added in US$'000,000; 2003): refined petroleum products 1,980; electronic products 1,696; food products 1,338. *Energy production (consumption):* electricity (kW-hr; 2006) 56,818,000,000 (56,818,000,000); coal (metric tons; 2006) 180,000 (3,600,000); lignite (metric tons; 2006) 3,072,000 (6,401,000); crude petroleum (barrels; 2006) 182,000 (78,262,000); petroleum products (metric tons; 2006) 9,823,000 (11,852,000); natural gas (cu m; 2006) 2,969,000,000 (2,969,000,000). **Selected balance of payments data.** Receipts from (US$'000,000): tourism (2007) 4,931; remittances (2008) 18,643; foreign direct investment (FDI; 2005–07 avg.) 2,568. Disbursements for (US$'000,000): tourism (2007) 1,615; remittances (2008) 44; FDI (2005–07 avg.) 1,245. **Gross national income** (2008): US$170,410,000,000 (US$1,890 per capita). **Public debt** (external, outstanding; June 2008): US$35,019,000,000. **Population economically active** (2007): total 36,434,000; activity rate 41% (participation rates: ages 15 and over, 63.6%; female [2006] 39.4%; unemployed [April 2007–March 2008] 7.2%).

## Foreign trade

**Imports** (2006; c.i.f.): US$54,078,000,000 (electronic components 33.6%; crude petroleum 14.1%; chemical products 7.4%; parts for office machines and computers 6.6%; food products 5.9%). *Major import sources:* US 16.2%; Japan 14.2%; Singapore 8.4%; Taiwan 7.9%; China 7.2%. **Exports** (2006; f.o.b.): US$47,410,000,000 (microcircuits and transistors 35.8%; office machines and computers and parts 17.2%; wearing apparel and accessories 5.5%; food products 3.8%). *Major export destinations:* US 18.3%; Japan 16.7%; Netherlands 10.1%; China 9.8%; Hong Kong 7.8%.

## Transport and communications

**Transport.** *Railroads* (2004): route length 897 km; passenger-km 83,400,000; metric ton-km cargo (2000) 660,000,000. *Roads* (2003): total length 200,037 km (paved 10%). *Vehicles* (2007): passenger cars 751,100; trucks and buses 311,400. *Air transport* (2008): passenger-km 17,868,000,000; metric ton-km cargo 265,380,000. **Communications,** in total units (units per 1,000 persons). Telephone landlines (2008): 3,905,000 (43); cellular telephone subscribers (2008): 68,102,000 (754); personal computers (2005): 4,521,000 (54); total Internet users (2008): 5,618,000 (62); broadband Internet subscribers (2007): 968,000 (11).

## Education and health

**Educational attainment** (2000). Percentage of population ages 25 and over having: no formal school-

ing/unknown 6.1%; primary education 38.5%; incomplete secondary 12.5%; complete secondary 17.2%; technical 5.9%; incomplete undergraduate 11.8%; complete undergraduate 7.3%; graduate 0.7%. **Literacy** (2003): total population ages 15 and over literate 92.6%. **Health** (2007): physicians (2005) 98,210 (1 per 865 persons); hospital beds 92,561 (1 per 956 persons); infant mortality rate per 1,000 live births 21.9; undernourished population (2003–05) 13,300,000 (16% of total population based on the consumption of a minimum daily requirement of 1,750 calories).

## Military

**Total active duty personnel** (November 2008): 106,000 (army 62.3%, navy 22.6%, air force 15.1%). **Military expenditure as percentage of GDP** (2008): 0.7%; per capita expenditure US$12.

## Background

Waves of diverse immigrants from the Asian mainland occupied the Philippines in ancient times. Ferdinand Magellan arrived in 1521. The islands were colonized by the Spanish, who retained control until the islands were ceded to the US in 1898 following the Spanish-American War. The Commonwealth of the Philippines was established in 1935 to prepare the country for political and economic independence, which was delayed by World War II and the Japanese invasion. The islands were liberated by US forces during 1944–45, and the Republic of the Philippines was proclaimed in 1946, with a government patterned on that of the US. In 1965 Ferdinand Marcos was elected president. He declared martial law in 1972, and it lasted until 1981. After 20 years of dictatorial rule, he was driven from power in 1986. Corazon Aquino became president and instituted democratic rule. The government has tried to come to terms with Muslim independence fighters in the south by establishing the Muslim Mindanao autonomous region in Mindanao and nearby islands, but violent conflict continued into the 21st century.

## Recent Developments

A long dispute between the Philippines and China escalated in 2011 over tiny islands in a portion of the South China Sea that the Philippines announced in June it had renamed the West Philippine Sea. China, however, claimed the entire South China Sea, including areas off the coasts of five other countries that may contain petroleum and natural gas beneath major shipping lanes. This led to several naval incidents between China and the Philippines during 2011. In March two Chinese patrol boats harassed an oil-exploration vessel sent by the Philippines to Reed Bank, an area claimed by the Philippines. The Philippines also accused Chinese forces of having shot at Filipino fishermen and having marked some islands as Chinese property. Pres. Benigno S. Aquino III ordered an improvement in the Philippines' limited ability to defend the islands. Armed forces—mostly using half-century-old equipment—were to be modernized with US help, he said. As a start, a decommissioned US Coast Guard patrol vessel was acquired. In December some 1,250 people died and

---

*1 metric ton = about 1.1 short tons;    1 kilometer = 0.6 mi (statute);    1 metric ton-km cargo = about 0.68 short ton-mi cargo;    c.i.f.: cost, insurance, and freight;    f.o.b.: free on board*

hundreds were missing after storms produced flash floods that devastated parts of Mindanao in the south.

Internet resource: <www.nscb.gov.ph>.

# Poland

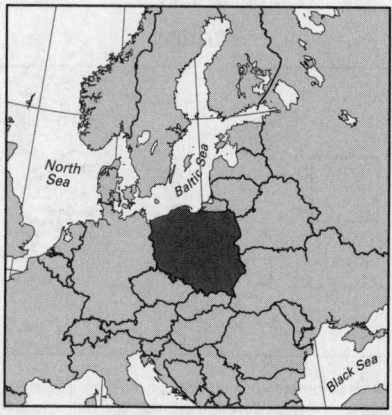

**Official name:** Rzeczpospolita Polska (Republic of Poland). **Form of government:** unitary multiparty republic with two legislative houses (Senate [100]; Sejm [460]). **Head of state:** President Bronisław Komorowski (from 2010). **Head of government:** Prime Minister Donald Tusk (from 2007). **Capital:** Warsaw. **Official language:** Polish. **Official religion:** none (Roman Catholicism has special recognition per 1997 concordat with Vatican City). **Monetary unit:** 1 złoty (zł) = 100 groszy; valuation (2 Jul 2012) US$1 = zł 3.35.

## Demography

**Area:** 120,726 sq mi, 312,679 sq km. **Population** (2011): 38,216,000. **Density** (2011): persons per sq mi 316.6, persons per sq km 122.2. **Urban** (2010): 60.9%. **Sex distribution** (2008): male 48.29%; female 51.71%. **Age breakdown** (2008): under 15, 15.2%; 15–29, 23.4%; 30–44, 20.7%; 45–59, 22.1%; 60–74, 12.4%; 75–84, 5.0%; 85 and over, 1.2%. **Ethnic composition** (2000): Polish 90.0%; Ukrainian 4.0%; German 4.0%; Belarusian 0.5%; Kashubian 0.4%; other 1.1%. **Religious affiliation** (2007): Roman Catholic 88.6%; other Catholic 0.1%; Polish Orthodox 1.3%; Protestant 0.4%; Jehovah's Witness 0.3%; other (mostly nonreligious) 9.3%. **Major cities** (2008): Warsaw 1,709,781; Krakow 754,624; Lodz 747,152; Wroclaw 632,162; Poznan 557,264. **Location:** central Europe, bordering the Baltic Sea, the Russian exclave of Kaliningrad, Lithuania, Belarus, Ukraine, Slovakia, Czech Republic, and Germany.

## Vital statistics

**Birth rate** per 1,000 population (2008): 10.9 (world avg. 20.3); within marriage 80.1%. **Death rate** per 1,000 population (2008): 10.0 (world avg. 8.5). **Total fertility rate** (avg. births per childbearing woman; 2008): 1.39. **Life expectancy** at birth (2008): male 71.3 years; female 80.0 years.

## National economy

**Budget** (2008). *Revenue:* zł 253,547,000,000 (VAT 40.1%; excise tax 19.9%; income tax 15.2%; corporate taxes 10.7%). *Expenditures:* zł 277,893,-000,000 (social security and welfare 29.6%; public debt 9.0%; national defense 5.0%; education 4.8%; public safety 4.5%). **Gross national income** (2008): US$453,034,000,000 (US$11,880 per capita). **Production** (metric tons except as noted). *Agriculture and fishing* (2008): potatoes 10,462,000, wheat 9,275,000, sugar beets 8,715,000, sour cherries 202,000, currants 197,000; *livestock* (number of live animals; 2009) 14,279,000 pigs, 5,700,000 cattle, (2007) 1,450,000 beehives; fisheries production (2007) 187,448 (from aquaculture 19%). *Mining and quarrying* (2007): sulfur (2008–09) 494,800; copper ore (metal content) 505,900; silver (metal content) 1,250. *Manufacturing* (value of sales in zł '000,000; 2008): food products 127,127; transportation equipment 94,790; mineral fuels 59,077. *Energy production (consumption):* electricity ('000,000 kW-hr; 2008–09) 151,968 ([2007] 154,000); coal ('000 metric tons; 2008–09) 81,441 ([2007] 85,337); lignite ('000 metric tons; 2008–09) 59,322 ([2007] 57,528); crude petroleum (barrels; 2008) 5,593,000 ([2007] 148,538,000); petroleum products (metric tons; 2008–09) 26,507,000 ([2007] 25,322,000); natural gas (cu m; 2008–09) 5,263,280,900 ([2007] 16,549,000,000). **Public debt** (external, outstanding; August 2009): US$53,287,900,000. **Population economically active** (2008): total 17,202,000; activity rate of total population 45.1% (participation rates: ages 15–64, 64.4%; female 45.2%; unemployed [October 2008–September 2009] 10.4%). **Selected balance of payments data.** Receipts from (US$'000,-000): tourism (2007) 10,599; remittances (2008) 10,727; foreign direct investment (FDI; 2005–07 avg.) 15,714. Disbursements for (US$'000,000): tourism (2007) 7,753; remittances (2008) 1,716; FDI (2005–07 avg.) 5,210.

## Foreign trade

**Imports** (2008; c.i.f.): zł 497,028,300,000 (electrical equipment 13.2%; chemical products 13.0%; mineral fuels 11.2%; transportation equipment 11.2%; machinery and apparatus 11.0%; base and fabricated metals 10.9%). *Major import sources:* Germany 23.0%; Russia 9.7%; China 8.1%; Italy 6.5%; France 4.7%. **Exports** (2008; f.o.b.): zł 405,383,100,000 (transportation equipment 17.4%; base and fabricated metals 12.9%; electrical equipment 12.4%; machinery and apparatus 12.3%; food products 10.1%; chemical products 5.9%; furniture 5.7%). *Major export destinations:* Germany 25.0%; France 6.2%; Italy 6.0%; UK 5.8%; Czech Republic 5.7%.

## Transport and communications

**Transport.** *Railroads* (2008): length 20,196 km; passenger-km 20,389,000,000; metric ton-km cargo 52,043,000,000. *Roads* (2007; public roads only): total length 383,100 km (paved 68%). *Vehicles* (2008): passenger cars 16,080,000; trucks and buses 2,802,000. *Air transport* (2008): passenger-km 9,438,000,000; metric ton-km cargo 106,-000,000. **Communications,** in total units (units per 1,000 persons). Telephone landlines (2008): 8,690,000 (228); cellular telephone subscribers (2008): 44,086,000 (1,156); personal computers

(2004): 7,362,000 (191); total Internet users (2008): 18,679,000 (490); broadband Internet subscribers (2008): 4,791,000 (126).

## Education and health

**Educational attainment** (2007). Percentage of population ages 13 and over having: no formal schooling/incomplete primary education 2.0%; complete primary 20.2%; lower secondary/vocational 27.9%; upper secondary and postsecondary 33.4%; university 16.5%. **Literacy** (2008): virtually 100%. **Health** (2007): physicians 78,229 (1 per 487 persons); hospital beds 227,845 (1 per 167 persons); infant mortality rate per 1,000 live births (2008) 5.6; undernourished population (2002–04) less than 2.5% of total population.

## Military

**Total active duty personnel** (November 2008): 121,808 (army 51.5%, navy 8.9%, air force 19.2%, joint staff 20.4%). **Military expenditure as percentage of GDP** (2008): 1.8%; per capita expenditure US$224.

## Background

Established as a kingdom in 922 under Mieszko I, Poland united with Lithuania in 1386 under the Jagiellon dynasty (1386–1572) to become the dominant power in east-central Europe. In 1466 it wrested western and eastern Prussia from the Teutonic Order, and its lands eventually stretched to the Black Sea. Wars with Sweden and Russia in the late 17th century led to the loss of considerable territory. In 1697 the electors of Saxony became kings of Poland, virtually ending Polish independence. In the late 18th century, Poland was divided among Prussia, Russia, and Austria. After 1815 the former Polish lands came under Russian domination, and from 1863 Poland was a Russian province. After World War I, an independent Poland was established by the Allies. The invasion of Poland in 1939 by the USSR and Germany precipitated World War II, during which the Nazis sought to purge its culture and its large Jewish population. Reoccupied by Soviet forces in 1945, it was controlled by a Soviet-dominated government from 1947. In the 1980s the Solidarity labor movement led by Lech Walesa achieved major political reforms, and free elections were held in 1989. An economic austerity program instituted in 1990 sped the transition to a market economy. Poland became a member of NATO in 1999 and the EU in 2004.

## Recent Developments

The economy of Poland continued to grow in 2011, with an estimated increase of 3.8%. In December the country's inflation rate stood at 4.6%, while the unemployment rate was 12.5%, slightly higher than the December 2010 figure. The government continued to express a commitment to adopting the euro, even though Greece's economic crisis dampened Polish enthusiasm for the common currency. The government did, however, refuse to set a new target date for adoption until the economic situation had stabilized.

Despite the economic slowdown in much of Europe, Poland was still perceived as a relatively safe haven in terms of economic development, a view that was supported by the country's decision not to use the US$20.5 billion flexible credit line established for it in 2009 by the International Monetary Fund.

**Internet resource:** <www.stat.gov.pl>.

# Portugal

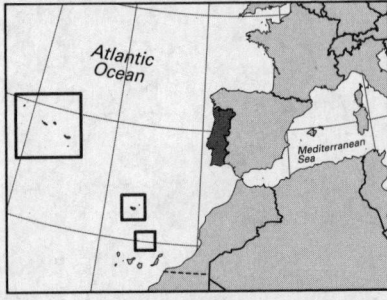

**Official name:** República Portuguesa (Portuguese Republic). **Form of government:** republic with one legislative house (Assembly of the Republic [230]). **Head of state:** President Aníbal Cavaco Silva (from 2006). **Head of government:** Prime Minister Pedro Passos Coelho (from 2011). **Capital:** Lisbon. **Official language:** Portuguese. **Official religion:** none (a 2004 concordat with the Vatican acknowledges the special role of the Roman Catholic Church in Portugal). **Monetary unit:** 1 euro (€) = 100 cents; valuation (2 Jul 2012) US$1 = €0.79.

## Demography

**Area:** 35,558 sq mi, 92,094 sq km. **Population** (2011): 10,555,000. **Density** (2011): persons per sq mi 296.8, persons per sq km 114.6. **Urban** (2009): 60.1%. **Sex distribution** (2008): male 48.40%, female 51.60%. **Age breakdown** (2005): under 15, 15.7%; 15–29, 20.4%; 30–44, 22.6%; 45–59, 19.2%; 60–74, 14.8%; 75–84, 5.9%; 85 and over, 1.4%. **Ethnic composition** (2000): Portuguese 91.9%; mixed race people from Angola, Mozambique, and Cape Verde 1.6%; Brazilian 1.4%; Marrano 1.2%; other European 1.2%; Han Chinese 0.9%; other 1.8%. **Religious affiliation** (2000): Christian 92.4%, of which Roman Catholic 87.4%, independent Christian 2.7%, Protestant 1.3%, other Christian 1.0%; nonreligious/atheist 6.5%; Buddhist 0.6%; other 0.5%. **Major cities** (2001): Lisbon 564,657 (urban agglomeration [2005] 2,761,000); Porto 263,131 (urban agglomeration [2005] 1,309,000); Braga 164,192; Coimbra 148,443; Funchal 103,961. **Location:** southwestern Europe, bordering Spain and the North Atlantic Ocean.

## Vital statistics

**Birth rate** per 1,000 population (2008): 9.8 (world avg. 20.3); within marriage 63.8%. **Death rate** per

---

*1 metric ton = about 1.1 short tons;    1 kilometer = 0.6 mi (statute);    1 metric ton-km cargo = about 0.68 short ton-mi cargo;    c.i.f.: cost, insurance, and freight;    f.o.b.: free on board*

1,000 population (2008): 9.8 (world avg. 8.5). **Total fertility rate** (avg. births per childbearing woman; 2008): 1.37. **Life expectancy** at birth (2008): male 75.5 years; female 81.7 years.

## National economy

**Budget** (2005). *Revenue:* €56,498,000,000 (tax revenue 56.2%, of which taxes of goods and services 33.7%, income tax 20.3%; social contributions 32.9%). *Expenditures:* €65,096,000,000 (social protection 35.6%; education 16.1%; health 15.9%; public order 4.5%; defense 3.2%). **Public debt** (2007): US$158,000,000,000. **Production** (metric tons except as noted). *Agriculture and fishing* (2007): grapes 1,050,000, tomatoes 1,000,000, corn (maize) 646,500, olives 375,000, cork (2008) 165,000; livestock (number of live animals) 3,549,000 sheep, 2,295,450 pigs, 1,407,270 cattle; fisheries production 260,275 (from aquaculture 3%). *Mining and quarrying* (2007): marble (2006) 837,000; kaolin (2006) 167,792; copper (metal content) 90,247; tungsten (metal content) 1,067. *Manufacturing* (value added in US$'000,000; 2003): food products 2,148; cement, tiles, and ceramics 1,611; fabricated metal products 1,536. *Energy production (consumption):* electricity (kW-hr; 2006) 49,041,000,000 (54,482,000,000); coal (metric tons; 2006) none (5,467,000); crude petroleum (barrels; 2006) none (97,108,000); petroleum products (metric tons; 2006) 12,036,000 (10,851,000); natural gas (cu m; 2006) none (4,339,000,000). **Population economically active** (2006): total 5,587,300; activity rate of total population 52.5% (participation rates: ages 15–64, 73.9%; female 46.6%; unemployed [2008] 7.6%). **Gross national income** (2008): US$218,405,000,000 (US$20,560 per capita). **Selected balance of payments data.** Receipts from (US$'000,000): tourism (2007) 10,162; remittances (2008) 4,057; foreign direct investment (FDI; 2005–07 avg.) 6,956. Disbursements for (US$'000,000): tourism (2007) 3,922; remittances (2008) 1,410; FDI (2005–07 avg.) 5,100.

## Foreign trade

**Imports** (2006; c.i.f.): €53,162,000,000 (machinery and apparatus 18.7%; chemical products 10.9%; motor vehicles 10.3%; crude petroleum 9.5%; food products 9.3%). *Major import sources* (2007): Spain 29.5%; Germany 12.9%; France 8.4%; Italy 5.2%; Netherlands 4.5%. **Exports** (2006; f.o.b.): €34,561,000,000 (machinery and apparatus and electronics 18.6%; textiles, wearing apparel, and footwear 14.2%; motor vehicles and parts 12.5%; base and fabricated metals 7.4%; chemical products 6.5%; food products 4.5%). *Major export destinations* (2007): Spain 27.1%; Germany 12.9%; France 12.3%; UK 5.9%; US 4.8%.

## Transport and communications

**Transport.** *Railroads* (2007): length 2,838 km; passenger-km 3,987,000,000; metric ton-km cargo 2,586,000,000. *Roads* (2005): total length 76,802 km (paved [2004] 86%). *Vehicles* (2006): passenger cars 5,234,477; trucks and buses 148,706. *Air transport* (2008): passenger-km 22,860,000,000; metric ton-km cargo 344,628,000. **Communications**, in total units (units per 1,000 persons). Telephone landlines (2008): 4,121,000 (386); cellular telephone subscribers (2008): 14,910,000 (1,396); personal computers (2007): 1,823,000 (172); total Internet users (2008): 4,451,000 (417); broadband Internet subscribers (2008): 1,692,000 (159).

## Education and health

**Educational attainment** (2002). Percentage of population ages 25–64 having: no formal schooling through complete primary 67%; complete lower secondary 13%; complete upper secondary 11%; higher 9%. **Literacy** (2002): total population ages 15 and over literate 92.5%; males literate 95.2%; females literate 90.3%. **Health** (2007): physicians 37,904 (1 per 280 persons); hospital beds 36,178 (1 per 294 persons); infant mortality rate per 1,000 live births (2008) 3.3; undernourished population (2002–04) less than 2.5% of total population.

## Military

**Total active duty personnel** (November 2008): 42,910 (army 62.2%, navy 21.2%, air force 16.6%); US troops (November 2008): 792. **Military expenditure as percentage of GDP** (2007): 1.5%; per capita expenditure US$319.

## Background

Celtic peoples settled the Iberian Peninsula in the 1st millennium BC. They were conquered about 140 BC by the Romans, who ruled until the 5th century AD, when the area was invaded by Germanic tribes. A Muslim invasion in 711 left only the northern part of Portugal in Christian hands. In 1139 it became the kingdom of Portugal and expanded as it reconquered the Muslim-held sectors. The boundaries of modern continental Portugal were completed in 1270 under King Afonso III. In the 15th and 16th centuries, exploration took Portuguese navigators to Africa, India, Indonesia, China, the Middle East, and South America, where colonies were established. António de Oliveira Salazar ruled Portugal as a dictator in the mid-20th century; he died in office in 1970, and his successor was ousted in a coup in 1974. A new constitution was adopted in 1976 (revised 1982), and civilian rule resumed. The government returned Macau, its last overseas territory, to Chinese rule in 1999. Portugal was a charter member of NATO and is a member of the EU.

## Recent Developments

Portugal's political and economic crisis came to a head in 2011 as the government struggled to put together a credible package to fix the country's huge fiscal imbalances and reduce the budget deficit. In May the government followed Greece and Ireland in seeking outside economic help and called for a bailout, agreeing to negotiate financial assistance from the EU, the European Central Bank, and the IMF. The deal would provide Portugal with €78 billion (US$116 billion) over three years. In exchange, Portugal agreed to apply tough economic measures designed to slash the deficit by cutting public spending and raising taxes. The austerity measures were dramatic—the bailout required Portugal to reduce its deficit to 5.9% of GDP in 2011, from more than 9.0% in 2010. Taxes were pushed higher. One-off measures were introduced, notably the decision to cancel the Christmas bonus for state employees. The outlook for Portugal over the following two years was for continued recession as the austerity effects worked their way through the economy.

Internet resource: <www.ine.pt>.

# Qatar

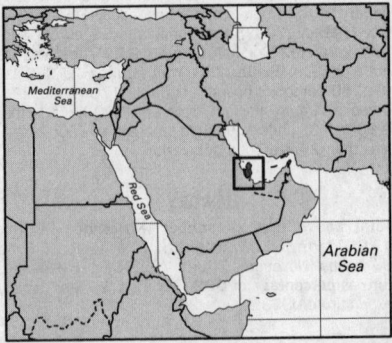

**Official name:** Dawlat Qatar (State of Qatar). **Form of government:** constitutional emirate with one advisory body (Advisory Council [35]). **Head of state and government:** Emir Sheikh Hamad ibn Khalifah al-Thani (from 1995), assisted by Prime Minister Sheikh Hamad ibn Jassim ibn Jabr al-Thani (from 2007). **Capital:** Doha. **Official language:** Arabic. **Official religion:** Islam. **Monetary unit:** 1 Qatari riyal (QR) = 100 dirhams; valuation (2 Jul 2012) US$1 = QR 3.64.

## Demography

**Area:** 4,468 sq mi, 11,571 sq km. **Population** (2011): 1,624,000. **Density** (2011): persons per sq mi 363.5, persons per sq km 140.4. **Urban** (2009): 95.8%. **Sex distribution** (2007): male 75.60%; female 24.40%. **Age breakdown** (2005): under 15, 21.8%; 15–29, 25.5%; 30–44, 33.7%; 45–59, 16.3%; 60–74, 2.4%; 75 and over, 0.3%. **Ethnic composition** (2000): Arab 52.5%, of which Palestinian 13.4%, Qatari 13.3%, Lebanese 10.4%, Syrian 9.4%; Persian 16.5%; Indo-Pakistani 15.2%; black African 9.5%; other 6.3%. **Religious affiliation** (2000): Muslim 83%, of which Sunni 73%, Shi'i 10%; Christian 10%, of which Roman Catholic 6%; Hindu 3%; Buddhist 2%; nonreligious 2%. **Major cities** (2004): Al-Dawhah (Doha) 339,847; Al-Rayyan 258,193; Al-Wakrah 26,993; Umm Salal Muhammad 25,413; Al-Khawr 18,036. **Location:** the Middle East, bordering the Persian Gulf and Saudi Arabia.

## Vital statistics

**Birth rate** per 1,000 population (2008): 11.9 (world avg. 20.3). **Death rate** per 1,000 population (2008): 1.3 (world avg. 8.5). **Total fertility rate** (avg. births per childbearing woman; 2005): 2.80. **Life ex-**

pectancy at birth (2005): male 74.4 years; female 75.8 years.

## National economy

**Budget** (2007–08). *Revenue:* QR 117,790,000,000 (petroleum and natural gas revenue 60.1%; investment income 25.8%; corporate taxes 7.6%). *Expenditures:* QR 84,727,000,000 (public utilities 11.4%; defense 7.5%; communications 5.6%; health 5.2%; education 5.1%; roads 3.2%; interest payments 2.2%). **Production** (metric tons except as noted). *Agriculture and fishing* (2007): dates 21,000, tomatoes 5,400, barley 5,000; livestock (number of live animals) 160,000 goats, 120,000 sheep, 14,000 camels; fisheries production 15,226 (from aquaculture, negligible). *Mining and quarrying* (2007): limestone 1,100,000; gypsum, sand and gravel, and clay are also produced. *Manufacturing* (value added in QR '000,000; 2005): refined petroleum products 4,502; chemical products 2,168; base metals 1,959. *Energy production (consumption):* electricity (kW-hr; 2006) 15,325,000,000 (15,325,000,000); crude petroleum (barrels; 2007) 308,600,000 ([2006] 41,797,000); petroleum products (metric tons; 2006) 4,723,000 (2,059,000); natural gas (cu m; 2006) 49,500,000,000 (19,092,000,000). **Population economically active** (2004): total 444,133; activity rate of total population 59.7% (participation rates: ages 15 and over, 77.1%; female 15.1%; unemployed 1.5%). **Gross national income** (2008): US$113,984,000,000 (US$88,990 per capita). **Selected balance of payments data.** Receipts from (US$'000,000): tourism (2006) 874; foreign direct investment (FDI; 2005–07 avg.) 865. Disbursements for (US$'000,000): tourism (2006) 3,751; remittances (2006–07) 5,000; FDI (2005–07 avg.) 1,914.

## Foreign trade

**Imports** (2006; c.i.f.): US$16,440,000,000 (nonelectrical machinery and equipment 23.5%; iron and steel 13.7%; electrical machinery and apparatus [including parts] 8.6%; motor vehicles 6.8%; chemical products 5.1%; fabricated metal products 4.9%). *Major import sources:* Japan 12.0%; US 9.9%; Germany 9.3%; Italy 9.3%; UAE 6.0%. **Exports** (2006; f.o.b.): US$34,051,000,000 (crude petroleum 46.9%; liquefied natural gas 34.8%; refined petroleum products 4.6%; liquefied propane and butane 3.4%; polyethylene 3.3%; urea 2.0%). *Major export destinations:* Japan 41.5%; South Korea 13.9%; Singapore 9.5%; India 4.9%; UAE 4.3%.

## Transport and communications

**Transport.** *Railroads:* none. *Roads* (2006): total length 7,790 km. *Vehicles* (2004): passenger cars 265,609; trucks and buses 114,115. *Air transport* (2008): passenger-km 36,204,000,000; metric ton-km cargo 1,639,000,000. **Communications,** in total units (units per 1,000 persons). Telephone landlines (2008): 263,000 (206); cellular telephone subscribers (2008): 1,683,000 (1,314); personal computers (2005): 145,000 (182); total Internet users (2008): 436,000 (340); broadband Internet subscribers (2008): 103,000 (81).

*1 metric ton = about 1.1 short tons;   1 kilometer = 0.6 mi (statute);   1 metric ton-km cargo = about 0.68 short ton-mi cargo;   c.i.f.: cost, insurance, and freight;   f.o.b.: free on board*

## Education and health

Educational attainment (2004). Percentage of population ages 10 and over having: no formal education/unknown 34.9%, of which illiterate 10.2%; primary 13.0%; preparatory (lower secondary) 16.2%; secondary 20.0%; postsecondary 15.9%. Literacy (2006): total population ages 15 and over literate 89.0%; males literate 89.1%; females literate 88.6%. Health (2007): physicians (public sector only) 1,775 (1 per 691 persons); hospital beds (public sector only) 1,651 (1 per 743 persons); infant mortality rate per 1,000 live births (2008) 7.7.

## Military

Total active duty personnel (November 2008): 11,800 (army 72.0%, navy 15.3%, air force 12.7%); US troops (November 2008): 444. Military expenditure as percentage of GDP (2007): 1.5%; per capita expenditure US$889.

## Background

Qatar was partly controlled by Bahrain in the 18th and 19th centuries and was part of the Ottoman Empire until World War I. In 1916 it became a British protectorate. Oil was discovered in 1939, and the country rapidly modernized. Qatar declared independence in 1971, when the British protectorate ended. In 1991 it served as a base for air strikes against Iraq in the Persian Gulf War.

## Recent Developments

Qatar served as a regional diplomatic arbiter and would-be peacemaker in 2011. The country was in the forefront in persuading the Arab League to support an international no-fly zone over Libya. With its fellow Gulf Cooperation Council members, Qatar also sought to end the violence that erupted in neighboring Bahrain and Yemen, pledged US$10 billion in investments for Egypt in the wake of the ousting of Pres. Hosni Mubarak by antiregime protesters, and recalled its ambassador from Damascus to protest the Syrian government's violence against its dissenting citizens.

Internet resource: <www.qsa.gov.qa>.

# Romania

Official name: Romania. Form of government: unitary republic with two legislative houses (Senate [137]; Chamber of Deputies [334]). Head of state: President Traian Basescu (from 2004). Head of government: Prime Minister Victor Ponta (from 2012). Capital: Bucharest. Official language: Romanian. Official religion: none. Monetary unit: 1 Romanian (new) leu (RON; plural lei) = 100 bani; valuation (2 Jul 2012) US$1 = 3.54 (new) lei.

## Demography

Area: 92,043 sq mi, 238,391 sq km. Population (2011): 21,393,000. Density (2011): persons per sq mi 232.4, persons per sq km 89.7. Urban (2010): 55.1%. Sex distribution (2008): male 48.71%; female 51.29%. Age breakdown (2008): under 15, 15.2%; 15–29, 22.0%; 30–44, 23.3%; 45–59,

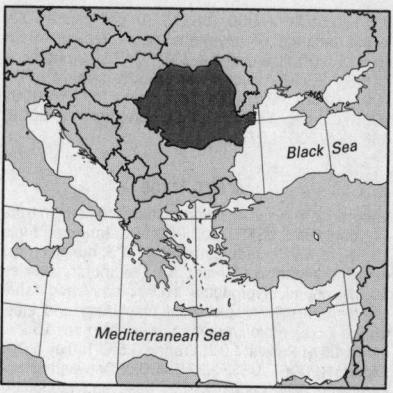

19.8%; 60–74, 13.5%; 75–84, 5.2%; 85 and over, 1.0%. Ethnic composition (2002): Romanian 89.5%; Hungarian 6.6%; Rom (Gypsy) 2.5%; Ukrainian 0.3%; German 0.3%; other 0.8%. Religious affiliation (2002): Romanian Orthodox 86.7%; Protestant 6.3%; Roman Catholic 4.7%; Greek Catholic 0.9%; Muslim 0.3%; other 1.1%. Major cities (2008): Bucharest 1,944,367; Timisoara 311,586; Iasi 308,843; Cluj-Napoca 306,474; Constanta 302,171. Location: southeastern Europe, bordering Ukraine, Moldova, the Black Sea, Bulgaria, Serbia, and Hungary.

## Vital statistics

Birth rate per 1,000 population (2008): 10.3 (world avg. 20.3); within marriage 72.6%. Death rate per 1,000 population (2008): 11.8 (world avg. 8.5). Total fertility rate (avg. births per childbearing woman; 2008): 1.35. Life expectancy at birth (2008): male 69.5 years; female 76.7 years.

## National economy

Budget (in US$'000,000; 2009). Revenue: 50,780. Expenditures: 61,510. Public debt (external, outstanding; June 2009): US$13,768,100,000. Population economically active (2008): total 9,944,700; activity rate 46.2% (participation rates: ages 15–64, 62.9%; female 44.4%; unemployed [September 2008–August 2009] 5.2%). Production (metric tons except as noted). Agriculture and fishing (2008): corn (maize) 7,849,000, wheat 7,181,000, potatoes 3,649,000, sunflower seeds 1,170,000; livestock (number of live animals) 8,882,000 sheep, 6,174,000 pigs, 2,684,000 cattle; fisheries production (2007) 16,496 (from aquaculture 63%). Mining and quarrying (2006; metal content of mine output): copper 12,200; zinc 9,574; lead 7,500. Manufacturing (value added in US$'000,000; 2006): food products 1,333; wearing apparel 1,257; transportation equipment 978. Energy production (consumption): electricity (kW-hr; 2008–09) 61,415,000,000 ([2006] 58,424,000,000); coal (metric tons; 2008–09) 2,356,000 ([2006] 2,796,000); lignite (metric tons; 2008–09) 32,251,000 (31,941,000); crude petroleum (barrels; 2008–09) 33,250,000 ([2006] 106,585,200); petroleum products (metric tons; 2008–09) 12,985,000 ([2006] 8,904,000); natural gas (cu m; 2008–09) 9,594,400,000 ([2008] 16,920,000,000). Gross national income (2008):

US\$170,560,000,000 (US\$7,930 per capita). **Selected balance of payments data.** Receipts from (US\$'000,000): tourism (2007) 1,467; remittances (2008) 9,395; foreign direct investment (FDI; 2005–07 avg.) 9,208. Disbursements for (US\$'000,-000): tourism (2007) 1,535; remittances (2008) 436; FDI (2005–07 avg.) 110.

## Foreign trade

**Imports** (2006; c.i.f. in commodities and f.o.b. in trading partners): US\$51,106,000,000 (mineral fuels 13.5%, of which crude petroleum 7.7%; nonelectrical machinery and equipment 11.1%; motor vehicles 10.6%; chemical products 10.6%; base and fabricated metals 9.7%; electrical machinery and electronics 7.5%). *Major import sources:* Germany 15.2%; Italy 14.6%; Russia 7.9%; France 6.5%; Turkey 5.0%. **Exports** (2006): US\$32,336,000,000 (wearing apparel and accessories 13.7%; base and fabricated metals 12.6%; refined petroleum products 8.9%; nonelectrical machinery and equipment 8.0%; motor vehicles and parts 6.2%; insulated wire and fiber-optic cables 6.0%; footwear 5.3%). *Major export destinations:* Italy 18.1%; Germany 15.7%; Turkey 7.7%; France 7.5%; Hungary 4.9%.

## Transport and communications

**Transport.** *Railroads* (2008): route length 10,788 km; passenger-km 6,958,000; metric ton-km cargo 15,000,000,000. *Roads* (2004; public roads only): length 79,454 km (paved 26%). *Vehicles* (2008): cars 4,027,000; trucks and buses 687,000. *Air transport* (2008–09): passenger-km 3,835,000,000; metric ton-km cargo 5,466,000,000. **Communications,** in total units (units per 1,000 persons). Telephone landlines (2008): 5,036,000 (236); cellular telephone subscribers (2008): 24,467,000 (1,145); personal computers (2007) 4,137,000 (192); total Internet users (2008): 6,132,000 (287); broadband Internet subscribers (2008): 2,510,000 (118).

## Education and health

**Educational attainment** (2002). Percentage of population ages 10 and over having: no formal schooling 5.5%; primary education 20.1%; lower secondary 27.6%; upper secondary/vocational 36.7%; higher vocational 3.0%; university 7.1%. **Literacy** (2007): total population ages 15 and over literate 97.6%; males literate 98.3%; females literate 96.9%. **Health** (2008): physicians 50,238 (1 per 428 persons); hospital beds 137,984 (1 per 156 persons); infant mortality rate per 1,000 live births 11.0; undernourished population (2002–04) less than 2.5% of total population.

## Military

**Total active duty personnel** (November 2008): 73,200 (army 58.8%, navy 8.9%, air force 13.9%, joint staff 18.4%). **Military expenditure as percentage of GDP** (2007): 1.9%; per capita expenditure US\$146.

## Background

Romania was formed in 1862 by the unification of the principalities Moldavia and Walachia, which had once been part of the ancient country of Dacia. During World War I, Romania sided with the Allies and doubled its territory in 1918 with the addition of Transylvania, Bukovina, and Bessarabia. Allied with Germany in World War II, it was occupied by Soviet troops in 1944 and became a satellite country of the USSR in 1948. During the 1960s Romania's foreign policy was frequently independent of the Soviet Union's. The communist regime of Nicolae Ceausescu was overthrown in 1989, and free elections were held in 1990. In 2004 it joined NATO, and in 2007 it became a member of the EU.

## Recent Developments

The Netherlands and Finland refused to allow Romania to join the visa-free Schengen zone over fears that organized crime and corruption could be exported westward, and the decision badly strained their relations in 2011. Romania pointed to a crackdown on bribe taking in the customs service and other antigraft efforts. In a move that was viewed as possibly retaliatory, in September Romania turned away 15 truckloads of flowers and seed imports from the Netherlands on suspicion of contamination with harmful bacteria in what became known as "the Tulip War." Resentment grew in Romania over the readiness of other EU members to restrict membership benefits after Romania had agreed to rapidly liberalize its economy, enabling top western European firms to acquire control of many of its strategic industries.

**Internet resource:** <www.insse.ro>.

# Russia

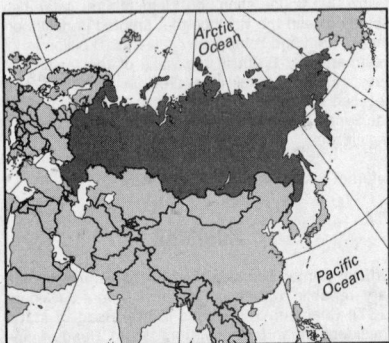

**Official name:** Rossiyskaya Federatsiya (Russian Federation). **Form of government:** federal multiparty republic with two legislative houses (Federation Council [178]; State Duma [450]). **Head of state:** President Vladimir Putin (from 2012). **Head of government:** Prime Minister Dmitry Medvedev (from 2012). **Capital:** Moscow. **Official language:** Russian. **Official religion:** none. **Monetary unit:** 1 ruble (RUB) = 100 kopecks; valuation (2 Jul 2012) market rate, US\$1 = RUB 32.59.

---

*1 metric ton = about 1.1 short tons;    1 kilometer = 0.6 mi (statute);    1 metric ton-km cargo = about 0.68 short ton-mi cargo;    c.i.f.: cost, insurance, and freight;    f.o.b.: free on board*

## Demography

**Area:** 6,601,700 sq mi, 17,098,200 sq km. **Population** (2011): 142,707,000. **Density** (2011): persons per sq mi 21.6, persons per sq km 8.3. **Urban** (2010): 73.7%. **Sex distribution** (2007): male 46.22%; female 53.78%. **Age breakdown** (2007): under 15, 14.6%; 15–29, 23.9%; 30–44, 21.3%; 45–59, 22.8%; 60–74, 11.9%; 75–84, 4.7%; 85 and over, 0.8%. **Ethnic composition** (2002): Russian 79.82%; Tatar 3.83%; Ukrainian 2.03%; Bashkir 1.15%; Chuvash 1.13%; Chechen 0.94%; Armenian 0.78%; Mordvin 0.58%; Belarusian 0.56%; Avar 0.52%; Kazakh 0.45%; Udmurt 0.44%; Azerbaijani 0.43%; Mari 0.42%; German 0.41%; Kabardinian 0.36%; Ossetian 0.35%; Dargin 0.35%; Buryat 0.31%; Sakha 0.31%; other 4.83%. **Religious affiliation** (2005): Christian 58.4%, of which Russian Orthodox 53.1%, Roman Catholic 1.0%, Ukrainian Orthodox 0.9%, Protestant 0.9%; Muslim 8.2%; traditional beliefs 0.8%; Jewish 0.6%; nonreligious 25.8%; atheist 5.0%; other 1.2%. **Major cities** (2007): Moscow 10,470,318; St. Petersburg 4,568,047; Novosibirsk 1,390,513; Yekaterinburg 1,322,954; Nizhny Novgorod 1,274,708; Samara 1,135,422; Omsk 1,131,100; Kazan 1,120,238; Chelyabinsk 1,092,495; Rostov-na-Donu 1,048,714; Ufa 1,021,458. **Location:** eastern Europe and northern Asia, bordering the Arctic Ocean, the North Pacific Ocean, North Korea, China, Mongolia, Kazakhstan, the Caspian Sea, Azerbaijan, Georgia, the Black Sea, Ukraine, Belarus, Latvia, Estonia, Finland, and Norway; the exclave of Kaliningrad on the Baltic Sea borders Lithuania and Poland. **Migration** (2006): immigrants 186,380; emigrants 54,061. **Refugees** (2007): 159,500, of which from Afghanistan 84,500, Georgia 45,000.

## Vital statistics

**Birth rate** per 1,000 population (2008): 12.1 (world avg. 20.3); within marriage 73.1%. **Death rate** per 1,000 population (2008): 14.7 (world avg. 8.5). **Total fertility rate** (avg. births per childbearing woman; 2008): 1.51. **Life expectancy** at birth (2008): male 61.7 years; female 74.2 years.

## Social indicators

**Educational attainment** (2002). Percentage of population ages 15 and over having: no formal schooling 2.1%; primary education 7.7%; some secondary 18.1%; complete secondary/basic vocational 53.0%; incomplete higher 3.1%; complete higher 16.0%, of which advanced degrees 0.3%. **Quality of working life** (2006). Average workweek (2004): 40 hours. Annual rate per 100,000 workers of: injury or accident 290; industrial illness 16.0; death 11.8. Average working days lost to labor strikes per 1,000 employees 0.2. **Social participation.** Trade union membership in total workforce (2003) 45%. **Social deviance.** Offense rate per 100,000 population (2007) for: murder and attempted murder 15.6; rape and attempted rape 4.9; serious injury 33.3; burglary 207.6; drug abuse 162.6; robbery 31.9; theft 1,102.7. Incidence per 100,000 population of: suicide (2007) 29.0.

## National economy

**Public debt** (external, outstanding; March 2008): US$35,200,000,000. **Budget** (2007). *Revenue:* RUB 7,443,900,000,000 (VAT 30.0%; taxes on natural resources 15.0%; corporate taxes 8.5%; income tax 5.2%). *Expenditures:* RUB 6,531,400,000,000 (transfers 29.7%; social and cultural services 14.1%; defense 12.8%; national economy 11.2%; public security 10.3%). **Gross national income** (2008): US$1,364,500,000,000 (US$9,620 per capita). **Production** (metric tons except as noted). *Agriculture and fishing* (2007): wheat 49,389,860, potatoes 36,784,200, sugar beets 29,000,000, barley 15,663,110 (world rank: 1), sunflower seeds 5,656,500 (world rank: 1), oats 5,407,000 (world rank: 1), cabbages 4,054,000, corn (maize) 3,953,240, rye 3,910,290 (world rank: 1), tomatoes 2,393,000, apples 2,211,000, carrots and turnips 1,900,000, dry onions 1,770,000, currants 600,000 (world rank: 1), raspberries (2005) 175,000 (world rank: 1; sour cherries 153,000 (world rank: 1); livestock (number of live animals) 21,466,000 cattle, 17,508,000 sheep, 15,793,000 pigs, camels (2008) 6,356; fisheries production 3,559,717 (from aquaculture 3%); aquatic plants production 28,594 (from aquaculture 1%). *Mining and quarrying* (2006): nickel (metal content) 320,000 (world rank: 1); platinum-group metals 138,300 (world rank: 2), of which palladium 96,800 (world rank: 1); mica 100,000 (world rank: 2); gem diamonds 23,400,000 carats (world rank: 2); vanadium (metal content) 15,100 (world rank: 3); industrial diamonds 15,000,000 carats (world rank: 3); iron ore (metal content) 59,100,000 (world rank: 5); cobalt (metal content) 5,100 (world rank: 5); copper ore (metal content) 725,000 (world rank: 6); molybdenum (metal content) 3,100 (world rank: 6); gold 159,340 kg (world rank: 7). *Manufacturing* (value added in US$'000,000; 2005): refined petroleum products 28,950; food products 12,942; iron and steel 11,904; nonferrous base metals 9,981; base chemical products 8,524; cement, bricks, and ceramics 4,892; beverages 4,532; general purpose machinery 4,075; motor vehicles 3,423; fabricated metal products 2,831; special purpose machinery 2,802; rubber products 2,313; paints, soaps, and pharmaceuticals 2,155; professional and scientific equipment 2,151; paper products 1,982; publishing 1,733. *Energy production (consumption):* electricity (kW-hr; 2007) 1,015,872,000,000 ([2006] 979,-973,000,000); coal (metric tons; 2007) 242,-100,000 ([2006] 145,771,000); lignite (metric tons; 2007) 72,200,000 ([2006] 73,929,000); crude petroleum (barrels; 2007) 3,568,000,000 ([2006] 1,523,000,000); petroleum products (metric tons; 2006) 197,412,000 (101,794,000); natural gas (cu m; 2007) 654,000,000,000 ([2006] 362,393,-000,000). **Population economically active** (2006): total 74,146,000; activity rate of total population 52.0% (participation rates: ages 15–64, 73.0%; female 49.4%; unemployed [October 2007] 6.1%). **Selected balance of payments data.** Receipts from (US$'000,000): tourism (2007) 9,607; remittances (2008) 6,033; foreign direct investment (FDI; 2005–07 avg.) 32,583. Disbursements for (US$'000,000): tourism (2007) 22,258; remittances (2008) 26,145; FDI (2005–07 avg.) 27,190.

## Foreign trade

**Imports** (2006; c.i.f.): US$137,728,000,000 (machinery and apparatus 27.6%, of which telecommunications equipment and television receivers 6.3%, general industrial machinery 6.2%, specialized machinery 5.4%, electrical machinery and electronics 5.3%; motor vehicles and parts 13.4%; chemical products 12.2%, of which pharmaceuticals and medicine 4.6%; food products 11.9%; base and fabricated metals 6.9%, of which iron and steel 3.6%. *Major import sources:* Germany 13.4%; China 9.4%; Ukraine 6.7%; Japan 5.7%; Belarus 5.0%; South Korea 4.9%; US 4.7%; France 4.3%; Italy 4.2%; Finland 2.9%. **Exports** (2006; f.o.b.): US$301,551,-000,000 (crude petroleum 32.1%; refined petroleum products 14.7%; natural gas 14.2%; nonferrous base metals 6.2%, of which aluminum 2.5%, nickel 2.0%, copper 1.5%; iron and steel 5.7%; chemical products 3.8%, of which fertilizers 1.4%; machinery and apparatus 2.4%; coal and coke 1.5%; food products 1.2%). *Major export destinations:* Netherlands 11.9%; Italy 8.3%; Germany 8.1%; China 5.2%; Ukraine 5.0%; Turkey 4.7%; Belarus 4.3%; Switzerland 4.0%; Poland 3.8%; UK 3.4%.

## Transport and communications

**Transport.** *Railroads* (2007): length (2007) 85,000 km; passenger-km 174,100,000,000; metric ton-km cargo 2,090,000,000,000. *Roads* (2006): total length 854,000 km (paved 85%). *Vehicles* (2007): passenger cars 29,249,000; trucks and buses 5,591,000. *Air transport* (2006–07): passenger-km 97,510,000,000; metric ton-km cargo 2,980,-000,000. **Communications,** in total units (units per 1,000 persons). Telephone landlines (2008): 44,200,000 (313); cellular telephone subscribers (2008): 187,500,000 (1,326); personal computers (2005): 17,400,000 (121); total Internet users (2008): 45,400,000 (321); broadband Internet subscribers (2008): 9,280,000 (66).

## Education and health

**Health** (2007): physicians 707,000 (1 per 201 persons); hospital beds 1,522,000 (1 per 93 persons); infant mortality rate per 1,000 live births (2008) 8.5; undernourished population (2002–04) 3,900,000 (3% of total population based on the consumption of a minimum daily requirement of 1,980 calories).

## Military

**Total active duty personnel** (November 2008): 1,027,000 (army 38.5%, navy 13.8%, air force 15.6%, strategic deterrent forces 7.8%, command and support 24.3%); troops abroad 31,713, of which in Ukraine 13,300, in Georgia 7,600, in Tajikistan 5,500, in Armenia 3,214 (an additional 449,000 personnel in paramilitary forces include railway troops, special construction troops, federal border guards, interior troops, and other federal guard units). **Military expenditure as percentage of GDP** (2007): 2.5%; per capita expenditure US$256.

## Background

The region between the Dniester and Volga rivers was inhabited from ancient times by various peoples, including the Slavs. The area was overrun from the 8th century BC to the 6th century AD by successive nomadic peoples, including the Sythians, Sarmatians,

Goths, Huns, and Avars. Kievan Rus, a confederation of principalities ruled from Kiev, emerged in the 10th century. It lost supremacy in the 11th and 12th centuries to independent principalities, including Novgorod and Vladimir. Novgorod ascended in the north and was the only Russian principality to escape the domination of the Mongol Golden Horde in the 13th century. In the 14th–15th centuries, the princes of Moscow gradually overthrew the Mongols. Under Ivan IV Russia began to expand. The Romanov dynasty arose in 1613. Expansion continued under Peter I (the Great) and Catherine II (the Great). The area was invaded by Napoleon in 1812; after his defeat, Russia received most of the grand duchy of Warsaw (1815). Russia annexed Georgia, Armenia, and other Caucasian territories in the 19th century. The Russian southward advance against the Ottoman Empire was of key importance to Europe. Russia was defeated in the Crimean War. It sold Alaska to the US in 1867. Russia's defeat in the Russo-Japanese War led to an unsuccessful uprising in 1905. In World War I it fought against the Central Powers.

The Russian Revolution that overthrew the czarist regime in 1917 marked the beginning of a government of soviets (councils). The Bolsheviks brought the main part of the former empire under communist control and organized it as the Russian Soviet Federated Socialist Republic (RSFSR; coextensive with present-day Russia). The RSFSR joined other soviet republics in 1922 to form the Union of Soviet Socialist Republics (USSR). Although it fought with the Allies in World War II, after the war tensions with the West led to the decades-long Cold War. Upon the dissolution of the USSR in 1991, the RSFSR was renamed Russia and became the leading member of the Commonwealth of Independent States. It adopted a new constitution in 1993. During the 1990s and into the 21st century, it struggled on several fronts, beset with economic difficulties, political corruption, and independence movements.

## Recent Developments

In September 2011, Pres. Dmitry Medvedev announced that he was nominating Prime Minister Vladimir Putin to be the party's presidential candidate in the elections set for March 2012. In that way Medvedev ended months of increasingly tense speculation over whether he himself would stand for a second presidential term. In an article in the newspaper *Izvestiya* in October 2011, Putin called for a new "Eurasian Union." He proposed that the existing Russia-Belarus-Kazakhstan Customs Union gradually expand to include other former Soviet states and develop into a "bridge between Europe and the dynamic Asia-Pacific region." That month Putin unexpectedly announced that Russia and seven other former Soviet republics had signed a free-trade agreement, which scrapped export and import tariffs on a range of goods. Putin's popularity with the public declined slowly but steadily throughout the year—but even so, he was elected for his third presidential term.

In November 2011, Russia and Georgia reached a compromise agreement that would allow Russia to complete its 18-year-long effort to join the World Trade Organization, and on 16 December Russia was invited to join. Thanks to the "reset" begun after US Pres. Barack Obama took office, relations between

---

*1 metric ton = about 1.1 short tons;    1 kilometer = 0.6 mi (statute);    1 metric ton-km cargo = about 0.68 short ton-mi cargo;    c.i.f.: cost, insurance, and freight;    f.o.b.: free on board*

Moscow and Washington remained cooperative. The year began well, with the entry into force in February of the New START (Strategic Arms Reduction Talks) between Russia and the US. Disagreements between the two countries remained, however, over US plans for ballistic missile defense. Moscow called on Washington to provide it with a legally binding guarantee that any US installation of a ballistic missile defense system would not weaken Russia's own system of strategic deterrence. In November Medvedev warned that failure by the US and its allies to take Moscow's concerns into consideration could spark a new arms race and announced the inauguration of an early-warning radar system in the Baltic exclave of Kaliningrad. At a NATO summit in Chicago in May 2012, however, NATO leaders announced that the first phase of the defense plan—integrating satellites, a radar base in Turkey, and a US warship in the Mediterranean—had been made functional.

Internet resource: <www.gks.ru>.

# Rwanda

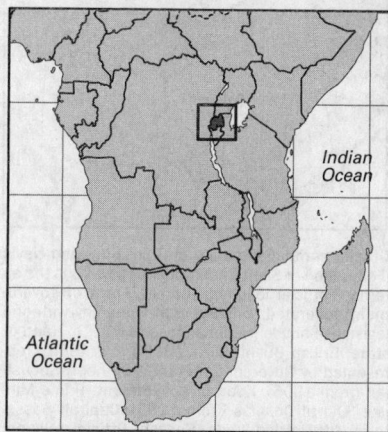

**Official name:** Repubulika y'u Rwanda (Rwanda); République Rwandaise (French); Republic of Rwanda (English). **Form of government:** multiparty republic with two legislative houses (Senate [26]; Chamber of Deputies [80]). **Head of state and government:** President Maj. Gen. Paul Kagame (from 2000), assisted by Prime Minister Pierre Damien Habumuremyi (from 2011). **Capital:** Kigali. **Official languages:** Rwanda; French; English. **Official religion:** none. **Monetary unit:** 1 Rwandan franc (RF); valuation (2 Jul 2012) US$1 = RF 612.43.

## Demography

**Area:** 10,185 sq mi, 26,379 sq km. **Population** (2011): 10,943,000. **Density** (2011; based on area excluding Rwandan part of Lake Kivu): persons per sq mi 1,120, persons per sq km 432.3. **Urban** (2009): 18.6%. **Sex distribution** (2008): male 49.75%; female 50.25%. **Age breakdown** (2008): under 15, 42.4%; 15–29, 29.6%; 30–44, 16.0%; 45–59, 8.2%; 60–74, 3.0%; 75–84, 0.7%; 85 and over, 0.1%. **Ethnic composition** (2002): Hutu 85%;

Tutsi 14%; Twa 1%. **Religious affiliation** (2005): Roman Catholic 44%; Protestant 25%; Muslim 13%; other 18%. **Major cities** (2002): Kigali (urban agglomeration; 2007) 860,000; Gitarama 84,669; Butare 77,449; Ruhengeri 71,511; Gisenyi 67,766. **Location:** east-central Africa, bordering Uganda, Tanzania, Burundi, and the Democratic Republic of the Congo.

## Vital statistics

**Birth rate** per 1,000 population (2008): 38.9 (world avg. 20.3). **Death rate** per 1,000 population (2008): 11.1 (world avg. 8.5). **Total fertility rate** (avg. births per childbearing woman; 2008): 5.25. **Life expectancy** at birth (2008): male 54.6 years; female 57.1 years.

## National economy

**Budget** (2008). *Revenue:* RF 660,800,000,000 (grants 42.3%; taxes on goods and services 24.4%; income tax 18.6%; nontax revenue 7.9%; import and export duties 6.6%). *Expenditures:* RF 649,700,000,000 (current expenditures 56.7%; capital expenditures 41.2%; net lending 2.1%). **Public debt** (external, outstanding; 2008): US$656,800,000. **Production** (metric tons except as noted). *Agriculture and fishing* (2007): plantains 2,580,000, potatoes 1,200,000, sweet potatoes 940,000, tea 19,000, coffee 18,900, pyrethrum 15; livestock (number of live animals) 1,300,000 goats, 950,000 cattle, 470,000 sheep; fisheries production 13,088 (from aquaculture 31%). *Mining and quarrying* (2007): cassiterite (tin content) 3,100; tungsten (wolframite content) 1,534; niobium 80,000 kg; tantalum 50,000 kg. *Manufacturing* (value added in RF '000,000; 2008): beverages and tobacco products 24,300; food products 16,200; furniture and unspecified products 13,200. *Energy production (consumption):* electricity (kW-hr; 2008) 194,000,000 ([2006] 220,-000,000); petroleum products (metric tons; 2006) none (190,000); natural gas (cu m; 2007) none ([2006] 615,000). **Population economically active** (2006): total 4,325,000; activity rate of total population 45.7% (participation rates: ages 15–64, 81.5%; female 53.4%). **Gross national income** (2008): US$3,955,000,000 (US$410 per capita). **Selected balance of payments data.** Receipts from (US$'000,000): tourism (2007) 65; remittances (2008) 51; foreign direct investment (FDI; 2005–07 avg.) 32; official development assistance (2007) 713. Disbursements for (US$'000,000): tourism (2007) 69; remittances (2008) 68; FDI (2006–07 avg.) 13.

## Foreign trade

**Imports** (2007; c.i.f.): US$696,900,000 (machinery and apparatus 17.8%; motor vehicles and parts 12.9%; food products 9.6%; refined petroleum products 8.5%; medicaments 6.8%). *Major import sources:* Kenya 17.8%; Uganda 14.0%; UAE 7.8%; Tanzania 6.8%; Belgium 6.3%. **Exports** (2008; f.o.b.): US$261,800,000 (coffee 17.9%; cassiterite [major ore of tin] 15.7%; tea 15.3%; columbite/tantalite 14.2%; tungsten 4.9%). *Major export destinations* (2007): Kenya 18.7%; UK 18.7%; Belgium 14.0%; Hong Kong 12.5%; Switzerland 7.2%.

## Transport and communications

**Transport.** *Railroads:* none. *Roads* (2004): total length 14,008 km (paved 19%). *Vehicles* (2008): passenger cars 21,350; trucks and buses 16,470. *Air transport* (2006; Kigali airport only): passengers embarked and disembarked 180,000; cargo loaded and unloaded (2000) 4,300 metric tons. **Communications**, in total units (units per 1,000 persons). Telephone landlines (2008): 17,000 (1.7); cellular telephone subscribers (2008): 1,323,000 (136); personal computers (2007): 28,000 (3); total Internet users (2008): 300,000 (31); broadband Internet subscribers (2008): 4,200 (0.4).

## Education and health

**Educational attainment** (2005). Percentage of population ages 15–49 having: no formal education/unknown 21.4%; primary education 68.2%; secondary 9.6%; higher 0.8%. **Literacy** (2007): percentage of total population ages 15 and over literate 74.7%; males literate 79.3%; females literate 70.2%. **Health** (2007): physicians 540 (1 per 17,509 persons); hospital beds 14,246 (1 per 664 persons); infant mortality rate per 1,000 live births (2008) 55.9; undernourished population (2002–04) 2,800,000 (33% of total population based on the consumption of a minimum daily requirement of 1,750 calories).

## Military

**Total active duty personnel** (November 2008): 33,000 (army 97.0%, air force 3.0%). **Military expenditure as percentage of GDP** (2007): 2.1%; per capita expenditure US$7.

## Background

Originally inhabited by the Twa, a Pygmy people, Rwanda became home to the Hutu, who were well established there when the Tutsi appeared in the 14th century. The Tutsi conquered the Hutu and in the 15th century founded a kingdom near Kigali. The Belgians occupied Rwanda in 1916, and the League of Nations created Ruanda-Urundi as a Belgian mandate in 1923. The Tutsi retained their dominance until shortly before Rwanda reached independence in 1962, when the Hutu took control of the government and stripped the Tutsi of much of their land. Many Tutsi fled Rwanda, and the Hutu dominated the country's political system, waging sporadic civil wars until mid-1994, when the death of the country's leader in a plane crash—apparently shot down—led to massive violence. The Tutsi-led Rwandan Patriotic Front took over the country by force after the massacre of almost one million Tutsi and Tutsi sympathizers by the Hutu. A transitional government was replaced in 2003 following the country's first multiparty elections.

## Recent Developments

The International Criminal Tribunal for Rwanda (ICTR) in Arusha, Tanzania, responsible for trying the alleged leaders of the 1994 genocide, returned verdicts against several notorious suspects in 2011. Pauline Nyiramasuhuko (former minister for family and women's affairs) and her son, Arsene Ntahobali (a former militia leader), received life sentences for their roles in the abduction, murder, or rape of hundreds of ethnic Tutsis. Several others received sentences ranging from 25 to 35 years, including former ministers Justin Mugenzi and Prosper Mugiraneza. The ICTR Appeals Chamber reduced the life sentences of former military leaders Théoneste Bagosora and Anatole Nsengiyumva to 35 and 15 years, respectively.

**Internet resource:** <www.statistics.gov.rw>.

# Saint Kitts and Nevis

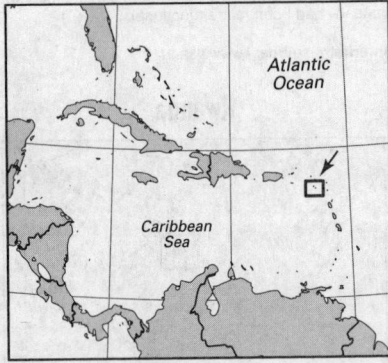

**Official name:** Federation of Saint Kitts and Nevis (Federation of Saint Christopher and Nevis is the alternate official long-form name). **Form of government:** federated constitutional monarchy with one legislative house (National Assembly [15]). **Head of state:** British Queen Elizabeth II (from 1952), represented by Governor-General Sir Cuthbert Sebastian (from 1996). **Head of government:** Prime Minister Denzil Douglas (from 1995). **Capital:** Basseterre. **Official language:** English. **Official religion:** none. **Monetary unit:** 1 Eastern Caribbean dollar (EC$) = 100 cents; valuation (2 Jul 2012) US$1 = EC$2.70.

## Demography

**Area:** 104.0 sq mi, 269.0 sq km. **Population** (2011): 50,300. **Density** (2011): persons per sq mi 483.7, persons per sq km 187.0. **Urban** (2010): 32.7%. **Sex distribution** (2008): male 49.70%; female 50.30%. **Age breakdown** (2008): under 15, 26.7%; 15–29, 25.9%; 30–44, 19.8%; 45–59, 17.3%; 60–74, 6.3%; 75–84, 2.9%; 85 and over, 1.1%. **Ethnic composition** (2000): black 90.4%; mulatto 5.0%; Indo-Pakistani 3.0%; white 1.0%; other 0.6%. **Religious affiliation** (2005): Protestant 75%, of which Anglican 24%, Methodist 23%; Roman Catholic 11%; other 14%. **Major towns** (2006): Basseterre 12,900; Charlestown 1,500; St. Paul's 1,200. **Location:** islands in the Caribbean Sea, between the US Virgin Islands and Antigua and Barbuda.

---

*1 metric ton = about 1.1 short tons;    1 kilometer = 0.6 mi (statute);    1 metric ton-km cargo = about 0.68 short ton-mi cargo;    c.i.f.: cost, insurance, and freight;    f.o.b.: free on board*

## Vital statistics

**Birth rate** per 1,000 population (2008): 17.7 (world avg. 20.3). **Death rate** per 1,000 population (2008): 8.2 (world avg. 8.5). **Total fertility rate** (avg. births per childbearing woman; 2008): 2.28. **Life expectancy** at birth (2008): male 70.1 years; female 78.0 years.

## National economy

**Budget** (2008). *Revenue:* EC$641,200,000 (tax revenue 64.9%, of which taxes on international trade 30.3%, taxes on income and profits 20.5%, taxes on domestic goods and services 13.1%; nontax revenue 18.4%; grants 8.4%). *Expenditures:* EC$634,-400,000 (current expenditures 87.8%, of which interest payments 20.6%; development expenditures 12.2%). **Production** (metric tons except as noted). *Agriculture and fishing* (2007): sugarcane (2005) 100,000, coconuts 1,000, pineapples (2006) 55; livestock (number of live animals) 16,000 goats, 12,600 sheep, 4,850 cattle; fisheries production 450 (from aquaculture, negligible). *Mining and quarrying:* excavation of sand and crushed stone for local use. *Manufacturing* (2003): raw sugar 22,000; carbonated beverages (2002) 32,000 hectoliters; beer (2002) 20,000 hectoliters; other manufactures include electronic components, garments, and cement. *Energy production (consumption):* electricity (kW-hr; 2006) 135,000,000 (135,000,000); petroleum products (metric tons; 2006) none (77,000). **Gross national income** (2008): US$539,000,000 (US$10,960 per capita). **Public debt** (external, outstanding; 2007): US$272,000,000. **Population economically active** (1995): total 18,170; activity rate of total population 41.7% (participation rates [1991]: ages 15–64, 70.5%; female 44.4%; unemployed [2006] 5.1%). **Selected balance of payments data.** Receipts from (US$'000,000): tourism (2007) 106; remittances (2008) 37; foreign direct investment (2005–07 avg.) 115; official development assistance (2007) 3. Disbursements for (US$'000,000): tourism (2007) 15; remittances (2008) 6.

## Foreign trade

**Imports** (2006; c.i.f.): US$249,500,000 (machinery and apparatus 23.1%, of which electrical machinery and parts 10.6%; food products 15.5%; base and fabricated metals 9.2%; refined petroleum products 6.6%; motor vehicles 6.5%). *Major import sources:* US 58.3%; Trinidad and Tobago 12.5%; UK 5.3%; Japan 4.3%; Canada 2.6%. **Exports** (2006; f.o.b.): US$39,700,000 (electrical switches 43.8%; telecommunications equipment and parts 25.4%; generators 9.8%; beverages [primarily bottled water and beer] 5.5%). *Major export destinations:* US 89.3%; UK 2.3%; Trinidad and Tobago 1.5%.

## Transport and communications

**Transport.** *Railroads* (2003): length 58 km. *Roads* (2002): total length 383 km (paved [2001] 44%). *Vehicles* (2002): passenger cars 6,900; trucks and buses 2,500. *Air transport* (2001; Saint Kitts airport only): passenger arrivals 135,237, passenger departures 134,937; cargo handled 1,802. **Communications,** in total units (units per 1,000 persons). Telephone landlines (2008): 20,000 (400); cellular telephone subscribers (2008): 80,000 (1,567); personal computers (2004): 11,000 (226); total Internet users (2008): 16,000 (313); broadband Internet subscribers (2008): 11,000 (217).

## Education and health

**Educational attainment** (1991). Percentage of population ages 25 and over having: no formal schooling/unknown 6.8%; primary education 45.9%; secondary 38.4%; higher 8.9%. **Literacy** (2004): total population ages 15 and over literate 97.8%. **Health** (2008): physicians (2005) 62 (1 per 796 persons); hospital beds 208 (1 per 247 persons); infant mortality rate per 1,000 live births 14.3; undernourished population (2002–04) 5,000 (10% of total population based on the consumption of a minimum daily requirement of 1,910 calories).

## Military

**Total active duty personnel** (2006): the defense force includes coast guard and police units.

## Background

Saint Kitts became the first British colony in the West Indies in 1623. Anglo-French rivalry grew in the 17th century and lasted more than a century. In 1783, by the Treaty of Versailles, the islands became wholly British possessions. They were united with Anguilla from 1882 to 1980 but became an independent federation within the British Commonwealth in 1983.

## Recent Developments

Saint Kitts and Nevis's Prime Minister Denzil Douglas hailed an economic union between Antigua and Barbuda, Dominica, Grenada, St. Lucia, and St. Vincent and the Grenadines, which came into force in January 2011. The union was expected to allow the free movement of people, goods, services, and capital.

**Internet resource:** <www.stkittsnevishta.org>.

# Saint Lucia

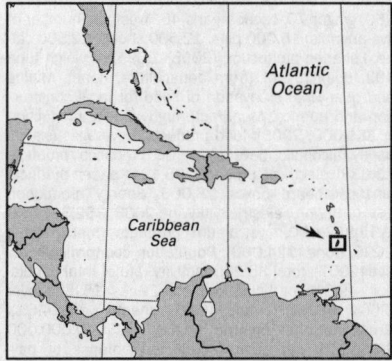

**Official name:** Saint Lucia. **Form of government:** constitutional monarchy with two legislative houses (Senate [11]; House of Assembly [18]). **Head of state:** British Queen Elizabeth II (from 1952), represented by Governor-General Dame Pearlette Louisy (from 1997). **Head of government:** Prime Minister Kenny Anthony (from 2011). **Capital:** Castries. **Official language:** English. **Official religion:** none. **Monetary unit:** 1 Eastern Caribbean dollar (EC$) = 100 cents; valuation (2 Jul 2012) US$1 = EC$2.70.

## Demography

**Area:** 238.0 sq mi, 617.0 sq km. **Population** (2011): 167,000. **Density** (2011): persons per sq mi 701.7, persons per sq km 270.7. **Urban** (2009): 27.9%. **Sex distribution** (2008): male 49.01%; female 50.99%. **Age breakdown** (2008): under 15, 26.4%; 15–29, 28.9%; 30–44, 21.6%; 45–59, 13.7%; 60–74, 6.6%; 75 and over, 2.8%. **Ethnic composition** (2000): black 50%; mulatto 44%; East Indian 3%; white 1%; other 2%. **Religious affiliation** (2001): Roman Catholic 67.5%; Protestant 22.0%, of which Seventh-day Adventist 8.4%, Pentecostal 5.6%; Rastafarian 2.1%; nonreligious 4.5%; other 3.9%. **Major towns** (2006): Castries 65,000; Vieux Fort 4,600; Micoud 3,400. **Location:** island between the Caribbean Sea and North Atlantic Ocean, north of Saint Vincent and the Grenadines.

## Vital statistics

**Birth rate** per 1,000 population (2008): 13.7 (world avg. 20.3); within marriage 14.0%. **Death rate** per 1,000 population (2008): 7.6 (world avg. 8.5). **Total fertility rate** (avg. births per childbearing woman; 2008): 2.2. **Life expectancy** at birth (2008): male 72.0 years; female 75.8 years.

## National economy

**Budget** (2008–09). *Revenue:* EC$815,950,000 (tax revenue 90.3%, of which consumption taxes 17.5%, corporate taxes 13.9%, import duties 12.7%, income tax 9.3%; nontax revenue 6.4%; grants 3.3%). *Expenditures:* EC$959,100,000 (current expenditures 67.8%, of which wages and salaries 31.8%, interest payments 9.5%; capital expenditures 32.2%). **Public debt** (external, outstanding; January 2009): US$372,-950,000. **Production** (metric tons except as noted). *Agriculture and fishing* (2007): bananas (2008) 38,359, coconuts 14,000, plantains 750, pepper 260, ginger 70, cacao beans 40; livestock (number of live animals) 15,000 pigs, 12,500 sheep, 12,500 cattle; fisheries production (2008) 1,695, of which tuna 492, dolphin 341 (from aquaculture, none). *Mining and quarrying:* excavation of sand for local construction and pumice. *Manufacturing* (value of production in EC$'000; 2008): food products, beverages (significantly alcoholic beverages), and tobacco products 73,638; electrical products 35,121; paper products and cardboard boxes 28,066. *Energy production (consumption):* electricity (kW-hr; 2008) 352,337,000 (352,337,000); petroleum products (metric tons; 2006) none (124,000). **Population economically active** (2007): total 85,260; activity rate of total population 49.8% (participation rates: ages 15 and over [2004] 68.6%; female 46.6%; unemployed 14.6%). **Gross national income** (2008): US$940,000,000 (US$5,530 per capita). **Selected balance of payments data.** Receipts from (US$'000;2008): tourism (2007) 296; remittances (2008) 31; foreign direct in-

vestment (2005–07 avg.) 191; official development assistance (2007) 24. Disbursements for (US$'000,000): tourism (2007) 41; remittances (2008) 4.

## Foreign trade

**Imports** (2006; c.i.f.): US$592,300,000 (food products 15.9%; machinery and apparatus 15.3%; motor vehicles 10.2%; chemical products 6.9%; base and fabricated metals 6.2%; refined petroleum products 5.7%). *Major import sources:* US 39.2%; Trinidad and Tobago 16.8%; UK 6.9%; Japan 6.3%; Barbados 4.4%. **Exports** (2005; f.o.b.): US$64,200,000 (bananas 24.1%; beer 16.2%; refined petroleum products 15.4%; nonelectrical machinery and equipment 6.7%; paperboard cartons 5.1%). *Major export destinations* (2005): UK 26.0%; Trinidad and Tobago 22.4%; US 14.0%; Barbados 10.1%; Grenada 5.1%.

## Transport and communications

**Transport.** *Railroads:* none. *Roads* (2002): total length 1,210 km (paved 5%). *Vehicles* (2008): passenger cars 38,504; trucks and buses 11,577. *Air transport* (2008; Castries and Vieux Fort airports only): passenger arrivals and departures 872,032; cargo unloaded and loaded 3,363 metric tons. **Communications,** in total units (units per 1,000 persons). Telephone landlines (2008): 49,000 (240); cellular telephone subscribers (2008): 170,000 (995); personal computers (2004): 26,000 (173); total Internet users (2008): 100,000 (587); broadband Internet subscribers (2008): 14,000 (82).

## Education and health

**Educational attainment** (2007). Percentage of population ages 15 and over having: no formal schooling/unknown 8.8%; incomplete primary education 5.6%; complete primary 43.1%; secondary 32.0%; higher vocational 7.1%; university 3.4%. **Literacy** (2004): 94.8%. **Health** (2008): physicians (2005) 83 (1 per 1,983 persons); hospital beds 470 (1 per 374 persons); infant mortality rate per 1,000 live births 25.2; undernourished population (2002–04) 8,000 (5% of total population based on the consumption of a minimum daily requirement of 1,900 calories).

## Military

**Total active duty personnel** (2006): none; a 300-member police force includes a specially trained paramilitary unit and a coast guard unit.

## Background

Caribs replaced early Arawak inhabitants on the island about AD 800–1300. Settled by the French in 1650, it was ceded to Great Britain in 1814 and became one of the Windward Islands in 1871. It became fully independent as Saint Lucia in 1979. The economy is based on agriculture and tourism.

## Recent Developments

Saint Lucia's police commissioner, Vernon Francois, in March 2011 strongly denied the existence of an al-

*1 metric ton = about 1.1 short tons;     1 kilometer = 0.6 mi (statute);     1 metric ton-km cargo = about 0.68 short ton-mi cargo;     c.i.f.: cost, insurance, and freight;     f.o.b.: free on board*

leged "hit list" of known criminals being pursued by a "death squad" within the Royal Saint Lucia Police Force. The allegations came after the killing of five suspects by police in the preceding months during a crime crackdown known as Operation Restore Confidence.

Internet resource: <www.stats.gov.lc>.

# Saint Vincent and the Grenadines

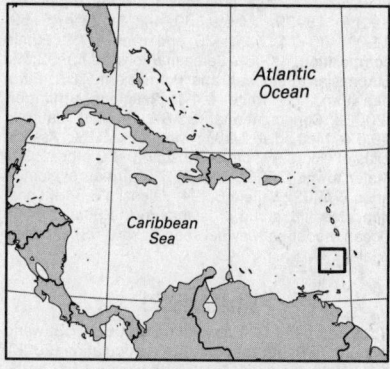

**Official name:** Saint Vincent and the Grenadines. **Form of government:** constitutional monarchy with one legislative house (House of Assembly [23]). **Head of state:** British Queen Elizabeth II (from 1952), represented by Governor-General Sir Frederick Ballantyne (from 2002). **Head of government:** Prime Minister Ralph Gonsalves (from 2001). **Capital:** Kingstown. **Official language:** English. **Official religion:** none. **Monetary unit:** 1 Eastern Caribbean dollar (EC$) = 100 cents; valuation (2 Jul 2012) US$1 = EC$2.70.

## Demography

**Area:** 150.3 sq mi, 389.3 sq km. **Population** (2011): 101,000. **Density** (2011): persons per sq mi 673.3, persons per sq km 259.6. **Urban** (2009): 48.6%. **Sex distribution** (2007): male 50.61%; female 49.39%. **Age breakdown** (2007): under 15, 27.3%; 15–29, 26.2%; 30–44, 21.6%; 45–59, 14.6%; 60–74, 7.1%; 75–84, 2.6%; 85 and over, 0.6%. **Ethnic composition** (2000): black 65.1%; mixed black-white 19.9%; Indo-Pakistani 5.5%; British 3.0%; black-Amerindian 2.0%; other 4.5%. **Religious affiliation** (2000): Protestant 47.0%; unaffiliated Christian 20.3%; independent Christian 11.7%; Roman Catholic 8.8%; Hindu 3.4%; Spiritist 1.8%; Muslim 1.5%; nonreligious 2.3%; other 3.2%. **Major cities** (2006): Kingstown 18,200; Georgetown 1,700; Byera 1,400. **Location:** islands in the Caribbean Sea, north of Trinidad and Tobago.

## Vital statistics

**Birth rate** per 1,000 population (2007): 16.0 (world avg. 20.3); (2003) within marriage 15.6%. **Death rate** per 1,000 population (2007): 6.9 (world avg. 8.5). **Total fertility rate** (avg. births per childbearing woman; 2007): 2.06. **Life expectancy** at birth (2007): male 71.4 years; female 75.0 years.

## National economy

**Budget** (2008). *Revenue:* EC$525,000,000 (tax revenue 84.2%, of which VAT 28.7%, tax on international trade 19.0%, income tax 10.7%, corporate taxes 8.9%; nontax revenue 7.9%; grants 7.6%). *Expenditures:* EC$558,500,000 (current expenditures 78.2%; development expenditures 21.8%). **Production** (metric tons except as noted). *Agriculture and fishing* (2007): bananas 51,000, sugarcane 20,000, roots and tubers (significantly eddoes and dasheens [varieties of taro roots]) 15,320, nutmegs 160, soursops and papayas are also grown; livestock (number of live animals) 12,000 sheep, 9,150 pigs, 7,200 goats; fisheries production 5,250 (from aquaculture, none). *Mining and quarrying:* sand and gravel for local use. *Manufacturing* (value added in EC$'000,000; 2000): beverages and tobacco products 17.4; food products 15.6; paper products and publishing 3.6. *Energy production (consumption):* electricity (kW-hr; 2008) 139,000,000 ([2006] 127,000,000); petroleum products (metric tons; 2006) none (64,000). **Selected balance of payments data.** Receipts from (US$'000,000): tourism (2008) 90; remittances (2007) 31; foreign direct investment (2005–07 avg.) 80; official development assistance (2007) 66. Disbursements for (US$'000,000): tourism (2007) 17; remittances (2007) 7. **Gross national income** (2008): US$561,000,000 (US$5,140 per capita). **Population economically active** (2006): total 58,000; activity rate of total population 48.3% (participation rates: ages 15–64, 75.3%; female 41.4%). **Public debt** (external, outstanding; December 2008): US$210,600,000.

## Foreign trade

**Imports** (2008; c.i.f.): US$373,200,000 (machinery and apparatus 23.1%; food products and beverages 22.6%; refined petroleum products 12.5%). *Major import sources* (2006): US 32.7%; Trinidad and Tobago 25.9%; UK 7.1%; Japan 3.9%; Canada 3.6%. **Exports** (2008; f.o.b.): US$52,200,000 (food products 61.7%, of which bananas 15.9%, wheat flour 15.1%, rice 12.1%, roots and tubers 7.1%; machinery and apparatus 23.0%, of which telecommunications equipment 10.7%). *Major export destinations* (2008): Grenada 18.2%; Trinidad and Tobago 17.4%; St. Lucia 14.8%; Barbados 10.7%; UK 9.0%.

## Transport and communications

**Transport.** *Railroads:* none. *Roads* (2004): total length 829 km (paved 70%). *Vehicles* (2008): passenger cars 9,247; trucks and buses 13,019. *Air transport* (2003): passenger arrivals 133,769; passenger departures 137,899. **Communications,** in total units (units per 1,000 persons). Telephone landlines (2008): 23,000 (217); cellular telephone subscribers (2008): 130,000 (1,239); personal computers (2005): 16,000 (152); total Internet users (2008): 66,000 (629); broadband Internet subscribers (2008): 9,400 (90).

## Education and health

**Educational attainment** (2001). Percentage of employed population having: no formal schooling/unknown 1.7%; primary education 55.6%; secondary

27.3%; higher vocational 15.1%; university 0.3%. Literacy (2004): total population ages 15 and over literate 88.1%. **Health:** physicians (2005) 72 (1 per 1,458 persons); hospital beds (2008) 280 (1 per 375 persons); infant mortality rate per 1,000 live births (2007) 16.1; undernourished population (2002–04) 10,000 (10% of total population based on the consumption of a minimum daily requirement of 1,900 calories).

## Military

Total active duty personnel (November 2007): none; a paramilitary includes coast guard and police units.

## Background

The French and the British contested for control of Saint Vincent and the Grenadines until 1763, when it was ceded to England by the Treaty of Paris. The original inhabitants, the Caribs, recognized British sovereignty but revolted in 1795. Most of the Caribs were deported; many who remained were killed in volcanic eruptions in 1812 and 1902. In 1969 Saint Vincent and the Grenadines became a self-governing state in association with the United Kingdom, and in 1979 it achieved full independence.

## Recent Developments

In 2011, Saint Vincent and the Grenadines continued its recovery from the destruction caused by Hurricane Tomas in October 2010—estimated to amount to at least 5% of GDP. In January the country received an interest-free loan of roughly US$3.25 million from the IMF, and the World Bank extended US$5 million in interest-free credit.

Internet resource: <http://discoversvg.com>.

## Samoa

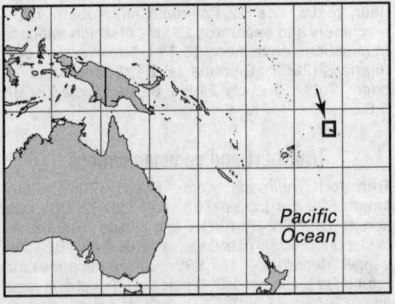

*Pacific Ocean*

**Official name:** Malo Sa'oloto Tuto'atasi o Samoa (Samoan); Independent State of Samoa (English). **Form of government:** mix of parliamentary democracy and Samoan customs with one legislative house (Legislative Assembly [49]). **Head of state:** Head of State Tuiatua Tupua Tamasese Efi (from 2007). **Head of government:** Prime Minister Tuilaepa Sailele Malielegaoi (from 1998). **Capital:** Apia. **Official languages:** Samoan; English. **Official religion:** none. **Monetary unit:** 1 tala (SAT) = 100 sene; valuation (2 Jul 2012) US$1 = SAT 2.28.

## Demography

**Area:** 1,075 sq mi, 2,785 sq km. **Population** (2011): 184,000. **Density** (2011): persons per sq mi 171.2, persons per sq km 66.1. **Urban** (2009): 20.4%. **Sex distribution** (2006): male 51.83%; female 48.17%. **Age breakdown** (2006): under 15, 39.3%; 15–29, 24.6%; 30–44, 18.2%; 45–59, 11.0%; 60–74, 5.2%; 75 and over, 1.7%. **Ethnic composition** (2006): Samoan (Polynesian) 92.6%; Euronesian (European and Polynesian) 7.0%; European and US white 0.4%. **Religious affiliation** (2006): Congregational 33.8%; Roman Catholic 19.6%; Methodist 14.3%; Mormon 13.3%; Assemblies of God 6.9%; other Christian 9.8%; other 2.3%. **Major towns** (2006): Apia 37,237 (urban agglomeration 60,702); Vaitele 6,294; Faleasi'u 3,548. **Location:** Oceania, group of islands in the South Pacific Ocean, about halfway between Hawaii (US) and New Zealand.

## Vital statistics

**Birth rate** per 1,000 population (2006): 27.3 (world avg. 20.3). **Death rate** per 1,000 population (2006): 4.0 (world avg. 8.5). **Total fertility rate** (avg. births per childbearing woman; 2006): 4.2. **Life expectancy** at birth (2006): male 71.5 years; female 74.2 years.

## National economy

**Budget** (2005–06). *Revenue:* SAT 387,200,000 (tax revenue 70.5%, of which VAT 28.0%, excise taxes 17.8%, income tax 12.2%; grants 18.6%; nontax revenue 10.9%). *Expenditures:* SAT 391,700,000 (current expenditures 72.0%, of which general services 22.9%, economic services 14.4%, education 14.1%, health 12.1%; development expenditures 22.0%). **Public debt** (external, outstanding; March 2008): US$192,000,000. **Production** (metric tons except as noted). *Agriculture and fishing* (2007): coconuts 146,000, bananas 23,000, taro 17,600, noni (fruit known locally as *nonu*; also known as Indian mulberry), n.a.; livestock (number of live animals) 202,000 pigs, 29,000 cattle; fisheries production 4,609 (from aquaculture, negligible). *Manufacturing* (value of manufactured exports in SAT '000; 2006–07): beer 3,520; noni juice 3,130; coconut cream 2,130. *Energy production (consumption):* electricity (kW-hr; 2006) 113,000,000 (90,000,000); petroleum products (metric tons; 2006) none (51,000). **Population economically active** (2003): total 64,000; activity rate of total population 35% (participation rates: ages 15–64, 63%; female 32%; unemployed [2006] 1.1%). **Gross national income** (2008): US$504,000,000 (US$2,780 per capita). **Selected balance of payments data.** Receipts from (US$'000,000): tourism (2007–08) 110; remittances (2008) 139; foreign direct investment (FDI; 2005–07 avg.) 8; official development assistance (2007) −31. Disbursements for (US$'000,000): tourism (2007) 5; remittances (2008) 13; FDI (2005–07 avg.) 1.

## Foreign trade

**Imports** (2007): SAT 593,000,000 (refined petroleum products 20.6%; products for government 5.1%). *Major import sources* (2005–06): New Zealand 29.3%; Australia 18.8%; US 10.6%; Fiji 7.0%; China 5.3%. **Exports** (2007): SAT 36,000,000 (fresh fish 55.3%; noni juice 10.6%; beer 8.6%; coconut cream 6.5%; noni fruit 1.9%). *Major export destinations* (2005–06): American Samoa 49.1%; US 32.6%; New Zealand 9.4%; Australia 3.4%; Japan 3.1%.

## Transport and communications

**Transport.** *Railroads:* none. *Roads* (2001): total length 2,337 km (paved 14%). *Vehicles* (2005): passenger cars 4,638; trucks and buses 4,894. *Air transport* (2004; Polynesian Airlines only): passenger-km 326,090,000; metric ton-km cargo 2,709,000. **Communications**, in total units (units per 1,000 persons). Telephone landlines (2008): 29,000 (161); cellular telephone subscribers (2008): 124,000 (493); personal computers (2005): 4,000 (22); total Internet users (2008): 9,000 (50); broadband Internet subscribers (2005): 100 (0.5).

## Education and health

**Educational attainment** (2002). Percentage of population ages 25 and over having: no formal schooling 1.8%; primary education 32.4%; secondary 55.4%; higher 10.4%. **Literacy** (2003): total population ages 16 and over literate 99.7%. **Health** (2005): physicians 50 (1 per 3,570 persons); hospital beds 229 (1 per 780 persons); infant mortality rate per 1,000 live births (2006) 20.4; undernourished population (2002–04) 7,000 (4% of total population based on the consumption of a minimum daily requirement of 1,870 calories).

## Military

No military forces are maintained; informal defense ties exist with New Zealand, and Australia assists with maritime surveillance training.

## Background

Polynesians inhabited the islands of the Samoan archipelago for thousands of years before they were visited by Europeans in the 18th century. Control of the islands was contested by the US, Britain, and Germany until 1899, when they were divided between the US and Germany. In 1914 Western Samoa was occupied by New Zealand, which received it as a League of Nations mandate in 1920. After World War II, it became a UN trust territory administered by New Zealand, and it achieved independence in 1962. In 1997 the word Western was dropped from the country's name.

## Recent Developments

Tourism continued to grow, and new hotels and other tourism-related businesses were producing much-needed employment for Samoan youth in 2011. Increasing Chinese demand for nonu juice and kava, New Zealand interest in Samoa's chili sauce and organic products, and a plan to use biomass to produce energy looked likely to stimulate opportunities for growers of those commodities, reducing traditional dependence on taro exports.

**Internet resource:** <www.visitsamoa.ws>.

# San Marino

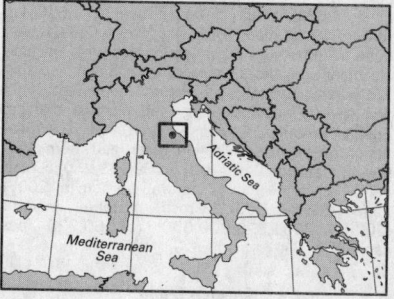

**Official name:** Repubblica di San Marino (Republic of San Marino). **Form of government:** unitary multiparty republic with one legislative house (Great and General Council [60]). **Heads of state and government:** two captains-regent who serve six-month terms beginning in April and October. **Capital:** San Marino. **Official language:** Italian. **Official religion:** none. **Monetary unit:** 1 euro (€) = 100 cents; valuation (2 Jul 2012) US$1 = €0.79 (San Marino uses the euro as its official currency, even though it is not a member of the EU).

## Demography

**Area:** 23.63 sq mi, 61.20 sq km. **Population** (2011): 32,000. **Density** (2011): persons per sq mi 1,354.2, persons per sq km 522.9. **Urban** (2010): 93.8%. **Sex distribution** (2008): male 49.07%; female 50.93%. **Age breakdown** (2008): under 15, 15.0%; 15–29, 14.9%; 30–44, 26.4%; 45–59, 21.5%; 60–74, 14.1%; 75–84, 5.8%; 85 and over, 2.3%. **Ethnic composition** (2006): Sammarinesi 87.0%; Italian 11.4%; other 1.6%. **Religious affiliation** (2000): Roman Catholic 88.7%; other Christian 3.5%; nonreligious 5.1%; other 2.7%. **Major municipalities** (2008): Serravalle 10,051; Borgo Maggiore 6,198; San Marino 4,376. **Location:** southern Europe, surrounded by Italy.

## Vital statistics

**Birth rate** per 1,000 population (2008): 11.2 (world avg. 20.3); within marriage 77.9%. **Death rate** per 1,000 population (2008): 6.1 (world avg. 8.5). **Total fertility rate** (avg. births per childbearing woman; 2008): 1.50. **Life expectancy** at birth (2008): male 80.1 years; female 85.7 years.

## National economy

**Budget** (2005). *Revenue:* €504,800,000 (VAT 23.6%; social contributions 21.3%; income tax 20.2%). *Expenditures:* €433,100,000 (wages and salaries 35.4%; social benefits 30.5%). **Public debt** (2003): US$52,900,000. **Tourism:** number of visitor arrivals (2008) 2,111,736. **Population economically active** (2008): total 22,708; activity rate of total population 73.2% (participation rates: ages 15–64 [2002] 72.1%; female 42.0%; unemployed 3.1%). **Production** (metric tons except as noted). *Agriculture and fishing:* small amounts of wheat, grapes, and barley; livestock (number of live animals; 2005) 991 cattle, 91 sheep, 32 pigs. *Quarrying:* building stone is an important export product. *Manufacturing* (2005): processed meats 283,674 kg, of which beef 270,616 kg; veal 8,549 kg, pork 3,615 kg; cheese 56,610 kg; butter 8,110 kg; other major products include electrical appliances, musical instruments, printing ink, paint, cosmetics, furniture, floor tiles, gold and silver jewelry, clothing, and postage stamps. *Energy production (consumption):* all electrical power is imported via electrical grid from Italy (kW-hr; consumption [2007] 239,983,250); crude petroleum, none (none); natural gas (cu m; 2007) none (52,785,000). **Gross national income** (2008): US$1,899,900,000 (US$60,925 per capita).

### Foreign trade

**Imports** (2005): US$2,582,000,000 (manufactured goods of all kinds, refined petroleum products, natural gas, electricity, and gold). *Major import source* (2004): significantly Italy (a customs union with Italy has existed since 1862). **Exports** (2005): US$2,531,000,000 (electronics, postage stamps, leather products, ceramics, wine, wood products, and building stone). *Major export destinations* (2004): Italy 90% (a customs union with Italy has existed since 1862).

### Transport and communications

**Transport.** *Railroads:* none. *Roads* (2001): total length 252 km. *Vehicles* (2008): passenger cars 34,025; trucks and buses 6,370. *Air transport:* a heliport provides passenger and cargo service between San Marino and Rimini, Italy, during the summer months. **Communications,** in total units (units per 1,000 persons). Telephone landlines (2008): 21,000 (683); cellular telephone subscribers (2008): 24,000 (797); personal computers (2003): 23,000 (819); total Internet users (2008): 21,000 (545); broadband Internet subscribers (2008): 4,900 (157).

### Education and health

**Educational attainment** (2007). Percentage of population ages 15 and over having: basic literacy or primary education 55.3%; secondary or vocational 34.5%; higher degree 10.2%. **Literacy** (2001): total population ages 15 and over literate 98.7%; males literate 98.9%; females literate 98.4%. **Health** (2002): physicians 117 (1 per 230 persons); hospital beds 134 (1 per 191 persons); infant mortality rate per 1,000 live births (2008) 2.9.

### Military

**Total active duty personnel:** none; defense is the responsibility of Italy; a small voluntary military force performs ceremonial duties and provides limited assistance to police.

### Background

According to tradition, San Marino was founded in the early 4th century AD by St. Marinus. By the 12th century it had developed into a commune and remained independent despite challenges from neighboring rulers, including the Malatesta family in nearby Rimini, Italy. San Marino survived the Renaissance as a relic of the self-governing Italian city-state and remained an independent republic after the unification of Italy in 1861. It is one of the smallest republics in the world, and it may be the oldest one in Europe.

### Recent Developments

It was alarming in 2011 to discover, following investigations by the Italian police, that powerful criminal organizations from Naples were well integrated into San Marino's financial fabric and could allegedly manipulate the country's political system. Evidently such distorted financial conditions were detrimental to the overall economy; during the year 7% of all San Marino companies closed.

**Internet resource:**
<www.statistica.sm/on-line/en/Home.html>.

# Sao Tome and Principe

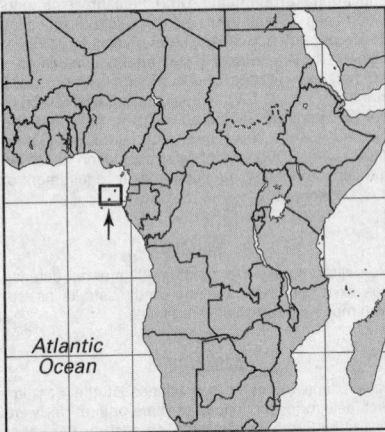

*Atlantic Ocean*

**Official name:** República Democrática de São Tomé e Príncipe (Democratic Republic of Sao Tome and Principe). **Form of government:** multiparty republic with one legislative house (National Assembly [55]). **Head of state:** President Manuel Pinto da Costa (from 2011). **Head of government:** Prime Minister Patrice Trovoada (from 2010). **Capital:** São Tomé. **Official language:** Portuguese. **Official religion:** none. **Monetary unit:** 1 dobra (Db) = 100 cêntimos; valuation (2 Jul 2012) US$1 = Db 19,210.00.

### Demography

**Area:** 386 sq mi, 1,001 sq km. **Population** (2011): 169,000. **Density** (2011): persons per sq mi 437.8,

---

*1 metric ton = about 1.1 short tons;    1 kilometer = 0.6 mi (statute);    1 metric ton-km cargo = about 0.68 short ton-mi cargo;    c.i.f.: cost, insurance, and freight;    f.o.b.: free on board*

persons per sq km 168.8. **Urban** (2008): 60.8%. **Sex distribution** (2006): male 48.63%, female 51.37%. **Age breakdown** (2006): under 15, 41.2%; 15–29, 30.8%; 30–44, 14.6%; 45–59, 7.8%; 60–74, 4.1%; 75 and over, 1.5%. **Ethnic composition** (2000): black-white admixture 79.5%; Fang 10.0%; Angolares (descendants of former Angolan slaves) 7.6%; Portuguese 1.9%; other 1.0%. **Religious affiliation** (2005): Roman Catholic 80%; Protestant 15%; Muslim 3%; other 2%. **Major urban agglomerations** (2001): São Tomé 49,957; Neves 6,635; Santana 6,228. **Location:** islands in the Gulf of Guinea, straddling the Equator west of Gabon.

## Vital statistics

**Birth rate** per 1,000 population (2008): 31.8 (world avg. 20.3). **Death rate** per 1,000 population (2008): 7.4 (world avg. 8.5). **Total fertility rate** (avg. births per childbearing woman; 2006): 5.62. **Life expectancy** at birth (2006): male 63.5 years; female 68.5 years.

## National economy

**Budget** (2007). *Revenue:* Db 3,144,000,000,000 (grants 75.0%; petroleum exploration bonuses 13.1%; tax revenue 10.2%; nontax revenue 1.7%). *Expenditures:* Db 780,000,000,000 (current expenditures 64.9%; capital expenditures 28.6%). **Public debt** (external, outstanding; October 2008): US$109,000,000. **Production** (metric tons except as noted). *Agriculture and fishing* (2007): oil palm fruit 40,000, coconuts 28,000, taro 27,000, cacao beans 3,500, cinnamon 30, coffee 20; livestock (number of live animals) 5,000 goats, 4,600 cattle, 350,000 chickens; fisheries production 4,150 (from aquaculture, none). *Mining and quarrying:* limited quarrying of clay and volcanic rock. *Manufacturing* (2007): small processing plants produce beer, soft drinks, soap, and textiles. *Energy production (consumption):* electricity (kW-hr; 2006) 19,000,000 (19,000,000); petroleum products (metric tons; 2006) none (34,000). **Population economically active** (2006): total 53,266; activity rate of total population 35.1% (participation rates: ages 15–64, 59.5%; female 41.6%). **Gross national income** (2008): US$164,000,000 (US$1,020 per capita). **Selected balance of payments data.** Receipts from (US$'000,000): tourism (2007) 3.4; remittances (2008) 2; foreign direct investment (FDI; 2005–07 avg.) 30; official development assistance (2007) 36. Disbursements for (US$'000,000): tourism (2007) 0.1; remittances (2008) 1; FDI (2005–07 avg.) 7.

## Foreign trade

**Imports** (2008): US$114,094,000 (mineral fuels 23.3%; food products 19.7%; machinery and apparatus 14.1%; transportation equipment 7.9%; construction materials 7.2%). *Major import sources:* Portugal 61.3%; Angola 22.9%; Gabon 3.0%; Nigeria 2.3%. **Exports** (2008): US$5,631,000 (cacao beans 89.4%; coconuts 0.6%; coffee 0.2%). *Major export destinations:* Portugal 49.2%; Netherlands 28.2%; Belgium 7.9%; France 6.8%.

## Transport and communications

**Transport.** *Railroads:* none. *Roads* (2000): total length 320 km (paved 68%). *Vehicles* (1996): pas-senger cars 4,040; trucks and buses 1,540. *Air transport* (2004): passenger-km 8,000,000. **Communications,** in total units (units per 1,000 persons). Telephone landlines (2008): 7,700 (48); cellular telephone subscribers (2008): 49,000 (306); personal computers (2005): 6,000 (38); total Internet users (2008): 25,000 (155); broadband Internet subscribers (2007): 2,500 (16).

## Education and health

**Educational attainment** (2001). Percentage of population ages 25 and over having: no formal schooling/unknown 22.9%; primary education 41.4%; lower secondary 25.0%; upper secondary/vocational 8.8%; higher 1.9%. **Literacy** (2006): total population ages 15 and over literate 85%; males literate 92%; females literate 78%. **Health** (2006): physicians 58 (1 per 2,621 persons); hospital beds (2003) 474 (1 per 313 persons); infant mortality rate per 1,000 live births 43.9; undernourished population (2002–04) 15,000 (10% of total population based on the consumption of a minimum daily requirement of 1,770 calories).

## Military

**Total active duty personnel** (2005): 460 (army and coast guard 65.2%; presidential guard 34.8%). **Military expenditure as percentage of GDP** (2005): 1.2%; per capita expenditure US$4.

## Background

First visited by European navigators in the 1470s, the islands of São Tomé and Príncipe were colonized by the Portuguese in the 16th century and were used in the trade and transshipment of slaves. Sugarcane and cacao were the main cash crops. The islands became an overseas province of Portugal in 1951 and achieved independence in 1975. Príncipe became autonomous in 1995. During recent decades the country's economy has been heavily dependent on international assistance.

## Recent Developments

Sao Tome and Principe remained highly dependent on foreign aid and agriculture in 2011 despite the vast oil fields that had been discovered offshore. Most of the population remained very poor, and a challenge for the government would be to bring the oil onstream. In February 2012 Russian oil company Gunvor announced plans to build a loading terminal and oil storage facility in the country.

**Internet resource:** <www.saotome.st>.

# Saudi Arabia

**Official name:** Al-Mamlakah al-ʻArabiyah al-Suʻudiyah (Kingdom of Saudi Arabia). **Form of government:** monarchy, assisted by the Consultative Council consisting of 150 appointed members. **Head of state and government:** King ʻAbd Allah (from 2005). **Capital:** Riyadh. **Official language:** Arabic. **Official religion:** Islam. **Monetary unit:** 1 Saudi riyal (SR) = 100 halala; valuation (2 Jul 2012) US$1 = SR 3.75.

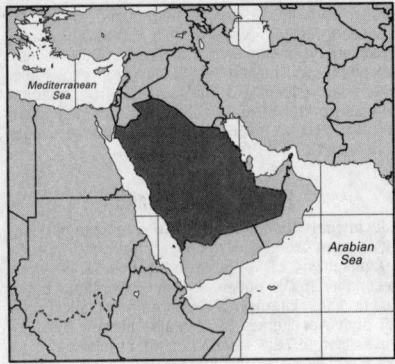

## Demography

**Area:** 830,000 sq mi, 2,149,690 sq km. **Population** (2011): 28,572,000. **Density** (2011): persons per sq mi 34.4, persons per sq km 13.3. **Urban** (2009): 81.9%. **Sex distribution** (2008): male 55.20%; female 44.80%. **Age breakdown** (2008): under 15, 32.3%; 15–29, 27.1%; 30–44, 25.5%; 45–59, 10.8%; 60–74, 3.3%; 75 and over, 1.0%. **Ethnic composition** (2005): Saudi Arab 74%; expatriates 26%, of which Indian 5%, Bangladeshi 3.5%, Pakistani 3.5%, Filipino 3%, Egyptian 3%, Palestinian 1%, other 7%. **Religious affiliation** (2000): Muslim 94%, of which Sunni 84%, Shiʿi 10%; Christian 3.5%, of which Roman Catholic 3%; Hindu 1%; nonreligious/other 1.5%. **Major urban agglomerations** (2007): Riyadh 4,465,000; Jiddah 3,012,000; Mecca 1,385,000; Medina 1,010,000; Al-Dammam 822,000. **Location:** the Middle East, bordering Iraq, Kuwait, the Persian Gulf, Qatar, the UAE, Oman, Yemen, the Red Sea, the Gulf of Aqaba, and Jordan.

## Vital statistics

**Birth rate** per 1,000 population (2008): 24.1 (world avg. 20.3). **Death rate** per 1,000 population (2008): 3.9 (world avg. 8.5). **Total fertility rate** (avg. births per childbearing woman; 2008): 3.10. **Life expectancy** at birth (2007): male 70.9 years; female 75.3 years.

## National economy

**Budget** (2008). *Revenue:* SR 1,100,993,000,000 (petroleum revenues 89.3%). *Expenditures:* SR 520,069,000,000 (current expenditures 74.8%; capital expenditures 25.2%). **National debt** (public only; January 2009): US$62,649,000,000. **Production** (metric tons except as noted). *Agriculture and fishing* (2007): wheat 2,700,000, alfalfa (2006) 1,644,661, dates 970,000; livestock (number of live animals) 7,000,000 sheep, 2,200,000 goats, 372,000 cattle, 260,000 camels; fisheries production 88,410 (from aquaculture 21%). *Mining and quarrying* (2008): gypsum 2,300,000; silver 7,513 kg; gold 4,139 kg. *Manufacturing* (value added in US$'000,000; 2006): industrial chemical products 6,207; food products 4,447; glass products 2,078; refined petroleum products (1998) 1,806. *Energy production (consump-*

*tion):* electricity (kW-hr; 2008) 181,097,000,000 (179,272,185,000); crude petroleum (barrels; 2008–09) 3,210,100,000 ([2008] 838,400,000); petroleum products (metric tons; 2006) 114,-437,000 (68,194,000); natural gas (cu m; 2008) 80,440,000,000 (80,440,000,000). **Population economically active** (2007): total 8,229,665, of which 4,029,966 Saudi workers and 4,199,699 foreign nationals; activity rate of total population 34.0% (participation rates: ages 15–64, 51.8%; female 15.4%; unemployed [2008] 5.0%). **Gross national income** (2008): US$471,692,446,000 (US$18,718 per capita). **Selected balance of payments data.** Receipts from (US$'000,000): tourism (2008) 9,756; foreign direct investment (FDI; 2005–07 avg.) 18,236. Disbursements for (US$'000,000): tourism (2008) 5,891; remittances (2008) 16,068; FDI (2005–07 avg.) 4,816.

## Foreign trade

**Imports** (2008; c.i.f.): SR 431,753,000,000 (machinery and apparatus 27.2%; transportation equipment 18.0%; base and fabricated metals 15.3%; food products and live animals 14.4%; chemical products 12.3%). *Major import sources:* US 13.7%; China 11.0%; Japan 8.2%; Germany 7.4%; South Korea 4.5%. **Exports** (2008; f.o.b.): SR 1,175,354,-000,000 (crude petroleum 78.8%; refined petroleum products 10.8%; other mineral fuels [mostly natural gas] 5.3%). *Major export destinations:* US 16.3%; Japan 15.2%; China 8.9%; South Korea 8.6%; India 7.3%.

## Transport and communications

**Transport.** *Railroads* (2007): route length (2008) 1,423 km; passenger-km 343,000,000; metric ton-km cargo 1,257,000,000. *Roads* (2008): total length 183,925 km (paved 29%). *Vehicles* (2001): passenger cars 4,452,793; trucks and buses 4,110,271. *Air transport* (2008; scheduled flights on Saudi Arabian Airlines only): passenger-km 27,736,000,000; metric ton-km cargo 1,391,000,000. **Communications,** in total units (units per 1,000 persons). Telephone landlines (2008): 4,100,000 (163); cellular telephone subscribers (2008): 36,000,000 (1,429); personal computers (2005): 8,184,000 (354); total Internet users (2008): 7,762,000 (308); broadband Internet subscribers (2008): 1,048,000 (42).

## Education and health

**Educational attainment** (2007). Percentage of Saudi ([2000] non-Saudi) population ages 10 and over who: are illiterate 13.7% (12.1%); are literate/have primary education 34.0% (40.6%); have some/completed secondary 42.1% (36.0%); have at least begun university 10.2% (11.3%). **Literacy** (2007): percentage of total population ages 15 and over literate 85.0%; males literate 89.1%; females literate 79.4%. **Health** (2007): physicians 47,919 (1 per 506 persons); hospital beds 53,519 (1 per 453 persons); infant mortality rate per 1,000 live births 17.9; undernourished population (2002–04) 1,000,000 (4% of total population based on the consumption of a minimum daily requirement of 1,860 calories).

---

*1 metric ton = about 1.1 short tons;    1 kilometer = 0.6 mi (statute);    1 metric ton-km cargo = about 0.68 short ton-mi cargo;    c.i.f.: cost, insurance, and freight;    f.o.b.: free on board*

## Military

Total active duty personnel (November 2008): 221,500 (army 33.9%, navy 6.1%, air force 9.0%, air defense forces 1.8%, industrial security force 4.1%, national guard 45.1%); US troops (November 2008): 287. Military expenditure as percentage of GDP (2008): 8.6%; per capita expenditure US$1,540.

## Background

Saudi Arabia is the historical home of Islam, founded by Muhammad in Medina in 622. During medieval times, local and foreign rulers fought for control of the Arabian Peninsula; in 1517 the Ottomans prevailed. In the 18th–19th centuries Islamic leaders supporting religious reform struggled to regain Saudi territory, all of which was restored by 1904. The British held Saudi lands as a protectorate from 1915 to 1927; then they acknowledged the sovereignty of the Kingdom of the Hejaz and Najd. The two kingdoms were unified as the Kingdom of Saudi Arabia in 1932. Since World War II, it has supported the Palestinian cause in the Middle East and maintained close ties with the US.

## Recent Developments

Saudi Arabia was seriously affected in 2011 by the Arab Spring, a wave of mass protests in Arab countries. In February and March, wary of possible unrest in Saudi Arabia, King 'Abd Allah announced two programs, with a combined cost of US$130 billion, that would provide for massive social spending and handouts. After witnessing the sudden collapse of rulers in both Egypt and Tunisia, Saudi Arabia—along with the UAE and Kuwait—sent troops to Bahrain in March to help crush pro-democracy protests there. In March and April, Saudi Arabia attempted to broker a peace deal in Yemen. In September, King 'Abd Allah announced that women would have the right to run and vote in municipal elections, starting in 2015. He also canceled an order from a religious court calling for a woman to receive 10 lashes for having disobeyed a law prohibiting females from driving cars.

Internet resource: <www.cdsi.gov.sa/english>.

# Senegal

Official name: République du Sénégal (Republic of Senegal). Form of government: multiparty republic with two legislative houses (Senate [100]; National Assembly [150]). Head of state and government: President Macky Sall (from 2012), assisted by Prime Minister Abdoul Mbaye (from 2012). Capital: Dakar. Official language: French. Official religion: none. Monetary unit: 1 CFA franc (CFAF) = 100 centimes; valuation (2 Jul 2012) US$1 = CFAF 521.26

## Demography

Area: 75,955 sq mi, 196,722 sq km. Population (2011): 12,644,000. Density (2011): persons per sq mi 166.5, persons per sq km 64.3. Urban (2009): 42.6%. Sex distribution (2006): male 49.99%; female 50.01%. Age breakdown (2006): under 15, 42.2%; 15–29, 28.4%; 30–44, 16.0%; 45–59,

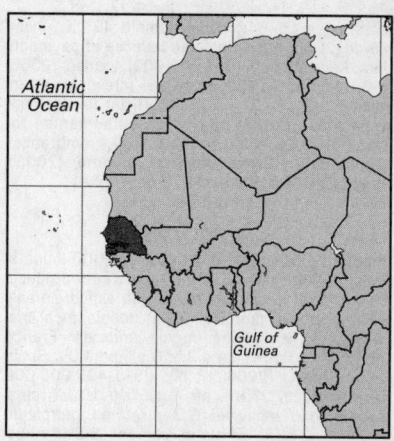

8.7%; 60–74, 3.9%; 75–84, 0.7%; 85 and over, 0.1%. Ethnic composition (2000): Wolof 34.6%; Peul (Fulani) and Tukulor 27.1%; Serer 12.0%; Malinke (Mandingo) 9.7%; other 16.6%. Religious affiliation (2005): Muslim 94%; Christian (mostly Roman Catholic) 4%; other 2%. Major cities (2007): Dakar (urban agglomeration) 2,243,400; Touba 529,200; Thiès 263,500; Kaolack 186,000; Mbour 181,800. Location: western Africa, bordering Mauritania, Mali, Guinea, Guinea-Bissau, the North Atlantic Ocean, and The Gambia.

## Vital statistics

Birth rate per 1,000 population (2008): 34.5 (world avg. 20.3). Death rate per 1,000 population (2008): 8.9 (world avg. 8.5). Total fertility rate (avg. births per childbearing woman; 2006): 5.13. Life expectancy at birth (2006): male 55.0 years; female 57.7 years.

## National economy

Budget (2008). Revenue: CFAF 1,350,900,000,000 (tax revenue 86.0%; grants 10.5%; nontax revenue 3.5%). Expenditures: CFAF 1,678,561,000,000 (current expenditures 67.1%; development expenditures 32.9%). Public debt (external, outstanding; 2007): US$2,029,000,000. Production (metric tons except as noted). Agriculture and fishing (2008): cassava 918,117, sugarcane 836,000, peanuts (groundnuts) 646,964, seed cotton 45,000; livestock (number of live animals) 5,241,352 sheep, 4,470,562 goats, 3,207,697 cattle, 4,634 camels; fisheries production (2007) 421,517 (from aquaculture, negligible). Mining and quarrying (2007): calcium phosphate (crude rock) 691,000. Manufacturing (value added in US$'000,000; 2002): food products 108; industrial chemical products 70; cement, bricks, and ceramics 31. Energy production (consumption): electricity (kW-hr; 2006) 2,433,000,000 (2,433,000,000); coal (metric tons; 2006) none (167,000); crude petroleum (barrels; 2006) none (2,419,000); petroleum products (metric tons; 2006) 336,000 (775,000); natural gas (cu m; 2006) 12,380,000 (12,380,000). Population economically active (2003): total 4,383,000; activity rate of total population 39.4% (participation rates: ages 15–64, 71.5%; female 42.0%; unemployed [2005] 40%). **Selected balance of payments data.** Receipts from (US$'000,000): tourism (2006) 250; remittances (2008) 1,288; foreign direct investment (2005–07 avg.) 114; official development assistance (2007) 843. Disbursements for (US$'000,000): tourism (2006) 54; remittances (2008) 143. **Gross national income** (2008): US$11,825,000,000 (US$970 per capita).

## Foreign trade

**Imports** (2006; c.i.f.): US$3,671,000,000 (mineral fuels 25.9%, of which refined petroleum products 18.4%; food products 19.0%, of which cereals 8.8%; chemical products 9.4%; nonelectrical machinery 9.0%). *Major import sources:* France 24.4%; UK 6.0%; China 4.3%; Thailand 4.0%; Spain 3.8%. **Exports** (2006; f.o.b.): US$1,492,000,000 (food products 27.8%, of which fish 10.7%, crustaceans and mollusks 6.9%; refined petroleum products 24.3%; portland cement 5.3%; phosphoric acid and related products 5.2%). *Major export destinations:* Mali 20.2%; bunker and ships' stores 16.2%; France 7.6%; The Gambia 5.6%; India 5.3%.

## Transport and communications

**Transport.** *Railroads* (2004): route length (2005) 906 km; passenger-km 122,000,000; metric ton-km cargo 358,000,000. *Roads* (2006): total length 14,805 km (paved 29%). *Vehicles* (2007): passenger cars 187,998; trucks and buses 64,537. *Air transport* (2006; Air Sénégal International only): passenger-km 937,000,000; metric ton-km cargo, none. **Communications,** in total units (units per 1,000 persons). Telephone landlines (2008): 238,000 (19); cellular telephone subscribers (2008): 5,389,000 (441); personal computers (2005): 250,000 (21); total Internet users (2008): 1,020,000 (84); broadband Internet subscribers (2008): 47,000 (3.9).

## Education and health

**Educational attainment** (2005). Percentage of population ages 25 and over having: no formal schooling/unknown 70.0%; incomplete primary education 13.0%; complete primary 3.7%; incomplete secondary 9.5%; complete secondary 1.4%; higher 2.4%. **Literacy** (2007): percentage of total population ages 15 and over literate 44.0%; males literate 53.4%; females literate 34.9%. **Health:** physicians (2005) 693 (1 per 17,115 persons); hospital beds (1998) 3,582 (1 per 2,500 persons); infant mortality rate per 1,000 live births (2006) 61.4; undernourished population (2003–05) 3,000,000 (26% of total population based on the consumption of a minimum daily requirement of 1,770 calories).

## Military

**Total active duty personnel** (November 2008): 13,620 (army 87.4%, navy 7.0%, air force 5.6%); French troops (November 2008): 841. **Military expenditure as percentage of GDP** (2007): 1.6%; per capita expenditure US$16.

## Background

Links between the peoples of Senegal and North Africa were established in the 10th century AD. Islam was introduced in the 11th century, though animism retained a hold on the country into the 19th century. The Portuguese explored the coast in 1445, and in 1638 the French established a trading post—the Europeans exported slaves, ivory, and gold from Senegal. The French gained control over the coast in the early 19th century, checking the expansion of the Tukulor empire; in 1895 Senegal became part of French West Africa. Its inhabitants were made French citizens in 1946, and it became an overseas territory of France. It became an autonomous republic in 1958 and was federated with Mali in 1959–60. It became an independent state in 1960. In 1982 it entered a confederation with The Gambia, called Senegambia, which was dissolved in 1989. Separatists fighting in the south since the early 1980s signed a peace accord with the government in 2004.

## Recent Developments

Protests against unemployment and constant power outages were widespread in Senegal in the summer of 2011. In Mbour rioters torched government buildings in June, including those of the state electricity company. After a period of relative calm, the Casamance region saw a resurgence of violence by some rebel factions late in the year.

**Internet resource:** <www.senegal-tourism.com>.

# Serbia

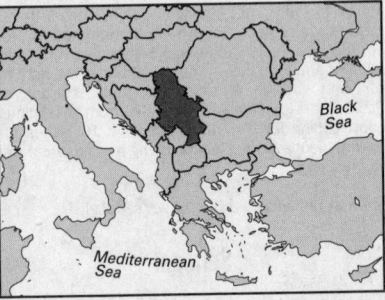

*Some of these statistics include Kosovo, which declared its independence in February 2008.* **Official name:** Republika Srbija (Republic of Serbia). **Form of government:** republic with one legislative house (National Assembly [250]). **Head of state:** President Tomislav Nikolic (from 2012). **Head of government:** Prime Minister Mirko Cvetkovic (from 2008). **Capital:** Belgrade. **Official language:** Serbian. **Official religion:** none. **Monetary unit:** 1 Serbian dinar (CSD) = 100 paras; valuation (2 Jul 2012) US$1 = CSD 91.72.

## Demography

**Area:** 29,922 sq mi, 77,498 sq km. **Population** (2011): 7,262,000. **Density** (2011): persons per sq

---

*1 metric ton = about 1.1 short tons;    1 kilometer = 0.6 mi (statute);    1 metric ton-km cargo = about 0.68 short ton-mi cargo;    c.i.f.: cost, insurance, and freight;    f.o.b.: free on board*

mi 242.7, persons per sq km 93.7. **Urban** (2009): 55.7%. **Sex distribution** (2007): male 48.62%; female 51.38%. **Age breakdown** (2007): under 15, 15.8%; 15–29, 19.7%; 30–44, 20.4%; 45–59, 22.4%; 60–74, 14.9%; 75–84, 5.9%; 85 and over, 0.9%. **Ethnic composition** (2002): Serb 82.9%; Hungarian 3.9%; Bosniak 1.8%; Rom (Gypsy) 1.4%; Yugoslav 1.1%; Croat 0.9%; Montenegrin 0.9%; other 7.1%. **Religious affiliation** (2002): Orthodox 85.0%; Roman Catholic 5.5%; Muslim 3.2%; Protestant 1.1%; other 5.2%. **Major cities** (2002): Belgrade (urban agglomeration) 1,120,092; Novi Sad 191,405; Nis 173,724; Kragujevac 146,373; Subotica 99,981. **Location:** southeastern Europe, bordering Romania, Bulgaria, Macedonia, Kosovo, Montenegro, Bosnia and Herzegovina, Croatia, and Hungary.

## Vital statistics

**Birth rate** per 1,000 population (2008): 9.4 (world avg. 20.3); (2007) within marriage 77.7%. **Death rate** per 1,000 population (2008): 14.0 (world avg. 8.5). **Total fertility rate** (avg. births per childbearing woman; 2007): 1.40. **Life expectancy** at birth (2008): male 71.1 years; female 76.3 years.

## National economy

**Budget** (2007). *Revenue:* CSD 913,488,000,000 (tax revenue 58.8%; social contributions 34.3%; nontax revenue 6.9%). *Expenditures:* CSD 935,-573,000,000 (social protection 38.2%; health 15.5%; economic affairs 11.3%; general public services 9.7%; education 8.1%; public order 6.1%; defense 6.1%). **Public debt** (external, outstanding; August 2009): US$9,803,000,000. **Population economically active** (2007): total 3,267,100; activity rate of total population 43.4% (participation rates: ages 15–64, 62.7%; female 44.0%; unemployed [September 2008–August 2009] 29.7%). **Production** (metric tons except as noted). *Agriculture and fishing* (2007; includes Kosovo): corn (maize) 3,904,825, sugar beets 3,206,380, wheat 1,863,811, sunflower seeds 294,502; livestock (number of live animals) 3,998,927 pigs, 1,106,000 cattle; fisheries production (includes Kosovo) 9,159 (from aquaculture 71%). *Mining and quarrying* (2007): copper (metal content) 32,000; silver (metal content) 4,150; selenium 7,500 kg. *Manufacturing* (value added in CSD '000,000 in constant prices of 2002; 2006): food products and beverages 52,302; chemical products 23,813; cement, bricks, and ceramics 11,532. *Energy production (consumption):* electricity (kW-hr; 2008) 37,392,000,000 ([2006] 35,671,000,000); coal (metric tons; 2008) 72,000 ([2006] 160,000); lignite (metric tons; 2008) 38,520,000 ([2006] 37,367,000); crude petroleum (barrels; 2008) 4,660,000 ([2006] 23,000,000); petroleum products (metric tons; 2006) 2,488,000 (3,588,000); natural gas (cu m; 2007) 271,000,000 ([2006] 2,374,000,000). **Gross national income** (2008): US$41,929,000,000 (US$5,710 per capita). **Selected balance of payments data.** Receipts from (US$'000,000): tourism (2007) 866; remittances (2008) 5,538; foreign direct investment (FDI; 2005–07 avg.) 3,073; official development assistance (2007) 834. Disbursements for (US$'000,-000): tourism (2007) 1,042; remittances (2008) 254; FDI (2005–07 avg.) 361.

## Foreign trade

**Imports** (2007; c.i.f.): US$18,554,000,000 (machinery and apparatus 20.3%; mineral fuels 17.2%; chemical products 14.0%; base metals 9.0%; motor vehicles 8.2%). *Major import sources:* Russia 14.2%; Germany 11.8%; Italy 9.7%; China 7.4%; Hungary 3.9%. **Exports** (2007; f.o.b.): US$8,825,000,000 (food products 15.4%, of which fruits and vegetables 5.3%; iron and steel 12.4%; machinery and apparatus 11.3%; nonferrous metals 7.9%). *Major export destinations:* Italy 12.4%; Bosnia and Herzegovina 11.8%; Montenegro 10.8%; Germany 10.6%; Russia 5.1%.

## Transport and communications

**Transport.** *Railroads* (2006): route length (2004) 3,809 km; passenger-km 684,000,000; metric ton-km cargo 4,232,000,000. *Roads* (2007): total length 39,184 km (paved [2006] 62%). *Vehicles* (2007): passenger cars 1,491,216; trucks and buses 164,566. *Air transport* (2008; Jat Airways only): passenger-km 1,434,000,000; metric ton-km cargo 3,492,000. **Communications,** in total units (units per 1,000 persons). Telephone landlines (2008): 3,085,000 (420); cellular telephone subscribers (2008): 9,619,000 (1,309); personal computers (2007): 1,801,000 (244); total Internet users (2008): 2,361,000 (321); broadband Internet subscribers (2008): 451,000 (61).

## Education and health

**Educational attainment** (2002). Percentage of population ages 15 and over having: no formal education/unknown 7.8%; incomplete primary education 16.2%; complete primary 23.9%; secondary 41.1%; higher 11.0%. **Health** (2007): physicians (public health institutions only) 20,066 (1 per 368 persons); hospital beds (public health institutions only) 41,100 (1 per 180 persons); infant mortality rate per 1,000 live births (2008) 6.7; undernourished population (2002–04; includes Kosovo and Montenegro) 900,000 (9% of total population based on the consumption of a minimum daily requirement of 2,000 calories).

## Military

**Total active duty personnel** (November 2008): 24,257 (army 46.1%, air force/air defense 17.1%, training/ministry of defense 36.8%). **Military expenditure as percentage of GDP** (2008) 2.1%; per capita expenditure US$128.

## Background

The Kingdom of the Serbs, Croats, and Slovenes was created after the collapse of Austria-Hungary at the end of World War I. The country signed treaties with Czechoslovakia and Romania in 1920–21, marking the beginning of the Little Entente. In 1929 an absolute monarchy was established, the country's name was changed to Yugoslavia, and it was divided into regions without regard to ethnic boundaries. Axis powers invaded Yugoslavia in 1941, and German, Italian, Hungarian, and Bulgarian troops occupied it for the rest of World War II. In 1945 the Socialist Federal Republic of Yugoslavia was established; it included the republics of Bosnia and Herzegovina, Croatia, Macedonia, Montenegro, Serbia, and Slovenia. Its independent form of communism under Josip

Broz Tito's leadership provoked the USSR. Internal ethnic tensions flared up in the 1980s, causing the country's ultimate collapse. In 1991–92 independence was declared by Croatia, Slovenia, Macedonia, and Bosnia and Herzegovina; the new Federal Republic of Yugoslavia (containing roughly 45% of the population and 40% of the area of its predecessor) was proclaimed by Serbia and Montenegro. Fueled by long-standing ethnic tensions, hostilities continued into the 1990s. Despite the approval of the Dayton Peace Agreement (1995), sporadic fighting continued and was followed in 1998–99 by Serbian repression and expulsion of ethnic populations in the province of Kosovo. In September–October 2000, the battered nation of Yugoslavia ended the autocratic rule of Pres. Slobodan Milosevic. In April 2001 he was arrested and in June extradited to The Hague to stand trial for war crimes, genocide, and crimes against humanity committed during the fighting in Kosovo. In February 2003 the government accepted a new state charter and changed the name of the country from Yugoslavia to Serbia and Montenegro. Henceforth, defense, international political and economic relations, and human rights matters would be handled centrally, while all other functions would be run from the republican capitals, Belgrade and Podgorica, respectively. A provision was included for both states to vote on independence after three years; Serbia declared its independence in June 2006, shortly after Montenegro severed its federal union with Serbia. In 2008 Kosovo formally seceded, but Serbia refused to recognize it as an independent country.

## Recent Developments

The European Commission's report for 2011, noting Serbia's significant progress toward bringing about the "stability of institutions guaranteeing democracy, rule of law, human rights and respect for and protection of minorities," recommended that Serbia become an official EU candidate country. In May, Ratko Mladic, commander of the Bosnian Serb forces during the 1992–95 war in Bosnia and Herzegovina, was arrested in Serbia. Indicted by the UN's International Criminal Tribunal for the Former Yugoslavia in 1995 on charges of genocide, war crimes, and crimes against humanity, he was held pending trial at The Hague. Serbia's actions here, too, were seen as moves in the right direction regarding negotiations over the country's EU membership drive. In February 2012, Serbia agreed to manage its border jointly with Kosovo, and in March EU members voted to grant Serbia candidate status.

Internet resource:
<http://webrzs.stat.gov.rs/WebSite>.

# Seychelles

**Official name:** Repiblik Sesel (Creole); République des Seychelles (French); Republic of Seychelles (English). **Form of government:** multiparty republic with one legislative house (National Assembly [34]). **Head of state and government:** President James Michel (from 2004). **Capital:** Victoria. **Official languages:** none (Creole, French, and English are national languages per the constitution). **Official religion:** none.

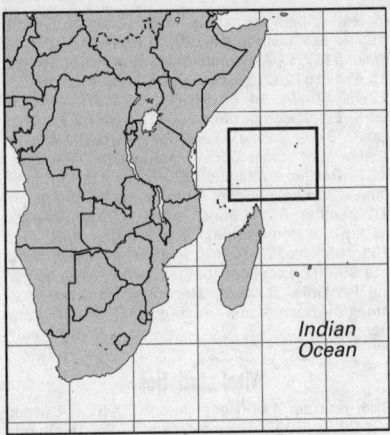

Indian Ocean

**Monetary unit:** 1 Seychelles rupee (roupi; SR) = 100 cents; valuation (2 Jul 2012) US$1 = SR 14.46.

## Demography

**Area:** 174.4 sq mi, 451.7 sq km. **Population** (2011): 92,000. **Density** (2011): persons per sq mi 527.5, persons per sq km 203.7. **Urban** (2009): 54.8%. **Sex distribution** (2008): male 51.75%; female 48.25%. **Age breakdown** (2008): under 15, 22.7%; 15–29, 26.0%; 30–44, 24.5%; 45–59, 16.2%; 60–74, 7.3%; 75 and over, 3.3%. **Ethnic composition** (2000): Seychellois Creole (mixture of Asian, African, and European) 93.2%; British 3.0%; French 1.8%; Chinese 0.5%; Indian 0.3%; other 1.2%. **Religious affiliation** (2002): Roman Catholic 82.3%; Anglican 6.4%; other Christian 4.5%; Hindu 2.1%; Muslim 1.1%; other 3.6%. **Major towns** (2006): Victoria 22,600; Anse Royale (2004) 3,800. **Location:** group of islands in the Indian Ocean, northeast of Madagascar.

## Vital statistics

**Birth rate** per 1,000 population (2007): 17.6 (world avg. 20.3); within marriage 20.8%. **Death rate** per 1,000 population (2007): 7.4 (world avg. 8.5). **Total fertility rate** (avg. births per childbearing woman; 2007): 2.24. **Life expectancy** at birth (2007): male 68.9 years; female 77.7 years.

## National economy

**Budget** (2007). *Revenue:* SR 2,487,300,000 (tax revenue 64.7%, of which taxes on goods and services 37.2%, taxes on international trade 13.0%; social contributions 18.1%). *Expenditures:* SR 2,854,-900,000 (social protection 21.5%; public debt interest charges 14.5%; education 9.9%; health 7.0%; public order 4.8%; defense 3.9%). **Public debt** (2008): US$254,000,000. **Gross national income** (2008): US$889,000,000 (US$10,290 per capita). **Production** (metric tons except as noted). *Agriculture and fishing* (2007): coconuts 3,200, bananas 2,000, cinnamon 315; livestock (number of live animals) 18,700 pigs, 5,200 goats, 575,000 chickens; fish-

*1 metric ton = about 1.1 short tons;    1 kilometer = 0.6 mi (statute);    1 metric ton-km cargo = about 0.68 short ton-mi cargo;    c.i.f.: cost, insurance, and freight;    f.o.b.: free on board*

eries production 66,239 (from aquaculture 6%). *Mining and quarrying* (2007): granite 149,000. *Manufacturing* (2006): canned tuna 40,222; fish meal 14,821; copra 253. *Energy production (consumption):* electricity (kW-hr; 2006) 251,000,000 (227,000,000); petroleum products (metric tons; 2006) none (243,000). **Population economically active** (2002): total 43,859; activity rate of total population 53.6% (participation rates: ages 15–64, 80.1%; female [1997] 47.6%; unemployed [2006] 2.6%). **Selected balance of payments data.** Receipts from (US$'000,000): tourism (2007) 278; remittances (2008) 12; foreign direct investment (FDI; 2005–07 avg.) 160; official development assistance (2007) 3. Disbursements for (US$'000,000): tourism (2007) 40; remittances (2008) 21; FDI (2005–07 avg.) 8.

## Foreign trade

**Imports** (2007; c.i.f.): SR 5,728,000,000 (mineral fuels 25.1%; machinery and apparatus 22.4%; food products 19.5%, of which marine products 11.9%; transportation equipment 4.1%; iron and steel 3.4%). *Major import sources:* Saudi Arabia 24.8%; Germany 9.5%; Singapore 8.5%; France 7.8%; Spain 6.6%. **Exports** (2007; f.o.b.): SR 2,435,000,000 (domestic exports 55.3%, of which canned tuna 50.6%, fish meal 1.2%; medicine and medical appliances 1.2%; reexports 44.7%, of which refined petroleum products to ships and aircraft 43.1%). *Major export destinations* (domestic exports only): UK 40.1%; France 34.7%; Italy 10.0%; Germany 3.2%.

## Transport and communications

**Transport.** *Railroads:* none. *Roads* (2006): total length 502 km (paved 96%). *Vehicles* (2006): passenger cars 7,070; trucks and buses 2,796. *Air transport* (2006–07; Air Seychelles only): passenger-km 1,593,000,000; metric ton-km cargo 31,000,000. **Communications,** in total units (units per 1,000 persons). Telephone landlines (2008): 22,000 (266); cellular telephone subscribers (2008): 94,000 (1,115); personal computers (2005): 16,000 (193); total Internet users (2008): 68,000 (382); broadband Internet subscribers (2008): 3,400 (41).

## Education and health

**Educational attainment** (2003). Percentage of population ages 12 and over having: less than primary or primary education 23.2%; secondary 73.4%; higher 3.4%. **Literacy** (2006): total population ages 15 and over literate 91.8%; males literate 91.4%; females literate 92.3%. **Health** (2007): physicians 91 (1 per 934 persons); hospital beds 401 (1 per 212 persons); infant mortality rate per 1,000 live births 10.7; undernourished population (2002–04) 7,000 (9% of total population based on the consumption of a minimum daily requirement of 1,810 calories).

## Military

**Total active duty personnel** (November 2008): 200 (army 100%); there is also a 450-member paramilitary, which includes both a coast guard and a national guard. **Military expenditure as percentage of GDP** (2007): 1.9%; per capita expenditure US$129.

## Background

The first recorded landing on the uninhabited Seychelles was made in 1609 by an expedition of the British East India Co. The archipelago was claimed by the French in 1756 and surrendered to the British in 1810. Seychelles became a British crown colony in 1903 and a republic within the Commonwealth in 1976. A one-party socialist state since 1979, Seychelles returned to democracy with the return of multiparty politics and the promulgation of a new constitution in 1993.

## Recent Developments

Diplomatic cables leaked in 2011 (part of WikiLeaks) indicated that a secret US military base had been built in Seychelles in 2009. It was alleged to be part of ongoing antipiracy activities but also as a drone-launching site for counterterrorism operations in the region.

**Internet resource:** <www.nsb.gov.sc>.

# Sierra Leone

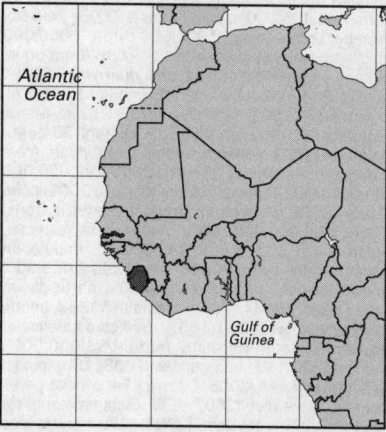

Atlantic Ocean

Gulf of Guinea

**Official name:** Republic of Sierra Leone. **Form of government:** republic with one legislative house (Parliament [124]). **Head of state and government:** President Ernest Bai Koroma (from 2007). **Capital:** Freetown. **Official language:** English. **Official religion:** none. **Monetary unit:** 1 leone (Le) = 100 cents; valuation (2 Jul 2012) US$1 = Le 4,328.23.

## Demography

**Area:** 27,699 sq mi, 71,740 sq km. **Population** (2011): 5,997,000. **Density** (2011): persons per sq mi 216.5, persons per sq km 83.6. **Urban** (2010): 38.4%. **Sex distribution** (2005): male 49.23%; female 50.77%. **Age breakdown** (2005): under 15, 42.8%; 15–29, 26.1%; 30–44, 16.0%; 45–59, 9.6%; 60–74, 4.7%; 75–84, 0.7%; 85 and over, 0.1%. **Ethnic composition** (2000): Mende 26.0%; Temne 24.6%; Limba 7.1%; Kuranko 5.5%; Kono 4.2%; Fulani 3.8%; Bullom-Sherbro 3.5%; other 25.3%. **Reli-**

**gious affiliation** (2005): Muslim 65%; Christian 25%; traditional beliefs/other 10%. **Major towns** (2006): Freetown 818,700; Bo 181,800; Kenema 148,800; Makeni 90,400; Koidu 87,300. **Location:** western Africa, bordering Guinea, Liberia, and the North Atlantic Ocean.

## Vital statistics

**Birth rate** per 1,000 population (2008): 45.8 (world avg. 20.3). **Death rate** per 1,000 population (2008): 21.8 (world avg. 8.5). **Total fertility rate** (avg. births per childbearing woman; 2005): 6.49. **Life expectancy** at birth (2005): male 40.1 years; female 43.5 years.

## National economy

**Budget** (2007). *Revenue:* Le 1,179,000,000,000 (grants 42.7%; import duties 21.8%; corporate taxes 7.7%; income tax 7.1%; excise duties on refined petroleum products 6.6%). *Expenditures:* Le 1,222,-000,000,000 (current expenditures 63.4%; capital expenditures 36.6%). **Gross national income** (2008): US$1,785,000,000 (US$320 per capita). **Production** (metric tons except as noted). *Agriculture and fishing* (2007): rice 650,000, cassava 370,000, oil palm fruit 195,000, cacao beans 12,000; livestock (number of live animals) 300,000 cattle, 7,500,000 chickens; fisheries production 144,535 (from aquaculture, negligible). *Mining and quarrying* (2008): bauxite 954,370; rutile 78,910; ilmenite 17,260; diamonds 371,290 carats; gold (2007) 212 kg. *Manufacturing* (2006): soap 467,360; cement 234,440; paint 142,730 gallons. *Energy production (consumption):* electricity (kW-hr; 2006) 99,000,000 (99,000,000); crude petroleum (barrels; 2006) none (1,980,000); petroleum products (metric tons; 2006) 166,000 (200,000). **Public debt** (external, outstanding; 2007): US$308,000,000. **Population economically active** (2003–04): total 2,005,900; activity rate of total population 40.0% (participation rates: ages 15–64, 68.2%; female 53.6%; unofficially unemployed [2007] 65%). **Selected balance of payments data.** Receipts from (US$'000,000): tourism (2007) 22; remittances (2008) 150; foreign direct investment (2005–07 avg.) 74; official development assistance (2007) 535. Disbursements for (US$'000,000): tourism (2007) 14; remittances (2008) 136.

## Foreign trade

**Imports** (2007; c.i.f.): Le 1,333,189,000,000 (mineral fuels 37.7%; machinery and transportation equipment 16.8%; food products 15.2%, of which rice 5.4%). *Major import sources* (2005): Germany 19%; Côte d'Ivoire 11%; UK 8%; US 7%; China 6%. **Exports** (2007; f.o.b.): Le 733,407,000,000 (diamonds 57.8%; rutile 15.5%; bauxite 13.3%; cocoa 4.6%; gold 1.2%). *Major export destinations:* Belgium 49.5%; US 20.6%; Netherlands 4.6%; Canada 4.0%.

## Transport and communications

**Transport.** *Railroads* (2002; Marampa Mineral Railway; there are no passenger railways): length 84 km. *Roads* (2002): total length 11,300 km (paved 8%).

*Vehicles* (2007): passenger cars 16,396; trucks and buses 14,444. *Air transport* (2004): passenger-km 85,000,000; metric ton-km cargo 8,000,000. **Communications,** in total units (units per 1,000 persons). Telephone landlines (2008): 32,000 (5.7); cellular telephone subscribers (2008): 1,009,000 (181); personal computers (1999): 100; total Internet users (2008): 14,000 (2.5).

## Education and health

**Educational attainment** (2004). Percentage of total population having: no formal schooling 62.2%; primary education 24.6%; lower secondary 6.4%; upper secondary 4.2%; vocational 2.0%; higher 0.6%. **Literacy** (2007): total population ages 15 and over literate 38.1%; males literate 50.0%; females literate 26.8%. **Health:** physicians (2004) 168 (1 per 32,083 persons); hospital beds (2001) 2,770 (1 per 1,698 persons); infant mortality rate per 1,000 live births (2005) 163.0; undernourished population (2003–05) 2,500,000 (47% of total population based on the consumption of a minimum daily requirement of 1,750 calories).

## Military

**Total active duty personnel** (November 2008): c. 10,500 (army 98%, navy 2%, air force, none). **Military expenditure as percentage of GDP** (2007): 1.7%; per capita expenditure US$5.

## Background

The earliest inhabitants of Sierra Leone were probably the Buloms; the Mende and Temne peoples arrived in the 15th century. The coastal region was visited by the Portuguese in the 15th century, and by 1495 there was a Portuguese fort on the site of modern Freetown. European ships visited the coast regularly to trade for slaves and ivory, and the English built trading posts on offshore islands in the 17th century. British abolitionists and philanthropists founded Freetown in 1787 as a private venture for freed and runaway slaves. In 1808 the coastal settlement became a British colony. The region became a British protectorate in 1896. It achieved independence in 1961 and became a republic in 1971. Since independence Sierra Leone experienced a series of military coups. An 11-year civil war, which was marked by horrific atrocities and further devastated the country, ended in 2002.

## Recent Developments

In 2011, Sierra Leone made notable progress in restoring democracy and socioeconomic programs. According to the 2011 Mo Ibrahim Index of African Governance, Sierra Leone rose three places to number 30 of 53 countries for governance quality. Expanded road and bridge construction throughout the country facilitated internal trade and movement. The free health care program increased the number of children receiving health care by 214%, reduced maternal mortalities, and diminished malaria deaths in children treated in hospitals by 85%.

**Internet resource:** <www.welcometosierraleone.sl>.

*1 metric ton = about 1.1 short tons;   1 kilometer = 0.6 mi (statute);   1 metric ton-km cargo = about 0.68 short ton-mi cargo;   c.i.f.: cost, insurance, and freight;   f.o.b.: free on board*

# Singapore

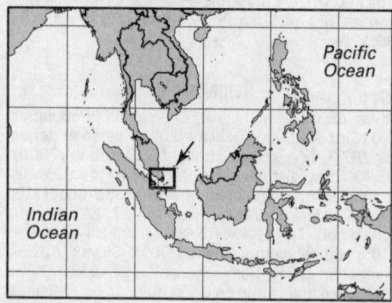

Pacific Ocean

Indian Ocean

**Official name:** Xinjiapo Gongheguo (Mandarin Chinese); Republik Singapura (Malay); Cingkappur Kudiyarasu (Tamil); Republic of Singapore (English). **Form of government:** unitary multiparty republic with one legislative house (Parliament [99]). **Head of state:** President Tony Tan (from 2011). **Head of state government:** Prime Minister Lee Hsien Loong (from 2004). **Capital:** Singapore. **Official languages:** Mandarin Chinese; Malay; Tamil; English. **Official religion:** none. **Monetary unit:** 1 Singapore dollar (S$) = 100 cents; valuation (2 Jul 2012) US$1 = S$1.27.

## Demography

**Area:** 274.2 sq mi, 710.2 sq km. **Population** (2011): 5,182,000. **Density** (2011): persons per sq mi 18,899, persons per sq km 7,297. **Urban:** (2011): 100%. **Sex distribution** (2009): male 49.41%; female 50.59%. **Age breakdown** (2009): under 15, 17.9%; 15–29, 20.9%; 30–44, 24.8%; 45–59, 23.0%; 60–74, 10.0%; 75–84, 2.6%; 85 and over, 0.8%. **Ethnic composition** (2009): Chinese 74.2%; Malay 13.4%; Indian 9.2%; other 3.2%. **Religious affiliation** (2000): Buddhist/Taoist/Chinese folk-religionist 51.0%; Muslim 14.9%; Christian 14.6%; Hindu 4.0%; traditional beliefs 0.6%; nonreligious 14.9%. **Location:** southeastern Asia, islands between Malaysia and Indonesia.

## Vital statistics

**Birth rate** per 1,000 population (2008): 10.2 (world avg. 20.3). **Death rate** per 1,000 population (2008): 4.4 (world avg. 8.5). **Total fertility rate** (avg. births per childbearing woman; 2008): 1.28. **Life expectancy** at birth (2008): male 78.4 years; female 83.2 years.

## National economy

**Budget** (2008). *Revenue:* S$41,376,700,000 (income tax 44.9%; goods and services tax 16.0%; fees and charges 9.0%; assets taxes 7.0%; customs and excise duties 5.0%). *Expenditures:* S$37,470,200,000 (security and external relations 36.3%; education 19.5%; health 6.1%; community development 3.1%). **Production** (metric tons except as noted). *Agriculture and fishing* (2008): vegetables 18,967, orchids (roughly 15% of the world market) and other ornamental plants are cultivated for export; livestock (number of live animals) 260,000 pigs, 2,000,000 chickens; fisheries production (2007) 8,025 (from aquaculture 56%); aquarium fish farming is also an important economic pursuit—Singapore produces roughly 30% of

the world's ornamental fish. *Quarrying:* limestone, n.a. *Manufacturing* (value added in S$'000,000; 2008): pharmaceuticals 9,443; professional and scientific equipment 7,898; semiconductors 7,894; refined petroleum products and petrochemicals 2,639. *Energy production (consumption):* electricity (kW-hr; 2008–09) 40,964,000,000 ([2008] 37,940,300,000); crude petroleum (barrels; 2008) 3,121,845 (327,040,000); petroleum products (metric tons; 2006) 36,501,000 (7,781,000); natural gas (cu m; 2008) none (8,270,000,000). **Gross national income** (2008): US$168,227,000,000 (US$34,760 per capita). **Population economically active** (2008): total 1,928,300; activity rate of total population 52.9% (participation rates: ages 15–64, 71.7%; female 43.3%; unemployed [October 2008–September 2009] 3.1%). **Public debt** (2006): US$122,000,000,000. **Selected balance of payments data.** Receipts from (US$'000,000): tourism (2007) 8,680; foreign direct investment (FDI; 2005–07 avg.) 20,937. Disbursements for (US$'000,000): tourism (2007) 11,844; FDI (2005–07 avg.) 10,495.

## Foreign trade

**Imports** (2008; c.i.f.): S$450,892,600,000 (crude petroleum and refined petroleum products 27.4%; nonelectrical machinery and equipment 16.1%; integrated circuits 13.4%; other electronics 10.2%; chemical products 5.3%; base metals 4.2%). *Major import sources:* Malaysia 11.9%; US 11.7%; China 10.6%; Japan 8.1%; South Korea 5.6%. **Exports** (2008; f.o.b.): S$476,762,100,000 (crude petroleum and refined petroleum products 24.1%; integrated circuits 16.8%; nonelectrical machinery and equipment 14.3%; other electronics 13.2%; chemical products 10.2%). *Major export destinations:* Malaysia 12.1%; Indonesia 10.6%; Hong Kong 10.4%; China 9.2%; US 7.0%.

## Transport and communications

**Transport.** *Railroads* (2006): length 39 km. *Roads* (2008; public roads only): total length 3,325 km (paved 100%). *Vehicles* (2009): passenger cars 566,520; trucks and buses 173,178. *Air transport* (2008–09): passenger-km 92,249,000,000; metric ton-km cargo 6,845,262,000. **Communications,** in total units (units per 1,000 persons). Telephone landlines (2008): 1,857,000 (402); cellular telephone subscribers (2008): 6,376,000 (1,382); personal computers (2007): 3,409,000 (743); total Internet users (2008): 3,370,000 (730); broadband Internet subscribers (2008): 1,003,000 (217).

## Education and health

**Educational attainment** (2005). Percentage of population ages 15 and over having: no schooling 16.4%; primary education 22.0%; lower secondary 21.3%; upper secondary 15.1%; technical 8.2%; university 17.0%. **Literacy** (2008): total population ages 15 and over literate 96.0%. **Health** (2008): physicians 7,841 (1 per 617 persons); hospital beds 11,457 (1 per 422 persons); infant mortality rate per 1,000 live births 2.1.

## Military

**Total active duty personnel** (November 2008): 72,500 (army 69.0%, navy 12.4%, air force 18.6%). **Military expenditure as percentage of GDP** (2008): 4.1%; per capita expenditure US$1,517.

## Background

Long inhabited by fishermen and pirates, Singapore was an outpost of the Sumatran empire of Srivijaya until the 14th century, when it passed to Java and then to Siam. It became part of the Malacca empire in the 15th century. In the 16th century the Portuguese controlled the area, followed by the Dutch. In 1819 Singapore was ceded to the British East India Co., becoming part of the Straits Settlements and the center of British colonial activity in Southeast Asia. The Japanese occupied the islands in 1942–45. In 1946 it became a crown colony. It achieved full internal self-government in 1959, became a part of Malaysia in 1963, and gained independence in 1965. It is influential in the affairs of the Association of Southeast Asian Nations and has become a regional economic powerhouse. The country's dominant voice in politics for 30 years after independence was Lee Kuan Yew.

## Recent Developments

In May 2011, in its worst showing in a general election since independence in 1965, Singapore's ruling People's Action Party lost a record 6 seats out of 87 contested and garnered a vote share of only 60.1%. A week later, in what Prime Minister Lee Hsien Loong billed as an "epochal change," Lee Kuan Yew, Singapore's founding prime minister (1959–90), and Goh Chok Tong, prime minister from 1990 to 2004, both stepped down from the cabinet. It was a tacit admission that their continued presence there hampered new approaches and styles of governance.

Internet resource: <www.singstat.gov.sg>.

## Slovakia

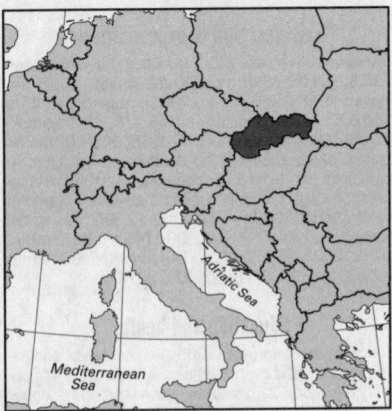

**Official name:** Slovenska republika (Slovak Republic). **Form of government:** unitary multiparty republic with one legislative house (National Council [150]). **Head of state:** President Ivan Gasparovic (from 2004). **Head of government:** Prime Minister Robert Fico (from 2012). **Capital:** Bratislava. **Official language:** Slovak. **Official religion:** none. Mon-

etary unit: 1 euro (€) = 100 cents; valuation (2 Jul 2012) US$1 = €0.79 (the euro replaced the Slovak koruna [Sk] on 1 Jan 2009, at the rate of €1 = Sk 30.126).

## Demography

**Area:** 18,932 sq mi, 49,034 sq km. **Population** (2011): 5,440,000. **Density** (2011): persons per sq mi 287.3, persons per sq km 110.9. **Urban** (2006): 55.4%. **Sex distribution** (2008): male 48.52%; female 51.48%. **Age breakdown** (2008): under 15, 16.3%; 15–29, 24.0%; 30–44, 22.2%; 45–59, 21.1%; 60–74, 11.4%; 75–84, 4.0%; 85 and over, 1.0%. **Ethnic composition** (2001): Slovak 85.8%; Hungarian 9.7%; Rom (Gypsy) 1.7%; Czech 0.8%; Ruthenian and Ukrainian 0.7%; other 1.3%. **Religious affiliation** (2001): Roman Catholic 68.9%; Protestant 9.2%, of which Lutheran 6.9%, Reformed Christian 2.0%; Greek Catholic 4.1%; Eastern Orthodox 0.9%; nonreligious 13.0%; other 3.9%. **Major cities** (2007): Bratislava 426,927; Kosice 234,237; Presov 91,498; Zilina 85,370; Nitra 84,444. **Location:** central Europe, bordering Poland, Ukraine, Hungary, Austria, and the Czech Republic.

## Vital statistics

**Birth rate** per 1,000 population (2008): 10.6 (world avg. 20.3); within marriage 69.9%. **Death rate** per 1,000 population (2008): 9.8 (world avg. 8.5). **Total fertility rate** (avg. births per childbearing woman; 2008): 1.33. **Life expectancy** at birth (2008): male 70.9 years; female 78.7 years.

## National economy

**Budget** (2007). *Revenue:* Sk 546,660,000,000 (tax revenue 47.9%, of which taxes on goods and services 35.6%; social security contributions 39.8%; nontax revenue 10.9%; grants 1.4%). *Expenditures:* Sk 580,610,000,000 (social protection 33.0%; health 20.0%; general administration 18.9%; economic affairs 11.8%; police 5.9%; defense 4.5%; education 3.7%). **Production** (metric tons except as noted). *Agriculture and fishing* (2007): wheat 1,440,637, sugar beets 855,343, barley 695,042, sunflower seeds 135,376; livestock (number of live animals) 1,104,830 pigs, 507,820 cattle; fisheries production 4,071 (from aquaculture 29%). *Mining and quarrying* (2007): magnesite 457,763; kaolin 30,000; barite 13,000. *Manufacturing* (value added in US$'000,000; 2006): fabricated metal products 1,200; nonelectrical machinery and apparatus 1,165; motor vehicles and parts 1,000. *Energy production (consumption):* electricity (kW-hr; 2008) 28,908,000,000 ([2006] 29,087,000,000); coal (metric tons; 2006) none (5,148,000); lignite (metric tons; 2008) 2,412,000 ([2006] 3,168,000); crude petroleum (barrels; 2007) 170,000 ([2006] 41,-400,000); petroleum products (metric tons; 2006) 5,330,000 (2,953,000); natural gas (cu m; 2007) 142,000,000 ([2006] 6,411,000,000). **Population economically active** (2008): total 2,691,200; activity rate of total population 49.8% (participation rates: ages 15–64, 68.9%; female 44.7%; unemployed [July 2008–June 2009] 9.1%). **Public debt** (external, outstanding; December 2008): US$10,313,000,000.

Gross national income (2008): US$78,607,000,000 (US$14,540 per capita). **Selected balance of payments data.** Receipts from (US$'000,000): tourism (2007) 2,026; remittances (2008) 1,500; foreign direct investment (FDI; 2005–07 avg.) 3,179. Disbursements for (US$'000,000): tourism (2007) 1,533; remittances (2008) 73; FDI (2005–07 avg.) 303.

## Foreign trade

**Imports** (2007): US$57,754,000,000 (machinery and apparatus 29.6%, of which telecommunications equipment and parts 9.6%; motor vehicles and parts 13.8%; mineral fuels 11.0%; base and fabricated metals 10.3%; chemical products 8.7%). *Major import sources:* Germany 19.9%; Czech Republic 11.5%; Russia 9.4%; Hungary 5.4%; China 5.2%. **Exports** (2008): US$57,802,000,000 (machinery and apparatus 28.7%, of which color television receivers 10.3%; motor vehicles and parts 24.3%, of which passenger cars 17.9%; base and fabricated metals 12.9%, of which iron and steel 7.5%; refined petroleum products 4.5%). *Major export destinations:* Germany 21.5%; Czech Republic 12.4%; France 6.8%; Italy 6.4%; Poland 6.2%.

## Transport and communications

**Transport.** *Railroads* (2006): length 3,658 km; passenger-km 2,213,000,000; metric ton-km cargo 9,988,000,000. *Roads* (2006): total length 43,770 km (paved 87%). *Vehicles* (2007): passenger cars 1,468,616; trucks and buses 255,089. *Air transport* (2008; SkyEurope airlines only): passenger-km 3,733,000,000; metric ton-km cargo, none. **Communications,** in total units (units per 1,000 persons). Telephone landlines (2008): 1,098,000 (203); cellular telephone subscribers (2008): 5,520,000 (1,021); personal computers (2007): 2,774,000 (514); total Internet users (2008): 2,771,000 (513); broadband Internet subscribers (2008): 619,000 (114).

## Education and health

**Educational attainment** (2007). Percentage of population ages 25–64 having: primary education 1%; lower secondary 12%; upper secondary 73%; higher vocational 1%; university 13%. **Literacy** (2007): total population ages 15 and over literate nearly 100%. **Health:** physicians (2006) 17,031 (1 per 317 persons); hospital beds (2007) 36,426 (1 per 148 persons); infant mortality rate per 1,000 live births (2008) 5.9; undernourished population (2002–04) 400,000 (7% of total population based on the consumption of a minimum daily requirement of 2,030 calories).

## Military

**Total active duty personnel** (November 2008): 17,445 (army 41.8%, air force 24.0%, headquarters staff 13.3%, support/training 20.9%). **Military expenditure as percentage of GDP** (2008): 1.5%; per capita expenditure US$255.

## Background

Slovakia was inhabited in the first centuries AD by Illyrian, Celtic, and Germanic tribes. Slovaks settled there around the 6th century. It became part of Great Moravia in the 9th century but was conquered by the Magyars c. 907. It remained in the kingdom of Hungary until the end of World War I, when the Slovaks joined the Czechs to form the new state of Czechoslovakia in 1918. Slovakia was nominally independent under German protection in 1939–45. After the expulsion of the Germans, Slovakia joined a reconstituted Czechoslovakia, which came under Soviet domination in 1948. In 1969 a partnership between the Czechs and the Slovaks established the Slovak Socialist Republic. The fall of the communist regime in 1989 led to a revival of interest in autonomy, and Slovakia became an independent nation in 1993. It joined both NATO and the EU in 2004.

## Recent Developments

Slovakia's economy in 2011 continued to recover from the 2009 downturn. In the first quarter of 2011, GDP returned to its precrisis level, and for the year, GDP grew 5.3%. Industrial output and exports were the biggest drivers of growth. Though there were signs of weakening by midyear, as the European debt crisis heightened, Slovakia's reliance on Germany as a key export market helped to guarantee stability. Household demand in Slovakia remained weak in 2011 owing to fiscal consolidation measures and high inflation. Despite public-sector job cuts, total employment rose substantially in 2011, and the unemployment rate dropped to 13.5%.

**Internet resource:** <http://portal.statistics.sk>.

# Slovenia

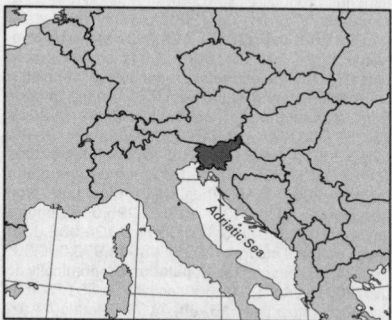

**Official name:** Republika Slovenija (Republic of Slovenia). **Form of government:** unitary multiparty republic with two legislative houses (National Council [40]; National Assembly [90]). **Head of state:** President Danilo Turk (from 2007). **Head of government:** Prime Minister Janez Jansa (from 2012). **Capital:** Ljubljana. **Official language:** Slovene. **Official religion:** none. **Monetary unit:** 1 euro (€) = 100 cents; valuation (2 Jul 2012) US$1 = €0.79.

## Demography

**Area:** 7,827 sq mi, 20,273 sq km. **Population** (2011): 2,052,000. **Density** (2011): persons per sq mi 262.2, persons per sq km 101.2. **Urban** (2009): 49.6%. **Sex distribution** (2008): male 49.64%; female 50.36%. **Age breakdown** (2007): under 15,

13.9%; 15–29, 20.0%; 30–44, 22.6%; 45–59, 22.4%; 60–74, 14.1%; 75–84, 5.7%; 85 and over, 1.3%. **Ethnic composition** (2002): Slovene 91.2%; Serb 2.2%; Croat 2.0%; Bosniak (Muslim) 1.8%; other 2.8%. **Religious affiliation** (2002): Roman Catholic 57.8%; Muslim 2.4%; Orthodox 2.3%; Protestant 0.8%; nonreligious/atheist 10.2%; other 26.5%. **Major cities** (2008): Ljubljana 268,423; Maribor 96,408; Celje 38,047; Kranj 36,357; Velenje 25,935. **Location:** southeastern Europe, bordering Austria, Hungary, Croatia, the Adriatic Sea, and Italy.

## Vital statistics

**Birth rate** per 1,000 population (2008): 10.8 (world avg. 20.3); within marriage 47.1%. **Death rate** per 1,000 population (2008): 9.1 (world avg. 8.5). **Total fertility rate** (avg. births per childbearing woman; 2008): 1.53. **Life expectancy** at birth (2007): male 75.0 years; female 82.3 years.

## National economy

**Budget** (2007). *Revenue:* €13,658,091,000 (tax revenue 59.7%, of which taxes on goods and services 32.9%, income tax 13.2%; social security contributions 33.7%; nontax revenue 5.2%; other [including grants] 1.4%). *Expenditures:* €13,092,376,000 (current expenditures 88.8%, of which social protection 46.9%; wages and salaries 21.5%; capital expenditures 11.2%). **Public debt** (2007): US$10,875,‐000,000. **Production** (metric tons except as noted). *Agriculture and fishing* (2007): corn (maize) 308,259, sugar beets 260,000, wheat 133,339, hops 2,157; livestock (number of live animals) 575,120 pigs, 451,293 cattle, 212,000 beehives; fisheries production 2,463 (from aquaculture 55%). *Mining and quarrying* (2007): sand and gravel 11,008,600; salt (2005) 125,000. *Manufacturing* (value added in €'000,000; 2007): chemical products 971; fabricated metal products 961; nonelectrical machinery and equipment 776. *Energy production (consumption):* electricity (kW-hr; 2008) 15,357,000,000 (12,945,000,000); coal (metric tons; 2006) none (46,000); lignite (metric tons; 2008) 4,032,000 (4,161,000); crude petroleum (barrels; 2007) 2,199 (negligible); petroleum products (metric tons; 2007) none (2,296,000); natural gas (cu m; 2007) 3,400,000 (1,124,000,000). **Gross national income** (2008): US$48,973,000,000 (US$24,010 per capita). **Population economically active** (2007): total 1,041,600; activity rate 51.8% (participation rates: ages 15–64, 71.7%; female 46.0%; unemployed [2008] 7.0%). **Selected balance of payments data.** Receipts from (US$'000,000): tourism (2007) 2,218; remittances (2008) 331; foreign direct investment (FDI; 2005–07 avg.) 883. Disbursements for (US$'000,000): tourism (2007) 1,103; remittances (2008) 371; FDI (2005–07 avg.) 1,038.

## Foreign trade

**Imports** (2007; c.i.f.): €21,487,000,000 (base and fabricated metals 14.1%; motor vehicles 13.2%; chemical products 12.1%; nonelectrical machinery and equipment 10.6%; mineral fuels 9.4%; food products 5.6%). *Major import sources:* Germany 19.4%; Italy 18.3%; Austria 12.5%; France 5.4%; Croatia 4.0%.

**Exports** (2007; f.o.b.): €19,385,000,000 (motor vehicles and parts 15.9%; base and fabricated metals 13.6%; nonelectrical machinery and equipment 12.5%; electrical machinery, electronics, and parts 9.6%; medicine and pharmaceuticals 7.2%; furniture 4.3%). *Major export destinations:* Germany 18.9%; Italy 13.2%; Croatia 8.1%; Austria 7.8%; France 6.5%.

## Transport and communications

**Transport.** *Railroads* (2008): length 1,228 km; passenger-km 834,000,000; metric ton-km cargo 3,520,000,000. *Roads* (2006): total length 38,562 km (paved 100%). *Vehicles* (2008): passenger cars 1,045,183; trucks and buses 83,909. *Air transport* (2008): passenger-km 1,008,000,000; metric ton-km cargo 1,944,000. **Communications,** in total units (units per 1,000 persons). Telephone landlines (2008): 1,010,000 (501); cellular telephone subscribers (2008): 2,055,000 (1,020); personal computers (2007): 850,000 (425); total Internet users (2008): 1,126,000 (559); broadband Internet subscribers (2008): 427,000 (212).

## Education and health

**Educational attainment** (2006). Percentage of population ages 15 and over having: no formal schooling through complete primary education 27.7%; secondary 6.0%; vocational 55.1%; some higher 2.9%; undergraduate 7.1%; advanced degree 1.2%. **Literacy** (2007): total population ages 15 and over literate, virtually 100%. **Health** (2007): physicians 4,441 (1 per 453 persons); hospital beds 9,414 (1 per 214 persons); infant mortality rate per 1,000 live births (2008) 2.4; undernourished population (2002–04) 60,000 (3% of total population based on the consumption of a minimum daily requirement of 1,990 calories).

## Military

**Total active duty personnel** (November 2008): 7,200 (army 100%). **Military expenditure as percentage of GNI** (2007): 1.7%; per capita expenditure US$373.

## Background

The Slovenes settled the region in the 6th century AD. In the 8th century it was incorporated into the Frankish empire of Charlemagne, and in the 10th century it came under Germany as part of the Holy Roman Empire. Except for 1809–14, when Napoleon ruled the area, most of the lands belonged to Austria until the formation of the Kingdom of Serbs, Croats, and Slovenes in 1918. It became a constituent republic of Yugoslavia in 1946. In 1990 Slovenia held the first contested multiparty elections in Yugoslavia since before World War II. In 1991 it seceded from Yugoslavia. Subsequently it sought to privatize the economy and build ties with Western Europe, joining both the EU and NATO in 2004.

## Recent Developments

Political uncertainty complicated efforts in 2011 to put Slovenia's economy back on track. Inflation for the year stood at only 1.8%, and the value of exports

---

*1 metric ton = about 1.1 short tons;  1 kilometer = 0.6 mi (statute);  1 metric ton-km cargo = about 0.68 short ton-mi cargo;  c.i.f.: cost, insurance, and freight;  f.o.b.: free on board*

rose by 17.9%. The unemployment rate, however, retreated from 12.3% (the highest rate since 2000) at the beginning of the year only to 12.1% by year's end. In September the government's economic growth forecast was revised downward from 2.2% to 1.5%, with spending to be reduced by US$500 million to deal with a loss of revenue. By the end of the year, the economy's growth had been revised again, to only 0.6%.

Internet resource: <www.stat.si/eng/index.asp>.

# Solomon Islands

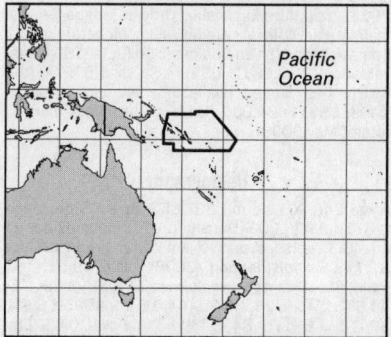

Pacific
Ocean

**Official name:** Solomon Islands. **Form of government:** constitutional monarchy with one legislative house (National Parliament [50]). **Head of state:** British Queen Elizabeth II (from 1952), represented by Governor-General Sir Frank Kabui (from 2009). **Head of government:** Prime Minister Gordon Darcy Lilo (from 2011). **Capital:** Honiara. **Official language:** English. **Official religion:** none. **Monetary unit:** 1 Solomon Islands dollar (SI$) = 100 cents; valuation (2 Jul 2012) US$1 = SI$7.06.

## Demography

**Area:** 10,954 sq mi, 28,370 sq km. **Population** (2011): 535,000. **Density** (2011): persons per sq mi 48.8, persons per sq km 18.9. **Urban** (2009): 18.2%. **Sex distribution** (2008): male 50.63%; female 49.37%. **Age breakdown** (2008): under 15, 40.1%; 15–29, 29.4%; 30–44, 17.4%; 45–59, 8.0%; 60–74, 4.0%; 75–84, 1.0%; 85 and over, 0.1%. **Ethnic composition** (2002): Melanesian 93.0%; Polynesian 4.0%; Micronesian 1.5%; other 1.5%. **Religious affiliation** (2005): Protestant 70%, of which Anglican 32%, Adventist 10%; Roman Catholic 18%; traditional beliefs 5%; other 7%. **Major towns** (2006): Honiara 57,400; Gizo 6,300; Auki 4,400. **Location:** Oceania, island group in the South Pacific Ocean, east of Papua New Guinea.

## Vital statistics

**Birth rate** per 1,000 population (2008): 28.5 (world avg. 20.3). **Death rate** per 1,000 population (2008): 3.8 (world avg. 8.5). **Total fertility rate** (avg. births per childbearing woman; 2008): 3.65. **Life expectancy** at birth (2008): male 70.9 years; female 76.1 years.

## National economy

**Budget** (2006). *Revenue:* SI$946,200,000 (tax revenue 73.0%, of which VAT 17.9%, logging duties 13.6%, import duties 9.3%, corporate taxes 8.2%; nontax revenue 13.9%; grants 13.1%). *Expenditures:* SI$911,100,000 (current expenditures 90.5%, of which wages and salaries 27.3%, debt service 13.9%; capital expenditures 9.5%). **Public debt** (external, outstanding; 2007): US$147,-300,000. **Gross national income** (2008): US$598,-000,000 (US$1,180 per capita). **Population economically active** (2006): total 201,000; activity rate of total population 41.0% (participation rates: ages 15 and over 68.8%; female 38.3%; unemployed [2003] 15.2%). **Production** (metric tons except as noted). *Agriculture and fishing* (2007): coconuts 276,000, oil palm fruit 155,000, sweet potatoes 86,000, cacao beans 5,300; livestock (number of live animals) 54,000 pigs, 13,600 cattle, 235,000 chickens; fisheries production 31,272 (from aquaculture, negligible); aquatic plants production 120 (from aquaculture 100%). *Mining and quarrying* (2005): gold 10 kg. *Manufacturing* (2006): coconut oil 59,000; vegetable oils and fats (2002) 50,000; copra 21,214. *Energy production (consumption):* electricity (kW-hr; 2008) 78,000,000 (57,000,000); petroleum products (metric tons; 2006) none (58,000). **Selected balance of payments data.** Receipts from (US$'000,000): tourism (2007) 4; remittances (2008) 20; foreign direct investment (2005–07 avg.) 26; official development assistance (2007) 248. Disbursements for (US$'000,000): tourism (2007) 8; remittances (2008) 3.

## Foreign trade

**Imports** (2006; c.i.f.): US$250,613,000 (machinery and transportation equipment 24.7%; petroleum [all forms] 21.7%; food products 14.1%; construction materials 10.0%; chemical products 5.2%). *Major import sources:* Australia 25.3%; Singapore 23.4%; Japan 7.8%; New Zealand 5.0%; Fiji 4.2%. **Exports** (2007; f.o.b.): US$156,008,000 (logs 63.7%; palm oil 8.6%; frozen fish 7.2%; cacao beans 5.8%; copra 3.7%; sawn wood 3.2%). *Major export destinations* (2006): China 45.7%; South Korea 14.0%; Japan 8.5%; Thailand 4.4%; Philippines 4.0%.

## Transport and communications

**Transport.** *Railroads:* none. *Roads* (2007): total length 1,500 km (paved 2.7%). *Vehicles* (1993): passenger cars 2,052; trucks and buses 2,574. *Air transport* (2006; Solomon Airlines only): passenger-km 74,870,000; metric ton-km cargo 648,000. **Communications,** in total units (units per 1,000 persons). Telephone landlines (2008): 8,000 (16); cellular telephone subscribers (2008): 14,000 (27); personal computers (2005): 22,000 (47); total Internet users (2008): 10,000 (20); broadband Internet subscribers (2008): 1,500 (2.9).

## Education and health

**Educational attainment** (2005–06). Percentage of population ages 15 and over having: no schooling/unknown 15.6%; primary education 46.7%; secondary 32.8%; vocational 4.0%; higher 0.9%. **Literacy** (2004): total population ages 15 and over literate 76.6%. **Health** (2005): physicians 89 (1 per 5,293 persons);

hospital beds 691 (1 per 682 persons); infant mortality rate per 1,000 live births (2008) 19.7; undernourished population (2002–04) 90,000 (21% of total population based on the consumption of a minimum daily requirement of 1,780 calories).

## Military

Total active duty personnel (2008): none; 200–300 military troops and police in an Australian-led multinational regional intervention force (from mid-2003) maintain civil and political order.

## Background

The Solomon Islands were settled c. 2000 BC by Austronesian people. Visited by the Spanish in AD 1568, the islands were subsequently explored by the French and the British. They came under British protection in 1893. During World War II, the Japanese invasion of 1942 ignited three years of the most bitter fighting in the Pacific, particularly on Guadalcanal. The protectorate became self-governing in 1976 and fully independent in 1978. In the late 20th and early 21st centuries, ethnic tensions led to political instability; a multinational force led by Australia helped restore order.

## Recent Developments

The Regional Assistance Mission to Solomon Islands (RAMSI) continued its activities in the Solomon Islands in 2011, maintaining order and providing technical aid to the government. In eight years in the country, RAMSI had trained 2,000 civil servants, overseen the introduction of competition in the telecommunications market, and provided stability that spurred the growth of foreign investment.

Internet resource: <www.visitsolomons.com.sb>.

# Somalia

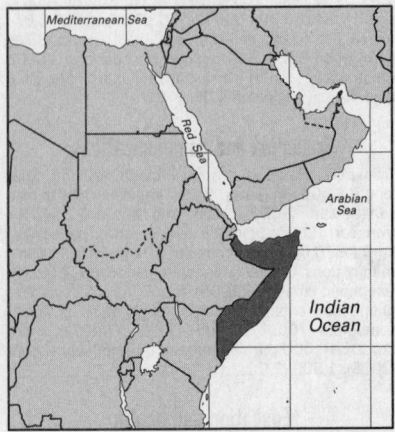

Proclamation of the "Republic of Somaliland" in May 1991 on territory corresponding to the former British Somaliland (which unified with the former Italian Trust Territory of Somalia to form Somalia in 1960) had not received international recognition as of 2012. This entity represented about a quarter of Somalia's territory. **Official name:** Soomaaliya (Somali); Al-Sumal (Arabic) (Somalia). **Form of government:** transitional regime (the "new transitional government" from October 2004 lacked effective control in mid-2012) with one legislative house (Transitional Federal Parliament [550]), At present Somalia is divided into three autonomous regions: Somaliland in the northwest, Puntland in the northeast, and Somalia in the south. **Head of state and government:** President Sheikh Sharif Sheikh Ahmed (from 2009), assisted by Prime Minister Abdeweli Mohamed Ali (from 2011). **Capital:** Mogadishu. **Official languages:** Somali; Arabic. **Official religion:** Islam. **Monetary unit:** 1 Somali shilling (Shilin Soomaali; So.Sh.) = 100 cents; valuation (2 Jul 2012) US$1 = So.Sh. 1,579.00 (the So.Sh. had limited availability and circulation in 2009; US$1 = 34,000 So.Sh. at the "black market" rate of May 2008).

## Demography

**Area:** 246,201 sq mi, 637,657 sq km. **Population** (2011): 9,926,000. **Density** (2011): persons per sq mi 40.3, persons per sq km 15.6. **Urban** (2011): 37.7%. **Sex distribution** (2008): male 49.57%; female 50.43%. **Age breakdown** (2005): under 15, 44.6%; 15–29, 26.3%; 30–44, 16.1%; 45–59, 8.6%; 60–74, 3.6%; 75–84, 0.7%; 85 and over, 0.1%. **Ethnic composition** (2000): Somali 92.4%; Arab 2.2%; Afar 1.3%; other 4.1%. **Religious affiliation** (2005): Muslim (nearly all Sunni) 99%; other 1%. **Major cities** (2008): Mogadishu (2007) 1,100,000; Hargeysa 436,232; Burao 151,451; Belet Weyne 108,125; Boosaaso 108,016. **Location:** the Horn of Africa, bordering Djibouti, the Gulf of Aden, the Indian Ocean, Kenya, and Ethiopia.

## Vital statistics

**Birth rate** per 1,000 population (2005): 45.0 (world avg. 20.3). **Death rate** per 1,000 population (2005): 16.0 (world avg. 8.5). **Total fertility rate** (avg. births per childbearing woman; 2005): 6.45. **Life expectancy** at birth (2005): male 48.0 years; female 51.0 years.

## National economy

**Budget:** n.a. UN assistance (2007): US$175,000,000, of which food aid US$50,000,000. **Public debt** (external, outstanding; 2007): US$1,979,000,000. **Production** (metric tons except as noted). *Agriculture and fishing* (2007): sugarcane 215,000, corn (maize) 99,000, cassava 82,000, sesame seed 30,000; other tree/bush products include khat, frankincense, and myrrh; livestock (number of live animals) 13,100,000 sheep, 12,700,000 goats, 7,000,000 camels, 5,350,000 cattle; fisheries production 30,000 (from aquaculture, none). *Mining and quarrying* (2007): small quantities of gemstones (including garnet and opal) and salt. *Manufacturing:* small manufacturers produce textiles, handicrafts, and processed meat. *Energy production (consumption):* electricity (kW-hr; 2006)

1 metric ton = about 1.1 short tons;   1 kilometer = 0.6 mi (statute);   1 metric ton-km cargo = about 0.68 short ton-mi cargo;   c.i.f.: cost, insurance, and freight;   f.o.b.: free on board

295,000,000 (295,000,000); crude petroleum (barrels; 2006) none (425,000); petroleum products (metric tons; 2006) 176,000 (174,000). **Population economically active** (2006): total 3,343,000; activity rate of total population 39.6% (participation rates: ages 15 and over, 72.1%; female 38.8%). **Gross national income** (2008): US$2,570,000,000 (US$288 per capita). **Selected balance of payments data.** Receipts from (US$'000,000): remittances (2008) 1,000; foreign direct investment (2005–07 avg.) 87; official development assistance (2007) 384.

## Foreign trade

**Imports** (2007): US$793,000,000 (agricultural products 48.1%, of which sugar [all forms] 12.3%, cereals 12.0%, vegetable and animal oils 6.6%). *Major import sources* (2008): Djibouti 29%; India 12%; Kenya 8%; US 6%; Oman 6%. **Exports** (2007): US$299,000,000 (goats 12.0%; sheep 6.4%; cattle 5.5%; other agricultural products 1.4%). *Major export destinations* (2008): UAE 56%; Yemen 21%; Saudi Arabia 4%.

## Transport and communications

**Transport.** *Railroads:* none. *Roads* (2003): total length 22,000 km (paved 12%). *Air transport* (2003; four Somaliland airports only): passenger arrivals 50,096, passenger departures 41,979; cargo unloaded 3,817 metric tons, cargo loaded 152 metric tons. **Communications,** in total units (units per 1,000 persons). Telephone landlines (2008): 100,000 (11); cellular telephone subscribers (2008): 627,000 (70); personal computers (2007): 79,000 (9); total Internet users (2008): 102,000 (11).

## Education and health

**Literacy** (2002): percentage of total population ages 15 and over literate 19.2%; males literate 25.1%; females literate 13.1%. **Health:** physicians, n.a. (in 2008, 18 doctors graduated from a Somali medical institution for the first time since 1990); infant mortality rate per 1,000 live births (2005) 110.1.

## Military

**Total active duty personnel:** none; Ethiopian forces backing the transitional government fought Islamic extremists from December 2006 to December 2008 and from June 2009 onward; AU peacekeeping troops (September 2009): 4,300.

## Background

Muslim Arabs and Persians first established trading posts along the coasts of Somalia in the 7th–10th centuries. By the 10th century Somali nomads occupied the area inland from the Gulf of Aden, and the south and west were inhabited by various groups of pastoral Oromo peoples. Intensive European exploration began after the British occupation of Aden in 1839, and in the late 19th century Britain and Italy set up protectorates in the region. During World War II the Italians invaded British Somaliland (1940); a year later British troops retook the area, and Britain administered the region until 1950, when Italian Somaliland became a UN trust territory. In 1960 it was united with the former British Somaliland, and the two became the independent Republic of Somalia. Since then it has suffered political and civil strife, including military dictatorship, civil war, drought, and famine. In 1991 a Republic of Somaliland was proclaimed by a breakaway group on territory corresponding to the former British Somaliland, and in 1998 the autonomous region of Puntland in the northeast was self-proclaimed; neither received international recognition, but both were more stable than the rest of Somalia. Several attempts have been made to end the conflict and create a new central government, but the country subsequently remained in turmoil. Incidents of piracy increased along the country's coast in the early 21st century and were the focus of international concern.

## Recent Developments

In 2011, Somalia's Transitional Federal Government (TFG) continued to battle al-Shabaab, an Islamic extremist movement with ties to al-Qaeda that controlled much of Mogadishu and southern Somalia for the first half of the year. By August al-Shabaab had been driven from Mogadishu by a combined TFG/African Union force. In early October fighting spilled over the Kenyan border. The Kenyan government responded by sending troops into Somalia (this was Kenya's first military invasion of another country). In late 2011, Ethiopian troops also crossed into Somalia to battle the group, and by mid-2012, al-Shabaab's sphere of control was severely limited. In 2012, Somalia moved to establish a new central government, as the TFG's charter ended in August.

**Internet resource:** <www.unsomalia.net>.

# South Africa

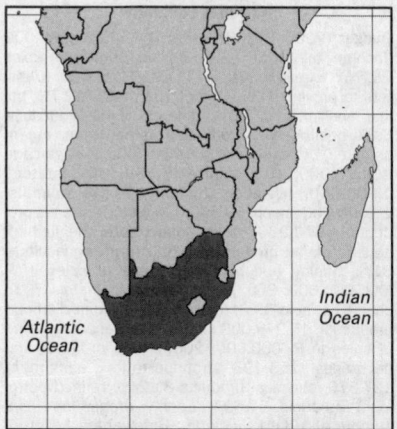

**Official name:** Republic of South Africa. **Form of government:** multiparty republic with two legislative houses (National Council of Provinces [90]; National Assembly [400]). **Head of state and government:** President Jacob Zuma (from 2009). **Capitals** (de facto): Pretoria/Tshwane (executive); Bloemfontein/Mangaung (judicial); Cape Town (legislative). **Official languages:** Afrikaans; English; Ndebele; Pedi;

Sotho; Swazi; Tsonga; Tswana; Venda; Xhosa; Zulu. **Official religion:** none. **Monetary unit:** 1 rand (R) = 100 cents; valuation (2 Jul 2012) US$1 = R 8.17.

## Demography

**Area:** 471,359 sq mi, 1,220,813 sq km. **Population** (2011): 50,587,000. **Density** (2011): persons per sq mi 107.3, persons per sq km 41.4. **Urban** (2010): 61.7%. **Sex distribution** (2009): male 48.40%; female 51.60%. **Age breakdown** (2009): under 15, 31.4%; 15–29, 29.5%; 30–44, 19.5%; 45–59, 12.0%; 60–74, 6.0%; 75 and over, 1.6%. **Ethnic composition** (2009): black 79.3%, of which Zulu 24%, Xhosa 18%, Pedi 9%, Tswana 8%, Sotho 8%, Tsonga 4%, Swazi 3%, other black 5%; white 9.1%; mixed white/black 9.0%; Asian/other 2.6%. **Religious affiliation** (2005): independent Christian 37.1%, of which Zion Christian 9.5%; Protestant 26.1%; traditional beliefs 8.9%; Roman Catholic 6.7%; Muslim 2.5%; Hindu 2.4%; nonreligious 3.0%; other 13.3%. **Major urban agglomerations** (2007): Johannesburg 3,435,000; Cape Town 3,215,000; Ekurhuleni (East Rand) 2,986,000; eThekwini (Durban) 2,729,000; Tshwane (Pretoria) 1,338,000. **Location:** southern Africa, bordering Namibia, Botswana, Zimbabwe, Mozambique, Swaziland, and the Indian and South Atlantic oceans; wholly contained within South Africa is the country of Lesotho.

## Vital statistics

**Birth rate** per 1,000 population (2005): 23.2 (world avg. 20.3). **Death rate** per 1,000 population (2005): 14.2 (world avg. 8.5). **Total fertility rate** (avg. births per childbearing woman; 2009): 2.38. **Life expectancy** at birth (2009): male 53.5 years; female 57.2 years.

## National economy

**Budget** (2005–06). *Revenue:* R 411,085,100,000 (income tax 30.6%; VAT 28.0%; corporate taxes 23.5%). *Expenditures:* R 417,819,200,000 (transfers to provinces 36.0%; debt payments 12.7%; police and prisons 9.0%; defense 5.4%; education 3.0%; health 2.4%). *Production* (in metric tons except as noted). *Agriculture and fishing* (2007): sugarcane 20,500,000, corn (maize) 7,338,738, potatoes 1,900,000; livestock (number of live animals) 25,000,000 sheep, 13,500,000 cattle; fisheries production 673,360 (from aquaculture, negligible); aquatic plants production 9,600 (from aquaculture 31%). *Mining and quarrying* (value of sales in R '000,000,000; 2007): platinum-group metals 79.9; coal 43.1; gold 39.0; iron ore 13.4; rough diamond production 15,249,000 carats. *Manufacturing* (value of sales in R '000,000; 2005): food products and beverages 153,496; transportation equipment 137,870; chemical products 81,240; refined petroleum products 57,697. *Energy production (consumption)* (data include Botswana, Lesotho, Namibia, and Swaziland): electricity (kW-hr; 2006) 256,882,000,000 (257,454,000,000); coal (metric tons; 2006) 246,236,000 (178,336,000); crude petroleum (barrels; 2006) 10,198,000 (180,640,000); petroleum products (metric tons; 2006) 27,024,000 (21,042,000); natural gas (cu m; 2006) 1,936,-000,000 (4,551,000,000). **Population economically active** (2007): total 17,232,000; activity rate of total population 36.0% (participation rates: ages 15–64, 56.7%; female 46.1%; unemployed 21.0%). **Gross national income** (2008): US$283,310,-000,000 (US$5,820 per capita). **Public debt** (external, outstanding; 2007): US$13,868,000,000. **Selected balance of payments data.** Receipts from (US$'000,000): tourism (2007) 8,443; remittances (2008) 823; foreign direct investment (FDI; 2005–07 avg.) 3,936; official development assistance (2006) 718. Disbursements for (US$'000,-000): tourism (2007) 3,927; remittances (2008) 1,133; FDI (2005–07 avg.) 3,794.

## Foreign trade

**Imports** (2006): US$69,185,000,000 (machinery and apparatus 26.5%; crude petroleum 13.9%; motor vehicles 9.6%; chemical products 8.9%). *Major import sources:* Germany 12.5%; China 10.0%; US 7.6%; Japan 6.5%; Saudi Arabia 5.3%. **Exports** (2006): US$53,170,000,000 (excluding gold export earnings estimated at US$5,400,000,000) (platinum-group metals 15.3%; iron and steel 10.8%; motor vehicles 9.0%; metal ores 7.4%; coal 6.0%; pumps and compressors 4.7%; diamonds 4.6%). *Major export destinations:* Japan 11.9%; US 11.5%; UK 8.8%; Germany 7.5%; Netherlands 5.2%.

## Transport and communications

**Transport.** *Railroads* (2001): route length (2005) 20,872 km; passenger-km 3,930,000,000; metric ton-km cargo 106,786,000,000. *Roads* (2002): length 362,099 km (paved 20%). *Vehicles* (2005): passenger cars 4,574,972; trucks and buses 2,112,601. *Air transport* (2007): passenger-km 27,576,000,000; metric ton-km cargo 935,-600,000. **Communications,** in total units (units per 1,000 persons). Telephone landlines (2008): 4,425,000 (89); cellular telephone subscribers (2008): 45,000,000 (906); personal computers (2005): 3,966,000 (85); total Internet users (2008): 4,187,000 (84); broadband Internet subscribers (2007): 378,000 (7.8).

## Education and health

**Educational attainment** (2006). Percentage of population ages 20 and over having: no formal schooling 10.4%; some primary education 21.1%; complete primary/some secondary 34.0%; complete secondary 24.9%; higher 9.1%. **Literacy** (2007): total population ages 15 and over literate 87.8%. **Health:** physicians (2006) 33,220 (1 per 1,427 persons); hospital beds (2004) 153,465 (1 per 303 persons); infant mortality rate per 1,000 live births (2009) 45.7; undernourished population (2002–04) less than 2.5% of total population.

## Military

**Total active duty personnel** (November 2008): 62,082 (army 59.8%, navy 10.1%, air force 17.2%, military health service 12.9%). **Military expenditure as percentage of GDP** (2007): 1.4%; per capita expenditure US$78.

*1 metric ton = about 1.1 short tons;    1 kilometer = 0.6 mi (statute);    1 metric ton-km cargo = about 0.68 short ton-mi cargo;    c.i.f.: cost, insurance, and freight;    f.o.b.: free on board*

## Background

San and Khoikhoi peoples roamed southern Africa as hunters and gatherers in the Stone Age, and the latter had developed a pastoralist culture by the time of European contact. By the 14th century AD, Bantu-speaking peoples had settled in the area and developed gold and copper mining and an active East African trade. In 1652 the Dutch established a colony at the Cape of Good Hope; the Dutch settlers became known as Boers and later as Afrikaners, after their Afrikaans language. In 1795 British forces captured the Cape, and in the 1830s, to escape British rule, Dutch settlers began the Great Trek northward and established the independent Boer republics of the Orange Free State and the South African Republic (later the Transvaal region), which the British annexed as colonies by 1902 as a result of the 30-month-long Boer War. In 1910 the British colonies of Cape Colony, Transvaal, Natal, and Orange River were unified into the new Union of South Africa. It became independent and withdrew from the Commonwealth in 1961. Throughout the 20th century, South African politics were dominated by the issue of maintaining white supremacy over the country's black majority, and in 1948 apartheid was formally instituted. Faced by increasing worldwide condemnation, it began dismantling the apartheid laws in 1990. In free elections in 1994, Nelson Mandela became the country's first black president. The country also rejoined the Commonwealth in 1994. A permanent nonracial constitution was promulgated in 1997.

## Recent Developments

A record number of working days (more than 27 million) were lost in South Africa in 2011 as a result of strikes that broke out in midyear. Striking employees included those in the metal, mine, food, petroleum, engineering, packaging, catering, and municipal industries. Job creation was the central focus of the 2011 budget, with 100 billion rand direct spending on plans for employment and skills training. The economy grew by 3.1% for the year. Despite this economic growth, the unemployment rate increased to 25.7% in the second quarter of 2011. (It did decline to 23.9% in the fourth quarter.) In January inflation was up slightly (3.7%) from December 2010 (3.5%), but by November it had increased to 6.1%.

Internet resource: <www.statssa.gov.za>.

# Spain

**Official name:** Reino de España (Kingdom of Spain). **Form of government:** constitutional monarchy with two legislative houses (Senate [264]; Congress of Deputies [350]). **Head of state:** King Juan Carlos I (from 1975). **Head of government:** Prime Minister Mariano Rajoy (from 2011). **Capital:** Madrid. **Official language:** Castilian Spanish (per constitution, Euskera [Basque], Catalan, Galician, and all other Spanish languages are also official in their autonomous communities). **Official religion:** none. **Monetary unit:** 1 euro (€) = 100 cents; valuation (2 Jul 2012) US$1 = €0.79.

## Demography

**Area:** 195,364 sq mi, 505,991 sq km. **Population** (2011): 47,215,000. **Density** (2011): persons per sq

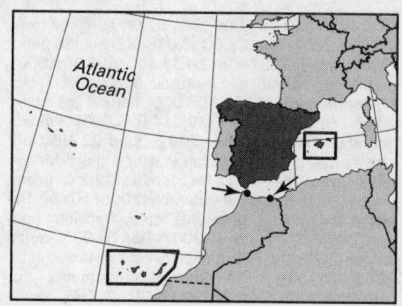

mi 241.7, persons per sq km 93.3. **Urban** (2009): 77.2%. **Sex distribution** (2008): male 49.38%; female 50.62%. **Age breakdown** (2008): under 15, 14.7%; 15–29, 18.9%; 30–44, 25.4%; 45–59, 19.2%; 60–74, 13.4%; 75–84, 6.3%; 85 and over, 2.1%. **Ethnic composition** (2000): Spaniard 44.9%; Catalonian 28.0%; Galician 8.2%; Basque 5.5%; Aragonese 5.0%; Rom (Gypsy) 2.0%; other 6.4%. **Religious affiliation** (2006): Roman Catholic 77%, of which practicing weekly 19%; Muslim 2.5%; Protestant 1%; other (mostly nonreligious) 19.5%. **Major cities** (2008): Madrid 3,213,271 (urban agglomeration [2007] 5,764,000); Barcelona 1,615,908 (urban agglomeration [2007] 5,057,000); Valencia 807,200; Sevilla 699,759; Zaragoza 666,129. **Location:** southwestern Europe, bordering France, Andorra, the Mediterranean Sea, the British overseas territory of Gibraltar, the Atlantic Ocean, and Portugal; the North African exclaves of Ceuta and Melilla border Morocco.

## Vital statistics

**Birth rate** per 1,000 population (2008): 11.4 (world avg. 20.3); within marriage 67.9%. **Death rate** per 1,000 population (2008): 8.5 (world avg. 8.5). **Total fertility rate** (avg. births per childbearing woman; 2008): 1.46. **Life expectancy** at birth (2008): male 79.1 years; female 85.2 years.

## National economy

**Budget** (2007). *Revenue:* €297,701,000,000 (tax revenue 49.1%; social contributions 45.6%). *Expenditures:* €270,293,000,000 (social protection 45.3%; debt service 4.9%; public safety 4.1%; defense 4.0%; health 1.6%; education 0.6%). **Public debt** (2007): US$520,918,000,000. **Gross national income** (2008): US$1,456,488,000,000 (US$31,960 per capita). **Production** (metric tons except as noted). *Agriculture and fishing:* barley 11,684,000, wheat 6,376,900, grapes 6,013,000, olives 5,787,600, oranges 2,691,400, sunflower seeds 743,400, almonds 201,100, garlic 142,400; livestock (number of live animals) 26,034,000 pigs, 21,847,050 sheep, 6,456,350 cattle, 2,500,000 beehives; fisheries production 1,089,922 (from aquaculture 26%). *Mining and quarrying* (2007): slate 1,200,000; sepiolite 800,000; fluorite 132,753; gold 3,100 kg. *Manufacturing* (value added in US$'000,000; 2004): food products 15,786; fabricated metal products 15,717; transportation equipment 14,508. *Energy production (consumption):* electricity (kW-hr; 2007–08) 303,278,000,000 (279,709,000,000); coal (metric tons; 2007) 10,995,000 (36,281,000); lignite (metric tons; 2007) 6,016,000 (6,016,000); crude petroleum (barrels; 2007–08) 1,133,400 (453,309,900); petroleum products (metric tons; 2007–08) 55,886,000 ([2006] 60,308,000); natural gas (cu m; 2007–08) 15,447,500 (39,414,926,000). **Population economically active** (2007): total 22,189,900; activity rate of total population 49.7% (participation rates: ages 16–64, 72.6%; female 42.3%; unemployed [October 2007–September 2008] 10.0%). **Selected balance of payments data.** Receipts from (US$'000,000): tourism (2007–08) 62,905; remittances (2008) 11,772; foreign direct investment (FDI; 2005–07 avg.) 35,098. Disbursements for (US$'000,000): tourism (2007–08) 21,277; remittances (2008) 14,656; FDI (2005–07 avg.) 87,228.

## Foreign trade

**Imports** (2006; c.i.f.): €263,024,000,000 (machinery and apparatus 19.7%; mineral fuels 15.7%; motor vehicles and parts 14.6%; chemical products 11.0%; base and fabricated metals 7.6%). *Major import sources* (2007): Germany 15.2%; France 12.2%; Italy 8.7%; China 6.7%; UK 4.7%. **Exports** (2006; f.o.b.): €170,628,000,000 (motor vehicles and parts 20.7%; machinery and apparatus 15.2%; food products 10.9%, of which fruits and vegetables 5.8%; base and fabricated metals 8.9%). *Major export destinations* (2007): France 18.6%; Germany 10.8%; Portugal 8.6%; Italy 8.5%; UK 7.5%.

## Transport and communications

**Transport.** *Railroads* (2007–08): route length (2006) 15,212 km; passenger-km 22,794,600,000; metric ton-km cargo 10,839,100,000. *Roads* (2006): length 681,224 km (paved 100%). *Vehicles* (2008): cars 21,440,700; trucks, vans, and buses 5,273,000. *Air transport* (2007–08): passenger-km 81,252,000,000; metric ton-km cargo 1,169,204,000. **Communications**, in total units (units per 1,000 persons). Telephone landlines (2008): 20,200,000 (454); cellular telephone subscribers (2008): 49,678,000 (1,117); personal computers (2007): 17,646,000 (393); total Internet users (2008): 25,240,000 (567); broadband Internet subscribers (2008): 8,995,000 (202).

## Education and health

**Educational attainment** (2007). Percentage of population ages 16 and over having: no formal schooling through incomplete primary education 11.6%; complete primary 20.9%; secondary 44.4%; undergraduate degree 14.2%; graduate degree 8.9%. **Literacy** (2003): total population ages 15 and over literate 97.9%; males literate 98.7%; females literate 97.2%. **Health** (2008): physicians 213,977 (1 per 214 persons); hospital beds (2007) 160,292 (1 per 283 persons); infant mortality rate per 1,000 live births 3.5; undernourished population (2002–04) less than 2.5% of total population.

## Military

**Total active duty personnel** (November 2008): 221,750 (army 43.1%, navy 10.5%, air force 9.4%, joint 4.3%,

civil guard 32.7%). **Military expenditure as percentage of GDP** (2008): 0.7%; per capita expenditure US$241.

## Background

Remains of Stone Age populations dating back some 35,000 years have been found in Spain. Celtic peoples arrived in the 9th century BC, followed by the Romans, who dominated Spain from about 200 BC until the Visigoth invasion in the early 5th century AD. In the early 8th century, most of the peninsula fell to Muslims (Moors) from North Africa, and it remained under their control until it was gradually reconquered by the Christian kingdoms of Castile, Aragon, and Portugal. Spain was reunited in 1479 following the marriage of Ferdinand II (of Aragon) and Isabella I (of Castile). The last Muslim kingdom, Granada, was reconquered in 1492, and around this time Spain also established a colonial empire in the Americas. In 1516 the throne passed to the Habsburgs, whose rule ended in 1700 when Philip V became the first Bourbon king of Spain. His ascendancy caused the War of the Spanish Succession, which resulted in the loss of numerous European possessions and sparked revolution in most of Spain's American colonies. Spain lost its remaining overseas possessions to the US in the Spanish-American War (1898). It became a republic in 1931. The Spanish Civil War (1936–39) ended in victory for the Nationalists under Gen. Francisco Franco, who ruled as dictator until his death in 1975. His successor as head of state, King Juan Carlos I, restored the monarchy; a new constitution in 1978 established a parliamentary monarchy. Spain joined NATO in 1982 and the European Community in 1986. In the late 20th and early 21st centuries, Basque separatists continued to resort to violence as they pressed for independence, but it was Islamic militants who were responsible for the 11 Mar 2004 bombings in Madrid that killed 191 people—the worst terrorist incident in Europe since World War II.

## Recent Developments

During the first half of 2011, optimists took a hopeful view regarding the Spanish economy as a result of a slight upturn in exports, a booming tourist season, and a reduction in the deficit that had been spurred by austerity measures introduced in 2010. Any illusions of a swift recovery were shattered in the summer by the onset of the European sovereign-debt crisis, however. The Spanish economy grew only 2.1% for the year, and the unemployment rate stood at 22.8%, with youth unemployment particularly worrisome. In July 2012, Spain accepted a €100 billion (US$123 billion) bailout from a group of EU countries led by Germany. Overshadowed by the economic meltdown, the declarations in January 2011 of a permanent, general, and verifiable cease-fire and on 20 October of "the complete cessation of armed activity" by Euskadi Ta Askatasuna (ETA) offered the prospect of a definitive end to the organization's 40-year armed struggle for Basque independence. The conflict had claimed nearly 850 lives, and though there had been a dozen broken cease-fires, many Spaniards believed that ETA was committed to peace.

Internet resource:
<www.ine.es/en/welcome_en.htm>.

---

*1 metric ton = about 1.1 short tons;    1 kilometer = 0.6 mi (statute);    1 metric ton-km cargo = about 0.68 short ton-mi cargo;    c.i.f.: cost, insurance, and freight;    f.o.b.: free on board*

# Sri Lanka

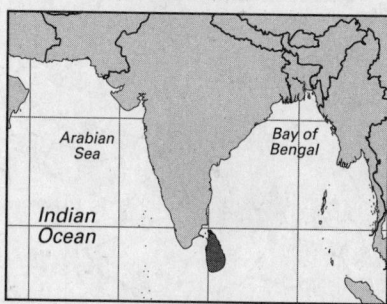

**Official name:** Sri Lanka Prajatantrika Samajavadi Janarajaya (Sinhala); Ilangai Jananayaka Socialisa Kudiarasu (Tamil) (Democratic Socialist Republic of Sri Lanka). **Form of government:** unitary multiparty republic with one legislative house (Parliament [225]). **Head of state and government:** President Mahinda Rajapakse (from 2005), assisted by Prime Minister D.M. Jayaratne (from 2010). **Capitals:** Colombo (executive and judicial); Sri Jayewardenepura Kotte (Colombo suburb; legislative). **Official languages:** Sinhala; Tamil (English has official status as "the link language" between Sinhala and Tamil). **Official religion:** none (Buddhism has special recognition). **Monetary unit:** 1 Sri Lankan rupee (LKR) = 100 cents; valuation (2 Jul 2012) US$1 = LKR 133.75.

## Demography

**Area:** 25,332 sq mi, 65,610 sq km. **Population** (2011): 21,045,000. **Density** (2011): persons per sq mi 830.8, persons per sq km 320.8. **Urban** (2009): 14.3%. **Sex distribution** (2008): male 49.36%; female 50.64%. **Age breakdown** (2008): under 15, 26.3%; 15–29, 27.0%; 30–44, 22.0%; 45–59, 15.4%; 60–74, 7.1%; 75 and over, 2.2%. **Ethnic composition** (2001): Sinhalese 81.9%; Tamil 9.4%; Sri Lankan Moor 8.0%; other 0.7%. **Religious affiliation** (2005): Buddhist 70%; Hindu 15%; Christian (mostly Roman Catholic) 8%; Muslim (nearly all Sunni) 7%. **Major cities** (2007): Colombo 672,743 (greater Colombo [2004] 2,490,300); Dehiwala–Mount Lavinia 219,827; Moratuwa 185,668; Jaffna 151,612; Negombo 150,364. **Location:** island in the Indian Ocean, southeast of India.

## Vital statistics

**Birth rate** per 1,000 population (2008): 18.8 (world avg. 20.3). **Death rate** per 1,000 population (2008): 5.9 (world avg. 8.5). **Total fertility rate** (avg. births per childbearing woman; 2008): 1.88. **Life expectancy** at birth (2008): male 68.8 years; female 76.3 years.

## National economy

**Budget** (2008). *Revenue:* LKR 775,477,000,000 (tax revenue 84.2%, of which VAT 32.5%, excises 15.8%; nontax revenue 12.1%; foreign grants 3.7%). *Expenditures:* LKR 1,516,330,000,000 (debt service 38.5%; transfers 15.9%; wages and salaries 11.1%). **Selected balance of payments data.** Receipts from (US$'000,000): tourism (2008) 320; remittances (2008) 2,947; foreign direct investment (FDI; 2005–07 avg.) 427; official development assistance (2007) 589. Disbursements for (US$'000,000): tourism (2007) 393; remittances (2008) 385; FDI (2005–07 avg.) 54. **Production** (metric tons except as noted). *Agriculture and fishing* (2008): rice 3,875,000, coconuts (2007) 954,000, sugarcane 799,447, tea 318,470, natural rubber 129,240, peppercorns 22,870, cinnamon 13,430, ginger 10,053; livestock (number of live animals) 1,196,000 cattle, 319,000 buffalo; fisheries production (2007) 317,988 (from aquaculture 3%). *Mining and quarrying* (2008): kaolin 11,000; graphite 10,000; sapphires 770,000 carats; rubies 23,000 carats; diamonds, n.a. *Manufacturing* (value added in LKR '000,000; 2008): food products, beverages, and tobacco products 348,358; textiles and wearing apparel 147,822; rubber and plastic products 60,680; coal and refined petroleum products 42,666. *Energy production (consumption):* electricity (kW-hr; 2008–09) 9,727,000,000 ([2006] 9,389,000,000); coal (metric tons; 2006) none (95,000); crude petroleum (barrels; 2006) none (15,766,800); petroleum products (metric tons; 2006) 1,875,000 (3,409,000). **Gross national income** (2008): US$35,854,000,000 (US$1,790 per capita). **Public debt** (external, outstanding; June 2009): US$12,737,600,000. **Population economically active** (2008): total 7,568,700; activity rate 37.7% (participation rates: ages 15–59 [2000] 60.6%; female 36.1%; unemployed [May 2008–April 2009] 5.2%).

## Foreign trade

**Imports** (2007; c.i.f.): LKR 1,251,135,000,000 (cotton yarn and textiles 14.4%; machinery and apparatus 13.9%; refined petroleum products 13.0%; crude petroleum 9.1%; food products and beverages 7.3%; base metals 7.3%). *Major import sources:* India 22.3%; Singapore 9.6%; China 7.9%; Iran 7.2%; Hong Kong 6.2%. **Exports** (2007; f.o.b.): LKR 856,808,000,000 (garments 40.6%; tea 13.3%, of which black 11.5%; gemstones 5.7%, of which diamonds 4.5%; rubber tires 4.5%; coconut products 1.8%; fish 1.6%; rubber products 1.4%; cinnamon 1.0%). *Major export destinations:* US 24.5%; UK 12.7%; India 6.4%; Germany 5.5%; Belgium 5.0%.

## Transport and communications

**Transport.** *Railroads* (2008–09): route length (2007) 1,449 km; passenger-km 4,515,916,000; metric ton-km cargo 115,313,000. *Roads* (2003): total length 97,286 km (paved 81%). *Vehicles* (2008): passenger cars 381,448; trucks and buses 552,474. *Air transport* (2008–09): passenger-km 8,248,000,000; metric ton-km cargo 300,611,000. **Communications,** in total units (units per 1,000 persons). Telephone landlines (2008): 3,446,000 (172); cellular telephone subscribers (2008): 11,083,000 (552); personal computers (2005): 734,000 (35); total Internet users (2008): 1,164,000 (58); broadband Internet subscribers (2008): 102,000 (5.1).

## Education and health

**Literacy** (2007): percentage of population ages 5 and over literate 91.5%; males literate 93.2%; females literate 89.9%. **Health** (2007): physicians 11,023 (1 per 1,804 persons); hospital beds 68,694 (1 per 289 persons); infant mortality rate per 1,000 live births (2006) 11.0; undernourished population (2002–04) 4,200,000 (22% of total population based on the consumption of a minimum daily requirement of 1,860 calories).

## Military

**Total active duty personnel** (November 2008): 150,900 (army 78.1%, navy 9.9%, air force 12.0%). **Military expenditure as percentage of GDP** (2008): 3.6%; per capita expenditure US$77.

## Background

The Sinhalese people of Sri Lanka (Ceylon) probably originated with the blending of aboriginal inhabitants and migrating Indo-Aryans from India about the 5th century BC. The Tamils were later immigrants from Dravidian India, migrating over a period from the early centuries AD to about 1200. Buddhism was introduced during the 3rd century BC. As Buddhism spread, the Sinhalese kingdom extended its political control over Ceylon but lost it to invaders from southern India in the 10th century AD. Between 1200 and 1505 Sinhalese power gravitated to southwestern Ceylon, while a southern Indian dynasty seized power in the north and established the Tamil kingdom in the 14th century. Foreign invasions from India, China, and Malaya occurred in the 13th–15th centuries. In 1505 the Portuguese arrived, and by 1619 they controlled most of the island. The Sinhalese enlisted the Dutch to help oust the Portuguese and eventually came under the control of the Dutch East India Co., which relinquished power in 1796 to the British. In 1802 Ceylon became a crown colony, gaining independence in 1948. It became the Republic of Sri Lanka in 1972 and took its current name in 1978. Civil strife between Tamil and Sinhalese groups has beset the country in recent years, with the Tamils demanding a separate autonomous state in northern Sri Lanka. A prolonged insurrection by the Liberation Tigers of Tamil Eelam (LTTE; Tamil Tigers) guerrilla group was defeated by government forces in 2009.

## Recent Developments

In 2011, Sri Lanka continued to recover from its 26-year civil war. Economic growth, which had slowed in recent years because of the global recession, began to accelerate rapidly. GDP was expected to rise by at least 8.0% in 2011, despite floods in January that displaced more than a million people and damaged crops. Major economic issues included continued poverty, unemployment, the reconstruction of war-damaged areas, and persistent inflation. Nevertheless, an IMF mission to Sri Lanka in August–September pronounced macroeconomic conditions there satisfactory and stated that monetary and fiscal policies were appropriate.

**Internet resource:** <www.statistics.gov.lk>.

# Sudan

**Official name:** Jumhuriyat al-Sudan (Republic of the Sudan). **Form of government:** military-backed interim

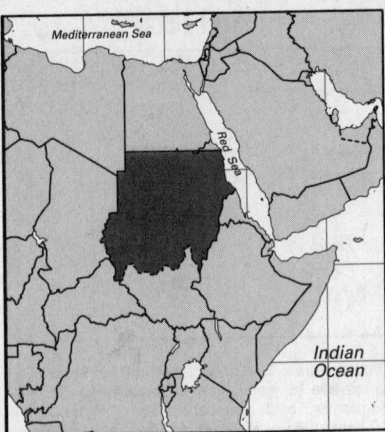

regime with two legislative houses (Council of States [32]; National Assembly [354]). **Head of state and government:** President Omar Hassan Ahmad al-Bashir (from 1989). **Capitals:** Khartoum (executive); Omdurman (legislative). **Official languages:** Arabic; English. **Official religion:** Islamic law and custom are applicable to Muslims only. **Monetary unit:** Sudanese pound (SDG); valuation (2 Jul 2012) US$1 = SDG 2.68.

## Demography

**Area:** 712,280 sq mi, 1,844,797 sq km. **Population** (2011): 36,787,000. **Density** (2011): persons per sq mi 51.6, persons per sq km 19.9. *The statistics that follow may include data for South Sudan.* **Urban** (2009): 39.4%. **Sex distribution** (2008): male 51.27%; female 48.73%. **Age breakdown** (2008): under 15, 42.6%; 15–29, 27.7%; 30–44, 16.8%; 45–59, 7.7%; 60–74, 3.8%; 75–84, 1.0%; 85 and over, 0.4%. **Ethnic composition** (2003): black 52%; Arab 39%; Beja 6%; foreigners 2%; other 1%. **Religious affiliation** (2005): Sunni Muslim 68.4%; traditional beliefs 10.8%; Roman Catholic 9.5%; Protestant 8.8%, of which Anglican 5.4%; other 2.5%. **Major cities** (2008): Khartoum 1,410,858 (urban agglomeration [2008] 4,272,728); Omdurman 1,849,659; Khartoum North 1,012,211; Nyala 492,984; Port Sudan 394,561. **Location:** northeastern Africa, bordering Egypt, the Red Sea, Eritrea, Ethiopia, South Sudan, the Central African Republic, Chad, and Libya.

## Vital statistics

**Birth rate** per 1,000 population (2006): 35.3 (world avg. 20.3). **Death rate** per 1,000 population (2006): 15.2 (world avg. 8.5). **Total fertility rate** (avg. births per childbearing woman; 2006): 4.79. **Life expectancy** at birth (2006): male 47.1 years; female 48.8 years.

## National economy

**Budget** (2008). *Revenue:* SDG 26,424,000,000 (nontax revenue 68.8%, of which export receipts for

*1 metric ton = about 1.1 short tons;   1 kilometer = 0.6 mi (statute);   1 metric ton-km cargo = about 0.68 short ton-mi cargo;   c.i.f.: cost, insurance, and freight;   f.o.b.: free on board*

crude petroleum 52.3%; tax revenue 29.0%, of which taxes on goods and services 18.0%; grants 2.2%). *Expenditures:* SDG 24,331,000,000 (federal government 52.5%; transfers to: Southern Sudan 25.3%; northern states 22.2%). **Public debt** (external, outstanding; 2007): US$12,337,000,000. **Gross national income** (2008): US$46,520,000,000 (US$1,130 per capita). **Production** (metric tons except as noted). *Agriculture and fishing* (2007): sugarcane 7,500,000, sorghum 5,048,000, millet 792,000, dates 330,000, sesame seeds 260,000, seed cotton 240,000, gum arabic (2006–07) 11,242; livestock (number of live animals) 49,000,000 sheep, 42,000,000 goats, 39,500,000 cattle, 3,700,000 camels; fisheries production 67,459 (from aquaculture 3%). *Mining and quarrying* (2007): marble 26,000 cu m; gold 2,787 kg. *Manufacturing* (2006): diesel 1,817,000; flour 1,200,000; benzene 1,139,000. *Energy production (consumption):* electricity (kW-hr; 2007) 5,021,000,000 (3,836,000,000); crude petroleum (barrels; 2008) 174,400,000 ([2006] 35,500,000); petroleum products (metric tons; 2006) 4,943,000 (3,714,000). **Population economically active** (2006): total 11,504,000; activity rate of total population 30.5% (participation rates: ages 15–64, 52.0%; female 30.3%). **Selected balance of payments data.** Receipts from (US$'000,000): tourism (2007) 262; remittances (2008) 1,850; foreign direct investment (2005–07 avg.) 2,761; official development assistance (2007) 2,104. Disbursements for (US$'000,000): tourism (2007) 1,477; remittances (2008) 2.

### Foreign trade

**Imports** (2008; c.i.f.): US$9,351,000,000 (machinery and apparatus 32.7%; transportation equipment 11.9%; wheat and wheat flour 7.6%; refined petroleum products 7.6%). *Major import sources:* China 23.1%; India 9.5%; Saudi Arabia 8.0%; UAE 6.7%; Italy 3.3%. **Exports** (2008; f.o.b.): US$11,670,000,000 (crude petroleum 92.9%; refined petroleum products 2.1%; sesame seeds 1.2%; gold 1.0%; cotton 0.5%; gum arabic 0.5%; livestock [mainly sheep and camels] 0.4%). *Major export destinations:* China 75.0%; Japan 9.7%; UAE 4.1%; Saudi Arabia 0.9%.

### Transport and communications

**Transport.** *Railroads* (2006): route length 4,578 km; passenger-km 49,000,000; metric ton-km cargo 893,000,000. *Roads* (2000): total length 11,900 km (paved 36%). *Vehicles* (2002): passenger cars 47,300; trucks and buses 62,500. *Air transport* (2004): passenger-km 758,000,000; metric ton-km cargo (including the weight of passengers and mail) 100,000,000. **Communications,** in total units (units per 1,000 persons). Telephone landlines (2008): 356,000 (8.6); cellular telephone subscribers (2008): 11,186,000 (271); personal computers (2007): 4,528,000 (112); total Internet users (2008): 3,800,000 (92); broadband Internet subscribers (2007): 43,000 (1.1).

### Education and health

**Literacy** (2003): total population ages 15 and over literate 60.9%; males literate 71.6%; females literate 50.4%. **Health** (2007): physicians 9,573 (1 per 4,224

persons); hospital beds 27,438 (1 per 1,474 persons); infant mortality rate per 1,000 live births (2006) 96.8; undernourished population (2002–04) 8,700,000 (26% of total population based on the consumption of a minimum daily requirement of 1,840 calories).

## Military

**Total active duty personnel** (November 2008): 109,300 (army 96.1%, navy 1.2%, air force 2.7%); foreign troops (September 2009): Southern Sudan—UN peacekeeping force 8,800; Darfur—African Union/UN hybrid peacekeeping force 14,600. **Military expenditure as percentage of GDP** (2005): 1.8%; per capita expenditure US$13.

## Background

From the end of the 4th millennium BC, Nubia (now northern Sudan) periodically came under Egyptian rule, and it was part of the kingdom of Cush from the 11th century BC to the 4th century AD. Christian missionaries converted the area's three principal kingdoms during the 6th century; these black Christian kingdoms coexisted with their Muslim Arab neighbors in Egypt for centuries, until the influx of Arab immigrants brought about their collapse in the 13th–15th centuries. Egypt had conquered all of the Sudan region by 1874 and encouraged British interference there; this aroused Muslim opposition and led to the revolt of al-Mahdi, who captured Khartoum in 1885 and established a Muslim theocracy in the Sudan that lasted until 1898, when Mahdist forces were defeated by the British. The British ruled, generally in partnership with Egypt, until the region achieved independence in 1956. Since then the country has fluctuated between ineffective parliamentary government and unstable military rule, with the distraction of long-running civil wars (1955–72; 1983–2005) between the northern-based government and non-Muslim southern rebels. This led to famines and the displacement of millions of people. Meanwhile, fighting broke out in 2003 between non-Arab Muslims in the Darfur region of western Sudan and government-backed Arab militias known as Janjaweed; tens of thousands of people were killed and hundreds of thousands more were displaced. In 2011, the southern Sudanese population voted overwhelmingly in favor of independence from the north and seceded on 9 July.

## Recent Developments

In Sudan, 2011 was dominated by the secession of its southern region in July. Despite considerable apprehension, Sudan abided by the terms of the 2005 Comprehensive Peace Agreement (CPA) and accepted the overwhelming majority vote of the South Sudanese for secession in the January referendum. The Sudanese president, Omar al-Bashir, attended the 9 July independence day celebrations and the swearing in of Salva Kiir Mayardit, South Sudan's new president. Southern Sudanese independence had profound implications for Sudan's politics, economy, and security. Rebel militias in Southern Kordofan and Blue Nile states stepped up activities against the Khartoum government. As in the earlier case of Darfur, the

Khartoum government launched a brutal campaign to quell resistance in those states. By December more than 400,000 people had been displaced. Meanwhile, Sudan faced the task of restructuring its political and economic landscape. Three-quarters of the oil that had hitherto fueled its prosperity derived from the south. Under the 2005 CPA, the two Sudans had shared equally the revenue generated from southern oil, but under the new order northern policy makers calculated a 36% shortfall in their budget. They expected to replace much of this through negotiations concerning South Sudan payments for access to the north's pipelines, refineries, and export terminal. In March 2012, Qatar pledged US$2 billion in investments to the Khartoum government.

Internet resource: <http://cbs.gov.sd>.

# Sudan, South

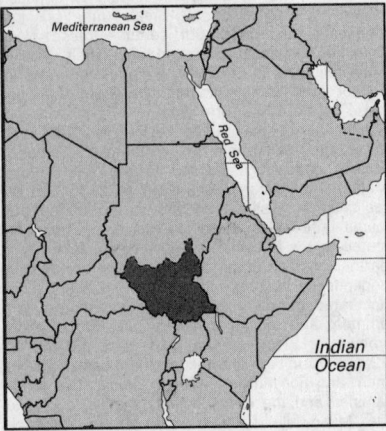

Official name: Republic of South Sudan. Form of government: republic with two legislative houses (National Legislative Assembly [332]; Council of States [50]). Head of state and government: President Salva Kiir (from 2011). Capital: Juba (the transfer of the capital to Ramciel, to be implemented in phases, was approved in late 2011). Official language: English. Official religion: none. Monetary unit: South Sudan pound (SSP); valuation (24 May 2012) US$1 = SSP 3.10 (the SSP was introduced 18 Jul 2011 and valued at 1 SSP = 1 Sudanese pound [SDG]; the US dollar, along with the currencies of Kenya, Ethiopia, and Uganda, also circulate in South Sudan.

## Demography

Area: 248,777 sq mi, 644,330 sq km. Population (2011): 9,150,000. Density (2011): persons per sq mi 36.8, persons per sq km 14.2. Urban (2011): 17.0%. Sex distribution (2008): male 51.90%; female 48.10%. Age breakdown (2008): under 15, 44.4%; 15–29, 27.7%; 30–44, 16.5%; 45–59, 7.3%;

60–74, 3.1%; 75–84, 0.7%; 85 and over, 0.3%. Ethnic composition (2008): Dinka 38%; Nuer 17%; Zande 10%; Bari 10%; Shilluk/Anywa 10%; Arab 4%; other 11%. Religious affiliation (2010): Christian, roughly 60% (significantly Roman Catholic, Anglican, and Presbyterian); remainder, roughly 40%. Major towns (2008): Yei 111,268; Yambio 105,881; Juba 82,346; Aweil 59,217; Bentiu 41,328. Location: northeastern Africa, bordering Sudan, Ethiopia, Kenya, Uganda, the Democratic Republic of the Congo, and the Central African Republic.

## Vital statistics

Birth rate per 1,000 population: n.a. (world avg. 19.2). Death rate per 1,000 population: n.a. (world avg. 8.2). Total fertility rate (avg. births per childbearing woman; 2009): 6.79. Life expectancy at birth (2009): 42 years.

## National economy

Budget (2009). Revenue: SDG 6,276,000,000 (oil-sharing revenue with Khartoum governmental authority [including arrears and Abyei oil share] 65.7%; grants 32.4%; personal income tax 1.4%; customs/VAT/other 0.5%). Public debt (external, outstanding): n.a. Gross national income (2007): US$718,000,000 (US$90 per capita). Production (metric tons except as noted). Agriculture and fishing (2010): cereals (mostly sorghum [also corn (maize), millet, and rice]) 695,000; other crops include cassava, peanuts (groundnuts), sweet potatoes, okra, cowpeas, tomatoes, and onions; livestock (number of live animals) 14,000,000 goats, 13,000,000 sheep, 11,000,000 cattle; fisheries production, n.a. Mining and quarrying (2010): negligible excluding oil extraction (marble quarrying is historically an important activity). Manufacturing (2010): beer and soft drink production began in 2010; other limited production includes roofing tiles. Energy production (consumption): electricity, n.a. (n.a.); coal, none (none); crude petroleum (barrels; 2009) 147,000,000 (n.a.); petroleum products, n.a. (n.a.); natural gas, none (none). Population economically active: n.a. Selected balance of payments data. Receipts from (US$'000,000): tourism, n.a.; remittances, n.a.; foreign direct investment (FDI), n.a.; official development assistance, n.a. Disbursements for (US$'000,000): tourism, n.a.; remittances, n.a.; FDI, n.a.

## Foreign trade

Imports (2009): n.a. Major import sources: n.a. Exports (2009): nearly all crude petroleum. Major export destinations: n.a.

## Transport and communications

Transport. Railroads (2010): route length 243 km; passenger-km, none; metric ton-km cargo, none. Roads (paved only; 2010): total length 50 km. Vehicles: passenger cars, n.a.; trucks and buses, n.a. Air transport: n.a. Communications, in total units (units per 1,000 persons). Telephone landlines (2010): n.a.; cellular telephone subscribers (2010): n.a.; personal computers (2010): n.a.; total Internet

*1 metric ton = about 1.1 short tons; 1 kilometer = 0.6 mi (statute); 1 metric ton-km cargo = about 0.68 short ton-mi cargo; c.i.f.: cost, insurance, and freight; f.o.b.: free on board*

users (2010): n.a.; broadband Internet subscribers (2010): n.a.

## Education and health

**Literacy** (2009): total population ages 15 and over literate 27%; males literate 40%; females literate 16%. **Health** (2010): physicians 34 ([foreign doctors are excluded from this total] 1 per 262,000 persons); hospital beds, n.a.; infant mortality rate per 1,000 live births (2009) 1.2; undernourished population (2009) 4,090,000 (47% of total population based on the consumption of a minimum daily requirement of 1,717 calories).

## Military

**Total active duty personnel:** UN peacekeeping personnel (October 2010): troops 9,451; police 655. **Military expenditure as percentage of GDP:** n.a.

## Background

From the end of the 4th millennium BC, Nubia (now northern Sudan) periodically came under Egyptian rule, and it was part of the kingdom of Cush from the 11th century BC to the 4th century AD. Christian missionaries converted the area's three principal kingdoms during the 6th century; these black Christian kingdoms coexisted with their Muslim Arab neighbors in Egypt for centuries, until the influx of Arab immigrants brought about their collapse in the 13th–15th centuries. Settled by many of its current ethnic groups during the 15th–19th centuries, the country has long been associated with Sudan, its neighbor to the north, despite the fact that Islam and the Arabic language tended to dominate in the north while older African languages and cultures were predominant in the south. By the end of the 19th century, both the north and the south—collectively considered the Sudan—were under British-Egyptian colonial rule. The existing differences between the two regions, exacerbated by the disparate level of development that occurred under colonial administration, made it difficult for Sudan to be effectively ruled as one country upon achieving independence in 1956. In fact, fears of marginalization by the north led to a civil war that began in 1955, months prior to actual independence. The initial conflict and the fears that fueled it were inflamed by northern leaders who hoped to impose unity upon the nascent country by imposing Islamic law and culture throughout the south. Fighting subsided with the 1972 Addis Ababa Agreement but resumed in 1983 and continued until 2005, when the Comprehensive Peace Agreement was signed. The agreement fostered a tenuous peace between the north and the south and granted southern Sudan semiautonomous status and the promise of a referendum on independence to be held in six years. The vote took place in January 2011 and was almost unanimous in supporting independence; the country of South Sudan was declared on 9 July 2011.

## Recent Developments

South Sudan raised its flag as Africa's newest independent country on 9 Jul 2011. Unfortunately, it faced a fragile future and numerous challenges. It ranked among the poorest countries on the UN Human Development Index. Interethnic rivalry was a massive problem—in January 2012, a raid by one village against a rival village with whom there was a history of cattle stealing left as many as 3,000 dead. In addition, the government inherited a series of disputes with Sudan over oil and national boundaries. Oil accounted for more than 95% of South Sudan's revenue and, prior to secession, some 75% of Sudan's. In May 2011, Sudanese troops occupied the Abyei region, an oil-producing borderland area, and in November bombed sites in South Sudan's Unity and Upper Nile states, both oil-producing areas. However, South Sudan signed two pipeline deals in early 2012—one with Kenya and another with Ethiopia and Djibouti—giving the appearance that the country was near to gaining control of its vital petroleum industry. As well, China pledged US$8 billion in development assistance to South Sudan in April.

**Internet resource:** <http://ssnbs.org>.

# Suriname

**Official name:** Republiek Suriname (Republic of Suriname). **Form of government:** multiparty republic with one legislative house (National Assembly [51]). **Head of state and government:** President Dési Bouterse (from 2010). **Capital:** Paramaribo. **Official language:** Dutch. **Official religion:** none. **Monetary unit:** 1 Suriname dollar (SRD) = 100 cents; valuation (2 Jul 2012) US$1 = SRD 3.30.

## Demography

**Area:** 63,251 sq mi, 163,820 sq km. **Population** (2011): 529,000. **Density** (2011): persons per sq mi 8.4, persons per sq km 3.2. **Urban** (2009): 68.9%. **Sex distribution** (2006): male 49.71%; female 50.29%. **Age breakdown** (2006): under 15, 28.5%; 15–29, 26.8%; 30–44, 24.3%; 45–59, 12.0%; 60–74, 6.2%; 75 and over, 2.2%. **Ethnic composition** (2004): Indo-Pakistani ("Hindustani") 27.4%; Suriname Creole ("Afro-Surinamese") 17.7%; Maroon (descendants of runaway slaves living in the interior) 14.7%; Javanese ("Indonesian") 14.6%; mixed race 12.5%; Amerindian 1.5%; other

11.6%. **Religious affiliation** (2004): Christian (mostly Roman Catholic and Moravian) 40.7%; Hindu 19.9%; Muslim 13.5%; nonreligious 4.4%; traditional beliefs 3.3%; other 2.5%; unknown 15.7%. **Major towns** (2004): Paramaribo 242,946; Nieuw Nickerie 13,842; Nieuw Amsterdam 5,489. **Location:** northern South America, bordering the North Atlantic Ocean, French Guiana, Brazil, and Guyana.

## Vital statistics

**Birth rate** per 1,000 population (2006): 17.6 (world avg. 20.3). **Death rate** per 1,000 population (2006): 5.5 (world avg. 8.5). **Total fertility rate** (avg. births per childbearing woman; 2006): 2.05. **Life expectancy** at birth (2006): male 70.3 years; female 75.8 years.

## National economy

**Budget** (2007). *Revenue:* SRD 2,002,000,000 (tax revenue 79.1%, of which corporate taxes 22.0%, taxes on international trade 21.5%, income tax 15.4%; nontax revenue 16.0%; grants 4.9%). *Expenditures:* SRD 1,806,500,000 (current expenditures 87.5%, of which wages and salaries 37.6%, transfers 12.0%, debt interest 5.2%; capital expenditures 12.5%). **Production** (metric tons except as noted). *Agriculture and fishing* (2007): rice 195,000, sugarcane 120,000, bananas 44,000; livestock (number of live animals) 137,000 cattle, 24,500 pigs, 3,800,000 chickens; fisheries production 29,679 (from aquaculture 1%). *Mining and quarrying* (2007): bauxite 5,331,000; alumina 2,152,000; gold 9,362 kg (recorded production; unrecorded production may be as high as 30,000 kg). *Manufacturing* (value of production at factor cost in SRG; 1993): food products 992,000,000; beverages 558,000,000; tobacco products 369,000,000. *Energy production (consumption):* electricity (kW-hr; 2006) 1,618,000,000 (1,618,000,000); crude petroleum (barrels; 2006) 4,800,000 (3,478,000); petroleum products (metric tons; 2006) 401,000 (624,000). **Population economically active** (2004): total 173,130; activity rate of total population 35.1% (participation rates: ages 15–64, 56.0%; female 36.7%; unemployed 9.5%). **Gross national income** (2008): US$2,570,000,000 (US$4,990 per capita). **Public debt** (external, outstanding; 2007): US$161,100,000. **Selected balance of payments data.** Receipts from (US$'000,000): tourism (2007) 67; remittances (2008) 140; foreign direct investment (FDI; 2005–07 avg.) 346; official development assistance (2007) 151. Disbursements for (US$'000,000): tourism (2007) 22; remittances (2008) 65.

## Foreign trade

**Imports** (2005; c.i.f.): US$1,099,900,000 (machinery and transportation equipment 26.8%; mineral fuels 15.6%; food products 9.1%; chemical products 6.9%). *Major import sources* (2007): US 31.7%; Netherlands 20.4%; Trinidad and Tobago 17.9%; China 5.5%; Japan 3.6%. **Exports** (2005; f.o.b.): US$929,100,000 (alumina 48.1%; gold 36.4%; shrimp and fish 6.1%; crude petroleum 5.8%; rice

1.5%). *Major export destinations* (2007): Canada 23.0%; Norway 14.4%; US 12.1%; Trinidad and Tobago 7.2%; France 5.4%.

## Transport and communications

**Transport.** *Railroads:* none. *Roads* (2003): total length 4,304 km (paved 26%). *Vehicles* (2006): passenger cars 81,778; trucks and buses 28,774. *Air transport* (2008; Surinam Airways only): passenger-km 958,323,000; metric ton-km cargo 25,794,000. **Communications,** in total units (units per 1,000 persons). Telephone landlines (2008): 82,000 (158); cellular telephone subscribers (2008): 416,000 (808); personal computers (2001): 20,000 (45); total Internet users (2008): 50,000 (97); broadband Internet subscribers (2008): 5,800 (11).

## Education and health

**Literacy** (2004): total population ages 15 and over literate 89.6%; males literate 92.0%; females literate 87.2%. **Health:** physicians (2001) 236 (1 per 2,000 persons); hospital beds (2005) 1,797 (1 per 278 persons); infant mortality rate per 1,000 live births (2006) 20.8; undernourished population (2002–04) 40,000 (8% of total population based on the consumption of a minimum daily requirement of 1,910 calories).

## Military

**Total active duty personnel** (November 2008): 1,840 (all services are officially part of the army) (army 76.1%, navy 13.0%, air force 10.9%). **Military expenditure as percentage of GDP** (2007): 1.0%; per capita expenditure US$43.

## Background

Suriname was inhabited by various native peoples prior to European settlement. Spanish explorers claimed it in 1593, but the Dutch began to settle there in 1602, followed by the English in 1651. It was ceded to the Dutch in 1667, and in 1682 the Dutch West India Co. introduced coffee and sugarcane plantations and African slaves to cultivate them. Slavery was abolished in 1863, and indentured servants were brought from China, Java, and India to work the plantations, adding to the population mix. Except for brief interludes of British rule (1799–1802, 1804–15), it remained a Dutch colony. It gained internal autonomy in 1954 and independence in 1975. A military coup in 1980 ended civilian control until the electorate approved a new constitution in 1987. Military control resumed after a coup in 1990. Elections were held in 1992, and democratic government returned. By the early 21st century, a vast criminal economy, including drug trafficking and gold smuggling, had developed.

## Recent Developments

Former dictator and convicted narcotics trafficker Dési Bouterse completed a full year as the president of Suriname in 2011, which proved to be less

*1 metric ton = about 1.1 short tons; 1 kilometer = 0.6 mi (statute); 1 metric ton-km cargo = about 0.68 short ton-mi cargo; c.i.f.: cost, insurance, and freight; f.o.b.: free on board*

disastrous than many observers had expected. GDP grew by 4%. The independent central bank imposed fiscal austerity measures, which helped to cushion the negative impact of rising inflation. Controversy arose in April 2012, however, when Suriname's legislators granted Bouterse immunity for past crimes, ending a murder investigation against him.

Internet resource: <www.surinametourism.net>.

# Swaziland

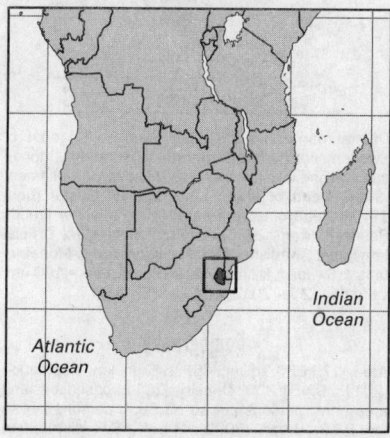

Indian Ocean

Atlantic Ocean

**Official name:** Umbuso weSwatini (Swati); Kingdom of Swaziland (English). **Form of government:** monarchy with two legislative houses (Senate [30]; House of Assembly [66]). **Head of state and government:** King Mswati III (from 1986), assisted by Prime Minister Barnabas Sibusiso Dlamini (from 2008). **Capitals:** Mbabane (administrative and judicial); Lobamba (legislative); Lozitha and Ludzidzini are royal residences that have national symbolic significance. **Official languages:** Swati (Swazi); English. **Official religion:** none. **Monetary unit:** 1 lilangeni (plural emalangeni [E]) = 100 cents; valuation (2 Jul 2012) US$1 = E 8.17.

## Demography

**Area:** 6,704 sq mi, 17,364 sq km. **Population** (2011): 1,203,000. **Density** (2011): persons per sq mi 179.4, persons per sq km 69.3. **Urban** (2010): 21.4%. **Sex distribution** (2008): male 49.60%; female 50.40%. **Age breakdown** (2008): under 15, 38.9%; 15–29, 31.5%; 30–44, 15.8%; 45–59, 8.6%; 60–74, 4.2%; 75–84, 0.9%; 85 and over, 0.1%. **Ethnic composition** (2000): Swazi 82.3%; Zulu 9.6%; Tsonga 2.3%; Afrikaner 1.4%; mixed (black-white) 1.0%; other 3.4%. **Religious affiliation** (2006): Protestant 35%; syncretistic Christianity/traditional beliefs 30%; Roman Catholic 25%; Muslim 1%; other (including Baha'i and Mormon) 9%. **Major towns** (2006): Manzini (urban agglomeration) 115,200; Mbabane 78,700; Lobamba 11,000; Big Bend 10,400; Malkerns 10,000. **Location:** southern Africa, bordering South Africa and Mozambique.

## Vital statistics

**Birth rate** per 1,000 population (2008): 29.1 (world avg. 20.3). **Death rate** per 1,000 population (2008): 14.9 (world avg. 8.5). **Total fertility rate** (avg. births per childbearing woman; 2008): 3.45. **Life expectancy** at birth (2008): male 47.8 years; female 48.2 years.

## National economy

**Budget** (2008–09). *Revenue:* E 9,208,400,000 (receipts from the Customs Union of Southern Africa 65.3%; income tax 10.9%; sales taxes 8.2%; corporate taxes 5.8%). *Expenditures:* E 9,538,-000,000 (general administration 31.5%; education 19.9%; transportation and communications 11.8%; police and defense 11.0%; agriculture 9.2%; health 8.8%). **Public debt** (external; March 2009): US$379,700,000. **Gross national income** (2008): US$2,945,000,000 (US$2,520 per capita). **Population economically active** (2006): total 337,200; activity rate of total population 32.8% (unemployed, 30%). **Production** (metric tons except as noted). *Agriculture and fishing* (2007): sugarcane 5,000,000, corn (maize) 68,000, grapefruit and pomelos 37,000; livestock (number of live animals) 585,000 cattle, 276,000 goats, 3,200,000 chickens; fisheries production 70 (from aquaculture, negligible). *Mining and quarrying* (2008): ferrovanadium 500; crushed stone 300,000 cu m. *Manufacturing* (value of exports in US$'000; 2007): wearing apparel and accessories (2002) 173,500; sugar 159,821; unbleached wood pulp 97,099. *Energy production (consumption):* electricity (kW-hr; 2008) 212,-000,000 (1,001,700,000); coal (metric tons; 2008) 250,000 ([2007] 223,000). **Selected balance of payments data.** Receipts from (US$'000,000): tourism (2007) 32; remittances (2008) 100; foreign direct investment (2005–07 avg.) 8; official development assistance (2007) 63. Disbursements for (US$'000,000): tourism (2007) 51; remittances (2008) 8.

## Foreign trade

**Imports** (2007; c.i.f.): US$1,164,200,000 (food products 18.2%, of which cereals and flour 7.6%; chemical products 13.6%; refined petroleum products 13.4%; machinery and apparatus 12.5%; motor vehicles and parts 6.5%). *Major import sources:* South Africa 92.9%; Namibia 2.2%; Lesotho 1.4%. **Exports** (2007; f.o.b.): US$1,082,-300,000 (essential oils for food and beverage industries 29.4%; food products 21.0%, of which raw sugar 14.1%; silicates 19.9%; wearing apparel and accessories 4.4%; organic chemical products 4.3%; rough and sawn wood 4.2%). *Major export destinations:* South Africa 45.2%; Botswana 31.6%; UK 14.2%; US 3.2%.

## Transport and communications

**Transport.** *Railroads* (2006): route length 301 km; passenger-km, n.a. (passenger service is for tourists and private charter only); metric ton-km cargo (2004) 710,000,000. *Roads* (2002): total length 3,594 km (paved 30%). *Vehicles* (2003): passenger cars 44,113; trucks and buses 47,761. **Communications,** in total units (units per 1,000 persons). Telephone landlines (2008): 44,000 (33); cellular telephone subscribers (2008): 457,000 (346); personal computers (2006): 47,000 (37); total Internet users (2008): 48,000 (37).

## Education and health

**Educational attainment** (2006–07). Percentage of population ages 25 and over having: no formal schooling/unknown 23.5%; incomplete primary education 23.9%; complete primary 10.1%; incomplete/complete secondary 33.6%; higher 8.9%. **Literacy** (2007): total population ages 15 and over literate 84.0%; males literate 84.7%; females literate 83.4%. **Health:** physicians (2004) 171 (1 per 7,240 persons); hospital beds (2006) 2,688 (1 per 476 persons); infant mortality rate per 1,000 live births (2008) 72.4; undernourished population (2002–04) 250,000 (22% of total population based on the consumption of a minimum daily requirement of 1,840 calories).

## Military

**Total active duty personnel** (2006): 3,000. **Military expenditure as percentage of GDP** (2004): 1.8%; per capita expenditure US$39.

## Background

Stone tools and rock paintings indicate prehistoric habitation in the region, but it was not settled until the Bantu-speaking Swazi people migrated there in the 18th century. The British gained control in the 19th century after the Swazi king sought their aid against the Zulus. Following the South African War, the British governor of Transvaal administered Swaziland; his powers were transferred to the British high commissioner in 1906. In 1949 the British rejected the Union of South Africa's request to control Swaziland. The country gained limited self-government in 1963 and achieved independence in 1968. In the 1970s new constitutions were framed based on the supreme authority of the king. During the 1990s forces demanding democracy arose, but the kingdom remained in place. In 2005 a new constitution was signed that contained a bill of rights. Swaziland has one of the highest rates of HIV infection in the world.

## Recent Developments

Swaziland faced serious financial challenges in 2011 that resulted in cash-flow problems for all government ministries as well as the state-supported University of Swaziland. In response to these pecuniary woes, the newly operational Swaziland Revenue Authority (SRA) began its efforts to become "a highly efficient and modern revenue collection agency." The financial situation grew worse, however, and in November the IMF declared that it was critical. Unemployment and poverty, like corruption, remained a major challenge. There was some optimism in 2012, however, that the SRA's introduction of a VAT would alleviate some of the government's financial problems.

**Internet resource:** <www.tourismswaziland.com>.

# Sweden

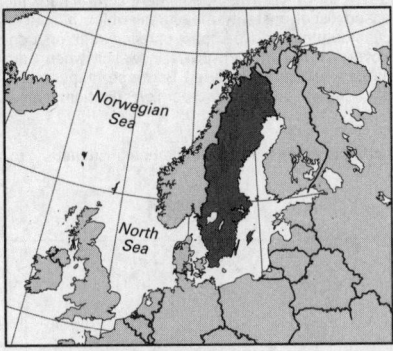

**Official name:** Konungariket Sverige (Kingdom of Sweden). **Form of government:** constitutional monarchy with one legislative house (Riksdag, or Parliament [349]). **Head of state:** King Carl XVI Gustaf (from 1973). **Head of government:** Prime Minister Fredrik Reinfeldt (from 2006). **Capital:** Stockholm. **Official language:** Swedish. **Official religion:** none. **Monetary unit:** 1 Swedish krona (SEK; plural kronor) = 100 ore; valuation (2 Jul 2012) US$1 = SEK 6.94.

## Demography

**Area:** 173,860 sq mi, 450,295 sq km. **Population** (2011): 9,451,000. **Density** (2011; based on land area only): persons per sq mi 59.7, persons per sq km 23.0. **Urban** (2009): 84.6%. **Sex distribution** (2008): male 49.74%; female 50.26%. **Age breakdown** (2008): under 15, 16.7%; 15–29, 19.3%; 30–44, 20.4%; 45–59, 19.1%; 60–74, 15.9%; 75–89, 7.8%; 90 and over, 0.8%. **Ethnic composition** (2008): Swedish 86.2%; other European 7.9%, of which Finnish 1.9%; Asian 3.9%, of which Iraqi 1.2%; other 2.0%. **Religious affiliation** (2005): Church of Sweden (including nonpracticing) 77%; other Protestant 4.5%; Muslim 4%; Roman Catholic 1.5%; Orthodox 1%; other 12%. **Major cities** (2008): Stockholm 810,120; Göteborg 500,197; Malmö 286,535; Uppsala 190,668; Linköping 141,863. **Location:** northern Europe, bordering Finland, the Gulf of Bothnia, the Baltic Sea, and Norway.

## Vital statistics

**Birth rate** per 1,000 population (2008): 11.8 (world avg. 20.3); (2008) within marriage 45.4%. **Death rate** per 1,000 population (2008): 9.9 (world avg. 8.5). **Total fertility rate** (avg. births per childbearing woman; 2008): 1.91. **Life expectancy** at birth (2008): male 79.1 years; female 83.2 years.

## National economy

**Budget** (2007). *Revenue:* SEK 857,200,000,000 (current revenue 95.2%, of which tax revenue 87.7%; capital revenue 2.1%). *Expenditures:* SEK 768,604,000,000 (social insurance 37.6%; defense 6.0%; health 5.9%; education 5.7%; debt service 5.4%). **Public debt** (October 2009):

US$157,935,000,000. **Production** (metric tons except as noted). *Agriculture and fishing* (2008): wheat 2,241,600, sugar beets 1,975,000, barley 1,671,600; livestock (number of live animals) 1,609,289 pigs, 1,558,381 cattle, 524,780 sheep, (2006) 254,893 reindeer; fisheries production (2007) 243,618 (from aquaculture 2%). *Mining and quarrying* (metal content; 2007): iron ore 16,100,000; zinc 214,576; copper 62,905; silver 323,171 kg. *Manufacturing* (value added in SEK '000,000 at constant prices of 2000; 2007): electrical machinery, telecommunications equipment, and electronics 243,346; transportation equipment 81,295; nonelectrical machinery 70,506. *Energy production (consumption):* electricity (kW-hr; 2008–09) 136,553,000,000 ([2008] 159,114,000,000); coal (metric tons; 2006) none (3,235,000); crude petroleum (barrels; 2008) none (128,417,950); petroleum products (metric tons; 2006) 17,682,000 (11,-390,000); natural gas (cu m; 2008) none (913,000,000). **Gross national income** (2008): US$469,744,000,000 (US$50,940 per capita). **Population economically active** (2008): total 4,898,000; activity rate of total population 53.2% (participation rates: ages 15–74, 71.2%; female 47.4%; unemployed [October 2009] 8.1%). **Selected balance of payments data.** Receipts from (US$'000,000): tourism (2007) 12,004; remittances (2008) 822; foreign direct investment (FDI; 2005–07 avg.) 18,094. Disbursements for (US$'000,000): tourism (2007) 13,972; remittances (2008) 912; FDI (2005–07 avg.) 28,747.

## Foreign trade

**Imports** (2006; c.i.f.): SEK 908,300,000,000 (motor vehicles 10.9%; crude petroleum and refined petroleum products 10.8%; nonelectrical machinery and equipment 10.1%; office machines and telecommunications equipment 9.9%; base metals 6.8%). *Major import sources:* Germany 17.9%; Denmark 9.4%; Norway 8.7%; Netherlands 6.3%; UK 6.2%. **Exports** (2006; f.o.b.): SEK 1,067,600,000,000 (nonelectrical machinery and equipment 14.4%; motor vehicles 13.6%; telecommunications equipment 8.5%; paper products 6.8%; medicines and pharmaceuticals 6.0%; iron and steel 5.7%). *Major export destinations:* Germany 9.9%; US 9.4%; Norway 9.3%; UK 7.2%; Denmark 7.0%.

## Transport and communications

**Transport.** *Railroads* (2006): length (2008) 11,633 km; passenger-km 9,642,000,000; metric ton-km cargo 22,271,000,000. *Roads* (2008): total length 425,440 km (paved 33%). *Vehicles* (2008): passenger cars 4,270,031; trucks and buses 522,313. *Air transport* (2008–09): passenger-km 4,721,000,000; metric ton-km cargo 1,603,000. **Communications,** in total units (units per 1,000 persons). Telephone landlines (2008): 5,323,000 (578); cellular telephone subscribers (2008): 10,892,000 (1,183); personal computers (2005): 7,548,000 (836); total Internet users (2008): 8,086,000 (878); broadband Internet subscribers (2008): 3,791,000 (412).

## Education and health

**Educational attainment** (2008). Percentage of population ages 16–74 having: incomplete or complete primary education 7.6%; lower secondary 15.0%; upper secondary 44.5%; vocational and higher 30.9%; unknown 2.0%. **Health** (2007): physicians 29,400 (1 per 311 persons); hospital beds 26,184 (1 per 349 persons); infant mortality rate per 1,000 live births (2008) 2.5; undernourished population (2002–04) less than 2.5% of total population.

## Military

**Total active duty personnel** (November 2008): 16,900 (army 60.4%, navy 18.3%, air force 21.3%); reserve 262,000. **Military expenditure as percentage of GDP** (2008): 1.2%; per capita expenditure US$570.

## Background

The first inhabitants of Sweden were apparently hunters who crossed the land bridge from Europe c. 9000 BC. During the Viking era (9th–10th centuries AD) the Swedes controlled river trade in eastern Europe between the Baltic Sea and the Black Sea and also raided western European lands. Sweden was loosely united and Christianized in the 11th–12th centuries. It conquered the Finns in the 12th century and in the 14th united with Norway and Denmark under a single monarchy. It broke away in 1523 under Gustav I Vasa. In the 17th century it emerged as a great European power in the Baltic region, but its dominance declined after its defeat in the Second Northern War (1700–21). Sweden became a constitutional monarchy in 1809 and united with Norway in 1814; it acknowledged Norwegian independence in 1905. It maintained its neutrality during both world wars. It was a charter member of the UN but abstained from membership in the European Union until 1995 and in NATO altogether. A new constitution drafted in 1975 reduced the monarch's role to that of ceremonial head of state. By the early 21st century, Sweden had emerged as a European center of telecommunications and information technology.

## Recent Developments

Sweden enjoyed strong public finances in 2011, and at 40% of GDP its national debt was among the lowest in Europe (the EU average was 80% of GDP). While the country needed neither budget cuts nor other drastic measures to bolster its own economy, it could not escape the economic turmoil elsewhere, especially in Europe, which remained the main export market for Swedish manufactures. In an effort to prepare for the worst, the government decided to postpone promised tax relief for wage earners and retirees.

**Internet resource:** <www.scb.se>.

# Switzerland

**Official name:** Confédération Suisse (French); Schweizerische Eidgenossenschaft (German); Confederazione Svizzera (Italian); Confederaziun Svizra (Romansh) (Swiss Confederation). **Form of government:** federal state with two legislative houses (Council of States [46]; National Council [200]). **Head of state and government:** President Eveline Widmer-Schlumpf (from 2012). **Capitals:** Bern (administrative); Lausanne (judicial). **Official languages:** French;

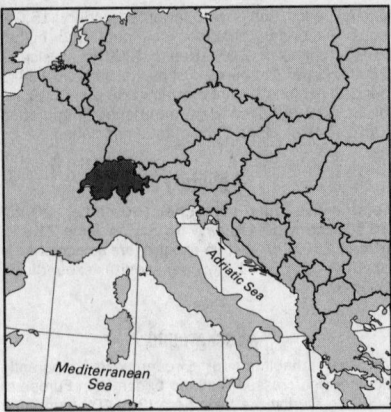

German; Italian; Romansh (locally). **Official religion:** none. **Monetary unit:** 1 Swiss franc (CHF) = 100 centimes; valuation (2 Jul 2012) US$1 = CHF 0.95.

## Demography

**Area:** 15,940 sq mi, 41,285 sq km. **Population** (2011): 7,913,000. **Density** (2011): persons per sq mi 496.4, persons per sq km 191.7. **Urban** (2009): 73.6%. **Sex distribution** (2007): male 49.08%; female 50.92%. **Age breakdown** (2007): under 15, 15.5%; 15–29, 18.3%; 30–44, 23.0%; 45–59, 20.9%; 60–74, 14.4%; 75–84, 5.7%; 85 and over, 2.2%. **National composition** (2007): Swiss 78.9%; Italian 3.8%; German 2.7%; Serb/Montenegrin 2.5%; Portuguese 2.4%; Turkish 1.0%; other 8.7%. **Religious affiliation** (2000): Roman Catholic 41.8%; Protestant 33.0%; Muslim 4.3%; Orthodox 1.8%; Jewish 0.2%; other Christian 2.7%; nonreligious 11.1%; other 0.8%; unknown 4.3%. **Major urban agglomerations** (2007): Zürich 1,132,200; Geneva 503,600; Basel 489,900; Bern 346,300; Lausanne 317,000. **Location:** central Europe, bordering Germany, Austria, Liechtenstein, Italy, and France.

## Vital statistics

**Birth rate** per 1,000 population (2008): 10.1 (world avg. 20.3); within marriage 83.0%. **Death rate** per 1,000 population (2008): 8.1 (world avg. 8.5). **Total fertility rate** (avg. births per childbearing woman; 2008): 1.48. **Life expectancy** at birth (2008): male 79.7 years; female 84.4 years.

## National economy

**Budget** (combined federal, cantonal, and communal budgets; 2007). *Revenue:* CHF 165,097,000,000 (tax revenue 59.1%, of which taxes on income and wealth 39.6%; nontax revenue 22.2%; social security obligations 18.7%). *Expenditures:* CHF 170,738,000,000 (social security 19.0%; social welfare 16.2%; education 16.2%; health 11.3%; transportation 8.4%; defense 2.9%). **Production** (metric tons except as noted). *Agriculture and fish-*ing (2007): sugar beets 1,584,000, wheat 562,200, potatoes 490,000; livestock (number of live animals) 1,650,000 pigs, 1,565,000 cattle; fisheries production 2,594 (from aquaculture 47%). *Mining and quarrying* (2007): salt 560,000. *Manufacturing* (value added in CHF '000,000; 2006): chemical products and refined petroleum products 18,260; professional and scientific equipment and watches 13,488; nonelectrical machinery and equipment 12,804. *Energy production (consumption):* electricity (kW-hr; 2007) 65,918,000,000 ([2006] 66,741,000,000); coal (metric tons; 2006) none (152,000); crude petroleum (barrels; 2006) none (39,800,000); petroleum products (metric tons; 2006) 5,418,000 (10,924,000); natural gas (cu m; 2006) none (3,226,000,000). **Population economically active** (2006): total 4,220,000; activity rate of total population 55.8% (participation rates: ages 15–64, 81.2%; female 45.7%; unemployed [May 2007–April 2008] 2.6%). **Gross national income** (2008): US$498,534,000,000 (US$65,330 per capita). **Public debt** (December 2006): US$188,701,000,000. **Selected balance of payments data.** Receipts from (US$'000,000): tourism (2007) 12,185; remittances (2008) 2,358; foreign direct investment (FDI; 2005–07 avg.) 21,708. Disbursements for (US$'000,000): tourism (2007) 10,265; remittances (2008) 18,954; FDI (2005–07 avg.) 57,429.

## Foreign trade

**Imports** (2006; c.i.f.): CHF 177,287,000,000 (machinery and apparatus 18.8%; medicine and pharmaceuticals 10.5%; base and fabricated metals [excluding gold] 10.2%; mineral fuels 7.9%; motor vehicles 6.5%). *Major import sources* (2008): Germany 34.7%; Italy 11.4%; France 9.7%; US 5.1%; Netherlands 4.8%. **Exports** (2006; f.o.b.): CHF 185,382,000,000 (medicine and pharmaceuticals 21.1%; nonelectrical machinery and equipment 15.1%; wrist watches 6.9%; organic chemical products 6.8%). *Major export destinations* (2008): Germany 20.3%; US 9.4%; Italy 8.8%; France 8.6%; UK 4.7%.

## Transport and communications

**Transport.** *Railroads* (2005): length (2006) 5,062 km; passenger-km 16,144,000,000; metric ton-km cargo 10,149,000,000. *Roads* (2006): total length 71,353 km. *Vehicles* (2007): passenger cars 3,955,787; trucks and buses 324,153. *Air transport* (2008): passenger-km 28,140,000,000; metric ton-km cargo 1,142,000,000. **Communications,** in total units (units per 1,000 persons). Telephone landlines (2008): 4,835,000 (641); cellular telephone subscribers (2008): 8,897,000 (1,180); personal computers (2007): 6,977,000 (918); total Internet users (2008): 5,739,000 (761); broadband Internet subscribers (2008): 2,576,000 (342).

## Education and health

**Educational attainment** (2008). Percentage of resident Swiss and resident alien population ages 25–64 having: compulsory education 13.2%; secondary 53.1%; higher 33.7%. **Health:** physicians

(2005) 28,251 (1 per 263 persons); hospital beds (2006) 40,347 (1 per 185 persons); infant mortality rate per 1,000 live births (2008) 4.0; undernourished population (2002–04) less than 2.5% of total population.

## Military

**Total active duty personnel** (November 2008): 22,823; additionally, there are 218,200 reservists and an 85,000-member civil defense force. **Military expenditure as percentage of GDP** (2008): 0.9%; per capita expenditure US$515.

## Background

The original inhabitants of Switzerland were the Helvetians, who were conquered by the Romans in the 1st century BC. Germanic tribes penetrated the region from the 3rd to the 6th century AD, and Muslim and Magyar raiders ventured in during the 10th century. It came under the Holy Roman Empire in the 11th century. In 1291 three cantons formed an anti-Habsburg league that became the nucleus of the Swiss Confederation. It was a center of the Reformation, which divided the confederation and led to a period of political and religious conflict. The French organized Switzerland as the Helvetic Republic in 1798. In 1815 the Congress of Vienna recognized Swiss independence and guaranteed its neutrality. A new federal state was formed in 1848 with Bern as the capital. It remained neutral in both world wars and thereafter. It joined the European Free Trade Association in 1960, but it has opted against joining the European Union. It joined the United Nations in 2002.

## Recent Developments

Switzerland, which was not a member of the EU, was spared the acute financial crises experienced elsewhere on the continent. Swiss exports and key economic sectors such as tourism were, however, battered by the strengthening of the Swiss franc, which became a safe haven from the euro zone's debt crisis. (The Swiss franc nearly touched parity with the euro in early August.) Switzerland continued to make progress in shaking off its reputation as a tax haven by exchanging tax data with other countries. It managed to stay off the Organisation for Economic Co-operation and Development's "grey list" of uncooperative countries, though a review of its performance found that there was still room for greater transparency. In an effort to prove that it was no longer a refuge for dictators' ill-gotten gains, Switzerland moved rapidly during the "Arab Spring" to freeze assets belonging to the erstwhile leaders of Tunisia, Egypt, and Libya. The historically neutral country also aligned itself with the EU to impose sanctions against Syria.

**Internet resource:** <www.bfs.admin.ch>.

# Syria

**Official name:** Al-Jumhuriyah al-ʿArabiyah al-Suriyah (Syrian Arab Republic). **Form of government:** unitary multiparty republic with one legislative house (People's Assembly [250]). **Head of state and government:** President Bashar al-Assad (from 2000). **Capital:** Damascus. **Official language:** Arabic. **Official religion:** none (Islam is the required religion of the

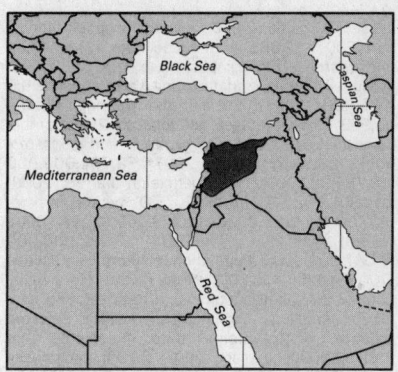

head of state and is the basis of the legal system). **Monetary unit:** 1 Syrian pound (S.P) = 100 piastres; valuation (2 Jul 2012) US$1 = S.P 63.93.

## Demography

**Area:** 71,498 sq mi, 185,180 sq km. **Population** (2011): 20,766,000 (includes 1,005,000 Iraqi refugees and 460,000 long-term Palestinian refugees in early 2011). **Density** (2011): persons per sq mi 290.4, persons per sq km 112.1. **Urban** (2010): 53.5%. **Sex distribution** (2008): male 50.85%; female 49.15%. **Age breakdown** (2008): under 15, 37.0%; 15–29, 30.8%; 30–44, 17.8%; 45–59, 9.1%; 60–74, 4.0%; 75–84, 1.1%; 85 and over, 0.2%. **Ethnic composition** (2000): Syrian Arab 74.9%; Bedouin Arab 7.4%; Kurd 7.3%; Palestinian Arab 3.9%; Armenian 2.7%; other 3.8%. **Religious affiliation** (2000): Muslim 86%, of which Sunni 74%, ʿAlawite (Shiʿi) 11%; Christian 8%, of which Orthodox 5%, Roman Catholic 2%; Druze 3%; nonreligious/atheist 3%. **Major cities** (2004): Aleppo 2,181,061; Damascus 1,552,161; Hims (Homs) 750,501; Hamah 467,807; Latakia 424,392. **Location:** the Middle East, bordering Turkey, Iraq, Jordan, Israel, Lebanon, and the Mediterranean Sea.

## Vital statistics

**Birth rate** per 1,000 population (2008): 25.6 (world avg. 20.3). **Death rate** per 1,000 population (2008): 3.7 (world avg. 8.5). **Total fertility rate** (avg. births per childbearing woman; 2008): 3.23. **Life expectancy** at birth (2008): male 71.6 years; female 76.4 years.

## National economy

**Budget** (2007). *Revenue:* S.P 458,571,000,000 (nonpetroleum nontax revenues 30.0%; petroleum royalties and taxes 21.7%; nonpetroleum tax on income and profits 16.2%; taxes on international trade 7.3%). *Expenditures:* S.P 520,531,000,000 (current expenditures 62.6%; capital expenditures 37.4%). **Public debt** (external, outstanding; 2008): US$5,678,-000,000. **Gross national income** (2008): US$44,-439,000,000 (US$2,090 per capita). **Production** (metric tons except as noted). *Agriculture and fishing* (2008): wheat 4,041,100, sugar beets 1,150,000, seed cotton 711,497, olives 495,310, almonds 76,093, pistachios 52,066; livestock (number of live animals) 22,865,400 sheep, 1,561,260 goats,

1,168,330 cattle, 24,500 camels; fisheries production (2007) 17,881 (from aquaculture 47%). *Mining and quarrying* (2007): phosphate rock 3,678,000; gypsum 447,900. *Manufacturing* (value added in S.P '000,000; 2007): textiles and wearing apparel 35,953; food, beverages, and tobacco 28,975; fabricated metals 20,003. *Energy production (consumption):* electricity (kW-hr; 2007) 38,784,000,000 (38,784,000,000); crude petroleum (barrels; 2008) 134,800,000 ([2006] 95,700,000); petroleum products (metric tons; 2006) 11,229,000 (11,988,000); natural gas (cu m; 2006) 6,087,000,000 (6,087,000,000). **Population economically active** (2007): total 5,400,800; activity rate of total population 27.5% (participation rates: ages 15 and over 45.7%; female 15.7%; unemployed 8.4%). **Selected balance of payments data.** Receipts from (US$'000,000): tourism (2007) 3,199; remittances (2008) 850; foreign direct investment (FDI; 2005–07 avg.) 662; official development assistance (2007) 75. Disbursements for (US$'000,000): tourism (2007) 719; remittances (2008) 235; FDI (2005–07 avg.) 57.

## Foreign trade

**Imports** (2006; c.i.f.): US$11,488,000,000 (refined petroleum products 24.4%; food products 10.7%; motor vehicles 8.6%; iron and steel 8.3%; nonelectrical machinery and equipment 7.3%). *Major import sources:* Russia 10.2%; China 6.5%; Ukraine 5.3%; Egypt 5.2%; Saudi Arabia 5.1%. **Exports** (2006; f.o.b.): US$10,919,000,000 (crude petroleum 33.6%; food products and live animals 14.9%, of which vegetables and fruit 6.0%; wearing apparel and accessories 7.9%; textile yarn, fabrics, and made-up articles 7.5%; refined petroleum products 6.7%). *Major export destinations* (2007): Italy 23.7%; France 11.5%; Saudi Arabia 10.6%; Iraq 5.6%; Turkey 5.2%.

## Transport and communications

**Transport.** *Railroads* (2007): length 2,833 km; passenger-km 744,110,000; metric ton-km cargo 2,550,742,000. *Roads* (2007): total length 55,041 km (paved 93%). *Vehicles* (2007): passenger cars 446,132; trucks and buses 566,976. *Air transport* (2008; SyrianAir only): passenger-km 2,448,000,000; metric ton-km cargo (2006) 16,000,000. **Communications**, in total units (units per 1,000 persons). Telephone landlines (2008): 3,633,000 (170); cellular telephone subscribers (2008): 7,056,000 (331); personal computers (2007): 1,844,000 (90); total Internet users (2008): 3,565,000 (167); broadband Internet subscribers (2008): 11,000 (0.5).

## Education and health

**Educational attainment** (2003–04). Percentage of population having: no formal education (illiterate) 14.3%; no formal education (literate) 9.9%; primary education 45.8%; secondary 22.5%; incomplete higher 3.9%; higher 3.6%. **Literacy** (2005): percentage of population ages 15 and over literate 78.4%; males literate 90.6%; females literate 66.1%. **Health** (2007): physicians 29,506 (1 per 694 persons); hospital beds 28,750 (1 per 713 persons); infant mortality rate per 1,000 live births (2008) 17.3; undernourished population (2002–04) 600,000 (4% of

total population based on the consumption of a minimum daily requirement of 1,840 calories).

## Military

**Total active duty personnel** (November 2008): 292,600 (army 73.5%, navy 2.6%, air force 10.3%, air defense 13.6%); UN peacekeeping troops in Golan Heights (June 2009): 1,043. **Military expenditure as percentage of GDP** (2007): 3.9%; per capita expenditure US$68.

## Background

Syria has been inhabited for several thousand years. From the 3rd millennium BC it was under the control variously of Sumerians, Akkadians, Amorites, Egyptians, Hittites, Assyrians, and Babylonians. In the 6th century BC it became part of the Persian Achaemenian dynasty, which fell to Alexander the Great in 330 BC. Seleucid rulers governed it from 301 BC to c. 164 BC; Parthians and Nabataean Arabs then divided the region. It flourished as a Roman province (64 BC–AD 300) and as part of the Byzantine Empire (300–634) until Muslims invaded and established control. It came under the Ottoman Empire in 1516, which held it, except for brief rules by Egypt, until the British invaded in World War I. After the war it became a French mandate; it achieved independence in 1945. It united with Egypt in the United Arab Republic (1958–61). During the Six-Day War (1967), it lost the Golan Heights to Israel. Syrian troops frequently clashed with Israeli troops in Lebanon during the 1980s and '90s. Hafez al-Assad's long and harsh regime (1971–2000) was marked also by antagonism toward Syria's neighbors Turkey and Iraq.

## Recent Developments

In March 2011, antigovernment protests broke out in Syria, inspired by a wave of similar demonstrations elsewhere in the Middle East and North Africa. Security forces responded with violence. Pres. Bashar al-Assad, in a speech before the country's legislature, claimed that the protests had been instigated by a foreign conspiracy, but he acknowledged the legitimacy of some of the protesters' concerns. In April the cabinet repealed Syria's emergency law, which had been in place for 48 years, and dissolved a special court used to try defendants accused of challenging the government. However, as protests intensified and spread to additional cities, there was an escalation in the use of violence by Syrian security forces. International condemnation of the Syrian government mounted. Nonetheless, in February 2012, the Syrian army began a sustained assault on Homs, bombarding opposition-held neighborhoods with artillery over a period of several weeks. The Arab League and the UN jointly appointed Kofi Annan, a former secretary-general of the United Nations, as a peace envoy for Syria. A drop in violence in mid-April following implementation of a UN-sponsored cease-fire eroded within days, however. Many nations withdrew their ambassadors from Syria in May in response to continuing violence. It was estimated in July that some 19,000 people had been killed in the conflict, which the Red Cross officially classified a civil war.

**Internet resource:** <www.cbssyr.org/index-EN.htm>.

---

*1 metric ton = about 1.1 short tons;    1 kilometer = 0.6 mi (statute);    1 metric ton-km cargo = about 0.68 short ton-mi cargo;    c.i.f.: cost, insurance, and freight;    f.o.b.: free on board*

# Taiwan

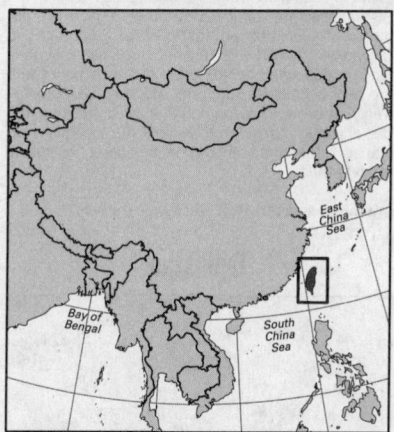

**Official name:** Chung-hua Min-kuo (Republic of China). **Form of government:** multiparty republic with one legislative house (Legislative Yuan [113]). **Head of state:** President Ma Ying-jeou (from 2008). **Head of government:** Premier Sean Chen (from 2012). **Seat of government:** Taipei. **Official language:** Mandarin Chinese. **Official religion:** none. **Monetary unit:** 1 New Taiwan dollar (NT$) = 100 cents; valuation (2 Jul 2012) US$1 = NT$29.90

## Demography

**Area:** 13,973 sq mi, 36,191 sq km. **Population** (2011): 23,190,000. **Density** (2011): persons per sq mi 1,659.6, persons per sq km 640.8. **Urban** (2005): 81%. **Sex distribution** (2007): male 50.57%; female 49.43%. **Age breakdown** (2007): under 15, 17.6%; 15–29, 23.2%; 30–44, 24.4%; 45–59, 21.2%; 60–74, 9.3%; 75–84, 3.5%; 85 and over, 0.8%. **Ethnic composition** (2003): Taiwanese 84%; mainland Chinese 14%; indigenous tribal peoples 2%, of which Ami 0.6%. **Religious affiliation** (2002): Buddhism 23.8%; Taoism 19.7%; Christian 4.5%, of which Protestant 2.6%, Roman Catholic 1.3%; I-kuan Tao 3.7% (syncretistic religion); Muslim 0.6%; other (mostly Chinese folk-religionist or non-religious) 47.7%. **Major cities (metropolitan areas)** (2007): Taipei 2,629,269 (6,698,319); Kao-hsiung 1,520,555 (2,767,655); T'ai-chung 1,055,898 (2,218,527); T'ao-yüan 391,822 (1,905,973); T'ai-nan 764,658 (1,255,-450). **Location:** island between the East China Sea, the Philippine Sea, and the South China Sea, north of the Philippines and southeast of mainland China.

## Vital statistics

**Birth rate** per 1,000 population (2008): 8.6 (world avg. 20.3); (2007) within marriage 95.6%. **Death rate** per 1,000 population (2008): 6.2 (world avg. 8.5). **Total fertility rate** (avg. births per childbearing woman; 2008): 1.05. **Life expectancy** at birth (2007): male 75.1 years; female 81.9 years.

## National economy

**Budget** (2006; general government). *Revenue:* NT$2,172,436,000,000 (tax revenue 71.7%; income from public enterprises 14.3%; fees 4.2%). *Expenditures:* NT$2,261,958,000,000 (education, science, and culture 21.6%; economic development 17.0%; general administration 15.3%; social welfare 13.6%; defense 10.5%). **Population economically active** (2006): total 10,522,000; activity rate of total population 46.3% (participation rates: ages 15–64, 57.9%; female 42.4%; unemployed [2007] 3.9%). **Production** (metric tons except as noted). *Agriculture and fishing* (2007): rice 1,363,458, pineapples 476,811, bamboo shoots 291,709, betel nuts 134,497; livestock (number of live animals; 2006) 7,068,621 pigs, 134,793 cattle; fisheries production 1,498,197 (from aquaculture 22%). *Mining and quarrying* (2008): marble 25,811,000. *Manufacturing* (value added in NT$'000,000,000; 2006): electronic parts and components 610; base metals 288; base chemical products 230; refined petroleum products and coal 206. *Energy production (consumption):* electricity (kW-hr; 2005) 210,300,000,000 (201,580,-000,000); coal (metric tons; 2006) none (66,000,000); crude petroleum (barrels; 2007) 292,000 ([2006] 347,000,000); natural gas (cu m; 2007) 396,000,000 (11,298,000,000). **Gross national income** (2008): US$401,806,000,000 (US$17,542 per capita). **Selected balance of payments data.** Receipts from (US$'000,000): tourism (2007) 5,137; remittances (2006) 355; foreign direct investment (FDI; 2005–07 avg.) 5,737. Disbursements for (US$'000,000): tourism (2007) 9,070; remittances (2006) 1,370; FDI (2005–07 avg.) 8,178.

## Foreign trade

**Imports** (2007; c.i.f.): US$219,252,000,000 (mineral fuels 20.9%; electronic parts and components 16.6%; base and fabricated metals 12.1%; chemical products 11.3%). *Major import sources:* Japan 21.0%; US 12.1%; China 11.3%; South Korea 6.9%; Saudi Arabia 4.5%. **Exports** (2007; f.o.b.): US$246,-677,000,000 (nonelectrical machinery, electrical machinery, and electronic goods 47.8%; base and fabricated metals 11.3%; precision instruments, watches, and musical instruments 8.1%; plastics and rubber products 7.7%). *Major export destinations:* China 21.0%; Hong Kong 15.4%; US 13.0%; Japan 6.5%; Singapore 4.3%.

## Transport and communications

**Transport.** *Railroads* (2008; Taiwan Railway Administration only): route length (2006) 1,118 km; passenger-km 19,066,000,000; metric ton-km cargo 933,000,000. *Roads* (2006): total length 39,286 km. *Vehicles* (2008): passenger cars 5,674,000; trucks and buses 1,000,000. *Air transport* (2006; China Airlines, EVA, and Far Eastern Air transport only): passenger-km 59,108,000,000; metric ton-km cargo 11,470,000,000. **Communications,** in total units (units per 1,000 persons). Telephone landlines (2008): 14,273,000 (620); cellular telephone subscribers (2008): 25,413,000 (1,103); personal computers (2005): 13,098,000 (575); total Internet users (2008): 15,143,000 (657); broadband Internet subscribers (2008): 5,024,000 (218).

## Education and health

**Educational attainment** (2003). Percentage of population ages 15 and over having: no formal schooling 4.6%; primary 19.8%; vocational 23.7%; secondary 26.8%; some college 12.0%; higher 13.1%. **Literacy** (2007): population ages 15 and over literate 97.6%. **Health** (2007): physicians 35,849 (excludes 4,862 doctors of traditional Chinese medicine) (1 per 639 persons); hospital beds 150,628 (1 per 152 persons); infant mortality rate per 1,000 live births 4.7.

## Military

**Total active duty personnel** (November 2008): 290,000 (army 69.0%, navy 15.5%, air force 15.5%); reserve 1,657,000. **Military expenditure as percentage of GDP** (2008): 2.4%; per capita expenditure US$456.

## Background

Known to the Chinese as early as the 7th century, Taiwan was widely settled by them early in the 17th century. In 1646 the Dutch seized control of the island, only to be ousted in 1661 by a large influx of Chinese refugees from the Ming dynasty. Taiwan fell to the Manchus in 1683 and was not open to Europeans again until 1858. In 1895 it was ceded to Japan following the Sino-Japanese War. A Japanese military center in World War II, it was frequently bombed by US planes. After Japan's defeat it was returned to China, which was then governed by the Nationalists. When the Communists took over mainland China in 1949, the Nationalist government fled to Taiwan and made it their seat of government, with Gen. Chiang Kai-shek as president. In 1954 he and the US signed a mutual defense treaty, and Taiwan received US support for almost three decades, developing its economy in spectacular fashion. It was recognized by many noncommunist countries as the representative of all China until 1971, when it was replaced in the UN by the People's Republic of China. Martial law was lifted in Taiwan in 1987 and travel restrictions with mainland China were removed in 1988. In 1989 opposition parties were legalized. The relationship with the mainland became increasingly close in the 1990s.

## Recent Developments

Taiwan's GDP grew by an estimated 4.4% in 2011, but the economy showed clear signs of cooling in the second half of the year in response to the European debt crisis and political uncertainty. Unemployment dropped to 4.4%. The crowning achievement of Pres. Ma Ying-jeou's China policy had been the Economic Cooperation Framework Agreement (ECFA), signed with China in 2010. Although Taiwan's exports under the ECFA increased by 12.3% in 2011, that rate was lower than the 17.5% annual increase reached in 2006–08 before the global financial downturn. Chinese tourism to Taiwan held steady at more than 1.2 million arrivals in 2011. In September Chinese students were allowed to enroll as full-time degree students in Taiwan. President Ma's government gingerly tried to step away from China by signaling Taiwan's willingness to join the US-proposed Trans-Pacific Partnership pact. The US, meanwhile, announced controversial arms sales to Taiwan worth US$5.85 billion, including upgrades for Taiwan's aging fighter jets. China was upset with the deal because it supported no arms sales to Taiwan. Taiwan was disappointed, as well, because the US originally considered selling the country new planes rather than upgrading the ones Taiwan already owned.

**Internet resource:** <http://eng.stat.gov.tw>.

# Tajikistan

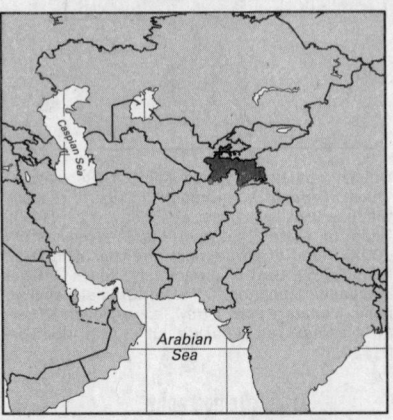

**Official name:** Jumhurii Tojikiston (Republic of Tajikistan). **Form of government:** republic with two legislative houses (National Assembly [34]; Assembly of Representatives [63]). **Head of state:** President Imomalii Rakhmon (from 1994). **Head of government:** Prime Minister Akil Akilov (from 1999). **Capital:** Dushanbe. **Official language:** Tajik. **Official religion:** none. **Monetary unit:** 1 somoni (TJS) = 100 dirams; valuation (2 Jul 2012) US$1 = TJS 4.76.

## Demography

**Area:** 55,300 sq mi, 143,100 sq km. **Population** (2011): 7,681,000. **Density** (2011): persons per sq mi 138.9, persons per sq km 53.7. **Urban** (2010): 26.5%. **Sex distribution** (2007): male 49.74%; female 50.26%. **Age breakdown** (2007): under 15, 35.0%; 15–29, 31.5%; 30–44, 18.8%; 45–59, 9.7%; 60–74, 3.8%; 75 and over, 1.2%. **Ethnic composition** (2000): Tajik 80.0%; Uzbek 15.3%; Russian 1.1%; Tatar 0.3%; other 3.3%. **Religious affiliation** (2005): Sunni Muslim 78%; Shi'i Muslim 6%; nonreligious 12%; other (mostly Christian) 4%. **Major cities** (2007): Dushanbe 679,400; Khujand 155,900; Kulyab 93,900; Kurgan-Tyube 71,000; Istaravshan (Ura-Tyube) 60,200. **Location:** central Asia, bordering Kyrgyzstan, China, Afghanistan, and Uzbekistan.

---

*1 metric ton = about 1.1 short tons; 1 kilometer = 0.6 mi (statute); 1 metric ton-km cargo = about 0.68 short ton-mi cargo; c.i.f.: cost, insurance, and freight; f.o.b.: free on board*

## Vital statistics

**Birth rate** per 1,000 population (2007): 27.3 (world avg. 20.3). **Death rate** per 1,000 population (2007): 7.0 (world avg. 8.5). **Total fertility rate** (avg. births per childbearing woman; 2007): 3.09. **Life expectancy** at birth (2007): male 61.6 years; female 67.8 years.

## National economy

**Budget** (2008). *Revenue:* TJS 3,436,000,000 (tax revenue 95.8%; nontax revenue 4.2%). *Expenditures:* TJS 5,058,000,000 (current expenditures 54.5%; capital expenditures 43.8%; net lending 1.7%). **Production** (metric tons except as noted). *Agriculture and fishing* (2007): potatoes 659,900, wheat 612,000, raw seed cotton 419,700; livestock (number of live animals) 1,922,000 sheep, 1,418,000 cattle, 1,250,000 goats, 42,000 camels; fisheries production 172 (from aquaculture 15%). *Mining and quarrying* (2006): antimony (metal content) 2,000; silver 5,000 kg; gold 3,000 kg. *Manufacturing* (value of production in TJS '000,000 at constant prices of 1998; 2007): nonferrous metals (nearly all aluminum) 585,103; food products 301,156; textiles 209,375. *Energy production (consumption):* electricity (kW-hr; 2008) 16,127,000,000 ([2007] 17,600,000,000); coal (metric tons; 2008) 216,000 ([2006] 94,000); lignite (metric tons; 2006) 15,000 (15,000); crude petroleum (barrels; 2008) 185,000 ([2006] 117,000); petroleum products (metric tons; 2006) none (1,542,000); natural gas (cu m; 2008) 12,000,000 (510,000,000). **Population economically active** (2007): total 2,201,000; activity rate of total population 30.5% (participation rates: ages 15–62 [male], 15–57 [female] 51.7%; female [2004] 41.7%; officially unemployed 2.3%). **Selected balance of payments data.** Receipts from (US$'000,000): tourism (2004) 1.0; remittances (2008) 1,750; foreign direct investment (2005–07 avg.) 265; official development assistance (2007) 221. Disbursements for (US$'000,000): tourism (2004) 3.0; remittances (2008) 184. **Gross national income** (2008): US$4,074,000,000 (US$600 per capita). **Public debt** (external, outstanding; 2007): US$1,065,000,000.

## Foreign trade

**Imports** (2007; c.i.f.): US$2,547,000,000 (refined petroleum products 10.8%; grain and flour 5.3%; electricity 2.6%; natural gas 2.6%; other [significantly alumina] 78.7%). *Major import sources* (2008): China 25.9%; Russia 24.8%; Kazakhstan 10.6%; Uzbekistan 6.8%; Turkey 5.4%. **Exports** (2007; f.o.b.): US$1,468,000,000 (cotton fiber 9.4%; electricity 4.1%; other [significantly aluminum] 86.5%). *Major export destinations* (2008): Israel 39.6%; Turkey 8.7%; Russia 7.6%; Italy 7.4%; Norway 7.2%.

## Transport and communications

**Transport.** *Railroads* (2005): length (2006) 482 km; passenger-km 46,000,000; metric ton-km cargo 1,066,000,000. *Roads* (2000): total length 27,767 km (paved [1996] 83%). *Vehicles* (2007): passenger cars 192,973; trucks and buses 64,324. *Air transport* (2005; Tajikistan Airlines only): passenger-km 1,030,000,000; metric ton-km cargo 7,031,000. **Communications**, in total units (units per 1,000 persons). Telephone landlines (2008): 360,000 (53); cellular telephone subscribers (2008): 2,459,000 (360); personal computers (2007): 87,000 (13); total Internet users (2008): 600,000 (88).

## Education and health

**Literacy** (2007): percentage of total population ages 15 and over literate, virtually 100%. **Health** (2007): physicians 13,400 (1 per 505 persons); hospital beds 38,800 (1 per 175 persons); infant mortality rate per 1,000 live births 43.6; undernourished population (2002–04) 3,500,000 (56% of total population based on the consumption of a minimum daily requirement of 1,910 calories).

## Military

**Total active duty personnel** (November 2008): 8,800 (army 83%, air force 17%); Russian troops (November 2008): 5,500. **Military expenditure as percentage of GDP** (2007): 2.4%; per capita expenditure US$13.

## Background

Settled by the Persians c. the 6th century BC, Tajikistan was part of the empires of the Persians and of Alexander the Great and his successors. In the 7th–8th centuries AD it was conquered by the Arabs, who introduced Islam. The Uzbeks controlled the region in the 15th–18th centuries. In the 1860s Russia took over much of Tajikistan. In 1924 it became an autonomous republic under the administration of the Uzbek Soviet Socialist Republic, and it gained republic status in 1929. It achieved independence with the collapse of the Soviet Union in 1991. Civil war raged through much of the 1990s between government forces and an opposition of mostly Islamic forces. Peace was achieved in 1997.

## Recent Developments

Tajikistan's relations with Russia intensified in 2011, reaching a high point during a Commonwealth of Independent States summit at the beginning of September with an agreement on a Russian military presence in Tajikistan for the next 49 years. In lieu of rent for the facilities used by Russian forces, Tajikistan was to receive military technology and training. Russian authorities were eager for Russian border troops to return to the Tajik border, but despite pressure from Moscow, Tajikistan resisted the Russian proposals. Iran also was eager to intensify relations with Persian-speaking Tajikistan. In September, Iranian Pres. Mahmoud Ahmadinejad formally opened the Iranian-financed Sangtuda-2 power plant, which would make a huge contribution to solving Tajikistan's energy problems.

**Internet resource:** <www.stat.tj/en>.

# Tanzania

**Official name:** Jamhuri ya Muungano wa Tanzania (Swahili); United Republic of Tanzania (English). **Form of government:** unitary multiparty republic with one

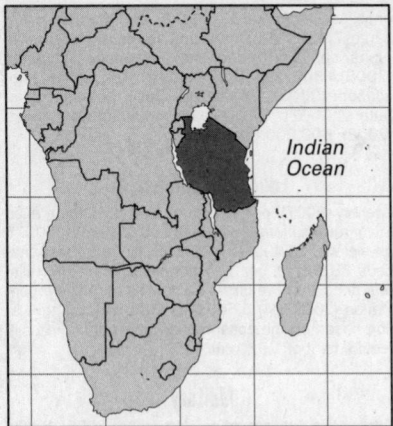

Indian Ocean

legislative house (National Assembly [357]). **Head of state and government:** President Jakaya Kikwete (from 2005). **Capital:** Dar es Salaam (Dodoma is the capital designate). **Official languages:** Swahili; English. **Official religion:** none. **Monetary unit:** 1 Tanzanian shilling (TZS) = 100 cents; valuation (2 Jul 2012) US$1 = TZS 1,576.00.

## Demography

**Area:** 364,901 sq mi, 945,090 sq km. **Population** (2011): 45,030,000. **Density** (2011; based on land area only): persons per sq mi 123.7, persons per sq km 51.0. **Urban** (2008): 25.6%. **Sex distribution** (2006): male 49.46%; female 50.54%. **Age breakdown** (2006): under 15, 44.3%; 15–29, 29.1%; 30–44, 14.6%; 45–59, 7.6%; 60–74, 3.6%; 75–84, 0.7%; 85 and over, 0.1%. **Ethnolinguistic composition** (2000): 130 different Bantu tribes 95%, of which Sukuma 9.5%, Hehe and Bena 4.5%, Gogo 4.4%, Haya 4.2%, Nyamwezi 3.6%, Makonde 3.3%, Chagga 3.0%, Ha 2.9%; other 5%. **Religious affiliation** (2005): Muslim 35%, of which Sunni 30%, Shi'i 5%; Christian 35%; other (significantly traditional beliefs) 30%; Zanzibar only is 99% Muslim. **Major urban areas** (2006): Dar es Salaam 2,805,500; Mwanza 458,100; Zanzibar (Unguja) 422,300; Arusha 362,900; Mbeya 304,200. **Location:** eastern Africa, bordering Kenya, the Indian Ocean, Mozambique, Malawi, Zambia, the Democratic Republic of the Congo, Burundi, Rwanda, and Uganda.

## Vital statistics

**Birth rate** per 1,000 population (2008): 38.3 (world avg. 20.3). **Death rate** per 1,000 population (2008): 12.6 (world avg. 8.5). **Total fertility rate** (avg. births per childbearing woman; 2006): 4.93. **Life expectancy** at birth (2006): male 48.5 years; female 50.9 years.

## National economy

**Budget** (2006–07). *Revenue:* TZS 3,691,247,-900,000 (tax revenue 68.5%, of which excise tax 27.6%, income tax 19.4%; nontax revenue 5.7%). *Expenditures:* TZS 4,474,680,900,000 (current expenditures 70.1%, of which interest payments on debt 4.8%; capital expenditures 29.9%). **Gross national income** (2008; mainland Tanzania only): US$18,350,000,000 (US$440 per capita). **Public debt** (external, outstanding; 2007): US$3,684,000,000. **Production** (metric tons except as noted). *Agriculture and fishing* (2007): cassava 6,600,000, corn (maize) 3,400,-000, rice 1,240,000, cashew nuts 92,000, tobacco leaves 53,000, coffee 52,000, cloves 9,900; livestock (number of live animals) 18,000,000 cattle, 12,550,000 goats, 3,550,000 sheep; fisheries production 328,827 (from aquaculture, negligible). *Mining and quarrying* (2007): gold 40,193 kg; garnets 5,900 kg; tanzanites 3,400 kg; rubies 2,700 kg; diamonds 282,786 carats. *Manufacturing* (2005): cement 1,281,-000; wheat flour 347,296; sugar 202,200; konyagi (a Tanzanian liquor) 41,050 hectoliters. *Energy production (consumption):* electricity (kW-hr; 2006) 2,776,000,000 (2,899,000,000); coal (metric tons; 2006) 80,000 (80,000); petroleum products (metric tons; 2006) none (1,216,000); natural gas (cu m; 2006) 374,000,000 (374,000,000). **Population economically active** (2002): total 14,841,000; activity rate of total population 43.1% (participation rates: ages 10 and over, 64.9%; female 48.0%; officially unemployed 3.7%). **Selected balance of payments data.** Receipts from (US$'000,000): tourism (2007) 1,037; remittances (2008) 15; foreign direct investment (2005–07 avg.) 563; official development assistance (2007) 2,811. Disbursements for (US$'000,000): tourism (2007) 645; remittances (2008) 46.

## Foreign trade

**Imports** (2006; c.i.f.): TZS 5,558,000,000,000 (refined petroleum products 23.7%; nonelectrical machinery and equipment 12.0%; chemical products 11.5%; motor vehicles 9.9%; food products 6.5%). *Major import sources* (2008): UAE 12.4%; India 11.9%; South Africa 11.0%; China 9.9%; Singapore 6.1%. **Exports** (2006; f.o.b.): TZS 2,116,000,000,000 (gold 34.9%; other metal ores [including copper and silver] 11.0%; fish 10.2%; tobacco products 6.2%; vegetables and fruit 4.7%; coffee 4.3%). *Major export destinations* (2008): Switzerland 20.8%; Kenya 8.6%; South Africa 8.5%; China 8.2%; India 6.3%.

## Transport and communications

**Transport.** *Railroads* (2003): length (2001) 3,690 km; passenger-km 1,305,000,000; metric ton-km cargo 4,461,000,000. *Roads* (2008): length 78,892 km (paved 6%). *Vehicles* (2007): passenger cars 80,913; trucks and buses 393,005. *Air transport* (2008): passenger-km 156,000,000; metric ton-km cargo 1,452,000. **Communications**, in total units (units per 1,000 persons). Telephone landlines (2008): 124,000 (2.9); cellular telephone subscribers (2008): 13,007,000 (306); personal computers (2005): 356,000 (9.3); total Internet users (2008): 520,000 (12).

*1 metric ton = about 1.1 short tons; 1 kilometer = 0.6 mi (statute); 1 metric ton-km cargo = about 0.68 short ton-mi cargo; c.i.f.: cost, insurance, and freight; f.o.b.: free on board*

## Education and health

**Educational attainment** (2002). Percentage of population ages 25 and over having: no formal schooling/unknown 49.6%; primary education 44.0%; secondary 5.5%; postsecondary 0.9%. **Literacy** (2007): percentage of population ages 15 and over literate 72.3%; males literate 79.0%; females literate 65.9%. **Health** (2002): physicians 822 (1 per 42,085 persons); hospital beds 36,853 (1 per 939 persons); infant mortality rate per 1,000 live births (2006) 73.0; undernourished population (2003–05) 13,000,000 (35% of total population based on the consumption of a minimum daily requirement of 1,730 calories).

## Military

**Total active duty personnel** (November 2008): 27,000 (army 85.2%, navy 3.7%, air force 11.1%). **Military expenditure as percentage of GDP** (2007): 1.1%; per capita expenditure US$4.

## Background

Inhabited from the 1st millennium BC, Tanzania was occupied by Arab and Indian traders and Bantu-speaking peoples by the 10th century AD. The Portuguese gained control of the coastline in the late 15th century, but they were driven out by the Arabs of Oman and Zanzibar in the late 18th century. German colonists entered the area in the 1880s, and in 1891 the Germans declared the region a protectorate as German East Africa. In World War I, Britain captured the German holdings, which became a British mandate (1920) under the name Tanganyika. Britain retained control of the region after World War II when it became a UN trust territory (1947). Tanganyika gained independence in 1961 and became a republic in 1962. In 1964 it united with Zanzibar under the name Tanzania. The country subsequently experienced both political and economic struggles; it held its first multiparty elections in 1995.

## Recent Developments

Transparency International's East African Bribery Index 2011 ranked Tanzania as the third most corrupt country in the region, behind Burundi and Uganda. Financial malfeasance was rampant in the police force, the judiciary and the courts, immigration services, government ministries, and other official bodies. On a positive note, however, late in June environmentalists and the East African tourist industry breathed a sigh of relief when the government changed its plan to build a highway across the Serengeti National Park to a southern route from Serengeti to Mukoma. The initial northern route would have interfered with the Serengeti–Maasai Mara ecosystem, especially the wildebeest migration route, a major attraction to the region.

Internet resource: <www.nbs.go.tz>.

# Thailand

**Official name:** Ratcha Anachak Thai (Kingdom of Thailand). **Form of government:** constitutional monarchy with two legislative houses (Senate [150]; House of Representatives [500]). **Head of state:**

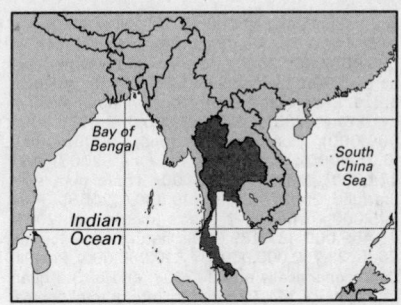

King Bhumibol Adulyadej (from 1946). **Head of government:** Prime Minister Yingluck Shinawatra (from 2011). **Capital:** Bangkok. **Official language:** Thai. **Official religion:** none. **Monetary unit:** 1 baht (THB) = 100 satang; valuation (2 Jul 2012) US$1 = THB 31.60.

## Demography

**Area:** 198,117 sq mi, 513,120 sq km. **Population** (2011): 65,856,000. **Density** (2011): persons per sq mi 332.4, persons per sq km 128.3. **Urban** (2009): 33.6%. **Sex distribution** (2008): male 49.44%; female 50.56%. **Age breakdown** (2008): under 15, 21.2%; 15–29, 23.9%; 30–44, 24.5%; 45–59, 18.2%; 60–74, 9.2%; 75–89, 2.9%; 90 and over, 0.1%. **Ethnic composition** (2000): Tai peoples 81.4%, of which Thai (Siamese) 34.9%, Lao 26.5%; Han Chinese 10.6%; Malay 3.7%; Khmer 1.9%; other 2.4%. **Religious affiliation** (2005): Buddhist 83%; Muslim (nearly all Sunni) 9%; traditional beliefs 2.5%; nonreligious 2%; other (significantly Christian) 3.5%. **Major cities** (2000): Bangkok (2007) 6,704,000; Samut Prakan 378,741; Nonthaburi 291,555; Udon Thani 222,425; Nakhon Ratchasima 204,641. **Location:** southeastern Asia, bordering Laos, Cambodia, the Gulf of Thailand, Malaysia, and Myanmar (Burma).

## Vital statistics

**Birth rate** per 1,000 population (2008): 13.6 (world avg. 20.3). **Death rate** per 1,000 population (2008): 7.1 (world avg. 8.5). **Total fertility rate** (avg. births per childbearing woman; 2008): 1.64. **Life expectancy** at birth (2008): male 70.5 years; female 75.3 years.

## National economy

**Budget** (2008). *Revenue:* THB 1,839,600,000,000 (tax revenue 89.9%, of which VAT 27.4%, corporate taxes 25.0%, excise tax 15.1%, income tax 11.1%; nontax revenue 10.1%). *Expenditures:* THB 1,633,-300,000,000 (current expenditures 79.9%; capital expenditures 20.1%). **Production** (metric tons except as noted). *Agriculture and fishing* (2008): sugarcane 76,018,410, rice 32,119,350, cassava 23,809,670, natural rubber 3,166,840; livestock (number of live animals) 7,845,346 pigs, 6,699,-999 cattle, 1,699,469 buffalo; fisheries production (2007) 3,858,815 (from aquaculture 36%). *Mining and quarrying* (2007): gypsum (2008) 8,500,401; dolomite 1,123,425; feldspar 684,668; zinc [metal content] 32,921; gemstones (significantly rubies and sapphires) 102,000 carats; silver 7,400 kg; gold 3,000 kg. *Manufacturing* (value added in US$'000,000; 2000): textiles and wearing apparel 1,905; electronics 1,817; food products 1,311. *Energy production (consumption):* electricity (kW-hr; 2007) 142,538,000,000 (138,609,-000,000); coal (metric tons; 2006) none (6,252,000); lignite (metric tons; 2008) 18,-171,950 ([2006] 18,852,000); crude petroleum (barrels; 2008–09) 79,899,830 ([2008] 340,-545,000); petroleum products (metric tons; 2006) 43,459,000 (37,489,000); natural gas (cu m; 2008) 28,760,000,000 (37,310,000,000). **Population economically active** (2008; end of 3rd quarter): total 38,344,700; activity rate of total population 58.5% (participation rates: ages 15–59, 79.3%; female 46.0%; unemployed [April 2008–March 2009] 1.5%. **Gross national income** (2008): US$191,650,000,000 (US$2,840 per capita). **Public debt** (external, outstanding; 2007): US$9,841,000,000. **Selected balance of payments data.** Receipts from (US$'000,000): tourism (2007) 16,667; remittances (2008) 1,800; foreign direct investment (FDI; 2006–08 avg.) 10,258. Disbursements for (US$'000,000): tourism (2007) 5,143; FDI (2005–07 avg.) 1,097.

## Foreign trade

**Imports** (2008; c.i.f.): THB 5,946,311,060,000 (mineral fuels 20.7%, of which crude petroleum 16.2%; chemical products 10.1%; electronic parts 8.5%; electrical machinery and equipment 8.3%; iron and steel 7.6%; nonelectrical machinery and equipment 6.5%; fabricated metal products 5.7%). *Major import sources:* Japan 18.8%; China 11.3%; US 6.4%; UAE 6.2%; Malaysia 5.4%. **Exports** (2008; f.o.b.): THB 5,851,371,140,000 (computers and parts 9.4%; transportation equipment 9.4%; agricultural products 9.0%; integrated circuits and parts 8.7%; electrical machinery and equipment 6.8%; refined petroleum products 5.4%; nonelectrical machinery and equipment 4.9%). *Major export destinations:* US 11.4%; Japan 11.3%; China 9.1%; Singapore 5.7%; Hong Kong 5.7%.

## Transport and communications

**Transport.** *Railroads* (2008): route length 4,071 km; passenger-km 8,570,000,000; metric ton-km cargo 3,139,000,000. *Roads* (2007): total length 51,538 km (paved 99%). *Vehicles* (2007): passenger cars 3,560,222; trucks and buses 3,615,153. *Air transport* (2008–09): passenger-km 51,-852,000,000; metric ton-km cargo 2,050,-901,000. **Communications,** in total units (units per 1,000 persons). Telephone landlines (2008): 7,024,000 (104); cellular telephone subscribers (2008): 62,000,000 (920); personal computers (2007): 4,039,000 (62); total Internet users (2008): 16,100,000 (239); broadband Internet subscribers (2008): 950,000 (14).

## Education and health

**Educational attainment** (2007). Percentage of employed population having: no formal schooling/un-known 5.4%; incomplete primary education 32.4%; complete primary 21.2%; lower secondary 29.6%; upper secondary/higher 11.4%. **Literacy** (2007): population ages 15 and over literate 94.1%; males literate 95.9%; females literate 92.6%. **Health** (2005): physicians 19,546 (1 per 3,287 persons); hospital beds 134,016 (1 per 470 persons); infant mortality rate per 1,000 live births (2008) 18.1; undernourished population (2002–04) 13,800,000 (22% of total population based on the consumption of a minimum daily requirement of 1,870 calories).

## Military

**Total active duty personnel** (November 2008): 306,600 (army 62.0%, navy 23.0%, air force 15.0%). **Military expenditure as percentage of GDP** (2007): 1.4%; per capita expenditure US$51.

## Background

The region of Thailand has been occupied continuously for 20,000 years. It was part of the Mon and Khmer kingdoms from the 9th century AD. Thai-speaking peoples emigrated from China in the 10th century. During the 13th century two Thai states emerged: the Sukhothai kingdom, founded about 1220 after a successful revolt against the Khmer, and Chiang Mai, founded in 1296 after the defeat of the Mon. In 1350 the Thai kingdom of Ayutthaya succeeded Sukhothai. The Burmese were its most powerful rivals, occupying it briefly in the 16th century and destroying the kingdom in 1767. The Chakri dynasty came to power in 1782, moving the capital to Bangkok and extending the empire along the Malay Peninsula and into Laos and Cambodia. The country was named Siam in 1856. Though Western influence increased during the 19th century, Siam's rulers avoided colonization by granting concessions to European countries; it was the only Southeast Asian nation able to do so. In 1917 it entered World War I on the side of the Allies. It became a constitutional monarchy following a military coup in 1932 and was officially renamed Thailand in 1939. It was occupied by Japan in World War II. It participated in the Korean War as a UN forces member and was allied with South Vietnam in the Vietnam War. The country subsequently became a regional economic powerhouse, though serious social problems also emerged, including a growing gap between rich and poor and a major AIDS epidemic.

## Recent Developments

In 2011, Thailand focused on the general election held in July, following the dissolution in May of the parliament by unelected Prime Minister Abhisit Vejjajiva. The dissolution came a year after Abhisit's bloody crackdown on the antigovernment demonstrations organized by the United Front for Democracy Against Dictatorship, popularly known as red shirts. The election was a fierce contest between Abhisit and Yingluck Shinawatra, the younger sister of former prime minister Thaksin Shinawatra (2001–06). Yingluck's party won a majority, sweeping seats in rural areas where her brother remained

*1 metric ton = about 1.1 short tons;    1 kilometer = 0.6 mi (statute);    1 metric ton-km cargo = about 0.68 short ton-mi cargo;    c.i.f.: cost, insurance, and freight;    f.o.b.: free on board*

popular for policies he had implemented to benefit the poor while in office. Subsequently, Yingluck assumed office in August as Thailand's first female prime minister. She vowed to achieve national reconciliation in the country, which had remained sharply divided between the urban rich and the rural poor following the 2006 coup that ousted Thaksin.

Internet resource: <http://web.nso.go.th>.

# Togo

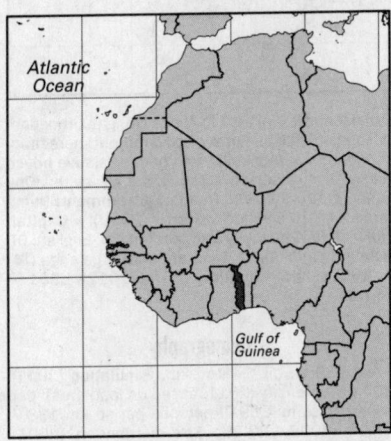

Atlantic Ocean

Gulf of Guinea

**Official name:** République Togolaise (Togolese Republic). **Form of government:** multiparty republic with one legislative house (National Assembly [81]). **Head of state and government:** President Faure Gnassingbé (from 2005), assisted by Prime Minister Kwesi Ahoomey-Zunu (from 2012). **Capital:** Lomé. **Official language:** French. **Official religion:** none. **Monetary unit:** 1 CFA franc (CFAF) = 100 centimes; valuation (2 Jul 2012) US$1 = CFAF 521.26.

## Demography

**Area:** 21,853 sq mi, 56,600 sq km. **Population** (2011): 5,830,000. **Density** (2011): persons per sq mi 266.8, persons per sq km 103.0. **Urban** (2010): 37.4%. **Sex distribution** (2008): male 49.12%; female 50.88%. **Age breakdown** (2008): under 15, 41.6%; 15–29, 30.0%; 30–44, 15.9%; 45–59, 8.1%; 60–74, 3.6%; 75–84, 0.7%; 85 and over, 0.1%. **Ethnic composition** (2000): Ewe 22.2%; Kabre 13.4%; Wachi 10.0%; Mina 5.6%; Kotokoli 5.6%; Bimoba 5.2%; Losso 4.0%; Gurma 3.4%; Lamba 3.2%; Adja 3.0%; other 24.4%. **Religious affiliation** (2004): Christian 47.2%, of which Roman Catholic 27.8%, Protestant 9.5%, independent and other Christian 9.9%; traditional beliefs 33.0%; Muslim 13.7%; nonreligious 4.9%; other 1.2%. **Major cities** (2005): Lomé 921,000 (urban agglomeration [2007] 1,452,000); Sokodé 106,300; Kara 100,400; Atakpamé 72,700; Kpalimé 71,400. **Location:** western Africa, bordering Burkina Faso, Benin, the Atlantic Ocean, and Ghana.

## Vital statistics

**Birth rate** per 1,000 population (2008): 36.7 (world avg. 20.3). **Death rate** per 1,000 population (2008): 9.1 (world avg. 8.5). **Total fertility rate** (avg. births per childbearing woman; 2008): 4.85. **Life expectancy** at birth (2008): male 57.0 years; female 61.6 years.

## National economy

**Budget** (2008). *Revenue:* CFAF 249,900,000,000 (tax revenue 84.5%, of which taxes on international trade 66.5%; grants 11.7%; nontax revenue 3.8%). *Expenditures:* CFAF 253,300,000,000 (current expenditures 80.2%; capital expenditures 19.8%). **Production** (metric tons except as noted). *Agriculture and fishing* (2008): cassava 881,011, yams 638,087, corn (maize) 595,311, cacao beans 80,000, seed cotton 32,500; livestock (number of live animals) 2,001,500 sheep, 1,508,100 goats, 582,400 pigs; fisheries production (2007) 24,905 (from aquaculture 20%). *Mining and quarrying* (2007): limestone 2,400,000; phosphate rock (2008; gross weight) 686,472; diamonds 17,362 carats. *Manufacturing* (value added in CFAF '000,000; 2006): food products, beverages, and tobacco products 33,800; bricks, cement, and ceramics 19,300; base and fabricated metals 10,800. *Energy production (consumption):* electricity (kW-hr; 2006) 221,000,000 (726,000,000); petroleum products (metric tons; 2006) none (268,000). **Population economically active** (2006): total 2,521,000; activity rate of total population 39.3% (participation rates: ages 15–64, 70.0%; female 38.4%; unemployed [2004] 32%). **Gross national income** (2008): US$2,607,000,000 (US$400 per capita). **Public debt** (external, outstanding; 2007): US$1,655,000,000. **Selected balance of payments data.** Receipts from (US$'000,000): tourism (2006) 21; remittances (2008) 229; foreign direct investment (2005–07 avg.) 74; official development assistance (2007) 121. Disbursements for (US$'000,000): tourism (2006) 5; remittances (2008) 35.

## Foreign trade

**Imports** (2007; c.i.f.): US$787,100,000 (refined petroleum products 26.7%; food products 10.6%, of which cereals 5.2%; machinery and apparatus 9.4%; cement clinker 7.9%; medicinal and pharmaceutical products 6.2%). *Major import sources:* France 19.2%; China 15.8%; Netherlands 11.1%; US 4.2%; Belgium 3.7%. **Exports** (2007; f.o.b.): US$280,000,000 (portland cement 24.1%; cement clinker 19.6%; iron and steel 12.5%; crude fertilizer 11.2%; food products 9.5%; cotton 8.9%). *Major export destinations:* Niger 12.7%; Benin 10.9%; India 9.8%; Burkina Faso 9.8%; Mali 7.1%.

## Transport and communications

**Transport.** *Railroads* (2006): route length 568 km; passenger-km, none; metric ton-km cargo (2001) 440,000,000. *Roads* (2001): total length 7,500 km (paved 24%). *Vehicles* (2007): passenger cars 10,611; trucks and buses 2,412. **Communications,** in total units (units per 1,000 persons). Telephone landlines (2008): 141,000

(24); cellular telephone subscribers (2008): 1,547,000 (264); personal computers (2007): 171,000 (30); total Internet users (2008): 350,000 (60); broadband Internet subscribers (2008): 1,900 (0.3).

## Education and health

**Educational attainment** (1998). Percentage of population ages 25 and over having: no formal education/unknown 57.2%; primary education 24.5%; secondary and higher 18.3%. **Literacy** (2007): total population ages 15 and over literate 65.8%; males literate 79.1%; females literate 52.8%. **Health:** physicians (2004) 225 (1 per 23,364 persons); hospital beds (2005) 4,862 (1 per 1,111 persons); infant mortality rate per 1,000 live births (2008) 58.2; undernourished population (2002–04) 1,200,000 (24% of total population based on the consumption of a minimum daily requirement of 1,830 calories).

## Military

**Total active duty personnel** (November 2008): 8,550 (army 94.7%, navy 2.3%, air force 3.0%). **Military expenditure as percentage of GDP** (2007): 1.6%; per capita expenditure US$7.

## Background

Until 1884 what is now Togo was an intermediate zone between the black African military states of Asante and Dahomey, and its various ethnic groups lived in general isolation from each other. In 1884 it became part of the Togoland German protectorate, which was occupied by British and French forces in 1914. In 1922 the League of Nations assigned eastern Togoland to France and the western portion to Britain. In 1946 the British and French governments placed the territories under UN trusteeship. Ten years later British Togoland was incorporated into the Gold Coast, and French Togoland became an autonomous republic within the French Union. Togo gained independence in 1960. It suspended its constitution in 1967–80. A multiparty constitution was approved in 1992, but the political situation remained unstable.

## Recent Developments

In late February 2011, ceremonies marked the agreement to construct two joint border posts between Togo and the neighboring countries of Ghana to the west and Benin to the east. The project was sponsored jointly by the EU and the Economic and Monetary Union of West Africa and was designed to facilitate inter-African trade, leading eventually to a free-trade zone. The Truth, Justice, and Reconciliation Commission, investigating the political violence that gripped Togo between 1958 and 2005, began hearings in September. More than 20,000 depositions had been taken by the commission.

**Internet resource:** <www.togo-tourisme.com>.

# Tonga

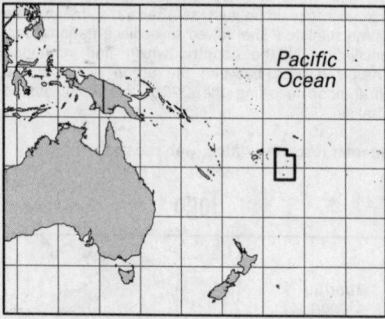

**Official name:** Fakatu'i 'o Tonga (Tongan); Kingdom of Tonga (English). **Form of government:** hereditary constitutional monarchy with one legislative house (Legislative Assembly [28]). **Head of state:** King Tupou VI (from 2012). **Head of government:** Prime Minister Tu'ivakano (from 2010). **Capital:** Nuku'alofa. **Official languages:** Tongan; English. **Official religion:** none. **Monetary unit:** 1 pa'anga (T$) = 100 seniti; valuation (2 Jul 2012) US$1 = T$1.73.

## Demography

**Area:** 289 sq mi, 748 sq km. **Population** (2011): 104,000. **Density** (2011; based on land area): persons per sq mi 359.0, persons per sq km 138.7. **Urban** (2006): 23.2%. **Sex distribution** (2006): male 50.76%; female 49.24%. **Age breakdown** (2006): under 15, 38.2%; 15–29, 26.3%; 30–44, 17.2%; 45–59, 10.1%; 60–74, 6.1%; 75 and over, 2.1%. **Ethnic composition** (2006): Tongan 96.6%; Tongan/other 1.6%; white 0.6%; Chinese 0.4%; other 0.8%. **Religious affiliation** (2006): Protestant 64.9%, of which Methodist-related denominations 55.9%; Mormon 16.8%; Roman Catholic 15.6%; Baha'i 0.7%; unknown 1.4%; other 0.6%. **Major towns** (2006): Nuku'alofa 23,658 (Greater Nuku'alofa 34,311); Neiafu 4,123; Haveloloto 3,405. **Location:** Oceania, archipelago in the South Pacific Ocean between Hawaii (US) and New Zealand.

## Vital statistics

**Birth rate** per 1,000 population (2008): 25.3 (world avg. 20.3). **Death rate** per 1,000 population (2008): 5.7 (world avg. 8.5). **Total fertility rate** (avg. births per childbearing woman; 2008): 3.76. **Life expectancy** at birth (2008): male 72.4 years; female 74.4 years.

## National economy

**Budget** (2005–06). *Revenue:* T$172,446,000 (tax revenue 72.9%; grants 15.1%; nontax revenue 12.0%). *Expenditures:* T$166,031,000 (current expenditures 93.0%; development expenditures 7.0%). **Public debt** (external, outstanding; 2007): US$89,600,000. **Gross national income** (2008):

---

*1 metric ton = about 1.1 short tons; 1 kilometer = 0.6 mi (statute); 1 metric ton-km cargo = about 0.68 short ton-mi cargo; c.i.f.: cost, insurance, and freight; f.o.b.: free on board*

US$265,000,000 (US$2,560 per capita). **Production** (metric tons except as noted). *Agriculture and fishing* (2007): coconuts 58,500, pumpkins, squash, and gourds 21,000, cassava 9,700, yams 4,700, plantains 3,300, vanilla 150; livestock (number of live animals) 81,200 pigs, 12,600 goats, 11,500 horses; fisheries production 2,549 (from aquaculture, negligible); aquatic plants production 107 (from aquaculture, negligible). *Mining and quarrying:* coral and sand for local use. *Manufacturing* (value of production in T$'000; 2005): food products and beverages 19,722; bricks, cement, and ceramics 4,109; chemical products 2,044. *Energy production (consumption):* electricity (kW-hr; 2008) 55,000,000 (47,000,000); petroleum products (metric tons; 2006) none (56,000). **Population economically active** (2003): total 36,450; activity rate 34.1% (participation rates: ages 15–64 (1996) 60.4%; female 41.9%; unemployed 5.2%). **Selected balance of payments data.** Receipts from (US$'000,000): tourism (2007) 15; remittances (2008) 100; foreign direct investment (2005–07 avg.) 17; official development assistance (2007) 30. Disbursements for (US$'000,000): tourism (2007) 10; remittances (2008) 12.

### Foreign trade

**Imports** (2006–07; c.i.f.): T$245,200,000 (food products and beverages 31.4%; refined petroleum products 29.5%; machinery and transportation equipment 14.2%). *Major import sources:* New Zealand 33.5%; Fiji 27.3%; Australia 13.8%; US 10.3%. **Exports** (2006–07; f.o.b.): T$20,900,000 (fish 40.2%; squash 26.8%; root crops 13.9%; kava 6.7%). *Major export destinations:* Japan 35.2%; New Zealand 20.2%; US 12.2%; Australia 6.1%.

### Transport and communications

**Transport.** *Railroads:* none. *Roads* (2000): total length 680 km (paved 27%). *Vehicles* (2004): passenger cars 7,705; trucks and buses 5,297. *Air transport* (2002): passenger-km 14,000,000; metric ton-km cargo 1,000,000. **Communications**, in total units (units per 1,000 persons). Telephone landlines (2008): 26,000 (247); cellular telephone subscribers (2008): 51,000 (487); personal computers (2005): 5,000 (50); total Internet users (2008): 8,400 (81); broadband Internet subscribers (2008): 700 (7).

### Education and health

**Educational attainment** (2006). Percentage of population ages 25 and over having: no formal schooling/unknown 1.8%; primary education 29.5%; lower secondary 46.7%; upper secondary 11.0%; higher 11.0%, of which university 3.6%. **Literacy** (2007): percentage of population ages 15 and over literate, virtually 100%. **Health** (2004): physicians 41 (1 per 2,447 persons); hospital beds 296 (1 per 332 persons); infant mortality rate per 1,000 live births (2006) 20.0.

### Military

**Total active duty personnel** (October 2007): 450-member force includes air and coast guard elements.

Tonga has defense cooperation agreements with both Australia and New Zealand. **Military expenditure as percentage of GDP** (2004): 1.0%; per capita expenditure US$23.

## Background

Tonga was inhabited at least 3,000 years ago by people of the Lapita culture. The Tongans developed a stratified social system headed by a paramount ruler whose dominion by the 13th century extended as far as the Hawaiian Islands. The Dutch visited the islands in the 17th century; in 1773 Capt. James Cook arrived and named the archipelago the Friendly Islands. The modern kingdom was established during the reign (1845–93) of King George Tupou I. It became a British protectorate in 1900. This was dissolved in 1970 when Tonga, the only ancient kingdom surviving from the pre-European period in Polynesia, achieved complete independence within the Commonwealth. King George Tupou V ceded much of the monarchy's formerly absolute power in 2008 and agreed to make most governmental decisions in consultation with the prime minister.

## Recent Developments

Relations with Fiji became strained in May 2011 when the Tongan navy assisted Lieut. Col. Ratu Tevita Ului lakeba Mara, a senior Fijian soldier and a critic of the Fijian military government, as he fled Fiji by sea. Tonga denied Fiji's extradition petitions and provided Mara with a passport, which allowed him to travel through the region.

**Internet resource:** <www.pmo.gov.to>.

# Trinidad and Tobago

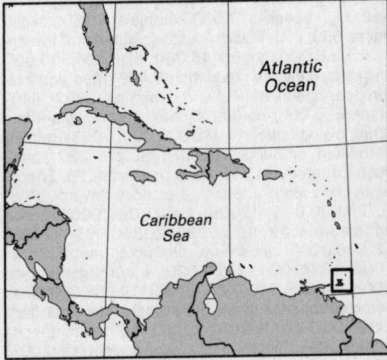

**Official name:** Republic of Trinidad and Tobago. **Form of government:** multiparty republic with two legislative houses (Senate [31]; House of Representatives [42]). **Head of state:** President George Maxwell Richards (from 2003). **Head of government:** Prime Minister Kamla Persad-Bissessar (from 2010). **Capital:** Port of Spain. **Official language:** English. **Official religion:** none. **Monetary unit:** 1 Trinidad and Tobago dollar (TT$) = 100 cents; valuation (2 Jul 2012) US$1 = TT$6.42.

## Demography

**Area:** 1,990 sq mi, 5,155 sq km. **Population** (2011): 1,325,000. **Density** (2011): persons per sq mi 665.8, persons per sq km 257.0. **Urban** (2010): 13.9%. **Sex distribution** (2007): male 50.59%; female 49.41%. **Age breakdown** (2007): under 15, 20.1%; 15–29, 28.3%; 30–44, 21.8%; 45–59, 18.7%; 60–74, 8.4%; 75–84, 2.2%; 85 and over, 0.5%. **Ethnic composition** (2000): black 39.2%; East Indian 38.6%; mixed 16.3%; Chinese 1.6%; white 1.0%; other 3.3%. **Religious affiliation** (2005): Roman Catholic 29%; Hindu 24%; Protestant 19%; independent and other Christian 7%; Muslim 7%; nonreligious 2%; other 12%. **Major towns** (2006): Port of Spain 49,800 (greater Port of Spain [2004] 264,000); Chaguanas 73,100; San Juan 57,100; San Fernando 56,600; Arima 35,600. **Location:** islands northeast of Venezuela, between the North Atlantic Ocean and the Caribbean Sea.

## Vital statistics

**Birth rate** per 1,000 population (2008): 14.1 (world avg. 20.3). **Death rate** per 1,000 population (2008): 7.7 (world avg. 8.5). **Total fertility rate** (avg. births per childbearing woman; 2007): 1.73. **Life expectancy** at birth (2007): male 67.6 years; female 73.5 years.

## National economy

**Budget** (2008). *Revenue:* TT$55,584,400,000 (taxes on petroleum and natural gas corporations 47.5%; nonoil corporate taxes 12.1%; VAT 11.9%; income tax 7.5%; nontax revenue 4.8%; import duties 4.3%). *Expenditures:* TT$45,767,000,000 (current expenditures 78.0%; development expenditures and net lending 22.0%). **Production** (metric tons except as noted). *Agriculture and fishing* (2007): sugarcane 358,000, bananas 7,000, oranges 5,250, cacao beans 639, coffee 250; livestock (number of live animals) 60,000 goats, 45,000 pigs, 28,500,000 chickens; fisheries production 8,406 (from aquaculture, negligible). *Mining and quarrying* (2007): limestone 850,000; natural asphalt 16,200. *Manufacturing* (value added in US$'000,000; 2003): refined petroleum products and natural gas 732; base chemical products 515; food products 129. *Energy production (consumption):* electricity (kW-hr; 2008) 7,760,000,000 ([2006] 6,901,000,000); crude petroleum (barrels; 2008) 41,800,000 ([2006] 56,500,000); petroleum products (metric tons; 2006) 8,093,000 (1,209,000); natural gas (cu m; 2008) 41,839,000,000 ([2006] 14,688,000,000). **Selected balance of payments data.** Receipts from (US$'000,000): tourism (2007) 463; remittances (2008) 109; official development assistance (2007) 18; foreign direct investment (FDI; 2005–07 avg.) 921. Disbursements for (US$'000,000): tourism (2007) 94; FDI (2005–07 avg.) 330. **Gross national income** (2008): US$22,123,000,000 (US$16,540 per capita). **Population economically active** (2008): total 626,600; activity rate of total population 48% (participation rates: ages 15–64, 70.2%; female 41.5%; unemployed 4.6%). **Public debt** (external, outstanding; March 2009): US$1,494,000,000.

## Foreign trade

**Imports** (2007; c.i.f.): US$7,663,000,000 (crude petroleum 31.0%; nonelectrical machinery and equipment 11.4%; base and fabricated metals 8.6%; food products 7.1%; iron ore agglomerates 5.8%; motor vehicles 5.5%). *Major import sources:* US 25.1%; Brazil 10.6%; Colombia 8.8%; Gabon 6.8%; Republic of the Congo 5.7%. **Exports** (2007; f.o.b.): US$13,396,000,000 (liquefied natural gas 30.8%; refined petroleum products 16.2%; crude petroleum 12.8%; ammonia 8.9%; methanol 7.2%). *Major export destinations:* US 57.7%; Jamaica 4.6%; Spain 4.0%; Dominican Republic 2.6%; Germany 2.2%.

## Transport and communications

**Transport.** *Railroads:* none. *Roads* (2000): total length 8,320 km (paved 51%). *Vehicles* (2005): passenger cars 320,000; trucks and buses 71,000. *Air transport* (2008; Caribbean Airlines only): passenger-km 2,285,000,000; metric ton-km cargo 19,696,000. **Communications,** in total units (units per 1,000 persons). Telephone landlines (2008): 307,000 (236); cellular telephone subscribers (2008): 1,505,000 (1,155); personal computers (2007): 172,000 (132); total Internet users (2008): 227,000 (174); broadband Internet subscribers (2007): 36,000 (27).

## Education and health

**Educational attainment** (2000). Percentage of population ages 15 and over having: no formal schooling/unknown 8.0%; primary education 35.4%; secondary 52.0%; university 4.6%. **Literacy** (2002): total population ages 15 and over literate 98.5%; males literate 99.0%; females literate 97.9%. **Health** (2008): physicians 1,735 (1 per 751 persons); hospital beds 3,499 (1 per 372 persons); infant mortality rate per 1,000 live births (2007) 32.2; undernourished population (2002–04) 130,000 (10% of total population based on the consumption of a minimum daily requirement of 1,950 calories).

## Military

**Total active duty personnel** (November 2008): 4,063 (army 73.8%, coast guard 26.2%). **Military expenditure as percentage of GNI** (2007): 0.3%; per capita expenditure US$42.

## Background

When Christopher Columbus visited Trinidad in 1498, it was inhabited by the Arawak Indians; Caribs inhabited Tobago. The islands were settled by the Spanish in the 16th century. In the 17th and 18th centuries African slaves were imported for plantation labor to replace the original Indian population, which had been worked to death by the Spanish. Trinidad was surrendered to the British in 1797. The British attempted to settle Tobago in 1721, but the French captured the island in 1781 and transformed it into a sugar-producing colony; the British acquired it in 1802. After slavery ended

---

*1 metric ton = about 1.1 short tons;    1 kilometer = 0.6 mi (statute);    1 metric ton-km cargo = about 0.68 short ton-mi cargo;    c.i.f.: cost, insurance, and freight;    f.o.b.: free on board*

in the islands in 1834–38, immigrants from India were brought in to work the plantations. The islands of Trinidad and Tobago were administratively combined in 1889. Granted limited self-government in 1925, the islands became an independent state within the Commonwealth in 1962 and a republic in 1976. Political unrest was followed in 1990 by an attempted Muslim fundamentalist coup against the government. Since the beginning of the 21st century, Trinidad and Tobago has continued its rapid pace of industrial development, which included building liquefied natural gas plants and steel smelters.

## Recent Developments

Trinidad and Tobago's economy continued to benefit significantly in 2011 from the country's exploitation of offshore natural gas deposits. In order to search for additional offshore gas reserves in a previously unexplored region, the government in July awarded three deepwater blocks in the Atlantic Ocean off the east coast of the country.

Internet resource: <www.cso.gov.tt>.

# Tunisia

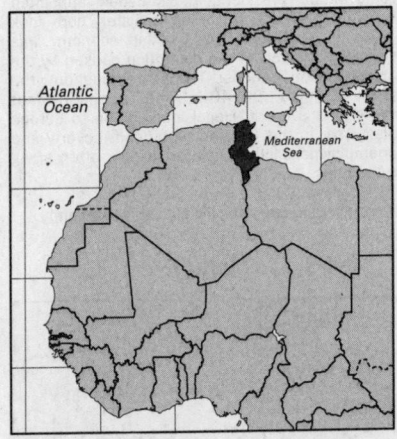

**Official name:** Al-Jumhuriyyah al-Tunisiyyah (Tunisian Republic). **Form of government:** interim regime with one interim legislative house (Constituent Assembly [217]). **Head of state:** President Moncef Marzouki (from 2011). **Head of government:** Prime Minister Hamadi Jebali (from 2011). **Capital:** Tunis. **Official language:** Arabic. **Official religion:** Islam. **Monetary unit:** 1 dinar (TND) = 1,000 millimes; valuation (2 Jul 2012) US$1 = TND 1.59.

## Demography

**Area:** 63,170 sq mi, 163,610 sq km. **Population** (2011): 10,594,000. **Density** (2011): persons per sq mi 167.7, persons per sq km 64.8. **Urban** (2009): 66.9%. **Sex distribution** (2008): male 50.30%; female 49.70%. **Age breakdown** (2005): under 15, 25.9%; 15–29, 30.1%; 30–44, 22.1%; 45–59,

13.2%; 60–74, 6.6%; 75–84, 1.8%; 85 and over, 0.3%. **Ethnic composition** (2000): Tunisian Arab 67.2%; Bedouin Arab 26.6%; Algerian Arab 2.4%; Amazigh (Berber) 1.4%; other 2.4%. **Religious affiliation** (2005): Muslim 99%, of which Sunni 97%; other 1%. **Major cities** (2004): Tunis (2007) 745,000; Safaqis 265,131; Al-Arianah 240,749; Susah 173,047; Ettadhamen 118,487. **Location:** northern Africa, bordering the Mediterranean Sea, Libya, and Algeria.

## Vital statistics

**Birth rate** per 1,000 population (2008–09): 15.3 (world avg. 20.3). **Death rate** per 1,000 population (2008–09): 4.3 (world avg. 8.5). **Total fertility rate** (avg. births per childbearing woman; 2007): 2.03. **Life expectancy** at birth (2007): male 72.4 years; female 76.3 years.

## National economy

**Budget** (2007). *Revenue:* TND 13,880,700,000 (tax revenue 68.6%, of which VAT 19.2%, income tax 9.8%; grants and loans 17.5%; nontax revenue 13.9%). *Expenditures:* TND 15,089,-000,000 (social services 40.9%; debt service 26.0%; economic services 17.4%). **Production** (metric tons except as noted). *Agriculture and fishing* (2008): tomatoes 1,200,000, olives 1,000,000, wheat 918,800, chilies and peppers 291,000, dates 127,000, almonds (2007) 58,000; livestock (live animals; 2007) 7,618,350 sheep, 1,550,650 goats, 710,130 cattle, 230,000 camels; fisheries production 92,982 (from aquaculture [2007] 3%). *Mining and quarrying* (2008–09): phosphate rock 8,017,200; iron ore 178,900. *Manufacturing* (value added in TND '000,000; 2008): crude petroleum, refined petroleum products, and natural gas 4,033; electrical machinery and equipment 2,144; textiles, leather, and wearing apparel 2,133. *Energy production (consumption):* electricity (kW-hr; 2008–09) 13,854,200,000 (11,861,200,000); crude petroleum (barrels; 2008–09) 31,975,500 (12,739,100); petroleum products (metric tons; 2008–09) 1,710,800 (3,336,900); natural gas (cu m; 2008–09) 2,789,000,000 (4,256,900,000). **Population economically active** (2008): total 3,677,700; activity rate of total population 36.2% (participation rates: ages 15 and over [2007] 46.8%; female [2007] 25.3%; unemployed 14.2%). **Gross national income** (2008): US$33,998,000,000 (US$3,290 per capita). **Public debt** (external, outstanding; June 2009): US$14,673,200,000. **Selected balance of payments data.** Receipts from (US$'000,000): tourism (2008) 2,658; remittances (2008) 1,870; foreign direct investment (FDI; 2005–07 avg.) 1,904; official development assistance (2007) 310. Disbursements for (US$'000,000): tourism (2007) 437; remittances (2008) 15; FDI (2005–07 avg.) 22.

## Foreign trade

**Imports** (2008; c.i.f.): TND 30,241,200,000 (mineral fuels 16.2%, of which refined petroleum products 10.2%; textiles and wearing apparel 13.5%, of which fabric 7.0%; food products 11.0%; chemical products 8.2%; base metals 6.8%; transportation equipment 6.7%). *Major import sources:* France 18.5%; Italy 17.2%; Germany 7.0%; Libya 4.4%; Spain 3.9%. **Exports** (2008; f.o.b.): TND 23,673,000,000 (textiles and wearing apparel 25.8%, of which clothing 19.3%; mineral fuels 17.2%, of which crude petroleum 13.6%, refined petroleum products 3.6%; electrical machinery and equipment 16.3%; phosphate products [mostly fertilizers] 12.3%; food products 9.1%). *Major export destinations:* France 28.5%; Italy 20.6%; Germany 6.9%; Spain 4.9%; UK 4.6%.

## Transport and communications

**Transport.** *Railroads* (2008–09): route length (2008) 2,165 km; passenger-km 1,509,700,000; metric ton-km cargo 1,854,200,000. *Roads* (2004): total length 19,232 km (paved 66%). *Vehicles* (2004): passenger cars 825,990; trucks and buses 119,064. *Air transport* (2008): passenger-km 3,357,000,000; metric ton-km cargo 15,380,000. **Communications**, in total units (units per 1,000 persons): Telephone landlines (2008): 1,239,000 (122); cellular telephone subscribers (2008): 8,602,000 (846); personal computers (2008): 997,000 (98); total Internet users (2008): 2,800,000 (275); broadband Internet subscribers (2008): 227,000 (22).

## Education and health

**Educational attainment** (2005). Percentage of population ages 10 and over having: no formal schooling 22.0%; primary education 36.5%; secondary 33.1%; higher 8.4%. **Literacy** (2007): total population ages 10 and over literate 77.9%; males literate 87.0%; females literate 68.7%. **Health** (2008): physicians (2007) 10,554 (1 per 969 persons); hospital beds 18,851 (1 per 539 persons); infant mortality rate per 1,000 live births 19.3; undernourished population (2002–04) less than 2.5% of total population.

## Military

**Total active duty personnel** (November 2008): 35,800 (army 75.4%, navy 13.4%, air force 11.2%). **Military expenditure as percentage of GDP** (2007): 1.3%; per capita expenditure US$47.

## Background

From the 12th century BC the Phoenicians had a series of trading posts on the northern African coast. By the 6th century BC, the Carthaginian kingdom encompassed most of present-day Tunisia. The Romans ruled from 146 BC until the Muslim Arab invasions in the mid-7th century AD. The area was fought over, won, and lost by many, including the Abbasids, the Almohads, the Spanish, and the Ottoman Turks, who finally conquered it in 1574 and held it until the late 19th century. For a time it maintained autonomy as the French, the British, and the Italians contended for the region. In 1881 Tunisia became a French protectorate. In World War II, US and British forces captured it (1943) to end a brief German occupation. In 1956 France granted it full independence; Habib Bourguiba as-

sumed power and remained in power until he was forced from office in 1987. His successor, Zine al-Abidine Ben Ali, continued with a similar authoritarian-style rule until 2011, when he stepped down amid an unprecedented level of unrest in the country.

## Recent Developments

The self-immolation of Mohamed Bouazizi in December 2010 ushered in a series of demonstrations throughout Tunisia that on 14 Jan 2011 led to the hurried departure of Pres. Zine al-Abidine Ben Ali from power. Accompanied by his immediate family, he fled into exile in Saudi Arabia. At the end of February, veteran politician Beji Caid Sebsi formed a transitional government, which was able to plan for elections in October to form a constituent assembly that would elect an interim president and draw up a new constitution. In 2011 many new and previously banned political parties emerged, eventually totaling 103 separate movements. Constituent Assembly elections were held in October to determine the composition of the 217-member body. The well-organized Nahdah Party won 90 seats with more than 40% of the vote. The Constituent Assembly began holding meetings in November. It elected Moncef Marzouki interim president, and Marzouki appointed Hamadi Jebali interim prime minister; both took office in December. The Tunisian economy was seriously affected by the disruption caused by the mass demonstrations. Tourism throughout the year declined 30–40%, and unemployment soared. As a result, illegal immigration to Europe also rose. In the Tunisian hinterland, poverty and unemployment led to violent clashes, often along tribal lines.

**Internet resource:** <www.ins.nat.tn/indexen.php>.

# Turkey

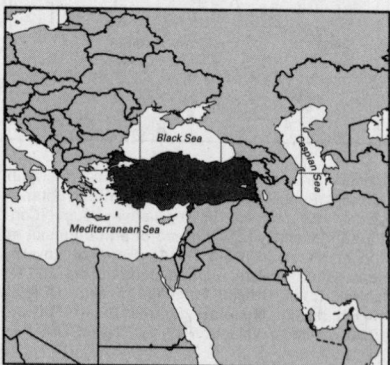

**Official name:** Turkiye Cumhuriyeti (Republic of Turkey). **Form of government:** multiparty republic with one legislative house (Grand National Assembly of Turkey [550]). **Head of state:** President Abdullah Gul (from 2007). **Head of government:** Prime Minister

---

*1 metric ton = about 1.1 short tons;   1 kilometer = 0.6 mi (statute);   1 metric ton-km cargo = about 0.68 short ton-mi cargo;   c.i.f.: cost, insurance, and freight;   f.o.b.: free on board*

Recep Tayyip Erdogan (from 2003). **Capital:** Ankara. **Official language:** Turkish. **Official religion:** none. **Monetary unit:** 1 Turkish lira (TL) = 100 kurus; valuation (2 Jul 2012) US$1 = TL 1.81 (the New Turkish lira [YTL] was removed from circulation on 1 Jan 2010, to be replaced by the Turkish lira [TL]).

## Demography

**Area:** 303,224 sq mi, 785,347 sq km. **Population** (2011): 74,306,000. **Density** (2011): persons per sq mi 245.1, persons per sq km 94.6. **Urban** (2009): 69.2%. **Sex distribution** (2008): male 50.20%; female 49.80%. **Age breakdown** (2008): under 15, 26.3%; 15–29, 26.5%; 30–44, 22.2%; 45–59, 15.1%; 60–74, 7.2%; 75–84, 2.4%; 85 and over, 0.3%. **Ethnic composition** (2000): Turk 65.1%; Kurd 18.9%; Crimean Tatar 7.2%; Arab 1.8%; Azerbaijani 1.0%; Yoruk 1.0%; other 5.0%. **Religious affiliation** (2005): Muslim 97.5%, of which Sunni 82.5%, Shiʿi (mostly nonorthodox Alevi) 15.0%; nonreligious 2.0%; other (mostly Christian) 0.5%. **Major cities** (2007): Istanbul 10,757,327; Ankara 3,763,591; Izmir 2,606,294; Bursa 1,431,172; Adana 1,366,027. **Location:** southwestern Asia and southeastern Europe, bordering the Black Sea, Georgia, Armenia, Azerbaijan, Iran, Iraq, Syria, the Mediterranean Sea, Greece, and Bulgaria.

## Vital statistics

**Birth rate** per 1,000 population (2008): 17.9 (world avg. 20.3). **Death rate** per 1,000 population (2008): 6.4 (world avg. 8.5). **Total fertility rate** (avg. births per childbearing woman; 2008): 2.14. **Life expectancy** at birth (2008): male 71.4 years; female 75.8 years.

## National economy

**Budget** (2007). *Revenue:* YTL 218,858,000,000 (tax revenue 72.1%, of which taxes on goods and services 42.2%, income tax 16.2%; nontax revenue and grants 27.9%). *Expenditures:* YTL 206,965,000,000 (public debt transactions 24.1%; other 75.9%). **Production** (in '000 metric tons except as noted). *Agriculture and fishing* (2008): wheat 17,782, sugar beets 15,488, tomatoes 10,985, barley 5,923, corn (maize) 4,274, potatoes 4,225, grapes 3,918, apples 2,504, seed cotton 1,820, olives 1,464, sunflower seeds 992, hazelnuts 801, chickpeas 518, cherries 338, walnuts 171, pistachios 120, tobacco 100; livestock (number of live animals) 23,974,600 sheep, 11,036,753 cattle, (2007) 191,066 angora goats, 1,057 camels; fisheries production (2007) 772 (from aquaculture 18%). *Mining and quarrying* (2007): magnesite 2,100; refined borates 1,093; chromite 466; copper ore (metal content) 49; marble 2,802,000 cu m; silver 198,000 kg. *Manufacturing* (value added in US$'000,000; 2005): food products 8,800; telecommunications equipment, electronics 7,450; chemical products 7,400; base metals 7,000; motor vehicles and parts 6,500; textiles 6,100. *Energy production (consumption):* electricity (kW-hr; 2008) 198,600,000,000 ([2006] 174,636,000,000); coal (metric tons; 2008) 3,340,000 ([2006] 22,800,000); lignite (metric tons; 2008) 86,100,000 ([2006] 60,800,000); crude petroleum (barrels; 2008) 15,600,000 ([2006] 194,100,000); petroleum products (metric tons; 2006) 21,563,000

(24,383,000); natural gas (cu m; 2007) 906,000,000 (36,586,000,000). **Population economically active** (2006): total 24,775,000; activity rate of total population 34.2% (participation rates: ages 15–64, 51.1%; female 26.1%; unemployed [July 2008–June 2009] 13.1%). **Gross national income** (2008): US$690,706,000,000 (US$9,340 per capita). **Public debt** (external, outstanding; December 2008): US$74,917,000,000. **Selected balance of payments data.** Receipts from (US$'000,000): tourism (2007) 18,487; remittances (2008) 1,360; foreign direct investment (FDI; 2005–07 avg.) 17,350; official development assistance (2007) 797. Disbursements for (US$'000,000): tourism (2007) 3,260; remittances (2008) 111; FDI (2005–07 avg.) 1,365.

## Foreign trade

**Imports** (2007; c.i.f.): US$170,057,000,000 (machinery and apparatus 21.1%; mineral fuels 20.6%; base and fabricated metals 15.2%; transportation equipment 8.5%). *Major import sources:* Russia 13.8%; Germany 10.3%; China 7.8%; Italy 5.9%; US 4.8%. **Exports** (2007; f.o.b.): US$107,213,000,000 (textiles and wearing apparel 21.4%; transportation equipment 17.0%; machinery and apparatus 15.1%; base and fabricated metals 14.6%; vegetables, fruits, and nuts 4.1%). *Major export destinations:* Germany 11.2%; UK 8.1%; Italy 7.0%; France 5.6%; Russia 4.4%.

## Transport and communications

**Transport.** *Railroads* (2007): length 8,697 km; passenger-km 5,553,000; metric ton-km cargo 9,921,000,000. *Roads* (2006): total length 427,099 km (paved [2004] 45%). *Vehicles* (2007): passenger cars 6,472,156; trucks and buses 3,181,390. *Air transport* (2008: Atlasjet, Turkish, Pegasus, and Onur airlines only): passenger-km 51,183,000,000; metric ton-km cargo 533,-501,000. **Communications,** in total units (units per 1,000 persons). Telephone landlines (2008): 17,502,000 (246); cellular telephone subscribers (2008): 65,824,000 (926); personal computers (2007): 4,207,000 (60); total Internet users (2008): 24,483,000 (345); broadband Internet subscribers (2008): 5,750,000 (81).

## Education and health

**Educational attainment** (2007). Percentage of population ages 25–64 having: no formal schooling through primary education 61%; lower secondary 10%; upper secondary 18%; university 11%. **Literacy** (2006): total population ages 15 and over literate 88.1%; males literate 96.0%; females literate 80.4%. **Health:** physicians (2006) 114,583 (1 per 604 persons); hospital beds (2007) 184,983 (1 per 379 persons); infant mortality rate per 1,000 live births (2008) 16.0; undernourished population (2002–04) 2,100,000 (3% of total population based on the consumption of a minimum daily requirement of 1,970 calories).

## Military

**Total active duty personnel** (November 2008): 510,600 (army 78.7%, navy 9.5%, air force 11.8%);

Turkish troops in the Turkish Republic of Northern Cyprus (November 2008): 36,000; US troops in Turkey (November 2008): 1,570. **Military expenditure as percentage of GDP** (2007): 2.1%; per capita expenditure US$195.

## Background

Turkey's early history corresponds to that of Asia Minor, the Byzantine Empire, and the Ottoman Empire. Byzantine rule emerged when Constantine the Great made Constantinople (now Istanbul) his capital. The Ottoman Empire, begun in the 12th century, dominated for more than 600 years; it ended in 1918 after the Young Turk revolt. Under the leadership of Mustafa Kemal Ataturk, a republic was proclaimed in 1923, and the caliphate was abolished in 1924. Turkey remained neutral throughout most of World War II, siding with the Allies in 1945. It has since alternated between civil and military governments and has had several conflicts with Greece over Cyprus. The early 21st century saw political and civic turmoil between fundamentalist Muslims and secularists and ongoing violent conflict with Kurdish separatists.

## Recent Developments

Turkey downgraded its diplomatic relations and ended defense cooperation with Israel in 2011, following the killing of nine Turkish activists by Israeli commandos enforcing the blockade of Gaza the previous year. Speaking at the UN, Prime Minister Recep Tayyip Erdogan advocated the immediate recognition of Palestinian statehood. Turkey's relationship with France deteriorated after the introduction of a French law that criminalized the denial of recognized genocide, including the killing of Armenians by Turks in 1915. Turkey protested the law, which passed in January 2012, by recalling its ambassador and freezing all economic and military ties with France. In December 2011, Erdogan accused France of having committed genocide during Algeria's struggle for independence, claiming that the French killed up to 15% of the Algerian population. The militants of the Kurdistan Workers' Party (PKK), listed as a terrorist organization in the EU and the US, continued their attacks against Turkey as the government failed to deal with their demands for Kurdish as a language of instruction in schools and for autonomy for Kurdish-majority provinces in southeastern Turkey. In retaliation for the killing of 13 soldiers in July and of another 24 in October, the Turkish air force launched air strikes against the PKK's base in the mountains of northern Iraq.

**Internet resource:** <www.turkstat.gov.tr>.

# Turkmenistan

**Official name:** Turkmenistan. **Form of government:** unitary republic with one legislative house (Mejlis, or Assembly [125]). **Head of state and government:** President Gurbanguly Berdymukhammedov (from 2006). **Capital:** Ashgabat. **Official language:** Turkmen. **Official religion:** none. **Monetary unit:** 1 (new)

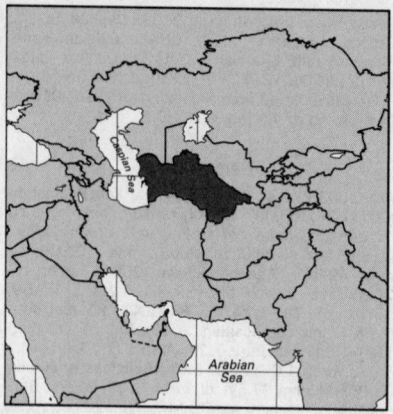

manat (TMT) = 100 tennesi; valuation (2 Jul 2012) US$1 = TMT 2.85 (the [new] manat replaced the [old] manat 1 Jan 2009, at the rate of [new] TMT 1 = [old] TMM 5,000).

## Demography

**Area:** 189,657 sq mi, 491,210 sq km. **Population** (2011): 4,998,000. **Density** (2011): persons per sq mi 26.4, persons per sq km 10.2. **Urban** (2008): 48.2%. **Sex distribution** (2005): male 49.24%; female 50.76%. **Age breakdown** (2005): under 15, 31.8%; 15–29, 30.0%; 30–44, 20.6%; 45–59, 11.4%; 60–74, 4.6%; 75–84, 1.4%; 85 and over, 0.2%. **Ethnic composition** (2000): Turkmen 79.2%; Uzbek 9.0%; Russian 3.0%; Kazakh 2.5%; Tatar 1.1%; other 5.2%. **Religious affiliation** (2000): Muslim (mostly Sunni) 87.2%; Russian Orthodox 1.7%; non-religious 9.0%; other 2.1%. **Major cities** (2004): Ashgabat (2007) 744,000; Turkmenabat 256,000; Dasoguz 210,000; Mary 159,000; Balkanabat 139,000. **Location:** central Asia, bordering Kazakhstan, Uzbekistan, Afghanistan, Iran, and the Caspian Sea.

## Vital statistics

**Birth rate** per 1,000 population (2008): 21.8 (world avg. 20.3); (1998) within marriage 96.2%. **Death rate** per 1,000 population (2008): 8.2 (world avg. 8.5). **Total fertility rate** (avg. births per childbearing woman; 2008): 2.48. **Life expectancy** at birth (2008): male 59.1 years; female 67.4 years.

## National economy

**Budget** (2006; excluding significant amounts of extra-budgetary funds). *Revenue:* TMM 22,474,-000,000,000 (tax revenue 93.8%; nontax revenue 6.2%). *Expenditures:* TMM 16,631,000,000,000 (current expenditures 94.2%; development expenditures 5.8%). **Public debt** (external, outstanding; 2007): US$648,000,000. **Production** (metric tons except as noted). *Agriculture and fishing* (2007): wheat 2,700,000, seed cotton 946,000, tomatoes 256,000; livestock (number of live animals)

---

*1 metric ton = about 1.1 short tons;    1 kilometer = 0.6 mi (statute);    1 metric ton-km cargo = about 0.68 short ton-mi cargo;    c.i.f.: cost, insurance, and freight;    f.o.b.: free on board*

15,500,000 sheep, 1,948,000 cattle; fisheries production 15,016 (from aquaculture, negligible). *Mining and quarrying* (2006): iodine 270,000, salt 215,000, gypsum 100,000. *Manufacturing* (2004): distillate fuel (gas-diesel oil) 2,511,000; residual fuel oils 1,745,000; motor spirits (gasoline) 1,265,000. *Energy production (consumption):* electricity (kW-hr; 2006) 13,650,000,000 (12,310,-000,000); crude petroleum (barrels; 2007) 65,700,000 (40,200,000); petroleum products (metric tons; 2006) 7,702,000 (4,191,000); natural gas (cu m; 2006) 62,000,000,000 (14,677,000,000). **Population economically active** (2006): total 2,181,000; activity rate of total population 44.5% (participation rates: ages 15–64, 68.5%; female 46.9%; unofficially unemployed [2004] 60%). **Gross national income** (2008): US$14,260,000,000 (US$2,840 per capita). **Selected balance of payments data.** Receipts from (US$'000,000): foreign direct investment (2005–07 avg.) 651; official development assistance (2007) 28.

## Foreign trade

**Imports** (2003; c.i.f.): US$2,450,000,000 (machinery and transportation equipment 45.9%; chemical products 11.1%; food products 5.3%). *Major import sources* (2007): UAE 15%; Turkey 11%; China 10%; Ukraine 9%; Russia 8%. **Exports** (2003; f.o.b.): US$3,720,000,000 (natural gas 49.7%; petrochemicals 18.3%; crude petroleum 8.9%; cotton fiber 3.2%; cotton yarn 2.2%). *Major export destinations* (2007): Ukraine 49%; Iran 18%; Azerbaijan 5%; Turkey 5%.

## Transport and communications

**Transport.** *Railroads* (2006): length 2,980 km; (1999) passenger-km 701,000,000; (2002) metric ton-km cargo 7,476,000,000. *Roads* (2001): total length 22,000 km (paved 82%). *Vehicles* (1995): passenger cars 220,000; trucks and buses 58,200. *Air transport* (2005; Turkmenistan Airlines only): passenger-km 1,913,000,000; metric ton-km cargo 25,997,000. **Communications**, in total units (units per 1,000 persons). Telephone landlines (2008): 478,000 (95); cellular telephone subscribers (2008): 1,135,000 (225); personal computers (2005): 348,000 (72); total Internet users (2008): 75,000 (15).

## Education and health

**Educational attainment** (2000), Percentage of population ages 25 and over having: no formal schooling/unknown 3.2%; incomplete primary to complete standard secondary education 60.1%; vocational secondary 23.5%; higher 13.2%. **Literacy** (2007): total population ages 15 and over literate, virtually 100%. **Health** (2006): physicians 12,210 (1 per 387 persons); hospital beds 20,296 (1 per 233 persons); infant mortality rate per 1,000 live births 55.2; undernourished population (2003–05) 300,000 (6% of total population based on the consumption of a minimum daily requirement of 1,880 calories).

## Military

**Total active duty personnel** (November 2008): 22,000 (army 84.1%, navy 2.3%, air force 13.6%). **Military expenditure as percentage of GDP** (2007): 1.7%; per capita expenditure US$44.

## Background

The earliest traces of human settlement in central Asia, dating back to Paleolithic times, have been found in Turkmenistan. The nomadic, tribal Turkmen probably entered the area in the 11th century AD. They were conquered by the Russians in the early 1880s, and the region became part of Russian Turkistan. It was organized as the Turkmen Soviet Socialist Republic in 1924 and became a constituent republic of the USSR in 1925. The country gained full independence from the USSR in 1991 under the name Turkmenistan. It experienced years of economic difficulty until oil and gas production was more fully developed.

## Recent Developments

Turkmenistan continued to be a difficult partner for the international community in 2011. Although officially supportive of NATO coalition activities in Afghanistan, as of late 2011, the country was still refusing involvement in land transport via the Northern Distribution Network. In late May, during a visit of Afghan Pres. Hamid Karzai to Ashgabat, cooperation agreements were signed on a wide range of issues, including transport and communications and the acceleration of construction of a Turkmen-Afghan-Pakistani-Indian gas pipeline. Despite the efforts of European diplomats, Turkmen participation in the proposed Nabucco gas pipeline remained uncertain, partly because of the unpredictable behavior of Turkmenistan's absolute ruler, Pres. Gurbanguly Berdymukhammedov. During a visit to the country in September by the Organization for Security and Co-operation in Europe (OSCE), Dunja Mijatovic, the representative on freedom of the media, appealed for the Turkmen authorities to ease restrictions on the media and permit greater Internet access.

**Internet resource:** <www.turkmenistanembassy.org>.

# Tuvalu

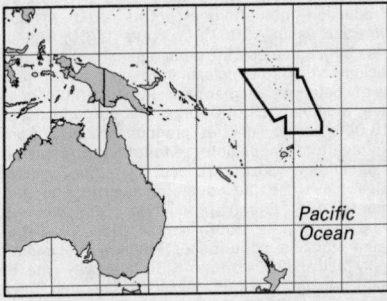

*Pacific Ocean*

**Official name:** Tuvalu. **Form of government:** constitutional monarchy with one legislative house (Parliament [15]). **Head of state:** British Queen Elizabeth II (from 1952), represented by Governor-General Iakoba Taeia Italeli (from 2010). **Head of government:** Prime Minister Willy Telavi (from 2010). **Capi-**

tal: government offices are at Vaiaku. **Official language:** none. **Official religion:** none. **Monetary units:** 1 Tuvaluan dollar ($T) = 1 Australian dollar ($A) = 100 Tuvaluan and Australian cents; valuation (2 Jul 2012) US$1 = $T 0.98.

## Demography

**Area:** 9.90 sq mi, 25.63 sq km. **Population** (2011): 11,200. **Density** (2011): persons per sq mi 1,131.3, persons per sq km 437.0. **Urban** (2010): 50.4%. **Sex distribution** (2009): male 49.73%; female 50.27%. **Age breakdown** (2007): under 15, 29.7%; 15–29, 27.9%; 30–44, 20.0%; 45–59, 14.9%; 60–74, 5.7%; 75 and over, 1.8%. **Ethnic composition** (2004–05): Tuvaluan (Polynesian) 95.1%; mixed (Tuvaluan/other) 3.4%; I-Kiribati 1.1%; other 0.4%. **Religious affiliation** (2002): Christian 97.0%, of which Church of Tuvalu (Congregational) 91.0%, Seventh-day Adventist 2.0%, Roman Catholic 1.0%; Baha'i 1.9%; other 1.1%. **Major villages** (2002): Alapi 1,024; Fakaifou 1,007; Vaiaku 516. **Location:** Oceania, group of islands in the South Pacific Ocean, east of Papua New Guinea.

## Vital statistics

**Birth rate** per 1,000 population (2008): 21.8 (world avg. 20.3); (2005) within marriage 92.7%. **Death rate** per 1,000 population (2008): 9.5 (world avg. 8.5). **Total fertility rate** (avg. births per childbearing woman; 2008): 3.70. **Life expectancy** at birth (2007): male 66.4 years; female 71.0 years.

## National economy

**Budget** (2007). *Revenue:* $A 19,126,000 (tax revenue 33.1%; nontax revenue [including remittances from phosphate miners in Nauru and seafarers on German ships, rentals of fishing resources to Japan, Taiwan, and the US, and the leasing of the country's Internet domain "tv."] 48.1%; grants 18.8%). *Expenditures:* $A23,-682,000 (current expenditures 91.6%; development expenditures 8.4%). **Public debt** (external; 2007): US$8,600,000. **Gross national income** (2008): US$31,800,000 (US$2,889 per capita). **Production** (metric tons except as noted). *Agriculture and fishing* (2007): coconuts 1,700, vegetables 540, bananas 280; other agricultural products include breadfruit, *pulaka* (taro), pandanus fruit, sweet potatoes, and pawpaws; livestock (number of live animals) 13,600 pigs, 45,000 chickens, 15,000 ducks; fisheries production 2,201 (from aquaculture, negligible). *Manufacturing* (value added in $A '000; 2002): local cigarettes 755; cottage industries (including handicrafts and garments) 158. *Energy production (consumption):* electricity (kW-hr; 2006) n.a. (4,235,100); petroleum products, none (none). **Population economically active** (2004): total 4,302; activity rate of total population 44.8% (participation rates: ages 15 and over [2002] 58.2%; female [2002] 43.4%; unemployed 16.3%). **Selected balance of payments data.** Receipts from (US$'000,000): tourism (1998) 0.2; remittances (2007) 1.5; foreign direct investment (FDI; 2005–07 avg.) 2; official development assistance (2007) 12.

## Foreign trade

**Imports** (2007; c.i.f.): $A 18,386,120 (food products [including live animals] 30.2%; mineral fuels 16.1%, of which diesel fuel 9.1%; telecommunications equipment 4.4%; wearing apparel 4.1%; base and fabricated metals 3.9%; wood products 3.4%). *Major import sources:* Australia 24.9%; Fiji 24.6%; Singapore 13.5%; New Zealand 11.3%; China 7.7%. **Exports** (2007; f.o.b.): $A 109,413 ([2005] precision instruments 18.6%; machinery and apparatus 17.4%; base and fabricated metals 15.4%; wood products 12.5%; transportation equipment 11.6%). *Major export destinations:* Fiji 93.1%; El Salvador 4.6%; New Zealand 2.2%; UK 0.1%.

## Transport and communications

**Transport.** *Railroads:* none. *Roads* (2002): total length 8 km (paved 100%). *Vehicles* (2007): passenger cars 15; trucks and buses 2. **Communications,** in total units (units per 1,000 persons). Telephone landlines (2008): 1,500 (136); cellular telephone subscribers (2008): 2,000 (182); total Internet users (2008): 4,200 (382); broadband Internet subscribers (2007): 400 (37).

## Education and health

**Educational attainment** (2004–05). Percentage of population ages 15 and over having: no formal education/unknown 8.8%; primary education 52.4%; secondary 29.8%; higher 9.0%. **Literacy** (2004): total population literate 95%. **Health:** physicians (2008) 7 (1 per 1,573 persons); hospital beds (2001) 56 (1 per 170 persons); infant mortality rate per 1,000 live births (2007) 19.5.

## Military

**Total active duty personnel:** none; Tuvalu has nonformal security arrangements with Australia and New Zealand.

## Background

The original Polynesian settlers of Tuvalu probably came mainly from Samoa or Tonga. The islands were sighted by the Spanish in the 16th century. Europeans settled there in the 19th century and intermarried with Tuvaluans. During this period Peruvian slave traders, known as "blackbirders," decimated the population. In 1856 the US claimed the four southern islands for guano mining. Missionaries from Europe arrived in 1865 and rapidly converted the islanders to Christianity. In 1892 Tuvalu joined the British Gilbert Islands, a protectorate that became the Gilbert and Ellice Islands Colony in 1916. Tuvaluans voted in 1974 for separation from the Gilberts (now Kiribati), whose people are Micronesian. Tuvalu gained independence in 1978, and in 1979 the US relinquished its claims. Elections were held in 1981, and a revised

---

*1 metric ton = about 1.1 short tons;   1 kilometer = 0.6 mi (statute);   1 metric ton-km cargo = about 0.68 short ton-mi cargo;   c.i.f.: cost, insurance, and freight;   f.o.b.: free on board*

constitution was adopted in 1986. In recent decades, the government has tried to find overseas job opportunities for its citizens. In the early 21st century, rising sea levels in the South Pacific began to degrade Tuvalu's coasts and to contaminate its freshwater aquifers, leading to fears that the islands might become uninhabitable within several decades.

### Recent Developments

A prolonged drought caused by La Niña's extended presence in the area caused not only freshwater deficiencies but also crop failures and consequent food shortages in Tuvalu in 2011. After the second driest year in 78 years, Tuvalu faced disastrous freshwater shortages and began rationing.

Internet resource: <www.timelesstuvalu.com>.

# Uganda

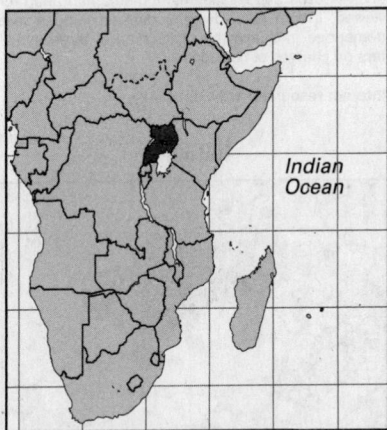

**Official name:** Republic of Uganda. **Form of government:** multiparty republic with one legislative house (Parliament [386]). **Head of state and government:** President Yoweri Museveni (from 1986), assisted by Prime Minister Amama Mbabazi (from 2011). **Capital:** Kampala. **Official languages:** English; Swahili. **Official religion:** none. **Monetary unit:** 1 Ugandan shilling (UGX) = 100 cents; valuation (2 Jul 2012) US$1 = UGX 2,475.00.

### Demography

**Area:** 93,263 sq mi, 241,551 sq km. **Population** (2011): 34,509,000. **Density** (2011; based on land area only): persons per sq mi 447.3, persons per sq km 172.7. **Urban** (2009): 14.8%. **Sex distribution** (2009): male 48.71%; female 51.29%. **Age breakdown** (2009): under 15, 50.2%; 15–29, 27.2%; 30–44, 13.9%; 45–59, 6.3%; 60–74, 2.1%; 75 and over, 0.3%. **Ethnolinguistic composition** (2002): Ganda 17.3%; Nkole 9.8%; Soga 8.6%; Kiga 7.0%; Teso 6.6%; Lango 6.2%; Acholi 4.8%; Gisu 4.7%. **Religious affiliation** (2002): Christian 85.3%, of which Roman Catholic 41.9%,

Anglican 35.9%, Pentecostal 4.6%, Seventh-day Adventist 1.5%; Muslim 12.1%; traditional beliefs 1.0%; nonreligious 0.9%; other 0.7%. **Major cities** (2009): Kampala 1,533,600; Kira 164,700; Gulu 146,600; Lira 102,200; Mbale 86,200. **Location:** eastern Africa, bordering South Sudan, Kenya, Tanzania, Rwanda, and the Democratic Republic of the Congo.

### Vital statistics

**Birth rate** per 1,000 population (2008): 48.2 (world avg. 20.3). **Death rate** per 1,000 population (2008): 12.3 (world avg. 8.5). **Total fertility rate** (avg. births per childbearing woman; 2008): 6.81. **Life expectancy** at birth (2008): male 51.3 years; female 53.4 years.

### National economy

**Budget** (2006–07). *Revenue:* UGX 3,574,000,-000,000 (tax revenue 63.3%, of which VAT and sales tax 21.7%, petroleum taxes 10.1%, income tax 6.9%; grants 25.4%; nontax revenue 11.3%). *Expenditures:* UGX 4,031,900,000,000 (current expenditures 60.6%, of which public administration 14.7%, defense 9.3%, public order 4.6%, education 3.9%, health 2.3%; capital expenditures 39.4%). **Public debt** (external, outstanding; January 2009): US$1,-835,000,000. **Production** (metric tons except as noted). *Agriculture and fishing* (2008): plantains 9,371,000, cassava 5,072,000, sweet potatoes 2,707,000, coffee 211,762, sesame 173,000, pigeon peas 90,000, cowpeas 79,000, tobacco 29,040; livestock (number of live animals) 8,523,000 goats, 7,398,000 cattle, 2,186,000 pigs; fisheries production (2007) 551,110 (from aquaculture 9%). *Mining and quarrying* (2007): cobalt 698; columbite-tantalite (ore and concentrate) 275 kg. *Manufacturing* (value added in US$'000,000; 2002): food products 109; chemical products 59; beverages 53; tobacco products 15. *Energy production (consumption):* electricity (kW-hr; 2007) 2,256,000,000 (2,068,000,000); crude petroleum (barrels; 2008) none (4,745,000); petroleum products (metric tons; 2006) none (766,000). **Gross national income** (2008): US$13,254,-000,000 (US$420 per capita). **Population economically active** (2005–06): total 10,848,000; activity rate of total population 37.2% (participation rates: ages 15 and older, 81.6%; female 51.4%; officially unemployed 1.9%). **Selected balance of payments data.** Receipts from (US$'000,000): tourism (2007) 356; remittances (2008) 489; foreign direct investment (2005–07 avg.) 383; official development assistance (2007) 1,728. Disbursements for (US$'000,000): tourism (2007) 112; remittances (2008) 281.

### Foreign trade

**Imports** (2008; c.i.f.): US$4,525,859,000 (refined petroleum products 18.5%; chemical products 14.1%; food products 11.7%, of which cereals 3.8%; electrical machinery and equipment 11.4%; nonelectrical machinery and equipment 8.5%; transportation equipment 7.8%; base metals 7.4%). *Major import sources:* UAE 11.4%; Kenya 11.3%; India 10.4%; China 8.1%; South Africa 6.7%. **Exports** (2008; f.o.b.): US$1,724,300,000 (food products and beverages 49.6%, of which coffee 23.4%, fresh fish 7.2%; base metals 6.2%; electrical machinery and equipment 5.1%; cement, bricks, and ceramics 5.0%; tobacco products 4.0%). *Major export destinations:* Sudan 14.3%; Kenya 9.5%; Switzerland 9.0%; Rwanda 7.9%; UAE 7.4%.

## Transport and communications

**Transport.** *Railroads* (2008): route length 1,244 km; metric ton-km cargo (2005) 185,559,000. *Roads* (2008; national roads only): total length 10,965 km (paved 28%). *Vehicles* (2008): passenger cars 90,856; trucks and buses 137,290. *Air transport* (2004): passenger-km 272,000,000; metric ton-km cargo 27,000,000. **Communications,** in total units (units per 1,000 persons). Telephone landlines (2008): 169,000 (5.3); cellular telephone subscribers (2008): 8,555,000 (270); personal computers (2005): 300,000 (10); total Internet users (2008): 2,500,000 (79); broadband Internet subscribers (2008): 4,800 (0.2).

## Education and health

**Educational attainment** (2005–06). Percentage of population ages 15 and over having: no formal schooling/unknown 20.0%; incomplete primary education 43.3%; complete primary 14.1%; incomplete secondary 18.1%; complete secondary (some higher) 1.1%; complete higher (including vocational) 3.4%. **Literacy** (2007): population ages 15 and over literate 73.2%; males literate 81.7%; females literate 64.8%. **Health:** physicians (2004) 2,209 (1 per 11,947 persons); hospital beds (2006) 32,617 (1 per 909 persons); infant mortality rate per 1,000 live births (2008) 66.0; undernourished population (2002–04) 4,800,000 (19% of total population based on the consumption of a minimum daily requirement of 1,770 calories).

## Military

**Total active duty personnel** (November 2008): 45,000 (army 100%); Ugandan peacekeeping troops in Somalia (November 2008): 1,700. **Military expenditure as percentage of GDP** (2007): 2.2%; per capita expenditure US$8.

## Background

By the 19th century, the region around Uganda comprised several separate kingdoms inhabited by various peoples, including Bantu- and Nilotic-speaking tribes. Arab traders reached the area in the 1840s. The native kingdom of Buganda was visited by the first European explorers in 1862. Protestant and Roman Catholic missionaries arrived in the 1870s, and the development of religious factions led to persecution and civil strife. In 1894 Buganda was formally proclaimed a British protectorate. As Uganda, it gained its independence in 1962, and in 1967 it adopted a republican constitution. The civilian government was overthrown in 1971 and replaced by a military regime under Idi Amin. His invasion of Tanzania in late 1978 resulted in the collapse of his regime. In 1985 the civilian government was again deposed by the military, which in turn was overthrown in 1986. A con-

stituent assembly enacted a new constitution in 1995.

## Recent Developments

In February 2011, Ugandan voters returned Yoweri Museveni for his fourth presidential term with a resounding 68.4% of the votes. Museveni's victory rested in part on the steady economic growth and stability achieved by the development policies of his administration. The IMF estimated that economic growth rose to 6.1% from 5.8% in 2010. Policy makers looked forward to an oil boom in 2012 to accelerate growth, raise the country to middle-income status, possibly create half a million jobs, and nearly double the annual per capita income to US$800. Unfortunately, such optimism soured in October when legislators forced a recall of Parliament to consider matters relating to the nascent oil industry. After a dramatic debate, Parliament demanded an end to secrecy relating to oil agreements and voted to freeze activities in the oil industry until a petroleum law had been passed and existing agreements had been reviewed. It also passed nonbinding resolutions that demanded inter alia the resignation of three ministers on charges of corruption.

**Internet resource:** <www.ubos.org>.

# Ukraine

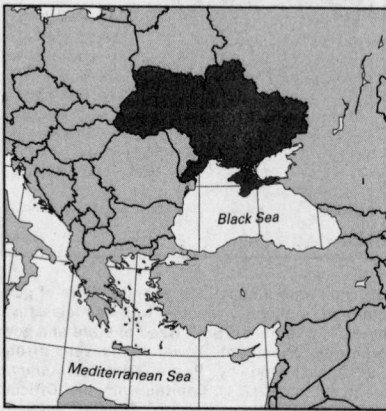

**Official name:** Ukrayina (Ukraine). **Form of government:** unitary multiparty republic with a single legislative house (Supreme Council [450]). **Head of state:** President Viktor Yanukovych (from 2010). **Head of government:** Prime Minister Mykola Azarov (from 2010). **Capital:** Kiev (Kyiv). **Official language:** Ukrainian. **Official religion:** none. **Monetary unit:** 1 hryvnya (UAH) = 100 kopiykas; valuation (2 Jul 2012) US$1 = UAH 8.08.

## Demography

**Area:** 233,062 sq mi, 603,628 sq km. **Population** (2011): 45,672,000. **Density** (2011): persons per

---

*1 metric ton = about 1.1 short tons; 1 kilometer = 0.6 mi (statute); 1 metric ton-km cargo = about 0.68 short ton-mi cargo; c.i.f.: cost, insurance, and freight; f.o.b.: free on board*

sq mi 196.0, persons per sq km 75.7. **Urban** (2011): 68.7%. **Sex distribution** (2005): male 45.97%; female 54.03%. **Age breakdown** (2006): under 15, 14.3%; 15–29, 23.0%; 30–44, 21.1%; 45–59, 21.2%; 60–74, 14.1%; 75–84, 5.5%; 85 and over, 0.8%. **Ethnic composition** (2001): Ukrainian 77.8%; Russian 17.3%; Belarusian 0.6%; Moldovan 0.5%; Crimean Tatar 0.5%; other 3.3%. **Religious affiliation** (2004): Ukrainian Orthodox, of which "Kiev patriarchy" 19%, "no particular patriarchy" 16%, "Moscow patriarchy" 9%, Ukrainian Autocephalous Orthodox 2%; Ukrainian Catholic 6%; Protestant 2%; Latin Catholic 2%; Muslim 1%; Jewish 0.5%; nonreligious/atheist/other 42.5%. **Major cities** (2008): Kiev 2,765,531; Kharkiv 1,455,964; Dnipropetrovsk 1,017,514; Odesa (Odessa) 1,008,627; Donetsk 974,598. **Location:** eastern Europe, bordering Belarus, Russia, the Black Sea, Romania, Moldova, Hungary, Slovakia, and Poland.

## Vital statistics

**Birth rate** per 1,000 population (2008): 11.1 (world avg. 20.3); within marriage 79.1%. **Death rate** per 1,000 population (2008): 16.4 (world avg. 8.6). **Total fertility rate** (avg. births per childbearing woman; 2007): 1.30. **Life expectancy** at birth (2007): male 62.5 years; female 74.2 years.

## National economy

**Budget** (2007). *Revenue:* UAH 165,942,000,000 (tax revenue 70.3%, of which VAT 35.8%, tax on profits of enterprises 20.5%, excise tax 6.3%; nontax revenue 25.4%). *Expenditures:* UAH 174,236,-000,000 (social security 16.8%; education and health 13.4%; transportation and communications 6.7%; energy and construction 4.7%; agriculture 4.6%). **Public debt** (external; April 2008): US$15,100,000,000. **Production** (metric tons except as noted). *Agriculture and fishing* (2007): potatoes 19,102,300, sugar beets 16,978,000, wheat 13,800,000, sunflower seeds 4,173,700, sour cherries 126,000; livestock (number of live animals) 8,055,000 pigs, 6,175,400 cattle, 145,600,000 chickens; fisheries production 241,349 (from aquaculture 12%). *Mining and quarrying* (2006): iron ore (2007) 77,952,000; manganese (metal content) 550,000; ilmenite concentrate 470,000. *Manufacturing* (value of sales in UAH '000,000,000; 2007): base and fabricated metals 157.5; food products, beverages, and tobacco products 110.0; coke and refined petroleum products 52.5. *Energy production (consumption):* electricity (kW-hr; 2007) 195,230,000,000 ([2006] 182,944,000,000); coal (metric tons; 2007) 58,742,000 ([2006] 68,470,000); crude petroleum (barrels; 2007) 31,700,000 ([2006] 100,960,000); petroleum products (metric tons; 2006) 13,941,000 (13,133,000); natural gas (cu m; 2007) 20,200,000,000 ([2006] 69,445,600,000). **Population economically active** (2005): total 22,280,800; activity rate of total population 47% (participation rates [2003]: ages 15–64, 65.8%; female 48.9%; unemployed [2007] 6.9%. **Gross national income** (2008): US$148,643,000,000 (US$3,210 per capita). **Selected balance of payments data.** Receipts from (US$'000,000): tourism (2007) 4,597; remittances (2008) 5,769; foreign di-

rect investment (FDI; 2005–07 avg.) 7,768; official development assistance (2007) 405. Disbursements for (US$'000,000): tourism (2007) 3,293; remittances (2008) 54.

## Foreign trade

**Imports** (2006; c.i.f.): US$45,022,000,000 (machinery and apparatus 17.7%; crude petroleum 15.2%; chemical products 12.1%; natural gas 10.6%; motor vehicles and parts 10.5%). *Major import sources:* Russia 30.6%; Germany 9.5%; Turkmenistan 7.8%; China 5.1%; Poland 4.7%. **Exports** (2006; f.o.b.): US$38,368,000,000 (iron and steel 38.5%, of which ingots 11.4%; machinery and apparatus 8.8%; crude petroleum 5.0%; cereals 3.9%; metal ore and scrap metal 3.9%). *Major export destinations:* Russia 22.5%; Italy 6.5%; Turkey 6.2%; Poland 3.5%; Germany 3.3%.

## Transport and communications

**Transport.** *Railroads* (2008): length 21,700 km; passenger-km 53,100,000,000; metric ton-km cargo 257,000,000,000. *Roads* (2008): total length 169,500 km (paved 98%). *Vehicles* (2005): passenger cars 5,538,972; trucks and buses 490,495. *Air transport* (2008): passenger-km 6,528,000,000; metric ton-km cargo 63,360,000,000. **Communications,** in total units (units per 1,000 persons). Telephone landlines (2008): 13,177,000 (287); cellular telephone subscribers (2008): 55,695,000 (1,211); total Internet users (2008): 10,354,000 (225); broadband Internet subscribers (2008): 1,600,000 (35).

## Education and health

**Educational attainment** (2001). Percentage of population ages 25 and over having: no formal schooling 0.7%; incomplete primary education 2.8%; complete primary/incomplete secondary 22.7%; complete secondary 35.9%; incomplete higher 21.7%; complete higher 16.2%. **Literacy** (2004): total population ages 15 and over literate, virtually 100%. **Health** (2006): physicians 225,000 (1 per 208 persons); hospital beds 444,000 (1 per 105 persons); infant mortality rate per 1,000 live births (2008) 9.9; undernourished population (2002–04) less than 2.5% of total population.

## Military

**Total active duty personnel** (November 2008): 129,925 (army 54.5%, air force/air defense 34.8%, navy 10.7%); reserve 1,000,000; Russian naval forces at Sevastopol (November 2008): 13,000. **Military expenditure as percentage of GDP** (2008): 1.7%; per capita expenditure US$66.

## Background

The area around Ukraine was invaded and occupied in the 1st millennium BC by the Cimmerians, Scythians, and Sarmatians and in the 1st millennium AD by the Goths, Huns, Bulgars, Avars, Khazars, and Magyars. Slavic tribes settled there after the 4th century. Kiev was the chief town of Kievan Rus. The Mongol conquest in the mid-13th century decisively ended Kievan power. Ruled by Lithuania in the 14th century and Poland in the 16th century, it fell to

Russian rule in the 18th century. The Ukrainian National Republic, established in 1917, declared its independence from Soviet Russia in 1918 but was reconquered in 1919; it was made the Ukrainian Soviet Socialist Republic of the USSR in 1922. The northwestern region was held by Poland from 1919 to 1939. Ukraine suffered a severe famine in 1932–33 under Soviet leader Joseph Stalin; over five million Ukrainians died of starvation. Overrun by Axis armies in 1941 in World War II, it was further devastated before being retaken by the Soviets in 1944. It was the site of the 1986 accident in Chernobyl, at a Soviet-built nuclear power plant. Ukraine declared independence in 1991. The turmoil it experienced in the 1990s as it attempted to implement economic and political reforms culminated in the disputed presidential election of 2004; mass protests over the results came to be known as the Orange Revolution.

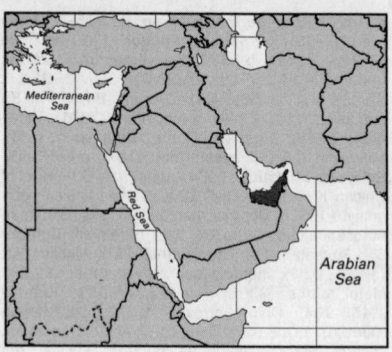

## Recent Developments

Ukrainian economic growth was estimated to be 5.2% in 2011, with inflation projected at 8.9%, but the economy in general was in difficulty. In March the IMF froze its quarterly payment to Ukraine of US$1.5 billion because of the country's failure to meet its agreed economic targets. In September Ukraine's foreign-currency reserves dropped by 8.3% to US$35 billion, which led the country to seek new loans. In late October an IMF mission arrived in Ukraine to discuss revisions to the standby program and a potential allocation of US$3 billion in credit. According to the International Organization for Migration, an estimated 6.5 million Ukrainians were working abroad. The average domestic wage in September was 2,700 hryvnia (about US$337), but it averaged much lower in western regions. Ukraine's outlook for long-term foreign and currency default ratings was revised from "positive" to "stable" by Fitch in October. The 25th anniversary of the Chernobyl disaster occurred on 26 April. A commemorative ceremony was held at the site of the abandoned nuclear plant, and a conference in Kiev attracted many world leaders. In September US Secretary of State Hillary Clinton and Ukrainian Foreign Minister Kostiantyn Hryshchenko signed a memorandum of understanding on nuclear security whereby the US would provide technical and financial assistance for the elimination of Ukraine's enriched uranium and for the improvement of civil nuclear research enterprises.

Internet resource: <www.ukrstat.gov.ua>.

# United Arab Emirates

Official name: Al-Imarat al-ʿArabiyah al-Muttahidah (United Arab Emirates). Form of government: federation of seven emirates with one advisory body (Federal National Council [40]). Head of state: President Sheikh Khalifah ibn Zayid al-Nahyan (from 2004). Head of government: Prime Minister Sheikh Muhammad ibn Rashid al-Maktum (from 2006). Capital: Abu Dhabi. Official language: Arabic. Official religion: Islam. Monetary unit: 1 UAE dirham (AED) = 100 fils; valuation (2 Jul 2012) US$1 = AED 3.67.

## Demography

Area: 32,280 sq mi, 83,600 sq km. Population (2011): 7,891,000. Density (2011): persons per sq mi 244.5, persons per sq km 94.4. Urban (2008): 80.0%. Sex distribution (2008): male 68.96%; female 31.04%. Age breakdown (2008): under 15, 19.1%; 15–29, 32.3%; 30–44, 36.6%; 45–59, 10.5%; 60–74, 1.2%; 75 and over, 0.3%. Ethnic composition (2000): Arab 48.1%, of which UAE Arab 12.2%, UAE Bedouin 9.4%, Egyptian Arab 6.2%, Omani Arab 4.1%, Saudi Arab 4.0%; South Asian 35.7%, of which Pashtun 7.1%, Balochi 7.1%, Malayali 7.1%; Persian 5.0%; Filipino 3.4%; white 2.4%; other 5.4%. Religious affiliation (2005): Muslim 62% (mostly Sunni); Hindu 21%; Christian 9%; Buddhist 4%; other 4%. Major cities (2006): Dubai 1,354,980; Sharjah 685,000; Abu Dhabi 630,000; Al-ʿAyn 350,000; ʿAjman 202,244. Location: the Middle East, bordering the Persian Gulf, the Gulf of Oman, Oman, and Saudi Arabia.

## Vital statistics

Birth rate per 1,000 population (2007): 16.1 (world avg. 20.3). Death rate per 1,000 population (2007): 2.2 (world avg. 8.5). Total fertility rate (avg. births per childbearing woman; 2007): 2.43. Life expectancy at birth (2007): male 73.2 years; female 78.3 years.

## National economy

Budget (2007). Revenue: AED 228,750,000,000 (royalties on hydrocarbons 77.1%; tax revenue 6.0%). Expenditures: AED 159,726,000,000 (current expenditures 76.0%; loans, net equity, and foreign grants 13.2%; development expenditures 10.8%). Gross national income (2008): US$272,053,000,000 (US$57,094 per capita). Public debt (2008): US$117,000,000,000. Production (metric tons except as noted). Agriculture and fishing (2007): dates 755,000, tomatoes 215,000, alfalfa for forage and silage (2005) 210,000; livestock (number of live animals) 1,570,000 goats, 615,000 sheep, 260,000 camels; fisheries production 87,570 (from aquaculture 1%). Mining and quarrying (2007): gypsum 150,000; lime 60,000. Manufacturing (2007): cement 15,000,000; aluminum 890,000;

1 metric ton = about 1.1 short tons;    1 kilometer = 0.6 mi (statute);    1 metric ton-km cargo = about 0.68 short ton-mi cargo;    c.i.f.: cost, insurance, and freight;    f.o.b.: free on board

steel 90,000; refined and unrefined gold (total foreign trade value) US$19,000,000,000; worked and unworked diamonds (total foreign trade value) US$11,230,000,000. *Energy production (consumption):* electricity (kW-hr; 2007) 76,532,000,000 (74,717,000,000); crude petroleum (barrels; 2008) 978,600,000 ([2006] 135,100,000); petroleum products (metric tons; 2006) 21,592,000 (10,071,000); natural gas (cu m; 2008) 50,200,-000,000 ([2007] 38,900,000,000). **Population economically active** (2005): total 2,559,668; activity rate of total population 54.6% (participation rates: ages 15–64, 78.1%; female 13.5%; unemployed [2008] 4%). **Selected balance of payments data.** Receipts from (US$'000,000): tourism (2008) 7,162; foreign direct investment (FDI; 2005–07 avg.) 12,320. Disbursements for (US$'000,000): tourism (2008) 13,288; remittances (2007) 5,000; FDI (2005–07 avg.) 7,089.

### Foreign trade

**Imports** (2006; c.i.f.): US$97,864,000,000 (machinery and apparatus 19.4%; base and fabricated metals 9.9%; motor vehicles 8.1%; gold 7.6%; food products 5.4%). *Major import sources* (2008): China 13.2%; India 10.4%; US 8.8%; Germany 6.5%; Japan 6.1%. **Exports** (2006; f.o.b.): US$142,505,000,000 (crude petroleum 37.9%; refined petroleum products 11.4%; gold [not jewelry] 3.4%; motor vehicles and parts 2.5%; natural gas 1.7%; telecommunications equipment 1.4%; diamonds 1.3%). *Major export destinations* (2008): Japan 23.0%; South Korea 9.4%; India 7.9%; Iran 6.5%; Thailand 5.3%.

### Transport and communications

**Transport.** *Railroads:* none. *Roads* (2008): total length (paved roads only) 4,080 km. *Vehicles* (2007): passenger cars 1,279,098; trucks and buses 48,205. *Air transport* (2007): passenger-km 90,-530,000,000; metric ton-km cargo 5,497,149,000. **Communications,** in total units (units per 1,000 persons). Telephone landlines (2008): 1,508,000 (317); cellular telephone subscribers (2008): 9,358,000 (1,964); personal computers (2006): 1,396,000 (330); total Internet users (2008): 2,922,000 (613); broadband Internet subscribers (2008): 529,000 (111).

### Education and health

**Educational attainment** (2005). Percentage of population ages 10 and over having: no formal schooling (illiterate/unknown) 9.4%, (literate) 13.9%; primary education 14.6%; incomplete/complete secondary 43.7%; postsecondary 4.0%; undergraduate 12.8%; graduate 1.6%. **Literacy** (2007): total population ages 10 and over literate 90.4%; males literate 90.9%; females literate 89.2%. **Health** (2007): physicians 8,662 (1 per 518 persons); hospital beds 8,348 (1 per 538 persons); infant mortality rate per 1,000 live births 7.8; undernourished population (2002–04) less than 2.5% of total population.

### Military

**Total active duty personnel** (November 2008): 51,000 (army 86.3%, navy 4.9%, air force 8.8%); US troops (June 2009): 104; French military base for up to 500 troops officially opened in May 2009. **Military expenditure as percentage of GDP** (2007): 5.5%; per capita expenditure US$2,246.

### Background

The Persian Gulf was the location of important trading centers as early as Sumerian times. Its people converted to Islam in Muhammad's lifetime. The Portuguese entered the region in the early 16th century, and the British East India Company arrived about 100 years later. In 1820 the British exacted a peace treaty with local rulers along the coast of the eastern Arabian Peninsula. The area formerly called the Pirate Coast became known as the Trucial Coast. In 1892 the rulers agreed to entrust foreign relations to Britain. Though the British administered the region from 1853, they never assumed sovereignty; each state maintained full internal control. The states formed the Trucial States Council in 1960. In 1971 the sheikhs terminated defense treaties with Britain and established the six-member federation. Ras al-Khaymah joined it in 1972. The United Arab Emirates (UAE) aided coalition forces against Iraq in the Persian Gulf War (1990–91).

### Recent Developments

The UAE did not experience the popular uprisings that shook the rest of the Arab world in 2011. Despite the Shi'ite uprising in neighboring Bahrain, UAE Shi'ites, constituting 15% of the native population, generally remained calm. In March, when the Bahraini government asked the UAE for military support against the Shi'ite opposition, the UAE sent some 500 police officers. In February the UAE was one of the first countries to support a rebellion in Libya against the regime of Muammar al-Qaddafi, offering the rebels military and financial aid.

**Internet resource:** <www.economy.ae>.

# United Kingdom

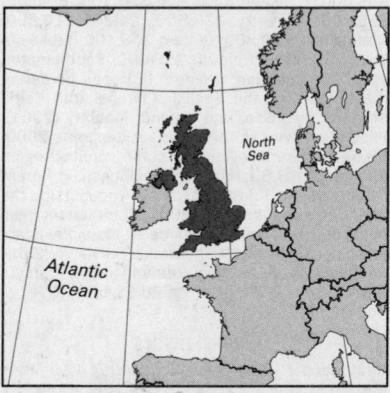

**Official name:** United Kingdom of Great Britain and Northern Ireland. **Form of government:** constitutional monarchy with two legislative houses (House of Lords [827]; House of Commons [650]). **Head of state:** Queen Elizabeth II (from 1952). **Head of government:** Prime Minister David Cameron (from 2010). **Capital:** London. **Official languages:** English (also Scots Gaelic in Scotland and Welsh in Wales). **Official religion:** none (the Church of England is "established" [protected by the state but not "official"]; the Church of Scotland is "national" [with exclusive jurisdiction in spiritual matters]; there is no established church in Northern Ireland or Wales). **Monetary unit:** 1 pound sterling (£) = 100 new pence; valuation (2 Jul 2012) US$1 = £0.64.

## Demography

**Area:** 93,851 sq mi, 243,073 sq km (England 50,302 sq mi, 130,281 sq km; Wales 8,005 sq mi, 20,732 sq km; Scotland 30,087 sq mi, 77,925 sq km; Northern Ireland 5,457 sq mi, 14,135 sq km). **Population** (2011): 62,675,000. **Density** (2011): persons per sq mi 667.8, persons per sq km 257.8. **Urban** (2011): 79.6%. **Sex distribution** (2008): male 49.12%; female 50.88%. **Age breakdown** (2007): under 15, 17.6%; 15–29, 19.9%; 30–44, 21.6%; 45–59, 19.2%; 60–74, 14.0%; 75–84, 5.6%; 85 and over, 2.1%. **Ethnic composition** (2007): white 86.8%, of which British 81.6%; Asian 5.3%, of which Indian 2.0%, Pakistani 1.6%, Bangladeshi 0.6%, Chinese 0.4%; black 2.5%, of which from Africa 1.3%, from the Caribbean 1.1%; mixed race 1.1%; other 4.3%. **Religious affiliation** (2001): Christian 71.8%, of which Anglican-identified 29%, other Protestant-identified (significantly Presbyterian) 14%, Roman Catholic-identified 10%; Muslim 2.8%; Hindu 1.0%; Sikh 0.6%; Jewish 0.5%; nonreligious 15.0%; other 8.3%. **Major cities (urban agglomerations)** (2008 [2007]): London 7,619,800 (8,567,000); Birmingham 1,010,400 (2,285,000); Manchester 465,900 (2,230,000); Leeds 477,600 (1,529,000); Glasgow 637,000 (1,160,000); Newcastle upon Tyne 200,200 (882,000); Liverpool 464,200 (811,000); Bristol 465,500; Sheffield 458,100; Edinburgh 452,200; Leicester 348,000; Kingston upon Hull 320,100; Bradford 315,100; Coventry 312,500; Cardiff 310,800; Nottingham 273,300; Belfast 268,400; Stoke-on-Trent 258,600; Plymouth 256,000; Southampton 252,700. **Location:** western Europe, bordering the North Sea, the English Channel, the Celtic Sea, the Irish Sea, and Ireland. **Mobility** (2001). Population living in the same residence as 2000, 88.6%; different residence, same country/region (of the UK) 8.6%; different residence, different country/region (of the UK) 2.1%; from outside the UK 0.7%. **Immigration** (2007): permanent residents 527,000, from Bangladesh, India, Pakistan, and Sri Lanka 16.9%; Australia 3.0%; US 2.8%; South Africa 2.5%; New Zealand 1.5%; Canada 0.8%; other 72.5%, of which EU 31.5%.

## Vital statistics

**Birth rate** per 1,000 population (2008): 12.9 (world avg. 20.3); within marriage 54.6%. **Death rate** per 1,000 population (2008): 9.4 (world avg. 8.5). **Total fertility rate** (avg. births per childbearing woman; 2008): 1.94. **Life expectancy** at birth (2007): male 77.6 years; female 81.7 years.

## Social indicators

**Educational attainment** (2007). Percentage of population ages 25–64 having: unknown through lower secondary education 13%; upper secondary 55%; higher 32%, of which at least some university 22%. **Quality of working life.** Average full-time workweek (hours; 2008): male 39.0, female 33.8. Annual rate per 100,000 workers for (2007–08): injury or accident 474.1; death 0.8. Proportion of employed labor force insured for damages or income loss resulting from (2004): injury 100%; permanent disability 100%; death 100%. Average days lost to labor stoppages per 1,000 employee workdays (2008): 28. **Social participation.** Population ages 16 and over participating in voluntary work (2001; Great Britain [England, Scotland, and Wales] only): 39%. Trade union membership in total workforce (2007–08) 26%. Percentage of population attending weekly church services (2001) 8%. **Social deviance** (2008–09; England and Wales only). Offense rate per 100,000 population for: theft and handling stolen goods 2,714; criminal damage 1,520; violence against a person 1,467; burglary 1,207; drug offenses 394; fraud and forgery 265; robbery 130; sex offenses 84. **Leisure** (2008). Favorite leisure activities: watching television, videos, and DVDs, listening to the radio, watching sporting events, and attending the cinema; the common free-time activity outside of the home is a visit to the pub; favorite sporting activities: for men—walking, golf, snooker, and billiards, for women—walking, swimming, fitness classes, and yoga. **Material well-being** (2007). Households possessing: automobile 75%, of which two cars 25%, three cars 6%; refrigerator/freezer 97%; washing machine 96%; central heating 95%; digital, cable, or satellite television receiver 77%; computer 70%; Internet connection 61%; dishwasher 37%.

## National economy

**Budget** (2007–08). *Revenue:* £548,000,000,000 (income tax 26.9%; production and import taxes 24.1%; social security contributions 18.3%). *Expenditures:* £557,800,000,000 (social protection 33.5%; health 18.4%; education 14.1%; defense 6.1%; public order 5.8%). **Public debt** (December 2008): US$1,155,620,000,000. **Production** (metric tons except as noted). *Agriculture and fishing* (2008): wheat 17,227,000, sugar beets 7,500,000, barley 6,144,000, potatoes 5,999,000, rapeseed 1,973,030, oats 784,000, carrots 732,400, onions 349,200, apples 242,900, cauliflower 118,500, mushrooms and truffles 43,752; livestock (number of live animals) 33,131,000 sheep, 10,107,000 cattle, 4,714,000 pigs; fisheries production (2007) 793,894 (from aquaculture 22%). *Mining and quarrying* (2007): sand and gravel 95,000,000; rock salt 2,000,000; china clay (kaolin) 1,671,000; slate 870,000; potash 716,000. *Manufacturing* (value added in

*1 metric ton = about 1.1 short tons;    1 kilometer = 0.6 mi (statute);    1 metric ton-km cargo = about 0.68 short ton-mi cargo;    c.i.f.: cost, insurance, and freight;    f.o.b.: free on board*

US$'000,000; 2006): chemical products 42,400; food products and beverages 39,100; nonelectrical machinery and equipment 26,000; printing and publishing 24,800; fabricated metal products 23,900; motor vehicles and parts 19,400; rubber and plastic products 13,300; bricks, cement, and ceramics 11,800; radio, television, and communications equipment 11,800. **Gross national income** (2008): US$2,787,159,000,000 (US$45,390 per capita). *Energy production (consumption):* electricity (kW-hr; 2008–09) 347,214,000,000 ([2007] 345,800,000,000); coal (metric tons; 2008–09) 18,321,000 ([2008] 58,900,000); crude petroleum (barrels; 2008–09) 481,183,700 ([2008] 568,- 909,000); petroleum products (metric tons; 2008) 80,435,000 (70,249,000); natural gas (cu m; 2008–09) 78,306,700,000 ([2008] 108,143,- 200,000). **Population economically active** (2008): total 31,118,000; activity rate of total population 50.7% (participation rates: ages 16 and over, 62.5%; female 45.8%; unemployed [April 2008– March 2009] 6.2%). **Selected balance of payments data.** Receipts from (US$'000,000): tourism (2007) 37,690; remittances (2008) 8,234; foreign direct investment (FDI; 2005–07 avg.) 183,352. Disbursements for (US$'000,000): tourism (2007) 72,436; remittances (2008) 5,048; FDI (2005–07 avg.) 144,188.

## Foreign trade

**Imports** (2008; c.i.f.): £343,964,000,000 (mineral fuels 13.9%, of which crude petroleum and refined petroleum products 10.8%; electrical machinery and equipment 13.8%; transportation equipment 12.9%; chemical products 11.0%, of which pharmaceuticals 3.2%; nonelectrical machinery and equipment 8.4%; food products and live animals 7.4%; wearing apparel 3.8%; base metals 3.8%). *Major import sources:* Germany 13.0%; Netherlands 7.5%; US 7.5%; China 6.7%; France 6.7%; Norway 6.3%; Belgium and Luxembourg 5.0%; Italy 4.0%; Ireland 3.6%; Spain 3.1%. **Exports** (2008; f.o.b.): £251,088,000,000 (chemical products 17.5%, of which pharmaceuticals 6.9%; mineral fuels 13.9%, of which crude petroleum and refined petroleum products 12.6%; nonelectrical machinery and equipment 12.8%; transportation equipment 12.6%; electrical machinery and equipment 10.1%; base metals 5.5%; food products and live animals 3.5%). *Major export destinations:* US 13.9%; Germany 11.2%; Netherlands 7.8%; Ireland 7.6%; France 7.2%; Belgium and Luxembourg 5.3%; Spain 4.1%; Italy 3.7%; Sweden 2.1%; China 2.0%.

## Transport and communications

**Transport.** *Railroads* (2007–08): length (2008) 16,454 km; passenger-km (Great Britain [England, Scotland, and Wales] only) 49,007,000,000; metric ton-km cargo (Great Britain [England, Scotland, and Wales] only) 21,200,000,000. *Roads* (2008; Great Britain [England, Scotland, and Wales] only): total length 394,467 km (paved 100%). *Vehicles* (2008; Great Britain [England, Scotland, and Wales] only): passenger cars 30,324,000, trucks and buses (2004) 3,522,424. *Air transport* (2008–09): passenger-km 229,710,000,000; metric ton-km cargo 6,029,510,000. **Communications,** in total units (units per 1,000 persons). Telephone

landlines (2008): 33,209,000 (542); cellular telephone subscribers (2008): 77,361,000 (1,263); personal computers (2006): 48,591,000 (802); total Internet users (2008): 46,684,000 (762); broadband Internet subscribers (2008): 17,276,- 000 (282).

## Education and health

**Literacy** (2006): total population literate, about 99%. **Health** (2008): physicians (England and Scotland only) 138,878 (1 per 405 persons); hospital beds (2007) 208,413 (1 per 293 persons); infant mortality rate per 1,000 live births 4.7; undernourished population (2002–04) less than 2.5% of total population.

## Military

**Total active duty personnel** (November 2008): 160,280 (army 59.7%, navy 19.3%, air force 21.0%); reserve 199,280); UK troops deployed abroad (November 2008): 41,700; US troops in the UK (July 2009): 9,367. **Military expenditure as percentage of GDP** (2008): 2.3%; per capita expenditure US$972.

## Background

The early pre-Roman inhabitants of Britain were Celtic-speaking peoples, including the Brythonic people of Wales, the Picts of Scotland, and the Britons of Britain. Celts also settled in Ireland about 500 BC. Julius Caesar invaded and took control of the area in 55–54 BC. The Roman province of Britannia endured until the 5th century AD and included present-day England and Wales. Germanic tribes, including Angles, Saxons, and Jutes, invaded Britain in the 5th century. The invasions had little effect on the Celtic peoples of Wales and Scotland. Christianity began to flourish in the 6th century. During the 8th–9th centuries, Vikings, particularly Danes, raided the coasts of Britain. In the late 9th century Alfred the Great repelled a Danish invasion, which helped bring about the unification of England under Athelstan. The Scots attained dominance in Scotland, which was finally unified under Malcolm II (1005–34).

William of Normandy took England in 1066. The Norman kings established a strong central government and feudal state. The French language of the Norman rulers eventually merged with the Anglo-Saxon of the common people to form the English language. From the 11th century, Scotland came under the influence of the English throne. Henry II conquered Ireland in the late 12th century. His sons Richard I and John had conflicts with the clergy and nobles, and eventually John was forced to grant the nobles concessions in the Magna Carta (1215). The concept of community of the realm developed during the 13th century, providing the foundation for parliamentary government. During the reign of Edward I, statute law developed to supplement English common law, and the first Parliament was convened. In 1314 Robert the Bruce won independence for Scotland.

The Tudors became the ruling family of England following the Wars of the Roses (1455–85). Henry VIII established the Church of England and made Wales part of his realm. The reign of Elizabeth I began a period of colonial expansion; 1588 brought the defeat of the Spanish Armada. In 1603 James VI of Scotland ascended to the English throne, becoming James I, and established a personal union of the two kingdoms.

The English Civil Wars erupted in 1642 between Royalists and Parliamentarians, ending in the execution of Charles I (1649). After 11 years of Puritan rule under Oliver Cromwell and his son (1649-60), the monarchy was restored with Charles II. In 1707 England and Scotland assented to the Act of Union, forming the kingdom of Great Britain. The Hanoverians ascended to the English throne in 1714, when George Louis, elector of Hanover, became George I of Great Britain. During the reign of George III, Great Britain's American colonies won independence (1783). This was followed by a period of war with revolutionary France and later with the empire of Napoleon (1789-1815). In 1801 legislation united Great Britain with Ireland to create the United Kingdom of Great Britain and Ireland. Britain was the birthplace of the Industrial Revolution in the late 18th century, and it remained the world's foremost economic power until the late 19th century. During the reign of Queen Victoria, Britain's colonial expansion reached its zenith, though the older dominions, including Canada and Australia, were granted independence (1867 and 1901, respectively).

The UK entered World War I allied with France and Russia in 1914. Following the war, revolutionary disorder erupted in Ireland, and in 1921 the Irish Free State was granted dominion status. The six counties of Ulster, however, remained in the UK as Northern Ireland. The UK entered World War II in 1939. Following the war the Irish Free State became the Irish Republic and left the Commonwealth. India gained independence from the UK in 1947. Throughout the postwar period and into the 1970s, the UK continued to grant independence to its overseas colonies and dependencies. With UN forces, it participated in the Korean War (1950-53). In 1956 it intervened militarily in Egypt during the Suez Crisis. It joined the European Economic Community, a forerunner of the European Union, in 1973. In 1982 it defeated Argentina in the Falkland Islands War. As a result of continuing social strife in Northern Ireland, it joined with Ireland in several peace initiatives, which eventually resulted in an agreement to establish an assembly in Northern Ireland. In 1997 referenda approved in Scotland and Wales devolved power to both countries, though both remained part of the UK. In 1991 the UK joined an international coalition to reverse Iraq's conquest of Kuwait. In 2003 the UK and the US attacked Iraq and overthrew the government of Saddam Hussein. Terrorist bombings in London on 7 Jul 2005 killed more than 50 people.

## Recent Developments

Millions of people were granted a brief respite from Britain's problems in 2011 by the marriage on 29 April of Prince William—the eldest son of Prince Charles, the heir to the throne—to Catherine Middleton. The day was made a public holiday, and thousands of people crowded the streets to join in the celebration. Queen Elizabeth II, William's grandmother, granted the young couple the titles of duke and duchess of Cambridge on their wedding day. Their marriage reopened a simmering controversy over whether the law of primogeniture—which held that the British crown passed to the eldest male child of the monarch—should be changed. Prime Minister David Cameron consulted the other 15 countries that also had the British monarch as their head of state, and they agreed in October, at a meeting of Commonwealth leaders in Australia, to change the rules so that the crown would in future pass to the first-born child, regardless of sex, and also lift the more than 300-year-old ban on a British monarch's marrying a Roman Catholic.

The recovery in the UK's economy faltered in 2011. Growth of about 1.0% over the year was too slow to prevent a rise in unemployment to 2.6 million, or roughly 8.0% of the labor force—the highest figure since 1994. The UK's economy—previously the sixth largest in the world—was surpassed by Brazil's economy in 2011. Treasury Minister Danny Alexander in June announced that the retirement age, traditionally 60 for most public-sector workers, would rise in stages to 66 by 2020. Another measure, designed to encourage more people to delay retirement, came into effect in October, when it became illegal for companies to force employees to retire. In the first quarter of 2012, the UK officially returned to recession, contracting 0.3%.

The UK played a significant role in Libya in 2011. Cameron joined with French Pres. Nicolas Sarkozy to secure NATO and UN support for a no-fly zone to prevent Libyan forces from attacking civilians, and they visited Libya's newly liberated capital, Tripoli, in September. The UK's eight-year military presence in Iraq came to an end on 22 May with the conclusion of a Royal Navy mission to train Iraqi sailors. Queen Elizabeth made a state visit to Ireland in May, the first such trip by a British monarch since Ireland seceded from the UK in 1922. Her visit was both symbolically important and immensely popular in Ireland. Celebrations for her Diamond Jubilee—commemorating her 60-year reign—took place in June 2012. In late summer London hosted the Olympic Games for the first time since 1948.

Internet resource: <www.statistics.gov.uk>.

# United States

Official name: United States of America. Form of government: federal republic with two legislative houses (Senate [100]; House of Representatives [435, excluding 5 nonvoting delegates from the District of Columbia, the US Virgin Islands, American Samoa, the Northern Mariana Islands, and Guam and a nonvoting resident commissioner from Puerto Rico]). Head of state and government: President Barack Obama (from 2009). Capital: Washington DC. Official language: none. Official religion: none. Monetary unit: 1 US dollar (US$) = 100 cents.

## Demography

Area: 3,678,190 sq mi, 9,526,468 sq km; inland water area equals 86,409 sq mi (223,798 sq km), and Great Lakes water area equals 59,959 sq mi

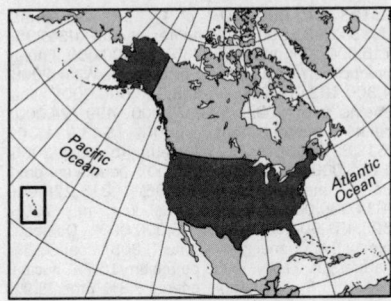

(155,293 sq km). **Population** (2011): 313,387,000. **Density** (2011; based on land area only): persons per sq mi 88.7, persons per sq km 34.3. **Urban** (2011): 82.4%. **Sex distribution** (2005): male 49.26%; female 50.74%. **Age breakdown** (2005): under 15, 20.5%; 15–29, 20.9%; 30–44, 21.6%; 45–59, 20.2%; 60–74, 10.7%; 75–84, 4.4%; 85 and over, 1.7%. **Population by race and Hispanic origin** (persons of Hispanic origin may be of any race) (2006): non-Hispanic white 66.4%; Hispanic 14.8%; non-Hispanic black 12.8%; Asian and Pacific Islander 4.6%; American Indian and Eskimo 1.0%; other 0.4%. **Religious affiliation** (2005): Christian 83.3%, of which independent Christian 23.2%, Roman Catholic 19.6%, Protestant (including Anglican) 18.9%, unaffiliated Christian 16.5%, Orthodox 1.8%, other Christian (primarily Mormon and Jehovah's Witness) 3.3%; Jewish 1.9%; Muslim 1.6%; Buddhist 0.9%; New Religionists 0.5%; Hindu 0.4%; traditional beliefs 0.4%; Baha'i 0.3%; Sikh 0.1%; nonreligious 9.8%; atheist 0.5%; other 0.3%. **Mobility** (2005). Reported gross percentage of population living in the same residence as in 2004: 86%; different residence, same county 8%; different county, same state 3%; different state 3%; moved from abroad 1%. **Place of birth** (2007): native-born 259,545,000 (87.4%); foreign-born 37,279,000 (12.6%), of which (2004) Mexico 10,011,000, the Philippines 1,222,000, China and Hong Kong 1,067,000, India 1,007,000, Cuba 952,000, Vietnam 863,000, El Salvador 765,000, South Korea 701,000. **Immigration** (2007–08): permanent immigrants admitted 1,107,126, from Mexico 17.2%, China 7.3%, India 5.7%, Philippines 4.9%, Cuba 4.5%, Dominican Republic 2.9%, Vietnam 2.8%, Colombia 2.7%, South Korea 2.4%, Haiti 2.3%, Pakistan 1.8%, El Salvador 1.8%, Jamaica 1.7%, other 42.0%. Refugees (2005) 380,000. **Location**: North America, bordering Canada, the North Atlantic Ocean, the Gulf of Mexico, Mexico, and the North Pacific Ocean; the outlying state of Alaska nearly touches eastern Russia and borders the Arctic Ocean, Canada, and the North Pacific Ocean; Hawaii is an island group in the North Pacific Ocean.

## Vital statistics

**Birth rate** per 1,000 population (2008): 14.0 (world avg. 20.3); within marriage (2006) 64.2%. **Death rate** per 1,000 population (2008): 8.1 (world avg. 8.5). **Total fertility rate** (avg. births per childbearing woman; 2007): 2.09. **Life expectancy** at birth (2005): male 75.2 years, of which white male 78.3 years, black male 69.5 years; female 80.4 years, of which white female 80.8 years, black female 76.5 years.

## Social indicators

**Educational attainment** (2007). Percentage of population ages 25 and over having: unknown/primary and incomplete secondary education 14.3%; secondary 31.6%; some postsecondary 25.3%; 4-year higher degree 18.9%; advanced degree 9.9%. Number of earned degrees (2006): associate's degree 713,066; bachelor's degree 1,485,242; master's degree 594,065; doctor's degree 56,067; first-professional degrees (in fields such as medicine, theology, and law) 87,655. **Quality of working life** (2006). Average workweek (2007): 41.3 hours. Annual death rate per 100,000 workers: 3.4; leading causes of occupational deaths: transportation incidents 42%, assaults and violent acts 13%, falls 14%, struck by object 10%. Annual occupational injury rate per 100,000 workers: 4.4. Average duration of journey to work (2006): 25.0 minutes (private automobile 86.7%, of which drive alone 76.0%, carpool 10.7%; take public transportation 4.8%; walk 2.5%; work at home 4.0%; other 2.0%). Rate per 1,000 employed workers of discouraged workers (unemployed no longer seeking work): 3.1. **Access to services** (2005). Proportion of occupied dwellings having access to: electricity 100%; safe public water supply 100%; public sewage collection 79.8%; septic tanks 20.2%. **Social participation** (2007). Population ages 16 and over volunteering for an organization 26.2%; median annual hours 52. Trade union membership in total workforce 12.1%. **Social deviance** (2007). Offense rate per 100,000 population for: murder 5.6; rape 30.0; robbery 147.6; aggravated assault 283.8; motor-vehicle theft 363.3; burglary and housebreaking 722.5; larceny-theft 2,177.8; drug-abuse violation (2005) 560.1; drunkenness (2003) 149.1. Estimated drug and substance users (population ages 12 and over; 2005): cigarettes 24.9%; binge alcohol (drinking five or more drinks on the same occasion on at least one day in the past 30 days) 22.7%; marijuana or hashish 6.0%. Rate per 100,000 population of suicide (2005): 10.7. **Leisure** (2006). Favorite leisure activities (percentage of total population ages 18 and over that undertook activity at least once in the previous year): dining out 48.6%, entertaining friends or relatives at home 40.2%, reading books 38.7%, barbecuing 33.9%, going to the beach 22.9%. **Material well-being** (2005). Occupied dwellings with householder possessing: automobiles, trucks, or vans 91.5%, 1 car with or without trucks or vans 47.5%, 2 cars 23.9%, only trucks and vans 12.7%, no cars, trucks, or vans 8.5%, 3 or more cars 7.4%; telephone 97.1%; television receiver 98.2%; video 90.2%; washing machine 82.0%; clothes dryer 79.1%; air conditioner 89.5%; cable television 67.5%; personal computers (2003) 61.8%; Internet connections (2003) 54.6%; broadband Internet (2003) 19.9%. **Recreational expenditures** (2006): US$791,100,000,000 (television and radio receivers, computers, and video equipment 19.2%; golfing, bowling, and other participatory activities 14.6%; sports supplies 10.0%; nondurable toys and sports equipment 9.0%; magazines, newspapers, and sheet music 5.7%; books and maps 5.5%).

## National economy

**Budget** (2009). *Revenue:* US$2,699,900,000,000 (income tax 46.6%; social-insurance taxes and contributions 35.1%; corporate taxes 12.6%). *Expenditures:* US$3,107,400,000,000 (social security and medicare 37.4%; defense 21.7%; health 9.6%; interest on debt 8.4%). *Total outstanding national debt* (September 2009): US$11,898,000,000,000, of which debt held by the public US$7,552,000,000,000, intragovernment holdings US$4,346,000,000,000. **Gross national income** (2008): US$14,466,112,000,000 (US$47,580 per capita). **Production.** *Agriculture and fishing* (value of production in US$'000,000 except as noted; 2007): corn (maize) 52,090, soybeans 26,752, wheat 13,669, alfalfa hay 8,972, cotton 5,197, grapes 3,381, potatoes 3,198, lettuce 2,751, apples 2,398, almonds 2,325, rice 2,274, tomatoes 2,179, oranges 2,111, sorghum 1,951, strawberries 1,746, sugar beets (2006) 1,526, tobacco 1,310, cottonseed 1,061, mushrooms 956, sugarcane (2006) 897, barley 852, onions 840, broccoli 764, peanuts (groundnuts) 763, cherries 651, carrots 614, sunflowers 607, blueberries 589, peppers 588, walnuts (2006) 564, pistachios 549, peaches 499, watermelons 476, cabbage 413, lemons 403, pecans 376, sweet potatoes 374, pears 346, cantaloupe 313; livestock (number of live animals; 2008) 96,669,000 cattle, 65,110,000 pigs, 9,500,000 horses, 6,100,000 sheep, 2,050,000,000 chickens; fisheries production 5,293,877 metric tons (from aquaculture 10%); aquatic plants production 2,272 (from aquaculture, none). *Metals mining* (metal content in metric tons unless otherwise noted; 2008): molybdenum 61,400 (world rank: 1); beryllium 155 (world rank: 1); copper 1,310,000 (world rank: 2); lead 440,000 (world rank: 3); gold 230,000 kg (world rank: 3); zinc 770,000 (world rank: 4); palladium 12,400 kg (world rank: 4); platinum 3,700 kg (world rank: 5); iron 54,000,000 (world rank: 7); silver 1,120,000 kg (world rank: 7). *Nonmetals mining* (metric tons; 2008): diatomite 653,000 (world rank: 1); bromine 235,000 (world rank: 1); boron (2006) 1,150,000 (world rank: 2); perlite 449,000 (world rank: 2); kyanite 90,000 (world rank: 2); vermiculite 100,000 (world rank: 3); barite 615,000 (world rank: 3); silicon 166,000 (world rank: 5); feldspar 600,000 (world rank: 6). *Quarrying* (metric tons; 2008): gypsum 12,700,000 (world rank: 2); salt 46,000,000 (world rank: 2); phosphate rock 30,900,000 (world rank: 2); lime 19,800,000 (world rank: 2). *Manufacturing* (value added in US$'000,000; 2005): chemical products 328,440, of which pharmaceuticals and medicine 124,586; transportation equipment 254,665, of which motor vehicle parts 81,600, motor vehicles 78,772, aerospace products and parts 71,221; food products 235,673; electronics 226,319, of which navigational, measuring, medical, and scientific equipment 68,730, computers and related components 36,407, communications equipment 32,413; fabricated metal products 154,928; nonelectrical machinery and equipment 142,438; refined petroleum products and coal 117,541; plastic and rubber products 96,348; beverages and tobacco products 80,716; base metals 77,179; paper products 75,889; cement, bricks, and ceramics 64,545; printing and publishing 58,930; electrical machinery and equipment 54,318; furniture 46,801; wood products 44,763; textiles 32,395. *Construction* (completed; 2006): private

US$937,047,000,000, of which residential US$641,332,000,000, nonresidential US$295,715,000,000; public US$255,191,000,000. *Energy production (consumption):* electricity (kW-hr; 2006) 4,300,103,000,000 (4,318,523,000,000); coal (metric tons; 2006) 523,971,000 (499,724,000); lignite (metric tons; 2006) 543,931,000 (517,337,000); crude petroleum (barrels; 2006) 1,857,000,000 (5,802,000,000); petroleum products (metric tons; 2006) 815,278,000 (834,999,000); natural gas (cu m; 2006) 525,481,000,000 (610,698,000,000). Domestic production of energy by source (2005): coal 33.3%, natural gas 27.2%, crude petroleum 15.7%, nuclear power 11.8%, renewable energy 8.8%, other 3.2%. *Energy consumption by source* (2007): crude petroleum and refined petroleum products 39.8%, natural gas 23.3%, coal 22.4%, nuclear electric power 8.3%, hydroelectric and thermal 3.2%, other renewable energy 3.0%; by end use: industrial 32.0%, residential and commercial 39.3%, transportation 28.7%. **Population economically active** (December 2009): total 153,059,000 (civilian population only); activity rate of total population 49.6% (participation rates: ages 16–64, 64.6%; female [2007] 46.5%; unemployed 10.0%). **Selected balance of payments data.** Receipts from (US$'000,000): tourism (2007) 119,223; remittances (2008) 3,049; foreign direct investment (FDI; 2005–07 avg.) 191,438. Disbursements for (US$'000,000): tourism (2007) 81,092; remittances (2008) 47,182; FDI (2005–07 avg.) 183,606. Number of foreign visitors (2007) 56,716,277 (17,735,000 from Canada, 15,089,000 from Mexico, 11,406,000 from Europe); number of nationals traveling abroad (2007) 64,052,000 (19,453,000 to Mexico, 13,371,000 to Canada, 12,304,000 to Europe).

## Foreign trade

**Imports** (2008): US$2,100,141,200,000 (crude petroleum and refined petroleum products 21.1%; motor vehicles 9.1%; chemical products 8.4%; telecommunications equipment 6.3%; electrical machinery and equipment 5.4%; computers and office equipment 4.6%; wearing apparel 3.8%; industrial machinery 3.2%; food products and beverages 3.2%). *Major import sources:* China 16.1%; Canada 16.0%; Mexico 10.3%; Japan 6.6%; Germany 4.6%; UK 2.8%; Saudi Arabia 2.6%; Venezuela 2.4%; South Korea 2.3%; France 2.1%; Nigeria 1.8%; Taiwan 1.7%; Italy 1.7%; Ireland 1.5%; Malaysia 1.5%. **Exports** (2008): US$1,300,135,700,000 (transportation equipment 14.2%, of which motor vehicles and parts 8.2%; chemical products 13.8%; electrical machinery and equipment 8.1%; agricultural commodities 6.6%; mineral fuels 5.9%; crude materials [inedible] 5.9%; power-generating machinery 4.5%; general industrial machinery 4.5%; specialized industrial machinery 4.3%; scientific and precision equipment 3.9%; computers and office equipment 3.5%; telecommunications equipment 3.2%). *Major export destinations:* Canada 20.1%; Mexico 11.7%; China 5.5%; Japan 5.1%; Germany 4.2%; UK 4.1%; Netherlands 3.1%; South Korea 2.7%; Brazil 2.5%; France 2.2%; Singapore 2.2%; Taiwan 1.9%; Australia 1.7%; Hong Kong 1.7%; Switzerland 1.7%.

*1 metric ton = about 1.1 short tons;   1 kilometer = 0.6 mi (statute);   1 metric ton-km cargo = about 0.68 short ton-mi cargo;   c.i.f.: cost, insurance, and freight;   f.o.b.: free on board*

## Transport and communications

**Transport.** *Railroads* (2006): route length 151,947 km, of which Amtrak operates 34,733 km; (2004) passenger-km 41,574,000,000; metric ton-km cargo 2,835,000,000,000. *Roads* (2008): total length 6,531,276 km (paved 67%). *Vehicles* (2007): passenger cars 135,933,000; trucks and buses 111,331,000. *Merchant marine* (2006): vessels (1,000 gross tons and over) 625; total deadweight tonnage 10,172,000. *Navigable channels* (2004) 41,843 km. *Oil pipeline length* (2005) 210,824 km; *gas pipeline length* (2004; excluding service pipelines) 2,353,300 km. *Air transport* (2007): passenger-km 1,334,199,200,000; metric ton-km cargo 43,104,300,000. *Certified route passenger/cargo air carriers* (2005) 80; operating revenue (US$'000,000; 2007) 173,104; operating expenses (US$'000,000; 2007) 163,894. **Communications,** in total units (units per 1,000 persons). Telephone landlines (2008): 150,000,000 (481); cellular telephone subscribers (2008): 270,500,000 (868); personal computers (2005): 223,810,000 (755); total Internet users (2008): 230,630,000 (740); broadband Internet subscribers (2008): 79,014,000 (254).

## Education and health

**Literacy** (2003): percentage of population ages 16 and over: "illiterate" (able to perform no more than the most simple literacy skills—14% [30,000,000 people]); "basically literate" (able to perform simple and everyday literacy activities—29% [63,000,000 people]); "intermediately and proficiently literate" (able to perform moderately challenging to complex literacy activities—57% [123,000,000 people]). An additional 6,500,000 people were not interviewed for this 2003 survey because they did not speak English or had cognitive or mental disabilities. **Food** (2005): daily per capita caloric intake 3,754 (vegetable products 72.2%, animal products 27.8%); 143% of FAO recommended minimum requirement. Per capita consumption of major food groups (kilograms annually; 2005): milk 256.4; fresh vegetables 125.5; cereal products 177.2; fresh fruits 122.7; red meat 62.7; potatoes 54.7; poultry products 55.8; fats and oil 31.6; sugar 30.2; fish and shellfish 23.4; undernourished population (2002–04) less than 2.5% of total population. **Health** (2006): doctors of medicine 921,900 (1 per 329 persons), of which office-based practice 560,400—male 72.2%; female 27.8% (including specialties in internal medicine 16.9%, general and family practice 10.1%, pediatrics 8.1%, obstetrics and gynecology 4.6%, psychiatry 4.5%, anesthesiology 4.5%, general surgery 4.1%, emergency medicine 3.3%, diagnostic radiology 2.7%, orthopedic surgery 2.6%, cardiovascular diseases 2.4%, pathology 2.1%, ophthalmology 2.0%); doctors of osteopathy (2008) 64,000; nurses 2,417,150 (1 per 123 persons); dentists (2007) 184,000 (1 per 1,639 persons); hospital beds 947,000 (1 per 315 persons), of which nonfederal 95.3% (community hospitals 84.7%, psychiatric 8.9%, long-term general and special 1.7%; federal 4.9%; infant mortality rate per 1,000 live births (2008) 6.5.

## Military

**Total active duty personnel** (November 2009): 1,417,747 (army 38.7%, navy 23.4%, air force 23.5%, marines 14.4%, coast guard [November 2008] 2.6%). *Total reserve duty personnel* (November 2008): 979,378 (army 55.9%, navy 12.9%, air force 19.5%, marines 10.6%, coast guard 1.1%). **Military expenditure as percentage of GDP** (2008): 4.2%; per capita expenditure US$1,994. *Major overseas deployment* (December 2008): 283,589, of which in support of Operation Iraqi Freedom 63%, in support of Operation Enduring Freedom (in Afghanistan) 11%. *Foreign military sales deliveries* (September 2004–September 2007): US$35,611,000,000, of which to Israel 11.5%, to Egypt 11.1%, to Taiwan 9.2%, to Saudi Arabia 8.6%, to Poland 5.6%, to Japan 5.2%, to South Korea 5.1%, to Australia 4.2%.

## Background

The territory that is now the United States was originally inhabited for several thousand years by numerous American Indian peoples who had probably emigrated from Asia. European exploration and settlement from the 16th century began displacement of the Indians. The first permanent European settlement, by the Spanish, was at St. Augustine FL in 1565; the British settled Jamestown VA (1607), Plymouth MA (1620), Maryland (1632), and Pennsylvania (1681). They took New York, New Jersey, and Delaware from the Dutch in 1664, a year after the Carolinas had been granted to British noblemen. The British defeat of the French in 1763 ensured British political control over the 13 colonies.

Political unrest caused by British colonial policy culminated in the American Revolution (1775–83) and the Declaration of Independence (1776). The US was first organized under the Articles of Confederation (1781) and then finally under the Constitution (1787) as a federal republic. Boundaries extended west to the Mississippi River, excluding Spanish Florida. Land acquired from France by the Louisiana Purchase (1803) nearly doubled the country's territory. The US fought the War of 1812 with the British and acquired Florida from Spain in 1819. In 1830 it legalized removal of American Indians to lands west of the Mississippi River. Settlement expanded to the West Coast in the mid-19th century, especially after the discovery of gold in California in 1848. Victory in the Mexican-American War (1846–48) brought the territory of seven more future states (including California and Texas) into US hands. The northwestern boundary was established by treaty with Great Britain in 1846. The US acquired southern Arizona by the Gadsden Purchase (1853). It suffered disunity during the conflict between the slavery-based plantation economy in the South and the free industrial and agricultural economy in the North, culminating in the American Civil War (1861–65) and the abolition of slavery under the 13th Amendment.

After Reconstruction (1865–77), the US experienced rapid growth, urbanization, industrial development, and European immigration. In 1877 it authorized allotment of Indian reservation land to individual tribesmen, resulting in widespread loss of land to whites. By the beginning of the 20th century, it had acquired outlying territories, including Alaska, the Midway Islands, the Hawaiian Islands, the Philippines, Puerto Rico, Guam, Wake Island, American Samoa, the Panama Canal Zone, and part of the Virgin Islands. The US participated in World War I during 1917–18. It granted suffrage to women in 1920 and citizenship to American Indians in 1924. The stock market crash of 1929 led to the Great Depression. The US entered World War II after the Japanese bombing of Pearl Harbor (7 Dec 1941). The explosion of the first atomic bomb (6 Aug 1945), on Hiroshima, Japan, brought about the end of the war and set the US apart as a military power. After the war the US was involved in the reconstruction of Europe and Japan and embroiled in a rivalry with the Soviet Union that became known as the Cold War. It participated in the Korean War (1950–53). In 1952 it granted autonomous commonwealth status to Puerto Rico.

Racial segregation in schools was declared unconstitutional in 1954. Alaska and Hawaii were made states in 1959, bringing the total to 50. In 1964 Congress passed the Civil Rights Act and authorized full-scale intervention in the Vietnam War. The mid- to late 1960s were marked by widespread civil disorder, including race riots and antiwar demonstrations. The US accomplished the first manned lunar landing in 1969. All US troops were withdrawn from Vietnam by 1973. With the dissolution of the Soviet Union in 1991, the US assumed the status of sole world superpower. The US led a coalition of forces against Iraq in the Persian Gulf War (1990–91). Administration of the Panama Canal was turned over to Panama in 1999. After the September 11 attacks on the US in 2001 destroyed the World Trade Center and part of the Pentagon, the US attacked Afghanistan's Taliban government for harboring and refusing to extradite the mastermind of the terrorist acts, Osama bin Laden. In 2003 the US attacked Iraq, with British support, and overthrew the government of Saddam Hussein; the US then found itself engaged in protracted wars in both Iraq and Afghanistan. In 2008 the US economy was rocked by a financial crisis brought about largely by the collapse of the housing market. As the crisis rippled worldwide, recession and a slow recovery followed in the US.

## Recent Developments

In its least-productive year in recent history, the US Congress approved only 80 new public measures in 2011, the lowest number since World War II. The deadlock resulted after a Republican majority took control of the House of Representatives in January, having vowed to stop and even undo Pres. Barack Obama's agenda. However, the White House successfully pushed Congress to approve free-trade agreements with Colombia, Panama, and South Korea. The agreement with South Korea was the largest new trade pact since the North American Free Trade Agreement (NAFTA). In October the first Mexican truck cleared to haul loads into the US interior under NAFTA's mandate entered the country. This was controversial because labor leaders claimed that Mexican safety rules and training were not as vigorous as were those in the US.

For the first three quarters of 2011, GDP grew at a woeful 1.8% or less, and though economic activity accelerated in the fourth quarter (with growth of 3.0%), first-quarter 2012 growth fell back, to 1.9%. It was estimated that more than 30% of borrowers held mortgages that were greater than the value of their homes. Even so, economic reports indicated a more robust recovery might be under way. In April 2012, the unemployment rate dropped to 8.1%, its lowest level in 35 months, and the US saw a monthly budget surplus for the first time in nearly three years.

The hostile US relationship with Iran deteriorated further as international efforts to prevent the development of nuclear weapons in that country met with continued Iranian intransigence. Late in the year, the US, Britain, and Canada imposed strict sanctions on the Iranian government, banking, and energy production. Iran retaliated by threatening to blockade the vital Strait of Hormuz. In November a drone conducting surveillance over Iran fell into Iranian hands largely intact in a major propaganda victory. Iran claimed that its computer specialists had hacked into the control system of the drone, effectively hijacking it and forcing it to land. The US continued its diplomatic chess game with China. After China arranged to set up a military outpost in far-off Seychelles, ostensibly to help counter Indian Ocean piracy, Obama announced a new US-Australian military arrangement, which began with the permanent detachment of a US Marine brigade to Darwin, on Australia's northern shore. In July 2011, in a case joined by the US, the WTO found that controls China put in 2010 on its export of rare-earth minerals, which are used in developing technologies such as computer and mobile-device components and hybrid and electric cars, violated WTO rules. Nonetheless, in December 2011, China announced that it would again cut its rare-earth export quota. In March 2012, the EU, Japan, and the US filed another, related complaint with the WTO. In September 2011, the US agreed to upgrade Taiwan's fleet of F-16 military jets rather than sell the country 66 new ones, but in May 2012 the US House of Representatives passed legislation that would require the US government to sell Taiwan the new planes, in addition to the upgrades.

On 2 May 2011, a US Navy SEAL team invaded a walled compound in Pakistan—located near the Pakistani army's chief officer-training academy—and killed Osama bin Laden, the mastermind of the September 11 attacks. The incident further strained the already-tenuous US relationship with Islamic Pakistan, which had long been suspected of playing both sides in the war on Muslim extremism. Rankled by the US failure to alert it to the bin Laden raid, the Pakistani government allowed Chinese technicians to inspect a technologically advanced US helicopter abandoned by the raiders. Late in the year, in an apparent case of mistaken targeting, NATO aircraft killed 24 Pakistani soldiers manning a border station near Afghanistan. In response the Pakistani government shut down one of the key routes used to supply NATO forces in Afghanistan. In June 2012, NATO signed an agreement with Kazakhstan, Kyrgyzstan, and Uzbekistan to remove war matériel through their territories ahead of the scheduled 2014 withdrawal of foreign troops from Afghanistan. In May, the US and Afghanistan signed a strategic partnership agreement that laid out the conditions for continued US aid as well as the stationing of military forces in Afghanistan after the 2014 withdrawal. In late December 2011, the departure of the final US troops from Iraq brought an end to a nearly nine-year conflict that had cost the US some US$800 billion and 4,400 lives.

Internet resource: <www.fedstats.gov>.

# Uruguay

Official name: República Oriental del Uruguay (Oriental Republic of Uruguay). Form of government: republic with two legislative houses (Senate [31]; Chamber of Representatives [99]). Head of state and government: President José Alberto Mujica Cordano (from 2010). Capital: Montevideo. Official language: Spanish. Official religion: none. Monetary unit: 1 peso uruguayo (UYU) = 100 centésimos; valuation (2 Jul 2012) US$1 = UYU 21.75.

## Demography

Area: 68,679 sq mi, 177,879 sq km. Population (2011): 3,380,000. Density (2011): persons per sq mi 49.2, persons per sq km 19.0. Urban (2010): 92.5%. Sex distribution (2007): male 48.30%; female 51.70%. Age breakdown (2007): under 15, 23.4%; 15–29, 22.8%; 30–44, 19.6%; 45–59, 16.5%; 60–74, 11.5%; 75–84, 4.7%; 85 and over, 1.5%. Ethnic composition (2006): white (mostly Spanish, Italian, or mixed Spanish-Italian) 87.4%; black/part-black 8.4%; Amerindian/part-Amerindian 3.0%; other 1.2%. Religious affiliation (2004): Roman Catholic 54%; Protestant 11%; Mormon 3%; Jewish 0.8%; nonreligious/atheist 26%; other 5.2%. Major cities (2004): Montevideo 1,269,552; Salto 99,072; Paysandú 73,272; Las Piedras 69,222; Rivera 64,426. Location: southern South America, bordering Brazil, the South Atlantic Ocean, and Argentina.

## Vital statistics

Birth rate per 1,000 population (2008): 14.6 (world avg. 20.3); (2002) within marriage 42.9%. Death rate per 1,000 population (2008): 9.4 (world avg. 8.5). Total fertility rate (avg. births per childbearing woman; 2007): 2.02. Life expectancy at birth (2008): male 72.4 years; female 79.7 years.

## National economy

Budget (2006). Revenue: UYU 111,321,000,000 (taxes on goods and services 59.1%; corporate taxes 12.3%; property taxes 7.1%; nontax revenue 6.7%; income tax 5.6%). Expenditures: UYU 117,225,-000,000 (social security and welfare 27.6%; government transfers including debt servicing 20.7%; public administration 13.9%; education 12.3%; health 7.4%; defense 4.4%). Production (metric tons except as noted). Agriculture and fishing (2007): rice 1,200,000, soybeans 800,000, wheat 620,000, sunflower seeds 60,000, honey 13,200; livestock (number of live animals) 12,000,000 cattle, 11,000,000 sheep; fisheries production 108,750 (from aquaculture, negligible). Mining and quarrying (2007): limestone 1,200,000; clays 82,200; gold 2,820 kg. Manufacturing (value added in UYU '000,000; 2005): food products and beverages 17,390; refined petroleum products 5,945; textiles, hides, and leather goods 4,633. Energy production (consumption): electricity (kW-hr; 2006) 5,618,000,000 (8,437,000,000); coal (metric tons; 2006) none (2,000); crude petroleum (barrels; 2006) none (13,900,000); petroleum products (metric tons; 2006) 1,758,000 (1,889,000); natural gas (cu m; 2006) none (110,000,000). Population economically active (2006): total 1,580,400; activity rate 47.7% (participation rates: ages 14–64, 72.7%; female 43.5%; unemployed [2007] 9.2%). Gross national income (2008): US$27,536,000,000 (US$8,260 per capita). Public debt (external, outstanding; 2007): US$9,616,000,000. Selected balance of payments data. Receipts from (US$'000,000): tourism (2007) 809; remittances (2008) 104; foreign direct investment (FDI; 2005–07 avg.) 1,042; official development assistance (2007) 34. Disbursements for (US$'000,000): tourism (2007) 239; remittances (2008) 5; FDI (2005–07 avg.) 13.

## Foreign trade

Imports (2006; c.i.f.): US$4,775,000,000 (crude petroleum and refined petroleum products 27.5%; machinery and appliances 16.0%; chemical products 12.7%; food products, beverages, and tobacco products 8.7%; transportation equipment 7.4%). Major import sources: Argentina 22.6%; Brazil 22.6%; Venezuela 12.6%; China 7.3%; US 6.8%. Exports (2006; f.o.b.): US$3,952,000,000 (beef 23.7%; hides and leather goods 8.6%; dairy products, eggs, and honey 6.9%; textiles and wearing apparel 6.8%; rice 5.5%; plastics and rubber products 5.1%). Major export destinations: Brazil 14.7%; US 13.2%; Argentina 7.6%; Russia 5.7%; Germany 4.2%.

## Transport and communications

Transport. Railroads (2006): route length 2,073 km; passenger-km (2004) 11,000,000; metric ton-km cargo (2005) 331,000,000. Roads (2007): length 16,398 km (paved 22%). Vehicles (2006): passenger cars 553,204; trucks and buses 91,007. Air transport (2008; PLUNA only): passenger-km 809,094,000; metric ton-km cargo, none. Commu-

**nications,** in total units (units per 1,000 persons). Telephone landlines (2008): 959,000 (286); cellular telephone subscribers (2008): 3,308,000 (1,047); personal computers (2005): 450,000 (135); total Internet users (2008): 1,340,000 (400); broadband Internet subscribers (2008): 245,000 (73).

## Education and health

**Educational attainment** (2006). Percentage of population ages 25 and over having: no formal schooling 1.9%; incomplete primary education 15.1%; complete primary 25.8%; incomplete secondary 20.8%; complete secondary 17.6%; incomplete higher 7.2%; complete higher 11.6%. **Literacy** (2003): population ages 15 and over literate 98.0%; males literate 97.6%; females literate 98.4%. **Health:** physicians (2006) 13,603 (1 per 245 persons); hospital beds (2003) 6,661 (1 per 499 persons); infant mortality rate per 1,000 live births (2007) 12.0; undernourished population (2002–04) less than 2.5% of total population.

## Military

**Total active duty personnel** (November 2008): 25,382 (army 66.6%, navy/coast guard 21.6%, air force 11.8%). **Military expenditure as percentage of GDP** (2007): 1.3%; per capita expenditure US$91.

## Background

The Spanish navigator Juan Díaz de Solís sailed into the Río de la Plata in 1516. The Portuguese established Colonia in 1680. Subsequently, the Spanish established Montevideo in 1726, driving the Portuguese from their settlement; 50 years later Uruguay became part of the Viceroyalty of the Río de la Plata. It gained independence from Spain in 1811. The Portuguese regained it in 1821, incorporating it into Brazil as a province. A revolt against Brazil in 1825 led to its being recognized as an independent state in 1828. It battled Paraguay in 1865–70. For much of World War II, Uruguay remained neutral. The presidential office was abolished in 1951 but restored in 1966. A military coup occurred in 1973, but the country returned to civilian rule in 1985. The 1990s brought a general upturn in the economy, largely the result of reform measures and membership in Mercosul, the Southern Common Market, from 1991.

## Recent Developments

In 2011, Pres. José Mujica's second year in office, Uruguay continued to enjoy a solid economy and international respect for its political stability. Inflation for the year was only 5.2%, unemployment stood at a historic low at 5.3%, and GDP was estimated to grow by 6.3% for the year—the ninth straight year of economic growth. Moreover, exports were at record levels, and tourism became the single-greatest source of foreign exchange. Politically, a conflict erupted in November, when the teachers union and local school boards rejected a pilot project for edu-

cational reform that had been painstakingly negotiated. President Mujica promised to take a firm stand to see that the reform project was implemented.

**Internet resource:** <www.turismo.gub.uy>.

# Uzbekistan

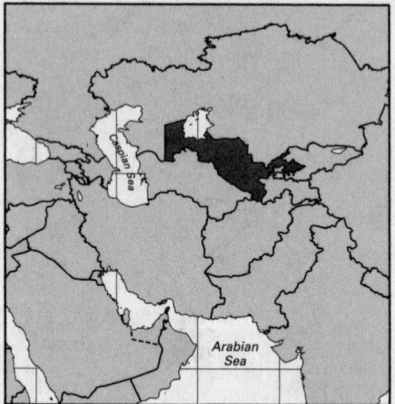

**Official name:** Uzbekiston Respublikasi (Republic of Uzbekistan). **Form of government:** republic with two legislative houses (Senate [100]; Legislative Chamber [150]). **Head of state and government:** President Islam Karimov (from 1990), assisted by Prime Minister Shavkat Mirziyayev (from 2003). **Capital:** Tashkent (Toshkent). **Official language:** Uzbek. **Official religion:** none. **Monetary unit:** sum (UZS; plural sumy); valuation (2 Jul 2012) US$1 = UZS 1,884.75.

## Demography

**Area:** 171,469 sq mi, 444,103 sq km. **Population** (2011): 28,129,000. **Density** (2011): persons per sq mi 164.0, persons per sq km 63.3. **Urban** (2010): 51.5%. **Sex distribution** (2006): male 49.56%; female 50.44%. **Age breakdown** (2006): under 15, 32.9%; 15–29, 30.3%; 30–44, 19.6%; 45–59, 11.2%; 60–74, 4.3%; 75 and over, 1.7%. **Ethnic composition** (2000): Uzbek 78.3%; Tajik 4.7%; Kazakh 4.1%; Tatar 3.3%; Russian 2.5%; Karakalpak 2.1%; other 5.0%. **Religious affiliation** (2000): Muslim (mostly Sunni) 76.2%; Russian Orthodox 0.8%; Jewish 0.2%; nonreligious 18.1%; other 4.7%. **Major cities** (2007): Tashkent (Toshkent) 1,959,190; Namangan 446,237; Andijon 321,622; Samarkand 312,863; Bukhara 249,037. **Location:** central Asia, bordering Kazakhstan, Kyrgyzstan, Tajikistan, Afghanistan, and Turkmenistan.

## Vital statistics

**Birth rate** per 1,000 population (2008): 23.6 (world avg. 20.3). **Death rate** per 1,000 population (2008):

*1 metric ton = about 1.1 short tons; 1 kilometer = 0.6 mi (statute); 1 metric ton-km cargo = about 0.68 short ton-mi cargo; c.i.f.: cost, insurance, and freight; f.o.b.: free on board*

5.0 (world avg. 8.5). **Total fertility rate** (avg. births per childbearing woman; 2006): 2.91. **Life expectancy** at birth (2006): male 61.2 years; female 68.1 years.

## National economy

**Budget** (2006; general government consolidated budget). *Revenue:* UZS 6,406,000,000,000 (taxes on income and profits 20.2%; VAT 17.3%; taxes on property and resources 12.2%; excise taxes 10.2%). *Expenditures:* UZS 6,331,000,000,000 (health and education 34.4%; social security 27.0%; national economy 9.0%; centralized investments 8.1%). **Public debt** (external, outstanding; 2007): US$3,086,000,000. **Production** (metric tons except as noted). *Agriculture and fishing* (2007): wheat 5,900,000, seed cotton 3,300,000, tomatoes 1,327,000, raw silk 487; livestock (number of live animals) 10,450,000 sheep, 7,042,500 cattle, 1,974,300 goats, 16,500 camels; fisheries production 6,226 (from aquaculture 55%). *Mining and quarrying* (metal content; 2006): copper 115,000; uranium 2,260; gold (all forms) 85,000 kg. *Manufacturing* (value of production in UZS '000,000,000; 2006): nonferrous metals 2,705; mineral fuels 2,487; machinery and metalworking products 1,986. *Energy production (consumption):* electricity (kW-hr; 2008) 50,100,000,000 ([2006] 47,000,000,000); lignite (metric tons; 2006) 3,126,000 (3,050,000); crude petroleum (barrels; 2006) 39,465,000 (24,078,000); petroleum products (metric tons; 2006) 4,685,000 (4,461,000); natural gas (cu m; 2006) 62,500,000,000 (48,400,000,000). **Population economically active** (2004): total 9,945,500; activity rate of total population 38.7% (participation rates [2001]: ages 16–59 [male], 16–54 [female] 70.4%; female 44.0%; unemployed [official rate; 2007] 0.8%). **Gross national income** (2008): US$24,738,000,000 (US$910 per capita). **Selected balance of payments data.** Receipts from (US$'000,000): tourism (2007) 51; remittances (2005) 790; foreign direct investment (2005–07 avg.) 182; official development assistance (2007) 166.

## Foreign trade

**Imports** (2006; c.i.f.): US$4,395,900,000 (machinery and metalworking products 40.3%; chemical products 15.0%; base metals 10.4%; food products 8.1%). *Major import sources:* Russia 27.8%; South Korea 15.2%; China 10.4%; Kazakhstan 7.3%; Germany 7.1%. **Exports** (2006; f.o.b.): US$6,389,800,000 (cotton fiber 17.2%; energy products [including natural gas and crude petroleum] 13.1%; base metals 12.9%; machinery and apparatus 10.1%; gold, n.a.; uranium, n.a.). *Major export destinations:* Russia 23.7%; Poland 11.7%; China 10.4%; Turkey 7.7%; Kazakhstan 5.9%.

## Transport and communications

**Transport.** *Railroads* (2008): length (2006) 3,950 km; passenger-km 2,500,000,000; metric ton-km cargo 23,400,000,000. *Roads* (2005): total length 84,400 km (paved 85%). *Vehicles* (1994): passenger cars 865,300; buses 14,500. *Air transport* (2008): passenger-km 5,600,000,000; metric ton-km cargo 83,300,000. **Communica-**

**tions,** in total units (units per 1,000 persons). Telephone landlines (2008): 1,850,000 (68); cellular telephone subscribers (2008): 12,734,000 (468); total Internet users (2008): 2,469,000 (91); broadband Internet subscribers (2008): 66,000 (2.4).

## Education and health

**Educational attainment** (2002). Percentage of population ages 25 and over having: no formal education/unknown 2.5%; incomplete primary education 9.0%; primary 7.3%; secondary 66.0%; higher 15.2%. **Literacy** (2003): percentage of total population ages 15 and over literate, virtually 100%. **Health** (2005): physicians 70,159 (1 per 371 persons); hospital beds 135,143 (1 per 193 persons); infant mortality rate per 1,000 live births (2008) 12.6; undernourished population (2003–05) 3,600,000 (14% of total population based on the consumption of a minimum daily requirement of 1,870 calories).

## Military

**Total active duty personnel** (November 2008): 67,000 (army 74.6%, air force 25.4%); German troops (November 2008): 163. **Military expenditure as percentage of GDP** (2007): 0.5%; per capita expenditure US$3.

## Background

Genghis Khan's grandson Shibaqan received the territory of Uzbekistan as his inheritance in the 13th century AD. His Mongols ruled over nearly 100 mainly Turkic tribes, who would eventually intermarry with the Mongols to form the Uzbeks and other Turkic peoples of central Asia. In the early 16th century, a federation of Mongol-Uzbeks invaded and occupied settled regions, including an area called Transoxania that would become the Uzbeks' permanent homeland. By the early 19th century the region was dominated by the khanates of Khiva, Bukhara, and Quqon, all of which eventually succumbed to Russian domination. The Uzbek Soviet Socialist Republic was created in 1924. In June 1990 Uzbekistan became the first Central Asian republic to declare sovereignty. It achieved full independence from the USSR in 1991. During the 1990s its economy was considered the strongest in Central Asia, though its political system was deemed harsh.

## Recent Developments

In September 2011 the US Congress voted to remove restrictions that had been imposed in 2004 on military aid to Uzbekistan because of the country's poor human rights record. Human Rights Watch, however, had appealed for the restrictions to remain intact, claiming that the Uzbek human rights record had hardly improved. That month more than 60 prominent international clothing firms signed a pledge to boycott Uzbek cotton because of the use of child labor in its production. While Uzbek officials denied that children were being forced into the cotton fields, human rights activists were detained for photographing child cotton pickers. The boycott threatened to have serious consequences for Uzbekistan's foreign currency earnings, though the country was increasingly shipping cotton to the Middle East and Asia. US officials' eagerness to remove the restrictions indicated the importance of Uzbek support for the Northern Distribution Network (NDN), which supplied the NATO military in Afghanistan. An unidentified US official was quoted as saying that the objective of providing military aid was to ensure that Uzbekistan could defend itself if it was attacked for its support of the NDN.

Internet resource: <www.stat.uz/en>.

# Vanuatu

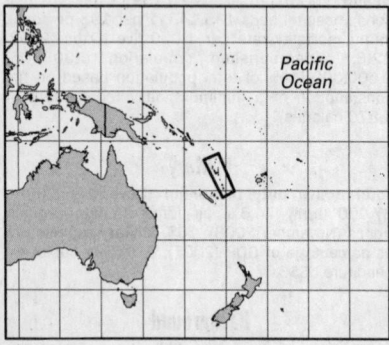

Pacific
Ocean

Official name: Ripablik blong Vanuatu (Bislama); République de Vanuatu (French); Republic of Vanuatu (English). Form of government: republic with a single legislative house (Parliament [52]). Head of state: President Iolu Abil (from 2009). Head of government: Prime Minister Sato Kilman (from 2011). Capital: Port-Vila. Official languages: Bislama; French; English. Official religion: none. Monetary unit: vatu (Vt); valuation (2 Jul 2012) US$1 = Vt 94.85.

## Demography

Area: 4,707 sq mi, 12,190 sq km. Population (2011): 251,000. Density (2011): persons per sq mi 53.3, persons per sq km 20.6. Urban (2010): 25.6%. Sex distribution (2009): male 51.27%; female 48.73%. Age breakdown (2005): under 15, 40.1%; 15–29, 27.7%; 30–44, 17.5%; 45–59, 9.7%; 60–74, 4.1%; 75 and over, 0.9%. Ethnic composition (1999): Ni-Vanuatu (Melanesian) 98.7%; European and other Pacific Islanders 1.3%. Religious affiliation (2005): Protestant 70%, of which Presbyterian 32%, Anglican 13%, Adventist 11%; Roman Catholic 13%; traditional beliefs (significantly the John Frum cargo cult) 5%; other 12%. Major towns (2009): Port-Vila 45,694; Luganville 13,484; Norsup (2006) 3,000. Location: Oceania, island group between the South Pacific Ocean and the Coral Sea.

## Vital statistics

Birth rate per 1,000 population (2008): 31.1 (world avg. 20.3). Death rate per 1,000 population (2008): 5.5 (world avg. 8.5). Total fertility rate (avg. births per childbearing woman; 2008): 4.40. Life expectancy at birth (2008): male 65.6 years; female 69.0 years.

## National economy

Budget (2008). Revenue: Vt 16,997,000,000 (tax revenue 69.5%, of which VAT 26.9%, import duties 22.5%; grants 23.4%; nontax revenue 7.1%). Expenditures: Vt 15,121,000,000 (current expenditures 77.6%; development expenditures 22.4%). Production (metric tons except as noted). Agriculture and fishing (2007): coconuts 322,000, copra 21,644, bananas 14,500, cacao beans 1,400, kava (2004) 825; livestock (number of live animals) 174,137 cattle, 88,694 pigs, 8,792 goats; fisheries production 85,387 (from aquaculture, negligible). Mining and quarrying: small quantities of coral-reef limestone, crushed stone, sand, and gravel. Manufacturing (value added in Vt '000,000; 1995): food products, beverages, and tobacco products 645; wood products 423; fabricated metal products 377. Energy production (consumption): electricity (kW-hr; 2008) 55,000,000 (55,000,000); petroleum products (metric tons; 2006) none (30,000). Population economically active (2006): total 112,000; activity rate of total population 50.7% (participation rates: ages 15–64, 84.3%; female 46.4%; officially unemployed [1999] 1.7%). Gross national income (2008): US$539,000,000 (US$2,330 per capita). Public debt (external, outstanding; 2007): US$71,600,000. Selected balance of payments data. Receipts from (US$'000,000): tourism (2007) 119; remittances (2008) 7; foreign direct investment (FDI; 2005–07 avg.) 30; official development assistance (2007) 57. Disbursements for (US$'000,000): tourism (2007) 11; remittances (2008) 3; FDI (2005–07 avg.) 1.

## Foreign trade

Imports (2008; c.i.f.): Vt 29,023,000,000 (machinery and transportation equipment 30.7%; mineral fuels 16.6%; food products and live animals 15.3%; chemical products 7.0%). Major import sources (2007): Australia 31.1%; New Zealand 16.8%; Singapore 12.4%; Fiji 9.1%; China 6.6%. Exports (2008; f.o.b.): Vt 4,249,000,000 (domestic exports 84.4%, of which copra 25.3%, coconut oil 17.1%, kava 11.5%, beef 9.1%, cocoa 5.6%; reexports 15.6%). Major export destinations (2007): Philippines 14.0%; New Caledonia 9.7%; Fiji 6.7%; Japan 5.4%; Singapore 5.4%.

## Transport and communications

Transport. Railroads: none. Roads (2000): total length 1,070 km (paved 24%). Vehicles (2001): passenger cars 2,600; trucks and buses 4,400. Air transport (2008; Air Vanuatu only): passenger-km 457,518,000; metric ton-km cargo 1,714,000. Communications, in total units (units per 1,000 persons). Telephone landlines (2008): 10,000 (44); cellular telephone subscribers (2008): 36,000 (154); personal computers

*1 metric ton = about 1.1 short tons;    1 kilometer = 0.6 mi (statute);    1 metric ton-km cargo = about 0.68 short ton-mi cargo;    c.i.f.: cost, insurance, and freight;    f.o.b.: free on board*

(2005): 3,000 (14); total Internet users (2008): 17,000 (73); broadband Internet subscribers (2007): 100 (0.4).

## Education and health

**Educational attainment** (1999). Percentage of population ages 15 and over having: no formal schooling 18.0%; incomplete primary education 20.6%; completed primary 35.5%; some secondary 12.2%; completed secondary 8.5%; higher 5.2%, of which university 1.3%. **Literacy** (2007): total population ages 15 and over literate, 74%. **Health** (2005): physicians (2008) 26 (1 per 9,000 persons); hospital beds 885 (1 per 244 persons); infant mortality rate per 1,000 live births 55.2; undernourished population (2002–04) 20,000 (11% of total population based on the consumption of a minimum daily requirement of 1,790 calories).

## Military

**Total active duty personnel** (2008): none; Australia and New Zealand assist paramilitary forces through defense assistance programs.

## Background

The islands of Vanuatu were inhabited for at least 3,000 years by Melanesian peoples before being discovered in 1606 by the Portuguese. They were rediscovered by French navigator Louis-Antoine de Bougainville in 1768 and then explored by English mariner Capt. James Cook in 1774 and named the New Hebrides. Sandalwood merchants and European missionaries arrived in the mid-19th century; they were followed by British and French cotton planters. Control of the islands was sought by both the French and the British, who agreed in 1906 to form a condominium government. During World War II a major Allied naval base was on Espíritu Santo; the island group escaped Japanese invasion. The New Hebrides became the independent Republic of Vanuatu in 1980. Much of the nation's housing was ravaged by a hurricane in 1987.

## Recent Developments

Vanuatu's economy remained strong in 2011. Remittances from horticultural and viticultural seasonal workers employed in Australia and New Zealand through government programs helped support the Vanuatu economy. In addition, Vanuatu established a trade office in Hong Kong to encourage foreign (primarily Chinese) companies to register in Vanuatu. In October the WTO approved Vanuatu's accession, but ratification was delayed by domestic opposition to membership. Membership in the international organization was approved in December, though controversy remained.

**Internet resource:** <www.vnso.gov.vu>.

# Vatican City State

**Official name:** State of the Vatican City (Holy See). **Form of government:** ecclesiastical. **Head of state:** Pope Benedict XVI (from 2005). **Head of govern-**

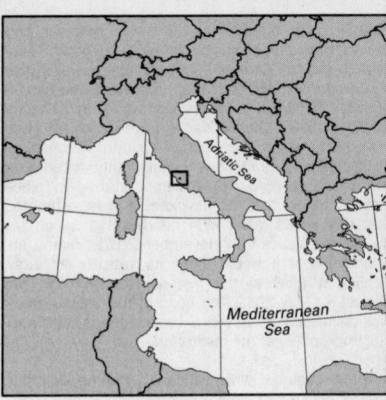

ment: Secretary of State Tarcisio Cardinal Bertone (from 2006). **Capital:** Vatican City. **Languages:** Italian; Latin. **Religion:** Roman Catholic. **Monetary unit:** 1 euro (€) = 100 cents; valuation (2 Jul 2012) US$1 = €0.79 (Vatican City uses the euro as its official currency, even though it is not a member of the EU).

## Demography

**Area:** 0.17 sq mi, 0.44 sq km. **Population** (2010): 800. **Density** (2010): persons per sq mi 4,706, persons per sq km 1,818. **Location:** southern Europe, within the commune of Rome, Italy. **Annual budget:** US$209,000,000. **Industries:** banking and finance; printing; production of a small amount of mosaics and uniforms; tourism.

## Background

Vatican City, the independent papal state, is the smallest independent state in the world. Its medieval and Renaissance walls form its boundaries except on the southeast, at St. Peter's Square. Within the walls is a miniature nation, with its own diplomatic missions, newspaper, post office, radio station, banking system, army of more than 100 Swiss Guards, and publishing house. Extraterritoriality of the state extends to Castel Gandolfo, summer home of the Pope, and to several churches and palaces in Rome proper. Its independent sovereignty was recognized in the Lateran Treaty of 1929. The pope has absolute executive, legislative, and judicial powers within the city. He appoints the members of the Vatican's government organs, which are separate from those of the Holy See. The state's many imposing buildings include St. Peter's Basilica, the Vatican Palace, and the Vatican Museums. Frescoes by Michelangelo and Pinturicchio (in the Sistine Chapel) and Raphael's Stanze are also there. The Vatican Library contains a priceless collection of manuscripts from the pre-Christian and Christian eras. Vatican City was designated a UNESCO World Heritage site in 1984.

## Recent Developments

The Vatican in 2011 reported that in the previous year it had showed a budget surplus for the first time in four years, notwithstanding a dip in donations and transfers from the international dioceses to the

Holy See. The budget was still small, however, and the Vatican called on governments in other countries to provide financial support for such activities as Roman Catholic education, a system that served almost 60 million students worldwide. In February 2012, however, the Vatican received grim financial news. Italy, which like much of Western Europe was struggling with a financial crisis, announced that the Vatican's property-tax-exempt status, in place since 2005, would be revoked. It was estimated that this would result in a nearly US$1 billion tax bill for the Vatican. In November 2011, Ireland announced that it would close its Vatican embassy, dealing a blow to the historic relations the two shared. In May 2012, the head of the Vatican Bank was dismissed after several investigations into financial impropriety at the institution.

Internet resource: <www.vatican.va/phome_en.htm>.

# Venezuela

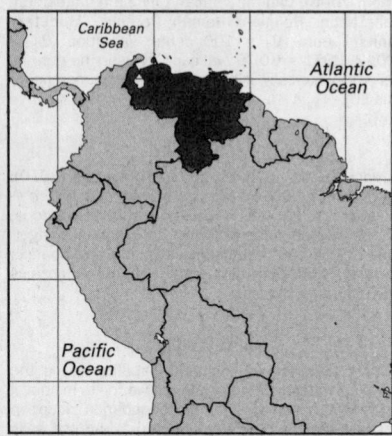

**Official name:** República Bolivariana de Venezuela (Bolivarian Republic of Venezuela). **Form of government:** federal multiparty republic with one legislative house (National Assembly [165]). **Head of state and government:** President Hugo Chávez Frías (from 2002). **Capital:** Caracas. **Official language:** Spanish (31 indigenous Indian languages are also official). **Official religion:** none. **Monetary unit:** 1 bolívar fuerte (VEF) = 100 céntimos; valuation (2 Jul 2012) US$1 = VEF 4.29 (the bolívar fuerte replaced the bolívar [VEB] 1 Jan 2008, at the rate of 1 VEF = VEB 1,000).

## Demography

**Area:** 353,841 sq mi, 916,445 sq km. **Population** (2011): 29,437,000. **Density** (2011): persons per sq mi 83.2, persons per sq km 32.1. **Urban** (2009): 93.7%. **Sex distribution** (2007): male 50.19%; female 49.81%. **Age breakdown** (2006): under 15, 32.1%; 15–29, 26.9%; 30–44, 20.5%; 45–59, 13.2%; 60–74, 5.5%; 75–84, 1.5%; 85 and over,

0.3%. **Ethnic composition** (2000): mestizo 63.7%; local white 20.0%; local black 10.0%; other white 3.3%; Amerindian 1.3%; other 1.7%. **Religious affiliation** (2005): Roman Catholic 84.5%; Protestant 4.0%; other 11.5%. **Major cities (urban agglomerations)** (2009 [2007]): Caracas 2,097,400 (2,985,000); Maracaibo 1,891,800 (2,072,000); Valencia 1,408,400 (1,770,000); Barquisimeto 1,018,900 (1,116,000); Ciudad Guayana 789,500. **Location:** northern South America, bordering the Caribbean Sea, the North Atlantic Ocean, Guyana, Brazil, and Colombia.

## Vital statistics

**Birth rate** per 1,000 population (2007): 21.5 (world avg. 20.3). **Death rate** per 1,000 population (2007): 5.1 (world avg. 8.5). **Total fertility rate** (avg. births per childbearing woman; 2007): 2.58. **Life expectancy** at birth (2007): male 70.7 years; female 76.6 years.

## National economy

**Budget** (2006). *Revenue:* VEB 117,326,000,000,000 (petroleum income 52.9%, of which royalties 37.5%, taxes 13.0%; nonpetroleum income 47.1%, of which VAT 22.4%). *Expenditures:* VEB 117,255,000,000,000 (current expenditures 75.0%; development expenditures 22.8%; other 2.2%). **Production** (metric tons except as noted). *Agriculture and fishing* (2007): sugarcane 9,300,000, corn (maize) 2,104,000, rice 800,000; livestock (number of live animals) 16,700,000 cattle, 120,000,000 chickens; fisheries production 477,210 (from aquaculture 5%). *Mining and quarrying* (2008): iron ore (metal content) 15,200,000; bauxite 5,500,000; phosphate rock 400,000; gold 10,100 kg; gem diamonds 45,000 carats. *Manufacturing* (value added in VEB '000,000,000; 2004): food products 8,122; iron and steel 3,022; refined petroleum products 2,890. *Energy production (consumption):* electricity (kW-hr; 2006) 110,357,000,000 (109,815,000,000); coal (metric tons; 2006) 7,338,000 (52,000); crude petroleum (barrels; 2008) 874,000,000 ([2006] 371,000,000); petroleum products (metric tons; 2006) 58,031,000 (26,320,000); natural gas (cu m; 2006) 24,530,000,000 (24,530,000,000). **Selected balance of payments data.** Receipts from (US$'000,000): tourism (2007) 817; remittances (2008) 130; foreign direct investment (FDI; 2005–07 avg.) 882; official development assistance (2007) 71. Disbursements for (US$'000,000): tourism (2007) 1,394; remittances (2008) 771; FDI (2005–07 avg.) 1,827. **Gross national income** (2008): US$257,794,000,000 (US$9,230 per capita). **Public debt** (external, outstanding; 2007): US$27,494,000,000. **Population economically active** (2006): total 12,379,700; activity rate 45.9% (participation rates: ages 15–64, 68.7%; female 38.6%; unemployed [July 2006–June 2007] 9.4%).

## Foreign trade

**Imports** (2006): US$30,559,000,000 (machinery and apparatus 26.6%; motor vehicles 12.1%;

*1 metric ton = about 1.1 short tons;　1 kilometer = 0.6 mi (statute);　1 metric ton-km cargo = about 0.68 short ton-mi cargo;　c.i.f.: cost, insurance, and freight;　f.o.b.: free on board*

chemical products 11.0%; food products 5.9%). *Major import sources:* US 30.6%; Colombia 10.2%; Brazil 10.1%; Mexico 5.9%; China 4.9%. **Exports** (2006): US$61,385,000,000 (crude petroleum 91.6%; iron and steel 2.8%; aluminum 1.7%; organic chemical products 0.6%). *Major export destinations:* US 46.2%; Netherlands Antilles 13.5%; China 3.2%.

## Transport and communications

**Transport.** *Railroads* (2008): route length 806 km; metric ton-km cargo (2004) 22,000,000. *Roads* (2004): total length 96,200 km (paved 34%). *Vehicles* (2007): passenger cars 2,952,129; trucks and buses 1,091,883. *Air transport* (2005): passenger-km 2,578,700,000; metric ton-km cargo 2,100,000. **Communications,** in total units (units per 1,000 persons). Telephone landlines (2008): 6,304,000 (224); cellular telephone subscribers (2008): 27,084,000 (963); personal computers (2005): 2,475,000 (98); total Internet users (2008): 7,167,000 (255); broadband Internet subscribers (2008): 1,330,000 (47).

## Education and health

**Educational attainment** (2003). Percentage of head-of-household population having: no formal schooling 10.2%; primary education or less 38.5%; some secondary 36.9%; completed secondary/higher 14.4%. **Literacy** (2003): total population ages 15 and over literate, 93.0%. **Health** (2003): physicians 35,756 (1 per 722 persons); hospital beds 74,866 (1 per 345 persons); infant mortality rate per 1,000 live births (2006) 23.0; undernourished population (2003–05) 3,200,000 (12% of total population based on the consumption of a minimum daily requirement of 1,830 calories).

## Military

**Total active duty personnel** (November 2008): 115,000 (army 54.8%, navy 15.2%, air force 10.0%, national guard 20.0%). **Military expenditure as percentage of GDP** (2007): 1.2%; per capita expenditure US$101.

## Background

In 1498 Christopher Columbus sighted Venezuela; in 1499 the navigators Alonso de Ojeda, Amerigo Vespucci, and Juan de la Cosa traced the coast. A Spanish missionary established the first European settlement at Cumaná in about 1520. In 1718 it was included in the Viceroyalty of New Granada and was made a captaincy general in 1731. Venezuelan Creoles led by Francisco de Miranda and Simón Bolívar spearheaded the South American independence movement, and though Venezuela declared independence from Spain in 1811, that status was not assured until 1821. Military dictators generally ruled the country from 1830 until the overthrow of Marcos Pérez Jiménez in 1958. A new constitution adopted in 1961 marked the beginning of democracy. As a founding member of OPEC, Venezuela enjoyed relative economic prosperity from oil production during the 1970s, and its economy has remained dependent on the world petroleum market. The leftist president Hugo Chávez promulgated a new constitution in 1999, and he was reelected in 2002. Despite an increase in oil prices in the early 21st century, the country experienced great political turmoil.

## Recent Developments

Even though a newly elected National Assembly took office in January 2011, Pres. Hugo Chávez of Venezuela used the special powers given to him for 18 months by the outgoing Assembly in December 2010 to legislate unilaterally in 2011. With these powers Chávez was able to end the autonomy of the central bank, increase the influence of communes, and establish military districts to enforce government policies in regions of strong resistance. The government increased its expropriation of farms and urban land. Chávez's ongoing crusade to build multinational Latin American organizations that excluded the United States bore fruit in December when 33 countries formed the Community of Latin American and Caribbean States (CELAC) without the US or Canada. Although the organization was structured as an annual summit without a permanent headquarters or secretariat, it sought to increase regional trade and integration. The Bolivarian Alliance of the Americas (ALBA), a group of seven countries governed by anticapitalist populist leaders, was another element of Chávez's strategy.

**Internet resource:**
<www.venezuelatuya.com/indexeng.htm>.

# Vietnam

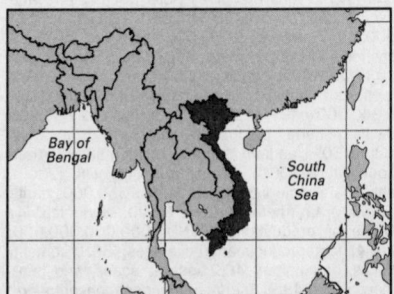

**Official name:** Cong Hoa Xa Hoi Chu Nghia Viet Nam (Socialist Republic of Vietnam). **Form of government:** socialist republic with one legislative house (National Assembly [500]). **Head of state:** President Truong Tan Sang (from 2011). **Head of government:** Prime Minister Nguyen Tan Dung (from 2006). **Capital:** Hanoi. **Official language:** Vietnamese. **Official religion:** none. **Monetary unit:** 1 dong (VND) = 10 hao = 100 xu; valuation (2 Jul 2012) US$1 = VND 20,895.00.

## Demography

**Area:** 127,882 sq mi, 331,212 sq km. **Population** (2011): 88,145,000. **Density** (2011): persons per sq mi 689.3, persons per sq km 266.1. **Urban** (2009): 29.6%. **Sex distribution** (2009): male 49.52%; female 50.48%. **Age breakdown** (2008): under 15,

26.6%; 15–29, 29.8%; 30–44, 22.2%; 45–59, 13.8%; 60–74, 5.3%; 75–84, 1.9%; 85 and over, 0.4%. **Ethnic composition** (1999): Vietnamese 86.2%; Tho (Tay) 1.9%; Montagnards 1.7%; Thai 1.7%; Muong 1.5%; Khmer 1.4%; Nung 1.1%; Miao (Hmong) 1.0%; Dao 0.8%; other 2.7%. **Religious affiliation** (2005): Buddhist 48%; New-Religionist (mostly Cao Dai and Hoa Hao) 11%; traditional beliefs 10%; Roman Catholic 7%; Protestant 1%; nonreligious/atheist 20%; other 3%. **Major cities (urban agglomerations)** (2009 [2007]): Ho Chi Minh City 5,929,479; Hanoi 2,632,087 (4,723,000); Haiphong 847,058 (2,129,000); Da Nang 770,499. **Location:** southeastern Asia, bordering China, the Gulf of Tonkin, the South China Sea, the Gulf of Thailand, Cambodia, and Laos.

## Vital statistics

**Birth rate** per 1,000 population (2008): 18.1 (world avg. 20.3). **Death rate** per 1,000 population (2008): 6.0 (world avg. 8.5). **Total fertility rate** (avg. births per childbearing woman; 2008): 2.02. **Life expectancy** at birth (2008): male 69.0 years; female 74.2 years.

## National economy

**Budget** (2008). *Revenue:* VND 323,000,000,000,000 (tax revenue 89.0%, of which petroleum related 20.3%; nontax revenue 9.9%; grants 1.1%). *Expenditures:* VND 364,000,000,000,000 (current expenditures 72.6%; capital expenditures 27.4%). **Public debt** (external, outstanding; 2007): US$19,372,000,000. **Gross national income** (2008): US$77,031,000,000 (US$890 per capita). **Production** (metric tons except as noted). *Agriculture and fishing* (2007): rice 35,566,800, sugarcane 16,000,000, cassava 8,900,000, coffee 1,060,000, cashews 961,000, natural rubber 550,000, tea 153,000, black pepper 82,000, cinnamon 9,500; livestock (number of live animals) 26,500,000 pigs, 6,840,000 cattle, 2,921,100 buffalo, 62,800,000 ducks; fisheries production 4,277,900 (from aquaculture 50%); aquatic plants production 38,000 (from aquaculture 100%). *Mining and quarrying* (2007): phosphate rock 1,360,000; kaolin 650,000; barite 120,000; tin (metal content) 3,500. *Manufacturing* (value of production in VND '000,000,000,000; 2004): food products and beverages 156.1; cement, bricks, and pottery 46.2; paints, soaps, and pharmaceuticals 43.9. *Energy production (consumption):* electricity (kW-hr; 2007) 66,900,000,000 ([2006] 56,494,000,000); coal (metric tons; 2007) 41,200,000 ([2006] 15,700,000); crude petroleum (barrels; 2008) 100,800,000 ([2006] negligible); petroleum products (metric tons; 2006) 483,000,000 (11,743,000); natural gas (cu m; 2007) 6,834,000,000 ([2006] 5,953,000,000). **Population economically active** (2004): total 43,242,000; activity rate of total population 52.9% (participation rates: ages 15–64, 77.7%; female 49.0%; unemployed [2008] 4.7%). **Selected balance of payments data.** Receipts from (US$'000,000): tourism (2006) 3,200; remittances (2008) 7,200; foreign direct investment (FDI; 2005–07 avg.) 3,707; official development assistance (2007) 2,497. Disbursements for (US$'000,000): FDI (2005–07 avg.) 100.

## Foreign trade

**Imports** (2006; c.i.f.): US$44,891,000,000 (machinery and apparatus 21.3%; chemical products 14.0%; refined petroleum products 13.9%; textile yarn, fabrics, and made-up articles 8.9%; iron and steel 7.7%). *Major import sources:* China 16.5%; Singapore 14.0%; Taiwan 10.7%; Japan 10.5%; South Korea 8.7%. **Exports** (2006; f.o.b.): US$39,826,000,000 (crude petroleum 20.9%; garments and accessories 14.0%; footwear 9.2%; furniture 4.5%; electrical machinery and equipment 3.7%; crustaceans 3.3%; rice 3.2%; coffee 3.1%; natural rubber 2.9%). *Major export destinations* (2007): US 20.8%; Japan 12.5%; Australia 7.8%; China 7.5%; Singapore 4.6%.

## Transport and communications

**Transport.** *Railroads* (2007): route length (2005) 2,600 km; passenger-km 4,659,000,000; metric ton-km cargo 3,883,000,000. *Roads* (2007): total length 160,089 km (paved 48%). *Vehicles* (2007): passenger cars 1,146,312. *Air transport* (2008): passenger-km 15,768,000,000; metric ton-km cargo 295,764,000. **Communications,** in total units (units per 1,000 persons). Telephone landlines (2008): 29,591,000 (338); cellular telephone subscribers (2008): 70,000,000 (799); personal computers (2007): 8,306,000 (96); total Internet users (2008): 20,834,000 (238); broadband Internet subscribers (2008): 2,049,000 (23).

## Education and health

**Educational attainment** (1999). Percentage of population ages 18 and over having: no formal education 9.0%; primary education 29.2%; lower secondary 32.5%; upper secondary 24.9%; incomplete/complete higher 4.3%; advanced degree 0.1%. **Literacy** (2003): percentage of population ages 15 and over literate 94.0%; males literate 95.8%; females literate 92.3%. **Health** (2007): physicians 54,798 (1 per 1,579 persons); hospital beds 210,800 (1 per 410 persons); infant mortality rate per 1,000 live births (2008) 23.0; undernourished population (2002–04) 13,000,000 (16% of total population based on the consumption of a minimum daily requirement of 1,840 calories).

## Military

**Total active duty personnel** (November 2008): 455,000 (army 90.5%, navy 2.9%, air force 6.6%). **Military expenditure as percentage of GDP** (2007): 5.3%; per capita expenditure US$43.

## Background

A distinct Vietnamese group began to emerge c. 200 BC in the independent kingdom of Nam Viet, which was annexed to China in the 1st century BC. The Vietnamese were under continuous Chinese control until the 10th century AD. The southern region was gradually overrun by Vietnamese from the north in the late 15th century. The area was divided into two parts in the early 17th century, with the northern part known as Tonkin and the southern

---

*1 metric ton = about 1.1 short tons;    1 kilometer = 0.6 mi (statute);    1 metric ton-km cargo = about 0.68 short ton-mi cargo;    c.i.f.: cost, insurance, and freight;    f.o.b.: free on board*

part as Cochin China. In 1802 the northern and southern parts of Vietnam were unified under a single dynasty. Following several years of attempted French colonial expansion in the region, the French captured Saigon in 1859 and later the rest of the area, controlling it until World War II. The Japanese occupied Vietnam in 1940–45 and declared it independent at the end of World War II, a move the French opposed. The French and Vietnamese fought the First Indochina War until French forces with US financial backing were defeated at Dien Bien Phu in 1954; evacuation of French troops ensued. Following an international conference at Geneva, Vietnam was partitioned along the 17th parallel, with the northern part under Ho Chi Minh and the southern part under Bao Dai; the partition was to be temporary, but the reunification elections scheduled for 1956 were never held. Bao Dai declared the independence of South Vietnam (Republic of Vietnam), while the Communists established North Vietnam (Democratic Republic of Vietnam). The activities of North Vietnamese guerrillas and pro-communist rebels in South Vietnam led to US intervention and the Vietnam War. A cease-fire agreement was signed in 1973, and US troops were withdrawn. The civil war soon resumed, and in 1975 North Vietnam invaded South Vietnam and the South Vietnamese government collapsed. In 1976 the two Vietnams were united as the Socialist Republic of Vietnam. From the mid-1980s the government enacted a series of economic reforms and began to open up to Asian and Western nations. In 1995 the US officially normalized relations with Vietnam.

## Recent Developments

The territorial dispute between Vietnam and China in the South China Sea heated up in 2011 as a result of altercations involving Chinese navy patrol boats and Vietnamese oil-exploration vessels in May and June. In June the Vietnamese navy conducted well-publicized live-fire exercises. China hosted a visit by Secretary-General Nguyen Phu Trong, the chair of the National Assembly Standing Committee, in October, during which an agreement on basic principles guiding the settlement of sea issues was reached, including proposals for joint economic development and biannual border negotiations. In September Vietnam signed a memorandum on defense cooperation with the United States. It was also announced in New Delhi that Vietnam had awarded an oil-exploration contract to an Indian company and that India was considering selling cruise missiles to Vietnam.

Internet resource: <www.gso.gov.vn>.

# Yemen

**Official name:** Al-Jumhuriyah al-Yamaniyah (Republic of Yemen). **Form of government:** multiparty republic with two legislative houses (Consultative Council [111]; House of Representatives [301]). **Head of state:** President ʻAbd Rabbuh Mansur Hadi (from 2012). **Head of government:** Prime Minister Muhammad Salim Basindwah (from 2011). **Capital:** Sanaa. **Official language:** Arabic. **Official religion:** Islam. **Monetary unit:** 1 Yemeni rial (YR) = 100 fils; valuation (2 Jul 2012): US$1 = YR 215.05.

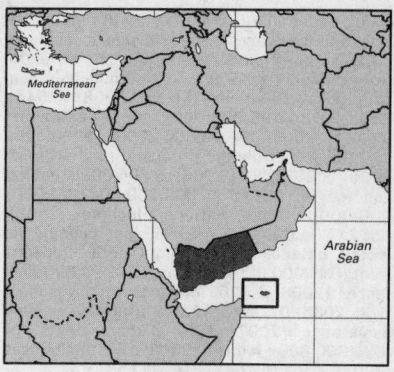

## Demography

**Area:** 203,891 sq mi, 528,076 sq km. **Population** (2011): 24,800,000. **Density** (2011): persons per sq mi 121.6, persons per sq km 47.0. **Urban** (2009): 31.2%. **Sex distribution** (2008): male 50.81%; female 49.19%. **Age breakdown** (2008): under 15, 44.3%; 15–29, 29.9%; 30–44, 14.0%; 45–59, 7.8%; 60–74, 3.1%; 75 and over, 0.9%. **Ethnic composition** (2000): Arab 92.8%; Somali 3.7%; black 1.1%; Indo-Pakistani 1.0%; other 1.4%. **Religious affiliation** (2005): Muslim nearly 100%, of which Sunni 58%, Shiʻi 42%. **Major cities** (2004): Sanaa (2007) 2,006,619; Aden 588,938; Taʻizz 466,968; Al-Hudaydah 409,994; Ibb 212,992. **Location:** the Middle East, bordering Saudi Arabia, Oman, the Arabian Sea, the Gulf of Aden, and the Red Sea.

## Vital statistics

**Birth rate** per 1,000 population (2008): 36.2 (world avg. 20.3). **Death rate** per 1,000 population (2008): 7.7 (world avg. 8.5). **Total fertility rate** (avg. births per childbearing woman; 2008): 5.20. **Life expectancy** at birth (2008): male 60.7 years; female 64.7 years.

## National economy

**Budget** (2007). *Revenue:* YR 1,406,400,000,000 (petroleum revenue 69.1%; tax revenue 21.9%; nontax revenue and grants 9.0%). *Expenditures:* YR 1,748,300,000,000 (transfers and subsidies 29.7%; wages and salaries 27.9%; interest on debt 5.7%). **Public debt** (external, outstanding; January 2009): US$5,977,000,000. **Population economically active** (2008): total 5,206,000; activity rate of total population 23.4% (participation rates: ages 15 and older, 42.7%; female 11.8%; unemployed 15.0%). **Production** (metric tons except as noted). *Agriculture and fishing* (2008): mangoes 387,906, sorghum 376,728, alfalfa 290,370, khat (qat) 165,668 [khat (qat) contributes roughly 2.5% of total GDP; khat cultivation employs nearly 15% of the labor force), dates 55,204, chickpeas 54,000, sesame 23,895; livestock (number of live animals) 8,889,000 sheep, 8,708,000 goats, 1,531,000 cattle, 373,000 camels; fisheries production 132,062 (from aquaculture, none). *Mining and quarrying* (2007): salt 100,000; gypsum 44,000. *Manufacturing* (value added in YR '000,000; 2008): food products and beverages 112,090; plastic products 60,299; paper products 46,850; refined petroleum products 10,509. *Energy production (consumption):* electricity (kW-hr; 2008) 6,545,-830,000 (4,496,700,000); crude petroleum (barrels; 2008–09) 102,041,700 ([2006] 29,-150,000); petroleum products (metric tons; 2008) 3,307,000 ([2006] 5,394,000); natural gas (cu m; 2007) 25,000,000,000 (25,000,-000,000). **Gross national income** (2008): US$21,901,000,000 (US$950 per capita). **Selected balance of payments data.** Receipts from (US$'000,000): tourism (2007) 425; remittances (2008) 1,420; foreign direct investment (FDI; 2005–07 avg.) 428; official development assistance (2007) 225. Disbursements for (US$'000,000): tourism (2008) 184; remittances (2008) 319; FDI (2005–07 avg.) 58.

## Foreign trade

**Imports** (2008; c.i.f.): YR 2,087,876,317,000 (crude petroleum and refined petroleum products 29.1%; food products and live animals 22.3%, of which grains 13.2%; transportation equipment 7.0%; base and fabricated metals 6.5%; chemical products 6.4%). *Major import sources:* UAE 28.9%; China 7.0%; Saudi Arabia 6.7%; Kuwait 6.4%; India 3.9%. **Exports** (2008; f.o.b.): YR 1,519,162,467,000 (refined petroleum products 77.3%; crude petroleum 9.9%; food products and live animals 5.0%, of which fish 2.6%; transportation equipment 1.9%; chemical products 1.7%). *Major export destinations:* China 31.1%; Thailand 23.8%; UAE 9.5%; India 8.0%; South Korea 6.3%.

## Transport and communications

**Transport.** *Railroads:* none. *Roads* (2007): total length 71,300 km (paved 9%). *Vehicles* (2004): passenger cars 522,437; trucks and buses 506,766. *Air transport* (2007): passenger-km (2004) 2,473,000,000; metric ton-km cargo 41,000,000. **Communications,** in total units (units per 1,000 persons). Telephone landlines (2008): 1,117,000 (49); cellular telephone subscribers (2008): 3,700,000 (161); personal computers (2006): 587,000 (28); total Internet users (2008): 370,000 (16).

## Education and health

**Educational attainment** (2005–06). Percentage of population ages 10 and over having: no formal schooling/unknown 42.3%; reading and writing ability 33.6%; primary education 13.1%; secondary 8.7%; higher 2.3%. **Literacy** (2007): percentage of total population ages 15 and over literate 58.9%; males literate 77.0%; females literate 40.5%. **Health** (2008): physicians 6,187 (1 per 3,592 persons); hospital beds 15,184 (1 per 1,464 persons); infant mortality rate per 1,000 live births 60.1; undernourished population (2002–04) 7,600,000 (38% of total population based on the consumption of a minimum daily requirement of 1,770 calories).

## Military

**Total active duty personnel** (November 2008): 66,700 (army 90.0%, navy 2.5%, air force/air defense 7.5%). **Military expenditure as percentage of GDP** (2007): 4.2%; per capita expenditure US$42.

## Background

Yemen was the home of ancient Minaean, Sabaean, and Himyarite kingdoms. The Romans invaded the region in the 1st century AD. In the 6th century, it was conquered by Ethiopians and Persians. Following conversion to Islam in the 7th century, it was ruled nominally under a caliphate. The Egyptian Ayyubid dynasty ruled there from 1173 to 1229, after which the region passed to the Rasulids. From 1517 through 1918, the Ottoman Empire maintained varying degrees of control, especially in the northwestern section. A boundary agreement was reached in 1934 between the northwestern imam-controlled territory, which subsequently became the Yemen Arab Republic (North Yemen), and the southeastern British-controlled territory, which subsequently became the People's Democratic Republic of Yemen (South Yemen). Relations between the two Yemens remained tense and were marked by conflict throughout the 1970s and 1980s. Reaching an accord, the two officially united as the Republic of Yemen in 1990. Its 1993 elections were the first free, multiparty general elections held in the Arabian Peninsula, and they were the first in which women participated. In 1994, after a two-month civil war, a new constitution was approved.

## Recent Developments

Inspired by the uprisings in Tunisia and Egypt, Yemeni protesters rallied in February 2011 to demand democratic reforms and an end to the nearly 33-year rule of Pres. ʿAli ʿAbd Allah Salih. The first protesters were mainly students, young people, and intellectuals, but in March they were joined by tribal forces and army units that had defected. As demonstrations continued, the government used force to suppress the revolt, killing and injuring thousands. A US-supported Gulf Cooperation Council (GCC) initiative to ease Salih out of power failed. In June an attack on Salih's compound left him badly injured. He was flown to Saudi Arabia for treatment, returning to Yemen in September. On November 23 Salih signed the GCC plan, transferring his powers to his vice president, ʿAbd Rabbuh Mansur Hadi. In December, Muhammad Basindwah became prime minister.

**Internet resource:** <www.cso-yemen.org>.

# Zambia

**Official name:** Republic of Zambia. **Form of government:** multiparty republic with one legislative house (National Assembly [158]). **Head of state and government:** President Michael Sata (from 2011). **Capital:** Lusaka. **Official language:** English. **Official religion:** none (Zambia is a Christian

*1 metric ton = about 1.1 short tons;   1 kilometer = 0.6 mi (statute);   1 metric ton-km cargo = about 0.68 short ton-mi cargo;   c.i.f.: cost, insurance, and freight;   f.o.b.: free on board*

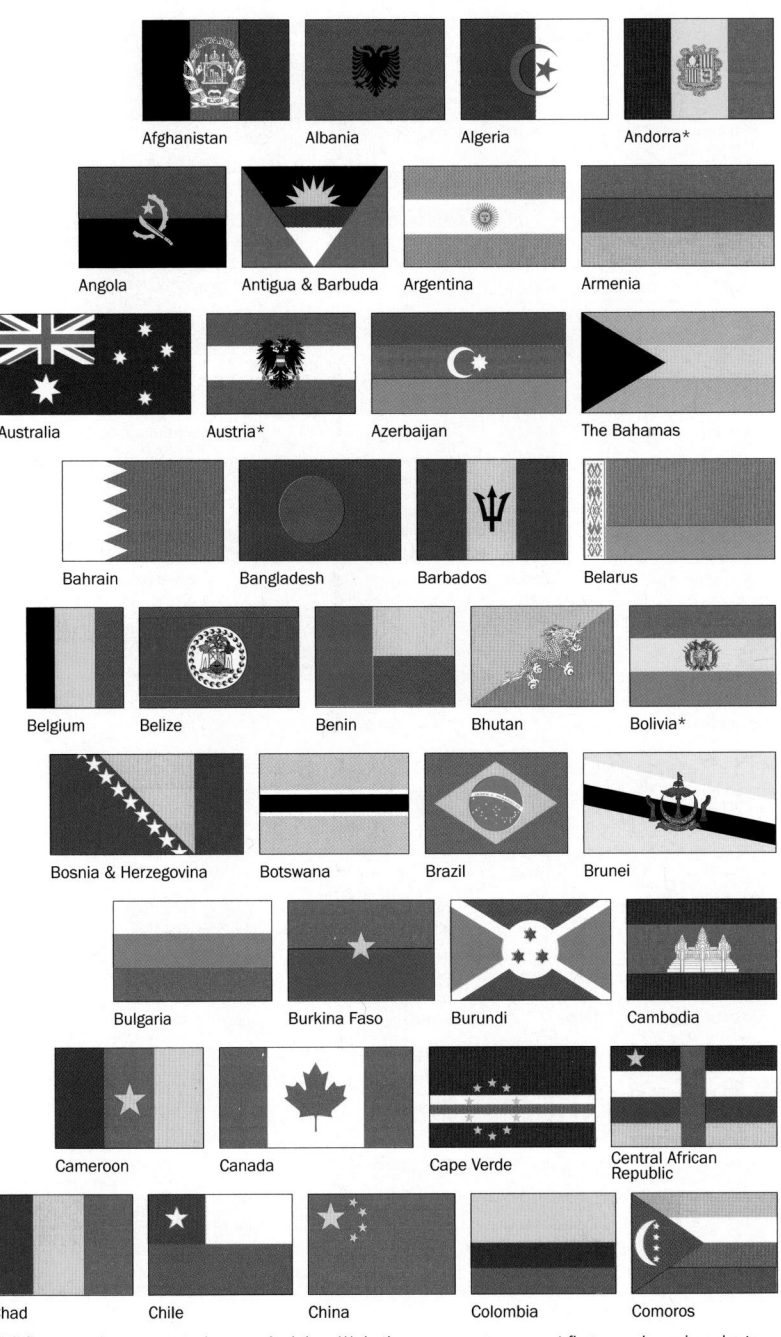

Afghanistan

Albania

Algeria

Andorra*

Angola

Antigua & Barbuda

Argentina

Armenia

Australia

Austria*

Azerbaijan

The Bahamas

Bahrain

Bangladesh

Barbados

Belarus

Belgium

Belize

Benin

Bhutan

Bolivia*

Bosnia & Herzegovina

Botswana

Brazil

Brunei

Bulgaria

Burkina Faso

Burundi

Cambodia

Cameroon

Canada

Cape Verde

Central African Republic

Chad

Chile

China

Colombia

Comoros

Civil flags are shown except where marked thus (*); in these cases, government flags are shown in order to illustrate emblems. Both styles are official national flags.

Plate 2 FLAGS OF THE WORLD

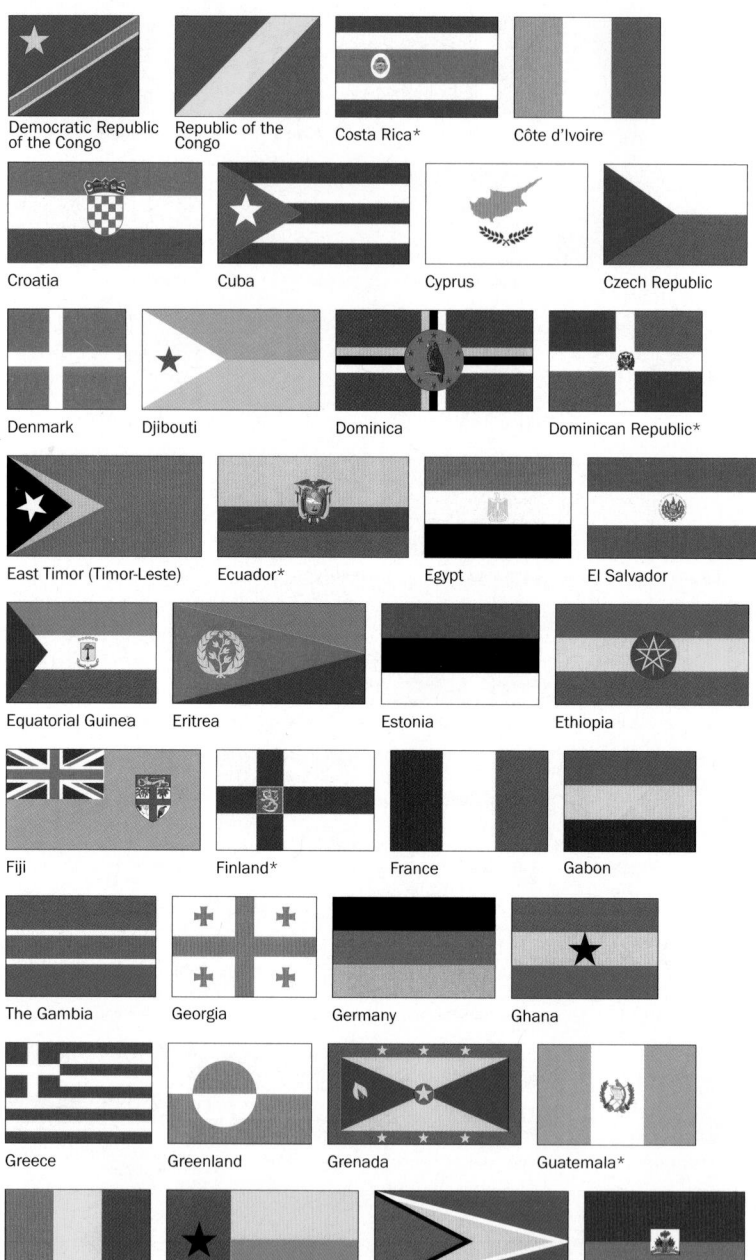

Democratic Republic of the Congo

Republic of the Congo

Costa Rica*

Côte d'Ivoire

Croatia

Cuba

Cyprus

Czech Republic

Denmark

Djibouti

Dominica

Dominican Republic*

East Timor (Timor-Leste)

Ecuador*

Egypt

El Salvador

Equatorial Guinea

Eritrea

Estonia

Ethiopia

Fiji

Finland*

France

Gabon

The Gambia

Georgia

Germany

Ghana

Greece

Greenland

Grenada

Guatemala*

Guinea

Guinea-Bissau

Guyana

Haiti*

Civil flags are shown except where marked thus (*); in these cases, government flags are shown in order to illustrate emblems. Both styles are official national flags.

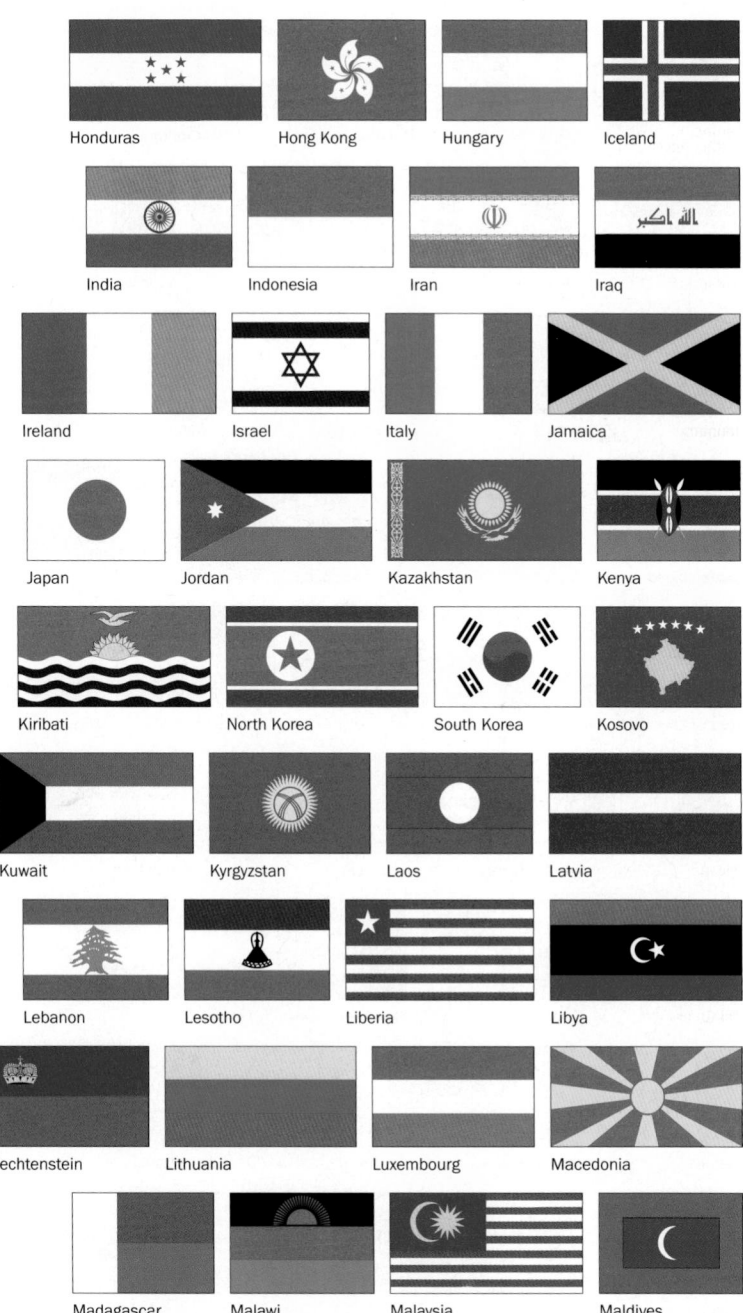

Honduras  Hong Kong  Hungary  Iceland

India  Indonesia  Iran  Iraq

Ireland  Israel  Italy  Jamaica

Japan  Jordan  Kazakhstan  Kenya

Kiribati  North Korea  South Korea  Kosovo

Kuwait  Kyrgyzstan  Laos  Latvia

Lebanon  Lesotho  Liberia  Libya

Liechtenstein  Lithuania  Luxembourg  Macedonia

Madagascar  Malawi  Malaysia  Maldives

Civil flags are shown except where marked thus (*); in these cases, government flags are shown in order to illustrate emblems. Both styles are official national flags.

Plate 4 FLAGS OF THE WORLD

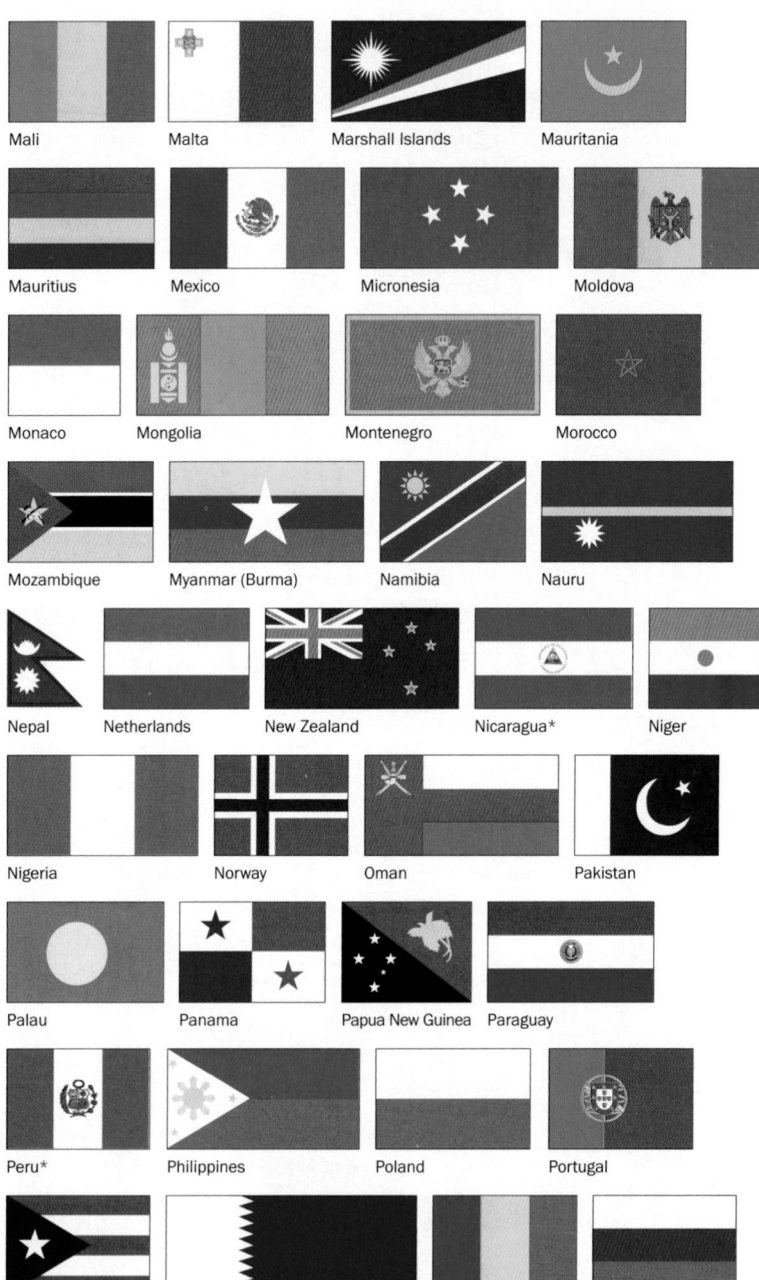

Mali    Malta    Marshall Islands    Mauritania

Mauritius    Mexico    Micronesia    Moldova

Monaco    Mongolia    Montenegro    Morocco

Mozambique    Myanmar (Burma)    Namibia    Nauru

Nepal    Netherlands    New Zealand    Nicaragua*    Niger

Nigeria    Norway    Oman    Pakistan

Palau    Panama    Papua New Guinea    Paraguay

Peru*    Philippines    Poland    Portugal

Puerto Rico    Qatar    Romania    Russia

Civil flags are shown except where marked thus (*); in these cases, government flags are shown in order to illustrate emblems. Both styles are official national flags.

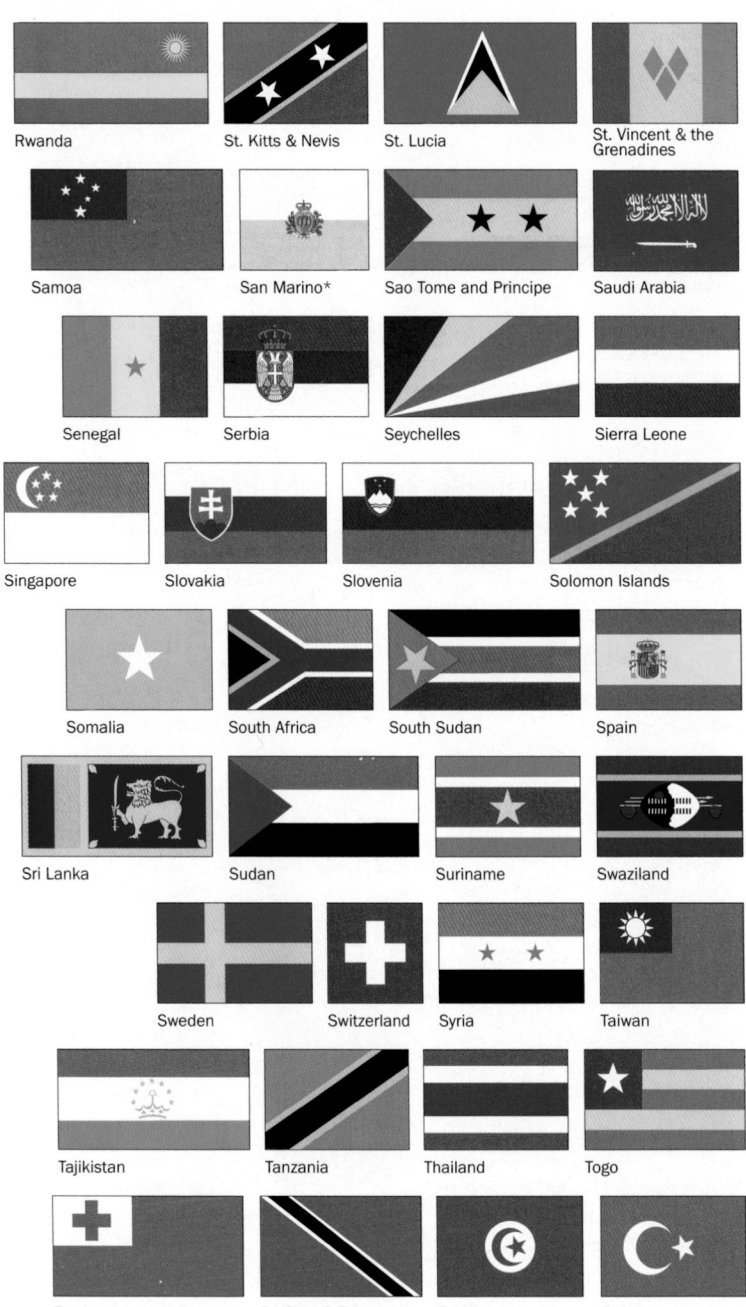

Rwanda

St. Kitts & Nevis

St. Lucia

St. Vincent & the Grenadines

Samoa

San Marino*

Sao Tome and Principe

Saudi Arabia

Senegal

Serbia

Seychelles

Sierra Leone

Singapore

Slovakia

Slovenia

Solomon Islands

Somalia

South Africa

South Sudan

Spain

Sri Lanka

Sudan

Suriname

Swaziland

Sweden

Switzerland

Syria

Taiwan

Tajikistan

Tanzania

Thailand

Togo

Tonga

Trinidad & Tobago

Tunisia

Turkey

Civil flags are shown except where marked thus (*); in these cases, government flags are shown in order to illustrate emblems. Both styles are official national flags.

Plate 6  FLAGS OF THE WORLD

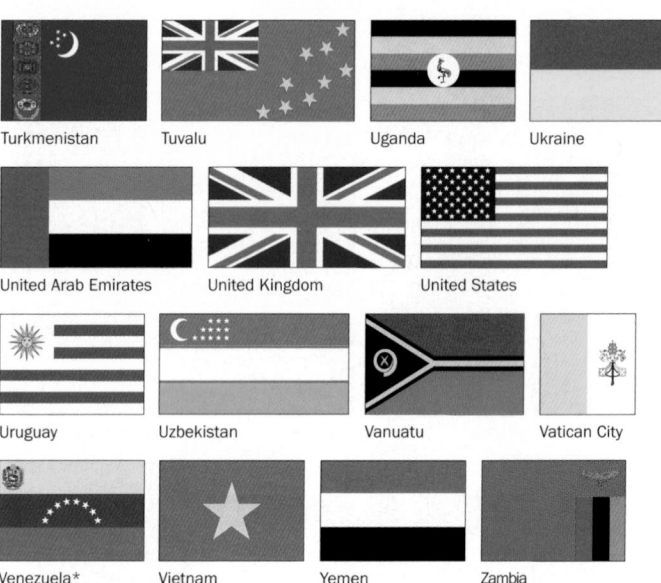

Turkmenistan     Tuvalu          Uganda          Ukraine

United Arab Emirates     United Kingdom     United States

Uruguay          Uzbekistan      Vanuatu         Vatican City

Venezuela*       Vietnam         Yemen           Zambia

Zimbabwe

Civil flags are shown except where marked thus (*); in these cases, government flags are shown in order to illustrate emblems. Both styles are official national flags.

## World Religions

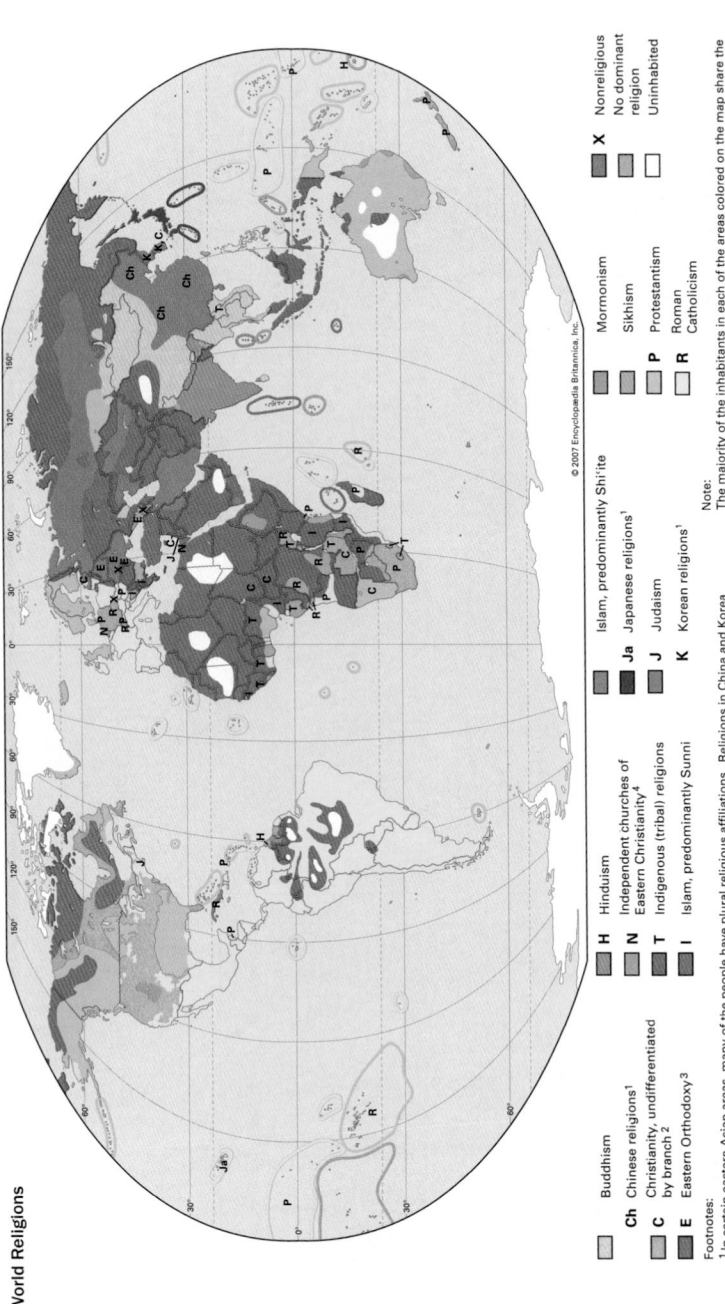

© 2007 Encyclopædia Britannica, Inc.

**Legend:**

- Buddhism
- **Ch** Chinese religions[1]
- **C** Christianity, undifferentiated by branch[2]
- **E** Eastern Orthodoxy[3]
- Hinduism
- **N** Independent churches of Eastern Christianity[4]
- **T** Indigenous (tribal) religions
- **I** Islam, predominantly Sunni
- Islam, predominantly Shi'ite
- **Ja** Japanese religions[1]
- **J** Judaism
- **K** Korean religions[1]
- Mormonism
- Sikhism
- **P** Protestantism
- **R** Roman Catholicism
- **X** Nonreligious
- No dominant religion
- Uninhabited

**Note:**
The majority of the inhabitants in each of the areas colored on the map share the religious tradition indicated. Letter symbols show religious traditions shared by at least 25 percent of the inhabitants within areas no smaller than 1,000 square miles. Therefore minority religions of city dwellers have generally not been represented.

**Footnotes:**

[1] In certain eastern Asian areas, many of the people have plural religious affiliations. Religions in China and Korea include Buddhism, Taoism, Confucianism, and folk cults. The Japanese religions include Shinto and Buddhism.
[2] Chiefly mingled Protestantism and Roman Catholicism, neither predominant.
[3] Including Greek and Russian Orthodox Christianity.
[4] Including Armenian, Coptic, Ethiopian, East and West Syrian.

## THE WORLD

CITIES

- City
- National capital
- Other capital
- Other administrative centre

BOUNDARIES

International

Robinson Projection

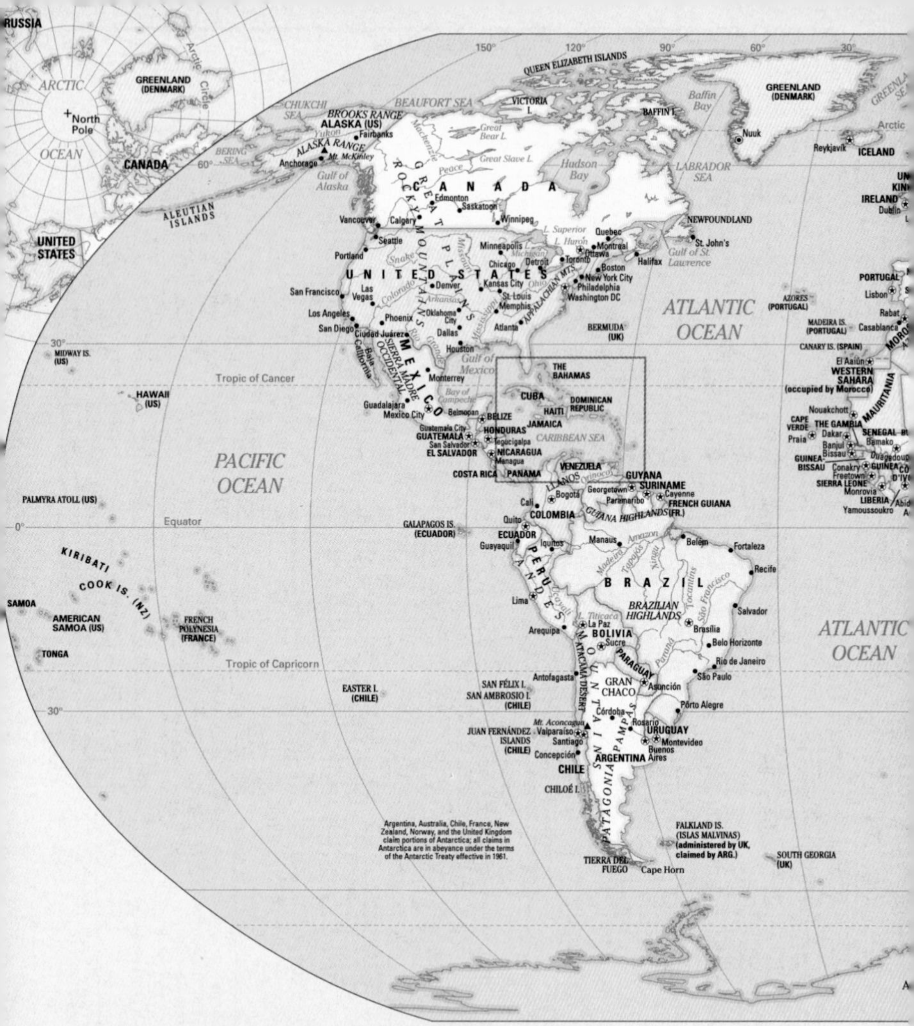

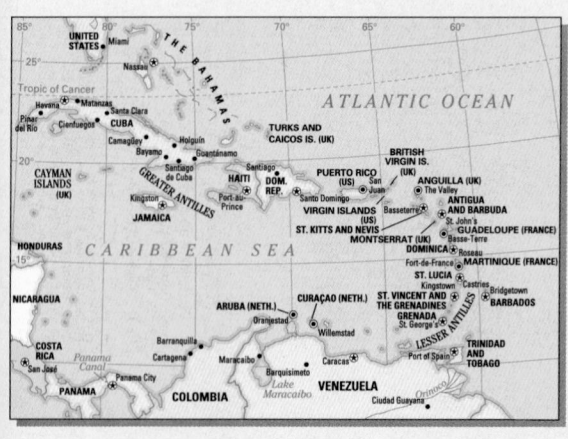

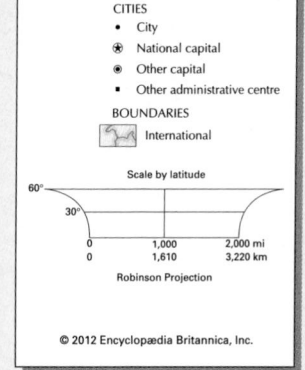

ARCTIC OCEAN
FRANZ JOSEF LAND
SVALBARD (NORWAY)
NOVAYA ZEMLYA
KARA SEA
URAL MOUNTAINS
NEW SIBERIAN IS.
EAST SIBERIAN SEA
VERKHOYANSK MTS.
KOLYMA MTS.
SWEDEN
FINLAND
Arkhangelsk
WEST SIBERIAN PLAIN
R U S S I A
Yakutsk
ESTONIA
LATVIA
LITHUANIA
Nizhny Novgorod
Moscow
Perm
Kazan
Yekaterinburg
Ufa
Chelyabinsk
Samara
Volgograd
Omsk
Novosibirsk
Krasnoyarsk
Novokuznetsk
Barnaul
Lake Baikal
STANOVOY MTS.
Irkutsk
Chita
KAMCHATKA PEN.
SEA OF OKHOTSK
BERING SEA
SAKHALIN I.
POLAND
BELARUS
CZECH REP.
SLOVAKIA
UKRAINE
MOLDOVA
AUS.
HUNG.
ROMANIA
SERBIA
BULG.
ITALY
GREECE
TURKEY
CYPRUS
BLACK SEA
GEORGIA
ARMENIA
AZERBAIJAN
Astana
KAZAKHSTAN
Lake Balqash
ARAL SEA
CASPIAN SEA
UZBEKISTAN
TURKMENISTAN
Tashkent
Bishkek
KYRGYZSTAN
Dushanbe
TAJIKISTAN
TIEN SHAN
Ulaanbaatar
MONGOLIA
GOBI DESERT
Khabarovsk
Harbin
Vladivostok
Shenyang
NORTH KOREA
P'yongyang
Beijing
Tianjin
Seoul
SOUTH KOREA
HOKKAIDO
JAPAN
HONSHU
Tokyo
Pusan
Osaka
KYUSHU
SHIKOKU
PACIFIC OCEAN
KUNLUN MTS.
C H I N A
TUNISIA
MEDITERRANEAN SEA
SYRIA
LEBANON
ISRAEL
Tripoli
IRAQ
JORDAN
I R A N
ZAGROS MOUNTAINS
AFGHANISTAN
Kabul
PLATEAU OF TIBET
Lanzhou
Xi'an
Islamabad
Lahore
HIMALAYAS
Mt. Everest
Lhasa
Nanjing
Shanghai
LIBYA
EGYPT
KUWAIT
BAHRAIN
SAUDI ARABIA
QATAR
UAE
Persian Gulf
PAKISTAN
Delhi
New Delhi
NEPAL
Kathmandu
BHUTAN
Thimphu
Chongqing
Wuhan
TAIWAN
Taipei
Kao-hsiung
SAHARA
L. Nasser
RED SEA
TIBESTI MTS.
RUB' AL-KHALI DESERT
OMAN
Karachi
INDIA
BANGLADESH
Dhaka
Kolkata
Ahmadabad
Mumbai
Nagpur
MYANMAR
Nay Pyi Taw
Yangon
LAOS
Hanoi
SOUTH CHINA SEA
PHILIPPINE SEA
NIGER
CHAD
SUDAN
ERITREA
YEMEN
Gulf of Aden
ARABIAN SEA
Bay of Bengal
Hyderabad
THAILAND
Vientiane
Bangkok
VIETNAM
LUZON
Quezon City/Manila
Saipan
NORTHERN MARIANA IS. (US)
L. Chad
DJIBOUTI
SOCOTRA I. (YEMEN)
Bangalore
Chennai
ANDAMAN IS. (INDIA)
CAMBODIA
Phnom Penh
Ho Chi Minh City
PHILIPPINES
GUAM (US)
NIGERIA
Abuja
CAMEROON
CENTRAL AFRICAN REPUBLIC
Bangui
SOUTH SUDAN
Addis Ababa
ETHIOPIA
ETHIOPIAN PLATEAU
SOMALIA
Colombo
SRI LANKA
NICOBAR IS. (INDIA)
Melekeok
MINDANAO
PALAU
FEDERATED STATES OF MICRONESIA
Palikir
MARSHALL IS.
Majuro
Yaounde
REP. OF THE CONGO
GABON
UGANDA
Kampala
RWANDA
Mogadishu
MALDIVES
Male
Medan
Kuala Lumpur
BRUNEI
Bandar Seri Begawan
MALAYSIA
SINGAPORE
Tarawa (Bairiki)
KIRIBATI
Brazzaville
DEM. REP. OF THE CONGO
KENYA
Nairobi
Kilimanjaro
Lake Victoria
SUMATRA
BORNEO
Kinshasa
BURUNDI
TANZANIA
Dodoma
Dar es Salaam
Lake Tanganyika
Victoria
SEYCHELLES
BRITISH INDIAN OCEAN TERRITORY (U.K.)
Palembang
I N D O N E S I A
CELEBES
NEW GUINEA
PAPUA NEW GUINEA
SOLOMON ISLANDS
Luanda
ANGOLA
MALAWI
Lake Nyasa
Moroni
COMOROS
Jakarta
Bandung
Semarang
Surabaya
JAVA
EAST TIMOR (TIMOR-LESTE)
ARAFURA SEA
Port Moresby
Honiara
TUVALU
Vaiaku (Funafuti)
ZAMBIA
Lusaka
Lilongwe
Harare
ZIMBABWE
MOZAMBIQUE
Mozambique Channel
Antananarivo
MADAGASCAR
INDIAN OCEAN
COCOS IS. (AUSTRALIA)
ARNHEM LAND
Great Barrier Reef
CORAL SEA
VANUATU
Port-Vila
ÉFATÉ
FIJI
Suva
NAMIBIA
Windhoek
NAMIB DESERT
BOTSWANA
Gaborone
Pretoria
Maputo
Mbabane
Johannesburg
SWAZILAND
MAURITIUS
Port Louis
RÉUNION (FRANCE)
GREAT SANDY DESERT
GREAT ARTESIAN BASIN
GREAT DIVIDING RANGE
NEW CALEDONIA (FRANCE)
Bloemfontein
LESOTHO
Maseru
SOUTH AFRICA
Cape Town
Cape of Good Hope
A U S T R A L I A
GREAT VICTORIA DESERT
Brisbane
Perth
Darling
Great Australian Bight
Adelaide
Sydney
Canberra
Melbourne
AMSTERDAM I. (FRANCE)
SAINT PAUL I. (FRANCE)
Auckland
NEW ZEALAND
Wellington
TASMANIA
Hobart
TASMAN SEA
CROZET IS. (FRANCE)
PRINCE EDWARD IS. (SOUTH AFRICA)
KERGUELEN IS. (FRANCE)
AUCKLAND IS. (NZ)
30°
60°
90°
120°
150°
WEDDELL SEA
QUEEN MAUD LAND
Antarctic Circle
ANTARCTIC PEN.
Ronne Ice Shelf
ANTARCTICA
MARIE BYRD LAND
South Pole
Ross Ice Shelf
ROSS SEA
WILKES LAND

NORWAY
Oslo
SWEDEN
FINLAND
Helsinki
Lake Ladoga
St. Petersburg
NORTH SEA
Stockholm
Tallinn
ESTONIA
RUSSIA
DENMARK
Copenhagen
BALTIC SEA
Riga
LATVIA
Moscow
RUSSIA
LITHUANIA
Vilnius
Minsk
NETHERLANDS
Hamburg
Amsterdam
Berlin
POLAND
BELARUS
Brussels
BELGIUM
GERMANY
Warsaw
Łódź
Homyel
Luxembourg
LUXEMBOURG
Prague
CZECH REPUBLIC
Kraków
UKRAINE
Kiev
Kharkiv
LIECHTENSTEIN
Vienna
SLOVAKIA
Dnipropetrovsk
Bern
Zürich
Munich
Bratislava
Vaduz
AUSTRIA
Budapest
MOLDOVA
Donetsk
SWITZ.
ALPS
Ljubljana
HUNGARY
Chişinău
Odessa
Lyon
Turin
Milan
SLOVENIA
Zagreb
CROATIA
ROMANIA
CRIMEAN PEN.
BOSNIA AND HERZEGOVINA
SAN MARINO
SERBIA
Belgrade
Bucharest
MONACO
Sarajevo
BLACK SEA
CORSICA (FRANCE)
ITALY
MONT.
KOS.
Priština
Danube
Sofia
Podgorica
BULGARIA
Rome
Adriatic Sea
Cetinje
Tiranë
Skopje
Istanbul
SARDINIA (ITALY)
ALBANIA
MACEDONIA
Ankara
TURKEY
GREECE
İzmir
Athens
SICILY (ITALY)
MALTA
MEDITERRANEAN SEA
CYPRUS
0°
10°
20°
30°
40°
50°
55°
60°

CROATIA
ROMANIA
CRIMEAN PEN.
KAZAKHSTAN
ARAL SEA
Sarajevo
SERBIA
Belgrade
Bucharest
RUSSIA
BOS. HER.
MONT.
KOS.
Priština
Sofia
BLACK SEA
Cetinje
Podgorica
BULGARIA
Skopje
CASPIAN SEA
UZBEKISTAN
ITALY
Tiranë
ALBANIA
MACEDONIA
Istanbul
Samsun
GEORGIA
Tbilisi
Bursa
Ankara
Yerevan
AZERBAIJAN
Baku
TURKMENISTAN
GREECE
Eskişehir
TURKEY
Kayseri
ARMENIA
Ashgabat
Athens
İzmir
Diyarbakır
Tabrīz
SICILY (ITALY)
Antalya
Gaziantep
Mersin
Aleppo
Mosul
CYPRUS
Nicosia
SYRIA
Tehrān
Mashhad
Beirut
Dayr al-Zawr
Euphrates
MEDITERRANEAN SEA
LEBANON
Damascus
Baghdad
IRAN
ISRAEL
Amman
AFGHANISTAN
Banghāzī
Alexandria
Jerusalem
West Bank*
IRAQ
Tigris
Ahvāz
Eşfahān
Cairo
JORDAN
Suez Canal
Gaza Strip*
Basra
Kuwait
KUWAIT
Shīrāz
LIBYA
Tabūk
Sabhā
EGYPT
BAHRAIN
Manama
OMAN
Buraydah
Persian Gulf
Nile
Riyadh
Doha
Abu Dhabi
Lake Nasser
Aswān
Medina
SAUDI ARABIA
QATAR
Al-Fujayrah
Muscat
TIBESTI MTS.
Jiddah
Mecca
UNITED ARAB EMIRATES
RED SEA
S A H A R A
Port Sudan
OMAN
Largeau
ERITREA
Asmara
YEMEN
ARABIAN SEA
Lake Chad
CHAD
Khartoum
SUDAN
Sanaa
Al-Mukallā
Ta'izz
DJIBOUTI
Gulf of Aden
N'Djamena
ETHIOPIA
Djibouti
* Final status to be determined.
20°
30°
40°
50°
60°

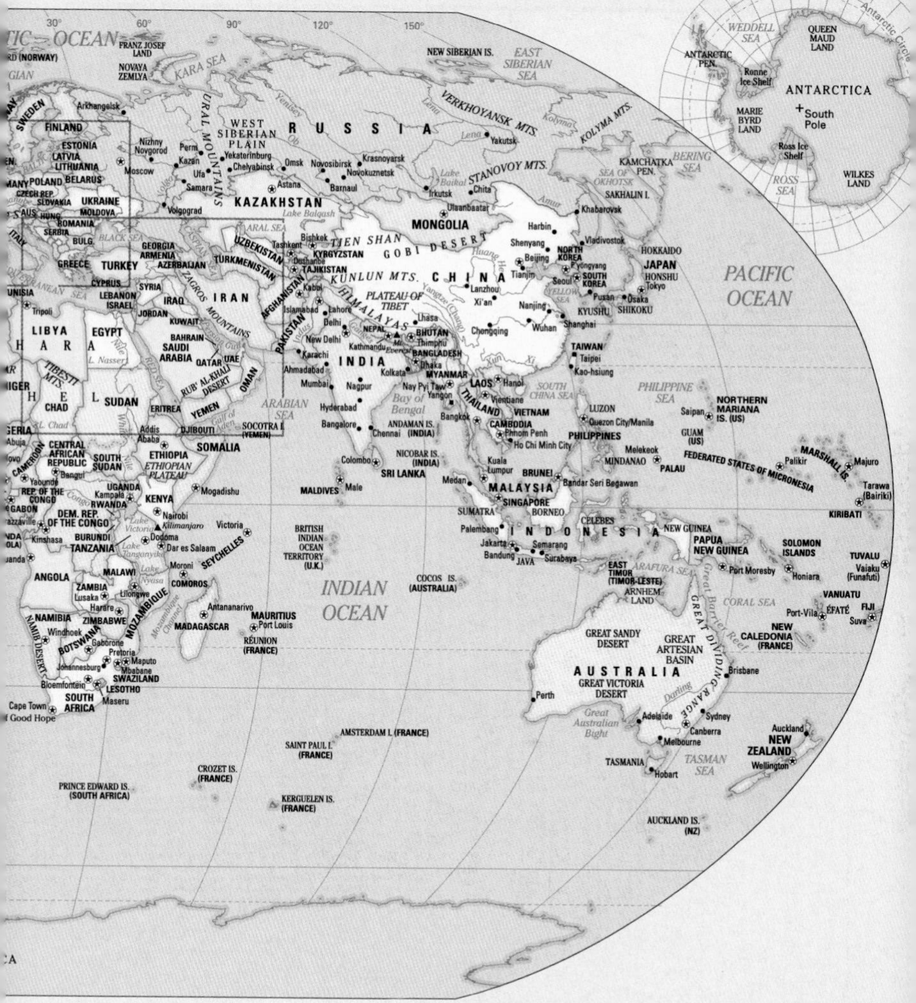

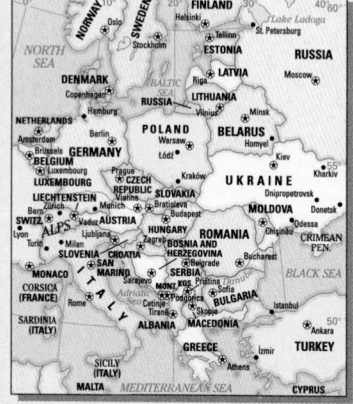

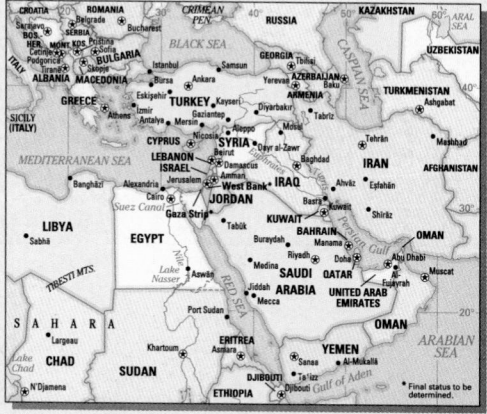

Plate 10 WORLD MAPS

## Africa

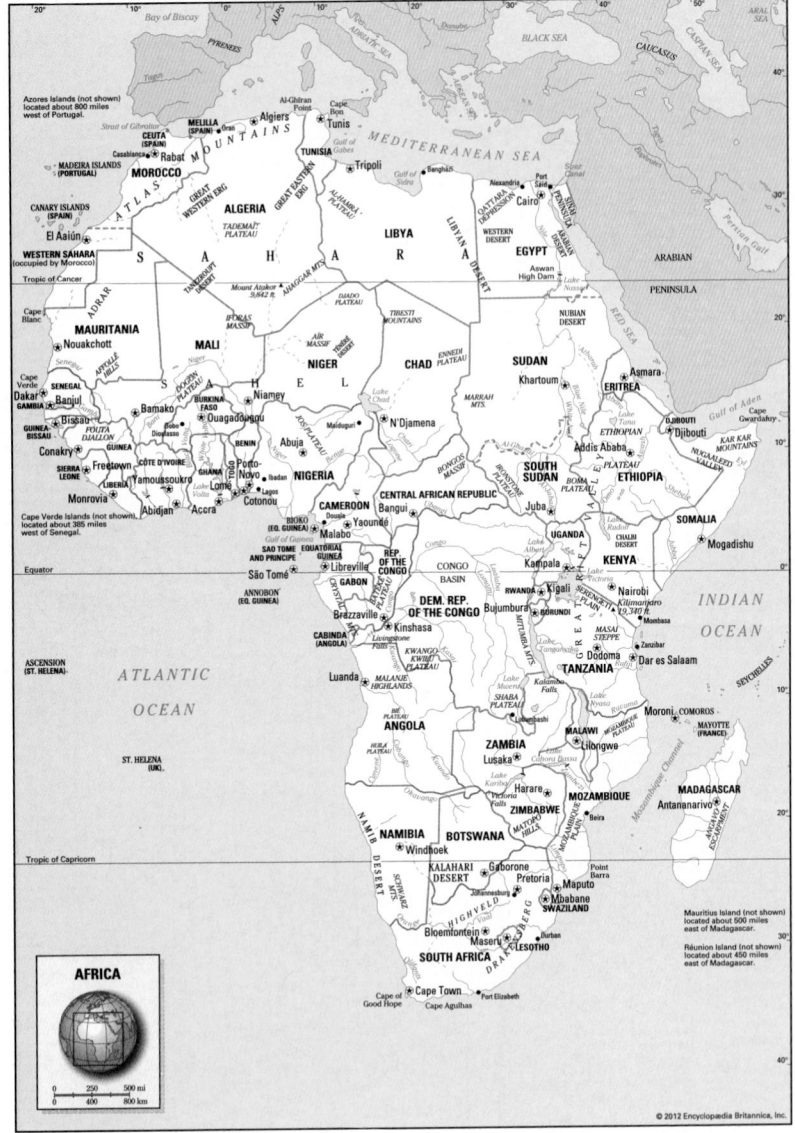

© 2012 Encyclopædia Britannica, Inc.

## Asia

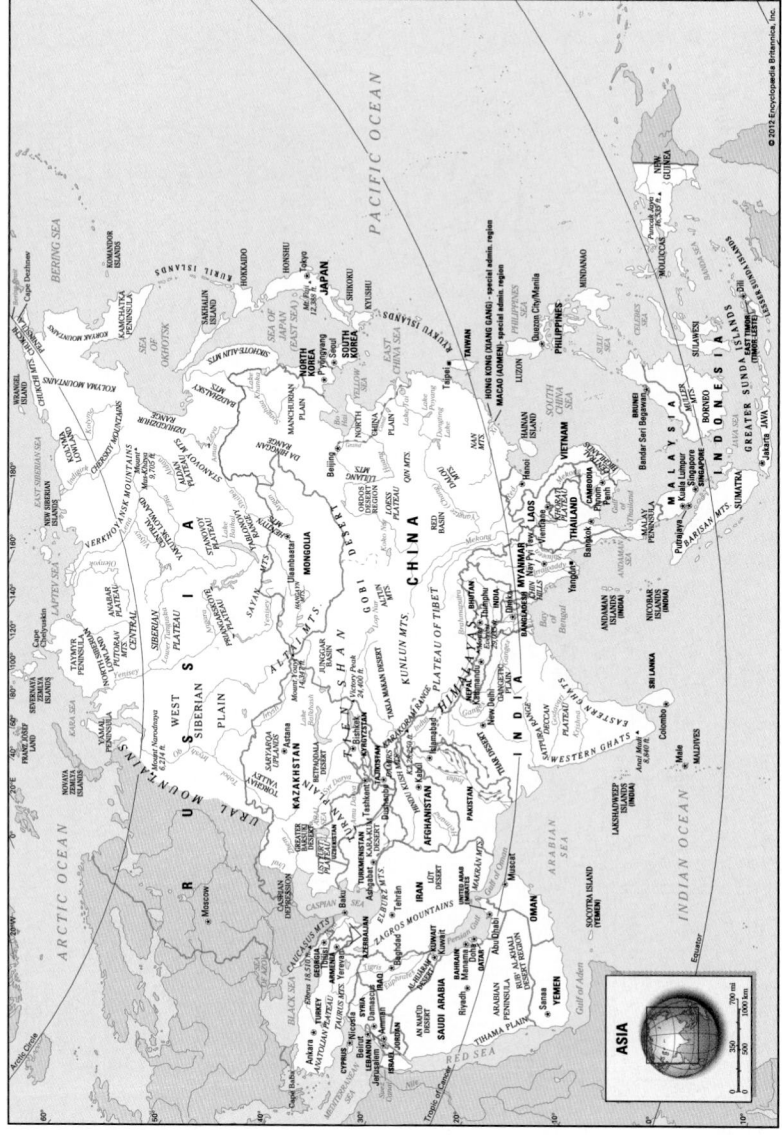

Plate 12

# WORLD MAPS

## Europe

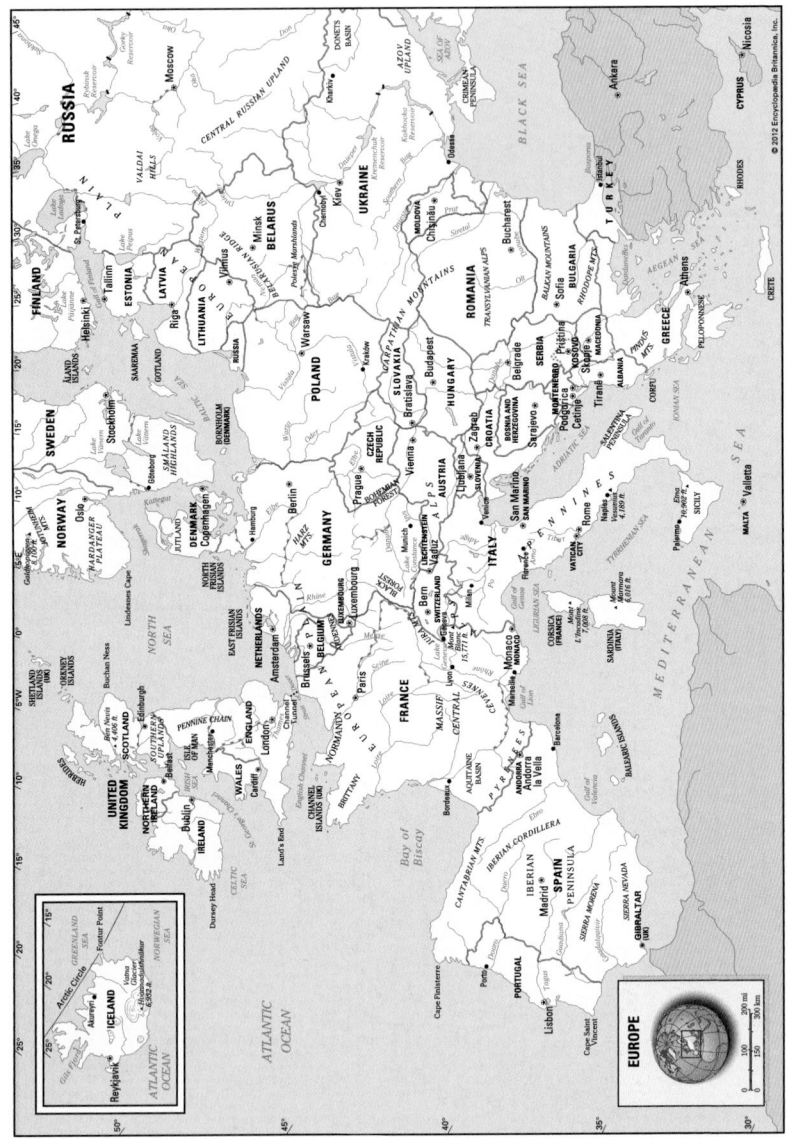

## North America

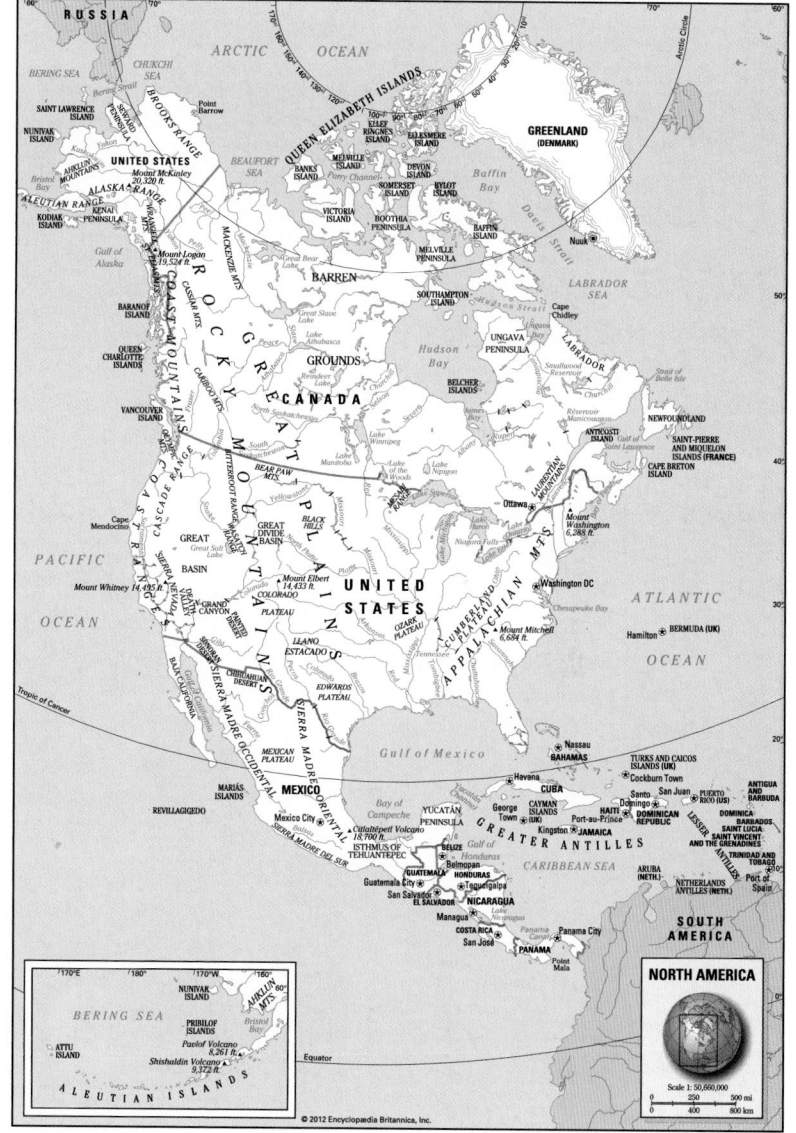

© 2012 Encyclopædia Britannica, Inc.

**Plate 14**          **WORLD MAPS**

## South America

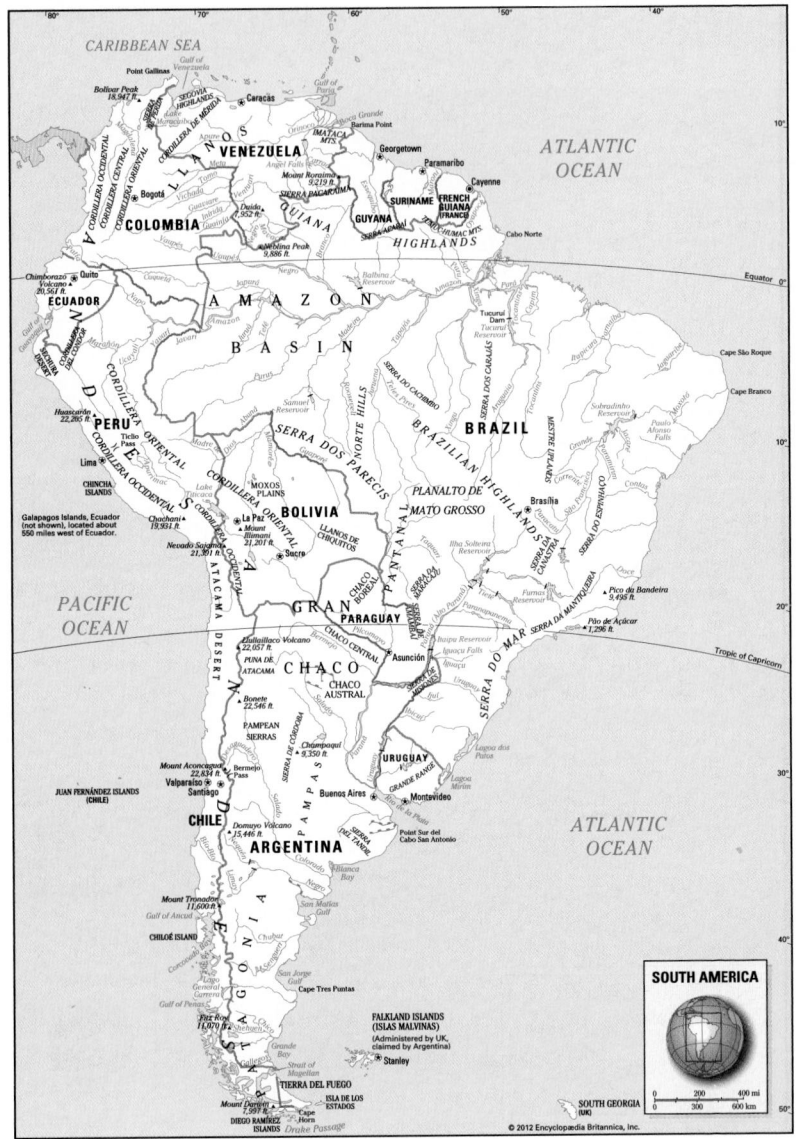

## Australia

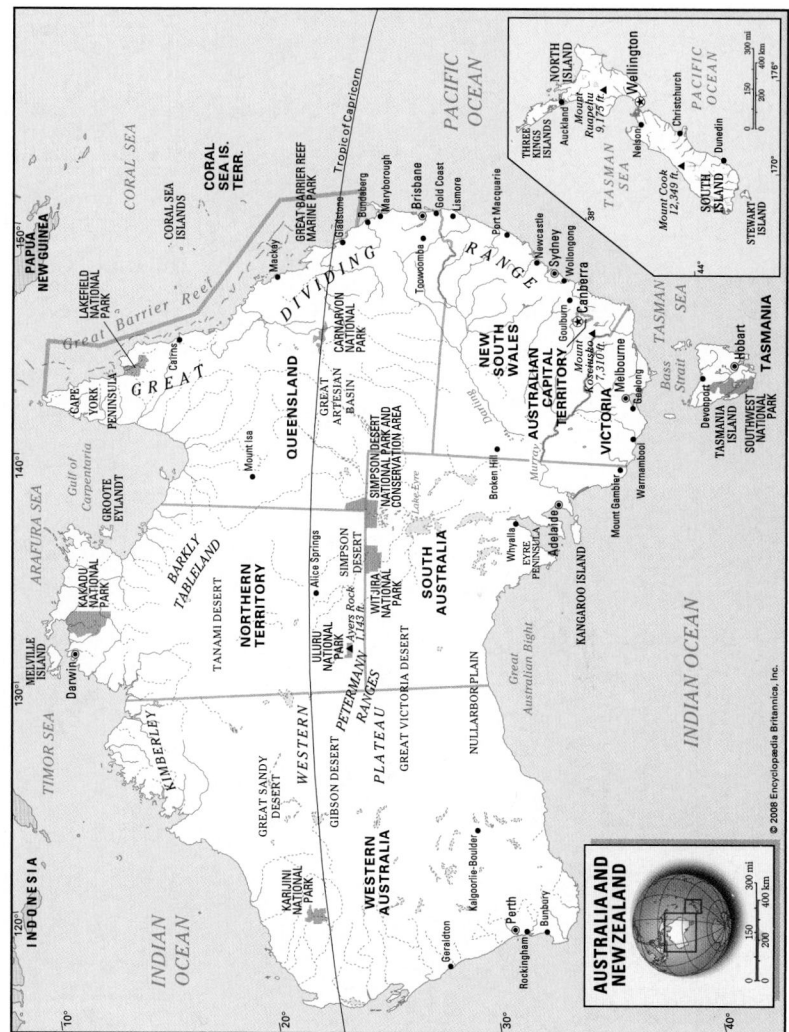

Plate 16

# WORLD MAPS

## Oceania/Pacific Islands

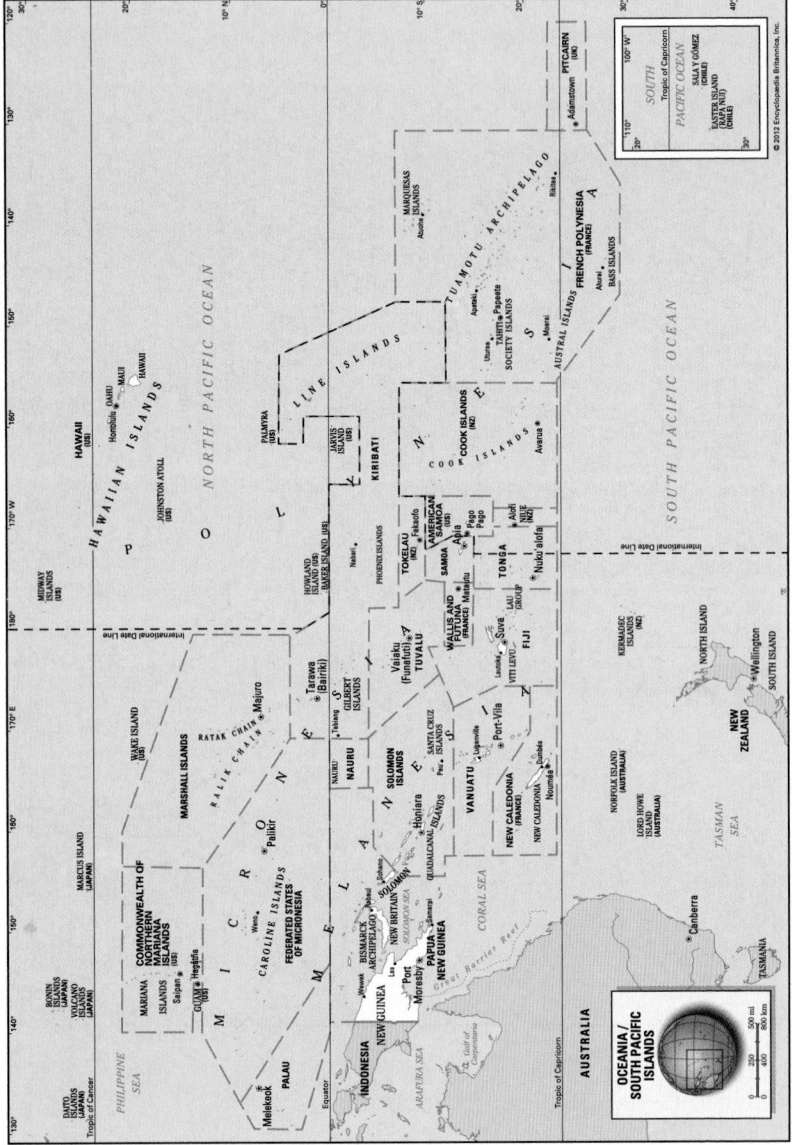

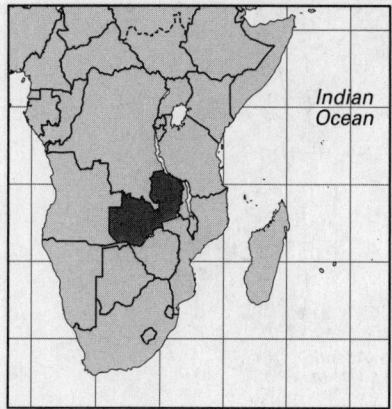

Indian
Ocean

nation per the preamble of a constitutional amendment). **Monetary unit:** 1 Zambian kwacha (K) = 100 ngwee; valuation (2 Jul 2012) US$1 = K 5,135.00.

## Demography

**Area:** 290,585 sq mi, 752,612 sq km. **Population** (2011): 13,306,000. **Density** (2011): persons per sq mi 45.8, persons per sq km 17.7. **Urban** (2010): 35.7%. **Sex distribution** (2005): male 49.75%; female 50.25%. **Age breakdown** (2005): under 15, 46.2%; 15–29, 30.6%; 30–44, 13.4%; 45–59, 6.1%; 60–74, 3.0%; 75–84, 0.6%; 85 and over, 0.1%. **Ethnic composition** (2000): Bemba 21.5%; Tonga 11.3%; Lozi 5.2%; Nsenga 5.1%; Tumbuka 4.3%; Ngoni 3.8%; Chewa 2.9%; other 45.9%. **Religious affiliation** (2000): Christian 82.4%, of which Roman Catholic 29.7%, Protestant (including Anglican) 28.2%, independent Christian 15.2%, unaffiliated Christian 5.5%; traditional beliefs 14.3%; Baha'i 1.8%; Muslim 1.1%; other 0.4%. **Major cities** (2006): Lusaka 1,306,600; Kitwe 408,300; Ndola 398,100; Kabwe 191,100; Chingola 148,600. **Location:** southern Africa, bordering Tanzania, Malawi, Mozambique, Zimbabwe, Botswana, Namibia, Angola, and the Democratic Republic of the Congo.

## Vital statistics

**Birth rate** per 1,000 population (2008): 38.8 (world avg. 20.3). **Death rate** per 1,000 population (2008): 18.5 (world avg. 8.5). **Total fertility rate** (avg. births per childbearing woman; 2006): 5.39. **Life expectancy** at birth (2006): male 38.0 years; female 38.2 years.

## National economy

**Budget** (2007). *Revenue:* K 10,094,600,000,000 (tax revenue 77.3%, of which income tax 33.1%, VAT 24.1%; grants 20.4%; nontax revenue 2.3%). *Expenditures:* K 12,034,400,000,000 (education 16.9%; economic affairs 14.1%; housing and community amenities 12.2%; defense 8.2%; public order 6.8%; public debt 6.0%; health 3.8%). **Production** (metric tons except as noted). *Agriculture and fishing* (2007): sugarcane 2,500,000, corn

(maize) 1,366,158, cassava 940,000, seed cotton 160,000, sunflower seeds 8,200, fresh-cut flowers (value of sales; 2000) US$21,000,000; livestock (number of live animals) 2,610,000 cattle, 1,275,000 goats, 340,000 pigs; fisheries production 70,125 (from aquaculture 7%). *Mining and quarrying* (2007): copper (metal content) 520,000; cobalt (metal content) 7,600; amethyst 1,200,000 kg; emeralds 2,500 kg. *Manufacturing* (2005): cement 435,000; refined copper 399,000; vegetable oils (2001) 11,800; refined cobalt 5,422. *Energy production (consumption):* electricity (kW-hr; 2006) 9,385,000,000 (9,130,000,000); coal (metric tons; 2006) 244,000 (171,000); crude petroleum (barrels; 2006) none (4,266,000); petroleum products (metric tons; 2006) 525,000 (577,000). **Selected balance of payments data.** Receipts from (US$'000,000): tourism (2007) 138; remittances (2008) 59; foreign direct investment (FDI; 2005–07 avg.) 652; official development assistance (2007) 1,045. Disbursements for (US$'000,000): tourism (2007) 56; remittances (2008) 124. **Population economically active** (2000): total 3,165,200; activity rate of total population 32.0% (participation rates: ages 12–64, 55.8%; female 41.3%; unemployed 12.7%). **Gross national income** (2008): US$11,986,000,000 (US$950 per capita). **Public debt** (external, outstanding; 2007): US$1,136,000,000.

## Foreign trade

**Imports** (2006; c.i.f.): US$3,074,000,000 (machinery and apparatus 29.7%, of which industrial machinery and equipment 19.5%; chemical products 14.6%; crude petroleum 13.6%; motor vehicles 10.0%). *Major import sources:* South Africa 47.0%; UAE 10.4%; Zimbabwe 5.7%; Norway 4.0%; UK 3.7%. **Exports** (2006; f.o.b.): US$3,770,000,000 (refined copper 67.9%; copper ore and concentrate 11.2%; cobalt 3.8%; food products 3.8%). *Major export destinations:* Switzerland 39.8%; South Africa 11.0%; Thailand 7.7%; China 6.8%; Egypt 4.2%.

## Transport and communications

**Transport.** *Railroads* (1998): length (2006) 2,157 km; passenger-km 586,000,000; metric ton-km cargo 702,000,000. *Roads* (2001): total length 91,440 km (paved 22%). *Vehicles* (2008): passenger cars 172,670; trucks and buses 91,835. *Air transport* (2006; Zambian Airways Limited only): passenger-km 56,609,000; metric ton-km cargo, none. **Communications,** in total units (units per 1,000 persons). Telephone landlines (2008): 91,000 (7.2); cellular telephone subscribers (2008): 3,539,000 (280); personal computers (2005): 131,000 (11); total Internet users (2008): 700,000 (56); broadband Internet subscribers (2007): 5,700 (0.4).

## Education and health

**Educational attainment** (2001–02). Percentage of population ages 15 and over having: no formal schooling/unknown 14.7%; some primary education 33.4%; completed primary 19.7%; some secondary 22.0%; completed secondary 5.9%; higher 4.3%. **Literacy** (2007): population ages 15 and over literate

83.5%; males literate 88.5%; females literate 78.6%. **Health** (2004): physicians 1,264 (1 per 8,672 persons); hospital beds 21,924 (1 per 500 persons); infant mortality rate per 1,000 live births (2008) 90.4; undernourished population (2003–05) 5,100,000 (40% of total population based on the consumption of a minimum daily requirement of 1,750 calories).

## Military

**Total active duty personnel** (November 2008): 15,100 (army 89.4%; navy, none; air force 10.6%). **Military expenditure as percentage of GDP** (2007): 2.2%; per capita expenditure US$20.

## Background

Archaeological evidence suggests that early humans roamed present-day Zambia one to two million years ago. Ancestors of the modern Tonga tribe reached the region early in the 2nd millennium BC, but other modern peoples from Congo and Angola reached the country only in the 17th and 18th centuries AD. Portuguese trading missions were established early in the 18th century. Emissaries of Cecil Rhodes and the British South Africa Co. concluded treaties with most of the Zambian chiefs during the 1890s. The company administered the region known as Northern Rhodesia until 1924, when it became a British protectorate. It was part of the Central African Federation of Rhodesia and Nyasaland in 1953–63. In 1964 Northern Rhodesia became the independent republic of Zambia. A constitutional amendment was passed in 1990 allowing opposition parties; the following years were filled with political tension.

## Recent Developments

Michael Sata, popularly known as "King Cobra" and the flag bearer of the Patriotic Front, came from behind to win the September 2011 presidential election in Zambia. His surprise victory ended two decades of rule by the Movement for Multiparty Democracy. As president, Sata faced the difficult task of implementing his campaign promises: creating new employment opportunities; raising workers' wages, especially those of miners; and curtailing rampant corruption. Of crucial importance was economic policy related to Chinese investment and trade, especially in the mining sector. In October he dismissed many senior officials, including the heads of the armed forces, the police, the Anti-Corruption Commission, and other key agencies. In addition, investigations into existing government contracts were announced.

**Internet resource:** <www.zamstats.gov.zm>.

# Zimbabwe

**Official name:** Republic of Zimbabwe. **Form of government:** transitional regime with two legislative houses (Senate [100]; House of Assembly [214]). **Heads of state and government:** President Robert Mugabe (from 1987), assisted by Prime Minister Morgan Tsvangirai (from 2009). Capital: Harare. **Official language:** English. **Official religion:** none. **Monetary**

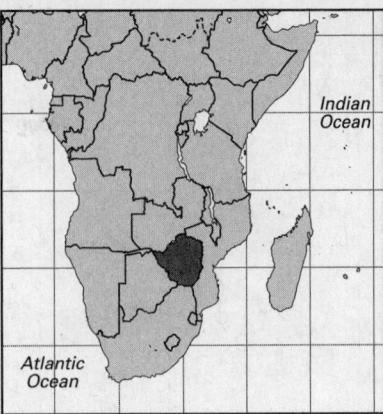

**unit:** 1 (redenominated) Zimbabwe dollar (Z$) = 100 cents; the use of the Zimbabwe dollar as legal currency was suspended indefinitely on 12 Apr 2009, because of long-term hyperinflation. Multiple foreign currencies (including the US dollar and South African rand) became legal tender in January 2009.

## Demography

**Area:** 150,872 sq mi, 390,757 sq km. **Population** (2011): 12,084,000 (includes some 3 million Zimbabweans living outside of the country, many of whom are in South Africa). **Density** (2011): persons per sq mi 80.1, persons per sq km 30.9. **Urban** (2010): 38.3%. **Sex distribution** (2008): male 47.40%; female 52.60%. **Age breakdown** (2008): under 15, 43.9%; 15–29, 28.8%; 30–44, 13.9%; 45–59, 7.9%; 60–74, 4.1%; 75 and over, 1.4%. **Ethnic composition** (2003): Shona 71%; Ndebele 16%; other African 11%; white 1%; mixed race/Asian 1%. **Religious affiliation** (2005): African independent Christian 38%; traditional beliefs 25%; Protestant 14%; Roman Catholic 8%; Muslim 1%; other (mostly unaffiliated Christian) 14%. **Major cities** (2002): Harare (2007) 1,572,000; Bulawayo 676,787; Chitungwiza 321,782; Mutare 170,106; Gweru 141,260. **Location:** southern Africa, bordering Mozambique, South Africa, Botswana, Namibia, and Zambia.

## Vital statistics

**Birth rate** per 1,000 population (2008): 31.6 (world avg. 20.3). **Death rate** per 1,000 population (2008): 17.3 (world avg. 8.5). **Total fertility rate** (avg. births per childbearing woman; 2008): 3.72. **Life expectancy** at birth (2008): male 45.1 years; female 43.5 years.

## National economy

**Budget** (2008). *Revenue:* US$133,000,000 (tax revenue 96.2%, of which customs duties 33.8%, VAT 24.1%, income tax 16.5%, corporate taxes 13.5%; nontax revenue 3.8%). *Expenditures:* US$255,-000,000 (current expenditures 94.5%, of which debt service 54.5%, wages and salaries 20.4%, transfer

*1 metric ton = about 1.1 short tons;    1 kilometer = 0.6 mi (statute);    1 metric ton-km cargo = about 0.68 short ton-mi cargo;    c.i.f.: cost, insurance, and freight;    f.o.b.: free on board*

payments 7.1%; capital expenditures 5.5%). **Public debt** (external, outstanding; 2007): US$3,735,-000,000. **Population economically active** (2008): total 5,836,000; activity rate of total population 46.8% (participation rates: ages 15–64 [2003] 74.0%; female 43.2%; unofficially unemployed [2009] 95.0%). **Production** (metric tons except as noted). *Agriculture and fishing* (2007): sugarcane 3,600,000, corn (maize) 952,600, seed cotton 235,000; livestock (number of live animals) 5,400,000 cattle, 3,000,000 goats, 630,000 pigs; fisheries production 12,950 (from aquaculture 19%). *Mining and quarrying* (2007): chromite 650,000; asbestos 100,000; nickel (metal content) 7,100; cobalt (metal content) 50; platinum-group metals (palladium, platinum, rhodium, ruthenium, and iridium) 11,150 kg; gold 6,750 kg; diamonds 695,015 carats. *Manufacturing* (value added in US$'000,000; 1998): beverages 171; food products 148; textiles 99. *Energy production (consumption):* electricity (kW-hr; 2008) 8,890,000,000 (10,890,-000,000); coal (metric tons; 2006) 3,447,000 (3,521,000); petroleum products (metric tons; 2006) none (624,000). **Gross national income** (2008): US$3,892,117,285 (US$312 per capita). **Selected balance of payments data.** Receipts from (US$'000,000): tourism (2007) 365; remittances (2008) 361; foreign direct investment (FDI; 2005–07 avg.) 71; official development assistance (2007) 465. Disbursements for (US$'000,000): tourism (1998) 131; FDI (2005–07 avg.) 1.3.

## Foreign trade

**Imports** (2007; c.i.f.): US$3,594,400,000 (refined petroleum products 15.7%; chemical products 12.6%; transportation equipment 9.3%; food products and live animals 7.9%; base metals 4.7%). *Major import sources:* South Africa 42.8%; Botswana 11.4%; China 5.7%; Mozambique 4.8%; Malawi 4.8%. **Exports** (2007; f.o.b.): US$3,310,-200,000 (base metals 18.8%, of which iron and steel 12.6%; nickel 5.9%; machinery and apparatus 10.7%, of which transportation equipment 5.4%; food products and live animals 8.6%; beverages and tobacco products 8.4%; textile fibers 4.0%). *Major export destinations:* South Africa 37.4%; Mozambique 13.0%; UK 7.4%; Botswana 6.1%; Netherlands 4.6%.

## Transport and communications

**Transport.** *Railroads:* route length (2008) 3,077 km; passenger-km (1998) 408,223,000; metric ton-km cargo (2004) 1,377,000. *Roads* (2002): total length 97,267 km (paved 19%). *Vehicles* (2002): passenger cars 570,866; trucks and buses 84,456. *Air transport:* passenger-km (2006; Air Zimbabwe only) 671,185,000; metric ton-km cargo (2007) 8,000,000. **Communications,** in total units (units per 1,000 persons). Telephone landlines (2008): 348,000 (28); cellular telephone subscribers (2008): 1,655,000 (133); personal computers (2007): 1,257,000 (101); total Internet users (2008): 1,421,000 (114); broadband Internet subscribers (2008): 17,000 (1.4).

## Education and health

**Educational attainment** (2005–06). Percentage of population ages 25 and over having: no formal schooling/unknown 13.6%; incomplete primary education 32.8%; complete primary 5.1%; incomplete secondary 42.0%; complete secondary 1.2%; vocational/higher 5.3%. **Literacy** (2007): percentage of total population ages 15 and over literate 92.8%; males literate 95.8%; females literate 89.9%. **Health:** physicians (2004) 2,086 (1 per 5,792 persons); hospital beds (2006) 37,377 (1 per 333 persons); infant mortality rate per 1,000 live births (2008) 33.9; undernourished population (2002–04) 6,000,000 (47% of total population based on the consumption of a minimum daily requirement of 1,840 calories).

## Military

**Total active duty personnel** (November 2008): 29,000 (army 86.2%; navy, none; air force 13.8%). **Military expenditure as percentage of GDP** (2005): 2.3%; per capita expenditure US$11.

## Background

Remains of Stone Age cultures dating back 500,000 years have been found in the Zimbabwe area. The first Bantu-speaking peoples reached it during the 5th–10th centuries AD, driving the San (Bushmen) inhabitants into the desert. A second migration of Bantu speakers began about 1830. During this period the British and the Afrikaners moved up from the south, and the area came under the administration of the British South Africa Co. in 1889–1923. Called Southern Rhodesia (1911–64), it became a self-governing British colony in 1923. The colony united in 1953 with Nyasaland (Malawi) and Northern Rhodesia (Zambia) to form the Central African Federation of Rhodesia and Nyasaland. The federation dissolved in 1963, and Southern Rhodesia reverted to its former colonial status; beginning in 1964 it called itself Rhodesia. In 1965 it issued a unilateral declaration of independence considered illegal by the British government, which led to economic sanctions against it. The country proclaimed itself a republic in 1970. In 1979 it instituted limited majority rule and changed its name to Zimbabwe Rhodesia. It was granted independence by Britain in 1980 and became Zimbabwe. A multiparty system was established in 1990. The economy began to experience a decline in the 1990s that accelerated dramatically in the 2000s. In 2008 long-simmering political tensions between the ruling party and the opposition led to a hotly contested presidential election that sparked a protracted political crisis and exacerbated the country's economic troubles and deteriorating health and welfare conditions. An agreement for a power-sharing government, reached in September 2008, was implemented in February 2009.

## Recent Developments

Economic life remained difficult for ordinary Zimbabweans in 2011; four out of five people had no form of modern employment. The production of food and export crops had still not recovered the levels realized before the government accelerated its land-redistribution strategy in the early 21st century. HIV/AIDS had reduced life expectancy for women to 34 years. Meanwhile, new diamond-mining activities produced substantial new wealth for a favored sector of the population. In November the countries making up the Kimberley Process Certification Scheme, which oversees the effort to eliminate the sale of conflict diamonds, cleared Zimbabwe to again export limited amounts of diamonds, ending a worldwide embargo.

Internet resource: <www.zimstat.co.zw>.

# Antarctica

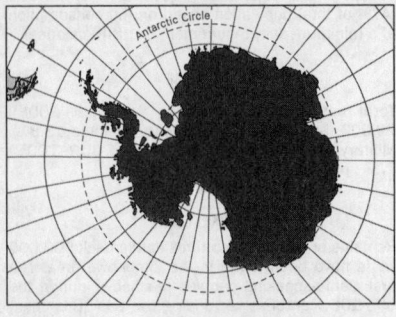

## Background

The Russian F.G. von Bellingshausen, the Englishman Edward Bransfield, and the American Nathaniel Palmer all claimed first sightings of the continent in 1820. The period from the 1760s to 1900 was dominated by the exploration of Antarctic and subantarctic seas. In the early 20th century, the "heroic era" of Antarctic exploration, Robert Scott and, later, Ernest Shackleton made expeditions deep into the interior. Roald Amundsen reached the South Pole in December 1911, and Scott followed in 1912. The first half of the 20th century was also Antarctica's colonial period. Seven nations claimed sectors of the continent, while many other nations carried out explorations. In 1957–58, 12 nations established over 50 stations on the continent for cooperative study. In 1961 the Antarctic Treaty, which reserved Antarctica for free and nonpolitical scientific study, was enacted. A 1991 agreement imposed a 50-year ban on mineral exploitation.

## Recent Developments

The hole in the atmosphere's ozone layer that forms above Antarctica during the austral spring in September 2011 reached its peak size of 25.9 million sq km (10 million sq mi). Australian scientists, however, believed that they had evidence that the hole was becoming smaller, something that most scientists had not expected to see until after 2020. At the 34th Antarctic Treaty Consultative Meeting, held in Buenos Aires in June and July, approximately 350 diplomats, Antarctic program managers, and polar scientists from 48 countries gathered to discuss environmental and management issues. During the 2010–11 austral summer, 33,824 tourists visited the continent, with some 33,438 arriving by ship. Compared with 2009–10, the number of tourists decreased by 8.3%, primarily because several cruises were canceled after the International Maritime Organization ban on

using heavy fuel oil in the Antarctic Treaty area took effect in August.

Internet resource: <www.coolantarctica.com>.

# Arctic Regions

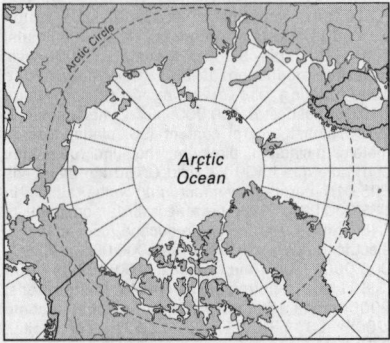

The Arctic regions may be defined in physical terms (astronomical [north of the Arctic Circle], climatic [above the 10 °C (50 °F) July isotherm], or vegetational [above the northern limit of the tree line]) or in human terms (the territory inhabited by the circumpolar cultures—Inuit [Eskimo] and Aleut in North America and Russia, Sami [Lapp] in northern Scandinavia and Russia, and 29 other peoples of the Russian North, Siberia, and East Asia). The region includes portions of Canada, the United States, Russia, Finland, Sweden, Norway, Iceland, and Greenland (part of Denmark). The Arctic Ocean, 14.09 million sq km (5.44 million sq mi) in area, constitutes about two-thirds of the region. The land area consists of permanent ice cap, tundra, or boreal forest (taiga). The population of peoples belonging to the circumpolar cultures in 2011 is about 530,000. The warming of the north continued to have a profound impact on all dimensions of the Arctic in 2011. As the Greenland ice sheet (the world's second largest) melted, both fresh water and icebergs were released to the North Atlantic Ocean. In the spring of 2011, a massive 250-sq-km (100-sq-mi) iceberg approached the northeastern coast of Canada. Warm surface temperatures were accompanied by cooling in the upper atmosphere of the high north. The prolonged low temperatures in the stratosphere activated ozone-depleting chemicals and produced the first significant ozone hole ever recorded over the Arctic. For the first time, a Suezmax-class tanker (i.e., the largest vessel that can transit the Suez Canal) sailed from Europe to Asia along the Northeast Passage. In addition, a new speed record was set when two tankers crossed the Russian Arctic in only eight days. Also set in 2011 was a record for the volume of goods shipped through the Arctic: more than 800,000 metric tons, which was a fivefold increase over 2010. Demand for metallic-mineral commodities rose in 2011, and mining in the north boomed. Two abandoned iron-ore mines were reopened in Norway, and as conditions changed, the possibility of locating a mine in the high Arctic became viable.

*1 metric ton = about 1.1 short tons;    1 kilometer = 0.6 mi (statute);    1 metric ton-km cargo = about 0.68 short ton-mi cargo;    c.i.f.: cost, insurance, and freight;    f.o.b.: free on board*

# Membership in International Organizations

**African Union (AU)**
Founded: 1963. **Members:** 53 countries of Africa (all except Morocco), Western Sahara (Madagascar was suspended in March 2009; Mali was suspended in March 2012; Guinea-Bissau was suspended in April 2012).
Web site: <www.africa-union.org>.

**Asia-Pacific Economic Cooperation (APEC)**
Founded: 1989. **Members:** Australia, Brunei, Canada, Chile, China, Hong Kong, Indonesia, Japan, Malaysia, Mexico, New Zealand, Papua New Guinea, Peru, Philippines, Republic of Korea, Russia, Singapore, Taiwan, Thailand, US, Vietnam.
Web site: <www.apec.org>.

**Association of Southeast Asian Nations (ASEAN)**
Founded: 1967. **Members:** Brunei, Cambodia, Indonesia, Laos, Malaysia, Myanmar (Burma), Philippines, Singapore, Thailand, Vietnam.
Web site: <www.aseansec.org>.

**Caribbean Community (Caricom)**
Founded: 1973. **Members:** Antigua and Barbuda, The Bahamas, Barbados, Belize, Dominica, Grenada, Guyana, Haiti, Jamaica, Montserrat, Saint Kitts and Nevis, Saint Lucia, Saint Vincent and the Grenadines, Suriname, Trinidad and Tobago; associate members Anguilla, Bermuda, British Virgin Islands, Cayman Islands, Turks and Caicos Islands.
Web site: <www.caricom.org>.

**Commonwealth (also called Commonwealth of Nations)**
Founded: 1931. **Members:** United Kingdom and 53 other countries, all of which (except Mozambique) were once under British rule or administratively connected to another member country (Fiji was suspended in September 2009; Nauru is a member in arrears).
Web site: <www.thecommonwealth.org>.

**Commonwealth of Independent States (CIS)**
Founded: 1991. **Members:** Armenia, Azerbaijan, Belarus, Kazakhstan, Kyrgyzstan, Moldova, Russia, Tajikistan, Turkmenistan, Ukraine, Uzbekistan.
Web site: <www.cisstat.com>.

**Community of Portuguese Language Countries (CPLP)**
Founded: 1996. **Members:** Angola, Brazil, Cape Verde, East Timor (Timor-Leste), Guinea-Bissau, Mozambique, Portugal, Sao Tome and Principe; observer states Equatorial Guinea, Mauritius, Senegal.
Web site: <www.cplp.org>.

**Economic Community of West African States (ECOWAS)**
Founded: 1975. **Members:** Benin, Burkina Faso, Cape Verde, Côte d'Ivoire, The Gambia, Ghana, Guinea, Guinea-Bissau, Liberia, Mali, Niger, Nigeria, Senegal, Sierra Leone, Togo (Mali was suspended in March 2012); observer state Chad.
Web site: <www.ecowas.int>.

**European Union (EU)**
Founded: 1950. **Members:** Austria, Belgium, Bulgaria, Cyprus, Czech Republic, Denmark, Estonia, Finland, France, Germany, Greece, Hungary, Ireland, Italy, Latvia, Lithuania, Luxembourg, Malta, Netherlands, Poland, Portugal, Romania, Slovakia, Slovenia, Spain, Sweden, UK.
Web site: <http://europa.eu>.

**Group of Twenty (G20)**
Founded: 1999. **Members:** Argentina, Australia, Brazil, Canada, China, France, Germany, India, Indonesia, Italy, Japan, Mexico, Republic of Korea, Russia, Saudi Arabia, South Africa, Turkey, UK, US, European Union.
Web site: <www.g20.org>.

**Gulf Cooperation Council (GCC)**
Founded: 1981. **Members:** Bahrain, Kuwait, Oman, Qatar, Saudi Arabia, UAE.
Web site: <www.gcc-sg.org/eng/index.html>.

**League of Arab States (LAS; also called Arab League)**
Founded: 1945. **Members:** Algeria, Bahrain, Comoros, Djibouti, Egypt, Iraq, Jordan, Kuwait, Lebanon, Libya, Mauritania, Morocco, Oman, Palestinian Authority, Qatar, Saudi Arabia, Somalia, Sudan, Syria, Tunisia, UAE, Yemen; observer states Brazil, Eritrea, India, Venezuela (Syria was suspended in November 2011).
Web site: <www.arableagueonline.org>.

**North Atlantic Treaty Organization (NATO)**
Founded: 1949. **Members:** Albania, Belgium, Bulgaria, Canada, Croatia, Czech Republic, Denmark, Estonia, France, Germany, Greece, Hungary, Iceland, Italy, Latvia, Lithuania, Luxembourg, Netherlands, Norway, Poland, Portugal, Romania, Slovakia, Slovenia, Spain, Turkey, UK, US.
Web site: <www.nato.int>.

**Organisation for Economic Co-operation and Development (OECD)**
Founded: 1961. **Members:** Australia, Austria, Belgium, Canada, Chile, Czech Republic, Denmark, Estonia, Finland, France, Germany, Greece, Hungary, Iceland, Ireland, Israel, Italy, Japan, Luxembourg, Mexico, Netherlands, New Zealand, Norway, Poland, Portugal, Republic of Korea, Slovakia, Slovenia, Spain, Sweden, Switzerland, Turkey, UK, US.
Web site: <www.oecd.org>.

**Organization for Security and Co-operation in Europe (OSCE)**
Founded: 1972. **Members:** 54 countries of Europe and Central Asia, plus Canada and the US.
Web site: <www.osce.org>.

**Organization of American States (OAS)**
Founded: 1948. **Members:** all 35 independent countries of the Western Hemisphere; 68 permanent observer states (including the EU).
Web site: <www.oas.org>.

**Organisation of Islamic Cooperation (OIC)**
Founded: 1969. **Members:** 56 Islamic countries (mainly in Africa and Asia), Palestinian Authority (Syria was suspended in August 2012); observer states Bosnia and Herzegovina, Central African Republic, Russia, Thailand, Turkish Republic of Northern Cyprus.
Web site: <www.oic-oci.org>.

# Membership in International Organizations (continued)

**Organization of the Petroleum Exporting Countries (OPEC)**
**Founded:** 1960. **Members:** Algeria, Angola, Ecuador, Iran, Iraq, Kuwait, Libya, Nigeria, Qatar, Saudi Arabia, UAE, Venezuela.
**Web site:** <www.opec.org>.

**Secretariat of the Pacific Community (SPC)**
**Founded:** 1947. **Members:** American Samoa, Australia, Cook Islands, Federated States of Micronesia, Fiji, France, French Polynesia, Guam, Kiribati, Marshall Islands, Nauru, New Caledonia, New Zealand, Niue, Northern Mariana Islands, Palau, Papua New Guinea, Pitcairn Islands, Samoa, Solomon Islands, Tokelau, Tonga, Tuvalu, US, Vanuatu, Wallis and Futuna.
**Web site:** <www.spc.int>.

**Southern African Development Community (SADC)**
**Founded:** 1979. **Members:** Angola, Botswana, Democratic Republic of the Congo, Lesotho, Madagascar, Malawi, Mauritius, Mozambique, Namibia, Seychelles, South Africa, Swaziland, Tanzania, Zambia, Zimbabwe (Madagascar was suspended in March 2009).
**Web site:** <www.sadc.int>.

**Union of South American Nations (UNASUR/UNASUL)**
**Founded:** 2004. **Members:** Argentina, Bolivia, Brazil, Chile, Colombia, Ecuador, Guyana, Paraguay, Peru, Suriname, Uruguay, Venezuela.
**Web site:** <www.comunidadandina.org>.

**World Trade Organization (WTO)**
**Founded:** 1995. **Members:** 155 member countries worldwide; 29 observer states as of May 2012.
**Web site:** <www.wto.org>.

## United Nations Membership by Date of Admission

| COUNTRY | DATE OF ADMISSION | COUNTRY | DATE OF ADMISSION | COUNTRY | DATE OF ADMISSION |
|---|---|---|---|---|---|
| Argentina | 24 Oct 1945 | Ecuador | 21 Dec 1945 | Gabon | 20 Sep 1960 |
| Belarus | 24 Oct 1945 | Iraq | 21 Dec 1945 | Madagascar | 20 Sep 1960 |
| Brazil | 24 Oct 1945 | Belgium | 27 Dec 1945 | Niger | 20 Sep 1960 |
| Chile | 24 Oct 1945 | Afghanistan | 19 Nov 1946 | Somalia | 20 Sep 1960 |
| China[1] | 24 Oct 1945 | Iceland | 19 Nov 1946 | Togo | 20 Sep 1960 |
| Cuba | 24 Oct 1945 | Sweden | 19 Nov 1946 | Mali | 28 Sep 1960 |
| Denmark | 24 Oct 1945 | Thailand | 16 Dec 1946 | Senegal | 28 Sep 1960 |
| Dominican Rep. | 24 Oct 1945 | Pakistan | 30 Sep 1947 | Nigeria | 7 Oct 1960 |
| Egypt | 24 Oct 1945 | Yemen | 30 Sep 1947 | Sierra Leone | 27 Sep 1961 |
| El Salvador | 24 Oct 1945 | Myanmar | 19 Apr 1948 | Mauritania | 27 Oct 1961 |
| France | 24 Oct 1945 | Israel | 11 May 1949 | Mongolia | 27 Oct 1961 |
| Haiti | 24 Oct 1945 | Indonesia | 28 Sep 1950 | Tanzania | 14 Dec 1961 |
| Iran | 24 Oct 1945 | Albania | 14 Dec 1955 | Burundi | 18 Sep 1962 |
| Lebanon | 24 Oct 1945 | Austria | 14 Dec 1955 | Jamaica | 18 Sep 1962 |
| Luxembourg | 24 Oct 1945 | Bulgaria | 14 Dec 1955 | Rwanda | 18 Sep 1962 |
| New Zealand | 24 Oct 1945 | Cambodia | 14 Dec 1955 | Trinidad and Tobago | 18 Sep 1962 |
| Nicaragua | 24 Oct 1945 | Finland | 14 Dec 1955 | Algeria | 8 Oct 1962 |
| Paraguay | 24 Oct 1945 | Hungary | 14 Dec 1955 | Uganda | 25 Oct 1962 |
| Philippines | 24 Oct 1945 | Ireland | 14 Dec 1955 | Kuwait | 14 May 1963 |
| Poland | 24 Oct 1945 | Italy | 14 Dec 1955 | Kenya | 16 Dec 1963 |
| USSR (later Russia) | 24 Oct 1945 | Jersey | 14 Dec 1955 | Malawi | 1 Dec 1964 |
| Saudi Arabia | 24 Oct 1945 | Jordan | 14 Dec 1955 | Malta | 1 Dec 1964 |
| Syria | 24 Oct 1945 | Laos | 14 Dec 1955 | Zambia | 1 Dec 1964 |
| Turkey | 24 Oct 1945 | Libya | 14 Dec 1955 | The Gambia | 21 Sep 1965 |
| Ukraine | 24 Oct 1945 | Nepal | 14 Dec 1955 | Maldives | 21 Sep 1965 |
| UK | 24 Oct 1945 | Portugal | 14 Dec 1955 | Singapore | 21 Sep 1965 |
| US | 24 Oct 1945 | Romania | 14 Dec 1955 | Guyana | 20 Sep 1966 |
| Greece | 25 Oct 1945 | Spain | 14 Dec 1955 | Lesotho | 17 Oct 1966 |
| India | 30 Oct 1945 | Sri Lanka | 14 Dec 1955 | Botswana | 17 Oct 1966 |
| Peru | 31 Oct 1945 | Morocco | 12 Nov 1956 | Barbados | 9 Dec 1966 |
| Australia | 1 Nov 1945 | Sudan | 12 Nov 1956 | Mauritius | 24 Apr 1968 |
| Costa Rica | 2 Nov 1945 | Tunisia | 12 Nov 1956 | Swaziland | 24 Sep 1968 |
| Liberia | 2 Nov 1945 | Japan | 18 Dec 1956 | Equatorial Guinea | 12 Nov 1968 |
| Colombia | 5 Nov 1945 | Ghana | 8 Mar 1957 | Fiji | 13 Oct 1970 |
| Mexico | 7 Nov 1945 | Malaysia | 17 Sep 1957 | Bahrain | 21 Sep 1971 |
| South Africa | 7 Nov 1945 | Guinea | 12 Dec 1958 | Bhutan | 21 Sep 1971 |
| Canada | 9 Nov 1945 | Benin | 20 Sep 1960 | Qatar | 21 Sep 1971 |
| Ethiopia | 13 Nov 1945 | Burkina Faso | 20 Sep 1960 | Oman | 7 Oct 1971 |
| Panama | 13 Nov 1945 | Cameroon | 20 Sep 1960 | United Arab Emirates | 9 Dec 1971 |
| Bolivia | 14 Nov 1945 | Central African Rep. | 20 Sep 1960 | The Bahamas | 18 Sep 1973 |
| Venezuela | 15 Nov 1945 | Chad | 20 Sep 1960 | Germany | 18 Sep 1973 |
| Guatemala | 21 Nov 1945 | Dem. Rep. of the Congo | 20 Sep 1960 | Bangladesh | 17 Sep 1974 |
| Norway | 27 Nov 1945 | | | Grenada | 17 Sep 1974 |
| Netherlands | 10 Dec 1945 | Rep. of the Congo | 20 Sep 1960 | Guinea-Bissau | 17 Sep 1974 |
| Honduras | 17 Dec 1945 | Côte d'Ivoire | 20 Sep 1960 | Cape Verde | 16 Sep 1975 |
| Uruguay | 18 Dec 1945 | Cyprus | 20 Sep 1960 | Mozambique | 16 Sep 1975 |

# United Nations Membership by Date of Admission (continued)

| COUNTRY | DATE OF ADMISSION | COUNTRY | DATE OF ADMISSION | COUNTRY | DATE OF ADMISSION |
|---|---|---|---|---|---|
| Sao Tome and Principe | 16 Sep 1975 | Namibia | 23 Apr 1990 | Croatia | 22 May 1992 |
| Papua New Guinea | 10 Oct 1975 | Liechtenstein | 18 Sep 1990 | Slovenia | 22 May 1992 |
| Comoros | 12 Nov 1975 | Estonia | 17 Sep 1991 | Georgia | 31 Jul 1992 |
| Suriname | 4 Dec 1975 | Dem. People's Republic of Korea | 17 Sep 1991 | Czech Republic | 19 Jan 1993 |
| Seychelles | 21 Sep 1976 | | | Slovakia | 19 Jan 1993 |
| Angola | 1 Dec 1976 | Republic of Korea | 17 Sep 1991 | Macedonia[2] | 8 Apr 1993 |
| Samoa | 15 Dec 1976 | Latvia | 17 Sep 1991 | Eritrea | 28 May 1993 |
| Djibouti | 20 Sep 1977 | Lithuania | 17 Sep 1991 | Monaco | 28 May 1993 |
| Vietnam | 20 Sep 1977 | Marshall Islands | 17 Sep 1991 | Andorra | 28 Jul 1993 |
| Solomon Islands | 19 Sep 1978 | Federated States of Micronesia | 17 Sep 1991 | Palau | 15 Dec 1994 |
| Dominica | 18 Dec 1978 | | | Kiribati | 14 Sep 1999 |
| St. Lucia | 18 Sep 1979 | Armenia | 2 Mar 1992 | Nauru | 14 Sep 1999 |
| Zimbabwe | 25 Aug 1980 | Azerbaijan | 2 Mar 1992 | Tonga | 14 Sep 1999 |
| St. Vincent and the Grenadines | 16 Sep 1980 | Kazakhstan | 2 Mar 1992 | Tuvalu | 5 Sep 2000 |
| | | Kyrgyzstan | 2 Mar 1992 | Serbia | 1 Nov 2000 |
| Vanuatu | 15 Sep 1981 | Moldova | 2 Mar 1992 | Switzerland | 10 Sep 2002 |
| Belize | 25 Sep 1981 | San Marino | 2 Mar 1992 | East Timor (Timor-Leste) | 27 Sep 2002 |
| Antigua and Barbuda | 11 Nov 1981 | Tajikistan | 2 Mar 1992 | | |
| | | Turkmenistan | 2 Mar 1992 | Montenegro | 28 Jun 2006 |
| | | Uzbekistan | 2 Mar 1992 | South Sudan | 14 Jul 2011 |
| St. Kitts and Nevis | 23 Sep 1983 | Bosnia and Herzegovina | 22 May 1992 | | |
| Brunei | 21 Sep 1984 | | | | |

[1]The Republic of China (Taiwan) held the seat until 25 Oct 1971, when UN Res. 2758 gave the membership and a seat on the Security Council to the People's Republic of China. [2]Macedonia is known in the UN as The Former Yugoslav Republic of Macedonia.

# Secretaries-General of the United Nations

The UN General Assembly appoints the Secretary-General to a five-year term on the recommendation of the 15-member Security Council; permanent members of the Security Council have veto power over nominees. The Secretary-General balances diverse and sometimes conflicting duties in the various roles of diplomat, advocate, administrator, and civil servant. The Secretary-General has a broad mandate, being able to marshal resources and advocacy on issues as various as peace efforts around the globe and disease prevention and treatment. United Nations Web site: <www.un.org>.

| SECRETARY-GENERAL | TERM | SECRETARY-GENERAL | TERM |
|---|---|---|---|
| Sir Gladwyn Jebb (acting) (UK) | 1945–1946 | Javier Pérez de Cuéllar (Peru) | 1982–1991 |
| Trygve Lie (Norway) | 1946–1952 | Boutros Boutros-Ghali (Egypt) | 1992–1996 |
| Dag Hammarskjöld (Sweden) | 1953–1961 | Kofi Annan (Ghana) | 1997–2006 |
| U Thant (Burma, now Myanmar) | 1962–1971 | Ban Ki-moon (Republic of Korea) | 2007– |
| Kurt Waldheim (Austria) | 1972–1981 | | |

# International Criminal Court

The International Criminal Court (ICC) was established by the Rome Statute of the International Criminal Court on 17 Jul 1998. The statute that created the ICC went into force on 1 Jul 2002; the court was fully operational as of July 2003. As of 1 Jul 2012, the ICC has 121 member countries.

**President**
Song Sang-Hyun (Republic of Korea)

**First Vice President**
Sanji Mmasenono Monageng (Botswana)

**Second Vice President**
Cuno Tarfusser (Italy)

**Chief Prosecutor**
Fatou Bensouda (The Gambia)

**Registrar**
Silvana Arbia (Italy)

**Judges**
List A—elected as experts in criminal law and procedure
Joyce Aluoch (Kenya)
Anthony T. Carmona (Trinidad and Tobago)
Bruno Cotte (France)
Fatoumata Dembele Diarra (Mali)
Chile Eboe-Osuji (Nigeria)
Silvia Alejandra Fernández de Gurmendi (Argentina)
Robert Fremr (Czech Republic)
Adrian Fulford (United Kingdom)
Olga Herrera Carbuccia (Dominican Republic)
Howard Morrison (United Kingdom)
Elizabeth Odio Benito (Costa Rica)
Song Sang-Hyun (Republic of Korea)
Sylvia Steiner (Brazil)

## International Criminal Court (continued)

**Judges—List A (continued)**
Cuno Tarfusser (Italy)
Ekaterina Trendafilova (Bulgaria)
Christine Van den Wyngaert (Belgium)

*List B—elected as experts in international law and human rights law*
René Blattmann (Bolivia)
Miriam Defensor-Santiago (Philippines)

**Judges—List B (continued)**
Hans-Peter Kaul (Germany)
Erkki Kourula (Finland)
Akua Kuenyehia (Ghana)
Sanji Mmasenono Monageng (Botswana)
Kuniko Ozaki (Japan)
Anita Usacka (Latvia)

# Rulers and Regimes

## Europe

### Roman Emperors

Overlapping reigns denote corulers. Diocletian (284–305) laid the foundation for the Byzantine Empire in the East when he appointed Maximian (286–305) to rule over the Western portion of the empire. Rome thus remained a unified state but was divided administratively. Theodosius I (379–395) was the last emperor to rule over a unified Roman Empire. When he died, Rome split into Eastern and Western empires. For a complete list of the Eastern emperors after the fall of Rome, *see* "Byzantine Empire."

| REIGN | BYNAME | FULL NAME |
|---|---|---|
| 27 BC–AD 14 | Augustus | Caesar Augustus |
| 14–37 | Tiberius | Tiberius Caesar Augustus |
| 37–41 | Caligula | Gaius Caesar Augustus Germanicus |
| 41–54 | Claudius | Tiberius Claudius Caesar Augustus Germanicus |
| 54–68 | Nero | Nero Claudius Caesar Augustus Germanicus |
| 68–69 | Galba | Servius Galba Caesar Augustus |
| 69 | Otho | Marcus Otho Caesar Augustus |
| 69 | Vitellius | Aulus Vitellius Germanicus |
| 69–79 | Vespasian | Caesar Vespasianus Augustus |
| 79–81 | Titus | Titus Vespasianus Augustus |
| 81–96 | Domitian | Caesar Domitianus Augustus |
| 96–98 | Nerva | Nerva Caesar Augustus |
| 98–117 | Trajan | Caesar Nerva Traianus Augustus |
| 117–138 | Hadrian | Caesar Traianus Hadrianus Augustus |
| 138–161 | Antoninus Pius | Caesar Titus Aelius Hadrianus Antoninus Augustus Pius |
| 161–180 | Marcus Aurelius | Marcus Aurelius Antoninus |
| 161–169 | Lucius Verus | Lucius Aurelius Verus |
| 177–192 | Commodus | Lucius Aelius Aurelius Commodus |
| 193 | Pertinax | Publius Helvius Pertinax |
| 193 | Didius Julianus | Marcus Didius Severus Julianus |
| 193–211 | Septimius Severus | Lucius Septimius Severus Pertinax |
| 198–217 | Caracalla | Marcus Aurelius Severus Antoninus |
| 209–212 | Geta | Publius Septimius Geta |
| 217–218 | Macrinus | Marcus Opellius Severus Macrinus |
| 218–222 | Elagabalus | Sacerdos dei invicti solis Elagabali Marcus Aurelius Antoninus |
| 222–235 | Alexander Severus | Marcus Aurelius Severus Alexander |
| 235–238 | Maximin | Gaius Julius Verus Maximinus |
| 238 | Gordian I | Marcus Antonius Gordianus Sempronianus Romanus Africanus |
| 238 | Gordian II | Marcus Antonius Gordianus Sempronianus Romanus Africanus |
| 238 | Maximus | Marcus Clodius Pupienus Maximus |
| 238 | Balbinus | Decius Caelius Calvinus Balbinus |
| 238–244 | Gordian III | Marcus Antonius Gordianus |
| 244–249 | Philip | |
| 249–251 | Decius | Galus Messius Quintus Trianus Decius |
| 251 | Hostilian | Gaius Valens Hostilianus Messius Quintus |
| 251–253 | Gallus | Gaius Vibius Trebonianus Gallus |
| 253 | Aemilian | Marcus Aemilius Aemilianus |
| 253–260 | Valerian | Publius Licinius Valerianus |
| 253–268 | Gallienus | Publius Licinius Egnatius Gallienus |
| 268–270 | Claudius II Gothicus | Marcus Aurelius Valerius Claudius |
| 269–270 | Quintillus | Marcus Aurelius Claudius Quintillus |
| 270–275 | Aurelian | Lucius Domitius Aurelianus |
| 275–276 | Tacitus | Marcus Claudius Tacitus |

## Roman Emperors (continued)

| REIGN | BYNAME | FULL NAME |
|---|---|---|
| 276 | Florian | Marcus Annius Florianus |
| 276–282 | Probus | Marcus Aurelius Probus |
| 282–283 | Carus | Marcus Aurelius Carus |
| 283–285 | Carinus | Marcus Aurelius Carinus |
| 283–284 | Numerian | Marcus Aurelius Numerius Numerianus |
| 284–305[1] | Diocletian | Gaius Aurelius Valerius Diocletianus |
| 286–305[2] | Maximian | Marcus Aurelius Valerius Maximianus Heraclius |
| 305–311[1] | Galerius | Gaius Galerius Valerius Maximianus |
| 305–306[2] | Constantius I Chlorus | Flavius Valerius Constantius |
| 306–307[2] | Severus | Flavius Valerius Severus |
| 306–312[2] | Maxentius | Marcus Aurelius Valerius Maxentius |
| 308–324[1] | Licinius | Valerius Licinianus Licinius |
| 312–337[2] | Constantine I | Flavius Valerius Constantinus |
| 337–340[2] | Constantine II | Flavius Claudius [or Julius] Constantinus |
| 337–350[2] | Constans I | Flavius Julius Constans |
| 337–361[2] | Constantius II | Flavius Julius [or Valerius] Constantius |
| 350–353[2] | Magnentius | Flavius Magnus Magnentius |
| 361–363[2] | Julian | Flavius Claudius Julianus |
| 363–364[2] | Jovian | Flavius Jovianus |
| 364–375[2] | Valentinian I | Flavius Valentinianus |
| 364–378[1] | Valens | Flavius Valens |
| 365–366[1] | Procopius | |
| 375–383[2] | Gratian | Flavius Gratianus Augustus |
| 375–392[2] | Valentinian II | Flavius Valentinianus |
| 379–395[2] | Theodosius I | Flavius Theodosius |
| 395–408[1] | Arcadius | Flavius Arcadius |
| 395–423[2] | Honorius | Flavius Honorius |
| 408–450[1] | Theodosius II | |
| 421[2] | Constantius III | |
| 425–455[2] | Valentinian III | Flavius Placidius Valentinianus |
| 450–457[1] | Marcian | Marcianus |
| 455[2] | Petronius Maximus | Flavius Ancius Petronius Maximus |
| 455–456[2] | Avitus | Flavius Maccilius Eparchus Avitus |
| 457–474[1] | Leo I | Leo Thrax Magnus |
| 457–461[2] | Majorian | Julius Valerius Majorianus |
| 461–467[2] | Libius Severus | Libius Severianus Severus |
| 467–472[2] | Anthemius | Procopius Anthemius |
| 472[2] | Olybrius | Anicius Olybrius |
| 473–474[2] | Glycerius | |
| 474–475[2] | Julius Nepos | |
| 474[1] | Leo II | |
| 474–491[1] | Zeno | |
| 475–476[2] | Romulus Augustulus | Flavius Momyllus Romulus Augustulus |

[1]Ruled in the East only.    [2]Ruled in the West only.

## Sovereigns of Britain

| SOVEREIGN | DYNASTY OR HOUSE | REIGN | SOVEREIGN | DYNASTY OR HOUSE | REIGN |
|---|---|---|---|---|---|
| **Kings of Wessex (West Saxons)** | | | **Sovereigns of England (continued)** | | |
| Egbert | Saxon | 802–839 | Ethelred II the Unready (Aethelred) | Saxon | 978–1013 |
| Aethelwulf (Ethelwulf) | Saxon | 839–856/858 | Sweyn Forkbeard | Danish | 1013–14 |
| Aethelbald (Ethelbald) | Saxon | 855/856–860 | Ethelred II the Unready (restored) | Saxon | 1014–16 |
| Aethelberht (Ethelbert) | Saxon | 860–865/866 | | | |
| Aethelred I (Ethelred) | Saxon | 865/866–871 | Edmund II Ironside | Saxon | 1016 |
| Alfred the Great | Saxon | 871–899 | Canute | Danish | 1016–35 |
| Edward the Elder | Saxon | 899–924 | Harold I Harefoot | Danish | 1035–40 |
| | | | Hardecanute | Danish | 1040–42 |
| **Sovereigns of England** | | | Edward the Confessor | Saxon | 1042–66 |
| Athelstan[1] | Saxon | 925–939 | Harold II | Saxon | 1066 |
| Edmund I | Saxon | 939–946 | William I the Conqueror | Norman | 1066–87 |
| Eadred (Edred) | Saxon | 946–955 | William II | Norman | 1087–1100 |
| Eadwig (Edwy) | Saxon | 955–959 | Henry I | Norman | 1100–35 |
| Edgar | Saxon | 959–975 | Stephen | Blois | 1135–54 |
| Edward the Martyr | Saxon | 975–978 | | | |

## Sovereigns of Britain (continued)

| SOVEREIGN | DYNASTY OR HOUSE | REIGN |
|---|---|---|
| **Sovereigns of England (continued)** | | |
| Henry II | Plantagenet | 1154–89 |
| Richard I | Plantagenet | 1189–99 |
| John | Plantagenet | 1199–1216 |
| Henry III | Plantagenet | 1216–72 |
| Edward I | Plantagenet | 1272–1307 |
| Edward II | Plantagenet | 1307–27 |
| Edward III | Plantagenet | 1327–77 |
| Richard II | Plantagenet | 1377–99 |
| Henry IV | Plantagenet: Lancaster | 1399–1413 |
| Henry V | Plantagenet: Lancaster | 1413–22 |
| Henry VI | Plantagenet: Lancaster | 1422–61 |
| Edward IV | Plantagenet: York | 1461–70 |
| Henry VI (restored) | Plantagenet: Lancaster | 1470–71 |
| Edward IV (restored) | Plantagenet: York | 1471–83 |
| Edward V | Plantagenet: York | 1483 |
| Richard III | Plantagenet: York | 1483–85 |
| Henry VII | Tudor | 1483–1509 |
| Henry VIII | Tudor | 1509–47 |
| Edward VI | Tudor | 1547–53 |
| Mary I | Tudor | 1553–58 |
| Elizabeth I | Tudor | 1558–1603 |

| SOVEREIGN | DYNASTY OR HOUSE | REIGN |
|---|---|---|
| **Sovereigns of Great Britain and the United Kingdom[2, 3]** | | |
| James I (VI of Scotland)[2] | Stuart | 1603–25 |
| Charles I | Stuart | 1625–49 |
| **Commonwealth** | | |
| Oliver Cromwell, Lord Protector | | 1653–58 |
| Richard Cromwell, Lord Protector | | 1658–59 |
| **Sovereigns of Great Britain and the United Kingdom (restored)** | | |
| Charles II | Stuart | 1660–85 |
| James II | Stuart | 1685–88 |
| William III and Mary II[4] | Orange/ Stuart | 1689–1702 |
| Anne | Stuart | 1702–14 |
| George I | Hanover | 1714–27 |
| George II | Hanover | 1727–60 |
| George III[3] | Hanover | 1760–1820 |
| George IV[5] | Hanover | 1820–30 |
| William IV | Hanover | 1830–37 |
| Victoria | Hanover | 1837–1901 |
| Edward VII | Saxe-Coburg-Gotha | 1901–10 |
| George V[6] | Windsor | 1910–36 |
| Edward VIII[7] | Windsor | 1936 |
| George VI | Windsor | 1936–52 |
| Elizabeth II | Windsor | 1952– |

[1]Athelstan was king of Wessex and the first king of all England. [2]James VI of Scotland became also James I of England in 1603. Upon accession to the English throne he styled himself "King of Great Britain" and was so proclaimed. Legally, however, he and his successors held separate English and Scottish kingships until the Act of Union of 1707, when the two kingdoms were united as the Kingdom of Great Britain. [3]The United Kingdom was formed on 1 Jan 1801, with the union of Great Britain and Ireland. After 1801 George III was styled "King of the United Kingdom of Great Britain and Ireland." [4]William and Mary, as husband and wife, reigned jointly until Mary's death in 1694. William then reigned alone until his own death in 1702. [5]George IV was regent from 5 Feb 1811. [6]In 1917, during World War I, George V changed the name of his house from Saxe-Coburg-Gotha to Windsor. [7]Edward VIII succeeded upon the death of his father, George V, on 20 Jan 1936, but abdicated on 11 Dec 1936, before coronation.

## British Prime Ministers

The origin of the term prime minister and the question of to whom it should originally be applied have long been issues of scholarly and political debate. Although the term was used as early as the reign of Queen Anne (1702–14), it acquired wider currency during the reign of George II (1727–60), when it began to be used as a term of reproach toward Robert Walpole. The title prime minister did not become official until 1905, to refer to the leader of a government.

Before the development of the Conservative and Liberal parties in the mid-19th century, parties in Britain were, for the most part, simply alliances of prominent groups or aristocratic families. The designations Whig and Tory tend often to be approximate. In all cases, the party designation is that of the prime minister; he or she might lead a coalition government, as did David Lloyd George and Winston Churchill (in his first term).

| PRIME MINISTER | PARTY | TERM |
|---|---|---|
| Robert Walpole | Whig | 1721–42 |
| Spencer Compton | Whig | 1742–43 |
| Henry Pelham | Whig | 1743–54 |
| Thomas Pelham-Holles | Whig | 1754–56 |
| William Cavendish | Whig | 1756–57 |
| Thomas Pelham-Holles | Whig | 1757–62 |
| John Stuart | | 1762–63 |
| George Grenville | | 1763–65 |
| Charles Watson Wentworth | Whig | 1765–66 |
| William Pitt | | 1766–68 |
| Augustus Henry Fitzroy | | 1768–70 |

| PRIME MINISTER | PARTY | TERM |
|---|---|---|
| Frederick North | | 1770–82 |
| Charles Watson Wentworth | Whig | 1782 |
| William Petty-Fitzmaurice | | 1782–83 |
| William Henry Cavendish-Bentinck | Whig | 1783 |
| William Pitt | Tory | 1783–1801 |
| Henry Addington | Tory | 1801–04 |
| William Pitt | Tory | 1804–06 |
| William Wyndham Grenville | | 1806–07 |

## British Prime Ministers (continued)

| PRIME MINISTER | PARTY | TERM | PRIME MINISTER | PARTY | TERM |
|---|---|---|---|---|---|
| William Henry Cavendish-Bentinck | Whig | 1807–09 | Archibald Philip Primrose | Liberal | 1894–95 |
| Spencer Perceval | Tory | 1809–12 | Robert Cecil | Conservative | 1895–1902 |
| Robert Banks Jenkinson | Tory | 1812–27 | Arthur James Balfour | Conservative | 1902–05 |
| George Canning | Tory | 1827 | Henry Campbell-Bannerman | Liberal | 1905–08 |
| Frederick John Robinson | Tory | 1827–28 | H.H. Asquith | Liberal | 1908–16 |
| Arthur Wellesley | Tory | 1828–30 | David Lloyd George | Liberal | 1916–22 |
| Charles Grey | Whig | 1830–34 | Bonar Law | Conservative | 1922–23 |
| William Lamb | Whig | 1834 | Stanley Baldwin | Conservative | 1923–24 |
| Arthur Wellesley | Tory | 1834 | Ramsay Macdonald | Labour | 1924 |
| Robert Peel | Tory | 1834–35 | Stanley Baldwin | Conservative | 1924–29 |
| William Lamb | Whig | 1835–41 | Ramsay Macdonald | Labour | 1929–35 |
| Robert Peel | Conservative | 1841–46 | Stanley Baldwin | Conservative | 1935–37 |
| John Russell | Whig-Liberal | 1846–52 | Neville Chamberlain | Conservative | 1937–40 |
| Edward Geoffrey Stanley | Conservative | 1852 | Winston Churchill | Conservative | 1940–45 |
| George Hamilton-Gordon | | 1852–55 | Clement Attlee | Labour | 1945–51 |
| Henry John Temple | Liberal | 1855–58 | Winston Churchill | Conservative | 1951–55 |
| Edward Geoffrey Stanley | Conservative | 1858–59 | Anthony Eden | Conservative | 1955–57 |
| Henry John Temple | Liberal | 1859–65 | Harold Macmillan | Conservative | 1957–63 |
| John Russell | Liberal | 1865–66 | Alec Douglas-Home | Conservative | 1963–64 |
| Edward Geoffrey Stanley | Conservative | 1866–68 | Harold Wilson | Labour | 1964–70 |
| Benjamin Disraeli | Conservative | 1868 | Edward Heath | Conservative | 1970–74 |
| William Ewart Gladstone | Liberal | 1868–74 | Harold Wilson | Labour | 1974–76 |
| Benjamin Disraeli | Conservative | 1874–80 | James Callaghan | Labour | 1976–79 |
| William Ewart Gladstone | Liberal | 1880–85 | Margaret Thatcher | Conservative | 1979–90 |
| Robert Cecil | Conservative | 1885–86 | John Major | Conservative | 1990–97 |
| William Ewart Gladstone | Liberal | 1886 | Tony Blair | Labour | 1997–2007 |
| Robert Cecil | Conservative | 1886–92 | Gordon Brown | Labour | 2007–10 |
| William Ewart Gladstone | Liberal | 1892–94 | David Cameron | Conservative | 2010– |

## Rulers of France

| RULER | REIGN | RULER | REIGN |
|---|---|---|---|
| **Carolingian dynasty** | | **Capetian dynasty (continued)** | |
| Pippin III the Short | 751–768 | Louis VI | 1108–37 |
| Charles I (Charlemagne, Kingdom of the Franks) | 768–814 | Louis VII | 1137–80 |
| | | Philip II (Philippe) | 1180–1223 |
| Louis I (Kingdom of the Franks) | 814–840 | Louis VIII | 1223–26 |
| *civil war* | 840–843 | Louis IX (Saint Louis) | 1226–70 |
| Charles II (Kingdom of the West Franks) | 843–877 | Philip III (Philippe) | 1270–85 |
| Louis II (Kingdom of the West Franks) | 877–879 | Philip IV (Philippe) | 1285–1314 |
| Louis III (Kingdom of the West Franks) | 879–882 | Louis X | 1314–16 |
| Carloman (Kingdom of the West Franks) | 879–884 | John I (Jean) | 1316 |
| Charles (III) (Charles III, Holy Roman Empire) | 884–887 | Philip V (Philippe) | 1316–22 |
| | | Charles IV | 1322–28 |
| **Robertian (Capetian) dynasty** | | **Valois dynasty** | |
| Eudes | 888–898 | Philip VI (Philippe) | 1328–50 |
| | | John II (Jean) | 1350–64 |
| **Carolingian dynasty** | | Charles V | 1364–80 |
| Charles III | 893/898–923 | Charles VI | 1380–1422 |
| | | Charles VII | 1422–61 |
| **Robertian (Capetian) dynasty** | | Louis XI | 1461–83 |
| Robert I | 922–923 | Charles VIII | 1483–98 |
| Rudolf (Raoul, or Rodolphe) | 923–936 | | |
| | | **Valois dynasty (Orléans branch)** | |
| **Carolingian dynasty** | | Louis XII | 1498–1515 |
| Louis IV | 936–954 | | |
| Lothair (Lothaire) | 954–986 | **Valois dynasty (Angoulême branch)** | |
| Louis V | 986–987 | Francis I (François) | 1515–47 |
| | | Henry II (Henri) | 1547–59 |
| **Capetian dynasty** | | Francis II (François) | 1559–60 |
| Hugh Capet (Hugues Capet) | 987–996 | Charles IX | 1560–74 |
| Robert II | 996–1031 | Henry III (Henri) | 1574–89 |
| Henry I (Henri) | 1031–60 | | |
| Philip I (Philippe) | 1060–1108 | | |

## Rulers of France (continued)

| RULER | REIGN |
|---|---|
| **House of Bourbon** | |
| Henry IV (Henri) | 1589–1610 |
| Louis XIII | 1610–43 |
| Louis XIV | 1643–1715 |
| Louis XV | 1715–74 |
| Louis XVI | 1774–92 |
| Louis (XVII) | 1793–95 |
| **First Republic** | |
| National Convention | 1792–95 |
| Directorate | 1795–99 |
| Consulate (Napoléon Bonaparte) | 1799–1804 |
| **First Empire (emperors)** | |
| Napoleon I (Napoléon Bonaparte) | 1804–14, 1815 |
| Napoleon (II) | 1815 |
| **House of Bourbon** | |
| Louis XVIII | 1814–24 |
| Charles X | 1824–30 |
| **House of Orléans** | |
| Louis-Philippe | 1830–48 |
| **Second Republic (president)** | |
| Louis-Napoléon Bonaparte | 1848–52 |
| **Second Empire (emperor)** | |
| Napoleon III (Louis-Napoléon Bonaparte) | 1852–70 |

| RULER | REIGN |
|---|---|
| **Third Republic (presidents)** | |
| Adolphe Thiers | 1871–73 |
| Marie-Edmé-Patrice-Maurice | 1873–79 |
| Jules Grévy | 1879–87 |
| Sadi Carnot | 1887–94 |
| Jean Casimir-Périer | 1894–95 |
| Félix Faure | 1895–99 |
| Émile Loubet | 1899–1906 |
| Armand Fallières | 1906–13 |
| Raymond Poincaré | 1913–20 |
| Paul Deschanel | 1920 |
| Alexandre Millerand | 1920–24 |
| Gaston Doumergue | 1924–31 |
| Paul Doumer | 1931–32 |
| Albert Lebrun | 1932–40 |
| **French State (État Français, or Vichy France)** | |
| Philippe Pétain | 1940–44 |
| **Provisional government** | 1944–47 |
| **Fourth Republic (presidents)** | |
| Vincent Auriol | 1947–54 |
| René Coty | 1954–59 |
| **Fifth Republic (presidents)** | |
| Charles de Gaulle | 1959–69 |
| Georges Pompidou | 1969–74 |
| Valéry Giscard d'Estaing | 1974–81 |
| François Mitterrand | 1981–95 |
| Jacques Chirac | 1995–2007 |
| Nicolas Sarkozy | 2007–12 |
| François Hollande | 2012– |

## Rulers of Germany

On 25 Jul 1806 the Confederation of the Rhine was founded, with Karl Theodor von Dalberg as prince primate (1806–13). After the dissolution of the Rhine Confederation, the German Confederation followed in 1815. In 1867 the governing structure became the North German Confederation, and in 1871 the German Reich. For rulers of Germany before the Confederation of the Rhine, see Holy Roman Emperors.

| RULER | REIGN OR TERM |
|---|---|
| **Emperors** | |
| **Hohenzollern dynasty** | |
| Wilhelm I | 1871–88 |
| Friedrich III | 1888 |
| Wilhelm II | 1888–1918 |
| **Presidents** | |
| Richard Müller | 1918 |
| Robert Leinert | 1918–19 |
| Wilhelm Pfannkuch | 1919 |
| Eduard David | 1919 |
| Friedrich Ebert | 1919–25 |
| Paul von Hindenburg | 1925–34 |
| Adolf Hitler (Führer) | 1934–45 |
| Karl Dönitz | 1945 |
| **Chancellors** | |
| Otto Fürst von Bismarck | 1871–90 |
| Leo Graf von Caprivi | 1890–94 |
| Chlodwig Fürst zu Hohenlohe-Schillingsfürst | 1894–1900 |
| Bernhard Graf Fürst von Bülow | 1900–09 |
| Theobald von Bethmann Hollweg | 1909–17 |
| Georg Michaelis | 1917 |

| RULER | REIGN OR TERM |
|---|---|
| **Chancellors (continued)** | |
| Georg Graf von Hertling | 1917–18 |
| Maximilian Prinz von Baden | 1918 |
| Friedrich Ebert | 1918 |
| Philipp Scheidemann | 1919 |
| Gustav Bauer | 1919–20 |
| Wolfgang Kapp (in rebellion) | 1920 |
| Hermann Müller | 1920 |
| Konstantin Fehrenbach | 1920–21 |
| Joseph Wirth | 1921–22 |
| Wilhelm Cuno | 1922–23 |
| Gustav Stresemann | 1923 |
| Wilhelm Marx | 1923–24 |
| Hans Luther | 1925–26 |
| Wilhelm Marx | 1926–28 |
| Hermann Müller | 1928–30 |
| Heinrich Brüning | 1930–32 |
| Franz von Papen | 1932 |
| Kurt von Schleicher | 1932–33 |
| Adolf Hitler | 1933–45 |
| Joseph Goebbels | 1945 |
| Lutz Graf Schwerin von Krosigk (chairman of interim government) | 1945 |

# Rulers of Germany (continued)

**Allied occupation**                                        1945–49

## German Democratic Republic (East Germany)[1]

| Presidents | | Chairmen of the Council of State (continued) | |
|---|---|---|---|
| Wilhelm Pieck | 1949–60 | Willi Stoph | 1973–76 |
| | | Erich Honecker | 1976–89 |
| **Chairmen of the Council of State** | | Egon Krenz | 1989 |
| Walter Ulbricht | 1960–73 | Sabine Bergmann-Pohl | 1990 |

## Federal Republic of Germany (West Germany)[1]

| Presidents | | Chancellors | |
|---|---|---|---|
| Theodor Heuss | 1949–59 | Konrad Adenauer | 1949–63 |
| Heinrich Lübke | 1959–69 | Ludwig Erhard | 1963–66 |
| Gustav Heinemann | 1969–74 | Kurt Georg Kiesinger | 1966–69 |
| Walter Scheel | 1974–79 | Willy Brandt | 1969–74 |
| Karl Carstens | 1979–84 | Helmut Schmidt | 1974–82 |
| Richard von Weizsäcker | 1984–94 | Helmut Kohl | 1982–98 |
| Roman Herzog | 1994–99 | Gerhard Schröder | 1998–2005 |
| Johannes Rau | 1999–2004 | Angela Merkel | 2005– |
| Horst Köhler | 2004– | | |

[1]After World War II, Germany was split into four occupational zones, governed by the French, British, American, and Soviet powers. The Western zones were merged and, on 23 May 1949, became the independent Federal Republic of Germany. On 7 October of the same year, the Soviet zone was proclaimed the German Democratic Republic. On 3 Oct 1990, the latter was incorporated into the Federal Republic of Germany.

# Holy Roman Emperors

*The Holy Roman Empire encompassed a varying complex of lands in Western and Central Europe. Ruled over by Frankish and then German kings, the empire officially dissolved on 6 Aug 1806, when Francis II resigned his title.*

| EMPEROR | REIGN | EMPEROR | REIGN |
|---|---|---|---|
| **Carolingian dynasty** | | **Salian dynasty (continued)** | |
| Charlemagne (Charles I) | 800–814 | Henry IV | 1056–1106 |
| Louis I | 814–840 | Rival claimants: | |
| *Civil War* | 840–843 | Rudolf | 1077–80 |
| Lothair I | 843–855 | Hermann | 1081–93 |
| Louis II | 855–875 | Conrad | 1093–1101 |
| Charles II | 875–877 | Henry V | 1105/06–25 |
| *Interregnum* | 877–881 | | |
| Charles III | 881–887 | **House of Supplinburg** | |
| *interregnum* | 887–891 | Lothair II | 1125–37 |
| | | | |
| **House of Spoleto** | | **House of Hohenstaufen** | |
| Guy | 891–894 | Conrad III | 1138–52 |
| Lambert | 894–898 | Frederick I (Barbarossa) | 1152–90 |
| | | Henry VI | 1190–97 |
| **Carolingian dynasty** | | Philip | 1198–1208 |
| Arnulf | 896–899 | | |
| Louis III | 901–905 | **Welf dynasty** | |
| | | Otto IV | 1198–1214 |
| **House of Franconia** | | | |
| Conrad I | 911–918 | **House of Hohenstaufen** | |
| | | Frederick II | 1215–50 |
| **Carolingian dynasty** | | Rival claimants: | |
| Berengar | 915–924 | Henry (VII) | 1220–35 |
| | | Henry Raspe | 1246–47 |
| **House of Saxony (Liudolfings)** | | William of Holland | 1247–56 |
| Henry I | 919–936 | Conrad IV | 1250–54 |
| Otto I | 936–973 | *Great Interregnum* | 1254–73 |
| Otto II | 973–983 | Richard | 1257–72 |
| Otto III | 983–1002 | Alfonso (Alfonso X of Castile) | 1257–75 |
| Henry II | 1002–24 | | |
| | | **House of Habsburg** | |
| **Salian dynasty** | | Rudolf I | 1273–91 |
| Conrad II | 1024–39 | | |
| Henry III | 1039–56 | | |

# Holy Roman Emperors (continued)

| EMPEROR | REIGN |
|---|---|
| **House of Nassau** | |
| Adolf | 1292–98 |
| | |
| **House of Habsburg** | |
| Albert I | 1298–1308 |
| | |
| **House of Luxembourg** | |
| Henry VII | 1308–13 |
| | |
| **House of Habsburg** | |
| Frederick (III) | 1314–26 |
| | |
| **House of Wittelsbach** | |
| Louis IV | 1314–46 |
| | |
| **House of Luxembourg** | |
| Charles IV | 1346–78 |
| Wenceslas | 1378–1400 |
| | |
| **House of Wittelsbach** | |
| Rupert | 1400–10 |
| | |
| **House of Luxembourg** | |
| Jobst | 1410–11 |
| Sigismund | 1410–37 |

| EMPEROR | REIGN |
|---|---|
| **House of Habsburg** | |
| Albert II | 1438–39 |
| Frederick III | 1440–93 |
| Maximilian I | 1493–1519 |
| Charles V | 1519–56 |
| Ferdinand I | 1556–64 |
| Maximilian II | 1564–76 |
| Rudolf II | 1576–1612 |
| Matthias | 1612–19 |
| Ferdinand II | 1619–37 |
| Ferdinand III | 1637–57 |
| Leopold I | 1658–1705 |
| Joseph I | 1705–11 |
| Charles VI | 1711–40 |
| | |
| **House of Wittelsbach** | |
| Charles VII | 1742–45 |
| | |
| **House of Habsburg** | |
| Francis I | 1745–65 |
| Joseph II | 1765–90 |
| Leopold II | 1790–92 |
| Francis II | 1792–1806 |

# Rulers of Russia[1]

| RULER | REIGN |
|---|---|
| **Princes and Grand Princes of Moscow** | |
| **(Muscovy): Danilovich dynasty[2]** | |
| Daniel (son of Alexander Nevsky) | c. 1276–1303 |
| Yury | 1303–25 |
| Ivan I | 1325–40 |
| Semyon (Simeon) | 1340–53 |
| Ivan II | 1353–59 |
| Dmitry Donskoy | 1359–89 |
| Vasily I | 1389–1425 |
| Vasily II | 1425–62 |
| Ivan III | 1462–1505 |
| Vasily III | 1505–33 |
| Ivan IV | 1533–47 |
| | |
| **Tsars of Russia: Danilovich dynasty** | |
| Ivan IV | 1547–84 |
| Fyodor I | 1584–98 |
| | |
| **Tsars of Russia: Time of Troubles** | |
| Boris Godunov | 1598–1605 |
| Fyodor II | 1605 |
| False Dmitry | 1605–06 |
| Vasily (IV) | 1606–10 |
| | |
| Interregnum | 1610–12 |
| | |
| **Tsars and Empresses of Russia and the** | |
| **Russian Empire: Romanov dynasty[3]** | |
| Michael III | 1613–45 |
| Alexis | 1645–76 |
| Fyodor III | 1676–82 |
| Peter I (Ivan V coruler 1682–96) | 1682–1725 |
| Catherine I | 1725–27 |

| RULER | REIGN |
|---|---|
| **Tsars and Empresses of Russia and the** | |
| **Russian Empire: Romanov dynasty[3] (continued)** | |
| Peter II | 1727–30 |
| Anna | 1730–40 |
| Ivan VI | 1740–41 |
| Elizabeth | 1741–61 (O.S.) |
| Peter III[4] | 1761–62 (O.S.) |
| Catherine II | 1762–96 |
| Paul | 1796–1801 |
| Alexander I | 1801–25 |
| Nicholas I | 1825–55 |
| Alexander II | 1855–81 |
| Alexander III | 1881–94 |
| Nicholas II | 1894–1917 |
| | |
| **Provisional government** | 1917 |
| | |
| **Chairmen (or First Secretaries) of the** | |
| **Communist Party of the Soviet Union** | |
| Vladimir Lenin | 1917–24 |
| Joseph Stalin | 1924–53 |
| Georgy Malenkov | 1953 |
| Nikita Khrushchev | 1953–64 |
| Leonid Brezhnev | 1964–82 |
| Yury Andropov | 1982–84 |
| Konstantin Chernenko | 1984–85 |
| Mikhail Gorbachev | 1985–91 |
| | |
| **Presidents of Russia** | |
| Boris Yeltsin | 1990–99 |
| Vladimir Putin | 2000–08 |
| Dmitry Medvedev | 2008–12 |
| Vladimir Putin | 2012– |

[1]*This table includes leaders of Muscovy, Russia, the Russian Empire, and the Soviet Union.* [2]*The Danilovich dynasty is a late branch of the Rurik dynasty, named after its progenitor, Daniel.* [3]*On 22 Oct (Old Style) 1721, Peter I the Great took the title of "emperor." However, despite the official titling, conventional usage took an odd*

# Rulers of Russia[1] (continued)

turn. Every male sovereign continued usually to be called tsar, but every female sovereign was conventionally called empress. [4]The direct line of the Romanov dynasty came to an end in 1761 with the death of Elizabeth, daughter of Peter I, but subsequent rulers of the "Holstein-Gottorp dynasty" (the first, Peter III, was son of Charles Frederick, duke of Holstein-Gottorp, and Anna, daughter of Peter I) took the family name of Romanov.

# Middle East

## Byzantine Emperors

The Byzantine Empire comprised what was previously the eastern half of the Roman Empire. It survived for nearly 1,000 years after the western half had crumbled into various feudal kingdoms; it finally fell to Ottoman Turkish onslaughts in 1453. For emperors of the Eastern Roman Empire (at Constantinople) before the fall of Rome, see "Roman Emperors."

| EMPEROR | REIGN |
| --- | --- |
| Zeno | 474–491 |
| Anastasius I | 491–518 |
| Justin I | 518–527 |
| Justinian I | 527–565 |
| Justin II | 565–578 |
| Tiberius II Constantine | 578–582 |
| Maurice Tiberius | 582–602 |
| Phocas | 602–610 |
| Heraclius | 610–641 |
| Heraclius Constantine | 641 |
| Heraclonas (or Heraclius) | 641 |
| Constans II (Constantine Pogonatus) | 641–668 |
| Constantine IV | 668–685 |
| Justinian II Rhinotmetus | 685–695 |
| Leontius | 695–698 |
| Tiberius III | 698–705 |
| Justinian II Rhinotmetus (restored) | 705–711 |
| Philippicus | 711–713 |
| Anastasius II | 713–715 |
| Theodosius III | 715–717 |
| Leo III | 717–741 |
| Constantine V Copronymus | 741–775 |
| Leo IV | 775–780 |
| Constantine VI | 780–797 |
| Irene (empress) | 797–802 |
| Nicephorus I | 802–811 |
| Stauracius | 811 |
| Michael I Rhangabe | 811–813 |
| Leo V | 813–820 |
| Michael II Balbus | 820–829 |
| Theophilus | 829–842 |
| Michael III | 842–867 |
| Basil I | 867–886 |
| Leo VI | 886–912 |
| Alexander | 912–913 |
| Constantine VII Porphyrogenitus | 913–959 |
| Romanus I Lecapenus | 920–944 |
| Romanus II | 959–963 |
| Nicephorus II Phocas | 963–969 |
| John I Tzimisces | 969–976 |
| Basil II Bulgaroctonus | 976–1025 |
| Constantine VIII | 1025–28 |
| Romanus III Argyrus | 1028–34 |
| Michael IV | 1034–41 |
| Michael V Calaphates | 1041–42 |
| Zoe (empress) | 1042–56 |
| Constantine IX Monomachus | 1042–55 |

| EMPEROR | REIGN |
| --- | --- |
| Theodora (empress) | 1055–56 |
| Michael VI Stratioticus | 1056–57 |
| Isaac I Comnenus | 1057–59 |
| Constantine X Ducas | 1059–67 |
| Romanus IV Diogenes | 1067–71 |
| Michael VII Ducas | 1071–78 |
| Nicephorus III Botaniates | 1078–81 |
| Alexius I Comnenus | 1081–1118 |
| John II Comnenus | 1118–43 |
| Manuel I Comnenus | 1143–80 |
| Alexius II Comnenus | 1180–83 |
| Andronicus I Comnenus | 1183–85 |
| Isaac II Angelus | 1185–95 |
| Alexius III Angelus | 1195–1203 |
| Isaac II Angelus (restored) and Alexius IV Angelus (joint ruler) | 1203–04 |
| Alexius V Ducas Murtzuphlus | 1204 |

**Latin emperors**

| | |
| --- | --- |
| Baldwin I | 1204–06 |
| Henry | 1206–16 |
| Peter | 1217 |
| Yolande (empress) | 1217–19 |
| Robert | 1221–28 |
| Baldwin II | 1228–61 |
| John | 1231–37 |

**Nicaean emperors**

| | |
| --- | --- |
| Constantine (XI) Lascaris | 1204–05? |
| Theodore I Lascaris | 1205?–22 |
| John III Ducas Vatatzes | 1222–54 |
| Theodore II Lascaris | 1254–58 |
| John IV Lascaris | 1258–61 |

**Greek emperors restored**

| | |
| --- | --- |
| Michael VIII Palaeologus | 1261–82 |
| Andronicus II Palaeologus | 1282–1328 |
| Andronicus III Palaeologus | 1328–41 |
| John V Palaeologus | 1341–76 |
| John VI Cantacuzenus | 1347–54 |
| Andronicus IV Palaeologus | 1376–79 |
| John V Palaeologus (restored) | 1379–90 |
| John VII Palaeologus | 1390 |
| John V Palaeologus (restored) | 1390–91 |
| Manuel II Palaeologus | 1391–1425 |
| John VIII Palaeologus | 1421–48 |
| Constantine XI Palaeologus | 1449–53 |

# Caliphs

When Muhammad died on 8 Jun 632, Abu Bakr, his father-in-law, succeeded to his political and administrative functions. He and his three immediate successors are known as the "perfect" or "rightly guided" caliphs. After them, the title was borne by the 14 Umayyad caliphs of Damascus (from 661–750) and subsequently by the 38 'Abbasid caliphs of Baghdad (both are named after their clans of origin). The empire of the caliphate grew rapidly through conquest during its first two centuries to include most of southwestern Asia, North Africa, and Spain. 'Abbasid power ended in 945,

when the Buyids took Baghdad under their rule. They retained the 'Abbasid caliphs as figureheads; other dynasties in Central Asia and the Ganges River basin acknowledged the 'Abbasid caliphs as spiritual leaders. The Fatimids, however, proclaimed a new caliphate in 920 in their capital of al-Mahdiyah in Tunisia; it lasted until 1171, by which time opposition within the sect caused it to disintegrate. 'Abbasid authority was partially restored in the 12th century, but the caliphate ceased to exist with the Mongol destruction of Baghdad in 1258. Some principal caliphs are listed below.

| CALIPH | REIGN |
| --- | --- |
| "Perfect" caliphs | |
| Abu Bakr | 632–634 |
| 'Umar I | 634–644 |
| 'Uthman ibn 'Affan | 644–656 |
| 'Ali | 656–661 |
| | |
| Umayyad caliphs (Damascus) | |
| Mu'awiyah I | 661–680 |
| 'Abd al-Malik | 685–705 |
| al-Walid | 705–715 |
| Hisham | 724–743 |
| Marwan II | 744–750 |
| | |
| 'Abbasid caliphs (Baghdad) | |
| al-Saffah | 749–754 |
| Harun al-Rashid | 786–809 |
| al-Mamun | 813–833 |

| CALIPH | REIGN |
| --- | --- |
| Fatimid caliphs (al-Mahdiyah) | |
| al-Mahdi | 909–934 |
| al-Qaim | 934–946 |
| al-Mansur | 946–953 |
| al-Mu'izz | 953–975 |
| al-Hakim | 996–1021 |
| al-Mustansir | 1036–94 |
| al-Musta'li | 1094–1101 |
| | |
| 'Abbasid caliph (Baghdad) | |
| al-Nasir | 1180–1225 |

# Sultans of the Ottoman Empire

One of the most powerful states in the world during the 15th and 16th centuries, the Ottoman empire was created by Turkish tribes in Anatolia and spanned more than 600 years. It came to an end in 1922, when it was replaced by the Turkish Republic and various successor states in southeastern Europe and the Middle East. At its height

the empire included most of southeastern Europe, the Middle East as far east as Iraq, North Africa as far west as Algeria, and most of the Arabian Peninsula. The term Ottoman is a dynastic appellation derived from Osman (Arabic: 'Uthman), the nomadic Turkmen chief who founded both the dynasty and the empire.

| SULTAN | REIGN |
| --- | --- |
| Osman I | c. 1300–1324 |
| Orhan | 1324–1360 |
| Murad I | 1360–1389 |
| Bayezid I | 1389–1402 |
| Mehmed I | 1413–1421 |
| Murad II | 1421–1444 |
| Mehmed II | 1444–1446 |
| Murad II (second reign) | 1446–1451 |
| Mehmed II (second reign) | 1451–1481 |
| Bayezid II | 1481–1512 |
| Selim I | 1512–1520 |
| Suleyman I | 1520–1566 |
| Selim II | 1566–1574 |
| Murad III | 1574–1595 |
| Mehmed III | 1595–1603 |
| Ahmed I | 1603–1617 |
| Mustafa I | 1617–1618 |
| Osman II | 1618–1622 |
| Mustafa I (second reign) | 1622–1623 |
| Murad IV | 1623–1640 |

| SULTAN | REIGN |
| --- | --- |
| Ibrahim | 1640–1648 |
| Mehmed IV | 1648–1687 |
| Suleyman II | 1687–1691 |
| Ahmed II | 1691–1695 |
| Mustafa II | 1695–1703 |
| Ahmed III | 1703–1730 |
| Mahmud I | 1730–1754 |
| Osman III | 1754–1757 |
| Mustafa III | 1757–1774 |
| Abdulhamid I | 1774–1789 |
| Selim III | 1789–1807 |
| Mustafa IV | 1807–1808 |
| Mahmud II | 1808–1839 |
| Abdulmecid I | 1839–1861 |
| Abdulaziz | 1861–1876 |
| Murad V | 1876 |
| Abdulhamid II | 1876–1909 |
| Mehmed V | 1909–1918 |
| Mehmed VI | 1918–1922 |

# Persian Dynasties

*Dates given are approximate and may overlap.*

| DYNASTY/KINGDOM | PERIOD | DYNASTY/KINGDOM | PERIOD |
|---|---|---|---|
| Median | 728–550 BC | Seljuqs | 1038–1157 |
| Achaemenian | 559–330 BC | Mongols[4] | 1220–1335 |
| Hellenistic period of Alexander and the Seleucids[1] | 330 BC–247 BC | Timurids and Ottoman Turks | 1380–1501 |
| | | Safavid | 1502–1736 |
| Parthian period (Arsacid dynasty)[2] | 247 BC–AD 224 | Afghan interlude | 1723–36 |
| Sasanian | 224–651 | Nader Shah | 1736–47 |
| Arab invasion and the advent of Islam | 640–829 | Zand | 1750–79 |
| | | Qajars | 1794–1925 |
| Iranian intermezzo[3] | 821–1055 | Pahlavi | 1925–79 |

[1]Dates from the death of Darius III, the last Achaemenian king, and the invasion of Alexander the Great. [2]Dates from the year in which the Parnian chief Arsaces first battled the Seleucids. [3]Includes the Tahirid, Samanid, Ghaznavids, and Buyid dynasties. [4]Mainly the Il-Khanid dynasty (1256–1353).

# Asia

## Indian Dynasties

*Dates given are approximations.*

| DYNASTY | LOCATION | DATES | DYNASTY | LOCATION | DATES |
|---|---|---|---|---|---|
| Nanda | Ganges Valley | 400 BC | Pala | Bengal | 800–1100 |
| Maurya | India, barring the area south of Mysore (Karnataka) | 400–200 BC | Pratihara | western India and upper Ganges Valley | 900–1100 |
| | | | Rastrakuta | western and central Deccan | 800–1100 |
| Indo-Greeks | northern India | 200–100 BC | | | |
| Sunga | Ganges Valley and parts of central India | 200–100 BC | Cola | Tamil Nadu | 900–1300 |
| | | | Candella | Bundelkhand | 1000–1200 |
| | | | Cauhan | Rajasthan | 1000–1200 |
| Satavahana | northern Deccan | 100 BC–AD 300 | Caulukya | Gujarat | 1000–1300 |
| Saka | western India | 100 BC–AD 400 | Paramara | western and central India | 1000–1100 |
| Kusana | northern India and Central Asia | AD 100–300 | Later Calukya | western and central Deccan | 1000–1200 |
| Gupta | northern India | 400–600 | | | |
| Harsa | northern India | 700 | Hoysala | central and southern Deccan | 1200–1400 |
| Pallava | Tamil Nadu | 400–900 | | | |
| Calukya | western and central Deccan | 600–800 | Yadava | northern Deccan | 1200–1300 |
| | | | Pandya | Tamil Nadu | 1300–1400 |

## Japanese Historical Periods and Rulers

| PERIOD | DATES | PERIOD | DATES |
|---|---|---|---|
| Asuka | 552–710 | Muromachi (or Ashikaga) | 1338–1573 |
| Nara | 710–784 | Azuchi-Momoyama | 1574–1600 |
| Heian | 794–1185 | Edo (or Tokugawa) | 1603–1867 |
| Kamakura | 1192–1333 | Meiji | 1868–1912 |

Reign dates for the first 28 sovereigns (Jimmu through Senka) are taken from the *Nihon shoki* ("Chronicles of Japan"). The first 14 sovereigns are considered legendary, and while the next 14 are known to have existed, their exact reign dates have not been verified historically. When the year of actual accession and year of formal coronation are different, the latter is placed in parentheses after the former. If the two events took place in the same year, no special notation is used. If only the coronation year is known, it is placed in parentheses.

| EMPEROR | REIGN | EMPEROR | REIGN |
|---|---|---|---|
| Jimmu | (660)–585 BC | Kogen | (214)–158 BC |
| Suizei | (581)–549 BC | Kaika | 158–98 BC |
| Annei | 549–511 BC | Sujin | (97)–30 BC |
| Itoku | (510)–477 BC | Suinin | (29 BC)–AD 70 |
| Kosho | (475)–393 BC | Keiko | (71)–130 |
| Koan | (392)–291 BC | Seimu | (131)–190 |
| Korei | (290)–215 BC | Chuai | (192)–200 |

## Japanese Historical Periods and Rulers (continued)

| EMPEROR | REIGN |
|---|---|
| Jingu Kogo (regent) | 201–269 |
| Ojin | (270)–310 |
| Nintoku | (313)–399 |
| Richu | (400)–405 |
| Hanzei | (406)–410 |
| Ingyo | (412)–453 |
| Anko | 453–456 |
| Yuryaku | 456–479 |
| Seinei | (480)–484 |
| Kenzo | (485)–487 |
| Ninken | (488)–498 |
| Buretsu | 498–506 |
| Keitai | (507)–531 |
| Ankan | 531 (534)–535 |
| Senka | 535–539 |
| Kimmei | 539–571 |
| Bidatsu | (572)–585 |
| Yomei | 585–587 |
| Sushun | 587–592 |
| Suiko (empress regnant) | 593–628 |
| Jomei | (629)–641 |
| Kogyoku (empress regnant) | (642)–645 |
| Kotoku | 645–654 |
| Saimei (empress regnant: Kogyoku rethroned) | (655)–661 |
| Tenji | 661 (668)–672 |
| Kobun | 672 |
| Temmu | 672 (673)–686 |
| Jito (empress regnant) | 686 (690)–697 |
| Mommu | 697–707 |
| Gemmei (empress regnant) | 707–715 |
| Gensho (empress regnant) | 715–724 |
| Shomu | 724–749 |
| Koken (empress regnant) | 749–758 |
| Junnin | 758–764 |
| Shotoku (empress regnant: Koken rethroned) | 764 (765)–770 |
| Konin | 770–781 |
| Kammu | 781–806 |
| Heizei | 806–809 |
| Saga | 809–823 |
| Junna | 823–833 |
| Nimmyo | 833–850 |
| Montoku | 850–858 |
| Seiwa | 858–876 |
| Yozei | 876 (877)–884 |
| Koko | 884–887 |
| Uda | 887–897 |
| Daigo | 897–930 |
| Suzaku | 930–946 |
| Murakami | 946–967 |
| Reizei | 967–969 |
| En'yu | 969–984 |
| Kazan | 984–986 |
| Ichijo | 986–1011 |
| Sanjo | 1011–16 |
| Go-Ichijo | 1016–36 |
| Go-Suzaku | 1036–45 |
| Go-Reizei | 1045–68 |
| Go-Sanjo | 1068–72 |
| Shirakawa | 1072–86 |
| Horikawa | 1086–1107 |

| EMPEROR | REIGN |
|---|---|
| Toba | 1107–23 |
| Sutoku | 1123–41 |
| Konoe | 1141–55 |
| Go-Shirakawa | 1155–58 |
| Nijo | 1158–65 |
| Rokujo | 1165–68 |
| Takakura | 1168–80 |
| Antoku | 1180–85[1] |
| Go-Toba | 1183 (1184)–98 |
| Tsuchimikado | 1198–1210 |
| Juntoku | 1210 (1211)–21 |
| Chukyo | 1221 |
| Goshirakawa | 1221 (1222)–32 |
| Shijo | 1232 (1233)–42 |
| Go-Saga | 1242–46 |
| Go-Fukakusa | 1246–59/60 |
| Kameyama | 1259/60–74 |
| Gouda | 1274–87 |
| Fushimi | 1287 (1288)–98 |
| Go-Fushimi | 1298–1301 |
| Go-Nijo | 1301–08 |
| Hanazono | 1308–18 |
| Go-Daigo | 1318–39 |
| Go-Murakami | 1339–68 |
| Chokei | 1368–83 |
| Go-Kameyama | 1383–92 |

**The Northern court[2]**

| EMPEROR | REIGN |
|---|---|
| Kogon | 1331 (1332)–33 |
| Komyo | 1336 (1337/38)–48 |
| Suko | 1348 (1349/50)–51 |
| Go-Kogon | 1351 (1353/54)–71 |
| Go-Enyu | 1371 (1374/75)–82 |
| Go-Komatsu | 1382–92 |
| Go-Komatsu | 1392–1412 |
| Shoko | 1412 (1414)–28 |
| Go-Hanazono | 1428 (1429/30)–64 |
| Go-Tsuchimikado | 1464 (1465/66)–1500 |
| Go-Kashiwabara | 1500 (1521)–26 |
| Go-Nara | 1526 (1536)–57 |
| Ogimachi | 1557 (1560)–86 |
| Go-Yozei | 1586 (1587)–1611 |
| Go-Mizunoo | 1611–29 |
| Meisho (empress regnant) | 1629 (1630)–43 |
| Go-Komyo | 1643–54 |
| Go-Sai | 1654/55 (1656)–63 |
| Reigen | 1663–87 |
| Higashiyama | 1687–1709 |
| Nakamikado | 1709 (1710)–35 |
| Sakuramachi | 1735–47 |
| Momozono | 1747–62 |
| Go-Sakuramachi (empress regnant) | 1762 (1763)–71 |
| Go-Momozono | 1771–79 |
| Kokaku | 1780–1817 |
| Ninko | 1817–46 |
| Komei | 1846 (1847)–66 |
| Meiji (personal name: Mutsuhito; era name: Meiji) | 1867 (1868)–1912 |
| Taisho (personal name: Yoshihito; era name: Taisho) | 1912 (1915)–26 |
| Hirohito (era name: Showa) | 1926 (1928)–1989 |
| Akihito (era name: Heisei) | 1989 (1990)– |

[1]Antoku's reign overlaps that of Go-Toba. Go-Toba was placed on the throne by the Minamoto clan after the rival Taira clan had fled Kyoto with Antoku.   [2]From 1336 until 1392 Japan witnessed the spectacle of two contending Imperial courts—the Southern court of Go-Daigo and his descendants, whose sphere of influence was restricted to the immediate vicinity of the Yoshino Mountains, and the Northern court of Kogon and his descendants, which was under the domination of the Ashikaga family.

## Chinese Dynasties

*Dates given for early dynasties are approximate and may overlap.*

| DYNASTY | ALTERNATE NAME | DATES | DYNASTY | ALTERNATE NAME | DATES |
|---|---|---|---|---|---|
| Hsia[1] | Xia | c. 2205–1766 BC | Six Dynasties[2] (continued) | | |
| Shang | | c. 1760–1030 BC | Southern Qi | | 479–502 |
| Western Zhou | Chou | c. 1050–771 BC | Southern Liang | | 502–57 |
| Eastern Zhou | Chou | c. 771–255 BC | Southern Chen | | 557–89 |
| Qin | Ch'in | 221–206 BC | Sui | | 581–618 |
| Han | | 206 BC–AD 220 | T'ang | Tang | 618–907 |
| Western Jin | Chin | 265–317 | Five Dynasties[3] | Ten Kingdoms[3] | 907–960 |
| Eastern Jin[2] | Chin | 317–420 | Sung | Song | 960–1279 |
| Six Dynasties[2] | | 220–589 | Yüan | Yuan, Mongol | 1206–1368 |
| Wu | | 222–80 | Ming | | 1368–1644 |
| Eastern Jin[2] | | 317–420 | Ch'ing | Qing, Manchu | 1644–1911/12 |
| Liusong | | 420–79 | | | |

[1]The Hsia Dynasty is mentioned in legends but is of undetermined historicity.   [2]Between the fall of the Han and the establishment of the Sui, China was divided into two societies, northern and southern. The Six Dynasties had their capital at Nanjing in the south. The Eastern Jin is considered one of these six dynasties and so is listed twice. [3]Period of time between the fall of the T'ang dynasty and the founding of the Sung dynasty, when five would-be dynasties followed one another in quick succession in North China. The era is also known as the period of the Ten Kingdoms because 10 regimes dominated separate regions of South China during the same period.

## Leaders of the People's Republic of China Since 1949

**Chinese Communist Party leaders**

| NAME | TITLE | DATES |
|---|---|---|
| Mao Zedong | CCP chairman | 1949–1976 |
| Hua Guofeng | CCP chairman | 1976–1981 |
| Hu Yaobang | CCP chairman; after September 1982, general secretary of the CCP | 1981–1987 |
| Zhao Ziyang | CCP general secretary | 1987–1989 |
| Jiang Zemin | CCP general secretary | 1989–2002 |
| Hu Jintao | CCP general secretary | 2002– |

**premiers**

| NAME | DATES |
|---|---|
| Zhou Enlai | 1949–1976 |
| Hua Guofeng | 1976–1980 |
| Zhao Ziyang | 1980–1987 |
| Li Peng | 1987–1998 |
| Zhu Rongji | 1998–2003 |
| Wen Jiabao | 2003– |

*Note: although he held no top party or state position, Deng Xiaoping was de facto leader of China from 1977 to 1997.*

## Dalai Lamas

The Dalai Lama is the head of the dominant Dge-lugs-pa (Yellow Hat) order of Tibetan Buddhists and, until 1959, was both spiritual and temporal ruler of Tibet. In accordance with the belief in reincarnate lamas, which began to develop in the 14th century, the successors of the first Dalai Lama were considered his rebirths and came to be regarded as physical manifestations of the compassionate bodhisattva ("buddha-to-be"), Avalokitesvara.

| DALAI LAMA | NAME | LIVED | DALAI LAMA | NAME | LIVED |
|---|---|---|---|---|---|
| first | Dge-'dun-grub-pa | 1391–1475 | eighth | 'Jam-dpal-rgya-mtsho | 1758–1804 |
| second | Dge-'dun-rgya-mtsho | 1475–1542 | ninth | Lung-rtogs-rgya-mtsho | 1806–1815[1] |
| third | Bsod-nams-rgya-mtsho | 1543–1588 | tenth | Tshul-khrims-rgya-mtsho | 1816–1837[1] |
| fourth | Yon-tan-rgya-mtsho | 1589–1617 | eleventh | Mkhas-grub-rgya-mtsho | 1838–1856[1] |
| fifth | Ngag-dbang-rgya-mtsho | 1617–1682 | twelfth | 'Phrin-las-rgya-mtsho | 1856–1875[1] |
| sixth | Tshangs-dbyangs-rgya-mtsho | 1683–1706 | thirteenth | Thub-bstan-rgya-mtsho | 1875–1933[2] |
| seventh | Bskal-bzang-rgya-mtsho | 1708–1757 | fourteenth | Bstan-'dzin-rgya-mtsho | 1935–[3] |

[1]Dalai Lamas 9–12 all died young, and the country was ruled by regencies.   [2]Reigned as head of a sovereign state from 1912.   [3]Ruled from exile in Dharmsala, India, from 1960.

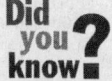

**Did you know?** The Oxford University Press in 2010 released its first new revision of the Zulu-English dictionary in more than 40 years. Zulu, one of the 11 official languages of South Africa, is spoken by tens of millions of people. Previous editions of the resource contain no vocabulary from the period since the end of the system of apartheid in 1994.

# The Americas

## Pre-Columbian Civilizations

Various aboriginal American Indian cultures evolved in Meso-America (part of Mexico and Central America) and the Andean region (western South America) prior to Spanish exploration and conquest in the 16th century. These pre-Columbian civilizations were extraordinary developments in human society and culture, characterized by kingdoms and empires, great monuments and cities, and refinements in the arts, metallurgy, and writing. Dates given below are approximations.

| CULTURE | LOCATION | DATES |
|---|---|---|
| **Meso-American civilizations** | | |
| Olmec | Gulf coast of southern Mexico | 1150 BC–800 BC |
| Zapotec | Oaxaca, particularly Monte Albán | 500 BC–AD 900 |
| Totonac | east-central Mexico | 500 BC–AD 900 |
| Teotihuacán | Teotihuacán, in the Valley of Mexico | AD 400–600 |
| Maya | southern Mexico and Guatemala | 250–900 |
| Toltec | central Mexico | 900–1200 |
| Aztec | central and southern Mexico | 1400–early 1500s |
| | | |
| **Andean civilizations** | | |
| Nazca | southern coast of Peru | 200 BC–AD 600 |
| Recuay | northern highlands of Peru | 200 BC–AD 600 |
| Tiwanaku | Lake Titicaca, Bolivia | 200 BC–AD 1000 |
| Moche (Mochica) | northern coast of Peru | AD 1–700 |
| Inca | Pacific coast of South America | 1100–1532 |

# Africa

## Historic Sub-Saharan African States

| STATE | LOCATION IN PRESENT-DAY COUNTRIES | FLOURISHED |
|---|---|---|
| Aksumite kingdom | Ethiopia, Sudan | 1st–10th centuries |
| Asante empire | Ghana | 18th–19th centuries |
| Basuto kingdom | Lesotho | 19th century |
| Benin kingdom | Nigeria | 12th–19th centuries |
| kingdom of Buganda | Uganda | 14th–20th centuries |
| kingdom of Bunyoro | Uganda | 15th–19th centuries |
| kingdom of Burundi | Burundi | 17th–20th centuries |
| kingdom of Dahomey | Benin | 17th–19th centuries |
| Darfur | Sudan | 17th–19th centuries |
| kingdom of Dongola | Sudan | 7th–14th centuries |
| Fulani empire | Cameroon, Niger, Nigeria | 19th–20th centuries |
| Ghana empire | Mali, Mauritania | 4th–13th centuries |
| Hausa states | Nigeria | 14th–19th centuries |
| Kanem-Bornu | Nigeria, Chad, Cameroon, Niger, Libya | 9th–19th centuries |
| Kongo kingdom | Angola, Dem. Rep. of Congo | 14th–17th centuries |
| Kuba kingdom | Dem. Rep. of Congo | 17th–19th centuries |
| kingdom of Kush | Egypt, Sudan | c. 850 BC–c. AD 325 |
| Luba empire | Dem Rep. of Congo | 16th–19th centuries |
| Lunda empire | Dem. Rep. of Congo, Angola, Zambia | 17th–19th centuries |
| Mali empire | Mali, Mauritania, Senegal, Gambia, Guinea-Bissau | 13th–16th centuries |
| Ndongo kingdom | Angola | 14th–17th centuries |
| kingdom of Nubia | Egypt, Sudan | 4th–7th centuries |
| Oyo empire | Nigeria | 16th–19th centuries |
| Rozwi empire | Zimbabwe, Botswana | 17th–19th centuries |
| Shewa empire | Ethiopia | 15th–19th centuries |
| Songhai empire | Nigeria, Niger | 6th–17th centuries |
| Tukulor empire | Mali | 19th century |
| Wolof empire | Senegal | 14th–19th centuries |
| Zeng empire | Somalia, Kenya, Tanzania, Mozambique | 10th–16th centuries |
| Zulu kingdom | South Africa | 19th century |

# Populations

## Largest Urban Agglomerations

*Agglomerations include a central city and associated neighboring communities.*
*Source: <www.citypopulation.de>.*

| RANK | AGGLOMERATION | COUNTRY | POPULATION (JANUARY 2012) | RANK | AGGLOMERATION | COUNTRY | POPULATION (JANUARY 2012) |
|---|---|---|---|---|---|---|---|
| 1 | Tokyo | Japan | 34,400,000 | 15 | Beijing | China | 16,300,000 |
| 2 | Guangzhou | China | 25,600,000 | 16 | Moscow | Russia | 16,100,000 |
| 3 | Seoul | Republic of Korea | 25,300,000 | 17 | Cairo | Egypt | 15,600,000 |
| | | | | | Kolkata (Calcutta) | India | 15,600,000 |
| 4 | Shanghai | China | 25,100,000 | 19 | Buenos Aires | Argentina | 14,200,000 |
| 5 | Mexico City | Mexico | 23,100,000 | 20 | Dhaka | Bangladesh | 13,900,000 |
| 6 | Delhi | India | 22,900,000 | 21 | Bangkok | Thailand | 13,700,000 |
| 7 | New York City | US | 22,000,000 | 22 | Tehran | Iran | 13,400,000 |
| 8 | São Paulo | Brazil | 21,000,000 | 23 | Istanbul | Turkey | 13,300,000 |
| 9 | Mumbai (Bombay) | India | 20,700,000 | 24 | Rio de Janeiro | Brazil | 12,700,000 |
| | | | | 25 | London | UK | 12,600,000 |
| 10 | Manila | Philippines | 20,500,000 | 26 | Lagos | Nigeria | 12,500,000 |
| 11 | Jakarta | Indonesia | 18,800,000 | 27 | Paris | France | 10,600,000 |
| 12 | Los Angeles | US | 18,100,000 | 28 | Tianjin | China | 9,800,000 |
| 13 | Karachi | Pakistan | 17,200,000 | 29 | Chicago | US | 9,750,000 |
| 14 | Osaka | Japan | 16,800,000 | | Shenzhen | China | 9,750,000 |

## Migration of Foreigners into Selected Countries

*Percentages of foreign-born populations in selected Organisation for Economic Co-operation and Development countries. N/A means not available. Source: <www.oecd.org>.*

| COUNTRY | FOREIGN-BORN AS % OF TOTAL POPULATION 2000 | 2009 | COUNTRY | FOREIGN-BORN AS % OF TOTAL POPULATION 2000 | 2009 |
|---|---|---|---|---|---|
| Luxembourg | 33.2 | 36.9 | France | 10.1 | 11.6 |
| Australia | 23.0 | 26.5 | UK | 7.9 | 11.3 |
| Switzerland | 21.9 | 26.3 | Netherlands | 10.1 | 11.1 |
| New Zealand | 17.2 | 22.7 | Norway | 6.8 | 10.9 |
| Canada | 17.4 | 19.6 | Denmark | 5.8 | 7.5 |
| Ireland | 8.7 | 17.2 | Czech Republic | 4.2 | 6.4 |
| Austria | 10.4 | 15.5 | Portugal | 5.1 | 6.3 |
| Sweden | 11.3 | 14.4 | Belgium | 10.3 | 13.0[1] |
| Spain | 4.9 | 14.3 | Greece | 10.3[2] | N/A |
| Germany | 12.5 | 12.9 | Italy | 2.5[2] | N/A |
| US | 11.0 | 12.7 | Slovakia | N/A | 8.2[3] |

[1]2007. [2]2001. [3]2008.

## Persons of Concern Worldwide

*The Office of the UN High Commissioner for Refugees (UNHCR) attempts to ease the plight of various "persons of concern," including refugees and asylum seekers. Detail may not add to total given because of statistical discrepancy. Sources: UNHCR, Global Trends 2011; Internal Displacement Monitoring Centre.*

**Persons of Concern to UNHCR by Region and Category (estimates as of 1 Jan 2012)**

| REGION | REFUGEES | ASYLUM SEEKERS | RETURNED REFUGEES | INTERNALLY DISPLACED PERSONS (IDPs)[1] | STATELESS AND OTHER | TOTAL[2] |
|---|---|---|---|---|---|---|
| Asia and Oceania | 5,138,870 | 88,618 | 144,074 | 5,302,437 | 3,892,230 | 14,566,229 |
| Africa | 2,924,091 | 390,715 | 386,483 | 9,157,328 | 195,452 | 13,054,069 |
| Europe | 1,534,415 | 312,701 | 1,321 | 371,108 | 801,247 | 3,020,792 |
| Northern America | 429,646 | 53,573 | — | — | — | 483,219 |
| Latin America and the Caribbean | 377,784 | 49,677 | 29 | 3,888,309 | 20 | 4,315,819 |
| total[2] | 10,404,806 | 895,284 | 531,907 | 18,719,182 | 4,888,949 | 35,440,128 |

# Persons of Concern Worldwide (continued)

**Total Number of Refugees (estimates as of 1 January of each year)**

| YEAR | REFUGEES | YEAR | REFUGEES |
|---|---|---|---|
| 2003 | 10,389,600 | 2008 | 11,390,670 |
| 2004 | 9,671,800 | 2009 | 10,478,621 |
| 2005 | 9,236,500 | 2010 | 10,396,540 |
| 2006 | 8,394,400 | 2011 | 10,549,686 |
| 2007 | 9,877,700 | 2012 | 10,404,806 |

**Origin of Major Refugee Populations[3] (estimates as of 1 Jan 2012)**

| COUNTRY OF ORIGIN | TOTAL | COUNTRY OF ORIGIN | TOTAL |
|---|---|---|---|
| Afghanistan | 2,664,436 | Myanmar (Burma) | 414,626 |
| Iraq | 1,428,308 | Colombia | 395,949 |
| Somalia | 1,077,048 | Vietnam | 337,829 |
| Sudan | 500,014 | Eritrea | 251,954 |
| Democratic Republic of the Congo | 491,481 | China | 190,384 |

**Host Country of Major Refugee Populations (estimates as of 1 Jan 2012)**

| COUNTRY OF ASYLUM | TOTAL | COUNTRY OF ASYLUM | TOTAL |
|---|---|---|---|
| Pakistan | 1,702,700 | Jordan | 451,009 |
| Iran | 886,468 | Chad | 366,494 |
| Syria | 755,445 | China | 301,170 |
| Germany | 571,685 | Ethiopia | 288,844 |
| Kenya | 566,487 | United States | 264,763 |

**Internally Displaced Persons (estimates as of 1 Jan 2012)**

| COUNTRY | TOTAL | COUNTRY | TOTAL |
|---|---|---|---|
| Colombia | 3,876,000–5,281,000 | Georgia | 257,000 |
| Iraq | 2,300,000–2,600,000 | Kenya | 250,000 |
| Sudan | 2,200,000 | Côte d'Ivoire | 247,000 |
| Democratic Republic of the Congo | 1,710,000 | Serbia | 225,000 |
| Somalia | 1,460,000 | Cyprus | 208,000 |
| Turkey | 954,000–1,201,000 | Indonesia | 180,000 |
| Pakistan | 900,000 | Mexico | 160,000 |
| Azerbaijan | 599,000 | Libya | 154,000 |
| Syria | 589,000 | Peru | 150,000 |
| India | 506,000 | Chad | 126,000 |
| Yemen | 463,500 | Sri Lanka | 125,000 |
| Afghanistan | 450,000 | Bosnia and Herzegovina | 113,000 |
| Myanmar (Burma) | 450,000 | Central African Republic | 105,000 |

[1]Data include only those IDPs to whom UNHCR extends protection and/or assistance. Data include 3,245,804 returned IDPs.  [2]Includes unlisted returned IDPs and various unclassified persons.  [3]A separate mandate of the UN Relief and Works Agency for Palestine Refugees (UNRWA) on 1 Jan 2012 covered some 4,800,000 Palestinians. Palestinian refugees in the West Bank and the Gaza Strip outside of the UNRWA mandate numbered 94,150 on 1 Jan 2012.

# Language

## Most Widely Spoken Languages

*Listing the languages spoken by approximately 1% of humankind (those spoken by more than 60,000,000 people), this table enumerates speakers of each tongue as a primary language. Source: Ethnologue: Languages of the World (2009), M. Paul Lewis, editor.*

| LANGUAGE | NUMBER OF SPEAKERS (MILLIONS) | % OF WORLD POPULATION (APPROXIMATE) | LANGUAGE FAMILY |
|---|---|---|---|
| Mandarin | 845 | 12.4 | Sino-Tibetan (Chinese) |
| Spanish | 329 | 4.8 | Indo-European (Romance) |
| English | 328 | 4.8 | Indo-European (Germanic) |

## Most Widely Spoken Languages (continued)

| LANGUAGE | NUMBER OF SPEAKERS (MILLIONS) | % OF WORLD POPULATION (APPROXIMATE) | LANGUAGE FAMILY |
|---|---|---|---|
| Arabic | 221 | 3.3 | Afro-Asiatic (Semitic) |
| Hindi[1] | 182 | 2.7 | Indo-European (Indo-Aryan) |
| Bengali | 181 | 2.7 | Indo-European (Indo-Aryan) |
| Portuguese | 178 | 2.6 | Indo-European (Romance) |
| Russian | 144 | 2.1 | Indo-European (Slavic) |
| Japanese | 122 | 1.8 | isolated language |
| Punjabi | 91 | 1.3 | Indo-European (Indo-Aryan) |
| German | 90 | 1.3 | Indo-European (Germanic) |
| Javanese | 85 | 1.2 | Austronesian (Malayo-Polynesian) |
| Wu | 77 | 1.1 | Sino-Tibetan (Chinese) |
| Telugu | 70 | 1.0 | Dravidian |
| Vietnamese | 69 | 1.0 | Mon-Khmer (Vietic) |
| Marathi | 68 | 1.0 | Indo-European (Indo-Aryan) |
| French | 68 | 1.0 | Indo-European (Romance) |
| Korean | 66 | 1.0 | isolated language |
| Tamil | 66 | 1.0 | Dravidian |
| Italian | 62 | 0.9 | Indo-European (Romance) |
| Urdu[1] | 61 | 0.9 | Indo-European (Indo-Aryan) |

[1]*Although Hindi and Urdu use different writing systems, these languages are branches of Hindustani and are orally mutually intelligible.*

## English Neologisms

*New entries from Merriam-Webster's Collegiate Dictionary, 11th ed. (2013). The date in parentheses is the date of the word's earliest recorded use in English. Italics are used to signify new definitions of established words.*

**aha moment** *n* (1939): a moment of sudden realization, inspiration, insight, recognition, or comprehension

**brain cramp** *n* (1982): an instance of temporary mental confusion resulting in an error or lapse of judgment

**bucket list** *n* (2006): a list of things that one has not done before but wants to do before dying

**cloud computing** *n* (2006): the practice of storing regularly used computer data on multiple servers that can be accessed through the Internet

**copernicium** *n* (2009): a short-lived artificially produced radioactive element that has 112 protons

**craft beer** *n* (1986): a specialty beer produced in limited quantities: MICROBREW

**earworm** *n* (1802) **1:** CORN EARWORM **2:** a song or melody that keeps repeating in one's mind

**energy drink** *n* (1904): a usually carbonated beverage that typically contains caffeine and other ingredients (as taurine and ginseng) intended to increase the drinker's energy

**e-reader** *n* (1999): a handheld electronic device designed to be used for reading e-books and similar material

**f-bomb** *n* (1988): the word *fuck*—used metaphorically as a euphemism

**flexitarian** *n* (1998): one whose normally meatless diet occasionally includes meat or fish

**game changer** *n* (1993): a newly introduced element or factor that changes an existing situation or activity in a significant way

**gassed** *adj* (1919) ...**2** *slang:* drained of energy: SPENT, EXHAUSTED

**gastropub** *n* (1996): a pub, bar, or tavern that also offers meals of high quality

**geocaching** *n* (2000): a game in which players are given the geographical coordinates of a cache of items which they search for with a GPS device

**life coach** *n* (1986): an advisor who helps people make decisions, set and reach goals, or deal with problems

**man cave** *n* (1992): a room or space (as in a basement) designed according to the taste of the man of the house to be used as his personal area for hobbies and leisure activities

**mash-up** *n* (1859): something created by combining elements from two or more sources: as **a:** a piece of music created by digitally overlaying an instrumental track with a vocal track from a different recording **b:** a movie or video having characters or situations from other sources **c:** a Web service or application that integrates data and functionalities from various online sources

**obesogenic** *adj* (1986): promoting excessive weight gain: producing obesity

**sexting** *n* (2007): the sending of sexually explicit messages or images by cell phone

**shovel-ready** *adj* (1998) *of a construction project or site:* ready for the start of work

**systemic risk** *n* (1982): the risk that the failure of one financial institution (as a bank) could cause other interconnected institutions to fail and harm the economy as a whole

**tipping point** *n* (1959): the critical point in a situation, process, or system beyond which a significant and often unstoppable effect or change takes place

**toxic** *adj* (1664) ...**4:** relating to or being an asset that has lost so much value that it cannot be sold on the market

**underwater** *adj* (1627) ...**3:** having, relating to, or being a mortgage loan for which more is owed than the property securing the loan is worth

# Scholarship

## National Libraries of the World

The national libraries listed below are generally open to the public. National libraries are usually the primary repository for a nation's printed works. Sources: "National Libraries of the World: An Address List," IFLA Publications; *International Dictionary of Library Histories*, 2001, Fitzroy Dearborn Publishers.

| LIBRARY | LOCATION | YEAR FOUNDED[1] | SPECIAL COLLECTIONS, ARCHIVES, PAPERS |
|---|---|---|---|
| Biblioteca Nacional de España | Madrid, Spain | 1836 | manuscripts, Miguel de Cervantes |
| Biblioteca Nacional de México | Mexico City | 1867 | Jesuit works, early Mexican printing |
| Biblioteca Nacional de Portugal | Lisbon | 1796 | Luís de Camões, Desiderius Erasmus |
| Biblioteca Nacional de Venezuela | Caracas | 1833 | politics and diplomacy, Simón Bolívar |
| Biblioteca Nazionale Centrale di Firenze | Florence, Italy | 1861 | Reformation, Galileo Galilei |
| Biblioteca Nazionale Centrale di Roma | Rome, Italy | 1876 | Jesuit collections, Gabriele D'Annunzio |
| Biblioteka Narodowa | Warsaw, Poland | 1928 | engravings, music |
| Bibliotheca Alexandrina | Alexandria, Egypt | 2002[2] | ancient manuscripts, Egyptian heritage |
| Bibliothèque Nationale de France | Paris | 1461 | Denis Diderot, Jean-Paul Sartre |
| British Library | London | 1973[3] | Charles Dickens, George B. Shaw |
| Deutsche Nationalbibliothek Frankfurt am Main | Germany | 2006 | bibliographies, exile literature (1933–45) |
| Deutsche Nationalbibliothek Leipzig | Germany | 2006 | socialism, Anne-Frank-Shoah-Bibliothek |
| Fundação Biblioteca Nacional | Rio de Janeiro, Brazil | 1810 | botany, Latin American music |
| Jewish National and University Library | Jerusalem, Israel | 1892 | world Jewish history, Albert Einstein |
| Koninklijke Bibliotheek | The Hague, Netherlands | 1798 | Hugo Grotius, Constantijn Huygens |
| Library and Archives Canada | Ottawa | 2004 | hockey, portraits of Canadians |
| Library of Congress | Washington DC | 1800 | Americana, folk music, early motion pictures |
| National Agricultural Library | Beltsville MD | 1962 | research reports |
| National Diet Library[4] | Tokyo, Japan | 1948 | Japanese culture, Allied occupation |
| National Library of Australia | Canberra | 1960 | Asian and Pacific area |
| National Library of China[5] | Beijing | 1909 | art, early communism |
| National Library of Education | Washington DC | 1994 | research reports |
| National Library of Greece[6] | Athens | 1866[7] | incunabula |
| National Library of India | Kolkata (Calcutta) | 1903 | rare journals of vernacular languages |
| National Library of Ireland | Dublin | 1877 | biography, Gaelic manuscripts |
| National Library of Medicine | Bethesda MD | 1956 | history of medicine |
| National Library of New Zealand[8] | Wellington | 1965 | European exploration, missionary activity |
| National Library of Pakistan | Islamabad | 1993 | manuscripts, censuses |
| National Library of Russia[9] | St. Petersburg | 1795 | rare books, Russian history |
| National Library of Scotland | Edinburgh | 1925 | mountaineering, witchcraft |
| National Library of South Africa | Pretoria; Cape Town | 1999 | Africana, cookery |
| National Library of Sweden[10] | Stockholm | 1661 | Scandinavian cartography and manuscripts |
| National Library of Wales | Aberystwyth | 1907 | publications of overseas Welsh settlements |

[1]*In present institutional form.* [2]*Originally founded in the 3rd century BC.* [3]*Originally founded in 1753 as the British Museum Library.* [4]*Kokuritsu Kokkai Toshokan.* [5]*Zhongguo Guojia Tushuguan.* [6]*Ethnike Bibliotheke tes Hellados.* [7]*Originally founded in 1832 as the Public Library.* [8]*Te Puna Matauranga o Aotearoa.* [9]*Rossyskaya Natsionalnaya Biblioteka.* [10]*Kungliga Biblioteket.*

## World Education Profile

This table provides comparative data about the education systems in selected countries. Definitions as well as information gathering and reporting methods vary widely from country to country, so the statistics presented here are not always exactly comparable. Some statistics are rounded estimates.

**Compulsory education** = the number of years of education and ages of pupils required by the system; **enrollment ratio** for primary and secondary education = the actual number of children attending primary school or secondary school as a percentage of all children in the primary school or secondary school age group as defined by the country (number may exceed 100%); **enrollment ratio** for higher education = the total enrollment in higher education, regardless of age, as a percentage of all persons of school-leaving age to five years thereafter; **student/teacher ratio** = the number of pupils or students per teacher at each level; **expenditure** = the total public expenditure on education as a percentage of GDP in 2009.

Sources: *Encyclopædia Britannica World Data*, 2012; UNESCO Institute for Statistics; World Bank.

## World Education Profile (continued)

| COUNTRY | YEAR | % LITERACY RATE OF THOSE 15 AND OLDER | | | COMPULSORY EDUCATION | | ENROLLMENT RATIO (2010) | | | STUDENT/TEACHER RATIO (2010) | | | EXPEN-DITURE |
|---|---|---|---|---|---|---|---|---|---|---|---|---|---|
| | | TOTAL | M | F | YEARS # | AGES | PRI. | SEC. | HIGHER | PRI. | SEC. | HIGHER | |
| **Africa** | | | | | | | | | | | | | |
| Egypt | 2010 | 72.0 | 80.3 | 63.5 | 9 | 6–14 | 101 | 72 | 32 | 26.3 | 13.5 | 29.4[1] | 3.8[2] |
| Kenya | 2010 | 87.4 | 90.6 | 84.2 | 8 | 6–13 | 113[1] | 60[1] | 4[1] | 46.8[1] | 29.7[1] | 24.6[3] | 6.7[4] |
| Nigeria | 2010 | 61.3 | 72.1 | 50.4 | 9 | 6–14 | 83 | 44 | 10[3] | 36.0 | 33.1 | 34.8[5] | — |
| South Africa | 2008 | 89.0 | 89.9 | 88.1 | 9 | 7–15 | 102[1] | 94[1] | 15[6] | 30.7[1] | 25.0[1] | 16.8[6] | 6.0[4] |
| **Asia** | | | | | | | | | | | | | |
| China | 2010 | 94.3 | 97.1 | 91.3 | 9 | 6–14 | 111 | 81 | 26 | 16.8 | 15.5 | 19.9 | — |
| India | 2007 | 66.0 | 76.9 | 54.5 | 9 | 6–14 | 116[2] | 63 | 18 | 40.2[5] | 25.3 | 18.6[5] | 3.2[7] |
| Indonesia | 2009 | 92.6 | 95.6 | 89.7 | 9 | 7–15 | 118 | 77 | 23 | 16.0 | 12.2 | 18.4 | 3.0[4] |
| Iran | 2008 | 85.0 | 89.3 | 80.7 | 8 | 6–13 | 114 | 91 | 43 | 20.3[1] | 20.3[6] | 21.8 | 4.7[4] |
| Japan | 2009 | 100 | 100 | 100 | 9 | 6–14 | 103 | 102 | 60 | 17.8 | 11.9 | 7.3 | 3.8[4] |
| Turkey | 2009 | 90.8 | 96.4 | 85.3 | 9 | 6–14 | 102[1] | 78[1] | 46[1] | 22.5 | 20.5 | 27.4[1] | 3.1[5] |
| **Europe** | | | | | | | | | | | | | |
| France | 2003 | 99.0 | 99.0 | 99.0 | 11 | 6–16 | 110 | 113 | 55[1] | 17.8 | 12.7 | 19.6[2] | 5.9 |
| Germany | 2003 | 99.0 | 99.0 | 99.0 | 13 | 6–18 | 102 | 103 | 51[8] | 12.7 | 12.9 | 12.1[7] | 4.6[2] |
| Italy | 2010 | 98.9 | 99.2 | 98.7 | 9 | 6–14 | 102 | 100 | 66[1] | 10.3[6] | 10.1[6] | 18.2[1] | 4.7 |
| Russia | 2010 | 99.6 | 99.7 | 99.5 | 10 | 6–15 | 99[1] | 89[1] | 76[1] | 18.1[1] | 8.5[1] | 13.9[1] | 4.1[2] |
| United Kingdom | 2006 | 100 | 100 | 100 | 12 | 5–16 | 106[1] | 102[1] | 59[1] | 18.0[1] | 14.3[2] | 17.5[1] | 5.6 |
| **Latin America** | | | | | | | | | | | | | |
| Argentina | 2010 | 97.8 | 97.8 | 97.8 | 13 | 5–17 | 118[1] | 89[1] | 71[1] | 16.3[2] | 10.9[2] | 16.8[1] | 6.0 |
| Brazil | 2009 | 90.3 | 90.2 | 90.4 | 9 | 6–14 | 127[2] | 101[2] | 34[2] | 22.2 | 16.7 | 19.0 | 5.7 |
| Cuba | 2010 | 99.8 | 99.8 | 99.8 | 9 | 6–14 | 101[9] | 90[9] | 95 | 9.1[9] | 9.0[9] | 5.2 | 12.9[4] |
| Mexico | 2010 | 93.1 | 94.4 | 91.9 | 11 | 4–14 | 114 | 89 | 28 | 28.1 | 17.9 | 9.2 | 5.3 |
| **Northern America** | | | | | | | | | | | | | |
| Canada | 2006 | 100 | 100 | 100 | 11 | 6–16 | 99[2] | 101[2] | 53[5] | 17.4[10] | 17.7[10] | 9.5[11] | 4.8[2] |
| United States | 2003 | 99.0 | 99.0 | 99.0 | 12 | 6–17 | 102 | 96 | 95 | 13.6 | 13.8 | 14.2 | 5.4 |
| **Oceania** | | | | | | | | | | | | | |
| Australia | 2006 | 100 | 100 | 100 | 11 | 5–15 | 105 | 131 | 80 | 16.0[7] | 12.1[7] | 10.6[3] | 5.1 |

[1]2009 data.   [2]2008 data.   [3]2005 data.   [4]2010 data.   [5]2004 data.   [6]2007 data.   [7]2006 data.   [8]2003 data.   [9]2011 data.   [10]2000 data.   [11]2002 data.

# Religion

## Chronological List of Popes

According to Roman Catholic doctrine, the pope is the successor of **St. Peter**, who was head of the Apostles. The pope thus is seen to have full and supreme power of jurisdiction over the universal church in matters of faith and morals, as well as in church discipline and government. Until the 4th century, the popes were usually known only as bishops of Rome. From 1309–77, the popes' seat was at Avignon, France. In the table, **antipopes**, who opposed the legitimately elected bishop of Rome and endeavored to secure the papal throne, are listed in italics. The elections of several antipopes are greatly obscured by incomplete or biased records, and at times even their contemporaries could not decide who was the true pope. It is impossible, therefore, to establish an absolutely definitive list of antipopes.

| POPE | REIGN | POPE | REIGN | POPE | REIGN |
|---|---|---|---|---|---|
| Peter | ?–c. 64 | Eleutherius | c. 175–189 | Dionysius | 259–268 |
| Linus | c. 67–76/79 | Victor I | c. 189–199 | Felix I | 269–274 |
| Anacletus | 76–88 or 79–91 | Zephyrinus | c. 199–217 | Eutychian | 275–283 |
| | | Calixtus I (Callistus) | 217?–222 | Gaius | 283–296 |
| Clement I | 88–97 or 92–101 | *Hippolytus* | 217, 218–235 | Marcellinus | 291/296–304 |
| Evaristus | c. 97–c. 107 | Urban I | 222–230 | Marcellus I | 308–309 |
| Alexander I | 105–115 or 109–119 | Pontian | 230–235 | Eusebius | 309/310 |
| | | Anterus | 235–236 | Miltiades (Melchiades) | 311–314 |
| Sixtus I | c. 115–c. 125 | Fabian | 236–250 | Sylvester I | 314–335 |
| Telesphorus | c. 125–c. 136 | Cornelius | 251–253 | Mark | 336 |
| Hyginus | c. 136–c. 140 | *Novatian* | 251 | Julius I | 337–352 |
| Pius I | c. 140–155 | Lucius I | 253–254 | Liberius | 352–366 |
| Anicetus | c. 155–c. 166 | Stephen I | 254–257 | *Felix (II)* | 355–358 |
| Soter | c. 166–c. 175 | Sixtus II | 257–258 | Damasus I | 366–384 |

# Chronological List of Popes (continued)

| POPE | REIGN | POPE | REIGN | POPE | REIGN |
|------|-------|------|-------|------|-------|
| *Ursinus* | 366–367 | Adrian I | 772–795 | Benedict IX | 1047–48 |
| Siricius | 384–399 | Leo III | 795–816 | (3rd time) | |
| Anastasius I | 399–401 | Stephen IV (or V)[2] | 816–817 | Damasus II | 1048 |
| Innocent I | 401–417 | Paschal I | 817–824 | Leo IX | 1049–54 |
| Zosimus | 417–418 | Eugenius II | 824–827 | Victor II | 1055–57 |
| Boniface I | 418–422 | Valentine | 827 | Stephen IX (or X)[2] | 1057–58 |
| *Eulalius* | 418–419 | Gregory IV | 827–844 | *Benedict X* | 1058–59 |
| Celestine I | 422–432 | *John* | 844 | Nicholas II | 1059–61 |
| Sixtus III | 432–440 | Sergius II | 844–847 | Alexander II | 1061–73 |
| Leo I | 440–461 | Leo IV | 847–855 | *Honorius (II)* | 1061–72 |
| Hilary | 461–468 | Benedict III | 855–858 | Gregory VII | 1073–85 |
| Simplicius | 468–483 | *Anastasius* | 855 | *Clement (III)* | 1080–1100 |
| Felix III (or II)[1] | 483–492 | *(Anastasius* | | Victor III | 1086–87 |
| Gelasius I | 492–496 | *the Librarian)* | | Urban II | 1088–99 |
| Anastasius II | 496–498 | Nicholas I | 858–867 | Paschal II | 1099–1118 |
| Symmachus | 498–514 | Adrian II | 867–872 | *Theodoric* | 1100–02 |
| *Laurentius* | 498, 501– | John VIII | 872–882 | *Albert (Aleric)* | 1102 |
| | c. 505/507 | Marinus I | 882–884 | *Sylvester (IV)* | 1105–11 |
| Hormisdas | 514–523 | Adrian III | 884–885 | Gelasius II | 1118–19 |
| John I | 523–526 | Stephen V (or VI)[2] | 885–891 | *Gregory (VIII)* | 1118–21 |
| Felix IV (or III)[1] | 526–530 | Formosus | 891–896 | Calixtus II | 1119–24 |
| *Dioscorus* | 530 | Boniface VI | 896 | (Callistus) | |
| Boniface II | 530–532 | Stephen VI (or VII)[2] | 896 | Honorius II | 1124–30 |
| John II | 533–535 | Romanus | 897 | *Celestine (II)* | 1124 |
| Agapetus I | 535–536 | Theodore II | 897 | Innocent II | 1130–43 |
| Silverius | 536–537 | John IX | 898–900 | *Anacletus (II)* | 1130–38 |
| Vigilius | 537–555 | Benedict IV | 900 | *Victor (IV)* | 1138 |
| Pelagius I | 556–561 | Leo V | 903 | Celestine II | 1143–44 |
| John III | 561–574 | *Christopher* | 903–904 | Lucius II | 1144–45 |
| Benedict I | 575–579 | Sergius III | 904–911 | Eugenius III | 1145–53 |
| Pelagius II | 579–590 | Anastasius III | 911–913 | Anastasius IV | 1153–54 |
| Gregory I | 590–604 | Lando | 913–914 | Adrian IV | 1154–59 |
| Sabinian | 604–606 | John X | 914–928 | Alexander III | 1159–81 |
| Boniface III | 604 | Leo VI | 928 | *Victor (IV)* | 1159–64 |
| Boniface IV | 608–615 | Stephen VII (or VIII)[2] | 929–931 | *Paschal (III)* | 1164–68 |
| Deusdedit | 615–618 | John XI | 931–935 | *Calixtus (III)* | 1168–78 |
| (Adeodatus I) | | Leo VII | 936–939 | *Innocent (III)* | 1179–80 |
| Boniface V | 619–625 | Stephen VIII (or IX)[2] | 939–942 | Lucius III | 1181–85 |
| Honorius I | 625–638 | Marinus II | 942–946 | Urban III | 1185–87 |
| Severinus | 640 | Agapetus II | 946–955 | Gregory VIII | 1187 |
| John IV | 640–642 | John XII | 955–964 | Clement III | 1187–91 |
| Theodore I | 642–649 | Leo VIII[3] | 963–965 | Celestine III | 1191–98 |
| Martin I | 649–655 | Benedict V[3] | 964–966? | Innocent III | 1198–1216 |
| Eugenius I | 654–657 | John XIII | 965–972 | Honorius III | 1216–27 |
| Vitalian | 657–672 | Benedict VI | 973–974 | Gregory IX | 1227–41 |
| Adeodatus II | 672–676 | *Boniface VII* | 974 | Celestine IV | 1241 |
| Donus | 676–678 | *(1st time)* | | Innocent IV | 1243–54 |
| Agatho | 678–681 | Benedict VII | 974–983 | Alexander IV | 1254–61 |
| Leo II | 682–683 | John XIV | 983–984 | Urban IV | 1261–64 |
| Benedict II | 684–685 | *Boniface VII* | 984–985 | Clement IV | 1265–68 |
| John V | 685–686 | *(2nd time)* | | Gregory X | 1271–76 |
| Conon | 686–687 | John XV (or XVI)[4] | 985–996 | Innocent V | 1276 |
| Sergius I | 687–701 | Gregory V | 996–999 | Adrian V | 1276 |
| *Theodore* | 687 | *John XVI (or XVII)[4]* | 997–998 | John XXI[4] | 1276–77 |
| *Paschal* | 687 | Sylvester II | 999–1003 | Nicholas III | 1277–80 |
| John VI | 701–705 | John XVII (or XVIII)[4] | 1003 | Martin IV[5] | 1281–85 |
| John VII | 705–707 | John XVIII (or XIX)[4] | 1004–09 | Honorius IV | 1285–87 |
| Sisinnius | 708 | Sergius IV | 1009–12 | Nicholas IV | 1288–92 |
| Constantine | 708–715 | *Gregory (VI)* | 1012 | Celestine V | 1294 |
| Gregory II | 715–731 | Benedict VIII | 1012–24 | Boniface VIII | 1294–1303 |
| Gregory III | 731–741 | John XIX (or XX)[4] | 1024–32 | Benedict XI | 1303–04 |
| Zacharias (Zachary) | 741–752 | Benedict IX | 1032–44 | Clement V (at | 1305–14 |
| Stephen (II)[2] | 752 | *(1st time)* | | Avignon from | |
| Stephen II (or III)[2] | 752–757 | Sylvester III | 1045 | 1309) | |
| Paul I | 757–767 | Benedict IX | 1045 | John XXII[4] | 1316–34 |
| Constantine (II) | 767–768 | *(2nd time)* | | (at Avignon) | |
| *Philip* | 768 | Gregory VI | 1045–46 | *Nicholas (V)* | 1328–30 |
| Stephen III (or IV)[2] | 768–772 | Clement II | 1046–47 | *(at Rome)* | |

## Chronological List of Popes (continued)

| POPE | REIGN | POPE | REIGN | POPE | REIGN |
|---|---|---|---|---|---|
| Benedict XII | 1334–42 | Calixtus III | 1455–58 | Alexander VII | 1655–67 |
| (at Avignon) | | (Callistus) | | Clement IX | 1667–69 |
| Clement VI | 1342–52 | Pius II | 1458–64 | Clement X | 1670–76 |
| (at Avignon) | | Paul II | 1464–71 | Innocent XI | 1676–89 |
| Innocent VI | 1352–62 | Sixtus IV | 1471–84 | Alexander VIII | 1689–91 |
| (at Avignon) | | Innocent VIII | 1484–92 | Innocent XII | 1691–1700 |
| Urban V | 1362–70 | Alexander VI | 1492–1503 | Clement XI | 1700–21 |
| (at Avignon) | | Pius III | 1503 | Innocent XIII | 1721–24 |
| Gregory XI | 1370–78 | Julius II | 1503–13 | Benedict XIII | 1724–30 |
| (at Avignon, then | | Leo X | 1513–21 | Clement XII | 1730–40 |
| Rome from 1377) | | Adrian VI | 1522–23 | Benedict XIV | 1740–58 |
| Urban VI | 1378–89 | Clement VII | 1523–34 | Clement XIII | 1758–69 |
| Clement (VII) | 1378–94 | Paul III | 1534–49 | Clement XIV | 1769–74 |
| (at Avignon) | | Julius III | 1550–55 | Pius VI | 1775–99 |
| Boniface IX | 1389–1404 | Marcellus II | 1555 | Pius VII | 1800–23 |
| Benedict (XIII) | 1394–1423 | Paul IV | 1555–59 | Leo XII | 1823–29 |
| (at Avignon) | | Pius IV | 1559–65 | Pius VIII | 1829–30 |
| Innocent VII | 1404–06 | Pius V | 1566–72 | Gregory XVI | 1831–46 |
| Gregory XII | 1406–15 | Gregory XIII | 1572–85 | Pius IX | 1846–78 |
| Alexander (V) | 1409–10 | Sixtus V | 1585–90 | Leo XIII | 1878–1903 |
| (at Bologna) | | Urban VII | 1590 | Pius X | 1903–14 |
| John (XXIII) | 1410–15 | Gregory XIV | 1590–91 | Benedict XV | 1914–22 |
| (at Bologna) | | Innocent IX | 1591 | Pius XI | 1922–39 |
| Martin V[5] | 1417–31 | Clement VIII | 1592–1605 | Pius XII | 1939–58 |
| Clement (VIII) | 1423–29 | Leo XI | 1605 | John XXIII | 1958–63 |
| Eugenius IV | 1431–47 | Paul V | 1605–21 | Paul VI | 1963–78 |
| Felix (V) (Amadeus | 1439–49 | Gregory XV | 1621–23 | John Paul I | 1978 |
| VIII of Savoy) | | Urban VIII | 1623–44 | John Paul II | 1978–2005 |
| Nicholas V | 1447–55 | Innocent X | 1644–55 | Benedict XVI | 2005– |

[1]The higher number is used if Felix (II), who reigned from 355 to 358 and is ordinarily classed as an antipope, is counted as a pope. [2]Though elected on 23 Mar 752, Stephen (II) died two days later before he could be consecrated and thus is ordinarily not counted. The issue has made the numbering of subsequent Stephens somewhat irregular. [3]Either Leo VIII or Benedict V may be considered an antipope. [4]A confusion in the numbering of popes named John after John XIV (reigned 983–984) resulted because some 11th-century historians mistakenly believed that there had been a pope named John between antipope Boniface VII and the true John XV (reigned 985–996). Therefore they mistakenly numbered the real popes John XV to XIX as John XVI to XX. These popes have since customarily been renumbered XV to XIX, but John XXI and John XXII continue to bear numbers that they themselves formally adopted on the assumption that there had indeed been 20 Johns before them. In current numbering there thus exists no pope by the name of John XX. [5]In the 13th century the papal chancery misread the names of the two popes Marinus as Martin, and as a result of this error Simon de Brie in 1281 assumed the name of Pope Martin IV instead of Martin II. The enumeration has not been corrected, and thus there exist no Martin II and Martin III.

# World Religions

At the beginning of the 21st century, one-third of the world's population is Christian, one-fifth is Muslim, one-eighth is Hindu, and one-eighth is nonreligious. Most people living in Europe and the Americas are Christian, while the vast majority of Muslims and Hindus are found in Asia. The plurality of Christians are Roman Catholics, of Muslims are Sunnis, and of Hindus are Vaishnavites. Africa hosts slightly more Christians than Muslims, with much of the rest of the population listed as ethnic religionists, which describes followers of local, tribal, animistic, or shamanistic religions.

In addition to the adherents of the predominant world religions (Christianity, Islam, Hinduism), there are small but noticeable percentages of Chinese folk religionists, Buddhists, other ethnic religionists, atheists, and new religionists. Among adherents of the remaining distinct religions, Sikhs, Spiritists, Jews, Baha'is, Confucianists, Jains, Shintoists, Daoists (Taoists), and Zoroastrians each make up less than one-half of one percent of religious adherents.

## Christianity

Christianity traces its origins to the 1st century AD and to Jesus of Nazareth, whom it affirms to be the chosen one (Christ) of God. Geographically the most widely diffused of all faiths, it has a constituency of more than two billion people. Its largest groups are the Roman Catholic Church, the Eastern Orthodox churches, and the Protestant churches; in addition, there are several independent churches of Eastern Christianity as well as numerous sects throughout the world.

Christianity's sacred scripture is the Bible, particularly the New Testament. Its principal tenets are that Jesus is the son of God (the second figure of the Holy Trinity), that God's love for the world is the essential component of his being, and that Jesus died to redeem humankind.

Christianity was originally a movement of Jews who accepted Jesus as the Messiah, but the movement (continued on page 511)

# The 2012 Annual Megacensus of Religions

*Todd M. Johnson, Brian J. Grim, and Peter F. Crossing*

Each year since 1750, a steadily increasing volume of new statistical data on religious adherents has been generated. Much of this is uncovered in decennial governmental censuses: half the countries of the world have long asked their populations to state their religions, if any, and they still do today. Another major source of data each year comes from membership reports undertaken by many religious headquarters. For example, each year almost all Christian denominations ask and answer statistical questions about their members. A third annual source is a large number

## Worldwide Adherents of All Religions by Six Continental Areas, mid-2012

| | AFRICA | ASIA | EUROPE | LATIN AMERICA |
|---|---|---|---|---|
| Christians | 519,501,000 | 358,211,000 | 581,360,000 | 556,946,000 |
| Affiliated | 494,057,000 | 354,051,000 | 560,757,000 | 550,680,000 |
| Roman Catholics | 189,983,000 | 141,740,000 | 278,115,000 | 494,205,000 |
| Protestants | 144,846,000 | 90,044,000 | 67,598,000 | 60,896,000 |
| Independents | 109,049,000 | 136,487,000 | 10,824,000 | 40,519,000 |
| Orthodox | 45,192,000 | 18,720,000 | 204,008,000 | 1,083,000 |
| Anglicans | 53,522,000 | 876,000 | 26,435,000 | 877,000 |
| Marginal Christians | 4,245,000 | 3,230,000 | 4,136,000 | 11,757,000 |
| *Doubly affiliated* | *−52,780,000* | *−37,046,000* | *−30,359,000* | *−58,657,000* |
| Unaffiliated | 25,444,000 | 4,160,000 | 20,603,000 | 6,266,000 |
| Muslims | 444,868,000 | 1,115,159,900 | 41,949,000 | 1,556,000 |
| Hindus | 3,054,000 | 959,711,000 | 1,200,000 | 776,000 |
| Agnostics | 6,862,000 | 503,989,000 | 93,415,100 | 18,889,910 |
| Buddhists | 263,000 | 496,787,000 | 1,803,000 | 775,000 |
| Chinese folk-religionists | 137,000 | 435,455,000 | 444,000 | 194,000 |
| Ethnoreligionists | 92,039,000 | 148,934,000 | 1,168,000 | 3,717,000 |
| Atheists | 589,000 | 114,647,000 | 15,349,000 | 2,981,000 |
| New religionists | 117,000 | 59,227,000 | 366,000 | 1,773,000 |
| Sikhs | 77,000 | 23,466,000 | 572,000 | 7,300 |
| Jews | 135,000 | 6,307,000 | 1,928,000 | 977,000 |
| Spiritists · | 2,700 | 2,100 | 145,000 | 13,527,000 |
| Daoists (Taoists) | 0 | 8,526,000 | 0 | 0 |
| Confucianists | 20,400 | 8,107,000 | 15,800 | 490 |
| Baha'is | 2,246,000 | 3,516,000 | 160,000 | 925,000 |
| Jains | 98,900 | 5,227,000 | 19,300 | 1,400 |
| Shintoists | 0 | 2,695,000 | 0 | 7,900 |
| Zoroastrians | 1,000 | 169,000 | 5,800 | 0 |
| Other religionists | 85,000 | 225,000 | 275,000 | 120,000 |
| **Total population** | **1,070,096,000** | **4,250,361,000** | **740,175,000** | **603,174,000** |

**Continents.** These follow current UN demographic terminology, which divides the world into the six major areas shown above. *See* United Nations, *World Population Prospects: The 2010 Revision* (New York: UN, 2011), with populations of all continents, regions, and countries covering the period 1950–2100, with 100 variables for every country each year.

**Change rate.** This column documents the annual change in 2012 (calculated as an average annual change from 2005 to 2010) in worldwide religious and nonreligious adherents. Note that from 2005 to 2010 the annual growth of world population was 1.17%, or a net increase of 77,851,200 persons per year.

**Countries.** The last column enumerates sovereign and nonsovereign countries in which each religion or religious grouping has a numerically significant and organized following.

**Adherents.** As defined in the 1948 Universal Declaration of Human Rights, a person's religion is what he or she professes, confesses, or states that it is. Totals are enumerated for each of the world's 232 countries using recent censuses, polls, surveys, yearbooks, reports, Web sites, literature, and other data. See the World Christian Database <www.worldchristiandatabase.org> and World Religion Database <www.worldreligiondatabase.org> for more detail. Religions (including agnostics and atheists) are ranked in order of worldwide size in mid-2012.

**Agnostics.** Persons professing no religion (unaffiliated), nonbelievers, freethinkers, uninterested, or dereligionized secularists indifferent to all religion but not atheists.

**Atheists.** Persons professing atheism, skepticism, disbelief, or irreligion, including the militantly antireligious (opposed to all religion). A flurry of recent books have outlined the Western philosophical and scientific basis for atheism. Ironically, the vast majority of atheists today are found in Asia (primarily Chinese communists).

**Buddhists.** 56% Mahayana, 38% Theravada (Hinayana), 6% Tantrayana (Lamaism).

**Chinese folk-religionists.** Followers of a unique complex of beliefs and practices that may include universism (yin/yang cosmology with dualities earth/heaven, evil/good, darkness/light), ancestor cult, Confucian ethics, divination, festivals, folk religion, goddess worship, household gods, local deities, mediums, metaphysics, monasteries, neo-Confucianism, popular religion, sacrifices, shamans, spirit-writing, and Daoist (Taoist) and Buddhist elements.

of surveys and polls taken around the world, many without a primary focus on religion but containing valuable information on religion. Together, these three major sources of data constitute a massive annual collection of data on religion, although decentralized and uncoordinated. These data are analyzed, evaluated, and reconciled, resulting in the two tables below. The first table summarizes worldwide adherents by religion. The second goes into more detail for the United States of America. For the first time, this year, three research projects offer support and additional information on the fig-

ures reported below. First, the World Religion Database offers sources and analysis of religious dynamics for every country. Second, a new book by Todd M. Johnson and Brian J. Grim both reports on and explains the methodology used in counting religious adherents around the world—*The World's Religions in Figures: An Introduction to International Religious Demography*. Third, the Pew Forum on Religion and Public Life continues to publish reports that offer depth to our sources and analysis.

Detail may not add to total given because of rounding.

| NORTHERN AMERICA | OCEANIA | WORLD | % | CHANGE RATE (%) | NUMBER OF COUNTRIES |
|---|---|---|---|---|---|
| 275,189,000 | 28,632,000 | 2,319,839,000 | 32.9 | 1.28 | 232 |
| 225,856,000 | 24,291,000 | 2,209,692,000 | 31.3 | 1.31 | 232 |
| 87,732,000 | 9,075,000 | 1,200,850,000 | 17.0 | 1.34 | 232 |
| 59,356,000 | 7,885,000 | 430,625,000 | 6.1 | 1.54 | 229 |
| 58,557,000 | 1,297,000 | 356,733,000 | 5.1 | 2.10 | 221 |
| 7,594,000 | 1,008,000 | 277,605,000 | 3.9 | 0.41 | 137 |
| 2,764,000 | 4,829,000 | 89,303,000 | 1.3 | 1.48 | 162 |
| 12,098,000 | 684,000 | 36,150,000 | 0.5 | 1.74 | 217 |
| −2,245,000 | −487,000 | −181,574,000 | −2.6 | 2.36 | 182 |
| 49,333,000 | 4,341,000 | 110,147,000 | 1.6 | 0.64 | 227 |
| 5,091,000 | 577,000 | 1,609,200,900 | 22.8 | 1.82 | 213 |
| 1,897,000 | 526,000 | 967,164,000 | 13.7 | 1.31 | 144 |
| 49,987,900 | 5,910,400 | 679,054,310 | 9.6 | 0.31 | 231 |
| 4,549,000 | 607,000 | 504,784,000 | 7.2 | 0.98 | 152 |
| 797,000 | 106,000 | 437,133,000 | 6.2 | 0.29 | 120 |
| 1,232,000 | 383,000 | 247,473,000 | 3.5 | 0.99 | 146 |
| 2,245,000 | 516,000 | 136,327,000 | 1.9 | −0.06 | 221 |
| 1,737,000 | 107,000 | 63,327,000 | 0.9 | 0.25 | 119 |
| 620,000 | 51,100 | 24,793,400 | 0.4 | 1.51 | 64 |
| 5,525,000 | 121,000 | 14,993,000 | 0.2 | 0.71 | 147 |
| 248,000 | 8,100 | 13,932,900 | 0.2 | 0.84 | 57 |
| 12,500 | 4,700 | 8,543,200 | 0.1 | 0.67 | 6 |
| 0 | 51,000 | 8,194,690 | 0.1 | 0.39 | 17 |
| 587,000 | 116,000 | 7,550,000 | 0.1 | 1.59 | 222 |
| 103,000 | 3,000 | 5,452,600 | 0.1 | 1.27 | 19 |
| 63,300 | 0 | 2,766,200 | 0.0 | 0.09 | 8 |
| 21,300 | 2,700 | 199,800 | 0.0 | 0.62 | 27 |
| 690,000 | 12,000 | 1,407,000 | 0.0 | 1.31 | 79 |
| **350,595,000** | **37,734,000** | **7,052,135,000** | **100.0** | **1.17** | **232** |

**Christians.** Followers of Jesus Christ, enumerated here under **Affiliated**, those affiliated with churches (church members, with names written on church rolls, usually total number of baptized persons including children baptized, dedicated, or undedicated): total in 2012 being 2,209,692,000, shown above divided among the six standardized ecclesiastical megablocs and with (negative and italicized) figures for those **Doubly affiliated** persons (all who are baptized members of two denominations) and **Unaffiliated**, who are persons professing or confessing in censuses or polls to be Christians though not so affiliated. **Independents.** This term here denotes members of Christian churches and networks that regard themselves as postdenominationalist and neoapostolic and thus independent of historical, mainstream, organized, institutionalized, confessional, denominationalist Christianity. **Marginal Christians.** Members of denominations who define themselves as Christians but on the margins of organized mainstream Christianity (e.g., Unitarians, Mormons, Jehovah's Witnesses, Christian Science, and Religious Science).

**Confucianists.** Chinese and non-Chinese followers of Confucius and Confucianism, mostly neo-Confucianists in East and Southeast Asia and Korean Confucianists in Korea.

**Ethnoreligionists.** Followers of local, tribal, animistic, or shamanistic religions, with members restricted to one ethnic group.

**Hindus.** 68% Vaishnavites, 27% Shaivites, 5% Saktists and neo-Hindus and reform Hindus.

**Jews.** Adherents of Judaism. For detailed data on "core" Jewish population, *see* the annual "World Jewish Populations" article in the American Jewish Committee's *American Jewish Year Book*.

**Muslims.** 86% Sunnites, 13% Shi'ites, 1% other schools.

**New religionists.** Followers of Asian 20th-century neoreligions, neoreligious movements, radical new crisis religions, and non-Christian syncretistic mass religions.

**Other religionists.** Including a handful of religions, quasi-religions, pseudoreligions, parareligions, religious or mystic systems, and religious and semireligious brotherhoods of numerous varieties.

**Total population.** UN medium variant figures for mid-2012, as given in *World Population Prospects: The 2010 Revision*.

## Religious Adherents in the United States of America, 1900–2010

*For categories not described below, see notes to Worldwide Adherents of All Religions, pp. 508–09.*

| | 1900 | % | MID-1970 | % | MID-1990 | % |
|---|---|---|---|---|---|---|
| Christians | 73,260,000 | 96.4 | 189,873,000 | 90.6 | 216,161,600 | 85.3 |
|   Affiliated | 54,425,000 | 71.6 | 152,752,300 | 72.9 | 174,682,600 | 69.0 |
|     Roman Catholics | 10,775,000 | 14.2 | 48,305,000 | 23.1 | 56,500,000 | 22.3 |
|     Independents | 5,850,000 | 7.7 | 33,656,000 | 16.1 | 42,900,000 | 16.9 |
|     Protestants | 35,000,000 | 46.1 | 57,185,000 | 27.3 | 60,216,000 | 23.8 |
|     Marginal Christians | 800,000 | 1.1 | 6,114,000 | 2.9 | 8,440,000 | 3.3 |
|     Orthodox | 400,000 | 0.5 | 4,395,000 | 2.1 | 5,150,000 | 2.0 |
|     Anglicans | 1,600,000 | 2.1 | 3,196,000 | 1.5 | 2,450,000 | 1.0 |
|     *Doubly affiliated* | *0* | *0.0* | *−98,700* | *0.0* | *−973,400* | *−0.4* |
|     *Evangelicals* | *32,068,000* | *42.2* | *33,625,000* | *16.1* | *38,400,000* | *15.2* |
|     *evangelicals* | *11,000,000* | *14.5* | *45,500,000* | *21.7* | *85,656,000* | *33.8* |
|   Unaffiliated | 18,835,000 | 24.8 | 37,120,700 | 17.7 | 41,479,000 | 16.4 |
| Agnostics | 1,000,000 | 1.3 | 10,270,000 | 4.9 | 21,442,000 | 8.5 |
| Jews | 1,500,000 | 2.0 | 6,700,000 | 3.2 | 5,535,000 | 2.2 |
| Muslims | 10,000 | 0.0 | 800,000 | 0.4 | 3,300,000 | 1.3 |
|   Black Muslims | 0 | 0.0 | 200,000 | 0.1 | 1,250,000 | 0.5 |
| Buddhists | 30,000 | 0.0 | 200,000 | 0.1 | 1,880,000 | 0.7 |
| New religionists | 10,000 | 0.0 | 560,000 | 0.3 | 1,155,000 | 0.5 |
| Hindus | 1,000 | 0.0 | 100,000 | 0.0 | 750,000 | 0.3 |
| Atheists | 1,000 | 0.0 | 200,000 | 0.1 | 770,000 | 0.3 |
| Ethnoreligionists | 100,000 | 0.1 | 70,000 | 0.0 | 780,000 | 0.3 |
| Baha'is | 2,800 | 0.0 | 138,000 | 0.1 | 600,000 | 0.2 |
| Sikhs | 0 | 0.0 | 10,000 | 0.0 | 160,000 | 0.1 |
| Spiritists | 0 | 0.0 | 0 | 0.0 | 120,000 | 0.0 |
| Chinese folk-religionists | 70,000 | 0.1 | 90,000 | 0.0 | 76,000 | 0.0 |
| Shintoists | 0 | 0.0 | 3,000 | 0.0 | 5,000 | 0.0 |
| Zoroastrians | 0 | 0.0 | 0 | 0.0 | 50,000 | 0.0 |
| Daoists (Taoists) | 0 | 0.0 | 0 | 0.0 | 14,400 | 0.0 |
| Jains | 0 | 0.0 | 0 | 0.0 | 10,000 | 0.0 |
| Other religionists | 10,200 | 0.0 | 450,000 | 0.2 | 530,000 | 0.2 |
| **US population** | **75,995,000** | **100.0** | **209,464,000** | **100.0** | **253,339,000** | **100.0** |

**Methodology.** This table extracts and analyzes a microcosm of the world religion table. It depicts the United States, the country with the largest number of adherents to Christianity, the world's largest religion. Statistics at five points in time from 1900 to 2010 are presented. Each religion's **Annual Change** for 2000–2010 is also analyzed by **Natural** increase (births minus deaths, plus immigrants minus emigrants) per year and **Conversion** increase (converts in minus converts out) per year, which together constitute the **Total** increase per year. **Rate** increase is then computed as percentage per year.

**Structure.** Vertically the table lists 30 major religious categories. The major categories (including nonreligious) in the US are listed with largest (Christians) first. Indented names of groups in the "Adherents" column are subcategories of the groups above them and are also counted in these unindented totals, so they should not be added twice into the column total. Figures in italics draw adherents from all categories of Christians above and so cannot be added together with them. Figures for Christians are built upon detailed head counts by churches, often to the last digit. Totals are then rounded to the nearest 1,000. Because of rounding, the corresponding percentage figures may sometimes not total exactly to 100%. Religions are ranked in order of size in 2010.

**Christians.** All persons who profess publicly to follow Jesus Christ as God and Savior. This category is subdivided into **Affiliated** (church members) and **Unaffiliated** (nominal) Christians (professing Christians not affiliated with any church). *See also* the note on Christians below the world religion table. The first six lines under "Affiliated Christians" are ranked by size in 2010 for each of the six megablocs (Anglican, Independent, Marginal Christian, Orthodox, Protestant, Roman Catholic).

**Evangelicals/evangelicals.** These two designations—italicized and enumerated separately here—cut across all of the six Christian traditions or ecclesiastical blocs listed above and should be considered separately from them. The **Evangelicals** (capitalized "E") are mainly Protestant churches, agencies, and individuals who call themselves by this term (for example, members of the National Association of Evangelicals); they usually emphasize 5 or more of 7, 9, or 21 fundamental doctrines (salvation by faith, personal acceptance, verbal inspiration of Scripture, depravity of man, Virgin Birth, miracles of Christ, atonement, evangelism, Second Advent, et al.). The **evangelicals** (lowercase "e") are Christians of evangelical conviction from all traditions who are committed to the evangel (gospel) and involved in personal witness and mission in the world.

**Jews.** Core Jewish population relating to Judaism, excluding Jewish persons professing a different religion.

**Other categories.** Definitions are as given under the world religion table.

| MID-2000 | % | MID-2010 | % | ANNUAL CHANGE, 2000–2010 | | | |
| --- | --- | --- | --- | --- | --- | --- | --- |
| | | | | NATURAL | CONVERSION | TOTAL | RATE (%) |
| 231,989,200 | 82.1 | 247,943,900 | 79.9 | 2,290,200 | −694,700 | 1,595,500 | 0.67 |
| 189,716,000 | 67.2 | 202,953,000 | 65.4 | 1,872,900 | −549,200 | 1,323,700 | 0.68 |
| 62,970,000 | 22.3 | 70,656,000 | 22.8 | 621,600 | 147,000 | 768,600 | 1.16 |
| 52,749,000 | 18.7 | 56,858,000 | 18.3 | 520,700 | −109,800 | 410,900 | 0.75 |
| 56,921,000 | 20.1 | 56,008,000 | 18.0 | 561,900 | −653,200 | −91,300 | −0.16 |
| 10,080,000 | 3.6 | 11,305,000 | 3.6 | 99,500 | 23,000 | 122,500 | 1.15 |
| 5,595,000 | 2.0 | 6,386,000 | 2.1 | 55,200 | 23,900 | 79,100 | 1.33 |
| 2,300,000 | 0.8 | 2,191,000 | 0.7 | 22,700 | −33,600 | −10,900 | −0.48 |
| *−899,000* | *−0.3* | *−451,000* | *−0.1* | *−8,900* | *53,700* | *44,800* | *−6.67* |
| *41,520,000* | *14.7* | *44,752,000* | *14.4* | *409,900* | *−86,700* | *323,200* | *0.75* |
| *95,900,000* | *33.9* | *102,759,000* | *33.1* | *946,700* | *−260,800* | *685,900* | *0.69* |
| 42,273,200 | 15.0 | 44,990,900 | 14.5 | 417,300 | −145,500 | 271,800 | 0.63 |
| 31,467,000 | 11.1 | 41,889,000 | 13.5 | 310,600 | 731,600 | 1,042,200 | 2.90 |
| 5,341,000 | 1.9 | 5,122,000 | 1.7 | 52,700 | −74,600 | −21,900 | −0.42 |
| 3,722,000 | 1.3 | 4,106,000 | 1.3 | 36,700 | 1,700 | 38,400 | 0.99 |
| 1,650,000 | 0.6 | 1,850,000 | 0.6 | 16,300 | 3,700 | 20,000 | 1.15 |
| 3,456,000 | 1.2 | 3,955,000 | 1.3 | 34,100 | 15,800 | 49,900 | 1.36 |
| 1,475,000 | 0.5 | 1,624,000 | 0.5 | 14,600 | 300 | 14,900 | 0.97 |
| 1,222,000 | 0.4 | 1,445,000 | 0.5 | 12,100 | 10,200 | 22,300 | 1.69 |
| 1,156,000 | 0.4 | 1,310,000 | 0.4 | 11,400 | 4,000 | 15,400 | 1.26 |
| 970,000 | 0.3 | 1,085,000 | 0.3 | 9,600 | 1,900 | 11,500 | 1.13 |
| 431,000 | 0.2 | 513,000 | 0.2 | 4,300 | 3,900 | 8,200 | 1.76 |
| 237,000 | 0.1 | 279,000 | 0.1 | 2,300 | 1,900 | 4,200 | 1.64 |
| 193,000 | 0.1 | 225,000 | 0.1 | 1,900 | 1,300 | 3,200 | 1.55 |
| 98,900 | 0.0 | 109,000 | 0.0 | 1,000 | 0 | 1,000 | 0.98 |
| 73,400 | 0.0 | 85,400 | 0.0 | 700 | 500 | 1,200 | 1.53 |
| 57,100 | 0.0 | 62,700 | 0.0 | 600 | 0 | 600 | 0.94 |
| 16,100 | 0.0 | 17,600 | 0.0 | 200 | 0 | 200 | 0.89 |
| 11,300 | 0.0 | 12,400 | 0.0 | 100 | 0 | 100 | 0.93 |
| 580,000 | 0.2 | 600,000 | 0.2 | 5,700 | −3,700 | 2,000 | 0.34 |
| **282,496,000** | **100.0** | **310,384,000** | **100.0** | **2,789,000** | **0** | **2,789,000** | **0.95** |

## World Religions (continued)

(continued from page 507)
quickly became predominantly Gentile. Nearly all Christian churches have an ordained clergy, who lead group worship services and are viewed as intermediaries between the laity and the divine in some churches. Most Christian churches administer at least two sacraments: baptism and the Lord's Supper.

### Islam
Islam is a religion that originated in the Middle East and was promulgated by the Prophet Muhammad in Arabia in the 7th century AD. The Arabic term *islam,* literally "surrender," illuminates the fundamental religious idea of Islam—that the believer (called a Muslim, from the active particle of *islam*) accepts "surrender to the will of Allah" (Arabic: "God"). Allah's will is made known through the sacred scriptures, the Qur'an, which Allah revealed to his messenger, Muhammad. In Islam, Muhammad is considered the last of a series of prophets (including Adam, Noah, Jesus, and others), and his message simultaneously consummates and abrogates the "revelations" attributed to earlier prophets.

The religious obligations of all Muslims are summed up in the Five Pillars of Islam. The fundamental concept in Islam is the Shari'ah, or Law, which embraces the total way of life commanded by God. Observant Muslims pray five times a day and join in community worship on Fridays at the mosque, where worship is led by an imam. Every believer is required to make a pilgrimage to Mecca, the holiest city, at least once in a lifetime, barring poverty or physical incapacity. The month of Ramadan is set aside for fasting. Jihad, considered a sixth pillar by some sects, is not accepted by most of the Islamic community as a call to wage physical war against unbelievers.

Divisions occurred early in Islam, brought about by disputes over the succession to the caliphate, resulting in various sects (Sunnis, Shi'ites, Isma'ilis, Sufis). From the 19th century, the concept of the Islamic community inspired Muslim peoples to cast off Western colonial rule, and in the late 20th century fundamentalist movements toppled a number of secular Middle Eastern governments. A movement of African American Muslims emerged in the 20th century in the US.

### Hinduism
Hinduism is the oldest of the world's major religions, dating back more than 3,000 years, though its present forms are of more recent origin. It evolved from Vedism, the religion of the Indo-European peoples who settled in India at the end of the 2nd millennium BC. The vast majority of the world's Hindus live in India, though significant minorities may be found in Pakistan and Sri Lanka, and smaller numbers live in Myanmar (Burma), South Africa, Trinidad, Europe, and the US.

Though the various Hindu sects each rely on their own set of scriptures, they all revere the ancient Vedas, which were brought to India by Aryan invaders after 1200 BC. The philosophical Vedic texts called the Upanishads explore the search for knowledge that will allow mankind to escape the cycle of reincarnation. Fundamental to Hinduism is the belief in a cosmic principle of ultimate reality, called brahman, and its identity with the individual soul, or atman. All creatures go through a cycle of rebirth, or samsara, which can be

# World Religions (continued)

broken only by spiritual self-realization, after which liberation, or moksha, is attained. The principle of karma determines a being's status within the cycle of rebirth.

The greatest Hindu deities are Brahma, Vishnu, and Shiva. The major sources of classical mythology are the Mahabharata (which includes the Bhagavadgita, the most important religious text of Hinduism), the Ramayana, and the Puranas. The hierarchical social structure of the caste system is important in Hinduism; it is supported by the principle of dharma. During the 20th century Hinduism was blended with Indian nationalism to become a potent political force. **Buddhism**, a religion concentrated in Asia with some representation in North America, was founded by the Buddha (Siddhartha Gautama, or Gotama) in northeast India in the 5th century BC. By adhering to the Buddha's teachings, the believer can alleviate suffering through an understanding of the transitory nature of existence, in the hopes of achieving enlightenment. Distinct from Buddhism, **Shinto** is the indigenous religion of Japan and has no founder, sacred scriptures, or fixed dogmas. Also based in Asia, **Chinese folk religions** worship local deities and teach ancestor worship and divination. They also adhere to Confucian ethics, though statistically only non-Chinese (mostly Korean) followers of Confucius, a Chinese philosopher of the 6th century BC, are categorized as followers of **Confucianism**. Confucianism is not an organized religion as much as it is a political and social ideology. Also in the Confucian tradition,

adherents of **Daoism** seek the correct path of human conduct and an understanding of the Absolute Dao. **Zoroastrianism** is an ancient pre-Islamic religion of Iran that survives there and in India. It was founded by the Iranian prophet Zoroaster in the 6th century BC and has both monotheistic and dualistic features. Also founded in Iran is the **Baha'i** faith, created as a universal religion in the mid-19th century AD for the worship of Baha' Ullah and his forerunner, the Bab; it has no priesthood or formal sacraments and is chiefly concerned with social ethics.

**Jainism** was founded in India in the 6th century BC by Vardhamana, or Mahavira, a monastic reformer in the Vedic, or early Hindu, tradition. Jainism emphasizes a path to spiritual purity and enlightenment through a disciplined mode of life founded upon the tradition of ahimsa, nonviolence to all living creatures.

**Sikhism** is a monotheistic religion founded in the late 15th century AD in India, historically associated with the Punjab region, though it includes representation in Europe and North America.

**Judaism**, like Christianity and Islam, is monotheistic and maintains the manifestation of God in human events, particularly through Moses in the Torah at Mount Sinai in the 13th century BC. Jews, who come together in both religious and ethnic communities, have worldwide representation, with the greatest concentration in North America and the Middle East. **New Religious Movements** and non-Christian syncretistic mass religions also have significant followings.

# Terrorism

## International Terrorist Organizations

*Below is the US Department of State list of Foreign Terrorist Organizations issued on 27 Jan 2012. Translations and acronyms are given in bold parenthetically; unofficial names and acronyms follow and are not in bold.*

**Abu Nidal Organization (ANO)** (Fatah Revolutionary Council, Arab Revolutionary Brigades, Black September)
    **founded** in 1974 as a splinter group from the Palestinian Liberation Organization (PLO)
        **country or region of operation:** Middle East, primarily Iraq and Lebanon; has also operated in Asia and Europe
        **primary goals:** elimination of Israel, establishment of a Palestinian state
**Abu Sayyaf Group (ASG)**
    **founded** in the early 1990s as a splinter group from Moro National Liberation Front by Abdurajak Abubakar Janjalani; mainly made up of semiautonomous factions
        **country or region of operation:** Philippines, Malaysia
        **primary goals:** establishment of an independent Islamic state in the southern Philippines
**Ansar al-Islam (AAI, Partisans of Islam)**
    **founded** in 2001 as an offshoot of the Islamic Movement in Iraqi Kurdistan by Najmeddin Faraj Ahmed
        **country or region of operation:** Iraq
        **primary goals:** establishment of an Islamic state in the Kurdish areas of northern Iraq
**al-Aqsa Martyrs Brigade (AAMS)**
    **founded** in 2000 as an offshoot of Fatah; diffuse cell-based leadership structure
        **country or region of operation:** Gaza Strip, West Bank, Israel
        **primary goals:** establishment of a Palestinian state with Jerusalem as its capital
**Army of Islam (AOI)**
    **founded** in 2005; led by Mumtaz Dughmush
        **country or region of operation:** Gaza Strip
        **primary goals:** removal of Israeli forces from the Palestinian occupied territories
**Asbat al-Ansar**
    **founded** in the late 1980s; led by Abou Mahjan, aka Abdel Karim al-Saadi
        **country or region of operation:** Lebanon
        **primary goals:** replacement of secular Lebanese government with an Islamic state
**AUM Shinrikyo (AUM Supreme Truth, Aleph)**
    **founded** in 1987 by Shoko Asahara; led by Fumihiro Joyu
        **country or region of operation:** Japan
        **primary goals:** takeover of Japan and the world

## International Terrorist Organizations (continued)

**Basque Fatherland and Liberty (Euzkadi Ta Askatasuna, ETA)**
   founded in 1959; allegedly led by Jurdan Martitegi Lizaso (arrested in April 2009)
   country or region of operation: Basque autonomous regions of northern Spain and southwestern France
   primary goals: establishment of an independent Basque state based on Marxism
**Communist Party of the Philippines/New People's Army (CPP/NPA)**
   founded in 1969 as a Maoist movement; led from exile by José María Sisón
   country or region of operation: Philippines
   primary goals: overthrow of the Philippine government
**Continuity Irish Republican Army (CIRA)**
   founded in 1994 as a splinter group of Irish Republican Army (IRA) after the latter declared its first cease-fire
   country or region of operation: Northern Ireland, Republic of Ireland
   primary goals: removal of British forces from Northern Ireland
**Hamas (Islamic Resistance Movement)**
   founded in 1987 by Sheikh Ahmed Yasin as an offshoot of Muslim Brotherhood; led by Khalid Mesha
   country or region of operation: Gaza Strip, West Bank, Israel; also present throughout the Middle East
   primary goals: elimination of Israel, establishment of an Islamic Palestinian state
**Harakat ul-Jihad-i-Islami (HUJI)**
   founded in 1980
   country or region of operation: South Asia; primarily in India and Pakistan
   primary goals: liberation of Kashmir and its accession to Pakistan
**Harakat ul-Jihad-i-Islami/Bangladesh (HUJI-B)**
   founded in the 1990s; affiliated with al-Qaeda
   country or region of operation: Bangladesh
   primary goals: establishment of Bangladesh as an Islamic state
**Harakat ul-Mujahidin (HUM) (Movement of Holy Warriors)**
   founded in the mid-1980s or early 1990s; led by Farooq Kashmiri
   country or region of operation: the Kashmir region of Pakistan and India
   primary goals: establishment of Kashmir as part of an Islamic state
**Hezbollah (Party of God) (Islamic Jihad for the Liberation of Palestine, Revolutionary Justice Organization)**
   founded in 1982
   country or region of operation: Lebanon; also has cells worldwide
   primary goals: establishment of Islamic rule in Lebanon, elimination of Israel, liberation of occupied Arab lands
**Indian Mujahideen (IM)**
   founded in the mid-2000s
   country or region of operation: India
   primary goals: establishment of an Islamic caliphate across South Asia
**Islamic Jihad Group (IJG) (IJU, Islamic Jihad Union)**
   founded in 2004; offshoot of Islamic Movement of Uzbekistan (IMU)
   country or region of operation: Central Asia
   primary goals: replacement of the secular Uzbek government with an Islamic state
**Islamic Movement of Uzbekistan (IMU)**
   founded in 1996
   country or region of operation: primarily Uzbekistan, Tajikistan, Kyrgyzstan, Afghanistan, Iran, and Pakistan
   primary goals: replacement of the secular Uzbek government with an Islamic state
**Jaish-e-Mohammed (JEM) (Army of Muhammad)**
   founded in 2000 as a spin-off from Harakat ul-Mujahidin; led by Maulana Masood Azhar
   country or region of operation: South Asia, primarily Pakistan and India
   primary goals: establishment of Pakistani control over India-administered Kashmir
**al-Jama'ah al-Islamiyah (Islamic Group, IG)**
   founded in the late 1970s; spiritual leader Sheikh Umar Abd al-Rahman
   country or region of operation: Egypt; also operates in several countries worldwide
   primary goals: replacement of Egyptian government with an Islamic state
**Jemaah Anshorut Tauhid (JAT)**
   founded in 2008 by Abu Bakar Baasyir
   country or region of operation: Indonesia
   primary goals: establishment of an Islamic caliphate in Indonesia
**Jemaah Islamiyah (JI)**
   founded in the mid-1990s as a successor to Darul Islam; led by Abu Bakar Baasyir
   country or region of operation: Southeast Asia, particularly Indonesia, Singapore, and Malaysia
   primary goals: establishment of a pan-Islamic state in Southeast Asia
**Jundallah (God's Soldiers)**
   founded in 2003; led by al-Hajj Mohammed Dhahir Baluch
   country or region of operation: Iran
   primary goals: protection of the rights of the Baluchi minority in Iran
**Kahane Chai (Kach)**
   founded in 1971 by Meir Kahane; Kahane Chai founded as follow-up group after Meir's assassination in 1990
   country or region of operation: Israel, West Bank
   primary goals: expansion of Israel, removal of Palestinians

## International Terrorist Organizations (continued)

**Kata'ib Hizballah (KH)** (Hezbollah Brigades)
   founded in 2007
   **country or region of operation:** Iraq
   **primary goals:** expulsion of American and allied forces from Iraq
**Kongra-Gel (KGK)** (formerly Kurdistan Workers' Party, PKK, KADEK)
   founded in 1974; led by Abdullah Ocalan (imprisoned since 1999)
   **country or region of operation:** Turkey; also operates in Europe and the Middle East
   **primary goals:** establishment of independent Kurdish state
**Lashkar-e-Taiba (LT, Army of the Righteous)**
   founded in 1990; led by Abdul Wahid Kashmiri
   **country or region of operation:** South Asia, primarily Pakistan and India
   **primary goals:** establishment of Pakistani control over India-administered Kashmir
**Lashkar I Jhangvi (LJ)**
   founded in 1996; decentralized leadership structure
   **country or region of operation:** Pakistan
   **primary goals:** replacement of the Pakistani government with an Islamic state
**Liberation Tigers of Tamil Eelam (LTTE)**
   founded in 1976; led by Velupillai Prabhakaran (until his death in May 2009)
   **country or region of operation:** Sri Lanka
   **primary goals:** establishment of an independent Tamil state
**Libyan Islamic Fighting Group (LIFG)**
   founded in 1995 among Libyans who had fought against Soviet forces in Afghanistan; led by Anas Sebai
   **country or region of operation:** Libya, various Middle Eastern and European countries
   **primary goals:** overthrow of the government of Libyan leader Muammar al-Qaddafi
**Moroccan Islamic Combatant Group (GICM)**
   founded in the 1990s as an offshoot of the Moroccan organization Shabiba Islamiya (Islamic Youth)
   **country or region of operation:** Afghanistan, Belgium, Denmark, Egypt, France, Morocco, Spain, Turkey, UK
   **primary goals:** creation of an Islamic state in Morocco
**Mojahedin-e Khalq Organization (MEK)**
   founded in the 1960s; led by Maryam and Masud Rajavi
   **country or region of operation:** Iran, Iraq
   **primary goals:** establishment of a secular government in Iran
**National Liberation Army (ELN)**
   founded in 1965; led by Nicolas Rodríguez Bautista
   **country or region of operation:** Colombia
   **primary goals:** replacement of the ruling Colombian government with a Marxist state
**Palestine Liberation Front (PLF)**
   founded in the mid-1970s as splinter group from PFLP–GC
   **country or region of operation:** Israel, Iraq
   **primary goals:** elimination of Israel, establishment of a Palestinian state
**Palestinian Islamic Jihad (PIJ)**
   founded in the 1970s; most active faction led by Ramadan Shallah
   **country or region of operation:** primarily Israel, West Bank, Gaza Strip, Lebanon, and Syria
   **primary goals:** elimination of Israel, establishment of an Islamic Palestinian state
**Popular Front for the Liberation of Palestine (PFLP)**
   founded in 1967 by George Habash; led by Ahmed Sadat (imprisoned by Israel since 2006)
   **country or region of operation:** Syria, Lebanon, Israel, West Bank, Gaza Strip
   **primary goals:** revitalization of the PLO, opposition to peace negotiations with Israel
**Popular Front for the Liberation of Palestine–General Command (PFLP–GC)**
   founded in 1968 as splinter group from PFLP; led by Ahmad Jibril
   **country or region of operation:** Syria, Lebanon, Israel, West Bank, Gaza Strip
   **primary goals:** opposition to the PLO and to peace negotiations with Israel
**al-Qaeda (AQ)**
   founded in the late 1980s; established and led until his death in 2011 by Osama bin Laden
   **country or region of operation:** worldwide
   **primary goals:** establishment of worldwide Islamic rule, overthrow of non-Islamic governments, expulsion of
   Western influences from Muslim states, killing of US citizens
**al-Qaeda Organization in the Arabian Peninsula (AQAP)** (formerly al-Qaeda in Yemen)
   founded in 2009; led by Nasir al-Wahishi
   **country or region of operation:** Yemen and Saudi Arabia
   **primary goals:** establishment of an Islamic state on the Arabian Peninsula
**al-Qaeda Organization in the Islamic Maghreb** (formerly Salafist Group for Call and Combat, GSPC)
   founded in 1996 as a splinter of the Armed Islamic Group; led by Abou Mossaab Abdelouadoud
   **country or region of operation:** primarily Algeria, with significant activity elsewhere in North Africa and in Europe
   **primary goals:** replacement of the Algerian government with an Islamic state
**Real IRA (RIRA)** (True IRA)
   founded in 1998 as a splinter group of the Irish Republican Army (IRA)
   **country or region of operation:** Northern Ireland; also elsewhere in Great Britain and in Ireland
   **primary goals:** removal of British forces from Northern Ireland, unification of Ireland

## International Terrorist Organizations (continued)

**Revolutionary Armed Forces of Colombia (FARC)**
    founded in 1964 as the military branch of the Colombian Communist Party; governed by a group led by Timochenko and including six others
    **country or region of operation:** Colombia; also some operations in Venezuela, Ecuador, and Panama
    **primary goals:** replacement of the ruling Colombian government with a Marxist state

**Revolutionary Organization 17 November (17N)**
    founded in 1975; allegedly led by Alexandros Giotopoulos (imprisoned in Greece since 2002)
    **country or region of operation:** Greece, primarily Athens
    **primary goals:** elimination of US military bases in Greece, removal of Turkish forces from Cyprus, opposition to capitalism and NATO/EU membership

**Revolutionary People's Liberation Party/Front (DHKP/C)** (Devrimci Sol, Revolutionary Left, Dev Sol)
    founded in 1978 as a splinter group from Turkish People's Liberation Party/Front
    **country or region of operation:** Turkey, primarily Istanbul
    **primary goals:** promotion of Marxism, opposition to US and NATO

**Revolutionary Struggle (RS, Epanastatikos Aghonas, EA)**
    founded in 2003; leadership unknown
    **country or region of operation:** Greece
    **primary goals:** opposition to Greece's political and economic climate

**al-Shabaab**
    founded in 2006 by fighters from the recently ousted Islamic Courts Union
    **country or region of operation:** Somalia
    **primary goals:** ejection of foreign troops from Somalia, reestablishment of an Islamic government in the country

**Shining Path (Sendero Luminoso, SL)**
    founded in the late 1960s by Abimael Guzman; led by Macario Ala
    **country or region of operation:** Peru, primarily rural areas
    **primary goals:** replacement of the Peruvian government with a communist state

**Tanzim Qaidat al-Jihad fi Bilad al-Rafidayn (QJBR, AQI, al-Qaeda in Iraq)** (formerly Jamaat al-Tawhid waal-Jihad, JTJ, al-Zarqawi Network)
    founded in April 2004 by Abu Musab al-Zarqawi shortly after the commencement of Operation Iraqi Freedom (OIF); adopted current name in October 2004 after merging with Osama bin Laden's al-Qaeda
    **country or region of operation:** Iraq
    **primary goals:** expulsion of OIF coalition from Iraq, establishment of Islamic state in Iraq

**Tehrik-e Taliban Pakistan (TTP)**
    founded in 2007; led by Hakimullah Mehsud
    **country or region of operation:** Pakistan
    **primary goals:** overthrow of the Pakistani government

**United Self-Defense Forces of Colombia (Autodefensas Unidas de Colombia, AUC)**
    founded in 1997 as an umbrella organization of paramilitary groups
    **country or region of operation:** Colombia
    **primary goals:** opposition to and defense against leftist guerrilla groups

# Military Affairs

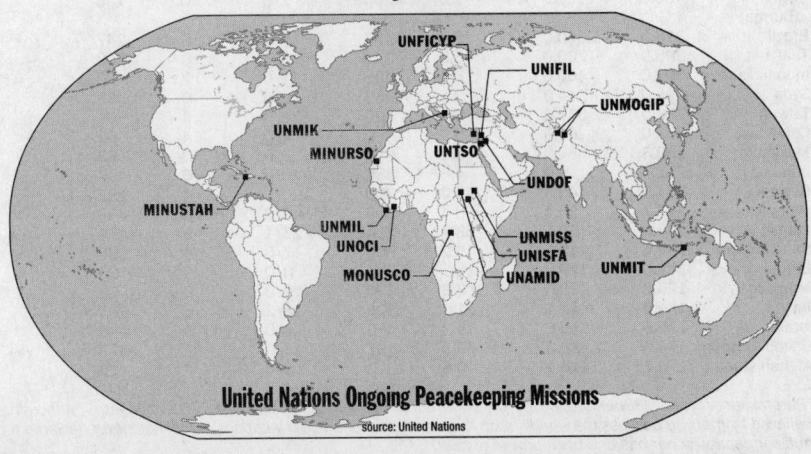

## United Nations Ongoing Peacekeeping Missions

source: United Nations

# United Nations Ongoing Peacekeeping Missions (continued)

**MINURSO** United Nations Mission for the Referendum in Western Sahara—since April 1991 (233)

**MINUSTAH** United Nations Stabilization Mission in Haiti—since June 2004 (11,109)

**MONUSCO** United Nations Organization Stabilization Mission in the Democratic Republic of the Congo—since June 2010 (19,060)

**UNAMID** African Union–United Nations Hybrid Operation in Darfur—since July 2007 (23,257)

**UNDOF** United Nations Disengagement Observer Force (in the Golan Heights)—since May 1974 (1,043)

**UNFICYP** United Nations Peacekeeping Force in Cyprus—since March 1964 (926)

**UNIFIL** United Nations Interim Force in Lebanon—since March 1978 (12,001)

**UNISFA** United Nations Interim Security Force for Abyei—since June 2011 (3,800)

**UNMIK** United Nations Interim Administration Mission in Kosovo—since June 1999 (16)

**UNMIL** United Nations Mission in Liberia—since September 2003 (9,185)

**UNMISS** United Nations Mission in the Republic of South Sudan—since July 2011 (5,484)

**UNMIT** United Nations Integrated Mission in Timor-Leste—since August 2006 (1,259)

**UNMOGIP** United Nations Military Observer Group in India and Pakistan—since January 1949 (38)

**UNOCI** United Nations Operation in Côte d'Ivoire—since April 2004 (10,988)

**UNTSO** United Nations Truce Supervision Organization (in the Middle East)—since May 1948 (149)

*Parenthetical figures indicate military personnel as of 29 Feb 2012. Civilian forces are not included in this table.*

# Nations with Largest Armed Forces

*The top 30 countries in terms of active-personnel military strength are included. Personnel numbers are in thousands ('000) and reflect November 2011 data; spending totals are from 2011 budgets except where noted. Source: The International Institute for Strategic Studies, The Military Balance 2012.*

| COUNTRY | MILITARY PERSONNEL | | DEFENSE SPENDING (US$ BILLIONS) | BATTLE TANKS | MAJOR WARSHIPS/ CARRIERS | SUB-MARINES | COMBAT AIRCRAFT | STRATEGIC NUCLEAR WEAPONS |
|---|---|---|---|---|---|---|---|---|
| | ACTIVE | RESERVES | | | | | | |
| China | 2,285.0 | 510.0 | 89.8 | 8,324+ | 78/0 | 71 | 2,004 | yes |
| United States | 1,569.4 | 865.4 | 739.3 | 6,302 | 122/11 | 71 | 3,591 | yes |
| India | 1,325.0 | 1,155.0 | 31.9 | 3,233+ | 21/1 | 15 | 829 | yes |
| D.P.R. Korea | 1,190.0 | 5,700.0[1] | 4.4[2] | 4,060+ | 3/0 | 72 | 603 | yes |
| Russia | 956.0 | 20,000.0 | 68.0 | 3,319+ | 32/1 | 65 | 1,909 | yes |
| Rep. of Korea | 655.0 | 4,500.0 | 28.5 | 2,514 | 28/0 | 23 | 398 | |
| Pakistan | 642.0 | 304.0[1] | 5.2 | 2,411+ | 10/0 | 8 | 460 | yes |
| Iran | 523.0 | 350.0 | 12.0 | 1,743+ | 0/0 | 23 | 339 | |
| Turkey | 510.6 | 378.7 | 10.3 | 4,503 | 18/0 | 14 | 338+ | |
| Vietnam | 482.0 | 5,000.0 | 2.7 | 1,935 | 2/0 | 2 | 235 | |
| Egypt | 438.5 | 479.0 | 4.2 | 2,412 | 8/0 | 4 | 589 | |
| Myanmar (Burma) | 406.0 | 107.3[1] | 2.0 | 265 | 1/0 | 0 | 136 | |
| Brazil | 318.5 | 1,340.0 | 36.6 | 437 | 15/1 | 5 | 247 | |
| Thailand | 305.9 | 200.0 | 5.5 | 748 | 10/1 | 0 | 202 | |
| Indonesia | 302.0 | 400.0 | 5.4 | 405 | 11/0 | 2 | 69 | |
| Syria | 295.0 | 314.0 | 2.1 | 4,950 | 0/0 | 0 | 365 | |
| Taiwan | 290.0 | 1,657.0 | 9.9 | 1,420 | 26/0 | 4 | 501 | |
| Colombia | 283.0 | 61.9 | 5.6 | 0 | 4/0 | 4 | 82 | |
| Mexico | 280.3 | 87.3 | 5.2 | 0 | 7/0 | 0 | 83 | |
| Iraq | 271.4 | 0.0 | 4.8 | 336+ | 0/0 | 0 | 3 | |
| Germany | 251.5 | 40.4 | 44.2 | 350 | 20/0 | 4 | 182 | |
| Japan | 247.7 | 56.4 | 58.4 | 806 | 48/2 | 18 | 466 | |
| France | 238.6 | 33.7 | 58.8 | 254 | 25/1 | 9 | 479 | yes |
| Saudi Arabia | 233.5 | 15.5[1] | 46.2 | 565 | 7/0 | 0 | 296 | |
| Eritrea | 201.8 | 120.0 | 0.1[3] | 270 | 0/0 | 0 | 20 | |
| Morocco | 195.8 | 150.0 | 3.3 | 496 | 3/0 | 0 | 72 | |
| Italy | 184.5 | 42.1 | 21.0 | 320 | 18/2 | 6 | 263 | |
| Israel | 176.5 | 565.0 | 15.3 | 480 | 0/0 | 3 | 440 | [4] |
| United Kingdom | 174.0 | 82.3 | 63.7 | 227 | 18/0 | 11 | 377 | yes |
| Afghanistan | 170.7 | 136.1[1] | 0.6 | 0 | 0/0 | 0 | 0 | |

[1]*Paramilitary forces.*    [2]*Spending based on 2009 budget.*    [3]*Spending based on 2010 budget.*    [4]*Although believed by many to possess the world's sixth largest arsenal of nuclear weapons, Israel has never declared a nuclear capability nor has one been proven to exist.*

# United States

## Privacy in Public

*by Massimo Calabresi, TIME*

Walking the streets of New York City in 1949, E.B. White observed that a person could find the "gift of privacy" amid the crowds. More than 60 years later, the US Supreme Court decided that White's paradox may literally be true. On 23 Jan 2012, the court said the FBI violated the Fourth Amendment's guarantee against unreasonable search and seizure when it used global-positioning-system signals to track a suspected drug dealer for four weeks without a valid warrant, even though the cops monitored only where the suspect went on public streets. Thanks to that decision, for the first time in American history there is now a legal right to privacy in public.

How much privacy? That's still in flux. In the GPS-tracking case, the justices couldn't decide how much protection the Constitution gives Americans in public; they could agree only that the FBI had gone too far. But cases are coming up that will define the new privacy more clearly, and state and federal officials are working to fill in the contours.

In a pending case from Texas, the Fifth Circuit Court of Appeals will decide whether the police have the right to search, without a warrant, historical data from cell-phone companies showing the movements of phones' owners. Senator Al Franken of Minnesota has introduced a bill that would limit what wireless carriers can do with GPS data. "People have a fundamental right to control their private information," Franken said. On 22 Feb 2012, the White House unveiled privacy guidelines meant as a blueprint for legislators and companies struggling to agree on how and when Americans can be tracked in public on the Internet.

The idea that we have any privacy in public is new. Over the years, the courts have found that Americans voluntarily gave up their Fourth Amendment protections almost as soon as they left their homes: garbage dropped at the curb was fair game for the cops, and—though you may not have contemplated your phone company's sharing its files—information given openly to businesses was deemed public knowledge too. But now, as cell phones, GPS devices, and Web browsers generate massive amounts of digital information about us and make it available to others, the minute details of what used to be our private lives are collected and stored as never before.

The McKinsey Global Institute estimated that 15 out of 17 sectors of the US economy have more data stored per company than does the Library of Congress, and in the US health care market alone, there is potentially US$300 billion in annual value to be squeezed from those vast stores, McKinsey says. The upshot: much of this information from our daily interactions with retailers, communications companies, and service providers is available not only to private companies that can make money off it but to law enforcement as well.

In the GPS case, the Supreme Court justices found two things to worry about. First, they were concerned about how much information was being collected. The government's ability to track citizens "24 hours a day anyplace you go that's not your home" without a warrant necessarily breached Americans' "expectation of privacy," Justice Elena Kagan said in oral arguments in the GPS case. Four other justices agreed, including the conservative George W. Bush appointee Samuel Alito.

Justice Sonia Sotomayor went further, saying Americans aren't worried only about how much information about them is collected; they are also concerned about who gets access to it, even if they appear to waive their right to keep it private. "I for one doubt that people would accept without complaint the warrantless disclosure to the Government [by an Internet-service provider] of a list of every Web site they had visited in the last week, or month, or year," Sotomayor wrote.

The Justice Department and other law-enforcement officials argue that once cops have probable cause to think a crime is being committed in public, they shouldn't have to get a warrant; in any case, they say, most Americans are happy to give up their privacy in exchange for safety or to save time or money. The law is still largely on the cops' side.

Five Supreme Court justices found in the GPS-tracking case that it was Americans' expectations of privacy that would define what privacy should be: if you and most of your friends are comfortable revealing details of your daily life in public, you'll be setting the legal bar for privacy low. And the fact is, Americans do want some of what they're getting in exchange for technology's intrusion into their private lives. Anyone who's avoided a rush-hour bottleneck thanks to traffic-monitoring software can see the benefit of instant analysis of shared GPS signals. Airport body scanners aside, the post-9/11 era has seen the growing use of technologies like security cameras and facial recognition in public places, with little backlash from citizens concerned about their privacy.

Still, as the Supreme Court suggests, drawing lines is important because the data banks keep swelling, making their contents irresistible to some. In December 2011 a company called Carrier IQ said the FBI had asked for access to data the company collects from software installed on more than 141 million cell phones, including what numbers and text the owners type in and where the phones, and their owners, travel during the day.

On 19 Jan 2012, the FBI's Strategic Information and Operations Center asked tech companies how much it would cost to build software that would search, monitor, and report on individuals using Twitter, Facebook, Myspace, and other Web sites. The FBI is rolling out facial-recognition software to check individuals against criminal databases; the Department of Homeland Security already uses facial recognition at major public events like the Super Bowl.

Once outsiders can use that data to create what Chief Justice John Roberts called a "mosaic" of who you are, the pressure for safeguards may grow. All the technology is delivering to us in public not just the gift of privacy E.B. White wrote about but the right to it as well.

# United States History
## United States Chronology

**1492** Christopher Columbus, sailing under the Spanish flag, arrives in the Americas, 12 October.

**1513** Ponce de León of Spain lands in Florida and gives that region its name.

**1534** France sends Jacques Cartier to find a route to the Far East; he explores along the St. Lawrence River, and France lays claim to part of North America.

**1541** Hernando de Soto of Spain sights the Mississippi River near the location of present-day Memphis.

**1565** St. Augustine, the oldest permanent settlement in the US, is founded by Spaniards.

**1587** A party under John White lands at Roanoke Island (now in North Carolina); when White returns three years later, the entire settlement has disappeared.

**1607** The English make the first permanent settlement in the New World at Jamestown; Virginia becomes the first of the 13 English colonies.

**1619** The first representative assembly in America, the House of Burgesses, meets in Virginia.

**1620** Pilgrims from the ship *Mayflower* found a settlement at Plymouth.

**1649** The Act Concerning Religion passed by Maryland's legislature is the first law of religious toleration in the English colonies.

**1682** The Sieur de La Salle explores the lower Mississippi valley and claims the entire region for France.

**1733** Georgia, the 13th and last of the English colonies in America, is founded.

**1754** The French and Indian War between France and England begins in America.

**1763** The Treaty of Paris ends the French and Indian War; Florida is ceded to Britain.

**1765** The Quartering Act and the Stamp Act anger Americans; nine colonies are represented at the Stamp Act Congress.

**1770** British troops fire on a crowd, killing five people in the so-called Boston Massacre.

**1773** The Boston Tea Party, the first action in a chain leading to war with Britain, takes place.

**1774** The First Continental Congress meets at Philadelphia and protests the five Intolerable Acts.

**1775** The battles of Lexington and Concord and Bunker Hill occur; the Second Continental Congress meets.

**1776** The Declaration of Independence is adopted.

**1778-79** Gen. George Rogers Clark leads a victorious expedition into the Northwest Territory.

**1781** George Washington accepts the surrender of Charles Cornwallis at Yorktown VA; the Articles of Confederation become the government of the US.

**1783** A treaty of peace with Great Britain is signed at Paris, formally ending the Revolutionary War.

**1787** The Northwest Territory is organized by Congress; a convention meets to draft a new constitution.

**1788** The US Constitution is ratified by the necessary nine states to ensure adoption.

**1789** The new US government goes into effect; Washington is inaugurated president; the first Congress meets in New York City.

**1791** The Bill of Rights is added to the Constitution; Vermont is the first new state admitted to the Union.

**1793** Eli Whitney invents the cotton gin, which leads to large-scale cotton growing in the South.

**1800** The national capital is moved from Philadelphia to Washington DC.

**1803** Louisiana is purchased from France; the Supreme Court makes its *Marbury* v. *Madison* decision, establishing judicial review; Congress halts the importation of slaves into the US after 1807.

**1804-06** Meriwether Lewis and William Clark blaze an overland trail to the Pacific and return.

**1807** Robert Fulton's steamboat makes a successful journey from New York City to Albany NY.

**1812-14** The US maintains its independence in a conflict with Britain, the War of 1812.

**1820** The Missouri Compromise settles the problem of slavery in new states for the next 30 years.

**1823** The Monroe Doctrine warns European nations that the US will protect the Americas.

**1825** The Erie Canal, from the Hudson River to the Great Lakes, becomes a great water highway.

**1829** The inauguration of Pres. Andrew Jackson introduces the era of Jacksonian Democracy.

**1843** The first migration begins on the Oregon Trail.

**1845** Texas is annexed and admitted as a state.

**1846** The Oregon boundary dispute is settled with Britain; the Mexican War begins.

**1847** Brigham Young leads a party of Mormons into the Salt Lake valley, Utah.

**1848** The Mexican War ends; the US gains possession of the California and New Mexico regions.

**1849** The gold rush to California begins.

**1850** The Compromise of 1850 admits California as a free state, postponing war between the North and South.

**1853** The Gadsden Purchase adds 117,935 sq km (45,535 sq mi) to what is now the southwestern US.

**1854** The Republican Party is organized in opposition to slavery.

**1857** The Dred Scott decision of the Supreme Court declares that the Missouri Compromise is illegal.

**1860** Abraham Lincoln is elected president; South Carolina secedes from the Union.

**1861** The Confederate States of America is formed; the Civil War begins; telegraph links New York City with San Francisco.

**1862** Gen. Ulysses S. Grant launches a Union attack in the West; the Confederate invasion of Maryland is halted at Antietam; the Homestead Act grants 160 acres to any settler.

**1863** Federal forces win decisive battles at Gettysburg PA, Vicksburg MS, and Chattanooga TN; the Emancipation Proclamation is delivered.

**1864** Gen. William Tecumseh Sherman captures Atlanta and marches across Georgia.

**1865** Gen. Robert E. Lee surrenders to Grant at Appomattox (VA) Court House, ending the Civil War; Lincoln is assassinated.

**1867** Reconstruction acts impose military rule on the South; Alaska is purchased from Russia.

**1869** The first transcontinental railroad is completed as two lines meet at Promontory UT.

**1876** The telephone is invented; the Centennial Exposition in Philadelphia celebrates the 100th birthday of the US.

**1877** The withdrawal of the last federal troops from the South ends the Reconstruction period.

**1879** The first practical electric light is invented by Thomas A. Edison.

**1884-85** The first skyscraper, the Home Insurance Building, is erected in Chicago.

**1886** The American Federation of Labor (AFL) is organized; its first president is Samuel Gompers.

**1887** The Interstate Commerce Act is adopted to control railroads that cross state lines.

**1889–90** The first pan-American conference is held, in Washington DC.

**1890** The Sherman Anti-Trust Act is passed in an effort to curb the growth of monopolies.

**1896** Henry Ford's first car is unveiled.

**1898** The US wins the Spanish-American War and gains the Philippines, Puerto Rico, and Guam.

**1903** The air age begins with the successful airplane flight by the Wright brothers.

**1906** The Federal Food and Drug Act is passed to protect the public from impure food and drugs.

**1913** Federal income tax is authorized by The 16th Amendment.

**1914** The Panama Canal is opened under the control of the US; World War I breaks out in Europe; Pres. Woodrow Wilson appeals for neutrality in the US.

**1915** A German submarine sinks the British ship *Lusitania* with the loss of 124 American lives; a telephone line is established coast-to-coast.

**1917** The US declares war against Germany.

**1918** Pres. Wilson proposes "Fourteen Points" as the basis for peace; Americans fight at Château-Thierry, Belleau Wood, Saint-Mihiel, and Argonne Forest in France; an armistice ends the war.

**1919** The US Senate rejects the League of Nations; prohibition is established by the 18th Amendment.

**1920** The right to vote is given to women by the 19th Amendment.

**1921** National immigration quotas are introduced.

**1921–22** The Washington Conference restricts warship construction among the chief naval powers.

**1924** The army plane *Chicago* makes the first flight around the world.

**1927** Charles A. Lindbergh makes the first nonstop solo flight across the Atlantic.

**1928** The Kellogg-Briand Pact outlaws war.

**1929** The stock market reaches a new high and then crashes; the panic marks the beginning of the Great Depression; millions of workers are unemployed.

**1932** Franklin Delano Roosevelt is elected president.

**1933** The New Deal is launched; the gold standard is suspended; bank deposits are insured; the Tennessee Valley Authority is organized; the 21st Amendment repeals prohibition.

**1934** Congress tightens control over securities, passes the first Reciprocal Trade Agreement Act, and launches the federal housing program.

**1935** The National Labor Relations (Wagner) Act guarantees collective bargaining to labor; the Congress of Industrial Organizations (CIO) is founded; the Social Security Act is passed.

**1936** The Boulder Dam (now Hoover Dam) is completed across the Colorado River.

**1938** The Fair Labor Standards Act provides a federal yardstick for wages and hours of workers.

**1939** Germany invades Poland, beginning World War II.

**1940** The US begins a huge rearmament program; the first peacetime draft takes effect.

**1941** The Japanese attack on Pearl Harbor, Hawaii, brings the US into World War II.

**1942** Americans launch a counteroffensive in the Pacific; the Allies invade North Africa.

**1943** The invasion of Italy is the Allies' first landing on the European continent.

**1944** The Allies launch the greatest sea-to-land assault in history in the invasion of France; the GI Bill of Rights is passed.

**1945** Germany surrenders, 8 May; the US drops atomic bombs on Japan at Hiroshima, 6 August, and Nagasaki, 9 August; Japan surrenders, 2 September; the Cold War begins between the US and the Soviet Union (USSR).

**1946** The Atomic Energy Commission is created.

**1947** The Truman Doctrine, offering aid to counter communism in Greece and Turkey, is declared; the Department of Defense consolidates the army, navy, and air force.

**1948** The European Recovery Program is enacted.

**1949** The Fair Deal program of social reform is announced; the US and its allies force the USSR to lift the Berlin blockade; the North Atlantic Treaty Organization (NATO) is founded.

**1950** The US and several other members of the UN send military forces to the aid of the Republic of Korea; bitter war develops.

**1951** A two-term limit is put on the presidency by ratification of the 22nd Amendment.

**1952** The US and its allies end the occupation of West Germany.

**1953** The Korean War ends; the Department of Health, Education, and Welfare becomes the 10th cabinet post.

**1954** Racial segregation of public schools is declared illegal by the Supreme Court.

**1955** The Jonas Salk poliomyelitis vaccine is proved successful.

**1956** Legislation is passed providing funding for the US Interstate Highway System.

**1957** The Eisenhower Doctrine to strengthen the US position in the Middle East is adopted.

**1958** The first US artificial Earth satellite is launched; the US joins the International Atomic Energy Agency.

**1959** Alaska becomes the 49th state, Hawaii the 50th.

**1960** A US spy plane is downed over the USSR, leading to the capture of Francis Gary Powers.

**1961** The CIA is involved in an unsuccessful invasion of Cuba at the Bay of Pigs; Alan Shepard becomes the first American to make spaceflight.

**1962** The Cuban missile crisis erupts; the Soviets remove missiles from Cuba at the urging of the US.

**1963** The March on Washington for Jobs and Freedom takes place; Pres. John F. Kennedy is assassinated in Dallas TX; a nuclear test-ban treaty is signed.

**1964** The landmark Civil Rights Act is passed.

**1965** US combat forces fight in Vietnam; the Medicare Act is signed; the Department of Housing and Urban Development becomes the 11th cabinet post.

**1966** The Department of Transportation becomes the 12th cabinet post.

**1967** The 25th Amendment to the Constitution provides for presidential succession.

**1968** The assassinations of Martin Luther King, Jr., and Robert F. Kennedy provoke riots.

**1969** US astronauts land on the Moon.

**1970** Four students at Kent State University in Ohio are killed by National Guard soldiers during anti-Vietnam War protests.

**1971** The 26th Amendment to the Constitution gives 18-year-olds the right to vote in all elections.

**1972** Pres. Richard M. Nixon visits China and the USSR.

**1973** The US withdraws its troops from Vietnam; gas prices soar as OPEC raises the price of oil 400%.

**1974** The Watergate Scandal and the threat of impeachment force Nixon to resign.

**1977** The Department of Energy becomes a new cabinet post; a treaty is signed to return the Panama Canal to Panama by the year 2000.

**1978** Pres. Jimmy Carter hosts the Camp David talks between Israel's Menachem Begin and Egypt's Anwar el-Sadat.

**1979** Militants seize 66 American hostages in a takeover of the US embassy in Iran.

**1980** The Department of Health, Education, and Welfare is separated into the Department of Health and Human Services and the Department of Education.

**1981** Sandra Day O'Connor is appointed the first woman Supreme Court justice.

**1983** Pres. Ronald Reagan announces the Star Wars missile-defense program; the US invades Grenada.

**1985** A summit between Reagan and Soviet leader Mikhail Gorbachev is held in Geneva, Switzerland.

**1986** The space shuttle *Challenger* explodes shortly after liftoff; the US bombs targets in Libya.

**1987** The Iran-Contra hearings are held; the stock market collapses; Reagan and Gorbachev sign the Intermediate-Range Nuclear Forces (INF) Treaty.

**1988** The Department of Veterans Affairs is approved as a cabinet post.

**1989** The *Exxon Valdez* supertanker spills 10 million gallons of crude oil off the Alaskan coast; the US invades Panama; the Berlin Wall ceases to divide the two Germanys, signaling the end of the Cold War.

**1990** US troops are sent to Saudi Arabia in response to Iraq's invasion of Kuwait.

**1991** A brief war leads to the Iraqi surrender and withdrawal from Kuwait; the USSR comes apart.

**1992** The North American Free Trade Agreement (NAFTA) is signed by the US, Canada, and Mexico.

**1993** Janet Reno becomes the first woman attorney general; the World Trade Center in New York City is bombed.

**1995** Timothy McVeigh detonates a bomb in a terrorist attack on the Alfred P. Murrah Federal Building in Oklahoma City, killing 168 people.

**1998** Pres. Bill Clinton is impeached for perjury and obstruction of justice; he is acquitted by the Senate the following year.

**2000** The results of the presidential election are challenged by Vice Pres. Al Gore; the US Supreme Court overrules the Florida Supreme Court's order for a statewide manual recount of ballots; George W. Bush wins the presidency.

**2001** On 11 September, two hijacked airplanes demolish the World Trade Center in New York City, another crashes into the Pentagon outside Washington DC, and a fourth crashes in the southern Pennsylvania countryside; Pres. Bush calls for a global "war on terror" and sends US troops into Afghanistan, eventually displacing the Taliban regime, which sheltered Osama bin Laden and his al-Qaeda network, thought to be behind the terror attacks.

**2002** Republicans take control of both houses of Congress, holding both the legislative and executive branches of government for the first time since 1952.

**2003** The US launches a war to depose the Saddam Hussein regime in Iraq and takes control of the country after just weeks of fighting; Congress passes a US$350 billion tax cut; the Department of Homeland Security is created as a cabinet post.

**2004** Scandal erupts with the publication of photos of prisoner abuse at Abu Ghraib prison in Iraq; the independent 9/11 Commission finds no credible evidence of a connection between Iraq and al-Qaeda's attacks of 11 Sep 2001; Bush is reelected president.

**2005** Hurricane Katrina strikes the Gulf Coast, destroying much of New Orleans and killing more than 1,500 people.

**2006** Conservative lawyer John G. Roberts, Jr., is appointed to the Supreme Court as chief justice; Democrats gain control of both houses of Congress.

**2007** In an effort to quell a persistent insurrection against the US-backed government of Iraq, Pres. Bush orders a "surge" of 20,000 additional US troops.

**2008** A crisis in the subprime mortgage industry, leading to foreclosures and falling home values, together with record-high prices of petroleum, pushes the US economy into recession.

**2009** In a historic ceremony on 20 January, Barack Obama is sworn in as the first African American president of the United States; two of the Big Three automobile manufacturers—Chrysler and General Motors—declare bankruptcy; American troops meet the 30 June deadline to withdraw from Iraqi cities under an agreement that calls for all American forces to leave Iraq by the end of 2011.

**2010** Congress repeals "Don't Ask, Don't Tell," allowing homosexuals to serve openly in the military; the war in Afghanistan becomes the longest in US history; a deep-water oil-drilling platform explodes in US waters in the Gulf of Mexico, causing a leak of as much as 2.5 million gallons of oil into the gulf per day, creating one of the world's worst environmental disasters; Congress passes the Patient Protection and Affordable Care Act, also known as "Obamacare."

**2011** After being sought for more than a decade, Osama bin Laden is discovered living in the Pakistani city of Abbottabad; after a brief firefight, he is shot and killed by US special forces soldiers; the last space shuttle mission concludes on 21 July, ending the 30-year NASA program; the last US combat troops leave Iraq, ending an almost nine-year war.

**2012** Major online protests undermine support for anti-piracy legislation in Congress; Pres. Obama publicly supports same-sex marriage, becoming the first US president to do so; the Supreme Court upholds the constitutionality of Obamacare.

# Important Documents in US History

## Mayflower Compact

*On 21 Nov 1620 (11 November, Old Style), 41 male passengers on the Mayflower signed the following compact prior to their landing at Plymouth (now Massachusetts). The compact resulted from the fear that some members of the company might leave the group and settle on their own. The Mayflower Compact bound the signers into a body politic for the purpose of forming a government and pledged them to abide by any laws and regulations that would later by established. The document was not a constitution but rather an adaptation of the usual church covenant to a civil situation. It became the foundation of Plymouth's government.*

In the name of God, Amen.

We whose names are underwritten, the loyal subjects of our dread sovereign Lord, King James, by the grace of God, of Great Britain, France and Ireland king, defender of the faith, etc., having undertaken, for the glory of God, and advancement of the Christian faith, and honor of our king and country, a voyage to plant the first colony in the Northern parts of Virginia, do by these presents solemnly and mutually in the presence of God, and one of another, covenant and combine ourselves together into a civil body politic, for our better ordering and preservation and furtherance of the ends aforesaid; and by virtue

hereof to enact, constitute, and frame such just and equal laws, ordinances, acts, constitutions, and offices, from time to time, as shall be thought most meet and convenient for the general good of the colony, unto which we promise all due submission and obedience.

In witness whereof we have hereunder subscribed our names at Cape-Cod the 11 of November, in the year of the reign of our sovereign lord, King James, of England, France, and Ireland the eighteenth, and of Scotland the fifty-fourth. Anno Domine 1620.

## Declaration of Independence

*On 4 Jul 1776 the Continental Congress officially adopted the Declaration of Independence. Two days before, the Congress had "unanimously" voted (with New York abstaining) to be free and independent from Britain. The Declaration of Independence was written largely by Thomas Jefferson. After modifications by the Congress, the document was prepared and voted upon. New York delegates voted to accept it on 15 July, and on 19 July the Congress ordered the document to be engrossed as "The Unanimous Declaration of the Thirteen United States of America." It was accordingly put on parchment, and members of the Congress present on 2 August affixed their signatures to this parchment copy on that day, and others later. The last signer was Thomas McKean of Delaware, whose name was not placed on the document before 1777.*

The Unanimous Declaration of the Thirteen United States of America

When in the Course of human events, it becomes necessary for one people to dissolve the political bands which have connected them with another, and to assume among the powers of the earth, the separate and equal station to which the Laws of Nature and of Nature's God entitle them, a decent respect to the opinions of mankind requires that they should declare the causes which impel them to the separation.—We hold these truths to be self-evident, that all men are created equal, that they are endowed by their Creator with certain unalienable Rights, that among these are Life, Liberty and the pursuit of Happiness.—That to secure these rights, Governments are instituted among Men, deriving their just powers from the consent of the governed,—That whenever any Form of Government becomes destructive of these ends, it is the Right of the People to alter or to abolish it, and to institute new Government, laying its foundation on such principles and organizing its powers in such form, as to them shall seem most likely to effect their Safety and Happiness.

Prudence, indeed, will dictate that Governments long established should not be changed for light and transient causes; and accordingly all experience hath shown, that mankind are more disposed to suffer, while evils are sufferable, than to right themselves by abolishing the forms to which they are accustomed. But when a long train of abuses and usurpations, pursuing invariably the same Object evinces a design to reduce them under absolute Despotism, it is their right, it is their duty, to throw off such Government, and to provide new Guards for their future security.— Such has been the patient sufferance of these Colonies; and such is now the necessity which constrains them to alter their former Systems of Government. The history of the present King of Great Britain is a history of repeated injuries and usurpations, all having in direct object the establishment of an absolute Tyranny over these States.

To prove this, let Facts be submitted to a candid world.—He has refused his Assent to Laws, the most

wholesome and necessary for the public good.—He has forbidden his Governors to pass Laws of immediate and pressing importance, unless suspended in their operation till his Assent should be obtained; and when so suspended, he has utterly neglected to attend to them.—He has refused to pass other Laws for the accommodation of large districts of people, unless those people would relinquish the right of Representation in the Legislature, a right inestimable to them and formidable to tyrants only.—He has called together legislative bodies at places unusual, uncomfortable, and distant from the depository of their public Records, for the sole purpose of fatiguing them into compliance with his measures.—He has dissolved Representative Houses repeatedly, for opposing with manly firmness his invasions on the rights of the people.—He has refused for a long time, after such dissolutions, to cause others to be elected; whereby the Legislative powers, incapable of Annihilation, have returned to the People at large for their exercise; the State remaining in the mean time exposed to all the dangers of invasion from without, and convulsions within.—He has endeavoured to prevent the population of these States; for that purpose obstructing the Laws for Naturalization of Foreigners; refusing to pass others to encourage their migration hither, and raising the conditions of new Appropriations of Lands.—He has obstructed the Administration of Justice, by refusing his Assent to Laws for establishing Judiciary powers.—He has made judges dependent on his Will alone, for the tenure of their offices, and the amount and payment of their salaries.—He has erected a multitude of New Offices, and sent hither swarms of Officers to harrass our people, and eat out their substance.—He has kept among us, in times of peace, Standing Armies, without the Consent of our legislatures.—He has affected to render the Military independent of and superior to the Civil power.—He has combined with others to subject us to a jurisdiction foreign to our constitution, and unacknowledged by our laws; giving his Assent to their Acts of pretended Legislation:—For quartering large bodies of armed troops among us:—For protecting them, by a mock Trial, from punishment for any Murders which they should commit on the Inhabitants of these States:—For cutting off our Trade with all parts of the world:—For imposing Taxes on us without our Consent:—For depriving us in many cases, of the benefits of Trial by Jury:—For transporting us beyond Seas to be tried for pretended offences:—For abolishing the free System of English Laws in a neighbouring Province, establishing therein an Arbitrary government, and enlarging its Boundaries so as to render it at once an example and fit instrument for introducing the same absolute rule into these Colonies:—For taking away our Charters, abolishing our most valuable Laws, and altering fundamentally the Forms of our Governments:—For suspending our own Legislatures, and declaring themselves invested with power to legislate for us in all cases whatsoever.—He has abdicated Government here, by declaring us out of his Protection and waging War against us.—He has plundered our seas, ravaged our Coasts, burnt our towns, and destroyed the lives of our people.—He is at this time transporting large Armies of foreign Mercenaries to compleat the works of death, desolation and tyranny, already begun with circumstances of Cruelty & perfidy scarcely paralleled in the most barbarous ages, and totally unworthy the Head of a civilized nation.—He has constrained our fellow Citizens taken Captive on the high Seas to bear Arms against their Country, to become the executioners of their friends and Brethren, or to fall themselves by their Hands.—He has excited domestic insurrections amongst us, and has endeavoured to bring on the inhabitants of our frontiers, the merciless Indian Savages, whose known rule of warfare, is an undistinguished destruction of all ages, sexes and conditions. In every stage of these Oppressions We have Petitioned for Redress in the most humble terms: Our repeated Petitions have been answered only by repeated injury. A Prince, whose character is thus marked by every act which may define a Tyrant, is unfit to be the ruler of a free people. Nor have We been wanting in attentions to our Brittish brethren. We have warned them from time to time of attempts by their legislature to extend an unwarrantable jurisdiction over us. We have reminded them of the circumstances of our emigration and settlement here. We have appealed to their native justice and magnanimity, and we have conjured them by the ties of our common kindred to disavow these usurpations, which, would inevitably interrupt our connections and correspondence. They too have been deaf to the voice of justice and of consanguinity. We must, therefore, acquiesce in the necessity, which denounces our Separation, and hold them, as we hold the rest of mankind. Enemies in War, in Peace Friends.—

We, therefore, the Representatives of the United States of America, in General Congress, Assembled, appealing to the Supreme Judge of the world for the rectitude of our intentions, do, in the Name, and by Authority of the good People of these Colonies, solemnly publish and declare, That these United Colonies are, and of Right ought to be Free and Independent States; that they are Absolved from all Allegiance to the British Crown, and that all political connection between them and the State of Great Britain, is and ought to be totally dissolved; and that as Free and Independent States, they have full Power to levy War, conclude Peace, contract Alliances, establish Commerce, and to do all other Acts and Things which Independent States may of right do.—And for the support of this Declaration, with a firm reliance on the protection of Divine Providence, we mutually pledge to each other our Lives, our Fortunes and our sacred Honor.

## Signers of the Declaration of Independence

**Connecticut**
Samuel Huntington
Roger Sherman
William Williams
Oliver Wolcott

**Delaware**
Thomas McKean
George Read
Caesar Rodney

**Georgia**
Button Gwinnett
Lyman Hall
George Walton

**Maryland**
Charles Carroll
Samuel Chase
William Paca
Thomas Stone

**Massachusetts**
John Adams
Samuel Adams
Elbridge Gerry
John Hancock
Robert Treat Paine

**New Hampshire**
Josiah Bartlett
Matthew Thornton
William Whipple

**New Jersey**
Abraham Clark
John Hart
Francis Hopkinson
Richard Stockton
John Witherspoon

**New York**
William Floyd
Francis Lewis
Philip Livingston
Lewis Morris

**North Carolina**
Joseph Hewes
William Hooper
John Penn

**Pennsylvania**
George Clymer
Benjamin Franklin
Robert Morris
John Morton
George Ross
Benjamin Rush
James Smith
George Taylor
James Wilson

**Rhode Island**
William Ellery
Stephen Hopkins

**South Carolina**
Thomas Heyward, Jr.
Thomas Lynch, Jr.
Arthur Middleton
Edward Rutledge

**Virginia**
Carter Braxton
Thomas Jefferson
Benjamin Harrison
Francis Lightfoot Lee
Richard Henry Lee
Thomas Nelson, Jr.
George Wythe

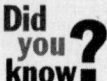

**Did you know?** The Young Men's Christian Association was founded in 1844 in London and became known throughout the world as the YMCA. In 2010, the United States branch officially changed its name to "the Y," adopting the even briefer nickname that had evolved for the association over the decades.

# The Constitution of the United States

*The Constitution was written during the summer of 1787 in Philadelphia by 55 delegates to a Constitutional Convention that was called ostensibly to amend the Articles of Confederation. It was submitted for ratification to the 13 states on 28 Sep 1787. In June 1788, after the Constitution had been ratified by nine states (as required by Article VII), Congress set 4 Mar 1789 as the date for the new government to commence proceedings.*

## Preamble

We the People of the United States, in Order to form a more perfect Union, establish Justice, insure domestic Tranquility, provide for common defence, promote the general Welfare, and secure the Blessings of Liberty to ourselves and our Posterity, do ordain and establish this Constitution for the United States of America.

## Article I

### Section 1—

All legislative Powers herein granted shall be vested in a Congress of the United States, which shall consist of a Senate and House of Representatives.

### Section 2—

The House of Representatives shall be composed of Members chosen every second Year by the People of the several States, and the Electors in each State shall have the Qualifications requisite for Electors of the most numerous Branch of the State Legislature.

No Person shall be a Representative who shall not have attained to the Age of twenty five Years, and been seven Years a Citizen of the United States, and who shall not, when elected, be an Inhabitant of that State in which he shall be chosen.

Representatives and direct Taxes shall be apportioned among the several States which may be included within this Union, according to their respective Numbers, which shall be determined by adding to the whole Number of free Persons, including those bound to Service for a Term of Years, and excluding Indians not taxed, three fifths of all other Persons. The actual Enumeration shall be made within three Years after the first Meeting of the Congress of the United States, and within every subsequent Term of ten Years, in such Manner as they shall by Law direct. The Number of Representatives shall not exceed one for every thirty Thousand, but each State shall have at Least one Representative; and until such enumeration shall be made, the State of New Hampshire shall be entitled to chuse three, Massachusetts eight, Rhode-Island and Providence Plantations one, Connecticut five, New-York six, New Jersey four, Pennsylvania eight, Delaware one, Maryland six, Virginia ten, North Carolina five, South Carolina five, and Georgia three.

When vacancies happen in the Representation from any State, the Executive Authority thereof shall issue Writs of Election to fill such Vacancies.

The House of Representatives shall chuse their speaker and other Officers; and shall have the sole Power of Impeachment.

### Section 3—

The Senate of the United States shall be composed of two Senators from each State, chosen by the Legislature thereof for six Years; and each Senator shall have one Vote.

Immediately after they shall be assembled in Consequence of the first Election, they shall be divided as equally as may be into three Classes. The Seats of the Senators of the first Class shall be vacated at the Expiration of the second Year, of the second Class at the Expiration of the fourth Year, and of the third Class at the Expiration of the sixth Year, so that one third may be chosen every second Year; and if Vacancies happen by Resignation, or otherwise, during the Recess of the Legislature of any State, the Executive thereof may make temporary Appointments until the next Meeting of the Legislature, which shall then fill such Vacancies.

No Person shall be a Senator who shall not have attained to the Age of thirty Years, and been nine Years a Citizen of the United States, and who shall not, when elected, be an Inhabitant of that State for which he shall be chosen.

The Vice President of the United States shall be President of the Senate, but shall have no Vote, unless they be equally divided.

The Senate shall chuse their other Officers, and also a President pro tempore, in the Absence of the Vice President, or when he shall exercise the Office of President of the United States.

The Senate shall have the sole Power to try all Impeachments. When sitting for that Purpose, they shall be on Oath or Affirmation. When the President of the United States is tried, the Chief Justice shall preside: And no Person shall be convicted without the concurrence of two thirds of the Members present. Judgment in Cases of Impeachment shaLl not extend further than to removal from Office, and disqualification to hold and enjoy any Office of honor, Trust or Profit under the United States: but the Party convicted shall nevertheless be liable and subject to Indictment, Trial, Judgment and Punishment, according to law.

### Section 4—

The Times, Places and Manner of holding Elections for Senators and Representatives, shall be prescribed in each State by the Legislature thereof; but the Congress may at any time by Law make or alter such Regulations, except as to the Places of chusing Senators.

The Congress shall assemble at least once in every Year, and such Meeting shall be on the first Monday in December, unless they shall by Law appoint a different Day.

### Section 5—

Each House shall be the Judge of the Elections, Returns and Qualifications of its own Members, and a Majority of each shall constitute a Quorum to do business; but a smaller Number may adjourn from day to day, and may be authorized to compel the Attendance of absent Members, in such Manner, and under such Penalties as each House may provide.

Each House may determine the Rules of its Proceedings, punish its Members for disorderly Behaviour, and, with the Concurrence of two thirds, expel a Member.

Each House shall keep a journal of its Proceedings, and from time to time publish the same, excepting such Parts as may in their Judgment require Secrecy; and the yeas and Nays of the Members of either House on any question shall, at the Desire of one fifth of those Present, be entered on the journal.

Neither House, during the Session of Congress, shall, without the Consent of the other, adjourn for more than three days, nor to any other place than that in which the two Houses shall be sitting.

## Section 6—

The Senators and Representatives shall receive a Compensation for their Services, to be ascertained by Law, and paid out of the Treasury of the United States. They shall in all Cases, except Treason, Felony and Breach of the Peace, be privileged from Arrest during their Attendance at the Session of their respective Houses, and in going to and returning from the same; and for any Speech or Debate in either House, they shall not be questioned in any other Place.

No Senator or Representative shall, during the Time for which he was elected, be appointed to any civil Office under the Authority of the United States, which shall have been created, or the Emoluments whereof shall have been encreased during such time; and no Person holding any Office under the United States, shall be a Member of either House during his Continuance in Office.

## Section 7—

All Bills for raising Revenue shall originate in the House of Representatives; but the Senate may propose or concur with Amendments as on other Bills.

Every Bill which shall have passed the House of Representatives and the Senate, shall, before it become a Law, be presented to the President of the United States; If he approve he shall sign it, but if not he shall return it, with his Objections to that House in which it shall have originated, who shall enter the Objections at large on their Journal, and proceed to reconsider it. If after such Reconsideration two thirds of that House shall agree to pass the Bill, it shall be sent, together with the Objections, to the other House, by which it shall likewise be reconsidered, and if approved by two thirds of that House, it shall become a Law. But in all such Cases the Votes of both Houses shall be determined by yeas and Nays, and the Names of the Persons voting for and against the Bill shall be entered on the Journal of each House respectively. If any Bill shall not be returned by the President within ten Days (Sundays excepted) after it shall have been presented to him, the Same shall be a Law, in like Manner as if he had signed it, unless the Congress by their Adjournment prevent its Return, in which Case it shall not be a Law.

Every Order, Resolution, or Vote to which the Concurrence of the Senate and House of Representatives may be necessary (except on a question of Adjournment) shall be presented to the President of the United States; and before the Same shall take Effect, shall be approved by him, or being disapproved by him, shall be repassed by two thirds of the Senate and House of Representatives, according to the Rules and Limitations prescribed in the Case of a Bill.

## Section 8—

The Congress shall have Power To lay and collect Taxes, Duties, Imposts and Excises, to pay the Debts and provide for the common Defence and general Welfare of the United States; but all Duties, Imposts and Excises shall be uniform throughout the United States;

To borrow Money on the credit of the United States;

To regulate Commerce with foreign Nations, and among the several States, and with the Indian Tribes;

To establish an uniform Rule of Naturalization, and uniform Laws on the subject of Bankruptcies throughout the United States;

To coin Money, regulate the Value thereof, and of foreign Coin, and fix the Standard of Weights and Measures;

To provide for the Punishment of counterfeiting the Securities and current Coin of the United States;

To establish Post Offices and post Roads;

To promote the Progress of Science and useful Arts, by securing for limited Times to Authors and Inventors the exclusive Right to their respective Writings and Discoveries;

To constitute Tribunals inferior to the supreme Court;

To define and punish Piracies and Felonies committed on the high Seas, and Offences against the Law of Nations;

To declare War, grant Letters of Marque and Reprisal, and make rules concerning Captures on Land and Water;

To raise and support Armies, but no Appropriation of Money to that Use shall be for a longer Term than two Years;

To provide and maintain a Navy;

To make Rules for the Government and Regulation of the land and naval Forces;

To provide for calling forth the Militia to execute the Laws of the Union, suppress Insurrections and repel Invasions;

To provide for organizing, arming, and disciplining, the Militia, and for governing such Part of them as may be employed in the Service of the United States, reserving to the States respectively, the Appointment of the Officers, and the Authority of training the Militia according to the discipline prescribed by Congress;

To exercise exclusive Legislation in all Cases whatsoever, over such District (not exceeding ten Miles square), as may, by Cession of particular States, and the Acceptance of Congress, become the Seat of the Government of the United States, and to exercise like Authority over all Places purchased by the Consent of the Legislature of the State in which the Same shall be for the Erection of Forts, Magazines, Arsenals, dock-Yards, and other needful Buildings; — And

To make all Laws which shall be necessary and proper for carying into Execution the foregoing Powers, and all other Powers vested by this Constitution in the Government of the United States, or in any Department or Officer thereof.

## Section 9—

The Migration or Importation of such Persons as any of the States now existing shall think proper to admit, shall not be prohibited by the Congress prior to the Year one thousand eight hundred and eight, but a Tax or duty may be imposed on such Importation, not exceeding ten dollars for each Person.

The Privilege of the Writ of Habeas Corpus shall not be suspended, unless when in Cases of Rebellion or Invasion the public Safety may require it.

No Bill of Attainder or ex post facto Law shall be passed.

No Capitation, or other direct, Tax shall be laid, unless in Proportion to the Census or Enumeration herein before directed to be taken.

No Tax or Duty shall be laid on Articles exported from any State.

No Preference shall be given by any Regulation of Commerce or Revenue to the Ports of one State over those of another; nor shall Vessels bound to, or from, one State, be obliged to enter, clear or pay Duties in another.

No money shall be drawn from the Treasury, but in Consequence of Appropriations made by Law; and a regular Statement and Account of the Receipts and Expenditures of all public Money shall be published from time to time.

No Title of Nobility shall be granted by the United States: And no Person holding any Office of Profit or Trust under them, shall, without the Consent of the Congress, accept of any present, Emolument, Office, or Title, of any kind whatever, from any King, Prince, or foreign State.

## Section 10—

No State shall enter into any Treaty, Alliance, or Confederation; grant Letters of Marque and Reprisal; coin Money; emit Bills of Credit; make any Thing but gold and silver Coin a Tender in Payment of Debts; pass any Bill of Attainder, ex post facto Law, or Law impairing the Obligation of Contracts, or grant any Title of Nobility.

No State shall, without the Consent of the Congress, lay any Imposts or Duties on Imports or Exports, except what may be absolutely necessary for executing it's inspection Laws: and the net Produce of all Duties and Imposts, laid by any State on Imports or Exports, shall be for the Use of the Treasury of the United States; and all such Laws shall be subject to the Revision and Controul of the Congress.

No State shall, without the Consent of Congress, lay any Duty of Tonnage, keep Troops, or Ships of War in time of Peace, enter into any Agreement or Compact with another State, or with a foreign Power, or engage in War, unless actually invaded, or in such imminent Danger as will not admit of delay.

## Article II
### Section 1—

The executive Power shall be vested in a President of the United States of America. He shall hold his Office during the Term of four Years, and, together with the Vice President, chosen for the same Term, be elected, as follows

Each State shall appoint, in such Manner as the Legislature thereof may direct, a Number of Electors, equal to the whole Number of Senators and Representatives to which the State may be entitled in the Congress: but no Senator or Representative, or Person holding an Office of Trust or Profit under the United States, shall be appointed an Elector.

The Electors shall meet in their respective States, and vote by Ballot for two Persons, of whom one at least shall not be an Inhabitant of the same State with themselves. And they shall make a List of all the Persons voted for, and of the Number of Votes for each; which List they shall sign and certify, and transmit sealed to the Seat of the Government of the United States, directed to the President of the Senate. The President of the Senate shall, in the Presence of the Senate and House of Representatives, open all the Certificates, and the Votes shall then be counted. The Person having the greatest Number of Votes shall be the President, if such Number be a Majority of the whole Number of Electors appointed; and if there be more than one who have such Majority, and have an equal Number of Votes, then the House of Representatives shall immediately chuse by Ballot one of them for President: and if no Person have a Majority, then from the five highest on the List the said House shall in like Manner chuse the President. But in chusing the President, the Votes shall be taken by States, the Representation from each State having one Vote; A quorum for this Purpose shall consist of a Member or Members from two thirds of the States, and a Majority of all the States shall be necessary to a Choice. In every Case, after the Choice of the President, the Person having the greatest Number of Votes of the Electors shall be the Vice President. But if there should remain two or more who have equal Votes, the Senate shall chuse from them by Ballot the Vice President.

The Congress may determine the Time of chusing the Electors, and the Day on which they shall give their Votes; which Day shall be the same throughout the United States.

No Person except a natural born Citizen, or a Citizen of the United States, at the time of the Adoption of this Constitution, shall be eligible to the Office of President; neither shall any Person be eligible to that Office who shall not have attained to the Age of thirty five Years, and been fourteen Years a Resident within the United States.

In Case of the Removal of the President from Office, or of his Death, Resignation, or Inability to discharge the Powers and Duties of the said Office, the Same shall devolve on the Vice President, and the Congress may by Law provide for the Case of Removal, Death, Resignation or Inability, both of the President and Vice President, declaring what Officer shall then act as President, and such Officer shall act accordingly, until the Disability be removed, or a President shall be elected.

The President shall, at stated Times, receive for his Services, a Compensation, which shall neither be encreased nor diminished during the Period for which he shall have been elected, and he shall not receive within that Period any other Emolument from the United States, or any of them.

Before he enter on the Execution of his Office, he shall take the following Oath or Affirmation: "I do solemnly swear (or affirm) that I will faithfully execute the Office of President of the United States, and will to the best of my Ability, preserve, protect and defend the Constitution of the United States."

### Section 2—

The President shall be Commander in Chief of the Army and Navy of the United States, and of the Militia of the several States, when called into the actual Service of the United States; he may require the Opinion, in writing, of the principal Officer in each of the executive Departments, upon any Subject relating to the Duties of their respective Offices, and he shall have Power to grant Reprieves and Pardons for Offences against the United States, except in Cases of Impeachment.

He shall have Power, by and with the Advice and Consent of the Senate, to make Treaties, provided two thirds of the Senators present concur; and he shall nominate, and by and with the Advice and Consent of the Senate, shall appoint Ambassadors, other public Ministers and Consuls, Judges of the supreme Court, and all other Officers of the United States, whose Appointments are not herein otherwise provided for, and which shall be established by Law: but the Congress may by Law vest the Appointment of such inferior Officers, as they think proper, in the President alone, in the Courts of Law, or in the Heads of Departments.

The President shall have Power to fill up all Vacancies that may happen during the Recess of the Senate, by granting Commissions which shall expire at the End of their next Session.

### Section 3—

He shall from time to time give to the Congress Information of the State of the Union, and recommend to their Consideration such Measures as he shall judge necessary and expedient; he may, on extraordinary Occasions, convene both Houses, or either of them, and in Case of Disagreement between them, with Respect to the Time of Adjournment, he may adjourn them to such Time as he shall think proper; he shall receive Ambassadors and other public Ministers; he shall take Care that the Laws be faithfully executed, and shall Commission all the Officers of the United States.

### Section 4—

The President, Vice President and all civil Officers of the United States, shall be removed from Office on Impeachment for, and Conviction of, Treason, Bribery, or other High Crimes and Misdemeanors.

### Article III

### Section 1—

The judicial Power of the United States, shall be vested in one supreme Court, and in such inferior Courts as the Congress may from time to time ordain and establish. The Judges, both of the supreme and inferior Courts, shall hold their Offices during good Behaviour, and shall, at stated Times, receive for their Services, a Compensation, which shall not be diminished during their Continuance in Office.

### Section 2—

The judicial Power shall extend to all Cases, in Law and Equity, arising under this Constitution, the Laws of the United States, and Treaties made, or which shall be made, under their Authority; — to all Cases affecting Ambassadors, other public Ministers and Consuls; — to all Cases of admiralty and maritime jurisdiction; — to Controversies to which the United States shall be a Party; — to Controversies between two or more States;-between a State and Citizens of another State; — between Citizens of different States; — between Citizens of the same State claiming Lands under Grants of different States, and between a State, or the Citizens thereof, and foreign States, Citizens or Subjects.

In all Cases affecting Ambassadors, other public Ministers and Consuls, and those in which a State shall be Party, the supreme Court shall have original Jurisdiction. In all the other Cases before mentioned, the supreme Court shall have appellate Jurisdiction, both as to Law and Fact, with such Exceptions, and under such Regulations as the Congress shall make.

The Trial of all Crimes, except in Cases of Impeachment, shall be by Jury; and such Trial shall be held in the State where the said Crimes shall have been committed; but when not committed within any State, the Trial shall be at such Place or Places as the Congress may by Law have directed.

### Section 3—

Treason against the United States, shall consist only in levying War against them, or in adhering to their Enemies, giving them Aid and Comfort. No Person shall be convicted of Treason unless on the Testimony of two Witnesses to the same overt Act, or on Confession in open Court.

The Congress shall have Power to declare the Punishment of Treason, but no Attainder of Treason shall work Corruption of Blood, or Forfeiture except during the Life of the Person attainted.

### Article IV

### Section 1—

Full Faith and Credit shall be given in each State to the public Acts, Records, and judicial Proceedings of every other State. And the Congress may by general Laws prescribe the Manner in which such Acts, Records and Proceedings shall be proved, and the Effect thereof.

### Section 2—

The Citizens of each State shall be entitled to all Privileges and Immunities of Citizens in the several States.

A person charged in any State with Treason, Felony, or other Crime, who shall flee from justice, and be found in another State, shall on Demand of the executive Authority of the State from which he fled, be delivered up, to be removed to the State having Jurisdiction of the Crime.

No Person held to Service or Labour in one State, under the Laws thereof, escaping into another, shall in Consequence of any Law or Regulation therein, be discharged from such Service or Labour, but shall be delivered upon on Claim of the Party to whom such Service or Labour may be due.

### Section 3—

New States may be admitted by the Congress into this Union; but no new State shall be formed or erected within the Jurisdiction of any other State; nor any State be formed by the Junction of two or more States, or Parts of States, without the Consent of the Legislatures of the States concerned as well as of the Congress.

The Congress shall have Power to dispose of and make all needful Rules and Regulations respecting the Territory or other Property belonging to the United States; and nothing in this Constitution shall be so construed as to Prejudice any Claims of the United States, or of any particular State.

### Section 4—

The United States shall guarantee to every State in this Union a Republican Form of Government, and shall protect each of them against Invasion; and on Application of the Legislature, or of the Executive (when the Legislature cannot be convened) against domestic Violence.

### Article V

The Congress, whenever two thirds of both Houses shall deem it necessary, shall propose Amendments to this Constitution, or, on the Application of the Legislatures of two thirds of the several States, shall call a Convention for proposing Amendments, which, in either Case, shall be valid to all Intents and Purposes, as Part of this Constitution, when ratified by the Legislatures of three fourths of the several States, or by Conventions in three fourths thereof, as the one or the other Mode of Ratification may be proposed by the Congress; Provided that no Amendment which may be made prior to the Year One thousand eight hundred and eight shall in any Manner affect the first and fourth Clauses in the Ninth Section of the first

Article; and that no State, without its Consent, shall be deprived of its equal Suffrage in the Senate.

### Article VI

All Debts contracted and Engagements entered into, before the Adoption of this Constitution, shall be as valid against the United States under this Constitution, as under the Confederation.

This Constitution, and the Laws of the United States which shall be made in Pursuance thereof; and all Treaties made, or which shall be made, under the Authority of the United States, shall be the supreme Law of the Land; and the Judges in every State shall be bound thereby, any Thing in the Constitution or Laws of any State to the Contrary notwithstanding.

The Senators and Representatives before mentioned, and the Members of the several State Legislatures, and all executive and judicial Officers, both of the United States and of the several States, shall be bound by Oath or Affirmation, to support this Constitution; but no religious Test shall ever be required as a Qualification to any Office or public Trust under the United States.

### Article VII

The Ratification of the Conventions of nine States, shall be sufficient for the Establishment of this Constitution between the States so ratifying the Same.

Done in Convention by the Unanimous Consent of the States present the Seventeenth Day of September in the Year of our Lord one thousand seven hundred and Eighty seven and of the Independence of the United States of America the Twelfth IN WITNESS whereof We have hereunto subscribed our Names,

G⁰ Washington—
*Presidᵗ. and deputy from Virginia*

*New Hampshire*
John Langdon
Nicholas Gilman

*Massachusetts*
Nathaniel Gorham
Rufus King

*Connecticut*
Wm. Saml. Johnson
Roger Sherman

*New York*
Alexander Hamilton

*New Jersey*
Wil: Livingston
David Brearley
Wm. Paterson
Jona: Dayton

*Pennsylvania*
B. Franklin
Thomas Mifflin
Robᵗ Morris
Geo. Clymer
Thos. FitzSimons
Jared Ingersoll
James Wilson
Gouv Morris

*Delaware*
Geo: Read
Gunning Bedford jun
John Dickinson
Richard Bassett
Jaco: Broom

*Maryland*
James McHenry
Dan of Sᵗ Thos. Jenifer
Danⁱ Carroll

*Virginia*
John Blair—
James Madison Jr.

*North Carolina*
Wm. Blount
Rich'd Dobbs Spaight
Hu Williamson

*South Carolina*
J. Rutledge
Charles Cotesworth Pinckney
Charles Pinckney
Pierce Butler

*Georgia*
William Few
Abr Baldwin

Attest:
William Jackson, *Secretary*

[*Rhode Island and the Providence Plantations*
Rhode Island did not send delegates to the Constitutional Convention.]

## Bill of Rights

*The first 10 amendments to the Constitution were adopted as a single unit on 15 Dec 1791. Together, they constitute a collection of mutually reinforcing guarantees of individual rights and of limitations on federal and state governments.*

### Amendment I

Congress shall make no law respecting an establishment of religion, or prohibiting the free exercise thereof; or abridging the freedom of speech, or of the press; or the right of the people peaceably to assemble, and to petition the Government for a redress of grievances.

### Amendment II

A well regulated Militia, being necessary to the security of a free State, the right of the people to keep and bear Arms, shall not be infringed.

### Amendment III

No Soldier shall, in time of peace be quartered in any house, without the consent of the Owner, nor in time of war, but in a manner to be prescribed by law.

### Amendment IV

The right of the People to be secure in their persons, houses, papers, and effects, against unreasonable searches and seizures, shall not be violated, and no Warrants shall issue, but upon probable cause, supported by Oath or affirmation, and particularity describing the place to be searched, and the persons or things to be seized.

### Amendment V

No person shall be held to answer for a capital, or otherwise infamous crime, unless on a presentment or indictment of a Grand Jury, except in cases arising in the land or naval forces, or in the Militia, when in actual service in time of War or public danger; nor shall any person be subject for the same offence to be twice put in jeopardy of life or limb; nor shall be compelled in any criminal case to be a witness against himself, nor be deprived of life, liberty, or property, without due process of law; nor shall private property be taken for public use, without just compensation.

### Amendment VI

In all criminal prosecutions, the accused shall enjoy the right to a speedy and public trial, by an impartial jury of the State and district wherein the crime shall have been committed, which district shall have been previously ascertained by law, and to be informed of the nature and cause of the accusation; to be confronted with the witnesses against him; to have compulsory process for obtaining witnesses in his favor, and to have Assistance of Counsel for his defence.

### Amendment VII

In Suits at common law, where the value in controversy shall exceed twenty dollars, the right of trial by jury shall be preserved, and no fact tried by a jury, shall be otherwise re-examined in any Court of the United States, than according to the rules of the common law.

### Amendment VIII

Excessive bail shall not be required, nor excessive fines imposed, nor cruel and unusual punishments inflicted.

### Amendment IX

The enumeration in the Constitution, of certain rights, shall not be construed to deny or disparage others retained by the people.

### Amendment X

The powers not delegated to the United States by the Constitution, nor prohibited by it to the States, are reserved to the States respectively, or to the people.

## Further Amendments

### Amendment XI
(ratified 7 Feb 1795)

The Judicial power of the United States shall not be construed to extend to any suit in law or equity, commenced or prosecuted against one of the United States by Citizens of another State, or by Citizens or Subjects of any Foreign State.

### Amendment XII
(ratified 15 Jun 1804)

The Electors shall meet in their respective states and vote by ballot for President and Vice-President, one of whom, at least, shall not be an inhabitant of the same state with themselves; they shall name in their ballots the person voted for as President, and in distinct ballots the person voted for as Vice-President, and they shall make distinct lists of all persons voted for as President, and of all persons voted for as Vice-President, and of the number of votes for each, which lists they shall sign and certify, and transmit sealed to the seat of the government of the United States, directed to the President of the Senate; — The President of the Senate shall, in the presence of the Senate and House of Representatives, open all the certificates and the votes shall then be counted; — The person having the greatest number of votes for President, shall be the President, if such number be a majority of the whole number of Electors appointed; and if no person have such majority, then from the persons having the highest numbers not exceeding three on the list of those voted for as President, the House of Representatives shall choose immediately, by ballot, the President. But in choosing the President, the votes shall be taken by states, the representation from each state having one vote; a quorum for this purpose shall consist of a member or members from two-thirds of the states, and a majority of all the states shall be necessary to a choice. And if the House of Representatives shall not choose a President whenever the right of choice shall devolve upon then, before the fourth day of March next following, then the Vice-President shall act as President, as in the case of the death or other constitutional disability of the President. — The person having the greatest number of votes as Vice-President, shall be the Vice-President, if such number be a majority of the whole number of Electors appointed, and if no person have a majority, then from the two highest numbers on the list, the Senate shall choose the Vice-President; a quorum for the purpose shall consist of two-thirds of the whole number of Senators, and a majority of the whole number shall be necessary to a choice. But no person constitutionally ineligible to the office of President shall be eligible to that of Vice-President of the United States.

### Amendment XIII
(ratified 6 Dec 1865)

Section 1—

Neither slavery nor involuntary servitude, except as a punishment for crime whereof the party shall have been duly convicted, shall exist within the United States, or any place subject to their jurisdiction.

Section 2—

Congress shall have power to enforce this article by appropriate legislation.

### Amendment XIV
(ratified 9 Jul 1868)

Section 1—

All persons born or naturalized in the United States, and subject to the jurisdiction thereof, are citizens of the United States and of the State wherein they reside. No State shall make or enforce any law which shall abridge the privileges or immunities of citizens of the United States; nor shall any State deprive any person of life, liberty, or property, without due process of law; nor deny to any person within its jurisdiction the equal protection of the laws.

### Section 2—

Representatives shall be apportioned among the several States according to their respective numbers, counting the whole number of persons in each State, excluding Indians not taxed. But when the right to vote at any election for the choice of electors for President and Vice President of the United States, Representatives in Congress, the Executive and Judicial officers of a State, or the members of the Legislature thereof, is denied to any of the male inhabitants of such State, being twenty-one years of age, and citizens of the United States, or in any way abridged, except for participation in rebellion, or other crime, the basis of representation therein shall be reduced in the proportion which the number of such male citizens shall bear to the whole number of male citizens twenty-one years of age in such State.

### Section 3—

No person shall be a Senator or Representative in Congress, or elector of President and Vice President, or hold any office, civil or military, under the United States, or under any State, who, having previously taken an oath, as a member of Congress, or as an officer of the United States, or as a member of any State legislature, or as an executive or judicial officer of any State, to support the Constitution of the United States, shall have engaged in insurrection or rebellion against the same, or given aid or comfort to the enemies thereof. But Congress may by a vote of two-thirds of each House, remove such disability.

### Section 4—

The validity of the public debt of the United States, authorized by law, including debts incurred for payment of pensions and bounties for services in suppressing insurrection or rebellion, shall not be questioned. But neither the United States nor any State shall assume or pay any debt or obligation incurred in aid of insurrection or rebellion against the United States, or any claim for the loss or emancipation of any slave; but all such debts, obligations and claims shall be held illegal and void.

### Section 5—

The Congress shall have power to enforce, by appropriate legislation, the provisions of this article.

### Amendment XV
(ratified 8 Feb 1870)

### Section 1—

The right of citizens of the United States to vote shall not be denied or abridged by the United States or by any State on account of race, color, or previous condition of servitude.

### Section 2—

The Congress shall have power to enforce this article by appropriate legislation.

### Amendment XVI
(ratified 3 Feb 1913)

The Congress shall have power to lay and collect taxes on incomes, from whatever source derived, without apportionment among the several States, and without regard to any census or enumeration.

### Amendment XVII
(ratified 13 Feb 1913)

The Senate of the United States shall be composed of two Senators from each State, elected by the people thereof for six years; and each Senator shall have one vote. The electors in each State shall have the qualifications requisite for electors of the most numerous branch of the State legislatures.

When vacancies happen in the representation of any State in the Senate, the executive authority of such State shall issue writs of election to fill such vacancies: Provided, That the legislature of any State may empower the executive thereof to make temporary appointments until the people fill the vacancies by election as the legislature may direct.

This amendment shall not be so construed as to affect the election or term of any Senator chosen before it becomes valid as part of the Constitution.

### Amendment XVIII
(ratified 16 Jan 1919; repealed 5 Dec 1933
by Amendment XXI)

### Section 1—

After one year from the ratification of this article the manufacture, sale, or transportation of intoxicating liquors within, the importation thereof into, or the exportation thereof from the United States and all territory subject to the jurisdiction thereof for beverage purposes is hereby prohibited.

### Section 2—

The Congress and the several States shall have concurrent power to enforce this article by appropriate legislation.

### Section 3—

This article shall be inoperative unless it shall have been ratified as an amendment to the Constitution by the legislatures of the several States as provided in the Constitution, within seven years from the date of the submission hereof to the States by the Congress.

### Amendment XIX
(ratified 18 Aug 1920)

The right of citizens of the United States to vote shall not be denied or abridged by the United States or by any State on account of sex.

Congress shall have power to enforce this article by appropriate legislation.

### Amendment XX
(ratified 23 Jan 1933)

### Section 1—

The terms of the President and Vice President shall end at noon on the 20th day of January, and the terms of Senators and Representatives at noon on the 3d day of January, of the years in which such terms would have ended if this article had not been ratified; and the terms of their successors shall then begin.

### Section 2—

The Congress shall assemble at least once in every year, and such meeting shall begin at noon on the 3d day of January, unless they shall by law appoint a different day.

### Section 3—

If, at the time fixed for the beginning of the term of the President, the President elect shall have died, the Vice President elect shall become President. If a President shall not have been chosen before the time fixed for the beginning of his term, or if the President elect shall have failed to qualify, then the Vice President elect shall act as President until a President shall have qualified; and the Congress may by law provide for the case wherein neither a President elect nor a Vice President elect shall have qualified, declaring who shall then act as President, or the manner in which one who is to act shall be selected, and such person shall act accordingly until a President or Vice President shall have qualified.

**Section 4—**
The Congress may by law provide for the case of the death of any of the persons from whom the House of Representatives may choose a President whenever the right of choice shall have devolved upon them, and for the case of the death of any of the persons from whom the Senate may choose a Vice President whenever the right of choice shall have devolved upon them.

**Section 5—**
Sections 1 and 2 shall take effect on the 15th day of October following the ratification of this article.

**Section 6—**
This article shall be inoperative unless it shall have been ratified as an amendment to the Constitution by the legislatures of three-fourths of the several States within seven years from the date of its submission.

## Amendment XXI
(ratified 5 Dec 1933)

**Section 1—**
The eighteenth article of amendment to the Constitution of the United States is hereby repealed.

**Section 2—**
The transportation or importation into any State, Territory, or possession of the United States for delivery or use therein of intoxicating liquors, in violation of the laws thereof, is hereby prohibited.

**Section 3—**
This article shall be inoperative unless it shall have been ratified as an amendment to the Constitution by conventions in the several States, as provided in the Constitution, within seven years from the date of the submission hereof to the States by the Congress.

## Amendment XXII
(ratified 27 Feb 1951)

**Section 1—**
No person shall be elected to the office of the President more than twice, and no person who has held the office of President, or acted as President, for more than two years of a term to which some other person was elected President shall be elected to the office of the President more than once. But this Article shall not apply to any person holding the office of President when this Article was proposed by the Congress, and shall not prevent any person who may be holding the office of President, or acting as President, during the term within which this Article becomes operative from holding the office of President or acting as President during the remainder of such term.

**Section 2—**
This Article shall be inoperative unless it shall have been ratified as an amendment to the Constitution by the legislatures of three-fourths of the several States within seven years from the date of its submission to the States by the Congress.

## Amendment XXIII
(ratified 29 Mar 1961)

**Section 1—**
The District constituting the seat of Government of the United States shall appoint in such manner as the Congress may direct:
A number of electors of President and Vice President equal to the whole number of Senators and Representatives in Congress to which the District would be entitled if it were a State, but in no event more than the least populous State; they shall be in addition to those appointed by the States, but they shall be considered, for the purposes of the election of President and Vice President, to be electors appointed by a State; and they shall meet in the District and perform such duties as provided by the twelfth article of amendment.

**Section 2—**
The Congress shall have power to enforce this article by appropriate legislation.

## Amendment XXIV
(ratified 23 Jan 1964)

**Section 1—**
The right of citizens of the United States to vote in any primary or other election for President or Vice President, for electors for President or Vice President, or for Senator or Representative in Congress, shall not be denied or abridged by the United States or any State by reason of failure to pay any poll tax or other tax.

**Section 2—**
The Congress shall have power to enforce this article by appropriate legislation.

## Amendment XXV
(ratified 23 Jan 1967)

**Section 1—**
In case of the removal of the President from office or of his death or resignation, the Vice President shall become President.

**Section 2—**
Whenever there is a vacancy in the office of the Vice President, the President shall nominate a Vice President who shall take office upon confirmation by a majority vote of both Houses of Congress.

**Section 3—**
Whenever the President transmits to the President pro tempore of the Senate and the Speaker of the House of Representatives his written declaration that he is unable to discharge the powers and duties of his office, and until he transmits to them a written declaration to the contrary, such powers and duties shall be discharged by the Vice President as Acting President.

**Section 4—**
Whenever the Vice president and a majority of either the principal officers of the executive departments or of such other body as Congress may by law provide, transmit to the President pro tempore of the Senate and the Speaker of the House of Representatives their written declaration that the President is unable to discharge the powers and duties of his office, the Vice President shall immediately assume the powers and duties of the office as Acting President.

Thereafter, when the President transmits to the President pro tempore of the Senate and the Speaker of the House of Representatives his written declaration that no inability exists, he shall resume the powers and duties of his office unless the Vice President and a majority of either the principal officers of the executive department or of such other body as Congress may by law provide, transmit within four days to the President pro tempore of the Senate and the Speaker of the House of Representatives their written declaration that the President is unable to discharge the powers and duties of his office. Thereupon Congress shall decide the issue, assembling within forty-eight hours for that purpose if not in session. If the Congress, within twenty-one days after receipt of the latter written declaration, or, if Congress is not in session, within twenty-one days after Congress is required to assemble, determines by two-thirds vote of both Houses that the President is unable to discharge the powers and duties of his office, the Vice President shall continue to discharge the same as Acting President; otherwise, the President shall resume the powers and duties of his office.

### Amendment XXVI
(ratified 1 Jul 1971)

**Section 1—**
The right of citizens of the United States, who are eighteen years of age or older, to vote shall not be denied or abridged by the United States or by any State on account of age.

**Section 2—**
The Congress shall have power to enforce this article by appropriate legislation.

### Amendment XXVII
(ratified 7 May 1992)

No law, varying the compensation for the services of the Senators and Representatives, shall take effect, until an election of representatives shall have intervened.

---

## Confederate States and Secession Dates

In the months following Abraham Lincoln's election as president in 1860, seven states of the Deep South held conventions and approved secession, thus precipitating the Civil War. After the attack on Fort Sumter SC on 12 Apr 1861, Virginia, Arkansas, North Carolina, and Tennessee also seceded (Tennessee was the only state to hold a popular referendum without a convention on secession). The Confederacy operated as a separate government, with Jefferson Davis as president and Alexander H. Stephens as vice president. Its principal goals were the preservation of states' rights and the institution of slavery. Although it enjoyed a series of military victories in the first two years of fighting, the surrender at Appomattox VA by Gen. Robert E. Lee on 9 Apr 1865 signaled its dissolution.

| STATE | DATE | STATE | DATE | STATE | DATE |
|---|---|---|---|---|---|
| South Carolina | 20 Dec 1860 | Georgia | 19 Jan 1861 | Arkansas | 6 May 1861 |
| Mississippi | 9 Jan 1861 | Louisiana | 26 Jan 1861 | North Carolina | 20 May 1861 |
| Florida | 10 Jan 1861 | Texas | 1 Feb 1861 | Tennessee | 8 Jun 1861 |
| Alabama | 11 Jan 1861 | Virginia | 17 Apr 1861 | | |

---

## Emancipation Proclamation

*The Emancipation Proclamation was issued by Pres. Abraham Lincoln and freed the slaves of the Confederate states in rebellion against the Union. After the Battle of Antietam (17 Sep 1862), Lincoln issued his proclamation calling on the revolted states to return to their allegiance before the next year, otherwise their slaves would be declared free men. No state returned, and the threatened declaration was issued on 1 Jan 1863.*

By the President of the United States of America:

A Proclamation.

Whereas, on the twenty-second day of September, in the year of our Lord one thousand eight hundred and sixty-two, a proclamation was issued by the President of the United States, containing, among other things, the following, to wit:

"That on the first day of January, in the year of our Lord one thousand eight hundred and sixty-three, all persons held as slaves within any State or designated part of a State, the people whereof shall then be in rebellion against the United States, shall be then, thenceforward, and forever free; and the Executive Government of the United States, including the military and naval authority thereof, will recognize and maintain the freedom of such persons, and will do no act or acts to repress such persons, or any of them, in any efforts they may make for their actual freedom.

"That the Executive will, on the first day of January aforesaid, by proclamation, designate the States and parts of States, if any, in which the people thereof, respectively, shall then be in rebellion against the United States; and the fact that any State, or the people thereof, shall on that day be, in good faith, represented in the Congress of the United States by members chosen thereto at elections wherein a majority of the qualified voters of such State shall have participated, shall, in the absence of strong countervailing testimony, be deemed conclusive evidence that such State, and the people thereof, are not then in rebellion against the United States."

Now, therefore I, Abraham Lincoln, President of the United States, by virtue of the power in me vested as Commander-in-Chief, of the Army and Navy of the

United States in time of actual armed rebellion against the authority and government of the United States, and as a fit and necessary war measure for suppressing said rebellion, do, on this first day of January, in the year of our Lord one thousand eight hundred and sixty-three, and in accordance with my purpose so to do publicly proclaimed for the full period of one hundred days, from the day first above mentioned, order and designate as the States and parts of States wherein the people thereof respectively, are this day in rebellion against the United States, the following, to wit:

Arkansas, Texas, Louisiana, (except the Parishes of St. Bernard, Plaquemines, Jefferson, St. John, St. Charles, St. James Ascension, Assumption, Terrebonne, Lafourche, St. Mary, St. Martin, and Orleans, including the City of New Orleans) Mississippi, Alabama, Florida, Georgia, South Carolina, North Carolina, and Virginia, (except the forty-eight counties designated as West Virginia, and also the counties of Berkley, Accomac, Northampton, Elizabeth City, York, Princess Ann, and Norfolk, including the cities of Norfolk and Portsmouth[]], and which excepted parts, are for the present, left precisely as if this proclamation were not issued.

And by virtue of the power, and for the purpose aforesaid, I do order and declare that all persons held as slaves within said designated States, and parts of States, are, and henceforward shall be free; and that the Executive government of the United States, including the military and naval authorities thereof, will recognize and maintain the freedom of said persons.

And I hereby enjoin upon the people so declared to be free to abstain from all violence, unless in necessary self-defence; and I recommend to them that, in all cases when allowed, they labor faithfully for reasonable wages.

And I further declare and make known, that such persons of suitable condition, will be received into the armed service of the United States to garrison forts, positions, stations, and other places, and to man vessels of all sorts in said service.

And upon this act, sincerely believed to be an act of justice, warranted by the Constitution, upon military necessity, I invoke the considerate judgment of mankind, and the gracious favor of Almighty God.

In witness whereof, I have hereunto set my hand and caused the seal of the United States to be affixed.

Done at the City of Washington, this first day of January, in the year of our Lord one thousand eight hundred and sixty three, and of the Independence of the United States of America the eighty-seventh.

By the President: Abraham Lincoln.
William H. Seward, Secretary of State.

## Gettysburg Address

*On 19 Nov 1863, Pres. Abraham Lincoln delivered this speech at the consecration of the National Cemetery at Gettysburg PA, the site of one of the most decisive battles of the American Civil War.*

Four score and seven years ago our fathers brought forth on this continent a new nation, conceived in Liberty, and dedicated to the proposition that all men are created equal. Now we are engaged in a great civil war, testing whether that nation or any nation so conceived and so dedicated, can long endure. We are met on a great battle-field of that war. We have come to dedicate a portion of that field, as a final resting place for those who here gave their lives that that nation might live. It is altogether fitting and proper that we should do this. But, in a larger sense, we can not dedicate—we can not consecrate—we can not hallow—this ground. The brave men, living and dead, who struggled here, have consecrated it, far above our poor power to add or detract. The world will little note, nor long remember what we say here, but it can never forget what they did here. It is for us the living, rather, to be dedicated here to the unfinished work which they who fought here have thus far so nobly advanced. It is rather for us to be here dedicated to the great task remaining before us—that from these honored dead we take increased devotion to that cause for which they gave the last full measure of devotion—that we here highly resolve that these dead shall not have died in vain—that this nation, under God, shall have a new birth of freedom—and that government of the people, by the people, for the people, shall not perish from the earth.

# Government

## The US Presidency at a Glance

|   | PRESIDENT | POLITICAL PARTY | TIME IN OFFICE | VICE PRESIDENT |
|---|---|---|---|---|
| 1 | George Washington | Federalist | 1789–1797 | John Adams |
| 2 | John Adams | Federalist | 1797–1801 | Thomas Jefferson |
| 3 | Thomas Jefferson | Jeffersonian Republican | 1801–1809 | Aaron Burr George Clinton |
| 4 | James Madison | Jeffersonian Republican | 1809–1817 | George Clinton Elbridge Gerry |
| 5 | James Monroe | Jeffersonian Republican | 1817–1825 | Daniel D. Tompkins |
| 6 | John Quincy Adams | National Republican | 1825–1829 | John C. Calhoun |

## The US Presidency at a Glance (continued)

| | PRESIDENT | POLITICAL PARTY | TIME IN OFFICE | VICE PRESIDENT |
|---|---|---|---|---|
| 7 | Andrew Jackson | Democratic | 1829–1837 | John C. Calhoun<br>Martin Van Buren |
| 8 | Martin Van Buren | Democratic | 1837–1841 | Richard M. Johnson |
| 9 | William Henry Harrison* | Whig | 4 Mar–4 Apr 1841 | John Tyler |
| 10 | John Tyler | Whig | 1841–1845 | none |
| 11 | James K. Polk | Democratic | 1845–1849 | George Mifflin Dallas |
| 12 | Zachary Taylor* | Whig | 1849–1850 | Millard Fillmore |
| 13 | Millard Fillmore | Whig | 1850–1853 | none |
| 14 | Franklin Pierce | Democratic | 1853–1857 | William Rufus de Vane King |
| 15 | James Buchanan | Democratic | 1857–1861 | John C. Breckinridge |
| 16 | Abraham Lincoln*† | Republican | 1861–1865 | Hannibal Hamlin<br>Andrew Johnson |
| 17 | Andrew Johnson | Democratic (Union) | 1865–1869 | none |
| 18 | Ulysses S. Grant | Republican | 1869–1877 | Schuyler Colfax<br>Henry Wilson |
| 19 | Rutherford B. Hayes | Republican | 1877–1881 | William A. Wheeler |
| 20 | James A. Garfield*† | Republican | 4 Mar–19 Sep 1881 | Chester A. Arthur |
| 21 | Chester A. Arthur | Republican | 1881–1885 | none |
| 22 | Grover Cleveland | Democratic | 1885–1889 | Thomas A. Hendricks |
| 23 | Benjamin Harrison | Republican | 1889–1893 | Levi Parons Morton |
| 24 | Grover Cleveland | Democratic | 1893–1897 | Adlai E. Stevenson |
| 25 | William McKinley*† | Republican | 1897–1901 | Garret A. Hobart<br>Theodore Roosevelt |
| 26 | Theodore Roosevelt | Republican | 1901–1909 | Charles Warren Fairbanks |
| 27 | William Howard Taft | Republican | 1909–1913 | James Schoolcraft Sherman |
| 28 | Woodrow Wilson | Democratic | 1913–1921 | Thomas R. Marshall |
| 29 | Warren G. Harding* | Republican | 1921–1923 | Calvin Coolidge |
| 30 | Calvin Coolidge | Republican | 1923–1929 | Charles G. Dawes |
| 31 | Herbert Hoover | Republican | 1929–1933 | Charles Curtis |
| 32 | Franklin D. Roosevelt* | Democratic | 1933–1945 | John Nance Garner<br>Henry A. Wallace<br>Harry S. Truman |
| 33 | Harry S. Truman | Democratic | 1945–1953 | Alben W. Barkley |
| 34 | Dwight D. Eisenhower | Republican | 1953–1961 | Richard M. Nixon |
| 35 | John F. Kennedy*† | Democratic | 1961–1963 | Lyndon B. Johnson |
| 36 | Lyndon B. Johnson | Democratic | 1963–1969 | Hubert H. Humphrey |
| 37 | Richard M. Nixon** | Republican | 1969–1974 | Spiro T. Agnew<br>Gerald R. Ford |
| 38 | Gerald R. Ford | Republican | 1974–1977 | Nelson A. Rockefeller |
| 39 | Jimmy Carter | Democratic | 1977–1981 | Walter F. Mondale |
| 40 | Ronald Reagan | Republican | 1981–1989 | George H.W. Bush |
| 41 | George H.W. Bush | Republican | 1989–1993 | Dan Quayle |
| 42 | Bill Clinton | Democratic | 1993–2001 | Albert Gore |
| 43 | George W. Bush | Republican | 2001–2009 | Richard B. Cheney |
| 44 | Barack Obama | Democratic | 2009– | Joe Biden |

*Died in office. **Resigned from office. †Assassinated.

# US Presidential Biographies

**George Washington** (22 Feb [11 Feb, Old Style] 1732, Westmoreland county VA–14 Dec 1799, Mount Vernon, in Fairfax county VA), American Revolutionary commander-in-chief (1775–83) and first president of the US (1789–97). Born into a wealthy family, he inherited his brother's estate at Mount Vernon, including 18 slaves whose ranks grew to 49 by 1760. In the French and Indian War he was commissioned a colonel and sent to the Ohio Territory, and later he became commander of all Virginia forces, entrusted with defending the western frontier (1755–58). He resigned to manage his estate and in 1759 married Martha Dandridge Custis (1731–1802), a widow. He served in the House of Burgesses (1759–74), where he supported the colonists' cause, and in the Continental Congress (1774–75). In 1775 he was elected to command the Continental Army. In the ensuing American Revolution, he proved a brilliant commander and stalwart leader despite several defeats. With the war effectively ended by the capture of Yorktown (1781), he resigned his commission and returned to Mount Vernon. He was a delegate to and presiding officer of the Constitutional Convention (1787) and helped secure ratification of the Constitution in Virginia. When the state electors met to select the first president (1789), Washington was the unanimous choice. He formed a cabinet to balance sectional and political differences but was committed to a strong central government.

Elected to a second term, he followed a middle course between the political factions that became the Federalist Party and Democratic Party. He proclaimed a policy of neutrality in the war between Britain and France (1793) and sent troops to suppress the Whiskey Rebellion (1794). He declined to serve a third term, setting a 144-year precedent, and retired in 1797. Known as the "father of his country," he is regarded as one of the greatest figures in US history.

**John Adams** (30 Oct [19 Oct, Old Style] 1735, Braintree [now in Quincy] MA—4 Jul 1826, Quincy MA), first vice president (1789–97) and second president (1797–1801) of the US. He practiced law in Boston and in 1764 married Abigail Smith. Active in the American independence movement, he was elected to the Massachusetts legislature and served as a delegate to the Continental Congress (1774–78), where he was appointed to a committee with Thomas Jefferson and others to draft the Declaration of Independence. He served as a diplomat in France, The Netherlands, and England (1778–88). In the first US presidential election, he received the second largest number of votes and became vice president under George Washington. Adams's term as president was marked by controversy over his signing the Alien and Sedition Acts in 1798 and by his alliance with the conservative Federalist Party. In 1800 he was defeated for reelection by Thomas Jefferson and retired to live a secluded life in Massachusetts. In 1812 he began an illuminating correspondence with Jefferson. Both men died on 4 Jul 1826, the Declaration's 50th anniversary. Pres. John Quincy Adams was his son.

**Thomas Jefferson** (13 Apr [2 Apr, Old Style] 1743, Shadwell VA—4 Jul 1826, Monticello VA), third president of the US (1801–9). He was a planter and lawyer from 1767, as well as a slaveholder. While a member of the House of Burgesses (1769–75), he initiated the Committee of Correspondence (1773) with Richard Henry Lee and Patrick Henry. In 1774 he wrote the influential *Summary View of the Rights of British America*, stating that the British Parliament had no authority to legislate for the colonies. A delegate to the Second Continental Congress, he was appointed to the committee to draft the Declaration of Independence and became its primary author. He was elected governor of Virginia (1779–81) but was unable to organize effective opposition when British forces invaded the colony (1780–81). Again a member of the Continental Congress (1783–85), he proposed territorial provisions later incorporated in the Northwest Ordinances. He became minister to France (1785–89), and George Washington made him secretary of state (1790–93). He soon became embroiled in conflict with Alexander Hamilton over their opposing interpretations of the Constitution. This led to the rise of factions and political parties, with Jefferson representing the Democratic-Republicans. He served as vice president (1797–1801) but opposed the Alien and Sedition Acts enacted under Pres. John Adams. In 1801 he became president after an electoral-vote tie with Aaron Burr was settled by the House of Representatives. Jefferson oversaw the Louisiana Purchase and authorized the Lewis and Clark Expedition. He sought to avoid involvement in the Napoleonic Wars by signing the Embargo Act. He retired to his plantation, Monticello, where he pursued his many interests in science, philosophy, and architecture, and in 1819 he founded and designed the University of Virginia. In January 2000, the Thomas Jefferson Memorial Foundation accepted the conclusion, supported by DNA evidence, that Jefferson had fathered at least one, and perhaps as many as six, children with Sally Hemings, one of his house slaves.

**James Madison** (16 Mar [5 Mar, Old Style] 1751, Port Conway VA—28 Jun 1836, Montpelier VA), fourth president of the US (1809–17). At the Constitutional Convention (1787), his active participation and his careful notes on the debates earned him the title "father of the Constitution." To promote ratification, he collaborated with Alexander Hamilton and John Jay on the Federalist papers. In the House of Representatives (1789–97), he sponsored the Bill of Rights, was a leading Jeffersonian Republican, and split with Hamilton over funding state war debts. He was appointed secretary of state (1801–09) by Thomas Jefferson, with whom he developed US foreign policy. Elected president in 1808, he was occupied by the trade and shipping embargo problems caused by France and Britain that led to the War of 1812. He was reelected in 1812; his second term was marked principally by the war, during which he reinvigorated the Army. He retired to his Virginia estate, Montpelier, with his wife, Dolley (1768–1849), whose political acumen he had long prized. He served as rector of the University of Virginia until his death (1826–36).

**James Monroe** (28 Apr 1758, Westmoreland county VA—4 Jul 1831, New York NY), fifth president of the US (1817–25). He fought in the American Revolution and studied law under Thomas Jefferson. He became minister to France (1794–96), where he misled the French about US politics and was recalled. He served as governor of Virginia (1799–1802). President Jefferson sent him to France to help negotiate the Louisiana Purchase (1803), then named him minister to Britain (1803–07). He returned to Virginia and became governor (1811), but he resigned to become US secretary of state (1811–17) and secretary of war (1814–15). He served two terms as president, presiding in a period that became known as the Era of Good Feelings. He oversaw the First Seminole War (1817–18) and the acquisition of the Floridas (1819–21) and signed the Missouri Compromise (1820). With Secretary of State John Quincy Adams, he developed the principles of US foreign policy later called the Monroe Doctrine.

**John Quincy Adams** (11 Jul 1767, Braintree [now in Quincy] MA—23 Feb 1848, Washington DC), sixth president of the US (1825–29). He was the eldest son of Pres. John Adams and Abigail. He accompanied his father to Europe on diplomatic missions (1778–80) and was later appointed minister to The Netherlands (1794) and Prussia (1797). In 1801 he returned to Massachusetts and served in the Senate (1803–8). Resuming his diplomatic service, he became minister to Russia (1809–11) and Britain (1815–17). Appointed secretary of state (1817–24), he was instrumental in acquiring Florida from Spain and in drafting the Monroe Doctrine. He was one of three candidates in the 1824 presidential election, in which none received a majority of the electoral votes, though Andrew Jackson received a plurality. The decision went to the House of Representatives, where Adams received crucial support from Henry Clay and the electoral votes necessary to elect him president. He appointed Clay secretary of state, which further angered Jackson. Adams's presidency was unsuccessful; when he ran for reelection, Jackson defeated him. In 1830 he was elected to the House of Representatives, where he served until his death. He was outspoken in his opposition to slavery and in 1839 proposed a constitutional amendment forbidding slavery in any new state admitted to the Union. In 1841 he successfully defended the slaves in the *Amistad* mutiny case.

**Andrew Jackson** (15 Mar 1767, Waxhaws region, South Carolina—8 Jun 1845, the Hermitage, near Nashville TN), seventh president of the US (1829–37). He fought briefly in the American Revolution near his frontier home, where his family was killed. He studied law and in 1788 was appointed prosecuting attorney for western North Carolina. When the region became the state of Tennessee, he was elected to the House of Representatives (1796–97) and Senate (1797–98). He served on the state supreme court (1798–1804) and in 1802 was elected major general of the Tennessee militia. When the War of 1812 began, he offered the US the services of his 50,000-volunteer militia. He was sent to fight the Creek Indians in Mississippi Territory. After a lengthy battle (1813–14), he defeated them at the Battle of Horseshoe Bend. After capturing Pensacola FL from the British-allied Spanish, he marched overland to engage the British in Louisiana. A decisive victory at the Battle of New Orleans made him a national hero, dubbed "Old Hickory" by the press. After US acquisition of Florida, he was named governor of the territory (1821). In 1828 Jackson defeated Adams after a fierce campaign and became the first president elected from west of the Appalachian Mountains. He replaced many federal officeholders with his supporters, a process that became known as the spoils system. He pursued a policy of moving Native Americans westward with the Indian Removal Acts. During his tenure a strong Democratic Party developed that led to a vigorous two-party system.

**Martin Van Buren** (5 Dec 1782, Kinderhook NY—24 Jul 1862, Kinderhook NY), eighth president of the US (1837–41). He practiced law and served in the NY state senate (1812–20) and as state attorney general (1816–19). He was elected to the US Senate (1821–28), where he supported states' rights and opposed a strong central government. After John Quincy Adams became president, Van Buren joined with Andrew Jackson and others to form a group that later became the Democratic Party. He was elected governor of New York (1828) but resigned to become US secretary of state (1829–31). He was nominated for vice president at the first Democratic Party convention (1832) and served under Jackson (1833–37). As Jackson's chosen successor, he defeated William H. Harrison to win the 1836 election. His presidency was marked by an economic depression, the Maine-Canada border dispute, the Second Seminole War in Florida, and debate over the annexation of Texas. He was defeated in his bid for reelection and failed to win the Democratic nomination in 1844 because of his antislavery views. In 1848 he was nominated for president by the Free Soil Party but failed to win the election and retired.

**William Henry Harrison** (9 Feb 1773, Charles City county VA—4 Apr 1841, Washington DC), ninth president of the US (1841). Born into a political family, he enlisted in the army at 18 and served under Anthony Wayne at the Battle of Fallen Timbers. In 1798 he became secretary of the Northwest Territories and in 1800 governor of the new Indiana Territory. In response to pressure from white settlers, he negotiated treaties with the Native Americans that ceded millions of acres of land to the US. When the chief Tecumseh organized an uprising in 1811, Harrison led a US force to defeat the Indians at the Battle of Tippecanoe, a victory that largely established his reputation in the public mind. In the War of 1812 he was made a brigadier general and defeated the British and their Indian allies at the Battle of the Thames in Ontario. He served in the House of Representatives (1816–19) and Senate (1825–28). As the Whig party candidate in the 1836 presidential election, he lost narrowly. In 1840 he and his running mate, John Tyler, won election with a slogan emphasizing Harrison's frontier triumph: "Tippecanoe and Tyler too!" The 68-year-old Harrison delivered his inaugural speech without a hat or overcoat in a cold drizzle, contracted pneumonia, and died one month later, the first president to die in office.

**John Tyler** (29 Mar 1790, Charles City county VA—18 Jan 1862, Richmond VA), 10th president of the US (1841–45). He practiced law before serving as governor of Virginia (1825–27). In the House of Representatives (1817–21) and Senate (1827–36), he was a states-rights supporter. Though a slaveholder, he sought to prohibit the slave trade in the District of Columbia, provided Maryland and Virginia concurred. He resigned from the Senate rather than acquiesce to state instructions to change his vote on a censure of Pres. Andrew Jackson. After breaking with the Democratic Party, he was nominated by the Whig Party for vice president under William Henry Harrison. They won the 1840 election, carefully avoiding the issues and stressing party loyalty and the slogan "Tippecanoe and Tyler too!" Harrison died a month after taking office, and Tyler became the first to attain the presidency "by accident." He vetoed a national bank bill supported by the Whigs, and all but one member of the cabinet resigned, leaving him without party support. Nonetheless, he reorganized the navy, settled the second of the Seminole Wars in Florida, and oversaw the annexation of Texas. Committed to states' rights but opposed to secession, he organized the Washington Peace Conference (1861) to resolve sectional differences.

**James Knox Polk** (2 Nov 1795, Mecklenburg county NC—15 Jun 1849, Nashville TN), 11th president of the US (1845–49). He became a lawyer in Tennessee and a friend and supporter of Andrew Jackson, who helped Polk win election to the House of Representatives (1825–39). He left the House to become governor of Tennessee (1839–41). At the deadlocked 1844 Democratic convention Polk was nominated as the compromise candidate; he is considered the first dark-horse presidential candidate. A proponent of western expansion, he campaigned with the slogan "Fifty-four Forty or Fight," to bring a solution to the Oregon Question. Elected at 49, the youngest president to that time, he successfully concluded the Oregon border dispute with Britain (1846) and secured passage of the Walker Tariff Act (1846), which lowered import duties and helped foreign trade. He led the prosecution of the Mexican-American War, which resulted in large territorial gains but reopened the debate over the extension of slavery. His administration established the US Naval Academy and the Smithsonian Institution, oversaw revision of the treasury system, and proclaimed the validity of the Monroe Doctrine. He died three months after leaving office.

**Zachary Taylor** (24 Nov 1784, Montebello VA–9 Jul 1850, Washington DC), 12th president of the US (1849–50). Born in Virginia, he grew up on the Kentucky frontier. He fought in the War of 1812, the Black Hawk War (1832), and the Second Seminole War in Florida (1835–42), earning the nickname "Old Rough-and-Ready" for his indifference to hardship. Sent to Texas in anticipation of war with Mexico, he defeated the Mexican invaders at the Battles of Palo Alto and Resaca de la Palma (1846). After the Mexican-American War formally began, he captured Monterrey and granted the Mexican army an eight-week armistice. Displeased, Pres. James Polk moved Taylor's best troops to serve under Winfield Scott in the invasion of Veracruz. Taylor ignored orders to remain in Monterrey and marched south to defeat a large Mexican force at the Battle of Buena Vista (1847). He became a national hero and won the presidency as the Whig candidate (1848). His brief term was marked by a controversy over the new territories that produced the Compromise of 1850. He died, probably of cholera, after only 16 months in office.

**Millard Fillmore** (7 Jan 1800, Locke Township NY–8 Mar 1874, Buffalo NY), 13th president of the US (1850–53). Born into poverty, he became an indentured apprentice at 15. Initially identified with the Anti-Masonic Party (1828–34), he followed his political mentor, Thurlow Weed, to the Whigs and was soon a leader of the party's northern wing. He served in the House of Representatives (1833–35, 1837–43), where he became a follower of Henry Clay. In 1848 the Whigs nominated Fillmore as vice president, and he was elected with Zachary Taylor. He became president on Taylor's death in 1850. Though he abhorred slavery, he supported the Compromise of 1850 and insisted on federal enforcement of the Fugitive Slave Act. His stand, which alienated the North, led to his defeat by Winfield Scott at the Whigs' nominating convention in 1852 and effectively led to the death of the party. In 1853 he sent Matthew Perry with a US fleet to Japan, forcing its isolationist government to enter into trade and diplomatic relations. He was nominated for president by the third-party Know-Nothing Party in 1856, but he was defeated by Democrat James Buchanan.

**Franklin Pierce** (23 Nov 1804, Hillsboro NH–8 Oct 1869, Concord NH), 14th president of the US (1853–57). He served in the House of Representatives (1833–37) and Senate (1837–42) and briefly fought in the Mexican-American War. At the deadlocked Democratic convention of 1852, he was nominated as the compromise candidate; though largely unknown nationally, he unexpectedly trounced Winfield Scott in the general election. For the sake of harmony and business prosperity, he was inclined to oppose antislavery agitation so as to placate Southern opinion. He promoted US territorial expansion, resulting in the diplomatic controversy of the Ostend Manifesto, which urged the seizure of Cuba from Spain. He encouraged plans for a transcontinental railroad and approved the Gadsden Purchase. To promote northwestern migration and conciliate sectional demands, he approved the Kansas-Nebraska Act but was unable to settle the resultant problems. Defeated for renomination by James Buchanan in 1856, he retired from politics.

**James Buchanan** (23 Apr 1791, near Mercersburg PA–1 Jun 1868, near Lancaster PA), 15th president of the US (1857–61). He served in the House of Representatives (1821–31), as minister to Russia (1832–34), and in the Senate (1834–45). He was secretary of state in James Polk's cabinet (1845–49). As minister to Britain (1853–56), he helped draft the Ostend Manifesto. In 1856 he secured the Democratic nomination and election as president, defeating John C. Fremont. He equivocated on the question of Kansas's status as a slaveholding state, and the ensuing split within his party allowed Abraham Lincoln to win the election of 1860. He denounced the secession of South Carolina following the election and sent reinforcements to Fort Sumter, but he failed to respond further to the mounting crisis.

**Abraham Lincoln** (12 Feb 1809, near Hodgenville KY–15 Apr 1865, Washington DC), 16th president of the US (1861–65). Born in a Kentucky log cabin, he moved to Indiana in 1816 and to Illinois in 1830. He worked as a storekeeper, rail-splitter, postmaster, and surveyor and then enlisted as a volunteer in the Black Hawk War and became a captain. Though largely self-taught, he practiced law in Springfield IL and served in the state legislature (1834–40). He was elected as a Whig to the House of Representatives (1847–49). He later became one of the state's most successful lawyers, noted for his shrewdness and honesty (earning him the nickname "Honest Abe"). In 1856 he joined the Republican Party, which nominated him as its candidate in the 1858 Senate election. In a series of seven debates with Stephen A. Douglas (the Lincoln-Douglas Debates), he argued against the extension of slavery into the territories, though not against slavery itself. Although morally opposed to slavery, he was not an abolitionist. During the campaign, he attempted to rebut Douglas's charge that he was a dangerous radical by reassuring audiences that he did not favor political equality for blacks. Despite his loss in the election, the debates brought him national attention. He again ran against Douglas in the 1860 presidential election, which he won by a large margin. But the South opposed his position on slavery in the territories, and before his inauguration seven Southern states had seceeded from the Union. The ensuing American Civil War completely consumed Lincoln's administration. He excelled as a wartime leader, combining statecraft and overall command of the armies with what some have called military genius. However, his abrogation of some civil liberties, especially the writ of habeas corpus, and the closing of several newspapers by his generals disturbed both Democrats and Republicans. To unite the North and influence foreign opinion, he issued the Emancipation Proclamation (1863); his Gettysburg Address (1863) further ennobled the war's purpose. His platform for reelection in 1864 included passage of the 13th Amendment outlawing slavery (ratified 1865), and he easily defeated George B. McClellan. At his second inaugural, with victory in sight, he spoke of moderation in reconstructing the South and building a harmonious Union. On 14 April, five days after the war ended, he was shot by John Wilkes Booth and soon after died.

**Andrew Johnson** (29 Dec 1808, Raleigh NC–31 Jul 1875, near Carter Station TN), 17th president of the US (1865–69). Born in North Carolina and reared in Tennessee, he organized a working-man's party and was elected to the state legislature (1835–43). He served in the House of Representatives (1843–53) and as governor of Tennessee (1853–57). Elected to the Senate (1857–62), he opposed antislavery agitation, but in 1860 he opposed Southern secession, even after Tennessee seceded in 1861, and during the Civil War he was the only Southern senator who refused to join the Confederacy. In 1862 he was appointed military governor of Tennessee, then under Union control. In 1864 he ran for vice president with Pres. Abraham Lincoln; he assumed the presidency after Lincoln's assassination. During Reconstruction he favored a moderate policy that readmitted former Confederate states to the Union with few provisions for reform or civil rights for freedmen. In 1867 the Radical Republicans in Congress passed civil rights legislation and established the Freedmen's Bureau. His veto angered Congress, which passed the Tenure of Office Act requiring congressional approval for the removal of any civil officers. In 1868, in defiance of the act, Johnson dismissed secretary of war Edwin M. Stanton, an ally of the Radicals, and the House responded by impeaching the president for the first time in US history. In the subsequent Senate trial, the charges proved weak and the necessary two-thirds vote needed for conviction failed by one vote. Johnson remained in office until 1869, but his effectiveness had ended. He returned to Tennessee, where he won reelection to the Senate shortly before he died.

**Ulysses S. Grant** (Hiram Ulysses Grant; 27 Apr 1822, Point Pleasant OH—23 Jul 1885, Mount McGregor NY), 18th president of the US (1869–77). He served in the Mexican-American War under Zachary Taylor. Allegations that he became a drunkard after the war, though never proved, would affect his reputation. When the Civil War began (1861), he was appointed brigadier general; his 1862 attack on Ft. Donelson in Tennessee produced the first major Union victory. He drove off a Confederate attack at Shiloh but was criticized for heavy Union losses. He devised the campaign to take the stronghold of Vicksburg MS in 1863, cutting the Confederacy in half from east to west. Following his victory at the Battle of Chattanooga in 1864, he was appointed commander of the Union army. While William T. Sherman made his famous march across Georgia, Grant attacked Robert E. Lee's forces in Virginia, bringing the war to an end in 1865. His successful Republican presidential campaign made him, at 46, the youngest man yet elected president. His two terms were marred by administrative inaction and political scandal involving members of his cabinet, including the Crédit Mobilier scandal and the Whiskey Ring operation. He supported amnesty for Confederate leaders and protection for black civil rights. His veto of a bill to increase the amount of legal tender (1874) diminished the currency crisis in the next 25 years. His memoirs were published by his friend Mark Twain.

**Rutherford Birchard Hayes** (4 Oct 1822, Delaware OH—17 Jan 1893, Fremont OH), 19th president of the US (1877–81). After fighting in the Union army, he served in the House of Representatives (1865–67). As governor of Ohio (1868–72, 1875–76), he advocated a sound currency backed by gold. In 1876 he won the Republican nomination for president. His opponent, Samuel Tilden, won a larger popular vote, but Hayes's managers contested the electoral-vote returns in four states, and a special

Electoral Commission awarded the election to Hayes. As part of a secret compromise reached with Southerners, he withdrew the remaining federal troops from the South, ending Reconstruction, and promised not to interfere with elections there, ensuring the return of white Democratic supremacy. At the request of state governors, he used federal troops against strikers in the railroad strikes of 1877. He declined to run for a second term.

**James Abram Garfield** (19 Nov 1831, near Orange [in Cuyahoga county] OH—19 Sep 1881, Elberon [now in Long Branch] NJ), 20th president of the US (1881). In the Civil War he led the 42nd Ohio Volunteers and fought at Shiloh and Chickamauga. He resigned as a major general to serve in the House of Representatives (1863–80). A Radical Republican during Reconstruction, he was the House Republican leader from 1876 to 1880, when he was elected to the Senate. At the 1880 Republican nominating convention, the delegates supporting Ulysses S. Grant and James Blaine became deadlocked. On the 36th ballot, Garfield was nominated as a compromise presidential candidate, with Chester Arthur as vice president, and he won by a narrow margin. His term was brief—less than 150 days. On 2 July he was shot at Washington's railroad station by Charles J. Guiteau, an Arthur supporter. He died on 19 September after 11 weeks of public debate over the ambiguous constitutional conditions for presidential succession (later clarified by the 20th and 25th Amendments).

**Chester Alan Arthur** (5 Oct 1829, North Fairfield VT—18 Nov 1886, New York NY), 21st president of the US (1881–85). Active in New York City Republican politics, he was appointed customs collector for the port of New York (1871–78), an office long known for its employment of the spoils system. He conducted the business of the office with integrity but continued to pad its payroll with loyalists of Sen. Roscoe Conkling. At the Republican National Convention in 1880, Arthur was the compromise choice for vice president on the ticket with James Garfield, and he became president upon Garfield's assassination. As president, Arthur displayed unexpected independence by vetoing measures that rewarded political patronage and signing the Pendleton Act, which created a civil-service system based on merit. He also recommended the appropriations for rebuilding the navy toward the strength it later achieved in the Spanish-American War (1898), but he failed to win his party's nomination for a second term.

**(Stephen) Grover Cleveland** (18 Mar 1837, Caldwell NJ—24 Jun 1908, Princeton NJ), 22nd and 24th president of the US (1885–89, 1893–97). As mayor of Buffalo NY (1881–82), he was known as a foe of corruption. As governor of New York (1883–85), he earned the hostility of Tammany Hall with his independence, but in 1884 he won the Democratic nomination for president and the election. The first Democratic president since 1856, he supported civil-service reform and opposed high protective tariffs, which became an issue in the 1888 election, when he was narrowly defeated by Benjamin Harrison. In 1892 he was reelected by a huge popular plurality. In 1893 he attributed the US's severe economic depression to the Sherman Silver Purchase Act of 1890 and strongly urged Congress to repeal the act. By 1896, however, supporters of the Free Silver Movement controlled the

Democratic Party, which nominated William Jennings Bryan instead of Cleveland for president.

**Benjamin Harrison** (20 Aug 1833, North Bend OH—13 Mar 1901, Indianapolis IN), 23rd president of the US (1889–93). The grandson of Pres. William H. Harrison, he served in the Union army in the Civil War, rising to brigadier general. He served a term in the Senate (1881–87) and, even though he lost reelection, was nominated for president by the Republicans. He went on to defeat the incumbent, Grover Cleveland, who lost despite winning more of the popular vote. As president, his domestic policy was marked by passage of the Sherman Antitrust Act, and his foreign policy expanded US influence abroad. His administration oversaw the conference that led to the establishment of the Pan-American Union, resisted pressure to abandon US interests in the Samoa Islands (1889), and negotiated a treaty with Britain in the Bering Sea Dispute (1891). He was defeated for reelection by Cleveland in 1892. In 1898–99 he was the leading counsel for Venezuela in its boundary dispute with Britain.

**William McKinley** (29 Jan 1843, Niles OH—14 Sep 1901, Buffalo NY), 25th president of the US (1897–1901). He served in the Civil War as an aide to Col. Rutherford B. Hayes, who later encouraged his political career. He was elected to the House of Representatives (1877–91), where he sponsored the McKinley Tariff of 1890, and he served as elected governor of Ohio (1892–96). In 1896 he won the Republican presidential nomination and the general election, defeating William Jennings Bryan. He was soon embroiled in events in Cuba and responses to the sinking of the USS *Maine*, which led to the Spanish-American War. At the war's end, he advocated US dependency status for the Philippines, Puerto Rico, and other former Spanish territories. He again defeated Bryan by a large majority in 1900. In Buffalo NY on 6 Sep 1901, he was fatally shot by an anarchist, Leon Czolgosz.

**Theodore Roosevelt** (27 Oct 1858, New York NY—6 Jan 1919, Oyster Bay NY), 26th president of the US (1901–09). He was elected to the New York legislature in 1882, where he became a Republican leader opposed to the Democratic political machine, and he went on to serve on the US Civil Service Commission (1889–95) and as head of New York City's board of police commissioners (1895–97). A supporter of William McKinley, he served as assistant secretary of the navy (1897–98). When the Spanish-American War was declared, he resigned to organize a cavalry unit, the Rough Riders. He returned to New York a hero and was elected governor in 1899. As the Republican vice-presidential nominee, he took office when McKinley was reelected, and he became president on McKinley's assassination in 1901. One of his early initiatives was to urge enforcement of the Sherman Antitrust Act against business monopolies. He won election in his own right in 1904, and at his urging, Congress regulated railroad rates and passed the Pure Food and Drug Act and Meat Inspection Act (both 1906) to provide new consumer protections. He set aside national forests, parks, and mineral, oil, and coal lands for conservation. For mediating an end to the Russo-Japanese War, he received the 1906 Nobel Peace Prize. He secured a treaty with Panama for construction of a trans-isthmus canal. Declining to seek reelection, he secured the nomination for William H. Taft. He tried to win the Republican presidential nomination

in 1912; when he was rejected, he organized the Bull Moose Party and ran on a policy of New Nationalism, but he failed to win the election.

**William Howard Taft** (15 Sep 1857, Cincinnati OH—8 Mar 1930, Washington DC), 27th president of the US (1909–13). He served as US solicitor general (1890–92) and as US appellate judge (1892–1900). He was appointed head of the Philippine Commission to set up a civilian government in the islands and was its first civilian governor (1901–04). He served as US secretary of war (1904–08) under Pres. Theodore Roosevelt, who supported Taft's nomination for president in 1908. He won the election but became allied with the conservative Republicans, causing a rift with party progressives. He was again the nominee in 1912, but the split with Roosevelt and the Bull Moose Party resulted in the electoral victory of Woodrow Wilson. Taft later was a supporter of the League of Nations. As chief justice of the Supreme Court (1921–30), he secured passage of the Judges Act of 1925, which gave the Court wider discretion in accepting cases.

**(Thomas) Woodrow Wilson** (28 Dec 1856, Staunton VA—3 Feb 1924, Washington DC), 28th president of the US (1913–21). He taught political science at Princeton University (1890–1902) and was its president (1902–10). With the support of progressives, he was elected governor of New Jersey. His reform measures attracted national attention, and he became the Democratic presidential nominee in 1912. His campaign emphasized the progressive measures of his New Freedom policy, and he defeated Theodore Roosevelt and William H. Taft to win the presidency. As president, he approved legislation that created the Federal Reserve System, established the Federal Trade Commission, and strengthened labor unions. In foreign affairs he promoted self-government for the Philippines and sought to contain the Mexican civil war. He maintained US neutrality in World War I, offering to mediate a settlement and initiate peace negotiations. Campaigning on the theme that he had "kept us out of war," he was narrowly reelected in 1916, defeating Charles Evans Hughes. Germany's continued submarine attacks on unarmed passenger ships caused Wilson to ask for a declaration of war in April 1917. In a continuing effort to negotiate a peace agreement, he led the US delegation to the Paris Peace Conference, where he attempted to stand on his original principles but was forced to compromise by the demands of various countries. The Treaty of Versailles faced opposition in the Senate from the Republican majority. In search of popular support for the treaty and its League of Nations, Wilson began a cross-country speaking tour, but he collapsed and returned to Washington DC, where a stroke left him partially paralyzed. He rejected any attempts to compromise his version of the League of Nations and as a result eventually urged his Senate followers to vote against ratification of the treaty, which was defeated in 1920. He was awarded the 1919 Nobel Peace Prize for his work on the League of Nations.

**Warren Gamaliel Harding** (2 Nov 1865, Caledonia [now Blooming Grove] OH—2 Aug 1923, San Francisco CA), 29th president of the US (1921–23). He served successively as Ohio state senator (1899–1902), lieutenant governor (1903–04), and US senator (1915–21), supporting conservative policies. At the deadlocked 1920 Republican presidential convention, he was chosen as the compromise candidate. Pledging a "return to normalcy" after World War I, he defeated James Cox with over 60% of the popular vote, the largest margin to that time. On his recommendation Congress established a budget system for the federal government, passed a high protective tariff, revised wartime taxes, and restricted immigration. His ill-advised cabinet and patronage appointments led to the Teapot Dome Scandal and characterized his administration as corrupt. While in Alaska he received word of the corruption about to be exposed and headed back. He arrived in San Francisco exhausted, reportedly suffering from food poisoning and other ills, and died there under unclear circumstances, to be succeeded by his vice president, Calvin Coolidge.

**(John) Calvin Coolidge** (4 Jul 1872, Plymouth VT–5 Jan 1933, Northampton MA), 30th president of the US (1923–29). He served as lieutenant governor of Massachusetts before being elected governor in 1918. He gained national attention by calling out the state guard during the Boston police strike in 1919. At the 1920 Republican convention, "Silent Cal" was nominated for vice president on Warren G. Harding's winning ticket. When Harding died in office in 1923, Coolidge became president. He restored confidence in an administration discredited by scandals and won the presidential election in 1924, defeating Robert La Follette. His presidency was marked by apparent prosperity. Congress maintained a high protective tariff and instituted tax reductions that favored capital. Coolidge declined to run for a second full term. His conservative policies of domestic and international inaction have come to symbolize the era between World War I and the Great Depression.

**Herbert Hoover** (10 Aug 1874, West Branch IA–20 Oct 1964, New York NY), 31st president of the US (1929–33). He headed Allied relief operations in England and Belgium prior to World War I, at which time he was appointed national food administrator (1917–19) and instituted programs that furnished food to famine-stricken areas of Europe. Appointed secretary of commerce (1921–27), he oversaw commissions to build Boulder (later Hoover) Dam and the St. Lawrence Seaway. In 1928, as the Republican presidential candidate, he soundly defeated Alfred E. Smith. His hopes for a "New Day" program were quickly overwhelmed by the Great Depression. As a believer in individual freedom, he vetoed bills to create a federal unemployment agency and to fund public-works projects, instead favoring private charity. In 1932 he finally allowed relief to farmers through the Reconstruction Finance Corp., but he was overwhelmingly defeated in 1932 by Franklin Roosevelt.

**Franklin Delano Roosevelt** (30 Jan 1882, Hyde Park NY–12 Apr 1945, Warm Springs GA), 32nd president of the US (1933–45). He was attracted to politics as an admirer of his cousin Pres. Theodore Roosevelt and became active in the Democratic Party. In 1905 he married distant cousin Eleanor Roosevelt, who would become a valued adviser in future years. He served as assistant secretary of the navy (1913–20). In 1920 he was nominated for vice president. The next year he was stricken with polio; though unable to walk, he remained active in politics. As governor of New York (1929–33), he set up the first state relief agency in the US. In 1932 he won the Democratic presidential nomination and

easily defeated Pres. Herbert Hoover. In his inaugural address to a nation of more than 13 million unemployed, he pronounced that "the only thing we have to fear is fear itself." Congress passed most of the changes he sought in his New Deal program in the first hundred days of his term. He was overwhelmingly reelected in 1936 over Alf Landon. By the late 1930s economic recovery had slowed, but Roosevelt was more concerned with the growing threat of war. In 1940 he was reelected to an unprecedented third term, defeating Wendell Willkie. He maintained US neutrality toward the war in Europe but approved the principle of lend-lease and in 1941 met with Winston Churchill to draft the Atlantic Charter. With US entry into World War II, he mobilized industry for military production and formed an alliance with Britain and the Soviet Union; he met with Churchill and Joseph Stalin to form war policy at Tehran (1943) and Yalta (1945). Despite declining health, he won reelection for a fourth term against Thomas Dewey (1944) but served only briefly before his death.

**Harry S. Truman** (8 May 1884, Lamar MO–26 Dec 1972, Kansas City MO), 33rd president of the US (1945–53). He served with distinction in World War I, and he later entered Democratic Party politics in Missouri. His reputation for honesty and good management gained him bipartisan support. In the Senate (1935–45), he led a committee that exposed fraud in defense production. In 1944 he was chosen to replace the incumbent Henry Wallace as vice-presidential nominee and was elected with Pres. Franklin Roosevelt. After only 82 days as vice president, he became president on Roosevelt's death (April 1945). He quickly made final arrangements for the San Francisco charter-writing meeting of the UN; helped arrange Germany's unconditional surrender on 8 May, which ended World War II in Europe; and in July attended the Potsdam Conference. The Pacific war ended officially on 2 September, after he ordered atomic bombs dropped on Hiroshima and Nagasaki; his justification was a report that 500,000 US troops would be lost in a conventional invasion of Japan. He announced the Truman Doctrine to aid Greece and Turkey (1947), established the Central Intelligence Agency, and pressed for passage of the Marshall Plan to aid European countries. In 1948 he defeated Thomas Dewey to gain reelection. He hewed to a foreign policy of containment to restrict the Soviet Union's sphere of influence and initiated the Berlin airlift and the NATO pact of 1949. In the Korean War he sent troops under Gen. Douglas MacArthur to head the United Nations forces. Though he was often criticized during his presidency, Truman's reputation grew steadily in later years.

**Dwight David Eisenhower** (14 Oct 1890, Denison TX–28 Mar 1969, Washington DC), 34th president of the US (1953–61). He graduated from West Point (1915) and then served in the Panama Canal Zone (1922–24) and in the Philippines under Douglas MacArthur (1935–39). In World War II, Gen. George Marshall chose him to command US forces in Europe (1942). After planning the invasions of North Africa, Sicily, and Italy, he was appointed supreme commander of Allied forces (1943). He planned the Normandy campaign (1944) and the conduct of the war in Europe until the German surrender (1945). He was promoted to five-star general (1944) and was named army chief of staff in 1945 and supreme commander of NATO in 1951. Both

Democrats and Republicans courted Eisenhower as a presidential candidate; in 1952, as the Republican candidate, he defeated Adlai Stevenson with the largest popular vote up to that time. He defeated Stevenson again in 1956 in an even larger landslide. His achievements included efforts to contain communism with the Eisenhower Doctrine. He sent federal troops to Little Rock AR to enforce integration of a city high school (1957). When the Soviet Union launched Sputnik 1 (1957), he was criticized for having failed to develop the US space program and responded by creating NASA (1958). In his last weeks in office the US broke diplomatic relations with Cuba.

**John Fitzgerald Kennedy** (29 May 1917, Brookline MA—22 Nov 1963, Dallas TX), 35th president of the US (1961–63). He joined the navy in World War II, where he earned medals for heroism. Elected to the House of Representatives (1947–53) and the Senate (1953–60), he supported social legislation and became increasingly committed to civil rights legislation. In 1960 he won the Democratic nomination for president; after a vigorous campaign, managed by his brother Robert F. Kennedy, he narrowly defeated Richard Nixon. He was the youngest person and the first Roman Catholic elected president. In his inaugural address he called on Americans to "ask not what your country can do for you, ask what you can do for your country." He proposed tax-reform and civil rights legislation but received little congressional support. He established the Peace Corps and the Alliance for Progress. His foreign policy began with the abortive Bay of Pigs invasion (1961), which emboldened the Soviet Union to move missiles to Cuba, sparking the Cuban missile crisis. In 1963 he successfully concluded the Nuclear Test-Ban Treaty. In November 1963 he was assassinated by a sniper, allegedly Lee Harvey Oswald, while riding in a motorcade in Dallas. The killing is considered the most notorious political murder of the 20th century. Kennedy's youth, energy, and charming family brought him world adulation and sparked the idealism of a generation, for whom the Kennedy White House became known as "Camelot."

**Lyndon Baines Johnson** (27 Aug 1908, Gillespie county TX—22 Jan 1973, San Antonio TX), 36th president of the US (1963–69). He won a seat in the House of Representatives (1937–49) as the New Deal was under conservative attack. His loyalty impressed Pres. Franklin Roosevelt, who made Johnson a protégé. He won election to the Senate in 1949 in a vicious campaign that saw fraud on both sides. As Democratic whip (1951–55) and majority leader (1955–61), he developed a talent for consensus building among dissident factions with methods both tactful and ruthless. He was largely responsible for passage of the civil rights bills of 1957 and 1960, the first in the 20th century. In 1960 he was elected vice president; he became president after the assassination of John F. Kennedy. In his first few months in office he won from Congress passage of a huge quantity of important civil rights, tax-reduction, antipoverty, and conservation legislation. He defeated Barry Goldwater in the 1964 election by the largest popular majority to that time and announced his Great Society program, which never came to fruition because of the escalation of US involvement in the Vietnam War, beginning with the Gulf of Tonkin Resolution. His approval ratings diminished markedly and led to his decision not to seek reelection in 1968.

**Richard Milhous Nixon** (9 Jan 1913, Yorba Linda CA—22 Apr 1994, New York NY), 37th president of the US (1969–74). After serving in World War II, he was elected to the House of Representatives in 1947, employing harsh campaign tactics, and to the Senate in 1951, again following a bitter campaign. He won the vice presidency in 1952 on a ticket with Dwight D. Eisenhower; they were reelected easily in 1956. As presidential candidate in 1960, he lost narrowly to John F. Kennedy. He reentered politics by running for president in 1968, and he defeated Hubert H. Humphrey with his "Southern strategy" of seeking votes from Southern and Western conservatives in both parties. As president, he began to gradually withdraw US military forces in an effort to end the Vietnam War while ordering the secret bombing of North Vietnamese military centers in Laos and Cambodia, which drew widespread protest. Economic problems included the largest US budget to date, and in 1971 Nixon established unprecedented peacetime controls on wages and prices. He won reelection in 1972 with a landslide victory over George McGovern. Assisted by Henry A. Kissinger, he concluded the Vietnam War. He reopened communications with China and made a state visit there. On his visit to the Soviet Union, the first by a US president, he signed the bilateral Strategic Arms Limitation Talks (SALT) agreements. The Watergate Scandal overshadowed his second term; his complicity in efforts to cover up his involvement and the likelihood of impeachment led to his becoming, in August 1974, the first president to resign from office.

**Gerald Rudolph Ford, Jr.** (Leslie Lynch King, Jr.; 14 Jul 1913, Omaha NE—26 Dec 2006, Rancho Mirage CA), 38th president of the US (1974–77). He served in the House of Representatives (1948–73), becoming minority leader in 1965. After Spiro Agnew resigned as vice president in 1973, Richard Nixon nominated Ford to fill the vacant post. When the Watergate Scandal forced Nixon's departure, Ford became the first president who had not been elected to either the vice presidency or the presidency. A month later he pardoned Nixon; to counter widespread outrage, he voluntarily appeared before a House subcommittee to explain his action. His administration gradually lowered the high inflation rate it inherited. Ford's relations with the Democratic-controlled Congress were typified by his more than 50 vetoes, of which more than 40 were sustained. In the final days of the Vietnam War in 1975, he ordered an airlift of 237,000 anticommunist Vietnamese refugees, most of whom came to the US. Reaction against Watergate contributed to his defeat by James Earl Carter, Jr., in 1976.

**James Earl Carter, Jr.** (1 Oct 1924, Plains GA), 39th president of the US (1977–81). As governor (1971–75) he opened Georgia's government offices to blacks and women and introduced stricter budgeting procedures for state agencies. In 1976, though lacking a national political base or major backing, he won the Democratic nomination and the presidency, defeating the sitting president, Gerald Ford. As president, Carter helped negotiate a peace treaty between Egypt and Israel, signed a treaty with Panama to make the Panama Canal a neutral zone after 1999, and established full diplomatic relations with China. In 1979-80 the Iran hostage crisis became a major political liability. He responded forcefully to the USSR's invasion of

Afghanistan in 1979, embargoing the shipment of US grain to that country and leading a boycott of the 1980 Summer Olympics in Moscow. Hampered by high inflation and a recession engineered to tame it, he lost his bid for reelection to Ronald Reagan. He subsequently became involved in international diplomatic negotiations and helped oversee elections in countries with insecure democratic traditions. Carter was awarded the Nobel Peace Prize in 2002.

**Ronald Wilson Reagan** (6 Feb 1911, Tampico IL—5 Jun 2004, Bel Air CA), 40th president of the US (1981–89). In his career as a Hollywood movie actor, he had roles in 50 films and was twice president of the Screen Actors Guild (1947–52, 1959–60). Having gradually changed his political affiliation from liberal Democrat to conservative Republican, he served as governor of California (1967–75). In 1980 he defeated incumbent Pres. Jimmy Carter to become president. Shortly after taking office, he was wounded in an assassination attempt. Reagan adopted supply-side economics to promote rapid economic growth and reduce the federal deficit. Congress approved most of his proposals in 1981, which succeeded in lowering inflation but doubled the national debt by 1986. He began the largest peacetime military buildup in US history and in 1983 proposed construction of the Strategic Defense Initiative to place antimissile technology in space. His foreign policy decisions included signing the Intermediate-Range Nuclear Forces (INF) Treaty to restrict intermediate-range nuclear weapons and invading Grenada. In 1984 Reagan defeated Walter Mondale in a landslide for reelection. Details of his administration's involvement in the Iran-Contra Affair emerged in 1986 and significantly weakened his popularity and authority. Though his intellectual capacity for governing was often disparaged (and in 1994 he revealed that he had Alzheimer disease), his artful communication skills enabled him to pursue numerous conservative policies with conspicuous success.

**George Herbert Walker Bush** (12 Jun 1924, Milton MA), 41st president of the US (1989–93). He served in World War II, graduated from Yale University, and started an oil business in Texas. He served in the House of Representatives (1966–70) as a Republican. He then served as ambassador to the UN (1971–72), chief liaison to China (1974–76), and head of the CIA (1976–77). In 1980 he ran for president but lost the nomination to Ronald Reagan. Bush served as vice president with Reagan (1981–89), whom he succeeded as president, defeating Michael Dukakis. He made no dramatic departures from Reagan's policies. In 1989 he ordered a brief military invasion of Panama, which toppled that country's leader, Gen. Manuel Noriega. He helped impose a UN-approved embargo against Iraq in 1990 to force its withdrawal from Kuwait. When Iraq refused, he authorized a US-led air offensive that began the Persian Gulf War. Despite general approval of his foreign policy, an economic recession led to his defeat by Bill Clinton in 1992. His son George W. Bush was elected president in 2000 and reelected in 2004.

**William Jefferson Clinton** (William Jefferson Blythe III; 19 Aug 1946, Hope AR), 42nd president of the US (1993–2001). He served as state attorney general (1977–79) and served several terms as governor (1979–81, 1983–92), during which he reformed Arkansas's educational system and encouraged the growth of industry through favorable tax policies. He won the Democratic presidential nomination in 1992, after withstanding charges of personal impropriety, and defeated the incumbent, George H.W. Bush. As president he obtained approval of the North American Free Trade Agreement (NAFTA) in 1993. He and his wife, Hillary Rodham Clinton, strongly advocated their plan to overhaul the US health care system, but Congress rejected it. He committed US forces to a peacekeeping initiative in Bosnia and Herzegovina. In 1994 the Democrats lost control of Congress for the first time since 1954. Clinton defeated Robert Dole to win reelection in 1996. He faced renewed charges of personal impropriety, this time involving Monica Lewinsky, and as a result, in 1998 he became the second president in history to be impeached. Charged with perjury and obstruction of justice, he was acquitted at his Senate trial in 1999. His two terms saw sustained economic growth and successive budget surpluses, the first in three decades.

**George Walker Bush** (6 Jul 1946, New Haven CT), 43rd president of the US (2001–09). The eldest child of Pres. George H.W. Bush, he served as governor of Texas (1995–2000). Despite losing the national popular vote to Vice President Al Gore by more than 500,000 votes in 2000, he gained the electoral college and the presidency when a Supreme Court ruling ended a recount of ballots in Florida. His response to the terrorist attacks on 11 Sep 2001 gave shape to his administration. The invasion of Iraq by US-led forces in March 2003 was followed by a problematic occupation during which a burgeoning insurgency threatened Iraqi efforts to stabilize a democratically elected government. Bush won reelection in 2004. The loss of Republican control of Congress in elections in November 2006 limited his power to steer legislation to passage at the end of his time in the White House.

**Barack Hussein Obama II** (4 Aug 1961, Honolulu HI), 44th president of the US (from 2009). He graduated from Columbia University (1983) and magna cum laude from Harvard Law School (1991), where he was the first African American to serve as president of the *Harvard Law Review*. He served as a community organizer on Chicago's largely impoverished Far South Side and lectured in constitutional law at the University of Chicago. He was elected (1996) to the Illinois Senate as a member of the Democratic Party. In 2004 he was elected to the US Senate, the third African American to be elected to that body since the end of Reconstruction. He quickly became a major national political figure. In 2008 Obama won an upset victory in the Democratic primary over US senator and former first lady Hillary Clinton to become the Democratic presidential nominee. He easily defeated Republican candidate John McCain to become the first African American president, capturing nearly 53 percent of the popular vote and 365 electoral votes. Not only did he hold all the states that John Kerry had won in the 2004 election, but he also captured a number of states (e.g., Colorado, Florida, Nevada, Ohio, and Virginia) that the Republicans had carried in the previous two presidential elections. He is the author of two books, the memoir *Dreams from My Father* (1995) and *The Audacity of Hope* (2006), a mainstream polemic on his vision for the United States.

# US Presidents' Spouses and Children

*Maiden names of the presidents' wives appear in small capital letters.*

| DATE OF MARRIAGE | PRESIDENTS, SPOUSES, AND CHILDREN |
|---|---|

**George Washington**
6 Jan 1759    **Martha DANDRIDGE Custis** (2 Jun 1731–22 May 1802)
no children

**John Adams**
25 Oct 1764    **Abigail SMITH** (22 Nov 1744–28 Oct 1818)
▸ Abigail Amelia Adams (1765–1813), ▸ John Quincy Adams (1767–1848), ▸ Susanna Adams (1768–70), ▸ Charles Adams (1770–1800), ▸ Thomas Boylston Adams (1772–1832)

**Thomas Jefferson**
1 Jan 1772    **Martha WAYLES Skelton** (30 Oct 1748–6 Sep 1782)
▸ Martha Washington Jefferson (1772–1836), ▸ Jane Randolph Jefferson (1774–75), ▸ infant son (1777), ▸ Mary Jefferson (1778–1804), ▸ Lucy Elizabeth Jefferson (1780–81), ▸ Lucy Elizabeth Jefferson (1782–84)

**James Madison**
15 Sep 1794    **Dolley PAYNE Todd** (20 May 1768–12 Jul 1849)
no children

**James Monroe**
16 Feb 1786    **Elizabeth KORTRIGHT** (30 Jun 1768–23 Sep 1830)
▸ Eliza Kortright Monroe (1786–1835), ▸ James Spence Monroe (1799–1800), ▸ Maria Hester Monroe (1803–50)

**John Quincy Adams**
26 Jul 1797    **Louisa Catherine JOHNSON** (12 Feb 1775–15 May 1852)
▸ George Washington Adams (1801–29), ▸ John Adams (1803–34), ▸ Charles Francis Adams (1807–86), ▸ Louisa Catherine Adams (1811–12)

**Andrew Jackson**
Aug 1791    **Rachel DONELSON Robards** (15? Jun 1767–22 Dec 1828)
no children

**Martin Van Buren**
21 Feb 1807    **Hannah HOES** (8 Mar 1783–5 Feb 1819)
▸ Abraham Van Buren (1807–73), ▸ John Van Buren (1810–66), ▸ Martin Van Buren (1812–55), ▸ Smith Thompson Van Buren (1817–76)

**William Henry Harrison**
25 Nov 1795    **Anna Tuthill SYMMES** (25 Jul 1775–25 Feb 1864)
▸ Elizabeth Bassett Harrison (1796–1846), ▸ John Cleves Symmes Harrison (1798–1830), ▸ Lucy Singleton Harrison (1800–26), ▸ William Henry Harrison (1802–38), ▸ John Scott Harrison (1804–78), ▸ Benjamin Harrison (1806–40), ▸ Mary Symmes Harrison (1809–42), ▸ Carter Bassett Harrison (1811–39), ▸ Anna Tuthill Harrison (1813–65), ▸ James Findlay Harrison (1814–17)

**John Tyler**
29 Mar 1813    **Letitia CHRISTIAN** (12 Nov 1790–10 Sep 1842)
▸ Mary Tyler (1815–48), ▸ Robert Tyler (1816–77), ▸ John Tyler (1819–96), ▸ Letitia Tyler (1821–1907), ▸ Elizabeth Tyler (1823–50), ▸ Anne Contesse Tyler (1825), ▸ Alice Tyler (1827–54), ▸ Tazewell Tyler (1830–74)
26 Jun 1844    **Julia GARDINER** (4 May 1820–10 Jul 1889)
▸ David Gardiner Tyler (1846–1927), ▸ John Alexander Tyler (1848–83), ▸ Julia Gardiner Tyler (1849?–71), ▸ Lachlan Tyler (1851–1902), ▸ Lyon Gardiner Tyler (1853–1935), ▸ Robert Fitzwalter Tyler (1856–1927), ▸ Pearl Tyler (1860–1947)

**James K. Polk**
1 Jan 1824    **Sarah CHILDRESS** (4 Sep 1803–14 Aug 1891)
no children

**Zachary Taylor**
21 Jun 1810    **Margaret Mackall SMITH** (21 Sep 1788–14 Aug 1852)
▸ Anne Margaret Mackall Taylor (1811–75), ▸ Sarah Knox Taylor (1814–35), ▸ Octavia Pannel Taylor (1816–20), ▸ Margaret Smith Taylor (1819–20), ▸ Mary Elizabeth Taylor (1824–1909), ▸ Richard Taylor (1826–79)

## US Presidents' Spouses and Children (continued)

| DATE OF MARRIAGE | PRESIDENTS, SPOUSES, AND CHILDREN |
|---|---|

**Millard Fillmore**

5 Feb 1826 **Abigail Powers** (13 Mar 1798–30 Mar 1853)
▶ Millard Powers Fillmore (1828–89), ▶ Mary Abigail Fillmore (1832–54)

10 Feb 1858 **Caroline Carmichael McIntosh** (21 Oct 1813–11 Aug 1881)
no children

**Franklin Pierce**

10 Nov 1834 **Jane Means Appleton** (12 Mar 1806–2 Dec 1863)
▶ Franklin Pierce (1836), ▶ Frank Robert Pierce (1839–43), ▶ Benjamin Pierce (1841–53)

**James Buchanan**
never married

**Abraham Lincoln**

4 Nov 1842 **Mary Ann Todd** (13 Dec 1818–16 Jul 1882)
▶ Robert Todd Lincoln (1843–1926), ▶ Edward Baker Lincoln (1846–50), ▶ William Wallace Lincoln (1850–62), ▶ Thomas Lincoln (1853–71)

**Andrew Johnson**

17 May 1827 **Eliza McCardle** (4 Oct 1810–15 Jan 1876)
▶ Martha Johnson (1828–1901), ▶ Charles Johnson (1830–63), ▶ Mary Johnson (1832–83), ▶ Robert Johnson (1834–69), ▶ Andrew Johnson (1852–79)

**Ulysses S. Grant**

22 Aug 1848 **Julia Boggs Dent** (26 Jan 1826–14 Dec 1902)
▶ Frederick Dent Grant (1850–1912), ▶ Ulysses Simpson Grant (1852–1929), ▶ Ellen Wrenshall Grant (1855–1922), ▶ Jesse Root Grant (1858–1934)

**Rutherford B. Hayes**

30 Dec 1852 **Lucy Ware Webb** (28 Aug 1831–25 Jun 1889)
▶ Birchard Austin Hayes (1853–1926), ▶ James Webb Cook Hayes (1856–1934), ▶ Rutherford Platt Hayes (1858–1927), ▶ Joseph Thompson Hayes (1861–63), ▶ George Crook Hayes (1864–66), ▶ Frances Hayes (1867–1950), ▶ Scott Russell Hayes (1871–1923), ▶ Manning Force Hayes (1873–74)

**James A. Garfield**

11 Nov 1858 **Lucretia Rudolph** (19 Apr 1832–13 Mar 1918)
▶ Eliza Arabella Garfield (1860–63), ▶ Harry Augustus Garfield (1863–1942), ▶ James Rudolph Garfield (1865–1950), ▶ Mary Garfield (1867–1947), ▶ Irvin McDowell Garfield (1870–1951), ▶ Abram Garfield (1872–1958), ▶ Edward Garfield (1874–76)

**Chester A. Arthur**

25 Oct 1859 **Ellen Lewis Herndon** (30 Aug 1837–12 Jan 1880)
▶ William Lewis Herndon Arthur (1860–63), ▶ Chester Alan Arthur (1864–1937), ▶ Ellen Herndon Arthur (1871–1915)

**Grover Cleveland**

2 Jun 1886 **Frances Folsom** (21 Jul 1864–29 Oct 1947)
▶ Ruth Cleveland (1891–1904), ▶ Esther Cleveland (1893–1980), ▶ Marion Cleveland (1895–1977), ▶ Richard Folsom Cleveland (1897–1974), ▶ Francis Grover Cleveland (1903–95)

**Benjamin Harrison**

20 Oct 1853 **Caroline Lavinia Scott** (1 Oct 1832–25 Oct 1892)
▶ Russell Benjamin Harrison (1854–1936), ▶ Mary Scott Harrison (1858–1930)

6 Apr 1896 **Mary Scott Lord Dimmick** (30 Apr 1858–5 Jan 1948)
▶ Elizabeth Harrison (1897–1955)

**William McKinley**

25 Jan 1871 **Ida Saxton** (8 Jun 1847–26 May 1907)
▶ Katherine McKinley (1871–75), ▶ Ida McKinley (1873)

## US Presidents' Spouses and Children (continued)

| DATE OF MARRIAGE | PRESIDENTS, SPOUSES, AND CHILDREN |
|---|---|
| | **Theodore Roosevelt** |
| 27 Oct 1880 | **Alice Hathaway LEE** (29 Jul 1861–14 Feb 1884) |
| | ▸ Alice Lee Roosevelt (1884–1980) |
| 2 Dec 1886 | **Edith Kermit CAROW** (6 Aug 1861–30 Sep 1948) |
| | ▸ Theodore Roosevelt (1887–1944), ▸ Kermit Roosevelt (1889–1943), ▸ Ethel Carow Roosevelt (1891–1977), ▸ Archibald Bulloch Roosevelt (1894–1979), ▸ Quentin Roosevelt (1897–1918) |
| | |
| | **William Howard Taft** |
| 19 Jun 1886 | **Helen HERRON** (2 Jun 1861–22 May 1943) |
| | ▸ Robert Alphonso Taft (1889–1953), ▸ Helen Herron Taft (1891–1987), ▸ Charles Phelps Taft (1897–1983) |
| | |
| | **Woodrow Wilson** |
| 24 Jun 1885 | **Ellen Louise AXSON** (15 May 1860–6 Aug 1914) |
| | ▸ Margaret Woodrow Wilson (1886–1944), ▸ Jessie Woodrow Wilson (1887–1933), ▸ Eleanor Randolph Wilson (1889–1967) |
| 18 Dec 1915 | **Edith BOLLING Galt** (15 Oct 1872–28 Dec 1961) |
| | no children |
| | |
| | **Warren G. Harding** |
| 8 Jul 1891 | **Florence Mabel KLING DeWolfe** (15 Aug 1860–21 Nov 1924) |
| | no children |
| | |
| | **Calvin Coolidge** |
| 4 Oct 1905 | **Grace Anna GOODHUE** (3 Jan 1879–8 Jul 1957) |
| | ▸ John Coolidge (1906–2000), ▸ Calvin Coolidge (1908–24) |
| | |
| | **Herbert Hoover** |
| 10 Feb 1899 | **Lou HENRY** (29 Mar 1874–7 Jan 1944) |
| | ▸ Herbert Clark Hoover (1903–69), ▸ Allan Henry Hoover (1907–93) |
| | |
| | **Franklin D. Roosevelt** |
| 17 Mar 1905 | **Anna Eleanor (Eleanor) ROOSEVELT** (11 Oct 1884–7 Nov 1962) |
| | ▸ Anna Eleanor Roosevelt (1906–75), ▸ James Roosevelt (1907–91), ▸ Franklin Delano Roosevelt (1909), ▸ Elliott Roosevelt (1910–90), ▸ Franklin Delano Roosevelt (1914–88), ▸ John Aspinwall Roosevelt (1916–81) |
| | |
| | **Harry S. Truman** |
| 28 Jun 1919 | **Elizabeth Virginia (Bess) WALLACE** (13 Feb 1885–18 Oct 1982) |
| | ▸ Mary Margaret Truman (1924–2008) |
| | |
| | **Dwight D. Eisenhower** |
| 1 Jul 1916 | **Mamie Geneva DOUD** (14 Nov 1896–1 Nov 1979) |
| | ▸ Doud Dwight Eisenhower (1917–21), ▸ John Sheldon Doud Eisenhower (1922–  ) |
| | |
| | **John F. Kennedy** |
| 12 Sep 1953 | **Jacqueline Lee BOUVIER** (28 Jul 1929–19 May 1994) |
| | ▸ Caroline Bouvier Kennedy (1957–  ), ▸ John Fitzgerald Kennedy (1960–99), ▸ Patrick Bouvier Kennedy (1963) |
| | |
| | **Lyndon B. Johnson** |
| 17 Nov 1934 | **Claudia Alta (Lady Bird) TAYLOR** (22 Dec 1912–11 Jul 2007) |
| | ▸ Lynda Bird Johnson (1944–  ), ▸ Luci Baines Johnson (1947–  ) |
| | |
| | **Richard M. Nixon** |
| 21 Jun 1940 | **Thelma Catherine (Pat) RYAN** (16 Mar 1912–22 Jun 1993) |
| | ▸ Patricia Nixon (1946–  ), ▸ Julie Nixon (1948–  ) |
| | |
| | **Gerald R. Ford** |
| 15 Oct 1948 | **Elizabeth Ann (Betty) BLOOMER Warren** (8 Apr 1918–8 Jul 2011) |
| | ▸ Michael Gerald Ford (1950–  ), ▸ John Gardner Ford (1952–  ), ▸ Steven Meigs Ford (1956–  ), ▸ Susan Elizabeth Ford (1957–  ) |
| | |
| | **Jimmy Carter** |
| 7 Jul 1946 | **Eleanor Rosalynn (Rosalynn) SMITH** (18 Aug 1927–  ) |
| | ▸ John William Carter (1947–  ), ▸ James Earl Carter (1950–  ), ▸ Donnel Jeffrey Carter (1952–  ), ▸ Amy Lynn Carter (1967–  ) |

## US Presidents' Spouses and Children (continued)

| DATE OF MARRIAGE | PRESIDENTS, SPOUSES, AND CHILDREN |
|---|---|

**Ronald Reagan**

24 Jan 1940 **Jane Wyman (née Sarah Jane MAYFIELD [FULKS])** (5 Jan 1917–10 Sep 2007)
▶ Maureen Elizabeth Reagan (1941–2001), ▶ Michael Edward Reagan (1945–  ),
▶ Christine Reagan (1947)

4 Mar 1952 **Nancy Davis (née Anne Frances ROBBINS)** (6 Jul 1921–  )
▶ Patricia Ann Reagan (1952–  ), ▶ Ronald Prescott Reagan (1958–  )

**George H.W. Bush**

6 Jan 1945 **Barbara PIERCE** (8 Jun 1925–  )
▶ George Walker Bush (1946–  ), ▶ Pauline Robinson Bush (1949–53), ▶ John Ellis
Bush (1953–  ), ▶ Neil Mallon Bush (1955–  ), ▶ Marvin Pierce Bush (1956–  ),
▶ Dorothy Walker Bush (1959–  )

**Bill Clinton**

11 Oct 1975 **Hillary Diane RODHAM** (26 Oct 1947–  )
▶ Chelsea Victoria Clinton (1980–  )

**George W. Bush**

5 Nov 1977 **Laura Lane WELCH** (4 Nov 1946–  )
▶ Barbara Pierce Bush (1981–  ), ▶ Jenna Bush (1981–  )

**Barack Obama**

18 Oct 1992 **Michelle LaVaughn ROBINSON** (17 Jan 1964–  )
▶ Malia Ann Obama (1998–  ), ▶ Natasha Obama (2001–  )

---

**Did you know?** The bicentennial of the founding of the West Florida Republic took place in 2010. Not included in the Louisiana Purchase, the "Florida parishes" revolted against the Spanish government in Baton Rouge and declared their independence in September 1810. Proclaiming St. Francisville as their capital, the citizens of West Florida elected Fulwar Skipwith as their president. After a period of 74 days, the republic was forcibly annexed to the United States.

---

## US Presidential Cabinets

The cabinet is composed of the heads of executive departments chosen by the president with the consent of the Senate. Cabinet officials do not hold seats in Congress and are not regulated by the US Constitution, which makes no mention of such a body. The existence of the cabinet is a matter of custom dating back to George Washington, who consulted regularly with his department heads as a group. Original dates of service are given for officials appointed midterm and for newly created posts. Interim officials are not listed. Presidencies and new positions are indicated in bold.

### George Washington

**30 APR 1789–3 MARCH 1793 (TERM 1)**

| | |
|---|---|
| State | Thomas Jefferson |
| Treasury | Alexander Hamilton |
| War | Henry Knox |
| Attorney General | Edmund Randolph |

**4 MAR 1793–3 MAR 1797 (TERM 2)**

| | |
|---|---|
| State | Thomas Jefferson; Edmund Randolph (2 Jan 1794); Timothy Pickering (20 Aug 1795) |
| Treasury | Alexander Hamilton; Oliver Wolcott, Jr. (2 Feb 1795) |
| War | Henry Knox; Timothy Pickering (2 Jan 1795); James McHenry (6 Feb 1796) |
| Attorney General | Edmund Randolph; William Bradford (29 Jan 1794); Charles Lee (10 Dec 1795) |

### John Adams

**4 MAR 1797–3 MAR 1801**

| | |
|---|---|
| State | Timothy Pickering; John Marshall (6 Jun 1800) |
| Treasury | Oliver Wolcott, Jr.; Samuel Dexter (1 Jan 1801) |
| War | James McHenry; Samuel Dexter (12 Jun 1800) |
| **Navy** | Benjamin Stoddert (18 Jun 1798) |
| Attorney General | Charles Lee |

# US Presidential Cabinets (continued)

### Thomas Jefferson

**4 MAR 1801–3 MAR 1805 (TERM 1)**

| | |
|---|---|
| State | James Madison |
| Treasury | Samuel Dexter; Albert Gallatin (14 May 1801) |
| War | Henry Dearborn |
| Navy | Benjamin Stoddert; Robert Smith (27 Jul 1801) |
| Attorney General | Levi Lincoln |

**4 MAR 1805–3 MAR 1809 (TERM 2)**

| | |
|---|---|
| State | James Madison |
| Treasury | Albert Gallatin |
| War | Henry Dearborn |
| Navy | Robert Smith |
| Attorney General | John Breckenridge; Caesar Augustus Rodney (20 Jan 1807) |

### James Madison

**4 MAR 1809–3 MAR 1813 (TERM 1)**

| | |
|---|---|
| State | Robert Smith |
| Treasury | Albert Gallatin |
| War | John Smith; William Eustis (8 Apr 1809); John Armstrong (5 Feb 1813) |
| Navy | Robert Smith; Paul Hamilton (15 May 1809); William Jones (19 Jan 1813) |
| Attorney General | Caesar Augustus Rodney; William Pinkney (6 Jan 1812) |

**4 MAR 1813–3 MAR 1817 (TERM 2)**

| | |
|---|---|
| State | James Monroe |
| Treasury | Albert Gallatin; George Washington Campbell (9 Feb 1814); Alexander James Dallas (14 Oct 1814); William Harris Crawford (22 Oct 1816) |
| War | John Armstrong; James Monroe (1 Oct 1814); William Harris Crawford (8 Aug 1815) |
| Navy | William Jones; Benjamin Williams Crowninshield (16 Jan 1815) |
| Attorney General | William Pinkney; Richard Rush (11 Feb 1814) |

### James Monroe

**4 MAR 1817–3 MAR 1821 (TERM 1)**

| | |
|---|---|
| State | John Quincy Adams |
| Treasury | William Harris Crawford |
| War | John C. Calhoun |
| Navy | Benjamin Williams Crowninshield; Smith Thompson (1 Jan 1819) |
| Attorney General | Richard Rush; William Wirt (15 Nov 1817) |

**4 MAR 1821–3 MAR 1825 (TERM 2)**

| | |
|---|---|
| State | John Quincy Adams |
| Treasury | William Harris Crawford |
| War | John C. Calhoun |
| Navy | Smith Thompson; Samuel Lewis Southard (16 Sep 1823) |
| Attorney General | William Wirt |

### John Quincy Adams

**4 MAR 1825–3 MAR 1829**

| | |
|---|---|
| State | Henry Clay |
| Treasury | Richard Rush |
| War | James Barbour; Peter Buell Porter (21 Jun 1828) |
| Navy | Samuel Lewis Southard |
| Attorney General | William Wirt |

### Andrew Jackson

**4 MAR 1829–3 MAR 1833 (TERM 1)**

| | |
|---|---|
| State | Martin Van Buren; Edward Livingston (24 May 1831) |
| Treasury | Samuel Delucenna Ingham; Louis McLane (8 Aug 1831) |
| War | John Henry Eaton; Lewis Cass (8 Aug 1831) |
| Navy | John Branch; Levi Woodbury (23 May 1831) |
| Attorney General | John Macpherson Berrien; Roger Brooke Taney (20 Jul 1831) |

# US Presidential Cabinets (continued)

### Andrew Jackson (continued)

**4 MAR 1833–3 MAR 1837 (TERM 2)**

| | |
|---|---|
| State | Edward Livingston; Louis McLane (29 May 1833); John Forsyth (1 Jul 1834) |
| Treasury | Louis McLane; William John Duane (1 Jun 1833); Roger Brooke Taney (23 Sep 1833); Levi Woodbury (1 Jul 1834) |
| War | Lewis Cass |
| Navy | Levi Woodbury; Mahlon Dickerson (30 Jun 1834) |
| Attorney General | Roger Brooke Taney; Benjamin Franklin Butler (18 Nov 1833) |

### Martin Van Buren

**4 MAR 1837–3 MAR 1841**

| | |
|---|---|
| State | John Forsyth |
| Treasury | Levi Woodbury |
| War | Joel Roberts Poinsett |
| Navy | Mahlon Dickerson; James Kirke Paulding (1 Jul 1838) |
| Attorney General | Benjamin Franklin Butler; Felix Grundy (1 Sep 1838); Henry Dilworth Gilpin (11 Jan 1840) |

### William Henry Harrison

**4 MAR 1841–4 APR 1841**

| | |
|---|---|
| State | Daniel Webster |
| Treasury | Thomas Ewing |
| War | John Bell |
| Navy | George Edmund Badger |
| Attorney General | John Jordan Crittenden |

### John Tyler

**6 APR 1841–3 MAR 1845**

| | |
|---|---|
| State | Daniel Webster; Abel Parker Upshur (24 Jul 1843); John C. Calhoun (1 Apr 1844) |
| Treasury | Thomas Ewing; Walter Forward (13 Sep 1841); John Canfield Spencer (8 Mar 1843); George Mortimer Bibb (4 Jul 1844) |
| War | John Bell; John Canfield Spencer (12 Oct 1841); James Madison Porter (8 Mar 1843); William Wilkins (20 Feb 1844) |
| Navy | George Edmund Badger; Abel Parker Upshur (11 Oct 1841); David Henshaw (24 Jul 1843); Thomas Walker Gilmer (19 Feb 1844); John Young Mason (26 Mar 1844) |
| Attorney General | John Jordan Crittenden; Hugh Swinton Legaré (20 Sep 1841); John Nelson (1 Jul 1843) |

### James K. Polk

**4 MAR 1845–3 MAR 1849**

| | |
|---|---|
| State | James Buchanan |
| Treasury | Robert James Walker |
| War | William Learned Marcy |
| Navy | George Bancroft; John Young Mason (9 Sep 1846) |
| Attorney General | John Young Mason; Nathan Clifford (17 Oct 1846); Isaac Toucey (29 Jun 1848) |

### Zachary Taylor

**4 MAR 1849–9 JUL 1850**

| | |
|---|---|
| State | John Middleton Clayton |
| Treasury | William Morris Meredith |
| War | George Washington Crawford |
| Navy | William Ballard Preston |
| Attorney General | Reverdy Johnson |
| **Interior** | Thomas Ewing (8 Mar 1849) |

### Millard Fillmore

**10 JUL 1850–3 MAR 1853**

| | |
|---|---|
| State | Daniel Webster; Edward Everett (6 Nov 1852) |
| Treasury | Thomas Corwin |
| War | George Washington Crawford; Charles Magill Conrad (15 Aug 1850) |
| Navy | William Alexander Graham; John Pendleton Kennedy (26 Jul 1852) |
| Attorney General | Reverdy Johnson; John Jordan Crittenden (14 Aug 1850) |
| Interior | Thomas Ewing; Thomas McKean Thompson McKennan (15 Aug 1850); Alexander Hugh Holmes Stuart (16 Sep 1850) |

## US Presidential Cabinets (continued)

### Franklin Pierce

**4 MAR 1853–3 MAR 1857**

| | |
|---|---|
| State | William Learned Marcy |
| Treasury | James Guthrie |
| War | Jefferson Davis |
| Navy | James Cochran Dobbin |
| Attorney General | Caleb Cushing |
| Interior | Robert McClelland |

### James Buchanan

**4 MAR 1857–3 MAR 1861**

| | |
|---|---|
| State | Lewis Cass; Jeremiah Sullivan Black (17 Dec 1860) |
| Treasury | Howell Cobb; Philip Francis Thomas (12 Dec 1860); John Adams Dix (15 Jan 1861) |
| War | John Buchanan Floyd |
| Navy | Isaac Toucey |
| Attorney General | Jeremiah Sullivan Black; Edwin McMasters Stanton (22 Dec 1860) |
| Interior | Jacob Thompson |

### Abraham Lincoln

**4 MAR 1861–3 MAR 1865 (TERM 1)**

| | |
|---|---|
| State | William Henry Seward |
| Treasury | Salmon Portland Chase; William Pitt Fessenden (5 Jul 1864) |
| War | Simon Cameron; Edwin McMasters Stanton (20 Jun 1862) |
| Navy | Gideon Welles |
| Attorney General | Edward Bates; James Speed (5 Dec 1864) |
| Interior | Caleb Blood Smith; John Palmer Usher (8 Jan 1863) |

**4 MAR 1865–15 APR 1865 (TERM 2)**

| | |
|---|---|
| State | William Henry Seward |
| Treasury | Hugh McCulloch |
| War | Edwin McMasters Stanton |
| Navy | Gideon Welles |
| Attorney General | James Speed |
| Interior | John Palmer Usher |

### Andrew Johnson

**15 APR 1865–3 MAR 1869**

| | |
|---|---|
| State | William Henry Seward |
| Treasury | Hugh McCulloch |
| War | Edwin McMasters Stanton; John McAllister Schofield (1 Jun 1868) |
| Navy | Gideon Welles |
| Attorney General | James Speed; Henry Stanbery (23 Jul 1866); William Maxwell Evarts (20 Jul 1868) |
| Interior | John Palmer Usher; James Harlan (15 May 1865); Orville Hickman Browning (1 Sep 1866) |

### Ulysses S. Grant

**4 MAR 1869–3 MAR 1873 (TERM 1)**

| | |
|---|---|
| State | Elihu Benjamin Washburne; Hamilton Fish (17 Mar 1869) |
| Treasury | George Sewall Boutwell |
| War | John Aaron Rawlins; William Tecumseh Sherman (11 Sep 1869); William Worth Belknap (1 Nov 1869) |
| Navy | Adolph Edward Borie; George Maxwell Robeson (25 Jun 1869) |
| Attorney General | Ebenezer Rockwood Hoar; Amos Tappan Akerman (8 Jul 1870); George Henry Williams (10 Jan 1872) |
| Interior | Jacob Dolson Cox; Columbus Delano (1 Nov 1870) |

**4 MAR 1873–3 MAR 1877 (TERM 2)**

| | |
|---|---|
| State | Hamilton Fish |
| Treasury | William Adams Richardson; Benjamin Helm Bristow (4 Jun 1874); Lot Myrick Morrill (7 Jul 1876) |
| War | William Worth Belknap; Alphonso Taft (11 Mar 1876); James Donald Cameron (1 Jun 1876) |
| Navy | George Maxwell Robeson |
| Attorney General | George Henry Williams; Edward Pierrepont (15 May 1875); Alphonso Taft (1 Jun 1876) |
| Interior | Columbus Delano; Zachariah Chandler (19 Oct 1875) |

## US Presidential Cabinets (continued)

### Rutherford B. Hayes

**4 MAR 1877–3 MAR 1881**

| | |
|---|---|
| State | William Maxwell Evarts |
| Treasury | John Sherman |
| War | George Washington McCrary; Alexander Ramsey (12 Dec 1879) |
| Navy | Richard Wigginton Thompson; Nathan Goff, Jr. (6 Jan 1881) |
| Attorney General | Charles Devens |
| Interior | Carl Schurz |

### James A. Garfield

**4 MAR 1881–19 SEP 1881**

| | |
|---|---|
| State | James Gillespie Blaine |
| Treasury | William Windom |
| War | Robert Todd Lincoln |
| Attorney General | (Isaac) Wayne MacVeagh |
| Navy | William Henry Hunt |
| Interior | Samuel Jordan Kirkwood |

### Chester A. Arthur

**20 SEP 1881–3 MAR 1885**

| | |
|---|---|
| State | James Gillespie Blaine; Frederick Theodore Frelinghuysen (19 Dec 1881) |
| Treasury | William Windom; Charles James Folger (14 Nov 1881); Walter Quintin Gresham (24 Sep 1884); Hugh McCulloch (31 Oct 1884) |
| War | Robert Todd Lincoln |
| Navy | William Henry Hunt; William Eaton Chandler (17 Apr 1882) |
| Attorney General | (Isaac) Wayne MacVeagh; Benjamin Harris Brewster (3 Jan 1882) |
| Interior | Samuel Jordan Kirkwood; Henry Moore Teller (17 Apr 1882) |

### Grover Cleveland

**4 MAR 1885–3 MAR 1889**

| | |
|---|---|
| State | Thomas Francis Bayard |
| Treasury | Daniel Manning; Charles Stebbins Fairchild (1 Apr 1887) |
| War | William Crowninshield Endicott |
| Navy | William Collins Whitney |
| Attorney General | Augustus Hill Garland |
| Interior | Lucius Quintus Cincinnatus Lamar; William Freeman Vilas (16 Jan 1888) |
| **Agriculture** | Norman Jay Colman (13 Feb 1889) |

### Benjamin Harrison

**4 MAR 1889–3 MAR 1893**

| | |
|---|---|
| State | James Gillespie Blaine; John Watson Foster (29 Jun 1892) |
| Treasury | William Windom; Charles Foster (24 Feb 1891) |
| War | Redfield Proctor; Stephen Benton Elkins (24 Dec 1891) |
| Navy | Benjamin Franklin Tracy |
| Attorney General | William Henry Harrison Miller |
| Interior | John Willock Noble |
| Agriculture | Jeremiah McLain Rusk |

### Grover Cleveland

**4 MAR 1893–3 MAR 1897**

| | |
|---|---|
| State | Walter Quintin Gresham; Richard Olney (10 Jun 1895) |
| Treasury | John Griffin Carlisle |
| War | Daniel Scott Lamont |
| Navy | Hilary Abner Herbert |
| Attorney General | Richard Olney; Judson Harmon (11 Jun 1895) |
| Interior | Hoke Smith; David Rowland Francis (4 Sep 1896) |
| Agriculture | Julius Sterling Morton |

### William McKinley

**4 MAR 1897–3 MAR 1901 (TERM 1)**

| | |
|---|---|
| State | John Sherman; William Rufus Day (28 Apr 1898); John Hay (30 Sep 1898) |
| Treasury | Lyman Judson |
| War | Russell Alexander Alger; Elihu Root (1 Aug 1899) |
| Navy | John Davis Long |
| Attorney General | Joseph McKenna; John William Griggs (1 Feb 1898) |
| Interior | Cornelius Newton Bliss; Ethan Allen Hitchcock (20 Feb 1899) |
| Agriculture | James Wilson |

## US Presidential Cabinets (continued)

### William McKinley (continued)

**4 MAR 1901–14 SEP 1901 (TERM 2)**

| | |
|---|---|
| State | John Hay |
| Treasury | Lyman Judson Gage |
| War | Elihu Root |
| Navy | John Davis Long |
| Attorney General | John William Griggs; Philander Chase Knox (10 Apr 1901) |
| Interior | Ethan Allen Hitchcock |
| Agriculture | James Wilson |

### Theodore Roosevelt

**14 SEP 1901–3 MAR 1905 (TERM 1)**

| | |
|---|---|
| State | John Hay |
| Treasury | Lyman Judson Gage; Leslie Mortier Shaw (1 Feb 1902) |
| War | Elihu Root; William Howard Taft (1 Feb 1904) |
| Navy | John Davis Long; William Henry Moody (1 May 1902); Paul Morton (1 Jul 1904) |
| Attorney General | Philander Chase Knox; William Henry Moody (1 Jul 1904) |
| Interior | Ethan Allen Hitchcock |
| Agriculture | James Wilson |
| **Commerce and Labor** | George Bruce Cortelyou (16 Feb 1903); Victor Howard Metcalf (1 Jul 1904) |

**4 MAR 1905–3 MAR 1909 (TERM 2)**

| | |
|---|---|
| State | John Hay; Elihu Root (19 Jul 1905); Robert Bacon (27 Jan 1909) |
| Treasury | Leslie Mortier Shaw; George Bruce Cortelyou (4 Mar 1907) |
| War | William Howard Taft; Luke Edward Wright (1 Jul 1908) |
| Navy | Paul Morton; Charles Joseph Bonaparte (1 Jul 1905); Victor Howard Metcalf (17 Dec 1906); Truman Handy Newberry (1 Dec 1908) |
| Attorney General | William Henry Moody; Charles Joseph Bonaparte (17 Dec 1906) |
| Interior | Ethan Allen Hitchcock; James Rudolph Garfield (4 Mar 1907) |
| Agriculture | James Wilson |
| Commerce and Labor | Victor Howard Metcalf; Oscar Solomon Straus (17 Dec 1906) |

### William Howard Taft

**4 MAR 1909–3 MAR 1913**

| | |
|---|---|
| State | Philander Chase Knox |
| Treasury | Franklin MacVeagh |
| War | Jacob McGavock Dickinson; Henry Lewis Stimson (22 May 1911) |
| Navy | George von Lengerke Meyer |
| Attorney General | George Woodward Wickersham |
| Interior | Richard Achilles Ballinger; Walter Lowrie Fisher (7 Mar 1911) |
| Agriculture | James Wilson |
| Commerce and Labor | Charles Nagel |

### Woodrow Wilson

**4 MAR 1913–3 MAR 1917 (TERM 1)**

| | |
|---|---|
| State | William Jennings Bryan; Robert Lansing (23 Jun 1915) |
| Treasury | William Gibbs McAdoo |
| War | Lindley Miller Garrison; Newton Diehl Baker (9 Mar 1916) |
| Navy | Josephus Daniels |
| Attorney General | James Clark McReynolds; Thomas Watt Gregory (3 Sep 1914) |
| Interior | Franklin Knight Lane |
| Agriculture | David Franklin Houston |
| **Commerce** | William Cox Redfield |
| **Labor** | William Bauchop Wilson |

**4 MAR 1917–3 MAR 1921 (TERM 2)**

| | |
|---|---|
| State | Robert Lansing; Bainbridge Colby (23 Mar 1920) |
| Treasury | William Gibbs McAdoo; Carter Glass (16 Dec 1918); David Franklin Houston (2 Feb 1920) |
| War | Newton Diehl Baker |
| Navy | Josephus Daniels |
| Attorney General | Thomas Watt Gregory; Alexander Mitchell Palmer (5 Mar 1919) |
| Interior | Franklin Knight Lane; John Barton Payne (13 Mar 1920) |
| Agriculture | David Franklin Houston; Edwin Thomas Meredith (2 Feb 1920) |
| Commerce | William Cox Redfield; Joshua Willis Alexander (16 Dec 1919) |
| Labor | William Bauchop Wilson |

# US Presidential Cabinets (continued)

### Warren G. Harding

**4 MAR 1921–2 AUG 1923**

| | |
|---|---|
| State | Charles Evans Hughes |
| Treasury | Andrew William Mellon |
| War | John Wingate Weeks |
| Navy | Edwin Denby |
| Attorney General | Harry Micajah Daugherty |
| Interior | Albert Bacon Fall; Hubert Work (5 Mar 1923) |
| Agriculture | Henry Cantwell Wallace |
| Commerce | Herbert Hoover |
| Labor | James John Davis |

### Calvin Coolidge

**3 AUG 1923–3 MAR 1925 (TERM 1)**

| | |
|---|---|
| State | Charles Evans Hughes |
| Treasury | Andrew William Mellon |
| War | John Wingate Weeks |
| Navy | Edwin Denby; Curtis Dwight Wilbur (18 Mar 1924) |
| Attorney General | Harry Micajah Daugherty; Harlan Fiske Stone (9 Apr 1924) |
| Interior | Hubert Work |
| Agriculture | Henry Cantwell Wallace; Howard Mason Gore (21 Nov 1924) |
| Commerce | Herbert Hoover |
| Labor | James John Davis |

**4 MAR 1925–3 MAR 1929 (TERM 2)**

| | |
|---|---|
| State | Frank Billings Kellogg |
| Treasury | Andrew William Mellon |
| War | John Wingate Weeks; Dwight Filley Davis (14 Oct 1925) |
| Navy | Curtis Dwight Wilbur |
| Attorney General | John Garibaldi Sargent |
| Interior | Hubert Work; Roy Owen West (21 Jan 1929) |
| Agriculture | William Marion Jardine |
| Commerce | Herbert Hoover; William Fairfield Whiting (11 Dec 1928) |
| Labor | James John Davis |

### Herbert Hoover

**4 MAR 1929–3 MAR 1933**

| | |
|---|---|
| State | Henry Lewis Stimson |
| Treasury | Andrew William Mellon; Ogden Livingston Mills (13 Feb 1932) |
| War | James William Good; Patrick Jay Hurley (9 Dec 1929) |
| Navy | Charles Francis Adams |
| Attorney General | William De Witt Mitchell |
| Interior | Ray Lyman Wilbur |
| Agriculture | Arthur Mastick Hyde |
| Commerce | Robert Patterson Lamont; Roy Dikeman Chapin (14 Dec 1932) |
| Labor | James John Davis; William Nuckles Doak (9 Dec 1930) |

### Franklin D. Roosevelt

**4 MAR 1933–20 JAN 1937 (TERM 1)**

| | |
|---|---|
| State | Cordell Hull |
| Treasury | William Hartman Woodin; Henry Morgenthau, Jr. (8 Jan 1934) |
| War | George Henry Dern |
| Navy | Claude Augustus Swanson |
| Attorney General | Homer Stille Cummings |
| Interior | Harold LeClaire Ickes |
| Agriculture | Henry Agard Wallace |
| Commerce | Daniel Calhoun Roper |
| Labor | Frances Perkins |

**20 JAN 1937–20 JAN 1941 (TERM 2)**

| | |
|---|---|
| State | Cordell Hull |
| Treasury | Henry Morgenthau, Jr. |
| War | Harry Hines Woodring; Henry Lewis Stimson (10 Jul 1940) |
| Attorney General | Homer Stille Cummings; Frank Murphy (17 Jan 1939); Robert Houghwout Jackson (18 Jan 1940) |
| Navy | Claude Augustus Swanson; Charles Edison (11 Jan 1940); Frank Knox (10 Jul 1940) |
| Interior | Harold LeClaire Ickes |
| Agriculture | Henry Agard Wallace; Claude Raymond Wickard (5 Sep 1940) |

# US Presidential Cabinets (continued)

### Franklin D. Roosevelt (continued)

**20 JAN 1937–20 JAN 1941 (TERM 2) (CONTINUED)**

| | |
|---|---|
| Commerce | Daniel Calhoun Roper; Harry Lloyd Hopkins (23 Jan 1939); Jesse Holman Jones (19 Sep 1940) |
| Labor | Frances Perkins |

**20 JAN 1941–20 JAN 1945 (TERM 3)**

| | |
|---|---|
| State | Cordell Hull; Edward Reilly Stettinius (1 Dec 1944) |
| Treasury | Henry Morgenthau, Jr. |
| War | Henry Lewis Stimson |
| Navy | Frank Knox; James Vincent Forrestal (18 May 1944) |
| Attorney General | Robert Houghwout Jackson; Francis Biddle (5 Sep 1941) |
| Interior | Harold LeClaire Ickes |
| Agriculture | Claude Raymond Wickard |
| Commerce | Jesse Holman Jones |
| Labor | Frances Perkins |

**20 JAN 1945–12 APR 1945 (TERM 4)**

| | |
|---|---|
| State | Edward Reilly Stettinius |
| Treasury | Henry Morgenthau, Jr. |
| War | Henry Lewis Stimson |
| Navy | James Vincent Forrestal |
| Attorney General | Francis Biddle |
| Interior | Harold LeClaire Ickes |
| Agriculture | Claude Raymond Wickard |
| Commerce | Jesse Holman Jones; Henry Agard Wallace (2 Mar 1945) |
| Labor | Frances Perkins |

### Harry S. Truman

**12 APR 1945–20 JAN 1949 (TERM 1)**

| | |
|---|---|
| State | Edward Reilly Stettinius; James Francis Byrnes (3 Jul 1945); George Catlett Marshall (21 Jan 1947) |
| Treasury | Henry Morgenthau, Jr.; Frederick Moore (23 Jul 1945); John Wesley Snyder (25 Jun 1946) |
| War | Henry Lewis Stimson; Robert Porter Patterson (27 Sep 1945); Kenneth Claiborne Royall (25 Jul 1947–17 Sep 1947) |
| **Defense** | James Vincent Forrestal (17 Sep 1947) |
| Navy | James Vincent Forrestal (–17 Sep 1947) |
| Attorney General | Francis Biddle; Thomas Campbell Clark (1 Jul 1945) |
| Interior | Harold LeClaire Ickes; Julius Albert Krug (18 Mar 1946) |
| Agriculture | Claude Raymond Wickard; Clinton Presba Anderson (30 Jun 1945); Charles Franklin Brannan (2 Jun 1948) |
| Commerce | Henry Agard Wallace; William Averell Harriman (28 Jan 1947); Charles Sawyer (6 May 1948) |
| Labor | Frances Perkins; Lewis Baxter Schwellenbach (1 Jul 1945) |

**20 JAN 1949–20 JAN 1953 (TERM 2)**

| | |
|---|---|
| State | Dean Gooderham Acheson |
| Treasury | John Wesley Snyder |
| Defense | James Vincent Forrestal; Louis Arthur Johnson (28 Mar 1949); George Catlett Marshall (21 Sep 1950); Robert Abercrombie Lovett (17 Sep 1951) |
| Attorney General | Thomas Campbell Clark; James Howard McGrath (24 Aug 1949) |
| Interior | Julius Albert Krug; Oscar Littleton Chapman (19 Jan 1950) |
| Agriculture | Charles Franklin Brannan |
| Commerce | Charles Sawyer |
| Labor | Maurice Joseph Tobin |

### Dwight D. Eisenhower

**20 JAN 1953–20 JAN 1957 (TERM 1)**

| | |
|---|---|
| State | John Foster Dulles |
| Treasury | George Magoffin Humphrey |
| Defense | Charles Erwin Wilson |
| Attorney General | Herbert Brownell |
| Interior | Douglas McKay; Frederick Andrew Seaton (8 Jun 1956) |
| Agriculture | Ezra Taft Benson |
| Commerce | Sinclair Weeks |
| Labor | Martin Patrick Durkin; James Paul Mitchell (9 Oct 1953) |
| **Health, Education, and Welfare** | Oveta Culp Hobby (11 Apr 1953); Marion Bayard Folson (1 Aug 1955) |

# US Presidential Cabinets (continued)

### Dwight D. Eisenhower (continued)

**20 JAN 1957–20 JAN 1961 (TERM 2)**

| | |
|---|---|
| State | John Foster Dulles; Christian Archibald Herter (22 Apr 1959) |
| Treasury | George Magoffin Humphrey; Robert Bernard Anderson (29 Jul 1957) |
| Defense | Charles Erwin Wilson; Neil Hosler McElroy (9 Oct 1957); Thomas Sovereign Gates, Jr. (2 Dec 1959) |
| Attorney General | Herbert Brownell, Jr.; William Pierce Rogers (27 Jan 1958) |
| Interior | Frederick Andrew Seaton |
| Agriculture | Ezra Taft Benson |
| Commerce | Sinclair Weeks; Frederick Henry Mueller (10 Aug 1959) |
| Labor | James Paul Mitchell |
| Health, Education, and Welfare | Marion Bayard Folsom; Arthur Sherwood Flemming (1 Aug 1958) |

### John F. Kennedy

**20 JAN 1961–22 NOV 1963**

| | |
|---|---|
| State | David Dean Rusk |
| Treasury | C. Douglas Dillon |
| Defense | Robert S. McNamara |
| Attorney General | Robert F. Kennedy |
| Interior | Stewart L. Udall |
| Agriculture | Orville Lothrop Freeman |
| Commerce | Luther H. Hodges |
| Labor | Arthur J. Goldberg; W. Willard Wirtz (25 Sep 1962) |
| Health, Education, and Welfare | Abraham Ribicoff; Anthony J. Celebrezze (31 Jul 1962) |

### Lyndon B. Johnson

**22 NOV 1963–20 JAN 1965 (TERM 1)**

| | |
|---|---|
| State | David Dean Rusk |
| Treasury | C. Douglas Dillon |
| Defense | Robert S. McNamara |
| Attorney General | Robert F. Kennedy |
| Interior | Stewart L. Udall |
| Agriculture | Orville Lothrop Freeman |
| Commerce | Luther H. Hodges |
| Labor | W. Willard Wirtz |
| Health, Education, and Welfare | Anthony J. Celebrezze |

**20 JAN 1965–20 JAN 1969 (TERM 2)**

| | |
|---|---|
| State | David Dean Rusk |
| Treasury | C. Douglas Dillon; Henry H. Fowler (1 Apr 1965); Joseph W. Barr (21 Dec 1968) |
| Defense | Robert S. McNamara; Clark M. Clifford (1 Mar 1968) |
| Attorney General | Nicholas Katzenbach; Ramsey Clark (10 Mar 1967) |
| Interior | Stewart L. Udall |
| Agriculture | Orville Lothrop Freeman |
| Commerce | John T. Connor; Alexander B. Trowbridge (14 Jun 1967); C.R. Smith (6 Mar 1968) |
| Labor | W. Willard Wirtz |
| Health, Education, and Welfare | Anthony J. Celebrezze; John W. Gardner (18 Aug 1965); Wilbur J. Cohen (9 May 1968) |
| Housing and Urban Development | Robert C. Weaver (18 Jan 1966); Robert C. Wood (7 Jan 1969) |
| Transportation | Alan Stephenson Boyd (16 Jan 1967) |

### Richard M. Nixon

**20 JAN 1969–20 JAN 1973 (TERM 1)**

| | |
|---|---|
| State | William Pierce Rogers |
| Treasury | David M. Kennedy; John B. Connally (11 Feb 1971); George P. Shultz (12 Jun 1972) |
| Defense | Melvin R. Laird |
| Attorney General | John N. Mitchell; Richard G. Kleindienst (12 Jun 1972) |
| Interior | Walter Hickel; Rogers C.B. Morton (29 Jan 1971) |
| Agriculture | Clifford Morris Hardin; Earl Lauer Butz (2 Dec 1971) |
| Commerce | Maurice H. Stans; Peter G. Peterson (21 Feb 1972) |
| Labor | George P. Shultz; James D. Hodgson (2 Jul 1970) |
| Health, Education, and Welfare | Robert H. Finch; Elliot L. Richardson (24 Jun 1970) |
| Housing and Urban Development | George W. Romney |
| Transportation | John Anthony Volpe |

## US Presidential Cabinets (continued)

### Richard M. Nixon (continued)

**20 JAN 1973–9 AUG 1974 (TERM 2)**

| | |
|---|---|
| State | William Pierce Rogers; Henry Alfred Kissinger (22 Sep 1973) |
| Treasury | George P. Shultz; William E. Simon (8 May 1974) |
| Defense | Elliot L. Richardson; James R. Schlesinger (2 Jul 1973) |
| Attorney General | Richard G. Kleindienst; Elliot L. Richardson (25 May 1973); William B. Saxbe (4 Jan 1974) |
| Interior | Rogers C.B. Morton |
| Agriculture | Earl Lauer Butz |
| Commerce | Frederick B. Dent |
| Labor | Peter J. Brennan |
| Health, Education, and Welfare | Caspar W. Weinberger |
| Housing and Urban Development | James T. Lynn |
| Transportation | Claude Stout Brinegar |

### Gerald R. Ford

**9 AUG 1974–20 JAN 1977**

| | |
|---|---|
| State | Henry Alfred Kissinger |
| Treasury | William E. Simon |
| Defense | James R. Schlesinger; Donald H. Rumsfeld (20 Nov 1975) |
| Attorney General | William B. Saxbe; Edward H. Levi (7 Feb 1975) |
| Interior | Rogers C.B. Morton; Stanley K. Hathaway (13 Jun 1975); Thomas S. Kleppe (17 Oct 1975) |
| Agriculture | Earl Lauer Butz; John Albert Knebel (4 Nov 1976) |
| Commerce | Frederick B. Dent; Rogers C.B. Morton (1 May 1975); Elliot L. Richardson (2 Feb 1976) |
| Labor | Peter J. Brennan; John T. Dunlop (18 Mar 1975); W.J. Usery, Jr. (10 Feb 1976) |
| Health, Education, and Welfare | Caspar W. Weinberger; David Mathews (8 Aug 1975) |
| Housing and Urban Development | James T. Lynn; Carla A. Hills (10 Mar 1975) |
| Transportation | Claude Stout Brinegar; William Thaddeus Coleman, Jr. (7 Mar 1975) |

### Jimmy Carter

**20 JAN 1977–20 JAN 1981**

| | |
|---|---|
| State | Cyrus Roberts Vance; Edmund Sixtus Muskie (8 May 1980) |
| Treasury | W. Michael Blumenthal; G. William Miller (6 Aug 1979) |
| Defense | Harold Brown |
| Attorney General | Griffin B. Bell; Benjamin R. Civiletti (16 Aug 1979) |
| Interior | Cecil D. Andrus |
| Agriculture | Robert Selmer Bergland |
| Commerce | Juanita M. Kreps; Philip M. Klutznick (9 Jan 1980) |
| Labor | Ray Marshall |
| Health, Education, and Welfare | Joseph A. Califano, Jr.; Patricia Roberts Harris (3 Aug 1979–4 May 1980) |
| **Health and Human Services** | Patricia Roberts Harris (4 May 1980) |
| Housing and Urban Development | Patricia Roberts Harris; Moon Landrieu (24 Sep 1979) |
| Transportation | Brockman Adams; Neil Edward Goldschmidt (24 Sep 1979) |
| **Energy** | James R. Schlesinger (1 Oct 1977); Charles W. Duncan, Jr. (24 Aug 1979) |
| **Education** | Shirley M. Hufstedler (6 Dec 1979) |

### Ronald Reagan

**20 JAN 1981–20 JAN 1985 (TERM 1)**

| | |
|---|---|
| State | Alexander Meigs Haig, Jr.; George P. Shultz (16 Jul 1982) |
| Treasury | Donald T. Regan |
| Defense | Caspar W. Weinberger |
| Attorney General | William French Smith |
| Interior | James G. Watt; William P. Clark (21 Nov 1983) |
| Agriculture | John Rusling Block |
| Commerce | Malcolm Baldrige |
| Labor | Raymond J. Donovan |
| Health and Human Services | Richard S. Schweiker; Margaret M. Heckler (9 Mar 1983) |
| Housing and Urban Development | Samuel R. Pierce, Jr. |
| Transportation | Andrew Lindsay Lewis, Jr.; Elizabeth Hanford Dole (7 Feb 1983) |
| Energy | James B. Edwards; Donald Paul Hodel (8 Dec 1982) |
| Education | Terrel H. Bell |

**20 JAN 1985–20 JAN 1989 (TERM 2)**

| | |
|---|---|
| State | George P. Shultz |
| Treasury | James A. Baker III; Nicholas F. Brady (18 Aug 1988) |

## US Presidential Cabinets (continued)

### Ronald Reagan (continued)

**20 JAN 1985–20 JAN 1989 (TERM 2) (CONTINUED)**

| | |
|---|---|
| Defense | Caspar W. Weinberger; Frank C. Carlucci (21 Nov 1987) |
| Attorney General | William French Smith; Edwin Meese III (25 Feb 1985); Richard Thornburgh (11 Aug 1988) |
| Interior | Donald Paul Hodel |
| Agriculture | John Rusling Block; Richard Edmund Lyng (7 Mar 1986) |
| Commerce | Malcolm Baldrige; C. William Verity (19 Oct 1987) |
| Labor | Raymond J. Donovan; William E. Brock (29 Apr 1985); Ann Dore McLaughlin (17 Dec 1987) |
| Health and Human Services | Margaret M. Heckler; Otis R. Bowen (13 Dec 1985) |
| Housing and Urban Development | Samuel R. Pierce, Jr. |
| Transportation | Elizabeth Hanford Dole; James Horace Burnley IV (3 Dec 1987) |
| Energy | John S. Herrington |
| Education | William J. Bennett; Lauro F. Cavazos, Jr. (20 Sep 1988) |

### George H.W. Bush

**20 JAN 1989–20 JAN 1993**

| | |
|---|---|
| State | James A. Baker III; Lawrence Sidney Eagleburger (8 Dec 1992) |
| Treasury | Nicholas F. Brady |
| Defense | Richard B. Cheney |
| Attorney General | Richard Thornburgh; William Barr (20 Nov 1991) |
| Interior | Manuel Lujan, Jr. |
| Agriculture | Clayton Keith Yeutter; Edward Rell Madigan (7 Mar 1991) |
| Commerce | Robert A. Mosbacher; Barbara H. Franklin (27 Feb 1992) |
| Labor | Elizabeth Hanford Dole; Lynn Morley Martin (7 Feb 1991) |
| Health and Human Services | Louis W. Sullivan |
| Housing and Urban Development | Jack F. Kemp |
| Transportation | Samuel Knox Skinner; Andrew Hill Card, Jr. (22 Jan 1992) |
| Energy | James D. Watkins |
| Education | Lauro F. Cavazos, Jr.; Lamar Alexander (14 Mar 1991) |
| **Veterans Affairs** | Edward J. Derwinski (15 Mar 1989) |

### Bill Clinton

**20 JAN 1993–20 JAN 1997 (TERM 1)**

| | |
|---|---|
| State | Warren Minor Christopher |
| Treasury | Lloyd M. Bentsen; Robert E. Rubin (10 Jan 1995) |
| Defense | Les Aspin; William J. Perry (3 Feb 1994) |
| Attorney General | Janet Reno |
| Interior | Bruce Babbitt |
| Agriculture | Alphonso Michael Espy; Daniel Robert Glickman (30 Mar 1995) |
| Commerce | Ronald H. Brown; Mickey Kantor (12 Apr 1996) |
| Labor | Robert B. Reich |
| Health and Human Services | Donna E. Shalala |
| Housing and Urban Development | Henry G. Cisneros |
| Transportation | Federico Fabian Peña |
| Energy | Hazel R. O'Leary |
| Education | Richard W. Riley |
| Veterans Affairs | Jesse Brown |

**20 JAN 1997–20 JAN 2001 (TERM 2)**

| | |
|---|---|
| State | Madeleine Korbel Albright |
| Treasury | Robert E. Rubin; Lawrence H. Summers (2 Jul 1999) |
| Defense | William S. Cohen |
| Attorney General | Janet Reno |
| Interior | Bruce Babbitt |
| Agriculture | Daniel Robert Glickman |
| Commerce | William M. Daley; Norman Y. Mineta (21 Jul 2000) |
| Labor | Alexis Herman |
| Health and Human Services | Donna E. Shalala |
| Housing and Urban Development | Andrew M. Cuomo |
| Transportation | Rodney Earl Slater |
| Energy | Federico Fabian Peña; Bill Richardson (18 Aug 1998) |
| Education | Richard W. Riley |
| Veterans Affairs | Togo D. West, Jr. |

## US Presidential Cabinets (continued)

### George W. Bush

**20 JAN 2001–20 JAN 2005 (TERM 1)**

| | |
|---|---|
| State | Colin L. Powell |
| Treasury | Paul H. O'Neill; John W. Snow (3 Feb 2003) |
| Defense | Donald H. Rumsfeld |
| Attorney General | John Ashcroft |
| Interior | Gale A. Norton |
| Agriculture | Ann M. Veneman |
| Commerce | Donald L. Evans |
| Labor | Elaine L. Chao |
| Health and Human Services | Tommy G. Thompson |
| Housing and Urban Development | Mel Martinez; Alphonso Jackson (1 Apr 2004) |
| Transportation | Norman Y. Mineta |
| Energy | Spencer Abraham |
| Education | Rod Paige |
| Veterans Affairs | Anthony J. Principi |
| **Homeland Security** | Tom Ridge (8 Oct 2001) |

**20 JAN 2005–20 JAN 2009 (TERM 2)**

| | |
|---|---|
| State | Condoleezza Rice |
| Treasury | John W. Snow; Henry M. Paulson, Jr. (10 Jul 2006) |
| Defense | Donald Rumsfeld; Robert M. Gates (18 Dec 2006) |
| Attorney General | Alberto R. Gonzales; Michael Mukasey (9 Nov 2007) |
| Interior | Gale A. Norton; Dirk Kempthorne (26 May 2006) |
| Agriculture | Mike Johanns; Ed Schafer (28 Jan 2008) |
| Commerce | Carlos M. Gutierrez |
| Labor | Elaine L. Chao |
| Health and Human Services | Michael O. Leavitt |
| Housing and Urban Development | Alphonso Jackson; Steve Preston (5 Jun 2008) |
| Transportation | Norman Y. Mineta; Mary E. Peters (30 Sep 2006) |
| Energy | Samuel W. Bodman |
| Education | Margaret Spellings |
| Veterans Affairs | R. James Nicholson; James B. Peake (20 Dec 2007) |
| Homeland Security | Michael Chertoff |

### Barack Obama

**20 JAN 2009–**

| | | WEB SITE |
|---|---|---|
| State | Hillary Clinton | <www.state.gov> |
| Treasury | Tim Geithner | <www.treasury.gov> |
| Defense | Robert M. Gates; Leon Panetta (1 Jul 2011) | <www.defense.gov> |
| Attorney General | Eric Holder | <www.justice.gov> |
| Interior | Ken Salazar | <www.doi.gov> |
| Agriculture | Tom Vilsack | <www.usda.gov> |
| Commerce | Gary Locke; Rebecca M. Blank (acting) (1 Aug 2011); John Bryson (21 Oct 2011); Rebecca M. Blank (acting) (21 Jun 2012) | <www.commerce.gov> |
| Labor | Hilda Solis | <www.dol.gov> |
| Health and Human Services | Kathleen Sebelius | <www.hhs.gov> |
| Housing and Urban Development | Shaun Donovan | <portal.hud.gov> |
| Transportation | Ray LaHood | <www.dot.gov> |
| Energy | Steven Chu | <energy.gov> |
| Education | Arne Duncan | <www.ed.gov> |
| Veterans Affairs | Eric Shinseki | <www.va.gov> |
| Homeland Security | Janet Napolitano | <www.dhs.gov> |

Additionally, the White House lists the following as cabinet-rank members: Vice President Joe Biden, Chief of Staff Jacob Lew, Environmental Protection Agency Administrator Lisa P. Jackson, US Trade Representative Ron Kirk, Office of Management and Budget Director Jeffrey Zients (acting), Council of Economic Advisers Chair Alan Krueger, and United States Ambassador to the United Nations Susan Rice.

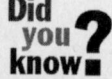

**Did you know?**

According to the US Census Bureau, by 2010 there were more Hispanics of Puerto Rican origin living in the 50 US states and Washington DC than there were living in Puerto Rico itself. The 2010 census results showed that there were some 4.6 million Hispanics of Puerto Rican origin in the US compared to 3.7 million on the island of Puerto Rico. Of those living in the US, almost one-third had been born in Puerto Rico.

# United States Supreme Court

## Justices of the Supreme Court of the United States

*Listed under presidents who made appointments (bold). Chief justices' names appear in italics.*

| NAME | TERM OF SERVICE[1] |
|---|---|
| **George Washington** | |
| *John Jay* | 1789–95 |
| James Wilson | 1789–98 |
| John Rutledge | 1790–91 |
| William Cushing | 1790–1810 |
| John Blair | 1790–96 |
| James Iredell | 1790–99 |
| Thomas Johnson | 1792–93 |
| William Paterson | 1793–1806 |
| *John Rutledge[2]* | 1795 |
| Samuel Chase | 1796–1811 |
| *Oliver Ellsworth* | 1796–1800 |
| **John Adams** | |
| Bushrod Washington | 1799–1829 |
| Alfred Moore | 1800–04 |
| *John Marshall* | 1801–35 |
| **Thomas Jefferson** | |
| William Johnson | 1804–34 |
| Brockholst Livingston | 1807–23 |
| Thomas Todd | 1807–26 |
| **James Madison** | |
| Gabriel Duvall | 1811–35 |
| Joseph Story | 1812–45 |
| **James Monroe** | |
| Smith Thompson | 1823–43 |
| **John Quincy Adams** | |
| Robert Trimble | 1826–28 |
| **Andrew Jackson** | |
| John McLean | 1830–61 |
| Henry Baldwin | 1830–44 |
| James M. Wayne | 1835–67 |
| *Roger Brooke Taney* | 1836–64 |
| Philip P. Barbour | 1836–41 |
| **Martin Van Buren** | |
| John Catron | 1837–65 |
| John McKinley | 1838–52 |
| Peter V. Daniel | 1842–60 |
| **John Tyler** | |
| Samuel Nelson | 1845–72 |
| **James K. Polk** | |
| Levi Woodbury | 1845–51 |
| Robert C. Grier | 1846–70 |
| **Millard Fillmore** | |
| Benjamin R. Curtis | 1851–57 |
| **Franklin Pierce** | |
| John Archibald Campbell | 1853–61 |
| **James Buchanan** | |
| Nathan Clifford | 1858–81 |
| **Abraham Lincoln** | |
| Noah H. Swayne | 1862–81 |
| Samuel Freeman Miller | 1862–90 |
| David Davis | 1862–77 |
| Stephen Johnson Field | 1863–97 |
| *Salmon P. Chase* | 1864–73 |

| NAME | TERM OF SERVICE[1] |
|---|---|
| **Ulysses S. Grant** | |
| William Strong | 1870–80 |
| Joseph P. Bradley | 1870–92 |
| Ward Hunt | 1873–82 |
| *Morrison Remick Waite* | 1874–88 |
| **Rutherford B. Hayes** | |
| John Marshall Harlan | 1877–1911 |
| William B. Woods | 1881–87 |
| **James A. Garfield** | |
| Stanley Matthews | 1881–89 |
| **Chester A. Arthur** | |
| Horace Gray | 1882–1902 |
| Samuel Blatchford | 1882–93 |
| **Grover Cleveland** | |
| Lucius Q.C. Lamar | 1888–93 |
| *Melville Weston Fuller* | 1888–1910 |
| **Benjamin Harrison** | |
| David J. Brewer | 1890–1910 |
| Henry B. Brown | 1891–1906 |
| George Shiras, Jr. | 1892–1903 |
| Howell E. Jackson | 1893–95 |
| **Grover Cleveland** | |
| Edward Douglass White | 1894–1910 |
| Rufus Wheeler Peckham | 1896–1909 |
| **William McKinley** | |
| Joseph McKenna | 1898–1925 |
| **Theodore Roosevelt** | |
| Oliver Wendell Holmes | 1902–32 |
| William R. Day | 1903–22 |
| William H. Moody | 1906–10 |
| **William Howard Taft** | |
| Horace H. Lurton | 1910–14 |
| Charles Evans Hughes | 1910–16 |
| Willis Van Devanter | 1911–37 |
| Joseph R. Lamar | 1911–16 |
| *Edward Douglass White* | 1910–21 |
| Mahlon Pitney | 1912–22 |
| **Woodrow Wilson** | |
| James C. McReynolds | 1914–41 |
| Louis Brandeis | 1916–39 |
| John H. Clarke | 1916–22 |
| **Warren G. Harding** | |
| *William Howard Taft* | 1921–30 |
| George Sutherland | 1922–38 |
| Pierce Butler | 1923–39 |
| Edward T. Sanford | 1923–30 |
| **Calvin Coolidge** | |
| Harlan Fiske Stone | 1925–41 |
| **Herbert Hoover** | |
| *Charles Evans Hughes* | 1930–41 |
| Owen Roberts | 1930–45 |
| Benjamin N. Cardozo | 1932–38 |

| NAME | TERM OF SERVICE[1] |
|---|---|
| **Franklin D. Roosevelt** | |
| Hugo L. Black | 1937–71 |
| Stanley F. Reed | 1938–57 |
| Felix Frankfurter | 1939–62 |
| William O. Douglas | 1939–75 |
| Frank Murphy | 1940–49 |
| *Harlan Fiske Stone* | 1941–46 |
| James F. Byrnes | 1941–42 |
| Robert H. Jackson | 1941–54 |
| Wiley B. Rutledge | 1943–49 |
| **Harry S. Truman** | |
| Harold H. Burton | 1945–58 |
| *Fred M. Vinson* | 1946–53 |
| Tom C. Clark | 1949–67 |
| Sherman Minton | 1949–56 |
| **Dwight D. Eisenhower** | |
| *Earl Warren* | 1953–69 |
| John Marshall Harlan | 1955–71 |
| William J. Brennan, Jr. | 1956–90 |
| Charles E. Whittaker | 1957–62 |
| Potter Stewart | 1958–81 |
| **John F. Kennedy** | |
| Byron R. White | 1962–93 |
| Arthur J. Goldberg | 1962–65 |
| **Lyndon B. Johnson** | |
| Abe Fortas | 1965–69 |
| Thurgood Marshall | 1967–91 |
| **Richard M. Nixon** | |
| *Warren E. Burger* | 1969–86 |
| Harry A. Blackmun | 1970–94 |
| Lewis F. Powell, Jr. | 1972–87 |
| William H. Rehnquist | 1972–86 |
| **Gerald Ford** | |
| John Paul Stevens | 1975–2010 |
| **Ronald Reagan** | |
| Sandra Day O'Connor | 1981–2006 |
| *William H. Rehnquist* | 1986–2005 |
| Antonin Scalia | 1986– |
| Anthony M. Kennedy | 1988– |
| **George H.W. Bush** | |
| David H. Souter | 1990–2009 |
| Clarence Thomas | 1991– |
| **Bill Clinton** | |
| Ruth Bader Ginsburg | 1993– |
| Stephen G. Breyer | 1994– |
| **George W. Bush** | |
| *John G. Roberts* | 2005– |
| Samuel Anthony Alito, Jr. | 2006– |
| **Barack Obama** | |
| Sonia Sotomayor | 2009– |
| Elena Kagan | 2010– |

[1]The year the justice took the judicial oath is here used as the beginning date of service, for until that oath is taken the justice is not vested with the prerogatives of the office. Justices, however, receive their commissions ("letters patent") before taking their oaths—in some instances, in the preceding year. [2]John Rutledge was acting chief justice; the US Senate refused to confirm him.

# Milestones of US Supreme Court Jurisprudence

*Information includes cases' short names, citation, year of release, and a short description of the Supreme Court's findings and importance for US law.*

**Marbury v. Madison, 5 U.S. 137 (1803):** the first instance in which the high court declared an act of Congress (the Judiciary Act of 1789) to be unconstitutional, thus establishing judicial review.

**Martin v. Hunter's Lessee, 14 U.S. 304 (1816):** asserted the US Supreme Court's power of appellate review of state Supreme Court decisions.

**McCulloch v. Maryland, 17 U.S. 316 (1819):** recognized the legitimacy of incidental or implied powers of the national legislature under the constitution, and ruled that the supremacy of the laws of Congress allowed it the power to incorporate a national bank free from state infringement.

**Gibbons v. Ogden, 22 U.S. 1 (1824):** held that a state law requiring a state license to operate a steamboat through a multi-state waterway infringed upon Congress's power as the sole regulator of interstate commerce and was, therefore, unconstitutional.

**Dred Scott v. Sandford, 60 U.S. 393 (1857):** ruled that blacks, free or enslaved, were not citizens under the Constitution, and further determined that only states, and not Congress or territorial governments, had the power to prohibit slavery, thus overturning the Missouri Compromise of 1820 and legalizing slavery in all US territories.

**Plessy v. Ferguson, 163 U.S. 537 (1896):** ruled that state laws that required racial segregation in "separate but equal" public facilities were constitutional and did not violate the Thirteenth or Fourteenth Amendments to the Constitution, paving the way for decades of racial segregation in the South.

**Lochner v. New York, 198 U.S. 45 (1905):** found that a state labor law limiting the number of hours in the work week violated due process because the "right of contract between the employer and employees" is protected under the Fourteenth Amendment.

**Standard Oil Co. of New Jersey et al. v. United States, 221 U.S. 1 (1911):** ruled that the activities of the Standard Oil Company of New Jersey, a holding company that through its subsidiaries controlled most of the US petroleum industry, constituted an undue restraint of trade and ordered the company's dissolution under the Sherman Antitrust Act.

**Brown v. Board of Education of Topeka, 349 U.S. 294 (1954):** ruled that racial segregation in public schools violated the Fourteenth Amendment, overturning the doctrine of "separate but equal" facilities reached in Plessy v. Ferguson.

**Mapp v. Ohio, 367 U.S. 643 (1961):** found that the Fourth Amendment prohibition of unreasonable search and seizure, and the inadmissibility of evidence obtained in violation of it, applied to state as well as to federal government.

**Gideon v. Wainwright, 372 U.S. 335 (1963):** guaranteed a defendant's right to legal counsel by overturning the Florida conviction of Clarence Gideon because he was denied free counsel during trial.

**New York Times Co. v. Sullivan, 376 U.S. 254 (1964):** protected the press from the prospects of large damage awards in libel cases by requiring that "actual malice" be demonstrated; public officials who sue for damages must prove that a falsehood had been issued with knowledge that it was false or in reckless disregard of whether it was false or not.

**Heart of Atlanta Motel v. United States, 379 U.S. 241; Katzenbach v. McClung, 379 U.S. 294 (1964):** upheld Title II of the Civil Rights Act of 1964 (which prohibits segregation or discrimination in places of public accommodation involved in interstate commerce) in the cases of an Atlanta motel and a Birmingham AL restaurant, both of which discriminated against blacks. The court ruled that both engaged in transactions affecting interstate commerce, and thus were within the purview of congressional regulation, and that the Civil Rights Act itself was constitutional.

**Miranda v. Arizona, 384 U.S. 436 (1966):** ruled that the prosecution may not use statements made by a person in police custody unless minimum procedural safeguards were followed and established guidelines to guarantee arrested persons' Fifth Amendment right not to be compelled to incriminate themselves. These guidelines included informing arrestees prior to questioning that they have the right to remain silent, that anything they say may be used against them as evidence, and that they have the right to the counsel of an attorney.

**Loving v. Virginia, 388 U.S. 1 (1967):** declared that antimiscegenation laws (prohibitions of interracial marriage) have no legitimate purpose and thus violate the Fourteenth Amendment.

**New York Times Co. v. United States, 403 U.S. 713 (1971):** in what was known as the "Pentagon Papers" case, the court vacated a US Justice Department injunction that restrained newspapers from publishing excerpts of a top-secret report on the Vietnam War, ruling that such prior restraint of the press was subject to a "heavy burden of...justification," which the government failed to meet.

**Roe v. Wade, 410 U.S. 113 (1973):** held that overly restrictive state regulation of abortion is unconstitutional. In balancing the "compelling state interest[s]" in protecting the health of pregnant women and the potential life of fetuses, the court ruled that regulation of abortion could begin no sooner than about the end of the first trimester, with increasing regulation permissible in the second and third trimesters; the state's interest in protecting the fetus was found to increase with the fetus's "capability for meaningful life outside the mother's womb."

**Gregg v. Georgia, 428 U.S. 153; Proffitt v. Florida, 428 U.S. 242; Jurek v. Texas, 428 U.S. 262 (1976):** ruled that the death penalty, in and of itself, does not violate the Eighth Amendment if applied under certain guidelines in first-degree murder cases.

**Cruzan by Cruzan v. Director, Missouri Department of Health, 497 U.S. 261 (1990):** found that, in the absence of "clear and convincing evidence" of a person's desire to refuse medical treatment or not to live on life support, a state could require that such treatment continue.

**Planned Parenthood of Southeastern Pennsylvania v. Casey, 505 U.S. 833 (1992):** softened the ruling in Roe v. Wade by finding that some state regulation of abortion prior to fetal viability, including a 24-hour waiting period, mandatory counseling, and a parental-consent requirement for minors, is permissible as long as the regulations do not place an "undue burden" on the woman.

**Romer v. Evans, 517 U.S. 620 (1996):** invalidated a Colorado referendum passed by popular vote that prohibited conferral of protected status on the basis of sexual orientation; the court ruled that the referendum was overbroad and violated the Fourteenth Amendment of the US Constitution.

*Boy Scouts of America* v. *Dale*, 530 U.S. 640 (2000): ruled that the Boy Scouts, because it is a private organization, was within its rights when it dismissed a scoutmaster expressly because of his avowed homosexuality. The court reasoned that a state statute banning discrimination on the basis of sexual orientation in places of public accommodation was outweighed by the Scouts' First Amendment right to freedom of association.

*Bush* v. *Gore*, 531 U.S. 98 (2000): stopped the manual recounts, then under way in certain Florida counties at the demand of Al Gore, of disputed ballots from the November 2000 presidential election on the grounds that inconsistent vote-counting standards among the several counties involved amounted to a violation of the Fourteenth Amendment's equal protection clause. Because George W. Bush at the time led Al Gore in the number of officially recognized Florida votes, the decision meant that he would win the state and thus the general election, despite having lost the popular vote.

*Atkins* v. *Virginia*, 536 U.S. 304 (2002): ruled that the death penalty, when applied to mentally retarded individuals, constitutes a "cruel and unusual punishment" prohibited by the Eighth Amendment.

*Lockyer* v. *Andrade*, 538 U.S. 63; *Ewing* v. *California*, 538 U.S. 11 (2003): upheld a "three-strikes" law that imposes long prison sentences for a third offense, even nonviolent crimes.

*United States* v. *American Library Association*, 539 U.S. 194 (2003): upheld the Children's Internet Protection Act, which conditions access to federal grants and subsidies upon the installation of antipornography filters on all Internet-connected computers.

*Lawrence* v. *Texas*, 539 U.S. 558 (2003): explicitly overruling *Bowers* v. *Hardwick*, 478 U.S. 186 (1986), the court declared that gay men and lesbians are "entitled to respect for their private lives" under the due process clause of the Fourteenth Amendment and rendered unconstitutional state statutes outlawing sex between adults of the same gender.

*Gratz* v. *Bollinger*, 539 U.S. 244 (2003): ruled that the affirmative action methodology of the University of Michigan's undergraduate admissions process, which awarded points for status as a racial minority, was not "narrowly tailored to achieve educational diversity" and thus was unconstitutional.

*Blakely* v. *Washington*, 542 U.S. 296 (2004): held that the Washington state system permitting judges to make independent findings that increase a convicted defendant's sentence beyond the ordinary range for the crime violated the Sixth Amendment guarantee of a right to trial by jury and to a higher standard of proof.

*Hamdi* v. *Rumsfeld*, 542 U.S. 507; *Rasul* v. *Bush*, 542 U.S. 466 (2004): ruled that while Congress may empower the executive branch to detain even US citizens as enemy combatants, any enemy combatant in US custody may challenge detention as illegal in federal court with the assistance of counsel. The court declared that "a state of war is not a blank check for the president when it comes to the rights of the nation's citizens."

*United States* v. *Booker* and *United States* v. *Fanfan*, 543 U.S. 220 (2005): ruled that mandatory federal sentencing guidelines violated defendants' Sixth Amendment right to jury trials because they require judges to make decisions affecting prison time.

*Roper* v. *Simmons*, 543 U.S. 551 (2005): held that the execution of a felon who had committed a capital crime while a juvenile violates the Eighth Amendment prohibition of cruel and unusual punishment, noting that "the State cannot extinguish [the juvenile defendant's] life and his potential to attain a mature understanding of his own humanity."

*Kelo* v. *City of New London*, 545 U.S. 469 (2005): found that governmental entities may exercise the power of eminent domain over private property and cede the property to private developers to promote economic growth.

*Hamdan* v. *Rumsfeld*, 548 U.S. 557 (2006): ruled that the government's special military commissions were not lawful courts. The commissions were to have tried some of the prisoners who had been captured in the "global war on terror."

*Gonzales* v. *Carhart*, 550 U.S. 124 (2007): held that a federal law banning dilation and extraction—or "partial-birth"—abortion was not unconstitutional.

*Parents Involved in Community Schools* v. *Seattle School District No. 1*, 551 U.S. 701 (2007): held that using a student's race in determining the availability of a spot at a desired school, even for the purpose of preventing resegregation, violated the 14th Amendment.

*District of Columbia* v. *Heller*, 554 U.S. 290 (2008): ruled that citizens have the right to bear arms without the need to be in service to a militia. This decision struck down a Washington DC handgun ban and threatened scores of other such bans nationwide.

*Boumediene* v. *Bush*, 553 U.S. 723 (2008): ruled that foreign prisoners held at Guantánamo Bay, Cuba, have the right to challenge their detention in US courts.

*District Attorney's Office for the Third Judicial District* v. *Osborne*, 557 U.S. ___ (2009): ruled that persons convicted of crimes do not have the constitutionally protected right to order advanced post-conviction DNA testing of evidence, even in the face of technological advances that may prove the innocence of the convicted person.

*McDonald* v. *City of Chicago*, 561 U.S. ___ (2010): extended *District of Columbia* v. *Heller* in holding that the Second Amendment protection of the right to bear arms applies to state and local governments as well as to the federal government, calling into question the constitutionality of a Chicago handgun ban.

*Citizens United* v. *Federal Election Commission*, 558 U.S. 50 (2010): struck down a provision of the Federal Election Campaign Act (1971) that prohibited corporate and union expenditures in connection with political elections and a provision of the Bipartisan Campaign Reform Act (2002) that banned direct corporate or union funding of political ads.

*Snyder* v. *Phelps*, 562 U.S. ___ (2011): held that First Amendment protection extends to even inflammatory or hurtful speech if that speech deals with a matter of public concern and does not interfere with the rights of assembled private citizens nearby.

*Wal-Mart Stores, Inc.* v. *Dukes*, 564 U.S. ___ (2011): ruled that plaintiffs could not join in a class-action suit in which the only commonality was their sex.

*Brown* v. *Entertainment Merchants Association*, 564 U.S. ___ (2011): affirmed that the ban on the rental or the sale of violent video games to minors violated the First Amendment. In so affirming the justices avoided the necessity of creating a new kind of speech that is to be left unprotected under the Constitution—as obscenity currently is.

*National Federation of Independent Business* v. *Sebelius*, 567 U.S. ___ (2012): upheld the individual mandate of the Patient Protection and Affordable Care Act under Congress's power to tax but struck down a provision of the Medicaid expansion that threatened states with removal of all Medicaid funding if they did not participate in the expansion.

*Miller* v. *Alabama*, 567 U.S. ___ (2012): ruled that state laws mandating life imprisonment without parole for juvenile homicide offenders violate the Eighth Amendment's protection against cruel and unusual punishment.

*Arizona* v. *United States*, 567 U.S. ___ (2012): struck down three key sections of Arizona immigration law, finding that warrantless arrests of suspected illegal aliens and criminal penalties for employing illegal aliens and unregistered aliens are preempted by federal law and thus cannot stand.

# United States Congress

*Parties: Democratic (D); Republican (R); Independent (I).*

## Senate, 112th Congress

*Party totals: **Democrats:** 51; **Republicans:** 47; **Independents:** 2.*

According to Article I, Section 3 of the US Constitution, a US senator must be at least 30 years old, must reside in the state he or she represents at the time of the election, and must have been a citizen of the United States for at least nine years. Voters elect two senators from each state; terms are for six years and begin on 3 January. Each current senator's annual salary is US$174,000. The majority and minority leaders and the president pro tempore receive US$193,400 per year.

**Senate leadership**

| | |
|---|---|
| president: | Joe Biden |
| president pro tempore: | Daniel K. Inouye |
| majority leader: | Harry Reid |
| minority leader: | Mitch McConnell |
| asst. majority leader (majority whip): | Dick Durbin |
| asst. minority leader (minority whip): | Jon Kyl |

**US Senate Web site:** <www.senate.gov>.

| STATE | NAME (PARTY) | SERVICE BEGAN | TERM ENDS |
|---|---|---|---|
| Alabama | Richard Shelby (R) | 1987 | 2011 |
| | Jeff Sessions (R) | 1997 | 2015 |
| Alaska | Lisa Murkowski (R) | 2002 | 2011 |
| | Mark Begich (D) | 2009 | 2015 |
| Arizona | John McCain (R) | 1987 | 2011 |
| | Jon Kyl (R) | 1995 | 2013 |
| Arkansas | Mark Pryor (D) | 2003 | 2015 |
| | John Boozman (R) | 2011 | 2017 |
| California | Dianne Feinstein (D) | 1992[1] | 2013 |
| | Barbara Boxer (D) | 1993 | 2011 |
| Colorado | Mark Udall (D) | 2009 | 2015 |
| | Michael F. Bennet (D) | 2009[2] | 2011 |
| Connecticut | Joe Lieberman (ID) | 1989 | 2013 |
| | Richard Blumenthal (D) | 2011 | 2017 |
| Delaware | Tom Carper (D) | 2001 | 2013 |
| | Christopher A. Coons (D) | 2010[3] | 2015 |
| Florida | Bill Nelson (D) | 2001 | 2013 |
| | Marco Rubio (R) | 2011 | 2017 |
| Georgia | Saxby Chambliss (R) | 2003 | 2015 |
| | Johnny Isakson (R) | 2005 | 2011 |
| Hawaii | Daniel K. Inouye (D) | 1963 | 2011 |
| | Daniel K. Akaka (D) | 1990[4] | 2013 |
| Idaho | Mike Crapo (R) | 1999 | 2011 |
| | James E. Risch (R) | 2009 | 2015 |
| Illinois | Dick Durbin (D) | 1997 | 2015 |
| | Mark Kirk (R) | 2010[5] | 2017 |
| Indiana | Richard G. Lugar (R) | 1977 | 2013 |
| | Daniel Coats (R) | 1999[6] | 2017 |
| Iowa | Chuck Grassley (R) | 1981 | 2011 |
| | Tom Harkin (D) | 1985 | 2015 |
| Kansas | Pat Roberts (R) | 1997 | 2015 |
| | Jerry Moran (R) | 2011 | 2017 |
| Kentucky | Mitch McConnell (R) | 1985 | 2015 |
| | Rand Paul (R) | 2011 | 2017 |
| Louisiana | Mary L. Landrieu (D) | 1997 | 2015 |
| | David Vitter (R) | 2005 | 2011 |
| Maine | Olympia J. Snowe (R) | 1995 | 2013 |
| | Susan Collins (R) | 1997 | 2015 |
| Maryland | Barbara Mikulski (D) | 1987 | 2011 |
| | Benjamin L. Cardin (D) | 2007 | 2013 |

## Senate, 112th Congress (continued)

| STATE | NAME (PARTY) | SERVICE BEGAN | TERM ENDS |
|---|---|---|---|
| Massachusetts | John Kerry (D) | 1985 | 2015 |
| | Scott Brown (R) | 2010[7] | 2013 |
| Michigan | Carl Levin (D) | 1979 | 2015 |
| | Debbie Stabenow (D) | 2001 | 2013 |
| Minnesota | Amy Klobuchar (D) | 2007 | 2013 |
| | Al Franken (D) | 2009 | 2015 |
| Mississippi | Thad Cochran (R) | 1979 | 2015 |
| | Roger Wicker (R) | 2007[8] | 2015 |
| Missouri | Claire McCaskill (D) | 2007 | 2013 |
| | Roy Blunt (R) | 2011 | 2017 |
| Montana | Max Baucus (D) | 1979 | 2015 |
| | Jon Tester (D) | 2007 | 2013 |
| Nebraska | Ben Nelson (D) | 2001 | 2013 |
| | Mike Johanns (R) | 2009 | 2015 |
| Nevada | Harry Reid (D) | 1987 | 2011 |
| | Dean Heller (R) | 2011[9] | 2013 |
| New Hampshire | Jeanne Shaheen (D) | 2009 | 2015 |
| | Kelly Ayotte (R) | 2011 | 2017 |
| New Jersey | Frank R. Lautenberg (D) | 2003 | 2015 |
| | Robert Menendez (D) | 2006[10] | 2013 |
| New Mexico | Jeff Bingaman (D) | 1983 | 2013 |
| | Tom Udall (D) | 2009 | 2015 |
| New York | Charles E. Schumer (D) | 1999 | 2011 |
| | Kirsten Gillibrand (D) | 2009[11] | 2011 |
| North Carolina | Richard Burr (R) | 2005 | 2011 |
| | Kay Hagan (D) | 2009 | 2015 |
| North Dakota | Kent Conrad (D) | 1987 | 2013 |
| | John Hoeven (R) | 2011 | 2017 |
| Ohio | Sherrod Brown (D) | 2007 | 2013 |
| | Rob Portman (R) | 2011 | 2017 |
| Oklahoma | James M. Inhofe (R) | 1994[12] | 2015 |
| | Tom Coburn (R) | 2005 | 2011 |
| Oregon | Ron Wyden (D) | 1996[13] | 2011 |
| | Jeff Merkley (D) | 2009 | 2015 |
| Pennsylvania | Robert P. Casey (D) | 2007 | 2013 |
| | Patrick J. Toomey (R) | 2011 | 2017 |
| Rhode Island | Jack Reed (D) | 1997 | 2015 |
| | Sheldon Whitehouse (D) | 2007 | 2013 |
| South Carolina | Lindsey Graham (R) | 2003 | 2015 |
| | Jim DeMint (R) | 2005 | 2011 |
| South Dakota | Tim Johnson (D) | 1997 | 2015 |
| | John Thune (R) | 2005 | 2011 |
| Tennessee | Lamar Alexander (R) | 2003 | 2015 |
| | Bob Corker (R) | 2007 | 2013 |
| Texas | Kay Bailey Hutchison (R) | 1993[14] | 2013 |
| | John Cornyn (R) | 2002 | 2015 |
| Utah | Orrin G. Hatch (R) | 1977 | 2013 |
| | Mike Lee (R) | 2011 | 2017 |
| Vermont | Patrick Leahy (D) | 1975 | 2011 |
| | Bernie Sanders (I) | 2007 | 2013 |
| Virginia | Jim Webb (D) | 2007 | 2013 |
| | Mark R. Warner (D) | 2009 | 2015 |
| Washington | Patty Murray (D) | 1993 | 2011 |
| | Maria Cantwell (D) | 2001 | 2013 |
| West Virginia | Jay Rockefeller (D) | 1985 | 2015 |
| | Joe Manchin III (D) | 2010[15] | 2013 |
| Wisconsin | Herb Kohl (D) | 1989 | 2013 |
| | Ron Johnson (R) | 2010 | 2017 |
| Wyoming | Mike Enzi (R) | 1997 | 2015 |
| | John Barrasso (R) | 2007[16] | 2015 |

[1]*Dianne Feinstein was elected in November 1992 to complete the term of Pete Wilson, who resigned in 1991 to become California's governor.* [2]*Michael F. Bennet was appointed in January 2009 to complete the term of Ken Salazar, who resigned to become secretary of the interior.* [3]*Christopher A. Coons was elected in November 2010 to replace Ted Kaufman, who was appointed in January 2009 to replace Joe Biden, who resigned to become vice president.* [4]*Daniel K. Akaka was appointed in April 1990 and took office in May 1990 to fill the vacancy caused by the death of Spark M. Matsunaga.* [5]*Mark Kirk was elected in November 2010 to replace Roland W. Burris, who was appointed in December 2008 and took office in January 2009 to replace Barack Obama, who resigned*

## Senate, 112th Congress (continued)

to become president.  [6]Daniel Coats did not serve 3 Jan 1999–3 Jan 2011.  [7]Scott Brown was elected in January 2010 to fill the vacancy caused by the death of Edward M. Kennedy.  [8]Roger Wicker was appointed in December 2007 to fill the vacancy caused by the resignation of Trent Lott.  [9]Dean Heller was appointed in May 2011 to replace John Ensign, who resigned.  [10]Robert Menendez was appointed in January 2006 to fill the vacancy caused by the resignation of Jon S. Corzine.  [11]Kirsten Gillibrand was appointed in January 2009 to replace Hillary Rodham Clinton, who resigned to become secretary of state.  [12]James M. Inhofe was elected in November 1994 to complete the term of David Boren, who resigned to become president of the University of Oklahoma.  [13]Ron Wyden was elected in January 1996 to complete the term of Bob Packwood, who resigned in 1995.  [14]Kay Bailey Hutchison was elected in June 1993 to complete the term of Lloyd Bentsen, Jr., who resigned to become secretary of the treasury.  [15]Joe Manchin III was elected in November 2010 to replace Carte Goodwin, who was appointed in July 2010 to fill the vacancy caused by the death of Robert C. Byrd.  [16]John Barrasso was appointed in June 2007 to fill the vacancy caused by the death of Craig Thomas.

## Senate Standing Committees

| COMMITTEE | CHAIRMAN (PARTY–STATE) | RANKING MINORITY MEMBER (PARTY–STATE) | NUMBER OF MEMBERS MAJORITY[1] | MINORITY | NUMBER OF SUBCOMMITTEES |
|---|---|---|---|---|---|
| Agriculture, Nutrition, and Forestry | Debbie Stabenow (D-MI) | Pat Roberts (R-KA) | 11 | 10 | 5 |
| Appropriations | Daniel K. Inouye (D-HI) | Thad Cochran (R-MS) | 16 | 14 | 12 |
| Armed Services | Carl Levin (D-MI) | John McCain (R-AZ) | 14 | 12 | 6 |
| Banking, Housing, and Urban Affairs | Tim Johnson (D-SD) | Richard Shelby (R-AL) | 12 | 10 | 5 |
| Budget | Kent Conrad (D-ND) | Jeff Sessions (R-AL) | 12 | 11 | none |
| Commerce, Science, and Transportation | Jay Rockefeller (D-WV) | Kay Bailey Hutchison (R-TX) | 13 | 12 | 7 |
| Energy and Natural Resources | Jeff Bingaman (D-NM) | Lisa Murkowski (R-AK) | 12 | 10 | 4 |
| Environment and Public Works | Barbara Boxer (D-CA) | James M. Inhofe (R-OK) | 10 | 8 | 7 |
| Finance | Max Baucus (D-MT) | Orrin G. Hatch (R-UT) | 13 | 11 | 6 |
| Foreign Relations | John Kerry (D-MA) | Richard G. Lugar (R-IN) | 10 | 9 | 7 |
| Health, Education, Labor, and Pensions | Tom Harkin (D-IA) | Mike Enzi (R-WY) | 12 | 10 | 3 |
| Homeland Security and Governmental Affairs | Joe Lieberman (ID-CT) | Susan Collins (R-ME) | 9 | 8 | 5 |
| Judiciary | Patrick Leahy (D-VT) | Chuck Grassley (R-IA) | 10 | 8 | 6 |
| Rules and Administration | Charles E. Schumer (D-NY) | Lamar Alexander (R-TN) | 10 | 8 | none |
| Small Business and Entrepreneurship | Mary L. Landrieu (D-LA) | Olympia J. Snowe (R-ME) | 10 | 9 | none |
| Veterans' Affairs | Patty Murray (D-WA) | Richard Burr (R-NC) | 8 | 7 | none |

[1]Joe Lieberman and Bernie Sanders are Independents but caucus with the Democratic Party.

## Senate Special, Select, and Other Committees

| COMMITTEE | CHAIRMAN (PARTY–STATE) | RANKING MINORITY MEMBER (PARTY–STATE) | NUMBER OF MEMBERS MAJORITY | MINORITY |
|---|---|---|---|---|
| Special Committee on Aging | Herb Kohl (D-WI) | Bob Corker (R-TN) | 11 | 10 |
| Select Committee on Ethics | Barbara Boxer (D-CA) | Johnny Isakson (R-GA) | 3 | 3 |
| Committee on Indian Affairs | Daniel K. Akaka (D-HI) | John Barrasso (R-WY) | 8 | 6 |
| Select Committee on Intelligence | Dianne Feinstein (D-CA) | Saxby Chambliss (R-GA) | 10 | 9 |

## House of Representatives, 112th Congress

*Party totals: **Republicans** 240, **Democrats** 191; vacancies: 4.*

According to Article I, Section 2 of the US Constitution, a US representative must be at least 25 years old, must reside in the state he or she represents at the time of the election, and must have been a citizen of the United States for at least seven years. Each state is entitled to at least one representative, with additional seats apportioned based on population. Each congressperson originally represented 30,000 people; the range in 2010 was from 493,352 (Louisiana 2nd district) to 1,043,855 (Nevada 3rd district) persons per representative. Terms are for two years and begin on 3 January (unless otherwise noted). The current representative's salary is US$174,000 per year. The majority and minority leaders receive US$193,400 per year; the speaker of the House receives US$223,500 per year.

American Samoa, the District of Columbia, Guam, the Northern Mariana Islands, and the Virgin Islands

## House of Representatives, 112th Congress (continued)

elect delegates; Puerto Rico elects a resident commissioner. Their formal duties are the same, but the resident commissioner serves a four-year term. They may participate in debate and serve on committees but are not permitted to vote.

Numbers preceding the names refer to districts. Certain states gained (+) or lost (−) districts by reapportionment since the 107th Congress.

**House leadership**

| | |
|---|---|
| speaker of the House: | John A. Boehner |
| majority leader: | Eric Cantor |
| minority leader: | Nancy Pelosi |
| majority whip: | Kevin McCarthy |
| minority whip: | Steny H. Hoyer |

US House Web site: <www.house.gov>.

| STATE | REPRESENTATIVES | SERVICE BEGAN |
|---|---|---|
| Alabama | 1. Jo Bonner (R) | Jan 2003 |
| | 2. Martha Roby (R) | Jan 2011 |
| | 3. Mike Rogers (R) | Jan 2003 |
| | 4. Robert B. Aderholt.(R) | Jan 1997 |
| | 5. Mo Brooks (R) | Jan 2011 |
| | 6. Spencer Bachus (R) | Jan 1993 |
| | 7. Terri Sewell (D) | Jan 2011 |
| | | |
| Alaska | Don Young (R) | Mar 1973 |
| | | |
| Arizona (+2) | 1. Paul Gosar (R) | Jan 2011 |
| | 2. Trent Franks (R) | Jan 2003 |
| | 3. Ben Quayle (R) | Jan 2011 |
| | 4. Ed Pastor (D) | Sep 1991 |
| | 5. David Schweikert (R) | Jan 2011 |
| | 6. Jeff Flake (R) | Jan 2001 |
| | 7. Raúl M. Grijalva (D) | Jan 2003 |
| | 8. Ron Barber (D)[1] | Jun 2012 |
| | | |
| Arkansas | 1. Rick Crawford (R) | Jan 2011 |
| | 2. Tim Griffin (R) | Jan 2011 |
| | 3. Steve Womack (R) | Jan 2011 |
| | 4. Mike Ross (D) | Jan 2001 |
| | | |
| California (+1) | 1. Mike Thompson (D) | Jan 1999 |
| | 2. Wally Herger (R) | Jan 1987 |
| | 3. Daniel E. Lungren (R) | Jan 2005 |
| | 4. Tom McClintock (R) | Jan 2009 |
| | 5. Doris O. Matsui (D)[2] | Mar 2005 |
| | 6. Lynn C. Woolsey (D) | Jan 1993 |
| | 7. George Miller (D) | Jan 1975 |
| | 8. Nancy Pelosi (D) | Jun 1987 |
| | 9. Barbara Lee (D) | Apr 1998 |
| | 10. John Garamendi (D)[3] | Nov 2009 |
| | 11. Jerry McNerney (D) | Jan 2007 |
| | 12. Jackie Speier (D)[4] | Apr 2008 |
| | 13. Fortney ("Pete") Stark (D) | Jan 1973 |
| | 14. Anna G. Eshoo (D) | Jan 1993 |
| | 15. Michael M. Honda (D) | Jan 2001 |
| | 16. Zoe Lofgren (D) | Jan 1995 |
| | 17. Sam Farr (D) | Jun 1993 |
| | 18. Dennis A. Cardoza (D) | Jan 2003 |
| | 19. Jeff Denham (R) | Jan 2011 |
| | 20. Jim Costa (D) | Jan 2005 |
| | 21. Devin Nunes (R) | Jan 2003 |
| | 22. Kevin McCarthy (R) | Jan 2007 |
| | 23. Lois Capps (D) | Mar 1998 |
| | 24. Elton Gallegly (R) | Jan 1987 |
| | 25. Howard P. ("Buck") McKeon (R) | Jan 1993 |
| | 26. David Dreier (R) | Jan 1981 |
| | 27. Brad Sherman (D) | Jan 1997 |
| | 28. Howard L. Berman (D) | Jan 1983 |
| | 29. Adam B. Schiff (D) | Jan 2001 |
| | 30. Henry A. Waxman (D) | Jan 1975 |
| | 31. Xavier Becerra (D) | Jan 1993 |
| | 32. Judy Chu (D)[5] | Jul 2009 |
| | 33. Karen Bass (D) | Jan 2011 |
| | 34. Lucille Roybal-Allard (D) | Jan 1993 |

| STATE | REPRESENTATIVES | SERVICE BEGAN |
|---|---|---|
| California (cont.) | 35. Maxine Waters (D) | Jan 1991 |
| | 36. Janice Hahn (D)[6] | Jul 2011 |
| | 37. Laura Richardson (D)[7] | Sep 2007 |
| | 38. Grace F. Napolitano (D) | Jan 1999 |
| | 39. Linda T. Sánchez (D) | Jan 2003 |
| | 40. Edward R. Royce (R) | Jan 1993 |
| | 41. Jerry Lewis (R) | Jan 1979 |
| | 42. Gary G. Miller (R) | Jan 1999 |
| | 43. Joe Baca (D) | Nov 1999 |
| | 44. Ken Calvert (R) | Jan 1993 |
| | 45. Mary Bono Mack (R) | Apr 1998 |
| | 46. Dana Rohrabacher (R) | Jan 1989 |
| | 47. Loretta Sanchez (D) | Jan 1997 |
| | 48. John Campbell (R)[8] | Dec 2005 |
| | 49. Darrell E. Issa (R) | Jan 2001 |
| | 50. Brian P. Bilbray (R)[9] | Jan 1995 |
| | 51. Bob Filner (D) | Jan 1993 |
| | 52. Duncan Hunter (R) | Jan 2009 |
| | 53. Susan A. Davis (D) | Jan 2001 |
| | | |
| Colorado (+1) | 1. Diana DeGette (D) | Jan 1997 |
| | 2. Jared Polis (D) | Jan 2009 |
| | 3. Scott Tipton (R) | Jan 2011 |
| | 4. Cory Gardner (R) | Jan 2011 |
| | 5. Doug Lamborn (R) | Jan 2007 |
| | 6. Mike Coffman (R) | Jan 2009 |
| | 7. Ed Perlmutter (D) | Jan 2007 |
| | | |
| Connecticut (−1) | 1. John B. Larson (D) | Jan 1999 |
| | 2. Joe Courtney (D) | Jan 2007 |
| | 3. Rosa L. DeLauro (D) | Jan 1991 |
| | 4. James A. Himes (D) | Jan 2009 |
| | 5. Christopher S. Murphy (D) | Jan 2007 |
| | | |
| Delaware | John C. Carney, Jr. (D) | Jan 2011 |
| | | |
| Florida (+2) | 1. Jeff Miller (R)[10] | Oct 2001 |
| | 2. Steve Southerland (R) | Jan 2011 |
| | 3. Corrine Brown (D) | Jan 1993 |
| | 4. Ander Crenshaw (R) | Jan 2001 |
| | 5. Richard Nugent (R) | Jan 2011 |
| | 6. Cliff Stearns (R) | Jan 1989 |
| | 7. John L. Mica (R) | Jan 1993 |
| | 8. Daniel Webster (R) | Jan 2011 |
| | 9. Gus M. Bilirakis (R) | Jan 2007 |
| | 10. C.W. Bill Young (R) | Jan 1971 |
| | 11. Kathy Castor (D) | Jan 2007 |
| | 12. Dennis Ross (R) | Jan 2011 |
| | 13. Vern Buchanan (R) | Jan 2007 |
| | 14. Connie Mack (R) | Jan 2005 |
| | 15. Bill Posey (R) | Jan 2009 |
| | 16. Thomas J. Rooney (R) | Jan 2009 |
| | 17. Frederica Wilson (R) | Jan 2011 |
| | 18. Ileana Ros-Lehtinen (R) | Aug 1989 |
| | 19. Theodore E. Deutch (D)[11] | Apr 2010 |
| | 20. Debbie Wasserman Schultz (D) | Jan 2005 |
| | 21. Mario Diaz-Balart (R) | Jan 2003 |
| | 22. Allen West (R) | Jan 2011 |

## House of Representatives, 112th Congress (continued)

| STATE | REPRESENTATIVES | SERVICE BEGAN |
|---|---|---|
| Florida (cont.) | 23. Alcee L. Hastings (D) | Jan 1993 |
| | 24. Sandy Adams (R) | Jan 2011 |
| | 25. David Rivera (R) | Jan 2011 |
| Georgia (+2) | 1. Jack Kingston (R) | Jan 1993 |
| | 2. Sanford D. Bishop, Jr. (D) | Jan 1993 |
| | 3. Lynn A. Westmoreland (R) | Jan 2005 |
| | 4. Henry C. ("Hank") Johnson, Jr. (D) | Jan 2007 |
| | 5. John Lewis (D) | Jan 1987 |
| | 6. Tom Price (R) | Feb 2005 |
| | 7. Rob Woodall (R) | Jan 2011 |
| | 8. Austin Scott (R) | Jan 2011 |
| | 9. Tom Graves (R)[12] | Jun 2010 |
| | 10. Paul C. Broun (R)[13] | Jul 2007 |
| | 11. Phil Gingrey (R) | Jan 2003 |
| | 12. John Barrow (D) | Jan 2005 |
| | 13. David Scott (D) | Jan 2003 |
| Hawaii | 1. Colleen Hanabusa (D) | Jan 2011 |
| | 2. Mazie K. Hirono (D) | Jan 2007 |
| Idaho | 1. Rául Labrador (R) | Jan 2011 |
| | 2. Michael K. Simpson (R) | Jan 1999 |
| Illinois (−1) | 1. Bobby L. Rush (D) | Jan 1993 |
| | 2. Jesse L. Jackson, Jr. (D) | Dec 1995 |
| | 3. Daniel Lipinski (D) | Jan 2005 |
| | 4. Luis V. Gutierrez (D) | Jan 1993 |
| | 5. Mike Quigley (D)[14] | Apr 2009 |
| | 6. Peter J. Roskam (R) | Jan 2007 |
| | 7. Danny K. Davis (D) | Jan 1997 |
| | 8. Joe Walsh (R) | Jan 2011 |
| | 9. Janice D. Schakowsky (D) | Jan 1999 |
| | 10. Robert Dold (R) | Jan 2011 |
| | 11. Adam Kinzinger (R) | Jan 2011 |
| | 12. Jerry F. Costello (D) | Aug 1988 |
| | 13. Judy Biggert (R) | Jan 1999 |
| | 14. Randy Hultgren (R) | Jan 2011 |
| | 15. Timothy V. Johnson (R) | Jan 2001 |
| | 16. Donald A. Manzullo (R) | Jan 1993 |
| | 17. Bobby Schilling (R) | Jan 2011 |
| | 18. Aaron Schock (R) | Jan 2009 |
| | 19. John Shimkus (R) | Jan 1997 |
| Indiana (−1) | 1. Peter J. Visclosky (D) | Jan 1985 |
| | 2. Joe Donnelly (D) | Jan 2007 |
| | 3. Marlin Stutzman (R)[15] | Nov 2010 |
| | 4. Todd Rokita (R) | Jan 2011 |
| | 5. Dan Burton (R) | Jan 1983 |
| | 6. Mike Pence (R) | Jan 2001 |
| | 7. André Carson (D)[16] | Mar 2008 |
| | 8. Larry Bucshon (R) | Jan 2011 |
| | 9. Todd Young (R) | Jan 2011 |
| Iowa | 1. Bruce L. Braley (D) | Jan 2007 |
| | 2. David Loebsack (D) | Jan 2007 |
| | 3. Leonard L. Boswell (D) | Jan 1997 |
| | 4. Tom Latham (R) | Jan 1995 |
| | 5. Steve King (R) | Jan 2003 |
| Kansas | 1. Tim Huelskamp (R) | Jan 2011 |
| | 2. Lynn Jenkins (R) | Jan 2009 |
| | 3. Kevin Yoder (R) | Jan 2011 |
| | 4. Mike Pompeo (R) | Jan 2011 |
| Kentucky | 1. Ed Whitfield (R) | Jan 1995 |
| | 2. Brett Guthrie (R) | Jan 2009 |

| STATE | REPRESENTATIVES | SERVICE BEGAN |
|---|---|---|
| Kentucky (cont.) | 3. John A. Yarmuth (D) | Jan 2007 |
| | 4. vacant[17] | |
| | 5. Harold Rogers (R) | Jan 1981 |
| | 6. Ben Chandler (D)[18] | Feb 2004 |
| Louisiana | 1. Steve Scalise (R)[19] | May 2008 |
| | 2. Cedric Richmond (D) | Jan 2011 |
| | 3. Jeffrey M. Landry (R) | Jan 2011 |
| | 4. John Fleming (R) | Jan 2009 |
| | 5. Rodney Alexander (R) | Jan 2003 |
| | 6. Bill Cassidy (R) | Jan 2009 |
| | 7. Charles W. Boustany, Jr. (R) | Jan 2005 |
| Maine | 1. Chellie Pingree (D) | Jan 2009 |
| | 2. Michael H. Michaud (D) | Jan 2003 |
| Maryland | 1. Andy Harris (R) | Jan 2011 |
| | 2. C.A. ("Dutch") Ruppersberger (D) | Jan 2003 |
| | 3. John P. Sarbanes (D) | Jan 2007 |
| | 4. Donna F. Edwards (D)[20] | Jun 2008 |
| | 5. Steny H. Hoyer (D) | May 1981 |
| | 6. Roscoe G. Bartlett (R) | Jan 1993 |
| | 7. Elijah E. Cummings (D) | Apr 1996 |
| | 8. Chris Van Hollen (D) | Jan 2003 |
| Massa-chusetts | 1. John W. Olver (D) | Jun 1991 |
| | 2. Richard E. Neal (D) | Jan 1989 |
| | 3. James P. McGovern (D) | Jan 1997 |
| | 4. Barney Frank (D) | Jan 1981 |
| | 5. Niki Tsongas (D)[21] | Oct 2007 |
| | 6. John F. Tierney (D) | Jan 1997 |
| | 7. Edward J. Markey (D) | Nov 1976 |
| | 8. Michael E. Capuano (D) | Jan 1999 |
| | 9. Stephen F. Lynch (D)[22] | Oct 2001 |
| | 10. William R. Keating (D) | Jan 2011 |
| Michigan (−1) | 1. Dan Benishek (R) | Jan 2011 |
| | 2. Bill Huizenga (R) | Jan 2011 |
| | 3. Justin Amash (R) | Jan 2011 |
| | 4. Dave Camp (R) | Jan 1991 |
| | 5. Dale E. Kildee (D) | Jan 1977 |
| | 6. Fred Upton (R) | Jan 1987 |
| | 7. Tim Walberg (R)[23] | Jan 2007 |
| | 8. Mike Rogers (R) | Jan 2001 |
| | 9. Gary C. Peters (D) | Jan 2009 |
| | 10. Candice S. Miller (R) | Jan 2003 |
| | 11. vacant[24] | |
| | 12. Sander M. Levin (D) | Jan 1983 |
| | 13. Hansen Clarke (D) | Jan 2011 |
| | 14. John Conyers, Jr. (D) | Jan 1965 |
| | 15. John D. Dingell (D) | Dec 1955 |
| Minnesota | 1. Timothy J. Walz (D) | Jan 2007 |
| | 2. John Kline (R) | Jan 2003 |
| | 3. Erik Paulsen (R) | Jan 2009 |
| | 4. Betty McCollum (D) | Jan 2001 |
| | 5. Keith Ellison (D) | Jan 2007 |
| | 6. Michele Bachmann (R) | Jan 2007 |
| | 7. Collin C. Peterson (D) | Jan 1991 |
| | 8. Chip Cravaack (R) | Jan 2011 |
| Mississippi (−1) | 1. Alan Nunnelee (R) | Jan 2011 |
| | 2. Bennie G. Thompson (D) | Apr 1993 |
| | 3. Gregg Harper (R) | Jan 2009 |
| | 4. Steven Palazzo (R) | Jan 2011 |

## House of Representatives, 112th Congress (continued)

| STATE | REPRESENTATIVES | SERVICE BEGAN |
|---|---|---|
| Missouri | 1. William Lacy Clay (D) | Jan 2001 |
| | 2. W. Todd Akin (R) | Jan 2001 |
| | 3. Russ Carnahan (D) | Jan 2005 |
| | 4. Vicky Hartzler (R) | Jan 2011 |
| | 5. Emanuel Cleaver (D) | Jan 2005 |
| | 6. Sam Graves (R) | Jan 2001 |
| | 7. Billy Long (R) | Jan 2011 |
| | 8. Jo Ann Emerson (R) | Nov 1996 |
| | 9. Blaine Luetkemeyer (R) | Jan 2009 |
| Montana | Denny Rehberg (R) | Jan 2001 |
| Nebraska | 1. Jeff Fortenberry (R) | Jan 2005 |
| | 2. Lee Terry (R) | Jan 1999 |
| | 3. Adrian Smith (R) | Jan 2007 |
| Nevada (+1) | 1. Shelley Berkley (D) | Jan 1999 |
| | 2. Mark E. Amodei (R)[25] | Sep 2011 |
| | 3. Joe Heck (R) | Jan 2011 |
| New Hampshire | 1. Frank Guinta (R) | Jan 2011 |
| | 2. Charles F. Bass (R)[26] | Jan 1995 |
| New Jersey | 1. Robert E. Andrews (D) | Nov 1990 |
| | 2. Frank A. LoBiondo (R) | Jan 1995 |
| | 3. Jon Runyan (R) | Jan 2011 |
| | 4. Christopher H. Smith (R) | Jan 1981 |
| | 5. Scott Garrett (R) | Jan 2003 |
| | 6. Frank Pallone, Jr. (D) | Nov 1988 |
| | 7. Leonard Lance (R) | Jan 2009 |
| | 8. Bill Pascrell, Jr. (D) | Jan 1997 |
| | 9. Steven R. Rothman (D) | Jan 1997 |
| | 10. *vacant*[27] | |
| | 11. Rodney P. Freling-huysen (R) | Jan 1995 |
| | 12. Rush D. Holt (D) | Jan 1999 |
| | 13. Albio Sires (D)[28] | Nov 2006 |
| New Mexico | 1. Martin Heinrich (D) | Jan 2009 |
| | 2. Stevan Pearce (R)[29] | Jan 2003 |
| | 3. Ben Ray Luján (D) | Jan 2009 |
| New York (−2) | 1. Timothy H. Bishop (D) | Jan 2003 |
| | 2. Steve Israel (D) | Jan 2001 |
| | 3. Peter T. King (R) | Jan 1993 |
| | 4. Carolyn McCarthy (D) | Jan 1997 |
| | 5. Gary L. Ackerman (D) | Mar 1983 |
| | 6. Gregory W. Meeks (D) | Feb 1998 |
| | 7. Joseph Crowley (D) | Jan 1999 |
| | 8. Jerrold Nadler (D) | Nov 1992 |
| | 9. Robert L. Turner (R)[30] | Sep 2011 |
| | 10. Edolphus Towns (D) | Jan 1983 |
| | 11. Yvette D. Clarke (D) | Jan 2007 |
| | 12. Nydia M. Velázquez (D) | Jan 1993 |
| | 13. Michael G. Grimm (R) | Jan 2011 |
| | 14. Carolyn B. Maloney (D) | Jan 1993 |
| | 15. Charles B. Rangel (D) | Jan 1971 |
| | 16. José E. Serrano (D) | Mar 1990 |
| | 17. Eliot L. Engel (D) | Jan 1989 |
| | 18. Nita M. Lowey (D) | Jan 1989 |
| | 19. Nan Hayworth (R) | Jan 2011 |
| | 20. Christopher Gibson (R) | Jan 2011 |
| | 21. Paul Tonko (D) | Jan 2009 |
| | 22. Maurice D. Hinchey (D) | Jan 1993 |
| | 23. William Owens (D)[31] | Nov 2009 |
| | 24. Richard Hanna (R) | Jan 2011 |
| | 25. Ann Marie Buerkle (R) | Jan 2011 |
| | 26. Kathy Hochul (D)[32] | Jun 2011 |

| STATE | REPRESENTATIVES | SERVICE BEGAN |
|---|---|---|
| New York (cont.) | 27. Brian Higgins (D) | Jan 2005 |
| | 28. Louise McIntosh Slaughter (D) | Jan 1987 |
| | 29. Tom Reed (R)[33] | Nov 2010 |
| North Carolina (+1) | 1. G.K. Butterfield (D)[34] | Jul 2004 |
| | 2. Renee Ellmers (R) | Jan 2011 |
| | 3. Walter B. Jones (R) | Jan 1995 |
| | 4. David E. Price (D) | Jan 1997 |
| | 5. Virginia Foxx (R) | Jan 2005 |
| | 6. Howard Coble (R) | Jan 1985 |
| | 7. Mike McIntyre (D) | Jan 1997 |
| | 8. Larry Kissell (D) | Jan 2009 |
| | 9. Sue Wilkins Myrick (R) | Jan 1995 |
| | 10. Patrick T. McHenry (R) | Jan 2005 |
| | 11. Heath Shuler (D) | Jan 2007 |
| | 12. Melvin L. Watt (D) | Jan 1993 |
| | 13. Brad Miller (D) | Jan 2003 |
| North Dakota | Rick Berg (R) | Jan 2011 |
| Ohio (−1) | 1. Steve Chabot (R)[35] | Jan 1995 |
| | 2. Jean Schmidt (R) | Sep 2005 |
| | 3. Michael R. Turner (R) | Jan 2003 |
| | 4. Jim Jordan (R) | Jan 2007 |
| | 5. Robert E. Latta (R)[36] | Dec 2007 |
| | 6. Bill Johnson (R) | Jan 2011 |
| | 7. Steve Austria (R) | Jan 2009 |
| | 8. John A. Boehner (R) | Jan 1991 |
| | 9. Marcy Kaptur (D) | Jan 1983 |
| | 10. Dennis J. Kucinich (D) | Jan 1997 |
| | 11. Marcia L. Fudge (D)[37] | Nov 2008 |
| | 12. Patrick J. Tiberi (R) | Jan 2001 |
| | 13. Betty Sutton (D) | Jan 2007 |
| | 14. Steven C. LaTourette (R) | Jan 1995 |
| | 15. Steve Stivers (R) | Jan 2011 |
| | 16. Jim Renacci (R) | Jan 2011 |
| | 17. Tim Ryan (D) | Jan 2003 |
| | 18. Bob Gibbs (R) | Jan 2011 |
| Oklahoma (−1) | 1. John Sullivan (R)[38] | Feb 2002 |
| | 2. Dan Boren (D) | Jan 2005 |
| | 3. Frank D. Lucas (R) | May 1994 |
| | 4. Tom Cole (R) | Jan 2003 |
| | 5. James Lankford (R) | Jan 2011 |
| Oregon | 1. Suzanne Bonamici (D)[39] | Feb 2012 |
| | 2. Greg Walden (R) | Jan 1999 |
| | 3. Earl Blumenauer (D) | May 1996 |
| | 4. Peter A. DeFazio (D) | Jan 1987 |
| | 5. Kurt Schrader (D) | Jan 2009 |
| Pennsylvania (−2) | 1. Robert A. Brady (D) | May 1998 |
| | 2. Chaka Fattah (D) | Jan 1995 |
| | 3. Mike Kelly (R) | Jan 2011 |
| | 4. Jason Altmire (D) | Jan 2007 |
| | 5. Glenn Thompson (R) | Jan 2009 |
| | 6. Jim Gerlach (R) | Jan 2003 |
| | 7. Patrick Meehan (R) | Jan 2011 |
| | 8. Michael G. Fitzpatrick (R)[40] | Jan 2005 |
| | 9. Bill Shuster (R) | May 2001 |
| | 10. Tom Marino (R) | Jan 2011 |
| | 11. Lou Barletta (R) | Jan 2011 |
| | 12. Mark S. Critz (D)[41] | May 2010 |
| | 13. Allyson Y. Schwartz (D) | Jan 2005 |
| | 14. Michael F. Doyle (D) | Jan 1995 |
| | 15. Charles W. Dent (R) | Jan 2005 |

## House of Representatives, 112th Congress (continued)

| STATE | REPRESENTATIVES | SERVICE BEGAN | STATE | REPRESENTATIVES | SERVICE BEGAN |
|---|---|---|---|---|---|
| Penn- | 16. Joseph R. Pitts (R) | Jan 1997 | Texas | 26. Michael C. Burgess (R) | Jan 2003 |
| sylvania | 17. Tim Holden (D) | Jan 1993 | (cont.) | 27. Blake Farenthold (R) | Jan 2011 |
| (cont.) | 18. Tim Murphy (R) | Jan 2003 | | 28. Henry Cuellar (D) | Jan 2005 |
| | 19. Todd Russell Platts (R) | Jan 2001 | | 29. Gene Green (D) | Jan 1993 |
| | | | | 30. Eddie Bernice | Jan 1993 |
| Rhode | 1. David N. Cicilline (D) | Jan 2011 | | Johnson (D) | |
| Island | 2. James R. Langevin (D) | Jan 2001 | | 31. John R. Carter (R) | Jan 2003 |
| | | | | 32. Pete Sessions (R) | Jan 1997 |
| South | 1. Tim Scott (R) | Jan 2011 | | | |
| Carolina | 2. Joe Wilson (R)[42] | Dec 2001 | Utah | 1. Rob Bishop (R) | Jan 2003 |
| | 3. Jeff Duncan (R) | Jan 2011 | | 2. Jim Matheson (D) | Jan 2001 |
| | 4. Trey Gowdy (R) | Jan 2011 | | 3. Jason Chaffetz (R) | Jan 2009 |
| | 5. Mick Mulvaney (R) | Jan 2011 | | | |
| | 6. James E. Clyburn (D) | Jan 1993 | Vermont | Peter Welch (D) | Jan 2007 |
| South | Kristi Noem (R) | Jan 2011 | Virginia | 1. Robert J. Wittman (R)[45] | Dec 2007 |
| Dakota | | | | 2. E. Scott Rigell (R) | Jan 2011 |
| | | | | 3. Robert C. ("Bobby") | Jan 1993 |
| Tennessee | 1. David P. Roe (R) | Jan 2009 | | Scott (D) | |
| | 2. John J. Duncan, Jr. (R) | Nov 1988 | | 4. J. Randy Forbes (R)[46] | Jun 2001 |
| | 3. Chuck Fleischmann (R) | Jan 2011 | | 5. Robert Hurt (R) | Jan 2011 |
| | 4. Scott DesJarlais (R) | Jan 2011 | | 6. Bob Goodlatte (R) | Jan 1993 |
| | 5. Jim Cooper (D)[43] | Jan 1983 | | 7. Eric Cantor (R) | Jan 2001 |
| | 6. Diane Black (R) | Jan 2011 | | 8. James P. Moran (D) | Jan 1991 |
| | 7. Marsha Blackburn (R) | Jan 2003 | | 9. H. Morgan Griffith (R) | Jan 2011 |
| | 8. Stephen Lee Fincher (R) | Jan 2011 | | 10. Frank R. Wolf (R) | Jan 1981 |
| | 9. Steve Cohen (D) | Jan 2007 | | 11. Gerald E. Connolly (D) | Jan 2009 |
| Texas | 1. Louie Gohmert (R) | Jan 2005 | Washington | 1. vacant[47] | |
| (+2) | 2. Ted Poe (R) | Jan 2005 | | 2. Rick Larsen (D) | Jan 2001 |
| | 3. Sam Johnson (R) | May 1991 | | 3. Jaime Herrera Beutler (R) | Jan 2011 |
| | 4. Ralph M. Hall (R) | Jan 1981 | | 4. Doc Hastings (R) | Jan 1995 |
| | 5. Jeb Hensarling (R) | Jan 2003 | | 5. Cathy McMorris | Jan 2005 |
| | 6. Joe Barton (R) | Jan 1985 | | Rodgers (R) | |
| | 7. John Abney Culberson (R) | Jan 2001 | | 6. Norman D. Dicks (D) | Jan 1977 |
| | 8. Kevin Brady (R) | Jan 1997 | | 7. Jim McDermott (D) | Jan 1989 |
| | 9. Al Green (D) | Jan 2005 | | 8. David G. Reichert (R) | Jan 2005 |
| | 10. Michael T. McCaul (R) | Jan 2005 | | 9. Adam Smith (D) | Jan 1997 |
| | 11. K. Michael Conaway (R) | Jan 2005 | | | |
| | 12. Kay Granger (R) | Jan 1997 | West Virginia | 1. David McKinley (R) | Jan 2011 |
| | 13. Mac Thornberry (R) | Jan 1995 | | 2. Shelley Moore Capito (R) | Jan 2001 |
| | 14. Ron Paul (R) | Jan 1997 | | 3. Nick J. Rahall II (D) | Jan 1977 |
| | 15. Rubén Hinojosa (D) | Jan 1997 | | | |
| | 16. Silvestre Reyes (D) | Jan 1997 | Wisconsin | 1. Paul Ryan (R) | Jan 1999 |
| | 17. Bill Flores (R) | Jan 2011 | (−1) | 2. Tammy Baldwin (D) | Jan 1999 |
| | 18. Sheila Jackson-Lee (D) | Jan 1995 | | 3. Ron Kind (D) | Jan 1997 |
| | 19. Randy Neugebauer (R)[44] | Jun 2003 | | 4. Gwen Moore (D) | Jan 2005 |
| | 20. Charles A. Gonzalez (D) | Jan 1999 | | 5. F. James Sensen- | Jan 1979 |
| | 21. Lamar Smith (R) | Jan 1987 | | brenner, Jr. (R) | |
| | 22. Pete Olson (R) | Jan 2009 | | 6. Thomas E. Petri (R) | Apr 1979 |
| | 23. Francisco (Quico) | Jan 2011 | | 7. Sean Duffy (R) | Jan 2011 |
| | Canseco (R) | | | 8. Reid Ribble (R) | Jan 2011 |
| | 24. Kenny Marchant (R) | Jan 2005 | | | |
| | 25. Lloyd Doggett (D) | Jan 2005 | Wyoming | Cynthia M. Lummis (R) | Jan 2009 |

| JURISDICTION | REPRESENTATIVES | SERVICE BEGAN |
|---|---|---|
| American Samoa | (Delegate) Eni F.H. Faleomavaega (D) | Jan 1989 |
| District of Columbia | (Delegate) Eleanor Holmes Norton (D) | Jan 1991 |
| Guam | (Delegate) Madeleine Z. Bordallo (D) | Jan 2003 |
| Northern Mariana Islands | (Delegate) Gregorio Kilili Camacho Sablan (D) | Jan 2009 |
| Puerto Rico | (Resident Commissioner) Pedro R. Pierluisi (New Progressive) | Jan 2009 |
| US Virgin Islands | (Delegate) Donna M. Christensen (D) | Jan 1997 |

[1]*Ron Barber was elected 12 Jun 2012 following the resignation of Gabrielle Giffords.* [2]*Doris O. Matsui was elected 8 Mar 2005 following the death of Robert T. Matsui.* [3]*John Garamendi was elected 3 Nov 2009 following the resignation of Ellen O. Tauscher.* [4]*Jackie Speier was elected 8 Apr 2008 following the death of Tom Lantos.* [5]*Judy Chu was elected 14 Jul 2009 following the resignation of Hilda L. Solis.* [6]*Janice Hahn*

## House of Representatives, 112th Congress (continued)

was elected 12 Jul 2011 following the resignation of Jane Harman. [7]Laura Richardson was elected 21 Aug 2007 following the death of Juanita Millender-McDonald. [8]John Campbell was elected 6 Dec 2005 following the resignation of Christopher Cox. [9]Brian P. Bilbray did not serve 3 Jan 2001–6 Jun 2005. He was elected 6 Jun 2005 following the resignation of Randall ("Duke") Cunningham. [10]Jeff Miller was elected 16 Oct 2001 following the resignation of Joe Scarborough. [11]Theodore Deutch was elected 13 Apr 2010 following the resignation of Robert Wexler. [12]Tom Graves was elected 8 Jun 2010 following the resignation of Nathan Deal. [13]Paul C. Broun was elected 17 Jul 2007 following the death of Charlie Norwood. [14]Mike Quigley was elected 7 Apr 2009 following the resignation of Rahm Emanuel. [15]Marlin Stutzman was elected 2 Nov 2010 following the resignation of Mark Souder. [16]André Carson was elected 11 Mar 2008 following the death of Julia Carson. [17]Vacant following the resignation of Geoff Davis, 31 Jul 2012. [18]Ben Chandler was elected 17 Feb 2004 following the resignation of Ernie Fletcher. [19]Steve Scalise was elected 3 May 2008 following the resignation of Bobby Jindal. [20]Donna F. Edwards was elected 17 Jun 2007 following the resignation of Albert Russell Wynn. [21]Niki Tsongas was elected 16 Oct 2007 following the resignation of Martin T. Meehan. [22]Stephen F. Lynch was elected 16 Oct 2001 following the death of John Joseph Moakley. [23]Tim Walberg did not serve 3 Jan 2009–3 Jan 2011. [24]Vacant following the resignation of Thaddeus McCotter, 6 Jul 2012. [25]Mark E. Amodei was elected 13 Sep 2011 following the resignation of Dean Heller. [26]Charles F. Bass did not serve 3 Jan 2007–3 Jan 2011. [27]Vacant following the death of Donald M. Payne, 6 Mar 2012. [28]Albio Sires was elected 7 Nov 2006 following the resignation of Robert Menendez. [29]Stevan Pearce did not serve 3 Jan 2009–3 Jan 2011. [30]Robert L. Turner was elected 13 Sep 2011 following the resignation of Anthony D. Weiner. [31]William Owens was elected 3 Nov 2009 following the resignation of John McHugh. [32]Kathy Hochul was elected 24 May 2011 and sworn in 1 Jun 2011 following the resignation of Christopher John Lee. [33]Tom Reed was elected 2 Nov 2010 following the resignation of Eric J.J. Massa. [34]G.K. Butterfield was elected 20 Jul 2004 following the resignation of Frank Ballance. [35]Steve Chabot did not serve 3 Jan 2009–3 Jan 2011. [36]Robert E. Latta was elected 11 Dec 2007 following the death of Paul E. Gillmor. [37]Marcia L. Fudge was elected 18 Nov 2008 following the death of Stephanie Tubbs Jones. [38]John Sullivan was elected 8 Jan 2002 following the resignation of Steve Largent. [39]Suzanne Bonamici was elected 31 Jan 2012 following the resignation of David Wu. [40]Michael G. Fitzpatrick did not serve 3 Jan 2007–3 Jan 2011. [41]Mark S. Critz was elected 18 May 2010 following the death of John P. Murtha. [42]Joe Wilson was elected 18 Dec 2001 following the death of Floyd Spence. [43]Jim Cooper did not serve 3 Jan 1995–3 Jan 2003. [44]Randy Neugebauer was elected 3 Jun 2003 following the resignation of Larry Combest. [45]Robert J. Wittman was elected 11 Dec 2007 following the death of Jo Ann Davis. [46]J. Randy Forbes was elected 19 Jun 2001 following the death of Norman Sisisky. [47]Vacant following the resignation of Jay Inslee, 20 Mar 2012.

## House of Representatives Standing and Select Committees

| COMMITTEE | CHAIRMAN (PARTY-STATE) | RANKING MINORITY MEMBER (PARTY-STATE) | NUMBER OF MEMBERS MAJORITY | MINORITY | NUMBER OF SUBCOMMITTEES |
|---|---|---|---|---|---|
| Agriculture | Frank D. Lucas (R-OK) | Collin C. Peterson (D-MN) | 26 | 20 | 6 |
| Appropriations | Harold Rogers (R-KY) | Norman D. Dicks (D-WA) | 29 | 21 | 12 |
| Armed Services | Howard P. "Buck" McKeon (R-CA) | Adam Smith (D-WA) | 35 | 27 | 7 |
| Budget | Paul Ryan (R-WI) | Chris Van Hollen (D-MD) | 22 | 16 | none |
| Education and the Workforce | John Kline (R-MN) | George Miller (D-CA) | 23 | 17 | 4 |
| Energy and Commerce | Fred Upton (R-MI) | Henry A. Waxman (D-CA) | 31 | 23 | 6 |
| Ethics | Jo Bonner (R-AL) | Linda T. Sánchez (D-CA) | 5 | 5 | none |
| Financial Services | Spencer Bachus (R-AL) | Barney Frank (D-MA) | 34 | 27 | 6 |
| Foreign Affairs | Ileana Ros-Lehtinen (R-FL) | Howard L. Berman (D-CA) | 26 | 20 | 7 |
| Homeland Security | Peter T. King (R-NY) | Bennie G. Thompson (D-MS) | 19 | 14 | 6 |
| House Administration | Daniel E. Lungren (R-CA) | Robert A. Brady (D-PA) | 6 | 3 | 2 |
| Judiciary | Lamar Smith (R-TX) | John Conyers, Jr. (D-MI) | 23 | 16 | 5 |
| Natural Resources | Doc Hastings (R-WA) | Edward J. Markey (D-MA) | 27 | 21 | 5 |
| Oversight and Government Reform | Darrell E. Issa (R-CA) | Elijah E. Cummings (D-MD) | 23 | 17 | 7 |
| Rules | David Dreier (R-CA) | Louise McIntosh Slaughter (D-NY) | 9 | 4 | 2 |
| Science, Space, and Technology | Ralph M. Hall (R-TX) | Eddie Bernice Johnson (D-TX) | 23 | 17 | 5 |
| Small Business | Sam Graves (R-MO) | Nydia M. Velázquez (D-NY) | 15 | 11 | 5 |
| Transportation and Infrastructure | John L. Mica (R-FL) | Nick J. Rahall II (D-WV) | 33 | 26 | 6 |
| Veterans' Affairs | Jeff Miller (R-FL) | Bob Filner (D-CA) | 15 | 11 | 4 |
| Ways and Means | Dave Camp (R-MI) | Sander M. Levin (D-MI) | 22 | 15 | 6 |
| Permanent Select Committee on Intelligence | Mike Rogers (R-MI) | C.A. ("Dutch") Ruppersberger (D-MD) | 12 | 8 | 3 |

# Joint Committees of Congress

The joint committees of Congress include members from both the Senate and the House of Representatives. They function as overseeing entities but do not have the power to approve appropriations or legislation. Chairmanship of the Joint Economic Committee is determined by seniority and alternates between the Senate and the House every Congress. The Joint Committee on the Library of Congress is evenly made up of members from the House Administration Committee and the Senate Rules and Administration Committee. Chairmanship and vice-chairmanship of the Joint Committee on Printing alternate between the House and the Senate every Congress. The Joint Committee on Taxation is composed of five members from the Senate Committee on Finance and five members from the House Committee on Ways and Means (three majority and two minority members from each).

| COMMITTEE | CHAIRMAN (PARTY-STATE) | VICE-CHAIRMAN (PARTY-STATE) | NUMBER OF MEMBERS | |
|---|---|---|---|---|
| | | | DEMOCRATIC | REPUBLICAN |
| Economic | Sen. Robert P. Casey (D-PA) | Rep. Kevin Brady (R-TX) | 10 | 10 |
| Library | Sen. Charles E. Schumer (D-NY) | Rep. Gregg Harper (R-MS) | 5 | 5 |
| Printing | Rep. Gregg Harper (R-MS) | Sen. Charles E. Schumer (D-NY) | 5 | 5 |
| Taxation | Sen. Max Baucus (D-MT) | Rep. Dave Camp (R-MI) | 5 | 5 |

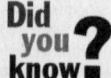

**Did you know?** The nonlethal TASER stun gun uses compressed gas to send two electrodes connected by a wire toward a target. If these attach themselves to the skin or clothing of the target, a charge of up to 50,000 volts is delivered, momentarily incapacitating the target. TASER stands for Thomas A. Swift Electric Rifle, named after the young protagonist in a series of science fiction novels from the early 20th century.

# Electoral Votes by State

Each state receives one electoral vote for each of its representatives and one for each of its two senators, ensuring at least three votes for each state, as the Constitution guarantees at least one representative regardless of population. Allocations are based on the 2010 census and are applicable for subsequent elections.

*Total: 538; Majority needed to elect president and vice president: 270*

| STATE | NUMBER OF VOTES | STATE | NUMBER OF VOTES | STATE | NUMBER OF VOTES |
|---|---|---|---|---|---|
| Alabama | 9 | Kentucky | 8 | North Dakota | 3 |
| Alaska | 3 | Louisiana | 8 | Ohio | 18 |
| Arizona | 11 | Maine | 4 | Oklahoma | 7 |
| Arkansas | 6 | Maryland | 10 | Oregon | 7 |
| California | 55 | Massachusetts | 11 | Pennsylvania | 20 |
| Colorado | 9 | Michigan | 16 | Rhode Island | 4 |
| Connecticut | 7 | Minnesota | 10 | South Carolina | 9 |
| Delaware | 3 | Mississippi | 6 | South Dakota | 3 |
| District of Columbia | 3 | Missouri | 10 | Tennessee | 11 |
| Florida | 29 | Montana | 3 | Texas | 38 |
| Georgia | 16 | Nebraska | 5 | Utah | 6 |
| Hawaii | 4 | Nevada | 6 | Vermont | 3 |
| Idaho | 4 | New Hampshire | 4 | Virginia | 13 |
| Illinois | 20 | New Jersey | 14 | Washington | 12 |
| Indiana | 11 | New Mexico | 5 | West Virginia | 5 |
| Iowa | 6 | New York | 29 | Wisconsin | 10 |
| Kansas | 6 | North Carolina | 15 | Wyoming | 3 |

# Congressional Apportionment

*The US Constitution requires a decennial census to determine the apportionment of representatives for each state in the House of Representatives.*

| STATE | REPRESENTATIVES | STATE | REPRESENTATIVES | STATE | REPRESENTATIVES |
|---|---|---|---|---|---|
| Alabama | 7 | Georgia | 14 | Maine | 2 |
| Alaska | 1 | Hawaii | 2 | Maryland | 8 |
| Arizona | 9 | Idaho | 2 | Massachusetts | 9 |
| Arkansas | 4 | Illinois | 18 | Michigan | 14 |
| California | 53 | Indiana | 9 | Minnesota | 8 |
| Colorado | 7 | Iowa | 4 | Mississippi | 4 |
| Connecticut | 5 | Kansas | 4 | Missouri | 8 |
| Delaware | 1 | Kentucky | 6 | Montana | 1 |
| Florida | 27 | Louisiana | 6 | Nebraska | 3 |

## Congressional Apportionment (continued)

| STATE | REPRESENTATIVES | STATE | REPRESENTATIVES | STATE | REPRESENTATIVES |
|---|---|---|---|---|---|
| Nevada | 4 | Oklahoma | 5 | Utah | 4 |
| New Hampshire | 2 | Oregon | 5 | Vermont | 1 |
| New Jersey | 12 | Pennsylvania | 18 | Virginia | 11 |
| New Mexico | 3 | Rhode Island | 2 | Washington | 10 |
| New York | 27 | South Carolina | 7 | West Virginia | 3 |
| North Carolina | 13 | South Dakota | 1 | Wisconsin | 8 |
| North Dakota | 1 | Tennessee | 9 | Wyoming | 1 |
| Ohio | 16 | Texas | 36 | **Total** | **435** |

# United States Military Affairs

## US Military Leadership

| | |
|---|---|
| **President, Commander in Chief:** | Barack Obama (20 Jan 2009) |
| **Secretary of Defense:** | Leon E. Panetta (1 Jul 2011) |
| **Chairman, Joint Chiefs of Staff:** | Gen. Martin Dempsey (1 Oct 2011) |
| **Vice Chairman, Joint Chiefs of Staff:** | Adm. James A. Winnefeld, Jr. (4 Aug 2011) |

| RANK/POSITION | NAME (DATE ASSUMED POST) |
|---|---|
| **Army** | |
| Chief of Staff | Gen. Raymond T. Odierno (7 Sep 2011) |
| Vice Chief of Staff | Gen. Lloyd J. Austin III (31 Jan 2012) |
| Sergeant Major | Raymond F. Chandler III (1 Mar 2011) |
| Sec. of the Army | John M. McHugh (21 Sep 2009) |
| Under Sec. of the Army | Joseph W. Westphal (21 Sep 2009) |
| **Navy** | |
| Chief of Naval Operations | Adm. Jonathan W. Greenert (23 Sep 2011) |
| Vice Chief of Naval Operations | Adm. Mark Ferguson (22 Aug 2011) |
| Master Chief Petty Officer | Rick D. West (12 Dec 2008) |
| Sec. of the Navy | Ray Mabus (19 May 2009) |
| Under Sec. of the Navy | Robert O. Work (19 May 2009) |

| RANK/POSITION | NAME (DATE ASSUMED POST) |
|---|---|
| **Air Force** | |
| Chief of Staff | Gen. Norton A. Schwartz (12 Aug 2008) |
| Vice Chief of Staff | Gen. Philip M. Breedlove (14 Jan 2011) |
| Chief Master Sgt. | James A. Roy (30 Jun 2009) |
| Sec. of the Air Force | Michael B. Donley (2 Oct 2008) |
| Under Sec. of the Air Force | Erin C. Conaton (4 Mar 2010) |
| **Marine Corps** | |
| Commandant | Gen. James F. Amos (22 Oct 2010) |
| Asst. Commandant | Gen. Joseph F. Dunford, Jr. (23 Oct 2010) |
| Sergeant Major | Micheal P. Barrett (9 Jun 2011) |
| **Coast Guard** | |
| Commandant | Adm. Robert J. Papp, Jr. (25 May 2010) |
| Vice Commandant | Vice Adm. Sally Brice-O'Hara (24 May 2010) |
| Dep. Commandant for Mission Control | Vice Adm. John P. Currier (August 2009) |
| Master Chief Petty Officer | Michael P. Leavitt (21 May 2010) |

## Unified Combatant Commands

The Unified Combatant Commands provide operational control of US combat forces and are organized geographically to a significant extent. Unified Commanders receive orders through the chairman of the Joint Chiefs of Staff. Although the number of commands may vary, each command must be composed of forces from at least two of the armed services. Information is current as of April 2012.

| COMMAND | HEADQUARTERS | COMMANDER |
|---|---|---|
| US European Command | Stuttgart-Vaihingen, Germany | Adm. James G. Stavridis, USN |
| US Pacific Command | Camp H.M. Smith, Hawaii | Adm. Samuel J. Locklear III, USN |
| US Southern Command | Doral FL | Gen. Douglas M. Fraser, USAF |
| US Central Command | MacDill Air Force Base, Florida | Gen. James N. Mattis, USMC |
| US Northern Command | Peterson Air Force Base, Colorado | Gen. Charles H. Jacoby, Jr., USA |
| US Special Operations Command | MacDill Air Force Base, Florida | Adm. William H. McRaven, USN |
| US Transportation Command | Scott Air Force Base, Illinois | Gen. William M. Fraser III, USAF |
| US Strategic Command | Offutt Air Force Base, Nebraska | Gen. C. Robert Kehler, USAF |
| US Africa Command | Stuttgart-Möhringen, Germany | Gen. Carter F. Ham, USA |

# North Atlantic Treaty Organization (NATO) International Commands

*The NATO military command structure comprises two main strategic commands, Allied Command Operations (ACO) and Allied Command Transformation (ACT), which works closely with the US Joint Forces Command. Their subordinate centers, also listed, change as their security measures evolve.*

**ALLIED COMMAND OPERATIONS (ACO)**
Headquarters: Casteau, Belgium
Supreme Allied Commander, Europe (SACEUR):
Adm. James G. Stavridis, USN (2 Jul 2009– )

**SUBORDINATE OPERATIONAL COMMANDS**
Allied Joint Force Command (JFC) Brunssum,
JFC Headquarters: Brunssum, Netherlands
Commander in Chief: Gen. Wolf Langheld (Army,
Germany) (29 Sep 2010– )

Allied Joint Force Command (JFC) Naples,
JFC Headquarters: Naples, Italy
Commander in Chief: Adm. Bruce W. Clingan (USN)
(24 Feb 2012– )

Allied Joint Command (JC) Lisbon,
JC Headquarters: Oeiras, Portugal
Commander in Chief: Gen. Philippe Stoltz (Army,
France) (20 Jul 2009– )

**ALLIED COMMAND TRANSFORMATION (ACT)**
Headquarters: Norfolk VA
Supreme Allied Commander, Transformation (SACT):
Gen. Stéphane Abrial (Air Force, France)
(29 Jul 2009– )

**SUBORDINATE CENTERS AND SCHOOLS**
Joint Analysis and Lessons Learned Centre (JALLC),
Monsanto, Portugal
Joint Force Training Centre (JFTC), Bydgoszcz, Poland
Joint Warfare Centre (JWC), Stavanger, Norway
NATO Communications and Information Systems
School (NCISS), Latina, Italy
NATO Defense College (NDC), Rome, Italy
NATO Maritime Interdiction Operational Training
Centre (NMIOTC), Chania, Greece
NATO School, Oberammergau, Germany
NATO Undersea Research Centre (NURC), La Spezia,
Italy

# Chairmen of the Joint Chiefs of Staff

The 1949 amendments to the National Security Act of 1947 created the position of chairman of the Joint Chiefs of Staff, the principal military adviser to the president, the secretary of defense, and the National Security Council. The president appoints the chairman for a two-year term with the advice and consent of the Senate. In 1986 the chairman's eligibility for service increased from two to three reappointments (there is no limit on reappointment during wartime). The Joint Chiefs of Staff consist of the chairman, a vice chairman, the chief of staff of the Army, the chief of staff of the Air Force, the chief of naval operations, and the commandant of the Marine Corps. Acting chairmen are not included in this table.

| NAME | MILITARY BRANCH | DATES OF SERVICE |
|---|---|---|
| Gen. of the Army Omar N. Bradley | US Army | 16 Aug 1949–14 Aug 1953 |
| Adm. Arthur W. Radford | US Navy | 15 Aug 1953–14 Aug 1957 |
| Gen. Nathan F. Twining | US Air Force | 15 Aug 1957–30 Sep 1960 |
| Gen. Lyman L. Lemnitzer | US Army | 1 Oct 1960–30 Sep 1962 |
| Gen. Maxwell D. Taylor | US Army | 1 Oct 1962–1 Jul 1964 |
| Gen. Earle G. Wheeler | US Army | 3 Jul 1964–1 Jul 1970 |
| Adm. Thomas H. Moorer | US Navy | 2 Jul 1970–30 Jun 1974 |
| Gen. George S. Brown | US Air Force | 1 Jul 1974–20 Jun 1978 |
| Gen. David C. Jones | US Air Force | 21 Jun 1978–17 Jun 1982 |
| Gen. John W. Vessey, Jr. | US Army | 18 Jun 1982–30 Sep 1985 |
| Adm. William J. Crowe, Jr. | US Navy | 1 Oct 1985–30 Sep 1989 |
| Gen. Colin L. Powell | US Army | 1 Oct 1989–30 Sep 1993 |
| Gen. John M. Shalikashvili | US Army | 25 Oct 1993–30 Sep 1997 |
| Gen. Harry Shelton | US Army | 1 Oct 1997–30 Sep 2001 |
| Gen. Richard B. Myers | US Air Force | 1 Oct 2001–29 Sep 2005 |
| Gen. Peter Pace | US Marine Corps | 30 Sep 2005–30 Sep 2007 |
| Adm. Mike Mullen | US Navy | 1 Oct 2007–30 Sep 2011 |
| Gen. Martin Dempsey | US Army | 1 Oct 2011– |

# Worldwide Deployment of the US Military

*Deployments of active duty military personnel as of 1 Jan 2012. Regional totals include countries and areas not shown in the table. Source: US Department of Defense.*

| COUNTRY/REGIONAL AREA | TOTAL | ARMY | NAVY | MARINE CORPS | AIR FORCE |
|---|---|---|---|---|---|
| US and territories[1] | | | | | |
| contiguous US | 1,017,418 | 446,734 | 194,019 | 119,266 | 257,399 |
| Alaska | 21,308 | 13,854 | 46 | 19 | 7,389 |

## Worldwide Deployment of the US Military (continued)

| COUNTRY/REGIONAL AREA | TOTAL | ARMY | NAVY | MARINE CORPS | AIR FORCE |
|---|---|---|---|---|---|
| US and territories[1] (continued) | | | | | |
| Hawaii | 42,502 | 22,632 | 8,781 | 6,147 | 4,942 |
| Guam | 4,272 | 58 | 1,980 | 196 | 2,038 |
| Puerto Rico | 179 | 102 | 25 | 23 | 29 |
| transients | 50,627 | 7,918 | 6,447 | 31,363 | 4,899 |
| afloat | 81,588 | 0 | 81,588 | 0 | 0 |
| **total ashore and afloat** | **1,217,901** | **491,298** | **292,887** | **157,016** | **276,700** |
| | | | | | |
| Europe | | | | | |
| Belgium | 1,207 | 646 | 96 | 31 | 434 |
| Germany[1] | 53,526 | 38,233 | 485 | 364 | 14,444 |
| Greece | 379 | 9 | 327 | 7 | 36 |
| Greenland | 122 | 0 | 0 | 0 | 122 |
| Italy[1] | 10,817 | 3,176 | 3,374 | 79 | 4,188 |
| Netherlands | 392 | 173 | 15 | 13 | 191 |
| Portugal | 700 | 18 | 24 | 7 | 651 |
| Spain | 1,481 | 74 | 902 | 142 | 363 |
| Turkey | 1,504 | 53 | 6 | 13 | 1,432 |
| United Kingdom[1] | 9,317 | 336 | 304 | 66 | 8,611 |
| afloat | 408 | 0 | 408 | 0 | 0 |
| **total ashore and afloat** | **80,370** | **42,822** | **5,985** | **913** | **30,650** |
| | | | | | |
| East Asia and Pacific | | | | | |
| Australia | 185 | 26 | 69 | 30 | 60 |
| Japan[1] | 36,708 | 2,501 | 6,766 | 14,951 | 12,490 |
| Philippines | 174 | 11 | 8 | 146 | 9 |
| Singapore | 150 | 7 | 113 | 16 | 14 |
| Thailand | 125 | 41 | 8 | 50 | 26 |
| afloat | 13,618 | 0 | 11,495 | 2,123 | 0 |
| **total ashore and afloat** | **51,170** | **2,647** | **18,495** | **17,405** | **12,623** |
| | | | | | |
| Africa, Near East, and South Asia | | | | | |
| Afghanistan (Operation Enduring Freedom)[2] | 102,200 | 68,100 | 4,600 | 18,900 | 10,600 |
| Iraq (Operation New Dawn)[2] | 49,800 | 18,400 | 17,000 | 2,900 | 11,500 |
| Bahrain | 2,135 | 21 | 1,812 | 272 | 30 |
| Diego Garcia | 303 | 0 | 265 | 0 | 38 |
| Djibouti | 192 | 1 | 0 | 191 | 0 |
| Egypt | 238 | 167 | 22 | 23 | 26 |
| Qatar | 596 | 370 | 4 | 30 | 192 |
| Saudi Arabia | 270 | 146 | 20 | 28 | 76 |
| United Arab Emirates | 175 | 6 | 12 | 69 | 88 |
| afloat | 600 | 0 | 600 | 0 | 0 |
| **total ashore and afloat (excluding Iraq and Afghanistan)** | **5,113** | **823** | **2,767** | **976** | **547** |
| | | | | | |
| Western Hemisphere | | | | | |
| Canada | 135 | 8 | 33 | 9 | 85 |
| Cuba (Guantánamo Bay) | 954 | 343 | 481 | 130 | 0 |
| Honduras | 357 | 209 | 1 | 7 | 140 |
| **total ashore and afloat** | **1,970** | **701** | **648** | **328** | **293** |
| | | | | | |
| all foreign countries (excluding Iraq and Afghanistan) | | | | | |
| ashore | 181,606 | 67,273 | 17,223 | 41,086 | 56,024 |
| afloat | 14,642 | 0 | 12,519 | 2,123 | 0 |
| **total ashore and afloat** | **196,248** | **67,273** | **29,742** | **43,209** | **56,024** |
| | | | | | |
| worldwide (excluding Iraq and Afghanistan) | | | | | |
| ashore | 1,317,919 | 558,571 | 228,522 | 198,102 | 332,724 |
| afloat | 96,230 | 0 | 94,107 | 2,123 | 0 |
| **total ashore and afloat** | **1,414,149** | **558,571** | **322,629** | **200,225** | **332,724** |

[1]Includes service members deployed to Operation New Dawn and Operation Enduring Freedom.    [2]Includes deployed Reserve/National Guard.

## Number of Living US Veterans[1]

Source: Statistical Abstract of the United States: 2012.

| AGE IN YEARS | KOREAN CONFLICT | VIETNAM ERA | GULF WAR[2] | TOTAL WARTIME[3,4] | TOTAL PEACETIME | TOTAL VETERANS[4] |
|---|---|---|---|---|---|---|
| under 35 | — | — | 1,964,000 | 1,964,000 | — | 1,964,000 |
| 35–39 | — | — | 996,000 | 996,000 | 26,000 | 1,023,000 |
| 40–44 | — | — | 1,033,000 | 1,033,000 | 429,000 | 1,461,000 |
| 45–49 | — | — | 692,000 | 692,000 | 1,098,000 | 1,790,000 |
| 50–54 | — | 189,000 | 477,000 | 648,000 | 1,274,000 | 1,922,000 |
| 55–59 | — | 1,415,000 | 312,000 | 1,589,000 | 416,000 | 2,005,000 |
| 60–64 | — | 3,153,000 | 184,000 | 3,208,000 | 119,000 | 3,327,000 |
| 65 and over | 2,449,000 | 2,770,000 | 78,000 | 6,735,000 | 2,430,000 | 9,166,000 |
| female, total | 61,000 | 251,000 | 918,000 | 1,295,000 | 545,000 | 1,840,000 |
| total[5,6] | 2,448,000 | 7,526,000 | 5,737,000 | 16,866,000 | 5,792,000 | 22,658,000 |

[1]As of 30 Sep 2010. Includes those living outside of the US. Estimated. [2]Service from 2 Aug 1990 to the present. [3]Veterans who served in more than one wartime period are counted only once. [4]Includes an estimated 1,981,000 veterans of World War II, all 75 or over, of which 98,000 are female. [5]Total includes female veterans. [6]Detail may not add to total given because of rounding.

## US Casualties of War

Data prior to World War I are based on incomplete records. Casualty data exclude personnel captured or missing in action. N/A means not available. Sources: US Department of Defense and US Coast Guard.

| WAR | SERVICE BRANCH | NUMBER OF COMBATANTS | CASUALTIES | | | |
|---|---|---|---|---|---|---|
| | | | WOUNDED[1] | BATTLE DEATHS | OTHER DEATHS | TOTAL DEATHS |
| Revolutionary War | Army | N/A | 6,004 | 4,044 | N/A | N/A |
| (1775–83) | Navy | N/A | 114 | 342 | N/A | N/A |
| | Marines | N/A | 70 | 49 | N/A | N/A |
| | total | 184,000–250,000[2] | 6,188 | 4,435 | 20,000[2] | 24,435 |
| War of 1812 | Army | N/A | 4,000 | 1,950 | N/A | N/A |
| (1812–15) | Navy | N/A | 439 | 265 | N/A | N/A |
| | Marines | N/A | 66 | 45 | N/A | N/A |
| | Coast Guard | 100 | N/A | 0 | N/A | N/A |
| | total | 286,830 | 4,505[3] | 2,260 | N/A | N/A |
| Indian Wars (about 1817–98) | total | 106,000[2] | N/A | 1,000[2] | N/A | N/A |
| Mexican-American War | Army | N/A | 4,102 | 1,721 | 11,550 | 13,271 |
| (1846–48) | Navy | N/A | 3 | 1 | N/A | 1 |
| | Marines | N/A | 47 | 11 | N/A | 11 |
| | Coast Guard | 71 | N/A | N/A | N/A | N/A |
| | total | 78,789 | 4,152[3] | 1,733[3] | 11,550[3] | 13,283 |
| Civil War (1861–65) | Army | 2,128,948 | 280,040 | 138,154 | 221,374 | 359,528 |
| Union | Navy | 84,415[4] | 1,710 | 2,112 | 2,411 | 4,523 |
| | Marines | N/A | 131 | 148 | 312 | 460 |
| | Coast Guard | 219 | N/A | 1 | N/A | N/A |
| | total | 2,213,582 | 281,881[3] | 140,415 | 224,097[3] | 364,511[3] |
| Confederate[5] | total | 600,000–1,500,000 | 137,000[2] | 74,524 | 124,000[2] | 198,524 |
| Spanish-American War | Army | 280,564 | 1,594 | 369 | 2,061 | 2,430 |
| (1898) | Navy | 22,875 | 47 | 10 | N/A | 10 |
| | Marines | 3,321 | 21 | 6 | N/A | 6 |
| | Coast Guard | 660 | N/A | 0 | N/A | 0 |
| | total | 307,420 | 1,662[3] | 385 | 2,061[3] | 2,446[3] |
| World War I | Army[6] | 4,057,101 | 193,663 | 50,510 | 55,868 | 106,378 |
| (1917–18) | Navy | 599,051 | 819 | 431 | 6,856 | 7,287 |
| | Marines | 78,839 | 9,520 | 2,461 | 390 | 2,851 |
| | Coast Guard | 8,835 | N/A | 111 | 81 | 192 |
| | total | 4,743,826 | 204,002[3] | 53,513 | 63,195 | 116,708 |
| World War II | Army[6] | 11,260,000 | 565,861 | 234,874 | 83,400 | 318,274 |
| (1941–46) | Navy | 4,183,466 | 37,778 | 36,950 | 25,664 | 62,614 |
| | Marines | 669,100 | 67,207 | 19,733 | 4,778 | 24,511 |
| | Coast Guard | 241,093 | N/A | 574 | 1,343 | 1,917 |
| | total | 16,353,659 | 670,846[3] | 292,131 | 115,185 | 407,316 |
| Korean War | Army | 2,834,000 | 77,596 | 27,731 | 2,125 | 29,856 |
| (1950–53) | Navy | 1,177,000 | 1,576 | 503 | 154 | 657 |
| | Marines | 424,000 | 23,744 | 4,267 | 242 | 4,509 |

## US Casualties of War (continued)

| WAR | SERVICE BRANCH | NUMBER OF COMBATANTS | WOUNDED[1] | BATTLE DEATHS | OTHER DEATHS | TOTAL DEATHS |
|---|---|---|---|---|---|---|
| Korean War | Air Force | 1,285,000 | 368 | 1,238 | 314 | 1,552 |
| (1950–53) (cont.) | Coast Guard | 8,500[7] | 0 | 0 | 0 | 0 |
| | total | 5,764,143 | 103,284 | 33,739 | 2,835 | 36,574 |
| Vietnam War | Army | 4,368,000 | 96,802 | 30,963 | 7,261 | 38,224 |
| (1964–73) | Navy | 1,842,000 | 4,178 | 1,631 | 935 | 2,566 |
| | Marines | 794,000 | 51,392 | 13,095 | 1,749 | 14,844 |
| | Air Force | 1,740,000 | 931 | 1,745 | 841 | 2,586 |
| | Coast Guard | 8,000 | 60 | 7 | N/A | 7 |
| | total | 8,752,000 | 153,363[8] | 47,441 | 10,786[3] | 58,227 |
| Persian Gulf War[9] | Army | 782,000 | 354 | 98 | 126 | 224 |
| (1990–91) | Navy[10] | 669,000 | 12 | 6 | 50 | 56 |
| | Marines | 213,000 | 92 | 24 | 44 | 68 |
| | Air Force | 561,000 | 9 | 20 | 15 | 35 |
| | Coast Guard | N/A | N/A | N/A | N/A | N/A |
| | total | 2,225,000 | 467 | 148 | 235 | 383 |
| War on Terrorism[11] | Army | N/A | 10,369 | 1,045 | 257 | 1,302 |
| (2001– ) | Navy[10] | N/A | 298 | 70 | 30 | 100 |
| | Marines | N/A | 4,319 | 325 | 70 | 395 |
| | Air Force | N/A | 336 | 50 | 30 | 80 |
| | Coast Guard | N/A | N/A | N/A | N/A | N/A |
| | total | N/A | 15,322 | 1,490 | 387 | 1,877 |
| Iraq War[12] | Army | N/A | 22,217 | 2,535 | 697 | 3,232 |
| (2003– ) | Navy[10] | N/A | 637 | 64 | 39 | 103 |
| | Marines | N/A | 8,622 | 851 | 171 | 1,022 |
| | Air Force | N/A | 446 | 29 | 22 | 51 |
| | Coast Guard | N/A | N/A | N/A | N/A | N/A |
| | Airlines | N/A | N/A | N/A | N/A | N/A |
| | total | N/A | 31,922 | 3,479 | 929 | 4,408 |

other[13]

[1]Data in this column account for the total number of wounds, except for Marine Corps data for World War II, the Spanish-American War, and earlier wars, which represent the number of combatants wounded. [2]Estimate. [3]Excluding unavailable data from one or more service branches. [4]Includes the Marine Corps. [5]US service members only. [6]Includes air service. [7]Number eligible for Korean Service Medal. [8]Excludes 150,341 wounded who did not require hospital care. [9]Data for military personnel serving in the theater of operation. [10]Includes Coast Guard. [11]Operation Enduring Freedom; data for 7 Oct 2001–6 Feb 2012. [12]Operation Iraqi Freedom; data for 19 Mar 2003–6 Feb 2012. [13]US casualties of other military operations: in Grenada (1983) 119 wounded, 19 battle deaths; in Panama (1989) 324 wounded, 23 battle deaths; in Somalia (1992–94) 153 wounded, 43 battle deaths.

## Leading Department of Defense Contractors

Top 40 Department of Defense contractors listed according to net value of prime contract awards, fiscal year 2010. Source: <https://www.fpds.gov>.

| RANK | CONTRACTOR | AMOUNT (US$) |
|---|---|---|
| 1 | Lockheed Martin | 29,054,980,518 |
| 2 | Boeing | 18,047,585,923 |
| 3 | Northrop Grumman | 15,574,347,189 |
| 4 | General Dynamics | 14,558,853,585 |
| 5 | Raytheon | 14,511,228,999 |
| 6 | Oshkosh | 7,223,976,311 |
| 7 | L-3 Communications Holdings | 6,834,329,137 |
| 8 | United Technologies | 6,814,361,100 |
| 9 | BAE Systems | 6,155,689,602 |
| 10 | SAIC | 4,862,950,839 |
| 11 | Cerberus Capital Management | 3,874,962,534 |
| 12 | KBR[1] | 3,571,649,246 |
| 13 | Humana | 3,248,725,848 |
| 14 | General Electric | 2,960,989,096 |
| 15 | Health Net | 2,960,589,395 |
| 16 | Computer Sciences | 2,789,942,771 |
| 17 | Bell Boeing Joint Project Office | 2,752,694,557 |
| 18 | TriWest Healthcare Alliance | 2,721,404,316 |

| RANK | CONTRACTOR | AMOUNT (US$) |
|---|---|---|
| 19 | Government of Canada | 2,653,702,764 |
| 20 | Booz Allen Hamilton Holding | 2,581,724,977 |
| 21 | ITT | 2,551,980,239 |
| 22 | Harris | 2,526,898,953 |
| 23 | CACI International | 2,359,957,377 |
| 24 | Textron | 2,194,238,669 |
| 25 | URS | 2,143,344,731 |
| 26 | Supreme Group Holding | 2,122,754,640 |
| 27 | Bechtel Group | 2,105,585,976 |
| 28 | Abu Dhabi National Oil | 1,895,207,544 |
| 29 | Navistar International | 1,867,806,085 |
| 30 | Fluor | 1,847,134,882 |
| 31 | General Atomic Technologies | 1,806,791,704 |
| 32 | Honeywell International | 1,690,894,804 |
| 33 | Evergreen International Airlines | 1,612,054,324 |
| 34 | Alliant Techsystems | 1,531,189,717 |
| 35 | Finmeccanica S.p.A. | 1,478,813,172 |
| 36 | Mantech International | 1,460,591,224 |

## Leading Department of Defense Contractors (continued)

| RANK | CONTRACTOR | AMOUNT (US$) | RANK | CONTRACTOR | AMOUNT (US$) |
|------|-----------|-------------|------|-----------|-------------|
| 37 | Fedex | 1,408,687,215 | 39 | Amerisourcebergen | 1,307,349,144 |
| 38 | Rockwell Collins | 1,366,236,162 | 40 | Public Warehousing | 1,302,596,361 |

[1]Until April 2007 KBR was a subsidiary of Halliburton.

## CIA Directors

*The National Security Act of 26 Jul 1947 established the Central Intelligence Agency (CIA) on 18 Sep 1947. Acting and interim directors are not included in this table.*

| NAME | DATES OF SERVICE | NAME | DATES OF SERVICE |
|------|-----------------|------|-----------------|
| Rear Adm. Sidney W. Souers, USNR | 23 Jan 1946–9 Jun 1946 | George H.W. Bush | 30 Jan 1976–20 Jan 1977 |
| Lt. Gen. Hoyt S. Vandenberg, USA | 10 Jun 1946–30 Apr 1947 | Adm. Stansfield Turner, USN | 9 Mar 1977–20 Jan 1981 |
| Rear Adm. Roscoe H. Hillenkoetter, USN | 1 May 1947–6 Oct 1950 | William J. Casey | 28 Jan 1981–29 Jan 1987 |
| | | William H. Webster | 26 May 1987–31 Aug 1991 |
| Gen. Walter Bedell Smith, USA | 7 Oct 1950–9 Feb 1953 | Robert M. Gates | 6 Nov 1991–20 Jan 1993 |
| Allen W. Dulles | 26 Feb 1953–28 Nov 1961 | R. James Woolsey | 5 Feb 1993–10 Jan 1995 |
| John A. McCone | 29 Nov 1961–27 Apr 1965 | John M. Deutch | 10 May 1995–15 Dec 1996 |
| Vice Adm. William F. Raborn, Jr., USN | 28 Apr 1965–29 Jun 1966 | George J. Tenet | 11 Jul 1997–11 Jul 2004 |
| | | Porter J. Goss | 24 Sep 2004–26 May 2006 |
| Richard M. Helms | 30 Jun 1966–1 Feb 1973 | Gen. Michael V. Hayden, USAF | 30 May 2006–12 Feb 2009 |
| James R. Schlesinger | 2 Feb 1973–2 Jul 1973 | Leon E. Panetta | 13 Feb 2009–30 Jun 2011 |
| William E. Colby | 4 Sep 1973–29 Jan 1976 | David H. Petraeus | 6 Sep 2011– |

## National Security Council (NSC)

*The National Security Act of 1947 established the NSC to advise the president on issues relating to national security.*

| | |
|---|---|
| chair | Barack Obama (president) |
| members | Joe Biden (vice president) |
| | Hillary Clinton (secretary of state) |
| | Leon E. Panetta (secretary of defense) |
| | Steven Chu (secretary of energy) |
| | Tim Geithner (secretary of the treasury) |
| | Eric Holder (attorney general) |
| | Janet Napolitano (secretary of homeland security) |
| | Susan Rice (US ambassador to the United Nations) |
| | Jack Lew (chief of staff to the president) |
| | Thomas E. Donilon (assistant to the president for national security affairs) |
| military adviser | Martin Dempsey (chairman of the Joint Chiefs of Staff) |
| intelligence adviser | James Clapper (director of national intelligence) |
| additional participants[1] | Kathryn Ruemmler (counsel to the president) |
| | Denis McDonough (deputy assistant to the president for national security affairs) |

In 1953 Pres. Dwight D. Eisenhower established the office of assistant to the president for national security affairs (commonly referred to as the national security advisor). Holders of this office are listed below.

| NAME | DATES OF SERVICE | NAME | DATES OF SERVICE |
|------|-----------------|------|-----------------|
| Robert Cutler | 23 Mar 1953–1 Apr 1955 | Robert C. McFarlane | 17 Oct 1983–3 Dec 1985 |
| Dillon Anderson | 2 Apr 1955–1 Sep 1956 | John M. Poindexter | 4 Dec 1985–25 Nov 1986 |
| Robert Cutler | 7 Jan 1957–23 Jun 1958 | Frank C. Carlucci | 2 Dec 1986–22 Nov 1987 |
| Gordon Gray | 24 Jun 1958–13 Jan 1961 | Colin L. Powell | 23 Nov 1987–19 Jan 1989 |
| McGeorge Bundy | 20 Jan 1961–28 Feb 1966 | Brent Scowcroft | 20 Jan 1989–19 Jan 1993 |
| Walt W. Rostow | 1 Apr 1966–1 Dec 1968 | W. Anthony Lake | 20 Jan 1993–13 Mar 1997 |
| Henry A. Kissinger | 2 Dec 1968–2 Nov 1975[2] | Samuel R. Berger | 14 Mar 1997–20 Jan 2001 |
| Brent Scowcroft | 3 Nov 1975–19 Jan 1977 | Condoleezza Rice | 22 Jan 2001–25 Jan 2005 |
| Zbigniew Brzezinski | 20 Jan 1977–20 Jan 1981 | Stephen Hadley | 26 Jan 2005–19 Jan 2009 |
| Richard V. Allen | 21 Jan 1981–4 Jan 1982 | James L. Jones | 20 Jan 2009–8 Oct 2010 |
| William P. Clark | 4 Jan 1982–16 Oct 1983 | Thomas E. Donilon | 8 Oct 2010– |

[1]Regular attendees include the secretary of commerce, the US trade representative, the assistant to the president for economic policy, the chair of the Council of Economic Advisers, and the assistant to the president for homeland security and counterterrorism. [2]Kissinger served concurrently as secretary of state from 21 Sep 1973.

# United States Population

## US Population by Race, Sex, Median Age, and Residence

*Numbers are in thousands ('000) except for the median age figures and the residency percentages. N/A means not available. Source: US Census Bureau.*

| YEAR | RACE | | | SEX | | MEDIAN AGE | RESIDENCE[2] | |
| --- | --- | --- | --- | --- | --- | --- | --- | --- |
| | WHITE | BLACK | OTHER[1] | MALE | FEMALE | | URBAN (%) | RURAL (%) |
| 1790 | 3,172 | 757 | N/A | N/A | N/A | N/A | 5.1 | 94.9 |
| 1800 | 4,306 | 1,002 | N/A | N/A | N/A | N/A | 6.1 | 93.9 |
| 1810 | 5,862 | 1,378 | N/A | N/A | N/A | N/A | 7.3 | 92.7 |
| 1820 | 7,867 | 1,772 | N/A | 4,897 | 4,742 | 16.7 | 7.2 | 92.8 |
| 1830 | 10,537 | 2,329 | N/A | 6,532 | 6,334 | 17.2 | 8.8 | 91.2 |
| 1840 | 14,196 | 2,874 | N/A | 8,689 | 8,381 | 17.8 | 10.8 | 89.2 |
| 1850 | 19,553 | 3,639 | N/A | 11,838 | 11,354 | 18.9 | 15.4 | 84.6 |
| 1860 | 26,923 | 4,442 | 79 | 16,085 | 15,358 | 19.4 | 19.8 | 80.2 |
| 1870 | 34,337 | 5,392 | 89 | 19,494 | 19,065 | 20.2 | 25.7 | 74.3 |
| 1880 | 43,403 | 6,581 | 172 | 25,519 | 24,637 | 20.9 | 28.2 | 71.8 |
| 1890 | 55,101 | 7,489 | 358 | 32,237 | 30,711 | 22.0 | 35.1 | 64.9 |
| 1900 | 66,809 | 8,834 | 351 | 38,816 | 37,178 | 22.9 | 39.6 | 60.4 |
| 1910 | 81,732 | 9,828 | 413 | 47,332 | 44,640 | 24.1 | 45.6 | 54.4 |
| 1920 | 94,821 | 10,463 | 427 | 53,900 | 51,810 | 25.3 | 51.2 | 48.8 |
| 1930 | 110,287 | 11,891 | 597 | 62,137 | 60,638 | 26.4 | 56.1 | 43.9 |
| 1940 | 118,215 | 12,866 | 589 | 66,062 | 65,608 | 29.0 | 56.5 | 43.5 |
| 1950 | 134,942 | 15,042 | 713 | 74,833 | 75,864 | 30.2 | 64.0 | 36.0 |
| 1960 | 158,832 | 18,872 | 1,620 | 88,331 | 90,992 | 29.5 | 69.9 | 30.1 |
| 1970 | 178,098 | 22,581 | 2,557 | 98,926 | 104,309 | 28.0 | 73.6 | 26.3 |
| 1980 | 194,713 | 26,683 | 5,150 | 110,053 | 116,493 | 30.0 | 73.7 | 26.3 |
| 1990 | 199,686 | 29,986 | 9,233 | 121,271 | 127,494 | 32.8 | 78.0 | 22.0 |
| 2000 | 211,461 | 34,658 | 13,118 | 138,054 | 143,368 | 35.3 | 79.0 | 21.0 |
| 2010 | 223,553 | 38,929 | 27,156 | 151,781 | 156,964 | 37.2 | 82.3 | 17.7 |
| 2011 | 243,470 | 40,751 | 27,371 | 153,291 | 158,301 | 37.3 | 82.4 | 17.6 |

[1]*"Other" refers to Asians, Native Hawaiians, other Pacific Islanders, American Indians, Alaska Natives, and those belonging to two or more races. Data for Alaska and Hawaii are not included until 1960, the first census after they became states in 1959.*   [2]*The census definitions for urban and rural areas have changed through the decades.*

## US Population by Race and Hispanic Origin

Census 2000 was the first US census in which individuals could report themselves as being of more than one race. For the comparison between these census results and the 2011 data, this table uses the 2000 census information that was revised in April 2000. Hispanic or Latino people may be of any race.

Source: US Census Bureau.

| RACE | 2000 CENSUS NUMBER | % | 2011 NUMBER | % | % DIFFERENCE 2000/2011 |
| --- | --- | --- | --- | --- | --- |
| white | 211,460,626 | 75.1 | 243,470,497 | 78.1 | +15.1 |
| black or African American | 34,658,190 | 12.3 | 40,750,746 | 13.1 | +17.6 |
| American Indian or Alaska Native | 2,475,956 | 0.9 | 3,814,772 | 1.2 | +54.1 |
| Asian | 10,242,998 | 3.6 | 15,578,383 | 5.0 | +52.1 |
| Native Hawaiian or other Pacific Islander | 398,835 | 0.1 | 692,091 | 0.2 | +73.5 |
| some other race | 15,359,073 | 5.5 | [1] | [1] | [1] |
| two or more races | 6,826,228 | 2.4 | 7,285,428 | 2.3 | +6.7 |
| **total population** | **281,421,906** | **100.0[2]** | **311,591,917** | **100.0[2]** | **+10.7** |

| HISPANIC OR LATINO POPULATION | 2000 CENSUS NUMBER | % | 2011 NUMBER | % | % DIFFERENCE 2000/2011 |
| --- | --- | --- | --- | --- | --- |
| Hispanic or Latino (of any race) | 35,305,818 | 12.5 | 52,045,277 | 16.7 | +47.4 |
| not Hispanic or Latino | 246,116,088 | 87.5 | 259,546,640 | 83.3 | +5.5 |
| **total population** | **281,421,906** | **100.0** | **311,591,917** | **100.0** | **+10.7** |

[1]*Responses of "some other race" have been modified and not included in summed totals since the 2010 census.*   [2]*Detail does not add to total given because of rounding.*

## State Populations, 1790–2010

*Resident population of the states and the District of Columbia. Numbers are in thousands ('000)[1].*
*Source: US Census Bureau.*

| STATE | 1790 | 1800 | 1810 | 1820 | 1830 | 1840 | 1850 | 1860 | 1870 | 1880 | 1890 | 1900 |
|---|---|---|---|---|---|---|---|---|---|---|---|---|
| AL |  | 1 | 9 | 128 | 310 | 591 | 772 | 964 | 997 | 1,263 | 1,513 | 1,829 |
| AK |  |  |  |  |  |  |  |  |  | 33 | 32 | 64 |
| AZ |  |  |  |  |  |  |  |  | 10 | 40 | 88 | 123 |
| AR |  |  | 1 | 14 | 30 | 98 | 210 | 435 | 484 | 803 | 1,128 | 1,312 |
| CA |  |  |  |  |  |  | 93 | 380 | 560 | 865 | 1,213 | 1,485 |
| CO |  |  |  |  |  |  |  | 34 | 40 | 194 | 413 | 540 |
| CT | 238 | 251 | 262 | 275 | 298 | 310 | 371 | 460 | 537 | 623 | 746 | 908 |
| DE | 59 | 64 | 73 | 73 | 77 | 78 | 92 | 112 | 125 | 147 | 168 | 185 |
| DC |  | 8 | 15 | 23 | 30 | 34 | 52 | 75 | 132 | 178 | 230 | 279 |
| FL |  |  |  |  | 35 | 54 | 87 | 140 | 188 | 269 | 391 | 529 |
| GA | 83 | 163 | 252 | 341 | 517 | 691 | 906 | 1,057 | 1,184 | 1,542 | 1,837 | 2,216 |
| HI |  |  |  |  |  |  |  |  |  |  |  | 154 |
| ID |  |  |  |  |  |  |  |  | 15 | 33 | 89 | 162 |
| IL |  |  | 12 | 55 | 157 | 476 | 851 | 1,712 | 2,540 | 3,078 | 3,826 | 4,822 |
| IN |  | 6 | 25 | 147 | 343 | 686 | 988 | 1,350 | 1,681 | 1,978 | 2,192 | 2,516 |
| IA |  |  |  |  |  | 43 | 192 | 675 | 1,194 | 1,625 | 1,912 | 2,232 |
| KS |  |  |  |  |  |  |  | 107 | 364 | 996 | 1,428 | 1,470 |
| KY | 74 | 221 | 407 | 564 | 688 | 780 | 982 | 1,156 | 1,321 | 1,649 | 1,859 | 2,147 |
| LA |  |  | 77 | 153 | 216 | 352 | 518 | 708 | 727 | 940 | 1,119 | 1,382 |
| ME | 97 | 152 | 229 | 298 | 399 | 502 | 583 | 628 | 627 | 649 | 661 | 694 |
| MD | 320 | 342 | 381 | 407 | 447 | 470 | 583 | 687 | 781 | 935 | 1,042 | 1,188 |
| MA | 379 | 423 | 472 | 523 | 610 | 738 | 995 | 1,231 | 1,457 | 1,783 | 2,239 | 2,805 |
| MI |  |  | 5 | 9 | 32 | 212 | 398 | 749 | 1,184 | 1,637 | 2,094 | 2,421 |
| MN |  |  |  |  |  |  | 6 | 172 | 440 | 781 | 1,310 | 1,751 |
| MS |  | 8 | 31 | 75 | 137 | 376 | 607 | 791 | 828 | 1,132 | 1,290 | 1,551 |
| MO |  |  | 20 | 67 | 140 | 384 | 682 | 1,182 | 1,721 | 2,168 | 2,679 | 3,107 |
| MT |  |  |  |  |  |  |  |  | 21 | 39 | 143 | 243 |
| NE |  |  |  |  |  |  |  | 29 | 123 | 452 | 1,063 | 1,066 |
| NV |  |  |  |  |  |  |  | 7 | 42 | 62 | 47 | 42 |
| NH | 142 | 184 | 214 | 244 | 269 | 285 | 318 | 326 | 318 | 347 | 377 | 412 |
| NJ | 184 | 211 | 246 | 278 | 321 | 373 | 490 | 672 | 906 | 1,131 | 1,445 | 1,884 |
| NM |  |  |  |  |  |  | 62 | 94 | 92 | 120 | 160 | 195 |
| NY | 340 | 589 | 959 | 1,373 | 1,919 | 2,429 | 3,097 | 3,881 | 4,383 | 5,083 | 6,003 | 7,269 |
| NC | 394 | 478 | 556 | 639 | 738 | 753 | 869 | 993 | 1,071 | 1,400 | 1,618 | 1,894 |
| ND |  |  |  |  |  |  |  |  | 5 | 2 | 37 | 191 | 319 |
| OH |  | 45 | 231 | 581 | 938 | 1,519 | 1,980 | 2,340 | 2,665 | 3,198 | 3,672 | 4,158 |
| OK |  |  |  |  |  |  |  |  |  |  | 259 | 790 |
| OR |  |  |  |  |  |  | 12 | 52 | 91 | 175 | 318 | 414 |
| PA | 434 | 602 | 810 | 1,049 | 1,348 | 1,724 | 2,312 | 2,906 | 3,522 | 4,283 | 5,258 | 6,302 |
| RI | 69 | 69 | 77 | 83 | 97 | 109 | 148 | 175 | 217 | 277 | 346 | 429 |
| SC | 249 | 346 | 415 | 503 | 581 | 594 | 669 | 704 | 706 | 996 | 1,151 | 1,340 |
| SD |  |  |  |  |  |  |  |  | 12 | 98 | 349 | 402 |
| TN | 36 | 106 | 262 | 423 | 682 | 829 | 1,003 | 1,110 | 1,259 | 1,542 | 1,768 | 2,021 |
| TX |  |  |  |  |  |  | 213 | 604 | 819 | 1,592 | 2,236 | 3,049 |
| UT |  |  |  |  |  |  | 11 | 40 | 87 | 144 | 211 | 277 |
| VT | 85 | 154 | 218 | 236 | 281 | 292 | 314 | 315 | 331 | 332 | 332 | 344 |
| VA | 692 | 808 | 878 | 938 | 1,044 | 1,025 | 1,119 | 1,220 | 1,225 | 1,513 | 1,656 | 1,854 |
| WA |  |  |  |  |  |  | 1 | 12 | 24 | 75 | 357 | 518 |
| WV | 56 | 79 | 105 | 137 | 177 | 225 | 302 | 377 | 442 | 618 | 763 | 959 |
| WI |  |  |  |  |  | 31 | 305 | 776 | 1,055 | 1,315 | 1,693 | 2,069 |
| WY |  |  |  |  |  |  |  |  | 9 | 21 | 63 | 93 |
| US total[2] | 3,929 | 5,308 | 7,240 | 9,638 | 12,866 | 17,069 | 23,192 | 31,443 | 39,818[3] | 50,156 | 62,948 | 75,995 |

[1]*Detail may not add to total given because of rounding.* [2]*Data for Alaska and Hawaii are not included until 1960,*

## State Populations, 1790–2010 (continued)

| 1910 | 1920 | 1930 | 1940 | 1950 | 1960 | 1970 | 1980 | 1990 | 2000 | 2010 |
|---|---|---|---|---|---|---|---|---|---|---|
| 2,138 | 2,348 | 2,646 | 2,833 | 3,062 | 3,267 | 3,444 | 3,894 | 4,040 | 4,447 | 4,785 |
| 64 | 55 | 59 | 73 | 129 | 226 | 300 | 402 | 550 | 627 | 714 |
| 204 | 334 | 436 | 499 | 750 | 1,302 | 1,771 | 2,718 | 3,665 | 5,131 | 6,413 |
| 1,574 | 1,752 | 1,854 | 1,949 | 1,910 | 1,786 | 1,923 | 2,286 | 2,351 | 2,673 | 2,922 |
| 2,378 | 3,427 | 5,677 | 6,907 | 10,586 | 15,717 | 19,953 | 23,668 | 29,811 | 33,872 | 37,338 |
| | | | | | | | | | | |
| 799 | 940 | 1,036 | 1,123 | 1,325 | 1,754 | 2,207 | 2,890 | 3,294 | 4,301 | 5,048 |
| 1,115 | 1,381 | 1,607 | 1,709 | 2,007 | 2,535 | 3,032 | 3,108 | 3,287 | 3,406 | 3,575 |
| 202 | 223 | 238 | 267 | 318 | 446 | 548 | 594 | 666 | 784 | 900 |
| 331 | 438 | 487 | 663 | 802 | 764 | 757 | 638 | 607 | 572 | 605 |
| 753 | 968 | 1,468 | 1,897 | 2,771 | 4,952 | 6,789 | 9,746 | 12,938 | 15,982 | 18,839 |
| | | | | | | | | | | |
| 2,609 | 2,896 | 2,909 | 3,124 | 3,445 | 3,943 | 4,590 | 5,463 | 6,478 | 8,186 | 9,712 |
| 192 | 256 | 368 | 423 | 500 | 633 | 769 | 965 | 1,108 | 1,212 | 1,363 |
| 326 | 432 | 445 | 525 | 589 | 667 | 713 | 944 | 1,007 | 1,294 | 1,571 |
| 5,639 | 6,485 | 7,631 | 7,897 | 8,712 | 10,081 | 11,114 | 11,427 | 11,431 | 12,419 | 12,842 |
| 2,701 | 2,930 | 3,239 | 3,428 | 3,934 | 4,662 | 5,194 | 5,490 | 5,544 | 6,080 | 6,491 |
| | | | | | | | | | | |
| 2,225 | 2,404 | 2,471 | 2,538 | 2,621 | 2,758 | 2,824 | 2,914 | 2,777 | 2,926 | 3,050 |
| 1,691 | 1,769 | 1,881 | 1,801 | 1,905 | 2,179 | 2,247 | 2,364 | 2,478 | 2,688 | 2,859 |
| 2,290 | 2,417 | 2,615 | 2,846 | 2,945 | 3,038 | 3,219 | 3,661 | 3,687 | 4,042 | 4,347 |
| 1,656 | 1,799 | 2,102 | 2,364 | 2,684 | 3,257 | 3,641 | 4,206 | 4,222 | 4,469 | 4,545 |
| 742 | 768 | 797 | 847 | 914 | 969 | 992 | 1,125 | 1,228 | 1,275 | 1,327 |
| | | | | | | | | | | |
| 1,295 | 1,450 | 1,632 | 1,821 | 2,343 | 3,101 | 3,922 | 4,217 | 4,781 | 5,296 | 5,786 |
| 3,366 | 3,852 | 4,250 | 4,317 | 4,691 | 5,149 | 5,689 | 5,737 | 6,016 | 6,349 | 6,555 |
| 2,810 | 3,668 | 4,842 | 5,256 | 6,372 | 7,823 | 8,875 | 9,262 | 9,295 | 9,938 | 9,877 |
| 2,076 | 2,387 | 2,564 | 2,792 | 2,982 | 3,414 | 3,805 | 4,076 | 4,376 | 4,919 | 5,311 |
| 1,797 | 1,791 | 2,010 | 2,184 | 2,179 | 2,178 | 2,217 | 2,521 | 2,575 | 2,845 | 2,970 |
| | | | | | | | | | | |
| 3,293 | 3,404 | 3,629 | 3,785 | 3,955 | 4,320 | 4,677 | 4,917 | 5,117 | 5,595 | 5,996 |
| 376 | 549 | 538 | 559 | 591 | 675 | 694 | 787 | 799 | 902 | 991 |
| 1,192 | 1,296 | 1,378 | 1,316 | 1,326 | 1,411 | 1,483 | 1,570 | 1,578 | 1,711 | 1,830 |
| 82 | 77 | 91 | 110 | 160 | 285 | 489 | 800 | 1,202 | 1,998 | 2,704 |
| 431 | 443 | 465 | 492 | 533 | 607 | 738 | 921 | 1,109 | 1,236 | 1,317 |
| | | | | | | | | | | |
| 2,537 | 3,156 | 4,041 | 4,160 | 4,835 | 6,067 | 7,168 | 7,365 | 7,748 | 8,414 | 8,800 |
| 327 | 360 | 423 | 532 | 681 | 951 | 1,016 | 1,303 | 1,515 | 1,819 | 2,066 |
| 9,114 | 10,385 | 12,588 | 13,479 | 14,830 | 16,782 | 18,237 | 17,558 | 17,991 | 18,976 | 19,395 |
| 2,206 | 2,559 | 3,170 | 3,572 | 4,062 | 4,556 | 5,082 | 5,882 | 6,632 | 8,049 | 9,560 |
| 577 | 647 | 681 | 642 | 620 | 632 | 618 | 653 | 639 | 642 | 675 |
| | | | | | | | | | | |
| 4,767 | 5,759 | 6,647 | 6,908 | 7,947 | 9,706 | 10,652 | 10,798 | 10,847 | 11,353 | 11,538 |
| 1,657 | 2,028 | 2,396 | 2,336 | 2,233 | 2,328 | 2,559 | 3,025 | 3,146 | 3,451 | 3,760 |
| 673 | 783 | 954 | 1,090 | 1,521 | 1,769 | 2,091 | 2,633 | 2,842 | 3,421 | 3,838 |
| 7,665 | 8,720 | 9,631 | 9,900 | 10,498 | 11,319 | 11,794 | 11,864 | 11,883 | 12,281 | 12,718 |
| 543 | 604 | 687 | 713 | 792 | 859 | 947 | 947 | 1,003 | 1,048 | 1,053 |
| | | | | | | | | | | |
| 1,515 | 1,684 | 1,739 | 1,900 | 2,117 | 2,383 | 2,591 | 3,122 | 3,486 | 4,012 | 4,637 |
| 584 | 637 | 693 | 643 | 653 | 681 | 666 | 691 | 696 | 755 | 817 |
| 2,185 | 2,338 | 2,617 | 2,916 | 3,292 | 3,567 | 3,924 | 4,591 | 4,877 | 5,689 | 6,357 |
| 3,897 | 4,663 | 5,825 | 6,415 | 7,711 | 9,580 | 11,197 | 14,229 | 16,986 | 20,852 | 25,253 |
| 373 | 449 | 508 | 550 | 689 | 891 | 1,059 | 1,461 | 1,723 | 2,233 | 2,775 |
| | | | | | | | | | | |
| 356 | 352 | 360 | 359 | 378 | 390 | 444 | 511 | 563 | 609 | 626 |
| 2,062 | 2,309 | 2,422 | 2,678 | 3,319 | 3,967 | 4,648 | 5,347 | 6,189 | 7,079 | 8,024 |
| 1,142 | 1,357 | 1,563 | 1,736 | 2,379 | 2,853 | 3,409 | 4,132 | 4,867 | 5,894 | 6,743 |
| 1,221 | 1,464 | 1,729 | 1,902 | 2,006 | 1,860 | 1,744 | 1,950 | 1,793 | 1,808 | 1,854 |
| 2,334 | 2,632 | 2,939 | 3,138 | 3,435 | 3,952 | 4,418 | 4,706 | 4,892 | 5,364 | 5,692 |
| 146 | 194 | 226 | 251 | 291 | 330 | 332 | 470 | 454 | 494 | 565 |
| | | | | | | | | | | |
| 91,972 | 105,711 | 122,775 | 131,669 | 150,697 | 179,323 | 203,302[3] | 226,546[3] | 248,791[3] | 281,422[3] | 309,330[3] |

the first census after they became states in 1959. [3]Figures were revised by the Census Bureau after the census.

## Population of US Territories

*Total midyear population. Source: US Census Bureau.*

| YEAR | PUERTO RICO | GUAM | VIRGIN ISLANDS | AMERICAN SAMOA | NORTHERN MARIANA ISLANDS |
|------|-------------|---------|----------------|----------------|--------------------------|
| 1960 | 2,358,000 | 66,900 | 32,500 | 20,000 | 8,861 |
| 1965 | 2,596,774 | 74,100 | 43,500 | 24,600 | 10,465 |
| 1970 | 2,721,754 | 86,470 | 63,476 | 27,267 | 12,359 |
| 1975 | 2,935,124 | 102,110 | 94,484 | 29,640 | 14,938 |
| 1980 | 3,209,648 | 106,869 | 99,636 | 32,418 | 16,890 |
| 1985 | 3,382,106 | 120,615 | 100,760 | 38,633 | 21,386 |
| 1990 | 3,536,910 | 134,125 | 103,963 | 47,199 | 44,037 |
| 1995 | 3,683,103 | 144,190 | 107,817 | 53,906 | 57,229 |
| 2000 | 3,814,413 | 155,324 | 108,639 | 57,771 | 69,706 |
| 2005 | 3,910,722 | 168,614 | 109,599 | 62,399 | 70,636 |
| 2012 | 3,998,905 | 185,674 | 109,574 | 68,061 | 44,582 |

## Foreign-Born Population in the US, 1850–2010

The foreign-born population consists of persons born outside the United States to parents who were not US citizens. Populations of Alaska and Hawaii were included starting in 1960. In 1850 and 1860 data, the entire slave population was considered native-born.

Source: *Statistical Abstract of the United States: 2012.*

| YEAR | POPULATION TOTAL | FOREIGN-BORN | % OF TOTAL | YEAR | POPULATION TOTAL | FOREIGN-BORN | % OF TOTAL |
|------|------------------|--------------|------------|------|------------------|--------------|------------|
| 1850 | 23,191,876 | 2,244,602 | 9.7 | 1940 | 131,669,275 | 11,594,896 | 8.8 |
| 1860 | 31,443,321 | 4,138,697 | 13.2 | 1950 | 150,216,110 | 10,347,395 | 6.9 |
| 1870 | 38,558,371 | 5,567,229 | 14.4 | 1960 | 179,325,671 | 9,738,091 | 5.4 |
| 1880 | 50,155,783 | 6,679,943 | 13.3 | 1970 | 203,210,158 | 9,619,302 | 4.7 |
| 1890 | 62,622,250 | 9,249,547 | 14.8 | 1980 | 226,545,805 | 14,079,906 | 6.2 |
| 1900 | 75,994,575 | 10,341,276 | 13.6 | 1990 | 248,709,873 | 19,767,316 | 7.9 |
| 1910 | 91,972,266 | 13,515,886 | 14.7 | 2000 | 281,421,906 | 31,107,889 | 11.1 |
| 1920 | 105,710,620 | 13,920,692 | 13.2 | 2009[1] | 306,170,830 | 36,750,000 | 12.0 |
| 1930 | 122,775,046 | 14,204,149 | 11.6 | 2010[1] | 308,779,455 | 37,606,000 | 12.2 |

[1] As of March.

## Total Immigrants Admitted to the US, 1901–2011

Numbers shown include only immigrant aliens admitted for permanent residence and are for fiscal years. Currently the fiscal year begins 1 October and ends 30 September. Prior to 1976, the fiscal year began 1 July and ended 30 June.

Source: <www.dhs.gov>.

| YEAR | NUMBER | YEAR | NUMBER | YEAR | NUMBER | YEAR | NUMBER |
|------|--------|------|--------|------|--------|------|--------|
| 1901 | 487,918 | 1911 | 878,587 | 1921 | 805,228 | 1931 | 97,139 |
| 1902 | 648,743 | 1912 | 838,172 | 1922 | 309,556 | 1932 | 35,576 |
| 1903 | 857,046 | 1913 | 1,197,892 | 1923 | 522,919 | 1933 | 23,068 |
| 1904 | 812,870 | 1914 | 1,218,480 | 1924 | 706,896 | 1934 | 29,470 |
| 1905 | 1,026,499 | 1915 | 326,700 | 1925 | 294,314 | 1935 | 34,956 |
| 1906 | 1,100,735 | 1916 | 298,826 | 1926 | 304,488 | 1936 | 36,329 |
| 1907 | 1,285,349 | 1917 | 295,403 | 1927 | 335,175 | 1937 | 50,244 |
| 1908 | 782,870 | 1918 | 110,618 | 1928 | 307,255 | 1938 | 67,895 |
| 1909 | 751,786 | 1919 | 141,132 | 1929 | 279,678 | 1939 | 82,998 |
| 1910 | 1,041,570 | 1920 | 430,001 | 1930 | 241,700 | 1940 | 70,756 |
| totals 1901–10 | 8,795,386 | 1911–20 | 5,735,811 | 1921–30 | 4,107,209 | 1931–40 | 528,431 |

| YEAR | NUMBER | YEAR | NUMBER | YEAR | NUMBER | YEAR | NUMBER |
|------|--------|------|--------|------|--------|------|--------|
| 1941 | 51,776 | 1951 | 205,717 | 1961 | 271,344 | 1971 | 370,478 |
| 1942 | 28,781 | 1952 | 265,520 | 1962 | 283,763 | 1972 | 384,685 |
| 1943 | 23,725 | 1953 | 170,434 | 1963 | 306,260 | 1973 | 398,515 |
| 1944 | 28,551 | 1954 | 208,177 | 1964 | 292,248 | 1974 | 393,919 |
| 1945 | 38,119 | 1955 | 237,790 | 1965 | 296,697 | 1975 | 385,378 |
| 1946 | 108,721 | 1956 | 321,625 | 1966 | 323,040 | 1976[1] | 499,093 |
| 1947 | 147,292 | 1957 | 326,867 | 1967 | 361,972 | 1977 | 458,755 |
| 1948 | 170,570 | 1958 | 253,265 | 1968 | 454,448 | 1978 | 589,810 |
| 1949 | 188,317 | 1959 | 260,686 | 1969 | 358,579 | 1979 | 394,244 |
| 1950 | 249,187 | 1960 | 265,398 | 1970 | 373,326 | 1980 | 524,295 |
| totals 1941–50 | 1,035,039 | 1951–60 | 2,515,479 | 1961–70 | 3,321,677 | 1971–80 | 4,399,172 |

## Total Immigrants Admitted to the US, 1901–2011 (continued)

| YEAR | NUMBER | YEAR | NUMBER | YEAR | NUMBER | YEAR | NUMBER |
|---|---|---|---|---|---|---|---|
| 1981 | 595,014 | 1991 | 1,826,595 | 2001 | 1,058,902 | 2011 | 1,062,040 |
| 1982 | 533,624 | 1992 | 973,445 | 2002 | 1,059,356 | | |
| 1983 | 550,052 | 1993 | 903,916 | 2003 | 703,542 | | |
| 1984 | 541,811 | 1994 | 803,993 | 2004 | 957,883 | | |
| 1985 | 568,149 | 1995 | 720,177 | 2005 | 1,122,257 | | |
| 1986 | 600,027 | 1996 | 915,560 | 2006 | 1,266,129 | | |
| 1987 | 599,889 | 1997 | 797,847 | 2007 | 1,052,415 | | |
| 1988 | 641,346 | 1998 | 653,206 | 2008 | 1,107,126 | | |
| 1989 | 1,090,172 | 1999 | 644,787 | 2009 | 1,130,818 | | |
| 1990 | 1,535,872 | 2000 | 841,002 | 2010 | 1,042,625 | | |
| totals 1981–90 | 7,255,956 | 1991–2000 | 9,080,528 | 2001–10 | 10,501,053 | 2011 | 1,062,040 |

totals 1901–2011: 58,337,781

[1]Includes the 15 months from 1 Jul 1975 through 30 Sep 1976.

## Immigrants Admitted to the US by State of Residence and Country of Birth
Fiscal year 2011. Korea used to designate both North and South Korea.
Source: <www.dhs.gov>.

| STATE OF RESIDENCE | TOTAL IMMIGRANTS | TOP FIVE COUNTRIES OF BIRTH (NUMBER OF IMMIGRANTS) |
|---|---|---|
| Alabama | 4,063 | Korea (389), Mexico (375), China (317), India (317), Philippines (242) |
| Alaska | 1,799 | Philippines (690), Dominican Republic (98), Mexico (70), Korea (67), China (47) |
| Arizona | 20,333 | Mexico (8,347), Iraq (1,294), India (988), Philippines (842), China (687) |
| Arkansas | 2,874 | Mexico (946), India (278), El Salvador (205), China (171), Philippines (151) |
| California | 210,591 | Mexico (49,774), China (23,117), Philippines (22,797), India (15,061), Vietnam (12,213) |
| Colorado | 13,547 | Mexico (3,372), China (734), Ethiopia (659), Vietnam (503), Myanmar (Burma) (496) |
| Connecticut | 12,577 | India (1,108), Jamaica (1,081), Dominican Republic (779), China (734), Poland (478) |
| Delaware | 2,355 | India (362), China (222), Mexico (158), Philippines (126), Kenya (108) |
| District of Columbia | 2,724 | Ethiopia (545), El Salvador (241), China (122), Cameroon (100), Dominican Republic (87) |
| Florida | 109,229 | Cuba (29,700), Haiti (11,446), Colombia (8,161), Jamaica (5,605), Venezuela (4,954) |
| Georgia | 27,015 | Mexico (2,763), India (2,311), Korea (1,521), China (1,260), Vietnam (1,113) |
| Hawaii | 7,296 | Philippines (4,399), China (864), Japan (493), Korea (233), Vietnam (158) |
| Idaho | 2,602 | Mexico (715), Iraq (192), Bhutan (190), China (134), Philippines (114) |
| Illinois | 38,325 | Mexico (7,334), India (4,532), China (2,816), Philippines (2,260), Poland (2,191) |
| Indiana | 8,262 | Myanmar (Burma) (1,277), Mexico (1,198), India (643), China (561), Philippines (350) |
| Iowa | 4,624 | Mexico (780), Myanmar (Burma) (544), Vietnam (277), China (245), India (242) |
| Kansas | 5,086 | Mexico (1,348), Myanmar (Burma) (324), Vietnam (318), India (308), China (273) |
| Kentucky | 5,403 | Cuba (561), Myanmar (Burma) (400), Mexico (382), Iraq (352), China (302) |
| Louisiana | 4,226 | Vietnam (401), China (337), Mexico (337), Honduras (235), Philippines (232) |
| Maine | 1,467 | Iraq (136), China (124), Somalia (118), Kenya (86), Canada (74) |
| Maryland | 25,778 | India (1,744), Cameroon (1,582), China (1,494), El Salvador (1,472), Nigeria (1,402) |
| Massachusetts | 32,236 | Dominican Republic (3,889), China (2,959), India (2,139), Haiti (1,916), Brazil (1,808) |
| Michigan | 18,347 | Iraq (3,326), India (1,602), Mexico (1,113), China (1,010), Bangladesh (862) |
| Minnesota | 12,389 | Somalia (1,157), Ethiopia (968), Mexico (779), Kenya (777), India (767) |
| Mississippi | 1,666 | Mexico (265), India (154), Vietnam (144), China (128), Philippines (119) |
| Missouri | 7,048 | Mexico (617), India (525), China (516), Iraq (349), Philippines (341) |
| Montana | 511 | Philippines (60), Canada (50), China (49), Mexico (27), Germany (24) |

## Immigrants Admitted to the US by State of Residence and Country of Birth (continued)

| STATE OF RESIDENCE | TOTAL IMMIGRANTS | TOP FIVE COUNTRIES OF BIRTH (NUMBER OF IMMIGRANTS) |
|---|---|---|
| Nebraska | 4,535 | Mexico (911), Myanmar (Burma) (445), Vietnam (280), Thailand (254), Somalia (239) |
| Nevada | 10,449 | Mexico (2,444), Philippines (1,950), Cuba (690), China (689), Ethiopia (484) |
| New Hampshire | 2,478 | Bhutan (340), India (231), Nepal (179), China (126), Dominican Republic (122) |
| New Jersey | 55,547 | India (8,341), Dominican Republic (7,229), Colombia (2,564), China (2,503), Philippines (2,352) |
| New Mexico | 3,767 | Mexico (1,981), Philippines (204), Vietnam (147), China (137), Cuba (104) |
| New York | 148,426 | China (27,358), Dominican Republic (22,154), Bangladesh (8,727), Jamaica (6,503), India (4,805) |
| North Carolina | 17,571 | Mexico (1,996), India (1,325), China (1,119), Vietnam (952), Myanmar (Burma) (805) |
| North Dakota | 948 | Bhutan (153), Iraq (78), Nepal (75), Canada (61), Philippines (42) |
| Ohio | 13,857 | India (1,557), China (1,065), Mexico (558), Ghana (528), Philippines (525) |
| Oklahoma | 4,503 | Mexico (1,251), Vietnam (311), India (281), China (276), Myanmar (Burma) (240) |
| Oregon | 7,694 | Mexico (1,462), China (722), Vietnam (643), India (487), Philippines (363) |
| Pennsylvania | 25,397 | India (2,396), China (2,227), Dominican Republic (2,024), Bhutan (1,036), Vietnam (940) |
| Rhode Island | 3,681 | Dominican Republic (1,028), Guatemala (268), Cape Verde (265), Colombia (197), Liberia (143) |
| South Carolina | 4,216 | Mexico (467), India (301), China (294), Colombia (250), Philippines (236) |
| South Dakota | 1,337 | Ethiopia (136), Myanmar (Burma) (127), Thailand (86), Bhutan (84), Eritrea (64) |
| Tennessee | 8,279 | Mexico (887), Egypt (622), India (613), China (510), Iraq (423) |
| Texas | 94,481 | Mexico (36,648), India (5,907), Vietnam (4,546), China (3,365), Philippines (2,475) |
| Utah | 6,426 | Mexico (1,422), Peru (335), China (298), Bhutan (268), Iraq (263) |
| Vermont | 943 | Bhutan (142), Canada (67), Nepal (65), China (51), India (51), Somalia (51) |
| Virginia | 27,767 | India (2,909), El Salvador (1,524), Ethiopia (1,426), China (1,405), Philippines (1,385) |
| Washington | 23,789 | Mexico (2,446), India (2,168), Philippines (2,025), China (1,962), Vietnam (1,838) |
| West Virginia | 830 | China (74), Philippines (65), India (54), Myanmar (Burma) (36), United Kingdom (29) |
| Wisconsin | 6,245 | Mexico (1,146), India (647), China (431), Myanmar (Burma) (265), Philippines (226) |
| Wyoming | 420 | Mexico (107), China (27), Philippines (21), India (19), United Kingdom (16) |

## Americans 65 and Older, 1900–2012

*Data for Hawaii and Alaska are included after 1950. Source: US Census Bureau.*

| CENSUS YEAR | NUMBER OF PEOPLE 65 AND OLDER | % OF TOTAL POPULATION | CENSUS YEAR | NUMBER OF PEOPLE 65 AND OLDER | % OF TOTAL POPULATION |
|---|---|---|---|---|---|
| 1900 | 3,080,498 | 4.1 | 1970 | 20,065,502 | 9.8 |
| 1910 | 3,949,524 | 4.3 | 1980 | 25,549,427 | 11.3 |
| 1920 | 4,933,215 | 4.7 | 1990 | 31,241,831 | 12.6 |
| 1930 | 6,633,805 | 5.4 | 2000 | 34,991,753 | 12.4 |
| 1940 | 9,019,314 | 6.8 | 2010 | 40,267,984 | 13.0 |
| 1950 | 12,269,537 | 8.1 | 2012 | 42,477,704 | 13.5 |
| 1960 | 16,559,580 | 9.2 | | | |

## Poverty Level by State, 1980–2010

*Source: US Census Bureau. Detail may not add to total given because of rounding.*

| STATE | % OF PEOPLE IN POVERTY | | | NUMBER OF PEOPLE IN POVERTY ('000) | | |
|---|---|---|---|---|---|---|
| | 1980 | 1990 | 2010 | 1980 | 1990 | 2010 |
| Alabama | 21.2 | 19.2 | 18.9 | 810 | 779 | 883 |
| Alaska | 9.6 | 11.4 | 11.0 | 36 | 57 | 77 |

## Poverty Level by State, 1980–2010 (continued)

| STATE | % OF PEOPLE IN POVERTY | | | NUMBER OF PEOPLE IN POVERTY ('000) | | |
|---|---|---|---|---|---|---|
| | 1980 | 1990 | 2010 | 1980 | 1990 | 2010 |
| Arizona | 12.8 | 13.7 | 17.6 | 354 | 484 | 1,105 |
| Arkansas | 21.5 | 19.6 | 18.7 | 484 | 472 | 530 |
| California | 11.0 | 13.9 | 15.8 | 2,619 | 4,128 | 5,785 |
| Colorado | 8.6 | 13.7 | 13.2 | 247 | 461 | 652 |
| Connecticut | 8.3 | 6.0 | 10.1 | 255 | 196 | 349 |
| Delaware | 11.8 | 6.9 | 11.9 | 68 | 48 | 104 |
| District of Columbia | 20.9 | 21.1 | 18.8 | 131 | 120 | 107 |
| Florida | 16.7 | 14.4 | 16.5 | 1,692 | 1,896 | 3,049 |
| Georgia | 13.9 | 15.8 | 18.0 | 727 | 1,001 | 1,698 |
| Hawaii | 8.5 | 11.0 | 11.1 | 81 | 121 | 147 |
| Idaho | 14.7 | 14.9 | 15.8 | 138 | 157 | 244 |
| Illinois | 12.3 | 13.7 | 13.8 | 1,386 | 1,606 | 1,732 |
| Indiana | 11.8 | 13.0 | 15.3 | 645 | 714 | 960 |
| Iowa | 10.8 | 10.4 | 12.5 | 311 | 289 | 369 |
| Kansas | 9.4 | 10.3 | 13.5 | 215 | 259 | 375 |
| Kentucky | 19.3 | 17.3 | 18.9 | 701 | 628 | 796 |
| Louisiana | 20.3 | 23.6 | 18.8 | 868 | 952 | 832 |
| Maine | 14.6 | 13.1 | 13.1 | 158 | 162 | 169 |
| Maryland | 9.5 | 9.9 | 9.9 | 389 | 468 | 560 |
| Massachusetts | 9.5 | 10.7 | 11.4 | 542 | 626 | 725 |
| Michigan | 12.9 | 14.3 | 16.7 | 1,194 | 1,315 | 1,614 |
| Minnesota | 8.7 | 12.0 | 11.5 | 342 | 524 | 595 |
| Mississippi | 24.3 | 25.7 | 22.4 | 591 | 684 | 644 |
| Missouri | 13.0 | 13.4 | 15.3 | 625 | 700 | 888 |
| Montana | 13.2 | 16.3 | 15.2 | 102 | 134 | 146 |
| Nebraska | 13.0 | 10.3 | 12.6 | 199 | 167 | 225 |
| Nevada | 8.3 | 9.8 | 14.8 | 70 | 119 | 394 |
| New Hampshire | 7.0 | 6.3 | 8.6 | 63 | 68 | 110 |
| New Jersey | 9.0 | 9.2 | 10.2 | 659 | 711 | 884 |
| New Mexico | 20.6 | 20.9 | 19.8 | 268 | 319 | 401 |
| New York | 13.8 | 14.3 | 15.0 | 2,391 | 2,571 | 2,841 |
| North Carolina | 15.0 | 13.0 | 17.4 | 877 | 829 | 1,619 |
| North Dakota | 15.5 | 13.7 | 12.5 | 99 | 87 | 81 |
| Ohio | 9.8 | 11.5 | 15.8 | 1,046 | 1,256 | 1,771 |
| Oklahoma | 13.9 | 15.6 | 16.8 | 406 | 481 | 613 |
| Oregon | 11.5 | 9.2 | 15.8 | 309 | 267 | 597 |
| Pennsylvania | 9.8 | 11.0 | 13.4 | 1,142 | 1,328 | 1,645 |
| Rhode Island | 10.7 | 7.5 | 14.1 | 97 | 71 | 143 |
| South Carolina | 16.8 | 16.2 | 18.1 | 534 | 548 | 814 |
| South Dakota | 18.8 | 13.3 | 14.6 | 127 | 93 | 115 |
| Tennessee | 19.6 | 16.9 | 17.8 | 884 | 833 | 1,103 |
| Texas | 15.7 | 15.9 | 17.9 | 2,247 | 2,684 | 4,411 |
| Utah | 10.0 | 8.2 | 13.3 | 148 | 143 | 363 |
| Vermont | 12.0 | 10.9 | 12.4 | 62 | 61 | 75 |
| Virginia | 12.4 | 11.1 | 11.1 | 647 | 705 | 866 |
| Washington | 12.7 | 8.9 | 13.5 | 538 | 434 | 890 |
| West Virginia | 15.2 | 18.1 | 18.2 | 297 | 328 | 327 |
| Wisconsin | 8.5 | 9.3 | 13.2 | 403 | 448 | 732 |
| Wyoming | 10.4 | 11.0 | 11.4 | 49 | 51 | 63 |
| all US | 13.0 | 13.5 | 15.3 | 29,272 | 33,585 | 46,216 |

## Poverty Level by Race, 2010

*Source: US Census Bureau. Detail may not add to total given because of rounding and because Hispanic people may be of any race.*

| RACE | NUMBER OF PEOPLE IN POVERTY ('000) 2010 | % OF PEOPLE IN POVERTY 2010 |
|---|---|---|
| White | 31,650 | 13.0 |
| Black | 10,675 | 27.4 |
| Asian | 1,729 | 12.1 |
| Other[1] | 2,126 | 22.7 |
| Hispanic | 13,243 | 26.6 |
| TOTAL | 46,180 | 15.1 |

[1]*Includes Pacific Islanders and Native Americans.*

# States and Other Areas of the United States

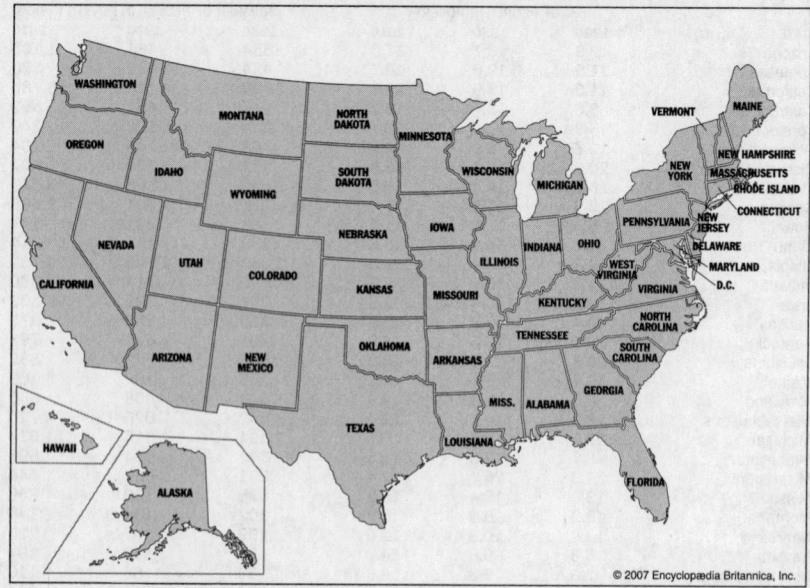

© 2007 Encyclopædia Britannica, Inc.

## Alabama

**Name:** Alabama, from the Choctaw language, meaning "thicket clearers." **Nickname:** Heart of Dixie. **Capital:** Montgomery. **Rank:** population: 23rd; area: 30th. **Motto:** "Audemus jura nostra defendere" ("We dare defend our rights"). **Song:** "Alabama," words by Julia S. Tutwiler and music by Edna Gockel Gussen. **Amphibian:** Red Hills salamander. **Bird:** yellowhammer. **Fish:** largemouth bass (freshwater); tarpon (saltwater). **Flower:** camellia. **Fossil:** *Basilosaurus cetoides*. **Gemstone:** star blue quartz. **Insect:** monarch butterfly. **Mineral:** hematite. **Reptile:** Alabama red-bellied turtle. **Rock:** marble. **Tree:** southern longleaf pine.

### Natural features

**Land area:** 51,701 sq mi, 133,905 sq km. **Mountain ranges:** Appalachian, Raccoon, Lookout. **Highest point:** Cheaha Mountain, 734 m (2,407 ft). **Largest lake:** Lake Guntersville. **Major rivers:** Mobile, Alabama, Tombigbee, Tennessee, Chattahoochee. **Natural regions:** the Appalachian Plateau, extending across the north-central region; Interior Low Plateaus, far north; Valley and Ridge Province, covering the east; Coastal Plain, covering the southern half of the state. **Land use:** forest, 64.4%; agricultural, 7.5%; pasture, 0.2%; other, 27.9%.

### People

**Population** (2011): 4,802,740; persons per sq mi 92.9, persons per sq km 35.9. **Vital statistics** (2010; per 1,000 population): birth rate, 12.6; death rate, 10.0; marriage rate, 8.2; divorce rate, 4.4. **Major cities** (2010): Birmingham 212,237; Montgomery 205,764; Mobile 195,111; Huntsville 180,105; Tuscaloosa 90,468.

### Government

**Statehood:** entered the Union on 14 Dec 1819 as the 22nd state. **State constitution:** adopted 1901. **Representation in US Congress:** 2 senators; 7 representatives. **Electoral college:** 9 votes. **Political divisions:** 67 counties.

### Economy

**Employment** (2008): services 30.6%; government 15.6%; trade 14.4%; finance, insurance, real estate 13.8%; manufacturing 11.1%. **Production** (2010): finance, insurance, real estate 22.7%; government 17.1%; manufacturing 16.3%; services 16.2%; trade 12.7%. **Chief agricultural products:** *Crops:* cotton, corn (maize), soybeans, peanuts (groundnuts), potatoes, sweet potatoes, peaches, pecans, winter wheat. *Livestock:* cattle and calves, poultry, hogs. *Fish catch:* catfish, shrimp, crab, mussels, oysters. **Chief manufactured products:** food products; textiles; wearing apparel; wood products; mobile homes; refined petroleum products; plastics and rubber products; base metals.

**Internet resources:** <www.alabama.travel>; <www.alabama.gov>.

## Alaska

**Name:** Alaska, from the Aleut words *alaxsxa* and *alaxsxix*, meaning "mainland" or "great land." **Nickname:** The Last Frontier. **Capital:** Juneau. **Rank:** population: 47th; area: 1st. **Motto:** "North to the future." **Song:** "Alaska's Flag," words by Marie Drake and music by Elinor Dusenbury. **Bird:** willow ptarmigan. **Fish:** giant king salmon. **Flower:** forget-me-not. **Fossil:** *Mammuthus primigenius* (woolly mammoth). **Gemstone:** jade. **Insect:** four-spot skimmer dragonfly. **Mammal:** moose. **Marine mammal:** bowhead whale. **Mineral:** gold. **Tree:** sitka spruce.

## Natural features

**Land area:** 590,693 sq mi, 1,529,888 sq km. **Mountain ranges:** Wrangell, Chugach, Alaska, Brooks, Aleutian, Boundary. **Highest point:** Mt. McKinley (Denali), 6,194 m (20,320 ft). **Largest lake:** Iliamna Lake. **Major rivers:** Yukon, Porcupine, Tanana, Koyukuk, Noataks. **Natural regions:** panhandle, a narrow strip of land that includes portions of the Coast Mountains; coastal archipelago and the Gulf of Alaska islands; the Alaska Peninsula and Aleutian island chain that separates the North Pacific from the Bering Sea; the Alaska Range, extending across the south-central region; the Interior Plateau, including the basin of the Yukon River, the central plains and tablelands of the interior, the Seward Peninsula to the west, and the Brooks Range, sometimes called the North Slope, to the north; the Arctic Coastal Plain, a treeless region of tundra lying at the northernmost edge of the state; tundra-covered islands of the Bering Sea. **Land use:** forest, 24.1%; pasture, 0.0%; other, 75.9%.

## People

**Population** (2011): 722,718; persons per sq mi 1.2, person per sq km 0.5. **Vital statistics** (2010; per 1,000 population): birth rate, 16.1; death rate, 5.2; marriage rate, 8.0; divorce rate, 4.7. **Major cities** (2010): Anchorage 291,826; Fairbanks 31,535; **Juneau 31,275;** Sitka 8,881; Ketchikan 8,050.

## Government

**Statehood:** entered the Union on 3 Jan 1959 as the 49th state. **State constitution:** adopted 1956. **Representation in US Congress:** 2 senators; 1 representative. **Electoral college:** 3 votes. **Political divisions:** 16 boroughs.

## Economy

**Employment** (2008): services 28.9%; government 23.5%; finance, insurance, real estate 12.0%; trade 11.9%; transportation, public utilities 7.7%. **Production** (2010): mining 25.5%; government 18.7%; finance, insurance, real estate 16.5%; transportation, public utilities 12.5%; services 12.3%. **Chief agricultural products:** *Crops:* hay, milk, potatoes, timber. *Livestock:* cattle and calves, pigs. *Fish catch:* salmon, herring, groundfish, shellfish, crab, shrimp. **Chief manufactured products:** processed fish and seafood (fresh, frozen, canned, and cured); wood products; paper products; transportation products.

**Internet resources:** <www.travelalaska.com>; <www.alaska.gov>.

# Arizona

**Name:** Arizona, derived from the Basque term for "place of oaks" or "the good oak tree." **Nickname:**
Grand Canyon State. **Capital:** Phoenix. **Rank:** population: 16th; area: 6th. **Motto:** "Ditat Deus" ("God enriches"). **Song:** "Arizona March Song," words by Margaret Rowe Clifford and music by Maurice Blumenthal. **Amphibian:** Arizona treefrog. **Bird:** cactus wren. **Fish:** Arizona trout. **Flower:** saguaro blossom. **Fossil:** petrified wood. **Gemstone:** turquoise. **Mammal:** ringtail. **Reptile:** Arizona ridgenose rattlesnake. **Tree:** palo verde.

## Natural features

**Land area:** 113,991 sq mi, 295,235 sq km. **Mountain ranges:** Black, Gila Bend, Chuska, Hualapai, San Francisco, White. **Highest point:** Humphreys Peak, 3,851 m (12,633 ft). **Largest lake:** Lake Roosevelt. **Major rivers:** Colorado, Little Colorado, Verde, Salt, Gila. **Natural regions:** the Colorado Plateaus, northeast third of the state, include the Grand Canyon and the Painted Desert; the Basin and Range Province, south, east, central, and northwest, includes the Sonoran Desert in the southwest corner and part of the Great Basin Desert to the northwest. **Land use:** pasture, 44.2%; forest, 5.7%; agricultural, 1.3%; other, 48.8%.

## People

**Population** (2011): 6,482,505; persons per sq mi 56.9, persons per sq km 22.0. **Vital statistics** (2010; per 1,000 population): birth rate, 13.9; death rate, 7.3; marriage rate, 5.9; divorce rate, 3.5. **Major cities** (2010): **Phoenix 1,445,632;** Tucson 520,116; Mesa 439,041; Chandler 236,123; Glendale 226,721; Scottsdale 217,385; Gilbert 208,453; Tempe 161,719.

## Government

**Statehood:** entered the Union on 14 Feb 1912 as the 48th state. **State constitution:** adopted 1911. **Representation in US Congress:** 2 senators; 9 representatives. **Electoral college:** 11 votes. **Political divisions:** 15 counties.

## Economy

**Employment** (2008): services 33.6%; finance, insurance, real estate 18.9%; trade 14.9%; government 13.3%; construction 7.2%. **Production** (2010): finance, insurance, real estate 30.2%; services 19.7%; government 13.6%; trade 13.3%; manufacturing 8.0%. **Chief agricultural products:** *Crops:* cotton and cottonseed, wheat, sorghum, hay, barley, corn (maize), potatoes, grapes, apples, dairy products. *Livestock:* cattle and calves, hogs and pigs, sheep and lambs, angora goats. **Chief manufactured products:** semiconductors; telecommunications equipment; electrical equipment; transportation equipment; soap products; nonferrous metal products.

**Internet resources:** <www.arizonaguide.com>; <http://az.gov>.

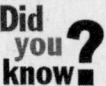

**Did you know?** Oraibi, a Hopi pueblo (village) in northern Arizona, is thought by some to be the oldest continuously occupied settlement in the United States.

*For details about state governments, see pages 608–613; for energy data, see pages 627–628.*

# Arkansas

**Name:** Arkansas, from *akansea,* an Illinois Indian word describing the Quapaw tribe (also known as the Arkansaw), meaning "people who live downstream." **Nickname:** Natural State. **Capital:** Little Rock. **Rank:** population: 32nd; area: 27th. **Motto:** "Regnat populus" ("The people rule"). **Songs:** "Arkansas," words and music by Wayland Holyfield; "Oh, Arkansas," words and music by by Terry Rose and Gary Klaff. **Bird:** mockingbird. **Flower:** apple blossom. **Gemstone:** diamond. **Insect:** honeybee. **Mammal:** white-tailed deer. **Mineral:** quartz crystal. **Rock:** bauxite. **Tree:** pine tree.

## Natural features

**Land area:** 53,179 sq mi, 137,733 sq km. **Mountain ranges:** Ozark, Ouachita. **Highest point:** Mt. Magazine, 839 m (2,753 ft). **Largest lake:** Lake Chicot. **Major rivers:** Arkansas, Red, Ouachita, White. **Natural regions:** the Ozark Plateaus, including the Boston Mountains, north and northwest regions; the Ouachita Province, including the Arkansas valley and the Ouachita Mountains, central region; the Coastal Plain, extends from southwest to northeast. **Land use:** forest, 44.1%; agricultural, 22.1%; pasture, 0.1%; other, 33.7%.

## People

**Population** (2011): 2,937,979; persons per sq mi 55.2, persons per sq km 21.3. **Vital statistics** (2010; per 1,000 population): birth rate, 13.2; death rate, 9.9; marriage rate, 10.8; divorce rate, 5.7. **Major cities** (2010): **Little Rock 193,524;** Fort Smith 86,209; Fayetteville 73,580; Springdale 69,797; Jonesboro 67,263.

## Government

**Statehood:** entered the Union on 15 Jun 1836 as the 25th state. **State constitution:** adopted 1874. **Representation in US Congress:** 2 senators; 4 representatives. **Electoral college:** 6 votes. **Political divisions:** 75 counties.

## Economy

**Employment** (2008): services 29.3%; government 14.5%; trade 13.7%; finance, insurance, real estate 12.6%; manufacturing 11.7%. **Production** (2010): finance, insurance, real estate 21.8%; services 16.1%; manufacturing 14.7%; government 14.6%; trade 13.9%. **Chief agricultural products:** *Crops:* corn (maize), cotton, soybeans, wheat, apples, blueberries, grapes, peaches, pecans, strawberries. *Livestock:* cattle and calves, hogs and pigs, poultry. *Fish catch:* catfish. **Chief manufactured products:** food products; lumber and paper products; refined petroleum products; chemical products; plastic and rubber products; base metals; fabricated metal products; machinery and apparatus; transportation equipment.

**Internet resources:** <www.arkansas.com>; <www.arkansas.gov>.

# California

**Name:** California, from unknown origins. **Nickname:** Golden State. **Capital:** Sacramento. **Rank:** population: 1st; area: 3rd. **Motto:** "Eureka" ("I have found it"). **Song:** "I Love You, California," words by F.B. Silverwood and music by A.F. Frankenstein. **Bird:** California quail. **Fish:** golden trout (freshwater); garibaldi (saltwater). **Flower:** California poppy. **Fossil:** sabertooth cat. **Gemstone:** benitoite. **Insect:** California dogface butterfly. **Mammal:** California grizzly bear. **Marine mammal:** California gray whale. **Mineral:** gold. **Reptile:** desert tortoise. **Rock:** serpentine. **Tree:** California redwood.

## Natural features

**Land area:** 158,608 sq mi, 410,793 sq km. **Mountain ranges:** Coast, Sierra Nevada, Cascade, Santa Lucia, Klamath, Tehachapi, San Gabriel, San Bernardino. **Highest point:** Mt. Whitney, 4,418 m (14,494 ft). **Largest lake:** Lake Tahoe. **Major rivers:** Colorado, Sacramento, Pit, San Joaquin. **Natural regions:** Basin and Range Province, northeast corner, also eastern border with Arizona and southern Nevada; Cascade-Sierra Mountains, running from north to south along the east-central region; Pacific Border Province, west, including the Coast Ranges to the west, the Klamath Mountains to the north, the Los Angeles Ranges to the south, and the California Trough (commonly referred to as the Central Valley) to the east; Lower Californian Province, southwestern tip. **Land use:** pasture, 17.5%; forest, 13.7%; agricultural, 9.3%; other, 59.5%.

## People

**Population** (2011): 37,691,912; persons per sq mi 237.6, persons per sq km 91.8. **Vital statistics** (2010; per 1,000 population): birth rate, 13.7; death rate, 6.3; marriage rate, 5.8; divorce rate (2001), 6.6. **Major cities** (2010): Los Angeles 3,792,621; San Diego 1,307,402; San Jose 945,942; San Francisco 805,235; Fresno 494,665; **Sacramento 466,488;** Long Beach 462,257; Oakland 390,724.

## Government

**Statehood:** entered the Union on 9 Sep 1850 as the 31st state. **State constitution:** adopted 1879. **Representation in US Congress:** 2 senators; 53 representatives. **Electoral college:** 55 votes. **Political divisions:** 58 counties.

## Economy

**Employment** (2008): services 32.5%; finance, insurance, real estate 19.7%; trade 13.7%; government 13.1%; manufacturing 7.2%. **Production** (2010): finance, insurance, real estate 32.2%; services 16.6%; government 11.6%; manufacturing 11.6%; trade 11.3%. **Chief agricultural products:** *Crops:* wheat, oats, rice, apples, apricots, cherries, grapes, olives, peaches, pears, strawberries, onions, lima beans, artichokes, broccoli, snap beans, dairy products, eggs. *Livestock:* cattle and calves, sheep and lambs. *Fish catch:* bonito, halibut, mackerel, groundfish, rockfish (Pacific red snapper), sablefish (black cod), soles and sand dabs, sardines, white sea bass, shark, swordfish, tuna, crab, California spiny lobster, Pacific Ocean shrimp, prawns, squid. **Chief manufactured products:** food products; soft drinks; beer and wine; textiles; wearing apparel; lumber and wood products; paper products; printing; refined petroleum products; asphalt; chemical products; plastic and rubber products; glass products; construction materials; base metals; fabricated metal products; machinery and apparatus; telecommunications equipment; semiconductors and computers; electronics; transportation equipment; furniture; medical equipment; sporting goods.

Internet resources: <www.visitcalifornia.com>; <www.ca.gov>.

## Colorado

Name: Colorado, from a Spanish word meaning "red." Nickname: Centennial State. Capital: Denver. Rank: population: 22nd; area: 8th. Motto: "Nil sine numine" ("Nothing without Providence"). Songs: "Where the Columbines Grow," words and music by A.J. Flynn; "Rocky Mountain High," words and music by John Denver. Bird: lark bunting. Fish: greenback cutthroat trout. Flower: white and lavender columbine. Fossil: stegosaurus. Gemstone: aquamarine. Insect: Colorado hairstreak butterfly. Mammal: Rocky Mountain bighorn sheep. Tree: Colorado blue spruce.

### Natural features

Land area: 104,095 sq mi, 269,605 sq km. Mountain ranges: Rocky, Front, Medicine Bow, Park, Rabbit Ears, San Juan, Sangre de Cristo, Sawatch. Highest point: Mt. Elbert, 4,399 m (14,433 ft). Largest lakes: Blue Mesa Reservoir (man-made); Grand Lake (natural). Major rivers: Colorado, Arkansas, South Platte, Rio Grande. Natural regions: the Great Plains Province, eastern half of state, includes the High Plains to the east, Colorado Piedmont to the west, and Raton Section to the south; Southern Rocky Mountains, running down the middle of the state; Middle Rocky Mountains and Wyoming Basin, northwest corner; Colorado Plateau, western and southwestern border, include the Uinta Basin to the north, the Canyon Lands in the middle, and the Navajo Section to the south. Land use: pasture, 37.2%; agricultural, 12.5%; forest, 4.9%; other, 45.4%.

### People

Population (2011): 5,116,796; persons per sq mi 49.2, persons per sq km 19.0. Vital statistics (2010; per 1,000 population): birth rate, 13.2; death rate, 6.3; marriage rate, 6.9; divorce rate, 4.3. Major cities (2010): Denver 600,158; Colorado Springs 416,427; Aurora 325,078; Fort Collins 143,986; Lakewood 142,980.

### Government

Statehood: entered the Union on 1 Aug 1876 as the 38th state. State constitution: adopted 1876. Representation in US Congress: 2 senators; 7 representatives. Electoral college: 9 votes. Political divisions: 64 counties.

### Economy

Employment (2008): services 31.1%; finance, insurance, real estate 21.1%; trade 13.3%; government 13.3%; construction 7.6%. Production (2010): finance, insurance, real estate 30.8%; services 16.8%; government 13.0%; transportation, public utilities 12.9%; trade 10.4%. Chief agricultural products: *Crops:* millet, corn (maize), potatoes, onions, sugar beets, sunflowers, wheat, dairy products, eggs, greenhouse products. *Livestock:* cattle and calves, hogs and pigs, sheep and lambs. Chief manufactured products: meat products; beverages; printing; semiconductors; computer and electronic products.

Internet resources: <www.colorado.com>; <www.colorado.gov>.

**Did you know?** Colorado's Rocky Mountains, which make up part of the North American Cordillera stretching more than 3,000 miles from Alaska to Mexico, contain some of the highest peaks in North America. The most impressive of these, perhaps, are the "Fourteeners," which is the name that mountain climbers give to the peaks that top 14,000 feet. In the state of Colorado, there are more than 50 "Fourteeners."

## Connecticut

Name: Connecticut, from the Algonquian Indian word *Quinnehtukqut,* meaning "land on the long tidal river." Nickname: Constitution State. Capital: Hartford. Rank: population: 29th; area: 48th. Motto: "Qui transtulit sustinet" ("He who transplanted still sustains"). Song: "Yankee Doodle," words and music from folk tradition. Bird: robin. Flower: mountain laurel. Fossil: *Eubrontes giganteus.* Insect: praying mantis. Mammal: sperm whale. Mineral: garnet. Shellfish: eastern oyster. Tree: white oak.

### Natural features

Land area: 5,004 sq mi, 12,960 sq km. Mountain range: Berkshire Hills. Highest point: Mt. Frissell, 725 m (2,380 ft). Largest lake: Candlewood Lake. Major rivers: Connecticut, Housatonic, Thames. Natural regions: the New England Province covers the state, divided into the Western Upland, Central Lowland (Connecticut Valley), and Eastern Upland. Land use: forest, 53.4%; agricultural, 5.4%; other, 41.2%.

### People

Population (2011): 3,580,709; persons per sq mi 715.6, persons per sq km 276.3. Vital statistics (2010; per 1,000 population): birth rate, 11.0; death rate, 8.0; marriage rate, 5.6; divorce rate, 2.9. Major cities (2010): Bridgeport 144,229; New Haven 129,779; Hartford 124,775; Stamford 122,643; Waterbury 110,366.

### Government

Statehood: entered the Union on 9 Jan 1788 as the 5th state. State constitution: adopted 1965. Representation in US Congress: 2 senators; 5 representatives. Electoral college: 7 votes. Political divisions: 8 counties.

*For details about state governments, see pages 608–613; for energy data, see pages 627–628.*

## Economy

**Employment** (2008): services 33.4%; finance, insurance, real estate 21.8%; trade 13.5%; government 11.9%; manufacturing 8.6%. **Production** (2010): finance, insurance, real estate 43.0%; services 16.5%; manufacturing 10.9%; government 10.0%; trade 10.0%. **Chief agricultural products:** *Crops:* corn (maize), silage, hay, tobacco, apples, pears, dairy products, eggs. *Livestock:* poultry, cattle and calves, sheep and lambs, horses. *Fish catch:* lobster, clams, oysters, shad. **Chief manufactured products:** printing; pharmaceutical products; soap and cleaning products; plastic products; fabricated metal products; machinery and apparatus; telecommunications equipment; electronics; aerospace products; aircraft engines.

**Internet resources:** <www.ctvisit.com>; <www.ct.gov>.

# Delaware

**Name:** Delaware, from Delaware River and Bay; named in turn for Sir Thomas West, Baron De La Warr. **Nickname:** First State. **Capital:** Dover. **Rank:** population: 45th; area: 49th. **Motto:** "Liberty and independence." **Song:** "Our Delaware," words by George B. Hynson and music by Will M.S. Brown. **Bird:** Blue Hen chicken. **Fish:** weakfish. **Flower:** peach blossom. **Insect:** ladybug. **Mineral:** sillimanite. **Tree:** American holly.

## Natural features

**Land area:** 2,023 sq mi, 5,240 sq km. **Highest point:** Ebright Azimuth, 137 m (448 ft). **Largest lake:** Red Mill Pond. **Major rivers:** Delaware, Nanticoke, Pocomoke. **Natural regions:** the Piedmont Province, including the Piedmont Upland, covers the northernmost tip of the state; the remainder consists of the Coastal Plain. **Land use:** agricultural, 29.8%; forest, 22.2%; other, 48.0%.

## People

**Population** (2011): 907,135; persons per sq mi 448.4, persons per sq km 173.1. **Vital statistics** (2010; per 1,000 population): birth rate, 12.6; death rate, 8.6; marriage rate, 5.2; divorce rate, 3.5. **Major cities** (2010): Wilmington 70,851; **Dover 36,047;** Newark 31,454; Middletown 18,871; Smyrna 10,023.

## Government

**Statehood:** entered the Union on 7 Dec 1787 as the 1st state. **State constitution:** adopted 1897. **Representation in US Congress:** 2 senators; 1 representative. **Electoral college:** 3 votes. **Political divisions:** 3 counties.

## Economy

**Employment** (2008): services 32.3%; finance, insurance, real estate 22.7%; trade 14.2%; government 12.9%; construction 6.7%. **Production** (2010): finance, insurance, real estate 56.3%; services 12.6%; government 9.3%; trade 7.3%; manufacturing 6.8%. **Chief agricultural products:** *Crops:* corn (maize), soybeans, wheat, barley, peas, dairy products. *Livestock:* poultry, cattle and calves, hogs. *Fish catch:* crustaceans, crab, clams. **Chief manufactured products:** chemical products; food products; paper products;

rubber and plastics products; fabricated metal products; printing.

**Internet resources:** <www.visitdelaware.com>; <www.delaware.gov>.

# District of Columbia

**Name:** District of Columbia, named in honor of Christopher Columbus. **Motto:** "Justitia omnibus" ("Justice for all"). **Bird:** woodthrush. **Flower:** American Beauty rose. **Tree:** scarlet oak.

## Natural features

**Land area:** 68 sq mi, 176 sq km. **Major river:** Potomac.

## People

**Population** (2011): 617,996; persons per sq mi 9,088.2, persons per sq km 3,511.3. **Vital statistics:** (2010; per 1,000 population): birth rate, 15.2; death rate, 7.8; marriage rate, 7.6; divorce rate, 2.8.

## Government

**Representation in US Congress:** 1 congressional delegate. **Political divisions:** 8 wards.

## Economy

**Employment** (2008): services 37.8%; government 31.0%; finance, insurance, real estate 21.7%; transportation, public utilities 4.0%; trade 3.4%. **Production** (2010): government 35.2%; finance, insurance, real estate 34.7%; services 20.5%; transportation, public utilities 6.5%; trade 2.0%. **Chief manufactured products:** printing and publishing products.

**Internet resources:** <http://washington.org>; <http://dc.gov>.

# Florida

**Name:** Florida, in honor of Pascua Florida ("feast of the flowers"), Spain's Easter celebration. **Nickname:** Sunshine State. **Capital:** Tallahassee. **Rank:** population: 4th; area: 23rd. **Motto:** "In God we trust." **Song:** "Old Folks at Home" ("Swanee River"), words and music by Stephen Foster. **Bird:** mockingbird. **Butterfly:** zebra longwing. **Fish:** sailfish (saltwater); largemouth bass (freshwater). **Flower:** orange blossom. **Gemstone:** moonstone. **Animal:** Florida panther. **Marine mammal:** manatee. **Saltwater mammal:** porpoise. **Reptile:** alligator. **Rock:** agatized coral. **Tree:** sabal palm.

## Natural features

**Land area:** 58,976 sq mi, 152,747 sq km. **Highest point:** Britton Hill 105 m (345 ft). **Largest lake:** Lake Okeechobee. **Major rivers:** Kissimmee, Suwannee, St. Johns, Caloosahatchee, Indian. **Natural regions:** Western Highlands, a region at the westernmost end of the panhandle; Marianna Lowlands, east of the Western Highlands; Tallahassee Hills, covering the northern border with Georgia; Central Highlands, extending down the middle two-thirds of the peninsula;

Coastal Lowlands, curving along the eastern, southern, and western coasts of the peninsula; the Everglades, far southern quarter of the peninsula. **Land use:** forest, 33.9%; agricultural, 7.7%; pasture, 7.2%; other, 51.2%.

## People

**Population** (2011): 19,057,542; persons per sq mi 323.1, persons per sq km 124.8. **Vital statistics** (2010; per 1,000 population): birth rate, 11.4; death rate, 9.2; marriage rate, 7.3; divorce rate, 4.4. **Major cities** (2010): Jacksonville 821,784; Miami 399,457; Tampa 335,709; St. Petersburg 244,769; Orlando 238,300; Hialeah 224,669; **Tallahassee 181,376;** Fort Lauderdale 165,521.

## Government

**Statehood:** entered the Union on 3 Mar 1845 as the 27th state. **State constitution:** adopted 1968. **Representation in US Congress:** 2 senators; 27 representatives. **Electoral college:** 29 votes. **Political divisions:** 67 counties.

## Economy

**Employment** (2008): services 37.3%; finance, insurance, real estate 18.8%; trade 14.8%; government 11.6%; construction 6.8%. **Production** (2010): finance, insurance, real estate 32.4%; services 21.3%; trade 13.6%; government 12.7%; transportation, public utilities 9.4%. **Chief agricultural products:** *Crops:* citrus fruit, cotton, peanuts (groundnuts), soybeans, sugarcane, tobacco, honey, dairy products, eggs, nursery plants and flowers. *Livestock:* cattle and calves, poultry, hogs and pigs. *Fish catch:* catfish, crab, shrimp, oysters. **Chief manufactured products:** food products; soft drinks; wearing apparel; paper products; pesticides and fertilizers; agricultural chemicals; plastic products; construction materials; fabricated metal products; machinery and apparatus; telecommunications equipment; semiconductors; electronics; aerospace products; airplane engines; ships and boats; medical and surgical equipment.

**Internet resources:** <www.visitflorida.com>; <www.myflorida.com>.

# Georgia

**Name:** Georgia, named for George II, king of England at the time the colony of Georgia was founded. **Nicknames:** Empire State of the South; Peach State. **Capital:** Atlanta. **Rank:** population: 9th; area: 24th. **Mottoes:** "Wisdom, justice, and moderation"; "Agriculture and commerce, 1776." **Song:** "Georgia on My Mind," words by Stuart Gorrell and music by Hoagy Carmichael. **Bird:** brown thrasher. **Fish:** largemouth bass. **Flower:** Cherokee rose. **Fossil:** shark tooth. **Gemstone:** quartz. **Insect:** honeybee. **Marine mammal:** right whale. **Mineral:** staurolite. **Reptile:** gopher tortoise. **Tree:** live oak.

## Natural features

**Land area:** 58,921 sq mi, 152,605 sq km. **Mountain range:** Blue Ridge. **Highest point:** Brasstown Bald, 1,458 m (4,784 ft). **Largest lake:** Lanier. **Major**

**rivers:** Chattahoochee, Flint, Apalachicola, Ocmulgee, Oconee. **Natural regions:** Blue Ridge Province, north-central edge; Valley and Ridge Province, northwest corner; Piedmont Province, northern half of state; Coastal Plain, southern half of state, divided into the Sea Island Section (southeast) and the East Gulf Coastal Plain (southwest). **Land use:** forest, 58.0%; agricultural, 11.0%; other, 31.0%.

## People

**Population** (2011): 9,815,210; persons per sq mi 166.6, persons per sq km 64.3. **Vital statistics** (2010; per 1,000 population): birth rate, 13.8; death rate, 7.4; marriage rate, 7.3; divorce rate (2001), 3.8. **Major cities** (2010): **Atlanta 420,003;** Augusta 195,844; Columbus 189,885; Savannah 136,286; Athens 115,452.

## Government

**Statehood:** entered the Union on 2 Jan 1788 as the 4th state. **State constitution:** adopted 1982. **Representation in US Congress:** 2 senators; 14 representatives. **Electoral college:** 16 votes. **Political divisions:** 159 counties.

## Economy

**Employment** (2008): services 32.3%; finance, insurance, real estate 16.4%; government 14.5%; trade 14.5%; manufacturing 7.7%. **Production** (2010): finance, insurance, real estate 26.8%; services 17.1%; government 13.9%; trade 13.6%; transportation, public utilities 12.6%. **Chief agricultural products:** *Crops:* peanuts (groundnuts), pecans, cotton and cottonseed, tobacco, peaches, apples, blueberries, grapes, honey, dairy products. *Livestock:* poultry, pigs, cattle and calves. *Fish catch:* catfish, trout. **Chief manufactured products:** food products; soft drinks; textiles; wood products; paper products; chemical products; transportation equipment.

**Internet resources:** <www.exploregeorgia.org>; <http://georgia.gov>.

# Hawaii

**Name:** Hawaii, from the Polynesian Hawaiki, the name for the ancestral home of Polynesians. **Nickname:** Aloha State. **Capital:** Honolulu. **Rank:** population: 40th; area: 47th. **Motto:** "Ua mau ke ea o ka aina i ka pono" ("The life of the land is perpetuated in righteousness"). **Song:** "Hawai'i Pono'i" ("Our Hawaii"), words by King David Kalakaua and music by Henry Berger. **Bird:** nene, or Hawaiian goose. **Fish:** rectangular triggerfish. **Flower:** yellow hibiscus. **Gemstone:** black coral. **Marine mammal:** humpback whale. **Tree:** candlenut.

## Natural features

**Land area:** 6,468 sq mi, 16,752 sq km; the eight largest islands: *Hawaii:* 4,030 sq mi, 10,438 sq km; *Maui:* 728 sq mi, 1,886 sq km; *Oahu:* 597 sq mi, 1,546 sq km; *Kauai:* 552 sq mi, 1,430 sq km; *Molokai:* 261 sq mi, 676 sq km; *Lanai:* 140 sq mi,

*For details about state governments, see pages 608–613; for energy data, see pages 627–628.*

363 sq km; *Niihau:* 70 sq mi, 180 sq km; *Kahoolawe:* 45 sq mi, 117 sq km. **Mountain ranges:** Koolau, Waianae (both Oahu). **Highest point:** Mauna Kea (Hawaii), 4,205 m (13,796 ft). **Major rivers:** Wailuku (Hawaii); Waimea, Hanalei (Kauai). **Natural regions:** The eight major islands at the eastern end of the 1,500-mile-long chain of islands are, from west to east, Niihau, Kauai, Oahu, Molokai, Lanai, Kahoolawe, Maui, and Hawaii; each island contains regions of mountains, deeps, ridges, and wide beaches; active volcanoes are found on the island of Hawaii. **Land use:** forest, 28.9%; pasture, 23.4%; agricultural, 7.1%; other, 40.6%.

## People

**Population** (2011): Total, 1,374,810; persons per sq mi 212.6, persons per sq km 82.1. **Vital statistics** (2010; per 1,000 population): birth rate, 14.0; death rate, 7.1; marriage rate, 17.6; divorce rate (2001), 3.8. **Major cities** (2010): Honolulu 387,170; Pearl City 47,698; Hilo 43,263; Kailua 38,635; Waipahu 38,216.

## Government

**Statehood:** entered the Union on 21 Aug 1959 as the 50th state. **State constitution:** adopted 1950. **Representation in US Congress:** 2 senators; 2 representatives. **Electoral college:** 4 votes. **Political divisions:** 4 counties.

## Economy

**Employment** (2008): services 37.0%; government 20.7%; finance, insurance, real estate 14.4%; trade 12.8%; construction 5.8%. **Production** (2010): finance, insurance, real estate 28.8%; government 23.8%; services 21.5%; trade 9.7%; transportation, public utilities 8.5%. **Chief agricultural products:** *Crops:* pineapples, sugarcane, cut flowers, macadamia nuts, coffee, dairy products, eggs. *Livestock:* cattle and calves. *Fish catch:* fish, shellfish. **Chief manufactured products:** food products, including processed sugar, canned pineapple, and preserved fruits and vegetables; wearing apparel; textiles; printing and publishing.

**Internet resources:** <www.hawaiitourismauthority.org>; <www.ehawaii.gov>.

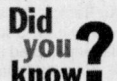

**Did you know?** Any island not named as part of a specific county in Hawaii is considered part of the city of Honolulu, making this the city with the longest borders in the entire world. Containing all of the islands in the Hawaiian and Pacific Islands National Wildlife Refuge, Honolulu officially stretches more than 1,300 miles.

# Idaho

**Name:** Idaho, from a Shoshone Indian phrase meaning "gem of the mountains." **Nickname:** Gem State. **Capital:** Boise. **Rank:** population: 39th; area: 14th. **Motto:** "Esto perpetua" ("It is forever"). **Song:** "Here We Have Idaho," words by McKinley Helm and Albert J. Tompkins and music by Sallie

Hume Douglas. **Bird:** mountain bluebird. **Fish:** cutthroat trout. **Flower:** syringa. **Fossil:** Hagerman horse fossil (*Equus simplicidens*). **Gemstone:** star garnet. **Horse:** Appaloosa. **Insect:** monarch butterfly. **Tree:** western white pine.

## Natural features

**Land area:** 83,569 sq mi, 216,443 sq km. **Mountain ranges:** Northern Rocky, Middle Rocky, Sawtooth, Pioneer, Continental Divide, Beaverhead, Clearwater, Bitterroot, Salmon River, Lost River, Lemhi. **Highest point:** Borah Peak, 3,859 m (12,662 ft). **Largest lake:** Lake Pend Oreille. **Major rivers:** Snake, Salmon. **Natural regions:** Northern Rocky Mountains, covering most of the northern half of the state; Columbia Plateau, extending across the south-central and southwestern regions; Great Basin region of the Basin and Range Province, southeast; Middle Rocky Mountains, extreme southeastern tip. **Land use:** pasture, 12.0%; agricultural, 10.2%; forest, 7.5%; other, 70.3%.

## People

**Population** (2011): 1,584,985; persons per sq mi 19.0, persons per sq km 7.3. **Vital statistics** (2010; per 1,000 population): birth rate, 14.8; death rate, 7.3; marriage rate, 8.8; divorce rate, 5.2. **Major cities** (2010): Boise 205,671; Nampa 81,557; Meridian 75,092; Idaho Falls 56,813; Pocatello 54,255.

## Government

**Statehood:** entered the Union on 3 Jul 1890 as the 43rd state. **State constitution:** adopted 1889. **Representation in US Congress:** 2 senators; 2 representatives. **Electoral college:** 4 votes. **Political divisions:** 44 counties.

## Economy

**Employment** (2008): services 29.5%; finance, insurance, real estate 15.8%; trade 14.9%; government 13.8%; construction 8.1%. **Production** (2010): finance, insurance, real estate 26.1%; services 17.0%; government 14.3%; trade 13.3%; manufacturing 10.8%. **Chief agricultural products:** *Crops:* potatoes, timber, sugar beets, alfalfa, Kentucky bluegrass seed, hops, onions, peas, honey, dairy products. *Livestock:* cattle and calves, sheep and lambs. *Fish catch:* trout. **Chief manufactured products:** food products; lumber and wood products; paper products; printing; chemical products; plastics and rubber products; cement, bricks, and ceramics; fabricated metal products; machinery and apparatus; computers and electronics.

**Internet resources:** <www.visitidaho.org>; <www.idaho.gov>.

# Illinois

**Name:** Illinois, from a Native American word meaning "tribe of superior men." **Nickname:** Prairie State. **Capital:** Springfield. **Rank:** population: 5th; area: 25th. **Motto:** "State sovereignty, national union." **Slogan:** Land of Lincoln. **Song:** "Illinois," words by Charles H. Chamberlain and music by Archibald

Johnston. **Bird:** cardinal. **Fish:** bluegill. **Flower:** violet. **Fossil:** Tully monster. **Insect:** monarch butterfly. **Mammal:** white-tailed deer. **Mineral:** fluorite. **Tree:** white oak.

## Natural features

**Land area:** 57,916 sq mi, 150,002 sq km. **Highest point:** Charles Mound, 376 m (1,235 ft). **Largest lake:** Carlyle Lake. **Major rivers:** Mississippi, Ohio, Wabash. **Natural regions:** Central Lowland, a region of sloping hills and broad, shallow river valleys covering almost the entire state; Ozark Plateaus, extreme southwest; Interior Low Plateaus and Coastal Plain, extreme southeastern tip. **Land use:** agricultural, 66.5%; forest, 11.0%; other, 22.5%.

## People

**Population** (2011): 12,869,257; persons per sq mi 222.2, persons per sq km 85.8. **Vital statistics** (2010; per 1,000 population): birth rate, 12.9; death rate, 7.8; marriage rate, 5.7; divorce rate, 2.6. **Major cities** (2010): Chicago 2,695,598; Aurora 197,899; Rockford 152,871; Joliet 147,433; Naperville 141,853; **Springfield 116,250.**

## Government

**Statehood:** entered the Union on 3 Dec 1818 as the 21st state. **State constitution:** adopted 1970. **Representation in US Congress:** 2 senators; 18 representatives. **Electoral college:** 20 votes. **Political divisions:** 102 counties.

## Economy

**Employment** (2008): services 33.6%; finance, insurance, real estate 18.7%; trade 14.1%; government 11.8%; manufacturing 8.9%. **Production** (2010): finance, insurance, real estate 34.5%; services 17.5%; manufacturing 12.9%; trade 11.8%; government 10.0%. **Chief agricultural products:** *Crops:* corn (maize), soybeans, wheat, oats, sorghum, apples, peaches, snap beans, sweet corn, potatoes, cabbage, dairy products, eggs. *Livestock:* pigs, cattle and calves, horses, poultry. **Chief manufactured products:** food products; beverages; textiles; leather goods; wearing apparel; wood products; paper products; printing; refined petroleum and coal products; asphalt; chemical products; plastics and rubber products; cement, bricks, and ceramics; base metals; fabricated metal products; machinery and apparatus; computers and electronics; transportation equipment.

**Internet resources:** <www.enjoyillinois.com>; <www2.illinois.gov>.

# Indiana

**Name:** Indiana, generally thought to mean "land of the Indians." **Nickname:** Hoosier State. **Capital:** Indianapolis. **Rank:** population: 15th; area: 38th. **Motto:** "The crossroads of America." **Song:** "On the Banks of the Wabash, Far Away," words and music by Paul Dresser. **Bird:** cardinal. **Flower:** peony. **Rock:** limestone. **Tree:** tulip tree (yellow poplar).

## Natural features

**Land area:** 36,417 sq mi, 94,320 sq km. **Highest point:** Hoosier Hill, 383 m (1,257 ft). **Largest lake:** Lake Monroe. **Major rivers:** Wabash, Ohio. **Natural regions:** Central Lowland comprises most of the state and includes the Eastern Lake Section to the north and the Till Plains in the center; Interior Low Plateaus, including the Highland Rim Section, cover the southern quarter of the state. **Land use:** agricultural, 57.5%; forest, 16.5%; other, 26.0%.

## People

**Population** (2011): 6,516,922; persons per sq mi 179.0, persons per sq km 69.1. **Vital statistics** (2010; per 1,000 population): birth rate, 12.9; death rate, 8.8; marriage rate, 6.3; divorce rate, N/A. **Major cities** (2010): **Indianapolis 820,445;** Fort Wayne 253,691; Evansville 117,429; South Bend 101,168; Hammond 80,830.

## Government

**Statehood:** entered the Union on 11 Dec 1816 as the 19th state. **State constitution:** adopted 1851. **Representation in US Congress:** 2 senators; 9 representatives. **Electoral college:** 11 votes. **Political divisions:** 92 counties.

## Economy

**Employment** (2008): services 32.3%; trade 14.4%; manufacturing 14.4%; finance, insurance, real estate 12.7%; government 12.3%. **Production** (2010): manufacturing 27.2%; finance, insurance, real estate 21.4%; services 17.2%; trade 11.1%; government 10.1%. **Chief agricultural products:** *Crops:* corn (maize), soybeans, wheat, popcorn, tobacco, peppermint, spearmint, blueberries, apples, eggs. *Livestock:* pigs, cattle and calves, poultry. **Chief manufactured products:** base metals; fabricated metal products; motor vehicle parts; machinery and apparatus; food products; dairy products; soft drinks; wood products; paper products; mobile homes.

**Internet resources:** <www.visitindiana.net>; <www.in.gov>.

# Iowa

**Name:** Iowa, named for the Iowa (or Ioway) Indians who once inhabited the area. **Nickname:** Hawkeye State. **Capital:** Des Moines. **Rank:** population: 30th; area: 26th. **Motto:** "Our liberties we prize and our rights we will maintain." **Song:** "The Song of Iowa," words by S.H.M. Byers, to the tune of "O Tannenbaum." **Bird:** eastern goldfinch. **Flower:** wild rose. **Rock:** geode. **Tree:** oak.

## Natural features

**Land area:** 56,273 sq mi, 145,746 sq km. **Highest point:** Hawkeye Point, 509 m (1,670 ft). **Largest lake:** Spirit Lake. **Major rivers:** Des Moines, Mississippi, Missouri, Big Sioux. **Natural regions:** overall, Central Lowland, including the Western Lake Section, north and central regions; Dissected Till Plains, south; Wisconsin

Driftless Section, northeast corner. **Land use:** agricultural, 70.8%; forest, 6.4%; other, 22.8%.

## People

**Population** (2011): 3,062,309; persons per sq mi 54.4, persons per sq km 21.0. **Vital statistics** (2010; per 1,000 population): birth rate, 12.7; death rate, 9.1; marriage rate, 6.9; divorce rate, 2.4. **Major cities** (2010): **Des Moines 203,433;** Cedar Rapids 126,326; Davenport 99,685; Sioux City 82,684; Waterloo 68,406.

## Government

**Statehood:** entered the Union on 28 Dec 1846 as the 29th state. **State constitution:** adopted 1857. **Representation in US Congress:** 2 senators; 4 representatives. **Electoral college:** 6 votes. **Political divisions:** 99 counties.

## Economy

**Employment** (2008): services 29.8%; trade 14.8%; finance, insurance, real estate 13.4%; government 13.2%; manufacturing 11.6%. **Production** (2010): finance, insurance, real estate 27.5%; manufacturing 17.8%; services 14.8%; government 11.5%; trade 11.4%. **Chief agricultural products:** *Crops:* corn (maize), soybeans, oats, milk, eggs, butter, honey, popcorn, sorghum. *Livestock:* poultry, hogs and pigs, beef cattle, sheep and lambs. **Chief manufactured products:** food products; dairy products; pesticides, fertilizers, and other agricultural chemicals; farm machinery; construction machinery; motor vehicle parts.

**Internet resources:** <www.traveliowa.com>; <www.iowa.gov>.

---

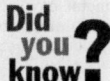

**Did you know?** The geodetic center of North America, the center point from which all maps of the continent base their coordinates and borders, was located in 1901 on Meade's Ranch in north-central Kansas. Some 40 miles north, near the town of Lebanon KS, lies the geographic center of the 48 coterminous US states.

## Kansas

**Name:** Kansas, from the Sioux word *kansa* ("people of the south wind") for the Native Americans who lived in the region. **Nickname:** Sunflower State. **Capital:** Topeka. **Rank:** population: 33rd; area: 15th. **Motto:** "Ad astra per aspera" ("To the stars through difficulties"). **Song:** "Home on the Range," words by Brewster Higley and music by Dan Kelly. **Amphibian:** barred tiger salamander. **Bird:** western meadowlark. **Flower:** wild native sunflower. **Insect:** honeybee. **Mammal:** American buffalo. **Reptile:** ornate box turtle. **Tree:** cottonwood.

## Natural features

**Land area:** 82,278 sq mi, 213,099 sq km. **Highest point:** Mt. Sunflower, 1,231 m (4,039 ft). **Largest lake:** Milford Lake. **Major rivers:** Kansas, Arkansas,

Big Blue, Republican, Solomon. **Natural regions:** the Great Plains Province, covering the western half of the state, consists of the High Plains to the west and the Plains Border to the east; the Central Lowland covers the eastern half of the state and consists of the Dissected Till Plains to the north and the Osage Plains to the south. **Land use:** agricultural, 50.3%; pasture, 30.1%; forest, 2.9%; other, 16.7%.

## People

**Population** (2011): 2,871,238; persons per sq mi 34.9, persons per sq km 13.5. **Vital statistics** (2010; per 1,000 population): birth rate, 14.2; death rate, 8.6; marriage rate, 6.4; divorce rate, 3.7. **Major cities** (2010): Wichita 382,368; Overland Park 173,372; Kansas City 145,786; **Topeka 127,473;** Olathe 125,872.

## Government

**Statehood:** entered the Union on 29 Jan 1861 as the 34th state. **State constitution:** adopted 1859. **Representation in US Congress:** 2 senators; 4 representatives. **Electoral college:** 6 votes. **Political divisions:** 105 counties.

## Economy

**Employment** (2008): services 29.4%; government 15.9%; finance, insurance, real estate 14.0%; trade 13.8%; manufacturing 10.3%. **Production** (2010): finance, insurance, real estate 23.1%; services 16.3%; government 15.3%; manufacturing 13.7%; trade 12.8%. **Chief agricultural products:** *Crops:* wheat, corn (maize), sorghum, soybeans, sunflower seed and oil, apples, peaches, pecans. *Livestock:* beef cattle, dairy cattle, hogs, sheep and lambs, horses and other equines. **Chief manufactured products:** food products; printing; refined petroleum products; soap and cleaning products; plastic products; aerospace products and parts; aircraft.

**Internet resources:** <www.travelks.com>; <www.kansas.gov>.

# Kentucky

**Name:** Kentucky, possibly from the Iroquois Indian word for "prairie." **Nickname:** Bluegrass State. **Capital:** Frankfort. **Rank:** population: 26th; area: 37th. **Motto:** "United we stand, divided we fall." **Song:** "My Old Kentucky Home," words and music by Stephen Foster. **Bird:** cardinal. **Butterfly:** viceroy butterfly. **Fish:** Kentucky bass. **Flower:** goldenrod. **Horse:** Thoroughbred. **Tree:** tulip poplar. **Wild animal:** gray squirrel.

## Natural features

**Land area:** 40,411 sq mi, 104,664 sq km. **Mountain ranges:** Cumberland, Pine. **Highest point:** Black Mountain, 1,263 m (4,145 ft). **Largest lake:** Kentucky Lake. **Major rivers:** Mississippi, Ohio, Big Sandy, Licking, Kentucky. **Natural regions:** Appalachian Plateau covers the eastern third of the state; Interior Low Plateaus, including the Highland Rim Section and the Lexington Plain, cover the remainder, with the exception of the Coastal Plain, which covers the extreme southwestern tip. **Land use:** forest, 40.6%; agricultural, 21.2%; other, 38.2%.

## People

**Population** (2011): 4,369,356; persons per sq mi 108.1, persons per sq km 41.7. **Vital statistics** (2010; per 1,000 population): birth rate, 12.9; death rate, 9.7; marriage rate, 7.4; divorce rate, 4.5. **Major cities** (2010): Louisville 597,337; Lexington 295,803; Bowling Green 58,067; Owensboro 57,265; Covington 40,640; **Frankfort 25,527.**

## Government

**Statehood:** entered the Union on 1 Jun 1792 as the 15th state. **State constitution:** adopted 1891. **Representation in US Congress:** 2 senators; 6 representatives. **Electoral college:** 8 votes. **Political divisions:** 120 counties.

## Economy

**Employment** (2008): services 30.3%; government 15.1%; trade 14.0%; finance, insurance, real estate 12.7%; manufacturing 10.4%. **Production** (2010): finance, insurance, real estate 20.4%; manufacturing 17.1%; services 17.0%; government 16.6%; trade 12.4%. **Chief agricultural products:** *Crops:* tobacco, soybeans, corn (maize), wheat, hay, sorghum, eggs, dairy products. *Livestock:* racing and show horses, beef cattle, dairy cattle, hogs, poultry, sheep and lambs. **Chief manufactured products:** food products; meatpacking; beverages; tobacco; wearing apparel; paper products; printing; chemical products; resin and synthetic rubber products; plastic products; iron and steel; aluminum; fabricated metal products; machinery; appliances; motor vehicles.

**Internet resources:** <www.kentuckytourism.com>; <http://kentucky.gov>.

# Louisiana

**Name:** Louisiana, named for Louis XIV, king of France. **Nickname:** Pelican State. **Capital:** Baton Rouge. **Rank:** population: 25th; area: 32nd. **Motto:** "Union, justice, and confidence." **Songs:** "Give Me Louisiana," words and music by Doralice Fontane; "You Are My Sunshine," words and music by Jimmy H. Davis and Charles Mitchell. **Amphibian:** green tree frog. **Bird:** brown pelican. **Crustacean:** crawfish. **Fish:** white perch (freshwater); spotted sea trout, or speckled trout (saltwater). **Flower:** magnolia. **Fossil:** petrified palmwood. **Gemstone:** agate. **Insect:** honeybee. **Mammal:** black bear. **Reptile:** alligator. **Tree:** bald cypress.

## Natural features

**Land area:** 47,632 sq mi, 123,366 sq km. **Highest point:** Driskill Mountain, 163 m (535 ft). **Largest lake:** Lake Pontchartrain. **Major rivers:** Mississippi, Red, Sabine. **Natural regions:** the entire state consists of the Coastal Plain and is divided into the West Gulf Coastal Plain to the west, the Mis-

sissippi Alluvial Plain to the northeast, and the East Gulf Coastal Plain in the southeast. **Land use:** forest, 42.5%; agricultural, 17.3%; pasture, 0.9%; other, 39.3%.

## People

**Population** (2011): 4,574,836; persons per sq mi 96.0, persons per sq km 37.1. **Vital statistics** (2010; per 1,000 population): birth rate, 13.8; death rate, 9.0; marriage rate, 6.9; divorce rate, N/A. **Major cities** (2010): New Orleans 343,829; **Baton Rouge 229,493;** Shreveport 199,311; Lafayette 120,623; Lake Charles 71,993.

## Government

**Statehood:** entered the Union on 30 Apr 1812 as the 18th state. **State constitution:** adopted 1974. **Representation in US Congress:** 2 senators; 6 representatives. **Electoral college:** 8 votes. **Political divisions:** 64 parishes.

## Economy

**Employment** (2008): services 33.0%; government 15.4%; finance, insurance, real estate 13.7%; trade 13.7%; construction 7.9%. **Production** (2010): finance, insurance, real estate 19.0%; manufacturing 18.1%; services 15.4%; mining 13.4%; government 10.9%. **Chief agricultural products:** *Crops:* soybeans, cotton, sorghum, sugarcane, rice, wheat, sweet potatoes, pecans, strawberries, peaches. *Livestock:* cattle and calves, chickens, hogs. *Fish catch:* catfish, crawfish, shrimp, oysters. **Chief manufactured products:** industrial chemicals; agricultural chemicals; plastics; refined petroleum products; cane sugar products; paper products; fabricated metal products; wood products; telecommunications equipment; ships, boats, and nautical equipment.

**Internet resources:** <www.louisianatravel.com>; <http://louisiana.gov>.

# Maine

**Name:** Maine, possibly named for the former French province of Maine, or used to distinguish the mainland portion of the territory from offshore islands. **Nickname:** Pine Tree State. **Capital:** Augusta. **Rank:** population: 41st; area: 39th. **Motto:** "Dirigo" ("I direct"). **Song:** "State of Maine Song," words and music by Roger Vinton Snow. **Bird:** chickadee. **Fish:** landlocked salmon. **Flower:** white pine cone and tassel. **Fossil:** *Pertica quadrifaria.* **Gemstone:** tourmaline. **Insect:** honeybee. **Mammal:** moose. **Tree:** white pine.

## Natural features

**Land area:** 33,123 sq mi, 85,788 sq km. **Mountain ranges:** Appalachian, Longfellow. **Highest point:** Mt. Katahdin, 1,606 m (5,268 ft). **Largest lake:** Moosehead Lake. **Major rivers:** Saco, Androscoggin, Kennebec, Penobscot, St. John's. **Natural regions:** entire state is part of the larger New England Province, subdivided into the White Moun-

*For details about state governments, see pages 608–613; for energy data, see pages 627–628.*

tain section (southwest), Seaboard Lowland Section (southeast coastline), and New England Upland Section (north and central regions). Land use: forest, 84.0%; agricultural, 1.8%; other 14.2%.

## People

Population (2011): 1,328,188; persons per sq mi 40.1, persons per sq km 15.5. Vital statistics (2010; per 1,000 population): birth rate, 9.8; death rate, 9.6; marriage rate, 7.1; divorce rate, 4.2. Major cities (2010): Portland 66,194; Lewiston 36,592; Bangor 33,039; South Portland 25,002; Auburn 23,055; Augusta 19,136.

## Government

Statehood: entered the Union on 15 Mar 1820 as the 23rd state. State constitution: adopted 1819. Representation in US Congress: 2 senators; 2 representatives. Electoral college: 4 votes. Political divisions: 16 counties.

## Economy

Employment (2008): services 34.6%; trade 15.4%; finance, insurance, real estate 13.8%; government 13.5%; manufacturing 7.6%. Production (2010): finance, insurance, real estate 27.3%; services 22.2%; government 14.3%; trade 13.1%; manufacturing 11.4%. Chief agricultural products: Crops: potatoes, blueberries, apples, cranberries, oats, honey, corn (maize), dairy products, eggs. Livestock: poultry, cattle and calves, sheep and lambs. Fish catch: salmon, rainbow trout, lobster, shrimp, crab, clams, haddock, cod, mackerel. Chief manufactured products: paper products; leather products; lumber and wood products; food products; semiconductors; wearing apparel; printing and publishing; plastic products; ships and boats.

Internet resources: <www.visitmaine.com>; <www.maine.gov>.

# Maryland

Name: Maryland, in honor of Henrietta Maria, queen of England at the time the colony of Maryland was founded. Nickname: Old Line State. Capital: Annapolis. Rank: population: 19th; area: 42nd. Motto: "Fatti maschii, parole femine" ("Manly deeds, womanly words"). Song: "Maryland, My Maryland," words by James Ryder Randall, to the tune of "O Tannenbaum." Bird: Baltimore oriole. Crustacean: Maryland blue crab. Dinosaur: Astrodon johnstoni. Fish: rockfish (striped bass). Flower: black-eyed Susan. Insect: Baltimore checkerspot. Reptile: diamondback terrapin. Tree: white oak.

## Natural features

Land area: 10,441 sq mi, 27,042 sq km. Mountain ranges: Allegheny, Appalachian. Highest point: Backbone Mountain, 1,024 m (3,360 ft). Largest lake: Deep Creek Lake. Major rivers: Potomac, Patuxent, Susquehanna. Natural regions: Coastal Plain, eastern half of the state, includes the Embayed Section near the southwest corner of the peninsula; Piedmont Province, central, includes the Piedmont Upland to the north and

the Piedmont Lowlands to the west; Blue Ridge Province, northwest; Valley and Ridge Province, part of western neck; Appalachian Plateau, extreme western neck. Land use: forest, 30.1%; agricultural, 19.3%; other, 50.6%.

## People

Population (2011): 5,828,289; persons per sq mi 558.2, persons per sq km 215.5. Vital statistics (2010; per 1,000 population): birth rate, 12.8; death rate, 7.5; marriage rate, 5.7; divorce rate, 2.8. Major cities (2010): Baltimore 620,961; Frederick 65,239; Rockville 61,209; Gaithersburg 59,933; Bowie 54,727; Annapolis 38,394.

## Government

Statehood: entered the Union on 28 Apr 1788 as the 7th state. State constitution: adopted 1867. Representation in US Congress: 2 senators; 8 representatives. Electoral college: 10 votes. Political divisions: 23 counties.

## Economy

Employment (2008): services 33.9%; finance, insurance, real estate 20.3%; government 15.9%; trade 13.2%; construction 7.2%. Production (2010): finance, insurance, real estate 35.0%; government 18.2%; services 18.2%; trade 10.0%; transportation, public utilities 8.0%. Chief agricultural products: Crops: corn (maize), soybeans, wheat, potatoes, tobacco, dairy products, eggs. Livestock: cattle and calves, pigs, poultry. Fish catch: hybrid striped bass, catfish, tilapia, trout, oysters, blue crab, other crustaceans, oysters, mollusks. Chief manufactured products: base metals; food products; transportation equipment, including motor vehicles and ships and boats; chemical products; plastics and rubber products; fabricated metal products; machinery and apparatus; computers and electronics.

Internet resources: <http://visitmaryland.org>; <www.maryland.gov>.

# Massachusetts

Name: Massachusetts, named for the Massachuset tribe of Native Americans who lived in the Great Blue Hill region south of Boston; the word massachuset means "near the great hill." Nickname: Bay State. Capital: Boston. Rank: population: 14th; area: 45th. Motto: "Ense petit placidam sub libertate quietem" ("By the sword we seek peace, but peace only under liberty"). Song: "All Hail to Massachusetts," words and music by Arthur J. Marsh. Bird: black-capped chickadee. Fish: cod. Flower: mayflower. Fossil: theropod dinosaur tracks. Gemstone: rhodonite. Insect: ladybug. Marine mammal: right whale. Mineral: babingtonite. Rock: Roxbury puddingstone. Tree: American elm.

## Natural features

Land area: 8,262 sq mi, 21,398 sq km. Mountain ranges: Berkshire Mountains, Hoosac Range, Taconic Range. Highest point: Mt. Greylock, 1,064 m (3,491 ft). Largest lake: Webster Lake. Major rivers: Connecticut, Charles, Merrimack, Housatonic,

Taunton. **Natural regions:** the New England Province, comprising most of the state, subdivided into the Taconic Section along the west, the New England Upland Section in the central region, and the Seaboard Lowland Section, covering the eastern third of the state; Coastal Plain, comprising the peninsula region. **Land use:** forest, 49.9%; agricultural, 4.7%; other, 45.4%.

## People

**Population** (2011): 6,587,536; persons per sq mi 797.3, persons per sq km 307.9. **Vital statistics** (2010; per 1,000 population): birth rate, 11.1; death rate, 8.0; marriage rate, 5.6; divorce rate, 2.5. **Major cities** (2010): **Boston 617,594;** Worcester 181,045; Springfield 153,060; Lowell 106,519; Cambridge 105,162.

## Government

**Statehood:** entered the Union on 6 Feb 1788 as the 6th state. **State constitution:** adopted 1780. **Representation in US Congress:** 2 senators; 9 representatives. **Electoral college:** 11 votes. **Political divisions:** 14 counties.

## Economy

**Employment** (2008): services 37.1%; finance, insurance, real estate 21.1%; trade 13.1%; government 10.6%; manufacturing 7.0%. **Production** (2010): finance, insurance, real estate 38.9%; services 21.5%; trade 9.6%; manufacturing 9.5%; government 9.0%. **Chief agricultural products:** *Crops:* tobacco, cranberries, potatoes, sweet corn, dairy products, eggs. *Livestock:* cattle and calves, poultry. *Fish catch:* lobster, crab, mollusks, oysters, quahogs, soft-shelled clams, scallops. **Chief manufactured products:** food products; dairy products; soft drinks; textiles; paper products; printing; pharmaceuticals; plastic products; cement, bricks, and ceramics; fabricated metal products.

**Internet resources:** <www.mass-vacation.com>; <www.mass.gov>.

# Michigan

**Name:** Michigan, from the Ojibwa Indian word *michi-gama,* meaning "large lake." **Nicknames:** Wolverine State; Great Lake State. **Capital:** Lansing. **Rank:** population: 8th; area: 11th. **Motto:** "Si quaeris peninsulam amoenam, circumspice" ("If you seek a pleasant peninsula, look around you"). **Song:** "Michigan, My Michigan," words by Giles Kavanagh and music by H.J. O'Reilly Clint. **Bird:** robin. **Fish:** brook trout. **Flower:** apple blossom. **Gemstone:** chlorastrolite. **Mammal:** white-tailed deer (game mammal). **Reptile:** painted turtle. **Rock:** Petoskey stone. **Tree:** white pine.

## Natural features

**Land area:** 96,713 sq mi, 250,486 sq km. **Highest point:** Mt. Arvon, 603 m (1,979 ft). **Largest lake:** Houghton Lake. **Major rivers:** Montreal, Brule, Menominee, St. Clair. **Natural regions:** the Central

Lowland, Eastern Lake Section, covers all of Lower Michigan and part of the Upper Peninsula region; the western half of the Upper Peninsula consists of Superior Upland, as do two small areas at the eastern end. **Land use:** forest, 44.7%; agricultural, 21.7%; other, 33.6%.

## People

**Population** (2011): 9,876,187; persons per sq mi 102.1, persons per sq km 39.4. **Vital statistics** (2010; per 1,000 population): birth rate, 11.6; death rate, 8.7; marriage rate, 5.5; divorce rate, 3.5. **Major cities** (2010): Detroit 713,777; Grand Rapids 188,040; Warren 134,056; Sterling Heights 129,699; **Lansing 114,297.**

## Government

**Statehood:** entered the Union on 26 Jan 1837 as the 26th state. **State constitution:** adopted 1963. **Representation in US Congress:** 2 senators; 14 representatives. **Electoral college:** 16 votes. **Political divisions:** 83 counties.

## Economy

**Employment** (2008): services 34.6%; finance, insurance, real estate 16.4%; trade 14.3%; government 12.3%; manufacturing 11.2%. **Production** (2010): finance, insurance, real estate 28.0%; services 18.5%; manufacturing 16.9%; trade 12.8%; government 12.2%. **Chief agricultural products:** *Crops:* apples, asparagus, blueberries, cherries, flowers, grapes and wine, honey, maple syrup, mint, plums. *Livestock:* beef cattle, dairy cattle, pigs, poultry, sheep and lambs. *Fish catch:* rainbow, brook, and brown trout, yellow perch, catfish. **Chief manufactured products:** motor vehicles; plastic products; pharmaceuticals; soaps; milled grain and dry cereals; agricultural machinery; furniture; dairy products; printing; electrical equipment.

**Internet resources:** <www.michigan.org>; <www.michigan.gov>.

# Minnesota

**Name:** Minnesota, from a Dakota Indian word meaning "sky-tinted water." **Nickname:** North Star State. **Capital:** St. Paul. **Rank:** population: 21st; area: 12th. **Motto:** "L'Étoile du nord" ("The star of the north"). **Song:** "Hail! Minnesota," first verse and music by Truman E. Rickard, second verse by Arthur E. Upson. **Bird:** common loon. **Fish:** walleye pike. **Flower:** pink and white lady slipper. **Gemstone:** Lake Superior agate. **Insect:** monarch butterfly. **Tree:** Norway pine.

## Natural features

**Land area:** 86,935 sq mi, 225,161 sq km. **Mountain ranges:** Mesabi, Vermillion, Cuyuna. **Highest point:** Eagle Mountain, 701 m (2,301 ft). **Largest lake:** Red Lake. **Major rivers:** Minnesota, St. Croix, Mississippi. **Natural regions:** Superior Upland, northeast corner; Central Lowland, covering most of the state; Western Lake Section, center; Dis-

*For details about state governments, see pages 608–613; for energy data, see pages 627–628.*

sected Till Plains, extreme southwest corner and south-central edge; Wisconsin Driftless Section, extreme southeast. **Land use:** agricultural, 39.1%; forest, 30.3%; other, 30.6%.

## People

**Population** (2011): 5,344,861; persons per sq mi 61.5, persons per sq km 23.7. **Vital statistics** (2010): per 1,000 population): birth rate, 12.9; death rate, 7.3; marriage rate, 5.3; divorce rate (2004), 2.8. **Major cities** (2010): Minneapolis 382,578; **St. Paul 285,068**; Rochester 106,769; Duluth 86,265; Bloomington 82,893.

## Government

**Statehood:** entered the Union on 11 May 1858 as the 32nd state. **State constitution:** adopted 1857. **Representation in US Congress:** 2 senators; 8 representatives. **Electoral college:** 10 votes. **Political divisions:** 87 counties.

## Economy

**Employment** (2008): services 32.8%; finance, insurance, real estate 17.7%; trade 14.4%; government 11.8%; manufacturing 9.8%. **Production** (2010): finance, insurance, real estate 32.4%; services 17.9%; manufacturing 13.2%; trade 12.0%; government 10.5%. **Chief agricultural products:** *Crops:* corn (maize), green peas, onions, apples, spring wheat, barley, potatoes, sugar beets, flaxseed, dairy products. *Livestock:* pigs, cattle and calves, poultry, sheep and lambs. **Chief manufactured products:** food products; malt beverages and other alcoholic products; dairy products; machinery and apparatus; computers and office machinery; electronics and electrical equipment; precision instruments; printing and publishing; information technology; lumber and wood products.

**Internet resources:** <www.exploreminnesota.com>; <www.state.mn.us>.

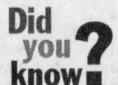

**Did you know?** The original name of Saint Paul, the capital of the state of Minnesota, was Pig's Eye Landing. Named after Pierre ("Pig's Eye") Parrant, a French-Canadian tavern owner who in 1838 made the first official land claim on the area, the community that was to become Minnesota's second largest city did not receive its current name until 1841.

# Mississippi

**Name:** Mississippi, from a Native American word meaning "great waters" or "father of waters." **Nickname:** Magnolia State. **Capital:** Jackson. **Rank:** population: 31st; area: 31st. **Motto:** "Virtute et armis" ("By valor and arms"). **Song:** "Go, Mississippi," words and music by Houston Davis. **Bird:** mockingbird. **Fish:** largemouth bass. **Flower:** magnolia. **Fossil:** prehistoric whale. **Insect:** honeybee. **Mammal:** white-tailed deer. **Marine mammal:** bottle-nosed dolphin (porpoise). **Rock:** petrified wood. **Tree:** magnolia tree.

## Natural features

**Land area:** 47,692 sq mi, 123,522 sq km. **Highest point:** Woodall Mountain, 246 m (806 ft). **Major rivers:** Mississippi, Pearl, Big Black, Yazoo, Tombigbee. **Natural regions:** the entire state consists of the Coastal Plain, subdivided into the Mississippi Alluvial Plain, in the west, and the East Gulf Coastal Plain, comprising the central and eastern regions. **Land use:** forest, 54.9%; agricultural, 16.3%; other, 28.8%.

## People

**Population** (2011): 2,978,512; persons per sq mi 62.5, persons per sq km 24.1. **Vital statistics** (2010): per 1,000 population): birth rate, 13.5; death rate, 9.8; marriage rate, 4.9; divorce rate, 4.3. **Major cities** (2010): **Jackson 173,514**; Gulfport 67,793; Southaven 48,982; Hattiesburg 45,989; Biloxi 44,054.

## Government

**Statehood:** entered the Union on 10 Dec 1817 as the 20th state. **State constitution:** adopted 1890. **Representation in US Congress:** 2 senators; 4 representatives. **Electoral college:** 6 votes. **Political divisions:** 82 counties.

## Economy

**Employment** (2008): services 30.1%; government 18.3%; trade 13.6%; finance, insurance, real estate 10.9%; manufacturing 10.6%. **Production** (2010): finance, insurance, real estate 18.6%; government 18.5%; services 17.3%; manufacturing 17.0%; trade 12.5%. **Chief agricultural products:** *Crops:* cotton, soybeans, rice, wheat, corn (maize), greenhouse and nursery plants, sweet potatoes, pecans. *Livestock:* cattle and calves. *Fish catch:* catfish, pearls, shrimp, oysters, crustaceans. **Chief manufactured products:** food products; transportation equipment; wearing apparel; textiles; electrical equipment; rubber products.

**Internet resources:** <www.visitmississippi.org>; <www.mississippi.gov>.

# Missouri

**Name:** Missouri, named for a Native American tribe that lived in the region; the name means "town of the large canoes." **Nickname:** Show Me State. **Capital:** Jefferson City. **Rank:** population: 18th; area: 20th. **Motto:** "Salus populi suprema lex esto" ("The welfare of the people shall be the supreme law"). **Song:** "Missouri Waltz," words by J.R. Shannon and music by John Valentine Eppel. **Aquatic animal:** paddlefish. **Bird:** bluebird. **Fish:** channel catfish. **Flower:** white hawthorn blossom. **Fossil:** crinoid. **Insect:** honeybee. **Mammal:** Missouri mule. **Mineral:** galena. **Rock:** mozarkite. **Tree:** flowering dogwood.

## Natural features

**Land area:** 69,703 sq mi, 180,530 sq km. **Mountain ranges:** Ozark Plateaus, St. Francois. **Highest point:** Taum Sauk Mountain, 540 m (1,772 ft). **Largest lake:** Truman Lake. **Major rivers:** Missouri, Mississippi, Des Plaines. **Natural regions:** Central Lowland, northwestern, subdivided into the Dissected Till Plains to the north and the Osage Plains to the west; Ozark Plateaus, including the Springfield-Salem Plateaus, southeast; Coastal Plain, including the Mississippi Alluvial Plain, extreme southeastern tip. **Land use:** agricultural, 30.7%; forest, 28.1%; pasture, 0.2%; other, 41.0%.

## People

**Population** (2011): 6,010,688; persons per sq mi 86.2, persons per sq km 33.3. **Vital statistics** (2010; per 1,000 population): birth rate, 12.8; death rate, 9.2; marriage rate, 6.5; divorce rate, 3.9. **Major cities** (2010): Kansas City 459,787; St. Louis 319,294; Springfield 159,498; Independence 116,830; Columbia 108,500; **Jefferson City 43,079.**

## Government

**Statehood:** entered the Union on 10 Aug 1821 as the 24th state. **State constitution:** adopted 1945. **Representation in US Congress:** 2 senators; 8 representatives. **Electoral college:** 10 votes. **Political divisions:** 114 counties.

## Economy

**Employment** (2008): services 32.3%; finance, insurance, real estate 16.2%; trade 14.3%; government 13.4%; manufacturing 8.2%. **Production** (2010): finance, insurance, real estate 26.2%; services 20.1%; government 13.0%; manufacturing 12.7%; trade 12.5%. **Chief agricultural products:** *Crops:* soybeans, corn (maize), cotton, rice, sorghum, wheat, dairy products. *Livestock:* cattle and calves, pigs, sheep and lambs, poultry. **Chief manufactured products:** industrial machinery; transportation equipment; food products; malt beverages and other alcoholic products; soft drinks; soaps and detergents; agricultural chemicals; pharmaceuticals; printing and publishing; base metals.

**Internet resources:** <www.visitmo.com>; <www.mo.gov>.

# Montana

**Name:** Montana, from the Spanish word *montaña* ("mountain," or "mountainous region"). **Nickname:** Treasure State. **Capital:** Helena. **Rank:** population: 44th; area: 4th. **Motto:** "Oro y plata" ("Gold and silver"). **Song:** "Montana," words by Charles C. Cohan and music by Joseph E. Howard. **Bird:** western meadowlark. **Fish:** cutthroat trout. **Flower:** bitterroot. **Fossil:** *Maiasaura.* **Gemstones:** agate; sapphire. **Mammal:** grizzly bear. **Tree:** ponderosa pine.

## Natural features

**Land area:** 147,039 sq mi, 380,829 sq km. **Mountain ranges:** Rocky, Grand Teton. **Highest point:** Granite Peak, 3,901 m (12,799 ft). **Largest lake:** Flathead Lake. **Major rivers:** Kootenai, Clark Fork, Flathead, Missouri, Yellowstone. **Natural regions:** Northern Rocky Mountains, western two-fifths of the state; Middle Rocky Mountains, small area along the south-central border; Missouri Plateau re-

gion of the Great Plains Province, eastern three-fifths of the state. **Land use:** pasture, 39.0%; agricultural, 15.4%; forest, 5.7%; other, 39.9%.

## People

**Population** (2011): 998,199; persons per sq mi 6.8, persons per sq km 2.6. **Vital statistics** (2010; per 1,000 population): birth rate, 12.2; death rate, 8.9; marriage rate, 7.4; divorce rate, 3.9. **Major cities** (2010): Billings 104,170; Missoula 66,788; Great Falls 58,505; Bozeman 37,280; Butte–Silver Bow 33,525; **Helena 28,190.**

## Government

**Statehood:** entered the Union on 8 Nov 1889 as the 41st state. **State constitution:** adopted 1972. **Representation in US Congress:** 2 senators; 1 representative. **Electoral college:** 3 votes. **Political divisions:** 56 counties.

## Economy

**Employment** (2008): services 32.7%; trade 14.6%; government 14.4%; finance, insurance, real estate 14.4%; construction 8.1%. **Production** (2010): finance, insurance, real estate 22.4%; services 20.0%; government 16.8%; trade 11.9%; transportation, public utilities 10.1%. **Chief agricultural products:** *Crops:* wheat, safflowers, sunflowers, mustard, sugar beets, grapes, garlic, potatoes, honey, cherries. *Livestock:* beef cattle, dairy cattle, sheep and lambs, poultry, horses, llamas. **Chief manufactured products:** food products; lumber and wood products; fabricated metal products; refined petroleum products; chemical products; cement, bricks, and ceramics; machinery and apparatus.

**Internet resources:** <www.visitmt.com>; <www.mt.gov>.

# Nebraska

**Name:** Nebraska, from the Oto Indian word *nebrathka*, meaning "flat water," a reference to the Platte River. **Nickname:** Cornhusker State. **Capital:** Lincoln. **Rank:** population: 38th; area: 16th. **Motto:** "Equality before the law." **Song:** "Beautiful Nebraska," words by Jim Fras and Guy Gage Miller and music by Jim Fras. **Bird:** western meadowlark. **Fish:** channel catfish. **Flower:** goldenrod. **Fossil:** mammoth. **Gemstone:** blue agate. **Insect:** honeybee. **Mammal:** white-tailed deer. **Rock:** prairie agate. **Tree:** cottonwood.

## Natural features

**Land area:** 77,349 sq mi, 200,333 sq km. **Highest point:** Panorama Point 1,653 m (5,424 ft). **Largest lake:** Lake McConaughy. **Major rivers:** Missouri, Platte, Elkhorn, Loup, Republican. **Natural regions:** Great Plains Province, western three-quarters of the state; Missouri Plateau, at the northern corners; High Plains, central and north central; Plains Border, southern border; Central Lowland, including the Dissected Till Plains, eastern quarter of the state. **Land use:** pasture, 46.6%; agricultural, 39.5%; forest, 1.6%; other, 12.3%.

*For details about state governments, see pages 608–613; for energy data, see pages 627–628.*

## People

**Population** (2011): 1,842,641; persons per sq mi 23.8, persons per sq km 9.2. **Vital statistics** (2010; per 1,000 population): birth rate, 14.2; death rate, 8.3; marriage rate, 6.6; divorce rate, 3.6. **Major cities** (2010): Omaha 408,958; **Lincoln 258,379**; Bellevue 50,137; Grand Island 48,520; Kearney 30,787.

## Government

**Statehood:** entered the Union on 1 Mar 1867 as the 37th state. **State constitution:** adopted 1875. **Representation in US Congress:** 2 senators; 3 representatives. **Electoral college:** 5 votes. **Political divisions:** 93 counties.

## Economy

**Employment** (2008): services 30.0%; finance, insurance, real estate 15.7%; trade 14.4%; government 13.8%; manufacturing 8.4%. **Production** (2010): finance, insurance, real estate 26.2%; services 15.3%; government 13.5%; manufacturing 12.1%; transportation, public utilities 11.6%. **Chief agricultural products:** *Crops:* corn (maize), soybeans, wheat, sorghum, dry beans, sugar beets. *Livestock:* beef cattle, dairy cattle, pigs, sheep and lambs, poultry. **Chief manufactured products:** food products, including canned and frozen fruits and vegetables, flour, cereal, grain products, and livestock feeds; beverages; dairy products; transportation equipment; printing and publishing; plastics and rubber goods; fabricated metal products; base metals.

**Internet resources:** <www.visitnebraska.gov>; <www.nebraska.gov>.

# Nevada

**Name:** Nevada, from the Spanish *nevada* ("snowclad"), a reference to the high mountain scenery of the Sierra Nevada on the southwestern border with California. **Nicknames:** Sagebrush State; Silver State. **Capital:** Carson City. **Rank:** population: 35th; area: 7th. **Motto:** "All for our country." **Song:** "Home Means Nevada," words and music by Bertha Raffeto. **Bird:** mountain bluebird. **Fish:** Lahontan cutthroat trout. **Flower:** sagebrush. **Fossil:** ichthyosaur. **Gemstones:** fire opal; turquoise. **Mammal:** desert bighorn sheep. **Metal:** silver. **Reptile:** desert tortoise. **Rock:** sandstone. **Trees:** single-leaf piñon; bristlecone pine.

## Natural features

**Land area:** 110,572 sq mi, 286,380 sq km. **Mountain ranges:** Snake, Schell Creek, Monitor, Toiyabe, Shoshone, Humboldt, Santa Rosa. **Highest point:** Boundary Peak, 4,006 m (13,143 ft). **Largest lakes:** Pyramid Lake (natural); Lake Mead (man-made). **Major rivers:** Humboldt, Truckee, Carson, Walker, Muddy. **Natural regions:** the Basin and Range Province covers all of the state, except for the southwestern corner, which consists of the Cascade-Sierra Mountains, and the northeastern corner, which comprises part of the Columbia Plateau. **Land use:** pasture, 11.7%; agricultural, 0.9%; forest, 0.4%; other, 87.0%.

## People

**Population** (2011): 2,723,322; persons per sq mi 24.6, persons per sq km 9.5. **Vital statistics** (2010; per 1,000 population): birth rate, 13.3; death rate, 7.3; marriage rate, 38.3; divorce rate, 5.9. **Major cities** (2010): Las Vegas 583,756; Henderson 257,729; Reno 225,221; North Las Vegas 216,961; Sparks 90,264; **Carson City 55,274.**

## Government

**Statehood:** entered the Union on 31 Oct 1864 as the 36th state. **State constitution:** adopted 1864. **Representation in US Congress:** 2 senators; 4 representatives. **Electoral college:** 6 votes. **Political divisions:** 16 counties; 1 independent city.

## Economy

**Employment** (2008): services 40.0%; finance, insurance, real estate 18.3%; trade 12.9%; government 10.6%; construction 8.5%. **Production** (2010): finance, insurance, real estate 31.4%; services 26.0%; government 11.1%; trade 10.1%; transportation, public utilities 7.6%. **Chief agricultural products:** *Crops:* wheat, corn (maize), potatoes, rye, alfalfa, barley, dairy products. *Livestock:* cattle and calves, horses, sheep and lambs, hogs, poultry. **Chief manufactured products:** food products, including candy and frozen desserts; dairy products; soft drinks; paper products; chemical products, notably pharmaceuticals; plastics; construction materials; machinery and apparatus, significantly agricultural equipment; printing and publishing.

**Internet resources:** <http://travelnevada.com>; <http://nv.gov>.

# New Hampshire

**Name:** New Hampshire, named for Hampshire, England, by Captain John Mason. **Nickname:** Granite State. **Capital:** Concord. **Rank:** population: 42nd; area: 44th. **Motto:** "Live free or die." **Songs:** "Old New Hampshire," words by John F. Holmes and music by Maurice Hoffmann; "New Hampshire, My New Hampshire," words by Julius Richelson and music by Walter P. Smith. **Amphibian:** red-spotted newt. **Bird:** purple finch. **Fish:** brook trout (freshwater); striped bass (saltwater). **Flower:** purple lilac. **Gemstone:** smoky quartz. **Insect:** ladybug. **Mammal:** white-tailed deer. **Mineral:** beryl. **Rock:** granite. **Tree:** white birch.

## Natural features

**Land area:** 9,280 sq mi, 24,035 sq km. **Mountain ranges:** White, Ossipee, Sandwich, Presidential. **Highest point:** Mt. Washington, 1,917 m (6,288 ft). **Largest lake:** Lake Winnipesaukee. **Major rivers:** Merrimack, Salmon Falls, Connecticut, Saco, Piscataqua. **Natural regions:** the New England Province covers the entire state and is subdivided into the White Mountain Section in the northern third, the New England Upland Section in the south-central region, and the Seaboard Lowland Section in the southeast corner. **Land use:** forest, 65.6%; agricultural, 2.1%; other, 32.3%.

## People

Population (2011): 1,318,194; persons per sq mi 142.0, persons per sq km 54.8. Vital statistics (2010; per 1,000 population): birth rate, 9.8; death rate, 7.7; marriage rate, 7.3; divorce rate, 3.8. Major cities (2010): Manchester 109,565; Nashua 86,494; Concord 42,695; Dover 29,987; Rochester 29,752.

## Government

Statehood: entered the Union on 21 Jun 1788 as the 9th state. State constitution: adopted 1784. Representation in US Congress: 2 senators; 2 representatives. Electoral college: 4 votes. Political divisions: 10 counties.

## Economy

Employment (2008): services 33.1%; trade 17.3%; finance, insurance, real estate 16.7%; government 11.2%; manufacturing 9.4%. Production (2010): finance, insurance, real estate 30.9%; services 21.7%; trade 13.5%; manufacturing 12.4%; government 10.6%. Chief agricultural products: Crops: apples, honey, ornamental horticulture, Christmas trees, dairy products, eggs, maple syrup. Livestock: horses, dairy cattle, sheep and lambs. Chief manufactured products: machinery and apparatus; computers and software; electrical equipment; semiconductors; food products; medical, surgical, and precision instruments; fabricated metal products; plastics and rubber products; printing and publishing; paper products.

Internet resources: <www.visitnh.gov>; <www.nh.gov>.

# New Jersey

Name: New Jersey, named for the island of Jersey in the English Channel. Nickname: Garden State. Capital: Trenton. Rank: population: 11th; area: 46th. Motto: "Liberty and prosperity." Bird: eastern goldfinch. Fish: brook trout. Flower: violet. Fossil: Hadrosaurus foulkii. Insect: honeybee. Mammal: horse. Tree: red oak.

## Natural features

Land area: 7,812 sq mi, 20,233 sq km. Mountain range: Appalachian. Highest point: Kittatinny Mountain, 550 m (1,803 ft). Largest lake: Lake Hopatcong. Major rivers: Delaware, Hudson, Passaic, Hackensack, Raritan. Natural regions: the Valley and Ridge Province, Middle Section, northwest corner; the New England Province, consisting of the New England Upland Section, east of the Valley and Ridge area; the Piedmont Province, including the Piedmont Lowlands, extending from the northeast corner to part of the border with Pennsylvania; the Coastal Plain, Embayed Section, southern half of the state. Land use: forest, 30.8%; agricultural, 10.1%; other, 59.1%.

## People

Population (2011): 8,821,155; persons per sq mi 1,129.2, persons per sq km 436.0. Vital statistics (2010; per 1,000 population): birth rate, 12.4; death rate, 7.9; marriage rate, 5.1; divorce rate, 3.0. Major cities (2010): Newark 277,140; Jersey City 247,597; Paterson 146,199; Elizabeth 124,969; Edison 99,967; Trenton 84,913.

## Government

Statehood: entered the Union on 18 Dec 1787 as the 3rd state. State constitution: adopted 1947. Representation in US Congress: 2 senators; 12 representatives. Electoral college: 14 votes. Political divisions: 21 counties.

## Economy

Employment (2008): services 32.3%; finance, insurance, real estate 21.8%; trade 15.3%; government 12.7%; transportation, public utilities 6.4%. Production (2010): finance, insurance, real estate 37.5%; services 17.0%; trade 13.3%; government 11.2%; transportation, public utilities 9.8%. Chief agricultural products: Crops: cranberries, blueberries, peaches, asparagus, bell peppers, spinach, sweet corn, escarole and endive, eggplants, nursery and greenhouse products. Livestock: horses, cattle, poultry. Fish catch: bluefish, tilefish, flounder, hake, shellfish. Chief manufactured products: chemical products, including pharmaceuticals; electronics and electrical equipment; telecommunications equipment; semiconductors; industrial equipment; refined petroleum products; fabricated metal products; cement, bricks, and ceramics; food products.

Internet resources: <www.visitnj.org>; <www.newjersey.gov>.

# New Mexico

Name: New Mexico, named for the country of Mexico. Nickname: Land of Enchantment. Capital: Santa Fe. Rank: population: 36th; area: 5th. Motto: "Crescit eundo" ("It grows as it goes"). Songs: "O, Fair New Mexico," words and music by Elizabeth Garrett; "Así es Nuevo Mexico," words and music by Amadeo Lucero. Bird: roadrunner. Fish: New Mexico cutthroat trout. Flower: yucca. Fossil: coelophysis. Gemstone: turquoise. Insect: tarantula hawk wasp. Tree: piñon pine.

## Natural features

Land area: 121,590 sq mi, 314,917 sq km. Mountain ranges: Rocky, Sangre de Cristo. Highest point: Wheeler Peak, 4,011 m (13,161 ft). Largest lake: Elephant Butte Reservoir. Major rivers: Rio Grande, Pecos, Canadian, San Juan, Gila. Natural regions: Great Plains Province, eastern third of the state, subdivided into the Raton Section to the north, the High Plains along the eastern edge, and the Pecos Valley to the west; Southern Rocky Mountains, north-central region; Colorado Plateau, northwest corner, including the Navajo Section and Datil Section; Basin and Range Province, central region and southwest corner, with the Sacramento Section to the east and the Mexican Highland to the south. Land use: pasture, 51.3%; forest, 7.0%; agricultural, 2.0%; other, 39.7%.

For details about state governments, see pages 608–613; for energy data, see pages 627–628.

## People

**Population** (2011): 2,082,224; persons per sq mi 17.1, persons per sq km 6.6. **Vital statistics** (2010; per 1,000 population): birth rate, 13.5; death rate, 7.7; marriage rate, 7.7; divorce rate, 4.0. **Major cities** (2010): Albuquerque 545,852; Las Cruces 97,618; Rio Rancho 87,521; **Santa Fe 67,947;** Roswell 48,366.

## Government

**Statehood:** entered the Union on 6 Jan 1912 as the 47th state. **State constitution:** adopted 1911. **Representation in US Congress:** 2 senators; 3 representatives. **Electoral college:** 5 votes. **Political divisions:** 33 counties.

## Economy

**Employment** (2008): services 31.9%; government 19.0%; finance, insurance, real estate 15.2%; trade 13.4%; construction 7.1%. **Production** (2010): finance, insurance, real estate 24.6%; government 19.9%; services 17.2%; trade 10.2%; mining 8.3%. **Chief agricultural products:** *Crops:* pecans, apples, potatoes, onions, chilies, peanuts (groundnuts), sorghum, corn (maize), wheat, eggs. *Livestock:* dairy cattle, beef cattle, poultry, sheep and lambs. **Chief manufactured products:** electronics; semiconductors; printing and publishing; food products.

**Internet resources:** <www.newmexico.org>; <www.newmexico.gov>.

# New York

**Name:** New York, named in honor of the English duke of York. **Nickname:** Empire State. **Capital:** Albany. **Rank:** population: 3rd; area: 28th. **Motto:** "Excelsior" ("Ever upward"). **Song:** "I Love New York," words and music by Steve Karmen. **Bird:** bluebird. **Fish:** brook trout. **Flower:** rose. **Fossil:** *Eurypterus remipes.* **Gemstone:** garnet. **Mammal:** beaver. **Tree:** sugar maple.

## Natural features

**Land area:** 53,095 sq mi, 137,515 sq km. **Mountain ranges:** Adirondack, Catskill, Shawangunk, Taconic. **Highest point:** Mt. Marcy, 1,629 m (5,344 ft). **Largest lake:** Oneida Lake. **Major rivers:** Hudson, Mohawk, Genesee, Oswego, Delaware. **Natural regions:** Central Lowland, Eastern Lake Section, extends along the northern coast of Lake Ontario; St. Lawrence Valley, Northern Section, extends along the northern border with Canada; Adirondack Province, northeast; Appalachian Plateau, including the Mohawks, Southern New York, and Catskill Sections, extends along the southern border with Pennsylvania and up halfway through the state; Valley and Ridge Province, southeastern edge bordering Connecticut and Massachusetts; Coastal Plain, Embayed Section, covers the islands of Manhattan and Long Island. **Land use:** forest, 56.1%; agricultural, 17.1%; other, 26.8%.

## People

**Population** (2011): 19,465,197; persons per sq mi 366.6, persons per sq km 141.5. **Vital statistics** (2010; per 1,000 population): birth rate, 12.5; death rate, 7.6; marriage rate, 6.5; divorce rate, 2.9. **Major**

**cities** (2010): New York 8,175,133; Buffalo 261,310; Rochester 210,565; Yonkers 195,976; Syracuse 145,170; **Albany 97,856.**

## Government

**Statehood:** entered the Union on 26 Jul 1788 as the 11th state. **State constitution:** adopted 1894. **Representation in US Congress:** 2 senators; 27 representatives. **Electoral college:** 29 votes. **Political divisions:** 62 counties.

## Economy

**Employment** (2008): services 35.8%; finance, insurance, real estate 21.2%; government 13.5%; trade 12.9%; transportation, public utilities 6.1%. **Production** (2010): finance, insurance, real estate 42.4%; services 17.8%; government 10.8%; transportation, public utilities 10.6%; trade 9.5%. **Chief agricultural products:** *Crops:* apples, cabbage, corn (maize), potatoes, onions, grapes, snap beans, cherries, strawberries, maple syrup, horticultural products, milk, other dairy products, eggs. *Livestock:* cattle and calves, chickens. **Chief manufactured products:** food products; chemical products; wearing apparel; base metals; machinery and apparatus; computers and software; scientific and measuring instruments; transportation equipment; electronics and electrical equipment; printing and publishing; biotechnology products.

**Internet resources:** <www.iloveny.com>; <www.ny.gov>.

# North Carolina

**Name:** North Carolina, named in honor of Charles I of England. **Nickname:** Old North State. **Capital:** Raleigh. **Rank:** population: 10th; area: 29th. **Motto:** "Esse quam videri" ("To be rather than to seem"). **Song:** "The Old North State," words by William Gaston, to the tune of a traditional German melody. **Bird:** cardinal. **Fish:** channel bass. **Flower:** dogwood. **Gemstone:** emerald. **Insect:** honeybee. **Mammal:** gray squirrel. **Reptile:** eastern box turtle. **Rock:** granite. **Tree:** pine.

## Natural features

**Land area:** 52,663 sq mi, 136,397 sq km. **Mountain ranges:** Appalachian, Great Smoky, Blue Ridge. **Highest point:** Mt. Mitchell, 2,037 m (6,684 ft). **Largest lake:** Lake Mattamuskeet. **Major rivers:** Roanoke, Yadkin, Pee Dee. **Natural regions:** Valley and Ridge Province, far western edge; Piedmont Province, consisting of the Piedmont Upland, extending in a southwest to northeast direction through the center of the state; Coastal Plain, eastern third, divided into the Sea Island Section to the south and the Embayed Section to the north. **Land use:** forest, 45.9%; agricultural, 16.4%; other, 37.7%.

## People

**Population** (2011): 9,656,401; persons per sq mi 183.4, persons per sq km 70.8. **Vital statistics** (2010; per 1,000 population): birth rate, 12.8; death rate, 8.3; marriage rate, 6.6; divorce rate, 3.8. **Major cities** (2010): Charlotte 731,424; **Raleigh 403,892;**

Greensboro 269,666; Winston-Salem 229,617; Durham 228,330; Fayetteville 200,564; Cary 135,234; Wilmington 106,476.

## Government

Statehood: entered the Union on 21 Nov 1789 as the 12th state. State constitution: adopted 1970. Representation in US Congress: 2 senators, 13 representatives. Electoral college: 15 votes. Political divisions: 100 counties.

## Economy

Employment (2008): services 31.9%; government 15.5%; finance, insurance, real estate 15.4%; trade 13.9%; manufacturing 9.8%. Production (2010): finance, insurance, real estate 28.9%; manufacturing 19.3%; services 15.4%; government 14.6%; trade 10.5%. Chief agricultural products: Crops: tobacco, peanuts (groundnuts), apples, blueberries, grapes, peaches, pecans, strawberries, sweet potatoes, Christmas trees. Livestock: cattle and calves, chickens, pigs, horses. Fish catch: catfish, trout. Chief manufactured products: textiles; cotton and synthetic fibers, yarns, and threads; cigarettes and tobacco products; chemical products; electronics and electrical equipment; furniture; lumber; paper products; food products.

Internet resources: <www.visitnc.com>; <www.ncgov.com>.

# North Dakota

Name: North Dakota, from the Dakota division of the Sioux, the Native American tribe that inhabited the plains before the arrival of Europeans; dakota may be the Sioux word· for "friend." Nickname: Peace Garden State. Capital: Bismarck. Rank: population: 48th; area: 18th. Motto: "Liberty and union now and forever, one and inseparable." Song: "North Dakota Hymn," words by James W. Foley and music by C.S. Putnam. Bird: western meadowlark. Fish: northern pike. Flower: wild prairie rose. Fossil: Teredo petrified wood. Tree: American elm.

## Natural features

Land area: 70,698 sq mi, 183,107 sq km. Highest point: White Butte, 1,069 m (3,506 ft). Largest lake: Devils Lake. Major rivers: Red, Souris, Missouri, Little Missouri, James. Natural regions: Central Lowland covers eastern half of the state, with the Western Lake Section lying in the east-central region; Great Plains Province covers western half of the state, including sections of the Missouri Plateau to the north and south. Land use: agricultural, 53.6%; pasture, 24.5%; forest, 1.0%; other, 20.9%.

## People

Population (2011): 683,932; persons per sq mi 9.7, persons per sq km 3.7. Vital statistics (2010; per 1,000 population): birth rate, 13.5; death rate, 8.8; marriage rate, 6.5; divorce rate, 3.1. Major cities (2010): Fargo 105,549; Bismarck 61,272; Grand Forks 52,838; Minot 40,888; West Fargo 25,830.

## Government

Statehood: entered the Union on 2 Nov 1889 as the 39th state. State constitution: adopted 1889. Representation in US Congress: 2 senators; 1 representative. Electoral college: 3 votes. Political divisions: 53 counties.

## Economy

Employment (2008): services 29.4%; government 16.3%; trade 15.2%; finance, insurance, real estate 12.9%; agriculture, forestry, fishing 7.2%. Production (2010): finance, insurance, real estate 21.6%; services 15.0%; government 13.7%; trade 13.7%; transportation, public utilities 10.0%. Chief agricultural products: Crops: spring wheat, durum wheat, flaxseed, canola, dry beans, sunflowers, barley, honey, potatoes, dairy products. Livestock: cattle and calves, sheep and lambs, pigs. Chief manufactured products: food products; wood products; refined petroleum products; transportation equipment; machinery and apparatus.

Internet resources: <www.ndtourism.com>; <www.nd.gov>.

Did you know■ A 12-foot-tall bronze statue of Sakakawea (Sacagawea), the Shoshone woman who traveled thousands of miles providing indispensable aid to the famous Lewis and Clark Expedition (1804–06), stands on the grounds of the North Dakota Heritage Center in Bismarck.

# Ohio

Name: Ohio, from an Iroquois Indian word meaning "great water." Nickname: Buckeye State. Capital: Columbus. Rank: population: 7th; area: 34th. Motto: "With God, all things are possible." Song: "Beautiful Ohio," words by Ballard MacDonald and music by Mary Earl. Bird: cardinal. Flower: red carnation. Fossil: Trilobite isotelus. Gemstone: flint. Insect: ladybug. Mammal: white-tailed deer. Reptile: black racer snake. Tree: Ohio buckeye.

## Natural features

Land area: 44,825 sq mi, 116,096 sq km. Highest point: Campbell Hill, 472 m (1,549 ft). Largest lake: Grand Lake St. Marys. Major rivers: Ohio, Maumee, Cuyahoga, Miami, Scioto. Natural regions: the Appalachian Plateau, eastern half of the state, includes the Southern New York Section to the north and the Kanawha Section to the east; the Central Lowlands, western half of the state, includes the Eastern Lake Section in the northwest corner, the Till Plains in the central region, and the Lexington Plain in the southwest. Land use: agricultural, 42.5%; forest, 27.3%; other, 30.2%.

## People

Population (2011): 11,544,951; persons per sq mi 257.6, persons per sq km 99.4. Vital statistics (2010; per 1,000 population): birth rate, 12.1; death rate, 9.4; marriage rate, 5.8; divorce rate, 3.4. **Major cities** (2010): **Columbus 787,033;** Cleveland 396,815; Cincinnati 296,943; Toledo 287,208; Akron 199,110; Dayton 141,527.

## Government

**Statehood:** entered the Union on 1 Mar 1803 as the 17th state. **State constitution:** adopted 1851. **Representation in US Congress:** 2 senators; 16 representatives. **Electoral college:** 18 votes. **Political divisions:** 88 counties.

## Economy

**Employment** (2008): services 33.7%; finance, insurance, real estate 15.8%; trade 14.4%; government 12.4%; manufacturing 11.2%. **Production** (2010): finance, insurance, real estate 28.7%; services 18.6%; manufacturing 16.7%; trade 12.4%; government 11.5%. **Chief agricultural products:** *Crops:* corn (maize), soybeans, grapes, apples, tobacco, winter wheat, dairy products, eggs, greenhouse and nursery products. *Livestock:* cattle and calves, hogs, poultry, goats. **Chief manufactured products:** machinery and apparatus; nonelectrical machinery; food products; transportation equipment; fabricated metal products; base metals; chemical products; rubber products.

**Internet resources:** <http://consumer.discoverohio.com>; <www.ohio.gov>.

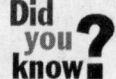

**Did you know?** Cambridge, Ohio's own John Glenn is famous for having been the first American astronaut to orbit Earth and later for serving four terms as a US senator from Ohio. Less known is the fact that in late 1998 Glenn returned to space on the space shuttle *Discovery,* at 77 becoming the oldest person ever to travel in space.

## Oklahoma

**Name:** Oklahoma, from two Choctaw Indian words: *okla,* meaning "people," and *humma,* meaning "red." **Nickname:** Sooner State. **Capital:** Oklahoma City. **Rank:** population: 28th; area: 19th. **Motto:** "Labor omnia vincit" ("Labor conquers all things"). **Song:** "Oklahoma," words by Oscar Hammerstein and music by Richard Rodgers. **Bird:** scissor-tailed flycatcher. **Fish:** white, or sand, bass. **Flower:** mistletoe. **Insect:** honeybee. **Mammal:** bison. **Reptile:** collared lizard (also known as the mountain boomer). **Rock:** rose rock. **Tree:** redbud.

### Natural features

**Land area:** 69,899 sq mi, 181,038 sq km. **Mountain ranges:** Ouachita, Arbuckle, Wichita, Sandstone Hills. **Highest point:** Black Mesa, 1,516 m (4,973 ft). **Largest lake:** Lake Eufaula. **Major rivers:** Arkansas, Red, Canadian. **Natural regions:** Great Plains Province, panhandle region, includes the High Plains to the west and the Plains Border to the east; Central Lowland, covering most of the state, includes the Osage Plains in the central region; West Gulf Coastal Plain, southeastern corner; Oua-

chita Province, east-central region, includes the Arkansas Valley in the center and the Ouachita Mountains to the south; Ozark Plateaus, northeast corner, include the Boston Mountains and Springfield-Salem Plateaus. **Land use:** pasture, 31.6%; agricultural, 20.1%; forest, 16.5%; other, 31.8%.

## People

**Population** (2011): 3,791,508; persons per sq mi 54.2, persons per sq km 20.9. **Vital statistics** (2010; per 1,000 population): birth rate, 14.2; death rate, 9.7; marriage rate, 7.2; divorce rate, 5.2. **Major cities** (2010): **Oklahoma City 579,999;** Tulsa 391,906; Norman 110,925; Broken Arrow 98,850; Lawton 96,867.

## Government

**Statehood:** entered the Union on 16 Nov 1907 as the 46th state. **State constitution:** adopted 1907. **Representation in US Congress:** 2 senators; 5 representatives. **Electoral college:** 7 votes. **Political divisions:** 77 counties.

## Economy

**Employment** (2008): services 30.2%; government 16.5%; finance, insurance, real estate 13.1%; trade 13.1%; manufacturing 7.2%. **Production** (2010): finance, insurance, real estate 20.2%; government 18.7%; services 15.8%; manufacturing 11.7%; trade 11.1%. **Chief agricultural products:** *Crops:* wheat, sorghum, soybeans, cotton, dairy products. *Livestock:* cattle and calves, poultry, hogs and pigs. **Chief manufactured products:** electronics and electrical equipment; telecommunications equipment; transportation equipment; food products; refined petroleum products.

**Internet resources:** <www.travelok.com>; <www.ok.gov>.

## Oregon

**Name:** Oregon, thought to be of Native American origin. **Nickname:** Beaver State. **Capital:** Salem. **Rank:** population: 27th; area: 10th. **Motto:** "Alis volat propiis" ("She flies with her own wings"). **Song:** "Oregon, My Oregon," words by J.A. Buchanan and music by Henry B. Murtagh. **Bird:** western meadowlark. **Fish:** chinook salmon. **Flower:** Oregon grape. **Gemstone:** Oregon sunstone. **Insect:** Oregon swallowtail. **Mammal:** beaver. **Rock:** thunder egg. **Tree:** Douglas fir.

### Natural features

**Land area:** 97,048 sq mi, 251,353 sq km. **Mountain ranges:** Coast, Klamath, Cascade, Blue, Wallowa. **Highest point:** Mt. Hood, 3,425 m (11,239 ft). **Largest lake:** Upper Klamath Lake. **Major rivers:** Snake, Owyhee, Columbia, Coquille. **Natural regions:** northern Rocky Mountains, northeastern corner, include the Blue Mountain Section; Columbia Plateau, north and north-central region, includes the Walla Walla Plateau in the central region, Harney Section to the south, and Payette Section to the southeast; Basin and Range Province, south-central border, includes the Great Basin; Cascade Sierra Mountains, west central region, include the Middle and Southern Cascades; Pacific

Border Province, western coast, includes the Klamath Mountains to the south, the Oregon Coast Range in the center and north, and the Puget Trough to the east. **Land use:** forest, 20.5%; pasture, 15.1%; agricultural, 6.0%; other, 58.4%.

## People

**Population** (2011): 3,871,859; persons per sq mi 39.9, persons per sq km 15.4. **Vital statistics** (2010; per 1,000 population): birth rate, 11.9; death rate, 8.3; marriage rate, 6.5; divorce rate, 4.0. **Major cities** (2010): Portland 583,776; Eugene 156,185; **Salem 154,637;** Gresham 105,594; Hillsboro 91,611.

## Government

**Statehood:** entered the Union on 14 Feb 1859 as the 33rd state. **State constitution:** adopted 1857. **Representation in US Congress:** 2 senators; 5 representatives. **Electoral college:** 7 votes. **Political divisions:** 36 counties.

## Economy

**Employment** (2008): services 32.7%; finance, insurance, real estate 15.9%; trade 14.4%; government 12.6%; manufacturing 9.0%. **Production** (2010): finance, insurance, real estate 25.2%; manufacturing 22.2%; services 16.4%; government 12.7%; trade 10.8%. **Chief agricultural products:** *Crops:* horticultural and nursery products, Christmas trees, pears, cherries, apples, hazelnuts, potatoes, mint, hops, sugar beets. *Livestock:* cattle and calves, horses, mink, poultry, sheep and lambs. *Fish catch:* tuna, salmon, shellfish, crab, shrimp. **Chief manufactured products:** lumber and wood products; food products; aircraft and spacecraft; semiconductors; computers.

Internet resources: <http://traveloregon.com>; <www.oregon.gov>.

# Pennsylvania

**Name:** Pennsylvania, named for Adm. Sir William Penn, father of the territory's founder, William Penn, and also including the Latin term *sylvania* ("woodlands"). **Nickname:** Keystone State. **Capital:** Harrisburg. **Rank:** population: 6th; area: 33rd. **Motto:** "Virtue, liberty, and independence." **Song:** "Pennsylvania," words and music by Eddie Khoury and Ronnie Bonner. **Bird:** ruffled grouse. **Fish:** brook trout. **Flower:** mountain laurel. **Fossil:** *Phacops rana.* **Insect:** firefly. **Mammal:** white-tailed deer. **Tree:** hemlock.

## Natural features

**Land area:** 46,055 sq mi, 119,282 sq km. **Mountain ranges:** Appalachian, Allegheny. **Highest point:** Mt. Davis, 979 m (3,213 ft). **Largest lake:** Raystown Lake. **Major rivers:** Delaware, Lehigh, Schuylkill, Susquehanna, Ohio. **Natural regions:** Central Lowland, Eastern Lake Section, extreme northwestern edge; Appalachian Plateau, including the Southern New York, Allegheny Mountain, and Kanawha sections, western

half of state; Valley and Ridge Province, central region, including portions of the Appalachian Mountains; Piedmont Province, comprising the Piedmont Lowlands and Upland, southeast corner; Coastal Plain, extreme southeast edge; New England Province, New England Upland Section, east-central border. **Land use:** forest, 53.9%; agricultural, 17.7%; other, 28.4%.

## People

**Population** (2011): 12,742,886; persons per sq mi 276.7, persons per sq km 106.8. **Vital statistics** (2010; per 1,000 population): birth rate, 11.2; death rate, 9.8; marriage rate, 5.3; divorce rate, 2.7. **Major cities** (2010): Philadelphia 1,526,006; Pittsburgh 305,704; Allentown 118,032; Erie 101,786; Reading 88,082; **Harrisburg 49,528.**

## Government

**Statehood:** entered the Union on 12 Dec 1787 as the 2nd state. **State constitution:** adopted 1968. **Representation in US Congress:** 2 senators, 18 representatives. **Electoral college:** 20 votes. **Political divisions:** 67 counties.

## Economy

**Employment** (2008): services 35.5%; finance, insurance, real estate 17.2%; trade 14.3%; government 11.0%; manufacturing 9.1%. **Production** (2010): finance, insurance, real estate 31.6%; services 20.3%; manufacturing 12.7%; trade 11.4%; government 10.3%. **Chief agricultural products:** *Crops:* mushrooms, apples, tobacco, grapes, peaches, cut flowers, dairy products. *Livestock:* cattle and calves, poultry, pigs, horses. **Chief manufactured products:** electronics; telecommunications equipment; semiconductors; chemical products; food products; base metals; machinery and apparatus; transportation equipment; paper products.

Internet resources: <www.visitpa.com>; <www.pa.gov>.

# Rhode Island

**Name:** Rhode Island, from the Greek island of Rhodes or the Dutch name *Roodt Eyland* ("Red Island"). **Nicknames:** Little Rhody; Ocean State. **Capital:** Providence. **Rank:** population: 43rd; area: 50th. **Motto:** "Hope." **Song:** "Rhode Island's It for Me," words by Charlie Hall and music by Maria Day. **Bird:** Rhode Island Red chicken. **Flower:** violet. **Mineral:** bowenite. **Rock:** cumberlandite.

## Natural features

**Land area:** 1,221 sq mi, 3,162 sq km. **Highest point:** Jerimoth Hill, 247 m (812 ft). **Largest lake:** Scituate Reservoir. **Major rivers:** Blackstone, Pawtuxet, Pawcatuck. **Natural regions:** the entire state is part of the New England Province, subdivided into the New England Upland (western two-thirds) and the Seaboard Lowland (eastern third). **Land use:** forest, 45.9%; agricultural, 2.5%; other, 51.6%.

*For details about state governments, see pages 608–613; for energy data, see pages 627–628.*

## People

**Population** (2011): 1,051,302; persons per sq mi 861.0, persons per sq km 332.5. **Vital statistics** (2010; per 1,000 population): birth rate, 10.6; death rate, 9.1; marriage rate, 5.8; divorce rate, 3.2. **Major cities** (2010): **Providence 178,042**; Warwick 82,672; Cranston 80,387; Pawtucket 71,148; East Providence 47,037.

## Government

**Statehood:** entered the Union on 29 May 1790 as the 13th state. **State constitution:** adopted 1986. **Representation in US Congress:** 2 senators; 2 representatives. **Electoral college:** 4 votes. **Political divisions:** 5 counties.

## Economy

**Employment** (2008): services 38.5%; finance, insurance, real estate 17.9%; trade 12.8%; government 12.2%; manufacturing 8.2%. **Production** (2010): finance, insurance, real estate 35.7%; services 21.4%; government 13.1%; trade 10.5%; manufacturing 8.0%. **Chief agricultural products:** *Crops:* apples, peaches, dairy products, eggs, potatoes. *Livestock:* poultry, cattle and calves, sheep and lambs. *Fish catch:* shellfish. **Chief manufactured products:** jewelry; silverware; textiles; fabricated metal products; electrical equipment; machinery and apparatus; surgical instruments; plastics.

**Internet resources:** <www.visitrhodeisland.com>; <www.ri.gov>.

# South Carolina

**Name:** South Carolina, named in honor of Charles I of England. **Nickname:** Palmetto State. **Capital:** Columbia. **Rank:** population: 24th; area: 40th. **Mottoes:** "Animis opibusque parati" ("Prepared in mind and resources"); *Dum Spiro Spero* (While I Breathe, I Hope). **Songs:** "Carolina," words by Henry Timrod and music by Anne Custis Burgess; "South Carolina on My Mind," words and music by Hank Martin and Buzz Arledge. **Amphibian:** spotted salamander. **Bird:** Carolina wren. **Fish:** striped bass. **Flower:** Carolina jessamine. **Gemstone:** amethyst. **Insect:** Carolina mantid. **Mammal:** white-tailed deer. **Reptile:** loggerhead turtle. **Rock:** blue granite. **Tree:** palmetto.

## Natural features

**Land area:** 31,114 sq mi, 80,585 sq km. **Mountain range:** Blue Ridge. **Highest point:** Sassafras Mountain, 1,085 m (3,560 ft). **Largest lake:** Lake Marion. **Major rivers:** Pee Dee, Savannah, Ashley, Combahee, Edisto. **Natural regions:** Coastal Plain covers the eastern two-thirds of the state and includes the Sea Island Section in the central region; Piedmont Province extends across the central and western region and includes the Piedmont Upland; Blue Ridge Province covers the far northwestern corner and includes the Southern Section. **Land use:** forest, 56.0%; agricultural, 11.9%; other, 32.1%.

## People

**Population** (2011): 4,679,230; persons per sq mi 150.4, persons per sq km 58.1. **Vital statistics**

(2010; per 1,000 population): birth rate, 12.6; death rate, 9.0; marriage rate, 7.4; divorce rate, 3.1. **Major cities** (2010): **Columbia 129,272**; Charleston 120,083; North Charleston 97,471; Mount Pleasant 67,843; Rock Hill 66,154.

## Government

**Statehood:** entered the Union on 23 May 1788 as the 8th state. **State constitution:** adopted 1895. **Representation in US Congress:** 2 senators; 7 representatives. **Electoral college:** 9 votes. **Political divisions:** 46 counties.

## Economy

**Employment** (2008): services 33.7%; government 15.6%; trade 14.1%; finance, insurance, real estate 14.0%; manufacturing 9.7%. **Production** (2010): finance, insurance, real estate 22.4%; services 18.1%; government 17.4%; manufacturing 16.4%; trade 12.9%. **Chief agricultural products:** *Crops:* tobacco, cotton, barley, peanuts (groundnuts), peaches, apples, pecans, sweet potatoes, snap beans, dairy products. *Livestock:* cattle and calves, chickens, pigs. *Fish catch:* marine fish, oysters, clams, shrimp. **Chief manufactured products:** chemical products, including pharmaceuticals and fertilizers; textiles; wearing apparel; machinery and apparatus; plastics and rubber products; paper and paperboard; electronics and electrical equipment; transportation equipment; lumber.

**Internet resources:** <www.discoversouthcarolina.com>; <www.sc.gov>.

# South Dakota

**Name:** South Dakota, from the Dakota division of the Sioux, the Native American tribe that inhabited the plains before the arrival of Europeans; *dakota* may be the Sioux word for "friend." **Nickname:** Mount Rushmore State. **Capital:** Pierre. **Rank:** population: 46th; area: 17th. **Motto:** "Under God the people rule." **Song:** "Hail! South Dakota," words and music by Deecort Hammitt. **Bird:** Chinese ring-necked pheasant. **Fish:** walleye. **Flower:** pasque. **Fossil:** triceratops. **Gemstone:** Fairburn agate. **Insect:** honeybee. **Mammal:** coyote. **Mineral:** rose quartz. **Tree:** Black Hills spruce.

## Natural features

**Land area:** 77,116 sq mi, 199,730 sq km. **Mountain range:** Black Hills. **Highest point:** Harney Peak, 2,207 m (7,242 ft). **Largest lake:** Lake Thompson. **Major rivers:** Big Sioux, Vermillion, James, Grand, Moreau. **Natural regions:** the Central Lowland, eastern third of the state, includes the Dissected Till Plains along the eastern edge and the Western Lake Section at the center; the Great Plains Province, western two-thirds of the state; the Black Hills, far west; the High Plains, southern border; the Missouri Plateau, west. **Land use:** pasture, 44.7%; agricultural, 34.6%; forest, 1.0%; other, 19.7%.

## People

**Population** (2011): 824,082; persons per sq mi 10.7, persons per sq km 4.1. **Vital statistics** (2010; per 1,000 population): birth rate, 14.5; death rate, 8.7; marriage rate, 7.3; divorce rate, 3.4. **Major cities**

(2010): Sioux Falls 153,888; Rapid City 67,956; Aberdeen 26,091; Brookings 22,056; Watertown 21,482; **Pierre 13,646.**

## Government

**Statehood:** entered the Union on 2 Nov 1889 as the 40th state. **State constitution:** adopted 1889. **Representation in US Congress:** 2 senators; 1 representative. **Electoral college:** 3 votes. **Political divisions:** 66 counties.

## Economy

**Employment** (2008): services 30.6%; trade 15.1%; government 14.4%; finance, insurance, real estate 14.2%; manufacturing 7.9%. **Production** (2010): finance, insurance, real estate 31.7%; services 16.3%; trade 12.5%; government 12.3%; manufacturing 8.9%. **Chief agricultural products:** Crops: corn (maize), wheat, sunflowers, dairy products, eggs, flaxseed, barley, rye. Livestock: cattle and calves, pigs, sheep and lambs. **Chief manufactured products:** machinery and apparatus; office machinery; computers; food products; electronics; printing and publishing; lumber; fabricated metal products; medical instruments; jewelry.

**Internet resources:** <www.travelsd.com>; <http://.sd. gov>.

 **Did you know?** The state of Tennessee was once called Franklin. Settlers from the east moved into the area in 1768, and by 1777 the territory had become Washington County, a part of North Carolina. In 1784 some of the settlers declared themselves independent of North Carolina and formed the State of Franklin, adopting their own constitution.

# Tennessee

**Name:** Tennessee, from Tanasi, a Cherokee Indian village. **Nickname:** Volunteer State. **Capital:** Nashville. **Rank:** population: 17th; area: 35th. **Motto:** "Agriculture and commerce." **Songs:** "My Homeland, Tennessee," words by Nell Grayson Taylor and music by Roy Lamont Smith; "When It's Iris Time in Tennessee," words and music by Willa Mae Waid; "The Tennessee Waltz," words and music by Redd Stewart and Pee Wee King; "Rocky Top," words and music by Boudleaux and Felice Bryant; "The Pride of Tennessee," words and music by Fred Congdon, Thomas Vaughn, and Carol Elliot. **Amphibian:** cave salamander. **Bird:** mockingbird. **Fish:** largemouth bass; channel catfish. **Flower:** iris. **Gemstone:** river pearl. **Insects:** firefly; ladybug. **Mammal:** raccoon. **Reptile:** box turtle. **Rocks:** limestone; agate. **Tree:** tulip poplar.

## Natural features

**Land area:** 42,145 sq mi, 109,155 sq km. **Mountain ranges:** Unaka, Great Smoky. **Highest point:** Clingmans Dome, 2,025 m (6,643 ft). **Largest lake:** Reelfoot. **Major rivers:** Tennessee, Cumberland, Mississippi. **Natural regions:** Blue Ridge Province, eastern border; Valley and Ridge Province, extending from southwest to northeast; Appalachian Plateau, central,

running from south to north, includes the Cumberland Plateau Section in the center and the Cumberland Mountain Section at the northern end; Interior Low Plateaus, west central, includes the Nashville Basin and Highland Rim Section. **Land use:** forest, 44.3%; agricultural, 17.6%; other, 38.1%.

## People

**Population** (2011): 6,403,353; persons per sq mi 151.9, persons per sq km 58.7. **Vital statistics** (2010; per 1,000 population): birth rate, 12.5; death rate, 9.4; marriage rate, 8.8; divorce rate, 4.2. **Major cities** (2010): Memphis 646,889; **Nashville 601,222;** Knoxville 178,874; Chattanooga 167,674; Clarksville 132,929.

## Government

**Statehood:** entered the Union on 1 Jun 1796 as the 16th state. **State constitution:** adopted 1870. **Representation in US Congress:** 2 senators; 9 representatives. **Electoral college:** 11 votes. **Political divisions:** 95 counties.

## Economy

**Employment** (2008): services 33.3%; trade 14.8%; finance, insurance, real estate 14.1%; government 12.1%; manufacturing 10.0%. **Production** (2010): finance, insurance, real estate 24.1%; services 22.1%; manufacturing 15.6%; trade 13.9%; government 12.1%. **Chief agricultural products:** Crops: cotton, tobacco, peaches, apples, tomatoes, snap beans, honey, dairy products, wheat, sorghum. Livestock: cattle and calves, poultry, hogs, sheep and lambs. **Fish catch:** catfish, trout. **Chief manufactured products:** transportation equipment, including motor vehicles, aircraft parts, and boats; chemical products; printing and publishing; electronics; lumber; paper products; wearing apparel; surgical instruments and supplies.

**Internet resources:** <www.tnvacation.com>; <www.tn. gov>.

# Texas

**Name:** Texas, from the Caddo Indian word thecas, meaning "allies" or "friends." **Nickname:** Lone Star State. **Capital:** Austin. **Rank:** population: 2nd; area: 2nd. **Motto:** "Friendship." **Song:** "Texas, Our Texas," words and music by William J. Marsh and Gladys Yoakum Wright. **Bird:** mockingbird. **Fish:** Guadalupe bass. **Flower:** bluebonnet. **Fossil:** pleurocoelus. **Gemstone:** Texas blue topaz. **Insect:** monarch butterfly. **Mammal:** Mexican free-tailed bat (flying); longhorn (large); armadillo (small). **Reptile:** horned lizard. **Rock:** petrified palmwood. **Tree:** pecan.

## Natural features

**Land area:** 266,833 sq mi, 691,094 sq km. **Mountain ranges:** Rocky, Guadalupe. **Highest point:** Guadalupe Peak, 2,667 m (8,749 ft). **Largest lake:** Caddo Lake. **Major rivers:** Red, Trinity, Brazos, Colorado, Rio Grande. **Natural regions:** Coastal Plain, southern and eastern regions, includes the West

*For details about state governments, see pages 608–613; for energy data, see pages 627–628.*

Gulf Coastal Plain near the east-central coast; Central Lowland, north central, includes the Osage Plains; Great Plains Province, extending from the panhandle across most of central and western Texas, includes the Edwards Plateau to the south, Pecos Valley to the west, High Plains to the north, and Central Texas Section; Basin and Range Province, extreme western region, comprises the Mexican Highland to the south and the Sacramento Section to the north. **Land use:** pasture, 56.2%; agricultural, 14.9%; forest, 6.2%; other, 22.7%.

## People

**Population** (2011): 25,674,681; persons per sq mi 96.2, persons per sq km 37.2. **Vital statistics** (2010; per 1,000 population): birth rate, 15.4; death rate, 6.6; marriage rate, 7.1; divorce rate, 3.3. **Major cities** (2010): Houston 2,099,451; San Antonio 1,327,407; Dallas 1,197,816; **Austin 790,390;** Fort Worth 741,206; El Paso 649,121; Arlington 365,438; Corpus Christi 305,215.

## Government

**Statehood:** entered the Union on 29 Dec 1845 as the 28th state. **State constitution:** adopted 1876. **Representation in US Congress:** 2 senators; 36 representatives. **Electoral college:** 38 votes. **Political divisions:** 254 counties.

## Economy

**Employment** (2008): services 31.0%; finance, insurance, real estate 16.6%; trade 14.2%; government 13.4%; construction 7.4%. **Production** (2010): finance, insurance, real estate 23.6%; services 15.3%; manufacturing 13.3%; trade 12.2%; government 11.8%. **Chief agricultural products:** *Crops:* cotton, apples, greenhouse and nursery products, corn (maize), sorghum, wheat, dairy products, eggs, rice. *Livestock:* cattle and calves, pigs, chickens. *Fish catch:* shrimp. **Chief manufactured products:** refined petroleum products; food products; computers; electronics; chemical products; plastics; wearing apparel; wood products; paper products; nonelectrical machinery; fabricated metal products; transportation equipment, including aerospace products and parts, aircraft parts, and motor vehicle parts.

**Internet resources:** <www.traveltex.com>; <www.texas.gov>.

# Utah

**Name:** Utah, named for the Ute Indian tribe; the word *ute* means "people of the mountains." **Nickname:** Beehive State. **Capital:** Salt Lake City. **Rank:** population: 34th; area: 13th. **Motto:** "Industry." **Song:** "Utah, This Is the Place," words by Sam and Gary Francis and music by Gary Francis. **Bird:** California seagull. **Fish:** Bonneville cutthroat trout. **Flower:** sego lily. **Fossil:** allosaurus. **Gemstone:** topaz. **Insect:** honeybee. **Mammal:** Rocky Mountain elk. **Mineral:** copper. **Rock:** coal. **Tree:** blue spruce.

## Natural features

**Land area:** 84,897 sq mi, 219,882 sq km. **Mountain ranges:** Uinta, Wasatch, Rocky. **Highest point:** Kings Peak, 4,123 m (13,528 ft). **Largest lake:** Great Salt Lake. **Major rivers:** Colorado, Green, Sevier. **Natural regions:** Basin and Range Province, western half of the state, includes the Great Salt Lake Desert and Bonneville Salt Flats to the north and the Great Basin to the south; Middle Rocky Mountains, northeast; Colorado Plateau, east-central and southeast regions, includes the Grand Canyon Section to the south, the High Plateaus of Utah and Canyon Lands in the center, the Navajo Section in the extreme southeast corner, and the Uinta Basin to the north. **Land use:** pasture, 19.6%; forest, 3.5%; agricultural, 3.1%; other, 73.8%.

## People

**Population** (2011): 2,817,222; persons per sq mi 33.2, persons per sq km 12.8. **Vital statistics** (2010; per 1,000 population): birth rate, 18.9; death rate, 5.3; marriage rate, 8.5; divorce rate, 3.7. **Major cities** (2010): **Salt Lake City 186,440;** West Valley City 129,480; Provo 112,488; West Jordan 103,712; Orem 88,328.

## Government

**Statehood:** entered the Union on 4 Jan 1896 as the 45th state. **State constitution:** adopted 1895. **Representation in US Congress:** 2 senators; 4 representatives. **Electoral college:** 6 votes. **Political divisions:** 29 counties.

## Economy

**Employment** (2008): services 29.1%; finance, insurance, real estate 20.0%; trade 14.2%; government 13.5%; manufacturing 7.9%. **Production** (2010): finance, insurance, real estate 29.4%; services 16.2%; government 14.0%; manufacturing 12.6%; trade 11.5%. **Chief agricultural products:** *Crops:* peaches, cherries, onions, dairy products. *Livestock:* cattle and calves, sheep and lambs, mink, poultry. *Fish catch:* trout. **Chief manufactured products:** machinery and apparatus; computers; office machinery; transportation equipment, including aerospace products, missile parts, and motor vehicle parts; surgical tools and electromedical equipment; food products.

**Internet resources:** <www.utah.com>; <www.utah.gov>.

# Vermont

**Name:** Vermont, from the French words *vert* and *mont,* meaning "green mountains." **Nickname:** Green Mountain State. **Capital:** Montpelier. **Rank:** population: 49th; area: 43rd. **Motto:** "Freedom and unity." **Song:** "These Green Mountains," words and music by Diane Martin. **Bird:** hermit thrush. **Flower:** red clover. **Insect:** honeybee. **Mammal:** Morgan horse. **Tree:** sugar maple.

## Natural features

**Land area:** 9,617 sq mi, 24,908 sq km. **Mountain ranges:** Green, Appalachian, Hoosac, Taconic. **Highest point:** Mt. Mansfield, 1,339 m (4,393 ft). **Largest lake:** Lake Champlain. **Major rivers:** Lamoille, Winooski, Otter Creek, Poultney, White. **Nat-**

ural regions: the New England Province, eastern two-thirds of the state, includes the Taconic Section to the south, the Green Mountain Section in the center, the New England Upland Section along the east-central edge, and the White Mountain Section in the far northeast corner; the St. Lawrence Valley, western edge of the state, includes the Champlain Section in the central portion; the Valley and Ridge Province, small section along the west-central edge, includes the Hudson Valley. **Land use:** forest, 67.1%; agricultural, 9.5%; other, 23.4%.

## People

**Population** (2011): 626,431; persons per sq mi 65.1, persons per sq km 25.1. **Vital statistics** (2010; per 1,000 population): birth rate, 9.9; death rate, 8.6; marriage rate, 9.3; divorce rate, 3.8. **Major cities** (2010): Burlington 42,417; South Burlington 17,904; Rutland 16,495; Essex Junction 9,271; Barre 9,052; **Montpelier 7,855.**

## Government

**Statehood:** entered the Union on 4 Mar 1791 as the 14th state. **State constitution:** adopted 1793. **Representation in US Congress:** 2 senators; 1 representative. **Electoral college:** 3 votes. **Political divisions:** 14 counties.

## Economy

**Employment** (2008): services 36.2%; trade 14.2%; government 13.1%; finance, insurance, real estate 12.9%; manufacturing 8.9%. **Production** (2010): finance, insurance, real estate 26.5%; services 22.7%; government 14.4%; trade 12.6%; manufacturing 11.1%. **Chief agricultural products:** *Crops:* apples, honey, greenhouse and nursery products, Christmas trees, maple syrup, dairy products, eggs. *Livestock:* cattle and calves, chickens, turkeys, sheep and lambs, horses. **Chief manufactured products:** electronics and electrical equipment; fabricated metal products; nonelectrical machinery; paper products; printing and publishing; food products; transportation equipment; lumber and wood products.

**Internet resources:** <www.travel-vermont.com>; <www.vermont.gov>.

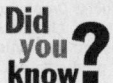

**Did you know?** Hampton Roads, Virginia, witnessed a battle on 9 Mar 1862 between USS *Monitor* and CSS *Virginia* (formerly USS *Merrimack*). The battle, which ended in a draw, featured the first combat between two iron-armored ships and ushered in the age of modern naval warfare.

# Virginia

**Name:** Virginia, named in honor of Elizabeth I of England, known as the Virgin Queen. **Nickname:** Old Dominion. **Capital:** Richmond. **Rank:** population: 12th; area: 36th. **Motto:** "Sic semper tyrannis" ("Thus ever to tyrants"). **Song:** "Carry Me Back to Old Virginia," words and music by James B. Bland. **Bird:** cardinal. **Fish:** brook trout. **Flower:** dogwood. **Fossil:** *Chesapecten jeffersonius.* **Insect:** tiger swallowtail butterfly. **Tree:** dogwood.

## Natural features

**Land area:** 40,599 sq mi, 105,151 sq km. **Mountain ranges:** Blue Ridge, Appalachian. **Highest point:** Mt. Rogers, 1,746 m (5,729 ft). **Largest lake:** Smith Mountain Lake. **Major rivers:** Potomac, Shenandoah, James, Roanoke. **Natural regions:** Coastal Plain, eastern region below the Potomac River; Piedmont Province, extending from the south-central border up to the border with Maryland, includes the Piedmont Upland and Piedmont Lowlands; Blue Ridge Province, west of the Piedmont Province; Valley and Ridge region, covering most of western Virginia, includes the Shenandoah Valley and Allegheny, Shenandoah, and Appalachian mountains; Appalachian Plateau, extreme western tip of the state, includes the Cumberland Mountain and Kanawha sections. **Land use:** forest, 48.7%; agricultural, 10.6%; other, 40.7%.

## People

**Population** (2011): 8,096,604; persons per sq mi 199.4, persons per sq km 77.0. **Vital statistics** (2010; per 1,000 population): birth rate, 12.9; death rate, 7.4; marriage rate, 6.8; divorce rate, 3.8. **Major cities** (2010): Virginia Beach 437,994; Norfolk 242,803; Chesapeake 222,209; **Richmond 204,214;** Newport News 180,719; Alexandria 139,966; Hampton 137,436.

## Government

**Statehood:** entered the Union on 26 Jun 1788 as the 10th state. **State constitution:** adopted 1970. **Representation in US Congress:** 2 senators; 11 representatives. **Electoral college:** 13 votes. **Political divisions:** 95 counties.

## Economy

**Employment** (2008): services 30.1%; finance, insurance, real estate 20.2%; government 17.7%; trade 12.9%; construction 6.7%. **Production** (2010): finance, insurance, real estate 35.8%; government 18.5%; services 14.8%; trade 9.0%; manufacturing 8.7%. **Chief agricultural products:** *Crops:* tobacco, soybeans, peanuts (groundnuts), cotton, apples, tomatoes, wheat, potatoes, honey. *Livestock:* chickens, turkeys, pigs, cattle and calves, sheep and lambs. *Fish catch:* clams, soft-shell and blue crabs, oysters, trout, catfish, hybrid striped bass. **Chief manufactured products:** electronics and electrical equipment; paper products; tobacco products; plastics and rubber products; chemical products; food products; printing and publishing.

**Internet resources:** <www.virginia.org>; <www.virginia.gov>.

# Washington

**Name:** Washington, named in honor of George Washington. **Nickname:** Evergreen State. **Capital:** Olympia. **Rank:** population: 13th; area: 21st. **Motto:** "Alki" ("By and by"). **Song:** "Washington My

*For details about state governments, see pages 608–613; for energy data, see pages 627–628.*

Home," words and music by Helen Davis. **Bird:** willow goldfinch. **Fish:** steelhead trout. **Flower:** coast rhododendron. **Fossil:** Columbian mammoth. **Gemstone:** petrified wood. **Insect:** green darner dragonfly. **Tree:** western hemlock.

## Natural features

**Land area:** 68,095 sq mi, 176,365 sq km. **Mountain ranges:** Olympic, Cascade, Blue. **Highest point:** Mt. Rainier, 4,392 m (14,410 ft). **Largest lake:** Moses Lake. **Major rivers:** Columbia, Pend Oreille, Snake, Yakima. **Natural regions:** Pacific Border Province, western quarter of the state, includes the Olympic Mountains to the west and the Puget Trough to the east; Cascade-Sierra Mountains, running north to south down center of state, include the Northern and Middle Cascades; Northern Rocky Mountains, northeast corner; Columbia Plateau, eastern, central, and southern regions, includes the Walla Walla Plateau in the center and the Blue Mountain Section in the southeast corner. **Land use:** forest, 28.9%; agricultural, 14.7%; pasture, 13.3%; other, 43.1%.

## People

**Population** (2011): 6,830,038; persons per sq mi 100.3, persons per sq km 38.7. **Vital statistics** (2010; per 1,000 population): birth rate, 12.9; death rate, 7.2; marriage rate, 6.0; divorce rate, 4.2. **Major cities** (2010): Seattle 608,660; Spokane 208,916; Tacoma 198,397; Vancouver 161,791; Bellevue 122,363; **Olympia 46,478.**

## Government

**Statehood:** entered the Union on 11 Nov 1889 as the 42nd state. **State constitution:** adopted 1889. **Representation in US Congress:** 2 senators; 10 representatives. **Electoral college:** 12 votes. **Political divisions:** 39 counties.

## Economy

**Employment** (2008): services 29.9%; finance, insurance, real estate 17.0%; government 15.6%; trade 13.8%; manufacturing 7.7%. **Production** (2010): finance, insurance, real estate 27.0%; services 15.9%; government 15.3%; transportation, public utilities 12.2%; trade 12.0%. **Chief agricultural products:** *Crops:* apples, peaches, pears, cherries, grapes, apricots, raspberries, asparagus, sweet corn, mint. *Livestock:* cattle and calves, chickens, turkeys, horses. *Fish catch:* oysters, clams, mussels, crab, shrimp, geoduck, sea cucumbers, salmon. **Chief manufactured products:** aerospace equipment; food products; forest products; advanced medical and technology products; aluminum products.

**Internet resources:** <www.experiencewa.com>; <http://access.wa.gov>.

# West Virginia

**Name:** West Virginia, named in honor of Elizabeth I of England, known as the Virgin Queen. **Nickname:** Mountain State. **Capital:** Charleston. **Rank:** population: 37th; area: 41st. **Motto:** "Montani semper liberi" ("Mountaineers are always free"). **Songs:** "This Is My West Virginia," words and music by Iris Bell; "West Virginia, My Home Sweet Home," words and music by Julian G. Hearne, Jr.; "The West Virginia Hills," words by Ellen King and music by H.E. Engle. **Bird:** cardinal. **Fish:** brook trout. **Flower:** rhododendron. **Gemstone:** West Virginia fossil coral. **Insect:** monarch butterfly. **Mammal:** black bear. **Tree:** sugar maple.

## Natural features

**Land area:** 24,230 sq mi, 62,755 sq km. **Mountain ranges:** Appalachian, Allegheny. **Highest point:** Spruce Knob, 1,482 m (4,863 ft). **Largest lake:** Summersville Lake. **Major rivers:** Ohio, Big Sandy, Guyandotte, Great Kanawha, Little Kanawha. **Natural regions:** the Valley and Ridge Province, eastern edge of the state, includes portions of the Shenandoah Mountains; the remainder of the state consists of the Appalachian Plateau and includes the Kanawha Section to the south, and the Allegheny Mountains in the northeast. **Land use:** forest, 68.1%; agricultural, 5.3%; other, 26.6%.

## People

**Population** (2011): 1,855,364; persons per sq mi 76.6, persons per sq km 29.6. **Vital statistics** (2010; per 1,000 population): birth rate, 11.0; death rate, 11.5; marriage rate, 6.7; divorce rate, 5.1. **Major cities** (2010): **Charleston 51,400;** Huntington 49,138; Parkersburg 31,492; Morgantown 29,660; Wheeling 28,486.

## Government

**Statehood:** entered the Union on 20 Jun 1863 as the 35th state. **State constitution:** adopted 1872. **Representation in US Congress:** 2 senators; 3 representatives. **Electoral college:** 5 votes. **Political divisions:** 55 counties.

## Economy

**Employment** (2008): services 33.1%; government 16.7%; trade 14.8%; finance, insurance, real estate 10.8%; manufacturing 6.3%. **Production** (2010): finance, insurance, real estate 18.8%; services 18.0%; government 17.6%; trade 11.5%; mining 11.1%. **Chief agricultural products:** *Crops:* apples, tobacco, peaches, dairy products. *Livestock:* cattle and calves, sheep and lambs, poultry. **Chief manufactured products:** chemical products; automobile parts; base metals; fabricated metal products; glassware; computer software; wood products; electrical equipment; machinery and apparatus.

**Internet resources:** <http://wvtourism.com>; <www.wv.gov>.

# Wisconsin

**Name:** Wisconsin, an anglicized version of a French rendering of the Algonquian Indian name *Meskousing,* said to mean "this stream of red stone." **Nickname:** Badger State. **Capital:** Madison. **Rank:** population: 20th; area: 22nd. **Motto:** "Forward." **Song:**

"On, Wisconsin," words and music by William T. Purdy. **Bird:** robin. **Fish:** muskellunge (muskie). **Flower:** wood violet. **Fossil:** trilobite. **Insect:** honeybee. **Mammal:** badger. **Mineral:** galena. **Rock:** red granite. **Tree:** sugar maple.

## Natural features

**Land area:** 65,496 sq mi, 169,634 sq km. **Mountain ranges:** Baraboo, Rib, Gogebic. **Highest point:** Timms Hill, 595 m (1,952 ft). **Largest lake:** Lake Winnebago. **Major rivers:** Wisconsin, St. Croix, Rock, Mississippi, Namekagon. **Natural regions:** Superior Upland, northern half of the state, divided into highland and lowland sections; Central Lowland, southern half of the state, divided into the Wisconsin Driftless Section to the west and the Eastern Lake Section to the east, with a section of the Till Plains occupying a small area at the southern border. **Land use:** forest, 40.4%; agricultural, 28.7%; other, 30.9%.

## People

**Population** (2011): 5,711,767; persons per sq mi 87.2, persons per sq km 33.7. **Vital statistics** (2010; per 1,000 population): birth rate, 12.0; death rate, 8.3; marriage rate, 5.3; divorce rate, 3.0. **Major cities** (2010): Milwaukee 594,833; **Madison 233,209;** Green Bay 104,057; Kenosha 99,218; Racine 78,860.

## Government

**Statehood:** entered the Union on 29 May 1848 as the 30th state. **State constitution:** adopted 1848. **Representation in US Congress:** 2 senators; 8 representatives. **Electoral college:** 10 votes. **Political divisions:** 72 counties.

## Economy

**Employment** (2008): services 31.3%; trade 14.6%; finance, insurance, real estate 14.4%; manufacturing 14.1%; government 11.9%. **Production** (2010): finance, insurance, real estate 27.8%; manufacturing 19.0%; services 17.8%; trade 11.6%; government 11.0%. **Chief agricultural products:** *Crops:* dairy products, corn (maize), honey, maple syrup, potatoes, strawberries, cherries, cranberries, Christmas trees, mint oil. **Livestock:** cattle and calves, hogs, mink. **Fish catch:** bass, trout, pike. **Chief manufactured products:** food products; beer; machinery and apparatus; paper products; fabricated metal products; transportation equipment; household appliances.

**Internet resources:** <www.travelwisconsin.com>; <www.wisconsin.gov>.

# Wyoming

**Name:** Wyoming, from a Delaware Indian word meaning "land of vast plains." **Nicknames:** Equality State; Cowboy State. **Capital:** Cheyenne. **Rank:** population: 50th; area: 9th. **Motto:** "Equal rights." **Song:** "Wyoming," words by Charles E. Winter and music by George E. Knapp. **Bird:** meadowlark. **Fish:** cutthroat trout. **Flower:** Indian paintbrush. **Fossil:** *Knightia.* **Gemstone:** jade. **Mammal:** bison. **Reptile:** horned toad. **Tree:** plains cottonwood.

## Natural features

**Land area:** 97,812 sq mi, 253,332 sq km. **Mountain ranges:** Rocky, Big Horn, Grand Teton, Wind River, Continental Divide, Sierra Madre, Washakie. **Highest point:** Gannett Peak, 4,207 m (13,804 ft). **Largest lake:** Yellowstone Lake. **Major rivers:** Snake, Colorado, Green, Columbia. **Natural regions:** Great Plains Province, eastern third of the state, includes the Black Hills in the northeast corner, the High Plains in the southwest corner, and the Missouri Plateau in the center; Wyoming Basin, central and southern regions; Southern Rocky Mountains, southern border; Middle Rocky Mountains, northwest third of the state, also cover a small area on the southern border; Northern Rocky Mountains, extreme northwestern tip of the state. **Land use:** pasture, 44.0%; agricultural, 3.5%; forest, 1.5%; other, 51.0%.

## People

**Population** (2011): 568,158; persons per sq mi 5.8, persons per sq km 2.2. **Vital statistics** (2010; per 1,000 population): birth rate, 13.4; death rate, 7.9; marriage rate, 7.6; divorce rate, 5.1. **Major cities** (2010): **Cheyenne 59,466;** Casper 55,316; Laramie 30,816; Gillette 29,087; Rock Springs 23,036.

## Government

**Statehood:** entered the Union on 10 Jul 1890 as the 44th state. **State constitution:** adopted 1889. **Representation in US Congress:** 2 senators; 1 representative. **Electoral college:** 3 votes. **Political divisions:** 23 counties.

## Economy

**Employment** (2008): services 26.0%; government 17.8%; finance, insurance, real estate 13.1%; trade 12.8%; construction 9.5%. **Production** (2010): mining 31.4%; finance, insurance, real estate 13.8%; government 13.4%; services 10.6%; trade 9.0%. **Chief agricultural products:** *Crops:* wheat, barley, sugar beets, corn (maize). **Livestock:** cattle and calves, sheep and lambs. **Chief manufactured products:** refined petroleum products; lumber and wood products; food products; fabricated metal products.

**Internet resources:** <www.wyomingtourism.org>; <www.wyoming.gov>.

 **Did you know?** Yellowstone National Park, the oldest national park in the world and one of the largest, was established by Congress in 1872 and lies mostly within the boundaries of Wyoming. In Yellowstone is Steamboat Geyser. The largest geyser in the world, it erupts and shoots a million gallons of water up to 300 feet into the air.

*For details about state governments, see pages 608–613; for energy data, see pages 627–628.*

# State Government

## Governors of US States and Territories

*Governors of New Hampshire and Vermont serve two-year terms; all others serve four-year terms. Parties: Democratic (D); Republican (R); Independent (I); New Progressive (NP); Covenant (C). Sources: National Governors Association; Council of State Governments.*

| STATE | GOVERNOR | IN OFFICE SINCE | PRESENT TERM EXPIRES |
|---|---|---|---|
| Alabama | Robert Bentley (R) | January 2011 | January 2015* |
| Alaska | Sean R. Parnell (R)[1] | July 2009 | December 2014* |
| Arizona | Jan Brewer (R)[2] | January 2009 | January 2015 |
| Arkansas | Mike Beebe (D) | January 2007 | January 2015 |
| California | Edmund "Jerry" Brown (D) | January 2011 | January 2015* |
| Colorado | John Hickenlooper (D) | January 2011 | January 2015* |
| Connecticut | Dan Malloy (D) | January 2011 | January 2015* |
| Delaware | Jack Markell (D) | January 2009 | January 2013* |
| Florida | Rick Scott (R) | January 2011 | January 2015* |
| Georgia | Nathan Deal (R) | January 2011 | January 2015* |
| Hawaii | Neil Abercrombie (D) | December 2010 | December 2014* |
| Idaho | C.L. "Butch" Otter (R) | January 2007 | January 2015* |
| Illinois | Pat Quinn (D)[3] | January 2009 | January 2015* |
| Indiana | Mitch Daniels (R) | January 2005 | January 2013 |
| Iowa | Terry Branstad (R) | January 2011 | January 2015* |
| Kansas | Sam Brownback (R) | January 2011 | January 2015* |
| Kentucky | Steve Beshear (D) | December 2007 | December 2015 |
| Louisiana | Bobby Jindal (R) | January 2008 | January 2016 |
| Maine | Paul LePage (R) | January 2011 | January 2015* |
| Maryland | Martin O'Malley (D) | January 2007 | January 2015 |
| Massachusetts | Deval Patrick (D) | January 2007 | January 2015* |
| Michigan | Rick Snyder (R) | January 2011 | January 2015* |
| Minnesota | Mark Dayton (D) | January 2011 | January 2015* |
| Mississippi | Phil Bryant (R) | January 2012 | January 2016* |
| Missouri | Jay Nixon (D) | January 2009 | January 2013* |
| Montana | Brian Schweitzer (D) | January 2005 | January 2013 |
| Nebraska | Dave Heineman (R)[4] | January 2005 | January 2015 |
| Nevada | Brian Sandoval (R) | January 2011 | January 2015* |
| New Hampshire | John Lynch (D) | January 2005 | January 2015* |
| New Jersey | Christopher J. Christie (R) | January 2010 | January 2014* |
| New Mexico | Susana Martinez (R) | January 2011 | January 2015* |
| New York | Andrew Cuomo (D) | January 2011 | January 2015* |
| North Carolina | Beverly Perdue (D) | January 2009 | January 2013* |
| North Dakota | Jack Dalrymple (R)[5] | December 2010 | December 2012* |
| Ohio | John Kasich (R) | January 2011 | January 2015* |
| Oklahoma | Mary Fallin (R) | January 2011 | January 2015* |
| Oregon | John Kitzhaber (D) | January 2011 | January 2015* |
| Pennsylvania | Tom Corbett (R) | January 2011 | January 2015* |
| Rhode Island | Lincoln Chafee (I) | January 2011 | January 2015* |
| South Carolina | Nikki Haley (R) | January 2011 | January 2015* |
| South Dakota | Dennis Daugaard (R) | January 2011 | January 2015* |
| Tennessee | Bill Haslam (R) | January 2011 | January 2015* |
| Texas | Rick Perry (R)[6] | December 2000 | January 2015* |
| Utah | Gary Herbert (R)[7] | August 2009 | January 2013* |
| Vermont | Peter Shumlin (D) | January 2011 | January 2013* |
| Virginia | Robert McDonnell (R) | January 2010 | January 2014 |
| Washington | Chris Gregoire (D) | January 2005 | January 2013* |
| West Virginia | Earl Ray Tomblin (D)[8] | November 2010 | January 2013* |
| Wisconsin | Scott Walker (R) | January 2011 | January 2015* |
| Wyoming | Matt Mead (R) | January 2011 | January 2015* |

| TERRITORY | GOVERNOR | IN OFFICE SINCE | PRESENT TERM EXPIRES |
|---|---|---|---|
| American Samoa | Togiola T.A. Tulafono (D)[9] | April 2003 | January 2013 |
| Guam | Eddie Calvo (R) | January 2011 | January 2015* |
| Northern Mariana Islands | Benígno Fitial (C) | January 2006 | January 2015 |
| Puerto Rico | Luis G. Fortuño (R) (NP) | January 2009 | January 2013* |
| Virgin Islands | John deJongh, Jr. (D) | January 2007 | January 2015 |

*Present governor is eligible for reelection.*

## Governors of US States and Territories (continued)

[1]Lieut. Gov. Sean R. Parnell became governor on 26 Jul 2009 following Sarah Palin's resignation. [2]Secretary of State Jan Brewer became governor on 21 Jan 2009 following Janet Napolitano's appointment to the office of US secretary of homeland security. [3]Lieut. Gov. Patrick Quinn became governor on 29 Jan 2009 following Rod Blagojevich's removal from office. [4]Lieut. Gov. Dave Heineman became governor on 21 Jan 2005 following Mike Johanns's appointment to the office of US secretary of agriculture. Gov. Heineman was elected to a full term in November 2006. [5]Lt. Gov. Dalrymple became governor on 21 Dec 2010 following John Hoeven's election to the US Senate. [6]Lieut. Gov. Rick Perry became governor in December 2000 following George W. Bush's election as president of the United States. Gov. Perry was elected to a full term in November 2002. [7]Lieut. Gov. Gary Herbert became governor on 10 Aug 2009 following the appointment of Jon M. Huntsman, Jr., as ambassador to China. [8]Senate president Earl Ray Tomblin became governor on 15 Nov 2010 following Joe Machin III's election to the US Senate. [9]Lieut. Gov. Togiola T.A. Tulafono became governor in April 2003 following the death of Gov. Tauese Sunia. Gov. Tulafono was elected to a full term in November 2004.

## State Officers and Legislatures

Sources: The Book of the States, vol. 44; CSG State Directory. Legislature figures are as of February 2012.
* designates an office that is filled by an appointed officeholder, for whom no political affiliation is given.

| STATE/OFFICE | OFFICEHOLDER | PAY[1] |
|---|---|---|
| **Alabama** | | |
| Governor | Robert Bentley (R) | US$119,950 |
| Lieut. Gov. | Kay Ivey (R) | US$134,592 |
| Sec. of State | Beth Chapman (R) | US$85,248 |
| Atty. Gen. | Luther Strange (R) | US$160,002 |
| Treasurer | Young Boozer III (R) | US$85,248 |
| Legislature | | |
| Senate | Dem: 12; Rep: 22; Ind: 1 | |
| House | Dem: 40; Rep: 65 | |
| **Alaska** | | |
| Governor | Sean R. Parnell (R) | US$145,000 |
| Lieut. Gov. | Mead Treadwell (R) | US$115,000 |
| Sec. of State[2] | | |
| Atty. Gen.* | Michael Geraghty | US$135,000 |
| Treasurer*[3] | Jerry Burnett (Deputy Revenue Commissioner) | US$119,328 |
| Legislature | | |
| Senate | Dem: 10; Rep: 10 | |
| House | Dem: 16; Rep: 24 | |
| **Arizona** | | |
| Governor | Jan Brewer (R) | US$95,000 |
| Lieut. Gov.[4] | | |
| Sec. of State | Ken Bennett (R) | US$70,000 |
| Atty. Gen. | Tom Horne (R) | US$90,000 |
| Treasurer | Doug Ducey (R) | US$70,000 |
| Legislature | | |
| Senate | Dem: 9; Rep: 21 | |
| House | Dem: 20; Rep: 40 | |
| **Arkansas** | | |
| Governor | Mike Beebe (D) | US$86,890 |
| Lieut. Gov. | Mark Darr (R) | US$41,896 |
| Sec. of State | Mark Martin (R) | US$54,305 |
| Atty. Gen. | Dustin McDaniel (D) | US$72,408 |
| Treasurer | Martha A. Shoffner (D) | US$54,305 |
| General Assembly | | |
| Senate | Dem: 20; Rep: 15 | |
| House | Dem: 54; Rep: 46 | |
| **California** | | |
| Governor | Edmund "Jerry" Brown (D) | US$173,987 |
| Lieut. Gov. | Gavin Newsom (D) | US$130,490 |
| Sec. of State | Debra Bowen (D) | US$130,490 |
| Atty. Gen. | Kamala Harris (D) | US$151,127 |
| Treasurer | Bill Lockyer (D) | US$139,189 |

| STATE/OFFICE | OFFICEHOLDER | PAY[1] |
|---|---|---|
| **California (continued)** | | |
| Legislature | | |
| Senate | Dem: 25; Rep: 15 | |
| Assembly | Dem: 52; Rep: 28 | |
| **Colorado** | | |
| Governor | John Hickenlooper (R) | US$90,000 |
| Lieut. Gov. | Joseph Garcia (D) | US$68,500 |
| Sec. of State | Scott Gessler (R) | US$68,500 |
| Atty. Gen. | John W. Suthers (R) | US$80,000 |
| Treasurer | Walker Stapleton (R) | US$68,500 |
| General Assembly | | |
| Senate | Dem: 20; Rep: 15 | |
| House | Dem: 32; Rep: 33 | |
| **Connecticut** | | |
| Governor | Dan Malloy (D) | US$150,000 |
| Lieut. Gov. | Nancy Wyman (D) | US$110,000 |
| Sec. of State | Denise Merrill (D) | US$110,000 |
| Atty. Gen. | George Jepsen (D) | US$110,000 |
| Treasurer | Denise L. Nappier (D) | US$110,000 |
| General Assembly | | |
| Senate | Dem: 22; Rep: 14 | |
| House | Dem: 99; Rep: 52 | |
| **Delaware** | | |
| Governor | Jack Markell (D) | US$171,000 |
| Lieut. Gov. | Matthew Denn (D) | US$77,775 |
| Sec. of State* | Jeffrey Bullock | US$126,327 |
| Atty. Gen. | Joseph Biden III (D) | US$143,769 |
| Treasurer | Chip Flowers (D) | US$112,250 |
| General Assembly | | |
| Senate | Dem: 14; Rep: 7 | |
| House | Dem: 26; Rep: 15 | |
| **Florida** | | |
| Governor | Rick Scott (R) | US$130,273 |
| Lieut. Gov. | Jennifer Carroll (R) | US$124,851 |
| Sec. of State* | Kenneth Detzner | US$140,000 |
| Atty. Gen. | Pam Bondi (R) | US$128,972 |
| Treasurer[3] | Jeff Atwater (R) (CFO) | US$128,972 |
| Legislature | | |
| Senate | Dem: 12; Rep: 28 | |
| House | Dem: 39; Rep: 81 | |
| **Georgia** | | |
| Governor | Nathan Deal (R) | US$139,339 |
| Lieut. Gov. | Casey Cagle (R) | US$91,609 |
| Sec. of State | Brian Kemp (R) | US$123,636 |
| Atty. Gen. | Sam Olens (R) | US$137,791 |

## State Officers and Legislatures (continued)

| STATE/OFFICE | OFFICEHOLDER | PAY[1] |
|---|---|---|
| **Georgia (continued)** | | |
| Treasurer*[3] | Thomas Hills (Director, Office of Treasury and Fiscal Services) | US$115,781 |
| General Assembly | | |
| Senate | Dem: 20; Rep: 36 | |
| House | Dem: 63; Rep: 115; Ind: 1; vacant: 1 | |
| | | |
| **Hawaii** | | |
| Governor | Neil Abercrombie (D) | US$117,312 |
| Lieut. Gov. | Brian Schatz (D) | US$114,420 |
| Sec. of State[2] | | |
| Atty. Gen.* | David Louie | US$114,420 |
| Treasurer*[3] | Kalbert Young (Director of Finance) | US$108,972 |
| Legislature | | |
| Senate | Dem: 24; Rep: 1 | |
| House | Dem: 42; Rep: 8; vacant: 1 | |
| | | |
| **Idaho** | | |
| Governor | C.L. "Butch" Otter (R) | US$115,348 |
| Lieut. Gov. | Brad Little (R) | US$30,400 |
| Sec. of State | Ben Ysursa (R) | US$93,756 |
| Atty. Gen. | Lawrence Wasden (R) | US$103,984 |
| Treasurer | Ron G. Crane (R) | US$93,756 |
| Legislature | | |
| Senate | Dem: 7; Rep: 28 | |
| House | Dem: 13; Rep: 57 | |
| | | |
| **Illinois** | | |
| Governor | Pat Quinn (D) | US$177,412 |
| Lieut. Gov. | Sheila Simon (D) | US$135,669 |
| Sec. of State | Jesse White (D) | US$156,541 |
| Atty. Gen. | Lisa Madigan (D) | US$156,541 |
| Treasurer | Dan Rutherford (R) | US$135,669 |
| General Assembly | | |
| Senate | Dem: 35; Rep: 24 | |
| House | Dem: 64; Rep: 54 | |
| | | |
| **Indiana** | | |
| Governor | Mitch Daniels (R) | US$107,881 |
| Lieut. Gov. | Becky Skillman (R) | US$84,031 |
| Sec. of State | Connie Lawson (R) | US$72,974 |
| Atty. Gen. | Greg Zoeller (R) | US$87,790 |
| Treasurer | Richard E. Mourdock (R) | US$72,974 |
| General Assembly | | |
| Senate | Dem: 13; Rep: 37 | |
| House | Dem: 40; Rep: 60 | |
| | | |
| **Iowa** | | |
| Governor | Terry Branstad (R) | US$130,000 |
| Lieut. Gov. | Kim Reynolds (R) | US$103,212 |
| Sec. of State | Matt Schultz (R) | US$103,212 |
| Atty. Gen. | Tom Miller (D) | US$123,669 |
| Treasurer | Michael L. Fitzgerald (D) | US$103,212 |
| General Assembly | | |
| Senate | Dem: 26; Rep: 24 | |
| House | Dem: 40; Rep: 60 | |
| | | |
| **Kansas** | | |
| Governor | Sam Brownback (R) | US$99,636 |
| Lieut. Gov. | Jeff Colyer (R) | US$54,000 |
| Sec. of State | Kris Kobach (R) | US$86,003 |
| Atty. Gen. | Derek Schmidt (R) | US$98,901 |
| Treasurer | Ron Estes (R) | US$86,003 |
| Legislature | | |
| Senate | Dem: 8; Rep: 32 | |
| House | Dem: 33; Rep: 92 | |

| STATE/OFFICE | OFFICEHOLDER | PAY[1] |
|---|---|---|
| **Kentucky** | | |
| Governor | Steve Beshear (D) | US$151,643 |
| Lieut. Gov. | Jerry Abramson (D) | US$113,615 |
| Sec. of State | Allison Lundergan Grimes (D) | US$113,615 |
| Atty. Gen. | Jack Conway (D) | US$113,615 |
| Treasurer | Todd Hollenbach (D) | US$113,615 |
| General Assembly | | |
| Senate | Dem: 15; Rep: 22; Ind: 1 | |
| House | Dem: 59; Rep: 40; vacant: 1 | |
| | | |
| **Louisiana** | | |
| Governor | Bobby Jindal (R) | US$130,000 |
| Lieut. Gov. | Jay Dardenne (R) | US$115,000 |
| Sec. of State | Tom Schedler (R) | US$115,000 |
| Atty. Gen. | James D. Caldwell (D) | US$115,000 |
| Treasurer | John Kennedy (R) | US$115,000 |
| Legislature | | |
| Senate | Dem: 15; Rep: 24 | |
| House | Dem: 45; Rep: 58; Ind: 2 | |
| | | |
| **Maine** | | |
| Governor | Paul LePage (R) | US$70,000 |
| Lieut. Gov.[5] | | |
| Sec. of State | Charles Summers (R) | US$69,264 |
| Atty. Gen. | William J. Schneider (R) | US$92,248 |
| Treasurer | Bruce Poliquin | US$69,264 |
| Legislature | | |
| Senate | Dem: 14; Rep: 20; unenrolled: 1 | |
| House | Dem: 72; Rep: 77; unenrolled: 1; vacant: 1 | |
| | | |
| **Maryland** | | |
| Governor | Martin O'Malley (D) | US$150,000 |
| Lieut. Gov. | Anthony G. Brown (D) | US$125,000 |
| Sec. of State* | John McDonough | US$87,500 |
| Atty. Gen. | Douglas F. Gansler (D) | US$125,000 |
| Treasurer | Nancy K. Kopp (D) | US$125,000 |
| General Assembly | | |
| Senate | Dem: 35; Rep: 12 | |
| House | Dem: 98; Rep: 43 | |
| | | |
| **Massachusetts** | | |
| Governor | Deval Patrick (D) | US$139,832 |
| Lieut. Gov. | Timothy Murray (D) | US$124,295 |
| Sec. of State | William F. Galvin (D) | US$130,262 |
| Atty. Gen. | Martha Coakley (D) | US$133,644 |
| Treasurer | Steve Grossman (D) | US$130,916 |
| General Court (legislature) | | |
| Senate | Dem: 36; Rep: 4 | |
| House | Dem: 125; Rep: 33; vacant: 2 | |
| | | |
| **Michigan** | | |
| Governor | Rick Snyder (R) | US$159,300 |
| Lieut. Gov. | Brian Calley (R) | US$111,510 |
| Sec. of State | Ruth Johnson (R) | US$124,410 |
| Atty. Gen. | Bill Schuette (R) | US$124,410 |
| Treasurer* | Andy Dillon | US$174,204 |
| Legislature | | |
| Senate | Dem: 12; Rep: 26 | |
| House | Dem: 46; Rep: 62; vacant: 2 | |
| | | |
| **Minnesota** | | |
| Governor | Mark Dayton (D) | US$120,303 |
| Lieut. Gov. | Yvonne Prettner Solon (D) | US$78,197 |
| Sec. of State | Mark Ritchie (D) | US$90,227 |
| Atty. Gen. | Lori Swanson (D) | US$114,288 |

# State Officers and Legislatures (continued)

| STATE/OFFICE | OFFICEHOLDER | PAY[1] |
|---|---|---|
| **Minnesota (continued)** | | |
| Treasurer*[3] | James Schowalter (Commissioner of Management and Budget) | US$108,388 |
| Legislature | | |
| Senate | Dem: 30; Rep: 37 | |
| House | Dem: 62; Rep: 72 | |
| **Mississippi** | | |
| Governor | Phil Bryant (R) | US$122,160 |
| Lieut. Gov. | Tate Reeves (R) | US$61,714 |
| Sec. of State | C. Delbert Hosemann, Jr. (R) | US$85,500 |
| Atty. Gen. | Jim Hood (D) | US$103,512 |
| Treasurer | Lynn Fitch (R) | US$85,500 |
| Legislature | | |
| Senate | Dem: 21; Rep: 31 | |
| House | Dem: 58; Rep: 64 | |
| **Missouri** | | |
| Governor | Jay Nixon (D) | US$133,821 |
| Lieut. Gov. | Peter Kinder (R) | US$86,484 |
| Sec. of State | Robin Carnahan (D) | US$107,746 |
| Atty. Gen. | Chris Koster (D) | US$116,437 |
| Treasurer | Clint Zweifel (D) | US$107,746 |
| General Assembly | | |
| Senate | Dem: 8; Rep: 26 | |
| House | Dem: 56; Rep: 106; vacant: 1 | |
| **Montana** | | |
| Governor | Brian Schweitzer (D) | US$108,167 |
| Lieut. Gov. | John Bohlinger (R) | US$86,362 |
| Sec. of State | Linda McCulloch (D) | US$86,018 |
| Atty. Gen. | Steve Bullock (D) | US$99,712 |
| Treasurer*[3] | Janet Kelly (Dir., Dept. of Administration) | US$96,967 |
| Legislature | | |
| Senate | Dem: 22; Rep: 28 | |
| House | Dem: 32; Rep: 68 | |
| **Nebraska** | | |
| Governor | Dave Heineman (R) | US$105,000 |
| Lieut. Gov. | Rick Sheehy (R) | US$75,000 |
| Sec. of State | John A. Gale (R) | US$85,000 |
| Atty. Gen. | Jon Bruning (R) | US$95,000 |
| Treasurer | Don Stenberg (R) | US$85,000 |
| Legislature (unicameral) | 49 nonpartisan members | |
| **Nevada** | | |
| Governor | Brian Sandoval (R) | US$141,000 |
| Lieut. Gov. | Brian K. Krolicki (R) | US$60,000 |
| Sec. of State | Ross Miller (D) | US$97,000 |
| Atty. Gen. | Catherine Cortez Masto (D) | US$133,000 |
| Treasurer | Kate Marshall (D) | US$97,000 |
| Legislature | | |
| Senate | Dem: 11; Rep: 10 | |
| Assembly | Dem: 26; Rep: 16 | |
| **New Hampshire** | | |
| Governor | John Lynch (D) | US$113,834 |
| Lieut. Gov.[5] | | |
| Sec. of State | William Gardner (D) | US$104,364 |
| Atty. Gen.* | Michael Delaney | US$110,114 |

| STATE/OFFICE | OFFICEHOLDER | PAY[1] |
|---|---|---|
| **New Hampshire (continued)** | | |
| Treasurer | Catherine Provencher | US$104,364 |
| General Court (legislature) | | |
| Senate | Dem: 5; Rep: 19 | |
| House | Dem: 104; Rep: 292; vacant: 4 | |
| **New Jersey** | | |
| Governor | Christopher J. Christie (R) | US$175,000 |
| Lieut. Gov. | Kim Guadagno (R) | US$141,000 |
| Sec. of State[2] | | |
| Atty. Gen.* | Jeffrey S. Chiesa | US$141,000 |
| Treasurer* | Andrew P. Sidamon-Eristoff | US$141,000 |
| Legislature | | |
| Senate | Dem: 24; Rep: 16 | |
| General Assembly | Dem: 47; Rep: 32; vacant: 1 | |
| **New Mexico** | | |
| Governor | Susana Martinez (R) | US$110,000 |
| Lieut. Gov. | John Sanchez (R) | US$85,000 |
| Sec. of State | Dianna Duran (R) | US$85,000 |
| Atty. Gen. | Gary K. King (D) | US$95,000 |
| Treasurer | James B. Lewis (D) | US$85,000 |
| Legislature | | |
| Senate | Dem: 28; Rep: 14 | |
| House | Dem: 36; Rep: 33; Ind: 1 | |
| **New York** | | |
| Governor | Andrew M. Cuomo (D) | US$179,000 |
| Lieut. Gov. | Robert Duffy (D) | US$151,500 |
| Sec. of State* | Cesar Perales | US$120,800 |
| Atty. Gen. | Eric Schneiderman (D) | US$151,500 |
| Treasurer* | Aida Brewer | US$127,000 |
| Legislature | | |
| Senate | Dem: 29; Rep: 32; vacant: 1 | |
| Assembly | Dem: 96; Rep: 49; Independence: 1; vacant: 4 | |
| **North Carolina** | | |
| Governor | Beverly Perdue (D) | US$139,590 |
| Lieut. Gov. | Walter Dalton (D) | US$123,198 |
| Sec. of State | Elaine F. Marshall (D) | US$123,198 |
| Atty. Gen. | Roy Cooper (D) | US$123,198 |
| Treasurer | Jane Cowell (D) | US$123,198 |
| General Assembly | | |
| Senate | Dem: 19; Rep: 31 | |
| House | Dem: 52; Rep: 68 | |
| **North Dakota** | | |
| Governor | Jack Dalrymple (R) | US$110,283 |
| Lieut. Gov. | Drew Wrigley (R) | US$85,614 |
| Sec. of State | Alvin A. Jaeger (R) | US$87,728 |
| Atty. Gen. | Wayne Stenehjem (R) | US$113,266 |
| Treasurer | Kelly Schmidt (R) | US$82,849 |
| Legislative Assembly | | |
| Senate | Dem: 12; Rep: 35 | |
| House | Dem: 25; Rep: 69 | |
| **Ohio** | | |
| Governor | John Kasich (R) | US$148,886 |
| Lieut. Gov. | Mary Taylor (R) | US$78,041 |
| Sec. of State | Jon Husted (R) | US$109,554 |
| Atty. Gen. | Mike Dewine (R) | US$109,986 |
| Treasurer | Josh Mandel (R) | US$109,986 |
| General Assembly | | |
| Senate | Dem: 10; Rep: 23 | |
| House | Dem: 40; Rep: 59 | |

## State Officers and Legislatures (continued)

| STATE/OFFICE | OFFICEHOLDER | PAY[1] |
|---|---|---|
| **Oklahoma** | | |
| Governor | Mary Fallin (R) | US$147,000 |
| Lieut. Gov. | Todd Lamb (R) | US$114,713 |
| Sec. of State* | Glenn Coffee | US$90,000 |
| Atty. Gen. | Scott Pruitt (R) | US$132,850 |
| Treasurer | Ken Miller (R) | US$114,713 |
| Legislature | | |
| Senate | Dem: 15; Rep: 31; vacant: 2 | |
| House | Dem: 33; Rep: 68 | |
| | | |
| **Oregon** | | |
| Governor | John Kitzhaber (D) | US$93,600 |
| Lieut. Gov.[4] | | |
| Sec. of State | Kate Brown (D) | US$72,000 |
| Atty. Gen. | John R. Kroger (D) | US$77,200 |
| Treasurer | Ted Wheeler (D) | US$72,000 |
| Legislative Assembly | | |
| Senate | Dem: 16; Rep: 14 | |
| House | Dem: 30; Rep: 30 | |
| | | |
| **Pennsylvania** | | |
| Governor | Tom Corbett (R) | US$183,255 |
| Lieut. Gov. | Jim Cawley (R) | US$153,907 |
| Sec. of State* | Carol Aichele | US$131,992 |
| Atty. Gen. | Linda L. Kelly (R) | US$152,443 |
| Treasurer | Robert McCord (D) | US$152,443 |
| General Assembly | | |
| Senate | Dem: 20; Rep: 30 | |
| House | Dem: 87; Rep: 110; vacant: 6 | |
| | | |
| **Rhode Island** | | |
| Governor | Lincoln Chafee (I) | US$129,210 |
| Lieut. Gov. | Elizabeth H. Roberts (D) | US$108,808 |
| Sec. of State | A. Ralph Mollis (D) | US$108,808 |
| Atty. Gen. | Peter Kilmartin (D) | US$115,610 |
| Treasurer | Gina Raimondo (D) | US$108,808 |
| General Assembly | | |
| Senate | Dem: 29; Rep: 8; Ind: 1 | |
| House | Dem: 65; Rep: 10 | |
| | | |
| **South Carolina** | | |
| Governor | Nikki Haley (R) | US$106,078 |
| Lieut. Gov. | Glen McConnell (R) | US$46,545 |
| Sec. of State | Mark Hammond (R) | US$92,007 |
| Atty. Gen. | Alan Wilson (R) | US$92,007 |
| Treasurer | Curtis Loftis (R) | US$92,007 |
| General Assembly | | |
| Senate | Dem: 19; Rep: 27 | |
| House | Dem: 48; Rep: 76 | |
| | | |
| **South Dakota** | | |
| Governor | Dennis Daugaard (R) | US$98,031 |
| Lieut. Gov. | Matt Michels (R) | US$120,000 |
| Sec. of State | Jason Gant (R) | US$78,363 |
| Atty. Gen. | Martin Jackley (R) | US$97,928 |
| Treasurer | Richard Sattgast (R) | US$78,363 |
| Legislature | | |
| Senate | Dem: 5; Rep: 30 | |
| House | Dem: 19; Rep: 50; Ind: 1 | |
| | | |
| **Tennessee** | | |
| Governor | Bill Haslam (R) | US$170,340 |
| Lieut. Gov.[6] | Ron Ramsey (R) | US$57,027 |
| Sec. of State | Tre Hargett (R) | US$182,800 |
| Atty. Gen.* | Robert E. Cooper, Jr. | US$167,976 |
| Treasurer | David H. Lillard, Jr. | US$182,880 |

| STATE/OFFICE | OFFICEHOLDER | PAY[1] |
|---|---|---|
| **Tennessee (continued)** | | |
| General Assembly | | |
| Senate | Dem: 13; Rep: 20 | |
| House | Dem: 34; Rep: 64; Carter County Rep: 1 | |
| | | |
| **Texas** | | |
| Governor | Rick Perry (R) | US$150,000 |
| Lieut. Gov. | David Dewhurst (R) | US$7,200 |
| Sec. of State* | Esperanza Andrade | US$125,880 |
| Atty. Gen. | Greg Abbott (R) | US$150,000 |
| Treasurer[3] | Susan Combs (R) (Comptroller) | US$150,000 |
| Legislature | | |
| Senate | Dem: 12; Rep: 19 | |
| House | Dem: 49; Rep: 101 | |
| | | |
| **Utah** | | |
| Governor | Gary Herbert (R) | US$109,470 |
| Lieut. Gov. | Greg Bell (R) | US$104,000 |
| Sec. of State[2] | | |
| Atty. Gen. | Mark Shurtleff (R) | US$98,509 |
| Treasurer | Richard K. Ellis (R) | US$104,000 |
| Legislature | | |
| Senate | Dem: 7; Rep: 22 | |
| House | Dem: 17; Rep: 58 | |
| | | |
| **Vermont** | | |
| Governor | Peter Shumlin (D) | US$142,542 |
| Lieut. Gov. | Phil Scott (R) | US$60,507 |
| Sec. of State | Jim Condos (D) | US$90,376 |
| Atty. Gen. | William H. Sorrell (D) | US$108,202 |
| Treasurer | Elizabeth Pearce (D) | US$90,376 |
| General Assembly | | |
| Senate | Dem: 21; Rep: 8; Progressive: 1 | |
| House | Dem: 94; Rep: 48; Ind: 3; Progressive: 5 | |
| | | |
| **Virginia** | | |
| Governor | Robert McDonnell (R) | US$175,000 |
| Lieut. Gov. | Bill Bolling (R) | US$36,321 |
| Sec. of State* | Janet Polarek | US$152,793 |
| Atty. Gen. | Ken Cuccinelli (R) | US$150,000 |
| Treasurer* | Manju Ganeriwala | US$157,249 |
| General Assembly | | |
| Senate | Dem: 20; Rep: 20 | |
| House | Dem: 32; Rep: 67; Ind: 1 | |
| | | |
| **Washington** | | |
| Governor | Chris Gregoire (D) | US$166,891 |
| Lieut. Gov. | Brad Owen (D) | US$91,129 |
| Sec. of State | Sam Reed (R) | US$116,950 |
| Atty. Gen. | Rob McKenna (R) | US$151,718 |
| Treasurer | James L. McIntire (D) | US$113,436 |
| Legislature | | |
| Senate | Dem: 27; Rep: 22 | |
| House | Dem: 56; Rep: 42 | |
| | | |
| **West Virginia** | | |
| Governor | Earl Ray Tomblin (D) | US$150,000 |
| Lieut. Gov.[7] | Jeffrey Kessler (D) | N/A |
| Sec. of State | Natalie Tennant (D) | US$95,000 |
| Atty. Gen. | Darrell V. McGraw, Jr. (D) | US$95,000 |
| Treasurer | John D. Perdue (D) | US$95,000 |
| Legislature | | |
| Senate | Dem: 28; Rep: 6 | |
| House | Dem: 65; Rep: 35 | |

## State Officers and Legislatures (continued)

| STATE/OFFICE | OFFICEHOLDER | PAY[1] | STATE/OFFICE | OFFICEHOLDER | PAY[1] |
|---|---|---|---|---|---|
| **Wisconsin** | | | **Wyoming** | | |
| Governor | Scott Walker (R) | US$144,423 | Governor | Matt Mead (R) | US$105,000 |
| Lieut. Gov. | Rebecca Kleefisch (R) | US$76,261 | Lieut. Gov.[4] | | |
| Sec. of State | Douglas La Follette (D) | US$68,556 | Sec. of State | Max Maxfield (R) | US$92,000 |
| Atty. Gen. | J.B. Van Hollen (R) | US$140,147 | Atty. Gen.* | Greg A. Phillips | US$137,150 |
| Treasurer | Kurt Schuller (R) | US$68,556 | Treasurer | Joseph B. Meyer (R) | US$92,000 |
| Legislature | | | Legislature | | |
| Senate | Dem: 16; Rep: 17 | | Senate | Dem: 4; Rep: 26 | |
| Assembly | Dem: 39; Rep: 59; Ind: 1 | | House | Dem: 10; Rep: 50 | |

[1]The salary rates are from April 2012.  [2]The lieutenant governor serves as secretary of state.  [3]No official state treasurer; the official in charge of the general treasury performs duties.  [4]The secretary of state assumes duties of lieutenant governor.  [5]No official lieutenant governor; the president of the Senate succeeds the governor.  [6]In Tennessee the speaker of the Senate and the lieutenant governor are one and the same.  [7]In West Virginia the president of the Senate and the lieutenant governor are one and the same.

# United States Cities

## US Urban Growth, 1850–2011

*Source: US Census Bureau.*

| RANK | CITY | 1850 | 1900 | 1950 | 1990 | 2000 | 2011 |
|---|---|---|---|---|---|---|---|
| 1 | New York NY[1] | 515,547 | 3,437,202 | 7,891,957 | 7,322,564 | 8,008,278 | 8,244,910 |
| 2 | Los Angeles CA | 1,610 | 102,479 | 1,970,358 | 3,485,398 | 3,694,820 | 3,819,702 |
| 3 | Chicago IL | 29,963 | 1,698,575 | 3,620,962 | 2,783,726 | 2,896,016 | 2,707,120 |
| 4 | Houston TX | 2,396 | 44,633 | 596,163 | 1,630,553 | 1,953,631 | 2,145,146 |
| 5 | Philadelphia PA[1] | 121,376 | 1,293,697 | 2,071,605 | 1,585,577 | 1,517,550 | 1,536,471 |
| 6 | Phoenix AZ | | 5,544 | 106,818 | 983,403 | 1,321,045 | 1,469,471 |
| 7 | San Antonio TX | 3,488 | 53,321 | 408,442 | 935,933 | 1,144,646 | 1,359,758 |
| 8 | San Diego CA | | 17,700 | 334,387 | 1,110,549 | 1,223,400 | 1,326,179 |
| 9 | Dallas TX | | 42,638 | 434,462 | 1,006,877 | 1,188,580 | 1,223,229 |
| 10 | San Jose CA | | 21,500 | 95,280 | 782,248 | 894,943 | 967,487 |
| 11 | Jacksonville FL | 1,045 | 28,429 | 204,517 | 635,230 | 735,617 | 827,908 |
| 12 | Indianapolis IN[1] | 8,091 | 169,164 | 427,173 | 731,726[2] | 781,870[2] | 827,609 |
| 13 | Austin TX | 629 | 22,258 | 132,459 | 465,622 | 656,562 | 820,611 |
| 14 | San Francisco CA[1] | 34,776 | 342,782 | 775,357 | 723,959 | 776,733 | 812,826 |
| 15 | Columbus OH | 17,882 | 125,560 | 375,901 | 632,910 | 711,470 | 797,434 |
| 16 | Fort Worth TX | | 26,688 | 278,778 | 447,619 | 534,694 | 758,738 |
| 17 | Charlotte NC | 1,065 | 18,091 | 134,042 | 395,934 | 540,828 | 751,087 |
| 18 | Detroit MI | 21,019 | 285,704 | 1,849,568 | 1,027,974 | 951,270 | 706,585 |
| 19 | El Paso TX | | 15,906 | 130,485 | 515,342 | 563,662 | 665,568 |
| 20 | Memphis TN | 8,841 | 102,320 | 396,000 | 610,337 | 650,100 | 652,050 |
| 21 | Boston MA | 136,881 | 560,892 | 801,444 | 574,283 | 589,141 | 625,087 |
| 22 | Seattle WA | | 80,671 | 467,591 | 516,259 | 563,374 | 620,778 |
| 23 | Denver CO[1] | | 133,859 | 415,786 | 467,610 | 554,636 | 619,968 |
| 24 | Baltimore MD | 169,054 | 508,957 | 949,708 | 736,014 | 651,154 | 619,493 |
| 25 | Nashville TN[1] | 10,165 | 80,865 | 174,307 | 488,374[2] | 545,524[2] | 609,644 |

[1]Cities with boundaries contiguous with their respective counties (year consolidated): New York (1683), Philadelphia (1854), San Francisco (1856), Indianapolis (1970), Nashville (1963), and Denver (1902).  [2]Figure represents the "balance," or the population of the consolidated city minus any semi-incorporated places located within the consolidated city.

## Fifteen Fastest-Growing Cities in the US

*Based on a population of 100,000 or more. Source: US Census Bureau.*

| CITY | POPULATION | | CHANGE (%) |
|---|---|---|---|
| | 1 APR 2010 | 1 JUL 2011 | |
| New Orleans LA | 343,829 | 360,740 | +4.9 |
| Round Rock TX | 99,887 | 104,664 | +4.8 |
| Austin TX | 790,390 | 820,611 | +3.8 |
| Plano TX | 259,841 | 269,776 | +3.8 |
| McKinney TX | 131,117 | 136,067 | +3.8 |

## Fifteen Fastest-Growing Cities in the US (continued)

| CITY | 1 APR 2010 | 1 JUL 2011 | CHANGE (%) |
|------|-----------|-----------|------------|
| Frisco TX | 116,989 | 121,387 | +3.8 |
| Denton TX | 113,383 | 117,187 | +3.4 |
| Denver CO | 600,158 | 619,968 | +3.3 |
| Cary NC | 135,234 | 139,633 | +3.2 |
| Raleigh NC | 403,892 | 416,468 | +3.1 |
| Alexandria VA | 139,966 | 144,301 | +3.1 |
| Tampa FL | 335,709 | 346,037 | +3.1 |
| McAllen TX | 129,877 | 133,742 | +3.0 |
| Carrollton TX | 119,097 | 122,640 | +3.0 |
| Atlanta GA | 420,003 | 432,427 | +3.0 |

## Fifteen Cities with the Greatest Population Losses in the US

*Based on a population of 100,000 or more. Source: US Census Bureau.*

| CITY | POPULATION 1 APR 2010 | POPULATION 1 JUL 2011 | CHANGE (%) | CITY | POPULATION 1 APR 2010 | POPULATION 1 JUL 2011 | CHANGE (%) |
|------|-----------|-----------|------------|------|-----------|-----------|------------|
| Detroit MI | 713,777 | 706,585 | −1.0 | St. Louis MO | 319,294 | 318,069 | −0.4 |
| Flint MI | 102,434 | 101,558 | −0.9 | Akron OH | 199,110 | 198,402 | −0.4 |
| Cleveland OH | 396,815 | 393,806 | −0.8 | Cincinnati OH | 296,950 | 296,223 | −0.2 |
| Hampton VA | 137,436 | 136,401 | −0.8 | Baltimore MD | 620,961 | 619,493 | −0.2 |
| Newport News VA | 180,719 | 179,611 | −0.6 | Waterbury CT | 110,366 | 110,189 | −0.2 |
| Wichita Falls TX | 104,553 | 103,931 | −0.6 | New Haven CT | 129,779 | 129,585 | −0.1 |
| Rockford IL | 152,871 | 152,222 | −0.4 | Buffalo NY | 261,310 | 261,025 | −0.1 |
| Toledo OH | 287,208 | 286,038 | −0.4 | | | | |

## Racial Makeup of the Fifteen Largest US Cities

Information is given in percent of the total population. The Hispanic or Latino category is listed for comparative purposes even though Hispanic or Latino people may be of any race; thus, the rows of racial percentages will not add up to 100 if the Hispanic or Latino entries are included. Data are preliminary.

Source: US Census Bureau, *2010 American Community Survey.*

| CITY | WHITE | BLACK OR AFRICAN AMERICAN | AMERICAN INDIAN AND ALASKA NATIVE | ASIAN | NATIVE HAWAIIAN AND OTHER PACIFIC ISLANDER | SOME OTHER RACE | TWO OR MORE RACES | HISPANIC OR LATINO | TOTAL POPULATION |
|------|-------|--------------------------|-----------------------------------|-------|--------------------------------------------|-----------------|-------------------|--------------------|------------------|
| New York NY | 44.6 | 25.0 | 0.4 | 12.8 | — | 14.0 | 3.1 | 28.7 | 8,184,899 |
| Los Angeles CA | 52.2 | 9.5 | 0.4 | 11.3 | 0.2 | 23.1 | 3.3 | 48.8 | 3,797,144 |
| Chicago IL | 46.5 | 33.6 | 0.2 | 5.6 | — | 12.3 | 1.7 | 28.3 | 2,698,831 |
| Houston TX | 56.6 | 23.7 | 0.5 | 6.2 | — | 11.4 | 1.4 | 43.6 | 2,107,208 |
| Philadelphia PA | 41.5 | 43.8 | 0.3 | 6.4 | — | 5.5 | 2.5 | 12.3 | 1,528,306 |
| Phoenix AZ | 77.9 | 6.9 | 1.7 | 2.9 | 0.2 | 7.6 | 2.8 | 39.4 | 1,449,481 |
| San Antonio TX | 76.0 | 6.2 | 0.9 | 2.2 | — | 12.2 | 2.4 | 64.0 | 1,334,359 |
| San Diego CA | 64.2 | 6.5 | 0.5 | 16.0 | 0.6 | 7.4 | 4.9 | 29.1 | 1,311,886 |
| Dallas TX | 53.3 | 24.7 | 0.4 | 2.8 | — | 16.6 | 2.2 | 42.6 | 1,202,797 |
| San Jose CA | 46.4 | 3.5 | 0.7 | 32.4 | 0.3 | 12.2 | 4.5 | 33.5 | 949,197 |
| Indianapolis IN | 63.5 | 27.7 | 0.3 | 2.1 | — | 3.8 | 2.6 | 9.5 | 824,199 |
| Jacksonville FL | 60.7 | 30.9 | 0.2 | 4.1 | — | 1.2 | 2.8 | 7.8 | 823,316 |
| San Francisco CA | 51.5 | 6.1 | 0.5 | 33.4 | 0.4 | 4.5 | 3.6 | 15.2 | 805,463 |
| Austin TX | 71.3 | 8.0 | 0.5 | 5.9 | — | 11.7 | 2.6 | 36.2 | 795,518 |
| Columbus OH | 62.8 | 27.8 | 0.2 | 4.5 | — | 1.6 | 3.0 | 5.5 | 789,939 |

— Less than 0.09 percent.   Detail may not add to total given because of rounding.

## Area and Zip Codes Web Sites

US telephone area codes and postal codes change frequently to accommodate telecommunications user patterns and expansions and shifts in patterns of business and residential development. Check local listings to determine whether to dial "1" before dialing outside of the area code or to dial the area code as well as the telephone number when dialing within the area code.

**Area codes:** <www.nanpa.com>.
**Zip codes:** <http://zip4.usps.com/zip4/welcome.jsp>.

# United States Law and Crime

## State Crime Rates, 2003–10

*Estimates of crimes reported to the police per 100,000 population.*

| STATE | 2003 TOTAL | 2004 TOTAL | 2005 TOTAL | 2006 TOTAL | 2007 TOTAL | 2008 TOTAL | 2009 TOTAL | 2010 TOTAL |
|---|---|---|---|---|---|---|---|---|
| AL | 4,475 | 4,452 | 4,324 | 4,361 | 4,420 | 4,536 | 4,222 | 3,895 |
| AK | 4,360 | 4,018 | 4,244 | 4,293 | 4,041 | 3,584 | 3,579 | 3,491 |
| AZ | 6,147 | 5,845 | 5,351 | 5,129 | 4,897 | 4,738 | 3,965 | 3,942 |
| AR | 4,088 | 4,512 | 4,585 | 4,519 | 4,483 | 4,339 | 4,291 | 4,064 |
| CA | 4,006 | 3,971 | 3,849 | 3,703 | 3,556 | 3,444 | 3,204 | 3,076 |
| CO | 4,299 | 4,293 | 4,436 | 3,843 | 3,354 | 3,192 | 3,004 | 3,005 |
| CT | 2,984 | 2,913 | 2,833 | 2,785 | 2,656 | 2,757 | 2,634 | 2,475 |
| DE | 4,090 | 3,732 | 3,744 | 4,099 | 4,059 | 4,289 | 3,986 | 4,069 |
| DC[1] | 7,489 | 6,230 | 6,206 | 6,162 | 6,328 | 6,542 | 6,091 | 6,109 |
| FL | 5,188 | 4,891 | 4,716 | 4,698 | 4,812 | 4,830 | 4,453 | 4,101 |
| GA | 4,715 | 4,722 | 4,621 | 4,360 | 4,394 | 4,494 | 4,093 | 4,044 |
| HI | 5,547 | 5,047 | 5,048 | 4,512 | 4,498 | 3,844 | 3,936 | 3,577 |
| ID | 3,175 | 3,039 | 2,955 | 2,666 | 2,486 | 2,330 | 2,217 | 2,217 |
| IL[2] | 3,844 | 3,729 | 3,632 | 3,561 | 3,469 | 3,458 | 3,234 | 3,116 |
| IN | 3,708 | 3,723 | 3,780 | 3,817 | 3,730 | 3,670 | 3,449 | 3,357 |
| IA | 3,254 | 3,176 | 3,125 | 3,086 | 2,910 | 2,705 | 2,588 | 2,516 |
| KS | 4,408 | 4,349 | 4,174 | 4,175 | 4,131 | 3,788 | 3,608 | 3,489 |
| KY | 2,759[2] | 2,783 | 2,797 | 2,808 | 2,813 | 2,880 | 2,771 | 2,794 |
| LA | 4,948 | 5,049 | 4,278 | 4,691 | 4,806 | 4,479 | 4,415 | 4,197 |
| ME | 2,559 | 2,514 | 2,525 | 2,634 | 2,547 | 2,570 | 2,523 | 2,601 |
| MD | 4,503 | 4,341 | 4,247 | 4,159 | 4,073 | 4,146 | 3,791 | 3,545 |
| MA | 3,036 | 2,919 | 2,821 | 2,838 | 2,823 | 2,849 | 2,761 | 2,817 |
| MI | 3,790 | 3,548 | 3,643 | 3,775 | 3,602 | 3,436 | 3,335 | 3,204 |
| MN[2] | 3,376 | 3,309 | 3,381 | 3,391 | 3,325 | 3,113 | 2,885 | 2,808 |
| MS | 4,031 | 3,774 | 3,539 | 3,507 | 3,492 | 3,225 | 3,235 | 3,255 |
| MO | 4,575 | 4,395 | 4,453 | 4,372 | 4,243 | 4,168 | 3,877 | 3,801 |
| MT | 3,461 | 3,230 | 3,424 | 2,941 | 3,053 | 2,861 | 2,718 | 2,816 |
| NE | 4,046 | 3,830 | 3,710 | 3,623 | 3,464 | 3,182 | 3,043 | 2,953 |
| NV | 4,903 | 4,823 | 4,848 | 4,830 | 4,528 | 4,172 | 3,758 | 3,435 |
| NH | 2,203 | 2,207 | 1,928 | 2,013 | 2,029 | 2,249 | 2,321 | 2,353 |
| NJ | 2,914 | 2,785 | 2,688 | 2,643 | 2,542 | 2,620 | 2,391 | 2,390 |
| NM | 4,756 | 4,885 | 4,851 | 4,580 | 4,390 | 4,559 | 4,355 | 4,024 |
| NY | 2,715 | 2,641 | 2,554 | 2,488 | 2,393 | 2,392 | 2,321 | 2,333 |
| NC | 4,725 | 4,608 | 4,543 | 4,596 | 4,554 | 4,511 | 4,072 | 3,811 |
| ND | 2,190 | 1,996 | 2,076 | 2,128 | 2,032 | 2,061 | 2,133 | 1,994 |
| OH | 3,984 | 4,015 | 4,014 | 4,029 | 3,798 | 3,760 | 3,603 | 3,560 |
| OK | 4,818 | 4,743 | 4,551 | 4,102 | 4,026 | 3,969 | 4,075 | 3,895 |
| OR | 5,061 | 4,929 | 4,687 | 3,952 | 3,814 | 3,539 | 3,222 | 3,265 |
| PA | 2,828 | 2,826 | 2,842 | 2,883 | 2,778 | 2,820 | 2,582 | 2,539 |
| RI | 3,281 | 3,131 | 2,970 | 2,814 | 2,850 | 3,090 | 2,863 | 2,813 |
| SC | 5,328 | 5,289 | 5,101 | 5,008 | 5,060 | 4,964 | 4,559 | 4,498 |
| SD | 2,177 | 2,106 | 1,952 | 1,791 | 1,822 | 1,847 | 1,905 | 2,121 |
| TN | 5,080 | 5,002 | 5,028 | 4,888 | 4,842 | 4,765 | 4,422 | 4,271 |
| TX | 5,153 | 5,035 | 4,862 | 4,598 | 4,632 | 4,494 | 4,506 | 4,233 |
| UT | 4,505 | 4,322 | 4,096 | 3,741 | 3,735 | 3,579 | 3,488 | 3,392 |
| VT | 2,343 | 2,420 | 2,400 | 2,441 | 2,447 | 2,674 | 2,533 | 2,413 |
| VA | 3,000 | 2,953 | 2,921 | 2,760 | 2,736 | 2,774 | 2,656 | 2,541 |
| WA | 5,102 | 5,193 | 5,239 | 4,826 | 4,364 | 4,090 | 3,998 | 4,020 |
| WV | 2,594 | 2,777 | 2,898 | 2,901 | 2,800 | 2,842 | 2,823 | 2,554 |
| WI | 3,101 | 2,873 | 2,902 | 3,102 | 3,129 | 3,030 | 2,865 | 2,756 |
| WY | 3,578 | 3,564 | 3,385 | 3,220 | 3,105 | 2,949 | 2,865 | 2,658 |
| US | 4,067 | 3,983 | 3,899 | 3,808 | 3,730 | 3,668 | 3,465 | 3,346 |

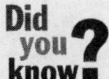

**Did you know?** For the first time ever, the United States in 2010 was the world's largest consumer of wine, accepting delivery of almost 330 million cases of wine in that year. France, which has historically been the world's leading wine consumer as well as a major producer, consumed almost 10 million cases less. Wine from California constituted more than 60% of the American consumption.

## State Crime Rates, 2003–10 (continued)

### 2010 CRIME RATES IN DETAIL

| | VIOLENT CRIME RATES | | | | | PROPERTY CRIME RATES | | | |
|---|---|---|---|---|---|---|---|---|---|
| STATE | MURDER[3] | FORCIBLE RAPE | AGGRAVATED ASSAULT | ROBBERY | TOTAL[4] | BURGLARY | LARCENY/ THEFT | MOTOR VEHICLE THEFT | TOTAL[4] |
| AL | 5.7 | 28.2 | 244 | 99.6 | 378 | 879 | 2,416 | 222 | 3,517 |
| AK | 4.4 | 75.0 | 476 | 83.6 | 639 | 437 | 2,187 | 228 | 2,853 |
| AZ | 6.4 | 33.9 | 259 | 109 | 408 | 794 | 2,403 | 337 | 3,534 |
| AR | 4.7 | 45.0 | 374 | 81.3 | 505 | 1,115 | 2,254 | 190 | 3,559 |
| CA | 4.9 | 22.4 | 257 | 156 | 441 | 614 | 1,612 | 409 | 2,636 |
| CO | 2.4 | 43.7 | 212 | 62.3 | 321 | 520 | 1,941 | 224 | 2,684 |
| CT | 3.6 | 16.3 | 162 | 99.4 | 281 | 425 | 1,581 | 188 | 2,193 |
| DE | 5.3 | 34.7 | 377 | 204 | 621 | 837 | 2,397 | 215 | 3,448 |
| DC[1] | 21.9 | 31.1 | 558 | 719 | 1,330 | 703 | 3,239 | 837 | 4,779 |
| FL | 5.2 | 28.6 | 370 | 139 | 542 | 900 | 2,438 | 221 | 3,558 |
| GA | 5.8 | 21.6 | 248 | 128 | 403 | 998 | 2,329 | 313 | 3,641 |
| HI | 1.8 | 26.8 | 157 | 77.5 | 263 | 637 | 2,302 | 375 | 3,314 |
| ID | 1.3 | 33.5 | 173 | 13.7 | 221 | 415 | 1,497 | 84.3 | 1,996 |
| IL[2] | 5.5 | 23.6 | 250 | 156 | 435 | 588 | 1,869 | 224 | 2,681 |
| IN | 4.5 | 27.2 | 187 | 95.9 | 315 | 727 | 2,113 | 202 | 3,042 |
| IA | 1.3 | 27.4 | 212 | 33.2 | 274 | 547 | 1,572 | 124 | 2,243 |
| KS | 3.5 | 38.8 | 273 | 54.1 | 369 | 680 | 2,229 | 211 | 3,120 |
| KY | 4.3 | 31.8 | 120 | 86.4 | 243 | 699 | 1,710 | 143 | 2,551 |
| LA | 11.2 | 27.2 | 396 | 115 | 549 | 1,002 | 2,427 | 218 | 3,648 |
| ME | 1.8 | 29.3 | 59.8 | 31.2 | 122 | 554 | 1,851 | 74.5 | 2,479 |
| MD | 7.4 | 21.3 | 328 | 192 | 548 | 633 | 2,052 | 313 | 2,997 |
| MA | 3.2 | 26.7 | 332 | 105 | 467 | 577 | 1,599 | 175 | 2,351 |
| MI | 5.7 | 47.3 | 321 | 116 | 490 | 747 | 1,690 | 277 | 2,714 |
| MN[2] | 1.8 | 33.9 | 136 | 63.9 | 236 | 460 | 1,950 | 162 | 2,572 |
| MS | 7.0 | 31.2 | 138 | 93.7 | 270 | 1,026 | 1,778 | 181 | 2,985 |
| MO | 7.0 | 23.9 | 322 | 102 | 455 | 735 | 2,343 | 268 | 3,346 |
| MT | 2.6 | 32.4 | 221 | 15.9 | 272 | 369 | 2,020 | 154 | 2,544 |
| NE | 3.0 | 36.8 | 184 | 56.1 | 280 | 456 | 2,019 | 198 | 2,673 |
| NV | 5.9 | 35.7 | 423 | 196 | 661 | 823 | 1,575 | 377 | 2,775 |
| NH | 1.0 | 31.3 | 100 | 34.3 | 167 | 413 | 1,700 | 73.5 | 2,186 |
| NJ | 4.2 | 11.2 | 158 | 134 | 308 | 441 | 1,465 | 177 | 2,082 |
| NM | 6.9 | 46.5 | 457 | 78.4 | 589 | 1,021 | 2,160 | 255 | 3,435 |
| NY | 4.5 | 14.3 | 226 | 147 | 392 | 335 | 1,500 | 105 | 1,941 |
| NC | 5.0 | 21.1 | 237 | 101 | 363 | 1,077 | 2,178 | 192 | 3,447 |
| ND | 1.5 | 35.2 | 175 | 13.4 | 225 | 292 | 1,349 | 128 | 1,769 |
| OH | 4.1 | 32.1 | 136 | 143 | 315 | 923 | 2,139 | 183 | 3,245 |
| OK | 5.2 | 38.7 | 347 | 89.0 | 480 | 999 | 2,145 | 272 | 3,416 |
| OR | 2.4 | 31.7 | 156 | 62.4 | 252 | 513 | 2,268 | 233 | 3,013 |
| PA | 5.2 | 26.9 | 205 | 129 | 366 | 434 | 1,607 | 131 | 2,173 |
| RI | 2.8 | 28.1 | 152 | 74.1 | 257 | 582 | 1,747 | 228 | 2,557 |
| SC | 6.1 | 31.7 | 452 | 108 | 598 | 998 | 2,617 | 285 | 3,900 |
| SD | 2.8 | 47.9 | 199 | 18.9 | 269 | 391 | 1,364 | 97.6 | 1,852 |
| TN | 5.6 | 33.7 | 442 | 132 | 613 | 1,012 | 2,412 | 234 | 3,658 |
| TX | 5.0 | 30.3 | 284 | 131 | 450 | 909 | 2,603 | 271 | 3,783 |
| UT | 1.9 | 34.3 | 131 | 45.9 | 213 | 543 | 2,421 | 215 | 3,180 |
| VT | 1.1 | 21.1 | 96.2 | 11.8 | 130 | 538 | 1,674 | 70.5 | 2,282 |
| VA | 4.6 | 19.1 | 119 | 70.7 | 214 | 383 | 1,813 | 132 | 2,327 |
| WA | 2.3 | 38.1 | 185 | 88.2 | 314 | 820 | 2,504 | 383 | 3,707 |
| WV | 3.3 | 19.1 | 248 | 44.7 | 315 | 581 | 1,532 | 127 | 2,240 |
| WI | 2.7 | 20.9 | 146 | 79.2 | 249 | 467 | 1,898 | 143 | 2,508 |
| WY | 1.4 | 29.1 | 152 | 13.5 | 196 | 381 | 1,975 | 105 | 2,462 |
| **Total US** | **4.8** | **27.5** | **252** | **119** | **404** | **700** | **2,004** | **239** | **2,942** |

[1]Up until 2008 includes reported offenses at the National Zoo and, from 2002 to 2008, offenses reported by the Metro Transit Police.   [2]Data are estimated or incomplete.   [3]Includes nonnegligent manslaughter.   [4]Detail may not add to total given because of rounding.

Source: Federal Bureau of Investigation, <http://www.fbi.gov>.

## Crime in the US, 1991–2010

This table presents the number of crimes reported in the seven categories that, with arson, are known as Part I crimes and are used by the Federal Bureau of Investigation to assess trends in criminality in the country.

Source: Federal Bureau of Investigation.

| | | VIOLENT CRIME | | | | PROPERTY CRIME | |
| | | FORCIBLE | | AGGRA-VATED | | LARCENY/ | MOTOR VEHICLE |
| YEAR | MURDER[1] | RAPE | ROBBERY | ASSAULT | BURGLARY | THEFT | THEFT |
|---|---|---|---|---|---|---|---|
| 1991 | 24,703 | 106,593 | 687,732 | 1,092,739 | 3,157,150 | 8,142,228 | 1,661,738 |
| 1992 | 23,760 | 109,062 | 672,478 | 1,126,974 | 2,979,884 | 7,915,199 | 1,610,834 |
| 1993 | 24,526 | 106,014 | 659,870 | 1,135,607 | 2,834,808 | 7,820,909 | 1,563,060 |
| 1994 | 23,326 | 102,216 | 618,949 | 1,113,179 | 2,712,774 | 7,879,812 | 1,539,287 |
| 1995 | 21,606 | 97,470 | 580,509 | 1,099,207 | 2,593,784 | 7,997,710 | 1,472,441 |
| 1996 | 19,645 | 96,252 | 535,594 | 1,037,049 | 2,506,400 | 7,904,685 | 1,394,238 |
| 1997 | 18,208 | 96,153 | 498,534 | 1,023,201 | 2,460,526 | 7,743,760 | 1,354,189 |
| 1998 | 16,974 | 93,144 | 447,186 | 976,583 | 2,332,735 | 7,376,311 | 1,242,781 |
| 1999 | 15,522 | 89,411 | 409,371 | 911,740 | 2,100,739 | 6,955,520 | 1,152,075 |
| 2000 | 15,586 | 90,178 | 408,016 | 911,706 | 2,050,992 | 6,971,590 | 1,160,002 |
| 2001 | 16,037 | 90,863 | 423,557 | 909,023 | 2,116,531 | 7,092,267 | 1,228,391 |
| 2002 | 16,229 | 95,235 | 420,806 | 891,407 | 2,151,252 | 7,057,379 | 1,246,646 |
| 2003 | 16,528 | 93,883 | 414,235 | 859,030 | 2,154,834 | 7,026,802 | 1,261,226 |
| 2004 | 16,148 | 95,089 | 401,470 | 847,381 | 2,144,446 | 6,937,089 | 1,237,851 |
| 2005 | 16,740 | 94,347 | 417,438 | 862,220 | 2,155,448 | 6,783,447 | 1,235,859 |
| 2006 | 17,309 | 94,472 | 449,246 | 874,096 | 2,194,993 | 6,626,363 | 1,198,245 |
| 2007 | 17,128 | 92,160 | 447,324 | 866,358 | 2,190,198 | 6,591,542 | 1,100,472 |
| 2008 | 16,465 | 90,750 | 443,563 | 843,683 | 2,228,887 | 6,586,206 | 959,059 |
| 2009 | 15,399 | 89,241 | 408,742 | 812,514 | 2,203,313 | 6,338,095 | 795,652 |
| 2010 | 14,748 | 84,767 | 367,832 | 778,901 | 2,159,878 | 6,185,867 | 737,142 |

### Crime trends: percent change in number of offenses[2]

| | | VIOLENT CRIME | | | | PROPERTY CRIME | |
| YEARS COMPARED | MURDER[1] | FORCIBLE RAPE | ROBBERY | AGGRA-VATED ASSAULT | BURGLARY | LARCENY/ THEFT | MOTOR VEHICLE THEFT |
|---|---|---|---|---|---|---|---|
| 2010/2009 | −4.2 | −5.0 | −10.0 | −4.1 | −2.0 | −2.4 | −7.4 |
| 2010/2006 | −14.8 | −10.3 | −18.1 | −10.9 | −1.6 | −6.6 | −38.5 |
| 2010/2001 | −8.0 | −6.7 | −13.2 | −14.3 | +2.0 | −12.8 | −40.0 |

[1]Includes the crime of nonnegligent manslaughter. [2]A minus sign indicates a decrease in crime; a plus sign indicates an increase.

## US Cities with Most and Fewest Violent Crimes

This table ranks cities with populations greater than 100,000 by the number of violent crimes reported during 2011. Source: Federal Bureau of Investigation, Preliminary Annual Uniform Crime Report, January to December 2011.

| CITIES | VIOLENT CRIMES[1] | MURDER | FORCIBLE RAPE | ROBBERY | AGGRAVATED ASSAULT | BURGLARY | LARCENY/ THEFT | CAR THEFT |
|---|---|---|---|---|---|---|---|---|
| **Most Violent Crimes** | | | | | | | | |
| New York NY | 51,209 | 515 | 1,092 | 19,773 | 29,829 | 18,159 | 112,864 | 9,434 |
| Chicago IL[2] | 26,813 | 430 | [2] | 13,975 | 12,408 | 26,420 | 72,373 | 19,446 |
| Houston TX | 20,892 | 198 | 771 | 8,054 | 11,869 | 27,459 | 68,596 | 12,281 |
| Los Angeles CA | 20,045 | 297 | 828 | 10,077 | 8,843 | 17,264 | 53,469 | 15,597 |
| Philadelphia PA | 18,268 | 324 | 833 | 8,246 | 8,865 | 12,057 | 40,113 | 7,447 |
| Detroit MI | 15,245 | 344 | 427 | 4,962 | 9,512 | 15,994 | 16,456 | 11,368 |
| Las Vegas NV | 10,810 | 79 | 651 | 3,493 | 6,587 | 12,662 | 21,977 | 6,787 |
| Memphis TN | 10,333 | 117 | 396 | 3,083 | 6,737 | 13,309 | 25,637 | 3,428 |
| Baltimore MD | 8,885 | 196 | 341 | 3,457 | 4,891 | 8,615 | 17,010 | 4,199 |
| Dallas TX | 8,330 | 133 | 428 | 4,066 | 3,703 | 18,727 | 35,148 | 7,984 |
| **Fewest Violent Crimes** | | | | | | | | |
| Temecula CA | 95 | 0 | 7 | 54 | 34 | 547 | 1,700 | 159 |
| Murrieta CA | 105 | 2 | 13 | 34 | 56 | 348 | 1,031 | 116 |
| Naperville IL | 112 | 2 | 4 | 24 | 82 | 300 | 1,768 | 42 |
| Round Rock TX | 115 | 2 | 25 | 39 | 49 | 394 | 2,001 | 51 |
| Simi Valley CA | 116 | 0 | 9 | 41 | 66 | 314 | 1,278 | 105 |
| Irvine CA | 120 | 2 | 11 | 40 | 67 | 513 | 2,649 | 118 |

## US Cities with Most and Fewest Violent Crimes (continued)

| CITIES | VIOLENT CRIMES[1] | MURDER | FORCIBLE RAPE | ROBBERY | AGGRAVATED ASSAULT | BURGLARY | LARCENY/ THEFT | CAR THEFT |
|---|---|---|---|---|---|---|---|---|
| Fewest Violent Crimes (continued) | | | | | | | | |
| Frisco TX | 122 | 3 | 6 | 23 | 90 | 483 | 1,878 | 99 |
| Amherst NY | 124 | 0 | 7 | 41 | 76 | 221 | 1,736 | 47 |
| Cary NC | 126 | 1 | 14 | 54 | 57 | 415 | 1,847 | 74 |
| Surprise AZ | 131 | 0 | 12 | 51 | 68 | 617 | 1,873 | 108 |

[1]Data for overall incidents of violent crimes are composites of data for murder, forcible rape, robbery, and aggravated assault.    [2]Data for forcible rape in Chicago are not available.

## Total Arrests in the US, 2010

Estimates for the year 2010. Source: Federal Bureau of Investigation, Crime in the United States, 2010.

| TYPE OF CRIME | NUMBER OF ARRESTS | TYPE OF CRIME | NUMBER OF ARRESTS |
|---|---|---|---|
| violent crime | | other crime types (continued) | |
| aggravated assault | 408,488 | drunkenness | 560,718 |
| robbery | 112,300 | vandalism | 252,753 |
| forcible rape | 20,088 | fraud | 187,887 |
| murder and nonnegligent manslaughter | 11,201 | weapons (carrying, possessing, etc.) | 159,020 |
| violent crime total | 552,077 | curfew and loitering law violations | 94,797 |
| | | offenses against the family and children | 111,062 |
| property crime | | stolen property (buying, receiving, possessing) | 94,802 |
| larceny/theft | 1,271,410 | runaways | n/a |
| burglary | 289,769 | forgery and counterfeiting | 78,101 |
| motor vehicle theft | 71,487 | sex offenses (except forcible rape and prostitution) | 72,628 |
| arson | 11,296 | prostitution and commercialized vice | 62,668 |
| property crime total | 1,643,962 | vagrancy | 32,033 |
| | | embezzlement | 16,616 |
| other crime types | | gambling | 9,941 |
| drug abuse violations | 1,638,846 | suspicion (not included in total) | 1,166 |
| driving under the influence | 1,412,223 | all other offenses (except traffic) | 3,720,402 |
| other assaults | 1,292,449 | total arrests | 13,120,947 |
| disorderly conduct | 615,172 | | |
| liquor laws | 512,790 | | |

## US State and Federal Prison Population

Source: US Bureau of Justice Statistics.

| STATE | NUMBER OF PRISONERS | | | | % CHANGE (31 DEC 2009 TO 31 DEC 2010) |
|---|---|---|---|---|---|
| | 31 DEC 1990 | 31 DEC 2000 | 31 DEC 2009 | 31 DEC 2010 | |
| Alabama | 15,665 | 26,332 | 31,874 | 31,764 | −0.3 |
| Alaska[1] | 2,622 | 4,173 | 5,285 | 5,597 | +5.9 |
| Arizona[2] | 14,261 | 26,510 | 40,627 | 40,130 | −1.2 |
| Arkansas | 7,322 | 11,915 | 15,208 | 16,204 | +6.5 |
| California | 97,309 | 163,001 | 171,275 | 165,062 | −3.6 |
| Colorado | 7,671 | 16,833 | 22,795 | 22,815 | +0.1 |
| Connecticut[1] | 10,500 | 18,355 | 19,716 | 19,321 | −2.0 |
| Delaware[1] | 3,471 | 6,921 | 6,794 | 6,598 | −2.9 |
| Florida | 44,387 | 71,319 | 103,915 | 104,306 | +0.4 |
| Georgia[2] | 22,411 | 44,232 | 53,371 | 49,164 | −7.9 |
| Hawaii[1] | 2,533 | 5,053 | 5,891 | 5,912 | +0.4 |
| Idaho | 1,961 | 5,535 | 7,400 | 7,431 | +0.4 |
| Illinois | 27,516 | 45,281 | 45,161 | 48,418 | +7.2 |
| Indiana | 12,736 | 20,125 | 28,808 | 28,028 | −2.7 |
| Iowa | 3,967 | 7,955 | 8,813 | 9,455 | +7.3 |
| Kansas | 5,775 | 8,344 | 8,641 | 9,051 | +4.7 |
| Kentucky | 9,023 | 14,919 | 21,638 | 20,544 | −5.1 |
| Louisiana | 18,599 | 35,207 | 39,780 | 39,445 | −0.8 |
| Maine | 1,523 | 1,679 | 2,206 | 2,154 | −2.4 |
| Maryland | 17,848 | 23,538 | 22,255 | 22,645 | +1.8 |
| Massachusetts | 8,345 | 10,722 | 11,316 | 11,312 | −0.0 |

## US State and Federal Prison Population (continued)

| STATE | NUMBER OF PRISONERS | | | | % CHANGE (31 DEC 2009 TO 31 DEC 2010) |
| --- | --- | --- | --- | --- | --- |
| | 31 DEC 1990 | 31 DEC 2000 | 31 DEC 2009 | 31 DEC 2010 | |
| Michigan | 34,267 | 47,718 | 45,478 | 44,113 | −3.0 |
| Minnesota | 3,176 | 6,238 | 9,986 | 9,796 | −1.9 |
| Mississippi | 8,375 | 20,241 | 21,482 | 21,067 | −1.9 |
| Missouri | 14,943 | 27,543 | 30,563 | 30,623 | +0.2 |
| Montana | 1,425 | 3,105 | 3,605 | 3,716 | +3.1 |
| Nebraska | 2,403 | 3,895 | 4,474 | 4,587 | +2.5 |
| Nevada | 5,322 | 10,063 | 12,482 | 12,653 | +1.4 |
| New Hampshire | 1,342 | 2,257 | 2,731 | 2,761 | +1.1 |
| New Jersey | 21,128 | 29,784 | 25,382 | 25,007 | −1.5 |
| New Mexico | 3,187 | 5,342 | 6,448 | 6,659 | +3.3 |
| New York | 54,895 | 70,199 | 58,687 | 56,656 | −3.5 |
| North Carolina | 18,411 | 31,266 | 40,529 | 40,116 | −1.0 |
| North Dakota | 483 | 1,076 | 1,486 | 1,487 | +0.1 |
| Ohio | 31,822 | 45,833 | 51,606 | 51,712 | +0.2 |
| Oklahoma | 12,285 | 23,181 | 26,397 | 26,252 | −0.5 |
| Oregon | 6,492 | 10,580 | 14,403 | 14,014 | −2.7 |
| Pennsylvania | 22,290 | 36,847 | 51,429 | 51,264 | −0.3 |
| Rhode Island[1] | 2,392 | 3,286 | 3,674 | 3,357 | −8.6 |
| South Carolina | 17,319 | 21,778 | 24,288 | 23,578 | −2.9 |
| South Dakota | 1,341 | 2,616 | 3,434 | 3,434 | +0.0 |
| Tennessee | 10,388 | 22,166 | 26,965 | 27,451 | +1.8 |
| Texas | 50,042 | 166,719 | 171,249 | 173,649 | +1.4 |
| Utah | 2,496 | 5,637 | 6,538 | 6,807 | +4.1 |
| Vermont[1] | 1,049 | 1,697 | 2,220 | 2,079 | −6.4 |
| Virginia | 17,593 | 30,168 | 38,092 | 37,410 | −1.8 |
| Washington | 7,995 | 14,915 | 18,233 | 18,235 | +0.0 |
| West Virginia | 1,565 | 3,856 | 6,367 | 6,681 | +4.9 |
| Wisconsin | 7,465 | 20,754 | 23,165 | 22,724 | −1.9 |
| Wyoming | 1,110 | 1,680 | 2,075 | 2,112 | +1.8 |
| | | | | | |
| state | 708,393 | 1,245,845 | 1,406,237 | 1,395,356 | −0.8 |
| federal[3] | 65,526 | 145,416 | 208,118 | 209,771 | +0.8 |
| | | | | | |
| **US total** | **773,919** | **1,391,261** | **1,614,355** | **1,605,127** | **−0.6** |

[1]Jails and prisons are part of an integrated system. Data include total jail and prison populations.    [2]Population figures are based on custody counts.    [3]As of the end of 2001, when the transfer of responsibility for sentenced felons from the District of Columbia to the Federal Bureau of Prisons was completed, the District of Columbia no longer operates a prison system, and its prisoners are from that date forward included in federal data only.

## Directors of the Federal Bureau of Investigation (FBI)

The FBI evolved from an unnamed force appointed by Attorney General Charles J. Bonaparte on 26 Jul 1908. It is the unit of the Department of Justice responsible for investigating foreign intelligence and terrorist activities and violations of federal criminal law. The president appoints the director of the FBI with confirmation from the Senate. Since J. Edgar Hoover's tenure, a director's term may not exceed 10 years. Acting directors are not included in this table.

| NAME | DATES OF SERVICE | NAME | DATES OF SERVICE |
| --- | --- | --- | --- |
| Stanley Finch | 26 Jul 1908–30 Apr 1912 | Clarence M. Kelley | 9 Jul 1973–15 Feb 1978 |
| Alexander Bruce Bielaski | 30 Apr 1912–10 Feb 1919 | William H. Webster | 23 Feb 1978–25 May 1987 |
| William J. Flynn | 1 Jul 1919–21 Aug 1921 | William S. Sessions | 2 Nov 1987–19 Jul 1993 |
| William J. Burns | 22 Aug 1921–14 Jun 1924 | Louis J. Freeh | 1 Sep 1993–25 Jun 2001 |
| J. Edgar Hoover | 10 Dec 1924–2 May 1972 | Robert S. Mueller, III | 4 Sep 2001– |

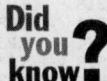
**Did you know?**

According to the research firm eMarketer, in 2010 spending on online advertising in the United States eclipsed spending from print newspaper advertising for the first time. Online advertising reached an estimated US$25.8 billion, while advertising in print newspapers declined to roughly US$22.8 billion. When online and print newspaper advertising were combined, however, spending totalled roughly US$25.7 billion.

# United States Society

## Average US Family Size, 1950–2010

Source: Statistical Abstract of the United States: 2012.

| YEAR | NUMBER OF FAMILIES ('000) | PEOPLE PER FAMILY (AVERAGE) | YEAR | NUMBER OF FAMILIES ('000) | PEOPLE PER FAMILY (AVERAGE) | YEAR | NUMBER OF FAMILIES ('000) | PEOPLE PER FAMILY (AVERAGE) |
|------|------|------|------|------|------|------|------|------|
| 1950 | 39,303 | 3.54 | 1970 | 51,586 | 3.58 | 1990 | 66,090 | 3.17 |
| 1955 | 41,951 | 3.59 | 1975 | 55,712 | 3.42 | 1995 | 69,305 | 3.19 |
| 1960 | 45,111 | 3.67 | 1980 | 59,550 | 3.29 | 2000 | 72,025 | 3.17 |
| 1965 | 47,956 | 3.70 | 1985 | 62,706 | 3.23 | 2010 | 78,833 | 3.16 |

## US Population by Age, 2012

Numbers are in thousands ('000). Source: US Census Bureau. Detail may not add to total given because of rounding.

| AGE | POPULATION NUMBER | (%) | AGE | POPULATION NUMBER | (%) |
|-----|------|-----|-----|------|-----|
| under 5 years | 21,222,135 | 6.8 | 55 to 64 years | 38,042,972 | 12.1 |
| 5 to 9 years | 20,942,698 | 6.7 | 65 to 74 years | 23,401,004 | 7.5 |
| 10 to 14 years | 20,605,798 | 6.6 | 75 years and over | 19,076,700 | 6.1 |
| 15 to 19 years | 21,139,064 | 6.7 | total population | 313,847,465 | 100 |
| 20 to 24 years | 22,146,988 | 7.1 | | | |
| 25 to 34 years | 42,517,547 | 13.5 | under 20 years | 83,909,695 | 26.7 |
| 35 to 44 years | 40,649,716 | 12.9 | 20 years and over | 229,937,770 | 73.3 |
| 45 to 54 years | 44,102,843 | 14.0 | 65 years and over | 42,477,704 | 13.5 |

## Living Arrangements of Children Under 18 in the US, 2011

Numbers in thousands ('000). Hispanics may be of any race. Detail may not add to total given because of rounding. Source: US Census Bureau.

| LIVING IN HOUSEHOLD WITH | RACE/ETHNICITY ALL RACES | WHITE | BLACK | HISPANIC |
|-----|-----|-----|-----|-----|
| both parents | 51,456 | 41,986 | 4,208 | 11,649 |
| mother only | 17,635 | 10,505 | 5,717 | 4,613 |
| father only | 2,628 | 2,052 | 387 | 479 |
| neither parent | 2,910 | 1,776 | 843 | 677 |
| total | 74,630 | 56,319 | 11,155 | 17,418 |

## Children Under 18 in the US Living Below the Poverty Level, 1985–2010

Numbers are in thousands ('000). Hispanics may be of any race.
N/A means not available.

Source: US Census Bureau. For the definition of the poverty level, see <www.census.gov/hhes/www/poverty/methods/definitions.html>.

| YEAR | % OF CHILDREN BELOW THE POVERTY LEVEL ALL[1] | WHITE[2] | BLACK | ASIAN/ PACIFIC ISLANDER | HISPANIC | NUMBER OF CHILDREN BELOW THE POVERTY LEVEL ALL[1] | WHITE[2] | BLACK | ASIAN/ PACIFIC ISLANDER | HISPANIC |
|------|------|------|------|------|------|------|------|------|------|------|
| 1985 | 20.7 | 12.8 | 43.6 | N/A | 40.3 | 13,010 | 5,745 | 4,157 | N/A | 2,606 |
| 1986 | 20.5 | 13.0 | 43.1 | N/A | 37.7 | 12,876 | 5,789 | 4,148 | N/A | 2,507 |
| 1987 | 20.3 | 11.8 | 45.1 | 23.5 | 39.3 | 12,843 | 5,230 | 4,385 | 455 | 2,670 |
| 1988 | 19.5 | 11.0 | 43.5 | 24.1 | 37.6 | 12,455 | 4,888 | 4,296 | 474 | 2,631 |
| 1989 | 19.6 | 11.5 | 43.7 | 19.8 | 36.2 | 12,590 | 5,110 | 4,375 | 392 | 2,603 |
| 1990 | 20.6 | 12.3 | 44.8 | 17.6 | 38.4 | 13,431 | 5,532 | 4,550 | 374 | 2,865 |
| 1991 | 21.8 | 13.1 | 45.9 | 17.5 | 40.4 | 14,341 | 5,918 | 4,755 | 360 | 3,094 |
| 1992 | 22.3 | 13.2 | 46.6 | 16.4 | 40.0 | 15,294 | 6,017 | 5,106 | 363 | 3,637 |
| 1993 | 22.7 | 13.6 | 46.1 | 18.2 | 40.9 | 15,727 | 6,255 | 5,125 | 375 | 3,873 |
| 1994 | 21.8 | 12.5 | 43.8 | 18.3 | 41.5 | 15,289 | 5,823 | 4,906 | 318 | 4,075 |
| 1995 | 20.8 | 11.2 | 41.9 | 19.5 | 40.0 | 14,665 | 5,115 | 4,761 | 564 | 4,080 |
| 1996 | 20.5 | 11.1 | 39.9 | 19.5 | 40.3 | 14,463 | 5,072 | 4,519 | 571 | 4,237 |
| 1997 | 19.9 | 11.4 | 37.2 | 20.3 | 36.8 | 14,113 | 5,204 | 4,225 | 628 | 3,972 |
| 1998 | 18.9 | 10.6 | 36.7 | 18.0 | 34.4 | 13,467 | 4,822 | 4,151 | 564 | 3,837 |
| 1999 | 16.9 | 9.4 | 33.2 | 11.9 | 30.3 | 12,280 | 4,155 | 3,813 | 381 | 3,693 |

## Children Under 18 in the US Living Below the Poverty Level, 1985–2010 (continued)

| | % OF CHILDREN BELOW THE POVERTY LEVEL | | | | | NUMBER OF CHILDREN BELOW THE POVERTY LEVEL | | | | |
| YEAR | ALL[1] | WHITE[2] | BLACK | ASIAN/ PACIFIC ISLANDER | HISPANIC | ALL[1] | WHITE[2] | BLACK | ASIAN/ PACIFIC ISLANDER | HISPANIC |
|---|---|---|---|---|---|---|---|---|---|---|
| 2000 | 16.2 | 9.1 | 31.2 | 12.7 | 28.4 | 11,587 | 4,018 | 3,581 | 420 | 3,522 |
| 2001 | 16.3 | 9.5 | 30.2 | 11.5 | 28.0 | 11,733 | 4,194 | 3,492 | 369 | 3,570 |
| 2002 | 16.7 | 9.4 | 32.3 | 12.2 | 28.6 | 12,133 | 4,090 | 3,645 | 351 | 3,782 |
| 2003 | 17.6 | 9.8 | 34.1 | 12.7 | 29.7 | 12,866 | 4,233 | 3,877 | 377 | 4,077 |
| 2004 | 17.8 | 10.5 | 33.7 | 10.1 | 28.9 | 13,041 | 4,519 | 3,788 | 305 | 4,098 |
| 2005 | 17.6 | 10.0 | 34.5 | 11.0 | 28.3 | 12,896 | 4,254 | 3,841 | 333 | 4,143 |
| 2006 | 17.4 | 10.0 | 33.4 | 12.5 | 26.9 | 12,827 | 4,208 | 3,777 | 391 | 4,072 |
| 2007 | 18.0 | 10.1 | 34.5 | 12.5 | 28.6 | 13,324 | 4,255 | 3,904 | 398 | 4,482 |
| 2008 | 19.0 | 10.6 | 34.7 | 15.5 | 30.6 | 14,068 | 4,364 | 3,878 | 514 | 5,010 |
| 2009 | 20.7 | 11.9 | 35.7 | 14.8 | 33.1 | 15,451 | 4,850 | 4,033 | 526 | 5,610 |
| 2010 | 22.0 | 12.4 | 39.1 | 15.0 | 35.0 | 16,401 | 5,002 | 4,362 | 664 | 6,110 |

[1]Includes other and unclassified.    [2]Excludes Hispanic population.

## US Adoptions of Foreign-Born Children

*Adoptions of foreign children by US citizens are tracked by the number of immigrant visas issued to orphans entering the US. Source: US Department of State.*

| TOP 10 COUNTRIES OF ORIGIN | ADOPTIONS FISCAL YEAR 2010 | 2011 | TOP 10 COUNTRIES OF ORIGIN | ADOPTIONS FISCAL YEAR 2010 | 2011 | TOTAL FOREIGN ADOPTIONS FISCAL YEAR | ADOPTIONS |
|---|---|---|---|---|---|---|---|
| 1  China | 3,401 | 2,589 | 6  Philippines | 214 | 230 | 2006 | 20,680 |
| 2  Ethiopia | 2,513 | 1,727 | 7  India | 243 | 228 | 2007 | 19,609 |
| 3  Russia | 1,082 | 970 | 8  Colombia | 235 | 216 | 2008 | 17,475 |
| 4  Rep. of Korea | 863 | 736 | 9  Uganda | 62 | 207 | 2009 | 12,753 |
| 5  Ukraine | 445 | 632 | 10  Taiwan | 285 | 205 | 2010 | 11,059 |
| | | | | | | 2011 | 9,320 |

## US Nursing Home Population

The data in these tables were gathered through interviews conducted for the most recent National Nursing Home Survey (2004) and through the publication *Health, United States, 2011*. Only those residents who described themselves as being of one race are included. Data on residents under the age of 65 are not available. Detail may not add to total given because of rounding.

Source: US National Center for Health Statistics.

| AGE AT INTERVIEW | TOTAL RESIDENTS | % | GENDER (2004) MALE | % | FEMALE | % |
|---|---|---|---|---|---|---|
| 65–74 | 174,100 | 13.2 | 75,400 | 22.4 | 98,800 | 10.1 |
| 75–84 | 468,700 | 35.6 | 140,900 | 41.8 | 327,800 | 33.4 |
| 85 and older | 674,500 | 51.2 | 120,600 | 35.8 | 553,900 | 56.5 |
| total | 1,317,300 | 100.0 | 336,900 | 100.0 | 980,400 | 100.0 |

| | RACE (2004) WHITE | % | BLACK | % |
|---|---|---|---|---|
| 65–74 | 134,200 | 11.7 | 34,500 | 23.7 |
| 75–84 | 405,800 | 35.3 | 54,600 | 37.6 |
| 85 and older | 608,900 | 53.0 | 56,300 | 38.7 |
| total | 1,148,900 | 100.0 | 145,400 | 100.0 |

| | RESIDENT LOCATION (1999) NORTHEAST | % | MIDWEST | % | SOUTH | % | WEST | % |
|---|---|---|---|---|---|---|---|---|
| 65–74 | 46,400 | 12.1 | 58,900 | 11.8 | 63,400 | 11.9 | 26,100 | 12.1 |
| 75–84 | 118,500 | 30.9 | 153,200 | 30.8 | 179,100 | 33.7 | 66,800 | 31.1 |
| 85 and older | 184,300 | 48.1 | 241,100 | 48.4 | 237,700 | 44.7 | 94,000 | 43.7 |
| total | 383,400 | 100.0 | 498,200 | 100.0 | 531,500 | 100.0 | 215,200 | 100.0 |

| | RESIDENT LOCATION (2010) NORTHEAST | % | MIDWEST | % | SOUTH | % | WEST | % |
|---|---|---|---|---|---|---|---|---|
| TOTAL RESIDENTS | 329,150 | 23.6 | 400,614 | 28.7 | 478,394 | 34.2 | 188,315 | 13.5 |

## Marital Status of US Population by Sex, 1960–2011

*The data in this table are taken from surveys of individuals 18 or over conducted by the US Census Bureau and exclude members of the armed forces except those living off post or with their families on post. Data exclude Alaska and Hawaii prior to 1960. Detail may not add to total given because of rounding.*
   *Source: US Census Bureau.*

| | TOTAL | | | | | | |
| | 1960 | 1970 | 1980 | 1990 | 2000 | 2010 | 2011 |
|---|---|---|---|---|---|---|---|
| Total individuals surveyed in hundred thousands ('000,000) | 125.5 | 132.5 | 159.5 | 181.8 | 201.8 | 229.1 | 231.1 |
| Percentage of individuals never married | 22.0 | 16.2 | 20.3 | 22.2 | 23.9 | 26.9 | 27.4 |
| Percentage of individuals married | 67.3 | 71.7 | 65.5 | 61.9 | 59.5 | 54.2 | 53.6 |
| Percentage of individuals widowed | 8.4 | 8.9 | 8.0 | 7.6 | 6.8 | 6.3 | 6.2 |
| Percentage of individuals divorced | 2.3 | 3.2 | 6.2 | 8.3 | 9.8 | 10.4 | 10.6 |
| Percentage of males never married | 25.3 | 18.9 | 23.8 | 25.8 | 27.0 | 30.4 | 30.6 |
| Percentage of males married | 69.1 | 75.3 | 68.4 | 64.3 | 61.5 | 55.9 | 55.2 |
| Percentage of males widowed | 3.7 | 3.3 | 2.6 | 2.7 | 2.7 | 2.7 | 2.6 |
| Percentage of males divorced | 1.9 | 2.5 | 5.2 | 7.2 | 8.8 | 9.0 | 9.5 |
| Percentage of females never married | 12.3 | 13.7 | 17.1 | 18.9 | 21.1 | 23.6 | 24.3 |
| Percentage of females married | 42.6 | 68.5 | 63.0 | 59.7 | 57.6 | 52.5 | 52.1 |
| Percentage of females widowed | 8.3 | 13.9 | 12.8 | 12.1 | 10.5 | 9.6 | 9.5 |
| Percentage of females divorced | 1.7 | 3.9 | 7.1 | 9.3 | 10.8 | 11.7 | 11.6 |

## Unmarried-Couple Households in the US

*Data based on Current Population Survey or American Community Survey except for census years of 1960 and 1970. 2009 data shown separately. Numbers in thousands ('000). Source: Statistical Abstract of the United States: 2012.*

| YEAR | TOTAL US HOUSEHOLDS | UNMARRIED-COUPLE HOUSEHOLDS (OPPOSITE SEX) | % OF TOTAL HOUSEHOLDS | NO CHILDREN UNDER 15 | WITH CHILDREN UNDER 15 |
|---|---|---|---|---|---|
| 1960 census | 52,799 | 439 | 0.8 | 242 | 197 |
| 1970 census | 63,401 | 523 | 0.8 | 327 | 196 |
| 1980 | 80,776 | 1,589 | 2.0 | 1,159 | 431 |
| 1985 | 86,789 | 1,983 | 2.3 | 1,380 | 603 |
| 1990 | 93,347 | 2,856 | 3.1 | 1,966 | 891 |
| 1995 | 98,990 | 3,668 | 3.7 | 2,349 | 1,319 |
| 2000 | 104,705 | 4,736 | 4.5 | 3,061 | 1,675 |

| UNMARRIED-COUPLE HOUSEHOLDS | 2009 |
|---|---|
| male householder/female partner | 3,053 |
| male householder/male partner | 280 |
| female householder/female partner | 301 |
| female householder/male partner | 2,868 |
| **unmarried-couple households** | **6,502** |
| **total households** | **113,616** |

# United States Education

## Educational Attainment in the US by Gender and Race

For persons ages 25 years old and older. Percentage rates for 1960, 1970, and 1980 are based on sample data from the decennial censuses. Rates for 1990, 2000, and 2010 are based on the Current Population Survey. N/A means not available.
   Source: US Census Bureau.

## Educational Attainment in the US by Gender and Race (continued)

### Percentage who had graduated from high school[1]

| YEAR | ALL RACES[2] | | WHITE | | BLACK | | ASIAN/PACIFIC ISLANDER | | HISPANIC[3] | |
|------|------|--------|------|--------|------|--------|------|--------|------|--------|
| | MALE | FEMALE | MALE | FEMALE | MALE | FEMALE | MALE | FEMALE | MALE | FEMALE |
| 1960 | 39.5 | 42.5 | 41.6 | 44.7 | 18.2 | 21.8 | N/A | N/A | N/A | N/A |
| 1970 | 51.9 | 52.8 | 54.0 | 55.0 | 30.1 | 32.5 | 61.3 | 63.1 | 37.9 | 34.2 |
| 1980 | 67.3 | 65.8 | 69.6 | 68.1 | 50.8 | 51.5 | 78.8 | 71.4 | 45.4 | 42.7 |
| 1990 | 77.7 | 77.5 | 79.1 | 79.0 | 65.8 | 66.5 | 84.0 | 77.2 | 50.3 | 51.3 |
| 2000 | 84.2 | 84.0 | 84.8 | 85.0 | 78.7 | 78.3 | 88.2 | 83.4 | 56.6 | 57.5 |
| 2010 | 86.6 | 87.6 | 86.9 | 88.2 | 83.6 | 84.6 | 91.2 | 87.0 | 61.4 | 64.4 |

### Percentage who had graduated from college[4]

| YEAR | ALL RACES[2] | | WHITE | | BLACK | | ASIAN/PACIFIC ISLANDER | | HISPANIC[3] | |
|------|------|--------|------|--------|------|--------|------|--------|------|--------|
| | MALE | FEMALE | MALE | FEMALE | MALE | FEMALE | MALE | FEMALE | MALE | FEMALE |
| 1960 | 9.7 | 5.8 | 10.3 | 6.0 | 2.8 | 3.3 | N/A | N/A | N/A | N/A |
| 1970 | 13.5 | 8.1 | 14.4 | 8.4 | 4.2 | 4.6 | 23.5 | 17.3 | 7.8 | 4.3 |
| 1980 | 20.1 | 12.8 | 21.3 | 13.3 | 8.4 | 8.3 | 39.8 | 27.0 | 9.4 | 6.0 |
| 1990 | 24.4 | 18.4 | 25.3 | 19.0 | 11.9 | 10.8 | 44.9 | 35.4 | 9.8 | 8.7 |
| 2000 | 27.8 | 23.6 | 28.5 | 23.9 | 16.3 | 16.7 | 47.6 | 40.7 | 10.7 | 10.6 |
| 2010 | 30.3 | 29.6 | 30.8 | 29.9 | 17.7 | 21.4 | 55.6 | 49.5 | 12.9 | 14.9 |

[1]Through 1990, finished four years or more of high school. [2]Includes races not shown separately in the table. [3]Hispanics may be of any race. [4]Through 1990, finished four years or more of college.

# National Spelling Bee

A spelling bee is a contest in which players attempt to spell correctly and aloud words assigned them by an impartial judge. Competition may be individual, with players eliminated when they misspell a word and the last remaining player being the winner, or between teams, the winner being the team with the most players remaining at the close of the contest. The spelling bee is an old custom that was revived in schools in the United States in the late 19th century and enjoyed a great vogue there and in Great Britain. In the US, local, regional, and national competitions continue to be held annually. The US National Spelling Bee was begun by the Louisville Courier-Journal newspaper in 1925, and it was taken over by Scripps Howard, Inc., in 1941. To qualify, spellers (who are sponsored by an organization, usually a newspaper) must meet 12 requirements, including that they have neither reached their 16th birthday nor passed beyond the eighth grade.

**National Spelling Bee Web site:** <www.spellingbee.com>.

| YEAR | CHAMPION | WINNING WORD |
|------|----------|-------------|
| 1925 | Frank Neuhauser, Courier-Journal (Louisville KY) | gladiolus |
| 1926 | Pauline Bell, Courier-Journal (Louisville KY) | cerise |
| 1927 | Dean Lucas, Akron Beacon Journal (Ohio) | abrogate |
| 1928 | Betty Robinson, South Bend News-Tribune (Indiana) | knack |
| 1929 | Virginia Hogan, Omaha World-Herald (Nebraska) | luxuriance |
| 1930 | Helen Jensen, Des Moines Register & Tribune (Iowa) | albumen |
| 1931 | Ward Randall, White Hall Register-Republican (Illinois) | foulard |
| 1932 | Dorothy Greenwald, Des Moines Register & Tribune (Iowa) | invulnerable[1] |
| 1933 | Alma Roach, Akron Beacon Journal (Ohio) | torsion |
| 1934 | Sarah Wilson, Portland Evening Express (Maine) | brethren |
| 1935 | Clara Mohler, Akron Beacon Journal (Ohio) | intelligible |
| 1936 | Jean Trowbridge, Des Moines Register & Tribune (Iowa) | eczema |
| 1937 | Waneeta Beckley, Courier-Journal (Louisville KY) | promiscuous |
| 1938 | Marian Richardson, Louisville Times (Kentucky) | sanitarium |
| 1939 | Elizabeth Ann Rice, Worcester Telegram & Gazette (Massachusetts) | canonical |
| 1940 | Laurel Kuykendall, Knoxville News-Sentinel (Tennessee) | therapy[1] |
| 1941 | Louis Edward Sissman, Detroit News (Michigan) | initials |
| 1942 | Richard Earnhart, El Paso Herald-Post (Texas) | sacrilegious |
| 1943–45 | | not held |
| 1946 | John McKinney, Des Moines Register & Tribune (Iowa) | semaphore |
| 1947 | Mattie Lou Pollard, Atlanta Journal (Georgia) | chlorophyll |
| 1948 | Jean Chappelear, Akron Beacon Journal (Ohio) | psychiatry |
| 1949 | Kim Calvin, Canton Repository (Ohio) | onerous |
| 1950 | Diana Reynard, Cleveland Press (Ohio); | meerschaum |
| | Colquitt Dean, Atlanta Journal (Georgia) (tied) | meticulosity |
| 1951 | Irving Belz, Memphis Press-Scimitar (Tennessee) | insouciant |

# National Spelling Bee (continued)

| YEAR | CHAMPION | WINNING WORD |
|------|----------|--------------|
| 1952 | Doris Ann Hall, *Winston-Salem Journal* (North Carolina) | vignette |
| 1953 | Elizabeth Hess, *Arizona Republic* (Phoenix AZ) | soubrette |
| 1954 | William Cashore, *Norristown Times Herald* (Pennsylvania) | transept |
| 1955 | Sandra Sloss, *St. Louis Globe-Democrat* (Missouri) | crustaceology |
| 1956 | Melody Sachko, *Pittsburgh Press* (Pennsylvania) | condominium |
| 1957 | Sandra Owen, *Canton Repository* (Ohio); | schappe[2] |
| | Dana Bennett, *Rocky Mountain News* (Denver CO) (tied) | |
| 1958 | Jolitta Schlehuber, *Topeka Daily Capital* (Kansas) | syllepsis |
| 1959 | Joel Montgomery, *Rocky Mountain News* (Denver CO) | catamaran |
| 1960 | Henry Feldman, *Knoxville News-Sentinel* (Tennessee) | eudaemonic |
| 1961 | John Capehart, *Tulsa Tribune* (Oklahoma) | smaragdine |
| 1962 | Nettie Crawford, *El Paso Herald-Post* (Texas); | esquamulose[2] |
| | Michael Day, *St. Louis Democrat* (Missouri) (tied) | |
| 1963 | Glen Van Slyke III, *Knoxville News-Sentinel* (Tennessee) | equipage |
| 1964 | William Kerek, *Akron Beacon Journal* (Ohio) | sycophant |
| 1965 | Michael Kerpan, Jr., *Tulsa Tribune* (Oklahoma) | eczema |
| 1966 | Robert A. Wake, *Houston Chronicle* (Texas) | ratoon |
| 1967 | Jennifer Reinke, *Omaha World-Herald* (Nebraska) | Chihuahua |
| 1968 | Robert L. Walters, *Topeka Daily Capital* (Kansas) | abalone |
| 1969 | Susan Yoachum, *Dallas Morning News* (Texas) | interlocutory |
| 1970 | Libby Childress, *Winston-Salem Journal & Sentinel* (North Carolina) | croissant |
| 1971 | Jonathan Knisely, *Philadelphia Bulletin* (Pennsylvania) | shalloon |
| 1972 | Robin Kral, *Lubbock Avalanche-Journal* (Texas) | macerate |
| 1973 | Barrie Trinkle, *Fort Worth Press* (Texas) | vouchsafe |
| 1974 | Julie Ann Junkin, *Birmingham Post-Herald* (Alabama) | hydrophyte |
| 1975 | Hugh Tosteson, *San Juan Star* (Puerto Rico) | incisor |
| 1976 | Tim Kneale, *Syracuse Herald Journal-American* (New York) | narcolepsy |
| 1977 | John Paola, *Pittsburgh Press* (Pennsylvania) | cambist |
| 1978 | Peg McCarthy, *Topeka Capital-Journal* (Kansas) | deification |
| 1979 | Katie Kerwin, *Rocky Mountain News* (Denver CO) | maculature |
| 1980 | Jacques Bailly, *Rocky Mountain News* (Denver CO) | elucubrate |
| 1981 | Paige Pipkin, *El Paso Herald-Post* (Texas) | sarcophagus |
| 1982 | Molly Dieveney, *Rocky Mountain News* (Denver CO) | psoriasis |
| 1983 | Blake Giddens, *El Paso Herald-Post* (Texas) | Purim |
| 1984 | Daniel Greenblatt, *Loudoun Times-Mirror* (Virginia) | luge |
| 1985 | Balu Natarajan, *Chicago Tribune* (Illinois) | milieu |
| 1986 | Jon Pennington, *Patriot News* (Harrisburg PA) | odontalgia |
| 1987 | Stephanie Petit, *Pittsburgh Press* (Pennsylvania) | staphylococci |
| 1988 | Rageshree Ramachandran, *Sacramento Bee* (California) | elegiacal |
| 1989 | Scott Isaacs, *Rocky Mountain News* (Denver CO) | spoliator |
| 1990 | Amy Marie Dimak, *Seattle Times* (Washington) | fibranne |
| 1991 | Joanne Lagatta, *Wisconsin State Journal* (Madison WI) | antipyretic |
| 1992 | Amanda Goad, *Richmond News Leader* (Virginia) | lyceum |
| 1993 | Geoff Hooper, *Commercial Appeal* (Memphis TN) | kamikaze |
| 1994 | Ned G. Andrews, *Knoxville News-Sentinel* (Tennessee) | antediluvian |
| 1995 | Justin Tyler Carroll, *Commercial Appeal* (Memphis TN) | xanthosis |
| 1996 | Wendy Guey, *Palm Beach Post* (Florida) | vivisepulture |
| 1997 | Rebecca Sealfon, *Daily News* (New York NY) | euonym |
| 1998 | Jody-Anne Maxwell, Phillips & Phillips Stationery Suppliers, Ltd. (Kingston, Jamaica) | chiaroscurist |
| 1999 | Nupur Lala, *Tampa Tribune* (Florida) | logorrhea |
| 2000 | George Abraham Thampy, *St. Louis Post-Dispatch* (Missouri) | demarche |
| 2001 | Sean Conley, *Aitkin Independent Age* (Minnesota) | succedaneum |
| 2002 | Pratyush Buddiga, *Rocky Mountain News* (Denver CO) | prospicience |
| 2003 | Sai R. Gunturi, *Dallas Morning News* (Texas) | pococurante |
| 2004 | David Tidmarsh, *South Bend Tribune* (Indiana) | autochthonous |
| 2005 | Anurag Kashyap, *San Diego Union-Tribune* (California) | appoggiatura |
| 2006 | Kerry Close, *Asbury Park Press/Home News Tribune* (New Jersey) | Ursprache |
| 2007 | Evan M. O'Dorney, *Contra Costa Times* (Walnut Creek CA) | serrefine |
| 2008 | Sameer Mishra, *Journal and Courier* (Lafayette IN) | guerdon |
| 2009 | Kavya Shivashankar, *Olathe News* (Kansas) | Laodicean |
| 2010 | Anamika Veeramani, *Plain Dealer* (Cleveland OH) | stromuhr |
| 2011 | Sukanya Roy, *Times Leader* (Wilkes-Barre PA) | cymotrichous |
| 2012 | Snigdha Nandipati, *San Diego Union-Tribune* (California) | guetapens |

[1]*It has not been independently verified that this was the winning, or final, word.*    [2]*Neither winning contestant spelled the winning word correctly, and the contest was declared a draw.*

# Business

## The End of Cash

*by Deirdre Van Dyk, TIME*

Walk into a store, submit your shopping list, and a map directs you to the peanut-butter-brittle ice cream you crave. When you get to the front of the line, just bump your phone on the reader and you also get a discount via an e-coupon you've downloaded. Or scan pictures of the lasagna, salad, and French bread you want for dinner from a Safeway ad as you wait for the train and pick up the bag on your way home. The surging popularity of the mobile wallet—a smart phone that also acts as credit card, checkbook, and shop-bot—is radically shifting shopping habits. It's the biggest thing in retail since the credit card got us talking about a cashless economy.

The driving force is communication: cash can't communicate, but phones can. Your alarm clock, radio, camera, landline, and GPS—even your laptop—have already been displaced by your phone. Why not the US$69 and four credit cards the average American carries? "Everything eventually migrates to the cell phone," says Scott Ellison, an analyst with IDC who tracks the mobile industry. "And when it moves, people tend to do a lot more of it."

Tammy Lam, 26, a p.r. executive in San Francisco, uses her T-Mobile HTC myTouch phone to pay for just about everything. "I ordered dinner from my local Thai on GrubHub while sitting on the bus on the way home from work last night. I bought all my Christmas presents on my phone. When friends and I are out, we use Groupon to buy a meal," said Lam, who uses her phone instead of her computer for shopping even when she's at home. And she prefers it to cards or bills when she's out. "I hate cash," Lam declared. She is an early adopter, but there are enough people like her to set off a mobile-wallet war that will escalate in years to come, converting billions of dollars' worth of transactions to cashless in the US$4 trillion retail economy.

Google, the company that changed online search, recently launched Google Wallet in partnership with Citibank, MasterCard, and Sprint's Nexus S 4G phone. PayPal, the company that solved secure online payment, is planning to announce 20 partnerships in 2012 designed to allow you to order ahead, self-check-out in stores, and simply use your phone number and a PIN to pay for purchases. Isis—a Verizon, AT&T, and T-Mobile wallet with Visa, AmEx, Discover, and MasterCard partnerships—launched in mid-2012 in Salt Lake City and Austin. Visa's own virtual wallet, V.Me, is also on deck. "Anything with an on switch could be a payment device," says Anuj Nayar, PayPal's communications director. And of course, everyone anticipates a move by Apple, whose stores are already processing sales through iPhones. Mark Beccue, a mobile analyst with ABI Research, told TIME: "They have such a loyal following, and they're so vertically integrated—they'll help move everything forward."

Mobile wallets work in different ways. Google and Isis rely on NFC, or near-field communication. Basically, this means the phone and the sales terminal talk to each other. The Subway sandwich chain is installing NFC in about 7,400 of its 25,000 locations; 219 Macy's and Bloomingdale's stores have it up and

running; Jamba Juice, OfficeMax, Coke vending machines, even New Jersey Transit trains are set up to take payments with a tap of your phone. Some of the more fantastic aspects of these schemes—like tapping a sign at Home Depot that automatically calls a service rep—require stores to be fitted with NFC equipment throughout, something that hasn't quite happened yet. But the pattern is set. "Consumers expect to use one click to buy just about anything," says Osama Bedier, vice president of payments at Google. "There are no checkout lines online."

Mobile wallets can also be your shop-bot, sniffing out exclusive offers—say, US$2 off oatmeal at Jamba Juice as you walk by. Not hungry? Save the coupon to the wallet, which will automatically activate it when you buy your next oatmeal. "Twenty years ago, we had zero need for digital payments," said Bedier. "But today you can't buy a song or a game or an app without them. Increasingly, it will be hard to get a lot of experiences on offer with just cash." There's something ironic about getting your money's worth only if you're not actually using money.

PayPal, with its 103 million account holders and 9 million merchants, is betting on the cloud: store your information and access it from any computer or phone. It has been buying up companies, at least a dozen in the past year, that specialize in bar code readers, inventory tracking, or offering location-based deals. And PayPal is working with retailers to put it all together in apps. Like Google, PayPal is building in loyalty cards and coupons and trying to wrap up other capabilities—like skip-the-line checkout at coffee shops, grocery stores, and home-improvement centers—before NFC is built in. "There is nothing you can imagine that isn't happening," said Scott Thompson, president of PayPal.

The goal is to reduce friction in retail. To solve the lunch-hour crunch at Pizza Express restaurants in London, for instance, PayPal created an app that allows customers to enter the number from their bill into their phone and then pay without waiting for a server to run a credit card. The potential glitch? If your cell service or wi-fi goes out, so does your ability to pay.

Certainly consumers seem ready to ditch paper and plastic. Thirty-two million banking customers are managing their money very comfortably on cell phones. Chase alone moves US$3 billion a year on mobiles with an app that allows you to deposit to checking via a cell-phone photograph or pay friends for your share of the moo-shu pork by phone transfer.

On an everyday level, the mobile wallet's big promise may lie in the little problems it can solve. "If it's a busy lunchtime and I can preorder and prepay at Chipotle, skipping that long line," says Charles Wilson, who helps companies with social-media strategies, "then it's a godsend." Or as Ed McLaughlin, head of emerging payments at MasterCard, says, cash will never go away but will only become less useful. "Cash is going to be like the postage stamp. If you aren't used to using it, it won't make a whole lot of sense why one would."

# US Economy

## Denominations of US Currency

### PAPER MONEY

| VALUE | PORTRAIT ON FRONT | DESIGN ON BACK | WHEN CIRCULATED |
|---|---|---|---|
| $1 | George Washington | Great Seal of US | 1929– |
| $2 | Thomas Jefferson | Monticello | 1929–75 |
| $2 | Thomas Jefferson | painting of the signing of the Declaration of Independence | 1976– |
| $5[1] | Abraham Lincoln | Lincoln Memorial | 2000– |
| $10[1] | Alexander Hamilton | US Treasury | 2000– |
| $20[1] | Andrew Jackson | White House | 1998– |
| $50[1] | Ulysses S. Grant | US Capitol | 1997– |
| $100[1] | Benjamin Franklin | Independence Hall | 1996– |
| $500 | William McKinley | ornate figure of value | 1929–69 |
| $1,000 | Grover Cleveland | ornate figure of value | 1929–69 |
| $5,000 | James Madison | ornate figure of value | 1929–69 |
| $10,000 | Salmon P. Chase | ornate figure of value | 1929–69 |
| $100,000[2] | Woodrow Wilson | ornate figure of value | — |

[1]Earlier versions issued starting in 1929 had same subjects as current version.     [2]Never issued to public.

### COINS

| VALUE | PORTRAIT ON FRONT | DESIGN ON BACK | WHEN CIRCULATED |
|---|---|---|---|
| 1¢ | Abraham Lincoln | "one cent" and wheat | 1909–58 |
| 1¢ | Abraham Lincoln | Lincoln Memorial | 1959–2008 |
| 1¢ | Abraham Lincoln | scenes from Lincoln's life | 2009 |
| 1¢ | Abraham Lincoln | Union shield with scroll | 2010 |
| 5¢ | Thomas Jefferson | Monticello | 1938–2003; 2006– |
| 5¢ | Thomas Jefferson | "Westward Journey" designs | 2004–05 |
| 10¢ | Franklin D. Roosevelt | torch | 1946– |
| 25¢ | George Washington | eagle | 1932–74; 1977–98 |
| 25¢ (bicentennial) | George Washington | colonial drummer | 1975–76 |
| 25¢ | George Washington | 50 state designs | 1999–2008 |
| 25¢ | George Washington | Washington DC, US territories designs | 2009 |
| 25¢ | George Washington | national parks and sites designs | 2010–21 |
| 50¢ | John F. Kennedy | presidential seal | 1964–74; 1977– |
| 50¢ (bicentennial) | John F. Kennedy | Independence Hall | 1975–76 |
| $1 | Dwight D. Eisenhower | eagle | 1971–74; 1977–78 |
| $1 (bicentennial) | Dwight D. Eisenhower | Liberty Bell and Moon | 1975–76 |
| $1 | Susan B. Anthony | eagle | 1979–81; 1999 |
| $1 | Sacagawea | eagle | 2000–06 |
| $1 | Sacagawea | Native American figure | 2009– |
| $1 | presidential portraits | Statue of Liberty | 2007–16 |

### 50 STATE QUARTERS PROGRAM

| STATE | WHEN ISSUED | STATE | WHEN ISSUED | STATE | WHEN ISSUED |
|---|---|---|---|---|---|
| Alabama | 2003 | Louisiana | 2002 | Ohio | 2002 |
| Alaska | 2008 | Maine | 2003 | Oklahoma | 2008 |
| Arizona | 2008 | Maryland | 2000 | Oregon | 2005 |
| Arkansas | 2003 | Massachusetts | 2000 | Pennsylvania | 1999 |
| California | 2005 | Michigan | 2004 | Rhode Island | 2001 |
| Colorado | 2006 | Minnesota | 2005 | South Carolina | 2000 |
| Connecticut | 1999 | Mississippi | 2002 | South Dakota | 2006 |
| Delaware | 1999 | Missouri | 2003 | Tennessee | 2002 |
| Florida | 2004 | Montana | 2007 | Texas | 2004 |
| Georgia | 1999 | Nebraska | 2006 | Utah | 2007 |
| Hawaii | 2008 | Nevada | 2006 | Vermont | 2001 |
| Idaho | 2007 | New Hampshire | 2000 | Virginia | 2000 |
| Illinois | 2003 | New Jersey | 1999 | Washington | 2007 |
| Indiana | 2002 | New Mexico | 2008 | West Virginia | 2005 |
| Iowa | 2004 | New York | 2001 | Wisconsin | 2004 |
| Kansas | 2005 | North Carolina | 2001 | Wyoming | 2007 |
| Kentucky | 2001 | North Dakota | 2006 | | |

### PRESIDENTIAL $1 COINS PROGRAM

| | |
|---|---|
| 2007 | George Washington, John Adams, Thomas Jefferson, James Madison |
| 2008 | James Monroe, John Quincy Adams, Andrew Jackson, Martin Van Buren |
| 2009 | William Henry Harrison, John Tyler, James K. Polk, Zachary Taylor |

## Denominations of US Currency (continued)
PRESIDENTIAL $1 COINS PROGRAM (CONTINUED)

| | |
|---|---|
| 2010 | Millard Fillmore, Franklin Pierce, James Buchanan, Abraham Lincoln |
| 2011 | Andrew Johnson, Ulysses S. Grant, Rutherford B. Hayes, James A. Garfield |
| 2012 | Chester A. Arthur, Grover Cleveland, Benjamin Harrison, Grover Cleveland |

## US Currency and Coins in Circulation

*Currency and coins outstanding and currency in circulation by denomination, 31 Dec 2011. Source: Treasury Bulletin, March 2012.*

| | TOTAL CURRENCY AND COINS | CURRENCY | COINS[1] |
|---|---|---|---|
| amounts in circulation | $1,075,793,739,508 | $1,034,503,194,982 | $41,290,544,526 |
| amounts held by: | | | |
| US Treasury | 150,241,926 | 31,732,202 | 118,509,724 |
| Federal Reserve Banks | 174,140,863,198 | 171,835,076,094 | 2,305,787,104 |
| total amounts outstanding | 1,250,084,844,632 | 1,206,370,003,278 | 43,714,841,354 |

| DENOMINATION | TOTAL CURRENCY IN CIRCULATION | FEDERAL RESERVE NOTES[2] | US NOTES | CURRENCY NO LONGER ISSUED |
|---|---|---|---|---|
| $1 | $ 9,998,620,182 | $ 9,856,744,780 | $ 143,503 | $141,731,899 |
| $2 | 1,896,675,820 | 1,764,702,530 | 131,960,718 | 12,572 |
| $5 | 11,797,697,010 | 11,663,689,520 | 108,388,810 | 25,618,680 |
| $10 | 17,190,041,190 | 17,169,419,320 | 6,300 | 20,615,570 |
| $20 | 141,082,184,080 | 141,062,075,740 | 3,840 | 20,104,500 |
| $50 | 69,606,248,700 | 69,594,748,850 | 500 | 11,499,350 |
| $100 | 782,618,890,900 | 782,596,899,400 | —[3] | 21,991,500 |
| $500 | 142,139,500 | 141,946,000 | 5,500 | 188,000 |
| $1,000 | 165,482,000 | 165,271,000 | 5,000 | 206,000 |
| $5,000 | 1,765,000 | 1,710,000 | — | 55,000 |
| $10,000 | 3,450,000 | 3,360,000 | — | 90,000 |
| fractional notes[4] | 600 | — | 90 | 510 |
| total currency | 1,034,503,194,982 | 1,034,020,567,140 | 240,514,261 | 242,113,581 |

[1]*Excludes coins sold to collectors at premium prices.*   [2]*Issued on or after 1 Jul 1929.*   [3]*Represents prior month adjustment.*   [4]*Represents value of certain partial denominations not presented for redemption.*

# Energy
## Energy Consumption by Source, 2010
*Figures represent '000,000,000,000 BTU.*
*Source: US Energy Information Administration, <www.eia.doe.gov>.*

| | PETROLEUM | NATURAL GAS | COAL | HYDRO-ELECTRIC POWER[1] | NUCLEAR ELECTRIC POWER | TOTAL[2] |
|---|---|---|---|---|---|---|
| Alabama | 554 | 547 | 719 | 85 | 397 | 2,301 |
| Alaska | 274 | 335 | 15 | 14 | 0 | 638 |
| Arizona | 508 | 337 | 458 | 65 | 326 | 1,693 |
| Arkansas | 341 | 275 | 294 | 36 | 157 | 1,102 |
| California | 3,463 | 2,326 | 55 | 326 | 337 | 6,507 |
| Colorado | 485 | 506 | 383 | 15 | 0 | 1,388 |
| Connecticut | 329 | 204 | 29 | 4 | 175 | 741 |
| Delaware | 91 | 56 | 30 | 0 | 0 | 177 |
| District of Columbia | 21 | 34 | [3] | 0 | 0 | 55 |
| Florida | 1,737 | 1,181 | 637 | 2 | 250 | 3,807 |
| Georgia | 1,052 | 541 | 768 | 32 | 350 | 2,744 |
| Hawaii | 234 | [3] | 17 | 1 | 0 | 252 |
| Idaho | 165 | 85 | 9 | 89 | 0 | 348 |
| Illinois | 1,230 | 935 | 1,069 | 1 | 1,005 | 4,241 |
| Indiana | 763 | 565 | 1,450 | 4 | 0 | 2,782 |
| Iowa | 421 | 279 | 494 | 9 | 47 | 1,249 |
| Kansas | 383 | 288 | 360 | 0 | 100 | 1,131 |
| Kentucky | 627 | 239 | 1,010 | 25 | 0 | 1,901 |
| Louisiana | 1,929 | 1,468 | 260 | 11 | 195 | 3,862 |
| Maine | 195 | 81 | 2 | 37 | 0 | 316 |
| Maryland | 505 | 214 | 266 | 16 | 146 | 1,147 |
| Massachusetts | 584 | 445 | 84 | 10 | 62 | 1,184 |
| Michigan | 813 | 759 | 749 | 12 | 310 | 2,643 |

## Energy Consumption by Source, 2010 (continued)

| | PETROLEUM | NATURAL GAS | COAL | HYDRO-ELECTRIC POWER[1] | NUCLEAR ELECTRIC POWER | TOTAL[2] |
|---|---|---|---|---|---|---|
| Minnesota | 612 | 427 | 315 | 8 | 141 | 1,504 |
| Mississippi | 422 | 438 | 149 | 0 | 101 | 1,109 |
| Missouri | 658 | 282 | 802 | 15 | 94 | 1,851 |
| Montana | 168 | 73 | 203 | 92 | 0 | 536 |
| Nebraska | 217 | 170 | 255 | 13 | 116 | 770 |
| Nevada | 236 | 268 | 80 | 21 | 0 | 605 |
| New Hampshire | 153 | 63 | 34 | 14 | 114 | 378 |
| New Jersey | 1,077 | 670 | 72 | [3] | 343 | 2,162 |
| New Mexico | 249 | 246 | 268 | 2 | 0 | 764 |
| New York | 1,324 | 1,224 | 167 | 249 | 438 | 3,402 |
| North Carolina | 825 | 309 | 749 | 46 | 426 | 2,355 |
| North Dakota | 150 | 64 | 410 | 20 | 0 | 644 |
| Ohio | 1,169 | 809 | 1,355 | 4 | 165 | 3.503 |
| Oklahoma | 491 | 697 | 346 | 27 | 0 | 1,562 |
| Oregon | 343 | 243 | 43 | 298 | 0 | 927 |
| Pennsylvania | 1,271 | 889 | 1,311 | 23 | 814 | 4,308 |
| Rhode Island | 92 | 96 | 0 | [3] | 0 | 188 |
| South Carolina | 508 | 226 | 405 | 23 | 543 | 1,705 |
| South Dakota | 115 | 72 | 39 | 51 | 0 | 277 |
| Tennessee | 681 | 260 | 516 | 79 | 290 | 1,826 |
| Texas | 5,752 | 3,459 | 1,609 | 12 | 432 | 11,263 |
| Utah | 266 | 229 | 356 | 7 | 0 | 858 |
| Vermont | 79 | 9 | 0 | 13 | 50 | 151 |
| Virginia | 818 | 386 | 346 | 15 | 278 | 1,842 |
| Washington | 739 | 295 | 95 | 666 | 97 | 1,891 |
| West Virginia | 201 | 122 | 848 | 13 | 0 | 1,183 |
| Wisconsin | 537 | 377 | 458 | 21 | 139 | 1,531 |
| Wyoming | 166 | 149 | 484 | 10 | 0 | 809 |
| total[2] | 36,021 | 24,249 | 20,869 | 2,539 | 8,434 | 92,111 |

[1]Data do not include results from pumped-storage hydroelectricity. [2]Detail may not add to total given because of rounding and the inclusion of energy that has not been allocated to a state. [3]Negligible.

# Travel and Tourism

## Passports, Visas, and Immunizations

With certain exceptions, a **passport** (also called a passport book) is required by law for all US citizens, including infants, to travel outside the United States and its territories. The exceptions of travel without passport to Mexico, Canada, Bermuda, and countries in the Caribbean were eliminated in 2007 by implementation of the Western Hemisphere Travel Initiative. A wallet-sized **passport card** was created as a more convenient, less expensive alternative to the passport book for reentry only into the US from those formerly exempt areas, except via air travel. A new passport card costs US$55 for persons ages 16 and older and US$40 for those under 16; the renewal fee is US$30. Passports can be applied for at more than 9,400 passport acceptance facilities nationwide, including most government facilities. State Department passport agencies accept applications only by appointment, usually from those in need of expedited service (two weeks or less). Passport agencies are located in Atlanta GA, Aurora CO, Boston MA, Buffalo NY, Chicago IL, Dallas TX, Detroit MI, El Paso TX, Honolulu HI, Hot Springs AR, Houston TX, Los Angeles CA, Miami FL, Minneapolis MN, New Orleans LA, New York NY, Norwalk CT, Philadelphia PA, Portsmouth NH, St. Albans VT, San Diego CA, San Francisco CA, Seattle WA, Tucson AZ, and Washington DC. Everyone must apply in person for his or her first passport; those issued to persons ages 16 and older may be renewed by mail if the person's expiring passport is undamaged and was issued no more than 15 years previously in current name. Appropriate paperwork should be submitted several months in advance of planned travel to allow for processing. Including a US$25 execution fee, new passport fees total US$135 for persons ages 16 and older and US$105 for those under 16; expedited service is an additional US$60. Renewal fees are US$110 for adults; minors must reapply in person at the cost of US$105. Passports are mailed to applicants in about six weeks or about two weeks for rush service. The status of a passport application may be checked online at <http://travel.state.gov/passport/status/status_2567.html> or by contacting the National Passport Information Center at 1-877-487-2778 (toll-free; automated information; representatives are available weekdays 8 AM to 10 PM ET, except federal holidays).

Applying in person for a passport requires submission of an application form; proof of US citizenship, such as a certified birth certificate; proof of identity, such as a driver's license; two identical recent 2×2-inch photographs; a social security number; and all applicable fees. Options for proving identity or citizenship are listed on the State Department Web site. A passport is valid for 10 years, or 5 years if issued to a person age 15

## Passports, Visas, and Immunizations (continued)

or younger. Renewing by mail requires submission of an application form, the most recent passport, two identical photographs, and applicable fees. Frequent travelers may request a passport with extra pages. A passport that is lost or stolen in a foreign country must immediately be reported to local police and the nearest US embassy or consulate to allow for the citizen's reentry into the US. Replacing a lost or stolen passport requires completion of a form reporting the loss or theft and an application for a new passport, as well as the usual documentation, photographs, and fees.

**Visas.** A visa is usually a stamp placed on a US passport by a foreign country's officials allowing the passport owner to visit that country. Travelers should check visa regulations and obtain visas where necessary before traveling to a foreign country. Visas may be acquired from the embassy or consulate of the intended destination and can be applied for by mail. Processing fees vary among countries.

**Immunizations.** Under regulations adopted by the World Health Organization, some countries require International Certificates of Vaccination against yellow fever. Other immunizations, such as those for tetanus and polio, should also be up-to-date. Preventive measures for malaria are recommended for some destinations. There are no immunization requirements for returning to the United States. Many countries require HIV/AIDS testing for work, study, or residence permits or for long-term stays.

For passport information, forms, and office locations, access the State Department Web site at <http://travel.state.gov/passport>. Entry requirements for foreign countries, including necessity of visas, immunizations, and HIV testing, are available at <http://travel.state.gov/travel/cis_pa_tw/cis/cis_4965.html>. Additional information on required or recommended health care measures can be obtained from the Centers for Disease Control and Prevention (CDC) at <www.cdc.gov/travel> or by calling 1-800-CDC-INFO; also helpful are local health departments and the publication *Health Information for International Travel,* available at the CDC Web site.

## Travelers to and from the US

Data for 2002 showed that overseas travel to the US dropped significantly during 2002, primarily as a response to the terrorist attacks of 11 Sep 2001. Since then, however, travel has rebounded at varying levels. Data for 2011 for all US resident travel to specific overseas countries are not available, but data for air travel to the various regions, as well as to Mexico and Canada, are presented below. Source: US Department of Commerce, International Trade Administration, Office of Travel and Tourism Industries.

**TOP COUNTRIES OF ORIGIN FOR VISITORS TO THE US (2011)**

| | | % CHANGE FROM 2010 |
|---|---|---|
| UK | 3,835,300 | −0.4 |
| Japan | 3,249,569 | −4.0 |
| Germany | 1,823,797 | +5.7 |
| Brazil | 1,508,279 | +25.9 |
| France | 1,504,182 | +12.1 |
| Republic of Korea | 1,145,216 | +3.4 |
| China[1] | 1,089,405 | +35.9 |
| Australia | 1,037,852 | +14.8 |
| Italy | 891,571 | +6.4 |
| Spain | 700,183 | +9.5 |
| **total overseas** | **27,883,157** | **+5.8** |
| Canada | 21,028,000 | +5.3 |
| Mexico | 13,414,000 | −0.4 |
| **total worldwide** | **62,325,157** | **+4.2** |

**REGIONAL DESTINATION OF US AIR TRAVELERS ABROAD (2011)**

| | | % CHANGE FROM 2010 |
|---|---|---|
| Europe | 10,825,923 | −2.5 |
| Caribbean | 6,031,974 | +5.5 |
| Asia | 4,135,648 | −14.9 |
| South America | 1,653,593 | −22.3 |
| Central America | 2,158,365 | −4.6 |
| Middle East | 1,346,896 | +0.6 |
| Oceania | 504,833 | −26.5 |
| Africa | 365,776 | −10.4 |
| **total overseas** | **27,023,008** | **−5.2** |
| Mexico | 5,537,383 | +2.9 |
| Canada | 3,518,788 | +1.5 |
| **total worldwide** | **36,079,179** | **−3.4** |

**TOP 10 STATES AND CITIES VISITED BY OVERSEAS VISITORS (2011)[2]**

| STATE | VISITORS/ IN THOUSANDS ('000) | % CHANGE FROM 2010 | CITY | VISITORS/ IN THOUSANDS ('000) | % CHANGE FROM 2010 |
|---|---|---|---|---|---|
| New York | 9,508 | +10.0 | New York NY | 9,285 | +9.7 |
| California | 6,134 | +9.2 | Los Angeles CA | 3,653 | +9.1 |
| Florida | 5,688 | −2.4 | Miami FL | 2,956 | −5.0 |
| Nevada | 2,872 | +14.7 | San Francisco CA | 2,872 | +9.0 |
| Hawaii | 2,286 | +7.1 | Las Vegas NV | 2,788 | +15.0 |
| Massachusetts | 1,422 | +10.1 | Orlando FL | 2,788 | +2.7 |
| Texas | 1,283 | +24.8 | Washington DC | 1,812 | +4.1 |
| Illinois | 1,255 | +5.8 | Honolulu HI | 1,785 | +9.2 |
| Guam[3] | 1,227 | −6.9 | Boston MA | 1,311 | +10.5 |
| New Jersey | 976 | +0.1 | Chicago IL | 1,199 | +5.7 |

[1]*Data for China include Hong Kong.* [2]*Excludes Canadian and Mexican visitors to the US.* [3]*Guam is a US territory. If Guam were excluded, Pennsylvania would rank 10th on the list with about 920,000 overseas visitors.*

## Customs Exemptions

Upon returning to the US from a foreign country, travelers must pay duty on items acquired outside the US if the value of the items is greater than the allowable exemption. The general exemption is US$800 per person, but it can also be US$200 or US$1,600, depending on the country or countries visited. Exemptions apply if the items are in the traveler's possession, are for the traveler's own use, and are declared to US Customs. The traveler must also have been out of the country for at least 48 hours (unless returning from Mexico or the US Virgin Islands) and must not have used any part of the exemption within the past 30 days; if one or both of these requirements does not apply, the allowable exemption drops to US$200 per person and includes additional restrictions. The general exemption of US$800 includes no more than 200 previously exported cigarettes, 100 cigars, and no more than one liter of alcoholic beverages. Cuban tobacco products are prohibited. Family members may combine their total exemptions in a joint declaration except under the US$200 exemption. The US$800 exemption also applies to travelers returning from any of 28 countries and dependencies in the Caribbean Basin or Andean Region but may include two liters of alcoholic beverages, as long as one of the liters was produced in one of these. The 28 countries and dependencies are Antigua and Barbuda, Aruba, The Bahamas, Barbados, Belize, Bolivia, the British Virgin Islands, Colombia, Costa Rica, Dominica, the Dominican Republic, Ecuador, El Salvador, Grenada, Guatemala, Guyana, Haiti, Honduras, Jamaica, Montserrat, the Netherlands Antilles, Nicaragua, Panama, Peru, Saint Kitts and Nevis, Saint Lucia, Saint Vincent and the Grenadines, and Trinidad and Tobago. A US$1,600 exemption applies to travelers returning from a trip that included the US Virgin Islands, American Samoa, or Guam and includes 1,000 cigarettes and five liters of alcoholic beverages; of this amount, 800 cigarettes and one liter of alcohol must be from one of the US islands. The US$1,600 exemption also applies to multi-country travel (such as a cruise) to a US possession and any of the 28 Caribbean Basin and Andean Region countries and dependencies, as long as no more than US$800 worth of goods was purchased in those locations.

Gifts valued at US$100 or less (US$200 or less for gifts sent from American Samoa, Guam, or the US Virgin Islands) may be sent to the US without duty as long as no single person receives more than this value within 24 hours. Alcoholic beverages may not be sent by mail; tobacco and alcohol-based perfumes worth more than US$5 are not included in the exemption. Travelers may ship goods home for personal use without duty if the value of the goods is US$200 or less and no single person receives more than this value within a day. This exemption increases to US$800 for goods from one of the 28 countries listed above and to US$1,600 for goods from American Samoa, Guam, or the US Virgin Islands.

Further customs information is available from the US Customs and Border Protection Web site at: <www.cbp.gov/xp/cgov/travel>.

## US State Department Travel Warnings

The State Department issues Travel Warnings when it is believed best for Americans to avoid certain countries in the interest of safety. It also releases Travel Alerts of more short-term hazards, such as terrorist threats or political coups, that may endanger American travelers; these include an expiration date when the announcement need no longer be heeded. The department also makes available Consular Information Sheets for all countries, which may discuss safety conditions not severe enough to require a travel warning. Current information can be found at <http://travel.state.gov>.

Travel Warnings were in effect on 20 Jul 2012 for: Afghanistan, Algeria, Burundi, the Central African Republic, Chad, Colombia, Côte d'Ivoire, the Democratic People's Republic of Korea, the Democratic Republic of the Congo, Eritrea, Guinea, Haiti, Iran, Iraq, Israel (including the West Bank and the Gaza Strip), Kenya, Lebanon, Libya, Mali, Mauritania, Mexico, Niger, Nigeria, Pakistan, the Philippines, Saudi Arabia, Somalia, South Sudan, Sudan, Syria, and Yemen.

Travel Alerts in effect on the same day included advisories for Bahrain and general notices alerting US citizens to the dangers of the hurricane season in the Atlantic and Pacific Oceans, the Caribbean Sea, and the Gulf of Mexico. A worldwide caution on the continuing threat of terrorist acts and violence against Americans was also in effect.

# Employment

## US Employment by Gender and Occupation

*Detail may not add to total given because of rounding. Source: US Bureau of Labor Statistics.*

| OCCUPATION | WORKERS 16 YEARS AND OLDER (NUMBERS IN '000) | | | | | |
|---|---|---|---|---|---|---|
| | TOTAL | | MEN | | WOMEN | |
| | 2010 | 2011 | 2010 | 2011 | 2010 | 2011 |
| management, professional, and related occupations | 51,743 | 52,547 | 25,070 | 25,552 | 26,673 | 26,995 |
| management, business, and financial-operations occupations | 20,938 | 21,589 | 11,945 | 12,275 | 8,993 | 9,314 |
| management occupations | 15,001 | 15,250 | 9,266 | 9,439 | 5,735 | 5,812 |
| business and financial-operations occupations | 5,937 | 6,339 | 2,679 | 2,837 | 3,258 | 3,503 |

## US Employment by Gender and Occupation (continued)

| OCCUPATION | WORKERS 16 YEARS AND OLDER (NUMBERS IN '000) | | | | | |
|---|---|---|---|---|---|---|
| | TOTAL | | MEN | | WOMEN | |
| | 2010 | 2011 | 2010 | 2011 | 2010 | 2011 |
| **management, professional, and related occupations (cont.)** | | | | | | |
| professional and related occupations | 30,805 | 30,957 | 13,125 | 13,277 | 17,680 | 17,681 |
| computer and mathematical occupations | 3,531 | 3,608 | 2,620 | 2,705 | 911 | 903 |
| architecture and engineering occupations | 2,619 | 2,785 | 2,282 | 2,406 | 337 | 379 |
| life, physical, and social-science occupations | 1,409 | 1,303 | 755 | 687 | 655 | 616 |
| community and social-services occupations | 2,337 | 2,352 | 836 | 835 | 1,500 | 1,518 |
| legal occupations | 1,716 | 1,770 | 878 | 889 | 838 | 881 |
| education, training, and library occupations | 8,628 | 8,619 | 2,261 | 2,274 | 6,367 | 6,345 |
| arts, design, entertainment, sports, and media occupations | 2,759 | 2,779 | 1,484 | 1,499 | 1,276 | 1,281 |
| health-care-practitioner and technical occupations | 7,805 | 7,740 | 2,009 | 1,982 | 5,796 | 5,758 |
| **service occupations** | 24,634 | 24,787 | 10,652 | 10,929 | 13,982 | 13,858 |
| health-care-support occupations | 3,332 | 3,359 | 370 | 413 | 2,962 | 2,945 |
| protective-service occupations | 3,289 | 3,210 | 2,587 | 2,546 | 703 | 664 |
| food-preparation and serving-related occupations | 7,660 | 7,747 | 3,439 | 3,534 | 4,221 | 4,213 |
| building- and grounds-cleaning and maintenance occupations | 5,328 | 5,492 | 3,164 | 3,359 | 2,164 | 2,133 |
| personal-care and service occupations | 5,024 | 4,979 | 1,092 | 1,077 | 3,932 | 3,902 |
| **sales and office occupations** | 33,433 | 33,066 | 12,419 | 12,450 | 21,015 | 20,616 |
| sales and related occupations | 15,386 | 15,330 | 7,703 | 7,733 | 7,683 | 7,597 |
| office and administrative-support occupations | 18,047 | 17,736 | 4,716 | 4,717 | 13,331 | 13,019 |
| **natural-resources, construction, and maintenance occupations** | 13,073 | 13,009 | 12,467 | 12,457 | 606 | 552 |
| farming, fishing, and forestry occupations | 987 | 1,001 | 755 | 785 | 231 | 216 |
| construction and extraction occupations | 7,175 | 7,125 | 6,990 | 6,962 | 185 | 163 |
| installation, maintenance, and repair occupations | 4,911 | 4,883 | 4,721 | 4,710 | 190 | 173 |
| **production, transportation, and material-moving occupations** | 16,180 | 16,461 | 12,751 | 12,902 | 3,429 | 3,558 |
| production occupations | 7,998 | 8,142 | 5,792 | 5,826 | 2,206 | 2,316 |
| transportation and material-moving occupations | 8,182 | 8,318 | 6,959 | 7,076 | 1,224 | 1,242 |
| **total** | 139,064 | 139,869 | 73,359 | 74,290 | 65,705 | 65,579 |

## US Federal Minimum Wage Rates, 1938–2012

*The table shows the actual minimum wage for the year in question and the value of that minimum wage adjusted for inflation in the year 2012. Source: US Department of Labor.*

| | minimum wage[1] | | | minimum wage[1] | | | minimum wage[1] | |
|---|---|---|---|---|---|---|---|---|
| YEAR | US DOLLARS | 2012 DOLLARS | YEAR | US DOLLARS | 2012 DOLLARS | YEAR | US DOLLARS | 2012 DOLLARS |
| 1938 | 0.25 | 4.02 | 1943 | 0.30 | 3.93 | 1948 | 0.40 | 3.76 |
| 1939 | 0.30 | 4.89 | 1944 | 0.30 | 3.86 | 1949 | 0.40 | 3.81 |
| 1940 | 0.30 | 4.86 | 1945 | 0.40 | 5.04 | 1950 | 0.75 | 7.05 |
| 1941 | 0.30 | 4.63 | 1946 | 0.40 | 4.65 | 1951 | 0.75 | 6.54 |
| 1942 | 0.30 | 4.17 | 1947 | 0.40 | 4.07 | 1952 | 0.75 | 6.42 |

## US Federal Minimum Wage Rates, 1938–2012 (continued)

| YEAR | minimum wage[1] US DOLLARS | 2012 DOLLARS | YEAR | minimum wage[1] US DOLLARS | 2012 DOLLARS | YEAR | minimum wage[1] US DOLLARS | 2012 DOLLARS |
|------|------|------|------|------|------|------|------|------|
| 1953 | 0.75 | 6.37 | 1973 | 1.60 | 8.17 | 1993 | 4.25 | 6.67 |
| 1954 | 0.75 | 6.32 | 1974 | 2.00 | 9.20 | 1994 | 4.25 | 6.50 |
| 1955 | 0.75 | 6.34 | 1975 | 2.10 | 8.85 | 1995 | 4.25 | 6.32 |
| 1956 | 1.00 | 8.33 | 1976 | 2.30 | 9.16 | 1996 | 4.75 | 6.86 |
| 1957 | 1.00 | 8.07 | 1977 | 2.30 | 8.60 | 1997 | 5.15 | 7.27 |
| 1958 | 1.00 | 7.84 | 1978 | 2.65 | 9.21 | 1998 | 5.15 | 7.16 |
| 1959 | 1.00 | 7.79 | 1979 | 2.90 | 9.05 | 1999 | 5.15 | 7.01 |
| 1960 | 1.00 | 7.66 | 1980 | 3.10 | 8.53 | 2000 | 5.15 | 6.78 |
| 1961 | 1.15 | 8.72 | 1981 | 3.35 | 8.35 | 2001 | 5.15 | 6.59 |
| 1962 | 1.15 | 8.63 | 1982 | 3.35 | 7.87 | 2002 | 5.15 | 6.49 |
| 1963 | 1.25 | 9.26 | 1983 | 3.35 | 7.62 | 2003 | 5.15 | 6.34 |
| 1964 | 1.25 | 9.14 | 1984 | 3.35 | 7.31 | 2004 | 5.15 | 6.18 |
| 1965 | 1.25 | 8.99 | 1985 | 3.35 | 7.06 | 2005 | 5.15 | 5.98 |
| 1966 | 1.25 | 8.74 | 1986 | 3.35 | 6.93 | 2006 | 5.15 | 5.79 |
| 1967 | 1.40 | 9.50 | 1987 | 3.35 | 6.68 | 2007 | 5.85 | 6.40 |
| 1968 | 1.60 | 10.42 | 1988 | 3.35 | 6.42 | 2008 | 6.55 | 6.90 |
| 1969 | 1.60 | 9.88 | 1989 | 3.35 | 6.12 | 2009 | 7.25 | 7.66 |
| 1970 | 1.60 | 9.35 | 1990 | 3.80 | 6.59 | 2010 | 7.25 | 7.54 |
| 1971 | 1.60 | 8.95 | 1991 | 4.25 | 7.07 | 2011 | 7.25 | 7.31 |
| 1972 | 1.60 | 8.68 | 1992 | 4.25 | 6.87 | 2012 | 7.25 | 7.25 |

[1] From 1938 to 1977, the minimum wage covered only interstate commerce workers. An amendment in 1961 set a lower minimum wage for retail and service enterprise workers as did a 1966 amendment that extended coverage to state and local employees in various sectors. Only from 1978 has the minimum wage covered all nonexempt workers.

## US Workers Earning the Minimum Wage

This table refers to wage and salary workers who were paid hourly rates in 2011, excluding the incorporated self-employed. The prevailing federal minimum wage was US$7.25. Workers earning less than minimum wage may have been working in jobs that are exempted from the minimum-wage provision of the Fair Labor Standards Act. Numbers are in thousands ('000) and may not add to total given because of rounding.

Source: US Bureau of Labor Statistics.

| WORKER CHARACTERISTICS | TOTAL NUMBER OF WORKERS | BELOW MINIMUM WAGE | AT MINIMUM WAGE | TOTAL NUMBER OF WORKERS AT OR BELOW MINIMUM WAGE NUMBER | % |
|---|---|---|---|---|---|
| **age** | | | | | |
| 16–24 years | 14,436 | 1,003 | 893 | 1,896 | 13.1 |
| 25 years and over | 59,490 | 1,149 | 784 | 1,933 | 3.2 |
| total (16 years and over) | 73,926 | 2,152 | 1,677 | 3,829 | 5.2 |
| **men** | | | | | |
| 16–24 years | 7,290 | 399 | 388 | 787 | 10.8 |
| 25 years and over | 29,167 | 387 | 260 | 647 | 2.2 |
| total (16 years and over) | 36,457 | 785 | 648 | 1,433 | 3.9 |
| **women** | | | | | |
| 16–24 years | 7,147 | 604 | 505 | 1,109 | 15.5 |
| 25 years and over | 30,323 | 762 | 524 | 1,286 | 4.2 |
| total (16 years and over) | 37,469 | 1,366 | 1,029 | 2,395 | 6.4 |
| **race and Hispanic or Latino ethnicity[1]** | | | | | |
| white (16 years and over) | 59,314 | 1,748 | 1,258 | 3,006 | 5.1 |
| black (16 years and over) | 9,523 | 253 | 324 | 577 | 6.1 |
| Asian (16 years and over) | 3,037 | 63 | 36 | 99 | 3.3 |
| Hispanic or Latino (16 years and over) | 13,264 | 380 | 340 | 720 | 5.4 |
| **full- and part-time workers[2]** | | | | | |
| full-time | 53,594 | 752 | 522 | 1,274 | 2.4 |
| part-time | 20,199 | 1,392 | 1,153 | 2,545 | 12.6 |

[1] Hispanics may be of any race and are also included in white, black, and Asian population groups. For this reason, data within this category do not add up to total.    [2] Full- and part-time workers are distinguished by the number of hours worked. These data do not add up to total because of a small number of multiple jobholders whose status on the principal job is unknown.

## Median Income by Educational and Social Variables

*This table refers to persons who worked full-time throughout the year and are 15 years old and older as of March of the following year. Median income dollar amounts are not adjusted for inflation. N/A means not available. Source: US Census Bureau.*

| | median income (US$) males | | | | median income (US$) females | | | |
|---|---|---|---|---|---|---|---|---|
| | 1980 | 1990 | 2000 | 2010 | 1980 | 1990 | 2000 | 2010 |
| full-time workers | 19,173 | 28,979 | 38,891 | 50,063 | 11,591 | 20,591 | 29,123 | 38,531 |
| **educational level[1]** | | | | | | | | |
| less than 9th grade | N/A | 10,319 | 14,131 | 16,237 | N/A | 6,268 | 8,546 | 10,658 |
| 9th to 12th grade (no diploma) | N/A | 14,736 | 18,915 | 19,243 | N/A | 7,055 | 10,063 | 12,063 |
| high school graduate | N/A | 21,546 | 27,480 | 30,232 | N/A | 10,818 | 15,153 | 17,830 |
| some college (no degree) | N/A | 26,591 | 33,319 | 36,082 | N/A | 13,963 | 20,166 | 22,772 |
| associate degree | N/A | 29,358 | 38,026 | 40,918 | N/A | 17,364 | 23,124 | 28,193 |
| bachelor's degree | N/A | 36,067 | 49,080 | 55,038 | N/A | 20,967 | 30,418 | 36,381 |
| master's degree | N/A | 43,125 | 59,732 | 69,378 | N/A | 29,747 | 40,619 | 48,556 |
| professional degree | N/A | 63,741 | 83,701 | 96,363 | N/A | 34,064 | 46,084 | 60,551 |
| doctoral degree | N/A | 51,845 | 71,271 | 85,963 | N/A | 37,242 | 51,460 | 70,375 |
| **race and origin[2, 3]** | | | | | | | | |
| white | 13,328 | 21,170 | 29,797 | 34,047 | 4,947 | 10,317 | 16,079 | 20,947 |
| white (non-Hispanic) | 13,681 | 21,958 | 31,508 | 37,037 | 4,980 | 10,581 | 16,665 | 21,754 |
| black | 8,009 | 12,868 | 21,343 | 23,203 | 4,580 | 8,328 | 15,881 | 19,700 |
| Hispanic origin | 9,659 | 13,470 | 19,498 | 22,233 | 4,405 | 7,532 | 12,248 | 16,269 |
| **age[2]** | | | | | | | | |
| 15 to 24 years | 4,597 | 6,319 | 9,546 | 9,959 | 3,124 | 4,902 | 7,360 | 8,765 |
| 25 to 34 years | 15,580 | 21,393 | 30,254 | 31,793 | 6,973 | 12,589 | 21,049 | 25,655 |
| 35 to 44 years | 20,037 | 29,773 | 37,922 | 42,252 | 6,465 | 14,504 | 22,077 | 29,447 |
| 45 to 54 years | 19,974 | 31,007 | 41,039 | 45,420 | 6,403 | 14,230 | 23,732 | 27,748 |
| 55 to 64 years | 15,914 | 24,804 | 34,189 | 41,197 | 4,926 | 9,400 | 16,920 | 25,502 |
| 65 years and over | 7,339 | 14,183 | 19,411 | 25,704 | 4,226 | 8,044 | 11,023 | 15,072 |
| all workers over age 14 | 12,530 | 20,293 | 28,343 | 32,137 | 4,920 | 10,070 | 16,063 | 20,831 |

[1]The income figures for the various educational levels are for workers 25 years old and over. Before 1991, the level of education categories used by the US Census Bureau differed from the categories presented in this table. Because of this, the 1980 figures for the median income by educational level are not completely comparable with the figures for later years. The figures presented in the 1990 column for educational levels are actually for 1991, the first year the educational categories listed in this table were used by the US Census Bureau.    [2]The figures presented in the 1980 column for race and origin and age pertain to civilian workers only.    [3]Hispanic people may be of any race.

## The 20 US Metropolitan Areas with the Highest Average Annual Per Capita Incomes

*Personal income is income received from all sources, including wages and salaries, property rental, transfers, and interest and dividends. Source: US Bureau of Economic Analysis.*

| METROPOLITAN AREA | ANNUAL INCOME (US$) 2009 | ANNUAL INCOME (US$) 2010[1] | INCOME CHANGE (%)[2] | METROPOLITAN AREA | ANNUAL INCOME (US$) 2009 | ANNUAL INCOME (US$) 2010[1] | INCOME CHANGE (%)[2] |
|---|---|---|---|---|---|---|---|
| Bridgeport, CT[3] | 74,010 | 76,070 | 2.8 | Trenton-Ewing, NJ | 52,066 | 53,484 | 2.7 |
| San Francisco, CA[4] | 60,203 | 61,208 | 1.7 | Barnstable, MA | 51,324 | 52,370 | 2.0 |
| Naples, FL[5] | 60,059 | 59,985 | -0.1 | Hartford, CT[11] | 50,105 | 51,291 | 2.4 |
| San Jose, CA[6] | 55,780 | 58,744 | 5.3 | Seattle-Tacoma-Bellevue, WA | 50,276 | 51,053 | 1.5 |
| Washington, DC, VA, MD, WV[7] | 56,797 | 57,671 | 1.5 | Boulder, CO | 49,743 | 50,697 | 1.9 |
| Midland, TX | 52,605 | 56,212 | 6.9 | Napa, CA | 49,573 | 49,808 | 0.5 |
| Boston, MA, NH[8] | 54,280 | 55,576 | 2.4 | Santa Cruz-Watsonville, CA | 48,429 | 49,346 | 1.9 |
| Sebastian, FL[9] | 55,543 | 55,179 | -0.7 | Baltimore-Towson, MD | 48,109 | 49,218 | 2.3 |
| New York, NY, NJ, PA[10] | 52,783 | 54,341 | 3.0 | North Port-Bradenton-Sarasota, FL | 47,836 | 47,860 | 0.1 |
| Casper, WY | 52,843 | 54,340 | 2.8 | New Haven-Milford, CT | 46,724 | 47,836 | 2.4 |

[1]Preliminary.    [2]Calculated from unrounded data.    [3]Includes Stamford and Norwalk.    [4]Includes Oakland and Fremont.    [5]Includes Marco Island.    [6]Includes Sunnyvale and Santa Clara.    [7]Includes Arlington and Alexandria.    [8]Includes Cambridge and Quincy.    [9]Includes Vero Beach.    [10]Includes northern New Jersey and Long Island.    [11]Includes West Hartford and East Hartford.

## US Civilian Federal Employment

Source: Statistical Abstract of the United States: 2012.

| AGENCIES | 1970 | 1980 | 1990 | 2000 | 2010 |
|---|---|---|---|---|---|
| legislative branch | 29,939 | 39,710 | 37,495 | 31,157 | 30,643 |
| judicial branch | 6,879 | 15,178 | 23,605 | 32,186 | 33,756 |
| executive branch | 2,829,495 | 2,820,978 | 3,067,167 | 2,644,758 | 2,776,744 |
| Executive Office of the President | 997 | 1,886 | 1,731 | 1,658 | 1,965 |
| executive departments | 1,772,363 | 1,716,970 | 2,065,542 | 1,592,200 | 1,937,291 |
| State | 40,042 | 23,497 | 25,288 | 27,983 | 39,016 |
| Treasury | 90,683 | 124,663 | 158,655 | 143,508 | 110,099 |
| Defense | 1,169,173 | 960,116 | 1,034,152 | 676,268 | 772,601 |
| Justice | 40,075 | 56,327 | 83,932 | 125,970 | 117,916 |
| Interior | 71,671 | 77,357 | 77,679 | 73,818 | 70,231 |
| Agriculture | 114,309 | 129,139 | 122,594 | 104,466 | 106,867 |
| Commerce[1] | 36,124 | 48,563 | 69,920 | 47,652 | 56,856 |
| Labor | 10,928 | 23,400 | 17,727 | 16,040 | 17,592 |
| Health and Human Services[2] | 110,186 | 155,662 | 123,959 | 62,605 | 69,839 |
| Housing and Urban Development | 15,046 | 16,964 | 13,596 | 10,319 | 9,585 |
| Transportation | 66,970 | 72,361 | 67,364 | 63,598 | 57,972 |
| Energy | 7,156 | 21,557 | 17,731 | 15,692 | 16,145 |
| Education | 0 | 7,364 | 4,771 | 4,734 | 4,452 |
| Veterans Affairs | 169,241 | 228,285 | 248,174 | 219,547 | 304,665 |
| Homeland Security | 0 | 0 | 0 | 0 | 183,455 |
| | | | | | |
| independent agencies[3, 4] | 1,056,135 | 1,102,122 | 999,894 | 1,050,900 | 837,488 |
| Board of Governors of the Federal Reserve System | N/A | N/A | 1,525 | 2,372 | 1,873 |
| Environmental Protection Agency | 0 | 14,715 | 17,123 | 18,036 | 18,740 |
| Equal Employment Opportunity Commission | 797 | 3,515 | 2,880 | 2,780 | 2,543 |
| Federal Communications Commission | N/A | N/A | 1,778 | 1,965 | 1,838 |
| Federal Deposit Insurance Corporation | 2,462 | 3,520 | 17,641 | 6,958 | 6,436 |
| Federal Trade Commission | N/A | N/A | 988 | 1,019 | 1,131 |
| General Services Administration[5] | 37,661 | 37,654 | 20,277 | 14,334 | 12,820 |
| National Aeronautics and Space Administration | 30,674 | 23,714 | 24,872 | 18,819 | 18,664 |
| National Archives and Records Administration | N/A | N/A | 3,120 | 2,702 | 3,523 |
| National Labor Relations Board | N/A | N/A | 2,263 | 2,054 | 1,715 |
| National Science Foundation | N/A | N/A | 1,318 | 1,247 | 1,474 |
| Nuclear Regulatory Commission | 0 | 3,283 | 3,353 | 2,858 | 4,240 |
| Office of Personnel Management | 5,513 | 8,280 | 6,636 | 3,780 | 5,892 |
| Peace Corps | N/A | N/A | 1,178 | 1,065 | 1,082 |
| Railroad Retirement Board | N/A | N/A | 1,772 | 1,176 | 981 |
| Securities and Exchange Commission | N/A | N/A | 2,302 | 2,955 | 3,917 |
| Small Business Administration | 4,397 | 5,804 | 5,128 | 4,150 | 4,037 |
| Smithsonian Institution | 2,547 | 4,403 | 5,092 | 5,065 | 4,984 |
| Social Security Administration[2] | N/A | N/A | N/A | 64,474 | 69,975 |
| Tennessee Valley Authority | 23,785 | 51,714 | 28,392 | 13,145 | 12,457 |
| US Information Agency | 10,156 | 8,138 | 8,555 | 2,436 | 1,953 |
| US International Development Cooperation Agency | 14,493 | 6,152 | 4,698 | 2,552 | 2,515 |
| US Postal Service | 721,183 | 660,014 | 816,886 | 860,726 | 643,420 |
| total, all agencies[3] | 2,866,313 | 2,875,866 | 3,128,267 | 2,708,101 | 2,841,143 |

N/A means not available.    [1]Data for 1990 and 2000 include census enumerators.    [2]Sizable decrease in 1995 owing to the Social Security Administration's becoming an independent agency.    [3]Includes other agencies not shown separately.    [4]The Defense Intelligence Agency was excluded as of November 1984 and the National Imagery and Mapping Agency as of October 1996. Entries for 1990, 2000, and 2010 exclude the Central Intelligence Agency and the National Security Agency.    [5]Entries for 1970 and 1980 include the National Archives and Records Administration, which became an independent agency in 1985.

## Strikes and Lockouts in the US

Strikes and lockouts are referred to as work stoppages by the Bureau of Labor Statistics. This table covers work stoppages since 1954 involving 1,000 workers or more. The number of workers and stoppages are for stoppages begun during that year. The number of days of work lost pertains to all strikes or lockouts in effect during the year, whether they began in that year or not. Percentage of working time pertains to all workers except those employed in private households, forestry, or fisheries. A minus sign (−) indicates a percentage less than 0.005.

Source: US Bureau of Labor Statistics.

## Strikes and Lockouts in the US (continued)

| | strikes and lockouts | | work time lost | | | strikes and lockouts | | work time lost | |
|---|---|---|---|---|---|---|---|---|---|
| YEAR | NUMBER | WORKERS INVOLVED ('000) | DAYS LOST ('000) | % OF WORKING TIME | YEAR | NUMBER | WORKERS INVOLVED ('000) | DAYS LOST ('000) | % OF WORKING TIME |
| 1954 | 265 | 1,075 | 16,630 | 0.13 | 1983 | 81 | 909 | 17,461 | 0.08 |
| 1955 | 363 | 2,055 | 21,180 | 0.16 | 1984 | 62 | 376 | 8,499 | 0.04 |
| 1956 | 287 | 1,370 | 26,840 | 0.20 | 1985 | 54 | 324 | 7,079 | 0.03 |
| 1957 | 279 | 887 | 10,340 | 0.07 | 1986 | 69 | 533 | 11,861 | 0.05 |
| 1958 | 332 | 1,587 | 17,900 | 0.13 | 1987 | 46 | 174 | 4,481 | 0.02 |
| 1959 | 245 | 1,381 | 60,850 | 0.43 | 1988 | 40 | 118 | 4,381 | 0.02 |
| 1960 | 222 | 896 | 13,260 | 0.09 | 1989 | 51 | 452 | 16,996 | 0.07 |
| 1961 | 195 | 1,031 | 10,140 | 0.07 | 1990 | 44 | 185 | 5,926 | 0.02 |
| 1962 | 211 | 793 | 11,760 | 0.08 | 1991 | 40 | 392 | 4,584 | 0.02 |
| 1963 | 181 | 512 | 10,020 | 0.07 | 1992 | 35 | 364 | 3,989 | 0.01 |
| 1964 | 246 | 1,183 | 16,220 | 0.11 | 1993 | 35 | 182 | 3,981 | 0.01 |
| 1965 | 268 | 999 | 15,140 | 0.10 | 1994 | 45 | 322 | 5,021 | 0.02 |
| 1966 | 321 | 1,300 | 16,000 | 0.10 | 1995 | 31 | 192 | 5,771 | 0.02 |
| 1967 | 381 | 2,192 | 31,320 | 0.18 | 1996 | 37 | 273 | 4,889 | 0.02 |
| 1968 | 392 | 1,855 | 35,367 | 0.20 | 1997 | 29 | 339 | 4,497 | 0.01 |
| 1969 | 412 | 1,576 | 29,397 | 0.16 | 1998 | 34 | 387 | 5,116 | 0.02 |
| 1970 | 381 | 2,468 | 52,761 | 0.29 | 1999 | 17 | 73 | 1,996 | 0.01 |
| 1971 | 298 | 2,516 | 35,538 | 0.19 | 2000 | 39 | 394 | 20,419 | 0.06 |
| 1972 | 250 | 975 | 16,764 | 0.09 | 2001 | 29 | 99 | 1,151 | – |
| 1973 | 317 | 1,400 | 16,260 | 0.08 | 2002 | 19 | 46 | 660 | – |
| 1974 | 424 | 1,796 | 31,809 | 0.16 | 2003 | 14 | 129 | 4,091 | 0.01 |
| 1975 | 235 | 965 | 17,563 | 0.09 | 2004 | 17 | 171 | 3,344 | 0.01 |
| 1976 | 231 | 1,519 | 23,962 | 0.12 | 2005 | 22 | 100 | 1,736 | 0.01 |
| 1977 | 298 | 1,212 | 21,258 | 0.10 | 2006 | 20 | 70 | 2,688 | 0.01 |
| 1978 | 219 | 1,006 | 23,774 | 0.11 | 2007 | 21 | 189 | 1,265 | – |
| 1979 | 235 | 1,021 | 20,409 | 0.09 | 2008 | 15 | 72 | 1,954 | 0.01 |
| 1980 | 187 | 795 | 20,844 | 0.09 | 2009 | 5 | 13 | 124 | – |
| 1981 | 145 | 729 | 16,908 | 0.07 | 2010 | 11 | 45 | 302 | – |
| 1982 | 96 | 656 | 9,061 | 0.04 | 2011 | 19 | 113 | 1,020 | – |

## US Trade Union Membership

Numbers are in thousands ('000). N/A means not available. Source: US Bureau of Labor Statistics.

| YEAR | NUMBER OF UNION MEMBERS | % OF TOTAL LABOR FORCE | YEAR | NUMBER OF UNION MEMBERS | % OF TOTAL LABOR FORCE | YEAR | NUMBER OF UNION MEMBERS | % OF TOTAL LABOR FORCE |
|---|---|---|---|---|---|---|---|---|
| 1900[1] | 791 | N/A | 1940 | 8,717 | 26.9 | 1980 | 20,095 | 23.0 |
| 1905 | 1,918 | N/A | 1945 | 14,322 | 35.5 | 1985 | 16,996 | 18.0 |
| 1910 | 2,116 | N/A | 1950 | 14,300[3] | 31.5 | 1990 | 16,740 | 16.1 |
| 1915 | 2,560 | N/A | 1955 | 16,802 | 33.2 | 1995 | 16,360 | 14.9 |
| 1920 | 5,034 | N/A | 1960 | 17,049 | 31.4 | 2000 | 16,258 | 13.5 |
| 1925 | 3,566 | N/A | 1965 | 17,299 | 28.4 | 2005 | 15,685 | 12.5 |
| 1930[2] | 3,401 | 11.6 | 1970 | 19,381 | 27.4 | 2010 | 14,715 | 11.9 |
| 1935 | 3,584 | 13.2 | 1977[4] | 19,335 | 23.8 | 2011 | 14,764 | 11.8 |

[1]Data from 1900 to 1925 include Canadian members whose union headquarters were in the US. [2]Agricultural workers were not included as part of the total labor force for the years from 1930 to 1970. [3]Rounded to nearest hundred thousand. [4]Data for 1975 are not available. Data for 1977 on include only employed union members.

## US Unemployment Rates

Unemployment rates of the civilian labor force ages 16 years and older. Source: US Bureau of Labor Statistics.

| YEAR | UNEMPLOYMENT RATE (%) | YEAR | UNEMPLOYMENT RATE (%) | YEAR | UNEMPLOYMENT RATE (%) | YEAR | UNEMPLOYMENT RATE (%) |
|---|---|---|---|---|---|---|---|
| 1950 | 5.29 | 1956 | 4.13 | 1962 | 5.54 | 1968 | 3.58 |
| 1951 | 3.31 | 1957 | 4.27 | 1963 | 5.67 | 1969 | 3.51 |
| 1952 | 3.03 | 1958 | 6.80 | 1964 | 5.18 | 1970 | 4.94 |
| 1953 | 2.91 | 1959 | 5.47 | 1965 | 4.52 | 1971 | 5.94 |
| 1954 | 5.55 | 1960 | 5.53 | 1966 | 3.79 | 1972 | 5.61 |
| 1955 | 4.39 | 1961 | 6.69 | 1967 | 3.85 | 1973 | 4.88 |

## US Unemployment Rates (continued)

| YEAR | UNEMPLOYMENT RATE (%) | YEAR | UNEMPLOYMENT RATE (%) | YEAR | UNEMPLOYMENT RATE (%) | YEAR | UNEMPLOYMENT RATE (%) |
|---|---|---|---|---|---|---|---|
| 1974 | 5.61 | 1984 | 7.52 | 1994 | 6.10 | 2004 | 5.53 |
| 1975 | 8.46 | 1985 | 7.20 | 1995 | 5.60 | 2005 | 5.08 |
| 1976 | 7.70 | 1986 | 6.99 | 1996 | 5.40 | 2006 | 4.62 |
| 1977 | 7.06 | 1987 | 6.19 | 1997 | 4.94 | 2007 | 4.62 |
| 1978 | 6.07 | 1988 | 5.51 | 1998 | 4.51 | 2008 | 5.78 |
| 1979 | 5.85 | 1989 | 5.27 | 1999 | 4.22 | 2009 | 9.25 |
| 1980 | 7.14 | 1990 | 5.60 | 2000 | 3.99 | 2010 | 9.63 |
| 1981 | 7.61 | 1991 | 6.83 | 2001 | 4.73 | 2011 | 8.95 |
| 1982 | 9.69 | 1992 | 7.50 | 2002 | 5.78 | | |
| 1983 | 9.61 | 1993 | 6.92 | 2003 | 5.99 | | |

## Social Characteristics of the Unemployed in the US

*Unemployment as a percentage of the civilian labor force. Source: US Bureau of Labor Statistics.*

| SOCIAL CHARACTERISTICS | UNEMPLOYMENT RATES BY YEAR (%) | | | | | | | | | |
|---|---|---|---|---|---|---|---|---|---|---|
| | 1975 | 1980 | 1985 | 1990 | 1995 | 2000 | 2005 | 2009 | 2010 | 2011 |
| **age (both sexes)** | | | | | | | | | | |
| 16 and over[1] | 19.9 | 17.8 | 18.6 | 15.5 | 17.3 | 13.1 | 5.1 | 9.3 | 9.6 | 8.9 |
| 25–54[2] | 6.0 | 5.1 | 5.6 | 4.4 | 4.3 | 3.0 | 4.1 | 8.3 | 8.6 | 7.9 |
| **sex (16 years and older)[3]** | | | | | | | | | | |
| men | 6.8 | 5.9 | 6.2 | 5.0 | 4.8 | 3.3 | 5.1 | 10.3 | 10.5 | 9.4 |
| women | 8.0 | 6.4 | 6.6 | 4.9 | 4.9 | 3.6 | 5.1 | 8.1 | 8.6 | 8.5 |
| **race/ethnicity** | | | | | | | | | | |
| white | 7.8 | 6.3 | 6.2 | 4.8 | 4.9 | 3.5 | 4.4 | 8.5 | 8.7 | 7.9 |
| black | 14.8 | 14.3 | 15.1 | 11.4 | 10.4 | 7.6 | 10.0 | 14.8 | 16.0 | 15.8 |
| Hispanic[4] | 12.2 | 10.1 | 10.5 | 8.2 | 9.3 | 5.7 | 6.0 | 12.1 | 12.5 | 11.5 |
| **overall unemployment** | 8.5 | 7.1 | 7.2 | 5.6 | 5.6 | 4.0 | 5.1 | 9.3 | 9.6 | 8.9 |

[1]Data for ages 16–19 until 2005.    [2]Data for ages 25 and older until 2005.    [3]Data for ages 20 years and older until 2005.    [4]Hispanics may be of any race and are included in both the white and black racial categories in this table.

## US Work-Related Fatalities by Cause

*Totals for major categories may include some subcategories not listed in the table. Detail may not add to total given because of rounding. Data for 2010 is preliminary. Source: US Bureau of Labor Statistics.*

| CAUSE OF FATALITY | 2005–09 NUMBER (AVG.) | 2010 NUMBER | 2010 (%) |
|---|---|---|---|
| **transportation incidents** | **2,246** | **1,766** | **38.8** |
| highway | 1,281 | 968 | 21.3 |
| collision between vehicles, mobile equipment | 625 | 501 | 11.0 |
| moving in same direction | 153 | 119 | 2.6 |
| moving in opposite directions, oncoming | 234 | 182 | 4.0 |
| moving in intersection | 122 | 102 | 2.2 |
| vehicle struck stationary object or equipment | 348 | 263 | 5.8 |
| noncollision | 289 | 195 | 4.3 |
| jackknifed or overturned—no collision | 248 | 173 | 3.8 |
| nonhighway (farm, industrial premises) | 305 | 272 | 6.0 |
| overturned | 159 | 154 | 3.4 |
| worker struck by a vehicle | 342 | 277 | 6.1 |
| railway accident | 53 | 44 | 1.0 |
| water vehicle accident | 83 | 52 | 1.1 |
| aircraft accident | 178 | 151 | 3.3 |
| **assaults and violent acts** | **819** | **808** | **17.8** |
| homicides | 561 | 506 | 11.1 |
| shooting | 447 | 401 | 8.8 |
| stabbing | 45 | 34 | 0.7 |
| self-inflicted injury | 222 | 258 | 5.7 |

## US Work-Related Fatalities by Cause (continued)

| CAUSE OF FATALITY | 2005–09 NUMBER (AVG.) | 2010 NUMBER | (%) |
|---|---|---|---|
| contact with objects and equipment | 919 | 732 | 16.1 |
| struck by object | 528 | 402 | 8.8 |
| struck by falling object | 345 | 263 | 5.8 |
| struck by flying object | 55 | 36 | 0.8 |
| caught in or compressed by equipment or objects | 278 | 224 | 4.9 |
| caught in running equipment or machinery | 126 | 90 | 2.0 |
| caught in or crushed in collapsing materials | 101 | 91 | 2.0 |
| falls | 758 | 635 | 14.0 |
| fall to lower level | 656 | 515 | 11.3 |
| fall from ladder | 128 | 129 | 2.8 |
| fall from roof | 148 | 117 | 2.6 |
| fall from scaffold, staging | 77 | 44 | 1.0 |
| fall on same level | 83 | 93 | 2.0 |
| exposure to harmful substances or environments | 478 | 409 | 9.0 |
| contact with electric current | 215 | 163 | 3.6 |
| contact with overhead power lines | 96 | 76 | 1.7 |
| contact with temperature extremes | 46 | 45 | 1.0 |
| exposure to caustic, noxious, or allergenic substances | 144 | 139 | 3.1 |
| inhalation of substance | 58 | 57 | 1.3 |
| oxygen deficiency | 70 | 60 | 1.3 |
| drowning, submersion | 55 | 45 | 1.0 |
| fires and explosions | 160 | 187 | 4.1 |
| total | 5,399 | 4,547 | 100 |

# Consumer Prices

The consumer price index (CPI) is used as an indicator of price changes in the goods and services purchased by US consumers. The information provided below is based on the purchases of a specific group of urban consumers who serve as a sample population representing more than 80% of the total US population. Each annual CPI is compared with the average index level of 100, which is a base number that represents the average price level for the 36-month period covering the years 1982, 1983, and 1984. A minus sign indicates a decrease.

Source: US Bureau of Labor Statistics.

## US Consumer Price Index, 1913–2011

This table presents the annual change in the Consumer Price Index (CPI) since 1913.

| YEAR | ANNUAL CPI | % ANNUAL CHANGE IN CPI | YEAR | ANNUAL CPI | % ANNUAL CHANGE IN CPI | YEAR | ANNUAL CPI | % ANNUAL CHANGE IN CPI |
|---|---|---|---|---|---|---|---|---|
| 1913 | 9.9 | . | 1930 | 16.7 | -2.3 | 1947 | 22.3 | 14.4 |
| 1914 | 10.0 | 1.0 | 1931 | 15.2 | -9.0 | 1948 | 24.1 | 8.1 |
| 1915 | 10.1 | 1.0 | 1932 | 13.7 | -9.9 | 1949 | 23.8 | -1.2 |
| 1916 | 10.9 | 7.9 | 1933 | 13.0 | -5.1 | 1950 | 24.1 | 1.3 |
| 1917 | 12.8 | 17.4 | 1934 | 13.4 | 3.1 | 1951 | 26.0 | 7.9 |
| 1918 | 15.1 | 18.0 | 1935 | 13.7 | 2.2 | 1952 | 26.5 | 1.9 |
| 1919 | 17.3 | 14.6 | 1936 | 13.9 | 1.5 | 1953 | 26.7 | 0.8 |
| 1920 | 20.0 | 15.6 | 1937 | 14.4 | 3.6 | 1954 | 26.9 | 0.7 |
| 1921 | 17.9 | -10.5 | 1938 | 14.1 | -2.1 | 1955 | 26.8 | -0.4 |
| 1922 | 16.8 | -6.1 | 1939 | 13.9 | -1.4 | 1956 | 27.2 | 1.5 |
| 1923 | 17.1 | 1.8 | 1940 | 14.0 | 0.7 | 1957 | 28.1 | 3.3 |
| 1924 | 17.1 | 0.0 | 1941 | 14.7 | 5.0 | 1958 | 28.9 | 2.8 |
| 1925 | 17.5 | 2.3 | 1942 | 16.3 | 10.9 | 1959 | 29.1 | 0.7 |
| 1926 | 17.7 | 1.1 | 1943 | 17.3 | 6.1 | 1960 | 29.6 | 1.7 |
| 1927 | 17.4 | -1.7 | 1944 | 17.6 | 1.7 | 1961 | 29.9 | 1.0 |
| 1928 | 17.1 | -1.7 | 1945 | 18.0 | 2.3 | 1962 | 30.2 | 1.0 |
| 1929 | 17.1 | 0.0 | 1946 | 19.5 | 8.3 | 1963 | 30.6 | 1.3 |

## US Consumer Price Index, 1913–2011 (continued)

| YEAR | ANNUAL CPI | % ANNUAL CHANGE IN CPI | YEAR | ANNUAL CPI | % ANNUAL CHANGE IN CPI | YEAR | ANNUAL CPI | % ANNUAL CHANGE IN CPI |
|---|---|---|---|---|---|---|---|---|
| 1964 | 31.0 | 1.3 | 1980 | 82.4 | 13.5 | 1996 | 156.9 | 3.0 |
| 1965 | 31.5 | 1.6 | 1981 | 90.9 | 10.3 | 1997 | 160.5 | 2.3 |
| 1966 | 32.4 | 2.9 | 1982 | 96.5 | 6.2 | 1998 | 163.0 | 1.6 |
| 1967 | 33.4 | 3.1 | 1983 | 99.6 | 3.2 | 1999 | 166.6 | 2.2 |
| 1968 | 34.8 | 4.2 | 1984 | 103.9 | 4.3 | 2000 | 172.2 | 3.4 |
| 1969 | 36.7 | 5.5 | 1985 | 107.6 | 3.6 | 2001 | 177.1 | 2.8 |
| 1970 | 38.8 | 5.7 | 1986 | 109.6 | 1.9 | 2002 | 179.9 | 1.6 |
| 1971 | 40.5 | 4.4 | 1987 | 113.6 | 3.6 | 2003 | 184.0 | 2.3 |
| 1972 | 41.8 | 3.2 | 1988 | 118.3 | 4.1 | 2004 | 188.9 | 2.7 |
| 1973 | 44.4 | 6.2 | 1989 | 124.0 | 4.8 | 2005 | 195.3 | 3.4 |
| 1974 | 49.3 | 11.0 | 1990 | 130.7 | 5.4 | 2006 | 201.6 | 3.2 |
| 1975 | 53.8 | 9.1 | 1991 | 136.2 | 4.2 | 2007 | 207.3 | 2.8 |
| 1976 | 56.9 | 5.8 | 1992 | 140.3 | 3.0 | 2008 | 215.3 | 3.8 |
| 1977 | 60.6 | 6.5 | 1993 | 144.5 | 3.0 | 2009 | 214.5 | −0.4 |
| 1978 | 65.2 | 7.6 | 1994 | 148.2 | 2.6 | 2010 | 218.1 | 1.6 |
| 1979 | 72.6 | 11.3 | 1995 | 152.4 | 2.8 | 2011 | 224.9 | 3.2 |

## US Consumer Price Indexes by Item Group, 1975–2011

*Source: US Bureau of Labor Statistics.*

| ITEM GROUP | CONSUMER PRICE INDEX | | | | | | | | |
|---|---|---|---|---|---|---|---|---|---|
| | 1975 | 1980 | 1985 | 1990 | 1995 | 2000 | 2005 | 2010 | 2011 |
| all items | 53.8 | 82.4 | 107.6 | 130.7 | 152.4 | 172.2 | 195.3 | 218.1 | 224.9 |
| commodities | 58.2 | 86.0 | 105.4 | 122.8 | 136.4 | 149.2 | 160.2 | 174.6 | 183.9 |
| energy | 42.1 | 86.0 | 101.6 | 102.1 | 105.2 | 124.6 | 177.1 | 211.4 | 243.9 |
| food | 59.8 | 86.8 | 105.6 | 132.4 | 148.4 | 167.8 | 190.7 | 219.6 | 227.8 |
| shelter | 48.8 | 81.0 | 109.8 | 140.0 | 165.7 | 193.4 | 224.4 | 248.4 | 251.6 |
| transportation | 50.1 | 83.1 | 106.4 | 120.5 | 139.1 | 153.3 | 173.9 | 193.4 | 212.4 |
| medical care | 47.5 | 74.9 | 113.5 | 162.8 | 220.5 | 260.8 | 323.2 | 388.4 | 400.3 |
| apparel | 72.5 | 90.9 | 105.0 | 124.1 | 132.0 | 129.6 | 119.5 | 119.5 | 122.1 |

| ITEM GROUP | % CHANGE IN CPI[1] | | | | | | | | |
|---|---|---|---|---|---|---|---|---|---|
| | 1975 | 1980 | 1985 | 1990 | 1995 | 2000 | 2005 | 2010 | 2011 |
| all items | 9.1 | 13.5 | 3.6 | 5.4 | 2.8 | 3.4 | 3.4 | 1.6 | 3.2 |
| commodities | 8.8 | 12.3 | 2.1 | 5.2 | 1.9 | 3.3 | 3.6 | 2.9 | 5.3 |
| energy | 10.5 | 30.9 | 0.7 | 8.3 | 0.6 | 16.9 | 17.0 | 9.5 | 15.4 |
| food | 8.5 | 8.6 | 2.3 | 5.8 | 2.8 | 2.3 | 2.4 | 0.8 | 3.7 |
| shelter | 9.9 | 17.6 | 5.6 | 5.4 | 3.2 | 3.3 | 2.6 | −0.4 | 1.3 |
| transportation | 9.4 | 17.9 | 2.6 | 5.6 | 3.6 | 6.2 | 6.6 | 7.9 | 9.8 |
| medical care | 12.0 | 11.0 | 6.3 | 9.0 | 4.5 | 4.1 | 4.2 | 3.4 | 3.0 |
| apparel | 4.5 | 7.1 | 2.8 | 4.6 | −1.0 | −1.3 | −0.7 | −0.5 | 2.2 |

[1]*Annual percent change from the preceding year.*

# US Budget

## US Public Debt

In order to fund governmental operations, the Department of the Treasury borrows money by selling Treasury bills, US savings bonds, and other securities to the public. The money borrowed by the Treasury is referred to as the public debt. A broader measure of the federal debt is known as the gross federal debt. It consists of the public debt plus money borrowed by federal agencies. The GDP is the gross domestic product. Data for 2010 and 2011 are estimates.

Source: US Office of Management and Budget.

| END OF FISCAL YEAR | PUBLIC DEBT (IN US$ MILLIONS) | % OF GDP | GROSS FEDERAL DEBT (IN US$ MILLIONS) | % OF GDP | END OF FISCAL YEAR | PUBLIC DEBT (IN US$ MILLIONS) | % OF GDP | GROSS FEDERAL DEBT (IN US$ MILLIONS) | % OF GDP |
|---|---|---|---|---|---|---|---|---|---|
| 1940 | 42,772 | 44.2 | 50,696 | 52.4 | 1960 | 236,840 | 45.6 | 290,525 | 56.0 |
| 1950 | 219,023 | 80.2 | 256,853 | 94.0 | 1970 | 283,198 | 28.0 | 380,921 | 37.6 |

## US Public Debt (continued)

| END OF FISCAL YEAR | PUBLIC DEBT (IN US$ MILLIONS) | % OF GDP | GROSS FEDERAL DEBT (IN US$ MILLIONS) | % OF GDP | END OF FISCAL YEAR | PUBLIC DEBT (IN US$ MILLIONS) | % OF GDP | GROSS FEDERAL DEBT (IN US$ MILLIONS) | % OF GDP |
|---|---|---|---|---|---|---|---|---|---|
| 1980 | 711,923 | 26.1 | 909,041 | 33.4 | 2009 | 7,544,707 | 53.0 | 11,875,851 | 83.4 |
| 1990 | 2,411,558 | 42.0 | 3,206,290 | 55.9 | 2010 | 9,297,653 | 63.6 | 13,786,615 | 94.3 |
| 2000 | 3,409,804 | 35.1 | 5,628,700 | 58.0 | 2011 | 10,498,325 | 68.6 | 15,144,029 | 99.0 |

## US Governmental Spending, 1800–2011

Entries for the years prior to 1933 are based on the administrative budget concept rather than on the unified budget concept. For a discussion of the unified budget concept and related topics, see <www.fms.treas.gov/bulletin/b2011_3ffotxt.doc>. The figures are in thousands ('000). A minus sign indicates a deficit.

Source: US Office of Management and Budget.

| YEAR[1] | FEDERAL INCOME | FEDERAL SPENDING | SURPLUS OR DEFICIT | YEAR[1] | FEDERAL INCOME | FEDERAL SPENDING | SURPLUS OR DEFICIT |
|---|---|---|---|---|---|---|---|
| 1800 | 10,849 | 10,786 | 63 | 1848 | 35,736 | 45,377 | −9,641 |
| 1801 | 12,935 | 9,395 | 3,541 | 1849 | 31,208 | 45,052 | −13,844 |
| 1802 | 14,996 | 7,862 | 7,134 | 1850 | 43,603 | 39,543 | 4,060 |
| 1803 | 11,064 | 7,852 | 3,212 | 1851 | 52,559 | 47,709 | 4,850 |
| 1804 | 11,826 | 8,719 | 3,107 | 1852 | 49,847 | 44,195 | 5,652 |
| 1805 | 13,561 | 10,506 | 3,054 | 1853 | 61,587 | 48,184 | 13,403 |
| 1806 | 15,560 | 9,804 | 5,756 | 1854 | 73,800 | 58,045 | 15,755 |
| 1807 | 16,398 | 8,354 | 8,044 | 1855 | 65,351 | 59,743 | 5,608 |
| 1808 | 17,061 | 9,932 | 7,128 | 1856 | 74,057 | 69,571 | 4,486 |
| 1809 | 7,773 | 10,281 | −2,507 | 1857 | 68,965 | 67,796 | 1,170 |
| 1810 | 9,384 | 8,157 | 1,228 | 1858 | 46,655 | 74,185 | −27,530 |
| 1811 | 14,424 | 8,058 | 6,365 | 1859 | 53,486 | 69,071 | −15,585 |
| 1812 | 9,801 | 20,281 | −10,480 | 1860 | 56,065 | 63,131 | −7,066 |
| 1813 | 14,340 | 31,682 | −17,341 | 1861 | 41,510 | 66,547 | −25,037 |
| 1814 | 11,182 | 34,721 | −23,539 | 1862 | 51,987 | 474,762 | −422,774 |
| 1815 | 15,729 | 32,708 | −16,979 | 1863 | 112,697 | 714,741 | −602,043 |
| 1816 | 47,678 | 30,587 | 17,091 | 1864 | 264,627 | 865,323 | −600,696 |
| 1817 | 33,099 | 21,844 | 11,255 | 1865 | 333,715 | 1,297,555 | −963,841 |
| 1818 | 21,585 | 19,825 | 1,760 | 1866 | 558,033 | 520,809 | 37,223 |
| 1819 | 24,603 | 21,464 | 3,140 | 1867 | 490,634 | 357,543 | 133,091 |
| 1820 | 17,881 | 18,261 | −380 | 1868 | 405,638 | 377,340 | 28,298 |
| 1821 | 14,573 | 15,811 | −1,237 | 1869 | 370,944 | 322,865 | 48,078 |
| 1822 | 20,232 | 15,000 | 5,232 | 1870 | 411,255 | 309,654 | 101,602 |
| 1823 | 20,541 | 14,707 | 5,834 | 1871 | 383,324 | 292,177 | 91,147 |
| 1824 | 19,381 | 20,327 | −945 | 1872 | 374,107 | 277,518 | 96,589 |
| 1825 | 21,841 | 15,857 | 5,984 | 1873 | 333,738 | 290,345 | 43,393 |
| 1826 | 25,260 | 17,036 | 8,225 | 1874 | 304,979 | 302,634 | 2,345 |
| 1827 | 22,966 | 16,139 | 6,827 | 1875 | 288,000 | 274,623 | 13,377 |
| 1828 | 24,764 | 16,395 | 8,369 | 1876 | 294,096 | 265,101 | 28,995 |
| 1829 | 24,828 | 15,203 | 9,624 | 1877 | 281,406 | 241,334 | 40,072 |
| 1830 | 24,844 | 15,143 | 9,701 | 1878 | 257,764 | 236,964 | 20,800 |
| 1831 | 28,527 | 15,248 | 13,279 | 1879 | 273,827 | 266,948 | 6,879 |
| 1832 | 31,866 | 17,289 | 14,577 | 1880 | 333,527 | 267,643 | 65,884 |
| 1833 | 33,948 | 23,018 | 10,931 | 1881 | 360,782 | 260,713 | 100,069 |
| 1834 | 21,792 | 18,628 | 3,164 | 1882 | 403,525 | 257,981 | 145,544 |
| 1835 | 35,430 | 17,573 | 17,857 | 1883 | 398,288 | 265,408 | 132,879 |
| 1836 | 50,827 | 30,868 | 19,959 | 1884 | 348,520 | 244,126 | 104,394 |
| 1837 | 24,954 | 37,243 | −12,289 | 1885 | 323,691 | 260,227 | 63,464 |
| 1838 | 26,303 | 33,865 | −7,562 | 1886 | 336,440 | 242,483 | 93,957 |
| 1839 | 31,483 | 26,899 | 4,584 | 1887 | 371,403 | 267,932 | 103,471 |
| 1840 | 19,480 | 24,318 | −4,837 | 1888 | 379,266 | 267,925 | 111,341 |
| 1841 | 16,860 | 26,566 | −9,706 | 1889 | 387,050 | 299,289 | 87,761 |
| 1842 | 19,976 | 25,206 | −5,230 | 1890 | 403,081 | 318,041 | 85,040 |
| 1843 | 8,303 | 11,858 | −3,555 | 1891 | 392,612 | 365,774 | 26,839 |
| 1844 | 29,321 | 22,338 | 6,984 | 1892 | 354,938 | 345,023 | 9,914 |
| 1845 | 29,970 | 22,937 | 7,033 | 1893 | 385,820 | 383,478 | 2,342 |
| 1846 | 29,700 | 27,767 | 1,933 | 1894 | 306,355 | 367,525 | −61,170 |
| 1847 | 26,496 | 57,281 | −30,786 | 1895 | 324,729 | 356,195 | −31,466 |

## US Governmental Spending, 1800–2011 (continued)

| YEAR[1] | FEDERAL INCOME | FEDERAL SPENDING | SURPLUS OR DEFICIT | YEAR[1] | FEDERAL INCOME | FEDERAL SPENDING | SURPLUS OR DEFICIT |
|---|---|---|---|---|---|---|---|
| 1896 | 338,142 | 352,179 | −14,037 | 1955 | 65,451,000 | 68,444,000 | −2,993,000 |
| 1897 | 347,722 | 365,774 | −18,052 | 1956 | 74,587,000 | 70,640,000 | 3,947,000 |
| 1898 | 405,321 | 443,369 | −38,047 | 1957 | 79,990,000 | 76,578,000 | 3,412,000 |
| 1899 | 515,961 | 605,072 | −89,112 | 1958 | 79,636,000 | 82,405,000 | −2,769,000 |
| 1900 | 567,241 | 520,861 | 46,380 | 1959 | 79,249,000 | 92,098,000 | −12,849,000 |
| 1901 | 587,685 | 524,617 | 63,068 | 1960 | 92,492,000 | 92,191,000 | 301,000 |
| 1902 | 562,478 | 485,234 | 77,244 | 1961 | 94,388,000 | 97,723,000 | −3,335,000 |
| 1903 | 561,881 | 517,006 | 44,875 | 1962 | 99,676,000 | 106,821,000 | −7,146,000 |
| 1904 | 541,087 | 583,660 | −42,573 | 1963 | 106,560,000 | 111,316,000 | −4,756,000 |
| 1905 | 544,275 | 567,279 | −23,004 | 1964 | 112,613,000 | 118,528,000 | −5,915,000 |
| 1906 | 594,984 | 570,202 | 24,782 | 1965 | 116,817,000 | 118,228,000 | −1,411,000 |
| 1907 | 665,860 | 579,129 | 86,732 | 1966 | 130,835,000 | 134,532,000 | −3,698,000 |
| 1908 | 601,862 | 659,196 | −57,334 | 1967 | 148,822,000 | 157,464,000 | −8,643,000 |
| 1909 | 604,320 | 693,744 | −89,423 | 1968 | 152,973,000 | 178,134,000 | −25,161,000 |
| 1910 | 675,512 | 693,617 | −18,105 | 1969 | 186,882,000 | 183,640,000 | 3,242,000 |
| 1911 | 701,833 | 691,202 | 10,631 | 1970 | 192,807,000 | 195,649,000 | −2,842,000 |
| 1912 | 692,609 | 689,881 | 2,728 | 1971 | 187,139,000 | 210,172,000 | −23,033,000 |
| 1913 | 714,463 | 714,864 | −401 | 1972 | 207,309,000 | 230,681,000 | −23,373,000 |
| 1914 | 725,117 | 725,525 | −408 | 1973 | 230,799,000 | 245,707,000 | −14,908,000 |
| 1915 | 683,417 | 746,093 | −62,676 | 1974 | 263,224,000 | 269,359,000 | −6,135,000 |
| 1916 | 761,445 | 712,967 | 48,478 | 1975 | 279,090,000 | 332,332,000 | −53,242,000 |
| 1917 | 1,100,500 | 1,953,857 | −853,357 | 1976 | 298,060,000 | 371,792,000 | −73,732,000 |
| 1918 | 3,645,240 | 12,677,359 | −9,032,120 | TQ | 81,232,000 | 95,975,000 | −14,744,000 |
| 1919 | 5,130,042 | 18,492,665 | −13,362,623 | 1977 | 355,559,000 | 409,218,000 | −53,659,000 |
| 1920 | 6,648,898 | 6,357,677 | 291,222 | 1978 | 399,561,000 | 458,746,000 | −59,185,000 |
| 1921 | 5,570,790 | 5,061,785 | 509,005 | 1979 | 463,302,000 | 504,028,000 | −40,726,000 |
| 1922 | 4,025,901 | 3,289,404 | 736,496 | 1980 | 517,112,000 | 590,941,000 | −73,830,000 |
| 1923 | 3,852,795 | 3,140,287 | 712,508 | 1981 | 599,272,000 | 678,241,000 | −78,968,000 |
| 1924 | 3,871,214 | 2,907,847 | 963,367 | 1982 | 617,766,000 | 745,743,000 | −127,977,000 |
| 1925 | 3,640,805 | 2,923,762 | 717,043 | 1983 | 600,562,000 | 808,364,000 | −207,802,000 |
| 1926 | 3,795,108 | 2,929,964 | 865,144 | 1984 | 666,438,000 | 851,805,000 | −185,367,000 |
| 1927 | 4,012,794 | 2,857,429 | 1,155,365 | 1985 | 734,037,000 | 946,344,000 | −212,308,000 |
| 1928 | 3,900,329 | 2,961,245 | 939,083 | 1986 | 769,155,000 | 990,382,000 | −221,227,000 |
| 1929 | 3,861,589 | 3,127,199 | 734,391 | 1987 | 854,288,000 | 1,004,017,000 | −149,730,000 |
| 1930 | 4,057,884 | 3,320,211 | 737,673 | 1988 | 909,238,000 | 1,064,416,000 | −155,178,000 |
| 1931 | 3,115,557 | 3,577,434 | −461,877 | 1989 | 991,105,000 | 1,143,744,000 | −152,639,000 |
| 1932 | 1,923,892 | 4,659,182 | −2,735,290 | 1990 | 1,031,958,000 | 1,252,994,000 | −221,036,000 |
| 1933 | 1,996,844 | 4,598,496 | −2,601,652 | 1991 | 1,054,988,000 | 1,324,226,000 | −269,238,000 |
| 1934 | 2,955,000 | 6,541,000 | −3,586,000 | 1992 | 1,091,208,000 | 1,381,529,000 | −290,321,000 |
| 1935 | 3,609,000 | 6,412,000 | −2,803,000 | 1993 | 1,154,335,000 | 1,409,386,000 | −255,051,000 |
| 1936 | 3,923,000 | 8,228,000 | −4,304,000 | 1994 | 1,258,566,000 | 1,461,753,000 | −203,186,000 |
| 1937 | 5,387,000 | 7,580,000 | −2,193,000 | 1995 | 1,351,790,000 | 1,515,742,000 | −163,952,000 |
| 1938 | 6,751,000 | 6,840,000 | −89,000 | 1996 | 1,453,053,000 | 1,560,484,000 | −107,431,000 |
| 1939 | 6,295,000 | 9,141,000 | −2,846,000 | 1997 | 1,579,232,000 | 1,601,116,000 | −21,884,000 |
| 1940 | 6,548,000 | 9,468,000 | −2,920,000 | 1998 | 1,721,728,000 | 1,652,458,000 | 69,270,000 |
| 1941 | 8,712,000 | 13,653,000 | −4,941,000 | 1999 | 1,827,452,000 | 1,701,842,000 | 125,610,000 |
| 1942 | 14,634,000 | 35,137,000 | −20,503,000 | 2000 | 2,025,191,000 | 1,788,950,000 | 236,241,000 |
| 1943 | 24,001,000 | 78,555,000 | −54,554,000 | 2001 | 1,991,082,000 | 1,862,846,000 | 128,236,000 |
| 1944 | 43,747,000 | 91,304,000 | −47,557,000 | 2002 | 1,853,136,000 | 2,010,894,000 | −157,758,000 |
| 1945 | 45,159,000 | 92,712,000 | −47,553,000 | 2003 | 1,782,314,000 | 2,159,899,000 | −377,585,000 |
| 1946 | 39,296,000 | 55,232,000 | −15,936,000 | 2004 | 1,880,114,000 | 2,292,841,000 | −412,727,000 |
| 1947 | 38,514,000 | 34,496,000 | 4,018,000 | 2005 | 2,153,611,000 | 2,471,957,000 | −318,346,000 |
| 1948 | 41,560,000 | 29,764,000 | 11,796,000 | 2006 | 2,406,869,000 | 2,655,050,000 | −248,181,000 |
| 1949 | 39,415,000 | 38,835,000 | 580,000 | 2007 | 2,567,985,000 | 2,728,686,000 | −160,701,000 |
| 1950 | 39,443,000 | 42,562,000 | −3,119,000 | 2008 | 2,523,991,000 | 2,982,544,000 | −458,553,000 |
| 1951 | 51,616,000 | 45,514,000 | 6,102,000 | 2009 | 2,104,989,000 | 3,517,677,000 | −1,412,688,000 |
| 1952 | 66,167,000 | 67,686,000 | −1,519,000 | 2010 | 2,162,724,000 | 3,456,213,000 | −1,293,489,000 |
| 1953 | 69,608,000 | 76,101,000 | −6,493,000 | 2011 | 2,303,466,000 | 3,603,061,000 | −1,299,595,000 |
| 1954 | 69,701,000 | 70,855,000 | −1,154,000 | | | | |

[1]The fiscal year ended on 31 December for the budgets from 1800 to 1842. It ended on 30 June for the budgets from 1844 through 1976 and on 30 September from fiscal year 1977. The budget figures for 1843 are for the period from 1 January to 30 June. The third quarter of 1976 was budgeted separately because of the change in the fiscal year calendar. It is referred to as the Transition Quarter (TQ).

## Annual National Average Terms on Conventional Single-Family Mortgages, 1982–2010

Source: Federal Housing Finance Agency Monthly Interest Rate Survey.

| YEAR | CONTRACT INTEREST RATE (%) | INITIAL FEES AND CHARGES (%) | EFFECTIVE INTEREST RATE (%) | TERM TO MATURITY (YEARS) | MORTGAGE AMOUNT (US$'000) | PURCHASE PRICE (US$'000) | LOAN-TO-PRICE RATIO (%) |
|---|---|---|---|---|---|---|---|
| 1982 | 14.73 | 2.65 | 15.31 | 25.6 | 55.0 | 78.4 | 72.9 |
| 1983 | 12.26 | 2.39 | 12.73 | 26.0 | 59.9 | 83.1 | 74.5 |
| 1984 | 11.99 | 2.57 | 12.48 | 26.8 | 64.5 | 86.6 | 77.0 |
| 1985 | 11.17 | 2.51 | 11.64 | 25.9 | 70.2 | 96.1 | 75.8 |
| 1986 | 9.79 | 2.21 | 10.18 | 25.6 | 79.3 | 110.6 | 74.1 |
| 1987 | 8.95 | 2.08 | 9.30 | 26.8 | 89.1 | 121.8 | 75.2 |
| 1988 | 8.98 | 1.96 | 9.30 | 27.7 | 97.4 | 131.6 | 76.0 |
| 1989 | 9.81 | 1.87 | 10.13 | 27.7 | 104.5 | 142.8 | 74.8 |
| 1990 | 9.74 | 1.79 | 10.05 | 27.0 | 104.0 | 142.6 | 74.7 |
| 1991 | 9.07 | 1.58 | 9.34 | 26.5 | 106.3 | 146.7 | 74.4 |
| 1992 | 7.83 | 1.58 | 8.11 | 25.4 | 108.7 | 146.4 | 76.6 |
| 1993 | 6.93 | 1.20 | 7.13 | 25.5 | 107.0 | 143.1 | 77.2 |
| 1994 | 7.31 | 1.10 | 7.49 | 27.1 | 109.9 | 142.0 | 79.9 |
| 1995 | 7.69 | 0.97 | 7.85 | 27.4 | 110.4 | 142.8 | 79.9 |
| 1996 | 7.58 | 0.97 | 7.74 | 26.9 | 118.7 | 155.1 | 79.0 |
| 1997 | 7.52 | 0.98 | 7.68 | 27.5 | 126.6 | 164.5 | 79.4 |
| 1998 | 6.97 | 0.85 | 7.10 | 27.8 | 131.8 | 173.4 | 78.9 |
| 1999 | 7.14 | 0.74 | 7.25 | 28.2 | 139.3 | 184.2 | 78.5 |
| 2000 | 7.86 | 0.67 | 7.96 | 28.7 | 148.3 | 198.9 | 77.8 |
| 2001 | 6.94 | 0.53 | 7.03 | 27.6 | 155.7 | 215.5 | 76.2 |
| 2002 | 6.44 | 0.46 | 6.51 | 27.3 | 163.4 | 231.2 | 75.1 |
| 2003 | 5.67 | 0.37 | 5.73 | 26.8 | 167.9 | 243.4 | 73.5 |
| 2004 | 5.68 | 0.40 | 5.74 | 27.9 | 185.5 | 262.0 | 74.9 |
| 2005 | 5.85 | 0.38 | 5.90 | 28.5 | 211.9 | 299.8 | 74.7 |
| 2006 | 6.54 | 0.41 | 6.60 | 29.0 | 222.9 | 307.1 | 76.6 |
| 2007 | 6.42 | 0.48 | 6.49 | 29.3 | 224.7 | 300.5 | 79.4 |
| 2008 | 6.06 | 0.53 | 6.14 | 28.4 | 219.8 | 306.1 | 76.9 |
| 2009 | 5.05 | 0.61 | 5.14 | 28.2 | 217.8 | 307.3 | 74.5 |
| 2010 | 4.81 | 0.73 | 4.91 | 27.7 | 215.8 | 304.9 | 74.0 |

## US Bankruptcy Filings

This table shows the number of business and consumer bankruptcy filings in the US since 1980. Bankruptcy is intended to give debtors a fresh start in managing their resources by cancelling many of their debts through a court order called a "discharge." It is also meant to give creditors a fair share of the money that the debtors can afford to pay back.

Businesses may file for bankruptcy under chapter 11 of the Internal Revenue Code. Chapter 11 offers protection from creditor demands to a business in debt so that its officers and managers have time to reorganize in order to fulfill obligations to creditors.

Individuals may file for bankruptcy under either chapter 7 of the Internal Revenue Code (under which debtors may liquidate assets with the supervision of a trustee in order to receive a nearly immediate discharge of debts) or chapter 13 (under which the debtor enters into a payment plan to repay debt out of future earnings over a three-to-five-year period, with the oversight of a trustee).

Source: American Bankruptcy Institute.

| YEAR | TOTAL FILINGS | BUSINESS FILINGS | CONSUMER FILINGS | CONSUMER FILINGS AS A PERCENTAGE OF TOTAL FILINGS |
|---|---|---|---|---|
| 1980 | 331,264 | 43,694 | 287,570 | 86.81% |
| 1985 | 412,510 | 71,277 | 341,233 | 82.72% |
| 1990 | 782,960 | 64,853 | 718,107 | 91.72% |
| 1995 | 926,601 | 51,959 | 874,642 | 94.39% |
| 2000 | 1,253,444 | 35,472 | 1,217,972 | 97.17% |
| 2001 | 1,492,129 | 40,099 | 1,452,030 | 97.31% |
| 2002 | 1,577,651 | 38,540 | 1,539,111 | 97.56% |
| 2003 | 1,660,245 | 35,037 | 1,625,208 | 97.89% |
| 2004 | 1,597,462 | 34,317 | 1,563,145 | 97.85% |
| 2005 | 2,078,415 | 39,201 | 2,039,214 | 98.11% |
| 2006 | 617,660 | 19,695 | 597,965 | 96.81% |
| 2007 | 850,912 | 28,322 | 822,590 | 96.67% |
| 2008 | 1,117,771 | 43,546 | 1,074,225 | 96.10% |
| 2009 | 1,473,675 | 60,837 | 1,412,838 | 95.87% |
| 2010 | 1,593,081 | 56,282 | 1,536,799 | 96.47% |
| 2011 | 1,410,653 | 47,806 | 1,362,847 | 96.61% |

# US Taxes

## US Federal Taxation Structure

This table shows the range of income taxes for various types of households in each tax bracket. In 2012 the standard deductions for most filers were US$5,950 for those submitting returns under status "single" and status "married filing separately," US$8,700 for those filing under status "head of household," and US$11,900 for those submitting returns under status "married filing jointly" or "qualifying widow(er) with dependent child." Source: US Department of the Treasury, Internal Revenue Service.

### Single — Schedule X
IF TAXABLE INCOME

| IS OVER | BUT NOT OVER | THEN THE TAX IS | PLUS | OF THE AMOUNT OVER |
|---|---|---|---|---|
| US$0 | US$8,700 | — | 10% | US$0 |
| US$8,700 | US$35,350 | US$870.00 | 15% | US$8,700 |
| US$35,350 | US$86,650 | US$4,867.50 | 25% | US$35,350 |
| US$86,650 | US$178,650 | US$17,442.50 | 28% | US$86,650 |
| US$178,650 | US$388,350 | US$43,482.50 | 33% | US$178,650 |
| US$388,350 | — | US$112,683.50 | 35% | US$388,350 |

### Married Filing Jointly or Qualifying Widow(er) — Schedule Y-1
IF TAXABLE INCOME

| IS OVER | BUT NOT OVER | THEN THE TAX IS | PLUS | OF THE AMOUNT OVER |
|---|---|---|---|---|
| US$0 | US$17,400 | — | 10% | US$0 |
| US$17,400 | US$70,700 | US$1,740.00 | 15% | US$17,400 |
| US$70,700 | US$142,700 | US$9,735.00 | 25% | US$70,700 |
| US$142,700 | US$217,450 | US$27,735.00 | 28% | US$142,700 |
| US$217,450 | US$388,350 | US$48,665.00 | 33% | US$217,450 |
| US$388,350 | — | US$105,062.00 | 35% | US$388,350 |

### Married Filing Separately — Schedule Y-2
IF TAXABLE INCOME

| IS OVER | BUT NOT OVER | THEN THE TAX IS | PLUS | OF THE AMOUNT OVER |
|---|---|---|---|---|
| US$0 | US$8,700 | — | 10% | US$0 |
| US$8,700 | US$35,350 | US$870.00 | 15% | US$8,700 |
| US$35,350 | US$71,350 | US$4,867.50 | 25% | US$35,350 |
| US$71,350 | US$108,725 | US$13,867.50 | 28% | US$71,350 |
| US$108,725 | US$194,175 | US$22,332.50 | 33% | US$108,725 |
| US$194,175 | — | US$52,531.00 | 35% | US$194,175 |

### Head of Household — Schedule Z
IF TAXABLE INCOME

| IS OVER | BUT NOT OVER | THEN THE TAX IS | PLUS | OF THE AMOUNT OVER |
|---|---|---|---|---|
| US$0 | US$12,400 | — | 10% | US$0 |
| US$12,400 | US$47,350 | US$1,240.00 | 15% | US$12,400 |
| US$47,350 | US$122,300 | US$6,482.50 | 25% | US$47,350 |
| US$122,300 | US$198,050 | US$25,220.00 | 28% | US$122,300 |
| US$198,050 | US$388,350 | US$46,430.00 | 33% | US$198,050 |
| US$388,350 | — | US$109,229.00 | 35% | US$388,350 |

## Individual Income Taxes by US State

*This table shows tax rates as of 1 Jan 2012 for tax year 2012. Tax rates are given in percentages; income brackets and personal exemptions are given in US$.*
*Source: Federation of Tax Administrators, <www.taxadmin.org/fta/rate/tax_stru.html>.*

| STATE | TAX RATES LOW | TAX RATES HIGH | NUMBER OF BRACKETS | INCOME BRACKETS LOW | INCOME BRACKETS HIGH | PERSONAL EXEMPTIONS SINGLE | PERSONAL EXEMPTIONS JOINT | PERSONAL EXEMPTIONS DEPENDENTS | FEDERAL TAX DEDUCTIBLE |
|---|---|---|---|---|---|---|---|---|---|
| AL | 2.0 | 5.0 | 3 | 500[1] | 3,001[1] | 1,500 | 3,000 | 500[2] | yes |
| AK | no state income tax | | | | | | | | |
| AZ | 2.59 | 4.54 | 5 | 10,000[1] | 150,001[1] | 2,100 | 4,200 | 2,100 | |
| AR[3] | 1.0 | 7.0 | 6 | 3,899 | 32,700 | 23[4] | 46[4] | 23[4] | |
| CA[3] | 1.0 | 9.3[5] | 6 | 7,316[1] | 48,029[1] | 102[4] | 204[4] | 315[4] | |
| CO | 4.63 | | 1 | ——flat rate—— | | 3,700[6] | 7,400[6] | 3,700[6] | |
| CT | 3.0 | 6.7 | 6 | 10,000[1] | 250,001[1] | 13,000[7] | 24,000[7] | 0 | |
| DE | 2.2 | 6.75 | 6 | 5,000 | 60,001 | 110[4] | 220[4] | 110[4] | |
| DC | 4.0 | 8.95 | 4 | 10,000 | 350,000 | 1,675 | 3,350 | 1,675 | |
| FL | no state income tax | | | | | | | | |
| GA | 1.0 | 6.0 | 6 | 750[8] | 7,001[8] | 2,700 | 5,400 | 3,000 | |
| HI | 1.4 | 11.00 | 12 | 2,400[1] | 200,001[1] | 1,040 | 2,080 | 1,040 | |

## Individual Income Taxes by US State (continued)

| STATE | TAX RATES LOW | HIGH | NUMBER OF BRACKETS | INCOME BRACKETS LOW | HIGH | PERSONAL EXEMPTIONS SINGLE | JOINT | DEPENDENTS | FEDERAL TAX DEDUCTIBLE |
|---|---|---|---|---|---|---|---|---|---|
| ID[3] | 1.6 | 7.8 | 8 | 1,338[1] | 26,760[1] | 3,700[6] | 7,400[6] | 3,700[6] | |
| IL | 5.0 | | 1 | ——flat rate—— | | 2,000 | 4,000 | 2,000 | |
| IN | 3.4 | | 1 | ——flat rate—— | | 1,000 | 2,000 | 2,500[9] | |
| IA[3] | 0.36 | 8.98 | 9 | 1,469 | 66,105 | 40[4] | 80[4] | 40[4] | yes |
| KS | 3.5 | 6.45 | 3 | 15,000[1] | 30,001[1] | 2,250 | 4,500 | 2,250 | |
| KY | 2.0 | 6.0 | 6 | 3,000 | 75,001 | 20[4] | 40[4] | 20[4] | |
| LA | 2.0 | 6.0 | 3 | 12,500[1] | 50,001[1] | 4,500[10] | 9,000[10] | 1,000 | yes |
| ME[3] | 2.0 | 8.5 | 4 | 5,100[1] | 20,350[1] | 2,850 | 5,700 | 2,850 | |
| MD | 2.0 | 5.5 | 7 | 1,000 | 500,001 | 3,200 | 6,400 | 3,200 | |
| MA[3] | 5.3 | | 1 | ——flat rate—— | | 4,400 | 8,800 | 1,000 | |
| MI[3] | 4.35 | | 1 | ——flat rate—— | | 3,600 | 7,200 | 4,200[11] | |
| MN[3] | 5.35 | 7.85 | 3 | 23,670[12] | 77,731[12] | 3,700[6] | 7,400[6] | 3,700[6] | |
| MS | 3.0 | 5.0 | 3 | 5,000 | 10,001 | 6,000 | 12,000 | 1,500 | |
| MO | 1.5 | 6.0 | 10 | 1,000 | 9,001 | 2,100 | 4,200 | 1,200 | yes[13] |
| MT[3] | 1.0 | 6.9 | 7 | 2,700 | 16,000 | 2,190 | 4,380 | 2,190 | yes[13] |
| NE[3] | 2.56 | 6.84 | 4 | 2,400[1] | 27,001[1] | 123[4] | 246[4] | 123[4] | |
| NV | no state income tax | | | | | | | | |
| NH | state income tax is on dividends and interest income only | | | | | | | | |
| NJ | 1.4 | 8.97 | 6 | 20,000[14] | 500,000[14] | 1,000 | 2,000 | 1,500 | |
| NM | 1.7 | 4.9 | 4 | 5,500[15] | 16,001[15] | 3,700[6] | 7,400[6] | 3,700[6] | |
| NY | 4.0 | 8.82 | 8 | 8,000[1] | 1,000,000[1] | 0 | 0 | 1,000 | |
| NC | 6.0 | 7.75 | 3 | 12,750[16] | 60,000[16] | 1,150 | 2,300 | 1,150 | |
| ND[3] | 1.51 | 3.99 | 5 | 35,350[17] | 388,350[17] | 3,700[6] | 7,400[6] | 3,700[6] | |
| OH[3] | 0.587 | 5.925 | 9 | 5,100 | 204,200 | 1,650[18] | 3,300[18] | 1,650[18] | |
| OK | 0.5 | 5.25 | 7 | 1,000[19] | 8,701[19] | 1,000 | 2,000 | 1,000 | |
| OR[3] | 5.0 | 9.9 | 4 | 2,000[1] | 125,000[1] | 183[4] | 366[4] | 183[4] | yes[13] |
| PA | 3.07 | | 1 | ——flat rate—— | | ——none—— | | | |
| RI[3] | 3.75 | 5.99 | 3 | 57,150 | 129,900 | 3,650 | 7,300 | 3,650 | |
| SC[3] | 0.0 | 7.0 | 6 | 2,800 | 14,000 | 3,700[6] | 7,400[6] | 3,700[6] | |
| SD | no state income tax | | | | | | | | |
| TN | state income tax is on dividends and interest income only | | | | | 1,250 | 2,500 | 0 | |
| TX | no state income tax | | | | | | | | |
| UT | 5.0 | | 1 | ——flat rate—— | | 20 | 20 | 20 | |
| VT[3] | 3.55 | 8.95 | 5 | 35,350[21] | 388,350[21] | 3,700[6] | 7,400[6] | 3,700[6] | |
| VA | 2.0 | 5.75 | 4 | 3,000 | 17,001 | 930 | 1,860 | 930 | |
| WA | no state income tax | | | | | | | | |
| WV | 3.0 | 6.5 | 5 | 10,000 | 60,000 | 2,000 | 4,000 | 2,000 | |
| WI[3] | 4.6 | 7.75 | 5 | 10,570[22] | 232,660[22] | 700 | 1,400 | 700 | |
| WY | no state income tax | | | | | | | | |

[1]For joint returns, taxes are twice the tax on half the couple's income.    [2]In Alabama the per-dependent exemption is US$1,000 for taxpayers with state adjusted gross income (AGI) of US$20,000 or less, US$500 with AGI from US$20,001 to US$100,000, and US$300 with AGI over US$100,000.    [3]Seventeen states have statutory provision for automatically adjusting to the rate of inflation the dollar values of the income tax brackets, standard deductions, and/or personal exemptions. Massachusetts, Michigan, and Nebraska index the personal exemption only. Oregon does not index the income brackets for US$125,000 and over. Because the inflation adjustments for 2012 are not yet available in some cases, the table may report the 2011 amounts.    [4]The personal exemption takes the form of a tax credit instead of a deduction.    [5]California imposes an additional 1% tax on taxable income over US$1 million, making the maximum rate 10.3% over US$1 million.    [6]These states use the personal exemption amounts provided in the federal Internal Revenue Code.    [7]Connecticut's personal exemption incorporates a standard deduction. An additional tax credit is allowed ranging from 75% to 0% based on state AGI. Exemption amounts are phased out for higher income taxpayers until they are eliminated for households earning over US$71,000.    [8]The Georgia income brackets reported are for single individuals. For married couples filing jointly, the same tax rates apply to income brackets ranging from US$1,000 to US$10,000.    [9]In Indiana, includes an additional exemption of US$1,500 for each dependent child.    [10]The amounts reported for Louisiana are a combined personal exemption–standard deduction.    [11]In Michigan, includes an additional exemption of US$600 for children age 18 and under. Tax rate scheduled to decrease to 4.25% on 1 Oct 2013.    [12]The income brackets reported for Minnesota are for single individuals. For married couples filing jointly, the same tax rates apply to income brackets ranging from US$34,590 to US$137,431.    [13]The deduction for federal income tax is limited to US$5,000 for individuals and US$10,000 for joint returns in Missouri and Montana, and to US$5,950 for all filers in Oregon.    [14]The New Jersey rates reported are for single individuals. For married couples filing jointly, the tax rates also range from 1.4% to 8.97%, with seven brackets and the same high and low income ranges.    [15]The income brackets reported for New Mexico are for single individuals. For married couples filing jointly, the same tax rates apply to income brackets ranging from US$8,000 to US$24,000.    [16]The income brackets reported for North Carolina are for single individuals. For married couples filing jointly, the same tax rates apply to income brackets ranging from US$21,250 to US$100,000.    [17]The income brackets reported for North Dakota are for single individuals. For married couples filing jointly, the same tax rates apply to income

## Individual Income Taxes by US State (continued)

brackets ranging from US$59,100 to US$388,350.    [18]Ohio provides an additional tax credit of US$20 per exemption. 2012 tax rates and brackets reported.    [19]The income brackets reported for Oklahoma are for single individuals. For married couples filing jointly, the same tax rates apply to income brackets ranging from US$2,000 to US$15,000.    [20]Utah provides a tax credit equal to 6% of the federal personal exemption amounts (an applicable standard deduction).    [21]Vermont's income brackets reported are for single individuals. For married couples filing jointly, the same tax rates apply to income brackets ranging from US$59,050 to US$388,350.    [22]The Wisconsin income brackets reported are for single individuals. For married couples filing jointly, the same tax rates apply to income brackets ranging from US$14,090 to US$310,210.

# World Economy

## Standardized Unemployment Rates in Selected Countries

Percentage of total labor force. N/A stands for not available. Sources: International Labour Organization; International Monetary Fund, International Financial Statistics, June 2012.

| COUNTRY | 2008 | 2009 | 2010 | 2011 | COUNTRY | 2008 | 2009 | 2010 | 2011 |
|---|---|---|---|---|---|---|---|---|---|
| Argentina | 7.9 | 8.7 | 7.8 | 7.5 | Japan | 4.0 | 5.1 | 5.1 | 4.6 |
| Australia | 4.3 | 5.6 | 5.2 | 5.1 | Korea, Rep. of | 3.2 | 3.6 | 3.7 | 3.4 |
| Brazil | 7.9 | 8.1 | 6.7 | 6.0 | Mexico | 4.0 | 5.5 | 5.4 | N/A |
| Canada | 6.1 | 8.3 | 8.0 | 7.5 | Russia | 6.2 | 8.4 | 7.5 | 6.6 |
| China | 4.1 | 4.3 | 4.1 | 4.1 | Saudi Arabia | 5.0 | N/A | N/A | N/A |
| France | 7.8 | 9.5 | 9.8 | 9.7 | South Africa | 22.9 | 23.9 | 24.9 | 24.9 |
| Germany | 7.5 | 7.8 | 7.1 | 5.9 | Turkey | 11.0 | 14.0 | 11.9 | 9.8 |
| India | N/A | N/A | N/A | N/A | UK | 5.7 | 7.6 | 7.9 | 8.1 |
| Indonesia | 8.1 | 7.4 | 7.1 | N/A | US | 5.8 | 9.3 | 9.6 | 9.0 |
| Italy | 6.7 | 7.8 | 8.4 | 8.4 | Euro zone | 7.6 | 9.6 | 10.1 | 10.2 |

## Consumer Price Change in Selected Countries

This table shows the change in consumer prices from the year previous, expressed in percent. The change in consumer prices is used as an indicator of inflation. An increase in percent from one year to the next indicates an increase in the overall price of certain goods and services purchased by the average consumer. A negative number indicates a decrease in consumer prices. Source: International Monetary Fund, International Financial Statistics, June 2012.

| COUNTRY | 2008 | 2009 | 2010 | 2011 | COUNTRY | 2008 | 2009 | 2010 | 2011 |
|---|---|---|---|---|---|---|---|---|---|
| Argentina | 8.6 | 6.3 | 10.8 | 9.5 | Japan | 1.4 | −1.3 | −0.7 | −0.3 |
| Australia | 4.4 | 1.8 | 2.8 | 3.4 | Korea, Rep. of | 4.7 | 2.8 | 3.0 | 4.0 |
| Brazil | 5.7 | 4.9 | 5.0 | 6.6 | Mexico | 5.1 | 5.3 | 4.2 | 3.4 |
| Canada | 2.4 | 0.3 | 1.8 | 2.9 | Russia | 14.1 | 11.7 | 6.9 | 8.4 |
| China | 5.9 | −0.7 | 3.3 | 5.4 | Saudi Arabia | 9.9 | 5.1 | 5.3 | 5.0 |
| France | 2.8 | 0.1 | 1.5 | 2.1 | South Africa | 11.5 | 7.1 | 4.3 | 5.0 |
| Germany | 2.6 | 0.3 | 1.1 | 2.3 | Turkey | 10.4 | 6.3 | 8.6 | 6.5 |
| India | 8.4 | 10.9 | 12.0 | 8.9 | UK | 3.6 | 2.2 | 3.3 | 4.5 |
| Indonesia | 9.8 | 4.8 | 5.1 | 5.4 | US | 3.8 | −0.4 | 1.6 | 3.2 |
| Italy | 3.4 | 0.8 | 1.5 | 2.7 | Euro zone | 3.3 | 0.3 | 1.6 | 2.7 |

## Real Gross Domestic Products of Selected Countries

Percent annual change. Source: World Bank, World Development Indicators, 2012.

| COUNTRY | 2008 | 2009 | 2010 | 2011 | COUNTRY | 2008 | 2009 | 2010 | 2011 |
|---|---|---|---|---|---|---|---|---|---|
| Argentina | 6.8 | 0.9 | 9.2 | 7.5 | Japan | −1.2 | −6.3 | 4.0 | −0.2 |
| Australia | 3.7 | 1.3 | 2.3 | 1.7 | Korea, Rep. of | 2.3 | 0.3 | 6.2 | 3.8 |
| Brazil | 5.2 | −0.6 | 7.5 | 2.9 | Mexico | 1.5 | −6.1 | 5.4 | 4.0 |
| Canada | 0.5 | −2.5 | 3.2 | 2.3 | Russia | 5.2 | −7.8 | 4.0 | 4.1 |
| China | 9.6 | 9.2 | 10.4 | 9.1 | Saudi Arabia | 4.2 | 0.6 | 3.8 | 5.0 |
| France | −0.1 | −2.7 | 1.5 | 1.6 | South Africa | 3.6 | −1.7 | 2.8 | 3.2 |
| Germany | 1.0 | −4.7 | 3.7 | 3.0 | Turkey | 0.7 | −4.8 | 9.0 | 7.9 |
| India | 4.9 | 9.1 | 8.8 | 7.0 | UK | −0.1 | −4.9 | 2.1 | 1.0 |
| Indonesia | 6.0 | 4.6 | 6.1 | 6.5 | US | 0.0 | −2.7 | 3.0 | 1.7 |
| Italy | −1.3 | −5.2 | 1.5 | 0.7 | Euro zone | 0.4 | −4.4 | 2.0 | 1.5 |

# Arts, Entertainment, & Leisure

## Control Freaks

*by Harry McCracken, TIME*

Hollywood has long specialized in artfully managed, highly profitable scarcity. A new film debuts in theaters. Months later, it arrives on DVD, Blu-ray, and pay-per-view. Next, on premium channels like Showtime. When the flick finally gets sliced to smithereens on some basic-cable station, you know that pretty much every last nickel has been squeezed out of it.

Reinventing this time-tested business model for the Internet age hasn't been easy. Increasingly, consumers want to watch whatever they want whenever and wherever they choose, on an array of gadgets—TVs, PCs, smart phones, and tablets. Studios and networks are working to make that happen, and despite the pesky holdouts (no *American Idol*, no regular-season NFL), the proportion of programming that's available online has never been higher. At the same time, content owners remain cautious about doing anything that might cause too many folks to switch off prime time, stop buying DVDs, or quit paying for cable.

In the coming years the way we watch TV will continue to be shaped by these conflicting agendas—innovation tempered by paranoia. "A lot's going to change," said Phillip Swann, president of the industry news site TVPredictions.com. "And it's all going to stay the same."

### The Netflix Dilemma

Just look at Netflix. The company that crushed the once mighty Blockbuster by mailing DVDs and dispensing with late fees now has more than 22 million customers streaming movies and TV shows over the Internet. Netflix has made its way onto more than 700 kinds of devices, including HDTVs, game consoles, smart phones, and tablets. It's also on middlemen like TiVo and the sandwich-size Roku, which offers access to tons of channels via the Internet.

Netflix is starting to view premium-cable channels as archrivals—and to act like them too. To shore up subscriptions, it is helping produce exclusive content, including an Americanized remake of the BBC series *House of Cards* in 2012 and new episodes of the canceled cult favorite *Arrested Development* in 2013. It will also start streaming DreamWorks cartoons before their cable debuts.

Netflix's new ambitions help explain why Starz terminated its distribution pact with the streaming service, a decision that will deprive Netflix subscribers of Disney and Sony releases starting in February. It's also why HBO (a subsidiary of TIME magazine's parent company, Time Warner) is adamantly uninterested in selling such shows as *Boardwalk Empire* and *Game of Thrones* to Netflix or Hulu, the streaming service that's a joint venture of all the major broadcast networks except CBS.

But the cable companies that aren't playing nice with third-party streamers like Netflix aren't trying to undo Internet TV; they're launching their own watch-us-anywhere services. HBO is ramping up HBO GO, which puts its current programming lineup and past seasons onto PCs, smart phones, and tablets. Starz says it's working on something similar. Comcast offers 65,000 on-demand choices from its Xfinity TV Web site and apps combined. And since none of these companies want to encourage consumers to dump cable TV altogether, they are making their Internet services available exclusively to people who pay for conventional cable. Cut the cord and the Net services go away too.

### Fractured Abundance

The broadcast networks' attitude toward online distribution is almost as passive-aggressive. In August 2011, Fox started protecting its prime-time-ad revenue by delaying free Hulu availability of its shows until eight days after their broadcast debut. Don't be startled if other networks, which currently put shows on Hulu as soon as 24 hours after their initial airing, make similar moves in 2012 and beyond.

Get ready, too, for Hollywood to introduce you to a technology called UltraViolet. Backed by all the major studios except Disney, it lets you buy a movie on DVD or Blu-ray and then unlock a digital copy for streaming and downloading. A handful of UltraViolet titles are already out, at the same price as standard discs; many more will appear in the future.

With no single video service offering anything close to a comprehensive selection, hardwaremakers are left trying to stitch multiple content deals into a coherent whole. Microsoft's recent software update for the Xbox 360, for instance, features ESPN, Hulu, Netflix, Verizon FiOS TV and other services, with more on the way. But the most interesting thing about the Xbox as a TV device isn't the wealth of stuff to watch. It's the pairing of Microsoft's search engine and spoken commands, like "Xbox Bing Breaking Bad," to help you hunt down a particular show.

All this fractured abundance can leave you pining for Internet TV that's genuinely easy to use. Even Apple, the grand master of simplification, hasn't introduced an iPod-like breakthrough. Its Apple TV box suffers from some of the same content and usability challenges that other products do.

Still, rumors persist that the company is building its own HDTV for release as early as fall 2012. A tantalizing passage in Walter Isaacson's book *Steve Jobs*, in which Apple's genius confides that he's "finally cracked" the code for making TV simple, has put the rumor mill into overdrive.

So for all the intriguing things that other companies are doing, many industry watchers are going to spend a good deal of time obsessing over unannounced, possibly imaginary Apple products. Steve Jobs may be gone, but the notion that he might yet transform TV is alive and well.

# Motion Pictures

## Academy Awards (Oscars), 2011

The Academy of Motion Picture Arts and Sciences, formed in 1927, first awarded the Academy Awards of Merit in 1929. The ceremony is held early in the year following the release of films under consideration; the latest Oscars were awarded 26 Feb 2012 in Los Angeles. Award: gold-plated statuette of a man with a sword. **Academy of Motion Picture Arts and Sciences Web site:** <www.oscars.org>.

| CATEGORY | WINNER |
|---|---|
| Motion picture of the year | *The Artist* (France/Belgium; Thomas Langmann, producer) |
| Director | Michel Hazanavicius (*The Artist,* France/Belgium) |
| Actor | Jean Dujardin (*The Artist,* France/Belgium) |
| Actress | Meryl Streep (*The Iron Lady,* UK/France) |
| Supporting actor | Christopher Plummer (*Beginners,* US) |
| Supporting actress | Octavia Spencer (*The Help,* US/India/United Arab Emirates) |
| Foreign-language film | *A Separation* (Iran; Asghar Farhadi, director) |
| Animated feature | *Rango* (US; Gore Verbinski, director) |
| Animated short | The Fantastic Flying Books of Mr. Morris Lessmore (US; William Joyce and Brandon Oldenburg, directors) |
| Live-action short | *The Shore* (UK; Terry George, director) |
| Documentary feature | *Undefeated* (US; T.J. Martin and Dan Lindsay, directors) |
| Documentary short | *Saving Face* (US/Pakistan; Daniel Junge, director) |
| Cinematography | Robert Richardson (*Hugo,* US) |
| Art direction | Dante Ferretti, production design; Francesca Lo Schiavo, set decoration (*Hugo,* US) |
| Film editing | Kirk Baxter and Angus Wall (*The Girl with the Dragon Tattoo,* US/Sweden/UK/Germany) |
| Costume design | Mark Bridges (*The Artist,* France/Belgium) |
| Makeup | Mark Coulier and J. Roy Helland (*The Iron Lady,* UK/France) |
| Original score | Ludovic Bource (*The Artist,* France/Belgium) |
| Original song | "Man or Muppet," Bret McKenzie (*The Muppets,* US) |
| Sound mixing | Tom Fleischman and John Midgley (*Hugo,* US) |
| Sound editing | Philip Stockton and Eugene Gearty (*Hugo,* US) |
| Visual effects | Rob Legato, Joss Williams, Ben Grossmann, and Alex Henning (*Hugo,* US) |
| Adapted screenplay | Alexander Payne, Nat Faxon, and Jim Rash (*The Descendants,* US) |
| Original screenplay | Woody Allen (*Midnight in Paris,* Spain/US) |

## Academy Awards (Oscars), 1928–2011

**BEST PICTURE**

1928  *Wings*
1929  *The Broadway Melody*
1930  *All Quiet on the Western Front*
1931  *Cimarron*
1932  *Grand Hotel*
1933  *Cavalcade*
1934  *It Happened One Night*
1935  *Mutiny on the Bounty*
1936  *The Great Ziegfeld*
1937  *The Life of Emile Zola*
1938  *You Can't Take It with You*
1939  *Gone with the Wind*
1940  *Rebecca*
1941  *How Green Was My Valley*
1942  *Mrs. Miniver*
1943  *Casablanca*
1944  *Going My Way*
1945  *The Lost Weekend*
1946  *The Best Years of Our Lives*
1947  *Gentleman's Agreement*
1948  *Hamlet*
1949  *All the King's Men*
1950  *All About Eve*
1951  *An American in Paris*
1952  *The Greatest Show on Earth*
1953  *From Here to Eternity*

**BEST PICTURE (CONTINUED)**

1954  *On the Waterfront*
1955  *Marty*
1956  *Around the World in 80 Days*
1957  *The Bridge on the River Kwai*
1958  *Gigi*
1959  *Ben-Hur*
1960  *The Apartment*
1961  *West Side Story*
1962  *Lawrence of Arabia*
1963  *Tom Jones*
1964  *My Fair Lady*
1965  *The Sound of Music*
1966  *A Man for All Seasons*
1967  *In the Heat of the Night*
1968  *Oliver!*
1969  *Midnight Cowboy*
1970  *Patton*
1971  *The French Connection*
1972  *The Godfather*
1973  *The Sting*
1974  *The Godfather Part II*
1975  *One Flew Over the Cuckoo's Nest*
1976  *Rocky*
1977  *Annie Hall*
1978  *The Deer Hunter*

**BEST PICTURE (CONTINUED)**

1979  *Kramer vs. Kramer*
1980  *Ordinary People*
1981  *Chariots of Fire*
1982  *Gandhi*
1983  *Terms of Endearment*
1984  *Amadeus*
1985  *Out of Africa*
1986  *Platoon*
1987  *The Last Emperor*
1988  *Rain Man*
1989  *Driving Miss Daisy*
1990  *Dances with Wolves*
1991  *The Silence of the Lambs*
1992  *Unforgiven*
1993  *Schindler's List*
1994  *Forrest Gump*
1995  *Braveheart*
1996  *The English Patient*
1997  *Titanic*
1998  *Shakespeare in Love*
1999  *American Beauty*
2000  *Gladiator*
2001  *A Beautiful Mind*
2002  *Chicago*
2003  *The Lord of the Rings: The Return of the King*

## Academy Awards (Oscars), 1928–2011 (continued)

**BEST PICTURE (CONTINUED)**
2004  *Million Dollar Baby*
2005  *Crash*
2006  *The Departed*

**BEST PICTURE (CONTINUED)**
2007  *No Country for Old Men*
2008  *Slumdog Millionaire*
2009  *The Hurt Locker*

**BEST PICTURE (CONTINUED)**
2010  *The King's Speech*
2011  *The Artist*

**BEST ACTOR**
1928  Emil Jannings (*The Last Command; The Way of All Flesh*)
1929  Warner Baxter (*In Old Arizona*)
1930  George Arliss (*Disraeli*)
1931  Lionel Barrymore (*A Free Soul*)
1932  Wallace Beery (*The Champ*); Fredric March (*Dr. Jekyll and Mr. Hyde*) (tied)
1933  Charles Laughton (*The Private Life of Henry VIII*)
1934  Clark Gable (*It Happened One Night*)
1935  Victor McLaglen (*The Informer*)
1936  Paul Muni (*The Story of Louis Pasteur*)
1937  Spencer Tracy (*Captains Courageous*)
1938  Spencer Tracy (*Boys Town*)
1939  Robert Donat (*Goodbye, Mr. Chips*)
1940  James Stewart (*The Philadelphia Story*)
1941  Gary Cooper (*Sergeant York*)
1942  James Cagney (*Yankee Doodle Dandy*)
1943  Paul Lukas (*Watch on the Rhine*)
1944  Bing Crosby (*Going My Way*)
1945  Ray Milland (*The Lost Weekend*)
1946  Fredric March (*The Best Years of Our Lives*)
1947  Ronald Colman (*A Double Life*)
1948  Laurence Olivier (*Hamlet*)
1949  Broderick Crawford (*All the King's Men*)
1950  José Ferrer (*Cyrano de Bergerac*)
1951  Humphrey Bogart (*The African Queen*)
1952  Gary Cooper (*High Noon*)
1953  William Holden (*Stalag 17*)
1954  Marlon Brando (*On the Waterfront*)
1955  Ernest Borgnine (*Marty*)
1956  Yul Brynner (*The King and I*)
1957  Alec Guinness (*The Bridge on the River Kwai*)
1958  David Niven (*Separate Tables*)
1959  Charlton Heston (*Ben-Hur*)
1960  Burt Lancaster (*Elmer Gantry*)
1961  Maximilian Schell (*Judgment at Nuremberg*)
1962  Gregory Peck (*To Kill a Mockingbird*)
1963  Sidney Poitier (*Lilies of the Field*)
1964  Rex Harrison (*My Fair Lady*)
1965  Lee Marvin (*Cat Ballou*)
1966  Paul Scofield (*A Man for All Seasons*)
1967  Rod Steiger (*In the Heat of the Night*)
1968  Cliff Robertson (*Charly*)
1969  John Wayne (*True Grit*)
1970  George C. Scott (*Patton*) (declined)
1971  Gene Hackman (*The French Connection*)
1972  Marlon Brando (*The Godfather*) (declined)
1973  Jack Lemmon (*Save the Tiger*)
1974  Art Carney (*Harry and Tonto*)
1975  Jack Nicholson (*One Flew Over the Cuckoo's Nest*)
1976  Peter Finch (*Network*)[1]
1977  Richard Dreyfuss (*The Goodbye Girl*)
1978  Jon Voight (*Coming Home*)
1979  Dustin Hoffman (*Kramer vs. Kramer*)
1980  Robert De Niro (*Raging Bull*)
1981  Henry Fonda (*On Golden Pond*)
1982  Ben Kingsley (*Gandhi*)
1983  Robert Duvall (*Tender Mercies*)
1984  F. Murray Abraham (*Amadeus*)
1985  William Hurt (*Kiss of the Spider Woman*)
1986  Paul Newman (*The Color of Money*)
1987  Michael Douglas (*Wall Street*)

**BEST ACTOR (CONTINUED)**
1988  Dustin Hoffman (*Rain Man*)
1989  Daniel Day-Lewis (*My Left Foot*)
1990  Jeremy Irons (*Reversal of Fortune*)
1991  Anthony Hopkins (*The Silence of the Lambs*)
1992  Al Pacino (*Scent of a Woman*)
1993  Tom Hanks (*Philadelphia*)
1994  Tom Hanks (*Forrest Gump*)
1995  Nicolas Cage (*Leaving Las Vegas*)
1996  Geoffrey Rush (*Shine*)
1997  Jack Nicholson (*As Good as It Gets*)
1998  Roberto Benigni (*Life Is Beautiful*)
1999  Kevin Spacey (*American Beauty*)
2000  Russell Crowe (*Gladiator*)
2001  Denzel Washington (*Training Day*)
2002  Adrien Brody (*The Pianist*)
2003  Sean Penn (*Mystic River*)
2004  Jamie Foxx (*Ray*)
2005  Philip Seymour Hoffman (*Capote*)
2006  Forest Whitaker (*The Last King of Scotland*)
2007  Daniel Day-Lewis (*There Will Be Blood*)
2008  Sean Penn (*Milk*)
2009  Jeff Bridges (*Crazy Heart*)
2010  Colin Firth (*The King's Speech*)
2011  Jean Dujardin (*The Artist*)

**BEST ACTRESS**
1928  Janet Gaynor (*7th Heaven; Street Angel; Sunrise*)
1929  Mary Pickford (*Coquette*)
1930  Norma Shearer (*The Divorcee*)
1931  Marie Dressler (*Min and Bill*)
1932  Helen Hayes (*The Sin of Madelon Claudet*)
1933  Katharine Hepburn (*Morning Glory*)
1934  Claudette Colbert (*It Happened One Night*)
1935  Bette Davis (*Dangerous*)
1936  Luise Rainer (*The Great Ziegfeld*)
1937  Luise Rainer (*The Good Earth*)
1938  Bette Davis (*Jezebel*)
1939  Vivien Leigh (*Gone with the Wind*)
1940  Ginger Rogers (*Kitty Foyle*)
1941  Joan Fontaine (*Suspicion*)
1942  Greer Garson (*Mrs. Miniver*)
1943  Jennifer Jones (*The Song of Bernadette*)
1944  Ingrid Bergman (*Gaslight*)
1945  Joan Crawford (*Mildred Pierce*)
1946  Olivia de Havilland (*To Each His Own*)
1947  Loretta Young (*The Farmer's Daughter*)
1948  Jane Wyman (*Johnny Belinda*)
1949  Olivia de Havilland (*The Heiress*)
1950  Judy Holliday (*Born Yesterday*)
1951  Vivien Leigh (*A Streetcar Named Desire*)
1952  Shirley Booth (*Come Back, Little Sheba*)
1953  Audrey Hepburn (*Roman Holiday*)
1954  Grace Kelly (*The Country Girl*)
1955  Anna Magnani (*The Rose Tattoo*)
1956  Ingrid Bergman (*Anastasia*)
1957  Joanne Woodward (*The Three Faces of Eve*)
1958  Susan Hayward (*I Want to Live!*)
1959  Simone Signoret (*Room at the Top*)
1960  Elizabeth Taylor (*Butterfield 8*)
1961  Sophia Loren (*Two Women*)
1962  Anne Bancroft (*The Miracle Worker*)
1963  Patricia Neal (*Hud*)

## Academy Awards (Oscars), 1928–2011 (continued)

**BEST ACTRESS (CONTINUED)**

1964 Julie Andrews (*Mary Poppins*)
1965 Julie Christie (*Darling*)
1966 Elizabeth Taylor (*Who's Afraid of Virginia Woolf?*)
1967 Katharine Hepburn (*Guess Who's Coming to Dinner*)
1968 Katharine Hepburn (*The Lion in Winter*); Barbra Streisand (*Funny Girl*) (tied)
1969 Maggie Smith (*The Prime of Miss Jean Brodie*)
1970 Glenda Jackson (*Women in Love*)
1971 Jane Fonda (*Klute*)
1972 Liza Minnelli (*Cabaret*)
1973 Glenda Jackson (*A Touch of Class*)
1974 Ellen Burstyn (*Alice Doesn't Live Here Anymore*)
1975 Louise Fletcher (*One Flew Over the Cuckoo's Nest*)
1976 Faye Dunaway (*Network*)
1977 Diane Keaton (*Annie Hall*)
1978 Jane Fonda (*Coming Home*)
1979 Sally Field (*Norma Rae*)
1980 Sissy Spacek (*Coal Miner's Daughter*)
1981 Katharine Hepburn (*On Golden Pond*)
1982 Meryl Streep (*Sophie's Choice*)
1983 Shirley MacLaine (*Terms of Endearment*)
1984 Sally Field (*Places in the Heart*)
1985 Geraldine Page (*The Trip to Bountiful*)
1986 Marlee Matlin (*Children of a Lesser God*)
1987 Cher (*Moonstruck*)
1988 Jodie Foster (*The Accused*)
1989 Jessica Tandy (*Driving Miss Daisy*)
1990 Kathy Bates (*Misery*)
1991 Jodie Foster (*The Silence of the Lambs*)
1992 Emma Thompson (*Howards End*)
1993 Holly Hunter (*The Piano*)
1994 Jessica Lange (*Blue Sky*)
1995 Susan Sarandon (*Dead Man Walking*)
1996 Frances McDormand (*Fargo*)
1997 Helen Hunt (*As Good as It Gets*)
1998 Gwyneth Paltrow (*Shakespeare in Love*)
1999 Hilary Swank (*Boys Don't Cry*)
2000 Julia Roberts (*Erin Brockovich*)
2001 Halle Berry (*Monster's Ball*)
2002 Nicole Kidman (*The Hours*)
2003 Charlize Theron (*Monster*)
2004 Hilary Swank (*Million Dollar Baby*)
2005 Reese Witherspoon (*Walk the Line*)
2006 Helen Mirren (*The Queen*)
2007 Marion Cotillard (*La Vie en rose*)
2008 Kate Winslet (*The Reader*)
2009 Sandra Bullock (*The Blind Side*)
2010 Natalie Portman (*Black Swan*)
2011 Meryl Streep (*The Iron Lady*)

**BEST SUPPORTING ACTOR**

1936 Walter Brennan (*Come and Get It*)
1937 Joseph Schildkraut (*The Life of Emile Zola*)
1938 Walter Brennan (*Kentucky*)
1939 Thomas Mitchell (*Stagecoach*)
1940 Walter Brennan (*The Westerner*)
1941 Donald Crisp (*How Green Was My Valley*)
1942 Van Heflin (*Johnny Eager*)
1943 Charles Coburn (*The More the Merrier*)
1944 Barry Fitzgerald (*Going My Way*)
1945 James Dunn (*A Tree Grows in Brooklyn*)
1946 Harold Russell (*The Best Years of Our Lives*)
1947 Edmund Gwenn (*Miracle on 34th Street*)
1948 Walter Huston (*The Treasure of the Sierra Madre*)

**BEST SUPPORTING ACTOR (CONTINUED)**

1949 Dean Jagger (*Twelve O'Clock High*)
1950 George Sanders (*All About Eve*)
1951 Karl Malden (*A Streetcar Named Desire*)
1952 Anthony Quinn (*Viva Zapata!*)
1953 Frank Sinatra (*From Here to Eternity*)
1954 Edmond O'Brien (*The Barefoot Contessa*)
1955 Jack Lemmon (*Mister Roberts*)
1956 Anthony Quinn (*Lust for Life*)
1957 Red Buttons (*Sayonara*)
1958 Burl Ives (*The Big Country*)
1959 Hugh Griffith (*Ben-Hur*)
1960 Peter Ustinov (*Spartacus*)
1961 George Chakiris (*West Side Story*)
1962 Ed Begley (*Sweet Bird of Youth*)
1963 Melvyn Douglas (*Hud*)
1964 Peter Ustinov (*Topkapi*)
1965 Martin Balsam (*A Thousand Clowns*)
1966 Walter Matthau (*The Fortune Cookie*)
1967 George Kennedy (*Cool Hand Luke*)
1968 Jack Albertson (*The Subject Was Roses*)
1969 Gig Young (*They Shoot Horses, Don't They?*)
1970 John Mills (*Ryan's Daughter*)
1971 Ben Johnson (*The Last Picture Show*)
1972 Joel Grey (*Cabaret*)
1973 John Houseman (*The Paper Chase*)
1974 Robert De Niro (*The Godfather Part II*)
1975 George Burns (*The Sunshine Boys*)
1976 Jason Robards (*All the President's Men*)
1977 Jason Robards (*Julia*)
1978 Christopher Walken (*The Deer Hunter*)
1979 Melvyn Douglas (*Being There*)
1980 Timothy Hutton (*Ordinary People*)
1981 John Gielgud (*Arthur*)
1982 Louis Gossett, Jr. (*An Officer and a Gentleman*)
1983 Jack Nicholson (*Terms of Endearment*)
1984 Haing S. Ngor (*The Killing Fields*)
1985 Don Ameche (*Cocoon*)
1986 Michael Caine (*Hannah and Her Sisters*)
1987 Sean Connery (*The Untouchables*)
1988 Kevin Kline (*A Fish Called Wanda*)
1989 Denzel Washington (*Glory*)
1990 Joe Pesci (*Goodfellas*)
1991 Jack Palance (*City Slickers*)
1992 Gene Hackman (*Unforgiven*)
1993 Tommy Lee Jones (*The Fugitive*)
1994 Martin Landau (*Ed Wood*)
1995 Kevin Spacey (*The Usual Suspects*)
1996 Cuba Gooding, Jr. (*Jerry Maguire*)
1997 Robin Williams (*Good Will Hunting*)
1998 James Coburn (*Affliction*)
1999 Michael Caine (*The Cider House Rules*)
2000 Benicio Del Toro (*Traffic*)
2001 Jim Broadbent (*Iris*)
2002 Chris Cooper (*Adaptation*)
2003 Tim Robbins (*Mystic River*)
2004 Morgan Freeman (*Million Dollar Baby*)
2005 George Clooney (*Syriana*)
2006 Alan Arkin (*Little Miss Sunshine*)
2007 Javier Bardem (*No Country for Old Men*)
2008 Heath Ledger (*The Dark Knight*)[1]
2009 Christoph Waltz (*Inglourious Basterds*)
2010 Christian Bale (*The Fighter*)
2011 Christopher Plummer (*Beginners*)

**BEST SUPPORTING ACTRESS**

1936 Gale Sondergaard (*Anthony Adverse*)
1937 Alice Brady (*In Old Chicago*)
1938 Fay Bainter (*Jezebel*)

# Academy Awards (Oscars), 1928–2011 (continued)

**BEST SUPPORTING ACTRESS (CONTINUED)**

1939 Hattie McDaniel (*Gone with the Wind*)
1940 Jane Darwell (*The Grapes of Wrath*)
1941 Mary Astor (*The Great Lie*)
1942 Teresa Wright (*Mrs. Miniver*)
1943 Katina Paxinou (*For Whom the Bell Tolls*)
1944 Ethel Barrymore (*None but the Lonely Heart*)
1945 Anne Revere (*National Velvet*)
1946 Anne Baxter (*The Razor's Edge*)
1947 Celeste Holm (*Gentleman's Agreement*)
1948 Claire Trevor (*Key Largo*)
1949 Mercedes McCambridge (*All the King's Men*)
1950 Josephine Hull (*Harvey*)
1951 Kim Hunter (*A Streetcar Named Desire*)
1952 Gloria Grahame (*The Bad and the Beautiful*)
1953 Donna Reed (*From Here to Eternity*)
1954 Eva Marie Saint (*On the Waterfront*)
1955 Jo Van Fleet (*East of Eden*)
1956 Dorothy Malone (*Written on the Wind*)
1957 Miyoshi Umeki (*Sayonara*)
1958 Wendy Hiller (*Separate Tables*)
1959 Shelley Winters (*The Diary of Anne Frank*)
1960 Shirley Jones (*Elmer Gantry*)
1961 Rita Moreno (*West Side Story*)
1962 Patty Duke (*The Miracle Worker*)
1963 Margaret Rutherford (*The V.I.P.s*)
1964 Lila Kedrova (*Zorba the Greek*)
1965 Shelley Winters (*A Patch of Blue*)
1966 Sandy Dennis (*Who's Afraid of Virginia Woolf?*)
1967 Estelle Parsons (*Bonnie and Clyde*)
1968 Ruth Gordon (*Rosemary's Baby*)
1969 Goldie Hawn (*Cactus Flower*)
1970 Helen Hayes (*Airport*)
1971 Cloris Leachman (*The Last Picture Show*)
1972 Eileen Heckart (*Butterflies Are Free*)
1973 Tatum O'Neal (*Paper Moon*)
1974 Ingrid Bergman (*Murder on the Orient Express*)
1975 Lee Grant (*Shampoo*)
1976 Beatrice Straight (*Network*)
1977 Vanessa Redgrave (*Julia*)
1978 Maggie Smith (*California Suite*)
1979 Meryl Streep (*Kramer vs. Kramer*)
1980 Mary Steenburgen (*Melvin and Howard*)
1981 Maureen Stapleton (*Reds*)
1982 Jessica Lange (*Tootsie*)
1983 Linda Hunt (*The Year of Living Dangerously*)
1984 Peggy Ashcroft (*A Passage to India*)
1985 Anjelica Huston (*Prizzi's Honor*)
1986 Dianne Wiest (*Hannah and Her Sisters*)
1987 Olympia Dukakis (*Moonstruck*)
1988 Geena Davis (*The Accidental Tourist*)
1989 Brenda Fricker (*My Left Foot*)
1990 Whoopi Goldberg (*Ghost*)
1991 Mercedes Ruehl (*The Fisher King*)
1992 Marisa Tomei (*My Cousin Vinny*)
1993 Anna Paquin (*The Piano*)
1994 Dianne Wiest (*Bullets over Broadway*)
1995 Mira Sorvino (*Mighty Aphrodite*)
1996 Juliette Binoche (*The English Patient*)
1997 Kim Basinger (*L.A. Confidential*)
1998 Judi Dench (*Shakespeare in Love*)
1999 Angelina Jolie (*Girl, Interrupted*)
2000 Marcia Gay Harden (*Pollock*)
2001 Jennifer Connelly (*A Beautiful Mind*)
2002 Catherine Zeta-Jones (*Chicago*)
2003 Renée Zellweger (*Cold Mountain*)
2004 Cate Blanchett (*The Aviator*)
2005 Rachel Weisz (*The Constant Gardener*)
2006 Jennifer Hudson (*Dreamgirls*)

**BEST SUPPORTING ACTRESS (CONTINUED)**

2007 Tilda Swinton (*Michael Clayton*)
2008 Penélope Cruz (*Vicky Cristina Barcelona*)
2009 Mo'Nique (*Precious: Based on the Novel "Push" by Sapphire*)
2010 Melissa Leo (*The Fighter*)
2011 Octavia Spencer (*The Help*)

**FOREIGN LANGUAGE FILM (AMERICAN TITLES)**

1947 *Shoe-Shine*
1948 *Monsieur Vincent*
1949 *The Bicycle Thief*
1950 *The Walls of Malapaga*
1951 *Rashomon*
1952 *Forbidden Games*
1953 not awarded
1954 *Gate of Hell*
1955 *Samurai, the Legend of Musashi*
1956 *La Strada*
1957 *The Nights of Cabiria*
1958 *My Uncle*
1959 *Black Orpheus*
1960 *The Virgin Spring*
1961 *Through a Glass Darkly*
1962 *Sundays and Cybele*
1963 *Federico Fellini's 8½*
1964 *Yesterday, Today, and Tomorrow*
1965 *The Shop on Main Street*
1966 *A Man and a Woman*
1967 *Closely Watched Trains*
1968 *War and Peace*
1969 *Z*
1970 *Investigation of a Citizen Above Suspicion*
1971 *The Garden of the Finzi-Continis*
1972 *The Discreet Charm of the Bourgeoisie*
1973 *Day for Night*
1974 *Amarcord*
1975 *Dersu Uzala*
1976 *Black and White in Color*
1977 *Madame Rosa*
1978 *Get Out Your Handkerchiefs*
1979 *The Tin Drum*
1980 *Moscow Does Not Believe in Tears*
1981 *Mephisto*
1982 *To Begin Again*
1983 *Fanny & Alexander*
1984 *Dangerous Moves*
1985 *The Official Story*
1986 *The Assault*
1987 *Babette's Feast*
1988 *Pelle the Conqueror*
1989 *Cinema Paradiso*
1990 *Journey of Hope*
1991 *Mediterraneo*
1992 *Indochine*
1993 *Belle Epoque*
1994 *Burnt by the Sun*
1995 *Antonia's Line*
1996 *Kolya*
1997 *Character*
1998 *Life Is Beautiful*
1999 *All About My Mother*
2000 *Crouching Tiger, Hidden Dragon*
2001 *No Man's Land*
2002 *Nowhere in Africa*
2003 *The Barbarian Invasions*
2004 *The Sea Inside*
2005 *Tsotsi*
2006 *The Lives of Others*

## Academy Awards (Oscars), 1928–2011 (continued)

**FOREIGN LANGUAGE FILM (AMERICAN TITLES) (CONTINUED)**

2007 *The Counterfeiters*
2008 *Departures*
2009 *The Secret in Their Eyes*
2010 *In a Better World*
2011 *A Separation*

**DIRECTING**

1928 Lewis Milestone (*Two Arabian Knights*); Frank Borzage (*7th Heaven*)
1929 Frank Lloyd (*The Divine Lady*)
1930 Lewis Milestone (*All Quiet on the Western Front*)
1931 Norman Taurog (*Skippy*)
1932 Frank Borzage (*Bad Girl*)
1933 Frank Lloyd (*Cavalcade*)
1934 Frank Capra (*It Happened One Night*)
1935 John Ford (*The Informer*)
1936 Frank Capra (*Mr. Deeds Goes to Town*)
1937 Leo McCarey (*The Awful Truth*)
1938 Frank Capra (*You Can't Take It with You*)
1939 Victor Fleming (*Gone with the Wind*)
1940 John Ford (*The Grapes of Wrath*)
1941 John Ford (*How Green Was My Valley*)
1942 William Wyler (*Mrs. Miniver*)
1943 Michael Curtiz (*Casablanca*)
1944 Leo McCarey (*Going My Way*)
1945 Billy Wilder (*The Lost Weekend*)
1946 William Wyler (*The Best Years of Our Lives*)
1947 Elia Kazan (*Gentleman's Agreement*)
1948 John Huston (*The Treasure of the Sierra Madre*)
1949 Joseph L. Mankiewicz (*A Letter to Three Wives*)
1950 Joseph L. Mankiewicz (*All About Eve*)
1951 George Stevens (*A Place in the Sun*)
1952 John Ford (*The Quiet Man*)
1953 Fred Zinnemann (*From Here to Eternity*)
1954 Elia Kazan (*On the Waterfront*)
1955 Delbert Mann (*Marty*)
1956 George Stevens (*Giant*)
1957 David Lean (*The Bridge on the River Kwai*)
1958 Vincente Minnelli (*Gigi*)
1959 William Wyler (*Ben-Hur*)
1960 Billy Wilder (*The Apartment*)
1961 Robert Wise, Jerome Robbins (*West Side Story*)
1962 David Lean (*Lawrence of Arabia*)
1963 Tony Richardson (*Tom Jones*)
1964 George Cukor (*My Fair Lady*)
1965 Robert Wise (*The Sound of Music*)
1966 Fred Zinnemann (*A Man for All Seasons*)
1967 Mike Nichols (*The Graduate*)
1968 Carol Reed (*Oliver!*)
1969 John Schlesinger (*Midnight Cowboy*)
1970 Franklin J. Schaffner (*Patton*)
1971 William Friedkin (*The French Connection*)
1972 Bob Fosse (*Cabaret*)
1973 George Roy Hill (*The Sting*)
1974 Francis Ford Coppola (*The Godfather Part II*)
1975 Milos Forman (*One Flew Over the Cuckoo's Nest*)
1976 John G. Avildsen (*Rocky*)
1977 Woody Allen (*Annie Hall*)
1978 Michael Cimino (*The Deer Hunter*)
1979 Robert Benton (*Kramer vs. Kramer*)
1980 Robert Redford (*Ordinary People*)
1981 Warren Beatty (*Reds*)
1982 Richard Attenborough (*Gandhi*)
1983 James L. Brooks (*Terms of Endearment*)
1984 Milos Forman (*Amadeus*)

**DIRECTING (CONTINUED)**

1985 Sydney Pollack (*Out of Africa*)
1986 Oliver Stone (*Platoon*)
1987 Bernardo Bertolucci (*The Last Emperor*)
1988 Barry Levinson (*Rain Man*)
1989 Oliver Stone (*Born on the Fourth of July*)
1990 Kevin Costner (*Dances with Wolves*)
1991 Jonathan Demme (*The Silence of the Lambs*)
1992 Clint Eastwood (*Unforgiven*)
1993 Steven Spielberg (*Schindler's List*)
1994 Robert Zemeckis (*Forrest Gump*)
1995 Mel Gibson (*Braveheart*)
1996 Anthony Minghella (*The English Patient*)
1997 James Cameron (*Titanic*)
1998 Steven Spielberg (*Saving Private Ryan*)
1999 Sam Mendes (*American Beauty*)
2000 Steven Soderbergh (*Traffic*)
2001 Ron Howard (*A Beautiful Mind*)
2002 Roman Polanski (*The Pianist*)
2003 Peter Jackson (*The Lord of the Rings: The Return of the King*)
2004 Clint Eastwood (*Million Dollar Baby*)
2005 Ang Lee (*Brokeback Mountain*)
2006 Martin Scorsese (*The Departed*)
2007 Joel Coen, Ethan Coen (*No Country for Old Men*)
2008 Danny Boyle (*Slumdog Millionaire*)
2009 Kathryn Bigelow (*The Hurt Locker*)
2010 Tom Hooper (*The King's Speech*)
2011 Michel Hazanavicius (*The Artist*)

**ADAPTED SCREENPLAY[2]**

1928 Benjamin Glazer (*7th Heaven*)
1929 Hans Kraly (*The Patriot*)
1930 no award given
1931 Howard Estabrook (*Cimarron*)
1932 Edwin Burke (*Bad Girl*)
1933 Victor Heerman, Sarah Y. Mason (*Little Women*)
1934 Robert Riskin (*It Happened One Night*)
1935 Dudley Nichols (*The Informer*)[3] (declined)
1936 Pierre Collings, Sheridan Gibney (*The Story of Louis Pasteur*)[3]
1937 Norman Reilly Raine, Heinz Herald, Geza Herczeg (*The Life of Emile Zola*)[3]
1938 George Bernard Shaw, W.P. Lipscomb, Cecil Lewis, Ian Dalrymple (*Pygmalion*)[3]
1939 Sidney Howard (*Gone with the Wind*)[1,3]
1940 Donald Ogden Stewart (*The Philadelphia Story*)[3]
1941 Sidney Buchman, Seton I. Miller (*Here Comes Mr. Jordan*)[3]
1942 George Froeschel, James Hilton, Claudine West, Arthur Wimperis (*Mrs. Miniver*)[3]
1943 Julius J. Epstein, Philip G. Epstein, Howard Koch (*Casablanca*)[3]
1944 Frank Butler, Frank Cavett (*Going My Way*)[3]
1945 Charles Brackett, Billy Wilder (*The Lost Weekend*)[3]
1946 Robert E. Sherwood (*The Best Years of Our Lives*)[3]
1947 George Seaton (*Miracle on 34th Street*)[3]
1948 John Huston (*The Treasure of the Sierra Madre*)[3]
1949 Joseph L. Mankiewicz (*A Letter to Three Wives*)[3]
1950 Joseph L. Mankiewicz (*All About Eve*)[3]
1951 Michael Wilson, Harry Brown (*A Place in the Sun*)[3]
1952 Charles Schnee (*The Bad and the Beautiful*)[3]
1953 Daniel Taradash (*From Here to Eternity*)[3]

# Academy Awards (Oscars), 1928–2011 (continued)

**ADAPTED SCREENPLAY[2] (CONTINUED)**

1954 George Seaton (*The Country Girl*)[3]
1955 Paddy Chayefsky (*Marty*)[3]
1956 James Poe, John Farrow, S.J. Perelman (*Around the World in 80 Days*)
1957 Michael Wilson[4], Carl Foreman[4] (Pierre Boulle, *The Bridge on the River Kwai*)
1958 Alan Jay Lerner (*Gigi*)
1959 Neil Paterson (*Room at the Top*)
1960 Richard Brooks (*Elmer Gantry*)
1961 Abby Mann (*Judgment at Nuremberg*)
1962 Horton Foote (*To Kill a Mockingbird*)
1963 John Osborne (*Tom Jones*)
1964 Edward Anhalt (*Becket*)
1965 Robert Bolt (*Doctor Zhivago*)
1966 Robert Bolt (*A Man for All Seasons*)
1967 Stirling Silliphant (*In the Heat of the Night*)
1968 James Goldman (*The Lion in Winter*)
1969 Waldo Salt (*Midnight Cowboy*)
1970 Ring Lardner, Jr. (*M\*A\*S\*H*)
1971 Ernest Tidyman (*The French Connection*)
1972 Mario Puzo, Francis Ford Coppola (*The Godfather*)
1973 William Peter Blatty (*The Exorcist*)
1974 Francis Ford Coppola, Mario Puzo (*The Godfather Part II*)
1975 Lawrence Hauben, Bo Goldman (*One Flew Over the Cuckoo's Nest*)
1976 William Goldman (*All the President's Men*)
1977 Alvin Sargent (*Julia*)
1978 Oliver Stone (*Midnight Express*)
1979 Robert Benton (*Kramer vs. Kramer*)
1980 Alvin Sargent (*Ordinary People*)
1981 Ernest Thompson (*On Golden Pond*)
1982 Costa-Gavras, Donald Stewart (*Missing*)
1983 James L. Brooks (*Terms of Endearment*)
1984 Peter Shaffer (*Amadeus*)
1985 Kurt Luedtke (*Out of Africa*)
1986 Ruth Prawer Jhabvala (*A Room with a View*)
1987 Mark Peploe, Bernardo Bertolucci (*The Last Emperor*)
1988 Christopher Hampton (*Dangerous Liaisons*)
1989 Alfred Uhry (*Driving Miss Daisy*)
1990 Michael Blake (*Dances with Wolves*)
1991 Ted Tally (*The Silence of the Lambs*)
1992 Ruth Prawer Jhabvala (*Howards End*)
1993 Steven Zaillian (*Schindler's List*)
1994 Eric Roth (*Forrest Gump*)
1995 Emma Thompson (*Sense and Sensibility*)
1996 Billy Bob Thornton (*Sling Blade*)
1997 Brian Helgeland, Curtis Hanson (*L.A. Confidential*)
1998 Bill Condon (*Gods and Monsters*)
1999 John Irving (*The Cider House Rules*)
2000 Stephen Gaghan (*Traffic*)
2001 Akiva Goldsman (*A Beautiful Mind*)
2002 Ronald Harwood (*The Pianist*)
2003 Fran Walsh, Philippa Boyens, Peter Jackson (*The Lord of the Rings: The Return of the King*)
2004 Alexander Payne, Jim Taylor (*Sideways*)
2005 Larry McMurtry, Diana Ossana (*Brokeback Mountain*)
2006 William Monahan (*The Departed*)
2007 Joel Coen, Ethan Coen (*No Country for Old Men*)
2008 Simon Beaufoy (*Slumdog Millionaire*)
2009 Geoffrey Fletcher (*Precious: Based on the Novel "Push" by Sapphire*)

**ADAPTED SCREENPLAY[2] (CONTINUED)**

2010 Aaron Sorkin (*The Social Network*)
2011 Alexander Payne, Nat Faxon, Jim Rash (*The Descendants*)

**ORIGINAL SCREENPLAY[2]**

1928 Ben Hecht (*Underworld*)[5]; Joseph Farnham (*The Fair Co-Ed; Laugh, Clown, Laugh; Telling the World*)[6]
1929 no award given
1930 Frances Marion (*The Big House*)
1931 John Monk Saunders (*The Dawn Patrol*)[5]
1932 Frances Marion (*The Champ*)[5]
1933 Robert Lord (*One Way Passage*)[5]
1934 Arthur Caesar (*Manhattan Melodrama*)[5]
1935 Ben Hecht, Charles MacArthur (*The Scoundrel*)[5]
1936 Pierre Collings, Sheridan Gibney (*The Story of Louis Pasteur*)[5]
1937 William A. Wellman, Robert Carson (*A Star Is Born*)[5]
1938 Eleanore Griffin, Dore Schary (*Boys Town*)[5]
1939 Lewis R. Foster (*Mr. Smith Goes to Washington*)[5]
1940 Benjamin Glazer, John S. Toldy (*Arise, My Love*)[5]; Preston Sturges (*The Great McGinty*)[7]
1941 Harry Segall (*Here Comes Mr. Jordan*)[5]; Herman J. Mankiewicz, Orson Welles (*Citizen Kane*)[7]
1942 Emeric Pressburger (*Forty-Ninth Parallel*)[5]; Michael Kanin, Ring Lardner, Jr. (*Woman of the Year*)[7]
1943 William Saroyan (*The Human Comedy*)[5]; Norman Krasna (*Princess O'Rourke*)[7]
1944 Leo McCarey (*Going My Way*)[5]; Lamar Trotti (*Wilson*)[7]
1945 Charles G. Booth (*The House on 92nd Street*)[5]; Richard Schweizer (*Marie-Louise*)[7]
1946 Clemence Dane (*Vacation from Marriage*)[5]; Muriel Box, Sydney Box (*The Seventh Veil*)[7]
1947 Valentine Davies (*Miracle on 34th Street*)[5]; Sidney Sheldon (*The Bachelor and the Bobby-Soxer*)[7]
1948 Richard Schweizer, David Wechsler (*The Search*)[5]
1949 Douglas Morrow (*The Stratton Story*)[5]; Robert Pirosh (*Battleground*)[7]
1950 Edna Anhalt, Edward Anhalt (*Panic in the Streets*)[5]; Charles Brackett, Billy Wilder, D.M. Marshman, Jr. (*Sunset Blvd.*)[7]
1951 Paul Dehn, James Bernard (*Seven Days to Noon*)[5]; Alan Jay Lerner (*An American in Paris*)[7]
1952 Fredric M. Frank, Theodore St. John, Frank Cavett (*The Greatest Show on Earth*)[5]; T.E.B. Clarke (*The Lavender Hill Mob*)[7]
1953 Dalton Trumbo[4] (Ian McLellan Hunter, *Roman Holiday*)[5]; Charles Brackett, Walter Reisch, Richard L. Breen (*Titanic*)[7]
1954 Philip Yordan (*Broken Lance*)[5]; Budd Schulberg (*On the Waterfront*)[7]
1955 Daniel Fuchs (*Love Me or Leave Me*)[5]; William Ludwig, Sonya Levien (*Interrupted Melody*)[7]
1956 Dalton Trumbo[4] (as Robert Rich, *The Brave One*)[5]; Albert Lamorisse (*The Red Balloon*)[7]
1957 George Wells (*Designing Woman*)
1958 Nedrick Young[4] (as Nathan E. Douglas), Harold Jacob Smith (*The Defiant Ones*)
1959 Russell Rouse, Clarence Greene, Stanley Shapiro, Maurice Richlin (*Pillow Talk*)

## Academy Awards (Oscars), 1928–2011 (continued)

ORIGINAL SCREENPLAY[2] (CONTINUED)

1960 Billy Wilder, I.A.L. Diamond (*The Apartment*)
1961 William Inge (*Splendor in the Grass*)
1962 Ennio de Concini, Alfredo Giannetti, Pietro Germi (*Divorce—Italian Style*)
1963 James R. Webb (*How the West Was Won*)
1964 S.H. Barnett, Peter Stone, Frank Tarloff (*Father Goose*)
1965 Frederic Raphael (*Darling*)
1966 Claude Lelouch, Pierre Uytterhoeven (*A Man and a Woman*)
1967 William Rose (*Guess Who's Coming to Dinner*)
1968 Mel Brooks (*The Producers*)
1969 William Goldman (*Butch Cassidy and the Sundance Kid*)
1970 Francis Ford Coppola, Edmund H. North (*Patton*)
1971 Paddy Chayefsky (*The Hospital*)
1972 Jeremy Larner (*The Candidate*)
1973 David S. Ward (*The Sting*)
1974 Robert Towne (*Chinatown*)
1975 Frank Pierson (*Dog Day Afternoon*)
1976 Paddy Chayefsky (*Network*)
1977 Woody Allen, Marshall Brickman (*Annie Hall*)
1978 Nancy Dowd, Waldo Salt, Robert C. Jones (*Coming Home*)
1979 Steve Tesich (*Breaking Away*)
1980 Bo Goldman (*Melvin and Howard*)
1981 Colin Welland (*Chariots of Fire*)
1982 John Briley (*Gandhi*)
1983 Horton Foote (*Tender Mercies*)
1984 Robert Benton (*Places in the Heart*)
1985 Earl W. Wallace, William Kelley, Pamela Wallace (*Witness*)
1986 Woody Allen (*Hannah and Her Sisters*)
1987 John Patrick Shanley (*Moonstruck*)
1988 Ronald Bass, Barry Morrow (*Rain Man*)
1989 Tom Schulman (*Dead Poets Society*)
1990 Bruce Joel Rubin (*Ghost*)
1991 Callie Khouri (*Thelma & Louise*)
1992 Neil Jordan (*The Crying Game*)
1993 Jane Campion (*The Piano*)
1994 Quentin Tarantino, Roger Avary (*Pulp Fiction*)
1995 Christopher McQuarrie (*The Usual Suspects*)
1996 Joel Coen, Ethan Coen (*Fargo*)
1997 Ben Affleck, Matt Damon (*Good Will Hunting*)
1998 Marc Norman, Tom Stoppard (*Shakespeare in Love*)
1999 Alan Ball (*American Beauty*)
2000 Cameron Crowe (*Almost Famous*)
2001 Julian Fellowes (*Gosford Park*)
2002 Pedro Almodóvar (*Talk to Her*)
2003 Sofia Coppola (*Lost in Translation*)
2004 Charlie Kaufman (*Eternal Sunshine of the Spotless Mind*)
2005 Paul Haggis, Bobby Moresco (*Crash*)
2006 Michael Arndt (*Little Miss Sunshine*)
2007 Diablo Cody (*Juno*)
2008 Dustin Lance Black (*Milk*)
2009 Mark Boal (*The Hurt Locker*)
2010 David Seidler (*The King's Speech*)
2011 Woody Allen (*Midnight in Paris*)

CINEMATOGRAPHY

1928 Charles Rosher, Karl Struss (*Sunrise*)
1929 Clyde De Vinna (*White Shadows in the South Seas*)
1930 Joseph T. Rucker, Willard Van Der Veer (*With Byrd at the South Pole*)

CINEMATOGRAPHY (CONTINUED)

1931 Floyd Crosby (*Tabu*)
1932 Lee Garmes (*Shanghai Express*)
1933 Charles Bryant Lang, Jr. (*A Farewell to Arms*)
1934 Victor Milner (*Cleopatra*)
1935 Hal Mohr (*A Midsummer Night's Dream*)
1936 Gaetano Gaudio (*Anthony Adverse*)
1937 Karl Freund (*The Good Earth*)
1938 Joseph Ruttenberg (*The Great Waltz*)
1939 Gregg Toland (*Wuthering Heights*)[8]; Ernest Haller, Ray Rennahan (*Gone with the Wind*)[9]
1940 George Barnes (*Rebecca*)[8]; Georges Perinal (*The Thief of Bagdad*)[9]
1941 Arthur Miller (*How Green Was My Valley*)[8]; Ernest Palmer, Ray Rennahan (*Blood and Sand*)[9]
1942 Joseph Ruttenberg (*Mrs. Miniver*)[8]; Leon Shamroy (*The Black Swan*)[9]
1943 Arthur Miller (*The Song of Bernadette*)[8]; Hal Mohr, W. Howard Greene (*The Phantom of the Opera*)[9]
1944 Joseph LaShelle (*Laura*)[8]; Leon Shamroy (*Wilson*)[9]
1945 Harry Stradling (*The Picture of Dorian Gray*)[8]; Leon Shamroy (*Leave Her to Heaven*)[9]
1946 Arthur Miller (*Anna and the King of Siam*)[8]; Charles Rosher, Leonard Smith, Arthur Arling (*The Yearling*)[9]
1947 Guy Green (*Great Expectations*)[8]; Jack Cardiff (*Black Narcissus*)[9]
1948 William Daniels (*The Naked City*)[8]; Joseph Valentine, William V. Skall, Winton Hoch (*Joan of Arc*)[9]
1949 Paul C. Vogel (*Battleground*)[8]; Winton Hoch (*She Wore a Yellow Ribbon*)[9]
1950 Robert Krasker (*The Third Man*)[8]; Robert Surtees (*King Solomon's Mines*)[9]
1951 William C. Mellor (*A Place in the Sun*)[8]; Alfred Gilks, John Alton (*An American in Paris*)[9]
1952 Robert Surtees (*The Bad and the Beautiful*)[8]; Winton C. Hoch, Archie Stout (*The Quiet Man*)[9]
1953 Burnett Guffey (*From Here to Eternity*)[8]; Loyal Griggs (*Shane*)[9]
1954 Boris Kaufman (*On the Waterfront*)[8]; Milton Krasner (*Three Coins in the Fountain*)[9]
1955 James Wong Howe (*The Rose Tattoo*)[8]; Robert Burks (*To Catch a Thief*)[9]
1956 Joseph Ruttenberg (*Somebody Up There Likes Me*)[8]; Lionel Lindon (*Around the World in 80 Days*)[9]
1957 Jack Hildyard (*The Bridge on the River Kwai*)
1958 Sam Leavitt (*The Defiant Ones*)[8]; Joseph Ruttenberg (*Gigi*)[9]
1959 William C. Mellor (*The Diary of Anne Frank*)[8]; Robert L. Surtees (*Ben-Hur*)[9]
1960 Freddie Francis (*Sons and Lovers*)[8]; Russell Metty (*Spartacus*)[9]
1961 Eugen Shuftan (*The Hustler*)[8]; Daniel L. Fapp (*West Side Story*)[9]
1962 Jean Bourgoin, Walter Wottitz (*The Longest Day*)[8]; Fred A. Young (*Lawrence of Arabia*)[9]
1963 James Wong Howe (*Hud*)[8]; Leon Shamroy (*Cleopatra*)[9]
1964 Walter Lassally (*Zorba the Greek*)[8]; Harry Stradling (*My Fair Lady*)[9]
1965 Ernest Laszlo (*Ship of Fools*)[8]; Freddie Young (*Doctor Zhivago*)[9]
1966 Haskell Wexler (*Who's Afraid of Virginia Woolf?*)[8]; Ted Moore (*A Man for All Seasons*)[9]

## Academy Awards (Oscars), 1928–2011 (continued)

CINEMATOGRAPHY (CONTINUED)

1967 Burnett Guffey (*Bonnie and Clyde*)
1968 Pasqualino De Santis (*Romeo and Juliet*)
1969 Conrad Hall (*Butch Cassidy and the Sundance Kid*)
1970 Freddie Young (*Ryan's Daughter*)
1971 Oswald Morris (*Fiddler on the Roof*)
1972 Geoffrey Unsworth (*Cabaret*)
1973 Sven Nykvist (*Cries and Whispers*)
1974 Fred Koenekamp, Joseph Biroc (*The Towering Inferno*)
1975 John Alcott (*Barry Lyndon*)
1976 Haskell Wexler (*Bound for Glory*)
1977 Vilmos Zsigmond (*Close Encounters of the Third Kind*)
1978 Nestor Almendros (*Days of Heaven*)
1979 Vittorio Storaro (*Apocalypse Now*)
1980 Geoffrey Unsworth[1], Ghislain Cloquet (*Tess*)
1981 Vittorio Storaro (*Reds*)
1982 Billy Williams, Ronnie Taylor (*Gandhi*)
1983 Sven Nykvist (*Fanny & Alexander*)
1984 Chris Menges (*The Killing Fields*)
1985 David Watkin (*Out of Africa*)
1986 Chris Menges (*The Mission*)
1987 Vittorio Storaro (*The Last Emperor*)
1988 Peter Biziou (*Mississippi Burning*)
1989 Freddie Francis (*Glory*)
1990 Dean Semler (*Dances with Wolves*)
1991 Robert Richardson (*JFK*)
1992 Philippe Rousselot (*A River Runs Through It*)
1993 Janusz Kaminski (*Schindler's List*)
1994 John Toll (*Legends of the Fall*)
1995 John Toll (*Braveheart*)
1996 John Seale (*The English Patient*)
1997 Russell Carpenter (*Titanic*)
1998 Janusz Kaminski (*Saving Private Ryan*)
1999 Conrad L. Hall (*American Beauty*)
2000 Peter Pau (*Crouching Tiger, Hidden Dragon*)
2001 Andrew Lesnie (*The Lord of the Rings: The Fellowship of the Ring*)
2002 Conrad L. Hall (*Road to Perdition*)[1]
2003 Russell Boyd (*Master and Commander: The Far Side of the World*)
2004 Robert Richardson (*The Aviator*)
2005 Dion Beebe (*Memoirs of a Geisha*)
2006 Guillermo Navarro (*Pan's Labyrinth*)
2007 Robert Elswit (*There Will Be Blood*)
2008 Anthony Dod Mantle (*Slumdog Millionaire*)
2009 Mauro Fiore (*Avatar*)
2010 Wally Pfister (*Inception*)
2011 Robert Richardson (*Hugo*)

VISUAL EFFECTS[10]

1939 Fred Sersen (*The Rains Came*)
1940 Lawrence Butler (*The Thief of Bagdad*)
1941 Farciot Edouart, Gordon Jennings (*I Wanted Wings*)
1942 Farciot Edouart, Gordon Jennings, William L. Pereira (*Reap the Wild Wind*)
1943 Fred Sersen (*Crash Dive*)
1944 A. Arnold Gillespie, Donald Jahraus, Warren Newcombe (*Thirty Seconds Over Tokyo*)
1945 John P. Fulton (*Wonder Man*)
1946 Thomas Howard (*Blithe Spirit*)
1947 A. Arnold Gillespie, Warren Newcombe (*Green Dolphin Street*)
1948 Paul Eagler, J. McMillan Johnson, Russell Shearman, Clarence Slifer (*Portrait of Jennie*)
1949 *Mighty Joe Young*

VISUAL EFFECTS[10] (CONTINUED)

1950 *Destination Moon*
1951 *When Worlds Collide*
1952 *Plymouth Adventure*
1953 *The War of the Worlds*
1954 *20,000 Leagues Under the Sea*
1955 *The Bridges at Toko-Ri*
1956 John Fulton (*The Ten Commandments*)
1957 [10]
1958 Tom Howard (*tom thumb*)
1959 A. Arnold Gillespie, Robert MacDonald (*Ben-Hur*)
1960 Gene Warren, Tim Baar (*The Time Machine*)
1961 Bill Warrington (*The Guns of Navarone*)
1962 Robert MacDonald (*The Longest Day*)
1963 Emil Kosa, Jr. (*Cleopatra*)
1964 Peter Ellenshaw, Hamilton Luske, Eustace Lycett (*Mary Poppins*)
1965 John Stears (*Thunderball*)
1966 Art Cruickshank (*Fantastic Voyage*)
1967 L.B. Abbott (*Doctor Dolittle*)
1968 Stanley Kubrick (*2001: A Space Odyssey*)
1969 Robbie Robertson (*Marooned*)
1970 A.D. Flowers, L.B. Abbott (*Tora! Tora! Tora!*)
1971 Alan Maley, Eustace Lycett, Danny Lee (*Bedknobs and Broomsticks*)
1972 L.B. Abbott, A.D. Flowers (*The Poseidon Adventure*)
1974 Frank Brendel, Glen Robinson, Albert Whitlock (*Earthquake*)
1975 Albert Whitlock, Glen Robinson (*The Hindenburg*)
1976 Carlo Rambaldi, Glen Robinson, Frank Van der Veer (*King Kong*); L.B. Abbott, Glen Robinson, Matthew Yuricich (*Logan's Run*)
1977 John Stears, John Dykstra, Richard Edlund, Grant McCune, Robert Blalack (*Star Wars*)
1978 Les Bowie[1], Colin Chilvers, Denys Coop, Roy Field, Derek Meddings, Zoran Perisic (*Superman*)
1979 H.R. Giger, Carlo Rambaldi, Brian Johnson, Nick Allder, Denys Ayling (*Alien*)
1980 Brian Johnson, Richard Edlund, Dennis Muren, Bruce Nicholson (*The Empire Strikes Back*)
1981 Richard Edlund, Kit West, Bruce Nicholson, Joe Johnston (*Raiders of the Lost Ark*)
1982 Carlo Rambaldi, Dennis Muren, Kenneth F. Smith (*E.T.: The Extra-Terrestrial*)
1983 Richard Edlund, Dennis Muren, Ken Ralston, Phil Tippet (*Return of the Jedi*)
1984 Dennis Muren, Michael McAlister, Lorne Peterson, George Gibbs (*Indiana Jones and the Temple of Doom*)
1985 Ken Ralston, Ralph McQuarrie, Scott Farrar, David Berry (*Cocoon*)
1986 Robert Skotak, Stan Winston, John Richardson, Suzanne Benson (*Aliens*)
1987 Dennis Muren, William George, Harley Jessup, Kenneth Smith (*Innerspace*)
1988 Ken Ralston, Richard Williams, Edward Jones, George Gibbs (*Who Framed Roger Rabbit*)
1989 John Bruno, Dennis Muren, Hoyt Yeatman, Dennis Skotak (*The Abyss*)
1990 Eric Brevig, Rob Bottin, Tim McGovern, Alex Funke (*Total Recall*)
1991 Robert Skotak (*Terminator 2: Judgment Day*)
1992 Ken Ralston, Doug Chiang, Doug Smythe, Tom Woodruff, Jr. (*Death Becomes Her*)

## Academy Awards (Oscars), 1928–2011 (continued)

**VISUAL EFFECTS[10] (CONTINUED)**

1993 Dennis Muren, Stan Winston, Phil Tippett, Michael Lantieri (*Jurassic Park*)

1994 Ken Ralston, George Murphy, Stephen Rosenbaum, Allen Hall (*Forrest Gump*)

1995 Scott E. Anderson, Charles Gibson, Neal Scanlan, John Cox (*Babe*)

1996 Volker Engel, Douglas Smith, Clay Pinney, Joseph Viskocil (*Independence Day*)

1997 Robert Legato, Mark Lasoff, Thomas L. Fisher, Michael Kanfer (*Titanic*)

1998 Joel Hynek, Nicholas Brooks, Stuart Robertson, Kevin Mack (*What Dreams May Come*)

1999 John Gaeta, Janek Sirrs, Steve Courtley, Jon Thum (*The Matrix*)

2000 John Nelson, Neil Corbould, Tim Burke, Rob Harvey (*Gladiator*)

2001 Jim Rygiel, Randall William Cook, Richard Taylor, Mark Stetson (*The Lord of the Rings: The Fellowship of the Ring*)

2002 Jim Rygiel, Joe Letteri, Randall William Cook, Alex Funke (*The Lord of the Rings: The Two Towers*)

2003 Jim Rygiel, Joe Letteri, Randall William Cook, Alex Funke (*The Lord of the Rings: The Return of the King*)

2004 John Dykstra, Scott Stokdyk, Anthony LaMolinara, John Frazier (*Spider-Man 2*)

2005 Joe Letteri, Brian Van't Hul, Christian Rivers, Richard Taylor (*King Kong*)

2006 John Knoll, Hal Hickel, Charles Gibson, Allen Hall (*Pirates of the Caribbean: Dead Man's Chest*)

2007 Michael Fink, Bill Westenhofer, Ben Morris, Trevor Wood (*The Golden Compass*)

2008 Eric Barba, Steve Preeg, Burt Dalton, Craig Barron (*The Curious Case of Benjamin Button*)

2009 Joe Letteri, Stephen Rosenbaum, Richard Baneham, Andrew R. Jones (*Avatar*)

2010 Paul Franklin, Chris Corbould, Andrew Lockley, Peter Bebb (*Inception*)

2011 Rob Legato, Joss Williams, Ben Grossmann, Alex Henning (*Hugo*)

**MAKEUP**

1981 Rick Baker (*An American Werewolf in London*)

1982 Sarah Monzani, Michele Burke (*Quest for Fire*)

1983 *no award given*

1984 Paul LeBlanc, Dick Smith (*Amadeus*)

1985 Michael Westmore, Zoltan Elek (*Mask*)

1986 Chris Walas, Stephan Dupuis (*The Fly*)

1987 Rick Baker (*Harry and the Hendersons*)

1988 Ve Neill, Steve La Porte, Robert Short (*Beetlejuice*)

1989 Manlio Rocchetti, Lynn Barber, Kevin Haney (*Driving Miss Daisy*)

1990 John Caglione, Jr., Doug Drexler (*Dick Tracy*)

1991 Stan Winston, Jeff Dawn (*Terminator 2: Judgment Day*)

1992 Greg Cannom, Michele Burke, Matthew W. Mungle (*Bram Stoker's Dracula*)

1993 Greg Cannom, Ve Neill, Yolanda Toussieng (*Mrs. Doubtfire*)

1994 Rick Baker, Ve Neill, Yolanda Toussieng (*Ed Wood*)

1995 Peter Frampton, Paul Pattison, Lois Burwell (*Braveheart*)

1996 Rick Baker, David L. Anderson (*The Nutty Professor*)

**MAKEUP (CONTINUED)**

1997 Rick Baker, David L. Anderson (*Men in Black*)

1998 Jenny Shircore (*Elizabeth*)

1999 Christine Blundell, Trefor Proud (*Topsy-Turvy*)

2000 Rick Baker, Gail Ryan (*Dr. Seuss' How the Grinch Stole Christmas*)

2001 Peter Owen, Richard Taylor (*The Lord of the Rings: The Fellowship of the Ring*)

2002 John Jackson, Beatrice Alba (*Frida*)

2003 Richard Taylor, Peter King (*The Lord of the Rings: The Return of the King*)

2004 Valli O'Reilly, Bill Corso (*Lemony Snicket's A Series of Unfortunate Events*)

2005 Howard Berger, Tami Lane (*The Chronicles of Narnia: The Lion, the Witch, and the Wardrobe*)

2006 David Martí, Montse Ribé (*Pan's Labyrinth*)

2007 Didier Lavergne, Jan Archibald (*La Vie en rose*)

2008 Greg Cannom (*The Curious Case of Benjamin Button*)

2009 Barney Burman, Mindy Hall, Joel Harlow (*Star Trek*)

2010 Rick Baker, Dave Elsey (*The Wolfman*)

2011 Mark Coulier, J. Roy Helland (*The Iron Lady*)

**ORIGINAL SCORE**

1938 Erich Wolfgang Korngold (*The Adventures of Robin Hood*)

1939 Herbert Stothart (*The Wizard of Oz*)

1940 Leigh Harline, Paul J. Smith, Ned Washington (*Pinocchio*)

1941 Bernard Herrmann (*All That Money Can Buy*)

1942 Max Steiner (*Now, Voyager*)

1943 Alfred Newman (*The Song of Bernadette*)

1944 Max Steiner (*Since You Went Away*)

1945 Miklós Rózsa (*Spellbound*)

1946 Hugo Friedhofer (*The Best Years of Our Lives*)

1947 Miklós Rózsa (*A Double Life*)

1948 Brian Easdale (*The Red Shoes*)

1949 Aaron Copland (*The Heiress*)

1950 Franz Waxman (*Sunset Blvd.*)

1951 Franz Waxman (*A Place in the Sun*)

1952 Dimitri Tiomkin (*High Noon*)

1953 Bronislau Kaper (*Lili*)

1954 Dimitri Tiomkin (*The High and the Mighty*)

1955 Alfred Newman (*Love Is a Many-Splendored Thing*)

1956 Victor Young (*Around the World in 80 Days*)[1]

1957 Malcolm Arnold (*The Bridge on the River Kwai*)[11]

1958 Dimitri Tiomkin (*The Old Man and The Sea*)

1959 Miklós Rózsa (*Ben-Hur*)

1960 Ernest Gold (*Exodus*)

1961 Henry Mancini (*Breakfast at Tiffany's*)

1962 Maurice Jarre (*Lawrence of Arabia*)

1963 John Addison (*Tom Jones*)

1964 Richard M. Sherman, Robert B. Sherman (*Mary Poppins*)

1965 Maurice Jarre (*Doctor Zhivago*)

1966 John Barry (*Born Free*)

1967 Elmer Bernstein (*Thoroughly Modern Millie*)

1968 John Barry (*The Lion in Winter*)[12]; John Green (*Oliver!*)[13]

1969 Burt Bacharach (*Butch Cassidy and the Sundance Kid*)[12]; Lennie Hayton, Lionel Newman (*Hello, Dolly!*)[13]

1970 Francis Lai (*Love Story*); The Beatles (*Let It Be*)[14]

1971 Michel Legrand (*Summer of '42*)

## Academy Awards (Oscars), 1928–2011 (continued)

ORIGINAL SCORE (CONTINUED)

1972 Charles Chaplin, Raymond Rasch[1], Larry Russell[1] (Limelight)
1973 Marvin Hamlisch (The Way We Were)
1974 Nino Rota, Carmine Coppola (The Godfather Part II)
1975 John Williams (Jaws)
1976 Jerry Goldsmith (The Omen)
1977 John Williams (Star Wars)
1978 Giorgio Moroder (Midnight Express)
1979 Georges Delerue (A Little Romance)
1980 Michael Gore (Fame)
1981 Vangelis (Chariots of Fire)
1982 John Williams (E.T.: The Extra-Terrestrial); Henry Mancini, Leslie Bricusse (Victor/Victoria)[14]
1983 Bill Conti (The Right Stuff); Michel Legrand, Alan Bergman, Marilyn Bergman (Yentl)[14]
1984 Maurice Jarre (A Passage to India); Prince (Purple Rain)[14]
1985 John Barry (Out of Africa)
1986 Herbie Hancock ('Round Midnight)
1987 Ryuichi Sakamoto, David Byrne, Cong Su (The Last Emperor)
1988 Dave Grusin (The Milagro Beanfield War)
1989 Alan Menken (The Little Mermaid)
1990 John Barry (Dances with Wolves)
1991 Alan Menken (Beauty and the Beast)
1992 Alan Menken (Aladdin)
1993 John Williams (Schindler's List)
1994 Hans Zimmer (The Lion King)
1995 Luis Enrique Bacalov (Il Postino)[12]; Alan Menken, Stephen Schwartz (Pocahontas)[15]
1996 Gabriel Yared (The English Patient)[12]; Rachel Portman (Emma)[15]
1997 James Horner (Titanic)[12]; Anne Dudley (The Full Monty)[15]
1998 Nicola Piovani (Life Is Beautiful)[12]; Stephen Warbeck (Shakespeare in Love)[15]
1999 John Corigliano (The Red Violin)
2000 Tan Dun (Crouching Tiger, Hidden Dragon)
2001 Howard Shore (The Lord of the Rings: The Fellowship of the Ring)
2002 Elliot Goldenthal (Frida)
2003 Howard Shore (The Lord of the Rings: The Return of the King)
2004 Jan A.P. Kaczmarek (Finding Neverland)
2005 Gustavo Santaolalla (Brokeback Mountain)
2006 Gustavo Santaolalla (Babel)
2007 Dario Marianelli (Atonement)
2008 A.R. Rahman (Slumdog Millionaire)
2009 Michael Giacchino (Up)
2010 Trent Reznor, Atticus Ross (The Social Network)
2011 Ludovic Bource (The Artist)

ORIGINAL SONG

1934 Con Conrad, Herb Magidson, "The Continental" (The Gay Divorcee)
1935 Harry Warren, Al Dubin, "Lullaby of Broadway" (Gold Diggers of 1935)
1936 Jerome Kern, Dorothy Fields, "The Way You Look Tonight" (Swing Time)
1937 Harry Owens, "Sweet Leilani" (Waikiki Wedding)
1938 Ralph Rainger, Leo Robin, "Thanks for the Memory" (The Big Broadcast of 1938)
1939 Harold Arlen, E.Y. Harburg, "Over the Rainbow" (The Wizard of Oz)
1940 Leigh Harline, Ned Washington, "When You Wish Upon a Star" (Pinocchio)

ORIGINAL SONG (CONTINUED)

1941 Jerome Kern, Oscar Hammerstein II, "The Last Time I Saw Paris" (Lady Be Good)
1942 Irving Berlin, "White Christmas" (Holiday Inn)
1943 Harry Warren, Mack Gordon, "You'll Never Know" (Hello, Frisco, Hello)
1944 James Van Heusen, Johnny Burke, "Swinging on a Star" (Going My Way)
1945 Richard Rodgers, Oscar Hammerstein II, "It Might As Well Be Spring" (State Fair)
1946 Harry Warren, Johnny Mercer, "On the Atchison, Topeka, and the Santa Fe" (The Harvey Girls)
1947 Allie Wrubel, Ray Gilbert, "Zip-a-dee-doo-dah" (Song of the South)
1948 Jay Livingston, Ray Evans, "Buttons and Bows" (The Paleface)
1949 Frank Loesser, "Baby, It's Cold Outside" (Neptune's Daughter)
1950 Ray Evans, Jay Livingston, "Mona Lisa" (Captain Carey, U.S.A.)
1951 Hoagy Carmichael, Johnny Mercer, "In The Cool, Cool, Cool of the Evening" (Here Comes the Groom)
1952 Dimitri Tiomkin, Ned Washington, "High Noon (Do Not Forsake Me, Oh My Darlin')" (High Noon)
1953 Sammy Fain, Paul Francis Webster, "Secret Love" (Calamity Jane)
1954 Jule Styne, Sammy Cahn, "Three Coins in the Fountain" (Three Coins in the Fountain)
1955 Sammy Fain, Paul Francis Webster, "Love Is a Many-Splendored Thing" (Love Is a Many-Splendored Thing)
1956 Jay Livingston, Ray Evans, "Whatever Will Be, Will Be (Que Sera, Sera)" (The Man Who Knew Too Much)
1957 James Van Heusen, Sammy Cahn, "All the Way" (The Joker Is Wild)
1958 Frederick Loewe, Alan Jay Lerner, "Gigi" (Gigi)
1959 James Van Heusen, Sammy Cahn, "High Hopes" (A Hole in the Head)
1960 Manos Hadjidakis, "Never on Sunday" (Never on Sunday)
1961 Henry Mancini, Johnny Mercer, "Moon River" (Breakfast at Tiffany's)
1962 Henry Mancini, Johnny Mercer, "Days of Wine and Roses" (Days of Wine and Roses)
1963 James Van Heusen, Sammy Cahn, "Call Me Irresponsible" (Papa's Delicate Condition)
1964 Richard M. Sherman, Robert B. Sherman, "Chim Chim Cher-ee" (Mary Poppins)
1965 Johnny Mandel, Paul Francis Webster, "The Shadow of Your Smile" (The Sandpiper)
1966 John Barry, Don Black, "Born Free" (Born Free)
1967 Leslie Bricusse, "Talk to the Animals" (Doctor Dolittle)
1968 Michel Legrand, Alan Bergman, Marilyn Bergman, "The Windmills of Your Mind" (The Thomas Crown Affair)
1969 Burt Bacharach, Hal David, "Raindrops Keep Fallin' On My Head" (Butch Cassidy and the Sundance Kid)
1970 Fred Karlin, Robb Royer (as Robb Wilson), James Griffin (as Arthur James), "For All We Know" (Lovers and Other Strangers)
1971 Isaac Hayes, "Theme from Shaft" (Shaft)

## Academy Awards (Oscars), 1928–2011 (continued)

**ORIGINAL SONG (CONTINUED)**

1972 Al Kasha, Joel Hirschhorn, "The Morning After" (*The Poseidon Adventure*)

1973 Marvin Hamlisch, Alan Bergman, Marilyn Bergman, "The Way We Were" (*The Way We Were*)

1974 Al Kasha, Joel Hirschhorn, "We May Never Love Like This Again" (*The Towering Inferno*)

1975 Keith Carradine, "I'm Easy" (*Nashville*)

1976 Barbra Streisand, Paul Williams, "Evergreen (Love Theme from *A Star Is Born*)" (*A Star Is Born*)

1977 Joseph Brooks, "You Light Up My Life" (*You Light Up My Life*)

1978 Paul Jabara, "Last Dance" (*Thank God It's Friday*)

1979 David Shire, Norman Gimbel, "It Goes Like It Goes" (*Norma Rae*)

1980 Michael Gore, Dean Pitchford, "Fame" (*Fame*)

1981 Burt Bacharach, Carole Bayer Sager, Christopher Cross, Peter Allen, "Arthur's Theme (Best That You Can Do)" (*Arthur*)

1982 Jack Nitzsche, Buffy Sainte-Marie, Will Jennings, "Up Where We Belong" (*An Officer and a Gentleman*)

1983 Giorgio Moroder, Keith Forsey, Irene Cara, "Flashdance...What a Feeling" (*Flashdance*)

1984 Stevie Wonder, "I Just Called To Say I Love You" (*The Woman in Red*)

1985 Lionel Richie, "Say You, Say Me" (*White Nights*)

1986 Giorgio Moroder, Tom Whitlock, "Take My Breath Away" (*Top Gun*)

1987 Franke Previte, John DeNicola, Donald Markowitz, "(I've Had) The Time of My Life" (*Dirty Dancing*)

1988 Carly Simon, "Let the River Run" (*Working Girl*)

1989 Alan Menken, Howard Ashman, "Under the Sea" (*The Little Mermaid*)

1990 Stephen Sondheim, "Sooner or Later (I Always Get My Man)" (*Dick Tracy*)

1991 Alan Menken, Howard Ashman[1], "Beauty and the Beast" (*Beauty and the Beast*)

**ORIGINAL SONG (CONTINUED)**

1992 Alan Menken, Tim Rice, "A Whole New World" (*Aladdin*)

1993 Bruce Springsteen, "Streets of Philadelphia" (*Philadelphia*)

1994 Elton John, Tim Rice, "Can You Feel the Love Tonight" (*The Lion King*)

1995 Alan Menken, Stephen Schwartz, "Colors of the Wind" (*Pocahontas*)

1996 Andrew Lloyd Webber, Tim Rice, "You Must Love Me" (*Evita*)

1997 James Horner, Will Jennings, "My Heart Will Go On" (*Titanic*)

1998 Stephen Schwartz, "When You Believe" (*The Prince of Egypt*)

1999 Phil Collins, "You'll Be in My Heart" (*Tarzan*)

2000 Bob Dylan, "Things Have Changed" (*Wonder Boys*)

2001 Randy Newman, "If I Didn't Have You" (*Monsters, Inc.*)

2002 Eminem, Jeff Bass, Luis Resto, "Lose Yourself" (*8 Mile*)

2003 Fran Walsh, Howard Shore, Annie Lennox, "Into the West" (*The Lord of the Rings: The Return of the King*)

2004 Jorge Drexler, "Al otro lado del río" (*The Motorcycle Diaries*)

2005 Jordan Houston, Cedric Coleman, Paul Beauregard, "It's Hard Out Here for a Pimp" (*Hustle & Flow*)

2006 Melissa Etheridge, "I Need To Wake Up" (*An Inconvenient Truth*)

2007 Glen Hansard, Marketa Irglova, "Falling Slowly" (*Once*)

2008 A.R. Rahman, Gulzar, "Jai Ho" (*Slumdog Millionaire*)

2009 Ryan Bingham, T Bone Burnett, "The Weary Kind (Theme from Crazy Heart)" (*Crazy Heart*)

2010 Randy Newman, "We Belong Together" (*Toy Story 3*)

2011 Bret McKenzie, "Man or Muppet" (*The Muppets*)

[1]*Posthumously.* [2]*The current screenplay categories were adopted for the 1957 awards. Until then, various separate writing awards were given for silent-film title writing, screenplay, story and screenplay, and motion picture story.* [3]*Screenplay (for script only).* [4]*Actual winner was blacklisted at the time of the award and the honored work was attributed to another name or person; pseudonym or nominal winner is listed in parentheses.* [5]*Motion picture story (for narrative only; also called original story).* [6]*Title writing.* [7]*Story and screenplay (for narrative and script; also called original screenplay).* [8]*Black and white.* [9]*Color.* [10]*Until 1963, both visual and sound effects were honored as special effects. Only those recipients honored for visual effects are listed here. In 1957 only a sound-effects engineer was honored.* [11]*Scoring.* [12]*Drama or not a musical.* [13]*Musical.* [14]*Song score.* [15]*Musical or comedy.*

## Golden Globe Awards, 2011

The Hollywood Foreign Press Association, a group of film critics for publications outside the US, began awarding prizes for outstanding American motion pictures and acting in 1944 and created the Golden Globe Awards in 1945. Over the years the prizes have expanded from recognizing only motion pictures and acting to include directing, screenwriting, film music scoring, foreign-language films, and television, as well as a number of other categories of achievement. The television network on which each winning series appears is given in parentheses. Prize: globe encircled by a strip of motion picture film, in gold.

   **Golden Globes/Hollywood Foreign Press Association Web site:** <www.goldenglobes.org>.

**Film**

Drama     *The Descendants* (US; director, Alexander Payne)

Musical/comedy     *The Artist* (France/Belgium; director, Michel Hazanavicius)

## Golden Globe Awards, 2011 (continued)

**Film (continued)**

| | |
|---|---|
| Director | Martin Scorsese (*Hugo,* US) |
| Actress, drama | Meryl Streep (*The Iron Lady,* UK/France) |
| Actor, drama | George Clooney (*The Descendants,* US) |
| Actress, musical/comedy | Michelle Williams (*My Week with Marilyn,* UK/US) |
| Actor, musical/comedy | Jean Dujardin (*The Artist,* France/Belgium) |
| Animated feature film | *The Adventures of Tintin* (US/New Zealand; director, Steven Spielberg) |
| Foreign-language film | *Jodaeiye Nader az Simin* (*A Separation*) (Iran; director, Asghar Farhadi) |
| Supporting actress | Octavia Spencer (*The Help,* US/India/United Arab Emirates) |
| Supporting actor | Christopher Plummer (*Beginners,* US) |
| Screenplay | Woody Allen (*Midnight in Paris,* Spain/US) |
| Original score | Ludovic Bource (*The Artist,* France/Belgium) |
| Original song | "Masterpiece" (*W.E.,* UK); music and lyrics, Madonna, Julie Frost, and Jimmy Harry |

**Television**

| | |
|---|---|
| Drama series | *Homeland* (Showtime) |
| Actress, drama series | Claire Danes (*Homeland*) |
| Actor, drama series | Kelsey Grammer (*Boss*) |
| Musical/comedy series | *Modern Family* (ABC) |
| Actress, musical/comedy series | Laura Dern (*Enlightened*) |
| Actor, musical/comedy series | Matt LeBlanc (*Episodes*) |
| Miniseries/movie made for TV | *Downton Abbey* (PBS) |
| Actress, miniseries/movie made for TV | Kate Winslet (*Mildred Pierce*) |
| Actor, miniseries/movie made for TV | Idris Elba (*Luther*) |
| Supporting actress, series/miniseries/movie | Jessica Lange (*American Horror Story*) |
| Supporting actor, series/miniseries/movie | Peter Dinklage (*Game of Thrones*) |

## Sundance Film Festival, 2012

Founded as the Utah/US Film Festival in Salt Lake City in 1978, the exhibition has traditionally focused on documentary and dramatic works from outside the Hollywood mainstream. It came under the auspices of actor Robert Redford's Sundance Institute in 1985 and is held every January in Park City UT.

**Sundance Institute Web site: <www.sundance.org>.**

| | |
|---|---|
| Grand Jury Prize, drama | *Beasts of the Southern Wild* (US; director, Benh Zeitlin) |
| Grand Jury Prize, documentary | *The House I Live In* (US; director, Eugene Jarecki) |
| World Cinema Jury Prize, drama | *Violeta Went to Heaven* (Chile/Argentina/Brazil/Spain; director, Andrés Wood) |
| World Cinema Jury Prize, documentary | *The Law in These Parts* (Israel; director, Ra'anan Alexandrowicz) |
| Audience Award, US drama | *The Surrogate* (director, Ben Lewin) |
| Audience Award, US documentary | *The Invisible War* (director, Kirby Dick) |
| World Cinema Audience Award, drama | *Valley of Saints* (India/US; director, Musa Syeed) |
| World Cinema Audience Award, documentary | *Searching for Sugar Man* (Sweden/UK; director, Malik Bendjelloul) |
| Directing Award, US drama | Ava DuVernay (*Middle of Nowhere*) |
| Directing Award, US documentary | Lauren Greenfield (*The Queen of Versailles*) |
| World Cinema Directing Award, drama | Mads Matthiesen (*Teddy Bear,* Denmark) |
| World Cinema Directing Award, documentary | Emad Burnat and Guy Davidi (*5 Broken Cameras,* Palestine/Israel/France) |
| Editing Award, US documentary | Enat Sidi (*Detropia*) |
| World Cinema Editing Award, documentary | Lisanne Pajot and James Swirsky (*Indie Game: The Movie,* Canada) |
| Cinematography Award, US drama | Ben Richardson (*Beasts of the Southern Wild*) |
| Cinematography Award, US documentary | Jeff Orlowski (*Chasing Ice*) |
| World Cinema Cinematography Award, drama | David Raedeker (*My Brother the Devil,* UK) |
| World Cinema Cinematography Award, documentary | Lars Skree (*Putin's Kiss,* Denmark) |
| World Cinema Screenwriting Award | Marialy Rivas, Camila Gutiérrez, Pedro Peirano, and Sebastián Sepúlveda (*Young & Wild,* Chile) |
| Waldo Salt Screenwriting Award | Derek Connolly (*Safety Not Guaranteed,* US) |
| Best of NEXT Audience Award | *Sleepwalk with Me* (US; director, Mike Birbiglia) |
| Special Jury Prize, US drama (for excellence in independent producing) | Jonathan Schwartz and Andrea Sperling (*Smashed* and *Nobody Walks*) |

## Sundance Film Festival, 2012 (continued)

| | |
|---|---|
| Special Jury Prize, US drama (for ensemble acting) | *The Surrogate* (director, Ben Lewin) |
| Special Jury Prize, US documentary (for agent of change) | Macky Alston (*Love Free or Die*) |
| Special Jury Prize, US documentary (for spirit of defiance) | Alison Klayman (*Ai Weiwei: Never Sorry,* China/US) |
| World Cinema Special Jury Prize, drama (for artistic vision) | Rasit Celikezer (*Can,* Turkey) |
| World Cinema Special Jury Prize, documentary (for its celebration of the artistic spirit) | Malik Bendjelloul (*Searching for Sugar Man,* Sweden/UK) |
| Jury Prize, short filmmaking | *Fishing Without Nets* (US; director, Cutter Hodierne) |
| Alfred P. Sloan Prize | *Robot & Frank* (US; director, Jake Schreier) and *Valley of Saints* (India/US; director, Musa Syeed) |

## Toronto International Film Festival, 2011

Founded in 1976, the Toronto International Film Festival is one of North America's best-attended exhibitions and a frequent forum for the premieres of major feature films. The festival, held in September, awards seven prizes, three of which are for Canadian films.
**Toronto International Film Festival Web site:** <www.tiff.net>.

| | |
|---|---|
| Canadian feature film | *Monsieur Lazhar* (director, Philippe Falardeau) |
| Canadian first feature film | *Edwin Boyd* (director, Nathan Morlando) |
| Canadian short film | *Doubles with Slight Pepper* (director, Ian Harnarine) |
| FIPRESCI Prize for Discovery | *Avalon* (Sweden; director, Axel Petersén) |
| FIPRESCI Prize for Special Presentations | *The First Man* (France/Algeria/Italy; director, Gianni Amelio) |
| People's Choice Award | *Where Do We Go Now?* (France/Lebanon/Italy/Egypt; director Nadine Labaki) |
| People's Choice Award–Documentary | *The Island President* (US; director, Jon Shenk) |
| People's Choice Award–Midnight Madness | *The Raid* (Indonesia; director, Gareth Evans) |

## Cannes International Film Festival, 2012

Established in 1946, the Cannes Festival is among the best-known and most influential film exhibitions in the world. A nine-member feature-film jury and a five-member short-film and Cinéfondation jury give awards to the best film (Palme d'Or) and other outstanding films (special jury prizes) in their respective categories. The Grand Prix goes to the feature film judged the most original, and the feature jury also chooses the winners of the performance, direction, and screenplay awards. The Caméra d'Or, for best first film, is awarded by a jury comprising film industry professionals and members of the moviegoing public. The Cinéfondation awards are for works of one hour or less by film-school students.

**Cannes Festival Web site:** <www.festival-cannes.fr>.

<u>feature films</u> ▶ **Palme d'Or:** *Amour* (*Love*) (France/Germany/Austria; director, Michael Haneke); ▶ **Grand Prix:** *Reality* (Italy/France; director, Matteo Garrone); ▶ **best actress:** Cristina Flutur, Cosmina Stratan (*Dupӑ Dealuri* [*Beyond the Hills*], Romania/France/Belgium); ▶ **best actor:** Mads Mikkelsen (*Jagten* [*The Hunt*], Denmark); ▶ **best director:** Carlos Reygadas (*Post Tenebras Lux,* Mexico/France/Germany/Netherlands); ▶ **best screenplay:** Cristian Mungiu (*Dupӑ Dealuri* [*Beyond the Hills*], Romania/France/Belgium); ▶ **jury prize:** *The Angels' Share* (UK/France/Belgium/Italy; director, Ken Loach); ▶ **Caméra d'Or:** *Beasts of the Southern Wild* (US; director, Benh Zeitlin)

<u>short films</u> ▶ **Palme d'Or:** *Sessiz-be deng* (*Silent*) (Turkey; director, L. Rezan Yesilbas)

<u>Cinéfondation</u> ▶ **1st prize:** *Doroga na* (*The Road To*) (Russia; director, Taisia Igumentseva); ▶ **2nd prize:** *Abigail* (US; director, Matthew James Reilly); ▶ **3rd prize:** *Los anfitriones* (*The Hosts*) (Cuba/Peru; director, Miguel Angel Moulet)

## Berlin International Film Festival, 2012

The Berlin International Film Festival (Internationale Filmfestspiele Berlin), held annually since 1951, comprises more than 20 separate competitions and juries emphasizing aspects of both worldwide and German cinema, each with their own prizes. The International Jury, made up of film-industry figures from across the globe, selects the winners of the Golden and Silver Bears, the festival's top awards.
**Berlin International Film Festival Web site:** <www.berlinale.de>.

## Berlin International Film Festival, 2012 (continued)

| | |
|---|---|
| Golden Bear | Cesare deve morire (Caesar Must Die) (Italy; directors, Paolo and Vittorio Taviani) |
| Jury Grand Prix (Silver Bear) | Csak a szél (Just the Wind) (Hungary/Germany/France; director, Bence Fliegauf) |
| Silver Bear, director | Christian Petzold (Barbara, Germany) |
| Silver Bear, actress | Rachel Mwanza (Rebelle [War Witch], Canada) |
| Silver Bear, actor | Mikkel Boe Følsgaard (En Kongelig Affære [A Royal Affair], Denmark/Czech Republic/Sweden/Germany) |
| Silver Bear, script | Nikolaj Arcel and Rasmus Heisterberg (En Kongelig Affære [A Royal Affair], Denmark/Czech Republic/Sweden/Germany) |
| Silver Bear, artistic contribution | Lutz Reitemeier (photography) (Bai lu yuan [White Deer Plain], China) |
| Alfred Bauer Prize (for a work of particular innovation) | Tabu (Portugal/Germany/Brazil/France; director, Miguel Gomes) |
| Ecumenical Jury prizes | Competition: Cesare deve morire (Caesar Must Die) (Italy; directors, Paolo and Vittorio Taviani); Panorama: Die Wand (The Wall) (Austria/Germany; director, Julian Roman Pölsler); Forum: La demora (The Delay) (Uruguay/Mexico/France; director, Rodrigo Plá) |
| FIPRESCI prizes | Competition: Tabu (Portugal/Germany/Brazil/France; director, Miguel Gomes); Panorama: L'Âge atomique (Atomic Age) (France; director, Héléna Klotz; Forum: Hemel (Netherlands; director, Sacha Polak) |
| Best First Feature Award | Kauwboy (Netherlands; director, Boudewijn Koole) |

## Worldwide Top-Grossing Films (Actual US Dollars)

As of 20 Aug 2012. Includes reissues. Source: <www.boxofficemojo.com>.

| | | ACTUAL US DOLLARS |
|---|---|---|
| 1 | Avatar (2009) | 2,782,300,000 |
| 2 | Titanic (1997) | 2,185,400,000 |
| 3 | Marvel's The Avengers (2012) | 1,481,500,000 |
| 4 | Harry Potter and the Deathly Hallows, Part II (2011) | 1,328,100,000 |
| 5 | Transformers: Dark of the Moon (2011) | 1,123,700,000 |
| 6 | The Lord of the Rings: The Return of the King (2003) | 1,119,900,000 |
| 7 | Pirates of the Caribbean: Dead Man's Chest (2006) | 1,066,200,000 |
| 8 | Toy Story 3 (2010) | 1,063,200,000 |
| 9 | Pirates of the Caribbean: On Stranger Tides (2011) | 1,043,900,000 |
| 10 | Star Wars: Episode I—The Phantom Menace (1999) | 1,027,000,000 |
| 11 | Alice in Wonderland (2010) | 1,024,300,000 |
| 12 | The Dark Knight (2008) | 1,003,000,000 |
| 13 | Harry Potter and the Sorcerer's Stone (2001) | 974,800,000 |
| 14 | Pirates of the Caribbean: At World's End (2007) | 963,400,000 |
| 15 | Harry Potter and the Deathly Hallows, Part I (2010) | 956,400,000 |
| 16 | The Lion King (1994) | 951,600,000 |
| 17 | Harry Potter and the Order of the Phoenix (2007) | 939,900,000 |
| 18 | Harry Potter and the Half-Blood Prince (2009) | 934,400,000 |
| 19 | The Lord of the Rings: The Two Towers (2002) | 926,000,000 |
| 20 | Shrek 2 (2004) | 919,800,000 |

## US Top-Grossing Films (Constant US Dollars, Estimated)

Admissions—the number of tickets sold to a movie—tell a different story from the raw dollars earned. While recent films have made hundreds of millions of dollars, only 2 of the top 10 films in terms of attendance were released after 1980. Includes reissues. Source: <www.boxofficemojo.com>.

| | | ADMISSIONS | 2012 US DOLLARS | ACTUAL US DOLLARS |
|---|---|---|---|---|
| 1 | Gone with the Wind (1939) | 202,044,600 | 1,620,397,900 | 198,676,459 |
| 2 | Star Wars (1977) | 178,119,600 | 1,428,519,200 | 460,998,007 |
| 3 | The Sound of Music (1965) | 142,415,400 | 1,142,171,300 | 158,671,368 |
| 4 | E.T.: The Extra-Terrestrial (1982) | 141,854,300 | 1,137,671,800 | 435,110,554 |
| 5 | Titanic (1997) | N/A | 1,087,949,000 | 658,672,302 |
| 6 | The Ten Commandments (1956) | 131,000,000 | 1,050,620,000 | 65,500,000 |
| 7 | Jaws (1975) | 128,078,800 | 1,027,192,100 | 260,000,000 |
| 8 | Doctor Zhivago (1965) | 124,135,500 | 995,566,400 | 111,721,910 |
| 9 | The Exorcist (1973) | 110,568,700 | 887,005,300 | 232,906,145 |
| 10 | Snow White and the Seven Dwarfs (1937) | 109,000,000 | 874,180,000 | 184,925,486 |

## Top US DVD Sales, 2011

Source: <www.the-numbers.com>.

1. Harry Potter and the Deadly Hallows, Part 1
2. Tangled
3. Harry Potter and the Deadly Hallows, Part 2
4. Cars 2
5. Bridesmaids
6. Rio
7. Megamind
8. The Help
9. Despicable Me
10. Red
11. Transformers: Dark of the Moon
12. The Hangover Part II
13. Inception
14. The King's Speech
15. Fast Five
16. Secretariat
17. The Twilight Saga: Eclipse
18. Beverly Hills Chihuahua 2
19. Due Date
20. Toy Story 3

# Television

## Emmy Awards, 2011

The Academy of Television Arts and Sciences gave out its first awards for excellence in television, named the Emmys after the nickname of an early television camera part, for the 1948 season.

Categories have evolved to include separate prime-time, daytime, and regional Emmy Awards. Award: statuette of a winged woman holding an atom.
**Emmy Awards Web site:** <www.emmys.tv/awards>.

Comedy: *Modern Family* (ABC)
Lead actor, comedy: Jim Parsons, *The Big Bang Theory* (CBS)
Lead actress, comedy: Melissa McCarthy, *Mike & Molly* (CBS)
Supporting actor, comedy: Ty Burrell, *Modern Family* (ABC)
Supporting actress, comedy: Julie Bowen, *Modern Family* (ABC)
Drama: *Mad Men* (AMC)
Lead actor, drama: Kyle Chandler, *Friday Night Lights* (DirecTV)
Lead actress, drama: Julianna Margulies, *The Good Wife* (CBS)

Supporting actor, drama: Peter Dinklage, *Game of Thrones* (HBO)
Supporting actress, drama: Margo Martindale, *Justified* (FX)
Miniseries: *Downton Abbey* (PBS)
Lead actor, miniseries or movie: Barry Pepper, *The Kennedys* (ReelzChannel)
Lead actress, miniseries or movie: Kate Winslet, *Mildred Pierce* (HBO)
Variety/music/comedy: *The Daily Show with Jon Stewart* (Comedy Central)
Nonfiction: *American Masters* (PBS)

## Emmy Awards, 1949–2011[1]

**1949**
Most popular program: *Pantomime Quiz,* KTLA
TV film: *Your Show Time: The Necklace*

**1950**
Live show: *The Ed Wynn Show,* KTTV
Kinescope show: *The Texaco Star Theater,* KNBH (NBC)
TV film: *The Life of Riley,* KNBH
Public service/cultural/educational: *Crusade in Europe,* KECA-TV/KTTV (ABC)
Children's: *Time for Beany,* KTLA

**1951**
Variety: *The Alan Young Show,* KTTV (CBS)
Drama: *Pulitzer Prize Playhouse,* KECA-TV (ABC)
Game/audience participation: *Truth or Consequences,* KTTV (CBS)
Children's: *Time for Beany,* KTLA
Educational: *KFI-TV University,* KFI-TV
Cultural: *Campus Chorus and Orchestra,* KTSL

**1952**
Variety: *Your Show of Shows* (NBC)
Comedy: *The Red Skelton Show* (NBC)
Drama: *Studio One* (CBS)

**1953**
Variety: *Your Show of Shows* (NBC)
Comedy: *I Love Lucy* (CBS)
Drama: *Robert Montgomery Presents* (NBC)
Mystery/action/adventure: *Dragnet* (NBC)
Public affairs: *See It Now* (CBS)
Audience participation/quiz/panel: *What's My Line?* (CBS)
Children's: *Time for Beany* (syndicated)

**1954**
Variety: *Omnibus* (CBS)
Comedy: *I Love Lucy* (CBS)
Drama: *The U.S. Steel Hour* (ABC)
Mystery/action/adventure: *Dragnet* (NBC)
Public affairs: *Victory at Sea* (NBC)
Audience participation/quiz/panel: *This Is Your Life* (NBC); *What's My Line?* (CBS)
Children's: *Kukla, Fran, and Ollie* (NBC)

**1955**
Variety: *Disneyland* (ABC)
Comedy: *Make Room for Daddy* (ABC)
Drama: *The U.S. Steel Hour* (ABC)
Mystery/intrigue: *Dragnet* (NBC)
Western/adventure: *Stories of the Century* (syndicated)

# Emmy Awards, 1949–2011[1] (continued)

## 1955 (continued)

Cultural/religious/educational: *Omnibus* (CBS)
Audience participation/quiz/panel: *This Is Your Life* (NBC)
Children's: *Lassie* (CBS)

## 1956

Variety: *The Ed Sullivan Show* (CBS)
Comedy: *The Phil Silvers Show: You'll Never Get Rich* (CBS)
Drama: *Producers' Showcase* (NBC)
Action/adventure: *Disneyland* (ABC)
Music: *Your Hit Parade* (NBC)
Documentary: *Omnibus* (CBS)
Audience participation: *The $64,000 Question* (CBS)
Children's: *Lassie* (CBS)

## 1957

Series (½ hr. or less): *The Phil Silvers Show: You'll Never Get Rich* (CBS)
Series (1 hr. or more): *Caesar's Hour* (NBC)
New series: *Playhouse 90* (CBS)

## 1958

Musical/variety/audience participation/quiz: *The Dinah Shore Chevy Show* (NBC)
Comedy: *The Phil Silvers Show: You'll Never Get Rich* (CBS)
Drama, continuing: *Gunsmoke* (CBS)
Drama, anthology: *Playhouse 90* (CBS)
New series: *The Seven Lively Arts* (CBS)
Public service: *Omnibus* (ABC/NBC)

## 1959

Musical/variety: *The Dinah Shore Chevy Show* (NBC)
Comedy: *The Jack Benny Show* (CBS)
Drama (<1 hr.): *Alcoa-Goodyear Playhouse* (NBC)
Drama (1 hr.+): *Playhouse 90* (CBS)
Western: *Maverick* (ABC)
News reporting: *The Huntley-Brinkley Report* (NBC)
Public service: *Omnibus* (NBC)
Panel/quiz/audience participation: *What's My Line?* (CBS)

## 1960

Variety: *The Fabulous Fifties* (CBS)
Humor: *Art Carney Special* (NBC)
Drama: *Playhouse 90* (CBS)
News: *The Huntley-Brinkley Report* (NBC)
Public affairs/education: *The Twentieth Century* (CBS)
Children's: *Huckleberry Hound* (syndicated)

## 1961

Variety: *Astaire Time* (NBC)
Humor: *The Jack Benny Show* (CBS)
Drama: *Hallmark Hall of Fame: Macbeth* (NBC)
News: *The Huntley-Brinkley Report* (NBC)
Public affairs/education: *The Twentieth Century* (CBS)
Children's: "Aaron Copland's Birthday Party," *Young People's Concert* (CBS)
Program of the year: *Hallmark Hall of Fame: Macbeth* (NBC)

## 1962

Variety: *The Garry Moore Show* (CBS)
Humor: *The Bob Newhart Show* (NBC)
Drama: *The Defenders* (CBS)
News: *The Huntley-Brinkley Report* (NBC)

## 1962 (continued)

Educational/public affairs: *David Brinkley's Journal* (NBC)
Children's: *New York Philharmonic Young People's Concerts with Leonard Bernstein* (CBS)
Program of the year: *Hallmark Hall of Fame: Victoria Regina* (NBC)

## 1963

Variety: *The Andy Williams Show* (NBC)
Humor: *The Dick Van Dyke Show* (CBS)
Drama: *The Defenders* (CBS)
News: *The Huntley-Brinkley Report* (NBC)
Commentary/public affairs: *David Brinkley's Journal* (NBC)
Documentary: *The Tunnel* (NBC)
Panel/quiz/aud. particip.: *The G.E. College Bowl* (CBS)
Children's: *Walt Disney's Wonderful World of Color* (NBC)
Program of the year: *The Tunnel* (NBC)

## 1964

Variety: *The Danny Kaye Show* (CBS)
Comedy: *The Dick Van Dyke Show* (CBS)
Drama: *The Defenders* (CBS)
News reports: *The Huntley-Brinkley Report* (NBC)
Commentary/public affairs: "Cuba—Part I: The Bay of Pigs" and "Cuba—Part II: The Missile Crisis," *NBC White Paper* (NBC)
Documentary: *The Making of the President 1960* (ABC)
Children's: *Discovery '63–'64* (ABC)
Program of the year: *The Making of the President 1960* (ABC)

## 1965

Entertainment: *The Dick Van Dyke Show* (CBS); *Hallmark Hall of Fame: The Magnificent Yankee* (NBC); *My Name Is Barbra* (CBS); "What Is Sonata Form?," *New York Philharmonic Young People's Concerts with Leonard Bernstein* (CBS)
News/docu./info./sports: "I, Leonardo da Vinci," *Saga of Western Man* (ABC); *The Louvre* (NBC)

## 1966

Variety: *The Andy Williams Show* (NBC)
Comedy: *The Dick Van Dyke Show* (CBS)
Drama: *The Fugitive* (ABC)

## 1967

Variety: *The Andy Williams Show* (NBC)
Comedy: *The Monkees* (NBC)
Drama: *Mission: Impossible* (CBS)

## 1968

Musical/variety: *Rowan and Martin's Laugh-In* (NBC)
Comedy: *Get Smart* (NBC)
Drama: *Mission: Impossible* (CBS)

## 1969

Variety/musical: *Rowan and Martin's Laugh-In* (NBC)
Comedy: *Get Smart* (NBC)
Drama: *NET Playhouse* (NET)

## 1970

Variety/musical: *The David Frost Show* (syndicated)
Comedy: *My World and Welcome to It* (NBC)
Drama: *Marcus Welby, M.D.* (ABC)

# Emmy Awards, 1949–2011[1] (continued)

**1971**
Comedy: *All in the Family* (CBS)
Drama: *The Bold Ones: The Senator* (NBC)
Variety, musical: *The Flip Wilson Show* (NBC)
Variety, talk: *The David Frost Show* (syndicated)
New series: *All in the Family* (CBS)

**1972**
Comedy: *All in the Family* (CBS)
Drama: *Masterpiece Theatre: Elizabeth R* (PBS)
Variety, musical: *The Carol Burnett Show* (CBS)
Variety, talk: *The Dick Cavett Show* (ABC)
New series: *Masterpiece Theatre: Elizabeth R* (PBS)

**1973**
Comedy: *All in the Family* (CBS)
Drama (continuing): *The Waltons* (CBS)
Drama/comedy (limited): *Masterpiece Theatre: Tom Brown's Schooldays* (PBS)
Variety, musical: *The Julie Andrews Hour* (ABC)
New series: *America* (NBC)

**1974**
Comedy: *M\*A\*S\*H* (CBS)
Drama: *Masterpiece Theatre: Upstairs, Downstairs* (PBS)
Limited series: *Columbo* (NBC)
Music/variety: *The Carol Burnett Show* (CBS)

**1975**
Comedy: *The Mary Tyler Moore Show* (CBS)
Drama: *Masterpiece Theatre: Upstairs, Downstairs* (PBS)
Limited series: *Benjamin Franklin* (CBS)
Comedy-variety/music: *The Carol Burnett Show* (CBS)

**1976**
Comedy: *The Mary Tyler Moore Show* (CBS)
Drama: *Police Story* (NBC)
Limited series: *Masterpiece Theatre: Upstairs, Downstairs* (PBS)
Comedy-variety/music: *NBC's Saturday Night* (NBC)

**1977**
Comedy: *The Mary Tyler Moore Show* (CBS)
Drama: *Masterpiece Theatre: Upstairs, Downstairs* (PBS)
Limited series: *Roots* (ABC)
Comedy-variety/music: *Van Dyke and Company* (NBC)

**1978**
Comedy: *All in the Family* (CBS)
Drama: *The Rockford Files* (NBC)
Limited series: *Holocaust* (NBC)
Comedy-variety/music: *The Muppet Show* (syndicated)
Informational: *The Body Human* (CBS)

**1979**
Comedy: *Taxi* (ABC)
Drama: *Lou Grant* (CBS)
Limited series: *Roots: The Next Generations* (ABC)

**1980**
Comedy: *Taxi* (ABC)
Drama: *Lou Grant* (CBS)
Limited series: *Edward & Mrs. Simpson* (syndicated)

**1981**
Comedy: *Taxi* (ABC)
Drama: *Hill Street Blues* (NBC)
Limited series: *Shogun* (NBC)
Informational: *Steve Allen's Meeting of Minds* (PBS)

**1982**
Comedy: *Barney Miller* (ABC)
Drama: *Hill Street Blues* (NBC)
Limited series: *Marco Polo* (NBC)
Informational: *Creativity with Bill Moyers* (PBS)

**1983**
Comedy: *Cheers* (NBC)
Drama: *Hill Street Blues* (NBC)
Limited series: *Nicholas Nickleby* (syndicated)
Informational: *The Barbara Walters Specials* (ABC)

**1984**
Comedy: *Cheers* (NBC)
Drama: *Hill Street Blues* (NBC)
Limited series: *American Playhouse: Concealed Enemies* (PBS)
Informational: *A Walk Through the 20th Century with Bill Moyers* (PBS)

**1985**
Comedy: *The Cosby Show* (NBC)
Drama: *Cagney & Lacey* (CBS)
Limited series: *Masterpiece Theatre: The Jewel in the Crown* (PBS)
Informational: *The Living Planet: A Portrait of the Earth* (PBS)

**1986**
Comedy: *The Golden Girls* (NBC)
Drama: *Cagney & Lacey* (CBS)
Miniseries: *Peter the Great* (NBC)
Informational: *Great Performances: Laurence Olivier—A Life* (PBS); *Planet Earth* (PBS)

**1987**
Comedy: *The Golden Girls* (NBC)
Drama: *L.A. Law* (NBC)
Miniseries: *A Year in the Life* (NBC)
Informational: *Smithsonian World* (PBS); *American Masters: Unknown Chaplin* (PBS)

**1988**
Comedy: *The Wonder Years* (ABC)
Drama: *thirtysomething* (ABC)
Miniseries: *The Murder of Mary Phagan* (NBC)
Informational: *American Masters: Buster Keaton: A Hard Act To Follow* (PBS); *Nature* (PBS)

**1989**
Comedy: *Cheers* (NBC)
Drama: *L.A. Law* (NBC)
Miniseries: *War and Remembrance* (ABC)
Informational: *Nature* (PBS)

**1990**
Comedy: *Murphy Brown* (CBS)
Drama: *L.A. Law* (NBC)
Miniseries: *Drug Wars: The Camarena Story* (NBC)
Variety/music/comedy: *In Living Color* (Fox)
Informational: *Smithsonian World* (PBS)

**1991**
Comedy: *Cheers* (NBC)
Drama: *L.A. Law* (NBC)
Miniseries: *Separate but Equal* (ABC)
Informational: *The Civil War* (PBS)

# Emmy Awards, 1949–2011[1] (continued)

**1992**
Comedy: *Murphy Brown* (CBS)
Drama: *Northern Exposure* (CBS)
Miniseries: *A Woman Named Jackie* (NBC)
Variety/music/comedy: *The Tonight Show Starring Johnny Carson* (NBC)
Informational: *MGM: When the Lion Roars* (TNT)

**1993**
Comedy: *Seinfeld* (NBC)
Drama: *Picket Fences* (CBS)
Miniseries: *Prime Suspect 2* (PBS)
Variety/music/comedy: *Saturday Night Live* (NBC)
Informational: *Healing and the Mind with Bill Moyers* (PBS)

**1994**
Comedy: *Frasier* (NBC)
Drama: *Picket Fences* (CBS)
Miniseries: *Prime Suspect 3* (PBS)
Variety/music/comedy: *Late Show with David Letterman* (CBS)
Informational: *Later with Bob Costas* (NBC)

**1995**
Comedy: *Frasier* (NBC)
Drama: *NYPD Blue* (ABC)
Miniseries: *Joseph* (TNT)
Variety/music/comedy: *The Tonight Show with Jay Leno* (NBC)
Informational: *Baseball* (PBS); *TV Nation* (NBC)

**1996**
Comedy: *Frasier* (NBC)
Drama: *ER* (NBC)
Miniseries: *Gulliver's Travels* (NBC)
Variety/music/comedy: *Dennis Miller Live* (HBO)
Informational: *Lost Civilizations* (NBC)

**1997**
Comedy: *Frasier* (NBC)
Drama: *Law & Order* (NBC)
Miniseries: *Prime Suspect 5: Errors of Judgment* (PBS)
Variety/music/comedy: *Tracey Takes On...* (HBO)
Informational: *Biography* (A&E); *The Great War and the Shaping of the 20th Century* (PBS)

**1998**
Comedy: *Frasier* (NBC)
Drama: *The Practice* (ABC)
Miniseries: *From the Earth to the Moon* (HBO)
Variety/music/comedy: *Late Show with David Letterman* (CBS)
Nonfiction: *The American Experience* (PBS)

**1999**
Comedy: *Ally McBeal* (Fox)
Drama: *The Practice* (ABC)
Miniseries: *Horatio Hornblower: The Even Chance* (A&E)
Variety/music/comedy: *Late Show with David Letterman* (CBS)
Nonfiction: *The American Experience* (PBS); *American Masters* (PBS)

**2000**
Comedy: *Will & Grace* (NBC)
Drama: *The West Wing* (NBC)
Miniseries: *The Corner* (HBO)

**2000 (continued)**
Variety/music/comedy: *Late Show with David Letterman* (CBS)
Nonfiction: *American Masters* (PBS)

**2001**
Comedy: *Sex and the City* (HBO)
Drama: *The West Wing* (NBC)
Miniseries: *Anne Frank* (ABC)
Variety/music/comedy: *Late Show with David Letterman* (CBS)
Nonfiction: *American Masters* (PBS)

**2002**
Comedy: *Friends* (NBC)
Drama: *The West Wing* (NBC)
Miniseries: *Band of Brothers* (HBO)
Variety/music/comedy: *Late Show with David Letterman* (CBS)
Nonfiction: *Biography* (A&E)

**2003**
Comedy: *Everybody Loves Raymond* (CBS)
Drama: *The West Wing* (NBC)
Miniseries: *Steven Spielberg Presents Taken* (Sci Fi)
Variety/music/comedy: *The Daily Show with Jon Stewart* (Comedy Central)
Nonfiction: *American Masters* (PBS)

**2004**
Comedy: *Arrested Development* (Fox)
Drama: *The Sopranos* (HBO)
Miniseries: *Angels in America* (HBO)
Variety/music/comedy: *The Daily Show with Jon Stewart* (Comedy Central)
Nonfiction: *American Masters* (PBS)

**2005**
Comedy: *Everybody Loves Raymond* (CBS)
Drama: *Lost* (ABC)
Miniseries: *Masterpiece Theatre: The Lost Prince* (PBS)
Variety/music/comedy: *The Daily Show with Jon Stewart* (Comedy Central)
Nonfiction: *Broadway: The American Musical* (PBS)

**2006**
Comedy: *The Office* (NBC)
Drama: *24* (Fox)
Miniseries: *Elizabeth I* (HBO)
Variety/music/comedy: *The Daily Show with Jon Stewart* (Comedy Central)
Nonfiction: *10 Days That Unexpectedly Changed America* (The History Channel)

**2007**
Comedy: *30 Rock* (NBC)
Drama: *The Sopranos* (HBO)
Miniseries: *Broken Trail* (AMC)
Variety/music/comedy: *The Daily Show with Jon Stewart* (Comedy Central)
Nonfiction: *Planet Earth* (Discovery Channel)

**2008**
Comedy: *30 Rock* (NBC)
Drama: *Mad Men* (AMC)
Miniseries: *John Adams* (HBO)

## Emmy Awards, 1949–2011[1] (continued)

**2008 (continued)**
Variety/music/comedy: *The Daily Show with Jon Stewart* (Comedy Central)
Nonfiction: *American Masters* (PBS); *This American Life* (Showtime)

**2009**
Comedy: *30 Rock* (NBC)
Drama: *Mad Men* (AMC)
Miniseries: *Little Dorrit* (PBS)
Variety/music/comedy: *The Daily Show with Jon Stewart* (Comedy Central)
Nonfiction: *American Masters* (PBS)

**2010**
Comedy: *Modern Family* (ABC)
Drama: *Mad Men* (AMC)

**2010 (continued)**
Miniseries: *The Pacific* (HBO)
Variety/music/comedy: *The Daily Show with Jon Stewart* (Comedy Central)
Nonfiction: *The National Parks: America's Best Idea* (PBS)

**2011**
Comedy: *Modern Family* (ABC)
Drama: *Mad Men* (AMC)
Miniseries: *Downton Abbey* (PBS)
Variety/music/comedy: *The Daily Show with Jon Stewart* (Comedy Central)
Nonfiction: *American Masters* (PBS)

[1]*From 1949 to 1958, awards were given for programs broadcast the previous year only; awards since have been given for programs broadcast in part of the previous year and in part of the year named.*

# Theater

## Tony Awards, 2012

The American Theatre Wing (ATW), established in 1939, created the Tony Awards, named for former ATW director Antoinette Perry, in 1947 to recognize distinguished achievement in the theater arts as presented on Broadway; since 1967 they have been presented in conjunction with the Broadway League (formerly the League of American Theatres and Producers), a trade association. Nominees are selected each May from among the year's new or newly revived Broadway shows; a body of some 700 current and former theater professionals, critics, and agents votes for the winners. The awards are presented in New York City in June. Prize: silver medallion, set in a base, depicting on one face the masks of tragedy and comedy and on the other the profile of Antoinette Perry.

**Tony Awards Web site:** <www.tonyawards.com>.

▶ **musical:** *Once* (book, Enda Walsh; music and lyrics, Glen Hansard and Markéta Irglová); ▶ **play:** *Clybourne Park* (playwright, Bruce Norris); ▶ **revival of a musical:** *The Gershwins' Porgy and Bess* (original book, Suzan-Lori Parks and Diedre Murray; music, George Gershwin; lyrics, DuBose Heyward, Dorothy Heyward, and Ira Gershwin); ▶ **revival of a play:** *Arthur Miller's Death of a Salesman* (playwright, Arthur Miller); ▶ **book, musical:** *Once*; ▶ **score:** Alan Menken and Jack Feldman (*Newsies, The Musical*); ▶ **leading actress, musical:** Audra McDonald (*The Gershwins' Porgy and Bess*); ▶ **leading actor, musical:** Steve Kazee (*Once*); ▶ **leading actress, play:** Nina Arianda (*Venus in Fur*); ▶ **leading actor, play:** James Corden (*One Man, Two Guvnors*); ▶ **featured actress, musical:** Judy Kaye (*Nice Work If You Can Get It*); ▶ **featured actor, musical:** Michael McGrath (*Nice Work If You Can Get It*); ▶ **featured actress, play:** Judith Light (*Other Desert Cities*); ▶ **featured actor, play:** Christian Borle (*Peter and the Starcatcher*); ▶ **direction, musical:** John Tiffany (*Once*); ▶ **direction, play:** Mike Nichols (*Arthur Miller's Death of a Salesman*); ▶ **costume design, musical:** Gregg Barnes (*Follies*); ▶ **costume design, play:** Paloma Young (*Peter and the Starcatcher*); ▶ **lighting design, musical:** Natasha Katz (*Once*); ▶ **lighting design, play:** Jeff Croiter (*Peter and the Starcatcher*); ▶ **scenic design, musical:** Bob Crowley (*Once*); ▶ **scenic design, play:** Donyale Werle (*Peter and the Starcatcher*); ▶ **sound design, musical:** Clive Goodwin (*Once*); ▶ **sound design, play:** Darron L. West (*Peter and the Starcatcher*); ▶ **orchestrations:** Martin Lowe (*Once*); ▶ **choreography:** Christopher Gattelli (*Newsies, The Musical*); ▶ **regional theater award:** Shakespeare Theatre Company, Washington DC; ▶ **lifetime achievement:** Emanuel Azenberg.

## Tony Awards, 1947–2012

| YEAR | BEST MUSICAL | BEST PLAY |
|---|---|---|
| 1947 | *not awarded* | *All My Sons* (Arthur Miller)[1] |
| 1948 | *not awarded* | *Mister Roberts* (Thomas Heggen and Joshua Logan) |
| 1949 | *Kiss Me, Kate* (book, Bella Spewack and Samuel Spewack; music and lyrics, Cole Porter) | *Death of a Salesman* (Arthur Miller) |
| 1950 | *South Pacific* (book, Oscar Hammerstein II and Joshua Logan; music, Richard Rodgers; lyrics, Oscar Hammerstein II) | *The Cocktail Party* (T.S. Eliot) |

## Tony Awards, 1947–2012 (continued)

| YEAR | BEST MUSICAL | BEST PLAY |
|---|---|---|
| 1951 | Guys and Dolls (book, Jo Swerling and Abe Burrows; music and lyrics, Frank Loesser) | The Rose Tattoo (Tennessee Williams) |
| 1952 | The King and I (book and lyrics, Oscar Hammerstein II; music, Richard Rodgers) | The Fourposter (Jan de Hartog) |
| 1953 | Wonderful Town (book, Joseph Fields and Jerome Chodorov; music, Leonard Bernstein; lyrics, Betty Comden and Adolph Green) | The Crucible (Arthur Miller) |
| 1954 | Kismet (book, Charles Lederer and Luther Davis; music, Alexander Borodin; adaptation and lyrics, Robert Wright and George Forrest) | The Teahouse of the August Moon (John Patrick) |
| 1955 | The Pajama Game (book, George Abbott and Richard Bissell; music and lyrics, Richard Adler and Jerry Ross) | The Desperate Hours (Joseph Hayes) |
| 1956 | Damn Yankees (book, George Abbott and Douglass Wallop; music and lyrics, Richard Adler and Jerry Ross) | The Diary of Anne Frank (Frances Goodrich and Albert Hackett) |
| 1957 | My Fair Lady (book and lyrics, Alan Jay Lerner; music, Frederick Loewe) | Long Day's Journey into Night (Eugene O'Neill) |
| 1958 | The Music Man (book, Meredith Willson and Franklin Lacey; music and lyrics, Meredith Willson) | Sunrise at Campobello (Dore Schary) |
| 1959 | Redhead (book, Herbert Fields, Dorothy Fields, Sidney Sheldon, and David Shaw; music, Albert Hague; lyrics, Dorothy Fields) | J.B. (Archibald MacLeish) |
| 1960 | The Sound of Music (book, Howard Lindsay and Russel Crouse; music, Richard Rodgers; lyrics, Oscar Hammerstein II); Fiorello! (book, Jerome Weidman and George Abbott; music, Jerry Brock; lyrics, Sheldon Harnick) (tied) | The Miracle Worker (William Gibson) |
| 1961 | Bye Bye Birdie (book, Michael Stewart; music, Charles Strouse; lyrics, Lee Adams) | Beckett (Jean Anouilh, translated by Lucienne Hill) |
| 1962 | How To Succeed in Business Without Really Trying (book, Abe Burrows, Jack Weinstock, and Willie Gilbert; music and lyrics, Frank Loesser) | A Man for All Seasons (Robert Bolt) |
| 1963 | A Funny Thing Happened on the Way to the Forum (book, Burt Shevelove and Larry Gelbart; music and lyrics, Stephen Sondheim) | Who's Afraid of Virginia Woolf? (Edward Albee) |
| 1964 | Hello, Dolly! (book, Michael Stewart; music and lyrics, Jerry Herman) | Luther (John Osborne) |
| 1965 | Fiddler on the Roof (book, Joseph Stein; music, Jerry Bock; lyrics, Sheldon Harnick) | The Subject Was Roses (Frank Gilroy) |
| 1966 | Man of La Mancha (book, Dale Wasserman; music, Mitch Leigh; lyrics, Joe Darion) | Marat/Sade (Peter Weiss, translated by Geoffrey Skelton) |
| 1967 | Cabaret (book, Joe Masteroff; music, John Kander; lyrics, Fred Ebb) | The Homecoming (Harold Pinter) |
| 1968 | Hallelujah, Baby! (book, Arthur Laurents; music, Jule Styne; lyrics, Betty Comden and Adolph Green) | Rosencrantz and Guildenstern Are Dead (Tom Stoppard) |
| 1969 | 1776 (book, Peter Stone; music and lyrics, Sherman Edwards) | The Great White Hope (Howard Sackler) |
| 1970 | Applause (book, Betty Comden and Adolph Green; music, Charles Strouse; lyrics, Lee Adams) | Borstal Boy (Frank McMahon) |
| 1971 | Company (book, George Furth; music and lyrics, Stephen Sondheim) | Sleuth (Anthony Shaffer) |
| 1972 | Two Gentlemen of Verona (book, John Guare and Mel Shapiro; music, Galt MacDermot; lyrics, John Guare) | Sticks and Bones (David Rabe) |
| 1973 | A Little Night Music (book, Hugh Wheeler; music and lyrics, Stephen Sondheim) | That Championship Season (Jason Miller) |
| 1974 | Raisin (book, Robert Nemiroff and Charlotte Zaltzberg; music, Judd Woldin; lyrics, Robert Brittan) | The River Niger (Joseph A. Walker) |
| 1975 | The Wiz (book, William F. Brown; music and lyrics, Charlie Smalls) | Equus (Peter Shaffer) |
| 1976 | A Chorus Line (book, James Kirkwood and Nicholas Dante; music, Marvin Hamlisch; lyrics, Edward Kleban) | Travesties (Tom Stoppard) |
| 1977 | Annie (book, Thomas Meehan; music, Charles Strouse; lyrics, Martin Charnin) | The Shadow Box (Michael Cristofer) |
| 1978 | Ain't Misbehavin' (book, Murray Horwitz and Richard Maltby, Jr.; music, Fats Waller; lyrics, Fats Waller and many others) | Da (Hugh Leonard) |
| 1979 | Sweeney Todd (book, Hugh Wheeler; music and lyrics, Stephen Sondheim) | The Elephant Man (Bernard Pomerance) |
| 1980 | Evita (book and lyrics, Tim Rice; music, Andrew Lloyd Webber) | Children of a Lesser God (Mark Medoff) |
| 1981 | 42nd Street (book, Michael Stewart and Mark Bramble; music, Harry Warren; lyrics, Al Dubin) | Amadeus (Peter Shaffer) |
| 1982 | Nine (book, Arthur Kopit; music and lyrics, Maury Yeston) | The Life and Adventures of Nicholas Nickleby (David Edgar) |
| 1983 | Cats (book and lyrics, T.S. Eliot; music, Andrew Lloyd Webber) | Torch Song Trilogy (Harvey Fierstein) |
| 1984 | La Cage aux folles (book, Harvey Fierstein; music and lyrics, Jerry Herman) | The Real Thing (Tom Stoppard) |

## Tony Awards, 1947–2012 (continued)

| YEAR | BEST MUSICAL | BEST PLAY |
|------|-------------|-----------|
| 1985 | *Big River* (book, William Hauptman; music and lyrics, Roger Miller) | *Biloxi Blues* (Neil Simon) |
| 1986 | *The Mystery of Edwin Drood* (book, music, and lyrics, Rupert Holmes) | *I'm Not Rappaport* (Herb Gardner) |
| 1987 | *Les Misérables* (book, Alain Boublil and Claude-Michel Schönberg; music, Claude-Michel Schönberg; lyrics, Herbert Kretzmer and Alain Boublil) | *Fences* (August Wilson) |
| 1988 | *The Phantom of the Opera* (book, Richard Stilgoe and Andrew Lloyd Webber; music, Andrew Lloyd Webber; lyrics, Charles Hart and Richard Stilgoe) | *M. Butterfly* (David Henry Hwang) |
| 1989 | *Jerome Robbins' Broadway* (compilation) | *The Heidi Chronicles* (Wendy Wasserstein) |
| 1990 | *City of Angels* (book, Larry Gelbart; music, Cy Coleman; lyrics, David Zippel) | *The Grapes of Wrath* (Frank Galati) |
| 1991 | *The Will Rogers Follies* (book, Peter Stone; music, Cy Coleman; lyrics, Betty Comden and Adolph Green) | *Lost in Yonkers* (Neil Simon) |
| 1992 | *Crazy for You* (book, Ken Ludwig; music and lyrics, George Gershwin and Ira Gershwin) | *Dancing at Lughnasa* (Brian Friel) |
| 1993 | *Kiss of the Spider Woman* (book, Terrence McNally; music, John Kander; lyrics, Fred Ebb) | *Angels in America: Millennium Approaches* (Tony Kushner) |
| 1994 | *Passion* (book, James Lapine; music and lyrics, Stephen Sondheim) | *Angels in America: Perestroika* (Tony Kushner) |
| 1995 | *Sunset Boulevard* (book and lyrics, Don Black and Christopher Hampton; music, Andrew Lloyd Webber) | *Love! Valour! Compassion!* (Terrence McNally) |
| 1996 | *Rent* (book, music, and lyrics, Jonathan Larson) | *Master Class* (Terrence McNally) |
| 1997 | *Titanic* (book, Peter Stone; music and lyrics, Maury Yeston) | *The Last Night of Ballyhoo* (Alfred Uhry) |
| 1998 | *The Lion King* (book, Roger Allers and Irene Mecchi; music and lyrics, Elton John, Tim Rice, and others) | *Art* (Yasmina Reza) |
| 1999 | *Fosse* (compilation) | *Side Man* (Warren Leight) |
| 2000 | *Contact* (book, John Weidman; music and lyrics, various artists) | *Copenhagen* (Michael Frayn) |
| 2001 | *The Producers* (book, Mel Brooks and Thomas Meehan; music and lyrics, Mel Brooks) | *Proof* (David Auburn) |
| 2002 | *Thoroughly Modern Millie* (book, Richard Morris and Dick Scanlan; music, Jeanine Tesori; lyrics, Dick Scanlan) | *The Goat, or Who Is Sylvia?* (Edward Albee) |
| 2003 | *Hairspray* (book, Mark O'Donnell and Thomas Meehan; music, Marc Shaiman; lyrics, Scott Wittman and Marc Shaiman) | *Take Me Out* (Richard Greenberg) |
| 2004 | *Avenue Q* (book, Jeff Whitty; music and lyrics, Robert Lopez and Jeff Marx) | *I Am My Own Wife* (Doug Wright) |
| 2005 | *Monty Python's Spamalot* (book, Eric Idle; music and lyrics, John Du Prez and Eric Idle) | *Doubt* (John Patrick Shanley) |
| 2006 | *Jersey Boys* (book, Marshall Brickman and Rick Elice; music, Bob Gaudio; lyrics, Bob Crewe) | *The History Boys* (Alan Bennett) |
| 2007 | *Spring Awakening* (book and lyrics, Steven Sater; music, Duncan Sheik) | *The Coast of Utopia* (Tom Stoppard) |
| 2008 | *In the Heights* (book, Quiara Alegría Hudes; music and lyrics, Lin-Manuel Miranda) | *August: Osage County* (Tracy Letts) |
| 2009 | *Billy Elliot: The Musical* (book and lyrics, Lee Hall; music, Elton John) | *God of Carnage* (Yasmina Reza) |
| 2010 | *Memphis* (book, Joe DiPietro; music, David Bryan; lyrics, Joe DiPietro and David Bryan) | *Red* (John Logan) |
| 2011 | *The Book of Mormon* (book, music, and lyrics, Trey Parker, Robert Lopez, and Matt Stone) | *War Horse* (Nick Stafford) |
| 2012 | *Once* (book, Enda Walsh; music and lyrics, Glen Hansard and Markéta Irglová) | *Clybourne Park* (Bruce Norris) |

[1]Awarded to playwright for Best Author.

## Longest-Running Broadway Shows

*As of 20 Aug 2012. Source: Internet Broadway Database, <www.ibdb.com>.*

| | SHOW | RUN | PERFORMANCES | | SHOW | RUN | PERFORMANCES |
|---|------|-----|-------------|---|------|-----|-------------|
| 1 | The Phantom of the Opera | 1988– | 10,217 | 6 | The Lion King | 1997– | 6,133 |
| | | | | 7 | Oh! Calcutta! (revival) | 1976–89 | 5,959 |
| 2 | Cats | 1982–2000 | 7,485 | 8 | Beauty and the Beast | 1994–2007 | 5,461 |
| 3 | Les Misérables | 1987–2003 | 6,680 | | | | |
| 4 | Chicago (revival) | 1996– | 6,544 | 9 | Rent | 1996–2008 | 5,123 |
| 5 | A Chorus Line | 1975–90 | 6,137 | 10 | Mamma Mia! | 2001– | 4,494 |

## Encyclopædia Britannica's Notable US Theater Companies

| COMPANY | LOCATION | ARTISTIC DIRECTOR (2012) |
|---|---|---|
| The Acting Company | New York NY | Margot Harley[1] |
| Actors Theatre of Louisville | Louisville KY | Les Waters |
| Alley Theatre | Houston TX | Gregory Boyd |
| American Conservatory Theater | San Francisco CA | Carey Perloff |
| American Repertory Theater | Cambridge MA | Diane Paulus |
| Arena Stage | Washington DC | Molly Smith |
| Asolo Repertory Theatre | Sarasota FL | Michael Donald Edwards[1] |
| Center Theatre Group | Los Angeles CA | Michael Ritchie |
| Chicago Shakespeare Theater | Chicago IL | Barbara Gaines |
| Denver Center Theatre Company | Denver CO | Kent Thompson |
| El Teatro Campesino | San Juan Bautista CA | Luis Valdez |
| Folger Theatre | Washington DC | Janet Alexander Griffin[2] |
| Goodman Theatre | Chicago IL | Robert Falls |
| Guthrie Theater | Minneapolis MN | Joe Dowling[3] |
| The Old Globe Theatre | San Diego CA | Michael G. Murphy[4] |
| Oregon Shakespeare Festival | Ashland OR | Bill Rauch |
| The Public Theater | New York NY | Oskar Eustis |
| Seattle Repertory Theatre | Seattle WA | Jerry Manning |
| Steppenwolf Theatre Company | Chicago IL | Martha Lavey |
| Yale Repertory Theatre | New Haven CT | James Bundy |

[1]Producing artistic director.   [2]Artistic producer.   [3]Director.   [4]Managing director.

# Music

## Grammy Awards, 2011

The Grammys, first awarded in 1958, recognize excellence in the recording industry without regard to record sales or chart position. Nominees and winners are selected by the members of the National Academy of Recording Arts and Sciences according to the members' areas of expertise. In addition to the four general categories (record, album, and song of the year and best new artist) for which all members are eligible to vote, for 2011 there were 78 categories in 29 fields, of which Academy members were permitted to vote in no more than 24 categories. Prizes for works released 1 Oct 2010–30 Sep 2011 were awarded in Los Angeles on 12 Feb 2012. Prize: gold miniature phonograph.

**Grammy Award Web site:** <www.grammy.com>.

category: winner (performer in parentheses for song-writing/production awards)

▸ **record (single) of the year:** "Rolling in the Deep," Adele; ▸ **album of the year:** 21, Adele; ▸ **song of the year:** "Rolling in the Deep," Adele Adkins and Paul Epworth, songwriters (Adele); ▸ **new artist:** Bon Iver; ▸ **pop solo performance:** "Someone like You," Adele; ▸ **pop duo/group performance:** "Body and Soul," Tony Bennett and Amy Winehouse; ▸ **pop instrumental album:** The Road from Memphis, Booker T. Jones; ▸ **pop vocal album:** 21, Adele; ▸ **dance recording:** "Scary Monsters and Nice Sprites," Skrillex; ▸ **dance/electronica album:** Scary Monsters and Nice Sprites, Skrillex; ▸ **pop vocal album, traditional:** Duets II, Tony Bennett and various artists; ▸ **rock performance:** "Walk," Foo Fighters; ▸ **hard rock/metal performance:** "White Limo," Foo Fighters; ▸ **rock song:** "Walk," Foo Fighters, songwriters (Foo Fighters); ▸ **rock album:** Wasting Light, Foo Fighters; ▸ **alternative music album:** Bon Iver, Bon Iver; ▸ **R&B performance:** "Is This Love," Corinne Bailey Rae; ▸ **R&B performance, traditional:** "Fool for You," Cee Lo Green and Melanie Fiona; ▸ **R&B song:** "Fool for You," Cee Lo Green, Melanie Hallim, and Jack Splash, songwriters (Cee Lo Green and Melanie Fiona); ▸ **R&B album:** F.A.M.E., Chris Brown; ▸ **rap performance:** "Otis," Jay-Z and Kanye West; ▸ **rap/sung collaboration:** "All of the Lights," Kanye West, Rihanna, Kid Cudi, and Fergie; ▸ **rap song:** "All of the Lights," Jeff Bhasker, Stacy Ferguson, Malik Jones, Warren Trotter, and Kanye West, songwriters (Kanye West, Rihanna, Kid Cudi, and Fergie); ▸ **rap album:** My Beautiful Dark Twisted Fantasy, Kanye West; ▸ **country solo performance:** "Mean," Taylor Swift; ▸ **country duo/group performance:** "Barton Hollow," The Civil Wars; ▸ **country song:** "Mean," Taylor Swift, songwriter (Taylor Swift); ▸ **country album:** Own the Night, Lady Antebellum; ▸ **new age album:** What's It All About, Pat Metheny; ▸ **jazz improvised solo:** "500 Miles High," Chick Corea; ▸ **jazz vocal album:** The Mosaic Project, Terri Lyne Carrington and various artists; ▸ **jazz instrumental album:** Forever, Corea, Clarke & White; ▸ **jazz album, large ensemble:** The Good Feeling, Christian McBride Big Band; ▸ **gospel/Christian music performance, contemporary:** "Jesus," Le'Andria Johnson; ▸ **gospel song:** "Hello Fear," Kirk Franklin, songwriter (Kirk Franklin); ▸ **Christian music song, contemporary:** "Blessings," Laura Story, songwriter (Laura Story); ▸ **gospel album:** Hello Fear, Kirk Franklin; ▸ **Christian music album, contemporary:** And If Our God Is for Us..., Chris Tomlin; ▸ **Latin album, pop/rock/urban:** Drama Y Luz, Maná; ▸ **regional Mexican/Tejano album:** Bicentenario, Pepe Aguilar;

# Grammy Awards, 2011 (continued)

▸ **Banda/Norteño album:** *Los Tigres del Norte and Friends,* Los Tigres del Norte; ▸ **Latin album, tropical:** *The Last Mambo,* Cachao; ▸ **Americana album:** *Ramble at the Ryman,* Levon Helm; ▸ **bluegrass album:** *Paper Airplane,* Alison Krauss and Union Station; ▸ **blues album:** *Revelator,* Tedeschi Trucks Band; ▸ **folk album:** *Barton Hollow,* The Civil Wars; ▸ **regional roots music album:** *Rebirth of New Orleans,* Rebirth Brass Band; ▸ **reggae album:** *Revelation, Part 1: The Root of Life,* Stephen Marley; ▸ **world music album:** *Tassili,* Tinariwen; ▸ **children's album:** *All About Bullies...Big and Small,* various artists; ▸ **spoken word album:** *If You Ask Me (And of Course You Won't),* Betty White; ▸ **comedy album:** *Hilarious,* Louis C.K.; ▸ **musical theater album:** *The Book of Mormon,* Josh Gad and Andrew Rannells, artists; Anne Garefino, Robert Lopez, Stephen Oremus, Trey Parker, Scott Rudin, and Matt Stone, producers; Robert Lopez, Trey Parker, and Matt Stone, composers/lyricists; ▸ **compilation soundtrack for visual media:** *Boardwalk Empire: Volume 1,* various artists; Stewart Lerman, Randall Poster, and Kevin Weaver, producers; ▸ **score soundtrack for visual media:** *The King's Speech,* Alexandre Desplat, composer; ▸ **song written for visual media:** "I See the Light" (from *Tangled*), Alan Menken and Glenn Slater, songwriters (Mandy Moore and Zachary Levi); ▸ **instrumental composition:** "Life in Eleven," Béla Fleck and Howard Levy, composers

(Béla Fleck and the Flecktones); ▸ **instrumental arrangement:** "Rhapsody in Blue," Gordon Goodwin, arranger (Gordon Goodwin's Big Phat Band); ▸ **instrumental arrangement accompanying vocalist(s):** "Who Can I Turn To (When Nobody Needs Me)," Jorge Calandrelli, arranger (Tony Bennett and Queen Latifah); ▸ **recording package:** "Scenes from the Suburbs," Caroline Robert, art director (Arcade Fire); ▸ **boxed/special limited edition package:** *The Promise: The Darkness on the Edge of Town Story,* Dave Bett and Michelle Holme, art directors (Bruce Springsteen); ▸ **historical album:** *Band on the Run,* Paul McCartney Archive Collection—Deluxe Edition, Paul McCartney, producer; ▸ **producer, nonclassical:** Paul Epworth; ▸ **producer, classical:** Judith Sherman; ▸ **orchestral performance:** *Brahms: Symphony No. 4,* Gustavo Dudamel, conductor (Los Angeles Philharmonic); ▸ **opera recording:** *Adams: Doctor Atomic,* Alan Gilbert, conductor; Meredith Arwady, Sasha Cooke, Richard Paul Fink, Gerald Finley, Thomas Glenn, and Eric Owens, soloists; Jay David Saks, producer (Metropolitan Opera Orchestra and Metropolitan Opera Chorus); ▸ **vocal solo, classical:** *Diva Divo,* Joyce DiDonato; ▸ **short-form music video:** "Rolling in the Deep," Adele; Sam Brown, director; Hannah Chandler, producer; ▸ **long-form music video:** "Foo Fighters: Back and Forth," Foo Fighters; James Moll, director; James Moll and Nigel Sinclair, producers

# Grammy Awards, 1958–2011

*The year denotes the period (from the fall of the previous year to the fall of the year named) for which the winning work or artist was recognized; the prizes are generally awarded during the following year.*

| YEAR | RECORD (SINGLE) OF THE YEAR | ALBUM OF THE YEAR | BEST NEW ARTIST |
|------|------|------|------|
| 1958 | "Nel blu dipinto di blu (Volare)," Domenico Modugno | *The Music from Peter Gunn,* Henry Mancini | not awarded |
| 1959 | "Mack the Knife," Bobby Darin | *Come Dance with Me,* Frank Sinatra | Bobby Darin |
| 1960 | "The Theme from *A Summer Place,*" Percy Faith | *The Button-Down Mind of Bob Newhart,* Bob Newhart | Bob Newhart |
| 1961 | "Moon River," Henry Mancini | *Judy at Carnegie Hall,* Judy Garland | Peter Nero |
| 1962 | "I Left My Heart in San Francisco," Tony Bennett | *The First Family,* Vaughn Meader | Robert Goulet |
| 1963 | "The Days of Wine and Roses," Henry Mancini | *The Barbra Streisand Album,* Barbra Streisand | Ward Swingle (The Swingle Singers) |
| 1964 | "The Girl from Ipanema," Stan Getz and Astrud Gilberto | *Getz/Gilberto,* Stan Getz and João Gilberto | The Beatles |
| 1965 | "A Taste of Honey," Herb Alpert | *September of My Years,* Frank Sinatra | Tom Jones |
| 1966 | "Strangers in the Night," Frank Sinatra | *A Man and His Music,* Frank Sinatra | not awarded |
| 1967 | "Up, Up, and Away," The 5th Dimension | *Sgt. Pepper's Lonely Hearts Club Band,* The Beatles | Bobbie Gentry |
| 1968 | "Mrs. Robinson," Simon & Garfunkel | *By the Time I Get to Phoenix,* Glen Campbell | José Feliciano |
| 1969 | "Aquarius/Let the Sunshine In," The 5th Dimension | *Blood, Sweat & Tears,* Blood, Sweat & Tears | Crosby, Stills & Nash |
| 1970 | "Bridge over Troubled Water," Simon & Garfunkel | *Bridge over Troubled Water,* Simon & Garfunkel | The Carpenters |
| 1971 | "It's Too Late," Carole King | *Tapestry,* Carole King | Carly Simon |
| 1972 | "The First Time Ever I Saw Your Face," Roberta Flack | *The Concert for Bangla Desh,* George Harrison and Friends | America |
| 1973 | "Killing Me Softly with His Song," Roberta Flack | *Innervisions,* Stevie Wonder | Bette Midler |
| 1974 | "I Honestly Love You," Olivia Newton-John | *Fulfillingness' First Finale,* Stevie Wonder | Marvin Hamlisch |
| 1975 | "Love Will Keep Us Together," Captain & Tennille | *Still Crazy After All These Years,* Paul Simon | Natalie Cole |
| 1976 | "This Masquerade," George Benson | *Songs in the Key of Life,* Stevie Wonder | Starland Vocal Band |

## Grammy Awards, 1958–2011 (continued)

| YEAR | RECORD (SINGLE) OF THE YEAR | ALBUM OF THE YEAR | BEST NEW ARTIST |
|------|------|------|------|
| 1977 | "Hotel California," The Eagles | *Rumours*, Fleetwood Mac | Debby Boone |
| 1978 | "Just the Way You Are," Billy Joel | *Saturday Night Fever*, The Bee Gees | A Taste of Honey |
| 1979 | "What a Fool Believes," The Doobie Brothers | *52nd Steet*, Billy Joel | Rickie Lee Jones |
| 1980 | "Sailing," Christopher Cross | *Christopher Cross*, Christopher Cross | Christopher Cross |
| 1981 | "Bette Davis Eyes," Kim Carnes | *Double Fantasy*, John Lennon and Yoko Ono | Sheena Easton |
| 1982 | "Rosanna," Toto | *Toto IV*, Toto | Men at Work |
| 1983 | "Beat It," Michael Jackson | *Thriller*, Michael Jackson | Culture Club |
| 1984 | "What's Love Got To Do with It," Tina Turner | *Can't Slow Down*, Lionel Richie | Cyndi Lauper |
| 1985 | "We Are the World," USA for Africa | *No Jacket Required*, Phil Collins | Sade |
| 1986 | "Higher Love," Steve Winwood | *Graceland*, Paul Simon | Bruce Hornsby and the Range |
| 1987 | "Graceland," Paul Simon | *The Joshua Tree*, U2 | Jody Watley |
| 1988 | "Don't Worry, Be Happy," Bobby McFerrin | *Faith*, George Michael | Tracy Chapman |
| 1989 | "Wind Beneath My Wings," Bette Midler | *Nick of Time*, Bonnie Raitt | Milli Vanilli (revoked) |
| 1990 | "Another Day in Paradise," Phil Collins | *Back on the Block*, Quincy Jones | Mariah Carey |
| 1991 | "Unforgettable," Natalie Cole with Nat King Cole | *Unforgettable: With Love*, Natalie Cole | Marc Cohn |
| 1992 | "Tears in Heaven," Eric Clapton | *Unplugged*, Eric Clapton | Arrested Development |
| 1993 | "I Will Always Love You," Whitney Houston | *The Bodyguard*, Whitney Houston | Toni Braxton |
| 1994 | "All I Wanna Do," Sheryl Crow | *MTV Unplugged*, Tony Bennett | Sheryl Crow |
| 1995 | "Kiss from a Rose," Seal | *Jagged Little Pill*, Alanis Morissette | Hootie and the Blowfish |
| 1996 | "Change the World," Eric Clapton | *Falling into You*, Celine Dion | LeAnn Rimes |
| 1997 | "Sunny Came Home," Shawn Colvin | *Time Out of Mind*, Bob Dylan | Paula Cole |
| 1998 | "My Heart Will Go On," Celine Dion | *The Miseducation of Lauryn Hill*, Lauryn Hill | Lauryn Hill |
| 1999 | "Smooth," Santana featuring Rob Thomas | *Supernatural*, Santana | Christina Aguilera |
| 2000 | "Beautiful Day," U2 | *Two Against Nature*, Steely Dan | Shelby Lynne |
| 2001 | "Walk On," U2 | *O Brother, Where Art Thou?*, various artists | Alicia Keys |
| 2002 | "Don't Know Why," Norah Jones | *Come Away with Me*, Norah Jones | Norah Jones |
| 2003 | "Clocks," Coldplay | *Speakerboxxx/The Love Below*, OutKast | Evanescence |
| 2004 | "Here We Go Again," Ray Charles and Norah Jones | *Genius Loves Company*, Ray Charles and various artists | Maroon 5 |
| 2005 | "Boulevard of Broken Dreams," Green Day | *How To Dismantle an Atomic Bomb*, U2 | John Legend |
| 2006 | "Not Ready To Make Nice," Dixie Chicks | *Taking the Long Way*, Dixie Chicks | Carrie Underwood |
| 2007 | "Rehab," Amy Winehouse | *River: The Joni Letters*, Herbie Hancock | Amy Winehouse |
| 2008 | "Please Read the Letter," Robert Plant and Alison Krauss | *Raising Sand*, Robert Plant and Alison Krauss | Adele |
| 2009 | "Use Somebody," Kings of Leon | *Fearless*, Taylor Swift | Zac Brown Band |
| 2010 | "Need You Now," Lady Antebellum | *The Suburbs*, Arcade Fire | Esperanza Spalding |
| 2011 | "Rolling in the Deep," Adele | *21*, Adele | Bon Iver |

## Eurovision Song Contest

The European Broadcasting Union (EBU), an association of television and radio companies from Europe and the Mediterranean, began the Eurovision Song Contest in 1956. Each EBU member country, along with several provisional participants, can nominate one original song per year, with a maximum length of three minutes. The winner is selected based on votes from fans and juries in each participating country. Prize: crystal microphone.
**Eurovision Song Contest Web site:** <www.eurovision.tv>.

YEAR · SONG, SONGWRITER(S) (PERFORMER, COUNTRY)
1956   "Refrain," Émile Gardaz, Géo Voumard (Lys Assia, Switzerland)
1957   "Net als toen," Willy van Hemert, Guus Jansen (Corry Brokken, Netherlands)
1958   "Dors mon amour," Pierre Delanoë, Hubert Giraud (André Claveau, France)

## Eurovision Song Contest (continued)

YEAR   SONG, SONGWRITER(S) (PERFORMER, COUNTRY)

1959   "Een beetje," Willy van Hemert, Dick Schallies (Teddy Scholten, Netherlands)
1960   "Tom Pillibi," Pierre Cour, André Popp (Jacqueline Boyer, France)
1961   "Nous les amoureux," Jacques Datin, Maurice Vidalin (Jean-Claude Pascal, Luxembourg)
1962   "Un Premier amour," Rolande Valade, Claude Henri Vic (Isabelle Aubret, France)
1963   "Dansevise," Sejr Volmer-Sørensen, Otto Francker (Grethe and Jørgen Ingmann, Denmark)
1964   "Non ho l'étà," Nicola Salerno (Gigliola Cinquetti, Italy)
1965   "Poupée de cire, poupée de son," Serge Gainsbourg (France Gall, Luxembourg)
1966   "Merci chérie," Udo Jürgens, Thomas Hörbiger (Udo Jürgens, Austria)
1967   "Puppet on a String," Bill Martin, Phil Coulter (Sandie Shaw, United Kingdom)
1968   "La, la, la," Ramón Arcusa, Manuel de la Calva (Massiel, Spain)
1969   "Vivo cantando," Aniano Alcalde, Maria José de Cerato (Salomé, Spain); "Boom Bang-a-Bang," Peter Warne,
       Alan Moorhouse (Lulu, United Kingdom); "De troubadour," Lenny Kuhr, David Hartsena (Lenny Kuhr,
       Netherlands); "Un Jour, un enfant," Eddy Marnay, Emile Stern (Frida Boccara, France) (four-way tie)
1970   "All Kinds of Everything," Derry Lindsay, Jackie Smith (Dana, Ireland)
1971   "Un Banc, un arbre, une rue," Yves Dessca, Jean-Pierre Bourtayre (Séverine, Monaco)
1972   "Après toi," Klaus Munro, Yves Dessca, Mario Panas (Vicky Leandros, Luxembourg)
1973   "Tu te reconnaîtras," Vline Buggy, Claude Morgan (Anne-Marie David, Luxembourg)
1974   "Waterloo," Stikkan Anderson, Benny Andersson, Björn Ulvaeus (ABBA, Sweden)
1975   "Ding-a-Dong," Will Luikinga, Eddy Ouwens, Dick Bakker (Teach-In, Netherlands)
1976   "Save Your Kisses for Me," Tony Hiller, Lee Sheriden, Martin Lee (Brotherhood of Man, United Kingdom)
1977   "L'Oiseau et l'enfant," José Gracy, Jean-Paul Cara (Marie Myriam, France)
1978   "A-Ba-Ni-Bi," Ehud Manor, Nurit Hirsh (Izhar Cohen and the Alphabeta, Israel)
1979   "Hallelujah," Shimrit Orr, Kobi Oshrat (Gali Atari and Milk and Honey, Israel)
1980   "What's Another Year," Shay Healy (Johnny Logan, Ireland)
1981   "Making Your Mind Up," Andy Hill, John Danter (Bucks Fizz, United Kingdom)
1982   "Ein bisschen Frieden," Bernd Meinunger, Ralph Siegel (Nicole, West Germany)
1983   "Si la vie est cadeau," Alain Garcia, Jean-Pierre Millers (Corinne Hermès, Luxembourg)
1984   "Diggi-loo diggi-ley," Britt Lindeborg, Torgny Söderberg (Herrey's, Sweden)
1985   "La det svinge," Rolf Løvland (Bobbysocks, Norway)
1986   "J'aime la vie," Marino Atria, Jean-Pierre Furnémont, Angelo Crisci (Sandra Kim, Belgium)
1987   "Hold Me Now," Sean Sherrard (Johnny Logan, Ireland)
1988   "Ne partez pas sans moi," Nella Martinetti, Atilla Sereftug (Céline Dion, Switzerland)
1989   "Rock Me," Stevo Cvikich, Rajko Dujmich (Riva, Yugoslavia)
1990   "Insieme: 1992," Toto Cutugno (Toto Cutugno, Italy)
1991   "Fångad av en stormvind," Stephan Berg (Carola, Sweden)
1992   "Why Me," Sean Sherrard (Linda Martin, Ireland)
1993   "In Your Eyes," Jimmy Walsh (Niamh Kavanagh, Ireland)
1994   "Rock 'n' Roll Kids," Brendan Graham (Paul Harrington and Charlie McGettigan, Ireland)
1995   "Nocturne," Petter Skavlan, Rolf Løvland (Secret Garden, Norway)
1996   "The Voice," Brendan Graham (Eimear Quinn, Ireland)
1997   "Love Shine a Light," Kimberley Rew (Katrina and the Waves, United Kingdom)
1998   "Diva," Yoav Ginay (Dana International, Israel)
1999   "Take Me to Your Heaven," Gert Lengstrand (Charlotte Nilsson, Sweden)
2000   "Fly on the Wings of Love," Jørgen Olsen (Olsen Brothers, Denmark)
2001   "Everybody," Maian-Anna Kärmas, Ivar Must (Tanel Padar, Dave Benton, and 2XL, Estonia)
2002   "I Wanna," Marija Naumova, Marats Samauskis (Marie N, Latvia)
2003   "Every Way That I Can," Demir Demirkan, Sertab Erener (Sertab Erener, Turkey)
2004   "Wild Dances," Ruslana Lyzhichko, Aleksandr Ksenofontov (Ruslana, Ukraine)
2005   "My Number One," Christos Dantis, Natalia Germanou (Helena Paparizou, Greece)
2006   "Hard Rock Hallelujah," LORDI (LORDI, Finland)
2007   "Molitva," Sasa Milosevic Mare (Marija Serifovic, Serbia)
2008   "Believe," Dima Bilan, Jim Beanz (Dima Bilan, Russia)
2009   "Fairytale," Alexander Rybak (Alexander Rybak, Norway)
2010   "Satellite," Julie Frost, John Gordon (Lena, Germany)
2011   "Running Scared," Stefan Örn, Sandra Bjurman, Iain Farquharson (Ell/Nikki, Azerbaijan)
2012   "Euphoria," Thomas G:son, Peter Boström (Loreen, Sweden)

## Brit Awards, 2012

*The British Phonographic Industry, a trade association of record companies, established the Brit Awards in 1977 to recognize pop acts from Great Britain and abroad. Prize: statuette.* **Web site:** *<www.brits.co.uk>.*

British male solo artist: Ed Sheeran
British female solo artist: Adele
British breakthrough act: Ed Sheeran
British group: Coldplay
MasterCard British album: Adele, *21*
International group: Foo Fighters

British single: One Direction, "What Makes You Beautiful"
International male solo artist: Bruno Mars
International female solo artist: Rihanna
International breakthrough act: Lana del Rey
Critics' choice: Emeli Sandé

## Country Music Association Awards, 2011

The Country Music Association began its annual awards ceremony in 1967 and made it the first nationally televised music awards show the following year. Ceremonies are held in November. Prize: hand-blown crystal statuette. **Country Music Association Awards Web site:** <www.cmaworld.com>.

▸ **entertainer of the year:** Taylor Swift; ▸ **female vocalist of the year:** Miranda Lambert; ▸ **male vocalist of the year:** Blake Shelton; ▸ **new artist of the year:** The Band Perry; ▸ **vocal duo of the year:** Sugarland; ▸ **vocal group of the year:** Lady Antebellum; ▸ **album of the year:** *My Kinda Party*, Jason Aldean; Michael Knox, producer; ▸ **song of the year:** "If I Die Young" (The Band Perry), Kimberly Perry, songwriter; ▸ **single of the year:** "If I Die Young," The Band Perry; Paul Worley, producer; ▸ **music video of the year:** "You and Tequila," Kenny Chesney featuring Grace Potter; Shaun Silva, director; ▸ **musical event of the year:** "Don't You Wanna Stay," Jason Aldean with Kelly Clarkson; ▸ **musician of the year:** Mac McAnally (guitar)

## All-Time Best-Selling Albums in the United States

*As of April 2012. Album sales are given only to the nearest million units, and in the case of a tie albums are listed alphabetically. Source: Recording Industry Association of America (RIAA), <www.riaa.com>.*

| | ALBUM | ARTIST | YEAR | | ALBUM | ARTIST | YEAR |
|---|---|---|---|---|---|---|---|
| 1 | Their Greatest Hits (1971–1975) | Eagles | 1976 | 28 | ...Baby One More Time | Britney Spears | 1999 |
| | Thriller | Michael Jackson | 1982 | | Backstreet Boys | Backstreet Boys | 1997 |
| 3 | Greatest Hits, Volume I & Volume II | Billy Joel | 1985 | | Bat out of Hell | Meat Loaf | 1977 |
| | untitled ("Led Zeppelin IV") | Led Zeppelin | 1971 | | Ropin' the Wind | Garth Brooks | 1991 |
| | | | | | Simon & Garfunkel's Greatest Hits | Simon & Garfunkel | 1972 |
| | The Wall | Pink Floyd | 1979 | 33 | Greatest Hits 1974–1978 | Steve Miller Band | 1978 |
| 6 | Back in Black | AC/DC | 1980 | | Live/1975–85 | Bruce Springsteen & the E Street Band | 1986 |
| 7 | Double Live | Garth Brooks | 1998 | | | | |
| 8 | Come On Over | Shania Twain | 1997 | | Millennium | Backstreet Boys | 1999 |
| 9 | The Beatles ("The White Album") | The Beatles | 1968 | | Purple Rain (soundtrack) | Prince and the Revolution | 1984 |
| | Rumours | Fleetwood Mac | 1977 | | Ten | Pearl Jam | 1991 |
| 11 | Appetite for Destruction | Guns N' Roses | 1987 | | Whitney Houston | Whitney Houston | 1985 |
| 12 | The Bodyguard (soundtrack) | Whitney Houston and various artists | 1992 | 39 | Abbey Road | The Beatles | 1969 |
| | | | | | Breathless | Kenny G | 1992 |
| | Boston | Boston | 1976 | | Forrest Gump (soundtrack) | various artists | 1994 |
| | 1967–70 | The Beatles | 1973 | | Hot Rocks 1964–1971 | The Rolling Stones | 1972 |
| | No Fences | Garth Brooks | 1990 | | | | |
| 16 | Cracked Rear View | Hootie & the Blowfish | 1994 | | Hysteria | Def Leppard | 1987 |
| | Greatest Hits | Elton John | 1974 | | Kenny Rogers' Greatest Hits | Kenny Rogers | 1980 |
| | Hotel California | Eagles | 1976 | | | | |
| | Jagged Little Pill | Alanis Morissette | 1995 | | Led Zeppelin II | Led Zeppelin | 1969 |
| | Physical Graffiti | Led Zeppelin | 1975 | | No Jacket Required | Phil Collins | 1985 |
| 21 | Born in the U.S.A. | Bruce Springsteen | 1984 | | Pieces of You | Jewel | 1995 |
| | Dark Side of the Moon | Pink Floyd | 1973 | | Slippery When Wet | Bon Jovi | 1986 |
| | Greatest Hits | Journey | 1988 | | II | Boyz II Men | 1994 |
| | Metallica | Metallica | 1991 | | Wide Open Spaces | Dixie Chicks | 1998 |
| | 1962–66 | The Beatles | 1973 | | The Woman in Me | Shania Twain | 1995 |
| | Saturday Night Fever (soundtrack) | The Bee Gees and various artists | 1977 | | Yourself or Someone Like You | Matchbox 20 | 1996 |
| | Supernatural | Santana | 1999 | | | | |

## Rock and Roll Hall of Fame

Music-industry professionals established the Rock and Roll Hall of Fame Foundation in 1983 in order to "recognize the contributions of those who have had a significant impact on the evolution, development, and perpetuation of rock and roll." Performers are eligible for induction 25 years after the release of their first record. The foundation's nominating committee compiles an annual list of eligible artists and distributes this list to about 1,000 rock experts throughout the world. Those performers receiving the highest number of votes, as well as at least 50% of the vote, are inducted. Special committees select inductees in other categories. Inductees for 2012 appear in **bold-face**.

**Rock and Roll Hall of Fame and Museum Web site:** <http://rockhall.com>.

## Rock and Roll Hall of Fame (continued)

**NAME (YEAR OF INDUCTION)**

ABBA (2010)
AC/DC (2003)
Paul Ackerman[1] (1995)
Aerosmith (2001)
The Allman Brothers Band (1995)
Herb Alpert and Jerry Moss[2] (2006)
The Animals (1994)
Louis Armstrong[3] (1990)
Chet Atkins[4] (2002)
LaVern Baker (1991)
Hank Ballard (1990)
The Band (1994)
Dave Bartholomew[1] (1991)
Frank Barsalona[2] (2005)
Ralph Bass[1] (1991)
The Beach Boys (1988)
**Beastie Boys (2012)**
The Beatles (1988)
Jeff Beck (2009)
The Bee Gees (1997)
Benny Benjamin[4] (2003)
Chuck Berry (1986)
Bill Black[4] (2009)
Black Sabbath (2006)
Chris Blackwell[1] (2001)
Otis Blackwell[1] (2010)
Hal Blaine[4] (2000)
Bobby "Blue" Bland (1992)
Blondie (2006)
**The Blue Caps (2012)**
Booker T. and the MG's (1992)
David Bowie (1996)
Charles Brown[3] (1999)
James Brown (1986)
Ruth Brown (1993)
Jackson Browne (2004)
Buffalo Springfield (1997)
Solomon Burke (2001)
James Burton[4] (2001)
The Byrds (1991)
Johnny Cash (1992)
Ray Charles (1986)
Leonard Chess[1] (1987)
Charlie Christian[3] (1990)
Eric Clapton (2000)
Dick Clark[1] (1993)
The Clash (2003)
Jimmy Cliff (2010)
The Coasters (1987)
Eddie Cochran (1987)
Leonard Cohen (2008)
Nat King Cole[3] (2000)
**The Comets (2012)**
Sam Cooke (1986)
Alice Cooper Band (2011)
Elvis Costello and the Attractions (2003)
Floyd Cramer[4] (2003)
Cream (1993)
Creedence Clearwater Revival (1993)
**The Crickets (2012)**
Crosby, Stills & Nash (1997)
Bobby Darin (1990)
The Dave Clark Five (2008)
Clive Davis[1] (2000)

Miles Davis (2006)
The Dells (2004)
Neil Diamond (2011)
Bo Diddley (1987)
Dion (1989)
Willie Dixon[3] (1994)
Fats Domino (1986)
Tom Donahue[1] (1996)
**Donovan (2012)**
The Doors (1993)
Steve Douglas[4] (2003)
**Tom Dowd[4] (2012)**
Dr. John (2011)
The Drifters (1988)
Bob Dylan (1988)
Eagles (1998)
Earth, Wind & Fire (2000)
Duane Eddy (1994)
Ahmet Ertegun[1] (1987)
Nesuhi Ertegun[2] (1991)
The Everly Brothers (1986)
**The Famous Flames (2012)**
Leo Fender[1] (1992)
The Flamingos (2001)
Fleetwood Mac (1998)
D.J. Fontana[4] (2009)
The Four Seasons (1990)
The Four Tops (1990)
Aretha Franklin (1987)
Alan Freed[1] (1986)
Milt Gabler[1] (1993)
Kenny Gamble and Leon Huff[1] (2008)
Marvin Gaye (1987)
David Geffen[1] (2010)
Genesis (2010)
Gerry Goffin and Carole King[1] (1990)
Berry Gordy, Jr.[1] (1988)
Bill Graham[1] (1992)
Grandmaster Flash and the Furious Five (2007)
Grateful Dead (1994)
Al Green (1995)
Ellie Greenwich and Jeff Barry[1] (2010)
**Guns N' Roses (2012)**
Woody Guthrie[3] (1988)
Buddy Guy (2005)
Bill Haley (1987)
John Hammond[2] (1986)
George Harrison (2004)
Isaac Hayes (2002)
The Jimi Hendrix Experience (1992)
Billie Holiday[3] (2000)
Holland, Dozier, and Holland[1] (1990)
The Hollies (2010)
Buddy Holly (1986)
Jac Holzman[1] (2011)
John Lee Hooker (1991)
Howlin' Wolf[3] (1991)
The Impressions (1991)
The Ink Spots[3] (1989)
The Isley Brothers (1992)
Mahalia Jackson[3] (1997)
Michael Jackson (2001)

Wanda Jackson[3] (2009)
The Jackson 5 (1997)
James Jamerson[4] (2000)
Elmore James[3] (1992)
Etta James (1993)
Jefferson Airplane (1996)
Billy Joel (1999)
Elton John (1994)
Little Willie John (1996)
**Glyn Johns[4] (2012)**
Johnnie Johnson[4] (2001)
Robert Johnson[3] (1986)
Janis Joplin (1995)
Louis Jordan[3] (1987)
B.B. King (1987)
**Freddie King[3] (2012)**
King Curtis[4] (2000)
The Kinks (1990)
**Don Kirshner[1] (2012)**
Gladys Knight and the Pips (1996)
Leadbelly[3] (1988)
Led Zeppelin (1995)
Brenda Lee (2002)
Jerry Leiber and Mike Stoller[1] (1987)
John Lennon (1994)
Jerry Lee Lewis (1986)
Little Anthony and the Imperials (2009)
Little Richard (1986)
Little Walter (2008)
Darlene Love (2011)
The Lovin' Spoonful (2000)
Frankie Lymon and the Teenagers (1993)
Lynyrd Skynyrd (2006)
Madonna (2008)
The Mamas and the Papas (1998)
Barry Mann and Cynthia Weil[1] (2010)
Bob Marley (1994)
Martha and the Vandellas (1995)
George Martin[1] (1999)
**Cosimo Matassa[4] (2012)**
Curtis Mayfield (1999)
Paul McCartney (1999)
Clyde McPhatter (1987)
John Mellencamp (2008)
Metallica (2009)
**The Midnighters (2012)**
**The Miracles (2012)**
Joni Mitchell (1997)
Bill Monroe[3] (1997)
The Moonglows (2000)
Van Morrison (1993)
Jelly Roll Morton[3] (1998)
Syd Nathan[1] (1997)
Ricky Nelson (1987)
**Laura Nyro (2012)**
The O'Jays (2005)
Spooner Oldham[4] (2009)
Roy Orbison (1987)
The Orioles[3] (1995)
Mo Ostin[1] (2003)
Johnny Otis[1] (1994)
Earl Palmer[4] (2000)

## Rock and Roll Hall of Fame (continued)

NAME (YEAR OF INDUCTION)
Parliament-Funkadelic (1997)
Les Paul[3] (1988)
Carl Perkins (1987)
Tom Petty and the Heartbreakers (2002)
Sam Phillips[1] (1986)
Wilson Pickett (1991)
Pink Floyd (1996)
Gene Pitney (2002)
The Platters (1990)
The Police (2003)
Doc Pomus[1] (1992)
Elvis Presley (1986)
The Pretenders (2005)
Lloyd Price (1998)
Prince (2004)
Professor Longhair[3] (1992)
Queen (2001)
Ma Rainey[3] (1990)
Bonnie Raitt (2000)
The Ramones (2002)
**Red Hot Chili Peppers (2012)**
Otis Redding (1989)
Jimmy Reed (1991)
R.E.M. (2007)
The Righteous Brothers (2003)
Smokey Robinson (1987)
Jimmie Rodgers[3] (1986)
The Rolling Stones (1989)
The Ronettes (2007)
Run-D.M.C. (2009)

NAME (YEAR OF INDUCTION)
Art Rupe[1] (2011)
Leon Russell[4] (2011)
Sam and Dave (1992)
Santana (1998)
Pete Seeger[3] (1996)
Bob Seger (2004)
The Sex Pistols (2006)
Del Shannon (1999)
The Shirelles (1996)
Mort Shuman[1] (2010)
Paul Simon (2001)
Simon & Garfunkel (1990)
Percy Sledge (2005)
Sly and the Family Stone (1993)
**The Small Faces/Faces (2012)**
Bessie Smith[3] (1989)
Patti Smith (2007)
The Soul Stirrers[3] (1989)
Phil Spector[1] (1989)
Dusty Springfield (1999)
Bruce Springsteen (1999)
The Staple Singers (1999)
Steely Dan (2001)
Seymour Stein[2] (2005)
Jim Stewart[1] (2002)
Rod Stewart (1994)
Jesse Stone[1] (2010)
The Stooges (2010)
The Supremes (1988)
Talking Heads (2002)

NAME (YEAR OF INDUCTION)
James Taylor (2000)
The Temptations (1989)
Allen Toussaint[1] (1998)
Traffic (2004)
Big Joe Turner (1987)
Ike and Tina Turner (1991)
U2 (2005)
Ritchie Valens (2001)
Van Halen (2007)
The Velvet Underground (1996)
The Ventures (2008)
Gene Vincent (1998)
Tom Waits (2011)
T-Bone Walker[3] (1987)
Dinah Washington[3] (1993)
Muddy Waters (1987)
Jann S. Wenner[2] (2004)
Jerry Wexler[1] (1987)
The Who (1990)
Hank Williams[3] (1987)
Bob Wills and His Texas Playboys[3] (1999)
Jackie Wilson (1987)
Bobby Womack (2009)
Stevie Wonder (1989)
Jimmy Yancey[3] (1986)
The Yardbirds (1992)
Neil Young (1995)
The (Young) Rascals (1997)
Frank Zappa (1995)
ZZ Top (2004)

[1]*Ahmet Ertegun Award (nonperformers).*     [2]*Lifetime Achievement.*     [3]*Early Influences.*     [4]*Sidemen.*

## Encyclopædia Britannica's World-Class Orchestras

| ORCHESTRA | LOCATION | FOUNDED | MUSIC DIRECTOR OR CONDUCTOR (2012) |
| --- | --- | --- | --- |
| Berliner Philharmoniker | Berlin, Germany | 1882 | Simon Rattle |
| Boston Symphony Orchestra | Boston MA | 1881 | *guest conductors* |
| Budapesti Fesztiválzenekar | Budapest, Hungary | 1983 | Iván Fischer |
| Ceská Filharmonie | Prague, Czech Republic | 1896 | Jiří Bělohlávek |
| Chicago Symphony Orchestra | Chicago IL | 1891 | Riccardo Muti |
| Cleveland Orchestra | Cleveland OH | 1918 | Franz Welser-Möst |
| Gewandhaus zu Leipzig | Leipzig, Germany | 1743 | Riccardo Chailly |
| Koninklijk Concertgebouworkest | Amsterdam, Netherlands | 1888 | Mariss Jansons |
| London Symphony Orchestra | London, England | 1904 | Valery Gergiev |
| Los Angeles Philharmonic | Los Angeles CA | 1919 | Gustavo Dudamel |
| New York Philharmonic | New York NY | 1842 | Alan Gilbert |
| Orchestre Symphonique de Montréal | Montreal, QC, Canada | 1934 | Kent Nagano |
| Philadelphia Orchestra | Philadelphia PA | 1900 | Yannick Nézet-Séguin |
| Philharmonia Orchestra | London, England | 1945 | Esa-Pekka Salonen |
| Russian National Orchestra | Moscow, Russia | 1990 | Mikhail Pletnev |
| Saint Petersburg Philharmonic | Saint Petersburg, Russia | 1882 | Yury Temirkanov |
| San Francisco Symphony | San Francisco CA | 1911 | Michael Tilson Thomas |
| Staatskapelle Dresden | Dresden, Germany | 1548 | Christian Thielemann |
| Symphonieorchester des Bayerischen Rundfunks | Munich, Germany | 1949 | Mariss Jansons |
| Wiener Philharmoniker | Vienna, Austria | 1842 | *guest conductors* |

## Encyclopædia Britannica's Top Opera Companies

| COMPANY | LOCATION | FOUNDED | GENERAL OR ARTISTIC DIRECTOR (2012) |
|---|---|---|---|
| Bayerische Staatsoper | Munich, Germany | 1653 | Nikolaus Bachler |
| Bolshoi Opera | Moscow, Russia | 1776 | Makvala Kasrashvili |
| Canadian Opera Company | Toronto, ON, Canada | 1950 | Alexander Neef |
| De Nederlandse Opera | Amsterdam, Netherlands | 1946 | Pierre Audi |
| Gran Teatre del Liceu | Barcelona, Spain | 1847 | Joan Francesc Marco |
| Lyric Opera of Chicago | Chicago IL | 1954 | Anthony Freud |
| Mariinsky Theatre (Kirov Opera) | St. Petersburg, Russia | 1783 | Valery Gergiev |
| Metropolitan Opera | New York NY | 1883 | Peter Gelb |
| Opera Australia | Sydney, NSW, and Melbourne, VIC, Australia | 1956 | Lyndon Terracini |
| Opéra National de Paris | Paris, France | 1669 | Nicolas Joel |
| Royal Opera | London, England | 1732 | Tony Hall[1] |
| San Francisco Opera | San Francisco CA | 1923 | David Gockley |
| Staatsoper Hamburg | Hamburg, Germany | 1678 | Simone Young |
| Teatro alla Scala (La Scala) | Milan, Italy | 1778 | Stéphane Lissner |
| Wiener Staatsoper | Vienna, Austria | 1869 | Franz Welser-Möst |

[1]Chief executive.

# Arts and Letters Awards

## Pulitzer Prizes

The Pulitzer Prizes are awarded annually by Columbia University, New York City, based on recommendations from the Pulitzer Prize Board, for works published or produced in the previous calendar year (for music, works must be performed or released between 16 January of the previous year and 15 January of the award year). The prizes, originally endowed by newspaper editor Joseph Pulitzer, were first awarded in 1917. There are currently 21 prizes presented. Most prizes include a US$10,000 cash award; the exception is the prize for public service in journalism, which is a gold medal.
**Pulitzer Prize Web site:** <www.pulitzer.org>.

### Journalism, 2012

| CATEGORY AND DESCRIPTION | WINNER | PUBLICATION | SUBJECT |
|---|---|---|---|
| Public Service: awarded to a newspaper for notable public service | staff | Philadelphia Inquirer | exploration of widespread violent crime in the city's school system |
| Breaking News Reporting: awarded for local reporting of breaking news | staff | Tuscaloosa News | in-depth reporting on the effects of a deadly tornado strike |
| Investigative Reporting: awarded to an individual or team for an investigative article or series | Michael J. Berens and Ken Armstrong | Seattle Times | investigation of a scandal-plagued methadone treatment |
| | Matt Apuzzo, Adam Goldman, Eileen Sullivan, and Chris Hawley | Associated Press | uncovering of a controversial NYPD spying program that focused on American Muslim communities |
| Explanatory Reporting: awarded for clarification of a difficult subject through clear communication of in-depth knowledge | David Kocieniewski | New York Times | examination of the American taxation system, which allows some of the nation's wealthiest to avoid paying taxes |
| Local Reporting: awarded for consistent, intelligent coverage of a particular topic | Sara Ganim and staff | Patriot-News (Harrisburg PA) | coverage of the Penn State football program's sex scandal |
| National Reporting: awarded for coverage of national news | David Wood | Huffington Post | exposure of the difficult conditions that wounded soldiers face in their recovery |
| International Reporting: awarded for coverage of international news | Jeffrey Gettleman | New York Times | reporting on the famines and military conflicts affecting East Africa |
| Feature Writing: awarded for original and concise writing of quality | Eli Sanders | The Stranger | story of a lesbian couple who are raped and stabbed by a man, leaving one dead |

## Journalism, 2012 (continued)

| CATEGORY AND DESCRIPTION | WINNER | PUBLICATION | SUBJECT |
|---|---|---|---|
| Commentary | Mary Schmich | Chicago Tribune | columns about Chicago known for down-to-earth style |
| Criticism | Wesley Morris | Boston Globe | critiques of a wide range of types of films |
| Editorial Writing: awarded for the ability to sway public opinion through solid reasoning, clear style, and "moral purpose" | no award | | |
| Editorial Cartooning: awarded for creative cartoons that display editorial effectiveness and superior drawing | Matt Wuerker | Politico | witty and original portfolio of cartoons, many dealing with the extreme partisan nature of Washington politics |
| Breaking News Photography: awarded for single or group and color or black-and-white photographs of breaking news | Massoud Hossaini | Agence France-Presse | heartbreaking photograph capturing the grief of a young girl in the immediate aftermath of a suicide bombing |
| Feature Photography: awarded for single or group and color or black-and-white feature photographs | Craig F. Walker | Denver Post | photographic documentation of the struggles of a veteran home from Iraq as he deals with PTSD |

## Letters, Drama, and Music

### Fiction
*Awarded for a work of fiction, preferably about American life, by an American author.*

| YEAR | TITLE | AUTHOR | YEAR | TITLE | AUTHOR |
|---|---|---|---|---|---|
| 1917 | no award | | 1948 | *Tales of the South Pacific* | James A. Michener |
| 1918 | *His Family* | Ernest Poole | 1949 | *Guard of Honor* | James Gould Cozzens |
| 1919 | *The Magnificent Ambersons* | Booth Tarkington | 1950 | *The Way West* | A.B. Guthrie, Jr. |
| 1920 | no award | | 1951 | *The Town* | Conrad Richter |
| 1921 | *The Age of Innocence* | Edith Wharton | 1952 | *The Caine Mutiny* | Herman Wouk |
| 1922 | *Alice Adams* | Booth Tarkington | 1953 | *The Old Man and the Sea* | Ernest Hemingway |
| 1923 | *One of Ours* | Willa Cather | 1954 | no award | |
| 1924 | *The Able McLaughlins* | Margaret Wilson | 1955 | *A Fable* | William Faulkner |
| 1925 | *So Big* | Edna Ferber | 1956 | *Andersonville* | MacKinlay Kantor |
| 1926 | *Arrowsmith* | Sinclair Lewis (declined) | 1957 | no award | |
| 1927 | *Early Autumn* | Louis Bromfield | 1958 | *A Death in the Family*[1] | James Agee |
| 1928 | *The Bridge of San Luis Rey* | Thornton Wilder | 1959 | *The Travels of Jaimie McPheeters* | Robert Lewis Taylor |
| 1929 | *Scarlet Sister Mary* | Julia Peterkin | 1960 | *Advise and Consent* | Allen Drury |
| 1930 | *Laughing Boy* | Oliver Lafarge | 1961 | *To Kill a Mockingbird* | Harper Lee |
| 1931 | *Years of Grace* | Margaret Ayer Barnes | 1962 | *The Edge of Sadness* | Edwin O'Connor |
| 1932 | *The Good Earth* | Pearl S. Buck | 1963 | *The Reivers* | William Faulkner |
| 1933 | *The Store* | T.S. Stribling | 1964 | no award | |
| 1934 | *Lamb in His Bosom* | Caroline Miller | 1965 | *The Keepers of the House* | Shirley Ann Grau |
| 1935 | *Now in November* | Josephine Winslow Johnson | 1966 | *Collected Stories* | Katherine Anne Porter |
| 1936 | *Honey in the Horn* | Harold L. Davis | 1967 | *The Fixer* | Bernard Malamud |
| 1937 | *Gone with the Wind* | Margaret Mitchell | 1968 | *The Confessions of Nat Turner* | William Styron |
| 1938 | *The Late George Apley* | John Phillips Marquand | 1969 | *House Made of Dawn* | N. Scott Momaday |
| 1939 | *The Yearling* | Marjorie Kinnan Rawlings | 1970 | *Collected Stories* | Jean Stafford |
| 1940 | *The Grapes of Wrath* | John Steinbeck | 1971 | no award | |
| 1941 | no award | | 1972 | *Angle of Repose* | Wallace Stegner |
| 1942 | *In This Our Life* | Ellen Glasgow | 1973 | *The Optimist's Daughter* | Eudora Welty |
| 1943 | *Dragon's Teeth* | Upton Sinclair | 1974 | no award | |
| 1944 | *Journey in the Dark* | Martin Flavin | 1975 | *The Killer Angels* | Michael Shaara |
| 1945 | *A Bell for Adano* | John Hersey | 1976 | *Humboldt's Gift* | Saul Bellow |
| 1946 | no award | | 1977 | no award | |
| 1947 | *All the King's Men* | Robert Penn Warren | | | |

## Letters, Drama, and Music (continued)

### Fiction (continued)

| YEAR | TITLE | AUTHOR | YEAR | TITLE | AUTHOR |
|---|---|---|---|---|---|
| 1978 | Elbow Room | James Alan McPherson | 1996 | Independence Day | Richard Ford |
| 1979 | The Stories of John Cheever | John Cheever | 1997 | Martin Dressler: The Tale of an American Dreamer | Steven Millhauser |
| 1980 | The Executioner's Song | Norman Mailer | 1998 | American Pastoral | Philip Roth |
| 1981 | A Confederacy of Dunces[1] | John Kennedy Toole | 1999 | The Hours | Michael Cunningham |
| 1982 | Rabbit Is Rich | John Updike | 2000 | Interpreter of Maladies | Jhumpa Lahiri |
| 1983 | The Color Purple | Alice Walker | 2001 | The Amazing Adventures of Kavalier and Clay | Michael Chabon |
| 1984 | Ironweed | William Kennedy | | | |
| 1985 | Foreign Affairs | Alison Lurie | 2002 | Empire Falls | Richard Russo |
| 1986 | Lonesome Dove | Larry McMurtry | 2003 | Middlesex | Jeffrey Eugenides |
| 1987 | A Summons to Memphis | Peter Taylor | 2004 | The Known World | Edward P. Jones |
| 1988 | Beloved | Toni Morrison | 2005 | Gilead | Marilynne Robinson |
| 1989 | Breathing Lessons | Anne Tyler | 2006 | March | Geraldine Brooks |
| 1990 | The Mambo Kings Play Songs of Love | Oscar Hijuelos | 2007 | The Road | Cormac McCarthy |
| | | | 2008 | The Brief Wondrous Life of Oscar Wao | Junot Díaz |
| 1991 | Rabbit at Rest | John Updike | | | |
| 1992 | A Thousand Acres | Jane Smiley | 2009 | Olive Kitteridge | Elizabeth Strout |
| 1993 | A Good Scent from a Strange Mountain | Robert Olen Butler | 2010 | Tinkers | Paul Harding |
| | | | 2011 | A Visit from the Goon Squad | Jennifer Egan |
| 1994 | The Shipping News | E. Annie Proulx | | | |
| 1995 | The Stone Diaries | Carol Shields | 2012 | no award | |

[1]Work published and prize awarded posthumously.

### Drama
*Awarded for a play, preferably about American life, by an American author.*

| YEAR | TITLE | AUTHOR | YEAR | TITLE | AUTHOR |
|---|---|---|---|---|---|
| 1917 | no award | | 1946 | State of the Union | Russel Crouse and Howard Lindsay |
| 1918 | Why Marry? | Jesse Lynch Williams | | | |
| 1919 | no award | | 1947 | no award | |
| 1920 | Beyond the Horizon | Eugene O'Neill | 1948 | A Streetcar Named Desire | Tennessee Williams |
| 1921 | Miss Lulu Bett | Zona Gale | | | |
| 1922 | Anna Christie | Eugene O'Neill | 1949 | Death of a Salesman | Arthur Miller |
| 1923 | Icebound | Owen Davis | 1950 | South Pacific | Richard Rodgers, Oscar Hammerstein II, and Joshua Logan |
| 1924 | Hell-Bent fer Heaven | Hatcher Hughes | | | |
| 1925 | They Knew What They Wanted | Sidney Howard | | | |
| 1926 | Craig's Wife | George Kelly | 1951 | no award | |
| 1927 | In Abraham's Bosom | Paul Green | 1952 | The Shrike | Joseph Kramm |
| 1928 | Strange Interlude | Eugene O'Neill | 1953 | Picnic | William Inge |
| 1929 | Street Scene | Elmer L. Rice | 1954 | The Teahouse of the August Moon | John Patrick |
| 1930 | The Green Pastures | Marc Connelly | | | |
| 1931 | Alison's House | Susan Glaspell | 1955 | Cat on a Hot Tin Roof | Tennessee Williams |
| 1932 | Of Thee I Sing | George S. Kaufman, Morrie Ryskind, and Ira Gershwin | | | |
| | | | 1956 | The Diary of Anne Frank | Albert Hackett and Frances Goodrich |
| 1933 | Both Your Houses | Maxwell Anderson | 1957 | Long Day's Journey into Night[1] | Eugene O'Neill |
| 1934 | Men in White | Sidney Kingsley | | | |
| 1935 | The Old Maid | Zoe Akins | 1958 | Look Homeward, Angel | Ketti Frings |
| 1936 | Idiot's Delight | Robert E. Sherwood | 1959 | J.B. | Archibald MacLeish |
| 1937 | You Can't Take It with You | Moss Hart and George S. Kaufman | | | |
| | | | 1960 | Fiorello! | Jerome Weidman, George Abbott, Jerry Bock, and Sheldon Harnick |
| 1938 | Our Town | Thornton Wilder | | | |
| 1939 | Abe Lincoln in Illinois | Robert E. Sherwood | | | |
| 1940 | The Time of Your Life | William Saroyan | 1961 | All the Way Home | Tad Mosel |
| 1941 | There Shall Be No Night | Robert E. Sherwood | 1962 | How To Succeed in Business Without Really Trying | Frank Loesser and Abe Burrows |
| 1942 | no award | | | | |
| 1943 | The Skin of Our Teeth | Thornton Wilder | | | |
| 1944 | no award | | 1963 | no award | |
| 1945 | Harvey | Mary Chase | 1964 | no award | |
| | | | 1965 | The Subject Was Roses | Frank D. Gilroy |

## Letters, Drama, and Music (continued)

### Drama (continued)

| YEAR | TITLE | AUTHOR | YEAR | TITLE | AUTHOR |
|------|-------|--------|------|-------|--------|
| 1966 | no award | | 1988 | Driving Miss Daisy | Alfred Uhry |
| 1967 | A Delicate Balance | Edward Albee | 1989 | The Heidi Chronicles | Wendy Wasserstein |
| 1968 | no award | | 1990 | The Piano Lesson | August Wilson |
| 1969 | The Great White Hope | Howard Sackler | 1991 | Lost in Yonkers | Neil Simon |
| 1970 | No Place To Be Somebody | Charles Gordone | 1992 | The Kentucky Cycle | Robert Schenkkan |
| 1971 | The Effect of Gamma Rays on Man-in-the-Moon Marigolds | Paul Zindel | 1993 | Angels in America: Millennium Approaches | Tony Kushner |
| 1972 | no award | | 1994 | Three Tall Women | Edward Albee |
| 1973 | That Championship Season | Jason Miller | 1995 | The Young Man from Atlanta | Horton Foote |
| 1974 | no award | | 1996 | Rent[1] | Jonathan Larson |
| 1975 | Seascape | Edward Albee | 1997 | no award | |
| 1976 | A Chorus Line | Michael Bennett, James Kirkwood, Nicholas Dante, Marvin Hamlisch, and Edward Kleban | 1998 | How I Learned To Drive | Paula Vogel |
| | | | 1999 | Wit | Margaret Edson |
| | | | 2000 | Dinner with Friends | Donald Margulies |
| | | | 2001 | Proof | David Auburn |
| | | | 2002 | Topdog/Underdog | Suzan-Lori Parks |
| | | | 2003 | Anna in the Tropics | Nilo Cruz |
| | | | 2004 | I Am My Own Wife | Doug Wright |
| 1977 | The Shadow Box | Michael Cristofer | 2005 | Doubt: A Parable | John Patrick Shanley |
| 1978 | The Gin Game | Donald L. Coburn | | | |
| 1979 | Buried Child | Sam Shepard | 2006 | no award | |
| 1980 | Talley's Folly | Lanford Wilson | 2007 | Rabbit Hole | David Lindsay-Abaire |
| 1981 | Crimes of the Heart | Beth Henley | | | |
| 1982 | A Soldier's Play | Charles Fuller | 2008 | August: Osage County | Tracy Letts |
| 1983 | 'Night, Mother | Marsha Norman | 2009 | Ruined | Lynn Nottage |
| 1984 | Glengarry Glen Ross | David Mamet | 2010 | Next to Normal | Tom Kitt and Brian Yorkey |
| 1985 | Sunday in the Park with George | Stephen Sondheim and James Lapine | | | |
| 1986 | no award | | 2011 | Clybourne Park | Bruce Norris |
| 1987 | Fences | August Wilson | 2012 | Water by the Spoonful | Quiara Alegría Hudes |

[1]Awarded posthumously

### History
Awarded for a work on the subject of American history.

| YEAR | TITLE | AUTHOR | YEAR | TITLE | AUTHOR |
|------|-------|--------|------|-------|--------|
| 1917 | With Americans of Past and Present Days | J.J. Jusserand | 1929 | The Organization and Administration of the Union Army, 1861–1865 | Fred Albert Shannon |
| 1918 | History of the Civil War, 1861–1865 | James Ford Rhodes | | | |
| 1919 | no award | | 1930 | The War of Independence | Claude H. Van Tyne |
| 1920 | The War with Mexico, 2 vols. | Justin H. Smith | | | |
| 1921 | The Victory at Sea | William Sowden Sims and Burton Jesse Hendrick | 1931 | The Coming of the War, 1914 | Bernadotte E. Schmitt |
| | | | 1932 | My Experiences in the World War | John J. Pershing |
| 1922 | The Founding of New England | James Truslow Adams | 1933 | The Significance of Sections in American History[1] | Frederick J. Turner |
| 1923 | The Supreme Court in United States History | Charles Warren | | | |
| 1924 | The American Revolution: A Constitutional Interpretation | Charles Howard McIlwain | 1934 | The People's Choice | Herbert Agar |
| | | | 1935 | The Colonial Period of American History | Charles McLean Andrews |
| | | | 1936 | A Constitutional History of the United States | Andrew C. McLaughlin |
| 1925 | History of the American Frontier | Frederic L. Paxson | 1937 | The Flowering of New England, 1815–1865 | Van Wyck Brooks |
| 1926 | A History of the United States | Edward Channing | 1938 | The Road to Reunion, 1865–1900 | Paul Herman Buck |
| 1927 | Pinckney's Treaty | Samuel Flagg Bemis | 1939 | A History of American Magazines | Frank Luther Mott |
| 1928 | Main Currents in American Thought, 2 vols. | Vernon Louis Parrington | 1940 | Abraham Lincoln: The War Years | Carl Sandburg |

# Letters, Drama, and Music (continued)

## History (continued)

| YEAR | TITLE | AUTHOR |
|------|-------|--------|
| 1941 | *The Atlantic Migration, 1607–1860* | Marcus Lee Hansen |
| 1942 | *Reveille in Washington, 1860–1865* | Margaret Leech |
| 1943 | *Paul Revere and the World He Lived In* | Esther Forbes |
| 1944 | *The Growth of American Thought* | Merle Curti |
| 1945 | *Unfinished Business* | Stephen Bonsal |
| 1946 | *The Age of Jackson* | Arthur M. Schlesinger, Jr. |
| 1947 | *Scientists Against Time* | James Phinney Baxter III |
| 1948 | *Across the Wide Missouri* | Bernard De Voto |
| 1949 | *The Disruption of American Democracy* | Roy Franklin Nichols |
| 1950 | *Art and Life in America* | Oliver W. Larkin |
| 1951 | *The Old Northwest: Pioneer Period, 1815–1840* | R. Carlyle Buley |
| 1952 | *The Uprooted* | Oscar Handlin |
| 1953 | *The Era of Good Feelings* | George Dangerfield |
| 1954 | *A Stillness at Appomattox* | Bruce Catton |
| 1955 | *Great River: The Rio Grande in North American History* | Paul Horgan |
| 1956 | *The Age of Reform* | Richard Hofstadter |
| 1957 | *Russia Leaves the War: Soviet-American Relations, 1917–1920* | George F. Kennan |
| 1958 | *Banks and Politics in America* | Bray Hammond |
| 1959 | *The Republican Era: 1869–1901* | Leonard D. White and Jean Schneider |
| 1960 | *In the Days of McKinley* | Margaret Leech |
| 1961 | *Between War and Peace: The Potsdam Conference* | Herbert Feis |
| 1962 | *The Triumphant Empire: Thunder-Clouds Gather in the West, 1763–1766* | Lawrence H. Gipson |
| 1963 | *Washington, Village and Capital, 1800–1878* | Constance McLaughlin Green |
| 1964 | *Puritan Village: The Formation of a New England Town* | Sumner Chilton Powell |
| 1965 | *The Greenback Era* | Irwin Unger |
| 1966 | *The Life of the Mind in America*[1] | Perry Miller |
| 1967 | *Exploration and Empire: The Explorer and the Scientist in the Winning of the American West* | William H. Goetzmann |
| 1968 | *The Ideological Origins of the American Revolution* | Bernard Bailyn |
| 1969 | *Origins of the Fifth Amendment* | Leonard W. Levy |
| 1970 | *Present at the Creation: My Years in the State Department* | Dean Acheson |
| 1971 | *Roosevelt: The Soldier of Freedom* | James MacGregor Burns |
| 1972 | *Neither Black nor White* | Carl N. Degler |
| 1973 | *People of Paradox: An Inquiry Concerning the Origins of American Civilization* | Michael Kammen |
| 1974 | *The Americans: The Democratic Experience* | Daniel J. Boorstin |
| 1975 | *Jefferson and His Time, vols. 1–5* | Dumas Malone |
| 1976 | *Lamy of Santa Fe* | Paul Horgan |
| 1977 | *The Impending Crisis, 1841–1867*[2] | David M. Potter and Don E. Fehrenbacher |
| 1978 | *The Visible Hand: The Managerial Revolution in American Business* | Alfred D. Chandler, Jr. |
| 1979 | *The Dred Scott Case* | Don E. Fehrenbacher |
| 1980 | *Been in the Storm So Long* | Leon F. Litwack |
| 1981 | *American Education: The National Experience, 1783–1876* | Lawrence A. Cremin |
| 1982 | *Mary Chesnut's Civil War* | C. Vann Woodward[3] |
| 1983 | *The Transformation of Virginia, 1740–1790* | Rhys L. Isaac |
| 1984 | no award | |
| 1985 | *Prophets of Regulation* | Thomas K. McCraw |
| 1986 | *The Heavens and the Earth: A Political History of the Space Age* | Walter A. McDougall |
| 1987 | *Voyagers to the West: A Passage in the Peopling of America on the Eve of the Revolution* | Bernard Bailyn |
| 1988 | *The Launching of Modern American Science, 1846–1876* | Robert V. Bruce |
| 1989 | *Battle Cry of Freedom: The Civil War Era* | James M. McPherson |
| | *Parting the Waters: America in the King Years, 1954–1963* | Taylor Branch |
| 1990 | *In Our Image: America's Empire in the Philippines* | Stanley Karnow |
| 1991 | *A Midwife's Tale* | Laurel Thatcher Ulrich |
| 1992 | *The Fate of Liberty: Abraham Lincoln and Civil Liberties* | Mark E. Neely, Jr. |
| 1993 | *The Radicalism of the American Revolution* | Gordon S. Wood |
| 1994 | no award | |
| 1995 | *No Ordinary Time: Franklin and Eleanor Roosevelt: The Home Front in World War II* | Doris Kearns Goodwin |
| 1996 | *William Cooper's Town: Power and Persuasion on the Frontier of the Early American Republic* | Alan Taylor |

## Letters, Drama, and Music (continued)

### History (continued)

| YEAR | TITLE | AUTHOR |
|---|---|---|
| 1997 | Original Meanings: Politics and Ideas in the Making of the Constitution | Jack N. Rakove |
| 1998 | Summer for the Gods: The Scopes Trial and America's Continuing Debate over Science and Religion | Edward J. Larson |
| 1999 | Gotham: A History of New York City to 1898 | Edwin G. Burrows and Mike Wallace |
| 2000 | Freedom from Fear: The American People in Depression and War, 1929–1945 | David M. Kennedy |
| 2001 | Founding Brothers: The Revolutionary Generation | Joseph J. Ellis |
| 2002 | The Metaphysical Club: A Story of Ideas in America | Louis Menand |
| 2003 | An Army at Dawn: The War in North Africa, 1942–1943 | Rick Atkinson |

| YEAR | TITLE | AUTHOR |
|---|---|---|
| 2004 | A Nation Under Our Feet: Black Political Struggles in the Rural South from Slavery to the Great Migration | Steven Hahn |
| 2005 | Washington's Crossing | David Hackett Fischer |
| 2006 | Polio: An American Story | David M. Oshinsky |
| 2007 | The Race Beat: The Press, the Civil Rights Struggle, and the Awakening of a Nation | Gene Roberts and Hank Klibanoff |
| 2008 | What Hath God Wrought: The Transformation of America, 1815–1848 | Daniel Walker Howe |
| 2009 | The Hemingses of Monticello: An American Family | Annette Gordon-Reed |
| 2010 | Lords of Finance: The Bankers Who Broke the World | Liaquat Ahamed |
| 2011 | The Fiery Trial: Abraham Lincoln and American Slavery | Eric Foner |
| 2012 | Malcolm X: A Life of Reinvention[1] | Manning Marable |

[1]Awarded posthumously.   [2]Potter died before completing the work; Fehrenbacher wrote the final chapters and edited it.   [3]Editor.

### Biography or Autobiography
*Awarded for a biography or autobiography by an American author.*

| YEAR | TITLE | AUTHOR |
|---|---|---|
| 1917 | Julia Ward Howe | Laura Elizabeth Howe Richards and Maude Howe Elliott; assisted by Florence Howe Hall |
| 1918 | Benjamin Franklin, Self-Revealed | William Cabell Bruce |
| 1919 | The Education of Henry Adams[1] | Henry Adams |
| 1920 | The Life of John Marshall, 4 vols. | Albert J. Beveridge |
| 1921 | The Americanization of Edward Bok | Edward Bok |
| 1922 | A Daughter of the Middle Border | Hamlin Garland |
| 1923 | The Life and Letters of Walter H. Page | Burton J. Hendrick |
| 1924 | From Immigrant to Inventor | Michael Idvorsky Pupin |
| 1925 | Barrett Wendell and His Letters | M.A. De Wolfe Howe |
| 1926 | The Life of Sir William Osler, 2 vols. | Harvey Cushing |
| 1927 | Whitman | Emory Holloway |
| 1928 | The American Orchestra and Theodore Thomas | Charles Edward Russell |
| 1929 | The Training of an American: The Earlier Life and Letters of Walter H. Page | Burton J. Hendrick |

| YEAR | TITLE | AUTHOR |
|---|---|---|
| 1930 | The Raven | Marquis James |
| 1931 | Charles W. Eliot | Henry James |
| 1932 | Theodore Roosevelt | Henry F. Pringle |
| 1933 | Grover Cleveland | Allan Nevins |
| 1934 | John Hay | Tyler Dennett |
| 1935 | R.E. Lee | Douglas S. Freeman |
| 1936 | The Thought and Character of William James | Ralph Barton Perry |
| 1937 | Hamilton Fish | Allan Nevins |
| 1938 | Andrew Jackson, 2 vols. | Marquis James |
| | Pedlar's Progress | Odell Shepard |
| 1939 | Benjamin Franklin | Carl Van Doren |
| 1940 | Woodrow Wilson, Life and Letters, vols. 7 and 8 | Ray Stannard Baker |
| 1941 | Jonathan Edwards | Ola Elizabeth Winslow |
| 1942 | Crusader in Crinoline | Forrest Wilson |
| 1943 | Admiral of the Ocean Sea | Samuel Eliot Morison |
| 1944 | The American Leonardo: The Life of Samuel F.B. Morse | Carleton Mabee |
| 1945 | George Bancroft: Brahmin Rebel | Russell Blaine Nye |
| 1946 | Son of the Wilderness | Linnie Marsh Wolfe |
| 1947 | The Autobiography of William Allen White | William Allen White |
| 1948 | Forgotten First Citizen: John Bigelow | Margaret Clapp |
| 1949 | Roosevelt and Hopkins | Robert E. Sherwood |

# Letters, Drama, and Music (continued)

<u>Biography or Autobiography</u> (continued)

| YEAR | TITLE | AUTHOR |
|------|-------|--------|
| 1950 | John Quincy Adams and the Foundations of American Foreign Policy | Samuel Flagg Bemis |
| 1951 | John C. Calhoun: American Portrait | Margaret Louise Coit |
| 1952 | Charles Evans Hughes | Merlo J. Pusey |
| 1953 | Edmund Pendleton, 1721–1803 | David J. Mays |
| 1954 | The Spirit of St. Louis | Charles A. Lindbergh |
| 1955 | The Taft Story | William S. White |
| 1956 | Benjamin Henry Latrobe | Talbot Faulkner Hamlin |
| 1957 | Profiles in Courage | John F. Kennedy |
| 1958 | George Washington, 7 vols.[2] | Douglas Southall Freeman, John Alexander Carroll, and Mary Wells Ashworth |
| 1959 | Woodrow Wilson, American Prophet | Arthur Walworth |
| 1960 | John Paul Jones | Samuel Eliot Morison |
| 1961 | Charles Sumner and the Coming of the Civil War | David Herbert Donald |
| 1962 | no award | |
| 1963 | Henry James | Leon Edel |
| 1964 | John Keats | Walter Jackson Bate |
| 1965 | Henry Adams, 3 vols. | Ernest Samuels |
| 1966 | A Thousand Days | Arthur M. Schlesinger, Jr. |
| 1967 | Mr. Clemens and Mark Twain | Justin Kaplan |
| 1968 | Memoirs | George F. Kennan |
| 1969 | The Man from New York: John Quinn and His Friends | Benjamin Lawrence Reid |
| 1970 | Huey Long | T. Harry Williams |
| 1971 | Robert Frost: The Years of Triumph, 1915–1938 | Lawrance Thompson |
| 1972 | Eleanor and Franklin | Joseph P. Lash |
| 1973 | Luce and His Empire | W.A. Swanberg |
| 1974 | O'Neill, Son and Artist | Louis Sheaffer |
| 1975 | The Power Broker: Robert Moses and the Fall of New York | Robert A. Caro |
| 1976 | Edith Wharton: A Biography | R.W.B. Lewis |
| 1977 | A Prince of Our Disorder: The Life of T.E. Lawrence | John E. Mack |
| 1978 | Samuel Johnson | Walter Jackson Bate |
| 1979 | Days of Sorrow and Pain: Leo Baeck and the Berlin Jews | Leonard Baker |
| 1980 | The Rise of Theodore Roosevelt | Edmund Morris |
| 1981 | Peter the Great: His Life and World | Robert K. Massie |
| 1982 | Grant: A Biography | William McFeely |

| YEAR | TITLE | AUTHOR |
|------|-------|--------|
| 1983 | Growing Up | Russell Baker |
| 1984 | Booker T. Washington: The Wizard of Tuskegee, 1901–1915 | Louis R. Harlan |
| 1985 | The Life and Times of Cotton Mather | Kenneth Silverman |
| 1986 | Louise Bogan: A Portrait | Elizabeth Frank |
| 1987 | Bearing the Cross: Martin Luther King, Jr., and the Southern Christian Leadership Conference | David J. Garrow |
| 1988 | Look Homeward: A Life of Thomas Wolfe | David Herbert Donald |
| 1989 | Oscar Wilde[1] | Richard Ellmann |
| 1990 | Machiavelli in Hell | Sebastian de Grazia |
| 1991 | Jackson Pollock | Steven Naifeh and Gregory White Smith |
| 1992 | Fortunate Son: The Healing of a Vietnam Vet | Lewis B. Puller, Jr. |
| 1993 | Truman | David McCullough |
| 1994 | W.E.B. Du Bois: Biography of a Race, 1868–1919 | David Levering Lewis |
| 1995 | Harriet Beecher Stowe: A Life | Joan D. Hedrick |
| 1996 | God: A Biography | Jack Miles |
| 1997 | Angela's Ashes: A Memoir | Frank McCourt |
| 1998 | Personal History | Katharine Graham |
| 1999 | Lindbergh | A. Scott Berg |
| 2000 | Vera (Mrs. Vladimir Nabokov) | Stacy Schiff |
| 2001 | W.E.B. Du Bois: The Fight for Equality and the American Century, 1919–1963 | David Levering Lewis |
| 2002 | John Adams | David McCullough |
| 2003 | Master of the Senate | Robert A. Caro |
| 2004 | Khrushchev: The Man and His Era | William Taubman |
| 2005 | De Kooning: An American Master | Mark Stevens and Annalyn Swan |
| 2006 | American Prometheus: The Triumph and Tragedy | Kai Bird and Martin J. Sherwin |
| 2007 | The Most Famous Man in America: The Biography of Henry Ward Beecher | Debby Applegate |
| 2008 | Eden's Outcasts: The Story of Louisa May Alcott and Her Father | John Matteson |
| 2009 | American Lion: Andrew Jackson in the White House | Jon Meacham |
| 2010 | The First Tycoon: The Epic Life of Cornelius Vanderbilt | T.J. Stiles |
| 2011 | Washington: A Life | Ron Chernow |
| 2012 | George F. Kennan: An American Life | John Lewis Gaddis |

[1]Awarded posthumously.  [2]Freeman died in 1953 after completing vols. 1–6; Carroll and Ashworth continued his work with vol. 7.

# Letters, Drama, and Music (continued)

## Poetry
*Awarded for a collection of original verse by an American author.*

| YEAR | TITLE | AUTHOR | YEAR | TITLE | AUTHOR |
|---|---|---|---|---|---|
| 1922 | Collected Poems | Edwin Arlington Robinson | 1963 | Pictures from Breughel[1] | William Carlos Williams |
| 1923 | The Ballad of the Harp-Weaver; A Few Figs from Thistles; eight sonnets in American Poetry, 1922: A Miscellany | Edna St. Vincent Millay | 1964 | At the End of the Open Road | Louis Simpson |
| | | | 1965 | 77 Dream Songs | John Berryman |
| | | | 1966 | Selected Poems | Richard Eberhart |
| 1924 | New Hampshire: A Poem with Notes and Grace Notes | Robert Frost | 1967 | Live or Die | Anne Sexton |
| | | | 1968 | The Hard Hours | Anthony Hecht |
| | | | 1969 | Of Being Numerous | George Oppen |
| 1925 | The Man Who Died Twice | Edwin Arlington Robinson | 1970 | Untitled Subjects | Richard Howard |
| | | | 1971 | The Carrier of Ladders | W.S. Merwin |
| 1926 | What's O'Clock[1] | Amy Lowell | 1972 | Collected Poems | James Wright |
| 1927 | Fiddler's Farewell | Leonora Speyer | 1973 | Up Country | Maxine Kumin |
| 1928 | Tristram | Edwin Arlington Robinson | 1974 | The Dolphin | Robert Lowell |
| | | | 1975 | Turtle Island | Gary Snyder |
| 1929 | John Brown's Body | Stephen Vincent Benét | 1976 | Self-Portrait in a Convex Mirror | John Ashbery |
| 1930 | Selected Poems | Conrad Aiken | 1977 | Divine Comedies | James Merrill |
| 1931 | Collected Poems | Robert Frost | 1978 | Collected Poems | Howard Nemerov |
| 1932 | The Flowering Stone | George Dillon | 1979 | Now and Then | Robert Penn Warren |
| 1933 | Conquistador | Archibald MacLeish | 1980 | Selected Poems | Donald Justice |
| 1934 | Collected Verse | Robert Hillyer | 1981 | The Morning of the Poem | James Schuyler |
| 1935 | Bright Ambush | Audrey Wurdemann | 1982 | The Collected Poems[2] | Sylvia Plath |
| 1936 | Strange Holiness | Robert P. Tristram Coffin | 1983 | Selected Poems | Galway Kinnell |
| | | | 1984 | American Primitive | Mary Oliver |
| 1937 | A Further Range | Robert Frost | 1985 | Yin | Carolyn Kizer |
| 1938 | Cold Morning Sky | Marya Zaturenska | 1986 | The Flying Change | Henry Taylor |
| 1939 | Selected Poems | John Gould Fletcher | 1987 | Thomas and Beulah | Rita Dove |
| | | | 1988 | Partial Accounts: New and Selected Poems | William Meredith |
| 1940 | Collected Poems | Mark Van Doren | | | |
| 1941 | Sunderland Capture | Leonard Bacon | 1989 | New and Collected Poems | Richard Wilbur |
| 1942 | The Dust Which Is God | William Rose Benét | | | |
| 1943 | A Witness Tree | Robert Frost | 1990 | The World Doesn't End | Charles Simic |
| 1944 | Western Star[1] | Stephen Vincent Benét | 1991 | Near Changes | Mona Van Duyn |
| | | | 1992 | Selected Poems | James Tate |
| 1945 | V-Letter and Other Poems | Karl Shapiro | 1993 | The Wild Iris | Louise Glück |
| 1946 | no award | | 1994 | Neon Vernacular: New and Selected Poems | Yusef Komunyakaa |
| 1947 | Lord Weary's Castle | Robert Lowell | | | |
| 1948 | The Age of Anxiety | W.H. Auden | 1995 | The Simple Truth | Philip Levine |
| 1949 | Terror and Decorum | Peter Viereck | 1996 | The Dream of the Unified Field | Jorie Graham |
| 1950 | Annie Allen | Gwendolyn Brooks | | | |
| 1951 | Complete Poems | Carl Sandburg | 1997 | Alive Together: New and Selected Poems | Lisel Mueller |
| 1952 | Collected Poems | Marianne Moore | | | |
| 1953 | Collected Poems, 1917–1952 | Archibald MacLeish | 1998 | Black Zodiac | Charles Wright |
| | | | 1999 | Blizzard of One | Mark Strand |
| 1954 | The Waking | Theodore Roethke | 2000 | Repair | C.K. Williams |
| 1955 | Collected Poems | Wallace Stevens | 2001 | Different Hours | Stephen Dunn |
| 1956 | Poems: North & South—A Cold Spring | Elizabeth Bishop | 2002 | Practical Gods | Carl Dennis |
| | | | 2003 | Moy Sand and Gravel | Paul Muldoon |
| 1957 | Things of This World | Richard Wilbur | 2004 | Walking to Martha's Vineyard | Franz Wright |
| 1958 | Promises: Poems 1954–1956 | Robert Penn Warren | | | |
| | | | 2005 | Delights & Shadows | Ted Kooser |
| 1959 | Selected Poems, 1928–1958 | Stanley Kunitz | 2006 | Late Wife | Claudia Emerson |
| | | | 2007 | Native Guard | Natasha Trethewey |
| 1960 | Heart's Needle | W.D. Snodgrass | 2008 | Time and Materials | Robert Hass |
| 1961 | Times Three: Selected Verse from Three Decades | Phyllis McGinley | | Failure | Philip Schultz |
| | | | 2009 | The Shadow of Sirius | W.S. Merwin |
| | | | 2010 | Versed | Rae Armantrout |
| 1962 | Poems | Alan Dugan | 2011 | The Best of It: New and Selected Poems | Kay Ryan |
| | | | 2012 | Life on Mars | Tracy K. Smith |

[1]*Awarded posthumously.*    [2]*Work published and prize awarded posthumously.*

## Letters, Drama, and Music (continued)

### General Nonfiction
*Awarded for a work of nonfiction, ineligible for any other category, by an American author.*

| YEAR | TITLE | AUTHOR |
|------|-------|--------|
| 1962 | *The Making of the President, 1960* | Theodore H. White |
| 1963 | *The Guns of August* | Barbara W. Tuchman |
| 1964 | *Anti-intellectualism in American Life* | Richard Hofstadter |
| 1965 | *O Strange New World* | Howard Mumford Jones |
| 1966 | *Wandering Through Winter* | Edwin Way Teale |
| 1967 | *The Problem of Slavery in Western Culture* | David Brion Davis |
| 1968 | *Rousseau and Revolution: A History of Civilization in France, England, and Germany from 1756 and in the Remainder of Europe from 1715 to 1789* | Will and Ariel Durant |
| 1969 | *The Armies of the Night* | Norman Mailer |
| | *So Human an Animal* | Rene Jules Dubos |
| 1970 | *Gandhi's Truth* | Erik H. Erikson |
| 1971 | *The Rising Sun* | John Toland |
| 1972 | *Stilwell and the American Experience in China, 1911–1945* | Barbara W. Tuchman |
| 1973 | *Fire in the Lake: The Vietnamese and the Americans in Vietnam* | Frances Fitzgerald |
| | *Children of Crisis, vols. 2 and 3* | Robert Coles |
| 1974 | *The Denial of Death*[1] | Ernest Becker |
| 1975 | *Pilgrim at Tinker Creek* | Annie Dillard |
| 1976 | *Why Survive?: Being Old in America* | Robert N. Butler |
| 1977 | *Beautiful Swimmers* | William W. Warner |
| 1978 | *The Dragons of Eden* | Carl Sagan |
| 1979 | *On Human Nature* | Edward O. Wilson |
| 1980 | *Gödel, Escher, Bach: An Eternal Golden Braid* | Douglas R. Hofstadter |
| 1981 | *Fin-de-Siècle Vienna: Politics and Culture* | Carl E. Schorske |
| 1982 | *The Soul of a New Machine* | Tracy Kidder |
| 1983 | *Is There No Place on Earth for Me?* | Susan Sheehan |
| 1984 | *The Social Transformation of American Medicine* | Paul Starr |
| 1985 | *The Good War: An Oral History of World War Two* | Studs Terkel |
| 1986 | *Common Ground: A Turbulent Decade in the Lives of Three American Families* | J. Anthony Lukas |
| | *Move Your Shadow: South Africa, Black and White* | Joseph Lelyveld |
| 1987 | *Arab and Jew: Wounded Spirits in a Promised Land* | David K. Shipler |
| 1988 | *The Making of the Atomic Bomb* | Richard Rhodes |
| 1989 | *A Bright Shining Lie: John Paul Vann and America in Vietnam* | Neil Sheehan |
| 1990 | *And Their Children After Them* | Dale Maharidge and Michael Williamson |
| 1991 | *The Ants* | Bert Holldobler and Edward O. Wilson |
| 1992 | *The Prize: The Epic Quest for Oil, Money, and Power* | Daniel Yergin |
| 1993 | *Lincoln at Gettysburg: The Words That Remade America* | Garry Wills |
| 1994 | *Lenin's Tomb: The Last Days of the Soviet Empire* | David Remnick |
| 1995 | *The Beak of the Finch: A Story of Evolution in Our Time* | Jonathan Weiner |
| 1996 | *The Haunted Land: Facing Europe's Ghosts After Communism* | Tina Rosenberg |
| 1997 | *Ashes to Ashes: America's Hundred-Year Cigarette War, the Public Health, and the Unabashed Triumph of Philip Morris* | Richard Kluger |
| 1998 | *Guns, Germs, and Steel* | Jared Diamond |
| 1999 | *Annals of the Former World* | John McPhee |
| 2000 | *Embracing Defeat: Japan in the Wake of World War II* | John W. Dower |
| 2001 | *Hirohito and the Making of Modern Japan* | Herbert P. Bix |
| 2002 | *Carry Me Home: Birmingham, Alabama, the Climactic Battle of the Civil Rights Revolution* | Diane McWhorter |
| 2003 | *"A Problem from Hell": America and the Age of Genocide* | Samantha Power |
| 2004 | *Gulag: A History* | Anne Applebaum |
| 2005 | *Ghost Wars* | Steve Coll |
| 2006 | *Imperial Reckoning: The Untold Story of Britain's Gulag in Kenya* | Caroline Elkins |
| 2007 | *The Looming Tower: Al-Qaeda and the Road to 9/11* | Lawrence Wright |
| 2008 | *The Years of Extermination: Nazi Germany and the Jews, 1939–1945* | Saul Friedländer |
| 2009 | *Slavery by Another Name: The Re-Enslavement of Black Americans from the Civil War to World War II* | Douglas A. Blackmon |
| 2010 | *The Dead Hand: The Untold Story of the Cold War Arms Race and Its Dangerous Legacy* | David E. Hoffman |
| 2011 | *The Emperor of All Maladies: A Biography of Cancer* | Siddhartha Mukherjee |
| 2012 | *The Swerve: How the World Became Modern* | Stephen Greenblatt |

[1]*Awarded posthumously.*

## Letters, Drama, and Music (continued)

### Music
*Awarded for a musical piece of "significant dimension" composed by an American and first performed or recorded in the United States between 16 January of the previous year and 15 January of the year of the award.*

| YEAR | TITLE | COMPOSER | YEAR | TITLE | COMPOSER |
|------|-------|----------|------|-------|----------|
| 1943 | Secular Cantata No. 2: A Free Song | William Schuman | 1981 | no award | |
| 1944 | Symphony No. 4, Opus 34 | Howard Hanson | 1982 | Concerto for Orchestra | Roger Sessions |
| 1945 | Appalachian Spring | Aaron Copland | 1983 | Symphony No. 1 (Three Movements for Orchestra) | Ellen Taaffe Zwilich |
| 1946 | The Canticle of the Sun | Leo Sowerby | | | |
| 1947 | Symphony No. 3 | Charles Ives | 1984 | "Canti del sole" for Tenor and Orchestra | Bernard Rands |
| 1948 | Symphony No. 3 | Walter Piston | | | |
| 1949 | music for the film Louisiana Story | Virgil Thomson | 1985 | Symphony RiverRun | Stephen Albert |
| | | | 1986 | Wind Quintet IV | George Perle |
| 1950 | The Consul | Gian Carlo Menotti | 1987 | The Flight into Egypt | John Harbison |
| 1951 | Giants in the Earth | Douglas S. Moore | 1988 | 12 New Etudes for Piano | William Bolcom |
| 1952 | Symphony Concertante | Gail Kubik | 1989 | Whispers out of Time | Roger Reynolds |
| 1953 | no award | | 1990 | "Duplicates": A Concerto for Two Pianos and Orchestra | Mel Powell |
| 1954 | Concerto for Two Pianos and Orchestra | Quincy Porter | | | |
| 1955 | The Saint of Bleecker Street | Gian Carlo Menotti | 1991 | Symphony | Shulamit Ran |
| | | | 1992 | The Face of the Night, the Heart of the Dark | Wayne Peterson |
| 1956 | Symphony No. 3 | Ernst Toch | | | |
| 1957 | Meditation on Ecclesiastes | Norman Dello Joio | 1993 | Trombone Concerto | Christopher Rouse |
| | | | 1994 | Of Reminiscences and Reflections | Gunther Schuller |
| 1958 | Vanessa | Samuel Barber | | | |
| 1959 | Concerto for Piano and Orchestra | John LaMontaine | 1995 | Stringmusic | Morton Gould |
| | | | 1996 | Lilacs, for Voice and Orchestra | George Walker |
| 1960 | Second String Quartet | Elliott Carter | | | |
| 1961 | Symphony No. 7 | Walter Piston | 1997 | Blood on the Fields | Wynton Marsalis |
| 1962 | The Crucible | Robert Ward | 1998 | String Quartet No. 2 (Musica Instrumentalis) | Aaron Jay Kernis |
| 1963 | Piano Concerto No. 1 | Samuel Barber | | | |
| 1964 | no award | | | | |
| 1965 | no award | | 1999 | Concerto for Flute, Strings, and Percussion | Melinda Wagner |
| 1966 | Variations for Orchestra | Leslie Bassett | | | |
| 1967 | Quartet No. 3 | Leon Kirchner | 2000 | Life Is a Dream, Opera in Three Acts: Act II, Concert Version | Lewis Spratlan |
| 1968 | Echoes of Time and the River | George Crumb | | | |
| 1969 | String Quartet No. 3 | Karel Husa | 2001 | Symphony No. 2 for String Orchestra | John Corigliano |
| 1970 | Time's Encomium | Charles Wuorinen | | | |
| 1971 | Synchronisms No. 6 for Piano and Electronic Sound | Mario Davidovsky | 2002 | Ice Field | Henry Brant |
| | | | 2003 | On the Transmigration of Souls | John Adams |
| 1972 | Windows | Jacob Druckman | | | |
| 1973 | String Quartet No. 3 | Elliott Carter | 2004 | Tempest Fantasy | Paul Moravec |
| 1974 | Notturno | Donald Martino | 2005 | Second Concerto for Orchestra | Steven Stucky |
| 1975 | From the Diary of Virginia Woolf | Dominick Argento | 2006 | Piano Concerto: "Chiavi in mano" | Yehudi Wyner |
| 1976 | Air Music | Ned Rorem | | | |
| 1977 | Visions of Terror and Wonder | Richard Wernick | 2007 | Sound Grammar | Ornette Coleman |
| | | | 2008 | The Little Match Girl Passion | David Lang |
| 1978 | Deja Vu for Percussion Quartet and Orchestra | Michael Colgrass | | | |
| | | | 2009 | Double Sextet | Steve Reich |
| 1979 | Aftertones of Infinity | Joseph Schwantner | 2010 | Violin Concerto | Jennifer Higdon |
| 1980 | In Memory of a Summer Day | David Del Tredici | 2011 | Madame White Snake | Zhou Long |
| | | | 2012 | Silent Night: Opera in Two Acts | Kevin Puts |

### Special Awards and Citations[1]

| YEAR | RECIPIENT | FOR | YEAR | RECIPIENT | FOR |
|------|-----------|-----|------|-----------|-----|
| 1987 | Joseph Pulitzer, Jr. | his contributions to journalism and letters | 1998 | George Gershwin[2] | centennial commemoration of his birth, celebrating his work in music |
| 1992 | Art Spiegelman | his graphic novel *Maus* | | | |
| 1996 | Herb Caen | his contributions as a voice of San Francisco | | | |

## Letters, Drama, and Music (continued)

**Special Awards and Citations[1] (continued)**

| YEAR | RECIPIENT | FOR | YEAR | RECIPIENT | FOR |
|------|-----------|-----|------|-----------|-----|
| 1999 | Duke Ellington[2] | centennial commemoration of his birth, celebrating his life's work in music | 2007 (cont.) | John Coltrane[2] | his contributions to jazz music |
| 2006 | Edmund S. Morgan | his life's work as an American historian | 2008 | Bob Dylan | his profound influence on pop culture and American music |
| | Thelonious Monk[2] | his contributions to jazz | 2010 | Hank Williams[2] | his role, as a songwriter and performer, in advancing country music |
| 2007 | Ray Bradbury | his contributions to science fiction and fantasy | | | |

[1]For the past 25 years.    [2]Awarded posthumously.

## National Book Awards

The National Book Awards were established in 1950 to honor exceptional books written by Americans. The awards recognize achievements in four genres: fiction, nonfiction, poetry, and young people's literature. A five-member judging panel chooses a winner for each genre. Award: US$10,000 cash and a bronze sculpture.

### Fiction

| YEAR | TITLE | AUTHOR |
|------|-------|--------|
| 1950 | The Man with the Golden Arm | Nelson Algren |
| 1951 | The Collected Stories of William Faulkner | William Faulkner |
| 1952 | From Here to Eternity | James Jones |
| 1953 | Invisible Man | Ralph Ellison |
| 1954 | The Adventures of Augie March | Saul Bellow |
| 1955 | A Fable | William Faulkner |
| 1956 | Ten North Frederick | John O'Hara |
| 1957 | The Field of Vision | Wright Morris |
| 1958 | The Wapshot Chronicle | John Cheever |
| 1959 | The Magic Barrel | Bernard Malamud |
| 1960 | Goodbye, Columbus | Philip Roth |
| 1961 | The Waters of Kronos | Conrad Richter |
| 1962 | The Moviegoer | Walker Percy |
| 1963 | Morte d'Urban | J.F. Powers |
| 1964 | The Centaur | John Updike |
| 1965 | Herzog | Saul Bellow |
| 1966 | The Collected Stories of Katherine Anne Porter | Katherine Anne Porter |
| 1967 | The Fixer | Bernard Malamud |
| 1968 | The Eighth Day | Thornton Wilder |
| 1969 | Steps | Jerzy Kosinski |
| 1970 | them | Joyce Carol Oates |
| 1971 | Mr. Sammler's Planet | Saul Bellow |
| 1972 | The Complete Stories | Flannery O'Connor |
| 1973 | Augustus | John Williams |
| | Chimera | John Barth |
| 1974 | A Crown of Feathers and Other Stories | Isaac Bashevis Singer |
| | Gravity's Rainbow | Thomas Pynchon |
| 1975 | Dog Soldiers: A Novel | Robert Stone |
| | The Hair of Harold Roux | Thomas Williams |
| 1976 | J.R. | William Gaddis |
| 1977 | The Spectator Bird | Wallace Stegner |
| 1978 | Blood Tie | Mary Lee Settle |

### Fiction (continued)

| YEAR | TITLE | AUTHOR |
|------|-------|--------|
| 1979 | Going After Cacciato | Tim O'Brien |
| 1980 | Sophie's Choice[1] | William Styron |
| 1981 | Plains Song[1] | Wright Morris |
| 1982 | Rabbit Is Rich[1] | John Updike |
| 1983 | The Color Purple[1] | Alice Walker |
| 1984 | Victory over Japan: A Book of Stories | Ellen Gilchrist |
| 1985 | White Noise | Don DeLillo |
| 1986 | World's Fair | E.L. Doctorow |
| 1987 | Paco's Story | Larry Heinemann |
| 1988 | Paris Trout | Pete Dexter |
| 1989 | Spartina | John Casey |
| 1990 | Middle Passage | Charles Johnson |
| 1991 | Mating | Norman Rush |
| 1992 | All the Pretty Horses | Cormac McCarthy |
| 1993 | The Shipping News | E. Annie Proulx |
| 1994 | A Frolic of His Own | William Gaddis |
| 1995 | Sabbath's Theater | Philip Roth |
| 1996 | Ship Fever | Andrea Barrett |
| 1997 | Cold Mountain | Charles Frazier |
| 1998 | Charming Billy | Alice McDermott |
| 1999 | Waiting | Ha Jin |
| 2000 | In America | Susan Sontag |
| 2001 | The Corrections | Jonathan Franzen |
| 2002 | Three Junes | Julia Glass |
| 2003 | The Great Fire | Shirley Hazzard |
| 2004 | The News from Paraguay | Lily Tuck |
| 2005 | Europe Central | William T. Vollmann |
| 2006 | The Echo Maker | Richard Powers |
| 2007 | Tree of Smoke | Denis Johnson |
| 2008 | Shadow Country | Peter Matthiessen |
| 2009 | Let the Great World Spin | Colum McCann |
| 2010 | Lord of Misrule | Jaimy Gordon |
| 2011 | Salvage the Bones | Jesmyn Ward |

### Nonfiction

| YEAR | TITLE | AUTHOR |
|------|-------|--------|
| 1950 | The Life of Ralph Waldo Emerson | Ralph L. Rusk |
| 1951 | Herman Melville | Newton Arvin |
| 1952 | The Sea Around Us | Rachel Carson |
| 1953 | The Course of Empire | Bernard A. De Voto |
| 1954 | A Stillness at Appomattox | Bruce Catton |

# National Book Awards (continued)

## Nonfiction (continued)

| YEAR | TITLE | AUTHOR |
|------|-------|--------|
| 1955 | *The Measure of Man: On Freedom, Human Values, Survival, and the Modern Temper* | Joseph Wood Krutch |
| 1956 | *American in Italy* | Herbert Kubly |
| 1957 | *Russia Leaves the War* | George F. Kennan |
| 1958 | *The Lion and the Throne: The Life and Times of Sir Edward Coke (1552–1634)* | Catherine Drinker Bowen |
| 1959 | *Mistress to an Age: A Life of Madame de Staël* | J. Christopher Herold |
| 1960 | *James Joyce* | Richard Ellmann |
| 1961 | *The Rise and Fall of the Third Reich: A History of Nazi Germany* | William L. Shirer |
| 1962 | *The City in History: Its Origins, Its Transformations, and Its Prospects* | Lewis Mumford |
| 1963 | *Henry James, Vol. II: The Conquest of London (1870–1881); Vol. III: The Middle Years (1882–1895)* | Leon Edel |
| 1964 | *The Rise of the West: A History of the Human Community[2]* | William H. McNeill |
| 1965 | *The Life of Lenin[2]* | Louis Fischer |
| 1966 | *A Thousand Days: John F. Kennedy in the White House[2]* | Arthur M. Schlesinger, Jr. |
| 1967 | *The Enlightenment: An Interpretation, Vol. I[2]* | Peter Gay |
| 1968 | *Memoirs: 1925–1950[2]* | George F. Kennan |
| 1969 | *White over Black: American Attitudes Toward the Negro, 1550–1812[2]* | Winthrop D. Jordan |
| 1970 | *Huey Long[2]* | T. Harry Williams |
| 1971 | *Roosevelt: The Soldier of Freedom[2]* | James MacGregor Burns |
| 1972 | *Eleanor and Franklin: The Story of Their Relationship, Based on Eleanor Roosevelt's Private Papers[3]* | Joseph P. Lash |
| 1973 | *George Washington, Vol. IV: Anguish and Farewell, 1793–1799[3]* | James Thomas Flexner |
| 1974 | *Macaulay: The Shaping of the Historian[4]* | John Clive |
| 1975 | *The Life of Emily Dickinson[3]* | Richard B. Sewall |
| 1976 | *The Problem of Slavery in the Age of Revolution, 1770–1823[2]* | David Brion Davis |
| 1977 | *Norman Thomas: The Last Idealist[5]* | W.A. Swanberg |
| 1978 | *Samuel Johnson[5]* | W. Jackson Bate |
| 1979 | *Robert Kennedy and His Times[5]* | Arthur M. Schlesinger, Jr. |
| 1980 | *The Right Stuff[6]* | Tom Wolfe |
| 1981 | *China Men[6]* | Maxine Hong Kingston |
| 1982 | *The Soul of a New Machine[6]* | Tracy Kidder |
| 1983 | *China: Alive in the Bitter Sea[6]* | Fox Butterfield |
| 1984 | *Andrew Jackson and the Course of American Democracy, 1833–1845* | Robert V. Remini |
| 1985 | *Common Ground: A Turbulent Decade in the Lives of Three American Families* | J. Anthony Lukas |
| 1986 | *Arctic Dreams* | Barry Lopez |
| 1987 | *The Making of the Atomic Bomb* | Richard Rhodes |
| 1988 | *A Bright Shining Lie: John Paul Vann and America in Vietnam* | Neil Sheehan |
| 1989 | *From Beirut to Jerusalem* | Thomas L. Friedman |
| 1990 | *The House of Morgan: An American Banking Dynasty and the Rise of Modern Finance* | Ron Chernow |
| 1991 | *Freedom* | Orlando Patterson |
| 1992 | *Becoming a Man: Half a Life Story* | Paul Monette |
| 1993 | *United States: Essays, 1952–1992* | Gore Vidal |
| 1994 | *How We Die: Reflections on Life's Final Chapter* | Sherwin B. Nuland |
| 1995 | *The Haunted Land: Facing Europe's Ghosts After Communism* | Tina Rosenberg |
| 1996 | *An American Requiem: God, My Father, and the War That Came Between Us* | James Carroll |
| 1997 | *American Sphinx: The Character of Thomas Jefferson* | Joseph J. Ellis |
| 1998 | *Slaves in the Family* | Edward Ball |
| 1999 | *Embracing Defeat: Japan in the Wake of World War II* | John W. Dower |
| 2000 | *In the Heart of the Sea: The Tragedy of the Whaleship Essex* | Nathaniel Philbrick |
| 2001 | *The Noonday Demon: An Atlas of Depression* | Andrew Solomon |
| 2002 | *Master of the Senate: The Years of Lyndon Johnson* | Robert A. Caro |
| 2003 | *Waiting for Snow in Havana* | Carlos Eire |
| 2004 | *Arc of Justice: A Saga of Race, Civil Rights, and Murder in the Jazz Age* | Kevin Boyle |
| 2005 | *The Year of Magical Thinking* | Joan Didion |
| 2006 | *The Worst Hard Time: The Untold Story of Those Who Survived the Great American Dust Bowl* | Timothy Egan |
| 2007 | *Legacy of Ashes: The History of the CIA* | Tim Weiner |
| 2008 | *The Hemingses of Monticello: An American Family* | Annette Gordon-Reed |
| 2009 | *The First Tycoon: The Epic Life of Cornelius Vanderbilt* | T.J. Stiles |
| 2010 | *Just Kids* | Patti Smith |
| 2011 | *The Swerve: How the World Became Modern* | Stephen Greenblatt |

## Poetry

| YEAR | TITLE | AUTHOR |
|------|-------|--------|
| 1950 | *Paterson: Book III and Selected Poems* | William Carlos Williams |
| 1951 | *The Auroras of Autumn* | Wallace Stevens |
| 1952 | *Collected Poems* | Marianne Moore |

# National Book Awards (continued)

## Poetry (continued)

| YEAR | TITLE | AUTHOR |
|---|---|---|
| 1953 | *Collected Poems, 1917–1952* | Archibald MacLeish |
| 1954 | *Collected Poems* | Conrad Aiken |
| 1955 | *The Collected Poems of Wallace Stevens* | Wallace Stevens |
| 1956 | *The Shield of Achilles* | W.H. Auden |
| 1957 | *Things of This World: Poems* | Richard Wilbur |
| 1958 | *Promises: Poems, 1954–1956* | Robert Penn Warren |
| 1959 | *Words for the Wind: The Collected Verse of Theodore Roethke* | Theodore Roethke |
| 1960 | *Life Studies* | Robert Lowell |
| 1961 | *The Woman at the Washington Zoo* | Randall Jarrell |
| 1962 | *Poems* | Alan Dugan |
| 1963 | *Traveling Through the Dark* | William Stafford |
| 1964 | *Selected Poems* | John Crowe Ransom |
| 1965 | *The Far Field* | Theodore Roethke |
| 1966 | *Buckdancer's Choice: Poems* | James Dickey |
| 1967 | *Nights and Days* | James Merrill |
| 1968 | *The Light Around the Body: Poems* | Robert Bly |
| 1969 | *His Toy, His Dream, His Rest: 308 Dream Songs* | John Berryman |
| 1970 | *The Complete Poems* | Elizabeth Bishop |
| 1971 | *To See, To Take: Poems* | Mona Van Duyn |
| 1972 | *The Collected Poems of Frank O'Hara* | Frank O'Hara |
|  | *Selected Poems* | Howard Moss |
| 1973 | *Collected Poems, 1951–1971* | A.R. Ammons |
| 1974 | *Diving into the Wreck: Poems, 1971–1972* | Adrienne Rich |
|  | *The Fall of America: Poems of These States* | Allen Ginsberg |
| 1975 | *Presentation Piece* | Marilyn Hacker |
| 1976 | *Self-Portrait in a Convex Mirror: Poems* | John Ashbery |
| 1977 | *Collected Poems, 1930–1976* | Richard Eberhart |
| 1978 | *The Collected Poems of Howard Nemerov* | Howard Nemerov |
| 1979 | *Mirabell: Books of Number* | James Merrill |
| 1980 | *Ashes: Poems New & Old* | Philip Levine |
| 1981 | *The Need to Hold Still* | Lisel Mueller |
| 1982 | *Life Supports: New and Collected Poems* | William Bronk |
| 1983 | *Country Music: Selected Early Poems* | Charles Wright |
| 1984 | *Selected Poems* | Galway Kinnell |
| 1985 | *Yin* | Carolyn Kizer |
| 1986 | *The Flying Change* | Henry Taylor |
| 1987 | *Thomas and Beulah* | Rita Dove |
| 1988 | *Partial Accounts: New and Selected Poems* | William Meredith |
| 1989 | *New and Collected Poems* | Richard Wilbur |
| 1990 | *The World Doesn't End* | Charles Simic |
| 1991 | *What Work Is: Poems* | Philip Levine |
| 1992 | *New and Selected Poems* | Mary Oliver |
| 1993 | *Garbage* | A.R. Ammons |
| 1994 | *Worshipful Company of Fletchers: Poems* | James Tate |
| 1995 | *Passing Through: The Later Poems, New and Selected* | Stanley Kunitz |
| 1996 | *Scrambled Eggs & Whiskey: Poems, 1991–1995* | Hayden Carruth |
| 1997 | *Effort at Speech: New and Selected Poems* | William Meredith |
| 1998 | *This Time: New and Selected Poems* | Gerald Stern |
| 1999 | *Vice: New and Selected Poems* | Ai |
| 2000 | *Blessing the Boats: New and Selected Poems, 1988–2000* | Lucille Clifton |
| 2001 | *Poems Seven: New and Complete Poetry* | Alan Dugan |
| 2002 | *In the Next Galaxy* | Ruth Stone |
| 2003 | *The Singing* | C.K. Williams |
| 2004 | *Door in the Mountain: New and Collected Poems, 1965–2003* | Jean Valentine |
| 2005 | *Migration: New and Selected Poems* | W.S. Merwin |
| 2006 | *Splay Anthem* | Nathaniel Mackey |
| 2007 | *Time and Materials* | Robert Hass |
| 2008 | *Fire to Fire: New and Collected Poems* | Mark Doty |
| 2009 | *Transcendental Studies: A Trilogy* | Keith Waldrop |
| 2010 | *Lighthead* | Terrance Hayes |
| 2011 | *Head Off & Split* | Nikky Finney |

## Young People's Literature

| YEAR | TITLE | AUTHOR |
|---|---|---|
| 1969 | *Journey from Peppermint Street* | Meindert De Jong |
| 1970 | *A Day of Pleasure: Stories of a Boy Growing Up in Warsaw*[7] | Isaac Bashevis Singer |
| 1971 | *The Marvelous Misadventures of Sebastian*[7] | Lloyd Alexander |

# National Book Awards (continued)

**Young People's Literature (continued)**

| YEAR | TITLE | AUTHOR |
|---|---|---|
| 1972 | The Slightly Irregular Fire Engine; or, The Hithering Thithering Djinn[7] | Donald Barthelme |
| 1973 | The Farthest Shore[7] | Ursula Le Guin |
| 1974 | The Court of the Stone Children[7] | Eleanor Cameron |
| 1975 | M.C. Higgins, the Great[7] | Virginia Hamilton |
| 1976 | Bert Breen's Barn | Walter D. Edmonds |
| 1977 | The Master Puppeteer | Katherine Paterson |
| 1978 | The View from the Oak: The Private Worlds of Other Creatures | Judith and Herbert Kohl |
| 1979 | The Great Gilly Hopkins | Katherine Paterson |
| 1980 | A Gathering of Days: A New England Girl's Journal, 1830–32[8] | Joan W. Blos |
| 1981 | The Night Swimmers[9] | Betsy Byars |
| 1982 | Westmark[9] | Lloyd Alexander |
| 1983 | Homesick: My Own Story[6] | Jean Fritz |
| 1996 | Parrot in the Oven: Mi Vida | Victor Martinez |
| 1997 | Dancing on the Edge | Han Nolan |
| 1998 | Holes | Louis Sachar |
| 1999 | When Zachary Beaver Came to Town | Kimberly Willis Holt |
| 2000 | Homeless Bird | Gloria Whelan |
| 2001 | True Believer | Virginia Euwer Wolff |
| 2002 | The House of the Scorpion | Nancy Farmer |
| 2003 | The Canning Season | Polly Horvath |
| 2004 | The Godless | Pete Hautman |
| 2005 | The Penderwicks | Jeanne Birdsall |
| 2006 | The Astonishing Life of Octavian Nothing, Traitor to the Nation, Vol. 1: The Pox Party | M.T. Anderson |
| 2007 | The Absolutely True Diary of a Part-Time Indian | Sherman Alexie |
| 2008 | What I Saw and How I Lied | Judy Blundell |
| 2009 | Claudette Colvin: Twice Toward Justice | Phillip Hoose |
| 2010 | Mockingbird | Kathryn Erskine |
| 2011 | Inside Out & Back Again | Thanhha Lai |

[1]Fiction (Hardcover).  [2]History and Biography (Nonfiction).  [3]Biography.  [4]History.  [5]Biography and Autobiography.  [6]General Nonfiction (Hardcover).  [7]Children's Books.  [8]Children's Books (Hardcover).  [9]Children's Books, Fiction (Hardcover).

# Newbery Medal

The American Library Association began awarding the John Newbery Medal in 1922 to the author of the most distinguished American children's book of the previous year. The award is named for John Newbery, the 18th-century English publisher who was among the first to publish books exclusively for children. Prize: inscribed bronze medal.

**ALA Newbery Medal Web site:**
<www.ala.org/alsc/awardsgrants/bookmedia/newberymedal/newberymedal>.

| YEAR | TITLE | AUTHOR |
|---|---|---|
| 1922 | The Story of Mankind | Hendrik Willem van Loon |
| 1923 | The Voyages of Doctor Dolittle | Hugh Lofting |
| 1924 | The Dark Frigate | Charles Hawes |
| 1925 | Tales from Silver Lands | Charles Finger |
| 1926 | Shen of the Sea | Arthur Bowie Chrisman |
| 1927 | Smoky, the Cowhorse | Will James |
| 1928 | Gay Neck, the Story of a Pigeon | Dhan Gopal Mukerji |
| 1929 | The Trumpeter of Krakow | Eric P. Kelly |
| 1930 | Hitty, Her First Hundred Years | Rachel Field |
| 1931 | The Cat Who Went to Heaven | Elizabeth Coatsworth |
| 1932 | Waterless Mountain | Laura Adams Armer |
| 1933 | Young Fu of the Upper Yangtze | Elizabeth Lewis |
| 1934 | Invincible Louisa: The Story of the Author of Little Women | Cornelia Meigs |
| 1935 | Dobry | Monica Shannon |
| 1936 | Caddie Woodlawn | Carol Ryrie Brink |
| 1937 | Roller Skates | Ruth Sawyer |
| 1938 | The White Stag | Kate Seredy |
| 1939 | Thimble Summer | Elizabeth Enright |
| 1940 | Daniel Boone | James Daugherty |
| 1941 | Call It Courage | Armstrong Sperry |
| 1942 | The Matchlock Gun | Walter Edmonds |
| 1943 | Adam of the Road | Elizabeth Janet Gray |
| 1944 | Johnny Tremain | Esther Forbes |
| 1945 | Rabbit Hill | Robert Lawson |
| 1946 | Strawberry Girl | Lois Lenski |
| 1947 | Miss Hickory | Carolyn Sherwin Bailey |
| 1948 | The Twenty-One Balloons | William Pène du Bois |
| 1949 | King of the Wind | Marguerite Henry |
| 1950 | The Door in the Wall | Marguerite de Angeli |
| 1951 | Amos Fortune, Free Man | Elizabeth Yates |
| 1952 | Ginger Pye | Eleanor Estes |

## Newbery Medal (continued)

| YEAR | TITLE | AUTHOR |
|------|-------|--------|
| 1953 | Secret of the Andes | Ann Nolan Clark |
| 1954 | ...And Now Miguel | Joseph Krumgold |
| 1955 | The Wheel on the School | Meindert De Jong |
| 1956 | Carry On, Mr. Bowditch | Jean Lee Latham |
| 1957 | Miracles on Maple Hill | Virginia Sorenson |
| 1958 | Rifles for Watie | Harold Keith |
| 1959 | The Witch of Blackbird Pond | Elizabeth George Speare |
| 1960 | Onion John | Joseph Krumgold |
| 1961 | Island of the Blue Dolphins | Scott O'Dell |
| 1962 | The Bronze Bow | Elizabeth George Speare |
| 1963 | A Wrinkle in Time | Madeleine L'Engle |
| 1964 | It's Like This, Cat | Emily Neville |
| 1965 | Shadow of a Bull | Maia Wojciechowska |
| 1966 | I, Juan de Pareja | Elizabeth Borton de Treviño |
| 1967 | Up a Road Slowly | Irene Hunt |
| 1968 | From the Mixed-Up Files of Mrs. Basil E. Frankweiler | E.L. Konigsburg |
| 1969 | The High King | Lloyd Alexander |
| 1970 | Sounder | William H. Armstrong |
| 1971 | Summer of the Swans | Betsy Byars |
| 1972 | Mrs. Frisby and the Rats of NIMH | Robert C. O'Brien |
| 1973 | Julie of the Wolves | Jean Craighead George |
| 1974 | The Slave Dancer | Paula Fox |
| 1975 | M.C. Higgins, the Great | Virginia Hamilton |
| 1976 | The Grey King | Susan Cooper |
| 1977 | Roll of Thunder, Hear My Cry | Mildred D. Taylor |
| 1978 | Bridge to Terabithia | Katherine Paterson |
| 1979 | The Westing Game | Ellen Raskin |
| 1980 | A Gathering of Days: A New England Girl's Journal, 1830–1832 | Joan W. Blos |
| 1981 | Jacob Have I Loved | Katherine Paterson |
| 1982 | A Visit to William Blake's Inn: Poems for Innocent and Experienced Travelers | Nancy Willard |

| YEAR | TITLE | AUTHOR |
|------|-------|--------|
| 1983 | Dicey's Song | Cynthia Voigt |
| 1984 | Dear Mr. Henshaw | Beverly Cleary |
| 1985 | The Hero and the Crown | Robin McKinley |
| 1986 | Sarah, Plain and Tall | Patricia MacLachlan |
| 1987 | The Whipping Boy | Sid Fleischman |
| 1988 | Lincoln: A Photo-biography | Russell Freedman |
| 1989 | Joyful Noise: Poems for Two Voices | Paul Fleischman |
| 1990 | Number the Stars | Lois Lowry |
| 1991 | Maniac Magee | Jerry Spinelli |
| 1992 | Shiloh | Phyllis Reynolds Naylor |
| 1993 | Missing May | Cynthia Rylant |
| 1994 | The Giver | Lois Lowry |
| 1995 | Walk Two Moons | Sharon Creech |
| 1996 | The Midwife's Apprentice | Karen Cushman |
| 1997 | The View from Saturday | E.L. Konigsburg |
| 1998 | Out of the Dust | Karen Hesse |
| 1999 | Holes | Louis Sachar |
| 2000 | Bud, Not Buddy | Christopher Paul Curtis |
| 2001 | A Year Down Yonder | Richard Peck |
| 2002 | A Single Shard | Linda Sue Park |
| 2003 | Crispin: The Cross of Lead | Avi |
| 2004 | The Tale of Despereaux: Being the Story of a Mouse, a Princess, Some Soup, and a Spool of Thread | Kate DiCamillo |
| 2005 | Kira-Kira | Cynthia Kadohata |
| 2006 | Criss Cross | Lynne Rae Perkins |
| 2007 | The Higher Power of Lucky | Susan Patron |
| 2008 | Good Masters! Sweet Ladies! Voices from a Medieval Village | Laura Amy Schlitz |
| 2009 | The Graveyard Book | Neil Gaiman |
| 2010 | When You Reach Me | Rebecca Stead |
| 2011 | Moon over Manifest | Clare Vanderpool |
| 2012 | Dead End in Norvelt | Jack Gantos |

## Caldecott Medal

The American Library Association (ALA) has awarded the Caldecott Medal—named for the 19th-century English illustrator Randolph Caldecott—annually since 1938 to "the artist of the most distinguished American picture book for children." If the author/reteller/translator/editor is someone other than the illustrator, that person's name appears in parentheses after that of the illustrator. Prize: inscribed bronze medal.

**Web site:** <www.ala.org/alsc/awardsgrants/bookmedia/caldecottmedal/caldecottmedal>.

| YEAR | TITLE | ILLUSTRATOR |
|------|-------|-------------|
| 1938 | Animals of the Bible: A Picture Book | Dorothy P. Lathrop (Helen Dean Fish) |
| 1939 | Mei Li | Thomas Handforth |
| 1940 | Abraham Lincoln | Ingri and Edgar Parin d'Aulaire |
| 1941 | They Were Strong and Good | Robert Lawson |
| 1942 | Make Way for Ducklings | Robert McCloskey |
| 1943 | The Little House | Virginia Lee Burton |
| 1944 | Many Moons | Louis Slobodkin (James Thurber) |
| 1945 | Prayer for a Child | Elizabeth Orton Jones (Rachel Field) |
| 1946 | The Rooster Crows | Maud and Miska Petersham |
| 1947 | The Little Island | Leonard Weisgard (Golden MacDonald, pseud. [Margaret Wise Brown]) |
| 1948 | White Snow, Bright Snow | Roger Duvoisin (Alvin Tresselt) |

## Caldecott Medal (continued)

| YEAR | TITLE | ILLUSTRATOR |
|------|-------|-------------|
| 1949 | The Big Snow | Berta and Elmer Hader |
| 1950 | Song of the Swallows | Leo Politi |
| 1951 | The Egg Tree | Katherine Milhous |
| 1952 | Finders Keepers | Nicolas, pseud. (Nicholas Mordvinoff) (Will, pseud. [William Lipkind]) |
| 1953 | The Biggest Bear | Lynd Ward |
| 1954 | Madeline's Rescue | Ludwig Bemelmans |
| 1955 | Cinderella, or the Little Glass Slipper | Marcia Brown (translated from Charles Perrault by Marcia Brown) |
| 1956 | Frog Went A-Courtin' | Feodor Rojankovsky (John Langstaff) |
| 1957 | A Tree Is Nice | Marc Simont (Janice Udry) |
| 1958 | Time of Wonder | Robert McCloskey |
| 1959 | Chanticleer and the Fox | Barbara Cooney (adapted from Chaucer's The Canterbury Tales by Barbara Cooney) |
| 1960 | Nine Days to Christmas | Marie Hall Ets (Marie Hall Ets and Aurora Labastida) |
| 1961 | Baboushka and the Three Kings | Nicolas Sidjakov (Ruth Robbins) |
| 1962 | Once a Mouse | Marcia Brown |
| 1963 | The Snowy Day | Ezra Jack Keats |
| 1964 | Where the Wild Things Are | Maurice Sendak |
| 1965 | May I Bring a Friend? | Beni Montresor (Beatrice Schenk de Regniers) |
| 1966 | Always Room for One More | Nonny Hogrogian (Sorche Nic Leodhas, pseud. [Leclair Alger]) |
| 1967 | Sam, Bangs & Moonshine | Evaline Ness |
| 1968 | Drummer Hoff | Ed Emberley (Barbara Emberley) |
| 1969 | The Fool of the World and the Flying Ship | Uri Shulevitz (Arthur Ransome) |
| 1970 | Sylvester and the Magic Pebble | William Steig |
| 1971 | A Story, a Story | Gail E. Haley |
| 1972 | One Fine Day | Nonny Hogrogian |
| 1973 | The Funny Little Woman | Blair Lent (Arlene Mosel) |
| 1974 | Duffy and the Devil | Margot Zemach (Harve Zemach) |
| 1975 | Arrow to the Sun | Gerald McDermott |
| 1976 | Why Mosquitoes Buzz in People's Ears | Leo and Diane Dillon (Verna Aardema) |
| 1977 | Ashanti to Zulu: African Traditions | Leo and Diane Dillon (Margaret Musgrove) |
| 1978 | Noah's Ark | Peter Spier |
| 1979 | The Girl Who Loved Wild Horses | Paul Goble |
| 1980 | Ox-Cart Man | Barbara Cooney (Donald Hall) |
| 1981 | Fables | Arnold Lobel |
| 1982 | Jumanji | Chris Van Allsburg |
| 1983 | Shadow | Marcia Brown (translated from Blaise Cendrars by Marcia Brown) |
| 1984 | The Glorious Flight: Across the Channel with Louis Blériot | Alice and Martin Provensen |
| 1985 | Saint George and the Dragon | Trina Schart Hyman (Margaret Hodges) |
| 1986 | The Polar Express | Chris Van Allsburg |
| 1987 | Hey, Al | Richard Egielski (Arthur Yorinks) |
| 1988 | Owl Moon | John Schoenherr (Jane Yolen) |
| 1989 | Song and Dance Man | Stephen Gammell (Karen Ackerman) |
| 1990 | Lon Po Po: A Red-Riding Hood Story from China | Ed Young |
| 1991 | Black and White | David Macaulay |
| 1992 | Tuesday | David Wiesner |
| 1993 | Mirette on the High Wire | Emily Arnold McCully |
| 1994 | Grandfather's Journey | Allen Say (Walter Lorraine) |
| 1995 | Smoky Night | David Diaz (Eve Bunting) |
| 1996 | Officer Buckle and Gloria | Peggy Rathmann |
| 1997 | Golem | David Wisniewski |
| 1998 | Rapunzel | Paul O. Zelinsky |
| 1999 | Snowflake Bentley | Mary Azarian (Jacqueline Briggs Martin) |
| 2000 | Joseph Had a Little Overcoat | Simms Taback |
| 2001 | So You Want To Be President? | David Small (Judith St. George) |
| 2002 | The Three Pigs | David Wiesner |
| 2003 | My Friend Rabbit | Eric Rohmann |
| 2004 | The Man Who Walked Between the Towers | Mordicai Gerstein |
| 2005 | Kitten's First Full Moon | Kevin Henkes |
| 2006 | The Hello, Goodbye Window | Chris Raschka (Norton Juster) |
| 2007 | Flotsam | David Wiesner |
| 2008 | The Invention of Hugo Cabret | Brian Selznick |
| 2009 | The House in the Night | Beth Krommes (Susan Marie Swanson) |
| 2010 | The Lion & the Mouse | Jerry Pinkney |

## Caldecott Medal (continued)

| YEAR | TITLE | ILLUSTRATOR |
|------|-------|-------------|
| 2011 | A Sick Day for Amos McGee | Erin E. Stead (Philip C. Stead) |
| 2012 | A Ball for Daisy | Chris Raschka |

## Coretta Scott King Award

Established in 1970, and since 1982 under the aegis of the American Library Association, the Coretta Scott King Award honors outstanding African American authors and illustrators of books for young people. The books must be original works that portray some aspect of the black experience. Only au-

thors were eligible for the award until 1974, and no illustrator awards were given in 1975–1977 and 1985. Prize: US$1,000, citation, honorarium, and encyclopedia set.

**Coretta Scott King Award Web site:**
<www.ala.org/emiert/cskbookawards>.

1970    Lillie Patterson, Martin Luther King, Jr.: Man of Peace

1971    Charlemae Rollins, Black Troubador: Langston Hughes

1972    Elton C. Fax, 17 Black Artists

1973    I Never Had It Made: The Autobiography of Jackie Robinson, as told to Alfred Duckett

1974    author: Sharon Bell Mathis, Ray Charles; illustrator: George Ford, Ray Charles

1975    author: Dorothy Robinson, The Legend of Africana

1976    author: Pearl Bailey, Duey's Tale

1977    author: James Haskins, The Story of Stevie Wonder

1978    author: Eloise Greenfield, Africa Dream; illustrator: Carole Byard, Africa Dream

1979    author: Ossie Davis, Escape to Freedom; illustrator: Tom Feelings, Something on My Mind

1980    author: Walter Dean Myers, The Young Landlords; illustrator: Carole Byard, Cornrows

1981    author: Sidney Poitier, This Life; illustrator: Ashley Bryan, Beat the Story Drum, Pum-Pum

1982    author: Mildred D. Taylor, Let the Circle Be Unbroken; illustrator: John Steptoe, Mother Crocodiletexas tech

1983    author: Virginia Hamilton, Sweet Whispers, Brother Rush; illustrator: Peter Mugabane, Black Child

1984    author: Lucille Clifton, Everett Anderson's Goodbye; illustrator: Pat Cummings, My Mama Needs Me

1985    author: Walter Dean Myers, Motown and Didi

1986    author: Virginia Hamilton, The People Could Fly: American Black Folktales; illustrator: Jerry Pinkney, The Patchwork Quilt

1987    author: Mildred Pitts Walter, Justin and the Best Biscuits in the World; illustrator: Jerry Pinkney, Half a Moon and One Whole Star

1988    author: Mildred D. Taylor, The Friendship; illustrator: John Steptoe, Mufaro's Beautiful Daughters: An African Tale

1989    author: Walter Dean Myers, Fallen Angels; illustrator: Jerry Pinkney, Mirandy and Brother Wind

1990    authors: Patricia C. and Frederick L. McKissack, A Long Hard Journey: The Story of the Pullman Porter; illustrator: Jan Spivey Gilchrist, Nathaniel Talking

1991    author: Mildred D. Taylor, The Road to Memphis; illustrators: Leo and Diane Dillon, Aida

1992    author: Walter Dean Myers, Now Is Your Time: The African American Struggle for Freedom; illustrator: Faith Ringgold, Tar Beach

1993    author: Patricia C. McKissack, Dark Thirty: Southern Tales of the Supernatural; illustrator: Kathleen Atkins Wilson, The Origin of Life on Earth: An African Creation Myth

1994    author: Angela Johnson, Toning the Sweep; illustrator: Tom Feelings, Soul Looks Back in Wonder

1995    authors: Patricia C. and Frederick L. McKissack, Christmas in the Big House, Christmas in the Quarters; illustrator: James Ransome, The Creation

1996    author: Virginia Hamilton, Her Stories; illustrator: Tom Feelings, The Middle Passage: White Ships/Black Cargo

1997    author: Walter Dean Myers, Slam; illustrator: Jerry Pinkney, Minty: A Story of Young Harriet Tubman

1998    author: Sharon M. Draper, Forged by Fire; illustrator: Javaka Steptoe, In Daddy's Arms I Am Tall: African Americans Celebrating Fathers

1999    author: Angela Johnson, Heaven; illustrator: Michele Wood, i see the rhythm

2000    author: Christopher Paul Curtis, Bud, Not Buddy; illustrator: Brian Pinkney, In the Time of the Drums

2001    author: Jacqueline Woodson, Miracle's Boys; illustrator: Bryan Collier, Uptown

2002    author: Mildred D. Taylor, The Land; illustrator: Jerry Pinkney, Goin' Someplace Special

2003    author: Nikki Grimes, Bronx Masquerade; illustrator: E.B. Lewis, Talkin' About Bessie: The Story of Aviator Elizabeth Coleman

2004    author: Angela Johnson, The First Part Last; illustrator: Ashley Bryan, Beautiful Blackbird

2005    author: Toni Morrison, Remember: The Journey to School Integration; illustrator: Kadir Nelson, Ellington Was Not a Street

2006    author: Julius Lester, Day of Tears: A Novel in Dialogue; illustrator: Bryan Collier, Rosa

2007    author: Sharon Draper, Copper Sun; illustrator: Kadir Nelson, Moses: When Harriet Tubman Led Her People to Freedom

2008    author: Christopher Paul Curtis, Elijah of Buxton; illustrator: Ashley Bryan, Let It Shine

2009    author: Kadir Nelson, We Are the Ship: The Story of Negro League Baseball; illustrator: Floyd Cooper, The Blacker the Berry

2010    author: Vaunda Micheaux Nelson, Bad News for Outlaws: The Remarkable Life of Bass Reeves, Deputy U.S. Marshal; illustrator: Charles R. Smith, Jr., My People

## Coretta Scott King Award (continued)

**2011**  author: Rita Williams-Garcia, *One Crazy Summer*; illustrator: Bryan Collier, *Dave the Potter: Artist, Poet, Slave*

**2012**  author: Kadir Nelson, *Heart and Soul: The Story of America and African Americans*; illustrator: Shane W. Evans, *Underground: Finding the Light to Freedom*

## Man Booker Prize

Awarded to the best full-length novel of the year written by a citizen of the Commonwealth, the Republic of Ireland, or Zimbabwe and published in the UK between 1 October and 30 September. Prize: £50,000 (about US$78,500). In 1993 Salman Rushdie was awarded the Booker of Bookers, a special award to mark 25 years of the Booker Prize, for *Midnight's Children*. In 2008 the Best of Bookers prize, to mark 40 years, was also won by *Midnight's Children*. In 2005 the Man Booker International Prize was created, to be awarded biennially to a living writer for outstanding lifetime achievement. Prize: £60,000 (about US$94,100). Albanian novelist Ismail Kadare won the first Man Booker International Prize. Nigerian author Chinua Achebe won the second in 2007. Canadian short-story writer Alice Munro was awarded the third in 2009. In 2011, American author Philip Roth won the fourth.

In 1969 and 1970, the prize was awarded to a novel published in the year previous to that in which the award was given. Since 1971 the prize has been awarded to a novel published within the listed year. Because the rule change precluded eligibility for some novels published in 1970 (those published before 1 October), the one-off Lost Man Booker Prize was devised in 2010 to honor such a novel. The winner was *Troubles* by J.G. Farrell.

Web site: <www.themanbookerprize.com>.

| YEAR | TITLE | AUTHOR | YEAR | TITLE | AUTHOR |
|---|---|---|---|---|---|
| 1969 | Something to Answer For | P.H. Newby | 1990 | Possession | A.S. Byatt |
| 1970 | The Elected Member | Bernice Rubens | 1991 | The Famished Road | Ben Okri |
| 1971 | In a Free State | V.S. Naipaul | 1992 | The English Patient | Michael Ondaatje |
| 1972 | G. | John Berger | 1992 | Sacred Hunger | Barry Unsworth |
| 1973 | The Siege of Krishnapur | J.G. Farrell | 1993 | Paddy Clarke Ha Ha Ha | Roddy Doyle |
| | | | 1994 | How Late It Was, How Late | James Kelman |
| 1974 | The Conservationist | Nadine Gordimer | 1995 | The Ghost Road | Pat Barker |
| 1974 | Holiday | Stanley Middleton | 1996 | Last Orders | Graham Swift |
| 1975 | Heat and Dust | Ruth Prawer Jhabvala | 1997 | The God of Small Things | Arundhati Roy |
| 1976 | Saville | David Storey | 1998 | Amsterdam | Ian McEwan |
| 1977 | Staying On | Paul Scott | 1999 | Disgrace | J.M. Coetzee |
| 1978 | The Sea, The Sea | Iris Murdoch | 2000 | The Blind Assassin | Margaret Atwood |
| 1979 | Offshore | Penelope Fitzgerald | 2001 | True History of the Kelly Gang | Peter Carey |
| 1980 | Rites of Passage | William Golding | | | |
| 1981 | Midnight's Children | Salman Rushdie | 2002 | Life of Pi | Yann Martel |
| 1982 | Schindler's Ark | Thomas Keneally | 2003 | Vernon God Little | DBC Pierre |
| 1983 | Life and Times of Michael K | J.M. Coetzee | 2004 | The Line of Beauty | Alan Hollinghurst |
| | | | 2005 | The Sea | John Banville |
| 1984 | Hotel du Lac | Anita Brookner | 2006 | The Inheritance of Loss | Kiran Desai |
| 1985 | The Bone People | Keri Hulme | 2007 | The Gathering | Anne Enright |
| 1986 | The Old Devils | Kingsley Amis | 2008 | The White Tiger | Aravind Adiga |
| 1987 | Moon Tiger | Penelope Lively | 2009 | Wolf Hall | Hilary Mantel |
| 1988 | Oscar and Lucinda | Peter Carey | 2010 | The Finkler Question | Howard Jacobson |
| 1989 | The Remains of the Day | Kazuo Ishiguro | 2011 | The Sense of an Ending | Julian Barnes |

## Costa Book Awards

The Whitbread Book Awards were inaugurated in 1971, and in 2006 Britain's Costa chain of coffee shops took over the prize. Since 1985, awards have been given in five categories: Novel, First Novel, Biography, Poetry, and Children's. From these a panel of judges chooses one overall winner—the Costa Book of the Year. The total prize fund is £55,000 (about US$86,300): each of the category award winners receives £5,000 (about US$7,800), and the Book of the Year winner receives an additional £30,000 (about US$47,100).

This list includes Novel award winners from 1971 to 1984 and Book of the Year winners from 1985 to 2011.

Costa Book Awards Web site: <www.costabookawards.com>.

| YEAR | TITLE | AUTHOR | YEAR | TITLE | AUTHOR |
|---|---|---|---|---|---|
| 1971 | The Destiny Waltz | Gerda Charles | 1974 | The Sacred and Profane Love Machine | Iris Murdoch |
| 1972 | The Bird of Night | Susan Hill | | | |
| 1973 | The Chip-Chip Gatherers | Shiva Naipaul | 1975 | Docherty | William McIlvanney |
| | | | 1976 | The Children of Dynmouth | William Trevor |

## Costa Book Awards (continued)

| YEAR | TITLE | AUTHOR | YEAR | TITLE | AUTHOR |
|------|-------|--------|------|-------|--------|
| 1977 | Injury Time | Beryl Bainbridge | 1996 | The Spirit Level | Seamus Heaney |
| 1978 | Picture Palace | Paul Theroux | 1997 | Tales from Ovid | Ted Hughes |
| 1979 | The Old Jest | Jennifer Johnston | 1998 | Birthday Letters | Ted Hughes |
| 1980 | How Far Can You Go? | David Lodge | 1999 | Beowulf | Seamus Heaney |
| 1981 | Silver's City | Maurice Leitch | 2000 | English Passengers | Matthew Kneale |
| 1982 | Young Shoulders | John Wain | 2001 | The Amber Spyglass | Philip Pullman |
| 1983 | Fools of Fortune | William Trevor | 2002 | Samuel Pepys: The Unequalled Self | Claire Tomalin |
| 1984 | Kruger's Alp | Christopher Hope | | | |
| 1985 | Elegies | Douglas Dunn | 2003 | The Curious Incident of the Dog in the Night-Time | Mark Haddon |
| 1986 | An Artist of the Floating World | Kazuo Ishiguro | | | |
| | | | 2004 | Small Island | Andrea Levy |
| 1987 | Under the Eye of the Clock | Christopher Nolan | 2005 | Matisse: The Master | Hilary Spurling |
| 1988 | The Comforts of Madness | Paul Sayer | 2006 | The Tenderness of Wolves | Stef Penney |
| 1989 | Coleridge: Early Visions | Richard Holmes | | | |
| 1990 | Hopeful Monsters | Nicholas Mosley | 2007 | Day | A.L. Kennedy |
| 1991 | A Life of Picasso | John Richardson | 2008 | The Secret Scripture | Sebastian Barry |
| 1992 | Swing Hammer Swing! | Jeff Torrington | 2009 | A Scattering | Christopher Reid |
| 1993 | Theory of War | Joan Brady | 2010 | Of Mutability | Jo Shapcott |
| 1994 | Felicia's Journey | William Trevor | 2011 | Pure | Andrew Miller |
| 1995 | Behind the Scenes at the Museum | Kate Atkinson | | | |

## Orange Prize for Fiction

Awarded to a work of published fiction written in English by a woman and published in the United Kingdom or Ireland. Prize: £30,000 (about US$47,100) and a bronze figurine called the "Bessie."
**Orange Prize for Fiction Web site:** <www.orangeprize.co.uk>.

| YEAR | TITLE | AUTHOR | YEAR | TITLE | AUTHOR |
|------|-------|--------|------|-------|--------|
| 1996 | A Spell of Winter | Helen Dunmore | 2005 | We Need To Talk About Kevin | Lionel Shriver |
| 1997 | Fugitive Pieces | Anne Michaels | | | |
| 1998 | Larry's Party | Carol Shields | 2006 | On Beauty | Zadie Smith |
| 1999 | A Crime in the Neighbourhood | Suzanne Berne | 2007 | Half of a Yellow Sun | Chimamanda Ngozi Adichie |
| 2000 | When I Lived in Modern Times | Linda Grant | | | |
| | | | 2008 | The Road Home | Rose Tremain |
| 2001 | The Idea of Perfection | Kate Grenville | 2009 | Home | Marilynne Robinson |
| 2002 | Bel Canto | Ann Patchett | 2010 | The Lacuna | Barbara Kingsolver |
| 2003 | Property | Valerie Martin | 2011 | The Tiger's Wife | Téa Obreht |
| 2004 | Small Island | Andrea Levy | 2012 | The Song of Achilles | Madeline Miller |

## Prix Goncourt

The Prix de l'Académie Goncourt was first awarded in 1903 from the estate of the brothers and French literary figures Edmond Huot de Goncourt (1822–1896) and Jules Huot de Goncourt (1830–1870) for a work of contemporary prose in French.
Prize: €10 (about US$13).

| YEAR | TITLE | AUTHOR | YEAR | TITLE | AUTHOR |
|------|-------|--------|------|-------|--------|
| 1903 | Force ennemie | John-Antoine Nau | 1915 | Gaspard | René Benjamin |
| 1904 | La Maternelle | Léon Frapié | 1916 | Le Feu | Henri Barbusse |
| 1905 | Les Civilisés | Claude Farrère | 1917 | La Flamme au poing | Henri Malherbe |
| 1906 | Dingley, l'illustre écrivain | Jérôme and Jean Tharaud | 1918 | Civilisation | Georges Duhamel |
| 1907 | Terres lorraines | Emile Moselly | 1919 | A l'ombre des jeunes filles en fleur | Marcel Proust |
| 1908 | Ecrit sur l'eau | Francis de Miomandre | 1920 | Nene | Ernest Pérochon |
| 1909 | En France | Marius-Ary Leblond | 1921 | Batouala | René Maran |
| 1910 | De Goupil à Margot | Louis Pergaud | 1922 | Le Vitriol de la lune; Le Martyre de l'obèse | Henri Béraud |
| 1911 | Monsieur des Lourdines | Alphonse de Chateaubriant | | | |
| 1912 | Les Filles de la pluie | André Savignon | 1923 | Rabevel; ou, le mal des ardents | Lucien Fabre |
| 1913 | Le Peuple de la mer | Marc Elder | 1924 | Le Chèvrefeuille; Le Purgatoire; Le Chapitre treize d'Athénée | Thierry Sandre · |
| 1914 | L'Appel du sol | Adrien Bertrand | | | |

## Prix Goncourt (continued)

| YEAR | TITLE | AUTHOR | YEAR | TITLE | AUTHOR |
|------|-------|--------|------|-------|--------|
| 1925 | Raboliot | Maurice Genevoix | 1969 | Creezy | Félicien Marceau |
| 1926 | Le Supplice de Phèdre | Henry Deberly | 1970 | Le Roi des Aulnes | Michel Tournier |
| 1927 | Jérôme, 60° latitude nord | Maurice Bedel | 1971 | Les Bêtises | Jacques Laurent |
| 1928 | Un Homme se penche sur son passé | Maurice Constantin-Weyer | 1972 | L'Épervier de Maheux | Jean Carrière |
| | | | 1973 | L'Ogre | Jacques Chessex |
| 1929 | L'Ordre | Marcel Arland | 1974 | La Dentellière | Pascal Lainé |
| 1930 | Malaisie | Henri Fauconnier | 1975 | La Vie devant soi | Emile Ajar (declined) |
| 1931 | Mal d'amour | Jean Fayard | 1976 | Les Flamboyants | Patrick Grainville |
| 1932 | Les Loups | Guy Mazeline | 1977 | John l'enfer | Didier Decoin |
| 1933 | La Condition humaine | André Malraux | 1978 | Rue des boutiques obscures | Patrick Modiano |
| 1934 | Capitaine Conan | Roger Vercel | | | |
| 1935 | Sang et lumières | Joseph Peyré | 1979 | Pélagie-la-charrette | Antonine Maillet |
| 1936 | L'Empreinte de Dieu | Maxence van der Meersch | 1980 | Le Jardin d'acclimatation | Yves Navarre |
| | | | 1981 | Anne Marie | Lucien Bodard |
| 1937 | Faux passeports | Charles Plisnier | 1982 | Dans la main de l'ange | Dominique Fernandez |
| 1938 | L'Araigne | Henri Troyat | | | |
| 1939 | Les Enfants gâtés | Philippe Hériat | 1983 | Les Égarés | Frédérick Tristan |
| 1940 | Les Grandes Vacances | Francis Ambrière | 1984 | L'Amant | Marguerite Duras |
| 1941 | Vent de Mars | Henri Pourrat | 1985 | Les Noces barbares | Yann Queffélec |
| 1942 | Pareil à des enfants | Bernard Marc | 1986 | Valet de nuit | Michel Host |
| 1943 | Passage de l'homme | Marius Grout | 1987 | La Nuit sacrée | Tahar Ben Jelloun |
| 1944 | Le Premier Accroc coûte 200 francs | Elsa Triolet | 1988 | L'Exposition coloniale | Erik Orsenna |
| | | | 1989 | Un Grand Pas vers le Bon Dieu | Jean Vautrin |
| 1945 | Mon village à l'heure allemande | Jean-Louis Bory | | | |
| | | | 1990 | Les Champs d'honneur | Jean Rouaud |
| 1946 | Histoire d'un fait divers | Jean-Jacques Gautier | 1991 | Les Filles du calvaire | Pierre Combescot |
| | | | 1992 | Texaco | Patrick Chamoiseau |
| 1947 | Les Forêts de la nuit | Jean-Louis Curtis | 1993 | La Rocher de Tanios | Amin Maalouf |
| 1948 | Les Grandes Familles | Maurice Druon | 1994 | Un Aller simple | Didier van Cauwelaert |
| 1949 | Week-end à Zuydcoote | Robert Merle | | | |
| 1950 | Les Jeux sauvages | Paul Colin | 1995 | Le Testament français | Andreï Makine |
| 1951 | Le Rivage des Syrtes | Julien Gracq (declined) | 1996 | Le Chasseur zéro | Pascale Roze |
| | | | 1997 | La Bataille | Patrick Rambaud |
| 1952 | Léon Morin, prêtre | Béatrice Beck | 1998 | Confidence pour confidence | Paule Constant |
| 1953 | Les Bêtes; Le Temps des morts | Pierre Gascar | | | |
| | | | 1999 | Je m'en vais | Jean Echenoz |
| 1954 | Mandarins | Simone de Beauvoir | 2000 | Ingrid Caven | Jean-Jacques Schuhl |
| 1955 | Les Eaux mêlées | Roger Ikor | 2001 | Rouge Brésil | Jean-Christophe Rufin |
| 1956 | Les Racines du ciel | Romain Gary | | | |
| 1957 | La Loi | Roger Vailland | 2002 | Les Ombres errantes | Pascal Quignard |
| 1958 | Saint Germain; ou, la négociation | Francis Walder | 2003 | La Maîtresse de Brecht | Jacques-Pierre Amette |
| 1959 | Le Dernier des justes | André Schwartz-Bart | 2004 | Le Soleil des Scorta | Laurent Gaudé |
| 1960 | Dieu est né en exil | Vintila Horia | 2005 | Trois jours chez ma mère | François Weyergans |
| 1961 | La Pitié de Dieu | Jean Cau | | | |
| 1962 | Les Bagages de sable | Anna Langfus | 2006 | Les Bienveillantes | Jonathan Littell |
| 1963 | Quand la mer se retire | Armand Lanoux | 2007 | Alabama Song | Gilles Leroy |
| 1964 | L'État sauvage | Georges Conchon | 2008 | Syngué sabour: pierre de patience | Atiq Rahimi |
| 1965 | L'Adoration | Jacques Borel | | | |
| 1966 | Oublier Palerme | Edmonde Charles-Roux | 2009 | Trois femmes puissantes | Marie NDiaye |
| 1967 | La Marge | André Pieyre de Mandiargues | 2010 | La Carte et le territoire | Michel Houellebecq |
| | | | 2011 | L'Art français de la guerre | Alexis Jenni |
| 1968 | Les Fruits de l'hiver | Bernard Clavel | | | |

## T.S. Eliot Prize

*Great Britain's Poetry Book Society awards the T.S. Eliot Prize to the best new collection of poetry published in the UK or the Republic of Ireland during the preceding year. The prize is £15,000 (about US$23,500).*

| YEAR | WORK | AUTHOR | COUNTRY |
|------|------|--------|---------|
| 1993 | First Language | Ciaran Carson | Ireland |
| 1994 | The Annals of Chile | Paul Muldoon | United Kingdom |
| 1995 | My Alexandria | Mark Doty | United States |
| 1996 | Subhuman Redneck Poems | Les Murray | Australia |
| 1997 | God's Gift to Women | Don Paterson | United Kingdom |

## T.S. Eliot Prize (continued)

| YEAR | WORK | AUTHOR | COUNTRY |
| --- | --- | --- | --- |
| 1998 | Birthday Letters | Ted Hughes | United Kingdom |
| 1999 | Billy's Rain | Hugo Williams | United Kingdom |
| 2000 | The Weather in Japan | Michael Longley | United Kingdom |
| 2001 | The Beauty of the Husband | Anne Carson | Canada |
| 2002 | Dart | Alice Oswald | United Kingdom |
| 2003 | Landing Light | Don Paterson | United Kingdom |
| 2004 | Reel | George Szirtes | United Kingdom |
| 2005 | Rapture | Carol Ann Duffy | United Kingdom |
| 2006 | District and Circle | Seamus Heaney | Ireland |
| 2007 | The Drowned Book | Sean O'Brien | United Kingdom |
| 2008 | Nigh-No-Place | Jen Hadfield | United Kingdom |
| 2009 | The Water Table | Philip Gross | United Kingdom |
| 2010 | White Egrets | Derek Walcott | St. Lucia |
| 2011 | Black Cat Bone | John Burnside | United Kingdom |

## Bollingen Prize in Poetry

The Bollingen Prize in Poetry is awarded biennially to the American poet whose work represents the highest achievement in the field of American poetry during the preceding two-year period. The committee considers published work, particularly work published during that preceding two-year period. Former winners of the US$100,000 prize are not eligible. **Web site:** <http://beinecke.library.yale.edu/bollingen>.

| YEAR | POET | YEAR | POET | YEAR | POET |
| --- | --- | --- | --- | --- | --- |
| 1948 | Ezra Pound | 1963 | Robert Frost | 1987 | Stanley Kunitz |
| 1949 | Wallace Stevens | 1965 | Horace Gregory | 1989 | Edgar Bowers |
| 1950 | John Crowe Ransom | 1967 | Robert Penn Warren | 1991 | Laura Riding Jackson |
| 1951 | Marianne Moore | 1969 | John Berryman | | Donald Justice |
| 1952 | Archibald MacLeish | | Karl Shapiro | 1993 | Mark Strand |
| | William Carlos Williams | 1971 | Richard Wilbur | 1995 | Kenneth Koch |
| 1953 | W.H. Auden | | Mona Van Duyn | 1997 | Gary Snyder |
| 1954 | Léonie Adams | 1973 | James Merrill | 1999 | Robert Creeley |
| | Louise Bogan | 1975 | A.R. Ammons | 2001 | Louise Glück |
| 1955 | Conrad Aiken | 1977 | David Ignatow | 2003 | Adrienne Rich |
| 1956 | Allen Tate | 1979 | W.S. Merwin | 2005 | Jay Wright |
| 1957 | E.E. Cummings | 1981 | May Swenson | 2007 | Frank Bidart |
| 1958 | Theodore Roethke | | Howard Nemerov | 2009 | Allen Grossman |
| 1959 | Delmore Schwartz | 1983 | Anthony Hecht | 2011 | Susan Howe |
| 1960 | Yvor Winters | | John Hollander | | |
| 1961 | Richard Eberhart | 1985 | John Ashbery | | |
| | John Hall Wheelock | | Fred Chappell | | |

## Pritzker Architecture Prize

The Pritzker Architecture Prize, awarded by the Hyatt Foundation since 1979, is given to an outstanding living architect for built work. Prize: US$100,000 and a bronze medallion. **Web site:** <www.pritzkerprize.com>.

| YEAR | NAME | COUNTRY | YEAR | NAME | COUNTRY |
| --- | --- | --- | --- | --- | --- |
| 1979 | Philip Johnson | United States | 1997 | Sverre Fehn | Norway |
| 1980 | Luis Barragán | Mexico | 1998 | Renzo Piano | Italy |
| 1981 | James Stirling | Great Britain | 1999 | Norman Foster | Great Britain |
| 1982 | Kevin Roche | United States | 2000 | Rem Koolhaas | Netherlands |
| 1983 | I.M. Pei | United States | 2001 | Jacques Herzog | Switzerland |
| 1984 | Richard Meier | United States | | Pierre de Meuron | Switzerland |
| 1985 | Hans Hollein | Austria | 2002 | Glenn Murcutt | Australia |
| 1986 | Gottfried Böhm | West Germany | 2003 | Jørn Utzon | Denmark |
| 1987 | Kenzo Tange | Japan | 2004 | Zaha Hadid | Great Britain |
| 1988 | Gordon Bunshaft | United States | 2005 | Thom Mayne | United States |
| | Oscar Niemeyer | Brazil | 2006 | Paulo Mendes da Rocha | Brazil |
| 1989 | Frank O. Gehry | United States | 2007 | Richard Rogers | Great Britain |
| 1990 | Aldo Rossi | Italy | 2008 | Jean Nouvel | France |
| 1991 | Robert Venturi | United States | 2009 | Peter Zumthor | Switzerland |
| 1992 | Alvaro Siza | Portugal | 2010 | Kazuyo Sejima | Japan |
| 1993 | Fumihiko Maki | Japan | | Ryue Nishizawa | Japan |
| 1994 | Christian de Portzamparc | France | 2011 | Eduardo Souto de Moura | Portugal |
| 1995 | Tadao Ando | Japan | 2012 | Wang Shu | China |
| 1996 | Rafael Moneo | Spain | | | |

# Sport

## Sport Coverage

The tables that follow contain information about the top contests of all the major sports that are international in character, as well as some professional and amateur sports that attract a huge national following—such as baseball in the United States and cricket in the United Kingdom, Australia, India, and the other Test match countries. In many sports the Olympic Games held every four years constitute the world championships; they are included in the listings below. In some cases circumstances such as marriage or divorce have changed the name of a winning athlete. The following tables give the name by which the athlete was known for the given year, resulting in instances in which the athlete may appear under two or more names in the same table. Similarly, if the citizenship of an athlete or name of the athlete's country changes, the tables reflect the accurate name for each given year.

## Sporting Codes for Countries
### Codes of the International Olympic Committee (IOC)

| | | | | | |
|---|---|---|---|---|---|
| AFG | Afghanistan | CUB | Cuba | KAZ | Kazakhstan |
| AHO | Netherlands Antilles | CYP | Cyprus | KEN | Kenya |
| ALB | Albania | CZE | Czech Republic | KGZ | Kyrgyzstan |
| ALG | Algeria | DEN | Denmark | KIR | Kiribati |
| AND | Andorra | DJI | Djibouti | KOR | Korea, Republic of |
| ANG | Angola | DMA | Dominica | | (South Korea) |
| ANT | Antigua and Barbuda | DOM | Dominican Republic | KOS | Kosovo |
| ARG | Argentina | ECU | Ecuador | KSA | Saudi Arabia |
| ARM | Armenia | EGY | Egypt | KUW | Kuwait |
| ARU | Aruba | ERI | Eritrea | LAO | Laos |
| ASA | American Samoa | ESA | El Salvador | LAT | Latvia |
| AUS | Australia | ESP | Spain | LBA | Libya |
| AUT | Austria | EST | Estonia | LBR | Liberia |
| AZE | Azerbaijan | ETH | Ethiopia | LCA | Saint Lucia |
| BAH | Bahamas, The | FIJ | Fiji | LES | Lesotho |
| BAN | Bangladesh | FIN | Finland | LIB | Lebanon |
| BAR | Barbados | FRA | France | LIE | Liechtenstein |
| BDI | Burundi | FSM | Micronesia, Federated | LTU | Lithuania |
| BEL | Belgium | | States of | LUX | Luxembourg |
| BEN | Benin | GAB | Gabon | MAD | Madagascar |
| BER | Bermuda | GAM | Gambia, The | MAR | Morocco |
| BHU | Bhutan | GBR | Great Britain | MAS | Malaysia |
| BIH | Bosnia and Herzegovina | GBS | Guinea-Bissau | MAW | Malawi |
| BIZ | Belize | GEO | Georgia | MDA | Moldova |
| BLR | Belarus | GEQ | Equatorial Guinea | MDV | Maldives |
| BOL | Bolivia | GER | Germany | MEX | Mexico |
| BOT | Botswana | GHA | Ghana | MGL | Mongolia |
| BRA | Brazil | GRE | Greece | MHL | Marshall Islands |
| BRN | Bahrain | GRN | Grenada | MKD | Macedonia[1] |
| BRU | Brunei | GUA | Guatemala | MLI | Mali |
| BUL | Bulgaria | GUI | Guinea | MLT | Malta |
| BUR | Burkina Faso | GUM | Guam | MNE | Montenegro |
| CAF | Central African Republic | GUY | Guyana | MON | Monaco |
| CAM | Cambodia | HAI | Haiti | MOZ | Mozambique |
| CAN | Canada | HKG | Hong Kong | MRI | Mauritius |
| CAY | Cayman Islands | HON | Honduras | MTN | Mauritania |
| CGO | Congo, Republic of the | HUN | Hungary | MYA | Myanmar (Burma) |
| CHA | Chad | INA | Indonesia | NAM | Namibia |
| CHI | Chile | IND | India | NCA | Nicaragua |
| CHN | China | IRI | Iran | NED | Netherlands |
| CIV | Côte d'Ivoire | IRL | Ireland | NEP | Nepal |
| CMR | Cameroon | IRQ | Iraq | NGR | Nigeria |
| COD | Congo, Democratic | ISL | Iceland | NIG | Niger |
| | Republic of the | ISR | Israel | NOR | Norway |
| COK | Cook Islands | ISV | US Virgin Islands | NRU | Nauru |
| COL | Colombia | ITA | Italy | NZL | New Zealand |
| COM | Comoros | IVB | British Virgin Islands | OMA | Oman |
| CPV | Cape Verde | JAM | Jamaica | PAK | Pakistan |
| CRC | Costa Rica | JOR | Jordan | PAN | Panama |
| CRO | Croatia | JPN | Japan | PAR | Paraguay |

# Sporting Codes for Countries (continued)
## Codes of the International Olympic Committee (IOC) (continued)

| | | | | | |
|---|---|---|---|---|---|
| PER | Peru | SLE | Sierra Leone | TOG | Togo |
| PHI | Philippines | SLO | Slovenia | TPE | Taiwan |
| PLE | Palestine | SMR | San Marino | TRI | Trinidad and Tobago |
| PLW | Palau | SOL | Solomon Islands | TUN | Tunisia |
| PNG | Papua New Guinea | SOM | Somalia | TUR | Turkey |
| POL | Poland | SRB | Serbia | TUV | Tuvalu |
| POR | Portugal | SRI | Sri Lanka | UAE | United Arab Emirates |
| PRK | Korea, Democratic | STP | Sao Tome and Principe | UGA | Uganda |
| | People's Republic of | SUD | Sudan | UKR | Ukraine |
| | (North Korea) | SUI | Switzerland | URU | Uruguay |
| PUR | Puerto Rico | SUR | Suriname | USA | United States |
| QAT | Qatar | SVK | Slovakia | UZB | Uzbekistan |
| ROU | Romania | SWE | Sweden | VAN | Vanuatu |
| RSA | South Africa | SWZ | Swaziland | VEN | Venezuela |
| RUS | Russia | SYR | Syria | VIE | Vietnam |
| RWA | Rwanda | TAN | Tanzania | VIN | Saint Vincent and |
| SAM | Samoa | TGA | Tonga | | the Grenadines |
| SEN | Senegal | THA | Thailand | YEM | Yemen |
| SEY | Seychelles | TJK | Tajikistan | ZAM | Zambia |
| SIN | Singapore | TKM | Turkmenistan | ZIM | Zimbabwe |
| SKN | Saint Kitts and Nevis | TLS | East Timor (Timor-Leste) | | |

## Historical and Other Country Codes

| | | | | | |
|---|---|---|---|---|---|
| ENG | England | GGY | Guernsey | TCH | Czechoslovakia |
| FRG | Germany, Federal Republic | IMN | Isle of Man | UNT | Unified Team[2] |
| | of (West Germany) | JEY | Jersey | URS | USSR |
| GDR | German Democratic | NIR | Northern Ireland | WAL | Wales |
| | Republic (East Germany) | SCO | Scotland | YUG | Yugoslavia |

[1]*Macedonia is known by the IOC as the Former Yugoslav Republic of Macedonia.*    [2]*The Unified Team consisted of athletes from the Commonwealth of Independent States plus Georgia.*

# The Olympic Games

By the 6th century BC several sporting festivals had achieved cultural importance in the Greek world. The most prominent among them were the Olympic Games at the city of Olympia, first recorded in 776 BC and held at four-year intervals thereafter. Those games, comprising many of the sports now included in the Summer Games, were abolished in AD 393 by the Roman emperor Theodosius I, probably because of their pagan associations. In 1887 the 24-year-old French aristocrat and educator Pierre, baron de Coubertin, conceived the idea of reviving the Olympic Games and spent seven years gathering support for his plan. At an international congress in 1894, his plan was accepted and the International Olympic Committee (IOC) was founded. The first modern Olympic Games were held in Athens in April 1896, with some 300 representatives from 13 nations competing. The revival led to the formation of international amateur sports organizations and national Olympic committees throughout the world.

The IOC is responsible for maintaining the regular celebration of the games, seeing that the games are carried out in a spirit of peace and intercultural communication, and promoting amateur sport throughout the world. IOC members may not accept from the government of their country, or from any other entity, instructions that compromise their independence.

The Olympic Games have come to be regarded as the world's foremost sports competition. Before the 1970s the Games were officially limited to amateurs, but since that time many events have been opened to professional athletes. In 1924 the Winter Games were created, and in 1986 the IOC voted to alternate the Winter and Summer Games every two years, beginning in 1994.

The games were canceled during the two world wars (1916, 1940, and 1944) and have frequently served as venues for the expression of political dissent. China refused to participate in the Summer Games from 1956 until 1984 because of Taiwan's participation; 26 nations boycotted the games in 1976 over the participation of New Zealand, some of whose athletes had competed in apartheid-era South Africa; the United States and some 60 other countries boycotted the 1980 games in Moscow to protest the Soviet invasion of Afghanistan, and the Communist bloc and Cuba in turn boycotted the 1984 Los Angeles games.

In light of the IOC's declared independence from political and financial interests, in 1998 the world was shocked by allegations of widespread corruption within the committee. Several committee members, it was found, had accepted bribes to approve the bid of Salt Lake City UT as the site for the 2002 Winter Games. Impropriety was also alleged for several previous bid committees. The IOC responded by expelling six members and in 1999 announced a number of wide-ranging reforms.

**IOC Web site:** <www.olympic.org>.

# Sites of the Modern Olympic Games

## Summer Games

| YEAR | LOCATION | YEAR | LOCATION | YEAR | LOCATION |
|---|---|---|---|---|---|
| 1896 | Athens, Greece | 1940-44 | *not held* | 1984 | Los Angeles CA |
| 1900 | Paris, France | 1948 | London, England | 1988 | Seoul, Republic of Korea |
| 1904 | St. Louis MO | 1952 | Helsinki, Finland | 1992 | Barcelona, Spain |
| 1908 | London, England | 1956 | Melbourne, VIC, | 1996 | Atlanta GA |
| 1912 | Stockholm, Sweden | | Australia | 2000 | Sydney, NSW, Australia |
| 1916 | *not held* | 1960 | Rome, Italy | 2004 | Athens, Greece |
| 1920 | Antwerp, Belgium | 1964 | Tokyo, Japan | 2008 | Beijing, China |
| 1924 | Paris, France | 1968 | Mexico City, Mexico | 2012 | London, England |
| 1928 | Amsterdam, Netherlands | 1972 | Munich, West Germany | 2016 | *scheduled to be held* |
| 1932 | Los Angeles CA | 1976 | Montreal, QC, Canada | | *5–21 August,* |
| 1936 | Berlin, Germany | 1980 | Moscow, USSR | | *Rio de Janeiro, Brazil* |

## Winter Games

| YEAR | LOCATION | YEAR | LOCATION | YEAR | LOCATION |
|---|---|---|---|---|---|
| 1924 | Chamonix, France | 1964 | Innsbruck, Austria | 2002 | Salt Lake City UT |
| 1928 | St. Moritz, Switzerland | 1968 | Grenoble, France | 2006 | Turin, Italy |
| 1932 | Lake Placid NY | 1972 | Sapporo, Japan | 2010 | Vancouver, BC, Canada |
| 1936 | Garmisch-Partenkirchen, | 1976 | Innsbruck, Austria | 2014 | *scheduled to be held* |
| | Germany | 1980 | Lake Placid NY | | *7–23 February, Sochi,* |
| 1940-44 | *not held* | 1984 | Sarajevo, Yugoslavia | | *Russia* |
| 1948 | St. Moritz, Switzerland | 1988 | Calgary, AB, Canada | 2018 | *scheduled to be held* |
| 1952 | Oslo, Norway | 1992 | Albertville, France | | *9–25 February,* |
| 1956 | Cortina d'Ampezzo, Italy | 1994 | Lillehammer, Norway | | *P'yongch'ang, Republic* |
| 1960 | Squaw Valley CA | 1998 | Nagano, Japan | | *of Korea* |

# Summer Olympic Games

*Gold-medal winners in all summer events since 1896. Note: East and West Germany fielded a joint all-Germany team in 1956, 1960, and 1964, abbreviated here as GER.*

## Archery

**MEN'S INDIVIDUAL**
| | |
|---|---|
| 1972 | John Williams (USA) |
| 1976 | Darrell Pace (USA) |
| 1980 | Tomi Poikolainen (FIN) |
| 1984 | Darrell Pace (USA) |
| 1988 | Jay Barrs (USA) |
| 1992 | Sebastien Flute (FRA) |
| 1996 | Justin Huish (USA) |
| 2000 | Simon Fairweather (AUS) |
| 2004 | Marco Galiazzo (ITA) |
| 2008 | Viktor Ruban (UKR) |
| 2012 | Oh Jin-Hyek (KOR) |

**AU CORDON DORÉ (50 METERS)**
1900   Henri Herouin (FRA)

**AU CORDON DORÉ (33 METERS)**
1900   Hubert van Innis (BEL)

**AU CHAPELET (50 METERS)**
1900   Eugène Mougin (FRA)

**SUR LA PERCHE À LA HERSE**
1900   Emmanuel Foulon (FRA)

**AU CHAPELET (33 METERS)**
1900   Hubert van Innis (BEL)

**SUR LA PERCHE À LA PYRAMIDE**
1900   Émile Grumiaux (FRA)

**DOUBLE AMERICAN ROUND**
1904   George Philip Bryant (USA)

## Archery (continued)

**(DOUBLE) YORK ROUND**
| | |
|---|---|
| 1904 | George Philip Bryant (USA) |
| 1908 | William Dod (GBR) |

**CONTINENTAL STYLE**
1908   Eugène G. Grizot (FRA)

**FIXED BIRD TARGET (SMALL)**
1920   Edmond van Moer (BEL)

**FIXED BIRD TARGET (LARGE)**
1920   Édouard Cloetens (BEL)

**MOVING BIRD TARGET (28 METERS)**
1920   Hubert van Innis (BEL)

**MOVING BIRD TARGET (33 METERS)**
1920   Hubert van Innis (BEL)

**MOVING BIRD TARGET (50 METERS)**
1920   Julien Brulé (FRA)

**WOMEN'S INDIVIDUAL**
| | |
|---|---|
| 1972 | Doreen Wilber (USA) |
| 1976 | Luann Ryon (USA) |
| 1980 | Ketevan Losaberidze (URS) |
| 1984 | Seo Hyang Soon (KOR) |
| 1988 | Kim Soo Nyung (KOR) |
| 1992 | Cho Youn Jeong (KOR) |
| 1996 | Kim Kyung-Wook (KOR) |
| 2000 | Yun Mi-Jin (KOR) |
| 2004 | Park Sung Hyun (KOR) |

# Summer Olympic Games (continued)

## Archery (continued)

### WOMEN'S INDIVIDUAL (CONTINUED)
2008 Zhang Juan Juan (CHN)
2012 Ki Bo-Bae (KOR)

### DOUBLE COLUMBIA ROUND
1904 Matilda Scott Howell (USA)

### (DOUBLE) NATIONAL ROUND
1904 Matilda Scott Howell (USA)
1908 Sybil Fenton "Queenie" Newall (GBR)

### MEN'S TEAM
1904 United States
1988 Republic of Korea
1992 Spain
1996 United States
2000 Republic of Korea
2004 Republic of Korea
2008 Republic of Korea
2012 Italy

### WOMEN'S TEAM
1904 United States
1988 Republic of Korea
1992 Republic of Korea
1996 Republic of Korea
2000 Republic of Korea
2004 Republic of Korea
2008 Republic of Korea
2012 South Korea

### FIXED TARGET (2 EVENTS)
1920 Belgium

### MOVING TARGET (28 METERS)
1920 The Netherlands

### MOVING TARGET (33 METERS)
1920 Belgium

### MOVING TARGET (50 METERS)
1920 Belgium

## Association Football (Soccer)[1]

### MEN
1900 Great Britain
1904 Canada
1908 Great Britain
1912 Great Britain
1920 Belgium
1924 Uruguay
1928 Uruguay
1936 Italy
1948 Sweden
1952 Hungary
1956 USSR
1960 Yugoslavia
1964 Hungary
1968 Hungary
1972 Poland
1976 East Germany
1980 Czechoslovakia
1984 France
1988 USSR
1992 Spain
1996 Nigeria
2000 Cameroon
2004 Argentina

## Association Football (Soccer)[1] (continued)

### MEN (CONTINUED)
2008 Argentina
2012 Mexico

### WOMEN
1996 United States
2000 Norway
2004 United States
2008 United States
2012 United States

## Athletics (Track and Field) (men)

| 60 METERS | | SEC |
|---|---|---|
| 1900 | Alvin Kraenzlein (USA) | 7 |
| 1904 | Archie Hahn (USA) | 7 |

| 100 METERS | | SEC |
|---|---|---|
| 1896 | Thomas Burke (USA) | 12.0 |
| 1900 | Francis Jarvis (USA) | 11.0 |
| 1904 | Archie Hahn (USA) | 11.0 |
| 1908 | Reginald Walker (RSA) | 10.8 |
| 1912 | Ralph Craig (USA) | 10.8 |
| 1920 | Charles Paddock (USA) | 10.8 |
| 1924 | Harold Abrahams (GBR) | 10.6 |
| 1928 | Percy Williams (CAN) | 10.8 |
| 1932 | Eddie Tolan (USA) | 10.3 |
| 1936 | Jesse Owens (USA) | 10.3 |
| 1948 | Harrison Dillard (USA) | 10.3 |
| 1952 | Lindy Remigino (USA) | 10.4 |
| 1956 | Robert Morrow (USA) | 10.5 |
| 1960 | Armin Hary (GER) | 10.2 |
| 1964 | Robert Hayes (USA) | 10.0 |
| 1968 | James Hines (USA) | 9.9 |
| 1972 | Valery Borzov (URS) | 10.14 |
| 1976 | Hasely Crawford (TRI) | 10.06 |
| 1980 | Allan Wells (GBR) | 10.25 |
| 1984 | Carl Lewis (USA) | 9.99 |
| 1988 | Carl Lewis (USA)[2] | 9.92 |
| 1992 | Linford Christie (GBR) | 9.96 |
| 1996 | Donovan Bailey (CAN) | 9.84 |
| 2000 | Maurice Greene (USA) | 9.87 |
| 2004 | Justin Gatlin (USA) | 9.85 |
| 2008 | Usain Bolt (JAM) | 9.69 |
| 2012 | Usain Bolt (JAM) | 9.63 |

| 200 METERS | | SEC |
|---|---|---|
| 1900 | Walter Tewksbury (USA) | 22.2 |
| 1904 | Archie Hahn (USA) | 21.6 |
| 1908 | Robert Kerr (CAN) | 22.6 |
| 1912 | Ralph Craig (USA) | 21.7 |
| 1920 | Allen Woodring (USA) | 22.0 |
| 1924 | Jackson Scholz (USA) | 21.6 |
| 1928 | Percy Williams (CAN) | 21.8 |
| 1932 | Eddie Tolan (USA) | 21.2 |
| 1936 | Jesse Owens (USA) | 20.7 |
| 1948 | Melvin Patton (USA) | 21.1 |
| 1952 | Andy Stanfield (USA) | 20.7 |
| 1956 | Robert Morrow (USA) | 20.6 |
| 1960 | Livio Berruti (ITA) | 20.5 |
| 1964 | Henry Carr (USA) | 20.3 |
| 1968 | Tommie Smith (USA) | 19.8 |
| 1972 | Valery Borzov (URS) | 20.00 |
| 1976 | Donald Quarrie (JAM) | 20.23 |
| 1980 | Pietro Mennea (ITA) | 20.19 |
| 1984 | Carl Lewis (USA) | 19.80 |
| 1988 | Joe DeLoach (USA) | 19.75 |
| 1992 | Mike Marsh (USA) | 20.01 |
| 1996 | Michael Johnson (USA) | 19.32 |

## Summer Olympic Games (continued)

### Athletics (Track and Field) (men) (continued)

| 200 METERS (CONTINUED) | | SEC |
|---|---|---|
| 2000 | Konstantinos Kenteris (GRE) | 20.09 |
| 2004 | Shawn Crawford (USA) | 19.79 |
| 2008 | Usain Bolt (JAM) | 19.30 |
| 2012 | Usain Bolt (JAM) | 19.32 |

| 400 METERS | | SEC |
|---|---|---|
| 1896 | Thomas Burke (USA) | 54.2 |
| 1900 | Maxwell Long (USA) | 49.4 |
| 1904 | Harry Hillman (USA) | 49.2 |
| 1908 | Wyndham Halswelle (GBR) | 50.0 |
| 1912 | Charles Reidpath (USA) | 48.2 |
| 1920 | Bevil Rudd (RSA) | 49.6 |
| 1924 | Eric Liddell (GBR) | 47.6 |
| 1928 | Raymond Barbuti (USA) | 47.8 |
| 1932 | William Carr (USA) | 46.2 |
| 1936 | Archie Williams (USA) | 46.5 |
| 1948 | Arthur Wint (JAM) | 46.2 |
| 1952 | Vincent George Rhoden (JAM) | 45.9 |
| 1956 | Charles Jenkins (USA) | 46.7 |
| 1960 | Otis Davis (USA) | 44.9 |
| 1964 | Michael Larrabee (USA) | 45.1 |
| 1968 | Lee Evans (USA) | 43.8 |
| 1972 | Vincent Matthews (USA) | 44.66 |
| 1976 | Alberto Juantorena (CUB) | 44.26 |
| 1980 | Viktor Markin (URS) | 44.60 |
| 1984 | Alonzo Babers (USA) | 44.27 |
| 1988 | Steven Lewis (USA) | 43.87 |
| 1992 | Quincy Watts (USA) | 43.50 |
| 1996 | Michael Johnson (USA) | 43.49 |
| 2000 | Michael Johnson (USA) | 43.84 |
| 2004 | Jeremy Wariner (USA) | 44.00 |
| 2008 | LaShawn Merritt (USA) | 43.75 |
| 2012 | Kirani James (GRN) | 43.94 |

| 800 METERS | | MIN:SEC |
|---|---|---|
| 1896 | Edwin Flack (AUS) | 2:11.0 |
| 1900 | Alfred Tysoe (GBR) | 2:01.2 |
| 1904 | James Lightbody (USA) | 1:56.0 |
| 1908 | Melvin Sheppard (USA) | 1:52.8 |
| 1912 | James Edward Meredith (USA) | 1:51.9 |
| 1920 | Albert Hill (GBR) | 1:53.4 |
| 1924 | Douglas Lowe (GBR) | 1:52.4 |
| 1928 | Douglas Lowe (GBR) | 1:51.8 |
| 1932 | Thomas Hampson (GBR) | 1:49.7 |
| 1936 | John Woodruff (USA) | 1:52.9 |
| 1948 | Malvin Whitfield (USA) | 1:49.2 |
| 1952 | Malvin Whitfield (USA) | 1:49.2 |
| 1956 | Thomas Courtney (USA) | 1:47.7 |
| 1960 | Peter Snell (NZL) | 1:46.3 |
| 1964 | Peter Snell (NZL) | 1:45.1 |
| 1968 | Ralph Doubell (AUS) | 1:44.3 |
| 1972 | David Wottle (USA) | 1:45.9 |
| 1976 | Alberto Juantorena (CUB) | 1:43.50 |
| 1980 | Steven Ovett (GBR) | 1:45.40 |
| 1984 | Joaquim Cruz (BRA) | 1:43.00 |
| 1988 | Paul Ereng (KEN) | 1:43.45 |
| 1992 | William Tanui (KEN) | 1:43.66 |
| 1996 | Vebjoern Rodal (NOR) | 1:42.58 |
| 2000 | Nils Schumann (GER) | 1:45.08 |
| 2004 | Yury Borzakovsky (RUS) | 1:44.45 |
| 2008 | Wilfred Bungei (KEN) | 1:44.65 |
| 2012 | David Rudisha (KEN) | 1:40.91 |

| 1,500 METERS | | MIN:SEC |
|---|---|---|
| 1896 | Edwin Flack (AUS) | 4:33.2 |
| 1900 | Charles Bennett (GBR) | 4:06.2 |
| 1904 | James Lightbody (USA) | 4:05.4 |

### Athletics (Track and Field) (men) (continued)

| 1,500 METERS (CONTINUED) | | MIN:SEC |
|---|---|---|
| 1908 | Melvin Sheppard (USA) | 4:03.4 |
| 1912 | Arnold Jackson (GBR) | 3:56.8 |
| 1920 | Albert Hill (GBR) | 4:01.8 |
| 1924 | Paavo Nurmi (FIN) | 3:53.6 |
| 1928 | Harry Larva (FIN) | 3:53.2 |
| 1932 | Luigi Beccali (ITA) | 3:51.2 |
| 1936 | John Lovelock (NZL) | 3:47.8 |
| 1948 | Henry Eriksson (SWE) | 3:49.8 |
| 1952 | Joseph Barthel (LUX) | 3:45.1 |
| 1956 | Ronald Delany (IRL) | 3:41.2 |
| 1960 | Herbert Elliott (AUS) | 3:35.6 |
| 1964 | Peter Snell (NZL) | 3:38.1 |
| 1968 | Hezekiah Kipchoge Keino (KEN) | 3:34.9 |
| 1972 | Pekka Vasala (FIN) | 3:36.3 |
| 1976 | John Walker (NZL) | 3:39.17 |
| 1980 | Sebastian Coe (GBR) | 3:38.40 |
| 1984 | Sebastian Coe (GBR) | 3:32.53 |
| 1988 | Peter Rono (KEN) | 3:35.96 |
| 1992 | Fermin Cacho Ruiz (ESP) | 3:40.12 |
| 1996 | Noureddine Morceli (ALG) | 3:35.78 |
| 2000 | Noah Ngeny (KEN) | 3:32.07 |
| 2004 | Hicham El Guerrouj (MAR) | 3:34.18 |
| 2008 | Asbel Kipruto Kiprop (KEN) | 3:33.11 |
| 2012 | Taoufik Makhloufi (ALG) | 3:34.08 |

| 5,000 METERS | | MIN:SEC |
|---|---|---|
| 1912 | Hannes Kolehmainen (FIN) | 14:36.6 |
| 1920 | Joseph Guillemot (FRA) | 14:55.6 |
| 1924 | Paavo Nurmi (FIN) | 14:31.2 |
| 1928 | Vilho Ritola (FIN) | 14:38.0 |
| 1932 | Lauri Lehtinen (FIN) | 14:30.0 |
| 1936 | Gunnar Höckert (FIN) | 14:22.2 |
| 1948 | Gaston Reiff (BEL) | 14:17.6 |
| 1952 | Emil Zatopek (TCH) | 14:06.6 |
| 1956 | Vladimir Kuts (URS) | 13:39.6 |
| 1960 | Murray Halberg (NZL) | 13:43.4 |
| 1964 | Robert Keyser Schul (USA) | 13:48.8 |
| 1968 | Mohamed Gammoudi (TUN) | 14:05.0 |
| 1972 | Lasse Viren (FIN) | 13:26.4 |
| 1976 | Lasse Viren (FIN) | 13:24.76 |
| 1980 | Miruts Yifter (ETH) | 13:21.00 |
| 1984 | Said Aouita (MAR) | 13:05.59 |
| 1988 | John Ngugi (KEN) | 13:11.70 |
| 1992 | Dieter Baumann (GER) | 13:12.52 |
| 1996 | Venuste Niyongabo (BDI) | 13:07.97 |
| 2000 | Million Wolde (ETH) | 13:35.49 |
| 2004 | Hicham El Guerrouj (MAR) | 13:14.39 |
| 2008 | Kenenisa Bekele (ETH) | 12:57.82 |
| 2012 | Mohamed Farah (GBR) | 13:41.66 |

| 5 MILES | | MIN:SEC |
|---|---|---|
| 1908 | Emil Voigt (GBR) | 25:11.2 |

| 10,000 METERS | | MIN:SEC |
|---|---|---|
| 1912 | Hannes Kolehmainen (FIN) | 31:20.8 |
| 1920 | Paavo Nurmi (FIN) | 31:45.8 |
| 1924 | Vilho Ritola (FIN) | 30:23.2 |
| 1928 | Paavo Nurmi (FIN) | 30:18.8 |
| 1932 | Janusz Kusocinski (POL) | 30:11.4 |
| 1936 | Ilmari Salminen (FIN) | 30:15.4 |
| 1948 | Emil Zatopek (TCH) | 29:59.6 |
| 1952 | Emil Zatopek (TCH) | 29:17.0 |
| 1956 | Vladimir Kuts (URS) | 28:45.6 |
| 1960 | Pyotr Bolotnikov (URS) | 28:32.2 |
| 1964 | William Mills (USA) | 28:24.4 |
| 1968 | Nabiba Temu (KEN) | 29:27.4 |
| 1972 | Lasse Viren (FIN) | 27:38.4 |

## Summer Olympic Games (continued)

### Athletics (Track and Field) (men) (continued)

| 10,000 METERS (CONTINUED) | | MIN:SEC |
|---|---|---|
| 1976 | Lasse Viren (FIN) | 27:40.38 |
| 1980 | Miruts Yifter (ETH) | 27:42.70 |
| 1984 | Alberto Cova (ITA) | 27:47.54 |
| 1988 | Brahim Boutaib (MAR) | 27:21.46 |
| 1992 | Khalid Skah (MAR) | 27:46.70 |
| 1996 | Haile Gebrselassie (ETH) | 27:07.34 |
| 2000 | Haile Gebrselassie (ETH) | 27:18.20 |
| 2004 | Kenenisa Bekele (ETH) | 27:05.10 |
| 2008 | Kenenisa Bekele (ETH) | 27:01.17 |
| 2012 | Mohamed Farah (GBR) | 27:30.42 |

| MARATHON | | HR:MIN:SEC |
|---|---|---|
| 1896 | Spiridon Louis (GRE) | 2:58:50.0 |
| 1900 | Michel Theato (FRA) | 2:59:45.0 |
| 1904 | Thomas Hicks (USA) | 3:28:53.0 |
| 1908 | John Hayes (USA) | 2:55:18.4 |
| 1912 | Kenneth McArthur (RSA) | 2:36:54.8 |
| 1920 | Hannes Kolehmainen (FIN) | 2:32:35.8 |
| 1924 | Albin Stenroos (FIN) | 2:41:22.6 |
| 1928 | Boughèra El Ouafi (FRA) | 2:32:57.0 |
| 1932 | Juan Carlos Zabala (ARG) | 2:31:36.0 |
| 1936 | Kitei Son (JPN) | 2:29:19.2 |
| 1948 | Delfo Cabrera (ARG) | 2:34:51.6 |
| 1952 | Emil Zatopek (TCH) | 2:23:03.2 |
| 1956 | Alain Mimoun-O-Kacha (FRA) | 2:25:00.0 |
| 1960 | Abebe Bikila (ETH) | 2:15:16.2 |
| 1964 | Abebe Bikila (ETH) | 2:12:11.2 |
| 1968 | Mamo Wolde (ETH) | 2:20:26.4 |
| 1972 | Frank Shorter (USA) | 2:12:19.8 |
| 1976 | Waldemar Cierpinski (GDR) | 2:09:55.0 |
| 1980 | Waldemar Cierpinski (GDR) | 2:11:03.0 |
| 1984 | Carlos Lopes (POR) | 2:09:21.0 |
| 1988 | Gelindo Bordin (ITA) | 2:10:32.0 |
| 1992 | Hwang Young-Cho (KOR) | 2:13:23.0 |
| 1996 | Josia Thugwane (RSA) | 2:12:36.0 |
| 2000 | Gezahgne Abera (ETH) | 2:10:11.0 |
| 2004 | Stefano Baldini (ITA) | 2:10:55.0 |
| 2008 | Samuel Kamau Wansiru (KEN) | 2:06:32.0 |
| 2012 | Stephen Kiprotich (UGA) | 2:08:01 |

| 110-METER HURDLES | | SEC |
|---|---|---|
| 1896[3] | Thomas Curtis (USA) | 17.6 |
| 1900 | Alvin Kraenzlein (USA) | 15.4 |
| 1904 | Frederick Schule (USA) | 16.0 |
| 1908 | Forrest Smithson (USA) | 15.0 |
| 1912 | Frederick Kelly (USA) | 15.1 |
| 1920 | Earl Thomson (CAN) | 14.8 |
| 1924 | Daniel Kinsey (USA) | 15.0 |
| 1928 | Sydney Atkinson (RSA) | 14.8 |
| 1932 | George Saling (USA) | 14.6 |
| 1936 | Forrest Towns (USA) | 14.2 |
| 1948 | William Porter (USA) | 13.9 |
| 1952 | Harrison Dillard (USA) | 13.7 |
| 1956 | Lee Calhoun (USA) | 13.5 |
| 1960 | Lee Calhoun (USA) | 13.8 |
| 1964 | Hayes Wendell Jones (USA) | 13.6 |
| 1968 | Willie Davenport (USA) | 13.3 |
| 1972 | Rodney Milburn (USA) | 13.24 |
| 1976 | Guy Drut (FRA) | 13.30 |
| 1980 | Thomas Munkelt (GDR) | 13.39 |
| 1984 | Roger Kingdom (USA) | 13.20 |
| 1988 | Roger Kingdom (USA) | 12.98 |
| 1992 | Mark McKoy (CAN) | 13.12 |
| 1996 | Allen Johnson (USA) | 12.95 |
| 2000 | Anier Garcia (CUB) | 13.00 |
| 2004 | Liu Xiang (CHN) | 12.91 |

### Athletics (Track and Field) (men) (continued)

| 110-METER HURDLES (CONTINUED) | | SEC |
|---|---|---|
| 2008 | Dayron Robles (CUB) | 12.93 |
| 2012 | Aries Merritt (USA) | 12.92 |

| 200-METER HURDLES | | SEC |
|---|---|---|
| 1900 | Alvin Kraenzlein (USA) | 25.4 |
| 1904 | Harry Hillman (USA) | 24.6 |

| 400-METER HURDLES | | SEC |
|---|---|---|
| 1900 | Walter Tewksbury (USA) | 57.6 |
| 1904[4] | Harry Hillman (USA) | 53.0 |
| 1908 | Charles Bacon (USA) | 55.0 |
| 1920 | Frank Loomis (USA) | 54.0 |
| 1924 | Frederick Morgan Taylor (USA) | 52.6 |
| 1928 | David George Burghley (GBR) | 53.4 |
| 1932 | Robert Tisdall (IRL) | 51.7 |
| 1936 | Glenn Hardin (USA) | 52.4 |
| 1948 | Roy Cochran (USA) | 51.1 |
| 1952 | Charles Moore (USA) | 50.8 |
| 1956 | Glenn Davis (USA) | 50.1 |
| 1960 | Glenn Davis (USA) | 49.3 |
| 1964 | Warren Cawley (USA) | 49.6 |
| 1968 | David Hemery (GBR) | 48.1 |
| 1972 | John Akii-Bua (UGA) | 47.82 |
| 1976 | Edwin Moses (USA) | 47.64 |
| 1980 | Volker Beck (GDR) | 48.70 |
| 1984 | Edwin Moses (USA) | 47.75 |
| 1988 | Andre Phillips (USA) | 47.19 |
| 1992 | Kevin Young (USA) | 46.78 |
| 1996 | Derrick Adkins (USA) | 47.54 |
| 2000 | Angelo Taylor (USA) | 47.50 |
| 2004 | Felix Sánchez (DOM) | 47.63 |
| 2008 | Angelo Taylor (USA) | 47.25 |
| 2012 | Felix Sanchez (DOM) | 47.63 |

| 2,500-METER STEEPLECHASE | | MIN:SEC |
|---|---|---|
| 1900 | George Orton (USA) | 7:34.4 |

| 2,590-METER STEEPLECHASE | | MIN:SEC |
|---|---|---|
| 1904 | James Lightbody (USA) | 7:39.6 |

| 3,000-METER STEEPLECHASE | | MIN:SEC |
|---|---|---|
| 1920 | Percy Hodge (GBR) | 10:00.4 |
| 1924 | Vilho Ritola (FIN) | 9:33.6 |
| 1928 | Toivo Loukola (FIN) | 9:21.8 |
| 1932 | Volmari Iso-Hollo (FIN) | 10:33.4[5] |
| 1936 | Volmari Iso-Hollo (FIN) | 9:03.8 |
| 1948 | Thore Sjöstrand (SWE) | 9:04.6 |
| 1952 | Horace Ashenfelter (USA) | 8:45.4 |
| 1956 | Christopher Brasher (GBR) | 8:41.2 |
| 1960 | Zdislaw Krzyszkowiak (POL) | 8:34.2 |
| 1964 | Gaston Roelants (BEL) | 8:30.8 |
| 1968 | Amos Biwott (KEN) | 8:51.0 |
| 1972 | Kipchoge Keino (KEN) | 8:23.6 |
| 1976 | Anders Gärderud (SWE) | 8:08.02 |
| 1980 | Bronislaw Malinowski (POL) | 8:09.70 |
| 1984 | Julius Korir (KEN) | 8:11.80 |
| 1988 | Julius Kariuki (KEN) | 8:05.51 |
| 1992 | Mathew Birir (KEN) | 8:08.84 |
| 1996 | Joseph Keter (KEN) | 8:07.12 |
| 2000 | Reuben Kosgei (KEN) | 8:21.43 |
| 2004 | Ezekiel Kemboi (KEN) | 8:05.81 |
| 2008 | Brimin Kiprop Kipruto (KEN) | 8:10.34 |
| 2012 | Ezekiel Kemboi (KEN) | 8:18.56 |

| 3,200-METER STEEPLECHASE | | MIN:SEC |
|---|---|---|
| 1908 | Arthur Russell (GBR) | 10:47.8 |

## Summer Olympic Games (continued)

### Athletics (Track and Field) (men) (continued)

| 3,000 METERS (TEAM) (TEAM/INDIVIDUAL WINNER) | MIN:SEC |
|---|---|
| 1912 | United States/Tell Berna | 8:44.6 |
| 1920 | United States/Horace Brown | 8:45.4 |
| 1924 | Finland/Paavo Nurmi | 8:32 |

| 3 MILES (TEAM) (TEAM/INDIVIDUAL WINNER) | MIN:SEC |
|---|---|
| 1908 | Great Britain/Joseph Deakin | 14:39.6 |

| 5,000 METERS (TEAM) (TEAM/INDIVIDUAL WINNER) | MIN:SEC |
|---|---|
| 1900 | Great Britain–Australia/Charles Bennett | 15:20 |

| 4 MILES (TEAM) (TEAM/INDIVIDUAL WINNER) | MIN:SEC |
|---|---|
| 1904 | United States/Arthur Newton | 21:17.8 |

| 4 × 100-METER RELAY | SEC |
|---|---|
| 1912 | Great Britain | 42.4 |
| 1920 | United States | 42.2 |
| 1924 | United States | 41.0 |
| 1928 | United States | 41.0 |
| 1932 | United States | 40.0 |
| 1936 | United States | 39.8 |
| 1948 | United States | 40.6 |
| 1952 | United States | 40.1 |
| 1956 | United States | 39.5 |
| 1960 | Germany | 39.5 |
| 1964 | United States | 39.0 |
| 1968 | United States | 38.2 |
| 1972 | United States | 38.19 |
| 1976 | United States | 38.33 |
| 1980 | USSR | 38.26 |
| 1984 | United States | 37.83 |
| 1988 | USSR | 38.19 |
| 1992 | United States | 37.40 |
| 1996 | Canada | 37.69 |
| 2000 | United States | 37.61 |
| 2004 | Great Britain | 38.07 |
| 2008 | Jamaica | 37.10 |
| 2012 | Jamaica | 36.84 |

| 4 × 400-METER RELAY | MIN:SEC |
|---|---|
| 1912 | United States | 3:16.6 |
| 1920 | Great Britain | 3:22.2 |
| 1924 | United States | 3:16.0 |
| 1928 | United States | 3:14.2 |
| 1932 | United States | 3:08.2 |
| 1936 | Great Britain | 3:09.0 |
| 1948 | United States | 3:10.4 |
| 1952 | Jamaica | 3:03.9 |
| 1956 | United States | 3:04.8 |
| 1960 | United States | 3:02.2 |
| 1964 | United States | 3:00.7 |
| 1968 | United States | 2:56.1 |
| 1972 | Kenya | 2:59.8 |
| 1976 | United States | 2:58.65 |
| 1980 | USSR | 3:01.08 |
| 1984 | United States | 2:57.91 |
| 1988 | United States | 2:56.16 |
| 1992 | United States | 2:55.74 |
| 1996 | United States | 2:55.99 |
| 2000 | Nigeria | 2:58.68 |
| 2004 | United States | 2:55.91 |
| 2008 | United States | 2:55.39 |
| 2012 | Bahamas | 2:56.72 |

| 1,600-METER RELAY (200 × 200 × 400 × 800 METERS) | MIN:SEC |
|---|---|
| 1908 | United States | 3:29.4 |

### Athletics (Track and Field) (men) (continued)

| 8,000-METER CROSS-COUNTRY | MIN:SEC |
|---|---|
| 1920 | Paavo Nurmi (FIN) | 27:15 |

| 10,000-METER CROSS-COUNTRY | MIN:SEC |
|---|---|
| 1924 | Paavo Nurmi (FIN) | 32:54.8 |

| 12,000-METER CROSS-COUNTRY | MIN:SEC |
|---|---|
| 1912 | Hannes Kolehmainen (FIN) | 45:11.6 |

| 3,000-METER WALK | MIN:SEC |
|---|---|
| 1920 | Ugo Frigerio (ITA) | 13:14.2 |

| 3,500-METER WALK | MIN:SEC |
|---|---|
| 1908 | George Larner (GBR) | 14:55 |

| 10,000-METER WALK | MIN:SEC |
|---|---|
| 1912 | George Goulding (CAN) | 46:28.4 |
| 1920 | Ugo Frigerio (ITA) | 48:06.2 |
| 1924 | Ugo Frigerio (ITA) | 47:49.0 |
| 1948 | John Mikaelsson (SWE) | 45:13.2 |
| 1952 | John Mikaelsson (SWE) | 45:02.8 |

| 10-MILE WALK | HR:MIN:SEC |
|---|---|
| 1908 | George Larner (GBR) | 1:15:57.4 |

| 20,000-METER WALK | HR:MIN:SEC |
|---|---|
| 1956 | Leonid Spirin (URS) | 1:31:27.4 |
| 1960 | Vladimir Golubnichy (URS) | 1:34:07.2 |
| 1964 | Kenneth Matthews (GBR) | 1:29:34.0 |
| 1968 | Vladimir Golubnichy (URS) | 1:33:58.4 |
| 1972 | Peter Frenkel (GDR) | 1:26:42.6 |
| 1976 | Daniel Bautista (MEX) | 1:24:40.6 |
| 1980 | Maurizio Damilano (ITA) | 1:23:35.5 |
| 1984 | Ernesto Canto (MEX) | 1:23:13.0 |
| 1988 | Jozef Pribilinec (TCH) | 1:19:57.0 |
| 1992 | Daniel Plaza Montero (ESP) | 1:21:45.0 |
| 1996 | Jefferson Pérez (ECU) | 1:20:07.0 |
| 2000 | Robert Korzeniowski (POL) | 1:18:59.0 |
| 2004 | Ivano Brugnetti (ITA) | 1:19:40.0 |
| 2008 | Valery Borchin (RUS) | 1:19:01.0 |
| 2012 | Chen Ding (CHN) | 1:18:46 |

| 50,000-METER WALK | HR:MIN:SEC |
|---|---|
| 1932 | Thomas Green (GBR) | 4:50:10.0 |
| 1936 | Harold Whitlock (GBR) | 4:30:41.4 |
| 1948 | John Ljunggren (SWE) | 4:41:52.0 |
| 1952 | Giuseppe Dordoni (ITA) | 4:28:07.8 |
| 1956 | Norman Read (NZL) | 4:30:42.8 |
| 1960 | Donald Thompson (GBR) | 4:25:30.0 |
| 1964 | Abdon Pamich (ITA) | 4:11:12.4 |
| 1968 | Christophe Höhne (GDR) | 4:20:13.6 |
| 1972 | Bernd Kannenberg (FRG) | 3:56:11.6 |
| 1980 | Hartwig Gauder (GDR) | 3:49:24.0 |
| 1984 | Raúl Gonzáles (MEX) | 3:47:26.0 |
| 1988 | Vyacheslav Ivanenko (URS) | 3:38:29.0 |
| 1992 | Andrey Perlov (UNT) | 3:50:13.0 |
| 1996 | Robert Korzeniowski (POL) | 3:43:03.0 |
| 2000 | Robert Korzeniowski (POL) | 3:42:22.0 |
| 2004 | Robert Korzeniowski (POL) | 3:38:46.0 |
| 2008 | Alex Schwazer (ITA) | 3:37:09.0 |
| 2012 | Sergey Kirdyapkin (RUS) | 3:35:59 |

| HIGH JUMP | METERS |
|---|---|
| 1896 | Ellery Clark (USA) | 1.81 |
| 1900 | Irving Baxter (USA) | 1.90 |
| 1904 | Samuel Jones (USA) | 1.80 |
| 1908 | Harry Porter (USA) | 1.90 |
| 1912 | Alma Richards (USA) | 1.93 |

# Summer Olympic Games (continued)

## Athletics (Track and Field) (men) (continued)

| HIGH JUMP (CONTINUED) | | METERS |
|---|---|---|
| 1920 | Richmond Landon (USA) | 1.93 |
| 1924 | Harold Osborn (USA) | 1.98 |
| 1928 | Robert King (USA) | 1.94 |
| 1932 | Duncan McNaughton (CAN) | 1.97 |
| 1936 | Cornelius Johnson (USA) | 2.03 |
| 1948 | John Winter (AUS) | 1.98 |
| 1952 | Walter Davis (USA) | 2.04 |
| 1956 | Charles Dumas (USA) | 2.12 |
| 1960 | Robert Shavlakadze (URS) | 2.16 |
| 1964 | Valery Brumel (URS) | 2.18 |
| 1968 | Richard Fosbury (USA) | 2.24 |
| 1972 | Yury Tarmak (URS) | 2.23 |
| 1976 | Jacek Wszola (POL) | 2.25 |
| 1980 | Gerd Wessig (GDR) | 2.36 |
| 1984 | Dietmar Mögenburg (FRG) | 2.35 |
| 1988 | Gennady Avdeyenko (URS) | 2.38 |
| 1992 | Javier Sotomayor (CUB) | 2.34 |
| 1996 | Charles Austin (USA) | 2.39 |
| 2000 | Sergey Klyugin (RUS) | 2.35 |
| 2004 | Stefan Holm (SWE) | 2.36 |
| 2008 | Andrey Silnov (RUS) | 2.36 |
| 2012 | Ivan Ukhov (RUS) | 2.38 |

| STANDING HIGH JUMP | | METERS |
|---|---|---|
| 1900 | Ray Ewry (USA) | 1.65 |
| 1904 | Ray Ewry (USA) | 1.60 |
| 1908 | Ray Ewry (USA) | 1.57 |
| 1912 | Platt Adams (USA) | 1.63 |

| POLE VAULT | | METERS |
|---|---|---|
| 1896 | William Welles Hoyt (USA) | 3.30 |
| 1900 | Irving Baxter (USA) | 3.30 |
| 1904 | Charles Dvorak (USA) | 3.50 |
| 1908 | Edward Cooke (USA); Alfred Gilbert (USA) (tied) | 3.71 |
| 1912 | Harry Babcock (USA) | 3.95 |
| 1920 | Frank Foss (USA) | 4.09 |
| 1924 | Lee Barnes (USA) | 3.95 |
| 1928 | Sabin Carr (USA) | 4.20 |
| 1932 | William Miller (USA) | 4.31 |
| 1936 | Earle Meadows (USA) | 4.35 |
| 1948 | Owen Guinn Smith (USA) | 4.30 |
| 1952 | Robert Richards (USA) | 4.55 |
| 1956 | Robert Richards (USA) | 4.56 |
| 1960 | Donald Bragg (USA) | 4.70 |
| 1964 | Fred Hansen (USA) | 5.10 |
| 1968 | Robert Seagren (USA) | 5.40 |
| 1972 | Wolfgang Nordwig (GDR) | 5.50 |
| 1976 | Tadeusz Slusarski (POL) | 5.50 |
| 1980 | Wladyslaw Kozakiewicz (POL) | 5.78 |
| 1984 | Pierre Quinon (FRA) | 5.75 |
| 1988 | Sergey Bubka (URS) | 5.90 |
| 1992 | Maksim Tarasov (UNT) | 5.80 |
| 1996 | Jean Galfione (FRA) | 5.92 |
| 2000 | Nick Hysong (USA) | 5.90 |
| 2004 | Timothy Mack (USA) | 5.95 |
| 2008 | Steve Hooker (AUS) | 5.96 |
| 2012 | Renaud Lavillenie (FRA) | 5.97 |

| LONG JUMP | | METERS |
|---|---|---|
| 1896 | Ellery Clark (USA) | 6.35 |
| 1900 | Alvin Kraenzlein (USA) | 7.18 |
| 1904 | Meyer Prinstein (USA) | 7.34 |
| 1908 | Francis Irons (USA) | 7.48 |
| 1912 | Albert Gutterson (USA) | 7.60 |
| 1920 | William Pettersson (SWE) | 7.15 |
| 1924 | William de Hart-Hubbard (USA) | 7.44 |

## Athletics (Track and Field) (men) (continued)

| LONG JUMP (CONTINUED) | | METERS |
|---|---|---|
| 1928 | Edward Hamm (USA) | 7.73 |
| 1932 | Edward Gordon (USA) | 7.64 |
| 1936 | Jesse Owens (USA) | 8.06 |
| 1948 | Willie Steele (USA) | 7.82 |
| 1952 | Jerome Biffle (USA) | 7.57 |
| 1956 | Gregory Bell (USA) | 7.83 |
| 1960 | Ralph Boston (USA) | 8.12 |
| 1964 | Lynn Davies (GBR) | 8.07 |
| 1968 | Robert Beamon (USA) | 8.90 |
| 1972 | Randy Williams (USA) | 8.24 |
| 1976 | Arnie Robinson (USA) | 8.35 |
| 1980 | Lutz Dombrowski (GDR) | 8.54 |
| 1984 | Carl Lewis (USA) | 8.54 |
| 1988 | Carl Lewis (USA) | 8.72 |
| 1992 | Carl Lewis (USA) | 8.67 |
| 1996 | Carl Lewis (USA) | 8.50 |
| 2000 | Ivan Pedroso (CUB) | 8.55 |
| 2004 | Dwight Phillips (USA) | 8.59 |
| 2008 | Irving Jahir Saladino Aranda (PAN) | 8.34 |
| 2012 | Greg Rutherford (GBR) | 8.31 |

| STANDING LONG JUMP | | METERS |
|---|---|---|
| 1900 | Ray Ewry (USA) | 3.21 |
| 1904 | Ray Ewry (USA) | 3.47 |
| 1908 | Ray Ewry (USA) | 3.33 |
| 1912 | Constantinos Tsiklitiras (GRE) | 3.37 |

| TRIPLE JUMP | | METERS |
|---|---|---|
| 1896 | James Connolly (USA) | 13.71 |
| 1900 | Myer Prinstein (USA) | 14.47 |
| 1904 | Myer Prinstein (USA) | 14.35 |
| 1908 | Timothy Ahearne (GBR) | 14.91 |
| 1912 | Gustaf Lindblom (SWE) | 14.76 |
| 1920 | Vilho Tuulos (FIN) | 14.50 |
| 1924 | Anthony Winter (AUS) | 15.53 |
| 1928 | Mikio Oda (JPN) | 15.21 |
| 1932 | Chuhei Nambu (JPN) | 15.72 |
| 1936 | Naoto Tajima (JPN) | 16.00 |
| 1948 | Arne Åhman (SWE) | 15.40 |
| 1952 | Adhemar Ferreira da Silva (BRA) | 16.22 |
| 1956 | Adhemar Ferreira da Silva (BRA) | 16.35 |
| 1960 | Josef Szmidt (POL) | 16.81 |
| 1964 | Josef Szmidt (POL) | 16.85 |
| 1968 | Viktor Saneyev (URS) | 17.39 |
| 1972 | Viktor Saneyev (URS) | 17.35 |
| 1976 | Viktor Saneyev (URS) | 17.29 |
| 1980 | Jaak Uudmae (URS) | 17.35 |
| 1984 | Al Joyner (USA) | 17.26 |
| 1988 | Khristo Markov (BUL) | 17.61 |
| 1992 | Michael Conley (USA) | 17.63 |
| 1996 | Kenny Harrison (USA) | 18.09 |
| 2000 | Jonathan Edwards (GBR) | 17.71 |
| 2004 | Christian Olsson (SWE) | 17.79 |
| 2008 | Nelson Évora (POR) | 17.67 |
| 2012 | Christian Taylor (USA) | 17.81 |

| STANDING TRIPLE JUMP | | METERS |
|---|---|---|
| 1900 | Ray Ewry (USA) | 10.58 |
| 1904 | Ray Ewry (USA) | 10.54 |

| SHOT PUT | | METERS |
|---|---|---|
| 1896 | Robert Garrett (USA) | 11.22 |
| 1900 | Richard Sheldon (USA) | 14.10 |
| 1904 | Ralph Rose (USA) | 14.81 |
| 1908 | Ralph Rose (USA) | 14.21 |
| 1912 | Patrick McDonald (USA) | 15.34 |
| 1920 | Frans Pörhölä (FIN) | 14.81 |

# Summer Olympic Games (continued)

## Athletics (Track and Field) (men) (continued)

| SHOT PUT (CONTINUED) | | METERS |
|---|---|---|
| 1924 | Lemuel Clarence Houser (USA) | 14.99 |
| 1928 | John Kuck (USA) | 15.87 |
| 1932 | Leo Sexton (USA) | 16.00 |
| 1936 | Hans Woellke (GER) | 16.20 |
| 1948 | Wilbur Thompson (USA) | 17.12 |
| 1952 | William Parry O'Brien (USA) | 17.41 |
| 1956 | William Parry O'Brien (USA) | 18.57 |
| 1960 | William Nieder (USA) | 19.68 |
| 1964 | Dallas Long (USA) | 20.33 |
| 1968 | Randy Matson (USA) | 20.54 |
| 1972 | Wladislaw Komar (POL) | 21.18 |
| 1976 | Udo Beyer (GDR) | 21.05 |
| 1980 | Vladimir Kiselyov (URS) | 21.35 |
| 1984 | Alessandro Andrei (ITA) | 21.26 |
| 1988 | Ulf Timmermann (GDR) | 22.47 |
| 1992 | Michael Stulce (USA) | 21.70 |
| 1996 | Randy Barnes (USA) | 21.62 |
| 2000 | Arsi Harju (FIN) | 21.29 |
| 2004 | Yury Bilonog (UKR) | 21.16 |
| 2008 | Tomasz Majewski (POL) | 21.51 |
| 2012 | Tomasz Majewski (POL) | 21.89 |

| SHOT PUT (TWO HANDS) | | METERS |
|---|---|---|
| 1912 | Ralph Rose (USA) | 27.7 |

| DISCUS THROW | | METERS |
|---|---|---|
| 1896 | Robert Garrett (USA) | 29.15 |
| 1900 | Rezso Bauer (HUN) | 36.04 |
| 1904 | Martin Sheridan (USA) | 39.28 |
| 1908 | Martin Sheridan (USA) | 40.89 |
| 1912 | Armas Taipale (FIN) | 45.21 |
| 1920 | Elmer Niklander (FIN) | 44.68 |
| 1924 | Lemuel Clarence Houser (USA) | 46.15 |
| 1928 | Lemuel Clarence Houser (USA) | 47.32 |
| 1932 | John Anderson (USA) | 49.49 |
| 1936 | Kenneth Carpenter (USA) | 50.48 |
| 1948 | Adolfo Consolini (ITA) | 52.78 |
| 1952 | Sim Iness (USA) | 55.03 |
| 1956 | Alfred Oerter (USA) | 56.36 |
| 1960 | Alfred Oerter (USA) | 59.18 |
| 1964 | Alfred Oerter (USA) | 61.00 |
| 1968 | Alfred Oerter (USA) | 64.78 |
| 1972 | Ludvig Danek (TCH) | 64.40 |
| 1976 | Mac Wilkins (USA) | 67.50 |
| 1980 | Viktor Rashchupkin (URS) | 66.64 |
| 1984 | Rolf Danneberg (FRG) | 66.60 |
| 1988 | Jürgen Schult (GDR) | 68.82 |
| 1992 | Romas Ubartas (LTU) | 65.12 |
| 1996 | Lars Riedel (GER) | 69.40 |
| 2000 | Virgilijus Alekna (LTU) | 69.30 |
| 2004 | Virgilijus Alekna (LTU)[2] | 69.89 |
| 2008 | Gerd Kanter (EST) | 68.82 |
| 2012 | Robert Harting (GER) | 68.27 |

| DISCUS (GREEK STYLE) | | METERS |
|---|---|---|
| 1908 | Martin Sheridan (USA) | 37.99 |

| DISCUS (TWO HANDS) | | METERS |
|---|---|---|
| 1912 | Armas Taipale (FIN) | 82.86 |

| HAMMER THROW | | METERS |
|---|---|---|
| 1900 | John Flanagan (USA) | 49.73 |
| 1904 | John Flanagan (USA) | 51.23 |
| 1908 | John Flanagan (USA) | 51.92 |
| 1912 | Matthew McGrath (USA) | 54.74 |
| 1920 | Patrick Ryan (USA) | 52.87 |
| 1924 | Frederick Tootell (USA) | 53.30 |

## Athletics (Track and Field) (men) (continued)

| HAMMER THROW (CONTINUED) | | METERS |
|---|---|---|
| 1928 | Patrick O'Callaghan (IRL) | 51.39 |
| 1932 | Patrick O'Callaghan (IRL) | 53.92 |
| 1936 | Karl Hein (GER) | 56.49 |
| 1948 | Imre Nemeth (HUN) | 56.07 |
| 1952 | Jozsef Csermak (HUN) | 60.34 |
| 1956 | Harold Connolly (USA) | 63.19 |
| 1960 | Vasily Rudenkov (URS) | 67.10 |
| 1964 | Romuald Klim (URS) | 69.74 |
| 1968 | Gyula Zsivotzky (HUN) | 73.36 |
| 1972 | Anatoly Bondarchuk (URS) | 75.50 |
| 1976 | Yury Sedykh (URS) | 77.52 |
| 1980 | Yury Sedykh (URS) | 81.80 |
| 1984 | Juha Tiainen (FIN) | 78.08 |
| 1988 | Sergey Litvinov (URS) | 84.80 |
| 1992 | Andrey Abduvaliyev (UNT) | 82.53 |
| 1996 | Balazs Kiss (HUN) | 81.24 |
| 2000 | Szymon Ziolkowski (POL) | 80.02 |
| 2004 | Koji Murofushi (JPN)[2] | 82.91 |
| 2008 | Primoz Kozmus (SLO) | 82.02 |
| 2012 | Krisztian Pars (HUN) | 80.59 |

| JAVELIN THROW | | METERS |
|---|---|---|
| 1908 | Eric Lemming (SWE) | 54.83 |
| 1912 | Eric Lemming (SWE) | 60.64 |
| 1920 | Jonni Myyrä (FIN) | 65.78 |
| 1924 | Jonni Myyrä (FIN) | 62.96 |
| 1928 | Erik Lundkvist (SWE) | 66.60 |
| 1932 | Matti Järvinen (FIN) | 72.71 |
| 1936 | Gerhard Stöck (GER) | 71.84 |
| 1948 | Kai Rautavaara (FIN) | 69.77 |
| 1952 | Cy Young (USA) | 73.78 |
| 1956 | Egil Danielson (NOR) | 85.71 |
| 1960 | Viktor Tsybulenko (URS) | 84.64 |
| 1964 | Pauli Nevala (FIN) | 82.66 |
| 1968 | Janis Lusis (URS) | 90.10 |
| 1972 | Klaus Wolfermann (FRG) | 90.48 |
| 1976 | Miklos Nemeth (HUN) | 94.58 |
| 1980 | Dainis Kula (URS) | 91.20 |
| 1984 | Arto Härkönen (FIN) | 86.76 |
| 1988 | Tapio Korjus (FIN) | 84.28 |
| 1992 | Jan Zelezny (TCH) | 89.66 |
| 1996 | Jan Zelezny (CZE) | 88.16 |
| 2000 | Jan Zelezny (CZE) | 90.17 |
| 2004 | Andreas Thorkildsen (NOR) | 86.50 |
| 2008 | Andreas Thorkildsen (NOR) | 90.57 |
| 2012 | Keshorn Walcott (TRI) | 84.58 |

| JAVELIN (FREESTYLE) | | METERS |
|---|---|---|
| 1908 | Eric Lemming (SWE) | 54.45 |

| JAVELIN (TWO HANDS) | | METERS |
|---|---|---|
| 1912 | Juho Saaristo (FIN) | 109.42 |

| 56-LB WEIGHT THROW | | METERS |
|---|---|---|
| 1904 | Étienne Desmarteau (CAN) | 10.46 |
| 1920 | Patrick McDonald (USA) | 11.26 |

| TUG-OF-WAR | |
|---|---|
| 1900 | Sweden-Denmark |
| 1904 | United States |
| 1908 | Great Britain |
| 1912 | Sweden |
| 1920 | Great Britain |

| TRIATHLON (LONG JUMP/SHOT PUT/100 YARDS) | |
|---|---|
| 1904 | Max Emmerich (USA) |

# Summer Olympic Games (continued)

## Athletics (Track and Field) (men) (continued)

### PENTATHLON
1912 Jim Thorpe (USA)[6]; Ferdinand Bie (NOR) (cowinners)
1920 Eero Lehtonen (FIN)
1924 Eero Lehtonen (FIN)

### DECATHLON
1904 Thomas Kiely (IRL)
1912 Jim Thorpe (USA)[6]; Hugo Wieslander (SWE) (cowinners)
1920 Helge Lövland (NOR)
1924 Harold Osborn (USA)
1928 Paavo Yrjölä (FIN)
1932 James Bausch (USA)
1936 Glenn Morris (USA)
1948 Robert Mathias (USA)
1952 Robert Mathias (USA)
1956 Milton Campbell (USA)
1960 Rafer Johnson (USA)
1964 Willi Holdorf (GER)
1968 William Toomey (USA)
1972 Nikolay Avilov (URS)
1976 Bruce Jenner (USA)
1980 Daley Thompson (GBR)
1984 Daley Thompson (GBR)
1988 Christian Schenk (GDR)
1992 Robert Zmelik (TCH)
1996 Dan O'Brien (USA)
2000 Erki Nool (EST)
2004 Roman Sebrle (CZE)
2008 Bryan Clay (USA)
2012 Ashton Eaton (USA)

## Athletics (Track and Field) (women)

### 100 METERS
|      |                                   | SEC   |
|------|-----------------------------------|-------|
| 1928 | Elizabeth Robinson (USA)          | 12.2  |
| 1932 | Stanislawa Walasiewicz (POL)      | 11.9  |
| 1936 | Helen Stephens (USA)              | 11.5  |
| 1948 | Francina Blankers-Koen (NED)      | 11.9  |
| 1952 | Marjorie Jackson (AUS)            | 11.5  |
| 1956 | Elizabeth Cuthbert (AUS)          | 11.5  |
| 1960 | Wilma Rudolph (USA)               | 11.0  |
| 1964 | Wyomia Tyus (USA)                 | 11.4  |
| 1968 | Wyomia Tyus (USA)                 | 11.0  |
| 1972 | Renate Stecher (GDR)              | 11.07 |
| 1976 | Annegret Richter (FRG)            | 11.08 |
| 1980 | Lyudmila Kondratyeva (URS)        | 11.06 |
| 1984 | Evelyn Ashford (USA)              | 10.97 |
| 1988 | Florence Griffith Joyner (USA)    | 10.54 |
| 1992 | Gail Devers (USA)                 | 10.82 |
| 1996 | Gail Devers (USA)                 | 10.94 |
| 2000 | *winner stripped of medal*        |       |
| 2004 | Yuliya Nesterenko (BLR)           | 10.93 |
| 2008 | Shelly-Ann Fraser (JAM)           | 10.78 |
| 2012 | Shelly-Ann Fraser-Pryce (JAM)     | 10.75 |

### 200 METERS
|      |                                 | SEC   |
|------|---------------------------------|-------|
| 1948 | Francina Blankers-Koen (NED)    | 24.4  |
| 1952 | Marjorie Jackson (AUS)          | 23.7  |
| 1956 | Elizabeth Cuthbert (AUS)        | 23.4  |
| 1960 | Wilma Rudolph (USA)             | 24.0  |
| 1964 | Edith Marie McGuire (USA)       | 23.0  |
| 1968 | Irena Szewinska (POL)           | 22.5  |
| 1972 | Renate Stecher (GDR)            | 22.40 |
| 1976 | Bärbel Eckert (GDR)             | 22.37 |
| 1980 | Bärbel Eckert-Wöckel (GDR)      | 22.03 |
| 1984 | Valerie Brisco-Hooks (USA)      | 21.81 |
| 1988 | Florence Griffith Joyner (USA)  | 21.34 |

## Athletics (Track and Field) (women) (continued)

### 200 METERS (CONTINUED)
|      |                                   | SEC   |
|------|-----------------------------------|-------|
| 1992 | Gwen Torrence (USA)               | 21.81 |
| 1996 | Marie-Jose Perec (FRA)            | 22.12 |
| 2000 | Pauline Davis-Thompson (BAH)[2]   | 22.27 |
| 2004 | Veronica Campbell (JAM)           | 22.05 |
| 2008 | Veronica Campbell-Brown (JAM)     | 21.74 |
| 2012 | Allyson Felix (USA)               | 21.88 |

### 400 METERS
|      |                                  | SEC   |
|------|----------------------------------|-------|
| 1964 | Elizabeth Cuthbert (AUS)         | 52.0  |
| 1968 | Colette Besson (FRA)             | 52.0  |
| 1972 | Monika Zehrt (GDR)               | 51.08 |
| 1976 | Irena Szewinska (POL)            | 49.29 |
| 1980 | Marita Koch (GDR)                | 48.88 |
| 1984 | Valerie Brisco-Hooks (USA)       | 48.83 |
| 1988 | Olga Bryzgina (URS)              | 48.65 |
| 1992 | Marie-Jose Perec (FRA)           | 48.83 |
| 1996 | Marie-Jose Perec (FRA)           | 48.25 |
| 2000 | Cathy Freeman (AUS)              | 49.11 |
| 2004 | Tonique Williams-Darling (BAH)   | 49.41 |
| 2008 | Christine Ohuruogu (GBR)         | 49.62 |
| 2012 | Sanya Richards-Ross (USA)        | 49.55 |

### 800 METERS
|      |                                  | MIN:SEC |
|------|----------------------------------|---------|
| 1928 | Lina Radke-Batschauer (GER)      | 2:16.8  |
| 1960 | Lyudmila Lysenko-Shevtsova (URS) | 2:04.3  |
| 1964 | Ann Packer (GBR)                 | 2:01.1  |
| 1968 | Madeline Manning (USA)           | 2:00.9  |
| 1972 | Hildegard Falck (FRG)            | 1:58.6  |
| 1976 | Tatyana Kazankina (URS)          | 1:54.94 |
| 1980 | Nadezhda Olizarenko (URS)        | 1:53.50 |
| 1984 | Doina Melinte (ROM)              | 1:57.60 |
| 1988 | Sigrun Wodars (GDR)              | 1:56.10 |
| 1992 | Ellen van Langen (NED)           | 1:55.54 |
| 1996 | Svetlana Masterkova (RUS)        | 1:57.73 |
| 2000 | Maria Mutola (MOZ)               | 1:56.15 |
| 2004 | Kelly Holmes (GBR)               | 1:56.38 |
| 2008 | Pamela Jelimo (KEN)              | 1:54.87 |
| 2012 | Mariya Savinova (RUS)            | 1:56.19 |

### 1,500 METERS
|      |                                | MIN:SEC |
|------|--------------------------------|---------|
| 1972 | Lyudmila Bragina (URS)         | 4:01.4  |
| 1976 | Tatyana Kazankina (URS)        | 4:05.48 |
| 1980 | Tatyana Kazankina (URS)        | 3:56.56 |
| 1984 | Gabriella Dorio (ITA)          | 4:03.25 |
| 1988 | Paula Ivan (ROM)               | 3:53.96 |
| 1992 | Hassiba Boulmerka (ALG)        | 3:55.30 |
| 1996 | Svetlana Masterkova (RUS)      | 4:00.83 |
| 2000 | Nouria Merah-Benida (ALG)      | 4:05.10 |
| 2004 | Kelly Holmes (GBR)             | 3:57.90 |
| 2008 | Nancy Jebet Langat (KEN)       | 4:00.23 |
| 2012 | Asli Cakir Alptekin (TUR)      | 4:10.23 |

### 3,000 METERS
|      |                                | MIN:SEC |
|------|--------------------------------|---------|
| 1984 | Maricica Puica (ROM)           | 8:35.96 |
| 1988 | Tatyana Samolenko (URS)        | 8:26.53 |
| 1992 | Yelena Romanova (UNT)          | 8:46.04 |

### 3,000-METER STEEPLECHASE
|      |                                  | MIN:SEC |
|------|----------------------------------|---------|
| 2008 | Gulnara Samitova-Galkina (RUS)   | 8:58.81 |
| 2012 | Yuliya Zaripova (RUS)            | 9:06.72 |

### 5,000 METERS
|      |                            | MIN:SEC  |
|------|----------------------------|----------|
| 1996 | Wang Jungxia (CHN)         | 14:59.88 |
| 2000 | Gabriela Szabo (ROM)       | 14:40.79 |
| 2004 | Meseret Defar (ETH)        | 14:45.65 |
| 2008 | Tirunesh Dibaba (ETH)      | 15:41.40 |
| 2012 | Meseret Defar (ETH)        | 15:04.25 |

# Summer Olympic Games (continued)

## Athletics (Track and Field) (women) (continued)

| 10,000 METERS | | MIN:SEC |
|---|---|---|
| 1988 | Olga Bondarenko (URS) | 31:05.21 |
| 1992 | Derartu Tulu (ETH) | 31:06.02 |
| 1996 | Fernanda Ribeiro (POR) | 31:01.63 |
| 2000 | Derartu Tulu (ETH) | 30:17.49 |
| 2004 | Xing Huina (CHN) | 30:24.36 |
| 2008 | Tirunesh Dibaba (ETH) | 29:54.66 |
| 2012 | Tirunesh Dibaba (ETH) | 30:20.75 |

| MARATHON | | HR:MIN:SEC |
|---|---|---|
| 1984 | Joan Benoit (USA) | 2:24:52 |
| 1988 | Rosa Mota (POR) | 2:25:40 |
| 1992 | Valentina Yegorova (UNT) | 2:32:41 |
| 1996 | Fatuma Roba (ETH) | 2:26:05 |
| 2000 | Naoko Takahashi (JPN) | 2:23:14 |
| 2004 | Mizuki Noguchi (JPN) | 2:26:20 |
| 2008 | Constantina Tomescu (ROM) | 2:26:44 |
| 2012 | Tiki Gelana (ETH) | 2:23:07 |

| 100-METER HURDLES[7] | | SEC |
|---|---|---|
| 1932 | Mildred "Babe" Didrikson (USA) | 11.7 |
| 1936 | Trebisonda Valla (ITA) | 11.7 |
| 1948 | Francina Blankers-Koen (NED) | 11.2 |
| 1952 | Shirley Strickland de La Hunty (AUS) | 10.9 |
| 1956 | Shirley Strickland de La Hunty (AUS) | 10.7 |
| 1960 | Irina Press (URS) | 10.8 |
| 1964 | Karin Balzer (GER) | 10.5 |
| 1968 | Maureen Caird (AUS) | 10.3 |
| 1972 | Annelie Ehrhardt (GDR) | 12.59 |
| 1976 | Johanna Schaller (GDR) | 12.77 |
| 1980 | Vera Komisova (URS) | 12.56 |
| 1984 | Benita Fitzgerald-Brown (USA) | 12.84 |
| 1988 | Iordanka Donkova (BUL) | 12.38 |
| 1992 | Paraskevi Patoulidou (GRE) | 12.64 |
| 1996 | Ludmila Engquist (SWE) | 12.58 |
| 2000 | Olga Shishigina (KAZ) | 12.65 |
| 2004 | Joanna Hayes (USA) | 12.37 |
| 2008 | Dawn Harper (USA) | 12.54 |
| 2012 | Sally Pearson (AUS) | 12.35 |

| 400-METER HURDLES | | SEC |
|---|---|---|
| 1984 | Nawal el Moutawakel (MAR) | 54.61 |
| 1988 | Debra Flintoff-King (AUS) | 53.17 |
| 1992 | Sally Gunnell (GBR) | 53.23 |
| 1996 | Deon Hemmings (JAM) | 52.82 |
| 2000 | Irina Privalova (RUS) | 53.02 |
| 2004 | Fani Halkia (GRE) | 52.82 |
| 2008 | Melaine Walker (JAM) | 52.64 |
| 2012 | Natalya Antyukh (RUS) | 52.70 |

| 4 × 100-METER RELAY | | SEC |
|---|---|---|
| 1928 | Canada | 48.4 |
| 1932 | United States | 47.0 |
| 1936 | United States | 46.9 |
| 1948 | The Netherlands | 47.5 |
| 1952 | United States | 45.9 |
| 1956 | Australia | 44.5 |
| 1960 | United States | 44.5 |
| 1964 | Poland | 43.6 |
| 1968 | United States | 42.8 |
| 1972 | West Germany | 42.81 |
| 1976 | East Germany | 42.55 |
| 1980 | East Germany | 41.60 |
| 1984 | United States | 41.65 |
| 1988 | United States | 41.98 |
| 1992 | United States | 42.11 |
| 1996 | United States | 41.95 |
| 2000 | The Bahamas | 41.95 |

## Athletics (Track and Field) (women) (continued)

| 4 × 100-METER RELAY (CONTINUED) | | SEC |
|---|---|---|
| 2004 | Jamaica | 41.73 |
| 2008 | Russia | 42.31 |
| 2012 | United States | 40.82 |

| 4 × 400-METER RELAY | | MIN:SEC |
|---|---|---|
| 1972 | East Germany | 3:23.0 |
| 1976 | East Germany | 3:19.23 |
| 1980 | USSR | 3:20.2 |
| 1984 | United States | 3:18.29 |
| 1988 | USSR | 3:15.18 |
| 1992 | Unified Team | 3:20.20 |
| 1996 | United States | 3:20.91 |
| 2000 | United States | 3:22:62 |
| 2004 | United States | 3:19.01. |
| 2008 | United States | 3:18.54 |
| 2012 | United States | 3:16.87 |

| 10,000-METER WALK | | MIN:SEC |
|---|---|---|
| 1992 | Chen Yueling (CHN) | 44:32 |
| 1996 | Yelena Nikolayeva (RUS) | 41:49 |

| 20,000-METER WALK | | HR:MIN:SEC |
|---|---|---|
| 2000 | Wang Liping (CHN) | 1:29:05 |
| 2004 | Athanasia Tsoumeleka (GRE) | 1:29:12 |
| 2008 | Olga Kaniskina (RUS) | 1:26:31 |
| 2012 | Yelena Lashmanova (RUS) | 1:25:02 |

| HIGH JUMP | | METERS |
|---|---|---|
| 1928 | Ethel Catherwood (CAN) | 1.59 |
| 1932 | Jean Shiley (USA) | 1.66 |
| 1936 | Ibolya Csak (HUN) | 1.60 |
| 1948 | Alice Coachman (USA) | 1.68 |
| 1952 | Esther Brand (RSA) | 1.67 |
| 1956 | Mildred Louise McDaniel (USA) | 1.76 |
| 1960 | Iolanda Balas (ROM) | 1.85 |
| 1964 | Iolanda Balas (ROM) | 1.90 |
| 1968 | Miloslava Rezkova (TCH) | 1.82 |
| 1972 | Ulrike Meyfarth (FRG) | 1.92 |
| 1976 | Rosemarie Ackermann (GDR) | 1.93 |
| 1980 | Sara Simeoni (ITA) | 1.97 |
| 1984 | Ulrike Meyfarth (FRG) | 2.02 |
| 1988 | Louise Ritter (USA) | 2.03 |
| 1992 | Heike Henkel (GER) | 2.02 |
| 1996 | Stefka Kostadinova (BUL) | 2.05 |
| 2000 | Yelena Yelesina (RUS) | 2.01 |
| 2004 | Yelena Slesarenko (RUS) | 2.06 |
| 2008 | Tia Hellebaut (BEL) | 2.05 |
| 2012 | Anna Chicherova (RUS) | 2.05 |

| POLE VAULT | | METERS |
|---|---|---|
| 2000 | Stacy Dragila (USA) | 4.60 |
| 2004 | Yelena Isinbayeva (RUS) | 4.91 |
| 2008 | Yelena Isinbayeva (RUS) | 5.05 |
| 2012 | Jennifer Suhr (USA) | 4.75 |

| LONG JUMP | | METERS |
|---|---|---|
| 1948 | Olga Gyarmati (HUN) | 5.69 |
| 1952 | Yvette Williams (NZL) | 6.24 |
| 1956 | Elzbieta Krzesinska (POL) | 6.35 |
| 1960 | Vera Krepkina (URS) | 6.37 |
| 1964 | Mary Rand (GBR) | 6.76 |
| 1968 | Viorica Viscopoleanu (ROM) | 6.82 |
| 1972 | Heidemarie Rosendahl (FRG) | 6.78 |
| 1976 | Angela Voigt (GDR) | 6.72 |
| 1980 | Tatyana Kolpakova (URS) | 7.06 |
| 1984 | Anisoara Stanciu (ROM) | 6.96 |
| 1988 | Jackie Joyner-Kersee (USA) | 7.40 |

# Summer Olympic Games (continued)

## Athletics (Track and Field) (women) (continued)

| LONG JUMP (CONTINUED) | METERS |
|---|---|
| 1992 Heike Drechsler (GER) | 7.14 |
| 1996 Chioma Ajunwa (NGR) | 7.12 |
| 2000 Heike Drechsler (GER) | 6.99 |
| 2004 Tatyana Lebedeva (RUS) | 7.07 |
| 2008 Maurren Higa Maggi (BRA) | 7.04 |
| 2012 Brittney Reese (USA) | 7.12 |

| TRIPLE JUMP | METERS |
|---|---|
| 1996 Inessa Kravets (UKR) | 15.33 |
| 2000 Tereza Marinova (BUL) | 15.20 |
| 2004 Françoise Mbango Etone (CMR) | 15.30 |
| 2008 Françoise Mbango Etone (CMR) | 15.39 |
| 2012 Olga Rypakova (KAZ) | 14.98 |

| SHOT PUT | METERS |
|---|---|
| 1948 Micheline Ostermeyer (FRA) | 13.75 |
| 1952 Galina Zybina (URS) | 15.28 |
| 1956 Tamara Tyshkevich (URS) | 16.59 |
| 1960 Tamara Press (URS) | 17.32 |
| 1964 Tamara Press (URS) | 18.14 |
| 1968 Margitta Gummel (GDR) | 19.61 |
| 1972 Nadezhda Chizhova (URS) | 21.03 |
| 1976 Ivanka Khristova (BUL) | 21.16 |
| 1980 Ilona Slupianek (GDR) | 22.41 |
| 1984 Claudia Losch (FRG) | 20.48 |
| 1988 Natalya Lisovskaya (URS) | 22.24 |
| 1992 Svetlana Krivalyova (UNT) | 21.06 |
| 1996 Astrid Kumbernuss (GER) | 20.56 |
| 2000 Yanina Korolchik (BLR) | 20.56 |
| 2004 Yumileidi Cumba (CUB)[2] | 19.59 |
| 2008 Valerie Vili (NZL) | 20.56 |
| 2012 Valerie Adams (NZL)[2] | 20.70 |

| DISCUS THROW | METERS |
|---|---|
| 1928 Halina Konopacka (POL) | 39.62 |
| 1932 Lillian Copeland (USA) | 40.58 |
| 1936 Gisela Mauermayer (GER) | 47.63 |
| 1948 Micheline Ostermeyer (FRA) | 41.92 |
| 1952 Nina Romashkova (URS) | 51.42 |
| 1956 Olga Fikotova (TCH) | 53.69 |
| 1960 Nina Ponomaryova-Romashkova (URS) | 55.10 |
| 1964 Tamara Press (URS) | 57.27 |
| 1968 Lia Manoliu (ROM) | 58.28 |
| 1972 Faina Melnik (URS) | 66.62 |
| 1976 Evelin Schlaak (GDR) | 69.00 |
| 1980 Evelin Schlaak Jahl (GDR) | 69.96 |
| 1984 Ria Stalman (NED) | 65.36 |
| 1988 Martina Hellmann (GDR) | 72.30 |
| 1992 Maritza Marten (CUB) | 70.06 |
| 1996 Ilke Wyludda (GER) | 69.66 |
| 2000 Ellina Zvereva (BLR) | 68.40 |
| 2004 Natalya Sadova (RUS) | 67.02 |
| 2008 Stephanie Brown Trafton (USA) | 64.74 |
| 2012 Sandra Perkovic (CRO) | 69.11 |

| HAMMER THROW | METERS |
|---|---|
| 2000 Kamila Skolimowska (POL) | 71.16 |
| 2004 Olga Kuzenkova (RUS) | 75.02 |
| 2008 Aksana Miankova (BLR) | 76.34 |
| 2012 Tatyana Lysenko (RUS) | 78.18 |

| JAVELIN THROW | METERS |
|---|---|
| 1932 Mildred "Babe" Didrikson (USA) | 43.68 |
| 1936 Tilly Fleischer (GER) | 45.18 |
| 1948 Hermine Bauma (AUT) | 45.57 |
| 1952 Dana Zatopkova (TCH) | 50.47 |
| 1956 Inese Jaunzeme (URS) | 53.86 |

## Athletics (Track and Field) (women) (continued)

| JAVELIN THROW (CONTINUED) | METERS |
|---|---|
| 1960 Elvira Ozolina (URS) | 55.98 |
| 1964 Mihaela Penes (ROM) | 60.54 |
| 1968 Angela Nemeth (HUN) | 60.36 |
| 1972 Ruth Fuchs (GDR) | 63.88 |
| 1976 Ruth Fuchs (GDR) | 65.94 |
| 1980 María Colón (CUB) | 68.40 |
| 1984 Tessa Sanderson (GBR) | 69.56 |
| 1988 Petra Felke (GDR) | 74.68 |
| 1992 Silke Renk (GER) | 68.34 |
| 1996 Heli Rantanen (FIN) | 67.94 |
| 2000 Trine Hattestad (NOR) | 68.91 |
| 2004 Osleidys Menéndez (CUB) | 71.53 |
| 2008 Barbora Spotakova (CZE) | 71.42 |
| 2012 Barbora Spotakova (CZE) | 69.55 |

| HEPTATHLON[B] | |
|---|---|
| 1964 Irina Press (URS) | |
| 1968 Ingrid Becker (FRG) | |
| 1972 Mary Peters (GBR) | |
| 1976 Siegrun Siegl (GDR) | |
| 1980 Nadezhda Tkachenko (URS) | |
| 1984 Glynis Nunn (AUS) | |
| 1988 Jackie Joyner-Kersee (USA) | |
| 1992 Jackie Joyner-Kersee (USA) | |
| 1996 Ghada Shouaa (SYR) | |
| 2000 Denise Lewis (GBR) | |
| 2004 Carolina Klüft (SWE) | |
| 2008 Nataliya Dobrynska (UKR) | |
| 2012 Jessica Ennis (GBR) | |

## Badminton

| MEN'S SINGLES | |
|---|---|
| 1992 Allan Budi Kusuma (INA) | |
| 1996 Poul-Erik Hoyer-Larsen (DEN) | |
| 2000 Ji Xinpeng (CHN) | |
| 2004 Taufik Hidayat (INA) | |
| 2008 Lin Dan (CHN) | |
| 2012 Lin Dan (CHN) | |

| MEN'S DOUBLES | |
|---|---|
| 1992 Republic of Korea | |
| 1996 Indonesia | |
| 2000 Indonesia | |
| 2004 Republic of Korea | |
| 2008 Indonesia | |
| 2012 China | |

| WOMEN'S SINGLES | |
|---|---|
| 1992 Susi Susanti (INA) | |
| 1996 Bang Soo-Hyun (KOR) | |
| 2000 Gong Zhichao (CHN) | |
| 2004 Zhang Ning (CHN) | |
| 2008 Zhang Ning (CHN) | |
| 2012 Li Xuerui (CHN) | |

| WOMEN'S DOUBLES | |
|---|---|
| 1992 Republic of Korea | |
| 1996 China | |
| 2000 China | |
| 2004 China | |
| 2008 China | |
| 2012 China | |

| MIXED DOUBLES | |
|---|---|
| 1996 Republic of Korea | |
| 2000 China | |
| 2004 China | |

## Summer Olympic Games (continued)

### Badminton (continued)

**MIXED DOUBLES (CONTINUED)**

| | |
|---|---|
| 2008 | Republic of Korea |
| 2012 | China |

### Baseball

| | |
|---|---|
| 1992 | Cuba |
| 1996 | Cuba |
| 2000 | United States |
| 2004 | Cuba |
| 2008 | Republic of Korea |

### Basketball

**MEN**

| | |
|---|---|
| 1936 | United States |
| 1948 | United States |
| 1952 | United States |
| 1956 | United States |
| 1960 | United States |
| 1964 | United States |
| 1968 | United States |
| 1972 | USSR |
| 1976 | United States |
| 1980 | Yugoslavia |
| 1984 | United States |
| 1988 | USSR |
| 1992 | United States |
| 1996 | United States |
| 2000 | United States |
| 2004 | Argentina |
| 2008 | United States |
| 2012 | United States |

**WOMEN**

| | |
|---|---|
| 1976 | USSR |
| 1980 | USSR |
| 1984 | United States |
| 1988 | United States |
| 1992 | Unified Team |
| 1996 | United States |
| 2000 | United States |
| 2004 | United States |
| 2008 | United States |
| 2012 | United States |

### Boxing (men)[9]

**49 KG (107.8 LB)**

| | |
|---|---|
| 1968 | Francisco Rodríguez (VEN) |
| 1972 | Gyorgy Gedo (HUN) |
| 1976 | Jorge Hernández (CUB) |
| 1980 | Shamil Sabyrov (URS) |
| 1984 | Paul Gonzales (USA) |
| 1988 | Ivailo Khristov (BUL) |
| 1992 | Rogelio Marcelo (CUB) |
| 1996 | Daniel Petrov Bojilov (BUL) |
| 2000 | Brahim Asloum (FRA) |
| 2004 | Yan Bhartelemy Varela (CUB) |
| 2008 | Zou Shiming (CHN) |
| 2012 | Zou Shiming (CHN) |

**52 KG (114.4 LB)**

| | |
|---|---|
| 1904 | George Finnegan (USA) |
| 1920 | Frank di Genaro (USA) |
| 1924 | Fidel La Barba (USA) |
| 1928 | Antal Kocsis (HUN) |
| 1932 | Istvan Enekes (HUN) |
| 1936 | Willi Kaiser (GER) |
| 1948 | Pascual Pérez (ARG) |
| 1952 | Nate Brooks (USA) |

### Boxing (men)[9] (continued)

**52 KG (114.4 LB) (CONTINUED)**

| | |
|---|---|
| 1956 | Terence Spinks (GBR) |
| 1960 | Gyula Torok (HUN) |
| 1964 | Fernando Atzori (ITA) |
| 1968 | Ricardo Delgado (MEX) |
| 1972 | Georgi Kostadinov (BUL) |
| 1976 | Leo Randolph (USA) |
| 1980 | Petar Lesov (BUL) |
| 1984 | Steven McCrory (USA) |
| 1988 | Kim Kwang Sun (KOR) |
| 1992 | Chol Choi Su (PRK) |
| 1996 | Maikro Romero (CUB) |
| 2000 | Wijan Ponlid (THA) |
| 2004 | Yuriorkis Gamboa Toledano (CUB) |
| 2008 | Somjit Jongjohor (THA) |
| 2012 | Robeisy Ramirez Carrazana (CUB) |

**56 KG (123.2 LB)**

| | |
|---|---|
| 1904 | Oliver Kirk (USA) |
| 1908 | Henry Thomas (GBR) |
| 1920 | Clarence Walker (RSA) |
| 1924 | William Smith (RSA) |
| 1928 | Vittorio Tamagnini (ITA) |
| 1932 | Horace Gwynne (CAN) |
| 1936 | Ulderico Sergo (ITA) |
| 1948 | Tibor Csik (HUN) |
| 1952 | Pentti Hämäläinen (FIN) |
| 1956 | Wolfgang Behrendt (GER) |
| 1960 | Oleg Grigoryev (URS) |
| 1964 | Takao Sakurai (JPN) |
| 1968 | Valery Sokolov (URS) |
| 1972 | Orlando Martínez (CUB) |
| 1976 | Gu Yong Jo (PRK) |
| 1980 | Juan Hernández (CUB) |
| 1984 | Maurizio Stecca (ITA) |
| 1988 | Kennedy McKinney (USA) |
| 1992 | Joel Casamayor (CUB) |
| 1996 | Istvan Kovacs (HUN) |
| 2000 | Guillermo Rigondeaux Ortiz (CUB) |
| 2004 | Guillermo Rigondeaux Ortiz (CUB) |
| 2008 | Badar-Uugan Enkhbat (MGL) |
| 2012 | Luke Campbell (GBR) |

**57 KG (125.4 LB)**

| | |
|---|---|
| 1904 | Oliver Kirk (USA) |
| 1908 | Richard Gunn (GBR) |
| 1920 | Paul Fritsch (FRA) |
| 1924 | John Fields (USA) |
| 1928 | Lambertus van Kleveren (NED) |
| 1932 | Carmelo Robledo (ARG) |
| 1936 | Oscar Casanovas (ARG) |
| 1948 | Ernesto Formenti (ITA) |
| 1952 | Jan Zachara (TCH) |
| 1956 | Vladimir Safronov (URS) |
| 1960 | Francesco Musso (ITA) |
| 1964 | Stanislav Stepashkin (URS) |
| 1968 | Antonio Roldan (MEX) |
| 1972 | Boris Kuznetsov (URS) |
| 1976 | Angel Herrera (CUB) |
| 1980 | Rudi Fink (GDR) |
| 1984 | Meldrick Taylor (USA) |
| 1988 | Giovanni Parisi (ITA) |
| 1992 | Andreas Tews (GER) |
| 1996 | Somluck Kamsing (THA) |
| 2000 | Bekzat Sattarkhanov (KAZ) |
| 2004 | Aleksey Tishchenko (RUS) |
| 2008 | Vasyl Lomachenko (UKR) |

## Summer Olympic Games (continued)

### Boxing (men)[9] (continued)

**60 KG (132 LB)**

| | |
|---|---|
| 1904 | Harry Spanger (USA) |
| 1908 | Frederick Grace (GBR) |
| 1920 | Samuel Mosberg (USA) |
| 1924 | Hans Nielsen (DEN) |
| 1928 | Carlo Orlandi (ITA) |
| 1932 | Lawrence Stevens (RSA) |
| 1936 | Imre Harangi (HUN) |
| 1948 | Gerald Dreyer (RSA) |
| 1952 | Aureliano Bolognesi (ITA) |
| 1956 | Richard McTaggart (GBR) |
| 1960 | Kazimierz Pazdzior (POL) |
| 1964 | Jozef Grudzien (POL) |
| 1968 | Ronnie Harris (USA) |
| 1972 | Jan Szczepanski (POL) |
| 1976 | Howard Davis (USA) |
| 1980 | Angel Herrera (CUB) |
| 1984 | Pernell Whitaker (USA) |
| 1988 | Andreas Zuelow (GDR) |
| 1992 | Oscar De La Hoya (USA) |
| 1996 | Hocine Soltani (ALG) |
| 2000 | Mario Kindelan (CUB) |
| 2004 | Mario César Kindelan Mesa (CUB) |
| 2008 | Aleksey Tishchenko (RUS) |
| 2012 | Vasyl Lomachenko (UKR) |

**64 KG (140.8 LB)**

| | |
|---|---|
| 1952 | Charles Adkins (USA) |
| 1956 | Vladimir Engibaryan (URS) |
| 1960 | Bohumil Nemecek (TCH) |
| 1964 | Jerzy Kulej (POL) |
| 1968 | Jerzy Kulej (POL) |
| 1972 | Ray Seales (USA) |
| 1976 | Ray Leonard (USA) |
| 1980 | Patrizio Oliva (ITA) |
| 1984 | Jerry Page (USA) |
| 1988 | Vyacheslav Yanovsky (URS) |
| 1992 | Héctor Vinent (CUB) |
| 1996 | Héctor Vinent (CUB) |
| 2000 | Mahamadkadyz Abdullayev (UZB) |
| 2004 | Manus Boonjumnong (THA) |
| 2008 | Félix Díaz (DOM) |
| 2012 | Roniel Iglesias Sotolongo (CUB) |

**69 KG (151.8 LB)**

| | |
|---|---|
| 1904 | Albert Young (USA) |
| 1920 | Julius Schneider (CAN) |
| 1924 | Jean Delarge (BEL) |
| 1928 | Edward Morgan (NZL) |
| 1932 | Edward Flynn (USA) |
| 1936 | Sten Suvio (FIN) |
| 1948 | Julius Torma (TCH) |
| 1952 | Zygmunt Chychla (POL) |
| 1956 | Nicolae Linca (ROM) |
| 1960 | Giovanni Benvenuti (ITA) |
| 1964 | Marian Kasprzyk (POL) |
| 1968 | Manfred Wolke (GDR) |
| 1972 | Emilio Correa (CUB) |
| 1976 | Jochen Bachfeld (GDR) |
| 1980 | Andres Aldama (CUB) |
| 1984 | Mark Breland (USA) |
| 1988 | Robert Wangila (KEN) |
| 1992 | Michael Carruth (IRL) |
| 1996 | Oleg Saytov (RUS) |
| 2000 | Oleg Saytov (RUS) |
| 2004 | Bakhtiyar Artayev (KAZ) |
| 2008 | Bakhyt Sarsekbayev (KAZ) |
| 2012 | Serik Sapiyev (KAZ) |

### Boxing (men)[9] (continued)

**71 KG (156.2 LB)**

| | |
|---|---|
| 1952 | Laszlo Papp (HUN) |
| 1956 | Laszlo Papp (HUN) |
| 1960 | Wilbert McClure (USA) |
| 1964 | Boris Lagutin (URS) |
| 1968 | Boris Lagutin (URS) |
| 1972 | Dieter Kottysch (FRG) |
| 1976 | Jerzy Rybicki (POL) |
| 1980 | Armando Martínez (CUB) |
| 1984 | Frank Tate (USA) |
| 1988 | Park Si Hun (KOR) |
| 1992 | Juan Lemus (CUB) |
| 1996 | David Reid (USA) |
| 2000 | Yermakhan Ibraimov (KAZ) |

**75 KG (165 LB)**

| | |
|---|---|
| 1904 | Charles Mayer (USA) |
| 1908 | John Douglas (GBR) |
| 1920 | Harry Mallin (GBR) |
| 1924 | Harry Mallin (GBR) |
| 1928 | Piero Toscani (ITA) |
| 1932 | Carmen Barth (USA) |
| 1936 | Jean Despeaux (FRA) |
| 1948 | Laszlo Papp (HUN) |
| 1952 | Floyd Patterson (USA) |
| 1956 | Gennady Shatkov (URS) |
| 1960 | Edward Crook (USA) |
| 1964 | Valery Popenchenko (URS) |
| 1968 | Christopher Finnegan (GBR) |
| 1972 | Vyatcheslav Lemeshev (URS) |
| 1976 | Michael Spinks (USA) |
| 1980 | Jose Gómez (CUB) |
| 1984 | Shin Joon Sup (KOR) |
| 1988 | Henry Maske (GDR) |
| 1992 | Ariel Hernández (CUB) |
| 1996 | Ariel Hernández (CUB) |
| 2000 | Jorge Gutiérrez (CUB) |
| 2004 | Gaydarbek Gaydarbekov (RUS) |
| 2008 | James Degale (GBR) |
| 2012 | Ryota Murata (JPN) |

**81 KG (178.2 LB)**

| | |
|---|---|
| 1920 | Edward Eagan (USA) |
| 1924 | Harry Mitchell (GBR) |
| 1928 | Viktor Avendano (ARG) |
| 1932 | David Carstens (RSA) |
| 1936 | Roger Michelot (FRA) |
| 1948 | George Hunter (RSA) |
| 1952 | Norvel Lee (USA) |
| 1956 | James Boyd (USA) |
| 1960 | Cassius Clay (USA) |
| 1964 | Cosimo Pinto (ITA) |
| 1968 | Dan Poznyak (URS) |
| 1972 | Mate Parlov (YUG) |
| 1976 | Leon Spinks (USA) |
| 1980 | Slobodan Kacar (YUG) |
| 1984 | Anton Josipovic (YUG) |
| 1988 | Andrew Maynard (USA) |
| 1992 | Torsten May (GER) |
| 1996 | Vasily Zhirov (KAZ) |
| 2000 | Aleksandr Lebzyak (RUS) |
| 2004 | Andre Ward (USA) |
| 2008 | Zhang Xiaoping (CHN) |
| 2012 | Egor Mekhontcev (RUS) |

**91 KG (200.2 LB)**

| | |
|---|---|
| 1904 | Samuel Berger (USA) |
| 1908 | Albert Oldman (GBR) |

# Summer Olympic Games (continued)

## Boxing (men)[9] (continued)

### 91 KG (200.2 LB) (CONTINUED)

| | | |
|---|---|---|
| 1920 | Ronald Rawson (GBR) | |
| 1924 | Otto Von Porat (NOR) | |
| 1928 | Arturo Rodriguez (ARG) | |
| 1932 | Alberto Santiago Lovell (ARG) | |
| 1936 | Herbert Runge (GER) | |
| 1948 | Rafael Iglesias (ARG) | |
| 1952 | Edward Sanders (USA) | |
| 1956 | Peter Rademacher (USA) | |
| 1960 | Franco de Piccoli (ITA) | |
| 1964 | Joseph Frazier (USA) | |
| 1968 | George Foreman (USA) | |
| 1972 | Teofilo Stevenson (CUB) | |
| 1976 | Teofilo Stevenson (CUB) | |
| 1980 | Teofilo Stevenson (CUB) | |
| 1984 | Henry Tillman (USA) | |
| 1988 | Ray Mercer (USA) | |
| 1992 | Félix Savon (CUB) | |
| 1996 | Félix Savon (CUB) | |
| 2000 | Félix Savon (CUB) | |
| 2004 | Odlanier Solis Fonte (CUB) | |
| 2008 | Rakhim Chakhkiyev (RUS) | |
| 2012 | Oleksandr Usyk (UKR) | |

### OVER 91 KG (OVER 200.2 LB)

| | |
|---|---|
| 1984 | Tyrell Biggs (USA) |
| 1988 | Lennox Lewis (CAN) |
| 1992 | Roberto Balado (CUB) |
| 1996 | Vladimir Klichko (UKR) |
| 2000 | Audley Harrison (GBR) |
| 2004 | Aleksandr Povetkin (RUS) |
| 2008 | Roberto Cammarelle (ITA) |
| 2012 | Anthony Joshua (GBR) |

## Boxing (women)

### 51 KG (112.2 LB)

| | |
|---|---|
| 2012 | Nicola Adams (GBR) |

### 60 KG (132 LB)

| | |
|---|---|
| 2012 | Katie Taylor (IRL) |

### 75 KG (165 LB)

| | |
|---|---|
| 2012 | Claressa Shields (USA) |

## Canoeing (men)

### KAYAK SINGLES (200 METERS)[10]

| | | MIN:SEC |
|---|---|---|
| 1976 | Vasile Diba (ROM) | 1:46.41 |
| 1980 | Vladimir Parfenovich (URS) | 1:43.43 |
| 1984 | Ian Ferguson (NZL) | 1:47.84 |
| 1988 | Zsolt Gyulay (HUN) | 1:44.82 |
| 1992 | Mikko Kolehmainen (FIN) | 1:40.34 |
| 1996 | Antonio Rossi (ITA) | 1:37.423 |
| 2000 | Knut Holmann (NOR) | 1:57.847 |
| 2004 | Adam van Koeverden (CAN) | 1:37.919 |
| 2008 | Ken Wallace (AUS) | 1:37.252 |
| 2012 | Ed McKeever (GBR) | 36.246 |

### KAYAK PAIRS (200 METERS)[10]

| | | MIN:SEC |
|---|---|---|
| 1976 | East Germany | 1:35.87 |
| 1980 | USSR | 1:32.38 |
| 1984 | New Zealand | 1:34.21 |
| 1988 | New Zealand | 1:33.98 |
| 1992 | Germany | 1:29.84 |
| 1996 | Germany | 1:28.697 |
| 2000 | Hungary | 1:47.050 |
| 2004 | Germany | 1:27.040 |
| 2008 | Spain | 1:28.736 |
| 2012 | Russia | 33.507 |

## Canoeing (men) (continued)

### KAYAK SINGLES (1,000 METERS)

| | | MIN:SEC |
|---|---|---|
| 1936 | Gregor Hradetzky (AUT) | 4:22.90 |
| 1948 | Gert Fredriksson (SWE) | 4:33.20 |
| 1952 | Gert Fredriksson (SWE) | 4:07.90 |
| 1956 | Gert Fredriksson (SWE) | 4:12.80 |
| 1960 | Erik Hansen (DEN) | 3:53.00 |
| 1964 | Rolf Peterson (SWE) | 3:57.13 |
| 1968 | Mihaly Hesz (HUN) | 4:03.58 |
| 1972 | Aleksandr Shaparenko (URS) | 3:48.06 |
| 1976 | Rüdiger Helm (GDR) | 3:48.20 |
| 1980 | Rüdiger Helm (GDR) | 3:48.77 |
| 1984 | Alan Thompson (NZL) | 3:45.73 |
| 1988 | Gregory Barton (USA) | 3:55.27 |
| 1992 | Clint Robinson (AUS) | 3:37.26 |
| 1996 | Knut Holmann (NOR) | 3:25.785 |
| 2000 | Knut Holmann (NOR) | 3:33.269 |
| 2004 | Eirik Veraas Larsen (NOR) | 3:25.897 |
| 2008 | Tim Brabants (GBR) | 3:26.323 |
| 2012 | Eirik Veras Larsen (NOR) | 3:26.462 |

### KAYAK PAIRS (1,000 METERS)

| | | MIN:SEC |
|---|---|---|
| 1936 | Austria | 4:03.80 |
| 1948 | Sweden | 4:07.30 |
| 1952 | Finland | 3:51.10 |
| 1956 | Germany | 3:49.60 |
| 1960 | Sweden | 3:34.70 |
| 1964 | Sweden | 3:38.54 |
| 1968 | USSR | 3:37.54 |
| 1972 | USSR | 3:31.23 |
| 1976 | USSR | 3:29.01 |
| 1980 | USSR | 3:26.72 |
| 1984 | Canada | 3:24.22 |
| 1988 | United States | 3:32.42 |
| 1992 | Germany | 3:16.10 |
| 1996 | Italy | 3:09.190 |
| 2000 | Italy | 3:14.461 |
| 2004 | Sweden | 3:18.420 |
| 2008 | Germany | 3:11.809 |
| 2012 | Hungary | 3:09.646 |

### KAYAK FOURS (1,000 METERS)

| | | MIN:SEC |
|---|---|---|
| 1964 | USSR | 3:14.67 |
| 1968 | Norway | 3:14.38 |
| 1972 | USSR | 3:14.02 |
| 1976 | USSR | 3:08.69 |
| 1980 | East Germany | 3:13.76 |
| 1984 | New Zealand | 3:02.28 |
| 1988 | Hungary | 3:00.20 |
| 1992 | Germany | 2:54.18 |
| 1996 | Germany | 2:51.528 |
| 2000 | Hungary | 2:55.188 |
| 2004 | Hungary | 2:56.919 |
| 2008 | Belarus | 2:55.714 |
| 2012 | Australia | 2:55.085 |

### KAYAK SINGLES (10,000 METERS)

| | | MIN:SEC |
|---|---|---|
| 1936 | Ernst Krebs (GER) | 46:01.6 |
| 1948 | Gert Fredriksson (SWE) | 50:47.7 |
| 1952 | Thorvald Strömberg (FIN) | 47:22.8 |
| 1956 | Gert Fredriksson (SWE) | 47:43.4 |

### KAYAK PAIRS (10,000 METERS)

| | | MIN:SEC |
|---|---|---|
| 1936 | Germany | 41:45.0 |
| 1948 | Sweden | 46:09.4 |
| 1952 | Finland | 44:21.3 |
| 1956 | Hungary | 43:37.0 |

# Summer Olympic Games (continued)

## Canoeing (men) (continued)

### COLLAPSIBLE KAYAK SINGLES (10,000 METERS)

| | | MIN:SEC |
|---|---|---|
| 1936 | Gregor Hradetzky (AUT) | 50:01.2 |

### COLLAPSIBLE KAYAK PAIRS (10,000 METERS)

| | | MIN:SEC |
|---|---|---|
| 1936 | Sweden | 45:48.9 |

### KAYAK SINGLES RELAY (1,500 METERS)

| | | MIN:SEC |
|---|---|---|
| 1960 | Germany | 7:39.43 |

### SLALOM KAYAK SINGLES

| | |
|---|---|
| 1972 | Siegbert Horn (GDR) |
| 1992 | Pierpaolo Ferrazzi (ITA) |
| 1996 | Oliver Fix (GER) |
| 2000 | Thomas Schmidt (GER) |
| 2004 | Benoit Peschier (FRA) |
| 2008 | Alexander Grimm (GER) |
| 2012 | Daniele Molmenti (ITA) |

### CANADIAN SINGLES (200 METERS)[10]

| | | MIN:SEC |
|---|---|---|
| 1976 | Aleksandr Rogov (URS) | 1:59.23 |
| 1980 | Sergey Postrekin (URS) | 1:53.37 |
| 1984 | Larry Cain (CAN) | 1:57.01 |
| 1988 | Olaf Heukrodt (GDR) | 1:56.42 |
| 1992 | Nikolay Bukhalov (BUL) | 1:51.15 |
| 1996 | Martin Doktor (CZE) | 1:49.934 |
| 2000 | Gyorgy Kolonics (HUN) | 2:24.813 |
| 2004 | Andreas Dittmer (GER) | 1:46.383 |
| 2008 | Maksim Opalev (RUS) | 1:47.140 |
| 2012 | Yuri Cheban (UKR) | 42.291 |

### CANADIAN PAIRS (500 METERS)

| | | MIN:SEC |
|---|---|---|
| 1976 | USSR | 1:45.81 |
| 1980 | Hungary | 1:43.39 |
| 1984 | Yugoslavia | 1:43.67 |
| 1988 | USSR | 1:41.77 |
| 1992 | Unified Team | 1:41.54 |
| 1996 | Hungary | 1:40.420 |
| 2000 | Hungary | 1:51.284 |
| 2004 | China | 1:40.278 |
| 2008 | China | 1:41.025 |

### CANADIAN SINGLES (1,000 METERS)

| | | MIN:SEC |
|---|---|---|
| 1936 | Francis Amyot (CAN) | 5:32.10 |
| 1948 | Josef Holecek (TCH) | 5:42.00 |
| 1952 | Josef Holecek (TCH) | 4:56.30 |
| 1956 | Leon Rottman (ROM) | 5:05.30 |
| 1960 | Janos Parti (HUN) | 4:33.03 |
| 1964 | Jürgen Eschert (GER) | 4:35.14 |
| 1968 | Tibor Tatai (HUN) | 4:36.14 |
| 1972 | Ivan Patzaichin (ROM) | 4:08.94 |
| 1976 | Matija Ljubek (YUG) | 4:09.51 |
| 1980 | Lyubomir Lyubenov (BUL) | 4:12.38 |
| 1984 | Ulrich Eicke (FRG) | 4:06.32 |
| 1988 | Ivans Klementyev (URS) | 4:12.78 |
| 1992 | Nikolay Bukhalov (BUL) | 4:05.92 |
| 1996 | Martin Doktor (CZE) | 3:54.418 |
| 2000 | Andreas Dittmer (GER) | 3:54.379 |
| 2004 | David Cal (ESP) | 3:46.201 |
| 2008 | Attila Sándor Vajda (HUN) | 3:50.467 |
| 2012 | Sebastian Brendel (GER) | 3:47.176 |

### CANADIAN PAIRS (1,000 METERS)

| | | MIN:SEC |
|---|---|---|
| 1936 | Czechoslovakia | 4:50.10 |
| 1948 | Czechoslovakia | 5:07.10 |
| 1952 | Denmark | 4:38.30 |
| 1956 | Romania | 4:47.40 |
| 1960 | USSR | 4:17.04 |
| 1964 | USSR | 4:04.65 |

## Canoeing (men) (continued)

### CANADIAN PAIRS (1,000 METERS) (CONTINUED)

| | | MIN:SEC |
|---|---|---|
| 1968 | Romania | 4:07.18 |
| 1972 | USSR | 3:52.60 |
| 1976 | USSR | 3:52.76 |
| 1980 | Romania | 3:47.65 |
| 1984 | Romania | 3:40.60 |
| 1988 | USSR | 3:48.36 |
| 1992 | Germany | 3:37.42 |
| 1996 | Germany | 3:31.870 |
| 2000 | Romania | 3:37.355 |
| 2004 | Germany | 3:41.802 |
| 2008 | Belarus | 3:36.365 |
| 2012 | Germany | 3:33.804 |

### CANADIAN SINGLES (10,000 METERS)

| | | MIN:SEC |
|---|---|---|
| 1948 | Frantisek Capek (TCH) | 62:05.2 |
| 1952 | Frank Havens (USA) | 57:41.1 |
| 1956 | Leon Rottman (ROM) | 56:41.0 |

### CANADIAN PAIRS (10,000 METERS)

| | | MIN:SEC |
|---|---|---|
| 1936 | Czechoslovakia | 50:35.5 |
| 1948 | United States | 55:55.4 |
| 1952 | France | 54:08.3 |
| 1956 | USSR | 54:02.4 |

### SLALOM CANADIAN SINGLES

| | |
|---|---|
| 1972 | Reinhard Eiben (GDR) |
| 1992 | Lukas Pollert (TCH) |
| 1996 | Michal Martikan (SVK) |
| 2000 | Tony Estanguet (FRA) |
| 2004 | Tony Estanguet (FRA) |
| 2008 | Michal Martikan (SVK) |
| 2012 | Tony Estanguet (FRA) |

### SLALOM CANADIAN PAIRS

| | |
|---|---|
| 1972 | East Germany |
| 1992 | United States |
| 1996 | France |
| 2000 | Slovakia |
| 2004 | Slovakia |
| 2008 | Slovakia |
| 2012 | Great Britain |

## Canoeing (women)

### KAYAK SINGLES (200 METERS)

| | | MIN:SEC |
|---|---|---|
| 2012 | Lisa Carrington (NZL) | 44.638 |

### KAYAK SINGLES (500 METERS)

| | | MIN:SEC |
|---|---|---|
| 1948 | Karen Hoff (DEN) | 2:31.90 |
| 1952 | Sylvi Saimo (FIN) | 2:18.40 |
| 1956 | Yelizaveta Dementyeva (URS) | 2:18.90 |
| 1960 | Antonina Seredina (URS) | 2:08.08 |
| 1964 | Lyudmila Khvedosyuk (URS) | 2:12.87 |
| 1968 | Lyudmila Pinayeva-Khvedosyuk (URS) | 2:11.09 |
| 1972 | Yuliya Ryabchinskaya (URS) | 2:03.17 |
| 1976 | Carola Zirzow (GDR) | 2:01.05 |
| 1980 | Birgit Fischer (GDR) | 1:57.96 |
| 1984 | Agneta Andersson (SWE) | 1:58.72 |
| 1988 | Vanya Gecheva (BUL) | 1:55.19 |
| 1992 | Birgit Fischer Schmidt (GER) | 1:51.60 |
| 1996 | Rita Koban (HUN) | 1:47.655 |
| 2000 | Josefa Idem Guerrini (ITA) | 2:13.848 |
| 2004 | Natasa Janics (HUN) | 1:47.741 |
| 2008 | Inna Osypenko-Radomska (UKR) | 1:50.673 |
| 2012 | Danuta Kozak (HUN) | 1:51.456 |

# Summer Olympic Games (continued)

## Canoeing (women) (continued)

### KAYAK PAIRS (500 METERS)

| | | MIN:SEC |
|---|---|---|
| 1960 | USSR | 1:54.76 |
| 1964 | Germany | 1:56.95 |
| 1968 | West Germany | 1:56.44 |
| 1972 | USSR | 1:53.50 |
| 1976 | USSR | 1:51.15 |
| 1980 | East Germany | 1:43.88 |
| 1984 | Sweden | 1:45.25 |
| 1988 | East Germany | 1:43.46 |
| 1992 | Germany | 1:40.29 |
| 1996 | Sweden | 1:39.329 |
| 2000 | Germany | 1:56.996 |
| 2004 | Hungary | 1:38.101 |
| 2008 | Hungary | 1:41.308 |
| 2012 | Germany | 1:42.213 |

### KAYAK FOURS (500 METERS)

| | | MIN:SEC |
|---|---|---|
| 1984 | Romania | 1:38.34 |
| 1988 | East Germany | 1:40.78 |
| 1992 | Hungary | 1:38.32 |
| 1996 | Germany | 1:31.077 |
| 2000 | Germany | 1:34.532 |
| 2004 | Germany | 1:34.340 |
| 2008 | Germany | 1:32.231 |
| 2012 | Hungary | 1:30.827 |

### SLALOM KAYAK SINGLES

| | |
|---|---|
| 1972 | Angelika Bahmann (GDR) |
| 1992 | Elisabeth Micheler (GER) |
| 1996 | Stepanka Hilgertova (CZE) |
| 2000 | Stepanka Hilgertova (CZE) |
| 2004 | Elena Kaliska (SVK) |
| 2008 | Elena Kaliska (SVK) |
| 2012 | Emilie Fer (FRA) |

## Cricket

| | |
|---|---|
| 1900 | Great Britain |

## Croquet

### SINGLES (ONE BALL)

| | |
|---|---|
| 1900 | Aumoitte (FRA) |

### SINGLES (TWO BALLS)

| | |
|---|---|
| 1900 | Waydelick (FRA) |

### DOUBLES

| | |
|---|---|
| 1900 | France |

## Cycling (men)

### 1,000-METER INDIVIDUAL SPRINT

| | |
|---|---|
| 1896[11] | Paul Masson (FRA) |
| 1900[11] | Georges Taillandier (FRA) |
| 1920 | Mauritius Peeters (NED) |
| 1924 | Lucien Michard (FRA) |
| 1928 | Roger Beaufrand (FRA) |
| 1932 | Jacobus Van Egmond (NED) |
| 1936 | Toni Merkens (GER) |
| 1948 | Mario Ghella (ITA) |
| 1952 | Enzo Sacchi (ITA) |
| 1956 | Michel Rousseau (FRA) |
| 1960 | Sante Gaiardoni (ITA) |
| 1964 | Giovanni Pettenella (ITA) |
| 1968 | Daniel Morelon (FRA) |
| 1972 | Daniel Morelon (FRA) |
| 1976 | Anton Tkac (TCH) |
| 1980 | Lutz Hesslich (GDR) |
| 1984 | Mark Gorski (USA) |
| 1988 | Lutz Hesslich (GDR) |

## Cycling (men) (continued)

### 1,000-METER INDIVIDUAL SPRINT (CONTINUED)

| | |
|---|---|
| 1992 | Jens Fiedler (GER) |
| 1996 | Jens Fiedler (GER) |
| 2000 | Marty Nothstein (USA) |
| 2004 | Ryan Bayley (AUS) |
| 2008 | Chris Hoy (GBR) |
| 2012 | Jason Kenny (GBR) |

### 1,000-METER TIME TRIAL

| | | MIN:SEC |
|---|---|---|
| 1896[12] | Paul Masson (FRA) | 24.0 |
| 1928 | Willy Falck-Hansen (DEN) | 1:14.4 |
| 1932 | Edgar Gray (AUS) | 1:13.0 |
| 1936 | Arie van Vliet (NED) | 1:12.0 |
| 1948 | Jacques Dupont (FRA) | 1:13.5 |
| 1952 | Russell Mockridge (AUS) | 1:11.1 |
| 1956 | Leandro Faggin (ITA) | 1:09.8 |
| 1960 | Sante Gaiardoni (ITA) | 1:07.27 |
| 1964 | Patrick Sercu (BEL) | 1:09.59 |
| 1968 | Pierre Trentin (FRA) | 1:03.91 |
| 1972 | Niels Fredborg (DEN) | 1:06.44 |
| 1976 | Klaus-Jürgen Grünke (GDR) | 1:05.927 |
| 1980 | Lothar Thoms (GDR) | 1:02.955 |
| 1984 | Fredy Schmidtke (FRG) | 1:06.104 |
| 1988 | Aleksandr Kirichenko (URS) | 1:04.499 |
| 1992 | José Moreno (ESP) | 1:03.342 |
| 1996 | Florian Rousseau (FRA) | 1:02.712 |
| 2000 | Jason Queally (GBR) | 1:01.609 |
| 2004 | Chris Hoy (GBR) | 1:00.711 |

### 1,500-METER TEAM PURSUIT

| | |
|---|---|
| 1900 | United States |

### 2,000 METERS

| | |
|---|---|
| 1904 | Marcus Hurley (USA) |

### 2,000-METER TANDEM

| | |
|---|---|
| 1908 | France |
| 1920 | Great Britain |
| 1924 | France |
| 1928 | The Netherlands |
| 1932 | France |
| 1936 | Germany |
| 1948 | Italy |
| 1952 | Australia |
| 1956 | Australia |
| 1960 | Italy |
| 1964 | Italy |
| 1968 | France |
| 1972 | USSR |

### INDIVIDUAL PURSUIT

| | |
|---|---|
| 1964 | Jiri Daler (TCH) |
| 1968 | Daniel Rebillard (FRA) |
| 1972 | Knut Knudsen (NOR) |
| 1976 | Gregor Braun (FRG) |
| 1980 | Robert Dill-Bondi (SUI) |
| 1984 | Steve Hegg (USA) |
| 1988 | Gintautas Umaras (URS) |
| 1992 | Christopher Boardman (GBR) |
| 1996 | Andrea Collinelli (ITA) |
| 2000 | Robert Bartko (GER) |
| 2004 | Bradley Wiggins (GBR) |
| 2008 | Bradley Wiggins (GBR) |

### TEAM PURSUIT

| | |
|---|---|
| 1908 | Great Britain |
| 1920 | Italy |
| 1924 | Italy |

# Summer Olympic Games (continued)

## Cycling (men) (continued)

**TEAM PURSUIT (CONTINUED)**

| | |
|---|---|
| 1928 | Italy |
| 1932 | Italy |
| 1936 | France |
| 1948 | France |
| 1952 | Italy |
| 1956 | Italy |
| 1960 | Italy |
| 1964 | Germany |
| 1968 | Denmark |
| 1972 | West Germany |
| 1976 | West Germany |
| 1980 | USSR |
| 1984 | Australia |
| 1988 | USSR |
| 1992 | Germany |
| 1996 | France |
| 2000 | Germany |
| 2004 | Australia |
| 2008 | Great Britain |
| 2012 | Great Britain |

| **5,000 METERS** | | **MIN:SEC** |
|---|---|---|
| 1908 | Benjamin Jones (GBR) | 8:36.2 |

| **10,000 METERS** | | **MIN:SEC** |
|---|---|---|
| 1896 | Paul Masson (FRA) | 17:54.2 |

| **20,000 METERS** | | **MIN:SEC** |
|---|---|---|
| 1908 | Charles Kingsbury (GBR) | 34:13.6 |

| **50,000 METERS** | | **HR:MIN:SEC** |
|---|---|---|
| 1920 | Henry George (BEL) | 1:16:43.2 |
| 1924 | Jacobus Willems (NED) | 1:18:24.0 |

| **100,000 METERS** | | **HR:MIN:SEC** |
|---|---|---|
| 1896 | Léon Flameng (FRA) | 3:08:19.2 |
| 1908 | Charles Bartlett (GBR) | 2:41:48.6 |

| **ONE-QUARTER MILE (440 YARDS)** | | **SEC** |
|---|---|---|
| 1904 | Marcus Hurley (USA) | 31.8 |

| **ONE-THIRD MILE (586⅔ YARDS)** | | **SEC** |
|---|---|---|
| 1904 | Marcus Hurley (USA) | 43.8 |

| **ONE-LAP TIME TRIAL (660 YARDS)** | | **SEC** |
|---|---|---|
| 1908 | Victor Johnson (GBR) | 51.2 |

| **ONE-HALF MILE (880 YARDS)** | | **MIN:SEC** |
|---|---|---|
| 1904 | Marcus Hurley (USA) | 1:09.0 |

| **1 MILE** | | **MIN:SEC** |
|---|---|---|
| 1904 | Marcus Hurley (USA) | 2:41.6 |

**1-MILE 1-FURLONG (1,980-YARD) TEAM PURSUIT**

| | |
|---|---|
| 1908 | Great Britain |

| **2 MILES** | | **MIN:SEC** |
|---|---|---|
| 1904 | Burton Downing (USA) | 4:58.0 |

| **5 MILES** | | **MIN:SEC** |
|---|---|---|
| 1904 | Charles Schlee (USA) | 13:08.2 |

**25 MILES**

| | |
|---|---|
| 1904 | Burton Downing (USA) |

**12 HOURS**

| | |
|---|---|
| 1896 | Adolf Schmal (AUT) |

## Cycling (men) (continued)

**INDIVIDUAL POINTS RACE**

| | |
|---|---|
| 1984 | Roger Ilegems (BEL) |
| 1988 | Dan Frost (DEN) |
| 1992 | Giovanni Lombardi (ITA) |
| 1996 | Silvio Martinello (ITA) |
| 2000 | Juan Llaneras (ESP) |
| 2004 | Mikhail Ignatyev (RUS) |
| 2008 | Joan Llaneras (ESP) |

| **KEIRIN** | | **SEC** |
|---|---|---|
| 2000 | Florian Rousseau (FRA) | 11.020 |
| 2004 | Ryan Bayley (AUS) | 10.601 |
| 2008 | Chris Hoy (GBR) | 10.450 |
| 2012 | Chris Hoy (GBR) | 10.306 |

**OMNIUM**

| | |
|---|---|
| 2012 | Lasse Norman Hansen (DEN) |

**MADISON**

| | |
|---|---|
| 2000 | Australia |
| 2004 | Australia |
| 2008 | Argentina |

| **TEAM SPRINT** | | **SEC** |
|---|---|---|
| 2000 | France | 44.233 |
| 2004 | Germany | 43.980 |
| 2008 | Great Britain | 43.128 |
| 2012 | Great Britain | 42.600 |

| **ROAD RACE (INDIVIDUAL)[13]** | | **HR:MIN:SEC** |
|---|---|---|
| 1896 | Aristidis Konstantinidis (GRE) | 3:22:31.0 |
| 1912 | Rudolph Lewis (RSA) | 10:42:39.0 |
| 1920 | Harry Stenqvist (SWE) | 4:40:01.8 |
| 1924 | Armand Blanchonnet (FRA) | 6:20:48.0 |
| 1928 | Henry Hansen (DEN) | 4:47:18.0 |
| 1932 | Attilio Pavesi (ITA) | 2:28:05.6 |
| 1936 | Robert Charpentier (FRA) | 2:33:05.0 |
| 1948 | Jose Beyaert (FRA) | 5:18:12.6 |
| 1952 | Andre Noyelle (BEL) | 5:06:03.4 |
| 1956 | Ercole Baldini (ITA) | 5:21:17.0 |
| 1960 | Viktor Kapitonov (URS) | 4:20:37.0 |
| 1964 | Mario Zanin (ITA) | 4:39:51.63 |
| 1968 | Pierfranco Vianelli (ITA) | 4:41:25.24 |
| 1972 | Hennie Kuiper (NED) | 4:14:37.0 |
| 1976 | Bernt Johansson (SWE) | 4:46:52.0 |
| 1980 | Sergey Sukhoruchenkov (URS) | 4:48:28.90 |
| 1984 | Alexei Grewal (USA) | 4:59:57.0 |
| 1988 | Olaf Ludwig (GDR) | 4:32:22.0 |
| 1992 | Fabio Casartelli (ITA) | 4:35:21.0 |
| 1996 | Pascal Richard (SUI) | 4:53:56.0 |
| 2000 | Jan Ullrich (GER) | 5:29:08.0 |
| 2004 | Paolo Bettini (ITA) | 5:41:44.0 |
| 2008 | Samuel Sánchez (ESP) | 6:23:49.0 |
| 2012 | Alexandr Vinokurov (KAZ) | 5:45:57 |

| **ROAD RACE (TEAM)** | | **HR:MIN:SEC** |
|---|---|---|
| 1912 | Sweden | 44:35:33.6 |
| 1920 | France | 19:16:43.2 |
| 1924 | France | 19:30:14 |
| 1928 | Denmark | 15:09:14 |
| 1932 | Italy | 7:27:15.2 |
| 1936 | France | 7:39:16.2 |
| 1948 | Belgium | 15:58:17.4 |
| 1952 | Belgium | 15:20:46.6 |
| 1956 | France | 5:21:17 |

| **ROAD TIME TRIAL (INDIVIDUAL)** | | **HR:MIN:SEC** |
|---|---|---|
| 1996 | Miguel Indurain (ESP) | 1:04:05 |

## Summer Olympic Games (continued)

### Cycling (men) (continued)

**ROAD TIME TRIAL (INDIVIDUAL) (CONTINUED)** — HR:MIN:SEC

| | | |
|---|---|---|
| 2000 | Vyacheslav Yekimov (RUS) | 57:40.42 |
| 2004 | Vyacheslav Yekimov (RUS)[2] | 57:50.58 |
| 2008 | Fabian Cancellara (SUI) | 1:02:11.43 |
| 2012 | Bradley Wiggins (GBR) | 50:39.54 |

**ROAD TIME TRIAL (TEAM)** — HR:MIN:SEC

| | | |
|---|---|---|
| 1960 | Italy | 2:14:33.53 |
| 1964 | The Netherlands | 2:26:31.19 |
| 1968 | The Netherlands | 2:07:49.06 |
| 1972 | USSR | 2:11:17.8 |
| 1976 | USSR | 2:08:53 |
| 1980 | USSR | 2:01:21.7 |
| 1984 | Italy | 1:58:28 |
| 1988 | East Germany | 1:57:47.7 |
| 1992 | Germany | 2:01:39 |

**MOUNTAIN BIKE** — HR:MIN:SEC

| | | |
|---|---|---|
| 1996 | Bart Jan Brentjens (NED) | 2:17:38 |
| 2000 | Miguel Martinez (FRA) | 2:09:2.50 |
| 2004 | Julien Absalon (FRA) | 2:15:02 |
| 2008 | Julien Absalon (FRA) | 1:55:59 |
| 2012 | Jaroslav Kulhavy (CZE) | 1:29:07 |

**MOTOCROSS/BMX** — SEC

| | | |
|---|---|---|
| 2008 | Maris Strombergs (LAT) | 36.190 |
| 2012 | Maris Strombergs (LAT) | 37.576 |

### Cycling (women)

**500-METER TIME TRIAL** — SEC

| | | |
|---|---|---|
| 2000 | Felicia Ballanger (FRA) | 34.140 |
| 2004 | Anna Meares (AUS) | 53.016 |

**1,000-METER INDIVIDUAL SPRINT**

| | |
|---|---|
| 1988 | Erika Salumae (URS) |
| 1992 | Erika Salumae (EST) |
| 1996 | Felicia Ballanger (FRA) |
| 2000 | Felicia Ballanger (FRA) |
| 2004 | Lori-Ann Muenzer (CAN) |
| 2008 | Victoria Pendleton (GBR) |

**INDIVIDUAL PURSUIT**

| | |
|---|---|
| 1992 | Petra Rossner (GER) |
| 1996 | Antonella Bellutti (ITA) |
| 2000 | Leontien Zijlaard–van Moorsel (NED) |
| 2004 | Sarah Ulmer (NZL) |
| 2008 | Rebecca Romero (GBR) |

**TEAM PURSUIT**

| | |
|---|---|
| 2012 | Great Britain |

**INDIVIDUAL POINTS RACE**

| | |
|---|---|
| 1996 | Nathalie Lancien (FRA) |
| 2000 | Antonella Bellutti (ITA) |
| 2004 | Olga Slyusareva (RUS) |
| 2008 | Marianne Vos (NED) |

**KEIRIN**

| | |
|---|---|
| 2012 | Victoria Pendleton (GBR) |

**OMNIUM**

| | |
|---|---|
| 2012 | Laura Trott (GBR) |

**SPRINT**

| | |
|---|---|
| 2012 | Anna Meares (AUS) |

**TEAM SPRINT**

| | |
|---|---|
| 2012 | Germany |

### Cycling (women) (continued)

**ROAD RACE (INDIVIDUAL)** — HR:MIN:SEC

| | | |
|---|---|---|
| 1984 | Connie Carpenter-Phinney (USA) | 2:11:14.0 |
| 1988 | Monique Knol (NED) | 2:00:52.0 |
| 1992 | Kathryn Watt (AUS) | 2:04:42.0 |
| 1996 | Jeannie Longo-Ciprelli (FRA) | 2:36:13.0 |
| 2000 | Leontien Zijlaard–van Moorsel (NED) | 3:06:31 |
| 2004 | Sara Carrigan (AUS) | 3:24:24 |
| 2008 | Nicole Cooke (GBR) | 3:32:24 |
| 2012 | Marianne Vos (NED) | 3:35:29 |

**ROAD TIME TRIAL (INDIVIDUAL)** — MIN:SEC

| | | |
|---|---|---|
| 1996 | Zulfiya Zabirova (RUS) | 36:40 |
| 2000 | Leontien Zijlaard–van Moorsel (NED) | 42:00.781 |
| 2004 | Leontien Zijlaard–van Moorsel (NED) | 31:11.53 |
| 2008 | Kristin Armstrong (USA) | 34:51.72 |
| 2012 | Kristin Armstrong (USA) | 37:34.82 |

**MOUNTAIN BIKE** — HR:MIN:SEC

| | | |
|---|---|---|
| 1996 | Paola Pezzo (ITA) | 1:50:51 |
| 2000 | Paola Pezzo (ITA) | 1:49:24.38 |
| 2004 | Gunn-Rita Dahle (NOR) | 1:56:51 |
| 2008 | Sabine Spitz (GER) | 1:45:11 |
| 2012 | Julie Bresset (FRA) | 1:30:52 |

**MOTOCROSS/BMX** — SEC

| | | |
|---|---|---|
| 2008 | Anne-Caroline Chausson (FRA) | 35.976 |
| 2012 | Mariana Pajon (COL) | 37.706 |

### Diving (men)

**3-METER SPRINGBOARD DIVING**

| | |
|---|---|
| 1908 | Albert Zürner (GER) |
| 1912 | Paul Günther (GER) |
| 1920 | Louis Kuehn (USA) |
| 1924 | Albert White (USA) |
| 1928 | Peter Desjardins (USA) |
| 1932 | Michael Galitzen (USA) |
| 1936 | Richard Degener (USA) |
| 1948 | Bruce Harlan (USA) |
| 1952 | David Browning (USA) |
| 1956 | Robert Clotworthy (USA) |
| 1960 | Gary Tobian (USA) |
| 1964 | Kenneth Sitzberger (USA) |
| 1968 | Bernie Wrightson (USA) |
| 1972 | Vladimir Vasin (URS) |
| 1976 | Philip Boggs (USA) |
| 1980 | Aleksandr Portnov (URS) |
| 1984 | Greg Louganis (USA) |
| 1988 | Greg Louganis (USA) |
| 1992 | Mark Edward Lenzi (USA) |
| 1996 | Xiong Ni (CHN) |
| 2000 | Xiong Ni (CHN) |
| 2004 | Peng Bo (CHN) |
| 2008 | He Chong (CHN) |
| 2012 | Ilya Zakharov (RUS) |

**10-METER PLATFORM (HIGH) DIVING**

| | |
|---|---|
| 1904 | George Sheldon (USA) |
| 1908 | Hjalmar Johansson (SWE) |
| 1912 | Erik Adlerz (SWE) |
| 1920 | Clarence Pinkston (USA) |
| 1924 | Albert White (USA) |
| 1928 | Peter Desjardins (USA) |
| 1932 | Harold Smith (USA) |
| 1936 | Marshall Wayne (USA) |
| 1948 | Samuel Lee (USA) |

# Summer Olympic Games (continued)

## Diving (men) (continued)

### 10-METER PLATFORM (HIGH) DIVING (CONTINUED)

1952　Samuel Lee (USA)
1956　Joaquin Capilla Perez (MEX)
1960　Robert Webster (USA)
1964　Robert Webster (USA)
1968　Klaus Dibiasi (ITA)
1972　Klaus Dibiasi (ITA)
1976　Klaus Dibiasi (ITA)
1980　Falk Hoffman (GDR)
1984　Greg Louganis (USA)
1988　Greg Louganis (USA)
1992　Sun Shuwei (CHN)
1996　Dmitry Sautin (RUS)
2000　Tian Liang (CHN)
2004　Hu Jia (CHN)
2008　Matt Mitcham (AUS)
2012　David Boudia (USA)

### 3-METER SYNCHRONIZED SPRINGBOARD DIVING

2000　China
2004　Greece
2008　China
2012　China

### 10-METER SYNCHRONIZED PLATFORM (HIGH) DIVING

2000　Russia
2004　China
2008　China
2012　China

### PLUNGE FOR DISTANCE

1904　William Paul Dickey (USA)

### PLAIN HIGH DIVING

1912　Erik Adlerz (SWE)
1920　Arvid Wallman (SWE)
1924　Richmond Eve (AUS)

## Diving (women)

### 3-METER SPRINGBOARD DIVING

1920　Aileen Riggin (USA)
1924　Elizabeth Becker-Pinkton (USA)
1928　Helen Meany (USA)
1932　Georgia Coleman (USA)
1936　Marjorie Gestring (USA)
1948　Victoria Draves (USA)
1952　Patricia McCormick (USA)
1956　Patricia McCormick (USA)
1960　Ingrid Krämer-Engel-Gulbin (GER)
1964　Ingrid Krämer-Engel-Gulbin (GER)
1968　Sue Gossick (USA)
1972　Micki King (USA)
1976　Jennifer Chandler (USA)
1980　Irina Kalinina (URS)
1984　Sylvie Bernier (CAN)
1988　Gao Min (CHN)
1992　Gao Min (CHN)
1996　Fu Mingxia (CHN)
2000　Fu Mingxia (CHN)
2004　Guo Jingjing (CHN)
2008　Guo Jingjing (CHN)
2012　Wu Minxia (CHN)

### 10-METER PLATFORM (HIGH) DIVING

1912　Greta Johansson (SWE)
1920　Stefani Fryland Clausen (DEN)
1924　Caroline Smith (USA)
1928　Elizabeth Anna Becker-Pinkston (USA)

## Diving (women) (continued)

### 10-METER PLATFORM (HIGH) DIVING (CONTINUED)

1932　Dorothy Poynton (USA)
1936　Dorothy Poynton-Hill (USA)
1948　Victoria Draves (USA)
1952　Patricia McCormick (USA)
1956　Patricia McCormick (USA)
1960　Ingrid Krämer-Engel-Gulbin (GER)
1964　Lesley Leigh Bush (USA)
1968　Milena Duchkova (TCH)
1972　Ulrika Knape (SWE)
1976　Yelena Vaytsekhovskaya (URS)
1980　Martina Jäschke (GDR)
1984　Zhou Ji-Hong (CHN)
1988　Xu Yan-Mei (CHN)
1992　Fu Mingxia (CHN)
1996　Fu Mingxia (CHN)
2000　Laura Wilkinson (USA)
2004　Chantelle Newbery (AUS)
2008　Chen Ruolin (CHN)
2012　Chen Ruolin (CHN)

### 3-METER SYNCHRONIZED SPRINGBOARD DIVING

2000　Russia
2004　China
2008　China
2012　Chna

### 10-METER SYNCHRONIZED PLATFORM (HIGH) DIVING

2000　China
2004　China
2008　China
2012　China

## Equestrian Sports

### GRAND PRIX (DRESSAGE) INDIVIDUAL

| Year | Winner | MOUNT |
|---|---|---|
| 1912 | Carl Bonde (SWE) | Emperor |
| 1920 | Janne Lundblad (SWE) | Uno |
| 1924 | Ernst Linder (SWE) | Piccolomini |
| 1928 | Carl Friedrich Freiherr von Langen-Parow (GER) | Draufgänger |
| 1932 | Xavier Lesage (FRA) | Taine |
| 1936 | Heinz Pollay (GER) | Kronos |
| 1948 | Hans Moser (SUI) | Hummer |
| 1952 | Henri St. Cyr (SWE) | Master Rufus |
| 1956 | Henri St. Cyr (SWE) | Juli |
| 1960 | Sergey Filatov (URS) | Absent |
| 1964 | Henri Chammartin (SUI) | Woermann |
| 1968 | Ivan Kizimov (URS) | Ikhor |
| 1972 | Liselott Linsenhoff (FRG) | Piaff |
| 1976 | Christine Stückelberger (SUI) | Granat |
| 1980 | Elisabeth Theurer (AUT) | Mon Cherie |
| 1984 | Reiner Klimke (FRG) | Ahlerich |
| 1988 | Nicole Uphoff (FRG) | Rembrandt 24 |
| 1992 | Nicole Uphoff (GER) | Rembrandt 24 |
| 1996 | Isabell Werth (GER) | Gigolo |
| 2000 | Anky van Grunsven (NED) | Bonfire |
| 2004 | Anky van Grunsven (NED) | Salinero |
| 2008 | Anky van Grunsven (NED) | Keltec Salinero |
| 2012 | Charlotte Dujardin (GBR) | Valegro |

### GRAND PRIX (DRESSAGE) TEAM

1928　Germany
1932　France
1936　Germany
1948　France
1952　Sweden
1956　Sweden
1964　Germany

# Summer Olympic Games (continued)

### Equestrian Sports (continued)

**GRAND PRIX (DRESSAGE) TEAM (CONTINUED)**

| | |
|---|---|
| 1968 | West Germany |
| 1972 | USSR |
| 1976 | West Germany |
| 1980 | USSR |
| 1984 | West Germany |
| 1988 | West Germany |
| 1992 | Germany |
| 1996 | Germany |
| 2000 | Germany |
| 2004 | Germany |
| 2008 | Germany |
| 2012 | Great Britain |

**GRAND PRIX (JUMPING) INDIVIDUAL** — MOUNT

| | | |
|---|---|---|
| 1900 | Aimé Haegeman (BEL) | Benton II |
| 1912 | Jean Cariou (FRA) | Mignon |
| 1920 | Tommaso Lequio di Assaba (ITA) | Trebecco |
| 1924 | Alphonse Gemuseus (SUI) | Lucette |
| 1928 | Frantisek Ventura (TCH) | Eliot |
| 1932 | Takeichi Nishi (JPN) | Uranus |
| 1936 | Kurt Hasse (GER) | Tora |
| 1948 | Humberto Mariles Cortés (MEX) | Arete |
| 1952 | Pierre Jonquères d'Oriola (FRA) | Ali Baba |
| 1956 | Hans-Günter Winkler (GER) | Halla |
| 1960 | Raimondo d'Inzeo (ITA) | Posillipo |
| 1964 | Pierre Jonquères d'Oriola (FRA) | Lutteur |
| 1968 | William Steinkraus (USA) | Snowbound |
| 1972 | Graziano Mancinelli (ITA) | Ambassador |
| 1976 | Alwin Schockemöhle (FRG) | Warwick Rex |
| 1980 | Jan Kowalczyk (POL) | Artemor |
| 1984 | Joe Fargis (USA) | Touch of Class |
| 1988 | Pierre Durand (FRA) | Jappeloup |
| 1992 | Ludger Beerbaum (GER) | Classic Touch |
| 1996 | Ulrich Kirchhoff (GER) | Jus des Pommes |
| 2000 | Jeroen Dubbeldam (NED) | Sjiem |
| 2004 | Rodrigo Pessoa (BRA)[2] | Baloubet du Rouet[2] |
| 2008 | Eric Lamaze (CAN) | Hickstead |
| 2012 | Steve Guerdat (SUI) | Nino des Buissonnets |

**GRAND PRIX (JUMPING) TEAM**

| | |
|---|---|
| 1912 | Sweden |
| 1920 | Sweden |
| 1924 | Sweden |
| 1928 | Spain |
| 1936 | Germany |
| 1948 | Mexico |
| 1952 | Great Britain |
| 1956 | Germany |
| 1960 | Germany |
| 1964 | Germany |
| 1968 | Canada |
| 1972 | West Germany |
| 1976 | France |
| 1980 | USSR |
| 1984 | United States |
| 1988 | West Germany |
| 1992 | The Netherlands |
| 1996 | Germany |
| 2000 | Germany |
| 2004 | United States[2] |
| 2008 | United States |
| 2012 | Great Britain |

**THREE-DAY EVENT (INDIVIDUAL)** — MOUNT

| | | |
|---|---|---|
| 1912 | Axel Nordlander (SWE) | Lady Artist |
| 1920 | Helmer Mörner (SWE) | Germania |
| 1924 | Adolph van der Voort van Zijp (NED) | Silver Piece |

### Equestrian Sports (continued)

**THREE-DAY EVENT (INDIVIDUAL) (CONTINUED)** — MOUNT

| | | |
|---|---|---|
| 1928 | Charles Pahud de Mortanges (NED) | Marcroix |
| 1932 | Charles Pahud de Mortanges (NED) | Marcroix |
| 1936 | Ludwig Stubbendorff (GER) | Nurmi |
| 1948 | Bernard Chevallier (FRA) | Aiglonne |
| 1952 | Hans von Blixen-Finecke, Jr. (SWE) | Jubal |
| 1956 | Petrus Kastenman (SWE) | Iluster |
| 1960 | Lawrence Morgan (AUS) | Salad Days |
| 1964 | Mauro Checcoli (ITA) | Surbean |
| 1968 | Jean-Jacques Goyon (FRA) | Pitou |
| 1972 | Richard Meade (GBR) | Laurieston |
| 1976 | Edmund Coffin (USA) | Bally-Cor |
| 1980 | Federico Euro Roman (ITA) | Rossinan |
| 1984 | Mark Todd (NZL) | Charisma |
| 1988 | Mark Todd (NZL) | Charisma |
| 1992 | Matthew Ryan (AUS) | Kibah Tic Toc |
| 1996 | Robert Blyth Tait (NZL) | Ready Teddy |
| 2000 | David O'Connor (USA) | Custom Made |
| 2004 | Leslie Law (GBR) | Shear L'Eau |
| 2008 | Hinrich Romeike (GER) | Marius |
| 2012 | Michael Jung (GER) | Sam |

**THREE-DAY EVENT (TEAM)**

| | |
|---|---|
| 1912 | Sweden |
| 1920 | Sweden |
| 1924 | The Netherlands |
| 1928 | The Netherlands |
| 1932 | United States |
| 1936 | Germany |
| 1948 | United States |
| 1952 | Sweden |
| 1956 | Great Britain |
| 1960 | Australia |
| 1964 | Italy |
| 1968 | Great Britain |
| 1972 | Great Britain |
| 1976 | United States |
| 1980 | USSR |
| 1984 | United States |
| 1988 | West Germany |
| 1992 | Australia |
| 1996 | Australia |
| 2000 | Australia |
| 2004 | France |
| 2008 | Germany |
| 2012 | Germany |

**HIGH JUMP** — MOUNT

| | | |
|---|---|---|
| 1900 | Dominique Maximien Gardéres (FRA); Gian Giorgio Trissino (ITA) (tied) | Canela; Oreste |

**LONG JUMP** — MOUNT

| | | |
|---|---|---|
| 1900 | Constant van Langhendonck (BEL) | Extra Dry |

**FIGURE RIDING (INDIVIDUAL)**

| | |
|---|---|
| 1920 | T. Bouckaert (BEL) |

**FIGURE RIDING (TEAM)**

| | |
|---|---|
| 1920 | Belgium |

### Fencing (men)

**FOIL (INDIVIDUAL)**

| | |
|---|---|
| 1896 | Eugène-Henri Gravelotte (FRA) |
| 1900 | Émile Coste (FRA) |
| 1904 | Ramón Fonst (CUB) |
| 1912 | Nedo Nadi (ITA) |
| 1920 | Nedo Nadi (ITA) |

# Summer Olympic Games (continued)

### Fencing (men) (continued)

**FOIL (INDIVIDUAL) (CONTINUED)**

| | |
|---|---|
| 1924 | Roger Ducret (FRA) |
| 1928 | Lucien Gaudin (FRA) |
| 1932 | Gustavo Marzi (ITA) |
| 1936 | Giulio Gaudini (ITA) |
| 1948 | Jehan Buhan (FRA) |
| 1952 | Christian d'Oriola (FRA) |
| 1956 | Christian d'Oriola (FRA) |
| 1960 | Viktor Zhdanovich (URS) |
| 1964 | Egon Franke (POL) |
| 1968 | Ion Drimba (ROM) |
| 1972 | Witold Woyda (POL) |
| 1976 | Fabio dal Zotto (ITA) |
| 1980 | Vladimir Smirnov (URS) |
| 1984 | Mauro Numa (ITA) |
| 1988 | Stefano Cerioni (ITA) |
| 1992 | Philippe Omnes (FRA) |
| 1996 | Alessandro Puccini (ITA) |
| 2000 | Kim Young Ho (KOR) |
| 2004 | Brice Guyart (FRA) |
| 2008 | Benjamin Philip Kleibrink (GER) |
| 2012 | Lei Sheng (CHN) |

**FOIL (TEAM)**

| | |
|---|---|
| 1904 | Cuba |
| 1920 | Italy |
| 1924 | France |
| 1928 | Italy |
| 1932 | France |
| 1936 | Italy |
| 1948 | France |
| 1952 | France |
| 1956 | Italy |
| 1960 | USSR |
| 1964 | USSR |
| 1968 | France |
| 1972 | Poland |
| 1976 | West Germany |
| 1980 | France |
| 1984 | Italy |
| 1988 | USSR |
| 1992 | Germany |
| 1996 | Russia |
| 2000 | France |
| 2004 | Italy |
| 2012 | Italy |

**INDIVIDUAL FOIL, PROFESSIONAL (MASTERS)**

| | |
|---|---|
| 1896 | Leon Pyrgos (GRE) |
| 1900 | Lucien Mérignac (FRA) |

**INDIVIDUAL FOIL, JUNIOR**

| | |
|---|---|
| 1904 | Arthur Fox (USA) |

**ÉPÉE (INDIVIDUAL)**

| | |
|---|---|
| 1900 | Ramón Fonst (CUB) |
| 1904 | Ramón Fonst (CUB) |
| 1908 | Gaston Alibert (FRA) |
| 1912 | Paul Anspach (BEL) |
| 1920 | Armand Massard (FRA) |
| 1924 | Charles Delporte (BEL) |
| 1928 | Lucien Gaudin (FRA) |
| 1932 | Giancarlo Cornaggia-Medici (ITA) |
| 1936 | Franco Riccardi (ITA) |
| 1948 | Luigi Cantone (ITA) |
| 1952 | Edoardo Mangiarotti (ITA) |
| 1956 | Carlo Pavesi (ITA) |
| 1960 | Giuseppe Delfino (ITA) |

### Fencing (men) (continued)

**ÉPÉE (INDIVIDUAL) (CONTINUED)**

| | |
|---|---|
| 1964 | Grigory Kriss (URS) |
| 1968 | Gyoso Kulcsar (HUN) |
| 1972 | Csaba Fenyvesi (HUN) |
| 1976 | Alexander Pusch (FRG) |
| 1980 | Johan Harmenberg (SWE) |
| 1984 | Philippe Boisse (FRA) |
| 1988 | Arnd Schmitt (FRG) |
| 1992 | Eric Srecki (FRA) |
| 1996 | Aleksandr Beketov (RUS) |
| 2000 | Pavel Kolobkov (RUS) |
| 2004 | Marcel Fischer (SUI) |
| 2008 | Matteo Tagliariol (ITA) |
| 2012 | Ruben Limardo Gascon (VEN) |

**ÉPÉE (TEAM)**

| | |
|---|---|
| 1908 | France |
| 1912 | Belgium |
| 1920 | Italy |
| 1924 | France |
| 1928 | Italy |
| 1932 | France |
| 1936 | Italy |
| 1948 | France |
| 1952 | Italy |
| 1956 | Italy |
| 1960 | Italy |
| 1964 | Hungary |
| 1968 | Hungary |
| 1972 | Hungary |
| 1976 | Sweden |
| 1980 | France |
| 1984 | West Germany |
| 1988 | France |
| 1992 | Germany |
| 1996 | Italy |
| 2000 | Italy |
| 2004 | France |
| 2008 | France |

**INDIVIDUAL ÉPÉE, PROFESSIONAL (MASTERS)**

| | |
|---|---|
| 1900 | Albert Ayat (FRA) |

**INDIVIDUAL ÉPÉE, OPEN (AMATEUR AND MASTERS)**

| | |
|---|---|
| 1900 | Albert Ayat (FRA) |

**SABRE (INDIVIDUAL)**

| | |
|---|---|
| 1896 | Ioannis Georgiadis (GRE) |
| 1900 | Georges de la Falaise (FRA) |
| 1904 | Manuel Díaz (CUB) |
| 1908 | Jeno Fuchs (HUN) |
| 1912 | Jeno Fuchs (HUN) |
| 1920 | Nedo Nadi (ITA) |
| 1924 | Sandor Posta (HUN) |
| 1928 | Odon Vitez Tersztyanszky (HUN) |
| 1932 | Gyorgy Piller (HUN) |
| 1936 | Endre Kabos (HUN) |
| 1948 | Aladar Gerevich (HUN) |
| 1952 | Pal Kovacs (HUN) |
| 1956 | Rudolph Karpati (HUN) |
| 1960 | Rudolph Karpati (HUN) |
| 1964 | Tibor Pezsa (HUN) |
| 1968 | Jerzy Pawlowski (POL) |
| 1972 | Viktor Sidyak (URS) |
| 1976 | Viktor Krovopuskov (URS) |
| 1980 | Viktor Krovopuskov (URS) |
| 1984 | Jean-François Lamour (FRA) |
| 1988 | Jean-François Lamour (FRA) |

## Summer Olympic Games (continued)

### Fencing (men) (continued)

**SABRE (INDIVIDUAL) (CONTINUED)**

| | |
|---|---|
| 1992 | Bence Szabo (HUN) |
| 1996 | Stanislav Pozdnyakov (RUS) |
| 2000 | Mihai Claudiu Covaliu (ROM) |
| 2004 | Aldo Montano (ITA) |
| 2008 | Zhong Man (CHN) |
| 2012 | Aron Szilagyi (HUN) |

**SABRE (TEAM)**

| | |
|---|---|
| 1908 | Hungary |
| 1912 | Hungary |
| 1920 | Italy |
| 1924 | Italy |
| 1928 | Hungary |
| 1932 | Hungary |
| 1936 | Hungary |
| 1948 | Hungary |
| 1952 | Hungary |
| 1956 | Hungary |
| 1960 | Hungary |
| 1964 | USSR |
| 1968 | USSR |
| 1972 | Italy |
| 1976 | USSR |
| 1980 | USSR |
| 1984 | Italy |
| 1988 | Hungary |
| 1992 | Unified Team |
| 1996 | Russia |
| 2000 | Russia |
| 2004 | France |
| 2008 | France |
| 2012 | South Korea |

**INDIVIDUAL SABRE, PROFESSIONAL (MASTERS)**

| | |
|---|---|
| 1900 | Antonio Conte (ITA) |

**SINGLE STICK**

| | |
|---|---|
| 1904 | Albertson Van Zo Post (CUB) |

### Fencing (women)

**FOIL (INDIVIDUAL)**

| | |
|---|---|
| 1924 | Ellen Osiier (DEN) |
| 1928 | Helene Mayer (GER) |
| 1932 | Ellen Preis (AUT) |
| 1936 | Ilona Schacherer-Elek (HUN) |
| 1948 | Ilona Elek (HUN) |
| 1952 | Irene Camber (ITA) |
| 1956 | Gillian Sheen (GBR) |
| 1960 | Adelheid Schmid (GER) |
| 1964 | Ildiko Ujlaki-Rejto (HUN) |
| 1968 | Yelena Novikova (URS) |
| 1972 | Antonella Ragno Lonzi (ITA) |
| 1976 | Ildiko Schwarczenberger (HUN) |
| 1980 | Pascale Trinquet (FRA) |
| 1984 | Jujie Luan (CHN) |
| 1988 | Anja Fichtel (FRG) |
| 1992 | Giovanna Trillini (ITA) |
| 1996 | Laura Gabriela Badea (ROM) |
| 2000 | Valentina Vezzali (ITA) |
| 2004 | Valentina Vezzali (ITA) |
| 2008 | Valentina Vezzali (ITA) |
| 2012 | Elisa Di Francisca (ITA) |

**FOIL (TEAM)**

| | |
|---|---|
| 1960 | USSR |
| 1964 | Hungary |
| 1968 | USSR |

### Fencing (women) (continued)

**FOIL (TEAM) (CONTINUED)**

| | |
|---|---|
| 1972 | USSR |
| 1976 | USSR |
| 1980 | France |
| 1984 | West Germany |
| 1988 | West Germany |
| 1992 | Italy |
| 1996 | Italy |
| 2000 | Italy |
| 2008 | Russia |
| 2012 | Italy |

**ÉPÉE (INDIVIDUAL)**

| | |
|---|---|
| 1996 | Laura Flessel (FRA) |
| 2000 | Timea Nagy (HUN) |
| 2004 | Timea Nagy (HUN) |
| 2008 | Britta Heidemann (GER) |
| 2012 | Yana Shemyakina (UKR) |

**ÉPÉE (TEAM)**

| | |
|---|---|
| 1996 | France |
| 2000 | Russia |
| 2004 | Russia |
| 2012 | China |

**SABRE (INDIVIDUAL)**

| | |
|---|---|
| 2004 | Mariel Zagunis (USA) |
| 2008 | Mariel Zagunis (USA) |
| 2012 | Kim Ji-Yeon (KOR) |

**SABRE (TEAM)**

| | |
|---|---|
| 2008 | Ukraine |

### Field Hockey

**MEN**

| | |
|---|---|
| 1908 | Great Britain |
| 1920 | Great Britain |
| 1928 | India |
| 1932 | India |
| 1936 | India |
| 1948 | India |
| 1952 | India |
| 1956 | India |
| 1960 | Pakistan |
| 1964 | India |
| 1968 | Pakistan |
| 1972 | West Germany |
| 1976 | New Zealand |
| 1980 | India |
| 1984 | Pakistan |
| 1988 | Great Britain |
| 1992 | Germany |
| 1996 | The Netherlands |
| 2000 | The Netherlands |
| 2004 | Australia |
| 2008 | Germany |
| 2012 | Germany |

**WOMEN**

| | |
|---|---|
| 1980 | Zimbabwe |
| 1984 | The Netherlands |
| 1988 | Australia |
| 1992 | Spain |
| 1996 | Australia |
| 2000 | Australia |
| 2004 | Germany |
| 2008 | The Netherlands |
| 2012 | The Netherlands |

# Summer Olympic Games (continued)

## Golf

**MEN, INDIVIDUAL**
1900  Charles Sands (USA)
1904  George Lyon (CAN)

**MEN, TEAM**
1904  United States

**WOMEN**
1900  Margaret Abbott (USA)

## Gymnastics (men)

**COMBINED, OR ALL-AROUND (INDIVIDUAL)**
1900  Gustave Sandras (FRA)
1904  Julius Lenhardt (USA)
1908  G. Alberto Braglia (ITA)
1912  G. Alberto Braglia (ITA)
1920  Giorgio Zampori (ITA)
1924  Leon Stukelj (YUG)
1928  Georges Miez (SUI)
1932  Romeo Neri (ITA)
1936  Karl-Alfred Schwarzmann (GER)
1948  Veikko Huhtanen (FIN)
1952  Viktor Chukarin (URS)
1956  Viktor Chukarin (URS)
1960  Boris Shakhlin (URS)
1964  Yukio Endo (JPN)
1968  Sawao Kato (JPN)
1972  Sawao Kato (JPN)
1976  Nikolay Andrianov (URS)
1980  Aleksandr Dityatin (URS)
1984  Koji Gushiken (JPN)
1988  Vladimir Artyomov (URS)
1992  Vitaly Shcherbo (UNT)
1996  Li Xiaosahuang (CHN)
2000  Aleksey Nemov (RUS)
2004  Paul Hamm (USA)
2008  Yang Wei (CHN)
2012  Kohei Uchimura (JPN)

**COMBINED, OR ALL-AROUND (TEAM)**
1920  Italy
1924  Italy
1928  Switzerland
1932  Italy
1936  Germany
1948  Finland
1952  USSR
1956  USSR
1960  Japan
1964  Japan
1968  Japan
1972  Japan
1976  Japan
1980  USSR
1984  United States
1988  USSR
1992  Unified Team
1996  Russia
2000  China
2004  Japan
2008  China
2012  China

**FLOOR EXERCISE**
1932  Istvan Pelle (HUN)
1936  Georges Miez (SUI)
1948  Ferenc Pataki (HUN)
1952  William Thoresson (SWE)

## Gymnastics (men) (continued)

**FLOOR EXERCISE (CONTINUED)**
1956  Valentin Muratov (URS)
1960  Nobuyuki Aihara (JPN)
1964  Franco Menichelli (ITA)
1968  Sawao Kato (JPN)
1972  Nikolay Andrianov (URS)
1976  Nikolay Andrianov (URS)
1980  Roland Brückner (GDR)
1984  Li Ning (CHN)
1988  Sergey Kharikov (URS)
1992  Li Xiaosahuang (CHN)
1996  Ioannis Melissanidis (GRE)
2000  Igors Vihrovs (LAT)
2004  Kyle Shewfelt (CAN)
2008  Zou Kai (CHN)
2012  Zou Kai (CHN)

**HORIZONTAL BAR**
1896  Hermann Weingärtner (GER)
1904  Anton Heida (USA); Edward Henning (USA) (tied)
1924  Leon Stukelj (YUG)
1928  Georges Miez (SUI)
1932  Dallas Bixler (USA)
1936  Aleksanteri Saarvala (FIN)
1948  Josef Stalder (SUI)
1952  Jack Günthard (SUI)
1956  Takashi Ono (JPN)
1960  Takashi Ono (JPN)
1964  Boris Shakhlin (URS)
1968  Mikhail Voronin (URS); Akinori Nakayama
        (JPN) (tied)
1972  Mitsuo Tsukahara (JPN)
1976  Mitsuo Tsukahara (JPN)
1980  Stoyan Delchev (BUL)
1984  Shinji Morisue (JPN)
1988  Vladimir Artyomov (URS); Valery Lyukin (URS)
        (tied)
1992  Trent Dimas (USA)
1996  Andreas Wecker (GER)
2000  Aleksey Nemov (RUS)
2004  Igor Cassina (ITA)
2008  Zou Kai (CHN)
2012  Epke Zonderland (NED)

**PARALLEL BARS**
1896  Alfred Flatow (GER)
1904  George Eyser (USA)
1924  August Güttinger (SUI)
1928  Ladislav Vacha (TCH)
1932  Romeo Neri (ITA)
1936  Konrad Frey (GER)
1948  Michael Reusch (SUI)
1952  Hans Eugster (SUI)
1956  Viktor Chukarin (URS)
1960  Boris Shakhlin (URS)
1964  Yukio Endo (JPN)
1968  Akinori Nakayama (JPN)
1972  Sawao Kato (JPN)
1976  Sawao Kato (JPN)
1980  Aleksandr Tkachyov (URS)
1984  Bart Conner (USA)
1988  Vladimir Artyomov (URS)
1992  Vitaly Shcherbo (UNT)
1996  Rustam Sharipov (UKR)
2000  Li Xiaopeng (CHN)
2004  Valery Goncharov (UKR)
2008  Li Xiaopeng (CHN)
2012  Feng Zhe (CHN)

# Summer Olympic Games (continued)

## Gymnastics (men) (continued)

### SIDE, OR POMMEL, HORSE
1896 Louis Zutter (SUI)
1904 Anton Heida (USA)
1924 Josef Wilhelm (SUI)
1928 Hermann Hänggi (SUI)
1932 Istvan Pelle (HUN)
1936 Konrad Frey (GER)
1948 Paavo Aaltonen (FIN); Veikko Huhtanen (FIN); Heikki Savolainen (FIN) (tied)
1952 Viktor Chukarin (URS)
1956 Boris Shakhlin (URS)
1960 Boris Shakhlin (URS); Eugen Ekman (FIN) (tied)
1964 Miroslav Cerar (YUG)
1968 Miroslav Cerar (YUG)
1972 Viktor Klimenko (URS)
1976 Zoltan Magyar (HUN)
1980 Zoltan Magyar (HUN)
1984 Li Ning (CHN); Peter Vidmar (USA) (tied)
1988 Lyubomir Geraskov (BUL); Zsolt Borkai (HUN); Dmitry Bilozerchev (URS) (tied)
1992 Vitaly Shcherbo (UNT); Pae Gil-su (PRK) (tied)
1996 Li Donghua (SUI)
2000 Marius Urzica (ROM)
2004 Teng Haibin (CHN)
2008 Xiao Qin (CHN)
2012 Krisztian Berki (HUN)

### LONG, OR VAULTING, HORSE
1896 Karl Schuhmann (GER)
1904 Anton Heida (USA); George Eyser (USA) (tied)
1924 Frank Kriz (USA)
1928 Eugen Mack (SUI)
1932 Savino Guglielmetti (ITA)
1936 Karl-Alfred Schnorzmann (GER)
1948 Paavo Johannes Aaltonen (FIN)
1952 Viktor Chukarin (URS)
1956 Valentin Muratov (URS); Helmut Bantz (GER) (tied)
1960 Takashi Ono (JPN); Boris Shakhlin (URS) (tied)
1964 Haruhiro Yamashita (JPN)
1968 Mikhail Voronin (URS)
1972 Klaus Köste (GDR)
1976 Nikolay Andrianov (URS)
1980 Nikolay Andrianov (URS)
1984 Lou Yun (CHN)
1988 Lou Yun (CHN)
1992 Vitaly Shcherbo (UNT)
1996 Aleksey Nemov (RUS)
2000 Gervasio Deferr (ESP)
2004 Gervasio Deferr (ESP)
2008 Leszek Blanik (POL)
2012 Yang Hak-Seon (KOR)

### RINGS
1896 Ioannis Mitropoulos (GRE)
1904 Hermann Glass (USA)
1924 Francesco Martino (ITA)
1928 Leon Stukelj (YUG)
1932 George Gulack (USA)
1936 Alois Hudec (TCH)
1948 Karl Frei (SUI)
1952 Grant Shaginyan (URS)
1956 Albert Azaryan (URS)
1960 Albert Azaryan (URS)
1964 Takuji Hayata (JPN)
1968 Akinori Nakayama (JPN)
1972 Akinori Nakayama (JPN)
1976 Nikolay Andrianov (URS)
1980 Aleksandr Dityatin (URS)

## Gymnastics (men) (continued)

### RINGS (CONTINUED)
1984 Li Ning (CHN); Koji Gushiken (JPN) (tied)
1988 Holger Behrendt (GDR); Dmitry Bilozerchev (URS) (tied)
1992 Vitaly Shcherbo (UNT)
1996 Yury Chechi (ITA)
2000 Szilveszter Csollany (HUN)
2004 Dimosthenis Tampakos (GRE)
2008 Chen Yibing (CHN)
2012 Arthur Nabarrete Zanetti (BRA)

### TRAMPOLINE
2000 Aleksandr Moskalenko (RUS)
2004 Yury Nikitin (UKR)
2008 Lu Chunlong (CHN)
2012 Dong Dong (CHN)

### ROPE CLIMBING
1896 Nicolaos Andriakopoulos (GRE)
1904 George Eyser (USA)
1924 Bedrich Supcik (TCH)
1932 Raymond Bass (USA)

### SWEDISH EXERCISES (TEAM)
1912 Sweden
1920 Sweden

### OPTIONAL EXERCISES (TEAM)
1912 Norway
1920 Denmark
1932 United States

### PARALLEL BARS (TEAM)
1896 Germany

### HORIZONTAL BARS (TEAM)
1896 Germany

### CLUB SWINGING
1904 Edward Hennig (USA)
1932 George Roth (USA)

### TUMBLING
1932 Rowland Wolfe (USA)

### COMBINED COMPETITION (7 APPARATUS)
1904 Anton Heida (USA)

### COMBINED COMPETITION (9 EVENTS)
1904 Adolf Spinnler (SUI)

### PRESCRIBED APPARATUS (TEAM)
1904 United States
1908 Sweden
1912 Italy
1952 Sweden
1956 Hungary

### MASS EXERCISES (TEAM)
1952 Finland

### SIDE HORSE (VAULTS)
1924 Albert Séguin (FRA)

## Gymnastics (women)

### COMBINED, OR ALL-AROUND (INDIVIDUAL)
1952 Mariya Gorokhovskaya (URS)
1956 Larisa Latynina (URS)

# Summer Olympic Games (continued)

## Gymnastics (women) (continued)

### COMBINED, OR ALL-AROUND (INDIVIDUAL) (CONTINUED)

1960    Larisa Latynina (URS)
1964    Vera Caslavska (TCH)
1968    Vera Caslavska (TCH)
1972    Lyudmila Turishcheva (URS)
1976    Nadia Comaneci (ROM)
1980    Yelena Davydova (URS)
1984    Mary Lou Retton (USA)
1988    Yelena Shushunova (URS)
1992    Tatyana Gutsu (UNT)
1996    Liliya Podkopayeva (UKR)
2000    Simona Amanar (ROM)[2]
2004    Carly Patterson (USA)
2008    Nastia Liukin (USA)
2012    Gabrielle Douglas (USA)

### COMBINED, OR ALL-AROUND (TEAM)

1928    The Netherlands
1936    Germany
1948    Czechoslovakia
1952    USSR
1956    USSR
1960    USSR
1964    USSR
1968    USSR
1972    USSR
1976    USSR
1980    USSR
1984    Romania
1988    USSR
1992    Unified Team
1996    United States
2000    Romania
2004    Romania
2008    China
2012    United States

### BALANCE BEAM

1952    Nina Bocharova (URS)
1956    Agnes Keleti (HUN)
1960    Eva Bosakova (TCH)
1964    Vera Caslavska (TCH)
1968    Natalya Kuchinskaya (URS)
1972    Olga Korbut (URS)
1976    Nadia Comaneci (ROM)
1980    Nadia Comaneci (ROM)
1984    Ecaterina Szabo (ROM); Simona Pauca
        (ROM) (tied)
1988    Daniela Silivas (ROM)
1992    Tatyana Lysenko (UNT)
1996    Shannon Miller (USA)
2000    Liu Xuan (CHN)
2004    Catalina Ponor (ROM)
2008    Shawn Johnson (USA)
2012    Deng Linlin (CHN)

### UNEVEN PARALLEL BARS

1952    Margit Korondi (HUN)
1956    Agnes Keleti (HUN)
1960    Polina Astakhova (URS)
1964    Polina Astakhova (URS)
1968    Vera Caslavska (TCH)
1972    Karin Janz (GDR)
1976    Nadia Comaneci (ROM)
1980    Maxi Gnauck (GDR)
1984    Julianne McNamara (USA); Ma Yanhong
        (CHN) (tied)
1988    Daniela Silivas (ROM)

## Gymnastics (women) (continued)

### UNEVEN PARALLEL BARS (CONTINUED)

1992    Li Lu (CHN)
1996    Svetlana Khorkina (RUS)
2000    Svetlana Khorkina (RUS)
2004    Emilie Lepennec (FRA)
2008    He Kexin (CHN)
2012    Aliya Mustafina (RUS)

### VAULT

1952    Yekaterina Kalinchuk (URS)
1956    Larisa Latynina (URS)
1960    Margarita Nikolayeva (URS)
1964    Vera Caslavska (TCH)
1968    Vera Caslavska (TCH)
1972    Karin Janz (GDR)
1976    Nelli Kim (URS)
1980    Natalya Shaposhnikova (URS)
1984    Ecaterina Szabo (ROM)
1988    Svetlana Boginskaya (URS)
1992    Henrietta Onodi (HUN); Lavinia Milosovici
        (ROM) (tied)
1996    Simona Amanar (ROM)
2000    Yelena Zamolodchikova (RUS)
2004    Monica Rosu (ROM)
2008    Hong Un Jong (PRK)
2012    Sandra Izbasa (ROU)

### FLOOR EXERCISE

1952    Agnes Keleti (HUN)
1956    Larisa Latynina (URS); Agnes Keleti (HUN) (tied)
1960    Larisa Latynina (URS)
1964    Larisa Latynina (URS)
1968    Vera Caslavska (TCH); Larissa Petrik (URS) (tied)
1972    Olga Korbut (URS)
1976    Nelli Kim (URS)
1980    Nadia Comaneci (ROM); Nelli Kim (URS) (tied)
1984    Ecaterina Szabo (ROM)
1988    Daniela Silivas (ROM)
1992    Lavinia Milosovici (ROM)
1996    Liliya Podkopayeva (UKR)
2000    Yelena Zamolodchikova (RUS)
2004    Catalina Ponor (ROM)
2008    Sandra Izbasa (ROM)
2012    Alexandra Raisman (USA)

### RHYTHMIC GYMNASTICS (INDIVIDUAL)

1984    Lori Fung (CAN)
1988    Marina Lobatch (URS)
1992    Aleksandra Timoshenko (UNT)
1996    Yekaterina Serebryanskaya (UKR)
2000    Yuliya Barsukova (RUS)
2004    Alina Kabayeva (RUS)
2008    Yevgeniya Kanayeva (RUS)
2012    Yevgeniya Kanayeva (RUS)

### RHYTHMIC GYMNASTICS (TEAM)

1996    Spain
2000    Russia
2004    Russia
2008    Russia
2012    Russia

### TRAMPOLINE

2000    Irina Karavayeva (RUS)
2004    Anna Dogonadze (GER)
2008    He Wenna (CHN)
2012    Rosannagh Maclennan (CAN)

## Summer Olympic Games (continued)

### Gymnastics (women) (continued)

**HAND APPARATUS (TEAM)**
1952 Sweden
1956 Hungary

### Handball (team)

**MEN**
1936[14] Germany
1972 Yugoslavia
1976 USSR
1980 East Germany
1984 Yugoslavia
1988 USSR
1992 Unified Team
1996 Croatia
2000 Russia
2004 Croatia
2008 France
2012 France

**WOMEN**
1976 USSR
1980 USSR
1984 Yugoslavia
1988 Republic of Korea
1992 Republic of Korea
1996 Denmark
2000 Denmark
2004 Denmark
2008 Norway
2012 Norway

**JEU DE PAUME (ROYAL TENNIS)**
1908 Jay Gould (USA)

### Judo (men)[15]

**60 KG (132 LB)**
1964 Takehide Nakatani (JPN)
1972 Takao Kawaguchi (JPN)
1976 Héctor Rodríguez (CUB)
1980 Thierry Rey (FRA)
1984 Shinji Hosokawa (JPN)
1988 Kim Jae-Yup (KOR)
1992 Nazim Guseynov (UNT)
1996 Tadahiro Nomura (JPN)
2000 Tadahiro Nomura (JPN)
2004 Tadahiro Nomura (JPN)
2008 Choi Min Ho (KOR)
2012 Arsen Galstyan (RUS)

**66 KG (145.2 LB)**
1980 Nikolay Solodukhin (URS)
1984 Yoshiyuki Matsuoka (JPN)
1988 Lee Kyung Ken (KOR)
1992 Rogerio Sampaio Cardoso (BRA)
1996 Udo Quellmalz (GER)
2000 Huseyin Ozkan (TUR)
2004 Masato Uchishiba (JPN)
2008 Masato Uchishiba (JPN)
2012 Lasha Shavdatuashvili (GEO)

**73 KG (160.6 LB)**
1972 Takao Kawaguchi (JPN)
1976 Héctor Rodríguez Torres (CUB)
1980 Ezio Gamba (ITA)
1984 Ahn Byeong Keun (KOR)
1988 Marc Alexandre (FRA)
1992 Toshihiko Koga (JPN)
1996 Kenzo Nakamura (JPN)

### Judo (men)[15] (continued)

**73 KG (160.6 LB) (CONTINUED)**
2000 Giuseppe Maddaloni (ITA)
2004 Lee Won Hee (KOR)
2008 Elnur Mammadli (AZE)
2012 Mansur Isayev (RUS)

**81 KG (178.2 LB)**
1972 Toyojazu Nomura (JPN)
1976 Vladimir Nevzorov (URS)
1980 Shota Khabareli (URS)
1984 Frank Wieneke (FRG)
1988 Waldemar Legien (POL)
1992 Hidehiko Yoshida (JPN)
1996 Djamel Bouras (FRA)
2000 Makoto Takimoto (JPN)
2004 Ilias Iliadis (GRE)
2008 Ole Bischof (GER)
2012 Kim Jae-Bum (KOR)

**90 KG (198 LB)**
1964 Isao Okano (JPN)
1972 Shinobu Sekine (JPN)
1976 Isamu Sonoda (JPN)
1980 Jürg Röthlisberger (SUI)
1984 Peter Seisenbacher (AUT)
1988 Peter Seisenbacher (AUT)
1992 Waldemar Legien (POL)
1996 Jeon Ki-Young (KOR)
2000 Mark Huizinga (NED)
2004 Zurab Zviadauri (GEO)
2008 Irakli Tsirekidze (GEO)
2012 Song Dae-Nam (KOR)

**100 KG (220 LB)**
1972 Shota Chochoshvili (URS)
1976 Kazuhiro Ninomiya (JPN)
1980 Robert van de Walle (BEL)
1984 Ha Young Zoo (KOR)
1988 Aurelio Miguel (BRA)
1992 Antal Kovacs (HUN)
1996 Pawel Nastula (POL)
2000 Kosei Inoue (JPN)
2004 Ihar Makarau (BLR)
2008 Tuvshinbayar Naidan (MGL)
2012 Tagir Khaibulayev (RUS)

**OVER 100 KG (220+ LB)**
1964 Isao Inokuma (JPN)
1972 Willem Ruska (NED)
1976 Sergey Novikov (URS)
1980 Angelo Parisi (FRA)
1984 Hitoshi Saito (JPN)
1988 Hitoshi Saito (JPN)
1992 David Khakhaleishvili (UNT)
1996 David Douillet (FRA)
2000 David Douillet (FRA)
2004 Keiji Suzuki (JPN)
2008 Satoshi Ishii (JPN)
2012 Teddy Riner (FRA)

**OPEN (NO WEIGHT LIMIT)**
1964 Antonius Johannes Geesink (NED)
1972 Willem Ruska (NED)
1976 Haruki Uemura (JPN)
1980 Dietmar Lorenz (GDR)
1984 Yasuhiro Yamashita (JPN)

# Summer Olympic Games (continued)

## Judo (women)[16]

**48 KG (105.6 LB)**
1992 Cecile Nowak (FRA)
1996 Kye Sun-Hi (PRK)
2000 Ryoko Tamura (JPN)
2004 Ryoko Tani (JPN)
2008 Alina Alexandra Dumitru (ROM)
2012 Sarah Menezes (BRA)

**52 KG (114.4 LB)**
1992 Almudena Muñoz Martínez (ESP)
1996 Marie-Claire Restoux (FRA)
2000 Legna Verdecia (CUB)
2004 Xian Dongmei (CHN)
2008 Xian Dongmei (CHN)
2012 An Kum-Ae (PRK)

**57 KG (125.4 LB)**
1992 Miriam Blasco Soto (ESP)
1996 Driulis González Morales (CUB)
2000 Isabel Fernández (ESP)
2004 Yvonne Bönisch (GER)
2008 Giulia Quintavalle (ITA)
2012 Kaori Matsumoto (JPN)

**63 KG (138.6 LB)**
1992 Catherine Fleury-Vachon (FRA)
1996 Yuko Emoto (JPN)
2000 Severine Vandenhende (FRA)
2004 Ayumi Tanimoto (JPN)
2008 Ayumi Tanimoto (JPN)
2012 Urska Zolnir (SLO)

**70 KG (154 LB)**
1992 Odalis Reve Jiménez (CUB)
1996 Cho Min-Sun (KOR)
2000 Sibelis Veranes (CUB)
2004 Masae Ueno (JPN)
2008 Masae Ueno (JPN)
2012 Lucie Decosse (FRA)

**78 KG (171.6 LB)**
1992 Kim Mi-Jung (KOR)
1996 Ulla Werbrouck (BEL)
2000 Tang Lin (CHN)
2004 Noriko Anno (JPN)
2008 Yang Xiuli (CHN)
2012 Kayla Harrison (USA)

**OVER 78 KG (171.6+ LB)**
1992 Zhuang Xiaoyan (CHN)
1996 Sun Fuming (CHN)
2000 Yuan Hua (CHN)
2004 Maki Tsukada (JPN)
2008 Tong Wen (CHN)
2012 Idalys Ortiz (CUB)

## Lacrosse
1904 Canada
1908 Canada

## Modern Pentathlon

**INDIVIDUAL (MEN)**
1912 Gösta Lilliehöök (SWE)
1920 Gustaf Dyrssen (SWE)
1924 Bo Lindman (SWE)
1928 Sven Thofelt (SWE)
1932 Johan Oxenstierna (SWE)
1936 Gotthardt Handrick (GER)

## Modern Pentathlon (continued)

**INDIVIDUAL (MEN) (CONTINUED)**
1948 William Grut (SWE)
1952 Lars-Goran Hall (SWE)
1956 Lars-Goran Hall (SWE)
1960 Ferenc Nemeth (HUN)
1964 Ferenc Torok (HUN)
1968 Björn Ferm (SWE)
1972 Andras Balczo (HUN)
1976 Janusz Pyciak-Peciak (POL)
1980 Anatoly Starostin (URS)
1984 Daniele Masala (ITA)
1988 Janos Martinek (HUN)
1992 Arkadiusz Skrzypaszek (POL)
1996 Aleksandr Parygin (KAZ)
2000 Dmitry Svatkovsky (RUS)
2004 Andrey Moiseyev (RUS)
2008 Andrey Moiseyev (RUS)
2012 David Svoboda (CZE)

**INDIVIDUAL (WOMEN)**
2000 Stephanie Cook (GBR)
2004 Zsuzsanna Voros (HUN)
2008 Lena Schöneborn (GER)
2012 Laura Asadauskaite (LTU)

**TEAM (MEN)**
1952 Hungary
1956 USSR
1960 Hungary
1964 USSR
1968 Hungary
1972 USSR
1976 Great Britain
1980 USSR
1984 Italy
1988 Hungary
1992 Poland

## Motorboat Racing

**OPEN CLASS, 40 NAUTICAL MILES**     **BOAT**
1908 Émile Thubron (FRA)     *Camille*

**8-METER CLASS, 40 NAUTICAL MILES**
1908 Thomas Thornycroft, Bernard     *Cyrinus*
     Redwood (GBR)

**UNDER 60-FOOT CLASS, 40 NAUTICAL MILES**
1908 Thomas Thornycroft, Bernard     *Cyrinus*
     Redwood (GBR)

## Polo
1900 Great Britain–United States
1908 Great Britain
1920 Great Britain
1924 Argentina
1936 Argentina

## Rackets

**SINGLES**
1908 Evan Noel (GBR)

**DOUBLES**
1908 Vane Pennell, John Jacob Astor (GBR)

## Roque
1904 Charles Jacobus (USA)

## Summer Olympic Games (continued)

### Rowing (men)[17]

| SINGLE SCULLS | | MIN:SEC |
|---|---|---|
| 1900 | Henri Barrelet (FRA) | 7:35.6 |
| 1904 | Frank Greer (USA) | 10:08.5 |
| 1908 | Harry Blackstaffe (GBR) | 9:26.0 |
| 1912 | William Kinnear (GBR) | 7:47.6 |
| 1920 | John Kelly, Sr. (USA) | 7:35.0 |
| 1924 | Jack Beresford (GBR) | 7:49.2 |
| 1928 | Henry Pearce (AUS) | 7:11.0 |
| 1932 | Henry Pearce (AUS) | 7:44.4 |
| 1936 | Gustav Schäfer (GER) | 8:21.5 |
| 1948 | Mervyn Wood (AUS) | 7:24.4 |
| 1952 | Yury Tyukalov (URS) | 8:12.8 |
| 1956 | Vyacheslav Ivanov (URS) | 8:02.5 |
| 1960 | Vyacheslav Ivanov (URS) | 7:13.96 |
| 1964 | Vyacheslav Ivanov (URS) | 8:22.51 |
| 1968 | Henri-Jan Wienese (NED) | 7:47.80 |
| 1972 | Yury Malyshev (URS) | 7:10.12 |
| 1976 | Pertti Karppinen (FIN) | 7:29.03 |
| 1980 | Pertti Karppinen (FIN) | 7:09.61 |
| 1984 | Pertti Karppinen (FIN) | 7:00.24 |
| 1988 | Thomas Lange (GDR) | 6:49.86 |
| 1992 | Thomas Lange (GER) | 6:51.40 |
| 1996 | Xeno Mueller (SUI) | 6:44.85 |
| 2000 | Robert Waddell (NZL) | 6:48.90 |
| 2004 | Olaf Tufte (NOR) | 6:49.30 |
| 2008 | Olaf Tufte (NOR) | 6:59.83 |
| 2012 | Mahe Drysdale (NZL) | 6:57.82 |

| DOUBLE SCULLS | | MIN:SEC |
|---|---|---|
| 1904 | United States | 10:03.2 |
| 1920 | United States | 7:09.0 |
| 1924 | United States | 6:34.0 |
| 1928 | United States | 6:41.4 |
| 1932 | United States | 7:17.4 |
| 1936 | Great Britain | 7:20.8 |
| 1948 | Great Britain | 6:51.3 |
| 1952 | Argentina | 7:32.2 |
| 1956 | USSR | 7:24.0 |
| 1960 | Czechoslovakia | 6:47.50 |
| 1964 | USSR | 7:10.66 |
| 1968 | USSR | 6:51.82 |
| 1972 | USSR | 7:01.77 |
| 1976 | Norway | 7:13.20 |
| 1980 | East Germany | 6:24.33 |
| 1984 | United States | 6:36.87 |
| 1988 | The Netherlands | 6:21.13 |
| 1992 | Australia | 6:17.32 |
| 1996 | Italy | 6:16.98 |
| 2000 | Slovenia | 6:16.63 |
| 2004 | France | 6:29.00 |
| 2008 | Australia | 6:27.77 |
| 2012 | New Zealand | 6:31.67 |

| FOUR SCULLS | | MIN:SEC |
|---|---|---|
| 1976 | East Germany | 6:18.65 |
| 1980 | East Germany | 5:49.81 |
| 1984 | West Germany | 5:57.55 |
| 1988 | Italy | 5:53.37 |
| 1992 | Germany | 5:45.17 |
| 1996 | Germany | 5:56.93 |
| 2000 | Italy | 5:45.56 |
| 2004 | Russia | 5:56.85 |
| 2008 | Poland | 5:41.33 |
| 2012 | Germany | 5:42.48 |

| LIGHTWEIGHT DOUBLE SCULLS | | MIN:SEC |
|---|---|---|
| 1996 | Switzerland | 6:23.47 |
| 2000 | Poland | 6:21.75 |

### Rowing (men)[17] (continued)

| LIGHTWEIGHT DOUBLE SCULLS (CONTINUED) | | MIN:SEC |
|---|---|---|
| 2004 | Poland | 6:20.93 |
| 2008 | Great Britain | 6:10.99 |
| 2012 | Denmark | 6:37.17 |

| PAIRS (WITHOUT COXSWAIN) | | MIN:SEC |
|---|---|---|
| 1904 | United States | 10:57.0 |
| 1908 | Great Britain | 9:41.0 |
| 1924 | The Netherlands | 8:19.4 |
| 1928 | Germany | 7:06.4 |
| 1932 | Great Britain | 8:00.0 |
| 1936 | Germany | 8:16.1 |
| 1948 | Great Britain | 7:21.1 |
| 1952 | United States | 8:20.7 |
| 1956 | United States | 7:55.4 |
| 1960 | USSR | 7:02.01 |
| 1964 | Canada | 7:32.94 |
| 1968 | East Germany | 7:26.56 |
| 1972 | East Germany | 6:53.16 |
| 1976 | East Germany | 7:23.31 |
| 1980 | East Germany | 6:48.01 |
| 1984 | Romania | 6:45.39 |
| 1988 | Great Britain | 6:36.84 |
| 1992 | Great Britain | 6:27.72 |
| 1996 | Great Britain | 6:20.09 |
| 2000 | France | 6:32.97 |
| 2004 | Australia | 6:30.76 |
| 2008 | Australia | 6:37.44 |
| 2012 | New Zealand | 6:16.65 |

| PAIRS (WITH COXSWAIN) | | MIN:SEC |
|---|---|---|
| 1900 | The Netherlands–France | 7:34.2 |
| 1920 | Italy | 7:56.0 |
| 1924 | Switzerland | 8:39.0 |
| 1928 | Switzerland | 7:42.6 |
| 1932 | United States | 8:25.8 |
| 1936 | Germany | 8:36.9 |
| 1948 | Denmark | 8:00.5 |
| 1952 | France | 8:28.6 |
| 1956 | United States | 8:26.1 |
| 1960 | Germany | 7:29.14 |
| 1964 | United States | 8:21.23 |
| 1968 | Italy | 8:04.81 |
| 1972 | East Germany | 7:17.25 |
| 1976 | East Germany | 7:58.99 |
| 1980 | East Germany | 7:02.54 |
| 1984 | Italy | 7:05.99 |
| 1988 | Italy | 6:58.79 |
| 1992 | Great Britain | 6:49.83 |

| LIGHTWEIGHT FOURS (WITHOUT COXSWAIN) | | MIN:SEC |
|---|---|---|
| 1996 | Denmark | 6:09.58 |
| 2000 | France | 6:01.68 |
| 2004 | Denmark | 6:01.39 |
| 2008 | Denmark | 5:47.76 |
| 2012 | South Africa | 6:02.84 |

| FOURS (WITHOUT COXSWAIN) | | MIN:SEC |
|---|---|---|
| 1900 | France | 7:11.0 |
| 1904 | United States | 9:53.8 |
| 1908 | Great Britain | 8:34.0 |
| 1920 | Great Britain | 7:08.6 |
| 1928 | Great Britain | 6:36.0 |
| 1932 | Great Britain | 6:58.2 |
| 1936 | Germany | 7:01.8 |
| 1948 | Italy | 6:39.0 |
| 1952 | Yugoslavia | 7:16.0 |
| 1956 | Canada | 7:08.8 |

# Summer Olympic Games (continued)

## Rowing (men)[17] (continued)

### FOURS (WITHOUT COXSWAIN) (CONTINUED)

| | | MIN:SEC |
|---|---|---|
| 1960 | United States | 6:26.26 |
| 1964 | Denmark | 6:59.30 |
| 1968 | East Germany | 6:39.18 |
| 1972 | East Germany | 6:24.27 |
| 1976 | East Germany | 6:37.42 |
| 1980 | East Germany | 6:08.17 |
| 1984 | New Zealand | 6:03.48 |
| 1988 | East Germany | 6:03.11 |
| 1992 | Australia | 5:55.04 |
| 1996 | Australia | 6:06.37 |
| 2000 | Great Britain | 5:56.24 |
| 2004 | Great Britain | 6:06.98 |
| 2008 | Great Britain | 6:06.57 |
| 2012 | Great Britain | 6:03.97 |

### FOURS (WITH COXSWAIN)

| | | MIN:SEC |
|---|---|---|
| 1900 | Germany | 5:59.0 |
| 1912 | Germany | 6:59.4 |
| 1920 | Switzerland | 6:54.0 |
| 1924 | Switzerland | 7:18.4 |
| 1928 | Italy | 6:47.8 |
| 1932 | Germany | 7:19.0 |
| 1936 | Germany | 7:16.2 |
| 1948 | United States | 6:50.3 |
| 1952 | Czechoslovakia | 7:33.4 |
| 1956 | Italy | 7:19.4 |
| 1960 | Germany | 6:39.12 |
| 1964 | Germany | 7:00.44 |
| 1968 | New Zealand | 6:45.62 |
| 1972 | West Germany | 6:31.85 |
| 1976 | USSR | 6:40.22 |
| 1980 | East Germany | 6:14.51 |
| 1984 | Great Britain | 6:18.64 |
| 1988 | East Germany | 6:10.74 |
| 1992 | Romania | 5:59.37 |

### FOURS, INRIGGERS (WITH COXSWAIN)

| | | MIN:SEC |
|---|---|---|
| 1912 | Denmark | 7:47.0 |

### EIGHTS (WITH COXSWAIN)

| | | MIN:SEC |
|---|---|---|
| 1900 | United States | 6:09.8 |
| 1904 | United States | 7:50.0 |
| 1908 | Great Britain | 7:52.0 |
| 1912 | Great Britain | 6:15.0 |
| 1920 | United States | 6:02.6 |
| 1924 | United States | 6:33.4 |
| 1928 | United States | 6:03.2 |
| 1932 | United States | 6:37.6 |
| 1936 | United States | 6:25.4 |
| 1948 | United States | 5:56.7 |
| 1952 | United States | 6:25.9 |
| 1956 | United States | 6:35.2 |
| 1960 | Germany | 5:57.18 |
| 1964 | United States | 6:18.23 |
| 1968 | West Germany | 6:07.00 |
| 1972 | New Zealand | 6:08.94 |
| 1976 | East Germany | 5:58.29 |
| 1980 | East Germany | 5:49.05 |
| 1984 | Canada | 5:41.32 |
| 1988 | West Germany | 5:46.05 |
| 1992 | Canada | 5:29.53 |
| 1996 | The Netherlands | 5:42.74 |
| 2000 | Great Britain | 5:33.08 |
| 2004 | United States | 5:42.48 |
| 2008 | Canada | 5:23.89 |
| 2012 | Germany | 5:48.75 |

## Rowing (women)[18]

### SINGLE SCULLS

| | | MIN:SEC |
|---|---|---|
| 1976 | Christine Scheiblich (GDR) | 4:05.56 |
| 1980 | Sanda Toma (ROM) | 3:40.69 |
| 1984 | Valeria Racila (ROM) | 3:40.68 |
| 1988 | Jutta Behrendt (GDR) | 7:47.19 |
| 1992 | Elisabeta Lipa (ROM) | 7:25.54 |
| 1996 | Yekaterina Khodotovich (BLR) | 7:32.21 |
| 2000 | Yekaterina Khodotovich Karsten (BLR) | 7:28.14 |
| 2004 | Katrin Rutschow-Stomporowski (GER) | 7:18.12 |
| 2008 | Rumyana Neykova (BUL) | 7:22.34 |
| 2012 | Miroslava Knapkova (CZE) | 7:54.37 |

### DOUBLE SCULLS

| | | MIN:SEC |
|---|---|---|
| 1976 | Bulgaria | 3:44.36 |
| 1980 | USSR | 3:16.27 |
| 1984 | Romania | 3:26.75 |
| 1988 | East Germany | 7:00.48 |
| 1992 | Germany | 6:49.00 |
| 1996 | Canada | 6:56.84 |
| 2000 | Germany | 6:55.44 |
| 2004 | New Zealand | 7:01.79 |
| 2008 | New Zealand | 7:07.32 |
| 2012 | Great Britain | 6:55.82 |

### LIGHTWEIGHT DOUBLE SCULLS

| | | MIN:SEC |
|---|---|---|
| 1996 | Romania | 7:12.78 |
| 2000 | Romania | 7:02.64 |
| 2004 | Romania | 6:56.05 |
| 2008 | The Netherlands | 6:54.74 |
| 2012 | Great Britain | 7:09.30 |

### FOUR SCULLS

| | | MIN:SEC |
|---|---|---|
| 1976 | East Germany | 3:29.99 |
| 1980 | East Germany | 3:15.32 |
| 1984 | Romania | 3:14.11 |
| 1988 | East Germany | 6:21.06 |
| 1992 | Germany | 6:20.18 |
| 1996 | Germany | 6:27.44 |
| 2000 | Germany | 6:19.58 |
| 2004 | Germany | 6:29.29 |
| 2008 | China | 6:16.06 |
| 2012 | Ukraine | 6:35.93 |

### PAIRS (WITHOUT COXSWAIN)

| | | MIN:SEC |
|---|---|---|
| 1976 | Bulgaria | 4:01.22 |
| 1980 | East Germany | 3:30.49 |
| 1984 | Romania | 3:32.60 |
| 1988 | Romania | 7:28.13 |
| 1992 | Canada | 7:06.22 |
| 1996 | Australia | 7:01.39 |
| 2000 | Romania | 7:11.00 |
| 2004 | Romania | 7:06.55 |
| 2008 | Romania | 7:20.60 |
| 2012 | Great Britain | 7:27.13 |

### FOURS (WITH COXSWAIN)

| | | MIN:SEC |
|---|---|---|
| 1976 | East Germany | 3:45.08 |
| 1980 | East Germany | 3:19.27 |
| 1984 | Romania | 3:19.3 |
| 1988 | East Germany | 6:56.0 |
| 1992[19] | Canada | 6:30.85 |

### EIGHTS (WITH COXSWAIN)

| | | MIN:SEC |
|---|---|---|
| 1976 | East Germany | 3:33.32 |
| 1980 | East Germany | 3:03.32 |
| 1984 | United States | 2:59.80 |
| 1988 | East Germany | 6:15.17 |

# Summer Olympic Games (continued)

## Rowing (women)[18] (continued)

**EIGHTS (WITH COXSWAIN) (CONTINUED)**     MIN:SEC

| | | |
|---|---|---|
| 1992 | Canada | 6:02.62 |
| 1996 | Romania | 6:19.73 |
| 2000 | Romania | 6:06.44 |
| 2004 | Romania | 6:17.70 |
| 2008 | United States | 6:05.34 |
| 2012 | United States | 6:10.59 |

## Rugby Football

| | |
|---|---|
| 1900 | France |
| 1908 | Australia |
| 1920 | United States |
| 1924 | United States |

## Sailing (Yachting)

**BOARDSAILING (WINDGLIDER/DIVISION II) (OPEN)**

| | |
|---|---|
| 1984 | Stephan van den Berg (NED) |
| 1988 | Anthony Bruce Kendall (NZL) |

**BOARDSAILING (RS:X[20]) (MEN)**

| | |
|---|---|
| 1992 | Franck David (FRA) |
| 1996 | Nikolaos Kaklamanakis (GRE) |
| 2000 | Christoph Sieber (AUT) |
| 2004 | Gal Fridman (ISR) |
| 2008 | Tom Ashley (NZL) |
| 2012 | Dorian van Rijsselberge (NED) |

**BOARDSAILING (RS:X[20]) (WOMEN)**

| | |
|---|---|
| 1992 | Barbara Anne Kendall (NZL) |
| 1996 | Lee Lai Shan (HKG) |
| 2000 | Alessandra Sensini (ITA) |
| 2004 | Faustine Merret (FRA) |
| 2008 | Yin Jian (CHN) |
| 2012 | Marina Alabau Neira (ESP) |

**SINGLE-HANDED DINGHY (LASER RADIAL) (WOMEN)**

| | |
|---|---|
| 1992 | Linda Andersen (NOR) |
| 1996 | Kristine Roug (DEN) |
| 2000 | Shirley Anne Robertson (GBR) |
| 2004 | Siren Sundby (NOR) |
| 2008 | Anna Tunnicliffe (USA) |
| 2012 | Xu Lijia (CHN) |

**SINGLE-HANDED DINGHY (LASER) (MEN[21])**

| | |
|---|---|
| 1996 | Robert Scheidt (BRA) |
| 2000 | Ben Ainslie (GBR) |
| 2004 | Robert Scheidt (BRA) |
| 2008 | Paul Goodison (GBR) |
| 2012 | Tom Slingsby (AUS) |

**SINGLE-HANDED DINGHY (FINN[22]) (OPEN[23])**

| | |
|---|---|
| 1924 | Léon Huybrechts (BEL) |
| 1928 | Sven Thorell (SWE) |
| 1932 | Jacques Lebrun (FRA) |
| 1936 | Daniel Kagchelland (NED) |
| 1948 | Paul Elvström (DEN) |
| 1952 | Paul Elvström (DEN) |
| 1956 | Paul Elvström (DEN) |
| 1960 | Paul Elvström (DEN) |
| 1964 | Wilhelm Kuhweide (GER) |
| 1968 | Valentin Mankin (URS) |
| 1972 | Serge Maury (FRA) |
| 1976 | Jochen Schümann (GDR) |
| 1980 | Esko Rechardt (FIN) |
| 1984 | Russell Coutts (NZL) |
| 1988 | José Luis Doreste (ESP) |
| 1992 | José van der Ploeg (ESP) |
| 1996 | Mateusz Kusznierewicz (POL) |

## Sailing (Yachting) (continued)

**SINGLE-HANDED DINGHY (FINN[22]) (OPEN[23]) (CONTINUED)**

| | |
|---|---|
| 2000 | Iain Percy (GBR) |
| 2004 | Ben Ainslie (GBR) |
| 2008 | Ben Ainslie (GBR) |
| 2012 | Ben Ainslie (GBR) |

**DOUBLE-HANDED DINGHY (470) (MEN)**

| | |
|---|---|
| 1976 | West Germany |
| 1980 | Brazil |
| 1984 | Spain |
| 1988 | France |
| 1992 | Spain |
| 1996 | Ukraine |
| 2000 | Australia |
| 2004 | United States |
| 2008 | Australia |
| 2012 | Australia |

**DOUBLE-HANDED DINGHY (470) (WOMEN)**

| | |
|---|---|
| 1988 | United States |
| 1992 | Spain |
| 1996 | Spain |
| 2000 | Australia |
| 2004 | Greece |
| 2008 | Australia |
| 2012 | New Zealand |

**ELLIOTT 6M (WOMEN)**

| | |
|---|---|
| 2012 | Spain |

**YNGLING (WOMEN)**

| | |
|---|---|
| 2004 | Great Britain |
| 2008 | Great Britain |

**HIGH-PERFORMANCE DINGHY (49ER) (OPEN)**

| | |
|---|---|
| 2000 | Finland |
| 2004 | Spain |
| 2008 | Denmark |
| 2012 | Australia |

**MULTIHULL (TORNADO) (OPEN)**

| | |
|---|---|
| 1976 | Great Britain |
| 1980 | Brazil |
| 1984 | New Zealand |
| 1988 | France |
| 1992 | France |
| 1996 | Spain |
| 2000 | Austria |
| 2004 | Austria |
| 2008 | Spain |

**FLEET/MATCH RACE KEELBOAT (SOLING) (OPEN)**

| | |
|---|---|
| 1972 | United States |
| 1976 | Denmark |
| 1980 | Denmark |
| 1984 | United States |
| 1988 | East Germany |
| 1992 | Denmark |
| 1996 | Germany |
| 2000 | Denmark |

**TWO-PERSON KEELBOAT (STAR) (MEN[24])**

| | |
|---|---|
| 1932 | United States |
| 1936 | Germany |
| 1948 | United States |
| 1952 | Italy |
| 1956 | United States |
| 1960 | USSR |

## Summer Olympic Games (continued)

### Sailing (Yachting) (continued)

**TWO-PERSON KEELBOAT (STAR) (MEN[24]) (CONTINUED)**

| | |
|---|---|
| 1964 | The Bahamas |
| 1968 | United States |
| 1972 | Australia |
| 1980 | USSR |
| 1984 | United States |
| 1988 | Great Britain |
| 1992 | United States |
| 1996 | Brazil |
| 2000 | United States |
| 2004 | Brazil |
| 2008 | Great Britain |
| 2012 | Sweden |

**40-METER CLASS**

| | |
|---|---|
| 1920 | Sweden |

**30-METER CLASS**

| | |
|---|---|
| 1920 | Sweden |

**12-METER CLASS**

| | |
|---|---|
| 1920 (old) | Norway |
| 1920 (new) | Norway |

**OVER-10-METER CLASS**

| | |
|---|---|
| 1900 | France |
| 1908 | Great Britain |
| 1912 | Norway |

**10-METER CLASS**

| | |
|---|---|
| 1900 | Germany |
| 1912 | Sweden |
| 1920 (old) | Norway |
| 1920 (new) | Norway |

**8-METER CLASS**

| | |
|---|---|
| 1900 | Great Britain |
| 1908 | Great Britain |
| 1912 | Norway |
| 1920 (old) | Norway |
| 1920 (new) | Norway |
| 1924 | Norway |
| 1928 | France |
| 1932 | United States |
| 1936 | Italy |

**7-METER CLASS**

| | |
|---|---|
| 1908 | Great Britain |
| 1920 (old) | Great Britain |

**6.5-METER CLASS**

| | |
|---|---|
| 1920 (new) | The Netherlands |

**6-METER CLASS**

| | |
|---|---|
| 1900 | Switzerland |
| 1908 | Great Britain |
| 1912 | France |
| 1920 (old) | Belgium |
| 1920 (new) | Norway |
| 1924 | Norway |
| 1928 | Norway |
| 1932 | Sweden |
| 1936 | Great Britain |
| 1948 | United States |
| 1952 | United States |

### Sailing (Yachting) (continued)

**5.5-METER CLASS**

| | |
|---|---|
| 1952 | United States |
| 1956 | Sweden |
| 1960 | United States |
| 1964 | Australia |
| 1968 | Sweden |

**18-FOOT CENTERBOARD BOAT**

| | |
|---|---|
| 1920 | Great Britain |

**12-FOOT CENTERBOARD BOAT**

| | |
|---|---|
| 1920 | The Netherlands |
| 1924 | Belgium |

**12-FOOT DINGHY**

| | |
|---|---|
| 1928 | Sweden |

**MONOTYPE CLASS**

| | |
|---|---|
| 1932 | France |

**MONOTYPE CLASS "NÜRNBERG"**

| | |
|---|---|
| 1936 | The Netherlands |

**SWALLOW**

| | |
|---|---|
| 1948 | Great Britain |

**FIREFLY**

| | |
|---|---|
| 1948 | Denmark |

**SHARPIE**

| | |
|---|---|
| 1956 | New Zealand |

**DRAGON**

| | |
|---|---|
| 1948 | Norway |
| 1952 | Norway |
| 1956 | Sweden |
| 1960 | Greece |
| 1964 | Denmark |
| 1968 | United States |
| 1972 | Australia |

**TEMPEST**

| | |
|---|---|
| 1972 | USSR |
| 1976 | Sweden |

**FLYING DUTCHMAN**

| | |
|---|---|
| 1960 | Norway |
| 1964 | New Zealand |
| 1968 | Great Britain |
| 1972 | Great Britain |
| 1976 | West Germany |
| 1980 | Spain |
| 1984 | United States |
| 1988 | Denmark |
| 1992 | Spain |

### Shooting (men)

**individual**

**TRAP (CLAY PIGEON)[25]**

| | |
|---|---|
| 1900 | Roger de Barbarin (FRA) |
| 1908 | Walter Ewing (CAN) |
| 1912 | James Graham (USA) |
| 1920 | Mark Arie (USA) |
| 1924 | Gyula Halasy (HUN) |
| 1952 | George Généreux (CAN) |
| 1956 | Galliano Rossini (ITA) |
| 1960 | Ion Dumitrescu (ROM) |
| 1964 | Ennio Mattarelli (ITA) |

# Summer Olympic Games (continued)

## Shooting (men) (continued)

### individual (continued)

**TRAP (CLAY PIGEON)[25] (CONTINUED)**

| | |
|---|---|
| 1968 | John Braithwaite (GBR) |
| 1972 | Angelo Scalzone (ITA) |
| 1976 | Donald Haldeman (USA) |
| 1980 | Luciano Giovannetti (ITA) |
| 1984 | Luciano Giovannetti (ITA) |
| 1988 | Donald Monakov (URS) |
| 1992 | Petr Hrdlicka (TCH) |
| 1996 | Michael Constantine Diamond (AUS) |
| 2000 | Michael Constantine Diamond (AUS) |
| 2004 | Aleksey Alipov (RUS) |
| 2008 | David Kostelecky (CZE) |
| 2012 | Giovanni Cernogoraz (CRO) |

**DOUBLE TRAP**

| | |
|---|---|
| 1996 | Russell Andrew Mark (AUS) |
| 2000 | Richard Faulds (GBR) |
| 2004 | Ahmed Almaktoum (UAE) |
| 2008 | Walton Eller (USA) |
| 2012 | Peter Wilson (GBR) |

**SKEET[26]**

| | |
|---|---|
| 1968 | Yevgeny Petrov (URS) |
| 1972 | Konrad Wirnhier (FRG) |
| 1976 | Josef Panacek (TCH) |
| 1980 | Hans Kjeld Rasmussen (DEN) |
| 1984 | Matthew Dryke (USA) |
| 1988 | Axel Wegner (GDR) |
| 1992 | Zhang Shan (CHN) |
| 1996 | Ennio Falco (ITA) |
| 2000 | Mykola Milchev (UKR) |
| 2004 | Andrea Benelli (ITA) |
| 2008 | Vincent Hancock (USA) |
| 2012 | Vincent Hancock (USA) |

**FREE PISTOL**

| | |
|---|---|
| 1896 | Sumner Paine (USA) |
| 1900 | Karl Konrad Röderer (SUI) |
| 1912 | Alfred Lane (USA) |
| 1920 | Carl Frederick (USA) |
| 1936 | Torsten Ullmann (SWE) |
| 1948 | Edwin Vásquez Cam (PER) |
| 1952 | Huelet Benner (USA) |
| 1956 | Pentti Tapio Linnosvuo (FIN) |
| 1960 | Aleksey Gushchin (URS) |
| 1964 | Väinö Johannes Markkanen (FIN) |
| 1968 | Grigory Kosykh (URS) |
| 1976 | Uwe Potteck (GDR) |
| 1980 | Aleksandr Melentev (URS) |
| 1984 | Xu Haifeng (CHN) |
| 1988 | Sorin Babii (ROM) |
| 1992 | Konstantin Lukachik (UNT) |
| 1996 | Boris Kokorev (RUS) |
| 2000 | Tanyu Kiryakov (BUL) |
| 2004 | Mikhail Nestruyev (RUS) |
| 2008 | Jin Jong-Oh (KOR) |
| 2012 | Jin Jong-Oh (KOR) |

**RAPID-FIRE PISTOL**

| | |
|---|---|
| 1896 | Joannis Phrangudis (GRE) |
| 1900 | Maurice Larrouy (FRA) |
| 1908 | Paul van Asbrock (BEL) |
| 1912 | Alfred Lane (USA) |
| 1920 | Guilherme Paraense (BRA) |
| 1924 | Henry Bailey (USA) |
| 1932 | Renzo Morigi (ITA) |
| 1936 | Cornelius van Oyen (GER) |

## Shooting (men) (continued)

### individual (continued)

**RAPID-FIRE PISTOL (CONTINUED)**

| | |
|---|---|
| 1948 | Karoly Takacs (HUN) |
| 1952 | Karoly Takacs (HUN) |
| 1956 | Stefan Petrescu (ROM) |
| 1960 | William McMillan (USA) |
| 1964 | Pentti Tapio Linnosvuo (FIN) |
| 1968 | Jozef Zapedzki (POL) |
| 1972 | Jozef Zapedzki (POL) |
| 1976 | Norbert Klaar (GDR) |
| 1980 | Corneliu Ion (ROM) |
| 1984 | Takeo Kamachi (JPN) |
| 1988 | Afanasy Kuzmin (URS) |
| 1992 | Ralf Schumann (GER) |
| 1996 | Ralf Schumann (GER) |
| 2000 | Sergey Alifirenko (RUS) |
| 2004 | Ralf Schumann (GER) |
| 2008 | Oleksandr Petriv (UKR) |
| 2012 | Leuris Pupo (CUB) |

**SMALL-BORE RIFLE (PRONE)**

| | |
|---|---|
| 1908 | Arthur Ashton Carnell (GBR) |
| 1912 | Frederick Hird (USA) |
| 1920 | Lawrence Nuesslein (USA) |
| 1924 | Pierre Coquelin de Lisle (FRA) |
| 1932 | Bertil Rönnmark (SWE) |
| 1936 | Willy Røgeberg (NOR) |
| 1948 | Arthur Cook (USA) |
| 1952 | Iosif Sarbu (ROM) |
| 1956 | Gerald Ouellette (CAN) |
| 1960 | Peter Kohnke (GER) |
| 1964 | Laszlo Hammerl (HUN) |
| 1968 | Jan Kurka (TCH) |
| 1972 | Ho Jun Li (PRK) |
| 1976 | Karlheinz Smieszek (FRG) |
| 1980 | Karoly Varga (HUN) |
| 1984 | Edward Etzel (USA) |
| 1988 | Miroslav Varga (TCH) |
| 1992 | Lee Eun Chul (KOR) |
| 1996 | Christian Klees (GER) |
| 2000 | Jonas Edman (SWE) |
| 2004 | Matthew Emmons (USA) |
| 2008 | Artur Ayvazian (UKR) |
| 2012 | Sergey Martynov (BLR) |

**SMALL-BORE RIFLE (3 POSITIONS)**

| | |
|---|---|
| 1952 | Erling Kongshaug (NOR) |
| 1956 | Anatoly Bogdanov (URS) |
| 1960 | Viktor Shamburkin (URS) |
| 1964 | Lones Wesley Wigger (USA) |
| 1968 | Bernd Klingner (FRG) |
| 1972 | John Writer (USA) |
| 1976 | Lanny Bassham (USA) |
| 1980 | Viktor Vlasov (URS) |
| 1984 | Malcolm Cooper (GBR) |
| 1988 | Malcolm Cooper (GBR) |
| 1992 | Gratchia Petikian (UNT) |
| 1996 | Jean-Pierre Amat (FRA) |
| 2000 | Rajmond Debevec (SLO) |
| 2004 | Jia Zhanbo (CHN) |
| 2008 | Qiu Jian (CHN) |
| 2012 | Niccolo Campriani (ITA) |

**10-METER RUNNING (GAME) TARGET**

| | |
|---|---|
| 1900 | Louis Debray (FRA) |
| 1972 | Yakov Zheleznyak (URS) |
| 1976 | Aleksandr Gazov (URS) |
| 1980 | Igor Sokolov (URS) |

# Summer Olympic Games (continued)

## Shooting (men) (continued)
### individual (continued)

**10-METER RUNNING (GAME) TARGET (CONTINUED)**
1984  Li Yuwei (CHN)
1988  Tor Heiestad (NOR)
1992  Michael Jakosits (GER)
1996  Yang Ling (CHN)
2000  Yang Ling (CHN)
2004  Manfred Kurzer (GER)

**AIR RIFLE**
1984  Philippe Heberle (FRA)
1988  Goran Maksimovic (YUG)
1992  Yury Fedkin (UNT)
1996  Artyom Khadzhibekov (RUS)
2000  Cai Yalin (CHN)
2004  Zhu Quinan (CHN)
2008  Abhinav Bindra (IND)
2012  Alin George Moldoveanu (ROU)

**AIR PISTOL**
1988  Tanyu Kiryakov (BUL)
1992  Wang Yifu (CHN)
1996  Roberto di Donna (ITA)
2000  Franck Dumoulin (FRA)
2004  Wang Yifu (CHN)
2008  Pang Wei (CHN)
2012  Jin Jong-Oh (KOR)

**FREE RIFLE (300 METERS, 3 POSITIONS)**
1908  Albert Helgerud (NOR)
1912  Paul René Colas (FRA)
1920  Morris Fisher (USA)
1924  Morris Fisher (USA)
1948  Emil Grünig (SUI)
1952  Anatoly Bogdanov (URS)
1956  Vasily Borisov (URS)
1960  Hubert Hammerer (AUT)
1964  Gary Lee Anderson (USA)
1968  Gary Lee Anderson (USA)
1972  Lones Wesley Wigger (USA)

**ARMY RIFLE (300 METERS, 3 POSITIONS)**
1896  Georgios Orphanidis (GRE)
1900  Emil Kellenberger (SUI)
1912  Sandor Prokop (HUN)

**ARMY RIFLE (200 METERS)**
1896  Pantelis Karasevdas (GRE)

**FREE RIFLE (1,000 YARDS PRONE)**
1908  Joshua Millner (GBR)

**FULL-BORE RIFLE (300 METERS STANDING)**
1900  Lars Madsen (DEN)

**FULL-BORE RIFLE (300 METERS KNEELING)**
1900  Konrad Staeheli (SUI)

**FULL-BORE RIFLE (300 METERS PRONE)**
1900  Achille Paroche (FRA)

**FULL-BORE RIFLE (300 METERS)**
1900  Emil Kellenberger (SUI)

**RIFLE (300 METERS, 2 POSITIONS)**
1920  Morris Fisher (USA)

## Shooting (men) (continued)
### individual (continued)

**RIFLE (300 METERS STANDING)**
1920  Carl Osburn (USA)

**RIFLE (300 METERS PRONE)**
1920  Otto Olsen (NOR)

**RIFLE (600 METERS PRONE)**
1920  Hugo Johansson (SWE)

**6-MILLIMETER SMALL GUN (OPEN REAR SIGHT)**
1900  C. Grosett (FRA)

**SMALL-BORE RIFLE (VANISHING TARGET)**
1908  William Styles (GBR)
1912  Wilhelm Carlberg (SWE)

**SMALL-BORE RIFLE (MOVING TARGET)**
1908  John Francis Fleming (GBR)

**RUNNING DEER (100 METERS SINGLE SHOT)**
1908  Oscar Swahn (SWE)
1912  Alfred Swahn (SWE)
1920  Otto Olsen (NOR)
1924  John Boles (USA)

**RUNNING DEER (100 METERS DOUBLE SHOT)**
1908  Walter Winans (USA)
1912  Ake Lundeberg (SWE)
1920  Ole Andreas Lilloe-Olsen (NOR)
1924  Ole Andreas Lilloe-Olsen (NOR)

**RUNNING DEER (100 METERS SINGLE AND DOUBLE SHOT)**
1952  John Larsen (NOR)
1956  Vitaly Romanenko (URS)

**LIVE PIGEON**
1900  Léon de Lunden (BEL)

**GAME SHOOTING**
1900  Donald Mackintosh (AUS)

**MILITARY REVOLVER (25 METERS)**
1896  John Paine (USA)

**REVOLVER AND PISTOL**
1900  Paul van Asbrock (BEL)
1908  Paul van Asbrock (BEL)
1912  Alfred Lane (USA)

**DUELING PISTOL**
1912  Alfred Lane (USA)

### team
**FREE RIFLE (300 METERS)**
1908  Norway
1912  Sweden

**ARMY RIFLE (300 METERS)**
1900  Norway

**ARMY RIFLE (ALL-AROUND)**
1900  United States
1908  United States
1912  United States

**FULL-BORE RIFLE (300 METERS)**
1900  Switzerland

## Summer Olympic Games (continued)

### Shooting (men) (continued)

**team (continued)**

**SMALL-BORE RIFLE**
| 1900 | Great Britain |
| 1908 | Great Britain |
| 1920 | United States |
| 1924 | France |

**SMALL-BORE RIFLE (VANISHING TARGET)**
| 1912 | Sweden |

**RIFLE (600 METERS PRONE)**
| 1920 | United States |

**RIFLE (300 METERS, 2 POSITIONS)**
| 1920 | United States |

**RIFLE (300 METERS STANDING)**
| 1920 | Denmark |

**RIFLE (300 METERS PRONE)**
| 1920 | United States |

**RIFLE (ALL-AROUND)**
| 1920 | United States |
| 1924 | United States |

**RUNNING DEER (SINGLE SHOT)**
| 1908 | Sweden |
| 1912 | Sweden |
| 1920 | Norway |
| 1924 | Norway |

**RUNNING DEER (DOUBLE SHOT)**
| 1920 | Norway |
| 1924 | Great Britain |

**CLAY PIGEON**
| 1900 | Great Britain |
| 1908 | Great Britain |
| 1912 | United States |
| 1920 | United States |
| 1924 | United States |

**REVOLVER**
| 1900 | Switzerland |

**PISTOL**
| 1920 | United States |
| 1924 | United States |

**REVOLVER AND PISTOL**
| 1900 | United States |
| 1908 | United States |
| 1912 | United States |
| 1920 | United States |

**DUELING PISTOL**
| 1912 | Sweden |

### Shooting (women)

**TRAP (CLAY PIGEON)**
| 2000 | Daina Gudzineviciute (LTU) |
| 2004 | Suzanne Balogh (AUS) |
| 2008 | Satu Mäkelä-Nummela (FIN) |
| 2012 | Jessica Rossi (ITA) |

### Shooting (women) (continued)

**DOUBLE TRAP**
| 1996 | Kimberly Rhode (USA) |
| 2000 | Pia Hansen (SWE) |
| 2004 | Kimberly Rhode (USA) |

**SKEET**
| 2000 | Zemfira Meftakhetdinova (AZE) |
| 2004 | Diana Igaly (HUN) |
| 2008 | Chiara Cainero (ITA) |
| 2012 | Kimberly Rhode (USA) |

**PISTOL**
| 1984 | Linda Thom (CAN) |
| 1988 | Nino Salukvadze (URS) |
| 1992 | Marina Logvinenko (UNT) |
| 1996 | Li Duihong (CHN) |
| 2000 | Mariya Zdravkova Grozdeva (BUL) |
| 2004 | Mariya Zdravkova Grozdeva (BUL) |
| 2008 | Chen Ying (CHN) |
| 2012 | Kim Jang-Mi (KOR) |

**SMALL-BORE RIFLE (3 POSITIONS)**
| 1984 | Wu Xiao-Xuan (CHN) |
| 1988 | Silvia Sperber (FRG) |
| 1992 | Launi Meili (USA) |
| 1996 | Aleksandra Ivosev (YUG) |
| 2000 | Renata Mauer (POL) |
| 2004 | Lyubov Galkina (RUS) |
| 2008 | Du Li (CHN) |
| 2012 | Jamie Lynn Gray (USA) |

**AIR RIFLE**
| 1984 | Pat Spurgin (USA) |
| 1988 | Irina Chilova (URS) |
| 1992 | Yeo Kab Soon (KOR) |
| 1996 | Renata Mauer (POL) |
| 2000 | Nancy Johnson (USA) |
| 2004 | Du Li (CHN) |
| 2008 | Katerina Emmons (CZE) |
| 2012 | Yi·Siling (CHN) |

**AIR PISTOL**
| 1988 | Jasna Sekaric (YUG) |
| 1992 | Marina Logvinenko (UNT) |
| 1996 | Olga Klochneva (RUS) |
| 2000 | Tao Luna (CHN) |
| 2004 | Olena Kostevych (UKR) |
| 2008 | Guo Wenjun (CHN) |
| 2012 | Guo Wenjun (CHN) |

### Softball
| 1996 | United States |
| 2000 | United States |
| 2004 | United States |
| 2008 | Japan |

### Swimming (men)

| 50-METER FREESTYLE | | SEC |
|---|---|---|
| 1988 | Matt Biondi (USA) | 22.14 |
| 1992 | Aleksandr Popov (UNT) | 21.91 |
| 1996 | Aleksandr Popov (RUS) | 22.13 |
| 2000 | Anthony Ervin (USA); Gary Hall, Jr. (USA) (tied) | 21.98 |
| 2004 | Gary Hall, Jr. (USA) | 21.93 |
| 2008 | César Cielo Filho (BRA) | 21.30 |
| 2012 | Florent Manaudou (FRA) | 21.34 |

## Summer Olympic Games (continued)

### Swimming (men) (continued)

| 100-METER FREESTYLE | MIN:SEC |
|---|---|
| 1896 Alfred Hajos (HUN) | 1:22.2 |
| 1904[27] Zoltan Halmay (HUN) | 1:02.8 |
| 1908 Charles Daniels (USA) | 1:05.6 |
| 1912 Duke Paoa Kahanamoku (USA) | 1:03.4 |
| 1920 Duke Paoa Kahanamoku (USA) | 1:00.4 |
| 1924 Johnny Weissmuller (USA) | 59.0 |
| 1928 Johnny Weissmuller (USA) | 58.6 |
| 1932 Yasuji Miyazaki (JPN) | 58.2 |
| 1936 Ferenc Csik (HUN) | 57.6 |
| 1948 Walter Ris (USA) | 57.3 |
| 1952 Clark Scholes (USA) | 57.4 |
| 1956 Jon Henricks (AUS) | 55.4 |
| 1960 John Devitt (AUS) | 55.2 |
| 1964 Donald Schollander (USA) | 53.4 |
| 1968 Michael Wenden (AUS) | 52.2 |
| 1972 Mark Spitz (USA) | 51.22 |
| 1976 Jim Montgomery (USA) | 49.99 |
| 1980 Jörg Woithe (GDR) | 50.40 |
| 1984 Ambrose Gaines (USA) | 49.80 |
| 1988 Matt Biondi (USA) | 48.63 |
| 1992 Aleksandr Popov (UNT) | 49.02 |
| 1996 Aleksandr Popov (RUS) | 48.74 |
| 2000 Pieter van den Hoogenband (NED) | 48.30 |
| 2004 Pieter van den Hoogenband (NED) | 48.17 |
| 2008 Alain Bernard (FRA) | 47.21 |
| 2012 Nathan Adrian (USA) | 47.52 |

| 100 METER FREESTYLE FOR SAILORS | MIN:SEC |
|---|---|
| 1896 Ioannis Malokinis (GRE) | 2:20.4 |

| 200-METER FREESTYLE | MIN:SEC |
|---|---|
| 1900 Fred Lane (AUS) | 2:25.2 |
| 1904[28] Charles Daniels (USA) | 2:44.2 |
| 1968 Michael Wenden (AUS) | 1:55.2 |
| 1972 Mark Spitz (USA) | 1:52.78 |
| 1976 Bruce Furniss (USA) | 1:50.29 |
| 1980 Sergey Koplyakov (URS) | 1:49.81 |
| 1984 Michael Gross (FRG) | 1:47.44 |
| 1988 Duncan Armstrong (AUS) | 1:47.25 |
| 1992 Yevgeny Sadovy (UNT) | 1:46.70 |
| 1996 Danyon Loader (NZL) | 1:47.63 |
| 2000 Pieter van den Hoogenband (NED) | 1:45.35 |
| 2004 Ian Thorpe (AUS) | 1:44.71 |
| 2008 Michael Phelps (USA) | 1:42.96 |
| 2012 Yannick Agnel (FRA) | 1:43.14 |

| 400-METER FREESTYLE | MIN:SEC |
|---|---|
| 1896[29] Paul Neumann (AUT) | 8:12.6 |
| 1904[30] Charles Daniels (USA) | 6:16.2 |
| 1908 Henry Taylor (GBR) | 5:36.8 |
| 1912 George Hodgson (CAN) | 5:24.4 |
| 1920 Norman Ross (USA) | 5:26.8 |
| 1924 Johnny Weissmuller (USA) | 5:04.2 |
| 1928 Victoriano Zorilla (ARG) | 5:01.6 |
| 1932 Clarence Crabbe (USA) | 4:48.4 |
| 1936 Jack Medica (USA) | 4:44.5 |
| 1948 William Smith (USA) | 4:41.0 |
| 1952 Jean Boiteux (FRA) | 4:30.7 |
| 1956 Murray Rose (AUS) | 4:27.3 |
| 1960 Murray Rose (AUS) | 4:18.3 |
| 1964 Donald Schollander (USA) | 4:12.2 |
| 1968 Michael Burton (USA) | 4:09.0 |
| 1972 Bradford Cooper (AUS)[2] | 4:00.27 |
| 1976 Brian Goodell (USA) | 3:51.93 |
| 1980 Vladimir Salnikov (URS) | 3:51.31 |
| 1984 George DiCarlo (USA) | 3:51.23 |
| 1988 Uwe Dassler (GDR) | 3:46.95 |

| 400-METER FREESTYLE (CONTINUED) | MIN:SEC |
|---|---|
| 1992 Yevgeny Sadovy (UNT) | 3:45.00 |
| 1996 Danyon Loader (NZL) | 3:47.97 |
| 2000 Ian Thorpe (AUS) | 3:40.59 |
| 2004 Ian Thorpe (AUS) | 3:43.10 |
| 2008 Park Tae Hwan (KOR) | 3:41.86 |
| 2012 Sun Yang (CHN) | 3:40.14 |

| 1,500-METER FREESTYLE | MIN:SEC |
|---|---|
| 1896[31] Alfred Hajos (HUN) | 18:22.2 |
| 1900[32] Johnny Arthur Jarvis (GBR) | 13:40.2 |
| 1904[33] Emil Rausch (GER) | 27:18.2 |
| 1908 Henry Taylor (GBR) | 22:48.4 |
| 1912 George Hodgson (CAN) | 22:00.0 |
| 1920 Norman Ross (USA) | 22:23.2 |
| 1924 Andrew Charlton (AUS) | 20:06.6 |
| 1928 Arne Borg (SWE) | 19:51.8 |
| 1932 Kusuo Kitamura (JPN) | 19:12.4 |
| 1936 Noburu Terada (JPN) | 19:13.7 |
| 1948 James McLane (USA) | 19:18.5 |
| 1952 Ford Konno (USA) | 18:30.0 |
| 1956 Murray Rose (AUS) | 17:58.9 |
| 1960 John Konrads (AUS) | 17:19.6 |
| 1964 Robert Windle (AUS) | 17:01.7 |
| 1968 Michael Burton (USA) | 16:38.9 |
| 1972 Michael Burton (USA) | 15:52.58 |
| 1976 Brian Goodell (USA) | 15:02.40 |
| 1980 Vladimir Salnikov (URS) | 14:58.27 |
| 1984 Michael O'Brien (USA) | 15:05.20 |
| 1988 Vladimir Salnikov (URS) | 15:00.40 |
| 1992 Kieren Perkins (AUS) | 14:43.48 |
| 1996 Kieren Perkins (AUS) | 14:56.40 |
| 2000 Grant Hackett (AUS) | 14:48.33 |
| 2004 Grant Hackett (AUS) | 14:43.40 |
| 2008 Oussama Mellouli (TUN) | 14:40.84 |
| 2012 Sun Yang (CHN) | 14:31.02 |

| 4,000-METER FREESTYLE | MIN:SEC |
|---|---|
| 1900 Johnny Arthur Jarvis (GBR) | 58:24 |

| 880-YARD FREESTYLE | MIN:SEC |
|---|---|
| 1904 Emil Rausch (GER) | 13:11.4 |

| 1-MILE FREESTYLE | MIN:SEC |
|---|---|
| 1904 Emil Rausch (GER) | 27:18.2 |

| 100-METER BUTTERFLY | SEC |
|---|---|
| 1968 Douglas Russell (USA) | 55.9 |
| 1972 Mark Spitz (USA) | 54.27 |
| 1976 Matt Vogel (USA) | 54.35 |
| 1980 Pär Arvidsson (SWE) | 54.92 |
| 1984 Michael Gross (FRG) | 53.08 |
| 1988 Anthony Nesty (SUR) | 53.00 |
| 1992 Pablo Morales (USA) | 53.32 |
| 1996 Denis Pankratov (RUS) | 52.27 |
| 2000 Lars Frölander (SWE) | 52.00 |
| 2004 Michael Phelps (USA) | 51.25 |
| 2008 Michael Phelps (USA) | 50.58 |
| 2012 Michael Phelps (USA) | 51.21 |

| 200-METER BUTTERFLY | MIN:SEC |
|---|---|
| 1956 William Yorzyk (USA) | 2:19.3 |
| 1960 Michael Troy (USA) | 2:12.8 |
| 1964 Kevin Berry (AUS) | 2:06.6 |
| 1968 Carl Robie (USA) | 2:08.7 |
| 1972 Mark Spitz (USA) | 2:00.70 |
| 1976 Mike Bruner (USA) | 1:59.23 |
| 1980 Sergey Fesenko (URS) | 1:59.76 |

## Summer Olympic Games (continued)

### Swimming (men) (continued)

**200-METER BUTTERFLY (CONTINUED)**

| | | MIN:SEC |
|---|---|---|
| 1984 | Jonathan Sieben (AUS) | 1:57.04 |
| 1988 | Michael Gross (FRG) | 1:56.94 |
| 1992 | Mel Stewart (USA) | 1:56.26 |
| 1996 | Denis Pankratov (RUS) | 1:56.51 |
| 2000 | Tom Malchow (USA) | 1:55.35 |
| 2004 | Michael Phelps (USA) | 1:54.04 |
| 2008 | Michael Phelps (USA) | 1:52.03 |
| 2012 | Chad le Clos (RSA) | 1:52.96 |

**100-METER BACKSTROKE**

| | | MIN:SEC |
|---|---|---|
| 1904³⁴ | Walter Brack (GER) | 1:16.8 |
| 1908 | Arno Bieberstein (GER) | 1:24.6 |
| 1912 | Harry Hebner (USA) | 1:21.2 |
| 1920 | Warren Paoa Kealoha (USA) | 1:15.2 |
| 1924 | Warren Paoa Kealoha (USA) | 1:13.2 |
| 1928 | George Kojac (USA) | 1:08.2 |
| 1932 | Masaji Kiyokawa (JPN) | 1:08.6 |
| 1936 | Adolph Kiefer (USA) | 1:05.9 |
| 1948 | Allen Stack (USA) | 1:06.4 |
| 1952 | Yoshinobu Oyakawa (JPN) | 1:05.4 |
| 1956 | David Theile (AUS) | 1:02.2 |
| 1960 | David Theile (AUS) | 1:01.9 |
| 1968 | Roland Matthes (GDR) | 58.7 |
| 1972 | Roland Matthes (GDR) | 56.58 |
| 1976 | John Naber (USA) | 55.49 |
| 1980 | Bengt Baron (SWE) | 56.53 |
| 1984 | Richard Carey (USA) | 55.79 |
| 1988 | Daichi Suzuki (JPN) | 55.05 |
| 1992 | Mark Tewksbury (CAN) | 53.98 |
| 1996 | Jeff Rouse (USA) | 54.10 |
| 2000 | Lenny Krayzelburg (USA) | 53.72 |
| 2004 | Aaron Peirsol (USA) | 54.06 |
| 2008 | Aaron Peirsol (USA) | 52.54 |
| 2012 | Matthew Grevers (USA) | 52.16 |

**200-METER BACKSTROKE**

| | | MIN:SEC |
|---|---|---|
| 1900 | Ernst Hoppenberg (GER) | 2:47.0 |
| 1964 | Jed Graef (USA) | 2:10.3 |
| 1968 | Roland Matthes (GDR) | 2:09.6 |
| 1972 | Roland Matthes (GDR) | 2:02.82 |
| 1976 | John Naber (USA) | 1:59.19 |
| 1980 | Sandor Wladar (HUN) | 2:01.93 |
| 1984 | Richard Carey (USA) | 2:00.23 |
| 1988 | Igor Polyansky (URS) | 1:59.37 |
| 1992 | Martin López-Zubero (ESP) | 1:58.47 |
| 1996 | Brad Bridgewater (USA) | 1:58.54 |
| 2000 | Lenny Krayzelburg (USA) | 1:56.76 |
| 2004 | Aaron Peirsol (USA) | 1:54.95 |
| 2008 | Ryan Lochte (USA) | 1:53.94 |
| 2012 | Tyler Clary (USA) | 1:53.41 |

**100-METER BREASTSTROKE**

| | | MIN:SEC |
|---|---|---|
| 1968 | Donald McKenzie (USA) | 1:07.7 |
| 1972 | Nobutaka Tagushi (JPN) | 1:04.94 |
| 1976 | John Hencken (USA) | 1:03.11 |
| 1980 | Duncan Goodhew (GBR) | 1:03.34 |
| 1984 | Steve Lundquist (USA) | 1:01.65 |
| 1988 | Adrian Moorhouse (GBR) | 1:02.04 |
| 1992 | Nelson Diebel (USA) | 1:01.50 |
| 1996 | Frederick Deburghgraeve (BEL) | 1:00.65 |
| 2000 | Domenico Fioravanti (ITA) | 1:00.46 |
| 2004 | Kosuke Kitajima (JPN) | 1:00.08 |
| 2008 | Kosuke Kitajima (JPN) | 0:58.91 |
| 2012 | Cameron van der Burgh (RSA) | 58.46 |

### Swimming (men) (continued)

**200-METER BREASTSTROKE**

| | | MIN:SEC |
|---|---|---|
| 1908 | Frederick Holman (GBR) | 3:09.2 |
| 1912 | Walter Bathe (GER) | 3:01.8 |
| 1920 | Hakan Malmroth (SWE) | 3:04.4 |
| 1924 | Robert Skelton (USA) | 2:56.6 |
| 1928 | Yoshiyuki Tsuruta (JPN) | 2:48.8 |
| 1932 | Yoshiyuki Tsuruta (JPN) | 2:45.4 |
| 1936 | Tetsuo Hamuro (JPN) | 2:42.5 |
| 1948 | Joseph Verdeur (USA) | 2:39.3 |
| 1952 | John Davies (AUS) | 2:34.4 |
| 1956 | Masaru Furukawa (JPN) | 2:34.7 |
| 1960 | William Mulliken (USA) | 2:37.4 |
| 1964 | Ian O'Brien (AUS) | 2:27.8 |
| 1968 | Felipe Muñoz (MEX) | 2:28.7 |
| 1972 | John Hencken (USA) | 2:21.55 |
| 1976 | David Wilkie (GBR) | 2:15.11 |
| 1980 | Robertas Zulpa (URS) | 2:15.85 |
| 1984 | Victor Davis (CAN) | 2:13.34 |
| 1988 | Jozsef Szabo (HUN) | 2:13.52 |
| 1992 | Mike Barrowman (USA) | 2:10.16 |
| 1996 | Norbert Rozsa (HUN) | 2:12.57 |
| 2000 | Domenico Fioravanti (ITA) | 2:10.87 |
| 2004 | Kosuke Kitajima (JPN) | 2:09.44 |
| 2008 | Kosuke Kitajima (JPN) | 2:07.64 |
| 2012 | Daniel Gyurta (HUN) | 2:07.28 |

**400-METER BREASTSTROKE**

| | | MIN:SEC |
|---|---|---|
| 1904³⁵ | Georg Zacharias (GER) | 7:23.6 |
| 1912 | Walter Bathe (GER) | 6:29.6 |
| 1920 | Hakan Malmroth (SWE) | 6:31.8 |

**200-YARD RELAY**

| | | MIN:SEC |
|---|---|---|
| 1904 | United States | 2:04.6 |

**200-METER INDIVIDUAL MEDLEY**

| | | MIN:SEC |
|---|---|---|
| 1968 | Charles Hickcox (USA) | 2:12.0 |
| 1972 | Gunnar Larsson (SWE) | 2:07.17 |
| 1984 | Alex Baumann (CAN) | 2:01.42 |
| 1988 | Tamas Darnyi (HUN) | 2:00.17 |
| 1992 | Tamas Darnyi (HUN) | 2:00.76 |
| 1996 | Attila Czene (HUN) | 1:59.91 |
| 2000 | Massimiliano Rosolino (ITA) | 1:58.98 |
| 2004 | Michael Phelps (USA) | 1:57.14 |
| 2008 | Michael Phelps (USA) | 1:54.23 |
| 2012 | Michael Phelps (USA) | 1:54.27 |

**400-METER INDIVIDUAL MEDLEY**

| | | MIN:SEC |
|---|---|---|
| 1964 | Richard William Roth (USA) | 4:45.4 |
| 1968 | Charles Hickcox (USA) | 4:48.4 |
| 1972 | Gunnar Larsson (SWE) | 4:31.98 |
| 1976 | Rod Strachan (USA) | 4:23.68 |
| 1980 | Aleksandr Sidorenko (URS) | 4:22.89 |
| 1984 | Alex Baumann (CAN) | 4:17.41 |
| 1988 | Tamas Darnyi (HUN) | 4:14.75 |
| 1992 | Tamas Darnyi (HUN) | 4:14.23 |
| 1996 | Tom Dolan (USA) | 4:14.90 |
| 2000 | Tom Dolan (USA) | 4:11.76 |
| 2004 | Michael Phelps (USA) | 4:08.26 |
| 2008 | Michael Phelps (USA) | 4:03.84 |
| 2012 | Ryan Lochte (USA) | 4:05.18 |

**4 × 100-METER MEDLEY RELAY**

| | | MIN:SEC |
|---|---|---|
| 1960 | United States | 4:05.4 |
| 1964 | United States | 3:58.4 |
| 1968 | United States | 3:54.9 |
| 1972 | United States | 3:48.16 |
| 1976 | United States | 3:42.22 |
| 1980 | Australia | 3:45.70 |

# Summer Olympic Games (continued)

## Swimming (men) (continued)

### 4 × 100-METER MEDLEY RELAY (CONTINUED)

| | | MIN:SEC |
|---|---|---|
| 1984 | United States | 3:39.30 |
| 1988 | United States | 3:36.93 |
| 1992 | United States | 3:36.93 |
| 1996 | United States | 3:34.84 |
| 2000 | United States | 3:33.73 |
| 2004 | United States | 3:30.68 |
| 2008 | United States | 3:29.34 |
| 2012 | United States | 3:29.35 |

### 4 × 100-METER FREESTYLE RELAY

| | | MIN:SEC |
|---|---|---|
| 1964 | United States | 3:33.2 |
| 1968 | United States | 3:31.7 |
| 1972 | United States | 3:26.42 |
| 1984 | United States | 3:19.03 |
| 1988 | United States | 3:16.53 |
| 1992 | United States | 3:16.74 |
| 1996 | United States | 3:15.41 |
| 2000 | Australia | 3:13.67 |
| 2004 | South Africa | 3:13.17 |
| 2008 | United States | 3:08.24 |
| 2012 | France | 3:09.93 |

### 4 × 200-METER FREESTYLE RELAY

| | | MIN:SEC |
|---|---|---|
| 1908 | Great Britain | 10:55.6 |
| 1912 | Australia | 10:11.2 |
| 1920 | United States | 10:04.4 |
| 1924 | United States | 9:53.4 |
| 1928 | United States | 9:36.2 |
| 1932 | Japan | 8:58.4 |
| 1936 | Japan | 8:51.5 |
| 1948 | United States | 8:46.0 |
| 1952 | United States | 8:31.1 |
| 1956 | Australia | 8:23.6 |
| 1960 | United States | 8:10.2 |
| 1964 | United States | 7:52.1 |
| 1968 | United States | 7:52.3 |
| 1972 | United States | 7:35.78 |
| 1976 | United States | 7:23.22 |
| 1980 | USSR | 7:23.50 |
| 1984 | United States | 7:15.69 |
| 1988 | United States | 7:12.51 |
| 1992 | Unified Team | 7:11.95 |
| 1996 | United States | 7:14.84 |
| 2000 | Australia | 7:07.05 |
| 2004 | United States | 7:07.33 |
| 2008 | United States | 6:58.56 |
| 2012 | United States | 6:59.70 |

### 60-METER UNDERWATER

| | | MIN:SEC (UNDERWATER) |
|---|---|---|
| 1900 | Charles de Vendeville (FRA) | 1:08.4 |

### 200-METER OBSTACLE

| | | MIN:SEC |
|---|---|---|
| 1900 | Frederick Lane (AUS) | 2:38.4 |

### 10-KM OPEN-WATER MARATHON

| | | HR:MIN:SEC |
|---|---|---|
| 2008 | Maarten van der Weijden (NED) | 1:51:51.6 |
| 2012 | Oussama Mellouli (TUN) | 1:49:55.1 |

## Swimming (women)

### 50-METER FREESTYLE

| | | SEC |
|---|---|---|
| 1988 | Kristin Otto (GDR) | 25.49 |
| 1992 | Yang Wenyi (CHN) | 24.79 |
| 1996 | Amy Van Dyken (USA) | 24.87 |
| 2000 | Inge de Bruijn (NED) | 24.32 |
| 2004 | Inge de Bruijn (NED) | 24.58 |
| 2008 | Britta Steffen (GER) | 24.06 |
| 2012 | Ranomi Kromowidjojo (NED) | 24.05 |

## Swimming (women) (continued)

### 100-METER FREESTYLE

| | | MIN:SEC |
|---|---|---|
| 1912 | Fanny Durack (AUS) | 1:22.2 |
| 1920 | Ethelda Bleibtrey (USA) | 1:13.6 |
| 1924 | Ethel Lackie (USA) | 1:12.4 |
| 1928 | Albina Osipowich (USA) | 1:11.0 |
| 1932 | Helene Madison (USA) | 1:06.8 |
| 1936 | Hendrika Mastenbroek (NED) | 1:05.9 |
| 1948 | Greta Andersen (DEN) | 1:06.3 |
| 1952 | Katalin Szoke (HUN) | 1:06.8 |
| 1956 | Dawn Fraser (AUS) | 1:02.0 |
| 1960 | Dawn Fraser (AUS) | 1:01.2 |
| 1964 | Dawn Fraser (AUS) | 59.5 |
| 1968 | Jan Henne (USA) | 1:00.0 |
| 1972 | Sandra Neilson (USA) | 58.59 |
| 1976 | Kornelia Ender (GDR) | 55.65 |
| 1980 | Barbara Krause (GDR) | 54.79 |
| 1984 | Carrie Steinseifer (USA); Nancy Hogshead (USA) (tied) | 55.92 |
| 1988 | Kristin Otto (GDR) | 54.93 |
| 1992 | Zhuang Yong (CHN) | 54.64 |
| 1996 | Le Jingyi (CHN) | 54.50 |
| 2000 | Inge de Bruijn (NED) | 53.83 |
| 2004 | Jodie Henry (AUS) | 53.84 |
| 2008 | Britta Steffen (GER) | 53.12 |
| 2012 | Ranomi Kromowidjojo (NED) | 53.00 |

### 200-METER FREESTYLE

| | | MIN:SEC |
|---|---|---|
| 1968 | Debbie Meyer (USA) | 2:10.5 |
| 1972 | Shane Gould (AUS) | 2:03.56 |
| 1976 | Kornelia Ender (GDR) | 1:59.26 |
| 1980 | Barbara Krause (GDR) | 1:58.33 |
| 1984 | Mary Wayte (USA) | 1:59.23 |
| 1988 | Heike Friedrich (GDR) | 1:57.65 |
| 1992 | Nicole Haislett (USA) | 1:57.90 |
| 1996 | Claudia Poll (CRC) | 1:58.16 |
| 2000 | Susie O'Neill (AUS) | 1:58.24 |
| 2004 | Camelia Potec (ROM) | 1:58.03 |
| 2008 | Federica Pellegrini (ITA) | 1:54.82 |
| 2012 | Allison Schmitt (USA) | 1:53.61 |

### 400-METER FREESTYLE

| | | MIN:SEC |
|---|---|---|
| 1920[36] | Ethelda Bleibtrey (USA) | 4:34.0 |
| 1924 | Martha Norelius (USA) | 6:02.2 |
| 1928 | Martha Norelius (USA) | 5:42.8 |
| 1932 | Helene Madison (USA) | 5:28.5 |
| 1936 | Hendrika Mastenbroek (NED) | 5:26.4 |
| 1948 | Ann Curtis (USA) | 5:17.8 |
| 1952 | Valeria Gyenge (HUN) | 5:12.1 |
| 1956 | Lorraine Crapp (AUS) | 4:54.6 |
| 1960 | Susan Christina von Saltza (USA) | 4:50.6 |
| 1964 | Virginia Duenkel (USA) | 4:43.3 |
| 1968 | Debbie Meyer (USA) | 4:31.8 |
| 1972 | Shane Gould (AUS) | 4:19.04 |
| 1976 | Petra Thümer (GDR) | 4:09.89 |
| 1980 | Ines Diers (GDR) | 4:08.76 |
| 1984 | Tiffany Cohen (USA) | 4:07.10 |
| 1988 | Janet Evans (USA) | 4:03.85 |
| 1992 | Dagmar Hase (GER) | 4:07.18 |
| 1996 | Michelle Smith (IRL) | 4:07.25 |
| 2000 | Brooke Bennett (USA) | 4:05.80 |
| 2004 | Laure Manaudou (FRA) | 4:05.34 |
| 2008 | Rebecca Adlington (GBR) | 4:03.22 |
| 2012 | Camille Muffat (FRA) | 4:01.45 |

### 800-METER FREESTYLE

| | | MIN:SEC |
|---|---|---|
| 1968 | Debbie Meyer (USA) | 9:24.0 |
| 1972 | Keena Rothhammer (USA) | 8:53.68 |
| 1976 | Petra Thümer (GDR) | 8:37.14 |

# Summer Olympic Games (continued)

## Swimming (women) (continued)

### 800-METER FREESTYLE (CONTINUED)

| | | MIN:SEC |
|---|---|---|
| 1980 | Michelle Ford (AUS) | 8:28.90 |
| 1984 | Tiffany Cohen (USA) | 8:24.95 |
| 1988 | Janet Evans (USA) | 8:20.20 |
| 1992 | Janet Evans (USA) | 8:25.52 |
| 1996 | Brooke Bennett (USA) | 8:27.89 |
| 2000 | Brooke Bennett (USA) | 8:19.67 |
| 2004 | Ai Shibata (JPN) | 8:24.54 |
| 2008 | Rebecca Adlington (GBR) | 8:14.10 |
| 2012 | Katie Ledecky (USA) | 8:14.63 |

### 100-METER BUTTERFLY

| | | MIN:SEC |
|---|---|---|
| 1956 | Shelley Mann (USA) | 1:11.0 |
| 1960 | Carolyn Schuler (USA) | 1:09.5 |
| 1964 | Sharon Stouder (USA) | 1:04.7 |
| 1968 | Lynette McClements (AUS) | 1:05.5 |
| 1972 | Mayumi Aoki (JPN) | 1:03.34 |
| 1976 | Kornelia Ender (GDR) | 1:00.13 |
| 1980 | Caren Metschuck (GDR) | 1:00.42 |
| 1984 | Mary Meagher (USA) | 59.26 |
| 1988 | Kristin Otto (GDR) | 59.00 |
| 1992 | Qian Hong (CHN) | 58.62 |
| 1996 | Amy Van Dyken (USA) | 59.13 |
| 2000 | Inge de Bruijn (NED) | 56.61 |
| 2004 | Petria Thomas (AUS) | 57.72 |
| 2008 | Lisbeth Lenton Trickett (AUS) | 56.73 |
| 2012 | Dana Vollmer (USA) | 55.98 |

### 200-METER BUTTERFLY

| | | MIN:SEC |
|---|---|---|
| 1968 | Aagje Kok (NED) | 2:24.7 |
| 1972 | Karen Moe (USA) | 2:15.57 |
| 1976 | Andrea Pollack (GDR) | 2:11.41 |
| 1980 | Ines Geissler (GDR) | 2:10.44 |
| 1984 | Mary Meagher (USA) | 2:06.90 |
| 1988 | Kathleen Nord (GDR) | 2:09.51 |
| 1992 | Summer Sanders (USA) | 2:08.67 |
| 1996 | Susie O'Neill (AUS) | 2:07.76 |
| 2000 | Misty Hyman (USA) | 2:05.88 |
| 2004 | Otylia Jedrzejczak (POL) | 2:06.05 |
| 2008 | Liu Zige (CHN) | 2:04.18 |
| 2012 | Jiao Liuyang (CHN) | 2:04.06 |

### 100-METER BACKSTROKE

| | | MIN:SEC |
|---|---|---|
| 1924 | Sybil Bauer (USA) | 1:23.2 |
| 1928 | Maria Braun (NED) | 1:22.0 |
| 1932 | Eleanor Holm (USA) | 1:19.4 |
| 1936 | Dina Senff (NED) | 1:18.9 |
| 1948 | Karen-Margrete Harup (DEN) | 1:14.4 |
| 1952 | Joan Harrison (RSA) | 1:14.3 |
| 1956 | Judith Grinham (GBR) | 1:12.9 |
| 1960 | Lynn Burke (USA) | 1:09.3 |
| 1964 | Cathy Ferguson (USA) | 1:07.7 |
| 1968 | Kaye Hall (USA) | 1:06.2 |
| 1972 | Melissa Belote (USA) | 1:05.78 |
| 1976 | Ulrike Richter (GDR) | 1:01.83 |
| 1980 | Rica Reinisch (GDR) | 1:00.86 |
| 1984 | Theresa Andrews (USA) | 1:02.55 |
| 1988 | Kristin Otto (GDR) | 1:00.89 |
| 1992 | Krisztina Egerszegi (HUN) | 1:00.68 |
| 1996 | Beth Botsford (USA) | 1:01.19 |
| 2000 | Diana Mocanu (ROM) | 1:00.21 |
| 2004 | Natalie Coughlin (USA) | 1:00.37 |
| 2008 | Natalie Coughlin (USA) | 0:58.96 |
| 2012 | Missy Franklin (USA) | 58.33 |

### 200-METER BACKSTROKE

| | | MIN:SEC |
|---|---|---|
| 1968 | Pokey Watson (USA) | 2:24.8 |
| 1972 | Melissa Belote (USA) | 2:19.19 |

## Swimming (women) (continued)

### 200-METER BACKSTROKE (CONTINUED)

| | | MIN:SEC |
|---|---|---|
| 1976 | Ulrike Richter (GDR) | 2:13.43 |
| 1980 | Rica Reinisch (GDR) | 2:11.77 |
| 1984 | Jolanda De Rover (NED) | 2:12.38 |
| 1988 | Krisztina Egerszegi (HUN) | 2:09.29 |
| 1992 | Krisztina Egerszegi (HUN) | 2:07.06 |
| 1996 | Krisztina Egerszegi (HUN) | 2:07.83 |
| 2000 | Diana Mocanu (ROM) | 2:08.16 |
| 2004 | Kirsty Coventry (ZIM) | 2:09.19 |
| 2008 | Kirsty Coventry (ZIM) | 2:05.24 |
| 2012 | Missy Franklin (USA) | 2:04.06 |

### 100-METER BREASTSTROKE

| | | MIN:SEC |
|---|---|---|
| 1968 | Djurdjica Bjedov (YUG) | 1:15.8 |
| 1972 | Cathy Carr (USA) | 1:13.58 |
| 1976 | Hannelore Anke (GDR) | 1:11.16 |
| 1980 | Ute Geveniger (GDR) | 1:10.22 |
| 1984 | Petra van Staveren (NED) | 1:09.88 |
| 1988 | Tanya Dangalakova (BUL) | 1:07.95 |
| 1992 | Yelena Rudkovskaya (UNT) | 1:08.00 |
| 1996 | Penelope Heyns (RSA) | 1:07.73 |
| 2000 | Megan Quann (USA) | 1:07.05 |
| 2004 | Luo Xuejuan (CHN) | 1:06.64 |
| 2008 | Leisel Jones (AUS) | 1:05.17 |
| 2012 | Ruta Meilutyte (LTU) | 1:05.47 |

### 200-METER BREASTSTROKE

| | | MIN:SEC |
|---|---|---|
| 1924 | Lucy Morton (GBR) | 3:33.2 |
| 1928 | Hilde Schrader (GER) | 3:12.6 |
| 1932 | Claire Dennis (AUS) | 3:06.3 |
| 1936 | Hideko Maehata (JPN) | 3:03.6 |
| 1948 | Petronella van Vliet (NED) | 2:57.2 |
| 1952 | Eva Szekely (HUN) | 2:51.7 |
| 1956 | Ursula Happe (GER) | 2:53.1 |
| 1960 | Anita Lonsbrough (GBR) | 2:49.5 |
| 1964 | Galina Prozumenshchikova-Stepanova (URS) | 2:46.4 |
| 1968 | Sharon Wichman (USA) | 2:44.4 |
| 1972 | Beverley Whitfield (AUS) | 2:41.71 |
| 1976 | Marina Koshevaya (URS) | 2:33.35 |
| 1980 | Lina Kachushite (URS) | 2:29.54 |
| 1984 | Anne Ottenbrite (CAN) | 2:30.38 |
| 1988 | Silke Hörner (GDR) | 2:26.71 |
| 1992 | Kyoko Iwasaki (JPN) | 2:26.65 |
| 1996 | Penelope Heyns (RSA) | 2:25.41 |
| 2000 | Agnes Kovacs (HUN) | 2:24.35 |
| 2004 | Amanda Beard (USA) | 2:23.37 |
| 2008 | Rebecca Soni (USA) | 2:20.22 |
| 2012 | Rebecca Soni (USA) | 2:19.59 |

### 200-METER INDIVIDUAL MEDLEY

| | | MIN:SEC |
|---|---|---|
| 1968 | Claudia Kolb (USA) | 2:24.7 |
| 1972 | Shane Gould (AUS) | 2:23.07 |
| 1984 | Tracy Caulkins (USA) | 2:12.64 |
| 1988 | Daniela Hunger (GDR) | 2:12.59 |
| 1992 | Lin Li (CHN) | 2:11.65 |
| 1996 | Michelle Smith (IRL) | 2:13.93 |
| 2000 | Yana Klochkova (UKR) | 2:10.68 |
| 2004 | Yana Klochkova (UKR) | 2:11.14 |
| 2008 | Stephanie Rice (AUS) | 2:08.45 |
| 2012 | Ye Shiwen (CHN) | 2:07.57 |

### 400-METER INDIVIDUAL MEDLEY

| | | MIN:SEC |
|---|---|---|
| 1964 | Donna De Varona (USA) | 5:18.7 |
| 1968 | Claudia Kolb (USA) | 5:08.5 |
| 1972 | Gail Neall (AUS) | 5:02.97 |
| 1976 | Ulrike Tauber (GDR) | 4:42.77 |
| 1980 | Petra Schneider (GDR) | 4:36.29 |

## Summer Olympic Games (continued)

### Swimming (women) (continued)

| 400-METER INDIVIDUAL MEDLEY (CONTINUED) | | MIN:SEC |
|---|---|---|
| 1984 | Tracy Caulkins (USA) | 4:39.24 |
| 1988 | Janet Evans (USA) | 4:37.76 |
| 1992 | Krisztina Egerszegi (HUN) | 4:36.54 |
| 1996 | Michelle Smith (IRL) | 4:39.18 |
| 2000 | Yana Klochkova (UKR) | 4:33.59 |
| 2004 | Yana Klochkova (UKR) | 4:34.83 |
| 2008 | Stephanie Rice (AUS) | 4:29.45 |
| 2012 | Ye Shiwen (CHN) | 4:28.43 |

| 4 × 100-METER MEDLEY RELAY | | MIN:SEC |
|---|---|---|
| 1960 | United States | 4:41.1 |
| 1964 | United States | 4:33.9 |
| 1968 | United States | 4:28.3 |
| 1972 | United States | 4:20.75 |
| 1976 | East Germany | 4:07.95 |
| 1980 | East Germany | 4:06.67 |
| 1984 | United States | 4:08.34 |
| 1988 | East Germany | 4:03.74 |
| 1992 | United States | 4:02.54 |
| 1996 | United States | 4:02.88 |
| 2000 | United States | 3:58.30 |
| 2004 | Australia | 3:57.32 |
| 2008 | Australia | 3:52.69 |
| 2012 | United States | 3:52.05 |

| 4 × 100-METER FREESTYLE RELAY | | MIN:SEC |
|---|---|---|
| 1912 | Great Britain | 5:52.8 |
| 1920 | United States | 5:11.6 |
| 1924 | United States | 4:58.8 |
| 1928 | United States | 4:47.6 |
| 1932 | United States | 4:38.0 |
| 1936 | The Netherlands | 4:36.0 |
| 1948 | United States | 4:29.2 |
| 1952 | Hungary | 4:24.4 |
| 1956 | Australia | 4:17.1 |
| 1960 | United States | 4:08.9 |
| 1964 | United States | 4:03.8 |
| 1968 | United States | 4:02.5 |
| 1972 | United States | 3:55.19 |
| 1976 | United States | 3:44.82 |
| 1980 | East Germany | 3:42.71 |
| 1984 | United States | 3:43.43 |
| 1988 | East Germany | 3:40.63 |
| 1992 | United States | 3:39.46 |
| 1996 | United States | 3:39.29 |
| 2000 | United States | 3:36.61 |
| 2004 | Australia | 3:35.94 |
| 2008 | The Netherlands | 3:33.76 |
| 2012 | Australia | 3:33.15 |

| 4 × 200-METER FREESTYLE RELAY | | MIN:SEC |
|---|---|---|
| 1996 | United States | 7:59.87 |
| 2000 | United States | 7:57.80 |
| 2004 | United States | 7:53.42 |
| 2008 | Australia | 7:44.31 |
| 2012 | United States | 7:42.92 |

| 10-KM OPEN-WATER MARATHON | | HR:MIN:SEC |
|---|---|---|
| 2008 | Larisa Ilchenko (RUS) | 1:59:27.7 |
| 2012 | Eva Risztov (HUN) | 1:57:38.2 |

### Synchronized Swimming

**INDIVIDUAL**

| 1984 | Tracie Ruiz (USA) |
|---|---|
| 1988 | Carolyn Waldo (CAN) |
| 1992 | Kristen Babb-Sprague (USA); Sylvie Fréchette (CAN)[37] |

### Synchronized Swimming (continued)

**DUET**

| 1984 | United States |
|---|---|
| 1988 | Canada |
| 1992 | United States |
| 2000 | Russia |
| 2004 | Russia |
| 2008 | Russia |
| 2012 | Russia |

**TEAM**

| 1996 | United States |
|---|---|
| 2000 | Russia |
| 2004 | Russia |
| 2008 | Russia |
| 2012 | Russia |

### Table Tennis (men)

**SINGLES**

| 1988 | Yoo Nam Kyu (KOR) |
|---|---|
| 1992 | Jan-Ove Waldner (SWE) |
| 1996 | Liu Guoliang (CHN) |
| 2000 | Kong Linghui (CHN) |
| 2004 | Ryu Seung Min (KOR) |
| 2008 | Ma Lin (CHN) |
| 2012 | Zhang Jike (CHN) |

**TEAM**

| 1988 | China |
|---|---|
| 1992 | China |
| 1996 | China |
| 2000 | China |
| 2004 | China |
| 2008 | China |
| 2012 | China |

### Table Tennis (women)

**SINGLES**

| 1988 | Chen Jing (CHN) |
|---|---|
| 1992 | Deng Yaping (CHN) |
| 1996 | Deng Yaping (CHN) |
| 2000 | Wang Nan (CHN) |
| 2004 | Zhang Yining (CHN) |
| 2008 | Zhang Yining (CHN) |
| 2012 | Li Xiaoxia (CHN) |

**TEAM**

| 1988 | Republic of Korea |
|---|---|
| 1992 | China |
| 1996 | China |
| 2000 | China |
| 2004 | China |
| 2008 | China |
| 2012 | China |

### Taekwondo (men)

**58 KG (127.6 LB)**

| 2000 | Michail Mouroutsos (GRE) |
|---|---|
| 2004 | Chu Mu Yen (TPE) |
| 2008 | Guillermo Pérez (MEX) |
| 2012 | Joel Gonzalez Bonilla (ESP) |

**68 KG (149.6 LB)**

| 2000 | Steven Lopez (USA) |
|---|---|
| 2004 | Hadi Saei Bonehkohal (IRI) |
| 2008 | Son Tae Jin (KOR) |
| 2012 | Servet Tazegul (TUR) |

## Summer Olympic Games (continued)

### Taekwondo (men) (continued)

**80 KG (176 LB)**

2000  Angel Valodia Matos (CUB)
2004  Steven Lopez (USA)
2008  Hadi Saei (IRI)
2012  Sebastian Eduardo Crismanich (ARG)

**OVER 80 KG (176+ LB)**

2000  Kim Kyong-Hun (KOR)
2004  Moon Sung Dae (KOR)
2008  Cha Dong Min (KOR)
2012  Carlo Molfetta (ITA)

### Taekwondo (women)

**49 KG (107.8 LB)**

2000  Lauren Burns (AUS)
2004  Chen Shih Hsin (TPE)
2008  Wu Jingyu (CHN)
2012  Wu Jingyu (CHN)

**57 KG (125.4 LB)**

2000  Jung Jae-Eun (KOR)
2004  Jang Ji Won (KOR)
2008  Lim Su Jeong (KOR)
2012  Jade Jones (GBR)

**67 KG (147.4 LB)**

2000  Lee Sun-Hee (KOR)
2004  Luo Wei (CHN)
2008  Hwang Kyung-Seon (KOR)
2012  Hwang Kyung-Seon (KOR)

**OVER 67 KG (147.4+ LB)**

2000  Chen Zhong (CHN)
2004  Chen Zhong (CHN)
2008  María del Rosario Espinoza (MEX)
2012  Milica Mandic (SRB)

### Tennis (men)

**SINGLES**

1896  John Pius Boland (GBR)
1900  Laurie Doherty (GBR)
1904  Beals Wright (USA)
1908  Josiah Ritchie (GBR)
1912  Charles Winslow (RSA)
1920  Louis Raymond (RSA)
1924  Vincent Richards (USA)
1988  Miloslav Mecir (TCH)
1992  Marc Rosset (SUI)
1996  Andre Agassi (USA)
2000  Yevgeny Kafelnikov (RUS)
2004  Nicolas Massu (CHI)
2008  Rafael Nadal (ESP)
2012  Andy Murray (GBR)

**DOUBLES**

1896  John Pius Boland (GBR), Friedrich Thraun (GER)
1900  Laurie Doherty, Reggie Doherty (GBR)
1904  Edgar Leonard, Beals Wright (USA)
1908  George Hillyard, Reggie Doherty (GBR)
1912  Harold Kitson, Charles Winslow (RSA)
1920  Oswald Noel Turnbull, Max Woosnam (GBR)
1924  Frank Hunter, Vincent Richards (USA)
1988  Kenneth Flach, Robert Seguso (USA)
1992  Boris Becker, Michael Stich (GER)
1996  Todd Woodbridge, Mark Woodforde (AUS)
2000  Sebastien Lareau, Daniel Nestor (CAN)
2004  Fernando Gonzalez, Nicolas Massu (CHI)

### Tennis (men) (continued)

**DOUBLES (CONTINUED)**

2008  Roger Federer, Stanislas Wawrinka (SUI)
2012  Bob Bryan, Mike Bryan (USA)

**MIXED DOUBLES**

1900  Charlotte Cooper, Reggie Doherty (GBR)
1912  Dora Köring, Heinrich Schomburgk (GER)
1920  Suzanne Lenglen, Max Décugis (FRA)
1924  Hazel Wightman, R. Norris Williams (USA)
2012  Victoria Azarenka, Max Mirnyi (BLR)

### Tennis (women)

**SINGLES**

1900  Charlotte Cooper (GBR)
1908  Dorothea Lambert Chambers (GBR)
1912  Marguerite Broquedis (FRA)
1920  Suzanne Lenglen (FRA)
1924  Helen Wills Moody (USA)
1988  Steffi Graf (FRG)
1992  Jennifer Capriati (USA)
1996  Lindsay Davenport (USA)
2000  Venus Williams (USA)
2004  Justine Henin-Hardenne (BEL)
2008  Yelena Dementyeva (RUS)
2012  Serena Williams (USA)

**DOUBLES**

1920  Winifred McNair, Kathleen McKane (GBR)
1924  Helen Wills Moody, Hazel Wightman (USA)
1988  Zina Garrison, Pam Shriver (USA)
1992  Gigi Fernández, Mary Joe Fernández (USA)
1996  Gigi Fernández, Mary Joe Fernández (USA)
2000  Serena Williams, Venus Williams (USA)
2004  Li Ting, Sun Tian Tian (CHN)
2008  Serena Williams, Venus Williams (USA)
2012  Serena Williams, Venus Williams (USA)

### Tennis—Covered Courts (Indoor Tennis)

**MEN'S SINGLES**

1908  Arthur Gore (GBR)
1912  André Gobert (FRA)

**MEN'S DOUBLES**

1908  Arthur Gore, Herbert Roper Barrett (GBR)
1912  Maurice Germot, André Gobert (FRA)

**WOMEN'S SINGLES**

1908  Gladys Eastlake-Smith (GBR)
1912  Edith Hannam (GBR)

**MIXED DOUBLES**

1912  Edith Hannam, Charles Dixon (GBR)

### Triathlon (swim/bike/run) (men)

2000  Simon Whitfield (CAN)
2004  Hamish Carter (NZL)
2008  Jan Frodeno (GER)
2012  Alistair Brownlee (GBR)

### Triathlon (swim/bike/run) (women)

2000  Brigitte McMahon (SUI)
2004  Kate Allen (AUT)
2008  Emma Snowsill (AUS)
2012  Nicola Spirig (SUI)

# Summer Olympic Games (continued)

## Volleyball (men)

**INDOOR**

| | |
|---|---|
| 1964 | USSR |
| 1968 | USSR |
| 1972 | Japan |
| 1976 | Poland |
| 1980 | USSR |
| 1984 | United States |
| 1988 | United States |
| 1992 | Brazil |
| 1996 | The Netherlands |
| 2000 | Yugoslavia |
| 2004 | Brazil |
| 2008 | United States |
| 2012 | Russia |

**BEACH**

| | |
|---|---|
| 1996 | United States |
| 2000 | United States |
| 2004 | Brazil |
| 2008 | United States |
| 2012 | Germany |

## Volleyball (women)

**INDOOR**

| | |
|---|---|
| 1964 | Japan |
| 1968 | USSR |
| 1972 | USSR |
| 1976 | Japan |
| 1980 | USSR |
| 1984 | China |
| 1988 | USSR |
| 1992 | Cuba |
| 1996 | Cuba |
| 2000 | Cuba |
| 2004 | China |
| 2008 | Brazil |
| 2012 | Brazil |

**BEACH**

| | |
|---|---|
| 1996 | Brazil |
| 2000 | Australia |
| 2004 | United States |
| 2008 | United States |
| 2012 | United States |

## Water Polo (men)

| | |
|---|---|
| 1900 | Great Britain |
| 1904 | United States |
| 1908 | Great Britain |
| 1912 | Great Britain |
| 1920 | Great Britain |
| 1924 | France |
| 1928 | Germany |
| 1932 | Hungary |
| 1936 | Hungary |
| 1948 | Italy |
| 1952 | Hungary |
| 1956 | Hungary |
| 1960 | Italy |
| 1964 | Hungary |
| 1968 | Yugoslavia |
| 1972 | USSR |
| 1976 | Hungary |
| 1980 | USSR |
| 1984 | Yugoslavia |
| 1988 | Yugoslavia |
| 1992 | Italy |
| 1996 | Spain |

## Water Polo (men) (continued)

| | |
|---|---|
| 2000 | Hungary |
| 2004 | Hungary |
| 2008 | Hungary |
| 2012 | Croatia |

## Water Polo (women)

| | |
|---|---|
| 2000 | Australia |
| 2004 | Italy |
| 2008 | The Netherlands |
| 2012 | United States |

## Weight Lifting (men)[38, 39]

**56 KG (123.2 LB)** — KG

| | | |
|---|---|---|
| 1972 | Zygmunt Smalcerz (POL) | 337.5 |
| 1976 | Aleksandr Varonin (URS) | 242.5 |
| 1980 | Kanybek Osmanaliyev (URS) | 245.0 |
| 1984 | Zeng Guoqiang (CHN) | 235.0 |
| 1988 | Sevdalin Marinov (BUL) | 270.0 |
| 1992 | Ivan Ivanov (BUL) | 265.0 |
| 1996 | Halil Mutlu (TUR) | 287.5 |
| 2000 | Halil Mutlu (TUR) | 305.0 |
| 2004 | Halil Mutlu (TUR) | 295.0 |
| 2008 | Long Qingquan (CHN) | 292.0 |
| 2012 | Om Yun Chol (PRK) | 293.0 |

**62 KG (136.4 LB)** — KG

| | | |
|---|---|---|
| 1948 | Joseph de Pietro (USA) | 307.5 |
| 1952 | Ivan Udodov (URS) | 315.0 |
| 1956 | Charles Vinci (USA) | 342.5 |
| 1960 | Charles Vinci (USA) | 345.0 |
| 1964 | Aleksey Vakhonin (URS) | 357.5 |
| 1968 | Mohammad Nassiri (IRI) | 367.5 |
| 1972 | Imre Foldi (HUN) | 377.5 |
| 1976 | Norair Nurikian (BUL) | 262.5 |
| 1980 | Daniel Núñez (CUB) | 275.0 |
| 1984 | Wu Shude (CHN) | 267.5 |
| 1988 | Oksen Mirzoyan (URS)[2] | 292.5 |
| 1992 | Chun Byung Kwan (KOR) | 287.5 |
| 1996 | Tang Ningsheng (CHN) | 307.5 |
| 2000 | Nikolay Pechalov (CRO) | 325.0 |
| 2004 | Shi Zhiyong (CHN) | 325.0 |
| 2008 | Zhang Xiangxiang (CHN) | 319.0 |
| 2012 | Kim Un Guk (PRK) | 327.0 |

**69 KG (151.8 LB)** — KG

| | | |
|---|---|---|
| 1920 | Frans de Haes (BEL) | 220.0 |
| 1924 | Pierino Gabetti (ITA) | 402.5[40] |
| 1928 | Franz Andrysek (AUT) | 287.5 |
| 1932 | Raymond Suvigny (FRA) | 287.5 |
| 1936 | Anthony Terlazzo (USA) | 312.5 |
| 1948 | Mahmoud Fayad (EGY) | 332.5 |
| 1952 | Rafael Chimishkyan (URS) | 337.5 |
| 1956 | Isaac Berger (USA) | 352.5 |
| 1960 | Yevgeny Minayev (URS) | 372.5 |
| 1964 | Yoshinobu Miyake (JPN) | 397.5 |
| 1968 | Yoshinobu Miyake (JPN) | 392.5 |
| 1972 | Norair Nurikian (BUL) | 402.5 |
| 1976 | Nikolay Kolesnikov (URS) | 285.0 |
| 1980 | Viktor Mazin (URS) | 290.0 |
| 1984 | Chen Weiqiang (CHN) | 282.5 |
| 1988 | Naim Suleymanoglu (TUR) | 342.5 |
| 1992 | Naim Suleymanoglu (TUR) | 320.0 |
| 1996 | Naim Suleymanoglu (TUR) | 335.0 |
| 2000 | Galabin Boevski (BUL) | 357.5 |
| 2004 | Zhang Guozheng (CHN) | 347.5 |
| 2008 | Liao Hui (CHN) | 348.0 |
| 2012 | Lin Qingfeng (CHN) | 344.0 |

## Summer Olympic Games (continued)

### Weight Lifting (men)[38, 39] (continued)

| 70 KG (154 LB) | | KG |
|---|---|---|
| 1920 | Alfred Neyland (EST) | 257.5 |
| 1924 | Edmond Décottignies (FRA) | 440.0[40] |
| 1928 | Kurt Helbig (GER); Hans Haas (AUT) (tied) | 322.5 |
| 1932 | René Duverger (FRA) | 325.0 |
| 1936 | Mohamed Ahmed Mesbah (EGY); Robert Fein (AUT) (tied) | 342.5 |
| 1948 | Ibrahim Shams (EGY) | 360.0 |
| 1952 | Tommy Kono (USA) | 362.5 |
| 1956 | Igor Rybak (URS) | 380.0 |
| 1960 | Viktor Bushuyev (URS) | 397.5 |
| 1964 | Waldemar Baszanowski (POL) | 432.5 |
| 1968 | Waldemar Baszanowski (POL) | 437.5 |
| 1972 | Mukharbi Kirzhinov (URS) | 460.0 |
| 1976 | Pyotr Korol (URS)[2] | 305.0 |
| 1980 | Yanko Rusev (BUL) | 342.5 |
| 1984 | Yao Jingyuan (CHN) | 320.0 |
| 1988 | Joachim Kunz (GDR)[2] | 340.0 |
| 1992 | Israil Militosyan (UNT) | 337.5 |
| 1996 | Zhan Xugang (CHN) | 357.5 |

| 77 KG (169.4 LB) | | KG |
|---|---|---|
| 1920 | Henri Gance (FRA) | 245.0 |
| 1924 | Carlo Galimberti (ITA) | 492.5[40] |
| 1928 | François Roger (FRA) | 335.0 |
| 1932 | Rudolf Ismayr (GER) | 345.0 |
| 1936 | Khadr el Thouni (EGY) | 387.5 |
| 1948 | Frank Spellman (USA) | 390.0 |
| 1952 | Peter George (USA) | 400.0 |
| 1956 | Fyodor Bogdanovsky (URS) | 420.0 |
| 1960 | Aleksandr Kurynov (URS) | 437.5 |
| 1964 | Hans Zdrazila (TCH) | 445.0 |
| 1968 | Viktor Kurentsov (URS) | 475.0 |
| 1972 | Iordan Bikov (BUL) | 485.0 |
| 1976 | Iordan Mitkov (BUL) | 335.0 |
| 1980 | Asen Zlatev (BUL) | 360.0 |
| 1984 | Karl-Heinz Radschinsky (FRG) | 340.0 |
| 1988 | Borislav Gidikov (BUL) | 375.0 |
| 1992 | Fyodor Kassapu (UNT) | 357.5 |
| 1996 | Pablo Lara (CUB) | 367.5 |
| 2000 | Zhan Xugang (CHN) | 367.5 |
| 2004 | Taner Sagir (TUR) | 375.0 |
| 2008 | Sa Jae Hyouk (KOR) | 366.0 |
| 2012 | Lu Xiaojun (CHN) | 379.0 |

| 85 KG (187 LB) | | KG |
|---|---|---|
| 1920 | Ernest Cadine (FRA) | 290.0 |
| 1924 | Charles Rigoulot (FRA) | 502.5[40] |
| 1928 | El Sayed Nosseir (EGY) | 355.0 |
| 1932 | Louis Hostin (FRA) | 365.0 |
| 1936 | Louis Hostin (FRA) | 372.5 |
| 1948 | Stanley Stanczyk (USA) | 417.5 |
| 1952 | Trofim Lomakin (URS) | 417.5 |
| 1956 | Tommy Kono (USA) | 447.5 |
| 1960 | Ireneusz Palinski (POL) | 442.5 |
| 1964 | Rudolph Plyukfelder (URS) | 475.0 |
| 1968 | Boris Selitsky (URS) | 485.0 |
| 1972 | Leif Jenssen (NOR) | 507.5 |
| 1976 | Valery Shary (URS) | 365.0 |
| 1980 | Yury Vardanyan (URS) | 400.0 |
| 1984 | Petre Becheru (ROM) | 355.0 |
| 1988 | Israil Arsamakov (URS) | 377.5 |
| 1992 | Pyrros Dimas (GRE) | 370.0 |
| 1996 | Pyrros Dimas (GRE) | 392.5 |
| 2000 | Pyrros Dimas (GRE) | 390.0 |
| 2004 | George Asanidze (GEO) | 382.5 |

### Weight Lifting (men)[38, 39] (continued)

| 85 KG (187 LB) (CONTINUED) | | KG |
|---|---|---|
| 2008 | Lu Yong (CHN) | 394.0 |
| 2012 | Adrian Edward Zielinski (POL) | 385.0 |

| 94 KG (206.8 LB) | | KG |
|---|---|---|
| 1952 | Norbert Schemansky (USA) | 445.0 |
| 1956 | Arkady Vorobyev (URS) | 462.5 |
| 1960 | Arkady Vorobyev (URS) | 472.5 |
| 1964 | Vladimir Golovanov (URS) | 487.5 |
| 1968 | Kaarlo Kangasniemi (FIN) | 517.5 |
| 1972 | Andon Nikolov (BUL) | 525.0 |
| 1976 | David Rigert (URS) | 382.5 |
| 1980 | Peter Baczako (HUN) | 377.5 |
| 1984 | Nicu Vlad (ROM) | 392.5 |
| 1988 | Anatoly Khrapaty (URS) | 412.5 |
| 1992 | Kakhi Kakhiashvili (UNT) | 412.5 |
| 1996 | Aleksey Petrov (RUS) | 402.5 |
| 2000 | Akakios Kakhiashvilis (GRE) | 405.0 |
| 2004 | Milen Dobrev (BUL) | 407.5 |
| 2008 | Ilya Ilyin (KAZ) | 406.0 |
| 2012 | Ilya Ilyin (KAZ) | 418.0 |

| 99 KG (217.8 LB) | | KG |
|---|---|---|
| 1980 | Ota Zaremba (TCH) | 395.0 |
| 1984 | Rolf Milser (FRG) | 385.0 |
| 1988 | Pavel Kuznetsov (URS) | 425.0 |
| 1992 | Viktor Tregubov (UNT) | 410.0 |
| 1996 | Akakios Kakhiashvilis (GRE) | 420.0 |

| 105 KG (231 LB) | | KG |
|---|---|---|
| 1972 | Jan Talts (URS) | 580.0 |
| 1976 | Yury Zaytsev (URS)[2] | 385.0 |
| 1980 | Leonid Taranenko (URS) | 422.5 |
| 1984 | Norberto Oberburger (ITA) | 390.0 |
| 1988 | Yury Zakharevitch (URS) | 455.0 |
| 1992 | Ronny Weller (GER) | 432.5 |
| 1996 | Timur Taymazov (UKR) | 430.0 |
| 2000 | Hossein Tavakoli (IRI) | 425.0 |
| 2004 | Dmitry Berestov (RUS) | 425.0 |
| 2008 | Andrei Aramnau (BLR) | 436.0 |
| 2012 | Oleksiy Torokhtiy (UKR) | 412.0 |

| OVER 105 KG (231+ LB) | | KG |
|---|---|---|
| 1920 | Filippo Bottino (ITA) | 265.5 |
| 1924 | Giuseppe Tonani (ITA) | 517.5[40] |
| 1928 | Josef Strassberger (GER) | 372.5 |
| 1932 | Jaroslav Skobla (TCH) | 380.0 |
| 1936 | Josef Manger (GER) | 410.0 |
| 1948 | John Davis (USA) | 452.5 |
| 1952 | John Davis (USA) | 460.0 |
| 1956 | Paul Anderson (USA) | 500.0 |
| 1960 | Yury Vlasov (URS) | 537.5 |
| 1964 | Leonid Zhabotinsky (URS) | 572.5 |
| 1968 | Leonid Zhabotinsky (URS) | 572.5 |
| 1972 | Vasily Alekseyev (URS) | 640.0 |
| 1976 | Vasily Alekseyev (URS) | 440.0 |
| 1980 | Sultan Rakhmanov (URS) | 440.0 |
| 1984 | Dinko Lukin (AUS) | 412.5 |
| 1988 | Aleksandr Kurlovich (URS) | 462.5 |
| 1992 | Aleksandr Kurlovich (UNT) | 450.0 |
| 1996 | Andrey Chemerkin (RUS) | 457.5 |
| 2000 | Hossein Reza Zadeh (IRI) | 472.5 |
| 2004 | Hossein Reza Zadeh (IRI) | 472.5 |
| 2008 | Matthias Steiner (GER) | 461.0 |
| 2012 | Behdad Salimikordasiabi (IRI) | 455.0 |

| ONE-HAND LIFT (UNLIMITED CLASS) | | KG |
|---|---|---|
| 1896 | Launceston Elliot (GBR) | 71.0 |

# Summer Olympic Games (continued)

## Weight Lifting (men)[38, 39] (continued)

**TWO-HAND LIFT (UNLIMITED CLASS)** KG

| | | |
|---|---|---|
| 1896 | Viggo Jensen (DEN) | 111.5 |
| 1904 | Perikles Kakousis (GRE) | 111.7 |

**ALL-AROUND DUMBBELLS (UNLIMITED CLASS)**

| | | |
|---|---|---|
| 1904 | Oscar Osthoff (USA) | |

## Weight Lifting (women)

**48 KG (105.6 LB)** KG

| | | |
|---|---|---|
| 2000 | Tara Nott (USA)[2] | 185.0 |
| 2004 | Nurcan Taylan (TUR) | 210.0 |
| 2008 | Chen Xiexia (CHN) | 212.0 |
| 2012 | Wang Mingjuan (CHN) | 205.0 |

**53 KG (116.6 LB)** KG

| | | |
|---|---|---|
| 2000 | Yang Xia (CHN) | 225.0 |
| 2004 | Udomporn Polsak (THA) | 222.5 |
| 2008 | Prapawadee Jaroenrattanatarakoon (THA) | 221.0 |
| 2012 | Zulfiya Chinshanlo (KAZ) | 226.0 |

**58 KG (127.6 LB)** KG

| | | |
|---|---|---|
| 2000 | Soraya Jiménez Mendívil (MEX) | 222.5 |
| 2004 | Chen Yanqing (CHN) | 237.5 |
| 2008 | Chen Yanqing (CHN) | 244.0 |
| 2012 | Li Xueying (CHN) | 246.0 |

**63 KG (138.6 LB)** KG

| | | |
|---|---|---|
| 2000 | Chen Xiaomin (CHN) | 242.5 |
| 2004 | Natalya Skakun (UKR) | 242.5 |
| 2008 | Pak Hyon Suk (PRK) | 241.0 |
| 2012 | Maiya Maneza (KAZ) | 245.0 |

**69 KG (151.8 LB)** KG

| | | |
|---|---|---|
| 2000 | Lin Weining (CHN) | 242.5 |
| 2004 | Liu Chunhong (CHN) | 275.0 |
| 2008 | Liu Chunhong (CHN) | 286.0 |
| 2012 | Rim Jong-Sim (PRK) | 261.0 |

**75 KG (165 LB)** KG

| | | |
|---|---|---|
| 2000 | Maria Isabel Urrutia (COL) | 245.0 |
| 2004 | Pawina Thongsuk (THA) | 272.5 |
| 2008 | Cao Lei (CHN) | 282.0 |
| 2012 | Svetlana Podobedova (KAZ) | 291.0 |

**OVER 75 KG (165+ LB)** KG

| | | |
|---|---|---|
| 2000 | Ding Meiyuan (CHN) | 300.0 |
| 2004 | Tang Gonghong (CHN) | 305.0 |
| 2008 | Jang Mi Ran (KOR) | 326.0 |
| 2012 | Zhou Lulu (CHN) | 333.0 |

## Wrestling—Freestyle (men)[38]

**48 KG (105.6 LB)**

| | |
|---|---|
| 1904 | Robert Curry (USA) |
| 1972 | Roman Dmitriyev (URS) |
| 1976 | Khassan Issaev (BUL) |
| 1980 | Claudio Pollio (ITA) |
| 1984 | Robert Weaver (USA) |
| 1988 | Takashi Kobayashi (JPN) |
| 1992 | Kim Il (PRK) |
| 1996 | Kim Il (PRK) |

**55 KG (121 LB)**

| | |
|---|---|
| 1904 | George Mehnert (USA) |
| 1948 | Lennart Viitala (FIN) |
| 1952 | Hasan Gemici (TUR) |
| 1956 | Mirian Tsalkalamanidze (URS) |
| 1960 | Ahmet Bilek (TUR) |

## Wrestling—Freestyle (men)[38]

**55 KG (121 LB) (CONTINUED)**

| | |
|---|---|
| 1964 | Yoshikatsu Yoshida (JPN) |
| 1968 | Shigeo Nakata (JPN) |
| 1972 | Kiyomi Kato (JPN) |
| 1976 | Yuji Takada (JPN) |
| 1980 | Anatoly Beloglazov (URS) |
| 1984 | Saban Trstena (YUG) |
| 1988 | Mitsuru Sato (JPN) |
| 1992 | Li Hak-son (PRK) |
| 1996 | Valentin Iordanov (BUL) |
| 2000 | Namig Amdullayev (AZE) |
| 2004 | Mavlet Batirov (RUS) |
| 2008 | Henry Cejudo (USA) |
| 2012 | Dzhamal Otarsultanov (RUS) |

**60 KG (132 LB)**

| | |
|---|---|
| 1904 | Isidor "Jack" Niflot (USA) |
| 1908 | George Mehnert (USA) |
| 1924 | Kustaa Pihlajamäki (FIN) |
| 1928 | Kaarlo Maakinen (FIN) |
| 1932 | Robert Pearce (USA) |
| 1936 | Odon Zombory (HUN) |
| 1948 | Nasuh Akar (TUR) |
| 1952 | Shohachi Ishii (JPN) |
| 1956 | Mustafa Dagistanli (TUR) |
| 1960 | Terence McCann (USA) |
| 1964 | Yojiro Uetake (JPN) |
| 1968 | Yojiro Uetake (JPN) |
| 1972 | Hideaki Yanagida (JPN) |
| 1976 | Vladimir Yumin (URS) |
| 1980 | Sergey Beloglazov (URS) |
| 1984 | Hideaki Tomiyama (JPN) |
| 1988 | Sergey Beloglazov (URS) |
| 1992 | Alejandro Puerto Diaz (CUB) |
| 1996 | Kendall Cross (USA) |
| 2000 | Alireza Dabir (IRI) |
| 2004 | Yandro Miguel Quintana (CUB) |
| 2008 | Mavlet Batirov (RUS) |
| 2012 | Toghrul Asgarov (AZE) |

**63 KG (138.6 LB)**

| | |
|---|---|
| 1904 | Benjamin Bradshaw (USA) |
| 1908 | George Dole (USA) |
| 1920 | Charles Ackerly (USA) |
| 1924 | Robin Reed (USA) |
| 1928 | Allie Morrison (USA) |
| 1932 | Hermanni Pihlajamäki (FIN) |
| 1936 | Kustaa Pihlajamäki (FIN) |
| 1948 | Gazanfer Bilge (TUR) |
| 1952 | Bayram Sit (TUR) |
| 1956 | Shozo Sasahara (JPN) |
| 1960 | Mustafa Dagistanli (TUR) |
| 1964 | Osamu Watanabe (JPN) |
| 1968 | Masaaki Kaneko (JPN) |
| 1972 | Zagalav Abdulbekov (URS) |
| 1976 | Yang Jung Mo (KOR) |
| 1980 | Magomedgasan Abushev (URS) |
| 1984 | Randy Lewis (USA) |
| 1988 | John Smith (USA) |
| 1992 | John Smith (USA) |
| 1996 | Tom Brands (USA) |
| 2000 | Murad Umakhanov (RUS) |

**66 KG (145.2 LB)**

| | |
|---|---|
| 1904 | Otto Roehm (USA) |
| 1908 | George de Relwyskow (GBR) |
| 1920 | Kaarlo "Kalle" Anttila (FIN) |
| 1924 | Russell Vis (USA) |

## Summer Olympic Games (continued)

### Wrestling—Freestyle (men)[38] (continued)

**66 KG (145.2 LB) (CONTINUED)**

| | |
|---|---|
| 1928 | Osvald Käpp (EST) |
| 1932 | Charles Pacome (FRA) |
| 1936 | Karoly Karpati (HUN) |
| 1948 | Celal Atik (TUR) |
| 1952 | Olle Anderberg (SWE) |
| 1956 | Emamali Habibi (IRI) |
| 1960 | Shelby Wilson (USA) |
| 1964 | Enio Valchev Dimov (BUL) |
| 1968 | Abdollah Movahed (IRI) |
| 1972 | Dan Gable (USA) |
| 1976 | Pavel Pinigin (URS) |
| 1980 | Saipulla Absaidov (URS) |
| 1984 | You In Tak (KOR) |
| 1988 | Arsen Fadzayev (URS) |
| 1992 | Arsen Fadzayev (UNT) |
| 1996 | Vadim Bogiyev (RUS) |
| 2000 | Daniel Igali (CAN) |
| 2004 | Elbrus Tedeyev (UKR) |
| 2008 | Ramazan Sahin (TUR) |
| 2012 | Tatsuhiro Yonemitsu (JPN) |

**74 KG (162.8 LB)**

| | |
|---|---|
| 1904 | Charles Eriksen (USA) |
| 1924 | Hermann Gehri (SUI) |
| 1928 | Arvo Haavisto (FIN) |
| 1932 | Jack van Bebber (USA) |
| 1936 | Frank Lewis (USA) |
| 1948 | Yasar Dogu (TUR) |
| 1952 | William Smith (USA) |
| 1956 | Mitsuo Ikeda (JPN) |
| 1960 | Douglas Blubaugh (USA) |
| 1964 | Ismail Ogan (TUR) |
| 1968 | Mahmut Atalay (TUR) |
| 1972 | Wayne Wells (USA) |
| 1976 | Jiichiro Date (JPN) |
| 1980 | Valentin Raychev (BUL) |
| 1984 | David Schultz (USA) |
| 1988 | Kenneth Monday (USA) |
| 1992 | Park Jang Soon (KOR) |
| 1996 | Buvaysa Saytiyev (RUS) |
| 2000 | Brandon Slay (USA)[2] |
| 2004 | Buvaysa Saytiyev (RUS) |
| 2008 | Buvaysa Saytiyev (RUS) |
| 2012 | Jordan Burroughs (USA) |

**84 KG (184.8 LB)**

| | |
|---|---|
| 1908 | Stanley Bacon (GBR) |
| 1920 | Eino Leino (FIN) |
| 1924 | Fritz Haggmann (SUI) |
| 1928 | Ernst Kyburz (SUI) |
| 1932 | Ivar Johansson (SWE) |
| 1936 | Émile Poilvé (FRA) |
| 1948 | Glen Brand (USA) |
| 1952 | David Tsimakurdze (URS) |
| 1956 | Nikola Stanchev (BUL) |
| 1960 | Hasan Gungor (TUR) |
| 1964 | Prodan Stoyanov Gardchev (BUL) |
| 1968 | Boris Gurevich (URS) |
| 1972 | Levan Tediashvili (URS) |
| 1976 | John Peterson (USA) |
| 1980 | Ismail Abilov (BUL) |
| 1984 | Mark Schultz (USA) |
| 1988 | Han Myung Woo (KOR) |
| 1992 | Kevin Jackson (USA) |
| 1996 | Khadshimurad Magomedov (RUS) |
| 2000 | Adam Saytev (RUS) |
| 2004 | Cael Sanderson (USA) |

### Wrestling—Freestyle (men)[38] (continued)

**84 KG (184.8 LB) (CONTINUED)**

| | |
|---|---|
| 2008 | Revazi Mindorashvili (GEO) |
| 2012 | Sharif Sharifov (AZE) |

**90 KG (198.5 LB)**

| | |
|---|---|
| 1920 | Anders Larsson (SWE) |
| 1924 | John Franklin Spellman (USA) |
| 1928 | Thure Sjöstedt (SWE) |
| 1932 | Peter Mehringer (USA) |
| 1936 | Knut Fridell (SWE) |
| 1948 | Henry Wittenberg (USA) |
| 1952 | Bror Wiking Palm (SWE) |
| 1956 | Gholam-Reza Takhti (IRI) |
| 1960 | Ismet Atli (TUR) |
| 1964 | Aleksandr Medved (URS) |
| 1968 | Ahmet Ayuk (TUR) |
| 1972 | Ben Peterson (USA) |
| 1976 | Levan Tediashvili (URS) |
| 1980 | Sanasar Oganesyan (URS) |
| 1984 | Ed Banach (USA) |
| 1988 | Macharbek Khadartsev (URS) |
| 1992 | Macharbek Khadartsev (UNT) |
| 1996 | Rasul Khadem Azghadi (IRI) |

**96 KG (211.2 LB)**

| | |
|---|---|
| 1896 | Karl Schumann (GER) |
| 1904 | Bernhuff Hansen (USA) |
| 1908 | George O'Kelly (GBR) |
| 1920 | Robert Rothe (SUI) |
| 1924 | Harry Steele (USA) |
| 1928 | Johan Richthoff (SWE) |
| 1932 | Johan Richthoff (SWE) |
| 1936 | Kristjan Palusalu (EST) |
| 1948 | Gyula Bobis (HUN) |
| 1952 | Arsen Mekokishvili (URS) |
| 1956 | Hamit Kaplan (TUR) |
| 1960 | Wilfried Dietrich (GER) |
| 1964 | Aleksandr Ivanitsky (URS) |
| 1968 | Aleksandr Medved (URS) |
| 1972 | Ivan Yarygin (URS) |
| 1976 | Ivan Yarygin (URS) |
| 1980 | Ilya Mate (URS) |
| 1984 | Lou Banach (USA) |
| 1988 | Vasile Puscasu (ROM) |
| 1992 | Leri Khabelov (UNT) |
| 1996 | Kurt Angle (USA) |
| 2000 | Sagid Murtasaliyev (RUS) |
| 2004 | Khajimurat Gatsalov (RUS) |
| 2008 | Shirvani Muradov (RUS) |
| 2012 | Jacob Varner (USA) |

**120 KG (264 LB)**

| | |
|---|---|
| 1972 | Aleksandr Medved (URS) |
| 1976 | Soslan Andiyev (URS) |
| 1980 | Soslan Andiyev (URS) |
| 1984 | Bruce Baumgartner (USA) |
| 1988 | David Gobedishvili (URS) |
| 1992 | Bruce Baumgartner (USA) |
| 1996 | Mahmut Demir (TUR) |
| 2000 | David Musulbes (RUS) |
| 2004 | Artur Taymazov (UZB) |
| 2008 | Artur Taymazov (UZB) |
| 2012 | Artur Taymazov (UZB) |

# Summer Olympic Games (continued)

## Wrestling—Freestyle (women)

**48 KG (105.6 LB)**
2004 Irini Merleni (UKR)
2008 Carol Huynh (CAN)
2012 Hitomi Obara (JPN)

**55 KG (121 LB)**
2004 Saori Yoshida (JPN)
2008 Saori Yoshida (JPN)
2012 Saori Yoshida (JPN)

**63 KG (138.6 LB)**
2004 Kaori Icho (JPN)
2008 Kaori Icho (JPN)
2012 Kaori Icho (JPN)

**72 KG (158 LB)**
2004 Wang Xu (CHN)
2008 Wang Jiao (CHN)
2012 Nataliya Vorobiyeva (RUS)

## Wrestling—Greco-Roman[38]

**48 KG (105.6 LB)**
1972 Gheorghe Berceanu (ROM)
1976 Aleksey Shumakov (URS)
1980 Zhaksylyk Ushkempirov (URS)
1984 Vincenzo Maenza (ITA)
1988 Vincenzo Maenza (ITA)
1992 Oleg Kucherenko (UNT)
1996 Sim Kwon-Ho (KOR)

**55 KG (121 LB)**
1948 Pietro Lombardi (ITA)
1952 Boris Gurevich (URS)
1956 Nikolay Solovyev (URS)
1960 Dumitru Pirvulescu (ROM)
1964 Tsutomu Hanahara (JPN)
1968 Petar Kirov (BUL)
1972 Petar Kirov (BUL)
1976 Vitaly Konstantinov (URS)
1980 Vakhtang Blagidze (URS)
1984 Atsuji Miyahara (JPN)
1988 Jon Ronningen (NOR)
1992 Jon Ronningen (NOR)
1996 Armen Nazaryan (ARM)
2000 Sim Kwon-Ho (KOR)
2004 Istvan Majoros (HUN)
2008 Nazyr Mankiyev (RUS)
2012 Hamid Mohammad Soryan Reihanpour (IRI)

**60 KG (132 LB)**
1924 Eduard Pûtsep (EST)
1928 Kurt Leucht (GER)
1932 Jakob Brendel (GER)
1936 Marton Lorincz (HUN)
1948 Kurt Pettersen (SWE)
1952 Imre Hodos (HUN)
1956 Konstantin Vyrupayev (URS)
1960 Oleg Karavayev (URS)
1964 Masamitsu Ichiguchi (JPN)
1968 Janos Varga (HUN)
1972 Rustem Kazakov (URS)
1976 Pertti Ukkola (FIN)
1980 Shamil Serikov (URS)
1984 Pasquale Passarelli (FRG)
1988 Andras Sike (HUN)
1992 An Han Bong (KOR)
1996 Yury Melnichenko (KAZ)
2000 Armen Nazarian (BUL)

## Wrestling—Greco-Roman[38] (continued)

**60 KG (132 LB) (CONTINUED)**
2004 Jung Ji Hyun (KOR)
2008 Islam-Beka Albiyev (RUS)
2012 Omid Haji Noroozi (IRI)

**63 KG (138.6 LB)**
1912 Kaarlo Koskelo (FIN)
1920 Oskar Friman (FIN)
1924 Kalle Anttila (FIN)
1928 Voldemar Väli (EST)
1932 Giovanni Gozzi (ITA)
1936 Yasar Erkan (TUR)
1948 Mehmet Oktav (TUR)
1952 Yakov Punkin (URS)
1956 Rauno Leonard Mäkinen (FIN)
1960 Muzahir Sille (TUR)
1964 Imre Polyak (HUN)
1968 Roman Rurua (URS)
1972 Georgi Markov (BUL)
1976 Kazimierz Lipien (POL)
1980 Stilianos Migiakis (GRE)
1984 Kim Weon Kee (KOR)
1988 Kamandar Madzhidov (URS)
1992 Akif Pirim (TUR)
1996 Wlodzimierz Zawadzki (POL)
2000 Varteres Samurgashev (RUS)

**66 KG (145.2 LB)**
1908 Enrico Porro (ITA)
1912 Eemil Väre (FIN)
1920 Eemil Väre (FIN)
1924 Oskar Friman (FIN)
1928 Lajos Keresztes (HUN)
1932 Erik Malmberg (SWE)
1936 Lauri Koskela (FIN)
1948 Karl Freij (SWE)
1952 Shazam Safin (URS)
1956 Kyösti Emil Lehtonen (FIN)
1960 Avtandil Koridze (URS)
1964 Kazim Ayvaz (TUR)
1968 Munji Mumemura (JPN)
1972 Shamil Khisamutdinov (URS)
1976 Suren Nalbandyan (URS)
1980 Stefan Rusu (ROM)
1984 Vlado Lisjak (YUG)
1988 Levon Dzhulfalakyan (URS)
1992 Attila Repka (HUN)
1996 Ryszard Wolny (POL)
2000 Filiberto Ascuy Aguilera (CUB)
2004 Farid Mansurov (AZE)
2008 Steeve Guénot (FRA)
2012 Kim Hyeon-Woo (KOR)

**74 KG (162.8 LB)**
1932 Ivar Johansson (SWE)
1936 Rudolf Svedberg (SWE)
1948 Erik Gösta Andersson (SWE)
1952 Miklos Szilvasi (HUN)
1956 Mithat Bayrak (TUR)
1960 Mithat Bayrak (TUR)
1964 Anatoly Kolesov (URS)
1968 Rudolf Vesper (GDR)
1972 Viteslav Macha (TCH)
1976 Anatoly Bykov (URS)
1980 Ferenc Kocsis (HUN)
1984 Jouko Salomaki (FIN)
1988 Kim Young Nam (KOR)
1992 Mnatsakan Iskandaryan (UNT)

## Summer Olympic Games (continued)

### Wrestling—Greco-Roman[38] (continued)

**74 KG (162.8 LB) (CONTINUED)**

| | |
|---|---|
| 1996 | Filiberto Ascuy Aguilera (CUB) |
| 2000 | Murat Kardanov (URS) |
| 2004 | Aleksandr Dokturishivili (UZB) |
| 2008 | Manuchar Kvirkelia (GEO) |
| 2012 | Roman Vlasov (RUS) |

**84 KG (184.8 LB)**

| | |
|---|---|
| 1908 | Frithiof Martenson (SWE) |
| 1912 | Claes Johansson (SWE) |
| 1920 | Carl Westergren (SWE) |
| 1924 | Edward Westerlund (FIN) |
| 1928 | Väinö Kokkinen (FIN) |
| 1932 | Väinö Kokkinen (FIN) |
| 1936 | Ivar Johansson (SWE) |
| 1948 | Axel Grönberg (SWE) |
| 1952 | Axel Grönberg (SWE) |
| 1956 | Givi Kartoziya (URS) |
| 1960 | Dimitar Dobrev (BUL) |
| 1964 | Branislav Simic (YUG) |
| 1968 | Lothar Metz (GDR) |
| 1972 | Csaba Hegedus (HUN) |
| 1976 | Momir Petkovic (YUG) |
| 1980 | Gennady Korban (URS) |
| 1984 | Ion Draica (ROM) |
| 1988 | Mikhail Mamiashvili (URS) |
| 1992 | Peter Farkas (HUN) |
| 1996 | Hamza Yerlikaya (TUR) |
| 2000 | Hamza Yerlikaya (TUR) |
| 2004 | Aleksey Mishin (RUS) |
| 2008 | Andrea Minguzzi (ITA) |
| 2012 | Alan Khugayev (RUS) |

**90 KG (198.5 LB)**

| | |
|---|---|
| 1908 | Verner Weckman (FIN) |
| 1912 | Anders Ahlgren (SWE) |
| 1920 | Claes Johansson (SWE) |
| 1924 | Carl Westergren (SWE) |
| 1928 | Ibrahim Moustafa (EGY) |
| 1932 | Rudolf Svensson (SWE) |
| 1936 | Axel Cadier (SWE) |
| 1948 | Karl-Erik Nilsson (SWE) |
| 1952 | Kelpo Olavi Gröndahl (FIN) |
| 1956 | Valentin Nikolayev (URS) |
| 1960 | Tevfik Kis (TUR) |
| 1964 | Boyan Radev (BUL) |
| 1968 | Boyan Radev (BUL) |
| 1972 | Valery Rezantsev (URS) |

### Wrestling—Greco-Roman[38] (continued)

**90 KG (198.5 LB) (CONTINUED)**

| | |
|---|---|
| 1976 | Valery Rezantsev (URS) |
| 1980 | Norbert Nottny (HUN) |
| 1984 | Steven Fraser (USA) |
| 1988 | Atanas Komchev (BUL) |
| 1992 | Maik Bullmann (GER) |
| 1996 | Vyacheslav Oleynyk (UKR) |

**96 KG (211.2 LB)**

| | |
|---|---|
| 1896 | Karl Schumann (GER) |
| 1908 | Richard Weisz (HUN) |
| 1912 | Yrjö Saarela (FIN) |
| 1920 | Adolf Lindfors (FIN) |
| 1924 | Henri Deglane (FRA) |
| 1928 | Rudolf Svensson (SWE) |
| 1932 | Carl Westergren (SWE) |
| 1936 | Kristjan Palusalu (EST) |
| 1948 | Ahmet Kirecci (TUR) |
| 1952 | Johannes Kotkas (URS) |
| 1956 | Anatoly Parfenov (URS) |
| 1960 | Ivan Bogdan (URS) |
| 1964 | Istvan Kozma (HUN) |
| 1968 | Istvan Kozma (HUN) |
| 1972 | Nicolae Martinescu (ROM) |
| 1976 | Nikolay Balboshin (URS) |
| 1980 | Georgi Raikov-Petkov (BUL) |
| 1984 | Vasile Andrei (ROM) |
| 1988 | Andrzej Wronski (POL) |
| 1992 | Héctor Milian (CUB) |
| 1996 | Andrzej Wronski (POL) |
| 2000 | Mikael Ljungberg (SWE) |
| 2004 | Karam Ibrahim (EGY) |
| 2008 | Aslanbek Khushtov (RUS) |
| 2012 | Ghasem Gholamreza Rezaei (IRI) |

**120 KG (264 LB)**

| | |
|---|---|
| 1972 | Anatoly Roshchin (URS) |
| 1976 | Aleksandr Kolchinsky (URS) |
| 1980 | Aleksandr Kolchinsky (URS) |
| 1984 | Jeffrey Blatnick (USA) |
| 1988 | Aleksandr Karelin (URS) |
| 1992 | Aleksandr Karelin (UNT) |
| 1996 | Aleksandr Karelin (RUS) |
| 2000 | Rulon Gardner (USA) |
| 2004 | Khasan Baroyev (RUS) |
| 2008 | Mijain López (CUB) |
| 2012 | Mijain López Nunez (CUB) |

[1]The competitions in 1900 and 1904 are said to be unofficial. [2]Winner after disqualification of top finisher for drug use. [3]100-meter event. [4]Hurdles were 2′ 6″ high, not 3′. [5]An extra lap of 460 meters was run in error. [6]Jim Thorpe was stripped of his gold medals in 1913 when it was discovered he had briefly competed as a professional athlete; in 1982 his gold medals were restored, and he was declared "cowinner" of the events. [7]80 meters from 1932 to 1968. [8]Pentathlon from 1964 to 1980. [9]Weight classifications have been revised numerous times. [10]500 meters until 2012. [11]2,000-meter event. [12]333.3-meter event. [13]Distance has varied from 87 to 320 km. [14]Held outdoors. [15]Weight classifications were changed in 1980 and 1996. [16]Weight classifications were changed in 2000. [17]The distances in men's rowing events have varied from time to time. In 1904 it was 2 miles; in 1908, 1.5 miles; from 1912 to 1936, 2,000 meters; in 1948, 1 mile 350 yards; and since 1952, 2,000 meters (1 mile 427 yards). [18]The distance in women's rowing events was 1,000 meters until 1988, at which time it became 2,000 meters. [19]Without coxswain. [20]From 2004. [21]Open from 1996 to 2004. [22]From 1952. [23]Men-only from 1924 to 2004. [24]Open from 1932 to 2004. [25]Open from 1968 to 1992. [26]Open from 1968 to 1992. [27]100 yards. [28]220 yards. [29]500 meters. [30]440 yards. [31]1,200 meters. [32]1,000 meters. [33]1 mile. [34]100 yards. [35]440 yards. [36]300 meters. [37]Fréchette's gold medal awarded in 1993 on basis of error in scoring. [38]Weight classifications have been revised numerous times, most recently after the 1996 Games. [39]In 1976 the press lift was removed, weights given thereafter being the total for the clean and jerk and the snatch. [40]Total of five lifts.

# Winter Olympic Games

*Gold medalists in all winter events since 1908; winter sports were not included in the three Olympic Games before 1908, and separate Winter Games were not held until 1924. Note: East and West Germany fielded a joint all-Germany team in 1956, 1960, and 1964, abbreviated here as GER.*

## Biathlon (men)

### 10 KM
| | | MIN:SEC |
|---|---|---|
| 1980 | Frank Ullrich (GDR) | 32:10.69 |
| 1984 | Eirik Kvalfoss (NOR) | 30:53.8 |
| 1988 | Frank-Peter Rötsch (GDR) | 25:08.1 |
| 1992 | Mark Kirchner (GER) | 26:02.3 |
| 1994 | Sergey Chepikov (RUS) | 28:07.0 |
| 1998 | Ole Einar Bjørndalen (NOR) | 27:16.2 |
| 2002 | Ole Einar Bjørndalen (NOR) | 24:51.3 |
| 2006 | Sven Fischer (GER) | 26:11.6 |
| 2010 | Vincent Jay (FRA) | 24:07.8 |

### 12.5-KM PURSUIT
| | | MIN:SEC |
|---|---|---|
| 2002 | Ole Einar Bjørndalen (NOR) | 32:34.6 |
| 2006 | Vincent Defrasne (FRA) | 35:20.2 |
| 2010 | Björn Ferry (SWE) | 33:38.4 |

### 15-KM MASS START
| | | MIN:SEC |
|---|---|---|
| 2006 | Michael Greis (GER) | 47:20.0 |
| 2010 | Yevgeny Ustyugov (RUS) | 35:35.7 |

### 20 KM
| | | HR:MIN:SEC |
|---|---|---|
| 1960 | Klas Lestander (SWE) | 1:33:21.6 |
| 1964 | Vladimir Melanin (URS) | 1:20:26.8 |
| 1968 | Magnar Solberg (NOR) | 1:13:45.9 |
| 1972 | Magnar Solberg (NOR) | 1:15:55.50 |
| 1976 | Nikolay Kruglov (URS) | 1:14:12.26 |
| 1980 | Anatoly Alyabyev (URS) | 1:08:16.31 |
| 1984 | Peter Angerer (FRG) | 1:11:52.70 |
| 1988 | Frank-Peter Rötsch (GDR) | 56:33.3 |
| 1992 | Yevgeny Redkin (UNT) | 57:34.4 |
| 1994 | Sergey Tarasov (RUS) | 57:25.3 |
| 1998 | Halvard Hanevold (NOR) | 56:16.4 |
| 2002 | Ole Einar Bjørndalen (NOR) | 51:03.3 |
| 2006 | Michael Greis (GER) | 54:23.0 |
| 2010 | Emil Hegle Svendsen (NOR) | 48:22.5 |

### 4 × 7.5-KM RELAY
| | | HR:MIN:SEC |
|---|---|---|
| 1968 | USSR | 2:13:02.4 |
| 1972 | USSR | 1:51:44.92 |
| 1976 | USSR | 1:57:55.64 |
| 1980 | USSR | 1:34:03.27 |
| 1984 | USSR | 1:38:51.70 |
| 1988 | USSR | 1:22:30.00 |
| 1992 | Germany | 1:24:43.5 |
| 1994 | Germany | 1:30:22.1 |
| 1998 | Germany | 1:19:43.3 |
| 2002 | Norway | 1:23:42.3 |
| 2006 | Germany | 1:21:51.5 |
| 2010 | Norway | 1:21:38.1 |

### MILITARY SKI PATROL
| | |
|---|---|
| 1924 | Switzerland |
| 1928 | Norway |
| 1936 | Italy |
| 1948 | Switzerland |

### DISTANCE SHOOTING
| | |
|---|---|
| 1936 | Georg Edenhauser (AUT) |

### ICE SHOOTING (TEAM)
| | |
|---|---|
| 1936 | Austria |

### TARGET SHOOTING
| | |
|---|---|
| 1936 | Ignaz Reiterer (AUT) |

## Biathlon (women)

### 7.5 KM
| | | MIN:SEC |
|---|---|---|
| 1992 | Anfisa Restsova (UNT) | 24:29.2 |
| 1994 | Myriam Bédard (CAN) | 26:08.8 |
| 1998 | Galina Kukleva (RUS) | 23:08.0 |
| 2002 | Kati Wilhelm (GER) | 20:41.4 |
| 2006 | Florence Baverel-Robert (FRA) | 22:31.4 |
| 2010 | Anastazia Kuzmina (SVK) | 19:55.6 |

### 10-KM PURSUIT
| | | MIN:SEC |
|---|---|---|
| 2002 | Olga Pyleva (RUS) | 31:07.7 |
| 2006 | Kati Wilhelm (GER) | 36:43.6 |
| 2010 | Magdalena Neuner (GER) | 30:16.0 |

### 12.5-KM MASS START
| | | MIN:SEC |
|---|---|---|
| 2006 | Anna Carin Olofsson (SWE) | 40:36.5 |
| 2010 | Magdalena Neuner (GER) | 35:19.6 |

### 15 KM
| | | MIN:SEC |
|---|---|---|
| 1992 | Antje Misersky (GER) | 51:47.2 |
| 1994 | Myriam Bédard (CAN) | 52:06.6 |
| 1998 | Ekaterina Dafovska (BUL) | 54:52.0 |
| 2002 | Andrea Henkel (GER) | 47:29.1 |
| 2006 | Svetlana Ishmuratova (RUS) | 49:24.1 |
| 2010 | Tora Berger (NOR) | 40:52.8 |

### 4 × 6-KM RELAY[1]
| | | HR:MIN:SEC |
|---|---|---|
| 1992 | France | 1:15:55.6 |
| 1994 | Russia | 1:47:19.5 |
| 1998 | Germany | 1:40:13.6 |
| 2002 | Germany | 1:27:55.0 |
| 2006 | Russia | 1:16:12.5 |
| 2010 | Russia | 1:09:36.3 |

## Bobsled

### TWO-MAN BOBSLED
| | | MIN:SEC |
|---|---|---|
| 1932 | United States | 8:14.74 |
| 1936 | United States | 5:29.29 |
| 1948 | Switzerland | 5:29.2 |
| 1952 | West Germany | 5:24.54 |
| 1956 | Italy | 5:30.14 |
| 1964 | Great Britain | 4:21.90 |
| 1968 | Italy | 4:41.54 |
| 1972 | West Germany | 4:57.07 |
| 1976 | East Germany | 3:44.42 |
| 1980 | Switzerland | 4:09.36 |
| 1984 | East Germany | 3:25.56 |
| 1988 | USSR | 3:53.48 |
| 1992 | Switzerland | 4:03.26 |
| 1994 | Switzerland | 3:30.81 |
| 1998 | Canada; Italy (tied) | 3:37.24 |
| 2002 | Germany | 3:10.11 |
| 2006 | Germany | 3:43.38 |
| 2010 | Germany | 3:26.65 |

### FOUR-MAN BOBSLED
| | | MIN:SEC |
|---|---|---|
| 1924 | Switzerland | 5:45.54 |
| 1928[2] | United States | 3:20.5 |
| 1932 | United States | 7:53.68 |
| 1936 | Switzerland | 5:19.85 |
| 1948 | United States | 5:20.1 |
| 1952 | West Germany | 5:07.84 |
| 1956 | Switzerland | 5:10.44 |
| 1964 | Canada | 4:14.46 |
| 1968 | Italy | 2:17.39 |

# Winter Olympic Games (continued)

## Bobsled (continued)

### FOUR-MAN BOBSLED (CONTINUED)

| | | MIN:SEC |
|---|---|---|
| 1972 | Switzerland | 4:43.07 |
| 1976 | East Germany | 3:40.43 |
| 1980 | East Germany | 3:59.92 |
| 1984 | East Germany | 3:20.22 |
| 1988 | Switzerland | 3:47.51 |
| 1992 | Austria | 3:53.90 |
| 1994 | Germany | 3:27.78 |
| 1998 | Germany | 2:39.41 |
| 2002 | Germany | 3:07.51 |
| 2006 | Germany | 3:40.42 |
| 2010 | United States | 3:24.46 |

### TWO-WOMAN BOBSLED

| | | MIN:SEC |
|---|---|---|
| 2002 | United States | 1:37.76 |
| 2006 | Germany | 3:49.98 |
| 2010 | Canada | 3:32.28 |

## Curling

### MEN

| | |
|---|---|
| 1924 | Great Britain |
| 1998 | Switzerland |
| 2002 | Norway |
| 2006 | Canada |
| 2010 | Canada |

### WOMEN

| | |
|---|---|
| 1998 | Canada |
| 2002 | Great Britain |
| 2006 | Sweden |
| 2010 | Sweden |

## Figure Skating

### MEN'S SINGLES

| | |
|---|---|
| 1908 | Ulrich Salchow (SWE) |
| 1920 | Gillis Gräfström (SWE) |
| 1924 | Gillis Gräfström (SWE) |
| 1928 | Gillis Gräfström (SWE) |
| 1932 | Karl Schäfer (AUT) |
| 1936 | Karl Schäfer (AUT) |
| 1948 | Richard Button (USA) |
| 1952 | Richard Button (USA) |
| 1956 | Hayes Alan Jenkins (USA) |
| 1960 | David Jenkins (USA) |
| 1964 | Manfred Schnelldorfer (GER) |
| 1968 | Wolfgang Schwarz (AUT) |
| 1972 | Ondrej Nepela (TCH) |
| 1976 | John Curry (GBR) |
| 1980 | Robin Cousins (GBR) |
| 1984 | Scott Hamilton (USA) |
| 1988 | Brian Boitano (USA) |
| 1992 | Viktor Petrenko (UNT) |
| 1994 | Aleksey Urmanov (RUS) |
| 1998 | Ilia Kulik (RUS) |
| 2002 | Aleksey Yagudin (RUS) |
| 2006 | Yevgeny Plushchenko (RUS) |
| 2010 | Evan Lysacek (USA) |

### WOMEN'S SINGLES

| | |
|---|---|
| 1908 | Madge Syers (GBR) |
| 1920 | Magda Julin-Mauroy (SWE) |
| 1924 | Herma Planck-Szabo (AUT) |
| 1928 | Sonja Henie (NOR) |
| 1932 | Sonja Henie (NOR) |
| 1936 | Sonja Henie (NOR) |
| 1948 | Barbara Ann Scott (CAN) |
| 1952 | Jeannette Altwegg (GBR) |
| 1956 | Tenley Albright (USA) |

## Figure Skating (continued)

### WOMEN'S SINGLES (CONTINUED)

| | |
|---|---|
| 1960 | Carol Heiss (USA) |
| 1964 | Sjoukje Dijkstra (NED) |
| 1968 | Peggy Fleming (USA) |
| 1972 | Beatrix Schuba (AUT) |
| 1976 | Dorothy Hamill (USA) |
| 1980 | Annett Potzsch (GDR) |
| 1984 | Katarina Witt (GDR) |
| 1988 | Katarina Witt (GDR) |
| 1992 | Kristi Yamaguchi (USA) |
| 1994 | Oksana Bayul (UKR) |
| 1998 | Tara Lipinski (USA) |
| 2002 | Sarah Hughes (USA) |
| 2006 | Shizuka Arakawa (JPN) |
| 2010 | Kim Yu-Na (KOR) |

### PAIRS

| | |
|---|---|
| 1908 | Anna Hübler, Heinrich Burger (GER) |
| 1920 | Ludoviga Jakobsson-Eilers, Walter Jakobsson (FIN) |
| 1924 | Helene Engelmann, Alfred Berger (AUT) |
| 1928 | Andrée Joly, Pierre Brunet (FRA) |
| 1932 | Andrée Brunet-Joly, Pierre Brunet (FRA) |
| 1936 | Maxi Herber, Ernst Baier (GER) |
| 1948 | Micheline Lannoy, Pierre Baugniet (BEL) |
| 1952 | Ria Falk, Paul Falk (FRG) |
| 1956 | Elisabeth Schwarz, Kurt Oppelt (AUT) |
| 1960 | Barbara Wagner, Robert Paul (CAN) |
| 1964 | Lyudmila Belousova, Oleg Protopopov (URS) |
| 1968 | Lyudmila Belousova, Oleg Protopopov (URS) |
| 1972 | Irina Rodnina, Aleksey Ulanov (URS) |
| 1976 | Irina Rodnina, Aleksandr Zaytsev (URS) |
| 1980 | Irina Rodnina, Aleksandr Zaytsev (URS) |
| 1984 | Yelena Valova, Oleg Vasilyev (URS) |
| 1988 | Yekaterina Gordeyeva, Sergey Grinkov (URS) |
| 1992 | Natalya Mishkutyonok, Artur Dmitriyev (UNT) |
| 1994 | Yekaterina Gordeyeva, Sergey Grinkov (RUS) |
| 1998 | Oksana Kazakova, Artur Dmitriyev (RUS) |
| 2002 | Yelena Berezhnaya, Anton Sikharulidze (RUS); Jamie Sale, David Pelletier (CAN) (shared) |
| 2006 | Tatyana Totmyanina, Maksim Marinin (RUS) |
| 2010 | Shen Xue, Zhao Hongbo (CHN) |

### ICE DANCING

| | |
|---|---|
| 1976 | Lyudmila Pakhomova, Aleksandr Gorshkov (URS) |
| 1980 | Natalya Linichuk, Gennady Karponosov (URS) |
| 1984 | Jayne Torvill, Christopher Dean (GBR) |
| 1988 | Natalya Bestemyanova, Andrey Bukin (URS) |
| 1992 | Marina Klimova, Sergey Ponomarenko (UNT) |
| 1994 | Oksana Grishchuk, Yevgeny Platov (RUS) |
| 1998 | Oksana Grishchuk, Yevgeny Platov (RUS) |
| 2002 | Marina Anissina, Gwendal Peizerat (FRA) |
| 2006 | Tatyana Navka, Roman Kostomarov (RUS) |
| 2010 | Tessa Virtue, Scott Moir (CAN) |

## Ice Hockey

### MEN

| | |
|---|---|
| 1920 | Canada |
| 1924 | Canada |
| 1928 | Canada |
| 1932 | Canada |
| 1936 | Great Britain |
| 1948 | Canada |
| 1952 | Canada |
| 1956 | USSR |
| 1960 | United States |

# Winter Olympic Games (continued)

## Ice Hockey (continued)

### MEN (CONTINUED)

| | |
|---|---|
| 1964 | USSR |
| 1968 | USSR |
| 1972 | USSR |
| 1976 | USSR |
| 1980 | United States |
| 1984 | USSR |
| 1988 | USSR |
| 1992 | Unified Team |
| 1994 | Sweden |
| 1998 | Czech Republic |
| 2002 | Canada |
| 2006 | Sweden |
| 2010 | Canada |

### WOMEN

| | |
|---|---|
| 1998 | United States |
| 2002 | Canada |
| 2006 | Canada |
| 2010 | Canada |

## Luge

### MEN'S SINGLES

| | | MIN:SEC |
|---|---|---|
| 1964 | Thomas Köhler (GER) | 3:26.77 |
| 1968 | Manfred Schmid (AUT) | 2:52.48 |
| 1972 | Wolfgang Schneidel (GDR) | 3:27.58 |
| 1976 | Detlef Guenther (GDR) | 3:27.688 |
| 1980 | Bernhard Glass (GDR) | 2:54.796 |
| 1984 | Paul Hildgartner (ITA) | 3:04.258 |
| 1988 | Jens Müller (GDR) | 3:05.548 |
| 1992 | Georg Hackl (GER) | 3:02.363 |
| 1994 | Georg Hackl (GER) | 3:21.571 |
| 1998 | Georg Hackl (GER) | 3:18.436 |
| 2002 | Armin Zöggeler (ITA) | 2:57.941 |
| 2006 | Armin Zöggeler (ITA) | 3:26.088 |
| 2010 | Felix Loch (GER) | 3:13.085 |

### MEN'S DOUBLES

| | | MIN:SEC |
|---|---|---|
| 1964 | Austria | 1:41.62 |
| 1968 | East Germany | 1:35.85 |
| 1972 | Italy; East Germany (tied) | 1:28.35 |
| 1976 | East Germany | 1:25.604 |
| 1980 | East Germany | 1:19.331 |
| 1984 | West Germany | 1:23.620 |
| 1988 | East Germany | 1:31.940 |
| 1992 | Germany | 1:32.053 |
| 1994 | Italy | 1:36.720 |
| 1998 | Germany | 1:41.105 |
| 2002 | Germany | 1:26.082 |
| 2006 | Austria | 1:34.497 |
| 2010 | Austria | 1:22.705 |

### WOMEN'S SINGLES

| | | MIN:SEC |
|---|---|---|
| 1964 | Ortrun Enderlein (GER) | 3:24.67 |
| 1968 | Erica Lechner (ITA) | 2:29.37 |
| 1972 | Anna-Maria Müller (GDR) | 2:59.18 |
| 1976 | Margit Schumann (GDR) | 2:50.621 |
| 1980 | Vera Zozulya (URS) | 2:36.537 |
| 1984 | Steffi Martin (GDR) | 2:46.570 |
| 1988 | Steffi Walter-Martin (GDR) | 3:03.973 |
| 1992 | Doris Neuner (AUT) | 3:06.696 |
| 1994 | Gerda Weissensteiner (ITA) | 3:15.517 |
| 1998 | Silke Kraushaar (GER) | 3:23.779 |
| 2002 | Sylke Otto (GER) | 2:52.464 |
| 2006 | Sylke Otto (GER) | 3:07.979 |
| 2010 | Tatjana Hüfner (GER) | 2:46.524 |

## Skeleton

### MEN

| | | MIN:SEC |
|---|---|---|
| 1928 | Jennison Heaton (USA) | 3:01.8 |
| 1948 | Nino Bibbia (ITA) | 5:23.2 |
| 2002 | Jim Shea (USA) | 1:41.96 |
| 2006 | Duff Gibson (CAN) | 1:55.88 |
| 2010 | Jon Montgomery (CAN) | 3:29.73 |

### WOMEN

| | | MIN:SEC |
|---|---|---|
| 2002 | Tristan Gale (USA) | 1:45.11 |
| 2006 | Maya Pedersen (SUI) | 1:59.83 |
| 2010 | Amy Williams (GBR) | 3:35.64 |

## Alpine Skiing (men)

### DOWNHILL

| | | MIN:SEC |
|---|---|---|
| 1948 | Henri Oreiller (FRA) | 2:55.0 |
| 1952 | Zeno Colò (ITA) | 2:30.8 |
| 1956 | Toni Sailer (AUT) | 2:52.2 |
| 1960 | Jean Vuarnet (FRA) | 2:06.0 |
| 1964 | Egon Zimmermann (AUT) | 2:18.16 |
| 1968 | Jean-Claude Killy (FRA) | 1:59.85 |
| 1972 | Bernhard Russi (SUI) | 1:51.43 |
| 1976 | Franz Klammer (AUT) | 1:45.73 |
| 1980 | Leonhard Stock (AUT) | 1:45.50 |
| 1984 | Bill Johnson (USA) | 1:45.59 |
| 1988 | Pirmin Zurbriggen (SUI) | 1:59.63 |
| 1992 | Patrick Ortlieb (AUT) | 1:50.37 |
| 1994 | Tommy Moe (USA) | 1:45.75 |
| 1998 | Jean-Luc Cretier (FRA) | 1:50.11 |
| 2002 | Fritz Strobl (AUT) | 1:39.13 |
| 2006 | Antoine Dénériaz (FRA) | 1:48.80 |
| 2010 | Didier Defago (SUI) | 1:54.31 |

### SLALOM

| | | MIN:SEC |
|---|---|---|
| 1948 | Edy Reinalter (SUI) | 2:10.3 |
| 1952 | Othmar Schneider (AUT) | 2:00.0 |
| 1956 | Toni Sailer (AUT) | 3:14.7 |
| 1960 | Ernst Hinterseer (AUT) | 2:08.9 |
| 1964 | Josef Stiegler (AUT) | 2:21.13 |
| 1968 | Jean-Claude Killy (FRA) | 1:39.73 |
| 1972 | Francisco Ochoa (ESP) | 1:49.27 |
| 1976 | Piero Gros (ITA) | 2:03.29 |
| 1980 | Ingemar Stenmark (SWE) | 1:44.26 |
| 1984 | Phil Mahre (USA) | 1:39.41 |
| 1988 | Alberto Tomba (ITA) | 1:39.47 |
| 1992 | Finn Christian Jagge (NOR) | 1:44.39 |
| 1994 | Thomas Stangassinger (AUT) | 2:02.02 |
| 1998 | Hans Petter Buraas (NOR) | 1:49.31 |
| 2002 | Jean-Pierre Vidal (FRA) | 1:41.06 |
| 2006 | Benjamin Raich (AUT) | 1:43.14 |
| 2010 | Giuliano Razzoli (ITA) | 1:39.32 |

### GIANT SLALOM

| | | MIN:SEC |
|---|---|---|
| 1952 | Stein Eriksen (NOR) | 2:25.0 |
| 1956 | Toni Sailer (AUT) | 3:00.1 |
| 1960 | Roger Staub (SUI) | 1:48.3 |
| 1964 | François Bonlieu (FRA) | 1:46.71 |
| 1968 | Jean-Claude Killy (FRA) | 3:29.28 |
| 1972 | Gustavo Thöni (ITA) | 3:09.62 |
| 1976 | Heini Hemmi (SUI) | 3:26.97 |
| 1980 | Ingemar Stenmark (SWE) | 2:40.74 |
| 1984 | Max Julen (SUI) | 2:41.18 |
| 1988 | Alberto Tomba (ITA) | 2:06.37 |
| 1992 | Alberto Tomba (ITA) | 2:06.98 |
| 1994 | Markus Wasmeier (GER) | 2:52.46 |
| 1998 | Hermann Maier (AUT) | 2:38.51 |
| 2002 | Stephan Eberharter (AUT) | 2:23.28 |
| 2006 | Benjamin Raich (AUT) | 2:35.00 |
| 2010 | Carlo Janka (SUI) | 2:37.83 |

# Winter Olympic Games (continued)

## Alpine Skiing (men) (continued)

### SUPERGIANT SLALOM

| | | MIN:SEC |
|---|---|---|
| 1988 | Franck Piccard (FRA) | 1:39.66 |
| 1992 | Kjetil André Aamodt (NOR) | 1:13.04 |
| 1994 | Markus Wasmeier (GER) | 1:32.53 |
| 1998 | Hermann Maier (AUT) | 1:34.82 |
| 2002 | Kjetil André Aamodt (NOR) | 1:21.58 |
| 2006 | Kjetil André Aamodt (NOR) | 1:30.65 |
| 2010 | Aksel Lund Svindal (NOR) | 1:30.34 |

### ALPINE COMBINED[3]

| | | MIN:SEC |
|---|---|---|
| 1936 | Franz Pfnür (GER) | |
| 1948 | Henri Oreiller (FRA) | |
| 1972 | Gustavo Thöni (ITA) | |
| 1976 | Gustavo Thöni (ITA) | |
| 1988 | Hubert Strolz (AUT) | |
| 1992 | Josef Polig (ITA) | |
| 1994 | Lasse Kjus (NOR) | 3:17.53 |
| 1998 | Mario Reiter (AUT) | 3:08.06 |
| 2002 | Kjetil André Aamodt (NOR) | 3:17.56 |
| 2006 | Ted Ligety (USA) | 3:09.35 |
| 2010 | Bode Miller (USA) | 2:44.92 |

## Alpine Skiing (women)

### DOWNHILL

| | | MIN:SEC |
|---|---|---|
| 1948 | Hedy Schlunegger (SUI) | 2:28.3 |
| 1952 | Trude Jochom-Beiser (AUT) | 1:47.1 |
| 1956 | Madeleine Berthod (SUI) | 1:40.7 |
| 1960 | Heidi Beibl (GER) | 1:37.6 |
| 1964 | Christl Haas (AUT) | 1:55.39 |
| 1968 | Olga Pall (AUT) | 1:40.87 |
| 1972 | Marie-Thérèse Nadig (SUI) | 1:36.68 |
| 1976 | Rosi Mittermaier (FRG) | 1:46.16 |
| 1980 | Annemarie Moser-Pröll (AUT) | 1:37.52 |
| 1984 | Michael Figini (SUI) | 1:13.36 |
| 1988 | Marina Kiehl (FRG) | 1:25.86 |
| 1992 | Kerrin Lee-Gartner (CAN) | 1:52.55 |
| 1994 | Katja Seizinger (GER) | 1:35.93 |
| 1998 | Katja Seizinger (GER) | 1:28.29 |
| 2002 | Carole Montillet (FRA) | 1:39.56 |
| 2006 | Michaela Dorfmeister (AUT) | 1:56.49 |
| 2010 | Lindsey Vonn (USA) | 1:44.19 |

### SLALOM

| | | MIN:SEC |
|---|---|---|
| 1948 | Gretchen Fraser (USA) | 1:57.2 |
| 1952 | Andrea Lawrence-Mead (USA) | 2:10.6 |
| 1956 | Renée Colliard (SUI) | 1:52.3 |
| 1960 | Anne Heggtveit (CAN) | 1:49.6 |
| 1964 | Christine Goitschel (FRA) | 1:29.86 |
| 1968 | Marielle Goitschel (FRA) | 1:59.85 |
| 1972 | Barbara Cochran (USA) | 1:31.24 |
| 1976 | Rosi Mittermaier (FRG) | 1:30.54 |
| 1980 | Hanni Wenzel (LIE) | 1:25.09 |
| 1984 | Paoletta Magoni (ITA) | 1:36.47 |
| 1988 | Vreni Schneider (SUI) | 1:36.69 |
| 1992 | Petra Kronberger (AUT) | 1:32.68 |
| 1994 | Vreni Schneider (SUI) | 1:56.01 |
| 1998 | Hilde Gerg (GER) | 1:32.40 |
| 2002 | Janica Kostelic (CRO) | 1:46.10 |
| 2006 | Anja Pärson (SWE) | 1:29.04 |
| 2010 | Maria Riesch (GER) | 1:42.89 |

### GIANT SLALOM

| | | MIN:SEC |
|---|---|---|
| 1952 | Andrea Lawrence-Mead (USA) | 2:06.8 |
| 1956 | Ossi Reichert (GER) | 1:56.5 |
| 1960 | Yvonne Rüegg (SUI) | 1:39.9 |
| 1964 | Marielle Goitschel (FRA) | 1:52.24 |
| 1968 | Nancy Greene (CAN) | 1:51.97 |
| 1972 | Marie-Thérèse Nadig (SUI) | 1:29.90 |

## Alpine Skiing (women) (continued)

### GIANT SLALOM (CONTINUED)

| | | MIN:SEC |
|---|---|---|
| 1976 | Kathy Kreiner (CAN) | 1:29.13 |
| 1980 | Hanni Wenzel (LIE) | 2:41.66 |
| 1984 | Debbie Armstrong (USA) | 2:20.98 |
| 1988 | Vreni Schneider (SUI) | 2:06.49 |
| 1992 | Pernilla Wiberg (SWE) | 2:12.74 |
| 1994 | Deborah Compagnoni (ITA) | 2:30.97 |
| 1998 | Deborah Compagnoni (ITA) | 2:50.59 |
| 2002 | Janica Kostelic (CRO) | 2:30.01 |
| 2006 | Julia Mancuso (USA) | 2:09.19 |
| 2010 | Viktoria Rebensburg (GER) | 2:27.11 |

### SUPERGIANT SLALOM

| | | MIN:SEC |
|---|---|---|
| 1988 | Sigrid Wolf (AUT) | 1:19.03 |
| 1992 | Deborah Compagnoni (ITA) | 1:21.22 |
| 1994 | Diann Roffe-Steinrotter (USA) | 1:22.15 |
| 1998 | Picabo Street (USA) | 1:18.02 |
| 2002 | Daniela Ceccarelli (ITA) | 1:13.59 |
| 2006 | Michaela Dorfmeister (AUT) | 1:32.47 |
| 2010 | Andrea Fischbacher (AUT) | 1:20.14 |

### ALPINE COMBINED[3]

| | | MIN:SEC |
|---|---|---|
| 1936 | Chrislt Cranz (GER) | |
| 1948 | Trude Beiser (AUT) | |
| 1972 | Annemarie Pröll (AUT) | |
| 1976 | Rosi Mittermaier (FRG) | |
| 1988 | Anita Wachter (AUT) | |
| 1992 | Petra Kronberger (AUT) | |
| 1994 | Pernilla Wiberg (SWE) | 3:05.16 |
| 1998 | Katja Seizinger (GER) | 2:40.74 |
| 2002 | Janica Kostelic (CRO) | 2:43.28 |
| 2006 | Janica Kostelic (CRO) | 2:51.08 |
| 2010 | Maria Riesch (GER) | 2:09.14 |

## Freestyle Skiing

### MEN'S MOGULS

| | |
|---|---|
| 1992 | Edgar Grospiron (FRA) |
| 1994 | Jean-Luc Brassard (CAN) |
| 1998 | Jonny Moseley (USA) |
| 2002 | Janne Lahtela (FIN) |
| 2006 | Dale Begg-Smith (AUS) |
| 2010 | Alexandre Bilodeau (CAN) |

### MEN'S AERIALS

| | |
|---|---|
| 1994 | Andreas Schönbächler (SUI) |
| 1998 | Eric Bergoust (USA) |
| 2002 | Ales Valenta (CZE) |
| 2006 | Han Xiaopeng (CHN) |
| 2010 | Alexey Grishin (BLR) |

### MEN'S SKI CROSS

| | |
|---|---|
| 2010 | Michael Schmid (SUI) |

### WOMEN'S MOGULS

| | |
|---|---|
| 1992 | Donna Weinbrecht (USA) |
| 1994 | Stine Lise Hattestad (NOR) |
| 1998 | Tae Satoya (JPN) |
| 2002 | Kari Traa (NOR) |
| 2006 | Jennifer Heil (CAN) |
| 2010 | Hannah Kearney (USA) |

### WOMEN'S AERIALS

| | |
|---|---|
| 1994 | Lina Cheryazova (UZB) |
| 1998 | Nikki Stone (USA) |
| 2002 | Alisa Camplin (AUS) |
| 2006 | Evelyne Leu (SUI) |
| 2010 | Lydia Lassila (AUS) |

# Winter Olympic Games (continued)

## Freestyle Skiing (continued)

**WOMEN'S SKI CROSS**

2010　Ashleigh McIvor (CAN)

## Nordic Skiing (men)

**1.5-KM CROSS-COUNTRY SPRINT**

| | | MIN:SEC |
|---|---|---|
| 2002 | Tor Arne Hetland (NOR) | 2:56.9 |
| 2006 | Björn Lind (SWE) | 2:26.5 |
| 2010 | Nikita Kriyukov (RUS) | 3:36.3 |

**TEAM SPRINT**

| | | MIN:SEC |
|---|---|---|
| 2006 | Sweden | 17:02.9 |
| 2010 | Norway | 19:1.0 |

**10-KM CROSS-COUNTRY**

| | | MIN:SEC |
|---|---|---|
| 1992 | Vegard Ulvang (NOR) | 27:36.0 |
| 1994 | Bjørn Daehlie (NOR) | 24:20.1 |
| 1998 | Bjørn Daehlie (NOR) | 27:24.5 |

**15-KM CROSS-COUNTRY[4]**

| | | HR:MIN:SEC |
|---|---|---|
| 1924 | Thorleif Haug (NOR) | 1:14:31.0 |
| 1928 | Johan Grøttumsbråten (NOR) | 1:37:01.0 |
| 1932 | Sven Utterström (SWE) | 1:23:07.0 |
| 1936 | Erik-August Larsson (SWE) | 1:14:38.0 |
| 1948 | Martin Lundström (SWE) | 1:13:50.0 |
| 1952 | Hallgeir Brenden (NOR) | 1:01:34.0 |
| 1956 | Hallgeir Brenden (NOR) | 49:39.0 |
| 1960 | Hakkon Brusveen (NOR) | 51:55.5 |
| 1964 | Eero Mäntyranta (FIN) | 50:54.1 |
| 1968 | Harald Grönningen (NOR) | 47:54.2 |
| 1972 | Sven-Ake Lundbäck (SWE) | 45:28.24 |
| 1976 | Nikolay Bazhukov (URS) | 43:58.47 |
| 1980 | Thomas Wassberg (SWE) | 41:57.63 |
| 1984 | Gunde Svan (SWE) | 41:25.60 |
| 1988 | Mikhail Devyatyarov (URS) | 41:18.9 |
| 1998 | Thomas Alsgaard (NOR) | 39:13.7 |
| 2002 | Andrus Veerpalu (EST) | 37:07.4 |
| 2006 | Andrus Veerpalu (EST) | 38:01.3 |
| 2010 | Dario Cologna (SUI) | 33:36.3 |

**COMBINED PURSUIT[5]**

| | | HR:MIN:SEC |
|---|---|---|
| 1992 | Bjørn Daehlie (NOR) | 1:05:37.9 |
| 1994 | Bjørn Daehlie (NOR) | 1:00:08.8 |
| 1998 | Thomas Alsgaard (NOR) | 1:07:01.7 |
| 2002 | Thomas Alsgaard (NOR); Frode Estil (NOR) (tied)[6] | 49:48.9 |
| 2006 | Yevgeny Dementyev (RUS) | 1:17:00.8 |
| 2010 | Marcus Hellner (SWE) | 1:15:11.4 |

**30-KM CROSS-COUNTRY**

| | | HR:MIN:SEC |
|---|---|---|
| 1956 | Veikko Hakulinen (FIN) | 1:44:06.0 |
| 1960 | Sixten Jernberg (SWE) | 1:51:03.9 |
| 1964 | Eero Mäntyranta (FIN) | 1:30:50.7 |
| 1968 | Franco Nones (ITA) | 1:35:39.2 |
| 1972 | Vyacheslav Vedenin (URS) | 1:36:31.15 |
| 1976 | Sergey Savelyev (URS) | 1:30:29.38 |
| 1980 | Nikolay Zimyatov (URS) | 1:27:02.80 |
| 1984 | Nikolay Zimyatov (URS) | 1:28:56.30 |
| 1988 | Aleksey Prokourorov (URS) | 1:24:26.3 |
| 1992 | Vegard Ulvang (NOR) | 1:22:27.8 |
| 1994 | Thomas Alsgaard (NOR) | 1:12:26.4 |
| 1998 | Mika Myllylä (FIN) | 1:33:56.0 |
| 2002 | Christian Hoffmann (AUT)[6] | 1:11:31.0 |

**50-KM CROSS-COUNTRY**

| | | HR:MIN:SEC |
|---|---|---|
| 1924 | Thorleif Haug (NOR) | 3:44:32.0 |
| 1928 | Per Erik Hedlund (SWE) | 4:52:03.3 |
| 1932 | Veli Saarinen (FIN) | 4:28:00.0 |
| 1936 | Elis Viklund (SWE) | 3:30:11.0 |

## Nordic Skiing (men) (continued)

**50-KM CROSS-COUNTRY (CONTINUED)**

| | | HR:MIN:SEC |
|---|---|---|
| 1948 | Nils Karlsson (SWE) | 3:47:48.0 |
| 1952 | Veikko Hakulinen (FIN) | 3:33:33.0 |
| 1956 | Sixten Jernberg (SWE) | 2:50:27.0 |
| 1960 | Kalevi Hämäläinen (FIN) | 2:59:06.3 |
| 1964 | Sixten Jernberg (SWE) | 2:43:52.6 |
| 1968 | Olle Ellefsäter (NOR) | 2:28:45.8 |
| 1972 | Pål Tyldum (NOR) | 2:43:14.75 |
| 1976 | Ivar Formo (NOR) | 2:37:30.05 |
| 1980 | Nikolay Zimyatov (URS) | 2:27:24.60 |
| 1984 | Thomas Wassberg (SWE) | 2:15:55.80 |
| 1988 | Gunde Svan (SWE) | 2:04:30.9 |
| 1992 | Bjørn Daehlie (NOR) | 2:03:41.5 |
| 1994 | Vladimir Smirnov (KAZ) | 2:07:20.3 |
| 1998 | Bjørn Daehlie (NOR) | 2:05:08.2 |
| 2002 | Mikhail Ivanov (RUS)[6] | 2:06:20.8 |
| 2006 | Giorgio Di Centa (ITA) | 2:06:11.8 |
| 2010 | Petter Northug (NOR) | 2:05:35.5 |

**4 × 10-KM RELAY**

| | | HR:MIN:SEC |
|---|---|---|
| 1936 | Finland | 2:41:33.0 |
| 1948 | Sweden | 2:32:08.0 |
| 1952 | Finland | 2:20:16.0 |
| 1956 | USSR | 2:15:30.0 |
| 1960 | Finland | 2:18:45.6 |
| 1964 | Sweden | 2:18:34.6 |
| 1968 | Norway | 2:08:33.5 |
| 1972 | USSR | 2:04:47.94 |
| 1976 | Finland | 2:07:59.72 |
| 1980 | USSR | 1:57:03.46 |
| 1984 | Sweden | 1:55:06.30 |
| 1988 | Sweden | 1:43:58.6 |
| 1992 | Norway | 1:39:26.0 |
| 1994 | Italy | 1:41:15.0 |
| 1998 | Norway | 1:40:55.7 |
| 2002 | Norway | 1:32:45.5 |
| 2006 | Italy | 1:43:45.7 |
| 2010 | Sweden | 1:45:05.4 |

**SKI JUMPING (70 METERS)[7]**

| 1924 | Jacob Tullin Thams (NOR) |
|---|---|
| 1928 | Alf Andersen (NOR) |
| 1932 | Birger Ruud (NOR) |
| 1936 | Birger Ruud (NOR) |
| 1948 | Petter Hugsted (NOR) |
| 1952 | Arnfinn Bergmann (NOR) |
| 1956 | Antti Hyvärinen (FIN) |
| 1960 | Helmut Recknagel (GER) |
| 1964 | Veikko Kankkonen (FIN) |
| 1968 | Jiri Raska (TCH) |
| 1972 | Yukio Kasaya (JPN) |
| 1976 | Hans-Georg Aschenbach (GDR) |
| 1980 | Toni Innauer (AUT) |
| 1984 | Jens Weissflog (GDR) |
| 1988 | Matti Nykänen (FIN) |

**SKI JUMPING (95 METERS)[7]**

| 1964 | Toralf Engan (NOR) |
|---|---|
| 1968 | Vladimir Belousov (URS) |
| 1972 | Wojciech Fortuna (POL) |
| 1976 | Karl Schnabl (AUT) |
| 1980 | Jens Tormanen (FIN) |
| 1984 | Matti Nykänen (FIN) |
| 1988 | Matti Nykänen (FIN) |
| 1992 | Ernst Vettori (AUT) |
| 1994 | Espen Bredesen (NOR) |
| 1998 | Jani Soininen (FIN) |
| 2002 | Simon Ammann (SUI) |

# Winter Olympic Games (continued)

## Nordic Skiing (men) (continued)

**SKI JUMPING (95 METERS)[7] (CONTINUED)**

| | |
|---|---|
| 2006 | Lars Bystøl (NOR) |
| 2010 | Simon Ammann (SUI) |

**SKI JUMPING (125 METERS)[7]**

| | |
|---|---|
| 1992 | Toni Nieminen (FIN) |
| 1994 | Jens Weissflog (GER) |
| 1998 | Kazuyoshi Funaki (JPN) |
| 2002 | Simon Ammann (SUI) |
| 2006 | Thomas Morgenstern (AUT) |
| 2010 | Simon Ammann (SUI) |

**NORDIC COMBINED SPRINT (7.5 KM)[8]**

| | |
|---|---|
| 2002 | Samppa Lajunen (FIN) |
| 2006 | Felix Gottwald (AUT) |

**NORDIC COMBINED INDIVIDUAL NORMAL HILL[8]**

| | |
|---|---|
| 2010 | Jason Lamy Chappuis (FRA) |

**NORDIC COMBINED INDIVIDUAL LARGE HILL[8]**

| | |
|---|---|
| 1924 | Thorleif Haug (NOR) |
| 1928 | Johan Grøttumsbråten (NOR) |
| 1932 | Johan Grøttumsbråten (NOR) |
| 1936 | Oddbjörn Hagen (NOR) |
| 1948 | Heikki Hasu (FIN) |
| 1952 | Simon Slåttvik (NOR) |
| 1956 | Sverre Stenersen (NOR) |
| 1960 | Georg Thoma (GER) |
| 1964 | Tormod Knutsen (NOR) |
| 1968 | Franz Keller (FRG) |
| 1972 | Ulrich Wehling (GDR) |
| 1976 | Ulrich Wehling (GDR) |
| 1980 | Ulrich Wehling (GDR) |
| 1984 | Tom Sandberg (NOR) |
| 1988 | Hippolyt Kempf (SUI) |
| 1992 | Fabrice Guy (FRA) |
| 1994 | Fred Børre Lundberg (NOR) |
| 1998 | Bjarte Engen Vik (NOR) |
| 2002 | Samppa Lajunen (FIN) |
| 2006 | Georg Hettich (GER) |
| 2010 | Bill Demong (USA) |

**TEAM SKI JUMPING (125 METERS)[9]**

| | |
|---|---|
| 1988 | Finland |
| 1992 | Finland |
| 1994 | Germany |
| 1998 | Japan |
| 2002 | Germany |
| 2006 | Austria |
| 2010 | Austria |

**NORDIC COMBINED TEAM RELAY**

| | |
|---|---|
| 1988 | West Germany |
| 1992 | Japan |
| 1994 | Japan |
| 1998 | Norway |
| 2002 | Finland |
| 2006 | Austria |
| 2010 | Austria |

## Nordic Skiing (women)

**1.5-KM CROSS-COUNTRY SPRINT**

| | | MIN:SEC |
|---|---|---|
| 2002 | Yuliya Chepalova (RUS) | 3:10.6 |
| 2006 | Chandra Crawford (CAN) | 2:12.3 |
| 2010 | Marit Bjørgen (NOR) | 3:39.2 |

## Nordic Skiing (women) (continued)

**TEAM SPRINT**

| | | MIN:SEC |
|---|---|---|
| 2006 | Sweden | 16:36.9 |
| 2010 | Germany | 18:03.7 |

**5-KM CROSS-COUNTRY**

| | | MIN:SEC |
|---|---|---|
| 1964 | Klavdiya Boyarskikh (URS) | 17:50.5 |
| 1968 | Toini Gustafsson (SWE) | 16:45.2 |
| 1972 | Galina Kulakova (URS) | 17:00.50 |
| 1976 | Helena Takalo (FIN) | 15:48.69 |
| 1980 | Raisa Smetanina (URS) | 15:06.92 |
| 1984 | Marja-Liisa Hämäläinen (FIN) | 17:04.00 |
| 1988 | Marjo Matikainen (FIN) | 15:04.00 |
| 1992 | Marjut Lukkarinen (FIN) | 14:13.8 |
| 1994 | Lyubov Yegorova (RUS) | 14:08.8 |
| 1998 | Larisa Lazutina (RUS) | 17:39.9 |

**10-KM CROSS-COUNTRY**

| | | MIN:SEC |
|---|---|---|
| 1952 | Lydia Wideman (FIN) | 41:40.0 |
| 1956 | Lyubov Kozyreva (URS) | 38:11.0 |
| 1960 | Mariya Gusakova (URS) | 39:46.6 |
| 1964 | Klavdiya Boyarskikh (URS) | 40:24.3 |
| 1968 | Toini Gustafsson (SWE) | 36:46.5 |
| 1972 | Galina Kulakova (URS) | 34:17.82 |
| 1976 | Raisa Smetanina (URS) | 30:13.41 |
| 1980 | Barbara Petzold (GDR) | 30:31.54 |
| 1984 | Marja-Liisa Hämäläinen (FIN) | 31:44.20 |
| 1988 | Vida Ventsene (URS) | 30:08.30 |
| 1998 | Larisa Lazutina (RUS) | 46:06.9 |
| 2002 | Bente Skari (NOR) | 28:05.6 |
| 2006 | Kristina Smigun (EST) | 27:51.4 |
| 2010 | Charlotte Kalla (SWE) | 24:58.4 |

**COMBINED PURSUIT[10]**

| | | MIN:SEC |
|---|---|---|
| 1992 | Lyubov Yegorova (UNT) | 40:08.4 |
| 1994 | Lyubov Yegorova (RUS) | 41:38.1 |
| 1998 | Larisa Lazutina (RUS) | 46:06.9 |
| 2002 | Beckie Scott (CAN)[6] | 25:09.9 |
| 2006 | Kristina Smigun (EST) | 42:48.7 |
| 2010 | Marit Bjørgen (NOR) | 39:58.1 |

**15-KM CROSS-COUNTRY**

| | | MIN:SEC |
|---|---|---|
| 1992 | Lyubov Yegorova (UNT) | 42:20.8 |
| 1994 | Manuela Di Centa (ITA) | 39:44.5 |
| 1998 | Olga Danilova (RUS) | 46:55.40 |
| 2002 | Stefania Belmondo (ITA) | 39:54.4 |

**20-KM CROSS-COUNTRY**

| | | HR:MIN:SEC |
|---|---|---|
| 1984 | Marja-Liisa Hämäläinen (FIN) | 1:01:45.0 |
| 1988 | Tamara Tikhonova (URS) | 55:53.6 |

**30-KM CROSS-COUNTRY**

| | | HR:MIN:SEC |
|---|---|---|
| 1992 | Stefania Belmondo (ITA) | 1:22:30.1 |
| 1994 | Manuela Di Centa (ITA) | 1:25:41.6 |
| 1998 | Yuliya Chepalova (RUS) | 1:22:01.5 |
| 2002 | Gabriella Paruzzi (ITA)[6] | 1:30:57.1 |
| 2006 | Katerina Neumannova (CZE) | 1:22:25.4 |
| 2010 | Justyna Kowalczyk (POL) | 1:30:33.7 |

**4 × 5-KM RELAY[11]**

| | | HR:MIN:SEC |
|---|---|---|
| 1956 | Finland | 1:09:01.0 |
| 1960 | Sweden | 1:04:21.4 |
| 1964 | USSR | 59:20.2 |
| 1968 | Norway | 57:30.0 |
| 1972 | USSR | 48:46.15 |
| 1976 | USSR | 1:07:49.75 |
| 1980 | East Germany | 1:02:11.10 |
| 1984 | Norway | 1:06:49.70 |
| 1988 | USSR | 59:51.10 |

# Winter Olympic Games (continued)

### Nordic Skiing (women) (continued)

**4 × 5-KM RELAY[11] (CONTINUED)**

| | | HR:MIN:SEC |
|---|---|---|
| 1992 | Unified Team | 59:34.8 |
| 1994 | Russia | 57:12.5 |
| 1998 | Russia | 55:13.5 |
| 2002 | Germany | 49:30.6 |
| 2006 | Russia | 54:47.7 |
| 2010 | Norway | 55:19.5 |

### Sled-dog Race

| | |
|---|---|
| 1932 | Emile St. Goddard (CAN) |

### Snowboarding (men)

**GIANT SLALOM**

| | |
|---|---|
| 1998 | Ross Rebagliati (CAN) |
| 2002 | Philipp Schoch (SUI) |
| 2006 | Philipp Schoch (SUI) |
| 2010 | Jasey Jay Anderson (CAN) |

**HALFPIPE**

| | |
|---|---|
| 1998 | Gian Simmen (SUI) |
| 2002 | Ross Powers (USA) |
| 2006 | Shaun White (USA) |
| 2010 | Shaun White (USA) |

**SNOWBOARDCROSS**

| | |
|---|---|
| 2006 | Seth Wescott (USA) |
| 2010 | Seth Wescott (USA) |

### Snowboarding (women)

**GIANT SLALOM**

| | |
|---|---|
| 1998 | Karine Ruby (FRA) |
| 2002 | Isabelle Blanc (FRA) |
| 2006 | Daniela Meuli (SUI) |
| 2010 | Nicolien Sauerbreij (NED) |

**HALFPIPE**

| | |
|---|---|
| 1998 | Nicola Thost (GER) |
| 2002 | Kelly Clark (USA) |
| 2006 | Hannah Teter (USA) |
| 2010 | Torah Bright (AUS) |

**SNOWBOARDCROSS**

| | |
|---|---|
| 2006 | Tanja Frieden (SUI) |
| 2010 | Maelle Ricker (CAN) |

### Speed Skating (men)

**500 METERS**

| | | SEC |
|---|---|---|
| 1924 | Charles Jewtraw (USA) | 44.0 |
| 1928 | Clas Thunberg (FIN); Bernt Evensen (NOR) (tied) | 43.4 |
| 1932 | John Shea (USA) | 43.4 |
| 1936 | Ivar Ballangrud (NOR) | 43.4 |
| 1948 | Finn Helgesen (NOR) | 43.1 |
| 1952 | Kenneth Henry (USA) | 43.2 |
| 1956 | Yevgeny Grishin (URS) | 40.2 |
| 1960 | Yevgeny Grishin (URS) | 40.2 |
| 1964 | Richard McDermott (USA) | 40.1 |
| 1968 | Erhard Keller (FRG) | 40.3 |
| 1972 | Erhard Keller (FRG) | 39.44 |
| 1976 | Yevgeny Kulikov (URS) | 39.17 |
| 1980 | Eric Heiden (USA) | 38.03 |
| 1984 | Sergey Fokichev (URS) | 38.19 |
| 1988 | Uwe-Jens Mey (GDR) | 36.45 |
| 1992 | Uwe-Jens Mey (GER) | 37.14 |
| 1994 | Aleksandr Golubyov (RUS) | 36.33 |
| 1998 | Hiroyasu Shimizu (JPN) | 71.35[12] |
| 2002 | Casey Fitzrandolph (USA) | 69.23[12] |

### Speed Skating (men) (continued)

**500 METERS (CONTINUED)**

| | | SEC |
|---|---|---|
| 2006 | Joey Cheek (USA) | 69.76[12] |
| 2010 | Mo Tae-Bum (KOR) | 69.82[12] |

**1,000 METERS**

| | | MIN:SEC |
|---|---|---|
| 1976 | Peter Mueller (USA) | 1:19.32 |
| 1980 | Eric Heiden (USA) | 1:15.18 |
| 1984 | Gaetan Boucher (CAN) | 1:15.80 |
| 1988 | Nikolay Gulyayev (URS) | 1:13.03 |
| 1992 | Olaf Zinke (GER) | 1:14.85 |
| 1994 | Dan Jansen (USA) | 1:12.43 |
| 1998 | Ids Postma (NED) | 1:10.71 |
| 2002 | Gerard van Velde (NED) | 1:07.18 |
| 2006 | Shani Davis (USA) | 1:08.89 |
| 2010 | Shani Davis (USA) | 1:08.94 |

**1,500 METERS**

| | | MIN:SEC |
|---|---|---|
| 1924 | Clas Thunberg (FIN) | 2:20.8 |
| 1928 | Clas Thunberg (FIN) | 2:21.1 |
| 1932 | John Shea (USA) | 2:57.5 |
| 1936 | Charles Mathisen (NOR) | 2:19.2 |
| 1948 | Sverre Farstad (NOR) | 2:17.6 |
| 1952 | Hjalmar Andersen (NOR) | 2:20.4 |
| 1956 | Yury Mikhaylov (URS); Yevgeny Grishin (URS) (tied) | 2:08.6 |
| 1960 | Yevgeny Grishin (URS); Roald Aas (NOR) (tied) | 2:10.4 |
| 1964 | Ants Antson (URS) | 2:10.3 |
| 1968 | Cornelis Verkerk (NED) | 2:03.4 |
| 1972 | Ard Schenk (NED) | 2:02.96 |
| 1976 | Jan Egil Storholt (NOR) | 1:59.38 |
| 1980 | Eric Heiden (USA) | 1:55.44 |
| 1984 | Gaetan Boucher (CAN) | 1:58.36 |
| 1988 | André Hoffmann (GDR) | 1:52.06 |
| 1992 | Johann Olav Koss (NOR) | 1:54.81 |
| 1994 | Johann Olav Koss (NOR) | 1:51.29 |
| 1998 | Ådne Søndrål (NOR) | 1:47.87 |
| 2002 | Derek Parra (USA) | 1:43.95 |
| 2006 | Enrico Fabris (ITA) | 1:45.97 |
| 2010 | Mark Tuitert (NED) | 1:45.57 |

**5,000 METERS**

| | | MIN:SEC |
|---|---|---|
| 1924 | Clas Thunberg (FIN) | 8:39.0 |
| 1928 | Ivar Ballangrud (NOR) | 8:50.5 |
| 1932 | Irving Jaffee (USA) | 9:40.8 |
| 1936 | Ivar Ballangrud (NOR) | 8:19.6 |
| 1948 | Reidar Liaklev (NOR) | 8:29.4 |
| 1952 | Hjalmar Andersen (NOR) | 8:10.6 |
| 1956 | Boris Shilkov (URS) | 7:48.7 |
| 1960 | Viktor Kosichkin (URS) | 7:51.3 |
| 1964 | Knut Johannesen (NOR) | 7:38.4 |
| 1968 | Fred Anton Maier (NOR) | 7:22.4 |
| 1972 | Ard Schenk (NED) | 7:23.61 |
| 1976 | Sten Stensen (NOR) | 7:24.48 |
| 1980 | Eric Heiden (USA) | 7:02.29 |
| 1984 | Thomas Gustafson (SWE) | 7:12.28 |
| 1988 | Thomas Gustafson (SWE) | 6:44.63 |
| 1992 | Geir Karlstad (NOR) | 6:59.97 |
| 1994 | Johann Olav Koss (NOR) | 6:34.96 |
| 1998 | Gianni Romme (NED) | 6:22.20 |
| 2002 | Jochem Uytdehaage (NED) | 6:14.66 |
| 2006 | Chad Hedrick (USA) | 6:14.68 |
| 2010 | Sven Kramer (NED) | 6:14.60 |

**10,000 METERS**

| | | MIN:SEC |
|---|---|---|
| 1924 | Julius Skutnabb (FIN) | 18:04.8 |
| 1932 | Irving Jaffee (USA) | 19:13.6 |
| 1936 | Ivar Ballangrud (NOR) | 17:24.3 |

# Winter Olympic Games (continued)

## Speed Skating (men) (continued)

### 10,000 METERS (CONTINUED)

| | | MIN:SEC |
|---|---|---|
| 1948 | Ake Seyffarth (SWE) | 17:26.3 |
| 1952 | Hjalmar Andersen (NOR) | 16:45.8 |
| 1956 | Sigvard Ericsson (SWE) | 16:35.9 |
| 1960 | Knut Johannesen (NOR) | 15:46.6 |
| 1964 | Jonny Nilsson (SWE) | 15:50.1 |
| 1968 | Johnny Höglin (SWE) | 15:23.6 |
| 1972 | Ard Schenk (NED) | 15:01.35 |
| 1976 | Piet Kleine (NED) | 14:50.59 |
| 1980 | Eric Heiden (USA) | 14:28.13 |
| 1984 | Igor Malkov (URS) | 14:39.90 |
| 1988 | Thomas Gustafson (SWE) | 13:48.20 |
| 1992 | Bart Veldkamp (NED) | 14:12.12 |
| 1994 | Johann Olav Koss (NOR) | 13:30.55 |
| 1998 | Gianni Romme (NED) | 13:15.33 |
| 2002 | Jochem Uytdehaage (NED) | 12:58.92 |
| 2006 | Bob de Jong (NED) | 13:01.57 |
| 2010 | Lee Seung-Hoon (KOR) | 12:58.55 |

### COMBINED SPEED SKATING

| | |
|---|---|
| 1924 | Clas Thunberg (FIN) |

### TEAM PURSUIT

| | | MIN:SEC |
|---|---|---|
| 2006 | Italy | 3:44.46 |
| 2010 | Canada | 3:41.37 |

## Speed Skating (women)

### 500 METERS

| | | SEC |
|---|---|---|
| 1960 | Helga Haase (GER) | 45.9 |
| 1964 | Lidiya Skoblikova (URS) | 45.0 |
| 1972 | Anne Henning (USA) | 43.33 |
| 1976 | Sheila Young (USA) | 42.76 |
| 1980 | Karin Enke (GDR) | 41.78 |
| 1984 | Christa Rothenburger (GDR) | 41.02 |
| 1988 | Bonnie Blair (USA) | 39.10 |
| 1992 | Bonnie Blair (USA) | 40.33 |
| 1994 | Bonnie Blair (USA) | 39.25 |
| 1998 | Catriona LeMay Doan (CAN) | 76.60[12] |
| 2002 | Catriona LeMay Doan (CAN) | 74.75[12] |
| 2006 | Svetlana Zhurova (RUS) | 76.57[12] |
| 2010 | Lee Sang-Hwa (KOR) | 76.09[12] |

### 1,000 METERS

| | | MIN:SEC |
|---|---|---|
| 1960 | Klara Guseva (URS) | 1:34.1 |
| 1964 | Lidiya Skoblikova (URS) | 1:32.6 |
| 1968 | Carolina Geijssen (NED) | 1:32.6 |
| 1972 | Monika Pflug (FRG) | 1:31.40 |
| 1976 | Tatyana Averina (URS) | 1:28.43 |
| 1980 | Natalya Petruseva (URS) | 1:24.10 |
| 1984 | Karin Enke (GDR) | 1:21.61 |
| 1988 | Christa Rothenburger (GDR) | 1:17.65 |
| 1992 | Bonnie Blair (USA) | 1:21.90 |
| 1994 | Bonnie Blair (USA) | 1:18.74 |
| 1998 | Marianne Timmer (NED) | 1:16.51 |
| 2002 | Chris Witty (USA) | 1:13.83 |
| 2006 | Marianne Timmer (NED) | 1:16.05 |
| 2010 | Christine Nesbitt (CAN) | 1:16.56 |

### 1,500 METERS

| | | MIN:SEC |
|---|---|---|
| 1960 | Lidiya Skoblikova (URS) | 2:25.2 |
| 1964 | Lidiya Skoblikova (URS) | 2:22.6 |
| 1968 | Kaija Mustonen (FIN) | 2:22.4 |
| 1972 | Dianne Holum (USA) | 2:20.85 |
| 1976 | Galina Stepanskaya (URS) | 2:16.58 |
| 1980 | Annie Borckink (NED) | 2:10.95 |
| 1984 | Karin Enke (GDR) | 2:03.42 |
| 1988 | Yvonne van Gennip (NED) | 2:00.68 |
| 1992 | Jacqueline Börner (GER) | 2:05.87 |

## Speed Skating (women) (continued)

### 1,500 METERS (CONTINUED)

| | | MIN:SEC |
|---|---|---|
| 1994 | Emese Hunyady (AUT) | 2:02.19 |
| 1998 | Marianne Timmer (NED) | 1:57.58 |
| 2002 | Anni Friesinger (GER) | 1:54.02 |
| 2006 | Cindy Klassen (CAN) | 1:55.27 |
| 2010 | Ireen Wüst (NED) | 1:56.89 |

### 3,000 METERS

| | | MIN:SEC |
|---|---|---|
| 1960 | Lidiya Skoblikova (URS) | 5:14.3 |
| 1964 | Lidiya Skoblikova (URS) | 5:14.9 |
| 1968 | Johanna Schut (NED) | 4:56.2 |
| 1972 | Christina Baas-Kaiser (NED) | 4:52.14 |
| 1976 | Tatyana Averina (URS) | 4:45.19 |
| 1980 | Björg Eva Jensen (NOR) | 4:32.13 |
| 1984 | Andrea Schöne (GDR) | 4:24.79 |
| 1988 | Yvonne van Gennip (NED) | 4:11.94 |
| 1992 | Gunda Niemann (GER) | 4:19.90 |
| 1994 | Svetlana Bazhanova (RUS) | 4:17.43 |
| 1998 | Gunda Niemann-Stirnemann (GER) | 4:07.29 |
| 2002 | Claudia Pechstein (GER) | 3:57.70 |
| 2006 | Ireen Wüst (NED) | 4:02.43 |
| 2010 | Martina Sablikova (CZE) | 4:02.53 |

### 5,000 METERS

| | | MIN:SEC |
|---|---|---|
| 1988 | Yvonne van Gennip (NED) | 7:14.13 |
| 1992 | Gunda Niemann (GER) | 7:31.57 |
| 1994 | Claudia Pechstein (GER) | 7:14.37 |
| 1998 | Claudia Pechstein (GER) | 6:59.61 |
| 2002 | Claudia Pechstein (GER) | 6:46.91 |
| 2006 | Clara Hughes (CAN) | 6:59.07 |
| 2010 | Martina Sablikova (CZE) | 6:50.91 |

### TEAM PURSUIT

| | | MIN:SEC |
|---|---|---|
| 2006 | Germany | 3:01.25 |
| 2010 | Germany | 3:02.82 |

## Short-Track Speed Skating (men)

### 500 METERS

| | | SEC |
|---|---|---|
| 1994 | Chae Ji-Hoon (KOR) | 43.45 |
| 1998 | Takafumi Nishitani (JPN) | 42.862 |
| 2002 | Marc Gagnon (CAN) | 41.802 |
| 2006 | Apolo Anton Ohno (USA) | 41.935 |
| 2010 | Charles Hamelin (CAN) | 40.981 |

### 1,000 METERS

| | | MIN:SEC |
|---|---|---|
| 1992 | Kim Ki-Hoon (KOR) | 1:30.76 |
| 1994 | Kim Ki-Hoon (KOR) | 1:34.57 |
| 1998 | Kim Dong Sung (KOR) | 1:32.428 |
| 2002 | Steven Bradbury (AUS) | 1:29.109 |
| 2006 | Ahn Hyun Soo (KOR) | 1:26.739 |
| 2010 | Lee Jung-Su (KOR) | 1:23.747 |

### 1,500 METERS

| | | MIN:SEC |
|---|---|---|
| 2002 | Apolo Anton Ohno (USA) | 2:18.541 |
| 2006 | Ahn Hyun Soo (KOR) | 2:25.341 |
| 2010 | Lee Jung-Su (KOR) | 2:17.611 |

### 5,000-METER RELAY

| | | MIN:SEC |
|---|---|---|
| 1992 | Republic of Korea | 7:14.02 |
| 1994 | Italy | 7:11.74 |
| 1998 | Canada | 7:06.075 |
| 2002 | Canada | 6:51.579 |
| 2006 | Republic of Korea | 6:43.376 |
| 2010 | Canada | 6:44.224 |

## Winter Olympic Games (continued)

### Short-Track Speed Skating (women)

| 500 METERS | | SEC |
|---|---|---|
| 1992 | Cathy Turner (USA) | 47.04 |
| 1994 | Cathy Turner (USA) | 45.98 |
| 1998 | Annie Perreault (CAN) | 46.568 |
| 2002 | Yang Yang (A) (CHN) | 44.187 |
| 2006 | Wang Meng (CHN) | 44.345 |
| 2010 | Wang Meng (CHN) | 43.048 |

| 1,000 METERS | | MIN:SEC |
|---|---|---|
| 1994 | Chun Lee-Kyung (KOR) | 1:36.87 |
| 1998 | Chun Lee-Kyung (KOR) | 1:42.776 |
| 2002 | Yang Yang (A) (CHN) | 1:36.391 |
| 2006 | Jin Sun Yu (KOR) | 1:32.859 |
| 2010 | Wang Meng (CHN) | 1:29.213 |

### Short-Track Speed Skating (women) (continued)

| 1,500 METERS | | MIN:SEC |
|---|---|---|
| 2002 | Ko Gi-Hyun (KOR) | 2:31.581 |
| 2006 | Jin Sun Yu (KOR) | 2:23.494 |
| 2010 | Zhou Yang (CHN) | 2:16.993 |

| 3,000-METER RELAY | | MIN:SEC |
|---|---|---|
| 1992 | Canada | 4:36.62 |
| 1994 | Republic of Korea | 4:26.64 |
| 1998 | Republic of Korea | 4:16.260 |
| 2002 | Republic of Korea | 4:12.793 |
| 2006 | Republic of Korea | 4:17.040 |
| 2010 | China | 4:06.610 |

### Winter Pentathlon[13]

| 1948 | Gustav Lindh (SWE) |
|---|---|

[1]In 1992 the relay was 3 × 7.5 km; from 1994 to 2002 it was 4 × 7.5 km.   [2]Five men.   [3]Competition scored on points until 1994.   [4]From 1924 to 1952, the event was 18 km.   [5]Results of a 10- or 15-km classical leg determine the starting order of a 10- or 15-km freestyle leg, the first finisher of which is the overall winner; each leg was 15 km in the 2010 Games.   [6]Winner after disqualification of top finisher for drug use.   [7]From 1924 to 1960 the jumping was held on one 70-meter hill. In 1964 there were two events, one on a 70-meter and the other on an 80-meter hill; from 1968 to 1988 there were 70-meter and 90-meter events; from 1992 to 2002 there were 90-meter and 120-meter events; and in 2006 there were 95-meter and 125-meter events.   [8]In 2010 the competition format was changed to consist of only individual normal hill and large hill.   [9]In 1988 the event was 90 meters; from 1992 to 2002 it was 120 meters.   [10]Results of a 5- or 7.5-km classical leg determine the starting order of a 5-, 7.5-, or 10-km freestyle leg, the first finisher of which is the overall winner; each leg was 7.5 km in the 2010 Games.   [11]From 1956 to 1972 the relay was 3 × 5 km.   [12]Combined time for two runs.   [13]Included elements of cross-country skiing, downhill skiing, shooting, fencing, and horse riding.

## XXX Summer Olympic Games (2012)

*The XXX Summer Games were held in London, England, 27 Jul–12 Aug 2012. Since the games, several athletes have been stripped of medals for having failed drug tests. New medalists are shown in this table.*

| EVENT | GOLD MEDALIST | PERFORMANCE | SILVER MEDALIST | BRONZE MEDALIST |
|---|---|---|---|---|
| **Archery** | | | | |
| Men's individual | Oh Jin-Hyek (KOR) | 115–108 | Takaharu Furukawa (JPN) | Dai Xiaoxiang (CHN) |
| Men's team | Italy | 219–218 | United States | South Korea |
| Women's individual | Ki Bo-Bae (KOR) | 135–129 | Aida Roman (MEX) | Mariana Avitia (MEX) |
| Women's team | South Korea | 210–209 | China | Japan |
| **Badminton** | | | | |
| Men's singles | Lin Dan (CHN) | 15–21, 21–10, 21–19 | Chong Wei Lee (MAS) | Chen Long (CHN) |
| Men's doubles | China | 21–16, 21–15 | Denmark | South Korea |
| Women's singles | Li Xuerui (CHN) | 21–15, 21–23, 21–17 | Wang Yihan (CHN) | Saina Nehwal (IND) |
| Women's doubles | China | 21–10, 25–23 | Japan | Russia |
| Mixed doubles | China | 21–11, 21–17 | China | Denmark |
| **Basketball** | | | | |
| Men | United States | 107–100 | Spain | Russia |
| Women | United States | 86–50 | France | Australia |
| **Boxing[1]** | | | | |
| **Men** | | | | |
| 49 kg (107.8 lb) | Zou Shiming (CHN) | | Kaeo Pongprayoon (THA) | Paddy Barnes (IRL); David Ayrapetyan (RUS) |
| 52 kg (114.4 lb) | Robeisy Ramirez Carrazana (CUB) | | Tugstsogt Nyambayar (MGL) | Michael Conlan (IRL); Misha Aloiyan (RUS) |
| 56 kg (123.2 lb) | Luke Campbell (GBR) | | John Nevin (IRL) | Satoshi Shimizu (JPN); Lazaro Alvarez Estrada (CUB) |
| 60 kg (132 lb) | Vasyl Lomachenko (UKR) | | Han Soon-Chul (KOR) | Yasniel Toledo Lopez (CUB); Evaldas Petrauskas (LTU) |

## XXX Summer Olympic Games (2012) (continued)

| EVENT | GOLD MEDALIST | PERFORMANCE | SILVER MEDALIST | BRONZE MEDALIST |
|---|---|---|---|---|
| **Boxing[1] (continued)** | | | | |
| **Men (continued)** | | | | |
| 64 kg (140.8 lb) | Roniel Iglesias Sotolongo (CUB) | | Denys Berinchyk (UKR) | Vincenzo Mangiacapre (ITA); Munkhe-Erdene Uranchimeg (MGL) |
| 69 kg (151.8 lb) | Serik Sapiyev (KAZ) | | Freddie Evans (GBR) | Andrey Zamkovoy (RUS); Taras Shelestyuk (UKR) |
| 75 kg (165 lb) | Ryota Murata (JPN) | | Esquiva Falcao Florentino (BRA) | Abbos Atoev (UZB); Anthony Ogogo (GBR) |
| 81 kg (178.2 lb) | Egor Mekhontcev (RUS) | | Adilbek Niyazymbetov (KAZ) | Yamaguchi Falcao Florentino (BRA); Oleksandr Gvozdyk (UKR) |
| 91 kg (200.2 lb) | Oleksandr Usyk (UKR) | | Clemente Russo (ITA) | Tervel Pulev (BUL); Teymur Mammadov (AZE) |
| 91+ kg (200.2+ lb) | Anthony Joshua (GBR) | | Roberto Cammarelle (ITA) | Ivan Dychko (KAZ); Magomedrasul Medzhidov (AZE) |
| **Women** | | | | |
| 51 kg (112.2 lb) | Nicola Adams (GBR) | | Ren Cancan (CHN) | Chungneijang Mery Kom Hmangte (IND); Marlen Esparza (USA) |
| 60 kg (132 lb) | Katie Taylor (IRL) | | Sofya Ochigava (RUS) | Mavzuna Chorieva (TJK); Adriana Araujo (BRA) |
| 75 kg (165 lb) | Claressa Shields (USA) | | Nadezda Torlopova (RUS) | Marina Volnova (KAZ); Li Jinzi (CHN) |
| **Canoeing** | | | | |
| **Men** | | | | |
| 200-m kayak singles | Ed McKeever (GBR) | 36.246 sec | Saul Craviotto Rivero (ESP) | Mark de Jonge (CAN) |
| 1,000-m kayak singles | Eirik Veras Larsen (NOR) | 3 min 26.462 sec | Adam van Koeverden (CAN) | Max Hoff (GER) |
| 200-m kayak pairs | Russia | 33.507 sec | Belarus | Great Britain |
| 1,000-m kayak pairs | Hungary | 3 min 09.646 sec | Portugal | Germany |
| 1,000-m kayak fours | Australia | 2 min 55.085 sec | Hungary | Czech Republic |
| Slalom kayak singles | Daniele Molmenti (ITA) | 93.43 pt | Vavrinec Hradilek (CZE) | Hannes Aigner (GER) |
| 200-m canoe singles | Yuri Cheban (UKR) | 42.291 sec | Jevgenij Shuklin (LTU) | Ivan Shtyl (RUS) |
| 1,000-m Canadian singles | Sebastian Brendel (GER) | 3 min 47.176 sec | David Cal Figueroa (ESP) | Mark Oldershaw (CAN) |
| 1,000-m Canadian pairs | Germany | 3 min 33.804 sec | Belarus | Russia |
| Slalom Canadian singles | Tony Estanguet (FRA) | 97.06 pt | Sideris Tasiadis (GER) | Michal Martikan (SVK) |
| Slalom Canadian pairs | Great Britain | 106.41 pt | Great Britain | Slovakia |
| **Women** | | | | |
| 200-m kayak singles | Lisa Carrington (NZL) | 44.638 sec | Inna Osypenko-Radomska (UKR) | Natasa Douchev-Janics (HUN) |
| 500-m kayak singles | Danuta Kozak (HUN) | 1 min 51.456 sec | Inna Osypenko-Radomska (UKR) | Bridgitte Hartley (RSA) |
| 500-m kayak pairs | Germany | 1 min 42.213 sec | Hungary | Poland |
| 500-m kayak fours | Hungary | 1 min 30.827 sec | Germany | Belarus |
| Slalom kayak singles | Emilie Fer (FRA) | 105.90 pt | Jessica Fox (AUS) | Maialen Chourraut (ESP) |
| **Cycling** | | | | |
| **Men** | | | | |
| Road race | Alexandr Vinokurov (KAZ) | 5 hr 45 min 57 sec | Rigoberto Uran Uran (COL) | Alexander Kristoff (NOR) |
| Individual road time trial | Bradley Wiggins (GBR) | 50 min 39.54 sec | Tony Martin (GER) | Christopher Froome (GBR) |
| Team pursuit | Great Britain | 3 min 51.659 sec[2] | Australia | New Zealand |
| Individual sprint | Jason Kenny (GBR) | | Gregory Bauge (FRA) | Shane Perkins (AUS) |

## XXX Summer Olympic Games (2012) (continued)

| EVENT | GOLD MEDALIST | PERFORMANCE | SILVER MEDALIST | BRONZE MEDALIST |
|---|---|---|---|---|
| **Cycling (continued)** | | | | |
| **Men (continued)** | | | | |
| Team sprint | Great Britain | | France | Germany |
| Keirin | Chris Hoy (GBR) | | Maximilian Levy (GER) | Simon van Velthoo- ven (NZL); Teun Mulder (NED) (tied) |
| Omnium | Lasse Norman Hansen (DEN) | 27 pt | Bryan Coquard (FRA) | Edward Clancy (GBR) |
| Mountain bike | Jaroslav Kulhavy (CZE) | 1 hr 29 min 07 sec | Nino Schurter (SUI) | Marco Aurelio Fontana (ITA) |
| Motocross/BMX | Maris Strombergs (LAT) | 37.576 sec | Sam Willoughby (AUS) | Carlos Mario Oquen- do Zabala (COL) |
| **Women** | | | | |
| Road race | Marianne Vos (NED) | 3 hr 35 min 29 sec | Elizabeth Armitstead (GBR) | Olga Zabelinskaya (RUS) |
| Individual road time trial | Kristin Armstrong (USA) | 37 min 34.82 sec | Judith Arndt (GER) | Olga Zabelinskaya (RUS) |
| Team pursuit | Great Britain | 3 min 15.669 sec | United States | Canada |
| Individual sprint | Anna Meares (AUS) | | Victoria Pendleton (GBR) | Guo Shuang (CHN) |
| Team sprint | Germany | | China | Australia |
| Keirin | Victoria Pendleton (GBR) | | Guo Shuang (CHN) | Lee Wai Sze (HKG) |
| Omnium | Laura Trott (GBR) | 18 pt | Sarah Hammer (USA) | Annette Edmondson (AUS) |
| Mountain bike | Julie Bresset (FRA) | 1 hr 30 min 52 sec | Sabine Spitz (GER) | Georgia Gould (USA) |
| Motocross/BMX | Mariana Pajon (COL) | 37.706 sec | Sarah Walker (NZL) | Laura Smulders (NED) |
| **Diving** | | | | |
| **Men** | | | | |
| 3-m springboard | Ilya Zakharov (RUS) | 555.90 pt | Qin Kai (CHN) | He Chong (CHN) |
| 10-m platform | David Boudia (USA) | 568.65 pt | Qiu Bo (CHN) | Thomas Daley (GBR) |
| 3-m synchronized springboard | China | 477.00 pt | Russia | United States |
| 10-m synchronized platform | China | 486.78 pt | Mexico | United States |
| **Women** | | | | |
| 3-m springboard | Wu Minxia (CHN) | 414.00 pt | He Zi (CHN) | Laura Sanchez Soto (MEX) |
| 10-m platform | Chen Ruolin (CHN) | 422.30 pt | Brittany Broben (AUS) | Pandelela Rinong Pamg (MAS) |
| 3-m synchronized springboard | China | 346.20 pt | United States | Canada |
| 10-m synchronized platform | China | 368.40 pt | Mexico | Canada |
| **Equestrian** | | | | |
| Individual 3-day event | Michael Jung (GER) | | Sara Algotsson Ostholt (SWE) | Sandra Auffarth (GER) |
| Team 3-day event | Germany | | Great Britain | New Zealand |
| Individual dressage | Charlotte Dujardin (GBR) | | Adelinde Cornelissen (NED) | Laura Bechtols- heimer (GBR) |
| Team dressage | Great Britain | | Germany | Netherlands |
| Individual jumping | Steve Guerdat (SUI) | | Gerco Schroder (NED) | Cian O'Connor (IRL) |
| Team jumping | Great Britain | | Netherlands | Saudi Arabia |
| **Fencing** | | | | |
| **Men** | | | | |
| Individual foil | Lei Sheng (CHN) | | Alaaeldin Abouelkassem (EGY) | Choi Byungchul (KOR) |
| Team foil | Italy | | Japan | Germany |
| Individual épée | Ruben Limardo Gascon (VEN) | | Bartosz Piasecki (NOR) | Jung Jin-Sun (KOR) |
| Individual sabre | Aron Szilagyi (HUN) | | Diego Occhiuzzi (ITA) | Nikolay Kovalev (RUS) |
| Team sabre | South Korea | | Romania | Italy |
| **Women** | | | | |
| Individual foil | Elisa Di Francisca (ITA) | | Arianna Errigo (ITA) | Valentina Vezzali (ITA) |
| Team foil | Italy | | Russia | South Korea |

## XXX Summer Olympic Games (2012) (continued)

| EVENT | GOLD MEDALIST | PERFORMANCE | SILVER MEDALIST | BRONZE MEDALIST |
|---|---|---|---|---|
| **Fencing (continued)** | | | | |
| **Women (continued)** | | | | |
| Individual épée | Yana Shemyakina (UKR) | | Britta Heidemann (GER) | Sun Yujie (CHN) |
| Team épée | China | | South Korea | United States |
| Individual sabre | Kim Ji-Yeon (KOR) | | Sofya Velikaya (RUS) | Olga Kharlan (UKR) |
| **Field Hockey** | | | | |
| Men | Germany | 2–1 | Netherlands | Australia |
| Women | Netherlands | 2–0 | Argentina | Great Britain |
| **Gymnastics** | | | | |
| **Men** | | | | |
| Team | China | 275.997 pt | Japan | Great Britain |
| All-around | Kohei Uchimura (JPN) | 92.690 pt | Marcel Nguyen (GER) | Danell Leyva (USA) |
| Floor exercise | Zou Kai (CHN) | 15.933 pt | Kohei Uchimura (JPN) | Denis Ablyazin (RUS) |
| Vault | Yang Hak-Seon (KOR) | 16.533 pt | Denis Ablyazin (RUS) | Igor Radivilov (UKR) |
| Pommel horse | Krisztian Berki (HUN) | 16.066 pt | Louis Smith (GBR) | Max Whitlock (GBR) |
| Rings | Arthur Nabarrete Zanetti (BRA) | 15.900 pt | Chen Yibing (CHN) | Matteo Morandi (ITA) |
| Parallel bars | Feng Zhe (CHN) | 15.966 pt | Marcel Nguyen (GER) | Hamilton Sabot (FRA) |
| Horizontal bar | Epke Zonderland (NED) | 16.533 pt | Fabian Hambuchen (GER) | Zou Kai (CHN) |
| Trampoline | Dong Dong (CHN) | 62.990 pt | Dmitry Ushakov (RUS) | Lu Chunlong (CHN) |
| **Women** | | | | |
| Team | United States | 183.596 pt | Russia | Romania |
| All-around | Gabrielle Douglas (USA) | 62.232 pt | Victoriya Komova (RUS) | Aliya Mustafina (RUS) |
| Floor exercise | Alexandra Raisman (USA) | 15.600 pt | Catalina Ponor (ROU) | Aliya Mustafina (RUS) |
| Vault | Sandra Izbasa (ROU) | 15.191 pt | McKayla Maroney (USA) | Maria Paseka (RUS) |
| Uneven bars | Aliya Mustafina (RUS) | 16.133 pt | He Kexin (CHN) | Elizabeth Tweddle (GBR) |
| Balance beam | Deng Linlin (CHN) | 15.600 pt | Sui Lu (CHN) | Alexandra Raisman (USA) |
| Trampoline | Rosannagh Maclennan (CAN) | 57.305 pt | Huang Shanshan (CHN) | He Wenna (CHN) |
| Individual rhythmic | Yevgeniya Kanayeva (RUS) | 116.900 pt | Dariya Dmitriyeva (RUS) | Liubou Charkashyna (BLR) |
| Team rhythmic | Russia | 57.000 pt | Belarus | Italy |
| **Handball (Team)** | | | | |
| Men | France | 10–8, 12–13 | Sweden | Croatia |
| Women | Norway | 13–10, 13–13 | Montenegro | Spain |
| **Judo[1]** | | | | |
| **Men** | | | | |
| 60 kg (132 lb) | Arsen Galstyan (RUS) | | Hiroaki Hiraoka (JPN) | Felipe Kitadai (BRA); Rishod Sobirov (UZB) |
| 66 kg (145.2 lb) | Lasha Shavdatuashvili (GEO) | | Miklos Ungvari (HUN) | Masashi Ebinuma (JPN); Cho Jun-Ho (KOR) |
| 73 kg (160.6 lb) | Mansur Isayev (RUS) | | Riki Nakaya (JPN) | Nyam-Ochir Sainjargal (MGL); Ugo Legrand (FRA) |
| 81 kg (178.2 lb) | Kim Jae-Bum (KOR) | | Ole Bischof (GER) | Ivan Nifontov (RUS); Antoine Valois-Fortier (CAN) |
| 90 kg (198 lb) | Song Dae-Nam (KOR) | | Asley Gonzalez (CUB) | Ilias Iliadis (GRE); Masashi Nishiyama (JPN) |
| 100 kg (220 lb) | Tagir Khaibulayev (RUS) | | Tuvshinbayar Naidan (MGL) | Dimitri Peters (GER); Henk Grol (NED) |
| 100+ kg (220+ lb) | Teddy Riner (FRA) | | Aleksandr Mikhaylin (RUS) | Andreas Toelzer (GER); Rafael Silva (BRA) |

## XXX Summer Olympic Games (2012) (continued)

| EVENT | GOLD MEDALIST | PERFORMANCE | SILVER MEDALIST | BRONZE MEDALIST |
|---|---|---|---|---|
| Judo[1] (continued) | | | | |
| **Women** | | | | |
| 48 kg (105.6 lb) | Sarah Menezes (BRA) | | Alina Dumitru (ROU) | Charline van Snick (BEL); Eva Csernoviczki (HUN) |
| 52 kg (114.4 lb) | An Kum-Ae (PRK) | | Yanet Bermoy Acosta (CUB) | Rosalba Forciniti (ITA); Priscilla Gneto (FRA) |
| 57 kg (125.4 lb) | Kaori Matsumoto (JPN) | | Corina Caprioriu (ROU) | Marti Malloy (USA); Automne Pavia (FRA) |
| 63 kg (138.6 lb) | Urska Zolnir (SLO) | | Xu Lili (CHN) | Yoshie Ueno (JPN); Gevrise Emane (FRA) |
| 70 kg (154 lb) | Lucie Decosse (FRA) | | Kerstin Thiele (GER) | Yuri Alvear (COL); Edith Bosch (NED) |
| 78 kg (171.6 lb) | Kayla Harrison (USA) | | Gemma Gibbons (GBR) | Audrey Tcheumeo (FRA); Mayra Aguiar (BRA) |
| 78+ kg (171.6 lb) | Idalys Ortiz (CUB) | | Mika Sugimoto (JPN) | Karina Bryant (GBR); Tong Wen (CHN) |
| **Modern Pentathlon** | | | | |
| Men | David Svoboda (CZE) | | Cao Zhongrong (CHN) | Adam Marosi (HUN) |
| Women | Laura Asadauskaite (LTU) | | Samantha Murray (GBR) | Yane Marques (BRA) |
| **Rowing** | | | | |
| **Men** | | | | |
| Single sculls | Mahe Drysdale (NZL) | 6 min 57.82 sec | Ondrej Synek (CZE) | Alan Campbell (GBR) |
| Double sculls | New Zealand | 6 min 31.67 sec | Italy | Slovenia |
| Quadruple sculls | Germany | 5 min 42.48 sec | Croatia | Australia |
| Coxless pairs (oars) | New Zealand | 6 min 16.65 sec | France | Great Britain |
| Coxless fours (oars) | Great Britain | 6 min 03.97 sec | Australia | United States |
| Eights | Germany | 5 min 48.75 sec | Canada | Great Britain |
| Lightweight double sculls | Denmark | 6 min 37.17 sec | Great Britain | New Zealand |
| Lightweight fours | South Africa | 6 min 02.84 sec | Great Britain | Denmark |
| **Women** | | | | |
| Single sculls | Miroslava Knapkova (CZE) | 7 min 54.37 sec | Fie Udby Erichsen (DEN) | Kim Crow (AUS) |
| Double sculls | Great Britain | 6 min 55.82 sec | Australia | Poland |
| Quadruple sculls | Ukraine | 6 min 35.93 sec | Germany | United States |
| Coxless pairs (oars) | Great Britain | 7 min 27.13 sec | Australia | New Zealand |
| Eights | United States | 6 min 10.59 sec | Canada | Netherlands |
| Lightweight double sculls | Great Britain | 7 min 09.30 sec | China | Greece |
| **Sailing** | | | | |
| Men's 470 | Australia | | Great Britain | Argentina |
| Women's 470 | New Zealand | | Great Britain | Netherlands |
| Men's RS:X | Dorian van Rijsselberge (NED) | | Nick Dempsey (GBR) | Przemyslaw Miarczynski (POL) |
| Women's RS:X | Marina Alabau Neira (ESP) | | Tuuli Petaja (FIN) | Zofia Noceti-Klepacka (POL) |
| Open Finn | Ben Ainslie (GBR) | | Jonas Hogh-Christensen (DEN) | Jonathan Lobert (FRA) |
| Open 49er | Australia | | New Zealand | Denmark |
| Men's Laser | Tom Slingsby (AUS) | | Pavlos Kontides (CYP) | Rasmus Myrgren (SWE) |
| Women's Laser Radial | Xu Lijia (CHN) | | Marit Bouwmeester (NED) | Evi Van Acker (BEL) |
| Men's Star | Sweden | | Great Britain | Brazil |
| Women's Elliott 6m | Spain | | Australia | Finland |

## XXX Summer Olympic Games (2012) (continued)

| EVENT | GOLD MEDALIST | PERFORMANCE | SILVER MEDALIST | BRONZE MEDALIST |
|---|---|---|---|---|
| **Shooting** | | | | |
| **Men** | | | | |
| Rapid-fire pistol | Leuris Pupo (CUB) | 34.0 pt² | Vijay Kumar (IND) | Ding Feng (CHN) |
| Free pistol | Jin Jong-Oh (KOR) | 662.0 pt | Choi Young-Rae (KOR) | Wang Zhiwei (CHN) |
| Air pistol | Jin Jong-Oh (KOR) | 688.2 pt | Iuca Tesconi (ITA) | Andrija Zlatic (SRB) |
| Small-bore (sport) rifle, 3 positions | Niccolo Campriani (ITA) | 1278.5 pt³ | Kim Jong-Hyun (KOR) | Matthew Emmons (USA) |
| Small-bore (sport) rifle, prone | Sergey Martynov (BLR) | 705.5 pt | Lionel Cox (BEL) | Rajmond Debevec (SLO) |
| Air rifle | Alin George Moldoveanu (ROU) | 702.1 pt | Niccolo Campriani (ITA) | Gagan Narang (IND) |
| Trap | Giovanni Cernogoraz (CRO) | 146.0 pt³ | Massimo Fabbrizi (ITA) | Fehaid Aldeehani (KUW) |
| Double trap | Peter Wilson (GBR) | 188.0 pt | Hakan Dahlby (SWE) | Vasily Mosin (RUS) |
| Skeet | Vincent Hancock (USA) | 148.0 pt³ | Anders Golding (DEN) | Nasser Al-Attiya (QAT) |
| **Women** | | | | |
| Pistol | Kim Jang-Mi (KOR) | 792.4 pt | Chen Ying (CHN) | Olena Kostevych (UKR) |
| Air pistol | Guo Wenjun (CHN) | 488.1 pt | Celine Goberville (FRA) | Olena Kostevych (UKR) |
| Small-bore (sport) rifle, 3 positions | Jamie Lynn Gray (USA) | 691.9 pt³ | Ivana Maksimovic (SRB) | Adela Sykorova (CZE) |
| Air rifle | Yi Siling (CHN) | 502.9 pt | Sylwia Bogacka (POL) | Yu Dan (CHN) |
| Trap | Jessica Rossi (ITA) | 99.0 pt² | Zuzana Stefecekova (SVK) | Delphine Reau (FRA) |
| Skeet | Kimberly Rhode (USA) | 99.0 pt² | Wei Ning (CHN) | Danka Bartekova (SVK) |
| **Soccer (Association Football)** | | | | |
| Men | Mexico | 2–1 | Brazil | South Korea |
| Women | United States | 2–1 | Japan | Canada |
| **Swimming** | | | | |
| **Men** | | | | |
| 50-m freestyle | Florent Manaudou (FRA) | 21.34 sec | Cullen Jones (USA) | César Cielo Filho (BRA) |
| 100-m freestyle | Nathan Adrian (USA) | 47.52 sec | James Magnussen (AUS) | Brent Hayden (CAN) |
| 200-m freestyle | Yannick Agnel (FRA) | 1 min 43.14 sec | Park Tae-Hwan (KOR); Sun Yang (CHN) (tied) | |
| 400-m freestyle | Sun Yang (CHN) | 3 min 40.14 sec³ | Park Tae-Hwan (KOR) | Peter Vanderkaay (USA) |
| 1,500-m freestyle | Sun Yang (CHN) | 14 min 31.02 sec² | Ryan Cochrane (CAN) | Oussama Mellouli (TUN) |
| 100-m backstroke | Matthew Grevers (USA) | 52.16 sec³ | Nick Thoman (USA) | Ryosuke Irie (JPN) |
| 200-m backstroke | Tyler Clary (USA) | 1 min 53.41 sec³ | Ryosuke Irie (JPN) | Ryan Lochte (USA) |
| 100-m breaststroke | Cameron van der Burgh (RSA) | 58.46 sec² | Christian Sprenger (AUS) | Brendan Hansen (USA) |
| 200-m breaststroke | Daniel Gyurta (HUN) | 2 min 07.28 sec² | Michael Jamieson (GBR) | Ryo Tateishi (JPN) |
| 100-m butterfly | Michael Phelps (USA) | 51.21 sec | Chad le Clos (RSA) | Yevgeny Korotyshkin (RUS) |
| 200-m butterfly | Chad le Clos (RSA) | 1 min 52.96 sec | Michael Phelps (USA) | Takeshi Matsuda (JPN) |
| 200-m individual medley | Michael Phelps (USA) | 1 min 54.27 sec | Ryan Lochte (USA) | Laszlo Cseh (HUN) |
| 400-m individual medley | Ryan Lochte (USA) | 4 min 05.18 sec | Thiago Pereira (BRA) | Kosuke Hagino (JPN) |
| 10-km open-water marathon | Oussama Mellouli (TUN) | 1 hr 49 min 55.1 sec | Thomas Lurz (GER) | Richard Weinberger (CAN) |
| 4 x 100-m freestyle relay | France | 3 min 09.93 sec | United States | Russia |
| 4 x 200-m freestyle relay | United States | 6 min 59.70 sec | France | China |
| 4 x 100-m medley relay | United States | 3 min 29.35 sec | Japan | Australia |
| **Women** | | | | |
| 50-m freestyle | Ranomi Kromowidjojo (NED) | 24.05 sec³ | Aliaksandra Herasimenia (BLR) | Marleen Veldhuis (NED) |
| 100-m freestyle | Ranomi Kromowidjojo (NED) | 53.00 sec³ | Aliaksandra Herasimenia (BLR) | Tang Yi (CHN) |

## XXX Summer Olympic Games (2012) (continued)

| EVENT | GOLD MEDALIST | PERFORMANCE | SILVER MEDALIST | BRONZE MEDALIST |
|---|---|---|---|---|
| **Swimming (continued)** | | | | |
| **Women (continued)** | | | | |
| 200-m freestyle | Allison Schmitt (USA) | 1 min 53.61 sec[3] | Camille Muffat (FRA) | Bronte Barratt (AUS) |
| 400-m freestyle | Camille Muffat (FRA) | 4 min 01.45 sec[3] | Allison Schmitt (USA) | Rebecca Adlington (GBR) |
| 800-m freestyle | Katie Ledecky (USA) | 8 min 14.63 sec | Mireia Belmonte Garcia (ESP) | Rebecca Adlington (GBR) |
| 100-m backstroke | Missy Franklin (USA) | 58.33 sec | Emily Seebohm (AUS) | Aya Terakawa (JPN) |
| 200-m backstroke | Missy Franklin (USA) | 2 min 04.06 sec[2] | Anastasiya Zueva (RUS) | Elizabeth Beisel (USA) |
| 100-m breaststroke | Ruta Meilutyte (LTU) | 1 min 05.47 sec | Rebecca Soni (USA) | Satomi Suzuki (JPN) |
| 200-m breaststroke | Rebecca Soni (USA) | 2 min 19.59 sec[2] | Satomi Suzuki (JPN) | Iuliya Efimova (RUS) |
| 100-m butterfly | Dana Vollmer (USA) | 55.98 sec[2] | Lu Ying (CHN) | Alicia Coutts (AUS) |
| 200-m butterfly | Jiao Liuyang (CHN) | 2 min 04.06 sec[3] | Mireia Belmonte Garcia (ESP) | Natsumi Hoshi (JPN) |
| 200-m individual medley | Ye Shiwen (CHN) | 2 min 07.57 sec[3] | Alicia Coutts (AUS) | Caitlin Leverenz (USA) |
| 400-m individual medley | Ye Shiwen (CHN) | 4 min 28.43 sec[2] | Elizabeth Beisel (USA) | Li Xuanxu (CHN) |
| 10-km open-water marathon | Eva Risztov (HUN) | 1 hr 57 min 38.20 sec | Haley Anderson (USA) | Martina Grimaldi (ITA) |
| 4 x 100-m freestyle relay | Australia | 3 min 33.15 sec[3] | Netherlands | United States |
| 4 x 200-m freestyle relay | United States | 7 min 42.92 sec[3] | Australia | France |
| 4 x 100-m medley relay | United States | 3 min 52.05 sec[2] | Australia | Japan |

| **Synchronized Swimming** | | | | |
|---|---|---|---|---|
| Duet | Russia | 197.100 pt | Spain | China |
| Team | Russia | 197.030 pt | China | Spain |

| **Table Tennis** | | | | |
|---|---|---|---|---|
| Men's singles | Zhang Jike (CHN) | 18–16, 11–5, 11–6, 10–12, 13–11 | Wang Hao (CHN) | Dimitrij Ovtcharov (GER) |
| Men's team | China | 3–0 | South Korea | Germany |
| Women's singles | Li Xiaoxia (CHN) | 11–8, 14–12, 8–11, 11–6, 11–4 | Ding Ning (CHN) | Feng Tianwei (SIN) |
| Women's team | China | 3–0 | Japan | Singapore |

| **Taekwondo[1]** | | | | |
|---|---|---|---|---|
| **Men** | | | | |
| 58 kg (127.6 lb) | Joel Gonzalez Bonilla (ESP) | | Lee Dae-Hoon (KOR) | Aleksey Denisenko (RUS); Oscar Munoz Oviedo (COL) |
| 68 kg (149.6 lb) | Servet Tazegul (TUR) | | Mohammad Bagheri Motamed (IRI) | Terrence Jennings (USA); Rohullah Nikpah (AFG) |
| 80 kg (176 lb) | Sebastian Eduardo Crismanich (ARG) | | Nicolas Garcia Hemme (ESP) | Lutalo Muhammad (GBR); Mauro Sarmiento (ITA) |
| 80+ kg (176+ lb) | Carlo Molfetta (ITA) | | Anthony Obame (GAB) | Robelis Despaigne (CUB); Liu Xiaobo (CHN) |
| **Women** | | | | |
| 49 kg (107.8 lb) | Wu Jingyu (CHN) | | Brigitte Yague Enrique (ESP) | Chanatip Sonkham (THA); Lucija Zaninovic (CRO) |
| 57 kg (125.4 lb) | Jade Jones (GBR) | | Hou Yuzhuo (CHN) | Marlene Harnois (FRA); Tseng Li-Cheng (TPE) |
| 67 kg (147.4 lb) | Hwang Kyung-Seon (KOR) | | Nur Tatar (TUR) | Paige McPherson (USA); Helena Fromm (GER) |
| 67+ kg (147.4+ lb) | Milica Mandic (SRB) | | Anne-Caroline Graffe (FRA) | Anastasiya Baryshnikova (RUS); Maria del Rosario Espinoza (MEX) |

## XXX Summer Olympic Games (2012) (continued)

| EVENT | GOLD MEDALIST | PERFORMANCE | SILVER MEDALIST | BRONZE MEDALIST |
|---|---|---|---|---|
| **Tennis** | | | | |
| Men's singles | Andy Murray (GBR) | 6–2, 6–1, 6–4 | Roger Federer (SUI) | Juan Martin del Potro (ARG) |
| Men's doubles | United States | 6–4, 7–6 | France 1 | France 2 |
| Women's singles | Serena Williams (USA) | 6–0, 6–1 | Mariya Sharapova (RUS) | Victoria Azarenka (BLR) |
| Women's doubles | United States | 6–4, 6–4 | Czech Republic | Russia |
| Mixed doubles | Belarus | 2–6, 6–3, 10–8 | Great Britain | United States |

**Track and Field (Athletics)**

| | | | | |
|---|---|---|---|---|
| **Men** | | | | |
| 100 m | Usain Bolt (JAM) | 9.63 sec[3] | Yohan Blake (JAM) | Justin Gatlin (USA) |
| 200 m | Usain Bolt (JAM) | 19.32 sec | Yohan Blake (JAM) | Warren Weir (JAM) |
| 400 m | Kirani James (GRN) | 43.94 sec | Luguelin Santos (DOM) | Lalonde Gordon (TRI) |
| 4 x 100-m relay | Jamaica | 36.84 sec[2] | United States | Trinidad and Tobago |
| 4 x 400-m relay | Bahamas | 2 min 56.72 sec | United States | Trinidad and Tobago |
| 800 m | David Rudisha (KEN) | 1 min 40.91 sec[2] | Nijel Amos (BOT) | Timothy Kitum (KEN) |
| 1,500 m | Taoufik Makhloufi (ALG) | 3 min 34.08 sec | Leonel Manzano (USA) | Abdalaati Iguider (MAR) |
| 5,000 m | Mohamed Farah (GBR) | 13 min 41.66 sec | Dejen Gebremeskel (ETH) | Thomas Pkemei Longosiwa (KEN) |
| 10,000 m | Mohamed Farah (GBR) | 27 min 30.42 sec | Galen Rupp (USA) | Tariku Bekele (ETH) |
| Marathon | Stephen Kiprotich (UGA) | 2 hr 08 min 01 sec | Abel Kirui (KEN) | Wilson Kipsang Kiprotich (KEN) |
| 110-m hurdles | Aries Merritt (USA) | 12.92 sec | Jason Richardson (USA) | Hansie Parchment (JAM) |
| 400-m hurdles | Felix Sanchez (DOM) | 47.63 sec | Michael Tinsley (USA) | Javier Culson (PUR) |
| 3,000-m steeple-chase | Ezekiel Kemboi (KEN) | 8 min 18.56 sec | Mahiedine Mekhissi-Benabbad (FRA) | Abel Kiprop Mutai (KEN) |
| 20,000-m walk | Chen Ding (CHN) | 1 hour 18 min 46 sec[3] | Erick Barrondo (GUA) | Wang Zhen (CHN) |
| 50,000-m walk | Sergey Kirdyapkin (RUS) | 3 hr 35 min 59 sec[3] | Jared Tallent (AUS) | Si Tianfeng (CHN) |
| High jump | Ivan Ukhov (RUS) | 2.38 m | Erik Kynard (USA) | Mutaz Essa Barshim (QAT); Derek Drouin (CAN); Robert Grabarz (GBR) (tied) |
| Long jump | Greg Rutherford (GBR) | 8.31 m | Mitchell Watt (AUS) | Will Claye (USA) |
| Triple jump | Christian Taylor (USA) | 17.81 m | Will Claye (USA) | Fabrizio Donato (ITA) |
| Pole vault | Renaud Lavillenie (FRA) | 5.97 m[3] | Bjorn Otto (GER) | Raphael Holzdeppe (GER) |
| Shot put | Tomasz Majewski (POL) | 21.89 m | David Storl (GER) | Reese Hoffa (USA) |
| Discus throw | Robert Harting (GER) | 68.27 m | Ehsan Hadadi (IRI) | Gerd Kanter (EST) |
| Javelin throw | Keshorn Walcott (TRI) | 84.58 m | Oleksandr Pyatnytsya (UKR) | Antti Ruuskanen (FIN) |
| Hammer throw | Krisztian Pars (HUN) | 80.59 m | Primoz Kozmus (SLO) | Koji Murofushi (JPN) |
| Decathlon | Ashton Eaton (USA) | 8,869 pt | Trey Hardee (USA) | Leonel Suárez (CUB) |
| **Women** | | | | |
| 100 m | Shelly-Ann Fraser-Pryce (JAM) | 10.75 sec | Carmelita Jeter (USA) | Veronica Campbell-Brown (JAM) |
| 200 m | Allyson Felix (USA) | 21.88 sec | Shelly-Ann Fraser-Pryce (JAM) | Carmelita Jeter (USA) |
| 400 m | Sanya Richards-Ross (USA) | 49.55 sec | Christine Ohuruogu (GBR) | DeeDee Trotter (USA) |
| 4 x 100-m relay | United States | 40.82 sec[2] | Jamaica | Ukraine |
| 4 x 400-m relay | United States | 3 min 16.87 sec | Russia | Jamaica |
| 800 m | Mariya Savinova (RUS) | 1 min 56.19 sec | Caster Semenya (RSA) | Yekaterina Poistogova (RUS) |
| 1,500 m | Asli Cakir Alptekin (TUR) | 4 min 10.23 sec | Gamze Bulut (TUR) | Maryam Yusuf Jamal (BRN) |
| 5,000 m | Meseret Defar (ETH) | 15 min 04.25 sec | Vivian Jepkemoi Cheruiyot (KEN) | Tirunesh Dibaba (ETH) |
| 10,000 m | Tirunesh Dibaba (ETH) | 30 min 20.75 sec | Sally Jepkosgei Kipyego (KEN) | Vivian Jepkemoi Cheruiyot (KEN) |
| Marathon | Tiki Gelana (ETH) | 2 hr 23 min 07 sec[3] | Priscah Jeptoo (KEN) | Tatyana Petrova Arkhipova (RUS) |
| 100-m hurdles | Sally Pearson (AUS) | 12.35 sec[3] | Dawn Harper (USA) | Kellie Wells (USA) |
| 400-m hurdles | Natalya Antyukh (RUS) | 52.70 sec | Lashinda Demus (USA) | Zuzana Hejnova (CZE) |

## XXX Summer Olympic Games (2012) (continued)

| EVENT | GOLD MEDALIST | PERFORMANCE | SILVER MEDALIST | BRONZE MEDALIST |
|---|---|---|---|---|
| **Track and Field (Athletics) (continued)** | | | | |
| **Women (continued)** | | | | |
| 3,000-m steeplechase | Yuliya Zaripova (RUS) | 9 min 06.72 sec[2] | Habiba Ghribi (TUN) | Sofia Assefa (ETH) |
| 20-km walk | Yelena Lashmanova (RUS) | 1 hr 25 min 02 sec[2] | Olga Kaniskina (RUS) | Qieyang Shenjie (CHN) |
| High jump | Anna Chicherova (RUS) | 2.05 m | Brigetta Barrett (USA) | Svetlana Shkolina (RUS) |
| Long jump | Brittney Reese (USA) | 7.12 m | Yelena Sokolova (RUS) | Janay Deloach (USA) |
| Triple jump | Olga Rypakova (KAZ) | 14.98 m | Caterine Ibarguen (COL) | Olha Saladuha (UKR) |
| Pole vault | Jennifer Suhr (USA) | 4.75 m | Yarisley Silva (CUB) | Yelena Isinbayeva (RUS) |
| Shot put | Valerie Adams (NZL)[4] | 20.70 m | Yevgeniya Kolodko (RUS) | Gong Lijiao (CHN) |
| Discus throw | Sandra Perkovic (CRO) | 69.11 m | Darya Pishchalnikova (RUS) | Li Yanfeng (CHN) |
| Javelin throw | Barbora Spotakova (CZE) | 69.55 m | Christina Obergfoll (GER) | Linda Stahl (GER) |
| Hammer throw | Tatyana Lysenko (RUS) | 78.18 m[3] | Anita Wlodarczyk (POL) | Betty Heidler (GER) |
| Heptathlon | Jessica Ennis (GBR) | 6,955 pt | Lilli Schwarzkopf (GER) | Tatyana Chernova (RUS) |
| **Triathlon** | | | | |
| Men | Alistair Brownlee (GBR) | 1 hr 46 min 25.00 sec | Javier Gomez (ESP) | Jonathan Brownlee (GBR) |
| Women | Nicola Spirig (SUI) | 1 hr 59 min 48.00 sec | Lisa Norden (SWE) | Erin Densham (GBR) |
| **Volleyball** | | | | |
| Men's indoor | Russia | 19–25, 20–25, 29–27, 25–22, 15–9 | Brazil | Italy |
| Women's indoor | Brazil | 11–25, 25–17, 25–20, 25–17 | United States | Japan |
| Men's beach | Germany | 23–21, 16–21, 16–14 | Brazil | Latvia |
| Women's beach | United States 1 | 21–16, 21–16 | United States 2 | Brazil |
| **Water Polo** | | | | |
| Men | Croatia | 8–6 | Italy | Serbia |
| Women | United States | 8–5 | Spain | Australia |
| **Weight Lifting** | | | | |
| **Men** | | | | |
| 56 kg (123.2 lb) | Om Yun Chol (PRK) | 293.0 kg[3] | Wu Jingbiao (CHN) | Valentin Hristov (AZE) |
| 62 kg (136.4 lb) | Kim Un Guk (PRK) | 327.0 kg[2] | Oscar Albeiro Figueroa Mosquera (COL) | Irawan Eko Yuli (INA) |
| 69 kg (151.8 lb) | Lin Qingfeng (CHN) | 344.0 kg | Triyatno Triyatno (INA) | Razvan Martin (ROU) |
| 77 kg (169.4 lb) | Lu Xiaojun (CHN) | 379.0 kg[2] | Lu Haojie (CHN) | Ivan Cambar Rodriguez (CUB) |
| 85 kg (187 lb) | Adrian Edward Zielinski (POL) | 385.0 kg | Apti Aukhadov (RUS) | Kianoush Rostami (IRI) |
| 94 kg (206.8 lb) | Ilya Ilyin (KAZ) | 418.0 kg[2] | Aleksandr Ivanov (RUS) | Anatoli Ciricu (MDA) |
| 105 kg (231 lb) | Oleksiy Torokhtiy (UKR) | 412.0 kg | Navab Nasirshelal (IRI) | Bartlomiej Wojciech Bonk (POL) |
| 105+ kg (231+ lb) | Behdad Salimikordasiabi (IRI) | 455.0 kg | Sajjad Anoushiravani Hamlabad (IRI) | Ruslan Albegov (RUS) |
| **Women** | | | | |
| 48 kg (105.6 lb) | Wang Mingjuan (CHN) | 205.0 kg | Hiromi Miyake (JPN) | Ryang Chun Hwa (PRK) |
| 53 kg (116.6 lb) | Zulfiya Chinshanlo (KAZ) | 226.0 kg | Hsu Shu-Ching (TPE) | Cristina Iovu (MDA) |
| 58 kg (127.6 lb) | Li Xueying (CHN) | 246.0 kg[3] | Pimsiri Sirikaew (THA) | Yuliya Kalina (UKR) |
| 63 kg (138.6 lb) | Maiya Maneza (KAZ) | 245.0 kg[3] | Svetlana Tsarukayeva (RUS) | Christine Girard (CAN) |
| 69 kg (151.8 lb) | Rim Jong-Sim (PRK) | 261.0 kg | Roxana Cocos (ROU) | Maryna Shkermankova (BLR) |
| 75 kg (165 lb) | Svetlana Podobedova (KAZ) | 291.0 kg[3] | Natalya Zabolotnaya (RUS) | Iryna Kulesha (BLR) |
| 75+ kg (165 lb) | Zhou Lulu (CHN) | 333.0 kg[2] | Tatyana Kashirina (RUS) | Hripsime Khurshudyan (ARM) |

## XXX Summer Olympic Games (2012) (continued)

| EVENT | GOLD MEDALIST | PERFORMANCE | SILVER MEDALIST | BRONZE MEDALIST |
|---|---|---|---|---|
| **Wrestling[1]** | | | | |
| **Freestyle** | | | | |
| **Men** | | | | |
| 55 kg (121 lb) | Dzhamal Otarsultanov (RUS) | | Vladimer Khinchegashvili (GEO) | Shinichi Yumoto (JPN); Yang Kyong-Il (PRK) |
| 60 kg (132 lb) | Toghrul Asgarov (AZE) | | Besik Kudukhov (RUS) | Yogeshwar Dutt (IND); Coleman Scott (USA) |
| 66 kg (145.2 lb) | Tatsuhiro Yonemitsu (JPN) | | Sushil Kumar (IND) | Livan Lopez Azcuy (CUB); Akzhurek Tanatarov (KAZ) |
| 74 kg (162.8 lb) | Jordan Burroughs (USA) | | Sadegh Saeed Goudarzi (IRI) | Denis Tsargush (RUS); Soslan Tigiev (UZB) |
| 84 kg (184.8 lb) | Sharif Sharifov (AZE) | | Jaime Yusept Espinal (PUR) | Ehsan Naser Iashgari (IRI); Dato Marsagishvili (GEO) |
| 96 kg (211.2 lb) | Jacob Varner (USA) | | Valerii Andriitsev (UKR) | Khetag Gazyumov (AZE); George Gogshelidze (GEO) |
| 120+ kg (264 lb) | Artur Taymazov (UZB) | | Davit Modzmanashvili (GEO) | Komeil Ghasemi (IRI); Bilyal Makhov (RUS) |
| **Women** | | | | |
| 48 kg (105.6 lb) | Hitomi Obara (JPN) | | Mariya Stadnyk (AZE) | Carol Huynh (CAN); Clarissa Chun (USA) |
| 55 kg (121 lb) | Saori Yoshida (JPN) | | Tonya Lynn Verbeek (CAN) | Jackeline Rentería Castillo (COL); Yuliya Ratkevich (AZE) |
| 63 kg (138.6 lb) | Kaori Icho (JPN) | | Jing Ruixue (CHN) | Battsetseg Sorozonbold (MGL); Lubov Volosova (RUS) |
| 72 kg (158.4 lb) | Nataliya Vorobiyeva (RUS) | | Stanka Zlateva Hristova (BUL) | Guzel Manyurova (KAZ); Maider Unda (ESP) |
| **Greco-Roman** | | | | |
| 55 kg (121 lb) | Hamid Mohammad Soryan Reihanpour (IRI) | | Rovshan Bayramov (AZE) | Peter Modos (HUN); Mingiyan Semenov (RUS) |
| 60 kg (132 lb) | Omid Haji Noroozi (IRI) | | Revaz Lashkhi (GEO) | Zaur Kuramagomedov (RUS); Ryutaro Matsumoto (JPN) |
| 66 kg (145.2 lb) | Kim Hyeon-Woo (KOR) | | Tamas Lorincz (HUN) | Steeve Guénot (FRA); Manuchar Tskhadaia (GEO) |
| 74 kg (162.8 lb) | Roman Vlasov (RUS) | | Arsen Julfalakyan (ARM) | Aleksandr Kazakevic (LTU); Emin Ahmadov (AZE) |
| 84 kg (184.8 lb) | Alan Khugayev (RUS) | | Karam Mohamed Gaber Ebrahim (EGY) | Danyal Gajiyev (KAZ); Damian Janikowski (POL) |
| 96 kg (211.2 lb) | Ghasem Gholamreza Rezaei (IRI) | | Rustam Totrov (RUS) | Artur Aleksanyan (ARM); Jimmy Lidberg (SWE) |
| 120 kg (264 lb) | Mijain López Nunez (CUB) | | Heiki Nabi (EST) | Riza Kayaalp (TUR); Johan Euren (SWE) |

[1]Two bronze medals awarded in each weight division. [2]World record. [3]Olympic record. [4]Winner after disqualification of top finisher for drug use.

## XXI Winter Olympic Games (2010)

*The XXI Winter Games were held in Vancouver, BC, Canada, 12–28 Feb 2010.*

| EVENT | GOLD MEDALIST | PERFORMANCE | SILVER MEDALIST | BRONZE MEDALIST |
|---|---|---|---|---|
| **Alpine Skiing** | | | | |
| **Men** | | | | |
| Downhill | Didier Defago (SUI) | 1 min 54.31 sec | Aksel Lund Svindal (NOR) | Bode Miller (USA) |
| Slalom | Giuliano Razzoli (ITA) | 1 min 39.32 sec | Ivica Kostelic (CRO) | Andre Myhrer (SWE) |

## XXI Winter Olympic Games (2010) (continued)

| EVENT | GOLD MEDALIST | PERFORMANCE | SILVER MEDALIST | BRONZE MEDALIST |
|---|---|---|---|---|
| **Alpine Skiing (continued)** | | | | |
| **Men (continued)** | | | | |
| Giant slalom | Carlo Janka (SUI) | 2 min 37.83 sec | Kjetil Jansrud (NOR) | Aksel Lund Svindal (NOR) |
| Supergiant slalom | Aksel Lund Svindal (NOR) | 1 min 30.34 sec | Bode Miller (USA) | Andrew Weibrecht (USA) |
| Alpine combined | Bode Miller (USA) | 2 min 44.92 sec | Ivica Kostelic (CRO) | Silvan Zurbriggen (SUI) |
| **Women** | | | | |
| Downhill | Lindsey Vonn (USA) | 1 min 44.19 sec | Julia Mancuso (USA) | Elisabeth Görgl (AUT) |
| Slalom | Maria Riesch (GER) | 1 min 42.89 sec | Marlies Schild (AUT) | Sarka Zahrobska (CZE) |
| Giant slalom | Viktoria Rebensburg (GER) | 2 min 27.11 sec | Tina Maze (SLO) | Elisabeth Görgl (AUT) |
| Supergiant slalom | Andrea Fischbacher (AUT) | 1 min 20.14 sec | Tina Maze (SLO) | Lindsey Vonn (USA) |
| Alpine combined | Maria Riesch (GER) | 2 min 09.14 sec | Julia Mancuso (USA) | Anja Pärson (SWE) |

| EVENT | GOLD MEDALIST | PERFORMANCE | SILVER MEDALIST | BRONZE MEDALIST |
|---|---|---|---|---|
| **Nordic Skiing** | | | | |
| **Men** | | | | |
| 1.5-km sprint | Nikita Kriyukov (RUS) | 3 min 36.3 sec | Aleksandr Panzhinskiy (RUS) | Petter Northug (NOR) |
| Team sprint | Øystein Pettersen, Petter Northug (NOR) | 19 min 01.0 sec | Tim Tscharnke, Axel Teichmann (GER) | Nikolay Morilov, Aleksey Petukhov (RUS) |
| 15-km classical | Dario Cologna (SUI) | 33 min 36.3 sec | Pietro Piller Cottrer (ITA) | Lukas Bauer (CZE) |
| 30-km pursuit | Marcus Hellner (SWE) | 1 hr 15 min 11.4 sec | Tobias Angerer (GER) | Johan Olsson (SWE) |
| 50-km freestyle, mass start | Petter Northug (NOR) | 2 hr 5 min 35.5 sec | Axel Teichmann (GER) | Johan Olsson (SWE) |
| 4 x 10-km relay | Sweden | 1 hr 45 min 05.4 sec | Norway | Czech Republic |
| 95-m ski jump | Simon Ammann (SUI) | 276.5 pt | Adam Malysz (POL) | Gregor Schlierenzauer (AUT) |
| 125-m ski jump | Simon Ammann (SUI) | 283.6 pt | Adam Malysz (POL) | Gregor Schlierenzauer (AUT) |
| 125-m team ski jump | Austria | 1,107.9 pt | Germany | Norway |
| Nordic combined normal hill | Jason Lamy Chappuis (FRA) | 25 min 01.1 sec | Johnny Spillane (USA) | Alessandro Pittin (ITA) |
| Nordic combined large hill | Bill Demong (USA) | 24 min 46.9 sec | Johnny Spillane (USA) | Bernhard Gruber (AUT) |
| Nordic combined team relay | Austria | 49 min 31.6 sec | United States | Germany |
| **Women** | | | | |
| 1.5-km sprint | Marit Bjørgen (NOR) | 3 min 39.2 sec | Justyna Kowalczyk (POL) | Petra Majdic (SLO) |
| Team sprint | Evi Sachenbacher-Stehle, Claudia Nystad (GER) | 18 min 03.7 sec | Charlotte Kalla, Anna Haag (SWE) | Irina Khazova, Nataliya Korosteleva (RUS) |
| 10-km classical | Charlotte Kalla (SWE) | 24 min 58.4 sec | Kristina Smigun-Vaehi (EST) | Marit Bjørgen (NOR) |
| 15-km pursuit | Marit Bjørgen (NOR) | 39 min 58.1 sec | Anna Haag (SWE) | Justyna Kowalczyk (POL) |
| 30-km freestyle, mass start | Justyna Kowalczyk (POL) | 1 hr 30 min 33.7 sec | Marit Bjørgen (NOR) | Aino-Kaisa Saarinen (FIN) |
| 4 x 5-km relay | Norway | 55 min 19.5 sec | Germany | Finland |

| EVENT | GOLD MEDALIST | PERFORMANCE | SILVER MEDALIST | BRONZE MEDALIST |
|---|---|---|---|---|
| **Biathlon** | | | | |
| **Men** | | | | |
| 10 km | Vincent Jay (FRA) | 24 min 07.8 sec | Emil Hegle Svendsen (NOR) | Jakov Fak (CRO) |
| 12.5-km pursuit | Björn Ferry (SWE) | 33 min 38.4 sec | Christoph Sumann (AUT) | Vincent Jay (FRA) |
| 20 km | Emil Hegle Svendsen (NOR) | 48 min 22.5 sec | Ole Einar Bjørndalen (NOR)[1], Sergey Novikov (BLR)[1] | |
| 4 x 7.5-km relay | Norway | 1 hr 21 min 38.1 sec | Austria | Russia |
| 15-km mass start | Yevgeny Ustyugov (RUS) | 35 min 35.7 sec | Martin Fourcade (FRA) | Pavol Hurajt (SVK) |

## XXI Winter Olympic Games (2010) (continued)

| EVENT | GOLD MEDALIST | PERFORMANCE | SILVER MEDALIST | BRONZE MEDALIST |
|---|---|---|---|---|
| **Biathlon (continued)** | | | | |
| **Women** | | | | |
| 7.5 km | Anastazia Kuzmina (SVK) | 19 min 55.6 sec | Magdalena Neuner (GER) | Marie Dorin (FRA) |
| 10-km pursuit | Magdalena Neuner (GER) | 30 min 16.0 sec | Anastazia Kuzmina (SVK) | Marie-Laure Brunet (FRA) |
| 15 km | Tora Berger (NOR) | 40 min 52.8 sec | Elena Khrustaleva (KAZ) | Darya Domracheva (BLR) |
| 4 x 6-km relay | Russia | 1 hr 09 min 36.3 sec | France | Germany |
| 12.5-km mass start | Magdalena Neuner (GER) | 35 min 19.6 sec | Olga Zaitseva (RUS) | Simone Hauswald (GER) |
| **Freestyle Skiing** | | | | |
| **Men** | | | | |
| Moguls | Alexandre Bilodeau (CAN) | 26.75 pt | Dale Begg-Smith (AUS) | Bryon Wilson (USA) |
| Aerials | Alexey Grishin (BLR) | 248.41 pt | Jeret Peterson (USA) | Liu Zhongqing (CHN) |
| Ski cross | Michael Schmid (SUI) | | Andreas Matt (AUT) | Audun Grønvold (NOR) |
| **Women** | | | | |
| Moguls | Hannah Kearney (USA) | 26.63 pt | Jennifer Heil (CAN) | Shannon Bahrke (USA) |
| Aerials | Lydia Lassila (AUS) | 214.74 pt | Li Nina (CHN) | Guo Xinxin (CHN) |
| Ski cross | Ashleigh McIvor (CAN) | | Hedda Berntsen (NOR) | Marion Josserand (FRA) |
| **Snowboarding** | | | | |
| **Men** | | | | |
| Giant slalom | Jasey Jay Anderson (CAN) | | Benjamin Karl (AUT) | Mathieu Bozzetto (FRA) |
| Halfpipe | Shaun White (USA) | 48.4 pt | Peetu Piiroinen (FIN) | Scott Lago (USA) |
| Snowboardcross | Seth Wescott (USA) | | Mike Robertson (CAN) | Tony Ramoin (FRA) |
| **Women** | | | | |
| Giant slalom | Nicolien Sauerbreij (NED) | | Yekaterina Ilyukhina (RUS) | Marion Kreiner (AUT) |
| Halfpipe | Torah Bright (AUS) | 45.0 pt | Hannah Teter (USA) | Kelly Clark (USA) |
| Snowboardcross | Maelle Ricker (CAN) | | Deborah Anthonioz (FRA) | Olivia Nobs (SUI) |
| **Figure Skating** | | | | |
| Men | Evan Lysacek (USA) | 257.67 pt | Yevgeny Plushchenko (RUS) | Daisuke Takahashi (JPN) |
| Women | Kim Yu-Na (KOR) | 228.56 pt | Mao Asada (JPN) | Joannie Rochette (CAN) |
| Pairs | Shen Xue, Zhao Hongbo (CHN) | 216.57 pt | Pang Qing, Tong Jian (CHN) | Aliona Savchenko, Robin Szolkowy (GER) |
| Ice dancing | Tessa Virtue, Scott Moir (CAN) | 221.57 pt | Meryl Davis, Charlie White (USA) | Oksana Domnina, Maksim Shabalin (RUS) |
| **Speed Skating** | | | | |
| **Men** | | | | |
| 500 m | Mo Tae-Bum (KOR) | 69.82 sec[2] | Keiichiro Nagashima (JPN) | Joji Kato (JPN) |
| 1,000 m | Shani Davis (USA) | 1 min 08.94 sec | Mo Tae-Bum (KOR) | Chad Hedrick (USA) |
| 1,500 m | Mark Tuitert (NED) | 1 min 45.57 sec | Shani Davis (USA) | Havard Bokko (NOR) |
| 5,000 m | Sven Kramer (NED) | 6 min 14.60 sec[3] | Lee Seung-Hoon (KOR) | Ivan Skobrev (RUS) |
| 10,000 m | Lee Seung-Hoon (KOR)[4] | 12 min 58.55 sec[3] | Ivan Skobrev (RUS) | Bob de Jong (NED) |
| Team pursuit | Canada | 3 min 41.37 sec | United States | Netherlands |
| **Women** | | | | |
| 500 m | Lee Sang-Hwa (KOR) | 76.09 sec[2] | Jenny Wolf (GER) | Wang Beixing (CHN) |
| 1,000 m | Christine Nesbitt (CAN) | 1 min 16.56 sec | Annette Gerritsen (NED) | Laurine van Riessen (NED) |

## XXI Winter Olympic Games (2010) (continued)

| EVENT | GOLD MEDALIST | PERFORMANCE | SILVER MEDALIST | BRONZE MEDALIST |
|---|---|---|---|---|
| **Speed Skating (continued)** | | | | |
| **Women (continued)** | | | | |
| 1,500 m | Ireen Wüst (NED) | 1 min 56.89 sec | Kristina Groves (CAN) | Martina Sablikova (CZE) |
| 3,000 m | Martina Sablikova (CZE) | 4 min 02.53 sec | Stephanie Beckert (GER) | Kristina Groves (CAN) |
| 5,000 m | Martina Sablikova (CZE) | 6 min 50.91 sec | Stephanie Beckert (GER) | Clara Hughes (CAN) |
| Team pursuit | Germany | 3 min 02.82 sec | Japan | Poland |
| **Short-Track Speed Skating** | | | | |
| **Men** | | | | |
| 500 m | Charles Hamelin (CAN) | 40.981 sec | Sung Si-Bak (KOR) | François-Louis Tremblay (CAN) |
| 1,000 m | Lee Jung-Su (KOR) | 1 min 23.747 sec[3] | Lee Ho-Suk (KOR) | Apolo Anton Ohno (USA) |
| 1,500 m | Lee Jung-Su (KOR) | 2 min 17.611 sec | Apolo Anton Ohno (USA) | J.R. Celski (USA) |
| 5,000-m relay | Canada | 6 min 44.224 sec | Republic of Korea | United States |
| **Women** | | | | |
| 500 m | Wang Meng (CHN) | 43.048 sec | Marianne St-Gelais (CAN) | Arianna Fontana (ITA) |
| 1,000 m | Wang Meng (CHN) | 1 min 29.213 sec | Katherine Reutter (USA) | Park Seung-Hi (KOR) |
| 1,500 m | Zhou Yang (CHN) | 2 min 16.993 sec[3] | Lee Eun-Byul (KOR) | Park Seung-Hi (KOR) |
| 3,000-m relay | China[4] | 4 min 06.610 sec[5] | Canada | United States |
| **Ice Hockey** | | | | |
| Men | Canada | 6–1–0 | United States | Finland |
| Women | Canada | 5–0–0 | United States | Finland |
| **Curling** | | | | |
| Men | Canada | 11–0–0 | Norway | Switzerland |
| Women | Sweden | 9–2–0 | Canada | China |
| **Bobsled** | | | | |
| Two-man | André Lange, Kevin Kuske (GER 1) | 3 min 26.65 sec | Thomas Florschütz, Richard Adjei (GER 2) | Aleksandr Zoubkov, Aleksey Voyevoda (RUS 1) |
| Four-man | Steven Holcomb, Steve Mesler, Curtis Tomasevicz, Justin Olsen (USA 1) | 3 min 24.46 sec | André Lange, Alexander Rödiger, Kevin Kuske, Martin Putze (GER 1) | Lyndon Rush, Chris Le Bihan, David Bissett, Lascelles Brown (CAN 1) |
| Two-woman | Kaillie Humphries, Heather Moyse (CAN 1) | 3 min 32.28 sec | Helen Upperton, Shelley-Ann Brown (CAN 2) | Erin Pac, Elana Meyers (USA 2) |
| **Luge** | | | | |
| Men's singles | Felix Loch (GER) | 3 min 13.085 sec | David Möller (GER) | Armin Zöggeler (ITA) |
| Men's doubles | Andreas Linger, Wolfgang Linger (AUT 1) | 1 min 22.705 sec | Andris Sics, Juris Sics (LAT 1) | Patric Leitner, Alexander Resch (GER 1) |
| Women's singles | Tatjana Hüfner (GER) | 2 min 46.524 sec | Nina Reithmayer (AUT) | Natalie Geisenberger (GER) |
| **Skeleton** | | | | |
| Men | Jon Montgomery (CAN) | 3 min 29.73 sec | Martins Dukurs (LAT) | Aleksandr Tretyakov (RUS) |
| Women | Amy Williams (GBR) | 3 min 35.64 sec | Kerstin Szymkowiak (GER) | Anja Huber (GER) |

[1]Tied for silver; no bronze awarded.    [2]Time is combined total of two heats.    [3]Olympic record.    [4]Original winner disqualified.    [5]World record.

# Special Olympics

The Special Olympics, an international program, provides individuals who have intellectual disabilities and are eight years of age or older with year-round sports training and athletic competition in a variety of Olympic-type summer and winter sports. Inaugurated in 1968, the Special Olympics is officially recognized by the International Olympic Committee. **International headquarters** are in Washington DC.

In the summer of 1962, with support from the Joseph P. Kennedy, Jr., Foundation, **Eunice Kennedy Shriver** (sister of Pres. John F. Kennedy) started a summer day camp at her home in Rockville MD for children with mental retardation. The Kennedy Foundation promoted the creation of dozens of similar camps in the United States and Canada. Special awards were developed for physical achievements, and by 1968 Shriver had persuaded the Chicago Park District to join with the Foundation in sponsoring a "Special Olympics," held at Soldier Field on 20 July. About 1,000 athletes from 26 US states and Canada participated. The games were such a success that, in December, Special Olympics, Inc. (now **Special Olympics International**), was founded, with chapters in the United States, Canada, and France. The first International Winter Special Olympics Games were held 5–11 Feb 1977 (in Steamboat Springs CO). The number of participating countries proliferated so that by 2012 there were chapters in more than 170 countries. More than 49,000 meets and tournaments are held worldwide each year, culminating in the Special Olympics World Games every two years, alternating between winter and summer sports.

**Special Olympics Web site:**
<www.specialolympics.org>.

# Automobile Racing

Of the various types of automobile races, the closed-circuit, or speedway, course was developed largely in the United States. A low-slung, fenderless (open-wheel) car—called an Indy car—is essential for this race; its suspension (i.e., its ability to hold the track) is as important to a car's performance as its turbo-charged engine. The **Indianapolis 500**—now the premier Indy car event—was first run in 1911. Often the chassis manufacturer is different from the engine manufacturer, resulting in cars identified, for example, as Brabham/Repcos, with the chassis maker listed first. The chassis maker receives any winnings.

Indy car racing began in 1909, when the American Automobile Association (AAA) began sponsoring a 24-race championship series, including three races at the newly opened Indianapolis Motor Speedway (IMS). In 1956 the United States Auto Club (**USAC**) was organized as the sport's governing body. In 1978 a new organization, Championship Auto Racing Teams, Inc. (**CART**), formed that sponsored its own series of races. In 1980 CART and USAC joined to form the Championship Racing League, which dissolved after five races. In 1994 the IMS announced a new Indy Racing League (**IRL**) to oversee the Indianapolis 500 beginning in 1996 and a new series of IRL races (leading to an annual drivers' championship) separate from those sponsored by CART.

The standard cars used for Grand Prix road (closed-highway) racing are called Formula One (or F-1) cars because they are built according to an evolving formula that was established after World War I by the Fédération Internationale de l'Automobile (**FIA**). Like the Indy car, the Formula One racer is open-wheeled and low-slung, but the F-1 is smaller and more maneuverable.

There are approximately 20 Grand Prix events held worldwide throughout the year. Drivers compete for the **World Championship of Drivers** (inaugurated in 1950), receiving a total number of points based on their placement in each of the official Grand Prix events. Many Grand Prix drivers participate in various endurance races, the most famous of which is the **Le Mans Grand Prix d'Endurance**.

The rally, established in 1907, is another popular racing event, with more than 35 yearly competitions raced over a specified route on public roads throughout the world. The classic occasion for rally racing is the **Rallye Automobile Monte-Carlo**, now started in various European cities with Monaco as its terminal point.

Stock-car racing, which began in the US in the first half of the 20th century, involves the racing of commercial cars that have been altered to increase their speed and maneuverability. The National Association for Stock Car Auto Racing (**NASCAR**) was founded in 1947, and it awarded the Winston Cup (1971–2003) to the driver who had earned the greatest number of points in a series of official NASCAR events over the stock-car racing season. In 2004 the competition was renamed the Nextel Cup, and from 2008 it is known as the Sprint Cup. The **Daytona 500** is the premiere event. In 1982 a platform for racing late model stock cars was developed through the Budweiser Late Model Sportsman Series, later (1984–2007) called the Busch Series and from 2008 known as the Nationwide Series. The Camping World Truck Series (founded as the Super Truck Series in 1995 and called the Craftsman Truck Series from 1996 through 2008) features race cars with bodies that mimic pickup trucks.

**Related Web sites:** Champ Car: <www.champcars.com>; USAC: <www.usacracing.com>; IRL: <www.indycar.com>; FIA: <www.fia.com>; Automobile Club de Monaco <www.acm.mc>; NASCAR: <www.nascar.com>.

## Formula One Grand Prix Race Results, 2011–12

*The season for the Formula One Grand Prix circuit is March–November.*

| RACE | DATE | LOCALE | WINNER (COUNTRY) | TIME (HR:MIN:SEC) |
|---|---|---|---|---|
| Belgian Grand Prix | 28 Aug 2011 | Spa-Francorchamps | Sebastian Vettel (GER) | 1:26:44.893 |
| Italian Grand Prix | 11 Sep 2011 | Monza | Sebastian Vettel (GER) | 1:20:46.172 |
| Singapore Grand Prix | 25 Sep 2011 | Singapore | Sebastian Vettel (GER) | 1:59:06.757 |

## Formula One Grand Prix Race Results, 2011–12 (continued)

| RACE | DATE | LOCALE | WINNER (COUNTRY) | TIME (HR:MIN:SEC) |
|------|------|--------|------------------|-------------------|
| Japanese Grand Prix | 9 Oct 2011 | Suzuka | Jenson Button (GBR) | 1:30:53.427 |
| Korean Grand Prix | 16 Oct 2011 | Yeongam | Sebastian Vettel (GER) | 1:38:01.994 |
| Indian Grand Prix | 30 Oct 2011 | New Delhi | Sebastian Vettel (GER) | 1:30:35.002 |
| Abu Dhabi Grand Prix | 13 Nov 2011 | Yas Marina | Lewis Hamilton (GBR) | 1:37:11.886 |
| Brazilian Grand Prix | 27 Nov 2011 | São Paulo | Mark Webber (AUS) | 1:32:17.464 |
| Australian Grand Prix | 18 Mar 2012 | Melbourne | Jenson Button (GBR) | 1:34:09.565 |
| Malaysian Grand Prix | 25 Mar 2012 | Kuala Lumpur | Fernando Alonso (ESP) | 2:44:51.812 |
| Chinese Grand Prix | 15 Apr 2012 | Shanghai | Nico Rosberg (GER) | 1:36:26.929 |
| Bahrainian Grand Prix | 22 Apr 2012 | Sakhir | Sebastian Vettel (GER) | 1:35:10.990 |
| Spanish Grand Prix | 13 May 2012 | Catalonia | Pastor Maldonado (VEN) | 1:39:09.145 |
| Monaco Grand Prix | 27 May 2012 | Monte-Carlo | Mark Webber (AUS) | 1:46:06.557 |
| Canadian Grand Prix | 10 Jun 2012 | Montreal | Lewis Hamilton (GBR) | 1:32:29.586 |
| European Grand Prix | 24 Jun 2012 | Valencia, Spain | Fernando Alonso (ESP) | 1:44:16.649 |
| British Grand Prix | 8 Jul 2012 | Silverstone | Mark Webber (AUS) | 1:25:11.288 |
| German Grand Prix | 22 Jul 2012 | Hockenheimring | Fernando Alonso (ESP) | 1:31:05.862 |
| Hungarian Grand Prix | 29 Jul 2012 | Budapest | Lewis Hamilton (GBR) | 1:41:05.503 |

## Indianapolis 500

*There was no competition in 1917–18 and 1942–45. Won by an American racer except as indicated.*

| YEAR | WINNER | AVG. SPEED (MPH) | YEAR | WINNER | AVG. SPEED (MPH) | YEAR | WINNER | AVG. SPEED (MPH) |
|------|--------|------------------|------|--------|------------------|------|--------|------------------|
| 1911 | Ray Harroun | 74.602 | 1954 | Bill Vukovich | 130.840 | 1989 | Emerson Fitti-paldi (BRA) | 167.581 |
| 1912 | Joe Dawson | 78.719 | 1955 | Robert Sweikert | 128.209 | 1990 | Arie Luyendyk (NED) | 185.984 |
| 1913 | Jules Goux (FRA) | 75.933 | 1956 | Pat Flaherty | 128.490 | 1991 | Rick Mears | 176.457 |
| 1914 | René Thomas (FRA) | 82.474 | 1957 | Sam Hanks | 135.601 | 1992 | Al Unser, Jr. | 134.479 |
| 1915 | Ralph DePalma | 89.840 | 1958 | Jimmy Bryan | 133.791 | 1993 | Emerson Fitti-paldi (BRA) | 157.207 |
| 1916[1] | Dario Resta (FRA) | 84.001 | 1959 | Rodger Ward | 135.857 | 1994 | Al Unser, Jr. | 160.872 |
| 1919 | Howdy Wilcox | 88.050 | 1960 | Jim Rathmann | 138.767 | 1995 | Jacques Ville-neuve (CAN) | 153.616 |
| 1920 | Gaston Chevrolet | 88.618 | 1961 | A.J. Foyt, Jr. | 139.131 | 1996 | Buddy Lazier | 147.956 |
| 1921 | Tommy Milton | 89.621 | 1962 | Rodger Ward | 140.293 | 1997 | Arie Luyendyk (NED) | 145.827 |
| 1922 | Jimmy Murphy | 94.484 | 1963 | Parnelli Jones | 143.137 | 1998 | Eddie Cheever, Jr. | 145.155 |
| 1923 | Tommy Milton | 90.954 | 1964 | A.J. Foyt, Jr. | 147.350 | 1999 | Kenny Bräck (SWE) | 153.176 |
| 1924[2] | L.L. Corum, Joe Boyer | 98.234 | 1965 | Jim Clark (GBR) | 150.686 | 2000 | Juan Montoya (COL) | 167.607 |
| 1925 | Peter DePaolo | 101.127 | 1966 | Graham Hill (GBR) | 144.317 | 2001 | Helio Castro-neves (BRA) | 153.601 |
| 1926[3] | Frank Lockhart | 95.904 | 1967 | A.J. Foyt, Jr. | 151.207 | 2002 | Helio Castro-neves (BRA) | 166.499 |
| 1927 | George Souders | 97.545 | 1968 | Bobby Unser | 152.882 | 2003 | Gil de Ferran (BRA) | 156.291 |
| 1928 | Louie Meyer | 99.482 | 1969 | Mario Andretti | 156.867 | 2004[3] | Buddy Rice | 138.518 |
| 1929 | Ray Keech | 97.585 | 1970 | Al Unser | 155.749 | 2005 | Dan Wheldon (GBR) | 157.603 |
| 1930 | Billy Arnold | 100.448 | 1971 | Al Unser | 157.735 | 2006 | Sam Hornish, Jr. | 157.085 |
| 1931 | Louis Schneider | 96.629 | 1972 | Mark Donohue | 162.962 | 2007 | Dario Franchitti (GBR) | 151.774 |
| 1932 | Fred Frame | 104.144 | 1973[3] | Gordon Johncock | 159.036 | 2008 | Scott Dixon (NZL) | 143.567 |
| 1933 | Louie Meyer | 104.162 | 1974 | Johnny Rutherford | 158.589 | 2009 | Helio Castro-neves (BRA) | 150.318 |
| 1934 | Bill Cummings | 104.863 | 1975[3] | Bobby Unser | 149.213 | 2010 | Dario Franchitti | 161.623 |
| 1935 | Kelly Petillo | 106.240 | 1976[3] | Johnny Rutherford | 148.725 | 2011 | Dan Wheldon (GBR) | 170.265 |
| 1936 | Louie Meyer | 109.069 | 1977 | A.J. Foyt, Jr. | 161.331 | 2012 | Dario Franchitti (GBR) | 167.734 |
| 1937 | Wilbur Shaw | 113.580 | 1978 | Al Unser | 161.363 |  |  |  |
| 1938 | Floyd Roberts | 117.200 | 1979 | Rick Mears | 158.899 |  |  |  |
| 1939 | Wilbur Shaw | 115.035 | 1980 | Johnny Rutherford | 142.862 |  |  |  |
| 1940 | Wilbur Shaw | 114.277 | 1981 | Bobby Unser | 139.084 |  |  |  |
| 1941[2] | Floyd Davis, Mauri Rose | 115.117 | 1982 | Gordon Johncock | 162.029 |  |  |  |
| 1946 | George Robson | 114.820 | 1983 | Tom Sneva | 162.117 |  |  |  |
| 1947 | Mauri Rose | 116.338 | 1984 | Rick Mears | 163.612 |  |  |  |
| 1948 | Mauri Rose | 119.814 | 1985 | Danny Sullivan | 152.982 |  |  |  |
| 1949 | Bill Holland | 121.327 | 1986 | Bobby Rahal | 170.722 |  |  |  |
| 1950[3] | Johnnie Parsons | 124.002 | 1987 | Al Unser | 162.175 |  |  |  |
| 1951 | Lee Wallard | 126.244 | 1988 | Rick Mears | 144.809 |  |  |  |
| 1952 | Troy Ruttman | 128.922 |  |  |  |  |  |  |
| 1953 | Bill Vukovich | 128.740 |  |  |  |  |  |  |

[1]Scheduled 300-mile race. [2]First driver named started the race but was replaced during the race by the second driver named. [3]Race stopped because of rain (in 1926 after 400 miles, in 1950 after 345 miles, in 1973 after 332.5 miles, in 1975 after 435 miles, in 1976 after 255 miles, in 2004 after 450 miles, and in 2007 after 415 miles).

## NASCAR Sprint Cup Champions

| YEAR | WINNER | YEAR | WINNER | YEAR | WINNER | YEAR | WINNER |
|------|--------|------|--------|------|--------|------|--------|
| 1949 | Red Byron | 1965 | Ned Jarrett | 1981 | Darrell Waltrip | 1997 | Jeff Gordon |
| 1950 | Bill Rexford | 1966 | David Pearson | 1982 | Darrell Waltrip | 1998 | Jeff Gordon |
| 1951 | Herb Thomas | 1967 | Richard Petty | 1983 | Bobby Allison | 1999 | Dale Jarrett |
| 1952 | Tim Flock | 1968 | David Pearson | 1984 | Terry Labonte | 2000 | Bobby Labonte |
| 1953 | Herb Thomas | 1969 | David Pearson | 1985 | Darrell Waltrip | 2001 | Jeff Gordon |
| 1954 | Lee Petty | 1970 | Bobby Isaac | 1986 | Dale Earnhardt | 2002 | Tony Stewart |
| 1955 | Tim Flock | 1971 | Richard Petty | 1987 | Dale Earnhardt | 2003 | Matt Kenseth |
| 1956 | Buck Baker | 1972 | Richard Petty | 1988 | Bill Elliott | 2004 | Kurt Busch |
| 1957 | Buck Baker | 1973 | Benny Parsons | 1989 | Rusty Wallace | 2005 | Tony Stewart |
| 1958 | Lee Petty | 1974 | Richard Petty | 1990 | Dale Earnhardt | 2006 | Jimmie Johnson |
| 1959 | Lee Petty | 1975 | Richard Petty | 1991 | Dale Earnhardt | 2007 | Jimmie Johnson |
| 1960 | Rex White | 1976 | Cale Yarborough | 1992 | Alan Kulwicki | 2008 | Jimmie Johnson |
| 1961 | Ned Jarrett | 1977 | Cale Yarborough | 1993 | Dale Earnhardt | 2009 | Jimmie Johnson |
| 1962 | Joe Weatherly | 1978 | Cale Yarborough | 1994 | Dale Earnhardt | 2010 | Jimmie Johnson |
| 1963 | Joe Weatherly | 1979 | Richard Petty | 1995 | Jeff Gordon | 2011 | Tony Stewart |
| 1964 | Richard Petty | 1980 | Dale Earnhardt | 1996 | Terry Labonte | | |

# Baseball

The sport of baseball—given its definitive form in the United States in the late 19th century—is popular throughout the world, though until 2006 it was organized internationally only for **Little League** players (children ages 5–18). Little League Baseball was founded in Pennsylvania in 1939. The first Little League World Series was in 1947, and the first Little League outside the US was organized in British Columbia in 1951. Baseball is especially popular in Japan and Latin America; it is also one of the national sports of the US.

On a **professional** level, the premier event of baseball in the US is the **World Series** of **Major League Baseball**, in which the first team to win four games wins the Series. In fact, the Series is not contested on an international level, but rather is played between the leading team of the **National League** (NL; formed 1876) and the leading team of the **American League** (AL; formed 1900

and including, from 1977, one Canadian team). In 2006 the inaugural World Baseball Classic, a competition featuring national teams, was held in Japan, Puerto Rico, and the US. The team from Japan beat Cuba's team in the finals. The second competition, held in 2009, also was won by Japan, this time defeating Korea.

Professional baseball began in Japan in 1936. Teams are organized into two leagues of six teams each. The seven-game **Japan Series**, first played in 1950, is contested between the leading team of the Central League (CL) and the leading team of the Pacific League (PL). The modern **Caribbean Series** began in 1970 with the winning team from each league in the Dominican Republic, Mexico, Puerto Rico, and Venezuela.

**Related Web sites:**
Major League Baseball: <http://mlb.mlb.com/index.-jsp>; Little League: <www.littleleague.org>.

## Major League Baseball Final Standings, 2011

### American League

| East Division CLUB | WON | LOST | GAMES BACK | Central Division CLUB | WON | LOST | GAMES BACK | West Division CLUB | WON | LOST | GAMES BACK |
|------|-----|------|------------|------|-----|------|------------|------|-----|------|------------|
| New York[1] | 97 | 65 | — | Detroit[1] | 95 | 67 | — | Texas[1] | 96 | 66 | — |
| Tampa Bay[1] | 91 | 71 | 6 | Cleveland | 80 | 82 | 15 | Los Angeles | 86 | 76 | 10 |
| Boston | 90 | 72 | 7 | Chicago | 79 | 83 | 16 | Oakland | 74 | 88 | 22 |
| Toronto | 81 | 81 | 16 | Kansas City | 71 | 91 | 24 | Seattle | 67 | 95 | 29 |
| Baltimore | 69 | 93 | 28 | Minnesota | 63 | 99 | 32 | | | | |

### National League

| East Division CLUB | WON | LOST | GAMES BACK | Central Division CLUB | WON | LOST | GAMES BACK | West Division CLUB | WON | LOST | GAMES BACK |
|------|-----|------|------------|------|-----|------|------------|------|-----|------|------------|
| Philadelphia[1] | 102 | 60 | — | Milwaukee[1] | 96 | 66 | — | Arizona[1] | 94 | 68 | — |
| Atlanta | 89 | 73 | 13 | St. Louis[1] | 90 | 72 | 6 | San Francisco | 86 | 76 | 8 |
| Washington | 80 | 81 | 21.5 | Cincinnati | 79 | 83 | 17 | Los Angeles | 82 | 79 | 11.5 |
| New York | 77 | 85 | 25 | Pittsburgh | 72 | 90 | 24 | Colorado | 73 | 89 | 21 |
| Florida | 72 | 90 | 30 | Chicago | 71 | 91 | 25 | San Diego | 71 | 91 | 23 |
| | | | | Houston | 56 | 106 | 40 | | | | |

[1]Gained play-off berth.

# World Series

| YEAR | WINNER | RUNNER-UP | RESULTS |
|------|--------|-----------|---------|
| 1903 | Boston Americans (AL) | Pittsburgh Pirates (NL) | 5–3 |
| 1904 | *not held* | | |
| 1905 | New York Giants (NL) | Philadelphia Athletics (AL) | 4–1 |
| 1906 | Chicago White Sox (AL) | Chicago Cubs (NL) | 4–2 |
| 1907 | Chicago Cubs (NL) | Detroit Tigers (AL) | 4–0[1] |
| 1908 | Chicago Cubs (NL) | Detroit Tigers (AL) | 4–1 |
| 1909 | Pittsburgh Pirates (NL) | Detroit Tigers (AL) | 4–3 |
| 1910 | Philadelphia Athletics (AL) | Chicago Cubs (NL) | 4–1 |
| 1911 | Philadelphia Athletics (AL) | New York Giants (NL) | 4–2 |
| 1912 | Boston Red Sox (AL) | New York Giants (NL) | 4–3[1] |
| 1913 | Philadelphia Athletics (AL) | New York Giants (NL) | 4–1 |
| 1914 | Boston Braves (NL) | Philadelphia Athletics (AL) | 4–0 |
| 1915 | Boston Red Sox (AL) | Philadelphia Phillies (NL) | 4–1 |
| 1916 | Boston Red Sox (AL) | Brooklyn Robins (NL) | 4–1 |
| 1917 | Chicago White Sox (AL) | New York Giants (NL) | 4–2 |
| 1918 | Boston Red Sox (AL) | Chicago Cubs (NL) | 4–2 |
| 1919 | Cincinnati Reds (NL) | Chicago White Sox (AL) | 5–3 |
| 1920 | Cleveland Indians (AL) | Brooklyn Robins (NL) | 5–2 |
| 1921 | New York Giants (NL) | New York Yankees (AL) | 5–3 |
| 1922 | New York Giants (NL) | New York Yankees (AL) | 4–0[1] |
| 1923 | New York Yankees (AL) | New York Giants (NL) | 4–2 |
| 1924 | Washington Senators (AL) | New York Giants (NL) | 4–3 |
| 1925 | Pittsburgh Pirates (NL) | Washington Senators (AL) | 4–3 |
| 1926 | St. Louis Cardinals (NL) | New York Yankees (AL) | 4–3 |
| 1927 | New York Yankees (AL) | Pittsburgh Pirates (NL) | 4–0 |
| 1928 | New York Yankees (AL) | St. Louis Cardinals (NL) | 4–0 |
| 1929 | Philadelphia Athletics (AL) | Chicago Cubs (NL) | 4–1 |
| 1930 | Philadelphia Athletics (AL) | St. Louis Cardinals (NL) | 4–2 |
| 1931 | St. Louis Cardinals (NL) | Philadelphia Athletics (AL) | 4–3 |
| 1932 | New York Yankees (AL) | Chicago Cubs (NL) | 4–0 |
| 1933 | New York Giants (NL) | Washington Senators (AL) | 4–1 |
| 1934 | St. Louis Cardinals (NL) | Detroit Tigers (AL) | 4–3 |
| 1935 | Detroit Tigers (AL) | Chicago Cubs (NL) | 4–2 |
| 1936 | New York Yankees (AL) | New York Giants (NL) | 4–2 |
| 1937 | New York Yankees (AL) | New York Giants (NL) | 4–1 |
| 1938 | New York Yankees (AL) | Chicago Cubs (NL) | 4–0 |
| 1939 | New York Yankees (AL) | Cincinnati Reds (NL) | 4–0 |
| 1940 | Cincinnati Reds (NL) | Detroit Tigers (AL) | 4–3 |
| 1941 | New York Yankees (AL) | Brooklyn Dodgers (NL) | 4–1 |
| 1942 | St. Louis Cardinals (NL) | New York Yankees (AL) | 4–1 |
| 1943 | New York Yankees (AL) | St. Louis Cardinals (NL) | 4–1 |
| 1944 | St. Louis Cardinals (NL) | St. Louis Browns (AL) | 4–2 |
| 1945 | Detroit Tigers (AL) | Chicago Cubs (NL) | 4–3 |
| 1946 | St. Louis Cardinals (NL) | Boston Red Sox (AL) | 4–3 |
| 1947 | New York Yankees (AL) | Brooklyn Dodgers (NL) | 4–3 |
| 1948 | Cleveland Indians (AL) | Boston Braves (NL) | 4–2 |
| 1949 | New York Yankees (AL) | Brooklyn Dodgers (NL) | 4–1 |
| 1950 | New York Yankees (AL) | Philadelphia Phillies (NL) | 4–0 |
| 1951 | New York Yankees (AL) | New York Giants (NL) | 4–2 |
| 1952 | New York Yankees (AL) | Brooklyn Dodgers (NL) | 4–3 |
| 1953 | New York Yankees (AL) | Brooklyn Dodgers (NL) | 4–2 |
| 1954 | New York Giants (NL) | Cleveland Indians (AL) | 4–0 |
| 1955 | Brooklyn Dodgers (NL) | New York Yankees (AL) | 4–3 |
| 1956 | New York Yankees (AL) | Brooklyn Dodgers (NL) | 4–3 |
| 1957 | Milwaukee Braves (NL) | New York Yankees (AL) | 4–3 |
| 1958 | New York Yankees (AL) | Milwaukee Braves (NL) | 4–3 |
| 1959 | Los Angeles Dodgers (NL) | Chicago White Sox (AL) | 4–2 |
| 1960 | Pittsburgh Pirates (NL) | New York Yankees (AL) | 4–3 |
| 1961 | New York Yankees (AL) | Cincinnati Reds (NL) | 4–1 |
| 1962 | New York Yankees (AL) | San Francisco Giants (NL) | 4–3 |
| 1963 | Los Angeles Dodgers (NL) | New York Yankees (AL) | 4–0 |
| 1964 | St. Louis Cardinals (NL) | New York Yankees (AL) | 4–3 |
| 1965 | Los Angeles Dodgers (NL) | Minnesota Twins (AL) | 4–3 |
| 1966 | Baltimore Orioles (AL) | Los Angeles Dodgers (NL) | 4–0 |
| 1967 | St. Louis Cardinals (NL) | Boston Red Sox (AL) | 4–3 |
| 1968 | Detroit Tigers (AL) | St. Louis Cardinals (NL) | 4–3 |
| 1969 | New York Mets (NL) | Baltimore Orioles (AL) | 4–1 |
| 1970 | Baltimore Orioles (AL) | Cincinnati Reds (NL) | 4–1 |

## World Series (continued)

| YEAR | WINNER | RUNNER-UP | RESULTS |
|------|--------|-----------|---------|
| 1971 | Pittsburgh Pirates (NL) | Baltimore Orioles (AL) | 4–3 |
| 1972 | Oakland Athletics (AL) | Cincinnati Reds (NL) | 4–3 |
| 1973 | Oakland Athletics (AL) | New York Mets (NL) | 4–3 |
| 1974 | Oakland Athletics (AL) | Los Angeles Dodgers (NL) | 4–1 |
| 1975 | Cincinnati Reds (NL) | Boston Red Sox (AL) | 4–3 |
| 1976 | Cincinnati Reds (NL) | New York Yankees (AL) | 4–0 |
| 1977 | New York Yankees (AL) | Los Angeles Dodgers (NL) | 4–2 |
| 1978 | New York Yankees (AL) | Los Angeles Dodgers (NL) | 4–2 |
| 1979 | Pittsburgh Pirates (NL) | Baltimore Orioles (AL) | 4–3 |
| 1980 | Philadelphia Phillies (NL) | Kansas City Royals (AL) | 4–2 |
| 1981 | Los Angeles Dodgers (NL) | New York Yankees (AL) | 4–2 |
| 1982 | St. Louis Cardinals (NL) | Milwaukee Brewers (AL) | 4–3 |
| 1983 | Baltimore Orioles (AL) | Philadelphia Phillies (NL) | 4–1 |
| 1984 | Detroit Tigers (AL) | San Diego Padres (NL) | 4–1 |
| 1985 | Kansas City Royals (AL) | St. Louis Cardinals (NL) | 4–3 |
| 1986 | New York Mets (NL) | Boston Red Sox (AL) | 4–3 |
| 1987 | Minnesota Twins (AL) | St. Louis Cardinals (NL) | 4–3 |
| 1988 | Los Angeles Dodgers (NL) | Oakland Athletics (AL) | 4–1 |
| 1989 | Oakland Athletics (AL) | San Francisco Giants (NL) | 4–0 |
| 1990 | Cincinnati Reds (NL) | Oakland Athletics (AL) | 4–0 |
| 1991 | Minnesota Twins (AL) | Atlanta Braves (NL) | 4–3 |
| 1992 | Toronto Blue Jays (AL) | Atlanta Braves (NL) | 4–2 |
| 1993 | Toronto Blue Jays (AL) | Philadelphia Phillies (NL) | 4–2 |
| 1994 | not held | | |
| 1995 | Atlanta Braves (NL) | Cleveland Indians (AL) | 4–2 |
| 1996 | New York Yankees (AL) | Atlanta Braves (NL) | 4–2 |
| 1997 | Florida Marlins (NL) | Cleveland Indians (AL) | 4–3 |
| 1998 | New York Yankees (AL) | San Diego Padres (NL) | 4–0 |
| 1999 | New York Yankees (AL) | Atlanta Braves (NL) | 4–0 |
| 2000 | New York Yankees (AL) | New York Mets (NL) | 4–1 |
| 2001 | Arizona Diamondbacks (NL) | New York Yankees (AL) | 4–3 |
| 2002 | Anaheim Angels (AL) | San Francisco Giants (NL) | 4–3 |
| 2003 | Florida Marlins (NL) | New York Yankees (AL) | 4–2 |
| 2004 | Boston Red Sox (AL) | St. Louis Cardinals (NL) | 4–0 |
| 2005 | Chicago White Sox (AL) | Houston Astros (NL) | 4–0 |
| 2006 | St. Louis Cardinals (NL) | Detroit Tigers (AL) | 4–1 |
| 2007 | Boston Red Sox (AL) | Colorado Rockies (NL) | 4–0 |
| 2008 | Philadelphia Phillies (NL) | Tampa Bay Rays (AL) | 4–1 |
| 2009 | New York Yankees (AL) | Philadelphia Phillies (NL) | 4–2 |
| 2010 | San Francisco Giants (NL) | Texas Rangers (AL) | 4–1 |
| 2011 | St. Louis Cardinals (NL) | Texas Rangers (AL) | 4–3 |

[1]Plus one tied game.

## Major League Baseball All-Time Records[1]

*Research courtesy of Baseball Almanac, <www.baseball-almanac.com>.*

| | PLAYERS/TEAMS | NUMBER | SEASON/DATE |
|--|---------------|--------|-------------|
| **Individual career records** | | | |
| Games played | Pete Rose | 3,562 | 1963–86 |
| Consecutive games played | Cal Ripken, Jr. | 2,632 | 1982–98 |
| Batting average[2] | Ty Cobb | .366 | 1905–28 |
| Hits | Pete Rose | 4,256 | 1963–86 |
| Doubles | Tris Speaker | 792 | 1907–28 |
| Triples | Sam Crawford | 309 | 1899–1917 |
| Home runs | Barry Bonds | 762 | 1986–2007 |
| Runs | Rickey Henderson | 2,295 | 1979–2003 |
| Runs batted in | Hank Aaron | 2,297 | 1954–76 |
| Walks (batting) | Barry Bonds | 2,558 | 1986–2007 |
| Stolen bases | Rickey Henderson | 1,406 | 1979–2003 |
| Wins (pitching) | Cy Young | 511 | 1890–1911 |
| Earned run average[3] | Ed Walsh | 1.82 | 1904–17 |
| Strikeouts (pitching) | Nolan Ryan | 5,714 | 1966–93 |
| Saves | Mariano Rivera[4] | 603 | 1995–2011 |
| No-hitters | Nolan Ryan | 7 | 1966–93 |
| Shutouts | Walter Johnson | 110 | 1907–27 |
| Wins (managing) | Connie Mack | 3,731 | 1894–96; 1901–50 |

## Major League Baseball All-Time Records[1] (continued)

| | PLAYERS/TEAMS | NUMBER | SEASON/DATE |
|---|---|---|---|
| **Individual season records** | | | |
| Batting average[5] | Hugh Duffy | .440 | 1894 |
| Hits | Ichiro Suzuki[4] | 262 | 2004 |
| Doubles | Earl Webb | 67 | 1931 |
| Triples | Chief Wilson | 36 | 1912 |
| Home runs | Barry Bonds | 73 | 2001 |
| Runs | Billy Hamilton | 192 | 1894 |
| Runs batted in | Hack Wilson | 191 | 1930 |
| Walks (batting) | Barry Bonds | 232 | 2004 |
| Stolen bases | Hugh Nicol | 138 | 1887 |
| Wins (pitching) | Charley Radbourn | 59 | 1884 |
| Earned run average[6] | Tim Keefe | 0.86 | 1880 |
| Strikeouts (pitching) | Matt Kilroy | 513 | 1886 |
| No-hitters | *5 players hold record* | 2 | |
| Saves | Francisco Rodriguez[4] | 62 | 2008 |
| Shutouts | George Bradley; Grover Alexander | 16 | 1876; 1916 |
| **Individual game records[7]** | | | |
| Hits | Wilbert Robinson; Rennie Stennett | 7 | 10 Jun 1892; 16 Sep 1975 |
| Doubles | *51 players hold record* | 4 | |
| Triples | George Strief; Bill Joyce | 4 | 25 Jun 1885; 18 May 1897 |
| Home runs | *12 players hold record* | 4 | |
| Runs | Guy Hecker | 7 | 15 Aug 1886 |
| Runs batted in | Jim Bottomley; Mark Whiten | 12 | 16 Sep 1924; 7 Sep 1993 |
| Walks (batting) | Walt Wilmot; Jimmie Foxx | 6 | 22 Aug 1891; 16 Jun 1938 |
| Stolen bases | George Gore; Billy Hamilton | 7 | 25 Jun 1881; 31 Aug 1894 |
| Strikeouts (pitching) | Roger Clemens (twice); Kerry Wood[4] | 20 | 29 Apr 1986 and 18 Sep 1996; 6 May 1998 |
| **Team season records** | | | |
| World Series titles | New York Yankees | 26 | |
| Consecutive World Series titles | New York Yankees | 5 | 1949–53 |
| Games won | Chicago Cubs; Seattle Mariners | 116 | 1906; 2001 |
| Highest winning percentage | St. Louis Maroons | .832 (94–19) | 1884 |
| Batting average | Philadelphia Phillies | .349 | 1894 |
| Doubles | Texas Rangers | 376 | 2008 |
| Triples | Baltimore Orioles | 153 | 1894 |
| Home runs | Seattle Mariners | 264 | 1997 |
| Runs | Boston Beaneaters | 1,220 | 1894 |
| Runs batted in | Boston Beaneaters | 1,043 | 1894 |
| Walks (batting) | Boston Red Sox | 835 | 1949 |
| Stolen bases | Philadelphia Athletics | 638 | 1887 |
| **Game records** | | | |
| Highest combined score | Chicago Cubs versus Philadelphia Phillies | 49 (26–23) | 25 Aug 1922 |
| Longest nine-inning game | New York Yankees versus Boston Red Sox | 4 hr 45 min | 18 Aug 2006 |
| Longest extra-inning game (time) | Chicago White Sox versus Milwaukee Brewers | 8 hr 6 min | 9 May 1984 |
| Longest extra-inning game (innings) | Brooklyn Dodgers versus Boston Braves | 26 innings | 1 May 1920 |

[1]*Through the end of the 2011 season.*    [2]*Minimum of 1,000 games played and 1,000 at-bats.*    [3]*Minimum of 2,000 innings pitched.*    [4]*Active in 2011.*    [5]*Minimum of 3.1 plate appearances per game played.*    [6]*Minimum of one inning pitched per game played.*    [7]*Nine-inning games only.*

## Caribbean Series

*Held since 1949. Table shows results for the past 10 years.*

| YEAR | WINNER | COUNTRY | YEAR | WINNER | COUNTRY |
|---|---|---|---|---|---|
| 2003 | Cibao Eagles | DOM | 2008 | Licey Tigers | DOM |
| 2004 | Licey Tigers | DOM | 2009 | Aragua Tigers | VEN |
| 2005 | Mazatlán Deer | MEX | 2010 | Escogido Lions | DOM |
| 2006 | Caracas Lions | VEN | 2011 | Obregón Yaquis | MEX |
| 2007 | Cibao Eagles | DOM | 2012 | Escogido Lions | DOM |

## Japan Series

*Held since 1950. Table shows results for the past 10 years.*

| YEAR | WINNER | YEAR | WINNER |
|------|--------|------|--------|
| 2002 | Yomiuri Giants (CL) | 2007 | Chunichi Dragons (CL) |
| 2003 | Fukuoka Daiei Hawks (PL) | 2008 | Saitama Seibu Lions (PL) |
| 2004 | Seibu Lions (PL) | 2009 | Yomiuri Giants (CL) |
| 2005 | Chiba Lotte Marines (PL) | 2010 | Chiba Lotte Marines (PL) |
| 2006 | Hokkaido Nippon Ham Fighters (PL) | 2011 | Fukuoka Softbank Hawks (PL) |

## Little League World Series

*The Little League World Series, first called the National Little League Tournament, was established in 1947. Table shows results for past 10 years.*

| YEAR | WINNING TEAM/HOME | RUNNER-UP | SCORE |
|------|-------------------|-----------|-------|
| 2003 | Musashi-Fuchu/Tokyo (JPN) | East Boynton Beach/Boynton Beach FL | 10-1 |
| 2004 | Pabao/Willemstad (AHO) | Conejo Valley/Thousand Oaks CA | 5-2 |
| 2005 | West Oahu/Ewa Beach HI | Pabao/Willemstad (AHO) | 7-6 |
| 2006 | Columbus Northern/Columbus GA | Kawaguchi/Kawaguchi City (JPN) | 2-1 |
| 2007 | Warner Robins American/Warner Robins GA | Tokyo Kitasuna/Tokyo (JPN) | 3-2 |
| 2008 | Waipio/Waipahu HI | Matamoros/Matamoros (MEX) | 12-3 |
| 2009 | Parkview/Chula Vista CA | Kuei-Shan/Taoyuan (TPE) | 6-3 |
| 2010 | Edogawa Minami/Tokyo (JPN) | Waipio/Waipahu HI | 4-1 |
| 2011 | Ocean View/Huntington Beach CA | Hamamatsu Minami/Hamamatsu (JPN) | 2-1 |
| 2012 | Kitasuna/Tokyo (JPN) | Goodlettsville/Goodlettsville TN | 12-2 |

# Basketball

American professional basketball is directed by the **National Basketball Association** (NBA; formed 1949). The NBA is divided into the Eastern and Western conferences (EC and WC; until 1970 the Eastern and Western divisions [ED and WD]), the top-ranking teams of which compete yearly for the championship. The **Women's National Basketball Association** (WNBA), also divided into an Eastern and a Western Conference (EC and WC), formed in 1997.

The **Fédération Internationale de Basketball** (FIBA; founded 1932) instituted world championships in 1950 for men and in 1953 for women. At the **collegiate** level in the United States, the most important event of the season is the **National Collegiate Athletic Association (NCAA) Championship**. The NCAA tournament was first contested by men in 1939. Women's college basketball was first played on an organized national level in 1972—in 1982 the NCAA held its first tournament for women.

**Related Web sites:** NBA: <www.nba.com>; WNBA: <www.wnba.com>; FIBA: <www.fiba.com>; NCAA: <www.ncaa.org>.

## National Basketball Association Final Standings, 2011–12

### EASTERN CONFERENCE

| Atlantic Division | WON | LOST | GAMES BACK | Central Division | WON | LOST | GAMES BACK | Southeast Division | WON | LOST | GAMES BACK |
|-------------------|-----|------|------------|------------------|-----|------|------------|--------------------|-----|------|------------|
| Boston[1] | 39 | 27 | — | Chicago[1] | 50 | 16 | — | Miami[1] | 46 | 20 | — |
| New York[1] | 36 | 30 | 3 | Indiana[1] | 42 | 24 | 8 | Atlanta[1] | 40 | 26 | 6 |
| Philadelphia[1] | 35 | 31 | 4 | Milwaukee | 31 | 35 | 19 | Orlando[1] | 37 | 29 | 9 |
| Toronto | 23 | 43 | 16 | Detroit | 25 | 41 | 25 | Washington | 20 | 46 | 26 |
| New Jersey | 22 | 44 | 17 | Cleveland | 21 | 45 | 29 | Charlotte | 7 | 59 | 39 |

### WESTERN CONFERENCE

| Northwest Division | WON | LOST | GAMES BACK | Pacific Division | WON | LOST | GAMES BACK | Southwest Division | WON | LOST | GAMES BACK |
|--------------------|-----|------|------------|------------------|-----|------|------------|--------------------|-----|------|------------|
| Oklahoma City[1] | 47 | 19 | — | L.A. Lakers[1] | 41 | 25 | — | San Antonio[1] | 50 | 16 | — |
| Denver[1] | 38 | 28 | 9 | L.A. Clippers[1] | 40 | 26 | 1 | Memphis[1] | 41 | 25 | 9 |
| Utah[1] | 36 | 30 | 11 | Phoenix | 33 | 33 | 8 | Dallas[1] | 36 | 30 | 14 |
| Portland | 28 | 38 | 19 | Golden State | 23 | 43 | 18 | Houston | 34 | 32 | 16 |
| Minnesota | 26 | 40 | 21 | Sacramento | 22 | 44 | 19 | New Orleans | 21 | 45 | 29 |

[1]Gained play-off berth.

## National Basketball Association Championship

| SEASON | WINNER | RUNNER-UP | RESULTS |
|---|---|---|---|
| 1949–50 | Minneapolis Lakers (CD)[1] | Syracuse Nationals (ED) | 4–2 |
| 1950–51 | Rochester Royals (WD) | New York Knickerbockers (ED) | 4–3 |
| 1951–52 | Minneapolis Lakers (WD) | New York Knickerbockers (ED) | 4–3 |
| 1952–53 | Minneapolis Lakers (WD) | New York Knickerbockers (ED) | 4–1 |
| 1953–54 | Minneapolis Lakers (WD) | Syracuse Nationals (ED) | 4–3 |
| 1954–55 | Syracuse Nationals (ED) | Fort Wayne Pistons (WD) | 4–3 |
| 1955–56 | Philadelphia Warriors (ED) | Fort Wayne Pistons (WD) | 4–1 |
| 1956–57 | Boston Celtics (ED) | St. Louis Hawks (WD) | 4–3 |
| 1957–58 | St. Louis Hawks (WD) | Boston Celtics (ED) | 4–2 |
| 1958–59 | Boston Celtics (ED) | Minneapolis Lakers (WD) | 4–0 |
| 1959–60 | Boston Celtics (ED) | St. Louis Hawks (WD) | 4–3 |
| 1960–61 | Boston Celtics (ED) | St. Louis Hawks (WD) | 4–1 |
| 1961–62 | Boston Celtics (ED) | Los Angeles Lakers (WD) | 4–3 |
| 1962–63 | Boston Celtics (ED) | Los Angeles Lakers (WD) | 4–2 |
| 1963–64 | Boston Celtics (ED) | San Francisco Warriors (WD) | 4–1 |
| 1964–65 | Boston Celtics (ED) | Los Angeles Lakers (WD) | 4–1 |
| 1965–66 | Boston Celtics (ED) | Los Angeles Lakers (WD) | 4–3 |
| 1966–67 | Philadelphia 76ers (ED) | San Francisco Warriors (WD) | 4–2 |
| 1967–68 | Boston Celtics (ED) | Los Angeles Lakers (WD) | 4–2 |
| 1968–69 | Boston Celtics (ED) | Los Angeles Lakers (WD) | 4–3 |
| 1969–70 | New York Knickerbockers (EC) | Los Angeles Lakers (WC) | 4–3 |
| 1970–71 | Milwaukee Bucks (WC) | Baltimore Bullets (EC) | 4–0 |
| 1971–72 | Los Angeles Lakers (WC) | New York Knickerbockers (EC) | 4–1 |
| 1972–73 | New York Knickerbockers (EC) | Los Angeles Lakers (WC) | 4–1 |
| 1973–74 | Boston Celtics (EC) | Milwaukee Bucks (WC) | 4–3 |
| 1974–75 | Golden State Warriors (WC) | Washington Bullets (EC) | 4–0 |
| 1975–76 | Boston Celtics (EC) | Phoenix Suns (WC) | 4–2 |
| 1976–77 | Portland Trail Blazers (WC) | Philadelphia 76ers (EC) | 4–2 |
| 1977–78 | Washington Bullets (EC) | Seattle SuperSonics (WC) | 4–3 |
| 1978–79 | Seattle SuperSonics (WC) | Washington Bullets (EC) | 4–1 |
| 1979–80 | Los Angeles Lakers (WC) | Philadelphia 76ers (EC) | 4–2 |
| 1980–81 | Boston Celtics (EC) | Houston Rockets (WC) | 4–2 |
| 1981–82 | Los Angeles Lakers (WC) | Philadelphia 76ers (EC) | 4–2 |
| 1982–83 | Philadelphia 76ers (EC) | Los Angeles Lakers (WC) | 4–0 |
| 1983–84 | Boston Celtics (EC) | Los Angeles Lakers (WC) | 4–3 |
| 1984–85 | Los Angeles Lakers (WC) | Boston Celtics (EC) | 4–2 |
| 1985–86 | Boston Celtics (EC) | Houston Rockets (WC) | 4–2 |
| 1986–87 | Los Angeles Lakers (WC) | Boston Celtics (EC) | 4–2 |
| 1987–88 | Los Angeles Lakers (WC) | Detroit Pistons (EC) | 4–3 |
| 1988–89 | Detroit Pistons (EC) | Los Angeles Lakers (WC) | 4–0 |
| 1989–90 | Detroit Pistons (EC) | Portland Trail Blazers (WC) | 4–1 |
| 1990–91 | Chicago Bulls (EC) | Los Angeles Lakers (WC) | 4–1 |
| 1991–92 | Chicago Bulls (EC) | Portland Trail Blazers (WC) | 4–2 |
| 1992–93 | Chicago Bulls (EC) | Phoenix Suns (WC) | 4–2 |
| 1993–94 | Houston Rockets (WC) | New York Knickerbockers (EC) | 4–3 |
| 1994–95 | Houston Rockets (WC) | Orlando Magic (EC) | 4–0 |
| 1995–96 | Chicago Bulls (EC) | Seattle SuperSonics (WC) | 4–2 |
| 1996–97 | Chicago Bulls (EC) | Utah Jazz (WC) | 4–2 |
| 1997–98 | Chicago Bulls (EC) | Utah Jazz (WC) | 4–2 |
| 1998–99 | San Antonio Spurs (WC) | New York Knickerbockers (EC) | 4–1 |
| 1999–2000 | Los Angeles Lakers (WC) | Indiana Pacers (EC) | 4–2 |
| 2000–01 | Los Angeles Lakers (WC) | Philadelphia 76ers (EC) | 4–1 |
| 2001–02 | Los Angeles Lakers (WC) | New Jersey Nets (EC) | 4–0 |
| 2002–03 | San Antonio Spurs (WC) | New Jersey Nets (EC) | 4–2 |
| 2003–04 | Detroit Pistons (EC) | Los Angeles Lakers (WC) | 4–1 |
| 2004–05 | San Antonio Spurs (WC) | Detroit Pistons (EC) | 4–3 |
| 2005–06 | Miami Heat (EC) | Dallas Mavericks (WC) | 4–2 |
| 2006–07 | San Antonio Spurs (WC) | Cleveland Cavaliers (EC) | 4–0 |
| 2007–08 | Boston Celtics (EC) | Los Angeles Lakers (WC) | 4–2 |
| 2008–09 | Los Angeles Lakers (WC) | Orlando Magic (EC) | 4–1 |
| 2009–10 | Los Angeles Lakers (WC) | Boston Celtics (EC) | 4–3 |
| 2010–11 | Dallas Mavericks (WC) | Miami Heat (EC) | 4–2 |
| 2011–12 | Miami Heat (EC) | Oklahoma City Thunder (WC) | 4–1 |

[1]In its inaugural season, the NBA had a third division, the Central Division (CD).

## National Basketball Association All-Time Records[1]

| | PLAYERS/TEAMS | NUMBER | SEASON/DATE |
|---|---|---|---|
| **Individual career records** | | | |
| Games played | Robert Parish | 1,611 | 1976-77—1996-97 |
| Points scored | Kareem Abdul-Jabbar | 38,387 | 1969-70—1988-89 |
| Most games, 50 or more points | Wilt Chamberlain | 118 | 1959-60—1972-73 |
| Most consecutive games, 10 or more points | Michael Jordan | 866 | 25 Mar 1986– 26 Dec 2001 |
| Field goals attempted | Kareem Abdul-Jabbar | 28,307 | 1969-70—1988-89 |
| Field goals made | Kareem Abdul-Jabbar | 15,837 | 1969-70—1988-89 |
| Field-goal percentage[2] | Artis Gilmore | .599 | 1976-77—1987-88 |
| Three-point field goals attempted | Ray Allen | 6,788 | 1996-97—2011-12 |
| Three-point field goals made | Ray Allen | 2,718 | 1996-97—2011-12 |
| Three-point field-goal percentage[3] | Steve Kerr | .454 | 1988-89—2002-03 |
| Free throws attempted | Karl Malone | 13,188 | 1985-86—2003-04 |
| Free throws made | Karl Malone | 9,787 | 1985-86—2003-04 |
| Free-throw percentage[4] | Mark Price | .904 | 1986-87—1997-98 |
| Assists | John Stockton | 15,806 | 1984-85—2002-03 |
| Rebounds | Wilt Chamberlain | 23,924 | 1959-60—1972-73 |
| Steals[5] | John Stockton | 3,265 | 1984-85—2002-03 |
| Blocked shots[5] | Hakeem Olajuwon | 3,830 | 1984-85—2001-02 |
| Wins (coaching) | Lenny Wilkens | 1,332 | 1969-70—2004-05, except 1972-1974 |
| **Individual season records** | | | |
| Points scored | Wilt Chamberlain | 4,029 | 1961-62 |
| Field goals attempted | Wilt Chamberlain | 3,159 | 1961-62 |
| Field goals made | Wilt Chamberlain | 1,597 | 1961-62 |
| Field-goal percentage | Wilt Chamberlain | .727 | 1972-73 |
| Three-point field goals attempted | George McCloud | 678 | 1995-96 |
| Three-point field goals made | Ray Allen | 269 | 2005-06 |
| Three-point field-goal percentage | Kyle Korver | .536 | 2009-10 |
| Free throws attempted | Wilt Chamberlain | 1,363 | 1961-62 |
| Free throws made | Jerry West | 840 | 1965-66 |
| Free-throw percentage | José Calderón | .981 | 2008-09 |
| Assists | John Stockton | 1,164 | 1990-91 |
| Rebounds | Wilt Chamberlain | 2,149 | 1960-61 |
| Steals[5] | Alvin Robertson | 301 | 1985-86 |
| Blocked shots[5] | Mark Eaton | 456 | 1984-85 |
| **Individual game records** | | | |
| Points scored | Wilt Chamberlain | 100 | 2 Mar 1962 |
| Field goals attempted | Wilt Chamberlain | 63 | 2 Mar 1962 |
| Field goals made | Wilt Chamberlain | 36 | 2 Mar 1962 |
| Three-point field goals attempted | Damon Stoudamire | 21 | 15 Apr 2005 |
| Three-point field goals made | Kobe Bryant; Donyell Marshall | 12 | 7 Jan 2003; 13 Mar 2005 |
| Free throws attempted | Dwight Howard | 39 | 12 Jan 2012 |
| Free throws made | Wilt Chamberlain; Adrian Dantley | 28 | 2 Mar 1962; 4 Jan 1984 |
| Assists | Scott Skiles | 30 | 30 Dec 1990 |
| Rebounds | Wilt Chamberlain | 55 | 24 Nov 1960 |
| Steals[5] | Larry Kenon; Kendall Gill | 11 | 26 Dec 1976; 3 Apr 1999 |
| Blocked shots[5] | Elmore Smith | 17 | 28 Oct 1973 |
| **Team records** | | | |
| Highest winning percentage (season) | Chicago Bulls | .878 (72-10) | 1995-96 |
| Consecutive games won | Los Angeles Lakers | 33 | 5 Nov 1971– 7 Jan 1972 |
| Championships | Boston Celtics | 17 | |
| Consecutive championships | Boston Celtics | 8 | 1959-66 |
| **Game records** | | | |
| Highest combined score | Detroit Pistons versus Denver Nuggets | 370 (186-184) | 13 Dec 1983 |
| Longest game (overtime periods) | Indianapolis Olympians versus Rochester Royals | 6 | 6 Jan 1951 |

[1]Through the end of the 2011-12 season.  [2]Minimum 2,000 made.  [3]Minimum 250 made.  [4]Minimum 1,200 made.  [5]Since 1973-74; before that season steals and blocked shots were not officially recorded by the NBA.

## Women's National Basketball Association Championship

| SEASON | WINNER | RUNNER-UP | RESULTS |
|---|---|---|---|
| 1997 | Houston Comets (EC) | New York Liberty (EC) | 1-0 |
| 1998 | Houston Comets (WC) | Phoenix Mercury (WC) | 2-1 |
| 1999 | Houston Comets (WC) | New York Liberty (EC) | 2-1 |
| 2000 | Houston Comets (WC) | New York Liberty (EC) | 2-0 |
| 2001 | Los Angeles Sparks (WC) | Charlotte Sting (EC) | 2-0 |
| 2002 | Los Angeles Sparks (WC) | New York Liberty (EC) | 2-0 |
| 2003 | Detroit Shock (EC) | Los Angeles Sparks (WC) | 2-1 |
| 2004 | Seattle Storm (WC) | Connecticut Sun (EC) | 2-1 |
| 2005 | Sacramento Monarchs (WC) | Connecticut Sun (EC) | 3-1 |
| 2006 | Detroit Shock (EC) | Sacramento Monarchs (WC) | 3-2 |
| 2007 | Phoenix Mercury (WC) | Detroit Shock (EC) | 3-2 |
| 2008 | Detroit Shock (EC) | San Antonio Silver Stars (WC) | 3-0 |
| 2009 | Phoenix Mercury (WC) | Indiana Fever (EC) | 3-2 |
| 2010 | Seattle Storm (WC) | Atlanta Dream (EC) | 3-0 |
| 2011 | Minnesota Lynx (WC) | Atlanta Dream (EC) | 3-0 |

## National Collegiate Athletic Association Basketball Championship—Men[1]

| YEAR | WINNER | RUNNER-UP | SCORE |
|---|---|---|---|
| 1939 | Oregon | Ohio State | 46-43 |
| 1940 | Indiana | Kansas | 60-42 |
| 1941 | Wisconsin | Washington State | 39-34 |
| 1942 | Stanford | Dartmouth | 53-38 |
| 1943 | Wyoming | Georgetown | 46-34 |
| 1944 | Utah | Dartmouth | 42-40 |
| 1945 | Oklahoma A&M | New York | 49-45 |
| 1946 | Oklahoma A&M | North Carolina | 43-40 |
| 1947 | Holy Cross (MA) | Oklahoma | 58-47 |
| 1948 | Kentucky | Baylor | 58-42 |
| 1949 | Kentucky | Oklahoma State | 46-36 |
| 1950 | City College of New York | Bradley | 71-68 |
| 1951 | Kentucky | Kansas State | 68-58 |
| 1952 | Kansas | St. John's (NY) | 80-63 |
| 1953 | Indiana | Kansas | 69-68 |
| 1954 | La Salle | Bradley | 92-76 |
| 1955 | San Francisco | La Salle | 77-63 |
| 1956 | San Francisco | Iowa | 83-71 |
| 1957 | North Carolina | Kansas | 54-53 |
| 1958 | Kentucky | Seattle | 84-72 |
| 1959 | California (Berkeley) | West Virginia | 71-70 |
| 1960 | Ohio State | California (Berkeley) | 75-55 |
| 1961 | Cincinnati | Ohio State | 70-65 |
| 1962 | Cincinnati | Ohio State | 71-59 |
| 1963 | Loyola (IL) | Cincinnati | 60-58 |
| 1964 | UCLA | Duke | 98-83 |
| 1965 | UCLA | Michigan | 91-80 |
| 1966 | Texas Western | Kentucky | 72-65 |
| 1967 | UCLA | Dayton | 79-64 |
| 1968 | UCLA | North Carolina | 78-55 |
| 1969 | UCLA | Purdue | 92-72 |
| 1970 | UCLA | Jacksonville | 80-69 |
| 1971 | UCLA | Villanova | 68-62 |
| 1972 | UCLA | Florida State | 81-76 |
| 1973 | UCLA | Memphis State | 87-66 |
| 1974 | North Carolina State | Marquette | 76-64 |
| 1975 | UCLA | Kentucky | 92-85 |

| YEAR | WINNER | RUNNER-UP | SCORE |
|---|---|---|---|
| 1976 | Indiana | Michigan | 86-68 |
| 1977 | Marquette | North Carolina | 67-59 |
| 1978 | Kentucky | Duke | 94-88 |
| 1979 | Michigan State | Indiana State | 75-64 |
| 1980 | Louisville | UCLA | 59-54 |
| 1981 | Indiana | North Carolina | 63-50 |
| 1982 | North Carolina | Georgetown | 63-62 |
| 1983 | North Carolina State | Houston | 54-52 |
| 1984 | Georgetown | Houston | 84-75 |
| 1985 | Villanova | Georgetown | 66-64 |
| 1986 | Louisville | Duke | 72-69 |
| 1987 | Indiana | Syracuse | 74-73 |
| 1988 | Kansas | Oklahoma | 83-79 |
| 1989 | Michigan | Seton Hall | 80-79 |
| 1990 | Nevada (Las Vegas) | Duke | 103-73 |
| 1991 | Duke | Kansas | 72-65 |
| 1992 | Duke | Michigan | 71-51 |
| 1993 | North Carolina | Michigan | 77-71 |
| 1994 | Arkansas | Duke | 76-72 |
| 1995 | UCLA | Arkansas | 89-78 |
| 1996 | Kentucky | Syracuse | 76-67 |
| 1997 | Arizona | Kentucky | 84-79 |
| 1998 | Kentucky | Utah | 78-69 |
| 1999 | Connecticut | Duke | 77-74 |
| 2000 | Michigan State | Florida | 89-76 |
| 2001 | Duke | Arizona | 82-72 |
| 2002 | Maryland | Indiana | 64-52 |
| 2003 | Syracuse | Kansas | 81-78 |
| 2004 | Connecticut | Georgia Tech | 82-73 |
| 2005 | North Carolina | Illinois | 75-70 |
| 2006 | Florida | UCLA | 73-57 |
| 2007 | Florida | Ohio State | 84-75 |
| 2008 | Kansas | Memphis[2] | 75-68 |
| 2009 | North Carolina | Michigan State | 89-72 |
| 2010 | Duke | Butler | 61-59 |
| 2011 | Connecticut | Butler | 53-41 |
| 2012 | Kentucky | Kansas | 67-59 |

[1]*University Division 1957-73, Division I from 1974.*    [2]*Memphis was stripped of this result in 2009 for NCAA rules violations.*

## National Collegiate Athletic Association Basketball Championship—Women[1]

| YEAR | WINNER | RUNNER-UP | SCORE | YEAR | WINNER | RUNNER-UP | SCORE |
|------|--------|-----------|-------|------|--------|-----------|-------|
| 1982 | Louisiana Tech | Cheyney State | 76-62 | 1998 | Tennessee | Louisiana Tech | 93-75 |
| 1983 | Southern California | Louisiana Tech | 69-67 | 1999 | Purdue | Duke | 62-45 |
| 1984 | Southern California | Tennessee | 72-61 | 2000 | Connecticut | Tennessee | 71-52 |
| 1985 | Old Dominion | Georgia | 70-65 | 2001 | Notre Dame | Purdue | 68-66 |
| 1986 | Texas | Southern California | 97-81 | 2002 | Connecticut | Oklahoma | 82-70 |
| 1987 | Tennessee | Louisiana Tech | 67-44 | 2003 | Connecticut | Tennessee | 73-68 |
| 1988 | Louisiana Tech | Auburn | 56-54 | 2004 | Connecticut | Tennessee | 70-61 |
| 1989 | Tennessee | Auburn | 76-60 | 2005 | Baylor | Michigan State | 84-62 |
| 1990 | Stanford | Auburn | 88-81 | 2006 | Maryland | Duke | 78-75 |
| 1991 | Tennessee | Virginia | 70-67 | 2007 | Tennessee | Rutgers | 59-46 |
| 1992 | Stanford | Western Kentucky | 78-62 | 2008 | Tennessee | Stanford | 64-48 |
| 1993 | Texas Tech | Ohio State | 84-82 | 2009 | Connecticut | Louisville | 76-54 |
| 1994 | North Carolina | Louisiana Tech | 60-59 | 2010 | Connecticut | Stanford | 53-47 |
| 1995 | Connecticut | Tennessee | 70-64 | 2011 | Texas A&M | Notre Dame | 76-70 |
| 1996 | Tennessee | Georgia | 83-65 | 2012 | Baylor | Notre Dame | 80-61 |
| 1997 | Tennessee | Old Dominion | 68-59 | | | | |

[1]Division I.

## FIBA World Championship—Men

| YEAR | WINNER | RUNNER-UP | YEAR | WINNER | RUNNER-UP |
|------|--------|-----------|------|--------|-----------|
| 1936[1] | United States | Canada | 1980[1] | Yugoslavia | Italy |
| 1948[1] | United States | France | 1982 | USSR | United States |
| 1950 | Argentina | United States | 1984[1] | United States | Spain |
| 1952[1] | United States | USSR | 1986 | United States | USSR |
| 1954 | United States | Brazil | 1988[1] | USSR | Yugoslavia |
| 1956[1] | United States | USSR | 1990 | Yugoslavia | USSR |
| 1959 | Brazil[2] | United States | 1992[1] | United States | Croatia |
| 1960[1] | United States | USSR | 1994 | United States | Russia |
| 1963 | Brazil | Yugoslavia | 1996[1] | United States | Yugoslavia |
| 1964[1] | United States | USSR | 1998 | Yugoslavia | Russia |
| 1967 | USSR | Yugoslavia | 2000[1] | United States | France |
| 1968[1] | United States | Yugoslavia | 2002 | Yugoslavia | Argentina |
| 1970 | Yugoslavia | Brazil | 2004[1] | Argentina | Italy |
| 1972[1] | USSR | United States | 2006 | Spain | Greece |
| 1974 | USSR | Yugoslavia | 2008[1] | United States | Spain |
| 1976[1] | United States | Yugoslavia | 2010 | United States | Turkey |
| 1978 | Yugoslavia | USSR | 2012[1] | United States | Spain |

[1]Olympic championships, recognized in this table as world championships (though not by FIBA). [2]Won by default.

## FIBA World Championship—Women

| YEAR | WINNER | RUNNER-UP | YEAR | WINNER | RUNNER-UP |
|------|--------|-----------|------|--------|-----------|
| 1953 | United States | Chile | 1988[1] | United States | Yugoslavia |
| 1957 | United States | USSR | 1990 | United States | Yugoslavia |
| 1959 | USSR | Bulgaria | 1992[1] | Unified Team | China |
| 1964 | USSR | Czechoslovakia | 1994 | Brazil | China |
| 1967 | USSR | Rep. of Korea | 1996[1] | United States | Brazil |
| 1971 | USSR | Czechoslovakia | 1998 | United States | Russia |
| 1975 | USSR | Japan | 2000[1] | United States | Australia |
| 1976[1] | USSR | United States | 2002 | United States | Russia |
| 1979 | United States | Rep. of Korea | 2004[1] | United States | Australia |
| 1980[1] | USSR | Bulgaria | 2006 | Australia | Russia |
| 1983 | USSR | United States | 2008[1] | United States | Australia |
| 1984[1] | United States | Rep. of Korea | 2010 | United States | Czech Republic |
| 1986 | United States | USSR | 2012[1] | United States | France |

[1]Olympic championships, recognized in this table as world championships (though not by FIBA).

# Cycling

By all accounts, the greatest cycling event of all is the annual **Tour de France** road race, founded in 1903. It is raced in stages over a distance usually exceeding 3,500 km (2,175 mi). From 1911 to 1929, distances exceeded 5,300 km (3,290 mi). A Tour de France for women was first held in 1984, over an 18-stage course of 991 km (616 mi). In addition to this and many other road races, there are yearly **road racing world championships**.

**Track racing** championships are also held. The oldest events of track racing are the **sprint** (in which only the last part of the race can actually be considered sprinting) and the **pursuit** (both a team and an individual event in which contestants start the race on opposite sides of the track and attempt to catch each other). **Mountain bike racing** and **cyclo-cross**, a cross-country bicycle race that requires cyclists to carry their bikes over parts of the course, developed in the latter part of the 20th century. World championships were established for these sports in 1997.

**International Cycling Union (Union Cycliste Internationale—UCI) Web site:** <www.uci.ch>.

## Cycling Champions, 2011–12

*In the case of multiday events, the concluding date is given.*

| EVENT | WINNER (COUNTRY) | | DATE |
|---|---|---|---|
| **World champions—mountain bikes** | | | **4 Sep 2011** |
| | **Men** | **Women** | |
| Cross-country | Jaroslav Kulhavy (CZE) | Catharine Pendrel (CAN) | |
| Downhill | Danny Hart (GBR) | Emmeline Ragot (FRA) | |
| **World champions—road** | | | **25 Sep 2011** |
| | **Men** | **Women** | |
| Individual road race | Mark Cavendish (GBR) | Giorgia Bronzini (ITA) | |
| Individual time trial | Tony Martin (GER) | Judith Arndt (GER) | |
| **World champions—cyclo-cross** | | | **29 Jan 2012** |
| | **Men** | **Women** | |
| | Niels Albert (BEL) | Marianne Vos (NED) | |
| **World champions—track** | | | **8 Apr 2012** |
| | **Men** | **Women** | |
| Individual pursuit | Michael Hepburn (AUS) | Alison Shanks (NZL) | |
| Individual sprint | Grégory Baugé (FRA) | Victoria Pendleton (GBR) | |
| 500-m time trial | — | Anna Meares (AUS) | |
| 1-km time trial | Stefan Nimke (GER) | — | |
| Points | Cameron Meyer (AUS) | Anastasia Chulkova (RUS) | |
| Team pursuit | Great Britain | Great Britain | |
| Team sprint | Australia | Germany | |
| Keirin | Chris Hoy (GBR) | Anna Meares (AUS) | |
| Madison | Kenny De Ketele, Gijs Van Hoecke (BEL) | — | |
| Scratch | Ben Swift (GBR) | Katarzyna Pawlowska (POL) | |
| Omnium | Glenn O'Shea (AUS) | Laura Trott (GBR) | |

| **Major elite road-race winners** | | |
|---|---|---|
| Tour of Spain (Vuelta a España) | Juan José Cobo (ESP) | 11 Sep 2011 |
| Tour of Lombardy (Giro di Lombardia) | Oliver Zaugg (SUI) | 15 Oct 2011 |
| Milan–San Remo | Simon Gerrans (AUS) | 17 Mar 2012 |
| Tour of Flanders (Ronde van Vlaanderen) | Tom Boonen (BEL) | 1 Apr 2012 |
| Paris–Roubaix | Tom Boonen (BEL) | 8 Apr 2012 |
| Tour of Romandie (Tour de Romandie) | Bradley Wiggins (GBR) | 29 Apr 2012 |
| Tour of Italy (Giro d'Italia) | Ryder Hesjedal (CAN) | 27 May 2012 |
| Tour of Switzerland (Tour de Suisse) | Rui Alberto Faria da Costa (POR) | 17 Jun 2012 |
| Tour de France | Bradley Wiggins (GBR) | 22 Jul 2012 |

## Tour de France

| YEAR | WINNER (COUNTRY) | LENGTH OF ROUTE (KM) | YEAR | WINNER (COUNTRY) | LENGTH OF ROUTE (KM) |
|---|---|---|---|---|---|
| 1903 | Maurice Garin (FRA) | 2,428 | 1909 | François Faber (LUX) | 4,507 |
| 1904 | Henri Cornet (FRA)[1] | 2,388 | 1910 | Octave Lapize (FRA) | 4,474 |
| 1905 | Louis Trousselier (FRA) | 2,975 | 1911 | Gustave Garrigou (FRA) | 5,344 |
| 1906 | René Pottier (FRA) | 4,637 | 1912 | Odile Defraye (BEL) | 5,319 |
| 1907 | Lucien Petit-Breton (FRA) | 4,488 | 1913 | Philippe Thys (BEL) | 5,387 |
| 1908 | Lucien Petit-Breton (FRA) | 4,487 | 1914 | Philippe Thys (BEL) | 5,405 |

## Tour de France (continued)

| YEAR | WINNER (COUNTRY) | LENGTH OF ROUTE (KM) | YEAR | WINNER (COUNTRY) | LENGTH OF ROUTE (KM) |
|---|---|---|---|---|---|
| 1915-18 | not held | | 1969 | Eddy Merckx (BEL) | 4,110 |
| 1919 | Firmin Lambot (BEL) | 5,560 | 1970 | Eddy Merckx (BEL) | 4,366 |
| 1920 | Philippe Thys (BEL) | 5,519 | 1971 | Eddy Merckx (BEL) | 3,689 |
| 1921 | Léon Scieur (BEL) | 5,484 | 1972 | Eddy Merckx (BEL) | 3,846 |
| 1922 | Firmin Lambot (BEL) | 5,375 | 1973 | Luis Ocaña (ESP) | 4,140 |
| 1923 | Henri Pélissier (FRA) | 5,386 | 1974 | Eddy Merckx (BEL) | 4,098 |
| 1924 | Ottavio Bottecchia (ITA) | 5,425 | 1975 | Bernard Thévenet (FRA) | 4,000 |
| 1925 | Ottavio Bottecchia (ITA) | 5,430 | 1976 | Lucien Van Impe (BEL) | 4,050 |
| 1926 | Lucien Buysse (BEL) | 5,745 | 1977 | Bernard Thévenet (FRA) | 4,098 |
| 1927 | Nicolas Frantz (LUX) | 5,341 | 1978 | Bernard Hinault (FRA) | 3,920 |
| 1928 | Nicolas Frantz (LUX) | 5,377 | 1979 | Bernard Hinault (FRA) | 3,719 |
| 1929 | Maurice De Waele (BEL) | 5,286 | 1980 | Joop Zoetemelk (NED) | 3,948 |
| 1930 | André Leducq (FRA) | 4,818 | 1981 | Bernard Hinault (FRA) | 3,765 |
| 1931 | Antonin Magne (FRA) | 5,095 | 1982 | Bernard Hinault (FRA) | 3,489 |
| 1932 | André Leducq (FRA) | 4,520 | 1983 | Laurent Fignon (FRA) | 3,568 |
| 1933 | Georges Speicher (FRA) | 4,395 | 1984 | Laurent Fignon (FRA) | 3,880 |
| 1934 | Antonin Magne (FRA) | 4,363 | 1985 | Bernard Hinault (FRA) | 4,100 |
| 1935 | Romain Maes (BEL) | 4,338 | 1986 | Greg LeMond (USA) | 4,091 |
| 1936 | Romain Maes (BEL) | 4,442 | 1987 | Stephen Roche (IRL) | 4,100 |
| 1937 | Roger Lapébie (FRA) | 4,415 | 1988 | Pedro Delgado (ESP) | 3,300 |
| 1938 | Gino Bartali (ITA) | 4,694 | 1989 | Greg LeMond (USA) | 3,215 |
| 1939 | Sylvere Maes (BEL) | 4,224 | 1990 | Greg LeMond (USA) | 3,399 |
| 1940-46 | not held | | 1991 | Miguel Indurain (ESP) | 3,935 |
| 1947 | Jean Robic (FRA) | 4,640 | 1992 | Miguel Indurain (ESP) | 3,983 |
| 1948 | Gino Bartali (ITA) | 4,922 | 1993 | Miguel Indurain (ESP) | 3,700 |
| 1949 | Fausto Coppi (ITA) | 4,808 | 1994 | Miguel Indurain (ESP) | 3,978 |
| 1950 | Ferdi Kubler (SUI) | 4,775 | 1995 | Miguel Indurain (ESP) | 3,635 |
| 1951 | Hugo Koblet (SUI) | 4,697 | 1996 | no winner[2] | 3,764 |
| 1952 | Fausto Coppi (ITA) | 4,807 | 1997 | Jan Ullrich (GER) | 3,944 |
| 1953 | Louison Bobet (FRA) | 4,479 | 1998 | Marco Pantani (ITA) | 3,831 |
| 1954 | Louison Bobet (FRA) | 4,469 | 1999 | Lance Armstrong (USA) | 3,687 |
| 1955 | Louison Bobet (FRA) | 4,855 | 2000 | Lance Armstrong (USA) | 3,663 |
| 1956 | Roger Walkowiak (FRA) | 4,496 | 2001 | Lance Armstrong (USA) | 3,454 |
| 1957 | Jacques Anquetil (FRA) | 4,686 | 2002 | Lance Armstrong (USA) | 3,272 |
| 1958 | Charly Gaul (LUX) | 4,319 | 2003 | Lance Armstrong (USA) | 3,428 |
| 1959 | Federico Bahamontes (ESP) | 4,355 | 2004 | Lance Armstrong (USA) | 3,391 |
| 1960 | Gastone Nencini (ITA) | 4,173 | 2005 | Lance Armstrong (USA) | 3,608 |
| 1961 | Jacques Anquetil (FRA) | 4,397 | 2006 | Óscar Pereiro (ESP)[3] | 3,657 |
| 1962 | Jacques Anquetil (FRA) | 4,274 | 2007 | Alberto Contador (ESP) | 3,550 |
| 1963 | Jacques Anquetil (FRA) | 4,137 | 2008 | Carlos Sastre (ESP) | 3,554 |
| 1964 | Jacques Anquetil (FRA) | 4,504 | 2009 | Alberto Contador (ESP) | 3,445 |
| 1965 | Felice Gimondi (ITA) | 4,183 | 2010 | Andy Schleck (LUX)[4] | 3,596 |
| 1966 | Lucien Aimar (FRA) | 4,303 | 2011 | Cadel Evans (AUS) | 3,431 |
| 1967 | Roger Pingeon (FRA) | 4,780 | 2012 | Bradley Wiggins (GBR) | 3,497 |
| 1968 | Jan Janssen (NED) | 4,662 | | | |

[1]Maurice Garin (FRA), the tour's first champion, finished first in the 1904 race, as well, but was later disqualified for having eaten illegally and for other, suspected offenses.   [2]The victory for Bjarne Riis (DEN) was invalidated after he admitted to having used illegal performance-enhancing drugs.   [3]Floyd Landis (USA) was stripped of the title after he was found to have had illegal performance-enhancing drugs in his system.   [4]Alberto Contador (ESP) was stripped of the title after he was found to have had illegal performance-enhancing drugs in his system.

# Football

Many types of games are known as football, among them association football (or soccer), gridiron football (or American football), Canadian football (or rugby football), Australian rules football (or footy), and rugby union and rugby league football (or rugger). Each of these games is unique, though some—such as US football and Canadian football—bear more than a little resemblance.

**American football—professional.** The National Football League (NFL) championship play-offs were organized in 1933. The American Football League (founded 1959) was a rival organization until 1970, when it merged with the NFL. The resulting reorganization added new teams (1976) and divided the reconstituted NFL into two conferences, the American Football Conference and the National Football Conference. (There

# Football (continued)

have been several expansions since.) The play-off winner in each conference contests the **Super Bowl**, the final game of the professional football season.

**American football—college.** Historically the national champion of college football has been informally selected by two rival opinion polls—one a survey of sportswriters (conducted by the Associated Press [AP] since 1936) and the other a survey of collegiate football coaches (begun in 1950 by the United Press [now United Press International (UPI)] and currently conducted by *USA Today*). Where polls designated different teams, both are listed. Desire for a clear-cut national champion led to the creation of the Bowl Championship Series (BCS) in 1999. The BCS uses a formula involving team records, strength of schedule, and rankings to determine the top two teams, who then meet in a **national championship game**. The site of the game annually shifts between the four major bowls—**Rose, Orange, Sugar**, and **Fiesta**. The Rose Bowl held its first game in 1902 in Pasadena CA. In 1935 the Sugar Bowl (played in New Orleans LA) and the Orange Bowl (played in Miami FL) were launched. The Fiesta Bowl (played in Phoenix AZ) began play in 1971.

**Canadian football—professional.** The rules of professional football in Canada have evolved for over 100 years based on the Canadian Rugby Union (formed in 1891). Until 1936 the Union included intercollegiate teams. In 1958 the Canadian Football League was formed, dividing into Eastern and Western conferences (in 1981 renamed divisions). The teams that win the division championships meet for the championship of the League, the **Grey Cup** (instituted in 1909).

**Australian football—professional.** Australian rules football, originally called Melbourne rules football, emerged in the state of Victoria in the late 1850s during the southern winter, when cricket was not played. The Victorian Football Association (formed in 1877) was supplanted by the Victorian Football League (formed in 1896), which was renamed the **Australian Football League** (AFL) in 1990 after two teams from outside Victoria were admitted in 1987. Currently, the eight AFL teams with the best records at the end of a 22-week season qualify for the play-offs. The first premiership Grand Final was played in 1886.

**Association football.** The game of association football is governed by the Fédération Internationale de Football Association (FIFA; founded in 1904). The quadrennial **FIFA World Cup** (established in 1930) was the first official internationally contested association football match. The popularity of the World Cup and, even earlier, the **Copa América** (1916) in South America led to the development of several regional cup competitions, including the European Champion Clubs' Cup (1955; discontinued after the 1992–93 season and superseded by the Union of European Football Associations [UEFA] Champions League), the **Asian Cup** (1956), the **African Cup of Nations** (1957), and the **Libertadores de América Cup** (1960). Competition for the **FIFA Women's World Cup** began in 1991. The **Major League Soccer Cup** in the US was launched in 1996.

**Rugby union football.** Rugby union football was open to amateurs only until 1995. The **Six Nations Championship** was first played in 1882 (as the Four Nations) and is now contested by England, Scotland, Wales, Ireland, France (since 1910), and Italy (since 2000). The international Test matches further include South Africa, New Zealand, and Australia. The International Amateur Rugby Federation (FIRA; now FIRA-AER) oversees rugby in 37 other (i.e., non-Test) countries. The chief international competition between rugby union clubs in the Southern Hemisphere is the tri-nation **Super 15** (Super 10 from 1993 to 1995, Super 12 from 1996 to 2005, and Super 14 from 2006 to 2010). Teams from Australia (five), South Africa (five), and New Zealand (five) play in a round-robin tournament. The **World Cup**, sponsored by the International Rugby Board (founded 1886), was inaugurated in 1987. The competition is held every four years.

**Rugby league football.** **Rugby League World Cup** competition began in 1954 between teams from Australia, France, Great Britain, and New Zealand. In 1975–77 it was known as the International Championship. The competition was then discontinued, but it revived during the 1980s and has been held irregularly since.

**Related Web sites:** National Football League (NFL): <www.nfl.com>; Canadian Football League (CFL): <www.cfl.ca>; Australian Football League (AFL): <www.afl.com.au>; Fédération Internationale de Football Association (FIFA): <www.fifa.com>; Union of European Football Associations (UEFA): <www.uefa.com>; Major League Soccer (MLS): <www.mlssoccer.com>; International Rugby Board (rugby union): <www.irb.com>; Rugby League International Federation: <www.rlif.org>; Super 15: <www.superxv.com>.

## National Football League Final Standings, 2011–12

### American Football Conference

**East Division**

| TEAM | WON | LOST | TIED |
|---|---|---|---|
| New England[1] | 13 | 3 | 0 |
| New York Jets | 8 | 8 | 0 |
| Miami | 6 | 10 | 0 |
| Buffalo | 6 | 10 | 0 |

**North Division**

| TEAM | WON | LOST | TIED |
|---|---|---|---|
| Baltimore[1] | 12 | 4 | 0 |
| Pittsburgh[1] | 12 | 4 | 0 |
| Cincinnati[1] | 9 | 7 | 0 |
| Cleveland | 4 | 12 | 0 |

**South Division**

| TEAM | WON | LOST | TIED |
|---|---|---|---|
| Houston[1] | 10 | 6 | 0 |
| Tennessee | 9 | 7 | 0 |
| Jacksonville | 5 | 11 | 0 |
| Indianapolis | 2 | 14 | 0 |

**West Division**

| TEAM | WON | LOST | TIED |
|---|---|---|---|
| Denver[1] | 8 | 8 | 0 |
| San Diego | 8 | 8 | 0 |
| Oakland | 8 | 8 | 0 |
| Kansas City | 7 | 9 | 0 |

## National Football League Final Standings, 2011–12 (continued)

### National Football Conference

**East Division**

| TEAM | WON | LOST | TIED |
|---|---|---|---|
| New York Giants[1] | 9 | 7 | 0 |
| Philadelphia | 8 | 8 | 0 |
| Dallas | 8 | 8 | 0 |
| Washington | 5 | 11 | 0 |

**South Division**

| TEAM | WON | LOST | TIED |
|---|---|---|---|
| New Orleans[1] | 13 | 3 | 0 |
| Atlanta[1] | 10 | 6 | 0 |
| Carolina | 6 | 10 | 0 |
| Tampa Bay | 4 | 12 | 0 |

**North Division**

| TEAM | WON | LOST | TIED |
|---|---|---|---|
| Green Bay[1] | 15 | 1 | 0 |
| Detroit[1] | 10 | 6 | 0 |
| Chicago | 8 | 8 | 0 |
| Minnesota | 3 | 13 | 0 |

**West Division**

| TEAM | WON | LOST | TIED |
|---|---|---|---|
| San Francisco[1] | 13 | 3 | 0 |
| Arizona | 8 | 8 | 0 |
| Seattle | 7 | 9 | 0 |
| St. Louis | 2 | 14 | 0 |

[1]Gained play-off berth.

## Super Bowl

*NFL-AFL championship 1966–70; NFL championship from 1970–71 season.*

| | SEASON | WINNER | RUNNER-UP | SCORE |
|---|---|---|---|---|
| I | 1966–67 | Green Bay Packers (NFL) | Kansas City Chiefs (AFL) | 35–10 |
| II | 1967–68 | Green Bay Packers (NFL) | Oakland Raiders (AFL) | 33–14 |
| III | 1968–69 | New York Jets (AFL) | Baltimore Colts (NFL) | 16–7 |
| IV | 1969–70 | Kansas City Chiefs (AFL) | Minnesota Vikings (NFL) | 23–7 |
| V | 1970–71 | Baltimore Colts (AFC) | Dallas Cowboys (NFC) | 16–13 |
| VI | 1971–72 | Dallas Cowboys (NFC) | Miami Dolphins (AFC) | 24–3 |
| VII | 1972–73 | Miami Dolphins (AFC) | Washington Redskins (NFC) | 14–7 |
| VIII | 1973–74 | Miami Dolphins (AFC) | Minnesota Vikings (NFC) | 24–7 |
| IX | 1974–75 | Pittsburgh Steelers (AFC) | Minnesota Vikings (NFC) | 16–6 |
| X | 1975–76 | Pittsburgh Steelers (AFC) | Dallas Cowboys (NFC) | 21–17 |
| XI | 1976–77 | Oakland Raiders (AFC) | Minnesota Vikings (NFC) | 32–14 |
| XII | 1977–78 | Dallas Cowboys (NFC) | Denver Broncos (AFC) | 27–10 |
| XIII | 1978–79 | Pittsburgh Steelers (AFC) | Dallas Cowboys (NFC) | 35–31 |
| XIV | 1979–80 | Pittsburgh Steelers (AFC) | Los Angeles Rams (NFC) | 31–19 |
| XV | 1980–81 | Oakland Raiders (AFC) | Philadelphia Eagles (NFC) | 27–10 |
| XVI | 1981–82 | San Francisco 49ers (NFC) | Cincinnati Bengals (AFC) | 26–21 |
| XVII | 1982–83 | Washington Redskins (NFC) | Miami Dolphins (AFC) | 27–17 |
| XVIII | 1983–84 | Los Angeles Raiders (AFC) | Washington Redskins (NFC) | 38–9 |
| XIX | 1984–85 | San Francisco 49ers (NFC) | Miami Dolphins (AFC) | 38–16 |
| XX | 1985–86 | Chicago Bears (NFC) | New England Patriots (AFC) | 46–10 |
| XXI | 1986–87 | New York Giants (NFC) | Denver Broncos (AFC) | 39–20 |
| XXII | 1987–88 | Washington Redskins (NFC) | Denver Broncos (AFC) | 42–10 |
| XXIII | 1988–89 | San Francisco 49ers (NFC) | Cincinnati Bengals (AFC) | 20–16 |
| XXIV | 1989–90 | San Francisco 49ers (NFC) | Denver Broncos (AFC) | 55–10 |
| XXV | 1990–91 | New York Giants (NFC) | Buffalo Bills (AFC) | 20–19 |
| XXVI | 1991–92 | Washington Redskins (NFC) | Buffalo Bills (AFC) | 37–24 |
| XXVII | 1992–93 | Dallas Cowboys (NFC) | Buffalo Bills (AFC) | 52–17 |
| XXVIII | 1993–94 | Dallas Cowboys (NFC) | Buffalo Bills (AFC) | 30–13 |
| XXIX | 1994–95 | San Francisco 49ers (NFC) | San Diego Chargers (AFC) | 49–26 |
| XXX | 1995–96 | Dallas Cowboys (NFC) | Pittsburgh Steelers (AFC) | 27–17 |
| XXXI | 1996–97 | Green Bay Packers (NFC) | New England Patriots (AFC) | 35–21 |
| XXXII | 1997–98 | Denver Broncos (AFC) | Green Bay Packers (NFC) | 31–24 |
| XXXIII | 1998–99 | Denver Broncos (AFC) | Atlanta Falcons (NFC) | 34–19 |
| XXXIV | 1999–2000 | St. Louis Rams (NFC) | Tennessee Titans (AFC) | 23–16 |
| XXXV | 2000–01 | Baltimore Ravens (AFC) | New York Giants (NFC) | 34–7 |
| XXXVI | 2001–02 | New England Patriots (AFC) | St. Louis Rams (NFC) | 20–17 |
| XXXVII | 2002–03 | Tampa Bay Buccaneers (NFC) | Oakland Raiders (AFC) | 48–21 |
| XXXVIII | 2003–04 | New England Patriots (AFC) | Carolina Panthers (NFC) | 32–29 |
| XXXIX | 2004–05 | New England Patriots (AFC) | Philadelphia Eagles (NFC) | 24–21 |
| XL | 2005–06 | Pittsburgh Steelers (AFC) | Seattle Seahawks (NFC) | 21–10 |
| XLI | 2006–07 | Indianapolis Colts (AFC) | Chicago Bears (NFC) | 29–17 |
| XLII | 2007–08 | New York Giants (NFC) | New England Patriots (AFC) | 17–14 |
| XLIII | 2008–09 | Pittsburgh Steelers (AFC) | Arizona Cardinals (NFC) | 27–23 |
| XLIV | 2009–10 | New Orleans Saints (NFC) | Indianapolis Colts (AFC) | 31–17 |
| XLV | 2010–11 | Green Bay Packers (NFC) | Pittsburgh Steelers (AFC) | 31–25 |
| XLVI | 2011–12 | New York Giants (NFC) | New England Patriots (AFC) | 21–17 |

## American Professional Football All-Time Records[1]

Research courtesy of Football Almanac, <www.football-almanac.com>.

| | PLAYERS/TEAMS | NUMBER | SEASON/DATE |
|---|---|---|---|
| **Individual career records** | | | |
| Total games | Morten Andersen | 382 | 1982–2007[2] |
| Total points | Morten Andersen | 2,544 | 1982–2007[2] |
| Touchdowns, total | Jerry Rice | 208 | 1985–2004 |
| Touchdowns, passing | Brett Favre | 508 | 1991–2010 |
| Touchdowns, receiving | Jerry Rice | 197 | 1985–2004 |
| Touchdowns, rushing | Emmitt Smith | 164 | 1990–2004 |
| Field goals made | Morten Andersen | 565 | 1982–2007[2] |
| Extra points made (kicked) | George Blanda | 943 | 1949–75, except 1959 |
| Passing yardage | Brett Favre | 71,838 | 1991–2010 |
| Passing completions | Brett Favre | 6,300 | 1991–2010 |
| Receiving yardage | Jerry Rice | 22,895 | 1985–2004 |
| Rushing yardage | Emmitt Smith | 18,355 | 1990–2004 |
| Interceptions (defense) | Paul Krause | 81 | 1964–79 |
| Sacks (defense)[3] | Bruce Smith | 200 | 1985–2003 |
| Coaching, total wins | Don Shula | 328 | 1963–95 |
| **Individual season records** | | | |
| Total points | LaDainian Tomlinson | 186 | 2006 |
| Touchdowns, total | LaDainian Tomlinson | 31 | 2006 |
| Touchdowns, passing | Tom Brady | 50 | 2007 |
| Touchdowns, receiving | Randy Moss | 23 | 2007 |
| Touchdowns, rushing | LaDainian Tomlinson | 28 | 2006 |
| Field goals made | Neil Rackers | 40 | 2005 |
| Extra points made (kicked) | Stephen Gostkowski | 74 | 2007 |
| Passing yardage | Drew Brees | 5,476 | 2011 |
| Receiving yardage | Jerry Rice | 1,848 | 1995 |
| Rushing yardage | Eric Dickerson | 2,105 | 1984 |
| Interceptions (defense) | Dick Lane | 14 | 1952 |
| Sacks (defense)[3] | Michael Strahan | 22.5 | 2001 |
| **Individual game records** | | | |
| Total points | Ernie Nevers | 40 | 28 Nov 1929 |
| Touchdowns, total | Ernie Nevers; Dub Jones; Gale Sayers | 6 | 28 Nov 1929; 25 Nov 1951; 12 Dec 1965 |
| Touchdowns, passing | Sid Luckman; Adrian Burk; George Blanda; Y.A. Tittle; Joe Kapp | 7 | 14 Nov 1943; 17 Oct 1954; 19 Nov 1961; 28 Oct 1962; 28 Sep 1969 |
| Touchdowns, receiving | Bob Shaw; Kellen Winslow; Jerry Rice | 5 | 2 Oct 1950; 22 Nov 1981; 14 Oct 1990 |
| Touchdowns, rushing | Ernie Nevers | 6 | 28 Nov 1929 |
| Field goals made | Rob Bironas | 8 | 21 Oct 2007 |
| Longest field goal | Tom Dempsey; Jason Elam; Sebastian Janikowski | 63 yd | 8 Nov 1970; 25 Oct 1998 12 Sep 2011 |
| Extra points made (kicked) | Pat Harder; Bob Waterfield; Charlie Gogolak | 9 | 17 Oct 1948; 22 Oct 1950; 27 Nov 1966 |
| Passing yardage | Norm Van Brocklin | 554 | 28 Sep 1951 |
| Receiving yardage | Willie Anderson | 336 | 26 Nov 1989 (overtime) |
| Rushing yardage | Adrian Peterson | 296 | 4 Nov 2007 |
| Longest run from scrimmage | Tony Dorsett | 99 yd | 3 Jan 1983 |
| Interceptions (defense) | *18 players hold record* | 4 | |
| Sacks (defense)[3] | Derrick Thomas | 7 | 11 Nov 1990 |
| **Team season records** | | | |
| League championships (including Super Bowls) | Green Bay Packers | 13 | |
| Super Bowl titles | Pittsburgh Steelers | 6 | |
| Consecutive Super Bowl titles | *7 teams hold record* | 2 | |

## American Professional Football All-Time Records[1] (continued)

**Team season records (continued)**

| | | | |
|---|---|---|---|
| Perfect regular season | New England Patriots; | 16 wins | 2007 |
| | Miami Dolphins; | 14 wins | 1972 |
| | Chicago Bears; | 13 wins | 1934 |
| | Chicago Bears | 11 wins | 1942 |
| Total points scored | New England Patriots | 589 | 2007 |
| Touchdowns, total | New England Patriots | 75 | 2007 |
| Touchdowns, passing | Indianapolis Colts | 51 | 2004 |
| Touchdowns, rushing | Green Bay Packers | 36 | 1962 |
| Field goals made | Arizona Cardinals | 43 | 2005 |
| Passing yardage | New Orleans Saints | 5,347 | 2011 |
| Rushing yardage | New England Patriots | 3,165 | 1978 |

**Game records**

| | | | |
|---|---|---|---|
| Highest total score | Washington Redskins versus New York Giants | 113 (72–41) | 27 Nov 1966 |
| Longest game | Miami Dolphins versus Kansas City Chiefs | 82:40 | 25 Dec 1971 (two overtimes) |

[1]Includes National Football League from 1920 through the 2011–12 season and American Football League from 1960 to 1969. [2]Except 2005. [3]Since 1982; before that year sacks were not officially recorded by the NFL.

## National Collegiate Athletic Association Football National Title[1]

| SEASON | CHAMPION | SEASON | CHAMPION | SEASON | CHAMPION |
|---|---|---|---|---|---|
| 1924–25 | Notre Dame | 1957–58 | Auburn (AP); Ohio | 1986–87 | Penn State |
| 1925–26 | Dartmouth | | State (UP) | 1987–88 | Miami (FL) |
| 1926–27 | Stanford | 1958–59 | Louisiana State | 1988–89 | Notre Dame |
| 1927–28 | Illinois | 1959–60 | Syracuse | 1989–90 | Miami (FL) |
| 1928–29 | Southern California | 1960–61 | Minnesota | 1990–91 | Colorado (AP); |
| 1929–30 | Notre Dame | 1961–62 | Alabama | | Georgia Tech (UPI) |
| 1930–31 | Notre Dame | 1962–63 | Southern California | 1991–92 | Miami (FL) (AP); |
| 1931–32 | Southern California | 1963–64 | Texas | | Washington (UPI) |
| 1932–33 | Michigan | 1964–65 | Alabama | 1992–93 | Alabama |
| 1933–34 | Michigan | 1965–66 | Alabama (AP); | 1993–94 | Florida State |
| 1934–35 | Minnesota | | Michigan State (UPI) | 1994–95 | Nebraska |
| 1935–36 | Southern Methodist | 1966–67 | Notre Dame | 1995–96 | Nebraska |
| 1936–37 | Minnesota | 1967–68 | Southern California | 1996–97 | Florida |
| 1937–38 | Pittsburgh | 1968–69 | Ohio State | 1997–98 | Michigan (AP); |
| 1938–39 | Texas Christian | 1969–70 | Texas | | Nebraska (USA |
| 1939–40 | Texas A&M | 1970–71 | Nebraska (AP); Texas | | Today/ESPN) |
| 1940–41 | Minnesota | | (UPI) | 1998–99 | Tennessee |
| 1941–42 | Minnesota | 1971–72 | Nebraska | 1999–2000 | Florida State |
| 1942–43 | Ohio State | 1972–73 | Southern California | 2000–01 | Oklahoma |
| 1943–44 | Notre Dame | 1973–74 | Notre Dame (AP); | 2001–02 | Miami (FL) |
| 1944–45 | Army | | Alabama (UPI) | 2002–03 | Ohio State |
| 1945–46 | Army | 1974–75 | Oklahoma (AP); South- | 2003–04 | Louisiana State |
| 1946–47 | Notre Dame | | ern California (UPI) | | (BCS); Southern |
| 1947–48 | Notre Dame | 1975–76 | Oklahoma | | California (AP) |
| 1948–49 | Michigan | 1976–77 | Pittsburgh | 2004–05 | Southern California |
| 1949–50 | Notre Dame | 1977–78 | Notre Dame | | (AP); BCS title va- |
| 1950–51 | Oklahoma | 1978–79 | Alabama (AP); South- | | cated for violations |
| 1951–52 | Tennessee | | ern California (UPI) | 2005–06 | Texas |
| 1952–53 | Michigan State | 1979–80 | Alabama | 2006–07 | Florida |
| 1953–54 | Maryland | 1980–81 | Georgia | 2007–08 | Louisiana State |
| 1954–55 | Ohio State (AP); | 1981–82 | Clemson | 2008–09 | Florida |
| | UCLA (UP) | 1982–83 | Penn State | 2009–10 | Alabama |
| 1955–56 | Oklahoma | 1983–84 | Miami (FL) | 2010–11 | Auburn |
| 1956–57 | Oklahoma | 1984–85 | Brigham Young | 2011–12 | Alabama |
| | | 1985–86 | Oklahoma | | |

[1]University Division 1956–73; Division I 1973–78; Division I-A 1978–2006; Football Bowl Subdivision from 2006.

## Rose Bowl

| SEASON | WINNER | RUNNER-UP | SCORE | SEASON | WINNER | RUNNER-UP | SCORE |
|---|---|---|---|---|---|---|---|
| 1901–02 | Michigan | Stanford | 49–0 | 1916–17 | Oregon | Pennsylvania | 14–0 |
| 1915–16 | Washington State | Brown | 14–0 | 1917–18 | Mare Island[1] | Camp Lewis[2] | 19–7 |

## Rose Bowl (continued)

| SEASON | WINNER | RUNNER-UP | SCORE |
|---|---|---|---|
| 1918–19 | Great Lakes³ | Mare Island¹ | 17–0 |
| 1919–20 | Harvard | Oregon | 7–6 |
| 1920–21 | California | Ohio State | 28–0 |
| 1921–22 | California | Washington and Jefferson | 0–0 |
| 1922–23 | Southern California | Penn State | 14–3 |
| 1923–24 | Washington | Navy | 14–14 |
| 1924–25 | Notre Dame | Stanford | 27–10 |
| 1925–26 | Alabama | Washington | 20–19 |
| 1926–27 | Alabama | Stanford | 7–7 |
| 1927–28 | Stanford | Pittsburgh | 7–6 |
| 1928–29 | Georgia Tech | California | 8–7 |
| 1929–30 | Southern California | Pittsburgh | 47–14 |
| 1930–31 | Alabama | Washington State | 24–0 |
| 1931–32 | Southern California | Tulane | 21–12 |
| 1932–33 | Southern California | Pittsburgh | 35–0 |
| 1933–34 | Columbia | Stanford | 7–0 |
| 1934–35 | Alabama | Stanford | 29–13 |
| 1935–36 | Stanford | Southern Methodist | 7–0 |
| 1936–37 | Pittsburgh | Washington | 21–0 |
| 1937–38 | California | Alabama | 13–0 |
| 1938–39 | Southern California | Duke | 7–3 |
| 1939–40 | Southern California | Tennessee | 14–0 |
| 1940–41 | Stanford | Nebraska | 21–13 |
| 1941–42 | Oregon State | Duke | 20–16 |
| 1942–43 | Georgia | UCLA | 9–0 |
| 1943–44 | Southern California | Washington | 29–0 |
| 1944–45 | Southern California | Tennessee | 25–0 |
| 1945–46 | Alabama | Southern California | 34–14 |
| 1946–47 | Illinois | UCLA | 45–14 |
| 1947–48 | Michigan | Southern California | 49–0 |
| 1948–49 | Northwestern | California | 20–14 |
| 1949–50 | Ohio State | California | 17–14 |
| 1950–51 | Michigan | California | 14–6 |
| 1951–52 | Illinois | Stanford | 40–7 |
| 1952–53 | Southern California | Wisconsin | 7–0 |
| 1953–54 | Michigan State | UCLA | 28–20 |
| 1954–55 | Ohio State | Southern California | 20–7 |
| 1955–56 | Michigan State | UCLA | 17–14 |
| 1956–57 | Iowa | Oregon State | 35–19 |
| 1957–58 | Ohio State | Oregon | 10–7 |
| 1958–59 | Iowa | California | 38–12 |
| 1959–60 | Washington | Wisconsin | 44–8 |
| 1960–61 | Washington | Minnesota | 17–7 |
| 1961–62 | Minnesota | UCLA | 21–3 |
| 1962–63 | Southern California | Wisconsin | 42–37 |
| 1963–64 | Illinois | Washington | 17–7 |
| 1964–65 | Michigan | Oregon State | 34–7 |
| 1965–66 | UCLA | Michigan State | 14–12 |
| 1966–67 | Purdue | Southern California | 14–13 |
| 1967–68 | Southern California | Indiana | 14–3 |
| 1968–69 | Ohio State | Southern California | 27–16 |
| 1969–70 | Southern California | Michigan | 10–3 |
| 1970–71 | Stanford | Ohio State | 27–17 |
| 1971–72 | Stanford | Michigan | 13–12 |
| 1972–73 | Southern California | Ohio State | 42–17 |
| 1973–74 | Ohio State | Southern California | 42–21 |
| 1974–75 | Southern California | Ohio State | 18–17 |
| 1975–76 | UCLA | Ohio State | 23–10 |
| 1976–77 | Southern California | Michigan | 14–6 |
| 1977–78 | Washington | Michigan | 27–20 |
| 1978–79 | Southern California | Michigan | 17–10 |
| 1979–80 | Southern California | Ohio State | 17–16 |
| 1980–81 | Michigan | Washington | 23–6 |
| 1981–82 | Washington | Iowa | 28–0 |
| 1982–83 | UCLA | Michigan | 24–14 |
| 1983–84 | UCLA | Illinois | 45–9 |
| 1984–85 | Southern California | Ohio State | 20–17 |
| 1985–86 | UCLA | Iowa | 45–28 |
| 1986–87 | Arizona State | Michigan | 22–15 |
| 1987–88 | Michigan State | Southern California | 20–17 |
| 1988–89 | Michigan | Southern California | 22–14 |
| 1989–90 | Southern California | Michigan | 17–10 |
| 1990–91 | Washington | Iowa | 46–34 |
| 1991–92 | Washington | Michigan | 34–14 |
| 1992–93 | Michigan | Washington | 38–31 |
| 1993–94 | Wisconsin | UCLA | 21–16 |
| 1994–95 | Penn State | Oregon | 38–20 |
| 1995–96 | Southern California | Northwestern | 41–32 |
| 1996–97 | Ohio State | Arizona State | 20–17 |
| 1997–98 | Michigan | Washington State | 21–16 |
| 1998–99 | Wisconsin | UCLA | 38–31 |
| 1999–2000 | Wisconsin | Stanford | 17–9 |
| 2000–01 | Washington | Purdue | 34–24 |
| 2001–02 | Miami (FL) | Nebraska | 37–14 |
| 2002–03 | Oklahoma | Washington State | 34–14 |
| 2003–04 | Southern California | Michigan | 28–14 |
| 2004–05 | Texas | Michigan | 38–37 |
| 2005–06 | Texas⁴ | | |
| 2006–07 | Southern California | Michigan | 32–18 |
| 2007–08 | Southern California | Illinois | 49–17 |
| 2008–09 | Southern California | Penn State | 38–24 |
| 2009–10 | Ohio State | Oregon | 26–17 |
| 2010–11 | Texas Christian | Wisconsin | 21–19 |
| 2011–12 | Oregon | Wisconsin | 45–38 |

¹US Marine Corps team. ²US Army team. ³US Navy team. ⁴Southern California's participation was vacated for rules violations.

## Orange Bowl

| SEASON | WINNER | RUNNER-UP | SCORE |
|---|---|---|---|
| 1934–35 | Bucknell | Miami (FL) | 26–0 |
| 1935–36 | Catholic | Mississippi | 20–19 |
| 1936–37 | Duquesne | Mississippi State | 13–12 |
| 1937–38 | Auburn | Michigan State | 6–0 |
| 1938–39 | Tennessee | Oklahoma | 17–0 |
| 1939–40 | Georgia Tech | Missouri | 21–7 |
| 1940–41 | Mississippi State | Georgetown | 14–7 |
| 1941–42 | Georgia | Texas Christian | 40–26 |
| 1942–43 | Alabama | Boston College | 37–21 |
| 1943–44 | Louisiana State | Texas A&M | 19–14 |
| 1944–45 | Tulsa | Georgia Tech | 26–12 |

## Orange Bowl (continued)

| SEASON | WINNER | RUNNER-UP | SCORE | SEASON | WINNER | RUNNER-UP | SCORE |
|--------|--------|-----------|-------|--------|--------|-----------|-------|
| 1945–46 | Miami (FL) | Holy Cross | 13–6 | 1979–80 | Oklahoma | Florida State | 24–7 |
| 1946–47 | Rice | Tennessee | 8–0 | 1980–81 | Oklahoma | Florida State | 18–17 |
| 1947–48 | Georgia Tech | Kansas | 20–14 | 1981–82 | Clemson | Nebraska | 22–15 |
| 1948–49 | Texas | Georgia | 41–28 | 1982–83 | Nebraska | Louisiana State | 21–20 |
| 1949–50 | Santa Clara | Kentucky | 21–13 | 1983–84 | Miami (FL) | Nebraska | 31–30 |
| 1950–51 | Clemson | Miami (FL) | 15–14 | 1984–85 | Washington | Oklahoma | 28–17 |
| 1951–52 | Georgia Tech | Baylor | 17–14 | 1985–86 | Oklahoma | Penn State | 25–10 |
| 1952–53 | Alabama | Syracuse | 61–6 | 1986–87 | Oklahoma | Arkansas | 42–8 |
| 1953–54 | Oklahoma | Maryland | 7–0 | 1987–88 | Miami (FL) | Oklahoma | 20–14 |
| 1954–55 | Duke | Nebraska | 34–7 | 1988–89 | Miami (FL) | Nebraska | 23–3 |
| 1955–56 | Oklahoma | Maryland | 20–6 | 1989–90 | Notre Dame | Colorado | 21–6 |
| 1956–57 | Colorado | Clemson | 27–21 | 1990–91 | Colorado | Notre Dame | 10–9 |
| 1957–58 | Oklahoma | Duke | 48–21 | 1991–92 | Miami (FL) | Nebraska | 22–0 |
| 1958–59 | Oklahoma | Syracuse | 21–6 | 1992–93 | Florida State | Nebraska | 27–14 |
| 1959–60 | Georgia | Missouri | 14–0 | 1993–94 | Florida State | Nebraska | 18–16 |
| 1960–61 | Missouri | Navy | 21–14 | 1994–95 | Nebraska | Miami | 24–17 |
| 1961–62 | Louisiana State | Colorado | 25–7 | 1995–96 | Florida State | Notre Dame | 31–26 |
| 1962–63 | Alabama | Oklahoma | 17–0 | 1996–97 | Nebraska | Virginia Tech | 41–21 |
| 1963–64 | Nebraska | Auburn | 13–7 | 1997–98 | Nebraska | Tennessee | 42–17 |
| 1964–65 | Texas | Alabama | 21–17 | 1998–99 | Florida | Syracuse | 31–10 |
| 1965–66 | Alabama | Nebraska | 39–28 | 1999–2000 | Michigan | Alabama | 35–34 |
| 1966–67 | Florida | Georgia Tech | 27–12 | 2000–01 | Oklahoma | Florida State | 13–2 |
| 1967–68 | Oklahoma | Tennessee | 26–24 | 2001–02 | Florida | Maryland | 56–23 |
| 1968–69 | Penn State | Kansas | 15–14 | 2002–03 | Southern | Iowa | 38–17 |
| 1969–70 | Penn State | Missouri | 10–3 | | California | | |
| 1970–71 | Nebraska | Louisiana State | 17–12 | 2003–04 | Miami (FL) | Florida State | 16–14 |
| 1971–72 | Nebraska | Alabama | 38–6 | 2004–05 | win vacated for rules violations | | |
| 1972–73 | Nebraska | Notre Dame | 40–6 | 2005–06 | Penn State | Florida State | 26–23 |
| 1973–74 | Penn State | Louisiana State | 16–9 | 2006–07 | Louisville | Wake Forest | 24–13 |
| 1974–75 | Notre Dame | Alabama | 13–11 | 2007–08 | Kansas | Virginia Tech | 24–21 |
| 1975–76 | Oklahoma | Michigan | 14–6 | 2008–09 | Virginia Tech | Cincinnati | 20–7 |
| 1976–77 | Ohio State | Colorado | 27–10 | 2009–10 | Iowa | Georgia Tech | 24–14 |
| 1977–78 | Arkansas | Oklahoma | 31–6 | 2010–11 | Stanford | Virginia Tech | 40–12 |
| 1978–79 | Oklahoma | Nebraska | 31–24 | 2011–12 | West Virginia | Clemson | 70–33 |

## Sugar Bowl

| SEASON | WINNER | RUNNER-UP | SCORE | SEASON | WINNER | RUNNER-UP | SCORE |
|--------|--------|-----------|-------|--------|--------|-----------|-------|
| 1934–35 | Tulane | Temple | 20–14 | 1963–64 | Alabama | Mississippi | 12–7 |
| 1935–36 | Texas Christian | Louisiana State | 3–2 | 1964–65 | Louisiana | Syracuse | 13–10 |
| 1936–37 | Santa Clara | Louisiana State | 21–14 | | State | | |
| 1937–38 | Santa Clara | Louisiana State | 6–0 | 1965–66 | Missouri | Florida | 20–18 |
| 1938–39 | Texas Christian | Carnegie Tech | 15–7 | 1966–67 | Alabama | Nebraska | 34–7 |
| 1939–40 | Texas A&M | Tulane | 14–13 | 1967–68 | Louisiana | Wyoming | 20–13 |
| 1940–41 | Boston College | Tennessee | 19–13 | | State | | |
| 1941–42 | Fordham | Missouri | 2–0 | 1968–69 | Arkansas | Georgia | 16–2 |
| 1942–43 | Tennessee | Tulsa | 14–7 | 1969–70 | Mississippi | Arkansas | 27–22 |
| 1943–44 | Georgia Tech | Tulsa | 20–18 | 1970–71 | Tennessee | Air Force | 34–13 |
| 1944–45 | Duke | Alabama | 29–26 | 1971–72 | Oklahoma | Auburn | 40–22 |
| 1945–46 | Oklahoma A&M | St. Mary's (CA) | 33–13 | 1972–73 | Oklahoma | Penn State | 14–0 |
| 1946–47 | Georgia | North Carolina | 20–10 | 1973–74 | Notre Dame | Alabama | 24–23 |
| 1947–48 | Texas | Alabama | 27–7 | 1974–75 | Nebraska | Florida | 13–10 |
| 1948–49 | Oklahoma | North Carolina | 14–6 | 1975–76 | Alabama | Penn State | 13–6 |
| 1949–50 | Oklahoma | Louisiana State | 35–0 | 1976–77 | Pittsburgh | Georgia | 27–3 |
| 1950–51 | Kentucky | Oklahoma | 13–7 | 1977–78 | Alabama | Ohio State | 35–6 |
| 1951–52 | Maryland | Tennessee | 28–13 | 1978–79 | Alabama | Penn State | 14–7 |
| 1952–53 | Georgia Tech | Mississippi | 24–7 | 1979–80 | Alabama | Arkansas | 24–9 |
| 1953–54 | Georgia Tech | West Virginia | 42–19 | 1980–81 | Georgia | Notre Dame | 17–10 |
| 1954–55 | Navy | Mississippi | 21–0 | 1981–82 | Pittsburgh | Georgia | 24–20 |
| 1955–56 | Georgia Tech | Pittsburgh | 7–0 | 1982–83 | Penn State | Georgia | 27–23 |
| 1956–57 | Baylor | Tennessee | 13–7 | 1983–84 | Auburn | Michigan | 9–7 |
| 1957–58 | Mississippi | Texas | 39–7 | 1984–85 | Nebraska | Louisiana State | 28–10 |
| 1958–59 | Louisiana State | Clemson | 7–0 | 1985–86 | Tennessee | Miami (FL) | 35–7 |
| 1959–60 | Mississippi | Louisiana State | 21–0 | 1986–87 | Nebraska | Louisiana State | 30–15 |
| 1960–61 | Mississippi | Rice | 14–6 | 1987–88 | Auburn | Syracuse | 16–16 |
| 1961–62 | Alabama | Arkansas | 10–3 | 1988–89 | Florida State | Auburn | 13–7 |
| 1962–63 | Mississippi | Arkansas | 17–13 | 1989–90 | Miami (FL) | Alabama | 33–25 |

## Sugar Bowl (continued)

| SEASON | WINNER | RUNNER-UP | SCORE | SEASON | WINNER | RUNNER-UP | SCORE |
|--------|--------|-----------|-------|--------|--------|-----------|-------|
| 1990–91 | Tennessee | Virginia | 23–22 | 2002–03 | Georgia | Florida State | 26–13 |
| 1991–92 | Notre Dame | Florida | 39–28 | 2003–04 | Louisiana State | Oklahoma | 21–14 |
| 1992–93 | Alabama | Miami (FL) | 34–13 | | | | |
| 1993–94 | Florida | West Virginia | 41–7 | 2004–05 | Auburn | Virginia Tech | 16–13 |
| 1994–95 | Florida State | Florida | 23–17 | 2005–06 | West Virginia | Georgia | 38–35 |
| 1995–96 | Virginia Tech | Texas | 28–10 | 2006–07 | Louisiana State | Notre Dame | 41–14 |
| 1996–97 | Florida | Florida State | 52–20 | | | | |
| 1997–98 | Florida State | Ohio State | 31–14 | 2007–08 | Georgia | Hawaii | 41–10 |
| 1998–99 | Ohio State | Texas A&M | 24–14 | 2008–09 | Utah | Alabama | 31–17 |
| 1999–2000 | Florida State | Virginia Tech | 46–29 | 2009–10 | Florida | Cincinnati | 51–24 |
| 2000–01 | Miami (FL) | Florida | 37–20 | 2010–11 | *win vacated for rules violations* | | |
| 2001–02 | Louisiana State | Illinois | 47–34 | 2011–12 | Michigan | Virginia Tech | 23–20 |

## Fiesta Bowl

| SEASON | WINNER | RUNNER-UP | SCORE | SEASON | WINNER | RUNNER-UP | SCORE |
|--------|--------|-----------|-------|--------|--------|-----------|-------|
| 1971–72 | Arizona State | Florida State | 45–38 | 1991–92 | Penn State | Tennessee | 42–17 |
| 1972–73 | Arizona State | Missouri | 49–35 | 1992–93 | Syracuse | Colorado | 26–22 |
| 1973–74 | Arizona State | Pittsburgh | 28–7 | 1993–94 | Arizona | Miami (FL) | 29–0 |
| 1974–75 | Oklahoma State | Brigham Young | 16–6 | 1994–95 | Colorado | Notre Dame | 41–24 |
| 1975–76 | Arizona State | Nebraska | 17–14 | 1995–96 | Nebraska | Florida | 62–24 |
| 1976–77 | Oklahoma | Wyoming | 41–7 | 1996–97 | Penn State | Texas | 38–15 |
| 1977–78 | Penn State | Arizona State | 42–30 | 1997–98 | Kansas State | Syracuse | 35–18 |
| 1978–79 | Arkansas | UCLA | 10–10 | 1998–99 | Tennessee | Florida State | 23–16 |
| 1979–80 | Pittsburgh | Arizona | 16–10 | 1999–2000 | Nebraska | Tennessee | 31–21 |
| 1980–81 | Penn State | Ohio State | 31–19 | 2000–01 | Oregon State | Notre Dame | 41–9 |
| 1981–82 | Penn State | Southern California | 26–10 | 2001–02 | Oregon | Colorado | 38–16 |
| | | | | 2002–03 | Ohio State | Miami (FL) | 31–24 |
| 1982–83 | Arizona State | Oklahoma | 32–21 | 2003–04 | Ohio State | Kansas State | 35–28 |
| 1983–84 | Ohio State | Pittsburgh | 28–23 | 2004–05 | Utah | Pittsburgh | 35–7 |
| 1984–85 | UCLA | Miami (FL) | 39–37 | 2005–06 | Ohio State | Notre Dame | 34–20 |
| 1985–86 | Michigan | Nebraska | 27–23 | 2006–07 | Boise State | Oklahoma | 43–42 |
| 1986–87 | Penn State | Miami (FL) | 14–10 | 2007–08 | West Virginia | Oklahoma | 48–28 |
| 1987–88 | Florida State | Nebraska | 31–28 | 2008–09 | Texas | Ohio State | 24–21 |
| 1988–89 | Notre Dame | West Virginia | 34–21 | 2009–10 | Boise State | Texas Christian | 17–10 |
| 1989–90 | Florida State | Nebraska | 41–17 | 2010–11 | Oklahoma | Connecticut | 48–20 |
| 1990–91 | Louisville | Alabama | 34–7 | 2011–12 | Oklahoma State | Stanford | 41–38 |

## Heisman Trophy

The Heisman Trophy goes yearly to the most outstanding college football player. Web site: <www.heisman.com>.

| YEAR | WINNER | COLLEGE | POSITION | YEAR | WINNER | COLLEGE | POSITION |
|------|--------|---------|----------|------|--------|---------|----------|
| 1935 | Jay Berwanger | Chicago | HB | 1957 | John David Crow | Texas A&M | HB |
| 1936 | Larry Kelley | Yale | E | 1958 | Pete Dawkins | Army | HB |
| 1937 | Clint Frank | Yale | HB | 1959 | Billy Cannon | Louisiana State | HB |
| 1938 | Davey O'Brien | Texas Christian | QB | 1960 | Joe Bellino | Navy | HB |
| 1939 | Nile Kinnick | Iowa | HB | 1961 | Ernie Davis | Syracuse | HB |
| 1940 | Tom Harmon | Michigan | HB | 1962 | Terry Baker | Oregon State | QB |
| 1941 | Bruce Smith | Minnesota | HB | 1963 | Roger Staubach | Navy | QB |
| 1942 | Frank Sinkwich | Georgia | HB | 1964 | John Huarte | Notre Dame | QB |
| 1943 | Angelo Bertelli | Notre Dame | QB | 1965 | Mike Garrett | Southern California | HB |
| 1944 | Les Horvath | Ohio State | QB | 1966 | Steve Spurrier | Florida | QB |
| 1945 | Felix Blanchard | Army | FB | 1967 | Gary Beban | UCLA | QB |
| 1946 | Glenn Davis | Army | HB | 1968 | O.J. Simpson | Southern California | HB |
| 1947 | John Lujack | Notre Dame | QB | 1969 | Steve Owens | Oklahoma | HB |
| 1948 | Doak Walker | Southern Methodist | HB | 1970 | Jim Plunkett | Stanford | QB |
| 1949 | Leon Hart | Notre Dame | E | 1971 | Pat Sullivan | Auburn | QB |
| 1950 | Vic Janowicz | Ohio State | HB | 1972 | Johnny Rodgers | Nebraska | RB |
| 1951 | Dick Kazmaier | Princeton | HB | 1973 | John Cappelletti | Penn State | HB |
| 1952 | Billy Vessels | Oklahoma | HB | 1974 | Archie Griffin | Ohio State | HB |
| 1953 | John Lattner | Notre Dame | HB | 1975 | Archie Griffin | Ohio State | HB |
| 1954 | Alan Ameche | Wisconsin | FB | 1976 | Tony Dorsett | Pittsburgh | HB |
| 1955 | Howard Cassady | Ohio State | HB | 1977 | Earl Campbell | Texas | HB |
| 1956 | Paul Hornung | Notre Dame | QB | 1978 | Billy Sims | Oklahoma | HB |

## Heisman Trophy (continued)

| YEAR | WINNER | COLLEGE | POSITION | YEAR | WINNER | COLLEGE | POSITION |
|------|--------|---------|----------|------|--------|---------|----------|
| 1979 | Charles White | Southern California | HB | 1996 | Danny Wuerffel | Florida | QB |
| 1980 | George Rogers | South Carolina | HB | 1997 | Charles Woodson | Michigan | DB |
| 1981 | Marcus Allen | Southern California | HB | 1998 | Ricky Williams | Texas | RB |
| 1982 | Herschel Walker | Georgia | HB | 1999 | Ron Dayne | Wisconsin | RB |
| 1983 | Mike Rozier | Nebraska | HB | 2000 | Chris Weinke | Florida State | QB |
| 1984 | Doug Flutie | Boston College | QB | 2001 | Eric Crouch | Nebraska | QB |
| 1985 | Bo Jackson | Auburn | HB | 2002 | Carson Palmer | Southern California | QB |
| 1986 | Vinny Testaverde | Miami (FL) | QB | 2003 | Jason White | Oklahoma | QB |
| 1987 | Tim Brown | Notre Dame | WR | 2004 | Matt Leinart | Southern California | QB |
| 1988 | Barry Sanders | Oklahoma State | RB | 2005 | Reggie Bush[1] | Southern California | RB |
| 1989 | Andre Ware | Houston | QB | 2006 | Troy Smith | Ohio State | QB |
| 1990 | Ty Detmer | Brigham Young | QB | 2007 | Tim Tebow | Florida | QB |
| 1991 | Desmond Howard | Michigan | WR | 2008 | Sam Bradford | Oklahoma | QB |
| 1992 | Gino Torretta | Miami | QB | 2009 | Mark Ingram | Alabama | RB |
| 1993 | Charlie Ward | Florida State | QB | 2010 | Cam Newton | Auburn | QB |
| 1994 | Rashaan Salaam | Colorado | TB | 2011 | Robert Griffin III | Baylor | QB |
| 1995 | Eddie George | Ohio State | RB | | | | |

[1]Reggie Bush relinquished his trophy in late 2010 after being stripped of his 2005 eligibility.

## Canadian Football League Grey Cup

*Held since 1909. Table shows results for the past 20 years.*

| YEAR | WINNER | RUNNER-UP | SCORE |
|------|--------|-----------|-------|
| 1992 | Calgary Stampeders (WD) | Winnipeg Blue Bombers (ED) | 24–10 |
| 1993 | Edmonton Eskimos (WD) | Winnipeg Blue Bombers (ED) | 33–23 |
| 1994 | British Columbia Lions (WD) | Baltimore Stallions (ED) | 26–23 |
| 1995[1] | Baltimore Stallions (SD) | Calgary Stampeders (ND) | 37–20 |
| 1996 | Toronto Argonauts (ED) | Edmonton Eskimos (WD) | 43–37 |
| 1997 | Toronto Argonauts (ED) | Saskatchewan Roughriders (WD) | 47–23 |
| 1998 | Calgary Stampeders (WD) | Hamilton Tiger-Cats (ED) | 26–24 |
| 1999 | Hamilton Tiger-Cats (ED) | Calgary Stampeders (WD) | 32–21 |
| 2000 | British Columbia Lions (WD) | Montreal Alouettes (ED) | 28–26 |
| 2001 | Calgary Stampeders (WD) | Winnipeg Blue Bombers (ED) | 27–19 |
| 2002 | Montreal Alouettes (ED) | Edmonton Eskimos (WD) | 25–16 |
| 2003 | Edmonton Eskimos (WD) | Montreal Alouettes (ED) | 34–22 |
| 2004 | Toronto Argonauts (ED) | British Columbia Lions (WD) | 27–19 |
| 2005 | Edmonton Eskimos (WD) | Montreal Alouettes (ED) | 38–35 |
| 2006 | British Columbia Lions (WD) | Montreal Alouettes (ED) | 25–14 |
| 2007 | Saskatchewan Roughriders (WD) | Winnipeg Blue Bombers (ED) | 23–19 |
| 2008 | Calgary Stampeders (WD) | Montreal Alouettes (ED) | 22–14 |
| 2009 | Montreal Alouettes (ED) | Saskatchewan Roughriders (WD) | 28–27 |
| 2010 | Montreal Alouettes (ED) | Saskatchewan Roughriders (WD) | 21–18 |
| 2011 | British Columbia Lions (WD) | Winnipeg Blue Bombers (ED) | 34–23 |

[1]In 1995 only, the divisions were reconfigured and renamed Northern and Southern in response to the inclusion of American teams in the CFL (1993–96).

## Australian Football League Final Standings, 2011[1]

*Teams that qualified for play-offs only.*

| TEAM | WON | LOST | TIED | POINTS | TEAM | WON | LOST | TIED | POINTS |
|------|-----|------|------|--------|------|-----|------|------|--------|
| Collingwood Magpies | 20 | 2 | 0 | 80 | Carlton Blues | 14 | 7 | 1 | 58 |
| Geelong Cats | 19 | 3 | 0 | 76 | St. Kilda Saints | 12 | 9 | 1 | 50 |
| Hawthorn Hawks | 18 | 4 | 0 | 72 | Sydney Swans | 12 | 9 | 1 | 50 |
| West Coast Eagles | 17 | 5 | 0 | 68 | Essendon Bombers | 11 | 10 | 1 | 46 |

[1]The Geelong Cats were the 2011 champions.

## Rugby World Cup

| YEAR | WINNER | RUNNER-UP | SCORE | YEAR | WINNER | RUNNER-UP | SCORE |
|------|--------|-----------|-------|------|--------|-----------|-------|
| 1987 | New Zealand | France | 29–9 | 1999 | Australia | France | 35–12 |
| 1991 | Australia | England | 12–6 | 2003 | England | Australia | 20–17 |
| 1995 | South Africa | New Zealand | 15–12 | 2007 | South Africa | England | 15–6 |

# Rugby League World Cup

| YEAR | WINNER | RUNNER-UP | SCORE | YEAR | WINNER | RUNNER-UP | SCORE |
|------|--------|-----------|-------|------|--------|-----------|-------|
| 1954 | Great Britain | France | 16–12 | 1977[3] | Australia | Great Britain | 13–12 |
| 1957 | Australia | Great Britain | [1] | 1988 | Australia | New Zealand | 25–12 |
| 1960 | Great Britain | Australia | [1] | 1992 | Australia | Great Britain | 10–6 |
| 1968 | Australia | France | 20–2 | 1995 | Australia | England | 16–8 |
| 1970 | Australia | Great Britain | 12–7 | 2000 | Australia | New Zealand | 40–12 |
| 1972 | Great Britain | Australia | 10–10[2] | 2008 | New Zealand | Australia | 34–20 |
| 1975[3] | Australia | England | [1] | | | | |

[1]Tournament played without a grand final match; winner determined by match points.   [2]Great Britain won on match points.   [3]Called International Championship from 1975 to 1977.

# Super 15 Rugby Final Standings, 2012[1]

Super 12 until 2006; Super 14 until 2011. Four points are awarded for a win and two for a draw; one bonus point is given for a loss by seven points or fewer and one for a team that scores four or more tries.

| TEAM (COUNTRY) | POINTS | W | L | D | BONUS | TEAM (COUNTRY) | POINTS | W | L | D | BONUS |
|----------------|--------|---|---|---|-------|----------------|--------|---|---|---|-------|
| Stormers (RSA) | 66 | 14 | 2 | 0 | 2 | Highlanders (NZL) | 50 | 9 | 7 | 0 | 2 |
| Chiefs (NZL) | 64 | 12 | 4 | 0 | 2 | Central Cheetahs (RSA) | 38 | 5 | 11 | 0 | 2 |
| Queensland Reds (AUS) | 58 | 11 | 5 | 0 | 2 | New South Wales | 35 | 4 | 12 | 0 | 2 |
| Crusaders (NZL) | 61 | 11 | 5 | 0 | 2 | Waratahs (AUS) | | | | | |
| Bulls (RSA) | 59 | 10 | 6 | 0 | 2 | Blues (NZL) | 32 | 4 | 12 | 0 | 2 |
| Sharks (RSA) | 59 | 10 | 6 | 0 | 2 | Melbourne Rebels (AUS) | 32 | 4 | 12 | 0 | 2 |
| Brumbies (AUS) | 58 | 10 | 6 | 0 | 2 | Western Force (AUS) | 27 | 3 | 13 | 0 | 2 |
| Hurricanes (NZL) | 57 | 10 | 6 | 0 | 2 | Lions (RSA) | 25 | 3 | 13 | 0 | 2 |

[1]The Chiefs were the 2012 champions.

# Six Nations Championship

Held since 1883; Five Nations in 1910–31 and 1947–99. Round-robin tournament, usually ending in April.

| YEAR | WINNER | YEAR | WINNER | YEAR | WINNER |
|------|--------|------|--------|------|--------|
| 1947 | England; Wales[1] | 1969 | Wales[3] | 1991 | England[2,3] |
| 1948 | Ireland[2,3] | 1970 | France; Wales[1] | 1992 | England[2,3] |
| 1949 | Ireland[3] | 1971 | Wales[2,3] | 1993 | France |
| 1950 | Wales[2,3] | 1972 | not completed | 1994 | Wales |
| 1951 | Ireland | 1973 | quintuple tie | 1995 | England[2,3] |
| 1952 | Wales[2,3] | 1974 | Ireland | 1996 | England[3] |
| 1953 | England | 1975 | Wales | 1997 | France[2,5] |
| 1954 | England[3]; France; Wales[1] | 1976 | Wales[2,3] | 1998 | France[2,5] |
| 1955 | France; Wales[1] | 1977 | France[2,4] | 1999 | Scotland |
| 1956 | Wales | 1978 | Wales[2,3] | 2000 | England |
| 1957 | England[2,3] | 1979 | Wales[3] | 2001 | England |
| 1958 | England | 1980 | England[2,3] | 2002 | France[2,5] |
| 1959 | France | 1981 | France[2] | 2003 | England[2,3] |
| 1960 | England[3]; France[1] | 1982 | Ireland[3] | 2004 | France[2,6] |
| 1961 | France | 1983 | France; Ireland[1] | 2005 | Wales[2,3] |
| 1962 | France | 1984 | Scotland[2,3] | 2006 | France[6] |
| 1963 | England | 1985 | Ireland[3] | 2007 | France[6] |
| 1964 | Scotland; Wales[1] | 1986 | France; Scotland[1] | 2008 | Wales[2,3] |
| 1965 | Wales[3] | 1987 | France[2] | 2009 | Ireland[2,3] |
| 1966 | Wales | 1988 | France; Wales[1,3] | 2010 | France[2] |
| 1967 | France | 1989 | France | 2011 | England |
| 1968 | France[2] | 1990 | Scotland[2,3] | 2012 | Wales[2,3] |

[1]Tied.   [2]Grand Slam winner (defeats all other competitors).   [3]Triple Crown winner (Home Nation [England, Ireland, Scotland, Wales] that defeats all three other Home Nations).   [4]Triple Crown won by Wales.   [5]Triple Crown won by England.   [6]Triple Crown won by Ireland.

# FIFA World Cup—Men

| YEAR | WINNER | RUNNER-UP | SCORE | YEAR | WINNER | RUNNER-UP | SCORE |
|------|--------|-----------|-------|------|--------|-----------|-------|
| 1930 | Uruguay | Argentina | 4–2 | 1954 | West Germany | Hungary | 3–2 |
| 1934 | Italy | Czechoslovakia | 2–1 | 1958 | Brazil | Sweden | 5–2 |
| 1938 | Italy | Hungary | 4–2 | 1962 | Brazil | Czechoslovakia | 3–1 |
| 1950 | Uruguay | Brazil | 2–1 | 1966 | England | West Germany | 4–2 |

## FIFA World Cup—Men (continued)

| YEAR | WINNER | RUNNER-UP | SCORE | YEAR | WINNER | RUNNER-UP | SCORE |
|------|--------|-----------|-------|------|--------|-----------|-------|
| 1970 | Brazil | Italy | 4–1 | 1994 | Brazil | Italy | 0–0 (3–2[1]) |
| 1974 | West Germany | Netherlands | 2–1 | 1998 | France | Brazil | 3–0 |
| 1978 | Argentina | Netherlands | 3–1 | 2002 | Brazil | Germany | 2–0 |
| 1982 | Italy | West Germany | 3–1 | 2006 | Italy | France | 1–1 (5–3[1]) |
| 1986 | Argentina | West Germany | 3–2 | 2010 | Spain | Netherlands | 1–0 |
| 1990 | West Germany | Argentina | 1–0 | | | | |

[1]Won in a penalty kick shoot-out.

## FIFA World Cup—Women

| YEAR | WINNER | RUNNER-UP | SCORE | YEAR | WINNER | RUNNER-UP | SCORE |
|------|--------|-----------|-------|------|--------|-----------|-------|
| 1991 | United States | Norway | 2–1 | 2003 | Germany | Sweden | 2–1 |
| 1995 | Norway | Germany | 2–0 | 2007 | Germany | Brazil | 2–0 |
| 1999 | United States | China | 0–0 (5–4[1]) | 2011 | Japan | United States | 2–2 (3–1[1]) |

[1]Won in a penalty kick shoot-out.

## UEFA Champions League

*Held since 1955 and known until 1992–93 as the European Champion Clubs' Cup; played on a knockout basis until 1992–93 and as a combination of group and knockout rounds since then. Table shows results for the past 20 years.*

| SEASON | WINNER (COUNTRY) | RUNNER-UP (COUNTRY) | SCORE |
|--------|------------------|---------------------|-------|
| 1992–93 | Olympique de Marseille (FRA) | AC Milan (ITA) | 1–0 |
| 1993–94 | AC Milan (ITA) | FC Barcelona (ESP) | 4–0 |
| 1994–95 | AFC Ajax (NED) | AC Milan (ITA) | 1–0 |
| 1995–96 | Juventus FC (ITA) | AFC Ajax (NED) | 1–1 (4–2[1]) |
| 1996–97 | BV Borussia Dortmund (GER) | Juventus FC (ITA) | 3–1 |
| 1997–98 | Real Madrid CF (ESP) | Juventus FC (ITA) | 1–0 |
| 1998–99 | Manchester United (ENG) | FC Bayern München (GER) | 2–1 |
| 1999–2000 | Real Madrid CF (ESP) | Valencia CF (ESP) | 3–0 |
| 2000–01 | FC Bayern München (GER) | Valencia CF (ESP) | 1–1 (5–4[1]) |
| 2001–02 | Real Madrid CF (ESP) | Bayer 04 Leverkusen (GER) | 2–1 |
| 2002–03 | AC Milan (ITA) | Juventus FC (ITA) | 0–0 (3–2[1]) |
| 2003–04 | FC Porto (POR) | AS Monaco (FRA) | 3–0 |
| 2004–05 | Liverpool FC (ENG) | AC Milan (ITA) | 3–3 (3–2[1]) |
| 2005–06 | FC Barcelona (ESP) | Arsenal FC (ENG) | 2–1 |
| 2006–07 | AC Milan (ITA) | Liverpool FC (ENG) | 2–1 |
| 2007–08 | Manchester United (ENG) | Chelsea FC (ENG) | 1–1 (6–5[1]) |
| 2008–09 | FC Barcelona (ESP) | Manchester United (ENG) | 2–0 |
| 2009–10 | FC Internazionale Milano (ITA) | FC Bayern München (GER) | 2–0 |
| 2010–11 | FC Barcelona (ESP) | Manchester United (ENG) | 3–1 |
| 2011–12 | Chelsea FC (ENG) | FC Bayern München (GER) | 1–1 (4–3[1]) |

[1]Won in a penalty kick shoot-out.

## UEFA European Championship

| YEAR | WINNER | RUNNER-UP | SCORE | YEAR | WINNER | RUNNER-UP | SCORE |
|------|--------|-----------|-------|------|--------|-----------|-------|
| 1960 | USSR | Yugoslavia | 2–1 | 1988 | Netherlands | USSR | 2–0 |
| 1964 | Spain | USSR | 2–1 | 1992 | Denmark | Germany | 2–0 |
| 1968 | Italy | Yugoslavia | 2–0 | 1996 | Germany | Czech Republic | 2–1 |
| 1972 | West Germany | USSR | 3–0 | 2000 | France | Italy | 2–1 |
| 1976 | Czechoslovakia | West Germany | 2–2 | 2004 | Greece | Portugal | 1–0 |
| 1980 | West Germany | Belgium | 2–1 | 2008 | Spain | Germany | 1–0 |
| 1984 | France | Spain | 2–0 | 2012 | Spain | Italy | 4–0 |

## UEFA Europa League

The UEFA Europa League is considered Europe's second most important football competition. Established in the 1971–72 season, the competition was restructured when the UEFA Cup Win-ners' Cup was abolished after the 1998–99 season and was named the UEFA Cup. Originally played on an entirely two-legged basis, since 1998 the competition has concluded with a single

## UEFA Europa League (continued)

match. The competition is open to top- and second-ranked teams in each country's league as well as to the winners of domestic cups. The competition was renamed in 2010.

| SEASON | WINNER (COUNTRY) | RUNNER-UP (COUNTRY) | SCORES |
|---|---|---|---|
| 1971–72 | Tottenham Hotspur FC (ENG) | Wolverhampton Wanderers FC (ENG) | 2–1, 1–1 |
| 1972–73 | Liverpool FC (ENG) | VfL Borussia Mönchengladbach (FRG) | 3–0, 0–2 |
| 1973–74 | Feyenoord (NED) | Tottenham Hotspur FC (ENG) | 2–2, 2–0 |
| 1974–75 | VfL Borussia Mönchengladbach (FRG) | FC Twente (NED) | 0–0, 5–1 |
| 1975–76 | Liverpool FC (ENG) | Club Brugge KV (BEL) | 3–2, 1–1 |
| 1976–77 | Juventus FC (ITA) | Athletic Club Bilbao (ESP) | 1–0, 1–2 |
| 1977–78 | PSV Eindhoven (NED) | SC Bastia (FRA) | 0–0, 3–0 |
| 1978–79 | VfL Borussia Mönchengladbach (FRG) | FK Crvena Zvezda Beograd (YUG) | 1–1, 1–0 |
| 1979–80 | Eintracht Frankfurt (FRG) | VfL Borussia Mönchengladbach (FRG) | 2–3, 1–0 |
| 1980–81 | Ipswich Town FC (ENG) | AZ Alkmaar (NED) | 3–0, 2–4 |
| 1981–82 | IFK Göteborg (SWE) | Hamburger SV (FRG) | 1–0, 3–0 |
| 1982–83 | RSC Anderlecht (BEL) | SL Benfica (POR) | 1–0, 1–1 |
| 1983–84 | Tottenham Hotspur FC (ENG) | RSC Anderlecht (BEL) | 1–1, 1–1 (4–3[1]) |
| 1984–85 | Real Madrid CF (ESP) | Videoton FCF (HUN) | 3–0, 0–1 |
| 1985–86 | Real Madrid CF (ESP) | 1. FC Köln (FRG) | 5–1, 0–2 |
| 1986–87 | IFK Göteborg (SWE) | Dundee United FC (SCO) | 1–0, 1–1 |
| 1987–88 | Bayer 04 Leverkusen (FRG) | RCD Espanyol (ESP) | 0–3, 3–0 (3–2[1]) |
| 1988–89 | SSC Napoli (ITA) | VfB Stuttgart (FRG) | 2–1, 3–3 |
| 1989–90 | Juventus FC (ITA) | AC Fiorentina (ITA) | 3–1, 0–0 |
| 1990–91 | Internazionale FC (ITA) | AS Roma (ITA) | 2–0, 0–1 |
| 1991–92 | AFC Ajax (NED) | Torino Calcio (ITA) | 2–2, 0–0 |
| 1992–93 | Juventus FC (ITA) | BV Borussia Dortmund (GER) | 3–1, 3–0 |
| 1993–94 | Internazionale FC (ITA) | SV Austria Salzburg (AUT) | 1–0, 1–0 |
| 1994–95 | Parma AC (ITA) | Juventus FC (ITA) | 1–0, 1–1 |
| 1995–96 | FC Bayern München (GER) | FC Girondins de Bordeaux (FRA) | 2–0, 3–1 |
| 1996–97 | FC Schalke 04 (GER) | Internazionale FC (ITA) | 1–0, 0–1 (4–1[1]) |
| 1997–98 | Internazionale FC (ITA) | SS Lazio (ITA) | 3–0 |
| 1998–99 | Parma AC (ITA) | Olympique de Marseille (FRA) | 3–0 |
| 1999–2000 | Galatasaray SK (TUR) | Arsenal FC (ENG) | 0–0 (4–1[1]) |
| 2000–01 | Liverpool FC (ENG) | Deportivo Alavés (ESP) | 5–4 |
| 2001–02 | Feyenoord (NED) | BV Borussia Dortmund (GER) | 3–2 |
| 2002–03 | FC Porto (POR) | Celtic FC (SCO) | 3–2[2] |
| 2003–04 | Valencia CF (ESP) | Olympique de Marseille (FRA) | 2–0 |
| 2004–05 | CSKA Moscow (RUS) | Sporting (POR) | 3–1 |
| 2005–06 | Sevilla FC (ESP) | Middlesbrough FC (ENG) | 4–0 |
| 2006–07 | Sevilla FC (ESP) | RCD Espanyol (ESP) | 2–2 (3–1[1]) |
| 2007–08 | FC Zenit St. Petersburg (RUS) | Rangers FC (SCO) | 2–0 |
| 2008–09 | Shakhtar Donetsk (UKR) | Werder Bremen (GER) | 2–1[2] |
| 2009–10 | Club Atlético de Madrid (ESP) | Fulham FC (ENG) | 2–1 |
| 2010–11 | FC Porto (POR) | SC Braga (POR) | 1–0 |
| 2011–12 | Club Atlético de Madrid (ESP) | Athletic Club Bilbao (ESP) | 3–0 |

[1]*Won in a penalty kick shoot-out.*   [2]*Won on "silver goal" in overtime.*

## Copa Libertadores de América

*Held since 1960. Table shows results for the past 20 years.*

| YEAR | WINNER (COUNTRY) | RUNNER-UP (COUNTRY) | SCORES |
|---|---|---|---|
| 1993 | São Paulo (BRA) | Universidad Católica (CHI) | 5–1, 0–2 |
| 1994 | Vélez Sársfield (ARG) | São Paulo (BRA) | 1–0, 0–1 (5–4[1]) |
| 1995 | Grêmio (BRA) | Atlético Nacional (COL) | 3–1, 1–1 |
| 1996 | River Plate (ARG) | América de Cali (COL) | 0–1, 2–0 |
| 1997 | Cruzeiro (BRA) | Sporting Cristal (PER) | 0–0, 1–0 |
| 1998 | Vasco da Gama (BRA) | Barcelona (ECU) | 2–0, 2–1 |
| 1999 | Palmeiras (BRA) | Deportiva Cali (COL) | 0–1, 2–1 (4–3[1]) |
| 2000 | Boca Juniors (ARG) | Palmeiras (BRA) | 2–2, 0–0 (4–2[1]) |
| 2001 | Boca Juniors (ARG) | Cruz Azul (MEX) | 1–0, 0–1 (3–1[1]) |
| 2002 | Olímpia (PAR) | São Caetano (BRA) | 0–1, 2–1 (4–2[1]) |
| 2003 | Boca Juniors (ARG) | Santos (BRA) | 2–0, 3–1 |
| 2004 | Once Caldas (COL) | Boca Juniors (ARG) | 0–0, 1–1 (2–0[1]) |

## Copa Libertadores de América (continued)

| YEAR | WINNER (COUNTRY) | RUNNER-UP (COUNTRY) | SCORES |
|------|------------------|---------------------|--------|
| 2005 | São Paulo (BRA) | Atlético Paranaense (BRA) | 1–1, 4–0 |
| 2006 | Internacional (BRA) | São Paulo (BRA) | 2–1, 2–2 |
| 2007 | Boca Juniors (ARG) | Grêmio (BRA) | 3–0, 2–0 |
| 2008 | Liga de Quito (ECU) | Fluminense (BRA) | 4–2, 1–3 (3–1[1]) |
| 2009 | Estudiantes de la Plata (ARG) | Cruzeiro (BRA) | 0–0, 2–1 |
| 2010 | Internacional (BRA) | Guadalajara (MEX) | 2–1, 3–2 |
| 2011 | Santos (BRA) | Peñarol (URU) | 0–0, 2–1 |
| 2012 | Corinthians (BRA) | Boca Juniors (ARG) | 1–1, 2–0 |

[1]Won in a penalty kick shoot-out.

## Copa América

*Held since 1916. Table shows results for past 20 years. The cup was contested by rounds in 1989 and 1991 and by a final championship match from 1993.*

| YEAR | WINNER | RUNNER-UP | SCORE | YEAR | WINNER | RUNNER-UP | SCORE |
|------|--------|-----------|-------|------|--------|-----------|-------|
| 1993 | Argentina | Mexico | 2–1 | 2001 | Colombia | Mexico | 1–0 |
| 1995 | Uruguay | Brazil | 1–1 (4–2[1]) | 2004 | Brazil | Argentina | 2–2 (2–0[1]) |
| 1997 | Brazil | Bolivia | 3–1 | 2007 | Brazil | Argentina | 3–0 |
| 1999 | Brazil | Uruguay | 3–0 | 2011 | Uruguay | Paraguay | 3–0 |

[1]Won in a penalty kick shoot-out.

## Asian Cup
*Scored on a points (percentage of wins) system until 1972.*

| YEAR | WINNER | RUNNER-UP | SCORE | YEAR | WINNER | RUNNER-UP | SCORE |
|------|--------|-----------|-------|------|--------|-----------|-------|
| 1956 | Rep. of Korea | Israel | 83.3 | 1988 | Saudi Arabia | Rep. of Korea | 0–0 (4–3[1]) |
| 1960 | Rep. of Korea | Israel | 100 | 1992 | Japan | Saudi Arabia | 1–0 |
| 1964 | Israel | India | 100 | 1996 | Saudi Arabia | United Arab Emirates | 0–0 (4–2[1]) |
| 1968 | Iran | Burma | 100 | 2000 | Japan | Saudi Arabia | 1–0 |
| 1972 | Iran | Rep. of Korea | 2–1 | 2004 | Japan | China | 3–1 |
| 1976 | Iran | Kuwait | 1–0 | 2007 | Iraq | Saudi Arabia | 1–0 |
| 1980 | Kuwait | Rep. of Korea | 3–0 | 2011 | Japan | Australia | 1–0 |
| 1984 | Saudi Arabia | China | 2–0 | | | | |

[1]Won in a penalty kick shoot-out.

## Africa Cup of Nations

| YEAR | WINNER | RUNNER-UP | SCORE | YEAR | WINNER | RUNNER-UP | SCORE |
|------|--------|-----------|-------|------|--------|-----------|-------|
| 1957 | Egypt | Ethiopia | 4–0 | 1986 | Egypt | Cameroon | 0–0 (5–4[3]) |
| 1959 | Egypt | The Sudan | 2–1 | 1988 | Cameroon | Nigeria | 1–0 |
| 1962 | Ethiopia | Egypt | 4–2 | 1990 | Algeria | Nigeria | 1–0 |
| 1963 | Ghana | The Sudan | 3–0 | 1992 | Côte d'Ivoire | Ghana | 0–0 (11–10[3]) |
| 1965 | Ghana | Tunisia | 3–2 | 1994 | Nigeria | Zambia | 2–1 |
| 1968 | Dem. Rep. of the Congo | Ghana | 1–0 | 1996 | South Africa | Tunisia | 2–0 |
| 1970 | The Sudan | Ghana | 1–0 | 1998 | Egypt | South Africa | 2–0 |
| 1972 | Rep. of the Congo | Mali | 3–2 | 2000 | Cameroon | Nigeria | 2–2 (4–3[3]) |
| 1974 | Zaire | Zambia | 2–2, 2–0[1] | 2002 | Cameroon | Senegal | 0–0 (3–2[3]) |
| 1976 | Morocco | Guinea | 1–1[2] | 2004 | Tunisia | Morocco | 2–1 |
| 1978 | Ghana | Uganda | 2–0 | 2006 | Egypt | Côte d'Ivoire | 0–0 (4–2[3]) |
| 1980 | Nigeria | Algeria | 3–0 | 2008 | Egypt | Cameroon | 1–0 |
| 1982 | Ghana | Libya | 1–1 (7–6[3]) | 2010 | Egypt | Ghana | 1–0 |
| 1984 | Cameroon | Nigeria | 3–1 | 2012 | Zambia | Côte d'Ivoire | 0–0 (8–7[3]) |

[1]Game replayed.  [2]Won via group format.  [3]Won in a penalty kick shoot-out.

## Major League Soccer Cup

| YEAR | WINNER | RUNNER-UP | SCORE | YEAR | WINNER | RUNNER-UP | SCORE |
|------|--------|-----------|-------|------|--------|-----------|-------|
| 1996 | DC United | Los Angeles Galaxy | 3–2 (OT) | 1998 | Chicago Fire | DC United | 2–0 |
| 1997 | DC United | Colorado Rapids | 2–1 | 1999 | DC United | Los Angeles Galaxy | 2–0 |

## Major League Soccer Cup (continued)

| YEAR | WINNER | RUNNER-UP | SCORE | YEAR | WINNER | RUNNER-UP | SCORE |
|------|--------|-----------|-------|------|--------|-----------|-------|
| 2000 | Kansas City Wizards | Chicago Fire | 1–0 | 2006 | Houston Dynamo | New England Revolution | 1–1 (4–3[1]) |
| 2001 | San Jose Earthquakes | Los Angeles Galaxy | 2–1 (OT) | 2007 | Houston Dynamo | New England Revolution | 2–1 |
| 2002 | Los Angeles Galaxy | New England Revolution | 1–0 | 2008 | Columbus Crew | New York Red Bulls | 3–1 |
| 2003 | San Jose Earthquakes | Chicago Fire | 4–2 | 2009 | Real Salt Lake | Los Angeles Galaxy | 1–1 (5–4[1]) |
| 2004 | DC United | Kansas City Wizards | 3–2 | 2010 | Colorado Rapids | FC Dallas | 2–1 |
| 2005 | Los Angeles Galaxy | New England Revolution | 1–0 (OT) | 2011 | Los Angeles Galaxy | Houston Dynamo | 1–0 |

[1]Won in a penalty kick shoot-out.

# Golf

In **individual events**, three of the four major men's golf championships, the **US and British Open tournaments** and the **Professional Golfers' Association Championship**, are played annually at a variety of golf courses over 72 holes, and each is preceded by qualifying rounds. The fourth major, the invitational **Masters Tournament**, is held annually at the Augusta [GA] National Golf Course. Events for amateurs include the **US and British Amateur championships**. In 2007 the **Professional Golf Association** (PGA) inaugurated the **FedExCup**, a season-long competition in which players accumulate points based on their performances in various PGA events (including the more heavily weighted majors) and participate in a four-week play-off and a final Tour Championship.

Women's golf has been around nearly as long as men's golf, but until the late 1940s, it was limited to amateurs, with the **US and British Amateur championships** being the major tournaments. The **US Women's Open Championship** was started in 1946,

and the **Ladies Professional Golf Association** (LPGA), which inaugurated the **LPGA Championship**, was formed in 1950. Since that time women's professional golf has flourished. In 1976 the **Women's British Open Championship** was added to the golf calendar, and in 1983 the Nabisco Dinah Shore (played since 1972 and renamed the **Kraft Nabisco Championship** in 2002) was designated the fourth women's major.

In **team events**, the **Ryder Cup** was originally a biennial match between male golfers from the US and Great Britain, but beginning in 1979 it was expanded into a biennial match between the United States and Europe. The **Solheim Cup**, the women's professional team tournament between the US and Europe, was played in even-numbered years from 1990 to 2002 and in odd-numbered years since 2003.

**Related Web sites:** United States Golf Association: <www.usga.org>; Professional Golf Association: <www.pgatour.com>; Ladies Professional Golf Association: <www.lpga.com>.

## FedExCup

In 2007 the PGA inaugurated the FedExCup, a season-long competition in which players accumulate points based on their performances in various PGA events throughout the year. In a standard (non-major) tournament, for instance, 3,513 points are awarded, with the winner receiving 500 points, a runner-up receiving 300 points, and so on. The four major tournaments and the Players Championship award 3,776 points, with 600 going to the winner. The cumulative total of points each player has received during the regular season determines that player's seed going into a four-tournament play-off at the end of the year, for which the top 125 players are eligible. A progressive cut through the first three of these play-off events determines the players who qualify for the final competition, the Tour Championship, which determines the FedExCup champion. The winner of each of the play-offs receives 2,500 points, the second-place finisher 1,500, and so on. The points are reset for the Tour Championship, with the leader at the end of the first three play-offs starting with 2,500 points, the player in second place receiving 2,250, and so on. The player with the most points at the end of the Tour Championship becomes the FedExCup champion and is awarded US$10 million, US$1 million of which is deferred into a retirement fund, making this the largest single bonus payout in professional sports. (In 2007 the entire US$10 million awarded to the winner was deferred.) Tiger Woods was the inaugural FedExCup champion. Vijay Singh of Fiji won the cup in 2008, and Woods repeated as champion in 2009. Jim Furyk won in 2010. Bill Haas was victorious in 2011.

## Masters Tournament

*Won by an American golfer except as indicated.*

| YEAR | WINNER | YEAR | WINNER | YEAR | WINNER |
|------|--------|------|--------|------|--------|
| 1934 | Horton Smith | 1936 | Horton Smith | 1938 | Henry Picard |
| 1935 | Gene Sarazen | 1937 | Byron Nelson | 1939 | Ralph Guldahl |

## Masters Tournament (continued)

| YEAR | WINNER | YEAR | WINNER | YEAR | WINNER |
|------|--------|------|--------|------|--------|
| 1940 | Jimmy Demaret | 1966 | Jack Nicklaus | 1990 | Nick Faldo (ENG) |
| 1941 | Craig Wood | 1967 | Gay Brewer | 1991 | Ian Woosnam (WAL) |
| 1942 | Byron Nelson | 1968 | Bob Goalby | 1992 | Fred Couples |
| 1943-45 | not held | 1969 | George Archer | 1993 | Bernhard Langer (GER) |
| 1946 | Herman Keiser | 1970 | Billy Casper | 1994 | José María Olazábal (ESP) |
| 1947 | Jimmy Demaret | 1971 | Charles Coody | 1995 | Ben Crenshaw |
| 1948 | Claude Harmon | 1972 | Jack Nicklaus | 1996 | Nick Faldo (ENG) |
| 1949 | Sam Snead | 1973 | Tommy Aaron | 1997 | Tiger Woods |
| 1950 | Jimmy Demaret | 1974 | Gary Player (RSA) | 1998 | Mark O'Meara |
| 1951 | Ben Hogan | 1975 | Jack Nicklaus | 1999 | José María Olazábal (ESP) |
| 1952 | Sam Snead | 1976 | Raymond Floyd | 2000 | Vijay Singh (FIJ) |
| 1953 | Ben Hogan | 1977 | Tom Watson | 2001 | Tiger Woods |
| 1954 | Sam Snead | 1978 | Gary Player (RSA) | 2002 | Tiger Woods |
| 1955 | Cary Middlecoff | 1979 | Fuzzy Zoeller | 2003 | Mike Weir (CAN) |
| 1956 | Jack Burke | 1980 | Seve Ballesteros (ESP) | 2004 | Phil Mickelson |
| 1957 | Doug Ford | 1981 | Tom Watson | 2005 | Tiger Woods |
| 1958 | Arnold Palmer | 1982 | Craig Stadler | 2006 | Phil Mickelson |
| 1959 | Art Wall | 1983 | Seve Ballesteros (ESP) | 2007 | Zach Johnson |
| 1960 | Arnold Palmer | 1984 | Ben Crenshaw | 2008 | Trevor Immelman (RSA) |
| 1961 | Gary Player (RSA) | 1985 | Bernhard Langer (FRG) | 2009 | Ángel Cabrera (ARG) |
| 1962 | Arnold Palmer | 1986 | Jack Nicklaus | 2010 | Phil Mickelson |
| 1963 | Jack Nicklaus | 1987 | Larry Mize | 2011 | Charl Schwartzel (RSA) |
| 1964 | Arnold Palmer | 1988 | Sandy Lyle (SCO) | 2012 | Bubba Watson |
| 1965 | Jack Nicklaus | 1989 | Nick Faldo (ENG) | | |

## United States Open Championship—Men

*Won by an American golfer except as indicated.*

| YEAR | WINNER | YEAR | WINNER | YEAR | WINNER |
|------|--------|------|--------|------|--------|
| 1895 | Horace Rawlins | 1934 | Olin Dutra | 1975 | Lou Graham |
| 1896 | James Foulis | 1935 | Sam Parks, Jr. | 1976 | Jerry Pate |
| 1897 | Joe Lloyd | 1936 | Tony Manero | 1977 | Hubert Green |
| 1898 | Fred Herd | 1937 | Ralph Guldahl | 1978 | Andy North |
| 1899 | Willie Smith | 1938 | Ralph Guldahl | 1979 | Hale Irwin |
| 1900 | Harry Vardon (ENG) | 1939 | Byron Nelson | 1980 | Jack Nicklaus |
| 1901 | Willie Anderson | 1940 | Lawson Little | 1981 | David Graham (AUS) |
| 1902 | Laurence Auchterlonie | 1941 | Craig Wood | 1982 | Tom Watson |
| 1903 | Willie Anderson | 1942-45 | not held | 1983 | Larry Nelson |
| 1904 | Willie Anderson | 1946 | Lloyd Mangrum | 1984 | Fuzzy Zoeller |
| 1905 | Willie Anderson | 1947 | Lew Worsham | 1985 | Andy North |
| 1906 | Alex Smith | 1948 | Ben Hogan | 1986 | Raymond Floyd |
| 1907 | Alex Ross | 1949 | Cary Middlecoff | 1987 | Scott Simpson |
| 1908 | Fred McLeod | 1950 | Ben Hogan | 1988 | Curtis Strange |
| 1909 | George Sargent | 1951 | Ben Hogan | 1989 | Curtis Strange |
| 1910 | Alex Smith | 1952 | Julius Boros | 1990 | Hale Irwin |
| 1911 | John J. McDermott | 1953 | Ben Hogan | 1991 | Payne Stewart |
| 1912 | John J. McDermott | 1954 | Ed Furgol | 1992 | Tom Kite |
| 1913 | Francis Ouimet | 1955 | Jack Fleck | 1993 | Lee Janzen |
| 1914 | Walter Hagen | 1956 | Cary Middlecoff | 1994 | Ernie Els (RSA) |
| 1915 | Jerome D. Travers | 1957 | Dick Mayer | 1995 | Corey Pavin |
| 1916 | Chick Evans | 1958 | Tommy Bolt | 1996 | Steve Jones |
| 1917-18 | not held | 1959 | Billy Casper | 1997 | Ernie Els (RSA) |
| 1919 | Walter Hagen | 1960 | Arnold Palmer | 1998 | Lee Janzen |
| 1920 | Edward Ray (ENG) | 1961 | Gene Littler | 1999 | Payne Stewart |
| 1921 | James M. Barnes | 1962 | Jack Nicklaus | 2000 | Tiger Woods |
| 1922 | Gene Sarazen | 1963 | Julius Boros | 2001 | Retief Goosen (RSA) |
| 1923 | Bobby Jones | 1964 | Ken Venturi | 2002 | Tiger Woods |
| 1924 | Cyril Walker | 1965 | Gary Player (RSA) | 2003 | Jim Furyk |
| 1925 | Willie MacFarlane, Jr. | 1966 | Billy Casper | 2004 | Retief Goosen (RSA) |
| 1926 | Bobby Jones | 1967 | Jack Nicklaus | 2005 | Michael Campbell (NZL) |
| 1927 | Tommy Armour | 1968 | Lee Trevino | 2006 | Geoff Ogilvy (AUS) |
| 1928 | Johnny Farrell | 1969 | Orville Moody | 2007 | Ángel Cabrera (ARG) |
| 1929 | Bobby Jones | 1970 | Tony Jacklin (ENG) | 2008 | Tiger Woods |
| 1930 | Bobby Jones | 1971 | Lee Trevino | 2009 | Lucas Glover |
| 1931 | Billy Burke | 1972 | Jack Nicklaus | 2010 | Graeme McDowell (NIR) |
| 1932 | Gene Sarazen | 1973 | Johnny Miller | 2011 | Rory McIlroy (NIR) |
| 1933 | John Goodman | 1974 | Hale Irwin | 2012 | Webb Simpson |

## British Open Tournament—Men

*Won by an English golfer unless otherwise indicated.*

| YEAR | WINNER | YEAR | WINNER | YEAR | WINNER |
|------|--------|------|--------|------|--------|
| 1860 | Willie Park, Sr. (SCO) | 1908 | James Braid (SCO) | 1965 | Peter Thomson (AUS) |
| 1861 | Tom Morris, Sr. (SCO) | 1909 | John H. Taylor | 1966 | Jack Nicklaus (USA) |
| 1862 | Tom Morris, Sr. (SCO) | 1910 | James Braid (SCO) | 1967 | Roberto de Vicenzo (ARG) |
| 1863 | Willie Park, Sr. (SCO) | 1911 | Harry Vardon (JEY) | 1968 | Gary Player (RSA) |
| 1864 | Tom Morris, Sr. (SCO) | 1912 | Ted Ray (JEY) | 1969 | Tony Jacklin |
| 1865 | Andrew Strath (SCO) | 1913 | John H. Taylor | 1970 | Jack Nicklaus (USA) |
| 1866 | Willie Park, Sr. (SCO) | 1914 | Harry Vardon (JEY) | 1971 | Lee Trevino (USA) |
| 1867 | Tom Morris, Sr. (SCO) | 1915–19 *not held* | | 1972 | Lee Trevino (USA) |
| 1868 | Tom Morris, Jr. (SCO) | 1920 | George Duncan (SCO) | 1973 | Tom Weiskopf (USA) |
| 1869 | Tom Morris, Jr. (SCO) | 1921 | Jock Hutchison (USA) | 1974 | Gary Player (RSA) |
| 1870 | Tom Morris, Jr. (SCO) | 1922 | Walter Hagen (USA) | 1975 | Tom Watson (USA) |
| 1871 | *not held* | 1923 | Arthur Havers | 1976 | Johnny Miller (USA) |
| 1872 | Tom Morris, Jr. (SCO) | 1924 | Walter Hagen (USA) | 1977 | Tom Watson (USA) |
| 1873 | Tom Kidd (SCO) | 1925 | James Barnes (USA) | 1978 | Jack Nicklaus (USA) |
| 1874 | Mungo Park (SCO) | 1926 | Bobby Jones (USA) | 1979 | Seve Ballesteros (ESP) |
| 1875 | Willie Park, Sr. (SCO) | 1927 | Bobby Jones (USA) | 1980 | Tom Watson (USA) |
| 1876 | Bob Martin (SCO) | 1928 | Walter Hagen (USA) | 1981 | Bill Rogers (USA) |
| 1877 | Jamie Anderson (SCO) | 1929 | Walter Hagen (USA) | 1982 | Tom Watson (USA) |
| 1878 | Jamie Anderson (SCO) | 1930 | Bobby Jones (USA) | 1983 | Tom Watson (USA) |
| 1879 | Jamie Anderson (SCO) | 1931 | Tommy Armour (USA) | 1984 | Seve Ballesteros (ESP) |
| 1880 | Robert Ferguson (SCO) | 1932 | Gene Sarazen (USA) | 1985 | Sandy Lyle (SCO) |
| 1881 | Robert Ferguson (SCO) | 1933 | Denny Shute (USA) | 1986 | Greg Norman (AUS) |
| 1882 | Robert Ferguson (SCO) | 1934 | Henry Cotton | 1987 | Nick Faldo |
| 1883 | Willie Fernie (SCO) | 1935 | Alfred Perry | 1988 | Seve Ballesteros (ESP) |
| 1884 | Jack Simpson (SCO) | 1936 | Alfred Padgham | 1989 | Mark Calcavecchia (USA) |
| 1885 | Bob Martin (SCO) | 1937 | Henry Cotton | 1990 | Nick Faldo |
| 1886 | David Brown (SCO) | 1938 | Reg A. Whitcombe | 1991 | Ian Baker-Finch (AUS) |
| 1887 | Willie Park, Jr. (SCO) | 1939 | Richard Burton | 1992 | Nick Faldo |
| 1888 | Jack Burns (SCO) | 1940–45 *not held* | | 1993 | Greg Norman (AUS) |
| 1889 | Willie Park, Jr. (SCO) | 1946 | Sam Snead (USA) | 1994 | Nick Price (ZIM) |
| 1890 | John Ball | 1947 | Fred Daly (NIR) | 1995 | John Daly (USA) |
| 1891 | Hugh Kirkaldy (SCO) | 1948 | Henry Cotton | 1996 | Tom Lehman (USA) |
| 1892 | Harold Hilton | 1949 | Bobby Locke (RSA) | 1997 | Justin Leonard (USA) |
| 1893 | William Auchterlonie (SCO) | 1950 | Bobby Locke (RSA) | 1998 | Mark O'Meara (USA) |
| 1894 | John H. Taylor | 1951 | Max Faulkner | 1999 | Paul Lawrie (SCO) |
| 1895 | John H. Taylor | 1952 | Bobby Locke (RSA) | 2000 | Tiger Woods (USA) |
| 1896 | Harry Vardon (JEY) | 1953 | Ben Hogan (USA) | 2001 | David Duval (USA) |
| 1897 | Harold Hilton | 1954 | Peter Thomson (AUS) | 2002 | Ernie Els (RSA) |
| 1898 | Harry Vardon (JEY) | 1955 | Peter Thomson (AUS) | 2003 | Ben Curtis (USA) |
| 1899 | Harry Vardon (JEY) | 1956 | Peter Thomson (AUS) | 2004 | Todd Hamilton (USA) |
| 1900 | John H. Taylor | 1957 | Bobby Locke (RSA) | 2005 | Tiger Woods (USA) |
| 1901 | James Braid (SCO) | 1958 | Peter Thomson (AUS) | 2006 | Tiger Woods (USA) |
| 1902 | Sandy Herd (SCO) | 1959 | Gary Player (RSA) | 2007 | Padraig Harrington (IRL) |
| 1903 | Harry Vardon (JEY) | 1960 | Kel Nagle (AUS) | 2008 | Padraig Harrington (IRL) |
| 1904 | Jack White (SCO) | 1961 | Arnold Palmer (USA) | 2009 | Stewart Cink (USA) |
| 1905 | James Braid (SCO) | 1962 | Arnold Palmer (USA) | 2010 | Louis Oosthuizen (RSA) |
| 1906 | James Braid (SCO) | 1963 | Bob Charles (NZL) | 2011 | Darren Clarke (NIR) |
| 1907 | Arnaud Massy (FRA) | 1964 | Tony Lema (USA) | 2012 | Ernie Els (RSA) |

## US Professional Golfers' Association (PGA) Championship

*Won by an American golfer except as indicated.*

| YEAR | WINNER | YEAR | WINNER | YEAR | WINNER |
|------|--------|------|--------|------|--------|
| 1916 | James M. Barnes | 1930 | Tommy Armour | 1943 | *not held* |
| 1917–18 *not held* | | 1931 | Tom Creavy | 1944 | Bob Hamilton |
| 1919 | James M. Barnes | 1932 | Olin Dutra | 1945 | Byron Nelson |
| 1920 | Jock Hutchison | 1933 | Gene Sarazen | 1946 | Ben Hogan |
| 1921 | Walter Hagen | 1934 | Paul Runyan | 1947 | Jim Ferrier |
| 1922 | Gene Sarazen | 1935 | Johnny Revolta | 1948 | Ben Hogan |
| 1923 | Gene Sarazen | 1936 | Denny Shute | 1949 | Sam Snead |
| 1924 | Walter Hagen | 1937 | Denny Shute | 1950 | Chandler Harper |
| 1925 | Walter Hagen | 1938 | Paul Runyan | 1951 | Sam Snead |
| 1926 | Walter Hagen | 1939 | Henry Picard | 1952 | Jim Turnesa |
| 1927 | Walter Hagen | 1940 | Byron Nelson | 1953 | Walter Burkemo |
| 1928 | Leo Diegel | 1941 | Vic Ghezzi | 1954 | Chick Harbert |
| 1929 | Leo Diegel | 1942 | Sam Snead | 1955 | Doug Ford |

## US Professional Golfers' Association (PGA) Championship (continued)

| YEAR | WINNER | YEAR | WINNER | YEAR | WINNER |
|------|--------|------|--------|------|--------|
| 1956 | Jack Burke | 1975 | Jack Nicklaus | 1994 | Nick Price (ZIM) |
| 1957 | Lionel Hebert | 1976 | Dave Stockton | 1995 | Steve Elkington (AUS) |
| 1958 | Dow Finsterwald | 1977 | Lanny Wadkins | 1996 | Mark Brooks |
| 1959 | Bob Rosburg | 1978 | John Mahaffey | 1997 | Davis Love III |
| 1960 | Jay Hebert | 1979 | David Graham (AUS) | 1998 | Vijay Singh (FIJ) |
| 1961 | Jerry Barber | 1980 | Jack Nicklaus | 1999 | Tiger Woods |
| 1962 | Gary Player (RSA) | 1981 | Larry Nelson | 2000 | Tiger Woods |
| 1963 | Jack Nicklaus | 1982 | Raymond Floyd | 2001 | David Toms |
| 1964 | Bobby Nichols | 1983 | Hal Sutton | 2002 | Rich Beems |
| 1965 | Dave Marr | 1984 | Lee Trevino | 2003 | Shaun Micheel |
| 1966 | Al Geiberger | 1985 | Hubert Green | 2004 | Vijay Singh (FIJ) |
| 1967 | Don January | 1986 | Bob Tway | 2005 | Phil Mickelson |
| 1968 | Julius Boros | 1987 | Larry Nelson | 2006 | Tiger Woods |
| 1969 | Raymond Floyd | 1988 | Jeff Sluman | 2007 | Tiger Woods |
| 1970 | Dave Stockton | 1989 | Payne Stewart | 2008 | Padraig Harrington (IRL) |
| 1971 | Jack Nicklaus | 1990 | Wayne Grady (AUS) | 2009 | Y.E. Yang (KOR) |
| 1972 | Gary Player (RSA) | 1991 | John Daly | 2010 | Martin Kaymer (GER) |
| 1973 | Jack Nicklaus | 1992 | Nick Price (ZIM) | 2011 | Keegan Bradley |
| 1974 | Lee Trevino | 1993 | Paul Azinger | 2012 | Rory McIlroy (NIR) |

## Kraft Nabisco Championship

*Won by an American golfer except as indicated.*

| YEAR | WINNER | YEAR | WINNER | YEAR | WINNER |
|------|--------|------|--------|------|--------|
| 1972 | Jane Blalock | 1986 | Pat Bradley | 2000 | Karrie Webb (AUS) |
| 1973 | Mickey Wright | 1987 | Betsy King | 2001 | Annika Sörenstam (SWE) |
| 1974 | Jo Ann Prentice | 1988 | Amy Alcott | 2002 | Annika Sörenstam (SWE) |
| 1975 | Sandra Palmer | 1989 | Juli Inkster | 2003 | Patricia Meunier-Lebouc (FRA) |
| 1976 | Judy Rankin | 1990 | Betsy King | | |
| 1977 | Kathy Whitworth | 1991 | Amy Alcott | 2004 | Grace Park (KOR) |
| 1978 | Sandra Post | 1992 | Dottie Mochrie | 2005 | Annika Sörenstam (SWE) |
| 1979 | Sandra Post | 1993 | Helen Alfredsson (SWE) | 2006 | Karrie Webb (AUS) |
| 1980 | Donna Caponi | 1994 | Donna Andrews | 2007 | Morgan Pressel |
| 1981 | Nancy Lopez | 1995 | Nanci Bowen | 2008 | Lorena Ochoa (MEX) |
| 1982 | Sally Little (RSA) | 1996 | Patty Sheehan | 2009 | Brittany Lincicome |
| 1983 | Amy Alcott | 1997 | Betsy King | 2010 | Yani Tseng (TPE) |
| 1984 | Juli Inkster | 1998 | Pat Hurst | 2011 | Stacy Lewis |
| 1985 | Alice Miller | 1999 | Dottie Pepper | 2012 | Sun Young Yoo (KOR) |

## Ladies Professional Golf Association (LPGA) Championship

*Won by an American golfer except as indicated.*

| YEAR | WINNER | YEAR | WINNER | YEAR | WINNER |
|------|--------|------|--------|------|--------|
| 1955 | Beverly Hanson | 1975 | Kathy Whitworth | 1995 | Kelly Robbins |
| 1956 | Marlene Hagge | 1976 | Betty Burfeindt | 1996 | Laura Davies (ENG) |
| 1957 | Louise Suggs | 1977 | Chako Higuchi | 1997 | Chris Johnson |
| 1958 | Mickey Wright | 1978 | Nancy Lopez | 1998 | Pak Se Ri (KOR) |
| 1959 | Betsy Rawls | 1979 | Donna Caponi | 1999 | Juli Inkster |
| 1960 | Mickey Wright | 1980 | Sally Little | 2000 | Juli Inkster |
| 1961 | Mickey Wright | 1981 | Donna Caponi | 2001 | Karrie Webb (AUS) |
| 1962 | Judy Kimball | 1982 | Jan Stephenson (AUS) | 2002 | Pak Se Ri (KOR) |
| 1963 | Mickey Wright | 1983 | Patty Sheehan | 2003 | Annika Sörenstam (SWE) |
| 1964 | Mary Mills | 1984 | Patty Sheehan | 2004 | Annika Sörenstam (SWE) |
| 1965 | Sandra Haynie | 1985 | Nancy Lopez | 2005 | Annika Sörenstam (SWE) |
| 1966 | Gloria Ehret | 1986 | Pat Bradley | 2006 | Pak Se Ri (KOR) |
| 1967 | Kathy Whitworth | 1987 | Jane Geddes | 2007 | Suzann Pettersen (NOR) |
| 1968 | Sandra Post | 1988 | Sherri Turner | 2008 | Yani Tseng (TPE) |
| 1969 | Betsy Rawls | 1989 | Nancy Lopez | 2009 | Anna Nordqvist (SWE) |
| 1970 | Shirley Englehorn | 1990 | Beth Daniel | 2010 | Cristie Kerr |
| 1971 | Kathy Whitworth | 1991 | Meg Mallon | 2011 | Yani Tseng (TPE) |
| 1972 | Kathy Ahern | 1992 | Betsy King | 2012 | Feng Shanshan (CHN) |
| 1973 | Mary Mills | 1993 | Patty Sheehan | | |
| 1974 | Sandra Haynie | 1994 | Laura Davies (ENG) | | |

## United States Women's Open Championship

*Won by an American golfer except as indicated.*

| YEAR | WINNER | YEAR | WINNER | YEAR | WINNER |
|------|--------|------|--------|------|--------|
| 1946 | Patty Berg | 1968 | Susie Berning | 1991 | Meg Mallon |
| 1947 | Betty Jameson | 1969 | Donna Caponi | 1992 | Patty Sheehan |
| 1948 | Babe Didrikson Zaharias | 1970 | Donna Caponi | 1993 | Lauri Merten |
| 1949 | Louise Suggs | 1971 | JoAnne Carner | 1994 | Patty Sheehan |
| 1950 | Babe Didrikson Zaharias | 1972 | Susie Berning | 1995 | Annika Sörenstam (SWE) |
| 1951 | Betsy Rawls | 1973 | Susie Berning | 1996 | Annika Sörenstam (SWE) |
| 1952 | Louise Suggs | 1974 | Sandra Haynie | 1997 | Alison Nicholas (ENG) |
| 1953 | Betsy Rawls | 1975 | Sandra Palmer | 1998 | Pak Se Ri (KOR) |
| 1954 | Babe Didrikson Zaharias | 1976 | JoAnne Carner | 1999 | Juli Inkster |
| 1955 | Fay Crocker | 1977 | Hollis Stacy | 2000 | Karrie Webb (AUS) |
| 1956 | Kathy Cornelius | 1978 | Hollis Stacy | 2001 | Karrie Webb (AUS) |
| 1957 | Betsy Rawls | 1979 | Jerilyn Britz | 2002 | Juli Inkster |
| 1958 | Mickey Wright | 1980 | Amy Alcott | 2003 | Hilary Lunke |
| 1959 | Mickey Wright | 1981 | Pat Bradley | 2004 | Meg Mallon |
| 1960 | Betsy Rawls | 1982 | Janet Anderson | 2005 | Birdie Kim (KOR) |
| 1961 | Mickey Wright | 1983 | Jan Stephenson (AUS) | 2006 | Annika Sörenstam (SWE) |
| 1962 | Murle Breer | 1984 | Hollis Stacy | 2007 | Cristie Kerr |
| 1963 | Mary Mills | 1985 | Kathy Baker | 2008 | Inbee Park (KOR) |
| 1964 | Mickey Wright | 1986 | Jane Geddes | 2009 | Ji Eun-Hee (KOR) |
| 1965 | Carol Mann | 1987 | Laura Davies (ENG) | 2010 | Paula Creamer |
| 1966 | Sandra Spuzich | 1988 | Liselotte Neumann (SWE) | 2011 | Ryu So-Yeon (KOR) |
| 1967 | Catherine Lacoste (FRA) | 1989 | Betsy King | 2012 | Choi Na-Yeon (KOR) |
|      |        | 1990 | Betsy King |      |        |

## Women's British Open Championship

*Won by an English golfer unless otherwise indicated.*

| YEAR | WINNER | YEAR | WINNER | YEAR | WINNER |
|------|--------|------|--------|------|--------|
| 1976 | Jenny Lee-Smith | 1988 | Corinne Dibnah (AUS) | 2000 | Sophie Gustafson (SWE) |
| 1977 | Vivien Saunders | 1989 | Jane Geddes (USA) | 2001 | Pak Se Ri (KOR) |
| 1978 | Janet Melville | 1990 | Helen Alfredsson (SWE) | 2002 | Karrie Webb (AUS) |
| 1979 | Alison Sheard (RSA) | 1991 | Penny Grice-Whittaker | 2003 | Annika Sörenstam (SWE) |
| 1980 | Debbie Massey (USA) | 1992 | Patty Sheehan (USA) | 2004 | Karen Stupples |
| 1981 | Debbie Massey (USA) | 1993 | Mardi Lunn (AUS) | 2005 | Jang Jeong (KOR) |
| 1982 | Marta Figueras-Dotti (ESP) | 1994 | Liselotte Neumann (SWE) | 2006 | Sherri Steinhauer (USA) |
| 1983 | *not held* | 1995 | Karrie Webb (AUS) | 2007 | Lorena Ochoa (MEX) |
| 1984 | Okamoto Ayako (JPN) | 1996 | Emilee Klein (USA) | 2008 | Ji Yai Shin (KOR) |
| 1985 | Betsy King (USA) | 1997 | Karrie Webb (AUS) | 2009 | Catriona Matthew (SCO) |
| 1986 | Laura Davies | 1998 | Sherri Steinhauer (USA) | 2010 | Yani Tseng (TPE) |
| 1987 | Alison Nicholas | 1999 | Sherri Steinhauer (USA) | 2011 | Yani Tseng (TPE) |

## Ryder Cup

| YEAR | RESULT | YEAR | RESULT |
|------|--------|------|--------|
| 1927 | United States 9½, Britain 2½ | 1973 | United States 19, Britain 13 |
| 1929 | Britain 7, United States 5 | 1975 | United States 21, Britain 11 |
| 1931 | United States 9, Britain 3 | 1977 | United States 12½, Britain 7½ |
| 1933 | Britain 6½, United States 5½ | 1979 | United States 17, Europe 11 |
| 1935 | United States 9, Britain 3 | 1981 | United States 18½, Europe 9½ |
| 1937 | United States 8, Britain 4 | 1983 | United States 14½, Europe 13½ |
| 1939–45 | *not held* | 1985 | Europe 16½, United States 11½ |
| 1947 | United States 11, Britain 1 | 1987 | Europe 15, United States 13 |
| 1949 | United States 7, Britain 5 | 1989 | Europe 14, United States 14 |
| 1951 | United States 9½, Britain 2½ | 1991 | United States 14½, Europe 13½ |
| 1953 | United States 6½, Britain 5½ | 1993 | United States 15, Europe 13 |
| 1955 | United States 8, Britain 4 | 1995 | Europe 14½, United States 13½ |
| 1957 | Britain 7½, United States 4½ | 1997 | Europe 14½, United States 13½ |
| 1959 | United States 8½, Britain 3½ | 1999 | United States 14½, Europe 13½ |
| 1961 | United States 14½, Britain 9½ | 2001 | *postponed until 2002* |
| 1963 | United States 23, Britain 9 | 2002 | Europe 15½, United States 12½ |
| 1965 | United States 19½, Britain 12½ | 2004 | Europe 18½, United States 9½ |
| 1967 | United States 23½, Britain 8½ | 2006 | Europe 18½, United States 9½ |
| 1969 | United States 16, Britain 16 | 2008 | United States 16½, Europe 11½ |
| 1971 | United States 18½, Britain 13½ | 2010 | Europe 14½, United States 13½ |

## Solheim Cup

| YEAR | RESULT | YEAR | RESULT |
|------|--------|------|--------|
| 1990 | United States 11½, Europe 4½ | 2002 | United States 15½, Europe 12½ |
| 1992 | Europe 11½, United States 6½ | 2003 | Europe 17½, United States 10½ |
| 1994 | United States 13, Europe 7 | 2005 | United States 15½, Europe 12½ |
| 1996 | United States 17, Europe 11 | 2007 | United States 16, Europe 12 |
| 1998 | United States 16, Europe 12 | 2009 | United States 16, Europe 12 |
| 2000 | Europe 14½, United States 11½ | 2011 | Europe 15, United States 13 |

## United States Amateur Championship—Men

*Won by an American golfer except as indicated. Table shows results for the past 20 years.*

| YEAR | WINNER | YEAR | WINNER | YEAR | WINNER |
|------|--------|------|--------|------|--------|
| 1993 | John Harris | 2000 | Jeff Quinney | 2007 | Colt Knost |
| 1994 | Tiger Woods | 2001 | Ben Dickerson | 2008 | Danny Lee (NZL) |
| 1995 | Tiger Woods | 2002 | Ricky Barnes | 2009 | Byeong-Hun An (KOR) |
| 1996 | Tiger Woods | 2003 | Nick Flanagan (AUS) | 2010 | Peter Uihlein |
| 1997 | Matt Kuchar | 2004 | Ryan Moore | 2011 | Kelly Kraft |
| 1998 | Hank Kuehne | 2005 | Edoardo Molinari (ITA) | 2012 | Steven Fox |
| 1999 | David Gossett | 2006 | Richie Ramsay (SCO) | | |

## British Amateur Championship—Men

*Held since 1885. Table shows results for the past 20 years. Won by an English golfer except as indicated.*

| YEAR | WINNER | YEAR | WINNER | YEAR | WINNER |
|------|--------|------|--------|------|--------|
| 1993 | Ian Pyman | 2000 | Mikko Ilonen (FIN) | 2007 | Drew Weaver (USA) |
| 1994 | Lee James | 2001 | Michael Hoey (NIR) | 2008 | Reinier Saxton (NED) |
| 1995 | Gordon Sherry (SCO) | 2002 | Alejandro Larrazábal (ESP) | 2009 | Matteo Manassero (ITA) |
| 1996 | Warren Bledon | 2003 | Gary Wolstenholme | 2010 | Jin Jeong (KOR) |
| 1997 | Craig Watson (SCO) | 2004 | Stuart Wilson (SCO) | 2011 | Bryden Macpherson (AUS) |
| 1998 | Sergio García (ESP) | 2005 | Brian McElhinney (IRL) | 2012 | Alan Dunbar (NIR) |
| 1999 | Graeme Storm | 2006 | Julien Guerrier (FRA) | | |

## United States Women's Amateur Championship

*Held since 1895. Table shows results for the past 20 years. Won by an American golfer except as indicated.*

| YEAR | WINNER | YEAR | WINNER | YEAR | WINNER |
|------|--------|------|--------|------|--------|
| 1993 | Jill McGill | 2000 | Marcy Newton | 2006 | Kimberly Kim |
| 1994 | Wendy Ward | 2001 | Meredith Duncan | 2007 | María José Uribe (COL) |
| 1995 | Kelli Kuehne | 2002 | Becky Lucidi | 2008 | Amanda Blumenherst |
| 1996 | Kelli Kuehne | 2003 | Virada Nirapath- | 2009 | Jennifer Song |
| 1997 | Silvia Cavalleri (ITA) | | pongporn (THA) | 2010 | Danielle Kang |
| 1998 | Grace Park | 2004 | Jane Park | 2011 | Danielle Kang |
| 1999 | Dorothy Delasin | 2005 | Morgan Pressel | 2012 | Lydia Ko (NZL) |

## Ladies' British Open Amateur Championship

*Held since 1893. Table shows results for the past 20 years. Won by an English golfer except as indicated.*

| YEAR | WINNER | YEAR | WINNER | YEAR | WINNER |
|------|--------|------|--------|------|--------|
| 1993 | Catriona Lambert (SCO) | 2000 | Rebecca Hudson | 2007 | Carlota Ciganda (ESP) |
| 1994 | Emma Duggleby | 2001 | Marta Prieto (ESP) | 2008 | Anna Nordqvist (SWE) |
| 1995 | Julie Wade Hall | 2002 | Rebecca Hudson | 2009 | Azahara Muñoz (ESP) |
| 1996 | Kelli Kuehne (USA) | 2003 | Elisa Serramia (ESP) | 2010 | Kelly Tidy |
| 1997 | Alison Rose (SCO) | 2004 | Louise Stahle (SWE) | 2011 | Lauren Taylor |
| 1998 | Kim Rostron | 2005 | Louise Stahle (SWE) | 2012 | Stephanie Meadow (NIR) |
| 1999 | Marine Monnet (FRA) | 2006 | Belén Mozo (ESP) | | |

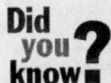

**Did you know?** The University of Connecticut set a major-college record on 21 Dec 2010 when they defeated Florida State's team to capture their famous streak by the John Wooden–coached men's UCLA basketball team from 1971 to 1974. Days later, on 30 December, Connecticut's streak came to an end at 90 straight victories after a defeat at the hands of Stanford University.

# Horse Racing

In the **oldest type** of horse racing, the rider sits astride the horse; in the other type of race, best known as **harness racing**, the driver sits in a sulky—a two-wheeled vehicle attached by shafts and traces to the horse. In the former type, a **Thoroughbred** horse is raced over either a track or a course of jumps and turns (**steeplechase**). Harness horses can be trotters or pacers and are Standardbred horses raced on a track.

**The English Thoroughbred classics.** The races are run by 3-year-old colts and fillies. **The Derby**, first run in 1780, is run at Epsom Downs, Surrey, over 1½ miles. **The Oaks** (for fillies only), also run at Epsom Downs, was first run in 1779; the oldest of the English races, however, is the **St. Leger** (1776). It is run over 1 mile 6½ furlongs at Doncaster, South Yorkshire. The **2,000 Guineas** (1809) is run over 1 mile at Newmarket, Suffolk. A horse that wins the Derby, the St. Leger, and the 2,000 Guineas all in one year is said to have won the **British Triple Crown**.

**The American Thoroughbred classics.** The **Kentucky Derby**, a **Triple Crown** event first run in 1875 and perhaps the best known of American horse races, is raced at Churchill Downs in Louisville KY, over a 10-furlong (1¼-mile) track. Another of the Triple Crown classics, the **Preakness Stakes**, was instituted in 1873; it is run over 9½ furlongs (1³⁄₁₆ miles) at Pimlico Race Course in Baltimore MD. The third Triple Crown event is the 12-furlong (1½-mile)

**Belmont Stakes**, established in 1867. It is run at Belmont Park Race Track, Long Island NY. All three events are for 3-year-old horses.

**Australian Thoroughbred racing.** The Victoria Racing Club's **Melbourne Cup**, first run in 1861, is one of the world's great handicap races. The day on which it is held (the first Tuesday in November) is a public holiday in Melbourne, VIC.

**Dubai World Cup**, first run in 1996, is the world's richest horse race (US$10 million in 2012). The 2,000-m (about 1¼-mi) race is held at the Meydan Racecourse in Dubai, United Arab Emirates, and is open to four-year-old and older Thoroughbred horses.

The **Grand National**, the world's most significant and widely followed **steeplechase** race, has been run annually at Aintree Racecourse near Liverpool, England, since 1839. The race, which includes 30 jumps, is run over a traditional distance of 4 miles 4 furlongs.

**Harness racing.** In the United States, the **Hambletonian Trot** is probably the most prestigious of harness races. It was established in 1926, was raced in New York, Kentucky, and Illinois, and is now run at the Meadowlands in New Jersey.

**Related Web sites:** US National Thoroughbred Racing Association: <www.ntra.com>; Fédération Equestre Internationale: <www.horsesport.org>; *Thoroughbred Times:* <www.thoroughbredtimes.com>; and *Racing Post:* <www.racingpost.com>.

## Major Thoroughbred Race Winners, 2011–12

### United States

| DATE | RACE | WINNER | JOCKEY |
|---|---|---|---|
| 6 Aug 2011 | Clement L. Hirsch Stakes | Ultra Blend | Tyler Baze |
| 6 Aug 2011 | Test Stakes | Turbulent Descent | David Romero Flores |
| 6 Aug 2011 | Whitney Invitational Handicap | Tizway | Rajiv Maragh |
| 13 Aug 2011 | Arlington Million | Cape Blanco | Jamie Spencer |
| 13 Aug 2011 | Beverly D. Stakes | Stacelita | Ramon Dominguez |
| 13 Aug 2011 | Secretariat Stakes | Treasure Beach | Colm O'Donoghue |
| 13 Aug 2011 | Sword Dancer Invitational Stakes | Winchester | Cornelio Velasquez |
| 14 Aug 2011 | John C. Mabee Stakes | Cozi Rosie | Garrett Gomez |
| 20 Aug 2011 | Alabama Stakes | Royal Delta | Jose Lezcano |
| 20 Aug 2011 | Del Mar Oaks | Summer Soiree | Gabriel Saez |
| 27 Aug 2011 | Ballerina Stakes | Hilda's Passion | Javier Castellano |
| 27 Aug 2011 | King's Bishop Stakes | Caleb's Posse | Rajiv Maragh |
| 27 Aug 2011 | Travers Stakes | Stay Thirsty | Javier Castellano |
| 28 Aug 2011 | Pacific Classic | Acclamation | Pat Valenzuela |
| 28 Aug 2011 | Pat O'Brien Stakes | The Factor | Martin Garcia |
| 3 Sep 2011 | Debutante Stakes | Weemissfrankie | Rafael Bejarano |
| 3 Sep 2011 | Forego Stakes | Jackson Bend | Corey Nakatani |
| 3 Sep 2011 | Personal Ensign Stakes | Ask the Moon | Javier Castellano |
| 3 Sep 2011 | Woodward Stakes | Havre de Grace | Ramon Dominguez |
| 4 Sep 2011 | Spinaway Stakes | Grace Hall | Ramon Dominguez |
| 5 Sep 2011 | Hopeful Stakes | Currency Swap | Rajiv Maragh |
| 7 Sep 2011 | Del Mar Futurity | Drill | Martin Garcia |
| 17 Sep 2011 | Garden City Stakes | Winter Memories | Javier Castellano |
| 1 Oct 2011 | Beldame Stakes | Havre de Grace | Ramon Dominguez |
| 1 Oct 2011 | Flower Bowl Invitational Stakes | Stacelita | Ramon Dominguez |
| 1 Oct 2011 | Goodwood Stakes | Game On Dude | Chantal Sutherland |
| 1 Oct 2011 | Jockey Club Gold Cup | Flat Out | Alex Solis |
| 1 Oct 2011 | Joe Hirsch Turf Classic Invitational | Cape Blanco | Jamie Spencer |
| 1 Oct 2011 | Lady's Secret Stakes | Zazu | Joel Rosario |
| 1 Oct 2011 | Norfolk Stakes | Creative Cause | Joel Rosario |
| 1 Oct 2011 | Vosburgh Invitational Stakes | Giant Ryan | Cornelio Velasquez |
| 1 Oct 2011 | Yellow Ribbon Stakes | Dubawi Heights | Joel Rosario |
| 2 Oct 2011 | Clement L. Hirsch Memorial Turf Championship | Acclamation | Pat Valenzuela |

## Major Thoroughbred Race Winners, 2011–12 (continued)

### United States (continued)

| DATE | RACE | WINNER | JOCKEY |
|---|---|---|---|
| 2 Oct 2011 | Oak Leaf Stakes | Weemissfrankie | Rafael Bejarano |
| 7 Oct 2011 | Darley Alcibiades Stakes | Stephanie's Kitten | John Velazquez |
| 8 Oct 2011 | Breeders' Futurity | Dullahan | Kent Desormeaux |
| 8 Oct 2011 | Champagne Stakes | Union Rags | Javier Castellano |
| 8 Oct 2011 | First Lady Stakes | Never Retreat | Julien Leparoux |
| 8 Oct 2011 | Frizette Stakes | My Miss Aurelia | Corey Nakatani |
| 8 Oct 2011 | Jamaica Handicap | Western Aristocrat | Corey Nakatani |
| 8 Oct 2011 | Turf Mile Stakes | Gio Ponti | Ramon Dominguez |
| 9 Oct 2011 | Spinster Stakes | Aruna | Ramon Dominguez |
| 15 Oct 2011 | Queen Elizabeth II Challenge Cup | Together | Colm O'Donoghue |
| 4 Nov 2011 | Breeders' Cup Filly and Mare Sprint | Musical Romance | Juan Leyva |
| 4 Nov 2011 | Breeders' Cup Filly and Mare Turf | Perfect Shirl | John Velazquez |
| 4 Nov 2011 | Breeders' Cup Juvenile Fillies | My Miss Aurelia | Corey Nakatani |
| 4 Nov 2011 | Breeders' Cup Juvenile Fillies Turf | Stephanie's Kitten | John Velazquez |
| 4 Nov 2011 | Breeders' Cup Juvenile Sprint | Secret Circle | Rafael Bejarano |
| 4 Nov 2011 | Breeders' Cup Ladies' Classic | Royal Delta | Jose Lezcano |
| 5 Nov 2011 | Breeders' Cup Classic | Drosselmeyer | Mike Smith |
| 5 Nov 2011 | Breeders' Cup Dirt Mile | Caleb's Posse | Rajiv Maragh |
| 5 Nov 2011 | Breeders' Cup Juvenile | Hansen | Ramon Dominguez |
| 5 Nov 2011 | Breeders' Cup Juvenile Turf | Wrote | Ryan Moore |
| 5 Nov 2011 | Breeders' Cup Marathon | Afleet Again | Cornelio Velasquez |
| 5 Nov 2011 | Breeders' Cup Mile | Court Vision | Robby Albarado |
| 5 Nov 2011 | Breeders' Cup Sprint | Amazombie | Mike Smith |
| 5 Nov 2011 | Breeders' Cup Turf | St Nicholas Abbey | Joseph O'Brien |
| 5 Nov 2011 | Breeders' Cup Turf Sprint | Regally Ready | Corey Nakatani |
| 25 Nov 2011 | Matriarch Stakes | Star Billing | Victor Espinoza |
| 26 Nov 2011 | Cigar Mile Handicap | To Honor and Serve | Jose Lezcano |
| 26 Nov 2011 | Citation Handicap | Jeranimo | Garrett Gomez |
| 26 Nov 2011 | Gazelle Stakes | Awesome Feather | Jeffrey Sanchez |
| 27 Nov 2011 | Hollywood Derby | Ultimate Eagle | Martin Pedroza |
| 10 Dec 2011 | Hollywood Starlet | Killer Graces | Joe Talamo |
| 17 Dec 2011 | CashCall Futurity | Liaison | Rafael Bejarano |
| 31 Dec 2011 | La Brea Stakes | Teddy's Promise | Victor Espinoza |
| 11 Feb 2012 | Donn Handicap | Hymn Book | John Velazquez |
| 11 Feb 2012 | Gulfstream Park Turf Handicap | Get Stormy | Ramon Dominguez |
| 3 Mar 2012 | Santa Anita Handicap | Ron the Greek | Jose Lezcano |
| 31 Mar 2012 | Florida Derby | Take Charge Indy | Calvin Borel |
| 7 Apr 2012 | Ashland Stakes | Karlovy Vary | James Graham |
| 7 Apr 2012 | Santa Anita Derby | I'll Have Another | Mario Gutierrez |
| 7 Apr 2012 | Wood Memorial Stakes | Gemologist | Javier Castellano |
| 12 Apr 2012 | Vinery Madison Stakes | Groupie Doll | Rajiv Maragh |
| 13 Apr 2012 | Apple Blossom Handicap | Plum Pretty | Rafael Bejarano |
| 13 Apr 2012 | Makers Mark Mile | Get Stormy | Javier Castellano |
| 14 Apr 2012 | Arkansas Derby | Bodemeister | Mike Smith |
| 14 Apr 2012 | Blue Grass Stakes | Dullahan | Kent Desormeaux |
| 4 May 2012 | Kentucky Oaks | Believe You Can | Rosie Napravnik |
| 5 May 2012 | Humana Distaff | Groupie Doll | Rajiv Maragh |
| 5 May 2012 | Kentucky Derby | I'll Have Another | Mario Gutierrez |
| 5 May 2012 | Woodford Reserve Turf Classic Stakes | Little Mike | Joe Bravo |
| 19 May 2012 | Preakness Stakes | I'll Have Another | Mario Gutierrez |
| 28 May 2012 | Acorn Stakes | Contested | Javier Castellano |
| 28 May 2012 | Metropolitan Handicap | Shackleford | John Velazquez |
| 9 Jun 2012 | Belmont Stakes | Union Rags | John Velazquez |
| 9 Jun 2012 | Just A Game Stakes | Tapitsfly | Ramon Dominguez |
| 9 Jun 2012 | Manhattan Handicap | Desert Blanc | Ramon Dominguez |
| 16 Jun 2012 | Stephen Foster Handicap | Ron the Greek | Jose Lezcano |
| 30 Jun 2012 | Shoemaker Mile Stakes | Jeranimo | Garrett Gomez |
| 7 Jul 2012 | Hollywood Gold Cup | Game On Dude | Chantal Sutherland |
| 7 Jul 2012 | Princess Rooney Handicap | Musical Romance | Juan Leyva |
| 7 Jul 2012 | United Nations Stakes | Turbo Compressor | Joe Bravo |
| 14 Jul 2012 | Man o' War Stakes | Point of Entry | Jose Lezcano |
| 21 Jul 2012 | Eddie Read Handicap | Acclamation | Pat Valenzuela |
| 28 Jul 2012 | Diana Stakes | Winter Memories | Javier Castellano |
| 29 Jul 2012 | Bing Crosby Stakes | Amazombie | Mike Smith |
| 29 Jul 2012 | Haskell Invitational | Paynter | Rafael Bejarano |

## Major Thoroughbred Race Winners, 2011–12 (continued)

### Canada

| DATE | RACE | WINNER | JOCKEY |
|---|---|---|---|
| 7 Aug 2011 | Breeders' Stakes | Pender Harbour | Luis Contreras |
| 18 Sep 2011 | Woodbine Mile | Turallure | Julien Leparoux |
| 16 Oct 2011 | Canadian International Stakes | Sarah Lynx | Christophe Soumillon |
| 16 Oct 2011 | E.P. Taylor Stakes | Miss Keller | John Velazquez |
| 16 Oct 2011 | Nearctic Stakes | Regally Ready | Corey Nakatani |
| 24 Jun 2012 | Queen's Plate Stakes | Strait of Dover | Justin Stein |
| 15 Jul 2012 | Prince of Wales Stakes | Dixie Strike | Patrick Husbands |

### England

| | | | |
|---|---|---|---|
| 17 Aug 2011 | Juddmonte International Stakes | Twice Over | Ian Mongan |
| 19 Aug 2011 | Nunthorpe Stakes | Margot Did | Hayley Turner |
| 10 Sep 2011 | St. Leger Stakes | Masked Marvel | William Buick |
| 15 Oct 2011 | Queen Elizabeth II Stakes | Frankel | Tom Queally |
| 5 May 2012 | 2,000 Guineas | Camelot | Joseph O'Brien |
| 6 May 2012 | 1,000 Guineas | Homecoming Queen | Ryan Moore |
| 2 Jun 2012 | The Derby | Camelot | Joseph O'Brien |
| 21 Jun 2012 | Ascot Gold Cup | Colour Vision | Frankie Dettori |
| 23 Jun 2012 | Diamond Jubilee Stakes | Black Caviar | Luke Nolen |
| 7 Jul 2012 | Coral-Eclipse Stakes | Nathaniel | William Buick |
| 21 Jul 2012 | King George VI and Queen Elizabeth Stakes | Danedream | Andrasch Starke |

### Ireland

| | | | |
|---|---|---|---|
| 3 Sep 2011 | Irish Champion Stakes | So You Think | Seamie Heffernan |
| 10 Sep 2011 | Irish St. Leger | Duncan[1] | Eddie Ahern |
| | | Jukebox Jury[1] | Johnny Murtagh |
| 26 May 2012 | Irish 2,000 Guineas | Power | Joseph O'Brien |
| 27 May 2012 | Irish 1,000 Guineas | Samitar | Martin Harley |
| 30 Jun 2012 | Irish Derby | Camelot | Joseph O'Brien |
| 22 Jul 2012 | Irish Oaks | Great Heavens | William Buick |

### France

| | | | |
|---|---|---|---|
| 15 Aug 2011 | Prix Jacques le Marois | Immortal Verse | Gerald Mosse |
| 2 Oct 2011 | Prix de l'Arc de Triomphe | Danedream | Andrasch Starke |
| 2 Oct 2011 | Prix Jean-Luc Lagardère (Grand Critérium) | Dabirsim | Frankie Dettori |
| 23 Oct 2011 | Prix Royal-Oak | Be Fabulous | Maxime Guyon |
| 29 Apr 2012 | Prix Ganay | Cirrus Des Aigles | Olivier Peslier |
| 13 May 2012 | Poule d'Essai des Poulains | Lucayan | Stephane Pasquier |
| 13 May 2012 | Poule d'Essai des Pouliches | Beauty Parlour | Christophe-Patrice Lemaire |
| 27 May 2012 | Prix Saint-Alary | Sagawara | Christophe-Patrice Lemaire |
| 17 Jun 2012 | Prix de Diane | Valyra | Johnny Murtagh |
| 24 Jun 2012 | Grand Prix de Saint-Cloud | Meandre | Maxime Guyon |
| 14 Jul 2012 | Grand Prix de Paris | Imperial Monarch | Joseph O'Brien |

### Germany

| | | | |
|---|---|---|---|
| 4 Sep 2011 | Grosser Preis von Baden | Danedream | Andrasch Starke |
| 25 Sep 2011 | Preis von Europa | Campanologist | Frankie Dettori |
| 1 Jul 2012 | Deutsches Derby | Pastorius | Terence Hellier |

### Italy

| | | | |
|---|---|---|---|
| 20 May 2012 | Derby Italiano | Feuerblitz | Robert Havlin |

### Australia

| | | | |
|---|---|---|---|
| 15 Oct 2011 | Caulfield Cup | Southern Speed | Craig Williams |
| 22 Oct 2011 | Cox Plate | Pinker Pinker | Craig Williams |
| 1 Nov 2011 | Melbourne Cup | Dunaden | Christophe-Patrice Lemaire |

### United Arab Emirates

| | | | |
|---|---|---|---|
| 31 Mar 2012 | Dubai Duty Free | Cityscape | James Doyle |
| 31 Mar 2012 | Dubai Golden Shaheen | Krypton Factor | Kieren Fallon |
| 31 Mar 2012 | Dubai Sheema Classic | Cirrus Des Aigles | Olivier Peslier |
| 31 Mar 2012 | Dubai World Cup | Monterosso | Mickael Barzalona |
| 31 Mar 2012 | Godolphin Mile | African Story | Frankie Dettori |
| 31 Mar 2012 | UAE Derby | Daddy Long Legs | Colm O'Donoghue |

## Major Thoroughbred Race Winners, 2011–12 (continued)

### Japan

| DATE | RACE | WINNER | JOCKEY |
|---|---|---|---|
| 27 Nov 2011 | Japan Cup | Buena Vista | Yasunari Iwata |

### Hong Kong

| | | | |
|---|---|---|---|
| 11 Dec 2011 | Hong Kong Cup | California Memory | Matthew Chadwick |
| 26 Feb 2012 | Hong Kong Gold Cup | Ambitious Dragon | Douglas Whyte |
| 29 Apr 2012 | Queen Elizabeth II Cup | Rulership | Umberto Rispoli |

[1]Dead heat.

## Kentucky Derby

| YEAR | HORSE | JOCKEY | YEAR | HORSE | JOCKEY |
|---|---|---|---|---|---|
| 1875 | Aristides | Oliver Lewis | 1928 | Reigh Count | Charles Lang |
| 1876 | Vagrant | Bobby Swim | 1929 | Clyde Van Dusen | Linus McAtee |
| 1877 | Baden-Baden | William Walker | 1930 | Gallant Fox | Earl Sande |
| 1878 | Day Star | Jimmy Carter | 1931 | Twenty Grand | Charles Kurtsinger |
| 1879 | Lord Murphy | Charlie Shauer | 1932 | Burgoo King | Eugene James |
| 1880 | Fonso | George Garret Lewis | 1933 | Brokers Tip | Don Meade |
| 1881 | Hindoo | James McLaughlin | 1934 | Cavalcade | Mack Garner |
| 1882 | Apollo | Babe Hurd | 1935 | Omaha | William Saunders |
| 1883 | Leonatus | William Donohue | 1936 | Bold Venture | Ira Hanford |
| 1884 | Buchanan | Isaac Murphy | 1937 | War Admiral | Charles Kurtsinger |
| 1885 | Joe Cotton | Erskine Henderson | 1938 | Lawrin | Eddie Arcaro |
| 1886 | Ben Ali | Paul Duffy | 1939 | Johnstown | James Stout |
| 1887 | Montrose | Isaac Lewis | 1940 | Gallahadion | Carroll Bierman |
| 1888 | Macbeth II | George Covington | 1941 | Whirlaway | Eddie Arcaro |
| 1889 | Spokane | Thomas Kiley | 1942 | Shut Out | Wayne D. Wright |
| 1890 | Riley | Isaac Murphy | 1943 | Count Fleet | John Longden |
| 1891 | Kingman | Isaac Murphy | 1944 | Pensive | Conn McCreary |
| 1892 | Azra | Alonzo Clayton | 1945 | Hoop Jr. | Eddie Arcaro |
| 1893 | Lookout | Eddie Kunze | 1946 | Assault | Warren Mehrtens |
| 1894 | Chant | Frank Goodale | 1947 | Jet Pilot | Eric Guerin |
| 1895 | Halma | James Perkins | 1948 | Citation | Eddie Arcaro |
| 1896 | Ben Brush | Willie Simms | 1949 | Ponder | Steve Brooks |
| 1897 | Typhoon II | Fred Garner | 1950 | Middleground | William Boland |
| 1898 | Plaudit | Willie Simms | 1951 | Count Turf | Conn McCreary |
| 1899 | Manuel | Fred Taral | 1952 | Hill Gail | Eddie Arcaro |
| 1900 | Lieut. Gibson | Jimmy Boland | 1953 | Dark Star | Henry Moreno |
| 1901 | His Eminence | James Winkfield | 1954 | Determine | Raymond York |
| 1902 | Alan-a-Dale | James Winkfield | 1955 | Swaps | William Shoemaker |
| 1903 | Judge Himes | Harold Booker | 1956 | Needles | David Erb |
| 1904 | Elwood | Frank Prior | 1957 | Iron Liege | William Hartack |
| 1905 | Agile | Jack Martin | 1958 | Tim Tam | Ismael Valenzuela |
| 1906 | Sir Huon | Roscoe Troxler | 1959 | Tomy Lee | William Shoemaker |
| 1907 | Pink Star | Andy Minder | 1960 | Venetian Way | William Hartack |
| 1908 | Stone Street | Arthur Pickens | 1961 | Carry Back | John Sellers |
| 1909 | Wintergreen | Vincent Powers | 1962 | Decidedly | William Hartack |
| 1910 | Donau | Fred Herbert | 1963 | Chateaugay | Braulio Baeza |
| 1911 | Meridian | George Archibald | 1964 | Northern Dancer | William Hartack |
| 1912 | Worth | Carroll Hugh Shilling | 1965 | Lucky Debonair | William Shoemaker |
| 1913 | Donerail | Roscoe Goose | 1966 | Kauai King | Don Brumfield |
| 1914 | Old Rosebud | John McCabe | 1967 | Proud Clarion | Robert Ussery |
| 1915 | Regret | Joe Notter | 1968 | Forward Pass | Ismael Valenzuela |
| 1916 | George Smith | John Loftus | 1969 | Majestic Prince | William Hartack |
| 1917 | Omar Khayyam | Charles Borel | 1970 | Dust Commander | Mike Manganello |
| 1918 | Exterminator | William Knapp | 1971 | Canonero II | Gustavo Avila |
| 1919 | Sir Barton | John Loftus | 1972 | Riva Ridge | Ron Turcotte |
| 1920 | Paul Jones | Ted Rice | 1973 | Secretariat[1] | Ron Turcotte |
| 1921 | Behave Yourself | Charles Thompson | 1974 | Cannonade | Angel Cordero, Jr. |
| 1922 | Morvich | Albert Johnson | 1975 | Foolish Pleasure | Jacinto Vasquez |
| 1923 | Zev | Earl Sande | 1976 | Bold Forbes | Angel Cordero, Jr. |
| 1924 | Black Gold | John D. Mooney | 1977 | Seattle Slew | Jean Cruguet |
| 1925 | Flying Ebony | Earl Sande | 1978 | Affirmed | Steve Cauthen |
| 1926 | Bubbling Over | Albert Johnson | 1979 | Spectacular Bid | Ronnie Franklin |
| 1927 | Whiskery | Linus McAtee | 1980 | Genuine Risk | Jacinto Vasquez |

## Kentucky Derby (continued)

| YEAR | HORSE | JOCKEY | YEAR | HORSE | JOCKEY |
|------|-------|--------|------|-------|--------|
| 1981 | Pleasant Colony | Jorge Velasquez | 1997 | Silver Charm | Gary Stevens |
| 1982 | Gato del Sol | Eddie Delahoussaye | 1998 | Real Quiet | Kent Desormeaux |
| 1983 | Sunny's Halo | Eddie Delahoussaye | 1999 | Charismatic | Chris Antley |
| 1984 | Swale | Laffit Pincay, Jr. | 2000 | Fusaichi Pegasus | Kent Desormeaux |
| 1985 | Spend a Buck | Angel Cordero, Jr. | 2001 | Monarchos | Jorge Chávez |
| 1986 | Ferdinand | William Shoemaker | 2002 | War Emblem | Victor Espinoza |
| 1987 | Alysheba | Chris McCarron | 2003 | Funny Cide | José Santos |
| 1988 | Winning Colors | Gary Stevens | 2004 | Smarty Jones | Stewart Elliott |
| 1989 | Sunday Silence | Patrick Valenzuela | 2005 | Giacomo | Mike Smith |
| 1990 | Unbridled | Craig Perret | 2006 | Barbaro | Edgar Prado |
| 1991 | Strike the Gold | Chris Antley | 2007 | Street Sense | Calvin Borel |
| 1992 | Lil E. Tee | Pat Day | 2008 | Big Brown | Kent Desormeaux |
| 1993 | Sea Hero | Jerry Bailey | 2009 | Mine That Bird | Calvin Borel |
| 1994 | Go for Gin | Chris McCarron | 2010 | Super Saver | Calvin Borel |
| 1995 | Thunder Gulch | Gary Stevens | 2011 | Animal Kingdom | John Velazquez |
| 1996 | Grindstone | Jerry Bailey | 2012 | I'll Have Another | Mario Gutierrez |

[1]Fastest time—1 min 59⅖ sec.

## Preakness Stakes

| YEAR | HORSE | JOCKEY | YEAR | HORSE | JOCKEY |
|------|-------|--------|------|-------|--------|
| 1873 | Survivor | George Barbee | 1919 | Sir Barton | John Loftus |
| 1874 | Culpepper | William Donohue | 1920 | Man o' War | Clarence Kummer |
| 1875 | Tom Ochiltree | Lloyd Hughes | 1921 | Broomspun | Frank Coltiletti |
| 1876 | Shirley | George Barbee | 1922 | Pillory | Louis Morris |
| 1877 | Cloverbrook | Cyrus Holloway | 1923 | Vigil | Benny Marinelli |
| 1878 | Duke of Magenta | Cyrus Holloway | 1924 | Nellie Morse | John Merimee |
| 1879 | Harold | Lloyd Hughes | 1925 | Coventry | Clarence Kummer |
| 1880 | Grenada | Lloyd Hughes | 1926 | Display | John Maiben |
| 1881 | Saunterer | T. Costello | 1927 | Bostonian | Alf J. "Whitey" Abel |
| 1882 | Vanguard | T. Costello | 1928 | Victorian | Raymond Workman |
| 1883 | Jacobus | George Barbee | 1929 | Dr. Freeland | Louis Schaefer |
| 1884 | Knight of Ellerslie | S. Fisher | 1930 | Gallant Fox | Earl Sande |
| 1885 | Tecumseh | James McLaughlin | 1931 | Mate | George Ellis |
| 1886 | The Bard | S. Fisher | 1932 | Burgoo King | Eugene James |
| 1887 | Dunboyne | William Donohue | 1933 | Head Play | Charles Kurtsinger |
| 1888 | Refund | Fred Littlefield | 1934 | High Quest | Robert Jones |
| 1889 | Buddhist | George Anderson | 1935 | Omaha | Willie Saunders |
| 1890 | Montague | W. Martin | 1936 | Bold Venture | George Woolf |
| 1891–93 | not held | | 1937 | War Admiral | Charles Kurtsinger |
| 1894 | Assignee | Fred Taral | 1938 | Dauber | Maurice Peters |
| 1895 | Belmar | Fred Taral | 1939 | Challedon | George Seabo |
| 1896 | Margrave | Henry Griffin | 1940 | Bimelech | Fred A. Smith |
| 1897 | Paul Kauvar | T. Thorpe | 1941 | Whirlaway | Eddie Arcaro |
| 1898 | Sly Fox | Willie Simms | 1942 | Alsab | Basil James |
| 1899 | Half Time | R. Clawson | 1943 | Count Fleet | John Longden |
| 1900 | Hindus | H. Spencer | 1944 | Pensive | Conn McCreary |
| 1901 | The Parader | Fred Landry | 1945 | Polynesian | Wayne D. Wright |
| 1902 | Old England | L. Jackson | 1946 | Assault | Warren Mehrtens |
| 1903 | Flocarline | W. Gannon | 1947 | Faultless | Doug Dodson |
| 1904 | Bryn Mawr | Eugene Hildebrand | 1948 | Citation | Eddie Arcaro |
| 1905 | Cairngorm | W. Davis | 1949 | Capot | Ted Atkinson |
| 1906 | Whimsical | Walter Miller | 1950 | Hill Prince | Eddie Arcaro |
| 1907 | Don Enrique | G. Mountain | 1951 | Bold | Eddie Arcaro |
| 1908 | Royal Tourist | Eddie Dugan | 1952 | Blue Man | Conn McCreary |
| 1909 | Effendi | Willie Doyle | 1953 | Native Dancer | Eric Guerin |
| 1910 | Layminster | Roy Estep | 1954 | Hasty Road | Johnny Adams |
| 1911 | Watervale | Eddie Dugan | 1955 | Nashua | Eddie Arcaro |
| 1912 | Colonel Holloway | Clarence Turner | 1956 | Fabius | William Hartack |
| 1913 | Buskin | James Butwell | 1957 | Bold Ruler | Eddie Arcaro |
| 1914 | Holiday | Andy Schuttinger | 1958 | Tim Tam | Ismael Valenzuela |
| 1915 | Rhine Maiden | Douglas Hoffman | 1959 | Royal Orbit | William Harmatz |
| 1916 | Damrosch | Linus McAtee | 1960 | Bally Ache | Robert Ussery |
| 1917 | Kalitan | Everett Haynes | 1961 | Carry Back | John Sellers |
| 1918[1] | War Cloud; Jack Hare, Jr. | John Loftus; Charles Peak | 1962 | Greek Money | John L. Rotz |
| | | | 1963 | Candy Spots | William Shoemaker |

## Preakness Stakes (continued)

| YEAR | HORSE | JOCKEY | YEAR | HORSE | JOCKEY |
|------|-------|--------|------|-------|--------|
| 1964 | Northern Dancer | William Hartack | 1989 | Sunday Silence | Patrick Valenzuela |
| 1965 | Tom Rolfe | Ron Turcotte | 1990 | Summer Squall | Pat Day |
| 1966 | Kauai King | Don Brumfield | 1991 | Hansel | Jerry Bailey |
| 1967 | Damascus | William Shoemaker | 1992 | Pine Bluff | Chris McCarron |
| 1968 | Forward Pass | Ismael Valenzuela | 1993 | Prairie Bayou | Mike Smith |
| 1969 | Majestic Prince | William Hartack | 1994 | Tabasco Cat | Pat Day |
| 1970 | Personality | Eddie Belmonte | 1995 | Timber Country | Pat Day |
| 1971 | Canonero II | Gustavo Avila | 1996 | Louis Quatorze | Pat Day |
| 1972 | Bee Bee Bee | Eldon Nelson | 1997 | Silver Charm | Gary Stevens |
| 1973 | Secretariat[2] | Ron Turcotte | 1998 | Real Quiet | Kent Desormeaux |
| 1974 | Little Current | Miguel Rivera | 1999 | Charismatic | Chris Antley |
| 1975 | Master Derby | Darrel McHague | 2000 | Red Bullet | Jerry Bailey |
| 1976 | Elocutionist | John Lively | 2001 | Point Given | Gary Stevens |
| 1977 | Seattle Slew | Jean Cruguet | 2002 | War Emblem | Victor Espinoza |
| 1978 | Affirmed | Steve Cauthen | 2003 | Funny Cide | José Santos |
| 1979 | Spectacular Bid | Ron Franklin | 2004 | Smarty Jones | Stewart Elliott |
| 1980 | Codex | Angel Cordero, Jr. | 2005 | Afleet Alex | Jeremy Rose |
| 1981 | Pleasant Colony | Jorge Velasquez | 2006 | Bernardini | Javier Castellano |
| 1982 | Aloma's Ruler | Jack Kaenel | 2007 | Curlin | Robby Albarado |
| 1983 | Deputed Testamony | Donald Miller | 2008 | Big Brown | Kent Desormeaux |
| 1984 | Gate Dancer | Angel Cordero, Jr. | 2009 | Rachel Alexandra | Calvin Borel |
| 1985 | Tank's Prospect | Pat Day | 2010 | Lookin At Lucky | Martin Garcia |
| 1986 | Snow Chief | Alex Solis | 2011 | Shackleford | Jesus Castanon |
| 1987 | Alysheba | Chris McCarron | 2012 | I'll Have Another | Mario Gutierrez |
| 1988 | Risen Star | Eddie Delahoussaye | | | |

[1]Run in two divisions in 1918 because of the large number of starters.    [2]Fastest time—1 min 53 sec.

## Belmont Stakes

| YEAR | HORSE | JOCKEY | YEAR | HORSE | JOCKEY |
|------|-------|--------|------|-------|--------|
| 1867 | Ruthless | Gilbert Patrick | 1903 | Africander | John Bullman |
| 1868 | General Duke | Bobby Swim | 1904 | Delhi | George Odom |
| 1869 | Fenian | Charley Miller | 1905 | Tanya | Eugene Hildebrand |
| 1870 | Kingfisher | Edward Brown | 1906 | Burgomaster | Lucien Lyne |
| 1871 | Harry Bassett | W. Miller | 1907 | Peter Pan | G. Mountain |
| 1872 | Joe Daniels | James Rowe | 1908 | Colin | Joe Notter |
| 1873 | Springbok | James Rowe | 1909 | Joe Madden | Eddie Dugan |
| 1874 | Saxon | George Barbee | 1910 | Sweep | James Butwell |
| 1875 | Calvin | Bobby Swim | 1911–12 | not held | |
| 1876 | Algerine | Billy Donohue | 1913 | Prince Eugene | Roscoe Troxler |
| 1877 | Cloverbrook | Cyrus Holloway | 1914 | Luke McLuke | Merritt Buxton |
| 1878 | Duke of Magenta | Lloyd Hughes | 1915 | The Finn | George Byrne |
| 1879 | Spendthrift | George Evans | 1916 | Friar Rock | Everett Haynes |
| 1880 | Grenada | Lloyd Hughes | 1917 | Hourless | James Butwell |
| 1881 | Saunterer | T. Costello | 1918 | Johren | Frank Robinson |
| 1882 | Forester | James McLaughlin | 1919 | Sir Barton | John Loftus |
| 1883 | George Kinney | James McLaughlin | 1920 | Man o' War | Clarence Kummer |
| 1884 | Panique | James McLaughlin | 1921 | Grey Lag | Earl Sande |
| 1885 | Tyrant | Paul Duffy | 1922 | Pillory | C.H. Miller |
| 1886 | Inspector B | James McLaughlin | 1923 | Zev | Earl Sande |
| 1887 | Hanover | James McLaughlin | 1924 | Mad Play | Earl Sande |
| 1888 | Sir Dixon | James McLaughlin | 1925 | American Flag | Albert Johnson |
| 1889 | Eric | W. Hayward | 1926 | Crusader | Albert Johnson |
| 1890 | Burlington | Shelby Barnes | 1927 | Chance Shot | Earl Sande |
| 1891 | Foxford | Edward Garrison | 1928 | Vito | Clarence Kummer |
| 1892 | Patron | W. Hayward | 1929 | Blue Larkspur | Mack Garner |
| 1893 | Comanche | Willie Simms | 1930 | Gallant Fox | Earl Sande |
| 1894 | Henry of Navarre | Willie Simms | 1931 | Twenty Grand | Charles Kurtsinger |
| 1895 | Belmar | Fred Taral | 1932 | Faireno | Tom Malley |
| 1896 | Hastings | Henry Griffin | 1933 | Hurryoff | Mack Garner |
| 1897 | Scottish Chieftain | J. Scherrer | 1934 | Peace Chance | Wayne D. Wright |
| 1898 | Bowling Brook | Fred Littlefield | 1935 | Omaha | Willie Saunders |
| 1899 | Jean Bereaud | R. Clawson | 1936 | Granville | James Stout |
| 1900 | Ildrim | Nash Turner | 1937 | War Admiral | Charles Kurtsinger |
| 1901 | Commando | H. Spencer | 1938 | Pasteurized | James Stout |
| 1902 | Masterman | John Bullman | 1939 | Johnstown | James Stout |

## Belmont Stakes (continued)

| YEAR | HORSE | JOCKEY | YEAR | HORSE | JOCKEY |
|------|-------|--------|------|-------|--------|
| 1940 | Bimelech | Fred A. Smith | 1977 | Seattle Slew | Jean Cruguet |
| 1941 | Whirlaway | Eddie Arcaro | 1978 | Affirmed | Steve Cauthen |
| 1942 | Shut Out | Eddie Arcaro | 1979 | Coastal | Ruben Hernandez |
| 1943 | Count Fleet | John Longden | 1980 | Temperence Hill | Eddie Maple |
| 1944 | Bounding Home | Gayle L. Smith | 1981 | Summing | George Martens |
| 1945 | Pavot | Eddie Arcaro | 1982 | Conquistador Cielo | Laffit Pincay, Jr. |
| 1946 | Assault | Warren Mehrtens | 1983 | Caveat | Laffit Pincay, Jr. |
| 1947 | Phalanx | Ruperto Donoso | 1984 | Swale | Laffit Pincay, Jr. |
| 1948 | Citation | Eddie Arcaro | 1985 | Creme Fraiche | Eddie Maple |
| 1949 | Capot | Ted Atkinson | 1986 | Danzig Connection | Chris McCarron |
| 1950 | Middleground | William Boland | 1987 | Bet Twice | Craig Perret |
| 1951 | Counterpoint | David Gorman | 1988 | Risen Star | Eddie Delahoussaye |
| 1952 | One Count | Eddie Arcaro | 1989 | Easy Goer | Pat Day |
| 1953 | Native Dancer | Eric Guerin | 1990 | Go and Go | Mick Kinane |
| 1954 | High Gun | Eric Guerin | 1991 | Hansel | Jerry Bailey |
| 1955 | Nashua | Eddie Arcaro | 1992 | A.P. Indy | Eddie Delahoussaye |
| 1956 | Needles | David Erb | 1993 | Colonial Affair | Julie Krone |
| 1957 | Gallant Man | William Shoemaker | 1994 | Tabasco Cat | Pat Day |
| 1958 | Cavan | Pete Anderson | 1995 | Thunder Gulch | Gary Stevens |
| 1959 | Sword Dancer | William Shoemaker | 1996 | Editor's Note | Rene Douglas |
| 1960 | Celtic Ash | William Hartack | 1997 | Touch Gold | Chris McCarron |
| 1961 | Sherluck | Braulio Baeza | 1998 | Victory Gallop | Gary Stevens |
| 1962 | Jaipur | William Shoemaker | 1999 | Lemon Drop Kid | José Santos |
| 1963 | Chateaugay | Braulio Baeza | 2000 | Commendable | Pat Day |
| 1964 | Quadrangle | Manuel Ycaza | 2001 | Point Given | Gary Stevens |
| 1965 | Hail to All | John Sellers | 2002 | Sarava | Edgar Prado |
| 1966 | Amberoid | William Boland | 2003 | Empire Maker | Jerry Bailey |
| 1967 | Damascus | William Shoemaker | 2004 | Birdstone | Edgar Prado |
| 1968 | Stage Door Johnny | Heliodoro Gustines | 2005 | Afleet Alex | Jeremy Rose |
| 1969 | Arts and Letters | Braulio Baeza | 2006 | Jazil | Fernando Jara |
| 1970 | High Echelon | John Rotz | 2007 | Rags to Riches | John Velazquez |
| 1971 | Pass Catcher | Walter Blum | 2008 | Da' Tara | Alan Garcia |
| 1972 | Riva Ridge | Ron Turcotte | 2009 | Summer Bird | Kent Desormeaux |
| 1973 | Secretariat[1] | Ron Turcotte | 2010 | Drosselmeyer | Mike Smith |
| 1974 | Little Current | Miguel Rivera | 2011 | Ruler On Ice | Jose Valdivia, Jr. |
| 1975 | Avatar | William Shoemaker | 2012 | Union Rags | John Velazquez |
| 1976 | Bold Forbes | Angel Cordero, Jr. | | | |

[1]Fastest time—2 min 24 sec.

## Triple Crown Champions—United States

| YEAR | HORSE | YEAR | HORSE | YEAR | HORSE | YEAR | HORSE |
|------|-------|------|-------|------|-------|------|-------|
| 1919 | Sir Barton | 1937 | War Admiral | 1946 | Assault | 1977 | Seattle Slew |
| 1930 | Gallant Fox | 1941 | Whirlaway | 1948 | Citation | 1978 | Affirmed |
| 1935 | Omaha | 1943 | Count Fleet | 1973 | Secretariat | | |

## Horse of the Year

A Horse of the Year was selected by the *Daily Racing Form* from 1936 to 1970 and by the Thoroughbred Racing Association beginning in 1950. From 1971 these two organizations, plus the National Turf Writers Association, founded the Eclipse Awards, of which the Horse of the Year is the most coveted.

| YEAR | HORSE | YEAR | HORSE | YEAR | HORSE | YEAR | HORSE |
|------|-------|------|-------|------|-------|------|-------|
| 1936 | Granville | 1948 | Citation | 1957 | Bold Ruler[1]; Dedicate[2] | 1967 | Damascus |
| 1937 | War Admiral | 1949 | Capot[1]; Coaltown[2] | 1958 | Round Table | 1968 | Dr. Fager |
| 1938 | Seabiscuit | | | 1959 | Sword Dancer | 1969 | Arts and Letters |
| 1939 | Challedon | 1950 | Hill Prince | 1960 | Kelso | 1970 | Fort Marcy[1]; Personality[2] |
| 1940 | Challedon | 1951 | Counterpoint | 1961 | Kelso | | |
| 1941 | Whirlaway | 1952 | One Count[1]; Native Dancer[2] | 1962 | Kelso | 1971 | Ack Ack |
| 1942 | Whirlaway | | | 1963 | Kelso | 1972 | Secretariat |
| 1943 | Count Fleet | 1953 | Tom Fool | 1964 | Kelso | 1973 | Secretariat |
| 1944 | Twilight Tear | 1954 | Native Dancer | 1965 | Roman Brother[1]; Moccasin[2] | 1974 | Forego |
| 1945 | Busher | 1955 | Nashua | | | 1975 | Forego |
| 1946 | Assault | 1956 | Swaps | 1966 | Buckpasser | 1976 | Forego |
| 1947 | Armed | | | | | 1977 | Seattle Slew |

## Horse of the Year (continued)

| YEAR | HORSE | YEAR | HORSE | YEAR | HORSE | YEAR | HORSE |
|---|---|---|---|---|---|---|---|
| 1978 | Affirmed | 1986 | Lady's Secret | 1995 | Cigar | 2004 | Ghostzapper |
| 1979 | Affirmed | 1987 | Ferdinand | 1996 | Cigar | 2005 | Saint Liam |
| 1980 | Spectacular Bid | 1988 | Alysheba | 1997 | Favorite Trick | 2006 | Invasor |
| 1981 | John Henry | 1989 | Sunday Silence | 1998 | Skip Away | 2007 | Curlin |
| 1982 | Conquistador | 1990 | Criminal Type | 1999 | Charismatic | 2008 | Curlin |
|  | Cielo | 1991 | Black Tie Affair | 2000 | Tiznow | 2009 | Rachel |
| 1983 | All Along | 1992 | A.P. Indy | 2001 | Point Given |  | Alexandra |
| 1984 | John Henry | 1993 | Kotashaan | 2002 | Azeri | 2010 | Zenyatta |
| 1985 | Spend a Buck | 1994 | Holy Bull | 2003 | Mineshaft | 2011 | Havre de Grace |

[1]Daily Racing Form.    [2]Thoroughbred Racing Association.

## 2,000 Guineas

*Held since 1809. Table shows the winners for the past 20 years.*

| YEAR | HORSE | JOCKEY | YEAR | HORSE | JOCKEY |
|---|---|---|---|---|---|
| 1993 | Zafonic | Pat Eddery | 2003 | Refuse To Bend | Pat Smullen |
| 1994 | Mister Baileys | Jason Weaver | 2004 | Haafhd | Richard Hills |
| 1995 | Pennekamp | Thierry Jarnet | 2005 | Footstepsinthesand | Kieren Fallon |
| 1996 | Mark of Esteem | Frankie Dettori | 2006 | George Washington | Kieren Fallon |
| 1997 | Entrepreneur | Mick Kinane | 2007 | Cockney Rebel | Olivier Peslier |
| 1998 | King of Kings | Mick Kinane | 2008 | Henrythenavigator | Johnny Murtagh |
| 1999 | Island Sands | Frankie Dettori | 2009 | Sea The Stars | Mick Kinane |
| 2000 | King's Best | Kieren Fallon | 2010 | Makfi | Christophe Lemaire |
| 2001 | Golan | Kieren Fallon | 2011 | Frankel | Tom Queally |
| 2002 | Rock of Gibraltar | Johnny Murtagh | 2012 | Camelot | Joseph O'Brien |

## The Derby

*Held since 1780. Table shows the winners for the past 20 years.*

| YEAR | HORSE | JOCKEY | YEAR | HORSE | JOCKEY |
|---|---|---|---|---|---|
| 1993 | Commander in Chief | Mick Kinane | 2003 | Kris Kin | Kieren Fallon |
| 1994 | Erhaab | Willie Carson | 2004 | North Light | Kieren Fallon |
| 1995 | Lammtarra | Walter R. Swinburn | 2005 | Motivator | Johnny Murtagh |
| 1996 | Shaamit | Michael Hills | 2006 | Sir Percy | Martin Dwyer |
| 1997 | Benny the Dip | Willie Ryan | 2007 | Authorized | Frankie Dettori |
| 1998 | High Rise | Olivier Peslier | 2008 | New Approach | Kevin Manning |
| 1999 | Oath | Kieren Fallon | 2009 | Sea The Stars | Mick Kinane |
| 2000 | Sinndar | Johnny Murtagh | 2010 | Workforce | Ryan Moore |
| 2001 | Galileo | Mick Kinane | 2011 | Pour Moi | Mickael Barzalona |
| 2002 | High Chaparral | Johnny Murtagh | 2012 | Camelot | Joseph O'Brien |

## St. Leger

*Held since 1776. Table shows the winners for the past 20 years.*

| YEAR | HORSE | JOCKEY | YEAR | HORSE | JOCKEY |
|---|---|---|---|---|---|
| 1992 | User Friendly | George Duffield | 2002 | Bollin Eric | Kevin Darley |
| 1993 | Bob's Return | Philip Robinson | 2003 | Brian Boru | Jamie Spencer |
| 1994 | Moonax | Pat Eddery | 2004 | Rule of Law | Kerrin McEvoy |
| 1995 | Classic Cliché | Frankie Dettori | 2005 | Scorpion | Frankie Dettori |
| 1996 | Shantou | Frankie Dettori | 2006 | Sixties Icon | Frankie Dettori |
| 1997 | Silver Patriarch | Pat Eddery | 2007 | Lucarno | Jimmy Fortune |
| 1998 | Nedawi | John Reid | 2008 | Conduit | Frankie Dettori |
| 1999 | Mutafaweq | Richard Hills | 2009 | Mastery | Ted Durcan |
| 2000 | Millenary | Richard Quinn | 2010 | Arctic Cosmos | William Buick |
| 2001 | Milan | Mick Kinane | 2011 | Masked Marvel | William Buick |

## Triple Crown Champions—British

| YEAR | WINNER | YEAR | WINNER | YEAR | WINNER | YEAR | WINNER |
|---|---|---|---|---|---|---|---|
| 1853 | West Australian | 1891 | Common | 1900 | Diamond Jubilee | 1918 | Gainsborough |
| 1865 | Gladiateur | 1893 | Isinglass | 1903 | Rock Sand | 1935 | Bahram |
| 1866 | Lord Lyon | 1897 | Galtee More | 1915 | Pommern | 1970 | Nijinsky |
| 1886 | Ormonde | 1899 | Flying Fox | 1917 | Gay Crusader |  |  |

# Melbourne Cup

*Held since 1861. Table shows the winners for the past 20 years.*

| YEAR | HORSE | JOCKEY | YEAR | HORSE | JOCKEY |
|------|-------|--------|------|-------|--------|
| 1992 | Subzero | Greg Hall | 2002 | Media Puzzle | Damien Oliver |
| 1993 | Vintage Crop | Mick Kinane | 2003 | Makybe Diva | Glen Boss |
| 1994 | Jeune | Wayne Harris | 2004 | Makybe Diva | Glen Boss |
| 1995 | Doriemus | Damien Oliver | 2005 | Makybe Diva | Glen Boss |
| 1996 | Saintly | Darren Beadman | 2006 | Delta Blues | Yasunari Iwata |
| 1997 | Might and Power | Jim Cassidy | 2007 | Efficient | Michael Rodd |
| 1998 | Jezabeel | Chris Munce | 2008 | Viewed | Blake Shinn |
| 1999 | Rogan Josh | John Marshall | 2009 | Shocking | Corey Brown |
| 2000 | Brew | Kerrin McEvoy | 2010 | Americain | Gerald Mosse |
| 2001 | Ethereal | Scott Seamer | 2011 | Dunaden | Christophe Lemaire |

# Dubai World Cup

| YEAR | HORSE | JOCKEY | YEAR | HORSE | JOCKEY |
|------|-------|--------|------|-------|--------|
| 1996 | Cigar | Jerry Bailey | 2005 | Roses in May | John Velazquez |
| 1997 | Singspiel | Jerry Bailey | 2006 | Electrocutionist | Frankie Dettori |
| 1998 | Silver Charm | Gary Stevens | 2007 | Invasor | Fernando Jara |
| 1999 | Almutawakel | Richard Hills | 2008 | Curlin | Robby Albarado |
| 2000 | Dubai Millennium | Frankie Dettori | 2009 | Well Armed | Aaron Gryder |
| 2001 | Captain Steve | Jerry Bailey | 2010 | Gloria De Campeao | Tiago Pereira |
| 2002 | Street Cry | Jerry Bailey | 2011 | Victoire Pisa | Mirco Demuro |
| 2003 | Moon Ballad | Frankie Dettori | 2012 | Opinion Poll | Frankie Dettori |
| 2004 | Pleasantly Perfect | Alex Solis | | | |

# Hambletonian Trot

| YEAR | HORSE | DRIVER | YEAR | HORSE | DRIVER |
|------|-------|--------|------|-------|--------|
| 1926 | Guy McKinney | Nat Ray | 1964 | Ayres | John Simpson, Sr. |
| 1927 | Iosola's Worthy | Marvin Childs | 1965 | Egyptian Candor | Adelbert Cameron |
| 1928 | Spencer | William H. Leese | 1966 | Kerry Way | Frank Ervin |
| 1929 | Walter Dear | Walter Cox | 1967 | Speedy Streak | Adelbert Cameron |
| 1930 | Hanover's Bertha | Thomas Berry | 1968 | Nevele Pride | Stanley Dancer |
| 1931 | Calumet Butler | Richard D. McMahon | 1969 | Lindy's Pride | Howard Beissinger |
| 1932 | The Marchioness | William Caton | 1970 | Timothy T. | John Simpson, Sr. |
| 1933 | Mary Reynolds | Ben White | 1971 | Speedy Crown | Howard Beissinger |
| 1934 | Lord Jim | Hugh M. Parshall | 1972 | Super Bowl | Stanley Dancer |
| 1935 | Greyhound | Scepter F. Palin | 1973 | Flirth | Ralph Baldwin |
| 1936 | Rosalind | Ben White | 1974 | Christopher T. | William Haughton |
| 1937 | Shirley Hanover | Henry Thomas | 1975 | Bonefish | Stanley Dancer |
| 1938 | McLin Hanover | Henry Thomas | 1976 | Steve Lobell | William Haughton |
| 1939 | Peter Astra | Hugh M. Parshall | 1977 | Green Speed | William Haughton |
| 1940 | Spencer Scott | Fred Egan | 1978 | Speedy Somolli | Howard Beissinger |
| 1941 | Bill Gallon | Lee Smith | 1979 | Legend Hanover | George Sholty |
| 1942 | The Ambassador | Ben White | 1980 | Burgomeister | William Haughton |
| 1943 | Volo Song | Ben White | 1981 | Shiaway St. Pat | Ray Remmen |
| 1944 | Yankee Maid | Henry Thomas | 1982 | Speed Bowl | Tom Haughton |
| 1945 | Titan Hanover | Harry Pownall, Sr. | 1983 | Duenna | Stanley Dancer |
| 1946 | Chestertown | Thomas Berry | 1984 | Historic Freight | Ben Webster |
| 1947 | Hoot Mon | Scepter F. Palin | 1985 | Prakas | William O'Donnell |
| 1948 | Demon Hanover | Harrison Hoyt | 1986 | Nuclear Kosmos | Ulf Thoresen |
| 1949 | Miss Tilly | Fred Egan | 1987 | Mack Lobell | John Campbell |
| 1950 | Lusty Song | Delvin Miller | 1988 | Armbro Goal | John Campbell |
| 1951 | Mainliner | Guy Crippen | 1989 | Park Avenue Joe; Probe (tied) | Ronald Waples; William Fahy |
| 1952 | Sharp Note | Bion Shively | | | |
| 1953 | Helicopter | Harry Harvey | 1990 | Harmonious | John Campbell |
| 1954 | Newport Dream | Adelbert Cameron | 1991 | Giant Victory | Jack Moiseyev |
| 1955 | Scott Frost | Joseph O'Brien | 1992 | Alf Palema | Mickey McNichol |
| 1956 | The Intruder | Ned Bower | 1993 | American Winner | Ron Pierce |
| 1957 | Hickory Smoke | John Simpson, Sr. | 1994 | Victory Dream | Michel Lachance |
| 1958 | Emily's Pride | Flave Nipe | 1995 | Tagliabue | John Campbell |
| 1959 | Diller Hanover | Frank Ervin | 1996 | Continentalvictory | Michel Lachance |
| 1960 | Blaze Hanover | Joseph O'Brien | 1997 | Malabar Man | Malvern Burroughs |
| 1961 | Harlan Dean | James Arthur | 1998 | Muscles Yankee | John Campbell |
| 1962 | A.C.'s Viking | Sanders Russell | 1999 | Self Possessed | Michel Lachance |
| 1963 | Speedy Scot | Ralph Baldwin | 2000 | Yankee Paco | Trevor Ritchie |

## Hambletonian Trot (continued)

| YEAR | HORSE | DRIVER | YEAR | HORSE | DRIVER |
|------|-------|--------|------|-------|--------|
| 2001 | Scarlet Knight | Stefan Melander | 2007 | Donato Hanover | Ron Pierce |
| 2002 | Chip Chip Hooray | Eric Ledford | 2008 | Deweycheatumnhowe | Ray Schnittker |
| 2003 | Amigo Hall | Michel Lachance | 2009 | Muscle Hill | Brian Sears |
| 2004 | Windsong's Legacy | Trond Smedshamer | 2010 | Muscle Massive | Ron Pierce |
| 2005 | Vivid Photo | Roger Hammer | 2011 | Broad Bahn | George Brennan |
| 2006 | Glidemaster | John Campbell | 2012 | Market Share | Tim Tetrick |

# Ice Hockey

The **National Hockey League** (NHL), which was organized in Canada in 1917, welcomed the first US team, the Boston Bruins, in 1924. Since 1926 the symbol of supremacy in professional hockey has been the **Stanley Cup,** which is awarded to the winner of a play-off that concludes the NHL season. The Stanley Cup was presented to amateur champions from 1893 to 1925. The **World Hockey Championships,** contested by national teams and sponsored by the **International Ice Hockey Federation** (IIHF; founded 1908), have been held since 1930 for men and since 1990 for women.

**Related Web sites:** National Hockey League: <www.nhl.com>; International Ice Hockey Federation: <www.iihf.com>.

## World Hockey Championship—Men

| YEAR | WINNER | YEAR | WINNER | YEAR | WINNER | YEAR | WINNER |
|------|--------|------|--------|------|--------|------|--------|
| 1920[1] | Canada | 1953 | Sweden | 1973 | USSR | 1993 | Russia |
| 1924[1] | Canada | 1954 | USSR | 1974 | USSR | 1994 | Canada |
| 1928[1] | Canada | 1955 | Canada | 1975 | USSR | 1995 | Finland |
| 1930 | Canada | 1956[1] | USSR | 1976 | Czechoslovakia | 1996 | Czech Republic |
| 1931 | Canada | 1957 | Sweden | 1977 | Czechoslovakia | 1997 | Canada |
| 1932[1] | Canada | 1958 | Canada | 1978 | USSR | 1998 | Sweden |
| 1933 | United States | 1959 | Canada | 1979 | USSR | 1999 | Czech Republic |
| 1934 | Canada | 1960[1] | United States | 1980 | *not held* | 2000 | Czech Republic |
| 1935 | Canada | 1961 | Canada | 1981 | USSR | 2001 | Czech Republic |
| 1936[1] | Great Britain | 1962 | Sweden | 1982 | USSR | 2002 | Slovakia |
| 1937 | Canada | 1963 | USSR | 1983 | USSR | 2003 | Canada |
| 1938 | Canada | 1964[1] | USSR | 1984 | *not held* | 2004 | Canada |
| 1939 | Canada | 1965 | USSR | 1985 | Czechoslovakia | 2005 | Czech Republic |
| 1940–46 | *not held* | 1966 | USSR | 1986 | USSR | 2006 | Sweden |
| 1947 | Czechoslovakia | 1967 | USSR | 1987 | Sweden | 2007 | Canada |
| 1948[1] | Canada | 1968[1] | USSR | 1988 | *not held* | 2008 | Russia |
| 1949 | Czechoslovakia | 1969 | USSR | 1989 | USSR | 2009 | Russia |
| 1950 | Canada | 1970 | USSR | 1990 | Sweden | 2010 | Czech Republic |
| 1951 | Canada | 1971 | USSR | 1991 | Sweden | 2011 | Finland |
| 1952[1] | Canada | 1972[2] | Czechoslovakia | 1992 | Sweden | 2012 | Russia |

[1]*Olympic championships, recognized in this table as world championships.* [2]*In 1972 a separate world championship was held for the first time in an Olympic year.*

## World Hockey Championship—Women

| YEAR | WINNER | YEAR | WINNER | YEAR | WINNER | YEAR | WINNER |
|------|--------|------|--------|------|--------|------|--------|
| 1990 | Canada | 1996 | *not held* | 2002[1] | Canada | 2008 | United States |
| 1991 | *not held* | 1997 | Canada | 2003 | *not held* | 2009 | United States |
| 1992 | Canada | 1998[1] | United States | 2004 | Canada | 2010[1] | Canada |
| 1993 | *not held* | 1999 | Canada | 2005 | United States | 2011 | United States |
| 1994 | Canada | 2000 | Canada | 2006[1] | Canada | 2012 | Canada |
| 1995 | *not held* | 2001 | Canada | 2007 | Canada | | |

[1]*Olympic championships, recognized in this table as world championships.*

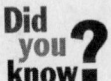

**Did you know?** In the 1930s, radio announcers would often describe a football field as being divided into squares, thus aiding listeners in the visualization of the game. The area just in front of the goal posts, in modern parlance called the "red zone," was known then as "square one." From this usage comes the modern expression "back to square one."

# National Hockey League Final Standings, 2011–12

## EASTERN CONFERENCE

### Northeast Division

| | WON | LOST | OTL[1] |
|---|---|---|---|
| Boston[2] | 49 | 29 | 4 |
| Ottawa[2] | 41 | 31 | 10 |
| Buffalo | 39 | 32 | 11 |
| Toronto | 35 | 37 | 10 |
| Montreal | 31 | 35 | 16 |

### Atlantic Division

| | WON | LOST | OTL[1] |
|---|---|---|---|
| New York Rangers[2] | 51 | 24 | 7 |
| Pittsburgh[2] | 51 | 25 | 6 |
| Philadelphia[2] | 47 | 26 | 9 |
| New Jersey[2] | 48 | 28 | 6 |
| New York Islanders | 34 | 37 | 11 |

### Southeast Division

| | WON | LOST | OTL[1] |
|---|---|---|---|
| Florida[2] | 38 | 26 | 18 |
| Washington[2] | 42 | 32 | 8 |
| Tampa Bay | 38 | 36 | 8 |
| Winnipeg | 37 | 35 | 10 |
| Carolina | 33 | 33 | 16 |

## WESTERN CONFERENCE

### Central Division

| | WON | LOST | OTL[1] |
|---|---|---|---|
| St. Louis[2] | 49 | 22 | 11 |
| Nashville[2] | 48 | 26 | 8 |
| Detroit[2] | 48 | 28 | 6 |
| Chicago[2] | 45 | 26 | 11 |
| Columbus | 29 | 46 | 7 |

### Northwest Division

| | WON | LOST | OTL[1] |
|---|---|---|---|
| Vancouver[2] | 51 | 22 | 9 |
| Calgary | 37 | 29 | 16 |
| Colorado | 41 | 35 | 6 |
| Minnesota | 35 | 36 | 11 |
| Edmonton | 32 | 40 | 10 |

### Pacific Division

| | WON | LOST | OTL[1] |
|---|---|---|---|
| Phoenix[2] | 42 | 27 | 13 |
| San Jose[2] | 43 | 29 | 10 |
| Los Angeles[2] | 40 | 27 | 15 |
| Dallas | 42 | 35 | 5 |
| Anaheim | 34 | 36 | 12 |

[1]Overtime losses, worth one point.   [2]Gained play-off berth.

## Stanley Cup

| YEAR | WINNER | RUNNER-UP | RESULTS |
|---|---|---|---|
| 1893 | Montreal Amateur Athletic Association | no challengers | |
| 1894 | Montreal Amateur Athletic Association | Ottawa Generals | 2-0 |
| 1895 | Montreal Victorias | no challengers | |
| 1896 | Winnipeg Victorias (Feb.); Montreal Victorias (Dec.) | Montreal Victorias (Feb.); Winnipeg Victorias (Dec.) | 1-0; 1-0 |
| 1897 | Montreal Victorias | Ottawa Capitals | 1-0 |
| 1898 | Montreal Victorias | no challengers | |
| 1899 | Montreal Victorias (Feb.); Montreal Shamrocks (March) | Winnipeg Victorias (Feb.); Queen's University (March) | 2-0; 1-0 |
| 1900 | Montreal Shamrocks | Winnipeg Victorias; Halifax Crescents | 2-1; 2-0 |
| 1901 | Winnipeg Victorias | Montreal Shamrocks | 2-0 |
| 1902 | Winnipeg Victorias (Jan.); Montreal Amateur Athletic Association (March) | Toronto Wellingtons (Jan.); Winnipeg Victorias (March) | 2-0; 2-1 |
| 1903 | Montreal Amateur Athletic Association (Feb.); Ottawa Silver Seven (March) | Winnipeg Victorias (Feb.); Montreal Victorias (March); Rat Portage Thistles (March) | 2-1; 1-0; 2-0 |
| 1904 | Ottawa Silver Seven | Winnipeg Rowing Club; Toronto Marlboros; Montreal Wanderers; Brandon Wheat Kings | 2-1; 2-0; 0-0 (tie); 2-0 |
| 1905 | Ottawa Silver Seven | Dawson City Nuggets; Rat Portage Thistles | 2-0; 2-1 |
| 1906 | Ottawa Silver Seven (Feb., March); Montreal Wanderers (March, Dec.) | Queen's University (Feb.); Smiths Falls (March); Ottawa Silver Seven (March); New Glasgow Cubs (Dec.) | 2-0; 2-0; 1-1; 2-0 |
| 1907 | Kenora Thistles (Jan.); Montreal Wanderers (March) | Montreal Wanderers (Jan.); Kenora Thistles (March) | 2-0; 1-1 |
| 1908 | Montreal Wanderers | Ottawa Victorias; Winnipeg Maple Leafs; Toronto Trolley Leaguers; Edmonton Eskimos | 2-0; 2-0; 1-0; 1-1 |
| 1909 | Ottawa Senators | no challengers | |
| 1910 | Ottawa Senators (Jan.); Montreal Wanderers (March) | Galt Professionals (Jan.); Edmonton Eskimos (Jan.); Berlin Union Jacks (March) | 2-0; 2-0; 1-0 |
| 1911 | Ottawa Senators | Port Arthur Bearcats; Galt Professionals | 1-0; 1-0 |
| 1912 | Quebec Bulldogs | Moncton Victorias | 2-0 |
| 1913 | Quebec Bulldogs[1] | Sydney Miners | 2-0 |
| 1914 | Toronto Blueshirts | Montreal Canadiens; Victoria Aristocrats | 1-1; 3-0 |
| 1915 | Vancouver Millionaires | Ottawa Senators | 3-0 |
| 1916 | Montreal Canadiens | Portland Rosebuds | 3-2 |
| 1917 | Seattle Metropolitans | Montreal Canadiens | 3-1 |
| 1918 | Toronto Arenas | Vancouver Millionaires | 3-2 |
| 1919 | no decision[2] | | |
| 1920 | Ottawa Senators | Seattle Metropolitans | 3-2 |
| 1921 | Ottawa Senators | Vancouver Millionaires | 3-2 |

# Stanley Cup (continued)

| YEAR | WINNER | RUNNER-UP | RESULTS |
|------|--------|-----------|---------|
| 1922 | Toronto St. Patricks | Vancouver Millionaires | 3-2 |
| 1923 | Ottawa Senators | Edmonton Eskimos | 2-0 |
| 1924 | Montreal Canadiens | Calgary Tigers | 2-0 |
| 1925 | Victoria Cougars | Montreal Canadiens | 3-1 |
| 1926 | Montreal Maroons | Victoria Cougars | 3-1 |
| 1927 | Ottawa Senators | Boston Bruins | 2-0 |
| 1928 | New York Rangers | Montreal Maroons | 3-2 |
| 1929 | Boston Bruins | New York Rangers | 2-0 |
| 1930 | Montreal Canadiens | Boston Bruins | 2-0 |
| 1931 | Montreal Canadiens | Chicago Black Hawks | 3-2 |
| 1932 | Toronto Maple Leafs | New York Rangers | 3-0 |
| 1933 | New York Rangers | Toronto Maple Leafs | 3-1 |
| 1934 | Chicago Black Hawks | Detroit Red Wings | 3-1 |
| 1935 | Montreal Maroons | Toronto Maple Leafs | 3-0 |
| 1936 | Detroit Red Wings | Toronto Maple Leafs | 3-1 |
| 1937 | Detroit Red Wings | New York Rangers | 3-2 |
| 1938 | Chicago Black Hawks | Toronto Maple Leafs | 3-1 |
| 1939 | Boston Bruins | Toronto Maple Leafs | 4-1 |
| 1940 | New York Rangers | Toronto Maple Leafs | 4-2 |
| 1941 | Boston Bruins | Detroit Red Wings | 4-0 |
| 1942 | Toronto Maple Leafs | Detroit Red Wings | 4-3 |
| 1943 | Detroit Red Wings | Boston Bruins | 4-0 |
| 1944 | Montreal Canadiens | Chicago Black Hawks | 4-0 |
| 1945 | Toronto Maple Leafs | Detroit Red Wings | 4-3 |
| 1946 | Montreal Canadiens | Boston Bruins | 4-1 |
| 1947 | Toronto Maple Leafs | Montreal Canadiens | 4-2 |
| 1948 | Toronto Maple Leafs | Detroit Red Wings | 4-0 |
| 1949 | Toronto Maple Leafs | Detroit Red Wings | 4-0 |
| 1950 | Detroit Red Wings | New York Rangers | 4-3 |
| 1951 | Toronto Maple Leafs | Montreal Canadiens | 4-1 |
| 1952 | Detroit Red Wings | Montreal Canadiens | 4-0 |
| 1953 | Montreal Canadiens | Boston Bruins | 4-1 |
| 1954 | Detroit Red Wings | Montreal Canadiens | 4-3 |
| 1955 | Detroit Red Wings | Montreal Canadiens | 4-3 |
| 1956 | Montreal Canadiens | Detroit Red Wings | 4-1 |
| 1957 | Montreal Canadiens | Boston Bruins | 4-1 |
| 1958 | Montreal Canadiens | Boston Bruins | 4-2 |
| 1959 | Montreal Canadiens | Toronto Maple Leafs | 4-1 |
| 1960 | Montreal Canadiens | Toronto Maple Leafs | 4-0 |
| 1961 | Chicago Black Hawks | Detroit Red Wings | 4-2 |
| 1962 | Toronto Maple Leafs | Chicago Black Hawks | 4-2 |
| 1963 | Toronto Maple Leafs | Detroit Red Wings | 4-1 |
| 1964 | Toronto Maple Leafs | Detroit Red Wings | 4-3 |
| 1965 | Montreal Canadiens | Chicago Black Hawks | 4-3 |
| 1966 | Montreal Canadiens | Detroit Red Wings | 4-2 |
| 1967 | Toronto Maple Leafs | Montreal Canadiens | 4-2 |
| 1968 | Montreal Canadiens | St. Louis Blues | 4-0 |
| 1969 | Montreal Canadiens | St. Louis Blues | 4-0 |
| 1970 | Boston Bruins | St. Louis Blues | 4-0 |
| 1971 | Montreal Canadiens | Chicago Black Hawks | 4-3 |
| 1972 | Boston Bruins | New York Rangers | 4-2 |
| 1973 | Montreal Canadiens | Chicago Black Hawks | 4-2 |
| 1974 | Philadelphia Flyers | Boston Bruins | 4-2 |
| 1975 | Philadelphia Flyers | Buffalo Sabres | 4-2 |
| 1976 | Montreal Canadiens | Philadelphia Flyers | 4-0 |
| 1977 | Montreal Canadiens | Boston Bruins | 4-0 |
| 1978 | Montreal Canadiens | Boston Bruins | 4-2 |
| 1979 | Montreal Canadiens | New York Rangers | 4-1 |
| 1980 | New York Islanders | Philadelphia Flyers | 4-2 |
| 1981 | New York Islanders | Minnesota North Stars | 4-1 |
| 1982 | New York Islanders | Vancouver Canucks | 4-0 |
| 1983 | New York Islanders | Edmonton Oilers | 4-0 |
| 1984 | Edmonton Oilers | New York Islanders | 4-1 |
| 1985 | Edmonton Oilers | Philadelphia Flyers | 4-1 |
| 1986 | Montreal Canadiens | Calgary Flames | 4-1 |
| 1987 | Edmonton Oilers | Philadelphia Flyers | 4-3 |
| 1988 | Edmonton Oilers | Boston Bruins | 4-0 |
| 1989 | Calgary Flames | Montreal Canadiens | 4-2 |

## Stanley Cup (continued)

| YEAR | WINNER | RUNNER-UP | RESULTS |
|------|--------|-----------|---------|
| 1990 | Edmonton Oilers | Boston Bruins | 4–1 |
| 1991 | Pittsburgh Penguins | Minnesota North Stars | 4–2 |
| 1992 | Pittsburgh Penguins | Chicago Blackhawks | 4–0 |
| 1993 | Montreal Canadiens | Los Angeles Kings | 4–1 |
| 1994 | New York Rangers | Vancouver Canucks | 4–3 |
| 1995 | New Jersey Devils | Detroit Red Wings | 4–0 |
| 1996 | Colorado Avalanche | Florida Panthers | 4–0 |
| 1997 | Detroit Red Wings | Philadelphia Flyers | 4–0 |
| 1998 | Detroit Red Wings | Washington Capitals | 4–0 |
| 1999 | Dallas Stars | Buffalo Sabres | 4–2 |
| 2000 | New Jersey Devils | Dallas Stars | 4–2 |
| 2001 | Colorado Avalanche | New Jersey Devils | 4–3 |
| 2002 | Detroit Red Wings | Carolina Hurricanes | 4–1 |
| 2003 | New Jersey Devils | Mighty Ducks of Anaheim | 4–3 |
| 2004 | Tampa Bay Lightning | Calgary Flames | 4–3 |
| 2005 | not held | | |
| 2006 | Carolina Hurricanes | Edmonton Oilers | 4–3 |
| 2007 | Anaheim Ducks | Ottawa Senators | 4–1 |
| 2008 | Detroit Red Wings | Pittsburgh Penguins | 4–2 |
| 2009 | Pittsburgh Penguins | Detroit Red Wings | 4–3 |
| 2010 | Chicago Blackhawks | Philadelphia Flyers | 4–2 |
| 2011 | Boston Bruins | Vancouver Canucks | 4–3 |
| 2012 | Los Angeles Kings | New Jersey Devils | 4–2 |

[1]Though Victoria defeated Quebec in challenge games, Victoria's win was not officially recognized.    [2]Series between Montreal Canadiens and Seattle Metropolitans called off because of flu epidemic.

# Marathon

The marathon is a long-distance footrace first held at the revival of the Olympic Games at Athens in 1896. It commemorates the legendary feat of a Greek soldier who, in 490 BC, is supposed to have run from Marathon to Athens, a distance of about 40 km (25 mi), to bring news of the Athenian victory over the Persians. In 1924 the **Olympic marathon distance** was standardized at 42,195 m, or 26 mi 385 yd. The marathon was added to the **women's Olympic program** in 1984. Because marathon courses are not of equal difficulty, the **International Association of Athletics Federations** does not list a world record for the event. One of the most prestigious marathons is the **Boston Marathon**, held annually since 1897. The **New York City Marathon** also attracts participants from many countries, as does the **Chicago Marathon**.

**Related Web sites:**

Boston Marathon: <www.bostonmarathon.org>;
New York City Marathon: <www.ingnycmarathon.org>;
Chicago Marathon: <www.chicagomarathon.com>.

## Boston Marathon

*Times are given in hours:minutes:seconds.*

### men

| YEAR | WINNER | TIME | YEAR | WINNER | TIME |
|------|--------|------|------|--------|------|
| 1897 | John J. McDermott (USA) | 2:55:10 | 1915 | Edouard Fabre (CAN) | 2:31:41 |
| 1898 | Ronald J. McDonald (CAN) | 2:42:00 | 1916 | Arthur V. Roth (USA) | 2:27:16 |
| 1899 | Lawrence J. Brignoli (USA) | 2:54:38 | 1917 | William K. Kennedy (USA) | 2:28:37 |
| 1900 | John J. Caffrey (CAN) | 2:39:44 | 1918 | not held | |
| 1901 | John J. Caffrey (CAN) | 2:29:23 | 1919 | Carl W.A. Linder (USA) | 2:29:13 |
| 1902 | Sammy A. Mellor (USA) | 2:43:12 | 1920 | Peter Trivoulides (USA) | 2:29:31 |
| 1903 | John C. Lorden (USA) | 2:41:29 | 1921 | Frank Zuna (USA) | 2:18:57 |
| 1904 | Michael Spring (USA) | 2:39:04 | 1922 | Clarence H. DeMar (USA) | 2:18:10 |
| 1905 | Frederick Lorz (USA) | 2:38:25 | 1923 | Clarence H. DeMar (USA) | 2:23:47 |
| 1906 | Tim Ford (USA) | 2:45:45 | 1924 | Clarence H. DeMar (USA) | 2:29:40 |
| 1907 | Thomas Longboat (CAN) | 2:24:24 | 1925 | Charles L. Mellor (USA) | 2:33:06 |
| 1908 | Thomas P. Morrissey (USA) | 2:25:43 | 1926 | John C. Miles (CAN) | 2:25:40 |
| 1909 | Henri Renaud (USA) | 2:53:36 | 1927 | Clarence H. DeMar (USA) | 2:40:22 |
| 1910 | Fred L. Cameron (CAN) | 2:28:52 | 1928 | Clarence H. DeMar (USA) | 2:37:07 |
| 1911 | Clarence H. DeMar (USA) | 2:21:39 | 1929 | John C. Miles (CAN) | 2:33:08 |
| 1912 | Michael J. Ryan (USA) | 2:21:18 | 1930 | Clarence H. DeMar (USA) | 2:34:48 |
| 1913 | Fritz Carlson (USA) | 2:25:14 | 1931 | James P. Hennigan (USA) | 2:46:45 |
| 1914 | James Duffy (CAN) | 2:25:01 | 1932 | Paul DeBruyn (GER) | 2:33:36 |

# Boston Marathon (continued)

## men (continued)

| YEAR | WINNER | TIME | YEAR | WINNER | TIME |
|------|--------|------|------|--------|------|
| 1933 | Leslie S. Pawson (USA) | 2:31:01 | 1973 | Jon Anderson (USA) | 2:16:03 |
| 1934 | Dave Komonen (CAN) | 2:32:53 | 1974 | Neil Cusack (USA) | 2:13:39 |
| 1935 | John A. Kelley (USA) | 2:32:07 | 1975 | Bill Rodgers (USA) | 2:09:55 |
| 1936 | Ellison M. Brown (USA) | 2:33:40 | 1976 | Jack Fultz (USA) | 2:20:19 |
| 1937 | Walter Young (CAN) | 2:33:20 | 1977 | Jerome Drayton (CAN) | 2:14:46 |
| 1938 | Leslie S. Pawson (USA) | 2:35:34 | 1978 | Bill Rodgers (USA) | 2:10:13 |
| 1939 | Ellison M. Brown (USA) | 2:28:51 | 1979 | Bill Rodgers (USA) | 2:09:27 |
| 1940 | Gerard Cote (CAN) | 2:28:28 | 1980 | Bill Rodgers (USA) | 2:12:11 |
| 1941 | Leslie S. Pawson (USA) | 2:30:38 | 1981 | Seko Toshihiko (JPN) | 2:09:26 |
| 1942 | Joe Smith (USA) | 2:26:51 | 1982 | Alberto Salazar (USA) | 2:08:51 |
| 1943 | Gerard Cote (CAN) | 2:28:25 | 1983 | Greg A. Meyer (USA) | 2:09:00 |
| 1944 | Gerard Cote (CAN) | 2:31:50 | 1984 | Geoff Smith (GBR) | 2:10:34 |
| 1945 | John A. Kelley (USA) | 2:30:40 | 1985 | Geoff Smith (GBR) | 2:14:05 |
| 1946 | Stylianos Kyriakides (GRE) | 2:29:27 | 1986 | Robert de Castella (AUS) | 2:07:51 |
| 1947 | Suh Yun Bok (KOR) | 2:25:39 | 1987 | Seko Toshihiko (JPN) | 2:11:50 |
| 1948 | Gerard Cote (CAN) | 2:31:02 | 1988 | Ibrahim Hussein (KEN) | 2:08:43 |
| 1949 | Karl G. Leandersson (SWE) | 2:31:50 | 1989 | Abebe Mekonnen (ETH) | 2:09:06 |
| 1950 | Ham Kee Yong (KOR) | 2:32:39 | 1990 | Gelindo Bordin (ITA) | 2:08:19 |
| 1951 | Tanaka Shigeki (JPN) | 2:27:45 | 1991 | Ibrahim Hussein (KEN) | 2:11:06 |
| 1952 | Doroteo Flores (GUA) | 2:31:53 | 1992 | Ibrahim Hussein (KEN) | 2:08:14 |
| 1953 | Yamada Keizo (JPN) | 2:18:51 | 1993 | Cosmas N'Deti (KEN) | 2:09:33 |
| 1954 | Veikko L. Karanen (FIN) | 2:20:39 | 1994 | Cosmas N'Deti (KEN) | 2:07:15 |
| 1955 | Hamamura Hideo (JPN) | 2:18:22 | 1995 | Cosmas N'Deti (KEN) | 2:09:22 |
| 1956 | Antti Viskari (FIN) | 2:14:14 | 1996 | Moses Tanui (KEN) | 2:09:16 |
| 1957 | John J. Kelley (USA) | 2:20:05 | 1997 | Lameck Aguta (KEN) | 2:10:34 |
| 1958 | Franjo Mihalic (YUG) | 2:25:54 | 1998 | Moses Tanui (KEN) | 2:07:34 |
| 1959 | Eino Oksanen (FIN) | 2:22:42 | 1999 | Joseph Chebet (KEN) | 2:09:52 |
| 1960 | Paavo Kotila (FIN) | 2:20:54 | 2000 | Elijah Lagat (KEN) | 2:09:47 |
| 1961 | Eino Oksanen (FIN) | 2:23:39 | 2001 | Lee Bong Ju (KOR) | 2:09:43 |
| 1962 | Eino Oksanen (FIN) | 2:23:48 | 2002 | Rodgers Rop (KEN) | 2:09:02 |
| 1963 | Aurele Vandendriessche (BEL) | 2:18:58 | 2003 | Robert Kipkoech Cheruiyot (KEN) | 2:10:11 |
| 1964 | Aurele Vandendriessche (BEL) | 2:19:59 | 2004 | Timothy Cherigat (KEN) | 2:10:37 |
| 1965 | Shigematsu Morio (JPN) | 2:16:33 | 2005 | Hailu Negussie (ETH) | 2:11:45 |
| 1966 | Kimihara Kenji (JPN) | 2:17:11 | 2006 | Robert Kipkoech Cheruiyot (KEN) | 2:07:14 |
| 1967 | David McKenzie (NZL) | 2:15:45 | 2007 | Robert Kipkoech Cheruiyot (KEN) | 2:14:13 |
| 1968 | Amby Burfoot (USA) | 2:22:17 | 2008 | Robert Kipkoech Cheruiyot (KEN) | 2:07:46 |
| 1969 | Unetani Yoshiaki (JPN) | 2:13:49 | 2009 | Deriba Merga (ETH) | 2:08:42 |
| 1970 | Ron Hill (GBR) | 2:10:30 | 2010 | Robert Kiprono Cheruiyot (KEN) | 2:05:52 |
| 1971 | Alvaro Mejia (COL) | 2:18:45 | 2011 | Geoffrey Mutai (KEN) | 2:03:02 |
| 1972 | Olavi Suomalainen (FIN) | 2:15:30 | 2012 | Wesley Korir (KEN) | 2:12:40 |

## women

| YEAR | WINNER | TIME | YEAR | WINNER | TIME |
|------|--------|------|------|--------|------|
| 1972 | Nina Kuscsik (USA) | 3:10:26 | 1993 | Olga Markova (RUS) | 2:25:27 |
| 1973 | Jacqueline Hansen (USA) | 3:05:59 | 1994 | Uta Pippig (GER) | 2:21:45 |
| 1974 | Michiko Gorman (USA) | 2:47:11 | 1995 | Uta Pippig (GER) | 2:25:11 |
| 1975 | Liane Winter (FRG) | 2:42:24 | 1996 | Uta Pippig (GER) | 2:27:12 |
| 1976 | Kim Merritt (USA) | 2:47:10 | 1997 | Fatuma Roba (ETH) | 2:26:23 |
| 1977 | Michiko Gorman (USA) | 2:46:22 | 1998 | Fatuma Roba (ETH) | 2:23:21 |
| 1978 | Gayle S. Barron (USA) | 2:44:52 | 1999 | Fatuma Roba (ETH) | 2:23:25 |
| 1979 | Joan Benoit (USA) | 2:35:15 | 2000 | Catherine Ndereba (KEN) | 2:26:11 |
| 1980 | Jacqueline Gareau (CAN) | 2:34:28 | 2001 | Catherine Ndereba (KEN) | 2:23:53 |
| 1981 | Allison Roe (NZL) | 2:26:46 | 2002 | Margaret Okayo (KEN) | 2:20:43 |
| 1982 | Charlotte Teske (FRG) | 2:29:33 | 2003 | Svetlana Zakharova (RUS) | 2:25:20 |
| 1983 | Joan Benoit (USA) | 2:22:42 | 2004 | Catherine Ndereba (KEN) | 2:24:27 |
| 1984 | Lorraine Moller (NZL) | 2:29:28 | 2005 | Catherine Ndereba (KEN) | 2:25:13 |
| 1985 | Lisa Larsen (USA) | 2:34:06 | 2006 | Rita Jeptoo (KEN) | 2:23:38 |
| 1986 | Ingrid Kristiansen (NOR) | 2:24:55 | 2007 | Lidiya Grigoryeva (RUS) | 2:29:18 |
| 1987 | Rosa Mota (POR) | 2:25:21 | 2008 | Dire Tune (ETH) | 2:25:25 |
| 1988 | Rosa Mota (POR) | 2:24:30 | 2009 | Salina Kosgei (KEN) | 2:32:16 |
| 1989 | Ingrid Kristiansen (NOR) | 2:24:33 | 2010 | Teyba Erkesso (ETH) | 2:26:11 |
| 1990 | Rosa Mota (POR) | 2:25:23 | 2011 | Caroline Kilel (KEN) | 2:22:36 |
| 1991 | Wanda Panfil (POL) | 2:24:18 | 2012 | Sharon Cherop (KEN) | 2:31:50 |
| 1992 | Olga Markova (RUS) | 2:23:43 | | | |

## New York City Marathon

*Times are given in hours:minutes:seconds.*

| YEAR | MEN | TIME | WOMEN | TIME |
|------|-----|------|-------|------|
| 1970 | Gary Muhrcke (USA) | 2:31:38 | no finisher | |
| 1971 | Norm Higgins (USA) | 2:22:54 | Beth Bonner (USA) | 2:55:22 |
| 1972 | Robert Karlin (USA) | 2:27:52 | Nina Kuscsik (USA) | 3:08:41 |
| 1973 | Tom Fleming (USA) | 2:21:54 | Nina Kuscsik (USA) | 2:57:07 |
| 1974 | Norbert Sander (USA) | 2:26:30 | Katherine Switzer (USA) | 3:07:29 |
| 1975 | Tom Fleming (USA) | 2:19:27 | Kim Merritt (USA) | 2:46:14 |
| 1976 | Bill Rodgers (USA) | 2:10:09 | Michiko Gorman (USA) | 2:39:11 |
| 1977 | Bill Rodgers (USA) | 2:11:28 | Michiko Gorman (USA) | 2:43:10 |
| 1978 | Bill Rodgers (USA) | 2:12:12 | Grete Waitz (NOR) | 2:32:30 |
| 1979 | Bill Rodgers (USA) | 2:11:42 | Grete Waitz (NOR) | 2:27:33 |
| 1980 | Alberto Salazar (USA) | 2:09:41 | Grete Waitz (NOR) | 2:25:41 |
| 1981 | Alberto Salazar (USA) | 2:08:13 | Allison Roe (NZL) | 2:25:29 |
| 1982 | Alberto Salazar (USA) | 2:09:29 | Grete Waitz (NOR) | 2:27:14 |
| 1983 | Rod Dixon (NZL) | 2:08:59 | Grete Waitz (NOR) | 2:27:00 |
| 1984 | Orlando Pizzolato (ITA) | 2:14:53 | Grete Waitz (NOR) | 2:29:30 |
| 1985 | Orlando Pizzolato (ITA) | 2:11:34 | Grete Waitz (NOR) | 2:28:34 |
| 1986 | Gianni Poli (ITA) | 2:11:06 | Grete Waitz (NOR) | 2:28:06 |
| 1987 | Ibrahim Hussein (KEN) | 2:11:01 | Priscilla Welch (GBR) | 2:30:17 |
| 1988 | Steve Jones (GBR) | 2:08:20 | Grete Waitz (NOR) | 2:28:07 |
| 1989 | Juma Ikangaa (TAN) | 2:08:01 | Ingrid Kristiansen (NOR) | 2:25:30 |
| 1990 | Douglas Wakiihuri (KEN) | 2:12:39 | Wanda Panfil (POL) | 2:30:45 |
| 1991 | Salvador Garcia (MEX) | 2:09:28 | Liz McColgan (GBR) | 2:27:23 |
| 1992 | Willie Mtolo (RSA) | 2:09:29 | Lisa Ondieki (AUS) | 2:24:40 |
| 1993 | Andrés Espinosa (MEX) | 2:10:04 | Uta Pippig (GER) | 2:26:24 |
| 1994 | German Silva (MEX) | 2:11:21 | Tegla Loroupe (KEN) | 2:27:37 |
| 1995 | German Silva (MEX) | 2:11:00 | Tegla Loroupe (KEN) | 2:28:06 |
| 1996 | Giacomo Leone (ITA) | 2:09:54 | Anuta Catuna (ROM) | 2:28:18 |
| 1997 | John Kagwe (KEN) | 2:08:12 | Franziska Rochat-Moser (SUI) | 2:28:43 |
| 1998 | John Kagwe (KEN) | 2:08:45 | Franca Fiacconi (ITA) | 2:25:17 |
| 1999 | Joseph Chebet (KEN) | 2:09:14 | Adriana Fernández (MEX) | 2:25:06 |
| 2000 | Abdelkhader El Mouaziz (MAR) | 2:10:09 | Lyudmila Petrova (RUS) | 2:25:45 |
| 2001 | Tesfaye Jifar (ETH) | 2:07:43 | Margaret Okayo (KEN) | 2:24:21 |
| 2002 | Rodgers Rop (KEN) | 2:08:07 | Joyce Chepchumba (KEN) | 2:25:56 |
| 2003 | Martin Lel (KEN) | 2:10:30 | Margaret Okayo (KEN) | 2:22:31 |
| 2004 | Hendrik Ramaala (RSA) | 2:09:28 | Paula Radcliffe (GBR) | 2:23:10 |
| 2005 | Paul Tergat (KEN) | 2:09:30 | Jelena Prokopcuka (LAT) | 2:24:41 |
| 2006 | Marílson Gomes dos Santos (BRA) | 2:09:58 | Jelena Prokopcuka (LAT) | 2:25:05 |
| 2007 | Martin Lel (KEN) | 2:09:04 | Paula Radcliffe (GBR) | 2:23:09 |
| 2008 | Marílson Gomes dos Santos (BRA) | 2:08:43 | Paula Radcliffe (GBR) | 2:23:56 |
| 2009 | Meb Keflezighi (USA) | 2:09:15 | Derartu Tulu (ETH) | 2:28:52 |
| 2010 | Gebre Gebremariam (ETH) | 2:08:14 | Edna Kiplagat (KEN) | 2:28:20 |
| 2011 | Geoffrey Mutai (KEN) | 2:05:06 | Firehiwot Dado (ETH) | 2:23:15 |

## Chicago Marathon

*Times are given in hours:minutes:seconds.*

| YEAR | MEN | TIME | WOMEN | TIME |
|------|-----|------|-------|------|
| 1977 | Dan Cloeter (USA) | 2:17:52 | Dorothy Doolittle (USA) | 2:50:47 |
| 1978 | Mark Stanforth (USA) | 2:19:20 | Lynae Larson (USA) | 2:59:25 |
| 1979 | Dan Cloeter (USA) | 2:23:20 | Laura Michalek (USA) | 3:15:45 |
| 1980 | Frank Richardson (USA) | 2:14:04 | Sue Petersen (USA) | 2:45:03 |
| 1981 | Philip Coppess (USA) | 2:16:13 | Tina Gandy (USA) | 2:49:39 |
| 1982 | Greg Meyer (USA) | 2:10:59 | Nancy Conz (USA) | 2:33:23 |
| 1983 | Joseph Nzau (KEN) | 2:09:44 | Rosa Mota (POR) | 2:31:12 |
| 1984 | Steve Jones (GBR) | 2:08:05 | Rosa Mota (POR) | 2:26:01 |
| 1985 | Steve Jones (GBR) | 2:07:13 | Joan Benoit Samuelson (USA) | 2:21:21 |
| 1986 | Toshihiko Seko (JPN) | 2:08:27 | Ingrid Kristiansen (NOR) | 2:27:08 |
| 1987 | not held | | | |
| 1988 | Alejandro Cruz (MEX) | 2:08:57 | Lisa Weidenbach (USA) | 2:29:17 |
| 1989 | Paul Davis-Hale (GBR) | 2:11:25 | Lisa Weidenbach (USA) | 2:28:15 |
| 1990 | Martín Pitayo (MEX) | 2:09:41 | Aurora Cunha (POR) | 2:30:11 |
| 1991 | Joseildo Rocha (BRA) | 2:14:33 | Midde Hamrin-Senorski (SWE) | 2:36:21 |
| 1992 | José César de Souza (BRA) | 2:16:14 | Linda Somers (USA) | 2:37:41 |
| 1993 | Luiz Antônio dos Santos (BRA) | 2:13:15 | Ritva Lemettinen (FIN) | 2:33:18 |
| 1994 | Luiz Antônio dos Santos (BRA) | 2:11:16 | Kristy Johnston (USA) | 2:31:34 |
| 1995 | Eamonn Martin (GBR) | 2:11:18 | Ritva Lemettinen (FIN) | 2:28:27 |
| 1996 | Paul Evans (GBR) | 2:08:52 | Marian Sutton (GBR) | 2:30:41 |

## Chicago Marathon (continued)

| YEAR | MEN | TIME | WOMEN | TIME |
|------|-----|------|-------|------|
| 1997 | Khalid Khannouchi (MAR) | 2:07:10 | Marian Sutton (GBR) | 2:29:03 |
| 1998 | Ondoro Osoro (KEN) | 2:06:54 | Joyce Chepchumba (KEN) | 2:23:57 |
| 1999 | Khalid Khannouchi (MAR) | 2:05:42 | Joyce Chepchumba (KEN) | 2:25:59 |
| 2000 | Khalid Khannouchi (USA) | 2:07:01 | Catherine Ndereba (KEN) | 2:21:33 |
| 2001 | Ben Kimondiu (KEN) | 2:08:52 | Catherine Ndereba (KEN) | 2:18:47 |
| 2002 | Khalid Khannouchi (USA) | 2:05:56 | Paula Radcliffe (GBR) | 2:17:18 |
| 2003 | Evans Rutto (KEN) | 2:05:50 | Svetlana Zakharova (RUS) | 2:23:07 |
| 2004 | Evans Rutto (KEN) | 2:06:16 | Constantina Tomescu-Dita (ROM) | 2:23:45 |
| 2005 | Felix Limo (KEN) | 2:07:02 | Deena Kastor (USA) | 2:21:25 |
| 2006 | Robert Kipkoech Cheruiyot (KEN) | 2:07:35 | Berhane Adere (ETH) | 2:20:42 |
| 2007 | Patrick Ivuti (KEN) | 2:11:11 | Berhane Adere (ETH) | 2:33:49 |
| 2008 | Evans Cheruiyot (KEN) | 2:06:25 | Lidiya Grigoryeva (RUS) | 2:27:17 |
| 2009 | Sammy Wanjiru (KEN) | 2:05:41 | Liliya Shobukhova (RUS) | 2:25:56 |
| 2010 | Sammy Wanjiru (KEN) | 2:06:24 | Liliya Shobukhova (RUS) | 2:20:25 |
| 2011 | Moses Mosop (KEN) | 2:05:37 | Liliya Shobukhova (RUS) | 2:18:20 |

# Skiing

The first internationally organized **skiing championships** took place in 1924. From 1924 to 1931 only **Nordic** competition was involved; **Alpine** championship events were added to world competition in 1931 and to the Olympics in 1936. **Events** include cross-country races, ski jumping, biathlon, and relay races (Nordic) and downhill and slalom skiing (Alpine). Since 1967, an **Alpine World Cup** has been presented to the competitor with the best combined downhill, slalom, giant slalom, and supergiant slalom (super-G) performance over a series of major contests. A **Nordic World Cup** for cross-country events has been awarded since 1979.

**International Ski Federation (FIS) Web site:** <www.fis-ski.com>.

## Alpine Skiing World Championships—Men
*Held since 1931. Table shows results for the past 20 years.*

**DOWNHILL**
| | |
|---|---|
| 1992[1] | Patrick Ortlieb (AUS) |
| 1993 | Urs Lehmann (SUI) |
| 1994[1] | Tommy Moe (USA) |
| 1995 | *not held* |
| 1996 | Patrick Ortlieb (AUS) |
| 1997 | Bruno Kernen (SUI) |
| 1998[1] | Jean-Luc Cretier (FRA) |
| 1999 | Hermann Maier (AUT) |
| 2001 | Hannes Trinkl (AUT) |
| 2002[1] | Fritz Strobl (AUT) |
| 2003 | Michael Walchhofer (AUT) |
| 2005 | Bode Miller (USA) |
| 2006[1] | Antoine Dénériaz (FRA) |
| 2007 | Aksel Lund Svindal (NOR) |
| 2009 | John Kucera (CAN) |
| 2010[1] | Didier Defago (SUI) |
| 2011 | Erik Guay (CAN) |

**COMBINED**
| | |
|---|---|
| 1992[1] | Josef Polig (ITA) |
| 1993 | Lasse Kjus (NOR) |
| 1994[1] | Lasse Kjus (NOR) |
| 1995 | *not held* |
| 1996 | Marc Girardelli (LUX) |
| 1997 | Kjetil André Aamodt (NOR) |
| 1998[1] | Mario Reiter (AUT) |
| 1999 | Kjetil André Aamodt (NOR) |
| 2001 | Kjetil André Aamodt (NOR) |
| 2002[1] | Kjetil André Aamodt (NOR) |
| 2003 | Bode Miller (USA) |
| 2005 | Benjamin Raich (AUT) |
| 2006[1] | Ted Ligety (USA) |

**COMBINED (CONTINUED)**
| | |
|---|---|
| 2007 | Daniel Albrecht (SUI) |
| 2009 | Aksel Lund Svindal (NOR) |
| 2010[1] | Bode Miller (USA) |
| 2011 | Aksel Lund Svindal (NOR) |

**SLALOM**
| | |
|---|---|
| 1993 | Kjetil André Aamodt (NOR) |
| 1994[1] | Thomas Stangassinger (AUT) |
| 1995 | *not held* |
| 1996 | Alberto Tomba (ITA) |
| 1997 | Tom Stiansen (NOR) |
| 1998[1] | Hans Petter Buraas (NOR) |
| 1999 | Kalle Palander (FIN) |
| 2001 | Mario Matt (AUT) |
| 2002[1] | Jean-Pierre Vidal (FRA) |
| 2003 | Ivica Kostelic (CRO) |
| 2005 | Benjamin Raich (AUT) |
| 2006[1] | Benjamin Raich (AUT) |
| 2007 | Mario Matt (AUT) |
| 2009 | Manfred Pranger (AUT) |
| 2010[1] | Giuliano Razzoli (ITA) |
| 2011 | Jean-Baptiste Grange (FRA) |

**GIANT SLALOM**
| | |
|---|---|
| 1992[1] | Alberto Tomba (ITA) |
| 1993 | Kjetil André Aamodt (NOR) |
| 1994[1] | Markus Wasmeier (GER) |
| 1995 | *not held* |
| 1996 | Alberto Tomba (ITA) |
| 1997 | Michael von Grünigen (SUI) |
| 1998[1] | Hermann Maier (AUT) |

**GIANT SLALOM (CONTINUED)**
| | |
|---|---|
| 1999 | Lasse Kjus (NOR) |
| 2001 | Michael von Grünigen (SUI) |
| 2002[1] | Stephan Eberharter (AUT) |
| 2003 | Bode Miller (USA) |
| 2005 | Hermann Maier (AUT) |
| 2006[1] | Benjamin Raich (AUT) |
| 2007 | Aksel Lund Svindal (NOR) |
| 2009 | Carlo Janka (SUI) |
| 2010[1] | Carlo Janka (SUI) |
| 2011 | Ted Ligety (USA) |

**SUPERGIANT SLALOM**
| | |
|---|---|
| 1992[1] | Kjetil André Aamodt (NOR) |
| 1993 | *not held* |
| 1994[1] | Markus Wasmeier (GER) |
| 1995 | *not held* |
| 1996 | Atle Skårdal (NOR) |
| 1997 | Atle Skårdal (NOR) |
| 1998[1] | Hermann Maier (AUT) |
| 1999 | Lasse Kjus (NOR), Hermann Maier (AUT) (tied) |
| 2001 | Daron Rahlves (USA) |
| 2002[1] | Kjetil André Aamodt (NOR) |
| 2003 | Stephan Eberharter (AUT) |
| 2005 | Bode Miller (USA) |
| 2006[1] | Kjetil André Aamodt (NOR) |
| 2007 | Patrick Staudacher (ITA) |
| 2009 | Didier Cuche (SUI) |
| 2010[1] | Aksel Lund Svindal (NOR) |
| 2011 | Christof Innerhofer (ITA) |

[1]*Olympic champions, recognized in this table as world champions (though not by FIS).*

# Alpine Skiing World Championships—Women

*Held since 1931. Table shows results for the past 20 years.*

**DOWNHILL**

| | |
|---|---|
| 1992[1] | Kerrin Lee-Gartner (CAN) |
| 1993 | Kate Pace (CAN) |
| 1994[1] | Katja Seizinger (GER) |
| 1995 | *not held* |
| 1996 | Picabo Street (USA) |
| 1997 | Hilary Lindh (USA) |
| 1998[1] | Katja Seizinger (GER) |
| 1999 | Renate Götschl (AUT) |
| 2001 | Michaela Dorfmeister (AUT) |
| 2002[1] | Carole Montillet (FRA) |
| 2003 | Mélanie Turgeon (CAN) |
| 2005 | Janica Kostelic (CRO) |
| 2006[1] | Michaela Dorfmeister (AUT) |
| 2007 | Anja Pärson (SWE) |
| 2009 | Lindsey Vonn (USA) |
| 2010[1] | Lindsey Vonn (USA) |
| 2011 | Elisabeth Görgl (AUT) |

**COMBINED**

| | |
|---|---|
| 1992[1] | Petra Kronberger (AUT) |
| 1993 | Miriam Vogt (GER) |
| 1994[1] | Pernilla Wiberg (SWE) |
| 1995 | *not held* |
| 1996 | Pernilla Wiberg (SWE) |
| 1997 | Renate Götschl (AUT) |
| 1998[1] | Katja Seizinger (GER) |
| 1999 | Pernilla Wiberg (SWE) |
| 2001 | Martina Ertl (GER) |
| 2002[1] | Janica Kostelic (CRO) |
| 2003 | Janica Kostelic (CRO) |
| 2005 | Janica Kostelic (CRO) |
| 2006[1] | Janica Kostelic (CRO) |
| 2007 | Anja Pärson (SWE) |
| 2009 | Kathrin Zettel (AUT) |

**COMBINED (CONTINUED)**

| | |
|---|---|
| 2010[1] | Maria Riesch (GER) |
| 2011 | Anna Fenninger (AUT) |

**SLALOM**

| | |
|---|---|
| 1992[1] | Petra Kronberger (AUT) |
| 1993 | Karin Buder (AUT) |
| 1994[1] | Vreni Schneider (SUI) |
| 1995 | *not held* |
| 1996 | Pernilla Wiberg (SWE) |
| 1997 | Deborah Compagnoni (ITA) |
| 1998[1] | Hilde Gerg (GER) |
| 1999 | Zali Steggall (AUS) |
| 2001 | Anja Pärson (SWE) |
| 2002[1] | Janica Kostelic (CRO) |
| 2003 | Janica Kostelic (CRO) |
| 2005 | Janica Kostelic (CRO) |
| 2006[1] | Anja Pärson (SWE) |
| 2007 | Sarka Zahrobska (CZE) |
| 2009 | Maria Riesch (GER) |
| 2010[1] | Maria Riesch (GER) |
| 2011 | Marlies Schild (AUT) |

**GIANT SLALOM**

| | |
|---|---|
| 1992[1] | Pernilla Wiberg (SWE) |
| 1993 | Carole Merle (FRA) |
| 1994[1] | Deborah Compagnoni (ITA) |
| 1995 | *not held* |
| 1996 | Deborah Compagnoni (ITA) |
| 1997 | Deborah Compagnoni (ITA) |
| 1998[1] | Deborah Compagnoni (ITA) |

**GIANT SLALOM (CONTINUED)**

| | |
|---|---|
| 1999 | Alexandra Meissnitzer (AUT) |
| 2001 | Sonja Nef (SUI) |
| 2002[1] | Janica Kostelic (CRO) |
| 2003 | Anja Pärson (SWE) |
| 2005 | Anja Pärson (SWE) |
| 2006[1] | Julia Mancuso (USA) |
| 2007 | Nicole Hosp (AUT) |
| 2009 | Kathrin Hölzl (GER) |
| 2010[1] | Viktoria Rebensburg (GER) |
| 2011 | Tina Maze (SLO) |

**SUPERGIANT SLALOM**

| | |
|---|---|
| 1992[1] | Deborah Compagnoni (ITA) |
| 1993 | Katja Seizinger (GER) |
| 1994[1] | Diann Roffe-Steinrotter (USA) |
| 1995 | *not held* |
| 1996 | Isolde Kostner (ITA) |
| 1997 | Isolde Kostner (ITA) |
| 1998[1] | Picabo Street (USA) |
| 1999 | Alexandra Meissnitzer (AUT) |
| 2001 | Régine Cavagnoud (FRA) |
| 2002[1] | Daniela Ceccarelli (ITA) |
| 2003 | Michaela Dorfmeister (AUT) |
| 2005 | Anja Pärson (SWE) |
| 2006[1] | Michaela Dorfmeister (AUT) |
| 2007 | Anja Pärson (SWE) |
| 2009 | Lindsey Vonn (USA) |
| 2010[1] | Andrea Fischbacher (AUT) |
| 2011 | Elisabeth Görgl (AUT) |

[1]*Olympic champions, recognized in this table as world champions (though not by FIS).*

# Alpine World Cup

*The winner is determined by the number of points awarded for finishes in various competitions during the season.*

| YEAR | MEN | WOMEN | YEAR | MEN | WOMEN |
|---|---|---|---|---|---|
| 1967 | Jean-Claude Killy (FRA) | Nancy Greene (CAN) | 1981 | Phil Mahre (USA) | Marie-Thérèse Nadig (SUI) |
| 1968 | Jean-Claude Killy (FRA) | Nancy Greene (CAN) | 1982 | Phil Mahre (USA) | Erika Hess (SUI) |
| 1969 | Karl Schranz (AUT) | Gertrude Gabl (AUT) | 1983 | Phil Mahre (USA) | Tamara McKinney (USA) |
| 1970 | Karl Schranz (AUT) | Michele Jacot (FRA) | | | |
| 1971 | Gustavo Thöni (ITA) | Annemarie Pröll (AUT) | 1984 | Pirmin Zurbriggen (SUI) | Erika Hess (SUI) |
| 1972 | Gustavo Thöni (ITA) | Annemarie Pröll (AUT) | 1985 | Marc Girardelli (LUX) | Michela Figini (SUI) |
| | | | 1986 | Marc Girardelli (LUX) | Maria Walliser (SUI) |
| 1973 | Gustavo Thöni (ITA) | Annemarie Pröll (AUT) | 1987 | Pirmin Zurbriggen (SUI) | Maria Walliser (SUI) |
| | | | 1988 | Pirmin Zurbriggen (SUI) | Michela Figini (SUI) |
| 1974 | Piero Gros (ITA) | Annemarie Moser-Pröll (AUT) | 1989 | Marc Girardelli (LUX) | Vreni Schneider (SUI) |
| 1975 | Gustavo Thöni (ITA) | Annemarie Moser-Pröll (AUT) | 1990 | Pirmin Zurbriggen (SUI) | Petra Kronberger (AUT) |
| 1976 | Ingemar Stenmark (SWE) | Rosi Mittermaier (FRG) | 1991 | Marc Girardelli (LUX) | Petra Kronberger (AUT) |
| 1977 | Ingemar Stenmark (SWE) | Lise-Marie Morerod (SUI) | 1992 | Paul Accola (SUI) | Petra Kronberger (AUT) |
| 1978 | Ingemar Stenmark (SWE) | Hanni Wenzel (LIE) | 1993 | Marc Girardelli (LUX) | Anita Wachter (AUT) |
| 1979 | Peter Luescher (SUI) | Annemarie Moser-Pröll (AUT) | 1994 | Kjetil André Aamodt (NOR) | Vreni Schneider (SUI) |
| | | | 1995 | Alberto Tomba (ITA) | Vreni Schneider (SUI) |
| 1980 | Andreas Wenzel (LIE) | Hanni Wenzel (LIE) | 1996 | Lasse Kjus (NOR) | Katja Seizinger (GER) |
| | | | 1997 | Luc Alphand (FRA) | Pernilla Wiberg (SWE) |

## Alpine World Cup (continued)

| YEAR | MEN | WOMEN | YEAR | MEN | WOMEN |
|---|---|---|---|---|---|
| 1998 | Hermann Maier (AUT) | Katja Seizinger (GER) | 2005 | Bode Miller (USA) | Anja Pärson (SWE) |
| 1999 | Lasse Kjus (NOR) | Alexandra Meiss-nitzer (AUT) | 2006 | Benjamin Raich (AUT) | Janica Kostelic (CRO) |
| | | | 2007 | Aksel Lund Svindal (NOR) | Nicole Hosp (AUT) |
| 2000 | Hermann Maier (AUT) | Renate Götschl (AUT) | | | |
| 2001 | Hermann Maier (AUT) | Janica Kostelic (CRO) | 2008 | Bode Miller (USA) | Lindsey Vonn (USA) |
| 2002 | Stephan Eberharter (AUT) | Michaela Dorf-meister (AUT) | 2009 | Aksel Lund Svindal (NOR) | Lindsey Vonn (USA) |
| 2003 | Stephan Eberharter (AUT) | Janica Kostelic (CRO) | 2010 | Carlo Janka (SUI) | Lindsey Vonn (USA) |
| | | | 2011 | Ivica Kostelic (CRO) | Maria Riesch (GER) |
| 2004 | Hermann Maier (AUT) | Anja Pärson (SWE) | 2012 | Marcel Hirscher (AUT) | Lindsey Vonn (USA) |

## Nordic Skiing World Championships—Men

*Held since 1924. Table shows results for the past 20 years.*

**INDIVIDUAL SPRINT**
2002[1] Tor Arne Hetland (NOR)
2003 Thobias Fredriksson (SWE)
2005 Vassily Rochev (RUS)
2006[1] Björn Lind (SWE)
2007 Jens Arne Svartedal (NOR)
2009 Ola Vigen Hattestad (NOR)
2010[1] Nikita Kriyukov (RUS)
2011 Marcus Hellner (SWE)

**10-KM CROSS-COUNTRY**[2]
1992[1] Vegard Ulvang (NOR)
1993 Sture Sivertsen (NOR)
1994[1] Björn Daehlie NOR)
1995 Vladimir Smirnov (KAZ)
1997 Björn Daehlie (NOR)
1998[1] Björn Daehlie (NOR)
1999 Mika Myllylä (FIN)

**15-KM CROSS-COUNTRY**[2,3]
1992[1] Björn Daehlie (NOR)
1993 Björn Daehlie (NOR)
1994[1] Björn Daehlie (NOR)
1995 Vladimir Smirnov (KAZ)
1997 Björn Daehlie (NOR)
1998[1] Thomas Alsgaard (NOR)
1999 Thomas Alsgaard (NOR)
2001 Per Elofsson (SWE)
2002[1] Andrus Veerpalu (EST)
2003 Axel Teichmann (GER)
2005 Pietro Piller Cottrer (ITA)
2006[1] Andrus Veerpalu (EST)
2007 Lars Berger (NOR)
2009 Andrus Veerpalu (EST)

**15-KM CROSS-COUNTRY**[2,3] **(CONT.)**
2010[1] Dario Cologna (SUI)
2011 Matti Heikkinen (FIN)

**COMBINED PURSUIT**[2]
2001 Per Elofsson (SWE)
2002[1] Thomas Alsgaard (NOR), Frode Estil (NOR) (tied)
2003 Per Elofsson (SWE)
2005 Vincent Vittoz (FRA)
2006[1] Yevgeny Dementyev (RUS)
2007 Axel Teichmann (GER)
2009 Petter Northug (NOR)
2010[1] Marcus Hellner (SWE)
2011 Petter Northug (NOR)

**30-KM CROSS-COUNTRY**
1992[1] Vegard Ulvang (NOR)
1993 Björn Daehlie (NOR)
1994[1] Thomas Alsgaard (NOR)
1995 Vladimir Smirnov (KAZ)
1997 Aleksey Prokurorov (RUS)
1998[1] Mika Myllylä (FIN)
1999 Mika Myllylä (FIN)
2001 Andrus Veerpalu (EST)
2002[1] Christian Hoffmann (AUT)
2003 Thomas Alsgaard (NOR)

**50-KM CROSS-COUNTRY**
1992[1] Björn Daehlie (NOR)
1993 Torgny Mogren (SWE)
1994 Vladimir Smirnov (KAZ)
1995 Silvio Fauner (ITA)
1997 Mika Myllylä (FIN)
1998[1] Björn Daehlie (NOR)
1999 Mika Myllylä (FIN)

**50-KM CROSS-COUNTRY (CONT.)**
2001 Johann Mühlegg (ESP)
2002[1] Mikhail Ivanov (RUS)
2003 Martin Koukal (CZE)
2005 Frode Estil (NOR)
2006[1] Giorgio Di Centa (ITA)
2007 Odd-Björn Hjelmeset (NOR)
2009 Petter Northug (NOR)
2010[1] Petter Northug (NOR)
2011 Petter Northug (NOR)

**TEAM SPRINT**
2005 Norway
2006[1] Sweden
2007 Italy
2009 Norway
2010[1] Norway
2011 Canada

**RELAY**[4]
1992[1] Norway
1993 Norway
1994[1] Italy
1995 Norway
1997 Norway
1998[1] Norway
1999 Austria
2001 Norway
2002[1] Norway
2003 Norway
2005 Norway
2006[1] Italy
2007 Norway
2009 Norway
2010[1] Sweden
2011 Norway

[1]*Olympic champions, recognized in this table as world champions (though not by FIS).* [2]*From 1991 to 1999, the 10-km event was held in tandem with the 15-km event; one event featured classical and the other freestyle technique. Medals were awarded for both races. Beginning in 2001 this pursuit race (skiers competing directly against each other rather than against the clock) led to one medal being awarded upon winning. The 10-km was discontinued, and the 15-km became a stand-alone event featuring classical technique. In 2001–03 the pursuit race featured two 10-km races; since then, two 15-km races.* [3]*18-km cross-country through 1952; 15-km thereafter.* [4]*Military relay until 1939; 40-km relay in 1948 and thereafter.*

## Nordic Skiing World Championships—Women

*Held since 1952. Table shows results for the past 20 years.*

**INDIVIDUAL SPRINT**
2001 Pirjo Manninen (FIN)
2002[1] Yuliya Chepalova (RUS)
2003 Marit Björgen (NOR)

**INDIVIDUAL SPRINT (CONT.)**
2005 Emilie Öhrstig (SWE)
2006[1] Chandra Crawford (CAN)
2007 Astrid Jacobsen (NOR)

**INDIVIDUAL SPRINT (CONT.)**
2009 Arianna Follis (ITA)
2010[1] Marit Björgen (NOR)
2011 Marit Björgen (NOR)

## Nordic Skiing World Championships—Women (continued)

**5-KM CROSS-COUNTRY[2]**

| | |
|---|---|
| 1992[1] | Marjut Lukkarinen (FIN) |
| 1993 | Larisa Lazutina (RUS) |
| 1994[1] | Lyubov Yegorova (RUS) |
| 1995 | Larisa Lazutina (RUS) |
| 1997 | Yelena Vyalbe (RUS) |
| 1998[1] | Larisa Lazutina (RUS) |
| 1999 | Bente Martinsen (NOR) |

**10-KM CROSS-COUNTRY[2]**

| | |
|---|---|
| 1992[1] | Lyubov Yegorova (UNT) |
| 1993 | Stefania Belmondo (ITA) |
| 1994[1] | Lyubov Yegorova (RUS) |
| 1995 | Larisa Lazutina (RUS) |
| 1997 | Stefania Belmondo (ITA) |
| 1998[1] | Larisa Lazutina (RUS) |
| 1999 | Stefania Belmondo (ITA) |
| 2001 | Bente Skari (NOR) |
| 2002[1] | Bente Skari (NOR) |
| 2003 | Bente Skari (NOR) |
| 2005 | Katerina Neumannova (CZE) |
| 2006[1] | Kristina Smigun (EST) |
| 2007 | Katerina Neumannova (CZE) |
| 2009 | Aino-Kaisa Saarinen (FIN) |
| 2010[1] | Charlotte Kalla (SWE) |
| 2011 | Marit Bjørgen (NOR) |

**COMBINED PURSUIT[2]**

| | |
|---|---|
| 2001 | Virpi Kuitunen (FIN) |
| 2002[1] | Beckie Scott (CAN) |
| 2003 | Kristina Smigun (EST) |

**COMBINED PURSUIT[2] (CONTINUED)**

| | |
|---|---|
| 2005 | Yuliya Chepalova (RUS) |
| 2006[1] | Kristina Smigun (EST) |
| 2007 | Olga Zavyalova (RUS) |
| 2009 | Justyna Kowalczyk (POL) |
| 2010[1] | Marit Bjørgen (NOR) |
| 2011 | Marit Bjørgen (NOR) |

**15-KM CROSS-COUNTRY**

| | |
|---|---|
| 1992[1] | Lyubov Yegorova (URS) |
| 1993 | Yelena Vyalbe (RUS) |
| 1994[1] | Manuela Di Centa (ITA) |
| 1995 | Larisa Lazutina (RUS) |
| 1997 | Yelena Vyalbe (RUS) |
| 1998[1] | Olga Danilova (RUS) |
| 1999 | Stefania Belmondo (ITA) |
| 2001 | Bente Skari (NOR) |
| 2002[1] | Stefania Belmondo (ITA) |
| 2003 | Bente Skari (NOR) |

**30-KM CROSS-COUNTRY**

| | |
|---|---|
| 1992[1] | Stefania Belmondo (ITA) |
| 1993 | Stefania Belmondo (ITA) |
| 1994[1] | Manuela Di Centa (ITA) |
| 1995 | Yelena Vyalbe (RUS) |
| 1997 | Yelena Vyalbe (RUS) |
| 1998[1] | Yulia Chepalova (RUS) |
| 1999 | Larisa Lazutina (RUS) |
| 2001 | *not held* |
| 2002[1] | Gabriella Paruzzi (ITA) |
| 2003 | Olga Savyalova (RUS) |
| 2005 | Marit Bjørgen (NOR) |
| 2006[1] | Katerina Neumannova (CZE) |
| 2007 | Virpi Kuitunen (FIN) |

**30-KM CROSS-COUNTRY (CONTINUED)**

| | |
|---|---|
| 2009 | Justyna Kowalczyk (POL) |
| 2010[1] | Justyna Kowalczyk (POL) |
| 2011 | Therese Johaug (NOR) |

**TEAM SPRINT**

| | |
|---|---|
| 2005 | Norway |
| 2006[1] | Sweden |
| 2007 | Finland |
| 2009 | Finland |
| 2010[1] | Germany |
| 2011 | Sweden |

**RELAY[3]**

| | |
|---|---|
| 1992[1] | Unified Team |
| 1993 | Russia |
| 1994[1] | Russia |
| 1995 | Russia |
| 1997 | Russia |
| 1998[1] | Russia |
| 1999 | Russia |
| 2001 | Russia |
| 2002[1] | Germany |
| 2003 | Germany |
| 2005 | Norway |
| 2006[1] | Russia |
| 2007 | Finland |
| 2009 | Finland |
| 2010[1] | Norway |
| 2011 | Norway |

**SKI JUMP**

| | |
|---|---|
| 2009 | Lindsey Van (USA) |
| 2011 | Daniela Iraschko (AUT) |

[1]*Olympic champions, recognized in this table as world champions (though not by FIS).* [2]*From 1991 to 1999, the 5-km event was held in tandem with the 10-km event; one event featured classical and the other freestyle technique. Medals were awarded for both races. Beginning in 2001 this pursuit race (skiers competing directly against each other rather than against the clock) led to one medal being awarded upon winning. The 5-km was discontinued, and the 10-km became a stand-alone event featuring classical technique. In 2001–03 the pursuit race featured two 5-km races; since then, two 7.5-km races.* [3]*15-km relay until 1974; 20-km in 1976 and thereafter.*

## Nordic Skiing World Championships—Nordic Combined

*The Nordic combined involves a 10-km cross-country race and ski jumping. Held since 1925. Table shows results for the past 20 years.*

| YEAR | COMBINED (NORMAL HILL)[1] | YEAR | COMBINED (LARGE HILL)[3] | YEAR | TEAM |
|---|---|---|---|---|---|
| 1992[2] | Fabrice Guy (FRA) | 1999 | Bjarte Engen Vik (NOR) | 1992[2] | Japan |
| 1993 | Kenji Ogiwara (JPN) | 2001 | Marko Baacke (GER) | 1993 | Japan |
| 1994[2] | Fred Børre Lundberg (NOR) | 2002[2] | Samppa Lajunen (FIN) | 1994[2] | Japan |
| 1995 | Fred Børre Lundberg (NOR) | 2003 | Johnny Spillane (USA) | 1995 | Japan |
| 1997 | Kenji Ogiwara (JPN) | 2005 | Ronny Ackermann (GER) | 1997 | Norway |
| 1998[2] | Bjarte Engen Vik (NOR) | 2006[2] | Felix Gottwald (AUT) | 1998[2] | Norway |
| 1999 | Bjarte Engen Vik (NOR) | 2007 | Hannu Manninen (FIN) | 1999 | Finland |
| 2001 | Bjarte Engen Vik (NOR) | 2009 | Bill Demong (USA) | 2001 | Norway |
| 2002[2] | Samppa Lajunen (FIN) | 2010[2] | Bill Demong (USA) | 2002[2] | Finland |
| 2003 | Ronny Ackermann (GER) | 2011 | Jason Lamy Chappuis (FRA) | 2003 | Austria |
| 2005 | Ronny Ackermann (GER) | | | 2005 | Norway |
| 2006[2] | Georg Hettich (GER) | | | 2006[2] | Austria |
| 2007 | Ronny Ackermann (GER) | YEAR | MASS START | 2007 | Finland |
| 2009 | Todd Lodwick (USA) | 2009 | Todd Lodwick (USA) | 2009 | Japan |
| 2010[2] | Jason Lamy Chappuis (FRA) | | | 2010[2] | Austria |
| 2011 | Eric Frenzel (GER) | | | 2011 | Austria[4] |

[1]*15-km cross-country race until 2009.* [2]*Olympic champions, recognized in this table as world champions (though not by FIS).* [3]*7.5-km cross-country race until 2009.* [4]*Large hill and normal hill competitions held and won by Austria in 2011.*

## Nordic Skiing World Championships—Ski Jump

*Men's events only. Held since 1924. Table shows results for the past 20 years.*

| YEAR | NORMAL HILL[1] |
|---|---|
| 1992[2] | Ernst Vettori (AUT) |
| 1993 | Masahiko Harada (JPN) |
| 1994[2] | Espen Bredesen (NOR) |
| 1995 | Takanobu Okabe (JPN) |
| 1997 | Janne Ahonen (FIN) |
| 1998[2] | Jani Soininen (FIN) |
| 1999 | Kazuyoshi Funaki (JPN) |
| 2001 | Adam Malysz (POL) |
| 2002[2] | Simon Ammann (SUI) |
| 2003 | Adam Malysz (POL) |
| 2005 | Rok Benkovic (SLO) |
| 2006[2] | Lars Bystøl (NOR) |
| 2007 | Adam Malysz (POL) |
| 2009 | Wolfgang Loitzl (AUT) |
| 2010[2] | Simon Ammann (SUI) |
| 2011 | Thomas Morgenstern (AUT) |

| YEAR | LARGE HILL[3] |
|---|---|
| 1992[2] | Toni Nieminen (FIN) |
| 1993 | Espen Bredesen (NOR) |

| YEAR | LARGE HILL[3] (CONTINUED) |
|---|---|
| 1994[2] | Jens Weissflog (GER) |
| 1995 | Tommy Ingebrigtsen (NOR) |
| 1997 | Masahiko Harada (JPN) |
| 1998[2] | Kazuyoshi Funaki (JPN) |
| 1999 | Martin Schmitt (GER) |
| 2001 | Martin Schmitt (GER) |
| 2002[2] | Simon Ammann (SUI) |
| 2003 | Adam Malysz (POL) |
| 2005 | Janne Ahonen (FIN) |
| 2006[2] | Thomas Morgenstern (AUT) |
| 2007 | Simon Ammann (SUI) |
| 2009 | Andreas Kuettel (SUI) |
| 2010[2] | Simon Ammann (SUI) |
| 2011 | Gregor Schlierenzauer (AUT) |

| YEAR | TEAM JUMP (NORMAL HILL[1]) |
|---|---|
| 2001 | Austria |
| 2005 | Austria |
| 2011 | Austria |

| YEAR | TEAM JUMP (LARGE HILL[3]) |
|---|---|
| 1992[2] | Finland |
| 1993 | Norway |
| 1994[2] | Germany |
| 1995 | Finland |
| 1997 | Finland |
| 1998[2] | Japan |
| 1999 | Germany |
| 2001 | Germany |
| 2002[2] | Germany |
| 2003 | Finland |
| 2005 | Austria |
| 2006[2] | Austria |
| 2007 | Austria |
| 2009 | Austria |
| 2010[2] | Austria |
| 2011 | Austria |

[1]The distance of the jump in the normal hill competition has varied over time; since 1992 it has been set at either 90 or 95 meters.   [2]Olympic champions, recognized in this table as world champions (though not by FIS).   [3]The distance of the jump in the large hill competition has varied over time; since 1992 it has been set at either 120 or 125 meters.

## Nordic World Cup

*The winner is determined by the number of points awarded for finishes in various competitions during the season.*

| YEAR | MEN | WOMEN |
|---|---|---|
| 1979 | Oddvar Braa (NOR) | Galina Kulakova (URS) |
| 1980 | not held | |
| 1981 | Aleksandr Zavyalov (URS) | Raisa Smetanina (URS) |
| 1982 | Bill Koch (USA) | Berit Aunli (NOR) |
| 1983 | Aleksandr Zavyalov (URS) | Marja-Liisa Hämäläinen (FIN) |
| 1984 | Gunde Svan (SWE) | Marja-Liisa Hämäläinen (FIN) |
| 1985 | Gunde Svan (SWE) | Anette Boe (NOR) |
| 1986 | Gunde Svan (SWE) | Marjo Matikainen (FIN) |
| 1987 | Torgny Mogren (SWE) | Marjo Matikainen (FIN) |
| 1988 | Gunde Svan (SWE) | Marjo Matikainen (FIN) |
| 1989 | Gunde Svan (SWE) | Yelena Vyalbe (URS) |
| 1990 | Vegard Ulvang (NOR) | Larisa Lazutina (URS) |
| 1991 | Vladimir Smirnov (URS) | Yelena Vyalbe (URS) |
| 1992 | Bjørn Daehlie (NOR) | Yelena Vyalbe (RUS) |
| 1993 | Bjørn Daehlie (NOR) | Lyudmila Yegorova (RUS) |
| 1994 | Vladimir Smirnov (KAZ) | Manuela Di Centa (ITA) |
| 1995 | Bjørn Daehlie (NOR) | Yelena Vyalbe (RUS) |
| 1996 | Bjørn Daehlie (NOR) | Manuela Di Centa (ITA) |
| 1997 | Bjørn Daehlie (NOR) | Yelena Vyalbe (RUS) |
| 1998 | Thomas Alsgaard (NOR) | Larisa Lazutina (RUS) |
| 1999 | Bjørn Daehlie (NOR) | Bente Martinsen (NOR) |
| 2000 | Johann Mühlegg (ESP) | Bente Skari-Martinsen (NOR) |
| 2001 | Per Elofsson (SWE) | Yuliya Chepalova (RUS) |
| 2002 | Per Elofsson (SWE) | Bente Skari (NOR) |
| 2003 | Mathias Fredriksson (SWE) | Bente Skari (NOR) |
| 2004 | Rene Sommerfeldt (GER) | Gabriella Paruzzi (ITA) |
| 2005 | Axel Teichmann (GER) | Marit Bjørgen (NOR) |
| 2006 | Tobias Angerer (GER) | Marit Bjørgen (NOR) |
| 2007 | Tobias Angerer (GER) | Virpi Kuitunen (FIN) |
| 2008 | Lukas Bauer (CZE) | Virpi Kuitunen (FIN) |
| 2009 | Dario Cologna (SUI) | Justyna Kowalczyk (POL) |
| 2010 | Petter Northug (NOR) | Justyna Kowalczyk (POL) |
| 2011 | Dario Cologna (SUI) | Justyna Kowalczyk (POL) |
| 2012 | Dario Cologna (SUI) | Marit Bjørgen (NOR) |

# Swimming

The **Fédération Internationale de Natation** (FINA), founded 1908) is the world governing body for amateur swimming. It held the first world swimming championships in 1973. After 1975 the FINA championships were held in non-Olympic, even-numbered years. (An exception was the 1991 championship.) Diving, synchronized (or synchro) swimming, and water polo events are included in the competition.

A distinction is made between **long-course** (50-m) and **short-course** (25-m) pools for purposes of record setting; world championships and other major contests were long held in 50-m pools, but now a separate short-course World Championship and World Cup take place.

**International Swimming Federation Web site:** <www.fina.org>.

# World Swimming and Diving Championships—Men
## swimming

**50-M FREESTYLE**
1986 Tom Jager (USA)
1991 Tom Jager (USA)
1994 Aleksandr Popov (RUS)
1998 Bill Pilczuk (USA)
2001 Anthony Ervin (USA)
2003 Aleksandr Popov (RUS)
2005 Roland Schoeman (RSA)
2007 Benjamin Wildman-
     Tobriner (USA)
2009 César Cielo Filho (BRA)
2011 César Cielo Filho (BRA)

**100-M FREESTYLE**
1973 Jim Montgomery (USA)
1975 Andy Coan (USA)
1978 David McCagg (USA)
1982 Jörg Woithe (GDR)
1986 Matt Biondi (USA)
1991 Matt Biondi (USA)
1994 Aleksandr Popov (RUS)
1998 Aleksandr Popov (RUS)
2001 Anthony Ervin (USA)
2003 Aleksandr Popov (RUS)
2005 Filippo Magnini (ITA)
2007 Filippo Magnini (ITA)
2009 César Cielo Filho (BRA)
2011 James Magnussen (AUS)

**200-M FREESTYLE**
1973 Jim Montgomery (USA)
1975 Tim Shaw (USA)
1978 Bill Forrester (USA)
1982 Michael Gross (FRG)
1986 Michael Gross (FRG)
1991 Giorgio Lamberti (ITA)
1994 Antti Kasvio (FIN)
1998 Michael Klim (AUS)
2001 Ian Thorpe (AUS)
2003 Ian Thorpe (AUS)
2005 Michael Phelps (USA)
2007 Michael Phelps (USA)
2009 Paul Biedermann (GER)
2011 Ryan Lochte (USA)

**400-M FREESTYLE**
1973 Rick DeMont (USA)
1975 Tim Shaw (USA)
1978 Vladimir Salnikov (URS)
1982 Vladimir Salnikov (URS)
1986 Rainer Henkel (FRG)
1991 Jörg Hoffmann (GER)
1994 Kieren Perkins (AUS)
1998 Ian Thorpe (AUS)
2001 Ian Thorpe (AUS)
2003 Ian Thorpe (AUS)
2005 Grant Hackett (AUS)
2007 Park Tae-Hwan (KOR)
2009 Paul Biedermann (GER)
2011 Park Tae-Hwan (KOR)

**800-M FREESTYLE**
2001 Ian Thorpe (AUS)
2003 Grant Hackett (AUS)
2005 Grant Hackett (AUS)
2007 Przemyslaw Stanczyk (POL)
2009 Zhang Lin (CHN)
2011 Sun Yang (CHN)

**1,500-M FREESTYLE**
1973 Steve Holland (AUS)
1975 Tim Shaw (USA)
1978 Vladimir Salnikov (URS)
1982 Vladimir Salnikov (URS)
1986 Rainer Henkel (FRG)
1991 Jörg Hoffmann (GER)
1994 Kieren Perkins (AUS)
1998 Grant Hackett (AUS)
2001 Grant Hackett (AUS)
2003 Grant Hackett (AUS)
2005 Grant Hackett (AUS)
2007 Mateusz Sawrymowicz
     (POL)
2009 Oussama Mellouli (TUN)
2011 Sun Yang (CHN)

**50-M BACKSTROKE**
2001 Randall Bal (USA)
2003 Thomas Rupprath (GER)
2005 Aristeidis Grigoriadis
     (GRE)
2007 Gerhard Zandberg (RSA)
2009 Liam Tancock (GBR)
2011 Liam Tancock (GBR)

**100-M BACKSTROKE**
1973 Roland Matthes (GDR)
1975 Roland Matthes (GDR)
1978 Bob Jackson (USA)
1982 Dirk Richter (GDR)
1986 Igor Polyansky (URS)
1991 Jeff Rouse (USA)
1994 Martin López-Zubero (ESP)
1998 Lenny Krayzelburg (USA)
2001 Matt Welsh (AUS)
2003 Aaron Peirsol (USA)
2005 Aaron Peirsol (USA)
2007 Aaron Peirsol (USA)
2009 Junya Koga (JPN)
2011 Jeremy Stravius (FRA)

**200-M BACKSTROKE**
1973 Roland Matthes (GDR)
1975 Zoltán Verrasztó (HUN)
1978 Jesse Vassallo (USA)
1982 Rick Carey (USA)
1986 Igor Polyansky (URS)
1991 Martin López-Zubero (ESP)
1994 Vladimir Selkov (RUS)
1998 Lenny Krayzelburg (USA)
2001 Aaron Peirsol (USA)
2003 Aaron Peirsol (USA)
2005 Aaron Peirsol (USA)
2007 Ryan Lochte (USA)
2009 Aaron Peirsol (USA)
2011 Ryan Lochte (USA)

**50-M BREASTSTROKE**
2001 Oleg Lisogor (UKR)
2003 James Gibson (GBR)
2005 Mark Warnecke (GER)
2007 Oleg Lisogor (UKR)
2009 Cameron van der Burgh
     (RSA)
2011 Felipe Franca da Silva
     (BRA)

**100-M BREASTSTROKE**
1973 John Hencken (USA)
1975 David Wilkie (GBR)
1978 Walter Kusch (FRG)
1982 Steve Lundquist (USA)
1986 Victor Davis (CAN)
1991 Norbert Rózsa (HUN)
1994 Norbert Rózsa (HUN)
1998 Fred Deburghgraeve (BEL)
2001 Roman Sloudnov (RUS)
2003 Kosuke Kitajima (JPN)
2005 Brendan Hansen (USA)
2007 Brendan Hansen (USA)
2009 Brenton Rickard (AUS)
2011 Alexander Dale Oen (NOR)

**200-M BREASTSTROKE**
1973 David Wilkie (GBR)
1975 David Wilkie (GBR)
1978 Nick Nevid (USA)
1982 Victor Davis (CAN)
1986 József Szabó (HUN)
1991 Mike Barrowman (USA)
1994 Norbert Rózsa (HUN)
1998 Kurt Grote (USA)
2001 Brendan Hansen (USA)
2003 Kosuke Kitajima (JPN)
2005 Brendan Hansen (USA)
2007 Kosuke Kitajima (JPN)
2009 Daniel Gyurta (HUN)
2011 Daniel Gyurta (HUN)

**50-M BUTTERFLY**
2001 Geoff Huegill (AUS)
2003 Matt Welsh (AUS)
2005 Roland Schoeman (RSA)
2007 Roland Schoeman (RSA)
2009 Milorad Cavic (SRB)
2011 César Cielo Filho (BRA)

**100-M BUTTERFLY**
1973 Bruce Robertson (CAN)
1975 Greg Jagenburg (USA)
1978 Joseph Bottom (USA)
1982 Matt Gribble (USA)
1986 Pablo Morales (USA)
1991 Anthony Nesty (SUR)
1994 Rafal Szukala (POL)
1998 Michael Klim (AUS)
2001 Lars Frölander (SWE)
2003 Ian Crocker (USA)
2005 Ian Crocker (USA)
2007 Michael Phelps (USA)
2009 Michael Phelps (USA)
2011 Michael Phelps (USA)

**200-M BUTTERFLY**
1973 Robin Backhaus (USA)
1975 Bill Forrester (USA)
1978 Mike Bruner (USA)
1982 Michael Gross (FRG)
1986 Michael Gross (FRG)
1991 Melvin Stewart (USA)
1994 Denis Pankratov (RUS)
1998 Denys Silantyev (UKR)
2001 Michael Phelps (USA)
2003 Michael Phelps (USA)
2005 Pawel Korzeniowski (POL)

## World Swimming and Diving Championships—Men (continued)

### swimming (continued)

**200-M BUTTERFLY (CONT.)**
2007 Michael Phelps (USA)
2009 Michael Phelps (USA)
2011 Michael Phelps (USA)

**200-M INDIVIDUAL MEDLEY**
1973 Gunnar Larsson (SWE)
1975 András Hargitay (HUN)
1978 Graham Smith (CAN)
1982 Aleksandr Sidorenko (URS)
1986 Tamás Darnyi (HUN)
1991 Tamás Darnyi (HUN)
1994 Jani Sievinen (FIN)
1998 Marcel Wouda (NED)
2001 Massimiliano Rosolino (ITA)
2003 Michael Phelps (USA)
2005 Michael Phelps (USA)
2007 Michael Phelps (USA)
2009 Ryan Lochte (USA)
2011 Ryan Lochte (USA)

**400-M INDIVIDUAL MEDLEY**
1973 András Hargitay (HUN)
1975 András Hargitay (HUN)
1978 Jesse Vassallo (USA)
1982 Ricardo Prado (BRA)
1986 Tamás Darnyi (HUN)
1991 Tamás Darnyi (HUN)
1994 Tom Dolan (USA)

**400-M INDIVIDUAL MEDLEY (CONT.)**
1998 Tom Dolan (USA)
2001 Alessio Boggiatto (ITA)
2003 Michael Phelps (USA)
2005 László Cseh (HUN)
2007 Michael Phelps (USA)
2009 Ryan Lochte (USA)
2011 Ryan Lochte (USA)

**4 × 100-M FREESTYLE RELAY**
1973 United States
1975 United States
1978 United States
1982 United States
1986 United States
1991 United States
1994 United States
1998 United States
2001 Australia
2003 Russia
2005 United States
2007 United States
2009 United States
2011 Australia

**4 × 200-M FREESTYLE RELAY**
1973 United States
1975 West Germany
1978 United States

**4 × 200-M FREESTYLE RELAY (CONT.)**
1982 United States
1986 East Germany
1991 Germany
1994 Sweden
1998 Australia
2001 Australia
2003 Australia
2005 United States
2007 United States
2009 United States
2011 United States

**4 × 100-M MEDLEY RELAY**
1973 United States
1975 United States
1978 United States
1982 United States
1986 United States
1991 United States
1994 United States
1998 Australia
2001 Australia
2003 Australia
2005 United States
2007 Australia
2009 United States
2011 United States

### diving

**1-M SPRINGBOARD**
1991 Edwin Jongejans (NED)
1994 Evan Stewart (ZIM)
1998 Yu Zhuocheng (CHN)
2001 Wang Feng (CHN)
2003 Xu Xiang (CHN)
2005 Alexandre Despatie (CAN)
2007 Luo Yutong (CHN)
2009 Qin Kai (CHN)
2011 Li Shixin (CHN)

**3-M SPRINGBOARD**
1973 Philip Boggs (USA)
1975 Philip Boggs (USA)
1978 Philip Boggs (USA)

**3-M SPRINGBOARD (CONTINUED)**
1982 Greg Louganis (USA)
1986 Greg Louganis (USA)
1991 Kent Ferguson (USA)
1994 Yu Zhuocheng (CHN)
1998 Dmitry Sautin (RUS)
2001 Dmitry Sautin (RUS)
2003 Aleksandr Dobrosok (RUS)
2005 Alexandre Despatie (CAN)
2007 Qin Kai (CHN)
2009 He Chong (CHN)
2011 He Chong (CHN)

**PLATFORM**
1973 Klaus Dibiasi (ITA)
1975 Klaus Dibiasi (ITA)
1978 Greg Louganis (USA)
1982 Greg Louganis (USA)
1986 Greg Louganis (USA)
1991 Sun Shuwei (CHN)
1994 Dmitry Sautin (RUS)
1998 Dmitry Sautin (RUS)
2001 Tian Liang (CHN)
2003 Alexandre Despatie (CAN)
2005 Hu Jia (CHN)
2007 Gleb Galperin (RUS)
2009 Thomas Daley (GBR)
2011 Qiu Bo (CHN)

## World Swimming and Diving Championships—Women

### swimming

**50-M FREESTYLE**
1986 Tamara Costache (ROM)
1991 Zhuang Yong (CHN)
1994 Le Jingyi (CHN)
1998 Amy Van Dyken (USA)
2001 Inge de Bruijn (NED)
2003 Inge de Bruijn (NED)
2005 Lisbeth Lenton (AUS)
2007 Lisbeth Lenton (AUS)
2009 Britta Steffen (GER)
2011 Therese Alshammar (SWE)

**100-M FREESTYLE**
1973 Kornelia Ender (GDR)
1975 Kornelia Ender (GDR)
1978 Barbara Krause (GDR)
1982 Birgit Meineke (GDR)

**100-M FREESTYLE (CONTINUED)**
1986 Kristin Otto (GDR)
1991 Nicole Haislett (USA)
1994 Le Jingyi (CHN)
1998 Jenny Thompson (USA)
2001 Inge de Bruijn (NED)
2003 Hanna-Maria Seppälä (FIN)
2005 Jodie Henry (AUS)
2007 Lisbeth Lenton (AUS)
2009 Britta Steffen (GER)
2011 Aliaksandra Herasimenia
(BLR); Jeanette Ottesen
(DEN) (tied)

**200-M FREESTYLE**
1973 Keena Rothhammer (USA)
1975 Shirley Babashoff (USA)

**200-M FREESTYLE (CONTINUED)**
1978 Cynthia Woodhead (USA)
1982 Annemarie Verstappen
(NED)
1986 Heike Friedrich (GDR)
1991 Hayley Lewis (AUS)
1994 Franziska van Almsick (GER)
1998 Claudia Poll (CRC)
2001 Giaan Rooney (AUS)
2003 Alena Popchanka (BLR)
2005 Solenne Figues (FRA)
2007 Laure Manaudou (FRA)
2009 Federica Pellegrini (ITA)
2011 Federica Pellegrini (ITA)

# World Swimming and Diving Championships—Women (continued)

## swimming (continued)

**400-M FREESTYLE**
1973   Heather Greenwood (USA)
1975   Shirley Babashoff (USA)
1978   Tracey Wickham (AUS)
1982   Carmela Schmidt (GDR)
1986   Heike Friedrich (GDR)
1991   Janet Evans (USA)
1994   Yang Aihua (CHN)
1998   Chen Yan (CHN)
2001   Yana Klochkova (UKR)
2003   Hannah Stockbauer (GER)
2005   Laure Manaudou (FRA)
2007   Laure Manaudou (FRA)
2009   Federica Pellegrini (ITA)
2011   Federica Pellegrini (ITA)

**800-M FREESTYLE**
1973   Novella Calligaris (ITA)
1975   Jenny Turrall (AUS)
1978   Tracey Wickham (AUS)
1982   Kim Linehan (USA)
1986   Astrid Strauss (GDR)
1991   Janet Evans (USA)
1994   Janet Evans (USA)
1998   Brooke Bennett (USA)
2001   Hannah Stockbauer (GER)
2003   Hannah Stockbauer (GER)
2005   Kate Ziegler (USA)
2007   Kate Ziegler (USA)
2009   Lotte Friis (DEN)
2011   Rebecca Adlington (GRB)

**1,500-M FREESTYLE**
2001   Hannah Stockbauer (GER)
2003   Hannah Stockbauer (GER)
2005   Kate Ziegler (USA)
2007   Kate Ziegler (USA)
2009   Alessia Filippi (ITA)
2011   Lotte Friis (DEN)

**50-M BREASTSTROKE**
2001   Luo Xuejuan (CHN)
2003   Luo Xuejuan (CHN)
2005   Jade Edmistone (AUS)
2007   Jessica Hardy (USA)
2009   Yuliya Yefimova (RUS)
2011   Jessica Hardy (USA)

**100-M BREASTSTROKE**
1973   Renate Vogel (GDR)
1975   Hannelore Anke (GDR)
1978   Yuliya Bogdanova (URS)
1982   Ute Geweniger (GDR)
1986   Sylvia Gerasch (GDR)
1991   Linley Frame (AUS)
1994   Samantha Riley (AUS)
1998   Kristy Kowal (USA)
2001   Luo Xuejuan (CHN)
2003   Luo Xuejuan (CHN)
2005   Leisel Jones (AUS)
2007   Leisel Jones (AUS)
2009   Rebecca Soni (USA)
2011   Rebecca Soni (USA)

**200-M BREASTSTROKE**
1973   Renate Vogel (GDR)
1975   Hannelore Anke (GDR)
1978   Lina Kachushite (URS)

**200-M BREASTSTROKE (CONTINUED)**
1982   Svetlana Varganova
         (URS)
1986   Silke Hörner (GDR)
1991   Yelena Volkova (URS)
1994   Samantha Riley (AUS)
1998   Agnes Kovacs (HUN)
2001   Agnes Kovacs (HUN)
2003   Amanda Beard (USA)
2005   Leisel Jones (AUS)
2007   Leisel Jones (AUS)
2009   Nadja Higl (SRB)
2011   Rebecca Soni (USA)

**50-M BUTTERFLY**
2001   Inge de Bruijn (NED)
2003   Inge de Bruijn (NED)
2005   Danni Miatke (AUS)
2007   Therese Alshammar (SWE)
2009   Marieke Guehrer (AUS)
2011   Inge Dekker (NED)

**100-M BUTTERFLY**
1973   Kornelia Ender (GDR)
1975   Kornelia Ender (GDR)
1978   Joan Pennington (USA)
1982   Mary Meagher (USA)
1986   Kornelia Gressler (GDR)
1991   Qian Hong (CHN)
1994   Liu Limin (CHN)
1998   Jenny Thompson (USA)
2001   Petria Thomas (AUS)
2003   Jenny Thompson (USA)
2005   Jessicah Schipper (AUS)
2007   Lisbeth Lenton (AUS)
2009   Sarah Sjöström (SWE)
2011   Dana Vollmer (USA)

**200-M BUTTERFLY**
1973   Rosemarie Kother (GDR)
1975   Rosemarie Kother (GDR)
1978   Tracy Caulkins (USA)
1982   Ines Geissler (GDR)
1986   Mary T. Meagher (USA)
1991   Summer Sanders (USA)
1994   Liu Limin (CHN)
1998   Susie O'Neill (AUS)
2001   Petria Thomas (AUS)
2003   Otylia Jedrzejczak (POL)
2005   Otylia Jedrzejczak (POL)
2007   Jessicah Schipper (AUS)
2009   Jessicah Schipper (AUS)
2011   Jiao Liuyang (CHN)

**50-M BACKSTROKE**
2001   Haley Cope (USA)
2003   Nina Zhivanevskaya (ESP)
2005   Giaan Rooney (AUS)
2007   Leila Vaziri (USA)
2009   Zhao Jing (CHN)
2011   Anastasia Zueva (RUS)

**100-M BACKSTROKE**
1973   Ulrike Richter (GDR)
1975   Ulrike Richter (GDR)
1978   Linda Jezek (USA)
1982   Kristin Otto (GDR)
1986   Betsy Mitchell (USA)

**100-M BACKSTROKE (CONTINUED)**
1991   Krisztina Egerszegi (HUN)
1994   He Cihong (CHN)
1998   Lea Maurer (USA)
2001   Natalie Coughlin (USA)
2003   Antje Buschschulte (GER)
2005   Kirsty Coventry (ZIM)
2007   Natalie Coughlin (USA)
2009   Gemma Spofforth (GBR)
2011   Zhao Jing (CHN)

**200-M BACKSTROKE**
1973   Melissa Belote (USA)
1975   Birgit Treiber (GDR)
1978   Linda Jezek (USA)
1982   Cornelia Sirch (GDR)
1986   Cornelia Sirch (GDR)
1991   Krisztina Egerszegi (HUN)
1994   He Cihong (CHN)
1998   Roxana Maracineanu (FRA)
2001   Diana Mocanu (ROM)
2003   Katy Sexton (GBR)
2005   Kirsty Coventry (ZIM)
2007   Margaret Hoelzer (USA)
2009   Kirsty Coventry (ZIM)
2011   Missy Franklin (USA)

**200-M INDIVIDUAL MEDLEY**
1973   Andrea Hubner (GDR)
1975   Kathy Heddy (USA)
1978   Tracy Caulkins (USA)
1982   Petra Schneider (GDR)
1986   Kristin Otto (GDR)
1991   Lin Li (CHN)
1994   Lu Bin (CHN)
1998   Wu Yanyan (CHN)
2001   Martha Bowen (USA)
2003   Yana Klochkova (UKR)
2005   Katie Hoff (USA)
2007   Katie Hoff (USA)
2009   Ariana Kukors (USA)
2011   Ye Shiwen (CHN)

**400-M INDIVIDUAL MEDLEY**
1973   Gudrun Wegner (GDR)
1975   Ulrike Tauber (GDR)
1978   Tracy Caulkins (USA)
1982   Petra Schneider (GDR)
1986   Kathleen Nord (GDR)
1991   Lin Li (CHN)
1994   Dai Guohong (CHN)
1998   Chen Yan (CHN)
2001   Yana Klochkova (UKR)
2003   Yana Klochkova (UKR)
2005   Katie Hoff (USA)
2007   Katie Hoff (USA)
2009   Katinka Hosszú (HUN)
2011   Elizabeth Beisel (USA)

**4 × 100-M FREESTYLE RELAY**
1973   East Germany
1975   East Germany
1978   United States
1982   East Germany
1986   East Germany
1991   United States
1994   China
1998   United States

## World Swimming and Diving Championships—Women (continued)
### swimming (continued)

**4 × 100-M FREESTYLE RELAY (CONT.)**
| | |
|---|---|
| 2001 | Germany |
| 2003 | United States |
| 2005 | Australia |
| 2007 | Australia |
| 2009 | Netherlands |
| 2011 | Netherlands |

**4 × 200-M FREESTYLE RELAY**
| | |
|---|---|
| 1986 | East Germany |
| 1991 | Germany |
| 1994 | China |
| 1998 | Germany |

**4 × 200-M FREESTYLE RELAY (CONT.)**
| | |
|---|---|
| 2001 | Great Britain |
| 2003 | United States |
| 2005 | United States |
| 2007 | United States |
| 2009 | China |
| 2011 | United States |

**4 × 100-M MEDLEY RELAY**
| | |
|---|---|
| 1973 | East Germany |
| 1975 | East Germany |
| 1978 | United States |
| 1982 | East Germany |

**4 × 100-M MEDLEY RELAY (CONT.)**
| | |
|---|---|
| 1986 | East Germany |
| 1991 | United States |
| 1994 | China |
| 1998 | United States |
| 2001 | Australia |
| 2003 | China |
| 2005 | Australia |
| 2007 | Australia |
| 2009 | China |
| 2011 | United States |

### diving

**1-M SPRINGBOARD**
| | |
|---|---|
| 1991 | Gao Min (CHN) |
| 1994 | Chen Lixia (CHN) |
| 1998 | Irina Lashko (RUS) |
| 2001 | Blythe Hartley (CAN) |
| 2003 | Irina Lashko (AUS) |
| 2005 | Blythe Hartley (CAN) |
| 2007 | He Zi (CHN) |
| 2009 | Yuliya Pakhalina (RUS) |
| 2011 | Shi Tingmao (CHN) |

**3-M SPRINGBOARD**
| | |
|---|---|
| 1973 | Christa Kohler (GDR) |
| 1975 | Irina Kalinina (URS) |
| 1978 | Irina Kalinina (URS) |

**3-M SPRINGBOARD (CONT.)**
| | |
|---|---|
| 1982 | Megan Neyer (USA) |
| 1986 | Gao Min (CHN) |
| 1991 | Gao Min (CHN) |
| 1994 | Tan Shuping (CHN) |
| 1998 | Yuliya Pakhalina (RUS) |
| 2001 | Guo Jingjing (CHN) |
| 2003 | Guo Jingjing (CHN) |
| 2005 | Guo Jingjing (CHN) |
| 2007 | Guo Jingjing (CHN) |
| 2009 | Guo Jingjing (CHN) |
| 2011 | Wu Minxia (CHN) |

**PLATFORM**
| | |
|---|---|
| 1973 | Ulrika Knape (SWE) |
| 1975 | Janet Ely (USA) |
| 1978 | Irina Kalinina (URS) |
| 1982 | Wendy Wyland (USA) |
| 1986 | Chen Lin (CHN) |
| 1991 | Fu Mingxia (CHN) |
| 1994 | Fu Mingxia (CHN) |
| 1998 | Olena Zhupina (UKR) |
| 2001 | Xu Mian (CHN) |
| 2003 | Emilie Heymans (CAN) |
| 2005 | Laura Wilkinson (USA) |
| 2007 | Wang Xin (CHN) |
| 2009 | Paola Espinosa (MEX) |
| 2011 | Chen Ruolin (CHN) |

## Swimming World Records—Long Course (50 m)
*Some records are awaiting FINA ratification as of 23 Aug 2012.*

### Men

| EVENT | RECORD HOLDER (COUNTRY) | PERFORMANCE | DATE |
|---|---|---|---|
| 50-m freestyle | César Cielo Filho (BRA) | 20.91 sec | 18 Dec 2009 |
| 100-m freestyle | César Cielo Filho (BRA) | 46.91 sec | 30 Jul 2009 |
| 200-m freestyle | Paul Biedermann (GER) | 1 min 42.00 sec | 28 Jul 2009 |
| 400-m freestyle | Paul Biedermann (GER) | 3 min 40.07 sec | 26 Jul 2009 |
| 800-m freestyle | Zhang Lin (CHN) | 7 min 32.12 sec | 29 Jul 2009 |
| 1,500-m freestyle | Yang Sun (CHN) | 14 min 34.14 sec | 31 Jul 2011 |
| 50-m backstroke | Liam Tancock (GBR) | 24.04 sec | 2 Aug 2009 |
| 100-m backstroke | Aaron Peirsol (USA) | 51.94 sec | 8 Jul 2009 |
| 200-m backstroke | Aaron Peirsol (USA) | 1 min 51.92 sec | 31 Jul 2009 |
| 50-m breaststroke | Cameron van der Burgh (RSA) | 26.67 sec | 29 Jul 2009 |
| 100-m breaststroke | Cameron van der Burgh (RSA) | 58.46 sec | 29 Jul 2012 |
| 200-m breaststroke | Daniel Gyurta (HUN) | 2 min 07.28 sec | 1 Aug 2012 |
| 50-m butterfly | Rafael Muñoz (ESP) | 22.43 sec | 5 Apr 2009 |
| 100-m butterfly | Michael Phelps (USA) | 49.82 sec | 1 Aug 2009 |
| 200-m butterfly | Michael Phelps (USA) | 1 min 51.51 sec | 29 Jul 2009 |
| 200-m individual medley | Ryan Lochte (USA) | 1 min 54.00 sec | 28 Jul 2011 |
| 400-m individual medley | Michael Phelps (USA) | 4 min 03.84 sec | 10 Aug 2008 |
| 4 × 100-m freestyle relay | United States (Michael Phelps, Garrett Weber-Gale, Cullen Jones, Jason Lezak) | 3 min 08.24 sec | 11 Aug 2008 |
| 4 × 200-m freestyle relay | United States (Michael Phelps, Ricky Berens, David Walters, Ryan Lochte) | 6 min 58.55 sec | 31 Jul 2009 |
| 4 × 100-m medley relay | United States (Aaron Peirsol, Eric Shanteau, Michael Phelps, David Walters) | 3 min 27.28 sec | 2 Aug 2009 |

### Women

| EVENT | RECORD HOLDER (COUNTRY) | PERFORMANCE | DATE |
|---|---|---|---|
| 50-m freestyle | Britta Steffen (GER) | 23.73 sec | 2 Aug 2009 |
| 100-m freestyle | Britta Steffen (GER) | 52.07 sec | 31 Jul 2009 |
| 200-m freestyle | Federica Pellegrini (ITA) | 1 min 52.98 sec | 29 Jul 2009 |
| 400-m freestyle | Federica Pellegrini (ITA) | 3 min 59.15 sec | 26 Jul 2009 |

## Swimming World Records—Long Course (50 m) (continued)

### Women (continued)

| EVENT | RECORD HOLDER (COUNTRY) | PERFORMANCE | DATE |
|---|---|---|---|
| 800-m freestyle | Rebecca Adlington (GBR) | 8 min 14.10 sec | 16 Aug 2008 |
| 1,500-m freestyle | Kate Ziegler (USA) | 15 min 42.54 sec | 17 Jun 2007 |
| 50-m backstroke | Zhao Jing (CHN) | 27.06 sec | 30 Jul 2009 |
| 100-m backstroke | Gemma Spofforth (GBR) | 58.12 sec | 28 Jul 2009 |
| 200-m backstroke | Kirsty Coventry (ZIM) | 2 min 04.81 sec | 1 Aug 2009 |
| 50-m breaststroke | Jessica Hardy (USA) | 29.80 sec | 7 Aug 2009 |
| 100-m breaststroke | Jessica Hardy (USA) | 1 min 04.45 sec | 7 Aug 2009 |
| 200-m breaststroke | Rebecca Soni (USA) | 2 min 19.59 sec | 2 Aug 2012 |
| 50-m butterfly | Therese Alshammar (SWE) | 25.07 sec | 31 Jul 2009 |
| 100-m butterfly | Dana Vollmer (USA) | 55.98 sec | 29 Jul 2012 |
| 200-m butterfly | Liu Zige (CHN) | 2 min 01.81 sec | 21 Oct 2009 |
| 200-m individual medley | Ariana Kukors (USA) | 2 min 06.15 sec | 27 Jul 2009 |
| 400-m individual medley | Ye Shiwen (CHN) | 4 min 28.43 sec | 28 Jul 2012 |
| 4 × 100-m freestyle relay | Netherlands (Inge Dekker, Ranomi Kromowidjojo, Femke Heemskerk, Marleen Veldhuis) | 3 min 31.72 sec | 26 Jul 2009 |
| 4 × 200-m freestyle relay | China (Yang Yu, Zhu Qian Wei, Liu Jing, Pang Jiaying) | 7 min 42.08 sec | 30 Jul 2009 |
| 4 × 100-m medley relay | China (Zhao Jing, Chen Huijia, Jiao Liuyang, Li Zhesi) | 3 min 52.19 sec | 1 Aug 2009 |

## Swimming World Records—Short Course (25 m)

*Some records are awaiting FINA ratification as of 23 Aug 2012.*

### Men

| EVENT | RECORD HOLDER (COUNTRY) | PERFORMANCE | DATE |
|---|---|---|---|
| 50-m freestyle | Roland Schoeman (RSA) | 20.30 sec | 8 Aug 2009 |
| 100-m freestyle | Amaury Leveaux (FRA) | 44.94 sec | 13 Dec 2008 |
| 200-m freestyle | Paul Biedermann (GER) | 1 min 39.37 sec | 15 Nov 2009 |
| 400-m freestyle | Paul Biedermann (GER) | 3 min 32.77 sec | 14 Nov 2009 |
| 800-m freestyle | Grant Hackett (AUS) | 7 min 23.42 sec | 20 Jul 2008 |
| 1,500-m freestyle | Grant Hackett (AUS) | 14 min 10.10 sec | 7 Aug 2001 |
| 50-m backstroke | Peter Marshall (USA) | 22.61 sec | 22 Nov 2009 |
| 100-m backstroke | Nick Thoman (USA) | 48.94 sec | 18 Dec 2009 |
| 200-m backstroke | Arkady Vyatchanin (RUS) | 1 min 46.11 sec | 15 Nov 2009 |
| 50-m breaststroke | Cameron van der Burgh (RSA) | 25.25 sec | 14 Nov 2009 |
| 100-m breaststroke | Cameron van der Burgh (RSA) | 55.61 sec | 15 Nov 2009 |
| 200-m breaststroke | Daniel Gyurta (HUN) | 2 min 00.67 sec | 13 Dec 2009 |
| 50-m butterfly | Steffen Deibler (GER) | 21.80 sec | 14 Nov 2009 |
| 100-m butterfly | Evgeny Korotyshkin (RUS) | 48.48 sec | 15 Nov 2009 |
| 200-m butterfly | Kaio Almeida (BRA) | 1 min 49.11 sec | 10 Nov 2009 |
| 100-m individual medley | Peter Mankoc (SLO) | 50.76 sec | 12 Dec 2009 |
| 200-m individual medley | Ryan Lochte (USA) | 1 min 50.08 sec | 17 Dec 2010 |
| 400-m individual medley | Ryan Lochte (USA) | 3 min 55.50 sec | 16 Dec 2010 |
| 4 × 100-m freestyle relay | United States (Nathan Adrian, Matt Grevers, Garrett Weber-Gale, Michael Phelps) | 3 min 03.30 sec | 19 Dec 2009 |
| 4 × 200-m freestyle relay | Russia (Nikita Lobintsev, Danila Izotov, Evgeny Lagunov, Alexander Sukhorukov) | 6 min 49.04 sec | 16 Dec 2010 |
| 4 × 100-m medley relay | Russia (Stanislav Donets, Sergey Geibel, Evgeny Korotyshkin, Danila Izotov) | 3 min 19.16 sec | 20 Dec 2009 |

### Women

| EVENT | RECORD HOLDER (COUNTRY) | PERFORMANCE | DATE |
|---|---|---|---|
| 50-m freestyle | Marleen Veldhuis (NED) | 23.25 sec | 13 Apr 2008 |
| 100-m freestyle | Lisbeth Trickett (AUS) | 51.01 sec | 10 Aug 2009 |
| 200-m freestyle | Federica Pellegrini (ITA) | 1 min 51.17 sec | 13 Dec 2009 |
| 400-m freestyle | Joanne Jackson (GBR) | 3 min 54.92 sec | 8 Aug 2009 |
| 800-m freestyle | Alessia Filippi (ITA) | 8 min 04.53 sec | 12 Dec 2008 |
| 1,500-m freestyle | Lotte Friis (DEN) | 15 min 28.65 sec | 28 Nov 2009 |
| 50-m backstroke | Sanja Jovanovic (CRO) | 25.70 sec | 12 Dec 2009 |
| 100-m backstroke | Shiho Sakai (JPN) | 55.23 sec | 15 Nov 2009 |
| 200-m backstroke | Missy Franklin (USA) | 2 min 00.03 sec | 22 Oct 2011 |
| 50-m breaststroke | Jessica Hardy (USA) | 28.80 sec | 15 Nov 2009 |
| 100-m breaststroke | Rebecca Soni (USA) | 1 min 02.70 sec | 19 Dec 2009 |
| 200-m breaststroke | Rebecca Soni (USA) | 2 min 14.57 sec | 18 Dec 2009 |

## Swimming World Records—Short Course (25 m) (continued)

### Women (continued)

| EVENT | RECORD HOLDER (COUNTRY) | PERFORMANCE | DATE |
|---|---|---|---|
| 50-m butterfly | Therese Alshammar (SWE) | 24.38 sec | 22 Nov 2009 |
| 100-m butterfly | Diane Bui-Duyet (FRA) | 55.05 sec | 12 Dec 2009 |
| 200-m butterfly | Liu Zige (CHN) | 2 min 00.78 sec | 15 Nov 2009 |
| 100-m individual medley | Hinkelien Schreuder (NED) | 57.74 sec | 15 Nov 2009 |
| 200-m individual medley | Julia Smit (USA) | 2 min 04.60 sec | 19 Dec 2009 |
| 400-m individual medley | Julia Smit (USA) | 4 min 21.04 sec | 18 Dec 2009 |
| 4 × 100-m freestyle relay | Netherlands (Hinkelien Schreuder, Ranomi Kromowidjojo, Inge Dekker, Marleen Veldhuis) | 3 min 28.22 sec | 19 Dec 2008 |
| 4 × 200-m freestyle relay | China (Chen Qian, Tang Yi, Liu Jing, Zhu Qianwei) | 7 min 35.94 sec | 15 Dec 2010 |
| 4 × 100-m medley relay | United States (Margaret Hoelzer, Jessica Hardy, Dana Vollmer, Amanda Weir) | 3 min 47.97 sec | 18 Dec 2009 |

# Tennis

Four events dominate world championship tennis. The first of these traditional **"Grand Slam"** events was the **All-England Lawn Tennis Championships** (better known as the **Wimbledon** Championships), founded in 1877. Its only event the first year was the men's singles championships; women first competed in 1884. Major tennis tournaments also sprang up in the **United States** (1881 for men; women's singles competition first officially added 1889), **France** (1891 for men; women's singles competition added 1897), and **Australia** (1905 for men; women's singles competition added 1922). Open tennis (open, that is, to both professionals and amateurs) became the rule in the Grand Slam tournaments in 1968. International team tennis was organized in 1900 with the institution of the **Davis Cup.** Men's teams competing for the Davis Cup play four singles matches and one doubles match in elimination rounds. The Wightman Cup was contested yearly between British and American women's teams from 1923 to 1989. The **International Tennis Federation** (ITF, formerly the International Lawn Tennis Federation; founded 1913) established the **Federation Cup** in 1963 (called the **Fed Cup** since 1994) for international women's team competition. It is also decided by elimination rounds of four singles and one doubles contest.

**Related Web sites:** International Tennis Federation: <www.itftennis.com>; ATP (formerly Association of Tennis Professionals): <www.atpworldtour.com>; Women's Tennis Association: <www.wtatennis.com>.

## Australian Open Tennis Championships—Singles

| YEAR | MEN | WOMEN |
|---|---|---|
| 1905 | Rodney Heath (AUS) | |
| 1906 | Tony Wilding (NZL) | |
| 1907 | Horace Rice (AUS) | |
| 1908 | Fred Alexander (USA) | |
| 1909 | Tony Wilding (NZL) | |
| 1910 | Rodney Heath (AUS) | |
| 1911 | Norman Brookes (AUS) | |
| 1912 | J. Cecil Parke (GBR) | |
| 1913 | E.F. Parker (AUS) | |
| 1914 | Pat O'Hara Wood (AUS) | |
| 1915 | Francis Lowe (GBR) | |
| 1916–18 | *not held* | |
| 1919 | A.R.F. Kingscote (GBR) | |
| 1920 | Pat O'Hara Wood (AUS) | |
| 1921 | Rhys Gemmell (AUS) | |
| 1922 | James Anderson (AUS) | Margaret Molesworth (AUS) |
| 1923 | Pat O'Hara Wood (AUS) | Margaret Molesworth (AUS) |
| 1924 | James Anderson (AUS) | Sylvia Lance (AUS) |
| 1925 | James Anderson (AUS) | Daphne Akhurst (AUS) |
| 1926 | John Hawkes (AUS) | Daphne Akhurst (AUS) |
| 1927 | Gerald Patterson (AUS) | Esna Boyd (AUS) |
| 1928 | Jean Borotra (FRA) | Daphne Akhurst (AUS) |
| 1929 | John Gregory (GBR) | Daphne Akhurst (AUS) |
| 1930 | Gar Moon (AUS) | Daphne Akhurst (AUS) |
| 1931 | Jack Crawford (AUS) | Coral Buttsworth (AUS) |
| 1932 | Jack Crawford (AUS) | Coral Buttsworth (AUS) |
| 1933 | Jack Crawford (AUS) | Joan Hartigan (AUS) |

## Australian Open Tennis Championships—Singles (continued)

| YEAR | MEN | WOMEN |
|------|-----|-------|
| 1934 | Fred Perry (GBR) | Joan Hartigan (AUS) |
| 1935 | Jack Crawford (AUS) | Dorothy Round (GBR) |
| 1936 | Adrian Quist (AUS) | Joan Hartigan (AUS) |
| 1937 | Vivian McGrath (AUS) | Nancye Wynne (AUS) |
| 1938 | Don Budge (USA) | Dorothy Bundy (USA) |
| 1939 | John Bromwich (AUS) | Emily Westacott (AUS) |
| 1940 | Adrian Quist (AUS) | Nancye Wynne (AUS) |
| 1941–45 | not held | |
| 1946 | John Bromwich (AUS) | Nancye Wynne Bolton (AUS) |
| 1947 | Dinny Pails (AUS) | Nancye Wynne Bolton (AUS) |
| 1948 | Adrian Quist (AUS) | Nancye Wynne Bolton (AUS) |
| 1949 | Frank Sedgman (AUS) | Doris Hart (USA) |
| 1950 | Frank Sedgman (AUS) | Louise Brough (USA) |
| 1951 | Dick Savitt (USA) | Nancye Wynne Bolton (AUS) |
| 1952 | Ken McGregor (AUS) | Thelma Long (AUS) |
| 1953 | Ken Rosewall (AUS) | Maureen Connolly (USA) |
| 1954 | Mervyn Rose (AUS) | Thelma Long (AUS) |
| 1955 | Ken Rosewall (AUS) | Beryl Penrose (AUS) |
| 1956 | Lew Hoad (AUS) | Mary Carter (AUS) |
| 1957 | Ashley Cooper (AUS) | Shirley Fry (USA) |
| 1958 | Ashley Cooper (AUS) | Angela Mortimer (GBR) |
| 1959 | Alex Olmedo (PER) | Mary Carter-Reitano (AUS) |
| 1960 | Rod Laver (AUS) | Margaret Smith (AUS) |
| 1961 | Roy Emerson (AUS) | Margaret Smith (AUS) |
| 1962 | Rod Laver (AUS) | Margaret Smith (AUS) |
| 1963 | Roy Emerson (AUS) | Margaret Smith (AUS) |
| 1964 | Roy Emerson (AUS) | Margaret Smith (AUS) |
| 1965 | Roy Emerson (AUS) | Margaret Smith (AUS) |
| 1966 | Roy Emerson (AUS) | Margaret Smith (AUS) |
| 1967 | Roy Emerson (AUS) | Nancy Richey (USA) |
| 1968 | Bill Bowrey (AUS) | Billie Jean King (USA) |
| 1969 | Rod Laver (AUS) | Margaret Smith Court (AUS) |
| 1970 | Arthur Ashe (USA) | Margaret Smith Court (AUS) |
| 1971 | Ken Rosewall (AUS) | Margaret Smith Court (AUS) |
| 1972 | Ken Rosewall (AUS) | Virginia Wade (GBR) |
| 1973 | John Newcombe (AUS) | Margaret Smith Court (AUS) |
| 1974 | Jimmy Connors (USA) | Evonne Goolagong (AUS) |
| 1975 | John Newcombe (AUS) | Evonne Goolagong (AUS) |
| 1976 | Mark Edmondson (AUS) | Evonne Goolagong Cawley (AUS) |
| 1977[1] | Roscoe Tanner (USA) | Kerry Reid (AUS) |
| 1977[1] | Vitas Gerulaitis (USA) | Evonne Goolagong Cawley (AUS) |
| 1978[2] | Guillermo Vilas (ARG) | Chris O'Neill (AUS) |
| 1979[2] | Guillermo Vilas (ARG) | Barbara Jordan (USA) |
| 1980[2] | Brian Teacher (USA) | Hana Mandlikova (TCH) |
| 1981[2] | Johan Kriek (RSA) | Martina Navratilova (USA) |
| 1982[2] | Johan Kriek (RSA) | Chris Evert Lloyd (USA) |
| 1983[2] | Mats Wilander (SWE) | Martina Navratilova (USA) |
| 1984[2] | Mats Wilander (SWE) | Chris Evert Lloyd (USA) |
| 1985[2] | Stefan Edberg (SWE) | Martina Navratilova (USA) |
| 1986 | not held | |
| 1987 | Stefan Edberg (SWE) | Hana Mandlikova (TCH) |
| 1988 | Mats Wilander (SWE) | Steffi Graf (FRG) |
| 1989 | Ivan Lendl (TCH) | Steffi Graf (FRG) |
| 1990 | Ivan Lendl (TCH) | Steffi Graf (FRG) |
| 1991 | Boris Becker (GER) | Monica Seles (YUG) |
| 1992 | Jim Courier (USA) | Monica Seles (YUG) |
| 1993 | Jim Courier (USA) | Monica Seles (YUG) |
| 1994 | Pete Sampras (USA) | Steffi Graf (GER) |
| 1995 | Andre Agassi (USA) | Mary Pierce (FRA) |
| 1996 | Boris Becker (GER) | Monica Seles (USA) |
| 1997 | Pete Sampras (USA) | Martina Hingis (SUI) |
| 1998 | Petr Korda (CZE) | Martina Hingis (SUI) |
| 1999 | Yevgeny Kafelnikov (RUS) | Martina Hingis (SUI) |
| 2000 | Andre Agassi (USA) | Lindsay Davenport (USA) |
| 2001 | Andre Agassi (USA) | Jennifer Capriati (USA) |
| 2002 | Thomas Johansson (SWE) | Jennifer Capriati (USA) |
| 2003 | Andre Agassi (USA) | Serena Williams (USA) |
| 2004 | Roger Federer (SUI) | Justine Henin-Hardenne (BEL) |

## Australian Open Tennis Championships—Singles (continued)

| YEAR | MEN | WOMEN |
|------|-----|-------|
| 2005 | Marat Safin (RUS) | Serena Williams (USA) |
| 2006 | Roger Federer (SUI) | Amélie Mauresmo (FRA) |
| 2007 | Roger Federer (SUI) | Serena Williams (USA) |
| 2008 | Novak Djokovic (SRB) | Mariya Sharapova (RUS) |
| 2009 | Rafael Nadal (ESP) | Serena Williams (USA) |
| 2010 | Roger Federer (SUI) | Serena Williams (USA) |
| 2011 | Novak Djokovic (SRB) | Kim Clijsters (BEL) |
| 2012 | Novak Djokovic (SRB) | Victoria Azarenka (BLR) |

[1]Tournament held in January and December. [2]Tournament held in December rather than January.

## Australian Open Tennis Championships—Doubles

| YEAR | MEN | WOMEN |
|------|-----|-------|
| 1905 | Tom Tachell, Randolph Lycett | |
| 1906 | Tony Wilding, Rodney Heath | |
| 1907 | Harry Parker, William Gregg | |
| 1908 | Fred Alexander, Alfred Dunlop | |
| 1909 | Ernie F. Parker, J.P. Keane | |
| 1910 | Horace Rice, Ashley Campbell | |
| 1911 | Rodney Heath, Randolph Lycett | |
| 1912 | J. Cecil Parke, Charles Dixon | |
| 1913 | Ernie F. Parker, Alf Hedemann | |
| 1905 | Tom Tachell, Randolph Lycett | |
| 1906 | Tony Wilding, Rodney Heath | |
| 1907 | Harry Parker, William Gregg | |
| 1908 | Fred Alexander, Alfred Dunlop | |
| 1909 | Ernie F. Parker, J.P. Keane | |
| 1910 | Horace Rice, Ashley Campbell | |
| 1911 | Rodney Heath, Randolph Lycett | |
| 1912 | J. Cecil Parke, Charles Dixon | |
| 1913 | Ernie F. Parker, Alf Hedemann | |
| 1914 | Ashley Campbell, Gerald Patterson | |
| 1915 | Horace Rice, Clarrie Todd | |
| 1916–18 | not held | |
| 1919 | Pat O'Hara Wood, Ron Thomas | |
| 1920 | Pat O'Hara Wood, Ron Thomas | |
| 1921 | S.H. Eaton-Rice, Rhys Gemmell | |
| 1922 | Gerald Patterson, John Hawkes | Esne Boyd, Marjorie Mountain |
| 1923 | Pat O'Hara Wood, Bert St. John | Esne Boyd, Sylvia Lance |
| 1924 | Norman Brookes, James Anderson | Daphne Akhurst, Sylvia Lance |
| 1925 | Gerald Patterson, Pat O'Hara Wood | Daphne Akhurst, Sylvia Lance Harper |
| 1926 | Gerald Patterson, John Hawkes | Meryl O'Hara Wood, Esne Boyd |
| 1927 | Gerald Patterson, John Hawkes | Meryl O'Hara Wood, Louise Bickerton |
| 1928 | Jean Borotra, Jacques Brugnon | Daphne Akhurst, Esne Boyd |
| 1929 | Jack Crawford, Harry Hopman | Daphne Akhurst, Louise Bickerton |
| 1930 | Jack Crawford, Harry Hopman | Margaret Molesworth, Emily Hood |
| 1931 | Charles Donohoe, Ray Dunlop | Daphne Akhurst Cozens, Louise Bickerton |
| 1932 | Jack Crawford, Gar Moon | Coral Buttsworth, Marjorie Cox Crawford |
| 1933 | Ellsworth Vines, Keith Gledhill | Margaret Molesworth, Emily Hood Westacott |
| 1934 | Fred Perry, George Hughes | Margaret Molesworth, Emily Hood Westacott |
| 1935 | Jack Crawford, Vivian McGrath | Evelyn Dearman, Nancy Lyle |
| 1936 | Adrian Quist, D.P. Turnbull | Thelma Coyne, Nancye Wynne |
| 1937 | Adrian Quist, D.P. Turnbull | Thelma Coyne, Nancye Wynne |
| 1938 | Adrian Quist, John Bromwich | Thelma Coyne, Nancye Wynne |
| 1939 | Adrian Quist, John Bromwich | Thelma Coyne, Nancye Wynne |
| 1940 | Adrian Quist, John Bromwich | Thelma Coyne, Nancye Wynne |
| 1941–45 | not held | |
| 1946 | Adrian Quist, John Bromwich | Joyce Fitch, Mary Bevis |
| 1947 | Adrian Quist, John Bromwich | Thelma Coyne Long, Nancye Wynne Bolton |
| 1948 | Adrian Quist, John Bromwich | Thelma Coyne Long, Nancye Wynne Bolton |
| 1949 | Adrian Quist, John Bromwich | Thelma Coyne Long, Nancye Wynne Bolton |
| 1950 | Adrian Quist, John Bromwich | Louise Brough, Doris Hart |
| 1951 | Ken McGregor, Frank Sedgman | Thelma Coyne Long, Nancye Wynne Bolton |
| 1952 | Ken McGregor, Frank Sedgman | Thelma Coyne Long, Nancye Wynne Bolton |
| 1953 | Lew Hoad, Ken Rosewall | Maureen Connolly, Julia Sampson |
| 1954 | Rex Hartwig, Mervyn Rose | Mary Bevis Hawton, Beryl Penrose |
| 1955 | Vic Seixas, Tony Trabert | Mary Bevis Hawton, Beryl Penrose |

## Australian Open Tennis Championships—Doubles (continued)

| YEAR | MEN | WOMEN |
|---|---|---|
| 1956 | Lew Hoad, Ken Rosewall | Mary Bevis Hawton, Thelma Coyne Long |
| 1957 | Lew Hoad, Neale Fraser | Althea Gibson, Shirley Fry |
| 1958 | Ashley Cooper, Neale Fraser | Mary Bevis Hawton, Thelma Coyne Long |
| 1959 | Rod Laver, Robert Mark | Sandra Reynolds, Renee Schuurman |
| 1960 | Rod Laver, Robert Mark | Maria Bueno, Christine Truman |
| 1961 | Rod Laver, Robert Mark | Mary Reitano, Margaret Smith |
| 1962 | Roy Emerson, Neale Fraser | Robyn Ebbern, Margaret Smith |
| 1963 | Bob Hewitt, Fred Stolle | Robyn Ebbern, Margaret Smith |
| 1964 | Bob Hewitt, Fred Stolle | Judy Tegart, Lesley Turner |
| 1965 | John Newcombe, Tony Roche | Margaret Smith, Lesley Turner |
| 1966 | Roy Emerson, Fred Stolle | Carole Graebner, Nancy Richey |
| 1967 | John Newcombe, Tony Roche | Judy Tegart, Lesley Turner |
| 1968 | Dick Crealy, Allan Stone | Karen Krantzcke, Karrie Melville |
| 1969 | Roy Emerson, Rod Laver | Margaret Smith Court, Judy Tegart |
| 1970 | Bob Lutz, Stan Smith | Margaret Smith Court, Judy Tegart Dalton |
| 1971 | John Newcombe, Tony Roche | Margaret Smith Court, Evonne Goolagong |
| 1972 | Owen Davidson, Ken Rosewall | Kerry Harris, Helen Gourlay |
| 1973 | Mal Anderson, John Newcombe | Margaret Smith Court, Virginia Wade |
| 1974 | Ross Case, Geoff Masters | Evonne Goolagong, Peggy Michel |
| 1975 | John Alexander, Phil Dent | Evonne Goolagong, Peggy Michel |
| 1976 | John Newcombe, Tony Roche | Evonne Goolagong Cawley, Helen Gourlay |
| 1977[1] | Arthur Ashe, Tony Roche | Dianne Fromholtz, Helen Gourlay |
| 1977[1] | Allan Stone, Ray Ruffels | Evonne Goolagong Cawley, Helen Gourlay Cawley; Mona Guerrant, Kerry Reid[2] |
| 1978[3] | Wojtek Fibak, Kim Warwick | Renata Tomanova, Betsy Nagelsen |
| 1979[3] | Peter McNamara, Paul McNamee | Judy Chaloner, Dianne Evers |
| 1980[3] | Kim Warwick, Mark Edmondson | Martina Navratilova, Betsy Nagelsen |
| 1981[3] | Kim Warwick, Mark Edmondson | Kathy Jordan, Anne Smith |
| 1982[3] | John Alexander, John Fitzgerald | Martina Navratilova, Pam Shriver |
| 1983[3] | Mark Edmondson, Paul McNamee | Martina Navratilova, Pam Shriver |
| 1984[3] | Mark Edmondson, Sherwood Stewart | Martina Navratilova, Pam Shriver |
| 1985[3] | Paul Annacone, Christo van Rensburg | Martina Navratilova, Pam Shriver |
| 1986 | not held | |
| 1987 | Stefan Edberg, Anders Järryd | Martina Navratilova, Pam Shriver |
| 1988 | Rick Leach, Jim Pugh | Martina Navratilova, Pam Shriver |
| 1989 | Rick Leach, Jim Pugh | Martina Navratilova, Pam Shriver |
| 1990 | Pieter Aldrich, Danie Visser | Jana Novotna, Helena Sukova |
| 1991 | Scott Davis, David Pate | Patty Fendick, Mary Joe Fernández |
| 1992 | Todd Woodbridge, Mark Woodforde | Arantxa Sánchez Vicario, Helena Sukova |
| 1993 | Danie Visser, Laurie Warder | Gigi Fernández, Natasha Zvereva |
| 1994 | Jacco Eltingh, Paul Haarhuis | Gigi Fernández, Natasha Zvereva |
| 1995 | Jared Palmer, Richey Reneberg | Arantxa Sánchez Vicario, Jana Novotna |
| 1996 | Stefan Edberg, Petr Korda | Arantxa Sánchez Vicario, Chanda Rubin |
| 1997 | Todd Woodbridge, Mark Woodforde | Martina Hingis, Natasha Zvereva |
| 1998 | Jonas Björkman, Jacco Eltingh | Martina Hingis, Mirjana Lucic |
| 1999 | Jonas Björkman, Patrick Rafter | Martina Hingis, Anna Kournikova |
| 2000 | Ellis Ferreira, Rick Leach | Lisa Raymond, Rennae Stubbs |
| 2001 | Jonas Björkman, Todd Woodbridge | Venus Williams, Serena Williams |
| 2002 | Mark Knowles, Daniel Nestor | Martina Hingis, Anna Kournikova |
| 2003 | Michaël Llodra, Fabrice Santoro | Venus Williams, Serena Williams |
| 2004 | Michaël Llodra, Fabrice Santoro | Virginia Ruano Pascual, Paola Suárez |
| 2005 | Wayne Black, Kevin Ullyett | Alicia Molik, Svetlana Kuznetsova |
| 2006 | Bob Bryan, Mike Bryan | Yan Zi, Zheng Jie |
| 2007 | Bob Bryan, Mike Bryan | Cara Black, Liezel Huber |
| 2008 | Jonathan Erlich, Andy Ram | Alona Bondarenko, Kateryna Bondarenko |
| 2009 | Bob Bryan, Mike Bryan | Venus Williams, Serena Williams |
| 2010 | Bob Bryan, Mike Bryan | Venus Williams, Serena Williams |
| 2011 | Bob Bryan, Mike Bryan | Gisela Dulko, Flavia Pennetta |
| 2012 | Leander Paes, Radek Stepanek | Svetlana Kuznetsova, Vera Zvonareva |

[1]Tournament held in January and December.    [2]Tie; finals rained out.    [3]Tournament held in December rather than January.

# French Open Tennis Championships—Singles

*From 1891 to 1924, only members of French tennis clubs were eligible to play in the French Championships. The table shows the winners only since 1925, when the tournament was opened to international competition.*

| YEAR | MEN | WOMEN |
|------|-----|-------|
| 1925 | René Lacoste (FRA) | Suzanne Lenglen (FRA) |
| 1926 | Henri Cochet (FRA) | Suzanne Lenglen (FRA) |
| 1927 | René Lacoste (FRA) | Kornelia Bouman (NED) |
| 1928 | Henri Cochet (FRA) | Helen Wills (USA) |
| 1929 | René Lacoste (FRA) | Helen Wills (USA) |
| 1930 | Henri Cochet (FRA) | Helen Wills Moody (USA) |
| 1931 | Jean Borotra (FRA) | Cilly Aussem (GER) |
| 1932 | Henri Cochet (FRA) | Helen Wills Moody (USA) |
| 1933 | John Crawford (AUS) | Margaret Scriven (GBR) |
| 1934 | Gottfried von Cramm (GER) | Margaret Scriven (GBR) |
| 1935 | Fred Perry (GBR) | Hilde Sperling (DEN) |
| 1936 | Gottfried von Cramm (GER) | Hilde Sperling (DEN) |
| 1937 | Henner Henkel (GER) | Hilde Sperling (DEN) |
| 1938 | Don Budge (USA) | Simone Mathieu (FRA) |
| 1939 | Don McNeill (USA) | Simone Mathieu (FRA) |
| 1940 | *not held* | *not held* |
| 1941 | Bernard Destremau (FRA) | *not held* |
| 1942 | Bernard Destremau (FRA) | *not held* |
| 1943 | Yvon Petra (FRA) | *not held* |
| 1944 | Yvon Petra (FRA) | *not held* |
| 1945 | Yvon Petra (FRA) | *not held* |
| 1946 | Marcel Bernard (FRA) | Margaret Osborne (USA) |
| 1947 | Joseph Asboth (HUN) | Patricia Todd (USA) |
| 1948 | Frank Parker (USA) | Nelly Landry (BEL) |
| 1949 | Frank Parker (USA) | Margaret Osborne duPont (USA) |
| 1950 | Budge Patty (USA) | Doris Hart (USA) |
| 1951 | Jaroslav Drobny (TCH) | Shirley Fry (USA) |
| 1952 | Jaroslav Drobny (TCH) | Doris Hart (USA) |
| 1953 | Ken Rosewall (AUS) | Maureen Connolly (USA) |
| 1954 | Tony Trabert (USA) | Maureen Connolly (USA) |
| 1955 | Tony Trabert (USA) | Angela Mortimer (GBR) |
| 1956 | Lew Hoad (AUS) | Althea Gibson (USA) |
| 1957 | Sven Davidson (SWE) | Shirley Bloomer (GBR) |
| 1958 | Mervyn Rose (AUS) | Zsuzsi Kormoczi (HUN) |
| 1959 | Nicola Pietrangeli (ITA) | Christine Truman (GBR) |
| 1960 | Nicola Pietrangeli (ITA) | Darlene Hard (USA) |
| 1961 | Manuel Santana (ESP) | Ann Haydon (GBR) |
| 1962 | Rod Laver (AUS) | Margaret Smith (AUS) |
| 1963 | Roy Emerson (AUS) | Lesley Turner (AUS) |
| 1964 | Manuel Santana (ESP) | Margaret Smith (AUS) |
| 1965 | Fred Stolle (AUS) | Lesley Turner (AUS) |
| 1966 | Tony Roche (AUS) | Ann Haydon Jones (GBR) |
| 1967 | Roy Emerson (AUS) | Françoise Durr (FRA) |
| 1968 | Ken Rosewall (AUS) | Nancy Richey (USA) |
| 1969 | Rod Laver (AUS) | Margaret Smith Court (AUS) |
| 1970 | Jan Kodes (TCH) | Margaret Smith Court (AUS) |
| 1971 | Jan Kodes (TCH) | Evonne Goolagong (AUS) |
| 1972 | Andres Gimeno (ESP) | Billie Jean King (USA) |
| 1973 | Ilie Nastase (ROM) | Margaret Smith Court (AUS) |
| 1974 | Björn Borg (SWE) | Chris Evert (USA) |
| 1975 | Björn Borg (SWE) | Chris Evert (USA) |
| 1976 | Adriano Panatta (ITA) | Sue Barker (USA) |
| 1977 | Guillermo Vilas (ARG) | Mima Jausovec (YUG) |
| 1978 | Björn Borg (SWE) | Virginia Ruzici (ROM) |
| 1979 | Björn Borg (SWE) | Chris Evert Lloyd (USA) |
| 1980 | Björn Borg (SWE) | Chris Evert Lloyd (USA) |
| 1981 | Björn Borg (SWE) | Hana Mandlikova (TCH) |
| 1982 | Mats Wilander (SWE) | Martina Navratilova (USA) |
| 1983 | Yannick Noah (FRA) | Chris Evert Lloyd (USA) |
| 1984 | Ivan Lendl (TCH) | Martina Navratilova (USA) |
| 1985 | Mats Wilander (SWE) | Chris Evert Lloyd (USA) |
| 1986 | Ivan Lendl (TCH) | Chris Evert Lloyd (USA) |
| 1987 | Ivan Lendl (TCH) | Steffi Graf (FRG) |
| 1988 | Mats Wilander (SWE) | Steffi Graf (FRG) |
| 1989 | Michael Chang (USA) | Arantxa Sánchez Vicario (ESP) |

## French Open Tennis Championships—Singles (continued)

| YEAR | MEN | WOMEN |
|---|---|---|
| 1990 | Andres Gómez (ECU) | Monica Seles (YUG) |
| 1991 | Jim Courier (USA) | Monica Seles (YUG) |
| 1992 | Jim Courier (USA) | Monica Seles (YUG) |
| 1993 | Sergi Bruguera (ESP) | Steffi Graf (GER) |
| 1994 | Sergi Bruguera (ESP) | Arantxa Sánchez Vicario (ESP) |
| 1995 | Thomas Muster (AUT) | Steffi Graf (GER) |
| 1996 | Yevgeny Kafelnikov (RUS) | Steffi Graf (GER) |
| 1997 | Gustavo Kuerten (BRA) | Iva Majoli (CRO) |
| 1998 | Carlos Moya (ESP) | Arantxa Sánchez Vicario (ESP) |
| 1999 | Andre Agassi (USA) | Steffi Graf (GER) |
| 2000 | Gustavo Kuerten (BRA) | Mary Pierce (FRA) |
| 2001 | Gustavo Kuerten (BRA) | Jennifer Capriati (USA) |
| 2002 | Albert Costa (ESP) | Serena Williams (USA) |
| 2003 | Juan Carlos Ferrero (ESP) | Justine Henin-Hardenne (BEL) |
| 2004 | Gastón Gaudio (ARG) | Anastasiya Myskina (RUS) |
| 2005 | Rafael Nadal (ESP) | Justine Henin-Hardenne (BEL) |
| 2006 | Rafael Nadal (ESP) | Justine Henin-Hardenne (BEL) |
| 2007 | Rafael Nadal (ESP) | Justine Henin (BEL) |
| 2008 | Rafael Nadal (ESP) | Ana Ivanovic (SRB) |
| 2009 | Roger Federer (SUI) | Svetlana Kuznetsova (RUS) |
| 2010 | Rafael Nadal (ESP) | Francesca Schiavone (ITA) |
| 2011 | Rafael Nadal (ESP) | Li Na (CHN) |
| 2012 | Rafael Nadal (ESP) | Mariya Sharapova (RUS) |

## French Open Tennis Championships—Doubles

| YEAR | MEN | WOMEN |
|---|---|---|
| 1925 | Jean Borotra, René Lacoste | Suzanne Lenglen, Didi Vlasto |
| 1926 | Vincent Richards, Howard Kinsey | Suzanne Lenglen, Didi Vlasto |
| 1927 | Henri Cochet, Jacques Brugnon | Irene Peacock, Bobby Heine |
| 1928 | Jean Borotra, Jacques Brugnon | Phoebe Watson, Eileen Bennett |
| 1929 | Jean Borotra, René Lacoste | Lili de Alvarez, Kea Bouman |
| 1930 | Henri Cochet, Jacques Brugnon | Helen Wills Moody, Elizabeth Ryan |
| 1931 | George Lott, John Van Ryn | Eileen Whittingstall, Betty Nuthall |
| 1932 | Henri Cochet, Jacques Brugnon | Helen Wills Moody, Elizabeth Ryan |
| 1933 | Pat Hughes, Fred Perry | Simone Mathieu, Elizabeth Ryan |
| 1934 | Jean Borotra, Jacques Brugnon | Simone Mathieu, Elizabeth Ryan |
| 1935 | Jack Crawford, Adrian Quist | Margaret Scriven, Kay Stammers |
| 1936 | Jean Borotra, Marcel Bernard | Simone Mathieu, Billie Yorke |
| 1937 | Gottfried von Cramm, Henner Henkel | Simone Mathieu, Billie Yorke |
| 1938 | Bernard Destremau, Yvon Petra | Simone Mathieu, Billie Yorke |
| 1939 | Don McNeill, Charles Harris | Simone Mathieu, Jadwiga Jedrzejowska |
| 1940-45 | not held | |
| 1946 | Marcel Bernard, Yvon Petra | Louise Brough, Margaret Osborne |
| 1947 | Eustace Fannin, Eric Sturgess | Louise Brough, Margaret Osborne |
| 1948 | Lennart Bergelin, Jaroslav Drobny | Doris Hart, Patricia Todd |
| 1949 | Pancho Gonzáles, Frank Parker | Louise Brough, Margaret Osborne duPont |
| 1950 | Billy Talbert, Tony Trabert | Doris Hart, Shirley Fry |
| 1951 | Ken McGregor, Frank Sedgman | Doris Hart, Shirley Fry |
| 1952 | Ken McGregor, Frank Sedgman | Doris Hart, Shirley Fry |
| 1953 | Lew Hoad, Ken Rosewall | Doris Hart, Shirley Fry |
| 1954 | Vic Seixas, Tony Trabert | Maureen Connolly, Nell Hopman |
| 1955 | Vic Seixas, Tony Trabert | Beverly Fleitz, Darlene Hard |
| 1956 | Don Candy, Robert Perry | Angela Buxton, Althea Gibson |
| 1957 | Mal Anderson, Ashley Cooper | Shirley Bloomer, Darlene Hard |
| 1958 | Ashley Cooper, Neale Fraser | Rosie Reyes, Yola Ramirez |
| 1959 | Nicola Pietrangeli, Orlando Sirola | Sandra Reynolds, Renee Schuurman |
| 1960 | Roy Emerson, Neale Fraser | Maria Bueno, Darlene Hard |
| 1961 | Roy Emerson, Rod Laver | Sandra Reynolds, Renee Schuurman |
| 1962 | Roy Emerson, Neale Fraser | Sandra Reynolds Price, Renee Schuurman |
| 1963 | Roy Emerson, Manuel Santana | Ann Haydon Jones, Renee Schuurman |
| 1964 | Roy Emerson, Ken Fletcher | Margaret Smith, Lesley Turner |
| 1965 | Roy Emerson, Fred Stolle | Margaret Smith, Lesley Turner |
| 1966 | Clark Graebner, Dennis Ralston | Margaret Smith, Judy Tegart |
| 1967 | John Newcombe, Tony Roche | Françoise Durr, Gail Sherriff |
| 1968 | Ken Rosewall, Fred Stolle | Françoise Durr, Ann Haydon Jones |
| 1969 | John Newcombe, Tony Roche | Françoise Durr, Ann Haydon Jones |
| 1970 | Ilie Nastase, Ion Tiriac | Françoise Durr, Gail Chanfreau |

## French Open Tennis Championships—Doubles (continued)

| YEAR | MEN | WOMEN |
|------|-----|-------|
| 1971 | Arthur Ashe, Marty Riessen | Françoise Durr, Gail Chanfreau |
| 1972 | Bob Hewitt, Frew McMillan | Billie Jean King, Betty Stove |
| 1973 | John Newcombe, Tom Okker | Margaret Smith Court, Virginia Wade |
| 1974 | Dick Crealy, Onny Parun | Chris Evert, Olga Morozova |
| 1975 | Brian Gottfried, Raúl Ramírez | Chris Evert, Martina Navratilova |
| 1976 | Fred McNair, Sherwood Stewart | Fiorella Bonicelli, Gail Lovera |
| 1977 | Brian Gottfried, Raúl Ramírez | Regina Marsikova, Pam Teeguarden |
| 1978 | Hank Pfister, Gene Mayer | Mima Jausovec, Virginia Ruzici |
| 1979 | Sandy Mayer, Gene Mayer | Wendy Turnbull, Betty Stove |
| 1980 | Victor Amaya, Hank Pfister | Kathy Jordan, Anne Smith |
| 1981 | Heinz Günthardt, Balázs Taróczy | Rosalyn Fairbank, Tanya Harford |
| 1982 | Sherwood Stewart, Ferdi Taygan | Martina Navratilova, Anne Smith |
| 1983 | Anders Järryd, Hans Simonsson | Rosalyn Fairbank, Candy Reynolds |
| 1984 | Henri Leconte, Yannick Noah | Martina Navratilova, Pam Shriver |
| 1985 | Kim Warwick, Mark Edmondson | Martina Navratilova, Pam Shriver |
| 1986 | John Fitzgerald, Tomas Smid | Martina Navratilova, Andrea Temesvari |
| 1987 | Robert Seguso, Anders Järryd | Martina Navratilova, Pam Shriver |
| 1988 | Emilio Sánchez, Andres Gómez | Martina Navratilova, Pam Shriver |
| 1989 | Jim Grabb, Patrick McEnroe | Larisa Savchenko, Natasha Zvereva |
| 1990 | Sergio Casal, Emilio Sánchez | Jana Novotna, Helena Sukova |
| 1991 | John Fitzgerald, Anders Järryd | Gigi Fernández, Jana Novotna |
| 1992 | Jacob Hlasek, Marc Rosset | Gigi Fernández, Natasha Zvereva |
| 1993 | Luke Jensen, Murphy Jensen | Gigi Fernández, Natasha Zvereva |
| 1994 | Byron Black, Jonathan Stark | Gigi Fernández, Natasha Zvereva |
| 1995 | Jacco Eltingh, Paul Haarhuis | Gigi Fernández, Natasha Zvereva |
| 1996 | Yevgeny Kafelnikov, Daniel Vacek | Lindsay Davenport, Mary Joe Fernández |
| 1997 | Yevgeny Kafelnikov, Daniel Vacek | Gigi Fernández, Natasha Zvereva |
| 1998 | Jacco Eltingh, Paul Haarhuis | Martina Hingis, Jana Novotna |
| 1999 | Mahesh Bhupathi, Leander Paes | Venus Williams, Serena Williams |
| 2000 | Todd Woodbridge, Mark Woodforde | Martina Hingis, Mary Pierce |
| 2001 | Mahesh Bhupathi, Leander Paes | Virginia Ruano Pascual, Paola Suárez |
| 2002 | Yevgeny Kafelnikov, Paul Haarhuis | Virginia Ruano Pascual, Paola Suárez |
| 2003 | Bob Bryan, Mike Bryan | Kim Clijsters, Ai Sugiyama |
| 2004 | Xavier Malisse, Olivier Rochus | Virginia Ruano Pascual, Paola Suárez |
| 2005 | Jonas Björkman, Max Mirnyi | Virginia Ruano Pascual, Paola Suárez |
| 2006 | Jonas Björkman, Max Mirnyi | Lisa Raymond, Samantha Stosur |
| 2007 | Mark Knowles, Daniel Nestor | Alicia Molik, Mara Santangelo |
| 2008 | Pablo Cuevas, Luis Horna | Anabel Medina Garrigues, Virginia Ruano Pascual |
| 2009 | Lukas Dlouhy, Leander Paes | Anabel Medina Garrigues, Virginia Ruano Pascual |
| 2010 | Nenad Zimonjic, Daniel Nestor | Venus Williams, Serena Williams |
| 2011 | Max Mirnyi, Daniel Nestor | Andrea Hlavackova, Lucie Hradecka |
| 2012 | Max Mirnyi, Daniel Nestor | Sara Errani, Roberta Vinci |

## All-England (Wimbledon) Tennis Championships—Singles

| YEAR | MEN | WOMEN |
|------|-----|-------|
| 1877 | Spencer Gore (GBR) | |
| 1878 | Frank Hadow (GBR) | |
| 1879 | John Hartley (GBR) | |
| 1880 | John Hartley (GBR) | |
| 1881 | William Renshaw (GBR) | |
| 1882 | William Renshaw (GBR) | |
| 1883 | William Renshaw (GBR) | |
| 1884 | William Renshaw (GBR) | Maud Watson (GBR) |
| 1885 | William Renshaw (GBR) | Maud Watson (GBR) |
| 1886 | William Renshaw (GBR) | Blanche Bingley (GBR) |
| 1887 | Herbert Lawford (GBR) | Lottie Dod (GBR) |
| 1888 | Ernest Renshaw (GBR) | Lottie Dod (GBR) |
| 1889 | William Renshaw (GBR) | Blanche Bingley Hillyard (GBR) |
| 1890 | William Hamilton (GBR) | Lena Rice (GBR) |
| 1891 | Wilfred Baddeley (GBR) | Lottie Dod (GBR) |
| 1892 | Wilfred Baddeley (GBR) | Lottie Dod (GBR) |
| 1893 | Joshua Pim (GBR) | Lottie Dod (GBR) |
| 1894 | Joshua Pim (GBR) | Blanche Bingley Hillyard (GBR) |
| 1895 | Wilfred Baddeley (GBR) | Charlotte Cooper (GBR) |
| 1896 | Harold Mahony (GBR) | Charlotte Cooper (GBR) |
| 1897 | Reggie Doherty (GBR) | Blanche Bingley Hillyard (GBR) |

## All-England (Wimbledon) Tennis Championships—Singles (continued)

| YEAR | MEN | WOMEN |
|------|-----|-------|
| 1898 | Reggie Doherty (GBR) | Charlotte Cooper (GBR) |
| 1899 | Reggie Doherty (GBR) | Blanche Bingley Hillyard (GBR) |
| 1900 | Reggie Doherty (GBR) | Blanche Bingley Hillyard (GBR) |
| 1901 | Arthur Gore (GBR) | Charlotte Cooper Sterry (GBR) |
| 1902 | Laurie Doherty (GBR) | Muriel Robb (GBR) |
| 1903 | Laurie Doherty (GBR) | Dorothea Douglass (GBR) |
| 1904 | Laurie Doherty (GBR) | Dorothea Douglass (GBR) |
| 1905 | Laurie Doherty (GBR) | May Sutton (USA) |
| 1906 | Laurie Doherty (GBR) | Dorothea Douglass (GBR) |
| 1907 | Norman Brookes (AUS) | May Sutton (USA) |
| 1908 | Arthur Gore (GBR) | Charlotte Cooper Sterry (GBR) |
| 1909 | Arthur Gore (GBR) | Dora Boothby (GBR) |
| 1910 | Tony Wilding (NZL) | Dorothea Lambert Chambers (GBR) |
| 1911 | Tony Wilding (NZL) | Dorothea Lambert Chambers (GBR) |
| 1912 | Tony Wilding (NZL) | Ethel Larcombe (GBR) |
| 1913 | Tony Wilding (NZL) | Dorothea Lambert Chambers (GBR) |
| 1914 | Norman Brookes (AUS) | Dorothea Lambert Chambers (GBR) |
| 1915–18 | *not held* | |
| 1919 | Gerald Patterson (AUS) | Suzanne Lenglen (FRA) |
| 1920 | Bill Tilden (USA) | Suzanne Lenglen (FRA) |
| 1921 | Bill Tilden (USA) | Suzanne Lenglen (FRA) |
| 1922 | Gerald Patterson (AUS) | Suzanne Lenglen (FRA) |
| 1923 | Bill Johnston (USA) | Suzanne Lenglen (FRA) |
| 1924 | Jean Borotra (FRA) | Kathleen McKane (GBR) |
| 1925 | René Lacoste (FRA) | Suzanne Lenglen (FRA) |
| 1926 | Jean Borotra (FRA) | Kathleen McKane Godfree (GBR) |
| 1927 | Henri Cochet (FRA) | Helen Wills (USA) |
| 1928 | René Lacoste (FRA) | Helen Wills (USA) |
| 1929 | Henri Cochet (FRA) | Helen Wills (USA) |
| 1930 | Bill Tilden (USA) | Helen Wills Moody (USA) |
| 1931 | Sidney Wood (USA) | Cilly Aussem (GER) |
| 1932 | Ellsworth Vines (USA) | Helen Wills Moody (USA) |
| 1933 | Jack Crawford (AUS) | Helen Wills Moody (USA) |
| 1934 | Fred Perry (GBR) | Dorothy Round (GBR) |
| 1935 | Fred Perry (GBR) | Helen Wills Moody (USA) |
| 1936 | Fred Perry (GBR) | Helen Jacobs (USA) |
| 1937 | Don Budge (USA) | Dorothy Round (GBR) |
| 1938 | Don Budge (USA) | Helen Wills Moody (USA) |
| 1939 | Bobby Riggs (USA) | Alice Marble (USA) |
| 1940–45 | *not held* | |
| 1946 | Yvon Petra (FRA) | Pauline Betz (USA) |
| 1947 | Jack Kramer (USA) | Margaret Osborne (USA) |
| 1948 | Bob Falkenburg (USA) | Louise Brough (USA) |
| 1949 | Ted Schroeder (USA) | Louise Brough (USA) |
| 1950 | Budge Patty (USA) | Louise Brough (USA) |
| 1951 | Dick Savitt (USA) | Doris Hart (USA) |
| 1952 | Frank Sedgman (AUS) | Maureen Connolly (USA) |
| 1953 | Vic Seixas (USA) | Maureen Connolly (USA) |
| 1954 | Jaroslav Drobny (TCH) | Maureen Connolly (USA) |
| 1955 | Tony Trabert (USA) | Louise Brough (USA) |
| 1956 | Lew Hoad (AUS) | Shirley Fry (USA) |
| 1957 | Lew Hoad (AUS) | Althea Gibson (USA) |
| 1958 | Ashley Cooper (AUS) | Althea Gibson (USA) |
| 1959 | Alex Olmedo (PER) | Maria Bueno (BRA) |
| 1960 | Neale Fraser (AUS) | Maria Bueno (BRA) |
| 1961 | Rod Laver (AUS) | Angela Mortimer (GBR) |
| 1962 | Rod Laver (AUS) | Karen Susman (USA) |
| 1963 | Chuck McKinley (USA) | Margaret Smith (AUS) |
| 1964 | Roy Emerson (AUS) | Maria Bueno (BRA) |
| 1965 | Roy Emerson (AUS) | Margaret Smith (AUS) |
| 1966 | Manuel Santana (ESP) | Billie Jean King (USA) |
| 1967 | John Newcombe (AUS) | Billie Jean King (USA) |
| 1968 | Rod Laver (AUS) | Billie Jean King (USA) |
| 1969 | Rod Laver (AUS) | Ann Jones (GBR) |
| 1970 | John Newcombe (AUS) | Margaret Smith Court (AUS) |
| 1971 | John Newcombe (AUS) | Evonne Goolagong (AUS) |
| 1972 | Stan Smith (USA) | Billie Jean King (USA) |
| 1973 | Jan Kodes (TCH) | Billie Jean King (USA) |

## All-England (Wimbledon) Tennis Championships—Singles (continued)

| YEAR | MEN | WOMEN |
|---|---|---|
| 1974 | Jimmy Connors (USA) | Chris Evert (USA) |
| 1975 | Arthur Ashe (USA) | Billie Jean King (USA) |
| 1976 | Björn Borg (SWE) | Chris Evert (USA) |
| 1977 | Björn Borg (SWE) | Virginia Wade (GBR) |
| 1978 | Björn Borg (SWE) | Martina Navratilova (TCH) |
| 1979 | Björn Borg (SWE) | Martina Navratilova (USA) |
| 1980 | Björn Borg (SWE) | Evonne Goolagong Cawley (AUS) |
| 1981 | John McEnroe (USA) | Chris Evert Lloyd (USA) |
| 1982 | Jimmy Connors (USA) | Martina Navratilova (USA) |
| 1983 | John McEnroe (USA) | Martina Navratilova (USA) |
| 1984 | John McEnroe (USA) | Martina Navratilova (USA) |
| 1985 | Boris Becker (FRG) | Martina Navratilova (USA) |
| 1986 | Boris Becker (FRG) | Martina Navratilova (USA) |
| 1987 | Pat Cash (AUS) | Martina Navratilova (USA) |
| 1988 | Stefan Edberg (SWE) | Steffi Graf (GDR) |
| 1989 | Boris Becker (FRG) | Steffi Graf (GDR) |
| 1990 | Stefan Edberg (SWE) | Martina Navratilova (USA) |
| 1991 | Michael Stich (GER) | Steffi Graf (GER) |
| 1992 | Andre Agassi (USA) | Steffi Graf (GER) |
| 1993 | Pete Sampras (USA) | Steffi Graf (GER) |
| 1994 | Pete Sampras (USA) | Conchita Martínez (ESP) |
| 1995 | Pete Sampras (USA) | Steffi Graf (GER) |
| 1996 | Richard Krajicek (NED) | Steffi Graf (GER) |
| 1997 | Pete Sampras (USA) | Martina Hingis (SUI) |
| 1998 | Pete Sampras (USA) | Jana Novotna (CZE) |
| 1999 | Pete Sampras (USA) | Lindsay Davenport (USA) |
| 2000 | Pete Sampras (USA) | Venus Williams (USA) |
| 2001 | Goran Ivanisevic (CRO) | Venus Williams (USA) |
| 2002 | Lleyton Hewitt (AUS) | Serena Williams (USA) |
| 2003 | Roger Federer (SUI) | Serena Williams (USA) |
| 2004 | Roger Federer (SUI) | Mariya Sharapova (RUS) |
| 2005 | Roger Federer (SUI) | Venus Williams (USA) |
| 2006 | Roger Federer (SUI) | Amélie Mauresmo (FRA) |
| 2007 | Roger Federer (SUI) | Venus Williams (USA) |
| 2008 | Rafael Nadal (ESP) | Venus WIlliams (USA) |
| 2009 | Roger Federer (SUI) | Serena Williams (USA) |
| 2010 | Rafael Nadal (ESP) | Serena Williams (USA) |
| 2011 | Novak Djokovic (SER) | Petra Kvitova (CZE) |
| 2012 | Roger Federer (SUI) | Serena Williams (USA) |

## All-England (Wimbledon) Tennis Championships—Doubles

| YEAR | MEN | WOMEN |
|---|---|---|
| 1879 | L.R. Erskine, H. Lawford | |
| 1880 | William Renshaw, Ernest Renshaw | |
| 1881 | William Renshaw, Ernest Renshaw | |
| 1882 | J.T. Hartley, R.T. Richardson | |
| 1883 | C.W. Grinstead, C.E. Welldon | |
| 1884 | William Renshaw, Ernest Renshaw | |
| 1885 | William Renshaw, Ernest Renshaw | |
| 1886 | William Renshaw, Ernest Renshaw | |
| 1887 | Herbert Wilberforce, P.B. Lyon | |
| 1888 | William Renshaw, Ernest Renshaw | |
| 1889 | William Renshaw, Ernest Renshaw | |
| 1890 | Joshua Pim, F.O. Stoker | |
| 1891 | Wilfred Baddeley, Herbert Baddeley | |
| 1892 | E.W. Lewis, H.S. Barlow | |
| 1893 | Joshua Pim, F.O. Stoker | |
| 1894 | Wilfred Baddeley, Herbert Baddeley | |
| 1895 | Wilfred Baddeley, Herbert Baddeley | |
| 1896 | Wilfred Baddeley, Herbert Baddeley | |
| 1897 | Reggie Doherty, Laurie Doherty | |
| 1898 | Reggie Doherty, Laurie Doherty | |
| 1899 | Reggie Doherty, Laurie Doherty | |
| 1900 | Reggie Doherty, Laurie Doherty | |
| 1901 | Reggie Doherty, Laurie Doherty | |
| 1902 | Sidney Smith, Frank Riseley | |
| 1903 | Reggie Doherty, Laurie Doherty | |

## All-England (Wimbledon) Tennis Championships—Doubles (continued)

| YEAR | MEN | WOMEN |
|---|---|---|
| 1904 | Reggie Doherty, Laurie Doherty | |
| 1905 | Reggie Doherty, Laurie Doherty | |
| 1906 | Sidney Smith, Frank Riseley | |
| 1907 | Norman Brookes, Tony Wilding | |
| 1908 | Tony Wilding, M.J.G. Ritchie | |
| 1909 | Arthur Gore, H. Roper Barrett | |
| 1910 | Tony Wilding, M.J.G. Ritchie | |
| 1911 | André Gobert, Max Decugis | |
| 1912 | H. Roper Barrett, Charles Dixon | |
| 1913 | H. Roper Barrett, Charles Dixon | Winifred McNair, Dora Boothby |
| 1914 | Norman Brookes, Tony Wilding | Elizabeth Ryan, Agatha Morton |
| 1915–18 | not held | |
| 1919 | R.V. Thomas, Pat O'Hara Wood | Suzanne Lenglen, Elizabeth Ryan |
| 1920 | Richard Williams, Chuck Garland | Suzanne Lenglen, Elizabeth Ryan |
| 1921 | Randolph Lycett, Max Woosnam | Suzanne Lenglen, Elizabeth Ryan |
| 1922 | James Anderson, Randolph Lycett | Suzanne Lenglen, Elizabeth Ryan |
| 1923 | Leslie Godfree, Randolph Lycett | Suzanne Lenglen, Elizabeth Ryan |
| 1924 | Frank Hunter, Vincent Richards | Hazel Wightman, Helen Wills |
| 1925 | Jean Borotra, René Lacoste | Suzanne Lenglen, Elizabeth Ryan |
| 1926 | Henri Cochet, Jacques Brugnon | Mary Browne, Elizabeth Ryan |
| 1927 | Bill Tilden, Frank Hunter | Helen Wills, Elizabeth Ryan |
| 1928 | Henri Cochet, Jacques Brugnon | Peggy Saunders, Phoebe Watson |
| 1929 | Wilmer Allison, John Van Ryn | Peggy Saunders Michell, Phoebe Watson |
| 1930 | Wilmer Allison, John Van Ryn | Helen Wills Moody, Elizabeth Ryan |
| 1931 | George Lott, John Van Ryn | Phyllis Mudford, Dorothy Barron |
| 1932 | Jean Borotra, Jacques Brugnon | Doris Metaxa, Josane Sigart |
| 1933 | Jean Borotra, Jacques Brugnon | Simone Mathieu, Elizabeth Ryan |
| 1934 | George Lott, Lester Stoefen | Simone Mathieu, Elizabeth Ryan |
| 1935 | Adrian Quist, Jack Crawford | Freda James, Kay Stammers |
| 1936 | Pat Hughes, Raymond Tuckey | Freda James, Kay Stammers |
| 1937 | Don Budge, Gene Mako | Simone Mathieu, Billie Yorke |
| 1938 | Don Budge, Gene Mako | Sarah Palfrey Fabyan, Alice Marble |
| 1939 | Bobby Riggs, Elwood Cooke | Sarah Palfrey Fabyan, Alice Marble |
| 1940–45 | not held | |
| 1946 | Jack Kramer, Tom Brown | Louise Brough, Margaret Osborne |
| 1947 | Jack Kramer, Bob Falkenburg | Patricia Todd, Doris Hart |
| 1948 | John Bromwich, Frank Sedgman | Louise Brough, Margaret Osborne duPont |
| 1949 | Pancho Gonzáles, Frank Parker | Louise Brough, Margaret Osborne duPont |
| 1950 | Adrian Quist, John Bromwich | Louise Brough, Margaret Osborne duPont |
| 1951 | Ken McGregor, Frank Sedgman | Doris Hart, Shirley Fry |
| 1952 | Ken McGregor, Frank Sedgman | Doris Hart, Shirley Fry |
| 1953 | Lew Hoad, Ken Rosewall | Doris Hart, Shirley Fry |
| 1954 | Rex Hartwig, Mervyn Rose | Louise Brough, Margaret Osborne duPont |
| 1955 | Rex Hartwig, Lew Hoad | Angela Mortimer, Anne Shilcock |
| 1956 | Lew Hoad, Ken Rosewall | Angela Buxton, Althea Gibson |
| 1957 | Budge Patty, Gardnar Mulloy | Althea Gibson, Darlene Hard |
| 1958 | Sven Davidson, Ulf Schmidt | Maria Bueno, Althea Gibson |
| 1959 | Roy Emerson, Neale Fraser | Jeanne Arth, Darlene Hard |
| 1960 | Rafael Osuna, Dennis Ralston | Maria Bueno, Darlene Hard |
| 1961 | Roy Emerson, Neale Fraser | Karen Hantze, Billie Jean Moffitt |
| 1962 | Bob Hewitt, Fred Stolle | Karen Hantze Susman, Billie Jean Moffitt |
| 1963 | Rafael Osuna, Antonio Palafox | Maria Bueno, Darlene Hard |
| 1964 | Bob Hewitt, Fred Stolle | Margaret Smith, Leslie Turner |
| 1965 | John Newcombe, Tony Roche | Maria Bueno, Billie Jean Moffitt |
| 1966 | John Newcombe, Ken Fletcher | Maria Bueno, Nancy Richey |
| 1967 | Bob Hewitt, Frew McMillan | Billie Jean King, Rosemary Casals |
| 1968 | John Newcombe, Tony Roche | Billie Jean King, Rosemary Casals |
| 1969 | John Newcombe, Tony Roche | Margaret Smith Court, Judy Tegart |
| 1970 | John Newcombe, Tony Roche | Billie Jean King, Rosemary Casals |
| 1971 | Roy Emerson, Rod Laver | Billie Jean King, Rosemary Casals |
| 1972 | Bob Hewitt, Frew McMillan | Billie Jean King, Betty Stove |
| 1973 | Jimmy Connors, Ilie Nastase | Billie Jean King, Rosemary Casals |
| 1974 | John Newcombe, Tony Roche | Evonne Goolagong, Peggy Michel |
| 1975 | Vitas Gerulaitis, Sandy Mayer | Ann Kiyomura, Kazuko Sawamatsu |
| 1976 | Brian Gottfried, Raúl Ramírez | Chris Evert, Martina Navratilova |
| 1977 | Ross Case, Geoff Masters | Helen Gourlay Cawley, Joanne Russell |
| 1978 | Bob Hewitt, Frew McMillan | Kerry Reid, Wendy Turnbull |
| 1979 | John McEnroe, Peter Fleming | Billie Jean King, Martina Navratilova |

## All-England (Wimbledon) Tennis Championships—Doubles (continued)

| YEAR | MEN | WOMEN |
|---|---|---|
| 1980 | Peter McNamara, Paul McNamee | Kathy Jordan, Anne Smith |
| 1981 | John McEnroe, Peter Fleming | Martina Navratilova, Pam Shriver |
| 1982 | Peter McNamara, Paul McNamee | Martina Navratilova, Pam Shriver |
| 1983 | John McEnroe, Peter Fleming | Martina Navratilova, Pam Shriver |
| 1984 | John McEnroe, Peter Fleming | Martina Navratilova, Pam Shriver |
| 1985 | Heinz Günthardt, Balázs Taróczy | Kathy Jordan, Elizabeth Smylie |
| 1986 | Joakim Nyström, Mats Wilander | Martina Navratilova, Pam Shriver |
| 1987 | Robert Seguso, Ken Flach | Claudia Kohde-Kilsch, Helena Sukova |
| 1988 | Robert Seguso, Ken Flach | Steffi Graf, Gabriela Sabatini |
| 1989 | John Fitzgerald, Anders Järryd | Jana Novotna, Helena Sukova |
| 1990 | Rick Leach, Jim Pugh | Jana Novotna, Helena Sukova |
| 1991 | John Fitzgerald, Anders Järryd | Larisa Savchenko, Natasha Zvereva |
| 1992 | John McEnroe, Michael Stich | Gigi Fernández, Natasha Zvereva |
| 1993 | Todd Woodbridge, Mark Woodforde | Gigi Fernández, Natasha Zvereva |
| 1994 | Todd Woodbridge, Mark Woodforde | Gigi Fernández, Natasha Zvereva |
| 1995 | Todd Woodbridge, Mark Woodforde | Arantxa Sánchez Vicario, Jana Novotna |
| 1996 | Todd Woodbridge, Mark Woodforde | Helena Sukova, Martina Hingis |
| 1997 | Todd Woodbridge, Mark Woodforde | Gigi Fernández, Natasha Zvereva |
| 1998 | Jacco Eltingh, Paul Haarhuis | Martina Hingis, Jana Novotna |
| 1999 | Mahesh Bhupathi, Leander Paes | Lindsay Davenport, Corina Morariu |
| 2000 | Todd Woodbridge, Mark Woodforde | Venus Williams, Serena Williams |
| 2001 | Donald Johnson, Jared Palmer | Lisa Raymond, Rennae Stubbs |
| 2002 | Jonas Björkman, Todd Woodbridge | Venus Williams, Serena Williams |
| 2003 | Jonas Björkman, Todd Woodbridge | Kim Clijsters, Ai Sugiyama |
| 2004 | Jonas Björkman, Todd Woodbridge | Cara Black, Rennae Stubbs |
| 2005 | Stephen Huss, Wesley Moodie | Cara Black, Liezel Huber |
| 2006 | Bob Bryan, Mike Bryan | Yan Zi, Zheng Jie |
| 2007 | Arnaud Clément, Michaël Llodra | Cara Black, Liezel Huber |
| 2008 | Daniel Nestor, Nenad Zimonjic | Venus Williams, Serena Williams |
| 2009 | Daniel Nestor, Nenad Zimonjic | Venus Williams, Serena Williams |
| 2010 | Jürgen Melzer, Philipp Petzschner | Vania King, Yaroslava Shvedova |
| 2011 | Bob Bryan, Mike Bryan | Kveta Peschke, Katarina Srebotnik |
| 2012 | Jonathan Marray, Frederik Nielsen | Venus Williams, Serena Williams |

## United States Open Tennis Championships—Singles

| YEAR | MEN | WOMEN |
|---|---|---|
| 1881 | Richard Sears (USA) | |
| 1882 | Richard Sears (USA) | |
| 1883 | Richard Sears (USA) | |
| 1884 | Richard Sears (USA) | |
| 1885 | Richard Sears (USA) | |
| 1886 | Richard Sears (USA) | |
| 1887 | Richard Sears (USA) | Ellen Hansell (USA) |
| 1888 | Henry Slocum, Jr. (USA) | Bertha Townsend (USA) |
| 1889 | Henry Slocum, Jr. (USA) | Bertha Townsend (USA) |
| 1890 | Oliver Campbell (USA) | Ellen Roosevelt (USA) |
| 1891 | Oliver Campbell (USA) | Mabel Cahill (USA) |
| 1892 | Oliver Campbell (USA) | Mabel Cahill (USA) |
| 1893 | Robert Wrenn (USA) | Aline Terry (USA) |
| 1894 | Robert Wrenn (USA) | Helen Helwig (USA) |
| 1895 | Fred Hovey (USA) | Juliette Atkinson (USA) |
| 1896 | Robert Wrenn (USA) | Elisabeth Moore (USA) |
| 1897 | Robert Wrenn (USA) | Juliette Atkinson (USA) |
| 1898 | Malcom Whitman (USA) | Juliette Atkinson (USA) |
| 1899 | Malcom Whitman (USA) | Marion Jones (USA) |
| 1900 | Malcom Whitman (USA) | Myrtle McAteer (USA) |
| 1901 | William Larned (USA) | Elisabeth Moore (USA) |
| 1902 | William Larned (USA) | Marion Jones (USA) |
| 1903 | Laurie Doherty (GBR) | Elisabeth Moore (USA) |
| 1904 | Holcombe Ward (USA) | May Sutton (USA) |
| 1905 | Beals Wright (USA) | Elisabeth Moore (USA) |
| 1906 | Bill Clothier (USA) | Helen Homans (USA) |
| 1907 | William Larned (USA) | Evelyn Sears (USA) |
| 1908 | William Larned (USA) | Maud Barger-Wallach (USA) |
| 1909 | William Larned (USA) | Hazel Hotchkiss (USA) |
| 1910 | William Larned (USA) | Hazel Hotchkiss (USA) |

## United States Open Tennis Championships—Singles (continued)

| YEAR | MEN | WOMEN |
|------|-----|-------|
| 1911 | William Larned (USA) | Hazel Hotchkiss (USA) |
| 1912 | Maurice McLoughlin (USA) | Mary Browne (USA) |
| 1913 | Maurice McLoughlin (USA) | Mary Browne (USA) |
| 1914 | R. Norris Williams (USA) | Mary Browne (USA) |
| 1915 | Bill Johnston (USA) | Molla Bjurstedt (NOR) |
| 1916 | R. Norris Williams (USA) | Molla Bjurstedt (NOR) |
| 1917 | Lindley Murray (USA) | Molla Bjurstedt (NOR) |
| 1918 | Lindley Murray (USA) | Molla Bjurstedt (NOR) |
| 1919 | Bill Johnston (USA) | Hazel Hotchkiss Wightman (USA) |
| 1920 | Bill Tilden (USA) | Molla Bjurstedt Mallory (USA) |
| 1921 | Bill Tilden (USA) | Molla Bjurstedt Mallory (USA) |
| 1922 | Bill Tilden (USA) | Molla Bjurstedt Mallory (USA) |
| 1923 | Bill Tilden (USA) | Helen Wills (USA) |
| 1924 | Bill Tilden (USA) | Helen Wills (USA) |
| 1925 | Bill Tilden (USA) | Helen Wills (USA) |
| 1926 | René Lacoste (FRA) | Molla Bjurstedt Mallory (USA) |
| 1927 | René Lacoste (FRA) | Helen Wills (USA) |
| 1928 | Henri Cochet (FRA) | Helen Wills (USA) |
| 1929 | Bill Tilden (USA) | Helen Wills (USA) |
| 1930 | John Doeg (USA) | Betty Nuthall (GBR) |
| 1931 | Ellsworth Vines (USA) | Helen Wills Moody (USA) |
| 1932 | Ellsworth Vines (USA) | Helen Jacobs (USA) |
| 1933 | Fred Perry (GBR) | Helen Jacobs (USA) |
| 1934 | Fred Perry (GBR) | Helen Jacobs (USA) |
| 1935 | Wilmer Allison (USA) | Helen Jacobs (USA) |
| 1936 | Fred Perry (GBR) | Alice Marble (USA) |
| 1937 | Don Budge (USA) | Anita Lizana (CHI) |
| 1938 | Don Budge (USA) | Alice Marble (USA) |
| 1939 | Bobby Riggs (USA) | Alice Marble (USA) |
| 1940 | Don McNeill (USA) | Alice Marble (USA) |
| 1941 | Bobby Riggs (USA) | Sarah Palfrey Cooke (USA) |
| 1942 | Ted Schroeder (USA) | Pauline Betz (USA) |
| 1943 | Joe Hunt (USA) | Pauline Betz (USA) |
| 1944 | Frank Parker (USA) | Pauline Betz (USA) |
| 1945 | Frank Parker (USA) | Sarah Palfrey Cooke (USA) |
| 1946 | Jack Kramer (USA) | Pauline Betz (USA) |
| 1947 | Jack Kramer (USA) | Louise Brough (USA) |
| 1948 | Pancho Gonzáles (USA) | Margaret du Pont (USA) |
| 1949 | Pancho Gonzáles (USA) | Margaret du Pont (USA) |
| 1950 | Arthur Larsen (USA) | Margaret du Pont (USA) |
| 1951 | Frank Sedgman (AUS) | Maureen Connolly (USA) |
| 1952 | Frank Sedgman (AUS) | Maureen Connolly (USA) |
| 1953 | Tony Trabert (USA) | Maureen Connolly (USA) |
| 1954 | Vic Seixas (USA) | Doris Hart (USA) |
| 1955 | Tony Trabert (USA) | Doris Hart (USA) |
| 1956 | Ken Rosewall (AUS) | Shirley Fry (USA) |
| 1957 | Mal Anderson (AUS) | Althea Gibson (USA) |
| 1958 | Ashley Cooper (AUS) | Althea Gibson (USA) |
| 1959 | Neale Fraser (AUS) | Maria Bueno (BRA) |
| 1960 | Neale Fraser (AUS) | Darlene Hard (USA) |
| 1961 | Roy Emerson (AUS) | Darlene Hard (USA) |
| 1962 | Rod Laver (AUS) | Margaret Smith (AUS) |
| 1963 | Rafael Osuna (MEX) | Maria Bueno (BRA) |
| 1964 | Roy Emerson (AUS) | Maria Bueno (BRA) |
| 1965 | Manuel Santana (ESP) | Margaret Smith (AUS) |
| 1966 | Fred Stolle (AUS) | Maria Bueno (BRA) |
| 1967 | John Newcombe (AUS) | Billie Jean King (USA) |
| 1968[1] | Arthur Ashe (USA) | Virginia Wade (GBR); Margaret Smith Court (AUS) |
| 1969[1] | Rod Laver (AUS); Stan Smith (USA) | Margaret Smith Court (AUS) |
| 1970 | Ken Rosewall (AUS) | Margaret Smith Court (AUS) |
| 1971 | Stan Smith (USA) | Billie Jean King (USA) |
| 1972 | Ilie Nastase (ROM) | Billie Jean King (USA) |
| 1973 | John Newcombe (AUS) | Margaret Smith Court (AUS) |
| 1974 | Jimmy Connors (USA) | Billie Jean King (USA) |
| 1975 | Manuel Orantes (ESP) | Chris Evert (USA) |
| 1976 | Jimmy Connors (USA) | Chris Evert (USA) |
| 1977 | Guillermo Vilas (ARG) | Chris Evert (USA) |

## United States Open Tennis Championships—Singles (continued)

| YEAR | MEN | WOMEN |
|---|---|---|
| 1978 | Jimmy Connors (USA) | Chris Evert (USA) |
| 1979 | John McEnroe (USA) | Tracy Austin (USA) |
| 1980 | John McEnroe (USA) | Chris Evert Lloyd (USA) |
| 1981 | John McEnroe (USA) | Tracy Austin (USA) |
| 1982 | Jimmy Connors (USA) | Chris Evert Lloyd (USA) |
| 1983 | Jimmy Connors (USA) | Martina Navratilova (USA) |
| 1984 | John McEnroe (USA) | Martina Navratilova (USA) |
| 1985 | Ivan Lendl (TCH) | Hana Mandlikova (TCH) |
| 1986 | Ivan Lendl (TCH) | Martina Navratilova (USA) |
| 1987 | Ivan Lendl (TCH) | Martina Navratilova (USA) |
| 1988 | Mats Wilander (SWE) | Steffi Graf (FRG) |
| 1989 | Boris Becker (FRG) | Steffi Graf (FRG) |
| 1990 | Pete Sampras (USA) | Gabriela Sabatini (ARG) |
| 1991 | Stefan Edberg (SWE) | Monica Seles (YUG) |
| 1992 | Stefan Edberg (SWE) | Monica Seles (YUG) |
| 1993 | Pete Sampras (USA) | Steffi Graf (GER) |
| 1994 | Andre Agassi (USA) | Arantxa Sánchez Vicario (ESP) |
| 1995 | Pete Sampras (USA) | Steffi Graf (GER) |
| 1996 | Pete Sampras (USA) | Steffi Graf (GER) |
| 1997 | Patrick Rafter (AUS) | Martina Hingis (SUI) |
| 1998 | Patrick Rafter (AUS) | Lindsay Davenport (USA) |
| 1999 | Andre Agassi (USA) | Serena Williams (USA) |
| 2000 | Marat Safin (RUS) | Venus Williams (USA) |
| 2001 | Lleyton Hewitt (AUS) | Venus Williams (USA) |
| 2002 | Pete Sampras (USA) | Serena Williams (USA) |
| 2003 | Andy Roddick (USA) | Justine Henin-Hardenne (BEL) |
| 2004 | Roger Federer (SUI) | Svetlana Kuznetsova (RUS) |
| 2005 | Roger Federer (SUI) | Kim Clijsters (BEL) |
| 2006 | Roger Federer (SUI) | Mariya Sharapova (RUS) |
| 2007 | Roger Federer (SUI) | Justine Henin (BEL) |
| 2008 | Roger Federer (SUI) | Serena Williams (USA) |
| 2009 | Juan Martín Del Potro (ARG) | Kim Clijsters (BEL) |
| 2010 | Rafael Nadal (ESP) | Kim Clijsters (BEL) |
| 2011 | Novak Djokovic (SRB) | Samantha Stosur (AUS) |
| 2012 | Andy Murray (SCO) | Serena Williams (USA) |

[1]In 1968 and 1969 both amateur and open championships were held. Ashe won both men's competitions in 1968; Smith won the amateur championship in 1969. Court won the women's amateur competition in 1968 and both championships in 1969. Thereafter the championships were open.

## United States Open Tennis Championships—Doubles

| YEAR | MEN | WOMEN |
|---|---|---|
| 1881 | Clarence Clark, Fred Taylor | |
| 1882 | Richard Sears, James Dwight | |
| 1883 | Richard Sears, James Dwight | |
| 1884 | Richard Sears, James Dwight | |
| 1885 | Richard Sears, Joseph Clark | |
| 1886 | Richard Sears, James Dwight | |
| 1887 | Richard Sears, James Dwight | |
| 1888 | Oliver Campbell, Valentine Hall | |
| 1889 | Henry Slocum, Howard Taylor | Bertha Townsend, Margarette Ballard |
| 1890 | Valentine Hall, Clarence Hobart | Ellen Roosevelt, Grace Roosevelt |
| 1891 | Oliver Campbell, Robert Huntington | Mabel Cahill, Mrs. W. Fellowes Morgan |
| 1892 | Oliver Campbell, Robert Huntington | Mabel Cahill, Adeline McKinley |
| 1893 | Clarence Hobart, Fred Hovey | Aline Terry, Hattie Butler |
| 1894 | Clarence Hobart, Fred Hovey | Helen Helwig, Juliette Atkinson |
| 1895 | Malcom Chace, Robert Wrenn | Helen Helwig, Juliette Atkinson |
| 1896 | Carr Neel, Samuel Neel | Elisabeth Moore, Juliette Atkinson |
| 1897 | Leo Ware, George Sheldon | Juliette Atkinson, Kathleen Atkinson |
| 1898 | Leo Ware, George Sheldon | Juliette Atkinson, Kathleen Atkinson |
| 1899 | Holcombe Ward, Dwight Davis | Jane Craven, Myrtle McAteer |
| 1900 | Holcombe Ward, Dwight Davis | Edith Parker, Hallie Champlin |
| 1901 | Holcombe Ward, Dwight Davis | Juliette Atkinson, Myrtle McAteer |
| 1902 | Reggie Doherty, Laurie Doherty | Juliette Atkinson, Marion Jones |
| 1903 | Reggie Doherty, Laurie Doherty | Elisabeth Moore, Carrie Neely |
| 1904 | Holcombe Ward, Beals Wright | Mary Sutton, Miriam Hall |
| 1905 | Holcombe Ward, Beals Wright | Helen Homans, Carrie Neely |

## United States Open Tennis Championships—Doubles (continued)

| YEAR | MEN | WOMEN |
|------|-----|-------|
| 1906 | Holcombe Ward, Beals Wright | Mrs. L.S. Coe, Mrs. D.S. Platt |
| 1907 | Fred Alexander, Harold Hackett | Marie Weimer, Carrie Neely |
| 1908 | Fred Alexander, Harold Hackett | Evelyn Sears, Margaret Curtis |
| 1909 | Fred Alexander, Harold Hackett | Hazel Hotchkiss, Edith Rotch |
| 1910 | Fred Alexander, Harold Hackett | Hazel Hotchkiss, Edith Rotch |
| 1911 | Raymond Little, Gustave Touchard | Hazel Hotchkiss, Eleanora Sears |
| 1912 | Maurice McLoughlin, Thomas Bundy | Dorothy Green, Mary Browne |
| 1913 | Maurice McLoughlin, Thomas Bundy | Mary Browne, Mrs. R.H. Williams |
| 1914 | Maurice McLoughlin, Thomas Bundy | Mary Browne, Mrs. R.H. Williams |
| 1915 | William Johnston, Clarence Griffin | Hazel Hotchkiss Wightman, Eleanora Sears |
| 1916 | William Johnston, Clarence Griffin | Molla Bjurstedt, Eleanora Sears |
| 1917 | Fred Alexander, Harold Throckmorton | Molla Bjurstedt, Eleanora Sears |
| 1918 | Bill Tilden, Vincent Richards | Marion Zinderstein, Eleanor Goss |
| 1919 | Norman Brookes, Gerald Patterson | Marion Zinderstein, Eleanor Goss |
| 1920 | William Johnston, Clarence Griffin | Marion Zinderstein, Eleanor Goss |
| 1921 | Bill Tilden, Vincent Richards | Mary Browne, Mrs. R.H. Williams |
| 1922 | Bill Tilden, Vincent Richards | Marion Zinderstein Jessup, Helen Wills |
| 1923 | Bill Tilden, Brian Norton | Kathleen McKane, Phyllis Covell |
| 1924 | Howard Kinsey, Robert Kinsey | Hazel Hotchkiss Wightman, Helen Wills |
| 1925 | Richard Williams, Vincent Richards | Mary Browne, Helen Wills |
| 1926 | Richard Williams, Vincent Richards | Elizabeth Ryan, Eleanor Goss |
| 1927 | Bill Tilden, Frank Hunter | Kathleen McKane Godfree, Ermyntrude Harvey |
| 1928 | George Lott, John Hennessey | Hazel Hotchkiss Wightman, Helen Wills |
| 1929 | George Lott, John Doeg | Phoebe Watson, Peggy Michell |
| 1930 | George Lott, John Doeg | Betty Nuthall, Sarah Palfrey |
| 1931 | Wilmer Allison, John Van Ryn | Betty Nuthall, Eileen Whittingstall |
| 1932 | Ellsworth Vines, Keith Gledhill | Helen Jacobs, Sarah Palfrey |
| 1933 | George Lott, Lester Stoefen | Betty Nuthall, Freda James |
| 1934 | George Lott, Lester Stoefen | Helen Jacobs, Sarah Palfrey |
| 1935 | Wilmer Allison, John Van Ryn | Helen Jacobs, Sarah Palfrey Fabyan |
| 1936 | Don Budge, Gene Mako | Marjorie Van Ryn, Carolin Babcock |
| 1937 | Gottfried von Cramm, Henner Henkel | Sarah Palfrey Fabyan, Alice Marble |
| 1938 | Don Budge, Gene Mako | Sarah Palfrey Fabyan, Alice Marble |
| 1939 | Adrian Quist, John Bromwich | Sarah Palfrey Fabyan, Alice Marble |
| 1940 | Jack Kramer, Ted Schroeder | Sarah Palfrey Fabyan, Alice Marble |
| 1941 | Jack Kramer, Ted Schroeder | Sarah Palfrey Cooke, Margaret Osborne |
| 1942 | Gardnar Mulloy, Billy Talbert | Louise Brough, Margaret Osborne |
| 1943 | Jack Kramer, Frank Parker | Louise Brough, Margaret Osborne |
| 1944 | Don McNeill, Bob Falkenburg | Louise Brough, Margaret Osborne |
| 1945 | Gardnar Mulloy, Billy Talbert | Louise Brough, Margaret Osborne |
| 1946 | Gardnar Mulloy, Billy Talbert | Louise Brough, Margaret Osborne |
| 1947 | Jack Kramer, Ted Schroeder | Louise Brough, Margaret Osborne |
| 1948 | Gardnar Mulloy, Billy Talbert | Louise Brough, Margaret Osborne du Pont |
| 1949 | John Bromwich, Billy Sidwell | Louise Brough, Margaret Osborne du Pont |
| 1950 | John Bromwich, Frank Sedgman | Louise Brough, Margaret Osborne du Pont |
| 1951 | Ken McGregor, Frank Sedgman | Doris Hart, Shirley Fry |
| 1952 | Mervyn Rose, Vic Seixas | Doris Hart, Shirley Fry |
| 1953 | Rex Hartwig, Mervyn Rose | Doris Hart, Shirley Fry |
| 1954 | Vic Seixas, Tony Trabert | Doris Hart, Shirley Fry |
| 1955 | Kosei Kamo, Atushi Miyagi | Louise Brough, Margaret Osborne du Pont |
| 1956 | Lew Hoad, Ken Rosewall | Louise Brough, Margaret Osborne du Pont |
| 1957 | Ashley Cooper, Neale Fraser | Louise Brough, Margaret Osborne du Pont |
| 1958 | Alex Olmedo, Hamilton Richardson | Jeanne Arth, Darlene Hard |
| 1959 | Roy Emerson, Neale Fraser | Jeanne Arth, Darlene Hard |
| 1960 | Roy Emerson, Neale Fraser | Maria Bueno, Darlene Hard |
| 1961 | Charles McKinley, Dennis Ralston | Darlene Hard, Lesley Turner |
| 1962 | Rafael Osuna, Antonio Palafox | Maria Bueno, Darlene Hard |
| 1963 | Charles McKinley, Dennis Ralston | Robyn Ebbern, Margaret Smith |
| 1964 | Charles McKinley, Dennis Ralston | Karen Susman, Billie Jean Moffitt |
| 1965 | Roy Emerson, Fred Stolle | Carole Caldwell Graebner, Nancy Richey |
| 1966 | Roy Emerson, Fred Stolle | Maria Bueno, Nancy Richey |
| 1967 | John Newcombe, Tony Roche | Billie Jean Moffitt King, Rosemary Casals |
| 1968[1] | Robert Lutz, Stan Smith | Maria Bueno, Margaret Smith Court |
| 1969[1] | Ken Rosewall, Fred Stolle; | Françoise Durr, Darlene Hard; |
|  | Dick Crealy, Allan Stone | Margaret Smith Court, Virginia Wade |
| 1970 | Pierre Barthes, Niki Pilic | Margaret Smith Court, Judy Dalton |
| 1971 | John Newcombe, Roger Taylor | Rosemary Casals, Judy Dalton |
| 1972 | Cliff Drysdale, Roger Taylor | Françoise Durr, Betty Stove |

## United States Open Tennis Championships—Doubles (continued)

| YEAR | MEN | WOMEN |
|------|-----|-------|
| 1973 | Owen Davidson, John Newcombe | Margaret Smith Court, Virginia Wade |
| 1974 | Robert Lutz, Stan Smith | Billie Jean King, Rosemary Casals |
| 1975 | Jimmy Connors, Ilie Nastase | Margaret Smith Court, Virginia Wade |
| 1976 | Tom Okker, Marty Riessen | Delina Boshoff, Ilana Kloss |
| 1977 | Bob Hewitt, Frew McMillan | Martina Navratilova, Betty Stove |
| 1978 | Robert Lutz, Stan Smith | Billie Jean King, Martina Navratilova |
| 1979 | John McEnroe, Peter Fleming | Wendy Turnbull, Betty Stove |
| 1980 | Robert Lutz, Stan Smith | Billie Jean King, Martina Navratilova |
| 1981 | John McEnroe, Peter Fleming | Kathy Jordan, Anne Smith |
| 1982 | Kevin Curren, Steve Denton | Rosemary Casals, Wendy Turnbull |
| 1983 | John McEnroe, Peter Fleming | Martina Navratilova, Pam Shriver |
| 1984 | John Fitzgerald, Tomas Smid | Martina Navratilova, Pam Shriver |
| 1985 | Robert Seguso, Ken Flach | Claudia Kohde-Kilsch, Helena Sukova |
| 1986 | Andres Gómez, Slobodan Zivojinovic | Martina Navratilova, Pam Shriver |
| 1987 | Stefan Edberg, Anders Järryd | Martina Navratilova, Pam Shriver |
| 1988 | Sergio Casal, Emilio Sánchez | Gigi Fernández, Robin White |
| 1989 | John McEnroe, Mark Woodforde | Martina Navratilova, Hana Mandlikova |
| 1990 | Pieter Aldrich, Danie Visser | Martina Navratilova, Gigi Fernández |
| 1991 | John Fitzgerald, Anders Järryd | Pam Shriver, Natasha Zvereva |
| 1992 | Jim Grabb, Richey Reneberg | Gigi Fernández, Natasha Zvereva |
| 1993 | Ken Flach, Rick Leach | Arantxa Sánchez Vicario, Helena Sukova |
| 1994 | Jacco Eltingh, Paul Haarhuis | Arantxa Sánchez Vicario, Jana Novotna |
| 1995 | Todd Woodbridge, Mark Woodforde | Gigi Fernández, Natasha Zvereva |
| 1996 | Todd Woodbridge, Mark Woodforde | Gigi Fernández, Natasha Zvereva |
| 1997 | Yevgeny Kafelnikov, Daniel Vacek | Lindsay Davenport, Jana Novotna |
| 1998 | Sandon Stolle, Cyril Suk | Martina Hingis, Jana Novotna |
| 1999 | Sébastien Lareau, Alex O'Brien | Venus Williams, Serena Williams |
| 2000 | Lleyton Hewitt, Max Mirnyi | Julie Halard-Decugis, Ai Sugiyama |
| 2001 | Wayne Black, Kevin Ullyet | Lisa Raymond, Rennae Stubbs |
| 2002 | Mahesh Bhupathi, Max Mirnyi | Virginia Ruano Pascual, Paola Suárez |
| 2003 | Jonas Björkman, Todd Woodbridge | Virginia Ruano Pascual, Paola Suárez |
| 2004 | Mark Knowles, Daniel Nestor | Virginia Ruano Pascual, Paola Suárez |
| 2005 | Bob Bryan, Mike Bryan | Lisa Raymond, Samantha Stosur |
| 2006 | Martin Damm, Leander Paes | Nathalie Dechy, Vera Zvonareva |
| 2007 | Simon Aspelin, Julian Knowle | Nathalie Dechy, Dinara Safina |
| 2008 | Bob Bryan, Mike Bryan | Cara Black, Liezel Huber |
| 2009 | Lukas Dlouhy, Leander Paes | Venus Williams, Serena Williams |
| 2010 | Bob Bryan, Mike Bryan | Vania King, Yaroslava Shvedova |
| 2011 | Jurgen Melzer, Philipp Petzschner | Liezel Huber, Lisa Raymond |
| 2012 | Bob Bryan, Mike Bryan | Sara Errani, Roberta Vinci |

[1]In 1968 and 1969 both amateur and open championships were held. Lutz and Smith won both men's competitions in 1968; Crealy and Stone took the men's amateur championships in 1969. Bueno and Court won both women's competitions in 1968; Court and Wade took the women's amateur championships in 1969. Thereafter the championships were open.

## Davis Cup

| YEAR | WINNER | RUNNER-UP | RESULTS | YEAR | WINNER | RUNNER-UP | RESULTS |
|------|--------|-----------|---------|------|--------|-----------|---------|
| 1900 | United States | British Isles[1] | 3-0 | 1921 | United States | Japan | 5-0 |
| 1901 | not held | | | 1922 | United States | Australasia[2] | 4-1 |
| 1902 | United States | British Isles[1] | 3-2 | 1923 | United States | Australasia[2] | 4-1 |
| 1903 | British Isles[1] | United States | 4-1 | 1924 | United States | Australia | 5-0 |
| 1904 | British Isles[1] | Belgium | 5-0 | 1925 | United States | France | 5-0 |
| 1905 | British Isles[1] | United States | 5-0 | 1926 | United States | France | 4-1 |
| 1906 | British Isles[1] | United States | 5-0 | 1927 | France | United States | 3-2 |
| 1907 | Australasia[2] | British Isles[1] | 3-2 | 1928 | France | United States | 4-1 |
| 1908 | Australasia[2] | United States | 3-2 | 1929 | France | United States | 3-2 |
| 1909 | Australasia[2] | United States | 5-0 | 1930 | France | United States | 4-1 |
| 1910 | not held | | | 1931 | France | Great Britain | 3-2 |
| 1911 | Australasia[2] | United States | 5-0 | 1932 | France | United States | 3-2 |
| 1912 | British Isles[1] | Australasia[2] | 3-2 | 1933 | Great Britain | France | 3-2 |
| 1913 | United States | Great Britain | 3-2 | 1934 | Great Britain | United States | 4-1 |
| 1914 | Australasia[2] | United States | 3-2 | 1935 | Great Britain | United States | 5-0 |
| 1915-18 | not held | | | 1936 | Great Britain | Australia | 3-2 |
| 1919 | Australasia[2] | Great Britain | 4-1 | 1937 | United States | Great Britain | 4-1 |
| 1920 | United States | Australasia[2] | 5-0 | 1938 | United States | Australia | 3-2 |

## Davis Cup (continued)

| YEAR | WINNER | RUNNER-UP | RESULTS | YEAR | WINNER | RUNNER-UP | RESULTS |
|---|---|---|---|---|---|---|---|
| 1939 | Australia | United States | 3-2 | 1979 | United States | Italy | 5-0 |
| 1940-45 | not held | | | 1980 | Czecho-slovakia | Italy | 4-1 |
| 1946 | United States | Australia | 5-0 | | | | |
| 1947 | United States | Australia | 4-1 | 1981 | United States | Argentina | 3-1 |
| 1948 | United States | Australia | 5-0 | 1982 | United States | France | 4-1 |
| 1949 | United States | Australia | 4-1 | 1983 | Australia | Sweden | 3-2 |
| 1950 | Australia | United States | 4-1 | 1984 | Sweden | United States | 4-1 |
| 1951 | Australia | United States | 3-2 | 1985 | Sweden | West Germany | 3-2 |
| 1952 | Australia | United States | 4-1 | 1986 | Australia | Sweden | 3-2 |
| 1953 | Australia | United States | 3-2 | 1987 | Sweden | India | 5-0 |
| 1954 | United States | Australia | 3-2 | 1988 | West Germany | Sweden | 4-1 |
| 1955 | Australia | United States | 5-0 | 1989 | West Germany | Sweden | 3-2 |
| 1956 | Australia | United States | 5-0 | 1990 | United States | Australia | 3-2 |
| 1957 | Australia | United States | 3-2 | 1991 | France | United States | 3-1 |
| 1958 | United States | Australia | 3-2 | 1992 | United States | Switzerland | 3-1 |
| 1959 | Australia | United States | 3-2 | 1993 | Germany | Australia | 4-1 |
| 1960 | Australia | Italy | 4-1 | 1994 | Sweden | Russia | 4-1 |
| 1961 | Australia | Italy | 5-0 | 1995 | United States | Russia | 3-2 |
| 1962 | Australia | Mexico | 5-0 | 1996 | France | Sweden | 3-2 |
| 1963 | United States | Australia | 3-2 | 1997 | Sweden | United States | 5-0 |
| 1964 | Australia | United States | 3-2 | 1998 | Sweden | Italy | 4-1 |
| 1965 | Australia | Spain | 4-1 | 1999 | Australia | France | 3-2 |
| 1966 | Australia | India | 4-1 | 2000 | Spain | Australia | 3-1 |
| 1967 | Australia | Spain | 4-1 | 2001 | France | Australia | 3-2 |
| 1968 | United States | Australia | 4-1 | 2002 | Russia | France | 3-2 |
| 1969 | United States | Romania | 5-0 | 2003 | Australia | Spain | 3-1 |
| 1970 | United States | West Germany | 5-0 | 2004 | Spain | United States | 3-2 |
| 1971 | United States | Romania | 3-2 | 2005 | Croatia | Slovakia | 3-2 |
| 1972 | United States | Romania | 3-2 | 2006 | Russia | Argentina | 3-2 |
| 1973 | Australia | United States | 5-0 | 2007 | United States | Russia | 4-1 |
| 1974 | South Africa | India | [3] | 2008 | Spain | Argentina | 3-1 |
| 1975 | Sweden | Czechoslovakia | 3-2 | 2009 | Spain | Czech Republic | 5-0 |
| 1976 | Italy | Chile | 4-1 | 2010 | Serbia | France | 3-2 |
| 1977 | Australia | Italy | 3-1 | 2011 | Spain | Argentina | 3-1 |
| 1978 | United States | Great Britain | 4-1 | | | | |

[1]Great Britain and Ireland.    [2]Australia and New Zealand.    [3]Won by forfeit; India withdrew from the final.

## Fed Cup

| YEAR | WINNER | RUNNER-UP | RESULTS | YEAR | WINNER | RUNNER-UP | RESULTS |
|---|---|---|---|---|---|---|---|
| 1963 | United States | Australia | 2-1 | 1988 | Czechoslovakia | USSR | 2-1 |
| 1964 | Australia | United States | 2-1 | 1989 | United States | Spain | 3-0 |
| 1965 | Australia | United States | 2-1 | 1990 | United States | USSR | 2-1 |
| 1966 | United States | West Germany | 3-0 | 1991 | Spain | United States | 2-1 |
| 1967 | United States | Great Britain | 2-0 | 1992 | Germany | Spain | 2-1 |
| 1968 | Australia | Netherlands | 3-0 | 1993 | Spain | Australia | 3-0 |
| 1969 | United States | Australia | 2-1 | 1994 | Spain | United States | 3-0 |
| 1970 | Australia | West Germany | 3-0 | 1995 | Spain | United States | 3-2 |
| 1971 | Australia | Great Britain | 3-0 | 1996 | United States | Spain | 5-0 |
| 1972 | South Africa | Great Britain | 2-1 | 1997 | France | Netherlands | 4-1 |
| 1973 | Australia | South Africa | 3-0 | 1998 | Spain | Switzerland | 3-2 |
| 1974 | Australia | United States | 2-1 | 1999 | United States | Russia | 4-1 |
| 1975 | Czechoslovakia | Australia | 3-0 | 2000 | United States | Spain | 5-0 |
| 1976 | United States | Australia | 2-1 | 2001 | Belgium | Russia | 2-1 |
| 1977 | United States | Australia | 2-1 | 2002 | Slovakia | Spain | 3-1 |
| 1978 | United States | Australia | 2-1 | 2003 | France | United States | 4-1 |
| 1979 | United States | Australia | 3-0 | 2004 | Russia | France | 3-2 |
| 1980 | United States | Australia | 3-0 | 2005 | Russia | France | 3-2 |
| 1981 | United States | Great Britain | 3-0 | 2006 | Italy | Belgium | 3-2 |
| 1982 | United States | West Germany | 3-0 | 2007 | Russia | Italy | 4-0 |
| 1983 | Czechoslovakia | West Germany | 2-1 | 2008 | Russia | Spain | 4-0 |
| 1984 | Czechoslovakia | Australia | 2-1 | 2009 | Italy | United States | 4-0 |
| 1985 | Czechoslovakia | United States | 2-1 | 2010 | Italy | United States | 3-1 |
| 1986 | United States | Czechoslovakia | 3-0 | 2011 | Czech Republic | Russia | 3-2 |
| 1987 | West Germany | United States | 2-1 | | | | |

# Track & Field

The world governing body for track and field, or athletics, is the **International Association of Athletics Federations** (IAAF), founded in 1912. The sport includes relay running, a number of individual running, jumping, and throwing events, and one event (the decathlon for men and the heptathlon for women) that includes all three activities. The best-known competition for most track-and-field athletics is the **Olympic Games** held every four years. In 1983 the first officially recognized non-Olympic world athletics championships were held.

**IAAF Web site:** <www.iaaf.org>.

## World Track & Field Championships—Men

**100 M**

| | |
|---|---|
| 1983 | Carl Lewis (USA) |
| 1987 | Carl Lewis (USA) |
| 1991 | Carl Lewis (USA) |
| 1993 | Linford Christie (GBR) |
| 1995 | Donovan Bailey (CAN) |
| 1997 | Maurice Greene (USA) |
| 1999 | Maurice Greene (USA) |
| 2001 | Maurice Greene (USA) |
| 2003 | Kim Collins (SKN) |
| 2005 | Justin Gatlin (USA) |
| 2007 | Tyson Gay (USA) |
| 2009 | Usain Bolt (JAM) |
| 2011 | Yohan Blake (JAM) |

**200 M**

| | |
|---|---|
| 1983 | Calvin Smith (USA) |
| 1987 | Calvin Smith (USA) |
| 1991 | Michael Johnson (USA) |
| 1993 | Frank Fredericks (NAM) |
| 1995 | Michael Johnson (USA) |
| 1997 | Ato Boldon (TRI) |
| 1999 | Maurice Greene (USA) |
| 2001 | Konstadinos Kederis (GRE) |
| 2003 | John Capel (USA) |
| 2005 | Justin Gatlin (USA) |
| 2007 | Tyson Gay (USA) |
| 2009 | Usain Bolt (JAM) |
| 2011 | Usain Bolt (JAM) |

**400 M**

| | |
|---|---|
| 1983 | Bert Cameron (JAM) |
| 1987 | Thomas Schoenlebe (GDR) |
| 1991 | Antonio Pettigrew (USA) |
| 1993 | Michael Johnson (USA) |
| 1995 | Michael Johnson (USA) |
| 1997 | Michael Johnson (USA) |
| 1999 | Michael Johnson (USA) |
| 2001 | Avard Moncur (BAH) |
| 2003 | Tyree Washington (USA) |
| 2005 | Jeremy Wariner (USA) |
| 2007 | Jeremy Wariner (USA) |
| 2009 | LaShawn Merritt (USA) |
| 2011 | Kirani James (GRN) |

**800 M**

| | |
|---|---|
| 1983 | Willi Wülbeck (FRG) |
| 1987 | Billy Konchellah (KEN) |
| 1991 | Billy Konchellah (KEN) |
| 1993 | Paul Ruto (KEN) |
| 1995 | Wilson Kipketer (DEN) |
| 1997 | Wilson Kipketer (DEN) |
| 1999 | Wilson Kipketer (DEN) |
| 2001 | André Bucher (SUI) |
| 2003 | Djabir Saïd-Guerni (ALG) |
| 2005 | Rashid Ramzi (BRN) |
| 2007 | Alfred Kirwa Yego (KEN) |
| 2009 | Mbulaeni Mulaudzi (RSA) |
| 2011 | David Lekuta Rudisha (KEN) |

**1,500 M**

| | |
|---|---|
| 1983 | Steve Cram (GBR) |
| 1987 | Abdi Bile (SOM) |
| 1991 | Noureddine Morceli (ALG) |
| 1993 | Noureddine Morceli (ALG) |
| 1995 | Noureddine Morceli (ALG) |
| 1997 | Hicham El Guerrouj (MAR) |
| 1999 | Hicham El Guerrouj (MAR) |
| 2001 | Hicham El Guerrouj (MAR) |
| 2003 | Hicham El Guerrouj (MAR) |
| 2005 | Rashid Ramzi (BRN) |
| 2007 | Bernard Lagat (USA) |
| 2009 | Yusuf Saad Kamel (BRN) |
| 2011 | Asbel Kiprop (KEN) |

**5,000 M**

| | |
|---|---|
| 1983 | Eamonn Coghlan (IRL) |
| 1987 | Said Aouita (MAR) |
| 1991 | Yobes Ondieki (KEN) |
| 1993 | Ismael Kirui (KEN) |
| 1995 | Ismael Kirui (KEN) |
| 1997 | Daniel Komen (KEN) |
| 1999 | Salah Hissou (MAR) |
| 2001 | Richard Limo (KEN) |
| 2003 | Eliud Kipchoge (KEN) |
| 2005 | Benjamin Limo (KEN) |
| 2007 | Bernard Lagat (USA) |
| 2009 | Kenenisa Bekele (ETH) |
| 2011 | Mohamed Farah (GBR) |

**10,000 M**

| | |
|---|---|
| 1983 | Alberto Cova (ITA) |
| 1987 | Paul Kipkoech (KEN) |
| 1991 | Moses Tanui (KEN) |
| 1993 | Haile Gebrselassie (ETH) |
| 1995 | Haile Gebrselassie (ETH) |
| 1997 | Haile Gebrselassie (ETH) |
| 1999 | Haile Gebrselassie (ETH) |
| 2001 | Charles Kamathi (KEN) |
| 2003 | Kenenisa Bekele (ETH) |
| 2005 | Kenenisa Bekele (ETH) |
| 2007 | Kenenisa Bekele (ETH) |
| 2009 | Kenenisa Bekele (ETH) |
| 2011 | Ibrahim Jeilan (ETH) |

**STEEPLECHASE**

| | |
|---|---|
| 1983 | Patriz Ilg (FRG) |
| 1987 | Francesco Panetta (ITA) |
| 1991 | Moses Kiptanui (KEN) |
| 1993 | Moses Kiptanui (KEN) |
| 1995 | Moses Kiptanui (KEN) |
| 1997 | Wilson Boit Kipketer (KEN) |
| 1999 | Christopher Koskei (KEN) |
| 2001 | Reuben Kosgei (KEN) |
| 2003 | Saif Saaeed Shaheen (QAT) |
| 2005 | Saif Saaeed Shaheen (QAT) |
| 2007 | Brimin Kiprop Kipruto (KEN) |
| 2009 | Ezekiel Kemboi (KEN) |
| 2011 | Ezekiel Kemboi (KEN) |

**110-M HURDLES**

| | |
|---|---|
| 1983 | Greg Foster (USA) |
| 1987 | Greg Foster (USA) |
| 1991 | Greg Foster (USA) |
| 1993 | Colin Jackson (GBR) |
| 1995 | Allen Johnson (USA) |
| 1997 | Allen Johnson (USA) |
| 1999 | Colin Jackson (GBR) |
| 2001 | Allen Johnson (USA) |
| 2003 | Allen Johnson (USA) |
| 2005 | Ladji Doucouré (FRA) |
| 2007 | Liu Xiang (CHN) |
| 2009 | Ryan Brathwaite (BAR) |
| 2011 | Jason Richardson (USA) |

**400-M HURDLES**

| | |
|---|---|
| 1983 | Edwin Moses (USA) |
| 1987 | Edwin Moses (USA) |
| 1991 | Samuel Matete (ZAM) |
| 1993 | Kevin Young (USA) |
| 1995 | Derrick Adkins (USA) |
| 1997 | Stéphane Diagana (FRA) |
| 1999 | Fabrizio Mori (ITA) |
| 2001 | Felix Sánchez (DOM) |
| 2003 | Felix Sánchez (DOM) |
| 2005 | Bershawn Jackson (USA) |
| 2007 | Kerron Clement (USA) |
| 2009 | Kerron Clement (USA) |
| 2011 | David Greene (GBR) |

**MARATHON**

| | |
|---|---|
| 1983 | Robert de Castella (AUS) |
| 1987 | Douglas Wakiihuri (KEN) |
| 1991 | Hiromi Taniguchi (JPN) |
| 1993 | Mark Plaatjes (USA) |
| 1995 | Martín Fiz (ESP) |
| 1997 | Abel Antón (ESP) |
| 1999 | Abel Antón (ESP) |
| 2001 | Gezahegne Abera (ETH) |
| 2003 | Jaouad Gharib (MAR) |
| 2005 | Jaouad Gharib (MAR) |
| 2007 | Luke Kibet (KEN) |
| 2009 | Abel Kirui (KEN) |
| 2011 | Abel Kirui (KEN) |

**20-KM WALK**

| | |
|---|---|
| 1983 | Ernesto Canto (MEX) |
| 1987 | Maurizio Damilano (ITA) |
| 1991 | Maurizio Damilano (ITA) |
| 1993 | Valentí Massana (ESP) |
| 1995 | Michele Didoni (ITA) |
| 1997 | Daniel García (MEX) |
| 1999 | Ilya Markov (RUS) |
| 2001 | Roman Rasskazov (RUS) |
| 2003 | Jefferson Pérez (ECU) |
| 2005 | Jefferson Pérez (ECU) |
| 2007 | Jefferson Pérez (ECU) |
| 2009 | Valeriy Borchin (RUS) |
| 2011 | Valeriy Borchin (RUS) |

## World Track & Field Championships—Men (continued)

**50-KM WALK**
1983 Ronald Weigel (GDR)
1987 Hartwig Gauder (GDR)
1991 Aleksandr Potashov (URS)
1993 Jesús Angel García (ESP)
1995 Valentin Kononen (FIN)
1997 Robert Korzeniowski (POL)
1999 Ivano Brugnetti (ITA)
2001 Robert Korzeniowski (POL)
2003 Robert Korzeniowski (POL)
2005 Sergey Kirdyapkin (RUS)
2007 Nathan Deakes (AUS)
2009 Sergey Kirdyapkin (RUS)
2011 Sergey Bakulin (RUS)

**4 × 100-M RELAY**
1983 United States
1987 United States
1991 United States
1993 United States
1995 Canada
1997 Canada
1999 United States
2001 South Africa
2003 United States
2005 France
2007 United States
2009 Jamaica
2011 Jamaica

**4 × 400-M RELAY**
1983 USSR
1987 United States
1991 United Kingdom
1993 United States
1995 United States
1997 Great Britain
1999 Poland
2001 The Bahamas
2003 France
2005 United States
2007 United States
2009 United States
2011 United States

**HIGH JUMP**
1983 Gennady Avdeyenko
     (URS)
1987 Patrik Sjöberg (SWE)
1991 Charles Austin (USA)
1993 Javier Sotomayor (CUB)
1995 Troy Kemp (BAH)
1997 Javier Sotomayor (CUB)
1999 Vyacheslav Voronin (RUS)
2001 Martin Buss (GER)
2003 Jacques Freitag (RSA)
2005 Yuri Krymarenko (UKR)
2007 Donald Thomas (BAH)
2009 Yaroslav Rybakov (RUS)
2011 Jesse Williams (USA)

**POLE VAULT**
1983 Sergey Bubka (URS)
1987 Sergey Bubka (URS)
1991 Sergey Bubka (URS)
1993 Sergey Bubka (UKR)
1995 Sergey Bubka (UKR)
1997 Sergey Bubka (UKR)
1999 Maksim Tarasov (RUS)
2001 Dmitri Markov (AUS)
2003 Giuseppe Gibilisco (ITA)
2005 Rens Blom (NED)
2007 Brad Walker (USA)
2009 Steven Hooker (AUS)
2011 Pawel Wojciechowski (POL)

**LONG JUMP**
1983 Carl Lewis (USA)
1987 Carl Lewis (USA)
1991 Mike Powell (USA)
1993 Mike Powell (USA)
1995 Iván Pedroso (CUB)
1997 Iván Pedroso (CUB)
1999 Iván Pedroso (CUB)
2001 Iván Pedroso (CUB)
2003 Dwight Phillips (USA)
2005 Dwight Phillips (USA)
2007 Irving Saladino (PAN)
2009 Dwight Phillips (USA)
2011 Dwight Phillips (USA)

**TRIPLE JUMP**
1983 Zdzislaw Hoffman (POL)
1987 Khristo Markov (BUL)
1991 Kenny Harrison (USA)
1993 Mike Conley (USA)
1995 Jonathan Edwards (GBR)
1997 Yoelbi Quesada (CUB)
1999 Charles Michael Friedek
     (GER)
2001 Jonathan Edwards (GBR)
2003 Christian Olsson (SWE)
2005 Walter Davis (USA)
2007 Nelson Évora (POR)
2009 Phillips Idowu (GBR)
2011 Christian Taylor (USA)

**SHOT PUT**
1983 Edward Sarul (POL)
1987 Werner Günthör (SUI)
1991 Werner Günthör (SUI)
1993 Werner Günthör (SUI)
1995 John Godina (USA)
1997 John Godina (USA)
1999 C.J. Hunter (USA)
2001 John Godina (USA)
2003 Andrey Mikhnevich (BLR)
2005 Adam Nelson (USA)
2007 Reese Hoffa (USA)
2009 Christian Cantwell (USA
2011 David Storl (GER)

**DISCUS THROW**
1983 Imrich Bugar (TCH)
1987 Jürgen Schult (GDR)
1991 Lars Riedel (GER)
1993 Lars Riedel (GER)
1995 Lars Riedel (GER)
1997 Lars Riedel (GER)
1999 Anthony Washington (USA)
2001 Lars Riedel (GER)
2003 Virgilijus Alekna (LTU)
2005 Virgilijus Alekna (LTU)
2007 Gerd Kanter (EST)
2009 Robert Harting (GER)
2011 Robert Harting (GER)

**HAMMER THROW**
1983 Sergey Litvinov (URS)
1987 Sergey Litvinov (URS)
1991 Yury Sedykh (URS)
1993 Andrey Abduvaliyev (TJK)
1995 Andrey Abduvaliyev (TJK)
1997 Heinz Weis (GER)
1999 Karsten Kobs (GER)
2001 Szymon Ziolkowski (POL)
2003 Ivan Tikhon (BLR)
2005 Ivan Tikhon (BLR)
2007 Ivan Tikhon (BLR)
2009 Primoz Kozmus (SLO)
2011 Koji Murofushi (JPN)

**JAVELIN THROW**
1983 Detlef Michel (GDR)
1987 Seppo Räty (FIN)
1991 Kimmo Kinnunen (FIN)
1993 Jan Zelezny (CZE)
1995 Jan Zelezny (CZE)
1997 Marius Corbett (RSA)
1999 Aki Parviainen (FIN)
2001 Jan Zelezny (CZE)
2003 Sergey Makarov (RUS)
2005 Andrus Varnik (EST)
2007 Tero Pitkämäki (FIN)
2009 Andreas Thorkildsen (NOR)
2011 Matthias de Zordo (GER)

**DECATHLON**
1983 Daley Thompson (GBR)
1987 Torsten Voss (GDR)
1991 Dan O'Brien (USA)
1993 Dan O'Brien (USA)
1995 Dan O'Brien (USA)
1997 Tomas Dvorak (CZE)
1999 Tomas Dvorak (CZE)
2001 Tomas Dvorak (CZE)
2003 Tom Pappas (USA)
2005 Bryan Clay (USA)
2007 Roman Sebrle (CZE)
2009 Trey Hardee (USA)
2011 Trey Hardee (USA)

## World Track & Field Championships—Women

**100 M**
1983 Marlies Göhr (GDR)
1987 Silke Gladisch (GDR)
1991 Katrin Krabbe (GER)
1993 Gail Devers (USA)
1995 Gwen Torrence (USA)

**100 M (CONTINUED)**
1997 Marion Jones (USA)
1999 Marion Jones (USA)
2001 Zhanna Pintusevich (UKR)
2003 Torri Edwards (USA)
2005 Lauryn Williams (USA)

**100 M (CONTINUED)**
2007 Veronica Campbell (JAM)
2009 Shelly-Ann Fraser (JAM)
2011 Carmelita Jeter (USA)

# World Track & Field Championships—Women (continued)

**200 M**
| | |
|---|---|
| 1983 | Marita Koch (GDR) |
| 1987 | Silke Gladisch (GDR) |
| 1991 | Katrin Krabbe (GER) |
| 1993 | Merlene Ottey (JAM) |
| 1995 | Merlene Ottey (JAM) |
| 1997 | Zhanna Pintusevich (UKR) |
| 1999 | Inger Miller (USA) |
| 2001 | Marion Jones (USA) |
| 2003 | Anastasiya Kapachinskaya (RUS) |
| 2005 | Allyson Felix (USA) |
| 2007 | Allyson Felix (USA) |
| 2009 | Allyson Felix (USA) |
| 2011 | Veronica Campbell-Brown (JAM) |

**400 M**
| | |
|---|---|
| 1983 | Jarmila Kratochvilova (TCH) |
| 1987 | Olga Bryzgina (URS) |
| 1991 | Marie-José Pérec (FRA) |
| 1993 | Jearl Miles (USA) |
| 1995 | Marie-José Pérec (FRA) |
| 1997 | Cathy Freeman (AUS) |
| 1999 | Cathy Freeman (AUS) |
| 2001 | Amy Mbacke Thiam (SEN) |
| 2003 | Ana Guevara (MEX) |
| 2005 | Tonique Williams-Darling (BAH) |
| 2007 | Christine Ohuruogu (GBR) |
| 2009 | Sanya Richards (USA) |
| 2011 | Amantle Montsho (BOT) |

**800 M**
| | |
|---|---|
| 1983 | Jarmila Kratochvilova (TCH) |
| 1987 | Sigrun Wodars (GDR) |
| 1991 | Liliya Nurutdinova (URS) |
| 1993 | Maria Mutola (MOZ) |
| 1995 | Ana Quirot (CUB) |
| 1997 | Ana Quirot (CUB) |
| 1999 | Ludmila Formanova (CZE) |
| 2001 | Maria Mutola (MOZ) |
| 2003 | Maria Mutola (MOZ) |
| 2005 | Zulia Calatayud (CUB) |
| 2007 | Janeth Jepkosgei (KEN) |
| 2009 | Caster Semenya (RSA) |
| 2011 | Mariya Savinova (RUS) |

**1,500 M**
| | |
|---|---|
| 1983 | Mary Decker (USA) |
| 1987 | Tatyana Samolenko (URS) |
| 1991 | Hassiba Boulmerka (ALG) |
| 1993 | Liu Dong (CHN) |
| 1995 | Hassiba Boulmerka (ALG) |
| 1997 | Carla Sacramento (POR) |
| 1999 | Svetlana Masterkova (RUS) |
| 2001 | Gabriela Szabo (ROM) |
| 2003 | Tatyana Tomashova (RUS) |
| 2005 | Tatyana Tomashova (RUS) |
| 2007 | Maryam Yusuf Jamal (BRN) |
| 2009 | Maryam Yusuf Jamal (BRN) |
| 2011 | Jennifer Simpson (USA) |

**5,000 M[1]**
| | |
|---|---|
| 1983 | Mary Decker (USA) |
| 1987 | Tatyana Samolenko (URS) |
| 1991 | Tatyana Dorovskikh (URS) |
| 1993 | Qu Yunxia (CHN) |
| 1995 | Sonia O'Sullivan (IRL) |

**5,000 M[1] (CONTINUED)**
| | |
|---|---|
| 1997 | Gabriela Szabo (ROM) |
| 1999 | Gabriela Szabo (ROM) |
| 2001 | Olga Yegorova (RUS) |
| 2003 | Tirunesh Dibaba (ETH) |
| 2005 | Tirunesh Dibaba (ETH) |
| 2007 | Meseret Defar (ETH) |
| 2009 | Vivian Cheruiyot (KEN) |
| 2011 | Vivian Cheruiyot (KEN) |

**10,000 M**
| | |
|---|---|
| 1987 | Ingrid Kristiansen (NOR) |
| 1991 | Liz McColgan (GBR) |
| 1993 | Wang Junxia (CHN) |
| 1995 | Fernanda Ribeiro (POR) |
| 1997 | Sally Barsosio (KEN) |
| 1999 | Gete Wami (ETH) |
| 2001 | Derartu Tulu (ETH) |
| 2003 | Berhane Adere (ETH) |
| 2005 | Tirunesh Dibaba (ETH) |
| 2007 | Tirunesh Dibaba (ETH) |
| 2009 | Linet Chepkwemoi Masai (KEN) |
| 2011 | Vivian Cheruiyot (KEN) |

**STEEPLECHASE**
| | |
|---|---|
| 2005 | Dorcus Inzikuru (UGA) |
| 2007 | Yekaterina Volkova (RUS) |
| 2009 | Marta Domínguez (ESP) |
| 2011 | Yuliya Zaripova (RUS) |

**100-M HURDLES**
| | |
|---|---|
| 1983 | Bettine Jahn (GDR) |
| 1987 | Ginka Zagorcheva (BUL) |
| 1991 | Ludmila Narozhilenko (URS) |
| 1993 | Gail Devers (USA) |
| 1995 | Gail Devers (USA) |
| 1997 | Ludmila Engquist (SWE) |
| 1999 | Gail Devers (USA) |
| 2001 | Anjanette Kirkland (USA) |
| 2003 | Perdita Felicien (CAN) |
| 2005 | Michelle Perry (USA) |
| 2007 | Michelle Perry (USA) |
| 2009 | Brigitte Foster-Hylton (JAM) |
| 2011 | Sally Pearson (AUS) |

**400-M HURDLES**
| | |
|---|---|
| 1983 | Yekaterina Fesenko (URS) |
| 1987 | Sabine Busch (GDR) |
| 1991 | Tatyana Ledovskaya (URS) |
| 1993 | Sally Gunnell (GBR) |
| 1995 | Kim Batten (USA) |
| 1997 | Nezha Bidouane (MAR) |
| 1999 | Daimí Pernía (CUB) |
| 2001 | Nezha Bidouane (MAR) |
| 2003 | Jana Pittman (AUS) |
| 2005 | Yuliya Pechonkina (RUS) |
| 2007 | Jana Rawlinson (AUS) |
| 2009 | Melanie Walker (JAM) |
| 2011 | Lashinda Demus (USA) |

**MARATHON**
| | |
|---|---|
| 1983 | Grete Waitz (NOR) |
| 1987 | Rosa Mota (POR) |
| 1991 | Wanda Panfil (POL) |
| 1993 | Asari Junko (JPN) |
| 1995 | Maria Machado (POR) |
| 1997 | Hiromi Suzuki (JPN) |

**MARATHON (CONTINUED)**
| | |
|---|---|
| 1999 | Jong Song Ok (PRK) |
| 2001 | Lidia Simon (ROM) |
| 2003 | Catherine Ndereba (KEN) |
| 2005 | Paula Radcliffe (GBR) |
| 2007 | Catherine Ndereba (KEN) |
| 2009 | Bai Xue (CHN) |
| 2011 | Edna Kiplagat (KEN) |

**10-KM WALK**
| | |
|---|---|
| 1987 | Irina Strakhova (URS) |
| 1991 | Alina Ivanova (URS) |
| 1993 | Sari Essayeh (FIN) |
| 1995 | Irina Stankina (RUS) |
| 1997 | Annarita Sidoti (ITA) |

**20-KM RACE WALK**
| | |
|---|---|
| 1999 | Liu Hongyu (CHN) |
| 2001 | Olimpiada Ivanova (RUS) |
| 2003 | Yelena Nikolayeva (RUS) |
| 2005 | Olimpiada Ivanova (RUS) |
| 2007 | Olga Kaniskina (RUS) |
| 2009 | Olga Kaniskina (RUS) |
| 2011 | Olga Kaniskina (RUS) |

**4 × 100-M RELAY**
| | |
|---|---|
| 1983 | East Germany |
| 1987 | United States |
| 1991 | Jamaica |
| 1993 | Russia |
| 1995 | United States |
| 1997 | United States |
| 1999 | Bahamas |
| 2001 | Germany |
| 2003 | France |
| 2005 | United States |
| 2007 | United States |
| 2009 | Jamaica |
| 2011 | United States |

**4 × 400-M RELAY**
| | |
|---|---|
| 1983 | East Germany |
| 1987 | East Germany |
| 1991 | USSR |
| 1993 | United States |
| 1995 | United States |
| 1997 | Germany |
| 1999 | Russia |
| 2001 | Jamaica |
| 2003 | United States |
| 2005 | Russia |
| 2007 | United States |
| 2009 | United States |
| 2011 | United States |

**HIGH JUMP**
| | |
|---|---|
| 1983 | Tamara Bykova (URS) |
| 1987 | Stefka Kostadinova (BUL) |
| 1991 | Heike Henkel (GER) |
| 1993 | Ioamnet Quintero (CUB) |
| 1995 | Stefka Kostadinova (BUL) |
| 1997 | Hanne Haugland (NOR) |
| 1999 | Inga Babakova (UKR) |
| 2001 | Hestrie Cloete (RSA) |
| 2003 | Hestrie Cloete (RSA) |
| 2005 | Kajsa Bergqvist (SWE) |
| 2007 | Blanka Vlasic (CRO) |
| 2009 | Blanka Vlasic (CRO) |
| 2011 | Anna Chicherova (RUS) |

## World Track & Field Championships—Women (continued)

**POLE VAULT**
1999  Stacy Dragila (USA)
2001  Stacy Dragila (USA)
2003  Svetlana Feofanova (RUS)
2005  Yelena Isinbayeva (RUS)
2007  Yelena Isinbayeva (RUS)
2009  Anna Rogowska (POL)
2011  Fabiana Murer (BRA)

**LONG JUMP**
1983  Heike Daute (GDR)
1987  Jackie Joyner-Kersee (USA)
1991  Jackie Joyner-Kersee (USA)
1993  Heike Drechsler (GER)
1995  Fiona May (ITA)
1997  Ludmila Galkina (RUS)
1999  Niurka Montalvo (ESP)
2001  Fiona May (ITA)
2003  Eunice Barber (FRA)
2005  Tianna Madison (USA)
2007  Tatyana Lebedeva (RUS)
2009  Brittney Reese (USA)
2011  Brittney Reese (USA)

**TRIPLE JUMP**
1993  Anna Biryukova (RUS)
1995  Inessa Kravets (UKR)
1997  Sarka Kasparkova (CZE)
1999  Paraskevi Tsiamita (GRE)
2001  Tatyana Lebedeva (RUS)
2003  Tatyana Lebedeva (RUS)
2005  Trecia Smith (JAM)
2007  Yargelis Savigne (CUB)
2009  Yargelis Savigne (CUB)
2011  Olha Saladuha (UKR)

**SHOT PUT**
1983  Helena Fibingerova (TCH)
1987  Natalya Lisovskaya (URS)
1991  Huang Zhihong (CHN)
1993  Huang Zhihong (CHN)
1995  Astrid Kumbernuss (GER)
1997  Astrid Kumbernuss (GER)
1999  Astrid Kumbernuss (GER)
2001  Yanina Korolchik (BLR)
2003  Svetlana Krivelyova (RUS)
2005  Nadezhda Ostapchuk (BLR)
2007  Valerie Vili (NZL)
2009  Valerie Vili (NZL)
2011  Valerie Adams (NZL)

**DISCUS THROW**
1983  Martina Opitz (GDR)
1987  Martina Hellmann (GDR)
1991  Tsvetanka Khristova (BUL)
1993  Olga Burova (RUS)
1995  Ellina Zvereva (BLR)
1997  Beatrice Faumuina (NZL)
1999  Franka Dietzsch (GER)
2001  Ellina Zvereva (BLR)
2003  Irina Yachenko (BLR)
2005  Franka Dietzsch (GER)
2007  Franka Dietzsch (GER)
2009  Dani Samuels (AUS)
2011  Li Yanfeng (CHN)

**HAMMER THROW**
1999  Mihaela Melinte (ROM)
2001  Yipsi Moreno (CUB)
2003  Yipsi Moreno (CUB)
2005  Olga Kuzenkova (RUS)

**HAMMER THROW (CONTINUED)**
2007  Betty Heidler (GER)
2009  Anita Wlodarczyk (POL)
2011  Tatyana Lysenko (RUS)

**JAVELIN THROW**
1983  Tiina Lillak (FIN)
1987  Fatima Whitbread (GBR)
1991  Xu Demei (CHN)
1993  Trine Hattestad (NOR)
1995  Natalya Shikolenko (BLR)
1997  Trine Hattestad (NOR)
1999  Mirela Tzelili (GRE)
2001  Osleidys Menéndez (CUB)
2003  Mirela Manjani (GRE)
2005  Osleidys Menéndez (CUB)
2007  Barbora Spotakova (CZE)
2009  Steffi Nerius (GER)
2011  Maria Abakumova (RUS)

**HEPTATHLON**
1983  Ramona Neubert (GDR)
1987  Jackie Joyner-Kersee (USA)
1991  Sabine Braun (GER)
1993  Jackie Joyner-Kersee (USA)
1995  Ghada Shouaa (SYR)
1997  Sabine Braun (GER)
1999  Eunice Barber (FRA)
2001  Yelena Prokhorova (RUS)
2003  Carolina Klüft (SWE)
2005  Carolina Klüft (SWE)
2007  Carolina Klüft (SWE)
2009  Jessica Ennis (GBR)
2011  Tatyana Chernova (RUS)

[1]3,000 m until 1995.

## Outdoor Track & Field World Records

### Men

| EVENT | RECORD HOLDER (COUNTRY) | PERFORMANCE | DATE |
|---|---|---|---|
| 100 m | Usain Bolt (JAM) | 9.58 sec | 16 Aug 2009 |
| 200 m | Usain Bolt (JAM) | 19.19 sec | 20 Aug 2009 |
| 400 m | Michael Johnson (USA) | 43.18 sec | 26 Aug 1999 |
| 800 m | David Lekuta Rudisha (KEN) | 1 min 41.01 sec | 29 Aug 2010 |
| 1,000 m | Noah Ngeny (KEN) | 2 min 11.96 sec | 5 Sep 1999 |
| 1,500 m | Hicham El Guerrouj (MAR) | 3 min 26.00 sec | 14 Jul 1998 |
| 1 mile | Hicham El Guerrouj (MAR) | 3 min 43.13 sec | 7 Jul 1999 |
| 3,000 m | Daniel Komen (KEN) | 7 min 20.67 sec | 1 Sep 1996 |
| 5,000 m | Kenenisa Bekele (ETH) | 12 min 37.35 sec | 31 May 2004 |
| 10,000 m | Kenenisa Bekele (ETH) | 26 min 17.53 sec | 26 Aug 2005 |
| Marathon[1] | Haile Gebrselassie (ETH) | 2 hr 3 min 59 sec | 28 Sep 2008 |
| 110-m hurdles | Dayron Robles (CUB) | 12.87 sec | 12 Jun 2008 |
| 400-m hurdles | Kevin Young (USA) | 46.78 sec | 6 Aug 1992 |
| 20-km walk | Vladimir Kanaykin (RUS) | 1 hr 17 min 16 sec | 29 Sep 2007 |
| 50-km walk | Denis Nizhegorodov (RUS) | 3 hr 34 min 14 sec | 11 May 2008 |
| Steeplechase | Saif Saaeed Shaheen (QAT) | 7 min 53.63 sec | 3 Sep 2004 |
| 4 × 100-m relay | Jamaica[2] | 37.04 sec | 4 Sep 2011 |
| 4 × 400-m relay | United States | 2 min 54.29 sec | 22 Aug 1993 |
| High jump | Javier Sotomayor (CUB) | 2.45 m (8 ft ½ in) | 27 Jul 1993 |
| Long jump | Mike Powell (USA) | 8.95 m (29 ft 4½ in) | 30 Aug 1991 |
| Triple jump | Jonathan Edwards (GBR) | 18.29 m (60 ft ¼ in) | 7 Aug 1995 |
| Pole vault | Sergey Bubka (UKR) | 6.14 m (20 ft 1¾ in) | 31 Jul 1994 |
| Shot put | Randy Barnes (USA) | 23.12 m (75 ft 10¼ in) | 20 May 1990 |
| Discus throw | Jürgen Schult (GDR) | 74.08 m (243 ft) | 6 Jun 1986 |
| Hammer throw | Yuriy Sedykh (URS) | 86.74 m (284 ft 7 in) | 30 Aug 1986 |
| Javelin throw | Jan Zelezny (CZE) | 98.48 m (323 ft 1 in) | 25 May 1996 |
| Decathlon | Ashton Eaton (USA)[2] | 9,039 points | 23 Jun 2012 |

## Outdoor Track & Field World Records (continued)

### Women

| EVENT | RECORD HOLDER (COUNTRY) | PERFORMANCE | DATE |
|---|---|---|---|
| 100 m | Florence Griffith-Joyner (USA) | 10.49 sec | 16 Jul 1988 |
| 200 m | Florence Griffith-Joyner (USA) | 21.34 sec | 29 Sep 1988 |
| 400 m | Marita Koch (GDR) | 47.60 sec | 6 Oct 1985 |
| 800 m | Jarmila Kratochvilova (TCH) | 1 min 53.28 sec | 26 Jul 1983 |
| 1,000 m | Svetlana Masterkova (RUS) | 2 min 28.98 sec | 23 Aug 1996 |
| 1,500 m | Qu Yunxia (CHN) | 3 min 50.46 sec | 11 Sep 1993 |
| 1 mile | Svetlana Masterkova (RUS) | 4 min 12.56 sec | 14 Aug 1996 |
| 3,000 m | Wang Junxia (CHN) | 8 min 06.11 sec | 13 Sep 1993 |
| 5,000 m | Tirunesh Dibaba (ETH) | 14 min 11.15 sec | 6 Jun 2008 |
| 10,000 m | Wang Junxia (CHN) | 29 min 31.78 sec | 8 Sep 1993 |
| Marathon[1] | Paula Radcliffe (GBR) | 2 hr 15 min 25 sec | 13 Apr 2003 |
| 100-m hurdles | Yordanka Donkova (BUL) | 12.21 sec | 20 Aug 1988 |
| 400-m hurdles | Yuliya Pechonkina (RUS) | 52.34 sec | 8 Aug 2003 |
| 20-km walk | Elena Lashmanova (RUS)[2] | 1 hr 25 min 02 sec | 11 Aug 2012 |
| Steeplechase | Gulnara Samitova-Galkina (RUS) | 8 min 58.81 sec | 17 Aug 2008 |
| 4 × 100-m relay | United States[2] | 40.82 sec | 10 Aug 2012 |
| 4 × 400-m relay | USSR | 3 min 15.17 sec | 1 Oct 1988 |
| High jump | Stefka Kostadinova (BUL) | 2.09 m (6 ft 10¼ in) | 30 Aug 1987 |
| Long jump | Galina Chistyakova (URS) | 7.52 m (24 ft 8¼ in) | 11 Jun 1988 |
| Triple jump | Inessa Kravets (UKR) | 15.50 m (50 ft 10¼ in) | 10 Aug 1995 |
| Pole vault | Yelena Isinbayeva (RUS) | 5.06 m (16 ft 7¼ in) | 28 Aug 2009 |
| Shot put | Natalya Lisovskaya (URS) | 22.63 m (74 ft 3 in) | 7 Jun 1987 |
| Discus throw | Gabriele Reinsch (GDR) | 76.80 m (252 ft) | 9 Jul 1988 |
| Hammer throw | Betty Heidler (GER) | 79.42 m (260 ft 6¾ in) | 21 May 2011 |
| Javelin throw | Barbora Spotakova (CZE) | 72.28 m (237 ft 2 in) | 13 Sep 2008 |
| Heptathlon | Jackie Joyner-Kersee (USA) | 7,291 points | 24 Sep 1988 |
| Decathlon | Austra Skujyte (LTU) | 8,358 points | 15 Apr 2005 |

[1]Not an officially ratified event; best performance on record.   [2]Awaiting IAAF ratification as of 23 Aug 2012.

## Indoor Track & Field World Records

### Men

| EVENT | RECORD HOLDER (COUNTRY) | PERFORMANCE | DATE |
|---|---|---|---|
| 50 m | Donovan Bailey (CAN) | 5.56 sec | 9 Feb 1996 |
| 60 m | Maurice Greene (USA) | 6.39 sec | 3 Feb 1998 |
| 200 m | Frank Fredericks (NAM) | 19.92 sec | 18 Feb 1996 |
| 400 m | Kerron Clement (USA) | 44.57 sec | 12 Mar 2005 |
| 800 m | Wilson Kipketer (DEN) | 1 min 42.67 sec | 9 Mar 1997 |
| 1,000 m | Wilson Kipketer (DEN) | 2 min 14.96 sec | 20 Feb 2000 |
| 1,500 m | Hicham El Guerrouj (MAR) | 3 min 31.18 sec | 2 Feb 1997 |
| 1 mile | Hicham El Guerrouj (MAR) | 3 min 48.45 sec | 12 Feb 1997 |
| 3,000 m | Daniel Komen (KEN) | 7 min 24.90 sec | 6 Feb 1998 |
| 5,000 m | Kenenisa Bekele (ETH) | 12 min 49.60 sec | 20 Feb 2004 |
| 50-m hurdles | Mark McKoy (CAN) | 6.25 sec | 5 Mar 1986 |
| 60-m hurdles | Colin Jackson (GBR) | 7.30 sec | 6 Mar 1994 |
| 5,000-m walk | Mikhail Shchennikov (RUS) | 18 min 07.08 sec | 14 Feb 1995 |
| 4 × 200-m relay | Great Britain and Northern Ireland | 1 min 22.11 sec | 3 Mar 1991 |
| 4 × 400-m relay | United States | 3 min 02.83 sec | 7 Mar 1999 |
| 4 × 800-m relay | United States | 7 min 13.94 sec | 6 Feb 2000 |
| High jump | Javier Sotomayor (CUB) | 2.43 m (7 ft 11½ in) | 4 Mar 1989 |
| Long jump | Carl Lewis (USA) | 8.79 m (28 ft 10 in) | 27 Jan 1984 |
| Triple jump | Teddy Tamgho (FRA) | 17.92 m (58 ft 9½ in) | 6 Mar 2011 |
| Pole vault | Sergey Bubka (UKR) | 6.15 m (20 ft 2¼ in) | 21 Feb 1993 |
| Shot put | Randy Barnes (USA) | 22.66 m (74 ft 4¼ in) | 20 Jan 1989 |
| Heptathlon | Ashton Eaton (USA) | 6,645 points | 10 Mar 2012 |

### Women

| EVENT | RECORD HOLDER (COUNTRY) | PERFORMANCE | DATE |
|---|---|---|---|
| 50 m | Irina Privalova (RUS) | 5.96 sec | 9 Feb 1995 |
| 60 m | Irina Privalova (RUS) | 6.92 sec | 11 Feb 1993 |
| 200 m | Merlene Ottey (JAM) | 21.87 sec | 13 Feb 1993 |
| 400 m | Jarmila Kratochvilova (TCH) | 49.59 sec | 7 Mar 1982 |
| 800 m | Jolanda Ceplak (SLO) | 1 min 55.82 sec | 3 Mar 2002 |
| 1,000 m | Maria Mutola (MOZ) | 2 min 30.94 sec | 25 Feb 1999 |
| 1,500 m | Yelena Soboleva (RUS) | 3 min 58.28 sec | 18 Feb 2006 |

## Indoor Track & Field World Records (continued)

### Women (continued)

| EVENT | RECORD HOLDER (COUNTRY) | PERFORMANCE | DATE |
|---|---|---|---|
| 1 mile | Doina Melinte (ROU) | 4 min 17.14 sec | 9 Feb 1990 |
| 3,000 m | Meseret Defar (ETH) | 8 min 23.72 sec | 3 Feb 2007 |
| 5,000 m | Meseret Defar (ETH) | 14 min 24.37 sec | 18 Feb 2009 |
| 50-m hurdles | Cornelia Oschkenat (GDR) | 6.58 sec | 20 Feb 1988 |
| 60-m hurdles | Susanna Kallur (SWE) | 7.68 sec | 10 Feb 2008 |
| 3,000-m walk | Claudia Stef (ROU) | 11 min 40.33 sec | 30 Jan 1999 |
| 4 × 200-m relay | Russia | 1 min 32.41 sec | 29 Jan 2005 |
| 4 × 400-m relay | Russia | 3 min 23.37 sec | 28 Jan 2006 |
| 4 × 800-m relay | Russia | 8 min 06.24 sec | 18 Feb 2011 |
| High jump | Kajsa Bergqvist (SWE) | 2.08 m (6 ft 10 in) | 4 Feb 2006 |
| Long jump | Heike Drechsler (GDR) | 7.37 m (24 ft 2¼ in) | 13 Feb 1988 |
| Triple jump | Tatyana Lebedeva (RUS) | 15.36 m (50 ft 4¾ in) | 6 Mar 2004 |
| Pole vault | Yelena Isinbayeva (RUS) | 5.01 m (16 ft 5¼ in) | 23 Feb 2012 |
| Shot put | Helena Fibingerova (TCH) | 22.50 m (73 ft 9¾ in) | 19 Feb 1977 |
| Pentathlon | Natallia Dobrynska (UKR) | 5,013 points | 9 Mar 2012 |

## Volleyball

World volleyball championships for men were inaugurated in 1949. Women's competition began in 1952. These biennial championships are organized by the Fédération Internationale de Volleyball (FIVB; founded 1947). Indoor volleyball has been included in the Olympic Games since 1964 and beach volleyball since 1996.

FIVB Web site: <www.fivb.org>.

### Volleyball World Championships

| YEAR | MEN | WOMEN | YEAR | MEN | WOMEN |
|---|---|---|---|---|---|
| 1949 | USSR | | 1984[1] | United States | China |
| 1952 | USSR | USSR | 1986 | United States | China |
| 1956 | Czechoslovakia | USSR | 1988[1] | United States | USSR |
| 1960 | USSR | USSR | 1990 | Italy | USSR |
| 1962 | USSR | Japan | 1992[1] | Brazil | Cuba |
| 1964[1] | USSR | Japan | 1994 | Italy | Cuba |
| 1966 | Czechoslovakia | not held | 1996[1] | Netherlands | Cuba |
| 1967 | not held | Japan | 1998 | Italy | Cuba |
| 1968[1] | USSR | USSR | 2000[1] | Yugoslavia | Cuba |
| 1970 | East Germany | USSR | 2002 | Brazil | Italy |
| 1972[1] | Japan | USSR | 2004[1] | Brazil | China |
| 1974 | Poland | Japan | 2006 | Brazil | Russia |
| 1976[1] | Poland | Japan | 2008[1] | United States | Brazil |
| 1978 | USSR | Cuba | 2010 | Brazil | Russia |
| 1980[1] | USSR | USSR | 2012[1] | Russia | Brazil |
| 1982 | USSR | China | | | |

[1]Olympic champions, recognized in this table as world champions (though not by FIVB).

### Beach Volleyball World Championships

Beach volleyball world championships, organized by the Fédération Internationale de Volleyball, were inaugurated in 1997 with teams of two, who compete biennially for their share of US$1 million. Beach volleyball has been included in the Olympic Games since 1996. FIVB Web site: <www.fivb.org>.

| YEAR | MEN | WOMEN |
|---|---|---|
| 1996[1] | Karch Kiraly/Kent Steffes (USA) | Jackie Silva/Sandra Pires (BRA) |
| 1997 | Guilherme Marques/Para Ferreira (BRA) | Jackie Silva/Sandra Pires (BRA) |
| 1999 | Emanuel Rego/José Loiola (BRA) | Shelda Bede/Adriana Behar (BRA) |
| 2000[1] | Dain Blaton/Eric Fonoimoana (USA) | Natalie Cook/Kerri-Ann Pottharst (AUS) |
| 2001 | Mariano Baracetti/Martín Conde (ARG) | Shelda Bede/Adriana Behar (BRA) |
| 2003 | Emanuel Rego/Ricardo Santos (BRA) | Misty May/Kerri Walsh (USA) |
| 2004[1] | Emanuel Rego/Ricardo Santos (BRA) | Misty May/Kerri Walsh (USA) |
| 2005 | Marcio Araujo/Fabio Magalhães (BRA) | Misty May-Treanor/Kerri Walsh (USA) |
| 2007 | Phil Dalhausser/Todd Rogers (USA) | Misty May-Treanor/Kerri Walsh (USA) |
| 2008[1] | Phil Dalhausser/Todd Rogers (USA) | Misty May-Treanor/Kerri Walsh (USA) |

## Beach Volleyball World Championships (continued)

| YEAR | MEN | WOMEN |
|---|---|---|
| 2009 | Julius Brink/Jonas Reckermann (GER) | Jen Kessy/April Ross (USA) |
| 2011 | Emanuel Rego/Alison Cerutti (BRA) | Juliana Felisberta Silva/Larissa Franca (BRA) |
| 2012[1] | Julius Brink/Jonas Reckermann (GER) | Misty May-Treanor/Kerri Walsh (USA) |

[1]*Olympic champions, recognized in this table as world champions.*

# Weight Lifting

World weight lifting is overseen by the **International Weightlifting Federation** (IWF; founded 1905). The first **men's international weight lifting competition** was held in London in 1891; the sport was also included in the first modern Olympic Games, in Athens in 1896. By the 1930s championship events consisted of the snatch, clean and jerk, and press (which was eliminated in 1972). **Women's world championships** have been held since 1987, and women's competition was added to the Olympics in 2000. In 1998 the IWF established **new weight classes** (eight for men and seven for women).

**IWF Web site:** <www.iwf.net>.

## World Weight Lifting Champions, 2011

### Men

| WEIGHT CLASS | WINNER (COUNTRY) | PERFORMANCE |
|---|---|---|
| 56 kg (123 lb) | Wu Jingbiao (CHN) | 292 kg (644 lb) |
| 62 kg (137 lb) | Zhang Jie (CHN) | 321 kg (708 lb) |
| 69 kg (152 lb) | Tang Deshang (CHN) | 341 kg (752 lb) |
| 77 kg (170 lb) | Lu Xiaojun (CHN) | 375 kg (827 lb) |
| 85 kg (187 lb) | Kianoush Rostami (IRI) | 382 kg (842 lb) |
| 94 kg (207 lb) | Ilya Ilyin (KAZ) | 407 kg (897 lb) |
| 105 kg (231 lb) | Khadzhimurat Akkaev (RUS) | 430 kg (948 lb) |
| 105+ kg (231+ lb) | Behdad Salimikordasiabi (IRI) | 464 kg (1,023 lb) |

### Women

| WEIGHT CLASS | WINNER (COUNTRY) | PERFORMANCE |
|---|---|---|
| 48 kg (106 lb) | Tian Yuan (CHN) | 207 kg (456 lb) |
| 53 kg (117 lb) | Zulfiya Chinshanlo (KAZ) | 227 kg (500 lb) |
| 58 kg (128 lb) | Nastassia Novikava (BLR) | 237 kg (522 lb) |
| 63 kg (139 lb) | Svetlana Tsarukaeva (RUS) | 255 kg (562 lb) |
| 69 kg (152 lb) | Oxana Slivenko (RUS) | 266 kg (586 lb) |
| 75 kg (165 lb) | Nadezhda Yevstyukhina (RUS) | 293 kg (646 lb) |
| 75+ kg (165+ lb) | Zhou Lulu (CHN) | 328 kg (723 lb) |

## Weight Lifting World Records

*Total weight for snatch and clean-and-jerk lifts.*

### Men

| WEIGHT CLASS | RECORD HOLDER (COUNTRY) | PERFORMANCE | DATE |
|---|---|---|---|
| 56 kg (123 lb) | Halil Mutlu (TUR) | 305 kg (672 lb) | 16 Sep 2000 |
| 62 kg (137 lb) | Kim Un Guk (PRK) | 327 kg (721 lb) | 30 Jul 2012 |
| 69 kg (152 lb) | Galabin Boevski (BUL) | 357 kg (787 lb) | 24 Nov 1999 |
| 77 kg (170 lb) | Lu Xiaojun (CHN) | 379 kg (836 lb) | 1 Aug 2012 |
| 85 kg (187 lb) | Lu Yong (CHN); | 394 kg (869 lb) | 15 Aug 2008; |
|  | Andrei Rybakov (BLR) |  | 15 Aug 2008 |
| 94 kg (207 lb) | Ilya Ilyin (KAZ) | 418 kg (922 lb) | 4 Aug 2012 |
| 105 kg (231.5 lb) | Andrei Aramnau (BLR) | 436 kg (961 lb) | 18 Aug 2008 |
| 105+ kg (231.5+ lb) | Hossein Rezazadeh (IRI) | 472 kg (1041 lb) | 26 Sep 2000 |

### Women

| WEIGHT CLASS | RECORD HOLDER (COUNTRY) | PERFORMANCE | DATE |
|---|---|---|---|
| 48 kg (106 lb) | Yang Lian (CHN) | 217 kg (478 lb) | 1 Oct 2006 |
| 53 kg (117 lb) | Li Ping (CHN) | 230 kg (507 lb) | 14 Nov 2010 |
| 58 kg (128 lb) | Chen Yanqing (CHN) | 251 kg (553 lb) | 3 Dec 2006 |
| 63 kg (139 lb) | Liu Haixia (CHN) | 257 kg (567 lb) | 23 Sep 2007 |
| 69 kg (152 lb) | Liu Chunhong (CHN) | 286 kg (631 lb) | 13 Aug 2008 |
| 75 kg (165 lb) | Natalya Zabolotnaya (RUS) | 296 kg (653 lb) | 17 Dec 2011 |
| 75+ kg (165+ lb) | Zhou Lulu (CHN) | 333 kg (734 lb) | 5 Aug 2012 |

# INDEX

Page numbers in **boldface** indicate main subject references; references in *italics* indicate illustrations.
Flags of the world are on plates 1–6, and maps of the world are on plates 7–16.

International Space Station, *or*
    ISS 151, 153
  chronology 13, 28
  space shuttle 8
International System of Units, *or*
    SI 144
international trade: *see under*
    individual nations by name
Internet 149, 150, 619
  chronology 13, 19, 21, 23, 27,
    28
  entertainment distribution
    models 645
  privacy rights 517
  US area and zip codes 614
  *see also* individual subjects for
    relevant Web sites
IOC: *see* International Olympic
    Committee
Iowa 589
  crime rates 615, 616
  currency: quarters 626
  electoral votes 568
  energy consumption 627
  government 608, 610
  immigration 579
  income taxes 643
  poverty level 581
  prison population 618
  state population 576
  US Congress 560, 564, 568
Iran 308
  armed forces of the world 516
  cell phone subscribers 150
  chronology 13, 15, 17, 18, 19,
    20, 21, 24, 27
  education 505
  *flags of the world Plate 3*
  Persian dynasties 497
  refugee population 502
Iraq 309
  Arab Spring 10
  armed forces of the world 516
  chronology 14, 16, 19, 22, 23,
    29
  *flags of the world Plate 3*
  internally displaced persons
    502
  refugee population 502
Iraq War, *or* Second Persian Gulf
    War 19
  US casualties 573
Ireland 311
  awards 691, 692, 693
  chronology 12, 25
  *flags of the world Plate 3*
  immigration 501
  literary awards 691, 692, 693
  Thoroughbred racing 796
Irish Sea 174
iron 183, 185
Isaacson, Walter 36
Ishioka, Eiko 81
Isis
  mobile wallets 625
Islam 508, 510, 511
  calendar 118
  caliphs 496
  holidays 119
  *world map Plate 7*
island 171

Israel 312
  armed forces of the world 516
  chronology 16, 19
  *flags of the world Plate 3*
ISS: *see* International Space
    Station
Italy 314
  armed forces of the world 516
  cell phone subscribers 150
  chronology 13, 15, 21, 27
  consumer price 644
  disasters 33, 34
  education 505
  *flags of the world Plate 3*
  gross domestic product 644
  horse racing 796
  immigration 501
  Roman emperors 488
  unemployment 644

# J

Jackson, Andrew 533, **535**, 542,
    546, 557, 626
Jainism 508, 510, 512
Jamaica 316
  *flags of the world Plate 3*
James, E. L. 35
James, Etta 82
James, LeBron 52
January
  astronomical phenomena 128
  civil holidays 122
Japan 317
  armed forces of the world
    516
  cell phone subscribers 150
  chronology 13, 15, 16, 21, 23,
    26
  consumer price 644
  disasters 32
  education 505
  *flags of the world Plate 3*
  gross domestic product 644
  holidays 120
  rulers and regimes 497
  Thoroughbred racing 797
  unemployment 644
  *world religions map Plate 7*
Japan Series 18, **769**
Japanese language 503
Jasmine Revolution 9
Jefferson, Thomas 521, 532,
    **534**, 542, 546, 557,
    626
Jenkins, Bill 82
Jesus Christ: *see* Christianity
Jew: *see* Judaism
Jewish Calendar **117**
Jobs, Steve 82, 645
Johnson, Andrew 533, **536**, 543,
    548, 627
Johnson, Lyndon B. 533, **540**,
    544, 553, 557
Joint Chiefs of Staff (US) **570**
Jonathan, Goodluck 36
Jones, Davy 82
Joosten, Kathryn 82
Jordan 320
  *flags of the world Plate 3*
  refugee population 502

journalism 11, 26
  Pulitzer Prize 674
JPMorgan Chase 28
Judaism 508, 510, 512
  calendar 117
  holidays 119
  *world map Plate 7*
judo 721, 753
Julian calendar, *or* Old Style
    calendar **117**, 121
July
  astronomical phenomena 129
  civil holidays 122
June
  astronomical phenomena 128
  civil holidays 122
Jupiter 137
  celestial bodies 131
  moons 138
  morning and evening stars
    130
  rings 139
  solar system superlatives 133

# K

Kansas 590
  crime rates 615, 616
  currency: quarters 626
  electoral votes 568
  energy consumption 627
  government 608, 610
  immigration 579
  income taxes 643
  poverty level 581
  prison population 618
  state population 576
  US Congress 560, 564, 568
Karzai, Ahmed Wali 82
Karzai, Hamid 54
Katzenbach, Nicholas 82
Kazakhstan 321
  *flags of the world Plate 3*
Keane, Bill 82
Kelly, David 82
kelvin 144
Kennedy, Anthony 35
Kennedy, John F. 533, **540**, 544,
    553, 557, 626
Kennedy, Mary Richardson 82
Kennedy Center Honors 19, **104**
Kenny, Enda 54
Kentucky 590
  crime rates 615, 616
  currency: quarters 626
  electoral votes 568
  energy consumption 627
  government 608, 610
  immigration 579
  income taxes 643
  poverty level 581
  prison population 618
  state population 576
  US Congress 560, 564, 568
Kentucky Derby 28, **797**
Kenya 16, 32, 33, **323**
  education 505
  *flags of the world Plate 3*
  internally displaced persons
    502
  refugee population 502